Compact Literature

READING ◼ REACTING ◼ WRITING

2016 MLA Update Edition

Compact Literature

READING ∷ REACTING ∷ WRITING

Ninth Edition
2016 MLA Update Edition

Laurie G. Kirszner
University of the Sciences, Emeritus

Stephen R. Mandell
Drexel University

CENGAGE
Learning·

Australia • Brazil • Mexico • Singapore • United Kingdom • United States

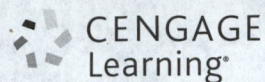

**Compact Literature:
Reading, Reacting, Writing,
Ninth Edition
2016 MLA Update Edition**
Laurie G. Kirszner,
Stephen R. Mandell

Product Director: Monica Eckman

Product Team Manager: Nicole Morinon

Product Manager: Kate Derrick

Senior Content Developer: Leslie Taggart

Content Developer: Karen Mauk

Associate Content Developer: Erin Bosco

Product Assistant: Claire Branman

Media Developer: Janine Tangney

Marketing Manager: Erin Parkins

Senior Content Project Manager: Michael Lepera

Senior Art Director: Marissa Falco

Manufacturing Planner: Betsy Donaghey

IP Analyst: Ann Hoffman

IP Project Manager: Farah Fard

Production Service/Compositor: Cenveo® Publisher Services

Text Designer: Cenveo® Publisher Services

Cover Designer: Sarah Bishins

Cover Image: © 2013 Aryana B. Londir

For product information and technology assistance, contact us at **Cengage Learning Customer & Sales Support, 1-800-354-9706**

For permission to use material from this text or product, submit all requests online at **www.cengage.com/permissions**. Further permissions questions can be emailed to **permissionrequest@cengage.com**.

Library of Congress Control Number: On file

ISBN: 978-1-337-28102-7

Cengage Learning
20 Channel Center Street
Boston, MA 02210
USA

Cengage Learning is a leading provider of customized learning solutions with employees residing in nearly 40 different countries and sales in more than 125 countries around the world. Find your local representative at **www.cengage.com**.

Cengage Learning products are represented in Canada by Nelson Education, Ltd.

To learn more about Cengage Learning Solutions, visit **www.cengage.com**.
Purchase any of our products at your local college store or at our preferred online store **www.cengagebrain.com**.

Printed in the United States of America

Print Number: 01   Print Year: 2017

BRIEF CONTENTS

CONTENTS

PART 1   A GUIDE TO WRITING ABOUT LITERATURE   1

1 Understanding Literature   2

Westminster Bridge, London
(1886) by Claude Thomas Stanfield Moore

2 Reading and Writing about Literature   16

Julia Alvarez

3   Approaching Assignments in Literature   36

Apache children at the Carlisle Indian Industrial School, Pennsylvania, 1886 (from student essay: "Dreaming of Home")

4   Thinking Critically about Your Writing   55

Major Premise: All tragic heroes have tragic flaws.
Minor Premise: Hamlet is a tragic hero.
Conclusion: Therefore, Hamlet has a tragic flaw.

Syllogism

5 Writing Literary Arguments   62

Film still from the DVD version of
Alice Walker's "Everyday Use"

6 Using Sources in Your Writing   78

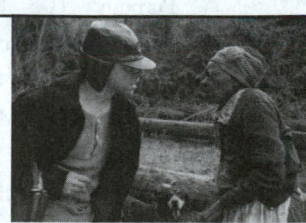

Scene from DVD of "A Worn Path"

7 Documenting Sources and Avoiding Plagiarism 90

To cite information from an online database, supply the publication information (including page numbers, if available) followed by the italicized name of the database and the DOI or URL. Include the date of access if the source is subject to change.

Luckenbilt, Trent. "Environmental Litigation: Down the Endless Corridor." *Environment,* 17 July 2001, pp. 34–42. *ABI / INFORM GLOBAL.*

31. A scholarly journal article from an online database
Schaefer, Richard J. "Editing Strategies in Television News Documentaries." *Journal of Communication,* vol. 47, no. 4, 1997, pp. 69–86. *InfoTrac OneFile Plus.*

32. A monthly magazine article from an online database
Livermore, Beth. "Meteorites on Ice." *Astronomy,* July 1993, pp. 54–58. *Expanded Academic ASAP Plus.*

33. A newspaper article from an online database
Meyer, Greg. "Answering Questions about the West Nile Virus." *Dayton Daily News,* 11 July 2002, pp. Z3–7. *LexisNexis.*

34. A reference book article from an online database
Laird, Judith. "Geoffrey Chaucer." *Cyclopedia of World Authors,* 1997. *MagillOnLiterature.* Accessed 2 Oct. 2010.

35. A dictionary definition from an online database
"Migraine." *Mosby's Medical, Nursing and Allied Health Dictionary,* 1998 ed., *Health Reference Center.*

Sample MLA works-cited entries

8 Writing Essay Exams about Literature 104

Key Words in Exam Questions		
Analyze	Describe	Interpret
Clarify	Discuss	Justify
Classify	Evaluate	Relate
Compare	Explain	Summarize
Contrast	Identify	Support
Define	Illustrate	Trace

Alberto Alvaro Ríos

Kate Chopin

Zadie Smith

Sherman Alexie

Edwidge Danticat

James Joyce

18   Symbol, Allegory, and Myth   407

Alice Walker

19   Theme   459

D(avid) H(erbert) Lawrence

20 Joyce Carol Oates's "Where Are You Going, Where Have You Been?": A Casebook for Reading, Research, and Writing   503

Joyce Carol Oates

21 Fiction for Further Reading   543

Edgar Allan Poe

Illustration of Trojan horse from Virgil's *Aenied*.

Seamus Heaney

27 Figures of Speech   758

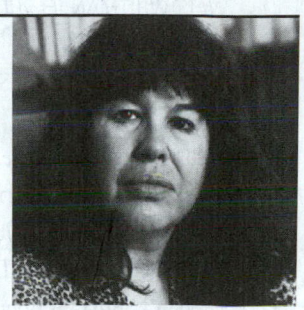

Marge Piercy

28 Sound 791

Emily Dickinson

24 Voice 675

Janice Mirikitani

E. E. Cummings

Jane Flanders

29 Form   813

Elizabeth Bishop

30   Symbol, Allegory, Allusion, Myth   852

W. H. Auden

31 | Discovering Themes in Poetry 882

Dylan Thomas

Langston Hughes

33 Poetry for Further Reading 952

Linda Pastan

Poetry Sampler: Poetry and Art   PS1

Detail from *Water Lilies* (1914–1917) by Claude Monet

August Wilson

Susan Glaspell

Appendix   Using Literary Criticism in Your Writing   1661

AUTHORS REPRESENTED BY MULTIPLE WORKS

PREFACE

In Alice Walker's short story "Everyday Use" (p. 426), two sisters—one rural and traditional, one urban and modern—compete for possession of two quilts that have been in their family for years. At the end of the story, the narrator's description of the quilts suggests their significance—as a link between the old and the new, between what was and what is:

> One was in the Lone Star pattern. The other was Walk Around the Mountain. In both of them were scraps of dresses that Grandma Dee had worn fifty and more years ago. Bits and pieces of Grandpa Jarrell's Paisley shirts. And one teeny faded blue piece, about the size of a penny matchbox, that was from Great Grandpa Eza's uniform that he wore in the Civil War. (431)

In a sense, *Compact Literature: Reading, Reacting, Writing* is a kind of literary quilt, one that places nontraditional works alongside classics, integrates the familiar with the unfamiliar, and invites students to see well-known works in new contexts. To convey this message, each edition of the book integrates imagery from a handmade quilt. The quilt designed for this new edition uses contemporary as well as traditional quilting techniques to reflect our own increased focus on contemporary and emerging writers as well as on writers from diverse cultures and backgrounds.

The ninth edition of *Compact Literature: Reading, Reacting, Writing*, like the previous editions, is designed to demystify the study of literature and to prepare students to explore the literary works collected here. Our goal in this edition remains what it has been from the start: to expand students' personal literary boundaries. To this end, we have fine-tuned the reading selections and expanded the pedagogical features that support the study of literature, acting in response to thoughtful comments from our reviewers and from our students. Having class-tested this book in our own literature classrooms, we have learned what kinds of selections and features best help our students to read, think about, understand, and write about literature in ways that make it meaningful to their lives in the twenty-first century.

To help instructors engage their students with literature and guide them in becoming better thinkers and writers, we have added new readings and enhanced key elements that have made *Compact Literature: Reading, Reacting, Writing* a classroom success.

Unparalleled Writing Coverage

The first college literature anthology to address writing as a major component of the introductory literature course, *Compact Literature: Reading, Reacting, Writing* begins with a comprehensive writing guide. **Part 1, "A Guide to Writing about Literature,"** consists of eight chapters that help students see writing about literature as a process of discovering, testing, and arguing about ideas. In addition, comprehensive writing coverage is integrated throughout the book in the following features:

- **A general introduction to the writing process** Chapter 2, "Reading and Writing about Literature," explains and illustrates the process of planning, drafting, and revising essays about literary works, concluding with an exercise asking students to evaluate and compare two student essays that examine the same three short stories.

- **Special treatment for writing about each genre** "Reading and Writing about Fiction" (Chapter 12), "Reading and Writing about Poetry" (Chapter 23), and "Reading and Writing about Drama" (Chapter 36) follow the writing process of students as they focus on works in each genre: Alberto Alvaro Ríos's short story "The Secret Lion" (p. 180); Seamus Heaney's poem "Digging" (p. 663) and Robert Hayden's poem "Those Winter Sundays" (p. 662); and Susan Glaspell's one-act play *Trifles* (p. 1604).

- **Two chapters on literary argument** Chapter 4, "Thinking Critically about Your Writing," and Chapter 5, "Writing Literary Arguments," help students to think critically about their writing and build convincing and insightful arguments about literary works. Chapter 5 takes students through the process of writing a literary argument and concludes with two annotated student essays.

- **Extensive research and documentation coverage** Tracing the research process of a student writing a short essay on Eudora Welty's "A Worn Path" (p. 463), Chapter 6, "Using Sources in Your Writing," includes extensive advice for conducting research both online and in print. Chapter 7, "Documenting Sources and Avoiding Plagiarism," includes strategies for avoiding plagiarism. Chapter 7 also includes the updated documentation guidelines put forth in the eighth edition of the *MLA Handbook* (2016). The style has been simplified to emphasize a common approach to a wide variety of source types, and the updated chapter introduces the new approach while continuing to offer numerous citation examples for students.

- **Thirteen complete model student essays** Because our own experience in the classroom has shown us that students often learn most easily from models, the text includes thirteen model student essays written in response to the kinds of topics that are frequently assigned in Introduction to Literature classes. Some of these model essays are source-based, and three are shown in multiple drafts along with annotations and commentary. In addition, an annotated sample student answer to an essay exam question appears in Chapter 8, "Writing Essay Exams about Literature."

- **Casebooks for reading, research, and writing** Three casebooks—on Joyce Carol Oates, Langston Hughes, and Susan Glaspell—feature seminal works by each writer accompanied by literary criticism, biographical essays, and other useful and interesting materials (song lyrics, photographs, newspaper articles, and so on), including visuals that enhance each work's appeal. Each casebook also includes discussion questions as well as writing prompts for essays that use sources. Students can use these casebooks to supplement their reading or as source material for a research project. By gathering research materials in a convenient, accessible format, these casebooks offer students a controlled, self-contained introduction to source-based writing as well as all the materials they need to begin a research project.

- **Checklists** Most chapter introductions end with a checklist designed to help students measure their understanding of concepts introduced in the chapter. These checklists can also guide students as they generate, explore, focus, and organize ideas for writing about works of literature.

- **Writing suggestions** Imaginative suggestions for essay topics are included at the end of each chapter to spark students' interest and inspire engaged writing.

Fresh, Balanced Selections

The short stories, poems, and plays collected in this book represent a balance of old and new as well as a wide variety of nations and cultures and a full range of writing styles.

- **Extensive selection of fiction** The fiction section includes not only perennial classics ("The Lottery," "A Rose for Emily," "The Cask of Amontillado") and stories we introduced to readers in the first edition, such as David Michael Kaplan's "Doe Season" and Charles Baxter's "Gryphon," but also a number of works never previously collected in a college literature anthology, such as Amanda Brown's "Love and Other Catastrophes: A Mix Tape." The 17 new stories that appear in this edition include several popular contemporary works, such as Lorrie Moore's "Referential" and Ed Park's "Slide to Unlock." In addition, Chapter 11, "Fiction Sampler: Graphic Fiction," engages students with visual examples from the literary canon.

- **Blend of contemporary and classic poetry** The poetry section balances works by classic poets (such as Robert Frost, Emily Dickinson, and Langston Hughes) with works by more contemporary poets (such as Linda Pastan and Francisco X. Alarcón) and also introduces students to exciting twenty-first-century works by poets such as Richard Blanco and Claire Lee. Now offering an even broader range of diverse works, the poetry section has been expanded with 57 new works by poets such as Agha Shahid Ali, Wendell Berry, Gwendolyn Brooks, Lewis Carroll, Sandra M. Castillo, Hart Crane, Rhina Espaillat, David Hernandez, Nancy Mercado, Deborah Paredez, Sylvia Plath, Lola Ridge, Jacob Saenz, Carl Sandburg, Virgil Suárez, May Swenson, Jean Toomer, and Pamela Spiro Wagner. In addition, unique visual glossary items appear throughout the poetry section, clarifying and illuminating unfamiliar terms and concepts within poems.

- **Varied selection of plays** The drama section juxtaposes classic selections—William Shakespeare's *Hamlet*, August Wilson's *Fences*, Milcha Sanchez-Scott's *The Cuban Swimmer*—with contemporary plays, such as David Auburn's *Proof* and David Ives's *The Blizzard*. Seven plays are new to the ninth edition, including Kimberly Pau's *Magic 8 Ball* and Michael Salomon's *The Date*.

- **Innovative "sampler" chapters** Chapter 10, "Fiction Sampler: The Short-Short Story"; Chapter 11, "Fiction Sampler: Graphic Fiction"; the full-color "Poetry Sampler: Poetry and Art"; and Chapter 36, "Drama Sampler: Ten-Minute Plays," showcase representative selections from four popular literary subgenres, introducing students to the variety and diversity of literature with brief, accessible works.

Film
Series

DVD

- **Integrated Fiction in Film coverage** "Fiction in Film" sections throughout Part 2 help students to understand the challenges of adapting fiction to film. Accompanying five short stories in the text, this integrated material includes still photos taken from DVDs of the following stories: John Updike's "A&P" (p. 238), Tillie Olsen's "I Stand Here Ironing" (p. 299), Alice Walker's "Everyday Use" (p. 426), Raymond Carver's "Cathedral" (p. 435), and Eudora Welty's "A Worn Path" (p. 463). The photos are followed by a series of questions that ask students to think critically about the decisions they would make if they were adapting each of the stories into a short film. (A marginal icon highlights each "Fiction in Film" section.)

- **Authors represented by multiple works** Many authors are represented in the book by more than one work—and, in some cases, by more than one literary genre. A list of all such works follows the book's table of contents, giving students an opportunity to see at a glance how a particular writer explores different themes, styles, and genres.

 Thorough Background Information

As we have learned in our classrooms over the years, part of helping students to demystify literature is helping them to understand the context in which the stories, poems, and plays were written. To achieve this goal, we continue to include contextual and background materials throughout the book in various forms:

- **Cultural context notes** A cultural context section follows each author headnote in the fiction and drama sections, providing vital background about the social and historical climate in which the work was written.

- **Accessible discussion of literary history** "Origins of Modern Fiction" in Chapter 9, "Understanding Fiction"; "Origins of Modern Poetry" in Chapter 22, "Understanding Poetry"; and "Origins of Modern Drama" in Chapter 34, "Understanding Drama," are fully illustrated with visuals that trace each genre's development and bring the history of literature to life.

 Other Pedagogical Features

A number of other pedagogical features appear throughout the text to prompt students to think critically about reading and to stimulate class discussions and energetic, thoughtful writing:

- **Introductory overview** Chapter 1, "Understanding Literature," presents an overview of some of the most important issues surrounding the study of literature, acquainting students with traditional literary themes as well as with the concept of the literary canon. The chapter also lays the groundwork for students' independent exploration of literary texts by discussing the processes of interpreting and evaluating literature, placing special emphasis on how readers' personal experiences affect meaning. Finally, the chapter examines the role of literary criticism and considers how critics' interpretations can help students expand their literary horizons.

- **Reading and Reacting questions** Reading and Reacting questions, including journal prompts, follow many selections throughout the text. These questions ask students to interpret and evaluate what they have read—sometimes encouraging them to make connections between the literary work being studied and other works in the text.

- **Critical Perspectives** Critical Perspective questions (included in most sets of Reading and Reacting questions) ask students to respond to analytical, interpretative, or evaluative comments that writers and critics have made about the work. This feature encourages students to apply their own critical thinking skills to literary criticism as well as to the work of literature itself.

- **Literary criticism appendix** The appendix, "Using Literary Criticism in Your Writing," explains and illustrates the key schools of literary criticism and shows how each can be applied to a typical student writing assignment inspired by a literary work.

- **Related Works** A Related Works section following the Reading and Reacting questions lists works linked (by theme, author, or genre) to the particular work under study. This feature encourages students to see connections between works by different writers, between works in different genres, or between two themes—connections they can explore in class discussion and in writing.

 ## A Full Package of Supplementary Materials

To support students and instructors who use the ninth edition of Compact *Literature: Reading, Reacting, Writing*, these ancillary materials are available from Cengage Learning:

- **Instructor's Resource Manual** A comprehensive instructor's manual provides all the materials necessary to support a variety of teaching styles. This resource includes discussion and activities for every short story, poem, and play in the anthology; a thematic table of contents; semester and quarter sample syllabi; and articles on the evolution of the literary canon and reader-response theory. In addition, many selections include a section called "Do Your Students Know?"—brief, entertaining notes that provide interesting, sometimes offbeat contextual information.

- **MindTap™ Literature** MindTap is a personalized teaching and learning experience with relevant assignments that guide students to analyze, apply, and improve thinking, allowing instructors to measure skills and outcomes with ease. By seamlessly integrating course material with videos, activities, apps, and much more, MindTap creates a unique learning path that fosters increased comprehension and efficiency.

 ## Acknowledgments

From start to finish, this book has been a true collaboration, not only with each other, but also with our students and colleagues. We have worked hard on this book, and many people have worked hard along with us.

We would like to begin by thanking our incredibly creative and talented Content Developer, Karen Mauk, who has always been there for us (and who we hope always will be there). She is one of a kind, and we are simply in awe of her abilities.

At Cengage, we thank Nicole Morinon, Product Team Manager; Kate Derrick, Product Manager; Leslie Taggart, Senior Content Developer; Erin Bosco, Associate Content Developer; Claire Branman, Product Assistant; Janine Tangney, Media Developer; and Michael Lepera, Content Project Manager. We also thank the team at Cenveo® Publisher Services, especially Karen Oemler, our talented Project Manager and Copyeditor.

We also very much appreciate the help we got on this project from William Coyle on the poetry selections and apparatus as well as the Instructor's Resource Manual and from Karen Mauk on updating the headnotes, footnotes, Cultural Contexts, and Critical Perspective questions.

We would like to thank the following reviewers of the ninth edition: Emory Abbott, Georgia Perimeter College; Lisa Angius, Farmingdale State College; Carolyn Ayers, Saint Mary's University of Minnesota; Alyce Baker, Lock Haven University of Pennsylvania; Annalisa Buerke, University of Northwestern—St. Paul; Robert Canipe, Catawba Valley Community College; Jill Channing, Mitchell Community College; Sheila Chase, Arkansas State University—Beebe; Sheryl Chisamore, SUNY—Ulster; Susan Chism, Greenville College; Ellen Feig, Bergen Community College; Joanne Gabel, Reading Area Community College; Barbara Goldstein, Hillsborough Community College; Joseph Granitto, Farmingdale State College; Michael Hedges, Horry-Georgetown Technical College; Margaret Hosty, Tarrant County College; Robert Hurd, Anne Arundel Community College; Kristin Jacobson, Richard Stockton College of New Jersey; Alyssa Johnson, Horry-Georgetown Technical College; Lisa Jones, Hillsborough Community College—Dale Mabry and Pasco- Hernando State College—West; Carol Kushner, Dutchess Community College; Pete Landino, Terra State Community College; Elizabeth Langemak, La Salle University; Richard Larschan, University of Massachusetts—Dartmouth; Dawn Lattin, Idaho State University; Andrea Laurencell Sheridan, SUNY—Orange; Kristin Le Veness, Nassau Community College; Angie Macri, Pulaski Technical College; Boyd Minner, Navarro College; Lisa Moslow, Erie Community College—North; Karen O'Donnell, Finger Lakes Community College; Paula Rash, Caldwell Community College and Technical Institute; Perimeter College; Joan Reeves, Northeast Alabama Community College; Shewanda Riley, Tarrant County College; Nancy Risch, Caldwell Community College and Technical Institute; Gregory Sargent, Quinsigamond Community College; James Scruton, Bethel University; Roy Seeger, University of South Carolina—Aiken; Amy Smith, Hilbert College; Susan St. Peters, Riverside City College; Karl Terryberry, Daemen College; Stephanie Tingley, Youngstown State University; Andrew Tomko, Bergen Community College; Heather Weiss, Technical College of the Lowcountry; Stephen Whited, Piedmont College; Winona Winkler Wendth, Quinsigamond Community College; and Kristy Wooten, Catawba Valley Community College.

We would also like to thank our families for being there when we needed them. And finally, we each thank the person on the other side of the ampersand for making our collaboration work one more time.

1 | A GUIDE TO WRITING ABOUT LITERATURE

CHAPTER 1

UNDERSTANDING LITERATURE

Westminster Bridge, London (1886) by Claude Thomas Stanfield Moore
Source: ©Fine Art Photographic Library/Corbis

 Imaginative Literature

Imaginative literature begins with a writer's need to convey a personal vision to readers. Consider, for example, how William Wordsworth uses language in these lines from his poem "Composed upon Westminster Bridge, September 3, 1802" (p. 1024):

> This City now doth, like a garment, wear
> The beauty of the morning; silent, bare,
> Ships, towers, domes, theatres, and temples lie
> Open unto the fields, and to the sky;
> All bright and glittering in the smokeless air.

Wordsworth does not try to present a picture of London that is topographically or sociologically accurate. Instead, by comparing the city at dawn to a person wearing a beautiful garment, he creates a striking picture that has its own kind of truth. By using a vivid, original comparison, the poet suggests the oneness of the city, nature, and himself.

Even when writers of imaginative literature use factual material—historical documents, newspaper stories, or personal experience, for example—their primary purpose is to present their own unique view of experience, one that has significance beyond the moment. (As the poet Ezra Pound said, "Literature is the news that *stays* news.") To convey their views of experience, these writers often manipulate facts—changing dates, creating characters and events, and inventing dialogue. For example, when Herman Melville wrote his nineteenth-century novella *Benito Cereno*, he drew many of his facts from an 1817 account of an actual slave revolt. In his story, he reproduces court records and uses plot details from this primary source—Amasa Delano's *Narrative of Voyages and Travels, in the Northern and Southern Hemispheres*—but he leaves out some incidents, and he adds material of his own. The result is an original work of literature. Wanting to do more than retell the original story, Melville used the factual material as "a skeleton of actual reality" on which he built a story that attacks the institution of slavery and examines the nature of truth.

Imaginative literature is more likely than other types of writing to include words chosen not only because they communicate the writer's ideas, but also because they are memorable. Using vivid imagery and evocative comparisons, writers of imaginative literature often stretch language to its limits. By relying on the multiple connotations of words and images, a work of imaginative literature encourages readers to see the possibilities of language and to move beyond the factual details of an event.

Even though imaginative literature can be divided into types called **genres**—fiction, poetry, and drama—the nature of literary genres varies greatly from culture to culture. In fact, some literary forms that Western readers take for granted are alien to other literary traditions. The sonnet, a fairly common poetic form in the West, is not a conventional literary form in Chinese or Arabic poetry. Similarly, the most popular theatrical entertainment in Japan since the mid-seventeenth century, the Kabuki play, has no counterpart in the West. (In a Kabuki play, which

© Geraint Lewis/Alamy

Kabuki performance of Shakespeare's *Twelfth Night*

includes stories, scenes, dances, music, acrobatics, and elaborate costumes and stage settings, all of the actors are men, some of whom play the parts of females. Many Kabuki plays have little plot and seem to be primarily concerned with spectacle. One feature of this form of drama is a walkway that extends from the stage through the audience to the back of the theater.)

Conventions of narrative organization and character development can also vary considerably from culture to culture, especially in literature derived from oral traditions. For example, narrative organization in some Native American stories (and, even more commonly, in some African stories) can be very different from what contemporary Western readers are accustomed to. Events may be arranged spatially instead of chronologically: first a story presents all the events that happened in one place, then it presents everything that happened in another location, and so on. Character development is also much less important in some traditional African and Native American stories than it is in modern short fiction. In fact, a character's name, description, and personality can change dramatically (and without warning) during the course of a story.

Despite such differences, the imaginative literature of all cultures has similar effects on readers: memorable characters, vivid descriptions, imaginative use of language, and compelling plots can fascinate and delight. Literature can take readers where they have never been before and, in so doing, can create a sense of adventure and wonder.

At another level, however, readers can find more than just pleasure or escape in literature. Beyond transporting readers out of their own lives and times, literature can enable them to see their lives and times more clearly. Whether a work of imaginative literature depicts a young girl as she experiences the disillusionment of adulthood for the first time, as in David Michael Kaplan's "Doe Season" (p. 472), or the thoughts and feelings of a soldier as he tries to come to terms with what he did during the Boer War, as in Thomas Hardy's "The Man He Killed," (p. 687), it can help readers to understand their own experiences and the experiences of others. In this sense, literature offers readers increased insight into the human condition. As the Chilean poet Pablo Neruda said, works of imaginative literature fulfill "the most ancient rites of our conscience in the awareness of being human and of believing in a common destiny."

 Conventional Themes

The **theme** of a work of literature—its central or dominant idea—is seldom stated explicitly. Instead, it is conveyed through the selection and arrangement of details; through the emphasis of certain words, events, or images; and through the actions and reactions of characters.

Although one central theme may dominate a literary work, many works explore a number of different themes or ideas. For example, the central theme of Mark Twain's *Adventures of Huckleberry Finn* might be the idea that an individual's innate sense of right and wrong is superior to society's artificial and sometimes unnatural values. The main character, Huck, gains a growing awareness of this idea by witnessing feuds, duels, and all manner of human folly. As a result, he makes a decision to help his friend Jim escape from slavery despite the fact that society, as well as his own conscience, condemns this action. However, *Huckleberry Finn* also examines other themes. Throughout his novel, Twain criticizes many of the ideas that prevailed in the pre–Civil War South, such as the racism and religious hypocrisy that pervaded the towns along the Mississippi.

A literary work can explore any theme; however, certain themes have become conventions—that is, they have reoccurred so often over the years that they have become familiar and accepted. One **conventional theme**—a character's loss of innocence—appears in the biblical story of Adam and Eve and later finds its way into works such as Nathaniel Hawthorne's 1835 short story "Young Goodman Brown" (p. 448) and James Joyce's 1914 short story "Araby" (p. 361). Another conventional theme—the conflict between an individual's values and the values of society—is examined in the ancient Greek play *Antigone* (p. 1484) by Sophocles. Almost two thousand years later, Norwegian playwright Henrik Ibsen deals with the same theme in *A Doll House* (p. 1138).

Other conventional themes examined in literary works include the individual's quest for spiritual enlightenment, the *carpe diem* ("seize the day") philosophy, the making of the artist, the nostalgia for a vanished past, the disillusionment of adulthood, the pain of love, the struggle of women for equality, the conflict between parents and children, the clash between civilization and the wilderness, the evils of unchecked ambition, the inevitability of fate, the impact of the past on the present, the conflict between human beings and machines, and the tension between the ideal and the actual realms of experience.

Many cultures explore similar themes, but writers from different cultures may develop these themes differently. A culture's history, a particular region's geography, or a country's social structure can suggest unique ways of developing conventional themes. In addition, the assumptions, concerns, values, ideals, and beliefs of a particular country or society—or of a particular group within that society—can help to determine the themes writers choose to explore and the manner in which they do so.

In American literature, for instance, familiar themes include the loss of innocence, rites of passage, childhood epiphanies, and the ability (or inability) to form relationships. American writers of color may use these themes to express their frustration with racism or to celebrate their

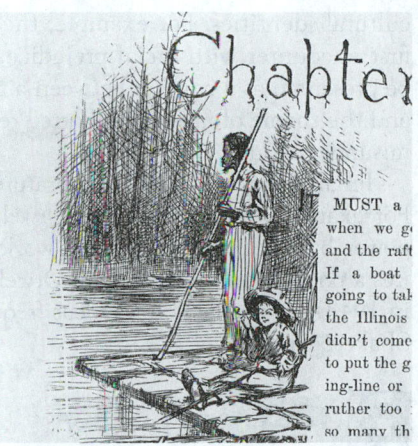

On the Raft, illustration from Mark Twain's *Adventures of Huckleberry Finn*
Source: Historical/Corbis

Detail of fresco showing expulsion of Adam and Eve from the Garden of Eden

© Iberfoto/The Image Works

cultural identities. For example, the theme of loss of innocence may be presented as a first encounter with racial prejudice; a conflict between the individual and society may be presented as a conflict between a minority view and the values of the dominant group; and the theme of failure or aborted relationships may be explored in a work about cultural misunderstandings.

Finally, modern works of literature sometimes treat conventional themes in new ways. For example, in *1984* George Orwell explores the negative consequences of unchecked power by creating a nightmare world in which the government controls and dehumanizes a population. Even though Orwell's novel is set in an imaginary future (it was written in 1948), its theme echoes ideas frequently examined in the plays of both Sophocles and Shakespeare.

 ## The Literary Canon

Originally, the term *canon* referred to the accepted list of books that made up the Christian Bible. More recently, the term **literary canon** has come to denote a group of works generally agreed upon by writers, teachers, and critics to be worth reading and studying. Over the years, as standards have changed, the definition of "good" literature has also changed, and the literary canon has been modified accordingly. For example, at various times, critics have characterized Shakespeare's plays as mundane, immoral, commonplace, and brilliant. The eighteenth-century critic Samuel Johnson said of Shakespeare that "in his comick scenes he is seldom very successful" and in tragedy "his performance seems constantly to be worse, as his labor is more." Many people find it difficult to believe that a writer whose name today is synonymous with great literature could ever have been judged so harshly. Like all aesthetic works, however, the plays of Shakespeare affect individuals in different periods of history and in different societies in different ways.

Some educators and literary scholars believe that the traditional literary canon, like a restricted club, arbitrarily admits some authors and excludes others. This fact is borne out, they say, by an examination of the literature curriculum that until recently was standard at many North American universities. This curriculum typically began with Homer, Plato, Dante, and Chaucer; progressed to Shakespeare, Milton, the eighteenth-century novel, the Romantics, and the Victorians; and ended with some of the "classics" of modern British and American literature. Most of the authors of these works are white and male, and their writing for the most part reflects Western values.

Missing from the literature courses in North American universities for many years were South American, African, and Asian writers. Students of American literature were not encouraged to consider the perspectives of women, of gay and lesbian writers, or of Latinos, Native Americans, or other ethnic or racial groups. During the past four decades, however, most universities have expanded the traditional canon by including more works by women, people of color, and writers from a variety of cultures. These additional works, studied alongside those representing the traditional canon, have opened up the curriculum and redefined the standards by which literature is judged.

One example of a literary work that challenged the traditional canon is "All about Suicide" by Luisa Valenzuela, an Argentinean writer. Currently, she is one of the most widely translated South American writers. This brief, shocking story is part of a large and growing body of literature from around the world that purposely violates our standard literary expectations to make its point—in this case, a point about the political realities of Argentina in the 1960s.

LUISA VALENZUELA (1938–   )

All about Suicide (1967)

Translated by Helen Lane

Ismael grabbed the gun and slowly rubbed it across his face. Then he pulled the trigger and there was a shot. Bang. One more person dead in the city. It's getting to be a vice. First he grabbed the revolver that was in a desk drawer, rubbed it gently across his face, put it to his temple, and pulled the trigger. Without saying a word. Bang. Dead.

Let's recapitulate: the office is grand, fit for a minister. The desk is ministerial too, and covered with a glass that must have reflected the scene, the shock. Ismael knew where the gun was, he'd hidden it there himself. So he didn't lose any time, all he had to do was open the right-hand drawer and stick his hand in. Then he got a good hold on it and rubbed it over his face with a certain pleasure before putting it to his temple and pulling the trigger. It was something almost sensual and quite unexpected. He hadn't even had time to think about it. A trivial gesture, and the gun had fired.

There's something missing: Ismael in the bar with a glass in his hand thinking over his future act and its possible consequences.

We must go back farther if we want to get at the truth: Ismael in the cradle crying because his diapers are dirty and nobody is changing him.

Not that far.

Ismael in the first grade fighting with a classmate who'll one day become a minister, his friend, a traitor.

No, Ismael in the ministry without being able to tell what he knew, forced to be silent. Ismael in the bar with the glass (his third) in his hand, and the irrevocable decision: better death.

Ismael pushing the revolving door at the entrance to the building, pushing the swinging door leading to the office section, saying good morning to the guard, opening the door of his office. Once in his office, seven steps to his desk. Terror, the act of opening the drawer, taking out the revolver, and rubbing it across his face, almost a single gesture and very quick. The act of putting it to his temple and pulling the trigger—another act, immediately following the previous one. Bang. Dead. And Ismael coming out of his office (the other man's office, the minister's) almost relieved, even though he can predict what awaits him.

*   *   *

In "All about Suicide," the author not only undercuts the reader's assumptions about the story but also about fiction itself. Is the story about suicide, as the title implies, or is it about something else? Should readers trust their preconceptions about the conventions of fiction, or should they begin to question the "rules"? By addressing questions such as these, Venezuela expands the boundaries of literature and invites readers to abandon easy assumptions about their world and their place within it.

5

Certainly canon revision is not without problems—for example, the possibility of including a work more for political or sociological reasons than for its literary merit. Nevertheless, if the debate about the literary canon has accomplished anything, it has revealed that the canon is not fixed and that many works formerly excluded—African American slave narratives and eighteenth-century women's diaries, for example—deserve to be read.

 ## Interpreting Literature

When you **interpret** a literary work, you explore its possible meanings. One commonly held idea about reading a literary work is that its meaning lies buried somewhere within it, waiting to be unearthed. This reasoning suggests that a clever reader has only to discover the author's intent to find out what a story or poem means, and that the one actual meaning of a work is hidden "between the lines," unaffected by a reader's experiences or interpretations. More recently, however, a different model of the reading process—one that takes into consideration the reader as well as the work he or she is interpreting—has emerged.

Many contemporary critics see the reading process as **interactive**. In other words, meaning is created through the reader's interaction with a text. Thus, the meaning of a particular work comes alive in the imagination of an individual reader, and no reader can determine a work's meaning without considering his or her own reaction to the text. Meaning, therefore, is created partly by what is supplied by a work and partly by what is supplied by the reader.

The most obvious thing a work supplies is **facts**, the information that enables a reader to follow the plot of a story, the action of a play, or the development of a poem. The work itself will provide factual details about the setting; about the characters' names, ages, and appearances; about the sequence of events; and about the emotions and attitudes of a poem's speaker, a story's narrator, or the characters in a play or story. This factual information cannot be ignored: if a play's stage directions identify its setting as nineteenth-century Norway or the forest of Arden, that is where the play is set.

In addition to facts, a work also conveys the social, political, class, and gender **attitudes** of the writer. Thus, a work may have an overt feminist or working-class bias or a subtle (or obvious) political agenda; it may confirm or challenge contemporary attitudes; it may communicate a writer's nostalgia for a vanished past or outrage at a corrupt present; it may take an elitist, distant view of characters and events or present a sympathetic perspective. A reader's understanding of these attitudes will contribute to his or her interpretation of the work.

Finally, a work also includes **assumptions** about literary conventions. A poet, for example, may have definite ideas about whether a poem should be rhymed or unrhymed or about whether a particular subject is appropriate or inappropriate for poetic treatment. Therefore, a knowledge of the literary conventions of a particular period or the preferences of a particular writer can provide a starting point for your interpretation of literature.

As a reader, you bring to a work your own **personal perspectives**. Your experiences, your beliefs, your ideas about the issues discussed in the work, and your assumptions about literature color your interpretations. In fact, nearly every literary work has somewhat different meanings for different people, depending on their age, gender, nationality, political and religious beliefs, ethnic background, social and economic class, education, knowledge, and personal experiences. Depending on your religious beliefs, for instance, you can react to a passage from the Old Testament as literal truth, symbolic truth, or fiction. Depending on your race, where you live, your biases, and the nature of your experience, a story about racial discrimination can strike you as accurate and realistic, exaggerated and unrealistic, or understated and restrained.

In a sense, then, the process of determining meaning is like a conversation, one in which both you and the text have a voice. Sometimes, by clearly dictating the terms of the discussion, the text determines the direction of the conversation; at other times, by using your knowledge and experience to interpret the text, you dominate. Thus, because every reading of a literary work is actually an interpretation, it is a mistake to look for a single "correct" reading.

The 1923 poem "Stopping by Woods on a Snowy Evening," by the American poet Robert Frost, illustrates how a single work can have more than one interpretation.

ROBERT FROST (1874–1963)

Stopping by Woods on a Snowy Evening (1923)

Whose woods these are I think I know.
His house is in the village though;
He will not see me stopping here
To watch his woods fill up with snow.

My little horse must think it queer   5
To stop without a farmhouse near
Between the woods and frozen lake
The darkest evening of the year.

He gives his harness bells a shake
To ask if there is some mistake.   10
The only other sound's the sweep
Of easy wind and downy flake.

The woods are lovely, dark and deep,
But I have promises to keep,
And miles to go before I sleep,   15
And miles to go before I sleep.

Readers may interpret the poem as being about the inevitability of death, as suggesting that the poet is tired or world weary, or as making a comment about duty and the need to persevere or about the conflicting pulls of life and art. Beyond these possibilities, readers' own associations of snow with quiet and sadness could lead them to define the mood of the poem as sorrowful or melancholy. Information about Robert Frost's life or his ideas about poetry could add to readers' understanding of the poem, and they might even develop ideas about the poem that are quite different from the poet's. In fact, on several occasions, Frost himself gave strikingly different—even contradictory—interpretations of "Stopping by Woods on a Snowy Evening," sometimes insisting that the poem had no hidden meaning and at other times saying that it required a good deal of explication. (Literary critics also disagree about its meaning.) When reading a work of literature, then, keep in mind that the meaning of the

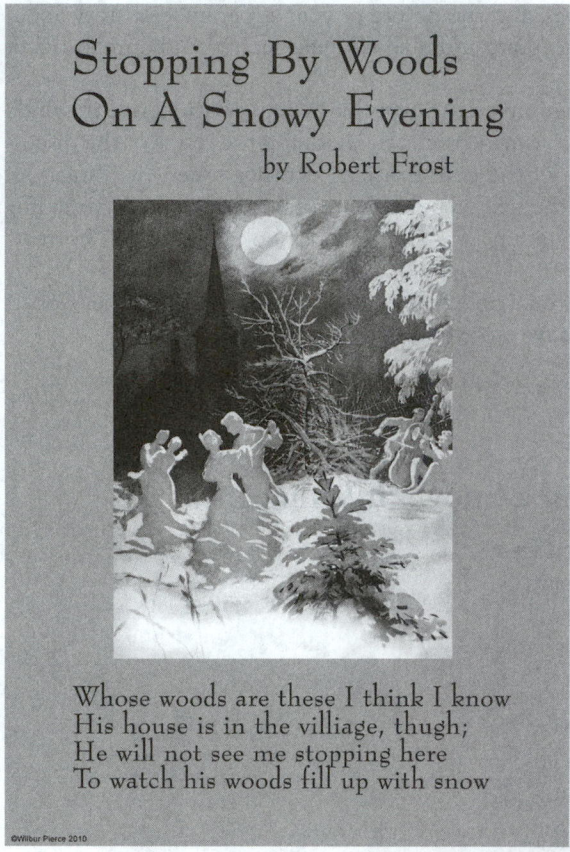

Stopping By Woods
On A Snowy Evening
by Robert Frost

Whose woods are these I think I know
His house is in the villiage, thugh;
He will not see me stopping here
To watch his woods fill up with snow

©Wilbur Pierce 2010

Opening pages from Susan Jeffers's illustrated children's book
Stopping by Woods on a Snowy Evening (1978)
akg-images/Universal Images Group

text is not fixed. Your best strategy is to open yourself up to the text's many possibilities and explore the full range of your responses.

Although no single reading of a literary work is "correct," some readings are more defensible than others. Like a scientific theory, a literary interpretation must have a basis in fact, and the text supplies the facts against which your interpretation should be judged. For example, after you read Shirley Jackson's "The Lottery" (p. 419), a 1948 short story in which a randomly chosen victim is stoned to death by her neighbors, it would be reasonable to conclude that the ceremonial aspects of the lottery suggest a pagan ritual. Your understanding of what a pagan ritual is, combined with your observation that a number of details in the text suggest ancient fertility rites, might lead you to this conclusion. Another possibility is that "The Lottery" provides a commentary on mob psychology. The way characters reinforce one another's violent tendencies lends support to this interpretation. However, the interpretation that the ritual of the lottery is a thinly veiled attack on the death penalty would be difficult to support. Certainly a character in the story is killed, but she is not accused of a crime, nor is she tried or convicted; in fact, the killing is random and seemingly without motivation. Still, although seeing "The Lottery" as a comment on the death penalty may be far-fetched, this interpretation could be a starting point. A second, closer reading of the story would allow you to explore other, more plausible, interpretations.

As you read, do not be afraid to develop unusual or creative interpretations. A **safe reading** of a work is likely to result in a dull essay that simply states the obvious, but an aggressive or **strong reading** of a work—one that challenges generally held assumptions—can lead to interesting and intellectually challenging conclusions. Even if your reading differs from established critics' interpretations, you should not automatically assume it has no merit. Your own special knowledge of the material discussed in the text—a regional practice, an ethnic custom, a personal experience—may give you a unique perspective from which to view the work. Whatever interpretation you make, be sure that you support it with specific references to the text. If your interpretation is based on your own experiences, explain those experiences and relate them clearly to the work you are discussing. As long as you can make a reasonable case, you have the right (and perhaps the obligation) to present your ideas. By doing so, you may give your fellow students and your instructor new insight into the work.

NOTE Keep in mind that some interpretations are *not* reasonable. You may contribute ideas based on your own perspectives, but you cannot ignore or contradict evidence in the text to suit your own biases. As you read and reread a text, continue to question and reexamine your judgments. The conversation between you and the text should be a dialogue, not a monologue or a shouting match.

Evaluating Literature

When you **evaluate** a work of literature, you do more than interpret it; you make a judgment about it. You reach conclusions not simply about whether the work is "good" or "bad," but also about how effectively the work presents itself to you, the reader. To evaluate a work, you **analyze** it, breaking it apart and considering its individual elements. As you evaluate a work of literature, remember that different works are designed to fulfill different needs—entertainment, education, or enlightenment, for example. Before you begin to evaluate a work, be sure you understand its purpose; then, follow these guidelines:

- *Consider how various literary elements function within a work.* Fiction may be divided into chapters and use flashbacks and foreshadowing; plays may be divided into scenes and acts and include dialogue and special staging techniques; poems may be divided into stanzas and use poetic devices such as rhyme and meter. Understanding the choices writers make about these and other literary elements can help you form judgments about a work. For example, why does Alberto Alvaro Ríos use a first-person narrator in his story "The Secret Lion" (p. 180)? Would the story have been different had it been told in the third person by a narrator who was not a character in the story? How does unusual staging contribute to the effect Milcha Sanchez-Scott achieves in her play *The Cuban Swimmer* (p. 1454)? How would a more realistic setting change the play? Naturally, you cannot focus on every element of a particular story, poem, or play. But you can and should focus on those aspects that determine your responses to a work. For this reason, elements such as the unusual stanzaic form in E. E. Cummings's poem "Buffalo Bill's" (p. 971) and the very specific stage directions in Arthur Miller's play *Death of a Salesman* (p. 1262) should be of special interest to you.

    As you read, then, you should ask questions. Do the characters in a short story seem real, or do they seem like cardboard cutouts? Are the images in a poem original and thought provoking, or are they clichéd? Are the stage directions of a play minimal or very detailed? The answers to these and other questions will help you to shape your evaluation.

- *Consider whether the literary elements of a work interact to achieve a common goal.* Good writers are like master cabinetmakers: their skill disguises the actual work that has gone into the process of creation. Thus, the elements of a well-crafted literary work often fit together in a way that conceals the craft of the writer. Consider the subtlety of the following stanza from the 1862 poem "Echo" by Christina Rossetti:

> Come to me in the silence of the night;
>   Come to me in the speaking silence of a dream;
> Come with soft round cheeks and eyes as bright
>   As sunlight on a stream;
>   Come back in tears,
> O memory, hope, love of finished years.

Throughout this stanza, Rossetti repeats words ("Come to me.../ Come with soft.../ Come back...") and initial consonants ("speaking silence"; "sunlight on a stream"), using sound to create an almost hypnotic mood. The rhyme scheme (*night/bright, dream/stream,* and *tears/years*) reinforces the mood by establishing a musical under-current that extends throughout the poem. Thus, this stanza is effective because its repeated words and sounds work together to create a single lyrical effect.

The chorus in *Oedipus the King* by Sophocles (p. 1467) also illustrates how the elements of a well-crafted work of literature function together. In ancient Greece, plays were performed by masked male actors who played both male and female roles. A chorus of fifteen men remained in a central circle called the *orchestra* and com-mented on and reacted to the action taking place around them. The chorus expresses the judgment of the community and acts as a moral guide for the audience. Once modern audiences grow accustomed to the presence of the chorus, it becomes an important part of the play. It neither distracts the audience nor intrudes on the action. In fact, eliminating the chorus would diminish the impact of the play.

- **Consider whether a work reinforces or calls into question your ideas about the world.** Works of **popular fiction**—those aimed at a mass audience—usually do little more than reassure readers that what they believe is correct. Catering to people's desires (for wealth or success, for example), to their prejudices, or to their fears, these works serve as escapes from life. More serious fiction, however, often goes against the grain, challenging cherished beliefs and leading readers to reexamine long-held assumptions. For instance, in the 1957 short story "Big Black Good Man" (p. 318), Richard Wright's protagonist, a night porter at a hotel, struggles with his consum-ing yet irrational fear of a "big black" sailor and with his inability to see beyond the sailor's size and color. Only at the end of the story do many readers see that they, like the night porter, have stereotyped and dehumanized the sailor.

- **Consider whether a work is intellectually challenging.** The extended comparison between the legs of a compass and two people in love in "A Valediction: Forbidding Mourning" (p. 768) by the seventeenth-century English poet John Donne, illustrates how effectively an image can communicate complex ideas to readers. Compressed into this comparison are ideas about the perfection of love, the pain of enforced separa-tion, and the difference between sexual and spiritual love. As intellectually challeng-ing as this extended comparison is, it is nonetheless accessible to the careful reader. After all, many people have used a compass to draw a circle and, therefore, are able to understand the relationship between the two legs of the compass (and the two lovers).

A fine line exists, however, between works that are intellectually challenging and those that are intentionally obscure. An intellectually challenging work requires effort from readers to unlock ideas that enrich and expand their understanding of themselves and the world. Although complex, the work gives readers a sense that they have gained something by putting forth the effort to interpret it. An intentionally obscure work exists solely to display a writer's erudition or intellectual idiosyncrasies. Allusions to other works and events are so numerous and confusing that the work may seem more like a private code than an effort to enlighten readers. Consider the following excerpt from "Canto LXXVI" by the twentieth-century American poet Ezra Pound:

> Le Paradis n'est pas artificiel
>> States of mind are inexplicable to us.
>> δακρυων δακρυων δακρυων
> L. P. gli onesti
>>> J'ai eu pitié des autres
> probablement pas assez, and at moments that suited my own
>> convenience
>>>> Le paradis n'est pas artificiel,
>>>> l'enfer non plus.
> Came Eurus as comforter
> and at sunset la pastorella dei suini
>> driving the pigs home, benecomata dea
>>> under the two-winged cloud
>>> as of less and more than a day

This passage contains lines in French, Greek, and Italian, as well as a reference to Eurus, the ancient Greek personification of the east wind, and the initials L. P. (Loomis Pound?). It demands a lot from readers; the question is whether the reward is worth the effort.

No hard-and-fast rule exists for determining whether a work is intellectually challenging or simply obscure. Just as a poem has no fixed meaning, it also has no fixed value. Some readers would say that the passage from "Canto LXXVI" is good, even great, poetry. Others would argue that those lines do not yield enough pleasure and insight to justify the effort needed to analyze them. As a reader, you must draw your own conclusions and justify them in a clear and reasonable way. Do not assume that just because a work is difficult, it is obscure. (Nor should you assume that all difficult works are great literature or that all accessible literature is trivial.) Some of the most beautiful and inspiring literary works demand a great deal of effort. Most readers would agree, however, that the time spent exploring such works yields tremendous rewards.

- *Consider whether a work gives you pleasure.* One of the primary reasons literature endures is that it gives readers enjoyment. As subjective as this assessment is, it is a starting point for critical judgment. When readers ask themselves what they liked about a work, why they liked it, or what they learned, they begin the process of evaluation. Although this process is largely uncritical, it can lead to an involvement with the work and to a valid critical response. When you encounter great literature, with all its complexities, you may lose sight of the idea of literature as a source of pleasure. But literature should touch you on a deep emotional or intellectual level. If it does not—despite its technical perfection—it fails to achieve one of its primary aims.

Using Literary Criticism

Sometimes your personal reactions and knowledge cannot give you enough insight into a literary work. For example, archaic language, references to mythology, historical allusions, and textual inconsistencies can make reading a work difficult. Similarly, an intellectual or philosophical movement such as Darwinism, Marxism, naturalism, structuralism, or feminism may influence a work, and if this is the case, you need some knowledge of the movement before you can interpret the work. In addition, you may not have the background to appreciate the technical or historical dimensions of a work. To increase your understanding, you may choose to read **literary criticism**—books and journal articles written by experts who describe, analyze, interpret, or evaluate a work of literature (see the appendix: "Using Literary Criticism in Your Writing"). Reading literary criticism enables you to expand your knowledge of a particular work and to participate in ongoing critical discussions about literature. In a sense, when you read literary criticism, you become part of a community of scholars who share their ideas and who are connected to one another through their writing.

Literary criticism is written by experts, but this does not mean you must always agree with it. You have to evaluate literary criticism just as you would any new opinion that you encounter. Not all criticism is sound, timely, or responsible (and not all literary criticism is pertinent to your assignment or useful for your purposes). Some critical comments will strike you as plausible; others will seem unfounded or biased.

Quite often, two critics will reach strikingly different conclusions about the quality or significance of the same work or writer, or they will interpret a character, a symbol, or even the entire work quite differently. The Fiction Casebook that begins on page 503 includes articles in which critics disagree in just this way. Although critics may disagree, their conflicting ideas can help you reach your own conclusions about a work. It is up to you to sort out the various opinions and decide which have merit and which do not.

NOTE If you use literary criticism in your own writing, keep in mind that your ideas, not the ideas of the critics, should dominate the discussion. The critical opinions you include should support your points and strengthen your argument. Also, remember that you must document all words and ideas that you borrow from your sources. If you do not, you will be committing **plagiarism**—presenting another person's words or ideas as if they were your own. (See Chapter 7 for information on documenting sources and avoiding plagiarism.)

✔ **CHECKLIST Evaluating Literary Criticism**

To help you evaluate literary criticism, consider the following questions:

▪ What is the main point of the text you are reading?

▪ Does the critic supply enough examples to support his or her conclusions?

- Does the critic acknowledge and refute the most obvious arguments against his or her position?

- Does the critic ignore any information in the text that might call his or her conclusions into question?

- Does the critic present historical information? biographical information? literary information? How does this information shed light on the work or works being discussed?

- Does the critic hold any beliefs that might interfere with his or her critical judgment?

- Does the critic slant the facts, or does he or she approach the text critically and objectively?

- Does the critic support conclusions with references to other sources? Does the critic provide documentation and a list of works cited?

- Does the critic take into consideration the most important critical books and articles on his or her subject? Are there works that should have been mentioned but were not?

- Do other critics mention the source you are reading? Do they agree or disagree with its conclusions?

- Is the critic identified with a particular critical school of thought—deconstruction or Marxism, for example? What perspective does this school of thought provide?

- Is the critic well known and respected?

- Is the critical work's publication date of any significance?

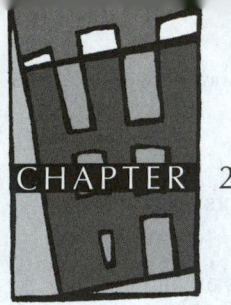

CHAPTER 2

READING AND WRITING ABOUT LITERATURE

 Reading Literature

Much of the time, reading is a passive process; readers expect the text to give them everything they need, and they do not expect to contribute much to the reading process. In contrast, **active reading** means participating in the reading process: thinking about what you read, asking questions, challenging ideas, and forming judgments. Active reading is excellent preparation for the discussion and writing you will do in college literature classes. And, because it helps you understand and appreciate the works you read, active reading will continue to be of value to you long after your formal classroom study of literature has ended.

Previewing

You begin active reading by **previewing** a work to get a general idea of what to look for later on, when you read it more carefully.

Start previewing by observing the work's most obvious visual characteristics. How long is a short story? How many acts and scenes does a play have? Is a poem divided into stanzas? The answers to these and similar questions will help you begin to notice more subtle aspects of the work's form. For example, previewing may reveal that a contemporary short story is presented entirely in a question-and-answer format, that it is organized as diary entries, or that it is divided into sections by headings. Previewing may identify poems that seem to lack formal structure, such as E. E. Cummings's unconventional "l(a" (p. 659); poems written in traditional forms (such as **sonnets**) or in experimental forms, such as Richard Blanco's **prose poem** "Mexican Almuerzo in New England" (p. 843); or **concrete poems,** such as George Herbert's "Easter Wings" (p. 847). Your awareness of these and other distinctive features at this point may help you gain insight into a work later on.

Perhaps the most distinctive visual element of a work is its title. Not only can the title give you a general idea of what the work is about, as straightforward titles like "Miss Brill" and "The Cask of Amontillado" do, but it can also call attention to a word or phrase that emphasizes an important idea. For example, the title of Amy Tan's short story "Two Kinds" (p. 639) refers to two kinds of daughters—Chinese and American—identifying the two perspectives that create the story's conflict. A title can also be an allusion to another work. Thus, *The Sound and the Fury*, the title of a novel by William Faulkner, alludes to a speech from Shakespeare's *Macbeth* that reinforces a major theme of the novel. Finally, a title can introduce a symbol that will gain meaning in the course of a work—as the quilt does in Alice Walker's "Everyday Use" (p. 426).

Other visual elements—such as paragraphing, capitalization, italics, and punctuation—can also provide clues about how to read a work. In William Faulkner's short story "Barn Burning" (p. 335), for instance, previewing would help you to notice passages in italic type, indicating the protagonist's thoughts, which occasionally interrupt the narrator's story.

Finally, previewing can enable you to identify some of the more obvious structural features of a work—how long a story is, how many acts a play has, or the shape of a poem, for example. Such features may or may not be important; at this stage, your goal is to observe, not to analyze or evaluate.

Previewing is a useful strategy not because it provides answers but because it suggests questions to ask later, as you read more closely. For instance, *why* does Faulkner use italics in "Barn Burning," and *why* does Herbert shape his poem like a pair of wings? Elements such as those described above will gain significance as you read more carefully.

Highlighting

When you read a work closely, you will notice additional, more subtle, elements that you may want to examine further. At this point, you should begin **highlighting**—physically marking the text to identify key words or details and to note relationships among ideas.

For example, you might notice that particular words or phrases are repeated, as in Tim O'Brien's short story "The Things They Carried" (p. 392), in which the word *carried* appears again and again. Because this word appears so frequently, and because it appears at key points in the story, it helps to reinforce a key theme: that soldiers carry heavy burdens and responsibilities in wartime. Repeated words and phrases are particularly important in poetry. In Dylan Thomas's "Do not go gentle into that good night" (p. 891), for example, the repetition of two of the poem's nineteen lines four times each enhances the poem's rhythmic, almost monotonous, cadence. As you read, highlight your text to identify such repeated words and phrases. Later, you can consider *why* these elements are repeated.

During the highlighting stage, you might also pay particular attention to **patterns of imagery** that can help you to interpret the work. When highlighting Robert Frost's "Stopping by Woods on a Snowy Evening" (p. 9), for instance, you might identify the related images of silence, cold, and darkness. Later on, you can consider their significance.

✔ **CHECKLIST   Using Highlighting Symbols**

When you highlight a text, try these strategies:

- Underline important ideas.
- Box or circle words, phrases, or images that you want to think more about.
- Put question marks beside confusing passages, unfamiliar references, or words that need to be defined.
- Circle related words, ideas, or images and draw lines or arrows to connect them.

continued on next page

- Number incidents that occur in sequence.
- Mark a key portion of the text with a vertical line in the margin.
- Star particularly important ideas.

   The following poem by Julia Alvarez has been highlighted by a student preparing to write about it. Notice how the student uses highlighting symbols to identify key ideas and patterns that she plans to examine later.

JULIA ALVAREZ (1950–   )

Dusting   (1984)

Each morning I wrote my name
On the dusty cabinet, then crossed
The dining table in script, scrawled
In capitals on the backs of chairs,
Practicing signatures like scales ?   5
While mother followed, squirting
Linseed from a burping can
Into a crumpled-up flannel.

She erased my fingerprints
From the bookshelf and rocker,   10
Polished mirrors on the desk
Scribbled with my alphabets.
My name was swallowed in the towel
With which she jeweled the table tops.
The grain surfaced in the oak   15
And the pine grew luminous.
But I refused with every mark
To be like her, anonymous.

The student boxes and stars words that she thinks are important ("polished" and "swallows"). In addition, she boxes a simile ("like scales") that she wants to think more about. She also circles two words ("erased" and "anonymous") that she believes express an important theme and draws an arrow to connect them. Finally, she underlines what she tentatively thinks are the poem's key ideas. When she rereads her poem, her highlighting will make it easier for her to react to and interpret the poem's ideas.

Annotating

As you highlight a text, you also **annotate** it, recording your reactions in the form of marginal notes. In these notes, you may define new words, identify **allusions** and patterns of language or imagery, summarize key events, list a work's possible themes, suggest a character's motivation, examine the possible significance of a particular symbol, or record questions that occur to you as you read. Ideally, your annotations will help you find ideas to write about.

The following paragraph from John Updike's 1961 short story "A&P" (p. 238) was highlighted and annotated by a student in an Introduction to Literature course who was responding to the question, "Why does Sammy really quit his job?"

Lengel sighs and begins to look very patient and old and gray. He's been a friend of my parents for years. "Sammy, you don't want to do this to your Mom and Dad," he tells me. It's true, I don't. But it seems to me that once you begin a gesture it's fatal not to go through with it. I fold the apron, "Sammy" stitched in red on the pocket, and put it on the counter, and drop the bow tie on top of it. The bow tie is theirs, if you've ever wondered. "You'll feel this for the rest of your life," Lengel* says, and I know that's true, too, but remembering how he made the pretty girl blush makes me so scrunchy inside I punch the No Sale tab and the machine whirs "pee-pul" and the drawer splats out. One advantage to this scene taking place in summer, I can follow this up with a clean exit, there's no fumbling around getting your coat and galoshes, I just saunter into the electric eye in my white shirt that my mother ironed the night before, and the door heaves itself open, and outside the sunshine is skating around on the asphalt.

Margin annotations:

Action isn't the Result of thought.

Sammy Reacts to the girl's embar-Rassment.

Need foR a clean exit— Romantic idea.

→ Romantic cowboy, but his mother iRons his shiRt (iRony).

Because the instructor had discussed the story in class and given students a specific assignment, these annotations are quite focused. In addition to highlighting important information, the student notes her reactions to the story and tries to interpret the main character's actions.

Sometimes, however, you annotate a work before you have decided on a topic. In fact, the process of reading and responding to the text can help you find a topic to write about. If you don't yet have a topic, your annotations are likely to be somewhat unfocused, so you will probably need to make additional annotations when your essay's direction is clearer.

 ## Writing about Literature

Writing about literature—or about anything else—is an idiosyncratic process during which many activities occur at once: as you write, you think of ideas; as you think of ideas, you clarify the focus of your essay; and as you clarify your focus, you reshape your paragraphs and sentences and refine your word choice. Even though this process may sound disorganized, it has three distinct stages: *planning, drafting,* and *revising and editing.*

Planning an Essay

Considering Your Audience

Sometimes you write primarily for yourself—for example, when you write a journal entry. At other times, you write for others. As you write an essay, consider the special requirements of your **audience**. Is your audience your classmates or your instructor? Can you assume your readers are familiar with your essay's topic and with any technical terms you will use, or should you include brief plot summaries or definitions of key terms? If your audience is your instructor, remember that he or she is a representative of a larger academic audience that expects accurate information, logical arguments, and a certain degree of stylistic fluency—as well as standard English and correct grammar, mechanics, and spelling. In addition, your instructor expects you to support your statements with specific information, to express yourself clearly and unambiguously, and to document your sources. In short, your instructor wants to see how clearly you think and whether you are able to arrange your ideas into a well-organized, coherent essay.

In addition to being a member of a general academic audience, your instructor is also a member of a particular community of scholars—in this case, those who study literature. By writing about literature, you engage in a dialogue with this community. For this reason, you need to follow certain specific **conventions**—procedures that by habitual use have become accepted practice. Many of the conventions that apply specifically to writing about literature—matters of style, format, and the like—are discussed in this book. (The checklist on p. 31 addresses some of these conventions.)

Understanding Your Purpose

Sometimes you write with a single **purpose** in mind. At other times, you may have more than one purpose. In general terms, you may write for any of the following three reasons:

1. *Writing to respond*   When you write to **respond**, your goal is to discover and express your reactions to a work. To record your responses, you engage in relatively informal

activities, such as brainstorming and journal writing (see pp. 22–23). As you write, you explore your own ideas, forming and re-forming your impressions of the work.

2. *Writing to interpret*   When you write to **interpret**, your aim is to explain a work's possible meanings. As you interpret a work of literature, you may summarize, give examples, or compare and contrast the work to other works or to your own experiences. Then, you may go on to analyze the work: as you discuss each of its elements, you put complex statements into your own words, define difficult concepts, and place ideas in context.

3. *Writing to evaluate*   When you write to **evaluate**, your purpose is to assess a work's literary merits. You may consider not only its aesthetic appeal but also its ability to retain that appeal over time and across national or cultural boundaries. As you write, you use your own critical sense and the opinions of experts to help you make judgments about the work.

 When you write a **literary argument**, your purpose is to **persuade**. See Chapter 5.

Choosing a Topic

When you write an essay about literature, you develop and support an idea about one or more literary works. Before you begin writing, you should make certain that you understand your assignment. Do you know how much time you have to complete your essay? Are you expected to rely on your own ideas, or are you able to consult outside sources? Is your essay to focus on a specific work or on a particular element of literature? Do you have to write on an assigned topic, or are you free to choose a topic? About how long should your essay be? Do you understand exactly what the assignment is asking you to do? Do you know what format to use?

Sometimes your assignment limits your options by telling you what you should discuss:

- Analyze Thomas Hardy's use of irony in his poem "The Man He Killed."
- Discuss Hawthorne's use of allegory in his short story "Young Goodman Brown."
- Explain Nora's actions at the end of Ibsen's *A Doll House*.

At other times, your instructor may give you few guidelines other than an essay's required length and format. In such situations, when you must choose a topic on your own, you can often find a topic by brainstorming or by writing journal entries. As you engage in these activities, keep in mind that you have many options to choose from:

- You can **explicate** a poem or a passage of a play or short story, doing a close reading and analyzing the text.
- You can **compare two works** of literature. (The Related Works lists that follow many of the selections in this book suggest possible connections.)
- You can **compare two characters** or discuss some trait those characters share.
- You can **trace a common theme**—jealousy, revenge, power, coming of age—in two or more works.
- You can **discuss a common subject**—war, love, nature—in two or more works.

- You can **analyze a single literary element** in one or more works—for instance, plot, point of view, or character development.
- You can **focus on a single aspect** of a literary element, such as the use of flashbacks, the effect of a shifting narrative perspective, or the role of a minor character.
- You can **apply a critical theory** to a work of literature—for instance, a feminist perspective to Tillie Olsen's "I Stand Here Ironing" (p. 299).
- You can **consider a work's cultural context**, examining connections between an issue treated in a work of literature—for instance, racism in Ralph Ellison's "Battle Royal" (p. 287) or postpartum psychosis in Charlotte Perkins Gilman's "The Yellow Wallpaper" (p. 379)—and that same issue as it is treated in professional journals or in the popular press.
- You can **examine some aspect of history or biography** and consider its relationship to a literary work—for instance, the influence of World War I on Wilfred Owen's poems.
- You can **explore a problem within a work and propose a possible solution**—for example, consider Montresor's possible motives for killing Fortunato in Edgar Allan Poe's "The Cask of Amontillado" (p. 328) and suggest the most likely one.
- You can **compare fiction and film**, exploring similarities and differences between a literary work and a film version of the work—for example, the different endings in Joyce Carol Oates's short story "Where Are You Going, Where Have You Been?" (p. 506) and *Smooth Talk*, the film version of the story.

Finding Something to Say

Once you have a topic, you have to find something to say about it. The ideas you came up with as you highlighted and annotated can help you formulate a statement that will be the central idea of your essay and will help you find material that can support that statement.

You can use a variety of strategies to find supporting material:

- You can **freewrite**—that is, write on a topic for a given period of time without pausing to consider style, structure, or content.
- You can discuss ideas with others—friends, classmates, instructors, parents, and so on.
- You can do research, either in print sources or online.

Two additional strategies—*brainstorming* and *keeping a journal*—are especially helpful at this stage of the writing process.

Brainstorming   When you **brainstorm**, you record ideas—single words, phrases, or sentences (in the form of statements or questions)—as they occur to you, moving as quickly as possible. Your starting point may be a general assignment, a particular work (or works) of literature, or a specific topic. You can brainstorm at any stage of the writing process—alone or with other students—and you can repeat this activity as often as you like.

A student preparing to write an essay on the relationships between children and parents in four poems brainstormed about each poem. The following excerpt from her notes shows her preliminary reactions to one of the four poems, Adrienne Rich's "A Woman Mourned by Daughters" (p. 890):

(Memory:) then and now

Then: leaf, straw, dead insect (= light);

ignored

Now: swollen, puffed up, weight (= heavy);

focus of attention controls their

movements.

＊ Kitchen = a "universe"

(Teaspoons, goblets, etc.) = concrete

representations of mother; also =

obligations, responsibilities (like

plants and father)

(weigh on them, keep them under her spell)

Milestones of past: weddings, being fed as

children, "You breathe upon us now"

PARADOX? (Dead, she breathes, has weight,

fills house and sky. Alive, she was a dead

insect, no one paid attention to her.)

Keeping a Journal You can record ideas in a journal (a notebook, a small notepad, or a computer file)—and, later, you can use these ideas in your essay. In a **journal**, you expand your marginal annotations, recording your responses to works you have read, noting questions, exploring emerging ideas, experimenting with possible essay topics, trying to paraphrase or summarize difficult concepts, or speculating about a work's ambiguities. A journal is the place to take chances, to try out ideas that may initially seem frivolous or irrelevant; here you can write until connections become clear or ideas crystallize.

As he prepared to write an essay analyzing the role of Jim—the "gentleman caller" who is invited to meet Laura, the shy, lonely sister of the protagonist in Tennessee Williams's 1945 play *The Glass Menagerie*—a student explored ideas in the following journal entry.

When he tells Laura that being disappointed is not the same as being discouraged, and that he's disappointed but not discouraged, Jim reveals his role as a symbol of the power of newness and change—a "bulldozer" that will clear out whatever is in its path, even delicate people like Laura. But the fact that he is disappointed shows Jim's human side. He has run into problems since high school, and these problems have blocked his progress toward a successful future. Working at the warehouse, Jim needs Tom's friendship to remind him of what he used to be (and what he still can be?), and this shows his insecurity. He isn't as sure of himself as he seems to be.

Seeing Connections

As you review your notes, you try to discover patterns—to see repeated images, similar characters, recurring words and phrases, and interrelated themes or ideas. Identifying these patterns can help you to decide which points to make in your essay and what information you will use to support these points.

A student preparing an essay about D. H. Lawrence's short story "The Rocking-Horse Winner" (p. 484) made the following list of related ideas.

Secrets
   Mother can't feel love
   Paul gambles
   Paul gives mother money
   Family lives beyond means
   Paul gets information from horse

Religion
   Gambling becomes like a religion
   They all worship money
   Specific references: "serious as a church"; "It's as if he had it from heaven"; "secret, religious voice"

Luck
   Father is unlucky
   Mother is desperate for luck
   Paul is lucky (ironic)

Deciding on a Thesis

When you are ready, you will express the main idea of your emerging essay in a **thesis statement**—an idea, usually expressed in a single sentence, that the rest of your essay will support. This idea should emerge logically out of your highlighting, annotating, brainstorming notes, journal entries, and lists of related ideas. Eventually, you will write a **thesis-and-support essay**: stating your thesis in your introduction, supporting the thesis in the body paragraphs of your essay, and reinforcing the thesis in your conclusion.

An effective thesis statement tells readers what your essay will discuss and how you will approach your material. For this reason, it should be precisely worded, making its point clear to your readers, and it should contain no vague words or imprecise phrases that will make it difficult for readers to follow your discussion.

In addition to being specific, your thesis statement should give your readers an accurate sense of the scope and direction of your essay. It should not make promises that you do not intend to fulfill or include extraneous details that might confuse your readers. If, for example, you are going to write an essay about the dominant image in a poem, your thesis should not imply that you will focus on the poem's setting or tone.

Remember that as you organize your ideas and as you write, you will probably modify and sharpen your thesis. Sometimes you will even begin planning your essay with one thesis in mind and end up with an entirely different one. If this happens, be sure to revise your body paragraphs so that they support your new thesis. If you find that your ideas about your topic are changing, don't be concerned; this is how the writing process works. (See p. 27 for more on stating a thesis.)

Preparing an Outline

Once you have decided on a thesis and have some idea how you will support it, you can begin to plan your essay's structure. At this stage of the writing process, an **outline** can help you to clarify your ideas and show how these ideas relate to one another.

A **scratch outline** is perhaps the most useful kind of outline for a short essay. An informal list of the main points you will discuss in your essay, a scratch outline is more focused than a simple list of related ideas because it presents ideas in the order in which they will be introduced. As its name implies, however, a scratch outline lacks the detail and the degree of organization of a more formal outline. The main purpose of a scratch outline is to give you a sense of the shape and order of your essay and thus enable you to begin writing.

A student writing a short essay on Edwin Arlington Robinson's use of irony in his poem "Miniver Cheevy" (p. 1010) used the following scratch outline as a guide.

Speaker's Attitude
    Ironic
    Cynical
    Critical

Diction
    Formal
    Detached

Allusions
    Thebes
    Camelot
    Priam
    Medici

Repeated Words
    "Miniver"
    "thought"

Regular Rhyme Scheme

Drafting an Essay

A first draft is a preliminary version of your essay, something to react to and revise. Even before you actually begin drafting your essay, however, you should review the material you have collected. To make sure you are ready to begin drafting, take the following three steps:

1. *Make sure you have collected enough information to support your thesis.* The points you make are only as convincing as the evidence you present to support them. As you read and take notes, you collect supporting examples from the work or works about which you are writing. How many of these examples you need to use in your draft depends on the scope of your thesis. In general, the broader your thesis, the more material you need to support it. For example, if you were supporting the rather narrow thesis that the speech of a certain character in one scene of a play reveals important information about his motivation, only a few examples would be needed. However, if you wanted to

support the broader thesis that Nora and Torvald Helmer in Henrik Ibsen's *A Doll House* (p. 1138) are trapped in their roles, you would need to present a wide range of examples.

2. *See if the work includes any details that contradict your thesis.*   Before you begin writing, test the validity of your thesis by looking for details that contradict it. For example, if you plan to support the thesis that in *A Doll House*, Ibsen makes a strong case for the rights of women, you should look for counterexamples. Can you find subtle hints in the play that suggest women should remain locked in their traditional roles and continue to defer to their fathers and husbands? If so, you will want to modify your thesis accordingly.

3. *Consider whether you need to use outside sources to help you support your thesis.*   You could, for example, strengthen the thesis that *A Doll House* challenged contemporary attitudes about marriage by including the information that when the play first opened, Ibsen was convinced by an apprehensive theater manager to write an alternative ending. In this new ending, Ibsen had Nora decide, after she stopped briefly to look in at her sleeping children, that she could not leave her family. Sometimes information from a source can even lead you to change your thesis. For example, after reading *A Doll House*, you might have decided that Ibsen's purpose was to make a strong case for the rights of women. In class, however, you might learn that Ibsen repeatedly said that his play was about the rights of all human beings, not just of women. This information could lead you to a thesis that suggests Torvald is just as trapped in his role as Nora is in hers. Naturally, Ibsen's interpretation of his own work does not invalidate your first judgment, but it does suggest another conclusion that is worth investigating.

After carefully evaluating the completeness, relevance, and validity of your supporting material, you can begin drafting your essay, using your scratch outline as a guide. In this first draft, your focus should be on the body of your essay; this is not the time to worry about constructing the "perfect" introduction and conclusion. (In fact, many writers, knowing that their ideas will change as they write, postpone writing these paragraphs until a later draft, preferring instead to begin simply by stating their thesis.) As you write, remember that your first draft will probably not be as clear as you would like it to be; still, it will enable you to see your ideas begin to take shape.

Revising and Editing an Essay

Revision

When you **revise**, you literally "re-see" your draft; sometimes you then go on to reorder and rewrite substantial portions of your essay. Before you are satisfied with your essay, you will probably write several drafts—each more closely focused and more coherent than the previous one.

Strategies for Revision

Two strategies can help you to revise your drafts: *peer review* and *a dialogue with your instructor*:

1. **Peer review** is a process in which students assess each other's work-in-progress. This activity may be carried out in informal sessions during which one student comments on another's draft, or it may be a formal process in which students respond

to specific questions on a form supplied by the instructor or participate in a discussion online. In either case, one student's reactions can help another student revise.

2. **A dialogue with your instructor**—in a face-to-face conference or by email—can give you a sense of how to proceed with your revision. Establishing such an oral or written dialogue can help you learn how to respond critically to your own writing, and your reactions to your instructor's comments on any draft can help you to clarify your essay's goals and write drafts that are increasingly consistent with these goals. (If your instructor is not available, try to schedule a conference with a writing center tutor.)

As you move through successive drafts, the task of revising your essay will be easier if you follow a systematic process. As you read and react to your essay, begin by assessing the effectiveness of the larger elements—for example, your thesis statement and your key supporting ideas—and then move on to examine increasingly smaller elements.

Thesis Statement First, reconsider your **thesis statement**. Is it carefully and precisely worded? Does it provide a realistic idea of what your essay will cover? Does it make a point that is worth supporting?

Vague: Many important reasons exist to explain why Margot Macomber's shooting of her husband was probably intentional.

Revised: Although Hemingway's text states that Margot Macomber "shot at the buffalo," a careful analysis of her relationship with her husband suggests that in fact she intended to kill him.

Vague: Dickens's characters are a lot like those of Addison and Steele.

Revised: With their familiar physical and moral traits, Charles Dickens's minor characters are similar to the "characters" created by the eighteenth-century essayists Joseph Addison and Richard Steele for the newspaper the *Spectator*.

Supporting Ideas Next, assess the appropriateness of your **supporting ideas**, considering whether you present enough support for your thesis and whether all the details you include are relevant to that thesis. Make sure you have supported your key points with specific, concrete examples from the work or works you are discussing, briefly summarizing key events, quoting dialogue or description, and describing characters or settings. Make certain, however, that your own ideas are central to the essay and that you have not substituted plot summary for analysis and interpretation. Your goal is to draw a conclusion about one or more works and to support that conclusion with pertinent details. If an event in a story you are analyzing supports a point you wish to make, include a *brief* summary; then, explain its relevance to the point you are making.

In the following excerpt from an essay on a short story by James Joyce, the first sentence briefly summarizes a key event, and the second sentence explains its significance.

> At the end of James Joyce's "Counterparts," when Farrington returns home after a day of frustration and abuse at work, his reaction is to strike out at his son Tom. This act shows that although he and his son are similarly victimized, Farrington is also the counterpart of his tyrannical boss.

Topic Sentences   Now, turn your attention to the **topic sentences** that present the main ideas of your body paragraphs. Make sure that each topic sentence is clearly worded and that it signals the direction of your discussion.

Be especially careful to avoid abstractions and vague generalities in topic sentences. Also avoid words and phrases like *involves, deals with, concerns, revolves around,* and *pertains to,* which are likely to make your topic sentences wordy and imprecise.

Vague: One similarity involves the dominance of the men by women. (What is the similarity?)

Revised: In both stories, a man is dominated by a woman.

Vague: There is one reason for the fact that Jay Gatsby remains a mystery. (What is the reason?)

Revised: Because *The Great Gatsby* is narrated by the outsider Nick Carraway, Jay Gatsby himself remains a mystery.

When revising topic sentences that are intended to move readers from one point (or one section of your essay) to another, be sure the relationship between the ideas they link is clear. A topic sentence should include transitions that look back at the previous paragraphs as well as ahead to the paragraph it introduces.

Unclear: Now, the poem's imagery will be discussed.

Revised: Another reason for the poem's effectiveness is its unusual imagery.

Unclear: The sheriff's wife is another interesting character.

Revised: Like her friend Mrs. Hale, the sheriff's wife also has mixed feelings about what Mrs. Wright has done.

Introduction and Conclusion   When you are satisfied with the body of your essay, you can turn your attention to your essay's *introduction* and *conclusion*.

The **introduction** of an essay about literature should identify the works to be discussed and their authors and indicate the emphasis of the discussion to follow. Depending on your purpose and on your essay's topic, you may want to provide some historical background or biographical information or briefly discuss the work in relation to similar works. Like all introductions, the one you write for an essay about literature should create interest in your topic and should include a clear thesis statement.

The following introduction, though acceptable for a first draft, is in need of revision.

Draft: *Revenge,* which is defined as "the chance to retaliate, get satisfaction, take vengeance, or inflict damage or injury in return for an injury, insult, etc.," is a major theme in many of the stories we have read. The stories that will be discussed here deal with a variety of ways to seek revenge. In my essay, I will consider some of these differences.

Although the student clearly identifies her essay's topic, she does not identify the works she will discuss or the particular point she will make about revenge. Her tired opening strategy, a dictionary definition, is not likely to create interest in her topic, and her announcement of her intention in the last sentence is awkward and unnecessary. The following revised introduction is much more effective.

Revised: In Edgar Allan Poe's "The Cask of Amontillado," Montresor vows revenge on Fortunato for an unspecified "insult"; in Ring Lardner's "Haircut," Paul, a young mentally challenged man, gets even with a cruel practical joker who has taunted him for years. Both of these stories present characters who seek revenge, and both stories end in murder. However, the murderers' motivations are presented very differently. In "Haircut," the narrator is unaware of the significance of many events, and his ignorance helps to create sympathy for the murderer; in "The Cask of Amontillado," where the narrator is actually the murderer, Montresor's inability to offer a convincing motive turns the reader against him.

In your **conclusion**, you reinforce your thesis and perhaps sum up your essay's main points; then, you make a graceful exit.

The conclusion that follows is acceptable for a first draft, but it needs further development.

Draft: Although the characters of Montresor and Paul were created by different authors at different times, they do have similar motives and goals. However, they are portrayed very differently.

The following revised conclusion reinforces the essay's main point, effectively incorporating a brief quotation from "The Cask of Amontillado":

Revised: What is significant is not whether each murderer's act is justified, but rather how each murderer, and each victim, is portrayed by the narrator. Montresor—driven by a thirst to avenge a "thousand injuries" as well as a final insult—is shown to be sadistic and unrepentant; in "Haircut," it is Jim, the victim, whose sadism and lack of remorse are revealed to the reader.

Sentences and Words Now, focus on the individual sentences and words of your essay. Begin by evaluating your **transitions**, the words and phrases that link sentences and paragraphs. Be sure that every necessary transitional element has been supplied and that each word or phrase you have selected accurately conveys the exact relationship (sequence, contradiction, and so on) between ideas.

When you are satisfied with the clarity and appropriateness of your essay's transitions, consider sentence variety and word choice:

- Be sure you have varied your sentence structure. You will bore your readers if all your sentences begin with the subject ("He . . . He . . ."; "The story . . . The story . . .").
- Make sure that all the words you have selected communicate your ideas accurately and that you have not used vague, inexact diction. For example, saying that a character is *bad* is not as helpful as describing him or her as *ruthless, conniving,* or *malicious.*
- Eliminate subjective expressions, such as *I think, in my opinion, I believe, it seems to me,* and *I feel.* These phrases weaken your essay by suggesting that its ideas are "only" your opinions and have no objective validity.

Documentation Make certain that all references to sources are integrated smoothly into your sentences and that all information that is not your own is documented appropriately. For specific information on using and documenting sources, see Chapter 7.

✔ **CHECKLIST Using Sources**

When you incorporate source material into your essays, follow these guidelines:

- ☐ Acknowledge all material from sources, including the literary work or works under discussion, using the documentation style of the Modern Language Association (MLA).

- ☐ Combine paraphrases, summaries, and quotations with your own interpretations, weaving quotations smoothly into your essay. Introduce the words or ideas of others with a phrase that identifies their source ("According to Richard Wright's biographer, . . ."), and end with appropriate parenthetical documentation.

- ☐ Use quotations *only* when something vital would be lost if you did not reproduce the author's exact words.

- ☐ Integrate short quotations (four lines or fewer of prose or three lines or fewer of poetry) smoothly into your essay. Use a slash (/) with one space on either side to separate lines of poetry. Be sure to enclose quotations in quotation marks.

- ☐ Set off quotations of more than four lines of prose or more than three lines of poetry by indenting one inch from the left-hand margin. Double-space, and do not use quotation marks. If you are quoting just one paragraph, do not indent the first line.

- ☐ Use ellipses—three spaced periods—to indicate that you have omitted material within a quotation (but never use ellipses at the beginning of a quoted passage).

- ☐ Use brackets to indicate that you have added words to a quotation: As Earl notes, "[Willie] is a modern-day Everyman" (201). Use brackets to alter a quotation so that it fits grammatically into your sentence: Wilson says that Miller "offer[s] audiences a dark view of the present" (74).

- ☐ Place commas and periods *inside* quotation marks: According to Robert Coles, the child could "make others smile."

- ☐ Place punctuation marks other than commas and periods *outside* quotation marks: What does Frost mean when he says, "a poem must ride on its own melting"? However, if the punctuation mark is part of the quoted material, place it *inside* the quotation marks: In "Mending Wall," Frost asks, "Why do they make good neighbors?"

- ☐ When citing part of a short story or novel, supply the page number (143). For a poem, supply line numbers (3-5), including the word *line* or *lines* in just the first reference. For a play, supply act, scene, and line numbers in arabic numerals (2.2.17-22).

- ☐ Include a works-cited list.

Editing and Proofreading

Once you have finished revising, you **edit**—that is, you make certain that your essay's grammar, punctuation, spelling, and mechanics are correct. Always run a spell check, but remember that you still have to **proofread**—look carefully for errors that the spell checker will not identify. These include homophones (*brake* incorrectly used instead of *break*), typos that create correctly spelled words (*work* instead of *word*), and words (such as a technical or foreign term or a writer's name) that may not be in your computer's dictionary. If you use a grammar checker, remember that although grammar programs may identify potential problems—long sentences, for example—they may not be able to determine whether a particular long sentence is grammatically correct (let alone stylistically pleasing). Always keep a style handbook nearby so that you can double-check any problems a spell checker or grammar checker highlights in your writing.

As you edit, pay particular attention to the special conventions of literary essays, some of which are addressed in the checklist below. When your editing is complete, give your essay a descriptive title. Before you print your final copy, be sure that its format conforms to your instructor's requirements.

✔ **CHECKLIST**   **Conventions of Writing about Literature**

When you write about works of literature, follow these guidelines:

- Use present-tense verbs when discussing works of literature: The character of Mrs. Mallard's husband is not developed. . . .

- Use past-tense verbs only when discussing historical events ("Owen's poem conveys the destructiveness of World War I, which at the time the poem was written was considered to be . . ."); when presenting historical or biographical data ("Her first novel, which was published in 1811 when Austen was thirty-six, . . ."); or when identifying events that occurred prior to the time of the story's main action ("Miss Emily is a recluse; since her father's death she has lived alone except for a servant").

- Avoid unnecessary plot summary. Your goal is to draw a conclusion about one or more works and to support that conclusion with pertinent details. If a plot detail supports a point you wish to make, a *brief* summary is acceptable. But remember, plot summary is no substitute for analysis.

- Use literary terms accurately. For example, be careful not to confuse *narrator* or *speaker* with *author;* feelings or opinions expressed by a narrator or character do not necessarily represent those of the author. You should not say, "In the poem's last stanza, Frost expresses his indecision" when you mean that the poem's *speaker* is indecisive.

- Italicize titles of novels and plays; place titles of short stories and poems within quotation marks.

- Refer to authors of literary works by their full names (*Edgar Allan Poe*) in your first reference to them and by their last names (*Poe*) in subsequent references. Never refer to authors by their first names, and never use titles that indicate marital status (*Flannery O'Connor* or *O'Connor*, never *Flannery* or *Miss O'Connor*).

- Be careful not to make sweeping or unrealistic claims. Remember that the support you present cannot "prove" that what you are saying is true, so choose verbs like *demonstrate*, *show*, *suggest*, and *indicate* rather than *prove*.

Exercise: Evaluating Two Student Essays

The following student essays, "Initiation into Adulthood" and "Hard Choices," were written for the same Introduction to Literature class. Both consider the initiation theme in the same three short stories: James Joyce's "Eveline," John Updike's "A&P" (p. 238), and William Faulkner's "Barn Burning" (p. 335). "Hard Choices" conforms to the conventions of writing about literature discussed in this chapter. "Initiation into Adulthood" does not.

Read the two essays. Then, guided by this chapter's discussion of writing about literature and by the checklists on pages 30–31 identify the features that make "Hard Choices" the more effective essay, and decide where "Initiation into Adulthood" needs further revision. Finally, suggest some possible revisions for "Hard Choices."

Initiation into Adulthood

At an early age, the main focus in a child's life is his parents. But as this child | *Introduction*
grows, he begins to get his own view of life, which may be, and usually is, different from that of his parents. Sooner or later, there will come a time in this child's life when he must stand up for what he truly believes in. At this point in his life, he can no longer be called a child, and he becomes part of the adult world. In literature, many stories—such | *Thesis statement*
as James Joyce's "Eveline," John Updike's "A&P," and William Faulkner's "Barn Burning"—focus on this initiation into adulthood.

James Joyce's "Eveline" is a story that describes a major turning point in a woman's | *Discussion of first story: "Eveline"*
life. At home, Eveline's life was very hard. She was responsible for keeping the house together and caring for the younger children after her mother's death. Unfortunately, the only thoughts that ran through her mind were thoughts of escape, of leaving her unhappy life and beginning a new life of her own. The night before she was to secretly leave with Frank on a boat to Buenos Ayres, a street organ playing reminded her of her promise to her dying mother to keep the home together as long as she could. She was now forced to make a decision between life with Frank and her present life, which didn't look wholly undesirable now that she was about to leave. The next night, just as she was about to step on the boat, she realized she could not leave. The making of this decision was in essence Eveline's initiation into adulthood.

John Updike's "A&P" presents the brief infatuation of a young boy, Sammy, and | *Discussion of second story: "A&P"*
the consequences that follow. Sammy's home was a small quiet town a few miles from the shore. He worked in the local A&P as a cashier, a job his father had gotten for him. One day, three girls in nothing but bathing suits walked through the front door. Immediately they caught Sammy's eye, especially the leader, the one he nicknamed "Queenie." After prancing through the store, they eventually came to Sammy's checkout with an unusual purchase. It was not long before they caught the attention of Mr. Lengel, the manager. Unpleasant words were

exchanged between the manager and Queenie pertaining to their inappropriate shopping attire. Before the girls left the store, Sammy told Lengel that he quit, hoping they would stop and watch him, their unsuspected hero. But they kept walking, and Sammy was faced with the decision of whether or not to follow through with his gesture. Knowing that it is "fatal" not to follow through with a gesture once you've started, he removed his apron and bow tie and walked out the door, realizing how hard the world was going to be to him hereafter. The making of this decision, to leave the mundane life of the A&P and enter the harsh world, was in essence Sammy's initiation into adulthood.

William Faulkner's "Barn Burning" is a story about Sarty Snopes, an innocent young boy who must make a decision between his family and his honor. Because Abner Snopes, Sarty's father, had so little, he tried to hurt those who had more than he had—often by burning down their barns. These acts forced the Snopes family to move around quite a bit. The last time Snopes burned a barn, he did it without warning his victim, making Sarty realize how cruel and dishonest his father really was. Because of this realization, Sarty decided to leave his family. This decision of Sarty's not to stick to his own blood was his initiation into adulthood.

Discussion of third story: "Barn Burning"

"Eveline," "A&P," and "Barn Burning" all deal with a youth maturing to adulthood in the process of deciding whether to stay unhappy or to go and seek a better life. Sammy and Sarty leave their unpleasant situations because of something done unfairly. Eveline, on the other hand, decides to stay, remembering a promise to her mother. The decisions of these characters presented in their respective stories are focal points in the literary works and pertain to initiation into adulthood.

Conclusion

Hard Choices

Although William Faulkner's "Barn Burning" focuses on a young boy in the American South, John Updike's "A&P" on a teenager in a town north of Boston, and James Joyce's "Eveline" on a young woman in Dublin, each of the three stories revolves around a decision the central character must make. These decisions are not easy ones; in all three cases, family loyalty competes with a desire for individual freedom. However, the difficult decision-making process helps each character to mature, and in this sense, all three works are initiation stories.

> Introduction
>
> Thesis statement

For Sarty Snopes in "Barn Burning," initiation into adulthood means coming to terms with his father's concept of revenge. Mr. Snopes believes that a person should take revenge himself if he cannot get justice in court. Revenge, for this bitter man, means burning down barns. Sarty knows that his father is doing wrong, but Mr. Snopes drills into his son's mind the idea that "You got to learn to stick to your own blood or you ain't going to have any blood to stick to you" (Faulkner 338), and for a long time Sarty believes him. Naturally, this blood tie makes Sarty's decision to leave his family extremely difficult. In the end, though, Sarty decides to reject his father's values and remain behind when his family moves.

> Discussion of first story: "Barn Burning"

Like Sarty, Sammy must choose between his values and his parents' values (reflected in his job at the supermarket). While Sammy is working in the A&P, he notices how much like sheep people are. Most customers have a routine life that they never consider changing, and Sammy does not want to end up like them. When three seemingly carefree girls enter the store and exhibit nonconformist behavior—such as going against the flow of people in the aisles, not having a grocery list, and wearing bathing suits—Sammy sees them as rebels, and he longs to escape through them from his humdrum world. In the end, he chooses to defend the girls and quit the job his parents helped him to get.

> Discussion of second story: "A&P"

Likewise, Eveline has to decide between a new life with her boyfriend, Frank, in South America and her dull, hard life at home with her father. The new life offers change and freedom, while her life at home is spent working and keeping house. Still, when given the chance to leave, she declines because she promised her dying mother to "keep the home together as long as she could" (Joyce 47).

> Discussion of third story: "Eveline"

All three characters enter adulthood by making difficult decisions. Sarty realizes that in order to grow, he must repudiate his father's wrongdoings. He stands up for his values and rejects his "blood." Sammy makes the same decision although with less extreme consequences: knowing that he will have to confront his parents, he still defends the three girls and stands up to his boss, rejecting a life of conformity and security. Unlike the other two, Eveline does not reject her parents' values. Instead, she decides to

> Comparative analysis of the three stories

sacrifice her own future by remaining with her father. She keeps her promise to her mother and puts her father before herself because she believes that caring for him is her duty.

Each of the three characters confronts a challenging future. Sarty must support himself and make a new life. Because he is very young and because he has no one to help him, his future is the most uncertain of the three. Unlike Sammy and Eveline, who still have homes, Sarty has only his judgment and his values to guide him. Sammy's future is less bleak but still unpredictable: he knows that the world will be a harder place for him from now on (Updike 238) because now he is a man of principle. Unlike the other two, Eveline knows exactly what her future holds: work, pain, and boredom. She has no fear or uncertainty—but no hope for a better tomorrow either.

> Further analysis of the three stories

"Barn Burning," "A&P," and "Eveline" are stories of initiation in which the main characters struggle with decisions that help them to grow up. All three consider giving up the known for the unknown, challenging their parents and becoming truly themselves, but only Sarty and Sammy actually do so. Both boys defy their parents and thus trade difficult lives for uncertain ones. Eveline, however, decides to stay on in her familiar life, choosing the known—however deadening—over the unknown. Still, all three, in confronting hard choices and deciding to do what their values tell them they must do, experience an initiation into adulthood.

> Conclusion

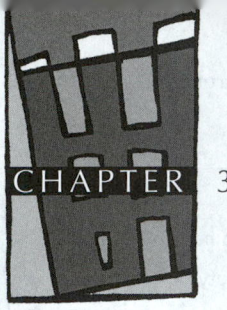

CHAPTER 3

APPROACHING ASSIGNMENTS IN LITERATURE

When you write an essay about literature, you have many options (some of these are listed in Chapter 2, pp. 16–35). Often, however, you will be asked to respond to one of five special assignments: to write a *response*, to write a *comparison-contrast essay*, to write an *explication*, to write a *character analysis*, or to write about a work's *cultural context*. The pages that follow offer guidelines for responding to each of these assignments as well as annotated model student essays.

 Writing a Response

When you write a **response**, you explore and explain your reactions to a short story, poem, or play by focusing on one or more of the work's elements to discover how they contribute to its overall effectiveness, meaning, and impact. For example, a controversial theme in a particular work may elicit a strong negative response, or a character's actions might amuse, enrage, or enlighten you. Probing your own personal reactions to various elements can help you begin to understand the work as a whole and bring the work to life in a meaningful way. As you consider how a particular literary work relates to others you have read and to your own experiences, you create your own interpretation of the work.

Eventually, you may develop a response into a longer, more formal essay. In fact, a response is often assigned as an initial step toward formulating a thesis statement for a more complex assignment. A response, sometimes written as a **journal entry** (see p. 23), is generally less formal than other types of writing about literature, and it can incorporate freewriting, brainstorming, and informal outlining techniques. Remember, however, that although your response may use an informal—even personal—style and tone, it cannot be based solely on your personal opinions. You must always include examples and details from the work to support your reactions to it.

✔ CHECKLIST   Writing a Response

When you write a response, consider these questions:

- Have you expressed your reactions directly and honestly?
- Have you focused on particular literary elements in the work, clearly explaining how they relate to its overall effectiveness?

- If your response analyzes more than one literary element, have you paid enough attention to each element?

- Do you use examples and details—including paraphrases and quotations—from the work to illustrate your points and to support your reactions?

- Have you followed your instructor's format and documentation guidelines?

Responding to a Short Story

The following is a student's response to questions about Tim O'Brien's story "The Things They Carried" (p. 392).

> At the end of the story, what has Lieutenant Cross learned? What more do you think he still has to learn?

(Note that this response does not include a works-cited list because the instructor did not require one for this informal assignment.)

Russell 1

Brad Russell

Professor Chu

English 102

12 January 2015

Response to Tim O'Brien's "The Things They Carried"

Tim O'Brien's "The Things They Carried" is a coming-of-age story, and Lieutenant Cross, a young soldier, learns the hard way that war can have serious consequences. Throughout the story, the narrator lists all the weapons and tools and mementos that the soldiers carry, and having to read about all the technical specifications of guns, ammunition, and other machinery that the men carry got to be really boring after a while, and I couldn't figure out why all this information was in the story. I looked forward to the short paragraphs about the men's emotions and the deeper impact of the war.

It didn't occur to me until I read the story a second time that what I was experiencing as a reader was similar to what Lieutenant Cross experiences. He feels the burden of all the monotonous details, and they prevent him from seeing the big picture. Some details show

Russell 2

how dull and uneventful war can be, like when the narrator describes "moving on to the next village, then other villages, where it would always be the same" (399). Other details are shocking; for example, the narrator describes in a flat, detached way how Norman Bowker carries around a dead Vietcong soldier's severed thumb that is "dark brown, rubbery to the touch" (398) and how when Ted Lavender gets shot, "[t]he cheekbone was gone" (398). I understand that all these details are supposed to show readers the heavy burden war places on the soldiers, but I wanted to get past the details. I wanted to know what these things and events mean to the men, and especially to Lieutenant Cross.

For a long time, Lieutenant Cross relies on the details of his job—and on his memories of home—to help him survive. He is unable to focus on the brutal reality of war, and he slips into daydreams about Martha and the New Jersey shore when he and his men are on long missions, or when they face danger (like when one of them gets picked to search out a tunnel they're about to destroy). Lieutenant Cross blames himself for Lavender's death because he was unable to focus on his men's safety and on the dangers all around them, but eventually he learns that blaming himself will not make the situation better or bring Ted Lavender back. What he needs to do now is stop focusing on the endless burdens he and his men carry, or on the monotony and pointlessness of the daily struggle to survive, or on "all the emotional baggage of men who might die" (402). Now, he has to focus on being a leader.

Lieutenant Cross finally realizes that war "was another world, where there were no pretty poems or midterm exams, a place where men died because of carelessness and gross stupidity" (404). He learns that he has to "dispense with love; it was not now a factor" (405). But I think Lieutenant Cross still has more to learn. What I learned while reading the story is that we *need* the "pretty poems" and "midterm exams" and especially the "love" that make us human; we need to carry these things with us to survive in times, such as wartime, when these things are absent. Although Lieutenant Cross doesn't realize it by the end of the story, he still must carry these memories with him in order to "[c]arry on" and to get back to a place where people are allowed to dream and love (405).

 ## Writing a Comparison-Contrast Essay

Writing a **comparison-contrast essay**, one of the most common assignments in literature classes, offers many possibilities. For example, you can compare two stories, two poems, or two plays—or you can cross genres, comparing a story with a poem or a play on a similar topic. Alternatively, you can compare two characters, two works by the same author, a poem to a work of fine art, a conventional print story to a graphic story, or a literary work to a film.

When you write a comparison-contrast essay, you look first for significant similarities between your two subjects. For example, two characters may have a similar motivation or similar goals or flaws; two stories may have similar settings; two plays may have similar plots; and two poems may have parallels in their use of sound or imagery. Once you have identified the key similarities, you can consider why these similarities are important and what they reveal about the works.

There are two ways to arrange material in a comparison-contrast essay. When you write a **point-by-point comparison**, you discuss one point of similarity at a time, alternating between subjects. When you write a **subject-by-subject comparison**, you approach each subject separately, discussing all your points first for one subject and then for the other. The outlines that follow illustrate how you could use either a point-by-point or a subject-by-subject strategy to support the same thesis statement:

> Both David Michael Kaplan's "Doe Season" and Alice Munro's "Boys and Girls" focus on a young girl who learns that her gender limits her and comes to accept that such limitations are inevitable.

Point-by-Point Comparison

First point: In both stories, the girls are tomboys who like being with their fathers.
  "Doe Season": Andy goes hunting with her father.
  "Boys and Girls": The narrator does farm chores with her father.

Second point: In both stories, the girls struggle against the expectations of others.
  "Doe Season": Mac and Charlie challenge Andy's right to hunt.
  "Boys and Girls": Narrator's mother expects her to do household chores.

Third point: In both stories, the girls learn that they are limited by their gender.
  "Doe Season": Andy shoots the deer but runs away, thinking of her mother.
  "Boys and Girls": The narrator fails to save the horse and realizes she is "only a girl."

Subject-by-Subject Comparison

First subject: "Doe Season"
  First point: Andy is a tomboy who is excited about going hunting with her father.
  Second point: Charlie and Mac challenge her right to hunt.
  Third point: Through her encounter with the deer, she learns that she is not as brave as she thought she was.

Second subject: "Boys and Girls"
  First point: Like Andy, the narrator likes being with her father and is glad not to be in the house with her mother.
  Second point: Like Andy, she is criticized by others.
  Third point: Like Andy, she learns through her encounter with an animal—in her case, the horse whose life she cannot save—that she is limited by her gender.

✔ **CHECKLIST**　Writing a Comparison-Contrast Essay

When you write a comparison-contrast essay, consider the following questions:

☐　Have you chosen two subjects that have significant similarities?

☐　Does your thesis statement identify the two subjects you are comparing and tell why they are alike (and perhaps also briefly acknowledge their differences)?

☐　Does your essay's structure follow either a point-by-point or a subject-by-subject pattern?

☐　Does each paragraph's topic sentence identify the subject you are discussing and the point you are focusing on in the paragraph?

☐　Do transitional words and phrases clearly lead readers from subject to subject and from point to point?

☐　Have you followed your instructor's format and documentation guidelines?

Comparing a Short Story and a Film

The following student essay, "Two Cathedrals," is a point-by-point comparison of Raymond Carver's short story "Cathedral" (p. 435) and a film version of the story.

Townsend 1

Jason Townsend

Professor Blair

English 102

8 January 2015

Two Cathedrals

    In many ways, the film version of Raymond Carver's "Cathedral" is very similar to the short story on which it is based. The plots are the same, the characters are the same, and much of the film's dialogue is taken directly from the story. Still, there are a number of [Thesis statement] differences in how the characters' relationships, and other important information, are presented, and these differences help to explain the very different impacts of the endings.

Townsend 2

Early in the story, the first-person narrator tells about his wife's first marriage. The subject comes up as part of his explanation of how his wife came to work for Robert, the blind man who is about to visit. But the narrator describes her first marriage in a way that raises questions about the strength of their current marriage, saying, "she was in love with the guy, and he was in love with her, etc." (436). In the film, however, the wife's first husband is not mentioned until after Robert's arrival. Here, the first husband is brought up to explain the wife's suicide attempt rather than to explain how she met Robert. As a result, the importance of the wife's first marriage is diminished in the film, and the possibility of her romantic connection with Robert is heightened. This relationship is reinforced in the movie when Robert reminisces about how they sometimes drank Scotch together at the end of the workday—a memory that does not exist in the story.

> First point of contrast: importance of past relationships

Throughout the story, the narrator has no name. In addition, he refuses to use the name of his wife's first husband, asking, "why should he have a name? he was the childhood sweetheart, and what more does he want?" (436). The wife is also unnamed. Only Robert has a name and, thus, only he has an identity, a distinctive self. However, in the film the wife calls the narrator "Ed" on one occasion; only she herself remains nameless. As a result, any notion that the story is about namelessness or identity is lost. Moreover, the wife's use of her husband's name in the film makes Robert's tendency to call him "Bub" hard to understand. In the story, this familiar usage makes sense, following logically from Robert's statement when they first meet: "'I feel like we've already met'" (438).

> Second point of contrast: use of names

For years, Robert and the wife have stayed in touch through an exchange of audio tapes, and these tapes have different purposes in the story and the film. In the story, this exchange of tapes is used to emphasize the relationship, or potential relationship, between Robert and the husband. The narrator concludes his discussion of the tapes with a memory of his wife and himself listening to a tape from Robert. The narrator says they were interrupted just as Robert was about to say what he thought of the husband: "'From what you've said about him, I can only conclude—.'" The husband never listened to Robert's conclusion; he admits, "I'd heard all I wanted to" (437). In the film, however, the tapes are used to emphasize the relationship between the husband and the wife. In a flashback in which the husband listens alone to a tape his wife had made for Robert, she tells Robert why she will probably remarry. The husband turns the recorder off in anger at the thought that he had been "settled for."

> Third point of contrast: role of audio tapes

Townsend 3

Robert's own marriage is also treated differently in the story and the film. In the story, the wife has two reasons for telling her husband about the death of Robert's wife. First, she uses it in connection with her attempt to make the husband's reaction to Robert a kind of test of their own relationship: "'If you love me,'" she tells him, "'you can do this for me'" (437). Second, she tells the story of Robert's wife dying as Robert held her hand to increase the husband's sympathy for Robert. In the film, however, Robert himself tells the husband and the wife about his wife's death, and he presents information that does not exist in the story at all. Robert says that at the end his wife "lost her voice" and could only communicate by squeezing his hand, one squeeze for "yes" and two for "no." This discussion of touch as a means of communication, absent in the story, tends to decrease the surprise (and, therefore, diminish the power) of the joined hands that draw the cathedral at the story's end.

> Fourth point of contrast: treatment of Robert's marriage

Robert's touching of the wife's face with his hands on her last day of work is merely described by the narrator of the story. The narrator reports that his wife wrote a poem about this experience that he did not think much of, although he admits, "Maybe I just don't understand poetry" (436). A flashback in the film actually shows Robert's hands feeling the features of the wife's face while the wife's voice reads the poem aloud. In short, what the reader of the story is encouraged to imagine is actually depicted in visual images and sound for a viewer of the film. The film's ability to show rather than suggesting is one of the things that makes the endings of the story and the film so different.

> Fifth point of contrast: showing vs. suggesting

In the story, the narrator looks for some ballpoint pens and a brown paper shopping bag in preparation for drawing a cathedral as Robert has suggested. When the narrator returns to the living room, he puts the paper bag on the coffee table and sits on the floor. At this point, the narrator says, "The blind man got down from the sofa and sat next to me on the carpet" (445). The description of the two men sitting together on the floor to draw almost suggests boys at play, childlike innocents who are more or less equals. In the film, however, the husband returns to the dining room and sits in a chair to work at the table. Robert stands behind him, blind but still "looking" over his shoulder, suggesting a teacher and a student or a parent and a child—people who are unequal.

> Sixth point of contrast: staging of drawing scene

The greatest single difference between the story and the film is the treatment of the actual picture of a cathedral that the men draw. Viewers of the film see it being drawn and see it in its finished state. When the husband—with his eyes still closed—judges the work he has done with Robert and says, "'It's really something,'" viewers know exactly what the picture looks like. Readers of the story, on the other hand,

> Last (and most important) point of contrast: treatment of cathedral picture

Townsend 4

must imagine the picture and the experience of creating the drawing—an experience that is, the narrator says, "like nothing else in my life up to now" (445). Their own inability to see the finished product makes it possible for readers to understand both the limitations and the power of Robert's blindness.

Because the story is about blindness and sight, the visual capabilities of the film   Conclusion are important. However, rather than strengthening the story, the film's visual images are to some extent intrusive. The substitution of an actual visual image of the cathedral for readers' own imagined image changes everything. In fact, those who read the story are more likely to understand Robert's perspective, and to sense what the narrator experienced, than those who see the film are.

Townsend 5

Works Cited

Carver, Raymond. "Cathedral." *Compact Literature: Reading, Reacting, Writing*, edited by Laurie
     G. Kirszner and Stephen R. Mandell, 9th ed., Wadsworth, 2016, pp. 435–45.
The Heinle Original Film Series in Literature: Raymond Carver's "Cathedral." Directed by Bruce R.
     Schwartz, Wadsworth, 2003.

NOTE

- For a model student essay that compares two poems, see "Digging for Memories" (p. 672).
- For possible topics for comparing a poem and a work of art, see the Poetry Sampler: Poetry and Art.
- For additional possibilities for comparison-contrast essays, see the "Related Works" lists that follow many of the selections in this book.

Writing an Explication

When you write an **explication** (of a poem, a short story, or a scene in a play), you do a close reading of a work or a portion of a work, carefully analyzing one or more of its elements. For example, you might decide to analyze a story's characters, symbols, or setting; a poem's language, rhyme scheme, meter, or form; or a play's dialogue or staging. One way to approach a work you wish to explicate is to apply the guidelines for reading fiction (pp. 179–80), poetry (p. 661), or drama (pp. 1085–1086) in a systematic way.

When you organize your material in an explication, you should proceed systematically. If you are focusing on a single element, analyze its importance in one section of the work at a time. If you are analyzing several elements, consider each—plot, setting, point of view, and so on—in turn. You will probably choose to group the less significant elements together in a single paragraph or section of your essay and perhaps devote several paragraphs to one particularly important element, carefully considering how symbols, for example, shed light on the work. For each element you discuss, you will give examples from the work you are explicating, quoting words, phrases, lines, and passages that illustrate each point you are making.

✔ **CHECKLIST**   **Writing an Explication**

When you write an explication, consider the following questions:

☐ Is the work (or section of a work) you have chosen sufficiently rich to support an explication?

☐ Does your thesis state the central point about the work that your explication supports?

☐ Do your topic sentences make clear which element (or elements) you are focusing on in each paragraph?

☐ Do you use quotations from the work to illustrate your points?

☐ Have you followed your instructor's format and documentation guidelines?

Explicating a Poem

The following student essay, "A Lingering Doubt," is an explication of Robert Frost's poem "The Road Not Taken" (p. 805).

Craff 1

Jeanette Craff

Professor Rosenberg

English 102

13 January 2015

A Lingering Doubt

Sometimes it is tempting to look back on a lifetime of choices and decisions and | Introduction |
to think, "What if? What if I had made a different choice? Would my life be better? worse? more interesting?" In Robert Frost's poem "The Road Not Taken," the speaker does just this: he looks back at a time in his life when he came to a fork in the road and chose one path over another. He tells readers that he "took the one less traveled by, / And that has made

Craff 2

all the difference" (lines 19-20). At first, this statement seems to suggest that the speaker is satisfied with the decision he made long ago. However, certain elements in the poem—its structure, its language, and even its title—suggest that the speaker is regretting his decision, not celebrating it.

Thesis
statement

The title of the poem, "The Road Not Taken," immediately suggests that the speaker is focusing not on the choice he *did* make long ago but on the road he chose *not* to take. The poem's language supports this interpretation. Frost begins his poem with the speaker recalling that "Two roads diverged in a yellow wood" and saying that he is "sorry [he] could not travel both" (1-2). The image Frost uses of the two roads diverging is an obvious metaphor for the choices a person has to make in the course of a lifetime. As a young man, the speaker was not aware of any major difference between the two roads. He says that he saw one as "just as fair" (6) as the other, and he uses words and phrases such as "equally" (11) and "really about the same" (10). However, in the third stanza of the poem, the older and wiser speaker, looking back on that period of his life, says that he still might take the other road "another day" (13). That the mature speaker still continues to examine a decision he made earlier in life suggests that he may not be completely satisfied with that decision.

Overview
of poem's
language
and theme

A close look at the poem suggests that it is the departures from the expected structure and meter that make its meaning clear. The poem is divided into four stanzas, each made up of five lines. The regular meter of these four stanzas conveys a sense of tranquility and certainty. The regularity of the poem's rhyme scheme (a, b, a, a, b) also contributes to the poem's natural fluidity. This fluidity is evident, for example, in the first stanza:

Analysis
of poem's
structure
and meter

> Two roads diverged in a yellow wood,
> And sorry I could not travel both
> And be one traveler, long I stood
> And looked down one as far as I could
> To where it bent in the undergrowth; (1-5)

Here, the end rhyme of lines 1, 3, and 4 and of lines 2 and 5, as well as the even line lengths (each line contains nine syllables), make the poem flow smoothly.

However, the poem does not maintain this fluidity. In other stanzas, lines range from eight to ten syllables, and the important final stanza ends with a line that is an awkward metrical departure from the rest of the poem:

Further
analysis
of poem's
structure
and meter

> I shall be telling this with a sigh
> Somewhere ages and ages hence:

Craft 3

> Two roads diverged in a wood, and I—
>
> I took the one less traveled by, And
>
> that has made all the difference. (16-20)

In this stanza, line 20 has nine syllables as lines 16 and 18 do, but unlike them, it also has an irregular meter ("And that has made all the difference"), which forces readers to hesitate on the word "all" before landing on "difference." This hesitation, coupled with the hesitation signaled by the dash that ends line 18, suggests the speaker's doubts about his decision. When the speaker was young, he did not notice any significant difference between the two roads, or the two life choices, presented to him. Now, looking back, he believes that there was a difference, and he may be lamenting the fact that he will never know where life would have taken him had he chosen differently.

Departure from expected meter is not the only strategy Frost uses to convey a sense of hesitation and an air of regret. Frost's choice of words also plays an important part [Analysis of poem's language] in helping readers understand the poem's theme. In the first stanza, for example, the speaker thinks back to the period of his life in which he had to choose between two separate paths, and he says that he was "sorry [he] could not travel both" (2). The word "sorry" helps to establish the tone of regret that pervades the poem.

In the second stanza, Frost begins to use words and phrases to convey indecision and doubt in the speaker's voice. The speaker attempts to pacify himself by saying that the road he chose had "perhaps the better claim" (7), but then he is quick to say that the passage of time has worn both roads "really about the same" (10). The words "perhaps" and "really" suggest indecision, and Frost's choice of these words helps to convey the doubt in the speaker's mind.

The speaker's sense of regret deepens in the third stanza as he continues to think back on his decision. When the speaker says, "Oh, I kept the first for another day!" (13), the word "Oh" expresses his regret. The exclamation point at the end of the statement helps reinforce the finality of his decision. When the speaker continues, "Yet knowing how way leads on to way, / I doubted if I should ever come back" (14-15), the word "Yet" is filled with uncertainty.

In the poem's final stanza, the speaker suddenly leaves his thoughts of the past and speaks in the future tense: "I shall be telling this [story] with a sigh" (16). Frost's use of the word "sigh" here is very revealing because it connotes resignation or regret. The speaker concludes, "Two roads diverged in a wood, and I— / I took the one less traveled by, / And that has made all the difference" (18-20). Both the dash and the repetition of the word "I" convey hesitation and thus communicate his lingering doubts over the decision he made long ago.

Graff 4

Conclusion

Although this doubt is evident throughout the poem, "The Road Not Taken" has frequently been interpreted as optimistic because of the speaker's final statement that the choice he made "has made all the difference" (20). However, "made all the difference" can be interpreted as neutral (or even negative) as well as positive, and so the speaker's statement at the end of the poem may actually be a statement of regret, not celebration. The "difference" mentioned in the final line has left a doubt in the speaker's mind, and, as Frost suggests in the title of his poem, the speaker is left thinking about the road he did not take—and will never be able to take.

Graff 5

Work Cited

Frost, Robert. "The Road Not Taken." *Compact Literature: Reading, Reacting, Writing*, edited by Laurie G. Kirszner and Stephen R. Mandell, 9th ed., Wadsworth, 2016, pp. 805-06.

Writing a Character Analysis

When you write a **character analysis** of a character in a short story or play, you can focus on a major or a minor character, examining the character's language, behavior, background, interaction with other characters, and reaction to his or her environment. Everything you are told about a character—and everything you can reasonably infer about him or her from words, actions, or appearance—can help you to understand the character. In your analysis, you can focus on the influences that shaped the character, the character's effect on others, how the character changes during the course of the story or play, or what motivates him or her to act (or not to act).

✔ **CHECKLIST   Writing a Character Analysis**

When you write a character analysis, consider the following questions:

☐ Have you chosen a character who is interesting enough to serve as the focus of your essay?

☐ Have you considered the character's background, words, actions, appearance, and interactions with others?

---

continued on next page

■ Have you considered how and why the character changes—or why he or she fails to change?

■ Have you considered how the work would be different if the character had made different choices?

■ Have you considered how the work would be different without the character?

■ Have you considered what motivates the character to act (or not to act)?

■ Have you followed your instructor's format and documentation guidelines?

Analyzing a Character in a Play

The following student essay, "Linda Loman: Breaking the Mold," analyzes a character in Arthur Miller's play *Death of a Salesman* (p. 1233).

Dube 1

Caroline Dube

Professor Nelson

English 1302

14 January 2015

Linda Loman: Breaking the Mold

In many ways, Linda Loman appears to play the part of the stereotypical dutiful and loving wife in Arthur Miller's *Death of a Salesman*. She eagerly greets her husband, ignores his shortcomings, and maintains an upbeat attitude, all while managing the bills, waxing the floors, and mending the clothes. Her kindness and infinite patience seem to establish her as a foil for Willy, with his turbulent temperament. In addition, most of her actions seem to be only reactions to the other characters in the play. However, a closer look at Linda reveals a more complex woman: a fully developed character with dreams, insights, and flashes of defiance.

> Thesis statement

Unlike stock characters, whose motivations seem transparent and obvious, Linda has dreams that are both complex and realistically human. The stage directions that introduce Linda describe her as sharing Willy's "turbulent longings" but lacking the temperament to pursue them (1236). It seems she has applied the wisdom she shares with Willy, that "life is a casting off," to her own cast-away dreams (1237). Linda's hopes seem more realistic than Willy's. She wants Biff to settle down, the mortgage to be paid off, and the members of her family to coexist happily. These modest aspirations are the product of Linda's

> Linda's hopes and dreams

Dube 2

long experience. The fact that Linda does not pursue unrealistic goals, as Willy does, does not make her a flat character (or even a less interesting one); instead, her weaknesses give her character a degree of depth and human realism.

At times, Linda takes on the role of family peacemaker—a role we would expect her to play consistently throughout the play if she were simply a stock character. But Linda breaks out of the obedient wife mode on several occasions. When Willy insists that she stop mending her stockings, Linda quietly puts them into her pocket to resume her mending later. When Biff and Happy show they are ashamed of their father, Linda fiercely lashes out at them in his defense, calling Happy a "philandering bum" and threatening to kick Biff out of the house for good (1259). Although at first she cannot bring herself to remove the rubber pipe that Willy used to attempt to commit suicide, Linda says she had finally decided to destroy the pipe when Biff removed it. She does not always have an opportunity to follow through on her threats, but Linda demonstrates clearly that she will not always follow orders—especially when she is protecting Willy.

> Linda's actions

Linda seems to be the cheerful voice of the family, but beneath the surface, she is keenly aware of the ongoing problems. She knows that Charley has been giving money to Willy every week, but she says nothing for fear of embarrassing Willy. She senses Willy's suicidal tendencies and even finds physical evidence of his plans. Linda is the first to raise doubts about Biff's plan to ask Mr. Oliver for money, suggesting that he may not remember Biff. Above all, Linda understands human nature and how the minds of those around her work. She gives an honest description of her husband and his situation:

> Linda's awareness of family problems

> I don't say he's a great man. Willy Loman never made a lot of money. His name was never in the paper. He's not the finest character that ever lived. But he's a human being, and a terrible thing is happening to him. So attention must be paid. (1258)

Linda sees past her sons' exaggerated lies and is not afraid to criticize them for their selfish choices. She pretends to be unaware of their shortcomings, but her seeming obliviousness is simply another layer in her multifaceted personality.

Linda appears to be the steadiest character in the play, providing stability for the other characters, but her constant brushing aside of problems actually makes her the most responsible for the ultimate tragedy of the play. She lies to Willy in order to soothe him, telling him he has "too much on the ball to worry about" (1238) and is "the handsomest man in the world" (1249). In the process, she allows him to continue believing in the unattainable dreams that ultimately lead him to self-destruct. She also makes exceptions for her sons, suggesting Willy can simply talk to Biff's teacher to change his grade

> Linda's failure to confront family problems

Dube 3

and encouraging Biff's business plans even when she knows he will not succeed. As a result, failure hits Biff hard because he has not been forced to think realistically.

In the end, Linda goes beyond the stereotypical boundaries of her role as ever-   Conclusion
supportive wife and mother. There are many layers to her character: beneath her simple goals of owning her home and living happily with her family lie years of disappointments and failed dreams. Hidden beneath her eagerness to please is her willingness to defy orders to defend her husband. And, although she seems not to notice what is going on, she is perceptive about the family's problems long before others show awareness. Her actions clearly show that she is more than a minor supporting character. Linda is deeply involved in the actions and impulses of the other characters in the play. As a fully developed character, she has complex motivations and human qualities (including faults) that set her apart from stock characters. As her son Happy notes, "They broke the mold when they made her" (1264).

Dube 4

Work Cited

Miller, Arthur. *Death of a Salesman. Compact Literature: Reading, Reacting, Writing*, edited by Laurie G. Kirszner and Stephen R. Mandell, 9th ed., Wadsworth, 2016, pp. 1233-1302.

 ## Writing about a Work's Cultural Context

When you explore the **cultural context** of a short story, poem, or play, you set the work in a particular time and place. Acknowledging that literary works do not exist in a vacuum, you consider factors such as the characters' social class and cultural or racial background as well as specific events that occurred at the time in which the story is set or written. You can also consider practices and situations that were characteristic of the time—for example, the wife's subservient role in Arthur Miller's *Death of a Salesman* (p. 1233) or racial discrimination in Richard Wright's "Big Black Good Man" (p. 318).

When you write your essay, you examine the connections between the work's cultural setting and the work itself, considering how particular situations and events influence the characters' actions. For example, you might see that a character in a story or play is limited—or inspired to act—by his or her race or class or gender or by a social movement, such as feminism, or by a particular event, such as a war. To set the work in context, you will probably need to do some research—perhaps reading contemporary newspapers, diaries, and letters as well as current critical interpretations of the cultural period on which you are focusing. You might even want to interview someone who lived through the events that influenced the work—for example, someone who lived through the Great Depression, which has a great impact on the lives of the characters in Tillie Olsen's "I Stand Here Ironing" (p. 299).

It usually makes sense to begin your essay with an overview to help orient readers who are not familiar with the work's background. You might also **explicate** the work (see p. 43), systematically exploring specific parallels between the historical setting and the work. Alternatively, you might focus on one character in a story or play, examining how that character is shaped by the events or conventions of a particular cultural time—for example, how Ab Snopes in William Faulkner's "Barn Burning" (p. 335) has been affected by the Civil War—and by his inferior station in life.

✔ **CHECKLIST** **Writing about a Work's Cultural Context**

When you write about a work's cultural context, consider the following questions:

- ☐ Is a particular figure or event is an important influence on the work?
- ☐ Is a particular cultural movement is an important influence on the work?
- ☐ Do you summarize and explain the relevant historical background?
- ☐ Do you clearly explain the relationship between the historical background and the literary work?
- ☐ Do you use examples and quotations from the literary work to illustrate specific parallels between the work of literature and its cultural context?
- ☐ Have you followed your instructor's format and documentation guidelines?

Writing about a Poem's Cultural Context

The following student essay, "Dreaming of Home," sets Louise Erdrich's poem "Indian Boarding School: The Runaways" (p. 986) in the context of the events that inspired it.

Monteleone 1

Matt Monteleone

Professor Kennedy

Composition 101

11 January 2015

Dreaming of Home

Louise Erdrich's poem "Indian Boarding School: The Runaways" describes the   [Introduction]
experiences of Native American children who have been sent to a US-government-sponsored boarding school. Although the experiences themselves are traumatic and heart wrenching,

Monteleone 2

the full impact of the poem comes only with an understanding of the United States
government's motivation for creating these schools and of their treatment of the Native
American children who lived there during the late nineteenth and early twentieth   Thesis
centuries. With this background, Erdrich's work becomes not only a moving description   statement
of the painful experience of Native American children at federal boarding schools, but also
a political statement about the treatment of Native Americans in the United States—and,
perhaps, a statement about the pain of forced cultural assimilation.

    "Indian Boarding School: The Runaways" relates the experience of Indian children   Explication
struggling to maintain their cultural identities and preserve their cherished memories   of poem's
of home despite a series of efforts to purge them of their Indian heritage. Erdrich   theme
uses haunting language to explain that, for these children, the world they once knew has
changed to such an extent that it exists only in their imaginations. Therefore, the children
can escape to their home only when they go to sleep—and dream. In the first stanza, the
narrator conveys her longing when she says, "Home's the place we head for in our sleep. /
Boxcars stumbling north in dreams / don't wait for us. We catch them on the run" (lines
1-3). At night, the children dream of making their way home. In the daytime, they are "cold
in regulation clothes" (11), forced to wear "dresses, long green ones" (17) and to engage in
"shameful" manual labor (19). To fight the assimilation being forced upon them, the children
have only their memories.

    By relating the experiences of these "runaways" and their dreams of home,   Transitional
Erdrich recreates the emotional experience of Native American children sent to the   paragraph
United States government's boarding schools. The history of these Indian schools further
explains the experience described in the poem and sheds light on the consequences of
America's policy of forced assimilation.

    During the late 1800s and early 1900s, the United States government sponsored   Back-
a variety of initiatives aimed at assimilating Native Americans into white culture.   ground:
Although some government officials genuinely believed that assimilation was the best   Rational-
way for Native Americans to live better, happier lives, this policy was grounded in the   ization for US govern-
assumption that white culture is superior to Indian culture. As a result, government   ment's
officials used a variety of methods to encourage assimilation, and the establishment of   Indian boarding schools
the non-reservation boarding school was one of them. According to the *Modern American
Poetry* website, the Carlisle Indian Industrial School, established in 1879 with 139 students
from the Rosebud and Pine Ridge nations, was one of the first of these schools. A description of
the Carlisle Indian Industrial School reveals that Erdrich's poem is rooted in actual events.

Monteleone 3

According to the Cumberland County Historical Society in Pennsylvania, where the Carlisle Industrial School was located, in 1879 General Richard Henry Pratt received permission from the United States government to use a former military base as the site of the first Indian boarding school. Although the school closed in 1918, Carlisle served as a model for many of the other Indian boarding schools around the United States. Consequently, an examination of its policies and practices will explain how most Indian boarding schools operated.

Background: History of Indian boarding schools

After receiving permission from the government, Pratt traveled to the Rosebud and Pine Ridge reservations to recruit students. According to an article in *Carlisle Indian Industrial School*, the chief of the Rosebud reservation, although initially reluctant, eventually agreed to send some children from the reservation to the school. Pratt soon convinced other Indian nations, including the Cheyenne, Kiowa, and Lakota, to send their children to the school as well. At the Carlisle school, the teachers used a variety of methods to "civilize" the Native American students. For example, as the *Modern American Poetry* website explains, students were given new names, their hair was cut, and they were forced to speak English instead of their tribal languages. As also noted in this article, members of the Lakota nation cut hair to symbolize mourning, so this practice was particularly upsetting to the Lakota children ("History"). Fig. 1 shows a group of Indian children at the Carlisle school. Like the girls being forced to wear long green dresses in Erdrich's poem, these Indian students are dressed in school uniforms, not in their native clothing.

Fig. 1. U.S. Army Signal Corps, "Apache children four months after arriving at the Carlisle Indian Industrial School in Pennsylvania." Owen Lindauer, "Archaeology of the Phoenix Indian School," *Archaeology*, 27 Mar. 1998, archive.archaeology.org/online/features/phoenix/.

Monteleone 4

Parents did not always send their children to Carlisle willingly. When Geronimo, chief of the Apache nation, was arrested, Pratt traveled to Fort Mario prison, where the Apache children were being held. Pratt then picked sixty-two of the children to be sent to Carlisle, despite pleas from their parents. In an effort to prevent them from leaving, several of the parents hid the children, but Pratt eventually found them, and the children were sent to the school ("History").

Erdrich closes her poem by explaining how the children try to remember their cultural heritage even as they are being forced to adopt the customs of white America:

> Our brushes cut the stone in watered arcs
>
> and in the soak frail outlines shiver clear
>
> a moment, things us kids pressed on the dark
>
> face before it hardened, pale, remembering
>
> delicate old injuries, the spines of names and leaves. (20-24)

Conclusion (poem set in cultural context)

The history of the Indian boarding schools, and how they worked to rid children of their Native American identities, clearly informs this poem. In this sense, Erdrich's work is not only literary; it is also political. By invoking an emotional response in her readers, Erdrich is able to expose a dark side of United States history and its treatment of Native Americans.

Monteleone 5

Works Cited

"Carlisle Indian Industrial School." *Cumberland County Historical Society*, historicalsociety.com/
    Template14.html#ciis_ancestors.

Erdrich, Louise. "Indian Boarding School: The Runaways." *Compact Literature: Reading,Reacting,
    Writing*, edited by Laurie G. Kirszner and Stephen R. Mandell, 9th ed., Wadsworth, 2016,
    p. 986.

Landis, Barbara. "About the *Carlisle Indian Industrial School*." *Modern American Poetry*, 1996,
    www.english.illinois.edu/maps/poets/a_f/erdrich/boarding/carlisle.htm.

Nelson, Cary. "About Indian Boarding Schools: Key Issues and Challenges." *Modern American
    Poetry*, www.english.illinois.edu/Maps/poets/a_f/erdrich/boarding/keyissues.htm.

CHAPTER 4

THINKING CRITICALLY ABOUT YOUR WRITING

As you write about literature, you should carefully assess the strength of the ideas you present to readers. This is especially true in **literary arguments**, essays in which you take a stand on a debatable topic and try to convince readers to accept your position (see Chapter 5). If you learn to **think critically** about your writing, you will be able to distinguish fact from opinion, evaluate the usefulness and appropriateness of your supporting evidence, and keep any biases you have out of your writing. Then, guided by the basic principles of inductive and deductive reasoning, you will be able to structure your literary argument in a way that will encourage readers to accept (or at least acknowledge) the strengths of your ideas.

 ## Distinguishing Fact from Opinion

A **fact** is a verifiable statement that something is true or that something occurred. An **opinion** is a personal judgment or belief that can never be substantiated beyond any doubt and is, therefore, debatable.

Fact: Langston Hughes mentions four rivers in his poem "The Negro Speaks of Rivers."

Opinion: Rivers have symbolic significance in Langston Hughes's poem "The Negro Speaks of Rivers."

An opinion may be *unsupported* or *supported.*

Unsupported Opinion: Rivers have symbolic significance in Langston Hughes's poem "The Negro Speaks of Rivers."

Supported Opinion: Rivers have symbolic significance in Langston Hughes's poem "The Negro Speaks of Rivers." In the poem, the speaker mentions four rivers—the Euphrates, the Congo, the Nile, and the Mississippi. According to the speaker, these rivers are as "ancient as the world and as old as the flow of human blood in human veins" (line 2). Through their associations with the black experience, these particular rivers are linked not only to the speaker's African roots but also to the racial situation in America at the time the poem was written.

As the above examples show, supported opinion is much more convincing than unsupported opinion.

Supporting Your Opinions

Your opinions can be supported with **examples**, **quotations**, or **expert opinion**.

Examples:

In the play *The Glass Menagerie*, Jim's focus on the future challenges Amanda's unrealistic romantic dreams of the past. For example, when Jim comes to dinner, she dreams of entertaining him in the old Southern tradition, but he talks enthusiastically of the promise the future holds.

Quotations:

Although Gertrude is queen of Denmark, she is also a devoted mother. In her efforts to console her son, she speaks tenderly: "Good Hamlet, cast thy knighted color off" (1.2.68). She also conveys her wisdom about life: "Thou know'st 'tis common,—all that live must die, / Passing through nature to eternity" (1.2.72-73).

Expert Opinion (from Literary Criticism):

Throughout the short story "The Yellow Wallpaper," a number of clues suggest that the narrator may be delusional. According to Sandra Gilbert and Susan Gubar in *Madwoman in the Attic: The Woman Writer and the Nineteenth-Century Literary Imagination*, the extent of the narrator's dislike for the wallpaper should serve as an early warning that she is not responding well to her treatment and that she may in fact be losing her mind (464).

 ## Evaluating Supporting Evidence

The examples, quotations, and opinions of literary critics that you use to support your statements constitute **evidence**. The more reliable your supporting evidence, the more willing your readers will be to accept a statement. Remember, though, that to be **reliable** the evidence you use must be *accurate, sufficient, representative,* and *relevant.*

For your evidence to be **accurate**, it must come from a trustworthy source. Such a source quotes *exactly* and does not present information out of context. It also presents examples, quotations, and expert opinion fairly, drawing them from other reliable sources. Finally, a trustworthy source includes full documentation for information it takes from other sources.

For your evidence to be **sufficient**, it must contain enough information to support your conclusions. It is not enough, for instance, to cite just one Joyce Carol Oates short story in an attempt to demonstrate that Oats's experiments with literary form and subject matter give her work universal appeal. Moreover, the opinions of a single literary critic, no matter how reputable, are not enough to support this position.

For your evidence to be **representative**, it must reflect a range of sources and viewpoints. You should not choose evidence that supports your thesis and ignore evidence that does not. For example, if you are making the point that the structure of Emily Dickinson's poems changed over the course of her career, you cannot disregard compelling evidence that, in fact, her poetic structure remained consistent over the years.

Finally, for your evidence to be **relevant**, it must apply to the work being discussed. For example, you cannot support the statement that Arthur Miller's *Death of a Salesman* critiques post–World War II American society by citing examples from Miller's *The Crucible*.

 ## Detecting Bias in Your Writing

A **bias** is an opinion, usually unfavorable, based on preconceived ideas rather than on evidence. As a critical thinker, you should be aware that your biases can sometimes lead you to see just what you want to see and to ignore evidence to the contrary.

Detecting Bias in Your Writing

When you write, be on the lookout for the following kinds of biases:

- **Slanted language:** Avoid slanted language—language that is inflammatory or confrontational. For example, do not say that a literary critic's article is stupid or that a character in a short story is immoral. Instead, use language that clearly and accurately conveys your ideas.
- **Biased tone:** Avoid using a tone that communicates bias toward your subject (for example, anger or sarcasm).
- **Stereotypes:** Avoid statements that perpetuate stereotypes. For example, be careful not to make unwarranted assumptions about gender roles or about a particular groups' attributes or shortcomings and then criticize characters on the basis of these generalizations. For example, saying that Andy in "Doe Season" gets what she deserves because a deer hunt is no place for girls stereotypes the character and reveals gender bias.
- **Preconceived ideas:** Don't let your own beliefs or attitudes prevent you from fairly evaluating a work of literature. For example, you may believe strongly that husbands and wives should be faithful to each other, but you should not let this belief prevent you from appreciating the literary strengths of Kate Chopin's "The Storm," a short story in which two characters commit adultery, apparently with no consequences.

 ## Understanding Logic

All argumentative essays, including literary arguments, rely on **logic**—inductive and deductive reasoning—to reach conclusions in a systematic way. If you understand the basic principles of inductive and deductive reasoning, you will be able to write clearer, more convincing essays.

Inductive Reasoning

Inductive reasoning is a process that moves from specific facts, observations, or experiences to a general conclusion. You use inductive reasoning in your writing when you want to lead readers from a series of specific observations to a general conclusion. You can see how inductive reasoning operates by studying the following list of statements about John Updike's short story "A&P":

- Sammy, the main character in "A&P," is nineteen and works as a cashier in a supermarket in a small New England town.
- Sammy sees the A&P's customers as sheep, with no individuality.
- Sammy's fellow workers include Stokesie, a married twenty-two-year-old with two children, and Lengel, the store manager.
- Stokesie and Lengel lead boring, predictable lives.
- On the day the story takes place, three girls in bathing suits walk into the store and change Sammy's life.
- Sammy fantasizes about the girls' lives and imagines what a party at one girl's home would be like.
- When Lengel scolds the girls for dressing inappropriately, Sammy abruptly quits his job.
- At the end of the story, Sammy realizes that although some people think he was foolish to quit his job, he did the right thing.

After reading the statements above, you can use inductive reasoning to reach a general conclusion about the theme of Updike's story: that someone who wants to escape a confining life must sometimes reject his community's values.

No matter how much evidence you present, however, an inductive conclusion is never certain, only probable. You arrive at an inductive conclusion by making an **inference**, a statement about the unknown based on the known. In order to bridge the gap that exists between your specific observations and your general conclusion, you have to make an **inductive leap**. If you have presented enough specific evidence, this gap will be relatively small and your readers will accept your conclusion. If the gap is too wide, your readers will accuse you of making a **hasty generalization**—a conclusion based on too little evidence.

Deductive Reasoning

Deductive reasoning is a process that moves from a general statement believed to be true or **self-evident** (so obvious that it needs no proof) to a specific conclusion. Writers use deductive reasoning when they think their audience is more likely to be influenced by logic than by evidence. The process of deduction has traditionally been illustrated by a **syllogism**, a three-part set of statements or propositions that includes a *major premise*, a *minor premise*, and a *conclusion*.

Major Premise: All tragic heroes have tragic flaws.

Minor Premise: Hamlet is a tragic hero.

Conclusion: Therefore, Hamlet has a tragic flaw.

The **major premise** of a syllogism makes a general statement that the writer believes to be true or self-evident. The **minor premise** presents a specific example of the belief that is stated in the major premise. If the reasoning is sound, the **conclusion** should follow from the two premises. (Note that the conclusion should introduce no terms that have not already appeared in the major and minor premises.) The advantage of a deductive argument is that if readers accept the premises, they must necessarily grant the conclusion.

A syllogism is **valid** when its conclusion logically follows from its premises. A syllogism is **true** when the information it contains is consistent with the facts. To be **sound**, a syllogism must be *both* valid and true. However, a syllogism can be valid without being true or true without being valid. The following syllogism, for example, is valid but not true.

> **Major Premise:** All poems contain rhymed lines.
>
> **Minor Premise:** Walt Whitman's "Had I the Choice" is a poem.
>
> **Conclusion:** Therefore, Walt Whitman's "Had I the Choice" contains rhymed lines.

This syllogism is valid. In the major premise, the phrase *all poems* establishes that the entire class *poems* contains rhymed lines. After Walt Whitman's "Had I the Choice" is identified as a poem, the conclusion that it contains rhymed lines logically follows. However, Whitman's poem, like many others, is unrhymed. Because the major premise of this syllogism is not true, no conclusion based on it can be true. For this reason, even though the logic of the syllogism is solid, its conclusion is not.

Toulmin Logic

Stephen Toulmin, a philosopher and rhetorician, has formulated another way to analyze arguments. According to Toulmin, the traditional syllogism, while useful for identifying flaws in logic, is not useful for analyzing arguments that occur in the real world. To address this shortcoming, Toulmin divides arguments into three parts: the *claim*, the *grounds*, and the *warrant*:

- **The claim** is your thesis, the main point that you want to make in your essay.
- **The grounds** are the facts, examples, and opinions of experts that support your claim. In essays about literature, the grounds can come from a work of literature or from literary criticism.
- **The warrant** is an assumption that underlies both the claim and the grounds. Keep in mind that some warrants are explicitly stated while others may be simply implied.

In its simplest terms, an argument following Toulmin's structure would look like this:

- **The claim:** Phoenix Jackson, the main character in Eudora Welty's "A Worn Path," challenges the racial restrictions of her community.
- **The grounds:** Phoenix Jackson defies the man with the gun; she asks a white woman to tie her shoe; she steals a nickel; she gets free medicine from the doctor.
- **The warrant:** At the time "A Worn Path" takes place, racial segregation limited the actions of African Americans.

Notice that the claim presents a specific situation; the warrant, however, is a general principle that could apply to a number of situations. In a sense, the warrant is similar to the major premise of a syllogism, and the claim is similar to the conclusion. The grounds consist of the evidence that supports the claim.

Recognizing Logical Fallacies

Logical fallacies are flawed arguments. A writer who inadvertently uses such fallacies is not thinking clearly or logically; a writer who intentionally uses them is trying to deceive readers. Learn to recognize them so you can avoid them when you write.

Common Logical Fallacies

When you read and when you write, watch out for the following logical fallacies:

- **Hasty Generalization:** A form of induction that reaches a conclusion on the basis of insufficient evidence. For example, one appearance of a river in a poem is not enough to support the statement that it is an important symbol. Several mentions, however, might justify this conclusion.
- **Sweeping Generalization:** A generalization that cannot be supported no matter how much evidence is supplied. For example, the statement "All literary critics like August Wilson's plays" is a sweeping generalization. Certainly, many critics like Wilson's plays, but it is virtually impossible to prove that all do. To avoid making statements that cannot be supported, qualify your statements with words such as *some, many, often,* or *most.*
- ***Ad Hominem* (Argument to the Person):** A fallacy that occurs when you attack a person rather than the issue, as in the following argument: "Many critics see imagism as a very important literary movement. However, the fact that its founder, Ezra Pound, was a Nazi sympathizer challenges that assessment." Although you may find Pound's Nazi sympathies repugnant, his political ideas are not relevant to your evaluation of imagism.
- **Non Sequitur:** A conclusion that does not logically follow from what comes before it, as in the following statement: "John Updike wrote critically acclaimed novels, so he must have been a gifted poet." It does not logically follow that just because Updike wrote good novels, he also wrote good poetry.
- **Either/Or Fallacy:** A fallacy that occurs when a complex issue is presented as if it has only two sides. If you ask your readers to consider whether a character is good or evil, you commit this fallacy. In fact, a complex character may possess both positive and negative qualities.
- **Begging the Question:** A fallacy that occurs when you present a debatable premise as if it were true, as in the following statement: "Hemingway's negative portrayals of women have caused his popularity to decline in recent years."

Hemingway's portrayals of women may be negative, but readers do not have to accept this statement as fact just because you say it is true. Before you can make a judgment based on this assertion, you must support it with examples from Hemingway's work as well as with statements from a fair range of literary critics.

- **Bandwagon:** A fallacy that occurs when you try to establish that something is true just because everyone believes it is. You commit this fallacy when you say, for example, that a certain literary work must be good because it is so popular.

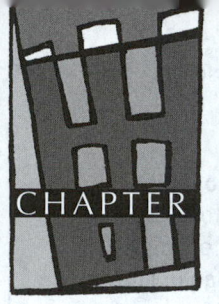

CHAPTER 5

WRITING LITERARY ARGUMENTS

Many of the essays you write about literature are **expository**—that is, you write to give information to readers. For example, you might discuss the rhyme or meter of a poem or examine the interaction of two characters in a play. Other essays you write, however, may be **literary arguments**—that is, you take a position on a debatable topic and attempt to change readers' minds about it. For example, you might argue that the boy's quest in James Joyce's short story "Araby" (p. 361) has symbolic meaning or that Sammy, the main character in John Updike's short story "A&P" (p. 238), is sexist.

When you write a literary argument, you follow the same process you do when you write any essay about a literary topic. However, because the purpose of an argument is to convince readers, you need to use some additional strategies to present your ideas.

 ## Planning a Literary Argument

Choosing a Topic

Your first step in writing a literary argument will be to decide on a topic to write about. Ideally, your topic should be one that you really want to explore further. It stands to reason that the more your topic interests you, the more willing you will be to do some serious research and some hard thinking.

Your topic should also be narrow enough for you to develop within your page limit. After all, in an argumentative essay, you will have to present your own ideas and supply convincing support while possibly also addressing opposing arguments. If your topic is too broad, you will not be able to discuss it in enough detail.

Finally, your topic should be interesting to your readers. Keep in mind that some topics—such as the significance of the wall in Robert Frost's poem "Mending Wall" (p. 988)—have been written about so often that you will probably not be able to say anything new or interesting about them. Instead of relying on an overused topic, choose one that allows you to write something original.

Developing an Argumentative Thesis

After you have chosen a topic, your next step is to develop an **argumentative thesis**—one that takes a strong stand on an issue. Because an argumentative essay attempts to change the way readers think, it should focus on a thesis about which reasonable people disagree. In other words, it must be **debatable**; that is, it must have at least two sides. A factual statement—one about which reasonable people do not disagree—is therefore not appropriate as a thesis for an argumentative essay.

> **Factual Statement:** Linda Loman is Willie's long-suffering wife in Arthur Miller's play *Death of a Salesman*.

> **Debatable Thesis:** More than a stereotype of the long-suffering wife, Linda Loman in Arthur Miller's play *Death of a Salesman* is a complex character.

One way to make sure that your thesis actually does take a stand is to try to formulate an **antithesis**—a statement that takes an arguable position opposite from yours. If you can construct an antithesis, you can be certain that your thesis statement is debatable. If you cannot, your thesis statement needs further revision.

> **Thesis Statement:** The last line of Richard Wright's short story "Big Black Good Man" indicates that Jim was fully aware all along of Olaf's deep-seated racial prejudice.

> **Antithesis:** The last line of Richard Wright's short story "Big Black Good Man" indicates that Jim remained unaware of Olaf's feelings toward him.

NOTE Your thesis statement is an assertion that your entire essay supports. Keep in mind, however, that you can never prove an argumentative thesis conclusively—if you could, there would be no argument. The best you can do is provide enough evidence to establish a high probability that your thesis is reasonable.

✔ **CHECKLIST   Developing an Argumentative Thesis**

To make sure you have an effective argumentative thesis, consider these questions:

☐ Does your thesis statement make clear to readers what position you are taking?

☐ Can you formulate an antithesis?

☐ Can you support your thesis with evidence from the text and from research?

Defining Your Terms

You should always define the key terms you use in your argument. For example, if you are using the term *narrator* in an essay, make sure that readers know whether you are referring to a first-person or a third-person narrator. In addition, you may need to clarify the difference between an **unreliable narrator**—someone who misrepresents or misinterprets events—and a **reliable narrator**—someone who accurately describes events. Without a clear definition of the terms you are using, readers may have a difficult time understanding the point you are making.

Defining Your Terms

Be especially careful to use precise terms in your thesis statement. Avoid vague and judgmental words, such as *wrong, bad, good, right*, and *immoral*.

Vague: The poem "Birmingham Sunday (September 15, 1963)" by Langston Hughes shows how bad racism can be.

Clearer: The poem "Birmingham Sunday (September 15, 1963)" by Langston Hughes makes a moving statement about how pervasive and dehumanizing racism can be.

Considering Your Audience

As you plan your essay, keep your audience in mind. For example, if you are writing about a work that has been discussed in class, you can assume that your readers are familiar with it; include plot summary only when it is needed to explain a point you are making. Keep in mind that you will be addressing an academic audience—your instructor and possibly some students. For this reason, you should be sure to follow the conventions of writing about literature as well as the conventions of standard written English. (For information on the conventions of writing about literature, see the checklist in Chapter 2, p. 31.)

When you write an argumentative essay, you should assume that you are addressing a **skeptical audience**—one that is not easily convinced. Remember, your thesis is debatable, so not everyone will agree with you—and even if your readers are sympathetic to your position, you cannot assume that they will accept your ideas without question.

The strategies you use to convince your readers will vary according to your relationship with them. Somewhat skeptical readers may need to see only that your argument is logical and that your evidence is solid. More skeptical readers, however, may need to see that you understand their reservations and that you concede some of their points. Of course, you may never be able to convince hostile readers that your conclusions are legitimate. The best you can hope for is that these readers will acknowledge the strengths of your argument even if they do not accept your conclusion.

Refuting Opposing Arguments

As you develop your literary argument, you may often need to **refute**—that is, to disprove or raise doubts about—opposing arguments by demonstrating that they are false, misguided, exaggerated, or illogical. By summarizing and refuting opposing views, you make opposing arguments seem less credible to readers; thus, you strengthen your case. When an opposing argument is so strong that it cannot be easily dismissed, however, you should acknowledge the strength of the argument and then point out its limitations.

Notice in the following paragraph how a student refutes the argument that Homer Barron, a character in William Faulkner's short story "A Rose for Emily," is gay.

Summary of opposing argument	A number of critics have suggested that Homer Barron, Miss Emily's suitor, is gay. Actually, there is some evidence in the story to support this interpretation. For example, the narrator points out that Homer "liked men" and that he was not "a marrying man" (Faulkner 224). In addition, the narrator describes Homer as wearing yellow gloves when he took Emily for drives. According to the critic William Greenslade, in the 1890s yellow was associated with homosexuality (24). This evidence does not in itself establish that Homer is gay, however. During the nineteenth century, many men preferred the company of other men (as many do today). This, in itself, did not mean they were gay. Neither does the fact that Homer wore yellow gloves. According to the narrator, Homer was a man who liked to dress well. It is certainly possible that he wore these gloves to impress Miss Emily, a woman he was trying to attract.
Acknowledgment of argument's strengths	
Refutation	

 Using Evidence Effectively

Supporting Your Literary Argument

Many literary arguments are built on **assertions**—statements made about a debatable topic—backed by **evidence**—supporting examples in the form of references to the text, quotations, and the opinions of literary critics. For example, if you stated that Torvald Helmer, Nora's husband in Henrik Ibsen's play *A Doll House*, is as much a victim of society as his wife is, you could support this assertion with relevant quotations and examples from the play. You could also paraphrase, summarize, or quote the ideas of literary critics who also hold this opinion. Remember, only assertions that are **self-evident** ("All plays include characters and dialogue.") or **factual** ("*A Doll House* was published in 1879.") need no supporting evidence. All other kinds of assertions require support.

Establishing Credibility

Some people bring **credibility** with them whenever they write. When a well-known literary critic evaluates the contributions of a particular writer, you can assume that he or she speaks with authority. (Although you might question the critic's opinions, you do not question his or her expertise.) But most people do not have this kind of credibility. When you write a literary argument, you must constantly work to establish credibility. You do this by *demonstrating knowledge, maintaining a reasonable tone,* and *presenting yourself as someone worth listening to.*

Demonstrating Knowledge One way to establish credibility is by presenting your own carefully considered ideas about a subject. A clear argument and compelling support can demonstrate to readers that you know what you are talking about.

You can also show readers that you have thoroughly researched your subject. By referring to important research sources and by providing accurate documentation for your information, you present evidence that you have done the necessary background reading. Including a range of sources—not just one or two—suggests that you are well acquainted with your subject. Remember, however, that questionable sources, inaccurate (or missing) documentation, and factual errors can undermine your credibility. For some readers, an undocumented quotation or even an incorrect date can call an entire argument into question.

Maintaining a Reasonable Tone Your **tone**—your attitude toward your readers or subject—is almost as important as the information you convey. Talk *to* your readers, not *at* them. If you lecture your readers or appear to talk down to them, you will alienate them. Generally speaking, readers are more likely to respond to a writer who seems fair and respectful than one who seems strident or condescending.

As you write your essay, use moderate language, and qualify your statements so that they seem reasonable. Avoid words and phrases such as *all, never, always, definitely,* and *in every case,* which can make your points seem simplistic, exaggerated, or unrealistic. Also, avoid absolute statements. For example, the statement, In "Doe Season," the ocean definitely symbolizes Andy's attachment to her mother, leaves no room for other possible interpretations. A more measured and accurate statement might be, In "Doe Season," the use of the ocean as a symbol suggests Andy's identification with her mother and her realization that she is becoming a woman.

Presenting Yourself as Someone Worth Listening To When you write a literary argument, you should present yourself as someone your readers will want to listen to. Make your argument confidently, and don't apologize for your views. For example, do not use phrases such as "In my opinion," "It seems to me," and "Although I am not an expert," which undercut your credibility. Be consistent, and be careful not to contradict yourself. Finally, avoid the use of *I* (unless you are asked to give your opinion or to write a response), and avoid slang and colloquialisms.

Being Fair

Because argument promotes one position over all others, it is seldom objective. However, college writing requires that you stay within the bounds of fairness and that you avoid **bias**—opinions based on preconceived ideas rather than on evidence (see p. 57). To make sure that the support for your argument is not misleading or distorted, follow these guidelines:

- *Avoid misrepresenting evidence.* You **misrepresent evidence** when you exaggerate the extent to which critical opinion supports your thesis. For example, don't try to make a weak case stronger than it actually is by saying that "many critics" think that something is so when only one or two do.

- *Avoid quoting out of context.* You **quote out of context** when you take a passage out of its original setting in order to distort its intended meaning. For example, you are quoting out of context if you say, Emily Dickinson's poems are so idiosyncratic that they do not appeal to readers when your source says, "Emily Dickinson's poems are so idiosyncratic that they do not appeal to readers *who are accustomed to safe, conventional subjects.*" By eliminating a key portion of the sentence, you unfairly alter the meaning of the original.

- *Avoid slanting.* When you select only information that supports your case and ignore information that does not, you are guilty of **slanting.** You can eliminate this problem by including a full range of examples, not just examples that support your thesis. Be sure to consult books and articles that represent a cross-section of critical opinion about your subject.

- *Avoid using unfair appeals.* Traditionally, writers of arguments use three types of appeals to influence readers: **logical appeals**, which address a reader's sense of reason, **emotional appeals**, which play on a reader's emotions, and **ethical appeals**, which emphasize the credibility of the writer. Problems arise, however, when these appeals are used unfairly. For example, writers can use **logical fallacies**—flawed arguments—to fool readers into thinking a conclusion is logical when it is not (see Chapter 4 for a discussion of logical fallacies). Writers can also use inappropriate emotional appeals— appeals to prejudice, for example—to influence readers. And finally, writers can undercut their credibility if they use questionable support—books and articles written by people who have little or no expertise on the topic. This is especially true when information is obtained from the Internet, where the credentials of the writer may be difficult or impossible to assess. If you want your readers to accept your position, you should be careful to avoid logical fallacies and unfair appeals.

Using Visuals as Evidence

Visuals—pictures, drawings, diagrams, and the like—can add a persuasive element to your essay. Because visual images have an immediate impact, they can sometimes make a strong literary argument even stronger. In a sense, visuals are another type of evidence that can support your thesis. For example, suppose you are writing an essay about the play *Trifles* in which you argue that Mrs. Wright's quilt is an important symbol in the play. In fact, your research leads you to conclude that the process of creating the quilt by piecing together its log cabin pattern parallels the process by which the two female characters in the play determine why Mrs. Wright murdered her husband. The addition of a photograph of a quilt with a log cabin pattern could not only eliminate several paragraphs of description but also help support your conclusion.

Of course, not all visuals will be appropriate or effective for a literary argument. Before using a visual, make certain it actually supports the point you want to make. If it does not, it will distract readers and undercut your argument. To ensure that readers understand the purpose of the visual, introduce it with a sentence that establishes its context; then, discuss its significance, paying particular attention to how it helps you make your point. Finally, be sure to include full documentation for any visual that is not your original creation. (See pp. 70, 71, and 75 for examples of visuals used as evidence in student essays.)

 ## Organizing a Literary Argument

In its simplest form, a literary argument—like any argumentative essay—consists of a thesis statement and supporting evidence. Literary arguments, however, frequently use additional strategies to win audience approval and to overcome potential opposition.

Elements of a Literary Argument

- **Introduction:** The introduction should orient readers to the subject of your essay, presenting the issue you will discuss and explaining its significance.
- **Thesis statement:** In most literary arguments, you will present your thesis statement in your introduction. However, if you think your readers may not be familiar with the issue you are discussing (or if it is very controversial), you may want to postpone stating your thesis until later in the essay.
- **Background:** In this section, you can survey critical opinion about your topic, perhaps pointing out the shortcomings of these opinions. You can also define key terms, review basic facts, or briefly summarize the plot of the work or works you will discuss.
- **Arguments in support of your thesis:** Here you present your arguments and the evidence to support them. It makes sense to move from the least controversial to the most controversial point or from the most familiar to the least familiar idea. In other words, you should begin with arguments that your readers are most likely to accept and then deal with those that require more discussion and more evidence.
- **Refutation of opposing arguments:** In a literary argument, you should summarize and refute the most obvious arguments against your thesis. If you do not address these opposing arguments, doubts about your position will remain in your readers' minds. If the opposing arguments are relatively weak, refute them after you have presented your own arguments. However, if the opposing arguments are strong, you may want to concede their strengths and discuss their limitations *before* you present your own arguments.
- **Conclusion:** Your conclusion will often restate your thesis as well as the major arguments you have made in support of it. Your conclusion can also summarize key points, remind readers of the weaknesses of opposing arguments, or underscore the logic of your position. Many writers like to end their essays with a strong last line—for example, a quotation or a memorable statement that they hope will stay with readers after they finish the essay.

Writing a Literary Argument

The following student essay and the one that begins on page 73 present literary arguments.

The first essay focuses on Dee, a character in Alice Walker's short story "Everyday Use." The student author supports her thesis with ideas she developed as she read the story and watched a DVD that dramatized it. She also includes information she found when she did research. (Note that her essay includes two visuals from a DVD version of the story.)

Chase 1

Margaret Chase

Professor Sierra

English 1001

6 January 2015

The Politics of "Everyday Use"

Alice Walker's "Everyday Use" focuses on a mother, Mrs. Johnson, and her two Introduction
daughters, Maggie and Dee, and how they view their heritage. The story's climax comes
when Mrs. Johnson rejects Dee's request to take a hand-stitched quilt with her so that she can
hang it on her wall. Knowing that Maggie will put the quilt to "everyday use," Dee is horrified,
and she tells her mother and Maggie that they do not understand their heritage. Although
many literary critics see Dee's desire for the quilt as materialistic and shallow, a closer Thesis statement
examination of this story, written in 1973, suggests a more positive interpretation of
Dee's character.

On the surface, "Everyday Use" is about two sisters, Dee and Maggie, and Background
Mrs. Johnson, their mother. Mrs. Johnson tells the reader that "Dee, . . . would always
look anyone in the eye. Hesitation was no part of her nature" (428). Unlike her sister Dee,
Maggie is shy and introverted. She is described as looking like a lame animal that has been run
over by a car. According to the narrator, "She has been like this, chin on chest,
eyes on ground, feet in shuffle" (428) ever since she was burned in a fire.

Unlike Dee, Mrs. Johnson never got an education. After second grade, she explains, the
school closed down. She says, "Don't ask me why: in 1927 colored asked fewer questions
than they do now" (428). Mrs. Johnson admits that she accepts the status quo even though
she knows that it is unjust. This admission further establishes the difference between Mrs.
Johnson and Dee: Mrs. Johnson has accepted her circumstances, while Dee has worked to
change hers. Their differences are illustrated in a film version of the story by their contrasting styles of dress. As shown in fig. 1, Dee and her boyfriend Hakim-a-barber dress Background continued
in clothes that celebrate their African heritage; Mrs. Johnson and Maggie dress in
plain, conservative clothing.

When Dee arrives home with her new boyfriend, other differences soon become obvious. As she eyes her mother's belongings and asks Mrs. Johnson if she can take the top
of the butter churn home with her, it is clear that she is materialistic. However, her years
away from home have also politicized her. Dee now wants to be called "Wangero" because
she believes (although mistakenly) that her given name comes

Chase 2

©Denna Bendall/Worn Path Productions

Fig. 1. Dee and Hakim-a-barber arrive at the family home; *The Wadsworth Original Film Series in Literature: "Everyday Use,"* directed by Bruce R. Schwartz, Wadsworth, 2005.

from whites who owned her ancestors. In addition, she talks about how a new day is dawning for African Americans.

The meaning and political importance of Dee's decision to adopt an African name and wear African clothing cannot be fully appreciated without a knowledge of the social and political context in which Walker wrote this story. Walker's own comments about this time period explain Dee's behavior and add meaning to it. In her interview with White, Walker explains that the late 1960s was a time of cultural and intellectual awakening for African Americans. Many turned ideologically and culturally to Africa, adopting the dress, hairstyles, and even the names of their African ancestors. Walker admits that as a young woman she too became interested in discovering her African heritage. (In fact, she herself was given the name *Wangero* during a visit to Kenya in the late 1960s.) Walker tells White that she considered keeping this new name but eventually realized that to do so would be to "dismiss" her family and her American heritage. When she researched her American family, she found that her great-great-grandmother had walked from Virginia to Georgia carrying two children. "If that's not a Walker," she says, "I don't know what is." Thus, Walker realized that, over

> First argument in support of thesis

time, African Americans had actually transformed the names they had originally taken from their enslavers. To respect the ancestors she knew, Walker says, she decided it was important to keep her given name.

Along with adopting symbols of their African heritage, many African Americans also elevated these symbols, such as the quilt shown in fig. 2, to the status of art. According to Salaam, one way of doing this was to put these objects in museums; another was to hang them on the walls of their homes. Such acts were aimed at convincing whites that African Americans had an old and rich culture and that, consequently, they deserved respect. These gestures were also meant to improve self-esteem and pride within black communities (Salaam 42-43).

> Second argument in support of thesis

©Suzanne English/Worn Path Productions

Fig. 2. Traditional hand-stitched quilt; Evelyn C. White, "Alice Walker: Stitches in Time," interview, *The Wadsworth Original Film Series in Literature: "Everyday Use,"* directed by Bruce R. Schwartz, Wadsworth, 2005.

Admittedly, as some critics have pointed out, Dee is more materialistic than political. For example, although Mrs. Johnson makes several statements throughout the story that suggest her admiration of Dee's defiant character, she also identifies incidents that highlight Dee's materialism and selfishness. When their first house burned down, Dee watched it burn while she stood under a tree with "a look of concentration" (428) rather than grief. Mrs. Johnson knows that Dee hated their small, dingy house, and she knows too that Dee was glad to see it destroyed. Furthermore, Walker acknowledges in an interview with her biographer, Evelyn C. White, that as she was writing the story, she imagined that Dee might even have set the fire that destroyed the house and scarred her

> Summary and refutation of opposing argument

sister. Even now, Dee is ashamed of the tin-roofed house her family lives in, and she has said that she would never bring her friends there. Mrs. Johnson has always known that Dee wanted "nice things" (428); even at sixteen, "she had a style of her own,: and knew what style was" (428). However, although Dee is materialistic and self-serving, she is also proud and strong willed. Knowing that she will encounter opposition wherever she goes, she works to establish power. Thus, her desire for the quilt can be seen as an attempt to establish herself and her African American culture in a society dominated by whites.

Even though Mrs. Johnson knows Dee wants the quilt, she gives it to Maggie. According to literary critics Houston Baker and Charlotte Pierce-Baker, when Mrs. Johnson decides to give the quilt to Maggie, she is challenging Dee's understanding of her heritage. Unlike Dee, Mrs. Johnson recognizes that quilts signify "sacred generations of women who have made their own special kind of beauty separate from the traditional artistic world" (qtd. in Piedmont-Marton 45). According to Baker and Pierce-Baker, Mrs. Johnson realizes that her daughter Maggie, whom she has long dismissed because of her quiet nature and shyness, understands the true meaning of the quilt in a way that Dee never will (Piedmont-Marton 45).

> Analysis of Mrs. Johnson's final act

Unlike Dee, Maggie has paid close attention to the traditions and skills of her mother and grandmother: she has actually learned to quilt. More important, by staying with her mother instead of going to school, she has gotten to know her family. She underscores this fact when she tells her mother that Dee can have the quilt because she does not need it to remember her grandmother. Even though Maggie's and Mrs. Johnson's understanding of heritage may be more emotionally profound than Dee's, it is important not to dismiss Dee's interest in elevating the quilt to the level of art. The political stakes of defining an object as art in the late 1960s and early 1970s were high, and the fight for equality went beyond basic civil rights.

Although there is much in the story that indicates Dee's materialism, her desire to hang the quilt should not be dismissed as selfish. Like Mrs. Johnson and Maggie, Dee is a complicated character. In 1973, when "Everyday Use" was written, displaying the quilt would have been not only a personal act, but also a political act—an act with important implications. The final message of "Everyday Use" may just be that an accurate understanding of the quilt (and, by extension, of African American culture) requires both views—Maggie's and Mrs. Johnson's "everyday use" and Dee's elevation of the quilt to art.

> Conclusion (restating thesis)

Chase 5

Works Cited

Piedmont-Marton, Elisabeth. "An Overview of 'Everyday Use.'" *Short Stories for Students,*
    vol. 2, 1997, pp. 42–45. *Literature Resource Center,* www.go.galegroup.com/ps/i.
    do?id=Gale%7CH1420002698&V=2.

Salaam, Kalamu Ya. "A Primer of the Black Arts Movement: Excerpts from *The Magic of Juju: An*
    Appreciation of the Black Arts Movement." *Black Renaissance / Renaissance Noire*, 2002,
    pp. 40–59.

Walker, Alice. "Alice Walker: Stitches in Time." Interview by Evelyn C. White, *The Wadsworth*
    Original Film Series in Literature: "Everyday Use," directed by Bruce R. Schwartz, Wad-
    sworth, 2005.

---. "Everyday Use." *Compact Literature: Reading, Reacting, Writing,* edited by Laurie G. Kirszner
    and Stephen R. Mandell, 9th ed., Wadsworth, 2016, pp. 427–33.

The following literary argument addresses the question of why video games should be considered literature. The student who wrote this essay supports her argument with her own experience with video games as well as with information that she found online and in her college library. (Note that her essay includes a visual from the video game *World of Warcraft* to illustrate one of her points.)

Linde 1

Danielle Linde

Professor Smith

English 1001

15 January 2015

The Literary Merit of Video Games

In recent years, some critics have begun to view video games not just as   Introduction
entertainment but also as a form of literature. While some claim that video games will
bring about the death of traditional literature, others argue that they will bring new life to
literature. More than one literary critic has observed that many of the games that are available
today have much in common with traditional forms of literature.

Linde 2

In fact, some video games create fictionalized worlds that share many of the characteristics of traditional literature. For this reason, video games should be given the respect they deserve and be considered a legitimate form of imaginative literature.

> Thesis statement

The basic function of video games is to tell a story. Critic Marie-Laure Ryan argues that "a text of fiction invites its readers to imagine a world" and that a video game presents the same experience to players. Like a traditional author of a literary work, a video game creator invents a world that can be inhabited by the imagination as players interact with the game. Ryan observes that players can "transport themselves in imagination from the world they regard as actual toward an alternative possible world—a virtual reality—which they regard as actual for the duration of their involvement in the text, game, or spectacle." Similarly, Geoffrey Rockwell refers to video games as a "form of fiction consumed through the computer" (345). Like fiction, these video games contain their own casts of characters, including heroes and villains the player can interact with or even become. In many ways, this experience is the same one a reader has when he or she chooses to identify with or disapprove of the characters in a novel.

> First argument in support of thesis

Like all forms of literature, video games create a world. Just like those of novels, the worlds of video games can mirror current events, as is the case with *Medal of Honor*, which takes place on the battlefields of Afghanistan, or they can be highly imaginative, such as the fantasy world of *World of Warcraft*. Just as many novels do, video games often contain allusions to mythology and history as well as to literary works—such as Dante's *Inferno* and Poe's "The Gold Bug." Critic Tanya Krzywinska points out that some parts of the narrative of *World of Warcraft* are based on classical myth, while others are based on the typical stories told in fantasy novels, and still others are based on events drawn from popular culture (124). She also notes that the narratives of games such as *World of Warcraft* which tend to have a hero who is in conflict with an evil villain and often feature magic, are similar to classical myths (126). Mythical creatures, such as the dragons that are common in video games (see fig. 1), are also common in fantasy literature and fairy tales.

> Second argument in support of thesis

Like novels, the plots of video games follow certain conventional patterns or plots. According to Krzywinska, "the primary and highly recognizable mythic pattern that informs and structures the game [*World of Warcraft*] is the epic hero quest, wherein various forces work to help and hinder the hero-player en route to achieving particular goals" (126). It is clear that in terms of both of setting and narrative, video games can bear striking similarities to conventional literary works.

> Third argument in support of thesis

Linde 3

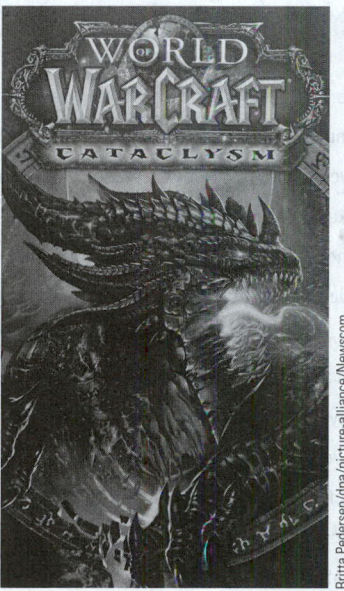

Britta Pedersen/dpa/picture-alliance/Newscom

Fig. 1. Screen shot from *World of Warcraft: Cataclysm; Blizzard Entertainment*, 2015, us.blizzard. com/en-us/games/music/wow-cataclysm.html.

Despite these similarities, however, some critics claim that video games are fundamentally different from literature, and for this reason should not be considered art, let alone literature. Roger Ebert, the celebrated film critic, says, "In principle, video games cannot be art." He expands his statement by focusing on the features that define art, calling it "the fruition of a long gestation." He concludes that video games have their origins in such artistic reflection but from commercial interests. Furthermore, Ebert argues that the fact that video games are an emerging form of media does not mean that they should not be judged by the same standards as other arts. His main point, however, is that video games are fundamentally different from art forms such as literature and film. "One obvious difference between art and games," he says, "is that you can win a game. It has rules, points, objectives, and an outcome". Although Ebert's analysis is fundamentally correct, he seems to ignore the many similarities that exist between literature and video games. Because video games have highly developed settings, characters, and plots, it does not seem unreasonable to see some video games as forms of literary expression.

Summary and refutation of opposing argument

Linde 4

The main difference between video games and traditional literature is the fact that games involve multimedia interaction. After all, novels do not come with control- lers, nor do they allow readers to choose what a character does next. Novelist Don Zancanella points out that "console game narratives are more of a mosaic than a linear recounting of time-ordered events" (99). Whereas a reader of a literary work is told a story, a video game player takes a direct role in determining the outcome of the story, making choices that can result in either a favorable or an unfavorable outcome. This more interactive model does not mean that video games are not literature. However, it does mean that they should be analyzed differently from traditional literature. Geoffrey Rockwell observes that because of their popularity and similarity to literature, video games require further attention and study. He concludes by saying that we need a "critical framework" for discussing video games (350). This new framework should take into consideration the specific types of interac- tion that make video games unique. For instance, in video games, characters can interact with a variety of other characters, creating an experience in which "consideration of multiple points of view is central to interpretation" (Zancanella 99). Clearly, as the study of video games as literature becomes more academically accepted, scholars will have to develop new, more suit- able ways of evaluating this genre.

Summary refutation of opposing argument

Despite some arguments to the contrary, video games have much in common with works of literature. Video games, like literature, serve the basic function of transporting read- ers to other worlds by creating characters, plots, and settings. Video games also draw from and contribute to the larger literary canon, frequently integrating references and allusions to literary works into their stories. As video games continue to increase in popularity and the variety of subjects covered by the games continues to grow, the value of studying the genre as a form of literature will become more obvious to both players and to critics. In ana- lyzing and evaluating video games, however, scholars will have to take into account the inter- activity and the less linear plots that characterize these games. The result will be not just new forms of criticism, but also new forms of games that will expand the definition of literature.

Conclusion (restating thesis)

Linde 5

Works Cited

Ebert, Roger. "Video Games Can Never Be Art." *Roger Ebert's Journal,* 16 Apr. 2010,
www.rogerebert.com/rogers-journal/video-games-can-never-be-art.

Krzywinska, Tanya. "World Creation and Lore: *World of Warcraft* as Rich Text." *Digital Culture,*
Play, and Identity: A Critical Anthology of World of Warcraft *Research,* edited by Hilde
Walker Corneliussen and Jill Rettberg, MIT P, 2008, pp. 123–42.

Rockwell, Geoffrey. "Gore Galore: Literary Theory and Computer Games." *Computers and the*
Humanities, vol. 36, no. 3, 2002, pp. 345–58.

Ryan, Marie-Laure. "Fictional Worlds in the Digital Age." *A Companion to Digital Literary Stud-*
ies, edited by Susan Schreibman and Ray Siemens, Blackwell, 2008. *Wiley Online Library,*
doi:10.1002/9781405177504.ch13.

Zancanella, Don, et al. "Computer Games as Literature." *English in the Digital Age: Informa-*
tion and Communications Technology (ICT) and the Teaching of English, edited by Andrew
Goodwyn, Continuum, 2000, pp. 87–102.

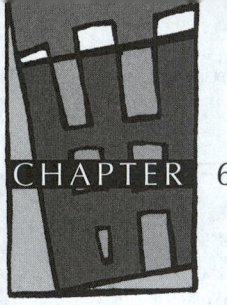

CHAPTER 6

USING SOURCES IN YOUR WRITING

When you write a an essay about a literary topic, you often do **research**, supplementing your own interpretations with information from other sources. These sources may include works of literature as well as books and journal articles by literary critics (see p. 79). You may get this information from print sources, from electronic databases in the library, or from the Internet. When you write an essay that uses sources, follow the process discussed in this chapter.

 Choosing a Topic

Your instructor may assign a topic or allow you to choose one. If you choose a topic, make sure it is narrow enough for your essay's length, the amount of time you have for writing, and the number of sources your instructor expects you to use.

Daniel Collins, a student in an Introduction to Literature course, was given three weeks to write a four- to six-page essay on one of the short stories the class had read. Daniel chose to write about Eudora Welty's short story "A Worn Path" because the main character, Phoenix Jackson, interested him. He knew, however, that he would have to narrow his topic before he could begin. In class, Daniel's instructor had asked some provocative questions about the significance of Phoenix Jackson's journey. Daniel thought that this topic might work well because he could explore it in a short essay and could complete the essay within the three-week time limit.

 Doing Exploratory Research

To see whether you will be able to find enough material about your topic, you should do some **exploratory research** by taking a quick survey of your resources. Your goal at this stage is to formulate a **research question**, the question that you want your research to answer. This question will help you decide which sources to look for, which to examine first, and which to skip entirely.

You can begin your exploratory research by consulting your library's **online central information system**. This system usually includes the library's **catalog** as well as a number of **databases**, such as *Readers' Guide to Periodical Literature Index* and *Humanities Index*. Then, if necessary, consult **general reference works** like encyclopedias and specialized dictionaries and browse your search engine's subject guides to get an overview of your subject.

You should also see what resources are available on the Internet. Try using more than one search engine—or a meta search engine like *Dogpile* or *MetaCrawler*—to determine if you can find appropriate materials for your project. For the most part, you can access the same types of resources on the Internet as you can in the library—for example, general encyclopedias, magazine articles, newspapers, and some scholarly journal articles. Keep in mind, however, that because of the nature of online publication and the ease with which some online texts can be altered, Internet sources need to be scrutinized carefully. Still, a preliminary survey of online resources can help you develop your research question.

When he surveyed his library's resources Daniel saw that his library's central information system included several books and a number of articles on Eudora Welty. He found two critical articles that discussed the significance of Phoenix Jackson's journey, and he hoped they would help him to understand why this character continued her journey despite all the hardships she encountered. However, he knew that he would have to do more than just summarize his sources; he would have to make a point about Phoenix's journey, one that he could support with examples from the story as well as from his research.

After looking at some additional sources on the Internet, Daniel came up with the following research question: What enabled Phoenix Jackson to continue her journey despite the many obstacles she faced?

 ## Narrowing Your Topic

As you survey your library and Internet resources, the titles of books and articles as well as discussions in general encyclopedias should help you to narrow your topic.

 ## Doing Focused Research

Once you have completed your exploratory research and formulated your research question, you are ready to begin **focused research**—the process of looking in the library and on the Internet for the specific information you need.

Library Research

Using the Library

The first step is to go back to the library and check out any books that you think will be useful. Then, consult **specialized reference works**—indexes, bibliographies, and specialized encyclopedias, for example—to find relevant articles. If you find print articles, photocopy them (and make sure to copy all the publication information you will need to document these sources).

Your library's databases (usually accessed through its website) will help you find information in periodicals. A **periodical** is a newspaper, magazine, or scholarly journal published at regular intervals. **Periodical databases** list articles from a selected group of periodicals. Although you may occasionally find scholarly articles on the Internet, the easiest (and most reliable) way to access scholarly journals is through the databases to which your college library subscribes. These databases are updated frequently, and the articles they include usually provide current, reliable information.

Choosing the right periodical database for your research is important. Each database has a different focus and lists different magazines or journals. In addition, some databases include just citations while others contain the full text of articles. Using the wrong database can lead to wasted time and frustration. For example, searching a database that focuses on business will not help you much if you are looking for information on a literary topic. Be sure to ask a reference librarian which database will be most helpful.

Frequently Used Periodical Databases

The following databases are useful for literary research.

EBSCOhost	Includes thousands of periodical articles on many subjects
Expanded Academic ASAP	Largely full-text database covering all subjects in thousnds of magazines and journals
FirstSearch	Includes full-text articles in many popular and scholarly periodicals
Project Muse	Contains full-text articles from over four hundred journals in the humanities and the social sciences

---

Evaluating Library Sources

Whenever you find a library source (print or electronic), take the time to **evaluate** it—to assess its usefulness and reliability.

✔ **CHECKLIST   Evaluating Library Sources**

To help you evaluate sources you find in the library, consider the following questions:

- *Does the source treat your topic in enough detail?* To be of real help, a book should include a section or a chapter on your topic. An article should have your topic as its central subject or at least one of its main concerns.

- *Is the source current?* Although currency is not as important for literary research as it is in the sciences, it should still be a consideration. Check the date of publication to see whether the information in a book or article is up to date.

- *Is the source respected?* A contemporary review of a source can help you make this assessment. You can find reviews in *Book Review Digest,* available in print and online.

> ■   *Is the source reliable?* Does the author support his or her opinions? Does the author include documentation? Does the author have a particular agenda to advance? Compare a few statements with a more neutral source—an encyclopedia or a textbook, for example—to see whether the author seems to be slanting facts. If you have difficulty making this assessment, ask your instructor or a reference librarian for help.

Internet Research

Using the Internet

As you can imagine, the Internet has revolutionized the way scholars conduct research, offering instant access to a host of useful sources. Keep in mind, however, that the Internet does not give you access to the large number of high-quality print and electronic sources that you can find in your college library.

Locating Sources

You can look for sources on the Internet in two ways:

1. You can look for Internet sources by entering a **keyword** (or words) into your search engine's search field. The search engine will identify any site in its database on which the keyword (or words) you have typed appears.

2. You can look for Internet sources by using **subject guides**—the lists of general subject areas provided by search engines such as *Yahoo!*, *About.com*, and *Google Directory*. Each of these subject areas will lead you to a more specific list until, eventually, you get to the topic you want.

Some search engines are more user friendly than others, some allow for more sophisticated searching, and some are more comprehensive. As you try out various search engines, you will eventually settle on one that you will turn to when you need to find information.

Some General-Purpose Search Engines

Bing   Bing is currently the third most-used search engine on the Web. It has a variety of specialized functions that sort responses into categories. By clicking on progressively narrower categories, you get more and more specific results. For some searches, a single "Best Match" response may appear. Excellent image- and video-search functions.

Excite   Searches more than 250 million websites.

Google	Considered by many to be the best search engine available. Accesses a large database that enables you to search for websites, images, discussion groups, and news stories.
Google Scholar	Enables you to search a broad range of scholarly literature, including peer-reviewed papers, books, abstracts, and technical reports as well as scholarly articles.
Yahoo!	A search tool that allows you to use either subject headings or keywords. Searches its own indexes as well as the Web.
Dogpile	A **metasearch engine** that searches several search engines simultaneously.

In addition to the general-purpose search engines listed above, you can use **specialized search engines**—search sites that are especially useful during focused research when you are looking for in-depth information about a specific topic.

Some Specialized Search Engines

Directory of Open-Access Journals <doaj.org>	This site offers access to over 2000 free, full-text, open-access journals.
Librarians' Index <lii.org>	A high-quality, reliable site designed for librarians
Thinkers.net <thinkers.net>	Discussions on literature and information about the publishing world
Voice of the Shuttle <vos.ucsb.edu>	Reliable in-depth research in the humanities

Evaluating Websites

Anyone can operate a website and thereby publish anything. For this reason, it is important to determine the quality of a website before you use it as a source. Asking the questions below will help you evaluate websites and the information they contain.

✔ **CHECKLIST   Evaluating Websites**

To help you evaluate websites, consider the following questions:

▪ *How credible is the person or organization responsible for the site?* Does the site list an author? Can you determine the author's expertise?

> ☐ *How accurate is the information on the website?* Is it free of factual, spelling, and grammatical errors? Can you verify the information by checking other sources? Does the site include documentation?
>
> ☐ *How balanced does the information on the website seem?* Does a business, political organization, or special interest group sponsor the site? Does the site express only one viewpoint?
>
> ☐ *How comprehensive is the website?* Does the site provide in-depth coverage, or is the information largely common knowledge?
>
> ☐ *How well maintained is the website?* Has it been active for a long period of time? Has the site been updated recently?

Daniel Collins, the student writing about Phoenix Jackson's journey, located everything he needed in his college library. He found two print articles about the Welty story, and he found two more articles in the *Humanities Index* database. Finally, a search of his library's online central information system revealed that among the library's holdings was a DVD dramatization of "A Worn Path" that included an interview with the author.

 ## Taking Notes

Once you have located your sources, you should record information that you think will be useful. There is no single correct way to take notes. Some writers store information in a computer file; others keep their notes on index cards. Still others take notes using an electronic note-taking tool like *Evernote* or *Springpad*. Whatever system you use, be sure to record the author's full name as well as *complete* publication information. You will need this information later on to compile your works-cited list (see p. 96).

When you take notes from a source, you have three options: you can *paraphrase, summarize,* or *quote.*

When you **paraphrase**, you put the author's main points into your own words, keeping the emphasis of the original. You paraphrase when you want to make a difficult or complex discussion accessible to readers so that you can comment on it or use it to support your own points. (For this reason, a paraphrase can sometimes be longer than the original.) Here is a passage from a critical article, followed by Daniel's paraphrase.

Original: The assumption that the grandson is dead helps explain Phoenix Jackson's stoical behavior in the doctor's office. She displays a "ceremonial stiffness" as she sits "bolt upright" staring "straight ahead, her face solemn and withdrawn into rigidity." This passiveness suggests her psychological dilemma—she cannot explain why she made the journey. Her attempt to blame the lapse of memory on her illiteracy is unconvincing. Her lack of education is hardly an excuse for forgetting her grandson, but it goes a long way toward explaining her inability to articulate her subconscious motives for her journey. (Bartel, Roland. "Life and Death in Eudora Welty's 'A Worn Path.'" *Studies in Short Fiction* 14 (1977): 288-90)

Paraphrase: As Roland Bartel points out in "Life and Death in Eudora Welty's 'A Worn Path,'" Phoenix Jackson's "stoical behavior" at the doctor's office makes sense if her grandson is actually dead. Although she says that her forgetfulness is due to her lack of education, Bartel does not accept this excuse. According to him, the fact that Phoenix is uneducated cannot fully explain her forgetting about her grandson—although it might explain why she cannot communicate her reasons for her trip (289).

When you write a **summary**, you also put an author's ideas into your own words, but in this case you convey just the main idea of a passage. (For this reason, a summary is always much shorter than the original.) Here is Daniel's Collins's summary of the passage from Bartel's article.

Summary: As Roland Bartel points out in "Life and Death in Eudora Welty's 'A Worn Path,'" Phoenix Jackson's actions make sense if we assume that her grandson is dead and that she does not have the verbal skills to explain why she made the trip (289).

When you **quote**, you reproduce a passage exactly, word for word and punctuation mark for punctuation mark, enclosing the entire passage in quotation marks. Because a large number of quotations will distract readers, use a quotation only when you think that the author's words will add something—memorable wording, for example—to your essay.

NOTE Remember to document all paraphrases, summaries, and quotations that you use in your essays. (See Chapter 7, Documenting Sources and Avoiding Plagiarism.)

Integrating Sources

To integrate a paraphrase, summary, or quotation smoothly into your essay, use a phrase that introduces your source and its author—*Bartel points out, according to Bartel, Bartel claims,* or *Bartel says,* for example. You can place this identifying phrase at various points in a sentence.

According to Roland Bartel, "The assumption that the grandson is dead helps explain Phoenix Jackson's stoical behavior in the doctor's office" (289).

"The assumption that the grandson is dead helps explain Phoenix Jackson's stoical behavior in the doctor's office," observes Roland Bartel in his article "Life and Death in Eudora Welty's 'A Worn Path'" (289).

"The assumption that the grandson is dead," notes the literary critic Roland Bartel, "helps explain Phoenix Jackson's stoical behavior in the doctor's office" (289).

EXERCISE Integrating Quotations

For each of the quotations below, write three sentences: one that integrates the complete quotation into your sentence, one that integrates part of the quotation into your sentence, and one that quotes just a distinctive word or phrase.

Example

- **Original quotation:** "But it seems to me that once you begin a gesture it's fatal not to go through with it" (Updike 242).
- **Sentence integrating complete quotation:** Readers understand Sammy's determination to stand up to Lengel when he says, "But it seems to me that once you begin a gesture it's fatal not to go through with it" (Updike 242).
- **Sentence integrating part of the quotation:** Sammy has mixed feelings about quitting his job but feels that "once you begin a gesture it's fatal not to go through with it" (Updike 242).
- **Sentence quoting one distinctive word:** Sammy considers changing his mind but decides that to do so would be "fatal" (Updike 242).

Quotations

- "We remembered all the young men her father had driven away, and we knew that with nothing left she would have to cling to that which had robbed her, as people will" (Faulkner 227).
- "And so the house came to be haunted by the unspoken phrase: *There must be more money! There must be more money!*" (Lawrence 485).
- "That moment she was mine, mine, fair" (Browning, line 36)
- "But I have promises to keep, / And miles to go before I sleep / and miles to go before I sleep" (Frost, lines 14–16).
- "We live close together and we live far apart. We all go through the same things—it's just a different kind of the same thing" (Glaspell 1614).

 ## Developing a Thesis Statement

After you have taken notes, review the information you have gathered, and use it to help you draft a **thesis statement**—a single sentence that states the main idea of your essay. You will support this thesis with a combination of your own ideas and the ideas you have drawn from your research.

After reviewing his notes, Daniel developed the following thesis statement about Eudora Welty's "A Worn Path."

> **Thesis Statement:** What is most important in the story is the spiritual and emotional strength of Phoenix Jackson and how this strength enables her to continue her journey.

As you draft and revise your essay, your thesis statement will probably change. At this point in the writing process, however, it gives your ideas focus and enables you to organize them into an outline.

Constructing a Formal Outline

Once you have a thesis statement, you can construct a **formal outline** that presents your main points and supporting details in the order you will discuss them. Begin by writing your thesis statement at the top of the page. Then, review your notes, and arrange them in the order in which you plan to use them. As you construct your outline, group these points under appropriate headings.

When it is completed, your formal outline will show you how much support you have for each of your points, and it will guide you as you write a draft of your essay. Your outline, which covers the body paragraphs of your essay, can be a **sentence outline**, in which each idea is expressed as a sentence, or a **topic outline**, in which each idea is expressed in a word or a short phrase.

After reviewing his notes, Daniel constructed the following topic outline. Notice that he uses roman numerals for first-level headings, capital letters for second-level headings, and arabic numerals for third-level headings. Notice too that all points in the outline are expressed in parallel terms.

Thesis Statement: What is most important in the story is the spiritual and emotional strength of Phoenix Jackson and how this strength enables her to continue her journey.

- I. Critical interpretations of "A Worn Path"
  - A. Heroic act of sacrifice
  - B. Journey of life
  - C. Religious pilgrimage
- II. Focus on journey
  - A. Jackson and her grandson
  - B. Nurse's question
  - C. Jackson's reply
- III. Jackson's character
  - A. Interaction between Jackson's character and journey
    1. Significance of Jackson's first name
    2. Jackson as a complex character
  - B. Jackson's physical problems
    1. Failing eyesight
    2. Difficulty walking
- IV. Jackson's spiritual strength
  - A. Belief in God
  - B. Child of nature
- V. Jackson's emotional strength
  - A. Love for grandson
  - B. Fearlessness and selflessness
  - C. Determination

 ## Drafting Your Essay

Once you have constructed your outline, you are ready to draft your essay. Follow your outline as you write, using your notes as the need arises.

Your essay's **introduction** will usually be a single paragraph. In addition to identifying the work (or works) you are writing about and stating your thesis, the introduction to an essay that uses sources may present an overview of your topic or necessary background information.

The **body** of your essay supports your thesis statement, with each of your paragraphs developing a single point. Support your points with examples from the literary work you are discussing as well as with summaries, paraphrases, and quotations from your sources. In addition, be sure to include your own observations and inferences.

Your essay's **conclusion**, usually a single paragraph (but sometimes more), restates your main points and reinforces your thesis statement.

Remember, the purpose of your first draft is to get ideas down on paper so that you can react to them. You should expect to revise, possibly writing several drafts.

The final draft of Daniel Collins's essay on Eudora Welty's "A Worn Path" (p. 463) appears on the pages that follow.

 ## Model Essay with MLA Documentation

Collins 1

Daniel Collins

Professor Smith

English 201

20 January 2015

And Again She Makes the Journey: Character and

Act in Eudora Welty's "A Worn Path"

Since it was published in 1940, Eudora Welty's "A Worn Path," the tale of an elderly black woman, Phoenix Jackson, traveling to the city to obtain medicine for her sick grandson, has been the subject of much critical interpretation. Critics have wondered about the meaning of the many death and rebirth symbols, including the scarecrow, which the old woman believes is a ghost; the buzzard who watches her travel; the skeleton-like branches that reach out to slow her; and her first name, Phoenix. Various critics have concluded that "A Worn Path" is either a "heroic act of sacrifice," "a parable for the journey of life," or "a religious pilgrimage" (Piwinski 40). It is certainly true that Phoenix Jackson's journey has symbolic significance. However, what is most important in the story is Phoenix Jackson's spiritual and emotional strength—and how this strength enables her to continue her journey.

Eudora Welty discusses Phoenix Jackson in an interview with Beth Henley. Welty points out that Jackson's first name refers to a mythical bird that dies and is reborn every five hundred years. She explains, however, that despite her symbolic name, Phoenix Jackson is more than a symbol: she is a complex character with human frailties and emotions.

Phoenix Jackson has a number of physical problems that make it difficult for her to perform daily tasks. Because of her age, she has failing eyesight, which distorts her perception of the objects she encounters during her journey. For example, Phoenix mistakes a patch of thorns for "a pretty little *green* bush" (464), and she believes a scarecrow is the ghost of a man. She also has difficulty walking, so she must use a cane; at one point, she is unable to bend and tie her own shoes. Because of these physical problems, readers might expect her to fail in her attempt to reach town; as the narrator points out, the journey is long and difficult. So what gives Phoenix Jackson the energy and endurance for the journey?

Although Phoenix Jackson's body is weak, she has great spiritual and emotional strength. According to James Saunders, her oneness with nature helps her overcome the challenges that she encounters (67). Because Phoenix Jackson is "a child of nature," her impaired vision, although it slows her journey, does not stop it. As Saunders explains, "mere human vision would not have been sufficient for the journey" (67). Instead, Phoenix Jackson relies on her spiritual connection with nature; thus, she warns various animals to "Keep out from under these feet . . . " (464). Her spiritual strength also comes from her belief in God—a quality seen when she refers to God watching her steal the hunter's nickel.

Phoenix Jackson's spiritual strength is matched by her emotional strength. Her love for her grandson drives her to endure any difficulty and to defy any danger. Therefore, throughout her journey, she demonstrates fearlessness and selflessness. For example, when the hunter threatens her with his gun, she tells him that she has faced worse dangers. And, despite her need for new shoes, she buys a paper windmill for her grandson instead.

In her interview with Beth Henley, Eudora Welty explains how she created Phoenix Jackson— outwardly frail and inwardly strong. Welty tells how she noticed an "old lady" slowly making her way across a "silent horizon,"[1] driven by an overwhelming need to reach her destination; as Welty says, "she had a purpose." Welty created Phoenix Jackson in the image of this determined woman. In order to underscore the character's strength, Welty had her make the journey to Natchez to get medication for her grandson. Because the act had to be performed repeatedly, the journey became a ritual that had to be completed at all costs. Thus, as Welty explains in the interview, the act of making the journey—not the journey itself—is the most significant element in the story.

In order to emphasize the importance of the journey, Welty gives little information about the daily life of the boy and his grandmother or about the illness for which the boy is being treated. Regardless of the boy's condition—or even whether he is alive or dead—Jackson must complete her journey. The nurse's statement—"The doctor said as long as you came to get it [the medicine], you could have it" (469)—reinforces the ritualistic nature of Jackson's journey, a journey that Bartel suggests is a "subconscious" act (289). Thus, Phoenix Jackson cannot answer the nurse's questions because she does not consciously know what forces her to make the journey. Nevertheless, next Saturday, Phoenix Jackson will again walk, and "will continue to do so, regardless of the difficulties facing her, along the worn path that leads through the wilderness of the Natchez Trace, cheerfully performing her labor of love" (Howard 84).

Collins 3

Clearly, the interaction of character (Phoenix Jackson) and act (the ritual journey in search of medication) is the most important element of Welty's story. By describing Phoenix Jackson's difficult encounters during her ritual journey to town, Welty emphasizes how spiritual and emotional strength can overcome physical frailty and how determination and fearlessness can overcome danger (Bethea 37). These moral messages become clear by the time Jackson reaches the doctor's office. The image of the elderly woman determinedly walking across the horizon, the image that prompted Welty to write the story, remains in the minds of readers.

Collins 4

Note

1. Unlike the written version of "A Worn Path," the DVD version of the short story ends not at the doctor's office but with a vision similar to the one that inspired Welty to write the story: the elderly African American woman silently walking along the horizon at dusk.

Collins 5

Works Cited

Bartel , Roland. "Life and Death in Eudora Welty's 'A Worn Path.'" *Studies in Short Fiction*, vol. 14, no. 1, 1977, pp. 288-90.

Bethea, Dean. "Phoenix Has No Coat: Historicity, Eschatology, and Sins of Omission in Eudora Welty's 'A Worn Path.'" *International Fiction Review*, vol. 27, no. 5, 2001, pp. 32-38, journals.lib.unb.ca/index.php/ifr/article/view/7689/8746.

Howard, Zelma Turner. *The Rhetoric of Eudora Welty's Short Stories*. UP of Mississippi, 1973.

Piwinski, David J. "Mistletoe in Eudora Welty's 'A Worn Path.'" *ANQ: A Quarterly Journal of Short Articles, Notes and Reviews*, vol. 16, no. 1, 2003, pp. 40-43. *Taylor and Francis Online*, doi:10.1080/08957690309598188.

Saunders, James Robert. "'A Worn Path': The Eternal Quest of Welty's Phoenix Jackson." *Southern Literary Journal*, vol. 25, no. 1, 1992, pp. 62-73.

Welty, Eudora. Interview by Beth Henley. *The Heinle Original Film Series in Literature: Eudora Welty's "A Worn Path."* Directed by Bruce R. Schwartz. Wadsworth, 2003.

---. " A Worn Path." *Compact Literature: Reading, Reacting, Writing*, edited by Laurie G. Kirszner and Stephen R. Mandell, 9th ed., Wadsworth, 2016, pp. 463-69.

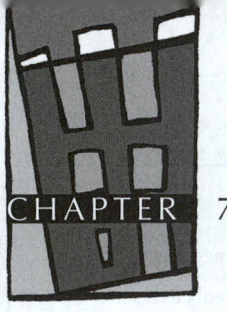

CHAPTER 7

DOCUMENTING SOURCES AND AVOIDING PLAGIARISM

Documentation is the formal acknowledgment of the sources in a an essay. This chapter explains and illustrates the documentation style recommended by the Modern Language Association (MLA), the style used by students of literature.

What to Document

In general, you must document the following types of information from a source (print or electronic):

- ***All word-for-word quotations from a source.*** Whenever you use a writer's exact words, you must document them. Even if you quote only a word or two within a paraphrase or summary, you must document the quoted words separately, after the final quotation marks.
- ***All ideas from a source that you put into your own words.*** Be sure to document all paraphrases or summaries of a source's ideas, including the author's judgments, conclusions, and debatable assertions.
- ***All visuals—tables, charts, and photographs—from a source.*** Because visuals are almost always someone's original creation, they must be documented.

NOTE Certain items do not require documentation: **common knowledge** (information most readers probably know), facts available from a variety of reference sources, familiar sayings and well-known quotations, and your own ideas and conclusions.

 Avoiding Plagiarism

Plagiarism is the presentation of another person's words or ideas as if they were your own. Most plagiarism is **unintentional plagiarism**—for example, pasting a passage from a downloaded document directly into your essay and forgetting to include quotation marks and documentation. However, there is a difference between an honest mistake and **intentional plagiarism**—for example, copying sentences from a journal article or submitting as your own an essay that someone else has written. The penalties for unintentional plagiarism may sometimes be severe, but intentional plagiarism is intellectual theft and is almost always dealt with harshly.

The guidelines that follow can help you avoid the most common mistakes that lead to unintentional plagiarism.

Document All Material That Requires Documentation

Original: In Oates's stories there are no safe relationships, but the most perilous of all possibilities is sex. Sex is always destructive. (Tierce, Mike, and John Michael Crafton. "Connie's Tambourine Man: A New Reading of Arnold Friend.")

Plagiarism: In many of Oates's stories, relationships—especially sexual relationships—are dangerous.

In the example above, the writer uses an idea from a source but does not include documentation. As a result, she gives readers the mistaken impression that the source's idea is actually her own.

Correct: Tierce and Crafton point out that in many of Oates's stories, relationships—especially sexual relationships—are dangerous (220).

Enclose Borrowed Words in Quotation Marks

Original: "The Yellow Wallpaper," which Gilman herself called "a description of a case of nervous breakdown," recalls in the first person the experiences of a woman who is evidently suffering from postpartum psychosis. (Gilbert, Sandra M., and Susan Gubar. *The Madwoman in the Attic: The Woman Writer and the Nineteenth-Century Literary Imagination.*)

Plagiarism: As Gilbert and Gubar point out, the narrator in "The Yellow Wallpaper" is evidently suffering from postpartum psychosis (212).

Even though the writer documents the passage, he uses the source's exact words without putting them in quotation marks.

Correct: As Gilbert and Gubar point out, the narrator in "The Yellow Wallpaper" is "evidently suffering from postpartum psychosis" (212).

Do Not Imitate a Source's Syntax and Phrasing

Original: Tennessee Williams's *The Glass Menagerie*, though it has achieved a firmly established position in the canon of American plays, is often distorted, if not misunderstood, by readers, directors, and audiences. (King, Thomas. "Irony and Distance in *The Glass Menagerie*.")

Plagiarism: Although *The Glass Menagerie* has a well-established place in the American theater, it is frequently misinterpreted by those who read it, direct it, and see it (King 125).

Although the student does not use the exact words of his source, he closely follows the sentence structure of the original and simply substitutes synonyms for the writer's key words. Remember, acceptable paraphrases and summaries do more than change words; they use original phrasing and syntax to convey the source's meaning.

> **Correct:** According to Thomas King, although *The Glass Menagerie* has become an American classic, it is still not fully appreciated (125).

Differentiate Your Words from Those of Your Source

> **Original:** At some colleges and universities, traditional survey courses of world and English literature . . . have been scrapped or diluted. . . . What replaces them is sometimes a mere option of electives, sometimes "multicultural" courses introducing material from Third World cultures and thinning out an already thin sampling of Western writings, and sometimes courses geared especially to issues of class, race, and gender. (Howe, Irving. "The Value of the Canon.")

> **Plagiarism:** At many universities, the Western literature survey courses have been edged out by courses that emphasize minority concerns. These courses are "thinning an already thin sampling of Western writings" in favor of "courses geared especially to issues of class, race, and gender" (Howe 40).

Because the student writer does not differentiate his ideas from those of his source, it appears that only the two quotations in the last sentence are borrowed when, in fact, the first sentence also borrows ideas from the original. The student should have identified the boundaries of the borrowed material by introducing it with an identifying phrase and ending with documentation. (Note that a quotation always requires its own documentation.)

> **Correct:** According to Irving Howe, at many universities the Western literature survey courses have been edged out by courses that emphasize minority concerns (40). These courses, says Howe, are "thinning an already thin sampling of Western writings" in favor of "courses geared especially to issues of class, race, and gender" (40).

NOTE   It is easy to become overwhelmed by any research project. For example, you can run out of time, lose track of your sources, or confuse your own ideas with those of your sources.

✔ **CHECKLIST   Avoiding Unintentional Plagiarism**

Any of these problems can result in unintentional plagiarism—to avoid this problem, keep the following suggestions in mind:

- *Formulate a research plan.* List the steps you intend follow and estimate how much time they will take.

- *Set up a schedule.* Set up a realistic schedule that allows you enough time to complete your assignment. Include extra time just in case any unexpected problems occur.

- *Ask for help.* If you run into trouble, don't panic; ask your instructor or a college reference librarian for help.

- *Don't paste downloaded text directly into your essay.* Summarize or paraphrase downloaded material that you intend to use. Boldface or highlight quotation marks to remind you that you are using the exact words of your sources.

- *Keep track of your sources.* Create one set of files for downloaded material and another set of files for your notes. Make sure you label and date these files so that you'll know what they contain and when they were created.

- *Record full documentation information for every source.* Make sure you have all the source information you will need to create your works-cited list.

- *Document your sources.* As you write your first draft, document each piece of information that comes from a source. Don't make the mistake of thinking you will be able to find this information later on. If you don't keep track of your sources as you draft, you may forget which words and ideas are your own and which require documentation.

- *Keep a list of the sources you are using.* Keep an up-to-date list of all the sources you are using. This list will enable you to create a works-cited list when you have finished writing your essay.

 ## Documenting Sources

MLA documentation has two main parts: parenthetical references in the body of the essay (in-text citations) and a works-cited list.* In addition, there may be content notes.

Parenthetical References in the Text

MLA documentation style uses parenthetical references within the text to refer to an alphabetical works-cited list at the end of the essay. A parenthetical reference should contain just enough information to guide readers to the appropriate entry in your works-cited list.

A typical parenthetical reference consists of the author's last name and a page number.

Gwendolyn Brooks uses the sonnet form to create poems that have a wide social and aesthetic range (Williams 972).

---

*For more information, see the *MLA Handbook,* 8th ed. (MLA, 2016). You can also consult the MLA website at style.mla.org.

✔ **CHECKLIST** **Guidelines for Punctuating Parenthetical References**

To punctuate parenthetical references correctly, follow these guidelines:

Paraphrases and Summaries

☐ Place the parenthetical reference *after* the last word of the sentence and *before* the final punctuation.

> In her poems, Brooks combines the pessimism of modernist poetry with the optimism of the Harlem Renaissance (Smith 978).

Direct Quotations Run in with the Text

☐ Place the parenthetical reference *after* the quotation marks and *before* the final punctuation.

> According to Gary Smith, Brooks's *A Street in Bronzeville* "conveys the primacy of suffering in the lives of poor Black women" (980).

> According to Gary Smith, the poems in *A Street in Bronzeville* "served notice that Brooks had learned her craft . . ." (978).

> Along with Thompson, we must ask, "Why did it take so long for critics to acknowledge that Gwendolyn Brooks is an important voice in twentieth-century American poetry" (123)?

Quotations Set Off from the Text

☐ Omit the quotation marks, and place the parenthetical reference one space *after* the final punctuation. (For guidelines for setting off long quotations, see p. 30.)

> For Gary Smith, the identity of Brooks's African American women is inextricably linked with their sense of race and poverty:
>> For Brooks, unlike the Renaissance poets, the victimization of poor Black women becomes not simply a minor chord but a predominant theme of *A Street in Bronzeville*. Few, if any, of her female characters are able to free themselves from a web of poverty that threatens to strangle their lives. (980)

If you mention the author's name or the title of the work in your essay, only a page reference is needed.

> According to Gladys Margaret Williams in "Gwendolyn Brooks's Way with the Sonnet," Brooks combines a sensitivity to poetic forms with a depth of emotion appropriate for her subject matter (972-73).

If you use more than one source by the same author, include a shortened title in the parenthetical reference.

> Brooks knows not only Shakespeare, Spenser, and Milton, but also the full range of African American poetry (Williams, "Brooks's Way" 972).

SAMPLE PARENTHETICAL REFERENCES

An entire work

When citing an entire work, state the name of the author in your essay instead of in a parenthetical reference.

August Wilson's play *Fences* treats many themes frequently expressed in modern drama.

A work by two authors

Myths cut across boundaries and cultural spheres and reappear in strikingly similar forms from country to country (Feldman and Richardson 124).

A work by three or more authors

State the last name of the first author, and use the abbreviation et al. (Latin for "and others") for the rest.

Hawthorne's short stories frequently use a combination of allegorical and symbolic methods (Guerin et al. 91).

A work in an anthology

In his essay "Flat and Round Characters," E. M. Forster distinguishes between one-dimensional characters and those that are well developed (Stevick 223-31).

Note that the parenthetical reference cites the anthology (edited by Stevick) that contains Forster's essay; full information about the anthology appears in the works-cited list.

A work with volume and page numbers

Critics consider *The Zoo Story* to be one of Albee's best plays (Eagleton 2: 17).

An indirect source

Use the abbreviation qtd. in ("quoted in") to indicate that the quoted material was not taken directly from the original source.

Wagner observed that myth and history stood before him "with opposing claims" (qtd. in Winkler 10).

A play with numbered lines

The parenthetical reference should contain the act, scene, and line numbers (in arabic numerals), separated by periods. When included in parenthetical references, titles of the books of the Bible and well-known literary works are often abbreviated—Gen. for Genesis and Ham. for Hamlet, for example.

"Give thy thoughts no tongue," says Polonius, "Nor any unproportioned thought his act" (*Ham.* 1.3.64-65).

A poem

Use a slash (/) to separate lines of poetry run in with the text. (The slash is preceded and followed by one space.) Use a double slash (//) to separate stanzas. The parenthetical reference should cite the lines quoted. Include the word line or lines in the first reference but just the numbers in subsequent references.

"I muse my life-long hate, and without flinch / I bear it nobly as I live my part," says the speaker in Claude McKay's bitterly ironic poem "The White City" (lines 3-4).

An electronic source

If you are citing a source from the Internet or from an online database, use page numbers if they are available. If the source uses paragraph, section, or screen numbers, use the abbreviation par. or sec. or the full word screen.

The earliest type of movie censoring came in the form of licensing fees, and in Deer River, Minnesota, "a licensing fee of $200 was deemed not excessive for a town of 1000" (Ernst, par. 20).

If an Internet source has no page, paragraph, section, or screen markers, cite the entire work. (When readers consult your works-cited list, they will be able to determine the nature of the source.)

In her article "Limited Horizons," Lynne Cheney says that schools do best when students read literature not for practical information but for its insights into the human condition.

Because of its parody of communism, the film *Antz* is actually an adult film masquerading as a child's tale (Clemin).

The Works-Cited List

Parenthetical references refer to a **works-cited list** that includes all the sources you refer to in your essay:

- Begin the works-cited list on a new page, continuing the page numbers of the essay. For example, if the text of the essay ends on page 6, the works-cited list will begin on page 7.
- Center the title Works Cited one inch from the top of the page.
- Arrange entries alphabetically, according to the last name of each author. Use the first word of the title if the author is unknown (articles—a, an, and the—at the beginning of a title are not considered first words).
- Double-space the entire works-cited list between and within entries.
- Begin typing each entry at the left margin, and indent subsequent lines one-half inch.
- Each works-cited entry has divisions between its core elements—author, title, and publishing information—separated by periods. If there is another source that "contains" the original published source (for example, a database or website containing a journal article), that information is also followed by a period. The *MLA Handbook* shows a single space after all end punctuation.

Following is a directory listing the sample MLA works-cited list entries that begin on page 98.

DIRECTORY OF MLA WORKS-CITED LIST ENTRIES

Print Sources: Entries for Articles

1. An article in a scholarly journal
2. An article in a magazine
3. An article in a daily newspaper
4. An article in a reference book

Print Sources: Entries for Books

5. A book by a single author
6. A book by two authors
7. A book by three or more authors
8. Two or more works by the same author
9. An edited book
10. A book with a volume number
11. A short story, poem, or play in a collection of the author's work
12. A short story in an anthology
13. A poem in an anthology
14. A play in an anthology
15. An essay in an anthology
16. More than one item from the same anthology
17. A translation

Entries for Other Sources

18. An interview
19. A lecture or an address

Electronic Sources: Entries from Internet Sites

20. A scholarly project or information database on the Internet
21. A document within a scholarly project or information database on the Internet
22. A personal site on the Internet
23. A book on the Internet
24. An article in a scholarly journal on the Internet
25. An article in an encyclopedia on the Internet
26. An article in a newspaper on the Internet
27. An article in a magazine on the Internet
28. A painting or photograph on the Internet
29. An email
30. A blog or online forum

Electronic Sources: Entries from Online Databases

31. A scholarly journal article from an online database
32. A monthly magazine article from an online database

33. A newspaper article from an online database
34. A reference book article from an online database
35. A dictionary definition from an online database

Entries for Other Electronic Sources

36. A nonperiodical publication on DVD-ROM or CD-ROM
37. A periodical publication on DVD-ROM or CD-ROM
38. A film, videocassette, DVD, or CD-ROM

MLA • Print Sources:
Entries for Articles

Article citations include the author's name; the title of the article (in quotation marks); the name of the periodical (italicized); the volume and issue numbers (if applicable; see the following); the month, if applicable (abbreviated, except for May, June, and July), and the year; and the pages on which the full article appears (with the abbreviations *p.* or *pp.*).

1. An article in a scholarly journal

Grossman, Robert. "The Grotesque in Faulkner's 'A Rose for Emily.'" *Mosaic*, vol. 20, no. 3, 1987,
     pp. 40-55.

In the citation above, no. 3 signifies issue 3. Note that some scholarly journals do not have volume numbers.

2. An article in a magazine

Milosz, Czeslaw. "A Lecture." *The New Yorker*, 22 June 1992, p. 32.

An article with no listed author is entered by title on the works-cited list.

"Solzhenitsyn: An Artist Becomes an Exile." *Time*, 25 Feb. 1974, pp. 34+.

3. An article in a daily newspaper

Oates, Joyce Carol. "When Characters from the Page Are Made Flesh on the Screen." *The New York Times*,
     23 Mar. 1986, late ed., pp. C1+.

Note that *C1+* indicates that the article begins on page 1 of Section C and continues on a subsequent page.

4. An article in a reference book

"Dance Theatre of Harlem." *The New Encyclopaedia Britannica: Micropaedia*, Encyclopaedia Britannica,
     2008.

Grimstead, David. "Fuller, Margaret Sarah." *Encyclopedia of American Biography*, edited by John A.
     Garraty, HarperCollins, 1996.

MLA • Print Sources: Entries for Books

Book citations include the author's name; book title and subtitle (italicized); and publication information (place, only if relevant; publisher; and date). Capitalize all major words in the title except articles, prepositions, and the *to* of an infinitive (unless it is the first or last word of the title or subtitle). Write publishers' names in full, with the following exceptions: Omit business words like *Company (Co.)*, *Corporation (Corp.)*, *Incorporated (Inc.)*, and *Limited (Ltd.)*. In the names of academic presses, replace *University Press* with *UP* (or, if the words are separated by other words or appear alone, replace them with *U* and *P: U of Chicago P, MIT P.*

5. A book by a single author

Kingston, Maxine Hong. *The Woman Warrior: Memoirs of a Girlhood among Ghosts*. Alfred A. Knopf, 1976.

6. A book by two authors

Feldman, Burton, and Robert D. Richardson. *The Rise of Modern Mythology*. Indiana UP, 1972.

Note that only the *first* author's name is in reverse order.

7. A book by three or more authors

Guerin, Wilfred, et al., editors. *A Handbook of Critical Approaches to Literature*. 5th ed., HarperCollins, 2004.

8. Two or more works by the same author

List two or more works by the same author in alphabetical order by *title*. Include the author's full name in the first entry; use three unspaced hyphens followed by a period to take the place of the author's name in second and subsequent entries.

Novoa, Juan-Bruce. *Chicano Authors: Inquiry by Interview*. U of Texas P, 1980.

---. "Themes in Rudolfo Anaya's Work." Literature Colloquium, New Mexico State U, Las Cruces, 11 Apr. 2002. Address.

9. An edited book

Oosthuizen, Ann, editor. *Sometimes When It Rains: Writings by South African Women*. Pandora, 1987.

10. A book with a volume number

When all the volumes of a multivolume work have the same title, list the number of the volume you used.

Eagleton, T. Allston. *A History of the New York Stage*. Vol. 2, Prentice Hall, 1987.

When each volume of a multivolume work has a separate title, list the title of the volume you used.

Durant, Will, and Ariel Durant. *The Age of Napoleon: A History of European Civilization from 1789 to 1815*. Simon & Schuster, 1975.

(*The Age of Napoleon* is volume 2 of *The Story of Civilization*. You need not provide documentation for the entire multivolume work unless this information is relevant to your essay.)

11. A short story, poem, or play in a collection of the author's work

Gordimer, Nadine. *"Once upon a Time." "Jump" and Other Stories*. Farrar, Straus and Giroux, 1991, pp. 23-30.

12. A short story in an anthology

Salinas, Marta. "The Scholarship Jacket." *Nosotros: Latina Literature Today*, edited by Maria del Carmen Boza et al., Bilingual, 1986, pp. 68-70.

13. A poem in an anthology

Simmerman, Jim. "Child's Grave, Hale County, Alabama." *The Pushcart Prize, X: Best of the Small Presses*, edited by Bill Henderson, Penguin, 1986, pp. 198-99.

14. A play in an anthology

Hughes, Langston. *Mother and Child. Black Drama Anthology*, edited by Woodie King and Ron Miller, New American Library, 1986, pp. 399-406.

15. An essay in an anthology

Forster, E. M. "Flat and Round Characters." *The Theory of the Novel*, edited by Philip Stevick, Free Press, 1980, pp. 223-31.

16. More than one item from the same anthology

If you are using more than one selection from an anthology, cite the anthology in a separate entry. Then, list each individual selection separately, including the author and title of the selection, the anthology editor's last name, and the inclusive page numbers.

Baxter, Charles. "Gryphon." Kirszner and Mandell, pp. 173-86.
Kirszner, Laurie G., and Stephen R. Mandell, editors. *Portable Literature: Reading, Reacting, Writing*. 9th ed., Cengage Learning, 2016.
Rich, Adrienne. "Living in Sin." Kirszner and Mandell, pp. 538-39.

17. A translation

Carpentier, Alejo. *Reasons of State*. Translated by Francis Partridge, W. W. Norton, 1976.

Entries for Other Sources

18. An interview

Brooks, Gwendolyn. "An Interview with Gwendolyn Brooks." *Triquarterly*, no. 60, 1984, pp. 405-10.

19. A lecture or an address

Novoa, Juan-Bruce. "Themes in Rudolfo Anaya's Work." Literature Colloquium, New Mexico State U, Las Cruces, 11 Apr. 2002. Address.

MLA • Electronic Sources: Entries from Internet Sites

MLA style recognizes that full publication information is not always available for electronic sources. Include in your citation whatever information you can reasonably obtain: the author or editor of the source (if available); the title of site (italicized); the version number of the source (if applicable); the name of the publisher (if available); and the date of electronic publication. MLA recommends including digital object identifiers (DOIs) or URLs, preferably permalinks (stable Internet addresses), in the works-cited list. The date of access may be included if there is a possibility that the source may change or be removed from the site, or if the source provides no date specifying when it was published.

20. A scholarly project or information database on the Internet

Nelson, Cary, editor. *Modern American Poetry*. Dept. of English, U of Illinois, Urbana-Champaign, 1999-2014, www.english.illinois.edu/maps/index.htm.

21. A document within a scholarly project or information database on the Internet

"D-Day: June 6th, 1944." *History.com*, History Channel, 1999, www.history.com/topics/world-war-ii/d-day.

22. A personal site on the Internet

Yerkes, James. *The Centaurian: John Updike Home Page*. Prexar, 15 June 2009, userpages.prexar.com/joyerkes. Accessed 19 June 2015.

23. A book on the Internet

Douglass, Frederick. *My Bondage and My Freedom*. Boston, 1855. *Google Book Search*, books.google.com/books?id=AbUgrcBdsncC&dq=editions:ISBN1593083572.

24. An article in a scholarly journal on the Internet

DeKoven, Marianne. "Utopias Limited: Post-Sixties and Postmodern American Fiction." *Modern Fiction Studies*, vol. 41, no. 1, 1995, pp. 75-97. *Project Muse*, doi: 10.1353/mfs.1995.0002.

25. An article in an encyclopedia on the Internet

"Hawthorne, Nathaniel." *Encyclopaedia Britannica Online*, 2010, www.britannica.com/biography/Nathaniel-Hawthorne.

26. An article in a newspaper on the Internet

Cave, Damien. "Election Day May Look Familiar." *The New York Times*, 28 Apr. 2008, www.nytimes.com/2008/04/28/us/politics/28voting.html?_r=0.

27. An article in a magazine on the Internet

Anolik, Lili. "How Joan Didion the Writer Became Joan Didion the Legend." *Vanity Fair*, Feb. 2016, www.vanityfair.com/culture/2016/02/joan-didion-writer-los-angeles.

28. A painting or photograph on the Internet

Lange, Dorothea. *Looking at Pictures*. 1936, Museum of Modern Art, New York. *MoMA*, www.moma.org/collection/artists/3373/.

29. An email

Mauk, Karen. "Re: Manuscript." Received by Stephanie Carpenter, 3 Mar. 2016.

30. A blog or online forum

Berg, Kirsten. "Bright Angel." *PowellsBooks.Blog*, 17 June 2009, www.powellsbook.blog.com. Accessed 18 June 2014.

MLA • Electronic Sources: Entries from Online Databases

To cite information from an online database, supply the publication information (including page numbers, if available) followed by the italicized name of the database and the DOI or URL. Include the date of access if the source is subject to change.

Witze, Alexandra. "Climate Change: Losing Greenland." *Nature*, 17 Apr. 2008, pp. 798-802. *ProQuest*, doi:10.1038/452798a.

31. A scholarly journal article from an online database

Schaefer, Richard J. "Editing Strategies in Television News Documentaries." *Journal of Communication*, vol. 47, no. 4, 1997, pp. 69-89, *InfoTrac OneFile Plus*, doi:10.1111/j.1460-2466.1997.tb02726.x.

32. A monthly magazine article from an online database

Livermore, Beth. "Meteorites on Ice." *Astronomy*, July 1993, pp. 54-58. *Expanded Academic ASAP Plus*, ezproxy.cut.columbiau/login?url=http://search.proquest.com.proxy.cul.columbia.edu.docview/215935960?accountid=10226.

33. A newspaper article from an online database

Meyer, Greg. "Answering Questions about the West Nile Virus." *Dayton Daily News*, 11 July 2002, pp. Z3-7. *LexisNexis*, ezproxy.cul.columbia.edu/login?url=search.proquest.com.ezproxy.cul.columbia.edu/docview/254487263?accountid=10226.

34. A reference book article from an online database

"Food Chain/Web." *Environmental Encyclopedia*, 2011. *Biography in Context*, ic.galegroup.com/ic/bic1/ReferenceDetailsPage/ReferenceDetailsWindow?failOverType=&query=&prodId=BIC1&windowstate=normal&contentModules=&display-query=&mode=view&displayGroupName=Reference&limiter=&currPage=&disableHighlighting=false&displayGroups=&sortBy=&search_within_results=&p=BIC1&action=e&catId=&activityType=&scanId=&documentId=GALE%7CCV2644150565&source=Bookmark&u=columbiau&jsid=79e21d41751c4f6bc5a337d3e22d61fa.

35. A dictionary definition from an online database

"Migraine." *Columbia Electronic Encyclopedia*, 6th ed. *Literary Reference Center*, web.a.ebscohost.com/ehost/detail/detail?vid=8&sid=a0d05779-c5ea-4daf-b800-1e0f8e09ecde%40sessionmgr4001&hid=4104&bdata=JnNpdGU9ZWhvc3QtbGl2ZQ%3d%3d#db=lfh&AN=39021787.

MLA • Electronic Sources: Entries for Other Electronic Sources

36. A nonperiodical publication on DVD-ROM or CD-ROM

"Windhover." *Concise Oxford English Dictionary*, 11th ed., Oxford UP, 2009.

37. A periodical publication on DVD-ROM or CD-ROM

Zurbach, Kate. "The Linguistic Roots of Three Terms." *Linguistic Quarterly*, vol. 30, 1994, pp. 12-47. *InfoTrac: Magazine Index Plus CD-ROM*.

38. A film, videocassette, DVD, or CD-ROM

The Heinle Original Film Series in Literature: Eudora Welty's "A Worn Path." Directed by Bruce R. Schwartz, DVD ed., Wadsworth, 2003.

NOTE Using information from Internet sources (especially blogs and online forums) can be risky. Contributors are not necessarily experts. Unless you can verify that the information you are obtaining from these sources is reliable, do not use it. You can check the reliability of an Internet source by asking your instructor or librarian for guidance.

Content Notes

Use **content notes**, indicated by a superscript (a raised number) in the text, to cite several sources at once or to provide commentary or explanations that do not fit smoothly into your essay. The full text of these notes appears on the first numbered page following the last page of the essay. (If your essay has no content notes, the works-cited page follows the last page of the essay.) Like works-cited entries, content notes are double-spaced within and between entries. However, the first line of each explanatory note is indented one-half inch, and subsequent lines are flush with the left-hand margin.

To Cite Several Sources

In the essay

Surprising as it may seem, there have been many attempts to define literature.[1]

In the note

1. For an overview of critical opinion, see Arnold 72; Eagleton 1-2; Howe 43-44; and Abrams 232-34.

To Provide Explanations

In the essay

In recent years, gothic novels have achieved great popularity.[3]

In the note

3. Gothic novels, works written in imitation of medieval romances, originally relied on supernatural occurrences. They flourished in the late eighteenth and early nineteenth centuries.

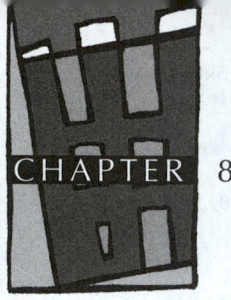

CHAPTER 8

WRITING ESSAY EXAMS
ABOUT LITERATURE

Taking exams is a skill that you have been developing throughout your career as a student. Both short-answer exams and essay exams require you to study, to recall what you know, and to budget your time carefully as you write your answers. Only essay questions, however, ask you to synthesize information and to arrange ideas in a series of clear, logically connected sentences and paragraphs. For this reason, taking essay exams requires writing skills. To write an essay exam—or even a paragraph-length response—you must do more than memorize facts; you must identify the relationships among them. In other words, you must **think critically** about your subject, and you must plan, draft, and revise an essay that clearly communicates your ideas to your audience.

 ## Planning an Essay Exam Answer

Because you are under pressure during an exam and tend to write quickly, you may be tempted to skip the planning and revision stages of the writing process. But if you write in a frenzy and hand in your exam without a second glance, you are likely to produce a disorganized (or even incoherent) answer. With careful planning, you can write an essay that demonstrates your understanding of the material.

Review Your Material

Be sure you know beforehand the scope and format of the exam. How much of your textbook and class notes will the exam cover—the entire semester's work or only the material covered since the last test? Will you have to answer every question, or will you be able to choose among alternatives? Will the exam test your ability to recall specific facts, or will it require you to demonstrate your understanding of the course material by drawing original conclusions?

Exams challenge you to recall and express in writing what you already know—what you have read, what you have heard in class, what you have reviewed in your notes. Before you even begin an exam, you must study: reread your textbook and class notes, highlight key points, and perhaps outline particularly important sections of your notes. When you prepare for a short-answer exam, you may memorize facts without analyzing their relationship to one another or their relationship to a body of knowledge as a whole: the definition of romanticism, the date of Queen Victoria's death, two examples of irony, four characteristics of a villanelle. When you prepare for an essay exam, however, you must do more than remember bits of information; you must also make connections among ideas.

When you are sure you know what to expect, try to anticipate the essay questions your instructor might ask. Try out likely questions on classmates, and see whether you can do some collaborative brainstorming to outline answers to possible questions. If you have time, you might even practice answering one or two in writing.

Consider Your Audience and Purpose

The audience for any exam is the instructor who prepared it. As you read the questions, think about what your instructor has emphasized in class. Although you may certainly arrange material in a new way or use it to make an original point, keep in mind that your purpose is to demonstrate that you understand the material, not to make clever remarks or introduce irrelevant information. In addition, you should make every effort to use the vocabulary of the discipline for which you are writing and to follow the specific **conventions** for writing about literature (p. 31).

Read Through the Entire Exam

Your time is usually limited when you take an exam, so plan carefully. How long should a "one-paragraph" or "essay-length" answer be? How much time should you devote to answering each question? The exam question itself may specify the time allotted for each answer, so look for that information. More often, the point value of each question or the number of questions on the exam indicates how much time to spend on each answer. If an essay question is worth 50 out of 100 points, for example, you will probably have to spend at least half of your time planning, writing, and revising your answer.

Before you begin to write, read the entire exam carefully to determine your priorities and your strategy. First, be sure that your copy of the test is complete and that you understand exactly what each question requires. If you need clarification, ask your instructor or proctor for help. Then, decide where to start. If there is more than one question on the exam, responding first to the one you feel most confident about is usually a good strategy. This approach ensures that you will not become bogged down responding to a question that baffles you and have too little time to write a strong answer to a question that you understand well.

Read Each Question Carefully

To write an effective answer, you need to understand the question. As you read any essay question, you may find it helpful to underline key words and important terms.

> Summarize in detail the contributions of American writers of the Harlem Renaissance, briefly outlining the contributions of artists and musicians.

Look carefully at the question's wording. If the question calls for a comparison and contrast of two works of literature, a description or analysis of *one* work, no matter how comprehensive, will not be acceptable. If a question asks for causes *and* effects, a discussion of causes alone will be insufficient.

Key Words in Exam Questions

Analyze	Describe	Interpret
Clarify	Discuss	Justify
Classify	Evaluate	Relate
Compare	Explain	Summarize
Contrast	Identify	Support
Define	Illustrate	Trace

As its key words indicate, the following question calls for a very specific kind of response.

Question

Identify <u>three differences</u> between the <u>hard-boiled detective story</u> and the <u>classical detective story</u>.

The following response to the question simply *identifies* three characteristics of *one* kind of detective story and is therefore not acceptable.

Unacceptable Answer

The hard-boiled detective story, popularized in *Black Mask* magazine in the 1930s and 1940s, is very different from the classical detective stories of Edgar Allan Poe or Agatha Christie. The hard-boiled stories feature a down-on-his-luck detective who is constantly tempted and betrayed. His world is dark and chaotic, and the crimes he tries to solve are not out-of-the-ordinary occurrences; they are the norm. These stories have no happy endings; even when the crime is solved, the world is still corrupt.

The answer below, which *contrasts* the two kinds of detective stories, is acceptable.

Acceptable Answer

The hard-boiled detective story differs from the classical detective story in its characters, its setting, and its plot. The classical detective is usually well educated and well off; he is aloof from the other characters and therefore can remain in total control of the situation. The hard-boiled detective, on the other hand, is typically a decent but down-on-his-luck man who is drawn into the chaos around him, constantly tempted and betrayed. In the orderly world of the classical detective, the crime is a temporary disruption. In the hard-boiled detective's dark and chaotic world, the crimes he tries to solve are the norm. In the classical detective story, order is restored at the end. Hard-boiled stories have no happy endings; even when the crime is solved, the world is still a corrupt and dangerous place.

Brainstorm to Find Ideas

Once you understand the question, you need to find something to say. Begin by **brainstorming**—quickly listing all of the relevant ideas you can remember about a topic. Then, identify the most important points on your list, and delete the others. A quick review of the exam question and your remaining ideas should lead you toward a workable thesis for your essay.

State Your Thesis

Often, you can rephrase the exam question as a **thesis statement**. For example, the question "Discuss in detail the contributions of American writers of the Harlem Renaissance, briefly outlining the contributions of artists and musicians" suggests the following thesis statement.

Effective Thesis Statement

Writers of the Harlem Renaissance—notably Richard Wright, Gwendolyn Brooks, Zora Neale Hurston, and Langston Hughes—made significant contributions to American literature; artists and musicians of the movement also left an important legacy.

An effective thesis statement addresses all aspects of the exam question but highlights only relevant concerns. The following thesis statements are not effective.

Vague Thesis Statement

The Harlem Renaissance produced many important writers, artists, and musicians.

Incomplete Thesis Statement

The writers of the Harlem Renaissance, such as Richard Wright, Gwendolyn Brooks, Zora Neale Hurston, and Langston Hughes, made significant contributions to American literature.

Irrelevant Thesis Statement

The writers of the Harlem Renaissance had a greater impact on American literature than the writers of the Beat generation, such as Jack Kerouac.

Make a Scratch Outline

Because time is limited, you should plan your answer before you write it. Therefore, once you have decided on a suitable thesis, you should make a **scratch outline** that lists the points you will use to support your thesis.

On the inside cover of your exam book, arrange your supporting points in the order in which you plan to discuss them. Once you have completed your outline, check it against the exam question to make certain it covers everything the question calls for—and *only* what the question calls for.

A scratch outline for an answer to the question "Discuss in detail the contributions of American writers of the Harlem Renaissance, briefly outlining the contributions of artists and musicians" might look like this.

Thesis statement: Writers of the Harlem Renaissance—notably Richard Wright, Gwendolyn Brooks, Zora Neale Hurston, and Langston Hughes—made significant contributions to American literature; artists and musicians of the movement also left an important legacy.

Writers

Wright—*Uncle Tom's Children, Black Boy, Native Son*
Brooks—poetry (classical forms; social issues)
Hurston—*Their Eyes Were Watching God*, essays, autobiography
Hughes—poetry (ballads, blues); "Simple" stories

Artists and Musicians
    Henry Tanner
    Duke Ellington

 ## Drafting and Revising an Essay Exam Answer

Referring to your outline, you can now begin to draft your answer. Don't bother crafting an elaborate or unusual **introduction**; your time is precious, and so is your reader's. A simple statement of your thesis that summarizes your answer is your best introductory strategy. This approach is efficient, and it reminds you to address the question directly.

To develop the **body** of the essay, follow your outline point by point, using specifically worded topic sentences to introduce your supporting points and clear transitions to indicate your progression from point to point (and to help your instructor see that you are answering the question in full). Such signals, along with parallel sentence structure and repeated words, will make your essay easy to follow.

The most effective **conclusion** for an essay exam is a clear, simple restatement of the thesis or a summary of the essay's main points.

Essay answers should be complete and detailed, but they should not contain irrelevant material. Every unnecessary fact or opinion increases your chance of error, so don't repeat yourself or volunteer unrequested information, and don't express your own feelings or opinions unless such information is specifically called for. Finally, be sure to support all your general statements with specific examples.

Don't forget to leave enough time to reread and revise what you have written. When you reread, try to view your answer from a fresh perspective. Is your thesis statement clearly worded? Does your essay support your thesis and answer the question? Are your facts correct, and are your ideas presented in a logical order? Review your topic sentences and transitions, and check sentence structure and word choice, spelling and punctuation. If a sentence—or even a whole paragraph—seems irrelevant, cross it out. If you suddenly remember something you want to add, you can insert a few additional words with a caret (^). Neatly insert a longer addition at the end of your answer, box it, and label it so your instructor will know where it belongs. Finally, be sure that you have written legibly and that you have not inadvertently left out any words.

Model Student Essay Exam Answer

The essay exam answer on pages 109–10 was written in response to the following question.

Question

> Analyze Kate Chopin's "The Story of an Hour," focusing on setting, point of view, character, and theme. Be sure to include relevant quotations to support your analysis.

As you read the following response to the exam question, note that the student writer does not include irrelevant information. She does not, for example, provide unnecessary plot summary or discuss the story's style; she covers only what the question asks for. Guided by the question's key words—*analyze, setting, point of view, character,* and *theme*—she devotes a paragraph to each of the four elements in turn, including relevant quotations to support her statements. (Note that students were given a copy of the story to refer to during the exam.)

Kate Chopin was one of the most influential feminist writers of the nineteenth century, and her views about gender roles and marriage are made clear in "The Story of An Hour." While the story is brief, it uses a variety of literary techniques to build up to a surprising ending that underscores the author's view of nineteenth-century marriage. Chopin uses setting, point of view, and character to lay the groundwork for a story that explores the themes that marriage limits individual freedom and that women can only be truly independent without husbands. Introduction

Thesis statement echoes wording of exam question

Chopin gives readers little information about the setting of "The Story of An Hour," which is Mrs. Mallard's home. The details that Chopin does reveal, however, provide insight into Mrs. Mallard's state of mind. The narrator describes the view out Mrs. Mallard's open window, of "the tops of trees that were all aquiver with the new spring life" (202). This image seems to be in conflict with the news that Mrs. Mallard has just received of her husband's death: it actually reveals her feelings of happiness and renewal. When the narrator observes "patches of blue sky showing here and there through the clouds" (202), it is not the clouds, a symbol of despair, that are being described but the patches of blue, which suggest hope and happiness. The sounds that Chopin describes are also full of life: Mrs. Mallard hears "a peddler . . . crying his wares" (202), "the notes of a distant song which some one was singing" (202), and "countless sparrows . . . twittering" (202). These images and sounds create a setting that expresses Mrs. Mallard's dreams of the future, of the "spring days, and summer days . . . that would be her own" (203). The uplifting scene the narrator describes suggests that Mr. Mallard's death is not a real tragedy. First element of analysis: setting

"The Story of an Hour" has a third-person point of view. The narrator conveys Mrs. Mallard's thoughts and emotions through statements such as "she saw beyond that bitter moment a long procession of years to come that would belong to her absolutely" (202). The narrator also shows us Mrs. Mallard as she is seen by others, such as the way she "carrie[s] herself unwittingly like a goddess of Victory" (203). Mrs. Mallard is the only character into whose mind the narrator sees; the others are only depicted through their actions and words. However, the narrator's omniscience does not end with Mrs. Mallard's death. Instead, the narrator is able to relate what happens "when the doctors came" (203), indicating that the story is told at some point after her death. Second element of analysis: point of view

The only well-developed character in "The Story of An Hour" is Mrs. Mallard. The other characters only advance the plot, and we do not get any sense of their thoughts or their personalities. Chopin reveals a great deal about Mrs. Mallard despite the short length of the story. At first, the narrator leads the reader to believe that Mrs. Mallard Third element of analysis: character is deeply distraught at the death of her husband, describing her "storm of grief" (202) and relating how she runs to her room alone to sob. However, this impression quickly shifts as the narrator reveals the sudden change that comes over Mrs. Mallard as she realizes what her husband's death will mean to her. Suddenly she is "free, free, free!" (202), and she rejoices at this knowledge, imagining all the new possibilities of her life. Once she believes that her husband is gone, she feels a great release, and it is the loss of this freedom that ultimately kills her.

Today, Kate Chopin is considered a feminist writer, and "The Story of An Hour" is ultimately based on the theme of female empowerment. Mrs. Mallard is clearly not a weak woman—in fact, the narrator notes that her face contains "a certain strength" (202). However, her life has been constrained by her marriage, and it is the imagined loss of this constraint that makes the news of her husband's apparent death fill her with joy. Her husband, the narrator notes, "never looked save with love upon her" (202), and this suggests that the relationship was not cruel or abusive. Nonetheless, to Mrs. Mallard her husband had represented a "powerful will bending her in that blind persistence with which men and women believe they have a right to impose a private will upon a fellow creature" (202).

> Fourth element of analysis: theme

In "The Story of an Hour," little background is given about the lives of the characters or the setting of the story. Though the omniscient narrator sees into the mind of Mrs. Mallard, readers really do not see the thoughts of other characters, and the story is too brief to reveal many details. The focus of the story is its theme, which Chopin explores with great economy. This is a story about marriage, which, as Chopin saw it, kept women from being free and independent beings.

> Conclusion

2 | FICTION

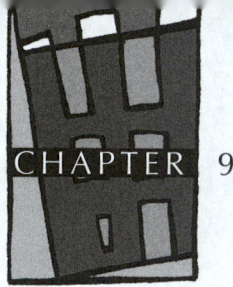

CHAPTER 9

UNDERSTANDING FICTION

A **narrative** tells a story by presenting events in some logical or orderly way. A work of **fiction** is a narrative that originates in the imagination of the author rather than in history or fact. Of course, some fiction—historical or autobiographical fiction, for example—focuses on real people and is grounded in actual events, but the way the characters interact, what they say, and how the plot unfolds are largely the author's invention.

Even before they know how to read, most people learn how narratives are structured. As children learn how to tell a story, they start to experiment with its form, learning the value of exaggerating, adding or deleting details, rearranging events, and bending facts. In other words, they learn how to *fictionalize* a narrative to achieve a desired effect. This kind of informal personal narrative is similar in many respects to more structured literary narratives.

 ## Origins of Modern Fiction

People have always had stories to tell, and as we evolved, so did our means of self-expression. Our early ancestors depicted the stories of their daily lives and beliefs in primitive drawings that used pictures as symbols. As language evolved, so too did our means of communicating—and our need to preserve what we understood to be our past.

Stories and songs emerged as an oral means of communicating and preserving the past: tales of heroic battles or struggles, myths, or religious beliefs. In a society that was not literate, and in a time before mass communication, the oral tradition enabled people to pass down these stories, usually in the form of long rhyming poems. These poems used various literary devices—including **rhyme** and **alliteration** as well as **anaphora** (the repetition of key words or phrases)—to make them easier to remember. Thus, the earliest works of fiction were in fact poetry.

Eventually written down, these extended narratives developed into **epics**—long narrative poems about heroic figures whose actions determine the fate of a nation or of an entire race. Homer's *Iliad* and *Odyssey*, the ancient Babylonian *Epic of Gilgamesh*, the Hindu *Bhagavad Gita*, and the Anglo-Saxon *Beowulf* are examples of epics. Many of the tales of the Old Testament also came out of this tradition. The setting of an epic is vast—sometimes worldwide or cosmic, including heaven and hell—and the action commonly involves a battle or a perilous journey. Quite often, divine beings participate in the action and influence the outcome of events, as they do in the Trojan War in the *Iliad* and in the founding of Rome in Virgil's *Aeneid*.

Engraving of Ulysses slaying Penelope's
suitors, from Homer's *Odyssey*
Source: ©Bettmann/Corbis

Engraving of the Trojan horse from Homer's *Odyssey*
Source: ©Bettmann/Corbis

During the Middle Ages, these early epics were supplanted by the **romance**. Written initially in verse and later in prose, the romance replaced the gods, goddesses, and central heroic characters of the epic with knights, kings, and damsels in distress. Events were controlled by enchantments rather than by the will of divine beings. The anonymously written *Sir Gawain and the Green Knight* and Thomas Malory's *Le Morte d'Arthur* are romances based on the legend of King Arthur and the Knights of the Round Table.

Other significant texts of the Middle Ages include Geoffrey Chaucer's *The Canterbury Tales* and Giovanni Boccaccio's *The Decameron*, both written in the fourteenth century. These two works are made up of poems and stories, respectively, integrated into a larger narrative framework. They share similarities with modern collections of linked short stories—stories set in the same town or featuring the same characters, such as Sherwood Anderson's 1919 *Winesburg, Ohio*, and Amy Tan's 1989 *The Joy Luck Club*.

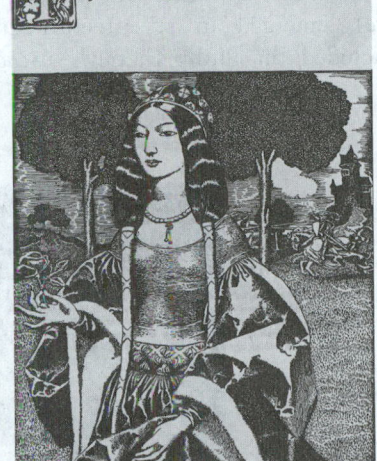

Portrait of Queen Guinevere, King Arthur's
wife and Sir Lancelot's mistress

The History of the Novel

The evolution of the **novel** has been a gradual but steady process. Early forms of literature share many of the characteristics of the novel (although not necessarily sharing its recog-

The First Printing Press.

Nineteenth-century woodcut depicting
Johannes Gutenberg's printing press

North Wind Picture Archives/Alamy

nizable form). Epics and romances, for instance, often had unified plots, developed characters, and complex themes, and in this way, they were precursors of what today we call the novel.

Perhaps the most notable event in the development of the novel, and of literature as a whole, was the invention of the printing press by Johannes Gutenberg in 1440. Before this milestone, printing was a costly and impractical process that was largely reserved for medical books and sacred texts. However, this invention made the production and distribution of longer works a practical possibility and forever expanded the scope of what we consider literature to be—and how we access it. In fact, the printing press was one of the factors that made the Renaissance possible. During this period, philosophy, science, literature, and the arts flowered. The **pastoral romance**, a prose tale set in an idealized rural world, and the **character**, a brief satirical sketch illustrating a type of personality, both became popular in Renaissance England. The **picaresque novel**, an episodic, often satirical work about a rogue or rascal (such as Miguel de Cervantes's *Don Quixote*), emerged in seventeenth-century Spain. Other notable Renaissance-era texts included Sir Philip Sidney's *Arcadia*, Edmund Spenser's *The Faerie Queen*, and John

©Timewatch Images/Alamy

An 1863 engraving by Gustave Doré depicting a scene from Miguel de
Cervantes's *Don Quixote*

Nineteenth-century woodcut by J. Mahoney depicting a scene from Charles Dickens's *Oliver Twist*

Bunyan's *The Pilgrim's Progress*. Each of these texts included features now associated with the novel—longer narratives, extended plots, the development of characters over time, and a hero/protagonist—and the form continued to evolve.

The English writer Daniel Defoe is commonly given credit for writing the first novel. His *Robinson Crusoe* (1719) is an episodic narrative similar to a picaresque but unified by a single setting as well as by a central character. Another early novel, Jonathan Swift's *Gulliver's Travels* (1726), is a satirical commentary on the undesirable outcomes of science. During this time, the **epistolary novel** also flourished. This kind of novel told a story in letters or included letters as a means of disseminating information. Samuel Richardson's *Clarissa* (1748) is an example from the eighteenth century; a contemporary example is Alice Walker's *The Color Purple* (1982).

By the nineteenth century, the novel had reached a high point in its development, and its influence and importance were widespread. During the Victorian era in England (1837–1901), many novels reflected the era's preoccupation with propriety and manners. The most notable examples of these **novels of manners** were Jane Austen's *Sense and Sensibility* (1811) and *Pride and Prejudice* (1813). Beyond the world of the aristocracy, members of the middle class clamored for novels that mirrored their own experiences, and writers such as George Eliot, Charles Dickens, William Thackeray, and Charlotte and Emily Brontë appealed to this desire by creating large fictional worlds populated by many different characters who reflected the

Scene from the 1931 film *Frankenstein*.

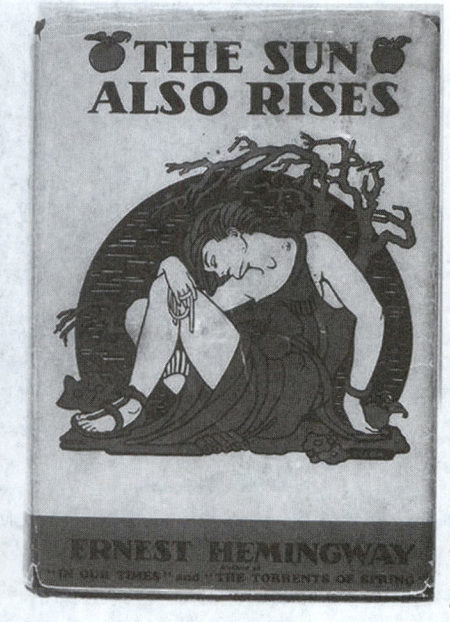

Courtesy, Charles Scribner's Sons, an imprint of Simon & Schuster

Courtesy, Charles Scribner's Sons, an imprint of Simon & Schuster

Cover images of *The Great Gatsby, The Sun Also Rises,* and *The Sound and the Fury*

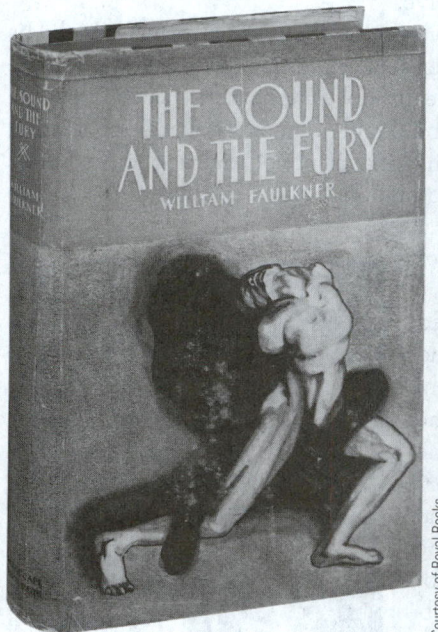

Courtesy of Royal Books

complexity—and at times the melodrama—of Victorian society. Other writers addressed the dire consequences of science and ambition, as Mary Wollstonecraft Shelley did in her Gothic tale *Frankenstein* (1817).

In the United States, the early nineteenth century was marked by novels that reflected the concerns of a growing country with burgeoning interests. James Fenimore Cooper (*Last of the Mohicans*) and Nathaniel Hawthorne (*The Scarlet Letter*) wrote historical fiction, while Herman Melville (*Moby-Dick*) examined good and evil, madness and sanity. **Realism**, which strove to portray everyday events and people in a realistic fashion, began in France with Honoré de Balzac and Gustav Flaubert and spread to the United States, influencing writers such as Henry James, Stephen Crane, and Mark Twain. Other nineteenth-century writers addressed social and even feminist themes in their work. In the United States, writers who addressed such concerns included Harriet Beecher Stowe (*Uncle Tom's Cabin*) and Kate Chopin (*The Awakening*). Meanwhile, in Russia, novelists such as Fyodor Dostoyevsky (*Crime and Punishment*) and Leo Tolstoy (*War and Peace*) examined the everyday lives, as well as the larger political struggles and triumphs, of their people.

The early twentieth century marked the beginning of a literary movement known as **modernism**, in which writers reacted to the increasing complexity of a changing world and mourned the passing of old ways under the pressures of modernity. World War I, urbanization, and the rise of industrialism all contributed to a sense that new ideas needed to be expressed in new ways, and writers such as James Joyce (*Ulysses*), Virginia Woolf (*To the Lighthouse*), and D. H. Lawrence (*Sons and Lovers*) experimented with both form and content.

In the United States, the Roaring Twenties and the Great Depression inspired numerous novelists who set out to write the "Great American Novel" and capture the culture and concerns of the times, often in very gritty and realistic ways. These authors included F. Scott Fitzgerald (*The Great Gatsby*), Ernest Hemingway (*The Sun Also Rises*), William Faulkner (*The Sound and the Fury*), and John Steinbeck (*The Grapes of Wrath*). A little later, novelists such as Richard Wright (*Native Son*) and Ralph Ellison (*Invisible Man*) made important literary contributions by addressing the sociopolitical climate for African Americans in a segregated society.

In the aftermath of modernism, a movement called **postmodernism** emerged. Postmodern artists reacted against the limitations imposed on them by modernist ideas as well as the carnage of World War II. Often, the search for meaning in a postmodern text became an end in itself, and in this way, a work's meaning became relative and subjective. Postmodern novelists, such as Donald Barthelme, Margaret Atwood, Thomas Pynchon, Salman Rushdie, and Kurt Vonnegut, confronted the fragmentation of society and rejected the idea of a unified plot or the possibility of a reliable narrator.

Contemporary fiction has been marked and influenced by the developments of the latter part of the twentieth century, including globalization, the rise of technology, and the advent of the Internet and the Age of Communication. As our ability to interact and communicate with other societies has increased exponentially, so too has our access to the literature of other cultures. Contemporary fiction is a world that mirrors the diversity of its participants in terms of form, content, theme, style, and language. There are many writers worthy of mention, as each culture makes its own invaluable contributions. Some particularly noteworthy contemporary writers include the Nobel Prize–winning novelists Orhan Pamuk, José Saramago, Doris Lessing, Gabriel García Márquez, Nadine Gordimer, Saul Bellow, Toni Morrison, and V. S. Naipul. As we continue into the twenty-first century, the only thing that remains certain about the future of the novel, and of fiction in general, is its past.

The History of the Short Story

Early precursors of the short story include **anecdotes, parables, fables, folk tales**, and **fairy tales**. What all of these forms have in common is brevity and a moral. The ones that have survived, such as "Cinderella" and Aesop's *Fables*, are contemporary versions of old, even ancient, tales that can be traced back centuries through many different cultures.

Folktales and fairy tales share many characteristics. First, they feature simple characters who illustrate a quality or trait that can be summed up in a few words. Much of the appeal of "Cinderella," for example, depends on the contrast between the selfish, sadistic stepsisters and the poor, gentle, victimized Cinderella. In addition, the folktale or fairy

©Bettmann/Corbis

Undated woodcut of Cinderella

tale has an obvious theme or **moral**—good triumphing over evil, for instance. The stories move directly to their conclusions, never interrupted by ingenious or unexpected plot twists. (Love is temporarily thwarted, but the prince eventually finds Cinderella and marries her.) Finally, these tales are anchored not in specific times or places but in "once upon a time" settings, green worlds of prehistory filled with royalty, talking animals, and magic.

The thematically linked stories in Giovanni Boccaccio's *The Decameron* and Geoffrey Chaucer's *The Canterbury Tales*, both written in the fourteenth century, were precursors of the modern short story. *Grimm's Fairy Tales* (1824–1826), an early collection of short narratives and folk stories, also helped to pave the way for the development of the genre, but it was not until the nineteenth century that the contemporary version of the short story emerged.

During the last quarter of the nineteenth century, a proliferation of literary and popular magazines and journals created a demand for short fiction (between 3,000 and 15,000 words) that could be published in their entirety rather than in serial installments, as most novels at the time were. Nathaniel Hawthorne's *Twice-Told Tales* (1842) and Edgar Allan Poe's *Tales of the Grotesque and Arabesque* (1836) were early collections of short stories. Americans in particular hungrily consumed the written word, and short stories soared in popularity. In fact, because the short story was embraced so readily and developed so quickly in the United States, it is commonly (although not quite accurately) thought of as an American literary form.

 ## Defining the Short Story

Like the novel, the short story evolved from various forms of narrative and has its roots in an oral tradition. However, whereas the novel is an extended piece of narrative fiction, the **short story** is distinguished by its relative brevity, which creates a specific set of expectations and possibilities as well as certain limitations. Unlike the novelist, the short story writer cannot devote a great deal of space to developing a highly complex plot or a large number of characters. As a result, the short story often begins close to or at the height of action and develops a limited number of characters. Usually focusing on a single incident, the writer develops one or more characters by showing their reactions to events. This attention to character development, as well as its detailed description of setting, is what distinguishes the short story from earlier short narrative forms.

In many contemporary short stories, a character experiences an **epiphany**, a moment of illumination in which something hidden or not understood becomes immediately clear. In other short stories, the thematic significance, or meaning, is communicated through the way in which the characters develop, or react. Regardless of the specifics of its format or its theme, a short story offers readers an open window to a world that they can enter—if only briefly.

The short story that follows, Ernest Hemingway's "Hills Like White Elephants" (1927), illustrates many of the characteristics of the modern **short story**. Although it is so brief that it might be more accurately called a **short-short story**, it uses its limited space to establish a distinct setting and develop two characters. From the story's first paragraph, readers know where the story takes place and whom it is about: "The American and the girl with him sat at a table in the shade, outside the building. It was very hot and the express from Barcelona would come in forty minutes." As time elapses and the man and woman wait for the train to Madrid, their strained dialogue reveals the tension between them and hints at the serious conflict they must resolve.

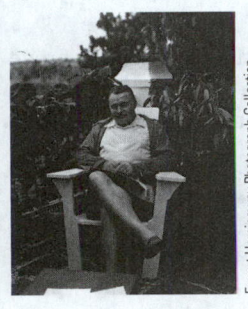

Ernest Hemingway Photograph Collection, John F. Kennedy Presidential Library and Museum, Boston.

ERNEST HEMINGWAY (1898–1961) grew up in Oak Park, Illinois, and after high school graduation began his writing career as a reporter on the *Kansas City Star*. While working as a volunteer ambulance driver in World War I, eighteen-year-old Hemingway was wounded. As Hemingway himself told the story, he was hit by machine-gun fire while carrying an Italian soldier to safety. (Hemingway biographer Michael Reynolds, however, reports that Hemingway was wounded when a mortar shell fell and killed the man next to him.)

Success for Hemingway came early, with publication of the short story collection *In Our Time* (1925) and his first and most acclaimed novel, *The Sun Also Rises* (1926), a portrait of a postwar "lost generation" of Americans adrift in Europe. This novel established Hemingway as a writer who was able to create fiction out of his own life experiences. *A Farewell to Arms* (1929) harks back to his war experiences; *For Whom the Bell Tolls* (1940) emerged out of his experiences as a journalist in Spain during the Spanish Civil War. Later in life, he made his home in Key West, Florida, and then in Cuba, where he wrote *The Old Man and the Sea* (1952). In 1954 he won the Nobel Prize in Literature. In 1961, plagued by poor health and mental illness—and perhaps also by the difficulty of living up to his own image—Hemingway took his own life.

Cultural Context At the time this story was written, Ernest Hemingway was part of a group of American expatriates living in Paris. Disillusioned by World War I and seeking a more bohemian lifestyle, free from the concerns of American materialism, this group of artists, intellectuals, poets, and writers were known as the "Lost Generation." Some of the group's most famous members included F. Scott Fitzgerald, Gertrude Stein, and John Dos Passos. The literary legacy they left behind is arguably one of the greatest of the twentieth century.

Hills Like White Elephants (1927)

The hills across the valley of the Ebro[1] were long and white. On this side there was no shade and no trees and the station was between two lines of rails in the sun. Close against the side of the station there was the warm shadow of the building and a curtain, made of strings of bamboo beads, hung across the open door into the bar, to keep out flies. The American and the girl with him sat at a table in the shade, outside the building. It was very hot and the express from Barcelona would come in forty minutes. It stopped at this junction for two minutes and went on to Madrid.

"What should we drink?" the girl asked. She had taken off her hat and put it on the table.

---

[1]*Ebro:* A river in northern Spain.

"It's pretty hot," the man said.

"Let's drink beer."

5 "Dos cervezas," the man said into the curtain.

"Big ones?" a woman asked from the doorway.

"Yes. Two big ones."

The woman brought two glasses of beer and two felt pads. She put the felt pads and the beer glasses on the table and looked at the man and the girl. The girl was looking off at the line of hills. They were white in the sun and the country was brown and dry.

"They look like white elephants," she said.

10 "I've never seen one," the man drank his beer.

"No, you wouldn't have."

"I might have," the man said. "Just because you say I wouldn't have doesn't prove anything."

The girl looked at the bead curtain. "They've painted something on it," she said. "What does it say?"

"Anis del Toro.² It's a drink."

15 "Could we try it?"

The man called "Listen" through the curtain. The woman came out from the bar.

"Four reales."³

"We want two Anis del Toro."

"With water?"

20 "Do you want it with water?"

"I don't know," the girl said. "Is it good with water?"

"It's all right."

"You want them with water?" asked the woman.

"Yes, with water."

25 "It tastes like licorice," the girl said and put the glass down.

"That's the way with everything."

"Yes," said the girl. "Everything tastes of licorice. Especially all the things you've waited so long for, like absinthe."⁴

"Oh, cut it out."

"You started it," the girl said. "I was being amused. I was having a fine time."

30 "Well, let's try and have a fine time."

"All right. I was trying. I said the mountains looked like white elephants. Wasn't that bright?"

"That was bright."

"I wanted to try this new drink. That's all we do, isn't it—look at things and try new drinks?"

"I guess so."

35 The girl looked across at the hills.

"They're lovely hills," she said. "They don't really look like white elephants. I just meant the coloring of their skin through the trees."

---

²*Anis del Toro:* Spanish for *bull's anisette*, a dark alcoholic drink made from anise, an herb that tastes like licorice.

³*reales:* Spanish coins.

⁴*absinthe:* A green alcoholic drink made from wormwood, anise, and other herbs.

"Should we have another drink?"

"All right."

The warm wind blew the bead curtain against the table.

"The beer's nice and cool," the man said.   40

"It's lovely," the girl said.

"It's really an awfully simple operation, Jig," the man said. "It's not really an operation at all."

The girl looked at the ground the table legs rested on.

"I know you wouldn't mind it, Jig. It's really not anything. It's just to let the air in."

The girl did not say anything.   45

"I'll go with you and I'll stay with you all the time. They just let the air in and then it's all perfectly natural."

"Then what will we do afterward?"

"We'll be fine afterward. Just like we were before."

"What makes you think so?"

"That's the only thing that bothers us. It's the only thing that's made us unhappy."   50

The girl looked at the bead curtain, put her hand out and took hold of two of the strings of beads.

"And you think then we'll be all right and be happy."

"I know we will. You don't have to be afraid. I've known lots of people that have done it."

"So have I," said the girl. "And afterward they were all so happy."

"Well," the man said, "if you don't want to you don't have to. I wouldn't have you   55
do it if you didn't want to. But I know it's perfectly simple."

"And you really want to?"

"I think it's the best thing to do. But I don't want you to do it if you don't really want to."

"And if I do it you'll be happy and things will be like they were and you'll love me?"

"I love you now. You know I love you."

"I know. But if I do it, then it will be nice again if I say things are like white el-   60
ephants, and you'll like it?"

"I'll love it. I love it now but I just can't think about it. You know how I get when I worry."

"If I do it you won't ever worry?"

"I won't worry about that because it's perfectly simple."

"Then I'll do it. Because I don't care about me."

"What do you mean?"   65

"I don't care about me."

"Well, I care about you."

"Oh, yes. But I don't care about me. And I'll do it and then everything will be fine."

"I don't want you to do it if you feel that way."

The girl stood up and walked to the end of the station. Across, on the other side,   70
were fields of grain and trees along the banks of the Ebro. Far away beyond the river, were mountains. The shadow of a cloud moved across the field of grain and she saw the river through the trees.

"And we could have all this," she said. "And we could have everything and every day we make it more impossible."

"What did you say?"

"I said we could have everything."

"We can have everything."

75   "No, we can't."

"We can have the whole world."

"No, we can't."

"We can go everywhere."

"No, we can't. It isn't ours any more."

80   "It's ours."

"No, it isn't. And once they take it away, you never get it back."

"But they haven't taken it away."

"We'll wait and see."

"Come on back in the shade," he said. "You mustn't feel that way."

85   "I don't feel any way," the girl said. "I just know things."

"I don't want you to do anything that you don't want to do—."

"Nor that isn't good for me," she said. "I know. Could we have another beer?"

"All right. But you've got to realize—"

"I realize," the girl said. "Can't we maybe stop talking?"

90   They sat down at the table and the girl looked across at the hills on the dry side of the valley and the man looked at her and at the table.

"You've got to realize," he said, "that I don't want you to do it if you don't want to. I'm perfectly willing to go through with it if it means anything to you."

"Doesn't it mean anything to you? We could get along."

"Of course it does. But I don't want anybody but you. I don't want anyone else. And I know it's perfectly simple."

"Yes, you know it's perfectly simple."

95   "It's all right for you to say that, but I do know it."

"Would you do something for me now?"

"I'd do anything for you."

"Would you please please please please please please please stop talking?"

He did not say anything but looked at the bags against the wall of the station. There were labels on them from all the hotels where they had spent nights.

100   "But I don't want you to," he said, "I don't care anything about it."

"I'll scream," the girl said.

The woman came out through the curtains with two glasses of beer and put them down on the damp felt pads. "The train comes in five minutes," she said.

"What did she say?" asked the girl.

"That the train is coming in five minutes."

105   The girl smiled brightly at the woman, to thank her.

"I'd better take the bags over to the other side of the station," the man said. She smiled at him.

"All right. Then come back and we'll finish the beer."

He picked up the two heavy bags and carried them around the station to the other tracks. He looked up the tracks but could not see the train. Coming back, he walked through the barroom, where people waiting for the train were drinking. He drank an Anis at the bar and looked at the people. They were all waiting reasonably for the train. He went out through the bead curtain. She was sitting at the table and smiled at him.

"Do you feel better?" he asked.

"I feel fine," she said. "There's nothing wrong with me. I feel fine."

* * *

Like many short stories, "Hills Like White Elephants" has a single setting, contains a straightforward plot, involves few characters, starts at the height of the action, and reaches its climax quickly. Even so, this story is anything but simple. From the beginning, readers can sense the tension that exists between the two characters, "the girl" and "the American." For almost half the story, they talk about anything except what concerns them most—the question of whether the girl should have an unspecified "simple operation"—presumably an abortion. When they finally confront the issue, the man trivializes the situation by saying that the procedure is "natural" and "not really an operation at all." Eventually, the girl pleads, "Would you please please please please please please stop talking?" She is clearly hurt by the American's condescending tone and is frightened by her circumstances. Although at the end of the story she assures him that she is "fine," they both sense that no matter what she decides to do, their relationship will never be the same. In this brief, seemingly uncomplicated story, Hemingway manages to convey, almost entirely through dialogue, the inability of the two main characters to communicate as well as the moral bankruptcy of their world.

The Boundaries of Fiction

As noted above, a **short story** is a work of fiction that is marked by its brevity, its relatively limited number of characters, its short time frame, and its ability to achieve thematic significance in a relatively short space. A **novella** (such as Franz Kafka's "The Metamorphosis" and Herman Melville's "Bartleby, the Scrivener") is an extended short story that shares some characteristics (for example, concentrated action) with a short story while retaining some qualities of a novel, including greater character development. At the other end of the spectrum are **short-short stories**, which are under 1,500 words (about five pages) in length. (Examples of those very brief stories are included in Chapter 10.) **Prose poems**, such as Richard Blanco's "Mexican Almuerzo in New England" (p. 843), are hybrid versions of literature that have characteristics of both prose (being written in paragraphs) and poetry (being written in verse form, often using imagery, meter, and rhyme to convey lyrical beauty). In addition, **graphic stories**—sometimes complete in themselves, sometimes part of longer works of **graphic fiction**—have proliferated in recent years. (Examples of such works are included in Chapter 11.)

Finally, the Internet—along with computers, smartphones, and tablets—offers numerous possibilities for arranging and disseminating texts. Currently, writers are experimenting with fictional forms that are every bit as revolutionary as those modernist works created by James Joyce, John Dos Passos, Virginia Woolf, and Gertrude Stein nearly a century ago. For example, "Black Box" (an excerpt appears below), a science fiction short story written by Pulitzer Prize–winning author Jennifer Egan, was originally presented as tweets over a ten-night period.

Some powerful men actually call their beauties "Beauty."

Contrary to reputation, there is a deep camaraderie among beauties.

If your Designated Mate is widely feared, the beauties at the house party where you've gone undercover to meet him will be especially kind.

Kindness feels good, even when it's based on a false notion of your identity and purpose.

Egan has also written a story in the form of a PowerPoint presentation. The writer Alex Epstein has created a story made up of Facebook photos, and other writers are experimenting with blog-post fiction as well as with stories on websites devoted to specific kinds of fiction—for example, flash fiction or graphic short stories. Perhaps the most experimental fictional form is **hypertext fiction**—stories, such as Catlin Fisher's "These Waves of Girls" and Paul La Farge's "Luminous Airplanes"—that contains text and links to pictures, film clips, and other texts. Readers create "paths" through hypertext stories by following links in any order they choose. In this way, a single work of hypertext fiction can contain many possible plots, and readers can move through them at will.

There are, it seems, as many different ways to tell a story as there are stories to be told. A short story may be comic or tragic; its subject may be growing up, marriage, crime and punishment, war, sexual awakening, death, or any number of other human concerns. The setting can be an imaginary world, the old West, rural America, the jungles of Uruguay, nineteenth-century Russia, precommunist China, or modern Egypt. The story may have a conventional form, with a definite beginning, middle, and end, or it may be structured as a letter, as a diary entry, or even as a collection of random notes. The story may use just words, or it may juxtapose conventional text with symbols, pictures, or empty space. The narrator of a story may be trustworthy or unreliable, involved in the action or a disinterested observer, sympathetic or deserving of scorn, extremely ignorant or highly insightful, limited in vision or able to see inside the minds of all the characters. As the selections in this anthology show, the possibilities of the short story are almost endless.

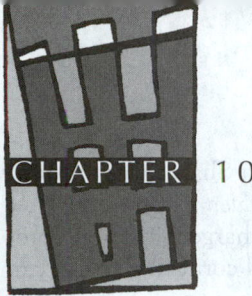

CHAPTER 10

FICTION SAMPLER:
THE SHORT-SHORT STORY

Julia Alvarez
AP Images/Ramon Espinosa

Stephen Graham Jones
Gary Isaacs

Ed Park
Sylvia Plachy

Jamaica Kincaid
Taro Yamasaki/The LIFE Images Collection/
Getty Images

This chapter focuses on the **short-short story**, a short story that is fewer than 1,500 words in length. Short-shorts are often divided into subcategories according to their overall length. For example, **micro fiction**, at approximately 250 words or fewer, is one of the shortest kinds of short-short fiction, followed by **flash fiction** (fewer than approximately 1,000 words) and then by **sudden fiction** (fewer than approximately 1,500 words). Short-shorts are sometimes also categorized according to how long they take to read or how long they take to write. Regardless of their individual characteristics, all short-short stories compress ideas into a small package and, to varying degrees, test the limits of the short story genre. Some short-shorts are quite conventional (that is, they include recognizable characters and have an identifiable beginning, middle, and end); others are experimental, perhaps lacking a definite setting or a clear plot. As defined by Robert Shapard (who, along with James Thomas, edited the short-short story collections *Sudden Fiction* and *New Sudden Fiction*), short-short stories are "Highly compressed, highly charged, insidious, protean, sudden, alarming, tantalizing"; they can "confer form on small corners of chaos, can do in a page what a novel does in two hundred." One of the most extreme examples is Ernest Hemingway's famous six-word story: "For sale: baby shoes, never worn."

The stories in this sampler represent a wide range of short-short fiction. Of the ten stories collected here, Julia Alvarez's "Snow" and Bret Anthony Johnston's "Encounters with Unexpected Animals" perhaps most closely resemble traditional short stories in that they develop familiar characters in recognizable settings. Similarly, Sandra Cisneros's "Pilón" explores a theme that is familiar in literary works: the narrator's attempt to recapture long-ago memories.

Other stories in this sampler are somewhat more experimental. Although their plots may unfold in conventional ways, their treatment of time is sometimes surprising. For example, in "Discovering America," Stephen Graham Jones summarizes the events of several years of the narrator's life in three pages; George Saunders's two-paragraph "Sticks" covers several decades; and Ed Park's "Slide to Unlock" unfolds in just a few minutes. Dave Eggers's "Accident" and Lydia Davis's "Television" are perhaps even more unpredictable: although they resemble conventional short stories in some respects, both maintain an unusual narrative distance through their unexpected use of point of view.

Finally, Jamaica Kincaid's "Girl," a **stream-of-consciousness monologue**, is unique in its style and form (the entire story is a single sentence), as is Amanda Brown's "Love and Other Catastrophes: A Mix Tape," consisting entirely of a list of song titles.

Despite their brevity, the stories in this chapter have much in common with the stories that appear elsewhere in this book. Each, in its own distinctive way, "tells a story."

JULIA ALVAREZ (1950–   ) was born in New York City. Soon after her birth, Alvarez's family relocated to the Dominican Republic, where they lived for ten years until they emigrated back to New York. Alvarez describes herself as "a Dominican, hyphen, American. . . . As a fiction writer, I find that the most exciting things happen in the realm of that hyphen—the place where two worlds collide or blend together." Alvarez's works explore the experiences and emotions of immigrants, particularly female Hispanic immigrants, as they struggle to redefine themselves in the context of a new culture. She has published many highly regarded works of fiction and poetry, including *Homecoming* (1984 and 1996), *How the García Girls Lost Their Accents* (1991), *In the Time of Butterflies* (1995), and *¡Yo!* (1997). She is also the author of the children's book *How Tía Lola Saved the Summer* (2011) and the memoir *A Wedding in Haiti* (2012). Alvarez is currently a writer-in-residence at Middlebury College in Vermont.

AP Images/Ramon Espinosa

Snow (1984)

Our first year in New York we rented a small apartment with a Catholic school nearby, taught by the Sisters of Charity, hefty women in long black gowns and bonnets that made them look peculiar, like dolls in mourning. I liked them a lot, especially my grandmotherly fourth grade teacher, Sister Zoe. I had a lovely name, she said, and she had me teach the whole class how to pronounce it. *Yo-Ian-da*. As the only immigrant in my class, I was put in a special seat in the first row by the window, apart from the other children so that Sister Zoe could tutor me without disturbing them. Slowly, she enunciated the new words I was to repeat: *laundromat, cornflakes, subway, snow*.

Soon I picked up enough English to understand holocaust was in the air. Sister Zoe explained to a wide-eyed classroom what was happening in Cuba. Russian missiles were being assembled, trained supposedly on New York City. President Kennedy, looking worried too, was on the television at home, explaining we might have to go to war against the Communists. At school, we had air-raid drills: an ominous bell would go off and we'd file into the hall, fall to the floor, cover our heads with our coats, and imagine our hair falling out, the bones in our arms going soft. At home, Mami and my sisters and I said a rosary for world peace. I heard new vocabulary: *nuclear bomb, radioactive fallout, bomb shelter*. Sister Zoe explained how it would happen. She drew a picture of a mushroom on the blackboard and dotted a flurry of chalkmarks for the dusty fallout that would kill us all.

The months grew cold, November, December. It was dark when I got up in the morning, frosty when I followed my breath to school. One morning as I sat at my desk daydreaming out the window, I saw dots in the air like the ones Sister Zoe had drawn— random at first, then lots and lots. I shrieked, "Bomb Bomb!" Sister Zoe jerked around, her full black skirt ballooning as she hurried to my side. A few girls began to cry.

But then Sister Zoe's shocked look faded. "Why, Yolanda dear, that's snow!" She laughed. "Snow."

"Snow," I repeated. I looked out the window warily. All my life I had heard about the white crystals that fell out of American skies in the winter. From my desk I watched the fine powder dust the sidewalk and parked cars below. Each flake was different, Sister Zoe said, like a person, irreplaceable and beautiful.

*   *   *

AMANDA BROWN (1981–   ), a graduate of Emerson College, co-owns the independent record label Not Not Fun. "Love and Other Catastrophes" was first published in 2002 in *Story Quarterly* and was reprinted in *The Best American Nonrequired Reading 2003*.

Love and Other Catastrophes: A Mix Tape (2002)

"All By Myself" (Eric Carmen). "Looking for Love" (Lou Reed). "I Wanna Dance With Somebody" (Whitney Houston). "Let's Dance" (David Bowie). "Let's Kiss" (Beat Happening). "Let's Talk About Sex" (Salt N' Pepa). "Like A Virgin" (Madonna). "We've Only Just Begun" (The Carpenters). "I Wanna Be Your Boyfriend" (The Ramones). "I'll Tumble 4 Ya" (Culture Club). "Head Over Heels" (The Go-Go's). "Nothing Compares To You" (Sinéad O'Connor). "My Girl" (The Temptations). "Could This Be Love?" (Bob Marley). "Love and Marriage" (Frank Sinatra). "White Wedding" (Billy Idol). "Stuck in the Middle with You" (Steelers Wheel). "Tempted" (The Squeeze). "There Goes My Baby" (The Drifters). "What's Going On?" (Marvin Gaye). "Where Did You Sleep Last Night?" (Leadbelly). "Whose Bed Have Your Boots Been Under?" (Shania Twain). "Jealous Guy" (John Lennon). "Your Cheatin' Heart" (Tammy Wynette). "Shot Through the Heart" (Bon Jovi). "Don't Go

Breaking My Heart" (Elton John and Kiki Dee). "My Achy Breaky Heart" (Billy Ray Cyrus). "Heartbreak Hotel" (Elvis Presley). "Stop, In the Name of Love" (The Supremes). "Try a Little Tenderness" (Otis Redding). "Try (Just a Little Bit Harder)" (Janis Joplin). "All Apologies" (Nirvana). "Hanging on the Telephone" (Blondie). "I Just Called to Say I Love You" (Stevie Wonder). "Love Will Keep Us Together" (Captain and Tennille). "Let's Stay Together" (Al Green). "It Ain't Over 'Till It's Over" (Lenny Kravitz). "What's Love Got To Do With It?" (Tina Turner). "You Don't Bring Me Flowers Anymore" (Barbara Streisand and Neil Diamond). "I Wish You Wouldn't Say That" (Talking Heads). "You're So Vain" (Carly Simon). "Love Is a Battlefield" (Pat Benatar). "Heaven Knows I'm Miserable Now" (The Smiths). "(Can't Get No) Satisfaction" (Rolling Stones). "Must Have Been Love (But It's Over Now)" (Roxette). "Breaking Up Is Hard to Do" (Neil Sedaka). "I Will Survive" (Gloria Gaynor). "Hit the Road, Jack" (Mary McCaslin and Jim Ringer). "These Boots Were Made for Walking" (Nancy Sinatra). "All Out of Love" (Air Supply). "All By Myself" (Eric Carmen).

*   *   *

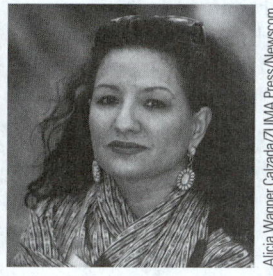

SANDRA CISNEROS (1954–   ) was born and raised in Chicago. Her fiction, poems, and essays explore Mexican–American heritage and identity. She is the author of *The House on Mango Street* (1983), *My Wicked Wicked Ways* (1987), *Woman Hollering Creek and Other Stories* (1991), *Loose Woman: Poems* (1994), and *Caramelo, or, Puro Cuento: A Novel* (2002). Cisneros is the recipient of numerous awards and fellowships, including a MacArthur Foundation Fellowship and two national Endowment of the Arts Fellowships for fiction and poetry.

Pilón (2002)

Like the Mexican grocer who gives you a pilón, *something extra tossed into your bag as a thank-you for your patronage just as you are leaving. I give you here another story in thanks for having listened to my* cuento[1] . . .

On Cinco de Mayo Street, in front of Café la Blanca, an organ grinder playing "Farolito." Out of a happy grief, people give coins for shaking awake the memory of a father, a beloved, a child whom God ran away with.

And it was as if that music stirred up things in a piece of my heart from a time I couldn't remember. From before. Not exactly a time, a feeling. The way sometimes one remembers a memory with the images blurred and rounded, but has forgotten the one thing that would draw it all into focus. In this case, I'd forgotten a mood. Not a mood—a state of being, to be more precise.

---

[1]*cuento:* Spanish for *story.*

How before my body wasn't my body. I didn't have a body. I was a being as close to a spirit as a spirit. I was a ball of light floating across the planet. I mean the me I was before puberty, that red Rio Bravo[2] you have to carry yourself over.

I don't know how it is with boys. I've never been a boy. But girls somewhere between the ages of, say, eight and puberty, girls forget they have bodies. It's the time she has trouble keeping herself clean, socks always drooping, knees pocked and bloody, hair crooked as a broom. She doesn't look in mirrors. She isn't aware of being watched. Not aware of her body causing men to look at her yet. There isn't the sense of the female body's volatility, its rude weight, the nuisance of dragging it about. There isn't the world to bully you with it, bludgeon you, condemn you to a life sentence of fear. It's the time when you look at a young girl and notice she is at her ugliest, but at the same time, at her happiest. She is a being as close to a spirit as a spirit.

Then that red Rubicon. The never going back there. To that country, I mean.   5

And I remember along with that feeling fluttering through the notes of "Farolito," so many things, so many, all at once, each distinct and separate, and all running together. The taste of a *caramelo* called Glorias on my tongue. At la Caleta beach, a girl with skin like *cajeta*, like goat-milk candy. The *caramelo* color of your skin after rising out of the Acapulco foam, salt water running down your hair and stinging the eyes, the raw ocean smell, and the ocean running out of your mouth and nose. My mother watering her dahlias with a hose and running a stream of water over her feet as well, Indian feet, thick and square, *como de barro*, like the red clay of Mexican pottery.

And I don't know how it is with anyone else, but for me these things, that song, that time, that place, are all bound together in a country I am homesick for, that doesn't exist anymore. That never existed. A country I invented. Like all emigrants caught between here and there.

*   *   *

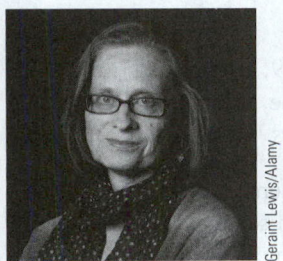

LYDIA DAVIS (1947–   ) has published one novel and seven story collections, including, most recently, *Can't and Won't* (2014). She is the recipient of the 2013 Man Booker International Prize as well as other awards and honors. The author of numerous short-short stories, Davis has also translated works by Maurice Blanchot, Michel Leiris, and Marcel Proust.

Geraint Lewis/Alamy

Television (1989)

1.

We have all these favorite shows coming on every evening. They say it will be exciting and it always is.

They give us hints of what is to come and then it comes and it is exciting.

If dead people walked outside our windows we would be no more excited.

We want to be part of it all.

---

[2] *Rio Bravo:* The Rio Grande river.

5   We want to be the people they talk to when they tell what is to come later in the evening and later in the week.

We listen to the ads until we are exhausted, punished with lists: they want us to buy so much, and we try, but we don't have a lot of money. Yet we can't help admiring the science of it all.

How can we ever be as sure as these people are sure? These women are women in control, as the women in my family are not.

Yet we believe in this world.

We believe these people are speaking to us.

10   Mother, for example, is in love with an anchorman. And my husband sits with his eyes on a certain young reporter and waits for the camera to draw back and reveal her breasts.

After the news we pick out a quiz show to watch and then a story of detective investigation.

The hours pass. Our hearts go on beating, now slow, now faster.

There is one quiz show which is particularly good. Each week the same man is the in the audience with his mouth tightly closed and tears in his eyes. His son is coming back on stage to answer more questions. The boy stands there blinking at the television camera. They will not let him go on answering questions if he wins the final sum of a hundred and twenty-eight thousand dollars. We don't care much about the boy and we don't like the mother, who smiles and shows her bad teeth, but we are moved by the father: his heavy lips, his wet eyes.

And so we turn off the telephone during this program and do not answer the knock at the door that rarely comes. We watch closely, and my husband now presses his lips together and then smiles so broadly that his eyes disappear, and as for me, I sit back like the mother with a sharp gaze, my mouth full of gold.

2.

15   It's not that I really think this show about Hawaiian policemen is very good, it's just that it seems more real than my own life.

Different routes through the evening: Channels 2, 2, 4, 7, 9, or channels 13, 13, 13, 2, 2, 4, etc. Sometimes it's the police dramas I want to see, other times the public television documentaries, such as one called *Swamp Critters*.

It's partly my isolation at night, the darkness outside, the silence outside, the increasing lateness of the hour, that makes the story on television seem so interesting. But the plot, too, has something to do with it: tonight a son comes back after many years and marries his father's wife. (She is not his mother.)

We pay a good deal of attention because these shows seem to be the work of so many smart and fashionable people.

I think it is a television sound beyond the wall, but it's the honking of wild geese flying south in the first dark of the evening.

20   You watch a young woman named Susan Smith with pearls around her neck sing the Canadian National Anthem before a hockey game. You listen to the end of the song, then you change the channel.

Or you watch Pete Seeger's legs bounce up and down in time to his *Reuben E. Lee* song, then change the channel.

It is not what you want to be doing. It is that you are passing the time.

You are waiting until it is a certain hour and you are in a certain condition so that you can go to sleep.

There is some real satisfaction in getting this information about the next day's weather—how fast the wind might blow and from what direction, when the rain might come, when the skies might clear—and the exact science of it is indicated by the words "40 percent" in "40 percent chance."

It all begins with the blue dot in the center of the dark screen, and this is when you can sense that these pictures will be coming to you from a long way off.

25

3.

Often, at the end of the day, when I am tired, my life seems to turn into a movie. I mean my real day moves into my real evening, but also moves away from me enough to be strange and a movie. It has by then become so complicated, so hard to understand, that I want to watch a different movie. I want to watch a movie made for TV, which will be simple and easy to understand, even if it involves disaster or disability or disease. It will skip over so much, it will skip over all the complications, knowing we will understand, so that major events will happen abruptly: a man may change his mind though it was firmly made up, and he may also fall in love suddenly. It will skip all the complications because there is not enough time to prepare for major events in the space of only one hour and twenty minutes, which also has to include commercial breaks, and we want major events.

One movie was about a woman professor with Alzheimer's disease; one was about an Olympic skier who lost a leg but learned to ski again. Tonight it was about a deaf man who fell in love with his speech therapist, as I knew he would because she was pretty, though not a good actress, and he was handsome, though deaf. He was deaf at the beginning of the movie and deaf again at the end, while in the middle he heard and learned to speak with a definite regional accent. In the space of one hour and twenty minutes, this man not only heard and fell deaf again but created a successful business through his own talent, was robbed of it through a company man's treachery, fell in love, kept his woman as far as the end of the movie, and lost his virginity, which seemed to be hard to lose if one was deaf and easier once one could hear.

All this was compressed into the very end of a day in my life that as the evening advanced had already moved away from me . . .

*   *   *

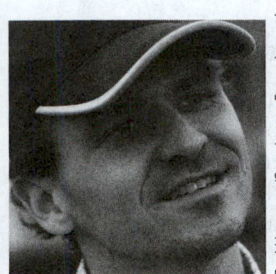

DAVE EGGERS (1970–   ) grew up near Chicago. In addition to many short stories, he has also published the memoir *A Heartbreaking Work of Staggering Genius* (2000), a finalist for the Pulitzer Prize, as well as several novels, including, most recently, *Your Fathers, Where Are They? And the Prophets, Do They Live Forever?* (2014). As the founder of McSweeney's (a literary group that publishes the journal *McSweeney's*, the magazine *The Believer*, and the DVD magazine *Wholphin*) and as editor of *The Best American Nonrequired Reading 2002, 2003*, and *2004*, Eggers has helped to popularize experimental, irreverent literature in print and electronic formats.

Accident (2005)

You all get out of your cars. You are alone in yours, and there are three teenagers in theirs, an older Camaro in new condition. The accident was your fault, and you walk over to tell them this. Walking over to their car, which you have ruined, it occurs to you that if the three teenagers are angry teenagers, this encounter could be very unpleasant. You pulled into an intersection, obstructing them, and their car hit yours. They have every right to be upset, or livid, or even violence-contemplating. As you approach, you see that their driver's side door won't open. The driver pushes against it, and you are reminded of scenes where drivers are stuck in submerged cars. Soon they all exit through the passenger side door and walk around the Camaro, inspecting the damage. None of them is hurt, but the car is wrecked. "Just bought this today," the driver says. He is 18, blond, average in all ways. "Today?" you ask. You are a bad person, you think. You also think: what a dorky car for a teenager to buy in 2005. "Yeah, today," he says, then sighs. You tell him that you are sorry. That you are so, so sorry. That it was your fault and that you will cover all costs. You exchange insurance information, and you find yourself, minute by minute, ever more thankful that none of these teenagers has punched you, or even made a remark about your being drunk, which you are not, or being stupid, which you are, often. You become more friendly with all of them, and you realize that you are much more connected to them, particularly to the driver, than possible in perhaps any other way. You have done him and his friends harm, in a way, and you jeopardized their health, and now you are so close you feel like you share a heart. He knows your name and you know his, and you almost killed him and, because you got so close to doing so but didn't, you want to fall on him, weeping, because you are so lonely, so lonely always, and all contact is contact, and all contact makes us so grateful we want to cry and dance and cry and cry. In a moment of clarity, you finally understand why boxers, who want so badly to hurt each other, can rest their heads on the shoulders of their opponents, can lean against one another like tired lovers, so thankful for a moment of peace.

*   *   *

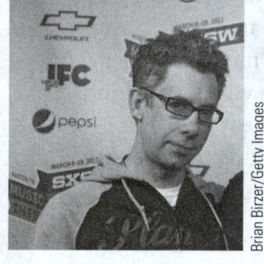

BRET ANTHONY JOHNSTON (1971–   ) is the director of creative writing at Harvard University. He is the author of the story collection *Corpus Christi* (2004), the documentary *Waiting for Lightning* (2012), and the novel *Remember Me Like This* (2014). Johnston has received several honors and prizes, including the Pushcart Prize, a National Endowment for the Arts Literature Fellowship, and the National Book Foundation 5 Under 35 award.

Encounters with Unexpected Animals (2012)

Lambright had surprised everyone by offering to drive his son's girlfriend home. The girl was three months shy of seventeen, two years older than Robbie. She'd been held back in school. Her driver's license was currently suspended. She had a reputation, a body, and a bar code tattooed on the back of her neck. Lambright sometimes glimpsed it when her green hair was ponytailed. She'd come over for supper this evening, and though she volunteered to help Robbie and his mother with the dishes, Lambright had said he'd best deliver her home, it being a school night. He knew this pleased his wife and Robbie, the notion of him giving the girl another chance.

Driving, Lambright thought the moon looked like a fingerprint of chalk. They headed south on Airline Road. A couple of miles and he'd turn right on Saratoga, then left onto Everhart, and eventually they'd enter Kings Crossing, the subdivision with pools and sprinkler systems. At supper, Robbie and the girl had told, in tandem, a story about playing hide-and-seek on the abandoned country club golf course. Hide-and-seek, Lambright thought, is that what y'all call it now? Then they started talking about wildlife. The girl had once seen a blue-and-gold macaw riding on the headrest of a man's passenger seat, and another time, in a pasture in the Rio Grande Valley, she'd spotted zebras grazing among cattle. Robbie's mother recalled finding goats in the tops of peach trees in her youth. Robbie told the story of visiting the strange neighborhood in San Antonio where the muster of peacocks lived, and it led the girl to confess her desire to get a fan of peacock feathers tattooed on her lower back. She wanted a tattoo of a busted magnifying glass hovering over the words FIX ME.

Lambright couldn't figure what she saw in his son. Until the girl started visiting, Robbie had superhero posters on his walls and a fleet of model airplanes suspended from the ceiling with fishing wire. Lambright had actually long been skeptical of the boy's room, worrying it looked too childish, worrying it confirmed what might be called "softness" of character. But now the walls were stripped and all that remained of the fighter fleet was the fishing-wire stubble on the ceiling.

Two weeks ago, one of his wife's necklaces disappeared. Last week, a bottle of her nerve pills. Then, over the weekend, he'd caught Robbie and the girl with a flask of whiskey in the backyard. She'd come to supper tonight to make amends.

Traffic was light. When he stopped at the intersection of Airline and Saratoga, the only headlights he saw were far off, like buoys in the bay. The turn signal dinged. He debated, then clicked it off. He accelerated straight across Saratoga.   5

"We were supposed to turn—"

"Scenic route," he said. "We'll visit a little."

But they didn't. There was only the low hum of the tires on the road, the noise of the truck pushing against the wind. Lambright hadn't contributed anything to the animal discussion earlier, but now he considered mentioning what he'd read a while back, how bald-eagle nests are often girded with cat collars, strung with the little bells and tags of lost pets. He stayed quiet, though. They were out near the horse stables now. The air smelled of alfalfa and manure. The streetlights had fallen away.

The girl said, "I didn't know you could get to Kings Crossing like this."

They crossed the narrow bridge over Oso Creek, then came into a clearing, a swath   10
of clay and patchy brush, gnarled mesquite trees.

He pulled onto the road's shoulder. Caliche pinged against the truck's chassis. He doused his headlights, and the scrub around them silvered, turned to moonscape. They were outside the city limits, miles from where the girl lived. He killed the engine.

"I know you have doubts about me. I know I'm not—"

"Cut him loose," Lambright said.

"Do what?"

"Give it a week, then tell him you've got someone else."   15

Her eyes scanned the night through the windshield. Maybe she was getting her bearings, calculating how far out they were. Cows lowed somewhere in the darkness. She said, "I love Rob—"

"You're a pretty girl. You've been to the rodeo a few times. You'll do all right. But not with him."

The chalky moon was in and out of clouds. A wind buffeted the truck and kicked up the odor of the brackish creek. The girl was picking at her cuticles, which made her look docile.

"Is there anything I can say here? Is there something you're wanting to hear?"

20   "You can say you'll quit him," Lambright said. "I'd like to have your word on that subject."

"And if I don't, you'll leave me on the side of the road?"

"We're just talking. We're sorting out a problem."

"Or you'll beat me up and throw me in the creek?"

"You're too much for him. He's overmatched."

25   "And so if I don't dump him, you'll, what, rape me? Murder me? Bury me in the dunes?"

"Lisa," he said, his tone pleasingly superior. He liked how much he sounded like a father.

Another wind blew, stiff and parched, rustling the trees. To Lambright, they appeared to shiver, like they'd gotten cold. A low cloud unspooled on the horizon. The cows were quiet.

"I see how you look at me, you know," she said, shifting toward him. She unbuckled her seat belt, the noise startlingly loud in the truck. Lambright's eyes went to the rearview mirror: no one around. She scooted an inch closer. Two inches. Three. He smelled lavender, her hair or cool skin. She said, "Everyone sees it. Nobody'll be surprised you drove me out here."

"I'm telling you to stay away from my son."

30   "In the middle of the night, in the middle of nowhere."

"There's no mystery here," Lambright said.

"Silly," she said.

"Do what?"

"I said you're silly. There's mystery all around us. Goats in trees. Macaws in cars."

35   Enough, Lambright thought. He cranked the ignition, switched on his headlights.

"A man who drives his son's underage girl into remote areas, that's awfully mysterious."

"Just win him loose," he said.

"A girl who flees the truck and comes home dirty and crying. What will she tell her parents? Her boyfriend? The man's depressed wife?"

"Just leave him be," he said. "That's the takeaway tonight."

40   "Will the police be called? Will they match the clay on her shoes to his tires?"

"Lisa—"

"Or will she keep it to herself? Will it be something she and the man always remember when they see each other? When she marries his son, when she bears his grandbabies? These are bona fide mysteries, Mr. Lambright."

"Lisa," he said. "Lisa, let's be clear."

But she was already out of the truck, sprinting toward the creek. She flashed through the brush and descended the bank, and Lambright was shocked by the languid swiftness with which she crossed the earth. Blood was surging in his veins, like he'd swerved to miss something in the road and his truck had just skidded to a stop and he didn't yet know if he was hurt, if the world was changed. The passenger door was open, the interior light burning, pooling. The girl jumped across the creek and bolted alongside it. She cut to and fro. He wanted to see her as an animal he'd managed to avoid, a rare and dangerous creature he'd describe for Robbie when he got home, but really her movement reminded him of a trickle of water tracking through pebbles. It stirred in him a floating sensation, the curious and scattered feeling of being born on waves or air or wings. He was disoriented, short of breath. He knew he was at the beginning of something, though just then he couldn't say exactly what.

*   *   *

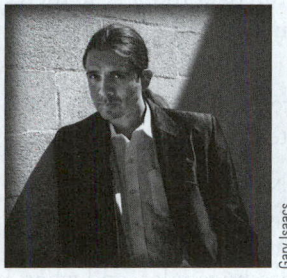

STEPHEN GRAHAM JONES (1972–   ) is a Blackfoot Native American who grew up in Texas. Currently a professor of English at the University of Colorado at Boulder, Jones has published five story collections and fifteen novels. His novel *The Last Final Girl* was recognized as the 2012 Novel of the Year by the online publication *This Is Horror*. The recipient of a National Endowment for the Arts Literature Fellowship, Jones also won the 2001 Independent Publishers Award for Multicultural Fiction.

Discovering America (2001)

Because I'm Indian in Tallahassee Florida the girl behind the counter feels compelled to pull the leather strap ($1.19 per foot) around her neck, show me her medicine pouch, how authentic it is. "Yeah," I say, "hmm," and don't tell her about the one-act play I'm writing, about this Indian in the gift shop at the bottom of Carlsbad Caverns. His name isn't Curio but that's what the lady calls him when she sighs into line with her Germanic accent and her Karl May[1] childhood. "You should do a rain dance or something," she tells him, she's never seen heat like this, like New Mexico. In the play she's sweating, he's sweating, and there's uncounted tons of rock above them, all this pressure.

In Tallahassee it rained all the time.

I stayed there for eleven months, nineteen days, and six hours.

Because I'm Indian at a party in Little Rock Arkansas, a group of students approaches me out of a back room of the house, ceremony still thick on their breath. In a shy voice their leader asks me what kind of animal my spirit helper is, and when I can't quite get enough tact into my mouth to answer, they make a show of respect, say they understand if I can't tell them, really. They tell me theirs, though: a grasshopper, a dragonfly, three wolves, and somewhere in there I become that tall, silent Indian in

---

[1] *Karl May:* German author (1842–1912).

Thomas Pynchon's "Mortality and Mercy in Vienna," right before he goes cannibalistic in the middle of an otherwise happening party. The working title of the play I'm still writing is *The Time That Indian Started Killing Everybody*, and standing there with my beer I don't revise it.

5   In Little Rock there were all kinds of bugs I hadn't seen before.
    I stayed there for five months, four days, and twenty-two hours.

Because I'm Indian in Odessa Texas the guy who picks me up off the side of the road asks me what kind. He's an oilfield worker. His dashboard is black with it. When I say *Blackfeet* he finishes for me with *Montana*, says yeah, he drilled up there for a while. Cold as hell. "Yeah," I say, thinking this is going to be an all right ride. He drives and tells me how when he was up there he used to ride a helicopter to the rig every morning, it was *that* cold. In trade I tell him how the National Guard had to airlift hay and supplies a couple of winters back. He nods as if this is all coming back to him, and then, with both arms draped over the wheel real casual, asks me if they still run over Indians up there? I turn to him and he explains the sport, even hangs a tire into the ditch to show me how it's done.

    In Odessa the butane pumps go all night, and it's hard to sleep.
    I stayed there for three months, fourteen days, and fourteen hours.

Because I'm Indian the guys at the warehouse in Clovis New Mexico add a single feather to the happy face that's been carved into the back of my locker ever since I got there. It's not like looking in a mirror. Every time it's not like looking in a mirror. My second week there we're sweeping rat droppings into huge piles, and when I lean over one to see what Butch is pointing at he slams his broom down, drives it all into my face. That weekend I start coughing it all up, become sure it's the hantavirus that's been killing Indians all over. My whole check goes into the pay phone, calling everyone, talking to them one last time, reading them my play, the part where Curio kills one of the gift-shop people the old way, which means he hits him across the face with a log of Copenhagen, then follows him down to finish it, out of mercy.

10   In Clovis they don't turn their trucks off so you can talk on the phone, so you have to scream.
    I stayed there for four weeks, one day, and two and a half hours.

Because I'm Indian in Carlsbad New Mexico the crew I'm working with calls me Chief, motions me over every time there's another animal track in the dirt. "I don't know," I tell them about the tracks, even though I do, and for a couple of hours we work in silence, up one row, down another. Once I find strange and cartoonish tracks in my row—traced with the sharp corner of a hoe—but I pretend to miss them, pretend no one's watching me miss them. All this pretending. Towards the end of the day I pass one of the crew and, without looking up, he asks if I've scalped anybody today, Chief?

    I unplant a weed from his row, look up for the briefest moment, long enough to say it: "Nobody you know." He doesn't laugh, and neither do I, and then later that night in a gas station I finish the play I started writing in Florida. It starts when the clerk wipes the sweat from his forehead, says how damn hot it is. And dry. I neither nod nor don't nod, just wait for him to say it.

In Carlsbad New Mexico the law is sluggish, slow to respond.

I stay there for sixteen hours, nine minutes, and fifty-two seconds, and when the rain comes it's not because I danced it up, but because I brought it with me.

*   *   *

Source: Taro Yamasaki//Time Life Pictures/ Getty Images

JAMAICA KINCAID (1949–   ) was born Elaine Potter Richardson on the island of Antigua, where she received a British education and was often at the top of her class. In early childhood, she was very close to her mother, but when her mother gave birth to three sons in quick succession, it altered their relationship forever. According to Kincaid, she was treated badly and neglected, and she left Antigua in 1965 to work as an au pair in Westchester county, near New York City. She went on to study photography at the New School for Social Research and attended Franconia College in New Hampshire for a year. In 1973, after having begun her writing career, she changed her name to Jamaica Kincaid because her family disapproved of her writing. She soon began writing a regular column for the *New Yorker*. Her best-known works include the novel *Annie John* (1986) and the nonfiction book *A Small Place* (1988), which criticizes British Colonialism in Antigua. Her most recent books include *Talk Stories* (2001), *Among Flowers: A Walk in the Himalaya* (2005), *My Favorite Tool* (2005), and *See Now Then* (2013).

Girl (1984)

Wash the white clothes on Monday and put them on the stone heap; wash the color clothes on Tuesday and put them on the clothesline to dry; don't walk barehead in the hot sun; cook pumpkin fritters in very hot sweet oil; soak your little clothes right after you take them off; when buying cotton to make yourself a nice blouse, be sure that it doesn't have gum on it, because that way it won't hold up well after a wash; soak salt fish overnight before you cook it; is it true that you sing benna[1] in Sunday School?; always eat your food in such a way that it won't turn someone else's stomach; on Sundays try to walk like a lady and not like the slut you are so bent on becoming; don't sing benna in Sunday School; you mustn't speak to wharf-rat boys, not even to give directions; don't eat fruits on the street—flies will follow you; *but I don't sing benna on Sundays at all and never in Sunday school!*; this is how to sew on a button; this is how to make a buttonhole for the button you have just sewed on; this is how to hem a dress when you see the hem coming down and so to prevent yourself from looking like the slut I know you are so bent on becoming; this is how you iron your father's khaki shirt so that it doesn't have a crease; this is how you iron your father's khaki pants so that they don't have a crease; this is how you grow okra—far from the house, because okra tree harbors red ants; when you are growing dasheen, make sure it gets plenty of water or else it makes your throat itch when you are eating it; this is how you sweep a corner; this is how you sweep a whole house; this is how you sweep a yard; this is how you smile to someone you don't like too much; this is

---

[1] *benna:* Calypso music.

how you smile to someone you don't like at all; this is how you smile to someone you like completely; this is how you set a table for tea; this is how you set a table for dinner; this is how you set a table for dinner with an important guest; this is how you set a table for lunch; this is how you set a table for breakfast; this is how to behave in the presence of men who don't know you very well, and this way they won't recognize immediately the slut I have warned you against becoming; be sure to wash every day, even if it is with your own spit; don't squat down to play marbles—you are not a boy, you know; don't pick people's flowers—you might catch something; don't throw stones at blackbirds, because it might not be a blackbird at all; this is how to make a bread pudding; this is how to make doukona;[2] this is how to make pepper pot; this is how to make a good medicine for a cold; this is how to make a good medicine to throw away a child before it even becomes a child; this is how to catch a fish; this is how to throw back a fish you don't like, and that way something bad won't fall on you; this is how to bully a man; this is how a man bullies you; this is how to love a man, and if this doesn't work there are other ways, and if they don't work don't feel too bad about giving up; this is how to spit up in the air if you feel like it, and this is how to move quick so that it doesn't fall on you; this is how to make ends meet; always squeeze bread to make sure it's fresh; *but what if the baker won't let me feel the bread?*; you mean to say that after all you are really going to be the kind of woman who the baker won't let near the bread?

* * *

ED PARK (1970–   ) teaches in the graduate writing program at Columbia University. An avid blogger and tweeter, Park has published numerous stories and short works of creative nonfiction. Recognized as one of *Time's* top ten fiction books of the year and one of *The Atlantic's* top ten pop culture moments of the decade, his 2008 novel *Personal Days* was a finalist for the PEN Hemingway Award, the Asian American Literary Award, and the John Sargent Sr. First Novel Prize.

Slide to Unlock (2013)

You cycle through your passwords. They tell the secret story. What's most important to you, the things you think can't be deciphered. Words and numbers stored in the lining of your heart.

Your daughter's name.

Your daughter's name backward.

Your daughter's name backward plus the year of her birth.

5   Your daughter's name backward plus the last two digits of the year of her birth.

Your daughter's name backward plus the current year.

They keep changing. They blur in the brain. Every day you punch in three or four of these memory strings to access the home laptop, the work laptop. The e-mail,

---

[2] *doukona:* Spicy plantain pudding.

the Facebook, the voice mail. Frequent-flyer account. Every week, you're asked to change at least one, to increase the security. You feel virtuous when the security meter changes from red to green.

Your home town backward.

Your home town plus the year you were born.

Your home town backward plus the year you were born.

Olaf Fub 1970.

There are hints when you forget. Mother's maiden name. First car, favorite color, elementary school.

First girl you kissed—that should be one.

First boy.

Can the hints just be the passwords?

Stop stalling.

First sex. You remember the day, month, year. The full year or just the last two digits?

First concert you attended.

Name of hospital where you were born.

You wonder who writes these prompts. Someone has to write them.

Tip: Never use the same password for more than one account.

Last four digits of first phone number.

Last four digits of first work number.

Your daughter's best friend's name backward.

Your boss's first name.

Your first boss's last name plus the year you were born.

If you could type out all your passwords, their entire silent history, they would fill a book you could read in a minute.

Last four digits of your cell backward.

Favorite sports team.

Favorite sports team backward.

Serbas.

Pet's name.

You knew a guy who had a dog named Serbas. You knew two guys with dogs named Serbas. They didn't like each other. The guys, that is. The dogs, who knows. You're pretty sure one was female, the other male.

Pet's name backward plus current year.

Favorite sibling—sibling who never let you down—plus last two digits of current year.

Mix of capitals and lowercase.

Six to eight characters long.

Ten to fourteen.

Stop stalling.

Mix of numerals and letters.

At least one symbol: #, %,*,!.!

Father's home town.

Mother's maiden name backward.

The girl at work you can't stop thinking about.
45   The girl at work plus current year.
The girl at work backward.
The girl at work backward and lowercase plus last two digits of current year.

Passwords mean nothing to the machine. The machine lets you in to do what you need to do. It doesn't judge. It doesn't care.

Your password appears as a row of dots.
50   Favorite film. But that keeps changing.
"Vertigo." "Groundhog Day."
Favorite actor.
Actress who first made you hard, backward, plus current year.
Best friend from high school.
Best friend from college.
55   *Stop stalling.*
Year you last saw your daughter.
Year you last saw your daughter plus her name.

There's a file on your work computer called passwords. But what if you forget the password to get into your work computer?

Her favorite toy.
60   What she named her bike.
First girl you dated in college backward and lowercase.
"The Shop Around the Corner." "Buffalo '66."
Date of first death in the family.
Grandfather's name backward plus birth year.
65   Year you finally started getting your shit together.
"Citizen Kane." "Ace Ventura: Pet Detective."
Year of First Communion plus name of priest.
Stop stalling.
Favorite author backward and lowercase with middle letter capped for no reason save randomness.
70   Street address of the house you grew up in.
Sibling you don't talk to.
Spouse of sibling you don't talk to, whom you text when you're drunk.
Stop stalling.

Your last name backward plus the day, month, and year you find yourself at an A.T.M. at the ass end of Hertel Avenue with the tip of a gun pressed between your shoulder blades, the gun in the hand of the guy who followed you from down the street, affecting a limp, a big guy in a black windbreaker and a Bills Starter cap, who stepped behind you, quiet as a shadow, the big guy with dead eyes behind five-dollar sunglasses who already has your phone and wallet and the bottle of wine you thought it would be a good idea to run out and get, at ten in the evening, she said she'd stay inside and you said you would hurry, and it was a good night for a walk, so, while you're at it, taking in the cool night air, why not get some cash for the week to come?
75   The big guy with the very hard gun who is saying *Password* and *Right now* and *Stop stalling.*

*   *   *

Eamonn McCabe/Getty Images

GEORGE SAUNDERS (1958–) teaches in the MFA program at Syracuse University and was named one of *Time's* 100 most influential people in the world. He has published several story and essay collections, including *Tenth of December* (2013), in which the following story appeared. Saunders is the recipient of a Guggenheim Fellowship, a MacArthur Fellowship, and an Academy Award from the American Academy of Arts and Letters.

Sticks (1995)

Every year Thanksgiving night we flocked out behind Dad as he dragged the Santa suit to the road and draped it over a kind of crucifix he'd built out of metal pole in the yard. Super Bowl week the pole was dressed in a jersey and Rod's helmet and Rod had to clear it with Dad if he wanted to take the helmet off. On Fourth of July the pole was Uncle Sam, on Veterans Day a soldier, on Halloween a ghost. The pole was Dad's one concession to glee. We were allowed a single Crayola from the box at a time. One Christmas Eve he shrieked at Kimmie for wasting an apple slice. He hovered over us as we poured ketchup, saying, Good enough good enough good enough. Birthday parties consisted of cupcakes, no ice cream. The first time I brought a date over she said, What's with your dad and that pole? and I sat there blinking.

We left home, married, had children of our own, found the seeds of meanness blooming also within us. Dad began dressing the pole with more complexity and less discernible logic. He draped some kind of fur over it on Groundhog Day and lugged out a floodlight to ensure a shadow. When an earthquake struck Chile he laid the pole on its side and spray-painted a rift in the earth. Mom died and he dressed the pole as Death and hung from the crossbar photos of Mom as a baby. We'd stop by and find odd talismans from his youth arranged around the base: army medals, theater tickets, old sweatshirts, tubes of Mom's makeup. One autumn he painted the pole bright yellow. He covered it with cotton swabs that winter for warmth and provided offspring by hammering in six crossed sticks around the yard. He ran lengths of string between the pole and the sticks, and taped to the string letters of apology, admissions of error, pleas for understanding, all written in a frantic hand on index cards. He painted a sign saying LOVE and hung it from the pole and another that said FORGIVE? and then he died in the hall with the radio on and we sold the house to a young couple who yanked out the pole and left it by the road on garbage day.

Reading and Reacting

1. Which of the stories in this chapter do you see as the most conventional? Which seems the *least* conventional? Why?

2. Does every story seem complete? What, if anything, seems to be missing from each story that might be present in a longer story?

3. If you were going to add material to "Snow" or "Sticks," what would you add? Why?

4. Some stories in this chapter—for example, "Encounters with Unexpected Animals"—include dialogue; others include none (or very little). How would these stories—for example, "Pilón"—be different if dialogue (or more dialogue) were added? What kind of dialogue would be useful?

5. **CRITICAL PERSPECTIVE** Writing for *Studies in Short Fiction*, William C. Hamlin describes the essential characteristics of the short-short story.

> Perhaps in no kind of fiction other than the short-short can Poe's "rules" for the "tale" be so fully adapted and realized. He wrote about organic unity and singleness of effect and the totality of that effect. In the short-short there is simply no room for sub-plotting, for Jamesian penetration, for slowly developing tensions, for any kind of byplay. The writer is trying to go from A to B in the shortest time consistent with purpose and reason. If he or she is successful, then the reader is richer by a minor masterpiece.

Do you think all the stories in this sampler meet Hamlin's criteria for success? Why or why not?

WRITING SUGGESTIONS: The Short-Short Story

1. Write a **response** (see Chapter 3) expressing your reactions to the ending of "Slide to Unlock."

2. Write an **explication** (see Chapter 3) of any short-short story in this chapter—or of a short-short story located elsewhere in this book—for example, Kate Chopin's "The Story of an Hour" (p. 201).

3. Write a **comparison-contrast essay** (see Chapter 3) comparing "Love and Other Catastrophes: A Mix Tape" with one of the love poems in Chapter 31.

4. Write a **comparison-contrast essay** comparing "Encounters with Unexpected Animals" to Joyce Carol Oates's "Where Are You Going, Where Have You Been?" (p. 506).

5. Write a **character analysis** (see Chapter 3) of the narrator in "Accident" or "Television."

6. Write an essay about the **cultural context** (see Chapter 3) of "Pilón," "Girl," or "Discovering America."

7. Write a "mix tape" story about an experience in your own life.

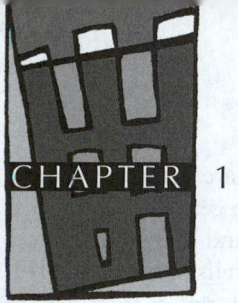

CHAPTER 11

FICTION SAMPLER: GRAPHIC FICTION

R. Crumb
Oscar White/Corbis

Art Spiegelman
Sean Gallup/Getty Images Entertainment/Getty Images

Marjane Satrapi
AP Images/Kirsty Wigglesworth

Gene Luen Yang
Gene Luen Yang

The term *graphic fiction* can be applied to a wide range of visual material, including individual and collected comics and cartoons. As graphic novelist Ivan Brunetti explains, when creating graphic fiction, "The cartoonist uses his own particular set of marks (or 'visual handwriting') to establish a consistent visual vocabulary in which to communicate experience, memory, and imagination—in short, the stuff of narratives."

Like the **short-short stories** (see p. 125), works of graphic fiction pack ideas into small spaces (in this case, the "cells" or "panels" on a page). While many graphic works are fictional narratives, others—such as graphic essays, biographies, autobiographies, historical accounts, and journalistic pieces—actually qualify as nonfiction. Works of graphic fiction appear in printed books, magazines, newspapers, and pamphlets, and many are published online as

Web comics. Two of today's most popular kinds of graphic fiction are **manga** (Japanese comics translated into English) and **superhero comic books**. In the genre's volatile history, graphic novels have taken various forms, appealing to popular and literary audiences alike. In fact, the genre is constantly being redefined. As graphic novelist Eddie Campbell argues, the graphic novel genre "signifies a movement rather than a form" as it strives "to take the form of the comic book, which has become an embarrassment, and raise it to a more ambitious and meaningful level."

Graphic fiction had its origins in comic strips. In the late nineteenth and early twentieth centuries, American newspapers started to feature comic strips that ranged in variety from popular, slapstick, and sci-fi (*The Yellow Kid*, 1895; *Happy Hooligan*, 1900; *Thimble Theatre* [later renamed *Popeye*], 1929; *Flash Gordon*, 1934) to literary and artistic (*Little Nemo*, 1905; *Krazy Kat*, 1913). Comic books, or collections of previously published comic strips, appeared in the mid 1930s, and shortly thereafter the superhero comic emerged and exploded. Comic book characters like Superman, Batman, Wonder Woman, and Captain Marvel began to dominate the genre in the 1940s, and contemporary superhero comics such as *Spider-Man* (1962) and *X-Men* (1963) have achieved international fame both in traditional print formats and in major motion pictures.

In response to the superhero subgenre, **underground** or **alternative comics** appeared in the 1960s, challenging the status quo and depicting taboo topics such as drugs and sex. These unconventional comics, created by artists such as Robert Crumb (1943–) and S. Clay Wilson (1941–), have experienced ups and downs throughout their sales history, unlike their consistently best-selling superhero counterparts. Alternative comics helped usher in the more acclaimed literary graphic novels of the 1980s and 1990s, including Art Spiegelman's Pulitzer Prize–winning *Maus* (1986) and Daniel Clowes's *Ghost World* (1993).

Will Eisner's *A Contract with God* (1978) is generally acknowledged to be the first graphic novel. Actually a collection of four short stories, the book displayed the label "graphic novel" on its cover, establishing this new genre as a literary form fundamentally different from mainstream comics. The graphic novel continues to evolve today in its attempt to contribute in fresh, new ways to the changing literary canon.

This chapter includes six works of graphic fiction, narratives that use words as well as images to tell their stories and weave together fiction, history, and memoir. Max Brooks's *The Harlem Hellfighters* recounts the struggles and triumphs of an African American army regiment in World War I; like the book as a whole, the two excerpts reprinted here juxtapose the men's courage in combat with the discrimination they faced at home. In "A Hunger Artist," R. Crumb reinterprets Franz Kafka's 1924 short story of the same name (see p. 592). The excerpt from Marjane

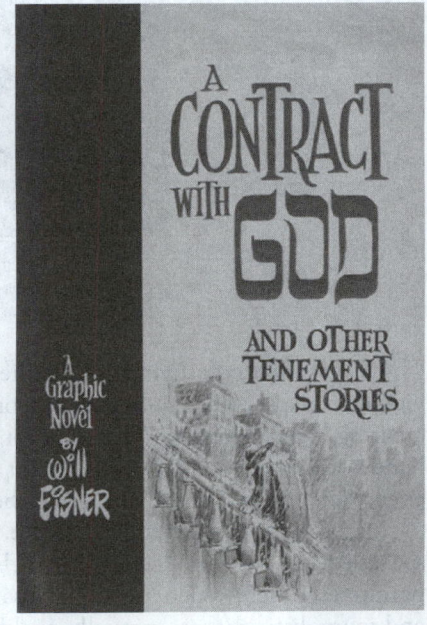

Cover image of the first graphic novel, Eisner's *A Contract with God* (1978)

Source: © Baronet Books 1978

Satrapi's *Persepolis* presents an episode from Satrapi's life as a rebellious child in Iran during the Islamic Revolution; in an excerpt from his Pulitzer Prize–winning book *Maus: A Survivor's Tale*, Art Spiegelman reimagines an episode from the life of his father, a Polish Jew who survived the Holocaust. In the excerpt from *Blankets*, Craig Thompson intertwines stories of family and the creative process. Finally, the brief excerpt from Gene Luen Yang's *American Born Chinese* explores the familiar American theme of reinvention through a young boy's struggles with his identity.

JStone/Shutterstock.com

MAX BROOKS (1972–   ) is the author of the 2006 novel *World War Z*, which was adapted into a film starring Brad Pitt. He has also published *The Zombie Survival Guide: Complete Protection from the Living Dead* (2003), *The Zombie Survival Guide: Recorded Attacks* (2009), and, most recently, *The Harlem Hellfighters* (2014), from which the following excerpts were taken.

Cultural Context   The 369th infantry regiment (nicknamed the Harlem Hellfighters by German soldiers) was an African American unit of the U.S. Army that fought in World Wars I and II. When the unit returned home from Europe in 1919 after a long and heroic tour of duty, they faced the same racial discrimination and violence that other African American citizens experienced at that time.

from The Harlem Hellfighters   (2014)

"THE HARLEM HELLFIGHTERS."

Another excerpt from The Harlem Hellfighters begins on the following page. ➤

IT'D BE A NICE STORY IF I COULD SAY THAT OUR PARADE OR EVEN OUR VICTORIES CHANGED THE WORLD OVERNIGHT, BUT TRUTH'S GOT AN UGLY WAY OF KILLIN' NICE STORIES. THE TRUTH IS THAT WE CAME HOME TO IGNORANCE, BITTERNESS, AND SOMETHIN' CALLED "THE RED SUMMER OF 1919," SOME OF THE WORST RACIAL VIOLENCE AMERICA'S EVER SEEN. THE TRUTH IS THAT OUR FIGHT, AND THE FIGHT OF THOSE WHO LOOKED UP TO US AS HEROES, DIDN'T END WITH THE "THE WAR TO END ALL WARS."

WAS IT ALL
FOR NOTHING?

ONLY IF WE'RE
FORGOTTEN

R. CRUMB (1943–   ) is widely acknowledged as the founder of the underground or alternative comics movement, which emerged in the 1960s as a reaction against the popular superhero comics that had, until then, dominated and defined the comic book genre. Crumb and his underground contemporaries, including Art Spiegelman (p. 166), depicted taboo topics such as drugs and sex in a medium that had previously been perceived as a children's genre. He created the infamously risqué illustrated character Fritz the Cat, among others. With works such as *Introducing Kafka* (1993), in which he illustrates Franz Kafka's life and work and from which the following selection is excerpted, Crumb helped to raise the graphic novel to the level of high art. His work appears in numerous collections, including the *R. Crumb Sketchbook* volumes (1978, 1981, 2005), *The Complete Crumb* volumes (2005 and 2013), and *The Sweeter Side of R. Crumb* (2010).

Cultural Context   Throughout history, people have been fascinated with the effects of fasting on the human body and mind. In the early twentieth century, carnivals and freak shows throughout Europe featured "hunger artists," such as the one depicted in the following graphic story, who voluntarily starved themselves for the public's entertainment. Carnival goers would watch hunger artists, who were considered to be more oddities than "artists," while they would sit in a cage and do menial tasks—or nothing at all. Large crowds would often form when hunger artists, for whatever reason, decided to end their fast and finally eat.

A Hunger Artist (1993)

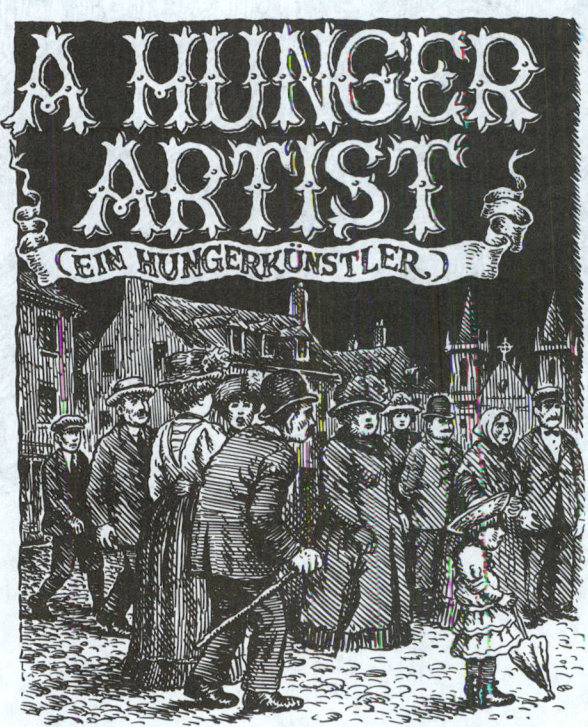

This graphic story starts on the next page. ➡

Source: ©1993 R. Crumb. Used by permission of Totem Books.

IN THE LAST FEW DECADES, THE INTEREST IN PROFESSIONAL HUNGER-ARTISTRY HAS GREATLY DIMINISHED. ONCE THE WHOLE TOWN CAME OUT TO SEE THE HUNGER-ARTIST. SOME EVEN BOUGHT SEASON TICKETS, AND AT NIGHT THE SCENE WAS BATHED IN THE LIGHT OF TORCHES.

GROUPS OF PROFESSIONAL WATCHERS, USUALLY BUTCHERS, WERE SENT TO WATCH HIM, IN CASE HE HAD SOME SECRET CACHE OF NOURISHMENT. BUT, DURING HIS FAST THE ARTISTE WOULD NEVER, EVEN UNDER COMPULSION, SWALLOW THE SMALLEST BIT OF FOOD; HIS PROFESSIONAL HONOR FORBADE IT. HE ALONE KNEW WHAT THE OTHERS DIDN'T: FASTING WAS THE EASIEST THING IN THE WORLD.

THE PERIOD OF FASTING WAS SET BY HIS IMPRESARIO AT FORTY DAYS MAXIMUM, BECAUSE AFTER THAT TIME THE PUBLIC BEGAN TO LOSE INTEREST. SO, ON THE FORTIETH DAY, WITH AN EXCITED CROWD FILLING THE ARENA AND A MILITARY BAND PLAYING, TWO YOUNG LADIES CAME TO LEAD THE HUNGER-ARTIST OUT OF HIS CAGE. WHEN THIS HAPPENED HE ALWAYS PUT UP SOME RESISTANCE...WHY STOP AFTER ONLY FORTY DAYS?!? WHY SHOULD THEY TAKE FROM HIM THE GLORY OF FASTING EVEN LONGER, OF SURPASSING EVEN HIMSELF TO REACH UNIMAGINABLE HEIGHTS, FOR HE SAW HIS ABILITY TO GO ON FASTING AS *UNLIMITED!*

Source: ©1993 R. Crumb. Used by permission of Totem Books.

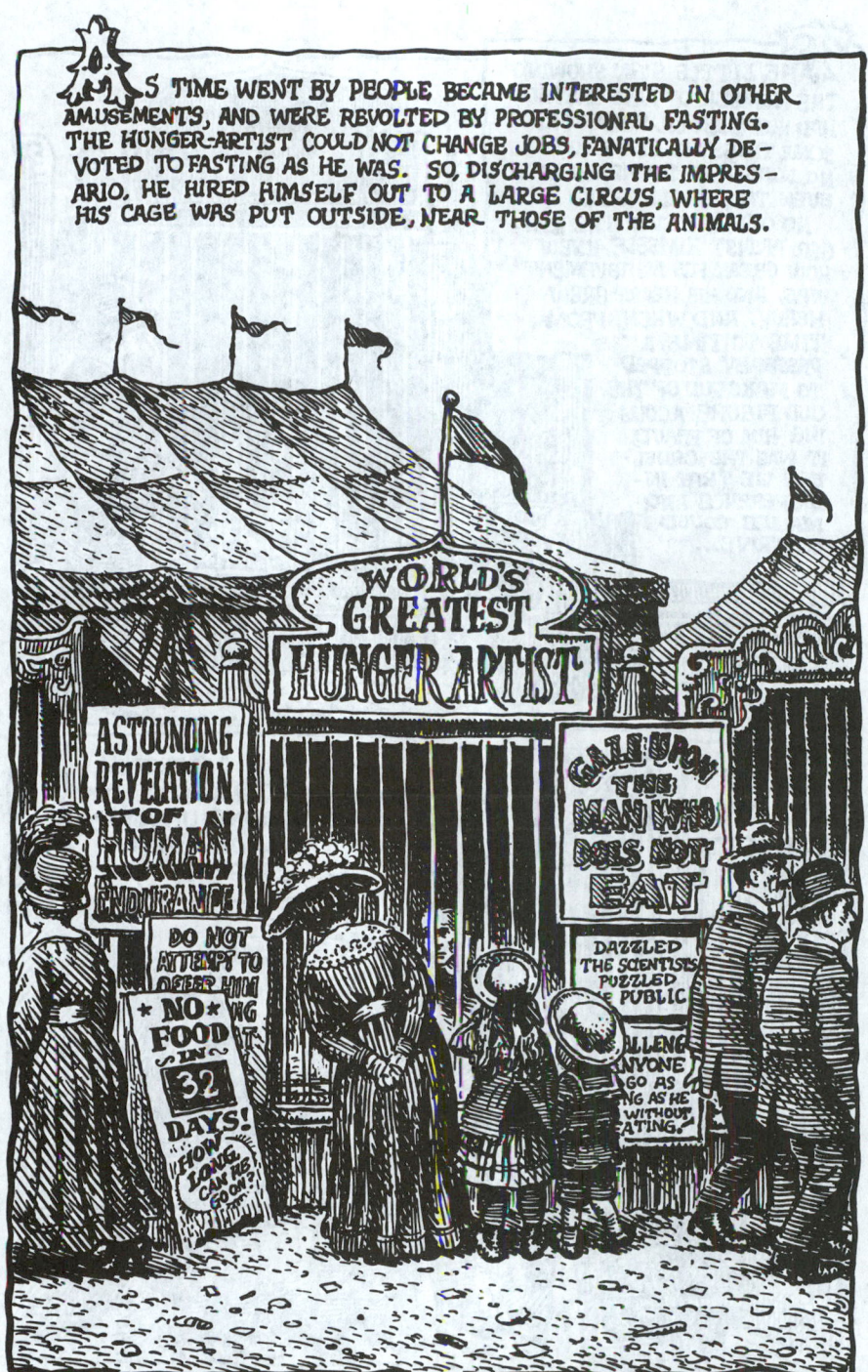

AS TIME WENT BY PEOPLE BECAME INTERESTED IN OTHER AMUSEMENTS, AND WERE REVOLTED BY PROFESSIONAL FASTING. THE HUNGER-ARTIST COULD NOT CHANGE JOBS, FANATICALLY DEVOTED TO FASTING AS HE WAS. SO, DISCHARGING THE IMPRESARIO, HE HIRED HIMSELF OUT TO A LARGE CIRCUS, WHERE HIS CAGE WAS PUT OUTSIDE, NEAR THOSE OF THE ANIMALS.

WORLD'S GREATEST HUNGER ARTIST

ASTOUNDING REVELATION OF HUMAN ENDURANCE

GAZE UPON THE MAN WHO DOES NOT EAT!

DO NOT ATTEMPT TO OFFER HIM ANYTHING

★ NO ★ FOOD IN 32 DAYS!

HOW LONG CAN HE GO ON?

DAZZLED THE SCIENTISTS! PUZZLED THE PUBLIC

CHALLENGE ANYONE TO GO AS LONG AS HE WITHOUT EATING!

VEN THE MOST THICK-SKINNED PEOPLE WERE RELIEVED TO SEE THIS WILD CREATURE THROWING HIM-SELF ABOUT IN THE CAGE THAT HAD SO LONG BEEN SO MISERABLE. WITHOUT ANY AFTERTHOUGHT HIS KEEPERS BROUGHT HIM ALL THE FOODS HE LIKED BEST.

E SEEMED NOT EVEN TO MISS HIS FREEDOM. HIS NOBLE BODY, FILLED OUT TO BURSTING WITH ALL IT NEEDED, CARRIED FREEDOM AROUND WITH IT, AS IF HELD IN ITS JAWS, AND THE LIFE FORCE CAME SO PASSIONATE-LY FROM HIS THROAT THAT THE SPECTA-TORS COULD HARDLY BEAR THE SIGHT OF IT. BUT THEY BRACED THEMSELVES, CROWD-ED ROUND THE CAGE, AND DID NOT WANT TO MOVE AWAY.

• ◈ •

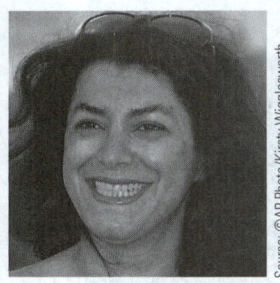

MARJANE SATRAPI (1969–), raised in Tehran, Iran, has published numerous graphic fiction books in both English and French, including the award-winning graphic memoir *Persepolis* (2003) and its sequel, *Persepolis 2* (2004). The *Persepolis* works, from which the following excerpt is taken, depict Satrapi's experiences growing up in Tehran during the Islamic Revolution and Iran's war with Iraq. Satrapi cowrote and codirected the animated feature film *Persepolis* (2007), which tied for a Special Jury Prize at the 2007 Cannes Film Festival and was nominated for an Academy Award for best animated feature film. Like *Persepolis*, Satrapi's graphic novel *Embroideries* (2005) also portrays the female experience in modern-day Iran.

Source: ©AP Photo/Kirsty Wigglesworth

Cultural Context   Persepolis was an ancient Persian city located in modern-day Iran. King of Persia from 522–486 B.C., Darius I named Persepolis the capital of Persia. The city is known for its monumental architecture, including several royal palaces and an audience hall, the ruins of which can still be seen today. Named after the ancient city, Satrapi's graphic novel, from which the following excerpt is taken, alludes to Iran's epic past and makes an ironic statement about the cultural climate of today.

from Persepolis   (2003)

Source: ©2003 Marjane Satrapi. Used courtesy of Pantheon Books at Random House.

This graphic story starts on the next page. ➡

FOR A YEAR NOW, THE FOOD SHORTAGE HAD BEEN RESOLVED BY THE GROWTH OF THE BLACK MARKET. HOWEVER, FINDING TAPES WAS A LITTLE MORE COMPLICATED. ON GANDHI AVENUE YOU COULD FIND THEM SOMETIMES.

ESTEVIE VONDER

ABBA, BEE GEES   YAZOO   JULIO IGLESIAS   JIKAEL MACKSON

PINK FLOYD

VIDEOS, MUSIC, CARDS, LIPSTICK, NAIL POLISH, CHESS SET, PANTYHOSE, CHOCOLATE, ...,...

I BOUGHT TWO TAPES: KIM WILDE AND CAMEL.

HOW MUCH?

110 TUMANS.

♪WE'RE THE KIDS IN AMERICA ♪WHOA...

YOU! STOP!

THEY WERE GUARDIANS OF THE REVOLUTION, THE WOMEN'S BRANCH. THIS GROUP HAD BEEN ADDED IN 1982, TO ARREST WOMEN WHO WERE IMPROPERLY VEILED. (LIKE ME, FOR EXAMPLE.)

Source: ©2003 Marjane Satrapi. Used courtesy of Pantheon Books at Random House.

AT THE COMMITTEE, THEY DIDN'T HAVE TO INFORM MY PARENTS. THEY COULD DETAIN ME FOR HOURS, OR FOR DAYS. I COULD BE WHIPPED. IN SHORT, ANYTHING COULD HAPPEN TO ME. IT WAS TIME FOR ACTION.

I'M SORRY MA'AM! I'LL NEVER DO IT AGAIN...

GET IN THE CAR!

MA'AM, MY MOTHER'S DEAD. MY STEPMOTHER IS REALLY CRUEL AND IF I DON'T GO HOME RIGHT AWAY, SHE'LL KILL ME...

SHE'LL BURN ME WITH THE CLOTHES IRON!

SHE'LL MAKE MY FATHER PUT ME IN AN ORPHANAGE

MAYBE SHE BELIEVED ME, MAYBE SHE JUST PRETENDED TO. BUT, MIRACULOUSLY, SHE LET ME GO.

BACK HOME...

MARJI! WHAT HAPPENED? HAVE YOU BEEN CRYING?

NO MOM. I'M JUST TIRED. I'M GOING TO MY ROOM.

THERE WAS NO WAY I COULD TELL THE TRUTH. SHE NEVER WOULD HAVE LET ME GO OUT ALONE AGAIN.

I GOT OFF PRETTY EASY, CONSIDERING. THE GUARDIANS OF THE REVOLUTION DIDN'T FIND MY TAPES.

♪ WE'RE THE KIDS IN AMERICA WHOAO ♪

TO EACH HIS OWN WAY OF CALMING DOWN.

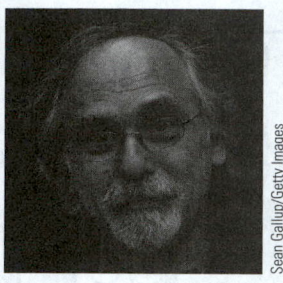

Sean Gallup/Getty Images Entertainment/Getty Images

ART SPIEGELMAN (1948–   ) was born in Stockholm, Sweden, and raised in Queens, New York. He is arguably one of the most influential comic artists of the underground movement, which began (thanks in large part to R. Crumb; see p. 151) in the 1960s. In collaboration with his wife, Spiegelman founded the comics magazine *RAW* in 1980, and his comics have been featured in such publications as the *New Yorker*, the *New York Times*, and the *Village Voice*. The following graphic story comes from his two-part masterpiece, the Pulitzer Prize–winning *Maus* (1986) and *Maus II* (1991), which are based on his parents' struggle for survival during the Holocaust. Collections of Spiegelman's work include *In the Shadow of No Towers* (2004), one of the *New York Times* Book Review's 100 Notable Books of 2004.

Cultural Context This graphic story depicts the heartrending process in which Jews were separated from their families and forced into concentration and death camps during the Nazi regime. Between 1933 and 1945, an estimated fifteen thousand camps throughout Nazi-occupied countries killed approximately 3.5 million people. The camps were originally established to incarcerate political adversaries, such as Communists and Social Democrats, but soon began imprisoning Jews, Jehovah's Witnesses, Gypsies, homosexuals, the mentally ill, and anyone who opposed the Nazi regime. Chelmno, the first of six death camps established in Poland, opened in 1941. At these camps, the Nazis carried out the systematic murder of millions of Jews and other innocent people.

from Maus (1973)

Art Spiegelman, from MAUS I. Copyright © 1973, 1980, 1982, 1983, 1984, 1985, 1986 by Art Spiegelman. Used by permission of Pantheon Books, a division of Random House, Inc.

This graphic story starts on the next page.

WHEN DID YOU FIRST HEAR ABOUT AUSCHWITZ?

RIGHT AWAY WE HEARD...

EVEN FROM THERE—FROM THAT OTHER WORLD—PEOPLE CAME BACK AND TOLD US.

BUT WE DIDN'T BELIEVE.

THEN THIS SAME NEWS CAME MORE AND MORE, SO WE BELIEVED. AND LATER ON, WE SAW ... EVEN WORSE!

AFTER WHAT HAPPENED TO THE GRANDPARENTS, IT WAS A FEW MONTHS QUIET. THEN IT CAME POSTERS EVERYWHERE AND SPEECHES FROM THE GEMEINDE[1]...

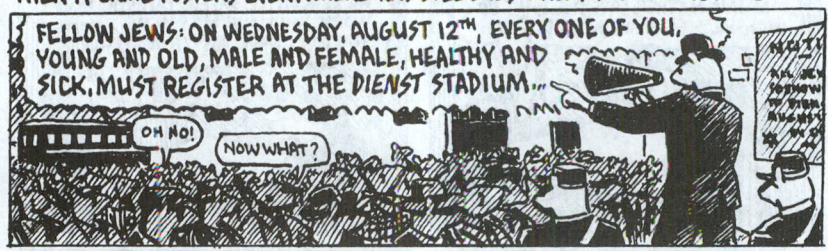

FELLOW JEWS: ON WEDNESDAY, AUGUST 12ᵀᴴ, EVERY ONE OF YOU, YOUNG AND OLD, MALE AND FEMALE, HEALTHY AND SICK, MUST REGISTER AT THE DIENST STADIUM...

OH NO!

NOW WHAT?

...THERE'S NO CAUSE FOR ALARM—IT'S ONLY A MATTER OF INSPECTING YOUR DOCUMENTS AND STAMPING THEM. THIS WILL PROTECT YOU AS CITIZENS OF THE REGION!...

I'M NOT GOING. IT'S A NAZI TRAP!...

EVERYBODY WAS WORRIED.

...AND OUR JEWISH COMMITTEE IS HELPING THOSE MURDERERS. GOD KNOWS WHAT WILL HAPPEN TO US AT THE STADIUM!

WELL, THEY JUST INSPECTED JEWISH DOCUMENTS IN SOME NEARBY TOWNS. IT WAS NO BIG DEAL.

ANYWAY, WE'VE **GOT** TO GO. WITHOUT LEGAL PAPERS, WE'RE LOST!

TO GO, IT WAS NO GOOD. BUT, NOT TO GO—IT WAS ALSO NO GOOD.

[1] *Gemeinde:* Local government in Germany.

EVERYONE CAME VERY NICE DRESSED. THEY TRIED SO THAT THEY WOULD LOOK YOUNG AND ABLE TO WORK, IN ORDER TO GET A GOOD STAMP ON THEIR PASSPORT.

WHEN WE WERE EVERYBODY INSIDE, GESTAPO WITH MACHINE GUNS SURROUNDED THE STADIUM.

LINE UP BY FAMILY AT THE TABLES TO REGISTER! QUICKLY!

THEN WAS A SELECTION, WITH PEOPLE SENT EITHER TO THE LEFT, EITHER TO THE RIGHT.

OLD PEOPLE, FAMILIES WITH LOTS OF KIDS, AND PEOPLE WITHOUT WORK CARDS ARE ALL GOING TO THE LEFT!

WE UNDERSTOOD THIS MUST BE VERY BAD.

ME AND ANJA CAME TO THE TABLE WHERE MY COUSIN WAS SITTING...

AH, YOU WORK AT THE CARPENTRY SHOP. GO TO THE RIGHT.

SO WE GOT STAMPED OUR PASSPORTS AND CAME QUICK TO THE GOOD SIDE OF THE STADIUM. THOSE THEY SENT LEFT, THEY DIDN'T GET ANY STAMP.

Art Spiegelman, from MAUS I. Copyright © 1973, 1980, 1982, 1983, 1984, 1985, 1986 by Art Spiegelman. Used by permission of Pantheon Books, a division of Random House, Inc.

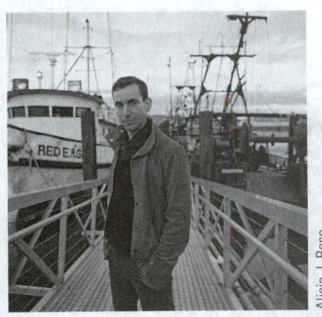

Alicia J. Rose

CRAIG THOMPSON (1975–   ) is the author of the graphic novels *Good-bye, Chunky Rice* (1999), *Blankets* (2003), *Carnet de Voyage* (2004) and *Habibi* (2011). His cover design for the 2007 album *Friend and Foe* by the rock band Menomena was nominated for a Grammy Award. The recipient of three Eisner Awards, four Harvey Awards, and two Ignatz Awards, Thompson is currently collaborating on a book project with French graphic novelist Edmond Baudoin.

Cultural Context In various cultures around the world, quilts (like the one in this excerpt and the one on the cover of this book) have been an important form of textile art, using scraps of fabric to depict a scene or to tell a story. They are often given as gifts to commemorate major life events or rites of passage, such as marriage or birth. From the bold colors and asymmetrical shapes of African American quilts to the intricate Japanese styles that were influenced by American designs, the range of quilting techniques is as vast as the backgrounds and interests of those who create them.

from Blankets (2003)

Another excerpt from Blankets begins on the following page.

GENE LUEN YANG (1973–   ) teaches for Hamline University's MFA Program in writing for children and young adults. He has published several graphic novels, including *American Born Chinese* (2006), from which the following excerpt was taken and which was the first graphic novel to win the American Library Association's Printz Award and to be nominated for a National Book Award. Yang has also been honored with two Eisner Awards.

Cultural Context This excerpt from *American Born Chinese* refers to the Transformers toys, which were originally developed by a Japanese company and purchased in 1984 by the American company Hasbro. Transformers are robot action figures with movable parts that can be shaped into animals as well as land and space vehicles. The toys have been popular among generations of children around the world and were spun off into a comic book series as well as TV shows and feature films. The young boy in this excerpt quotes two Transformers taglines, "Robot in Disguise" and "More than Meets the Eye." Here, the boy plays with the robot/truck as he plays with transforming his identity.

from American Born Chinese (2006)

Reading and Reacting

1. What specific visual elements establish the setting of the excerpt from *Persepolis* as harsh and restrictive for Marji? How do these visual elements help to move readers from one panel of the story to the next?
2. Write a plot summary of the excerpt from *Maus* or one of the excerpts from *The Harlem Hellfighters*. Include as much specific detail as you can.
3. Create a graphic fiction sequel (or prequel) to the excerpts from *Blankets* or the excerpt from *American Born Chinese*.
4. In *Maus*, the Jews are portrayed as mice, and the Nazis are depicted as cats. Why do you think Spiegelman chose to portray his characters as animals—and, specifically, as *these* animals? What does he gain (or lose) by doing so?
5. Do you see the title character in "The Hunger Artist" as a mentally ill fanatic or as a man of high principles? In what sense, if any, do you see him as an "artist"? How is he different from the people who come to see him?
6. **Critical Perspective** Writing for *Wilson Quarterly*, Ken Chen describes the relationship of graphic fiction to the broader literary canon in this way: "Because comics tradition-ally have been a pulp medium, they've been able to portray the world with a liberating strangeness, unconstrained by taste or codified literary standards." In what sense do the graphic stories in this sampler "portray the world with a liberating strangeness"? Do these stories break any literary rules?

WRITING SUGGESTIONS: Graphic Fiction

1. Write a **response** (see Chapter 3) expressing your reactions to the excerpt from *Maus*.
2. Write an **explication** (see Chapter 3) of the excerpt from *Blankets*.
3. Write a **comparison-contrast essay** (see Chapter 3) comparing the short story "A Hun-ger Artist" (p. 592) to the graphic fiction version of the story.
4. Write a **comparison-contrast essay** (see Chapter 3) comparing the excerpts from *The Harlem Hellfighters* to "The Things They Carried" (p. 392)—or to one of the war poems in Chapter 31.
5. Write a **character analysis** (see Chapter 3) of Marji in the excerpt from *Persepolis*.
6. Write an essay about the **cultural context** (see Chapter 3) of the excerpt from *Maus* or the excerpt from *American Born Chinese*.

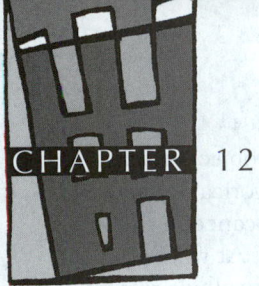

CHAPTER 12

READING AND WRITING ABOUT FICTION

Reading Fiction

As you read works of short fiction, you should pay careful attention to elements such as plot; character; setting; point of view; style, tone, and language; symbol, allegory, and myth; and theme. By looking closely at these elements, you will be able to understand and appreciate the story more fully. The following guidelines, designed to help you explore works of fiction, focus on issues that are examined in depth in chapters to come:

- *Consider the **plot** of the story.* How do the events in the story relate to one another, and how do they relate to the story as a whole? What conflicts occur in the story, and how are these conflicts developed or resolved? Does the story include any noteworthy plot devices, such as flashbacks or foreshadowing? (See Chapter 13.)
- *Analyze the **characters** in the story.* What are their most striking traits? How do these individuals interact with one another? What motivates them? Are the characters fully developed, or are they stereotypes whose sole purpose is to express a single trait (innocence, evil, generosity, and so on) or to move the plot along? (See Chapter 14.)
- *Identify the **setting** of the story.* During what time period, and in what geographic location, does the action of the story occur? How does the setting affect the characters' lives? How does it affect their relationships? Does the setting create a mood for the story? How does the setting reinforce the central ideas that the story examines? (See Chapter 15.)
- *Examine the narrative **point of view** of the story.* Who is telling the story? Is the story told by an outside narrator? Is the story told from the perspective of a character? If so, is this narrator a major character telling his or her own story or a minor character who witnesses events? How much does this narrator know about the events in the story? Does the narrator present an accurate picture of events? Does the narrator understand the full significance of the story he or she is telling? (See Chapter 16.)
- *Analyze the **style, tone**, and **language** of the story.* Does the writer make any unusual use of diction or syntax? Does the writer use imaginative figures of speech? patterns of imagery? What level of diction is associated with particular characters? What words or phrases are repeated throughout the work? Is the story's style plain or elaborate? Does the narrator's tone reveal his or her attitude toward characters or events? Is the tone of the story playful, humorous, ironic, satirical, serious, somber, solemn, bitter, condescending, formal, or informal—or does the tone convey some other attitude? (See Chapter 17.)

- *Focus on **symbol**, **allegory**, and **myth**.* Does the author use any objects or ideas symbolically? Are characters or objects in the story part of an allegorical framework? How does an object establish its symbolic or allegorical significance in the story? Are the symbols or allegorical figures conventional or unusual? At what points in the story do symbols or allegorical figures appear? Does the story allude to a myth? (See Chapter 18.)
- *Identify the **themes** of the story.* What is the central theme? How is this idea or concept expressed in the work? What elements of the story develop the central theme? How do character, plot, setting, point of view, and symbols reinforce the central theme? How does the title of the story contribute to readers' understanding of the central theme? What other themes are explored? (See Chapter 19.)

Active Reading

John Frei, a student in an Introduction to Literature course, was assigned to write a three- to four-page essay on a topic of his choice, focusing on any short story in this literature anthology, without consulting outside sources. After considering a number of possible choices, John selected Alberto Alvaro Ríos's "The Secret Lion."

Source: Courtesy of Alberto Alvaro Ríos

ALBERTO ALVARO RÍOS (1952–   ) was born and raised in the border town of Nogales, Arizona, the son of a Mexican father and an English mother. He is the author of ten books and chapbooks of poetry, including *Whispering to Fool the Wind* (1982), which won the American Academy of Poets Walt Whitman Award; *Teodoro Luna's Two Kisses* (1990); *The Smallest Muscle in the Human Body* (2002); *The Theater of Night* (2005); and *The Dangerous Shirt* (2009). His collections of short stories include *The Iguana Killer: Twelve Stories of the Heart* (1984), in which "The Secret Lion" appeared; *Pig Cookies and Other Stories* (1995), and *The Curtain of Trees* (1999). *Capirotada*, which was published in 1999, is a memoir about growing up on the Mexican border. Ríos is presently Regents' Professor of English at Arizona State University.

Reviewer Mary Logue, writing in the *Village Voice Literary Supplement*, observes that Ríos's writings "carry the feel of another world. . . . Ríos's tongue is both foreign and familiar," reflecting an upbringing "where one is neither in this country nor the other." In many of his stories, Ríos expresses the seeming "other-ness" of Anglo culture as seen through the eyes of Chicano children: a little boy frightened by the sight of his first snowfall or (as in "The Secret Lion") boys amazed by the otherworldly sight of "heaven." Through Ríos's children, we see our own world with new eyes.

Cultural Context With their rolling hills, freshwater ponds, lush greens, and fastidiously trimmed turf, golf courses are designed to convey a sense of wealth and comfort, typically providing recreation for the middle and upper classes. In a dry region—or even in a densely populated city—an irrigated, sculpted golf course may look like an oasis in the desert. The golf course that plays a role in this story is probably (like many others) part of a privately owned, exclusive country club.

The Secret Lion (1984)

I was twelve and in junior high school and something happened that we didn't have a name for, but it was there nonetheless like a lion, and roaring, roaring that way the biggest things do. Everything changed. Just that. Like the rug, the one that gets pulled—or better, like the tablecloth those magicians pull where the stuff on the table stays the same but the gasp! from the audience makes the staying-the-same part not matter. Like that.

What happened was there were teachers now, not just one teacher, teach-erz, and we felt personally abandoned somehow. When a person had all these teachers now, he didn't get taken care of the same way, even though six was more than one. Arithmetic went out the door when we walked in. And we saw girls now, but they weren't the same girls we used to know because we couldn't talk to them anymore, not the same way we used to, certainly not to Sandy, even though she was my neighbor, too. Not even to her. She just played the piano all the time. And there were words, oh there were words in junior high school, and we wanted to know what they were, and how a person did them—that's what school was supposed to be for. Only, in junior high school, school wasn't school, everything was backward-like. If you went up to a teacher and said the word to try and find out what it meant you got in trouble for saying it. So we didn't. And we figured it must have been that way about other stuff, too, so we never said anything about anything—we weren't stupid.

But my friend Sergio and I, we solved junior high school. We would come home from school on the bus, put our books away, change shoes, and go across the highway to the arroyo. It was the one place we were not supposed to go. So we did. This was, after all, what junior high had at least shown us. It was our river, though, our personal Mississippi, our friend from long back, and it was full of stories and all the branch forts we had built in it when we were still the Vikings of America, with our own symbol, which we had carved everywhere, even in the sand, which let the water take it. That was good, we had decided; whoever was at the end of this river would know about us.

At the very very top of our growing lungs, what we would do down there was shout every dirty word we could think of, in every combination we could come up with, and we would yell about girls, and all the things we wanted to do with them, as loud as we could—we didn't know what we wanted to do with them, just things—and we would yell about teachers, and how we loved some of them, like Miss Crevelone, and how we wanted to dissect some of them, making signs of the cross, like priests, and we would yell this stuff over and over because it felt good, we couldn't explain why, it just felt good and for the first time in our lives there was nobody to tell us we couldn't. So we did.

One Thursday we were walking along shouting this way, and the railroad, the Southern Pacific, which ran above and along the far side of the arroyo, had dropped a grinding ball down there, which was, we found out later, a cannonball thing used in mining. A bunch of them were put in a big vat which turned around and crushed the ore. One had been dropped, or thrown—what do caboose men do when they get bored—but it got down there regardless and as we were walking along yelling about one girl or another, a particular Claudia, we found it, one of these things, looked at it, picked it up, and got very very excited, and held it and passed it back and forth, and we were saying "Guythisis, this is, geeGuythis . . .": we had this perception about nature then, that nature is imperfect and that round things are perfect: we said "GuyGodthis is perfect, thisisthis is perfect, it's round, round and heavy, it'sit's the best thing we'veeverseen. Whatisit?" We didn't know. We just knew it was great. We just, whatever, we played with it, held it some more.

5

And then we had to decide what to do with it. We knew, because of a lot of things, that if we were going to take this and show it to anybody, this discovery, this best thing, was going to be taken away from us. That's the way it works with little kids, like all the polished quartz, the tons of it we had collected piece by piece over the years. Junior high kids too. If we took it home, my mother, we knew, was going to look at it and say "throw that dirty thing in the, get rid of it." Simple like, like that. "But ma it's the best thing I" "Getridofit." Simple.

So we didn't. Take it home. Instead, we came up with the answer. We dug a hole and buried it. And we marked it secretly. Lots of secret signs. And came back the next week to dig it up and, we didn't know, pass it around some more or something, but we didn't find it. We dug up that whole bank, and we never found it again. We tried.

Sergio and I talked about that ball or whatever it was when we couldn't find it. All we used were small words, neat, good. Kid words. What we were really saying, but didn't know the words, was how much that ball was like that place, that whole arroyo: couldn't tell anybody about it, didn't understand what it was, didn't have a name for it. It just felt good. It was just perfect in the way it was that place, that whole going to that place, that whole junior high school lion. It was just iron-heavy, it had no name, it felt good or not, we couldn't take it home to show our mothers, and once we buried it, it was gone forever.

The ball was gone, like the first reasons we had come to that arroyo years earlier, like the first time we had seen the arroyo, it was gone like everything else that had been taken away. This was not our first lesson. We stopped going to the arroyo after not finding the thing, the same way we had stopped going there years earlier and headed for the mountains. Nature seemed to keep pushing us around one way or another, teaching us the same thing every place we ended up. Nature's gang was tough that way, teaching us stuff.

10   When we were young we moved away from town, me and my family. Sergio's was already out there. Out in the wilds. Or at least the new place seemed like the wilds since everything looks bigger the smaller a man is. I was five, I guess, and we had moved three miles north of Nogales where we had lived, three miles north of the Mexican border. We looked across the highway in one direction and there was the arroyo; hills stood up in the other direction. Mountains, for a small man.

When the first summer came the very first place we went to was of course the one place we weren't supposed to go, the arroyo. We went down in there and found water running, summer rain water mostly, and we went swimming. But every third or fourth or fifth day, the sewage treatment plant that was, we found out, upstream, would release whatever it was that it released, and we would never know exactly what day that was, and a person really couldn't tell right off by looking at the water, not every time, not so a person could get out in time. So, we went swimming that summer and some days we had a lot of fun. Some days we didn't. We found a thousand ways to explain what happened on those other days, constructing elaborate stories about the neighborhood dogs, and hadn't she, my mother, miscalculated her step before, too? But she knew something was up because we'd come running into the house those days, wanting to take a shower, even—if this can be imagined—in the middle of the day.

That was the first time we stopped going to the arroyo. It taught us to look the other way. We decided, as the second side of summer came, we wanted to go into the mountains. They were still mountains then. We went running in one summer Thursday morning, my friend Sergio and I, into my mother's kitchen, and said, well, what'zin, what'zin those hills over there—we used her word so she'd understand us— and she said nothingdon'tworryaboutit. So we went out, and we weren't dumb, we thought with our eyes to each other, ohhoshe'stryingtokeepsomethingfromus. We knew adults.

We had read the books, after all; we knew about bridges and castles and wild-treacherousraging alligatormouth rivers. We wanted them. So we were going to go out and get them. We went back that morning into that kitchen and we said, "We're going out there, we're going into the hills, we're going away for three days, don't worry." She said, "All right."

"You know," I said to Sergio, "if we're going to go away for three days, well, we ought to at least pack a lunch."

But we were two young boys with no patience for what we thought at the time was mom-stuff: making sa-and-wiches. My mother didn't offer. So we got out little kid knapsacks that my mother had sewn for us, and into them we put the jar of mustard. A loaf of bread. Knivesforksplates, bottles of Coke, a can opener. This was lunch for the two of us. And we were weighed down, humped over to be strong enough to carry this stuff. But we started walking anyway, into the hills. We were going to eat berries and stuff otherwise. "Goodbye." My mom said that.

After the first hill we were dead. But we walked. My mother could still see us. And we kept walking. We walked until we got to where the sun is straight overhead, noon. That place. Where that is doesn't matter; it's time to eat. The truth is we weren't anywhere close to that place. We just agreed that the sun was overhead and that it was time to eat, and by tilting our heads a little we could make that the truth.

"We really ought to start looking for a place to eat."

"Yeah. Let's look for a good place to eat." We went back and forth saying that for fifteen minutes, making it lunchtime because that's what we always said back and forth before lunchtimes at home. "Yeah, I'm hungry all right." I nodded my head. "Yeah, I'm hungry all right too. I'm hungry." He nodded his head. I nodded my head back. After a good deal more nodding, we were ready, just as we came over a little hill. We hadn't found the mountains yet. This was a little hill.

And on the other side of this hill we found heaven.

It was just what we thought it would be.

Perfect. Heaven was green, like nothing else in Arizona. And it wasn't a cemetery or like that because we had seen cemeteries and they had gravestones and stuff and this didn't. This was perfect, had trees, lots of trees, had birds, like we had never seen before. It was like *The Wizard of Oz*, like when they got to Oz and everything was so green, so emerald, they had to wear those glasses, and we ran just like them, laughing, laughing that way we did that moment, and we went running down to this clearing in it all, hitting each other that good way we did.

We got down there, we kept laughing, we kept hitting each other, we unpacked our stuff, and we started acting "rich." We knew all about how to do that, like blowing on our nails, then rubbing them on our chests for the shine. We made our sandwiches, opened our Cokes, got out the rest of the stuff, the salt and pepper shakers. I found this particular hole and I put my Coke right into it, a perfect fit, and I called it my Coke-holder. I got down next to it on my back, because everyone knows that rich people eat lying down, and I got my sandwich in one hand and put my other arm around the Coke in its holder. When I wanted a drink, I lifted my neck a little, put out my lips, and tipped my Coke a little with the crook of my elbow. Ah.

We were there, lying down, eating our sandwiches, laughing, throwing bread at each other and out for the birds. This was heaven. We were laughing and we couldn't believe it. My mother was keeping something from us, ah ha, but we had found her out. We even found water over at the side of the clearing to wash our plates with—we had brought plates. Sergio started washing his plates when he was done, and I was being rich with my Coke, and this day in summer was right.

When suddenly these two men came, from around a corner of trees and the tallest grass we had ever seen. They had bags on their backs, leather bags, bags and sticks.

25   We didn't know what clubs were, but I learned later, like I learned about the grinding balls. The two men yelled at us. Most specifically, one wanted me to take my Coke out of my Coke-holder so he could sink his golf ball into it.

Something got taken away from us that moment. Heaven. We grew up a little bit, and couldn't go backward. We learned. No one had ever told us about golf. They had told us about heaven. And it went away. We got golf in exchange.

We went back to the arroyo for the rest of that summer, and tried to have fun the best we could. We learned to be ready for finding the grinding ball. We loved it, and when we buried it we knew what would happen. The truth is, we didn't look so hard for it. We were two boys and twelve summers then, and not stupid. Things get taken away.

We buried it because it was perfect. We didn't tell my mother, but together it was all we talked about, till we forgot. It was the lion.

*   *   *

Previewing

Student John Frei began the reading process by previewing his text. A quick glance at the story showed him that it was quite short (under five pages), that it was written in the first person ("I was twelve"), that it included dialogue as well as narrative, and that it had an interesting title.

Highlighting and Annotating

As he reread the story, John highlighted words and ideas that he thought might be useful to him, noted possible connections among ideas, and wrote down questions and comments as they occurred to him. During this process, he considered the meaning of the term *secret lion*, and he paid close attention to the narrator's voice. The highlighted and annotated passage that follows illustrates his responses to the last five paragraphs of the story.

When suddenly these two men came, from around a corner of trees and the tallest grass we had ever seen. They had bags on their backs, leather bags, bags and sticks.

pt. of
view

We didn't know what clubs were, <u>but I learned later, like I learned about the grinding balls.</u> The two men yelled at us. Most specifically, one wanted me to take my Coke out of my Coke-holder so he could sink his golf ball into it.

Heaven =
innocence
Golf =
adulthood
Things lose
their magic
+ special-
ness.

<u>Something got taken away from us that moment. Heaven. We grew up a little bit, and couldn't go backward. We learned. No one had ever told us about golf. They had told us about heaven. And it went away. We got golf in exchange.</u>

We went back to the arroyo for the rest of that summer, and tried to have fun the best we could. <u>We learned to be ready for finding the grinding ball. We loved it, and when we buried it we knew what would happen. The truth is, we didn't look so hard for it. We were two boys and twelve summers then, and not</u>

Loss of inno-
cence, trust,
belief in
perfection.

stupid. ⟨Things get taken away.⟩ ←

We buried it because it was perfect. We didn't tell my mother but together

⸢ball?

it was all we talked about, till we forgot. ⟨It⟩ was the ⟨lion.⟩

Lion=Knowledge that growing up=loss? or is lion growing up itself?

John's highlighting and annotation of the entire story suggested a number of interesting possibilities for his essay. First, he noticed that the story contrasts the narrator's childhood innocence with his adult knowledge. John's highlighting also identified some unusual stylistic features, such as words run together ("Getridofit") and the repetition of words like *neat* and *perfect*. Finally, he noticed that four items—the arroyo, the grinding ball, the golf course, and the lion—are mentioned again and again. This observation led him to suspect that these items—particularly the secret lion, prominently mentioned in the story's title—might have symbolic significance.

 ## Writing about Fiction

Planning an Essay

At this stage, John had not yet decided on a topic; however, his previewing, highlighting, and annotations had revealed some interesting ideas about style and point of view—and, possibly, about symbolism. Now, because his essay was to be no more than four pages long, he needed to select one element on which to concentrate.

Choosing a Topic

John decided to explore possible topics in his journal. Here are his journal entries on the story's style and point of view.

Style—Style is informal, with lots of contractions and slang terms like "neat." Words are run together. Most of the time, the boys combine words to indicate something unimportant to them. When they're packing the lunch, they include "knivesforksplates." They're not interested in packing the lunch—they just want to get to the "mountains." Packing lunch is very important to the mother, so she does the opposite of combining words: she breaks them down ("sa-and-wiches"). This style can get pretty annoying.

Point of view—We see the story through the eyes of the narrator, who is a character in the story. Sergio is developed along with the narrator as part of a "we." The characters are not really individuals—they function as "we" for most of the story. We don't see into the minds of the boys to any great extent. The narrator has a double perspective: he takes readers back to his childhood, and this helps us understand the boys' excitement and disappointment, but he also shows us how much more he knows now, so we know that, too.

John had no trouble writing paragraphs on style and point of view in his journal, but he ran out of ideas quickly; he knew that he did not have enough material for an essay about either of these two topics. However, when he started to write a journal entry about the symbolic significance of certain elements in the story, he found that he had a lot more to say. As a result, he chose "Symbols in 'The Secret Lion'" as his essay's topic. Here is his journal entry on symbolism.

Symbolism—The arroyo, the grinding ball, the golf course, and of course the secret lion all seem to mean something beyond their literal meanings as objects and places. (Maybe the "mountains" do too.) For one thing, they're all repeated over and over again. Also, they all seem to be related somehow to magic and perfection and surprise and expectation and idealism (and, later, to disillusionment and disappointment). If this is a story about growing up, these things could be related to that theme.

Finding Something to Say

Brainstorming   Once he decided to write about symbolism, John moved on to **brainstorm** about his topic, focusing on what he considered the story's most important—and most obvious—symbol: the secret lion itself.

(Lion) = "roaring, roaring that way the biggest things do"

EVERYTHING CHANGED   (= secret because it's

something they have to find

out on their own, not from

adults?)

(Tablecloth)-rug (=magic). "Staying-the-same part" is

most important—why?

(Arroyo:) not supposed to go (= rebellion)— Mississippi,

"friend from long back"; freedom. Place that doesn't

change.

(Grinding ball)— Perfection in imperfect world,

innocence in adult world. "Nature = imperfect," but

"round things = "perfect"— "the best thing." ("That

ball was like that place, that whole arroyo")

Buried and "gone forever"—"taken away" (like arroyo)

(Mountains:) "everything looks bigger the smaller

a man is"; hills = "Mountains for a small man."

(Mother calls them hills)

"perfect"   (Arroyo) = polluted with sewage (never know when it's

x3   coming)—went to mts. On other side of hills = golf course

(= heaven) "perfect"

＊Like Oz— green, emerald

＊Place to act "rich"

＊Men with clubs =

reality, future

(= end of innocence)

"Things get taken away" heaven, ball (something

buried and lost), arroyo

"We buried it because it was "perfect." . . . It

was the lion."

Lion = secret place inside us that still craves

childhood (as adults, we learn we have to keep it

buried, like ball). ＊How can a "roaring" lion be secret?

Seeing Connections

When John looked over his brainstorming notes in search of an organizing scheme for his essay, he saw that he had plenty of information about the secret lion, the arroyo, the grinding ball, and the golf course. His most obvious option was to discuss one item at a time, but he knew that he needed to find something that would tie the four separate items together. When he noticed that each item seemed to have different meanings at different periods of the boys' lives, he realized that his essay could discuss how these meanings change as the boys move from childhood to adolescence to adulthood. He experimented with this possibility as he grouped related details in the following lists.

The secret lion
Beginning: "raging beast" inside of them (6th grade class) = frustration, puberty
Beginning: "roaring, roaring that way the biggest things do"
Middle: "that whole junior high school lion"
End: Lion = greatness, something important (also = puberty?)
Also = great discoveries they expect to make in their lives.
End: "It was the lion."

Arroyo
Place that doesn't change (= childhood); constant in their changing lives. (But it changes too)
Mississippi—horizons
Freedom of childhood
Waste dump

Grinding ball
Perfection (in imperfect world)
Childhood innocence (in adult world)
Undiscovered knowledge?
Secrets of childhood (buried)
Something lost: "Things get taken away"

Golf course
Heaven—knowledge that there is no heaven, that it's a fraud, like the Wizard of Oz.
Adulthood—men with clubs
Scene of remembered humiliation
End of innocence (realization that it's just a golf course)

John's lists confirmed that the meanings of the four items did seem to change as the boys grew up. To the boys, the arroyo, the grinding ball, and the golf course are magical, but when they grow up, all three items lose their magic and became ordinary. The secret lion, however, seemed more complex than the other three items, and John knew that he would have to develop his ideas further before he could show how the lion's meaning changes and what these changes contribute to the story as a whole.

Deciding on a Thesis

With his ideas organized into lists that clarified some possible relationships among them, John began to see a central idea for his essay. He expressed this idea in a tentative **thesis statement**, a sentence that he could use to guide his essay's first draft.

The meanings of the story's key symbols change as the boys move from childhood to adolescence to adulthood, and these changes reveal corresponding changes in the boys' view of the world as they move from idealism to frustration to resignation.

Preparing an Outline

Even though his essay was to be short, John prepared a scratch outline that mapped out an arrangement for his ideas. He decided to discuss the four key symbols one by one, tracing each through the boys' childhood, adolescence, and adulthood. He planned to discuss the lion last because he saw it as the story's most important symbol. Looking back over all his notes, and paying close attention to his tentative thesis statement, John constructed this scratch outline.

Arroyo
    Mississippi
    Rebellion
    Waste dump

Grinding ball
    [Not yet discovered]
    Lost perfection
    "Things get taken away."

Golf course
    "Heaven"
    Humiliation
    Golf course

Lion
    [Not yet discovered]
    "roaring"; "raging beast"
    Just the lion

Drafting an Essay

Guided by his scratch outline, his tentative thesis statement, and his notes, John wrote the following first draft.

first draft

Symbols in "The Secret Lion"

"The Secret Lion" is a story that is rich in symbols. It is also a story about change. The meanings of the story's key symbols change as the boys move from childhood to adolescence to adulthood, and these changes reveal corresponding changes in the boys' view of the world as they move from idealism to frustration to resignation.

The arroyo, a dry gulch that can fill up with water, is special to the narrator and his friend Sergio when they are boys. Literally, it is a place to play. Symbolically, it is a place to rebel (they're not supposed to be there; they yell forbidden words). It could also symbolize all the discoveries they will make before they are completely grown up. To the young boys, the arroyo symbolizes a retreat from the disappointment of the golf course; it is their second choice. Later, it represents adventure, the uncertainty and unpredictability of adolescence, as illustrated by the fact that they cannot tell just by looking at it from the riverside whether the river was going to be tainted with sewage. When they are children, it is their Mississippi. When they are adolescents, it is a place to hang out and a symbol of adolescent rebellion; as an adult, the narrator looks back at it for what it was: an ordinary river polluted by sewage. The arroyo doesn't change, but the boys' view of it changes as they change.

At first, when they find the grinding ball, it stands for everything that is perfect and fascinating (and therefore forbidden and unattainable) in life. Like a child's life, it is perfect. They knew they couldn't keep it forever, just as they couldn't be children forever, so they buried it. When they tried to look for it again, they couldn't find it. They admit later that they don't look very hard. (People always wish they can find youth again, but they can't.) The ball represents perfection in an imperfect world, childhood innocence in an adult world. They hide it from their mother because they know she won't see it as perfect; she'll make them "getridofit" (182). They hide it because they want to retain the excitement of the undiscovered, but once they've used it and seen it and buried it, it's not new anymore. Even if they'd been able to find it, it would still be lost. To the adult narrator, it's just an ordinary object used in mining.

The golf course, which they wander into at age five, is, for a short period of time, "heaven" (183). It is lush and green and carefully cared for, and it is the opposite of the polluted arroyo. It is also another world, as mysterious as the Land of Oz. With the realization that it is not heaven to the golfers, the boys see what outsiders they really are. They may start "acting 'rich'" (183), but it will be just an act. There are no Coke-holders, no Oz, no heaven. The adolescents see the golf course as a scene of defeat and embarrassment, the setting for the confrontation that sent them back to the arroyo. To the adult, the golf course is just a golf course.

The secret lion is the most complex symbol in the story. In a sense it stands for the innocence of childhood, something we lose when we learn more. The lion symbolizes a great "roaring" disturbance (180). It is a change that unsettles everything for a brief time and then passes, leaving everything changed in irrevocable, indescribable ways. It symbolizes the boys' growing up: they are changed, but still the same people. The "secret lion" is that thing that

changes little boys into men. It is secret because no one notices it happening; by the time
it is noticed, the change has already occurred, and the little boy is gone forever. It is a lion
because it "roars" through the boy like a storm and causes all of the growing-up changes,
which can be "the biggest things" (180). In a more specific sense, the lion stands for puberty,
reflected in their rage and frustration when they shout profanity. In the beginning of the story,
the lion is rage (puberty, adolescence); in the middle, it suggests greatness (passing through
adolescence into manhood); at the end, it's just the lion—"It was the lion" (184)—without
any symbolic significance.

   By the time they bury the ball, they have already learned one lesson, and the force
of adulthood is pushing childhood aside. The golf course changes from heaven to shame to
golf course; the ball changes from a special, perfect thing to something ordinary; the arroyo
changes from grand river to polluted stream. Maybe it is the knowledge that life is not perfect,
the knowledge that comes from growing up, that is the secret lion.

First Draft: Commentary

Discussions with other students in a peer-review session helped to guide John's revision of
his first draft. The students' major criticism was that John's thesis seemed to make a complicated claim he could not support: that the development of all four symbols follows the three
stages of the boys' lives. One student pointed out that two of the four symbols (the grinding
ball and the secret lion) do not even enter the boys' lives until adolescence and that John's
treatment of the story's most prominent symbol—the lion—does not show it changing in any
significant way. The group agreed that he should simplify his thesis, focusing on the way the
four symbols all reflect the story's theme about the inevitability of change.

   John also met with his instructor, who suggested that he discuss the golf course first
because it is the setting for the event that occurs first in time and because the disillusionment
associated with it influences subsequent events. His instructor then expressed his concern
about John's tendency to engage in "symbol hunting." He suggested that rather than focusing
on finding equivalents for each of the four items ("the ball represents perfection," "the lion
stands for puberty," and so on), John should consider how these symbols work together to
communicate the story's theme. His instructor pointed out that in looking for neat equivalent values for each symbol, John was oversimplifying very complex ideas.

   After discussing his first draft with his classmates and his instructor, John made changes
in his essay's content and organization. In his next draft, he also planned to delete wordiness
and repetition; revise inconsistent verb tenses; add more specific references, including quotations, from the story; sharpen transitions and add clearer topic sentences; and reorganize
paragraphs to make logical and causal connections more obvious.

Revising and Editing an Essay

The revisions John decided to make are reflected in his second draft.

Symbols in "The Secret Lion"

"The Secret Lion" is a story about change. The first paragraph of the story gives a twelve-year-old's view of growing up: everything changes. When the child watches the magician, he is amazed at the "staying-the-same part" (181); adults focus on the tablecloth. As adults, we lose the ability to see the world through innocent eyes. We have the benefit of experience, confident the trick will work as long as the magician pulls the tablecloth in the proper way. The "staying-the-same part" is less important than the technique. In a story full of prominent symbols, the magician's trick does not seem very important, but all the key symbols, like the magician's trick, are about change. In fact, each of the story's key symbols highlights the theme of the inevitability of change that permeates the lives of the narrator and his friend Sergio.

The golf course is one such symbol. When the boys first see it, it is "heaven" (183). Lush and green and carefully cared for, it is completely different from the dry brown Arizona countryside and the polluted arroyo. In fact, to the boys it is another world, as mysterious as Oz—and just as unreal. Almost at once, the Emerald City becomes black and white again, the "Coke—holders" disappear, and the boys stop "acting 'rich'" (183). Heaven becomes a golf course, and the boys are changed forever.

The arroyo, a dry gulch that can fill up with water, is another symbol that reinforces the theme of the inevitability of change. It is a special place for the boys—a place to rebel, to shout forbidden words, to swim in waters polluted by a sewage treatment plant. Although it represents a retreat from the disillusionment of the golf course, clearly second choice, it is the boys' "personal Mississippi" (181), full of possibilities. Eventually, though, the arroyo too disappoints the boys, and they stop going there. "Nature seemed to keep pushing us around one way or another, teaching us the same thing every place we ended up" (182). The lesson they keep learning is that nothing is permanent.

The grinding ball, round and perfect, seems to suggest permanence and stability. But when the boys find it, they realize at once that they cannot keep it forever, just as they cannot remain children forever. Like a child's life, it is perfect but temporary. Burying it is their futile attempt to make time stand still, to preserve perfection in an imperfect world, innocence in an adult world, and they have already learned Nature's lesson well enough to know that this is not possible. They do not look very hard for the ball, but even if they'd been able to find it, the perfection and the innocence it represents would still be unattainable.

The secret lion, the most complex symbol, suggests the most profound kind of change: moving from innocence to experience, from childhood to adulthood. When the narrator is twelve, he says, "something happened that we didn't have a name for, but it was there nonetheless like a lion, and roaring, roaring that way the biggest things do. Everything changed" (180). School is different, girls are different, language is different. Innocence has been lost. The lion is associated with a great "roaring" disturbance, a change that unsettles everything for a brief time and then passes, leaving everything changed in irrevocable, indescribable ways. The secret lion is the thing that changes little boys into men. It is a lion because it "roars" through the boys like a storm; everything changes.

In an attempt to make things stay the same, to make time stand still, the boys bury the grinding ball "because it was perfect. . . . It was the lion" (184). The grinding ball is "like that place, that whole arroyo" (182): secret and perfect. In other words, the ball and the arroyo and the lion are all tightly connected. By the time the boys bury the ball, they have already learned one sad lesson and are on their way to adulthood. Heaven is just a golf course; the round, perfect object is only "a cannonball thing used in mining" (181); the arroyo is no Mississippi but only a polluted stream; and childhood does not last forever. "Things get taken away" (184), and this knowledge that things do not last is the secret lion.

Second Draft: Commentary

John felt satisfied with his second draft. His revised thesis statement was clearer and simpler than the one in his first draft; it was also convincingly supported, with clearly worded topic sentences introducing support paragraphs and connecting them to the thesis statement. The second draft was also a good deal less wordy and more focused than the first, notably in the paragraphs about the arroyo and the grinding ball, and the introduction and conclusion were more fully developed. Moreover, he had given up his search for the one true "meaning" of each symbol, focusing instead on the many possibilities of each.

Now, John felt ready to turn his attention to smaller items, such as grammar, mechanics, punctuation, and format. Specifically, he planned to eliminate contractions, to work quotations into his text more smoothly, to make his thesis statement more precise and his title more interesting, and to revise the language of his introduction and conclusion further.

Frei 1

John Frei

Professor Nyysola

English 102

16 February 2015

"The Secret Lion": Everything Changes

    The first paragraph of Alberto Alvaro Ríos's "The Secret Lion" presents a twelve-year-old's view of growing up: everything changes. When the magician pulls a tablecloth out from under a pile of dishes, the child is amazed at the "staying-the-same part" (181); adults focus on the tablecloth. As adults, we have the benefit of experience; we know the trick will work as long as the technique is correct. We gain confidence, but we lose our innocence, and we lose our sense of wonder. The price we pay for knowledge is a permanent sense of loss, and this trade-off is central to "The Secret Lion," a story whose key symbols reinforce its central theme: that change is inevitable and that change is always accompanied by loss.

    The golf course is one symbol that helps to convey this theme. When the boys first see the golf course, it is "heaven" (183). Lush and green and carefully tended, it is very different from the dry, brown Arizona landscape and the polluted arroyo. In fact, to the boys it is another world, as exotic as Oz and ultimately as unreal. Before long, the Emerald City becomes black and white again. They learn that there is no such thing as a "Coke-holder," that their "acting 'rich'" is just an act, and that their heaven is only a golf course (183). As the narrator acknowledges, "Something got taken away from us that moment. Heaven" (184).

    The arroyo, a dry gulch that can fill up with water, is another symbol that reflects the idea of the inevitability of change and of the loss that accompanies change. It is a special, Edenlike place for the boys—a place where they can rebel by shouting forbidden words and by swimming in forbidden waters. Although it represents a retreat from the disillusionment of the golf course, and it is clearly second choice, it is still their "personal Mississippi" (181), full of possibilities. Eventually, though, the arroyo too disappoints the boys, and they stop going there. As the narrator says, "Nature seemed to keep pushing us around one way or another, teaching us the same thing every place we ended up" (182). The lesson they keep learning is that nothing is permanent.

    The grinding ball, round and perfect, suggests permanence and stability. But when the boys find it, they realize at once that they cannot keep it forever, just as they cannot remain balanced forever between childhood and adulthood. Like a child's life, the ball is

---

Marginal annotations:

Opening paragraph identifies work and author. Parenthetical documentation identifies source of quotation.

Thesis statement

Topic sentence identifies one key symbol.

Topic sentence identifies another key symbol.

Topic sentence identifies another key symbol.

perfect but temporary. Burying it is their desperate attempt to stop time, to preserve perfection in an imperfect world, innocence in an adult world. But the boys are already twelve years old, and they have learned nature's lesson well enough to know that this action will not work. Even if they had been able to find the ball, the perfection and the innocence it suggests to them would still be unattainable. Perhaps that is why they do not try very hard to find it.

Like the story's other symbols, the secret lion itself suggests the most profound kind of change: the movement from innocence to experience, from childhood to adulthood, from expectation to disappointment to resignation. The narrator explains that when he was twelve, "something happened that we didn't have a name for, but it was there nonetheless like a lion, and roaring, roaring that way the biggest things do. Everything changed" (180). School was different, girls were different, language was different. Despite its loud roar, the lion remained paradoxically "secret," unnoticed until it passed. Like adolescence, the secret lion is a roaring disturbance that unsettles everything for a brief time and then passes, leaving everything changed.

In an attempt to make things stay the same, to make time stand still, the boys bury the grinding ball "because it was perfect. . . . It was the lion" (184). The grinding ball is "like that place, that whole arroyo" (182): secret and perfect. The ball and the arroyo and the lion are all perfect, but all, ironically, are temporary. The first paragraph of "The Secret Lion" tells us, "Everything changed" (180); by the last paragraph, we learn what this change means: "Things get taken away" (184). In other words, change implies loss. Heaven turns out to be just a golf course; the round, perfect object is only "a cannonball thing used in mining" (181); the arroyo is just a polluted stream; and childhood is just a phase. "Things get taken away," and this knowledge that things do not last is the lion, secret yet roaring.

Marginal note, left of second paragraph: Topic sentence identifies final (and most important) symbol.

Marginal note, left of third paragraph: Conclusion

Work Cited

Ríos, Alberto Alvaro. "The Secret Lion." *Compact Literature: Reading, Reacting, Writing*, edited by Laurie G. Kirszner and Stephen R. Mandell, 9th ed., Wadsworth, 2016, pp. 180–84.

Final Draft: Commentary

As John revised and edited his second draft, he made changes in word choice and sentence structure. He also changed his title and edited to eliminate errors in mechanics and punctuation. In this final draft, he made his thesis statement more precise than it was in the previous draft, to communicate the idea of the relationship between change and loss that is central to the essay. In addition, he worked all quoted material smoothly into his discussion, taking care to use quotations only when the author's words added something vital to the essay, and he added a works-cited page. Finally, John checked all his references to page numbers in the story so readers would be able to return to his source if necessary to check the accuracy and appropriateness of his quotations.

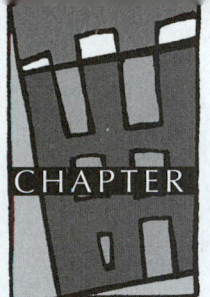

PLOT

Orhan Pamuk
LFI/Geoff Swaine/PhotoShot

William Faulkner
AP Images

Kate Chopin
Courtesy of Louisiana State University

Neil Gaiman
Allstar Picture Library / Alamy

Alfred Hitchcock's 1951 film *Strangers on a Train*, based on a suspense novel by Patricia Highsmith, offers an intriguing premise: two men, strangers, each can murder someone the other wishes dead; because they have no apparent connection to their victims, both can escape suspicion. Many people would describe this ingenious scheme as the film's "plot," but in fact it is simply the gimmick around which the complex plot revolves. Certainly a clever twist can be an important ingredient of a story's plot, but **plot** is more than "what happens": it is how what happens is revealed, the way in which a story's events are arranged.

197

Scene from Alfred Hitchcock's 1951 film *Strangers on a Train*
Source: ©Warner Bros./The Kobal Collection

Plot is shaped by causal connections—historical, social, and personal—by the inter-action between characters, and by the juxtaposition of events. In *Strangers on a Train*, the plot that unfolds is complex: one character directs the events and determines their order while the other character is drawn into the action against his will. The same ele-ments that enrich the plot of the film—unexpected events, conflict, suspense, flashbacks, foreshadowing—can also enrich the plot of a work of short fiction.

 ## Conflict

Readers' interest and involvement are heightened by a story's **conflict**, the struggle between opposing forces that emerges as the action develops. This conflict is a clash between the **protagonist**, a story's principal character, and an **antagonist**, someone or something pre-sented in opposition to the protagonist. Sometimes the antagonist is a villain; more often, it is a character who represents a conflicting point of view or advocates a course of action dif-ferent from the one the protagonist follows. Sometimes the antagonist is not a character at all but a situation (for instance, war or poverty) or an event (for example, a natural disaster, such as a flood or a storm) that challenges the protagonist. In some stories, the protagonist may struggle against a supernatural force, or the conflict may occur within a character's mind. It may, for example, be a struggle between two moral choices, such as whether to stay at home and care for an aging parent or to leave and make a new life.

 ## Stages of Plot

A work's plot explores one or more conflicts, moving from *exposition* through a series of *complications* to a *climax* and, finally, to a *resolution*.

During a story's **exposition**, the writer presents the basic information readers need to understand the events that follow. Typically, the exposition sets the story in motion: it establishes the scene, introduces the major characters, and perhaps suggests the major events or conflicts to come.

Sometimes a single sentence can present a story's exposition clearly and economically, giving readers information vital to their understanding of the plot that will unfold. For example, the opening sentence of Amy Tan's "Two Kinds" (p. 639)—"My mother believed you could be anything you wanted to be in America"—reveals an important trait of a central character. Similarly, the opening sentence of Shirley Jackson's "The Lottery" (p. 419)—"The morning of June 27th was clear and sunny, with the fresh warmth of a full-summer day; the flowers were blossoming profusely and the grass was richly green"—introduces the picture-perfect setting that is essential to the story's irony. At other times, as in John Updike's "A&P" (p. 238), a more fully developed exposition section establishes the story's setting, introduces the main characters, and suggests possible conflicts. Finally, in some experimental stories, a distinct exposition component may be absent, as it is in Luisa Valenzuela's "All about Suicide" (p. 7) and Amanda Brown's "Love and Other Catastrophes: A Mix Tape" (p. 127).

As the plot progresses, the story's conflict unfolds through a series of complications that eventually lead readers to the story's climax. As it develops, the story may include several crises. A **crisis** is a peak in the story's action, a moment of considerable tension or importance. The **climax** is the point of greatest tension or importance, the scene that presents a story's decisive action or event.

The final stage of plot, the **resolution** or **denouement** (French for "untying of the knot"), draws the action to a close and accounts for all remaining loose ends. Sometimes this resolution is achieved with the help of a *deus ex machina* (Latin for "god from a machine"), an intervention of some force or agent previously extraneous to the story—for example, the sudden arrival of a long-lost relative or a fortuitous inheritance, the discovery of a character's true identity, or a surprise last-minute rescue. Usually, however, the resolution is more plausible: all the events lead logically and convincingly (though not necessarily predictably) to the resolution. Sometimes the ending of a story is indefinite—that is, readers are not quite sure what the protagonist will do or what will happen next. This kind of resolution, although it may leave some readers feeling cheated, has its advantages: it mirrors the complexity of life, where closure rarely occurs, and it can keep readers involved in the story as they try to understand the significance of its ending or to decide how conflicts should have been resolved.

Order and Sequence

A writer may introduce a story's events in strict chronological order, presenting each event in the sequence in which it actually takes place. More often, however, especially in relatively modern fiction, writers do not introduce events chronologically. Instead, they present incidents out of expected order, or in no apparent order. For example, a writer may choose to begin *in medias res* (Latin for "in the midst of things"), starting with a key event and later going back in time to explain events that preceded it, as Tillie Olsen does in "I Stand Here Ironing" (p. 299). Or, a writer can decide to begin a work of fiction at the end and then move back to reconstruct events that led up to the final outcome, as William Faulkner does in "A Rose for Emily" (p. 224). Many sequences are possible as the writer manipulates events to create interest, suspense, confusion, shock, or some other effect.

Writers who wish to depart from strict chronological order can use *flashbacks* and *foreshadowing*. A **flashback** moves out of sequence to examine an event or situation that occurred before the time in which the story's action takes place. A character can remember an earlier event, or a story's narrator can re-create an earlier situation. For example, in Alberto Alvaro Ríos's "The Secret Lion" (p. 180), the adult narrator looks back at events that occurred when he was twelve years old and then moves further back in time to consider related events that occurred when he was five. In Edgar Allan Poe's "The Cask of Amontillado" (p. 328), the entire story is told as a flashback. Flashbacks are valuable because they can substitute for or supplement formal exposition by presenting background readers need to understand a story's events. One disadvantage of flashbacks is that if they interrupt the natural flow of events, they may be intrusive or distracting. Such distractions, however, can be an advantage if the writer wishes to reveal events gradually and subtly or to obscure causal links.

Foreshadowing is the introduction early in a story of comments, situations, events, characters, or objects that hint at things to come. Typically, a seemingly simple element—a chance remark, a natural occurrence, a trivial event—is eventually revealed to have great significance. For example, a dark cloud passing across the sky during a wedding can foreshadow future problems for the marriage. Foreshadowing allows a writer to hint provocatively at what is to come so that readers only gradually become aware of a particular detail's role in a story. Thus, foreshadowing helps readers sense what will occur and grow increasingly involved as they see the likelihood (or even the inevitability) of a particular outcome.

In addition to using conventional techniques like flashbacks and foreshadowing, writers may experiment with sequence by substantially tampering with—or even dispensing with—chronological order. (An example is the scrambled chronology of "A Rose for Emily.") In such instances, the experimental form enhances interest and encourages readers to become involved with the story as they work to untangle or reorder the events and determine their logical and causal connections.

In recent years, the Internet has given a new fluidity to the nature of plot, with readers actually able to participate in creating a story's plot. For more on such innovations, see page 124.

✔ **CHECKLIST**   **Writing about Plot**

☐ What happens in the story?

☐ Where does the story's formal exposition section end? What do readers learn about characters in this section? What do readers learn about setting? What possible conflicts are suggested here?

☐ What is the story's central conflict? What other conflicts are presented? Who is the protagonist? Who (or what) serves as the antagonist?

☐ Identify the story's crisis or crises.

☐ Identify the story's climax.

☐ How is the story's central conflict resolved? Is this resolution plausible? satisfying?

■ Which part of the story constitutes the resolution? Do any problems remain unresolved? Does any uncertainty remain? If so, does this uncertainty strengthen or weaken the story? Would another ending be more effective?

■ How are the story's events arranged? Are they presented in chronological order? What events are presented out of logical sequence? Does the story use foreshadowing? flashbacks? Are the causal connections between events clear? logical? If not, can you explain why?

Source: Courtesy of Louisiana State University

KATE CHOPIN (1851–1904) was born Katherine O'Flaherty, the daughter of a wealthy Irish-born merchant and his aristocratic Creole wife. She was married at nineteen to Oscar Chopin, a Louisiana cotton broker, who took her to live first in New Orleans and later on a plantation in central Louisiana. Chopin's representations of the Cane River region and its people in two volumes of short stories—*Bayou Folk* (1894) and *A Night in Arcadie* (1897)—are the foundation of her reputation as a local colorist, a writer dedicated to creating an accurate picture of a particular region and its people.

Her honest, sexually frank stories (many of them out of print for more than half a century) were rediscovered in the 1960s and 1970s, influencing a new generation of writers. Though she was a popular contributor of stories and sketches to the magazines of her day, Chopin scandalized many critics with her outspoken novel *The Awakening* (1899), in which a woman seeks sexual and emotional fulfillment with a man who is not her husband. The book was removed from the shelves of the public library in St. Louis, where Chopin was born.

"The Story of an Hour" depicts a brief event in a woman's life, but in this single hour, Chopin reveals both a lifetime's emotional torment and the momentary joy of freedom.

Cultural Context During her marriage, Chopin lived in Louisiana, the only civil-law state in the United States. Whereas the legal systems of all other states are based on common law, the laws of Louisiana have their roots in the Napoleonic Code, the civil code enacted in France in 1804 to regulate issues of property, marriage, and divorce. This patriarchal code favored the husband in all domestic affairs and left women without many legal or fiscal rights. In "The Story of an Hour," the concept of freedom is closely tied to the prospect of escaping these restrictions.

The Story of an Hour (1894)

Knowing that Mrs. Mallard was afflicted with a heart trouble, great care was taken to break to her as gently as possible the news of her husband's death.

It was her sister Josephine who told her, in broken sentences, veiled hints that revealed in half concealing. Her husband's friend Richards was there, too, near her. It was he who had been in the newspaper office when intelligence of the railroad disaster was received, with Brently Mallard's name leading the list of "killed." He had only taken the time to assure himself of its truth by a second telegram, and had hastened to forestall any less careful, less tender friend in bearing the sad message.

She did not hear the story as many women have heard the same, with a paralyzed inability to accept its significance. She wept at once, with sudden, wild abandonment, in her sister's arms. When the storm of grief had spent itself she went away to her room alone. She would have no one follow her.

There stood, facing the open window, a comfortable, roomy armchair. Into this she sank, pressed down by a physical exhaustion that haunted her body and seemed to reach into her soul.

5   She could see in the open square before her house the tops of trees that were all aquiver with the new spring life. The delicious breath of rain was in the air. In the street below a peddler was crying his wares. The notes of a distant song which some one was singing reached her faintly, and countless sparrows were twittering in the eaves.

There were patches of blue sky showing here and there through the clouds that had met and piled one above the other in the west facing her window.

She sat with her head thrown back upon the cushion of the chair, quite motionless, except when a sob came up into her throat and shook her, as a child who has cried itself to sleep continues to sob in its dreams.

She was young, with a fair, calm face, whose lines bespoke repression and even a certain strength. But now there was a dull stare in her eyes, whose gaze was fixed away off yonder on one of those patches of blue sky. It was not a glance of reflection, but rather indicated a suspension of intelligent thought.

There was something coming to her and she was waiting for it, fearfully. What was it? She did not know; it was too subtle and elusive to name. But she felt it, creeping out of the sky, reaching toward her through the sounds, the scents, the color that filled the air.

10   Now her bosom rose and fell tumultuously. She was beginning to recognize this thing that was approaching to possess her, and she was striving to beat it back with her will—as powerless as her two white slender hands would have been.

When she abandoned herself a little whispered word escaped her slightly parted lips. She said it over and over under her breath: "Free, free, free!" The vacant stare and the look of terror that had followed it went from her eyes. They stayed keen and bright. Her pulses beat fast, and the coursing blood warmed and relaxed every inch of her body.

She did not stop to ask if it were not a monstrous joy that held her. A clear and exalted perception enabled her to dismiss the suggestion as trivial.

She knew that she would weep again when she saw the kind, tender hands folded in death; the face that had never looked save with love upon her, fixed and gray and dead. But she saw beyond that bitter moment a long procession of years to come that would belong to her absolutely. And she opened and spread her arms out to them in welcome.

There would be no one to live for during those coming years; she would live for herself. There would be no powerful will bending her in that blind persistence with which men and women believe they have a right to impose a private will upon a fellow creature. A kind intention or a cruel intention made the act seem no less a crime as she looked upon it in that brief moment of illumination.

15   And yet she had loved him—sometimes. Often she had not. What did it matter! What could love, the unsolved mystery, count for in the face of this possession of self-assertion which she suddenly recognized as the strongest impulse of her being.

"Free! Body and soul free!" she kept whispering.

Josephine was kneeling before the closed door with her lips to the key-hole, imploring for admission. "Louise, open the door! I beg; open the door—you will make yourself ill. What are you doing, Louise? For heaven's sake open the door."

"Go away. I am not making myself ill." No; she was drinking in a very elixir of life through that open window.

Her fancy was running riot along those days ahead of her. Spring days, and summer days, and all sorts of days that would be her own. She breathed a quick prayer that life might be long. It was only yesterday she had thought with a shudder that life might be long.

She arose at length and opened the door to her sister's importunities. There was a feverish triumph in her eyes, and she carried herself unwittingly like a goddess of Victory. She clasped her sister's waist, and together they descended the stairs. Richards stood waiting for them at the bottom.

Some one was opening the front door with a latchkey. It was Brently Mallard who entered, a little travel-stained, composedly carrying his grip-sack and umbrella. He had been far from the scene of the accident, and did not even know there had been one. He stood amazed at Josephine's piercing cry; at Richards' quick motion to screen him from the view of his wife.

But Richards was too late.

When the doctors came they said she had died of heart disease—of joy that kills.

Reading and Reacting

1. The story's basic exposition is presented in its first two paragraphs. What additional information about character or setting would you like to know? Why do you suppose Chopin does not supply this information?

2. "The Story of an Hour" is a very economical story, with little action or dialogue. Do you see this economy as a strength or a weakness? Explain.

3. When "The Story of an Hour" was first published in *Vogue* magazine in 1894, the magazine's editors titled it "The Dream of an Hour." A film version, echoing the last words of the story, is called *The Joy That Kills*. Which of the three titles do you believe most accurately represents what happens in the story? Why?

4. Do you think Brently Mallard physically abused his wife? Did he love her? Did she love him? Exactly why was she so relieved to be rid of him? Can you answer any of these questions with certainty?

5. What is the nature of the conflict in this story? Who, or what, do you see as Mrs. Mallard's antagonist?

6. What emotions does Mrs. Mallard experience during the hour she spends alone in her room? What events do you imagine take place during this same period outside her room? outside her house?

7. Do you find the story's ending satisfying? believable? contrived?

8. Was the story's ending unexpected, or were you prepared for it? What elements in the story foreshadow this ending?

9. **Journal Entry** Rewrite the story's ending, substituting a few paragraphs of your own for the last three paragraphs.

10. **CRITICAL PERSPECTIVE** Kate Chopin is widely viewed today as an early feminist writer whose work often addressed the social injustices and inequalities that women faced during the second half of the nineteenth century. According to literary critic Elaine Showalter, "The Story of an Hour" was written during a period in which women writers were able to "reject the accommodating postures of femininity and to use literature to dramatize the ordeals of wronged womanhood."

Do you think this story rejects the "postures of femininity"? What "ordeals of wronged womanhood" are being dramatized here?

Related Works: "The Storm" (p. 273), "The Yellow Wallpaper" (p. 379), "If I should learn, in some quite casual way" (p. 775), "Women" (p. 846), *A Doll House* (p. 1138), *Trifles* (p. 1604)

ORHAN PAMUK (1952–   ) grew up in Istanbul, Turkey, the focus of his memoir *Istanbul: Memories and the City* (2003). Pamuk has published several novels and an essay collection, *Other Colors* (1999). He holds several honorary degrees from universities around the world and is the recipient of numerous awards and honors, including the 2006 Nobel Prize in Literature.

Cultural Context According to the Organization for Economic Cooperation and Development, two percent of global trade is in counterfeit goods, including handbags, shoes, watches, and pharmaceuticals. Some of the most popular handbag knockoffs are those imitating the brands Chanel, Coach, Gucci, Prada, Kate Spade, and Louis Vuitton. In this story, a character identifies a fake purse by its poor stitching. Other telltale signs of a counterfeit purse include cheap fabric or hardware and the use of colors that are not typical for a particular brand.

Distant Relations (2009)

Translated from the Turkish by Maureen Freely

The series of events and coincidences that would change my entire life began on April 27, 1975, when Sibel happened to spot a purse designed by the famous Jenny Colon in a shopwindow as we were walking along Valikonagi Avenue, enjoying the cool spring evening. Our formal engagement was not far off; we were tipsy and in high spirits. We'd just been to Fuaye, a posh new restaurant in Nisantasi; over dinner with my parents, we'd discussed at length the preparations for the engagement party, which was scheduled for the middle of June, so that Nurcihan, Sibel's friend since her days at the Lycée Notre Dame de Sion, in Paris, could come from France to attend. Sibel had long ago arranged for her engagement dress to be made by Silky Ismet, who was then the most expensive and sought-after dressmaker in Istanbul, and that evening Sibel and my mother discussed how they might sew on the pearls that my mother had given her for the dress. It was my future father-in-law's express wish that his only daughter's engagement party be as extravagant as a wedding, and my mother was delighted to help fulfill that wish as best she could. As for my father, he was charmed enough by the prospect of a daughter-in-law who had "studied at the Sorbonne," as was said in those days among the Istanbul bourgeoisie of any girl who had gone to Paris for any kind of education.

It was as I was walking Sibel home that evening, my arm wrapped lovingly around her sturdy shoulders, and thinking with pride how happy and lucky I was, that she said, "Oh, what a beautiful bag!" Though my mind was clouded by the wine I'd drunk at dinner, I took note of the purse and the name of the shop, and the next day I went back. In fact, I had never been one of those suave, chivalrous playboys who are always looking for the slightest excuse to buy women presents or send them flowers, though perhaps I longed to be. In those days, bored Westernized housewives in the affluent neighborhoods of Sisli, Nisantasi, and Bebek did not open "art galleries," as they did later, but ran boutiques, stocking them with trinkets and entire ensembles smuggled in their luggage from Paris and Milan or with copies of "the latest" dresses featured in imported magazines like *Elle* and *Vogue*, and selling these goods at ridiculously inflated prices to other rich housewives who were as bored as they were.

The proprietress of the Sanzelize (its name a transliteration of the legendary Parisian avenue), Senay Hanim, was a very distant relation on my mother's side, but she wasn't there when I walked into the boutique at around twelve and the small bronze double-knobbed camel bell jingled two notes that can still make my heart pound. It was a warm day, but inside the shop it was cool and dark. At first I thought that there was no one there, my eyes still adjusting to the gloom after the noonday sunlight. Then I felt my heart rise into my throat, with the force of an immense wave about to crash against the shore.

"I'd like to buy the handbag on the mannequin in the window," I managed to say, staggered by the sight of her.

"Do you mean the cream-colored Jenny Colon?"   5

When we came eye to eye, I immediately remembered her.

"The handbag on the mannequin in the window," I repeated dreamily.

"Oh, right," she said and walked over to the window. In a flash she had slipped off one of her high-heeled yellow pumps, extending her bare foot, whose nails she'd carefully painted red, onto the floor of the display area, and stretching her arm toward the mannequin. My eyes travelled from her empty shoe over her long bare legs. It wasn't even May yet, and they were already tanned.

Their length made her lacy yellow skirt seem even shorter. Hooking the bag, she returned to the counter and, with slender, dexterous fingers, removed the balls of crumpled tissue paper, showing me the inside of the zippered pocket, the two smaller pockets (both empty), and also a secret compartment, from which she produced a card inscribed "Jenny Colon," her whole demeanor suggesting mystery and seriousness, as if she were showing me something very personal.

"Hello, Füsun," I said. "You're all grown up! Perhaps you don't recognize me."   10

"Of course, Kemal, sir, I recognized you right away, but when I saw that you did not recognize me I thought it would be better not to disturb you."

There was a silence. I looked again at one of the pockets she had pointed to inside the bag. Her beauty, or her skirt, which was in fact too short, or something else altogether, had unsettled me, and I couldn't act naturally.

"Well . . . what are you up to these days?"

"I'm studying for my university entrance exams. And I come here every day, too. Here in the shop, I'm meeting lots of new people."

15   "That's wonderful. So, tell me, how much is this handbag?"

Furrowing her brow, she peered at the handwritten price tag on the bottom: "One thousand five hundred liras." (At the time, this would have been six months' pay for a junior civil servant.) "But I am sure Senay Hanim would want to offer you a special price. She's gone home for lunch and must be napping now, so I can't phone her. But if you could come by this evening . . ."

"It's not important," I said, and, taking out my wallet—a clumsy gesture that, later, Füsun often mimicked—I counted out the damp bills. Füsun wrapped the purse in paper, carefully but with evident inexperience, and then put it into a plastic bag. Throughout this process she knew that I was admiring her honey-hued arms and her quick, elegant gestures. When she politely handed me the shopping bag, I thanked her. "Please give my regards to Aunt Nesibe and your father," I said, having failed to remember his name in time. Then, for a moment, I paused: my ghost had left my body and was now, in some corner of Heaven, embracing Füsun and kissing her. I made quickly for the door. The bell jingled, and I heard a canary warbling. I went out into the street, glad to feel the heat. I was pleased with my purchase; I loved Sibel very much. I decided to forget this shop, and Füsun.

Nevertheless, at dinner that evening I mentioned to my mother that I had run into our distant relation Füsun while buying a handbag for Sibel.

"Oh, yes, Nesibe's daughter is working in that shop of Senay's, and what a shame it is!" my mother said. "They don't even visit us for the holidays anymore. That beauty contest put them in such an awkward spot. I walk past the shop every day, but I can't even bring myself to go inside and say hello to the poor girl—nor, in fact, does it even cross my mind. But when she was little, you know, I was very fond of her. When Nesibe came to sew, she'd come, too, sometimes. I'd get your toys out of the cupboard and, while her mother sewed, she'd play with them quietly. Nesibe's mother, Aunt Mihriver, may she rest in peace—she was such a wonderful person, too."

20   "Exactly how are we related?"

Because my father was watching television and paying us no mind, my mother launched into an elaborate story about her father, who was born the same year as Atatürk and, just like the founder of the Republic, attended Semsi Efendi School. It seems that long before my grandfather, Ethem Kemal, married my grandmother he had made a very hasty first marriage, at the age of twenty-three, to Füsun's great-grandmother, who was of Bosnian extraction, and who died in the Balkan wars, during the evacuation of Edirne. Though the unfortunate woman had not given Ethem Kemal children, she had already had a daughter, named Mihriver, by a poor sheikh, whom she'd married when she was "still a child." So Aunt Mihriver (Füsun's grandmother, who had been brought up by a very odd assortment of people) and her daughter, Nesibe Hanim (Füsun's mother), were not, strictly speaking, relatives; they were more like in-laws, and though my mother had always emphasized this she had still directed us to call the women from this far branch of the family "Aunt." During their last holiday visit, my mother had given these impoverished relations (who lived in the backstreets of Tesvikiye) an unusually chilly reception that had led to hurt feelings, because, two years earlier, Aunt Nesibe, without saying a word, had allowed her sixteen-year-old daughter, then a student at Nisantasi Lycée for Girls, to enter a beauty contest. My mother, on subsequently learning that Aunt Nesibe had in fact encouraged her daughter, even taking pride in this stunt, which should have caused her to feel only shame, had hardened her heart against Aunt Nesibe, whom she had once so loved and protected.

For her part, Aunt Nesibe had always esteemed my mother, who was twenty years older and had been supportive of her when she was a young woman going from house to house in Istanbul's most affluent neighborhoods, in search of work as a seamstress.

"They were desperately poor," my mother said. And, lest she exaggerate, she added, "Though they were hardly the only ones, my son—all of Turkey was poor in those days." My mother had recommended Aunt Nesibe to all her friends, and once a year (sometimes twice) she herself would call her to our house to sew a dress for some party or wedding.

Because these sewing visits almost always took place during school hours, I didn't see her much. But in 1957, at the end of August, my mother, urgently needing a dress for a wedding, had called Nesibe to our summer home, in Suadiye. Retiring to the back room on the second floor, overlooking the sea, she and Nesibe set themselves up next to the window, from which, peering between the fronds of the palm trees, they might see the rowboats and motorboats and the boys jumping off the pier. When Nesibe had unpacked her sewing box, whose lid was adorned with a view of Istanbul, they sat surrounded by her scissors, pins, measuring tape, thimbles, and swatches of lace and other material, complaining of the heat, the mosquitoes, and the strain of sewing under such pressure, joking like sisters, and staying up half the night to slave away on my mother's Singer sewing machine. I remember Bekri, the cook, bringing one glass of lemonade after another into that room (the hot air thick with the dust of velvet), because Nesibe, who was twenty and pregnant, was prone to cravings; when we all sat down to lunch, my mother would tell Bekri, half joking, "Whatever a pregnant woman desires, you must let her have, or else the child will turn out ugly!" And, with that in mind, I remember looking at Nesibe's small bump with a certain interest. That must have been my first awareness of Füsun's existence, though no one knew yet whether she was a girl or a boy.

"Nesibe didn't even inform her husband—she just lied about her daughter's age and entered her in that beauty contest," my mother said, fuming at the thought. "Thank God, she didn't win, so they were spared that public disgrace. If the school authorities had got wind of it, they would have expelled the girl. . . . She must have finished lycée by now. I don't expect that she'll be doing any further studies, but I'm not up to date, since they don't come to visit on holidays anymore. . . . Can there be anyone in this country who doesn't know what kind of girl, what kind of woman, enters a beauty contest? How did she behave with you?"

This was my mother's way of suggesting that Füsun had begun to sleep with men. I'd heard the same from my Nisantasi playboy friends when Füsun appeared in a photograph with the other finalists in the newspaper *Milliyet*, but as I'd found the whole thing embarrassing I tried to show no interest. After we both fell silent, my mother wagged her finger at me ominously and said, "Be careful! You're about to become

25

engaged to a very special, very charming, very lovely girl! Why don't you show me this purse you've bought her. Mümtaz!"—she was calling my father—"Look! Kemal's bought Sibel a purse!"

"Really?" my father said, his contented expression suggesting that he had seen and approved of the bag as a sign of how happy his son and his son's sweetheart were, though not once did he take his eyes off the screen.

Once I'd graduated from business school in America and completed my military service, my father demanded that I follow in my brother's footsteps and become a manager in his business, which was growing by leaps and bounds, and so when I was still very young he appointed me the general manager of Satsat, his distribution-and-export firm. Satsat had an inflated operating budget and made hefty profits, thanks not to me but to various accounting tricks by which profits from my father's other factories and businesses were funnelled into Satsat (which could be translated into English as "Sellsell"). I spent my days mastering the finer points of the business from worn-out accountants, twenty or thirty years my senior, and large-breasted lady clerks as old as my mother; mindful that I would not have been in charge if I weren't the owner's son, I tried to show some humility.

At quitting time, while buses and streetcars as old as Satsat's clerks rumbled down the avenue, shaking the building to its foundations, Sibel, my intended, would come to visit, and we would make love in my office. Despite her modern outlook and the feminist notions she had brought back from Europe, Sibel's ideas about secretaries were no different from my mother's. "Let's not make love here. It makes me feel like a secretary!" she'd say sometimes. But, as we proceeded to the leather sofa in the office, the real reason for her reserve—that Turkish girls, in those days, were afraid of sex before marriage—became obvious.

30   Little by little, sophisticated girls from wealthy Westernized families who had spent time in Europe were beginning to break this taboo and sleep with their boyfriends before marriage. Sibel, who occasionally boasted of being one of those "brave" girls, had first slept with me eleven months earlier. But, by this point, she felt that the arrangement had gone on long enough and it was about time we married. I do not want to exaggerate my fiancée's daring or make light of the sexual oppression of women, because it was only when Sibel saw that my "intentions were serious," when she was confident that I was "someone who could be trusted"—in other words, when she was absolutely sure that there would, in the end, be a wedding—that she gave herself to me. Believing myself a decent and responsible person, I had every intention of marrying her; but, even if I hadn't wished to, there was no question of my having a choice now that she had "given me her virginity." Before long, this burden cast a shadow over the common ground between us, which we were so proud of—the illusion of being "free and modern" (though, of course, we would never have used such words for ourselves), on account of having made love before marriage—and in a way this, too, brought us closer.

A similar shadow fell over us each time Sibel anxiously hinted that we should set a date soon, but there were also times when she and I were very happy, making love in the office, and I remember wrapping my arms around her in the dark, as the noise of traffic and rumbling buses rose from Halaskargazi Avenue, and telling myself how lucky I was, how content I would be for the rest of my life. Once, after our exertions, as I was stubbing out my cigarette in an ashtray bearing the Satsat logo, Sibel, sitting half naked on my secretary's chair, started tapping at the typewriter, and giggling over her impression of the dumb blonde who featured so prominently in the jokes and humor magazines of the time.

Over dinner at Fuaye on the evening of the day I bought the purse, I asked Sibel, "Wouldn't it be better if from now on we met in that flat my mother has in the Merhamet Apartments? It looks out over such a pretty garden."

"Are you expecting some delay in moving to our own house once we're married?" she asked.

"No, darling, I meant nothing of the sort."

"I don't want to skulk about in secret apartments, as if I were your mistress."   35

"You're right."

"Where did this idea come from, to meet in that apartment?"

"Never mind," I said. I looked at the cheerful crowd around me as I brought out the purse, still hidden in its plastic bag.

"What's this?" Sibel asked, sensing a present.

"A surprise! Open and see."   40

"Is it really?" When she opened the plastic bag and saw the purse, the childish joy on her face gave way first to a quizzical look, and then to a disappointment that she tried to hide.

"Do you remember?" I ventured. "When I was walking you home last night, you saw it in the window of that shop and admired it."

"Oh, yes. How thoughtful of you."

"I'm glad you like it. It will look so elegant on your arm at our engagement party."

"I hate to say it, but the purse I'm taking to our engagement party was chosen a   45
long time ago," Sibel said. "Oh, don't look so downcast! It was so thoughtful of you to go to all the effort of buying this lovely present for me. . . . All right then, just so you don't think I'm being unkind to you. I could never put this purse on my arm at our engagement party, because this purse is a fake!"

"What?"

"This is not a genuine Jenny Colon, my dear Kemal. It's an imitation."

"How can you tell?"

"Just by looking at it, dear. See the way the label is stitched to the leather? Now look at the stitching in this real Jenny Colon I bought in Paris. It's not for nothing that it's an exclusive brand in France and all over the world. She would never use such cheap thread."

For a moment, as I looked at the genuine stitching, I asked myself why my future   50
bride was taking such a triumphant tone. Sibel was the daughter of a retired ambassador who had long since sold off his pasha grandfather's land and was now penniless; technically, this made her the daughter of a civil servant, and this status sometimes caused her to feel uneasy and insecure. Whenever her anxieties overtook her, she would talk about her paternal grandmother, who had played the piano, or about her paternal grandfather, who had fought in the War of Independence, or she'd tell me how close her maternal grandfather had been to Sultan Abdülhamid. But her timidity moved me, and I loved her all the more for it. With the expansion of the textile and export trades in the early seventies, and the consequent tripling of Istanbul's

population, the price of land had skyrocketed throughout the city and particularly in neighborhoods like ours. Although my father's fortune, carried on this wave, had grown extravagantly over the past decade, increasing fivefold, our surname (Basmaci, "cloth printer") left no doubt that we owed our wealth to generations of cloth manufacture. It made me uneasy to be troubled by the "fake" purse, despite all our cumulative progress.

When she saw my spirits sink, Sibel caressed my hand. "How much did you pay for the bag?"

"Fifteen hundred liras," I said. "If you don't want it, I can exchange it tomorrow."

"Don't exchange it, darling. Ask for your money back, because they really cheated you."

"The owner of the shop is Senay Hanim, and we're distantly related!" I said, raising my eyebrows in dismay.

55 Sibel took back the bag, whose interiors I had been quietly exploring. "You're so knowledgeable, darling, so clever and cultured," she said, with a tender smile, "but you have absolutely no idea how easily women can trick you."

At noon the next day, I went back to the Sanzelize Boutique carrying the purse in the same plastic bag. The bell rang as I walked in, but once again the shop was so gloomy that at first I thought no one was there. In the strange silence of the ill-lit shop, the canary sang *chik-chik-chik*. Then I made out Füsun's shadow through a screen, between the leaves of a huge vase of cyclamens. She was waiting on a fat lady, who was trying on an outfit in the fitting room. This time, she was wearing a charming and flattering blouse, a print of hyacinths intertwined with leaves and wildflowers. When she looked around the screen and saw me, she smiled sweetly.

"You seem busy," I said, indicating the fitting room with my eyes.

"We're just about finished," she said, as if to imply that she and her customer were just talking idly at this point.

My eyes caught the canary, fluttering up and down in its cage, a pile of fashion magazines in the corner, and an assortment of accessories imported from Europe, but I couldn't fix my attention on anything. Much as I wanted to dismiss the feeling as ordinary, I could not deny the startling truth that when I looked at Füsun I saw someone familiar, someone I felt I knew intimately. She resembled me. The same sort of hair that grew curly and dark in childhood only to straighten as we grew older. On her, it was now a shade of blond, which, like her clear complexion, was complemented by her print blouse. I felt that I could easily put myself in her place, could understand her deeply. A painful memory came to me: my friends referring to her as "something out of *Playboy*." Could she have slept with them? "Return the purse, take your money, and run," I told myself. "You're about to become engaged to a wonderful girl." I turned to look outside, in the direction of Nisantasi Square, but soon Füsun's reflection appeared ghostlike in the smoky glass.

60 After the woman in the fitting room huffed and puffed her way out of a skirt and left without buying anything, Füsun folded up the rejected items and put them back where they belonged. "I saw you walking down the street yesterday evening," she said, turning up her beautiful lips. She was wearing a light-pink lipstick, sold under the brand name Misslyn, and though it was a common Turkish product, on her it looked exotic and alluring.

"When did you see me?" I asked.

"Early in the evening. You were with Sibel Hanim. I was walking down the side-walk on the other side of the street. Were you going out to eat?"

"Yes."

"You make a handsome couple!" she said, as the elderly do when taking pleasure in the sight of happy young people.

I did not ask her how she knew Sibel. "There's a small favor we'd like to ask of you," I said. As I took out the bag, I felt both embarrassment and panic. "We'd like to return this bag." 65

"Certainly. I'd be happy to exchange it for you. You might like these chic new gloves and we have this hat, which has just arrived from Paris. Sibel Hanim didn't like the bag?"

"I'd prefer not to exchange it," I said shamefacedly. "I'd like to ask for my money back."

I saw shock on her face, even some fear. "Why?" she asked.

"Apparently this bag is not a genuine Jenny Colon," I whispered. "It seems that it's a fake."

"What?" 70

"I don't really understand these things," I said helplessly.

"Nothing like that ever happens here!" she said in a harsh voice. "Do you want your money back right now?"

"Yes!" I blurted out.

She looked deeply pained. Dear God, I thought, why hadn't I just disposed of the bag and told Sibel I'd got the money back? "Look, this has nothing to do with you or Senay Hanim. We Turks, praise God, manage to make imitations of every European fashion," I said, struggling to smile. "For me—or should I say for us—it's enough for a bag to fulfill its function, to look lovely in a woman's hand. It's not important what the brand is, or who made it, or if it's an original." But Füsun, like me, didn't believe a word I was saying.

"No, I am going to give you your money back," she said in that same harsh voice. I looked down and remained silent, prepared to meet my fate, and ashamed of my brutishness. 75

Determined as she sounded, I sensed that Füsun could not do what she intended to do; there was something strange in the intensely embarrassing moment. She was looking at the till as if someone had put a spell on it, as if it were possessed by demons and she couldn't bring herself to touch it. When I saw her face redden and crinkle up, her eyes welling with tears, I panicked and drew two steps closer.

She began to cry softly. I have never worked out exactly how it happened, but I wrapped my arms around her and she leaned her head against my chest and wept. "Füsun, I'm so sorry," I whispered. I caressed her soft hair and her forehead. "Please, just forget this ever happened. It's a fake purse, that's all."

Like a child, she took a deep breath, sobbed once or twice, then burst into tears again. To touch her body and her beautiful arms, to feel her breasts pressed against my chest, to hold her like that, if only briefly, made my head spin. Perhaps it was because I was trying to repress my desire, stronger each time I touched her, that I conjured up the illusion that we had known each other for years, that we were already very close.

She was my sweet, inconsolable, grief-stricken, beautiful sister! For a moment—and perhaps because I knew that we were related, however distantly—her body, with its long limbs, fine bones, and fragile shoulders, reminded me of my own. Had I been a girl, had I been twelve years younger, this was what my body would have been like. "There's nothing to be upset about," I said, as I caressed her blond hair.

"I can't open the till to give you back your money," she explained. "Because when Senay Hanim goes home for lunch she locks it and takes the key with her, I'm ashamed to say." Leaning her head against my chest, she began to cry again, as I continued my careful and compassionate caressing of her hair. "I just work here to meet people and pass the time. It's not for the money," she said, sobbing.

80   "Working for money is nothing to be embarrassed about," I said stupidly, heartlessly.

"Yes," she said, like a dejected child. "My father is a retired teacher. . . . I turned eighteen two weeks ago, and I didn't want to be a burden."

Fearful of the sexual beast now threatening to rear its head, I took my hand from her hair. She understood at once and collected herself; we both stepped back.

"Please don't tell anyone I cried," she said, after rubbing her eyes.

"It's a promise," I said. "A solemn promise between friends, Füsun. We can trust each other with our secrets."

85   I saw her smile. "Let me leave the purse here," I said. "I can come back for the money later."

"Leave the bag if you wish, but it'd be better if you didn't come back here for the money. Senay Hanim will insist that it isn't a fake and you'll come to regret that you ever suggested otherwise."

"Then let's exchange it for something," I said.

"I can no longer do that," she said, sounding like a proud and tetchy girl.

"No, really, it's not important," I offered.

90   "But it is to me," she said firmly. "When Senay Hanim comes back to the shop, I'll get the money from her."

"I don't want that woman causing you any more upset," I replied.

"Don't worry, I've just worked out how to do it," she said with the faintest of smiles. "I'm going to say that Sibel Hanim already has exactly the same bag, and that's why she's returning it. Is that all right?"

"Wonderful idea," I said. "But why don't I say that to Senay Hanim?"

"No, don't you say anything to her," Füsun said emphatically. "Because she'll only try to trick you, to extract personal information from you. Don't come to the shop at all. I can leave the money with Aunt Vecihe."

95   "Oh, please, don't involve my mother in this. She's even nosier."

"Then where shall I leave your money?" Füsun asked, raising her eyebrows.

"At the Merhamet Apartments, 131 Tesvikiye Avenue, where my mother has a flat," I said. "Before I went to America, I used it as my hideout—I'd go there to study and listen to music. It's a delightful place that looks out over a garden in the back. . . . I still go there at lunchtime, between two and four, to catch up on paperwork."

"Of course. I can bring your money there. What's the apartment number?"

"Four," I whispered. I could barely get out the next three words, which seemed to die in my throat. "Second floor. Goodbye."

My heart had figured it all out and was beating madly. Before rushing outside, I 100
gathered up my strength and, pretending that nothing unusual had happened, gave
her one last look. Back in the street, my shame and guilt mixed with so many images
of bliss in the unseasonable warmth of that April afternoon that the very sidewalks of
Nisantasi seemed aglow with a mysterious yellow. My feet chose the shaded path, taking me under the eaves of the buildings and the blue-and-white striped awnings of the
shopwindows, and when, in one of those windows, I saw a yellow jug, I felt compelled
to go inside and buy it. Unlike any other object acquired so casually, this yellow jug
drew no comment from anyone during the twenty years that it sat on the table where
my mother and father and, later, my mother and I ate our meals. Every time I touched
the handle of that jug, I would remember those days when I first felt the misery that
was to turn me in on myself, leaving my mother to watch me in silence at dinner, her
eyes filled half with sadness, half with reproach.

Arriving home, I greeted my mother with a kiss; though pleased to see me early in
the afternoon, she was nevertheless surprised. I told her that I had bought the jug on a
whim, adding, "Could you give me the key to the Merhamet Apartments? Sometimes
the office gets so noisy I just can't concentrate. I was wondering if I might have better
luck at the apartment. It always worked when I was young."

My mother said, "It must be an inch thick with dust," but she went straight to her
room to fetch the key to the building, which was attached to the apartment key by a
red ribbon. "Do you remember that Kütahya vase with the red flowers?" she asked as
she handed me the keys. "I can't find it anywhere in the house, so can you check to
see if I took it over there? And don't work so hard. . . . Your father spent his whole
life working hard so that you young ones could have some fun in life. You deserve
to be happy. Take Sibel out and enjoy the spring air." Then, pressing the keys into
my hand, she gave me a strange look and said, "Be careful!" It was the look that she
would give us when we were children, to warn us that life held unsuspected dangers
that were far deeper and more treacherous than, for instance, failing to take proper
care of a key.

Reading and Reacting

1. The first paragraph presents the story's exposition. What information about characters
   and setting is revealed here? What essential information is not revealed?
2. Where else in the story is background information presented? What do readers learn from
   this information? Is all of this background essential to our understanding of the story, or
   could some be deleted?
3. Füsun is a "distant relation" (par. 18) of the narrator's family. To what other "distant relations" might the story's title refer? (For example, what other meanings might the words
   distant and *relations* suggest?)
4. In the opening paragraph, the narrator announces that a "series of events and coincidences" changed his life. What are these "events and coincidences"? How do you think
   they changed his life?
5. Identify some examples of the narrator's physical description of Füsun. How is Sibel
   described? What do these descriptions suggest about the way the narrator views the two
   women?

6. The purse that the narrator buys for Sibel turns out to be a fake. Given this development, do you see the purse as a symbol? Why, or why not? What might it symbolize?

7. In paragraph 17, the narrator refers to "a clumsy gesture that, later, Füsun often mimicked." What do the words *later* and *often* suggest here? In what sense is this reference an example of foreshadowing? What other examples of foreshadowing can you identify in the story?

8. In paragraph 59, the narrator says, "Much as I wanted to dismiss the feeling as ordinary, I could not deny the startling truth that when I looked at Füsun I saw someone familiar, someone I felt I knew intimately. She resembled me." What is the significance of this "feeling"—and of the similar observation the narrator makes in paragraph 78?

9. At the end of the story, why does the narrator's mother tell him to be careful? What does she know (or suspect)? Do you think she is right?

10. **JOURNAL ENTRY** How would you characterize the narrator's attitude about his job? How is it similar to his attitude toward Sibel?

11. **CRITICAL PERSPECTIVE** In her review of Pamuk's book *The Innocence of Objects*, Presca Ahn describes the role of "nostalgia" in Pamuk's fiction. In what sense is the narrator of "Distant Relations" nostalgic? What exactly is he longing for?

Related Works: "Gryphon" (p. 250), "The Girl with Bangs" (p. 262), "The Storm" (p. 273), "Araby" (p. 361), *Beauty* (p. 1087).

NEIL GAIMAN (1960–   ) grew up in England and currently lives in Minnesota. The author of numerous critically acclaimed stories, novels, and graphic fiction for children and adults, Gaiman is also a screenwriter, film director, and essayist. Largely dealing with fantasy and science fiction subjects, his work has been translated into numerous languages. Gaiman is also the author of the award-winning comics series *Sandman*. In discussing his novel *Anansi Boys* (2005), Gaiman provides a description that applies to much of his work: "It's a scary, funny sort of a story, which isn't exactly a thriller, and isn't really horror, and doesn't quite qualify as a ghost story (although it has at least one ghost in it), or a romantic comedy (although there are several romances in there, and it's certainly a comedy, except for the scary bits)."

Cultural Context   The concept of "aliens living among us" is a popular subject in the science fiction genre. Classic science fiction films that explore this theme include *The Day the Earth Stood Still* (originally released in 1951 and remade in 2008), *The Thing* (originally released in 1951 and remade in 1982 and 2011), *Invasion of the Body Snatchers* (1956), and *The Blob* (1958). More recent "aliens among us" films include *E.T.: The Extra-Terrestrial* (1982) and the *Men in Black* movies (1997, 2002, and 2012). While the classics tend to depict aliens as evil and scary, some of the newer films show the "human" side of our alien counterparts. In "How to Talk to Girls at Parties," Gaiman builds on this science fiction tradition by depicting young, enticing girls as aliens who forever change the male protagonists' attitudes toward lust and temptation.

How to Talk to Girls at Parties (2007)

"Come on," said Vic. "It'll be great."

"No, it won't," I said, although I'd lost this fight hours ago, and I knew it.

"It'll be brilliant," said Vic, for the hundredth time. "Girls! Girls! Girls!" He grinned with white teeth.

We both attended an all-boys' school in South London. While it would be a lie to say that we had no experience with girls—Vic seemed to have had many girlfriends, while I had kissed three of my sister's friends—it would, I think, be perfectly true to say that we both chiefly spoke to, interacted with, and only truly understood, other boys. Well, I did, anyway. It's hard to speak for someone else, and I've not seen Vic for thirty years. I'm not sure that I would know what to say to him now if I did.

We were walking the back streets that used to twine in a grimy maze behind East Croydon station—a friend had told Vic about a party, and Vic was determined to go whether I liked it or not, and I didn't. But my parents were away that week at a conference, and I was Vic's guest at his house, so I was trailing along beside him.

"It'll be the same as it always is," I said. "After an hour you'll be off somewhere snogging the prettiest girl at the party, and I'll be in the kitchen listening to somebody's mum going on about politics or poetry or something."

"You just have to *talk* to them," he said. "I think it's probably that road at the end here." He gestured cheerfully, swinging the bag with the bottle in it.

"Don't you know?"

"Alison gave me directions and I wrote them on a bit of paper, but I left it on the hall table. S'okay. I can find it."

"How?" Hope welled slowly up inside me.

"We walk down the road," he said, as if speaking to an idiot child. "And we look for the party. Easy."

I looked, but saw no party: just narrow houses with rusting cars or bikes in their concreted front gardens; and the dusty glass fronts of newsagents, which smelled of alien spices and sold everything from birthday cards and second-hand comics to the kind of magazines that were so pornographic that they were sold already sealed in plastic bags. I had been there when Vic had slipped one of those magazines beneath his sweater, but the owner caught him on the pavement outside and made him give it back.

We reached the end of the road and turned into a narrow street of terraced houses. Everything looked very still and empty in the Summer's evening. "It's all right for you," I said. "They fancy you. You don't actually *have* to talk to them." It was true: one urchin grin from Vic and he could have his pick of the room.

"Nah. S'not like that. You've just got to talk."

The times I had kissed my sister's friends I had not spoken to them. They had been around while my sister was off doing something elsewhere, and they had drifted into my orbit, and so I had kissed them. I do not remember any talking. I did not know what to say to girls, and I told him so.

"They're just girls," said Vic. "They don't come from another planet."

As we followed the curve of the road around, my hopes that the party would prove unfindable began to fade: a low pulsing noise, music muffled by walls and doors, could be heard from a house up ahead. It was eight in the evening, not that early if you aren't yet sixteen, and we weren't. Not quite.

I had parents who liked to know where I was, but I don't think Vic's parents cared that much. He was the youngest of five boys. That in itself seemed magical to me: I merely had two sisters, both younger than I was, and I felt both unique and lonely. I had wanted a brother as far back as I could remember. When I turned thirteen, I stopped wishing on falling stars or first stars, but back when I did, a brother was what I had wished for.

We went up the garden path, crazy paving leading us past a hedge and a solitary rose bush to a pebble-dashed facade. We rang the doorbell, and the door was opened by a girl. I could not have told you how old she was, which was one of the things about girls I had begun to hate: when you start out as kids you're just boys and girls, going through time at the same speed, and you're all five, or seven, or eleven, together. And then one day there's a lurch and the girls just sort of sprint off into the future ahead of you, and they know all about everything, and they have periods and breasts and makeup and God-only-knew-what-else—for I certainly didn't. The diagrams in biology textbooks were no substitute for being, in a very real sense, young adults. And the girls of our age were.

20   Vic and I weren't young adults, and I was beginning to suspect that even when I started needing to shave every day, instead of once every couple of weeks, I would still be way behind.

The girl said, "Hello?"

Vic said, "We're friends of Alison's." We had met Alison, all freckles and orange hair and a wicked smile, in Hamburg, on a German Exchange. The exchange organizers had sent some girls with us, from a local girls' school, to balance the sexes. The girls, our age, more or less, were raucous and funny, and had more or less adult boyfriends with cars and jobs and motorbikes and—in the case of one girl with crooked teeth and a raccoon coat, who spoke to me about it sadly at the end of a party in Hamburg, in, of course, the kitchen—a wife and kids.

"She isn't here," said the girl at the door. "No Alison,"

"Not to worry," said Vic, with an easy grin. "I'm Vic. This is Enn." A beat, and then the girl smiled back at him. Vic had a bottle of white wine in a plastic bag, removed from his parents' kitchen cabinet. "Where should I put this, then?"

25   She stood out of the way, letting us enter. "There's a kitchen in the back," she said. "Put it on the table there, with the other bottles." She had golden, wavy hair, and she was very beautiful. The hall was dim in the twilight, but I could see that she was beautiful.

"What's your name, then?" said Vic.

She told him it was Stella, and he grinned his crooked white grin and told her that that had to be the prettiest name he had ever heard. Smooth bastard. And what was worse was that he said it like he meant it.

Vic headed back to drop off the wine in the kitchen, and I looked into the front room, where the music was coming from. There were people dancing in there. Stella walked in, and she started to dance, swaying to the music all alone, and I watched her.

This was during the early days of punk. On our own record players we would play the Adverts and the Jam, the Stranglers and the Clash and the Sex Pistols. At other people's parties you'd hear ELO or 10cc or even Roxy Music. Maybe some Bowie, if you were lucky. During the German Exchange, the only LP that we had all been able to agree on was Neil Young's *Harvest*, and his song "Heart of Gold" had threaded through the trip like a refrain; *I crossed the ocean for a heart of gold.* . . .

30   The music playing in that front room wasn't anything I recognized. It sounded a bit like a German electronic pop group called Kraftwerk, and a bit like an LP I'd been given for my last birthday, of strange sounds made by the BBC Radiophonic

Workshop. The music had a beat, though, and the half-dozen girls in that room were moving gently to it, although I only looked at Stella. She shone.

Vic pushed past me, into the room. He was holding a can of lager. "There's booze back in the kitchen," he told me. He wandered over to Stella and he began to talk to her. I couldn't hear what they were saying over the music, but I knew that there was no room for me in that conversation.

I didn't like beer, not back then. I went off to see if there was something I wanted to drink. On the kitchen table stood a large bottle of Coca-Cola, and I poured myself a plastic tumblerful, and I didn't dare say anything to the pair of girls who were talking in the underlit kitchen. They were animated and utterly lovely. Each of them had very black skin and glossy hair and movie star clothes, and their accents were foreign, and each of them was out of my league.

I wandered, Coke in hand.

The house was deeper than it looked, larger and more complex than the two-up two-down model I had imagined. The rooms were underlit—I doubt there was a bulb of more than forty watts in the building—and each room I went into was inhabited: in my memory, inhabited only by girls. I did not go upstairs.

A girl was the only occupant of the conservatory. Her hair was so fair it was white, and long, and straight, and she sat at the glass-topped table, her hands clasped together, staring at the garden outside, and the gathering dusk. She seemed wistful. 35

"Do you mind if I sit here?" I asked, gesturing with my cup. She shook her head, and then followed it up with a shrug, to indicate that it was all the same to her. I sat down.

Vic walked past the conservatory door. He was talking to Stella, but he looked in at me, sitting at the table, wrapped in shyness and awkwardness, and he opened and closed his hand in a parody of a speaking mouth. *Talk.* Right.

"Are you from around here?" I asked the girl.

She shook her head. She wore a low-cut silvery top, and I tried not to stare at the swell of her breasts.

I said, "What's your name? I'm Enn." 40

"Wain's Wain," she said, or something that sounded like it. "I'm a second."

"That's uh. That's a different name."

She fixed me with huge liquid eyes. "It indicates that my progenitor was also Wain, and that I am obliged to report back to her. I may not breed."

"Ah. Well. Bit early for that anyway, isn't it?"

She unclasped her hands, raised them above the table, spread her fingers. "You see?" The little finger on her left hand was crooked, and it bifurcated at the top, splitting into two smaller fingertips. A minor deformity. "When I was finished a decision was needed. Would I be retained, or eliminated? I was fortunate that the decision was with me. Now, I travel, while my more perfect sisters remain at home in stasis. They were firsts. I am a second. 45

"Soon I must return to Wain, and tell her all I have seen. All my impressions of this place of yours."

"I don't actually live in Croydon," I said. "I don't come from here." I wondered if she was American. I had no idea what she was talking about.

"As you say," she agreed, "neither of us comes from here." She folded her six-fingered left hand beneath her right, as if tucking it out of sight. "I had expected it to be bigger, and cleaner, and more colorful. But still, it is a jewel."

She yawned, covered her mouth with her right hand, only for a moment, before it was back on the table again. "I grow weary of the journeying, and I wish sometimes that it would end. On a street in Rio, at Carnival, I saw them on a bridge, golden and tall and insect-eyed and winged, and elated I almost ran to greet them, before I saw that they were only people in costumes. I said to Hola Colt, 'Why do they try so hard to look like us?' and Hola Colt replied, 'Because they hate themselves, all shades of pink and brown, and so small.' It is what I experience, even me, and I am not grown. It is like a world of children, or of elves." Then she smiled and said, "It was a good thing they could not any of them see Hola Colt."

50   "Um," I said, "do you want to dance?"

She shook her head immediately. "It is not permitted," she said. "I can do nothing that might cause damage to property. I am Wain's."

"Would you like something to drink, then?"

"Water," she said.

I went back to the kitchen and poured myself another Coke, and filled a cup with water from the tap. From the kitchen back to the hall, and from there into the conservatory, but now it was quite empty.

55   I wondered if the girl had gone to the toilet, and if she might change her mind about dancing later. I walked back to the front room and stared in. The room was filling up. There were more girls dancing, and several lads I didn't know, who looked older than me and Vic. The lads and the girls all kept their distance, but Vic was holding Stella's hand as they danced, and when the song ended he put an arm around her, casually, almost proprietorially, to make sure that nobody else cut in.

I wondered if the girl I had been talking to in the conservatory was now upstairs, as she did not appear to be on the ground floor.

I walked into the living room, which was across the hall from the room where the people were dancing, and I sat down on the sofa. There was a girl sitting there already. She had dark hair, cut short and spiky, and a nervous manner.

Talk, I thought. "Um, this mug of water's going spare," I told her, "if you want it?"

She nodded, and reached out her hand and took the mug, extremely carefully, as if she were unused to taking things, as if she could trust neither her vision nor her hands.

60   "I love being a tourist," she said, and smiled hesitantly. She had a gap between her two front teeth, and she sipped the tap water as if she were an adult sipping a fine wine. "The last tour, we went to sun, and we swam in sunfire pools with the whales. We heard their histories and we shivered in the chill of the outer places, then we swam deepward where the heat churned and comforted us.

"I wanted to go back. This time, I wanted it. There was so much I had not seen. Instead we came to world. Do you like it?"

"Like what?"

She gestured vaguely to the room—the sofa, the armchairs, the curtains, the unused gas fire.

"It's all right, I suppose."

"I told them I did not wish to visit world," she said, "My parent-teacher was unimpressed. 'You will have much to learn,' it told me. I said 'I could learn more in sun, again. Or in the deeps. Jessa spun webs between galaxies. I want to do that.'

"But there was no reasoning with it, and I came to world. Parent-teacher engulfed me, and I was here, embodied in a decaying lump of meat hanging on a frame of calcium. As I incarnated I felt things deep inside me, fluttering and pumping and squishing. It was my first experience with pushing air through the mouth, vibrating the vocal cords on the way, and I used it to tell parent-teacher that I wished that I would die, which it acknowledged was the inevitable exit strategy from world."

There were black worry beads wrapped around her wrist, and she fiddled with them as she spoke. "But knowledge is there, in the meat," she said, "and I am resolved to learn from it."

We were sitting close at the center of the sofa now. I decided I should put an arm around her, but casually. I would extend my arm along the back of the sofa and eventually sort of creep it down, almost imperceptibly, until it was touching her. She said, "The thing with the liquid in the eyes, when the world blurs. Nobody told me, and I still do not understand. I have touched the folds of the Whisper and pulsed and flown with the tachyon[1] swans, and I still do not understand."

She wasn't the prettiest girl there, but she seemed nice enough, and she was a girl, anyway. I let my arm slide down a little, tentatively, so that it made contact with her back, and she did not tell me to take it away.

Vic called to me then, from the doorway. He was standing with his arm around Stella, protectively, waving at me. I tried to let him know, by shaking my head, that I was onto something, but he called my name, and, reluctantly, I got up from the sofa, and walked over to the door. "What?"

"Er. Look. The party," said Vic, apologetically. "It's not the one I thought it was. I've been talking to Stella and I figured it out. Well, she sort of explained it to me. We're at a different party."

"Christ. Are we in trouble? Do we have to go?"

Stella shook her head. He leaned down and kissed her, gently, on the lips. "You're just happy to have me here, aren't you darlin'?"

"You know I am," she told him.

He looked from her back to me, and he smiled his white smile: roguish, loveable, a little bit Artful Dodger, a little bit wide-boy Prince Charming. "Don't worry. They're all tourists here anyway. It's a foreign exchange thing, innit? Like when we all went to Germany."

"It is?"

"Enn. You got to *talk* to them. And that means you got to listen to them too. You understand?"

"I *did*. I already talked to a couple of them."

"You getting anywhere?"

"I was till you called me over."

"Sorry about that. Look, I just wanted to fill you in. Right?"

---

[1]tachyon: A hypothetical particle moving faster than light.

And he patted my arm and he walked away with Stella. Then, together, the two of them went up the stairs.

Understand me, all the girls at that party, in the twilight, were lovely; they all had perfect faces, but, more important than that, they had whatever strangeness of proportion, of oddness or humanity it is that makes a beauty something more than a shop-window dummy. Stella was the most lovely of any of them, but she, of course, was Vic's, and they were going upstairs together, and that was just how things would always be.

There were several people now sitting on the sofa, talking to the gap-toothed girl. Someone told a joke, and they all laughed. I would have had to push my way in there to sit next to her again, and it didn't look like she was expecting me back, or cared that I had gone, so I wandered out into the hall. I glanced in at the dancers and found myself wondering where the music was coming from. I couldn't see a record player or speakers.

85   From the hall I walked back to the kitchen.

Kitchens are good at parties. You never need an excuse to be there, and, on the good side, at this party I couldn't see any signs of someone's mum. I inspected the various bottles and cans on the kitchen table, then I poured a half an inch of Pernod into the bottom of my plastic cup, which I filled to the top with Coke. I dropped in a couple of ice cubes, and took a sip, relishing the sweet-shop tang of the drink.

"What's that you're drinking?" A girl's voice.

"It's Pernod," I told her. "It tastes like aniseed balls, only it's alcoholic." I didn't say that I only tried it because I'd heard someone in the crowd ask for a Pernod on a live Velvet Underground LP.

"Can I have one?" I poured another Pernod, topped it off with Coke, passed it to her. Her hair was a coppery auburn, and it tumbled around her head in ringlets. It's not a hair style you see much now, but you saw it a lot back then.

90   "What's your name?" I asked.

"Triolet," she said.

"Pretty name," I told her, although I wasn't sure that it was. She was pretty, though.

"It's a verse form," she said, proudly. "Like me."

"You're a poem?"

95   She smiled and looked down and away, perhaps bashfully. Her profile was almost flat—a perfect Grecian nose that came down from her forehead in a straight line. We did *Antigone* in the school theater the previous year. I was the messenger who brings Creon the news of Antigone's death. We wore half-masks that made us look like that. I thought of that play, looking at her face, in the kitchen, and I thought of Barry Smith's drawings of women in the *Conan* comics: five years later I would have thought of the Pre-Raphaelites, of Jane Morris and Lizzie Siddall. But I was only fifteen, then.

"You're a poem?" I repeated.

She chewed her lower lip. "If you want. I am a poem, or I am a pattern, or a race of people whose world was swallowed by the sea."

"Isn't it hard to be three things at the same time?"

"What's your name?"

"Enn."

"So you are Enn," she said. "And you are a male. And you are a biped. Is it hard to be three things at the same time?"

"But they aren't different things. I mean, they aren't contradictory." It was a word I had read many times but never said aloud before that night, and I put the stresses in the wrong places. Contradictory.

She wore a thin dress, made of a white, silky fabric. Her eyes were a pale green, a color that would now make me think of colored contact lenses; but this was thirty years ago; things were different then. I remember wondering about Vic and Stella, upstairs. By now, I was sure that they were in one of the bedrooms, and I envied Vic so much it hurt.

Still, I was talking to this girl, even if we were talking nonsense, even if her name wasn't really Triolet (my generation had not been given hippie names: all the Rainbows and the Sunshines and the Moons, they were only six, seven, eight years old back then). She said, "We knew that it would soon be over, and so we put it all into a poem, to tell the universe who we were, and why we were here, and what we said and did and thought and dreamed and yearned for. We wrapped our dreams in words and patterned the words so that they would live forever, unforgettable. Then we sent the poem as a pattern of flux, to wait in the heart of a star, beaming out its message in pulses and bursts and fuzzes across the electromagnetic spectrum, until the time when, on worlds a thousand sun systems distant, the pattern would be decoded and read, and it would become a poem once again."

"And then what happened?"

She looked at me with her green eyes, and it was as if she stared out at me from her own Antigone half-mask; but as if her pale green eyes were just a different, deeper, part of the mask. "You cannot hear a poem without it changing you," she told me. "They heard it, and it colonized them. It inherited them and it inhabited them, its rhythms becoming part of the way that they thought; its images permanently transmuting their metaphors; its verses, its outlook, its aspirations becoming their lives. Within a generation their children would be born already knowing the poem, and, sooner rather than later, as these things go, there were no more children born. There was no need for them, not any longer. There was only a poem, which took flesh and walked and spread itself across the vastness of the known."

I edged closer to her, so I could feel my leg pressing against hers. She seemed to welcome it: she put her hand on my arm, affectionately, and I felt a smile spreading across my face.

"There are places that we are welcomed," said Triolet, "and places where we are regarded as a noxious weed, or as a disease, something immediately to be quarantined and eliminated. But where does contagion end and art begin?"

"I don't know," I said, still smiling. I could hear the unfamiliar music as it pulsed and scattered and boomed in the front room.

She leaned into me then and—I suppose it was a kiss. . . . I suppose. She pressed her lips to my lips, anyway, and then, satisfied, she pulled back, as if she had now marked me as her own.

"Would you like to hear it?" she asked, and I nodded, unsure what she was offering me, but certain that I needed anything she was willing to give me.

She began to whisper something in my ear. It's the strangest thing about poetry—you can tell it's poetry, even if you don't speak the language. You can hear Homer's Greek without understanding a word, and you still know it's poetry. I've heard Polish poetry, and Iniut poetry, and I knew what it was without knowing. Her whisper was like that. I didn't know the language, but her words washed through me, perfect, and in my mind's eye I saw towers of glass and diamond; and people with eyes of the palest green; and, unstoppable, beneath every syllable, I could feel the relentless advance of the ocean.

Perhaps I kissed her properly. I don't remember. I know I wanted to.

And then Vic was shaking me violently. "Come on!" he was shouting. "Quickly. Come on!"

115   In my head I began to come back from a thousand miles away.

"Idiot. Come on. Just get a move on," he said, and he swore at me. There was fury in his voice.

For the first time that evening I recognized one of the songs being played in the front room. A sad saxophone wail followed by a cascade of liquid chords, a man's voice singing cut-up lyrics about the sons of the silent age. I wanted to stay and hear the song.

She said, "I am not finished. There is yet more of me."

"Sorry love," said Vic, but he wasn't smiling any longer. "There'll be another time," and he grabbed me by the elbow and he twisted and pulled, forcing me from the room. I did not resist. I knew from experience that Vic could beat the stuffing out me if he got it into his head to do so. He wouldn't do it unless he was upset or angry, but he was angry now.

120   Out into the front hall. As Vic pulled open the door, I looked back one last time, over my shoulder, hoping to see Triolet in the doorway to the kitchen, but she was not there. I saw Stella, though, at the top of the stairs. She was staring down at Vic, and I saw her face.

This all happened thirty years ago. I have forgotten much, and I will forget more, and in the end I will forget everything; yet, if I have any certainty of life beyond death, it is all wrapped up not in psalms or hymns, but in this one thing alone: I cannot believe that I will ever forget that moment, or forget the expression on Stella's face as she watched Vic hurrying away from her. Even in death I shall remember that.

Her clothes were in disarray, and there was makeup smudged across her face, and her eyes—

You wouldn't want to make a universe angry. I bet an angry universe would look at you with eyes like that.

We ran then, me and Vic, away from the party and the tourists and the twilight, ran as if a lightning storm was on our heels, a mad helterskelter dash down the confusion of streets, threading through the maze, and we did not look back, and we did not stop until we could not breathe; and then we stopped and panted, unable to run any longer. We were in pain. I held onto a wall, and Vic threw up, hard and long, in the gutter.

125   He wiped his mouth.

"She wasn't a—" He stopped.

He shook his head.

Then he said, "You know . . . I think there's a thing. When you've gone as far as you dare. And if you go any further, you wouldn't be *you* anymore? You'd be the person who'd done *that*? The places you just can't go . . . I think that happened to me tonight."

I thought I knew what he was saying, "Screw her, you mean?" I said.

He rammed a knuckle hard against my temple, and twisted it violently. I wondered   130
if I was going to have to fight him—and lose—but after a moment he lowered his hand and moved away from me, making a low, gulping noise.

I looked at him curiously, and I realized that he was crying: his face was scarlet; snot and tears ran down his cheeks. Vic was sobbing in the street, as unselfconsciously and heartbreakingly as a little boy.

He walked away from me then, shoulders heaving, and he hurried down the road so he was in front of me and I could no longer see his face. I wondered what had occurred in that upstairs room to make him behave like that, to scare him so, and I could not even begin to guess.

The streetlights came on, one by one. Vic stumbled on ahead, while I trudged down the street behind him in the dusk, my feet treading out the measure of a poem that, try as I might, I could not properly remember and would never be able to repeat.

Reading and Reacting

1. Consider the story's exposition. Where does it take place? What do we know about Enn? about Vic?
2. What is Enn's impression of Vic at the beginning of the story? Has it changed by the end? Explain.
3. In paragraph 7, Vic tells Enn that he needs to *talk* to girls if he is going to make any headway with them. Does Enn follow Vic's advice? Does the story actually explain or illustrate "how to talk to girls at parties"?
4. In paragraph 16, Vic says, "They're just girls, . . . They don't come from another planet." How does this statement foreshadow the events to come? What other instances of foreshadowing can you identify?
5. What is your initial reaction to Wain? to the dark-haired girl? to Triolet? How do your own reactions differ from Enn's? How do you explain why you respond differently?
6. Reread paragraph 119. Do you think the narrator is exaggerating when he says he will remember forever the expression on Stella's face?
7. In what respects is this a realistic story? In what respects is it *not* realistic? Is it an initiation story? Is it a horror story?
8. What, if anything, does this story say about the differences between male and female teenagers? Is the story about male–female social interactions, or is it about something else entirely?

9. **JOURNAL ENTRY** What do you think Vic sees at the end of the story that upsets him so much?

10. **CRITICAL PERSPECTIVE** Literary critic David Rudd describes Gaiman's children's novel *Coraline* (2003) as "a rich and powerful work that explores areas seen by many as inappropriate for children, although other critics, such as Bruno Bettelheim in *The Uses of*

Enchantment (1976), argue that children not only *want* to but *need* to explore matters that affect their lives, albeit in their own time and fashion (issues to do with death, sex, ontology, evil, desire, violence and so on)."

In what ways are Enn and Vic expressing their "need to explore matters that affect their lives" in "How to Talk to Girls at Parties"? How does this need help to drive the story's plot?

Related Works: "The Secret Lion" (p. 180), "Gryphon" (p. 250), "Oaks Park" (p. 413), "Young Goodman Brown" (p. 448), "Greasy Lake" (p. 569), "You Fit into Me" (p. 780), "Acquainted with the Night" (p. 987), "La Belle Dame Sans Merci: A Ballad" (p. 993), *Zombie Love* (p. 1079)

WILLIAM FAULKNER (1897–1962), winner of the 1949 Nobel Prize in Literature and the 1955 and 1963 Pulitzer Prizes for fiction, was a Southern writer whose work transcends the regional label. His nineteen novels, notably *The Sound and the Fury* (1929), *As I Lay Dying* (1930), *Light in August* (1932), *Absalom, Absalom!* (1936), and *The Reivers* (1962), explore a wide range of human experience—from high comedy to tragedy—as seen in the life of one community, the fictional Yoknapatawpha County (modeled on the area around Faulkner's own hometown of Oxford, Mississippi). Faulkner's Yoknapatawpha stories—a fascinating blend of complex Latinate prose and primitive Southern dialect—paint an extraordinary portrait of a community bound together by ties of blood, by a shared belief in moral "verities," and by an old grief (the Civil War). Faulkner's grandfather raised "Billy" on Civil War tales and local legends, including many about the "Old Colonel," the writer's great-grandfather, who was a colorful Confederate officer. Although Faulkner's stories elegize the agrarian virtues of the Old South, they look unflinchingly at that world's tragic flaw: the "peculiar institution" of slavery.

Local legends and gossip frequently served as the spark for Faulkner's stories. As John B. Cullen, writing in *Old Times in Faulkner Country*, notes, "A Rose for Emily," Faulkner's first nationally published short story, was based on the tale of Oxford's aristocratic "Miss Mary" Neilson, who married Captain Jack Hume, the charming Yankee foreman of a street-paving crew, over her family's shocked protests. According to Cullen, one of Faulkner's neighbors said he created his story "out of fears and rumors"—the dire predictions of what *might* happen if Mary Neilson married her Yankee.

Cultural Context For many years, the pre–Civil War South was idealized as a land of prosperous plantations, large white houses, cultured and gracious people, and a stable economy based on farming. Central to the myth of the Old South was an adherence to the code of chivalry and a belief in the natural superiority of the white aristocracy, led by men who made their fortunes by owning and running plantations that depended on slave labor. Once the South lost the Civil War, the idealized image of the Old South fell by the wayside, making room for the New South, which, like the North, was industrialized. In this story, Faulkner contrasts notions of the Old South and its decaying values with the newer ideas and innovations of the post-Reconstruction South.

A Rose for Emily (1930)

I

When Miss Emily Grierson died, our whole town went to her funeral: the men through a sort of respectful affection for a fallen monument, the women mostly out of curiosity to see the inside of her house, which no one save an old manservant—a combined gardener and cook—had seen in at least ten years.

It was a big, squarish frame house that had once been white, decorated with cupo-las[1] and spires[2] and scrolled balconies in the heavily lightsome style of the seventies, set on what had once been our most select street. But garages and cotton gins had encroached and obliterated even the august names of that neighborhood; only Miss Emily's house was left, lifting its stubborn and coquettish decay above the cotton wagons and the gasoline pumps—an eyesore among eyesores. And now Miss Emily had gone to join the representatives of those august names where they lay in the cedar-bemused cemetery among the ranked and anonymous graves of Union and Confederate soldiers who fell at the battle of Jefferson.

Alive, Miss Emily had been a tradition, a duty, and a care; a sort of hereditary obligation upon the town, dating from that day in 1894 when Colonel Sartoris, the mayor—he who fathered the edict that no Negro woman should appear on the streets without an apron—remitted her taxes, the dispensation dating from the death of her father on into perpetuity. Not that Miss Emily would have accepted charity. Colonel Sartoris invented an involved tale to the effect that Miss Emily's father had loaned money to the town, which the town, as a matter of business, preferred this way of repaying. Only a man of Colonel Sartoris' generation and thought could have invented it, and only a woman could have believed it.

When the next generation, with its more modern ideas, became mayors and alder-men, this arrangement created some little dissatisfaction. On the first of the year they mailed her a tax notice. February came, and there was no reply. They wrote her a formal letter, asking her to call at the sheriff's office at her convenience. A week later the mayor wrote her himself, offering to call or to send his car for her, and received in reply a note on paper of an archaic shape, in a thin, flowing calligraphy in faded ink, to the effect that she no longer went out at all. The tax notice was also enclosed, without comment.

They called a special meeting of the Board of Aldermen. A deputation waited upon her, knocked at the door through which no visitor had passed since she ceased giving china-painting lessons eight or ten years earlier. They were admitted by the old Negro into a dim hall from which a stairway mounted into still more shadow. It smelled of dust and disuse—a close, dank smell. The Negro led them into the parlor. It was furnished in heavy, leather-covered furniture. When the Negro opened the blinds of one window, they could see that the leather was cracked; and when they sat down, a faint dust rose sluggishly about their thighs, spinning with slow motes in the single sun-ray. On a tarnished gilt easel before the fireplace stood a crayon portrait of Miss Emily's father.

They rose when she entered—a small, fat woman in black, with a thin gold chain descending to her waist and vanishing into her belt, leaning on an ebony cane with a tarnished gold head. Her skeleton was small and spare; perhaps that was why what would have been merely plumpness in another was obesity in her. She looked bloated, like a body long submerged in motionless water, and of that pallid hue. Her eyes, lost in the fatty ridges of her face, looked like two small pieces of coal pressed

5

---

[1] *cupolas:* Rounded structures on roofs.

[2] *spires:* Tapered structures on roofs.

into a lump of dough as they moved from one face to another while the visitors stated their errand.

She did not ask them to sit. She just stood in the door and listened quietly until the spokesman came to a stumbling halt. Then they could hear the invisible watch ticking at the end of the gold chain.

Her voice was dry and cold. "I have no taxes in Jefferson. Colonel Sartoris explained it to me. Perhaps one of you can gain access to the city records and satisfy yourselves."

"But we have. We are the city authorities, Miss Emily. Didn't you get a notice from the sheriff, signed by him?"

10   "I received a paper, yes," Miss Emily said. "Perhaps he considers himself the sheriff . . . I have no taxes in Jefferson."

"But there is nothing on the books to show that, you see. We must go by the—"

"See Colonel Sartoris. I have no taxes in Jefferson."

"But, Miss Emily—"

"See Colonel Sartoris." (Colonel Sartoris had been dead almost ten years.) "I have no taxes in Jefferson. Tobe!" The Negro appeared. "Show these gentlemen out."

II

15   So she vanquished them, horse and foot, just as she had vanquished their fathers thirty years before about the smell. That was two years after her father's death and a short time after her sweetheart—the one we believed would marry her—had deserted her. After her father's death she went out very little; after her sweetheart went away, people hardly saw her at all. A few of the ladies had the temerity to call, but were not received, and the only sign of life about the place was the Negro man—a young man then—going in and out with a market basket.

"Just as if a man—any man—could keep a kitchen properly," the ladies said; so they were not surprised when the smell developed. It was another link between the gross, teeming world and the high and mighty Griersons.

A neighbor, a woman, complained to the mayor, Judge Stevens, eighty years old.

"But what will you have me do about it, madam?" he said.

"Why, send her word to stop it," the woman said. "Isn't there a law?"

20   "I'm sure that won't be necessary," Judge Stevens said. "It's probably just a snake or a rat that nigger of hers killed in the yard. I'll speak to him about it."

The next day he received two more complaints, one from a man who came in diffident deprecation. "We really must do something about it, Judge. I'd be the last one in the world to bother Miss Emily, but we've got to do something." That night the Board of Aldermen met—three graybeards and one younger man, a member of the rising generation.

"It's simple enough," he said. "Send her word to have her place cleaned up. Give her a certain time to do it in, and if she don't . . ."

"Dammit, sir," Judge Stevens said, "will you accuse a lady to her face of smelling bad?"

So the next night, after midnight, four men crossed Miss Emily's lawn and slunk about the house like burglars, sniffing along the base of the brickwork and at the cellar openings while one of them performed a regular sowing motion with his hand out of a sack slung from his shoulder. They broke open the cellar door and sprinkled lime there, and in all the outbuildings. As they recrossed the lawn, a window that had been dark was lighted and Miss Emily sat in it, the light behind her, and her upright torso motionless as that of an idol. They crept quietly across the lawn and into the shadow of the locusts that lined the street. After a week or two the smell went away.

That was when people had begun to feel really sorry for her. People in our town,   25
remembering how old lady Wyatt, her great-aunt, had gone completely crazy at last, believed that the Griersons held themselves a little too high for what they really were. None of the young men were quite good enough for Miss Emily and such. We had long thought of them as a tableau, Miss Emily a slender figure in white in the background, her father a spraddled silhouette in the foreground, his back to her and clutching a horsewhip, the two of them framed by the back-flung front door. So when she got to be thirty and was still single, we were not pleased exactly, but vindicated; even with insanity in the family she wouldn't have turned down all of her chances if they had really materialized.

When her father died, it got about that the house was all that was left to her; and in a way, people were glad. At last they could pity Miss Emily. Being left alone, and a pauper, she had become humanized. Now she too would know the old thrill and the old despair of a penny more or less.

The day after his death all the ladies prepared to call at the house and offer condolence and aid, as is our custom. Miss Emily met them at the door, dressed as usual and with no trace of grief on her face. She told them that her father was not dead. She did that for three days, with the ministers calling on her, and the doctors, trying to persuade her to let them dispose of the body. Just as they were about to resort to law and force, she broke down, and they buried her father quickly.

We did not say she was crazy then. We believed she had to do that. We remembered all the young men her father had driven away, and we knew that with nothing left, she would have to cling to that which had robbed her, as people will.

III

She was sick for a long time. When we saw her again, her hair was cut short, making her look like a girl, with a vague resemblance to those angels in colored church windows—sort of tragic and serene.

The town had just let the contracts for paving the sidewalks, and in the summer   30
after her father's death they began the work. The construction company came with niggers and mules and machinery, and a foreman named Homer Barron, a Yankee—a big, dark, ready man, with a big voice and eyes lighter than his face. The little boys would follow in groups to hear him cuss the niggers, and the niggers singing in time to the rise and fall of picks. Pretty soon he knew everybody in town. Whenever you heard a lot of laughing anywhere about the square, Homer Barron would be in the center of the group. Presently we began to see him and Miss Emily on Sunday afternoons driving in the yellow-wheeled buggy and the matched team of bays from the livery stable.

At first we were glad that Miss Emily would have an interest, because the ladies all said, "Of course a Grierson would not think seriously of a Northerner, a day laborer."

But there were still others, older people, who said that even grief could not cause a real lady to forget *noblesse oblige*[3]—without calling it *noblesse oblige*. They just said, "Poor Emily. Her kinsfolk should come to her." She had some kin in Alabama; but years ago her father had fallen out with them over the estate of old lady Wyatt, the crazy woman, and there was no communication between the two families. They had not even been represented at the funeral.

And as soon as the old people said, "Poor Emily," the whispering began. "Do you suppose it's really so?" they said to one another. "Of course it is. What else could . . ." This behind their hands; rustling of craned silk and satin behind jalousies[4] closed upon the sun of Sunday afternoon as the thin, swift clop-clop-clop of the matched team passed: "Poor Emily."

She carried her head high enough—even when we believed that she was fallen. It was as if she demanded more than ever the recognition of her dignity as the last Grierson; as if it had wanted that touch of earthiness to reaffirm her imperviousness. Like when she bought the rat poison, the arsenic. That was over a year after they had begun to say "Poor Emily," and while the two female cousins were visiting her.

"I want some poison," she said to the druggist. She was over thirty then, still a slight woman, though thinner than usual, with cold, haughty black eyes in a face the flesh of which was strained across the temples and about the eye-sockets as you imagine a lighthouse-keeper's face ought to look. "I want some poison," she said.

35   "Yes, Miss Emily. What kind? For rats and such? I'd recom—"

"I want the best you have. I don't care what kind."

The druggist named several. "They'll kill anything up to an elephant. But what you want is—"

"Arsenic," Miss Emily said. "Is that a good one?"

"Is . . . arsenic? Yes, ma'am. But what you want—"

40   "I want arsenic."

The druggist looked down at her. She looked back at him, erect, her face like a strained flag. "Why, of course," the druggist said. "If that's what you want. But the law requires you to tell what you are going to use it for."

Miss Emily just stared at him, her head tilted back in order to look him eye for eye, until he looked away and went and got the arsenic and wrapped it up. The Negro delivery boy brought her the package; the druggist didn't come back. When she opened the package at home there was written on the box, under the skull and bones: "For rats."

IV

So the next day we all said, "She will kill herself"; and we said it would be the best thing. When she had first begun to be seen with Homer Barron, we had said, "She will marry him." Then we said, "She will persuade him yet," because Homer himself had remarked—he liked men, and it was known that he drank with the younger men in the Elks' Club—that he was not a marrying man. Later we said, "Poor Emily" behind the jalousies as they passed on Sunday afternoon in the glittering buggy, Miss Emily

---

[3]*noblesse oblige:* The obligation of those of high birth or rank to behave honorably.

[4]*jalousies:* Blinds or shutters with adjustable horizontal slats.

with her head high and Homer Barron with his hat cocked and a cigar in his teeth, reins and whip in a yellow glove.

Then some of the ladies began to say that it was a disgrace to the town and a bad example to the young people. The men did not want to interfere, but at last the ladies forced the Baptist minister—Miss Emily's people were Episcopal—to call upon her. He would never divulge what happened during that interview, but he refused to go back again. The next Sunday they again drove about the streets, and the following day the minister's wife wrote to Miss Emily's relations in Alabama.

So she had blood-kin under her roof again and we sat back to watch develop-   45
ments. At first nothing happened. Then we were sure that they were to be married. We learned that Miss Emily had been to the jeweler's and ordered a man's toilet set in silver, with the letters H. B. on each piece. Two days later we learned that she had bought a complete outfit of men's clothing, including a nightshirt, and we said, "They are married." We were really glad. We were glad because the two female cousins were even more Grierson than Miss Emily had ever been.

So we were not surprised when Homer Barron—the streets had been finished some time since—was gone. We were a little disappointed that there was not a public blowing-off, but we believed that he had gone on to prepare for Miss Emily's coming, or to give her a chance to get rid of the cousins. (By that time it was a cabal, and we were all Miss Emily's allies to help circumvent the cousins.) Sure enough, after another week they departed. And, as we had expected all along, within three days Homer Barron was back in town. A neighbor saw the Negro man admit him at the kitchen door at dusk one evening.

And that was the last we saw of Homer Barron. And of Miss Emily for some time. The Negro man went in and out with the market basket, but the front door remained closed. Now and then we would see her at a window for a moment, as the men did that night when they sprinkled the lime, but for almost six months she did not appear on the streets. Then we knew that this was to be expected too; as if that quality of her father which had thwarted her woman's life so many times had been too virulent and too furious to die.

When we next saw Miss Emily, she had grown fat and her hair was turning gray. During the next few years it grew grayer and grayer until it attained an even pepper-and-salt iron-gray, when it ceased turning. Up to the day of her death at seventy-four it was still that vigorous iron-gray, like the hair of an active man.

From that time on her front door remained closed, save for a period of six or seven years, when she was about forty, during which she gave lessons in china-painting. She fitted up a studio in one of the downstairs rooms, where the daughters and granddaughters of Colonel Sartoris' contemporaries were sent to her with the same regularity and in the same spirit that they were sent to church on Sundays with a twenty-five-cent piece for the collection plate. Meanwhile her taxes had been remitted.

Then the newer generation became the backbone and the spirit of the town,   50
and the painting pupils grew up and fell away and did not send their children to her with boxes of color and tedious brushes and pictures cut from the ladies' magazines. The front door closed upon the last one and remained closed for good. When the town got free postal delivery, Miss Emily alone refused to let them

fasten the metal numbers above her door and attach a mailbox to it. She would not listen to them.

Daily, monthly, yearly we watched the Negro grow grayer and more stooped, going in and out with the market basket. Each December we sent her a tax notice, which would be returned by the post office a week later, unclaimed. Now and then we would see her in one of the downstairs windows—she had evidently shut up the top floor of the house—like the carven torso of an idol in a niche, looking or not looking at us, we could never tell which. Thus she passed from generation to generation—dear, inescapable, impervious, tranquil, and perverse.

And so she died. Fell ill in the house filled with dust and shadows, with only a doddering Negro man to wait on her. We did not even know she was sick; we had long since given up trying to get any information from the Negro. He talked to no one, probably not even to her, for his voice had grown harsh and rusty, as if from disuse.

She died in one of the downstairs rooms, in a heavy walnut bed with a curtain, her gray head propped on a pillow yellow and moldy with age and lack of sunlight.

V

The Negro met the first of the ladies at the front door and let them in, with their hushed, sibilant voices and their quick, curious glances, and then he disappeared. He walked right through the house and out the back and was not seen again.

55   The two female cousins came at once. They held the funeral on the second day, with the town coming to look at Miss Emily beneath a mass of bought flowers, with the crayon face of her father musing profoundly above the bier and the ladies sibilant and macabre; and the very old men—some in their brushed Confederate uniforms—on the porch and the lawn, talking of Miss Emily as if she had been a contemporary of theirs, believing that they had danced with her and courted her perhaps, confusing time with its mathematical progression, as the old do, to whom all the past is not a diminishing road but, instead, a huge meadow which no winter ever quite touches, divided from them now by the narrow bottle-neck of the most recent decade of years.

Already we knew that there was one room in that region above stairs which no one had seen in forty years, and which would have to be forced. They waited until Miss Emily was decently in the ground before they opened it.

The violence of breaking down the door seemed to fill this room with pervading dust. A thin, acrid pall as of the tomb seemed to lie everywhere upon this room decked and furnished as for a bridal: upon the valance curtains of faded rose color, upon the rose-shaded lights, upon the dressing table, upon the delicate array of crystal and the man's toilet things backed with tarnished silver, silver so tarnished that the monogram was obscured. Among them lay collar and tie, as if they had just been removed, which, lifted, left upon the surface a pale crescent in the dust. Upon a chair hung the suit, carefully folded; beneath it the two mute shoes and the discarded socks.

The man himself lay in the bed.

For a long while we just stood there, looking down at the profound and fleshless grin. The body had apparently once lain in the attitude of an embrace, but now the long sleep that outlasts love, that conquers even the grimace of love, had cuckolded him. What was left of him, rotted beneath what was left of the nightshirt, had become inextricable from the bed in which he lay; and upon him and upon the pillow beside him lay that even coating of the patient and biding dust.

Then we noticed that in the second pillow was the indentation of a head. One of us lifted something from it, and leaning forward, that faint and invisible dust dry and acrid in the nostrils, we saw a long strand of iron-gray hair.   50

Reading and Reacting

1. Arrange these events in the sequence in which they actually occur: Homer's arrival in town, the aldermen's visit, Emily's purchase of poison, Colonel Sartoris's decision to remit Emily's taxes, the development of the odor around Emily's house, Emily's father's death, the arrival of Emily's relatives, Homer's disappearance. Then, list the events in the sequence in which they are introduced in the story. Why do you suppose Faulkner presents these events out of their actual chronological order?

2. Despite the story's confusing sequence, many events are foreshadowed. Give some examples of this technique. How does foreshadowing enrich the story?

3. Where does the exposition end and the movement toward the story's climax begin? Where does the resolution stage begin?

4. Emily is clearly the story's protagonist. In the sense that he opposes her wishes, Homer is the antagonist. What other characters—or what larger forces—are in conflict with Emily?

5. Explain how each of these phrases moves the story's plot along: "So she vanquished them, horse and foot . . ." (par. 15); "After a week or two the smell went away" (par. 24); "And that was the last we saw of Homer Barron" (par. 47); "And so she died" (par. 52); "The man himself lay in the bed" (par. 58).

6. The narrator of the story is an observer, not a participant. Who might this narrator be? Do you think the narrator is male or female? How do you suppose the narrator might know so much about Emily? Why do you think the narrator uses *we* instead of *I*?

7. The original version of "A Rose for Emily" included a two-page deathbed scene revealing that Tobe, Emily's servant, has shared her terrible secret all these years and that Emily has left her house to him. Why do you think Faulkner deleted this scene? Do you think he made the right decision?

8. Some critics have suggested that Miss Emily Grierson is a kind of symbol of the Old South, with its outdated ideas of chivalry, formal manners, and tradition. In what sense is she also a victim of those values?

9. **JOURNAL ENTRY** When asked at a seminar at the University of Virginia about the meaning of the title "A Rose for Emily," Faulkner replied, "Oh, it's simply the poor woman had no life at all. Her father had kept her more or less locked up and then she had a lover who was about to quit her, she had to murder him. It was just 'A Rose for Emily'—that's all."

In another interview, asked the same question, he replied, "I pitied her and this was a salute, just as if you were to make a gesture, a salute, to anyone; to a woman you would hand a rose, as you would lift a cup of *sake* to a man." What do you make of Faulkner's responses? What else might the title suggest?

10. **CRITICAL PERSPECTIVE** In his essay "William Faulkner: An American Dickens," literary critic Leslie A. Fiedler characterizes Faulkner as "primarily . . . a sentimental writer; not a writer with the occasional vice of sentimentality, but one whose basic mode of experience is sentimental." Fiedler continues, "In a writer whose very method is self-indulgence, that sentimentality becomes sometimes downright embarrassing." Fiedler also notes Faulkner's "excesses of maudlin feelings and absurd indulgences in overripe rhetoric."

Do you think these criticisms apply to "A Rose for Emily"? If so, does the "vice of sentimentality" diminish the story, or do you agree with Fiedler—who calls Faulkner a "supereminently good 'bad' writer"—that the author is able to transcend these excesses?

Related Works: "Miss Brill" (p. 245), "Barn Burning" (p. 335), "Porphyria's Lover" (p. 696), "Richard Cory" (p. 1011), *Trifles* (p. 1604)

WRITING SUGGESTIONS: Plot

1. Write a sequel to "The Story of an Hour," telling the story in the voice of Brently Mallard. Use flashbacks to provide information about his view of the Mallards' marriage. Or, write a sequel to "Distant Relations," telling what happens in the days—and years—to come.

2. Find a newspaper or magazine article that presents a story that you find disturbing. Then, write a fictionalized version of the article in which you retell the story's events in a detached tone, without adding analysis or commentary. Expand the original article by creating additional characters and settings.

3. "The Story of an Hour" includes a *deus ex machina*, an outside force or agent that suddenly appears to change the course of events. Consider the possible effects of a *deus ex machina* on the other stories in this chapter. What might this outside force be in each story? How might it change the story's action? How plausible would such a dramatic turn of events be in each case?

4. Both "The Story of an Hour" and "How to Talk to Girls at Parties" create a dreamlike, disorienting atmosphere that has an unsettling effect on the protagonists. However, "The Story of an Hour" is essentially a realistic story while "How to Talk to Girls at Parties" is something quite different. Compare and contrast these two stories, focusing on how the stories' events affect the two protagonists and their perceptions of reality.

5. Read the following article from the January 30, 1987, *Philadelphia Inquirer*. After listing some similarities and differences between the events in the article's story and those in "A Rose for Emily," write an essay in which you discuss how the presentation of events differs. Can you draw any conclusions about the differences between journalistic and fictional treatments of similar incidents?

DICK POTHIER AND THOMAS J. GIBBONS JR.

A Woman's Wintry Death Leads to a Long-Dead Friend

For more than two years, Frances Dawson Hamilton lived with the body of her long-time companion, draping his skeletonized remains with palm fronds and rosary beads.

Yesterday, the 70-year-old woman was found frozen to death in the home in the 4500 block of Higbee Street where she had lived all her life—the last year without heat or hot water. Her body was found by police accompanying a city social worker who came bearing an order to have her taken to a hospital.

Police investigators said the body of Bernard J. Kelly, 84, was found in an upstairs bedroom of the two-story brick home in the Wissinoming section, on the twin bed where he apparently died at least two years ago.

Two beds had been pushed together, and Hamilton apparently had been sleeping beside Kelly's remains since he died of unknown causes, police said.

Kelly's remains were clothed in long johns and socks, investigators said. The body was draped with rosary beads and palm fronds, and on the bed near his body were two boxes of Valentine's Day candy.

"It was basically a funeral—we've seen it before in such cases," said one investigator who was at the scene but declined to be identified.

Neighbors and investigators said Hamilton and Kelly had lived together in the house for at least 15 years. Several neighbors said Hamilton came from an affluent family, was educated in Europe, and lived on a trust fund until a year or so ago.

Last winter, said John Wasniewski, Hamilton's next-door neighbor, the basement of the home was flooded and the heater destroyed. "There was no heat in that house last winter or this winter," he said.

An autopsy will be performed on Hamilton today, but she apparently froze to death sometime since Monday, when a friend spoke to her on the telephone, investigators said.

Over the last two years, neighbors said, Hamilton had become increasingly reclusive and irrational. Just last week, a city social worker summoned by a friend arranged for a Philadelphia Gas Works team to visit the home and try to repair the furnace—but she refused to let them in.

The friend was James Phillips, 44, of Horsham, a salesman for Apex Electric in Souderton.

In October 1985, he said, Hamilton visited the Frankford Avenue electrical shop where he was then working, told him that she had an electrical problem in her house and had no lights, and asked whether he could help.

Phillips said he visited the house, fixed the problem and gave her some light bulbs.

"She was really paranoid," Phillips said. "She believed that all her problems were from people doing things to her. For some reason or other, she took to me."

Phillips said that he began visiting her, taking her shopping and doing some shopping for her. But, he said, he never saw the body on the second floor.

Hamilton told him there was a man up there. "I thought it was a story she was telling to protect herself," Phillips said.

He provided her with electric heaters and also contacted a caseworker with the city's Department of Human Services whom Phillips identified as Albert Zbik.

Between the two of them, he said, "we got her through last winter." Phillips said Zbik helped her obtain food stamps and Social Security assistance.

When the snowstorm hit last week, Phillips became concerned because he knew Hamilton would have trouble getting food. On Saturday, he took her a plate of hot food and bought more food from a local store.

On Monday, she telephoned him. "I didn't like the way she sounded," he said. He called Zbik and told him he felt it was time that they forced her to go to a hospital.

Phillips said Zbik went to her home yesterday, carrying a form authorizing an involuntary admission to a hospital for observation or required medical treatment.

Phillips told police that he was never allowed above the first floor and was often told by Hamilton that "Bernie is not feeling well today."

Neighbors and police investigators said Kelly was last seen alive about two years ago, and appeared to be quite ill at the time.

"As recently as last month, I asked Frances how Bernard was and whether she should get a doctor, and she said it wasn't necessary. She said 'He's sick, but I'm taking care of him—I'm feeding him with an eyedropper,'" Wasniewski said.

"I told her in December that if he was that sick, she should call a doctor, but she'd say she was taking care of him very well," Wasniewski said.

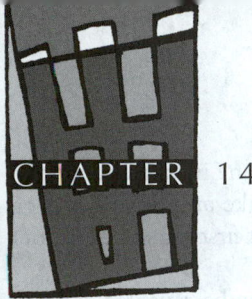

CHAPTER 14

CHARACTER

Katherine Mansfield
Bettmann/Corbis

Zadie Smith
AP Images/Sang Tan

John Updike
AP Images/Bill Uhrich

Charles Baxter
AP Images/Janet Hostetter

A **character** is a fictional representation of a person—usually (but not necessarily) a psychologically realistic depiction. Writers may develop characters through their actions, through their reactions to situations or to other characters, through their physical appearance, through their speech and gestures and expressions, and even through their names.

Generally speaking, characters' personality traits, as well as their appearances and their feelings and beliefs, are communicated to readers in two ways. First, readers can be *told* about characters. Third-person narrators can provide information about what characters are doing, saying, and thinking; what experiences they have had; what they look like; how they are dressed; and so on. Sometimes these narrators also offer analysis of and judgments about a character's behavior or motivation. Similarly, first-person narrators can tell us about themselves or about other characters. Thus, Sammy in John Updike's "A&P" (p. 238) tells readers what he thinks about his job and about the girls who come into the supermarket where he works. He also tells us what various characters look like and describes their actions, attitudes, speech, and gestures. (For more information about first-person narrators, see Chapter 16, "Point of View.")

Alternatively, aspects of a character's personality and beliefs may be revealed through his or her actions, dialogue, or thoughts. For instance, Sammy's vivid fantasies and his disapproval of his customers' lives suggest to readers that he is something of a nonconformist; however, Sammy himself does not actually tell us this.

 ## Round and Flat Characters

In his influential 1927 work *Aspects of the Novel*, English novelist E. M. Forster classifies characters as either **round** (well developed, closely involved in and responsive to the action) or **flat** (barely developed or stereotypical). To a great extent, these categories are still useful today. In an effective story, the major characters are usually complex and fully developed; if they are not, readers will not care what happens to them. Sometimes readers are encouraged to become involved with the characters, even to identify with them, and this empathy is possible only when we know something about the characters—their strengths and weaknesses, their likes and dislikes. In some cases, of course, a story can be effective even when its central characters are not well developed. Sometimes, in fact, a story's effectiveness is enhanced by an *absence* of character development, as in Shirley Jackson's "The Lottery" (p. 419).

Readers often expect characters to behave as "real people" in their situation might behave. Real people are not perfect, and realistic characters cannot be perfect either. The flaws that are revealed as round characters are developed—greed, gullibility, naïveté, shyness, a quick temper, or a lack of insight or judgment or tolerance or even intelligence— make them believable. In modern fiction, the protagonist is seldom if ever the noble "hero"; more often, he or she is at least partly a victim, someone to whom unpleasant things happen and someone who is sometimes ill-equipped to cope with events.

Unlike major characters, minor characters are frequently not well developed. Often they are flat, perhaps acting as *foils* for the protagonist. A **foil** is a supporting character whose role in the story is to highlight a major character by presenting a contrast with him or her. For instance, in "A&P," Stokesie, another young checkout clerk, is a foil for Sammy. Because he is a little older than Sammy and seems to have none of Sammy's imagination, restlessness, or nonconformity, Stokesie suggests what Sammy might become if he were to continue to work at the A&P. Some flat characters are **stock characters**, easily identifiable types who behave so predictably that readers can readily recognize them. The kindly old priest, the tough young bully, the ruthless business executive, and the reckless adventurer are all stock characters. Some flat characters can even be **caricatures**, characterized by a single dominant trait, such as miserliness, or even by one physical trait, such as nearsightedness.

 ## Dynamic and Static Characters

Characters may also be classified as either *dynamic* or *static*. A **dynamic character** grows and changes in the course of a story, developing as he or she reacts to events and to other characters. In "A&P," for instance, Sammy's decision to speak out in defense of the girls—as well as the events that lead him to do so—changes him. His view of the world has changed at the end of the story, and as a result his position in the world may change too. A **static character** may face the same challenges a dynamic character might face but will remain essentially unchanged: a static character who was selfish and arrogant will remain selfish and arrogant, regardless of the nature of the story's conflict. In the fairy tale "Cinderella," for example, the title character is as sweet and good-natured at the end of the story—despite her mistreatment by her family—as she is at the beginning. Her situation may have changed, but her character has not.

Whereas round characters tend to be dynamic, flat characters tend to be static. But even a very complex, well-developed major character may be static; sometimes, in fact, the point of a story may hinge on a character's inability to change. A familiar example is the title character in William Faulkner's "A Rose for Emily" (p. 224), who lives a wasted, empty life, at least in part because she is unwilling or unable to accept that the world around her and the people in it have changed.

A story's minor characters are often static; their growth is not usually relevant to the story's development. Moreover, we usually do not learn enough about a minor character's traits, thoughts, actions, or motivation to determine whether the character changes significantly.

 ## Motivation

Because round characters are complex, they are not always easy to understand. They may act unpredictably, just as real people do. They wrestle with decisions, resist or succumb to temptation, make mistakes, ask questions, search for answers, hope and dream, rejoice and despair. What is important is not whether we approve of a character's actions but whether those actions are *plausible*—whether the actions make sense in light of what we know about the character. We need to understand a character's **motivation**—the reasons behind his or her behavior—or we will not believe or accept that behavior. In "A&P" for instance, given Sammy's age, his dissatisfaction with his job, and his desire to impress the young woman he calls Queenie, the decision he makes at the end of the story is perfectly plausible. Without having established his motivation, Updike could not have expected readers to accept Sammy's actions.

Of course, even when readers get to know a character, they still are not able to predict how a complex, round character will behave in a given situation; only a flat character is predictable. The tension that develops as readers wait to see how a character will act or react, and thus how a story's conflict will be resolved, is what holds readers' interest and keeps them involved as a story's action unfolds.

✔ **CHECKLIST**   **Writing about Character**

    Who is the story's main character? Who are the other major characters?

    Who are the minor characters? What roles do they play in the story? How would the story be different without them?

continued on next page

- What do the major characters look like? Is their physical appearance important?

- What are the major characters' most notable personality traits?

- What are the major characters' likes and dislikes? their strengths and weaknesses?

- What are the main character's most strongly held feelings and beliefs?

- What are we told about the major characters' backgrounds and prior experiences? What can we infer?

- Are the characters round or flat?

- Are the characters dynamic or static?

- Does the story include any stock characters? Does any character serve as a foil?

- Do the characters act in a way that is consistent with how readers expect them to act?

- With which characters are readers likely to be most sympathetic? least sympathetic?

AP Images/Bill Ulrich

JOHN UPDIKE (1932–2009) was a prolific writer of novels, short stories, essays, poems, plays, and children's tales. Updike's earliest ambition was to be a cartoonist for the *New Yorker*. He attended Harvard hoping to draw cartoons for the *Harvard Lampoon*, studied drawing and fine art at Oxford, and in 1955 went to work for the *New Yorker*—not as a cartoonist but as a "Talk of the Town" reporter. Updike left the *New Yorker* after three years to write full time but continued to contribute stories, reviews, and essays to the magazine for over forty years. Among his novels are *Rabbit, Run* (1960), *The Centaur* (1963), *Rabbit Redux* (1971), *Rabbit Is Rich* (1981), *The Witches of Eastwick* (1985), and *Rabbit at Rest* (1990). His last novels are *Seek My Face* (2002), *Villages* (2004), *Of the Farm* (2004), *Terrorist* (2006), and *The Widows of Eastwick* (2008). In 1998, Updike received the National Book Foundation Medal for Distinguished Contribution to American Letters.

In early stories such as "A&P" (1961), Updike draws on memories of his childhood and teenage years for the sort of "small" scenes and stories for which he quickly became famous. "There is a great deal to be said about almost anything," Updike comments in an interview in *Contemporary Authors*. "All people can be equally interesting. . . . Now either nobody is a hero or everybody is. I vote for everybody. My subject is the American Protestant small-town middle class. I like middles. It is in middles that extremes clash."

Cultural Context The 1950s were a decade of prosperity for the United States. Soldiers returned from World War II, women who had worked in defense plants returned to their homes, and the population soared as a result of a "baby boom." Part of this prosperity manifested itself materially: Americans tried to "keep up with the Joneses" in terms of their possessions, and manufacturers raced to produce the latest consumer goods. Conformity became the norm, with the advent of mass-produced suburban tract houses and a conservative code of dress and behavior that dictated what was appropriate. This atmosphere is the context for the manager's disapproval in "A&P"—and Sammy's reaction foreshadows the mood of the rebellious generation to come.

A&P (1961)

Film Series

DVD
See p. 244
for film stills
from the
DVD
version
of this
story.

In walks these three girls in nothing but bathing suits. I'm in the third check-out slot, with my back to the door, so I don't see them until they're over by the bread. The one that caught my eye first was the one in the plaid green two-piece. She was a chunky kid, with a good tan and a sweet broad soft-looking can with those two crescents of white just under it, where the sun never seems to hit, at the top of the backs of her legs. I stood there with my hand on a box of Hi Ho crackers trying to remember if I rang it up or not. I ring it up again and the customer starts giving me hell. She's one of these cash-register-watchers, a witch about fifty with rouge on her cheekbones and no eyebrows, and I know it made her day to trip me up. She'd been watching cash registers for fifty years and probably never seen a mistake before.

By the time I got her feathers smoothed and her goodies into a bag—she gives me a little snort in passing, if she'd been born at the right time they would have burned her over in Salem—by the time I get her on her way the girls had circled around the bread and were coming back, without a push-cart, back my way along the counters, in the aisle between the check-outs and the Special bins. They didn't even have shoes on. There was this chunky one, with the two-piece—it was bright green and the seams on the bra were still sharp and her belly was still pretty pale so I guessed she just got it (the suit)—there was this one, with one of those chubby berry-faces, the lips all bunched together under her nose, this one, and a tall one, with black hair that hadn't quite frizzed right, and one of these sunburns right across under the eyes, and a chin that was too long—you know, the kind of girl other girls think is very "striking" and "attractive" but never quite makes it, as they very well know, which is why they like her so much—and then the third one, that wasn't quite so tall. She was the queen. She kind of led them, the other two peeking around and making their shoulders round. She didn't look around, not this queen, she just walked straight on slowly, on these long white prima-donna legs. She came down a little hard on her heels, as if she didn't walk in her bare feet that much, putting down her heels and then letting the weight move along to her toes as if she was testing the floor with every step, putting a little deliberate extra action into it. You never know for sure how girls' minds work (do you really think it's a mind in there or just a little buzz like a bee in a glass jar?) but you got the idea she had talked the other two into coming in here with her, and now she was showing them how to do it, walk slow and hold yourself straight.

She had on a kind of dirty-pink—beige maybe, I don't know—bathing suit with a little nubble all over it and, what got me, the straps were down. They were off her shoulders looped loose around the cool tops of her arms, and I guess as a result the suit had slipped a little on her, so all around the top of the cloth there was this shining rim. If it hadn't been there you wouldn't have known there could have been anything whiter than those shoulders. With the straps pushed off, there was nothing between the top of the suit and the top of her head except just *her*, this clean bare plane of the top of her chest down from the shoulder bones like a dented sheet of metal tilted in the light. I mean, it was more than pretty.

She had sort of oaky hair that the sun and salt had bleached, done up in a bun that was unravelling, and a kind of prim face. Walking into the A&P with your straps down, I suppose it's the only kind of face you *can* have. She held her head so high her neck, coming up out of those white shoulders, looked kind of stretched, but I didn't mind. The longer her neck was, the more of her there was.

5   She must have felt in the corner of her eye me and over my shoulder Stokesie in the second slot watching, but she didn't tip. Not this queen. She kept her eyes moving across the racks, and stopped, and turned so slow it made my stomach rub the inside of my apron, and buzzed to the other two, who kind of huddled against her for relief, and they all three of them went up the cat-and-dog-food-breakfast-cereal-macaroni-rice-raisins-seasonings-spreads-spaghetti-soft-drinks-crackers-and-cookies aisle. From the third slot I look straight up this aisle to the meat counter, and I watched them all the way. The fat one with the tan sort of fumbled with the cookies, but on second thought she put the packages back. The sheep pushing their carts down the aisle—the girls were walking against the usual traffic (not that we have one-way signs or anything)—were pretty hilarious. You could see them, when Queenie's white shoulders dawned on them, kind of jerk, or hop, or hiccup, but their eyes snapped back to their own baskets and on they pushed. I bet you could set off dynamite in an A&P and the people would by and large keep reaching and checking oatmeal off their lists and muttering "Let me see, there was a third thing, began with A, asparagus, no, ah, yes, applesauce!" or whatever it is they do mutter. But there was no doubt, this jiggled them. A few houseslaves in pin curlers even looked around after pushing their carts past to make sure what they had seen was correct.

You know, it's one thing to have a girl in a bathing suit down on the beach, where what with the glare nobody can look at each other much anyway, and another thing in the cool of the A&P, under the fluorescent lights, against all those stacked packages, with her feet paddling along naked over our checkerboard green-and-cream rubber-tile floor.

"Oh Daddy," Stokesie said beside me. "I feel so faint."

"Darling," I said. "Hold me tight." Stokesie's married, with two babies chalked up on his fuselage already, but as far as I can tell that's the only difference. He's twenty-two, and I was nineteen this April.

"Is it done?" he asks, the responsible married man finding his voice. I forgot to say he thinks he's going to be manager some sunny day, maybe in 1990 when it's called the Great Alexandrov and Petrooshki Tea Company or something.

10   What he meant was, our town is five miles from a beach, with a big summer colony out on the Point, but we're right in the middle of town, and the women generally put on a shirt or shorts or something before they get out of the car into the street. And anyway these are usually women with six children and varicose veins mapping their legs and nobody, including them, could care less. As I say, we're right in the middle of town, and if you stand at our front doors you can see two banks and the Congregational church and the newspaper store and three real-estate offices and about twenty-seven old freeloaders tearing up Central Street because the sewer broke again. It's not as if we're on the Cape; we're north of Boston and there's people in this town haven't seen the ocean for twenty years.

The girls had reached the meat counter and were asking McMahon something. He pointed, they pointed, and they shuffled out of sight behind a pyramid of Diet

Delight peaches. All that was left for us to see was old McMahon patting his mouth and looking after them sizing up their joints. Poor kids, I began to feel sorry for them, they couldn't help it.

Now here comes the sad part of the story, at least my family says it's sad but I don't think it's sad myself. The store's pretty empty, it being Thursday afternoon, so there was nothing much to do except lean on the register and wait for the girls to show up again. The whole store was like a pinball machine and I didn't know which tunnel they'd come out of. After a while they come around out of the far aisle, around the light bulbs, records at discount of the Caribbean Six or Tony Martin Sings or some such gunk you wonder they waste the wax on, sixpacks of candy bars, and plastic toys done up in cellophane that fall apart when a kid looks at them anyway. Around they come, Queenie still leading the way, and holding a little gray jar in her hand. Slots Three through Seven are unmanned and I could see her wondering between Stokes and me, but Stokesie with his usual luck draws an old party in baggy gray pants who stumbles up with four giant cans of pineapple juice (what do these bums *do* with all that pineapple juice? I've often asked myself) so the girls come to me. Queenie puts down the jar and I take it into my fingers icy cold. Kingfish Fancy Herring Snacks in Pure Sour Cream: 49. Now her hands are empty, not a ring or a bracelet, bare as God made them, and I wonder where the money's coming from. Still with that prim look she lifts a folded dollar bill out of the hollow at the center of her nubbled pink top. The jar went heavy in my hand. Really, I thought that was so cute.

Then everybody's luck begins to run out. Lengel comes in from haggling with a truck full of cabbages on the lot and is about to scuttle into that door marked MANAGER behind which he hides all day when the girls touch his eye. Lengel's pretty dreary, teaches Sunday school and the rest, but he doesn't miss that much. He comes over and says, "Girls, this isn't the beach."

Queenie blushes, though maybe it's just a brush of sunburn I was noticing for the first time, now that she was so close. "My mother asked me to pick up a jar of herring snacks." Her voice kind of startled me, the way voices do when you see the people first, coming out so flat and dumb yet kind of tony, too, the way it ticked over "pick up" and "snacks." All of a sudden I slid right down her voice into her living room. Her father and the other men were standing around in ice-cream coats and bow ties and the women were in sandals picking up herring snacks on toothpicks off a big plate and they were all holding drinks the color of water with olives and sprigs of mint in them. When my parents have somebody over they get lemonade and if it's a real racy affair Schlitz in tall glasses with "They'll Do It Every Time" cartoons stencilled on.

"That's all right," Lengel said. "But this isn't the beach." His repeating this struck me as funny, as if it had just occurred to him, and he had been thinking all these years the A&P was a great big dune and he was the head lifeguard. He didn't like my smiling—as I say he doesn't miss much—but he concentrates on giving the girls that sad Sunday-school-superintendent stare.

Queenie's blush is no sunburn now, and the plump one in plaid, that I liked better from the back—a really sweet can—pipes up, "We weren't doing any shopping. We just came in for the one thing."

15

"That makes no difference," Lengel tells her, and I could see from the way his eyes went that he hadn't noticed she was wearing a two-piece before. "We want you decently dressed when you come in here."

"We *are* decent," Queenie says suddenly, her lower lip pushing, getting sore now that she remembers her place, a place from which the crowd that runs the A&P must look pretty crummy. Fancy Herring Snacks flashed in her very blue eyes.

"Girls, I don't want to argue with you. After this come in here with your shoulders covered. It's our policy." He turns his back. That's policy for you. Policy is what the kingpins want. What the others want is juvenile delinquency.

20   All this while, the customers had been showing up with their carts but, you know, sheep, seeing a scene, they had all bunched up on Stokesie, who shook open a paper bag as gently as peeling a peach, not wanting to miss a word. I could feel in the silence everybody getting nervous, most of all Lengel, who asks me, "Sammy, have you rung up this purchase?"

I thought and said "No" but it wasn't about that I was thinking. I go through the punches, 4, 9, GROC, TOT—it's more complicated than you think, and after you do it often enough, it begins to make a little song, that you hear words to, in my case "Hello (*bing*) there, you (*gung*) hap-py *pee*-pul (*splat*)!"—the *splat* being the drawer flying out. I uncrease the bill, tenderly as you may imagine, it just having come from between the two smoothest scoops of vanilla I had ever known were there, and pass a half and a penny into her narrow pink palm, and nestle the herrings in a bag and twist its neck and hand it over, all the time thinking.

The girls, and who'd blame them, are in a hurry to get out, so I say "I quit" to Lengel quick enough for them to hear, hoping they'll stop and watch me, their unsuspected hero. They keep right on going, into the electric eye; the door flies open and they flicker across the lot to their car, Queenie and Plaid and Big Tall Goony-Goony (not that as raw material she was so bad), leaving me with Lengel and a kink in his eyebrow.

"Did you say something, Sammy?"

"I said I quit."

25   "I thought you did."

"You didn't have to embarrass them."

"It was they who were embarrassing us."

I started to say something that came out "Fiddle-de-doo." It's a saying of my grandmother's, and I know she would have been pleased.

"I don't think you know what you're saying," Lengel said.

30   "I know you don't," I said. "But I do." I pull the bow at the back of my apron and start shrugging it off my shoulders. A couple customers that had been heading for my slot begin to knock against each other, like scared pigs in a chute.

Lengel sighs and begins to look very patient and old and gray. He's been a friend of my parents for years. "Sammy, you don't want to do this to your Mom and Dad," he tells me. It's true, I don't. But it seems to me that once you begin a gesture it's fatal not to go through with it. I fold the apron, "Sammy" stitched in red on the pocket, and put it on the counter, and drop the bow tie on top of it. The bow tie is theirs, if you've ever wondered. "You'll feel this for the rest of your life," Lengel says, and I know that's true, too, but remembering how he made that pretty girl blush makes me so scrunchy inside I punch the No Sale tab and the machine whirs "pee-pul" and the drawer splats out. One advantage to this scene taking place in summer, I can follow this up with a clean exit, there's no fumbling around getting your coat and galoshes, I just saunter into the electric eye in my white shirt that my mother ironed the night before, and the door heaves itself open, and outside the sunshine is skating around the asphalt.

I look around for my girls, but they're gone, of course. There wasn't anybody but some young married screaming with her children about some candy they didn't get by the door of a powder-blue Falcon station wagon. Looking back in the big windows, over the bags of peat moss and aluminum lawn furniture stacked on the pavement, I could see Lengel in my place in the slot, checking the sheep through. His face was dark gray and his back stiff, as if he'd just had an injection of iron, and my stomach kind of fell as I felt how hard the world was going to be to me hereafter.

Reading and Reacting

1. Summarize the information Sammy gives readers about his tastes and background. Why is this exposition vital to the story's development?
2. List some of the most obvious physical characteristics of the A&P's customers. How do these characteristics make them foils for Queenie and her friends?
3. What is it about Queenie and her friends that appeals to Sammy?
4. Is Queenie a stock character? Explain.
5. What rules and conventions are customers expected to follow in a supermarket? How does the behavior of Queenie and her friends violate these rules?
6. Is the supermarket setting vital to the story? Could the story have been set in a car wash? in a fast-food restaurant? in a business office?
7. How accurate are Sammy's judgments about the other characters? How might the characters be portrayed if the story were told by Lengel?
8. Given what you learn about Sammy during the course of the story, what do you see as his *primary* motivation for quitting his job? What other factors motivate him?

9. JOURNAL ENTRY Where do you think Sammy will find himself in ten years? Why?

10. CRITICAL PERSPECTIVE In her 1976 book *The Necessary Blackness*, critic Mary Allen observes, "Updike's most tender reverence is reserved for women's bodies. The elegant style with which he describes female anatomy often becomes overwrought, as his descriptions do generally. But it always conveys wonder."

    In what passages in "A&P" does Updike (through Sammy) convey this sense of wonder? Do you think today's audience, reading the story more than fifty years after Updike wrote it, and more than thirty years after Allen's essay was published, would still see such passages as conveying "tender reverence"? Or do you think readers might now see Sammy (and, indeed, Updike) as sexist? How do you react to these passages?

Related Works: "A Supermarket in California" (p. 78), "How to Talk to Girls at Parties" (p. 214), "New York Day Women" (p. 348), "Araby" (p. 361), "Ex-Basketball Player" (p. 764), "The Road Not Taken" (p. 805), Short-Order Cook (p. 972), *"What Are You Going to Be?"* (p. 1062)

Fiction in Film: John Updike's "A&P"

Character is central to "A&P," and the DVD version of the story characterizes Sammy, Stokesie, Lengel, and Queenie and her friends visually as well as through their dialogue and actions. The supermarket setting—so vividly described in the story—also comes to life on the screen. The stills included here depict scenes that appear on the DVD.

Sammy at the cash register with a customer
Source: ©Steven Payne/Worn Path Productions

Queenie and her friends
Source: ©Steven Payne/Worn Path Productions

Interior of the A&P
Source: ©Steven Payne/Worn Path Productions

Mr. Lengel confronting the girls while Sammy watches
Source: ©Steven Payne/Worn Path Productions

Reading and Reacting

1. If you were making a film of "A&P," which scenes from the story would you consider essential? Which might you omit? Why?
2. Which minor characters would you include? Why?
3. Would you depict on screen any characters who are not described in the story—for example, Sammy's parents? If so, in what kind of scene would you introduce them?
4. How would you dramatize Sammy's fantasies about Queenie and her family (par. 14)?
5. Would you set the entire film inside the A&P, or would you create additional settings? For example, where might you set a scene designed to present background information about Sammy? a scene depicting events that might have followed the story?

6. If you were setting the film in the present (rather than in 1961), how would you depict Queenie and her friends? How would they look different from the girls pictured on page 244?

7. In a present-day film version of the story, which actor would you cast as Sammy? Queenie? Stokesie? Lengel?

KATHERINE MANSFIELD (1888–1923), one of the pioneers of the modern short story, was born in New Zealand and educated in England. Very much a "modern young woman," she began living on her own in London at the age of nineteen, soon publishing stories and book reviews in many of the most influential literary magazines of the day.

A short story writer of great versatility, Mansfield produced sparkling social comedies as well as more intellectually and technically complex works intended for "perceptive readers." According to one critic, her best works "[w]ith delicate plainness . . . present elusive moments of decision, defeat, and small triumph." Her last two story collections—*Bliss and Other Stories* (1920) and *The Garden Party and Other Stories* (1922)—were met with immediate critical acclaim, but Mansfield's career was cut short in 1923 when she died of complications from tuberculosis at the age of thirty-five.

One notable theme in Mansfield's work is the *dame seule*, the "woman alone," which provides the basis for the poignant "Miss Brill."

Cultural Context During the nineteenth century, the task of spinning wool was typically given to unmarried women as a way for them to earn their keep in the home. Thus, the term *spinster* came into existence. Over time, the word acquired a negative stereotype, conjuring up the image of a lonely, childless, frumpy middle-aged woman who longs to be like other "normal" women—wives and mothers. Today, the word *spinster* is rarely used, reflecting the changed perception of unmarried women and the wider lifestyle choices open to them.

Miss Brill (1922)

Although it was so brilliantly fine—the blue sky powdered with gold and great spots of light like white wine splashed over the Jardins Publiques[1]—Miss Brill was glad that she had decided on her fur. The air was motionless, but when you opened your mouth there was just a faint chill, like a chill from a glass of iced water before you sip, and now and again a leaf came drifting—from nowhere, from the sky. Miss Brill put up her hand and touched her fur. Dear little thing! It was nice to feel it again. She had taken it out of its box that afternoon, shaken out the moth-powder, given it a good brush, and rubbed the life back into the dim little eyes. "What has been happening to me?" said the sad little eyes. Oh, how sweet it was to see them snap at her again from the red eiderdown! . . . . But the nose, which was of some black composition, wasn't at all firm. It must have had a knock, somehow. Never mind—a little dab of black sealing-wax when the time came—when it was absolutely necessary. . . . Little rogue! Yes, she really felt like that about it. Little rogue biting its tail just by her left ear. She

---

[1] *Jardins Publiques:* "Public Gardens" (French).

could have taken it off and laid it on her lap and stroked it. She felt a tingling in her hands and arms, but that came from walking, she supposed. And when she breathed, something light and sad—no, not sad, exactly—something gentle seemed to move in her bosom.

There were a number of people out this afternoon, far more than last Sunday. And the band sounded louder and gayer. That was because the Season had begun. For although the band played all year round on Sundays, out of season it was never the same. It was like some one playing with only the family to listen; it didn't care how it played if there weren't any strangers present. Wasn't the conductor wearing a new coat, too? She was sure it was new. He scraped with his foot and flapped his arms like a rooster about to crow, and the bandsmen sitting in the green rotunda blew out their cheeks and glared at the music. Now there came a little "flutey" bit—very pretty!—a little chain of bright drops. She was sure it would be repeated. It was; she lifted her head and smiled.

Only two people shared her "special" seat: a fine old man in a velvet coat, his hands clasped over a huge carved walking-stick, and a big old woman, sitting upright, with a roll of knitting on her embroidered apron. They did not speak. This was disappointing, for Miss Brill always looked forward to the conversation. She had become really quite expert, she thought, at listening as though she didn't listen, at sitting in other people's lives just for a minute while they talked round her.

She glanced, sideways, at the old couple. Perhaps they would go soon. Last Sunday, too, hadn't been as interesting as usual. An Englishman and his wife, he wearing a dreadful Panama hat and she button boots. And she'd gone on the whole time about how she ought to wear spectacles; she knew she needed them; but that it was no good getting any; they'd be sure to break and they'd never keep on. And he'd been so patient. He'd suggested everything—gold rims, the kind that curved round your ears, little pads inside the bridge. No, nothing would please her. "They'll always be sliding down my nose!" Miss Brill wanted to shake her.

5   The old people sat on the bench, still as statues. Never mind, there was always the crowd to watch. To and fro, in front of the flower-beds and the band rotunda, the couples and groups paraded, stopped to talk, to greet, to buy a handful of flowers from the old beggar who had his tray fixed to the railings. Little children ran among them, swooping and laughing; little boys with big white silk bows under their chins, little girls, little French dolls, dressed up in velvet and lace. And sometimes a tiny staggerer came suddenly rocking into the open from under the trees, stopped, stared, as suddenly sat down "flop," until its small high-stepping mother, like a young hen, rushed scolding to its rescue. Other people sat on the benches and green chairs, but they were nearly always the same, Sunday after Sunday, and—Miss Brill had often noticed—there was something funny about nearly all of them. They were odd, silent, nearly all old, and from the way they stared they looked as though they'd just come from dark little rooms or even—even cupboards!

Behind the rotunda the slender trees with yellow leaves down drooping, and through them just a line of sea, and beyond the blue sky with gold-veined clouds.

Tum-tum-tum tiddle-um! tiddle-um! tum tiddley-um tum ta! blew the band.

Two young girls in red came by and two young soldiers in blue met them, and they laughed and paired and went off arm-in-arm. Two peasant women with funny straw hats passed, gravely, leading beautiful smoke-colored donkeys. A cold, pale nun hurried by. A beautiful woman came along and dropped her bunch of violets, and a little boy ran after to hand them to her, and she took them and threw them away as if they'd been poisoned. Dear me! Miss Brill didn't know whether to admire that or not! And now an ermine toque[2] and a gentleman in grey met just in front of her. He was tall, stiff, dignified, and she was wearing the ermine toque she'd bought when her hair was yellow. Now everything, her hair, her face, even her eyes, was the same color as the shabby ermine, and her hand, in its cleaned glove, lifted to dab her lips, was a tiny yellowish paw. Oh, she was so pleased to see him—delighted! She rather thought they were going to meet that afternoon. She described where she'd been—everywhere, here, there, along by the sea. The day was so charming—didn't he agree? And wouldn't he, perhaps? . . . But he shook his head, lighted a cigarette, slowly breathed a great deep puff into her face, and, even while she was still talking and laughing, flicked the match away and walked on. The ermine toque was alone; she smiled more brightly than ever. But even the band seemed to know what she was feeling and played more softly, played tenderly, and the drum beat, "The Brute! The Brute!" over and over. What would she do? What was going to happen now? But as Miss Brill wondered, the ermine toque turned, raised her hand as though she'd seen some one else, much nicer, just over there, and pattered away. And the band changed again and played more quickly, more gaily than ever, and the old couple on Miss Brill's seat got up and marched away, and such a funny old man with long whiskers hobbled along in time to the music and was nearly knocked over by four girls walking abreast.

Oh, how fascinating it was! How she enjoyed it! How she loved sitting here, watching it all! It was like a play. It was exactly like a play. Who could believe the sky at the back wasn't painted? But it wasn't till a little brown dog trotted on solemn and then slowly trotted off, like a little "theatre" dog, a little dog that had been drugged, that Miss Brill discovered what it was that made it so exciting. They were all on the stage. They weren't only the audience, not only looking on; they were acting. Even she had a part and came every Sunday. No doubt somebody would have noticed if she hadn't been there; she was part of the performance after all. How strange she'd never thought of it like that before! And yet it explained why she made such a point of starting from home at just the same time each week—so as not to be late for the performance—and it also explained why she had quite a queer, shy feeling at telling her English pupils how she spent her Sunday afternoons. No wonder! Miss Brill nearly laughed out loud. She was on the stage. She thought of the old invalid gentleman to whom she read the newspaper four afternoons a week while he slept in the garden. She had got quite used to the frail head on the cotton pillow, the hollowed eyes, the open mouth and the high pinched nose. If he'd been dead she mightn't have noticed for weeks; she wouldn't have minded. But suddenly he knew he was having the paper read to him by an actress! "An actress!" The old head lifted; two points of light quivered in the old eyes. "An actress—are ye?" And Miss Brill smoothed the newspaper as though it

---

[2]*ermine toque:* Small, close-fitting woman's hat made from the fur of an ermine, a type of weasel.

were the manuscript of her part and said gently: "Yes, I have been an actress for a long time."

10   The band had been having a rest. Now they started again. And what they played was warm, sunny, yet there was just a faint chill—a something, what was it?—not sadness—no, not sadness—a something that made you want to sing. The tune lifted, lifted, the light shone; and it seemed to Miss Brill that in another moment all of them, all the whole company, would begin singing. The young ones, the laughing ones who were moving together, they would begin, and the men's voices, very resolute and brave, would join them. And then she too, she too, and the others on the benches—they would come in with a kind of accompaniment—something low, that scarcely rose or fell, something so beautiful—moving. . . . And Miss Brill's eyes filled with tears and she looked smiling at all the other members of the company. Yes, we understand, we understand, she thought—though what they understood she didn't know.

Just at that moment a boy and a girl came and sat down where the old couple had been. They were beautifully dressed; they were in love. The hero and heroine, of course, just arrived from his father's yacht. And still soundlessly singing, still with that trembling smile, Miss Brill prepared to listen.

"No, not now," said the girl. "Not here, I can't."

"But why? Because of that stupid old thing at the end there?" asked the boy. "Why does she come here at all—who wants her? Why doesn't she keep her silly old mug at home?"

"It's her fu-fur which is so funny," giggled the girl. "It's exactly like a fried whiting."[3]

15   "Ah, be off with you!" said the boy in an angry whisper. Then: "Tell me, my petite chérie—"[4]

"No, not here," said the girl. "Not *yet*."

On her way home she usually bought a slice of honeycake at the baker's. It was her Sunday treat. Sometimes there was an almond in her slice, sometimes not. It made a great difference. If there was an almond it was like carrying home a tiny present—a surprise—something that might very well not have been there. She hurried on the almond Sundays and struck the match for the kettle in quite a dashing way.

But to-day she passed the baker's by, climbed the stairs, went into the little dark room—her room like a cupboard—and sat down on the red eiderdown. She sat there for a long time. The box that the fur came out of was on the bed. She unclasped the necklet quickly; quickly, without looking, laid it inside. But when she put the lid on she thought she heard something crying.

---

[3]*whiting:* Food fish related to the cod.

[4]*petite chérie:* "Little darling" (French).

Reading and Reacting

1. What specific details can you infer about Miss Brill's character (and, perhaps, about her life) from this statement: "She had become really quite expert, she thought, at listening as though she didn't listen, at sitting in other people's lives just for a minute while they talked round her" (par. 3)?

2. How do Miss Brill's observations of the people around her give us insight into her own character? Why do you suppose she doesn't interact with any of the people she observes?

3. In paragraph 9, Miss Brill realizes that the scene she observes is "exactly like a play" and that "Even she had a part and came every Sunday." What part does Miss Brill play? Is she a stock character in this play, or is she a three-dimensional character? Does she play a lead role or a supporting role?

4. What do you think Miss Brill means when she says, "I have been an actress for a long time" (par. 9)? What does this comment reveal about how she sees herself? Is her view of herself similar to or different from the view the other characters have of her?

5. What role does Miss Brill's fur piece play in the story? In what sense, if any, does it function as a character?

6. What happens in paragraphs 11–16 to break Miss Brill's mood? Why is the scene she observes so upsetting to her?

7. At the end of the story, has Miss Brill changed as a result of what she has overheard, or is she the same person she was at the beginning? Do you think she will return to the park the following Sunday?

8. The story's last paragraph describes Miss Brill's room as being "like a cupboard." Where else has this image appeared in the story? What does its reappearance in the conclusion tell us?

9. **JOURNAL ENTRY** Write a character sketch of Miss Brill, inventing a plausible family and personal history that might help to explain the character you see in the story.

10. **CRITICAL PERSPECTIVE** Critic Gillian Boddy, in *Katherine Mansfield: The Woman, The Writer*, offers the following analysis of Mansfield's fiction:

    > The story evolves through the characters' minds. The external narrator is almost eliminated. As so often in her work, the reader is dropped into the story and simply confronted by a particular situation. There is no preliminary establishing and identification of time and place. The reader is immediately involved; it is assumed that he or she has any necessary prerequisite knowledge and is, in a sense, part of the story too.

    Do you see this absence of conventional exposition as a problem in "Miss Brill"? Do you think the story would be more effective if Mansfield had supplied more preliminary information about setting and character? Or do you believe that what Boddy calls Mansfield's "concentration on a moment or episode" is a satisfactory substitute for the missing exposition, effectively shifting interest from "*what* happens" to "*why* it happens"?

Related Works: "No Face" (p. 577), "Rooming houses are old women" (p. 761), "Aunt Jennifer's Tigers" (p. 799), "After great pain, a formal feeling comes—" (p. 972), "Acquainted with the Night" (p. 987), *Trifles* (p. 1604)

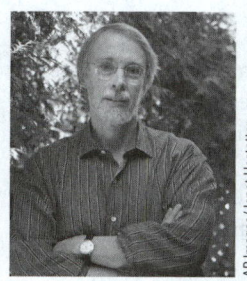

AP Images/Janet Hostetter

CHARLES BAXTER (1947–   ) was born in Minneapolis and educated at Macalester College and at the State University of New York, Buffalo. Currently teaching in the creative writing program at the University of Minnesota, Baxter is the author of six critically praised collections of short stories: *Harmony of the World* (1984), *Through the Safety Net* (1985), *A Relative Stranger: Stories* (1990), *Believers: A Novella and Stories* (1997), *Gryphon: New and Selected Stories* (2011), and *There's Something I Want You to Do* (2014). He is also the author of five novels, *First Light* (1987), *Shadow Play* (1993), *The Feast of Love* (2002), *Saul and Patsy* (2003), and *The Soul Thief* (2008), and one book of poetry, *Imaginary Paintings and Other Poems* (1989). Baxter has also written *Burning Down the House* (1997), a collection of essays on fiction.

Baxter's critics often mention the compassion he shows in writing about his fictional characters: a couple who lose their child, a hospital worker who wants to be famous, a tired businessman who really wants to paint. In many of his short stories in *Through the Safety Net* (in which "Gryphon" appeared), unexpected events jar Baxter's characters out of their routines, forcing them to consider different choices, to call on inner strength, or to swim against the tide of "middle America's" conventions.

Cultural Context One of the key elements of this story is a character's use of a deck of tarot cards to predict the future. Originating more than 500 years ago in northern Italy in a game called "Triumphs," the Tarot was quickly adopted as a tool for divining the future. With deep roots in the symbolism of medieval and Renaissance Europe, the Tarot is today the singular most popular tool for spiritual introspection and prophesy. While the death card in particular is often feared, many interpreters argue that it hardly ever points to literal death but rather symbolizes the ending of something significant and the beginning of something new. In "Gryphon," the accuracy of the Tarot's prediction is less important than the young students' reactions to it.

Gryphon (1985)

On Wednesday afternoon, between the geography lesson on ancient Egypt's hand-operated irrigation system and an art project that involved drawing a model city next to a mountain, our fourth-grade teacher, Mr. Hibler, developed a cough. This cough began with a series of muffled throat clearings and progressed to propulsive noises contained within Mr. Hibler's closed mouth. "Listen to him," Carol Peterson whispered to me. "He's gonna blow up." Mr. Hibler's laughter—dazed and infrequent—sounded a bit like his cough, but as we worked on our model cities we would look up, thinking he was enjoying a joke, and see Mr. Hibler's face turning red, his cheeks puffed out. This was not laughter. Twice he bent over, and his loose tie, like a plumb line, hung down straight from his neck as he exploded himself into a Kleenex. He would excuse himself, then go on coughing. "I'll bet you a dime," Carol Peterson whispered, "we get a substitute tomorrow."

Carol sat at the desk in front of mine and was a bad person—when she thought no one was looking she would blow her nose on notebook paper, then crumble it up and throw it into the wastebasket—but at times of crisis she spoke the truth. I knew I'd lose the dime.

"No deal," I said.

When Mr. Hibler stood us up in formation at the door just prior to the final bell, he was almost incapable of speech. "I'm sorry, boys and girls," he said. "I seem to be coming down with something."

"I hope you feel better tomorrow, Mr. Hibler," Bobby Kryzanowicz, the faultless brown-noser said, and I heard Carol Peterson's evil giggle. Then Mr. Hibler opened the door and we walked out to the buses, a clique of us starting noisily to hawk and cough as soon as we thought we were a few feet beyond Mr. Hibler's earshot.

Five Oaks being a rural community, and in Michigan, the supply of substitute teachers was limited to the town's unemployed community college graduates, a pool of about four mothers. These ladies fluttered, provided easeful class days, and nervously covered material we had mastered weeks earlier. Therefore it was a surprise when a woman we had never seen came into the class the next day, carrying a purple purse, a checkerboard lunchbox, and a few books. She put the books on one side of Mr. Hibler's desk and the lunchbox on the other, next to the Voice of Music phonograph. Three of us in the back of the room were playing with Heever, the chameleon that lived in the terrarium and on one of the plastic drapes, when she walked in.

She clapped her hands at us. "Little boys," she said, "why are you bent over together like that?" She didn't wait for us to answer. "Are you tormenting an animal? Put it back. Please sit down at your desks. I want no cabals this time of the day." We just stared at her. "Boys," she repeated, "I asked you to sit down."

I put the chameleon in his terrarium and felt my way to my desk, never taking my eyes off the woman. With white and green chalk, she had started to draw a tree on the left side of the blackboard. She didn't look usual. Furthermore, her tree was outsized, disproportionate, for some reason.

"This room needs a tree," she said, with one line drawing the suggestion of a leaf. "A large, leafy, shady, deciduous . . . oak."

Her fine, light hair had been done up in what I would learn years later was called a chignon, and she wore gold-rimmed glasses whose lenses seemed to have the faintest blue tint. Harold Knardahl, who sat across from me, whispered "Mars," and I nodded slowly, savoring the imminent weirdness of the day. The substitute drew another branch with an extravagant arm gesture, then turned around and said, "Good morning. I don't believe I said good morning to all of you yet."

Facing us, she was no special age—an adult is an adult—but her face had two prominent lines, descending vertically from the sides of her mouth to her chin. I knew where I had seen those lines before: *Pinocchio*. They were marionette lines. "You may stare at me," she said to us, as a few more kids from the last bus came into the room, their eyes fixed on her, "for a few more seconds, until the bell rings. Then I will permit no more staring. Looking I will permit. Staring, no. It is impolite to stare, and a sign of bad breeding. You cannot make a social effort while staring."

Harold Knardahl did not glance at me, or nudge, but I heard him whisper "Mars" again, trying to get more mileage out of his single joke with the kids who had just come in.

When everyone was seated, the substitute teacher finished her tree, put down her chalk fastidiously on the phonograph, brushed her hands, and faced us. "Good morning," she said. "I am Miss Ferenczi, your teacher for the day. I am fairly new to your community, and I don't believe any of you know me. I will therefore start by telling you a story about myself."

While we settled back, she launched into her tale. She said her grandfather had been a Hungarian prince; her mother had been born in some place called Flanders, had been a pianist, and had played concerts for people Miss Ferenczi referred to as "crowned heads." She gave us a knowing look. "Grieg," she said, "the Norwegian master, wrote a concerto for piano that was," she paused, "my mother's triumph at her debut concert in London." Her eyes searched the ceiling. Our eyes followed. Nothing up there but ceiling tile. "For reasons that I shall not go into, my family's fortunes took us to Detroit, then north to dreadful Saginaw, and now here I am in Five Oaks, as your substitute teacher, for today, Thursday, October the eleventh. I believe it will be a good day: All the forecasts coincide. We shall start with your reading lesson. Take out your reading book. I believe it is called *Broad Horizons*, or something along those lines."

15 Jeannie Vermeesch raised her hand. Miss Ferenczi nodded at her. "Mr. Hibler always starts the day with the Pledge of Allegiance," Jeannie whined.

"Oh, does he? In that case," Miss Ferenczi said, "you must know it *very* well by now, and we certainly need not spend our time on it. No, no allegiance pledging on the premises today, by my reckoning. Not with so much sunlight coming into the room. A pledge does not suit my mood." She glanced at her watch. "Time *is* flying. Take out *Broad Horizons*."

She disappointed us by giving us an ordinary lesson, complete with vocabulary word drills, comprehension questions, and recitation. She didn't seem to care for the material, however. She sighed every few minutes and rubbed her glasses with a frilly perfumed handkerchief that she withdrew, magician style, from her left sleeve.

After reading we moved on to arithmetic. It was my favorite time of the morning, when the lazy autumn sunlight dazzled its way through ribbons of clouds past the windows on the east side of the classroom, and crept across the linoleum floor. On the playground the first group of children, the kindergartners, were running on the quack grass just beyond the monkey bars. We were doing multiplication tables. Miss Ferenczi had made John Wazny stand up at his desk in the front row. He was supposed to go through the tables of six. From where I was sitting, I could smell the Vitalis soaked into John's plastered hair. He was doing fine until he came to six times eleven and six times twelve. "Six times eleven," he said, "is sixty-eight. Six times twelve is . . ." He put his fingers to his head, quickly and secretly sniffed his fingertips, and said, "seventy-two." Then he sat down.

"Fine," Miss Ferenczi said. "Well now. That was very good."

20 "Miss Ferenczi!" One of the Eddy twins was waving her hand desperately in the air. "Miss Ferenczi! Miss Ferenczi!"

"Yes?"

"John said that six times eleven is sixty-eight and you said he was right!"

"*Did* I?" She gazed at the class with a jolly look breaking across her marionette's face. "Did I say that? Well, what *is* six times eleven?"

"It's sixty-six!"

25 She nodded. "Yes. So it is. But, and I know some people will not entirely agree with me, at some times it is sixty-eight."

"When? When is it sixty-eight?"

We were all waiting.

"In higher mathematics, which you children do not yet understand, six times eleven can be considered to be sixty-eight." She laughed through her nose. "In higher mathematics numbers are . . . more fluid. The only thing a number does is contain a certain amount of something. Think of water. A cup is not the only way to measure a certain amount of water, is it?" We were staring, shaking our heads. "You could use saucepans or thimbles. In either case, the water *would be the same.* Perhaps," she started again, "it would be better for you to think that six times eleven is sixty-eight only when I am in the room."

"Why is it sixty-eight," Mark Poole asked, "when you're in the room?"

"Because it's more interesting that way," she said, smiling very rapidly behind her blue-tinted glasses. "Besides, I'm your substitute teacher, am I not?" We all nodded. "Well, then, think of six times eleven equals sixty-eight as a substitute fact."

"A substitute fact?"

"Yes." Then she looked at us carefully. "Do you think," she asked, "that anyone is going to be hurt by a substitute fact?"

We looked back at her.

"Will the plants on the windowsill be hurt?" We glanced at them. There were sensitive plants thriving in a green plastic tray, and several wilted ferns in small clay pots. "Your dogs and cats, or your moms and dads?" She waited. "So," she concluded, "what's the problem?"

"But it's wrong," Janice Weber said, "isn't it?"

"What's your name, young lady?"

"Janice Weber."

"And you think it's wrong, Janice?"

"I was just asking."

"Well, all right. You were just asking. I think we've spent enough time on this matter by now, don't you, class? You are free to think what you like. When your teacher, Mr. Hibler, returns, six times eleven will be sixty-six again, you can rest assured. And it will be that for the rest of your lives in Five Oaks. Too bad, eh?" She raised her eyebrows and glinted herself at us. "But for now, it wasn't. So much for that. Let us go to your assigned problems for today, as painstakingly outlined, I see, in Mr. Hibler's lesson plan. Take out a sheet of paper and write your names in the upper left-hand corner."

For the next half hour we did the rest of our arithmetic problems. We handed them in and went on to spelling, my worst subject. Spelling always came before lunch. We were taking spelling dictation and looking at the clock. "Thorough," Miss Ferenczi said. "Boundary." She walked in the aisles between the desks, holding the spelling book open and looking down at our papers. "Balcony." I clutched my pencil. Somehow, the way she said those words, they seemed foreign, Hungarian, mis-voweled and mis-consonanted. I stared down at what I had spelled. *Balconie.* I turned my pencil upside down and erased my mistake. *Balconey.* That looked better, but still incorrect. I cursed the world of spelling and tried erasing it again and saw the paper beginning to wear away. *Balkony.* Suddenly I felt a hand on my shoulder.

"I don't like that word either," Miss Ferenczi whispered, bent over, her mouth near my ear. "It's ugly. My feeling is, if you don't like a word, you don't have to use it." She straightened up, leaving behind a slight odor of Clorets.

At lunchtime we went out to get our trays of sloppy joes, peaches in heavy syrup, coconut cookies, and milk, and brought them back to the classroom, where Miss Ferenczi was sitting at the desk, eating a brown sticky thing she had unwrapped from tightly rubber-banded wax paper. "Miss Ferenczi," I said, raising my hand. "You don't have to eat with us. You can eat with the other teachers. There's a teachers' lounge," I ended up, "next to the principal's office."

"No, thank you," she said. "I prefer it here."

45   "We've got a room monitor," I said. "Mrs. Eddy." I pointed to where Mrs. Eddy, Joyce and Judy's mother, sat silently at the back of the room, doing her knitting.

"That's fine," Miss Ferenczi said. "But I shall continue to eat here, with you children. I prefer it," she repeated.

"How come?" Wayne Razmer asked without raising his hand.

"I talked with the other teachers before class this morning," Miss Ferenczi said, biting into her brown food. "There was a great rattling of the words for the fewness of ideas. I didn't care for their brand of hilarity. I don't like ditto machine jokes."

"Oh," Wayne said.

50   "What's that you're eating?" Maxine Sylvester asked, twitching her nose. "Is it food?"

"It most certainly *is* food. It's a stuffed fig. I had to drive almost down to Detroit to get it. I also bought some smoked sturgeon. And this," she said, lifting some green leaves out of her lunchbox, "is raw spinach, cleaned this morning before I came out here to the Garfield-Murry school."

"Why're you eating raw spinach?" Maxine asked.

"It's good for you," Miss Ferenczi said. "More stimulating than soda pop or smelling salts." I bit into my sloppy joe and stared blankly out the window. An almost invisible moon was faintly silvered in the daytime autumn sky. "As far as food is concerned," Miss Ferenczi was saying, "you have to shuffle the pack. Mix it up. Too many people eat . . . well, never mind."

"Miss Ferenczi," Carol Peterson said, "what are we going to do this afternoon?"

55   "Well," she said, looking down at Mr. Hibler's lesson plan, "I see that your teacher, Mr. Hibler, has you scheduled for a unit on the Egyptians." Carol groaned. "Yessss," Miss Ferenczi continued, "that is what we will do: the Egyptians. A remarkable people. Almost as remarkable as the Americans. But not quite." She lowered her head, did her quick smile, and went back to eating her spinach.

After noon recess we came back into the classroom and saw that Miss Ferenczi had drawn a pyramid on the blackboard, close to her oak tree. Some of us who had been playing baseball were messing around in the back of the room, dropping the bats and the gloves into the playground box, and I think that Ray Schontzeler had just slugged me when I heard Miss Ferenczi's high-pitched voice quavering with emotion. "Boys," she said, "come to order right this minute and take your seats. I do not wish to waste a minute of class time. Take out your geography books." We trudged to our desks and, still sweating, pulled out *Distant Lands and Their People.* "Turn to page forty-two." She waited for thirty seconds, then looked over at Kelly Munger. "Young man," she said, "why are you still fossicking in your desk?"

Kelly looked as if his foot had been stepped on. "Why am I what?"

"Why are you . . . burrowing in your desk like that?"

"I'm lookin' for the book, Miss Ferenczi."

Bobby Kryzanowicz, the faultless brown-noser who sat in the first row by choice, softly said, "His name is Kelly Munger. He can't ever find his stuff. He always does that."

"I don't care what his name is, especially after lunch," Miss Ferenczi said. "*Where is your book?*"

"I just found it." Kelly was peering into his desk and with both hands pulled at the book, shoveling along in front of it several pencils and crayons, which fell into his lap and then to the floor.

"I hate a mess," Miss Ferenczi said. "I hate a mess in a desk or a mind. It's . . . unsanitary. You wouldn't want your house at home to look like your desk at school, now, would you?" She didn't wait for an answer. "I should think not. A house at home should be as neat as human hands can make it. What were we talking about? Egypt. Page forty-two. I note from Mr. Hibler's lesson plan that you have been discussing the modes of Egyptian irrigation. Interesting, in my view, but not so interesting as what we are about to cover. The pyramids and Egyptian slave labor. A plus on one side, a minus on the other." We had our books open to page forty-two, where there was a picture of a pyramid, but Miss Ferenczi wasn't looking at the book. Instead, she was staring at some object just outside the window.

"Pyramids," Miss Ferenczi said, still looking past the window. "I want you to think about the pyramids. And what was inside. The bodies of the pharaohs, of course, and their attendant treasures. Scrolls. Perhaps," Miss Ferenczi said, with something gleeful but unsmiling in her face, "these scrolls were novels for the pharaohs, helping them to pass the time in their long voyage through the centuries. But then, I am joking." I was looking at the lines on Miss Ferenczi's face. "Pyramids," Miss Ferenczi went on, "were the repositories of special cosmic powers. The nature of a pyramid is to guide cosmic energy forces into a concentrated point. The Egyptians knew that; we have generally forgotten it. Did you know," she asked, walking to the side of the room so that she was standing by the coat closet, "that George Washington had Egyptian blood, from his grandmother? Certain features of the Constitution of the United States are notable for their Egyptian ideas."

Without glancing down at the book, she began to talk about the movement of souls in Egyptian religion. She said that when people die, their souls return to Earth in the form of carpenter ants or walnut trees, depending on how they behaved—"well or ill"—in life. She said that the Egyptians believed that people act the way they do because of magnetism produced by tidal forces in the solar system, forces produced by the sun and by its "planetary ally," Jupiter. Jupiter, she said, was a planet, as we had been told, but had "certain properties of stars." She was speaking very fast. She said that the Egyptians were great explorers and conquerors. She said that the greatest of all the conquerors, Genghis Khan, had had forty horses and forty young women killed on the site of his grave. We listened. No one tried to stop her. "I myself have been in Egypt," she said, "and have witnessed much dust and many brutalities." She said that an old man in Egypt who worked for a circus had personally shown her an animal in a cage, a monster, half bird and half lion. She said that this monster was called a gryphon and that she had heard about them but never seen them until she traveled to the outskirts of Cairo. She said that Egyptian astronomers had discovered the planet Saturn, but had not seen its rings. She said that the Egyptians were the first to discover that dogs, when they are ill, will not drink from rivers, but wait for rain, and hold their jaws open to catch it.

*   *   *

"She lies."

We were on the school bus home. I was sitting next to Carl Whiteside, who had bad breath and a huge collection of marbles. We were arguing. Carl thought she was lying. I said she wasn't, probably.

"I didn't believe that stuff about the bird," Carl said, "and what she told us about the pyramids? I didn't believe that either. She didn't know what she was talking about."

"Oh yeah?" I had liked her. She was strange. I thought I could nail him. "If she was lying," I said, "what'd she say that was a lie?"

70   "Six times eleven isn't sixty-eight. It isn't ever. It's sixty-six, I know for a fact."

"She said so. She admitted it. What else did she lie about?"

"I don't know," he said. "Stuff."

"What stuff?"

"Well." He swung his legs back and forth. "You ever see an animal that was half lion and half bird?" He crossed his arms. "It sounded real fakey to me."

75   "It could happen," I said. I had to improvise, to outrage him. "I read in this newspaper my mom bought in the IGA about this scientist, this mad scientist in the Swiss Alps, and he's been putting genes and chromosomes and stuff together in test tubes, and he combined a human being and a hamster." I waited, for effect. "It's called a humster."

"You never." Carl was staring at me, his mouth open, his terrible bad breath making its way toward me. "What newspaper was it?"

"The *National Enquirer*," I said, "that they sell next to the cash registers." When I saw his look of recognition, I knew I had bested him. "And this mad scientist," I said, "his name was, um, Dr. Frankenbush." I realized belatedly that this name was a mistake and waited for Carl to notice its resemblance to the name of the other famous mad master of permutations, but he only sat there.

"A man and a hamster?" He was staring at me, squinting, his mouth opening in distaste. "Jeez. What'd it look like?"

When the bus reached my stop, I took off down our dirt road and ran up through the back yard, kicking the tire swing for good luck. I dropped my books on the back steps so I could hug and kiss our dog, Mr. Selby. Then I hurried inside. I could smell Brussels sprouts cooking, my unfavorite vegetable. My mother was washing other vegetables in the kitchen sink, and my baby brother was hollering in his yellow playpen on the kitchen floor.

80   "Hi, Mom," I said, hopping around the playpen to kiss her, "Guess what?"

"I have no idea."

"We had this substitute today, Miss Ferenczi, and I'd never seen her before, and she had all these stories and ideas and stuff."

"Well. That's good." My mother looked out the window behind the sink, her eyes on the pine woods west of our house. Her face and hairstyle always reminded other people of Betty Crocker, whose picture was framed inside a gigantic spoon on the side of the Bisquick box; to me, though, my mother's face just looked white. "Listen, Tommy," she said, "go upstairs and pick your clothes off the bathroom floor, then go outside to the shed and put the shovel and ax away that your father left outside this morning."

"She said that six times eleven was sometimes sixty-eight!" I said. "And she said she once saw a monster that was half lion and half bird." I waited. "In Egypt, she said."

"Did you hear me?" my mother asked, raising her arm to wipe her forehead with the back of her hand. "You have chores to do."   85

"I know," I said. "I was just telling you about the substitute."

"It's very interesting," my mother said, quickly glancing down at me, "and we can talk about it later when your father gets home. But right now you have some work to do."

"Okay, Mom." I took a cookie out of the jar on the counter and was about to go outside when I had a thought. I ran into the living room, pulled out a dictionary next to the TV stand, and opened it to the G's. *Gryphon*: "variant of griffin." *Griffin*: "a fabulous beast with the head and wings of an eagle and the body of a lion." Fabulous was right. I shouted with triumph and ran outside to put my father's tools back in their place.

Miss Ferenczi was back the next day, slightly altered. She had pulled her hair down and twisted it into pigtails, with red rubber bands holding them tight one inch from the ends. She was wearing a green blouse and pink scarf, making her difficult to look at for a full class day. This time there was no pretense of doing a reading lesson or moving on to arithmetic. As soon as the bell rang, she simply began to talk.

She talked for forty minutes straight. There seemed to be less connection   90
between her ideas, but the ideas themselves were, as the dictionary would say, fabulous. She said she had heard of a huge jewel, in what she called the Antipodes, that was so brilliant that when the light shone into it at a certain angle it would blind whoever was looking at its center. She said that the biggest diamond in the world was cursed and had killed everyone who owned it, and that by a trick of fate it was called the Hope diamond. Diamonds are magic, she said, and this is why women wear them on their fingers, as a sign of the magic of womanhood. Men have strength, Miss Ferenczi said, but no true magic. That is why men fall in love with women but women do not fall in love with men; they just love being loved. George Washington had died because of a mistake he made about a diamond. Washington was not the first *true* President, but she did not say who was. In some places in the world, she said, men and women still live in the trees and eat monkeys for break-fast. Their doctors are magicians. At the bottom of the sea are creatures thin as pancakes which have never been studied by scientists because when you take them up to the air, the fish explode.

There was not a sound in the classroom, except for Miss Ferenczi's voice, and Donna DeShano's coughing. No one even went to the bathroom.

Beethoven, she said, had not been deaf; it was a trick to make himself famous, and it worked. As she talked, Miss Ferenczi's pigtails swung back and forth. There are trees in the world, she said, that eat meat: their leaves are sticky and close up on bugs like hands. She lifted her hands and brought them together, palm to palm. Venus, which most people think is the next closest planet to the sun, is not always closer, and, besides, it is the planet of greatest mystery because of its thick cloud cover. "I know what lies underneath those clouds," Miss Ferenczi said, and waited. After the silence, she said, "Angels. Angels live under those clouds." She said that angels were not invisible to everyone and were in fact smarter than most people. They did not dress in robes as was often claimed but instead wore formal evening clothes, as if they were about to attend a concert. Often angels *do* attend concerts and sit in the aisles where, she said, most people pay no attention to them. She said the most terrible angel had the shape of the Sphinx. "There is no running away from that one," she said. She said that unquenchable fires burn just under the surface of the earth in Ohio, and that the baby Mozart fainted dead away in his cradle when he first heard the sound of a trumpet. She said that someone named Narzim al Harrardim was the greatest writer who ever lived. She said that planets control behavior, and anyone conceived during a solar eclipse would be born with webbed feet.

"I know you children like to hear these things," she said, "these secrets, and that is why I am telling you all this." We nodded. It was better than doing comprehension questions for the readings in *Broad Horizons*.

"I will tell you one more story," she said, "and then we will have to do arithmetic." She leaned over, and her voice grew soft. "There is no death," she said. "You must never be afraid. Never. That which is, cannot die. It will change into different earthly and unearthly elements, but I know this as sure as I stand here in front of you, and I swear it: you must not be afraid. I have seen this truth with these eyes. I know it because in a dream God kissed me. Here." And she pointed with her right index finger to the side of her head, below the mouth, where the vertical lines were carved into her skin.

95   Absent-mindedly we all did our arithmetic problems. At recess the class was out on the playground, but no one was playing. We were all standing in small groups, talking about Miss Ferenczi. We didn't know if she was crazy, or what. I looked out beyond the playground, at the rusted cars piled in a small heap behind a clump of sumac, and I wanted to see shapes there, approaching me.

On the way home, Carl sat next to me again. He didn't say much, and I didn't either. At last he turned to me. "You know what she said about the leaves that close up on bugs?"

"Huh?"

"The leaves," Carl insisted. "The meat-eating plants. I know it's true. I saw it on television. The leaves have this icky glue that the plants have got smeared all over them and the insects can't get off, 'cause they're stuck. I saw it." He seemed demoralized. "She's tellin' the truth."

"Yeah."

100   "You think she's seen all those angels?"

I shrugged.

"I don't think she has," Carl informed me. "I think she made that part up."

"There's a tree," I suddenly said. I was looking out the window at the farms along County Road H. I knew every barn, every broken windmill, every fence, every anhydrous ammonia tank, by heart. "There's a tree that's . . . that I've seen . . ."

"Don't you try to do it," Carl said. "You'll just sound like a jerk."

I kissed my mother. She was standing in front of the stove. "How was your day?" she asked.   105

"Fine."

"Did you have Miss Ferenczi again?"

"Yeah."

"Well?"

"She was fine. Mom," I asked, "can I go to my room?"   110

"No," she said, "not until you've gone out to the vegetable garden and picked me a few tomatoes." She glanced at the sky. "I think it's going to rain. Skedaddle and do it now. Then you come back inside and watch your brother for a few minutes while I go upstairs. I need to clean up before dinner." She looked down at me. "You're looking a little pale, Tommy." She touched the back of her hand to my forehead and I felt her diamond ring against my skin. "Do you feel all right?"

"I'm fine," I said, and went out to pick the tomatoes.

Coughing mutedly, Mr. Hibler was back the next day, slipping lozenges into his mouth when his back was turned at forty-five minute intervals and asking us how much of the prepared lesson plan Miss Ferenczi had followed. Edith Atwater took the responsibility for the class of explaining to Mr. Hibler that the substitute hadn't always done exactly what he would have done, but we had worked hard even though she talked a lot. About what? he asked. All kinds of things, Edith said. I sort of forgot. To our relief, Mr. Hibler seemed not at all interested in what Miss Ferenczi had said to fill the day. He probably thought it was woman's talk; unserious and not suited for school. It was enough that he had a pile of arithmetic problems from us to correct.

For the next month, the sumac turned a distracting red in the field, and the sun traveled toward the southern sky, so that its rays reached Mr. Hibler's Halloween display on the bulletin board in the back of the room, fading the scarecrow with a pumpkin head from orange to tan. Every three days I measured how much farther the sun had moved toward the southern horizon by making small marks with my black Crayola on the north wall, ant-sized marks only I knew were there, inching west.

And then in early December, four days after the first permanent snowfall, she   115
appeared again in our classroom. The minute she came in the door, I felt my heart begin to pound. Once again, she was different: this time, her hair hung straight down and seemed hardly to have been combed. She hadn't brought her lunchbox with her, but she was carrying what seemed to be a small box. She greeted all of us and talked about the weather. Donna DeShano had to remind her to take her overcoat off.

When the bell to start the day finally rang, Miss Ferenczi looked out at all of us and said, "Children, I have enjoyed your company in the past, and today I am going to reward you." She held up the small box. "Do you know what this is?" She waited. "Of course you don't. It is a tarot pack."

Edith Atwater raised her hand. "What's a tarot pack, Miss Ferenczi?"

"It is used to tell fortunes," she said. "And that is what I shall do this morning. I shall tell your fortunes, as I have been taught to do."

"What's fortune?" Bobby Kryzanowicz asked.

120   "The future, young man. I shall tell you what your future will be. I can't do your whole future, of course. I shall have to limit myself to the five-card system, the wands, cups, swords, pentacles, and the higher arcanes. Now who wants to be first?"

There was a long silence. Then Carol Peterson raised her hand.

"All right," Miss Ferenczi said. She divided the pack into five smaller packs and walked back to Carol's desk, in front of mine. "Pick one card from each of these packs," she said. I saw that Carol had a four of cups, a six of swords, but I couldn't see the other cards. Miss Ferenczi studied the cards on Carol's desk for a minute. "Not bad," she said. "I do not see much higher education. Probably an early marriage. Many children. There's something bleak and dreary here, but I can't tell what. Perhaps just the tasks of a housewife life. I think you'll do very well, for the most part." She smiled at Carol, a smile with a certain lack of interest. "Who wants to be next?"

Carl Whiteside raised his hand slowly.

"Yes," Miss Ferenczi said, "let's do a boy." She walked over to where Carl sat. After he picked his five cards, she gazed at them for a long time. "Travel," she said. "Much distant travel. You might go into the Army. Not too much romantic interest here. A late marriage, if at all. Squabbles. But the Sun is in your major arcana, here, yes, that's a very good card." She giggled. "Maybe a good life."

125   Next I raised my hand, and she told me my future. She did the same with Bobby Kryzanowicz, Kelly Munger, Edith Atwater, and Kim Foor. Then she came to Wayne Razmer. He picked his five cards, and I could see that the Death card was one of them.

"What's your name?" Miss Ferenczi asked.

"Wayne."

"Well, Wayne," she said, "you will undergo a *great* metamorphosis, the greatest, before you become an adult. Your earthly element will leap away, into thin air, you sweet boy. This card, this nine of swords here, tells of suffering and desolation. And this ten of wands, well, that's certainly a heavy load."

"What about this one?" Wayne pointed to the Death card.

130   "That one? That one means you will die soon, my dear." She gathered up the cards. We were all looking at Wayne. "But do not fear," she said. "It's not really death, so much as change." She put the cards on Mr. Hibler's desk. "And now, let's do some arithmetic."

At lunchtime Wayne went to Mr. Faegre, the principal, and told him what Miss Ferenczi had done. During the noon recess, we saw Miss Ferenczi drive out of the parking lot in her green Rambler. I stood under the slide, listening to the other kids coasting down and landing in the little depressive bowl at the bottom. I was kicking stones and tugging at my hair right up to the moment when I saw Wayne come out to the playground. He smiled, the dead fool, and with the fingers of his right hand he was showing everyone how he had told on Miss Ferenczi.

I made my way toward Wayne, pushing myself past two girls from another class. He was watching me with his little pinhead eyes.

"You told," I shouted at him. "She was just kidding."

"She shouldn't have," he shouted back. "We were supposed to be doing arithmetic."

"She just scared you," I said. "You're a chicken. You're a chicken, Wayne. You are. 135
Scared of a little card," I singsonged.

Wayne fell at me, his two fists hammering down on my nose. I gave him a good one in the stomach and then I tried for his head. Aiming my fist, I saw that he was crying. I slugged him.

"She was right," I yelled. "She was always right! She told the truth!" Other kids were whooping. "You were just scared, that's all!"

And then large hands pulled at us, and it was my turn to speak to Mr. Faegre.

In the afternoon Miss Ferenczi was gone, and my nose was stuffed with cotton clotted with blood, and my lip had swelled, and our class had been combined with Mrs. Mantei's sixth-grade class for a crowded afternoon science unit on insect life in ditches and swamps. I knew where Mrs. Mantei lived: she had a new house trailer just down the road from us, at the Clearwater Park. She was no mystery. Somehow she and Mr. Bodine, the other fourth-grade teacher, had managed to fit forty-five desks into the room. Kelly Munger asked if Miss Ferenczi had been arrested, and Mrs. Mantei said no, of course not. All that afternoon, until the buses came to pick us up, we learned about field crickets and two-striped grasshoppers, water bugs, cicadas, mosquitoes, flies, and moths. We learned about insects' hard outer shell, the exoskeleton, and the usual parts of the mouth, including the labrum, mandible, maxilla, and glossa. We learned about compound eyes and the four-stage metamorphosis from egg to larva to pupa to adult. We learned something, but not much, about mating. Mrs. Mantei drew, very skillfully, the internal anatomy of the grasshopper on the blackboard. We learned about the dance of the honeybee, directing other bees in the hive to pollen. We found out about which insects were pests to man, and which were not. On lined white pieces of paper we made lists of insects we might actually see, then a list of insects too small to be clearly visible, such as fleas; Mrs. Mantei said that our assignment would be to memorize these lists for the next day, when Mr. Hibler would certainly return and test us on our knowledge.

Reading and Reacting

1. In classical mythology, a gryphon (also spelled *griffin*) is a monster that has the head and wings of an eagle and the body of a lion. Why is this story called "Gryphon"?
2. Describe Miss Ferenczi's physical appearance. Why is her appearance important to the story? How does it change as the story progresses?
3. How is Miss Ferenczi different from other teachers? from other substitute teachers? from other people in general? How is her differentness communicated to her pupils? to the story's readers?
4. What is the significance of the narrator's comment, in paragraph 11, that the lines on Miss Ferenczi's face remind him of Pinocchio?
5. Is Miss Ferenczi a round or a flat character? Explain.
6. In what sense is the narrator's mother a foil for Miss Ferenczi?

7. Why does the narrator defend Miss Ferenczi, first in his argument with Carl Whiteside and later on the playground? What does his attitude toward Miss Ferenczi reveal about his own character?

8. Are all of Miss Ferenczi's "substitute facts" lies, or is there some truth in what she says? Is she correct when she says that substitute facts cannot hurt anyone? Could it be argued that much of what is taught in schools today could be viewed as "substitute facts"?

9. **JOURNAL ENTRY** Is Miss Ferenczi a good teacher? Why or why not?

10. **CRITICAL PERSPECTIVE** Writing in the *New York Times Book Review*, critic William Ferguson characterizes *A Relative Stranger*, a more recent collection of Baxter's short stories than the one in which "Gryphon" appeared, as follows:

> The thirteen stories in *A Relative Stranger*, in all quietly accomplished, suggest a mysterious yet fundamental marriage of despair and joy. Though in one way or another each story ends in disillusionment, the road that leads to that dismal state is so richly peopled, so finely drawn, that the effect is oddly reassuring.

Do you think this characterization of Baxter's work in *A Relative Stranger* applies to "Gryphon" as well? For example, do you see a "marriage of despair and joy"? Do you find the story reassuring in any way, or does it convey only a sense of disillusionment?

Related Works: "The Secret Lion" (p. 180), "Distant Relations" (p. 204), "A&P" (p. 238), "A Worn Path" (p. 463), "When I Heard the Learn'd Astronomer" (p. 715), "On First Looking into Chapman's Homer" (p. 819), "Isla" (p. 860), *Proof* (p. 1180)

ZADIE SMITH (1975–   ), born in London as Sadie Smith, changed her name at a young age "because," she said in an interview, "it seemed right, exotic, different." The author of four novels, she has published short stories in such publications as the *New Yorker, McSweeney's,* and *Granta*. Her highly praised first novel, *White Teeth* (2000), winner of numerous awards, was later followed by *On Beauty* (2005), winner of the 2006 Orange Prize for Fiction. In 2009, she published a collection of essays, *Changing My Mind*. Smith wrote "The Girl with Bangs" in response to the song "Bangs" by They Might Be Giants.

AP Images/Sang Tan

Cultural Context As a cultural trend, bangs have come and gone and come again with American women throughout the latter part of the twentieth century and into the twenty-first century. The hairstyle has evolved from the long "mall bangs" of the 1960s, which start at the crown of the head, to a range of subtler styles used to frame the face. Today, popular styles of bangs among twenty- and thirty-something women include side-swept bangs, angled bangs, short choppy bangs, classic blunt bangs, straight bangs, super-short bangs, curly bangs, and eyebrow-skimming bangs. Celebrities helping to repopularize the look include Jessica Simpson, Lara Flynn Boyle, Kim Cattrall, Ashlee Simpson, Jennifer Lopez, Paris Hilton, and Nicole Richie.

The Girl with Bangs (2001)

I fell in love with a girl once. Some time ago, now. She had bangs. I was twenty years old at the time and prey to the usual rag-bag of foolish ideas. I believed, for example, that one might meet some sweet kid and like them a lot—maybe even marry them—while all the time allowing that kid to sleep with other kids, and that this could be done with no fuss at all, just a chuck under the chin, and no tears. I believed the majority of people to be bores, however you cut them; that the mark of their dullness was easy to spot (clothes, hair) and impossible to avoid, running right through them like a watermark. I had made mental notes, too, on other empty notions—the death of certain things (socialism, certain types of music, old people), the future of others (film, footwear, poetry)—but no one need be bored with those now. The only significant bit of nonsense I carried around in those days, the only one that came from the gut, if you like, was this feeling that a girl with soft black bangs falling into eyes the color of a Perrier bottle must be good news. Look at her palming the bangs away from her face, pressing them back along her hairline, only to have them fall forward again! I found this combination to be good, *intrinsically* good in both form and content, the same way you think of cherries (life is a bowl of; she was a real sweet) until the very center of one becomes lodged in your windpipe. I believed Charlotte Greaves and her bangs to be good news. But Charlotte was emphatically bad news, requiring only eight months to take me entirely apart; the kind of clinically efficient dismembering you see when a bright child gets his hand on some toy he assembled in the first place. I'd never dated a girl before, and she was bad news the way boys can never be, because with boys it's always possible to draw up a list of pros and cons, and see the matter rationally, from either side. But you could make a list of cons on Charlotte stretching to Azerbaijan,[1] and "her bangs" sitting solitary in the pros column would outweigh all objections. Boys are just boys after all, but sometimes girls *really seem to be* the turn of a pale wrist, or the sudden jut of a hip, or a clutch of very dark hair falling across a freckled forehead. I'm not saying that's what they really are. I'm just saying sometimes it seems that way, and that those details (a thigh mole, a full face flush, a scar the precise shape and size of a cashew nut) are so many hooks waiting to land you. In this case, it was those bangs, plush and dramatic, curtains opening on to a face one would queue up to see. All women have a backstage, of course, of course. Labyrinthine, many-roomed, no doubt, no doubt. But you come to see the show, that's all I'm saying.

I first set eyes on Charlotte when she was seeing a Belgian who lived across the hall from me in college. I'd see her first thing, shuffling around the communal bathroom looking a mess—undone, always, in every sense—with her T-shirt tucked in her knickers, a fag[2] hanging out of her mouth, some kind of toothpaste or maybe mouthwash residue by her lips and those bangs in her eyes. It was hard to understand why this Belgian, Maurice, had chosen to date her. He had this great accent, Maurice, *elaborately* French, like you couldn't *be* more French, and a jaw line that seemed in fashion at the time, and you could tick all the boxes vis-à-vis personal charms; Maurice was an impressive kind of a guy. Charlotte was the kind of woman who has only two bras, both of them gray. But after a while, if you paid attention, you came to realize that she had a look about her like she just got out of a bed, no matter what

---

[1] *Azerbaijan:* Country on the coast of the Caspian Sea, bordered by Russia, Armenia, and Iran.

[2] *fag:* Cigarette.

time of day you collided with her (she had a stalk of a walk, never looked where she was going, so you had no choice) and this tendency, if put under the heading "QUALITIES THAT GIRLS SOMETIMES HAVE," was a kind of poor relation of "BEDROOM EYES" or "LOOKS LIKE SHE'S THINKING ABOUT SEX ALL THE TIME"—and it worked. She seemed always to be stumbling away from someone else, toward you. A limping figure smiling widely, arms outstretched, dressed in rags, a smouldering city as backdrop. I had watched too many films, possibly. But still: a bundle of precious things thrown at you from a third-floor European window, wrapped loosely in a blanket, chosen frantically and at random by the well-meaning owner slung haphazardly from a burning building; launched at you; it could hurt, this bundle, but look! You have caught it! A little chipped, but otherwise fine. Look what you have saved! (You understand me, I know. This is how it feels. What is the purpose of metaphor, anyway, if not to describe women?)

Now, it came to pass that this Maurice was offered a well-paid TV job in Thailand as a newscaster, and he agonized, and weighed Charlotte in one hand and the money in the other and found he could not leave without the promise that she would wait for him. This promise she gave him, but he was still gone, and gone is gone, and that's where I came in. Not immediately—I am no thief—but by degrees, studying near her in the library, watching her hair make reading difficult. Sitting next to her at lunch watching the bangs go hither, and, I suppose, thither, as people swished by with their food trays. Befriending her friends and then her; making as many nice noises about Maurice as I could. I became a boy for the duration. I stood under the window with my open arms. I did all the old boy tricks. These tricks are not as difficult as some boys will have you believe, but they are indeed slow, and work only by a very gradual process of accumulation. You have sad moments when you wonder if there will ever be an end to it. But then, usually without warning, the hard work pays off. With Charlotte it went like this: she came by for an herbal tea one day, and I rolled a joint and then another and soon enough she was lying across my lap, spineless as a mollusk, and I had my fingers in those bangs—teasing them, as the hairdressers say—and we had begun.

Most of the time we spent together was in her room. At the beginning of an affair you've no need to be outside. And it was like a filthy cocoon, her room, ankle deep in rubbish; it was the kind of room that took you in and held you close. With no clocks and my watch lost and buried, we passed time by the degeneration of things, the rotting of fruit, the accumulation of bacteria, the rising-tideline of cigarettes in the vase we used to put them out. It was a quarter past this apple. The third Saturday in the month of that stain. These things were unpleasant and tiresome. And she was no intellectual; any book I gave her she treated like a kid treats a Christmas present—fascination for a day and then the quick pall of boredom; by the end of the week it was flung across the room and submerged; weeks later when we made love I'd find the spine of the novel sticking into the small of my back, paper cuts on my toes. There was no bed to speak of. There was just a bit of the floor that was marginally clearer than the rest of it. (But wait! Here she comes, falling in an impossible arc, and here I am by careful design in just the right spot, under the window, and here she is, landing and nothing is broken, and I cannot believe my luck. You understand me. Every time I looked at the bangs, the bad stuff went away.)

Again: I know it doesn't sound great, but let's not forget the bangs. Let us not forget that after a stand-up row, a real screaming match, she could look at me from underneath the distinct hairs, separated by sweat, and I had no more resistance. *Yes, you can leave the overturned plant pot where it is. Yes, Rousseau is an idiot if you say so.* So this is what it's like being a boy. The cobbled street, the hopeful arms hugging air. There is nothing you won't do.

Charlotte's exams were coming up. I begged her to look through her reading list once more, and plan some strategic line of attack, but she wanted to do it her way. Her way meant reading the same two books—Rousseau's *Social Contract* and Plato's *Republic* (her paper was to be on people, and the way they organize their lives, or the way they did, or the way they should, I don't remember; it had a technical title, I don't remember that either)—again and again, in the study room that sat in a quiet corner of the college. The study room was meant to be for everyone but since Charlotte had moved in, all others had gradually moved out. I recall one German graduate who stood his ground for a month or so, who cleared his throat regularly and pointedly picked up things that she had dropped—but she got to him, finally. Charlotte's papers all over the floor, Charlotte's old lunches on every table, Charlottes clothes and my clothes (now indistinguishable) thrown over every chair. People would come up to me in the bar and say, "Look, Charlotte did X. Could you please, for the love of God, stop Charlotte doing X, *please?*" and I would try, but Charlotte's bangs kept Charlotte in the world of Charlotte and she barely heard me. And now, please, before we go any further: tell me. Tell me if you've ever stood under a window and caught an unworthy bundle of chintz.[3] Gold plating that came off with one rub; faked signatures, worthless trinkets. Have you? Maybe the bait was different—not bangs, but deep pockets either side of the smile or unusually vivid eye pigmentation. Or some other bodily attribute (hair, skin, curves) that recalled in you some natural phenomenon (wheat, sea, cream). Some difference. So: have you? Have you ever been out with a girl like this?

Some time after Charlotte's exams, after the 2.2 that had been stalking her for so long finally pounced, there was a knock on the door. My door—I recall now that we were in my room that morning. I hauled on a dressing-gown and went to answer it. It was Maurice, tanned and dressed like one of the Beatles when they went to see the Maharashi,[4] a white suit with a Nehru collar, his own bangs and tousled hair, slightly long at the back. He looked terrific. He said, "Someone in ze bar says you might have an idea where Charlotte is. I need to see 'er—it is very urgent. Have you seen 'er?" I had seen her. She was in my bed, about five feet from where Maurice stood, but obscured by a partition wall. "No . . ." I said. "No, not this morning. She'll probably be in the hall for breakfast though, she usually is. So, Maurice! When did you get back?" He said, "All zat must come later. I 'ave to find Charlotte. I sink I am going to marry 'er." And I thought, *Christ, which bad movie am I in?*

I got Charlotte up, shook her, poured her into some clothes, and told her to run around the back of the college and get to the dining hall before Maurice. I saw her

---

[3] *chintz:* A usually brightly printed and glazed cotton fabric.
[4] *Maharashi:* Maharishi Mahesh Yogi (1911?–2008), Hindu religious leader revered by the British rock group the Beatles.

in my head, the moment the door closed—no great feat of imagination, I had seen her run before, like a naturally uncoordinated animal (a panda?) that somebody has just shot—I saw her dashing incompetently past the ancient walls, catching herself on ivy, tripping up steps, and finally falling through the swing doors, looking wildly round the dining hall like those movie time-travellers who know not in which period they have just landed. But still she managed it, apparently she got there in time, though as the whole world now knows, Maurice took one look at her strands matted against her forehead, running in line with the ridge-ways of sleep left by the pillows, and said, "You're sleeping with her?" (Or maybe, "You're sleeping with *her?*"—I don't know; this is all reported speech) and Charlotte, who, like a lot of low-maintenance women, cannot tell a lie, said "Er . . . yes. Yes" and then made that signal of feminine relief; bottom lip out, air blown upward; bangs all of a flutter.

Later that afternoon, Maurice came back round to my room, looking all the more noble, and seemingly determined to have a calm man-to-man "you see, I have returned to marry her / I will not stand in your way" type of a chat, which was very reasonable and English of him. I let him have it alone. I nodded when it seemed appropriate; sometimes I lifted my hands in protest but soon let them fall again. You can't fight it when you've been replaced: a simple side-step and here is some old/new Belgian guy standing in the cobbled street with his face upturned, and his arms wide open, judging the angles. I thought of this girl he wanted back, who had taken me apart piece by piece, causing me nothing but trouble, with her bangs and her antisocial behaviour. I was all (un)done, I realized. I sort of marvelled at the devotion he felt for her. From a thousand miles away, with a smoldering city as a backdrop, I watched him beg me to leave them both alone; tears in his eyes, the works. I agreed it was the best thing, all round. I had the impression that here was a girl who would be thrown from person to person over years, and each would think they had saved her by some miracle when in actual fact she was in no danger at all. Never even for a second.

10   He said, "Let us go, zen, and tell 'er the decision we have come to," and I said yes, let's, but when we got to Charlotte's room, someone else was putting his fingers through her curls. Charlotte was always one of those people for whom sex is available at all times—it just happens to her, quickly, and with a minimum of conversation. This guy was some other guy that she'd been sleeping with on the days when she wasn't with me. It had been going on for four months. This all came out later, naturally.

Would you believe he married her anyway? And not only that, he married her after she'd shaved her head that afternoon just to spite us. All of us—even the other guy no one had seen before. Maurice took a bald English woman with a strange lopsided walk and a temper like a gorgon back to Thailand and married her despite friends' complaints and the voluble protest of Aneepa Kapoor, who was the woman he read the news with. The anchorwoman, who had that Hitchcock style: hair tied back tight in a bun, a spiky nose and a vicious red mouth. The kind of woman who doesn't need catching. "Maurice," she said, "you *owe* me. You can't just throw four months away like it wasn't worth a bloody thing!" He emailed me about it. He admitted that he'd been stringing Aneepa along for a while, and she'd been expecting something at the end of it. For in the real world, or so it seems to me, it is almost always women and not men who are waiting under windows, and they are almost always disappointed. In this matter, Charlotte was unusual.

Reading and Reacting

1. At what point did you realize that the narrator was female? Do you think her feelings and behavior would have been any different if she were male?
2. What exactly is it about Charlotte that fascinates the narrator? Do you share this fascination?
3. What do we learn in paragraph 1 about the narrator's tastes, feelings, and beliefs? Is this information enough to explain her obsession with Charlotte?
4. Why do you think the narrator focuses on Charlotte's bangs? What other physical traits does Charlotte have?
5. In paragraph 2, the narrator characterizes Charlotte as "the kind of woman who has only two bras, both of them gray." What does this tell readers about Charlotte? What does the description of Charlotte's room in paragraph 4 reveal about her?
6. What role does Maurice play in the story? What do we know about him? Is he a flat or a round character? Is he essential to the story?
7. At the end of paragraph 4, the narrator tells us, "Every time I looked at the bangs, the bad stuff went away." What do you think this "bad stuff" is?
8. In the story's last lines, the narrator explains that "in the real world, or so it seems to me, it is almost always women and not men who are waiting under windows, and they are almost always disappointed. In this matter, Charlotte was unusual." What does the narrator mean? How do these words help to explain her infatuation with Charlotte?

9. **JOURNAL ENTRY** Write a farewell email to the narrator from Charlotte. Try to explain her feelings for the narrator as well as her motivation for shaving her head and for deciding to marry Maurice.

10. **CRITICAL PERSPECTIVE** Writing about Zadie Smith's novel *On Beauty*, Max Watman makes the following comments:

    > Smith's characters are expertly portrayed. . . . She can blow them up in all their chalky whites and lively pinks. She is one of the best character writers working. . . . *On Beauty* is one of the few contemporary novels that feels as if it is stuffed with fully formed people rather than tics and mannerisms.

    Do you think Charlotte in "The Girl with Bangs" is depicted as a "fully formed" person, or do you think she is really just "tics and mannerisms"?

Related Works: "Love and Other Catastrophes: A Mix Tape" (p. 127), "Araby" (p. 361), "My mistress' eyes are nothing like the sun" (p. 754), "Love is not all" (p. 821), "General Review of the Sex Situation" (p. 901), "She Walks in Beauty" (p. 967), *Beauty* (p. 1069), *The Date* (p. 1411)

WRITING SUGGESTIONS: Character

1. In both "A&P," and "Gryphon," the main characters (Sammy and Tommy, respectively) struggle against rules, authority figures, and inflexible social systems. Compare and contrast the struggles in which these two characters are engaged.
2. Write an essay in which you contrast the character of Miss Brill (p. 245) with the character of Emily Grierson in "A Rose for Emily" (p. 224) or with Phoenix Jackson in

"A Worn Path" (p. 463). Consider how each character interacts with those around her as well as how each seems to see her role or mission in the world.

3. Sammy, Miss Brill, and Miss Ferenczi all use their active imaginations to create scenarios that help get them through the day. None of them is able to sustain the illusion, however. As a result, all three find out how harsh reality can be. How are these scenarios alike, and how are they different? What steps could these three characters take to fit more comfortably into the worlds they inhabit? *Should* they take such steps? Are they able to do so?

4. Write an analysis of a minor character in one of this chapter's stories—for example, Stokesie in "A&P" or Maurice in "The Girl with Bangs."

5. In "A&P," "Gryphon," and "The Girl with Bangs," each narrator is fascinated by another character—Queenie, Miss Ferenczi, and Charlotte, respectively. What exactly is each narrator attracted to? How do you account for these almost obsessive attachments?

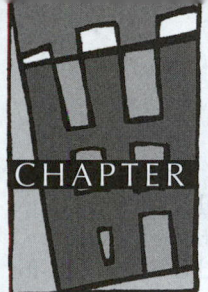

CHAPTER 15

SETTING

Ralph Ellison

Sherman Alexie

Tillie Olsen

The **setting** of a work of fiction establishes its historical, geographical, and physical context. *Where* a work is set—on a tropical island, in a dungeon, at a crowded party, in the woods—influences our reactions to the story's events and characters. *When* a work takes place—during the French Revolution, during the Vietnam War, today, or in the future—is equally important. Setting, however, is more than just the approximate time and place in which a work is set; setting also encompasses a wide variety of other elements.

Clearly, setting is more important in some works than in others. In some stories, no particular time or place is specified or even suggested, perhaps because the writer does not consider a specific setting to be important or because the writer wishes the story's events to seem timeless and universal. In other stories, a writer may provide only minimal information about setting, telling readers little more than where and when the action takes place. In many cases, however, a particular setting is vital to the story, perhaps influencing characters' feelings or behavior, as it does in the stories in this chapter.

Sometimes a story's central conflict is between the protagonist and the setting—for example, *Alice in Wonderland*, a Northerner in the South, an unsophisticated American tourist in an old European city, a sane person in a psychiatric hospital, a moral person in a corrupt environment, an immigrant in a new world, or a city dweller in the country. Such a conflict may drive the story's plot and also help to define the characters. A conflict between *events* and setting—for example, the arrival of a mysterious stranger in a typical suburban neighborhood, the intrusion of modern social ideas into an old-fashioned world, or the intrusion of a brutal murder into a peaceful village—can also enrich a story.

 ## Historical Setting

A particular historical period, and the events and customs associated with it, can be important to your understanding of a story; therefore, some knowledge of the period in which a story is set may be useful (or even essential) for readers. The historical setting establishes a story's social, cultural, economic, and political environment. Knowing, for instance, that Charlotte Perkins Gilman's "The Yellow Wallpaper" (p. 379) was written in the late nineteenth century, when doctors treated women as delicate and dependent creatures, helps to explain the narrator's emotional state. Likewise, it may be important to know that a story is set during a particularly volatile (or static) political era, during a time of permissive (or repressive) attitudes toward sex, during a war, or during a period of economic prosperity or recession. Any one of these factors may help to explain why events occur as well as why characters act (and react) as they do. Historical events or cultural norms may, for instance, limit or expand a character's options, and our knowledge of history may reveal to us a character's incompatibility with his or her milieu. For example, in F. Scott Fitzgerald's "Bernice Bobs Her Hair" (1920) set in the 1920s in a midwestern town, a young girl is goaded into cutting her long hair. To understand the significance of Bernice's act—and to understand the reactions of others to that act—readers must know that during that era only racy "society vampires," not nice girls from good families, bobbed their hair.

Knowing the approximate year or historical period during which a story takes place can help readers to better understand characters and events. This knowledge can explain forces that act on characters and account for their behavior, clarify circumstances that influence the story's action, and justify a writer's use of plot devices that might otherwise seem improbable. Thus, stories set before the development of modern transportation and communication networks may hinge on plot devices readers would not accept in a modern story. For example, in "Paul's Case," a 1904 story by Willa Cather, a young man who steals a large sum of money in Pittsburgh is able to spend several days enjoying his newfound wealth before the news of the theft reaches New York, where he has fled. In other stories, we see characters threatened by diseases that have now been eradicated (or subjected to outdated medical or psychiatric treatment) or constrained by social conventions very different from those that operate in our own society.

Geographical Setting

In addition to knowing *when* a work takes place, readers need to know *where* it takes place. Knowing whether a story is set in the United States, in Europe, or in a developing nation can help to explain anything from why language and customs are unfamiliar to us to why characters act in ways we find surprising or hold beliefs that are alien to us. Even in stories set in the United States, regional differences may account for differences in plot development and characters' motivation. For example, knowing that William Faulkner's "A Rose for Emily" (p. 224) is set in the post–Civil War American South helps to explain why the townspeople are so chivalrously protective of Miss Emily. Similarly, the fact that Bret Harte's classic story "The Outcasts of Poker Flat" (1869) is set in a California mining camp accounts for its varied cast of characters—including a gambler, a prostitute, and a traveling salesman.

The size of the town or city in which a story takes place may also be important. In a small town, for example, a character's problems are more likely to be subject to intense scrutiny by other characters, as they are in stories of small-town life such as "A Rose for Emily." In a large city, characters may be more likely to be isolated and anonymous, like Mrs. Miller in Truman Capote's gothic short story "Miriam" (1945), who is so lonely that she creates an imaginary companion. Characters may also be alienated by their big-city surroundings, as Gregor Samsa is in Franz Kafka's classic 1915 novella "The Metamorphosis," about a man who turns into a bug.

Of course, a story may not have a recognizable geographical setting: its location may not be specified, or it may be set in a fantasy world. Choosing unusual settings may free writers from the constraints placed on them by familiar environments, thus allowing them to experiment with situations and characters, unaffected by readers' expectations or associations with familiar settings.

 Physical Setting

Physical setting can influence a story's mood as well as its development. For example, *time of day* can be important. The gruesome murder described in Edgar Allan Poe's "The Cask of Amontillado" (p. 328) takes place in an appropriate setting: not just underground but in the darkness of night. Conversely, the horrifying events of Shirley Jackson's "The Lottery" (p. 419) take place in broad daylight, contrasting dramatically with the darkness of the society that permits—and even participates in—a shocking ritual. Many stories, of course, move through several time periods as the action unfolds, and changes in time may also be important. For instance, the approach of evening (or of dawn) can signal the end of a crisis in the plot.

Whether a story is set primarily *indoors* or *out-of-doors* may also be significant: characters may be physically constrained by a closed-in setting or liberated by an expansive landscape. Some interior settings may be psychologically limiting. For instance, the narrator in "The Yellow Wallpaper" feels suffocated by her room, whose ugly wallpaper comes to haunt her. In many of Poe's stories, the central character is trapped, physically or psychologically, in a confined, suffocating space. In other stories, an interior setting may have a symbolic function. For example, in "A Rose for Emily," the house is for Miss Emily a symbol of the

South's past glory as well as a refuge, a fortress, and a hiding place. Similarly, a building or house may represent society, with its rules, norms, and limitations, as in John Updike's "A&P" (p. 238), where the supermarket establishes social as well as physical limits.

Conversely, an outdoor setting can free a character from social norms of behavior, as it does for Ernest Hemingway's Nick Adams, a war veteran who, in "Big Two-Hearted River" (1925), finds order, comfort, and peace only when he is away from civilization. An outdoor setting can also expose characters to physical dangers, such as untamed wilderness, uncharted seas, and frighteningly empty open spaces, as is the case in Stephen Crane's "The Open Boat" (1897).

Weather can be another important aspect of setting. A storm can threaten a character's life or just make the character—and readers—*think* danger is present, distracting us from other, more subtle threats. Extreme weather conditions can make characters act irrationally or uncharacteristically, as in Kate Chopin's "The Storm" (p. 273), where a storm provides the story's complication and sets in motion the characters' actions. In numerous stories set in hostile landscapes, where extremes of heat and cold influence the action, weather may serve as a test for characters, as it does in Jack London's "To Build a Fire" (1908), in which the main character struggles unsuccessfully against the brutally cold, hostile environment of the Yukon.

The various physical attributes of setting combine to create a story's **atmosphere** or **mood**. In "The Cask of Amontillado," for example, several factors work together to create the story's eerie, intense atmosphere: it is nighttime; it is the hectic carnival season; and the catacombs are dark, damp, and filled with the bones of the narrator's ancestors. Sometimes the mood or atmosphere that is created helps to convey a story's central theme—as the ironic contrast between the pleasant atmosphere and the shocking events that unfold communicates the theme of "The Lottery." A story's atmosphere may also be linked to a character's mental state, perhaps reflecting his or her mood. For example, darkness and isolation can reflect a character's depression, whereas an idyllic, peaceful atmosphere can express a character's joy. And, of course, a story's atmosphere can also *influence* the characters' state of mind, causing them to react one way in a crowded, hectic city but to react very differently in a peaceful rural atmosphere.

✔ **CHECKLIST Writing about Setting**

☐ Is the setting specified or unspecified? Is it fully described or only suggested?

☐ Is the setting just background, or is it a key force in the story?

☐ Are any characters in conflict with their environment?

☐ How does the setting influence the story's plot? Does it cause characters to act?

☐ In what time period does the story take place? How can you tell? What social, political, or economic situations or events of the historical period might influence the story?

☐ In what geographical location is the story set? Is this location important to the story?

- At what time of day is the story set? Is time important to the development of the story?

- Is the story set primarily indoors or out-of-doors? What role does this aspect of the setting play in the story?

- What role do weather conditions play in the story?

- What kind of atmosphere or mood does the physical setting create?

- How does the story's atmosphere influence the characters? Does it affect (or reflect) their emotional state? Does it help to explain their motivation?

- Does the atmosphere change as the story progresses? Is this change significant?

KATE CHOPIN (1851–1904) (picture and biography on p. 201) wrote in a style that was realistic yet infused with a dense, sensual texture that was perhaps, in part, her artistic response to her memories of the exotic Louisiana bayou country. Like her contemporary Gustave Flaubert (Chopin's short novel *The Awakening* has often been called a "Creole *Bovary*"), Chopin used the physical world—as in the charged atmosphere of "The Storm"—to symbolize the inner truths of her characters' minds and hearts. Unlike Flaubert, however, she depicted sex not as a frantic and destructive force but as a joyous, elemental part of life. Apparently Kate Chopin knew how daring "The Storm" was: she never submitted it for publication.

Cultural Context   In the following story, which presumably takes place in Louisiana, the character Calixta expresses fear that the powerful storm will break the levees, the raised embankments kept in place to prevent the river from overflowing. In August 2005, more than one hundred years after this story was written, the levees in New Orleans gave way to the sheer force of Hurricane Katrina, which flooded the city, destroyed the area's economic and cultural foundation, and displaced hundreds of thousands of residents.

The Storm (c. 1899)

I

The leaves were so still that even Bibi thought it was going to rain. Bobinôt, who was accustomed to converse on terms of perfect equality with his little son, called the child's attention to certain sombre clouds that were rolling with sinister intention from the west, accompanied by a sullen, threatening roar. They were at Friedheimer's store and decided to remain there till the storm had passed. They sat within the door on two empty kegs. Bibi was four years old and looked very wise.

"Mama'll be 'fraid, yes," he suggested with blinking eyes.

"She'll shut the house. Maybe she got Sylvie helpin' her this evenin'," Bobinôt responded reassuringly.

"No; she ent got Sylvie. Sylvie was helpin' her yistiday," piped Bibi.

Bobinôt arose and going across to the counter purchased a can of shrimps, of which Calixta was very fond. Then he returned to his perch on the keg and sat stolidly holding the can of shrimps while the storm burst. It shook the wooden store and seemed to be ripping great furrows in the distant field. Bibi laid his little hand on his father's knee and was not afraid.

5

II

Calixta, at home, felt no uneasiness for their safety. She sat at a side window sewing furiously on a sewing machine. She was greatly occupied and did not notice the approaching storm. But she felt very warm and often stopped to mop her face on which the perspiration gathered in beads. She unfastened her white sacque at the throat. It began to grow dark, and suddenly realizing the situation she got up hurriedly and went about closing windows and doors.

Out on the small front gallery she had hung Bobinôt's Sunday clothes to air and she hastened out to gather them before the rain fell. As she stepped outside, Alcée Laballière rode in at the gate. She had not seen him very often since her marriage, and never alone. She stood there with Bobinôt's coat in her hands, and the big rain drops began to fall. Alcée rode his horse under the shelter of a side projection where the chickens had huddled and there were plows and a harrow piled up in the corner.

"May I come and wait on your gallery till the storm is over, Calixta?" he asked.

"Come 'long in, M'sieur Alcée."

His voice and her own startled her as if from a trance, and she seized Bobinôt's vest. Alcée, mounting to the porch, grabbed the trousers and snatched Bibi's braided jacket that was about to be carried away by a sudden gust of wind. He expressed an intention to remain outside, but it was soon apparent that he might as well have been out in the open: the water beat in upon the boards in driving sheets, and he went inside, closing the door after him. It was even necessary to put something beneath the door to keep the water out.

"My! what a rain! It's good two years sence it rain' like that," exclaimed Calixta as she rolled up a piece of bagging and Alcée helped her to thrust it beneath the crack.

She was a little fuller of figure than five years before when she married; but she had lost nothing of her vivacity. Her blue eyes still retained their melting quality; and her yellow hair, dishevelled by the wind and rain, kinked more stubbornly than ever about her ears and temples.

The rain beat upon the low, shingled roof with a force and clatter that threatened to break an entrance and deluge them there. They were in the dining room—the sitting room—the general utility room. Adjoining was her bed room, with Bibi's couch along side her own. The door stood open, and the room with its white, monumental bed, its closed shutters, looked dim and mysterious.

Alcée flung himself into a rocker and Calixta nervously began to gather up from the floor the lengths of a cotton sheet which she had been sewing.

"If this keeps up, *Dieu sait*[1] if the levees[2] goin' to stan' it!" she exclaimed.

"What have you got to do with the levees?"

"I got enough to do! An' there's Bobinôt with Bibi out in that storm—if he only didn't left Friedheimer's!"

"Let us hope, Calixta, that Bobinôt's got sense enough to come in out of a cyclone."

10

15

---

[1]*Dieu sait:* "God knows" (French).

[2]*levees:* Raised embankments designed to keep a river from overflowing.

She went and stood at the window with a greatly disturbed look on her face. She wiped the frame that was clouded with moisture. It was stiflingly hot. Alcée got up and joined her at the window, looking over her shoulder. The rain was coming down in sheets obscuring the view of far-off cabins and enveloping the distant wood in a gray mist. The playing of the lightning was incessant. A bolt struck a tall chinaberry tree at the edge of the field. It filled all visible space with a blinding glare and the crash seemed to invade the very boards they stood upon.

Calixta put her hands to her eyes, and with a cry, staggered backward. Alcée's arm encircled her, and for an instant he drew her close and spasmodically to him.   20

"Bonté!"[3] she cried, releasing herself from his encircling arm and retreating from the window, "the house'll go next! If I only knew w'ere Bibi was!" She would not compose herself; she would not be seated. Alcée clasped her shoulders and looked into her face. The contact of her warm, palpitating body when he had unthinkingly drawn her into his arms, had aroused all the old-time infatuation and desire for her flesh.

"Calixta," he said, "don't be frightened. Nothing can happen. The house is too low to be struck, with so many tall trees standing about. There! aren't you going to be quiet? say, aren't you?" He pushed her hair back from her face that was warm and steaming. Her lips were as red and moist as pomegranate seed. Her white neck and a glimpse of her full, firm bosom disturbed him powerfully. As she glanced up at him the fear in her liquid blue eyes had given place to a drowsy gleam that unconsciously betrayed a sensuous desire. He looked down into her eyes and there was nothing for him to do but to gather her lips in a kiss. It reminded him of Assumption.

"Do you remember—in Assumption, Calixta?" he asked in a low voice broken by passion. Oh! she remembered; for in Assumption he had kissed her and kissed and kissed her; until his senses would well nigh fail, and to save her he would resort to a desperate flight. If she was not an immaculate dove in those days, she was still inviolate; a passionate creature whose very defenselessness had made her defense, against which his honor forbade him to prevail. Now—well, now—her lips seemed in a manner free to be tasted, as well as her round, white throat and her whiter breasts.

They did not heed the crashing torrents, and the roar of the elements made her laugh as she lay in his arms. She was a revelation in that dim, mysterious chamber; as white as the couch she lay upon. Her firm, elastic flesh that was knowing for the first time its birthright, was like a creamy lily that the sun invites to contribute its breath and perfume to the undying life of the world.

The generous abundance of her passion, without guile or trickery, was like a   25
white flame which penetrated and found response in depths of his own sensuous nature that had never yet been reached.

When he touched her breasts they gave themselves up in quivering ecstasy, inviting his lips. Her mouth was a fountain of delight. And when he possessed her, they seemed to swoon together at the very borderland of life's mystery.

He stayed cushioned upon her, breathless, dazed, enervated, with his heart beating like a hammer upon her. With one hand she clasped his head, her lips

---

[3]Bonté: "Goodness!" (French).

lightly touching his forehead. The other hand stroked with a soothing rhythm his muscular shoulders.

The growl of the thunder was distant and passing away. The rain beat softly upon the shingles, inviting them to drowsiness and sleep. But they dared not yield.

The rain was over; and the sun was turning the glistening green world into a palace of gems. Calixta, on the gallery, watched Alcée ride away. He turned and smiled at her with a beaming face; and she lifted her pretty chin in the air and laughed aloud.

III

30   Bobinôt and Bibi, trudging home, stopped without at the cistern to make themselves presentable.

"My! Bibi, w'at will yo' mama say! You ought to be ashame'. You oughtn' put on those good pants. Look at 'em! An' that mud on yo' collar! How you got that mud on yo' collar, Bibi? I never saw such a boy!" Bibi was the picture of pathetic resignation. Bobinôt was the embodiment of serious solicitude as he strove to remove from his own person and his son's the signs of their tramp over heavy roads and through wet fields. He scraped the mud off Bibi's bare legs and feet with a stick and carefully removed all traces from his heavy brogans. Then, prepared for the worst—the meeting with an over-scrupulous housewife, they entered cautiously at the back door.

Calixta was preparing supper. She had set the table and was dripping coffee at the hearth. She sprang up as they came in.

"Oh, Bobinôt! You back! My! but I was uneasy. W'ere you been during the rain? An' Bibi? he ain't wet? he ain't hurt?" She had clasped Bibi and was kissing him effusively. Bobinôt's explanations and apologies which he had been composing all along the way, died on his lips as Calixta felt him to see if he were dry, and seemed to express nothing but satisfaction at their safe return.

"I brought you some shrimps, Calixta," offered Bobinôt, hauling the can from his ample side pocket and laying it on the table.

35   "Shrimps! Oh, Bobinôt! you too good fo' anything!" and she gave him a smacking kiss on the cheek that resounded. "*J'vous réponds*,[4] we'll have a feas' tonight! umph-umph!"

Bobinôt and Bibi began to relax and enjoy themselves, and when the three seated themselves at table they laughed much and so loud that anyone might have heard them as far away as Laballière's.

IV

Alcée Laballière wrote to his wife, Clarisse, that night. It was a loving letter, full of tender solicitude. He told her not to hurry back, but if she and the babies liked it at Biloxi, to stay a month longer. He was getting on nicely; and though he missed them, he was willing to bear the separation a while longer—realizing that their health and pleasure were the first things to be considered.

---

[4]*J'vous réponds*: "I tell you" (French).

V

As for Clarisse, she was charmed upon receiving her husband's letter. She and the babies were doing well. The society was agreeable; many of her old friends and acquaintances were at the bay. And the first free breath since her marriage seemed to restore the pleasant liberty of her maiden days. Devoted as she was to her husband, their intimate conjugal life was something which she was more than willing to forego for a while.

So the storm passed and everyone was happy.

Reading and Reacting

1. Trace the progress of the storm through the five parts of the story. Then, trace the stages of the story's plot. How does the progress of the storm parallel the developing plot?

2. How does the weather help to create the story's atmosphere? How would you characterize this atmosphere?

3. In Part I, the "sombre clouds . . . rolling with sinister intention" introduce the storm. In what sense does this description introduce the story's action as well?

4. In what respects does the storm *cause* the events of the story? List specific events that occur because of the storm. Is the presence of the storm essential to the story?

5. In what sense does the storm act as a character in the story?

6. The weather is the most obvious element of the story's setting. What other aspects of setting are important to the story?

7. After Part II, the storm is not mentioned again until the last line of the story. What signs of the storm remain in Parts III, IV, and V?

8. Besides referring to the weather, what else might the title suggest?

9. JOURNAL ENTRY The storm sets in motion the chain of events that leads to the characters' adultery. Do you think the storm excuses the characters in any way from responsibility for their actions?

10. CRITICAL PERSPECTIVE Kate Chopin is widely considered to be a regional, or "local color" writer. This term refers to writing in which descriptions of a particular geographic region are prominent. Local color writers strive to incorporate accurate speech patterns and dialects—as well as descriptions of local scenery, dress, and social customs—into their writing. Writing for the *Southern Literary Journal* and quoting Chopin critic Helen Taylor, Sylvia Bailey Shurbutt notes, "Of the regional stories, Taylor writes, ['Chopin's'] ironic and resonant use of historical, topographical, and mythical Louisiana materials . . . functions to interrogate both the Southern ideology of womanhood and contradictory constructions of Southern femininity in the 1890's.'"

In what respects is "The Storm" an example of local color writing? How does it challenge "the southern ideology of womanhood"?

Related Works: "Hills Like White Elephants" (p. 119), "Distant Relations" (p. 204), "Love is not all" (p. 821), "What lips my lips have kissed" (p. 899), "General Review of the Sex Situation" (p. 901), "Wild Nights—Wild Nights!" (p. 979)

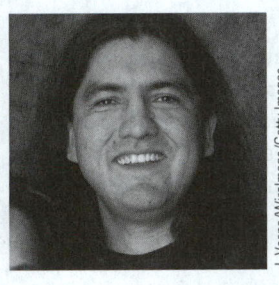

SHERMAN ALEXIE (1966–   ), a Spokane/Coeur d'Alene Indian, grew up on the Spokane Indian Reservation in Wellpinit, Washington, about fifty miles northwest of Spokane, where approximately 2,400 Spokane Tribal members live. Alexie has published short stories, novels, and poetry. He was named one of *Granta's* Best of Young American Novelists, and his first novel, *Reservation Blues* (1995), won the Before Columbus Foundation's American Book Award and the Murray Morgan Prize. His second novel, *Indian Killer* (1996), was named one of *People's* Best of Pages and was a *New York Times* Notable Book. "This Is What It Means to Say Phoenix, Arizona" (from his 1993 short story collection *The Lone Ranger and Tonto Fistfight in Heaven*) eventually became the movie *Smoke Signals*, which was released in 1998. His most recent books are the young adult novel *The Absolutely True Diary of a Part-Time Indian* (2007), for which he won the National Book Award for Young People's Literature; the novel *Flight* (2007); the story collection *Blasphemy* (2012); and the poetry collections *Face* (2009) and *What I've Stolen, What I've Earned* (2013).

Commenting on Native American culture, Alexie has said, "One of the biggest misconceptions about Indians is that we're stoic, but humor is an essential part of our culture." "This Is What It Means to Say Phoenix, Arizona" demonstrates this unique use of humor to transcend the harsh realities of life on the reservation and of the struggle to adapt to contemporary American life.

Cultural Context   The United States policy of creating Native American reservations can be traced back to the administration of President Ulysses S. Grant, who determined that establishing such reservations was the best way to handle the "Indian problem" between white settlers and the Native Americans they encountered. (Even supporters of Native Americans believed that they were incapable of assimilating into the wider American society and that only on reservations would they be able to survive as a people.) Today, about forty percent of America's 4.9 million Native Americans continue to live on reservations, where unemployment rates soar and more than twenty-eight percent of families live below the federal poverty line. At the same time, reservations are the one place where members of a tribe can live together and retain their culture, language, and heritage. The characters in "This Is What It Means to Say Phoenix, Arizona" experience both the positive and negative aspects of reservation life.

This Is What It Means to Say
Phoenix, Arizona (1993)

Just after Victor lost his job at the Bureau of Indian Affairs,[1] he also found out that his father had died of a heart attack in Phoenix, Arizona. Victor hadn't seen his father in a few years, had only talked to him on the telephone once or twice, but there still was a genetic pain, which was as real and immediate as a broken bone. Victor didn't have any money. Who does have money on a reservation, except the cigarette and fireworks salespeople? His father had a savings account waiting to be claimed, but Victor needed to find a way to get from Spokane to Phoenix. Victor's mother was just as poor as he was, and the rest of his family didn't have any use at all for him. So Victor called the tribal council.

---

[1] *Bureau of Indian Affairs:* The division of the U.S. Department of the Interior that manages Native American matters; the bureau is operated by government officials, not tribal leaders.

"Listen," Victor said. "My father just died. I need some money to get to Phoenix to make arrangements."

"Now Victor," the council said, "you know we're having a difficult time financially."

"But I thought the council had special funds set aside for stuff like this."

"Now, Victor, we do have some money available for the proper return of tribal members' bodies. But I don't think we have enough to bring your father all the way back from Phoenix."   5

"Well," Victor said. "It ain't going to cost all that much. He had to be cremated. Things were kind of ugly. He died of a heart attack in his trailer and nobody found him for a week. It was really hot, too. You get the picture."

"Now, Victor, we're sorry for your loss and the circumstances. But we can really only afford to give you one hundred dollars."

"That's not even enough for a plane ticket."

"Well, you might consider driving down to Phoenix."

"I don't have a car. Besides, I was going to drive my father's pickup back up here."   10

"Now, Victor," the council said, "we're sure there is somebody who could drive you to Phoenix. Or could anybody lend you the rest of the money?"

"You know there ain't nobody around with that kind of money."

"Well, we're sorry, Victor, but that's the best we can do."

Victor accepted the tribal council's offer. What else could he do? So he signed the proper papers, picked up his check, and walked over to the Trading Post to cash it.

While Victor stood in line, he watched Thomas Builds-the-Fire standing near the magazine rack talking to himself. Like he always did. Thomas was a storyteller whom nobody wanted to listen to. That's like being a dentist in a town where everybody has false teeth.   15

Victor and Thomas Builds-the-Fire were the same age, had grown up and played in the dirt together. Ever since Victor could remember, it was Thomas who had always had something to say.

Once, when they were seven years old, when Victor's father still lived with the family, Thomas closed his eyes and told Victor this story: "Your father's heart is weak. He is afraid of his own family. He is afraid of you. Late at night, he sits in the dark. Watches the television until there's nothing but that white noise. Sometimes he feels like he wants to buy a motorcycle and ride away. He wants to run and hide. He doesn't want to be found."

Thomas Builds-the-Fire had known that Victor's father was going to leave, known it before anyone. Now Victor stood in the Trading Post with a one-hundred-dollar check in his hand, wondering if Thomas knew that Victor's father was dead, if he knew what was going to happen next.

Just then, Thomas looked at Victor, smiled, and walked over to him.

"Victor, I'm sorry about your father," Thomas said.   20

"How did you know about it?" Victor asked.

"I heard it on the wind. I heard it from the birds. I felt it in the sunlight. Also, your mother was just in here crying."

"Oh," Victor said and looked around the Trading Post. All the other Indians stared, surprised that Victor was even talking to Thomas. Nobody talked to Thomas anymore because he told the same damn stories over and over again. Victor was embarrassed, but he thought that Thomas might be able to help him. Victor felt a sudden need for tradition.

"I can lend you the money you need," Thomas said suddenly. "But you have to take me with you."

25   "I can't take your money," Victor said. "I mean, I haven't hardly talked to you in years. We're not really friends anymore."

"I didn't say we were friends. I said you had to take me with you."

"Let me think about it."

Victor went home with his one hundred dollars and sat at the kitchen table. He held his head in his hands and thought about Thomas Builds-the-Fire, remembered little details, tears and scars, the bicycle they shared for a summer, so many stories.

*   *   *

Thomas Builds-the-Fire sat on the bicycle, waiting in Victor's yard. He was ten years old and skinny. His hair was dirty because it was the Fourth of July.

30   "Victor," Thomas yelled. "Hurry up. We're going to miss the fireworks."

After a few minutes, Victor ran out of his family's house, vaulted over the porch railing, and landed gracefully on the sidewalk.

Thomas gave him the bike and they headed for the fireworks. It was nearly dark and the fireworks were about to start.

"You know," Thomas said, "it's strange how us Indians celebrate the Fourth of July. It ain't like it was our independence everybody was fighting for."

"You think about things too much," Victor said. "It's just supposed to be fun. Maybe Junior will be there."

35   "Which Junior? Everybody on this reservation is named Junior."

The fireworks were small, hardly more than a few bottle rockets and a fountain. But it was enough for two Indian boys. Years later, they would need much more.

Afterward, sitting in the dark, fighting off mosquitoes, Victor turned to Thomas Builds-the-Fire.

"Hey," Victor said. "Tell me a story."

Thomas closed his eyes and told this story: "There were these two Indian boys who wanted to be warriors. But it was too late to be warriors in the old way. All the horses were gone. So the two Indian boys stole a car and drove to the city. They parked the stolen car in the front of the police station and then hitchhiked back home to the reservation. When they got back, all their friends cheered and their parents' eyes shone with pride. 'You were very brave,' everybody said to the two Indian boys. 'Very brave.'"

40   "Ya-hey," Victor said. "That's a good one. I wish I could be a warrior."

"Me too," Thomas said.

Victor sat at his kitchen table. He counted his one hundred dollars again and again. He knew he needed more to make it to Phoenix and back. He knew he needed Thomas Builds-the-Fire. So he put his money in his wallet and opened the front door to find Thomas on the porch.

"Ya-hey, Victor," Thomas said. "I knew you'd call me."

Thomas walked into the living room and sat down in Victor's favorite chair.

"I've got some money saved up," Thomas said. "It's enough to get us down there, but you have to get us back." 45

"I've got this hundred dollars," Victor said. "And my dad had a savings account I'm going to claim."

"How much in your dad's account?"

"Enough. A few hundred."

"Sounds good. When we leaving?"

When they were fifteen and had long since stopped being friends, Victor and Thomas 50 got into a fistfight. That is, Victor was really drunk and beat Thomas up for no reason at all. All the other Indian boys stood around and watched it happen. Junior was there and so were Lester, Seymour, and a lot of others.

The beating might have gone on until Thomas was dead if Norma Many Horses hadn't come along and stopped it.

"Hey, you boys," Norma yelled and jumped out of her car. "Leave him alone."

If it had been someone else, even another man, the Indian boys would've just ignored the warnings. But Norma was a warrior. She was powerful. She could have picked up any two of the boys and smashed their skulls together. But worse than that, she would have dragged them all over to some tepee and made them listen to some elder tell a dusty old story.

The Indian boys scattered, and Norma walked over to Thomas and picked him up.

"Hey, little man, are you O.K.?" she asked. 55

Thomas gave her a thumbs-up.

"Why they always picking on you?"

Thomas shook his head, closed his eyes, but no stories came to him, no words or music. He just wanted to go home, to lie in his bed and let his dreams tell the stories for him.

Thomas Builds-the-Fire and Victor sat next to each other in the airplane, coach section. A tiny white woman had the window seat. She was busy twisting her body into pretzels. She was flexible.

"I have to ask," Thomas said, and Victor closed his eyes in embarrassment. 60

"Don't," Victor said.

"Excuse me, miss," Thomas asked. "Are you a gymnast or something?"

"There's no something about it," she said. "I was first alternate on the 1980 Olympic team."

"Really?" Thomas asked.

"Really." 65

"I mean, you used to be a world-class athlete?" Thomas asked.

"My husband thinks I still am."

Thomas Builds-the-Fire smiled. She was a mental gymnast too. She pulled her leg straight up against her body so that she could've kissed her kneecap.

"I wish I could do that," Thomas said.

70   Victor was ready to jump out of the plane. Thomas, that crazy Indian storyteller with ratty old braids and broken teeth, was flirting with a beautiful Olympic gymnast. Nobody back home on the reservation would ever believe it.

"Well," the gymnast said. "It's easy. Try it."

Thomas grabbed at his leg and tried to pull it up into the same position as the gymnast's. He couldn't even come close, which made Victor and the gymnast laugh.

"Hey," she asked. "You two are Indian, right?"

"Full-blood," Victor said.

75   "Not me," Thomas said. "I'm half magician on my mother's side and half clown on my father's."

They all laughed.

"What are your names?" she asked.

"Victor and Thomas."

"Mine is Cathy. Pleased to meet you all."

80   The three of them talked for the duration of the flight. Cathy the gymnast complained about the government, how they screwed the 1980 Olympic team by boycotting the games.

"Sounds like you all got a lot in common with Indians," Thomas said.

Nobody laughed.

After the plane landed in Phoenix and they had all found their way to the terminal, Cathy the gymnast smiled and waved goodbye.

"She was really nice," Thomas said.

85   "Yeah, but everybody talks to everybody on airplanes," Victor said.

"You always used to tell me I think too much," Thomas said. "Now it sounds like you do."

"Maybe I caught it from you."

"Yeah."

Thomas and Victor rode in a taxi to the trailer where Victor's father had died.

90   "Listen," Victor said as they stopped in front of the trailer. "I never told you I was sorry for beating you up that time."

"Oh, it was nothing. We were just kids and you were drunk."

"Yeah, but I'm still sorry."

"That's all right."

Victor paid for the taxi, and the two of them stood in the hot Phoenix summer. They could smell the trailer.

95   "This ain't going to be nice," Victor said. "You don't have to go in."

"You're going to need help."

Victor walked to the front door and opened it. The stink rolled out and made them both gag. Victor's father had lain in that trailer for a week in hundred-degree temperatures before anyone had found him. And the only reason anyone found him was the smell. They needed dental records to identify him. That's exactly what the coroner said. They needed dental records.

"Oh, man," Victor said. "I don't know if I can do this."

"Well, then don't."

100   "But there might be something valuable in there."

"I thought his money was in the bank."

"It is: I was talking about pictures and letters and stuff like that."

"Oh," Thomas said as he held his breath and followed Victor into the trailer.

When Victor was twelve, he stepped into an underground wasps' nest. His foot was caught in the hole and no matter how hard he struggled, Victor couldn't pull free. He might have died there, stung a thousand times, if Thomas Builds-the-Fire had not come by.

"Run," Thomas yelled and pulled Victor's foot from the hole. They ran then, hard   105
as they ever had, faster than Billy Mills, faster than Jim Thorpe, faster than the wasps could fly.

Victor and Thomas ran until they couldn't breathe, ran until it was cold and dark outside, ran until they were lost and it took hours to find their way home. All the way back, Victor counted his stings.

"Seven," Victor said. "My lucky number."

*   *   *

Victor didn't find much to keep in the trailer. Only a photo album and a stereo. Everything else had that smell stuck in it or was useless anyway. "I guess this is all," Victor said. "It ain't much."

"Better than nothing," Thomas said.

"Yeah, and I do have the pickup."   110

"Yeah," Thomas said. "It's in good shape."

"Dad was good about that stuff."

"Yeah, I remember your dad."

"Really?" Victor asked. "What do you remember?"

Thomas Builds-the-Fire closed his eyes and told this story: "I remember when I had   115
this dream that told me to go to Spokane, to stand by the falls in the middle of the city and wait for a sign. I knew I had to go there but I didn't have a car. Didn't have a license. I was only thirteen. So I walked all the way, took me all day, and I finally made it to the falls. I stood there for an hour waiting. Then your dad came walking up. 'What the hell are you doing here?' he asked me. I said, 'Waiting for a vision.' Then your father said, 'All you're going to get here is mugged.' So he drove me over to Denny's, bought me dinner, and then drove me home to the reservation. For a long time, I was mad because I thought my dreams had lied to me. But they hadn't. Your dad was my vision. *Take care of each other* is what my dreams were saying. *Take care of each other*."

Victor was quiet for a long time. He searched his mind for memories of his father, found the good ones, found a few bad ones, added it all up, and smiled.

"My father never told me about finding you in Spokane," Victor said.

"He said he wouldn't tell anybody. Didn't want me to get in trouble. But he said I had to watch out for you as part of the deal."

"Really?"

"Really. Your father said you would need the help. He was right."   120

"That's why you came down here with me, isn't it?" Victor asked.

"I came because of your father."

Victor and Thomas climbed into the pickup, drove over to the bank, and claimed the three hundred dollars in the savings account.

Thomas Builds-the-Fire could fly.

125   Once, he jumped off the roof of the tribal school and flapped his arms like a crazy eagle. And he flew. For a second he hovered, suspended above all the other Indian boys, who were too smart or too scared to jump too.

"He's flying," Junior yelled, and Seymour was busy looking for the trick wires or mirrors. But it was real. As real as the dirt when Thomas lost altitude and crashed to the ground.

He broke his arm in two places.

"He broke his wing, he broke his wing, he broke his wing," all the Indian boys chanted as they ran off, flapping their wings, wishing they could fly too. They hated Thomas for his courage, his brief moment as a bird. Everybody has dreams about flying. Thomas flew.

One of his dreams came true for just a second, just enough to make it real.

                *   *   *

130 Victor's father, his ashes, fit in one wooden box with enough left over to fill a cardboard box.

"He always was a big man," Thomas said.

Victor carried part of his father out to the pickup, and Thomas carried the rest. They set him down carefully behind the seats, put a cowboy hat on the wooden box and a Dodgers cap on the cardboard box. That was the way it was supposed to be.

"Ready to head back home?" Victor asked.

"It's going to be a long drive."

135   "Yeah, take a couple days, maybe."

"We can take turns," Thomas said.

"O.K.," Victor said, but they didn't take turns. Victor drove for sixteen hours straight north, made it halfway up Nevada toward home before he finally pulled over.

"Hey, Thomas," Victor said. "You got to drive for a while."

"O.K."

140 Thomas Builds-the-Fire slid behind the wheel and started off down the road. All through Nevada, Thomas and Victor had been amazed at the lack of animal life, at the absence of water, of movement.

"Where is everything?" Victor had asked more than once.

Now, when Thomas was finally driving, they saw the first animal, maybe the only animal in Nevada. It was a long-eared jackrabbit.

"Look," Victor yelled. "It's alive."

Thomas and Victor were busy congratulating themselves on their discovery when the jackrabbit darted out into the road and under the wheels of the pickup.

145   "Stop the goddamn car," Victor yelled, and Thomas did stop and backed the pickup to the dead jackrabbit.

"Oh, man, he's dead," Victor said as he looked at the squashed animal.

"Really dead."

"The only thing alive in this whole state and we just killed it."

"I don't know," Thomas said. "I think it was suicide."

Victor looked around the desert, sniffed the air, felt the emptiness and loneliness, and nodded his head.   150

"Yeah," Victor said. "It had to be suicide."

"I can't believe this," Thomas said. "You drive for a thousand miles and there ain't even any bugs smashed on the windshield. I drive for ten seconds and kill the only living thing in Nevada."

"Yeah," Victor said. "Maybe I should drive."

"Maybe you should."

Thomas Builds-the-Fire walked through the corridors of the tribal school by him-   155
self. Nobody wanted to be anywhere near him because of all those stories. Story after story.

Thomas closed his eyes and this story came to him: "We are all given one thing by which our lives are measured, one determination. Mine are the stories that can change or not change the world. It doesn't matter which, as long as I continue to tell the stories. My father, he died on Okinawa[2] in World War II, died fighting for this country, which had tried to kill him for years. My mother, she died giving birth to me, died while I was still inside her. She pushed me out into the world with her last breath. I have no brothers or sisters. I have only my stories, which came to me before I even had the words to speak. I learned a thousand stories before I took my first thousand steps. They are all I have. It's all I can do."

Thomas Builds-the-Fire told his stories to all those who would stop and listen. He kept telling them long after people had stopped listening.

Victor and Thomas made it back to the reservation just as the sun was rising. It was the beginning of a new day on earth, but the same old shit on the reservation.

"Good morning," Thomas said.

"Good morning."   160

The tribe was waking up, ready for work, eating breakfast, reading the newspaper, just like everybody else does. Willene LeBret was out in her garden, wearing a bath-robe. She waved when Thomas and Victor drove by.

"Crazy Indians made it," she said to herself and went back to her roses.

Victor stopped the pickup in front of Thomas Builds-the-Fire's HUD[3] house. They both yawned, stretched a little, shook dust from their bodies.

"I'm tired," Victor said.

"Of everything," Thomas added.   165

They both searched for words to end the journey. Victor needed to thank Thomas for his help and for the money, and to make the promise to pay it all back.

"Don't worry about the money," Thomas said. "It don't make any difference anyhow."

---

[2]*Okinawa:* Largest island of the Ryukyus, a chain of Japanese islands in the western Pacific Ocean.

[3]*HUD:* The U.S. Department of Housing and Urban Development.

"Probably not, enit?"

"Nope."

170   Victor knew that Thomas would remain the crazy storyteller who talked to dogs and cars, who listened to the wind and pine trees. Victor knew that he couldn't really be friends with Thomas, even after all that had happened. It was cruel but it was real. As real as the ash, as Victor's father, sitting behind the seats.

"I know how it is," Thomas said. "I know you ain't going to treat me any better than you did before. I know your friends would give you too much shit about it."

Victor was ashamed of himself. Whatever happened to the tribal ties, the sense of community? The only real thing he shared with anybody was a bottle and broken dreams. He owed Thomas something, anything.

"Listen," Victor said and handed Thomas the cardboard box that contained half of his father. "I want you to have this."

Thomas took the ashes and smiled, closed his eyes, and told this story: "I'm going to travel to Spokane Falls one last time and toss these ashes into the water. And your father will rise like a salmon, leap over the bridge, over me, and find his way home. It will be beautiful. His teeth will shine like silver, like a rainbow. He will rise, Victor, he will rise."

175   Victor smiled.

"I was planning on doing the same thing with my half," Victor said. "But I didn't imagine my father looking anything like a salmon. I thought it'd be like cleaning the attic or something. Like letting things go after they've stopped having any use."

"Nothing stops, cousin," Thomas said. "Nothing stops."

Thomas Builds-the-Fire got out of the pickup and walked up his driveway. Victor started the pickup and began the drive home.

"Wait," Thomas yelled suddenly from his porch. "I just got to ask one favor."

180   Victor stopped the pickup, leaned out the window, and shouted back.

"What do you want?" he asked.

"Just one time when I'm telling a story somewhere, why don't you stop and listen?" Thomas asked.

"Just once?"

"Just once."

185   Victor waved his arms to let Thomas know that the deal was good. It was a fair trade. That's all Thomas had ever wanted from his whole life. So Victor drove his father's pickup toward home while Thomas went into his house, closed the door behind him, and heard a new story come to him in the silence afterward.

Reading and Reacting

1. In paragraph 1, readers are told that Victor lives on a reservation. What details elsewhere in the story establish this setting? What associations does this setting have for you? Do you think the story could take place anywhere else?

2. In addition to various locations on the reservation, the story's settings include an airplane, a trailer in Phoenix, and a road through Nevada. What does each of these settings contribute to the story's plot?

3. Is the scene on the plane necessary? intrusive? distracting? far-fetched?

4. How would you characterize the story's mood or atmosphere? How do Thomas's stories help to create this mood? How do they help to establish his character? Do you think the story should have included more of Thomas's stories?

5. Why do you suppose Victor and Thomas cannot be friends when they get back to the reservation? Why are they able to be friends when they are traveling to Phoenix?

6. Do the flashbacks to the two men's childhood add something vital to the story? What purpose do these flashbacks serve?

7. In Native American culture, the storyteller holds an important position, telling tales that transmit and preserve the tribe's basic beliefs. Do you think Thomas's stories serve such a function? Or, do you think that he is, as Victor characterizes him, simply "the crazy storyteller who talked to dogs and cars, who listened to the wind and pine trees" (par. 170)?

8. What do you think the story's title means?

9. **JOURNAL ENTRY** At the end of the story, when Thomas returns home, he hears "a new story come to him in the silence" after he closes the door. What kind of story do you think comes to him at this point?

10. **CRITICAL PERSPECTIVE** In the introduction to a collection of Native American literature, Clifford E. Trafzer, the collection's editor, discusses the unique characteristics of Native American writers:

> Due to their grounding in the oral tradition of their people, Native American writers do not follow the literary canon of the dominant society in their approach to short stories. Rather than focusing on one theme or character in a brief time frame, or using one geographical area, they often use multiple themes and characters with few boundaries of time or place. Their stories do not always follow a linear and clear path, and frequently the past and present, real and mythic, and conscious and unconscious are not distinguishable. Multidimensional characters are common, and involved stories usually lack absolute conclusions. Native American writers may also play tricks with language, deliberately misusing grammar, syntax, and spelling—sometimes in defiance of the dominant culture—in order to make English reflect the language of their peoples.

Do you think "This Is What It Means to Say Phoenix, Arizona" displays the characteristics Trafzer associates with Native American writers?

Related Works: "Discovering America" (p. 135), "Evolution" (p. 699), "Defending Walt Whitman" (p. 952), "Indian Boarding School: The Runaways" (p. 986)

RALPH ELLISON (1914–1994) was born in Oklahoma City, Oklahoma. After his father's death when Ellison was three, Ellison's mother took up work as a domestic servant to support herself and her son. Early on, Ellison developed an interest in literature and music. He enrolled as a musician at Tuskegee Institute in Alabama; then, in 1936, he moved to New York City, where he worked with the Federal Writer's Project. While there, Ellison met prominent African American writers Langston Hughes and Richard Wright, who encouraged his literary ambitions. He began to publish stories in journals and became an editor of *Negro Quarterly*. After serving in the Merchant Marines during World War II, Ellison returned to New York and taught literature at New York University for many years.

Ellison's first novel, *Invisible Man* (1952), was an instant success. The book—a semiautobiographical chronicle of a young African American man's search for intellectual identity—won the National Book Award for fiction and was listed in *Book Week* as the most distinguished American novel of the preceding twenty years. His short story "Battle Royal" was first published in 1948; it went on to become, in a slightly revised form, the opening chapter of *Invisible Man*. Ellison published two collections of essays, *Shadow and Act* (1964) and *Going to the Territories* (1986); his collected essays appeared in 1995. Ellison's second novel, *Juneteenth*, was planned as a trilogy, but after a large section of the novel burned in a fire in 1967, Ellison spent years reconstructing the text, only to leave it unfinished at his death. His manuscript, some two thousand pages, was edited by John Callahan and posthumously published in 1999.

Cultural Context The term *battle royal* refers to an ancient Roman contest in which a group of gladiators fought until only one remained alive. Due to the random and chaotic nature of these contests, the winners were determined more by luck than by martial skill. In the period before the Civil War, these contests often involved slaves fighting bare-fisted (and sometimes blindfolded) at boxing matches. Today, this form of combat is a staple of professional wrestling, but at the time this story was written, the battle royal was relegated to back rooms and more clandestine functions and almost always involved African Americans fighting in front of a white audience.

Battle Royal (1952)

It goes a long way back, some twenty years. All my life I had been looking for something, and everywhere I turned someone tried to tell me what it was. I accepted their answers too, though they were often in contradiction and even self-contradictory. I was naïve. I was looking for myself and asking everyone except myself questions which I, and only I, could answer. It took me a long time and much painful boomeranging of my expectations to achieve a realization everyone else appears to have been born with: That I am nobody but myself. But first I had to discover that I am an invisible man!

And yet I am no freak of nature, nor of history. I was in the cards, other things having been equal (or unequal) eighty-five years ago. I am not ashamed of my grandparents for having been slaves. I am only ashamed of myself for having at one time been ashamed. About eighty-five years ago they were told that they were free, united with others of our country in everything pertaining to the common good, and, in everything social, separate like the fingers of the hand. And they believed it. They exulted in it. They stayed in their place, worked hard, and brought up my father to do the same. But my grandfather is the one. He was an odd old guy, my grandfather, and I am told I take after him. It was he who caused the trouble. On his deathbed he called my father to him and said, "Son, after I'm gone I want you to keep up the good fight. I never told you, but our life is a war and I have been a traitor all my born days, a spy in the enemy's country ever since I give up my gun back in the Reconstruction. Live with your head in the lion's mouth. I want you to overcome 'em with yeses, undermine 'em with grins, agree 'em to death and destruction, let 'em swoller you till they vomit or bust wide open." They thought the old man had gone out of his mind. He had been the meekest of men. The younger children were rushed from the room, the shades drawn and the flame of the lamp turned so low that it sputtered on the wick like the old man's breathing. "Learn it to the younguns," he whispered fiercely; then he died.

But my folks were more alarmed over his last words than over his dying. It was as though he had not died at all, his words caused so much anxiety. I was warned emphatically to forget what he had said and, indeed, this is the first time it has been mentioned outside the family circle. It had a tremendous effect upon me, however. I could never be sure of what he meant. Grandfather had been a quiet old man who never made any trouble, yet on his deathbed he had called himself a traitor and a spy, and he had spoken of his meekness as a dangerous activity. It became a constant puzzle which lay unanswered in the back of my mind. And whenever things went well for me I remembered my grandfather and felt guilty and uncomfortable. It was as though I was carrying out his advice in spite of myself. And to make it worse, everyone loved me for it. I was praised by the most lily-white men of the town. I was considered an example of desirable conduct—just as my grandfather had been. And what puzzled me was that the old man had defined it as *treachery*. When I was praised for my conduct I felt a guilt that in some way I was doing something that was really against the wishes of the white folks, that if they had understood they would have desired me to act just the opposite, that I should have been sulky and mean, and that that really would have been what they wanted, even though they were fooled and thought they wanted me to act as I did. It made me afraid that some day they would look upon me as a traitor and I would be lost. Still I was more afraid to act any other way because they didn't like that at all. The old man's words were like a curse. On my graduation day I delivered an oration in which I showed that humility was the secret, indeed, the very essence of progress. (Not that I believed this—how could I, remembering my grandfather?—I only believed that it worked.) It was a great success. Everyone praised me and I was invited to give the speech at a gathering of the town's leading white citizens. It was a triumph for our whole community.

It was in the main ballroom of the leading hotel. When I got there I discovered that it was on the occasion of a smoker[1] and I was told that since I was to be there anyway I might as well take part in the battle royal to be fought by some of my schoolmates as part of the entertainment. The battle royal came first.

All of the town's big shots were there in their tuxedoes, wolfing down the buffet foods, drinking beer and whiskey and smoking black cigars. It was a large room with a high ceiling. Chairs were arranged in neat rows around three sides of a portable boxing ring. The fourth side was clear, revealing a gleaming space of polished floor. I had some misgivings over the battle royal, by the way. Not from a distaste for fighting, but because I didn't care too much for the other fellows who were to take part. They were tough guys who seemed to have no grandfather's curse worrying their minds. No one could mistake their toughness. And besides, I suspected that fighting a battle royal might detract from the dignity of my speech. In those pre-invisible days I visualized myself as a potential Booker T. Washington.[2] But the other fellows didn't care too much for me either, and there were nine of them. I felt superior to them in my way, and I didn't like the manner in which we were all crowded together into the servants'

5

---

[1]*smoker:* Informal men-only social gathering.

[2]*Booker T. Washington:* American educator (1856–1915), born into slavery, who gained an education after emancipation and in 1881 organized Tuskegee Institute, a vocational school for African Americans.

elevator. Nor did they like my being there. In fact, as the warmly lighted floors flashed past the elevator we had words over the fact that I, by taking part in the fight, had knocked one of their friends out of a night's work.

We were led out of the elevator through a rococo hall into an anteroom and told to get into our fighting togs. Each of us was issued a pair of boxing gloves and ushered out into the big mirrored hall, which we entered looking cautiously about us and whispering, lest we might accidentally be heard above the noise of the room. It was foggy with cigar smoke. And already the whiskey was taking effect. I was shocked to see some of the most important men of the town quite tipsy. They were all there—bankers, lawyers, judges, doctors, fire chiefs, teachers, merchants. Even one of the more fashionable pastors. Something we could not see was going on up front. A clarinet was vibrating sensuously and the men were standing up and moving eagerly forward. We were a small tight group, clustered together, our bare upper bodies touching and shining with anticipatory sweat; while up front the big shots were becoming increasingly excited over something we still could not see. Suddenly I heard the school superintendent, who had told me to come, yell, "Bring up the shines[3] gentlemen! Bring up the little shines!"

We were rushed up to the front of the ballroom, where it smelled even more strongly of tobacco and whiskey. Then we were pushed into place. I almost wet my pants. A sea of faces, some hostile, some amused, ringed around us, and in the center, facing us, stood a magnificent blonde—stark naked. There was dead silence. I felt a blast of cold air chill me. I tried to back away, but they were behind me and around me. Some of the boys stood with lowered heads, trembling. I felt a wave of irrational guilt and fear. My teeth chattered, my skin turned to goose flesh, my knees knocked. Yet I was strongly attracted and looked in spite of myself. Had the price of looking been blindness, I would have looked. The hair was yellow like that of a circus kewpie doll, the face heavily powdered and rouged, as though to form an abstract mask, the eyes hollow and smeared a cool blue, the color of a baboon's butt. I felt a desire to spit upon her as my eyes brushed slowly over her body. Her breasts were firm and round as the domes of East Indian temples, and I stood so close as to see the fine skin texture and beads of pearly perspiration glistening like dew around the pink and erected buds of her nipples. I wanted at one and the same time to run from the room, to sink through the floor, or go to her and cover her from my eyes and the eyes of the others with my body; to feel the soft thighs, to caress her and destroy her, to love her and murder her, to hide from her, and yet to stroke where below the small American flag tattooed upon her belly her thighs formed a capital V. I had a notion that of all in the room she saw only me with her impersonal eyes.

And then she began to dance, a slow sensuous movement; the smoke of a hundred cigars clinging to her like the thinnest of veils. She seemed like a fair bird-girl girdled in veils calling to me from the angry surface of some gray and threatening sea. I was transported. Then I became aware of the clarinet playing and the big shots yelling at us. Some threatened us if we looked and others if we did not. On my right I saw one boy faint. And now a man grabbed a silver pitcher from a table and stepped close as

---

[3]*shines:* A racial slur for African Americans.

he dashed ice water upon him and stood him up and forced two of us to support him as his head hung and moans issued from his thick bluish lips. Another boy began to plead to go home. He was the largest of the group, wearing dark red fighting trunks much too small to conceal the erection which projected from him as though in answer to the insinuating low-registered moaning of the clarinet. He tried to hide himself with his boxing gloves.

And all the while the blonde continued dancing, smiling faintly at the big shots who watched her with fascination, and faintly smiling at our fear. I noticed a certain merchant who followed her hungrily, his lips loose and drooling. He was a large man who wore diamond studs in a shirtfront which swelled with the ample paunch underneath, and each time the blonde swayed her undulating hips he ran his hand through the thin hair of his bald head and, with his arms upheld, his posture clumsy like that of an intoxicated panda, wound his belly in a slow and obscene grind. This creature was completely hypnotized. The music had quickened. As the dancer flung herself about with a detached expression on her face, the men began reaching out to touch her. I could see their beefy fingers sink into her soft flesh. Some of the others tried to stop them and she began to move around the floor in graceful circles, as they gave chase, slipping and sliding over the polished floor. It was mad. Chairs went crashing, drinks were spilt, as they ran laughing and howling after her. They caught her just as she reached a door, raised her from the floor, and tossed her as college boys are tossed at a hazing, and above her red, fixed-smiling lips I saw the terror and disgust in her eyes, almost like my own terror and that which I saw in some of the other boys. As I watched, they tossed her twice and her soft breasts seemed to flatten against the air and her legs flung wildly as she spun. Some of the more sober ones helped her to escape. And I started off the floor, heading for the anteroom with the rest of the boys.

Some were still crying and in hysteria. But as we tried to leave we were stopped   10
and ordered to get into the ring. There was nothing to do but what we were told. All ten of us climbed under the ropes and allowed ourselves to be blindfolded with broad bands of white cloth. One of the men seemed to feel a bit sympathetic and tried to cheer us up as we stood with our backs against the ropes. Some of us tried to grin. "See that boy over there?" one of the men said. "I want you to run across at the bell and give it to him right in the belly. If you don't get him, I'm going to get you. I don't like his looks." Each of us was told the same. The blindfolds were put on. Yet even then I had been going over my speech. In my mind each word was as bright as flame. I felt the cloth pressed into place, and frowned so that it would be loosened when I relaxed.

But now I felt a sudden fit of blind terror. I was unused to darkness. It was as though I had suddenly found myself in a dark room filled with poisonous cottonmouths. I could hear the bleary voices yelling insistently for the battle royal to begin.

"Get going in there!"

"Let me at that big nigger!"

I strained to pick up the school superintendent's voice, as though to squeeze some security out of that slightly more familiar sound.

"Let me at those black sonsabitches!" someone yelled.   15

"No, Jackson, no!" another voice yelled. "Here, somebody, help me hold Jack."

"I want to get at that ginger-colored nigger. Tear him limb from limb," the first voice yelled.

I stood against the ropes trembling. For in those days I was what they called ginger-colored, and he sounded as though he might crunch me between his teeth like a crisp ginger cookie.

Quite a struggle was going on. Chairs were being kicked about and I could hear voices grunting as with a terrific effort. I wanted to see, to see more desperately than ever before. But the blindfold was as tight as a thick skin-puckering scab and when I raised my gloved hands to push the layers of white aside a voice yelled, "Oh, no you don't! black bastard! Leave that alone!"

20 "Ring the bell before Jackson kills him a coon!" someone boomed in the sudden silence. And I heard the bell clang and the sound of the feet scuffling forward.

A glove smacked against my head. I pivoted, striking out stiffly as someone went past, and felt the jar ripple along the length of my arm to my shoulder. Then it seemed as though all nine of the boys had turned upon me at once. Blows pounded me from all sides while I struck out as best I could. So many blows landed upon me that I wondered if I were not the only blindfolded fighter in the ring, or if the man called Jackson hadn't succeeded in getting me after all.

Blindfolded, I could no longer control my motions. I had no dignity. I stumbled about like a baby or a drunken man. The smoke had become thicker and with each new blow it seemed to sear and further restrict my lungs. My saliva became like hot bitter glue. A glove connected with my head, filling my mouth with warm blood. It was everywhere. I could not tell if the moisture I felt upon my body was sweat or blood. A blow landed hard against the nape of my neck. I felt myself going over, my head hitting the floor. Streaks of blue light filled the black world behind the blindfold. I lay prone, pretending that I was knocked out, but felt myself seized by hands and yanked to my feet. "Get going, black boy! Mix it up!" My arms were like lead, my head smarting from blows. I managed to feel my way to the ropes and held on, trying to catch my breath. A glove landed in my midsection and I went over again, feeling as though the smoke had become a knife jabbed into my guts. Pushed this way and that by the legs milling around me, I finally pulled erect and discovered that I could see the black, sweat-washed forms weaving in the smoky-blue atmosphere like drunken dancers weaving to the rapid drum-like thuds of blows.

Everyone fought hysterically. It was complete anarchy. Everybody fought everybody else. No group fought together for long. Two, three, four, fought one, then turned to fight each other, were themselves attacked. Blows landed below the belt and in the kidney, with the gloves open as well as closed, and with my eye partly opened now there was not so much terror. I moved carefully, avoiding blows, although not too many to attract attention, fighting from group to group. The boys groped about like blind, cautious crabs crouching to protect their mid-sections, their heads pulled in short against their shoulders, their arms stretched nervously before them, with their fists testing the smoke-filled air like the knobbed feelers of hypersensitive snails. In one corner I glimpsed a boy violently punching the air and heard him scream in pain as he smashed his hand against a ring post. For a second I saw him bent over holding his hand, then going down as a blow caught his unprotected head. I played one group against the other, slipping in and throwing a punch then stepping out of range while pushing the others into the melee to take the blows blindly aimed at me. The smoke was agonizing and there were no rounds, no bells at three minute intervals to relieve our exhaustion. The room spun round me, a swirl of lights, smoke, sweating bodies surrounded by tense white faces. I bled from both nose and mouth, the blood spattering upon my chest.

The men kept yelling, "Slug him, black boy! Knock his guts out!"

"Uppercut him! Kill him! Kill that big boy!"   25

Taking a fake fall, I saw a boy going down heavily beside me as though we were felled by a single blow, saw a sneaker-clad foot shoot into his groin as the two who had knocked him down stumbled upon him. I rolled out of range, feeling a twinge of nausea.

The harder we fought the more threatening the men became. And yet, I had begun to worry about my speech again. How would it go? Would they recognize my ability? What would they give me?

I was fighting automatically and suddenly I noticed that one after another of the boys was leaving the ring. I was surprised, filled with panic, as though I had been left alone with an unknown danger. Then I understood. The boys had arranged it among themselves. It was the custom for the two men left in the ring to slug it out for the winner's prize. I discovered this too late. When the bell sounded two men in tuxedoes leaped into the ring and removed the blindfold. I found myself facing Tatlock, the biggest of the gang. I felt sick at my stomach. Hardly had the bell stopped ringing in my ears than it clanged again and I saw him moving swiftly toward me. Thinking of nothing else to do I hit him smash on the nose. He kept coming, bringing the rank sharp violence of stale sweat. His face was a black blank of a face, only his eyes alive— with hate of me and aglow with a feverish terror from what had happened to us all. I became anxious. I wanted to deliver my speech and he came at me as though he meant to beat it out of me. I smashed him again and again, taking his blows as they came. Then on a sudden impulse I struck him lightly and as we clinched, I whispered, "Fake like I knocked you out, you can have the prize."

"I'll break your behind," he whispered hoarsely.

"For *them*?"   30

"For *me*, sonofabitch!"

They were yelling for us to break it up and Tatlock spun me half around with a blow, and as a joggled camera sweeps in a reeling scene, I saw the howling red faces crouching tense beneath the cloud of blue-gray smoke. For a moment the world wavered, unraveled, flowed, then my head cleared and Tatlock bounced before me. That fluttering shadow before my eyes was his jabbing left hand. Then falling forward, my head against his damp shoulder, I whispered, "I'll make it five dollars more."

"Go to hell!"

But his muscles relaxed a trifle beneath my pressure and I breathed, "Seven!"

"Give it to your ma," he said, ripping me beneath the heart.   35

And while I still held him I butted him and moved away. I felt myself bombarded with punches. I fought back with hopeless desperation. I wanted to deliver my speech more than anything else in the world, because I felt that only these men could judge truly my ability, and now this stupid clown was ruining my chances. I began fighting carefully now, moving in to punch him and out again with my greater speed. A lucky blow to his chin and I had him going too—until I heard a loud voice yell, "I got my money on the big boy."

Hearing this, I almost dropped my guard. I was confused: Should I try to win against the voice out there? Would not this go against my speech, and was not this a moment for humility, for nonresistance? A blow to my head as I danced about sent my right eye popping like a jack-in-the-box and settled my dilemma. The room went red as I fell. It was a dream fall, my body languid and fastidious as to where to land, until the floor became impatient and smashed up to meet me. A moment later I came to. An hypnotic voice said FIVE emphatically. And I lay there, hazily watching a dark red spot of my own blood shaping itself into a butterfly, glistening and soaking into the soiled gray world of the canvas.

When the voice drawled TEN I was lifted up and dragged to a chair. I sat dazed. My eye pained and swelled with each throb of my pounding heart and I wondered if now I would be allowed to speak. I was wringing wet, my mouth still bleeding. We were grouped along the wall now. The other boys ignored me as they congratulated Tatlock and speculated as to how much they would be paid. One boy whimpered over his smashed hand. Looking up front, I saw attendants in white jackets rolling the portable ring away and placing a small square rug in the vacant space surrounded by chairs. Perhaps, I thought, I will stand on the rug to deliver my speech.

Then the M.C. called to us, "Come on up here boys and get your money."

40   We ran forward to where the men laughed and talked in their chairs, waiting. Everyone seemed friendly now.

"There it is on the rug," the man said. I saw the rug covered with coins of all dimensions and a few crumpled bills. But what excited me, scattered here and there, were the gold pieces.

"Boys, it's all yours," the man said. "You get all you grab."

"That's right, Sambo,"[4] a blond man said, winking at me confidentially.

I trembled with excitement, forgetting my pain. I would get the gold and the bills, I thought. I would use both hands. I would throw my body against the boys nearest me to block them from the gold.

45   "Get down around the rug now," the man commanded, "and don't anyone touch it until I give the signal."

"This ought to be good," I heard.

As told, we got around the square rug on our knees. Slowly the man raised his freckled hand as we followed it upward with our eyes.

I heard, "These niggers look like they're about to pray!"

Then, "Ready," the man said. "Go!"

50   I lunged for a yellow coin lying on the blue design of the carpet, touching it and sending a surprised shriek to join those rising around me. I tried frantically to remove my hand but could not let go. A hot, violent force tore through my body, shaking me like a wet rat. The rug was electrified. The hair bristled up on my head as I shook myself free. My muscles jumped, my nerves jangled, writhed. But I saw that this was not stopping the other boys. Laughing in fear and embarrassment, some were holding

---

[4]*Sambo:* A racial slur for blacks, referring to a character in a children's story.

back and scooping up the coins knocked off by the painful contortions of the others. The men roared above us as we struggled.

"Pick it up, goddamnit, pick it up!" someone called like a bass-voiced parrot. "Go on, get it!"

I crawled rapidly around the floor, picking up the coins, trying to avoid the coppers and to get greenbacks and the gold. Ignoring the shock by laughing, as I brushed the coins off quickly, I discovered that I could contain the electricity—a contradiction, but it works. Then the men began to push us onto the rug. Laughing embarrassedly, we struggled out of their hands and kept after the coins. We were all wet and slippery and hard to hold. Suddenly I saw a boy lifted into the air, glistening with sweat like a circus seal, and dropped, his wet back landing flush upon the charged rug, heard him yell and saw him literally dance upon his back, his elbows beating a frenzied tattoo upon the floor, his muscles twitching like the flesh of a horse stung by many flies. When he finally rolled off, his face was gray and no one stopped him when he ran from the floor amid booming laughter.

"Get the money," the M.C. called. "That's good hard American cash!"

And we snatched and grabbed, snatched and grabbed. I was careful not to come too close to the rug now, and when I felt the hot whiskey breath descend upon me like a cloud of foul air I reached out and grabbed the leg of a chair. It was occupied and I held on desperately.

"Leggo, nigger! Leggo!"

The huge face wavered down to mine as he tried to push me free. But my body was slippery and he was too drunk. It was Mr. Colcord, who owned a chain of movie houses and "entertainment palaces." Each time he grabbed me I slipped out of his hands. It became a real struggle. I feared the rug more than I did the drunk, so I held on, surprising myself for a moment by trying to topple *him* upon the rug. It was such an enormous idea that I found myself actually carrying it out. I tried not to be obvious, yet when I grabbed his leg, trying to tumble him out of the chair, he raised up roaring with laughter, and, looking at me with soberness dead in the eye, kicked me viciously in the chest. The chair leg flew out of my hand. I felt myself going and rolled. It was as though I had rolled through a bed of hot coals. It seemed a whole century would pass before I would roll free, a century in which I was seared through the deepest levels of my body to the fearful breath within me and the breath seared and heated to the point of explosion. It'll all be over in a flash, I thought as I rolled clear. It'll all be over in a flash.

But not yet, the men on the other side were waiting, red faces swollen as though from apoplexy as they bent forward in their chairs. Seeing their fingers coming toward me I rolled away as a fumbled football rolls off the receiver's fingertips, back into the coals. That time I luckily sent the rug sliding out of place and heard the coins ringing against the floor and the boys scuffling to pick them up and the M.C. calling, "All right, boys, that's all. Go get dressed and get your money."

I was limp as a dish rag. My back felt as though it had been beaten with wires.

When we had dressed the M.C. came in and gave us each five dollars, except Tatlock, who got ten for being last in the ring. Then he told us to leave. I was not to get a chance to deliver my speech, I thought. I was going out into the dim alley in despair when I was stopped and told to go back. I returned to the ballroom, where the men were pushing back their chairs and gathering in groups to talk.

55

60   The M.C. knocked on a table for quiet. "Gentlemen," he said, "we almost forgot an important part of the program. A most serious part, gentlemen. This boy was brought here to deliver a speech which he made at his graduation yesterday. . . ."

"Bravo!"

"I'm told that he is the smartest boy we've got out there in Greenwood. I'm told that he knows more big words than a pocket-sized dictionary."

Much applause and laughter.

"So now, gentlemen, I want you to give him your attention."

65   There was still laughter as I faced them, my mouth dry, my eye throbbing. I began slowly, but evidently my throat was tense, because they began shouting, "Louder! Louder!"

"We of the younger generation extol the wisdom of that great leader and educator," I shouted, "who first spoke these flaming words of wisdom: 'A ship lost at sea for many days suddenly sighted a friendly vessel. From the mast of the unfortunate vessel was seen a signal: "Water, water; we die of thirst!" The answer from the friendly vessel came back: "Cast down your bucket where you are." The captain of the distressed vessel, at last heeding the injunction, cast down his bucket, and it came up full of fresh sparkling water from the mouth of the Amazon River.' And like him I say, and in his words, 'To those of my race who depend upon bettering their condition in a foreign land, or who underestimate the importance of cultivating friendly relations with the Southern white man, who is his next-door neighbor, I would say: "Cast down your bucket where you are"—cast it down in making friends in every manly way of the people of all races by whom we are surrounded. . . .'"

I spoke automatically and with such fervor that I did not realize that the men were still talking and laughing until my dry mouth, filling up with blood from the cut, almost strangled me. I coughed, wanting to stop and go to one of the tall brass, sand filled spittoons to relieve myself, but a few of the men, especially the superintendent, were listening and I was afraid. So I gulped it down, blood, saliva and all, and continued. (What powers of endurance I had during those days! What enthusiasm! What a belief in the rightness of things!) I spoke even louder in spite of the pain. But still they talked and still they laughed, as though deaf with cotton in dirty ears. So I spoke with greater emotional emphasis. I closed my ears and swallowed blood until I was nauseated. The speech seemed a hundred times as long as before, but I could not leave out a single word. All had to be said, each memorized nuance considered, rendered. Nor was that all. Whenever I uttered a word of three or more syllables a group of voices would yell for me to repeat it. I used the phrase "social responsibility" and they yelled:

"What's the word you say, boy?"

"Social responsibility," I said.

70   "What?"

"Social . . ."

"Louder."

". . . responsibility."

"More!"

75   "Respon—"

"Repeat!"

"— sibility."

The room filled with the uproar of laughter until, no doubt, distracted by having to gulp down my blood, I made a mistake and yelled a phrase I had often seen denounced in newspaper editorials, heard debated in private.

"Social . . ."

"What?" they yelled.

". . . equality—"

The laughter hung smokelike in the sudden stillness. I opened my eyes, puzzled. Sounds of displeasure filled the room. The M.C. rushed forward. They shouted hostile phrases at me. But I did not understand.

A small dry mustached man in the front row blared out, "Say that slowly, son!"

"What sir?"

"What you just said!"

"Social responsibility, sir," I said.

"You weren't being smart, were you, boy?" he said, not unkindly.

"No, sir!"

"You sure that about 'equality' was a mistake?"

"Oh, yes, sir," I said. "I was swallowing blood."

"Well, you had better speak more slowly so we can understand. We mean to do right by you, but you've got to know your place at all times. All right, now, go on with your speech."

I was afraid. I wanted to leave but I wanted also to speak and I was afraid they'd snatch me down.

"Thank you, sir," I said, beginning where I had left off, and having them ignore me as before.

Yet when I finished there was a thunderous applause. I was surprised to see the superintendent come forth with a package wrapped in white tissue paper, and, gesturing for quiet, address the men.

"Gentlemen, you see that I did not overpraise this boy. He makes a good speech and some day he'll lead his people in the proper paths. And I don't have to tell you that that is important in these days and times. This is a good, smart boy, and so to encourage him in the right direction, in the name of the Board of Education I wish to present him a prize in the form of this . . ."

He paused, removing the tissue paper and revealing a gleaming calfskin brief case.

". . . in the form of this first-class article from Shad Whitmore's shop."

"Boy," he said, addressing me, "take this prize and keep it well. Consider it a badge of office. Prize it. Keep developing as you are and some day it will be filled with important papers that will help shape the destiny of your people."

I was so moved that I could hardly express my thanks. A rope of bloody saliva forming a shape like an undiscovered continent drooled upon the leather and I wiped it quickly away. I felt an importance that I had never dreamed.

"Open it and see what's inside," I was told.

My fingers a-tremble, I complied, smelling the fresh leather and finding an official-looking document inside. It was a scholarship to the state college for Negroes. My eyes filled with tears and I ran awkwardly off the floor.

I was overjoyed; I did not even mind when I discovered that the gold pieces I had scrambled for were brass pocket tokens advertising a certain make of automobile.

When I reached home everyone was excited. Next day the neighbors came to congratulate me. I even felt safe from grandfather, whose deathbed curse usually spoiled my triumphs. I stood beneath his photograph with my brief case in hand and smiled triumphantly into his stolid black peasant's face. It was a face that fascinated me. The eyes seemed to follow everywhere I went.

That night I dreamed I was at a circus with him and that he refused to laugh at the clowns no matter what they did. Then later he told me to open my brief case and read what was inside and I did, finding an official envelope stamped with the state seal; and inside the envelope I found another and another, endlessly, and I thought I would fall of weariness. "Them's years," he said. "Now open that one." And I did and in it I found an engraved document containing a short message in letters of gold. "Read it," my grandfather said. "Out loud."

105   "To Whom It May Concern," I intoned. "Keep This Nigger-Boy Running."

I awoke with the old man's laughter ringing in my ears.

(It was a dream I was to remember and dream again for many years after. But at the time I had no insight into its meaning. First I had to attend college.)

Reading and Reacting

1. "Battle Royal," the first chapter of Ellison's novel *Invisible Man* (1952), is set in the American South. How does the story's historical and geographical setting make possible the events that occur?

2. In paragraph 2, the narrator quotes his grandfather's deathbed statement. Why does the narrator think of his grandfather's words as a "curse" (par. 3)?

3. When the narrator is told he is expected to participate in the "battle royal," he feels that the battle will "detract from the dignity" of the speech he is to give (par. 5). Why, then, does he agree to take part in the fight? Why is he so intent on delivering his speech to the men assembled in the ballroom?

4. In his graduation speech, the narrator tells his audience that "humility [is] the secret, indeed, the very essence of progress" (par. 3). What do you suppose he means? How do you think his grandfather would feel about this statement?

5. Describe the physical setting (the sights, sounds, smells) of the ballroom. What is your emotional reaction to this setting?

6. Why is the narrator blindfolded before the fight? What effect does the blindfold have on him as a fighter? as a human being?

7. The superintendent tells the audience that the narrator will someday "lead his people in the proper paths" (par. 95). What "proper paths" do you think the superintendent has in mind?

8. Why do you think the narrator dreams about his grandfather after the fight? What do you think his dream means?

9. **JOURNAL ENTRY** Do you see the "battle royal" as a necessary evil, a hurdle the narrator has to leap over in order to win the college scholarship? Does the prize in any way make up for the humiliating ordeal? Do you think the narrator should (or even could) have turned down the scholarship?

10. CRITICAL PERSPECTIVE This story is set in the South in the 1940s, during a time of violent racism and "Jim Crow" laws that enforced legal segregation. Whites and blacks were not allowed equality on even the most fundamental levels, and this backdrop heightens the tension of the battle royal. Thomas F. Bertonneau offers this observation:

> The atmosphere is gladiatorial and orgiastic. Before the fight, for example, the businessmen make the protagonist and his compeers watch a lewd performance by a blonde stripper, which shocks and humiliates them. In the perverse ethos of Jim Crow, it also sets them up, because it embroils them willy-nilly in a racial-sexual scenario in which they fill the role of lascivious onlookers. On the street, should any of them stare at a white woman, stripper or bourgeoisie, he would run the risk of accusation and be under the lethal threat of the outraged mob. It is a formula for lynching.

In this scene in the story, what is the main attraction? Who is watching whom? In what ways is the scenario Bertonneau describes ironic? How does this irony contribute to the meaning of the story?

Related Works: from *The Harlem Hellfighters* (p. 145), "We Wear the Mask" (p. 728), "The Secretary Chant" (p. 767), "Yet Do I Marvel" (p. 869), "If We Must Die" (p. 1003), *Applicant* (p. 1091), *Fences* (p. 1548)

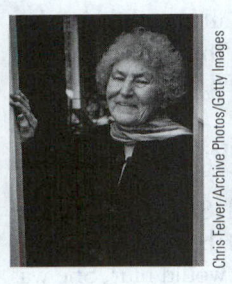

Chris Felver/Archive Photos/Getty Images

TILLIE OLSEN (1912 or 1913–2007) is known for her works of fiction about working-class Americans. Her short stories and one novel are inhabited by those she called the "despised people"—coal miners, farm laborers, packinghouse butchers, and housewives. Olsen was born in Nebraska into a working-class family. According to an account in her nonfiction work *Silences* (1978), she was inspired at age fifteen to write about working-class people when she read Rebecca Harding Davis's *Life in the Iron Mills*, a tale of the effects of industrialization on workers, in an 1861 issue of *Atlantic Monthly* bought for ten cents in a junk shop.

Shortly after she left high school, Olsen was jailed for helping to organize packinghouse workers. Motivated by her experiences, she began to write a novel, *Yonnondio*. Under her maiden name, Tillie Lerner, she published two poems, a short story, and part of her novel during the 1930s. After her marriage, she did not publish again for twenty-two years, spending her time raising four children and working at a variety of jobs. The collection of short stories *Tell Me a Riddle* (1961), which includes "I Stand Here Ironing" (originally titled "Help Her to Believe"), was published when she was fifty. Her only other work of fiction is *Yonnondio* (1974), which she pieced together from drafts she wrote in the 1930s and edited for publication in 1974.

In 1984, she edited *Mother to Daughter, Daughter to Mother: Mothers on Mothering*, a collection of poems, letters, short fiction, and diary excerpts written by famous and not-so-famous women, and in 1987, she collaborated with photographer Estelle Jussim on *Mothers & Daughters: An Exploration in Photographs*.

Cultural Context During the Great Depression of the 1930s, jobs were scarce throughout the United States, and many people who managed to keep their jobs were forced to take pay cuts. At the height of the Depression in 1933, almost twenty-five percent of the total workforce—more than eleven million people—were unemployed. The displacement of the American worker and the destruction of farming communities caused families such as the one in this story to split up or to migrate from their homes in search of work. In 1935, the Social Security Act established public assistance, unemployment insurance, and social security, which offered economic relief to American workers and their families.

Film Series

DVD
See
pp. 306–307
for film stills
from the
DVD
version
of this
story.

I Stand Here Ironing (1961)

I stand here ironing, and what you asked me moves tormented back and forth with the iron.

"I wish you would manage the time to come and talk with me about your daughter. I'm sure you can help me understand her. She's a youngster who needs help and whom I'm deeply interested in helping."

"Who needs help." . . . Even if I came, what good would it do? You think because I am her mother I have a key, or that in some way you could use me as a key? She has lived for nineteen years. There is all that life that has happened outside of me, beyond me.

And when is there time to remember, to sift, to weigh, to estimate, to total? I will start and there will be an interruption and I will have to gather it all together again. Or I will become engulfed with all I did or did not do, with what should have been and what cannot be helped.

5   She was a beautiful baby. The first and only one of our five that was beautiful at birth. You do not guess how new and uneasy her tenancy in her now-loveliness. You did not know her all those years she was thought homely, or see her poring over her baby pictures, making me tell her over and over how beautiful she had been—and would be, I would tell her—and was now, to the seeing eye. But the seeing eyes were few or nonexistent. Including mine.

I nursed her. They feel that's important nowadays. I nursed all the children, but with her, with all the fierce rigidity of first motherhood, I did like the books then said. Though her cries battered me to trembling and my breasts ached with swollenness, I waited till the clock decreed.

Why do I put that first? I do not even know if it matters, or if it explains anything.

She was a beautiful baby. She blew shining bubbles of sound. She loved motion, loved light, loved color and music and textures. She would lie on the floor in her blue overalls patting the surface so hard in ecstasy her hands and feet would blur. She was a miracle to me, but when she was eight months old I had to leave her daytimes with the woman downstairs to whom she was no miracle at all, for I worked or looked for work and for Emily's father, who "could no longer endure" (he wrote in his good-bye note) "sharing want with us."

I was nineteen. It was the pre-relief, pre-WPA[1] world of the depression. I would start running as soon as I got off the streetcar, running up the stairs, the place smelling sour, and awake or asleep to startle awake, when she saw me she would break into a clogged weeping that could not be comforted, a weeping I can hear yet.

10   After a while I found a job hashing at night so I could be with her days, and it was better. But it came to where I had to bring her to his family and leave her.

It took a long time to raise the money for her fare back. Then she got chicken pox and I had to wait longer. When she finally came, I hardly knew her, walking quick and

---

[1] *WPA*: The Works Progress Administration, created in 1935 as part of President Franklin D. Roosevelt's New Deal program. The purpose of the WPA (renamed the Works Projects Administration in 1939) was to provide jobs for the unemployed during the Great Depression.

nervous like her father, looking like her father, thin, and dressed in a shoddy red that yellowed her skin and glared at the pockmarks. All the baby loveliness gone.

She was two. Old enough for nursery school they said, and I did not know then what I know now—the fatigue of the long day, and the lacerations of group life in the kinds of nurseries that are only parking places for children.

Except that it would have made no difference if I had known. It was the only place there was. It was the only way we could be together, the only way I could hold a job.

And even without knowing, I knew. I knew the teacher that was evil because all these years it has curdled into my memory, the little boy hunched in the corner, her rasp, "why aren't you outside, because Alvin hits you? that's no reason, go out, scaredy." I knew Emily hated it even if she did not clutch and implore "don't go Mommy" like the other children, mornings.

She always had a reason why we should stay home. Momma, you look sick. 15
Momma, I feel sick. Momma, the teachers aren't there today, they're sick. Momma, we can't go, there was a fire there last night. Momma, it's a holiday today, no school, they told me.

But never a direct protest, never rebellion. I think of our others in their three-, four-year-oldness—the explosions, the tempers, the denunciations, the demands— and I feel suddenly ill. I put the iron down. What in me demanded that goodness in her? And what was the cost, the cost to her of such goodness?

The old man living in the back once said in his gentle way: "You should smile at Emily more when you look at her." What *was* in my face when I looked at her? I loved her. There were all the acts of love.

It was only with the others I remembered what he said, and it was the face of joy, and not of care or tightness or worry I turned to them—too late for Emily. She does not smile easily, let alone almost always as her brothers and sisters do. Her face is closed and sombre, but when she wants, how fluid. You must have seen it in her pantomimes, you spoke of her rare gift for comedy on the stage that rouses laughter out of the audience so dear they applaud and applaud and do not want to let her go.

Where does it come from, that comedy? There was none of it in her when she came back to me that second time, after I had had to send her away again. She had a new daddy now to learn to love, and I think perhaps it was a better time.

Except when we left her alone nights, telling ourselves she was old enough. 20

"Can't you go some other time, Mommy, like tomorrow?" she would ask. "Will it be just a little while you'll be gone? Do you promise?"

The time we came back, the front door open, the clock on the floor in the hall. She rigid awake. "It wasn't just a little while. I didn't cry. Three times I called you, just three times, and then I ran downstairs to open the door so you could come faster. The clock talked loud. I threw it away, it scared me what it talked."

She said the clock talked loud again that night I went to the hospital to have Susan. She was delirious with the fever that comes before red measles, but she was fully conscious all the week I was gone and the week after we were home when she could not come near the new baby or me.

She did not get well. She stayed skeleton thin, not wanting to eat, and night after night she had nightmares. She would call for me, and I would rouse from exhaustion to sleepily call back: "You're all right, darling, go to sleep, it's just a dream," and if she still called, in a sterner voice, "now go to sleep, Emily, there's nothing to hurt you." Twice, only twice, when I had to get up for Susan anyhow, I went in to sit with her.

25   Now when it is too late (as if she would let me hold and comfort her like I do the others) I get up and go to her at once at her moan or restless stirring. "Are you awake, Emily? Can I get you something?" And the answer is always the same: "No, I'm all right, go back to sleep, Mother."

They persuaded me at the clinic to send her away to a convalescent home in the country where "she can have the kind of food and care you can't manage for her, and you'll be free to concentrate on the new baby." They still send children to that place. I see pictures on the society page of sleek young women planning affairs to raise money for it, or dancing at the affairs, or decorating Easter eggs or filling Christmas stockings for the children.

They never have a picture of the children so I do not know if the girls still wear those gigantic red bows and the ravaged looks on the every other Sunday when parents can come to visit "unless otherwise notified"—as we were notified the first six weeks.

Oh it is a handsome place, green lawns and tall trees and fluted flower beds. High up on the balconies of each cottage the children stand, the girls in their red bows and white dresses, the boys in white suits and giant red ties. The parents stand below shrieking up to be heard and the children shriek down to be heard, and between them the invisible wall: "Not to Be Contaminated by Parental Germs or Physical Affection."

There was a tiny girl who always stood hand in hand with Emily. Her parents never came. One visit she was gone. "They moved her to Rose Cottage," Emily shouted in explanation. "They don't like you to love anybody here."

30   She wrote once a week, the labored writing of a seven-year-old. "I am fine. How is the baby. If I write my leter nicly I will have a star. Love." There never was a star. We wrote every other day, letters she could never hold or keep but only hear read—once. "We simply do not have room for children to keep any personal possessions," they patiently explained when we pieced one Sunday's shrieking together to plead how much it would mean to Emily, who loved so to keep things, to be allowed to keep her letters and cards.

Each visit she looked frailer. "She isn't eating," they told us.

(They had runny eggs for breakfast or mush with lumps, Emily said later, I'd hold it in my mouth and not swallow. Nothing ever tasted good, just when they had chicken.)

It took us eight months to get her released home, and only the fact that she gained back so little of her seven lost pounds convinced the social worker.

I used to try to hold and love her after she came back, but her body would stay stiff, and after a while she'd push away. She ate little. Food sickened her, and I think much of life too. Oh she had physical lightness and brightness, twinkling by on skates, bouncing like a ball up and down up and down over the jump rope, skimming over the hill; but these were momentary.

35   She fretted about her appearance, thin and dark and foreign-looking at a time when every little girl was supposed to look or thought she should look a chubby

blonde replica of Shirley Temple. The doorbell sometimes rang for her, but no one seemed to come and play in the house or be a best friend. Maybe because we moved so much.

There was a boy she loved painfully through two school semesters. Months later she told me how she had taken pennies from my purse to buy him candy. "Licorice was his favorite and I brought him some every day, but he still liked Jennifer better'n me. Why, Mommy?" The kind of question for which there is no answer.

School was a worry to her. She was not glib or quick in a world where glibness and quickness were easily confused with ability to learn. To her overworked and exasperated teachers she was an overconscientious "slow learner" who kept trying to catch up and was absent entirely too often.

I let her be absent, though sometimes the illness was imaginary. How different from my now-strictness about attendance with the others. I wasn't working. We had a new baby, I was home anyhow. Sometimes, after Susan grew old enough, I would keep her home from school, too, to have them all together.

Mostly Emily had asthma, and her breathing, harsh and labored, would fill the house with a curiously tranquil sound. I would bring the two old dresser mirrors and her boxes of collections to her bed. She would select beads and single earrings, bottle tops and shells, dried flowers and pebbles, old postcards and scraps, all sorts of odd-ments; then she and Susan would play Kingdom, setting up landscapes and furniture, peopling them with action.

Those were the only times of peaceful companionship between her and Susan. I have edged away from it, that poisonous feeling between them, that terrible balancing of hurts and needs I had to do between the two, and did so badly, those earlier years.

40

Oh there are conflicts between the others too, each one human, needing, demanding, hurting, taking—but only between Emily and Susan, no, Emily toward Susan that corroding resentment. It seems so obvious on the surface, yet it is not obvious. Susan, the second child, Susan, golden- and curly-haired and chubby, quick and articulate and assured, everything in appearance and manner Emily was not; Susan, not able to resist Emily's precious things, losing or sometimes clumsily breaking them; Susan telling jokes and riddles to company for applause while Emily sat silent (to say to me later: that was my riddle, Mother, I told it to Susan); Susan, who for all the five years' difference in age was just a year behind Emily in developing physically.

I am glad for that slow physical development that widened the difference between her and her contemporaries, though she suffered over it. She was too vulnerable for that terrible world of youthful competition, of preening and parading, of constant measuring of yourself against every other, of envy, "If I had that copper hair," "If I had that skin. . . ." She tormented herself enough about not looking like the others, there was enough of the unsureness, the having to be conscious of words before you speak, the constant caring—what are they thinking of me? without having it all magnified by the merciless physical drives.

Ronnie is calling. He is wet and I change him. It is rare there is such a cry now. That time of motherhood is almost behind me when the ear is not one's own but must always be racked and listening for the child cry, the child call. We sit for a while and I hold him, looking out over the city spread in charcoal with its soft aisles of light. "Shoogily," he breathes and curls closer. I carry him back to bed, asleep. Shoogily. A funny word, a family word, inherited from Emily, invented by her to say: *comfort*.

In this and other ways she leaves her seal, I say aloud. And startle at my saying it. What do I mean? What did I start to gather together, to try and make coherent? I was at the terrible, growing years. War years. I do not remember them well. I was working, there were four smaller ones now, there was not time for her. She had to help be a mother, and housekeeper, and shopper. She had to set her seal. Mornings of crisis and near hysteria trying to get lunches packed, hair combed, coats and shoes found, everyone to school or Child Care on time, the baby ready for transportation. And always the paper scribbled on by a smaller one, the book looked at by Susan then mislaid, the homework not done. Running out to that huge school where she was one, she was lost, she was a drop; suffering over the unpreparedness, stammering and unsure in her classes.

45   There was so little time left at night after the kids were bedded down. She would struggle over books, always eating (it was in those years she developed her enormous appetite that is legendary in our family) and I would be ironing, or preparing food for the next day, or writing V-mail[2] to Bill, or tending the baby. Sometimes, to make me laugh, or out of her despair, she would imitate happenings or types at school.

I think I said once: "Why don't you do something like this in the school amateur show?" One morning she phoned me at work, hardly understandable through the weeping: "Mother, I did it. I won, I won; they gave me first prize; they clapped and clapped and wouldn't let me go."

Now suddenly she was Somebody, and as imprisoned in her difference as she had been in anonymity.

She began to be asked to perform at other high schools, even in colleges, then at city and statewide affairs. The first one we went to, I only recognized her that first moment when thin, shy, she almost drowned herself into the curtains. Then: Was this Emily? The control, the command, the convulsing and deadly clowning, the spell, then the roaring, stamping audience, unwilling to let this rare and precious laughter out of their lives.

Afterwards: You ought to do something about her with a gift like that—but without money or knowing how, what does one do? We have left it all to her, and the gift has as often eddied inside, clogged and clotted, as been used and growing.

50   She is coming. She runs up the stairs two at a time with her light graceful step, and I know she is happy tonight. Whatever it was that occasioned your call did not happen today.

"Aren't you ever going to finish the ironing, Mother? Whistler painted his mother in a rocker. I'd have to paint mine standing over an ironing board." This is one of her communicative nights and she tells me everything and nothing as she fixes herself a plate of food out of the icebox.

---

[2]*V-mail:* Mail sent to or from members of the armed forces during World War II. Letters were reduced onto microfilm and enlarged and printed out at their destination.

She is so lovely. Why did you want me to come in at all? Why were you concerned? She will find her way.

She starts up the stairs to bed. "Don't get me up with the rest in the morning." "But I thought you were having midterms." "Oh, those," she comes back in, kisses me, and says quite lightly, "in a couple of years when we'll all be atom-dead they won't matter a bit."

She has said it before. She *believes* it. But because I have been dredging the past, and all that compounds a human being is so heavy and meaningful in me, I cannot endure it tonight.

I will never total it all. I will never come in to say: She was a child seldom smiled   55 at. Her father left me before she was a year old. I had to work her first six years when there was work, or I sent her home and to his relatives. There were years she had care she hated. She was dark and thin and foreign-looking in a world where the prestige went to blondeness and curly hair and dimples, she was slow where glibness was prized. She was a child of anxious, not proud, love. We were poor and could not afford for her the soil of easy growth. I was a young mother, I was a distracted mother. There were other children pushing up, demanding. Her younger sister seemed all that she was not. There were years she did not want me to touch her. She kept too much in herself, her life was such she had to keep too much in herself. My wisdom came too late. She has much to her and probably little will come of it. She is a child of her age, of depression, of war, of fear.

Let her be. So all that is in her will not bloom—but in how many does it? There is still enough left to live by. Only help her to know—help make it so there is cause for her to know—that she is more than this dress on the ironing board, helpless before the iron.

Reading and Reacting

1. "I Stand Here Ironing" focuses on incidents that took place in the "pre-relief, pre-WPA world" of the Depression (par. 9). In light of social, political, and economic changes that have occurred since the 1930s, do you think the events the story presents could occur today? Explain.

2. In what sense is the image of a mother at an ironing board appropriate for this story?

3. The narrator is overwhelmed by guilt. What does she believe she has done wrong? What, if anything, do *you* think she has done wrong? Do you think she has been a good mother? Why or why not?

4. Who, or what, do you blame for the narrator's problems? For example, do you blame Emily's father? the Depression? the social institutions and "experts" to which the narrator turns?

5. Do you see the narrator as a victim limited by the times in which she lives? Do you agree with the narrator that Emily is "a child of her age, of depression, of war, of fear" (par. 55)? Or do you believe both women have some control over their own destinies, regardless of the story's historical setting?

6. What do you think the narrator wants for her daughter? Do you think her goals for Emily are realistic? Why or why not?

7. Paragraph 28 describes the physical setting of the convalescent home to which Emily was sent. What does this description add to the story?

8. To whom do you think the mother is speaking in this story?

9. **JOURNAL ENTRY** Put yourself in Emily's position. What do you think she would like to tell her mother?

10. **CRITICAL PERSPECTIVE** Writing in *The Red Wheelbarrow*, psychologist Robert Coles discusses the complex family relationships depicted in "I Stand Here Ironing" and reaches an optimistic conclusion:

> But the child did not grow to be a mere victim of the kind so many of us these days are rather eager to recognize—a hopeless tangle of psychopathology. The growing child, even in her troubled moments, revealed herself to be persistent, demanding, and observant. In the complaints we make, in the "symptoms" we develop, we reveal our strengths as well as our weaknesses. The hurt child could summon her intelligence, exercise her will, smile and make others smile.

Do you agree with Coles's psychological evaluation of Emily? Do you find the story's ending as essentially uplifting as he seems to? Why or why not?

Related Works: "Everyday Use" (p. 426), "Two Kinds" (p. 639), "Those Winter Sundays" (p. 662), "Dusting" (p. 886), *Post-its* (p. 1176)

Fiction in Film: Tillie Olsen's "I Stand Here Ironing"

Setting is very important in "I Stand Here Ironing," whose events and emotions are rooted in a particular historical time: the years of the Great Depression. In the DVD version of the story, that time and mood are conveyed through specific, vivid images of Depression-era street scenes. The film also establishes the family's economic status, a key factor in the story, by showing how they are dressed and what their apartment looks like. The stills included here depict scenes that appear on the DVD.

Narrator (as a young woman) at ironing board
Source: ©Denna Bendall/Worn Path Productions

Emily as a child (in convalescent home)
Source: ©Denna Bendall/Worn Path Productions

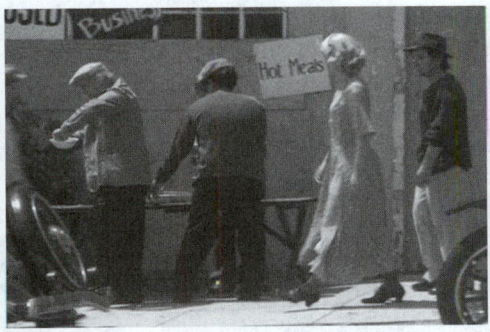

Street scene showing bread line
Source: ©Denna Bendall/Worn Path Productions

Emily performing at her school's amateur show
Source: ©Denna Bendall/Worn Path Productions

Reading and Reacting

1. The story does not describe the apartment in which Emily and her mother lived when she was a baby. How do you picture the apartment? If you were filming the story, how would you decorate and furnish it?

2. What other settings besides the apartment would you see as essential in a film version of the story? Why?

3. How would you convey the shifts in time presented in the story? For example, would you show the characters at different ages? Would you present certain scenes as flashbacks? If so, which scenes?

4. Would you include voice-over narration to reproduce the mother's voice, or would you have the story unfold without a narrator?

5. Where would you place the ironing board? Why? At what point (or points) in the story would you show the mother ironing?

6. The mother questions many of the decisions she made about Emily, and readers are left to decide whether she is a good mother. What scenes could a film version include to portray her as a good mother? as a neglectful mother?

7. Would your film be in color or in black and white? Why?

WRITING SUGGESTIONS: Setting

1. In "The Storm" and "I Stand Here Ironing," social constraints determined by the story's historical setting limit a woman's options. Explore the options each woman might reasonably exercise in order to break free of the limits that social institutions impose on her.

2. Write an essay in which you consider how "This Is What It Means to Say Phoenix, Arizona" would be different if its geographical and physical setting were changed to a setting of your choice. In your essay, examine the changes (in plot development as well as in the characters' conflicts, reactions, and motivation) that might occur as a result of the change in setting.

3. Select a story from another chapter, and write an essay in which you consider how setting affects its plot—for example, how it creates conflict or crisis, how it forces characters to act, or how it determines how the plot is resolved.

4. Both "The Storm" and "Battle Royal" use rich descriptive language to create a mood that dominates the story. Analyze this use of language in one of these stories, or explicate a short passage from each story and then compare the two passages.

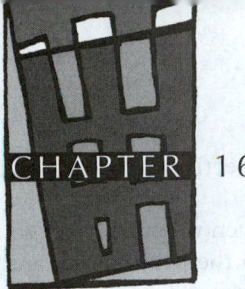

CHAPTER 16

POINT OF VIEW

Richard Wright
AP Images/Robert Kradin

Edwidge Danticat
AP Images/Laurent Rebours

Edgar Allan Poe
AP Images

One of the first choices writers make is who tells the story. This choice determines the story's **point of view**—the vantage point from which events are presented. The implications of this choice are far-reaching.

Consider the following scenario. Five people witness a crime and are questioned by the police. Their stories agree on certain points: a crime was committed, a body was found, and the crime occurred at noon. But in other ways their stories are different. The man who fled the scene was either tall or of average height; his hair was either dark or light; he either was carrying an object or was empty-handed. The events that led up to the crime and even the description of the crime itself are markedly different, depending on who tells the story. Thus, the **narrator**—the person telling the story—determines what details are included in the story and how they are arranged—in short, the plot. In addition, the perspective of the narrator affects the story's style, language, and themes.

The narrator of a work of fiction is not the same as the writer—even when a writer uses the first-person *I*. Writers create narrators to tell their stories. Often the personalities and opinions of narrators are far different from those of the author. The term **persona**—which literally means "mask"—is used for such narrators. By assuming this mask, a writer expands the creative possibilities of a work.

When deciding on a point of view for a work of fiction, a writer can choose to tell the story either in the **first person** or in the **third person**.

 ## First-Person Narrators

Sometimes the narrator is a character who uses the **first person** (*I* or sometimes *we*) to tell the story. Often this narrator is a **major character**—Sammy in John Updike's "A&P" (p. 238) and the boy in James Joyce's "Araby" (p. 361), for example—who tells his or her own story and is the focus of that story. Sometimes, however, a first-person narrator tells a story that is primarily about someone else. Such a narrator may be a **minor character** who plays a relatively small part in the story or simply an **observer** who reports events experienced or related by others. The narrator of William Faulkner's "A Rose for Emily" (p. 224), for example, is an unidentified witness to the story's events. By using *we* instead of *I*, this narrator speaks on behalf of all the town's residents, expressing their shared views of their neighbor, Emily Grierson, as the following excerpt illustrates:

> We did not say she was crazy then. We believed she had to do that. We remembered all the young men her father had driven away, and we knew that with nothing left, she would have to cling to that which had robbed her, as people will.

Writers gain a number of advantages when they use first-person narrators. First, they are able to present incidents convincingly. Readers are more willing to accept a statement like "My sister changed a lot after that day" than they are the impersonal observations of a third-person narrator. The first-person narrator also simplifies a writer's task of selecting details. Only the events and details that the narrator could actually have observed or experienced can be introduced into the story.

Another major advantage of first-person narrators is that their restricted view can create **irony**—a discrepancy between what is said and what readers believe to be true. Irony may be *dramatic*, *situational*, or *verbal*. **Dramatic irony** occurs when a narrator (or a character) perceives less than readers do; **situational irony** occurs when what happens is at odds with what readers are led to expect; **verbal irony** occurs when the narrator says one thing but actually means another.

"Gryphon," by Charles Baxter (p. 250), illustrates all three kinds of irony. Baxter creates **dramatic irony** when he has his main character see less than readers do. For example, at the end of the story, the young boy does not yet realize what readers already know—that he has learned more from Miss Ferenczi's way of teaching than from Mr. Hibler's. The setting of the story—a conventional school—creates **situational irony** because it contrasts with the unexpected events that unfold there. In addition, many of the narrator's comments create **verbal irony** because they convey the opposite of their literal meaning. At the end of the story, for example, after the substitute, Miss Ferenczi, has been fired, the narrator relates another teacher's comment that life will now return to "normal" and that their regular teacher will soon return to test them on their "knowledge." This comment is ironic in light of all Miss Ferenczi has done to redefine the narrator's ideas about "normal" education and about "knowledge."

Unreliable Narrators

Sometimes first-person narrators are self-serving, mistaken, confused, unstable, or even insane. These **unreliable narrators**, whether intentionally or unintentionally, misrepresent events and misdirect readers. In Edgar Allan Poe's "The Cask of Amontillado" (p. 328), for example, the narrator, Montresor, tells his story to justify a crime he committed fifty years before. Montresor's version of what happened is not accurate, and perceptive readers know it: his obvious self-deception, his sadistic manipulation of Fortunato, his detached description of the cold-blooded murder, and his lack of remorse lead readers to question his sanity and, therefore, to distrust his version of events. This distrust creates an ironic distance between readers and narrator.

The narrator of Charlotte Perkins Gilman's "The Yellow Wallpaper" (p. 379) is also an unreliable narrator. Suffering from "nervous depression," she unintentionally distorts the facts when she says that the shapes in her bedroom wallpaper are changing and moving. Moreover, she does not realize what is wrong with her or why, or how her husband's "good intentions" are hurting her. Readers, however, see the disparity between the narrator's interpretation of events and their own, and this irony enriches their understanding of the story.

Some narrators are unreliable because they are naive. Because they are immature, sheltered, or innocent of evil, these narrators are not aware of the significance of the events they are relating. Having the benefit of experience, readers interpret events differently from the way these narrators do. When we read a passage by a child narrator—such as the following one from J. D. Salinger's classic 1951 novel *The Catcher in the Rye*—we are aware of the narrator's innocence, and we know his interpretation of events is flawed:

> Anyway, I keep picturing all these little kids playing some game in this big field of rye and all. Thousands of little kids, and nobody's around—nobody big, I mean—except me. And I'm standing on the edge of some crazy cliff. What I have to do, I have to catch everybody if they start to go over the cliff—I mean if they're running and they don't look where they're going I have to come out from somewhere and catch them. I'd just be the catcher in the rye. . . .

The irony in the preceding passage comes from our knowledge that the naive narrator, Holden Caulfield, cannot stop children from growing up. Ultimately, they all fall off the "crazy cliff" and mature into adults. Although Holden is not aware of the futility of trying to protect children from the dangers of adulthood, readers know that his efforts are doomed from the start.

A naive narrator's background can also limit his or her ability to understand a situation. The narrator in Sherwood Anderson's 1922 short story "I'm a Fool," for example, lies to impress a rich girl he meets at a racetrack. At the end of the story, the boy regrets the fact that he lied, believing that if he had told the truth, he could have seen the girl again. The reader knows, however, that the narrator (a laborer at the racetrack) is deceiving himself because the social gap that separates him and the girl could never be bridged.

Keep in mind that all first-person narrators are, in a sense, unreliable because they present a situation as only one person sees it. When you read, you should look for discrepancies between a narrator's view of events and your own. Discovering that a story has an unreliable narrator enables you not only to question the accuracy of the narrative but also to recognize the irony in the narrator's version of events. In this way, you gain insight into the story and learn something about the writer's purpose.

Third-Person Narrators

Sometimes a writer uses the **third person** (*he, she, they*) to tell the story from the point of view of a narrator who is not a character. Third-person narrators fall into three categories: **omniscient**, **limited omniscient**, and **objective**.

Omniscient Narrators

Some third-person narrators are **omniscient** (all-knowing) narrators, moving at will from one character's mind to another's. One advantage of omniscient narrators is that they have none of the naïveté, dishonesty, gullibility, or mental instability that can characterize first-person narrators. In addition, because omniscient narrators are not characters in the story, their perception is not limited to what any one character can observe or comprehend. As a result, they can present a more inclusive view of events and characters than first-person narrators can.

Omniscient narrators can also convey their attitude toward their subject matter. For example, the omniscient narrator in the South African writer Nadine Gordimer's 1989 short story "Once upon a Time" uses sentence structure, word choice, repetition, and sarcasm to express disdain for the scene being described:

> In a house, in a suburb, in a city, there were a man and his wife who loved each other very much and were living happily ever after. They had a little boy, and they loved him very much. They had a cat and a dog that the little boy loved very much. They had a car and a caravan trailer for holidays, and a swimming-pool which was fenced so that the little boy and his playmates would not fall in and drown. They had a housemaid who was absolutely trustworthy and an itinerant gardener who was highly recommended by the neighbours. For when they began to live happily ever after they were warned, by that wise old witch, the husband's mother, not to take on anyone off the street.

Occasionally, omniscient narrators move not only in and out of the minds of the characters but also in and out of a **persona** (representing the voice of the author) who speaks directly to readers. This narrative technique was popular with writers during the eighteenth century, when the novel was a new literary form. It permitted writers to present themselves as masters of artifice, able to know and control all aspects of experience. Few contemporary writers would give themselves the license that Henry Fielding does in the following passage from *Tom Jones* (1749):

> And true it was that [Mr. Alworthy] did many of these things; but had he done nothing more I should have left him to have recorded his own merit on some fair freestone over the door of that hospital. Matters of a much more extraordinary kind are to be the subject of this history, or I should grossly misspend my time in writing so voluminous a work; and you

my sagacious friend, might with equal profit and pleasure travel through some pages which certain droll authors have been facetiously pleased to call *The History of England*.

A contemporary example of this type of omniscient point of view occurs in Ursula K. LeGuin's "The Ones Who Walk Away from Omelas." This story presents a description of a city that in the narrator's words is "like a city in a fairy tale." As the story proceeds, however, the description of Omelas changes, and the narrator's tone changes as well: "Do you believe? Do you accept the festival, the city, the joy? No? Then let me describe one more thing." By undercutting her own narrative, the narrator underscores the ironic theme of the story, which suggests that it is impossible for human beings to ever achieve an ideal society.

Limited Omniscient Narrators

Third-person narrators can have **limited omniscience**, focusing on only what a single character experiences. In other words, nothing is revealed that the character does not see, hear, feel, or think.

Limited omniscient narrators, like all third-person narrators, have certain advantages over first-person narrators. When a writer uses a first-person narrator, the narrator's personality and speech color the story, creating a personal or even an idiosyncratic narrative. Also, the first-person narrator's character flaws or lack of knowledge may limit his or her awareness of the significance of events. Limited omniscient narrators are more flexible: they take readers into a particular character's mind just as a first-person narrator does, but without the first-person narrator's subjectivity, self-deception, or naïveté. In the following example from Anne Tyler's "Teenage Wasteland" (1984), the limited omniscient narrator presents the story from the point of view of a single character, Daisy:

> Daisy and Matt sat silent, shocked. Matt rubbed his forehead with his fingertips. Imagine, Daisy thought, how they must look to Mr. Lanham: an overweight housewife in a cotton dress and a too-tall, too-thin insurance agent in a baggy, frayed suit. Failures, both of them—the kind of people who are always hurrying to catch up, missing the point of things that everyone else grasps at once. She wished she'd worn nylons instead of knee socks.

Here the point of view gives readers the impression that they are standing off to the side watching Daisy and her husband Matt. However, at the same time that we have the advantage of this objective view, we are also able to see into the mind of one character.

Objective Narrators

Third-person **objective narrators**, who tell a story from an objective (or dramatic) point of view, remain entirely outside the characters' minds. With objective narrators, events unfold the way they would in a play or a movie: narrators tell the story by presenting dialogue and recounting events; they do not reveal the characters' (or their own) thoughts or attitudes. Thus, they allow readers to interpret the actions of the characters without any interference. Ernest Hemingway uses the objective point of view in his short story "A Clean, Well-Lighted Place" (1933):

> The waiter took the brandy bottle and another saucer from the counter inside the café and marched out to the old man's table. He put down the saucer and poured the glass full of brandy.

"You should have killed yourself last week," he said to the deaf man. The old man motioned with his finger. "A little more," he said. The waiter poured on into the glass so that the brandy slopped over and ran down the stem into the top saucer of the pile. "Thank you," the old man said. The waiter took the bottle back inside the café. He sat down at the table with his colleague again.

The story's narrator is distant, seemingly emotionless, and this perspective is consistent with the author's purpose: for Hemingway, the attitude of the narrator reflects the stunned, almost anesthetized condition of people in the post–World War I world.

Selecting an Appropriate Point of View

The main criterion writers use when they decide on a point of view from which to tell a story is how the point of view they select will affect their narrative. The passages that follow illustrate the options available to writers.

Limited Omniscient Point of View

In the following passage from the short story "Doe Season" (p. 472), David Michael Kaplan uses a third-person limited omniscient narrator to tell the story of Andy, a nine-year-old girl who is going hunting with her father for the first time:

> They were always the same woods, she thought sleepily as they drove through the early morning darkness—deep and immense, covered with yesterday's snowfall, which had frozen overnight. They were the same woods that lay behind her house, *and they stretch all the way to here,* she thought, *for miles and miles, longer than I could walk in a day, or a week even, but they are still the same woods.* The thought made her feel good: it was like thinking of God; it was like thinking of the space between here and the moon; it was like thinking of all the foreign countries from her geography book where even now, Andy knew, people were going to bed, while they—she and her father and Charlie Spoon and Mac, Charlie's eleven-year-old son—were driving deeper into the Pennsylvania countryside, to go hunting.
>
> They had risen long before dawn. Her mother, yawning and not trying to hide her sleepiness, cooked them eggs and French toast. Her father smoked a cigarette and flicked ashes into his saucer while Andy listened, wondering *Why doesn't he come?* and *Won't he ever come?* until at last a car pulled into the graveled drive and honked. "That will be Charlie Spoon," her father said; he always said "Charlie Spoon," even though his real name was Spreun, because Charlie was, in a sense, shaped like a spoon, with a large head and a narrow waist and chest.

Here the limited omniscient point of view has the advantage of allowing the narrator to focus on the thoughts, fears, and reactions of the child while at the same time giving readers information about Andy that she herself is too immature or unsophisticated to know. Rather than simply presenting the thoughts of the child (represented in the story by italics), the third-person narrator makes connections between ideas and displays a level of language and a degree of insight that readers would not accept from Andy as a first-person narrator. In addition, the limited omniscient perspective enables the narrator to maintain some distance.

First-Person Point of View (Child)

Consider how different the passage would be if it were narrated by nine-year-old Andy:

> "I like the woods," I thought. "They're big and scary. I wonder if they're the same woods that are behind my house. They go on for miles. They're bigger than I could walk in a day, or a week even." It was neat to think that while we were driving into the woods people were going to bed in other countries.
>
> When I woke up this morning, I couldn't wait to go hunting. My mother was cooking breakfast, but all I could think of was, "When will he come?" and "Won't he ever come?" Finally, I heard a car honk. "That will be Charlie Spoon," my father said. I think he called him "Charlie Spoon" because he thought Charlie was shaped like a big spoon.

As a first-person narrator, nine-year-old Andy must have the voice of a child; moreover, she is restricted to only those observations that a nine-year-old could reasonably make. Because of these limitations, the passage lacks the level of vocabulary, syntax, and insight necessary to develop the central character and the themes of the story. This point of view could succeed only if Andy's words established an ironic contrast between her naive sensibility and the reality of the situation.

First-Person Point of View (Adult)

The writer could have avoided these problems and still gained the advantages of using a first-person narrator by having Andy tell her story as an adult looking back on a childhood experience. (This technique is used by James Joyce in "Araby" [p. 361], Charles Baxter in "Gryphon" [p. 250], and Alberto Alvaro Ríos in "The Secret Lion" [p. 180].)

> "They are always the same woods," I thought sleepily as we drove through the early morning darkness—deep and immense, covered with yesterday's snowfall, which had frozen overnight. "They're the same woods that lie behind my house, and they stretch all the way to here," I thought. I knew that they stretched for miles and miles, longer than I could walk in a day, or even in a week but that they were still the same woods. Knowing this made me feel good: I thought it was like thinking of God; it was like thinking of the space between that place and the moon; it was like thinking of all the foreign countries from my geography book where even then, I knew, people were going to bed, while we—my father and I and Charlie Spoon and Mac, Charlie's eleven-year-old son—were driving deeper into the Pennsylvania countryside, to go hunting.
>
> We had risen before dawn. My mother, who was yawning and not trying to hide her sleepiness, cooked us eggs and French toast. My father smoked a cigarette and flicked ashes into his saucer while I listened, wondering, "Why doesn't he come?" and "Won't he ever come?" until at last a car pulled into our driveway and honked. "That will be Charlie Spoon," my father said. He always said "Charlie Spoon," even though his real name was Spreun, because Charlie was, in a sense, shaped like a spoon, with a large head and a narrow waist and chest.

Although this passage presents the child's point of view, it does not use a child's voice; the language and scope of the passage are too sophisticated for a child. By using a mature style, the adult narrator considers ideas that a child could not possibly understand, such as the symbolic significance of the woods. In so doing, however, he sacrifices the objectivity and detachment that characterize the third-person limited omniscient narrator of the original story.

Omniscient Point of View

The writer could also have used an omniscient narrator to tell his story. In this case, the narrator would be free to reveal and comment not only on Andy's thoughts but also on those of her father, and possibly even on the thoughts of her mother and Charlie Spoon.

In the following passage, the omniscient narrator interprets the behavior of the characters and tells what each one is thinking.

> They were always the same woods, she thought sleepily as they drove through the early morning darkness—deep and immense, covered with yesterday's snowfall, which had frozen overnight. They were the same woods that lay behind her house, and they stretch all the way to here, she thought, for miles and miles, longer than I could walk in a day, or a week even, but they are still the same woods.
>
> They had risen before dawn. The mother, yawning and not trying to hide her sleepiness, cooked them eggs and French toast. She looked at her husband and her daughter and wondered if she was doing the right thing by allowing them to go hunting together. "After all," she thought, "he's not the most careful person. Will he watch her? Make sure that no harm comes to her?"
>
> The father smoked a cigarette and flicked ashes into his saucer. He was listening to the sounds of the early morning. "I know everything will be all right," he thought. "It's about time Andy went hunting. When I was her age. . . ." Andy listened, wondering *Why doesn't he come?* and *Won't he ever come?* until at last a car pulled into the graveled drive and honked. Suddenly the father cocked his head and said, "That will be Charlie Spoon."
>
> Andy thought it was funny that her father called Charlie "Spoon" even though his real name was Spreun, because Charlie was, in a sense, shaped like a spoon, with a large head and a narrow waist and chest.

Certainly this point of view has its advantages; for example, the wide scope of this perspective provides a great deal of information about the characters. However, the use of an omniscient point of view deprives the story of its focus on Andy.

Objective Point of View

Finally, the writer could have used an objective narrator. This point of view would eliminate all interpretation by the narrator and force readers to make judgments solely on the basis of what the characters say and do.

> Andy sat sleepily staring into her cereal. She played with the dry flakes of bran as they floated in the surface of the milk.
>
> Andy's mother, yawning, cooked them eggs and French toast. She looked at her husband and her daughter, paused for a second, and then went about what she was doing.
>
> Andy's father smoked a cigarette and flicked ashes into his saucer. He looked out the window and said, "I wonder where Charlie Spoon is?"
>
> Andy squirmed restlessly and repeatedly looked up at the clock that hung above the stove.

The disadvantage of this point of view is that it creates a great deal of distance between the characters and the readers. Instead of gaining the intimate knowledge of Andy that the limited omniscient point of view provides—knowledge even greater than she herself has—readers must infer what she thinks and feels without any help from the narrator.

✔ **CHECKLIST**   **Selecting an Appropriate Point of View: Review**

First-Person Narrators (use *I* or *WE*)

▶ *Major character telling his or her own story* "Every morning I lay on the floor in the front parlour watching her door." (James Joyce, "Araby")

▶ *Minor character as witness* "And so she died. . . . We did not even know she was sick; we had long since given up trying to get information. . . ." (William Faulkner, "A Rose for Emily")

Third-Person Narrators (use *HE*, *SHE*, and *THEY*)

▶ *Omniscient—able to move at will from character to character and comment about them* "In a house, in a suburb, in a city, there were a man and his wife who loved each other very much. . . ." (Nadine Gordimer, "Once upon a Time")

▶ *Limited omniscient—restricts focus to a single character* "The wagon went on. He did not know where they were going." (William Faulkner, "Barn Burning")

▶ *Objective (dramatic)—simply reports the dialogue and the actions of characters* "'You'll be drunk,' the waiter said. The old man looked at him. The waiter went away." (Ernest Hemingway, "A Clean, Well-Lighted Place")

✔ **CHECKLIST**   **Writing about Point of View**

☐ What is the dominant point of view from which the story is told?

☐ Is the narrator a character in the story? If so, is he or she a participant in the story's events or just a witness?

☐ Does the story's point of view create irony?

☐ If the story has a first-person narrator, is the narrator reliable or unreliable?

☐ If the story has a third-person narrator, is he or she omniscient? Does he or she have limited omniscience? Is the narrator objective?

☐ What are the advantages of the story's point of view? What are the disadvantages?

☐ Does the point of view remain consistent throughout the story, or does it shift?

☐ How might a different point of view change the story?

RICHARD WRIGHT (1908–1960) was born near Natchez, Mississippi, the son of sharecroppers. He had little formal schooling but as a young man was a voracious reader, especially of naturalistic fiction. Relocating to Chicago in the late 1920s, Wright worked as a postal clerk until 1935, when he joined the Federal Writers' Project. Deeply troubled by the economic and social oppression of African Americans, Wright joined the Communist Party in 1932, and his early poems and stories reflect a distinctly Marxist perspective. In 1944, he broke with the party because of its stifling effect on his creativity.

Wright began to reach a mainstream audience when a group of four long stories on the theme of racial oppression and violence was judged best manuscript in a contest sponsored by *Story* magazine; these stories were published as *Uncle Tom's Children* in 1938. Two years later, Wright published his most famous work, *Native Son*, an angry and brutal novel exploring the moral devastation wrought by a racist society. The autobiographical *Black Boy* was published in 1945. Wright eventually left the United States for Paris in protest against the treatment of African Americans in his native country. His later work was concerned with national independence movements in Africa and elsewhere in the third world.

The following story, published in the posthumous collection *Eight Men* (1961), is uncharacteristic of Wright's work in a number of ways—not least of which is that it is told through the eyes of a white protagonist.

Cultural Context In 1957, the year "Big Black Good Man" was written, President Dwight D. Eisenhower sent paratroopers to Little Rock, Arkansas, to forestall violence over desegregation of the public schools. The crisis began on September 2, when Governor Orval Faubus ordered the Arkansas National Guard to blockade Central High School in Little Rock to prevent the entrance of nine black students. On September 20, NAACP lawyers Thurgood Marshall and Wiley Brandon obtained an injunction from the federal district court that ordered the troops removed. On September 25, the students entered the school, escorted by members of the 101st Airborne Division of the United States Army.

Big Black Good Man (1957)

Through the open window Olaf Jenson could smell the sea and hear the occasional foghorn of a freighter; outside, rain pelted down through an August night, drumming softly upon the pavements of Copenhagen,[1] inducing drowsiness, bringing dreamy memory, relaxing the tired muscles of his work-wracked body. He sat slumped in a swivel chair with his legs outstretched and his feet propped atop an edge of his desk. An inch of white ash tipped the end of his brown cigar and now and then he inserted the end of the stogie[2] into his mouth and drew gently upon it, letting wisps of blue smoke eddy from the corners of his wide, thin lips. The watery gray irises behind the thick lenses of his eyeglasses gave him a look of abstraction, of absentmindedness, of an almost genial idiocy. He sighed, reached for his half-empty bottle of beer, and drained it into his glass and downed it with a long slow gulp, then licked his lips. Replacing the cigar, he slapped his right palm against his thigh and said half aloud:

---

[1] *Copenhagen:* The capital of Denmark.
[2] *stogie:* A cheap cigar.

"Well, I'll be sixty tomorrow. I'm not rich, but I'm not poor either . . . Really, I can't complain. Got good health. Traveled all over the world and had my share of girls when I was young . . . And my Karen's a good wife. I own my home. Got no debts. And I love digging in my garden in the spring . . . Grew the biggest carrots of anybody last year. Ain't saved much money, but what the hell . . . Money ain't everything. Got a good job. Night portering ain't too bad." He shook his head and yawned. "Karen and I could of had some children, though. Would of been good company . . . 'Specially for Karen. And I could of taught 'em languages . . . English, French, German, Danish, Dutch, Swedish, Norwegian, and Spanish . . ." He took the cigar out of his mouth and eyed the white ash critically. "Hell of a lot of good language learning did me . . . Never got anything out of it. But those ten years in New York were fun . . . Maybe I could of got rich if I'd stayed in America . . . Maybe. But I'm satisfied. You can't have everything."

Behind him the office door opened and a young man, a medical student occupying room number nine, entered.

"Good evening," the student said.

"Good evening," Olaf said, turning.   5

The student went to the keyboard and took hold of the round, brown knob that anchored his key.

"Rain, rain, rain," the student said.

"That's Denmark for you," Olaf smiled at him.

"This dampness keeps me clogged up like a drainpipe," the student complained.

"That's Denmark for you," Olaf repeated with a smile.   10

"Good night," the student said.

"Good night, son," Olaf sighed, watching the door close.

Well, my tenants are my children, Olaf told himself. Almost all of his children were in their rooms now . . . Only seventy-two and forty-four were missing . . . Seventy-two might've gone to Sweden . . . And forty-four was maybe staying at his girl's place tonight, like he sometimes did . . . He studied the pear-shaped blobs of hard rubber, reddish brown like ripe fruit, that hung from the keyboard, then glanced at his watch. Only room thirty, eighty-one, and one hundred and one were empty . . . And it was almost midnight. In a few moments he could take a nap. Nobody hardly ever came looking for accommodations after midnight, unless a stray freighter came in, bringing thirsty, women-hungry sailors. Olaf chuckled softly. Why in hell was I ever a sailor? The whole time I was at sea I was thinking and dreaming about women. Then why didn't I stay on land where women could be had? Hunh? Sailors are crazy . . .

But he liked sailors. They reminded him of his youth, and there was something so direct, simple, and childlike about them. They always said straight out what they wanted, and what they wanted was almost always women and whisky . . . "Well, there's no harm in that . . . Nothing could be more natural," Olaf sighed, looking thirstily at his empty beer bottle. No; he'd not drink any more tonight; he'd had enough; he'd go to sleep . . .

He was bending forward and loosening his shoelaces when he heard the office door crack open. He lifted his eyes, then sucked in his breath. He did not straighten; he just stared up and around at the huge black thing that filled the doorway. His reflexes   15 refused to function; it was not fear; it was just simple astonishment. He was staring at the biggest, strangest, and blackest man he'd ever seen in all his life.

"Good evening," the black giant said in a voice that filled the small office. "Say, you got a room?"

Olaf sat up slowly, not to answer but to look at this brooding black vision; it towered darkly some six and a half feet into the air, almost touching the ceiling, and its skin was so black that it had a bluish tint. And the sheer bulk of the man! . . . His chest bulged like a barrel; his rocklike and humped shoulders hinted of mountain ridges; the stomach ballooned like a threatening stone; and the legs were like telephone poles . . . The big black cloud of a man now lumbered into the office, bending to get its buffalolike head under the door frame, then advanced slowly upon Olaf, like a stormy sky descending.

"You got a room?" the big black man asked again in a resounding voice.

Olaf now noticed that the ebony giant was well dressed, carried a wonderful new suitcase, and wore black shoes that gleamed despite the raindrops that peppered their toes.

20   "You're American?" Olaf asked him.

"Yeah, man; sure," the black giant answered.

"Sailor?"

"Yeah. American Continental Lines."

Olaf had not answered the black man's question. It was not that the hotel did not admit men of color; Olaf took in all comers—blacks, yellows, whites, and browns . . . To Olaf, men were men, and, in his day, he'd worked and eaten and slept and fought with all kinds of men. But this particular black man . . . Well, he didn't seem human. Too big, too black, too loud, too direct, and probably too violent to boot . . . Olaf's five feet seven inches scarcely reached the black giant's shoulder and his frail body weighed less, perhaps, than one of the man's gigantic legs . . . There was something about the man's intense blackness and ungainly bigness that frightened and insulted Olaf; he felt as though this man had come here expressly to remind him how puny, how tiny, and how weak and how white he was. Olaf knew, while registering his reactions, that he was being irrational and foolish; yet, for the first time in his life, he was emotionally determined to refuse a man a room solely on the basis of the man's size and color . . . Olaf's lips parted as he groped for the right words in which to couch his refusal, but the black giant bent forward and boomed:

25   "I asked you if you got a room. I got to put up somewhere tonight, man."

"Yes, we got a room," Olaf murmured.

And at once he was ashamed and confused. Sheer fear had made him yield. And he seethed against himself for his involuntary weakness. Well, he'd look over his book and pretend that he'd made a mistake; he'd tell this hunk of blackness that there was really no free room in the hotel, and that he was so sorry . . . Then, just as he took out the hotel register to make believe that he was poring over it, a thick roll of American bank notes, crisp and green, was thrust under his nose.

"Keep this for me, will you?" the black giant commanded. "Cause I'm gonna get drunk tonight and I don't wanna lose it."

Olaf stared at the roll; it was huge, in denominations of fifties and hundreds. Olaf's eyes widened.

"How much is there?" he asked.

"Two thousand six hundred," the giant said. "Just put it into an envelope and write 'Jim' on it and lock it in your safe, hunh?"

The black mass of man had spoken in a manner that indicated that it was taking it for granted that Olaf would obey. Olaf was licked. Resentment clogged the pores of his wrinkled white skin. His hands trembled as he picked up the money. No; he couldn't refuse this man . . . The impulse to deny him was strong, but each time he was about to act upon it something thwarted him, made him shy off. He clutched about desperately for an idea. Oh yes, he could say that if he planned to stay for only one night, then he could not have the room, for it was against the policy of the hotel to rent rooms for only one night . . .

"How long are you staying? Just tonight?" Olaf asked.

"Naw. I'll be here for five or six days, I reckon," the giant answered off handedly.

"You take room number thirty," Olaf heard himself saying. "It's forty kroner a day."

"That's all right with me," the giant said.

With slow, stiff movements, Olaf put the money in the safe and then turned and stared helplessly up into the living, breathing blackness looming above him. Suddenly he became conscious of the outstretched palm of the black giant; he was silently demanding the key to the room. His eyes downcast, Olaf surrendered the key, marveling at the black man's tremendous hands . . . He could kill me with one blow, Olaf told himself in fear.

Feeling himself beaten, Olaf reached for the suitcase, but the black hand of the giant whisked it out of his grasp.

"That's too heavy for you, big boy; I'll take it," the giant said.

Olaf let him. He thinks I'm nothing . . . He led the way down the corridor, sensing the giant's lumbering presence behind him. Olaf opened the door of number thirty and stood politely to one side, allowing the black giant to enter. At once the room seemed like a doll's house, so dwarfed and filled and tiny it was with a great living blackness . . . Flinging his suitcase upon a chair, the giant turned. The two men looked directly at each other now. Olaf saw that the giant's eyes were tiny and red, buried, it seemed, in muscle and fat. Black cheeks spread, flat and broad, topping the wide and flaring nostrils. The mouth was the biggest that Olaf had ever seen on a human face; the lips were thick, pursed, parted, showing snow-white teeth. The black neck was like a bull's . . . The giant advanced upon Olaf and stood over him.

"I want a bottle of whiskey and a woman," he said. "Can you fix me up?"

"Yes," Olaf whispered, wild with anger and insult.

But what was he angry about? He'd had requests like this every night from all sorts of men and he was used to fulfilling them; he was a night porter in a cheap, water-front Copenhagen hotel that catered to sailors and students. Yes, men needed women, but this man, Olaf felt, ought to have a special sort of woman. He felt a deep and strange reluctance to phone any of the women whom he habitually sent to men. Yet he had promised. Could he lie and say that none was available? No. That sounded too fishy. The black giant sat upon the bed, staring straight before him. Olaf moved about quickly, pulling down the window shades, taking the pink coverlet off the bed, nudging the giant with his elbow to make him move as he did so . . . That's the way to treat 'im . . . Show 'im I ain't scared of 'im . . . But he was still seeking for an excuse to refuse. And he could think of nothing. He felt hypnotized, mentally immobilized. He stood hesitantly at the door.

"You send the whiskey and the woman quick, pal?" the black giant asked, rousing himself from a brooding stare.

45   "Yes," Olaf grunted, shutting the door.

Goddamn, Olaf sighed. He sat in his office at his desk before the phone. Why did *he* have to come here? . . . I'm not prejudiced . . . No, not at all . . . But . . . He couldn't think any more. God oughtn't make men as big and black as that . . . But what the hell was he worrying about? He'd sent women of all races to men of all colors . . . So why not a woman to the black giant? Oh, only if the man were small, brown, and intelligent-looking . . . Olaf felt trapped.

With a reflex movement of his hand, he picked up the phone and dialed Lena. She was big and strong and always cut him in for fifteen per cent instead of the usual ten per cent. Lena had four small children to feed and clothe. Lena was willing; she was, she said, coming over right now. She didn't give a good goddamn about how big and black the man was . . .

"Why you ask me that?" Lena wanted to know over the phone. "You never asked that before . . ."

"But this one is *big*," Olaf found himself saying.

50   "He's just a man," Lena told him, her voice singing stridently, laughingly over the wire. "You just leave that to me. You don't have to do anything. *I'll* handle 'im."

Lena had a key to the hotel door downstairs, but tonight Olaf stayed awake. He wanted to see her. Why? He didn't know. He stretched out on the sofa in his office, but sleep was far from him. When Lena arrived, he told her again how big and black the man was.

"You told me that over the phone," Lena reminded him.

Olaf said nothing. Lena flounced off on her errand of mercy. Olaf shut the office door, then opened it and left it ajar. But why? He didn't know. He lay upon the sofa and stared at the ceiling. He glanced at his watch; it was almost two o'clock . . . She's staying in there a long time . . . Ah, God, but he could do with a drink . . . Why was he so damned worked up and nervous about a nigger and a white whore? . . . He'd never been so upset in all his life. Before he knew it, he had drifted off to sleep. Then he heard the office door swinging creakingly open on its rusty hinges. Lena stood in it, grim and businesslike, her face scrubbed free of powder and rouge. Olaf scrambled to his feet, adjusting his eyeglasses, blinking.

"How was it?" he asked her in a confidential whisper.

55   Lena's eyes blazed.

"What the hell's that to you?" she snapped. "There's your cut," she said, flinging him his money, tossing it upon the covers of the sofa. "You're sure nosy tonight. You wanna take over my work?"

Olaf's pasty cheeks burned red.

"You go to hell," he said, slamming the door.

"I'll meet you there!" Lena's shouting voice reached him dimly.

60   He was being a fool; there was no doubt about it. But, try as he might, he could not shake off a primitive hate for that black mountain of energy, of muscle, of bone;

he envied the easy manner in which it moved with such a creeping and powerful motion; he winced at the booming and commanding voice that came to him when the tiny little eyes were not even looking at him; he shivered at the sight of those vast and clawlike hands that seemed always to hint of death . . .

Olaf kept his counsel. He never spoke to Karen about the sordid doings at the hotel. Such things were not for women like Karen. He knew instinctively that Karen would have been amazed had he told her that he was worried sick about a nigger and a blonde whore . . . No; he couldn't talk to anybody about it, not even the hard-bitten[3] old bitch who owned the hotel. She was concerned only about money; she didn't give a damn about how big and how black a client was as long as he paid his room rent.

Next evening, when Olaf arrived for duty, there was no sight or sound of the black giant. A little later after one o'clock in the morning he appeared, left his key, and went out wordlessly. A few moments past two the giant returned, took his key from the board, and paused.

"I want that Lena again tonight. And another bottle of whiskey," he said boomingly.

"I'll call her and see if she's in," Olaf said.

"Do that," the black giant said and was gone.

He thinks he's God, Olaf fumed. He picked up the phone and ordered Lena and a bottle of whiskey, and there was a taste of ashes in his mouth. On the third night came the same request: Lena and whiskey. When the black giant appeared on the fifth night, Olaf was about to make a sarcastic remark to the effect that maybe he ought to marry Lena, but he checked it in time . . . After all, he could kill me with one hand, he told himself.

Olaf was nervous and angry with himself for being nervous. Other black sailors came and asked for girls and Olaf sent them, but with none of the fear and loathing that he sent Lena and a bottle of whiskey to the giant . . . All right, the black giant's stay was almost up. He'd said that he was staying for five or six nights; tomorrow night was the sixth night and that ought to be the end of this nameless terror.

On the sixth night Olaf sat in his swivel chair with his bottle of beer and waited, his teeth on edge, his fingers drumming the desk. But what the hell am I fretting for? . . . The hell with 'im . . . Olaf sat and dozed. Occasionally he'd awaken and listen to the foghorns of freighters sounding as ships came and went in the misty Copenhagen harbor. He was half asleep when he felt a rough hand on his shoulder. He blinked his eyes open. The giant, black and vast and powerful, all but blotted out his vision.

"What I owe you, man?" the giant demanded. "And I want my money."

"Sure," Olaf said, relieved, but filled as always with fear of this living wall of black flesh.

With fumbling hands, he made out the bill and received payment, then gave the giant his roll of money, laying it on the desk so as not to let his hands touch the flesh of the black mountain. Well, his ordeal was over. It was past two o'clock in the morning.

65

70

---

[3] *hard-bitten:* Stubborn, tough.

Olaf even managed a wry smile and muttered a guttural "Thanks" for the generous tip that the giant tossed him.

Then a strange tension entered the office. The office door was shut and Olaf was alone with the black mass of power, yearning for it to leave. But the black mass of power stood still, immobile, looking down at Olaf. And Olaf could not, for the life of him, guess at what was transpiring in that mysterious black mind. The two of them simply stared at each other for a full two minutes, the giant's tiny little beady eyes blinking slowly as they seemed to measure and search Olaf's face. Olaf's vision dimmed for a second as terror seized him and he could feel a flush of heat overspread his body. Then Olaf sucked in his breath as the devil of blackness commanded:

"Stand up!"

Olaf was paralyzed. Sweat broke on his face. His worst premonitions about this black beast were coming true. This evil blackness was about to attack him, maybe kill him . . . Slowly Olaf shook his head, his terror permitting him to breathe:

75
"What're you talking about?"

"Stand up, I say!" the black giant bellowed.

As though hypnotized, Olaf tried to rise; then he felt the black paw of the beast helping him roughly to his feet.

They stood an inch apart. Olaf's pasty-white features were glued to the giant's swollen black face. The ebony ensemble of eyes and nose and mouth and cheeks looked down at Olaf, silently; then, with a slow and deliberate movement of his gorillalike arms, he lifted his mammoth hands to Olaf's throat. Olaf had long known and felt that this dreadful moment was coming; he felt trapped in a nightmare. He could not move. He wanted to scream, but could find no words. His lips refused to open; his tongue felt icy and inert. Then he knew that his end had come when the giant's black fingers slowly, softly encircled his throat while a horrible grin of delight broke out on the sooty face . . . Olaf lost control of the reflexes of his body and he felt a hot stickiness flooding his underwear . . . He stared without breathing, gazing into the grinning blackness of the face that was bent over him, feeling the black fingers caressing his throat and waiting to feel the sharp, stinging ache and pain of the bones in his neck being snapped, crushed . . . He knew all along that I hated 'im . . . Yes, and now he's going to kill me for it, Olaf told himself with despair.

The black fingers still circled Olaf's neck, not closing, but gently massaging it, as it were, moving to and fro, while the obscene face grinned into his. Olaf could feel the giant's warm breath blowing on his eyelashes and he felt like a chicken about to have its neck wrung and its body tossed to flip and flap dyingly in the dust of the barnyard . . . Then suddenly the black giant withdrew his fingers from Olaf's neck and stepped back a pace, still grinning. Olaf sighed, trembling, his body seeming to shrink; he waited. Shame sheeted him for the hot wetness that was in his trousers. Oh, God, he's teasing me . . . He's showing me how easily he can kill me . . . He swallowed, waiting, his eyes stones of gray.

80
The giant's barrel-like chest gave forth a low, rumbling chuckle of delight.

"You laugh?" Olaf asked whimperingly.

"Sure I laugh," the giant shouted.

"Please don't hurt me," Olaf managed to say.

"I wouldn't hurt you, boy," the giant said in a tone of mockery. "So long."

And he was gone. Olaf fell limply into the swivel chair and fought off los-   85
ing consciousness. Then he wept. He was showing me how easily he could kill
me . . . He made me shake with terror and then laughed and left . . . Slowly, Olaf
recovered, stood, then gave vent to a string of curses:

"Goddamn 'im! My gun's right there in the desk drawer; I should of shot 'im. Jesus,
I hope the ship he's on sinks . . . I hope he drowns and the sharks eat 'im . . ."

Later, he thought of going to the police, but sheer shame kept him back; and,
anyway, the giant was probably on board his ship by now. And he had to get home
and clean himself. Oh, Lord, what could he tell Karen? Yes, he would say that his
stomach had been upset . . . He'd change clothes and return to work. He phoned the
hotel owner that he was ill and wanted an hour off; the old bitch said that she was
coming right over and that poor Olaf could have the evening off.

Olaf went home and lied to Karen. Then he lay awake the rest of the night
dreaming of revenge. He saw that freighter on which the giant was sailing; he
saw it springing a dangerous leak and saw a torrent of sea water flooding, gushing
into all the compartments of the ship until it found the bunk in which the black
giant slept. Ah, yes, the foamy, surging waters would surprise that sleeping black
bastard of a giant and he would drown, gasping and choking like a trapped rat,
his tiny eyes bulging until they glittered red, the bitter water of the sea pounding
his lungs until they ached and finally burst . . . The ship would sink slowly to the
bottom of the cold, black, silent depths of the sea and a shark, a *white* one, would
glide aimlessly about the shut portholes until it found an open one and it would
slither inside and nose about until it found that swollen, rotting, stinking carcass
of the black beast and it would then begin to nibble at the decomposing mass of
tarlike flesh, eating the bones clean . . . Olaf always pictured the giant's bones as
being jet black and shining.

Once or twice, during these fantasies of cannibalistic revenge, Olaf felt a little guilty about all the many innocent people, women and children, all white and
blonde, who would have to go down into watery graves in order that that white shark
could devour the evil giant's black flesh . . . But, despite feelings of remorse, the fantasy lived persistently on, and when Olaf found himself alone, it would crowd and
cloud his mind to the exclusion of all else, affording him the only revenge he knew.
To make me suffer just for the pleasure of it, he fumed. Just to show me how strong
he was . . . Olaf learned how to hate, and got pleasure out of it.

Summer fled on wings of rain. Autumn flooded Denmark with color. Winter   90
made rain and snow fall on Copenhagen. Finally spring came, bringing violets and
roses. Olaf kept to his job. For many months he feared the return of the black giant.
But when a year had passed and the giant had not put in an appearance, Olaf allowed
his revenge fantasy to peter out, indulging in it only when recalling the shame that
the black monster had made him feel.

Then one rainy August night, a year later, Olaf sat drowsing at his desk, his
bottle of beer before him, tilting back in his swivel chair, his feet resting atop a
corner of his desk, his mind mulling over the more pleasant aspects of his life. The
office door cracked open. Olaf glanced boredly up and around. His heart jumped and
skipped a beat. The black nightmare of terror and shame that he had hoped that he
had lost forever was again upon him . . . Resplendently dressed, suitcase in hand,

the black looming mountain filled the doorway. Olaf's thin lips parted and a silent moan, half a curse, escaped them.

"Hi," the black giant boomed from the doorway.

Olaf could not reply. But a sudden resolve swept him: this time he would even the score. If this black beast came within so much as three feet of him, he would snatch his gun out of the drawer and shoot him dead, so help him God . . .

"No rooms tonight," Olaf heard himself announcing in a determined voice.

95   The black giant grinned; it was the same infernal grimace of delight and triumph that he had had when his damnable black fingers had been around his throat . . .

"Don't want no room tonight," the giant announced.

"Then what are you doing here?" Olaf asked in a loud but tremulous voice.

The giant swept toward Olaf and stood over him; and Olaf could not move, despite his oath to kill him . . .

"What do you want then?" Olaf demanded once more, ashamed that he could not lift his voice above a whisper.

100   The giant still grinned, then tossed what seemed the same suitcase upon Olaf's sofa and bent over it; he zippered it open with a sweep of his clawlike hand and rummaged in it, drawing forth a flat, gleaming white object done up in glowing cellophane. Olaf watched with lowered lids, wondering what trick was now being played on him. Then, before he could defend himself, the giant had whirled and again long, black, snakelike fingers were encircling Olaf's throat . . . Olaf stiffened, his right hand clawing blindly for the drawer where the gun was kept. But the giant was quick.

"Wait," he bellowed, pushing Olaf back from the desk.

The giant turned quickly to the sofa and, still holding his fingers in a wide circle that seemed a noose for Olaf's neck, he inserted the rounded fingers into the top of the flat, gleaming object. Olaf had the drawer open and his sweaty fingers were now touching the gun, but something made him freeze. The flat, gleaming object was a shirt and the black giant's circled fingers were fitting themselves into its neck . . .

"A perfect fit!" the giant shouted.

Olaf stared, trying to understand. His fingers loosened about the gun. A mixture of a laugh and a curse struggled in him. He watched the giant plunge his hands into the suitcase and pull out other flat, gleaming shirts.

105   "One, two, three, four, five, six," the black giant intoned, his voice crisp and businesslike. "Six nylon shirts. And they're all yours. One shirt for each time Lena came . . . See, Daddy-O?"

The black, cupped hands, filled with billowing nylon whiteness, were extended under Olaf's nose. Olaf eased his damp fingers from his gun and pushed the drawer closed, staring at the shirts and then at the black giant's grinning face.

"Don't you like 'em?" the giant asked.

Olaf began to laugh hysterically, then suddenly he was crying, his eyes so flooded with tears that the pile of dazzling nylon looked like snow in the dead of winter. Was this true? Could he believe it? Maybe this too was a trick? But, no. There were six shirts, all nylon, and the black giant had had Lena six nights.

"What's the matter with you, Daddy-O?" the giant asked. "You blowing your top? Laughing and crying . . ."

Olaf swallowed, dabbed his withered fists at his dimmed eyes; then he realized that   110
he had his glasses on. He took them off and dried his eyes and sat up. He sighed, the
tension and shame and fear and haunting dread of his fantasy went from him, and he
leaned limply back in his chair . . .

"Try one on," the giant ordered.

Olaf fumbled with the buttons of his shirt, let down his suspenders, and pulled
the shirt off. He donned a gleaming nylon one and the giant began buttoning it
for him.

"Perfect, Daddy-O," the giant said.

His spectacled face framed in sparkling nylon, Olaf sat with trembling lips. So
he'd not been trying to kill me after all.

"You want Lena, don't you?" he asked the giant in a soft whisper. "But I don't   115
know where she is. She never came back here after you left—"

"I know where Lena is," the giant told him. "We been writing to each other. I'm
going to her house. And, Daddy-O, I'm late." The giant zippered the suitcase shut
and stood a moment gazing down at Olaf, his tiny little red eyes blinking slowly.
Then Olaf realized that there was a compassion in that stare that he had never
seen before.

"And I thought you wanted to kill me," Olaf told him. "I was scared of you . . ."

"Me? Kill you?" the giant blinked. "When?"

"That night when you put your fingers around my throat—"

"What?" the giant asked, then roared with laughter. "Daddy-O, you're a funny   120
little man. I wouldn't hurt you. I like you. You a *good* man. You helped me."

Olaf smiled, clutching the pile of nylon shirts in his arms.

"You're a good man too," Olaf murmured. Then loudly, "You're a big black
good man."

"Daddy-O, you're crazy," the giant said.

He swept his suitcase from the sofa, spun on his heel, and was at the door in one
stride.

"Thanks!" Olaf cried after him.   125

The black giant paused, turned his vast black head, and flashed a grin.

"Daddy-O, drop dead," he said and was gone.

Reading and Reacting

1. Why do you suppose Wright presents events through Olaf's eyes? How would the story
be different if Jim told it?

2. This story was published in 1957. What attitudes about race does Wright expect his
American readers to have? Do these attitudes predispose readers to identify with Jim or
with Olaf? Explain.

3. Why does Olaf dislike Jim? What does the narrator mean in paragraph 24 when he says
that Jim's "intense blackness and ungainly bigness . . . frightened and insulted Olaf"?

4. In what ways do Jim's words and actions contribute to Olaf's fears? Do you think Olaf's
reactions are reasonable, or do you believe he is overreacting?

5. The sailor's name is hardly mentioned in the story. Why? List some words used to
describe Jim. Why are these words used? How do they affect your reaction to him?

6. Do you think the story's title is ironic? In what other respects is the story ironic?

7. Why do you think Wright set the story in Copenhagen? Could it have been set in the United States in 1957?

8. What do you think Jim thinks of Olaf? Do you suppose he realizes the effect he has on him? How do you explain Jim's last comment?

9. **JOURNAL ENTRY** What point do you think the story makes about racial prejudice? Do you think Wright seems optimistic or pessimistic about race relations in the United States?

10. **CRITICAL PERSPECTIVE** In his 1982 article "The Short Stories: *Uncle Tom's Children, Eight Men*," Edward Margolies notes that "Big Black Good Man" was somewhat of a departure for Wright:

> "Big Black Good Man," which first appeared in *Esquire* in 1957, is the last short story Wright published in his lifetime. Possibly it is the last he ever wrote. In any event it represents a more traditional approach to storytelling in that Wright here avoids confining himself exclusively to dialogue. On the other hand, "Big Black Good Man" deviates from the usual Wright short story. For one thing, the narrative, by Wright's standards at least, is practically pointless. Scarcely anything "happens." There is no violence, practically no external narrative action, and no change of milieu.

Do you agree that the story is "practically pointless"? If not, what point do you think the story makes?

Related Works: "Battle Royal" (p. 287), "The Cask of Amontillado" (p. 328), "We Wear the Mask" (p. 728), "The *Chicago Defender* Sends a Man to Little Rock" (p. 963), *Fences* (p. 1548)

EDGAR ALLAN POE (1809–1849) profoundly influenced many writers all over the world. His tales of psychological terror and the macabre, his hauntingly musical lyric poems, and his writings on the craft of poetry and short story writing affected the development of symbolic fiction, the modern detective story, and the gothic horror tale. In most of Poe's horror tales (as in "The Cask of Amontillado"), readers vicariously "live" the story through the first-person narrator who tells the tale.

Poe was born in 1809, the son of a talented English-born actress who, deserted by her actor husband, died of tuberculosis before her son's third birthday. Although Poe was raised in material comfort by foster parents in Richmond, Virginia, his life was increasingly uncertain: his foster mother loved him, but her husband became antagonistic. He kept the young Poe so short of money at the University of Virginia (and later at West Point) that Poe resorted to gambling to raise money for food and clothing. Finally, disgraced and debt-ridden, he left school.

Poe found work as a magazine editor, gaining recognition as a literary critic. In 1836, he married his frail thirteen-year-old cousin, Virginia Clemm. Poe produced many of his most famous stories and poems over the next few years, working feverishly to support his tubercular wife, but although his stories were widely admired, he never achieved financial success. His wife died in 1847. Less than two years after her death, Poe was found barely conscious on a Baltimore street; three days later, he was dead at age forty. To this day, the cause of Poe's death remains a mystery.

Cultural Context Throughout antiquity, catacombs, such as those in Poe's story, were used to bury the dead. Catacombs are underground cemeteries composed of passages with recesses for tombs. The early Christian catacombs of Rome, consisting of approximately forty known chambers located in a rough circle about three miles from the center of the city, are the most extensive of all known catacombs. (Besides being used for burial, these catacombs were also used by early Christians as a refuge from persecution.) Funeral feasts were often celebrated in family vaults on the day of burial and on anniversary dates of the deaths of loved ones.

The Cask of Amontillado (1846)

The thousand injuries of Fortunato I had borne as I best could, but when he ventured upon insult I vowed revenge. You, who so well know the nature of my soul, will not suppose, however, that I gave utterance to a threat. *At length* I would be avenged; this was a point definitely settled—but the very definitiveness with which it was resolved precluded the idea of risk. I must not only punish but punish with impunity. A wrong is unredressed when retribution overtakes its redresser. It is equally unredressed when the avenger fails to make himself felt as such to him who has done the wrong.

It must be understood that neither by word nor deed had I given Fortunato cause to doubt my good will. I continued, as was my wont, to smile in his face, and he did not perceive that my smile *now* was at the thought of his immolation.

He had a weak point—this Fortunato—although in other regards he was a man to be respected and even feared. He prided himself on his connoisseurship in wine. Few Italians have the true virtuoso spirit. For the most part their enthusiasm is adopted to suit the time and opportunity, to practise imposture upon the British and Austrian *millionaires*. In painting and gemmary, Fortunato, like his countrymen, was a quack, but in the matter of old wines he was sincere. In this respect I did not differ from him materially;—I was skillful in the Italian vintages myself, and bought largely whenever I could.

It was about dusk, one evening during the supreme madness of the carnival season, that I encountered my friend. He accosted me with excessive warmth, for he had been drinking much. The man wore motley.[1] He had on a tight-fitting parti-striped dress, and his head was surmounted by the conical cap and bells. I was so pleased to see him that I thought I should never have done wringing his hand.

I said to him—"My dear Fortunato, you are luckily met. How remarkably well 5 you are looking to-day. But I have received a pipe[2] of what passes for Amontillado,[3] and I have my doubts."

"How?" said he. "Amontillado? A pipe? Impossible! And in the middle of the carnival!"

"I have my doubts," I replied; "and I was silly enough to pay the full Amontillado price without consulting you in the matter. You were not to be found, and I was fearful of losing a bargain."

---

[1] *motley:* The many-colored attire of a court jester.

[2] *pipe:* In the United States and England, a cask containing a volume equal to 126 gallons.

[3] *Amontillado:* A pale, dry sherry; literally, a wine "from Montilla" (Spain).

"Amontillado!"

"I have my doubts."

10 "Amontillado!"

"And I must satisfy them."

"Amontillado!"

"As you are engaged, I am on my way to Luchresi. If any one has a critical turn it is he. He will tell me—"

"Luchresi cannot tell Amontillado from Sherry."

15 "And yet some fools will have it that his taste is a match for your own."

"Come, let us go."

"Whither?"

"To your vaults."

"My friend, no; I will not impose upon your good nature. I perceive you have an engagement. Luchresi—"

20 "I have no engagement;—come."

"My friend, no. It is not the engagement, but the severe cold with which I perceive you are afflicted. The vaults are insufferably damp. They are encrusted with nitre."[4]

"Let us go, nevertheless. The cold is merely nothing. Amontillado! You have been imposed upon. And as for Luchresi, he cannot distinguish Sherry from Amontillado."

Thus speaking, Fortunato possessed himself of my arm; and putting on a mask of black silk and drawing a *roquelaire*[5] closely about my person, I suffered him to hurry me to my palazzo.

There were no attendants at home; they had absconded to make merry in honor of the time. I had told them that I should not return until the morning, and had given them explicit orders not to stir from the house. These orders were sufficient, I well knew, to insure their immediate disappearance, one and all, as soon as my back was turned.

25 I took from their sconces two flambeaux, and giving one to Fortunato, bowed him through several suites of rooms to the archway that led into the vaults. I passed down a long and winding staircase, requesting him to be cautious as he followed. We came at length to the foot of the descent, and stood together upon the damp ground of the catacombs of the Montresors.

The gait of my friend was unsteady, and the bells upon his cap jingled as he strode.

"The pipe," he said.

"It is farther on," said I; "but observe the white web-work which gleams from these cavern walls."

He turned towards me, and looked into my eyes with two filmy orbs that distilled the rheum of intoxication.

30 "Nitre?" he asked at length.

"Nitre," I replied. "How long have you had that cough?"

---

[4]*nitre*: Mineral deposits.

[5]*roquelaire*: A short cloak.

"Ugh! ugh! ugh!—ugh! ugh! ugh!—ugh! ugh! ugh!—ugh! ugh! ugh!—ugh! ugh! ugh!"

My poor friend found it impossible to reply for many minutes.

"It is nothing," he said at last.

"Come," I said, with decision, "we will go back; your health is precious. You are rich, respected, admired, beloved; you are happy, as once I was. You are a man to be missed. For me it is no matter. We will go back; you will be ill, and I cannot be responsible. Besides, there is Luchresi—"

"Enough," he said; "the cough is a mere nothing; it will not kill me. I shall not die of a cough."

"True—true," I replied; "and, indeed, I had no intention of alarming you unnecessarily—but you should use all proper caution. A draught of this Médoc[6] will defend us from the damps."

Here I knocked off the neck of a bottle which I drew from a long row of its fellows that lay upon the mould.

"Drink," I said, presenting him the wine.

He raised it to his lips with a leer. He paused and nodded to me familiarly, while his bells jingled.

"I drink," he said, "to the buried that repose around us."

"And I to your long life."

He again took my arm, and we proceeded.

"These vaults," he said, "are extensive."

"The Montresors," I replied, "were a great and numerous family."

"I forget your arms."

"A huge human foot d'or, in a field azure; the foot crushes a serpent rampant whose fangs are imbedded in the heel."

"And the motto?"

"*Nemo me impune lacessit.*"[7]

"Good!" he said.

The wine sparkled in his eyes and the bells jingled. My own fancy grew warm with the Médoc. We had passed through long walls of piled skeletons, with casks and puncheons[8] intermingling, into the inmost recesses of the catacombs. I paused again, and this time I made bold to seize Fortunato by an arm above the elbow.

"The nitre!" I said; "see, it increases. It hangs like moss upon the vaults. We are below the river's bed. The drops of moisture trickle among the bones. Come, we will go back ere it is too late. Your cough—"

"It is nothing," he said; "let us go on. But first, another draught of the Médoc."

I broke and reached him a flagon of De Grâve.[9] He emptied it at a breath. His eyes flashed with a fierce light. He laughed and threw the bottle upwards with a gesticulation I did not understand.

---

[6]*Médoc:* A red wine from the Médoc district, near Bordeaux, France.

[7]"Nemo me impune lacessit": "No one insults me with impunity" (Latin); this is the legend on the royal coat of arms of Scotland.

[8]*puncheons:* Barrels.

[9]*De Grâve:* Correctly, "Graves," a light wine from the Bordeaux area.

55   I looked at him in surprise. He repeated the movement—a grotesque one.

"You do not comprehend?" he said.

"Not I," I replied.

"Then you are not of the brotherhood."

"How?"

60   "You are not of the masons."[10]

"Yes, yes," I said; "yes, yes."

"You? Impossible! A mason?"

"A mason," I replied.

"A sign," he said, "a sign."

65   "It is this," I answered, producing from beneath the folds of my *roquelaire* a trowel.

"You jest," he exclaimed, recoiling a few paces. "But let us proceed to the Amontillado."

"Be it so," I said, replacing the tool beneath the cloak and again offering him my arm. He leaned upon it heavily. We continued our route in search of the Amontillado. We passed through a range of low arches, descended, passed on, and descending again, arrived at a deep crypt, in which the foulness of the air caused our flambeaux rather to glow than flame.

At the most remote end of the crypt there appeared another less spacious. Its walls had been lined with human remains, piled to the vault overhead, in the fashion of the great catacombs of Paris. Three sides of this interior crypt were still ornamented in this manner. From the fourth side the bones had been thrown down, and lay promiscuously upon the earth, forming at one point a mound of some size. Within the wall thus exposed by the displacing of the bones, we perceived a still interior crypt or recess, in depth about four feet, in width three, in height six or seven. It seemed to have been constructed for no especial use within itself, but formed merely the interval between two of the colossal supports of the roof of the catacombs, and was backed by one of their circumscribing walls of solid granite.

It was in vain that Fortunato, uplifting his dull torch, endeavored to pry into the depth of the recess. Its termination the feeble light did not enable us to see.

70   "Proceed," I said; "herein is the Amontillado. As for Luchresi—"

"He is an ignoramus," interrupted my friend, as he stepped unsteadily forward, while I followed immediately at his heels. In an instant he had reached the extremity of the niche, and finding his progress arrested by the rock, stood stupidly bewildered. A moment more and I had fettered him to the granite. In its surface were two iron staples, distant from each other about two feet, horizontally. From one of these depended a short chain, from the other a padlock. Throwing the links about his waist, it was but the work of a few seconds to secure it. He was too much astounded to resist. Withdrawing the key I stepped back from the recess.

"Pass your hand," I said, "over the wall; you cannot help feeling the nitre. Indeed, it is *very* damp. Once more let me *implore* you to return. No? Then I must positively leave you. But I must first render you all the little attentions in my power."

---

[10]*masons:* Freemasons (members of a secret fraternity). The trowel is a symbol of their alleged origin as a guild of stonemasons.

"The Amontillado!" ejaculated my friend, not yet recovered from his astonishment.

"True," I replied; "the Amontillado."

As I said these words I busied myself among the pile of bones of which I have   75
before spoken. Throwing them aside, I soon uncovered a quantity of building stone
and mortar. With these materials and with the aid of my trowel, I began vigorously to
wall up the entrance of the niche.

I had scarcely laid the first tier of the masonry when I discovered that the intoxication of Fortunato had in a great measure worn off. The earliest indication I had of this
was a low moaning cry from the depth of the recess. It was *not* the cry of a drunken
man. There was a long and obstinate silence. I laid the second tier, and the third, and
the fourth; and then I heard the furious vibrations of the chain. The noise lasted for
several minutes, during which, that I might hearken to it with the more satisfaction,
I ceased my labors and sat down upon the bones. When at last the clanking subsided,
I resumed the trowel, and finished without interruption the fifth, the sixth, and the
seventh tier. The wall was now nearly upon a level with my breast. I again paused,
and holding the flambeaux over the mason-work, threw a few feeble rays upon the
figure within.

A succession of loud and shrill screams, bursting suddenly from the throat of the
chained form, seemed to thrust me violently back. For a brief moment I hesitated,
I trembled. Unsheathing my rapier, I began to grope with it about the recess; but the
thought of an instant reassured me. I placed my hand upon the solid fabric of the
catacombs, and felt satisfied. I reapproached the wall; I replied to the yells of him
who clamoured. I re-echoed, I aided, I surpassed them in volume and in strength.
I did this, and the clamourer grew still.

It was now midnight, and my task was drawing to a close. I had completed the
eighth, the ninth and the tenth tier. I had finished a portion of the last and the eleventh; there remained but a single stone to be fitted and plastered in. I struggled with
its weight; I placed it partially in its destined position. But now there came from out
the niche a low laugh that erected the hairs upon my head. It was succeeded by a
sad voice, which I had difficulty in recognizing as that of the noble Fortunato. The
voice said—

"Ha! ha! ha!—he! he! he!—a very good joke, indeed—an excellent jest. We will
have many a rich laugh about it at the palazzo—he! he! he!—over our wine—he! he!
he!"

"The Amontillado!" I said.   80

"He! he! he!—he! he! he!—yes, the Amontillado. But is it not getting late?
Will not they be awaiting us at the palazzo, the Lady Fortunato and the rest? Let us
be gone."

"Yes," I said, "let us be gone."

"For the love of God, Montresor!"

"Yes," I said, "for the love of God."

But to these words I hearkened in vain for a reply. I grew impatient. I called   85
aloud—

"Fortunato!"

No answer. I called again—

"Fortunato!"

No answer still. I thrust a torch through the remaining aperture and let it fall within. There came forth in return only a jingling of the bells. My heart grew sick on account of the dampness of the catacombs. I hastened to make an end of my labour. I forced the last stone into its position; I plastered it up. Against the new masonry I re-erected the old rampart of bones. For the half of a century no mortal has disturbed them. *In pace requiescat!*[11]

Reading and Reacting

1. Montresor cites a "thousand injuries" and an "insult" as his motives for murdering Fortunato. Given what you learn about the two men during the course of the story, what do you suppose the "injuries" and "insult" might be?

2. Do you find Montresor to be a reliable narrator? If not, what makes you question his version of events?

3. What is Montresor's concept of personal honor? Is it consistent or inconsistent with the values of contemporary American society? How relevant are the story's ideas about revenge and guilt to present-day society? Explain.

4. Does Fortunato ever understand why Montresor hates him? What is Fortunato's attitude toward Montresor?

5. What is the significance of Montresor's family coat of arms and motto? What is the significance of Fortunato's costume?

6. In what ways does Montresor manipulate Fortunato? What weaknesses does Montresor exploit?

7. Why does Montresor wait fifty years to tell his story? How might the story be different if he had told it the morning after the murder?

8. Why does Montresor wait for a reply before he puts the last stone in position? What do you think he wants Fortunato to say?

9. JOURNAL ENTRY Do you think the use of a first-person point of view makes you more sympathetic toward Montresor than you would be if his story were told by a third-person narrator? Why or why not?

10. CRITICAL PERSPECTIVE In his discussion of this story in *Edgar Allan Poe: A Study of the Short Fiction*, Charles E. May says, "We can legitimately hypothesize that the listener is a priest and that Montresor is an old man who is dying and making final confession. . . ."

    Do you agree or disagree with May's hypothesis? Do you think that Montresor has atoned for his sin? Who else could be listening to Montresor's story?

Related Works: "A Rose for Emily" (p. 224), "Porphyria's Lover" (p. 696), "The Wolf's Postscript to 'Little Red Riding Hood'" (p. 706), *Zombie Love* (p. 1079)

---

[11]In pace requiescat: "May he rest in peace" (Latin).

WILLIAM FAULKNER (1897–1962) (picture and biography on p. 224) "Barn Burning" (1939) marks the first appearance of the Snopes clan in Faulkner's fiction. These ruthless, conniving, and unappealing poor white tenant farmers and traders run roughshod over the aristocratic families of Yoknapatawpha County in three Faulkner novels: *The Hamlet* (1940), *The Town* (1957), and *The Mansion* (1959). According to Ben Wasson in *Count No Count*, Faulkner once told a friend that "somebody said I was a genius writer. The only thing I'd claim genius for is thinking up that name *Snopes*." In Southern literary circles, at least, the name "Snopes" still serves as a shorthand term for the graceless and greedy (but frequently successful) opportunists of the "New South."

Cultural Context Tenant farming is a system of agriculture in which workers (tenants) live on a landowner's property while providing labor. One form of tenant farming, which developed in the post–Civil War South, was known as sharecropping. Although white men, such as Ab Snopes, worked as sharecroppers, the majority of these workers were freed slaves. Sharecropping required a landowner to furnish land and housing, while a tenant supplied labor. In theory, sharecropping was supposed to benefit both the owners of the land and the people who farmed it. In practice, however, a sharecropper was lucky to end the year without owing money for seeds, tools, and so on to the landowner. As a result, a sharecropper would often find himself (and his family) tied to the land in a never-ending cycle of debt.

Barn Burning (1939)

The store in which the Justice of the Peace's court was sitting smelled of cheese. The boy, crouched on his nail keg at the back of the crowded room, knew he smelled cheese, and more: from where he sat he could see the ranked shelves close-packed with the solid, squat, dynamic shapes of tin cans whose labels his stomach read, not from the lettering which meant nothing to his mind but from the scarlet devils and the silver curve of fish—this, the cheese which he knew he smelled and the hermetic[1] meat which his intestines believed he smelled coming in intermittent gusts momentary and brief between the other constant one, the smell and sense just a little of fear because mostly of despair and grief, the old fierce pull of blood. He could not see the table where the Justice sat and before which his father and his father's enemy (*our enemy* he thought in that despair; *ourn! mine and hisn both! He's my father!*) stood, but he could hear them, the two of them that is, because his father had said no word yet:

"But what proof have you, Mr. Harris?"

"I told you. The hog got into my corn. I caught it up and sent it back to him. He had no fence that would hold it. I told him so, warned him. The next time I put the hog in my pen. When he came to get it I gave him enough wire to patch up his pen. The next time I put the hog up and kept it. I rode down to his house and saw the wire I gave him still rolled on to the spool in his yard. I told him he could have the hog when he paid me a dollar pound fee. That evening a nigger came with the dollar and got the hog. He was a strange nigger. He said, 'He say to tell you wood and hay kin burn.' I said, 'What?' 'That whut he say to tell you,' the nigger said. 'Wood and hay kin burn.' That night my barn burned. I got the stock out but I lost the barn."

"Where is the nigger? Have you got him?"

---

[1] *hermetic:* Canned.

5   "He was a strange nigger, I tell you. I don't know what became of him."

"But that's not proof. Don't you see that's not proof?"

"Get that boy up here. He knows." For a moment the boy thought too that the man meant his older brother until Harris said, "Not him. The little one. The boy," and, crouching, small for his age, small and wiry like his father, in patched and faded jeans even too small for him, with straight, uncombed, brown hair and eyes gray and wild as storm scud, he saw the men between himself and the table part and become a lane of grim faces, at the end of which he saw the Justice, a shabby, collarless, graying man in spectacles, beckoning him. He felt no floor under his bare feet; he seemed to walk beneath the palpable weight of the grim turning faces. His father, stiff in his black Sunday coat donned not for the trial but for the moving, did not even look at him. *He aims for me to lie,* he thought, again with that frantic grief and despair. *And I will have to do hit.*

"What's your name, boy?" the Justice said.

"Colonel Sartoris Snopes," the boy whispered.

10   "Hey?" the Justice said. "Talk louder. Colonel Sartoris? I reckon anybody named for Colonel Sartoris in this country can't help but tell the truth, can they?" The boy said nothing. *Enemy! Enemy!* he thought; for a moment he could not even see, could not see that the Justice's face was kindly nor discern that his voice was troubled when he spoke to the man named Harris: "Do you want me to question this boy?" But he could hear, and during those subsequent long seconds while there was absolutely no sound in the crowded little room save that of quiet and intent breathing it was as if he had swung outward at the end of a grape vine, over a ravine, and at the top of the swing had been caught in a prolonged instant of mesmerized gravity, weightless in time.

"No!" Harris said violently, explosively. "Damnation! Send him out of here!" Now time, the fluid world, rushed beneath him again, the voices coming to him again through the smell of cheese and sealed meat, the fear and despair and the old grief of blood:

"This case is closed. I can't find against you, Snopes, but I can give you advice. Leave this country and don't come back to it."

His father spoke for the first time, his voice cold and harsh, level, without emphasis: "I aim to. I don't figure to stay in a country among people who . . ." he said something unprintable and vile, addressed to no one.

"That'll do," the Justice said. "Take your wagon and get out of this country before dark. Case dismissed."

15   His father turned, and he followed the stiff black coat, the wiry figure walking a little stiffly from where a Confederate provost's man's[2] musket ball had taken him in the heel on a stolen horse thirty years ago, followed the two backs now, since his older brother had appeared from somewhere in the crowd, no taller than the father but thicker, chewing tobacco steadily, between the two lines of grim-faced men and out of the store and across the worn gallery and down the sagging steps and among the dogs and half-grown boys in the mild May dust, where as he passed a voice hissed:

---

[2]*provost's man's:* Military policeman's.

"Barn burner!"

Again he could not see, whirling; there was a face in a red haze, moonlike, bigger than the full moon, the owner of it half again his size, he leaping in the red haze toward the face, feeling no blow, feeling no shock when his head struck the earth, scrabbling up and leaping again, feeling no blow this time either and tasting no blood, scrabbling up to see the other boy in full flight and himself already leaping into pursuit as his father's hand jerked him back, the harsh, cold voice speaking above him: "Go get in the wagon."

It stood in a grove of locusts and mulberries across the road. His two hulking sisters in their Sunday dresses and his mother and her sister in calico and sunbonnets were already in it, sitting on and among the sorry residue of the dozen and more movings which even the boy could remember—the battered stove, the broken beds and chairs, the clock inlaid with mother-of-pearl, which would not run, stopped at some fourteen minutes past two o'clock of a dead and forgotten day and time, which had been his mother's dowry. She was crying, though when she saw him she drew her sleeve across her face and began to descend from the wagon. "Get back," the father said.

"He's hurt. I got to get some water and wash his . . ."

"Get back in the wagon," his father said. He got in too, over the tail-gate. His father mounted to the seat where the older brother already sat and struck the gaunt mules two savage blows with the peeled willow, but without heat. It was not even sadistic; it was exactly that same quality which in later years would cause his descendants to overrun the engine before putting a motor car into motion, striking and reining back in the same movement. The wagon went on, the store with its quiet crowd of grimly watching men dropped behind; a curve in the road hid it. *Forever* he thought. *Maybe he's done satisfied now, now that he has . . .* stopping himself, not to say it aloud even to himself. His mother's hand touched his shoulder.

"Does hit hurt?" she said.

"Naw," he said. "Hit don't hurt. Lemme be."

"Can't you wipe some of the blood off before hit dries?"

"I'll wash to-night," he said. "Lemme be, I tell you."

The wagon went on. He did not know where they were going. None of them ever did or ever asked, because it was always somewhere, always a house of sorts waiting for them a day or two days or even three days away. Likely his father had already arranged to make a crop on another farm before he . . . Again he had to stop himself. He (the father) always did. There was something about his wolf-like independence and even courage when the advantage was at least neutral which impressed strangers, as if they got from his latent ravening ferocity not so much a sense of dependability as a feeling that his ferocious conviction in the rightness of his own actions would be of advantage to all whose interest lay with his.

That night they camped, in a grove of oaks and beeches where a spring ran. The nights were still cool and they had a fire against it, of a rail lifted from a nearby fence and cut into lengths—a small fire, neat, niggard almost, a shrewd fire; such fires were his father's habit and custom always, even in freezing weather. Older, the boy might have remarked this and wondered why not a big one; why should not a man who had not only seen the waste and extravagance of war, but who had in his blood an inherent voracious prodigality with material not his own, have burned everything in sight? Then he might have gone a step farther and thought that that was the reason: that niggard blaze was the living fruit of nights passed during those four years in the woods hiding from all men, blue or gray, with his strings of horses (captured horses, he called them). And older still, he might have divined the true reason: that the element of fire spoke to some deep mainspring of his father's being, as the element of steel or of powder spoke to other men, as the one weapon for the preservation of integrity, else breath were not worth the breathing, and hence to be regarded with respect and used with discretion.

But he did not think this now and he had seen those same niggard blazes all his life. He merely ate his supper beside it and was already half asleep over his iron plate when his father called him, and once more he followed the stiff back, the stiff and ruthless limp, up the slope and on to the starlit road where, turning, he could see his father against the stars but without face or depth—a shape black, flat, and bloodless as though cut from tin in the iron folds of the frockcoat which had not been made for him, the voice harsh like tin and without heat like tin:

"You were fixing to tell them. You would have told him." He didn't answer. His father struck him with the flat of his hand on the side of the head, hard but without heat, exactly as he had struck the two mules at the store, exactly as he would strike either of them with any stick in order to kill a horse fly, his voice still without fear or anger: "You're getting to be a man. You got to learn. You got to learn to stick to your own blood or you ain't going to have any blood to stick to you. Do you think either of them, any man there this morning, would? Don't you know all they wanted was a chance to get at me because they knew I had them beat? Eh?" Later, twenty years later, he was to tell himself, "If I had said they wanted only truth, justice, he would have hit me again." But now he said nothing. He was not crying. He just stood there. "Answer me," his father said.

"Yes," he whispered. His father turned.

30   "Get on to bed. We'll be there tomorrow."

Tomorrow they were there. In the early afternoon the wagon stopped before a paintless two-room house identical almost with the dozen others it had stopped before even in the boy's ten years, and again, as on the other dozen occasions, his mother and aunt got down and began to unload the wagon, although his two sisters and his father and brother had not moved.

"Likely hit ain't fitten for hawgs," one of the sisters said.

"Nevertheless, fit it will and you'll hog it and like it," his father said. "Get out of them chairs and help your Ma unload."

The two sisters got down, big, bovine, in a flutter of cheap ribbons; one of them drew from the jumbled wagon bed a battered lantern, the other a worn broom. His father handed the reins to the older son and began to climb stiffly over the wheel. "When they get unloaded, take the team to the barn and feed them." Then he said, and at first the boy thought he was still speaking to his brother: "Come with me."

35   "Me?" he said.

"Yes," his father said. "You."

"Abner," his mother said. His father paused and looked back—the harsh level stare beneath the shaggy, graying, irascible brows.

"I reckon I'll have a word with the man that aims to begin tomorrow owning me body and soul for the next eight months."

They went back up the road. A week ago—or before last night, that is—he would have asked where they were going, but not now. His father had struck him before last night but never before had he paused afterward to explain why; it was as if the blow and the following calm, outrageous voice still rang, repercussed, divulging nothing to him save the terrible handicap of being young, the light weight of his few years, just heavy enough to prevent his soaring free of the world as it seemed to be ordered but not heavy enough to keep him footed solid in it, to resist it and try to change the course of its events.

Presently he could see the grove of oaks and cedars and the other flowering trees and shrubs, where the house would be, though not the house yet. They walked beside a fence massed with honeysuckle and Cherokee roses and came to a gate swinging open between two brick pillars, and now, beyond a sweep of drive, he saw the house for the first time and at that instant he forgot his father and the terror and despair both, and even when he remembered his father again (who had not stopped) the terror and despair did not return. Because, for all the twelve movings, they had sojourned until now in a poor country, a land of small farms and fields and houses, and he had never seen a house like this before. *Hit's big as a courthouse* he thought quietly, with a surge of peace and joy whose reason he could not have thought into words, being too young for that: *They are safe from him. People whose lives are a part of this peace and dignity are beyond his touch, he no more to them than a buzzing wasp: capable of stinging for a little moment but that's all; the spell of this peace and dignity rendering even the barns and stable and cribs which belong to it impervious to the puny flames he might contrive . . .* this, the peace and joy, ebbing for an instant as he looked again at the stiff black back, the stiff and implacable limp of the figure which was not dwarfed by the house, for the reason that it had never looked big anywhere and which now, against the serene columned backdrop, had more than ever that impervious quality of something cut ruthlessly from tin, depthless, as though, sidewise to the sun, it would cast no shadow. Watching him, the boy remarked the absolutely undeviating course which his father held and saw the stiff foot come squarely down in a pile of fresh droppings where a horse had stood in the drive and which his father could have avoided by a simple change of stride. But it ebbed only for a moment, though he could not have thought this into words either, walking on in the spell of the house, which he could even want but without envy, without sorrow, certainly never with that ravening and jealous rage which unknown to him walked in the ironlike black coat before him: *Maybe he will feel it too. Maybe it will even change him now from what maybe he couldn't help but be.*

They crossed the portico. Now he could hear his father's stiff foot as it came down on the boards with clocklike finality, a sound out of all proportion to the displacement of the body it bore and which was not dwarfed either by the white door before it, as though it had attained to a sort of vicious and ravening minimum not to be dwarfed by anything—the flat, wide, black hat, the formal coat of broadcloth which had once been black but which had now that friction-glazed greenish cast of the bodies of old house flies, the lifted sleeve which was too large, the lifted hand like a curled claw. The door opened so promptly that the boy knew the Negro must have been watching them all the time, an old man with neat grizzled hair, in a linen jacket, who stood barring the door with his body, saying, "Wipe yo foots, white man, fo you come in here. Major ain't home nohow."

"Get out of my way, nigger," his father said, without heat too, flinging the door back and the Negro also and entering, his hat still on his head. And now the boy saw the prints of the stiff foot on the doorjamb and saw them appear on the pale rug behind the machinelike deliberation of the foot which seemed to bear (or transmit) twice the weight which the body compassed. The Negro was shouting "Miss Lula! Miss Lula!" somewhere behind them, then the boy, deluged as though by a warm wave by a suave turn of carpeted stair and a pendant glitter of chandeliers and a mute gleam of gold frames, heard the swift feet and saw her too, a lady—perhaps he had never seen her like before either—in a gray, smooth gown with lace at the throat and an apron tied at the waist and the sleeves turned back, wiping cake or biscuit dough from her hands with a towel as she came up the hall, looking not at his father at all but at the tracks on the blond rug with an expression of incredulous amazement.

"I tried," the Negro cried, "I tole him to . . ."

"Will you please go away?" she said in a shaking voice. "Major de Spain is not at home. Will you please go away?"

45   His father had not spoken again. He did not speak again. He did not even look at her. He just stood stiff in the center of the rug, in his hat, the shaggy iron-gray brows twitching slightly above the pebble-colored eyes as he appeared to examine the house with brief deliberation. Then with the same deliberation he turned; the boy watched him pivot on the good leg and saw the stiff foot drag round the arc of the turning, leaving a final long and fading smear. His father never looked at it, he never once looked down at the rug. The Negro held the door. It closed behind them, upon the hysteric and indistinguishable woman-wail. His father stopped at the top of the steps and scraped his boot clean on the edge of it. At the gate he stopped again. He stood for a moment, planted stiffly on the stiff foot, looking back at the house. "Pretty and white, ain't it?" he said. "That's sweat. Nigger sweat. Maybe it ain't white enough yet to suit him. Maybe he wants to mix some white sweat with it."

Two hours later the boy was chopping wood behind the house within which his mother and aunt and the two sisters (the mother and aunt, not the two girls, he knew that; even at this distance and muffled by walls the flat loud voices of the two girls emanated an incorrigible idle inertia) were setting up the stove to prepare a meal, when he heard the hooves and saw the linen-clad man on a fine sorrel mare, whom he recognized even before he saw the rolled rug in front of the Negro youth following on a fat bay carriage horse—a suffused, angry face vanishing, still at full gallop, beyond the corner of the house where his father and brother were sitting in the two tilted chairs; and a moment later, almost before he could have put the axe down, he heard the hooves again and watched the sorrel mare go back out of the yard, already galloping again. Then his father began to shout one of the sisters' names, who presently emerged backward from the kitchen door dragging the rolled rug along the ground by one end while the other sister walked behind it.

"If you ain't going to tote, go on and set up the wash pot," the first said.

"You, Sarty!" the second shouted. "Set up the wash pot!" His father appeared at the door, framed against that shabbiness, as he had been against that other bland perfection, impervious to either, the mother's anxious face at his shoulder.

"Go on," the father said. "Pick it up." The two sisters stooped, broad, lethargic; stooping, they presented an incredible expanse of pale cloth and a flutter of tawdry ribbons.

"If I thought enough of a rug to have to git hit all the way from France I wouldn't keep hit where folks coming in would have to tromp on hit," the first said. They raised the rug.

"Abner," the mother said. "Let me do it."

"You go back and git dinner," his father said. "I'll tend to this."

From the woodpile through the rest of the afternoon the boy watched them, the rug spread flat in the dust beside the bubbling wash-pot, the two sisters stooping over it with that profound and lethargic reluctance, while the father stood over them in turn, implacable and grim, driving them though never raising his voice again. He could smell the harsh homemade lye[3] they were using; he saw his mother come to the door once and look toward them with an expression not anxious now but very like despair; he saw his father turn, and he fell to with the axe and saw from the corner of his eye his father raise from the ground a flattish fragment of field stone and examine it and return to the pot, and this time his mother actually spoke: "Abner. Abner. Please don't. Please, Abner."

Then he was done too. It was dusk; the whippoorwills had already begun. He could smell coffee from the room where they would presently eat the cold food remaining from the mid-afternoon meal, though when he entered the house he realized they were having coffee again probably because there was a fire on the hearth, before which the rug now lay spread over the backs of the two chairs. The tracks of his father's foot were gone. Where they had been were now long, water-cloudy scoriations resembling the sporadic course of a Lilliputian mowing machine.

It still hung there while they ate the cold food and then went to bed, scattered without order or claim up and down the two rooms, his mother in one bed, where his father would later lie, the older brother in the other, himself, the aunt, and the two sisters on pallets on the floor. But his father was not in bed yet. The last thing the boy remembered was the depthless, harsh silhouette of the hat and coat bending over the rug and it seemed to him that he had not even closed his eyes when the silhouette was standing over him, the fire almost dead behind it, the stiff foot prodding him awake. "Catch up the mule," his father said.

When he returned with the mule his father was standing in the black door, the rolled rug over his shoulder. "Ain't you going to ride?" he said.

"No. Give me your foot."

He bent his knee into his father's hand, the wiry, surprising power flowed smoothly, rising, he rising with it, on to the mule's bare back (they had owned a saddle once; the boy could remember it though not when or where) and with the same effortlessness his father swung the rug up in front of him. Now in the starlight they retraced the afternoon's path, up the dusty road rife with honeysuckle, through the gate and up the black tunnel to the drive to the lightless house, where he sat on the mule and felt the rough warp of the rug drag across his thighs and vanish.

---

[3]*lye:* A soap made from wood ashes and water, unsuitable for washing fine fabrics.

"Don't you want me to help?" he whispered. His father did not answer and now he heard again that stiff foot striking the hollow portico with that wooden and clock-like deliberation, that outrageous overstatement of the weight it carried. The rug, hunched, not flung (the boy could tell that even in the darkness) from his father's shoulder struck the angle of wall and floor with a sound unbelievably loud, thunderous, then the foot again, unhurried and enormous; a light came on in the house and the boy sat, tense, breathing steadily and quietly and just a little fast, though the foot itself did not increase its beat at all, descending the steps now; now the boy could see him.

60   "Don't you want to ride now?" he whispered. "We kin both ride now," the light within the house altering now, flaring up and sinking. *He's coming down the stairs now,* he thought. He had already ridden the mule up beside the horse block; presently his father was up behind him and he doubled the reins over and slashed the mule across the neck, but before the animal could begin to trot the hard, thin arm came round him, the hard, knotted hand jerking the mule back to a walk.

In the first red rays of the sun they were in the lot, putting plow gear on the mules. This time the sorrel mare was in the lot before he heard it at all, the rider collarless and even bareheaded, trembling, speaking in a shaking voice as the woman in the house had done, his father merely looking up once before stooping again to the hame[4] he was buckling, so that the man on the mare spoke to his stooping back:

"You must realize you have ruined that rug. Wasn't there anybody here, any of your women . . ." he ceased, shaking, the boy watching him, the older brother leaning now in the stable door, chewing, blinking slowly and steadily at nothing apparently. "It cost a hundred dollars. But you never had a hundred dollars. You never will. So I'm going to charge you twenty bushels of corn against your crop. I'll add it in your contract and when you come to the commissary you can sign it. That won't keep Mrs. de Spain quiet but maybe it will teach you to wipe your feet off before you enter her house again."

Then he was gone. The boy looked at his father, who still had not spoken or even looked up again, who was now adjusting the loggerhead in the hame.

"Pap," he said. His father looked at him—the inscrutable face, the shaggy brows beneath which the gray eyes glinted coldly. Suddenly the boy went toward him, fast, stopping as suddenly. "You done the best you could!" he cried. "If he wanted hit done different why didn't he wait and tell you how? He won't git no twenty bushels! He won't git none! We'll gether hit and hide hit! I kin watch . . ."

65   "Did you put the cutter back in that straight stock like I told you?"

"No, sir," he said.

"Then go do it."

That was Wednesday. During the rest of that week he worked steadily, at what was within his scope and some which was beyond it, with an industry that did not need to be driven nor even commanded twice; he had this from his mother, with the difference that some at least of what he did he liked to do, such as splitting wood with the half-size axe which his mother and aunt had earned, or saved money somehow, to

---

[4]*hame:* Harness.

present him with at Christmas. In company with the two older women (and on one afternoon, even one of the sisters), he built pens for the shoat and the cow which were a part of his father's contract with the landlord, and one afternoon, his father being absent, gone somewhere on one of the mules, he went to the field.

They were running a middle buster now, his brother holding the plow straight while he handled the reins, and walking beside the straining mule, the rich black soil shearing cool and damp against his bare ankles, he thought *Maybe this is the end of it. Maybe even that twenty bushels that seems hard to have to pay for just a rug will be a cheap price for him to stop forever and always from being what he used to be;* thinking, dreaming now, so that his brother had to speak sharply to him to mind the mule: *Maybe he even won't collect the twenty bushels. Maybe it will all add up and balance and vanish—corn, rug, fire; the terror and grief, the being pulled two ways like between two teams of horses—gone, done with for ever and ever.*

Then it was Saturday; he looked up from beneath the mule he was harnessing and saw his father in the black coat and hat. "Not that," his father said. "The wagon gear." And then, two hours later, sitting in the wagon bed behind his father and brother on the seat, the wagon accomplished a final curve, and he saw the weathered paint-less store with its tattered tobacco- and patent-medicine posters and the tethered wagons and saddle animals below the gallery. He mounted the gnawed steps behind his father and brother, and there again was the lane of quiet, watching faces for the three of them to walk through. He saw the man in spectacles sitting at the plank table and he did not need to be told this was a Justice of the Peace; he sent one glare of fierce, exultant, partisan defiance at the man in collar and cravat now, whom he had seen but twice before in his life, and that on a galloping horse, who now wore on his face an expression not of rage but of amazed unbelief which the boy could not have known was at the incredible circumstance of being sued by one of his own tenants, and came and stood against his father and cried at the Justice: "He ain't done it! He ain't burnt . . ."

"Go back to the wagon," his father said.

"Burnt?" the Justice said. "Do I understand this rug was burned too?"

"Does anybody here claim it was?" his father said. "Go back to the wagon." But he did not, he merely retreated to the rear of the room, crowded as that other had been, but not to sit down this time, instead, to stand pressing among the motionless bodies, listening to the voices:

"And you claim twenty bushels of corn is too high for the damage you did to the rug?"

"He brought the rug to me and said he wanted the tracks washed out of it. I washed the tracks out and took the rug back to him."

"But you didn't carry the rug back to him in the same condition it was in before you made the tracks on it."

His father did not answer, and now for perhaps half a minute there was no sound at all save that of breathing, the faint, steady suspiration of complete and intent listening.

"You decline to answer that, Mr. Snopes?" Again his father did not answer. "I'm going to find against you, Mr. Snopes. I'm going to find that you were responsible for the injury to Major de Spain's rug and hold you liable for it. But twenty bushels of corn seems a little high for a man in your circumstances to have to pay. Major de Spain claims it cost a hundred dollars. October corn will be worth about fifty cents. I figure that if Major de Spain can stand a ninety-five dollar loss on something he paid cash for, you can stand a five-dollar loss you haven't earned yet. I hold you in damages to Major de Spain to the amount of ten bushels of corn over and above your contract with him, to be paid to him out of your crop at gathering time. Court adjourned."

It had taken no time hardly, the morning was but half begun. He thought they would return home and perhaps back to the field, since they were late, far behind all other farmers. But instead his father passed on behind the wagon, merely indicating with his hand for the older brother to follow with it, and crossed the road toward the blacksmith shop opposite, pressing on after his father, overtaking him, speaking, whispering up at the harsh, calm face beneath the weathered hat: "He won't git no ten bushels neither. He won't git one. We'll . . ." until his father glanced for an instant down at him, the face absolutely calm, the grizzled eyebrows tangled above the cold eyes, the voice almost pleasant, almost gentle:

80

"You think so? Well, we'll wait till October anyway."

The matter of the wagon—the setting of a spoke or two and the tightening of the tires—did not take long either, the business of the tires accomplished by driving the wagon into the spring branch behind the shop and letting it stand there, the mules nuzzling into the water from time to time, and the boy on the seat with the idle reins, looking up the slope and through the sooty tunnel of the shed where the slow hammer rang and where his father sat on an upended cypress bolt, easily, either talking or listening, still sitting there when the boy brought the dripping wagon up out of the branch and halted it before the door.

"Take them on to the shade and hitch," his father said. He did so and returned. His father and the smith and a third man squatting on his heels inside the door were talking, about crops and animals; the boy, squatting too in the ammoniac dust and hoof-parings and scales of rust, heard his father tell a long and unhurried story out of the time before the birth of the older brother even when he had been a professional horsetrader. And then his father came up beside him where he stood before a tattered last year's circus poster on the other side of the store, gazing rapt and quiet at the scarlet horses, the incredible poisings and convolutions of tulle and tights and the painted leers of comedians, and said, "It's time to eat."

But not at home. Squatting beside his brother against the front wall, he watched his father emerge from the store and produce from a paper sack a segment of cheese and divide it carefully and deliberately into three with his pocket knife and produce crackers from the same sack. They all three squatted on the gallery and ate, slowly, without talking; then in the store again, they drank from a tin dipper tepid water smelling of the cedar bucket and of living beech trees. And still they did not go home. It was a horse lot this time, a tall rail fence upon and along which men stood and sat and out of which one by one horses were led, to be walked and trotted and then cantered back and forth along the road while the slow swapping and buying went on and the sun began to slant westward, they—the three of them—watching and listening, the older brother with his muddy eyes and his steady, inevitable tobacco, the father commenting now and then on certain of the animals, to no one in particular.

It was after sundown when they reached home. They ate supper by lamplight, then, sitting on the doorstep, the boy watched the night fully accomplish, listening to the whippoorwills and the frogs, when he heard his mother's voice: "Abner! No! No! Oh, God. Oh, God. Abner!" and he rose, whirled, and saw the altered light through the door where a candle stub now burned in a bottle neck on the table and his father, still in the hat and coat, at once formal and burlesque as though dressed carefully for some shabby and ceremonial violence, emptying the reservoir of the lamp back into the five-gallon kerosene can from which it had been filled, while the mother tugged at his arm until he shifted the lamp to the other hand and flung her back, not savagely or viciously, just hard, into the wall, her hands flung out against the wall for balance, her mouth open and in her face the same quality of hopeless despair as had been in her voice. Then his father saw him standing in the door.

"Go to the barn and get that can of oil we were oiling the wagon with," he said.   85
The boy did not move. Then he could speak.

"What . . ." he cried. "What are you . . ."

"Go get that oil," his father said. "Go."

Then he was moving, running, outside the house, toward the stable: this the old habit, the old blood which he had not been permitted to choose for himself, which had been bequeathed him willy nilly and which had run for so long (and who knew where, battening on what of outrage and savagery and lust) before it came to him. *I could keep on*, he thought. *I could run on and on and never look back, never need to see his face again. Only I can't. I can't*, the rusted can in his hand now, the liquid sploshing in it as he ran back to the house and into it, into the sound of his mother's weeping in the next room, and handed the can to his father.

"Ain't you going to even send a nigger?" he cried. "At least you sent a nigger before!"

This time his father didn't strike him. The hand came even faster than the blow   90
had, the same hand which had set the can on the table with almost excruciating care flashing from the can toward him too quick for him to follow it, gripping him by the back of his shirt and on to tiptoe before he had seen it quit the can, the face stooping at him in breathless and frozen ferocity, the cold, dead voice speaking over him to the older brother who leaned against the table, chewing with that steady, curious, sidewise motion of cows:

"Empty the can into the big one and go on. I'll catch up with you."

"Better tie him to the bedpost," the brother said.

"Do like I told you," the father said. Then the boy was moving, his bunched shirt and the hard, bony hand between his shoulderblades, his toes just touching the floor, across the room and into the other one, past the sisters sitting with spread heavy thighs in the two chairs over the cold hearth, and to where his mother and aunt sat side by side on the bed, the aunt's arms about his mother's shoulders.

"Hold him," the father said. The aunt made a startled movement. "Not you," the father said. "Lennie. Take hold of him. I want to see you do it." His mother took him by the wrist. "You'll hold him better than that. If he gets loose don't you know what he is going to do? He will go up yonder." He jerked his head toward the road. "Maybe I'd better tie him."

"I'll hold him," his mother whispered.   95

"See you do then." Then his father was gone, the stiff foot heavy and measured upon the boards, ceasing at last.

Then he began to struggle. His mother caught him in both arms, he jerking and wrenching at them. He would be stronger in the end, he knew that. But he had no time to wait for it. "Lemme go!" he cried. "I don't want to have to hit you!"

"Let him go!" the aunt said. "If he don't go, before God, I am going up there myself!"

"Don't you see I can't?" his mother cried. "Sarty! Sarty! No! No! Help me, Lizzie!"

100   Then he was free. His aunt grasped at him but it was too late. He whirled, running, his mother stumbled forward on to her knees behind him, crying to the nearest sister: "Catch him, Net! Catch him!" But that was too late too, the sister (the sisters were twins, born at the same time, yet either of them now gave the impression of being, encompassing as much living meat and volume and weight as any other two of the family) not yet having begun to rise from the chair, her head, face, alone merely turned, presenting to him in the flying instant an astonishing expanse of young female features untroubled by any surprise even, wearing only an expression of bovine interest. Then he was out of the room, out of the house, in the mild dust of the starlit road and the heavy rifeness of honeysuckle, the pale ribbon unspooling with terrific slowness under his running feet, reaching the gate at last and turning in, running, his heart and lungs drumming, on up the drive toward the lighted house, the lighted door. He did not knock, he burst in, sobbing for breath, incapable for the moment of speech; he saw the astonished face of the Negro in the linen jacket without knowing when the Negro had appeared.

"De Spain!" he cried, panted. "Where's . . ." then he saw the white man too emerging from a white door down the hall. "Barn!" he cried. "Barn!"

"What?" the white man said. "Barn?"

"Yes!" the boy cried. "Barn!"

"Catch him!" the white man shouted.

105   But it was too late this time too. The Negro grasped his shirt, but the entire sleeve, rotten with washing, carried away, and he was out that door too and in the drive again, and had actually never ceased to run even while he was screaming into the white man's face.

Behind him the white man was shouting, "My horse! Fetch my horse!" and he thought for an instant of cutting across the park and climbing the fence into the road, but he did not know the park nor how high the vine-massed fence might be and he dared not risk it. So he ran on down the drive, blood and breath roaring; presently he was in the road again though he could not see it. He could not hear either: the galloping mare was almost upon him before he heard her, and even then he held his course, as if the very urgency of his wild grief and need must in a moment more find him wings, waiting until the ultimate instant to hurl himself aside and into the weed-choked roadside ditch as the horse thundered past and on, for an instant in furious silhouette against the stars, the tranquil early summer night sky which, even before the shape of the horse and rider vanished, stained abruptly and violently upward: a long, swirling roar incredible and soundless, blotting the stars, and he springing up and into the road again, running again, knowing it was too late yet still running even after he heard the shot and, an instant later, two shots, pausing now without knowing he had ceased to run, crying "Pap! Pap!", running again before he knew he had begun to run, stumbling, tripping over something and scrabbling up again without ceasing to run, looking backward over his shoulder at the glare as he got up, running on among the invisible trees, panting, sobbing, "Father! Father!"

At midnight he was sitting on the crest of a hill. He did not know it was midnight and he did not know how far he had come. But there was no glare behind him now and he sat now, his back toward what he had called home for four days anyhow, his face toward the dark woods which he would enter when breath was strong again, small, shaking steadily in the chill darkness, hugging himself into the remainder of his thin, rotten shirt, the grief and despair now no longer terror and fear but just grief and despair. *Father. My father*, he thought. "He was brave!" he cried suddenly, aloud but not loud, no more than a whisper: "He was! He was in the war! He was in Colonel Sartoris' cav'ry!" not knowing that his father had gone to that war a private in the fine old European sense, wearing no uniform, admitting the authority of and giving fidelity to no man or army or flag, going to war as Malbrouck[5] himself did: for booty— it meant nothing and less than nothing to him if it were enemy booty or his own.

The slow constellations wheeled on. It would be dawn and then sunup after a while and he would be hungry. But that would be tomorrow and now he was only cold, and walking would cure that. His breathing was easier now and he decided to get up and go on, and then he found that he had been asleep because he knew it was almost dawn, the night almost over. He could tell that from the whippoorwills. They were everywhere now among the dark trees below him, constant and inflectioned and ceaseless, so that, as the instant for giving over to the day birds drew nearer and nearer, there was no interval at all between them. He got up. He was a little stiff, but walking would cure that too as it would the cold, and soon there would be the sun. He went on down the hill, toward the dark woods within which the liquid silver voices of the birds called unceasing—the rapid and urgent beating of the urgent and quiring heart of the late spring night. He did not look back.

Reading and Reacting

1. Is the third-person narrator of "Barn Burning" omniscient, or is his omniscience limited? Explain.
2. What is the point of view of the italicized passages? What do readers learn from them? Do they create irony? How would the story have been different without these passages?
3. "Barn Burning" includes a great deal of dialogue. How would you characterize the level of diction of this dialogue? What information about various characters does it provide?
4. What conflicts are presented in "Barn Burning"? Are any of these conflicts avoidable? Which, if any, are resolved in the story? Explain.
5. Why does Ab Snopes burn barns? Do you think his actions are justified? Explain your reasoning.
6. What role does the Civil War play in "Barn Burning"? What does Ab Snopes's behavior during the war tell readers about his character?

---

[5]*Malbrouck:* A character in a popular eighteenth-century nursery rhyme about a famous warrior.

7. In the First and Second books of Samuel in the Old Testament, Abner was a relative of King Saul and commander in chief of his armies. Abner supported King Saul against David and was killed as a result of his own jealousy and rage. What, if any, significance is there in the fact that Faulkner names Ab Snopes—loyal to no man, fighter "for booty, and father of the Snopes clan"—after this mighty biblical leader?

8. Why does Sarty Snopes insist that his father was brave? How does your knowledge of events unknown to the boy create **irony**?

9. JOURNAL ENTRY How would the story be different if it were told from Ab's point of view? From Sarty's? From the point of view of Ab's wife? From the point of view of a member of a community in which the Snopeses have lived?

10. CRITICAL PERSPECTIVE Critic Edmond L. Volpe argues in his article "'Barn Burning': A Definition of Evil" that "Barn Burning" is not really about the class conflict between the sharecropping Snopeses and landowners like the de Spains but rather about Sarty:

> The story is centered upon Sarty's emotional dilemma. His conflict would not have been altered in any way if the person whose barn Ab burns had been a simple poor farmer, rather than an aristocratic plantation owner. . . . Sarty's struggle is against the repressive and divisive force his father represents. The boy's anxiety is created by his awakening sense of his own individuality. Torn between strong emotional attachment to the parent and his growing need to assert his own identity, Sarty's crisis is psychological and his battle is being waged far below the level of his intellectual and moral awareness.

Do you believe "Barn Burning" is, as Volpe suggests, essentially a coming-of-age story, or do you believe it is about something else—class conflict, for example?

Related Works: "A Worn Path" (p. 463), "Baca Grande" (p. 723), "My Father as a Guitar" (p. 770), "Daddy" (p. 772), "Digging" (p. 886), *Fences* (p. 1548)

EDWIDGE DANTICAT (1969–   ) was born in Port-au-Prince, Haiti, and immigrated as a child with her parents to New York. Her work focuses largely on Haitian culture and the immigrant experience. In an interview, Danticat explained her motivation for writing the story collection *Krik? Krak!* (1995), a finalist for the National Book Award: "I wanted to raise the voice of a lot of the people that I knew growing up, and this was, for the most part . . . poor people who had extraordinary dreams but also very amazing obstacles." Winner of the 1995 Pushcart Short Story Prize and other fiction awards, Danticat has written the novels *The Dew Breaker* (2004) and *Claire of the Sea Light* (2013); the memoir *Brother, I'm Dying* (2007); the nonfiction collection *Create Dangerously: The Immigrant Artist at Work* (2010); and three young adult novels.

Cultural Context Haiti is a country that has been marked by authoritarian dictators, political unrest, crushing poverty, turbulent weather conditions, and a devastating earthquake in 2010 that killed over 230,000 people and injured another 300,000. These situations have led many Haitian immigrants to seek refuge in the United States. According to the 2009 American Community Survey, about 535,000 Haitians live in the United States, primarily in Florida and New York. In recent years, Haitian asylum seekers have encountered increased difficulty upon entering the United States, due in large part to the government's efforts to monitor immigration more closely after the 9/11 terrorist attacks.

New York Day Women (1991)

Today, walking down the street, I see my mother. She is strolling with a happy gait, her body thrust toward the DON'T WALK sign and the yellow taxicabs that make forty-five-degree turns on the corner of Madison and Fifty-seventh Street.

I have never seen her in this kind of neighborhood, peering into Chanel and Tiffany's and gawking at the jewels glowing in the Bulgari windows. My mother never shops outside of Brooklyn. She has never seen the advertising office where I work. She is afraid to take the subway, where you may meet those young black militant street preachers who curse black women for straightening their hair.

Yet, here she is, my mother, who I left at home that morning in her bathrobe, with pieces of newspapers twisted like rollers in her hair. My mother, who accuses me of random offenses as I dash out of the house.

*   *   *

Would you get up and give an old lady like me your subway seat? In this state of mind, I bet you don't even give up your seat to a pregnant lady.

*   *   *

My mother, who is often right about that. Sometimes I get up and give my seat. Other times, I don't. It all depends on how pregnant the woman is and whether or not she is with her boyfriend or husband and whether or not *he* is sitting down.   5

As my mother stands in front of Carnegie Hall, one taxi driver yells to another, "What do you think this is, a dance floor?"

My mother waits patiently for this dispute to be settled before crossing the street.

*   *   *

In Haiti when you get hit by a car, the owner of the car gets out and kicks you for getting blood on his bumper.

*   *   *

My mother who laughs when she says this and shows a large gap in her mouth where she lost three more molars to the dentist last week. My mother, who at fifty-nine, says dentures are okay.

*   *   *

You can take them out when they bother you. I'll like them. I'll like them fine.   10

*   *   *

Will it feel empty when Papa kisses you?

*   *   *

Oh no, he doesn't kiss me that way anymore.

*   *   *

My mother, who watches the lottery drawing every night on channel 11 without ever having played the numbers.

*   *   *

A third of that money is all I would need. We would pay the mortgage, and your father could stop driving that taxicab all over Brooklyn.

*   *   *

15   I follow my mother, mesmerized by the many possibilities of her journey. Even in a flowered dress, she is lost in a sea of pinstripes and gray suits, high heels and elegant short skirts, Reebok sneakers, dashing from building to building.

My mother, who won't go out to dinner with anyone.

*   *   *

If they want to eat with me, let them come to my house, even if I boil water and give it to them.

*   *   *

My mother, who talks to herself when she peels the skin off poultry.

*   *   *

Fat, you know, and cholesterol. Fat and cholesterol killed your aunt Hermine.

*   *   *

20   My mother, who makes jam with dried grapefruit peel and then puts in cinnamon bark that I always think is cockroaches in the jam. My mother, whom I have always bought household appliances for, on her birthday. A nice rice cooker, a blender.

I trail the red orchids in her dress and the heavy faux leather bag on her shoulders. Realizing the ferocious pace of my pursuit, I stop against a wall to rest. My mother keeps on walking as though she owns the sidewalk under her feet.

As she heads toward the Plaza Hotel, a bicycle messenger swings so close to her that I want to dash forward and rescue her, but she stands dead in her tracks and lets him ride around her and then goes on.

My mother stops at a corner hot-dog stand and asks for something. The vendor hands her a can of soda that she slips into her bag. She stops by another vendor selling sundresses for seven dollars each. I can tell that she is looking at an African print dress, contemplating my size. I think to myself, Please Ma, don't buy it. It would be just another thing that I would bury in the garage or give to Goodwill.

*   *   *

Why should we give to Goodwill when there are so many people back home who need clothes? We save our clothes for the relatives in Haiti.

*   *   *

Twenty years we have been saving all kinds of things for the relatives in Haiti.   25
I need the place in the garage for an exercise bike.

*   *   *

You are pretty enough to be a stewardess. Only dogs like bones.

*   *   *

This mother of mine, she stops at another hot-dog vendor's and buys a frankfurter that she eats on the street. I never knew that she ate frankfurters. With her blood pressure, she shouldn't eat anything with sodium. She has to be careful with her heart, this day woman.

*   *   *

I cannot just swallow salt. Salt is heavier than a hundred bags of shame.

*   *   *

She is slowing her pace, and now I am too close. If she turns around, she might see me. I let her walk into the park before I start to follow again.

My mother walks toward the sandbox in the middle of the park. There a woman   30
is waiting with a child. The woman is wearing a leotard with biker's shorts and has small weights in her hands. The woman kisses the child good-bye and surrenders him to my mother; then she bolts off, running on the cemented stretches in the park.

The child given to my mother has frizzy blond hair. His hand slips into hers easily, like he's known her for a long time. When he raises his face to look at my mother, it is as though he is looking at the sky.

My mother gives this child the soda that she bought from the vendor on the street corner. The child's face lights up as she puts a straw in the can for him. This seems to be a conspiracy just between the two of them.

My mother and the child sit and watch the other children play in the sandbox. The child pulls out a comic book from a knapsack with Big Bird on the back. My mother peers into his comic book. My mother, who taught herself to read as a little girl in Haiti from the books that her brothers brought home from school.

My mother, who has now lost six of her seven sisters in Ville Rose[1] and has never had the strength to return for their funerals.

*   *   *

35   **Many graves to kiss when I go back. Many graves to kiss.**

*   *   *

She throws away the empty soda can when the child is done with it. I wait and watch from a corner until the woman in the leotard and biker's shorts returns, sweaty and breathless, an hour later. My mother gives the woman back her child and strolls farther into the park.

I turn around and start to walk out of the park before my mother can see me. My lunch hour is long since gone. I have to hurry back to work. I walk through a cluster of joggers, then race to a *Sweden Tours* bus. I stand behind the bus and take a peek at my mother in the park. She is standing in a circle, chatting with a group of women who are taking other people's children on an afternoon outing. They look like a Third World Parent-Teacher Association meeting.

I quickly jump into a cab heading back to the office. Would Ma have said hello had she been the one to see me first?

As the cab races away from the park, it occurs to me that perhaps one day I would chase an old woman down a street by mistake and that old woman would be somebody else's mother, who I would have mistaken for mine.

*   *   *

40   **Day women come out when nobody expects them.**

*   *   *

Tonight on the subway, I will get up and give my seat to a pregnant woman or a lady about Ma's age.

My mother, who stuffs thimbles in her mouth and then blows up her cheeks like Dizzy Gillespie[2] while sewing yet another Raggedy Ann doll that she names Suzette after me.

*   *   *

I will have all these little Suzettes in case you never have any babies, which looks more and more like it is going to happen.

*   *   *

---

[1]*Ville Rose:* Fictional Haitian town.

[2]*Dizzy Gillespie:* American jazz trumpeter (1917–1993).

My mother who had me when she was thirty-three—*l'âge du Christ*—at the age that Christ died on the cross.

* * *

That's a blessing, believe you me, even if American doctors say by that time   45
you can make retarded babies.

* * *

My mother, who sews lace collars on my company softball T-shirts when she does my laundry.

* * *

Why can't you look like a lady playing softball?

* * *

My mother, who never went to any of my Parent-Teacher Association meetings when I was in school.

* * *

You're so good anyway. What are they going to tell me? I don't want to make
you ashamed of this day woman. Shame is heavier than a hundred bags of salt.

Reading and Reacting

1. Who is the narrator of the story? How does the narrative point of view shape the story?
2. How is the narrator different from her mother? What details in the story lead you to your conclusion?
3. The story consists of alternating passages—one in standard type and then one in bold-face type. How does the point of view of the story shift between these two kinds of passages?
4. The story begins when the narrator says, "Today, walking down the street, I see my mother." What motivates the narrator to follow her mother?
5. The narrator tells her story in the present tense. What would she have gained or lost by telling it in the past tense?
6. Why does the narrator hide from her mother? Why doesn't she greet her?
7. How would you characterize the relationship between the narrator and her mother?
8. In paragraph 28, the narrator's mother says, "Salt is heavier than a hundred bags of shame." However, the story ends with her saying, "Shame is heavier than a hundred bags of salt" (par. 49). What does she mean? What is the significance of this shift?
9. **JOURNAL ENTRY** Write a paragraph in which you define "day woman." Include some examples from the story to help you develop your definition.

10. CRITICAL PERSPECTIVE In a 2000 interview with the literary journal *Brick*, Edwidge Danticat explains how, as a Haitian immigrant living in the United States, she has a dualistic relationship with Haiti:

> I have come to terms with the fact that my relationship with Haiti is different than someone who lives there . . . I love being there, there's a kind of peace about it that I can't explain. But I realize that I'm not living, I'm staying for a certain period of time, at the end of which I travel back. And so, it's a relationship of insider/outsider.

How does "New York Day Women" convey the narrator's "insider/outsider" relationship with her mother and with Haiti?

Related Works: "Girl" (p. 137), "I Stand Here Ironing" (p. 299), "Two Kinds" (p. 639), "My Voice" (p. 685), "'Mexican' Is Not a Noun" (p. 720), "Those Winter Sundays" (p. 885), *The Cuban Swimmer* (p. 1416)

WRITING SUGGESTIONS: Point of View

1. How would Poe's "The Cask of Amontillado" be different if it were told by a minor character who observed the events? Rewrite the story from this point of view—or tell the story that precedes the story, explaining the "thousand injuries" and the "insult."
2. Assume that you are Jim, the sailor in "Big Black Good Man," and that you are keeping a journal of your travels. Write the journal entries for the time you spent in Copenhagen. Include your impressions of Olaf, Lena, the hotel, and anything else that caught your attention. Make sure you present your version of the key events described in the story—especially Olaf's reaction to you.
3. Both "The Cask of Amontillado" and "Barn Burning" deal with crimes that essentially go unpunished and with the emotions that accompany these crimes. In what sense does each story's use of point of view shape its treatment of the crime in question? For instance, how does point of view determine how much readers know about the motives for the crime, the crime's basic circumstances, and the extent to which the crime is justified?
4. Write a story in which you retell "New York Day Women" from the mother's point of view. Be true to the original story. Be sure to reveal what she is thinking at various points in the story.

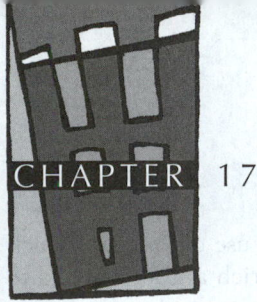

CHAPTER 17

STYLE, TONE, AND LANGUAGE

Charlotte Perkins Gilman
The Granger Collection, NYC

(Mary) Flannery O'Connor
AP Images

James Joyce
AP Images

Tim O'Brien
AP Images/David Pickoff

Style and Tone

One of the qualities that gives a work of literature its individuality is its **style**, the way in which a writer uses language, selecting and arranging words to say what he or she wants to say. Style encompasses elements such as word choice; syntax; sentence length and structure; and the presence, frequency, and prominence of imagery and figures of speech.

Closely related to style is **tone**, the attitude of the narrator or author of a work toward the subject matter, characters, or audience. Word choice and sentence structure help to create a work's tone, which may be intimate or distant, bitter or affectionate, straightforward or cautious, supportive or critical, respectful or condescending. (Tone may also be **ironic**; see Chapter 16, "Point of View," for a discussion of irony.)

The Uses of Language

Language offers almost limitless possibilities to a writer. Creative use of language (such as unusual word choice, word order, or sentence structure) can enrich a story and add to its overall effect. Sometimes, in fact, a writer's use of language can expand a story's possibilities through its very inventiveness. For example, James Joyce's innovative **stream-of-consciousness** style mimics thought, allowing ideas to run into one another as random associations are made so that readers may follow and participate in the thought processes of the narrator. Here is a stream-of-consciousness passage from Joyce's experimental 1922 novel *Ulysses*:

> frseeeeeeeefronnnng train somewhere whistling the strength those engines have in them like big giants and the water rolling all over and out of them all sides like the end of Loves old sweet sonnnng the poor men that have to be out all the night from their wives and families in those roasting engines stifling it was today. . . .

Skillfully used, language can enhance a story's other elements. It may, for example, help to create an atmosphere that is important to the story's plot or theme, as Kate Chopin's lush, rhythmic sentences help to create the sexually charged atmosphere of "The Storm" (p. 273)—an atmosphere that overpowers the characters and thus drives the plot. Language may also help to delineate character, perhaps by conveying a character's mental state to readers. For instance, the breathless, disjointed style of Edgar Allan Poe's "The Tell-Tale Heart" (p. 622) suggests the narrator's increasing emotional instability: "Was it possible they heard not? Almighty God!—no, no! They heard!—they suspected!—they *knew!*—they were making a mockery of my horror!"

In his 1925 short story "Big Two-Hearted River," Ernest Hemingway uses short, unconnected sentences to create a flat, emotionless prose style that reveals his character's alienation and fragility as he struggles to maintain control: "Now things were done. There had been this to do. Now it was done. It had been a hard trip. He was very tired. That was done. He had made his camp. He was settled. Nothing could touch him."

Language that places emphasis on the sounds and rhythm of words and sentences can also enrich a work of fiction. Consider the use of such language in the following sentence from James Joyce's "Araby" (p. 361):

> The light from the lamp opposite our door caught the white curve of her neck, lit up her hair that rested there and, falling, lit up the hand upon the railing.

Here the narrator is describing his first conversation with a girl who fascinates him, and the lyrical, almost musical language reflects his enchantment. Note in particular the **alliteration** (light/lamp; caught/curve; hair/hand), the repetition (lit up/lit up), and the rhyme (lit up her *hair*/that rested *there*) and **near rhyme** (falling/railing); these poetic devices weave the words of the sentence into a smooth, rhythmic whole.

Another example of this emphasis on sound may be found in the measured **parallelism** of this sentence from Nathaniel Hawthorne's 1843 story "The Birthmark":

> He had left his laboratory to the care of an assistant, cleared his fine countenance from the furnace smoke, washed the stain of acids from his fingers, and persuaded a beautiful woman to become his wife.

The style of this sentence, conveying methodical precision and order, reflects the compulsive personality of the character being described.

The following passage from Alberto Alvaro Ríos's story "The Secret Lion" (p. 180) illustrates the power of language to enrich a story:

> We had read the books, after all; we knew about bridges and castles and wildtreacherousraging alligatormouth rivers. We wanted them. So we were going to go out and get them. We went back that morning into that kitchen and we said, "We're going out there, we're going into the hills, we're going away for three days, don't worry." She said, "All right."
>
> "You know," I said to Sergio, "if we're going to go away for three days, well, we ought to at least pack a lunch."
>
> But we were two young boys with no patience for what we thought at the time was mom-stuff: making sa-and-wiches. My mother didn't offer. So we got out little kid knapsacks that my mother had sewn for us, and into them we put the jar of mustard. A loaf of bread. Knivesforksplates, bottles of Coke, a can opener. This was lunch for the two of us. And we were weighed down, humped over to be strong enough to carry this stuff. But we started walking anyway, into the hills. We were going to eat berries and stuff otherwise. "Goodbye." My mom said that.

Through language, the adult narrator of the preceding paragraphs recaptures the bravado of the boys in search of "wildtreacherousraging alligatormouth rivers" even as he suggests to readers that the boys are not going far. The story's use of language is original and inventive: words are blended together ("getridofit," "knivesforksplates"), linked to form new words ("mom-stuff"), and drawn out to mimic speech ("sa-and-wiches"). These experiments with language show the narrator's willingness to move back into a child's frame of reference while maintaining the advantage of distance. The adult narrator uses sentence fragments ("A loaf of bread."), colloquialisms ("kid," "mom," "stuff"), and contractions. He also includes conversational elements such as *you know* and *well* in the story's dialogue, accurately recreating the childhood scene even as he sees its folly and remains aware of the disillusionment that awaits him. Thus, the unique style permits the narrator to bring readers with him into the child's world while he maintains his adult stance: "But we were two young boys with no patience for what we thought at the time was mom-stuff. . . ."

Although many stylistic options are available to writers, a story's language must be consistent with the writer's purpose and with the effect he or she hopes to create. Just as writers may experiment with point of view or manipulate events to create a complex plot, so they can adjust language to suit a particular narrator or character or to convey a particular theme. In addition to the creative uses of language described above, writers also frequently experiment with *formal and informal diction*, *imagery*, and *figures of speech*.

Formal and Informal Diction

The level of diction—how formal or informal a story's language is—can reveal a good deal about a story's narrator and characters.

Formal diction is characterized by elaborate, complex sentences; a learned vocabulary; and a serious, objective, detached tone. It does not generally include contractions, shortened word forms (like *phone*), regional expressions, or slang, and it may substitute *one* or *we* for *I*. At its most extreme, formal language is stiff and stilted, far removed from everyday speech.

When formal diction is used by a narrator or by a character, it may indicate erudition, a high educational level, a superior social or professional position, or emotional detachment.

When one character's language is significantly more formal than others', he or she may seem old-fashioned or stuffy; when language is inappropriately elevated or complex, it may reveal the character to be pompous or ridiculous; when a narrator's language is noticeably more formal than that of the story's characters, the narrator may seem superior or even condescending. Thus, the choice of a particular level (or levels) of diction in a story can convey information about characters and about the narrator's attitude toward them.

The following passage from Hawthorne's "The Birthmark" illustrates formal style:

> In the latter part of the last century there lived a man of science, an eminent proficient in every branch of natural philosophy, who not long before our story opens had made experience of a spiritual affinity more attractive than any chemical one. He had left his laboratory to the care of an assistant, cleared his fine countenance from the furnace smoke, washed the stain of acids from his fingers, and persuaded a beautiful woman to become his wife. In those days when the comparatively recent discovery of electricity and other kindred mysteries of Nature seemed to open paths into the region of miracle, it was not unusual for the love of science to rival the love of woman in its depth and absorbing energy. The higher intellect, the imagination, the spirit, and even the heart might all find their congenial ailment in pursuits which, as some of their ardent votaries believed, would ascend from one step of powerful intelligence to another, until the philosopher should lay his hand on the secret of creative force and perhaps make new worlds for himself.

The long and complex sentences, learned vocabulary ("countenance," "ailment," "votaries"), and absence of colloquialisms suit Hawthorne's purpose well, recreating the formal language of the earlier era in which his story is set. The narrator is aloof and controlled, and his diction makes this clear to readers.

Informal diction, consistent with everyday speech, is characterized by slang, contractions, colloquial expressions like *you know* and *I mean*, shortened word forms, incomplete sentences, and a casual, conversational tone. A first-person narrator may use an informal style, or characters may speak informally; in either case, informal style tends to narrow the distance between readers and text.

One kind of informal language is illustrated in Joyce Carol Oates's "Where Are You Going, Where Have You Been?" (p. 506) by the casual, slangy style of the dialogue between the teenager Connie and her older stalker, Arnold Friend:

> "I ain't late, am I?" he said.
> "Who the hell do you think you are?" Connie said.
> "Toldja I'd be out, didn't I?"
> "I don't even know who you are."

Here, the level of the characters' diction is a key element of the story: because Arnold seems to speak Connie's language, she lets down her guard and becomes vulnerable to his advances.

Another kind of informal language is seen in the regionalisms and dialect used in Flannery O'Connor's "A Good Man Is Hard to Find" (p. 367), where speech patterns and individual words ("aloose"; "you all"; "britches") help to identify the region in which the characters live and their social class.

Informal diction may also include language readers find offensive. In such cases, a character's use of obscenities may suggest anything from crudeness to adolescent bravado, and the use of racial or ethnic slurs indicates that a character is insensitive or bigoted.

The following passage from John Updike's "A&P" (p. 238) illustrates informal style:

> She had sort of oaky hair that the sun and salt had bleached, done up in a bun that was unravelling, and a kind of prim face. Walking into the A&P with your straps down, I suppose it's the only kind of face you *can* have. She held her head so high her neck, coming out of those white shoulders, looked kind of stretched, but I didn't mind. The longer her neck was, the more of her there was.

Here, the first-person narrator, a nineteen-year-old supermarket checkout clerk, uses a conversational style, including colloquialisms ("sort of," "I suppose," "kind of"), contractions ("it's," "didn't"), and the imprecise, informal *you* ("Walking into the A&P with *your* straps down . . ."). The narrator uses neither elaborate syntax nor a learned vocabulary.

 ## Imagery

Imagery—words and phrases that describe what is seen, heard, smelled, tasted, or touched—can have a significant impact in a story. A writer may use a pattern of repeated imagery to convey a particular impression about a character or situation or to communicate or reinforce a story's theme. For example, a character's newly discovered sense of freedom or sexuality can be conveyed through repeated use of words and phrases suggesting blooming or ripening, as in the two stories in this text by Kate Chopin.

In T. Coraghessan Boyle's "Greasy Lake" (p. 569), the narrator's vivid description of Greasy Lake uses rich visual imagery to evoke a scene:

> Through the center of town, up the strip, past the housing developments and shopping malls, street lights giving way to the thin streaming illumination of the headlights, trees crowding the asphalt in a black unbroken wall: that was the way out to Greasy Lake. The Indians had called it Wakan, a reference to the clarity of its waters. Now it was fetid and murky, the mud banks glittering with broken glass and strewn with beer cans and the charred remains of bonfires. There was a single ravaged island a hundred yards from shore, so stripped of vegetation it looked as if the air force had strafed it. We went up to the lake because everyone went there, because we wanted to snuff the rich scent of possibility on the breeze, watch a girl take off her clothes and plunge into the festering murk, drink beer, smoke pot, howl at the stars, savor the incongruous full-throated roar of rock and roll against the primeval susurrus of frogs and crickets. This was nature.

By characterizing a bucolic natural setting with surprising words like "fetid," "murky," and "greasy" and unpleasant images such as the "glittering of broken glass," the "ravaged island," and the "charred remains of bonfires," Boyle creates a picture that is completely at odds with the traditional view of nature. The incongruous images are nevertheless perfectly consistent with the sordid events that take place at Greasy Lake.

 ## Figures of Speech

Figures of speech—such as *similes*, *metaphors*, and *personification*—can enrich a story, subtly revealing information about characters and themes.

By using **metaphors** and **similes**—figures of speech that compare two dissimilar items—writers can indicate a particular attitude toward characters and events. Thus, Flannery O'Connor's many grotesque similes in "A Good Man Is Hard to Find" help to dehumanize her characters; the children's mother, for instance, has a face "as broad and innocent as a cabbage." In Tillie Olsen's "I Stand Here Ironing" (p. 299), an extended metaphor in which a mother compares her daughter to a dress waiting to be ironed expresses the mother's attitude toward her child, effectively suggesting the daughter's vulnerability. Similes and metaphors are used throughout in Kate Chopin's "The Storm" (p. 273). In a scene of sexual awakening, Calixta's skin is "like a creamy lily," her passion is "like a white flame," and her mouth is "a fountain of delight"; these figures of speech add a lushness and sensuality to the story.

Personification—a figure of speech, closely related to metaphor, that endows inanimate objects or abstract ideas with life or with human characteristics—is used in "Araby" (p. 361), where houses, "conscious of decent lives within them, gazed at one another with brown imperturbable faces." This use of figurative language expands readers' vision of the story's setting and gives a dreamlike quality to the passage. (Other figures of speech, such as **hyperbole** and **understatement**, can also enrich works of fiction. See Chapter 27, "Figures of Speech," for further information.)

Allusions—references to familiar historical, cultural, literary, or biblical texts, figures, or events—may also expand readers' understanding and appreciation of a work. An allusion widens a work's context by bringing it into the context of a related subject or idea. For instance, in Charles Baxter's short story "Gryphon" (p. 250), the narrator's allusions to *Pinocchio* and Betty Crocker enable readers who recognize the references to gain a deeper understanding of what certain characters are really like. (For information on the use of allusion in poetry, see Chapter 30.)

NOTE In analyzing the use of language in a work of fiction, you may occasionally encounter unfamiliar allusions (or foreign words and phrases or regional expressions), particularly in works treating cultures and historical periods other than your own. Frequently, such language will be clarified by the context or by explanatory notes in your text. If it is not, always look up the meaning.

✔ **CHECKLIST   Writing about Style, Tone, and Language**

◻ Does the writer make any unusual creative use of word choice, word order, or sentence structure?

◻ Is the story's tone intimate? distant? ironic? How does the tone advance the writer's purpose?

◻ Does the style emphasize the sound and rhythm of language? For example, does the writer use alliteration and assonance? repetition and parallelism? What do such techniques add to the story?

◻ Is the level of diction generally formal, informal, or somewhere in between?

◻ Is there a difference between the diction used by the narrator and the diction used in the characters' speech? If so, what is the effect of this difference?

- Do any of the story's characters use regionalisms, colloquial language, or nonstandard speech? If so, what effect does this language have?

- What do different characters' levels of diction reveal about them?

- What kind of imagery predominates? Where, and why, is imagery used?

- Does the story develop a pattern of imagery? How does this pattern of imagery help to convey the story's themes?

- Does the story use simile and metaphor? personification? What is the effect of these figures of speech?

- Do figures of speech reinforce the story's themes? reveal information about characters?

- Does the story make any historical, literary, or biblical allusions? What do these allusions contribute to the story?

- Are any unfamiliar, obscure, or foreign words, phrases, or images used in the story? What do these words or expressions contribute to the story?

AP Images

JAMES JOYCE (1882–1941) was born in Dublin but lived his entire adult life in self-imposed exile from his native Ireland. Though his parents sent him to schools that trained young men for the priesthood, Joyce saw himself as a religious and artistic rebel and fled to Paris soon after graduation in 1902. Recalled briefly to Dublin by his mother's fatal illness, Joyce returned to the Continent in 1904, taking with him an uneducated Irish country girl named Nora Barnacle, who became his wife in 1931. In dreary quarters in Trieste, Zurich, and Paris, Joyce struggled to support a growing family, sometimes teaching classes in Berlitz language schools.

Though Joyce never again lived in Ireland, he continued to write about Dublin. Publication of *Dubliners* (1914), a collection of short stories that included "Araby," was delayed for seven years because the Irish publisher feared libel suits from local citizens who were thinly disguised as characters in the stories. Joyce's autobiographical *Portrait of the Artist as a Young Man* (1916) tells of a young writer's rejection of family, church, and country. *Ulysses* (1922), the comic tale of eighteen hours in the life of a wandering Dublin advertising salesman, was banned when the United States Post Office brought charges of obscenity against the book, and it remained banned in the United States and England for more than a decade. With *Ulysses*, Joyce began a revolutionary journey away from traditional techniques of plot and characterization to the interior monologues and stream-of-consciousness style that mark his last great novel, *Finnegans Wake* (1939).

Cultural Context In the early twentieth century, as world travel and the shipment of goods around the globe expanded at a dizzying pace, the West experienced a fascination with the "Orient." To peddle their wares, immigrants from the East established bazaars reminiscent of the ones in their homelands, displaying a dazzling array of spices, foods, and material goods. This exotic appeal to the senses, representing the allure of the distant and unknown, became a highlight of many towns and cities. In this story, the bazaar represents the allure of the strange and exotic for the young narrator.

Araby (1914)

North Richmond Street, being blind,[1] was a quiet street except at the hour when the Christian Brothers' School set the boys free. An uninhabited house of two storeys stood at the blind end, detached from its neighbours in a square ground. The other houses of the street, conscious of decent lives within them, gazed at one another with brown imperturbable faces.

The former tenant of our house, a priest, had died in the back drawing-room. Air, musty from having been long enclosed, hung in all the rooms, and the waste room behind the kitchen was littered with old useless papers. Among these I found a few paper-covered books, the pages of which were curled and damp: *The Abbot*, by Walter Scott, *The Devout Communicant* and *The Memoirs of Vidocq*.[2] I liked the last best because its leaves were yellow. The wild garden behind the house contained a central apple-tree and a few straggling bushes under one of which I found the late tenant's rusty bicycle-pump. He had been a very charitable priest; in his will he had left all his money to institutions and the furniture of his house to his sister.

When the short days of winter came dusk fell before we had well eaten our dinners. When we met in the street the houses had grown sombre. The space of sky above us was the colour of ever-changing violet and towards it the lamps of the street lifted their feeble lanterns. The cold air stung us and we played till our bodies glowed. Our shouts echoed in the silent street. The career of our play brought us through the dark muddy lanes behind the houses where we ran the gauntlet of the rough tribes from the cottages, to the back doors of the dark dripping gardens where odours arose from the ashpits, to the dark odorous stables where a coach-man smoothed and combed the horse or shook music from the buckled harness. When we returned to the street light from the kitchen windows had filled the areas. If my uncle was seen turning the corner we hid in the shadow until we had seen him safely housed. Or if Mangan's sister came out on the doorstep to call her brother in to his tea we watched her from our shadow peer up and down the street. We waited to see whether she would remain or go in and, if she remained, we left our shadow and walked up to Mangan's steps resignedly. She was waiting for us, her figure defined by the light from the half-opened door. Her brother always teased her before he obeyed and I stood by the railings looking at her. Her dress swung as she moved her body and the soft rope of her hair tossed from side to side.

Every morning I lay on the floor in the front parlour watching her door. The blind was pulled down to within an inch of the sash so that I could not be seen. When she came out on the doorstep my heart leaped. I ran to the hall, seized my books and followed her. I kept her brown figure always in my eye and, when we came near the point at which our ways diverged, I quickened my pace and passed her. This happened morning after morning. I had never spoken to her, except for a few casual words, and yet her name was like a summons to all my foolish blood.

---

[1] *blind*: Dead-end.

[2] *The Abbot . . . Vidocq*: Sir Walter Scott (1771–1832)—an English Romantic novelist; *The Devout Communicant*—a variant title for *Pious Meditations*, written by an eighteenth-century English Franciscan friar, Pacifus Baker; *The Memoirs of Vidocq*—an autobiography of François-Jules Vidocq (1775–1857), a French criminal turned police agent.

Her image accompanied me even in places the most hostile to romance. On Saturday evenings when my aunt went marketing I had to go to carry some of the parcels. We walked through the flaring streets, jostled by drunken men and bargaining women, amid the curses of labourers, the shrill litanies of shop-boys who stood on guard by the barrels of pigs' cheeks, the nasal chanting of street-singers, who sang a *come-all-you* about O'Donovan Rossa,[3] or a ballad about the troubles in our native land. These noises converged in a single sensation of life for me: I imagined that I bore my chalice safely through a throng of foes. Her name sprang to my lips at moments in strange prayers and praises which I myself did not understand. My eyes were often full of tears (I could not tell why) and at times a flood from my heart seemed to pour itself out into my bosom. I thought little of the future. I did not know whether I would ever speak to her or not or, if I spoke to her, how I could tell her of my confused adoration. But my body was like a harp and her words and gestures were like fingers running upon the wires.

One evening I went into the back drawing-room in which the priest had died. It was a dark rainy evening and there was no sound in the house. Through one of the broken panes I heard the rain impinge upon the earth, the fine incessant needles of water playing in the sodden beds. Some distant lamp or lighted window gleamed below me. I was thankful that I could see so little. All my senses seemed to desire to veil themselves and, feeling that I was about to slip from them, I pressed the palms of my hands together until they trembled, murmuring: "O love! O love!" many times.

At last she spoke to me. When she addressed the first words to me I was so confused that I did not know what to answer. She asked me was I going to *Araby*. I forgot whether I answered yes or no. It would be a splendid bazaar, she said she would love to go.

"And why can't you?" I asked.

While she spoke she turned a silver bracelet round and round her wrist. She could not go, she said, because there would be a retreat that week in her convent.[4] Her brother and two other boys were fighting for their caps and I was alone at the railings. She held one of the spikes, bowing her head towards me. The light from the lamp opposite our door caught the white curve of her neck, lit up her hair that rested there and, falling, lit up the hand upon the railing. It fell over one side of her dress and caught the white border of a petticoat, just visible as she stood at ease.

"It's well for you," she said.

"If I go," I said, "I will bring you something."

What innumerable follies laid waste my waking and sleeping thoughts after that evening! I wished to annihilate the tedious intervening days. I chafed against the work of school. At night in my bedroom and by day in the classroom her image came between me and the page I strove to read. The syllables of the word *Araby* were called to me through the silence in which my soul luxuriated and cast an Eastern enchantment over me. I asked for leave to go to the bazaar on Saturday night.

[3]*O'Donovan Rossa:* Any popular song beginning "Come all you gallant Irishmen . . ."; O'Donovan Rossa was an Irish nationalist who was banished in 1870 for advocating violent rebellion against the British.

[4]*convent:* Her convent school.

My aunt was surprised and hoped it was not some Freemason[5] affair. I answered few questions in class. I watched my master's face pass from amiability to sternness; he hoped I was not beginning to idle. I could not call my wandering thoughts together. I had hardly any patience with the serious work of life which, now that it stood between me and my desire, seemed to me child's play, ugly monotonous child's play.

On Saturday morning I reminded my uncle that I wished to go to the bazaar in the evening. He was fussing at the hallstand, looking for the hatbrush, and answered me curtly:

"Yes, boy, I know."

15   As he was in the hall I could not go into the front parlour and lie at the window. I left the house in bad humour and walked slowly towards the school. The air was pitilessly raw and already my heart misgave me.

When I came home to dinner my uncle had not yet been home. Still it was early. I sat staring at the clock for some time and, when its ticking began to irritate me, I left the room. I mounted the staircase and gained the upper part of the house. The high cold empty gloomy rooms liberated me and I went from room to room singing. From the front window I saw my companions playing below in the street. Their cries reached me weakened and indistinct and, leaning my forehead against the cool glass, I looked over at the dark house where she lived. I may have stood there for an hour, seeing nothing but the brown-clad figure cast by my imagination, touched discreetly by the lamplight at the curved neck, at the hand upon the railings and at the border below the dress.

When I came downstairs again I found Mrs. Mercer sitting at the fire. She was an old garrulous woman, a pawnbroker's widow, who collected used stamps for some pious purpose. I had to endure the gossip of the tea-table. The meal was prolonged beyond an hour and still my uncle did not come. Mrs. Mercer stood up to go: she was sorry she couldn't wait any longer, but it was after eight o'clock and she did not like to be out late, as the night air was bad for her. When she had gone I began to walk up and down the room, clenching my fists. My aunt said:

"I'm afraid you may put off your bazaar for this night of Our Lord."

At nine o'clock I heard my uncle's latchkey in the halldoor. I heard him talking to himself and heard the hallstand rocking when it had received the weight of his overcoat. I could interpret these signs. When he was midway through his dinner I asked him to give me the money to go to the bazaar. He had forgotten.

20   "The people are in bed and after their first sleep now," he said.

I did not smile. My aunt said to him energetically:

"Can't you give him the money and let him go? You've kept him late enough as it is."

My uncle said he was very sorry he had forgotten. He said he believed in the old saying: "All work and no play makes Jack a dull boy." He asked me where I was going and, when I had told him a second time he asked me did I know *The Arab's*

---

[5]*Freemason:* At the time the story takes place, many Catholics in Ireland thought the Masonic Order was a threat to the church.

Farewell to his Steed.[6] When I left the kitchen he was about to recite the opening lines of the piece to my aunt.

I held a florin tightly in my hand as I strode down Buckingham Street towards the station. The sight of the streets thronged with buyers and glaring with gas recalled to me the purpose of my journey. I took my seat in a third-class carriage of a deserted train. After an intolerable delay the train moved out of the station slowly. It crept onward among ruinous houses and over the twinkling river. At Westland Row Station a crowd of people pressed to the carriage doors; but the porters moved them back, saying that it was a special train for the bazaar. I remained alone in the bare carriage. In a few minutes the train drew up beside an improvised wooden platform. I passed out on to the road and saw by the lighted dial of a clock that it was ten minutes to ten. In front of me was a large building which displayed the magical name.

I could not find any sixpenny entrance and, fearing that the bazaar would be closed, I passed in quickly through a turnstile, handing a shilling to a weary-looking man. I found myself in a big hall girdled at half its height by a gallery. Nearly all the stalls were closed and the greater part of the hall was in darkness. I recognised a silence like that which pervades a church after a service. I walked into the centre of the bazaar timidly. A few people were gathered about the stalls which were still open. Before a curtain, over which the words *Café Chantant*[7] were written in coloured lamps, two men were counting money on a salver. I listened to the fall of the coins.   25

Remembering with difficulty why I had come I went over to one of the stalls and examined porcelain vases and flowered tea-sets. At the door of the stall a young lady was talking and laughing with two young gentlemen. I remarked their English accents and listened vaguely to their conversation.

"O, I never said such a thing!"

"O, but you did!"

"O, but I didn't!"

"Didn't she say that?"   30

"Yes. I heard her."

"O, there's a . . . fib!"

Observing me the young lady came over and asked me did I wish to buy anything. The tone of her voice was not encouraging; she seemed to have spoken to me out of a sense of duty. I looked humbly at the great jars that stood like eastern guards at either side of the dark entrance to the stall and murmured:

"No, thank you."

The young lady changed the position of one of the vases and went back to the two young men. They began to talk of the same subject. Once or twice the young lady glanced at me over her shoulder.   35

I lingered before her stall, though I knew my stay was useless, to make my interest in her wares seem the more real. Then I turned away slowly and walked down the middle of the bazaar. I allowed the two pennies to fall against the sixpence in my

---

[6]The Arab's Farewell to his Steed: A sentimental poem by Caroline Norton (1808–1877) that tells the story of a nomad's heartbreak after selling his much-loved horse.

[7]Café Chantant: A Paris café featuring musical entertainment.

pocket. I heard a voice call from one end of the gallery that the light was out. The upper part of the hall was now completely dark.

Gazing up into the darkness I saw myself as a creature driven and derided by vanity; and my eyes burned with anguish and anger.

Reading and Reacting

1. How would you characterize the story's level of diction? Is this level appropriate for a story about a young boy's experiences? Explain.

2. Identify several figures of speech in the story. Where is Joyce most likely to use this kind of language? Why?

3. What words and phrases express the boy's extreme idealism and romantic view of the world? How does such language help to communicate the story's major theme?

4. In paragraph 4, the narrator says, "her name was like a summons to all my foolish blood." In the story's last sentence, he sees himself as "a creature driven and derided by vanity." What other expressions does the narrator use to describe his feelings? How would you characterize these feelings?

5. How does the narrator's choice of words illustrate the contrast between his day-to-day life and the exotic promise of the bazaar?

6. What does each of the italicized words suggest: "We walked through the *flaring* streets" (par. 5); "I heard the rain *impinge* upon the earth" (par. 6); "I *chafed* against the work of school" (par. 12); "I found myself in a big hall *girdled* at half its height by a gallery" (par. 25)? What other examples of unexpected word choice can you identify in the story?

7. What is it about the events in this story that causes the narrator to remember them years later?

8. Identify words and phrases in the story that are associated with religion. What purpose do these references to religion serve? Do you think this pattern of words and phrases is intentional?

9. **JOURNAL ENTRY** Rewrite a brief passage from this story in the voice of the young boy. Use informal style, simple figures of speech, and vocabulary appropriate for a child.

10. **CRITICAL PERSPECTIVE** In *Notes on the American Short Story Today*, Richard Kostelanetz discusses the **epiphany**, one of Joyce's most significant contributions to literature:

> In Joyce's pervasively influential theory of the short story we remember, the fiction turned upon an epiphany, a moment of revelation in which, in [critic] Harry Levin's words, "amid the most encumbered circumstances it suddenly happens that the veil is lifted, the . . . mystery laid bare, and the ultimate secret of things made manifest." The epiphany, then, became a technique for jelling the narrative and locking the story's import into place. . . . What made this method revolutionary was the shifting of the focal point of the story from its end . . . to a spot within the body of the text, usually near (but not at) the end.

Where in "Araby" does the story's epiphany occur? Does it do all that Kostelanetz believes an epiphany should do? Do you think that—at least in the case of "Araby"—the epiphany may not be as significant a force as Kostelanetz suggests?

Related Works: "Snow" (p. 126), "The Secret Lion" (p. 180), "Distant Relations" (p. 204), "A&P" (p. 238), "Gryphon" (p. 250), "The Girl with Bangs" (p. 262), "Doe Season" (p. 472), "Shall I compare thee to a summer's day?" (p. 758), "How Do I Love Thee?" (p. 899), *Beauty* (p. 1087)

AP Images

FLANNERY O'CONNOR (1925–1964) was born to a prosperous Catholic family in Savannah, Georgia, and spent most of her adult life on a farm near the town of Milledgeville. She left the South to study writing at the University of Iowa, moving to New York to work on her first novel, *Wise Blood* (1952). On a train going south for Christmas, O'Connor became seriously ill; she was diagnosed as having lupus, the immune system disease that had killed her father and would cause O'Connor's death when she was only thirty-nine years old.

While her mother ran the farm, O'Connor spent mornings writing and afternoons wandering the fields with cane or crutches. Her short story collection *A Good Man Is Hard to Find* (1955) and an excellent French translation of *Wise Blood* established her international reputation, which was solidified with the publication of a second novel, *The Violent Bear It Away* (1960), and a posthumously published book of short stories, *Everything That Rises Must Converge* (1965).

O'Connor, said a friend, believed that an artist "should face all the truth down to the worst of it." Yet however dark, her stories are infused with grim humor and a fierce belief in the possibility of spiritual redemption, even for her most tortured characters. A line from her short story "A Good Man Is Hard to Find" says much about what O'Connor perceived about both natural things and her characters: "The trees were full of silver-white sunlight and the meanest of them sparkled." In O'Connor's work, the "meanest" things and people can sparkle, touched by a kind of holy madness and beauty.

Cultural Context   Some readers consider O'Connor a Christian writer, and indeed the Christian concepts of free will, original sin, and the need for spiritual redemption appear throughout her work. According to Christian theology, humanity was created with free will—the freedom to choose to obey or to disobey God, the freedom to follow right or wrong. Human beings fell from their original state of innocence, however, and this fall allowed sin and corruption to enter the world. Thus, a "good man"—one who is perfectly upright—is not simply "hard to find" but *impossible* to find: *all* have sinned and fall short of the glory of God, says the Bible (Romans 3.23). Because of that first disobedience (original sin), humanity stands in need of redemption—a reuniting with God—which, according to Christian theology, comes through Jesus Christ.

A Good Man Is Hard to Find (1955)

The grandmother didn't want to go to Florida. She wanted to visit some of her connections in east Tennessee and she was seizing at every chance to change Bailey's mind. Bailey was the son she lived with, her only boy. He was sitting on the edge of his chair at the table, bent over the orange sports section of the *Journal*. "Now look here, Bailey," she said, "see here, read this," and she stood with one hand on her thin hip and the other rattling the newspaper at his bald head. "Here this fellow that calls himself The Misfit is aloose from the Federal Pen and headed toward Florida and you read here what it says he did to these people. Just you read it. I wouldn't take my children in any direction with a criminal like that aloose in it. I couldn't answer to my conscience if I did."

Bailey didn't look up from his reading so she wheeled around then and faced the children's mother, a young woman in slacks, whose face was as broad and innocent as a cabbage and was tied around with a green headkerchief that had two points on the top like a rabbit's ears. She was sitting on the sofa, feeding the baby his apricots out of a jar. "The children have been to Florida before," the old lady said. "You all ought to take them somewhere else for a change so they would see different parts of the world and be broad. They never have been to east Tennessee."

The children's mother didn't seem to hear her but the eight-year-old boy, John Wesley, a stocky child with glasses, said, "If you don't want to go to Florida, why dontcha stay at home?" He and the little girl, June Star, were reading the funny papers on the floor.

"She wouldn't stay at home to be queen for a day," June Star said without raising her yellow head.

5   "Yes and what would you do if this fellow, the Misfit, caught you?" the grandmother asked.

"I'd smack his face," John Wesley said.

"She wouldn't stay at home for a million bucks," June Star said. "Afraid she'd miss something. She has to go everywhere we go."

"All right, Miss," the grandmother said. "Just remember that the next time you want me to curl your hair."

June Star said her hair was naturally curly.

10   The next morning the grandmother was the first one in the car, ready to go. She had her big black valise that looked like the head of a hippopotamus in one corner, and underneath it she was hiding a basket with Pitty Sing, the cat, in it. She didn't intend for the cat to be left alone in the house for three days because he would miss her too much and she was afraid he might brush against one of the gas burners and accidentally asphyxiate himself. Her son, Bailey, didn't like to arrive at a motel with a cat.

She sat in the middle of the back seat with John Wesley and June Star on either side of her. Bailey and the children's mother and the baby sat in front and they left Atlanta at eight forty-five with the mileage on the car at 55890. The grandmother wrote this down because she thought it would be interesting to say how many miles they had been when they got back. It took them twenty minutes to reach the outskirts of the city.

The old lady settled herself comfortably, removing her white cotton gloves and putting them up with her purse on the shelf in front of the back window. The children's mother still had on slacks and still had her head tied up in a green kerchief, but the grandmother had on a navy blue straw sailor hat with a bunch of white violets on the brim and a navy blue dress with a small white dot in the print. Her collars and cuffs were white organdy trimmed with lace and at her neckline she had pinned a purple spray of cloth violets containing a sachet. In case of an accident, anyone seeing her dead on the highway would know at once that she was a lady.

She said she thought it was going to be a good day for driving, neither too hot nor too cold, and she cautioned Bailey that the speed limit was fifty-five miles an hour and that the patrolmen hid themselves behind billboards and small clumps of trees and sped out after you before you had a chance to slow down. She pointed out interesting details of the scenery: Stone Mountain; the blue granite that in some places came up to both sides of the highway; the brilliant red clay banks slightly streaked with purple; and the various crops that made rows of green lace-work on the ground. The trees were full of silver-white sunlight and the meanest of them sparkled. The children were reading comic magazines and their mother had gone back to sleep.

"Let's go through Georgia fast so we won't have to look at it much," John Wesley said.

"If I were a little boy," said the grandmother, "I wouldn't talk about my native   15
state that way. Tennessee has the mountains and Georgia has the hills."

"Tennessee is just a hillbilly dumping ground," John Wesley said, "and Georgia
is a lousy state too."

"You said it," June Star said.

"In my time," said the grandmother, folding her thin veined fingers, "children
were more respectful of their native states and their parents and everything else.
People did right then. Oh look at the cute little pickaninny!" she said and pointed to
a Negro child standing in the door of a shack. "Wouldn't that make a picture, now?"
she asked and they all turned and looked at the little Negro out of the back window.
He waved.

"He didn't have any britches on," June Star said.

"He probably didn't have any," the grandmother explained. "Little niggers in   20
the country don't have things like we do. If I could paint, I'd paint that picture,"
she said.

The children exchanged comic books.

The grandmother offered to hold the baby and the children's mother passed him
over the front seat to her. She set him on her knee and bounced him and told him
about the things they were passing. She rolled her eyes and screwed up her mouth
and stuck her leathery thin face into his smooth bland one. Occasionally he gave her
a faraway smile. They passed a large cotton field with five or six graves fenced in the
middle of it, like a small island. "Look at the graveyard!" the grandmother said, pointing it out. "That was the old family burying ground. That belonged to the plantation."

"Where's the plantation?" John Wesley asked.

"Gone with the Wind,"[1] said the grandmother. "Ha. Ha."

When the children finished all the comic books they had brought, they opened   25
the lunch and ate it. The grandmother ate a peanut butter sandwich and an olive
and would not let the children throw the box and the paper napkins out the window. When there was nothing else to do they played a game by choosing a cloud
and making the other two guess what shape it suggested. John Wesley took one the
shape of a cow and June Star guessed a cow and John Wesley said, no, an automobile, and June Star said he didn't play fair, and they began to slap each other over
the grandmother.

The grandmother said she would tell them a story if they would keep quiet. When
she told a story, she rolled her eyes and waved her head and was very dramatic. She
said once when she was a maiden lady she had been courted by a Mr. Edgar Atkins
Teagarden from Jasper, Georgia. She said he was a very good-looking man and a
gentleman and that he brought her a watermelon every Saturday afternoon with
his initials cut in it, E. A. T. Well, one Saturday, she said, Mr. Teagarden brought
the watermelon and there was nobody at home and he left it on the front porch and
returned in his buggy to Jasper, but she never got the watermelon, she said, because a
nigger boy ate it when he saw the initials, E. A. T.! This story tickled John Wesley's
funny bone and he giggled and giggled but June Star didn't think it was any good.

---

[1] Gone with the Wind: Gone with the Wind is a 1936 novel by Margaret Mitchell about the Civil War.

She said she wouldn't marry a man that just brought her a watermelon on Saturday. The grandmother said she would have done well to marry Mr. Teagarden because he was a gentleman and had bought Coca-Cola stock when it first came out and that he died only a few years ago, a very wealthy man.

They stopped at The Tower for barbecued sandwiches. The Tower was a part stucco and part wood filling station and dance hall set in a clearing outside of Timothy. A fat man named Red Sammy Butts ran it and there were signs stuck here and there on the building and for miles up and down the highway saying, TRY RED SAMMY'S FAMOUS BARBECUE. NONE LIKE FAMOUS RED SAMMY'S! RED SAM! THE FAT BOY WITH THE HAPPY LAUGH. A VETERAN! RED SAMMY'S YOUR MAN!

Red Sammy was lying on the bare ground outside The Tower with his head under a truck while a gray monkey about a foot high, chained to a small chinaberry tree, chattered nearby. The monkey sprang back into the tree and got on the highest limb as soon as he saw the children jump out of the car and run toward him.

Inside, The Tower was a long dark room with a counter at one end and tables at the other and dancing space in the middle. They all sat down at a board table next to the nickelodeon and Red Sam's wife, a tall burnt-brown woman with hair and eyes lighter than her skin, came and took their order. The children's mother put a dime in the machine and played "The Tennessee Waltz," and the grandmother said that tune always made her want to dance. She asked Bailey if he would like to dance but he only glared at her. He didn't have a naturally sweet disposition like she did and trips made him nervous. The grandmother's brown eyes were very bright. She swayed her head from side to side and pretended she was dancing in her chair. June Star said play something she could tap to so the children's mother put in another dime and played a fast number and June Star stepped out onto the dance floor and did her tap routine.

30   "Ain't she cute?" Red Sam's wife said, leaning over the counter. "Would you like to come be my little girl?"

"No I certainly wouldn't," June Star said. "I wouldn't live in a broken-down place like this for a million bucks!" and she ran back to the table.

"Ain't she cute?" the woman repeated, stretching her mouth politely.

"Aren't you ashamed?" hissed the grandmother.

Red Sam came in and told his wife to quit lounging on the counter and hurry up with these people's order. His khaki trousers reached just to his hip bones and his stomach hung over them like a sack of meal swaying under his shirt. He came over and sat down at a table nearby and let out a combination sigh and yodel. "You can't win," he said. "You can't win," and he wiped his sweating red face off with a gray handkerchief. "These days you don't know who to trust," he said. "Ain't that the truth?"

35   "People are certainly not nice like they used to be," said the grandmother.

"Two fellers come in here last week," Red Sammy said, "driving a Chrysler. It was a old beat-up car but it was a good one and these boys looked all right to me. Said they worked at the mill and you know I let them fellers charge the gas they bought? Now why did I do that?"

"Because you're a good man!" the grandmother said at once.

"Yes'm, I suppose so," Red Sam said as if he were struck with this answer.

His wife brought the orders, carrying the five plates all at once without a tray, two in each hand and one balanced on her arm. "It isn't a soul in this green world of God's that you can trust," she said. "And I don't count nobody out of that, not nobody," she repeated, looking at Red Sammy.

"Did you read about that criminal, The Misfit, that's escaped?" asked the grandmother.

"I wouldn't be a bit surprised if he didn't attack this place right here," said the woman. "If he hears about it being here, I wouldn't be none surprised to see him. If he hears it's two cent in the cash register, I wouldn't be at all surprised if he . . ."

"That'll do," Red Sam said. "Go bring these people their Co'-Colas," and the woman went off to get the rest of the order.

"A good man is hard to find," Red Sammy said. "Everything is getting terrible. I remember the day you could go off and leave your screen door unlocked. Not no more."

He and the grandmother discussed better times. The old lady said that in her opinion Europe was entirely to blame for the way things were now. She said the way Europe acted you would think we were made of money and Red Sam said it was no use talking about it, she was exactly right. The children ran outside into the white sunlight and looked at the monkey in the lacy chinaberry tree. He was busy catching fleas on himself and biting each one carefully between his teeth as if it were a delicacy.

They drove off again into the hot afternoon. The grandmother took cat naps and woke up every few minutes with her own snoring. Outside of Toombsboro she woke up and recalled an old plantation that she had visited in this neighborhood once when she was a young lady. She said the house had six white columns across the front and that there was an avenue of oaks leading up to it and two little wooden trellis arbors on either side in front where you sat down with your suitor after a stroll in the garden. She recalled exactly which road to turn off to get to it. She knew that Bailey would not be willing to lose any time looking at an old house, but the more she talked about it, the more she wanted to see it once again and find out if the little twin arbors were still standing. "There was a secret panel in this house," she said craftily, not telling the truth but wishing that she were, "and the story went that all the family silver was hidden in it when Sherman came through but it was never found . . ."

"Hey!" John Wesley said. "Let's go see it! We'll find it! We'll poke all the woodwork and find it! Who lives there? Where do you turn off at? Hey Pop, can't we turn off there?"

"We never have seen a house with a secret panel!" June Star shrieked. "Let's go to the house with the secret panel! Hey Pop, can't we go see the house with the secret panel!"

"It's not far from here, I know," the grandmother said. "It wouldn't take over twenty minutes."

Bailey was looking straight ahead. His jaw was as rigid as a horseshoe. "No," he said.

The children began to yell and scream that they wanted to see the house with the secret panel. John Wesley kicked the back of the front seat and June Star hung over

40

45

50

her mother's shoulder and whined desperately into her ear that they never had any fun even on their vacation, that they could never do what THEY wanted to do. The baby began to scream and John Wesley kicked the back of the seat so hard that his father could feel the blows in his kidney.

"All right!" he shouted and drew the car to a stop at the side of the road. "Will you all shut up? Will you all just shut up for one second? If you don't shut up, we won't go anywhere."

"It would be very educational for them," the grandmother murmured.

"All right," Bailey said, "but get this: this is the only time we're going to stop for anything like this. This is the one and only time."

"The dirt road that you have to turn down is about a mile back," the grandmother directed. "I marked it when we passed."

55   "A dirt road," Bailey groaned.

After they had turned around and were headed toward the dirt road, the grandmother recalled other points about the house, the beautiful glass over the front doorway and the candle-lamp in the hall. John Wesley said that the secret panel was probably in the fireplace.

"You can't go inside this house," Bailey said. "You don't know who lives there."

"While you all talk to the people in front, I'll run around behind and get in a window," John Wesley suggested.

"We'll all stay in the car," his mother said.

60   They turned onto the dirt road and the car raced roughly along in a swirl of pink dust. The grandmother recalled the times when there were no paved roads and thirty miles was a day's journey. The dirt road was hilly and there were sudden washes in it and sharp curves on dangerous embankments. All at once they would be on a hill, looking down over the blue tops of trees for miles around, then the next minute, they would be in a red depression with the dust-coated trees looking down on them.

"This place had better turn up in a minute," Bailey said, "or I'm going to turn around."

The road looked as if no one had traveled on it in months.

"It's not much farther," the grandmother said and just as she said it, a horrible thought came to her. The thought was so embarrassing that she turned red in the face and her eyes dilated and her feet jumped up, upsetting her valise in the corner. The instant the valise moved, the newspaper top she had over the basket under it rose with a snarl and Pitty Sing, the cat, sprang onto Bailey's shoulder.

The children were thrown to the floor and their mother, clutching the baby, was thrown out the door onto the ground; the old lady was thrown into the front seat. The car turned over once and landed right-side-up in a gulch off the side of the road. Bailey remained in the driver's seat with the cat—gray-striped with a broad white face and an orange nose—clinging to his neck like a caterpillar.

65   As soon as the children saw they could move their arms and legs, they scrambled out of the car, shouting, "We've had an ACCIDENT!" The grandmother was curled up under the dashboard, hoping she was injured so that Bailey's wrath would not come down on her all at once. The horrible thought she had had before the accident was that the house she had remembered so vividly was not in Georgia but in Tennessee.

Bailey removed the cat from his neck with both hands and flung it out the window against the side of a pine tree. Then he got out of the car and started looking for the children's mother. She was sitting against the side of the red gutted ditch, holding the screaming baby, but she only had a cut down her face and a broken shoulder. "We've had an ACCIDENT!" the children screamed in a frenzy of delight.

"But nobody's killed," June Star said with disappointment as the grandmother limped out of the car, her hat still pinned to her head but the broken front brim standing up at a jaunty angle and the violet spray hanging off the side. They all sat down in the ditch, except the children, to recover from the shock. They were all shaking.

"Maybe a car will come along," said the children's mother hoarsely.

"I believe I have injured an organ," said the grandmother, pressing her side, but no one answered her. Bailey's teeth were clattering. He had on a yellow sport shirt with bright blue parrots designed in it and his face was as yellow as the shirt. The grandmother decided that she would not mention that the house was in Tennessee.

The road was about ten feet above and they could see only the tops of the trees on the other side of it. Behind the ditch they were sitting in there were more woods, tall and dark and deep. In a few minutes they saw a car some distance away on top of a hill, coming slowly as if the occupants were watching them. The grandmother stood up and waved both arms dramatically to attract their attention. The car continued to come on slowly, disappeared around a bend and appeared again, moving even slower, on top of the hill they had gone over. It was a big black battered hearse-like automobile. There were three men in it.

It came to a stop just over them and for some minutes, the driver looked down with a steady expressionless gaze to where they were sitting, and didn't speak. Then he turned his head and muttered something to the other two and they got out. One was a fat boy in black trousers and a red sweat shirt with a silver stallion embossed on the front of it. He moved around on the right side of them and stood staring, his mouth partly open in a kind of loose grin. The other had on khaki pants and a blue striped coat and a gray hat pulled down very low, hiding most of his face. He came around slowly on the left side. Neither spoke.

The driver got out of the car and stood by the side of it, looking down at them. He was an older man than the other two. His hair was just beginning to gray and he wore silver-rimmed spectacles that gave him a scholarly look. He had a long creased face and didn't have on any shirt or undershirt. He had on blue jeans that were too tight for him and was holding a black hat and a gun. The two boys also had guns.

"We've had an ACCIDENT!" the children screamed.

The grandmother had the peculiar feeling that the bespectacled man was someone she knew. His face was as familiar to her as if she had known him all her life but she could not recall who he was. He moved away from the car and began to come down the embankment, placing his feet carefully so that he wouldn't slip. He had on tan and white shoes and no socks, and his ankles were red and thin. "Good afternoon," he said. "I see you all had you a little spill."

"We turned over twice!" said the grandmother.

"Oncet," he corrected. "We seen it happen. Try their car and see will it run, Hiram," he said quietly to the boy with the gray hat.

"What you got that gun for?" John Wesley asked. "Watcha gonna do with that gun?"

"Lady," the man said to the children's mother, "would you mind calling them children to sit down by you? Children make me nervous. I want all you all to sit down right together there where you're at."

"What are you telling US what to do for?" June Star asked.

80   Behind them the line of woods gaped like a dark open mouth. "Come here," said their mother.

"Look here now," Bailey began suddenly, "we're in a predicament! We're in . . ."

The grandmother shrieked. She scrambled to her feet and stood staring. "You're The Misfit!" she said. "I recognized you at once!"

"Yes'm," the man said, smiling slightly as if he were pleased in spite of himself to be known, "but it would have been better for all of you, lady, if you hadn't of reckernized me."

Bailey turned his head sharply and said something to his mother that shocked even the children. The old lady began to cry and The Misfit reddened.

85   "Lady," he said, "don't you get upset. Sometimes a man says things he don't mean. I don't reckon he meant to talk to you thataway."

"You wouldn't shoot a lady, would you?" the grandmother said and removed a clean handkerchief from her cuff and began to slap at her eyes with it.

The Misfit pointed the toe of his shoe into the ground and made a little hole and then covered it up again. "I would hate to have to," he said.

"Listen," the grandmother almost screamed, "I know you're a good man. You don't look a bit like you have common blood. I know you must come from nice people!"

"Yes mam," he said, "finest people in the world." When he smiled he showed a row of strong white teeth. "God never made a finer woman than my mother and my daddy's heart was pure gold," he said. The boy with the red sweat shirt had come around behind them and was standing with his gun at his hip. The Misfit squatted down on the ground. "Watch them children, Bobby Lee," he said. "You know they make me nervous." He looked at the six of them huddled together in front of him and he seemed to be embarrassed as if he couldn't think of anything to say. "Ain't a cloud in the sky," he remarked, looking up at it. "Don't see no sun but don't see no cloud neither."

90   "Yes, it's a beautiful day," said the grandmother. "Listen," she said, "you shouldn't call yourself The Misfit because I know you're a good man at heart. I can just look at you and tell."

"Hush!" Bailey yelled. "Hush! Everybody shut up and let me handle this!" He was squatting in the position of a runner about to sprint forward but he didn't move.

"I pre-chate that, lady," The Misfit said and drew a little circle in the ground with the butt of his gun.

"It'll take a half a hour to fix this here car," Hiram called, looking over the raised hood of it.

"Well, first you and Bobby Lee get him and that little boy to step over yonder with you," The Misfit said, pointing to Bailey and John Wesley. "The boys want to ast you something," he said to Bailey. "Would you mind stepping back in them woods there with them?"

"Listen," Bailey began, "we're in a terrible predicament! Nobody realizes what this is," and his voice cracked. His eyes were as blue and intense as the parrots in his shirt and he remained perfectly still.

The grandmother reached up to adjust her hat brim as if she were going to the woods with him but it came off in her hand. She stood staring at it and after a second she let it fall on the ground. Hiram pulled Bailey up by the arm as if he were assisting an old man. John Wesley caught hold of his father's hand and Bobby Lee followed. They went off toward the woods and just as they reached the dark edge, Bailey turned and supporting himself against a gray naked pine trunk, he shouted, "I'll be back in a minute, Mamma, wait on me!"

"Come back this instant!" his mother shrilled but they all disappeared into the woods.

"Bailey Boy!" the grandmother called in a tragic voice but she found she was looking at The Misfit squatting on the ground in front of her. "I just know you're a good man," she said desperately. "You're not a bit common!"

"Nome, I ain't a good man," The Misfit said after a second as if he had considered her statement carefully, "but I ain't the worst in the world neither. My daddy said I was a different breed of dog from my brothers and sisters. 'You know,' Daddy said, 'it's some that can live their whole life out without asking about it and it's others has to know why it is, and this boy is one of the latters. He's going to be into everything!'" He put on his black hat and looked up suddenly and then away deep into the woods as if he were embarrassed again. "I'm sorry I don't have on a shirt before you ladies," he said, hunching his shoulders slightly. "We buried our clothes that we had on when we escaped and we're just making do until we can get better. We borrowed these from some folks we met," he explained.

"That's perfectly all right," the grandmother said. "Maybe Bailey has an extra shirt in his suitcase."

"I'll look and see terrectly," The Misfit said.

"Where are they taking him?" the children's mother screamed.

"Daddy was a card himself," The Misfit said. "You couldn't put anything over on him. He never got in trouble with the Authorities though. Just had the knack of handling them."

"You could be honest too if you'd only try," said the grandmother. "Think how wonderful it would be to settle down and live a comfortable life and not have to think about somebody chasing you all the time."

The Misfit kept scratching in the ground with the butt of his gun as if he were thinking about it. "Yes'm, somebody is always after you," he murmured.

The grandmother noticed how thin his shoulder blades were just behind his hat because she was standing up looking down on him. "Do you ever pray?" she asked.

He shook his head. All she saw was the black hat wiggle between his shoulder blades. "Nome," he said.

There was a pistol shot from the woods, followed closely by another. Then silence. The old lady's head jerked around. She could hear the wind move through the tree tops like a long satisfied insuck of breath. "Bailey Boy!" she called.

"I was a gospel singer for a while," The Misfit said. "I been most everything. Been in the arm service, both land and sea, at home and abroad, been twict married, been an undertaker, been with the railroads, plowed Mother Earth, been in a tornado, seen a man burnt alive oncet," and he looked up at the children's mother and the little girl who were sitting close together, their faces white and their eyes glassy; "I even seen a woman flogged," he said.

110   "Pray, pray," the grandmother began, "pray, pray . . ."

"I never was a bad boy that I remember of," The Misfit said in an almost dreamy voice, "but somewheres along the line I done something wrong and got sent to the penitentiary. I was buried alive," and he looked up and held her attention to him by a steady stare.

"That's when you should have started to pray," she said. "What did you do to get sent to the penitentiary that first time?"

"Turn to the right, it was a wall," The Misfit said, looking up again at the cloudless sky. "Turn to the left, it was a wall. Look up it was a ceiling, look down it was a floor. I forget what I done, lady. I set there and set there, trying to remember what it was I done and I ain't recalled it to this day. Oncet in a while, I would think it was coming to me, but it never come."

"Maybe they put you in by mistake," the old lady said vaguely.

115   "Nome," he said. "It wasn't no mistake. They had the papers on me."

"You must have stolen something," she said.

The Misfit sneered slightly. "Nobody had nothing I wanted," he said. "It was a head-doctor at the penitentiary said what I had done was kill my daddy but I known that for a lie. My daddy died in nineteen ought nineteen of the epidemic flu and I never had a thing to do with it. He was buried in the Mount Hopewell Baptist churchyard and you can go there and see for yourself."

"If you would pray," the old lady said, "Jesus would help you."

"That's right," The Misfit said.

120   "Well then, why don't you pray?" she asked trembling with delight suddenly.

"I don't want no hep," he said. "I'm doing all right by myself."

Bobby Lee and Hiram came ambling back from the woods. Bobby Lee was dragging a yellow shirt with bright blue parrots in it.

"Thow me that shirt, Bobby Lee," The Misfit said. The shirt came flying at him and landed on his shoulder and he put it on. The grandmother couldn't name what the shirt reminded her of. "No, lady," The Misfit said while he was buttoning it up, "I found out the crime don't matter. You can do one thing or you can do another, kill a man or take a tire off his car, because sooner or later you're going to forget what it was you done and just be punished for it."

The children's mother had begun to make heaving noises as if she couldn't get her breath. "Lady," he asked, "would you and that little girl like to step off yonder with Bobby Lee and Hiram and join your husband?"

125   "Yes, thank you," the mother said faintly. Her left arm dangled helplessly and she was holding the baby, who had gone to sleep, in the other. "Hep that lady up, Hiram," The Misfit said as she struggled to climb out of the ditch, "and Bobby Lee, you hold onto that little girl's hand."

"I don't want to hold hands with him," June Star said. "He reminds me of a pig."

The fat boy blushed and laughed and caught her by the arm and pulled her off into the woods after Hiram and her mother.

Alone with The Misfit, the grandmother found that she had lost her voice. There was not a cloud in the sky nor any sun. There was nothing around her but woods. She wanted to tell him that he must pray. She opened and closed her mouth several times before anything came out. Finally she found herself saying, "Jesus, Jesus," meaning, Jesus will help you, but the way she was saying it, it sounded as if she might be cursing.

"Yes'm," The Misfit said as if he agreed. "Jesus thown everything off balance. It was the same case with Him as with me except He hadn't committed any crime and they could prove I had committed one because they had the papers on me. Of course," he said, "they never shown me my papers. That's why I sign myself now. I said long ago, you get you a signature and sign everything you do and keep a copy of it. Then you'll know what you done and you can hold up the crime to the punishment and see do they match and in the end you'll have something to prove you ain't been treated right. I call myself The Misfit," he said, "because I can't make what all I done wrong fit what all I gone through in punishment."

There was a piercing scream from the woods, followed closely by a pistol report. "Does it seem right to you, lady, that one is punished a heap and another ain't punished at all?"   130

"Jesus!" the old lady cried. "You've got good blood! I know you wouldn't shoot a lady! I know you come from nice people! Pray! Jesus, you ought not to shoot a lady. I'll give you all the money I've got!"

"Lady," The Misfit said, looking beyond her far into the woods, "there never was a body that give the undertaker a tip."

There were two more pistol reports and the grandmother raised her head like a parched old turkey hen crying for water and called, "Bailey Boy, Bailey Boy!" as if her heart would break.

"Jesus was the only One that ever raised the dead," The Misfit continued, "and He shouldn't have done it. He thown everything off balance. If He did what He said, then it's nothing for you to do but thow away everything and follow Him, and if He didn't, then it's nothing for you to do but enjoy the few minutes you got left the best way you can—by killing somebody or burning down his house or doing some other meanness to him. No pleasure but meanness," he said and his voice became almost a snarl.

"Maybe He didn't raise the dead," the old lady mumbled, not knowing what she was saying and feeling so dizzy that she sank down in the ditch with her legs twisted under her.   135

"I wasn't there so I can't say He didn't," The Misfit said. "I wisht I had of been there," he said, hitting the ground with his fist. "It ain't right I wasn't there because if I had of been there I would of known. Listen, lady," he said in a high voice, "if I had of been there I would of known and I wouldn't be like I am now." His voice seemed about to crack and the grandmother's head cleared for an instant. She saw the man's face twisted close to her own as if he were going to cry and she murmured, "Why you're one of my babies. You're one of my own children!" She reached out and touched him on the shoulder. The Misfit sprang back as if a snake had bitten him and shot her three times through the chest. Then he put his gun down on the ground and took off his glasses and began to clean them.

Hiram and Bobby Lee returned from the woods and stood over the ditch, looking down at the grandmother who half sat and half lay in a puddle of blood with her legs crossed under her like a child's and her face smiling up at the cloudless sky.

Without his glasses, The Misfit's eyes were red-rimmed and pale and defenseless-looking. "Take her off and thow her where you thown the others," he said, picking up the cat that was rubbing itself against his leg.

"She was a talker, wasn't she?" Bobby Lee said, sliding down the ditch with a yodel.

140   "She would of been a good woman," The Misfit said, "if it had been somebody there to shoot her every minute of her life."

"Some fun!" Bobby Lee said.

"Shut up, Bobby Lee," The Misfit said. "It's no real pleasure in life."

Reading and Reacting

1. How are the style and tone of the narrator's voice different from those of the characters? What, if anything, is the significance of this difference?

2. The figures of speech used in this story sometimes create unflattering, even grotesque, pictures of the characters. Find several examples of such negative figures of speech. Why do you think O'Connor uses them?

3. What does the grandmother's use of the words *pickaninny* and *nigger* reveal about her? How are readers expected to reconcile this language with her very proper appearance and her preoccupation with manners? How does her use of these words affect your reaction to her?

4. Explain the **irony** in this statement: "In case of an accident, anyone seeing her dead on the highway would know at once that she was a lady" (par. 12).

5. How does The Misfit's dialect characterize him?

6. What does the **allusion** to *Gone with the Wind* (par. 24) contribute to the story?

7. How do the style and tone of the two-paragraph description of the three men in the car (pars. 71–72) help to prepare readers for the events that follow?

8. When The Misfit tells the grandmother about his life, his language takes on a measured, rhythmic quality: "Been in the arm service, both land and sea, at home and abroad, been twict married, been an undertaker, been with the railroads, plowed Mother Earth, been in a tornado, seen a man burnt alive oncet . . ." (par. 109). Find other examples of rhythmic repetition and parallelism in this character's speech. How does this style help to develop The Misfit's character?

9. JOURNAL ENTRY Why do you think the grandmother tells The Misfit that she recognizes him? Why does she fail to realize the danger of her remark?

10. CRITICAL PERSPECTIVE In his 2002 essay "Light and Shadow: Religious Grace in Two Stories by Flannery O'Connor," David Allen Cook writes:

> The literary works of Flannery O'Connor often contend that religious belief can only be consummated by direct confrontation with evil, and for those uncommitted and unprepared, tragedy seems inevitable. For O'Connor's religious "pretenders," a moment of religious grace—a revelation of Truth—often does come, but at a devastating price. In . . . "A Good

Man Is Hard to Find," we are presented with main characters that experience a deep epiphany after being spiritually challenged by the darker side of human nature.

In this story, who are the religious "pretenders," and who has true faith? What is the price of achieving a moment of religious grace? What role does violence play in this equation?

Related Works: "Accident" (p. 131), "Slide to Unlock" (p. 138), "The Lottery" (p. 419), "Bullet in the Brain" (p. 496), "Where Are You Going, Where Have You Been?" (p. 506), "Everything That Rises Must Converge" (p. 611), "The Tell-Tale Heart" (p. 622), "Hitler's First Photograph" (p. 709)

The Granger Collection, NYC

CHARLOTTE PERKINS GILMAN (1860–1935) was a prominent feminist and social thinker at the turn of the century. Her essays, lectures, and nonfiction works—such as *Women and Economics* (1898), *Concerning Children* (1900), and *The Man-Made World* (1911)—are forceful statements of Gilman's opinions on women's need for economic independence and social equality. Gilman is probably best known for three utopian feminist novels: *Moving the Mountain* (1911), *Herland* (1915; unpublished until 1978), and *With Her in Ourland* (1916). Her works are full of humor and satire. In *Herland*, for instance, a male sociologist (wandering in by accident from the outside world) is chagrined to find that the women of "Herland" want him as a friend, not a lover.

Although "The Yellow Wallpaper" (1982) is not typical of Gilman's other fiction, it is considered her artistic masterpiece. The terse, clinical precision of the writing, conveying the tightly wound and distraught mental state of the narrator, is particularly chilling when it is read with a knowledge of Gilman's personal history. In the 1880s, she met and married a young artist, Charles Walter Stetson. Following the birth of their daughter, she grew increasingly depressed and turned to a noted Philadelphia neurologist for help. Following the traditions of the time, he prescribed complete bed rest and mental inactivity—a treatment that, Gilman said later, drove her "so near the borderline of utter mental ruin that I could see over." "The Yellow Wallpaper" is not simply a psychological study. Like most of Gilman's work, it makes a point—in this case, about the dangers of women's utter dependence on a male interpretation of their needs.

Cultural Context Recent research indicates that one out of every ten new mothers becomes seriously depressed within six months after childbirth. This condition is known as postpartum depression, and its symptoms include severe feelings of sadness or emptiness, withdrawal from family and friends, a strong sense of failure or inadequacy, intense concern (or lack of concern) about the baby, and, in more serious cases, thoughts about suicide or fears of harming the baby. Today's treatments include medication and psychotherapy, but at the time of this story, the standard treatment was a "rest cure," in which the patient was placed in isolation and kept from distractions that were believed to be dangerous. For many patients (as for the narrator of this story), this "cure" was worse than the condition itself.

The Yellow Wallpaper (1892)

It is very seldom that mere ordinary people like John and myself secure ancestral halls for the summer.

A colonial mansion, a hereditary estate, I would say a haunted house, and reach the height of romantic felicity—but that would be asking too much of fate!

Still I will proudly declare that there is something queer about it.

Else, why should it be let so cheaply? And why have stood so long untenanted?

5   John laughs at me, of course, but one expects that in marriage.

John is practical in the extreme. He has no patience with faith, an intense horror of superstition, and he scoffs openly at any talk of things not to be felt and seen and put down in figures.

John is a physician, and *perhaps*—(I would not say it to a living soul, of course, but this is dead paper and a great relief to my mind—) *perhaps* that is one reason I do not get well faster.

You see he does not believe I am sick!

And what can one do?

10   If a physician of high standing, and one's own husband, assures friends and relatives that there is really nothing the matter with one but temporary nervous depression—a slight hysterical tendency—what is one to do?

My brother is also a physician, and also of high standing, and he says the same thing.

So I take phosphates or phosphites[1]—whichever it is, and tonics, and journeys, and air, and exercise, and am absolutely forbidden to "work" until I am well again.

Personally, I disagree with their ideas.

Personally, I believe that congenial work, with excitement and change, would do me good.

15   But what is one to do?

I did write for a while in spite of them; but it *does* exhaust me a good deal—having to be so sly about it, or else meet with heavy opposition.

I sometimes fancy that in my condition if I had less opposition and more society and stimulus—but John says the very worst thing I can do is to think about my condition, and I confess it always makes me feel bad.

So I will let it alone and talk about the house.

The most beautiful place! It is quite alone, standing well back from the road, quite three miles from the village. It makes me think of English places that you read about, for there are hedges and walls and gates that lock, and lots of separate little houses for the gardeners and people.

20   There is a *delicious* garden! I never saw such a garden—large and shady, full of box-bordered paths, and lined with long grape-covered arbors with seats under them.

There were greenhouses, too, but they are all broken now.

There was some legal trouble, I believe, something about the heirs and co-heirs; anyhow, the place has been empty for years.

That spoils my ghostliness, I am afraid, but I don't care—there is something strange about the house—I can feel it.

I even said so to John one moonlight evening, but he said what I felt was a *draught*, and shut the window.

---

[1] *phosphates or phosphites:* Both terms refer to salts of phosphorous acid. The narrator, however, means "phosphate," a carbonated beverage of water, flavoring, and a small amount of phosphoric acid.

I get unreasonably angry with John sometimes. I'm sure I never used to be so   25
sensitive. I think it is due to this nervous condition.

But John says if I feel so, I shall neglect proper self-control; so I take pains to
control myself—before him, at least, and that makes me very tired.

I don't like our room a bit. I wanted one downstairs that opened on the piazza and
had roses all over the window, and such pretty old-fashioned chintz hangings! But
John would not hear of it.

He said there was only one window and not room for two beds, and no near room
for him if he took another.

He is very careful and loving, and hardly lets me stir without special direction.

I have a schedule prescription for each hour in the day; he takes all care from me,   30
and so I feel basely ungrateful not to value it more.

He said we came here solely on my account, that I was to have perfect rest and all
the air I could get. "Your exercise depends on your strength, my dear," said he, "and
your food somewhat on your appetite; but air you can absorb all the time." So we took
the nursery at the top of the house.

It is a big, airy room, the whole floor nearly, with windows that look all ways,
and air and sunshine galore. It was nursery first and then playroom and gymnasium,
I should judge; for the windows are barred for little children, and there are rings and
things in the walls.

The paint and paper look as if a boys' school had used it. It is stripped off—the
paper—in great patches all around the head of my bed, about as far as I can reach, and
in a great place on the other side of the room low down. I never saw a worse paper in
my life.

One of those sprawling flamboyant patterns committing every artistic sin.

It is dull enough to confuse the eye in following, pronounced enough to con-   35
stantly irritate and provoke study, and when you follow the lame uncertain curves
for a little distance they suddenly commit suicide—plunge off at outrageous angles,
destroy themselves in unheard of contradictions.

The color is repellent, almost revolting; a smouldering unclean yellow, strangely
faded by the slow-turning sunlight.

It is a dull yet lurid orange in some places, a sickly sulphur tint in others.

No wonder the children hated it! I should hate it myself if I had to live in this
room long.

There comes John, and I must put this away,—he hates to have me write a word.

*   *   *

We have been here two weeks, and I haven't felt like writing before, since that   40
first day.

I am sitting by the window now, up in this atrocious nursery, and there is nothing
to hinder my writing as much as I please, save lack of strength.

John is away all day, and even some nights when his cases are serious.

I am glad my case is not serious!

But these nervous troubles are dreadfully depressing.

45   John does not know how much I really suffer. He knows there is no *reason* to suffer, and that satisfies him.

   Of course it is only nervousness. It does weigh on me so not to do my duty in any way!

   I meant to be such a help to John, such a real rest and comfort, and here I am a comparative burden already!

   Nobody would believe what an effort it is to do what little I am able,—to dress and entertain, and order things.

   It is fortunate Mary is so good with the baby. Such a dear baby!

50   And yet I *cannot* be with him, it makes me so nervous.

   I suppose John never was nervous in his life. He laughs at me so about this wallpaper!

   At first he meant to repaper the room, but afterwards he said that I was letting it get the better of me, and that nothing was worse for a nervous patient than to give way to such fancies.

   He said that after the wallpaper was changed it would be the heavy bedstead, and then the barred windows, and then that gate at the head of the stairs, and so on.

   "You know the place is doing you good," he said, "and really, dear, I don't care to renovate the house just for a three months' rental."

55   "Then do let us go downstairs," I said, "there are such pretty rooms there."

   Then he took me in his arms and called me a blessed little goose, and said he would go down cellar, if I wished, and have it whitewashed into the bargain.

   But he is right enough about the beds and windows and things.

   It is an airy and comfortable room as any one need wish, and, of course, I would not be so silly as to make him uncomfortable just for a whim.

   I'm really getting quite fond of the big room, all but that horrid paper.

60   Out of one window I can see the garden, those mysterious deep-shaded arbors, the riotous old-fashioned flowers, and bushes and gnarly trees.

   Out of another I get a lovely view of the bay and a little private wharf belonging to the estate. There is a beautiful shaded lane that runs down there from the house. I always fancy I see people walking in these numerous paths and arbors, but John has cautioned me not to give way to fancy in the least. He says that with my imaginative power and habit of story-making, a nervous weakness like mine is sure to lead to all manner of excited fancies, and that I ought to use my will and good sense to check the tendency. So I try.

   I think sometimes that if I were only well enough to write a little it would relieve the press of ideas and rest me.

   But I find I get pretty tired when I try.

   It is so discouraging not to have any advice and companionship about my work. When I get really well, John says we will ask Cousin Henry and Julia down for a long visit; but he says he would as soon put fireworks in my pillow-case as to let me have those stimulating people about now.

65   I wish I could get well faster.

   But I must not think about that. This paper looks to me as if it *knew* what a vicious influence it had!

There is a recurrent spot where the pattern lolls like a broken neck and two bulbous eyes stare at you upside down.

I get positively angry with the impertinence of it and the everlastingness. Up and down and sideways they crawl, and those absurd, unblinking eyes are everywhere. There is one place where two breadths didn't match, and the eyes go all up and down the line, one a little higher than the other.

I never saw so much expression in an inanimate thing before, and we all know how much expression they have! I used to lie awake as a child and get more entertainment and terror out of blank walls and plain furniture than most children could find in a toy-store.

I remember what a kindly wink the knobs of our big, old bureau used to have, and there was one chair that always seemed like a strong friend.

I used to feel that if any of the other things looked too fierce I could always hop into that chair and be safe.

The furniture in this room is no worse than inharmonious, however, for we had to bring it all from downstairs. I suppose when this was used as a playroom they had to take the nursery things out, and no wonder! I never saw such ravages as the children have made here.

The wallpaper, as I said before, is torn off in spots, and it sticketh closer than a brother—they must have had perseverance as well as hatred.

Then the floor is scratched and gouged and splintered, the plaster itself is dug out here and there, and this great heavy bed which is all we found in the room, looks as if it had been through the wars.

But I don't mind it a bit—only the paper.

There comes John's sister. Such a dear girl as she is, and so careful of me! I must not let her find me writing.

She is a perfect and enthusiastic housekeeper, and hopes for no better profession. I verily believe she thinks it is the writing which made me sick!

But I can write when she is out, and see her a long way off from these windows.

There is one that commands the road, a lovely shaded winding road, and one that just looks off over the country. A lovely country, too, full of great elms and velvet meadows.

This wallpaper has a kind of sub-pattern in a different shade, a particularly irritating one, for you can only see it in certain lights, and not clearly then.

But in the places where it isn't faded and where the sun is just so—I can see a strange, provoking, formless sort of figure, that seems to skulk about behind that silly and conspicuous front design.

There's sister on the stairs!

*   *   *

Well, the Fourth of July is over! The people are all gone and I am tired out. John thought it might do me good to see a little company, so we just had mother and Nellie and the children down for a week.

Of course I didn't do a thing. Jennie sees to everything now.

But it tired me all the same.

John says if I don't pick up faster he shall send me to Weir Mitchell[2] in the fall.

But I don't want to go there at all. I had a friend who was in his hands once, and she says he is just like John and my brother, only more so!

Besides, it is such an undertaking to go so far.

I don't feel as if it was worth while to turn my hand over for anything, and I'm getting dreadfully fretful and querulous.

90   I cry at nothing, and cry most of the time.

Of course I don't when John is here, or anybody else, but when I am alone.

And I am alone a good deal just now. John is kept in town very often by serious cases, and Jennie is good and lets me alone when I want her to.

So I walk a little in the garden or down that lovely lane, sit on the porch under the roses, and lie down up here a good deal.

I'm getting really fond of the room in spite of the wallpaper. Perhaps *because* of the wallpaper.

95   It dwells in my mind so!

I lie here on this great immovable bed—it is nailed down, I believe—and follow that pattern about by the hour. It is as good as gymnastics, I assure you. I start, we'll say, at the bottom, down in the corner over there where it has not been touched, and I determine for the thousandth time that I *will* follow that pointless pattern to some sort of a conclusion.

I know a little of the principle of design, and I know this thing was not arranged on any laws of radiation, or alternation, or repetition, or symmetry, or anything else that I ever heard of.

It is repeated, of course, by the breadths, but not otherwise.

Looked at in one way each breadth stands alone, the bloated curves and flourishes—a kind of "debased Romanesque" with *delirium tremens*[3] go waddling up and down in isolated columns of fatuity.

100   But, on the other hand, they connect diagonally, and the sprawling outlines run off in great slanting waves of optic horror, like a lot of wallowing seaweeds in full chase.

The whole thing goes horizontally, too, at least it seems so, and I exhaust myself in trying to distinguish the order of its going in that direction.

They have used a horizontal breadth for a frieze, and that adds wonderfully to the confusion.

There is one end of the room where it is almost intact, and there, when the cross-lights fade and the low sun shines directly upon it, I can almost fancy radiation after all,—the interminable grotesques seems to form around a common center and rush off in headlong plunges of equal distraction.

It makes me tired to follow it. I will take a nap I guess.

105   I don't know why I should write this.

I don't want to.

---

[2]*Weir Mitchell:* Silas Weir Mitchell (1829–1914), a Philadelphia neurologist-psychologist who introduced the "rest cure" for nervous diseases.

[3]delirium tremens: Mental confusion caused by alcohol poisoning and characterized by physical tremors and hallucinations.

I don't feel able.

And I know John would think it absurd. But I *must* say what I feel and think in some way—it is such a relief!

But the effort is getting to be greater than the relief.

Half the time now I am awfully lazy, and lie down ever so much.   110

John says I mustn't lose my strength, and has me take cod liver oil and lots of tonics and things, to say nothing of ale and wine and rare meat.

Dear John! He loves me very dearly, and hates to have me sick. I tried to have a real earnest reasonable talk with him the other day, and tell him how I wish he would let me go and make a visit to Cousin Henry and Julia.

But he said I wasn't able to go, nor able to stand it after I got there; and I did not make out a very good case for myself, for I was crying before I had finished.

It is getting to be a great effort for me to think straight. Just this nervous weakness I suppose.

And dear John gathered me up in his arms, and just carried me upstairs and laid   115
me on the bed, and sat by me and read to me till it tired my head.

He said I was his darling and his comfort and all he had, and that I must take care of myself for his sake, and keep well.

He says no one but myself can help me out of it, that I must use my will and self-control and not let any silly fancies run away with me.

There's one comfort, the baby is well and happy, and does not have to occupy this nursery with the horrid wallpaper.

If we had not used it, that blessed child would have! What a fortunate escape! Why, I wouldn't have a child of mine, an impressionable little thing, live in such a room for worlds.

I never thought of it before, but it is lucky that John kept me here after all, I can   120
stand it so much easier than a baby, you see.

Of course I never mention it to them any more—I am too wise,—but I keep watch of it all the same.

There are things in that paper that nobody knows but me, or ever will.

Behind that outside pattern the dim shapes get clearer every day.

It is always the same shape, only very numerous.

And it is like a woman stooping down and creeping about behind that pattern.   125
I don't like it a bit. I wonder—I begin to think—I wish John would take me away from here!

It is so hard to talk with John about my case, because he is so wise, and because he loves me so.

But I tried it last night.

It was moonlight. The moon shines in all around just as the sun does.

I hate to see it sometimes, it creeps so slowly, and always comes in by one window or another.

John was asleep and I hated to waken him, so I kept still and watched the moon-   130
light on that undulating wallpaper till I felt creepy.

The faint figure behind seemed to shake the pattern, just as if she wanted to get out.

I got up softly and went to feel and see if the paper *did* move, and when I came back John was awake.

"What is it, little girl?" he said. "Don't go walking about like that—you'll get cold."

I thought it was a good time to talk, so I told him that I really was not gaining here, and that I wished he would take me away.

135   "Why, darling!" said he, "our lease will be up in three weeks, and I can't see how to leave before.

"The repairs are not done at home, and I cannot possibly leave town just now. Of course if you were in any danger, I could and would, but you really are better, dear, whether you can see it or not. I am a doctor, dear, and I know. You are gaining flesh and color, your appetite is better, I feel really much easier about you."

"I don't weigh a bit more," said I, "nor as much; and my appetite may be better in the evening when you are here, but it is worse in the morning when you are away!"

"Bless her little heart!" said he with a big hug, "she shall be as sick as she pleases! But now let's improve the shining hours by going to sleep, and talk about it in the morning!"

"And you won't go away?" I asked gloomily.

140   "Why, how can I, dear? It is only three weeks more and then we will take a nice little trip of a few days while Jennie is getting the house ready. Really dear you are better!"

"Better in body perhaps—" I began, and stopped short, for he sat up straight and looked at me with such a stern, reproachful look that I could not say another word.

"My darling," said he, "I beg of you, for my sake and for our child's sake, as well as for your own, that you will never for one instant let that idea enter your mind! There is nothing so dangerous, so fascinating, to a temperament like yours. It is a false and foolish fancy. Can you not trust me as a physician when I tell you so?"

So of course I said no more on that score, and we went to sleep before long. He thought I was asleep first, but I wasn't, and lay there for hours trying to decide whether that front pattern and the back pattern really did move together or separately.

On a pattern like this, by daylight, there is a lack of sequence, a defiance of law, that is a constant irritant to a normal mind.

145   The color is hideous enough, and unreliable enough, and infuriating enough, but the pattern is torturing.

You think you have mastered it, but just as you get well underway in following, it turns back-somersault and there you are. It slaps you in the face, knocks you down, and tramples upon you. It is like a bad dream.

The outside pattern is a florid arabesque, reminding one of a fungus. If you can imagine a toadstool in joints, an interminable string of toadstools, budding and sprouting in endless convolutions—why, that is something like it.

That is, sometimes!

There is one marked peculiarity about this paper, a thing nobody seems to notice but myself, and that is that it changes as the light changes.

150   When the sun shoots in through the east window—I always watch for that first long, straight ray—it changes so quickly that I never can quite believe it.

That is why I watch it always.

By moonlight—the moon shines in all night when there is a moon—I wouldn't know it was the same paper.

At night in any kind of light, in twilight, candlelight, lamplight, and worst of all by moonlight, it becomes bars! The outside pattern I mean, and the woman behind it is as plain as can be.

I didn't realize for a long time what the thing was that showed behind, that dim sub-pattern, but now I am quite sure it is a woman.

By daylight she is subdued, quiet. I fancy it is the pattern that keeps her so still. It   155
is so puzzling. It keeps me quiet by the hour.

I lie down ever so much now. John says it is good for me, and to sleep all I can.

Indeed he started the habit by making me lie down for an hour after each meal.

It is a very bad habit I am convinced, for you see I don't sleep.

And that cultivates deceit, for I don't tell them I'm awake—O no!

The fact is I am getting a little afraid of John.   160

He seems very queer sometimes, and even Jennie has an inexplicable look.

It strikes me occasionally, just as a scientific hypothesis,—that perhaps it is the paper!

I have watched John when he did not know I was looking, and come into the room suddenly on the most innocent excuses, and I've caught him several times *looking at the paper!* And Jennie too. I caught Jennie with her hand on it once.

She didn't know I was in the room, and when I asked her in a quiet, a very quiet voice, with the most restrained manner possible, what she was doing with the paper— she turned around as if she had been caught stealing, and looked quite angry—asked me why I should frighten her so!

Then she said that the paper stained everything it touched, that she had found   165
yellow smooches on all my clothes and John's, and she wished we would be more careful!

Did not that sound innocent? But I know she was studying that pattern, and I am determined that nobody shall find it out but myself!

Life is very much more exciting now than it used to be. You see I have something more to expect, to look forward to, to watch. I really do eat better, and am more quiet than I was.

John is so pleased to see me improve! He laughed a little the other day, and said I seemed to be flourishing in spite of my wallpaper.

I turned it off with a laugh. I had no intention of telling him it was *because* of the wallpaper—he would make fun of me. He might even want to take me away.

I don't want to leave now until I have found it out. There is a week more, and   170
I think that will be enough.

I'm feeling ever so much better! I don't sleep much at night, for it is so interesting to watch developments; but I sleep a good deal in the daytime.

In the daytime it is tiresome and perplexing.

There are always new shoots on the fungus, and new shades of yellow all over it. I cannot keep count of them, though I have tried conscientiously.

It is the strangest yellow, that wallpaper! It makes me think of all the yellow things I ever saw—not beautiful ones like buttercups, but old foul, bad yellow things.

175   But there is something else about that paper—the smell! I noticed it the moment we came into the room, but with so much air and sun it was not bad. Now we have had a week of fog and rain, and whether the windows are open or not, the smell is here.

It creeps all over the house.

I find it hovering in the dining-room, skulking in the parlor, hiding in the hall, lying in wait for me on the stairs.

It gets into my hair.

Even when I go to ride, if I turn my head suddenly and surprise it—there is that smell!

180   Such a peculiar odor, too! I have spent hours in trying to analyze it, to find what it smelled like.

It is not bad—at first, and very gentle, but quite the subtlest, most enduring odor I ever met.

In this damp weather it is awful, I wake up in the night and find it hanging over me.

It used to disturb me at first. I thought seriously of burning the house—to reach the smell.

But now I am used to it. The only thing I can think of that it is like is the *color* of the paper! A yellow smell.

185   There is a very funny mark on this wall, low down, near the mop-board. A streak that runs round the room. It goes behind every piece of furniture, except the bed, a long, straight, even *smooch*, as if it had been rubbed over and over.

I wonder how it was done and who did it, and what they did it for. Round and round and round—round and round and round!—it makes me dizzy!

I really have discovered something at last.

Through watching so much at night, when it changes so, I have finally found out.

The front pattern *does* move—and no wonder! The woman behind shakes it!

190   Sometimes I think there are a great many women behind, and sometimes only one, and she crawls around fast, and her crawling shakes it all over.

Then in the very bright spots she keeps still, and in the very shady spots she just takes hold of the bars and shakes them hard.

And she is all the time trying to climb through. But nobody could climb through that pattern—it strangles so; I think that is why it has so many heads.

They get through, and then the pattern strangles them off and turns them upside down, and makes their eyes white!

If those heads were covered or taken off it would not be half so bad.

195   I think that woman gets out in the daytime!

And I'll tell you why—privately—I've seen her!

I can see her out of every one of my windows!

It is the same woman, I know, for she is always creeping, and most women do not creep by daylight.

I see her in that long shaded lane, creeping up and down. I see her in those dark grape arbors, creeping all around the garden.

I see her on that long road under the trees, creeping along, and when a carriage 200
comes she hides under the blackberry vines.

I don't blame her a bit. It must be very humiliating to be caught creeping by
daylight!

I always lock the door when I creep by daylight. I can't do it at night, for I know
John would suspect something at once.

And John is so queer now, that I don't want to irritate him. I wish he would
take another room! Besides, I don't want anybody to get that woman out at night
but myself.

I often wonder if I could see her out of all the windows at once.

But, turn as fast as I can, I can only see out of one at one time. 205

And though I always see her, she *may* be able to creep faster than I can turn!

I have watched her sometimes away off in the open country, creeping as fast as a
cloud shadow in a high wind.

If only that top pattern could be gotten off from the under one! I mean to try it, little
by little.

I have found out another funny thing, but I shan't tell it this time! It does not
do to trust people too much.

There are only two more days to get this paper off, and I believe John is beginning 210
to notice. I don't like the look in his eyes.

And I heard him ask Jennie a lot of professional questions about me. She had a
very good report to give.

She said I slept a good deal in the daytime.

John knows I don't sleep very well at night, for all I'm so quiet!

He asked me all sorts of questions, too, and pretended to be very loving and kind.

As if I couldn't see through him! 215

Still, I don't wonder he acts so, sleeping under this paper for three months.

It only interests me, but I feel sure John and Jennie are secretly affected by it.

*   *   *

Hurrah! This is the last day, but it is enough. John is to stay in town over night, and
won't be out until this evening.

Jennie wanted to sleep with me—the sly thing! But I told her I should undoubtedly
rest better for a night all alone.

That was clever, for really I wasn't alone a bit! As soon as it was moon-light 220
and that poor thing began to crawl and shake the pattern, I got up and ran to
help her.

I pulled and she shook, I shook and she pulled, and before morning we had peeled
off yards of that paper.

A strip about as high as my head and half around the room.

And then when the sun came and that awful pattern began to laugh at me,
I declared I would finish it to-day!

We go away to-morrow, and they are moving all my furniture down again to leave
things as they were before.

225   Jennie looked at the wall in amazement, but I told her merrily that I did it out of pure spite at the vicious thing.

She laughed and said she wouldn't mind doing it herself, but I must not get tired.

How she betrayed herself that time!

But I am here, and no person touches this paper but me,—not *alive*!

She tried to get me out of the room—it was too patent! But I said it was so quiet and empty and clean now that I believed I would lie down again and sleep all I could; and not to wake me even for dinner—I would call when I woke.

230   So now she is gone, and the servants are gone, and the things are gone, and there is nothing left but that great bedstead nailed down, with the canvas mattress we found on it.

We shall sleep downstairs to-night, and take the boat home tomorrow.

I quite enjoy the room, now it is bare again.

How those children did tear about here!

This bedstead is fairly gnawed!

235   But I must get to work.

I have locked the door and thrown the key down into the front path.

I don't want to go out, and I don't want to have anybody come in, till John comes.

I want to astonish him.

I've got a rope up here that even Jennie did not find. If that woman does get out, and tries to get away, I can tie her!

240   But I forgot I could not reach far without anything to stand on!

This bed will *not* move!

I tried to lift and push it until I was lame, and then I got so angry I bit off a little piece at one corner—but it hurt my teeth.

Then I peeled off all the paper I could reach standing on the floor. It sticks horribly and the pattern just enjoys it! All those strangled heads and bulbous eyes and waddling fungus growths just shriek with derision!

I am getting angry enough to do something desperate. To jump out of the window would be admirable exercise, but the bars are too strong even to try.

245   Besides I wouldn't do it. Of course not. I know well enough that a step like that is improper and might be misconstrued.

I don't like to *look* out of the windows even—there are so many of those creeping women, and they creep so fast.

I wonder if they come out of that wallpaper as I did?

But I am securely fastened now by my well-hidden rope—you don't get *me* out in the road there!

I suppose I shall have to get back behind the pattern when it comes night, and that is hard!

250   It is so pleasant to be out in this great room and creep around as I please!

I don't want to go outside. I won't, even if Jennie asks me to.

For outside you have to creep on the ground, and everything is green instead of yellow.

But here I can creep smoothly on the floor, and my shoulder just fits in that long smooch around the wall, so I cannot lose my way.

Why there's John at the door!

It is no use, young man, you can't open it!   255

How he does call and pound!

Now he's crying for an axe.

It would be a shame to break down that beautiful door!

"John dear!" said I in the gentlest voice, "the key is down by the front steps, under a plantain leaf!"

That silenced him for a few moments.   260

Then he said—very quietly indeed, "Open the door, my darling!"

"I can't," said I. "The key is down by the front door under a plantain leaf!"

And then I said it again, several times, very gently and slowly, and said it so often that he had to go and see, and he got it of course, and came in. He stopped short by the door.

"What is the matter?" he cried. "For God's sake, what are you doing!"

I kept on creeping just the same, but I looked at him over my shoulder.   265

"I've got out at last," said I, "in spite of you and Jane. And I've pulled off most of the paper, so you can't put me back!"

Now why should that man have fainted? But he did, and right across my path by the wall, so that I had to creep over him every time!

Reading and Reacting

1. The story's narrator, who has recently had a baby, is suffering from what her husband, a doctor, calls "temporary nervous depression—a slight hysterical tendency" (par. 10). How accurate is his diagnosis? Explain.

2. What do the following comments reveal about the narrator's situation: "John laughs at me, of course, but one expects that in marriage" (par. 5); "I must put this away,—he hates to have me write a word" (par. 39); "He laughs at me so about this wallpaper" (par. 51); "Then he took me in his arms and called me a blessed little goose" (par. 56)?

3. What is it about the house, the grounds, and her room that upsets the narrator?

4. What images and figures of speech does the narrator use to describe the wallpaper? To what extent do you think her descriptions are accurate? Which images do you think she sees, and which ones do you think she imagines?

5. How does the narrator's mood change as the story progresses? How does her language change?

6. How would you characterize the narrator's tone? Does she sound depressed? delusional? hysterical?

7. How do you explain the story's very short paragraphs? How do these short paragraphs help you to understand the narrator's mental state?

8. Study the story's punctuation—in particular, its use of dashes, question marks, and exclamation points. What does this use of punctuation contribute to the story?

9. JOURNAL ENTRY Do you think a present-day woman would respond differently to such advice from her husband or doctor? Explain.

10. CRITICAL PERSPECTIVE "The Yellow Wallpaper" was originally seen by some readers as a ghost story and was anthologized as such. More recently, critics have tended to interpret

the story from a feminist perspective, focusing on the way in which the nameless narrator is victimized by the men around her and by the values of the Victorian society they uphold. In the essay "An Unnecessary Maze of Sign-Reading," Mary Jacobus concludes that the overwhelmingly feminist perspective of recent criticism, though certainly valuable and enlightening, has overlooked other promising critical possibilities—for example, "the Gothic and uncanny elements present in the text."

If you were teaching "The Yellow Wallpaper," would you present it as a feminist story or as a chilling gothic ghost story? Do you think interpreting the story as a gothic horror tale precludes a feminist reading, or do you see the two interpretations as compatible?

Related Works: "The Story of an Hour" (p. 201), "Cinderella" (p. 700), "The Secretary Chant" (p. 767), "Daddy" (p. 772), *A Doll House* (p. 1113), *Trifles* (p. 1604)

AP Images/David Pickoff

TIM O'BRIEN (1946–   ) is sometimes described as a writer whose books are on the short list of essential fiction about the Vietnam War. After graduating *summa cum laude* from Macalester College in 1968, O'Brien was immediately drafted into the United States Army and sent to Vietnam, where he served with the 198th Infantry Brigade. He was promoted to sergeant and awarded a Purple Heart after receiving a shrapnel wound in a battle near My Lai. In 1970, after his discharge from the army, he attended Harvard graduate school to study government. He worked as a reporter for the *Washington Post* before pursuing a full-time career as a writer.

O'Brien's plots focus on danger, violence, courage, endurance, despair, and other topics often associated with war fiction, but he treats these topics with an emphasis on the contemporary dilemmas faced by those who may be unwilling participants in an unpopular war. O'Brien calls *If I Die in a Combat Zone, Box Me Up and Ship Me Home* (1979) a memoir because it relates his war experiences as a naive young college graduate who suddenly finds himself facing bullets and land mines rather than sitting behind a desk. *Northern Lights* (1975) concentrates on the wilderness survival experiences of two brothers, one of whom has just returned from the Vietnam War. A fantastic daydream of an American soldier, *Going after Cacciato* (1978) won a National Book Award. *The Things They Carried* (1990) is a quasi-fictional collection of interrelated stories that deal with a single platoon. *The Vietnam in Me* (1994) emphasizes the destructive effects of war on a soldier, even after he has returned home, and *In the Lake of the Woods* (1994) tells a dramatic story of a couple missing in Minnesota. O'Brien's most recent books are *Tomcat in Love* (1998) and *July, July* (2002).

Cultural Context United States involvement in the Vietnam War lasted from the early 1960s until the mid 1970s. By the war's end, more than 47,000 Americans had been killed in action, nearly 11,000 had died of other causes, and more than 303,000 had been wounded. Estimates of South Vietnamese army casualties range from 185,000 to 225,000 killed and 500,000 to 570,000 wounded. The North Vietnamese and the Viet Cong, the guerrilla force that fought against South Vietnam and the United States, lost about 900,000 troops. In addition, more than 1 million North and South Vietnamese civilians were killed during the war. In 1975, North Vietnam's communist forces defeated the South, and in 1976, North and South Vietnam reunified to form the Socialist Republic of Vietnam. By 2000, Vietnam had established diplomatic relations with most other nations around the world.

The Things They Carried (1986)

First Lieutenant Jimmy Cross carried letters from a girl named Martha, a junior at Mount Sebastian College in New Jersey. They were not love letters, but Lieutenant Cross was hoping, so he kept them folded in plastic at the bottom of his rucksack. In the late afternoon, after a day's march, he would dig his foxhole, wash his hands under a canteen, unwrap the letters, hold them with the tips of his fingers, and spend the last hour of light pretending. He would imagine romantic camping trips into the White Mountains in New Hampshire. He would sometimes taste the envelope flaps, knowing her tongue had been there. More than anything, he wanted Martha to love him as he loved her, but the letters were mostly chatty, elusive on the matter of love. She was a virgin, he was almost sure. She was an English major at Mount Sebastian, and she wrote beautifully about her professors and roommates and midterm exams, about her respect for Chaucer and her great affection for Virginia Woolf. She often quoted lines of poetry; she never mentioned the war, except to say, Jimmy, take care of yourself. The letters weighed ten ounces. They were signed "Love, Martha," but Lieutenant Cross understood that "Love" was only a way of signing and did not mean what he sometimes pretended it meant. At dusk, he would carefully return the letters to his rucksack. Slowly, a bit distracted, he would get up and move among his men, checking the perimeter, then at full dark he would return to his hole and watch the night and wonder if Martha was a virgin.

The things they carried were largely determined by necessity. Among the necessities or near necessities were P-38 can openers, pocket knives, heat tabs, wrist watches, dog tags, mosquito repellent, chewing gum, candy, cigarettes, salt tablets, packets of Kool-Aid, lighters, matches, sewing kits, Military Payment Certificates, C rations, and two or three canteens of water. Together, these items weighed between fifteen and twenty pounds, depending upon a man's habits or rate of metabolism. Henry Dobbins, who was a big man, carried extra rations; he was especially fond of canned peaches in heavy syrup over pound cake. Dave Jensen, who practiced field hygiene, carried a toothbrush, dental floss, and several hotel-size bars of soap he'd stolen on R&R in Sydney, Australia. Ted Lavender, who was scared, carried tranquilizers until he was shot in the head outside the village of Than Khe in mid-April. By necessity, and because it was SOP,[1] they all carried steel helmets that weighed five pounds including the liner and camouflage cover. They carried the standard fatigue jackets and trousers. Very few carried underwear. On their feet they carried jungle boots—2.1 pounds—and Dave Jensen carried three pairs of socks and a can of Dr. Scholl's foot powder as a precaution against trench foot. Until he was shot, Ted Lavender carried six or seven ounces of premium dope, which for him was a necessity. Mitchell Sanders, the RTO,[2] carried condoms. Norman Bowker carried a diary. Rat Kiley carried comic books. Kiowa, a devout Baptist, carried an illustrated New Testament that had been presented to him by his father, who taught Sunday school in Oklahoma City, Oklahoma. As a hedge

---

[1] *SOP:* Standard operating procedure.
[2] *RTO:* Radio telephone operator.

against bad times, however, Kiowa also carried his grandmother's distrust of the white man, his grandfather's old hunting hatchet. Necessity dictated. Because the land was mined and booby-trapped, it was SOP for each man to carry a steel-centered, nylon-covered flak jacket, which weighed 6.7 pounds, but which on hot days seemed much heavier. Because you could die so quickly, each man carried at least one large compress bandage, usually in the helmet band for easy access. Because the nights were cold, and because the monsoons were wet, each carried a green plastic poncho that could be used as a raincoat or ground sheet or makeshift tent. With its quilted liner, the poncho weighed almost two pounds, but it was worth every ounce. In April, for instance, when Ted Lavender was shot, they used his poncho to wrap him up, then to carry him across the paddy, then to lift him into the chopper that took him away.

They were called legs or grunts.

To carry something was to "hump" it, as when Lieutenant Jimmy Cross humped his love for Martha up the hills and through the swamps. In its intransitive form, "to hump" meant "to walk," or "to march," but it implied burdens far beyond the intransitive.

5   Almost everyone humped photographs. In his wallet, Lieutenant Cross carried two photographs of Martha. The first was a Kodachrome snapshot signed "Love," though he knew better. She stood against a brick wall. Her eyes were gray and neutral, her lips slightly open as she stared straight-on at the camera. At night, sometimes, Lieutenant Cross wondered who had taken the picture, because he knew she had boyfriends, because he loved her so much, and because he could see the shadow of the picture taker spreading out against the brick wall. The second photograph had been clipped from the 1968 Mount Sebastian yearbook. It was an action shot—women's volleyball—and Martha was bent horizontal to the floor, reaching, the palms of her hands in sharp focus, the tongue taut, the expression frank and competitive. There was no visible sweat. She wore white gym shorts. Her legs, he thought, were almost certainly the legs of a virgin, dry and without hair, the left knee cocked and carrying her entire weight, which was just over one hundred pounds. Lieutenant Cross remembered touching that left knee. A dark theater, he remembered, and the movie was *Bonnie and Clyde*, and Martha wore a tweed skirt, and during the final scene, when he touched her knee, she turned and looked at him in a sad, sober way that made him pull his hand back, but he would always remember the feel of the tweed skirt and the knee beneath it and the sound of the gunfire that killed Bonnie and Clyde, how embarrassing it was, how slow and oppressive. He remembered kissing her good night at the dorm door. Right then, he thought, he should've done something brave. He should've carried her up the stairs to her room and tied her to the bed and touched that left knee all night long. He should've risked it. Whenever he looked at the photographs, he thought of new things he should've done.

What they carried was partly a function of rank, partly of field specialty.

As a first lieutenant and platoon leader, Jimmy Cross carried a compass, maps, code books, binoculars, and a .45-caliber pistol that weighed 2.9 pounds fully loaded. He carried a strobe light and the responsibility for the lives of his men.

As an RTO, Mitchell Sanders carried the PRC-25 radio, a killer, twenty-six pounds with its battery.

As a medic, Rat Kiley carried a canvas satchel filled with morphine and plasma and malaria tablets and surgical tape and comic books and all the things a medic must carry, including M&M's for especially bad wounds, for a total weight of nearly twenty pounds.

As a big man, therefore a machine gunner, Henry Dobbins carried the M-60,   10 which weighed twenty-three pounds unloaded, but which was almost always loaded. In addition, Dobbins carried between ten and fifteen pounds of ammunition draped in belts across his chest and shoulders.

As PFCs or Spec 4s, most of them were common grunts and carried the standard M-16 gas-operated assault rifle. The weapon weighed 7.5 pounds unloaded, 8.2 pounds with its full twenty-round magazine. Depending on numerous factors, such as topography and psychology, the riflemen carried anywhere from twelve to twenty magazines, usually in cloth bandoliers, adding on another 8.4 pounds at minimum, fourteen pounds at maximum. When it was available, they also carried M-16 maintenance gear—rods and steel brushes and swabs and tubes of LSA oil—all of which weighed about a pound. Among the grunts, some carried the M-79 grenade launcher, 5.9 pounds unloaded, a reasonably light weapon except for the ammunition, which was heavy. A single round weighed ten ounces. The typical load was twenty-five rounds. But Ted Lavender, who was scared, carried thirty-four rounds when he was shot and killed outside Than Khe, and he went down under an exceptional burden, more than twenty pounds of ammunition, plus the flak jacket and helmet and rations and water and toilet paper and tranquilizers and all the rest, plus the unweighed fear. He was dead weight. There was no twitching or flopping. Kiowa, who saw it happen, said it was like watching a rock fall, or a big sandbag or something—just boom, then down—not like the movies where the dead guy rolls around and does fancy spins and goes ass over teakettle—not like that, Kiowa said, the poor bastard just flat-fuck fell. Boom. Down. Nothing else. It was a bright morning in mid-April. Lieutenant Cross felt the pain. He blamed himself. They stripped off Lavender's canteens and ammo, all the heavy things, and Rat Kiley said the obvious, the guy's dead, and Mitchell Sanders used his radio to report one U.S. KIA and to request a chopper. Then they wrapped Lavender in his poncho. They carried him out to a dry paddy, established security, and sat smoking the dead man's dope until the chopper came. Lieutenant Cross kept to himself. He pictured Martha's smooth young face, thinking he loved her more than anything, more than his men, and now Ted Lavender was dead because he loved her so much and could not stop thinking about her. When the dust-off arrived, they carried Lavender aboard. Afterward they burned Than Khe. They marched until dusk, then dug their holes, and that night Kiowa kept explaining how you had to be there, how fast it was, how the poor guy just dropped like so much concrete. Boom-down, he said. Like cement.

*   *   *

In addition to the three standard weapons—the M-60, M-16, and M-79—they carried whatever presented itself, or whatever seemed appropriate as a means of killing or staying alive. They carried catch-as-catch-can. At various times, in various situations, they carried M-14s and CAR-15s and Swedish Ks and grease guns and captured AK-47s and Chi-Coms and RPGs and Simonov carbines and black-market Uzis and .38-caliber Smith & Wesson handguns and 66 mm LAWs and shotguns and silencers and blackjacks and bayonets and C-4 plastic explosives. Lee Strunk carried a slingshot; a weapon of last resort, he called it. Mitchell Sanders carried brass knuckles. Kiowa carried his grandfather's feathered hatchet. Every third or fourth man carried a Claymore antipersonnel mine—3.5 pounds with its firing device. They all carried fragmentation grenades—fourteen ounces each. They all carried at least one M-18 colored smoke grenade—twenty-four ounces. Some carried CS or tear-gas grenades. Some carried white-phosphorus grenades. They carried all they could bear, and then some, including a silent awe for the terrible power of the things they carried.

In the first week of April, before Lavender died, Lieutenant Jimmy Cross received a good-luck charm from Martha. It was a simple pebble, an ounce at most. Smooth to the touch, it was a milky-white color with flecks of orange and violet, oval-shaped, like a miniature egg. In the accompanying letter, Martha wrote that she had found the pebble on the Jersey shoreline, precisely where the land touched water at high tide, where things came together but also separated. It was this separate-but-together quality, she wrote, that had inspired her to pick up the pebble and to carry it in her breast pocket for several days, where it seemed weightless, and then to send it through the mail, by air, as a token of her truest feelings for him. Lieutenant Cross found this romantic. But he wondered what her truest feelings were, exactly, and what she meant by separate-but-together. He wondered how the tides and waves had come into play on that afternoon along the Jersey shoreline when Martha saw the pebble and bent down to rescue it from geology. He imagined bare feet. Martha was a poet, with the poet's sensibilities, and her feet would be brown and bare, the toenails unpainted, the eyes chilly and somber like the ocean in March, and though it was painful, he wondered who had been with her that afternoon. He imagined a pair of shadows moving along the strip of sand where things came together but also separated. It was phantom jealousy, he knew, but he couldn't help himself. He loved her so much. On the march, through the hot days of early April, he carried the pebble in his mouth, turning it with his tongue, tasting sea salts and moisture. His mind wandered. He had difficulty keeping his attention on the war. On occasion he would yell at his men to spread out the column, to keep their eyes open, but then he would slip away into daydreams, just pretending, walking barefoot along the Jersey shore, with Martha, carrying nothing. He would feel himself rising. Sun and waves and gentle winds, all love and lightness.

What they carried varied by mission.

15 When a mission took them to the mountains, they carried mosquito netting, machetes, canvas tarps, and extra bug juice.

If a mission seemed especially hazardous, or if it involved a place they knew to be bad, they carried everything they could. In certain heavily mined AOs,[3] where the

---

[3] *AOs:* Areas of operation.

land was dense with Toe Poppers and Bouncing Betties, they took turns humping a twenty-eight-pound mine detector. With its headphones and big sensing plate, the equipment was a stress on the lower back and shoulders, awkward to handle, often useless because of the shrapnel in the earth, but they carried it anyway, partly for safety, partly for the illusion of safety.

On ambush, or other night missions, they carried peculiar little odds and ends. Kiowa always took along his New Testament and a pair of moccasins for silence. Dave Jensen carried night-sight vitamins high in carotin. Lee Strunk carried his slingshot; ammo, he claimed, would never be a problem. Rat Kiley carried brandy and M&M's. Until he was shot, Ted Lavender carried the starlight scope, which weighed 6.3 pounds with its aluminum carrying case. Henry Dobbins carried his girlfriend's panty-hose wrapped around his neck as a comforter. They all carried ghosts. When dark came, they would move out single file across the meadows and paddies to their ambush coordinates, where they would quietly set up the Claymores and lie down and spend the night waiting.

Other missions were more complicated and required special equipment. In mid-April, it was their mission to search out and destroy the elaborate tunnel complexes in the Than Khe area south of Chu Lai. To blow the tunnels, they carried one-pound blocks of pentrite high explosives, four blocks to a man, sixty-eight pounds in all. They carried wiring, detonators, and battery-powered clackers. Dave Jensen carried earplugs. Most often, before blowing the tunnels, they were ordered by higher command to search them, which was considered bad news, but by and large they just shrugged and carried out orders. Because he was a big man, Henry Dobbins was excused from tunnel duty. The others would draw numbers. Before Lavender died there were seventeen men in the platoon, and whoever drew the number seventeen would strip off his gear and crawl in head first with a flashlight and Lieutenant Cross's .45-caliber pistol. The rest of them would fan out as security. They would sit down or kneel, not facing the hole, listening to the ground beneath them, imagining cobwebs and ghosts, whatever was down there— the tunnel walls squeezing in—how the flashlight seemed impossibly heavy in the hand and how it was tunnel vision in the very strictest sense, compression in all ways, even time, and how you had to wiggle in—ass and elbows—a swallowed-up feeling—and how you found yourself worrying about odd things—will your flashlight go dead? Do rats carry rabies? If you screamed, how far would the sound carry? Would your buddies hear it? Would they have the courage to drag you out? In some respects, though not many, the waiting was worse than the tunnel itself. Imagination was a killer.

On April 16, when Lee Strunk drew the number seventeen, he laughed and muttered something and went down quickly. The morning was hot and very still. Not good, Kiowa said. He looked at the tunnel opening, then out across a dry paddy toward the village of Than Khe. Nothing moved. No clouds or birds or people. As they waited, the men smoked and drank Kool-Aid, not talking much, feeling sympathy for Lee Strunk but also feeling the luck of the draw. You win some, you lose some, said Mitchell Sanders, and sometimes you settle for a rain check. It was a tired line and no one laughed.

Henry Dobbins ate a tropical chocolate bar. Ted Lavender popped a tranquilizer and went off to pee.

20

After five minutes, Lieutenant Jimmy Cross moved to the tunnel, leaned down, and examined the darkness. Trouble, he thought—a cave-in maybe. And then suddenly, without willing it, he was thinking about Martha. The stresses and fractures, the quick collapse, the two of them buried alive under all that weight. Dense, crushing love. Kneeling, watching the hole, he tried to concentrate on Lee Strunk and the war, all the dangers, but his love was too much for him, he felt paralyzed, he wanted to sleep inside her lungs and breathe her blood and be smothered. He wanted her to be a virgin and not a virgin, all at once. He wanted to know her. Intimate secrets—why poetry? Why so sad? Why that grayness in her eyes? Why so alone? Not lonely, just alone—riding her bike across campus or sitting off by herself in the cafeteria. Even dancing, she danced alone—and it was the aloneness that filled him with love. He remembered telling her that one evening. How she nodded and looked away. And how, later, when he kissed her, she received the kiss without returning it, her eyes wide open, not afraid, not a virgin's eyes, just flat and uninvolved.

Lieutenant Cross gazed at the tunnel. But he was not there. He was buried with Martha under the white sand at the Jersey shore. They were pressed together, and the pebble in his mouth was her tongue. He was smiling. Vaguely, he was aware of how quiet the day was, the sullen paddies, yet he could not bring himself to worry about matters of security. He was beyond that. He was just a kid at war, in love. He was twenty-two years old. He couldn't help it.

A few moments later Lee Strunk crawled out of the tunnel. He came up grinning, filthy but alive. Lieutenant Cross nodded and closed his eyes while the others clapped Strunk on the back and made jokes about rising from the dead.

Worms, Rat Kiley said. Right out of the grave. Fuckin' zombie.

25   The men laughed. They all felt great relief.

Spook City, said Mitchell Sanders.

Lee Strunk made a funny ghost sound, a kind of moaning, yet very happy, and right then, when Strunk made that high happy moaning sound, when he went *Ahhooooo*, right then Ted Lavender was shot in the head on his way back from peeing. He lay with his mouth open. The teeth were broken. There was a swollen black bruise under his left eye. The cheekbone was gone. Oh shit, Rat Kiley said, the guy's dead. The guy's dead, he kept saying, which seemed profound—the guy's dead. I mean really.

The things they carried were determined to some extent by superstition. Lieutenant Cross carried his good-luck pebble. Dave Jensen carried a rabbit's foot. Norman Bowker, otherwise a very gentle person, carried a thumb that had been presented to him as a gift by Mitchell Sanders. The thumb was dark brown, rubbery to the touch, and weighed four ounces at most. It had been cut from a VC corpse, a boy of fifteen or sixteen. They'd found him at the bottom of an irrigation ditch, badly burned, flies in his mouth and eyes. The boy wore black shorts and sandals. At the time of his death he had been carrying a pouch of rice, a rifle, and three magazines of ammunition.

You want my opinion, Mitchell Sanders said, there's a definite moral here.

30   He put his hand on the dead boy's wrist. He was quiet for a time, as if counting a pulse, then he patted the stomach, almost affectionately, and used Kiowa's hunting hatchet to remove the thumb.

Henry Dobbins asked what the moral was.

Moral?

You know. *Moral.*

Sanders wrapped the thumb in toilet paper and handed it across to Norman Bowker. There was no blood. Smiling, he kicked the boy's head, watched the flies scatter, and said, It's like with that old TV show—Paladin. Have gun, will travel.

Henry Dobbins thought about it.

Yeah, well, he finally said. I don't see no moral.

There it *is*, man.

Fuck off.

They carried USO stationery and pencils and pens. They carried Sterno, safety pins, trip flares, signal flares, spools of wire, razor blades, chewing tobacco, liberated joss sticks and statuettes of the smiling Buddha, candles, grease pencils, *The Stars and Stripes*, fingernail clippers, Psy Ops leaflets, bush hats, bolos, and much more. Twice a week, when the resupply choppers came in, they carried hot chow in green Mermite cans and large canvas bags filled with iced beer and soda pop. They carried plastic water containers, each with a two-gallon capacity. Mitchell Sanders carried a set of starched tiger fatigues for special occasions. Henry Dobbins carried Black Flag insecticide. Dave Jensen carried empty sandbags that could be filled at night for added protection. Lee Strunk carried tanning lotion. Some things they carried in common. Taking turns, they carried the big PRC-77 scrambler radio, which weighed thirty pounds with its battery. They shared the weight of memory. They took up what others could no longer bear. Often, they carried each other, the wounded or weak. They carried infections. They carried chess sets, basketballs, Vietnamese-English dictionaries, insignia of rank, Bronze Stars and Purple Hearts, plastic cards imprinted with the Code of Conduct. They carried diseases, among them malaria and dysentery. They carried lice and ringworm and leeches and paddy algae and various rots and molds. They carried the land itself—Vietnam, the place, the soil—a powdery orange-red dust that covered their boots and fatigues and faces. They carried the sky. The whole atmosphere, they carried it, the humidity, the monsoons, the stink of fungus and decay, all of it, they carried gravity. They moved like mules. By daylight they took sniper fire, at night they were mortared, but it was not battle, it was just the endless march, village to village, without purpose, nothing won or lost. They marched for the sake of the march. They plodded along slowly, dumbly, leaning forward against the heat, unthinking, all blood and bone, simple grunts, soldiering with their legs, toiling up the hills and down into the paddies and across the rivers and up again and down, just humping, one step and then the next and then another, but no volition, no will, because it was automatic, it was anatomy, and the war was entirely a matter of posture and carriage, the hump was everything, a kind of inertia, a kind of emptiness, a dullness of desire and intellect and conscience and hope and human sensibility. Their principles were in their feet. Their calculations were biological. They had no sense of strategy or mission. They searched the villages without knowing what to look for, not caring, kicking over jars of rice, frisking children and old men, blowing tunnels, sometimes setting fires and sometimes not, then forming up and moving on to the next village, then other villages, where it would always be the same. They carried their own lives. The pressures were enormous.

35

In the heat of early afternoon, they would remove their helmets and flak jackets, walking bare, which was dangerous but which helped ease the strain. They would often discard things along the route of march. Purely for comfort, they would throw away rations, blow their Claymores and grenades, no matter, because by nightfall the resupply choppers would arrive with more of the same, then a day or two later still more, fresh watermelons and crates of ammunition and sunglasses and woolen sweaters—the resources were stunning—sparklers for the Fourth of July, colored eggs for Easter. It was the great American war chest—the fruits of science, the smokestacks, the canneries, the arsenals at Hartford, the Minnesota forests, the machine shops, the vast fields of corn and wheat—they carried like freight trains; they carried it on their backs and shoulders—and for all the ambiguities of Vietnam, all the mysteries and unknowns, there was at least the single abiding certainty that they would never be at a loss for things to carry.

                                   *   *   *

40   After the chopper took Lavender away, Lieutenant Jimmy Cross led his men into the village of Than Khe. They burned everything. They shot chickens and dogs, they trashed the village well, they called in artillery and watched the wreckage, then they marched for several hours through the hot afternoon, and then at dusk, while Kiowa explained how Lavender died, Lieutenant Cross found himself trembling.

He tried not to cry. With his entrenching tool, which weighed five pounds, he began digging a hole in the earth.

He felt shame. He hated himself. He had loved Martha more than his men, and as a consequence Lavender was now dead, and this was something he would have to carry like a stone in his stomach for the rest of the war.

All he could do was dig. He used his entrenching tool like an ax, slashing, feeling both love and hate, and then later, when it was full dark, he sat at the bottom of his foxhole and wept. It went on for a long while. In part, he was grieving for Ted Lavender, but mostly it was for Martha, and for himself, because she belonged to another world, which was not quite real, and because she was a junior at Mount Sebastian College in New Jersey, a poet and a virgin and uninvolved, and because he realized she did not love him and never would.

Like cement, Kiowa whispered in the dark. I swear to God—boom-down. Not a word.
45   I've heard this, said Norman Bowker.

A pisser, you know? Still zipping himself up. Zapped while zipping.

All right, fine. That's enough.

Yeah, but you had to see it, the guy just—

I *heard*, man. Cement. So why not shut the fuck *up*?
50   Kiowa shook his head sadly and glanced over at the hole where Lieutenant Jimmy Cross sat watching the night. The air was thick and wet. A warm, dense fog had settled over the paddies and there was the stillness that precedes rain.

After a time Kiowa sighed.

One thing for sure, he said. The Lieutenant's in some deep hurt. I mean that crying jag—the way he was carrying on—it wasn't fake or anything, it was real heavy-duty hurt. The man cares.

Sure, Norman Bowker said.

Say what you want, the man does care.

We all got problems. 55

Not Lavender.

No, I guess not, Bowker said. Do me a favor, though.

Shut up?

That's a smart Indian. Shut up.

Shrugging, Kiowa pulled off his boots. He wanted to say more, just to lighten up 60 his sleep, but instead he opened his New Testament and arranged it beneath his head as a pillow. The fog made things seem hollow and unattached. He tried not to think about Ted Lavender, but then he was thinking how fast it was, no drama, down and dead, and how it was hard to feel anything except surprise. It seemed un-Christian. He wished he could find some great sadness, or even anger, but the emotion wasn't there and he couldn't make it happen. Mostly he felt pleased to be alive. He liked the smell of the New Testament under his cheek, the leather and ink and paper and glue, whatever the chemicals were. He liked hearing the sounds of night. Even his fatigue, it felt fine, the stiff muscles and the prickly awareness of his own body, a floating feeling. He enjoyed not being dead. Lying there, Kiowa admired Lieutenant Jimmy Cross's capacity for grief. He wanted to share the man's pain, he wanted to care as Jimmy Cross cared. And yet when he closed his eyes, all he could think was Boom-down, and all he could feel was the pleasure of having his boots off and the fog curling in around him and the damp soil and the Bible smells and the plush comfort of night.

After a moment Norman Bowker sat up in the dark.

What the hell, he said. You want to talk, *talk*. Tell it to me.

Forget it.

No, man, go on. One thing I hate, it's a silent Indian.

For the most part they carried themselves with poise, a kind of dignity. Now and 65 then, however, there were times of panic, when they squealed or wanted to squeal but couldn't, when they twitched and made moaning sounds and covered their heads and said Dear Jesus and flopped around on the earth and fired their weapons blindly and cringed and sobbed and begged for the noise to stop and went wild and made stupid promises to themselves and to God and to their mothers and fathers, hoping not to die. In different ways, it happened to all of them. Afterward, when the firing ended, they would blink and peek up. They would touch their bodies, feeling shame, then quickly hiding it. They would force themselves to stand. As if in slow motion, frame by frame, the world would take on the old logic—absolute silence, then the wind, then sunlight, then voices. It was the burden of being alive. Awkwardly, the men would reassemble themselves, first in private, then in groups, becoming soldiers again. They would repair the leaks in their eyes. They would check for casualties, call in dust-offs, light cigarettes, try to smile, clear their throats and spit and begin cleaning their weapons. After a time someone would shake his head and say, No lie, I almost shit my pants, and someone else would laugh, which meant it was bad, yes, but the guy had obviously not shit his pants, it wasn't that bad, and in any case nobody would ever do such a thing and then go ahead and talk about it. They would squint into the dense, oppressive sunlight. For a few moments, perhaps, they would fall silent, lighting a joint and tracking its passage from man to man, inhaling, holding in the humiliation. Scary stuff, one of them might say. But then someone else would grin or flick his eyebrows and say, Roger-dodger, almost cut me a new asshole, *almost.*

There were numerous such poses. Some carried themselves with a sort of wistful resignation, others with pride or stiff soldierly discipline or good humor or macho zeal. They were afraid of dying but they were even more afraid to show it.

They found jokes to tell.

They used a hard vocabulary to contain the terrible softness. *Greased,* they'd say. *Offed, lit up,*[4] *zapped while zipping.*[5] It wasn't cruelty, just stage presence. They were actors and the war came at them in 3-D. When someone died, it wasn't quite dying, because in a curious way it seemed scripted, and because they had their lines mostly memorized, irony mixed with tragedy, and because they called it by other names, as if to encyst and destroy the reality of death itself. They kicked corpses. They cut off thumbs. They talked grunt lingo. They told stories about Ted Lavender's supply of tranquilizers, how the poor guy didn't feel a thing, how incredibly tranquil he was.

There's a moral here, said Mitchell Sanders.

70 They were waiting for Lavender's chopper, smoking the dead man's dope.

The moral's pretty obvious, Sanders said, and winked. Stay away from drugs. No joke, they'll ruin your day every time.

Cute, said Henry Dobbins.

Mind-blower, get it? Talk about wiggy—nothing left, just blood and brains.

They made themselves laugh.

75 There it is, they'd say, over and over, as if the repetition itself were an act of poise, a balance between crazy and almost crazy, knowing without going. There it is, which meant be cool, let it ride, because oh yeah, man, you can't change what can't be changed, there it is, there it absolutely and positively and fucking well *is.*

They were tough.

They carried all the emotional baggage of men who might die. Grief, terror, love, longing—these were intangibles, but the intangibles had their own mass and specific gravity, they had tangible weight. They carried shameful memories. They carried the common secret of cowardice barely restrained, the instinct to run or freeze or hide, and in many respects this was the heaviest burden of all, for it could never be put down, it required perfect balance and perfect posture. They carried their reputations. They carried the soldier's greatest fear, which was the fear of blushing. Men killed, and died, because they were embarrassed not to. It was what had brought them to the war in the first place, nothing positive, no dreams of glory or honor, just to avoid the blush of dishonor. They died so as not to die of embarrassment. They crawled into tunnels and walked point and advanced under fire. Each morning, despite the unknowns, they made their legs move. They endured. They kept humping. They did

---

[4]Offed, lit up: Killed.

[5]zapped while zipping: Killed while urinating.

not submit to the obvious alternative, which was simply to close the eyes and fall. So easy, really. Go limp and tumble to the ground and let the muscles unwind and not speak and not budge until your buddies picked you up and lifted you into the chopper that would roar and dip its nose and carry you off to the world. A mere matter of falling, yet no one ever fell. It was not courage, exactly; the object was not valor. Rather, they were too frightened to be cowards.

By and large they carried these things inside, maintaining the masks of composure. They sneered at sick call. They spoke bitterly about guys who had found release by shooting off their own toes or fingers. Pussies, they'd say. Candyasses. It was fierce, mocking talk, with only a trace of envy or awe, but even so, the image played itself out behind their eyes.

They imagined the muzzle against flesh. They imagined the quick, sweet pain, then the evacuation to Japan, then a hospital with warm beds and cute geisha nurses.

They dreamed of freedom birds.   80

At night, on guard, staring into the dark, they were carried away by jumbo jets. They felt the rush of takeoff. *Gone!* they yelled. And then velocity, wings and engines, a smiling stewardess—but it was more than a plane, it was a real bird, a big sleek silver bird with feathers and talons and high screeching. They were flying. The weights fell off, there was nothing to bear. They laughed and held on tight, feeling the cold slap of wind and altitude, soaring, thinking *It's over, I'm gone!*—they were naked, they were light and free—it was all lightness, bright and fast and buoyant, light as light, a helium buzz in the brain, a giddy bubbling in the lungs as they were taken up over the clouds and the war, beyond duty, beyond gravity and mortification and global entanglements—*Sin loi!* they yelled, *I'm sorry, motherfuckers, but I'm out of it, I'm goofed, I'm on a space cruise, I'm gone!*—and it was a restful, disencumbered sensation, just riding the light waves, sailing that big silver freedom bird over the mountains and oceans, over America, over the farms and great sleeping cities and cemeteries and highways and the golden arches of McDonald's. It was flight, a kind of fleeing, a kind of falling, falling higher and higher, spinning off the edge of the earth and beyond the sun and through the vast, silent vacuum where there were no burdens and where everything weighed exactly nothing. *Gone!* they screamed, *I'm sorry but I'm gone!* And so at night, not quite dreaming, they gave themselves over to lightness, they were carried, they were purely borne.

On the morning after Ted Lavender died, First Lieutenant Jimmy Cross crouched at the bottom of his foxhole and burned Martha's letters. Then he burned the two photographs. There was a steady rain falling, which made it difficult, but he used heat tabs and Sterno to build a small fire, screening it with his body, holding the photographs over the tight blue flame with the tips of his fingers.

He realized it was only a gesture. Stupid, he thought. Sentimental, too, but mostly just stupid.

Lavender was dead. You couldn't burn the blame.

Besides, the letters were in his head. And even now, without photographs, Lieu-   85
tenant Cross could see Martha playing volleyball in her white gym shorts and yellow T-shirt. He could see her moving in the rain.

When the fire died out, Lieutenant Cross pulled his poncho over his shoulders and ate breakfast from a can.

There was no great mystery, he decided.

In those burned letters Martha had never mentioned the war, except to say, Jimmy, take care of yourself. She wasn't involved. She signed the letters "Love," but it wasn't love, and all the fine lines and technicalities did not matter.

The morning came up wet and blurry. Everything seemed part of everything else, the fog and Martha and the deepening rain.

90   It was a war, after all.

Half smiling, Lieutenant Jimmy Cross took out his maps. He shook his head hard, as if to clear it, then bent forward and began planning the day's march. In ten minutes, or maybe twenty, he would rouse the men and they would pack up and head west, where the maps showed the country to be green and inviting. They would do what they had always done. The rain might add some weight, but otherwise it would be one more day layered upon all the other days.

He was realistic about it. There was that new hardness in his stomach.

No more fantasies, he told himself.

Henceforth, when he thought about Martha, it would be only to think that she belonged elsewhere. He would shut down the daydreams. This was not Mount Sebastian, it was another world, where there were no pretty poems or midterm exams, a place where men died because of carelessness and gross stupidity. Kiowa was right. Boom-down, and you were dead, never partly dead.

95   Briefly, in the rain, Lieutenant Cross saw Martha's gray eyes gazing back at him.

He understood.

It was very sad, he thought. The things men carried inside. The things men did or felt they had to do.

He almost nodded at her, but didn't.

Instead he went back to his maps. He was now determined to perform his duties firmly and without negligence. It wouldn't help Lavender, he knew that, but from this point on he would comport himself as a soldier. He would dispose of his good-luck pebble. Swallow it, maybe, or use Lee Strunk's slingshot, or just drop it along the trail. On the march he would impose strict field discipline. He would be careful to send out flank security, to prevent straggling or bunching up, to keep his troops moving at the proper pace and at the proper interval. He would insist on clean weapons. He would confiscate the remainder of Lavender's dope. Later in the day, perhaps, he would call the men together and speak to them plainly. He would accept the blame for what had happened to Ted Lavender. He would be a man about it. He would look them in the eyes, keeping his chin level, and he would issue the new SOPs in a calm, impersonal tone of voice, an officer's voice, leaving no room for argument or discussion. Commencing immediately, he'd tell them, they would no longer abandon equipment along the route of march. They would police up their acts. They would get their shit together, and keep it together, and maintain it neatly and in good working order.

100   He would not tolerate laxity. He would show strength, distancing himself.

Among the men there would be grumbling, of course, and maybe worse, because their days would seem longer and their loads heavier, but Lieutenant Cross reminded himself that his obligation was not to be loved but to lead. He would dispense with love; it was not now a factor. And if anyone quarreled or complained, he would simply tighten his lips and arrange his shoulders in the correct command posture. He might give a curt little nod. Or he might not. He might just shrug and say Carry on, then they would saddle up and form into a column and move out toward the villages west of Than Khe.

Reading and Reacting

1. Although the setting and the events described in "The Things They Carried" are dramatic and moving, the story's tone is often flat and emotionless. Give some examples. Why do you think the narrator adopts this kind of tone?

2. Consider the different meanings of the word *carry*, which can refer to burdens abstract or concrete as well as to things carried physically or emotionally, actively or passively. Give one or two examples of each of the different senses in which O'Brien uses the word. How does his repeated use of the word enrich the story?

3. A striking characteristic of the story's style is its thorough catalogs of the concrete, tangible "things" the soldiers carry. Why do you suppose such detailed lists are included? What does what each man carries tell you about him? In a less literal, more abstract sense, what else do these men "carry"?

4. One stylistic technique O'Brien uses is intentional repetition—of phrases ("they carried"); people's names and identifying details (Martha's virginity, for example); and pieces of equipment. What effect do you think O'Brien hopes to achieve through such repetition? Is he successful?

5. Interspersed among long paragraphs crammed with detail are short one- or two-sentence paragraphs. What function do these brief paragraphs serve?

6. What role does Martha play in the story? Why does Lieutenant Cross burn her letters?

7. In paragraph 68, the narrator says of the soldiers, "They used a hard vocabulary to contain the terrible softness." What do you think he means by this? Do you think this "hard vocabulary" is necessary? How does it affect your feelings about the characters?

8. Describing Lieutenant Cross's new sense of purpose in the story's final paragraph, the narrator uses the phrase "Carry on." Do you think the use of this phrase is linked in any way to the story's other uses of the word *carry*, or do you believe it is unrelated? Explain.

9. **JOURNAL ENTRY** "The Things They Carried" is a story about war. Do you think it is an antiwar story? Why or why not?

10. **CRITICAL PERSPECTIVE** In an essay about war memoirs, Clayton W. Lewis questions O'Brien's decision to present "the nightmare [he] faced in a Vietnam rice paddy" as fiction. Lewis believes that some of O'Brien's stories "dissolve into clever artifice" and, therefore, are not as effective as actual memoirs of the Vietnam experience would be. He concludes that "for all its brilliance and emotional grounding, [the stories do not] satisfy one's appetite to hear what happened rendered as it was experienced and remembered."

Do you think Lewis has a point? Or do you think O'Brien's "artifice" communicates his emotions and experiences more effectively than a straightforward memoir could? Explain your position.

Related Works: from *The Harlem Hellfighters* (p. 145), "Dulce et Decorum Est" (p. 902), "The Soldier" (p. 904), "Facing It" (p. 906), "Terza Rima" (p. 908).

WRITING SUGGESTIONS: Style, Tone, and Language

1. In "The Things They Carried," Tim O'Brien considers his characters' emotional and psychological burdens as well as the physical "things they carry." Applying O'Brien's criteria to "The Yellow Wallpaper," write an essay in which you consider what the narrator "carries" (and what her husband "carries") and why.

2. In all four of this chapter's stories, characters are trapped. Whether trapped by social roles, by circumstance, or by their own limitations, they are unable to escape their destinies. Explain what factors imprison each character; then, consider whether—and how—each might escape.

3. Imagine The Misfit in a prison cell, relating the violent incident at the end of "A Good Man Is Hard to Find" to another prisoner—or to a member of the clergy. Would his tone be boastful? regretful? apologetic? defiant? Would he use the elaborate poetic style he sometimes uses in the story or more straightforward language? Tell his version of the incident in his own words.

4. Both "Araby" and "The Things They Carried" deal, at least in part, with infatuation. Compare and contrast the infatuations described in the two stories. How does the language used by the narrators in the two stories communicate the two characters' fascination and subsequent disillusionment?

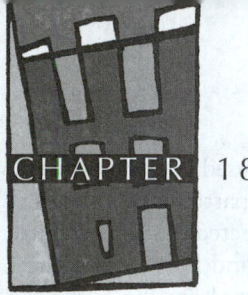

CHAPTER 18

SYMBOL, ALLEGORY, AND MYTH

Alice Walker
Monica Morgan/Getty Images

Shirley Jackson
AP Images

M. K. Hobson
Copyright M. K. Hobson 2014

Nathaniel Hawthorne
Mathew B. Brady/Bettmann/Corbis

Raymond Carver
Reg Innell/Getty Images

Symbol

A **symbol** is a person, object, action, place, or event that, in addition to its literal meaning, suggests a more complex meaning or range of meanings. **Universal** or **archetypal symbols**, such as the Old Man, the Mother, or the Grim Reaper, are so much a part of human experience that they suggest the same thing to most people. **Conventional symbols** are also likely to suggest the same thing to most people (a rose suggests love, a skull and crossbones denotes poison), provided the people share cultural and social assumptions. For this reason, conventional symbols are often used as a kind of shorthand in films and advertising, where they elicit predictable responses.

A conventional symbol, such as the stars and stripes of the American flag, can evoke powerful feelings of pride and patriotism in a group of people who share certain cultural assumptions, just as the maple leaf and the Union Jack can. Symbols used in works of literature can function in much the same way, enabling writers to convey particular emotions or messages with a high degree of predictability. Thus, spring can be expected to suggest rebirth and promise; autumn, declining years and powers; summer, youth and beauty. Because a writer expects a dark forest to evoke fear, or a rainbow to communicate hope, he or she can be quite confident in using such images to convey a particular idea or mood (provided the audience shares the writer's frame of reference).

Many symbols, however, suggest different things to different people, and different cultures may react differently to the same symbols. (In the United States, for example, an owl suggests wisdom; in India it suggests the opposite.) Thus, symbols enhance meaning, expanding the possibilities for interpretation and for readers' interaction with the text. Because they are so potentially rich, symbols have the power to open up a work of literature.

Literary Symbols

Both universal and conventional symbols can function as **literary symbols**—symbols that take on additional meanings in particular works. For instance, a watch or clock denotes time; as a conventional symbol, it suggests the passing of time; as a literary symbol in a particular work, it might also convey anything from a character's inability to recapture the past to the idea of time running out—or it might suggest something else.

Considering an object's symbolic significance can suggest a variety of ways to interpret a text. For instance, William Faulkner focuses attention on an unseen watch in a pivotal scene in "A Rose for Emily" (p. 224). The narrator first describes Emily Grierson as "a small, fat woman in black, with a thin gold chain descending to her waist and vanishing into her belt." Several sentences later, the narrator notes that Emily's visitors "could hear the invisible watch ticking at the end of the gold chain." Like these visitors, readers are drawn to the unseen watch as it ticks away. Because Emily is portrayed as a woman living in the past, readers can assume that the watch is intended to reinforce the impression that she cannot see that time (the watch) has moved on. The vivid picture of the pale, plump woman in the musty room with the watch invisibly ticking does indeed suggest that she is frozen in time and remains unaware of the progress around her. Thus, the symbol of the watch enriches both the depiction of character and the story's theme.

In "Barn Burning" (p. 335), another Faulkner story, the clock is a more complex symbol. The itinerant Snopes family is without financial security and apparently without a future. The clock the mother carries from shack to shack—"The clock inlaid with mother-of-pearl, which would not run, stopped at some fourteen minutes past two o'clock of a dead and forgotten day and time, which had been [Sarty's] mother's dowry"—is their only possession of value. The fact that the clock no longer works seems at first to suggest that time has run out for the family. On another level, the clock stands in stark contrast to Major de Spain's grand home, with its gold and glitter and Oriental rugs. Knowing that the clock was part of the mother's dowry, and that a dowry suggests a promise, readers may decide that the broken clock symbolizes lost hope. The fact that the mother still clings to the clock, however, could suggest just the opposite: her refusal to give up.

As you read, you should not try to find one exact equivalent for each symbol; that kind of search is reductive and unrewarding. Instead, consider the different meanings a symbol might suggest. Then, consider how these various interpretations enrich other elements of the story and the work as a whole.

Recognizing Symbols

When is a clock just a clock, and when is it also a symbol with a meaning (or meanings) beyond its literal significance? If a character waiting for a friend glances once at a watch to check the time, there is probably nothing symbolic about the watch or about the act of looking at it. If, however, the watch keeps appearing again and again in the story, at key moments; if the narrator devotes a good deal of time to describing it; if it is placed in a conspicuous physical location; if characters keep noticing it and commenting on its presence; if it is lost (or found) at a critical moment; if its function in some way parallels the development of plot or character (for instance, if it stops as a relationship ends or when a character dies); if the story's opening or closing paragraph focuses on the timepiece; or if the story is called "The Watch"—the watch most likely has symbolic significance. In other words, considering how an image is used, how often it is used, and when it appears will help you to determine whether or not it functions as a symbol.

Symbols expand the possible meanings of a story, thereby heightening interest and actively involving readers in the text. In "The Lottery" (p. 419), for example, the mysterious black box has symbolic significance. It is mentioned prominently and repeatedly, and it plays a pivotal role in the story's action. Of course, the black box is important on a purely literal level: it functions as a key component of the lottery. But the box has other associations as well, and it is these associations that suggest what its symbolic significance might be.

The black wooden box is very old, a relic of many past lotteries; the narrator observes that it represents tradition. It is also closed and closely guarded, suggesting mystery and uncertainty. It is shabby, "splintered badly along one side . . . and in places faded or stained," and this state of disrepair could suggest that the ritual it is part of has also deteriorated or that tradition itself has deteriorated. The box is also simple in construction and design, suggesting the primitive (and therefore perhaps outdated) nature of the ritual. Thus, this symbol encourages readers to probe the story for values and ideas, to consider and weigh the suitability of a variety of interpretations. It serves as a "hot spot" that invites questions, and the answers to these questions reinforce and enrich the story's theme.

 ## Allegory

An **allegory** communicates a doctrine, message, or moral principle by making it into a narrative in which the characters personify ideas, concepts, qualities, or other abstractions. Thus, an allegory is a story with two parallel and consistent levels of meaning—one literal and one figurative. The figurative level, which offers some moral or political lesson, is the story's main concern.

Whereas a symbol has multiple symbolic associations as well as a literal meaning, an **allegorical figure**—a character, object, place, or event in the allegory—has just one meaning within an **allegorical framework**, the set of ideas that conveys the allegory's message. (At the simplest level, for instance, one character can stand for good and another can stand for evil.) For this reason, allegorical figures do not open up a text to various interpretations the way symbols do. The allegorical figures are significant only because they represent something beyond their literal meaning in a fixed system. Because the purpose of allegory is to communicate a particular lesson, readers are not encouraged to speculate about the allegory's possible meanings; each element has only one equivalent, which readers must discover if they are to make sense of the story.

Naturally, the better a reader understands the political, religious, and literary assumptions of a writer (as well as the context of the work itself), the easier it will be to recognize the allegorical significance of his or her work. John Bunyan's *The Pilgrim's Progress*, for example, is a famous seventeenth-century allegory based on the Christian doctrine of salvation. In order to appreciate the complexity of Bunyan's work, readers would have to familiarize themselves with this doctrine.

One type of allegory, called a **beast fable**, is a short tale, usually including a moral, in which animals assume human characteristics. Aesop's fables are the best-known examples of beast fables. More recently, contemporary writers have used beast fables to satirize the political and social conditions of our time. In one such tale, "The Gentlemen of the Jungle" by the Kenyan writer Jomo Kenyatta, an elephant is allowed to put his trunk inside a man's hut during a rainstorm. Not content with keeping his trunk dry, the elephant pushes his entire body inside the hut, displacing the man. When the man protests, the elephant takes the matter to the lion, who appoints a Commission of Enquiry to settle the matter. Eventually, the man is forced not only to abandon his hut to the elephant but also to build new huts for all the animals on the Commission. Even so, the jealous animals occupy the man's new hut and begin fighting for space; while they are arguing, the man burns down the hut, animals and all. Like the tales told by Aesop, "The Gentlemen of the Jungle" has a moral: "Peace is costly," says the man as he walks away happily, "but it's worth the expense."

The following passage from Kenyatta's tale reveals how the allegorical figures work within the framework of the allegory:

> The elephant, obeying the command of his master (the lion), got busy with the other ministers to appoint a Commission of Enquiry. The following elders of the jungle were appointed to sit in the Commission: (1) Mr. Rhinoceros; (2) Mr. Buffalo; (3) Mr. Alligator; (4) The Rt. Hon. Mr. Fox to act as chairman; and (5) Mr. Leopard to act as Secretary of the Commission. On seeing the personnel, the man protested and asked if it was not necessary to include in this Commission a member from his side. But he was told that it was impossible, since no one from his side was well enough educated to understand the intricacy of jungle law.

From this excerpt, we can see that each character represents a particular idea. For example, the members of the Commission stand for bureaucratic smugness and inequity, and the man stands for the citizens who are victimized by the government. In order to fully understand the allegorical significance of each figure in this story, of course, readers would have to know something about government bureaucracies, colonialism in Africa, and possibly a specific historical event in Kenya.

Some works contain both symbolic elements *and* allegorical elements, as Nathaniel Hawthorne's "Young Goodman Brown" (p. 448) does. The names of the story's two main characters, "Goodman" and "Faith," suggest that they fit within an allegorical system of some sort: Young Goodman Brown represents a good person who, despite his best efforts, strays from the path of righteousness; his wife, Faith, represents the quality he must hold on to in order to avoid temptation. As characters, they have no significance outside of their allegorical functions. Other elements of the story, however, are not so clear-cut. The older man whom Young Goodman Brown meets in the woods carries a staff that has carved on it "the likeness of a great black snake, so curiously wrought, that it might almost be seen to twist and wriggle itself like a living serpent." This staff, carried by a Satanic figure who represents evil and temptation, suggests the snake in the Garden of Eden, an association that neatly fits into the allegorical framework of the story. Alternatively, however, the staff could suggest the "slippery," ever-changing nature of sin, the difficulty people have in perceiving sin, or even sexuality (which may explain Young Goodman Brown's susceptibility to temptation). This range of possible meanings suggests that the staff functions as a symbol (not an allegorical figure) that enriches Hawthorne's story.

Other stories work entirely on a symbolic level and contain no allegorical figures. "The Lottery," despite its moral overtones, is not an allegory because its characters, events, and objects are not arranged to serve one rigid, didactic purpose. In fact, many different interpretations have been suggested for this story. When it was first published in June 1948 in the *New Yorker*, some readers believed it to be a story about an actual custom or ritual. As author Shirley Jackson reports in her essay "Biography of a Story," even those who recognized it as fiction speculated about its meaning, seeing it as (among other things) an attack on prejudice; a criticism of society's need for a scapegoat; or a treatise on witchcraft, Christian martyrdom, or village gossip. The fact is that an allegorical interpretation will not account for every major character, object, and event in the story.

 ## Myth

Throughout history, human beings have been makers of myths. For the purpose of this discussion, a **myth** is a story that is central to a culture; it embodies the values on which a culture or society is built. Thus, myths are not synonymous with falsehoods or fairy tales. Rather, they are stories that contain ideas that inform a culture and that give that culture meaning. In this sense, then, both an ancient epic and a contemporary religious text can be considered myths.

Although many myths have to do with religion, myths are not limited to the theological. Myths explain everything from natural phenomena—such as the creation of the world—to the existence of human beings and the beginnings of agriculture. The importance of myths rests on their ability to embody a set of beliefs that unifies both individuals and the society in which they live. By examining myths, we can learn much about our own origins and about our most deeply held beliefs.

One of the most prevalent types of myth is the **creation myth**. Almost every culture has an explanation for how the earth, sun, and stars—not to mention people—came into being. According to the ancient Greeks, for example, the world began as an empty void from which Nyx, a bird with black wings, emerged. She laid a golden egg, and out of it arose Eros, the god of love. The two halves of the eggshell became the earth and the sky, who fell in love with each other and had many children and grandchildren. These offspring became the gods of the Greek pantheon, who eventually created human beings in their own likeness. Each of these gods had a role to play in the creation and maintenance of the world, and their actions—in particular, their constant meddling in the lives of people—comprise the myths of ancient Greece.

In various cultures all over the world, creation myths take different forms. According to the ancient Japanese, for example, the world emerged from a single seed, which grew to form a god who, in turn, created other gods and eventually the islands of Japan and their inhabitants. Several Native American tribes share common beliefs about "sky ancestors," who created the people on the planet.

In Western culture, the most recognizable creation myth appears in Genesis, the first book of the Old Testament. According to Genesis, God created the heavens and the earth as well as all living creatures—including Adam and Eve. Other stories are part of the oral tradition of Judaism and do not appear in Genesis. An example of such a story is the tale of Lilith, which emerged sometime between the eighth and eleventh centuries. According to this Hebrew myth, Lilith, who was created before Eve, was Adam's first wife. However, she refused to be subservient to Adam, and so she left Eden, eventually to be replaced by Eve. Talmudic tradition holds that she later mated with demons and gave birth to a legion of demonic offspring who inhabit the dark places of the earth.

The influence of mythology on literature is profound, and our contemporary understanding of narrative fiction owes a great deal to mythology. In fact, many of the short stories in this anthology contain allusions to myth. Consider, for example, the role of myth in "The Lottery," "Young Goodman Brown," and Raymond Carver's "Cathedral" (p. 435). In each of these short stories, myth is central to the characters' behavior, sensibility, and understanding of the world in which they live.

✔ **CHECKLIST   Writing about Symbol, Allegory, and Myth**

▪ Are any universal symbols used in the work? any conventional symbols? What is their function?

▪ Is any character, place, action, event, or object given unusual prominence or emphasis in the story? If so, does this element seem to have symbolic as well as literal significance?

▪ What possible meanings does each symbol suggest?

▪ How do symbols help to depict the story's characters?

▪ How do symbols help to characterize the story's setting?

▪ How do symbols help to advance the story's plot?

▪ Does the story have a moral or didactic purpose? What is the message, idea, or moral principle the story seeks to convey? Is the story an allegory?

▪ What equivalent may be assigned to each allegorical figure in the story?

▪ What is the allegorical framework of the story?

▪ Does the story combine allegorical figures and symbols? How do they work together in the story?

▪ Does the story have any references to myth? If so, what do these references contribute to the story's plot or theme?

Copyright M. K. Hobson 2014

M. K. HOBSON (1969–   ) is a pen name for Mary Catherine Koroloff, a fantasy and science fiction writer. The author of several stories and three novels, Hobson co hosts the fantasy fiction podcast *PodCastle*. She received honorable mention awards from *The Year's Best Fantasy and Horror* and *The Year's Best Science Fiction* as well as nominations for a Nebula Award and a Pushcart Prize. The following story appeared in *The Year's Best Dark Fantasy and Horror 2011*.

Cultural Context One of the country's oldest continuously operating amusement parks, Oaks Park opened in 1905 and is located in Portland, Oregon. Park attractions include more than twenty rides, a community stage for live entertainment, picnic grounds, and the largest roller skating rink in the United States. Although many of the park's rides have come and gone, the landmark Herschell–Spillman Noah's Ark carousel, built about a century ago, is still in operation.

Oaks Park (2010)

You are thirty-nine years old and you are a woman and a mother, and you've just avoided saying something to your husband that would cause a fight. Summer is almost over, though the days are still long and the evenings still warm and heavy with the sound of insects, and this makes you feel desperate, but you don't know why. You have a daughter who you already don't understand even though she is only twelve. Even your own life is puzzling to you, you move in a fog of mild discontent, whatever ability you ever had to make a decision or form an opinion lost to the endless consensus of family, the compromises of marriage, every day covering you like a sheet with holes cut out.

Your daughter has friends all over the neighborhood, tanned scuffed elastic creatures, each as wild and improbable as she. They are like another species. They come from nowhere, they come up from behind you and you never hear them coming. They all look alike. They lounge on couches inside dark cool houses hiding from daylight's glare, watching Nick for Teens and sipping Capri Suns, crushing packages of ramen and eating the crumbled noodles raw. They leave a trail of wrappers and crumbs. One day your daughter is prompted by her best girlfriend, a girl who looks exactly like your daughter, to ask "Can you take us to Oaks Park?" and you say "If you clean your room," knowing that she will never clean her room so you will never have to take her to Oaks Park.

Later, you hear your daughter talking to two more of her friends, a boy and a girl who look exactly like her, scraped knees and dark tanned skin and cornsilk hair and T-shirts that assert their unswerving allegiance to an anime show. They are all sitting in the shade of the porch, eating popsicles, dripping bright colored sugarwater on the worn treads.

"Oaks Park is haunted," one of them says. "Someone died there and the ghost wanders around."

You listen closely. You haven't heard this story before. You want to ask, *Who died there? Is there really a ghost? What does it look like?* But none of the kids on the porch have these questions, so they are not asked and not answered. The kids run into the

5

streets and seize their bikes, leaving behind wrappers and sticks and puddles of sugary sweetness for ants to swarm over.

You turn to the Internet.

Oaks Park is a modest amusement park located 3.5 miles (6 km) south of downtown Portland, Oregon in the United States.

The park was built by the Oregon Water Power and Railway Company and opened in 1905, when trolley parks were often constructed along streetcar lines.

The large wooden roller skating rink is open year-round. The centerpiece is the largest remaining pipe organ installed in a skating rink in the world.

10 *As of December 2005, Keith Fortune is at the organ's console providing music for skaters on Thursdays and Sundays.*

It's all ragtimey, bandstands and box lunches, women in gored skirts and men in straw boater hats. You find bits of information about the flyscreened dance-hall and how the floor of the roller skating rink is on floating pontoons so it can stay above water when the Willamette River floods. There is nothing about a dead child or a ghost. The absence of such information makes you feel better. The vague anxiety you have been feeling eases. Your husband comes home, and you avoid talking about something that would upset you both, and you make dinner and eat it in front of the television, closing the curtains against the summer sunlight that blazes long into the night.

The next day, you receive an email from a young man named Chuck. He works at Oaks Park. You've already forgotten that you emailed him—Internet time works like that. But when the message pops into your email box you suddenly remember filling out a web form marked "history questions." Your message was brief.

Is there a ghost that haunts Oaks Park?

Chuck's emailed reply is just as brief.

15 *Some people have reported seeing the ghost of a girl, about 12 years old. She's dressed in seventies-era clothing. She steals cotton candy from the snack bar and rides the rides. The Octopus is her favorite.*

Your fingers type a furious question in response:

Is she happy?

But you don't hit "send," because you know that Chuck won't know the answer and you already do.

The last time you went to Oaks Park you were twelve and it was 1977.

20 You remember riding in the back seat of the Dodge Dart, American steel bullying across the narrow Sellwood Bridge, sweltering heat pouring in through all four open windows.

Your hands are sticky and you are wearing Haggar shorts and a Garanimals T-shirt from the Sears Surplus over by Lloyd Center. Your hair is cornsilk blond and your skin is brown and scratched, scabs everywhere like a map of stars.

Your parents are brittle, recovering from a night-long fight. This is your reward, your battle pay, your assurance that everything in the world is perfect.

Your dad's profile is sleek and handsome and brutal. Your mom's face is soft and young beneath a smooth Dorothy Hamill[1] cut, her eyes watchful behind huge amber sunglasses. Your legs stick to the vinyl. "Hotel California" plays on the radio.

---

[1] *Dorothy Hamill:* American figure skater and 1976 Olympic champion.

Your parents park the car under knobby, diseased trees. The small parking lot seems like it's in the wrong place; you get to it by driving past a caretaker's shack and a shop with old ride parts jumbled before it. You approach the park from behind, like you're sneaking up on it, stepping carefully over cracked mounds where tree roots have broken the asphalt. You leave your parents behind to mutter between themselves. That's the only time they talk, these days—when they think you can't hear.

To get to the new rides you have to pass the old midway, abandoned attractions that have been shut down for years. The old buildings are regal in their decay, silvered wood and peeling paint, bulb-broken light fixtures clotted with nests and twigs, cottonwood fluff piled in unswept corners.

One tilting building has a gigantic round doorway, like a giant storm drain, all boarded up. You run up to it, peek through the boards, peer into the darkness. The cool air coming from inside smells of mold. Your parents call you away, to where the new rides are—the steel-spiderweb Ferris wheel, the carousel with its cracked menagerie of dragons and rabbits, the Erector Set roller-coaster of rusted bolts and oil-smeared wood. A vast go-kart track sprawls to the north, belching gas fumes and the smell of baking rubber; beyond it, a fetid river lowland, a swamp filled with abandoned cars and frayed tires. There's a neon sign for a ride called the Fly-O but the ride that's actually there is the Octopus, spinning arms swinging bulbous black seats like fists.

While you are standing in line to ride the Octopus, you see a boy and girl in the shade of the snack bar. She is wearing a halter-top and baby-blue shorts, and she has long smooth hair that gleams down her back. She has one thumb hooked in the top of her shorts, and a velour prize monkey under her arm. The boy has tight curly hair, and he is leaning against her, his thumbs stroking the sides of her ribs. You are eating popcorn. You don't understand them and you know, suddenly, that you don't want to understand them. You never want to understand them. Your father has gone off somewhere, and you are alone with your mother. You watch her watch them. She understands them. There is betrayal and regret on her face.

The sun is still beating down but you feel cold. The line is moving, and it is almost your turn to get on the Octopus, but you know that there are clouds coming in, and you know that it will rain, and it will get cold. Your parents will fight again and again and again. And school will start and you will have a new teacher in a room with waxed floors, and you will wear new clothes and then it will be Christmas and then spring and then summer again, and then high school and then college and then you will be far far away from here, far from where old wise buildings keep the order of time. You will be the girl with the straight shiny hair or you will be the curly haired boy in cutoffs, betrayed. You will be your parents. You will be thirty-nine years old, and a woman, and a mother, and nothing will make any sense but it will all hurt. You see it all in one shambling terrifying moment, you see that everything will go on and on, spinning.

You ride the Octopus with your mother. Then you run away.

You find a deserted place, trash-strewn nook behind the bumper cars near the old line of bathrooms. You hide there, legs drawn up to your chest. You rest your forehead on your knees, and you close your eyes.

You imagine a ghost, a shell, a hollow creature that can be buffeted and molded, pliant as your mother when your father's bulbous fists swing around and around, yielding as the girl with long smooth hair, the curly-haired boy looming over her like a cloud over the sun. You pretend someone else out into the world. You send her in your place.

You can't ever come back, you whisper to her. You tell yourself it's like a game. A game of hide and seek. You will hide from time and fear and betrayal and regret.

Someone else goes home in the car with your parents, someone new and formless, someone who feels no fear because she feels nothing. As insubstantial as mist, as air under a sheet. You will stay at Oaks Park. You will sleep during the hottest part of the day and at night, when the lights come on, the buildings will whisper their secrets to you and they will keep you safe forever.

You are thirty-nine years old and you are a woman and a mother.

35   You wake up after a night of unsettling dreams, whirling spinning dreams full of screaming and blurred lights and the smell of burnt sugar, and you have a fight with your husband. You tell him he's the worst decision you ever made. You tell him you wish you'd never married him. You tell him you never loved him. You tell him you hate him, and when you tell him this, you feel the sickening truth of it. You scream at each other for hours, and you're both late for work, and your daughter is late for school.

You drive her, and she cowers in the back seat and you feel, rather than see, the anxiety on her face. You understand it completely. You remember it, the fear of every-thing falling apart. The memory is strange and alien. It is a fear that is supposed to belong to someone else, someone like you.

You don't go in to work. You come home and sit on the couch in your front room, heat beating against the walls of the house. You draw curtains against it, you move the air with fans, but it's so terribly hot. You drowse, but every time you nod off you dream of boarded up buildings and peeling paint. The buildings are empty. You thought they held secrets, you thought they were wise. But they contain nothing. They are as empty as you are. You wake screaming.

Late in the afternoon, you drive to Oaks Park.

The air is still and sunny. You make the turn off the Sellwood Bridge at sunset, the dazzling light making your eyes tear. You drive along the road that leads to the park, fluff from the cottonwood trees glistening in the golden air. A stiff breeze from the Willamette[2] makes faded nylon pennants ripple. The lights have been turned on, but you can't see them, not yet.

40   Everything has changed. The big flat expanse of cracked blacktop where the go-karts used to be is now acres of smoothly paved parking. The swamp is now wetland and there are multi-use trails and urban hiking areas threaded throughout it. Every-thing is smaller. Most of the rides you remember are gone, even the Tilt-o-Whirl with its evil clown faces—you never liked it, it gave you a headache and made you feel sick and it smelled like diesel. The Erector Set roller-coaster has been replaced by something plastic and candy-colored that has a loop-de-loop. You pass what used to be the Haunted Mine, and remember that it used to scare you, but now it is called The Lewis and Clark Adventure and beavers jump out at you instead of skeletons. It's all bad hand-me-down Funtastic carnival rides with cheap graphics of secondhand superheroes. Alternative rock spews from the speakers.

---

[2]*Willamette:* The Willamette River in northwestern Oregon.

All the old boarded up rides are gone, razed. Where they once stood, picnic space has been cleared for corporate picnics and soccer team parties.

You buy popcorn from the snack bar. Made in China, it comes in a foil bag and is very stale. You sit on one of the old green wooden benches and wait for it to get dark.

You see her before she sees you. She's wearing Haggar shorts and a Garanimals shirt from Sears Surplus. She has a chunk of cotton candy in her hand. She's all eyes, wandering through the crowd in the watchful way of lost children, her brow creased with anxiety. You watch her until she sees you, watch her face light with perfect joy and relief. Feelings wrap around you like a winter coat. Anger. Resentment. Bitterness. Regret.

She runs to you, clutching grubby hands at your clothing. She buries a dirty face in your stomach and breaks, brave wary watchfulness dissolving into sobs. She wails and moans, a lost child found, and you pet her back and say soft soothing things to her. She clings to you, and people are watching, making sympathetic clucking sounds. You savor this moment. You hold onto it for as long as you can. You think of your daughter and you remember a million looks on her face that you couldn't interpret. You understand them all now. You remember a hundred times you hated your husband, your life, your job . . . even your own child.

I want to go home, she sobs into your stomach, *against your shirt. I want to go home.*　　45

You want to take her home. You want to put her in the back seat of your car; and let her fall asleep, exhausted by her ordeal. You would drive home, and when you got there, she would be gone, melted into the car; melted back into you. You would be whole again. Oaks Park would have one less ghost, and you would have one more.

And there would be another fight and another and another, and you would see the infinity of days stretch before you again, and you would see the looks your daughter gives you, and understand them for what they are—disgust, pity, shame. And maybe you would hurt her, hurt her so much that she would make her own ghost, and this whole terrible wheel would turn again, this carnival wheel, this gut-wrenching loop-de-loop.

You can't take her home.

Dread of what you will have to do makes all the small muscles in your body ache. You can't think about it. You will have to just do it. Your hands will have to rescue you.

You take her hand and walk. She is content to be pulled along, compliant and　　50
humbled, nose running. You are walking in the direction of the old parking lot at the back of the park. But you are really walking to the place behind the bumpercars, behind the bathrooms. It is the same as it was twenty-seven years ago, trash-strewn with the same trash, the same cottonwood fluff.

You pull her down beside you and you take her in your arms and hold her tight, cradling her for a few minutes more, telling her how brave she's been. She talks fast, sentences like broken sticks: she didn't mean to, it was just a game, she didn't mean to get lost, she was scared, she was looking for you.

You murmur *shh*, *shh* in her ear as your fingers find the kitchen knife you have brought from home.

You pull the knife across her smooth brown throat. She gushes, but it is not blood. She bleeds time, a million golden sunsets and white illuminated nights, and she bleeds fear, the shambling shadow of the eternal, dark and molasses-like. She bleeds regret.

She thrashes in your arms, making betrayed noises, animal noises. She deflates. She melts. Then she is nothing but a pile of dirty old clothes from Sears Surplus. You hide these beneath the trash.

55   Walking back to your car, you are trembling, but it is only a physical thing. Your mind is calm, and everything feels vague and unknowable again. Your accustomed numbness returns, and you know that everything will be all right.

She will stay at Oaks Park. She will ride the rides and steal cotton candy. But she will be someone else, someone new and formless, someone who feels all the terror that you should share. As insubstantial as mist, as air under a sheet. She will sleep during the hottest part of the day and at night when the lights come on, she will search watchfully through crowds for the mother she didn't mean to lose and a life she didn't mean to surrender.

You leave her to her haunts.

You return to yours.

Reading and Reacting

1. At the beginning of "Oaks Park," the narrator tells readers about herself. What information does she provide? How does this information set the stage for the rest of the story?

2. Explain the narrator's initial reaction to each of the following:

- Her husband
- Her daughter
- Her daughter's friends
- Oaks Park

3. Initially, the narrator claims that she hasn't heard the story of the ghost at Oaks Park. Do you believe her? What steps does she take to find out about the ghost? Why do you think she is so interested in this story?

4. At one level, "Oaks Park" is a story about relationships. How would you characterize the following relationships?

- The narrator and her daughter
- The narrator and her husband
- The narrator and her parents
- The narrator and the ghost

5. What elements in the story suggest that Oaks Park is a symbol? What does Oaks Park signify to the narrator? to readers?

6. In a **flashback**, the narrator tells about a time she visited Oaks Park with her parents. Does she describe this visit nostalgically or in some other way? Explain.

7. Why does the narrator run away from her mother? How does she create a "ghost"? Why does she tell the ghost, "You can't ever come back"?

8. Do you think that the ghost is a symbol? If not, why not? If so, what possible meanings could it suggest?

9. Later in the story, when the narrator drives to Oaks Park, she says, "Everything has changed." What does she mean?

10. Why does the narrator feel compelled to kill the ghost? What does the narrator mean when she says that the ghost "bleeds regret"?

11. **JOURNAL ENTRY** The story ends with the narrator saying, "You leave her [the ghost] to her haunts. You return to yours." What does she mean? In what sense is the narrator a ghost? What are her haunts?

12. **CRITICAL PERSPECTIVE** In an interview with *Locus* magazine, Hobson explains that her novels are based on the idea that "what the majority of people believe is what drives reality." Is the narrator's encounter with the ghost "real" or imagined? Explain.

Related Works: "Television" (p. 129), "How to Talk to Girls at Parties" (p. 214), "Halloween" (p. 580), "Gretel in Darkness" (p. 677), "The Wolf's Postscript to 'Little Red Riding Hood'" (p. 706), "The Raven" (p. 856), "The Centaur" (p. 871), *Magic 8 Ball* (p. 1073)

SHIRLEY JACKSON (1916–1965) is best known for her restrained tales of horror and the supernatural, most notably her novel *The Haunting of Hill House* (1959) and the short story "The Lottery" (1948). Among her other works are two novels dealing with multiple personalities—*The Bird's Nest* (1954) and *We Have Always Lived in the Castle* (1962)—and two collections of comic tales about her children and family life, *Life among the Savages* (1953) and *Raising Demons* (1957). A posthumous collection of stories, *Just an Ordinary Day* (1997), was published after the discovery of a box of some of Jackson's unpublished papers in a Vermont barn and her heirs' subsequent search for her other uncollected works.

AP Images

With her husband, literary critic Stanley Edgar Hyman, she settled in the small town of Bennington, Vermont, but was never accepted by the townspeople. "The Lottery" is set in much the same kind of small, parochial town. Despite the story's matter-of-fact tone and familiar setting, its publication in the *New Yorker* provoked a torrent of letters from enraged and shocked readers. In her quiet way, Jackson presented the underside of village life and revealed to readers the dark side of human nature. Future writers of gothic tales recognized their great debt to Jackson. Horror master Stephen King dedicated his book *Firestarter* "to Shirley Jackson, who never had to raise her voice."

Cultural Context "The Lottery" is sometimes seen as a protest against totalitarianism, a form of authoritarian government that permits no individual freedom. In *Eichmann in Jerusalem* (1963), political scientist Hannah Arendt (1906–1975) wrote about totalitarianism as it pertained to Nazi Germany and the Holocaust. Here, she introduced the concept of "the banality of evil," the potential in ordinary people to do evil things. Americans of the post–World War II era saw themselves as "good guys" defending the world against foreign evils. Jackson's story, written scarcely three years after the liberation of Auschwitz, told Americans something they did not want to hear—that the face of human evil could look just like their next-door neighbor.

The Lottery (1948)

The morning of June 27th was clear and sunny, with the fresh warmth of a full-summer day; the flowers were blossoming profusely and the grass was richly green. The people of the village began to gather in the square, between the post office and the bank, around ten o'clock; in some towns there were so many people that the lottery took two days and had to be started on June 26th, but in this village, where there were only about three hundred people, the whole lottery took less than two hours, so it could begin at ten o'clock in the morning and still be through in time to allow the villagers to get home for noon dinner.

The children assembled first, of course. School was recently over for the summer, and the feeling of liberty sat uneasily on most of them; they tended to gather together quietly for a while before they broke into boisterous play, and their talk was still of the classroom and the teacher, of books and reprimands. Bobby Martin had already stuffed his pockets full of stones, and the other boys soon followed his example, selecting the smoothest and roundest stones; Bobby and Harry Jones and Dickie Delacroix—the villagers pronounced this name "Dellacroy"—eventually made a great pile of stones in one corner of the square and guarded it against the raids of the other boys. The girls stood aside, talking among themselves, looking over their shoulders at the boys, and the very small children rolled in the dust or clung to the hands of their older brothers or sisters.

Soon the men began to gather, surveying their own children, speaking of planting and rain, tractors and taxes. They stood together, away from the pile of stones in the corner, and their jokes were quiet and they smiled rather than laughed. The women, wearing faded house dresses and sweaters, came shortly after their menfolk. They greeted one another and exchanged bits of gossip as they went to join their husbands. Soon the women, standing by their husbands, began to call to their children, and the children came reluctantly, having to be called four or five times. Bobby Martin ducked under his mother's grasping hand and ran, laughing, back to the pile of stones. His father spoke up sharply, and Bobby came quickly and took his place between his father and his oldest brother.

The lottery was conducted—as were the square dances, the teen-age club, the Halloween program—by Mr. Summers, who had time and energy to devote to civic activities. He was a round-faced, jovial man and he ran the coal business, and people were sorry for him, because he had no children and his wife was a scold. When he arrived in the square, carrying the black wooden box, there was a murmur of conversation among the villagers, and he waved and called, "Little late today, folks." The postmaster, Mr. Graves, followed him, carrying a three-legged stool, and the stool was put in the center of the square and Mr. Summers set the black box down on it. The villagers kept their distance, leaving a space between themselves and the stool, and when Mr. Summers said, "Some of you fellows want to give me a hand?" there was a hesitation before two men, Mr. Martin and his oldest son, Baxter, came forward to hold the box steady on the stool while Mr. Summers stirred up the papers inside it.

5   The original paraphernalia for the lottery had been lost long ago, and the black box now resting on the stool had been put into use even before Old Man Warner, the oldest man in town, was born. Mr. Summers spoke frequently to the villagers about making a new box, but no one liked to upset even as much tradition as was represented by the black box. There was a story that the present box had been made with some pieces of the box that had preceded it, the one that had been constructed when the first people settled down to make a village here. Every year, after the lottery, Mr. Summers began talking again about a new box, but every year the subject was allowed to fade off without anything's being done. The black box grew shabbier each year; by now it was no longer completely black but splintered badly along one side to show the original wood color, and in some places faded or stained.

Mr. Martin and his oldest son, Baxter, held the black box securely on the stool until Mr. Summers had stirred the papers thoroughly with his hand. Because so much of the ritual had been forgotten or discarded, Mr. Summers had been successful in having slips of paper substituted for the chips of wood that had been used for generations. Chips of wood, Mr. Summers had argued, had been all very well when the village was tiny, but now that the population was more than three hundred and likely to keep on growing, it was necessary to use something that would fit more easily into the black box. The night before the lottery, Mr. Summers and Mr. Graves made up the slips of paper and put them in the box, and it was then taken to the safe of Mr. Summers's coal company and locked up until Mr. Summers was ready to take it to the square next morning. The rest of the year, the box was put away, sometimes one place, sometimes another; it had spent one year in Mr. Graves's barn and another year underfoot in the post office, and sometimes it was set on a shelf in the Martin grocery and left there.

There was a great deal of fussing to be done before Mr. Summers declared the lottery open. There were the lists to make up—of heads of families, heads of households in each family, members of each household in each family. There was the proper swearing-in of Mr. Summers by the postmaster, as the official of the lottery; at one time, some people remembered, there had been a recital of some sort, performed by the official of the lottery, a perfunctory, tuneless chant that had been rattled off duly each year; some people believed that the official of the lottery used to stand just so when he said or sang it, others believed that he was supposed to walk among the people, but years and years ago this part of the ritual had been allowed to lapse. There had been, also, a ritual salute, which the official of the lottery had had to use in addressing each person who came up to draw from the box, but this also had changed with time, until now it was felt necessary only for the official to speak to each person approaching. Mr. Summers was very good at all this; in his clean white shirt and blue jeans, with one hand resting carelessly on the black box, he seemed very proper and important as he talked interminably to Mr. Graves and the Martins.

Just as Mr. Summers finally left off talking and turned to the assembled villagers, Mrs. Hutchinson came hurriedly along the path to the square, her sweater thrown over her shoulders, and slid into place in the back of the crowd. "Clean forgot what day it was," she said to Mrs. Delacroix, who stood next to her, and they both laughed softly. "Thought my old man was out back stacking wood," Mrs. Hutchinson went on, "and then I looked out the window and the kids was gone, and then I remembered it was the twenty-seventh and came a-running." She dried her hands on her apron, and Mrs. Delacroix said, "You're in time, though. They're still talking away up there."

Mrs. Hutchinson craned her neck to see through the crowd and found her husband and children standing near the front. She tapped Mrs. Delacroix on the arm as a farewell and began to make her way through the crowd. The people separated good-humoredly to let her through; two or three people said, in voices just loud enough to be heard across the crowd, "Here comes your Missus, Hutchinson," and "Bill, she made it after all." Mrs. Hutchinson reached her husband, and Mr. Summers, who had been waiting, said cheerfully, "Thought we were going to have to get on without you, Tessie." Mrs. Hutchinson said, grinning, "Wouldn't have me leave m'dishes in the sink, now, would you, Joe?," and soft laughter ran through the crowd as the people stirred back into position after Mrs. Hutchinson's arrival.

10   "Well, now," Mr. Summers said soberly, "guess we better get started, get this over with, so's we can go back to work. Anybody ain't here?"

"Dunbar," several people said. "Dunbar, Dunbar."

Mr. Summers consulted his list. "Clyde Dunbar," he said. "That's right. He's broke his leg, hasn't he? Who's drawing for him?"

"Me, I guess," a woman said, and Mr. Summers turned to look at her. "Wife draws for her husband," Mr. Summers said. "Don't you have a grown boy to do it for you, Janey?" Although Mr. Summers and everyone else in the village knew the answer perfectly well, it was the business of the official of the lottery to ask such questions formally. Mr. Summers waited with an expression of polite interest while Mrs. Dunbar answered.

"Horace's not but sixteen yet," Mrs. Dunbar said regretfully. "Guess I gotta fill in for the old man this year."

15   "Right," Mr. Summers said. He made a note on the list he was holding. Then he asked, "Watson boy drawing this year?"

A tall boy in the crowd raised his hand. "Here," he said. "I'm drawing for m'mother and me." He blinked his eyes nervously and ducked his head as several voices in the crowd said things like "Good fellow, Jack," and "Glad to see your mother's got a man to do it."

"Well," Mr. Summers said, "guess that's everyone. Old Man Warner make it?"

"Here," a voice said, and Mr. Summers nodded.

A sudden hush fell on the crowd as Mr. Summers cleared his throat and looked at the list. "All ready?" he called. "Now, I'll read the names—heads of families first—and the men come up and take a paper out of the box. Keep the paper folded in your hand without looking at it until everyone has had a turn. Everything clear?"

20   The people had done it so many times that they only half listened to the directions; most of them were quiet, wetting their lips, not looking around. Then Mr. Summers raised one hand high and said, "Adams." A man disengaged himself from the crowd and came forward. "Hi, Steve," Mr. Summers said, and Mr. Adams said, "Hi, Joe." They grinned at one another humorlessly and nervously. Then Mr. Adams reached into the black box and took out a folded paper. He held it firmly by one corner as he turned and went hastily back to his place in the crowd, where he stood a little apart from his family, not looking down at his hand.

"Allen," Mr. Summers said. "Anderson. . . . Bentham."

"Seems like there's no time at all between lotteries any more," Mrs. Delacroix said to Mrs. Graves in the back row. "Seems like we got through with the last one only last week."

"Time sure goes fast," Mrs. Graves said.

"Clark. . . . Delacroix."

25   "There goes my old man," Mrs. Delacroix said. She held her breath while her husband went forward.

"Dunbar," Mr. Summers said, and Mrs. Dunbar went steadily to the box while one of the women said, "Go on, Janey," and another said, "There she goes."

"We're next," Mrs. Graves said. She watched while Mr. Graves came around from the side of the box, greeted Mr. Summers gravely, and selected a slip of paper from the box. By now, all through the crowd there were men holding the small folded papers in their large hands, turning them over and over nervously. Mrs. Dunbar and her two sons stood together, Mrs. Dunbar holding the slip of paper.

"Harburt. . . . Hutchinson."

"Get up there, Bill," Mrs. Hutchinson said, and the people near her laughed.

"Jones." 30

"They do say," Mr. Adams said to Old Man Warner, who stood next to him, "that over in the north village they're talking of giving up the lottery."

Old Man Warner snorted. "Pack of crazy fools," he said. "Listening to the young folks, nothing's good enough for *them*. Next thing you know, they'll be wanting to go back to living in caves, nobody work any more, live *that* way for a while. Used to be a saying about 'Lottery in June, corn be heavy soon.' First thing you know, we'd all be eating stewed chickweed and acorns. There's *always* been a lottery," he added petulantly. "Bad enough to see young Joe Summers up there joking with everybody."

"Some places have already quit lotteries," Mrs. Adams said.

"Nothing but trouble in *that*," Old Man Warner said stoutly. "Pack of young fools."

"Martin." And Bobby Martin watched his father go forward. "Overdyke. . . . Percy." 35

"I wish they'd hurry," Mrs. Dunbar said to her older son. "I wish they'd hurry."

"They're almost through," her son said.

"You get ready to run tell Dad," Mrs. Dunbar said.

Mr. Summers called his own name and then stepped forward precisely and selected a slip from the box. Then he called, "Warner."

"Seventy-seventh year I been in the lottery," Old Man Warner said as he went 40
through the crowd. "Seventy-seventh time."

"Watson." The tall boy came awkwardly through the crowd. Someone said, "Don't be nervous, Jack," and Mr. Summers said, "Take your time, son."

"Zanini."

After that, there was a long pause, a breathless pause, until Mr. Summers, holding his slip of paper in the air, said, "All right, fellows." For a minute, no one moved, and then all the slips of paper were opened. Suddenly, all the women began to speak at once, saying, "Who is it?," "Who's got it?," "Is it the Dunbars?," "Is it the Watsons?" Then the voices began to say, "It's Hutchinson. It's Bill," "Bill Hutchinson's got it."

"Go tell your father," Mrs. Dunbar said to her older son.

People began to look around to see the Hutchinsons. Bill Hutchinson was standing 45
quiet, staring down at the paper in his hand. Suddenly, Tessie Hutchinson shouted to Mr. Summers, "You didn't give him time enough to take any paper he wanted. I saw you. It wasn't fair!"

"Be a good sport, Tessie," Mrs. Delacroix called, and Mrs. Graves said, "All of us took the same chance."

"Shut up, Tessie," Bill Hutchinson said.

"Well, everyone," Mr. Summers said, "that was done pretty fast, and now we've got to be hurrying a little more to get done in time." He consulted his next list. "Bill," he said, "you draw for the Hutchinson family. You got any other households in the Hutchinsons?"

"There's Don and Eva," Mrs. Hutchinson yelled, "Make *them* take their chance!"

"Daughters draw with their husbands' families, Tessie," Mr. Summers said gently. 50
"You know that as well as anyone else."

"It wasn't *fair*," Tessie said.

"I guess not, Joe," Bill Hutchinson said regretfully. "My daughter draws with her husband's family, that's only fair. And I've got no other family except the kids."

"Then, as far as drawing for families is concerned, it's you," Mr. Summers said in explanation, "and as far as drawing for households is concerned, that's you, too. Right?"

"Right," Bill Hutchinson said.

55   "How many kids, Bill?" Mr. Summers asked formally.

"Three," Bill Hutchinson said. "There's Bill, Jr., and Nancy, and little Dave. And Tessie and me."

"All right, then," Mr. Summers said. "Harry, you got their tickets back?"

Mr. Graves nodded and held up the slips of paper. "Put them in the box, then," Mr. Summers directed. "Take Bill's and put it in."

"I think we ought to start over," Mrs. Hutchinson said, as quietly as she could. "I tell you it wasn't *fair*. You didn't give him time enough to choose. *Everybody* saw that."

60   Mr. Graves had selected the five slips and put them in the box, and he dropped all the papers but those onto the ground, where the breeze caught them and lifted them off.

"Listen, everybody," Mrs. Hutchinson was saying to the people around her.

"Ready, Bill?" Mr. Summers asked, and Bill Hutchinson, with one quick glance around at his wife and children, nodded.

"Remember," Mr. Summers said, "take the slips and keep them folded until each person has taken one. Harry, you help little Dave." Mr. Graves took the hand of the little boy, who came willingly with him up to the box. "Take a paper out of the box, Davy," Mr. Summers said. Davy put his hand into the box and laughed. "Take just *one* paper," Mr. Summers said. "Harry, you hold it for him." Mr. Graves took the child's hand and removed the folded paper from the tight fist and held it while little Dave stood next to him and looked at him wonderingly.

"Nancy next," Mr. Summers said. Nancy was twelve, and her school friends breathed heavily as she went forward, switching her skirt, and took a slip daintily from the box. "Bill, Jr.," Mr. Summers said, and Billy, his face red and his feet overlarge, nearly knocked the box over as he got a paper out. "Tessie," Mr. Summers said. She hesitated for a minute, looking around defiantly, and then set her lips and went up to the box. She snatched a paper out and held it behind her.

65   "Bill," Mr. Summers said, and Bill Hutchinson reached into the box and felt around, bringing his hand out at last with the slip of paper in it.

The crowd was quiet. A girl whispered, "I hope it's not Nancy," and the sound of the whisper reached the edges of the crowd.

"It's not the way it used to be," Old Man Warner said clearly. "People ain't the way they used to be."

"All right," Mr. Summers said. "Open the papers. Harry, you open little Dave's."

Mr. Graves opened the slip of paper and there was a general sigh through the crowd as he held it up and everyone could see that it was blank. Nancy and Bill, Jr., opened theirs at the same time, and both beamed and laughed, turning around to the crowd and holding their slips of paper above their heads.

"Tessie," Mr. Summers said. There was a pause, and then Mr. Summers looked at   70
Bill Hutchinson, and Bill unfolded his paper and showed it. It was blank.

"It's Tessie," Mr. Summers said, and his voice was hushed. "Show us her paper,
Bill."

Bill Hutchinson went over to his wife and forced the slip of paper out of her hand.
It had a black spot on it, the black spot Mr. Summers had made the night before with
the heavy pencil in the coal-company office. Bill Hutchinson held it up, and there
was a stir in the crowd.

"All right, folks," Mr. Summers said. "Let's finish quickly."

Although the villagers had forgotten the ritual and lost the original black box,
they still remembered to use stones. The pile of stones the boys had made earlier was
ready; there were stones on the ground with the blowing scraps of paper that had come
out of the box. Mrs. Delacroix selected a stone so large she had to pick it up with both
hands and turned to Mrs. Dunbar. "Come on," she said. "Hurry up."

Mrs. Dunbar had small stones in both hands, and she said, gasping for breath, "I   75
can't run at all. You'll have to go ahead and I'll catch up with you."

The children had stones already, and someone gave little Davy Hutchinson a few
pebbles.

Tessie Hutchinson was in the center of a cleared space by now, and she held her
hands out desperately as the villagers moved in on her. "It isn't fair," she said. A stone
hit her on the side of the head.

Old Man Warner was saying, "Come on, come on, everyone." Steve Adams was in
the front of the crowd of villagers, with Mrs. Graves beside him.

"It isn't fair, it isn't right," Mrs. Hutchinson screamed, and then they were upon
her.

Reading and Reacting

1. What possible significance, beyond their literal meaning, might each of the following
   have:

   - The village square
   - Mrs. Hutchinson's apron
   - Old Man Warner
   - The slips of paper
   - The black spot

2. "The Lottery" takes place in summer, a conventional symbol that has a positive connotation. What does this setting contribute to the story's plot? to its atmosphere?

3. What, if anything, might the names *Graves, Adams, Summers,* and *Delacroix* signify in
   the context of this story? Do you think these names are intended to have any special
   significance? Why or why not?

4. What role do the children play in the ritual? How can you explain their presence in the
   story? Do they have any symbolic role?

5. What symbolic significance might be found in the way the characters are dressed? in their
   conversation?

6. In what sense is the story's title ironic?

7. Throughout the story, there is a general atmosphere of excitement. What indication is there of nervousness or apprehension?

8. Early in the story, the boys stuff their pockets with stones, foreshadowing the attack in the story's conclusion. What other examples of foreshadowing can you identify?

9. **JOURNAL ENTRY** How can a ritual like the lottery continue to be held year after year? Why does no one move to end it? Can you think of a modern-day counterpart to this lottery—a situation in which people continue to act in ways they know to be wrong rather than challenge the status quo? How can you account for such behavior?

10. **CRITICAL PERSPECTIVE** When "The Lottery" was published in the June 26, 1948, issue of the *New Yorker*, its effect was immediate. The story, as the critic Judy Oppenheimer notes in her book *Private Demons: The Life of Shirley Jackson*, "provoked an unprecedented outpouring of fury, horror, rage, disgust, and intense fascination." As a result, Jackson received hundreds of letters, which included (among others) the following interpretations of the story:

   - The story is an attack on small-town America.
   - The story is a parable about the perversion of democracy.
   - The story is a criticism of prejudice, particularly anti-Semitism.
   - The story has no point at all.

How plausible do you think each of these interpretations is? Which comes closest to your interpretation of the story? Why?

Related Works: "Young Goodman Brown" (p. 448), "Where Are You Going, Where Have You Been?" (p. 506), "Patterns" (p. 688), "Ballad of Birmingham" (p. 708), *Nine Ten* (p. 1108)

Monica Morgan/Getty Images

ALICE WALKER (1944–   ) was the youngest of eight children born to Willie Lee and Minnie Tallulah Grant Walker, sharecroppers who raised cotton. She left the rural South to attend Spelman College in Atlanta (1961–1963) and Sarah Lawrence College in Bronxville, New York (1963–1965).

In 1967, Walker moved to Mississippi, where she was supported in the writing of her first novel, *The Third Life of Grange Copeland* (1970), by a National Endowment for the Arts grant. Her short story "Everyday Use" was included in *Best American Short Stories 1973* and has been widely anthologized and studied. Other novels and collections of short stories followed, including *In Love & Trouble: Stories of Black Women* (1973), *Meridian* (1976), *You Can't Keep a Good Woman Down* (1981), *The Temple of My Familiar* (1989), *Possessing the Secret of Joy* (1993), *The Complete Stories* (1994), *By the Light of My Father's Smile* (1998), and *Now Is the Time to Open Your Heart* (2004). Her latest books include the essay collection *The Cushion in the Road* (2013) and the poetry collection *The World Will Follow Joy* (2013). Her third novel, *The Color Purple* (1982), won the American Book Award and a Pulitzer Prize and was made into an award-winning movie and a long-running Broadway play.

In the third year of her marriage, Walker took back her maiden name because she wanted to honor her great-great-great-grandmother who had walked, carrying her two children, from Virginia to Georgia. Walker's renaming is consistent with one of her goals in writing, which is to further the process of reconnecting people to their ancestors. She has said that "it is fatal to see yourself as separate" and that if people can reaffirm the past, they can "make a different future."

Cultural Context Quilting attained the status of art in Europe in the fourteenth century but reached its fullest development later in North America. By the end of the eighteenth century, the American quilt had taken on unique and distinctive features that separated it from quilts made in other parts of the world. For African Americans, quilting has particular significance. Some scholars think that during slavery, members of the Underground Railroad used quilts to send messages. One design, the Log Cabin, was hung outside to mark a house of refuge for fugitive slaves. Other quilts mapped escape routes out of a plantation or county, often by marking the stars that would act as a guide to freedom for those escaping at night. After the emancipation of slaves, quilts retained their cultural and historical significance, as the quilt in this story does.

Everyday Use (1973)

For Your Grandmama

Film Series

DVD

See p. 434 for film stills from the DVD version of this story.

I will wait for her in the yard that Maggie and I made so clean and wavy yesterday afternoon. A yard like this is more comfortable than most people know. It is not just a yard. It is like an extended living room. When the hard clay is swept clean as a floor and the fine sand around the edges lined with tiny, irregular grooves, anyone can come and sit and look up into the elm tree and wait for the breezes that never come inside the house.

Maggie will be nervous until after her sister goes: she will stand hopelessly in corners, homely and ashamed of the burn scars down her arms and legs, eying her sister with a mixture of envy and awe. She thinks her sister has held life always in the palm of one hand, that "no" is a word the world never learned to say to her.

You've no doubt seen those TV shows where the child who has "made it" is confronted, as a surprise, by her own mother and father, tottering in weakly from backstage. (A pleasant surprise, of course: What would they do if parent and child came on the show only to curse out and insult each other?) On TV mother and child embrace and smile into each other's faces. Sometimes the mother and father weep, the child wraps them in her arms and leans across the table to tell how she would not have made it without their help. I have seen these programs.

Sometimes I dream a dream in which Dee and I are suddenly brought together on a TV program of this sort. Out of a dark and soft-seated limousine I am ushered into a bright room filled with many people. There I meet a smiling, gray, sporty man like Johnny Carson who shakes my hand and tells me what a fine girl I have. Then we are on the stage and Dee is embracing me with tears in her eyes. She pins on my dress a large orchid, even though she has told me once that she thinks orchids are tacky flowers.

In real life I am a large, big-boned woman with rough, man-working hands. In the winter I wear flannel nightgowns to bed and overalls during the day. I can kill and clean a hog as mercilessly as a man. My fat keeps me hot in zero weather. I can work outside all day, breaking ice to get water for washing; I can eat pork liver cooked over the open fire minutes after it comes steaming from the hog. One winter I knocked a bull calf straight in the brain between the eyes with a sledge hammer and had the meat

5

hung up to chill before nightfall. But of course all this does not show on television. I am the way my daughter would want me to be: a hundred pounds lighter, my skin like an uncooked barley pancake. My hair glistens in the hot bright lights. Johnny Carson has much to do to keep up with my quick and witty tongue.

But that is a mistake. I know even before I wake up. Who ever knew a Johnson with a quick tongue? Who can even imagine me looking a strange white man in the eye? It seems to me I have talked to them always with one foot raised in flight, with my head turned in whichever way is farthest from them. Dee, though. She would always look anyone in the eye. Hesitation was no part of her nature.

"How do I look, Mama?" Maggie says, showing just enough of her thin body enveloped in pink skirt and red blouse for me to know she's there, almost hidden by the door.

"Come out into the yard," I say.

Have you ever seen a lame animal, perhaps a dog run over by some careless person rich enough to own a car, sidle up to someone who is ignorant enough to be kind to him? That is the way my Maggie walks. She has been like this, chin on chest, eyes on ground, feet in shuffle, ever since the fire that burned the other house to the ground.

10   Dee is lighter than Maggie, with nicer hair and a fuller figure. She's a woman now, though sometimes I forget. How long ago was it that the other house burned? Ten, twelve years? Sometimes I can still hear the flames and feel Maggie's arms sticking to me, her hair smoking and her dress falling off her in little black papery flakes. Her eyes seemed stretched open, blazed open by the flames reflected in them. And Dee. I see her standing off under the sweet gum tree she used to dig gum out of; a look of concentration on her face as she watched the last dingy gray board of the house fall in toward the red-hot brick chimney. Why don't you do a dance around the ashes? I'd wanted to ask her. She had hated the house that much.

I used to think she hated Maggie, too. But that was before we raised the money, the church and me, to send her to Augusta to school. She used to read to us without pity; forcing words, lies, other folks' habits, whole lives upon us two, sitting trapped and ignorant underneath her voice. She washed us in a river of make-believe, burned us with a lot of knowledge we didn't necessarily need to know. Pressed us to her with the serious way she read, to shove us away at just the moment, like dimwits, we seemed about to understand.

Dee wanted nice things. A yellow organdy dress to wear to her graduation from high school; black pumps to match a green suit she'd made from an old suit somebody gave me. She was determined to stare down any disaster in her efforts. Her eyelids would not flicker for minutes at a time. Often I fought off the temptation to shake her. At sixteen she had a style of her own, and knew what style was.

I never had an education myself. After second grade the school was closed down. Don't ask me why: in 1927 colored asked fewer questions than they do now. Sometimes Maggie reads to me. She stumbles along good-naturedly but can't see well. She knows she is not bright. Like good looks and money, quickness passed her by. She will marry John Thomas (who has mossy teeth in an earnest face) and then I'll be free to sit here and I guess just sing church songs to myself. Although I never was a good singer. Never could carry a tune. I was always better at a man's job. I used to love to milk till I was hooked in the side in '49. Cows are soothing and slow and don't bother you, unless you try to milk them the wrong way.

I have deliberately turned my back on the house. It is three rooms, just like the one that burned, except the roof is tin; they don't make shingle roofs any more. There are no real windows, just some holes cut in the sides, like the portholes in a ship, but not round and not square, with rawhide holding the shutters up on the outside. This house is in a pasture, too, like the other one. No doubt when Dee sees it she will want to tear it down. She wrote me once that no matter where we "choose" to live, she will manage to come see us. But she will never bring her friends. Maggie and I thought about this and Maggie asked me, "Mama, when did Dee ever *have* any friends?"

She had a few. Furtive boys in pink shirts hanging about on washday after school. Nervous girls who never laughed. Impressed with her they worshiped the well-turned phrase, the cute shape, the scalding humor that erupted like bubbles in lye. She read to them.

When she was courting Jimmy T she didn't have much time to pay to us, but turned all her faultfinding power on him. He *flew* to marry a cheap city girl from a family of ignorant flashy people. She hardly had time to recompose herself.

When she comes I will meet—but there they are!

Maggie attempts to make a dash for the house, in her shuffling way, but I stay her with my hand. "Come back here," I say. And she stops and tries to dig a well in the sand with her toe.

It is hard to see them clearly through the strong sun. But even the first glimpse of leg out of the car tells me it is Dee. Her feet were always neat-looking, as if God himself had shaped them with a certain style. From the other side of the car comes a short, stocky man. Hair is all over his head a foot long and hanging from his chin like a kinky mule tail. I hear Maggie suck in her breath. "Uhnnnh," is what it sounds like. Like when you see the wriggling end of a snake just in front of your foot on the road. "Uhnnnh."

Dee next. A dress down to the ground, in this hot weather. A dress so loud it hurts my eyes. There are yellows and oranges enough to throw back the light of the sun. I feel my whole face warming from the heat waves it throws out. Earrings gold, too, and hanging down to her shoulders. Bracelets dangling and making noises when she moves her arm up to shake the folds of the dress out of her armpits. The dress is loose and flows, and as she walks closer, I like it. I hear Maggie go "Uhnnnh" again. It is her sister's hair. It stands straight up like the wool on a sheep. It is black as night and around the edges are two long pigtails that rope about like small lizards disappearing behind her ears.

"Wa-su-zo-Tean-o!"[1] she says, coming on in that gliding way the dress makes her move. The short stocky fellow with the hair to his navel is all grinning and he follows up with "Asalamalakim,[2] my mother and sister!" He moves to hug Maggie but she falls back, right up against the back of my chair. I feel her trembling there and when I look up I see the perspiration falling off her chin.

15

20

---

[1] *Wa-su-zo-Tean-o:* A greeting in Swahili; Dee sounds it out one syllable at a time.

[2] *Asalamalakim:* A greeting in Arabic: "Peace be upon you."

"Don't get up," says Dee. Since I am stout it takes something of a push. You can see me trying to move a second or two before I make it. She turns, showing white heels through her sandals, and goes back to the car. Out she peeks next with a Polaroid.[3] She stoops down quickly and lines up picture after picture of me sitting there in front of the house with Maggie cowering behind me. She never takes a shot without making sure the house is included. When a cow comes nibbling around the edge of the yard she snaps it and me and Maggie *and* the house. Then she puts the Polaroid in the back seat of the car, and comes up and kisses me on the forehead.

Meanwhile Asalamalakim is going through motions with Maggie's hand. Maggie's hand is as limp as a fish, and probably as cold, despite the sweat, and she keeps trying to pull it back. It looks like Asalamalakim wants to shake hands but wants to do it fancy. Or maybe he don't know how people shake hands. Anyhow, he soon gives up on Maggie.

"Well," I say. "Dee."

25   "No, Mama," she says. "Not 'Dee,' Wangero Leewanika Kemanjo!"

"What happened to 'Dee'?" I wanted to know.

"She's dead," Wangero said. "I couldn't bear it any longer, being named after the people who oppress me."

"You know as well as me you was named after your aunt Dicie," I said. Dicie is my sister. She named Dee. We called her "Big Dee" after Dee was born.

"But who was *she* named after?" asked Wangero.

30   "I guess after Grandma Dee," I said.

"And who was she named after?" asked Wangero.

"Her mother," I said, and saw Wangero was getting tired. "That's about as far back as I can trace it," I said. Though, in fact, I probably could have carried it back beyond the Civil War through the branches.

"Well," said Asalamalakim, "there you are."

"Uhnnnh," I heard Maggie say.

35   "There I was not," I said, "before 'Dicie' cropped up in our family, so why should I try to trace it that far back?"

He just stood there grinning, looking down on me like somebody inspecting a Model A car. Every once in a while he and Wangero sent eye signals over my head.

"How do you pronounce this name?" I asked.

"You don't have to call me by it if you don't want to," said Wangero.

"Why shouldn't I?" I asked. "If that's what you want us to call you, we'll call you."

40   "I know it might sound awkward at first," said Wangero.

"I'll get used to it," I said. "Ream it out again."

Well, soon we got the name out of the way. Asalamalakim had a name twice as long and three times as hard. After I tripped over it two or three times he told me to just call him Hakim-a-barber. I wanted to ask him was he a barber, but I didn't really think he was, so I didn't ask.

"You must belong to those beef-cattle peoples down the road," I said. They said "Asalamalakim" when they met you, too, but they didn't shake hands. Always too

---

[3]*Polaroid:* A type of camera with self-developing film.

busy: feeding the cattle, fixing the fences, putting up salt-lick shelters, throwing down hay. When the white folks poisoned some of the herd the men stayed up all night with rifles in their hands. I walked a mile and a half just to see the sight.

Hakim-a-barber said, "I accept some of their doctrines, but farming and raising cattle is not my style." (They didn't tell me, and I didn't ask, whether Wangero [Dee] had really gone and married him.)

We sat down to eat and right away he said he didn't eat collards and pork was unclean. Wangero, though, went on through the chitlins and corn bread, the greens and everything else. She talked a blue streak over the sweet potatoes. Everything delighted her. Even the fact that we still used the benches her daddy made for the table when we couldn't afford to buy chairs.

"Oh, Mama!" she cried. Then turned to Hakim-a-barber. "I never knew how lovely these benches are. You can feel the rump prints," she said, running her hands underneath her and along the bench. Then she gave a sigh and her hand closed over Grandma Dee's butter dish. "That's it!" she said. "I knew there was something I wanted to ask you if I could have." She jumped up from the table and went over in the corner where the churn stood, the milk in it clabber by now. She looked at the churn and looked at it.

"This churn top is what I need," she said. "Didn't Uncle Buddy whittle it out of a tree you all used to have?"

"Yes," I said.

"Uh huh," she said happily. "And I want the dasher, too."

"Uncle Buddy whittle that, too?" asked the barber.

Dee (Wangero) looked up at me.

"Aunt Dee's first husband whittled the dash," said Maggie so low you almost couldn't hear her. "His name was Henry, but they called him Stash."

"Maggie's brain is like an elephant's," Wangero said, laughing. "I can use the churn top as a centerpiece for the alcove table," she said, sliding a plate over the churn, "and I'll think of something artistic to do with the dasher."

When she finished wrapping the dasher the handle stuck out. I took it for a moment in my hands. You didn't even have to look close to see where hands pushing the dasher up and down to make butter had left a kind of sink in the wood. In fact, there were a lot of small sinks; you could see where thumb and fingers had sunk into the wood. It was beautiful light yellow wood, from a tree that grew in the yard where Big Dee and Stash had lived.

After dinner Dee (Wangero) went to the trunk at the foot of my bed and started rifling through it. Maggie hung back in the kitchen over the dishpan. Out came Wangero with two quilts. They had been pieced by Grandma Dee and then Big Dee and me had hung them on the quilt frames on the front porch and quilted them. One was in the Lone Star pattern. The other was Walk Around the Mountain. In both of them were scraps of dresses Grandma Dee had worn fifty and more years ago. Bits and pieces of Grandpa Jarrell's Paisley shirts. And one teeny faded blue piece, about the size of a penny matchbox, that was from Great Grandpa Ezra's uniform that he wore in the Civil War.

"Mama," Wangero said sweet as a bird. "Can I have these old quilts?"

I heard something fall in the kitchen, and a minute later the kitchen door slammed.

45

50

55

"Why don't you take one or two of the others?" I asked. "These old things was just done by me and Big Dee from some tops your grandma pieced before she died."

"No," said Wangero. "I don't want those. They are stitched around the borders by machine."

60 "That'll make them last better," I said.

"That's not the point," said Wangero. "These are all pieces of dresses Grandma used to wear. She did all this stitching by hand. Imagine!" She held the quilts securely in her arms, stroking them.

"Some of the pieces, like those lavender ones, come from old clothes her mother handed down to her," I said, moving up to touch the quilts. Dee (Wangero) moved back just enough so that I couldn't reach the quilts. They already belonged to her.

"Imagine!" she breathed again, clutching them closely to her bosom.

"The truth is," I said, "I promised to give them quilts to Maggie, for when she marries John Thomas."

65 She gasped like a bee had stung her. "Maggie can't appreciate these quilts!" she said. "She'd probably be backward enough to put them to everyday use."

"I reckon she would," I said. "God knows I been saving 'em for long enough with nobody using 'em. I hope she will!" I didn't want to bring up how I had offered Dee (Wangero) a quilt when she went away to college. Then she had told me they were old-fashioned, out of style.

"But, they're *priceless!*" she was saying now, furiously; for she has a temper. "Maggie would put them on the bed and in five years they'd be in rags. Less than that!"

"She can always make some more," I said. "Maggie knows how to quilt."

Dee (Wangero) looked at me with hatred. "You just will not understand. The point is these quilts, *these* quilts!"

70 "Well," I said, stumped. "What would *you* do with them?"

"Hang them," she said. As if that was the only thing you *could* do with quilts.

Maggie by now was standing in the door. I could almost hear the sound her feet made as they scraped over each other.

"She can have them, Mama," she said, like somebody used to never winning anything, or having anything reserved for her. "I can 'member Grandma Dee without the quilts."

I looked at her hard. She had filled her bottom lip with checkerberry snuff and it gave her face a kind of dopey, hangdog look. It was Grandma Dee and Big Dee who taught her how to quilt herself. She stood there with her scarred hands hidden in the folds of her skirt. She looked at her sister with something like fear but she wasn't mad at her. This was Maggie's portion. This was the way she knew God to work.

75 When I looked at her like that something hit me in the top of my head and ran down to the soles of my feet. Just like when I'm in church and the spirit of God touches me and I get happy and shout. I did something I never had done before: hugged Maggie to me, then dragged her on into the room, snatched the quilts out of Miss Wangero's hands and dumped them into Maggie's lap. Maggie just sat there on my bed with her mouth open.

"Take one or two of the others," I said to Dee.

But she turned without a word and went out to Hakim-a-barber.

"You just don't understand," she said, as Maggie and I came out to the car.

"What don't I understand?" I wanted to know.

"Your heritage," she said. And then she turned to Maggie, kissed her, and said, 80 "You ought to try to make something of yourself, too, Maggie. It's really a new day for us. But from the way you and Mama still live you'd never know it."

She put on some sunglasses that hid everything above the tip of her nose and her chin.

Maggie smiled; maybe at the sunglasses. But a real smile, not scared. After we watched the car dust settle I asked Maggie to bring me a dip of snuff. And then the two of us sat there just enjoying, until it was time to go in the house and go to bed.

Reading and Reacting

1. In American culture, what does a patchwork quilt symbolize?

2. What is the literal meaning of the two quilts to Maggie and her mother? to Dee? What symbolic meaning, if any, do they have to Maggie and her mother? Do the quilts have any symbolic meaning to Dee?

3. How does the contrast between the two sisters' appearances, personalities, lifestyles, and feelings about the quilts help to convey the story's theme?

4. What does the name *Wangero* signify to Dee? to her mother and sister? Could the name be considered a symbol? Why or why not?

5. Why do you think Maggie gives the quilts to her sister?

6. What is Dee's opinion of her mother and sister? Do you agree with her assessment?

7. What does the story's title suggest to you? Is it ironic? What other titles would be effective?

8. Discuss the possible meanings, aside from their literal meanings, that each of the following suggest: the family's yard, Maggie's burn scars, the trunk in which the quilts are kept, Dee's Polaroid camera. What symbolic functions, if any, do these items serve in the story?

9. **JOURNAL ENTRY** What objects have the kind of symbolic value to you that the quilts have to Maggie? What gives these objects this value?

10. **CRITICAL PERSPECTIVE** In her article "The Black Woman Artist as Wayward," critic Barbara Christian characterizes "Everyday Use" as a story in which Alice Walker examines the "creative legacy" of ordinary African American women. According to Christian, the story "is about the use and misuse of the concept of heritage. The mother of two daughters, one selfish and stylish, the other scarred and caring, passes on to us its true definition."

   What definition of *heritage* does the mother attempt to pass on to her children? How is this definition like or unlike Dee's definition?

Related Works: "Discovering America" (p. 135), "Sonny's Blues" (p. 547), "Two Kinds" (p. 639), "Aunt Jennifer's Tigers" (p. 799), "Digging" (p. 886), *Beauty* (p. 1069), *Fences* (p. 1548), *Trifles* (p. 1604)

Fiction in Film: Alice Walker's "Everyday Use"

At the heart of "Everyday Use" (p. 426) is the quilt, a symbol, among other things, of family unity and racial pride. The story is set in 1973, at a time when many African Americans asserted their racial pride and their connections with Africa. In the DVD version of the story, Dee and her friend Hakim-a-barber do this by sporting Afros and by wearing African clothing. In contrast, Maggie and Mrs. Johnson, who show little sympathy for Dee's cause, dress in a simple style associated with the rural American South. Central to the story are several symbols: the house, the bench, the churn, and of course, the quilt. The stills reproduced here depict scenes that appear on the DVD.

Dee and Hakim-a-barber
Source: ©Suzanne English/Worn Path Productions

The quilt
Source: ©Suzanne English/Worn Path Productions

Maggie and Mrs. Johnson in front of their house
Source: ©Suzanne English/Worn Path Productions

Mrs. Johnson giving the quilt to Maggie
Source: ©Suzanne English/Worn Path Productions

Reading and Reacting

1. When you read "Everyday Use," how did you visualize the characters? How are the characters in the pictures above like or unlike those you imagined?
2. Mrs. Johnson, the narrator of "Everyday Use," not only tells the story but also adds her comments and insights. What aspects of her narrative could be dramatized in a film, and what parts would require a narrator's voice-over?

3. If you were making a film version of the story, how would you introduce the quilt? How would you emphasize its symbolic value?

4. How would you depict the house (inside and out)?

5. Would you use a flashback to show the fire? What would be gained and lost by actually showing—rather than telling about—this important event?

6. If you wanted to make a contemporary film of the story, what difficulties would you face? Which actor would you cast as Dee? Maggie? Hakim-a-barber? Mrs. Johnson?

7. In the story, Mrs. Johnson says that Dee is probably ashamed of her and Maggie as well as of their house. How would you make this apparent in a film version of the story?

RAYMOND CARVER (1938–1988) is one of the most influential and widely read writers of our time. He fashioned his stories from the stuff of common life uncommonly perceived. He married at nineteen and fathered two children by the time he was twenty; during this period, he also began to write. He received a degree from Humboldt State University and later from the University of Iowa. His first collection of stories, *Will You Please Be Quiet, Please* (1976), was nominated for a National Book Award. Five more collections of stories followed, including *Cathedral* (1983)—nominated for both a Pulitzer Prize and a National Book Critics Circle Award—and *Where I'm Calling From: New and Selected Stories* (1988). Carver was also the author of five books of poetry. In his last years, Carver was praised as the best American short story writer since Ernest Hemingway; novelist Robert Stone called him "a hero of perception." He was made an Honorary Doctor of Letters at the University of Hartford and was inducted into the American Academy and Institute of Arts and Letters.

Cultural Context A cathedral is the principal church of a bishop's diocese. As centers of religious authority, civic pomp, and communal worship, cathedrals began to be built in Europe around the year 1000. They flourished throughout the Middle Ages as the power of the Catholic Church grew. The lavish decoration and dazzling design of these structures were meant not only to celebrate God but also to honor those secular and religious authorities who had financed the construction of the buildings. Cathedrals—especially those built in the Gothic period, between 1200 and 1500—often featured pointed arches, flying buttresses, and high spires designed to lift worshipers' eyes toward heaven. Most of the great cathedrals took several generations to complete, and for this reason, the craftsmen who worked on them had no expectation of seeing them completed. Their reward was to contribute their labors to a project that was so uplifting that it inspired many of them to contribute without conditions or self-interest.

Cathedral (1983)

This blind man, an old friend of my wife's, he was on his way to spend the night. His wife had died. So he was visiting the dead wife's relatives in Connecticut. He called my wife from his in-laws'. Arrangements were made. He would come by train, a five-hour trip, and my wife would meet him at the station. She hadn't seen him since she worked for him one summer in Seattle ten years ago. But she and the blind man had kept in touch. They made tapes and mailed them back and forth. I wasn't enthusiastic about his visit. He was no one I knew. And his being blind bothered me. My idea of blindness came from the movies. In the movies, the blind moved slowly and never laughed. Sometimes they were led by seeing-eye dogs. A blind man in my house was not something I looked forward to.

**Film
Series**

DVD
See p. 447
for film stills
from the
DVD version
of this story.

That summer in Seattle she had needed a job. She didn't have any money. The man she was going to marry at the end of the summer was in officers' training school. He didn't have any money, either. But she was in love with the guy, and he was in love with her, etc. She'd seen something in the paper: HELP WANTED—*Reading to Blind Man*, and a telephone number. She phoned and went over, was hired on the spot. She'd worked with this blind man all summer. She read stuff to him, case studies, reports, that sort of thing. She helped him organize his little office in the county social-service department. They'd become good friends, my wife and the blind man. How do I know these things? She told me. And she told me something else. On her last day in the office, the blind man asked if he could touch her face. She agreed to this. She told me he touched his fingers to every part of her face, her nose—even her neck! She never forgot it. She even tried to write a poem about it. She was always trying to write a poem. She wrote a poem or two every year, usually after something really important had happened to her.

When we first started going out together, she showed me the poem. In the poem, she recalled his fingers and the way they had moved around over her face. In the poem, she talked about what she had felt at the time, about what went through her mind when the blind man touched her nose and lips. I can remember I didn't think much of the poem. Of course, I didn't tell her that. Maybe I just don't understand poetry. I admit it's not the first thing I reach for when I pick up something to read.

Anyway, this man who'd first enjoyed her favors, the officer-to-be, he'd been her childhood sweetheart. So okay. I'm saying that at the end of the summer she let the blind man run his hands over her face, said goodbye to him, married her childhood etc., who was now a commissioned officer, and she moved away from Seattle. But they'd kept in touch, she and the blind man. She made the first contact after a year or so. She called him up one night from an Air Force base in Alabama. She wanted to talk. They talked. He asked her to send a tape and tell him about her life. She did this. She sent the tape. On the tape, she told the blind man about her husband and about their life together in the military. She told the blind man she loved her husband but she didn't like it where they lived and she didn't like it that he was part of the military-industrial thing. She told the blind man she'd written a poem and he was in it. She told him that she was writing a poem about what it was like to be an Air Force officer's wife. The poem wasn't finished yet. She was still writing it. The blind man made a tape. He sent her the tape. She made a tape. This went on for years. My wife's officer was posted to one base and then another. She sent tapes from Moody AFB, McGuire, McConnell, and finally Travis,[1] near Sacramento, where one night she got to feeling lonely and cut off from people she kept losing in that moving-around life. She got to feeling she couldn't go it another step. She went in and swallowed all the pills and capsules in the medicine chest and washed them down with a bottle of gin. Then she got into a hot bath and passed out.

5   But instead of dying, she got sick. She threw up. Her officer—why should he have a name? he was the childhood sweetheart, and what more does he want?—came home from somewhere, found her, and called the ambulance. In time, she put it all on a tape

---

[1]*Moody . . . Travis:* United States Air Force bases.

and sent the tape to the blind man. Over the years, she put all kinds of stuff on tapes and sent the tapes off lickety-split. Next to writing a poem every year, I think it was her chief means of recreation. On one tape, she told the blind man she'd decided to live away from her officer for a time. On another tape, she told him about her divorce. She and I began going out, and of course she told her blind man about it. She told him everything, or so it seemed to me. Once she asked me if I'd like to hear the latest tape from the blind man. This was a year ago. I was on the tape, she said. So I said okay, I'd listen to it. I got us drinks and we settled down in the living room. We made ready to listen. First she inserted the tape into the player and adjusted a couple of dials. Then she pushed a lever. The tape squeaked and someone began to talk in this loud voice. She lowered the volume. After a few minutes of harmless chitchat, I heard my own name in the mouth of this stranger, this blind man I didn't even know! And then this: "From all you've said about him, I can only conclude—" But we were interrupted, a knock at the door, something, and we didn't ever get back to the tape. Maybe it was just as well. I'd heard all I wanted to.

Now this same blind man was coming to sleep in my house.

"Maybe I could take him bowling," I said to my wife. She was at the draining board doing scalloped potatoes. She put down the knife she was using and turned around.

"If you love me," she said, "you can do this for me. If you don't love me, okay. But if you had a friend, any friend, and the friend came to visit, I'd make him feel comfortable." She wiped her hands with the dish towel.

"I don't have any blind friends," I said.

"You don't have *any* friends," she said. "Period. Besides," she said, "goddamn it, his wife's just died! Don't you understand that? The man's lost his wife!"

I didn't answer. She'd told me a little about the blind man's wife. Her name was Beulah. Beulah! That's a name for a colored woman.

"Was his wife a Negro?" I asked.

"Are you crazy?" my wife said. "Have you just flipped or something?" She picked up a potato. I saw it hit the floor, then roll under the stove. "What's wrong with you?" she said. "Are you drunk?"

"I'm just asking," I said.

Right then my wife filled me in with more detail than I cared to know. I made a drink and sat at the kitchen table to listen. Pieces of the story began to fall into place.

Beulah had gone to work for the blind man the summer after my wife had stopped working for him. Pretty soon Beulah and the blind man had themselves a church wedding. It was a little wedding—who'd want to go to such a wedding in the first place?—just the two of them, plus the minister and the minister's wife. But it was a church wedding just the same. It was what Beulah had wanted, he'd said. But even then Beulah must have been carrying the cancer in her glands. After they had been inseparable for eight years—my wife's word, *inseparable*—Beulah's health went into a rapid decline. She died in a Seattle hospital room, the blind man sitting beside the bed and holding on to her hand. They'd married, lived and worked together, slept together—had sex, sure—and then the blind man had to bury her. All this without his having ever seen what the goddamned woman looked like. It was beyond my understanding. Hearing this, I felt sorry for the blind man for a little bit. And then I found myself thinking what a pitiful life this woman must have led. Imagine a woman

10

15

who could never see herself as she was seen in the eyes of her loved one. A woman who could go on day after day and never receive the smallest compliment from her beloved. A woman whose husband could never read the expression on her face, be it misery or something better. Someone who could wear makeup or not—what difference to him? She could, if she wanted, wear green eye-shadow around one eye, a straight pin in her nostril, yellow slacks, and purple shoes, no matter. And then to slip off into death, the blind man's hand on her hand, his blind eyes streaming tears—I'm imagining now—her last thought maybe this: that he never even knew what she looked like, and she on an express to the grave. Robert was left with a small insurance policy and a half of a twenty-peso Mexican coin. The other half of the coin went into the box with her. Pathetic.

So when the time rolled around, my wife went to the depot to pick him up. With nothing to do but wait—sure, I blamed him for that—I was having a drink and watching the TV when I heard the car pull into the drive. I got up from the sofa with my drink and went to the window to have a look.

I saw my wife laughing as she parked the car. I saw her get out of the car and shut the door. She was still wearing a smile. Just amazing. She went around to the other side of the car to where the blind man was already starting to get out. This blind man, feature this, he was wearing a full beard! A beard on a blind man! Too much, I say. The blind man reached into the backseat and dragged out a suitcase. My wife took his arm, shut the car door, and, talking all the way, moved him down the drive and then up the steps to the front porch. I turned off the TV. I finished my drink, rinsed the glass, dried my hands. Then I went to the door.

My wife said, "I want you to meet Robert. Robert, this is my husband. I've told you all about him." She was beaming. She had this blind man by his coat sleeve.

20   The blind man let go of his suitcase and up came his hand.

I took it. He squeezed hard, held my hand, and then he let it go.

"I feel like we've already met," he boomed.

"Likewise," I said. I didn't know what else to say. Then I said, "Welcome. I've heard a lot about you." We began to move then, a little group, from the porch into the living room, my wife guiding him by the arm. The blind man was carrying his suitcase in his other hand. My wife said things like, "To your left here, Robert. That's right. Now watch it, there's a chair. That's it. Sit down right here. This is the sofa. We just bought this sofa two weeks ago."

I started to say something about the old sofa. I'd liked that old sofa. But I didn't say anything. Then I wanted to say something else, small-talk, about the scenic ride along the Hudson.[2] How going *to* New York, you should sit on the right-hand side of the train, and coming *from* New York, the left-hand side.

25   "Did you have a good train ride?" I said. "Which side of the train did you sit on, by the way?"

"What a question, which side!" my wife said. "What's it matter which side?" she said.

"I just asked," I said.

---

[2] *Hudson:* A river in New York State.

"Right side," the blind man said. "I hadn't been on a train in nearly forty years. Not since I was a kid. With my folks. That's been a long time. I'd nearly forgotten the sensation. I have winter in my beard now," he said. "So I've been told, anyway. Do I look distinguished, my dear?" the blind man said to my wife.

"You look distinguished, Robert," she said. "Robert," she said. "Robert, it's just so good to see you."

My wife finally took her eyes off the blind man and looked at me. I had the feeling she didn't like what she saw. I shrugged.   30

I've never met, or personally known, anyone who was blind. This blind man was late forties, a heavy-set, balding man with stooped shoulders, as if he carried a great weight there. He wore brown slacks, brown shoes, a light-brown shirt, a tie, a sports coat. Spiffy. He also had this full beard. But he didn't use a cane and he didn't wear dark glasses. I'd always thought dark glasses were a must for the blind. Fact was, I wished he had a pair. At first glance, his eyes looked like anyone else's eyes. But if you looked close, there was something different about them. Too much white in the iris, for one thing, and the pupils seemed to move around in the sockets without his knowing it or being able to stop it. Creepy. As I stared at his face, I saw the left pupil turn in toward his nose while the other made an effort to keep in one place. But it was only an effort, for that eye was on the roam without his knowing it or wanting it to be.

I said, "Let me get you a drink. What's your pleasure? We have a little of everything. It's one of our pastimes."

"Bub, I'm a Scotch man myself," he said fast enough in this big voice.

"Right," I said. Bub! "Sure you are. I knew it."

He let his fingers touch his suitcase, which was sitting alongside the sofa. He was   35 taking his bearings. I didn't blame him for that.

"I'll move that up to your room," my wife said.

"No, that's fine," the blind man said loudly. "It can go up when I go up."

"A little water with the Scotch?" I said.

"Very little," he said.

"I knew it," I said.   40

He said, "Just a tad. The Irish actor, Barry Fitzgerald? I'm like that fellow. When I drink water, Fitzgerald said, I drink water. When I drink whiskey, I drink whiskey." My wife laughed. The blind man brought his hand up under his beard. He lifted his beard slowly and let it drop.

I did the drinks, three big glasses of Scotch with a splash of water in each. Then we made ourselves comfortable and talked about Robert's travels. First the long flight from the West Coast to Connecticut, we covered that. Then from Connecticut up here by train. We had another drink concerning that leg of the trip.

I remembered having read somewhere that the blind didn't smoke because, as speculation had it, they couldn't see the smoke they exhaled. I thought I knew that much and that much only about blind people. But this blind man smoked his cigarette down to the nubbin and then lit another one. This blind man filled his ashtray and my wife emptied it.

When we sat down at the table for dinner, we had another drink. My wife heaped Robert's plate with cube steak, scalloped potatoes, green beans. I buttered him up two slices of bread. I said, "Here's bread and butter for you." I swallowed some of my drink.

"Now let us pray," I said, and the blind man lowered his head. My wife looked at me, her mouth agape. "Pray the phone won't ring and the food doesn't get cold," I said.

45   We dug in. We ate everything there was to eat on the table. We ate like there was no tomorrow. We didn't talk. We ate. We scarfed. We grazed that table. We were into serious eating. The blind man had right away located his foods, he knew just where everything was on his plate. I watched with admiration as he used his knife and fork on the meat. He'd cut two pieces of meat, fork the meat into his mouth, and then go all out for the scalloped potatoes, the beans next, and then he'd tear off a hunk of buttered bread and eat that. He'd follow this up with a big drink of milk. It didn't seem to bother him to use his fingers once in a while, either.

We finished everything, including half a strawberry pie. For a few moments, we sat as if stunned. Sweat beaded on our faces. Finally, we got up from the table and left the dirty plates. We didn't look back. We took ourselves into the living room and sank into our places again. Robert and my wife sat on the sofa. I took the big chair. We had us two or three more drinks while they talked about the major things that had come to pass for them in the past ten years. For the most part, I just listened. Now and then I joined in. I didn't want him to think I'd left the room, and I didn't want her to think I was feeling left out. They talked of things that had happened to them—to them!—these past ten years. I waited in vain to hear my name on my wife's sweet lips: "And then my dear husband came into my life"—something like that. But I heard nothing of the sort. More talk of Robert. Robert had done a little of everything, it seemed, a regular blind jack-of-all-trades. But most recently he and his wife had had an Amway distributorship, from which, I gathered, they'd earned their living, such as it was. The blind man was also a ham radio operator.[3] He talked in his loud voice about conversations he'd had with fellow operators in Guam, in the Philippines, in Alaska, and even in Tahiti. He said he'd have a lot of friends there if he ever wanted to go visit those places. From time to time, he'd turn his blind face toward me, put his hand under his beard, ask me something. How long had I been in my present position? (Three years.) Did I like my work? (I didn't.) Was I going to stay with it? (What were the options?) Finally, when I thought he was beginning to run down, I got up and turned on the TV.

My wife looked at me with irritation. She was heading toward a boil. Then she looked at the blind man and said, "Robert, do you have a TV?"

The blind man said, "My dear, I have two TVs. I have a color set and a black-and-white thing, an old relic. It's funny, but if I turn the TV on, and I'm always turning it on, I turn on the color set. It's funny, don't you think?"

I didn't know what to say to that. I had absolutely nothing to say to that. No opinion. So I watched the news program and tried to listen to what the announcer was saying.

50   "This is a color TV," the blind man said. "Don't ask me how, but I can tell."

"We traded up a while ago," I said.

The blind man had another taste of his drink. He lifted his beard, sniffed it, and let it fall. He leaned forward on the sofa. He positioned his ashtray on the coffee table,

---

[3]*ham radio operator:* A licensed amateur radio operator.

then put the lighter to his cigarette. He leaned back on the sofa and crossed his legs at the ankles.

My wife covered her mouth, and then she yawned. She stretched. She said, "I think I'll go upstairs and put on my robe. I think I'll change into something else. Robert, you make yourself comfortable," she said.

"I'm comfortable," the blind man said.

"I want you to feel comfortable in this house," she said.

"I am comfortable," the blind man said.

After she'd left the room, he and I listened to the weather report and then to the sports roundup. By that time, she'd been gone so long I didn't know if she was going to come back. I thought she might have gone to bed. I wished she'd come back downstairs. I didn't want to be left alone with a blind man. I asked him if he wanted another drink, and he said sure. Then I asked if he wanted to smoke some dope with me. I said I'd just rolled a number. I hadn't, but I planned to do so in about two shakes.

"I'll try some with you," he said.

"Damn right," I said. "That's the stuff."

I got our drinks and sat down on the sofa with him. Then I rolled us two fat numbers. I lit one and passed it. I brought it to his fingers. He took it and inhaled.

"Hold it as long as you can," I said. I could tell he didn't know the first thing.

My wife came back downstairs wearing her pink robe and her pink slippers.

"What do I smell?" she said.

"We thought we'd have us some cannabis," I said.

My wife gave me a savage look. Then she looked at the blind man and said, "Robert, I didn't know you smoked."

He said, "I do now, my dear. There's a first time for everything. But I don't feel anything yet."

"This stuff is pretty mellow," I said. "This stuff is mild. It's dope you can reason with," I said. "It doesn't mess you up."

"Not much it doesn't, bub," he said, and laughed.

My wife sat on the sofa between the blind man and me. I passed her the number. She took it and toked[4] and then passed it back to me. "Which way is this going?" she said. Then she said, "I shouldn't be smoking this. I can hardly keep my eyes open as it is. That dinner did me in. I shouldn't have eaten so much."

"It was the strawberry pie," the blind man said. "That's what did it," he said, and he laughed his big laugh. Then he shook his head.

"There's more strawberry pie," I said.

"Do you want some more, Robert?" my wife said.

"Maybe in a little while," he said.

We gave our attention to the TV. My wife yawned again. She said, "Your bed is made up when you feel like going to bed, Robert. I know you must have had a long day. When you're ready to go to bed, say so." She pulled his arm. "Robert?"

He came to and said, "I've had a real nice time. This beats tapes, doesn't it?"

---

[4]*toked*: Inhaled.

I said, "Coming at you," and I put the number between his fingers. He inhaled, held the smoke, and then let it go. It was like he'd been doing it since he was nine years old.

"Thanks, bub," he said. "But I think this is all for me. I think I'm beginning to feel it," he said. He held the burning roach out for my wife.

"Same here," she said. "Ditto. Me, too." She took the roach and passed it to me. "I may just sit here for a while between you two guys with my eyes closed. But don't let me bother you, okay? Either one of you. If it bothers you, say so. Otherwise, I may just sit here with my eyes closed until you're ready to go to bed," she said. "Your bed's made up, Robert, when you're ready. It's right next to our room at the top of the stairs. We'll show you up when you're ready. You wake me up now, you guys, if I fall asleep." She said that and then she closed her eyes and went to sleep.

The news program ended. I got up and changed the channel. I sat back down on the sofa. I wished my wife hadn't pooped out. Her head lay across the back of the sofa, her mouth open. She'd turned so that her robe slipped away from her legs, exposing a juicy thigh. I reached to draw her robe back over her, and it was then that I glanced at the blind man. What the hell! I flipped the robe open again.

80   "You say when you want some strawberry pie," I said.

"I will," he said.

I said, "Are you tired? Do you want me to take you up to your bed? Are you ready to hit the hay?"

"Not yet," he said. "No, I'll stay up with you, bub. If that's all right. I'll stay up until you're ready to turn in. We haven't had a chance to talk. Know what I mean? I feel like me and her monopolized the evening." He lifted his beard and he let it fall. He picked up his cigarettes and his lighter.

"That's all right," I said. Then I said, "I'm glad for the company."

85   And I guess I was. Every night I smoked dope and stayed up as long as I could before I fell asleep. My wife and I hardly ever went to bed at the same time. When I did go to sleep, I had these dreams. Sometimes I'd wake up from one of them, my heart going crazy.

Something about the church and the Middle Ages was on the TV. Not your run-of-the-mill TV fare. I wanted to watch something else. I turned to the other channels. But there was nothing on them, either. So I turned back to the first channel and apologized.

"Bub, it's all right," the blind man said. "It's fine with me. Whatever you want to watch is okay. I'm always learning something. Learning never ends. It won't hurt me to learn something tonight. I got ears," he said.

We didn't say anything for a time. He was leaning forward with his head turned at me, his right ear aimed in the direction of the set. Very disconcerting. Now and then his eyelids drooped and then they snapped open again. Now and then he put his fingers into his beard and tugged, like he was thinking about something he was hearing on the television.

On the screen, a group of men wearing cowls was being set upon and tormented by men dressed in skeleton costumes and men dressed as devils. The men dressed as devils wore devil masks, horns, and long tails. This pageant was part of a procession. The Englishman who was narrating the thing said it took place in Spain once a year. I tried to explain to the blind man what was happening.

90 "Skeletons," he said. "I know about skeletons," he said, and nodded.

The TV showed this one cathedral. Then there was a long, slow look at another one. Finally, the picture switched to the famous one in Paris, with its flying buttresses[5] and its spires reaching up to the clouds. The camera pulled away to show the whole of the cathedral rising above the skyline.

There were times when the Englishman who was telling the thing would shut up, would simply let the camera move around the cathedrals. Or else the camera would tour the countryside, men in fields walking behind oxen. I waited as long as I could. Then I felt I had to say something. I said, "They're showing the outside of this cathedral now. Gargoyles. Little statues carved to look like monsters. Now I guess they're in Italy. Yeah, they're in Italy. There's paintings on the walls of this one church."

"Are those fresco[6] paintings, bub?" he asked, and he sipped from his drink.

I reached for my glass. But it was empty. I tried to remember what I could remember. "You're asking me are those frescoes?" I said. "That's a good question. I don't know."

The camera moved to a cathedral outside Lisbon.[7] The differences in the Portuguese cathedral compared with the French and Italian were not that great. But they were there. Mostly the interior stuff. Then something occurred to me, and I said, "Something has occurred to me. Do you have any idea what a cathedral is? What they look like, that is? Do you follow me? If somebody says cathedral to you, do you have any notion what they're talking about? Do you know the difference between that and a Baptist church, say?"

He let the smoke dribble from his mouth. "I know they took hundreds of workers fifty or a hundred years to build," he said. "I just heard the man say that, of course. I know generations of the same families worked on a cathedral. I heard him say that, too. The men who began their life's work on them, they never lived to see the completion of their work. In that wise, bub, they're no different from the rest of us, right?" He laughed. Then his eyelids drooped again. His head nodded. He seemed to be snoozing. Maybe he was imagining himself in Portugal. The TV was showing another cathedral now. This one was in Germany. The Englishman's voice droned on. "Cathedrals," the blind man said. He sat up and rolled his head back and forth. "If you want the truth, bub, that's about all I know. What I just said. What I heard him say. But maybe you could describe one to me? I wish you'd do it. I'd like that. If you want to know, I really don't have a good idea."

I stared hard at the shot of the cathedral on the TV. How could I even begin to describe it? But say my life depended on it. Say my life was being threatened by an insane guy who said I had to do it or else.

I stared some more at the cathedral before the picture flipped off into the countryside. There was no use. I turned to the blind man and said, "To begin with, they're very tall." I was looking around the room for clues. "They reach way up. Up and up. Toward the sky. They're so big, some of them, they have to have these supports. To help hold them up, so to speak. These supports are called buttresses. They remind me of viaducts,[8] for some reason. But maybe you don't know viaducts, either? Sometimes

95

---

[5] *flying buttresses:* Supports that are often connected to a building or structure by an arch.

[6] *fresco:* Painted plaster.

[7] *Lisbon:* The capital of Portugal.

[8] *viaducts:* Long, elevated roadways.

the cathedrals have devils and such carved into the front. Sometimes lords and ladies. Don't ask me why this is," I said.

He was nodding. The whole upper part of his body seemed to be moving back and forth.

100 "I'm not doing so good, am I?" I said.

He stopped nodding and leaned forward on the edge of the sofa. As he listened to me, he was running his fingers through his beard. I wasn't getting through to him, I could see that. But he waited for me to go on just the same. He nodded, like he was trying to encourage me. I tried to think what else to say. "They're really big," I said. "They're massive. They're built of stone. Marble, too, sometimes. In those olden days, when they built cathedrals, men wanted to be close to God. In those olden days, God was an important part of everyone's life. You could tell this from their cathedral-building. I'm sorry," I said, "but it looks like that's the best I can do for you. I'm just no good at it."

"That's all right, bub," the blind man said. "Hey, listen. I hope you don't mind my asking you. Can I ask you something? Let me ask you a simple question, yes or no. I'm just curious and there's no offense. You're my host. But let me ask if you are in any way religious? You don't mind my asking?"

I shook my head. He couldn't see that, though. A wink is the same as a nod to a blind man. "I guess I don't believe in it. In anything. Sometimes it's hard. You know what I'm saying?"

"Sure, I do," he said.

105 "Right," I said.

The Englishman was still holding forth. My wife sighed in her sleep. She drew a long breath and went on with her sleeping.

"You'll have to forgive me," I said. "But I can't tell you what a cathedral looks like. It just isn't in me to do it. I can't do any more than I've done."

The blind man sat very still, his head down, as he listened to me.

I said, "The truth is, cathedrals don't mean anything special to me. Nothing. Cathedrals. They're something to look at on late-night TV. That's all they are."

110 It wtas then that the blind man cleared his throat. He brought something up. He took a handkerchief from his back pocket. Then he said, "I get it, bub. It's okay. It happens. Don't worry about it," he said. "Hey, listen to me. Will you do me a favor? I got an idea. Why don't you find us some heavy paper? And a pen. We'll do something. We'll draw one together. Get us a pen and some heavy paper. Go on, bub, get the stuff," he said.

So I went upstairs. My legs felt like they didn't have any strength in them. They felt like they did after I'd done some running. In my wife's room, I looked around. I found some ballpoints in a little basket on her table. And then I tried to think where to look for the kind of paper he was talking about.

Downstairs, in the kitchen, I found a shopping bag with onion skins in the bottom of the bag. I emptied the bag and shook it. I brought it into the living room and sat down with it near his legs. I moved some things, smoothed the wrinkles from the bag, spread it out on the coffee table.

The blind man got down from the sofa and sat next to me on the carpet.

He ran his fingers over the paper. He went up and down the sides of the paper. The edges, even the edges. He fingered the corners.

"All right," he said. "All right, let's do her."

He found my hand, the hand with the pen. He closed his hand over my hand. "Go ahead, bub, draw," he said. "Draw. You'll see. I'll follow along with you. It'll be okay. Just begin now like I'm telling you. You'll see. Draw," the blind man said.

So I began. First I drew a box that looked like a house. It could have been the house I lived in. Then I put a roof on it. At either end of the roof, I drew spires. Crazy.

"Swell," he said. "Terrific. You're doing fine," he said. "Never thought anything like this could happen in your lifetime, did you, bub? Well, it's a strange life, we all know that. Go on now. Keep it up."

I put in windows with arches. I drew flying buttresses. I hung great doors. I couldn't stop. The TV station went off the air. I put down the pen and closed and opened my fingers. The blind man felt around over the paper. He moved the tips of his fingers over the paper, all over what I had drawn, and he nodded.

"Doing fine," the blind man said.

I took up the pen again, and he found my hand. I kept at it. I'm no artist. But I kept drawing just the same.

My wife opened up her eyes and gazed at us. She sat up on the sofa, her robe hanging open. She said, "What are you doing? Tell me, I want to know."

I didn't answer her.

The blind man said, "We're drawing a cathedral. Me and him are working on it. Press hard," he said to me. "That's right. That's good," he said. "Sure. You got it, bub, I can tell. You didn't think you could. But you can, can't you? You're cooking with gas now. You know what I'm saying? We're going to really have us something here in a minute. How's the old arm?" he said. "Put some people in there now. What's a cathedral without people?"

My wife said, "What's going on? Robert, what are you doing? What's going on?"

"It's all right," he said to her. "Close your eyes now," the blind man said to me.

I did it. I closed them just like he said.

"Are they closed?" he said. "Don't fudge."

"They're closed," I said.

"Keep them that way," he said. He said, "Don't stop now. Draw."

So we kept on with it. His fingers rode my fingers as my hand went over the paper. It was like nothing else in my life up to now.

Then he said, "I think that's it. I think you got it," he said. "Take a look. What do you think?"

But I had my eyes closed. I thought I'd keep them that way for a little longer. I thought it was something I ought to do.

"Well?" he said. "Are you looking?"

My eyes were still closed. I was in my house. I knew that. But I didn't feel like I
was inside anything.

"It's really something," I said.

Reading and Reacting

1. Who is the narrator? What do we know about him? Why does the impending visit by the blind man disturb him?

2. At several points in the story, the narrator's wife loses patience with him. What causes her displeasure? What do her reactions reveal about the wife? about the narrator?

3. Why did the narrator's wife leave her first husband? What qualities in the narrator might have led his wife to marry him?

4. Why is the narrator's wife so devoted to the blind man? What does she gain from her relationship with him?

5. According to the narrator, his wife never forgot the blind man's running his fingers over her face. Why is this experience so important to her?

6. Toward the end of the story, the blind man asks the narrator to describe a cathedral. Why is the narrator unable to do so? What does his inability to do so reveal about him?

7. Why does the blind man tell the narrator to close his eyes while he is drawing? What does he hope to teach him? What is the narrator able to "see" with his eyes shut that he cannot see with them open?

8. In paragraph 96, the blind man observes that the men who began work on a cathedral never lived to see it completed. In this way, he says, "they're no different from the rest of us." What does the cathedral symbolize to the blind man? What does it come to symbolize to the narrator?

9. JOURNAL ENTRY The blind man is an old friend of the narrator's wife. Why then does he focus on the narrator? In what way is the narrator's spiritual development the blind man's gift to the narrator's wife?

10. CRITICAL PERSPECTIVE Critic Kirk Nesset, in his discussion of "Cathedral," notes that the narrator becomes more open as the story progresses, and that this coming out is mirrored by the rhetoric of the story. Early on in the story, the narrator feels momentarily "sorry for the blind man," his insulated hardness beginning to soften. As the walls of his resentment noticeably crack, he watches with "admiration" as Robert eats, recognizing Robert's handicap to be "no impairment to his performance at the dinner table. . . . Like Robert, who is on a journey by train, dropping in on friends and relatives, trying to get over the loss of his wife, the narrator is also on a journey, one signaled by signposts in his language and played out by the events of the story he tells."

Do you agree that the narrator becomes more open? If so, can you cite any other instances where the words he chooses reflect this increasing openness?

Related Works: "Gryphon" (p. 250), "Doe Season" (p. 472), "When I Heard the Learn'd Astronomer" (p. 715), "The Value of Education" (p. 727), "On First Looking into Chapman's Homer" (p. 819), "Batter My Heart, Three-Personed God" (p. 979), "God's Grandeur" (p. 992)

Fiction in Film: Raymond Carver's "Cathedral"

Symbolism is important in the story "Cathedral" (p. 435). In the DVD version of the story, the narrator's encounter with his wife's blind friend, Robert, culminates in a symbolic event—the drawing of a cathedral. In addition, blindness becomes symbolic not only of Robert's condition but also of the narrator's—and, by extension, symbolic of the condition of all of humanity. The film clearly portrays the narrator's spiritual quest as well as the blind man's ability to guide him to salvation. The stills included here depict scenes that appear on the DVD.

Husband and wife on couch
Source: ©Howard Ksia/Worn Path Productions

Husband drawing (with eyes open)
Source: ©Howard Ksia/Worn Path Productions

The three characters sitting and eating
Source: ©Howard Ksia/Worn Path Productions

Husband drawing (with eyes shut) with wife and Robert beside him
Source: ©Howard Ksia/Worn Path Productions

Reading and Reacting

1. The first part of the story gives background information about the wife's relationship with Robert. How would you present this information in a film? Would you show it in a series of flashbacks, or would you have a narrator or one of the characters tell about it?
2. The husband has a number of preconceived ideas about blindness, and as a result, he does not look forward to having Robert visit him. How would you convey his discomfort in a film version of the story?

3. In the story, the wife is clearly uneasy about how her husband will react to Robert. How would you convey this emotion in the film?

4. Other than saying that Robert has a full beard, the narrator does not describe the characters in the story. If you were making a film, in what ways would your characters look different from the ones shown (p. 447)?

5. What information from the story would you consider essential for a film version? What information could you do without?

6. What scene could you add to show what took place after the story was over? Which characters would be in this new scene? What would they be doing?

Nathaniel: Mathew B. Brady/Bettmann/Corbis

NATHANIEL HAWTHORNE (1804–1864) was born in Salem, Massachusetts, the great-great-grandson of a judge who presided over the infamous Salem witch trials. After his sea captain father was killed on a voyage when Hawthorne was four years old, his childhood was one of genteel poverty. An uncle paid for his education at Bowdoin College in Maine, where Hawthorne's friends included a future president of the United States, Franklin Pierce, who in 1853 appointed him U.S. consul in Liverpool, England. Hawthorne published four novels—*The Scarlet Letter* (1850), *The House of the Seven Gables* (1851), *The Blithedale Romance* (1852), and *The Marble Faun* (1860)—and more than one hundred short stories and sketches.

Hawthorne referred to his own work as *romance*. He used this term to mean not an escape from reality but rather a method of confronting "the depths of our common nature" and "the truth of the heart." His stories probe the dark side of human nature and frequently paint a world that is virtuous on the surface but (as Young Goodman Brown comes to believe) "one stain of guilt, one mighty blood spot" beneath. Hawthorne's stories often emphasize the ambiguity of human experience. For example, the reader is left to wonder whether Goodman Brown actually saw a witch's coven or dreamed about the event. For Hawthorne, what is important is Brown's recognition that evil may be found everywhere. "Young Goodman Brown," as Hawthorne's neighbor and friend Herman Melville once said, is a tale "as deep as Dante."

Cultural Context   During the five months of the Salem witch trials of 1692, nineteen women and men accused of being witches were executed by hanging. The accusations began when a few young girls claimed they were possessed by the devil and accused three Salem women of witchcraft. As the hysteria grew throughout Massachusetts, the list of the accused grew as well. Eventually, 150 people were imprisoned before the governor dismissed the special witchcraft court and released the remaining twenty-two prisoners. It is in this historical setting that "Young Goodman Brown" takes place.

Young Goodman[1] Brown   (1835)

Young Goodman Brown came forth at sunset, into the street of Salem village, but put his head back, after crossing the threshold, to exchange a parting kiss with his young wife. And Faith, as the wife was aptly named, thrust her own pretty head into the street, letting the wind play with the pink ribbons of her cap, while she called to Goodman Brown.

---

[1]*Goodman:* A form of address, similar to *Mr.*, meaning "husband."

"Dearest heart," whispered she, softly and rather sadly, when her lips were close to his ear, "prithee, put off your journey until sunrise, and sleep in your own bed to-night. A lone woman is troubled with such dreams and such thoughts, that she's afeard of herself, sometimes. Pray, tarry with me this night, dear husband, of all nights in the year!"

"My love and my Faith," replied young Goodman Brown, "of all nights in the year, this one night must I tarry away from thee. My journey, as thou callest it, forth and back again, must needs be done 'twixt now and sunrise. What, my sweet, pretty wife, dost thou doubt me already, and we but three months married!"

"Then God bless you!" said Faith with the pink ribbons, "and may you find all well, when you come back."

"Amen!" cried Goodman Brown. "Say thy prayers, dear Faith, and go to bed at dusk, and no harm will come to thee."

So they parted; and the young man pursued his way, until, being about to turn the corner by the meeting-house, he looked back and saw the head of Faith still peeping after him, with a melancholy air, in spite of her pink ribbons.

"Poor little Faith!" thought he, for his heart smote him. "What a wretch am I, to leave her on such an errand! She talks of dreams, too. Methought, as she spoke, there was trouble in her face, as if a dream had warned her what work is to be done to-night. But no, no! 't would kill her to think it. Well; she's a blessed angel on earth; and after this one night, I'll cling to her skirts and follow her to Heaven."

With this excellent resolve for the future, Goodman Brown felt himself justified in making more haste on his present evil purpose. He had taken a dreary road, darkened by all the gloomiest trees of the forest, which barely stood aside to let the narrow path creep through, and closed immediately behind. It was as lonely as could be; and there is this peculiarity in such a solitude, that the traveller knows not who may be concealed by the innumerable trunks and the thick boughs overhead; so that, with lonely footsteps, he may yet be passing through an unseen multitude.

"There may be a devilish Indian behind every tree," said Goodman Brown to himself; and he glanced fearfully behind him, as he added, "What if the devil himself should be at my very elbow!"

His head being turned back, he passed a crook of the road, and looking forward again, beheld the figure of a man, in grave and decent attire, seated at the foot of an old tree. He arose at Goodman Brown's approach, and walked onward, side by side with him.

"You are late, Goodman Brown," said he. "The clock of the Old South[2] was striking, as I came through Boston; and that is full fifteen minutes agone."

"Faith kept me back awhile," replied the young man, with a tremor in his voice, caused by the sudden appearance of his companion, though not wholly unexpected.

It was now deep dusk in the forest, and deepest in that part of it where these two were journeying. As nearly as could be discerned, the second traveller was about fifty years old, apparently in the same rank of life as Goodman Brown, and bearing a considerable resemblance to him, though perhaps more in expression than features. Still,

5

10

---

[2] *Old South:* Old South Church in Boston, renowned meeting place for American patriots during the Revolution.

they might have been taken for father and son. And yet, though the elder person was as simply clad as the younger, and as simple in manner too, he had an indescribable air of one who knew the world, and would not have felt abashed at the governor's dinner-table, or in King William's[3] court, were it possible that his affairs should call him thither. But the only thing about him that could be fixed upon as remarkable, was his staff, which bore the likeness of a great black snake, so curiously wrought, that it might almost be seen to twist and wriggle itself like a living serpent. This, of course, must have been an ocular deception, assisted by the uncertain light.

"Come, Goodman Brown!" cried his fellow-traveller, "this is a dull pace for the beginning of a journey. Take my staff, if you are so soon weary."

15   "Friend," said the other, exchanging his slow pace for a full stop, "having kept covenant by meeting thee here, it is my purpose now to return whence I came. I have scruples, touching the matter thou wot'st[4] of."

"Sayest thou so?" replied he of the serpent, smiling apart. "Let us walk on, nevertheless, reasoning as we go, and if I convince thee not, thou shalt turn back. We are but a little way in the forest, yet."

"Too far, too far!" exclaimed the goodman, unconsciously resuming his walk. "My father never went into the woods on such an errand, nor his father before him. We have been a race of honest men and good Christians, since the days of the martyrs. And shall I be the first of the name of Brown that ever took this path and kept—"

"Such company, thou wouldst say," observed the elder person, interrupting his pause. "Well said, Goodman Brown! I have been as well acquainted with your family as with ever a one among the Puritans; and that's no trifle to say. I helped your grandfather, the constable, when he lashed the Quaker woman so smartly through the streets of Salem. And it was I that brought your father a pitch-pine knot, kindled at my own hearth, to set fire to an Indian village, in King Philip's war.[5] They were my good friends, both; and many a pleasant walk have we had along this path, and returned merrily after midnight. I would fain be friends with you, for their sake."

"If it be as thou sayest," replied Goodman Brown, "I marvel they never spoke of these matters. Or, verily, I marvel not, seeing that the least rumor of the sort would have driven them from New England. We are a people of prayer, and good works to boot, and abide no such wickedness."

20   "Wickedness or not," said the traveller with the twisted staff, "I have a very general acquaintance here in New England. The deacons of many a church have drunk the communion wine with me; the selectmen, of divers towns, make me their chairman; and a majority of the Great and General Court are firm supporters of my interest. The governor and I, too—but these are state secrets."

"Can this be so!" cried Goodman Brown, with a stare of amazement at his undisturbed companion. "Howbeit, I have nothing to do with the governor and council; they have their own ways, and are no rule for a simple husbandman like me. But, were I to go

---

[3]*King William:* William III, king of England from 1689 to 1702.

[4]*wot'st of:* Know of.

[5]*King Philip's war:* A war of Indian resistance led by Metacomet of the Wampanoags, known to the English as "King Philip." The war, intended to halt expansion of English settlers in Massachusetts, collapsed after Metacomet's death in August 1676.

on with thee, how should I meet the eye of that good old man, our minister, at Salem village? Oh, his voice would make me tremble, both Sabbath-day and lecture-day!"[6]

Thus far, the elder traveller had listened with due gravity, but now burst into a fit of irrepressible mirth, shaking himself so violently, that his snakelike staff actually seemed to wriggle in sympathy.

"Ha, ha, ha!" shouted he, again and again; then composing himself, "Well, go on, Goodman Brown, go on; but, prithee, don't kill me with laughing!"

"Well, then, to end the matter at once," said Goodman Brown, considerably net-tled, "there is my wife, Faith. It would break her dear little heart; and I'd rather break my own!"

"Nay, if that be the case," answered the other, "e'en go thy ways, Goodman Brown. I would not, for twenty old women like the one hobbling before us, that Faith should come to any harm."

As he spoke, he pointed his staff at a female figure on the path, in whom Good-man Brown recognized a very pious and exemplary dame, who had taught him his catechism in youth, and was still his moral and spiritual adviser, jointly with the minister and Deacon Gookin.

"A marvel, truly, that Goody[7] Cloyse should be so far in the wilderness, at night-fall!" said he. "But, with your leave, friend, I shall take a cut through the woods, until we have left this Christian woman behind. Being a stranger to you, she might ask whom I was consorting with, and whither I was going."

"Be it so," said his fellow-traveller. "Betake you to the woods, and let me keep the path."

Accordingly, the young man turned aside, but took care to watch his companion, who advanced softly along the road, until he had come within a staff's length of the old dame. She, meanwhile, was making the best of her way, with singular speed for so aged a woman, and mumbling some indistinct words, a prayer, doubtless, as she went. The traveller put forth his staff, and touched her withered neck with what seemed the serpent's tail.

"The devil!" screamed the pious old lady.

"Then Goody Cloyse knows her old friend?" observed the traveller, confronting her, and leaning on his writhing stick.

"Ah, forsooth, and is it your worship, indeed?" cried the good dame. "Yea, truly is it, and in the very image of my old gossip, Goodman Brown, the grandfather of the silly fellow that now is. But, would your worship believe it? my broomstick hath strangely disappeared, stolen, as I suspect, by that unhanged witch, Goody Cory, and that, too, when I was all anointed with the juice of smallage and cinque-foil and wolf's bane[8]—"

"Mingled with fine wheat and the fat of a new-born babe," said the shape of old Goodman Brown.

---

[6] *lecture-day:* The day of the midweek sermon, usually Thursday.

[7] *Goody:* A contraction of "Goodwife," a term of politeness used in addressing a woman of humble station. Goody Cloyse, like Goody Cory and Martha Carrier, who appear later in the story, was one of the Salem "witches" sentenced in 1692.

[8] *smallage . . . wolf's bane:* Plants believed to have magical powers. Smallage is wild celery.

"Ah, your worship knows the recipe," cried the old lady, cackling aloud. "So, as I was saying, being all ready for the meeting, and no horse to ride on, I made up my mind to foot it; for they tell me there is a nice young man to be taken into communion to-night. But now your good worship will lend me your arm, and we shall be there in a twinkling."

35   "That can hardly be," answered her friend. "I may not spare you my arm, Goody Cloyse, but here is my staff, if you will."

So saying, he threw it down at her feet, where, perhaps, it assumed life, being one of the rods which its owner had formerly lent to the Egyptian Magi. Of this fact, however, Goodman Brown could not take cognizance. He had cast his eyes in aston-ishment, and looking down again, beheld neither Goody Cloyse nor the serpentine staff, but his fellow-traveller alone, who waited for him as calmly as if nothing had happened.

"That old woman taught me my catechism!" said the young man; and there was a world of meaning in this simple comment.

They continued to walk onward, while the elder traveller exhorted his companion to make good speed and persevere in the path, discoursing so aptly, that his argu-ments seemed rather to spring up in the bosom of his auditor, than to be suggested by himself. As they went he plucked a branch of maple, to serve for a walking-stick, and began to strip it of the twigs and little boughs, which were wet with evening dew. The moment his fingers touched them, they became strangely withered and dried up, as with a week's sunshine. Thus the pair proceeded, at a good free pace, until suddenly, in a gloomy hollow of the road, Goodman Brown sat himself down on the stump of a tree, and refused to go any farther.

"Friend," said he, stubbornly, "my mind is made up. Not another step will I budge on this errand. What if a wretched old woman do choose to go to the devil, when I thought she was going to Heaven! Is that any reason why I should quit my dear Faith, and go after her?"

40   "You will think better of this by and by," said his acquaintance, composedly. "Sit here and rest yourself awhile; and when you feel like moving again, there is my staff to help you along."

Without more words, he threw his companion the maple stick, and was as speedily out of sight as if he had vanished into the deepening gloom. The young man sat a few moments by the roadside, applauding himself greatly, and thinking with how clear a conscience he should meet the minister, in his morning walk, nor shrink from the eye of good old Deacon Gookin. And what calm sleep would be his, that very night, which was to have been spent so wickedly, but purely and sweetly now, in the arms of Faith! Amidst these pleasant and praiseworthy meditations, Goodman Brown heard the tramp of horses along the road, and deemed it advisable to conceal himself within the verge of the forest, conscious of the guilty purpose that had brought him thither, though now so happily turned from it.

On came the hoof-tramps and the voices of the riders, two grave old voices, conversing soberly as they drew near. These mingled sounds appeared to pass along the road, within a few yards of the young man's hiding-place; but owing, doubtless, to the depth of the gloom, at that particular spot, neither the travellers nor their steeds were visible. Though their figures brushed the small boughs by the wayside, it could not be seen that they intercepted, even for a moment, the faint gleam from the strip of bright sky, athwart which they must have passed. Goodman Brown alternately crouched and stood on tiptoe, pulling aside the branches, and thrusting forth his head as far as he durst, without discerning so much as a shadow. It vexed him the more, because he could have sworn, were such a thing possible, that he recognized the voices of the minister and Deacon Gookin, jogging along quietly, as they were wont to do, when bound to some ordination or ecclesiastical council. While yet within hearing, one of the riders stopped to pluck a switch.

"Of the two, reverend Sir," said the voice like the deacon's, "I had rather miss an ordination dinner than to-night's meeting. They tell me that some of our community are to be here from Falmouth and beyond, and others from Connecticut and Rhode Island; besides several of the Indian powwows, who, after their fashion, know almost as much deviltry as the best of us. Moreover, there is a goodly young woman to be taken into communion."

"Mighty well, Deacon Gookin!" replied the solemn old tones of the minister. "Spur up, or we shall be late. Nothing can be done, you know, until I get on the ground."

The hoofs clattered again, and the voices, talking so strangely in the empty air, passed on through the forest, where no church had ever been gathered, nor solitary Christian prayed. Whither, then, could these holy men be journeying, so deep into the heathen wilderness? Young Goodman Brown caught hold of a tree, for support, being ready to sink down on the ground, faint and over-burthened with the heavy sickness of his heart. He looked up to the sky, doubting whether there really was a Heaven above him. Yet, there was the blue arch, and the stars brightening in it.

"With Heaven above, and Faith below, I will yet stand firm against the devil!" cried Goodman Brown.

While he still gazed upward, into the deep arch of the firmament, and had lifted his hands to pray, a cloud, though no wind was stirring, hurried across the zenith, and hid the brightening stars. The blue sky was still visible, except directly overhead, where this black mass of cloud was sweeping swiftly northward. Aloft in the air, as if from the depths of the cloud, came a confused and doubtful sound of voices. Once, the listener fancied that he could distinguish the accents of townspeople of his own, men and women, both pious and ungodly, many of whom he had met at the communion-table, and had seen others rioting at the tavern. The next moment, so indistinct were the sounds, he doubted whether he had heard aught but the murmur of the old forest, whispering without a wind. Then came a stronger swell of those familiar tones, heard daily in the sunshine, at Salem village, but never, until now, from a cloud at night. There was one voice, of a young woman, uttering lamentations, yet with an uncertain sorrow, and entreating for some favor, which, perhaps, it would grieve her to obtain. And all the unseen multitude, both saints and sinners, seemed to encourage her onward.

"Faith!" shouted Goodman Brown, in a voice of agony and desperation; and the echoes of the forest mocked him, crying—"Faith! Faith!" as if bewildered wretches were seeking her, all through the wilderness.

The cry of grief, rage, and terror was yet piercing the night, when the unhappy husband held his breath for a response. There was a scream, drowned immediately in a louder murmur of voices fading into far-off laughter, as the dark cloud swept

45

away, leaving the clear and silent sky above Goodman Brown. But something fluttered lightly down through the air, and caught on the branch of a tree. The young man seized it and beheld a pink ribbon.

50   "My Faith is gone!" cried he, after one stupefied moment. "There is no good on earth, and sin is but a name. Come, devil! for to thee is this world given."

And maddened with despair, so that he laughed loud and long, did Goodman Brown grasp his staff and set forth again, at such a rate, that he seemed to fly along the forest path, rather than to walk or run. The road grew wilder and drearier, and more faintly traced, and vanished at length, leaving him in the heart of the dark wilderness, still rushing onward, with the instinct that guides mortal man to evil. The whole forest was peopled with frightful sounds: the creaking of the trees, the howling of wild beasts, and the yell of Indians; while, sometimes, the wind tolled like a distant church bell, and sometimes gave a broad roar around the traveller, as if all Nature was laughing him to scorn. But he was himself the chief horror of the scene, and shrank not from its other horrors.

"Ha! ha! ha!" roared Goodman Brown, when the wind laughed at him. "Let us hear which will laugh loudest! Think not to frighten me with your deviltry! Come witch, come wizard, come Indian powwow, come devil himself! and here comes Goodman Brown. You may as well fear him as he fear you!"

In truth, all through the haunted forest, there could be nothing more frightful than the figure of Goodman Brown. On he flew, among the black pines, brandishing his staff with frenzied gestures, now giving vent to an inspiration of horrid blasphemy, and now shouting forth such laughter, as set all the echoes of the forest laughing like demons around him. The fiend in his own shape is less hideous, than when he rages in the breast of man. Thus sped the demoniac on his course, until, quivering among the trees, he saw a red light before him, as when the felled trunks and branches of a clearing have been set on fire, and throw up their lurid blaze against the sky, at the hour of midnight. He paused, in a lull of the tempest that had driven him onward, and heard the swell of what seemed a hymn, rolling solemnly from a distance, with the weight of many voices. He knew the tune. It was a familiar one in the choir of the village meeting-house. The verse died heavily away, and was lengthened by a chorus, not of human voices, but of all the sounds of the benighted wilderness, pealing in awful harmony together. Goodman Brown cried out; and his cry was lost to his own ear, by its unison with the cry of the desert.

In the interval of silence, he stole forward, until the light glared full upon his eyes. At one extremity of an open space, hemmed in by the dark wall of the forest, arose a rock, bearing some rude, natural resemblance either to an altar or a pulpit, and surrounded by four blazing pines, their tops aflame, their stems untouched, like candles at an evening meeting. The mass of foliage, that had overgrown the summit of the rock, was all on fire, blazing high into the night, and fitfully illuminating the whole field. Each pendent twig and leafy festoon was in a blaze. As the red light arose and fell, a numerous congregation alternately shone forth, then disappeared in shadow, and again grew, as it were, out of the darkness, peopling the heart of the solitary woods at once.

55   "A grave and dark-clad company!" quoth Goodman Brown.

In truth, they were such. Among them, quivering to-and-fro, between gloom and splendor, appeared faces that would be seen, next day, at the council-board of the province, and others which, Sabbath after Sabbath, looked devoutly heavenward, and benignantly over the crowded pews, from the holiest pulpits in the land. Some affirm, that the lady of the governor was there. At least, there were high dames well known to her, and wives of honored husbands, and widows a great multitude, and ancient maidens, all of excellent repute, and fair young girls, who trembled lest their mothers should espy them. Either the sudden gleams of light, flashing over the obscure field, bedazzled Goodman Brown, or he recognized a score of the church members of Salem village, famous for their especial sanctity. Good old Deacon Gookin had arrived, and waited at the skirts of that venerable saint, his reverend pastor. But, irreverently consorting with these grave, reputable, and pious people, these elders of the church, these chaste dames and dewy virgins, there were men of dissolute lives and women of spotted fame, wretches given over to all mean and filthy vice, and suspected even of horrid crimes. It was strange to see, that the good shrank not from the wicked, nor were the sinners abashed by the saints. Scattered, also, among their pale-faced enemies, were the Indian priests, or powwows, who had often scared their native forest with more hideous incantations than any known to English witchcraft.

"But, where is Faith?" thought Goodman Brown; and, as hope came into his heart, he trembled.

Another verse of the hymn arose, a slow and mournful strain, such as the pious love, but joined to words which expressed all that our nature can conceive of sin, and darkly hinted at far more. Unfathomable to mere mortals is the lore of fiends. Verse after verse was sung, and still the chorus of the desert swelled between, like the deepest tone of a mighty organ. And, with the final peal of that dreadful anthem, there came a sound, as if the roaring wind, the rushing streams, the howling beasts, and every other voice of the unconverted wilderness were mingling and according with the voice of guilty man, in homage to the prince of all. The four blazing pines threw up a loftier flame, and obscurely discovered shapes and visages of horror on the smoke-wreaths, above the impious assembly. At the same moment, the fire on the rock shot redly forth, and formed a glowing arch above its base, where now appeared a figure. With reverence be it spoken, the apparition bore no slight similitude, both in garb and manner, to some grave divine of the New England churches.

"Bring forth the converts!" cried a voice, that echoed through the field and rolled into the forest.

At the word, Goodman Brown stepped forth from the shadow of the trees, and approached the congregation, with whom he felt a loathful brotherhood, by the sympathy of all that was wicked in his heart. He could have well-nigh sworn, that the shape of his own dead father beckoned him to advance, looking downward from a smoke-wreath, while a woman, with dim features of despair, threw out her hand to warn him back. Was it his mother? But he had no power to retreat one step, nor to resist, even in thought, when the minister and good old Deacon Gookin seized his arms, and led him to the blazing rock. Thither came also the slender form of a veiled female, led between Goody Cloyse, that pious teacher of the catechism, and Martha Carrier, who had received the devil's promise to be queen of hell. A rampant hag was she! And there stood the proselytes, beneath the canopy of fire.

"Welcome, my children," said the dark figure, "to the communion of your race! Ye have found, thus young, your nature and your destiny. My children, look behind you!"

They turned; and flashing forth, as it were, in a sheet of flame, the fiend-worshippers were seen; the smile of welcome gleamed darkly on every visage.

"There," resumed the sable form, "are all whom ye have reverenced from youth. Ye deemed them holier than yourselves, and shrank from your own sin, contrasting it with their lives of righteousness and prayerful aspirations heavenward. Yet, here are they all, in my worshipping assembly! This night it shall be granted you to know their secret deeds; how hoary-bearded elders of the church have whispered wanton words to the young maids of their households; how many a woman, eager for widow's weeds, has given her husband a drink at bedtime, and let him sleep his last sleep in her bosom; how beardless youths have made haste to inherit their father's wealth; and how fair damsels—blush not, sweet ones!—have dug little graves in the garden, and bidden me, the sole guest, to an infant's funeral. By the sympathy of your human hearts for sin, ye shall scent out all the places—whether in church, bedchamber, street, field, or forest—where crime has been committed, and shall exult to behold the whole earth one stain of guilt, one mighty blood-spot. Far more than this! It shall be yours to penetrate, in every bosom, the deep mystery of sin, the fountain of all wicked arts, and which inexhaustibly supplies more evil impulses than human power—than my power, at its utmost!—can make manifest in deeds. And now, my children, look upon each other."

They did so; and, by the blaze of the hell-kindled torches, the wretched man beheld his Faith, and the wife her husband, trembling before that unhallowed altar.

65   "Lo! there ye stand, my children," said the figure, in a deep and solemn tone, almost sad, with its despairing awfulness, as if his once angelic nature could yet mourn for our miserable race. "Depending upon one another's hearts, ye had still hoped that virtue were not all a dream! Now are ye undeceived!—Evil is the nature of mankind. Evil must be your only happiness. Welcome, again, my children, to the communion of your race!"

"Welcome!" repeated the fiend-worshippers, in one cry of despair and triumph.

And there they stood, the only pair, as it seemed, who were yet hesitating on the verge of wickedness, in this dark world. A basin was hollowed, naturally, in the rock. Did it contain water, reddened by the lurid light? or was it blood? or, perchance, a liquid flame? Herein did the Shape of Evil dip his hand, and prepare to lay the mark of baptism upon their foreheads, that they might be partakers of the mystery of sin, more conscious of the secret guilt of others, both in deed and thought, than they could now be of their own. The husband cast one look at his pale wife, and Faith at him. What polluted wretches would the next glance show them to each other, shuddering alike at what they disclosed and what they saw!

"Faith! Faith!" cried the husband. "Look up to Heaven, and resist the Wicked One!"

Whether Faith obeyed, he knew not. Hardly had he spoken, when he found himself amid calm night and solitude, listening to a roar of the wind, which died heavily away through the forest. He staggered against the rock, and felt it chill and damp, while a hanging twig, that had been all on fire, besprinkled his cheek with the coldest dew.

70   The next morning, young Goodman Brown came slowly into the street of Salem village staring around him like a bewildered man. The good old minister was taking a walk along the grave-yard, to get an appetite for breakfast and meditate his sermon,

and bestowed a blessing, as he passed, on Goodman Brown. He shrank from the venerable saint, as if to avoid an anathema. Old Deacon Gookin was at domestic worship, and the holy words of his prayer were heard through the open window. "What God doth the wizard pray to?" quoth Goodman Brown. Goody Cloyse, that excellent old Christian, stood in the early sunshine, at her own lattice, catechising a little girl, who had brought her a pint of morning's milk. Goodman Brown snatched away the child, as from the grasp of the fiend himself. Turning the corner by the meeting-house, he spied the head of Faith, with the pink ribbons, gazing anxiously forth, and bursting into such joy at sight of him that she skipt along the street, and almost kissed her husband before the whole village. But Goodman Brown looked sternly and sadly into her face, and passed on without a greeting.

Had Goodman Brown fallen asleep in the forest, and only dreamed a wild dream of a witch-meeting?

Be it so, if you will. But, alas! it was a dream of evil omen for young Goodman Brown. A stern, a sad, a darkly meditative, a distrustful, if not a desperate man did he become, from the night of that fearful dream. On the Sabbath day, when the congregation were singing a holy psalm, he could not listen, because an anthem of sin rushed loudly upon his ear, and drowned all the blessed strain. When the minister spoke from the pulpit, with power and fervid eloquence, and with his hand on the open Bible, of the sacred truths of our religion, and of saint-like lives and triumphant deaths, and of future bliss or misery unutterable, then did Goodman Brown turn pale, dreading lest the roof should thunder down upon the gray blasphemer and his hearers. Often, awaking suddenly at midnight, he shrank from the bosom of Faith, and at morning or eventide, when the family knelt down at prayer, he scowled, and muttered to himself, and gazed sternly at his wife, and turned away. And when he had lived long, and was borne to his grave, a hoary corpse, followed by Faith, an aged woman, and children and grand-children, a goodly procession, besides neighbors not a few, they carved no hopeful verse upon his tombstone; for his dying hour was gloom.

Reading and Reacting

1. Who is the narrator of "Young Goodman Brown"? What advantages does the narrative point of view give the author?
2. What does young Goodman Brown mean when he says "of all nights in the year, this one night must I tarry away from thee" (par. 3)? What is important about *this* night, and why does Goodman Brown believe he must journey " 'twixt now and sunrise"?
3. Is Goodman Brown surprised to encounter the second traveler on the road, or does he seem to expect him? What is the significance of their encounter? What do you make of the fact that the stranger bears a strong resemblance to young Goodman Brown?
4. What sins are the various characters Goodman Brown meets in the woods guilty of committing?
5. "Young Goodman Brown" has two distinct settings: Salem and the woods. What are the differences between these settings? What significance does each setting have in the story?
6. Which figures in the story are allegorical, and which are symbols? On what evidence do you base your conclusions?
7. Why do the people gather in the woods? Why do they attend the ceremony?

8. Explain the change that takes place in young Goodman Brown at the end of the story. Why can he not listen to the singing of holy psalms or to the minister's sermons? What causes him to turn away from Faith and die in gloom?

9. **JOURNAL ENTRY** At the end of the story, the narrator suggests that Goodman Brown might have fallen asleep and imagined his encounter with the witches. Do you think the events in the story are all a dream?

10. **CRITICAL PERSPECTIVE** In *The Power of Blackness*, his classic study of nineteenth-century American writers, Harry Levin observes that Hawthorne had doubts about conventional religion. This, Levin believes, is why all efforts to read an enlightening theological message into Hawthorne's works are "doomed to failure."

    What comment do you think Hawthorne is making in "Young Goodman Brown" about religious faith?

Related Works: "Where Are You Going, Where Have You Been?" (p. 506), "Greasy Lake" (p. 569), "We Wear the Mask" (p. 728), "La Belle Dame sans Merci: A Ballad" (p. 993), *Zombie Love* (p. 1079), *Doubt: A Parable* (p. 1516).

WRITING SUGGESTIONS: Symbol, Allegory, and Myth

1. In "Cathedral" and "Young Goodman Brown," certain minor characters offer the possibility of salvation or healing. For example, in "Cathedral," The blind man holds out the possibility of healing to the narrator, and in "Young Goodman Brown," Faith offers her husband salvation from evil. Write an essay in which you examine the symbolic roles these characters play.

2. Strangers figure prominently in "Young Goodman Brown" and "Cathedral." Write an essay in which you discuss the possible symbolic significance of strangers in each story. If you like, you may also discuss Arnold Friend in "Where Are You Going, Where Have You Been?" (p. 506) or The Misfit in "A Good Man Is Hard to Find" (p. 367).

3. Write an essay in which you discuss the use of symbols in "Young Goodman Brown" or in "Oaks Park."

4. If Shirley Jackson had wished to write "The Lottery" as an allegory whose purpose was to expose the evils of Nazi Germany, what revisions would she have had to make to convey the dangers of blind obedience to authority? Consider the story's symbols, the characters (and their names), and the setting.

5. In literary works, objects can function as symbols. In this chapter, for example, the quilt in "Everyday Use" and the box in "The Lottery" take on symbolic significance. Write an essay in which you analyze objects that have symbolic significance in two or three of the stories in this text and discuss how these objects help to convey the main themes of the stories in which they appear.

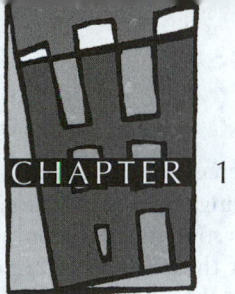

CHAPTER 19

THEME

David Michael Kaplan
Photography by Joyce Winer

Tobias Wolff
AP Images/Marty Lederhandler

Eudora Welty
Bettmann/Corbis

D(avid) H(erbert) Lawrence
Bettmann/CORBIS

The **theme** of a work of literature is its central or dominant idea. *Theme* is not the same as *plot* or *subject*, two terms with which it is sometimes confused. A summary of the **plot** of Tadeusz Borowski's "Silence," a story about survivors of the Holocaust, could be, "Prisoners are liberated from a concentration camp, and, despite the warnings of the American officer, they kill a captured German guard." The statement "'Silence' is about freed prisoners and a guard" could define the **subject** of the story. A statement of the **theme** of "Silence," however, has to do more than summarize its plot or define its subject; it has to convey the values and ideas expressed by the story.

Many effective stories are complex, expressing more than one theme, and "Silence" is no exception. You could say that "Silence" suggests that human beings have a need for vengeance. You could also say the story demonstrates that silence is sometimes the only response possible when people confront unspeakable horrors. Both these themes—and others—are expressed in the story, yet one theme seems to dominate: the idea that under extreme conditions, the oppressed can have the same capacity for evil as their oppressors.

When you write about theme, you need to do more than tell what happens in the story. The theme you identify should be a general idea that extends beyond the story and applies to the world outside fiction. Compare these two statements that a student wrote about Edgar Allan Poe's "The Cask of Amontillado" (p. 328):

Poe's "The Cask of Amontillado" is about a man who has an obsessive desire for revenge.

Poe's "The Cask of Amontillado" suggests that when the desire for revenge becomes obsessive, it can deprive individuals of all that makes them human.

The first statement merely tells what the story is about; the second statement identifies the story's theme, a general observation about humanity.

Granted, some short works (fairy tales or fables, for example) have themes that can only be expressed as **clichés**—overused phrases or expressions—or as **morals**—lessons dramatized by the work. The fairy tale "Cinderella," for example, expresses the clichéd theme that a virtuous girl who endures misfortune will eventually achieve her just reward; the fable "The Tortoise and the Hare" illustrates the moral "Slow and steady wins the race." Like "The Cask of Amontillado," however, the stories in this anthology have themes that are much more complex than clichés or morals.

 ## Interpreting Themes

Contemporary critical theory holds that the theme of a work of fiction is as much a creation of readers as it is of the writer. Readers' backgrounds, knowledge, values, and beliefs all play a part in determining the theme (or themes) they will identify in a work. Many readers, for example, will realize that David Michael Kaplan's story "Doe Season" (p. 472)—in which the main character goes hunting, kills her first deer, and is forced to confront suffering and death—expresses a conventional **initiation theme**, revealing growing up to be a disillusioning and painful process. Still, different readers bring different perspectives to the story and, in some cases, see different themes.

During a classroom discussion of "Doe Season," a student familiar with hunting saw more than his classmates did in the story's conventional initiation theme. He knew that in many states there really is a doe season. Shorter than the ten-day buck season, it allows hunters to control the size of the deer herd by killing females. This knowledge enabled the student to conclude that by the end of the story the female child's innocence is destroyed, just as the doe is.

Another student pointed out that the participation of Andy—a female who uses a male name—in hunting, a traditional male rite of passage, leads to her killing the deer and to her subsequent disillusionment. It also leads to her decision to abandon her nickname. By contrasting "Andrea" with "Andy," the story reveals the conflict between her "female" nature (illustrated by her compassion) and her desire to emulate the men to whom killing is a sport.

This interpretation led the student to conclude that the theme of "Doe Season" is that males and females must, by their natures, have very different outlooks on life.

Other students rejected the negative portrayal of the story's male characters that the preceding interpretation implies. They pointed out that the father is a sympathetic figure who is extremely supportive; he encourages and defends his daughter. He takes her hunting because he loves her, not because he wants to initiate her into life or to hurt her. One student mentioned that Andy's reaction (called *buck fever*) when she sees the doe is common in children who kill their first deer. In light of this information, several students concluded that far from being about irreconcilable male and female differences, "Doe Season" makes a statement about a young girl who is hunting for her own identity and who in the process discovers her mortality. Her father is therefore the agent who enables her to confront the inevitability of death, a fact she must accept if she is going to take her place in the adult world. In this sense, the theme of the story is the idea that in order to mature, a child must come to terms with the reality of death.

Different readers may see different themes in a story, but any interpretation of a theme must make sense in light of what is actually in the story. Evidence from the work, not just your own feelings or assumptions, must support your interpretation, and a single statement by a character is not usually enough in itself to reveal a story's theme. Therefore, you must present a cross-section of examples from the text to support your interpretation of the story's theme. If you say that the theme of James Joyce's "Araby" (p. 361) is that an innocent idealist is inevitably doomed to disillusionment, you have to find examples from the text to support this statement. You could begin with the title, concluding that the word *Araby* suggests idealistic dreams of exotic beauty that the boy tries to find when he goes to a bazaar. You could reinforce your interpretation by pointing out that the unattainable woman is a symbol of all that the boy wants so desperately to find. Finally, you could show how idealism is ultimately crushed by society: at the end of the story, the boy stands alone in the darkness and realizes that his dreams are childish fantasies. Although other readers may have different responses to "Araby," they will find your interpretation reasonable if you support it with enough examples.

 ## Identifying Themes

Every element of a story can shed light on its themes. As you analyze a short story, look for features that reveal and reinforce what you perceive to be the story's most important ideas.

- *The title can often provide insight into the theme or themes of a story.* The title of an F. Scott Fitzgerald story, "Babylon Revisited," emphasizes a major idea in the story— that Paris of the 1920s is like Babylon, the ancient city the Bible singles out as the epitome of evil and corruption. The story's protagonist, Charlie Wales, comes to realize that no matter how much money he lost after the 1929 stock market crash, he lost more—his wife and his daughter—during the boom, when he was in Paris. Charlie's search through his past—his return to "Babylon"—provides new meaning to his life and offers him at least a small bit of hope for the future.
- *Sometimes a narrator's or character's statement can reveal a theme.* For example, at the beginning of Alberto Alvaro Ríos's "The Secret Lion" (p. 180), the first-person narrator says, "I was twelve and in junior high school and something happened that we didn't have a name for, but it was there nonetheless like a lion, and roaring, roaring

that way the biggest things do. Everything changed." Although the narrator does not directly announce the story's theme, he suggests that the story will convey the idea that the price children pay for growing up is realizing that everything changes, that nothing stays the way it is.

- *The arrangement of events can suggest a story's theme*, as it does in an Ernest Hemingway story, "The Short Happy Life of Francis Macomber." At the beginning of the story, the title character is a coward who is stuck in an unhappy marriage. As the story progresses, he gradually learns the nature of courage and, finally, finds it in himself. At the moment of his triumph, however, Francis is shot by his wife; his "happy life" is short indeed. The way the events of the story are presented, through foreshadowing and flashbacks, reveals the connection between Macomber's marriage and his behavior as a hunter, and this connection in turn helps to reveal a possible theme: that sometimes courage can be more important than life itself.

- A *story's central conflict can offer clues to its theme*. For example, the main character in "The Yellow Wallpaper" (p. 379), a woman who has recently had a baby, is in conflict with the nineteenth-century society in which she lives. She is suffering from "temporary nervous depression," what doctors today recognize as postpartum depression. Following the practice of the time, her physician has ordered complete bed rest and has instructed her husband to deprive her of all mental and physical stimulation. This harsh treatment leads the narrator to lose her grasp on reality; eventually, she begins to hallucinate. The main conflict of the story is clearly between the woman and her society, controlled by men. This conflict communicates the central theme: that in nineteenth-century America, women are controlled not just by their husbands and the male medical establishment, but also by the society men have created.

- *The point of view of a story can shed light on its theme*. For instance, a writer's use of an unreliable first-person narrator can help to communicate the theme of a story. Thus, Montresor's self-serving first-person account of his crime in "The Cask of Amontillado"—along with his attempts to justify these actions—enables readers to understand the dangers of irrational anger and misplaced ideas about honor. The voice of a third-person narrator can also help to convey a story's theme. For example, the detachment of the narrator in Stephen Crane's Civil War novel *The Red Badge of Courage* reinforces the theme of the novel: that bravery, cowardice, war, and even life itself are insignificant when set beside the indifference of the universe.

- *Quite often a story's symbols—names, places, and objects—can suggest its theme*. For example, the rocking horse in D. H. Lawrence's "The Rocking-Horse Winner" (p. 484) can be seen as a symbol of the boy's desperate desire to remain a child. Interpreted in this way, it reinforces the theme that innocence cannot survive when it confronts adult greed and selfishness. Similarly, Hawthorne's "Young Goodman Brown" (p. 448) uses symbols such as the walking stick, the woods, sunset and night, and the vague shadows to develop one of its central themes: that once a person strays from the path of faith, evil is everywhere.

- *Finally, changes in a character can shed light on the theme or themes of the story*. The main character in Charles Baxter's "Gryphon" (p. 250), for example, eventually comes to realize that the "lies" his substitute teacher tells may be closer to the truth than the "facts" his other teachers present, and his changing attitude toward her helps to communicate the story's central theme about the nature of truth.

✔ **CHECKLIST   Writing about Theme**

▪ What is the central theme of the story?

▪ What other themes can you identify?

▪ Does the title of the story suggest a theme?

▪ Does the narrator, or any character, make statements that express or imply a theme?

▪ In what way does the arrangement of events in the story suggest a theme?

▪ In what way does the central conflict of the story suggest a theme?

▪ How does the point of view shed light on the story's central theme?

▪ Do any symbols suggest a theme?

▪ Do any characters in the story change in any significant way? Do these changes convey a particular theme?

Bettmann/Corbis

EUDORA WELTY (1909–2001) was born and raised in Jackson, Mississippi. After attending the Mississippi College for Women, the University of Wisconsin, and Columbia University (where she studied advertising), she returned to Jackson to pursue her long career as a writer, beginning as a journalist. In 1936, she wrote the first of her many short stories, which are gathered in *Collected Stories* (1980). Welty also wrote several novels, including *Delta Wedding* (1946), *Losing Battles* (1970), and the Pulitzer Prize–winning *The Optimist's Daughter* (1972). Her volume of memoirs, *One Writer's Beginnings* (1984), was a best-seller.

One of America's most accomplished writers, Welty focused much of her fiction on life in southern towns and villages peopled with dreamers, eccentrics, and close-knit families. Her sharply observed characters are sometimes presented with great humor, sometimes with poignant lyricism, but always with clarity and sympathy. "Of course any writer is in part all of his characters," she observed. "How otherwise would they be known to him, occur to him, become what they are?" In "A Worn Path," Welty creates a particularly memorable character in the tenacious Phoenix Jackson, and through her she explores a theme that transcends race and region.

Cultural Context During the 1930s, the years of the Great Depression, poverty and unemployment were widespread but were especially severe in isolated rural areas of the South. For the black population living in this poor and undeveloped region, difficult economic conditions were made worse by the system of segregation that prevented them from voting, receiving a good education, or enjoying the same rights and privileges as their white counterparts. Hoping to improve their situation, many African American families left the South and moved into northern and midwestern cities where there were better opportunities for education and employment. Others, like the protagonist of this story, remained in the South in an atmosphere of residual racism and oppression.

A Worn Path (1940)

Film
Series

DVD
See pp.
470–471
for film
stills from
the DVD
version
of this
story.

It was December—a bright frozen day in the early morning. Far out in the country there was an old Negro woman with her head tied in a red rag, coming along a path through the pinewoods. Her name was Phoenix Jackson. She was very old and small and she walked slowly in the dark pine shadows, moving a little from side to side in her steps, with the balanced heaviness and lightness of a pendulum in a grandfather clock. She carried a thin, small cane made from an umbrella, and with this she kept tapping the frozen earth in front of her. This made a grave and persistent noise in the still air, that seemed meditative like the chirping of a solitary little bird.

She wore a dark striped dress reaching down to her shoe tops, and an equally long apron of bleached sugar sacks, with a full pocket: all neat and tidy, but every time she took a step she might have fallen over her shoelaces, which dragged from her unlaced shoes. She looked straight ahead. Her eyes were blue with age. Her skin had a pattern all its own of numberless branching wrinkles and as though a whole little tree stood in the middle of her forehead, but a golden color ran underneath, and the two knobs of her cheeks were illumined by a yellow burning under the dark. Under the red rag her hair came down on her neck in the frailest of ringlets, still black, and with an odor like copper.

Now and then there was a quivering in the thicket. Old Phoenix said, "Out of my way, all you foxes, owls, beetles, jack rabbits, coons and wild animals! . . . Keep out from under these feet, little bob-whites. . . . Keep the big wild hogs out of my path. Don't let none of those come running my direction. I got a long way." Under her small black-freckled hand her cane, limber as a buggy whip, would switch at the brush as if to rouse up any hiding things.

On she went. The woods were deep and still. The sun made the pine needles almost too bright to look at, up where the wind rocked. The cones dropped as light as feathers. Down in the hollow was the mourning dove—it was not too late for him.

5   The path ran up a hill. "Seem like there is chains about my feet, time I get this far," she said, in the voice of argument old people keep to use with themselves. "Something always take a hold of me on this hill—pleads I should stay."

After she got to the top she turned and gave a full, severe look behind her where she had come. "Up through pines," she said at length. "Now down through oaks."

Her eyes opened their widest, and she started down gently. But before she got to the bottom of the hill a bush caught her dress.

Her fingers were busy and intent, but her skirts were full and long, so that before she could pull them free in one place they were caught in another. It was not possible to allow the dress to tear. "I in the thorny bush," she said. "Thorns, you doing your appointed work. Never want to let folks pass, no sir. Old eyes thought you was a pretty little *green* bush."

Finally, trembling all over, she stood free, and after a moment dared to stoop for her cane.

10   "Sun so high!" she cried, leaning back and looking, while the thick tears went over her eyes. "The time getting all gone here."

At the foot of this hill was a place where a log was laid across the creek.

"Now comes the trial," said Phoenix.

Putting her right foot out, she mounted the log and shut her eyes. Lifting her skirt, leveling her cane fiercely before her, like a festival figure in some parade, she began to march across. Then she opened her eyes and she was safe on the other side.

"I wasn't as old as I thought," she said.

But she sat down to rest. She spread her skirts on the bank around her and folded her hands over her knees. Up above her was a tree in a pearly cloud of mistletoe. She did not dare to close her eyes, and when a little boy brought her a plate with a slice of marble-cake on it she spoke to him. "That would be acceptable," she said. But when she went to take it there was just her own hand in the air. 15

So she left that tree, and had to go through a barbed-wire fence. There she had to creep and crawl, spreading her knees and stretching her fingers like a baby trying to climb the steps. But she talked loudly to herself: she could not let her dress be torn now, so late in the day, and she could not pay for having her arm or her leg sawed off if she got caught fast where she was.

At last she was safe through the fence and risen up out in the clearing. Big dead trees, like black men with one arm, were standing in the purple stalks of the withered cotton field. There sat a buzzard.

"Who you watching?"

In the furrow she made her way along.

"Glad this not the season for bulls," she said, looking sideways, "and the good Lord made his snakes to curl up and sleep in the winter. A pleasure I don't see no two-headed snake coming around that tree, where it come once. It took a while to get by him, back in the summer." 20

She passed through the old cotton and went into a field of dead corn. It whispered and shook and was taller than her head. "Through the maze now," she said, for there was no path.

Then there was something tall, black, and skinny there, moving before her.

At first she took it for a man. It could have been a man dancing in the field. But she stood still and listened, and it did not make a sound. It was as silent as a ghost.

"Ghost," she said sharply, "who be you the ghost of? For I have heard of nary death close by."

But there was no answer—only the ragged dancing in the wind. 25

She shut her eyes, reached out her hand, and touched a sleeve. She found a coat and inside that an emptiness, cold as ice.

"You scarecrow," she said. Her face lighted. "I ought to be shut up for good," she said with laughter. "My senses is gone. I too old. I the oldest people I ever know. Dance, old scarecrow," she said, "while I dancing with you."

She kicked her foot over the furrow, and with mouth drawn down, shook her head once or twice in a little strutting way. Some husks blew down and whirled in streamers about her skirts.

Then she went on, parting her way from side to side with the cane, through the whispering field. At last she came to the end, to a wagon track where the silver grass blew between the red ruts. The quail were walking around like pullets, seeming all dainty and unseen.

30   "Walk pretty," she said. "This is the easy place. This the easy going."

She followed the track, swaying through the quiet bare fields, through the little strings of trees silver in their dead leaves, past cabins silver from weather, with the doors and windows boarded shut, all like old women under a spell sitting there. "I walking in their sleep," she said, nodding her head vigorously.

In a ravine she went where a spring was silently flowing through a hollow log. Old Phoenix bent and drank. "Sweet-gum makes the water sweet," she said, and drank more. "Nobody know who made this well, for it was here when I was born."

The track crossed a swampy part where the moss hung as white as lace from every limb. "Sleep on, alligators, and blow your bubbles." Then the track went into the road.

Deep, deep the road went down between the high green-colored banks. Overhead the live-oaks met, and it was as dark as a cave.

35   A black dog with a lolling tongue came up out of the weeds by the ditch. She was meditating, and not ready, and when he came at her she only hit him a little with her cane. Over she went in the ditch, like a little puff of milkweed.

Down there, her senses drifted away. A dream visited her, and she reached her hand up, but nothing reached down and gave her a pull. So she lay there and presently went to talking. "Old woman," she said to herself, "that black dog come up out of the weeds to stall you off, and now there he sitting on his fine tail, smiling at you."

A white man finally came along and found her—a hunter, a young man, with his dog on a chain.

"Well, Granny!" he laughed. "What are you doing there?"

"Lying on my back like a June-bug waiting to be turned over, mister," she said, reaching up her hand.

40   He lifted her up, gave her a swing in the air, and set her down. "Anything broken, Granny?"

"No sir, them old dead weeds is springy enough," said Phoenix, when she had got her breath. "I thank you for your trouble."

"Where do you live, Granny?" he asked, while the two dogs were growling at each other.

"Away back yonder, sir, behind the ridge. You can't even see it from here."

"On your way home?"

45   "No sir, I going to town."

"Why, that's too far! That's as far as I walk when I come out myself, and I get something for my trouble." He patted the stuffed bag he carried, and there hung down a little closed claw. It was one of the bob-whites, with its beak hooked bitterly to show it was dead. "Now you go on home, Granny!"

"I bound to go to town, mister," said Phoenix. "The time come around."

He gave another laugh, filling the whole landscape. "I know you old colored people! Wouldn't miss going to town to see Santa Claus!"

But something held old Phoenix very still. The deep lines in her face went into a fierce and different radiation. Without warning, she had seen with her own eyes a flashing nickel fall out of the man's pocket onto the ground.

"How old are you, Granny?" he was saying.   50

"There is no telling, mister," she said, "no telling."

Then she gave a little cry and clapped her hands and said, "Git on away from here, dog! Look! Look at that dog!" She laughed as if in admiration. "He ain't scared of nobody. He a big black dog." She whispered, "Sic him!"

"Watch me get rid of that cur," said the man. "Sic him, Pete! Sic him!"

Phoenix heard the dogs fighting, and heard the man running and throwing sticks. She even heard a gunshot. But she was slowly bending forward by that time, further and further forward, the lid stretched down over her eyes, as if she were doing this in her sleep. Her chin was lowered almost to her knees. The yellow palm of her hand came out from the fold of her apron. Her fingers slid down and along the ground under the piece of money with the grace and care they would have in lifting an egg from under a setting hen. Then she slowly straightened up, she stood erect, and the nickel was in her apron pocket. A bird flew by. Her lips moved. "God watching me the whole time. I come to stealing."

The man came back, and his own dog panted about them. "Well, I scared him   55
off that time," he said, and then he laughed and lifted his gun and pointed it at Phoenix.

She stood straight and faced him.

"Doesn't the gun scare you?" he said, still pointing it.

"No, sir, I seen plenty go off closer by, in my day, and for less than what I done," she said, holding utterly still.

He smiled, and shouldered the gun. "Well, Granny," he said, "you must be a hundred years old, and scared of nothing. I'd give you a dime if I had any money with me. But you take my advice and stay home, and nothing will happen to you."

"I bound to go on my way, mister," said Phoenix. She inclined her head in the red   60
rag. Then they went in different directions, but she could hear the gun shooting again and again over the hill.

She walked on. The shadows hung from the oak trees to the road like curtains. Then she smelled wood-smoke, and smelled the river, and she saw a steeple and the cabins on their steep steps. Dozens of little black children whirled around her. There ahead was Natchez shining. Bells were ringing. She walked on.

In the paved city it was Christmas time. There were red and green electric lights strung and crisscrossed everywhere, and all turned on in the daytime. Old Phoenix would have been lost if she had not distrusted her eyesight and depended on her feet to know where to take her.

She paused quietly on the sidewalk where people were passing by. A lady came along in the crowd, carrying an armful of red-, green- and silver-wrapped presents; she gave off perfume like the red roses in hot summer, and Phoenix stopped her.

"Please, missy, will you lace up my shoe?" She held up her foot.

"What do you want, Grandma?"   65

"See my shoe," said Phoenix. "Do all right for out in the country, but wouldn't look right to go in a big building."

"Stand still then, Grandma," said the lady. She put her packages down on the sidewalk beside her and laced and tied both shoes tightly.

"Can't lace 'em with a cane," said Phoenix. "Thank you, missy. I doesn't mind asking a nice lady to tie up my shoe, when I gets out on the street."

Moving slowly and from side to side, she went into the big building, and into a tower of steps, where she walked up and around and around until her feet knew to stop.

70   She entered a door, and there she saw nailed up on the wall the document that had been stamped with the gold seal and framed in the gold frame, which matched the dream that was hung up in her head.

"Here I be," she said. There was a fixed and ceremonial stiffness over her body.

"A charity case, I suppose," said an attendant who sat at the desk before her.

But Phoenix only looked above her head. There was sweat on her face, the wrinkles in her face shone like a bright net.

"Speak up, Grandma," the woman said. "What's your name? We must have your history, you know. Have you been here before? What seems to be the trouble with you?"

75   Old Phoenix only gave a twitch to her face as if a fly were bothering her.

"Are you deaf?" cried the attendant.

But then the nurse came in.

"Oh, that's just old Aunt Phoenix," she said. "She doesn't come for herself—she has a little grandson. She makes these trips just as regular as clockwork. She lives away back off the Old Natchez Trace." She bent down. "Well, Aunt Phoenix, why don't you just take a seat? We won't keep you standing after your long trip." She pointed.

The old woman sat down, bolt upright in the chair.

80   "Now, how is the boy?" asked the nurse.

Old Phoenix did not speak.

"I said, how is the boy?"

But Phoenix only waited and stared straight ahead, her face very solemn and withdrawn into rigidity.

"Is his throat any better?" asked the nurse. "Aunt Phoenix, don't you hear me? Is your grandson's throat any better since the last time you came for the medicine?"

85   With her hands on her knees, the old woman waited, silent, erect and motionless, just as if she were in armor.

"You mustn't take up our time this way, Aunt Phoenix," the nurse said. "Tell us quickly about your grandson, and get it over. He isn't dead, is he?"

At last there came a flicker and then a flame of comprehension across her face, and she spoke.

"My grandson. It was my memory had left me. There I sat and forgot why I made my long trip."

"Forgot?" The nurse frowned. "After you came so far?"

90   Then Phoenix was like an old woman begging a dignified forgiveness for waking up frightened in the night. "I never did go to school, I was too old at the Surrender,"[1] she said in a soft voice. "I'm an old woman without an education. It was my memory fail me. My little grandson, he is just the same, and I forgot it in the coming."

---

[1]*the Surrender:* The surrender of General Robert E. Lee to General Ulysses S. Grant at the end of the Civil War, April 9, 1865.

"Throat never heals, does it?" said the nurse, speaking in a loud, sure voice to old Phoenix. By now she had a card with something written on it, a little list. "Yes. Swallowed lye. When was it?—January—two-three years ago—"

Phoenix spoke unasked now. "No, missy, he not dead, he just the same. Every little while his throat begin to close up again, and he not able to swallow. He not get his breath. He not able to help himself. So the time come around, and I go on another trip for the soothing medicine."

"All right. The doctor said as long as you came to get it, you could have it," said the nurse. "But it's an obstinate case."

"My little grandson, he sit up there in the house all wrapped up, waiting by himself," Phoenix went on. "We is the only two left in the world. He suffer and it don't seem to put him back at all. He got a sweet look. He going to last. He wear a little patch quilt and peep out holding his mouth open like a little bird. I remembers so plain now. I not going to forget him again, no, the whole enduring time. I could tell him from all the others in creation."

"All right." The nurse was trying to hush her now. She brought her a bottle of   95
medicine. "Charity," she said, making a check mark in a book.

Old Phoenix held the bottle close to her eyes, and then carefully put it into her pocket.

"I thank you," she said.

"It's Christmas time, Grandma," said the attendant. "Could I give you a few pennies out of my purse?"

"Five pennies is a nickel," said Phoenix stiffly.

"Here's a nickel," said the attendant.   100

Phoenix rose carefully and held out her hand. She received the nickel and then fished the other nickel out of her pocket and laid it beside the new one. She stared at her palm closely, with her head on one side.

Then she gave a tap with her cane on the floor.

"This is what come to me to do," she said. "I going to the store and buy my child a little windmill they sells, made out of paper. He going to find it hard to believe there such a thing in the world. I'll march myself back where he waiting, holding it straight up in this hand."

She lifted her free hand, gave a little nod, turned around, and walked out of the doctor's office. Then her slow step began on the stairs, going down.

Reading and Reacting

1. How does the first paragraph set the scene for the rest of the story? How does it foreshadow the events that will take place later on?
2. Traditionally, a **quest** is a journey in which a knight overcomes a series of obstacles in order to perform a prescribed feat. In what way is Phoenix's journey a quest? What obstacles does she face? What feat must she perform?
3. Because Phoenix is old, she has trouble seeing. What things does she have difficulty seeing? How do her mistakes shed light on her character? How do they contribute to the impact of the story?

4. What is the major theme of this story? What other themes are expressed?

5. A **phoenix** is a mythical bird that would live for five hundred years, be consumed by fire, and then rise from its own ashes. In what way is the name of this creature appropriate for the main character of this story?

6. Phoenix is not intimidated by the man with the gun and has no difficulty asking a white woman to tie her shoe. In spite of her pride and her strength of character, however, Phoenix has no qualms about stealing a nickel or taking charity from the doctor. How do you account for this apparent contradiction?

7. How do the various people Phoenix encounters react to her? Do they treat her with respect? with disdain? Why do you think they react the way they do?

8. In paragraph 90, Phoenix says that she is an old woman without an education. Even so, what knowledge does she seem to have that the other characters lack?

9. **Journal Entry** Could "A Worn Path" be seen as an **allegory**? If so, what might each of the characters represent?

10. **Critical Perspective** Writing about "A Worn Path," Eudora Welty said that the question she was asked most frequently by both students and teachers was whether Phoenix Jackson's grandson was actually dead. Here she attempts to answer this question:

    > I had not meant to mystify readers by withholding any fact; it is not a writer's business to tease. The story is told through Phoenix's mind and she undertakes her errand. As the author at one with the character as I tell it, I must assume that the boy is alive. As the reader, you are free to think as you like, of course; the story invites you to believe that no matter what happens, Phoenix for as long as she is able to walk and can hold to her purpose will make her journey.

    Do you think Phoenix's grandson is alive or dead? Why?

Related Works: "Miss Brill" (p. 245), "Araby" (p. 361), "Everyday Use" (p. 426), "We Wear the Mask" (p. 728), "The Negro Speaks of Rivers" (p. 916), "The Solitary Reaper" (p. 1026)

 Fiction in Film: Eudora Welty's "A Worn Path"

"A Worn Path" is a story about Phoenix Jackson, an elderly African American woman who repeatedly makes a long journey to town to get medicine for her ailing grandson. The theme of the story, however, is much more than the difficulty of Phoenix Jackson's journey. In one sense, Phoenix represents the strength of human spirit that perseveres regardless of the difficulties or the odds against success. In another sense, she represents African Americans in their long quest for integration and equal treatment. The DVD of "A Worn Path" presents the vivid incidents—both imaginary and real—that are described in the story. The stills included here depict scenes that appear on the DVD.

Phoenix and the hunter
Source: ©Bruce Schwartz/Worn Path Productions

Phoenix walking down the street in town
Source: ©Victoria Mihich/Worn Path Productions

Phoenix in the doctor's office
Source: ©James Patterson/Worn Path Productions

The film's last scene, with Phoenix, outlined against the
sky, walking back to her cabin
Source: ©Francisco Gonzales/Worn Path Productions

Reading and Reacting

1. If you were making a film of "A Worn Path," how would you show Phoenix's encounter with the thorn bush? the buzzard? the scarecrow?

2. How would you indicate which events actually took place and which are imaginary? For example, how would you show Phoenix's imaginary encounter with the boy who offers her a piece of cake?

3. How much would you show of Phoenix's encounter with the hunter? How would she react to the dog? How would you show her stealing the nickel? What would her reaction be when the hunter asked her if she was afraid of guns?

4. Which of the story's themes could you easily suggest in a film? Which would be more difficult to suggest?

5. The story takes place around Christmas. How would you indicate this setting in a film?

6. "A Worn Path" is set during the Depression near Natchez, Mississippi, a segregated city in the South. If you were making a film version of the story, how would you suggest this racial situation?

7. The story ends with Phoenix walking down the stairs of the doctor's office. The DVD ends with Phoenix walking home, outlined against the sky (shown on the previous page). Is the DVD's ending an improvement? Explain.

Photography by Joyce Winer

DAVID MICHAEL KAPLAN (1946–   ) is one of a group of American writers who, along with South American writers such as Gabriel García Márquez of Columbia, are called "magic realists." Magic realists work outside of the borders of traditional fantasy writing, seamlessly interweaving magical elements with detailed, realistically drawn "everyday" settings. These elements, says a reviewer of Kaplan's work, are invoked "to illuminate and underscore heightened moments of reality." The story "Doe Season," which appeared in Kaplan's debut collection, *Comfort* (1987), was included in *Best American Short Stories 1985.* Kaplan's first novel, *Skating in the Dark*, was published in 1991, and his writing text, *Revision: A Creative Approach to Writing and Re-writing Fiction*, was published in 1997. Kaplan teaches fiction writing at Loyola University Chicago.

Interestingly, the stories in *Comfort* break from classic "first-time author" tradition by sidestepping the autobiographical, young-man-comes-of-age theme. Instead, these stories are about young girls—or young women—coming to grips with parents (present or absent) and with loss and searching for ways to resolve their ambivalence about becoming women. In "Doe Season," Andy's surreal encounter with the doe may be a dream, but the beauty and horror of their meeting will affect the rest of her life.

Cultural Context   When European settlers first came to America, deer roamed freely from coast to coast, and the settlers hunted them to put meat on the table. Today, deer are hunted in a regulated fashion in order to control their numbers and maintain a balance in their population. Deer hunting has long been viewed as a coming-of-age ritual for young men—and, more recently, for young women first entering adulthood, like the protagonist in this story. It used to be the tradition that a young hunter who missed his first deer had his shirt-tail cut off; if he succeeded, his face was smeared with the blood of his first kill. Now few hunters observe these initiation rites.

Doe Season (1985)

They were always the same woods, she thought sleepily as they drove through the early morning darkness—deep and immense, covered with yesterday's snowfall, which had frozen overnight. They were the same woods that lay behind her house, *and they stretch all the way to here*, she thought, *for miles and miles, longer than I could walk in a day, or a week even, but they are still the same woods.* The thought made her feel good: it was like thinking of God; it was like thinking of the space between here and the moon; it was like thinking of all the foreign countries from her geography book where even now, Andy knew, people were g oing to bed, while they—she and her father and Charlie Spoon and Mac, Charlie's eleven-year-old son—were driving deeper into the Pennsylvania countryside, to go hunting.

They had risen long before dawn. Her mother, yawning and not trying to hide her sleepiness, cooked them eggs and French toast. Her father smoked a cigarette and flicked ashes into his saucer while Andy listened, wondering *Why doesn't he come?* and *Won't he ever come?* until at last a car pulled into the graveled drive and honked. "That will be Charlie Spoon," her father said; he always said "Charlie Spoon," even though his real name was Spreun, because Charlie was, in a sense, shaped like a spoon, with a large head and a narrow waist and chest.

Andy's mother kissed her and her father and said, "Well, have a good time" and "Be careful." Soon they were outside in the bitter dark, loading gear by the back-porch light, their breath steaming. The woods behind the house were then only a black streak against the wash of night.

Andy dozed in the car and woke to find that it was half light. Mac—also sleeping—had slid against her. She pushed him away and looked out the window. Her breath clouded the glass, and she was cold; the car's heater didn't work right. They were riding over gentle hills, the woods on both sides now—the same woods, she knew, because she had been watching the whole way, even while she slept. They had been in her dreams, and she had never lost sight of them.

Charlie Spoon was driving. "I don't understand why she's coming," he said to her 5
father. "How old is she anyway—eight?"

"Nine," her father replied. "She's small for her age."

"So—nine. What's the difference? She'll just add to the noise and get tired besides."

"No, she won't," her father said. "She can walk me to death. And she'll bring good luck, you'll see. Animals—I don't know how she does it, but they come right up to her. We go walking in the woods, and we'll spot more raccoons and possums and such than I ever see when I'm alone."

Charlie grunted.

"Besides, she's not a bad little shot, even if she doesn't hunt yet. She shoots the 10
.22 real good."

"Popgun," Charlie said, and snorted. "And target shooting ain't deer hunting."

"Well, she's not gonna be shooting anyway, Charlie," her father said. "Don't worry. She'll be no bother."

"I still don't know why she's coming," Charlie said.

"Because she wants to, and I want her to. Just like you and Mac. No difference."

Charlie turned onto a side road and after a mile or so slowed down. "That's it!" he 15
cried. He stopped, backed up, and entered a narrow dirt road almost hidden by trees. Five hundred yards down, the road ran parallel to a fenced-in field. Charlie parked in a cleared area deeply rutted by frozen tractor tracks. The gate was locked. *In the spring,* Andy thought, *there will be cows here, and a dog that chases them,* but now the field was unmarked and bare.

"This is it," Charlie Spoon declared. "Me and Mac was up here just two weeks ago, scouting it out, and there's deer. Mac saw the tracks."

"That's right," Mac said.

"Well, we'll just see about that," her father said, putting on his gloves. He turned to Andy. "How you doing, honeybun?"

"Just fine," she said.

Andy shivered and stamped as they unloaded: first the rifles, which they 20
unsheathed and checked, sliding the bolts, sighting through scopes, adjusting the

slings; then the gear, their food and tents and sleeping bags and stove stored in four backpacks—three big ones for Charlie Spoon and her father and Mac, and a day pack for her.

"That's about your size," Mac said, to tease her.

She reddened and said, "Mac, I can carry a pack big as yours any day." He laughed and pressed his knee against the back of hers, so that her leg buckled. "Cut it out," she said. She wanted to make an iceball and throw it at him, but she knew that her father and Charlie were anxious to get going, and she didn't want to displease them.

Mac slid under the gate, and they handed the packs over to him. Then they slid under and began walking across the field toward the same woods that ran all the way back to her home, where even now her mother was probably rising again to wash their breakfast dishes and make herself a fresh pot of coffee. *She is there, and we are here:* the thought satisfied Andy. There was no place else she would rather be.

Mac came up beside her. "Over there's Canada," he said, nodding toward the woods.

25   "Huh!" she said. "Not likely."

"I don't mean *right* over there. I mean farther up north. You think I'm dumb?"

Dumb as your father, she thought.

"Look at that," Mac said, pointing to a piece of cow dung lying on a spot scraped bare of snow. "A frozen meadow muffin." He picked it up and sailed it at her. "Catch!"

"Mac!" she yelled. His laugh was as gawky as he was. She walked faster. He seemed different today somehow, bundled in his yellow-and-black-checkered coat, a rifle in hand, his silly floppy hat not quite covering his ears. They all seemed different as she watched them trudge through the snow—Mac and her father and Charlie Spoon— bigger, maybe, as if the cold landscape enlarged rather than diminished them, so that they, the only figures in that landscape, took on size and meaning just by being there. If they weren't there, everything would be quieter, and the woods would be the same as before. *But they are here*, Andy thought, looking behind her at the boot prints in the snow, *and I am too, and so it's all different.*

30   "We'll go down to the cut where we found those deer tracks," Charlie said as they entered the woods. "Maybe we'll get lucky and get a late one coming through."

The woods descended into a gully. The snow was softer and deeper here, so that often Andy sank to her knees. Charlie and Mac worked the top of the gully while she and her father walked along the base some thirty yards behind them. "If they miss the first shot, we'll get the second," her father said, and she nodded as if she had known this all the time. She listened to the crunch of their boots, their breathing, and the drumming of a distant woodpecker. And the crackling. In winter the woods crackled as if everything were straining, ready to snap like dried chicken bones.

We are hunting, Andy thought. The cold air burned her nostrils.

They stopped to make lunch by a rock outcropping that protected them from the wind. Her father heated the bean soup her mother had made for them, and they ate it with bread already stiff from the cold. He and Charlie took a few pulls from a flask of Jim Beam while she scoured the plates with snow and repacked them. Then they all had coffee with sugar and powdered milk, and her father poured her a cup too.

"We won't tell your momma," he said, and Mac laughed. Andy held the cup the way her father did, not by the handle but around the rim. The coffee tasted smoky. She felt a little queasy, but she drank it all.

Charlie Spoon picked his teeth with a fingernail. "Now, you might've noticed one thing," he said.

"What's that?" her father asked.   35

"You might've noticed you don't hear no rifles. That's because there ain't no other hunters here. We've got the whole damn woods to ourselves. Now, I ask you—do I know how to find 'em?"

"We haven't seen deer yet, neither."

"Oh, we will," Charlie said, "but not for a while now." He leaned back against the rock. "Deer're sleeping, resting up for the evening feed."

"I seen a deer behind our house once, and it was afternoon," Andy said.

"Yeah, honey, but that was *before* deer season," Charlie said, grinning. "They know   40
something now. They're smart that way."

"That's right," Mac said.

Andy looked at her father—had she said something stupid?

"Well, Charlie," he said, "if they know so much, how come so many get themselves shot?"

"Them's the ones that don't *believe* what they know," Charlie replied. The men laughed. Andy hesitated, and then laughed with them.

They moved on, as much to keep warm as to find a deer. The wind became even   45
stronger. Blowing through the treetops, it sounded like the ocean, and once Andy thought she could smell salt air. But that was impossible; the ocean was *hundreds* of miles away, farther than Canada even. She and her parents had gone last summer to stay for a week at a motel on the New Jersey shore. That was the first time she'd seen the ocean, and it frightened her. It was huge and empty, yet always moving. Everything lay hidden. If you walked in it, you couldn't see how deep it was or what might be below; if you swam, something could pull you under and you'd never be seen again. Its musky, rank smell made her think of things dying. Her mother had floated beyond the breakers, calling to her to come in, but Andy wouldn't go farther than a few feet into the surf. Her mother swam and splashed with animal-like delight while her father, smiling shyly, held his white arms above the waist-deep water as if afraid to get them wet. Once a comber rolled over and sent them both tossing, and when her mother tried to stand up, the surf receding behind, Andy saw that her mother's swimsuit top had come off, so that her breasts swayed free, her nipples like two dark eyes. Embarrassed, Andy looked around: except for two women under a yellow umbrella farther up, the beach was empty. Her mother stood up unsteadily, regained her footing. Taking what seemed the longest time, she calmly refixed her top. Andy lay on the beach towel and closed her eyes. The sound of the surf made her head ache.

And now it was winter; the sky was already dimming, not just with the absence of light but with a mist that clung to the hunters' faces like cobwebs. They made camp early. Andy was chilled. When she stood still, she kept wiggling her toes to make sure they were there. Her father rubbed her arms and held her to him briefly, and that felt better. She unpacked the food while the others put up the tents.

"How about rounding us up some firewood, Mac?" Charlie asked.

"I'll do it," Andy said. Charlie looked at her thoughtfully and then handed her the canvas carrier.

There wasn't much wood on the ground, so it took her a while to get a good load. She was about a hundred yards from camp, near a cluster of high, lichen-covered boulders, when she saw through a crack in the rock a buck and two does walking gingerly, almost daintily, through the alder trees. She tried to hush her breathing as they passed not more than twenty yards away. There was nothing she could do. If she yelled, they'd be gone; by the time she got back to camp, they'd be gone. The buck stopped, nostrils quivering, tail up and alert. He looked directly at her. Still she didn't move, not one muscle. He was a beautiful buck, the color of late-turned maple leaves. Unafraid, he lowered his tail, and he and his does silently merged into the trees. Andy walked back to camp and dropped the firewood.

50   "I saw three deer," she said. "A buck and two does."

"Where?" Charlie Spoon cried, looking behind her as if they might have followed her into camp.

"In the woods yonder. They're gone now."

"Well, hell!" Charlie banged his coffee cup against his knee.

"Didn't I say she could find animals?" her father said, grinning.

55   "Too late to go after them," Charlie muttered. "It'll be dark in a quarter hour. Damn!"

"Damn," Mac echoed.

"They just walk right up to her," her father said.

"Well, leastwise this proves there's deer here." Charlie began snapping long branches into shorter ones. "You know, I think I'll stick with you," he told Andy, "since you're so good at finding deer and all. How'd that be?"

"Okay, I guess," Andy murmured. She hoped he was kidding; no way did she want to hunt with Charlie Spoon. Still, she was pleased he had said it.

60   Her father and Charlie took one tent, she and Mac the other. When they were in their sleeping bags, Mac said in the darkness, "I bet you really didn't see no deer, did you?"

She sighed. "I did, Mac. Why would I lie?"

"How big was the buck?"

"Four point. I counted."

Mac snorted.

65   "You just believe what you want, Mac," she said testily.

"Too bad it ain't buck season," he said. "Well, I got to go pee."

"So pee."

She heard him turn in his bag. "You ever see it?" he asked.

"It? What's 'it'?"

70   "It. A pecker."

"Sure," she lied.

"Whose? Your father's?"

She was uncomfortable. "No," she said.

"Well, whose then?"

75   "Oh I don't know! Leave me be, why don't you?"

"Didn't see a deer, didn't see a pecker," Mac said teasingly.

She didn't answer right away. Then she said, "My cousin Lewis. I saw his."

"Well, how old's he?"

"One and a half."

"Ha! A baby! A baby's is like a little worm. It ain't a real one at all."

If he says he'll show me his, she thought, *I'll kick him. I'll just get out of my bag and kick him.*

"I went hunting with my daddy and Versh and Danny Simmons last year in buck season," Mac said, "and we got ourselves one. And we hog-dressed the thing. You know what that is, don't you?"

"No," she said. She was confused. What was he talking about now?

"That's when you cut him open and take out all his guts, so the meat don't spoil. Makes him lighter to pack out, too."

She tried to imagine what the deer's guts might look like, pulled from the gaping hole. "What do you do with them?" she said. "The guts?"

"Oh, just leave 'em for the bears."

She ran her finger like a knife blade along her belly.

"When we left them on the ground," Mac said, "they smoked. Like they were cooking."

"Huh," she said.

"They cut off the deer's pecker, too, you know."

Andy imagined Lewis's pecker and shuddered. "Mac, you're disgusting."

He laughed. "Well, I gotta go pee." She heard him rustle out of his bag. "Broo!" he cried, flapping his arms. "It's cold!"

He makes so much noise, she thought, *just noise and more noise.*

Her father woke them before first light. He warned them to talk softly and said that they were going to the place where Andy had seen the deer, to try to cut them off on their way back from their night feeding. Andy couldn't shake off her sleep. Stuffing her sleeping bag into its sack seemed to take an hour, and tying her boots was the strangest thing she'd ever done. Charlie Spoon made hot chocolate and oatmeal with raisins. Andy closed her eyes and, between beats of her heart, listened to the breathing of the forest. *When I open my eyes, it will be lighter*, she decided. But when she did, it was still just as dark, except for the swaths of their flashlights and the hissing blue flame of the stove. *There has to be just one moment when it all changes from dark to light*, Andy thought. She had missed it yesterday, in the car; today she would watch more closely.

But when she remembered again, it was already first light and they had moved to the rocks by the deer trail and had set up shooting positions—Mac and Charlie Spoon on the up-trail side, she and her father behind them, some six feet up on a ledge. The day became brighter, the sun piercing the tall pines, raking the hunters, yet providing little warmth. Andy now smelled alder and pine and the slightly rotten odor of rock lichen. She rubbed her hand over the stone and considered that it must be very old, had probably been here before the giant pines, *before anyone was in these woods at all*. A chipmunk sniffed on a nearby branch. She aimed an imaginary rifle and pressed the trigger. The chipmunk froze, then scurried away. Her legs were cramping on the narrow ledge. Her father seemed to doze, one hand in his parka, the other cupped lightly around the rifle. She could smell his scent of old wool and leather. His cheeks were speckled with gray-black whiskers, and he worked his jaws slightly, as if chewing a small piece of gum.

Please let us get a deer, she prayed.

A branch snapped on the other side of the rock face. Her father's hand stiffened on the rifle, startling her—*He hasn't been sleeping at all*, she marveled—and then his jaw relaxed, as did the lines around his eyes, and she heard Charlie Spoon call, "Yo, don't shoot, it's us." He and Mac appeared from around the rock. They stopped beneath the ledge. Charlie solemnly crossed his arms.

"I don't believe we're gonna get any deer here," he said drily.

Andy's father lowered his rifle to Charlie and jumped down from the ledge. Then he reached up for Andy. She dropped into his arms and he set her gently on the ground.

100   Mac sidled up to her. "I knew you didn't see no deer," he said.

"Just because they don't come when you want 'em to don't mean she didn't see them," her father said.

Still, she felt bad. Her telling about the deer had caused them to spend the morning there, cold and expectant, with nothing to show for it.

They tramped through the woods for another two hours, not caring much about noise. Mac found some deer tracks, and they argued about how old they were. They split up for a while and then rejoined at an old logging road that deer might use, and followed it. The road crossed a stream, which had mostly frozen over but in a few spots still caught leaves and twigs in an icy swirl. They forded it by jumping from rock to rock. The road narrowed after that, and the woods thickened.

They stopped for lunch, heating up Charlie's wife's corn chowder. Andy's father cut squares of applesauce cake with his hunting knife and handed them to her and Mac, who ate his almost daintily. Andy could faintly taste knife oil on the cake. She was tired. She stretched her leg; the muscle that had cramped on the rock still ached.

105   "Might as well relax," her father said, as if reading her thoughts. "We won't find deer till suppertime."

Charlie Spoon leaned back against his pack and folded his hands across his stomach. "Well, even if we don't get a deer," he said expansively, "it's still great to be out here, breathe some fresh air, clomp around a bit. Get away from the house and the old lady." He winked at Mac, who looked away.

"That's what the woods are all about, anyway," Charlie said. "It's where the women don't want to go." He bowed his head toward Andy. "With your exception, of course, little lady." He helped himself to another piece of applesauce cake.

"She ain't a woman," Mac said.

"Well, she damn well's gonna be," Charlie said. He grinned at her. "Or will you? You're half a boy anyway. You go by a boy's name. What's your real name? Andrea, ain't it?"

110   "That's right," she said. She hoped that if she didn't look at him, Charlie would stop.

"Well, which do you like? Andy or Andrea?"

"Don't matter," she mumbled. "Either."

"She's always been Andy to me," her father said.

Charlie Spoon was still grinning. "So what are you gonna be, Andrea? A boy or a girl?"

"I'm a girl," she said.   115

"But you want to go hunting and fishing and everything, huh?"

"She can do whatever she likes," her father said.

"Hell, you might as well have just had a boy and be done with it!" Charlie exclaimed.

"That's funny," her father said, and chuckled. "That's just what her momma tells me."

They were looking at her, and she wanted to get away from them all, even from   120
her father, who chose to joke with them.

"I'm going to walk a bit," she said.

She heard them laughing as she walked down the logging trail. She flapped her arms; she whistled. *I don't care how much noise I make*, she thought. Two grouse flew from the underbrush, startling her. A little farther down, the trail ended in a clearing that enlarged into a frozen meadow; beyond it the woods began again. A few moldering posts were all that was left of a fence that had once enclosed the field. The low afternoon sunlight reflected brightly off the snow, so that Andy's eyes hurt. She squinted hard. A gust of wind blew across the field, stinging her face. And then, as if it had been waiting for her, the doe emerged from the trees opposite and stepped cautiously into the field. Andy watched: it stopped and stood quietly for what seemed a long time and then ambled across. It stopped again about seventy yards away and began to browse in a patch of sugar grass uncovered by the wind. Carefully, slowly, never taking her eyes from the doe, Andy walked backward, trying to step into the boot prints she'd already made. When she was far enough back into the woods, she turned and walked faster, her heart racing. *Please let it stay*, she prayed.

"There's doe in the field yonder," she told them.

They got their rifles and hurried down the trail.

"No use," her father said. "We're making too much noise any way you look at it."   125

"At least we got us the wind in our favor," Charlie Spoon said, breathing heavily.

But the doe was still there, grazing.

"Good Lord," Charlie whispered. He looked at her father. "Well, whose shot?"

"Andy spotted it," her father said in a low voice. "Let her shoot it."

"What!" Charlie's eyes widened.   130

Andy couldn't believe what her father had just said. She'd only shot tin cans and targets; she'd never even fired her father's .30-.30, and she'd never killed anything.

"I can't," she whispered.

"That's right, she can't," Charlie Spoon insisted. "She's not old enough and she don't have a license even if she was!"

"Well, who's to tell?" her father said in a low voice. "Nobody's going to know but us." He looked at her. "Do you want to shoot it, punkin?"

Why doesn't it hear us? she wondered. *Why doesn't it run away?* "I don't know,"   135
she said.

"Well, I'm sure as hell gonna shoot it," Charlie said. Her father grasped Charlie's rifle barrel and held it. His voice was steady.

"Andy's a good shot. It's her deer. She found it, not you. You'd still be sitting on your ass back in camp." He turned to her again. "Now—do you want to shoot it, Andy? Yes or no."

He was looking at her; they were all looking at her. Suddenly she was angry at the deer, who refused to hear them, who wouldn't run away even when it could. "I'll shoot it," she said. Charlie turned away in disgust.

She lay on the ground and pressed the rifle stock against her shoulder bone. The snow was cold through her parka; she smelled oil and wax and damp earth. She pulled off one glove with her teeth. "It sights just like the .22," her father said gently. "Cartridge's already chambered." As she had done so many times before, she sighted down the scope; now the doe was in the reticle. She moved the barrel until the cross hairs lined up. Her father was breathing beside her.

140 "Aim where the chest and legs meet, or a little above, punkin," he was saying calmly. "That's the killing shot."

But now, seeing it in the scope, Andy was hesitant. Her finger weakened on the trigger. Still, she nodded at what her father said and sighted again, the cross hairs lining up in exactly the same spot—the doe had hardly moved, its brownish-gray body outlined starkly against the blue-backed snow. *It doesn't know*, Andy thought. *It just doesn't know.* And as she looked, deer and snow and faraway trees flattened within the circular frame to become like a picture on a calendar, not real, and she felt calm, as if she had been dreaming everything—the day, the deer, the hunt itself. And she, finger on trigger, was only a part of that dream.

"Shoot!" Charlie hissed.

Through the scope she saw the deer look up, ears high and straining.

Charlie groaned, and just as he did, and just at the moment when Andy knew— *knew*—the doe would bound away, as if she could feel its haunches tensing and gathering power, she pulled the trigger. Later she would think, *I felt the recoil, I smelled the smoke, but I don't remember pulling the trigger.* Through the scope the deer seemed to shrink into itself, and then slowly knelt, hind legs first, head raised as if to cry out. It trembled, still straining to keep its head high, as if that alone would save it; failing, it collapsed, shuddered, and lay still.

145 "Whoee!" Mac cried.

"One shot! One shot!" her father yelled, clapping her on the back. Charlie Spoon was shaking his head and smiling dumbly.

"I told you she was a great little shot!" her father said. "I told you!" Mac danced and clapped his hands. She was dazed, not quite understanding what had happened. And then they were crossing the field toward the fallen doe, she walking dreamlike, the men laughing and joking, released now from the tension of silence and anticipation. Suddenly Mac pointed and cried out, "Look at that!"

The doe was rising, legs unsteady. They stared at it, unable to comprehend, and in that moment the doe regained its feet and looked at them, as if it too were trying to understand. Her father whistled softly. Charlie Spoon unslung his rifle and raised it to his shoulder, but the doe was already bounding away. His hurried shot missed, and the deer disappeared into the woods.

"Damn, damn, damn," he moaned.

"I don't believe it," her father said. "That deer was dead."   150

"Dead, hell!" Charlie yelled. "It was gutshot, that's all. Stunned and gutshot. Clean shot, my ass!"

What have I done? Andy thought.

Her father slung his rifle over his shoulder. "Well, let's go. It can't get too far."

"Hell, I've seen deer run ten miles gutshot," Charlie said. He waved his arms. "We may never find her!"

As they crossed the field, Mac came up to her and said in a low voice, "Gutshoot   155
a deer, you'll go to hell."

"Shut up, Mac," she said, her voice cracking. It was a terrible thing she had done, she knew. She couldn't bear to think of the doe in pain and frightened. *Please let it die,* she prayed.

But though they searched all the last hour of daylight, so that they had to recross the field and go up the logging trail in a twilight made even deeper by thick, smoky clouds, they didn't find the doe. They lost its trail almost immediately in the dense stands of alderberry and larch.

"I am cold, and I am tired," Charlie Spoon declared. "And if you ask me, that deer's in another county already."

"No one's asking you, Charlie," her father said.

They had a supper of hard salami and ham, bread, and the rest of the applesauce   160
cake. It seemed a bother to heat the coffee, so they had cold chocolate instead. Everyone turned in early.

"We'll find it in the morning, honeybun," her father said, as she went to her tent.

"I don't like to think of it suffering." She was almost in tears.

"It's dead already, punkin. Don't even think about it." He kissed her, his breath sour and his beard rough against her cheek.

Andy was sure she wouldn't get to sleep; the image of the doe falling, falling, then rising again, repeated itself whenever she closed her eyes. Then she heard an owl hoot and realized that it had awakened her, so she must have been asleep after all. She hoped the owl would hush, but instead it hooted louder. She wished her father or Charlie Spoon would wake up and do something about it, but no one moved in the other tent, and suddenly she was afraid that they had all decamped, wanting nothing more to do with her. She whispered, "Mac, Mac," to the sleeping bag where he should be, but no one answered. She tried to find the flashlight she always kept by her side, but couldn't, and she cried in panic, "Mac, are you there?" He mumbled something, and immediately she felt foolish and hoped he wouldn't reply.

When she awoke again, everything had changed. The owl was gone, the woods   165
were still, and she sensed light, blue and pale, light where before there had been none. *The moon must have come out,* she thought. And it was warm, too, warmer than it should have been. She got out of her sleeping bag and took off her parka—it was that warm. Mac was asleep, wheezing like an old man. She unzipped the tent and stepped outside.

The woods were more beautiful than she had ever seen them. The moon made everything ice-rimmed glimmer with a crystallized, immanent light, while underneath that ice the branches of trees were as stark as skeletons. She heard a crunching in the snow, the one sound in all that silence, and there, walking down the logging trail into their camp, was the doe. Its body, like everything around her, was silvered with frost and moonlight. It walked past the tent where her father and Charlie Spoon were sleeping and stopped no more than six feet from her. Andy saw that she had shot it, yes, had shot it cleanly, just where she thought she had, the wound a jagged, bloody hole in the doe's chest.

A heart shot, she thought.

The doe stepped closer, so that Andy, if she wished, could have reached out and touched it. It looked at her as if expecting her to do this, and so she did, running her hand, slowly at first, along the rough, matted fur, then down to the edge of the wound, where she stopped. The doe stood still. Hesitantly, Andy felt the edge of the wound. The torn flesh was sticky and warm. The wound parted under her touch. And then, almost without her knowing it, her fingers were within, probing, yet still the doe didn't move. Andy pressed deeper, through flesh and muscle and sinew, until her whole hand and more was inside the wound and she had found the doe's heart, warm and beating. She cupped it gently in her hand. *Alive*, she marveled. *Alive*.

The heart quickened under her touch, becoming warmer and warmer until it was hot enough to burn. In pain, Andy tried to remove her hand, but the wound closed about it and held her fast. Her hand was burning. She cried out in agony, sure they would all hear and come help, but they didn't. And then her hand pulled free, followed by a steaming rush of blood, more blood than she ever could have imagined—it covered her hand and arm, and she saw to her horror that her hand was steaming. She moaned and fell to her knees and plunged her hand into the snow. The doe looked at her gently and then turned and walked back up the trail.

170   In the morning, when she woke, Andy could still smell the blood, but she felt no pain. She looked at her hand. Even though it appeared unscathed, it felt weak and withered. She couldn't move it freely and was afraid the others would notice. *I will hide it in my jacket pocket*, she decided, *so nobody can see*. She ate the oatmeal that her father cooked and stayed apart from them all. No one spoke to her, and that suited her. A light snow began to fall. It was the last day of their hunting trip. She wanted to be home.

Her father dumped the dregs of his coffee. "Well, let's go look for her," he said.

Again they crossed the field. Andy lagged behind. She averted her eyes from the spot where the doe had fallen, already filling up with snow. Mac and Charlie entered the woods first, followed by her father. Andy remained in the field and considered the smear of gray sky, the nearby flock of crows pecking at unyielding stubble. *I will stay here*, she thought, *and not move for a long while*. But now someone—Mac—was yelling. Her father appeared at the woods' edge and waved for her to come. She ran and pushed through a brake of alderberry and larch. The thick underbrush scratched her face. For a moment she felt lost and looked wildly about. Then, where the brush thinned, she saw them standing quietly in the falling snow. They were staring down at the dead doe. A film covered its upturned eye, and its body was lightly dusted with snow.

"I told you she wouldn't get too far," Andy's father said triumphantly. "We must've just missed her yesterday. Too blind to see."

"We're just damn lucky no animal got to her last night," Charlie muttered.

Her father lifted the doe's foreleg. The wound was blood-clotted, brown, and   175
caked like frozen mud. "Clean shot," he said to Charlie. He grinned. "My little
girl."

Then he pulled out his knife, the blade gray as the morning. Mac whispered to
Andy, "Now watch this," while Charlie Spoon lifted the doe from behind by its
forelegs so that its head rested between his knees, its underside exposed. Her father's
knife sliced thickly from chest to belly to crotch, and Andy was running from them,
back to the field and across, scattering the crows who cawed and circled angrily. And
now they were all calling to her—Charlie Spoon and Mac and her father—crying
Andy, Andy (but that wasn't her name, she would no longer be called that); yet
louder than any of them was the wind blowing through the treetops, like the ocean
where her mother floated in green water, also calling *Come in, come in*, while all
around her roared the mocking of the terrible, now inevitable, sea.

Reading and Reacting

1. The initiation of a child into adulthood is a common literary theme. In this story, hunting is presented as an initiation rite. In what way is hunting an appropriate coming-of-
   age ritual?

2. Which characters are in conflict in this story? Which ideas are in conflict? How do
   these conflicts help to communicate the story's initiation theme?

3. In the story's opening paragraph and elsewhere, Andy finds comfort and reassurance
   in the idea that the woods are "always the same"; later in the story, she remembers the
   ocean, "huge and empty, yet always moving. Everything lay hidden . . ." (par. 45). How
   does the contrast between the woods and the ocean suggest the transition she must
   make from childhood to adulthood?

4. How do the references to blood support the story's initiation theme? Do they suggest
   other themes as well?

5. Throughout the story, references are made to Andy's ability to inspire the trust of
   animals. As her father says, "Animals—I don't know how she does it, but they come
   right up to her" (par. 8). How does his comment foreshadow later events?

6. Why does Andy pray that she and the others will get a deer? What makes her change
   her mind? How does the change in Andy's character help to convey the story's
   theme?

7. Andy's mother is not an active participant in the story's events. Still, she is important
   to the story. Why is her role important? How does paragraph 45 reveal the importance
   of the mother's role?

8. What has Andy learned as a result of her experience? What else do you think she still
   has to learn?

9. **JOURNAL ENTRY** How would the story be different if Andy were a boy? What would be
   the same?

10. **CRITICAL PERSPECTIVE** In a review of *Comfort*, the book in which "Doe Season"
    appears, Susan Wood makes the following observation:

The dozen or so stories in David Michael Kaplan's affecting first collection share a common focus on the extraordinary moments of recognition in ordinary lives. He is at his best suggesting how such moments may alter, for better or for worse, our relationships with those to whom we are most deeply bound—children, parents, lovers—in love and guilt.

At what point does "the extraordinary moment of recognition" occur in "Doe Season"? How does this moment alter Andy's relationship with both her parents?

Related Works: "Snow" (p. 126), from *Persepolis* (p. 162), "A&P" (p. 238), "The Girl with Bangs" (p. 262), "Greasy Lake" (p. 569), "The Lamb" (p. 960), "What Are You Going to Be?" (p. 1062), *Proof* (p. 1180)

D(AVID) H(ERBERT) LAWRENCE (1885–1930) was born in Nottinghamshire, England, the son of a coal miner and a schoolteacher. Determined to escape the harsh life of a miner, Lawrence taught for several years after graduating from high school. He soon began writing fiction and established himself in London literary circles.

During World War I, Lawrence and his wife were suspected of treason because of his pacifism and her connection to German aristocracy. Because Lawrence suffered from tuberculosis, he and his wife left England after the armistice in search of a healthier climate. They traveled in Australia, France, Italy, Mexico, and the United States throughout their lives.

Lawrence is recognized for his impassioned portrayal of our unconscious and instinctive natures. In his novel *Lady Chatterley's Lover* (1928), he attempted to incorporate explicit sexuality into English fiction, and the book was banned for years in Britain and the United States. His other novels include *Sons and Lovers* (1913), *The Rainbow* (1915), *Women in Love* (1921), and *The Plumed Serpent* (1926). Lawrence was also a gifted poet, essayist, travel writer, and short story writer, and his work strongly influenced other writers.

Lawrence's fascination with the struggle between the unconscious and the intellect is revealed in his short story "The Rocking-Horse Winner" (1920). Lawrence sets his story in a house full of secrets and weaves symbolism with elements of the fairy tale and the gothic to produce a tale that has often been the subject of literary debate.

Cultural Context   Horse racing in England has a long history, beginning with casual competitions organized by Roman soldiers in Yorkshire in A.D. 200. The first recorded horse race was run during the reign of Henry II in 1174. Today, horses can be raced over fences or hurdles (National Hunt Racing) or over unobstructed distances (flat racing). There are also cross-country races from point to point, which are called steeplechases. A derby, like the one mentioned in this story, usually denotes a race in which three-year-old horses compete. The name *derby* is derived from the Epsom Derby, which is still run at the Epsom racecourse and is named for Edward Smith Stanley, the twelfth Earl of Derby.

The Rocking-Horse Winner (1920)

There was a woman who was beautiful, who started with all the advantages, yet she had no luck. She married for love, and the love turned to dust. She had bonny children, yet she felt they had been thrust upon her, and she could not love them. They looked at her coldly, as if they were finding fault with her. And hurriedly she felt she must cover up some fault in herself. Yet what it was that she must cover up she never knew. Nevertheless, when her children were present, she always felt the centre of her heart go hard. This troubled her, and in her manner she was all the more gentle and anxious for her children, as if she loved them very much. Only she herself knew that at the centre of her heart was a hard little place that could not feel love, no, not for anybody. Everybody else said of her: "She is such a good mother. She adores her children." Only she herself, and her children themselves, knew it was not so. They read it in each other's eyes.

There were a boy and two little girls. They lived in a pleasant house, with a garden, and they had discreet servants, and felt themselves superior to anyone in the neighbourhood.

Although they lived in style, they felt always an anxiety in the house. There was never enough money. The mother had a small income, and the father had a small income, but not nearly enough for the social position which they had to keep up. The father went into town to some office. But though he had good prospects, these prospects never materialised. There was always the grinding sense of the shortage of money, though the style was always kept up.

At last the mother said: "I will see if *I* can't make something." But she did not know where to begin. She racked her brains, and tried this thing and the other, but could not find anything successful. The failure made deep lines come into her face. Her children were growing up, they would have to go to school. There must be more money, there must be more money. The father, who was always very handsome and expensive in his tastes, seemed as if he never *would* be able to do anything worth doing. And the mother, who had a great belief in herself, did not succeed any better, and her tastes were just as expensive.

And so the house came to be haunted by the unspoken phrase: *There must be more money! There must be more money!* The children could hear it all the time, though nobody said it aloud. They heard it at Christmas, when the expensive and splendid toys filled the nursery. Behind the shining modern rocking-horse, behind the smart doll's house, a voice would start whispering: "There *must* be more money! There *must* be more money!" And the children would stop playing, to listen for a moment. They would look into each other's eyes, to see if they had all heard. And each one saw in the eyes of the other two that they too had heard. "There *must* be more money! There *must* be more money!"   5

It came whispering from the springs of the still-swaying rocking-horse, and even the horse, bending his wooden, champing head, heard it. The big doll, sitting so pink and smirking in her new pram, could hear it quite plainly, and seemed to be smirking all the more self-consciously because of it. The foolish puppy, too, that took the place of the teddybear, he was looking so extraordinarily foolish for no other reason but that he heard the secret whisper all over the house: "There *must* be more money!"

Yet nobody ever said it aloud. The whisper was everywhere, and therefore no one spoke it. Just as no one ever says: "We are breathing!" in spite of the fact that breath is coming and going all the time.

"Mother," said the boy Paul one day, "why don't we keep a car of our own? Why do we always use uncle's, or else a taxi?"

"Because we're the poor members of the family," said the mother.

"But why *are* we, mother?"   10

"Well—I suppose," she said slowly and bitterly, "it's because your father has no luck."

The boy was silent for some time.

"Is luck money, mother?" he asked, rather timidly.

"No, Paul. Not quite. It's what causes you to have money."

15   "Oh!" said Paul vaguely. "I thought when Uncle Oscar said *filthy lucker*, it meant money."

"*Filthy lucre*[1] does mean money," said the mother. "But it's lucre, not luck."

"Oh!" said the boy. "Then what *is* luck, mother?"

"It's what causes you to have money. If you're lucky you have money. That's why it's better to be born lucky than rich. If you're rich, you may lose your money. But if you're lucky, you will always get more money."

"Oh! Will you? And is father not lucky?"

20   "Very unlucky, I should say," she said bitterly.

The boy watched her with unsure eyes.

"Why?" he asked.

"I don't know. Nobody ever knows why one person is lucky and another unlucky."

"Don't they? Nobody at all? Does *nobody* know?"

25   "Perhaps God. But He never tells."

"He ought to, then. And aren't you lucky either, mother?"

"I can't be, if I married an unlucky husband."

"But by yourself, aren't you?"

"I used to think I was, before I married. Now I think I am very unlucky indeed."

30   "Why?"

"Well—never mind! Perhaps I'm not really," she said.

The child looked at her to see if she meant it. But he saw, by the lines of her mouth, that she was only trying to hide something from him.

"Well, anyhow," he said stoutly, "I'm a lucky person."

"Why?" said his mother, with a sudden laugh.

35   He stared at her. He didn't even know why he had said it.

"God told me," he asserted, brazening it out.

"I hope He did, dear!" she said, again with a laugh, but rather bitter.

"He did, mother!"

"Excellent!" said the mother, using one of her husband's exclamations.

40   The boy saw she did not believe him; or rather, that she paid no attention to his assertion. This angered him somewhat, and made him want to compel her attention.

He went off by himself, vaguely, in a childish way, seeking for the clue to "luck." Absorbed, taking no heed of other people, he went about with a sort of stealth, seeking inwardly for luck. He wanted luck, he wanted it, he wanted it. When the two girls were playing dolls in the nursery, he would sit on his big rocking-horse, charging madly into space, with a frenzy that made the little girls peer at him uneasily. Wildly the horse careered, the waving dark hair of the boy tossed, his eyes had a strange glare in them. The little girls dared not speak to him.

---

[1] *filthy lucre:* An expression originating from Titus 1.11 in the Bible, meaning money acquired through deceit.

When he had ridden to the end of his mad little journey, he climbed down and stood in front of his rocking-horse, staring fixedly into its lowered face. Its red mouth was slightly open, its big eye was wide and glassy-bright.

"Now!" he would silently command the snorting steed. "Now, take me to where there is luck! Now take me!"

And he would slash the horse on the neck with the little whip he had asked Uncle Oscar for. He *knew* the horse could take him to where there was luck, if only he forced it. So he would mount again and start on his furious ride, hoping at last to get there. He knew he could get there.

"You'll break your horse, Paul!" said the nurse.   45

"He's always riding like that! I wish he'd leave off!" said his elder sister Joan.

But he only glared down on them in silence. Nurse gave him up. She could make nothing of him. Anyhow, he was growing beyond her.

One day his mother and his Uncle Oscar came in when he was on one of his furious rides. He did not speak to them.

"Hallo, you young jockey! Riding a winner?" said his uncle.

"Aren't you growing too big for a rocking-horse? You're not a very little boy any   50
longer, you know," said his mother.

But Paul only gave a blue glare from his big, rather close-set eyes. He would speak to nobody when he was in full tilt. His mother watched him with an anxious expression on her face.

At last he suddenly stopped forcing his horse into the mechanical gallop and slid down.

"Well, I got there!" he announced fiercely, his blue eyes still flaring, and his sturdy long legs straddling apart.

"Where did you get to?" asked his mother.

"Where I wanted to go," he flared back at her.   55

"That's right, son!" said Uncle Oscar. "Don't you stop till you get there. What's the horse's name?"

"He doesn't have a name," said the boy.

"Gets on without all right?" asked the uncle.

"Well, he has different names. He was called Sansovino last week."

"Sansovino, eh? Won the Ascot.[2] How did you know this name?"   60

"He always talks about horse-races with Bassett," said Joan.

The uncle was delighted to find that his small nephew was posted with all the racing news. Bassett, the young gardener, who had been wounded in the left foot in the war and had got his present job through Oscar Cresswell, whose batman[3] he had been, was a perfect blade of the "turf." He lived in the racing events, and the small boy lived with him.

Oscar Cresswell got it all from Bassett.

"Master Paul comes and asks me, so I can't do more than tell him, sir," said Bassett, his face terribly serious, as if he were speaking of religious matters.

---

[2]*the Ascot:* The annual horse race at Ascot Heath in England.

[3]*batman:* A British military officer's personal assistant.

65   "And does he ever put anything on a horse he fancies?"

"Well—I don't want to give him away—he's a young sport, a fine sport, sir. Would you mind asking him himself? He sort of takes a pleasure in it, and perhaps he'd feel I was giving him away, sir, if you don't mind."

Bassett was serious as a church.

The uncle went back to his nephew and took him off for a ride in the car.

"Say, Paul, old man, do you ever put anything on a horse?" the uncle asked.

70   The boy watched the handsome man closely.

"Why, do you think I oughtn't to?" he parried.

"Not a bit of it! I thought perhaps you might give me a tip for the Lincoln."[4]

The car sped on into the country, going down to Uncle Oscar's place in Hampshire.

"Honour bright?" said the nephew.

75   "Honour bright, son!" said the uncle.

"Well, then, Daffodil."

"Daffodil! I doubt it, sonny. What about Mirza?"

"I only know the winner," said the boy. "That's Daffodil."

"Daffodil, eh?"

80   There was a pause. Daffodil was an obscure horse comparatively.

"Uncle!"

"Yes, son?"

"You won't let it go any further, will you? I promised Bassett."

"Bassett be damned, old man! What's he got to do with it?"

85   "We're partners. We've been partners from the first. Uncle, he lent me my first five shillings, which I lost. I promised him, honour bright, it was only between me and him; only you gave me that ten-shilling note I started winning with, so I thought you were lucky. You won't let it go any further, will you?"

The boy gazed at his uncle from those big, hot, blue eyes, set rather close together. The uncle stirred and laughed uneasily.

"Right you are, son! I'll keep your tip private. Daffodil, eh? How much are you putting on him?"

"All except twenty pounds," said the boy. "I keep that in reserve."

The uncle thought it a good joke.

90   "You keep twenty pounds in reserve, do you, you young romancer? What are you betting, then?"

"I'm betting three hundred," said the boy gravely. "But it's between you and me, Uncle Oscar! Honour bright?"

The uncle burst into a roar of laughter.

"It's between you and me all right, you young Nat Gould,"[5] he said, laughing. "But where's your three hundred?"

"Bassett keeps it for me. We're partners."

95   "You are, are you! And what is Bassett putting on Daffodil?"

---

[4]*the Lincoln:* The Lincolnshire Handicap, a horse race.

[5]*Nat Gould:* Nathaniel Gould (1857–1919), British journalist and writer known for his stories about horse racing.

"He won't go quite as high as I do, I expect. Perhaps he'll go a hundred and fifty."

"What, pennies?" laughed the uncle.

"Pounds," said the child, with a surprised look at his uncle. "Bassett keeps a bigger reserve than I do."

Between wonder and amusement Uncle Oscar was silent. He pursued the matter no further, but he determined to take his nephew with him to the Lincoln races.

"Now, son," he said, "I'm putting twenty on Mirza, and I'll put five on for you on any horse you fancy. What's your pick?"   100

"Daffodil, uncle."

"No, not the fiver on Daffodil!"

"I should if it was my own fiver," said the child.

"Good! Good! Right you are! A fiver for me and a fiver for you on Daffodil."

The child had never been to a race-meeting before, and his eyes were blue fire.   105
He pursed his mouth tight and watched. A Frenchman just in front had put his money on Lancelot. Wild with excitement, he flayed his arms up and down, yelling "*Lancelot! Lancelot!*" in his French accent.

Daffodil came in first, Lancelot second, Mirza third. The child, flushed and with eyes blazing, was curiously serene. His uncle brought him four five-pound notes, four to one.

"What am I to do with these?" he cried, waving them before the boy's eyes.

"I suppose we'll talk to Bassett," said the boy. "I expect I have fifteen hundred now; and twenty in reserve; and this twenty."

His uncle studied him for some moments.

"Look here, son!" he said. "You're not serious about Bassett and that fifteen hun-   110
dred, are you?"

"Yes, I am. But it's between you and me, uncle. Honour bright?"

"Honour bright all right, son! But I must talk to Bassett."

"If you'd like to be a partner, uncle, with Bassett and me, we could all be partners. Only, you'd have to promise, honour bright, uncle, not to let it go beyond us three. Bassett and I are lucky, and you must be lucky, because it was your ten shillings I started winning with. . . ."

Uncle Oscar took both Bassett and Paul into Richmond Park for an afternoon, and there they talked.

"It's like this, you see, sir," Bassett said. "Master Paul would get me talking about   115
racing events, spinning yarns, you know, sir. And he was always keen on knowing if I'd made or if I'd lost. It's about a year since, now, that I put five shillings on Blush of Dawn for him: and we lost. Then the luck turned, with that ten shillings he had from you: that we put on Singhalese. And since that time, it's been pretty steady, all things considering. What do you say, Master Paul?"

"We're all right when we're sure," said Paul. "It's when we're not quite sure that we go down."

"Oh, but we're careful then," said Bassett.

"But when are you *sure*?" smiled Uncle Oscar.

"It's Master Paul, sir," said Bassett in a secret, religious voice. "It's as if he had it from heaven. Like Daffodil, now, for the Lincoln. That was as sure as eggs."

"Did you put anything on Daffodil?" asked Oscar Cresswell.   120

"Yes, sir. I made my bit."

"And my nephew?"

Bassett was obstinately silent, looking at Paul.

"I made twelve hundred, didn't I, Bassett? I told uncle I was putting three hundred on Daffodil."

125 "That's right," said Bassett, nodding.

"But where's the money?" asked the uncle.

"I keep it safe locked up, sir. Master Paul can have it any minute he likes to ask for it."

"What, fifteen hundred pounds?"

"And twenty! And *forty*, that is, with the twenty he made on the course."

130 "It's amazing!" said the uncle.

"If Master Paul offers you to be partners, sir, I would, if I were you: if you'll excuse me," said Bassett.

Oscar Cresswell thought about it.

"I'll see the money," he said.

They drove home again, and, sure enough, Bassett came round to the garden-house with fifteen hundred pounds in notes. The twenty pounds reserve was left with Joe Glee, in the Turf Commission deposit.

135 "You see, it's all right, uncle, when I'm *sure!* Then we go strong, for all we're worth. Don't we, Bassett?"

"We do that, Master Paul."

"And when are you sure?" said the uncle, laughing.

"Oh, well, sometimes I'm *absolutely* sure, like about Daffodil," said the boy; "and sometimes I have an idea; and sometimes I haven't even an idea, have I, Bassett? Then we're careful, because we mostly go down."

"You do, do you! And when you're sure, like about Daffodil, what makes you sure, sonny?"

140 "Oh, well, I don't know," said the boy uneasily. "I'm sure, you know, uncle; that's all."

"It's as if he had it from heaven, sir," Bassett reiterated.

"I should say so!" said the uncle.

But he became a partner. And when the Leger[6] was coming on Paul was "sure" about Lively Spark, which was a quite inconsiderable horse. The boy insisted on putting a thousand on the horse, Bassett went for five hundred, and Oscar Cresswell two hundred. Lively Spark came in first, and the betting had been ten to one against him. Paul had made ten thousand.

"You see," he said, "I was absolutely sure of him."

145 Even Oscar Cresswell had cleared two thousand.

"Look here, son," he said, "this sort of thing makes me nervous."

"It needn't, uncle! Perhaps I shan't be sure again for a long time."

"But what are you going to do with your money?" asked the uncle.

"Of course," said the boy, "I started it for mother. She said she had no luck, because father is unlucky, so I thought if *I* was lucky, it might stop whispering."

---

[6]*the Leger:* The St. Leger Stakes, a horse race.

"What might stop whispering?"

"Our house. I *hate* our house for whispering."

"What does it whisper?"

"Why—why"—the boy fidgeted—"why, I don't know. But it's always short of money, you know, uncle."

"I know it, son, I know it."

"You know people send mother writs,[7] don't you, uncle?"

"I'm afraid I do," said the uncle.

"And then the house whispers, like people laughing at you behind your back. It's awful, that is! I thought if I was lucky . . ."

"You might stop it," added the uncle.

The boy watched him with big blue eyes, that had an uncanny cold fire in them, and he said never a word.

"Well, then!" said the uncle. "What are we doing?"

"I shouldn't like mother to know I was lucky," said the boy.

"Why not, son?"

"She'd stop me."

"I don't think she would."

"Oh!"—and the boy writhed in an odd way—"I *don't* want her to know, uncle."

"All right, son! We'll manage it without her knowing."

They managed it very easily. Paul, at the other's suggestion, handed over five thousand pounds to his uncle, who deposited it with the family lawyer, who was then to inform Paul's mother that a relative had put five thousand pounds into his hands, which sum was to be paid out a thousand pounds at a time, on the mother's birthday, for the next five years.

"So she'll have a birthday present of a thousand pounds for five successive years," said Uncle Oscar. "I hope it won't make it all the harder for her later."

Paul's mother had her birthday in November. The house had been "whispering" worse than ever lately, and, even in spite of his luck, Paul could not bear up against it. He was very anxious to see the effect of the birthday letter, telling his mother about the thousand pounds.

When there were no visitors, Paul now took his meals with his parents, as he was beyond the nursery control. His mother went into town nearly every day. She had discovered that she had an odd knack of sketching furs and dress materials, so she worked secretly in the studio of a friend who was the chief "artist" for the leading drapers. She drew the figures of ladies in furs and ladies in silk and sequins for the newspaper advertisements. This young woman artist earned several thousand pounds a year, but Paul's mother only made several hundreds, and she was again dissatisfied. She so wanted to be first in something, and she did not succeed, even in making sketches for drapery advertisements.

She was down to breakfast on the morning of her birthday. Paul watched her face as she read her letters. He knew the lawyer's letter. As his mother read it, her face hardened and became more expressionless. Then a cold, determined look came on her mouth. She hid the letter under the pile of others, and said not a word about it.

---

[7]*writs:* Letters from creditors requesting payment.

"Didn't you have anything nice in the post for your birthday, mother?" said Paul.

"Quite moderately nice," she said, her voice cold and absent.

She went away to town without saying more.

175 But in the afternoon Uncle Oscar appeared. He said Paul's mother had had a long interview with the lawyer, asking if the whole five thousand could not be advanced at once, as she was in debt.

"What do you think, uncle?" asked the boy.

"I leave it to you, son."

"Oh, let her have it, then! We can get some more with the other," said the boy.

"A bird in the hand is worth two in the bush, laddie!" said Uncle Oscar.

180 "But I'm sure to *know* for the Grand National; or the Lincolnshire; or else the Derby.[8] I'm sure to know for *one* of them," said Paul.

So Uncle Oscar signed the agreement, and Paul's mother touched the whole five thousand. Then something very curious happened. The voices in the house suddenly went mad, like a chorus of frogs on a spring evening. There was certain new furnishings, and Paul had a tutor. He was *really* going to Eton, his father's school, in the following autumn. There were flowers in the winter, and a blossoming of the luxury Paul's mother had been used to. And yet the voices in the house, behind the sprays of mimosa and almond-blossom, and from under the piles of iridescent cushions, simply trilled and screamed in a sort of ecstasy: "There *must* be more money! Oh-h-h; there *must* be more money. Oh, now, now-w! Now-w-w— there *must* be more money!—more than ever! More than ever!"

It frightened Paul terribly. He studied away at his Latin and Greek with his tutor. But his intense hours were spent with Bassett. The Grand National had gone by: he had not "known," and had lost a hundred pounds. Summer was at hand. He was in agony for the Lincoln. But even for the Lincoln he didn't "know," and he lost fifty pounds. He became wild-eyed and strange, as if something were going to explode in him.

"Let it alone, son! Don't you bother about it!" urged Uncle Oscar. But it was as if the boy couldn't really hear what his uncle was saying.

"I've got to know for the Derby! I've got to know for the Derby!" the child reiterated, his big blue eyes blazing with a sort of madness.

185 His mother noticed how overwrought he was.

"You'd better go to the seaside. Wouldn't you like to go now to the seaside, instead of waiting? I think you'd better," she said, looking down at him anxiously, her heart curiously heavy because of him.

But the child lifted his uncanny blue eyes.

"I couldn't possibly go before the Derby, mother!" he said. "I couldn't possibly!"

"Why not?" she said, her voice becoming heavy when she was opposed. "Why not? You can still go from the seaside to see the Derby with your Uncle Oscar, if that's what you wish. No need for you to wait here. Besides, I think you care too much about these races. It's a bad sign. My family has been a gambling family, and

---

[8]*Grand National . . . Derby:* Famous British horse races. The Grand National is run at Aintree; the Derby, at Epsom Downs.

you won't know till you grow up how much damage it has done. But it has done damage. I shall have to send Bassett away, and ask Uncle Oscar not to talk racing to you, unless you promise to be reasonable about it: go away to the seaside and forget it. You're all nerves!"

"I'll do what you like, mother, so long as you don't send me away till after the   190
Derby," the boy said.

"Send you away from where? Just from this house?"

"Yes," he said, gazing at her.

"Why, you curious child, what makes you care about this house so much, suddenly? I never knew you loved it."

He gazed at her without speaking. He had a secret within a secret, something he had not divulged, even to Bassett or to his Uncle Oscar.

But his mother, after standing undecided and a little bit sullen for some   195
moments, said:

"Very well, then! Don't go to the seaside till after the Derby, if you don't wish it. But promise me you won't let your nerves go to pieces. Promise you won't think so much about horse-racing and *events*, as you call them!"

"Oh no," said the boy casually. "I won't think much about them, mother. You needn't worry. I wouldn't worry, mother, if I were you."

"If you were me and I were you," said his mother, "I wonder what we *should* do!"

"But you know you needn't worry, mother, don't you?" the boy repeated.

"I should be awfully glad to know it," she said wearily.   200

"Oh, well, you *can*, you know. I mean, you *ought* to know you needn't worry," he insisted.

"Ought I? Then I'll see about it," she said.

Paul's secret of secrets was his wooden horse, that which had no name. Since he was emancipated from a nurse and a nursery-governess, he had had his rocking-horse removed to his own bedroom at the top of the house.

"Surely you're too big for a rocking-horse!" his mother had remonstrated.

"Well, you see, mother, till I can have a *real* horse, I like to have *some* sort of   205
animal about," had been his quaint answer.

"Do you feel he keeps you company?" she laughed.

"Oh yes! He's very good, he always keeps me company, when I'm there," said Paul.

So the horse, rather shabby, stood in an arrested prance in the boy's bedroom.

The Derby was drawing near, and the boy grew more and more tense. He hardly heard what was spoken to him, he was very frail, and his eyes were really uncanny. His mother had sudden strange seizures of uneasiness about him. Sometimes, for half an hour, she would feel a sudden anxiety about him that was almost anguish. She wanted to rush to him at once, and know he was safe.

Two nights before the Derby, she was at a big party in town, when one of her   210
rushes of anxiety about her boy, her firstborn, gripped her heart till she could hardly speak. She fought with the feeling, might and main, for she believed in common sense. But it was too strong. She had to leave the dance and go downstairs to telephone to the country. The children's nursery-governess was terribly surprised and startled at being rung up in the night.

"Are the children all right, Miss Wilmot?"

"Oh yes, they are quite all right."

"Master Paul? Is he all right?"

"He went to bed as right as a trivet. Shall I run up and look at him?"

215   "No," said Paul's mother reluctantly. "No! Don't trouble. It's all right. Don't sit up. We shall be home fairly soon." She did not want her son's privacy intruded upon.

"Very good," said the governess.

It was about one o'clock when Paul's mother and father drove up to their house. All was still. Paul's mother went to her room and slipped off her white fur cloak. She had told her maid not to wait up for her. She heard her husband downstairs, mixing a whisky and soda.

And then, because of the strange anxiety at her heart, she stole upstairs to her son's room. Noiselessly she went along the upper corridor. Was there a faint noise? What was it?

She stood, with arrested muscles, outside his door, listening. There was a strange, heavy, and yet not loud noise. Her heart stood still. It was a soundless noise, yet rushing and powerful. Something huge, in violent, hushed motion. What was it? What in God's name was it? She ought to know. She felt that she knew the noise. She knew what it was.

220   Yet she could not place it. She couldn't say what it was. And on and on it went, like a madness.

Softly, frozen with anxiety and fear, she turned the door-handle.

The room was dark. Yet in the space near the window, she heard and saw something plunging to and fro. She gazed in fear and amazement.

Then suddenly she switched on the light, and saw her son, in his green pyjamas, madly surging on the rocking-horse. The blaze of light suddenly lit him up, as he urged the wooden horse, and lit her up, as she stood, blonde, in her dress of pale green and crystal, in the doorway.

"Paul!" she cried. "Whatever are you doing?"

225   "It's Malabar!" he screamed in a powerful, strange voice. "It's Malabar!"

His eyes blazed at her for one strange and senseless second, as he ceased urging his wooden horse. Then he fell with a crash to the ground, and she, all her tormented motherhood flooding upon her, rushed to gather him up.

But he was unconscious, and unconscious he remained, with some brain-fever. He talked and tossed, and his mother sat stonily by his side.

"Malabar! It's Malabar! Bassett, Bassett, I *know!* It's Malabar!"

So the child cried, trying to get up and urge the rocking-horse that gave him his inspiration.

230   "What does he mean by Malabar?" asked the heart-frozen mother.

"I don't know," said the father stonily.

"What does he mean by Malabar?" she asked her brother Oscar.

"It's one of the horses running for the Derby," was the answer.

And, in spite of himself, Oscar Cresswell spoke to Bassett, and himself put a thousand on Malabar: at fourteen to one.

235   The third day of the illness was critical: they were waiting for a change. The boy, with his rather long, curly hair, was tossing ceaselessly on the pillow. He neither

slept nor regained consciousness, and his eyes were like blue stones. His mother sat, feeling her heart had gone, turned actually into a stone.

In the evening, Oscar Cresswell did not come, but Bassett sent a message, saying could he come up for one moment, just one moment? Paul's mother was very angry at the intrusion, but on second thought she agreed. The boy was the same. Perhaps Bassett might bring him to consciousness.

The gardener, a shortish fellow with a little brown moustache and sharp little brown eyes, tiptoed into the room, touched his imaginary cap to Paul's mother, and stole to the bedside, staring with glittering, smallish eyes at the tossing, dying child.

"Master Paul!" he whispered. "Master Paul! Malabar came in first all right, a clean win. I did as you told me. You've made over seventy thousand pounds, you have; you've got over eighty thousand. Malabar came in all right, Master Paul."

"Malabar! Malabar! Did I say Malabar, mother? Did I say Malabar? Do you think I'm lucky, mother? I knew Malabar, didn't I? Over eighty thousand pounds! I call that lucky, don't you, mother? Over eighty thousand pounds! I knew, didn't I know I knew? Malabar came in all right. If I ride my horse till I'm sure, then I tell you, Bassett, you can go as high as you like. Did you go for all you were worth, Bassett?"

"I went a thousand on it, Master Paul."   240

"I never told you, mother, that if I can ride my horse, and *get there*, then I'm absolutely sure—oh, absolutely! Mother, did I ever tell you? I *am* lucky!"

"No, you never did," said his mother.

But the boy died in the night.

And even as he lay dead, his mother heard her brother's voice saying to her: "My God, Hester, you're eighty-odd thousand to the good, and a poor devil of a son to the bad. But, poor devil, poor devil, he's best gone out of a life where he rides his rocking-horse to find a winner."

Reading and Reacting

1. From what point of view is "The Rocking-Horse Winner" told? How does this point of view help to communicate the story's theme?

2. In what ways is "The Rocking-Horse Winner" like a fairy tale? How is it different?

3. Many fairy tales involve a hero who goes on a journey to search for something of great value. What journey does Paul go on? What thing of value does he search for? Is he successful?

4. In paragraph 5, the narrator says that the house is "haunted by the unspoken phrase: '*There must be more money!*'" In what way does this phrase "haunt" the house?

5. How would you characterize Paul's parents? his uncle? Bassett? Are they weak? evil? What motivates them?

6. Beginning in paragraph 11, Paul's mother attempts to define the word *luck*. According to her definition, is Paul lucky?

7. In what ways does Paul behave like other children? In what ways is he different? How do you account for these differences? How old do you think Paul is? Why is his age significant?

8. The rocking horse is an important literary **symbol** in the story. What possible meanings might the rocking horse suggest? In what ways does this symbol reinforce the story's theme?

9. What secrets do the various characters keep from one another? Why do they keep them? What do these secrets suggest about the story's theme?

10. How does Paul know who the winners will be? Does the rocking horse really tell him? Does he get his information "from heaven" as Bassett suggests (par. 119)? Or does he just guess?

11. JOURNAL ENTRY In your opinion, who or what is responsible for Paul's death?

12. CRITICAL PERSPECTIVE In a letter dated January 17, 1913, Lawrence wrote the following:

> My great religion is a belief in the blood, the flesh, as being wiser than the intellect. We can go wrong in our minds. But what our blood feels and believes and says, is always true. The intellect is only a bit and a bridle. What do I care about knowledge. All I want is to answer to my blood, direct, without fribbling intervention of mind, or moral, or what-not.

How does Lawrence's portrayal of Paul in "The Rocking-Horse Winner" support his belief in "the blood . . . being wiser than the intellect"? How does Lawrence remain true in this story to his metaphor of the intellect as "a bit and a bridle"?

Related Works: "Gretel in Darkness" (p. 677), "Suicide Note" (p. 683), "Birches" (p. 895), *Death of a Salesman* (p. 1233)

AP Images/Marty Lederhandler

TOBIAS WOLFF (1945–   ) is a novelist, short story writer, and editor whose work has appeared in the *Atlantic Monthly*, the *New Yorker*, and the *Paris Review*. The author of four story collections, two novels, and two memoirs, Wolff received a PEN/Faulkner Award for his first novel, *The Barracks Thief* (1984). His award-winning memoir *This Boy's Life* (1989), which chronicles his unstable childhood growing up with various abusive stepfathers, was adapted into the feature film of the same name. In addition to writing his own successful short fiction, Wolff has edited a collection of Anton Chekhov's short stories and two collections of American short stories.

Cultural Context Bank robberies are particularly prevalent in the southern and north central United States. According to the Bank Crime Statistics database, only twenty percent of the approximately seventy million dollars stolen each year from banks is recovered. On average, thieves steal less than $8,000 in a single robbery. Data also show, surprisingly, that violence and injury are generally uncommon in bank robberies, with only two percent of all robberies involving shootings. In recent years, the number of bank robberies has declined, while online crime has increased. Modern security measures, such as hidden cameras, silent alarms, exploding dye packs, and SWAT teams, make robbing brick-and-mortar banks very difficult. In addition, bank robbery is a federal crime and is severely punished. Today, the arrest rate for bank robbery is second only to that for murder.

Bullet in the Brain (1996)

Anders couldn't get to the bank until just before it closed, so of course the line was endless and he got stuck behind two women whose loud, stupid conversation put him in a murderous temper. He was never in the best of tempers anyway, Anders—a book critic known for the weary, elegant savagery with which he dispatched almost everything he reviewed.

With the line still doubled around the rope, one of the tellers stuck a "POSITION CLOSED" sign in her window and walked to the back of the bank, where she leaned against a desk and began to pass the time with a man shuffling papers. The women in front of Anders broke off their conversation and watched the teller with hatred. "Oh, that's nice," one of them said. She turned to Anders and added, confident of his accord, "One of those little human touches that keep us coming back for more."

Anders had conceived his own towering hatred of the teller, but he immediately turned it on the presumptuous crybaby in front of him. "Damned unfair," he said. "Tragic, really. If they're not chopping off the wrong leg, or bombing your ancestral village, they're closing their positions."

She stood her ground. "I didn't say it was tragic," she said. "I just think it's a pretty lousy way to treat your customers."

"Unforgivable," Anders said. "Heaven will take note."   5

She sucked in her cheeks but stared past him and said nothing. Anders saw that the other woman, her friend, was looking in the same direction. And then the tellers stopped what they were doing, and the customers slowly turned, and silence came over the bank. Two men wearing black ski masks and blue business suits were standing to the side of the door. One of them had a pistol pressed against the guard's neck. The guard's eyes were closed, and his lips were moving. The other man had a sawed-off shotgun. "Keep your big mouth shut!" the man with the pistol said, though no one had spoken a word. "One of you tellers hits the alarm, you're all dead meat. Got it?"

The tellers nodded.

"Oh, bravo," Anders said. "*Dead meat.*" He turned to the woman in front of him. "Great script, eh? The stern, brass-knuckled poetry of the dangerous classes."

She looked at him with drowning eyes.

The man with the shotgun pushed the guard to his knees. He handed up the shot-   10
gun to his partner and yanked the guard's wrists up behind his back and locked them together with a pair of handcuffs. He toppled him onto the floor with a kick between the shoulder blades. Then he took his shotgun back and went over to the security gate at the end of the counter. He was short and heavy and moved with peculiar slowness, even torpor. "Buzz him in," his partner said. The man with the shotgun opened the gate and sauntered along the line of tellers, handing each of them a Hefty bag. When he came to the empty position he looked over at the man with the pistol, who said, "Whose slot is that?"

Anders watched the teller. She put her hand to her throat and turned to the man she'd been talking to. He nodded. "Mine," she said.

"Then get your ugly ass in gear and fill that bag."

"There you go," Anders said to the woman in front of him. "Justice is done."

"Hey! Bright Boy! Did I tell you to talk?"

"No," Anders said.   15

"Then shut your trap."

"Did you hear that?" Anders said. "'Bright boy.' Right out of 'The Killers'."

"Please be quiet," the woman said.

"Hey, you deaf or what?" The man with the pistol walked over to Anders. He poked the weapon into Anders' gut. "You think I'm playing games?"

20   "No," Anders said, but the barrel tickled like a stiff finger and he had to fight back
the titters. He did this by making himself stare into the man's eyes, which were clearly
visible behind the holes in the mask: pale blue, and rawly red-rimmed. The man's
left eyelid kept twitching. He breathed out a piercing, ammoniac smell that shocked
Anders more than anything that had happened, and he was beginning to develop a
sense of unease when the man prodded him again with the pistol.

"You like me, bright boy?" he said. "You want to suck my dick?"

"No," Anders said.

"Then stop looking at me."

Anders fixed his gaze on the man's shiny wing-tip shoes.

25   "Not down there. Up there." He stuck the pistol under Anders' chin and pushed
it upward until Anders was looking at the ceiling.

Anders had never paid much attention to that part of the bank, a pompous
old building with marble floors and counters and pillars, and gilt scrollwork over
the tellers' cages. The domed ceiling had been decorated with mythological figures
whose fleshy, toga-draped ugliness Anders had taken in at a glance many years earlier and afterward declined to notice. Now he had no choice but to scrutinize the
painter's work. It was even worse than he remembered, and all of it executed with
the utmost gravity. The artist had a few tricks up his sleeve and used them again and
again—a certain rosy blush on the underside of the clouds, a coy backward glance on
the faces of the cupids and fauns. The ceiling was crowded with various dramas, but
the one that caught Anders' eye was Zeus and Europa[1]—portrayed, in this rendition,
as a bull ogling a cow from behind a haystack. To make the cow sexy, the painter had
canted her hips suggestively and given her long, droopy eyelashes through which she
gazed back at the bull with sultry welcome. The bull wore a smirk and his eyebrows
were arched. If there'd been a bubble coming out of his mouth, it would have said,
"Hubba hubba."

"What's so funny, bright boy?"

"Nothing."

"You think I'm comical? You think I'm some kind of clown?"

30   "No."

"You think you can fuck with me?"

"No."

"Fuck with me again, you're history. Capiche?"[2]

Anders burst out laughing. He covered his mouth with both hands and said, "I'm
sorry, I'm sorry," then snorted helplessly through his fingers and said, "Capiche—oh,
God, capiche," and at that the man with the pistol raised the pistol and shot Anders
right in the head.

35   The bullet smashed Anders' skull and ploughed through his brain and exited
behind his right ear, scattering shards of bone into the cerebral cortex, the corpus
callosum, back toward the basal ganglia, and down into the thalamus. But before all

---

[1]*Zeus and Europa:* According to Greek mythology, the god Zeus, as a white bull, seduced Europa, who in turn gave
birth to three sons.

[2]Capiche?: Americanized spelling of *capisci*, Italian for "Do You Understand?"

this occurred, the first appearance of the bullet in the cerebrum set off a cracking chain of ion transports and neuro-transmissions. Because of their peculiar origin these traced a peculiar pattern, flukishly calling to life a summer afternoon some forty years past, and long since lost to memory. After striking the cranium the bullet was moving at 900 feet per second, a pathetically sluggish, glacial pace compared to the synaptic lightning that flashed around it. Once in the brain, that is, the bullet came under the mediation of brain time, which gave Anders plenty of leisure to contemplate the scene that, in a phrase he would have abhorred, "passed before his eyes."

It is worth noting what Anders did not remember, given what he did remember. He did not remember his first lover, Sherry, or what he had most madly loved about her, before it came to irritate him—her unembarrassed carnality, and especially the cordial way she had with his unit, which she called Mr. Mole, as in, "Uh-oh, looks like Mr. Mole wants to play," and "Let's hide Mr. Mole!" Anders did not remember his wife, whom he had also loved before she exhausted him with her predictability, or his daughter, now a sullen professor of economics at Dartmouth. He did not remember standing just outside his daughter's door as she lectured her bear about his naughtiness and described the truly appalling punishments Paws would receive unless he changed his ways. He did not remember a single line of the hundreds of poems he had committed to memory in his youth so that he could give himself the shivers at will—not "Silent, upon a peak in Darien," or "My God, I heard this day," or "All my pretty ones? Did you say all? O hell-kite! All?" None of these did he remember; not one. Anders did not remember his dying mother saying of his father, "I should have stabbed him in his sleep."

He did not remember Professor Josephs telling his class how Athenian prisoners in Sicily had been released if they could recite Aeschylus,[3] and then reciting Aeschylus himself, right there, in the Greek. Anders did not remember how his eyes had burned at those sounds. He did not remember the surprise of seeing a college classmate's name on the jacket of a novel not long after they graduated, or the respect he had felt after reading the book. He did not remember the pleasure of giving respect.

Nor did Anders remember seeing a woman leap to her death from the building opposite his own just days after his daughter was born. He did not remember shouting, "Lord have mercy!" He did not remember deliberately crashing his father's car into a tree, or having his ribs kicked in by three policemen at an anti-war rally, or waking himself up with laughter. He did not remember when he began to regard the heap of books on his desk with boredom and dread, or when he grew angry at writers for writing them. He did not remember when everything began to remind him of something else.

This is what he remembered. Heat. A baseball field. Yellow grass, the whirr of insects, himself leaning against a tree as the boys of the neighborhood gather for a pickup game. He looks on as the others argue the relative genius of Mantle and Mays.[4]

---

[3] *Aeschylus:* Greek tragic dramatist (525/524 B.C.–456/455 B.C.).

[4] *Mantle and Mays:* American professional baseball players Mickey Mantle (1931–1995) and Willie Mays (1931–   ).

They have been worrying this subject all summer, and it has become tedious to Anders: an oppression, like the heat.

40   Then the last two boys arrive, Coyle and a cousin of his from Mississippi. Anders has never met Coyle's cousin before and will never see him again. He says hi with the rest but takes no further notice of him until they've chosen sides and someone asks the cousin what position he wants to play. "Shortstop," the boy says. "Short's the best position they is." Anders turns and looks at him. He wants to hear Coyle's cousin repeat what he's just said, but he knows better than to ask. The others will think he's being a jerk, ragging the kid for his grammar. But that isn't it, not at all—it's that Anders is strangely roused, elated, by those final two words, their pure unexpectedness and their music. He takes the field in a trance, repeating them to himself.

The bullet is already in the brain; it won't be outrun forever, or charmed to a halt. In the end it will do its work and leave the troubled skull behind, dragging its comet's tail of memory and hope and talent and love into the marble hall of commerce. That can't be helped. But for now Anders can still make time. Time for the shadows to lengthen on the grass, time for the tethered dog to bark at the flying ball, time for the boy in right field to smack his sweat-blackened mitt and softly chant, *They is, they is, they is.*

Reading and Reacting

1. According to the narrator, Anders is a book critic "known for the weary, elegant savagery with which he dispatched almost everything he reviewed" (par. 1). Why does Wolff begin his story with this statement? In what way does it set the stage for what follows?

2. In paragraphs 3–5, Anders has an exchange with a woman waiting in line with him. Why does the woman react to Anders's comments the way she does?

3. Why does Anders sarcastically refer to the bank robber's words as a "great script" (par. 8)? What does this remark reveal about him?

4. At one point in the story the bank robber sticks a gun under Anders's chin and forces his head up. As he looks up, Anders begins to mentally critique the artwork on the ceiling. What does this action tell you about him?

5. After repeatedly threatening him, one of the bank robbers tells Anders that if he laughs again, he will shoot him. Why does Anders burst out laughing?

6. What does the bank robber not understand about Anders? What does Anders not understand about the bank robber?

7. In his dying moments, what events does Anders not remember? What does the narrator mean when he says, "He did not remember when everything began to remind him of something else" (par. 38)?

8. As he is dying, what event does Anders remember? Why do you think he remembers this? What insight does this memory provide into Anders's character?

9. **JOURNAL ENTRY** What is your opinion of Anders before he is shot? Does your opinion of him change by the end of the story?

10. CRITICAL PERSPECTIVE Tobias Wolff, writing in his role as editor of *A Doctor's Visit* (1988), a collection of Anton Chekhov's short stories, makes the following observation:

> [Chekhov] gives an intuitive sense that the lives of his characters continue after the story, he does not forcibly bring things to a conclusion. . . . the moral arc of the story, though apparent, is not completed, the circle is not drawn; there is enough of it there, I think, for an imaginative and intelligent reader to continue to draw the circle.

Do you think that, despite Anders's death, Wolff resists "forcibly bring[ing] things to a conclusion" in "Bullet in the Brain"? What techniques in the final paragraph allow the story to continue on for the reader?

Related Works: "The Story of an Hour" (p. 201), "Miss Brill" (p. 245), "Baca Grande" (p. 723), "The Love Song of J. Alfred Prufrock" (p. 981)

WRITING SUGGESTIONS: Theme

1. Both Paul in "The Rocking-Horse Winner" and Andy in "Doe Season" experience traumatic events that, as children, they cannot fully understand or interpret. Write an essay in which you examine the limited nature of each character's view of events. Then, discuss how this limited view helps each author develop the main theme of his story.

2. Two of the stories in this chapter deal with characters who experience violence and death: Andy, in "Doe Season," kills her first deer, and Anders, in "Bullet in the Brain," is shot during a bank robbery. Write an essay in which you discuss the ways these characters respond to the violence they see. How do their reactions help develop the major theme of each of these stories?

3. Both "The Rocking-Horse Winner" and "A Worn Path" deal with characters who make journeys. What is the significance of each journey? How do the protagonists of these two stories overcome the obstacles they encounter? In what sense are these journeys symbolic as well as actual?

4. Like "Doe Season," the following poem focuses on a child's experience with hunting. Write an essay in which you contrast its central theme with the central theme of "Doe Season."

ROBERT HUFF (1924–1993)

Rainbow[1]

After the shot the driven feathers rock
In the air and are by sunlight trapped.
Their moment of descent is eloquent.

---

[1]publication date is not available.

It is the rainbow echo of a bird
Whose thunder, stopped, puts in my daughter's eyes   5
A question mark. She does not see the rainbow,
And the folding bird-fall was for her too quick.
It is about the stillness of the bird
Her eyes are asking. She is three years old;
Has cut her fingers; found blood tastes of salt;   10
But she has never witnessed quiet blood,
Nor ever seen before the peace of death.
I say: "The feathers—Look!" but she is torn
And wretched and draws back. And I am glad
That I have wounded her, have winged her heart,   15
And that she goes beyond my fathering.

CHAPTER 20

JOYCE CAROL OATES'S "WHERE ARE YOU GOING, WHERE HAVE YOU BEEN?": A CASEBOOK FOR READING, RESEARCH, AND WRITING

This chapter provides all the materials you will need to begin a research project about a work of fiction. It includes the following resources:

Background

Critical Perspectives

---

*Note that some of the critical articles in this casebook were written before the current MLA documentation style was adopted. See Chapter 7 for current MLA format.

Each of the sources in this casebook provides insights (sometimes contradictory ones) into the short story "Where Are You Going, Where Have You Been?" Other sources can also enrich your understanding of the work—for instance, other works by Oates, biographical data about the author, or stories by other writers dealing with similar themes. The film *Smooth Talk*, which is based on the story, and websites devoted to Oates and her work can also offer insight into the story.

Although no analytical or biographical source—not even the author's comments—can give you a magical key that will unlock a story's secrets, such sources can enhance your enjoyment and aid in your understanding of a work. They can also suggest topics that you can explore in writing.

In preparation for writing an essay on a topic of your choice about the story "Where Are You Going, Where Have You Been?" read the story and the accompanying source materials carefully. Then, consider the Reading and Reacting questions that follow the story (p. 517), and use your responses to help you find a topic that you can develop in a short essay. Be sure to include parenthetical documentation for any references to the story or to another source, and remember to enclose words that are not your own in quotation marks. For guidelines on evaluating literary criticism, see page 14; for guidelines on using source materials, see Chapter 6, "Using Sources in Your Writing," and Chapter 7, "Documenting Sources and Avoiding Plagiarism."

About the Author

Source: ©Nancy Kaszerman/ZUMA/CORBIS

JOYCE CAROL OATES (1938–   ) is one of contemporary America's most prolific novelists and short story writers. Oates first gained prominence in the 1960s with the publication of *A Garden of Earthly Delights* (1967), *Expensive People* (1968), and *them* (1969), which won the National Book Award. In these and other works, Oates explores the multilayered nature of American society, writing about urban slums, decaying rural communities, and exclusive suburbs in a dense and compellingly realistic prose style. In some of her novels, including *Bellefleur* (1980) and *Mysteries of Winterthurn* (1984), Oates reveals her deep fascination with the traditions of nineteenth-century gothic writers Edgar Allan Poe, Fyodor Dostoevski, Mary Shelley, and others. Oates's recent works include *Black Dahlia & White Rose* (2012), *Mudwoman* (2012), *Two or Three Things I Forgot to Tell You* (2012), *The Accursed* (2013), *Daddy Love* (2013), and *Lovely, Dark, Deep* (2014).

Born on June 16, 1938, Joyce Carol Oates grew up in the small hamlet of Millersport, near Lockport, New York, about ten miles east of Niagara Falls and twenty miles north of Buffalo. She is the eldest of three children (her sister Lynn, who is almost twenty years younger, has been institutionalized with autism since adolescence). Oates attended school in a one-room schoolhouse with other working-class children from the area. Her childhood was hard, yet she writes about it in a loving and respectful tone: "Though frequently denounced and often misunderstood by a somewhat genteel literary community, my writing is, at least in part, an attempt to memorialize my parents' vanished world; my parents' lives. Sometimes directly, sometimes in metaphor." Her childhood town, parents, siblings, relatives, and neighbors all appear in some form in three of Oates's books: *You Must Remember This* (1987) blends Buffalo and Lockport as its backdrop, along with the Erie Canal; *Marya: A Life* (1986) contains elements of Oates's mother's childhood as well as her own; and in *Wonderland* (1971), one of Oates's earliest novels, the main character stops off in Millersport and meets her family.

Oates is one of those writers who has always been a writer, and even before she could possibly know the alphabet, she drew and painted words. Once she did learn her letters, she was given a typewriter and learned how to use it, and she was soon writing book after book. She left her small town to attend Syracuse University on a scholarship and while there won the *Mademoiselle* fiction contest. She earned an MA in English at the University of Wisconsin. Oates moved to Detroit in 1962, during a time when social tensions were at the boiling point; Detroit was one of the first American cities to erupt in urban violence in the 1960s. Oates considers her time in Detroit to be significant, shaping her writing as well as her personal beliefs and political views.

Martin Luther King Jr., leading a civil rights march in Detroit, June 1963
© Bettman/Corbis

In 1968, Oates crossed the Detroit River to teach at the University of Windsor in Ontario, Canada. While teaching a full load of courses, she embarked on an extremely productive period of writing. In less than a decade, she wrote over twenty novels, and her audience grew along with her success. In 1978, she moved to Princeton, New Jersey, to accept a teaching position at Princeton University, where she taught until 2014.

Washington Post critic Susan Wood has written that Oates "attempts more than most of our writers . . . to explore the profound issues of evil and innocence, betrayal and revenge and atonement, as they are manifest in contemporary American experience. . . ." Although Oates frequently centers her novels on larger issues and moral questions, she can also focus on the private worlds of her characters, as in *Black Water* (1992).

Critics responding to Oates's work have called it violent, lurid, even depraved. Yet, asks Laura Z. Hobson in a review of Oates's 1981 novel, *Angel of Light*, "Would there be such a hullabaloo about the violence in her books if they had been written by a man? From her earliest books onward, reviewers too often struck an insulting tone of surprise: *What's a nice girl like you doing in a place like this?* [Oates] replies that in these violent times only tales of violence have reality. Well, maybe. But the critics' preoccupation with a single facet of her work ignores everything else: her inventiveness, her insider's knowledge of college life, her evocations of nature . . . her ability to tell a story, to write a spellbinder. . . ."

Oates's work changes as the landscape changes around her. Her earliest novels focused on rural characters who seemingly could have sprung from her hometown, and the dozens of books she wrote while in Detroit and

Ontario reveal the often harsh realities of those places and times. The novels she began to write in New Jersey went in an entirely new direction. Published in the 1980s, her series of ambitious gothic novels challenge established literary form and also envision a vastly different American identity and history from that of her earlier books. Later novels published under the pseudonyms Rosamond Smith and Lauren Kelly demonstrate Oates's unique ability to constantly recreate herself and her work. In short, her prolific career reveals an ability to experiment with new forms and subject matter, and it is exactly this ability that makes her universally appealing and that makes her books timeless as well as timebound.

  Story

Where Are You Going, Where Have You Been? (1966)

For Bob Dylan

Her name was Connie. She was fifteen and she had a quick nervous giggling habit of craning her neck to glance into mirrors, or checking other people's faces to make sure her own was all right. Her mother, who noticed everything and knew everything and who hadn't much reason any longer to look at her own face, always scolded Connie about it. "Stop gawking at yourself, who are you? You think you're so pretty?" she would say. Connie would raise her eye-brows at these familiar complaints and look right through her mother, into a shadowy vision of herself as she was right at that moment: she knew she was pretty and that was everything. Her mother had been pretty once too, if you could believe those old snapshots in the album, but now her looks were gone and that was why she was always after Connie.

"Why don't you keep your room clean like your sister? How've you got your hair fixed—what the hell stinks? Hair spray? You don't see your sister using that junk."

Her sister June was twenty-four and still lived at home. She was a secretary in the high school Connie attended, and if that wasn't bad enough—with her in the same building—she was so plain and chunky and steady that Connie had to hear her praised all the time by her mother and her mother's sisters. June did this, June did that, she saved money and helped clean the house and cooked and Connie couldn't do a thing, her mind was all filled with trashy daydreams. Their father was away at work most of the time and when he came home he wanted supper and he read the newspaper at supper and after supper he went to bed. He didn't bother talking much to them, but around his bent head Connie's mother kept picking at her until Connie wished her mother was dead and she herself was dead and it was all over. "She makes me want to throw up sometimes," she complained to her friends. She had a high, breathless, amused voice which made everything she said sound a little forced, whether it was sincere or not.

There was one good thing: June went places with girl friends of hers, girls who were just as plain and steady as she, and so when Connie wanted to do that her mother had no objections. The father of Connie's best girl friend drove the girls the three miles to town and left them off at a shopping plaza, so that they could walk through the stores or go to a movie, and when he came to pick them up again at eleven he never bothered to ask what they had done.

5

They must have been familiar sights, walking around that shopping plaza in their shorts and flat ballerina slippers that always scuffed the sidewalk, with charm bracelets jingling on their thin wrists; they would lean together to whisper and laugh secretly if someone passed by who amused or interested them. Connie had long dark blond hair that drew anyone's eye to it, and she wore part of it pulled up on her head and puffed out and the rest of it she let fall down her back. She wore a pull-over jersey blouse that looked one way when she was at home and another way when she was away from home. Everything about her had two sides to it, one for home and one for anywhere that was not home: her walk that could be childlike and bobbing, or languid enough to make anyone think she was hearing music in her head, her mouth which was pale and smirking most of the time, but bright and pink on these evenings out, her laugh which was cynical and drawling at home—"Ha, ha, very funny"—but high-pitched and nervous anywhere else, like the jingling of the charms on her bracelet.

Sometimes they did go shopping or to a movie, but sometimes they went across the highway, ducking fast across the busy road, to a drive-in restaurant where older kids hung out. The restaurant was shaped like a big bottle, though squatter than a real bottle, and on its cap was a revolving figure of a grinning boy who held a hamburger aloft. One night in mid-summer they ran across, breathless with daring, and right away someone leaned out a car window and invited them over, but it was just a boy from high school they didn't like. It made them feel good to be able to ignore him. They went up through the maze of parked and cruising cars to the bright-lit, fly-infested restaurant, their faces pleased and expectant as if they were entering a sacred building that loomed out of the night to give them what haven and what blessing they yearned for. They sat at the counter and crossed their legs at the ankles, their thin shoulders rigid with excitement, and listened to the music that made everything so good: the music was always in the background like music at a church service, it was something to depend upon.

A boy named Eddie came in to talk with them. He sat backwards on his stool, turning himself jerkily around in semi-circles and then stopping and turning again, and after a while he asked Connie if she would like something to eat. She said she did and so she tapped her friend's arm on her way out—her friend pulled her face up into a brave droll look—and Connie said she would meet her at eleven, across the way. "I just hate to leave her like that," Connie said earnestly, but the boy said that she wouldn't be alone for long. So they went out to his car and on the way Connie couldn't help but let her eyes wander over the windshields and faces all around her, her face gleaming with a joy that had nothing to do with Eddie or even this place; it might have been the music. She drew her shoulders up and sucked in her breath with the pure pleasure of being alive, and just at that moment she happened to glance at a face just a few feet from hers. It was a boy with shaggy black hair, in a convertible jalopy painted gold. He stared at her and then his lips widened into a grin. Connie slit her eyes at him and turned away, but she couldn't help glancing back and there he was still watching her. He wagged a finger and laughed and said, "Gonna get you, baby," and Connie turned away again without Eddie noticing anything.

She spent three hours with him, at the restaurant where they ate hamburgers and drank Cokes in wax cups that were always sweating, and then down an alley a mile or so away, and when he left her off at five to eleven only the movie house was still open at the plaza. Her girl friend was there, talking with a boy. When Connie came up the two girls smiled at each other and Connie said, "How was the movie?" and the girl said, "*You* should know." They rode off with the girl's father, sleepy and pleased, and Connie couldn't help but look at the darkened shopping plaza with its big empty parking lot and its signs that were faded and ghostly now, and over at the drive-in restaurant where cars were still circling tirelessly. She couldn't hear the music at this distance.

Next morning June asked her how the movie was and Connie said, "So-so."

10   She and that girl and occasionally another girl went out several times a week that way, and the rest of the time Connie spent around the house—it was summer vacation—getting in her mother's way and thinking, dreaming, about the boys she met. But all the boys fell back and dissolved into a single face that was not even a face, but an idea, a feeling, mixed up with the urgent insistent pounding of the music and the humid night air of July. Connie's mother kept dragging her back to the daylight by finding things for her to do or saying, suddenly, "What's this about the Pettinger girl?"

And Connie would say nervously, "Oh, her. That dope." She always drew thick clear lines between herself and such girls, and her mother was simple and kindly enough to believe her. Her mother was so simple, Connie thought, that it was maybe cruel to fool her so much. Her mother went scuffling around the house in old bedroom slippers and complained over the telephone to one sister about the other, then the other called up and the two of them complained about the third one. If June's name was mentioned her mother's tone was approving, and if Connie's name was mentioned it was disapproving. This did not really mean she disliked Connie and actually Connie thought that her mother preferred her to June because she was prettier, but the two of them kept up a pretense of exasperation, a sense that they were tugging and struggling over something of little value to either of them. Sometimes, over coffee, they were almost friends, but something would come up—some vexation that was like a fly buzzing suddenly around their heads—and their faces went hard with contempt.

One Sunday Connie got up at eleven—none of them bothered with church—and washed her hair so that it could dry all day long, in the sun. Her parents and sister were going to a barbecue at an aunt's house and Connie said no, she wasn't interested, rolling her eyes to let her mother know just what she thought of it. "Stay home alone then," her mother said sharply. Connie sat out back in a lawn chair and watched them drive away, her father quiet and bald, hunched around so that he could back the car out, her mother with a look that was still angry and not at all softened through the windshield, and in the back seat poor old June all dressed up as if she didn't know what a barbecue was, with all the running yelling kids and the flies. Connie sat with her eyes closed in the sun, dreaming and dazed with the warmth about her as if this were a kind of love, the caresses of love, and her mind slipped over onto thoughts of the boy she had been with the night before and how nice he had been, how sweet it always was, not the way someone like June would suppose but sweet, gentle, the way it was in movies and promised in songs; and when she opened her eyes she hardly knew where she was, the back yard ran off into weeds and a fence-line of trees and behind it the sky was perfectly blue and still. The asbestos "ranch house" that was now three years old startled her—it looked small. She shook her head as if to get awake.

It was too hot. She went inside the house and turned on the radio to drown out the quiet. She sat on the edge of her bed, barefoot, and listened for an hour and a half to a program called *XYZ Sunday Jamboree*, record after record of hard, fast, shrieking songs she sang along with, interspersed by exclamations from "Bobby King": "An' look here you girls at Napoleon's—Son and Charley want you to pay real close attention to this song coming up!"

And Connie paid close attention herself, bathed in a glow of slow-pulsed joy that seemed to rise mysteriously out of the music itself and lay languidly about the airless little room, breathed in and breathed out with each gentle rise and fall of her chest.

After a while she heard a car coming up the drive. She sat up at once, startled, because it couldn't be her father so soon. The gravel kept crunching all the way in from the road—the driveway was long—and Connie ran to the window. It was a car she didn't know. It was an open jalopy, painted a bright gold that caught the sunlight opaquely. Her heart began to pound and her fingers snatched at her hair, checking it, and she whispered "Christ. Christ," wondering how bad she looked. The car came to a stop at the side door and the horn sounded four short taps as if this were a signal Connie knew.

She went into the kitchen and approached the door slowly, then hung out the screen door, her bare toes curling down off the step. There were two boys in the car and now she recognized the driver: he had shaggy, shabby black hair that looked crazy as a wig and he was grinning at her.

"I ain't late, am I?" he said.

"Who the hell do you think you are?" Connie said.

"Toldja I'd be out, didn't I?"

"I don't even know who you are."

She spoke sullenly, careful to show no interest or pleasure, and he spoke in a fast bright monotone. Connie looked past him to the other boy, taking her time. He had fair brown hair, with a lock that fell onto his forehead. His sideburns gave him a fierce, embarrassed look, but so far he hadn't even bothered to glance at her. Both boys wore sunglasses. The driver's glasses were metallic and mirrored everything in miniature.

"You wanta come for a ride?" he said.

Connie smirked and let her hair fall loose over one shoulder.

"Don'tcha like my car? New paint job," he said. "Hey."

"What?"

"You're cute."

She pretended to fidget, chasing flies away from the door.

"Don'tcha believe me, or what?" he said.

"Look, I don't even know who you are," Connie said in disgust.

"Hey, Ellie's got a radio, see. Mine's broke down." He lifted his friend's arm and showed her the little transistor the boy was holding, and now Connie began to hear the music. It was the same program that was playing inside the house.

"Bobby King?" she said.

"I listen to him all the time. I think he's great."

"He's kind of great," Connie said reluctantly.

"Listen, that guy's *great*. He knows where the action is."

35   Connie blushed a little, because the glasses made it impossible for her to see just what this boy was looking at. She couldn't decide if she liked him or if he was just a jerk, and so she dawdled in the doorway and wouldn't come down or go back inside. She said, "What's all that stuff painted on your car?"

"Can'tcha read it?" He opened the door very carefully, as if he was afraid it might fall off. He slid out just as carefully, planting his feet firmly on the ground, the tiny metallic world in his glasses slowing down like gelatine hardening and in the midst of it Connie's bright green blouse. "This here is my name, to begin with," he said. ARNOLD FRIEND was written in tarlike black letters on the side, with a drawing of a round grinning face that reminded Connie of a pumpkin, except it wore sunglasses. "I wanta introduce myself, I'm Arnold Friend and that's my real name and I'm gonna be your friend, honey, and inside the car's Ellie Oscar, he's kinda shy." Ellie brought his transistor radio up to his shoulder and balanced it there. "Now these numbers are a secret code, honey," Arnold Friend explained. He read off the numbers 33, 19, 17 and raised his eyebrows at her to see what she thought of that, but she didn't think much of it. The left rear fender had been smashed and around it was written, on the gleaming gold background: DONE BY CRAZY WOMAN DRIVER. Connie had to laugh at that. Arnold Friend was pleased at her laughter and looked up at her. "Around the other side's a lot more—you wanta come and see them?"

"No."

"Why not?"

"Why should I?"

40   "Don'tcha wanta see what's on the car? Don'tcha wanta go for a ride?"

"I don't know."

"Why not?"

"I got things to do."

"Like what?"

45   "Things."

He laughed as if she had said something funny. He slapped his thighs. He was standing in a strange way, leaning back against the car as if he were balancing himself. He wasn't tall, only an inch or so taller than she would be if she came down to him. Connie liked the way he was dressed, which was the way all of them dressed: tight faded jeans stuffed into black, scuffed boots, a belt that pulled his waist in and showed how lean he was, and a white pull-over shirt that was a little soiled and showed the hard small muscles of his arms and shoulders. He looked as if he probably did hard work, lifting and carrying things. Even his neck looked muscular. And his face was a familiar face, somehow: the jaw and chin and cheeks slightly darkened, because he hadn't shaved for a day or two, and the nose long and hawk-like, sniffing as if she were a treat he was going to gobble up and it was all a joke.

"Connie, you ain't telling the truth. This is your day set aside for a ride with me and you know it," he said, still laughing. The way he straightened and recovered from his fit of laughing showed that it had been all fake.

"How do you know what my name is?" she said suspiciously.

"It's Connie."

50   "Maybe and maybe not."

"I know my Connie," he said, wagging his finger. Now she remembered him even better, back at the restaurant, and her cheeks warmed at the thought of how she sucked in her breath just at the moment she passed him—how she must have looked to him. And he had remembered her. "Ellie and I come out here especially for you," he said. "Ellie can sit in back. How about it?"

"Where?"

"Where what?"

"Where're we going?"

He looked at her. He took off the sunglasses and she saw how pale the skin around his eyes was, like holes that were not in shadow but instead in light. His eyes were chips of broken glass that catch the light in an amiable way. He smiled. It was as if the idea of going for a ride somewhere, to some place, was a new idea to him.

"Just for a ride, Connie sweetheart."

"I never said my name was Connie," she said.

"But I know what it is. I know your name and all about you, lots of things," Arnold Friend said. He had not moved yet but stood still leaning back against the side of his jalopy. "I took a special interest in you, such a pretty girl, and found out all about you like I know your parents and sister are gone somewheres and I know where and how long they're going to be gone, and I know who you were with last night, and your best girl friend's name is Betty. Right?"

He spoke in a simple lilting voice, exactly as if he were reciting the words to a song. His smile assured her that everything was fine. In the car Ellie turned up the volume on his radio and did not bother to look around at them.

"Ellie can sit in the back seat," Arnold Friend said. He indicated his friend with a casual jerk of his chin, as if Ellie did not count and she should not bother with him.

"How'd you find out all that stuff?" Connie said.

"Listen: Betty Schultz and Tony Fitch and Jimmy Pettinger and Nancy Pettinger," he said, in a chant. "Raymond Stanley and Bob Hutter—"

"Do you know all those kids?"

"I know everybody."

"Look, you're kidding. You're not from around here."

"Sure."

"But—how come we never saw you before?"

"Sure you saw me before," he said. He looked down at his boots, as if he were a little offended. "You just don't remember."

"I guess I'd remember you," Connie said.

"Yeah?" He looked up at this, beaming. He was pleased. He began to mark time with the music from Ellie's radio, tapping his fists lightly together. Connie looked away from his smile to the car, which was painted so bright it almost hurt her eyes to look at it. She looked at that name, ARNOLD FRIEND. And up at the front fender was an expression that was familiar—MAN THE FLYING SAUCERS. It was an expression kids had used the year before, but didn't use this year. She looked at it for a while as if the words meant something to her that she did not yet know.

"What're you thinking about? Huh?" Arnold Friend demanded. "Not worried about your hair blowing around in the car, are you?"

"No."

"Think I maybe can't drive good?"

"How do I know?"

75 "You're a hard girl to handle. How come?" he said. "Don't you know I'm your friend? Didn't you see me put my sign in the air when you walked by?"

"What sign?"

"My sign." And he drew an X in the air, leaning out toward her. They were maybe ten feet apart. After his hand fell back to his side the X was still in the air, almost visible. Connie let the screen door close and stood perfectly still inside it, listening to the music from her radio and the boy's blend together. She stared at Arnold Friend. He stood there so stiffly relaxed, pretending to be relaxed, with one hand idly on the door handle as if he were keeping himself up that way and had no intention of ever moving again. She recognized most things about him, the tight jeans that showed his thighs and buttocks and the greasy leather boots and the tight shirt, and even that slippery friendly smile of his, that sleepy dreamy smile that all the boys used to get across ideas they didn't want to put into words. She recognized all this and also the singsong way he talked, slightly mocking, kidding, but serious and a little melancholy, and she recognized the way he tapped one fist against the other in homage to the perpetual music behind him. But all these things did not come together.

She said suddenly, "Hey, how old are you?"

His smile faded. She could see then that he wasn't a kid, he was much older—thirty, maybe more. At this knowledge her heart began to pound faster.

80 "That's a crazy thing to ask. Can'tcha see I'm your own age?"

"Like hell you are."

"Or maybe a coupla years older, I'm eighteen."

"Eighteen?" she said doubtfully.

He grinned to reassure her and lines appeared at the corners of his mouth. His teeth were big and white. He grinned so broadly his eyes became slits and she saw how thick the lashes were, thick and black as if painted with a black tarlike material. Then he seemed to become embarrassed, abruptly, and looked over his shoulder at Ellie. "*Him*, he's crazy," he said. "Ain't he a riot, he's a nut, a real character." Ellie was still listening to the music. His sunglasses told nothing about what he was thinking. He wore a bright orange shirt unbuttoned halfway to show his chest, which was a pale, bluish chest and not muscular like Arnold Friend's. His shirt collar was turned up all around and the very tips of the collar pointed out past his chin as if they were protecting him. He was pressing the transistor radio up against his ear and sat there in a kind of daze, right in the sun.

85 "He's kinda strange," Connie said.

"Hey, she says you're kinda strange! Kinda strange!" Arnold Friend cried. He pounded on the car to get Ellie's attention. Ellie turned for the first time and Connie saw with shock that he wasn't a kid either—he had a fair, hairless face, cheeks reddened slightly as if the veins grew too close to the surface of his skin, the face of a forty-year-old baby. Connie felt a wave of dizziness rise in her at this sight and she stared at him as if waiting for something to change the shock of the moment, make it all right again. Ellie's lips kept shaping words, mumbling along with the words blasting in his ear.

"Maybe you two better go away," Connie said faintly.

"What? How come?" Arnold Friend cried. "We come out here to take you for a ride. It's Sunday." He had the voice of the man on the radio now. It was the same voice, Connie thought. "Don'tcha know it's Sunday all day and honey, no matter who you were with last night today you're with Arnold Friend and don't you forget it!—Maybe you better step out here," he said, and this last was in a different voice. It was a little flatter, as if the heat was finally getting to him.

"No. I got things to do."

"Hey."

"You two better leave."

"We ain't leaving until you come with us."

"Like hell I am—"

"Connie, don't fool around with me. I mean, I mean, don't fool *around*," he said, shaking his head. He laughed incredulously. He placed his sunglasses on top of his head, carefully, as if he were indeed wearing a wig, and brought the stems down behind his ears. Connie stared at him, another wave of dizziness and fear rising in her so that for a moment he wasn't even in focus but was just a blur, standing there against his gold car, and she had the idea that he had driven up the driveway all right but had come from nowhere before that and belonged nowhere and that everything about him and even about the music that was so familiar to her was only half real.

"If my father comes and sees you—"

"He ain't coming. He's at a barbecue."

"How do you know that?"

"Aunt Tillie's. Right now they're—uh—they're drinking. Sitting around," he said vaguely, squinting as if he were staring all the way to town and over to Aunt Tillie's backyard. Then the vision seemed to get clear and he nodded energetically. "Yeah. Sitting around. There's your sister in a blue dress, huh? And high heels, the poor sad bitch—nothing like you sweetheart! And your mother's helping some fat woman with the corn, they're cleaning the corn—husking the corn—"

"What fat woman?" Connie cried.

"How do I know what fat woman. I don't know every goddam fat woman in the world!" Arnold Friend laughed.

"Oh, that's Mrs. Hornby. . . . Who invited her?" Connie said. She felt a little light-headed. Her breath was coming quickly.

"She's too fat. I don't like them fat. I like them the way you are, honey," he said, smiling sleepily at her. They stared at each other for a while, through the screen door. He said softly, "Now what you're going to do is this: you're going to come out that door. You're going to sit up front with me and Ellie's going to sit in the back, the hell with Ellie, right? This isn't Ellie's date. You're my date. I'm your lover, honey."

"What? You're crazy—"

"Yes, I'm your lover. You don't know what that is but you will," he said. "I know that too. I know all about you. But look: it's real nice and you couldn't ask for nobody better than me, or more polite. I always keep my word. I'll tell you how it is, I'm always nice at first, the first time. I'll hold you so tight you won't think you have to try to get away or pretend anything because you'll know you can't. And I'll come inside you where it's all secret and you'll give in to me and you'll love me—"

90

95

100

105   "Shut up! You're crazy!" Connie said. She backed away from the door. She put her hands against her ears as if she'd heard something terrible, something not meant for her. "People don't talk like that, you're crazy," she muttered. Her heart was almost too big now for her chest and its pumping made sweat break out all over her. She looked out to see Arnold Friend pause and then take a step toward the porch lurching. He almost fell. But, like a clever drunken man, he managed to catch his balance. He wobbled in his high boots and grabbed hold of one of the porch posts.

"Honey?" he said. "You still listening?"

"Get the hell out of here!"

"Be nice, honey. Listen."

"I'm going to call the police—"

110   He wobbled again and out of the side of his mouth came a fast spat curse, an aside not meant for her to hear. But even this "Christ!" sounded forced. Then he began to smile again. She watched this smile come, awkward as if he were smiling from inside a mask. His whole face was a mask, she thought wildly, tanned down onto his throat but then running out as if he had plastered makeup on his face but had forgotten about his throat.

"Honey—? Listen, here's how it is. I always tell the truth and I promise you this: I ain't coming in that house after you."

"You better not! I'm going to call the police if you—if you don't—"

"Honey," he said, talking right through her voice, "honey, I'm not coming in there but you are coming out here. You know why?"

She was panting. The kitchen looked like a place she had never seen before, some room she had run inside but which wasn't good enough, wasn't going to help her. The kitchen window had never had a curtain, after three years, and there were dishes in the sink for her to do—probably—and if you ran your hand across the table you'd probably feel something sticky there.

115   "You listening, honey? Hey?"

"—going to call the police—"

"Soon as you touch the phone I don't need to keep my promise and can come inside. You won't want that."

She rushed forward and tried to lock the door. Her fingers were shaking. "But why lock it," Arnold Friend said gently, talking right into her face. "It's just a screen door. It's just nothing." One of his boots was at a strange angle, as if his foot wasn't in it. It pointed out to the left, bent at the ankle. "I mean, anybody can break through a screen door and glass and wood and iron or anything else if he needs to, anybody at all and specially Arnold Friend. If the place got lit up with a fire honey you'd come running out into my arms, right into my arms and safe at home—like you knew I was your lover and'd stopped fooling around. I don't mind a nice shy girl but I don't like no fooling around." Part of those words were spoken with a slight rhythmic lilt, and Connie somehow recognized them—the echo of a song from last year, about a girl rushing into her boy friend's arms and coming home again—

Connie stood barefoot on the linoleum floor, staring at him. "What do you want?" she whispered.

120   "I want you," he said.

"What?"

"Seen you that night and thought, that's the one, yes sir. I never needed to look any more."

"But my father's coming back. He's coming to get me. I had to wash my hair first—" She spoke in a dry, rapid voice, hardly raising it for him to hear.

"No, your daddy is not coming and yes, you had to wash your hair and you washed it for me. It's nice and shining and all for me, I thank you, sweetheart," he said, with a mock bow, but again he almost lost his balance. He had to bend and adjust his boots. Evidently his feet did not go all the way down; the boots must have been stuffed with something so that he would seem taller. Connie stared out at him and behind him Ellie in the car, who seemed to be looking off toward Connie's right, into nothing. This Ellie said, pulling the words out of the air one after another as if he were just discovering them, "You want me to pull out the phone?"

"Shut your mouth and keep it shut," Arnold Friend said, his face red from bending over or maybe from embarrassment because Connie had seen his boots. "This ain't none of your business."

"What—what are you doing? What do you want?" Connie said. "If I call the police they'll get you, they'll arrest you—"

"Promise was not to come in unless you touch that phone, and I'll keep that promise," he said. He resumed his erect position and tried to force his shoulders back. He sounded like a hero in a movie, declaring something important. He spoke too loudly and it was as if he were speaking to someone behind Connie. "I ain't made plans for coming in that house where I don't belong but just for you to come out to me, the way you should. Don't you know who I am?"

"You're crazy," she whispered. She backed away from the door but did not want to go into another part of the house, as if this would give him permission to come through the door. "What do you. . . . You're crazy, you . . ."

"Huh? What're you saying, honey?"

Her eyes darted everywhere in the kitchen. She could not remember what it was, this room.

"This is how it is, honey: you come out and we'll drive away, have a nice ride. But if you don't come out we're gonna wait till your people come home and then they're all going to get it."

"You want that telephone pulled out?" Ellie said. He held the radio away from his ear and grimaced, as if without the radio the air was too much for him.

"I toldja shut up, Ellie," Arnold Friend said, "you're deaf, get a hearing aid, right? Fix yourself up. This little girl's no trouble and's gonna be nice to me, so Ellie keep to yourself, this ain't your date—right? Don't hem in on me. Don't hog. Don't crush. Don't bird dog. Don't trail me," he said in a rapid meaningless voice, as if he were running through all the expressions he'd learned but was no longer sure which one of them was in style, then rushing on to new ones, making them up with his eyes closed, "Don't crawl under my fence, don't squeeze in my chipmunk hole, don't sniff my glue, suck my popsicle, keep your own greasy fingers on yourself!" He shaded his eyes and peered in at Connie, who was backed against the kitchen table. "Don't mind him honey he's just a creep. He's a dope. Right? I'm the boy for you and like I said you come out here nice like a lady and give me your hand, and nobody else gets hurt, I mean, your nice old bald-headed daddy and your mummy and your sister in her high heels. Because listen: why bring them in this?"

125

130

135   "Leave me alone," Connie whispered.

"Hey, you know that old woman down the road, the one with the chickens and stuff—you know her?"

"She's dead!"

"Dead? What? You know her?" Arnold Friend said.

"She's dead—"

"Don't you like her?"

140   "She's dead—she's—she isn't here any more—"

"But don't you like her, I mean, you got something against her? Some grudge or something?" Then his voice dipped as if he were conscious of a rudeness. He touched the sunglasses perched on top of his head as if to make sure they were still there. "Now you be a good girl."

"What are you going to do?"

"Just two things, or maybe three," Arnold Friend said. "But I promise it won't last long and you'll like me that way you get to like people you're close to. You will. It's all over for you here, so come on out. You don't want your people in any trouble, do you?"

She turned and bumped against a chair or something, hurting her leg, but she ran into the back room and picked up the telephone. Something roared in her ear, a tiny roaring, and she was so sick with fear that she could do nothing but listen to it—the telephone was clammy and very heavy and her fingers groped down to the dial but were too weak to touch it. She began to scream into the phone, into the roaring. She cried out, she cried for her mother, she felt her breath start jerking back and forth in her lungs as if it were something Arnold Friend were stabbing her with again and again with no tenderness. A noisy sorrowful wailing rose all about her and she was locked inside it the way she was locked inside the house.

145   After a while she could hear again. She was sitting on the floor with her wet back against the wall.

Arnold Friend was saying from the door, "That's a good girl. Put the phone back."

She kicked the phone away from her.

"No, honey. Pick it up. Put it back right."

She picked it up and put it back. The dial tone stopped.

150   "That's a good girl. Now you come outside."

She was hollow with what had been fear, but what was now just an emptiness. All that screaming had blasted it out of her. She sat, one leg cramped under her, and deep inside her brain was something like a pinpoint of light that kept going and would not let her relax. She thought, I'm not going to see my mother again. She thought, I'm not going to sleep in my bed again. Her bright green blouse was all wet.

Arnold Friend said, in a gentle-loud voice that was like a stage voice, "The place where you came from ain't there any more, and where you had in mind to go is cancelled out. This place you are now—inside your daddy's house—is nothing but a cardboard box I can knock down any time. You know that and always did know it. You hear me?"

She thought, I have got to think. I have to know what to do.

"We'll go out to a nice field, out in the country here where it smells so nice and it's sunny," Arnold Friend said. "I'll have my arms around you so you won't need to try to get away and I'll show you what love is like, what it does. The hell with this house!

It looks solid all right," he said. He ran a fingernail down the screen and the noise did not make Connie shiver, as it would have the day before. "Now put your hand on your heart, honey. Feel that? That feels solid too but we know better, be nice to me, be sweet like you can because what else is there for a girl like you but to be sweet and pretty and give in?—and get away before her people come back?"

She felt her pounding heart. Her hand seemed to enclose it. She thought for the first time in her life that it was nothing that was hers, that belonged to her, but just a pounding, living thing inside this body that wasn't really hers either.

"You don't want them to get hurt," Arnold Friend went on. "Now get up, honey. Get up all by yourself."

She stood.

"Now turn this way. That's right. Come over here to me—Ellie, put that away, didn't I tell you? You dope. You miserable creepy dope," Arnold Friend said. His words were not angry but only part of an incantation. The incantation was kindly. "Now come out through the kitchen to me honey and let's see a smile, try it, you're a brave sweet little girl and now they're eating corn and hotdogs cooked to bursting over an outdoor fire, and they don't know one thing about you and never did and honey you're better than them because not a one of them would have done this for you."

Connie felt the linoleum under her feet; it was cool. She brushed her hair back out of her eyes. Arnold Friend let go of the post tentatively and opened his arms for her, his elbows pointing in toward each other and his wrists limp, to show that this was an embarrassed embrace and a little mocking, he didn't want to make her self-conscious.

She put out her hand against the screen. She watched herself push the door slowly open as if she were safe back somewhere in the other doorway, watching this body and this head of long hair moving out into the sunlight where Arnold Friend waited.

"My sweet little blue-eyed girl," he said, in a half-sung sigh that had nothing to do with her brown eyes but was taken up just the same by the vast sunlit reaches of the land behind him and on all sides of him, so much land that Connie had never seen before and did not recognize except to know that she was going to it.

Reading and Reacting

1. Is Arnold Friend meant to be the devil? a rapist and murderer? Is he actually Bob Dylan? Or is he just a misunderstood social misfit who terrifies Connie more because of her innocence than because of his evil?

2. What **allusions** to fairy tales can you identify in the story? What do these allusions add to the story?

3. Many critical articles see "Where Are You Going, Where Have You Been?" as heavily symbolic, even allegorical, with elements of myth, dream, and fairy tale woven throughout. Do you think such analysis adds something vital to readers' understanding of the story, or do you think the story could be explained in much simpler terms?

4. Feminist critics might see this story as a familiar tale of a man who uses flattering seductive language followed by threats of physical violence to coerce a young woman into giving in to him. In what sense do you see this as a story of male power and female powerlessness?

5. Dark undertones aside, in what sense is this simply a story about the coming of age of a typical 1960s teenager?

6. What roles do music, sex, the weather, contemporary slang, and the characters' physical appearance play in the story?

7. Why do members of Connie's family make such brief appearances in the story? How might expanding their roles change the story?

8. Which aspects of teenage culture have changed in the nearly fifty years since Oates wrote the story? Which have stayed the same? Given the scope of these changes, is the story dated?

9. Most critics (like Oates herself) see the end of the story as alarmingly negative, suggesting rape and even murder. Do you see it this way?

10. Do you agree with Oates's view, expressed in her article below, that the differences in the endings of the 1985 film *Smooth Talk* (based on the story) and the story itself are justified by the differences between the 1960s and the 1980s?

11. **JOURNAL ENTRY** In what sense is the generation gap—the failure of one generation to understand another's culture, customs, and heroes—central to the story?

12. **CRITICAL PERSPECTIVE** According to *New York Times* book critic Michiko Kakutani, Joyce Carol Oates has several "fictional trademarks":

> [She has] a penchant for mixing the mundane and Gothic, the ordinary and sensationalistic; a fascination with the dark undercurrents of violence, eroticism and emotional chaos in American life, and a tendency to divide her characters' lives into a Before and After with one "unspeakable turn of destiny."

> In what sense do Kakutani's remarks apply to "Where Are You Going, Where Have You Been?" Do you see a fascination with "the dark undercurrents of . . . life" in this story? What is the "unspeakable turn of destiny" that divides Connie's life into a "Before and After"?

Related Works: "Encounters with Unexpected Animals" (p. 132), "A&P" (p. 238), "A Good Man Is Hard to Find" (p. 367), "The Lottery" (p. 419), "Young Goodman Brown" (p. 448), "Bullet in the Brain" (p. 496), "The Wolf's Postscript to 'Little Red Riding Hood'" (p. 706), "To His Coy Mistress" (p. 776), *Beauty* (p. 1069).

Sources

Background

JOYCE CAROL OATES

When Characters from the Page Are Made Flesh on the Screen*

Some years ago in the American Southwest there surfaced a tabloid psychopath known as "The Pied Piper of Tucson." I have forgotten his name but his specialty was

*_New York Times_ 23 Mar. 1986, sec 2:14. Print.

the seduction and occasional murder of teen-age girls. He may or may not have had actual accomplices, but his bizarre activities were known among a circle of teen-agers in the Tucson area; for some reason they kept his secrets, deliberately did not inform parents or police. It was this fact, not the fact of the mass murderer himself, that struck me at the time. And this was a pre-Manson time, this was early or mid-1960's.

The "Pied Piper" mimicked teen-agers in their talk, dress and behavior, but he was not a teen-ager—he was a man in his early 30's. Rather short, he stuffed rags in his leather boots to give himself height. (And sometimes walked unsteadily as a consequence: did none among his admiring constituency notice?) He charmed his victims, to the bewilderment of others who fancy themselves free of all lunatic attractions. "The Pied Piper of Tucson": a trashy dream, a tabloid archetype, sheer artifice, comedy, cartoon—surrounded, however improbably, and finally tragically, by real people. You think that, if you look twice, he won't be there. But there he is.

I don't remember any longer where I first read about "The Pied Piper"—very likely in *Life* magazine. I do recall deliberately not reading the full article because I didn't want to be distracted by too much detail. It was not after all the mass murderer himself who intrigued me, but the disturbing fact that a number of teen-agers—from "good" families—aided and abetted his crimes. This is the sort of thing authorities and responsible citizens invariably call "inexplicable" because they can't find explanations for it. *They* would not have fallen under this maniac's spell, after all.

An early draft of my short story "Where Are You Going, Where Have You Been?"— from which the current film "Smooth Talk" has been adapted by Joyce Chopra and Tom Cole—had the rather too explicit title "Death and the Maiden." It was cast in a mode of fiction to which I am still partial—indeed, every third or fourth story of mine is probably in this mode—"realistic allegory," it might be called. It is Hawthornian, romantic, shading into parable. Like the medieval German engraving from which my title was taken the story was minutely detailed yet clearly an allegory of the fatal attractions of death (or the devil). An innocent young girl is seduced by way of her own vanity; she mistakes death for erotic romance of a particularly American/trashy sort.

Laura Dern and Treat Williams in a still from the film *Smooth Talk* (1985)
International Spectrafilm/courtesy Everett Collection

5   In subsequent drafts the story changed its tone, its focus, its language, its title. It became "Where Are You Going, Where Have You Been?" Written at a time when the author was intrigued by the music of Bob Dylan, particularly the hauntingly elegiac song "It's All Over Now, Baby Blue," it was dedicated to Bob Dylan. The charismatic mass murderer drops into the background and his innocent victim, a 15-year-old, moves into the foreground. She becomes the true protagonist of the tale, courting and being courted by her fate, a self-styled 1950's pop figure, alternately absurd and winning.

There is no suggestion in the published story that "Arnold Friend" has seduced and murdered other young girls, or even that he necessarily intends to murder Connie. Is his interest "merely" sexual? (Nor is there anything about the complicity of other teen-agers. I saved that yet more provocative note for a current story, "Testimony.") Connie is shallow, vain, silly, hopeful, doomed—perhaps as I saw, and still see, myself?—but capable nonetheless of an unexpected gesture of heroism at the story's end.

Her smooth-talking seducer, who cannot lie, promises her that her family will be unharmed if she gives herself to him; and so she does. The story ends abruptly at the point of her "crossing over." We don't know the nature of her sacrifice, only that she is generous enough to make it.

In adapting a narrative so spare and thematically foreshortened as "Where Are You Going, Where Have You Been?" film director Joyce Chopra and screenwriter Tom Cole were required to do a good deal of filling in, expanding, inventing. Connie's story becomes lavishly, and lovingly, textured; she is not an allegorical figure so much as a "typical" teen-age girl (if Laura Dern, spectacularly good-looking, can be so defined).

Joyce Chopra, who has done documentary films on contemporary teen-age culture, and, yet more authoritatively, has an adolescent daughter of her own, creates in "Smooth Talk" a believable world for Connie to inhabit. Or worlds: as in the original story there is Connie-at-home, and there is Connie-with-her-friends. Two 15-year-old girls, two finely honed styles, two voices, sometimes but not often overlapping. It is one of the marvelous visual features of the film that we *see* Connie and her friends transform themselves, once they are safely free of parental observation. What freedom, what joy! The girls claim their true identities in the neighborhood shopping mall!

10   "Smooth Talk" is, in a way, as much Connie's mother's story as it is Connie's; its center of gravity, its emotional nexus, is frequently with the mother—played by Mary Kay Place. (Though the mother's sexual jealousy of her daughter is slighted in the film.) Connie's ambiguous relationship with her affable, somewhat mysterious father (played by Levon Helm) is an excellent touch: I had thought, subsequent to the story's publication, that I should have built up the father, suggesting, as subtly as I could, an attraction there paralleling the attraction Connie feels for her seducer Arnold Friend.

Treat Williams impersonates Arnold Friend as Arnold Friend impersonates—is it James Dean? James Dean regarding himself in mirrors, doing James Dean impersonations? Laura Dern is so right as "my" Connie that I may come to think I modeled the fictitious girl on her, in the way that writers frequently delude themselves about notions of causality.

My difficulties with "Smooth Talk" have primarily to do with my chronic hesitation—a justifiable shyness, I'm sure—about seeing/hearing work of mine abstracted from its contexture of language. All writers know that language is their subject; quirky word choices, patterns of rhythm, enigmatic pauses, punctuation marks. Where the quick-scanner sees "quick" writing, the writer conceals nine-tenths of his iceberg.

Of course we all have "real" subjects, and we will fight to the death to defend these subjects, but beneath the tale-telling it is the tale-telling that grips us so very fiercely: "the soul at the *white heat*" in Emily Dickinson's words. Because of this it is always an eerie experience for me, as a writer, to hear "my" dialogue floating back to me from the external world; particularly when it is surrounded, as of course it must be, by "other" dialogue I seem not to recall having written. Perhaps a panic reaction sets in—perhaps I worry that I might be responsible for knowing what "I" meant, in writing things "I" didn't write? Like a student who has handed in work not entirely his own, and dreads interrogation from his teacher?

It is startling too to *see* fictitious characters inhabiting, with such seeming aplomb, roles that until now seemed private, flat on the page. (I don't, like many of my writing colleagues, feel affronted, thinking, "*That* isn't how he/she looks!" I think instead, guiltily, "Is *that* how he/she really looks?")

I have also had a number of plays produced and so characteristically doubtful am I about intruding into my directors' territories that I nearly always abrogate my authority to them. The writer works in a single dimension, the director works in three. I assume that they are professionals to their fingertips; authorities in their medium as I am an authority (if I am) in mine. I would fiercely defend the placement of a semicolon in one of my novels, but I would probably have deferred fairly quickly to Joyce Chopra's decision to reverse the story's ending, turn it upside-down, in a sense, so that the film ends not with death, not with a sleepwalker's crossing-over to her fate, but upon a sense of reconciliation, rejuvenation. Laura Dern's Connie is no longer "my" Connie at the film's conclusion; she is very much alive, assertive, strong-willed—a girl, perhaps, of the mid-1980's, and not of the mid-1960's.

A girl's loss of virginity, bittersweet but not necessarily tragic. Not today. A girl's coming of age that involves her succumbing to, but then rejecting, the "trashy dreams" of her pop teen-age culture. "Where Are You Going, Where Have You Been?" deliberately betrays itself as allegorical in its conclusion: Death and Death's chariot (a funky souped-up convertible) have come for the Maiden. Awakening is, in the story's final lines, moving out into the sunlight where Arnold Friend waits:

> "My sweet little blue-eyed girl," he said, in a half-sung sigh that had nothing to do with (Connie's) brown eyes but was taken up just the same by the vast sunlit reaches of the land behind him and on all sides of him, so much land that Connie had never seen before and did not recognize except to know that she was going to it.

I quite understand that this is an unfilmable conclusion, and "Where Are You Going, Where Have You Been?" is in fact an unfilmable short story. But Joyce Chopra's "Smooth Talk" is an accomplished and sophisticated movie that attempts to do just that.

15

BOB DYLAN

It's All Over Now, Baby Blue*

You must leave now, take what you need you think will last
But whatever you wish to keep, you better grab it fast
Yonder stands your orphan with his gun
Crying like a fire in the sun.
Look out, the saints are comin' through   5
And it's all over now, baby blue.

The highway is for gamblers, better use your sins
Take what you have gathered from coincidence
The empty-handed painter from your streets
Is drawing crazy patterns on your sheets   10
This sky too is folding under you
And it's all over now, baby blue.

All your seasick sailors they are rowing home
Your empty-handed army men are going home
The lover who has just walked out your door   15
Has taken all his blankets from the floor
The carpet too is moving under you
And it's all over now, baby blue.

Leave your stepping stones behind, something calls for you
Forget the dead you've left, they will not follow you   20
The vagabond who's rapping at your door
Is standing in the clothes that you once wore
Strike another match, go start anew
And it's all over now, baby blue.

*Los Angeles: Warner Bros., 1965. Print.

The Pied Piper of Tucson

These photos show Charles Schmid (the real-life inspiration for Arnold Friend), three of his teenage victims, and the speedway where they hung out in the 1960s.

Murderer Charles H. Schmid Jr. after his arrest
Corbis

Charles Schmid's teenage victims Gretchen Fritz, Wendy Fritz, and Alleen Rowe
Bettmann/Corbis

Tucson's Speedway Boulevard (c. 1966), teenage hangout where
Schmid was often seen
Source: ©Bill Ray/Time Life Pictures/Getty Images

Schmid before his trial
Source: ©Bill Ray/Time Life Pictures/Getty Images

ANONYMOUS

The Pied Piper of Hamelin

Once upon a time . . . on the banks of a great river in the north of Germany lay a town called Hamelin. The citizens of Hamelin were honest folk who lived contentedly in their grey stone houses. The years went by, and the town grew very rich. Then one day, an extraordinary thing happened to disturb the peace. Hamelin had always had rats, and a lot too. But they had never been a danger, for the cats had always solved the rat problem in the usual way—by killing them. All at once, however, the rats began to multiply.

In the end, a black sea of rats swarmed over the whole town. First, they attacked the barns and storehouses, then, for lack of anything better, they gnawed the wood, cloth or anything at all. The one thing they didn't eat was metal. The terrified citizens flocked to plead with the town councillors to free them from the plague of rats. But the council had, for a long time, been sitting in the Mayor's room, trying to think of a plan.

Illustration of the Brothers Grimm version of the fairy tale "The Pied Piper of Hamelin"
Source: ©Bettmann/Corbis

"What we need is an army of cats!"

But all the cats were dead.

"We'll put down poisoned food then . . ."

But most of the food was already gone and even poison did not stop the rats.

"It just can't be done without help!" said the Mayor sadly.

Just then, while the citizens milled around outside, there was a loud knock at the door. "Who can that be?" the city fathers wondered uneasily, mindful of the angry crowds. They gingerly opened the door. And to their surprise, there stood a tall thin man dressed in brightly coloured clothes, with a long feather in his hat, and waving a gold pipe at them.

"I've freed other towns of beetles and bats," the stranger announced, "and for a thousand florins, I'll rid you of your rats!"

"A thousand florins!" exclaimed the Mayor. "We'll give you fifty thousand if you succeed!" At once the stranger hurried away, saying: "It's late now, but at dawn tomorrow, there won't be a rat left in Hamelin!"

The sun was still below the horizon, when the sound of a pipe wafted through the streets of Hamelin. The pied piper slowly made his way through the houses and behind him flocked the rats. Out they scampered from doors, windows and gutters, rats of every size, all after the piper. And as he played, the stranger marched down to the

5

10

river and straight into the water, up to his middle. Behind him swarmed the rats and every one was drowned and swept away by the current.

By the time the sun was high in the sky, there was not a single rat in the town. There was even greater delight at the town hall, until the piper tried to claim his payment.

"Fifty thousand florins?" exclaimed the councillors, "Never . . ."

"A thousand florins at least!" cried the pied piper angrily. But the Mayor broke in. "The rats are all dead now and they can never come back. So be grateful for fifty florins, or you'll not get even that . . ."

15   His eyes flashing with rage, the pied piper pointed a threatening finger at the Mayor.

"You'll bitterly regret ever breaking your promise," he said, and vanished.

A shiver of fear ran through the councillors, but the Mayor shrugged and said excitedly: "We've saved fifty thousand florins!"

That night, freed from the nightmare of the rats, the citizens of Hamelin slept more soundly than ever. And when the strange sound of piping wafted through the streets at dawn, only the children heard it. Drawn as by magic, they hurried out of their homes. Again, the pied piper paced through the town. This time, it was children of all sizes that flocked at his heels to the sound of his strange piping. The long procession soon left the town and made its way through the wood and across the forest till it reached the foot of a huge mountain. When the piper came to the dark rock, he played his pipe even louder still and a great door creaked open. Beyond lay a cave. In trooped the children behind the pied piper, and when the last child had gone into the darkness, the door creaked shut. A great landslide came down the mountain blocking the entrance to the cave forever. Only one little lame boy escaped this fate. It was he who told the anxious citizens, searching for their children, what had happened. And no matter what people did, the mountain never gave up its victims. Many years were to pass before the merry voices of other children would ring through the streets of Hamelin but the memory of the harsh lesson lingered in everyone's heart and was passed down from father to son through the centuries.

CHARLES PERRAULT

Little Red Riding Hood*

Once upon a time there was a little village girl, the prettiest that had ever been seen. Her mother doted on her. Her grandmother was even fonder, and made her a little red hood, which became her so well that everywhere she went by the name of Little Red Riding Hood.

One day her mother, who had just made and baked some cakes, said to her: "Go and see how your grandmother is, for I have been told that she is ill. Take her a cake and this little pot of butter."

*from *Little Red Riding Hood: A Casebook*. By Alan Dundes. Madison: U of Wisconsin P, 1989. Print.

Illustration from "Little Red Riding Hood"
Bettmann/Corbis

Little Red Riding Hood set off at once for the house of her grandmother, who lived in another village. On her way through a wood she met old Father Wolf. He would have very much liked to eat her, but dared not do so on account of some wood-cutters who were in the forest. He asked her where she was going. The poor child, not knowing that it was dangerous to stop and listen to a wolf, said: "I am going to see my grandmother, and am taking her a cake and a pot of butter which my mother has sent to her." "Does she live far away?" asked the Wolf. "Oh, yes," replied Little Red Riding Hood; "it is yonder by the mill which you can see right below there, and it is the first house in the village."

"Well now," said the Wolf, "I think I shall go and see her too. I will go by this path, and you by that path, and we will see who gets there first." The Wolf set off running with all his might by the shorter road, and the little girl continued on her way by the longer road. As she went she amused herself by gathering nuts, running after the butterflies, and making nosegays of the wild flowers which she found.

The Wolf was not long in reaching the grandmother's house. He knocked. Toc Toc. "Who is there?" "It is your granddaughter, Red Riding Hood," said the Wolf, disguising his voice, "and I bring you a cake and a little pot of butter as a present from my mother." The worthy grandmother was in bed, not being very well, and cried out to him: "Pull out the peg and the latch will fall." The Wolf drew out the peg and the door flew open. Then he sprang upon the poor old lady and ate her up in less than no time, for he had been more than three days without food. 5

After that he shut the door, lay down in the grandmother's bed, and waited for Little Red Riding Hood. Presently she came and knocked. Toc Toc.

"Who is there?"

Now Little Red Riding Hood on hearing the Wolf's gruff voice was at first frightened, but thinking that her grandmother had a bad cold, she replied: "It is your granddaughter, Red Riding Hood, and I bring you a cake and a little pot of butter from my mother."

Softening his voice, the Wolf called out to her: "Pull out the peg and the latch will fall." Little Red Riding Hood drew out the peg and the door flew open. When he saw her enter, the Wolf hid himself in the bed beneath the counterpane. "Put the cake and the little pot of butter on the bin," he said, "and come up on the bed with me."

Little Red Riding Hood took off her cloak, but when she climbed up on the bed she was astonished to see how her grandmother looked in her nightgown. 10

"Grandmother dear!" she exclaimed, "what big arms you have!"

"The better to embrace you, my child!"

"Grandmother dear, what big legs you have!"

"The better to run with, my child!"

15 "Grandmother dear, what big ears you have!"

"The better to hear with, my child!"

"Grandmother dear, what big eyes you have!"

"The better to see with, my child!"

"Grandmother dear, what big teeth you have!"

20 "The better to eat you with!"

With these words the wicked Wolf leapt upon Little Red Riding Hood and gobbled her up.

Moral

From this story one learns that children, especially young lasses, pretty, courteous and well-bred, do very wrong to listen to strangers, and it is not an unheard thing if the Wolf is thereby provided with his dinner. I say Wolf, for all wolves are not of the same sort; there is one kind with an amenable disposition—neither noisy, nor hateful, nor angry, but tame, obliging and gentle, following the young maids in the streets, even into their homes. Alas! Who does not know that these gentle wolves are of all such creatures the most dangerous!

Critical Perspectives

A. R. COULTHARD

Joyce Carol Oates's "Where Are You Going, Where Have You Been?" as Pure Realism*

The tendency among "Where Are You Going, Where Have You Been?" commentators is to equate Arnold Friend with the Devil himself and to "mysticize" the story into a dream allegory. This interpretation may have been largely inspired by the author's remark that "Arnold Friend is a fantastic figure: he is Death, he is the 'elf-knight' of the ballads, he is the Imagination, he is a Dream, he is a Lover, a Demon, and all that."[1] This is a lot of weight for one short man to carry. Arnold Friend is a fantastic character, but only in the slang sense of the word. Such sweeping pronouncements as Oates's, especially when a nonchalant "and all that" is appended, should be viewed with skepticism, and I suspect that the author was seizing upon an after-the-fact opportunity to make her story seem more "literary" than it really is. If so, I don't understand why. Joyce Carol Oates should have been content to let "Where Are You Going?" stand on its solid realism.

That Oates is operating in a realistic mode is indicated by Tom Quirk in an article so revealing that its main details are worth repeating here.[2] Quirk convincingly demonstrates that Oates closely modeled her story on Charles Schmid's murder of Alleen Rowe in the fall of 1965, just prior to the 1966 publication of "Where Are You Going?" in *Epoch*.[3] Though the murder was publicized in several popular news

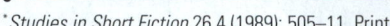

magazines, Quirk even identifies the one which Oates most likely used, noting that the *Life* account alone mentioned that Alleen, like Connie, has just washed her hair before her assailants arrived (416).

"Assailants" is also revealing, in that Schmid murdered two other young girls, but the killing of Rowe was the only one in which he had an accomplice. Schmid and his friend John Saunders raped and murdered Alleen Rowe, beating her to death and buried her in the desert outside Tucson, Arizona (416). Arnold Friend's creepy cohort Ellie Oscar was no doubt suggested to Oates by John Saunders.

The parallels between "Where Are You Going?" and the Rowe account are so numerous that Oates's borrowing is unquestionable. For instance, Alleen was fifteen at the time of her death, the same age as Connie. Either by accident or by design, the murderers caught her at home alone on a night when her mother was working, just as Connie is found in helpless circumstances in her own house (416).

But the most telling evidence is how faithfully Oates duplicated the bizarre facts about Charles Schmid in her characterization of Arnold Friend. When Schmid was arrested, he was twenty-three but still haunting teen hangouts. Like Friend, he was short (5'3") and muscular, and he tried to appear younger and to disguise his lack of height by dying his hair black, wearing pancake makeup, and stuffing rags and even crumpled cans into his black leather boots (414). He was also a rock-and-roll fan and identified Elvis as his "idol" (417). Schmid, like Arnold, even drove a garish gold-colored car (414).

But while the fact that Oates copied many of her details from the account of an actual murder suggests a realistic story, it does not prove that she did not transform Charles Schmid into a mystical Arnold Friend and, in so doing, mythologize "Where Are You Going?" What proves that she didn't is the story's consistent naturalism. Absolutely nothing occurs that can't be explained in purely literal terms or that isn't best explained so. Like all good stories, "Where Are You Going?" resonates in the mind, but its style is realistic, not allegorical. Its principle characters are not personifications of abstract qualities but a demented killer and giddy teen-aged girl. Arnold Friend does not appear in a dream but at Connie's kitchen door.

Joan D. Winslow would disagree with this view.[4] Winslow argues that Connie's "repressed fear, uncertainty, and guilt finally emerge in the shape of Arnold Friend" (268) and says that "The knowing reader can easily identify him as the devil" (267). But Connie's problem is that she has no sexual fear, uncertainty, or guilt, not even in repressed form. There is nothing psychologically complex about her. She is simply a pathetic teenager who isn't being reared very well. Her church is a "bright-lit, fly-infested"[5] drive-in restaurant, and her inspirational music is mind-numbing rock-and-roll, both middle-class cliches of the early sixties. Connie's father doesn't care where she has been, and her mother, who the story implies was much like Connie when she was younger, takes only a perfunctory interest in where she's going. When Connie blithely distances herself from the disreputable Pettinger girl, Connie's mother, "who noticed everything and knew everything" (821), pretends to accept her daughter's nice girl/bad girl distinction. Connie thinks that "it was maybe cruel to fool her so much" (823), but she isn't fooled. She just doesn't care. This is the stuff of sociological naturalism, not psychosexual allegory.

Winslow sees "Where Are You Going?" as a dream allegory[6] comparable to Hawthorne's "Young Goodman Brown" but the stories differ markedly in style. The dream possibility is pronounced in Hawthorne's story ("Had Goodman Brown fallen asleep in the forest, and only dreamed a wild dream of a witch-meeting?"), and several of its events, such as the vanishing of the Satanic initiation rite, cannot be explained except in terms of dream or fantasy. No such narrative signals or unreal occurrences appear in Oates's story.

Connie exists in a dream-like state but never in a dream. Her mother is right when she says that Connie's "mind was all filled with trashy daydreams" (821). Connie is never more than half awake to reality, but this is her natural mental state and not a temporary psychic phenomenon that conjures up Arnold Friend. Connie rides home from the mall "sleepy and pleased" (823) because she has sated her appetite for cheap diversion for another night. Her "dreams" are mundane teenage boy-girl reveries, enhanced by the hypnotic music she listens to constantly. She spends most of her waking hours "dreaming about the boys she met. But all the boys fell back and dissolved into a single face that was not even a face, but an idea, a feeling, mixed up with the urgent insistent pounding of the music" (823)—which is merely to say that Connie, like many teenagers, is in love with love.

10   Or maybe just sex. Not only is there nothing remotely fabulous about such daydreaming, but it may be inspired by a reality-based erotic impulse: "her mind slipped over onto thoughts of the boy she had been with the night before and how nice he had been, how sweet it always was . . ."(823). There is a good possibility that "it" refers to sexual intercourse. (That Arnold Friend likes to think his victim is a virgin doesn't mean this is so.) Connie is in her characteristic semi-conscious state on the fateful Sunday of Arnold Friend's visit. She has "sat with her eyes closed in the sun, dreaming and dazed with the warmth about her" (823), but she is merely indulging in her routine "trashy daydreams" about boys when Arnold arrives. He is not a dream but a brutal awakening.

Connie's dream-like state at the end of the story is of another type. It is the nightmare sense of unreality of a person who knows she is about to be murdered: "She thought, I'm not going to see my mother again. She thought, I'm not going to sleep in my bed again" (831). Her final trancelike compliance signals the acceptance of the inevitable. The atrocious thing that is happening to her renders her empty. She is in effect "out of body" from despair and shock: "She watched herself push the door slowly open . . . , watching this body and this head of long hair moving out into the sunlight where Arnold Friend waited" (832). Connie's psychological reaction to her impending death is realistically detailed and completely believable. Allegorizing it into a mere bad dream not only strains the text but takes the edge off the genuine horror of Connie's fate.

Just as Connie is no more and no less than the pathetic girl who is about to be murdered, Arnold Friend is simply the sick killer who is going to murder her. He doesn't "represent" anything, except the kind of creep a girl like Connie (or even a girl unlike Connie) might have the bad luck to attract. The story even implies that Arnold has killed, or at least raped, before. "[T]he numbers 33, 19, 17" painted on the car may be "a secret code" (825), as the miscreant himself boasts, but they are not demonic numerology. The numbers most likely are the ages of Arnold Friend's previous victims, suggested to Oates by the ages—seventeen, fifteen, and thirteen—of the girls killed by

Charles Schmid. Assuming that Friend has listed his victims in chronological order, the number sequence is revealing. He started with a woman near his own age, dropped down to the last teen year, then picked a girl two years younger than the previous one, which parallels Schmid's youth fetish. Connie fits perfectly into the descending two-year age difference of nineteen, seventeen, and now fifteen. (Schmid's thirteen-year-old would be next for Arnold.) For Friend's "secret code" Oates used two of the three ages of Charles Schmid's victims, all of whom were two years apart in age.

That Arnold Friend seems to possess Satanic powers in the form of supernatural knowledge of Connie and her family is also explicable on a purely realistic level. Even Tom Quirk credits him with "intimate, even satanic knowledge of her family's doings" (417), but Arnold really has no supernatural powers. He knows nothing about Connie that he could not have observed, learned by asking around, or guessed. That he knows about "that old woman down the road, the one with the chickens" (830) suggests that he has cased the neighborhood; that he doesn't know she has recently died—"Dead? What?" (830)—suggests the opposite of Satanic perception. It is true that when Connie tries to scare him off by saying that her father is due home, Arnold knows that the family is at a barbecue at Aunt Tillie's. But when Connie asks him how he knows this, his halting reply again suggests no mystical knowledge: "Right now they're—uh—they're drinking!" As Arnold continues, Oates's "stage directions" make it clear that he is improvising: "Sitting around; he said vaguely, squinting as if he were staring all the way to town and over to Aunt Tillie's backyard" (828). (Since Aunt Tillie's house is in town, it is quite possible that the cruising Arnold Friend has previously observed Connie's family—and maybe even Connie—there. Oates's locale seems a much smaller place than Charles Schmid's Tuscon, a fact which would explain how Arnold has even learned the name of Connie's aunt.) Then he says something which reveals he has in fact watched the family depart: "Yeah. Sitting around. There's your sister in a blue dress, huh? And high heels" (828). (If he has been this close, he could have overheard the family's destination and the aunt's name.)

The rest of Arnold Friend's "special knowledge" is simply guesswork, not all of it correct. He speculates that a family cookout is likely to have corn-on-the-cob (it may or may not) and that there is a "fat woman" present, an idea which startles Connie: "'What fat woman?' Connie cried." Friend, the omniscient Devil, replies, "How do I know what fat woman?" To complete this hint that Arnold's "powers" are totally fake, there isn't even a fat woman at the gathering. "Oh, that's Mrs. Hornsby" the shaken girl replies, then adds, "Who invited her?" (828). Arnold's scam has worked so well that Connie imagines an outsider at the barbecue, and then wonders why she is there!

Neither does Arnold Friend possess any supernatural knowledge about Connie. He boasts to her that "I know your name and all about you" (826), and then proves it by reciting a list of her friends. But his information would be easily available to anyone who frequents teen gathering places, as Arnold does. That Arnold has gone to the trouble of "researching" Connie merely emphasizes that he has had his eye on her for some time: "I took a special interest in you, such a pretty girl, and found out all about you" (826). When Arnold calls June "the poor sad bitch" (828), he correctly guesses Connie's attitude toward her plain older sister, but his conjecture is likely enough, considering what he knows of Connie's narcissism. It is hard to believe that Oates intended special powers for a character who can't even get current teen slang right:

15

Arnold runs through "all the expressions he'd learned but was no longer sure which one of them was in style . . ." (830).

Other so-called symbols of Arnold Friend as supernatural Demon are also better explained as the trappings of a pathological pervert. His "sign" (826), the X he draws in the air, is no arcane Satanic marking of Connie. It is, rather, the kind of banal, sexually aggressive gesture one would expect of an Arnold Friend, the body-language counterpart to his hackneyed "Gonna get you, baby" (822). Friend's clumsy boots do not hide "the cloven feet of the devil" as Joan Winslow contends (267) but the comically vain height-enhancing rags and cans of Charles Schmid. The phoney name of Arnold Friend does not bespeak Satan in disguise but is rather an ironically inappropriate alias, probably copied, as Quirk surmises, after Charles Schmid's pseudonym of Angel Rodriguez (415).

The only "demonic" power Arnold Friend possesses is the ability to use fear to ravage his victim's humanity, but such power is within the province of any heartless killer. During their final moments, Charles Schmid's young victims may well have experienced the same hopeless disorientation as Connie does. To reduce "Where Are You Going, Where Have You Been?" to a teen-age dream and to raise Arnold Friend to a superhuman Symbol is to rob the story of its elemental power. Arnold Friends do exist (Charles Schmid is proof of that), and the evil they do is not safely confined to the literary dreamworld.

Notes

[1]Oates made this statement to John R. Knott and Christopher R. Keaske in an interview published in the second edition of their textbook *Mirrors: An Introduction to Literature* (San Francisco: Canfield Press, 1975), p. 19. James H. Pickering and Jeffrey D. Hoeper quote it in the Instructor's Manual to the second edition of *Literature* (New York: Macmillan, 1986), p. 47. Gretchen Schulz and J. R. Rockwood also quote it on the opening page of their article "In Fairyland Without a Map: Connie's Exploration Inward in Joyce Carol Oates' 'Where Are You Going, Where Have You Been?'" (*Literature and Psychology* 30 [1978], 155–67); this article is a fanciful explication of "Where Are You Going?" as a modernized witches' brew of popular fairy tales: "Arnold Friend is the Woodcutter as well as the Wolf" (p. 163), and Connie is Snow White (p. 160), Cinderella and Rapunzel (p. 162), as well as Little Red Riding Hood (p. 163). Oates apparently blessed even this interpretation. Schulz says that she asked Oates at the 1976 MLA convention "if the many allusions to various fairy tales in 'Where Are You Going, Where Have You Been?' were intentional" and "She replied that they were" (p. 166, n. 9).

[2]"A Source for 'Where Are You Going, Where Have You Been?'" *Studies in Short Fiction*, 18, No.4 (1981), 413–19. Further citations are in the text.

[3]Oates mentioned this influence in the Knott and Keaske interview when she said that the story came to her "after reading about a killer in some Southwestern state" (p. 18), but the casual nature of this remark does not acknowledge the extent of the author's debt, a fact which Quirk's article makes plain.

[4]"The Stranger Within: Two Stories by Oates and Hawthorne," *Studies in Short Fiction*, 17, No. 3 (1980), 263–68. Further citations are in the text.

[5]"Where Are You Going, Where Have You Been?" in *Classic Short Fiction*, ed. Charles H. Bohner (Englewood Cliffs, NJ: Prentice-Hall, 1986), p. 822. Further citations are in the text.

[6]Marie Mitchell Olesen Urbanski also treats the story as an allegory in "Existential Allegory: Joyce Carol Oates's 'Where Are You Going Where Have You Been?'" (*Studies in Short Fiction*, 15, No. 2 [1978], 200–203), and Christina Marsden Gillis refers to "elements of fairy tale and dream" (p. 65) in "'Where Are You Going, Where Have You Been?': Seduction, Space, and a Fictional Mode" (*Studies in Short Fiction*, 18, No. 1[1981], 65–70).

LAURA KALPAKIAN

from a review of Where Are You Going, Where Have You Been?: Selected Early Stories*

In acknowledging her range, one must celebrate Ms. Oates's bravery. Range requires courage—and always did, though people perpetually insist things are worse now than they were thirty years ago. In any event and for a wide variety of reasons, current American literature seems self-consciously picketed off, writers hunkered over thimble-sized garden plots, No Trespassing signs stuck about tiny terrains of age or race, region, religion, gender, sexual persuasion, politics, each writer farming a tiny furrow: the pen as plow. Joyce Carol Oates, as these early stories [from the collection *Where Are You Going, Where Have You Been?: Selected Early Stories*] testify, has always declined to be pinned down to her plot, has kicked down the fences. She writes about the rich and poor, urban and rural, black and white, the literate, the tongue-tied, young and old, the primly conventional, the drugged, delinquent, and debilitated. They're all here. Moreover, they're cast out of the comfy old narrative conventions and into structures which demand more from the reader.

Given Ms. Oates's range of structure, character, and voice, we might ask ourselves what unites these pieces. Poured, all of them, into a vial, shaken, what might rise to the top? Drastic acts with drastic consequences, severed connections, doomed love, destructive sex, fear, evil, madness—but not much guilt. Oates's characters all twist about on short tethers, whatever the differences in their worldly circumstances. More often than not a single act or choice or instant plummets these characters not merely into the depths of despair, but into depravity and destruction. In "Upon the Sweeping Flood" (1966), we meet a complacent, well-to-do family man driving home from his father's funeral. Caught in a hurricane, he refuses to obey an order to evacuate and plunges into the maelstrom, thrust finally into the company of two unnamed, abandoned white-trash kids, a boy and a girl. The three survive the night, but in the morning the boy dies at the hands of this man who then lunges toward the girl—he can "already see himself grappling with her in the mud, forcing her down, tearing her ugly clothing from her body"—just as a rescue boat heaves into view. "Save me! Save me!" cries yesterday's prosperous bourgeois and today's murderer.

In the ironically titled "Love and Death" (1972), an equally short distance separates a man (again comfortable, conventional, unloved, and unflappable) from a previously unthinkable fate. Visiting his infirm father, he meets a prostitute he slept with years before, as a young man. Their versions of the past are different; hers is correct. Though he returns to his manicured life, the chance encounter evolves into an obsession, sucking him into abasement and humiliation.

The Southern Review 29.4 (Autumn1993): 802–08. Print.

At the conclusion of "In the Warehouse" (1973), the narrator tells us of her tidy married life in "a colonial house on a lane of colonial houses called Meadowbrook Lane." But as a twelve-year-old, she was bullied about by a stronger girl named Ronnie whose toughness sprung from a sort of delinquent passion and unfocused unhappiness. The narrator was completely cowed by Ronnie: "I have never thought about liking Ronnie. I have no choice. She has never given me the privilege of liking or disliking her and if she knew I was thinking such a thought, she would yank my hair out of my head." As the girls prowled the darkened loft of a deserted warehouse, Ronnie urged the narrator up the stairs, ordering, "Do it! Do it!" Atop the loft, the narrator pushed Ronnie, who was impaled on the machinery below and died in a pool of blood. The sleepy narrator then went home, went to bed. Eventually, she "[grew] out of the skinny little body that knocked the clumsy body down—and I have never felt sorry. Never any guilt."

5   The Joyce Carol Oates of these early stories believes that evil lurks everywhere, even in the sunniest lives, the ostensibly to-be-envied lives. The knowledge of this evil defines character for Oates—or, more to the point, the individual's reaction to this knowledge defines character. Oates cares nothing for justice, nor judgment, nor Christian virtue and Christian wickedness. There are only two possible responses to the darkness. One reaction is the murderer's cry, "Save me! Save me!", the wail of inescapable horror, the wish to be delivered. But there is no deliverance and there is no salvation. The narrator of "In the Warehouse" expresses for Oates the other possible reaction: "Never any guilt." She waits patiently to feel guilt for Ronnie's murder; but guilt, like a missed train, never arrives. In Oates's moral lexicon, the word "retribution" does not exist, nor "punishment," nor even anything so personal as "revenge." Evil is an impersonal, inescapable fact in every life. The central recognition of adulthood—no matter how old or young the character—is the recognition of this evil.

So omnipresent are the evil acts and consequences that Oates's characters seem often to be less created than enslaved by narrative: allegorical figures painted against realistic sunshine. In the title piece, "Where Are You Going, Where Have You Been?" (1970), for instance, there is a struggle between the menacing and cajoling Arnold Friend and the pubescent Connie. In the end Connie is, apparently, raped (in the Afterword Oates calls her "the presumably doomed Connie"). But Connie seems, despite the carefully drawn settings—shopping malls, drive-in restaurants, backyard barbecues—less a character than a cipher. She has no volition, no choices, and therefore it's hard to see her even as a victim. Instead, she suggests in her helplessness the awful inequalities of sex and power and violence. . . .

Emphatically in the stories in this volume, character and landscape serve the narrative rather than vice versa. Moreover, Joyce Carol Oates does not stoop to authorial pleading; she is neither pseudomaternal toward her characters nor pseudo-avuncular toward the reader, and she never importunes us with the unspoken: Please care for these characters. And, though the seasons are always noted and the geographical details of settings are always provided (including the oft-mentioned Detroit and its suburbs, as well as Erie County, New York), landscape in Oates's work seems dreamy, monochromatic, and unrealized—landscape as Tim Burton sometimes uses it in his movies. We may care about these characters or not, as we wish, but we are compelled by vigorous narrative through essentially indifferent landscapes. . . .

In Oates's stories there are no safe relationships, but the most perilous of all possibilities is sex. Sex is always destructive. In "Accomplished Desires" (1970), a two-edged narrative recounts the collision (and collusion) of two women: one a pretty college girl, vacuous but orderly, the other an accomplished woman poet married to a bullying professor. The wife is a prisoner in the upper reaches of her rented home; defeated by her home life, her three children, her inability to write, she drinks and looks out the high window. The smarmy husband not only beds the student but installs her as his secretary and housekeeper and moves her into his home to keep his life in order. According to the husband, this young woman "gets herself pregnant. On purpose." Because sages concerned with the state of modern literature await the professor's lecture at a meeting on the West Coast, the wife drives the student to an appointment with an abortionist. The women strike up a tentative, unspoken alliance (though not against the man, as we might have thought—or hoped). Indeed, the wife bows out of the struggle altogether, almost gracefully: a quiet overdose self-administered in a hotel room. The pretty former student, new wife—now, suddenly, a mother of four—finds herself prisoner in the upper reaches of the rented house, without the consolations of company or poetry or even gin.

Communication—especially sexual communication—is not only baffling and treacherous for Oates's characters; it often seems impossible. My personal favorite in this collection, "Translation" (1977), describes a middle-aged American academic who makes an official visit to an unnamed Central European country and is provided with a translator, Liebert. At a dreary communist cocktail party the American, Oliver, meets a woman whose beauty and fragility strike him to the very heart. He falls in love though he cannot even pronounce her name: "Alisa was as close as he could come to it." Oliver is euphoric, intoxicated, as he spends a memorable evening with her in a cafe (Liebert translating) where they speak of literature, politics, passion, history, and love. Oliver feels himself buoyed, enfolded, welcomed in a country where, in effect, he is a mute. The following day Liebert discreetly suggests that Alisa's roommate could be persuaded to leave overnight if she had train fare, which Oliver provides. But on the morning of the intended assignation, Oliver discovers he has been given a new translator. No explanations offered. No questions answered. This new man—obscene in every way—talks of the weather, smirks lewdly, arranges another cafe date with Alisa that evening. Through the new translator, Alisa inquires after Oliver's life in America, his financial assets, his cars, his wife. She eyeballs his watch. As Oliver leaves the country the next day, desperate for Liebert, he cries, "What shall I do for the rest of my life . . . ?"

No doubt the young and gifted writer of these stories found herself facing that same question. The dust-jacket photo for these selected early stories shows Ms. Oates circa 1965, her hair in the "flip" fashionable in that era, shoulders framed by a boat-necked dress. She regards the reader with the serene gaze of a high-school valedictorian. Not at all the look of a woman who willingly, knowingly smashes up the conventions of narrative. She does not look like the author who will unmask the evil of everyday life, who will see allegory in the backyard and real darkness among the metaphoric daisies. But she is.

10

LARRY RUBIN

Oates's "Where Are You Going, Where Have You Been?"*

In a recent essay Joyce M. Wegs brilliantly establishes the satanic identity of the sinister Arnold Friend, young Connie's abductor and probable rapist-murderer in Joyce Carol Oates's widely anthologized short story "Where Are You Going, Where Have You Been?"[1] On another level, the psychological level, she points out that Arnold is "the incarnation of Connie's unconscious erotic desires and dreams, but in uncontrollable nightmare form."[2] I would go a step further and suggest that, on still another level, the whole terrifying episode involving Arnold Friend is itself a dream—a fantasy that Connie falls into on a sleepy Sunday afternoon when she is left alone in the house and decides to spend the entire day drying her hair.[3] For those of her readers who don't believe in devils, Oates has made the willing suspension of disbelief somewhat easier by imparting to her story a dreamlike, unreal atmosphere that makes it possible for the reader to view Connie's scary encounter with Arnold as a dream-vision or "daymare"—one in which Connie's intense desire for total sexual experience runs headlong into her innate fear of such experience.[4] We must remember that Connie is only fifteen; and the collision is gorgeous.

First of all, for all the talk of sex and boys in the story, we have no clear evidence that Connie is not still a virgin. Sophisticated, yes—but only in the most superficial ways, involving the heightening of her physical charms. Even the brief time Connie spends with a boy named Eddie in an alley[5] seems, in context, more in keeping with smooching or even heavy petting than with triple-x sex. Indeed, her horror at Arnold Friend's direct solicitation ("I'll come inside you where it's all secret and you'll give in to me and you'll love me—" [p. 47]) would appear to be owing to her basic lack of full sexual experience. In the repeated references to rock music in the shopping center she frequents and on the radio, both in Arnold's car and her own house, we find a powerful source of erotic suggestion and of Connie's intensified teen-age hungers, true; but nowhere are we given to feel that she is a fully experienced woman. Rather, we experience her as a somewhat childish and silly narcissistic adolescent, one who feels put down by her more mature older sister (a librarian, and a perfect foil to Connie in her primness) and by her mother, who accuses her of "trashy daydreams" (p. 35). Actually, the trashy daydream involving Arnold may, in a sense, have a certain sobering effect on her frivolousness. Like Dante's dream-vision of Hell, it might improve the situation.

But such speculation begs the question, which is, *Is* it all a daydream? The first clue that we get that it *is* comes even before the Arnold Friend episode, when Oates tells us: "But all the boys fell back and dissolved into a single face that was not even a face but an idea, a feeling, mixed up with the urgent insistent pounding of the music and the humid night air of July" (p. 38). As we shall see, that music provides a key

---

Explicator 42.4 (1984): 57–60. Print.

link between her daydreams and their materialization in Arnold Friend. But first we have another important clue, in Connie's languid dreaminess when she is left alone in the house on that fateful, hot summer afternooon: "Connie sat with her eyes closed in the sun, dreaming and dazed with the warmth about her as if this were a kind of love, the caresses of 'love'. . . . She shook her head as if to get awake" (p. 39). Because it is so hot she goes inside and, sitting on the edge of her bed [N.B.], listens for an hour and a half to rock songs on the radio, "bathed in a glow of slow-pulsed joy that seemed to rise mysteriously out of the music itself and lay languidly about the airless little room, breathed in and out with each gentle rise and fall of her chest" (p. 39). At this point Oates starts a new paragraph to tell us that "After a while she heard a car coming up the drive" (p. 39). This is Arnold driving up, just when the author has described certain physiological sounds and motions that sound suspiciously like those of sleep.

If Arnold is indeed the devil—and he may well be, on the level so perspicaciously analyzed by Joyce Wegs—he is certainly a comical one, with his wig, incompletely made-up face, stuffed boots, and stumbling gait. In the *threat* he represents to Connie, of course, he is indeed a figure of evil, but with all this fakery, what Oates seems to be showing us is the absurd emptiness and falseness of sexual fulfillment. Connie fears she will be destroyed by Arnold, and the critics (like Wegs) have concentrated on the immediate level of *physical* death; what makes the story so rich, it seems to me, is the possibility of seeing her pending destruction as a *moral* phenomenon. Her compulsive sex drive will destroy her, Oates seems to tell us, but not simply physically (which, if that were all there were to it, would make the story merely a luscious gumdrop for gothic horror fans). It is the potential destruction of Connie as a *person*, on a humanistic level, that is the real source of power in this story, and it is through the protagonist's daydream of fearful sexual fulfillment that this horror is conveyed.

The fact that Connie recognizes the sensual music being broadcast on Arnold's car radio as being the same as that emanating from her own in the house (p. 41) provides another strong clue to his real nature—that of a dream-like projection of her erotic fantasies. His music and hers, Oates tells us, blend perfectly (p. 44), and indeed Arnold's voice is perceived by Connie as being the same as that of the disc jockey on the radio (p. 46). Thus the protagonist's inner state of consciousness is being given physical form by her imagination. We should recall that Connie's initial response to her first view of Arnold the night before, in the shopping center, was one of intense sexual excitement (p. 42); now she discovers how dangerous that excitement can be to her survival as a person. Instinctively she recoils; but the conflict between excitement and desire, on the one hand, and fear, on the other, leaves her will paralyzed, and she cannot even dial the phone for help (p. 52). Such physical paralysis in the face of oncoming danger is a phenomenon familiar to all dreamers, like being unable to run from the monster because your legs won't respond to your will.

Finally, the rather un-devil-like tribute that Arnold pays Connie as she finally succumbs to his threats against her family and goes out of the house to him—". . . you're better than them [her family] because not a one of them would have done this for you" (p. 53)—is exactly what poor, unappreciated Connie wants to hear. She is making a noble sacrifice, and in her dream she gives herself full credit for it.

The episode with Arnold Friend, then, may be viewed as the vehicle for fulfillment of Connie's deep-rooted desire for ultimate sexual gratification, a fearsome business which, for the uninitiated female, may involve destruction of the person. Unsophisticated as she is, Connie's subconscious is aware of this danger, and her dream conveys this conflict. Thus, Oates's achievement in this story lies in her ability to convey all these subtleties while still creating the illusion of a real-life experience.

Notes

[1] Joyce M. Wegs, "'Don't You Know Who I Am?' The Grotesque in Oates's 'Where Are You Going, Where Have You Been?'" in *Critical Essays on Joyce Carol Oates*, ed. Linda W. Wagner (Boston: G. K. Hall & Co., 1979), pp. 87–92. See also Joan D. Winslow, "The Stranger Within: Two Stories by Oates and Hawthorne," *Studies in Short Fiction*, 17 (1980), 263–68.

[2] Wegs, *Critical Essays*, p. 90.

[3] Winslow (*Stranger Within*, pp. 267–68), considers briefly the possibility of the Arnold Friend episode's being interpreted as a dream but focuses primarily on other similarities between Oates' story and Hawthorne's "Young Goodman Brown."

[4] Winslow (pp. 265–66) also discusses the virginal Connie's fear of total sexual experience.

[5] Joyce Carol Oates, "Where Are You Going, Where Have You Been?" in *The Wheel of Love and Other Stories* (New York: The Vanguard Press, 1970), p. 37. All subsequent references to the story are to this edition.

PETER DICKINSON

from Riding in Cars with Boys: Reconsidering *Smooth Talk**

Several critics have noted the importance of automobiles in both Oates's story and Chopra's film, that Connie, for example, "is always at the mercy of men who will come with a vehicle to take her away, to take her somewhere else" (Showalter 17), and that a car's "mobility is equated with sexual freedom for Connie" (Sumner 93–94). But few have actually tracked the various narrative and symbolic patterns established by the successive car rides Connie accepts from men in the film, nor made any serious attempt to link those patterns to a larger meta-analysis of female psycho-sexual development that Chopra might be embedding beneath the realist representations of her film. And yet, surely this is what we are invited to do from the opening sequence of the film, when Connie and her girlfriends accept a lift from an older man in a pick-up, a car ride that is bracketed syntagmatically by the driver's leering invitation to Jill to play him some tunes and his equally knowing thanking of all the girls, once he drops them off, for sharing their music with him. During this first car ride, Connie is crucially distanced from her friends via her position in the back of the pick-up. We clearly see her thrilling to the open air and the speed, raising her arms and whooping as the pick-up crosses a bridge, the first of several threshold images (including the road that separates the mall from Frank's Diner, the aforementioned screen door that separates Connie from Arnold, and so on) that recur throughout the film, all of which Connie will eventually cross.

Literature Film Quarterly 36.3 (2008): 208–14. Print.

Not long after this scene, following the debacle of the family dinner of tuna salad, Connie lingers outside the Wyatt house with her father, colluding in part over the fact that they are both in the doghouse with Mrs. Wyatt. Gazing at the stars, Connie sighs: "I can't wait till I'm old enough to drive." The car, which at this point Connie must rely on others to both provide and drive, is the literal means of escape from what she sees as the impossibly staid and dull existence of her suburban mom. But, as importantly, the car, as a ubiquitous symbol of sexual desire and fulfillment in North American pop culture, and when viewed explicitly through the lens of Freudian drive theory, binds Connie, in her primary narcissistic, or Oedipal, phase of ego formation, to her father, toward whom her id is instinctually, or unconsciously, channeling its libidinal energy.[1] Indeed, my argument for a more complex, psychological reading of Chopra's film rests, fundamentally, on the fact that each of the four ensuing rides Connie accepts in cars driven by men (I am purposefully excluding from this analysis the rides she takes in cars that are driven by the mothers of Laura or Jill) can be read as a stage in Connie's "object-cathexis," that is, what Freud would describe as the transferring of her libido from her father onto an external love object, which, through the necessary work of sublimation, succeeds in strengthening the ego, but which also, in giving birth to the super-ego, puts the sex drive on a possible collision course with the death drive (see Freud, *The Ego* 55–59).[2]

We see the start of this process in Connie's encounter with Jeff (William Ragsdale), the first of the boys she meets at Frank's Diner. Together they drive to a cliff-top lookout, where Connie repeats her longing to escape; but this time flight via an automobile is very explicitly associated with sex, as after uttering this line she leans in for a kiss with Jeff. However, death is never far away, for just prior to her departure from the restaurant with Jeff, Connie (unwittingly to her at the time) first encounters Arnold in the parking lot. Leaning against his car, he stops her short by saying "I'm watching you," then points his finger at her and makes a mysterious figure-eight sign in the air. This alerts us to the fact that from this point on, the car rides that Connie takes with men are going to be increasingly dangerous for her, both in terms of the potential consequences if she acts on her desires and, as importantly, if she does not act on those of her male companions. This is certainly the case with Eddie, the second of the boys Connie meets at Frank's, and with whom she ends up making out in an underground parking lot. There are no lovely vistas here, only anonymous concrete, and Eddie has only one thing on his mind. His almost-seduction of Connie—who tells him to stop because she is enjoying it too much—is one of the most erotically charged scenes in the film, and while he chivalrously accedes to Connie's sublimation of the goals of her "Object-libido" within those of her "ego-libido" (Freud, *Beyond* 59–60), thereby allowing her to preserve her virtue, the threat of sexual violence again frames the whole encounter. In particular, back at Frank's Diner, prior to going parking, Eddie threatens, only half-jokingly it appears, to give Connie "a fat lip" if she does not behave herself. And then on the long walk home after her date with Eddie, and Laura's parents' discovery of what the girls have been up to, Connie is passed on the road by a group of rowdy boys in a Mustang, who clearly hurl some offensive sexual taunts at her.

However, of even greater importance, I would argue, is the fact that Connie's second visit to Frank's Diner, and her subsequent sexual encounter with Eddie, are preceded by her nervous declaration to Laura that she may have seen her father drive by just as they were crossing the highway to go to the hamburger joint. As Freud writes of the special prohibitive nature of the super-ego in *The Ego and the Id*, it "retains the character of the father, while the more powerful the Oedipus complex was and the more rapidly it succumbed to repression [. . .] the stricter the domination of the super-ego over the ego later on—in the form of conscience or perhaps of an unconscious sense of guilt" (34–35). Sure enough, the next car ride Connie takes in the film, and the one that immediately precedes her climactic journey with Arnold, is with her father. Following her fight with her mother the next morning, Mr. Wyatt asks Connie to accompany him to the store to get charcoal briquettes for the barbecue at Aunt Til-lie's. Connie complains that she is still in her nightgown, but her father persuades her that she will not have to get out of the car. This detail is important, because symboli-cally it associates Connie with the dream-like space of sleep, or the fuzzy, disorienting realm of not-quite-waking. Just as important psychologically and imagistically, the representation of this child-woman (at once a little girl still in her nightie and a fully developed sexual being who should perhaps be more discreet in covering herself up) sharing the front seat of the car with her father inextricably links Connie's sexuality with her still in flux object-relations within the Wyatt family romance. In this regard, we get confirmation in this scene that Connie's father did in fact see her crossing the road to Frank's the night before, information that the two become complicit in keep-ing from Connie's mother. Viewed within the framework of Freudian psychoanalysis, what we are witnessing here is Connie's struggle, during the latency period of her psy-chosexual development, to cathect° herself from her father, transferring her primary identification to another love-object, and internalizing within her emergent super-ego the future force of his possible displeasure with her (see Freud, *The Ego* 29–31 and ff). Indeed, Oates herself has commented that one of the things she liked best about Chopra's adaptation was the subtext of "Connie's ambiguous relationship with her affable, somewhat mysterious father" that the director succeeded in bringing out from the story: "I had thought, subsequent to the story's publication, that I should have built up the father, suggesting, as subtly as I could, an attraction there paralleling the attraction Connie feels for her seducer, Arnold Friend" (*[Woman] Writer* 319).

5   And it is, of course, Arnold who steps into the emotional and psychological void consequent to this transitional phase in Connie's development, when her ego defenses are not yet fully formed and she is wont to confuse the competing pulls of the sex and death drives as each attempts to gain control of her libido. The car ride with her father still fresh in both Connie's and viewers' imaginations, Arnold's unex-pected arrival in his own wheels of fortune intrudes upon our respective unconscious desires. Love-object or agent of destruction? Friend or foe? We, like Connie, are ini-tially unable to read the screen Arnold's intentions (especially as charmingly played by Treat Williams) in part because cinema operates on the same pleasure principle as the id, mitigating to a degree any reaction formations we may erect to counter its seductive and soporific° effects. Chopra, I would argue, is aware of this. When Con-nie gets in the car with Arnold, we go with her. When the camera comes to rest on

---

° *cathact:* To emotionally detach.

° *soporific:* Sleep inducing.

the shiny grille of Arnold's car parked in the sunlit field described above, we cannot look away. And it is my contention that the film, in necessarily inviting us to project onto this scene an image of the very real sexual violence that is presumably occurring off-screen, is also projecting, through the image of the car—at once a love machine and a death-mobile—its own quasi-allegorization of the psychological violence that attends the dissolution of the Oedipus complex and the adolescent ego's consequent reorganization of its object-choices and identifications. As Arnold puts it to Connie in both the story and the film, "The place where you came from ain't there any more, and where you had in mind to go is cancelled out. This place you are now—inside your daddy's house—is nothing but a cardboard box I can knock down any time. You know that and always did know it" (Oates, "Where" 29).

Notes
[1]Freud develops and elaborates his theory of the drives—or "instincts"—as they structure the unconscious and the ego in most sustained terms in the following four works: *Three Essays on the Theory of Sexuality* (1905);" On Narcissism" (1914); *Beyond the Pleasure Principle* (1920); and *The Ego and the Id* (1923).

[2]While Marilyn C. Wesley has convincingly used Freudian theory to examine what she calls "the totality of Joyce Carol Oates's family fiction" (10) including "Where Are You Going, Where Have You Been?" no one has yet done the same to Chopra's film.

Works Cited

Freud. Sigmund. *Beyond the Pleasure Principle*. Vol. 18 of *The Standard Edition of the Complete Psycho-logical Works of Sigmund Freud*, 24 vols. Trans, and ed, James Starchy. London Hogarth, 1943 74. 1–64.

———, *The Ego and the Id* Vol. 19 of *The Standard Edition of the Complete Psychological Works of Sigmund Freud*. 1–66.

Oates, Joyce Carol. "Where Are You Going, Where Have You Been?" *Where Are You Going, Where Have You Been? Stories of Young America*. Greenwich Fawcett, 1974. 11–31.

———, "'Where Are You Going, Where Have You Been?' and *Smooth Talk*. Short Story into Film." *(Women) Writer: Occasion and Opportunities*. New York: Dutton, 1988. 316–21.

Showalter, Elaine. Introduction. *Where Are You Going, Where Have You Been?* Ed. Showalter. New Brunswick: Rutgers UP, 1995, 3–20.

Sumner, Rebecca. "Smoothing Out the Rough Spots: The Film Adaptation of 'Where Are You Going, Where Have You Been?'" *Vision /Re Vision Adapting Contemporary American Fiction by Women to Film*. Ed. Barbara Tepa Lupack. Bowling Green: Bowling Green State U Popular P, 1996. 85–100. (*Literature Film Quarterly* 36.3 (2008): 208–14)

Topics for Further Research

1. After consulting Bruno Bettelheim's classic book *The Uses of Enchantment* (as well as the other sources in this casebook) and after reading "Little Red Riding Hood" (p. 526) and "The Pied Piper of Hamelin" (p. 525), write an essay in which you consider the impor-tance of fairy tales in the story.

2. In her article "When Characters from the Page Are Made Flesh on the Screen" (p. 518), Oates refers to her use of "realistic allegory" as a mode of fiction that is

"Hawthornian . . . shading into parable" (par. 4). Research Hawthorne's views on allegory by reading some of his many essays on the subject, such as "The Custom House." Then, write an essay in which you consider how "Where Are You Going, Where Have You Been?" might be compared to Hawthorne's stories, such as "Young Goodman Brown" (p. 448), in terms of its portrayal of good, evil, and innocence. Try to identify elements in Oates's story that might be considered allegorical in the Hawthornian sense.

3. Oates has been described as a modern realist, and she herself has used the term "psychological realism" to describe her work. Research the history and emergence of literary realism in American literature. What elements of realism as it first appeared in literature at the end of the nineteenth century and the beginning of the twentieth century are found in Oates's work?

4. Critics often see Oates's short stories as gothic. Research the term *gothic* as it applies to works of literature. Then, write an essay in which you make the case for three of her stories, including "Where Are You Going, Where Have You Been?" and "Heat" (p. 603), as gothic works. You may also wish to discuss gothic stories by other writers—for example, Poe's "The Cask of Amontillado" (p. 328) and Flannery O'Connor's "A Good Man Is Hard to Find" (p. 367).

5. In the excerpt from her book review included in this casebook (p. 533) critic Laura Kalpakian takes a look at some of the themes of Oates's works as they are represented by her characters. Do some research to find out what other critics and reviewers have identified as recurring themes in Oates's work. Then, choose one of these themes, and write an essay discussing how three characters in Oates's stories illustrate the theme you have chosen.

6. Read some reviews of the 1985 film *Smooth Talk*, which was based on "Where Are You Going, Where Have You Been?" Do critics seem to agree with one or more of the critical interpretations of the character Arnold Friend presented in the sources in this casebook? Write an essay in which you examine whether critics seem to agree on how to "read" Arnold or whether there are widely divergent opinions about the character.

CHAPTER 21

FICTION FOR FURTHER READING

CHINUA ACHEBE (1930–2013)

Dead Man's Path (1953) (1972)

Michael Obi's hopes were fulfilled much earlier than he had expected. He was appointed headmaster of Ndume Central School in January 1949. It had always been an unprogressive school, so the Mission authorities decided to send a young and energetic man to run it. Obi accepted this responsibility with enthusiasm. He had many wonderful ideas and this was an opportunity to put them into practice. He had had sound secondary school education which designated him a "pivotal teacher" in the official records and set him apart from the other headmasters in the mission field. He was outspoken in his condemnation of the narrow views of these older and often less-educated ones.

"We shall make a good job of it, shan't we?" he asked his young wife when they first heard the joyful news of his promotion.

"We shall do our best," she replied. "We shall have such beautiful gardens and everything will be just *modern* and delightful . . ." In their two years of married life she had become completely infected by his passion for "modern methods" and his denigration of "these old and superannuated people in the teaching field who would be better employed as traders in the Onitsha market." She began to see herself already as the admired wife of the young headmaster, the queen of the school.

The wives of the other teachers would envy her position. She would set the fashion in everything . . . Then, suddenly, it occurred to her that there might not be other wives. Wavering between hope and fear, she asked her husband, looking anxiously at him.

"All our colleagues are young and unmarried," he said with enthusiasm which for once she did not share. "Which is a good thing," he continued.

"Why?"

"Why? They will give all their time and energy to the school."

Nancy was downcast. For a few minutes she became skeptical about the new school; but it was only for a few minutes. Her little personal misfortune could not blind her to her husband's happy prospects. She looked at him as he sat folded up in a chair. He was stoop-shouldered and looked frail. But he sometimes surprised people

5

with sudden bursts of physical energy. In his present posture, however, all his bodily strength seemed to have retired behind his deep-set eyes, giving them an extraordinary power of penetration. He was only twenty-six, but looked thirty or more. On the whole, he was not unhandsome.

"A penny for your thoughts, Mike," said Nancy after a while, imitating the woman's magazine she read.

10 "I was thinking what a grand opportunity we've got at last to show these people how a school should be run."

Ndume School was backward in every sense of the word. Mr. Obi put his whole life into the work, and his wife hers too. He had two aims. A high standard of teaching was insisted upon, and the school compound was to be turned into a place of beauty. Nancy's dream-gardens came to life with the coming of the rains, and blossomed. Beautiful hibiscus and allamanda hedges in brilliant red and yellow marked out the carefully tended school compound from the rank neighbor-hood bushes.

One evening as Obi was admiring his work he was scandalized to see an old woman from the village hobble right across the compound, through a marigold flower-bed and the hedges. On going up there he found faint signs of an almost disused path from the village across the school compound to the bush on the other side.

"It amazes me," said Obi to one of his teachers who had been three years in the school, "that you people allowed the villagers to make use of this footpath. It is simply incredible." He shook his head.

"The path," said the teacher apologetically, "appears to be very important to them. Although it is hardly used, it connects the village shrine with their place of burial."

15 "And what has that got to do with the school?" asked the headmaster.

"Well, I don't know," replied the other with a shrug of the shoulders. "But I remember there was a big row some time ago when we attempted to close it."

"That was some time ago. But it will not be used now," said Obi as he walked away. "What will the Government Education Officer think of this when he comes to inspect the school next week? The villagers might, for all I know, decide to use the schoolroom for pagan ritual during the inspection."

Heavy sticks were planted closely across the path at the two places where it entered and left the school premises. These were further strengthened with barbed wire.

Three days later the village priest of *Ani* called on the headmaster. He was an old man and walked with a slight stoop. He carried a stout walking-stick which he usually tapped on the floor, by way of emphasis, each time he made a new point in his argument.

20 "I have heard," he said after the usual exchange of cordialities, "that our ancestral footpath has recently been closed . . ."

"Yes," replied Mr. Obi. "We cannot allow people to make a highway of our school compound."

"Look here, my son," said the priest bringing down his walking-stick, "this path was here before you were born and before your father was born. The whole life of this village depends on it. Our dead relatives depart by it and our ancestors visit us by it. But most important, it is the path of children coming in to be born . . ."

Mr. Obi listened with a satisfied smile on his face.

"The whole purpose of our school," he said finally, "is to eradicate just such beliefs as that. Dead men do not require footpaths. The whole idea is just fantastic. Our duty is to teach your children to laugh at such ideas."

"What you say may be true," replied the priest, "but we follow the practices of our fathers. If you reopen the path we shall have nothing to quarrel about. What I always say is let the hawk perch and let the eagle perch." He rose to go.

25

"I am sorry," said the young headmaster. "But the school compound cannot be a thoroughfare. It is against our regulations. I would suggest your constructing another path, skirting our premises. We can even get our boys to help in building it. I don't suppose the ancestors will find the little detour too burdensome."

"I have no more words to say," said the old priest, already outside.

Two days later a young woman in the village died in childbed. A diviner was immediately consulted and he prescribed heavy sacrifices to propitiate ancestors insulted by the fence.

Obi woke up next morning among the ruins of his work. The beautiful hedges were torn up not just near the path but right round the school, the flowers trampled to death and one of the school buildings pulled down . . . That day, the white Supervisor came to inspect the school and wrote a nasty report on the state of the premises but more seriously about the "tribal-war situation developing between the school and the village, arising in part from the misguided zeal of the new headmaster."

MARGARET ATWOOD (1939–)

Happy Endings (1983)

John and Mary meet.
What happens next?
If you want a happy ending, try A.

A. John and Mary fall in love and get married. They both have worthwhile and remunerative jobs which they find stimulating and challenging. They buy a charming house. Real estate values go up. Eventually, when they can afford live-in help, they have two children, to whom they are devoted. The children turn out well. John and Mary have a stimulating and challenging sex life and worthwhile friends. They go on fun vacations together. They retire. They both have hobbies which they find stimulating and challenging. Eventually they die. This is the end of the story.

B. Mary falls in love with John but John doesn't fall in love with Mary. He merely uses her body for selfish pleasure and ego gratification of a tepid kind. He comes to her apartment twice a week and she cooks him dinner, you'll notice that he doesn't even consider her worth the price of a dinner out, and after he's eaten the dinner he fucks her and after that he falls asleep, while she does the dishes so he won't think she's untidy, having all those dirty dishes lying around, and puts

5

on fresh lipstick so she'll look good when he wakes up, but when he wakes up he doesn't even notice, he puts on his socks and his shorts and his pants and his shirt and his tie and his shoes, the reverse order from the one in which he took them off. He doesn't take off Mary's clothes, she takes them off herself, she acts as if she's dying for it every time, not because she likes sex exactly, she doesn't, but she wants John to think she does because if they do it often enough surely he'll get used to her, he'll come to depend on her and they will get married, but John goes out the door with hardly so much as a good-night and three days later he turns up at six o'clock and they do the whole thing over again.

Mary gets run-down. Crying is bad for your face, everyone knows that and so does Mary but she can't stop. People at work notice. Her friends tell her John is a rat, a pig, a dog, he isn't good enough for her, but she can't believe it. Inside John, she thinks, is another John, who is much nicer. This other John will emerge like a butterfly from a cocoon, a Jack from a box, a pit from a prune, if the first John is only squeezed enough.

One evening John complains about the food. He has never complained about the food before. Mary is hurt.

Her friends tell her they've seen him in a restaurant with another woman, whose name is Madge. It's not even Madge that finally gets to Mary: it's the restaurant. John has never taken Mary to a restaurant. Mary collects all the sleeping pills and aspirins she can find, and takes them and a half a bottle of sherry. You can see what kind of a woman she is by the fact that it's not even whiskey. She leaves a note for John. She hopes he'll discover her and get her to the hospital in time and repent and then they can get married, but this fails to happen and she dies.

John marries Madge and everything continues as in A.

10   C. John, who is an older man, falls in love with Mary, and Mary, who is only twenty-two, feels sorry for him because he's worried about his hair falling out. She sleeps with him even though she's not in love with him. She met him at work. She's in love with someone called James, who is twenty-two also and not yet ready to settle down.

John on the contrary settled down long ago: this is what is bothering him. John has a steady, respectable job and is getting ahead in his field, but Mary isn't impressed by him, she's impressed by James, who has a motorcycle and a fabulous record collection. But James is often away on his motorcycle, being free. Freedom isn't the same for girls, so in the meantime Mary spends Thursday evenings with John. Thursdays are the only days John can get away.

John is married to a woman called Madge and they have two children, a charming house which they bought just before the real estate values went up, and hobbies which they find stimulating and challenging, when they have the time. John tells Mary how important she is to him, but of course he can't leave his wife because a commitment is a commitment. He goes on about this more than is necessary and Mary finds it boring, but older men can keep it up longer so on the whole she has a fairly good time.

One day James breezes in on his motorcycle with some top-grade California hybrid and James and Mary get higher than you'd believe possible and they climb into bed. Everything becomes very underwater, but along comes John, who has a key to Mary's apartment. He finds them stoned and entwined. He's hardly in any position to be jealous, considering Madge, but nevertheless he's overcome with despair. Finally he's middle-aged, in two years he'll be bald as an egg and he can't stand it. He purchases a handgun, saying he needs it for target practice—this is the thin part of the plot, but it can be dealt with later—and shoots the two of them and himself.

Madge, after a suitable period of mourning, marries an understanding man called Fred and everything continues as in A, but under different names.

D. Fred and Madge have no problems. They get along exceptionally well and are good at working out any little difficulties that may arise. But their charming house is by the seashore and one day a giant tidal wave approaches. Real estate values go down. The rest of the story is about what caused the tidal wave and how they escape from it. They do, though thousands drown, but Fred and Madge are virtuous and lucky. Finally on high ground they clasp each other, wet and dripping and grateful, and continue as in A. | 15

E. Yes, but Fred has a bad heart. The rest of the story is about how kind and understanding they both are until Fred dies. Then Madge devotes herself to charity work until the end of A. If you like, it can be "Madge," "cancer," "guilty and confused," and "bird watching."

F. If you think this is all too bourgeois, make John a revolutionary and Mary a counterespionage agent and see how far that gets you. Remember, this is Canada. You'll still end up with A, though in between you may get a lustful brawling saga of passionate involvement, a chronicle of our times, sort of.

You'll have to face it, the endings are the same however you slice it. Don't be deluded by any other endings, they're all fake, either deliberately fake, with malicious intent to deceive, or just motivated by excessive optimism if not by downright sentimentality.

The only authentic ending is the one provided here:

John and Mary die. John and Mary die. John and Mary die.

So much for endings. Beginnings are always more fun. True connoisseurs, however, are known to favor the stretch in between, since it's the hardest to do anything with. | 20

That's about all that can be said for plots, which anyway are just one thing after another, a what and a what and a what.

Now try How and Why.

JAMES BALDWIN (1924–1987)

Sonny's Blues (1957)

I read about it in the paper, in the subway, on my way to work. I read it, and I couldn't believe it, and I read it again. Then perhaps I just stared at it, at the newsprint spelling out his name, spelling out the story. I stared at it in the swinging lights of the subway car, and in the faces and bodies of the people, and in my own face, trapped in the darkness which roared outside.

It was not to be believed and I kept telling myself that, as I walked from the subway station to the high school. And at the same time I couldn't doubt it. I was scared, scared for Sonny. He became real to me again. A great block of ice got settled in my belly and kept melting there slowly all day long, while I taught my classes algebra it was a special kind of ice. It kept melting, sending trickles of ice water all up and down my veins, but it never got less. Sometimes it hardened and seemed to expand until I felt my guts were going to come spilling out or that I was going to choke or scream. This would always be at a moment when I was remembering some specific thing Sonny had once said or done.

When he was about as old as the boys in my classes his face had been bright and open, there was a lot of copper in it; and he'd had wonderfully direct brown eyes, and great gentleness and privacy. I wondered what he looked like now. He had been picked up, the evening before, in a raid on an apartment downtown, for peddling and using heroin.

I couldn't believe it: but what I mean by that is that I couldn't find any room for it anywhere inside me. I had kept it outside me for a long time. I hadn't wanted to know. I had had suspicions, but I didn't name them, I kept putting them away. I told myself that Sonny was wild, but he wasn't crazy. And he'd always been a good boy, he hadn't ever turned hard or evil or disrespectful, the way kids can, so quick, so quick, especially in Harlem. I didn't want to believe that I'd ever see my brother going down, coming to nothing, all that light in his face gone out, in the condition I'd already seen so many others. Yet it had happened and here I was, talking about algebra to a lot of boys who might, every one of them for all I knew, be popping off needles every time they went to the head.[1] Maybe it did more for them than algebra could.

5   I was sure that the first time Sonny had ever had horse,[2] he couldn't have been much older than these boys were now. These boys, now, were living as we'd been living then, they were growing up with a rush and their heads bumped abruptly against the low ceiling of their actual possibilities. They were filled with rage. All they really knew were two darknesses, the darkness of their lives, which was now closing in on them, and the darkness of the movies, which had blinded them to that other darkness, and in which they now, vindictively, dreamed, at once more together than they were at any other time, and more alone.

When the last bell rang, the last class ended, I let out my breath. It seemed I'd been holding it for all that time. My clothes were wet—I may have looked as though I'd been sitting in a steam bath, all dressed up, all afternoon. I sat alone in the classroom a long time. I listened to the boys outside, downstairs, shouting and cursing and laughing. Their laughter struck me for perhaps the first time. It was not the joyous laughter which—God knows why—one associates with children. It was mocking and insular, its intent was to denigrate. It was disenchanted, and in this, also, lay the authority of their curses. Perhaps I was listening to them because I was thinking about my brother and in them I heard my brother. And myself.

One boy was whistling a tune, at once very complicated and very simple, it seemed to be pouring out of him as though he were a bird, and it sounded very cool

---

[1] *the head:* Restroom.

[2] *horse:* Heroin.

and moving through all that harsh, bright air, only just holding its own through all those other sounds.

I stood up and walked over to the window and looked down into the courtyard. It was the beginning of the spring and the sap was rising in the boys. A teacher passed through them every now and again, quickly, as though he or she couldn't wait to get out of that courtyard, to get those boys out of their sight and off their minds. I started collecting my stuff. I thought I'd better get home and talk to Isabel.

The courtyard was almost deserted by the time I got downstairs. I saw this boy standing in the shadow of a doorway, looking just like Sonny. I almost called his name. Then I saw that it wasn't Sonny, but somebody we used to know, a boy from around our block. He'd been Sonny's friend. He'd never been mine, having been too young for me, and, anyway, I'd never liked him. And now, even though he was a grown-up man, he still hung around that block, still spent hours on the street corners, was always high and raggy. I used to run into him from time to time and he'd often work around to asking me for a quarter or fifty cents. He always had some real good excuse, too, and I always gave it to him. I don't know why.

But now, abruptly, I hated him. I couldn't stand the way he looked at me, partly   10
like a dog, partly like a cunning child. I wanted to ask him what the hell he was doing in the school courtyard.

He sort of shuffled over to me, and he said, "I see you got the papers. So you already know about it."

"You mean about Sonny? Yes, I already know about it. How come they didn't get you?"

He grinned. It made him repulsive and it also brought to mind what he'd looked like as a kid. "I wasn't there. I stay away from them people."

"Good for you." I offered him a cigarette and I watched him through the smoke. "You come all the way down here just to tell me about Sonny?"

"That's right." He was sort of shaking his head and his eyes looked strange, as   15
though they were about to cross. The bright sun deadened his damp dark brown skin and it made his eyes look yellow and showed up the dirt in his kinked hair. He smelled funky. I moved a little away from him and I said, "Well, thanks. But I already know about it and I got to get home."

"I'll walk you a little ways," he said. We started walking. There were a couple of kids still loitering in the courtyard and one of them said goodnight to me and looked strangely at the boy beside me.

"What're you going to do?" he asked me. "I mean, about Sonny?"

"Look. I haven't seen Sonny for over a year, I'm not sure I'm going to do anything. Anyway, what the hell *can* I do?"

"That's right," he said quickly, "ain't nothing you can do. Can't much help old Sonny no more, I guess."

It was what I was thinking and so it seemed to me he had no right to say it.   20

"I'm surprised at Sonny, though," he went on—he had a funny way of talking, he looked straight ahead as though he were talking to himself—"I thought Sonny was a smart boy, I thought he was too smart to get hung."

"I guess he thought so too," I said sharply, "and that's how he got hung. And how about you? You're pretty goddamn smart, I bet."

Then he looked directly at me, just for a minute. "I ain't smart," he said. "If I was smart, I'd have reached for a pistol a long time ago."

"Look. Don't tell *me* your sad story, if it was up to me, I'd give you one." Then I felt guilty—guilty, probably, for never having supposed that the poor bastard *had* a story of his own, much less a sad one, and I asked, quickly, "What's going to happen to him now?"

25   He didn't answer this. He was off by himself some place.

"Funny thing," he said, and from his tone we might have been discussing the quickest way to get to Brooklyn, "when I saw the papers this morning, the first thing I asked myself was if I had anything to do with it. I felt sort of responsible."

I began to listen more carefully. The subway station was on the corner, just before us, and I stopped. He stopped, too. We were in front of a bar and he ducked slightly, peering in, but whoever he was looking for didn't seem to be there. The juke box was blasting away with something black and bouncy and I half watched the barmaid as she danced her way from the juke box to her place behind the bar. And I watched her face as she laughingly responded to something someone said to her, still keeping time to the music. When she smiled one saw the little girl, one sensed the doomed, still struggling woman beneath the battered face of the semi-whore.

"I never *give* Sonny nothing," the boy said finally, "but a long time ago I come to school high and Sonny asked me how it felt." He paused, I couldn't bear to watch him, I watched the barmaid, and I listened to the music which seemed to be causing the pavement to shake. "I told him it felt great." The music stopped, the barmaid paused and watched the juke box until the music began again. "It did."

All this was carrying me some place I didn't want to go. I certainly didn't want to know how it felt. It filled everything, the people, the houses, the music, the dark, quicksilver barmaid, with menace; and this menace was their reality.

30   "What's going to happen to him now?" I asked again.

"They'll send him away some place and they'll try to cure him." He shook his head. "Maybe he'll even think he's kicked the habit. Then they'll let him loose"—he gestured, throwing his cigarette into the gutter. "That's all."

"What do you mean, that's *all?*"

But I knew what he meant.

"I *mean*, that's *all*." He turned his head and looked at me, pulling down the corners of his mouth. "Don't you know what I mean?" he asked softly.

35   "How the hell *would* I know what you mean?" I almost whispered it, I don't know why.

"That's right," he said to the air, "how would *he* know what I mean?" He turned toward me again, patient and calm, and yet I somehow felt him shaking, shaking as though he were going to fall apart. I felt that ice in my guts again, the dread I'd felt all afternoon; and again I watched the barmaid, moving about the bar, washing glasses, and singing. "Listen. They'll let him out and then it'll just start all over again. That's what I mean."

"You mean—they'll let him out. And then he'll just start working his way back in again. You mean he'll never kick the habit. Is that what you mean?"

"That's right," he said, cheerfully. "*You* see what I mean."

"Tell me," I said at last, "why does he want to die? He must want to die, he's killing himself, why does he want to die?"

He looked at me in surprise. He licked his lips. "He don't want to die. He wants   40
to live. Don't nobody want to die, ever."

Then I wanted to ask him—too many things. He could not have answered, or if he had, I could not have borne the answers. I started walking. "Well, I guess it's none of my business."

"It's going to be rough on old Sonny," he said. We reached the subway station.

"This is your station?" he asked. I nodded. I took one step down. "Damn!" he said, suddenly. I looked up at him. He grinned again. "Damn it if I didn't leave all my money home. You ain't got a dollar on you, have you? Just for a couple of days is all."

All at once something inside gave and threatened to come pouring out of me. I didn't hate him any more. I felt that in another moment I'd start crying like a child.

"Sure," I said. "Don't sweat." I looked in my wallet and didn't have a dollar,   45
I only had a five. "Here," I said. "That hold you?"

He didn't look at it—he didn't want to look at it. A terrible, closed look came over his face, as though he were keeping the number on the bill a secret from him and me. "Thanks," he said, and now he was dying to see me go. "Don't worry about Sonny. Maybe I'll write him or something."

"Sure," I said. "You do that. So long."

"Be seeing you," he said. I went on down the steps.

And I didn't write Sonny or send him anything for a long time. When I finally did, it was just after my little girl died, and he wrote me back a letter which made me feel like a bastard.

Here's what he said: 50

> Dear brother,
>
> You don't know how much I needed to hear from you. I wanted to write you many a time but I dug how much I must have hurt you and so I didn't write. But now I feel like a man who's been trying to climb up out of some deep, real deep and funky hole and just saw the sun up there, outside I got to get outside.
>
> I can't tell you much about how I got here. I mean I don't know how to tell you. I guess I was afraid of something or I was trying to escape from something and you know I have never been very strong in the head (smile). I'm glad Mama and Daddy are dead and can't see what's happened to their son and I swear if I'd known what I was doing I would never have hurt you so, you and a lot of other fine people who were nice to me and who believed in me.
>
> I don't want you to think it had anything to do with me being a musician. It's more than that. Or maybe less than that. I can't get anything straight in my head down here and I try not to think about what's going to happen to me when I get outside again. Sometime I think I'm going to flip and *never* get outside and sometime I think I'll come straight back. I tell you one thing, though, I'd rather blow my brains out than go through this again. But that's what they all say, so they tell me. If I tell you when I'm coming to New York and if you could meet me, I sure

would appreciate it. Give my love to Isabel and the kids and I was sure sorry to hear about little Gracie. I wish I could be like Mama and say the Lord's will be done, but I don't know it seems to me that trouble is the one thing that never does get stopped and I don't know what good it does to blame it on the Lord. But maybe it does some good if you believe it.

Your brother,
Sonny

55

Then I kept in constant touch with him and I sent him whatever I could and I went to meet him when he came back to New York. When I saw him many things I thought I had forgotten came flooding back to me. This was because I had begun, finally, to wonder about Sonny, about the life that Sonny lived inside. This life, whatever it was, had made him older and thinner and it had deepened the distant stillness in which he had always moved. He looked very unlike my baby brother. Yet, when he smiled, when we shook hands, the baby brother I'd never known looked out from the depths of his private life, like an animal waiting to be coaxed into the light.

"How you been keeping?" he asked me.

"All right. And you?"

60 "Just fine." He was smiling all over his face. "It's good to see you again."

"It's good to see you."

The seven years difference in our ages lay between us like a chasm: I wondered if these years would ever operate between us as a bridge. I was remembering, and it made it hard to catch my breath, that I had been there when he was born; and I had heard the first words he had ever spoken. When he started to walk, he walked from our mother straight to me. I caught him just before he fell when he took the first steps he ever took in this world.

"How's Isabel?"

"Just fine. She's dying to see you."

65 "And the boys?"

"They're fine, too. They're anxious to see their uncle."

"Oh, come on. You know they don't remember me."

"Are you kidding? Of course they remember you."

He grinned again. We got into a taxi. We had a lot to say to each other, far too much to know how to begin.

70 As the taxi began to move, I asked, "You still want to go to India?"

He laughed. "You still remember that. Hell, no. This place is Indian enough for me."

"It used to belong to them," I said.

And he laughed again. "They damn sure knew what they were doing when they got rid of it."

Years ago, when he was around fourteen, he'd been all hipped on the idea of going to India. He read books about people sitting on rocks, naked, in all kinds of weather, but mostly bad, naturally, and walking barefoot through hot coals and arriving at wisdom. I used to say that it sounded to me as though they were getting away from wisdom as fast as they could. I think he sort of looked down on me for that.

75 "Do you mind," he asked, "if we have the driver drive alongside the park? On the west side—I haven't seen the city in so long."

"Of course not," I said. I was afraid that I might sound as though I were humoring him, but I hoped he wouldn't take it that way.

So we drove along, between the green of the park and the stony, lifeless elegance of hotels and apartment buildings, toward the vivid, killing streets of our childhood. These streets hadn't changed, though housing projects jutted up out of them now like rocks in the middle of a boiling sea. Most of the houses in which we had grown up had vanished, as had the stores from which we had stolen, the basements in which we had first tried sex, the rooftops from which we had hurled tin cans and bricks. But houses exactly like the houses of our past yet dominated the landscape, boys exactly like the boys we once had been found themselves smothering in these houses, came down into the streets for light and air and found themselves encircled by disaster. Some escaped the trap, most didn't. Those who got out always left something of themselves behind, as some animals amputate a leg and leave it in the trap. It might be said, perhaps, that I had escaped, after all, I was a school teacher; or that Sonny had, he hadn't lived in Harlem for years. Yet, as the cab moved uptown through streets which seemed, with a rush, to darken with dark people, and as I covertly studied Sonny's face, it came to me that what we both were seeking through our separate cab windows was that part of ourselves which had been left behind. It's always at the hour of trouble and confrontation that the missing member aches.

We hit 110th Street and started rolling up Lenox Avenue. And I'd known this avenue all my life, but it seemed to me again, as it had seemed on the day I'd first heard about Sonny's trouble, filled with a hidden menace which was its very breath of life.

"We almost there," said Sonny.

"Almost." We were both too nervous to say anything more.

We live in a housing project. It hasn't been up long. A few days after it was up it seemed uninhabitably new, now, of course, it's already rundown. It looks like a parody of the good, clean, faceless life—God knows the people who live in it do their best to make it a parody. The beat-looking grass lying around isn't enough to make their lives green, the hedges will never hold out the streets, and they know it. The big windows fool no one, they aren't big enough to make space out of no space. They don't bother with the windows, they watch the TV screen instead. The playground is most popular with the children who don't play at jacks, or skip rope, or roller skate, or swing, and they can be found in it after dark. We moved in partly because it's not too far from where I teach, and partly for the kids; but it's really just like the houses in which Sonny and I grew up. The same things happen, they'll have the same things to remember. The moment Sonny and I started into the house I had the feeling that I was simply bringing him back into the danger he had almost died trying to escape.

Sonny has never been talkative. So I don't know why I was sure he'd be dying to talk to me when supper was over the first night. Everything went fine, the oldest boy remembered him, and the youngest boy liked him, and Sonny had remembered to bring something for each of them; and Isabel, who is really much nicer than I am, more open and giving, had gone to a lot of trouble about dinner and was genuinely glad to see him. And she's always been able to tease Sonny in a way that I haven't. It was nice to see her face so vivid again and to hear her laugh and watch her make Sonny laugh. She wasn't, or, anyway, she didn't seem to be, at all uneasy or embarrassed. She chatted as though there were no subject which had to be avoided and she got Sonny

80

past his first, faint stiffness. And thank God she was there, for I was filled with that icy dread again. Everything I did seemed awkward to me, and everything I said sounded freighted with hidden meaning. I was trying to remember everything I'd heard about dope addiction and I couldn't help watching Sonny for signs. I wasn't doing it out of malice. I was trying to find out something about my brother. I was dying to hear him tell me he was safe.

"Safe!" my father grunted, whenever Mama suggested trying to move to a neighborhood which might be safer for children. "Safe, hell! Ain't no place safe for kids, nor nobody."

He always went on like this, but he wasn't, ever, really as bad as he sounded, not even on weekends, when he got drunk. As a matter of fact, he was always on the lookout for "something a little better," but he died before he found it. He died suddenly, during a drunken weekend in the middle of the war, when Sonny was fifteen. He and Sonny hadn't ever got on too well. And this was partly because Sonny was the apple of his father's eye. It was because he loved Sonny so much and was frightened for him, that he was always fighting with him. It doesn't do any good to fight with Sonny. Sonny just moves back, inside himself, where he can't be reached. But the principal reason that they never hit it off is that they were so much alike. Daddy was big and rough and loud-talking, just the opposite of Sonny, but they both had—that same privacy.

85   Mama tried to tell me something about this, just after Daddy died. I was home on leave from the army.

This was the last time I ever saw my mother alive. Just the same, this picture gets all mixed up in my mind with pictures I had of her when she was younger. The way I always see her is the way she used to be on a Sunday afternoon, say, when the old folks were talking after the big Sunday dinner. I always see her wearing pale blue. She'd be sitting on the sofa. And my father would be sitting in the easy chair, not far from her. And the living room would be full of church folks and relatives. There they sit, in chairs all around the living room, and the night is creeping up outside, but nobody knows it yet. You can see the darkness growing against the windowpanes and you hear the street noises every now and again, or maybe the jangling beat of a tambourine from one of the churches close by, but it's real quiet in the room. For a moment nobody's talking, but every face looks darkening, like the sky outside. And my mother rocks a little from the waist, and my father's eyes are closed. Everyone is looking at something a child can't see. For a minute they've forgotten the children. Maybe a kid is lying on the rug half asleep. Maybe somebody's got a kid in his lap and is absent-mindedly stroking the kid's head. Maybe there's a kid, quiet and big-eyed, curled up in a big chair in the corner. The silence, the darkness coming, and the darkness in the faces frighten the child obscurely. He hopes that the hand which strokes his forehead will never stop—will never die. He hopes that there will never come a time when the old folks won't be sitting around the living room, talking about where they've come from, and what they've seen, and what's happened to them and their kinfolk.

But something deep and watchful in the child knows that this is bound to end, is already ending. In a moment someone will get up and turn on the light. Then the old folks will remember the children and they won't talk any more that day. And when light fills the room, the child is filled with darkness. He knows that every time this happens he's moved just a little closer to that darkness outside. The darkness outside is what the old folks have been talking about. It's what they've come from. It's what they endure. The child knows that they won't talk any more because if he knows too much about what's happened to *them*, he'll know too much too soon, about what's going to happen to *him*.

The last time I talked to my mother, I remember I was restless. I wanted to get out and see Isabel. We weren't married then and we had a lot to straighten out between us.

There Mama sat, in black, by the window. She was humming an old church song, *Lord, you brought me from a long ways off.* Sonny was out somewhere. Mama kept watching the streets.

"I don't know," she said, "if I'll ever see you again, after you go off from here. But   90
I hope you'll remember the things I tried to teach you."

"Don't talk like that," I said, and smiled. "You'll be here a long time yet."

She smiled, too, but she said nothing. She was quiet for a long time. And I said, "Mama, don't you worry about nothing. I'll be writing all the time, and you be getting the checks. . . ."

"I want to talk to you about your brother," she said, suddenly. "If anything happens to me he ain't going to have nobody to look out for him."

"Mama," I said, "ain't nothing going to happen to you *or* Sonny. Sonny's all right. He's a good boy and he's got good sense."

"It ain't a question of his being a good boy," Mama said, "nor of his having good   95
sense. It ain't only the bad ones, nor yet the dumb ones that gets sucked under." She stopped, looking at me. "Your Daddy once had a brother," she said, and she smiled in a way that made me feel she was in pain. "You didn't never know that, did you?"

"No," I said, "I never knew that," and I watched her face.

"Oh, yes," she said, "your Daddy had a brother." She looked out of the window again. "I know you never saw your Daddy cry. But *I* did—many a time, through all these years."

I asked her, "What happened to his brother? How come nobody's ever talked about him?"

This was the first time I ever saw my mother look old.

"His brother got killed," she said, "when he was just a little younger than you are   100
now. I knew him. He was a fine boy. He was maybe a little full of the devil, but he didn't mean nobody no harm."

Then she stopped and the room was silent, exactly as it had sometimes been on those Sunday afternoons. Mama kept looking out into the streets.

"He used to have a job in the mill," she said, "and, like all young folks, he just liked to perform on Saturday nights. Saturday nights, him and your father would drift around to different places, go to dances and things like that, or just sit around with people they knew, and your father's brother would sing, he had a fine voice, and play along with himself on his guitar. Well, this particular Saturday night, him and your father was coming home from some place, and they were both a little drunk and there was a moon that night, it was bright like day. Your father's brother was feeling kind of good, and he was whistling to himself, and he had his guitar slung over his shoulder.

They was coming down a hill and beneath them was a road that turned off from the highway. Well, your father's brother, being always kind of frisky, decided to run down this hill, and he did, with that guitar banging and clanging behind him, and he ran across the road, and he was making water behind a tree. And your father was sort of amused at him and he was still coming down the hill, kind of slow. Then he heard a car motor and that same minute his brother stepped from behind the tree, into the road, in the moonlight. And he started to cross the road. And your father started to run down the hill, he says he don't know why. This car was full of white men. They was all drunk, and when they seen your father's brother they let out a great whoop and holler and they aimed the car straight at him. They was having fun, they just wanted to scare him, the way they do sometimes, you know. But they was drunk. And I guess the boy, being drunk, too, and scared, kind of lost his head. By the time he jumped it was too late. Your father says he heard his brother scream when the car rolled over him, and he heard the wood of that guitar when it give, and he heard them strings go flying, and he heard them white men shouting, and the car kept on a-going and it ain't stopped till this day. And, time your father got down the hill, his brother weren't nothing but blood and pulp."

Tears were gleaming on my mother's face. There wasn't anything I could say.

"He never mentioned it," she said, "because I never let him mention it before you children. Your Daddy was like a crazy man that night and for many a night thereafter. He says he never in his life seen anything as dark as that road after the lights of that car had gone away. Weren't nothing, weren't nobody on that road, just your Daddy and his brother and that busted guitar. Oh, yes. Your Daddy never did really get right again. Till the day he died he weren't sure but that every white man he saw was the man that killed his brother."

105   She stopped and took out her handkerchief and dried her eyes and looked at me.

"I ain't telling you all this," she said, "to make you scared or bitter or to make you hate nobody. I'm telling you this because you got a brother. And the world ain't changed."

I guess I didn't want to believe this. I guess she saw this in my face. She turned away from me, toward the window again, searching those streets.

"But I praise my Redeemer," she said at last, "that He called your Daddy home before me. I ain't saying it to throw no flowers at myself, but, I declare, it keeps me from feeling too cast down to know I helped your father get safely through this world. Your father always acted like he was the roughest, strongest man on earth. And everybody took him to be like that. But if he hadn't had me there—to see his tears!"

She was crying again. Still, I couldn't move. I said, "Lord, Lord, Mama, I didn't know it was like that."

110   "Oh, honey," she said, "there's a lot that you don't know. But you are going to find out." She stood up from the window and came over to me. "You got to hold on to your brother," she said, "and don't let him fall, no matter what it looks like is happening to him and no matter how evil you gets with him. You going to be evil with him many a time. But don't you forget what I told you, you hear?"

"I won't forget," I said. "Don't you worry, I won't forget. I won't let nothing happen to Sonny."

My mother smiled as though she was amused at something she saw in my face. Then, "You may not be able to stop nothing from happening. But you got to let him know you's *there*."

Two days later I was married, and then I was gone. And I had a lot of things on my mind and I pretty well forgot my promise to Mama until I got shipped home on a special furlough for her funeral.

And, after the funeral, with just Sonny and me alone in the empty kitchen, I tried to find out something about him.

"What do you want to do?" I asked him.

"I'm going to be a musician," he said.

For he had graduated, in the time I had been away, from dancing to the juke box to finding out who was playing what, and what they were doing with it, and he had bought himself a set of drums.

"You mean, you want to be a drummer?" I somehow had the feeling that being a drummer might be all right for other people but not for my brother Sonny.

"I don't think," he said, looking at me very gravely, "that I'll ever be a good drummer. But I think I can play a piano."

I frowned. I'd never played the role of the oldest brother quite so seriously before, had scarcely ever, in fact, *asked* Sonny a damn thing. I sensed myself in the presence of something I didn't really know how to handle, didn't understand. So I made my frown a little deeper as I asked: "What kind of musician do you want to be?"

He grinned. "How many kinds do you think there are?"

"Be *serious*," I said.

He laughed, throwing his head back, and then looked at me. "I *am* serious."

"Well, then, for Christ's sake, stop kidding around and answer a serious question. I mean, do you want to be a concert pianist, you want to play classical music and all that, or—or what?" Long before I finished he was laughing again. "For Christ's *sake*, Sonny!"

He sobered, but with difficulty. "I'm sorry. But you sound so—*scared*!" and he was off again.

"Well, you may think it's funny now, baby, but it's not going to be so funny when you have to make your living at it, let me tell you *that*." I was furious because I knew he was laughing at me and I didn't know why.

"No," he said, very sober now, and afraid, perhaps, that he'd hurt me, "I don't want to be a classical pianist. That isn't what interests me. I mean"—he paused, looking hard at me, as though his eyes would help me to understand, and then gestured helplessly, as though perhaps his hand would help—"I mean, I'll have a lot of studying to do, and I'll have to study *everything*, but, I mean, I want to play *with*—jazz musicians." He stopped. "I want to play jazz," he said.

Well, the word had never before sounded as heavy, as real, as it sounded that afternoon in Sonny's mouth. I just looked at him and I was probably frowning a real frown by this time. I simply couldn't see, why on earth he'd want to spend his time hanging around nightclubs, clowning around on bandstands, while people pushed each other around a dance floor. It seemed—beneath him, somehow. I had never thought about it before, had never been forced to, but I suppose I had always put jazz musicians in a class with what Daddy called "good-time people."

115

120

125

"Are you *serious?*"

130   "Hell, *yes*, I'm serious."

He looked more helpless than ever, and annoyed, and deeply hurt.

I suggested, helpfully: "You mean—like Louis Armstrong?"

His face closed as though I'd struck him. "No. I'm not talking about none of that old-time, down home crap."

"Well, look, Sonny, I'm sorry, don't get mad. I just don't altogether get it, that's all. Name somebody—you know, a jazz musician you admire."

135   "Bird."

"Who?"

"Bird! Charlie Parker![3] Don't they teach you nothing in the goddamn army?"

I lit a cigarette. I was surprised and then a little amused to discover that I was trembling. "I've been out of touch," I said. "You'll have to be patient with me. Now. Who's this Parker character?"

"He's just one of the greatest jazz musicians alive," said Sonny, sullenly, his hands in his pockets, his back to me. "Maybe *the* greatest," he added, bitterly, "that's probably why *you* never heard of him."

140   "All right," I said, "I'm ignorant. I'm sorry. I'll go out and buy all the cat's records right away, all right?"

"It don't," said Sonny, with dignity, "make any difference to me. I don't care what you listen to. Don't do me no favors."

I was beginning to realize that I'd never seen him so upset before. With another part of my mind I was thinking that this would probably turn out to be one of those things kids go through and that I shouldn't make it seem important by pushing it too hard. Still, I didn't think it would do any harm to ask: "Doesn't all this take a lot of time? Can you make a living at it?"

He turned back to me and half leaned, half sat, on the kitchen table. "Everything takes time," he said, "and—well, yes, sure, I can make a living at it. But what I don't seem to be able to make you understand is that it's the only thing I want to do."

"Well, Sonny," I said gently, "you know people can't always do exactly what they *want* to do—."

145   "No, I don't know that," said Sonny, surprising me. "I think people *ought* to do what they want to do, what else are they alive for?"

"You getting to be a big boy," I said desperately, "it's time you started thinking about your future."

"I'm thinking about my future," said Sonny, grimly "I think about it all the time."

I gave up. I decided, if he didn't change his mind, that we could always talk about it later. "In the meantime," I said, "you got to finish school." We had already decided that he'd have to move in with Isabel and her folks. I knew this wasn't the ideal arrangement because Isabel's folks are inclined to be dicty[4] and they hadn't especially

---

[3]*Bird Charlie Parker!* Charlie "Bird" Parker (1920–1955) is a renowned jazz saxophonist and composer who, with Dizzy Gillespie and others, developed the jazz style "bebop." He died of pneumonia and a bleeding ulcer, both of which were exacerbated by his addiction to narcotics and alcohol.

[4]*dicty:* Bossy.

wanted Isabel to marry me. But I didn't know what else to do. "And we have to get you fixed up at Isabel's."

There was a long silence. He moved from the kitchen table to the window. "That's a terrible idea. You know it yourself."

"Do you have a *better* idea?"

He just walked up and down the kitchen for a minute. He was as tall as I was. He had started to shave. I suddenly had the feeling that I didn't know him at all.

He stopped at the kitchen table and picked up my cigarettes. Looking at me with a kind of mocking, amused defiance, he put one between his lips. "You mind?"

"You smoking already?"

He lit the cigarette and nodded, watching me through the smoke. "I just wanted to see if I'd have the courage to smoke in front of you." He grinned and blew a great cloud of smoke to the ceiling. "It was easy." He looked at my face. "Come on, now. I bet you was smoking at my age, tell the truth."

I didn't say anything but the truth was on my face, and he laughed. But now there was something very strained in his laugh. "Sure. And I bet that ain't all you was doing."

He was frightening me a little. "Cut the crap," I said. "We already decided that you was going to go and live at Isabel's. Now what's got into you all of a sudden?"

"*You* decided it," he pointed out. "*I* didn't decide nothing." He stopped in front of me, leaning against the stove, arms loosely folded. "Look, brother. I don't want to stay in Harlem no more, I really don't." He was very earnest. He looked at me, then over toward the kitchen window. There was something in his eyes I'd never seen before, some thoughtfulness, some worry all his own. He rubbed the muscle of one arm. "It's time I was getting out of here."

"Where do you want to *go*, Sonny?"

"I want to join the army. Or the navy, I don't care. If I say I'm old enough, they'll believe me."

Then I got mad. It was because I was so scared. "You must be crazy. You goddamn fool, what he hell do you want to go and join the *army* for?"

"I just told you. To get out of Harlem."

"Sonny, you haven't even finished *school*. And if you really want to be a musician, how do you expect to study if you're in the *army?*"

He looked at me, trapped, and in anguish. "There's ways. I might be able to work out some kind of deal. Anyway, I'll have the G.I. Bill when I come out."

"*If* you come out." We stared at each other. "Sonny, please. Be reasonable. I know the setup is far from perfect. But we got to do the best we can."

"I ain't learning nothing in school," he said. "Even when I go." He turned away from me and opened the window and threw his cigarette out into the narrow alley. I watched his back. "At least, I ain't learning nothing you'd want me to learn." He slammed the window so hard I thought the glass would fly out, and turned back to me. "And I'm sick of the stink of these garbage cans!"

"Sonny," I said, "I know how you feel. But if you don't finish school now, you're going to be sorry later that you didn't." I grabbed him by the shoulders. "And you only got another year. It ain't so bad. And I'll come back and I swear I'll help you

150
155
160
165

do *whatever* you want to do. Just try to put up with it till I come back. Will you please do that? For me?"

He didn't answer and he wouldn't look at me.

"Sonny. You hear me?"

He pulled away. "I hear you. But you never hear anything I say."

170   I didn't know what to say to that. He looked out of the window and then back at me. "OK," he said, and sighed. "I'll try."

Then I said, trying to cheer him up a little, "They got a piano at Isabel's. You can practice on it."

And as a matter of fact, it did cheer him up for a minute. "That's right," he said to himself, "I forgot that." His face relaxed a little. But the worry, the thoughtfulness, played on it still, the way shadows play on a face which is staring into the fire.

But I thought I'd never hear the end of that piano. At first, Isabel would write me, saying how nice it was that Sonny was so serious about his music and how, as soon as he came in from school, or wherever he had been when he was supposed to be at school, he went straight to that piano and stayed there until suppertime. And, after supper, he went back to that piano and stayed there until everybody went to bed. He was at the piano all day Saturday and all day Sunday. Then he bought a record player and started playing records. He'd play one record over and over again, all day long sometimes, and he'd improvise along with it on the piano. Or he'd play one section of the record, one chord, one change, one progression, then he'd do it on the piano. Then back to the record. Then back to the piano.

Well, I really don't know how they stood it. Isabel finally confessed that it wasn't like living with a person at all, it was like living with sound. And the sound didn't make any sense to her, didn't make any sense to any of them—naturally. They began, in a way, to be afflicted by this presence that was living in their home. It was as though Sonny were some sort of god, or monster. He moved in an atmosphere which wasn't like theirs at all. They fed him and he ate, he washed himself, he walked in and out of their door; he certainly wasn't nasty or unpleasant or rude, Sonny isn't any of those things, but it was as though he were all wrapped up in some cloud, some fire, some vision all his own, and there wasn't any way to reach him.

175   At the same time, he wasn't really a man yet, he was still a child, and they had to watch out for him in all kinds of ways. They certainly couldn't throw him out. Neither did they dare to make a great scene about that piano because even they dimly sensed, as I sensed, from so many thousands of miles away, that Sonny was at that piano playing for his life.

But he hadn't been going to school. One day a letter came from the school board and Isabel's mother got it—there had, apparently, been other letters but Sonny had torn them up. This day, when Sonny came in, Isabel's mother showed him the letter and asked where he'd been spending his time. And she finally got it out of him that he'd been down in Greenwich Village, with musicians and other characters, in a white girl's apartment. And this scared her and she started to scream at him and what came up, once she began—though she denies it to this day—was what sacrifices they were making to give Sonny a decent home and how little he appreciated it.

Sonny didn't play the piano that day. By evening, Isabel's mother had calmed down but then there was the old man to deal with, and Isabel herself. Isabel says she did her best to be calm but she broke down and started crying. She says she just watched Sonny's face. She could tell, by watching him, what was happening with him. And what was happening was that they penetrated his cloud, they had reached him. Even if their fingers had been a thousand times more gentle than human fingers ever are, he could hardly help feeling that they had stripped him naked and were spitting on that nakedness. For he also had to see that his presence, that music, which was life or death to him, had been torture for them and that they had endured it, not at all for his sake, but only for mine. And Sonny couldn't take that. He can take it a little better today than he could then but he's still not very good at it and, frankly, I don't know anybody who is.

The silence of the next few days must have been louder than the sound of all the music ever played since time began. One morning, before she went to work, Isabel was in his room for something and she suddenly realized that all of his records were gone. And she knew for certain that he was gone. And he was. He went as far as the navy would carry him. He finally sent me a postcard from some place in Greece and that was the first I knew that Sonny was still alive. I didn't see him any more until we were both back in New York and the war had long been over.

He was a man by then, of course, but I wasn't willing to see it. He came by the house from time to time, but we fought almost every time we met. I didn't like the way he carried himself, loose and dreamlike all the time, and I didn't like his friends, and his music seemed to be merely an excuse for the life he led. It sounded just that weird and disordered.

Then we had a fight, a pretty awful fight, and I didn't see him for months. By and by I looked him up, where he was living, in a furnished room in the Village, and I tried to make it up. But there were lots of other people in the room and Sonny just lay on his bed, and he wouldn't come downstairs with me, and he treated these other people as though they were his family and I weren't. So I got mad and then he got mad, and then I told him that he might just as well be dead as live the way he was living. Then he stood up and he told me not to worry about him any more in life, that he *was* dead as far as I was concerned. Then he pushed me to the door and the other people looked on as though nothing were happening, and he slammed the door behind me. I stood in the hallway, staring at the door. I heard somebody laugh in the room and then the tears came to my eyes. I started down the steps, whistling to keep from crying, I kept whistling to myself, *You going to need me, baby, one of these cold, rainy days.*

180

I read about Sonny's trouble in the spring. Little Grace died in the fall. She was a beautiful little girl. But she only lived a little over two years. She died of polio and she suffered. She had a slight fever for a couple of days, but it didn't seem like anything and we just kept her in bed. And we would certainly have called the doctor, but the fever dropped, she seemed to be all right. So we thought it had just been a cold. Then, one day, she was up, playing. Isabel was in the kitchen fixing lunch for the two boys when they'd come in from school, and she heard Grace fall down in the living room. When you have a lot of children you don't always start running when one of them falls, unless they start screaming or something. And, this time, Gracie was quiet. Yet, Isabel says that when she heard that *thump* and then that silence, something happened to her to make her afraid. And she ran to the living room and there was little Grace on the floor, all twisted up, and the reason she hadn't screamed was that she couldn't get her breath. And when she did scream, it was the worst sound, Isabel says, that she'd ever heard in all her life, and she still hears it sometimes in her dreams. Isabel will sometimes wake me up with a low, moaning, strangling sound and I have to be quick to awaken her and hold her to me and where Isabel is weeping against me seems a mortal wound.

I think I may have written Sonny the very day that little Grace was buried. I was sitting in the living room in the dark, by myself, and I suddenly thought of Sonny. My trouble made his real.

One Saturday afternoon, when Sonny had been living with us, or anyway, been in our house, for nearly two weeks. I found myself wandering aimlessly about the living room, drinking from a can of beer, and trying to work up courage to search Sonny's room. He was out, he was usually out whenever I was home, and Isabel had taken the children to see their grandparents. Suddenly I was standing still in front of the living room window, watching Seventh Avenue. The idea of searching Sonny's room made me still. I scarcely dared to admit to myself what I'd be searching for. I didn't know what I'd do if I found it. Or if I didn't.

On the sidewalk across from me, near the entrance to a barbecue joint, some people were holding an old fashioned revival meeting. The barbecue cook, wearing a dirty white apron, his conked[5] hair reddish and metallic in the pale sun, and a cigarette between his lips, stood in the doorway, watching them. Kids and older people paused in their errands and stood there, along with some older men and a couple of very tough looking women who watched everything that happened on the avenue, as though they owned it, or were maybe owned by it. Well, they were watching this, too. The revival was being carried on by three sisters in black, and a brother. All they had were their voices and their Bibles and a tambourine. The brother was testifying[6] and while he testified two of the sisters stood together, seeming to say, amen, and the third sister walked around with the tambourine outstretched and a couple of people dropped coins into it. Then the brother's testimony ended and the sister who had been taking up the collection dumped the coins into her palm and transferred them to the pocket of her long black robe. Then she raised both hands, striking the tambourine against the air, and then against one hand, and she started to sing. And the two other sisters and the brother joined in.

185   It was strange, suddenly, to watch, though I had been seeing these meetings all my life. So, of course, had everybody else down there. Yet, they paused and watched and listened and I stood still at the window. *"'Tis the old ship of Zion,"* they sang, and the sister with the tambourine kept a steady, jangling beat, *"it has rescued many a thousand!"* Not a soul under the sound of their voices was hearing this song for the first time, not one of them had been rescued. Nor had they seen much in the way of rescue work being done around them. Neither did they especially believe in the holiness of the three sisters and the brother, they knew too much about them,

---

[5]*conked:* Chemically straightened and greased hair.

[6]*testifying:* Publicly proclaiming one's religious experience and belief.

knew where they lived, and how. The woman with the tambourine, whose voice dominated the air, whose face was bright with joy, was divided by very little from the woman who stood watching her, a cigarette between her heavy, chapped lips, her hair a cuckoo's nest, her face scarred and swollen from many beatings, and her black eyes glittering like coal. Perhaps they both knew this, which was why, when, as rarely, they addressed each other, they addressed each other as Sister. As the singing filled the air the watching, listening faces underwent a change, the eyes focusing on something within; the music seemed to soothe a poison out of them; and time seemed, nearly, to fall away from the sullen, belligerent, battered faces, as though they were fleeing back to their first condition, while dreaming of their last. The barbecue cook half shook his head and smiled, and dropped his cigarette and disappeared into his joint. A man fumbled in his pockets for change and stood holding it in his hand impatiently, as though he had just remembered a pressing appointment further up the avenue. He looked furious. Then I saw Sonny, standing on the edge of the crowd. He was carrying a wide, flat notebook with a green cover, and it made him look, from where I was standing, almost like a schoolboy. The coppery sun brought out the copper in his skin, he was very faintly smiling, standing very still. Then the singing stopped, the tambourine turned into a collection plate again. The furious man dropped in his coins and vanished, so did a couple of the women, and Sonny dropped some change in the plate, looking directly at the woman with a little smile. He started across the avenue, toward the house. He has a slow, loping walk, something like the way Harlem hipsters walk, only he's imposed on this his own half-beat. I had never really noticed it before.

I stayed at the window, both relieved and apprehensive. As Sonny disappeared from my sight, they began singing again. And they were still singing when his key turned in the lock.

"Hey," he said.

"Hey, yourself. You want some beer?"

"No. Well, maybe." But he came up to the window and stood beside me, looking out. "What a warm voice," he said.

They were singing *If I could only hear my mother pray again!*   190

"Yes," I said, "and she can sure beat that tambourine."

"But what a terrible song," he said, and laughed. He dropped his notebook on the sofa and disappeared into the kitchen. "Where's Isabel and the kids?"

"I think they went to see their grandparents. You hungry?"

"No." He came back into the living room with his can of beer. "You want to come some place with me tonight?"

I sensed, I don't know how, that I couldn't possibly say no. "Sure. Where?"   195

He sat down on the sofa and picked up his notebook and started leafing through it. "I'm going to sit in with some fellows in a joint in the Village."

"You mean, you're going to play, tonight?"

"That's right." He took a swallow of his beer and moved back to the window. He gave me a sidelong look. "If you can stand it."

"I'll try," I said.

He smiled to himself and we both watched as the meeting across the way broke   200
up. The three sisters and the brother, heads bowed, were singing *God be with you till*

we meet again. The faces around them were very quiet. Then the song ended. The small crowd dispersed. We watched the three women and the lone man walk slowly up the avenue.

"When she was singing before," said Sonny, abruptly, "her voice reminded me for a minute of what heroin feels like sometimes—when it's in your veins. It makes you feel sort of warm and cool at the same time. And distant. And—and sure." He sipped his beer, very deliberately not looking at me. I watched his face. "It makes you feel—in control. Sometimes you've got to have that feeling."

"Do you?" I sat down slowly in the easy chair.

"Sometimes." He went to the sofa and picked up his notebook again. "Some people do."

"In order," I asked, "to play?" And my voice was very ugly, full of contempt and anger.

205   "Well"—he looked at me with great, troubled eyes, as though, in fact, he hoped his eyes would tell me things he could never otherwise say—"they *think* so. And *if* they think so—!"

"And what do *you* think?" I asked.

He sat on the sofa and put his can of beer on the floor. "I don't know," he said, and I couldn't be sure if he were answering my question or pursuing his thoughts. His face didn't tell me. "It's not so much to *play*. It's to *stand* it, to be able to make it at all. On any level." He frowned and smiled! "In order to keep from shaking to pieces."

"But these friends of yours," I said, "they seem to shake themselves to pieces pretty goddamn fast."

"Maybe." He played with the notebook. And something told me that I should curb my tongue, that Sonny was doing his best to talk, that I should listen. "But of course you only know the ones that've gone to pieces. Some don't—or at least they haven't *yet* and that's just about all *any* of us can say. He paused. "And then there are some who just live, really, in hell, and they know it and they see what's happening and they go right on. I don't know." He sighed, dropped the notebook, folded his arms. "Some guys, you can tell from the way they play, they on something *all* the time. And you can see that, well, it makes something real for them. But of course," he picked up his beer from the floor and sipped it and put the can down again, "they *want* to, too, you've got to see that. Even some of them that say they don't—*some*, not all."

210   "And what about you?" I asked—I couldn't help it. "What about you? Do *you* want to?"

He stood up and walked to the window and I remained silent for a long time. Then he sighed. "Me," he said. Then: "While I was downstairs before, on my way here, listening to that woman sing, it struck me all of a sudden how much suffering she must have had to go through—to sing like that. It's *repulsive* to think you have to suffer that much."

I said: "But there's no way not to suffer—is there, Sonny?"

"I believe not," he said and smiled, "but that's never stopped anyone from trying." He looked at me. "Has it?" I realized, with this mocking look, that there stood between us, forever, beyond the power of time or forgiveness, the fact that I had held silence—so long!—when he had needed human speech to help him.

He turned back to the window. "No, there's no way not to suffer. But you try all kinds of ways to keep from drowning in it, to keep on top of it, and to make it seem—well, like *you*. Like you did something, all right, and now you're suffering for it. You know?" I said nothing. "Well you know," he said, impatiently, "why *do* people suffer? Maybe it's better to do something to give it a reason, *any* reason."

"But we just agreed," I said, "that there's no way not to suffer. Isn't it better, then, just to—take it?"

"But nobody just takes it," Sonny cried, "that's what I'm telling you! *Everybody* tries not to. You're just hung up on the way some people try—it's not *your* way!" 215

The hair on my face began to itch, my face felt wet. "That's not true," I said, "that's not true. I don't give a damn what other people do, I don't even care how they suffer. I just care how *you* suffer." And he looked at me. "Please believe me," I said, "I don't want to see you—die—trying not to suffer."

"I won't," he said flatly, "die trying not to suffer. At least, not any faster than anybody else."

"But there's no need," I said, trying to laugh, "is there? in killing yourself."

I wanted to say more, but I couldn't. I wanted to talk about will power and how life could be—well, beautiful. I wanted to say that it was all within; but was it? or, rather, wasn't that exactly the trouble? And I wanted to promise that I would never fail him again. But it would all have sounded—empty words and lies.

So I made the promise to myself and prayed that I would keep it. 220

"It's terrible sometimes, inside," he said, "that's what's the trouble. You walk these streets, black and funky and cold, and there's not really a living ass to talk to, and there's nothing shaking, and there's no way of getting it out—that storm inside. You can't talk it and you can't make love with it, and when you finally try to get with it and play it, you realize *nobody's* listening. So *you've* got to listen. You got to find a way to listen."

And then he walked away from the window and sat on the sofa again, as though all the wind had suddenly been knocked out of him. "Sometimes you'll do *anything* to play, even cut your mother's throat." He laughed and looked at me. "Or your brother's." Then he sobered. "Or your own." Then: "Don't worry. I'm all right now and I think I'll be all right. But I can't forget—where I've been. I don't mean just the physical place I've been, I mean where I've *been*. And *what* I've been."

"What have you been, Sonny?" I asked.

He smiled—but sat sideways on the sofa, his elbow resting on the back, his fingers playing with his mouth and chin, not looking at me. "I've been something I didn't recognize, didn't know, I could be. Didn't know anybody could be." He stopped, looking inward, looking helplessly young, looking old. "I'm not talking about it now because I feel *guilty* or anything like that—maybe it would be better if I did, I don't know. Anyway, I can't really talk about it. Not to you, not to anybody," and now he turned and faced me. "Sometimes, you know, and it was actually when I was most *out* of the world, I felt that I was in it, that I was *with* it, really, and I could *play* or I didn't really have to *play*, it just came out of me, it was there. And I don't know how I played, thinking about it now, but I know I did awful things, those times, sometimes, to people. Or it wasn't that I *did* anything to them—it was that they weren't real." He picked up the beer can; it was empty; he rolled it between his palms: "And other times—well, I needed a fix, I needed to find a place to lean, I needed to clear a space to *listen*—and I couldn't find it, and I—went crazy, I did terrible things to *me*, I was terrible *for* me." He began pressing the beer can between his hands, I watched the metal begin to give. It glittered, as he played with it like a knife, and I was afraid he would cut himself, but I said nothing. "Oh well, I can never tell you. I was all by myself at the bottom of something, stinking and sweating and crying and shaking, and I smelled it, you know? *my* stink, and I thought I'd die if I couldn't get away from it and yet, all the same, I knew that everything I was doing was just locking me in with it. And I didn't know," he paused, still flattening the beer can, "I didn't know, I still *don't* know, something kept telling me that maybe it was good to smell your own stink, but I didn't think that *that* was what I'd been trying to do—and—who can stand it?" and he abruptly dropped the ruined beer can, looking at me with a small, still smile, and then rose, walking to the window as though it were the lodestone rock. I watched his face, he watched the avenue. "I couldn't tell you when Mama died—but the reason I wanted to leave Harlem so bad was to get away from drugs. And then, when I ran away, that's what I was running from—really. When I came back, nothing had changed, I hadn't changed, I was just—older." And he stopped, drumming with his fingers on the windowpane. The sun had vanished, soon darkness would fall. I watched his face. "It can come again," he said, almost as though speaking to himself. Then he turned to me. "It can come again," he repeated. "I just want you to know that."

225   "All right," I said, at last. "So it can come again. All right."

He smiled, but the smile was sorrowful. "I had to try to tell you," he said.

"Yes," I said, "I understand that."

"You're my brother," he said, looking straight at me, and not smiling at all.

"Yes," I repeated, "yes I understand that."

230   He turned back to the window, looking out. "All that hatred down there," he said, "all that hatred and misery and love. It's a wonder it doesn't blow the avenue apart."

We went to the only nightclub on a short, dark street, downtown. We squeezed through the narrow, chattering, jampacked bar to the entrance of the big room, where the bandstand was. And we stood there for a moment, for the lights were very dim in this room and we couldn't see. Then, "Hello, boy," said the voice and an enormous black man, much older than Sonny or myself, erupted out of all that atmospheric lighting and put an arm around Sonny's shoulder. "I been sitting right here," he said, "waiting for you."

He had a big voice, too, and heads in the darkness turned toward us.

Sonny grinned and pulled a little away, and said, "Creole, this is my brother. I told you about him."

Creole shook my hand. "I'm glad to meet you, son," he said, and it was clear that he was glad to meet me *there*, for Sonny's sake. And he smiled: "You got a real musician in *your* family," and he took his arm from Sonny's shoulders and slapped him, lightly, affectionately, with the back of his hand.

235   "Well. Now I've heard it all," said a voice behind us. This was another musician, and a friend of Sonny's, a coal-black, cheerful-looking man, built close to the ground.

He immediately began confiding to me, at the top of his lungs, the most terrible things about Sonny, his teeth gleaming like a lighthouse and his laugh coming up out of him like the beginning of an earthquake. And it turned out that everyone at the bar knew Sonny, or almost everyone; some were musicians, working there, or nearby, or not working, some were simply hangers on, and some were there to hear Sonny play. I was introduced to all of them and they were all very polite to me. Yet, it was clear that, for them, I was only Sonny's brother. Here, I was in Sonny's world. Or, rather: his kingdom. Here, it was not even a question that his veins bore royal blood.

They were going to play soon and Creole installed me, by myself, at a table in a dark corner. Then I watched them, Creole, and the little black man, and Sonny, and the others, while they horsed around, standing just below the bandstand. The light from the bandstand spilled just a little short of them and watching them laughing and gesturing and moving about, I had the feeling that they, nevertheless, were being most careful not to step into that circle of light too suddenly; that if they moved into the light too suddenly, without thinking, they would perish in flame. Then, while I watched, one of them, the small black man, moved into the light and crossed the bandstand and started fooling around with his drums. Then—being funny and being, also, extremely ceremonious—Creole took Sonny by the arm and led him to the piano. A woman's voice called Sonny's name and a few hands started clapping. And Sonny, also being funny and being ceremonious, and so touched, I think, that he could have cried, but neither hiding it nor showing it, riding it like a man, grinned, and put both hands to his heart and bowed from the waist.

Creole then went to the bass fiddle and a lean, very bright-skinned brown man jumped up on the bandstand and picked up his horn. So there they were, and the atmosphere on the bandstand and in the room began to change and tighten. Someone stepped up to the microphone and announced them. Then there were all kinds of murmurs. Some people at the bar shushed others. The waitress ran around, frantically getting in the last orders, guys and chicks got closer to each other, and the lights on the bandstand, on the quartet, turned to a kind of indigo. Then they all looked different there. Creole looked about him for the last time, as though he were making certain that all his chickens were in the coop, and then he—jumped and struck the fiddle. And there they were.

All I know about music is that not many people ever really hear it. And even then, on the rare occasions when something opens within, and the music enters, what we mainly hear, or hear corroborated, are personal, private, vanishing evocations. But the man who creates the music is hearing something else, is dealing with the roar rising from the void and imposing order on it as it hits the air. What is evoked in him, then, is of another order, more terrible because it has no words, and triumphant, too, for that same reason. And his triumph, when he triumphs, is ours. I just watched Sonny's face. His face was troubled, he was working hard, but he wasn't with it. And I had the feeling that, in a way, everyone on the bandstand was waiting for him, both waiting for him and pushing him along. But as I began to watch Creole, I realized that it was Creole who held them all back. He had them on a short rein. Up there, keeping the heat with his whole body, wailing on the fiddle, with his eyes half closed, he was listening to everything, but he was listening to Sonny. He was having a dialogue with Sonny. He wanted Sonny to leave the shoreline and strike out for the deep water.

He was Sonny's witness that deep water and drowning were not the same thing—he had been there, and he knew. And he wanted Sonny to know. He was waiting for Sonny to do the things on the keys which would let Creole know that Sonny was in the water.

And, while Creole listened, Sonny moved, deep within, exactly like someone in torment. I had never before thought of how awful the relationship must be between the musician and his instrument. He has to fill it, this instrument, with the breath of life, his own. He has to make it do what he wants it to do. And a piano is just a piano. It's made out of so much wood and wires and little hammers and big ones, and Ivory. While there's only so much you can do with it, the only way to find this out is to try, to try and make it do everything.

240   And Sonny hadn't been near a piano for over a year. And he wasn't on much better terms with his life, not the life that stretched before him now. He and the piano stammered, started one way, got scared, stopped, started another way, panicked, marked time, started again, then seemed to have found a direction, panicked again, got stuck. And the face I saw on Sonny I'd never seen before. Everything had been burned out of it, and, at the same time, things usually hidden were being burned in, by the fire and fury of the battle which was occurring in him up there.

Yet, watching Creole's face as they neared the end of the first set, I had the feeling that something had happened, something I hadn't heard. Then they finished, there was scattered applause, and then, without an instant's warning, Creole started into something else, it was almost sardonic, it was *Am I Blue*.[7] And, as though he commanded, Sonny began to play. Something began to happen. And Creole let out the reins. The dry, low, black man said something awful on the drums, Creole answered, and the drums talked back. Then the horn insisted, sweet and high, slightly detached perhaps, and Creole listened, commenting now and then, dry, and driving, beautiful and calm and old. Then they all came together again, and Sonny was part of the family again. I could tell this from his face. He seemed to have found, right there beneath his fingers, a damn brand-new piano. It seemed that he couldn't get over it. Then, for a while, just being happy with Sonny, they seemed to be agreeing with him that brand-new pianos certainly were a gas.

Then Creole stepped forward to remind them that what they were playing was the blues. He hit something in all of them, he hit something in me, myself, and the music tightened and deepened, apprehension began to beat the air. Creole began to tell us what the blues were all about. They were not about anything very new. He and his boys up there were keeping it new, at the risk of ruin, destruction, madness, and death, in order to find new ways to make us listen. For, while the tale of how we suffer, and how we are delighted, and how we may triumph is never new, it always must be heard. There isn't any other tale to tell, it's the only light we've got in all this darkness.

And this tale, according to that face, that body, those strong hands on those strings, has another aspect in every country, and a new depth in every generation. Listen, Creole seemed to be saying, listen, Now these are Sonny's blues. He made the little black man on the drums know it, and the bright, brown man on the horn.

---

[7]Am I Blue: A jazz standard.

Creole wasn't trying any longer to get Sonny in the water. He was wishing him God-speed. Then he stepped back, very slowly, filling the air with the immense suggestion that Sonny speak for himself.

Then they all gathered around Sonny and Sonny played. Every now and again one of them seemed to say, amen. Sonny's fingers filled the air with life, his life. But that life contained so many others. And Sonny went all the way back, he really began with the spare, flat statement of the opening phrase of the song. Then he began to make it his. It was very beautiful because it wasn't hurried and it was no longer a lament. I seemed to hear with what burning he had made it his, and what burning we had yet to make it ours, how we could cease lamenting. Freedom lurked around us and I understood, at last, that he could help us to be free if we would listen, that he would never be free until we did. Yet, there was no battle in his face now, I heard what he had gone through, and would continue to go through until he came to rest in earth. He had made it his: that long line, of which we knew only Mama and Daddy. And he was giving it back, as everything must be given back, so that, passing through death, it can live forever. I saw my mother's face again, and felt, for the first time, how the stones of the road she had walked on must have bruised her feet. I saw the moonlit road where my father's brother died. And it brought something else back to me, and carried me past it, I saw my little girl again and felt Isabel's tears again, and I felt my own tears begin to rise. And I was yet aware that this was only a moment, that the world waited outside, as hungry as a tiger, and that trouble stretched above us, longer than the sky.

Then it was over. Creole and Sonny let out their breath, both soaking wet, and grinning. There was a lot of applause and some of it was real. In the dark, the girl came by and I asked her to take drinks to the bandstand. There was a long pause, while they talked up there in the indigo light and after awhile I saw the girl put a Scotch and milk on top of the piano for Sonny. He didn't seem to notice it, but just before they started playing again, he sipped from it and looked toward me, and nodded. Then he put it back on top of the piano. For me, then, as they began to play again, it glowed and shook above my brother's head like the very cup of trembling.[8]

T. CORAGHESSAN BOYLE (1948–   )

Greasy Lake (1985)

It's about a mile down on the dark side of Route 88.

—Bruce Springsteen

There was a time when courtesy and winning ways went out of style, when it was good to be bad, when you cultivated decadence like a taste. We were all dangerous characters then. We wore torn-up leather jackets, slouched around with toothpicks

---

[8]*Cup of trembling:* See Isaiah 51:17, 22–23: "Awake, awake, stand up, O Jerusalem, which hast drunk at the hand of the Lord the cup of his fury; thou hast drunken the dregs of the cup of trembling, and wrung them out . . . Behold, I have taken out of thine hand the cup of trembling, even the dregs of the cup of my fury; thou shalt no more drink it again: But I will put it into the hand of them that affect thee . . ."

in our mouths, sniffed glue and ether and what somebody claimed was cocaine. When we wheeled our parents' whining station wagons out into the street we left a patch of rubber half a block long. We drank gin and grape juice, Tango, Thunderbird, and Bali Hai. We were nineteen. We were bad. We read André Gide[1] and struck elaborate poses to show that we didn't give a shit about anything. At night, we went up to Greasy Lake.

Through the center of town, up the strip, past the housing developments and shopping malls, street lights giving way to the thin streaming illumination of the headlights, trees crowding the asphalt in a black unbroken wall: that was the way out to Greasy Lake. The Indians had called it Wakan, a reference to the clarity of its waters. Now it was fetid and murky, the mud banks glittering with broken glass and strewn with beer cans and the charred remains of bonfires. There was a single ravaged island a hundred yards from shore, so stripped of vegetation it looked as if the air force had strafed it. We went up to the lake because everyone went there, because we wanted to snuff the rich scent of possibility on the breeze, watch a girl take off her clothes and plunge into the festering murk, drink beer, smoke pot, howl at the stars, savor the incongruous full-throated roar of rock and roll against the primeval susurrus[2] of frogs and crickets. This was nature.

I was there one night, late, in the company of two dangerous characters. Digby wore a gold star in his right ear and allowed his father to pay his tuition at Cornell; Jeff was thinking of quitting school to become a painter/musician/head-shop proprietor. They were both expert in the social graces, quick with a sneer, able to manage a Ford with lousy shocks over a rutted and gutted blacktop road at eighty-five while rolling a joint as compact as a Tootsie Roll Pop stick. They could lounge against a bank of booming speakers and trade "man"s with the best of them or roll out across the dance floor as if their joints worked on bearings. They were slick and quick and they wore their mirror shades at breakfast and dinner, in the shower, in closets and caves. In short, they were bad.

I drove. Digby pounded the dashboard and shouted along with Toots & the Maytals while Jeff hung his head out the window and streaked the side of my mother's Bel Air with vomit. It was early June, the air soft as a hand on your cheek, the third night of summer vacation. The first two nights we'd been out till dawn, looking for something we never found. On this, the third night, we'd cruised the strip sixty-seven times, been in and out of every bar and club we could think of in a twenty-mile radius, stopped twice for bucket chicken and forty-cent hamburgers, debated going to a party at the house of a girl Jeff's sister knew, and chucked two dozen raw eggs at mailboxes and hitchhikers. It was 2:00 A.M.; the bars were closing. There was nothing to do but take a bottle of lemon-flavored gin up to Greasy Lake.

5   The taillights of a single car winked at us as we swung into the dirt lot with its tufts of weed and washboard corrugations; '57 Chevy, mint, metallic blue. On the far side of the lot, like the exoskeleton of some gaunt chrome insect, a chopper leaned against its

---

[1]*André Gide:* French novelist and critic (1869–1951) whose work—much of it semiautobiographical—examines the conflict between desire and discipline and shows individuals battling conventional morality.

[2]*susurrus:* A whispering or rustling sound.

kickstand. And that was it for excitement: some junkie half-wit biker and a car freak pumping his girlfriend. Whatever it was we were looking for, we weren't about to find it at Greasy Lake. Not that night.

But then all of a sudden Digby was fighting for the wheel. "Hey, that's Tony Lovett's car! Hey!" he shouted, while I stabbed at the brake pedal and the Bel Air nosed up to the gleaming bumper of the parked Chevy. Digby leaned on the horn, laughing, and instructed me to put my brights on. I flicked on the brights. This was hilarious. A joke. Tony would experience premature withdrawal and expect to be confronted by grim-looking state troopers with flashlights. We hit the horn, strobed the lights, and then jumped out of the car to press our witty faces to Tony's windows; for all we knew we might even catch a glimpse of some little fox's tit, and then we could slap backs with red-faced Tony, roughhouse a little, and go on to new heights of adventure and daring.

The first mistake, the one that opened the whole floodgate, was losing my grip on the keys. In the excitement, leaping from the car with the gin in one hand and a roach clip in the other, I spilled them in the grass—in the dark, rank, mysterious nighttime grass of Greasy Lake. This was a tactical error, as damaging and irreversible in its way as Westmoreland's decision to dig in at Khe Sanh.[3] I felt it like a jab of intuition, and I stopped there by the open door, peering vaguely into the night that puddled up round my feet.

The second mistake—and this was inextricably bound up with the first—was identifying the car as Tony Lovett's. Even before the very bad character in greasy jeans and engineer boots ripped out of the driver's door, I began to realize that this chrome blue was much lighter than the robin's-egg of Tony's car, and that Tony's car didn't have rear-mounted speakers. Judging from their expressions, Digby and Jeff were privately groping toward the same inevitable and unsettling conclusion as I was.

In any case, there was no reasoning with this bad greasy character—clearly he was a man of action. The first lusty Rockette[4] kick of his steel-toed boot caught me under the chin, chipped my favorite tooth, and left me sprawled in the dirt. Like a fool, I'd gone down on one knee to comb the stiff hacked grass for the keys, my mind making connections in the most dragged-out, testudineous[5] way, knowing that things had gone wrong, that I was in a lot of trouble, and that the lost ignition key was my grail and my salvation. The three or four succeeding blows were mainly absorbed by my right buttock and the tough piece of bone at the base of my spine.

Meanwhile, Digby vaulted the kissing bumpers and delivered a savage kung-fu   10
blow to the greasy character's collarbone. Digby had just finished a course in martial arts for phys-ed credit and had spent the better part of the past two nights telling us apocryphal tales of Bruce Lee types and of the raw power invested in lightning blows shot from coiled wrists, ankles, and elbows. The greasy character was unimpressed.

---

[3]*Khe Sanh:* In late 1967, North Vietnamese and Viet Cong forces mounted a strong attack against American troops at Khe Sanh, thereby causing General William C. Westmoreland, commander of United States forces in Vietnam, to "dig in" to defend an area of relatively little tactical importance.

[4]*Rockette:* The reference is to the Rockettes, a dance troupe at New York's Radio City Music Hall noted for precision and cancan-like high kicks.

[5]*testudineous:* Slow, like the pace of a tortoise.

He merely backed off a step, his face like a Toltec mask, and laid Digby out with a single whistling roundhouse blow. . . but by now Jeff had got into the act, and I was beginning to extricate myself from the dirt, a tinny compound of shock, rage, and impotence wadded in my throat.

Jeff was on the guy's back, biting at his ear. Digby was on the ground, cursing. I went for the tire iron I kept under the driver's seat. I kept it there because bad characters always keep tire irons under the driver's seat, for just such an occasion as this. Never mind that I hadn't been involved in a fight since sixth grade, when a kid with a sleepy eye and two streams of mucus depending from his nostrils hit me in the knee with a Louisville slugger,[6] never mind that I'd touched the tire iron exactly twice before, to change tires: it was there. And I went for it.

I was terrified. Blood was beating in my ears, my hands were shaking, my heart turning over like a dirtbike in the wrong gear. My antagonist was shirtless, and a single cord of muscle flashed across his chest as he bent forward to peel Jeff from his back like a wet overcoat. "Motherfucker," he spat, over and over, and I was aware in that instant that all four of us—Digby, Jeff, and myself included—were chanting "motherfucker, motherfucker," as if it were a battle cry. (What happened next? the detective asks the murderer from beneath the turned-down brim of his porkpie hat. I don't know, the murderer says, something came over me. Exactly.)

Digby poked the flat of his hand in the bad character's face and I came at him like a kamikaze, mindless, raging, stung with humiliation—the whole thing, from the initial boot in the chin to this murderous primal instant involving no more than sixty hyperventilating, gland-flooding seconds—I came at him and brought the tire iron down across his ear. The effect was instantaneous, astonishing. He was a stunt man and this was Hollywood, he was a big grimacing toothy balloon and I was a man with a straight pin. He collapsed. Wet his pants. Went loose in his boots.

A single second, big as a zeppelin, floated by. We were standing over him in a circle, gritting our teeth, jerking our necks, our limbs and hands and feet twitching with glandular discharges. No one said anything. We just stared down at the guy, the car freak, the lover, the bad greasy character laid low. Digby looked at me; so did Jeff. I was still holding the tire iron, a tuft of hair clinging to the crook like dandelion fluff, like down. Rattled, I dropped it in the dirt, already envisioning the headlines, the pitted faces of the police inquisitors, the gleam of handcuffs, clank of bars, the big black shadows rising from the back of the cell . . . when suddenly a raw torn shriek cut through me like all the juice in all the electric chairs in the country.

15   It was the fox. She was short, barefoot, dressed in panties and a man's shirt. "Animals!" she screamed, running at us with her fists clenched and wisps of blow-dried hair in her face. There was a silver chain round her ankle, and her toenails flashed in the glare of the headlights. I think it was the toenails that did it. Sure, the gin and the cannabis and even the Kentucky Fried may have had a hand in it, but it was the sight of those flaming toes that set us off—the toad emerging from the loaf in *Virgin Spring*,[7] lipstick smeared on a child: she was already tainted. We were on her

---

[6]*Louisville slugger:* A popular brand of baseball bat.
[7]*Virgin Spring:* A film by Swedish director Ingmar Bergman.

like Bergman's deranged brothers—see no evil, hear none, speak none—panting, wheezing, tearing at her clothes, grabbing for flesh. We were bad characters, and we were scared and hot and three steps over the line—anything could have happened.

It didn't.

Before we could pin her to the hood of the car, our eyes masked with lust and greed and the purest primal badness, a pair of headlights swung into the lot. There we were, dirty, bloody, guilty, dissociated from humanity and civilization, the first of the Ur-crimes[8] behind us, the second in progress, shreds of nylon panty and spandex brassiere dangling from our fingers, our flies open, lips licked—there we were, caught in the spotlight. Nailed.

We bolted. First for the car, and then, realizing we had no way of starting it, for the woods. I thought nothing. I thought escape. The headlights came at me like accusing fingers. I was gone.

Ram-bam-bam, across the parking lot, past the chopper and into the feculent undergrowth at the lake's edge, insects flying up in my face, weeds whipping, frogs and snakes and red-eyed turtles splashing off into the night: I was already ankle-deep in muck and tepid water and still going strong. Behind me, the girl's screams rose in intensity, disconsolate, incriminating, the screams of the Sabine women,[9] the Christian martyrs, Anne Frank[10] dragged from the garret. I kept going, pursued by those cries, imagining cops and bloodhounds. The water was up to my knees when I realized what I was doing: I was going to swim for it. Swim the breadth of Greasy Lake and hide myself in the thick clot of woods on the far side. They'd never find me there.

I was breathing in sobs, in gasps. The water lapped at my waist as I looked out over   20
the moon-burnished ripples, the mats of algae that clung to the surface like scabs. Digby and Jeff had vanished. I paused. Listened. The girl was quieter now, screams tapering to sobs, but there were male voices, angry, excited, and the high-pitched ticking of the second car's engine. I waded deeper, stealthy, hunted, the ooze sucking at my sneakers. As I was about to take the plunge—at the very instant I dropped my shoulder for the first slashing stroke—I blundered into something. Something unspeakable, obscene, something soft, wet, moss-grown. A patch of weed? A log? When I reached out to touch it, it gave like a rubber duck, it gave like flesh.

In one of those nasty little epiphanies for which we are prepared by films and TV and childhood visits to the funeral home to ponder the shrunken painted forms of dead grandparents, I understood what it was that bobbed there so inadmissibly in the dark. Understood, and stumbled back in horror and revulsion, my mind yanked in six different directions (I was nineteen, a mere child, an infant, and here in the space of five minutes I'd struck down one greasy character and blundered into the waterlogged

---

[8]*Ur-crimes:* Primitive crimes.

[9]*Sabine women:* According to legend, members of an ancient Italian tribe abducted by Romans who took them for wives. The "Rape of the Sabine Women" has been depicted by various artists, most notably by seventeenth-century French painter Nicolas Poussin.

[10]*Anne Frank:* German Jewish girl (1929–1945) whose family hid in an attic in Amsterdam during the Nazi occupation of the Netherlands. Frank, who along with her family was discovered by storm troopers and sent to die at the concentration camp at Belsen, is famous for her diary, which recounts her days in hiding. A new version of the diary containing five missing pages surfaced in 1998.

carcass of a second), thinking, The keys, the keys, why did I have to go and lose the keys? I stumbled back, but the muck took hold of my feet—a sneaker snagged, balance lost—and suddenly I was pitching face forward into the buoyant black mass, throwing out my hands in desperation while simultaneously conjuring the image of reeking frogs and muskrats revolving in slicks of their own deliquescing[11] juices. AAAAArrrgh! I shot from the water like a torpedo, the dead man rotating to expose a mossy beard and eyes cold as the moon. I must have shouted out, thrashing around in the weeds, because the voices behind me suddenly became animated.

"What was that?"

"It's them, it's them: they tried to, tried to . . . *rape* me!" Sobs.

A man's voice, flat Midwestern accent. "You sons a bitches, we'll kill you!"

25   Frogs, crickets.

Then another voice, harsh, *r*-less, Lower East Side: "Motherfucker!" I recognized the verbal virtuosity of the bad greasy character in the engineer boots. Tooth chipped, sneakers gone, coated in mud and slime and worse, crouching breathless in the weeds waiting to have my ass thoroughly and definitively kicked and fresh from the hideous stinking embrace of a three-days-dead-corpse, I suddenly felt a rush of joy and vindication: the son of a bitch was alive! Just as quickly, my bowels turned to ice. "Come on out of there, you pansy mothers!" the bad greasy character was screaming. He shouted curses till he was out of breath.

The crickets started up again, then the frogs. I held my breath. All at once there was a sound in the reeds, a swishing, a splash: thunk-a-thunk. They were throwing rocks. The frogs fell silent. I cradled my head. Swish, swish, thunk-a-thunk. A wedge of feldspar the size of a cue ball glanced off my knee. I bit my finger.

It was then that they turned to the car. I heard a door slam, a curse, and then the sound of the headlights shattering—almost a good-natured sound, celebratory, like corks popping from the necks of bottles. This was succeeded by the dull booming of the fenders, metal on metal, and then the icy crash of the windshield. I inched forward, elbows and knees, my belly pressed to the muck, thinking of guerrillas and commandos and *The Naked and the Dead.*[12] I parted the weeds and squinted the length of the parking lot.

The second car—it was a Trans-Am—was still running, its high beams washing the scene in a lurid stagy light. Tire iron flailing, the greasy bad character was laying into the side of my mother's Bel Air like an avenging demon, his shadow riding up the trunks of the trees. Whomp. Whomp. Whomp-whomp. The other two guys—blond types, in fraternity jackets—were helping out with tree branches and skull-sized boulders. One of them was gathering up bottles, rocks, muck, candy wrappers, used condoms, pop-tops, and other refuse and pitching it through the window on the driver's side. I could see the fox, a white bulb behind the windshield of the '57 Chevy. "Bobbie," she whined over the thumping, "come *on.*" The greasy character paused a moment, took one good swipe at the left taillight, and then heaved the tire iron halfway across the lake. Then he fired up the '57 and was gone.

---

[11] *deliquescing:* Melting.

[12] The Naked and the Dead: A popular and critically praised 1948 novel by Norman Mailer depicting Army life among U.S. soldiers during World War II.

Blond head nodded at blond head. One said something to the other, too low for   30
me to catch. They were no doubt thinking that in helping to annihilate my mother's
car they'd committed a fairly rash act, and thinking too that there were three bad
characters connected with that very car watching them from the woods. Perhaps
other possibilities occurred to them as well—police, jail cells, justices of the peace,
reparations, lawyers, irate parents, fraternal censure. Whatever they were thinking,
they suddenly dropped branches, bottles, and rocks and sprang for their car in unison,
as if they'd choreographed it. Five seconds. That's all it took. The engine shrieked,
the tires squealed, a cloud of dust rose from the rutted lot and then settled back on
darkness.

I don't know how long I lay there, the bad breath of decay all around me, my
jacket heavy as a bear, the primordial ooze subtly reconstituting itself to accommodate my upper thighs and testicles. My jaws ached, my knee throbbed, my coccyx[13]
was on fire. I contemplated suicide, wondered if I'd need bridgework, scraped the
recesses of my brain for some sort of excuse to give my parents—a tree had fallen on
the car, I was blindsided by a bread truck, hit and run, vandals had got to it while
we were playing chess at Digby's. Then I thought of the dead man. He was probably
the only person on the planet worse off than I was. I thought about him, fog on the
lake, insects chirring eerily, and felt the tug of fear, felt the darkness opening up
inside me like a set of jaws. Who was he, I wondered, this victim of time and circumstance bobbing sorrowfully in the lake at my back. The owner of the chopper, no
doubt, a bad older character come to this. Shot during a murky drug deal, drowned
while drunkenly frolicking in the lake. Another headline. My car was wrecked; he
was dead.

When the eastern half of the sky went from black to cobalt and the trees began to
separate themselves from the shadows, I pushed myself up from the mud and stepped
out into the open. By now the birds had begun to take over for the crickets, and dew
lay slick on the leaves. There was a smell in the air, raw and sweet at the same time,
the smell of the sun firing buds and opening blossoms. I contemplated the car. It lay
there like a wreck along the highway, like a steel sculpture left over from a vanished
civilization. Everything was still. This was nature.

I was circling the car, as dazed and bedraggled as the sole survivor of an air blitz,
when Digby and Jeff emerged from the trees behind me. Digby's face was crosshatched
with smears of dirt; Jeff's jacket was gone and his shirt was torn across the shoulder.
They slouched across the lot, looking sheepish, and silently came up beside me to
gape at the ravaged automobile. No one said a word. After a while Jeff swung open the
driver's door and began to scoop the broken glass and garbage off the seat. I looked at
Digby. He shrugged. "At least they didn't slash the tires," he said.

It was true: the tires were intact. There was no windshield, the headlights were
staved in, and the body looked as if it had been sledgehammered for a quarter a shot
at the county fair, but the tires were inflated to regulation pressure. The car was
drivable. In silence, all three of us bent to scrape the mud and shattered glass from
the interior. I said nothing about the biker. When we were finished, I reached in

---

[13]*coccyx*: Tailbone.

my pocket for the keys, experienced a nasty stab of recollection, cursed myself, and turned to search the grass. I spotted them almost immediately, no more than five feet from the open door, glinting like jewels in the first tapering shaft of sunlight. There was no reason to get philosophical about it: I eased into the seat and turned the engine over.

35 It was at that precise moment that the silver Mustang with the flame decals rumbled into the lot. All three of us froze; then Digby and Jeff slid into the car and slammed the door. We watched as the Mustang rocked and bobbed across the ruts and finally jerked to a halt beside the forlorn chopper at the far end of the lot. "Let's go," Digby said. I hesitated, the Bel Air wheezing beneath me.

Two girls emerged from the Mustang. Tight jeans, stiletto heels, hair like frozen fur. They bent over the motorcycle, paced back and forth aimlessly, glanced once or twice at us, and then ambled over to where the reeds sprang up in a green fence round the perimeter of the lake. One of them cupped her hands to her mouth. "Al," she called, "Hey, Al!"

"Come on," Digby hissed. "Let's get out of here."

But it was too late. The second girl was picking her way across the lot, unsteady on her heels, looking up at us and then away. She was older—twenty-five or -six—and as she came closer we could see there was something wrong with her: she was stoned or drunk, lurching now and waving her arms for balance. I gripped the steering wheel as if it were the ejection lever of a flaming jet, and Digby spat out my name, twice, terse and impatient.

"Hi," the girl said.

40 We looked at her like zombies, like war veterans, like deaf-and-dumb pencil peddlers.

She smiled, her lips cracked and dry. "Listen," she said, bending from the waist to look in the window, "you guys seen Al?" Her pupils were pinpoints, her eyes glass. She jerked her neck. "That's his bike over there—Al's. You seen him?"

Al. I didn't know what to say. I wanted to get out of the car and retch, I wanted to go home to my parents' house and crawl into bed. Digby poked me in the ribs. "We haven't seen anybody," I said.

The girl seemed to consider this, reaching out a slim veiny arm to brace herself against the car. "No matter," she said, slurring the *t*'s, "he'll turn up." And then, as if she'd just taken stock of the whole scene—the ravaged car and our battered faces, the desolation of the place—she said: "Hey, you guys look like some pretty bad characters—been fightin', huh?" We stared straight ahead, rigid as catatonics. She was fumbling in her pocket and muttering something. Finally she held out a handful of tablets in glassine wrappers: "Hey, you want to party, you want to do some of these with me and Sarah?"

I just looked at her. I thought I was going to cry. Digby broke the silence. "No, thanks," he said, leaning over me. "Some other time."

45 I put the car in gear and it inched forward with a groan, shaking off pellets of glass like an old dog shedding water after a bath, heaving over the ruts on its worn springs, creeping toward the highway. There was a sheen of sun on the lake. I looked back. The girl was still standing there, watching us, her shoulders slumped, hand outstretched.

JUNOT DÍAZ (1968–   )

No Face (1996)

In the morning he pulls on his mask and grinds his fist into his palm. He goes to the guanábana tree and does his pull-ups, nearly fifty now, and then he picks up the café dehuller and holds it to his chest for a forty count. His arms, chest and neck bulge and the skin around his temple draws tight, about to split. But no! He's unbeatable and drops the dehuller with a fat Yes. He knows that he should go but the morning fog covers everything and he listens to the roosters for a while. Then he hears his family stirring. Hurry up, he says to himself. He runs past his tío's land and with a glance he knows how many beans of café his tío has growing red, black and green on his conucos. He runs past the water hose and the pasture, and then he says FLIGHT and jumps up and his shadow knifes over the tops of the trees and he can see his family's fence and his mother washing his little brother, scrubbing his face and his feet.

The storekeepers toss water on the road to keep the dust down; he sweeps past them. No Face! a few yell out but he has no time for them. First he goes to the bars, searches the nearby ground for dropped change. Drunks sometimes sleep in the alleys so he moves quietly. He steps over the piss-holes and the vomit, wrinkles his nose at the stink. Today he finds enough coins in the tall crackling weeds to buy a bottle of soda or a johnnycake. He holds the coins tightly in his hands and under his mask he smiles.

At the hottest part of the day Lou lets him into the church with its bad roof and poor wiring and gives him café con leche and two hours of reading and writing. The books, the pen, the paper all come from the nearby school, donated by the teacher. Father Lou has small hands and bad eyes and twice he's gone to Canada for operations. Lou teaches him the English he'll need up north. I'm hungry. Where's the bathroom? I come from the Dominican Republic. Don't be scared.

After his lessons he buys Chiclets and goes to the house across from the church. The house has a gate and orange trees and a cobblestone path. A TV trills somewhere inside. He waits for the girl but she doesn't come out. Normally she'd peek out and see him. She'd make a TV with her hands. They both speak with their hands.

Do you want to watch? 5

He'd shake his head, put his hands out in front of him. He never went into casas ajenas. *No. I like being outside.*

I'd rather be inside where it's cool.

He'd stay until the cleaning woman, who also lived in the mountains, yelled from the kitchen, Stay away from here. Don't you have any shame? Then he'd grip the bars of the gate and pull them a bit apart, grunting, to show her who she was messing with.

Each week Padre Lou lets him buy a comic book. The priest takes him to the bookseller and stands in the street, guarding him, while he peruses the shelves.

Today be buys Kaliman, who takes no shit and wears a turban. If his face were 10 covered he'd be perfect.

*   *   *

He watches for opportunities from corners, away from people. He has his power of INVISIBILITY and no one can touch him. Even his tío, the one who guards the dams, strolls past and says nothing. Dogs can smell him though and a couple nuzzle his feet. He pushes them away since they can betray his location to his enemies. So many wish him to fall. So many wish him gone.

A viejo[1] needs help pushing his cart. A cat needs to be brought across the street.

Hey No Face! a motor driver yells. What the hell are you doing? You haven't started eating cats, have you?

He'll be eating kids next, another joins in.

15   Leave that cat alone, it's not yours.

He runs. It's late in the day and the shops are closing and even the motorbikes at each corner have dispersed, leaving oil stains and ruts in the dirt.

*   *   *

The ambush comes when he's trying to figure out if he can buy another johnnycake. Four boys tackle him and the coins jump out of his hand like grasshoppers. The fat boy with the single eyebrow sits on his chest and his breath flies out of him. The others stand over him and he's scared.

We're going to make you a girl, the fat one says and he can hear the words echoing through the meat of the fat boy's body. He wants to breathe but his lungs are as tight as pockets.

You ever been a girl before?

20   I betcha he hasn't. It ain't a lot of fun.

He says STRENGTH and the fat boy flies off him and he's running down the street and the others are following. You better leave him alone, the owner of the beauty shop says but no one ever listens to her, not since her husband left her for a Haitian. He makes it back to the church and slips inside and hides. The boys throw rocks against the door of the church but then Eliseo, the groundskeeper says, Boys, prepare for hell, and runs his machete on the sidewalk. Everything outside goes quiet. He sits down under a pew and waits for nighttime, when he can go back home to the smokehouse to sleep. He rubs the blood on his shorts, spits on the cut to get the dirt out.

Are you okay? Padre Lou asks.

I've been running out of energy.

Padre Lou sits down. He looks like one of those Cuban shopkeepers in his shorts and guayabera. He pats his hands together. I've been thinking about you up north. I'm trying to imagine you in the snow.

25   Snow won't bother me.

Snow bothers everybody.

Do they like wrestling?

Padre Lou laughs. Almost as much as we do, Except nobody gets cut up, not anymore.

He comes out from under the pew then and shows the priest his elbow. The priest sighs, Let's go take care of that, OK?

---

[1]*viejo:* Spanish for "old man."

Just don't use the red stuff.   30

We don't use the red stuff anymore. We have the white stuff now and it doesn't hurt.

I'll believe that when I see it.

*   *   *

No one has ever hidden it from him. They tell him the story over and over again, as though afraid that he might forget.

On some nights he opens his eyes and the pig has come back. Always huge and pale. Its hooves peg his chest down and he can smell the curdled bananas on its breath. Blunt teeth rip a strip from under his eye and the muscle revealed is delicious, like lechosa. He turns his head to save one side of his face; in some dreams he saves his right side and in some his left but in the worst ones he cannot turn his head, its mouth is like a pothole and nothing can escape it. When he awakens he's screaming and blood braids down his neck; he's bitten his tongue and it swells and he cannot sleep again until he tells himself to be a man.

*   *   *

Padre Lou borrows a Honda motorcycle and the two set out early in the morning. He   35
leans into the turns and Lou says, Don't do that too much. You'll tip us.

Nothing will happen to us! he yells.

The road to Ocoa is empty and the fincas[2] are dry and many of the farmsteads have been abandoned. On a bluff he sees a single black horse. It's eating a shrub and a garza[3] is perched on its back.

The clinic is crowded with bleeding people but a nurse with bleached hair brings them through to the front.

How are we today? the doctor says.

I'm fine, he says. When are you sending me away?   40

The doctor smiles and makes him remove his mask and then massages his face with his thumbs. The doctor has colorless food in his teeth. Have you had trouble swallowing?

No.

Breathing?

No.

Have you had any headaches? Does your throat ever hurt? Are you ever dizzy?   45

Never.

The doctor checks his eyes, his ears, and then listens to his breathing. Everything looks good, Lou.

I'm glad to hear that. Do you have a ballpark figure?

Well, the doctor says. We'll get him there eventually.

Padre Lou smiles and puts a hand on his shoulder. What do you think about that?   50

---

[2]*fincas:* Spanish for *farms.*

[3]*garza:* Spanish for *heron.*

He nods but doesn't know what he should think. He's scared of the operations and scared that nothing will change, that the Canadian doctors will fail like the santeras his mother hired, who called every spirit in the celestial directory for help. The room he's in is hot and dim and dusty and he's sweating and wishes he could lie under a table where no one can see. In the next room he met a boy whose skull plates had not closed all the way and a girl who didn't have arms and a baby whose face was huge and swollen and whose eyes were dripping pus.

You can see my brain, the boy said. All I have is this membrane thing and you can see right into it.

*   *   *

In the morning he wakes up hurting. From the doctor, from a fight he had outside the church. He goes outside, dizzy, and leans against the guanabana tree. His little brother Pesao is awake, flicking beans at the chickens, his little body bowed and perfect and when he rubs the four-year-old's head he feels the sores that have healed into yellow crusts. He aches to pick at them but the last time the blood had *gushed* and Pesao had *screamed.*

Where have you been? Pesao asks.

55   I've been fighting evil.

I want to do that.

You won't like it, he says.

Pesao looks at his face, giggles and flings another pebble at the hens, who scatter indignantly.

He watches the sun burn the mists from the fields and despite the heat the beans are thick and green and flexible in the breeze. His mother sees him on the way back from the outhouse. She goes to fetch his mask.

60   He's tired and aching but he looks out over the valley, and the way the land curves away to hide itself reminds him of the way Lou hides his dominos when they play. Go, she says, Before your father comes out.

He knows what happens when his father comes out. He pulls on his mask and feels the fleas stirring in the cloth. When she turns her back, he hides, blending into the weeds. He watches his mother hold Pesao's head gently under the faucet and when the water finally urges out from the pipe Pesao yells as if he's been given a present or a wish come true.

He runs, down towards town, never slipping or stumbling. Nobody's faster.

JAMES FRANCO (1978–   )

Halloween (2010)

Ten years ago, my sophomore year in high school, I killed a woman on Halloween.

I had been drinking at Ed Sales's house all afternoon, which I wasn't supposed to be doing because I was on probation. The probation rules said I was only allowed to drive to school and then right back home after school was out. But it was six months since I'd been arrested for being a minor under the influence, and my parents had become lax about the driving rules. On that Halloween Tuesday, instead of going home, I took some friends over to Ed's and we all got drunk.

His father was a mathematics professor at Stanford and his mother was a nurse, and neither of them came home until at least six but usually seven. His professor father had a great liquor cabinet. I had my first drink there when I was thirteen, and in the three years since then we had been taking from his cupboard and putting water back into the bottles. We could never get much from any one bottle because it would be too obvious; so we would take a little from all the bottles and mix everything into a punch like the bums did in *Cannery Row*.[1] I like that we did that, I liked thinking that we were like Mack and the boys, even though the punch tasted horrible. We'd usually mix it with grape juice, but it wouldn't help much.

We were all sitting in the backyard on a little picnic table that you might find at a park. His dad probably took it from the dump. He was always doing weird stuff like that to save money. Ed did it too, like scraping the mold off old bread and then eating it. His dad was a mathematics professor who smoked a pipe, every night. His teeth were yellow and crooked and horrible. Ed had a little pipe and he smoked tobacco with his dad at night. Ed was half Korean and half white because his mother was Korean and his dad was white from Gary, Indiana.

Outside, we were smoking weed in Ed's little tobacco pipe. We were all planning on going to Alice Wolfe's house later for the Halloween party, and we were getting ourselves revved up. I picked a fight with Nick Dobbs. I had seen him hanging around my girlfriend, Susan, and I didn't like it. I spotted them a couple times laughing in the corner of the library at school. I probably wouldn't have cared if he had been just one of those theater dorks that she was always planning events with, but he wasn't. He was a handsome skateboarder, and I had enough of the alcohol punch in me to start something.   5

"I heard you and Susan did acid. Why did you give my girlfriend acid?"

"She wanted it."

His eyes actually looked worried. It was not the reaction I was expecting. I suddenly felt powerful and a little bad for him at the same time. I probably couldn't have asked for a better reaction because I really wasn't a fighter, and this way, because he looked scared, I had beat him without having to fight him. I didn't like to see people intimidated, but this guilt made me turn meaner because I told him to apologize, and when he did, I demanded that he say it louder so that everyone could hear. I was pushing it a little and I could see him consider just taking a swing at me, but he apologized again slightly louder. Jack spoke up.

"What the fuck do you care, Ryan? She does acid and other drugs all the time, with all of us."

Well, I didn't like that. Funny how new facts pop up and make you doubt that   10
there's any goodness in life. Everyone pretends to be normal and be your friend, but underneath, everyone is living some other life you don't know about, and if only we had a camera on us at all times, we could go and watch each other's tapes and find out what each of us was really like. But then you'd have to watch girls go poo and boys trying to go down on themselves.

---

[1]*Cannery Row*: 1945 novel by American author John Steinbeck.

Then Ed's Korean mom came home. She was only about four foot ten, but we all got scared anyway. We heard the front door close inside the house, and Ed said, "My mom's home!" And we grabbed most of the cups and someone grabbed the punch and Ed grabbed his pipe and we all scrambled over the fence and jumped into my car. It was a Honda Accord I'd inherited from my father when things were better between us, and it was pretty small for eight people. There were two others in the front besides me and five in the back. Jack's elbow was in my face, and when I looked in the rearview, the back-seat was a jumble of arms and torsos and heads up against the ceiling. Nick wasn't in the car. He ran off somewhere to go and cry, I guess.

I raced out of there. It wasn't time for Alice's party so we had to find a place to go. The sun was going down, and there were already trick-or-treaters out with their parents. Everyone started getting rambunctious. It made it hard to drive with all the yelling and Jack's elbow in my face.

"Get that thing out of my face!"

Jack just laughed because there wasn't much he could do with his elbow. Everyone was talking very loudly, and the people that had saved their cups were trying to drink their punch and were spilling it all over the car. Then for some reason everyone started chanting, "Fuck Alice Wolfe, fuck Alice Wolfe, fuck the Wolfe!" We didn't know why we were saying it, at least I didn't, but it was really funny, and some of the guys were howling and everyone was feeling good from the drinks and about the escape and about the night ahead.

15   For some reason I was still driving fast. As if we were racing somewhere. I guess I just wanted to get this octopus of bodies out of the car as soon as possible, but it was also more fun to drive faster, as if we were really having a crazy adventure. I used to think of these escapades around the neighborhood as good life experience.

We decided to go to Eleanor Park to lie low before the party. There was a little community garden in the back of the park where people could grow their own vegetables, and there were some picnic tables there just like the one in Ed's backyard. We all sat down and continued what we had been doing at Ed's house. Ed went over and started picking baby tomatoes and carrots from the garden. They were small but tasted really good, and the carrots were soft and buttery tasting. Ivan went over and started kicking a trellis down, and everyone laughed because his foot went through it.

It was a simple existence, when I look back on it now I have friends who grew up in New York City, and the stories they have from their childhoods are amazing. Full of color and culture and danger. I envy them.

At about eight we went to Alice Wolfe's party. We had finished the punch in the park, and everyone was feeling even happier. The Wolfe chant started up again, but this time it was slurred. Now that we were close to the house, the chant began to take on meaning for me. It meant that we had little respect for Alice Wolfe and her friends. Yes, they were the prettiest, most popular girls in our class, but they weren't that pretty. And our chant meant that we were going to dominate them. We were going to go over there and do our best to get them alone and fuck them.

We had decided to go as monkeys. We had identical monkey masks that we'd stashed in the trunk. All eight of us wore one so no one could tell us apart. At Alice's it worked out great. It broke the ice because we could act as stupidly as we liked, and we ended up making the girls laugh a lot more than they usually did. I had a few more beers, and then I found myself talking on the back porch with Sandy Cooper.

"I know it's you, Ryan."   20

"Nooooo it's naaaaht." I was using a deep, doofusy kind of voice like Baloo from the *Jungle Book* movie.

"I'll pretend it's not you so if I get caught I won't get beat up by Susan."

"Whooooooo's Suuusaaan?"

"Shut up, Ryan."

I took the monkey mask off, and we made out for a bit in the backyard. Then I   25
figured that I had better call Susan because I said I was going to. She was going to a different, less cool party with her girlfriends because they weren't invited to Alice's. I needed to come up with an excuse not to meet her. I told Sandy to wait, and I went inside to use the phone.

I called Susan at her house.

"Took you long enough," she said.

"What?"

"You were supposed to call me two hours ago."

"Sorry, we were just over at the park and there wasn't a phone around."   30

"Good excuse."

"It's true. So you're still at home?"

"Yeah, we're just getting our costumes on."

"Who?"

"Me and Elizabeth and Jenny and Hart and Nick."   35

"Nick Dobbs? What's he doing there?"

"Putting his costume on. He and Hart are going to be the guys from *A Clockwork Orange*[2] with Terry and Pete."

"Why the fuck are you hanging out with Nick?"

"He's my friend."

"Yeah, getting real friendly in the library."   40

I hung up the phone. I told Jack and Ed that I was leaving, and I ran out to my car. The driveway and bushes were blurry as I ran. I got the car handle in my grip and opened the door. I got in and took off toward Susan's.

I was racing on my anger. On the righteousness of catching Nick with her. I had no clear plan for what I would do when I arrived, but I could see my fist going toward Nick's face. I had glimpses of Hart's angry face; I'd probably have to deal with him too. He was bigger than me. I'd probably have to reason with him after I kicked the shit out of Nick. I saw Susan's horrified reaction, and I felt buffeted on a hot wave of self-righteousness. The streets were fairly empty, and I accepted them as my personal roadway. My ordinary submission to traffic laws evaporated. I raced around corners without looking and shot through the phantom walls of the stoplights. The more recklessly I drove, the easier it was.

The Main Library passed on my left. I went through the red light at Embarcadero and Newell and passed Candice Brown's house on the right. Bitch, she cheated on her

---

[2]*A Clockwork Orange*: 1971 film by American director Stanley Kubrick.

boyfriend too. I shot down Newell, busting through neighborhood stop signs toward Jordan Middle School. At the school I screeched through the stop sign and around the corner to the right.

There was no time to do anything about the dark figure standing in the road. The car went right at it. There was a bump and the figure disappeared underneath the car. I realized I was already pressing the brakes when the car stopped ten yards away. I put the car in Park and pressed the button for the automatic window and stuck my body out the window to look back. The figure was lying facedown on the road. There was no one else around. Just the empty school on one side of the street and on the other some sycamores in shadow. Whoever the figure was couldn't have seen what kind of car raced into her. I took the moment and drove off before she started moving.

45   I was driving fast again, but I obeyed the street signs now. I didn't know where to go. My rage had dissipated into a little boy's fear for his safety. I couldn't go to Susan's, and I didn't want to go home because my father would see how drunk I was; but I wanted to get the car off the street. Ed's house was close, and I drove in that direction. The flaccid monkey mask in the passenger seat looked like it was grinning. It was an object from a different time. Alice Wolfe's house and Sandy Cooper were far away. The accident had drained the life from everything that had happened earlier.

Near Ed's, I parked the car very carefully under the shadow of a large tree. I got out and forced myself to look at the front of the car. There was only a small dent on the front of the hood where the head must have hit. I didn't see any blood. I realized I was only wearing a T-shirt, and I was shivering.

I knocked on Ed's door. Inside, someone grumbled, and then, finally, there were footsteps. Ed's professor father opened the door. At first only a little, and then he saw it was me and stuck his bald lightbulb head out and smiled, showing his bad teeth.

"Why, hello, Ryan. I thought you were some late trick-or-treaters, and I was about to tell them to go screw."

"Can I come in?"

50   "Uhh, sure. Is everything all right?"

I was still shivering.

"Yeah, I'm just drunk and I don't want to drive right now. I don't think it would be safe,"

I thought he would understand about being drunk better than my own father. My father was tired of my shit.

"Sure, come in," he said. He sat in his chair and I sat on the couch. Ed's mom wasn't there. The TV was on to the news, something about the Gulf War. Ed's dad took up his meerschaum[3] pipe and lit it.

55   "Would you like to smoke? Ed usually keeps his pipe here on the bookshelf, but I don't see it. Here, I have an extra."

He picked up another old pipe and loaded it with tobacco.

"Just suck a bit while you get it started or it will go out."

I did, and inhaled sweet-tasting tobacco.

"Where's Ed?" he said.

---

[3]*meerschaum:* A usually white mineral and common material for tobacco pipes.

"Oh, out with the guys, I guess."   60

"Chasing tail, no doubt."

This was funny because Ed wasn't the best guy with the ladies.

"Hope it works out for him," he said. "He's gone through all the tissues in the house." He laughed a high-pitched, too-big laugh. The longer I sat there, the more I calmed down. It meant no one was coming after me. My father would hardly notice the dent on the already beat-up car. I might get in a little trouble because I had kept the car and not gone home after school, but that would blow over. I would tell Susan that I got upset over Nick and went home.

After about an hour there was something on the news about the actor River Phoenix overdosing outside a club in LA. Then I decided to go.

"You sure you'll be all right?"   65

"Yeah, I feel okay now. Thanks, Mr. Sales."

I never told anyone about the accident. The *San Jose Mercury* ran a story about the woman the day after and so did the *Palo Alto Weekly*. She was a librarian and had been walking home from work. She lived alone.

My last couple of years of high school, I passed that corner a few times, and the little-boy terror came back. But eventually the feeling left. When I went back home from college to visit my parents, I'd drive past the corner, and it seemed like the accident only happened in a movie.

After my father died, I'd visit my mother at Christmas. One December, I passed the corner while driving my mother to the library. At first the corner didn't register. My mother was talking about the new children's book she was working on, and I was just listening to her when, halfway down the block, I remembered, "Oh yeah, that's where the accident happened."

GABRIEL GARCÍA MÁRQUEZ (1928–2014)

A Very Old Man with Enormous Wings (1968)

A Tale for Children

Translated from the Spanish by Gregory Rabassa

On the third day of rain they had killed so many crabs inside the house that Pelayo had to cross his drenched courtyard and throw them into the sea, because the newborn child had a temperature all night and they thought it was due to the stench. The world had been sad since Tuesday. Sea and sky were a single ash-gray thing and the sands of the beach, which on March nights glimmered like powdered light, had become a stew of mud and rotten shellfish. The light was so weak at noon that when Pelayo was coming back to the house after throwing away the crabs, it was hard for him to see what it was that was moving and groaning in the rear of the courtyard. He had to go very close to see that it was an old man, a very old man, lying face down in the mud, who, in spite of his tremendous efforts, couldn't get up, impeded by his enormous wings.

Frightened by that nightmare, Pelayo ran to get Elisenda, his wife, who was putting compresses on the sick child, and he took her to the rear of the courtyard. They both looked at the fallen body with mute stupor. He was dressed like a ragpicker.[1] There were only a few faded hairs left on his bald skull and very few teeth in his mouth, and his pitiful condition of a drenched great-grandfather had taken away any sense of grandeur he might have had. His huge buzzard wings, dirty and half-plucked, were forever entangled in the mud. They looked at him so long and so closely that Pelayo and Elisenda very soon overcame their surprise and in the end found him familiar. Then they dared speak to him, and he answered in an incomprehensible dialect with a strong sailor's voice. That was how they skipped over the inconvenience of the wings and quite intelligently concluded that he was a lonely castaway from some foreign ship wrecked by the storm. And yet, they called in a neighbor woman who knew everything about life and death to see him, and all she needed was one look to show them their mistake.

"He's an angel," she told them. "He must have been coming for the child, but the poor fellow is so old that the rain knocked him down."

On the following day everyone knew that a flesh-and-blood angel was held captive in Pelayo's house. Against the judgment of the wise neighbor woman, for whom angels in those times were the fugitive survivors of a celestial conspiracy, they did not have the heart to club him to death. Pelayo watched over him all afternoon from the kitchen, armed with his bailiff's club, and before going to bed he dragged him out of the mud and locked him up with the hens in the wire chicken coop. In the middle of the night, when the rain stopped, Pelayo and Elisenda were still killing crabs. A short time afterward the child woke up without a fever and with a desire to eat. Then they felt magnanimous and decided to put the angel on a raft with fresh water and provisions for three days and leave him to his fate on the high seas. But when they went out into the courtyard with the first light of dawn, they found the whole neighborhood in front of the chicken coop having fun with the angel, without the slightest reverence, tossing him things to eat through the openings in the wire as if he weren't a supernatural creature but a circus animal.

5   Father Gonzaga arrived before seven o'clock, alarmed by the strange news. By that time onlookers less frivolous than those at dawn had already arrived and they were making all kinds of conjectures concerning the captive's future. The simplest among them thought that he should be named mayor of the world. Others of sterner mind felt that he should be promoted to the rank of five-star general in order to win all wars. Some visionaries hoped that he could be put to stud in order to implant on earth a race of winged wise men who could take charge of the universe. But Father Gonzaga, before becoming a priest, had been a robust woodcutter. Standing by the wire, he reviewed his catechism[2] in an instant and asked them to open the door so that he could take a close look at that pitiful man who looked more like a huge decrepit hen among the fascinated chickens. He was lying in a corner drying his open wings in the sunlight among the fruit peels and breakfast leftovers that the

---

[1] *ragpicker:* Someone who makes a living collecting rags and other refuse.

[2] *catechism:* A book that summarizes the doctrines of Roman Catholicism in question-and-answer form.

early risers had thrown him. Alien to the impertinences of the world, he only lifted his antiquarian[3] eyes and murmured something in his dialect when Father Gonzaga went into the chicken coop and said good morning to him in Latin. The parish priest had his first suspicion of an imposter when he saw that he did not understand the language of God or know how to greet His ministers. Then he noticed that seen close up he was much too human; he had an unbearable smell of the outdoors, the back side of his wings was strewn with parasites and his main feathers had been mistreated by terrestrial winds, and nothing about him measured up to the proud dignity of angels. Then he came out of the chicken coop and in a brief sermon warned the curious against the risks of being ingenuous. He reminded them that the devil had the bad habit of making use of carnival tricks in order to confuse the unwary. He argued that if wings were not the essential element in determining the difference between a hawk and an airplane, they were even less so in the recognition of angels. Nevertheless, he promised to write a letter to his bishop so that the latter would write to his primate so that the latter would write to the Supreme Pontiff[4] in order to get the final verdict from the highest courts.

His prudence fell on sterile hearts. The news of the captive angel spread with such rapidity that after a few hours the courtyard had the bustle of a marketplace and they had to call in troops with fixed bayonets to disperse the mob that was about to knock the house down. Elisenda, her spine all twisted from sweeping up so much marketplace trash, then got the idea of fencing in the yard and charging five cents admission to see the angel.

The curious came from far away. A traveling carnival arrived with a flying acrobat who buzzed over the crowd several times, but no one paid any attention to him because his wings were not those of an angel but, rather, those of a sidereal[5] bat. The most unfortunate invalids on earth came in search of health: a poor woman who since childhood had been counting her heartbeats and had run out of numbers; a Portuguese man who couldn't sleep because the noise of the stars disturbed him; a sleepwalker who got up at night to undo the things he had done while awake; and many others with less serious ailments. In the midst of that shipwreck disorder that made the earth tremble, Pelayo and Elisenda were happy with fatigue, for in less than a week they had crammed their rooms with money and the line of pilgrims waiting their turn to enter still reached beyond the horizon.

The angel was the only one who took no part in his own act. He spent his time trying to get comfortable in his borrowed nest, befuddled by the hellish heat of the oil lamps and sacramental candles that had been placed along the wire. At first they tried to make him eat some mothballs, which, according to the wisdom of the wise neighbor woman, were the food prescribed for angels. But he turned them down, just as he turned down the papal lunches that the penitents brought him, and they never found out whether it was because he was an angel or because he was an old man that in the end he ate nothing but eggplant mush. His only supernatural

---

[3] *antiquarian:* Ancient.

[4] *the Supreme Pontiff:* The pope.

[5] *sidereal:* Relating to the stars.

virtue seemed to be patience. Especially during the first days, when the hens pecked at him, searching for the stellar parasites that proliferated in his wings, and the cripples pulled out feathers to touch their defective parts with, and even the most merciful threw stones at him, trying to get him to rise so they could see him standing. The only time they succeeded in arousing him was when they burned his side with an iron for branding steers, for he had been motionless for so many hours that they thought he was dead. He awoke with a start, ranting in his hermetic[6] language and with tears in his eyes, and he flapped his wings a couple of times, which brought on a whirlwind of chicken dung and lunar dust and a gale of panic that did not seem to be of this world. Although many thought that his reaction had been one not of rage but of pain, from then on they were careful not to annoy him, because the majority understood that his passivity was not that of a hero taking his ease but that of a cataclysm in repose.

Father Gonzaga held back the crowd's frivolity with formulas of maid-servant inspiration while awaiting the arrival of a final judgment on the nature of the captive. But the mail from Rome showed no sense of urgency. They spent their time finding out if the prisoner had a navel, if his dialect had any connection with Aramaic,[7] how many times he could fit on the head of a pin, or whether he wasn't just a Norwegian with wings. Those meager letters might have come and gone until the end of time if a providential event had not put an end to the priest's tribulations.

10   It so happened that during those days, among so many other carnival attractions, there arrived in town the traveling show of the woman who had been changed into a spider for having disobeyed her parents. The admission to see her was not only less than the admission to see the angel, but people were permitted to ask her all manner of questions about her absurd state and to examine her up and down so that no one would ever doubt the truth of her horror. She was a frightful tarantula the size of a ram and with the head of a sad maiden. What was most heart-rending, however, was not her outlandish shape but the sincere affliction with which she recounted the details of her misfortune. While still practically a child she had sneaked out of her parents' house to go to a dance, and while she was coming back through the woods after having danced all night without permission, a fearful thunderclap rent the sky in two and through the crack came the lightning bolt of brimstone that changed her into a spider. Her only nourishment came from the meatballs that charitable souls chose to toss into her mouth. A spectacle like that, full of so much human truth and with such a fearful lesson, was bound to defeat without even trying that of a haughty angel who scarcely deigned to look at mortals. Besides, the few miracles attributed to the angel showed a certain mental disorder, like the blind man who didn't recover his sight but grew three new teeth, or the paralytic who didn't get to walk but almost won the lottery, and the leper whose sores sprouted sunflowers. Those consolation miracles, which were more like mocking fun, had already ruined the angel's reputation when the woman who had been changed into a spider finally crushed him completely. That was how Father Gonzaga was cured forever of his insomnia and

---

[6]*hermetic:* Occult, magical.

[7]*Aramaic:* An ancient Middle Eastern language believed to have been the language spoken by Jesus.

Pelayo's courtyard went back to being as empty as during the time it had rained for three days and crabs walked through the bedrooms.

The owners of the house had no reason to lament. With the money they saved they built a two-story mansion with balconies and gardens and high netting so that crabs wouldn't get in during the winter, and with iron bars on the windows so that angels wouldn't get in. Pelayo also set up a rabbit warren close to town and gave up his job as bailiff for good, and Elisenda bought some satin pumps with high heels and many dresses of iridescent silk, the kind worn on Sunday by the most desirable women in those times. The chicken coop was the only thing that didn't receive any attention. If they washed it down with creolin[8] and burned tears of myrrh[9] inside it every so often, it was not in homage to the angel but to drive away the dungheap stench that still hung everywhere like a ghost and was turning the new house into an old one. At first, when the child learned to walk, they were careful that he not get too close to the chicken coop. But then they began to lose their fears and got used to the smell, and before the child got his second teeth he'd gone inside the chicken coop to play, where the wires were falling apart. The angel was no less standoffish with him than with other mortals, but he tolerated the most ingenious infamies with the patience of a dog who had no illusions. They both came down with chicken pox at the same time. The doctor who took care of the child couldn't resist the temptation to listen to the angel's heart, and he found so much whistling in the heart and so many sounds in his kidneys that it seemed impossible for him to be alive. What surprised him most, however, was the logic of his wings. They seemed so natural on that completely human organism that he couldn't understand why other men didn't have them too.

When the child began school it had been some time since the sun and rain had caused the collapse of the chicken coop. The angel went dragging himself about here and there like a stray dying man. They would drive him out of the bedroom with a broom and a moment later find him in the kitchen. He seemed to be in so many places at the same time that they grew to think that he'd been duplicated, that he was reproducing himself all through the house, and the exasperated and unhinged Elisenda shouted that it was awful living in that hell full of angels. He could scarcely eat and his antiquarian eyes had also become so foggy that he went about bumping into posts. All he had left were the bare cannulae[10] of his last feathers. Pelayo threw a blanket over him and extended him the charity of letting him sleep in the shed, and only then did they notice that he had a temperature at night, and was delirious with the tongue twisters of an old Norwegian. That was one of the few times they became alarmed, for they thought he was going to die and not even the wise neighbor woman had been able to tell them what to do with dead angels.

And yet he not only survived his worst winter, but seemed improved with the first sunny days. He remained motionless for several days in the farthest corner of the courtyard, where no one would see him, and at the beginning of December some

---

[8]*creolin:* A disinfectant.
[9]*myrrh:* A type of incense.
[10]*cannulae:* Quills.

large, stiff feathers began to grow on his wings, the feathers of a scarecrow, which looked more like another misfortune of decrepitude. But he must have known the reason for those changes, for he was quite careful that no one should notice them, that no one should hear the sea chanteys that he sometimes sang under the stars. One morning Elisenda was cutting some bunches of onions for lunch when a wind that seemed to come from the high seas blew into the kitchen. Then she went to the window and caught the angel in his first attempts at flight. They were so clumsy that his fingernails opened a furrow in the vegetable patch and he was on the point of knocking the shed down with the ungainly flapping that slipped on the light and couldn't get a grip on the air. But he did manage to gain altitude. Elisenda let out a sigh of relief, for herself and for him, when she saw him pass over the last houses, holding himself up in some way with the risky flapping of a senile vulture. She kept watching him even when she was through cutting the onions and she kept on watching until it was no longer possible for her to see him, because then he was no longer an annoyance in her life but an imaginary dot on the horizon of the sea.

HA JIN (1956–   )

The Bane of the Internet (2009)

My sister Yuchin and I used to write each other letters. It took more than ten days for the mail to reach Sichuan, and usually I wrote her once a month. After Yuchin married, she was often in trouble, but I no longer thought about her every day. Five years ago her marriage began falling apart. Her husband started an affair with his female boss and sometimes came home reeling drunk. One night he beat and kicked Yuchin so hard she miscarried. At my suggestion, she filed for divorce. Afterward she lived alone and seemed content. I urged her to find another man, because she was only twenty-six, but she said she was done with men for this life. Capable and with a degree in graphic design, she has been doing well and even bought her own apartment four years ago. I sent her two thousand dollars to help her with the down payment.

Last fall she began e-mailing me. At first it was exciting to chat with her every night. We stopped writing letters. I even stopped writing to my parents, because she lives near them and can report to them. Recently she said she wanted to buy a car. I had misgivings about that, though she had already paid off her mortgage. Our hometown is small. You can cross by bicycle in half an hour: a car was not a necessity for her. It's too expensive to keep an automobile there—the gas, the insurance, the registration, the maintenance, the tolls cost a fortune. I told her I didn't have a car even though I had to commute to work from Brooklyn to Flushing. But she got it into her head that she must have a car because most of her friends had cars. She wrote: "I want to let that man see how well I'm doing." She was referring to her ex-husband. I urged her to wipe him out of her mind as if he had never existed. Indifference is the strongest contempt. For a few weeks she didn't raise the topic again.

Then she told me that she had just passed the road test, bribing the officer with five hundred yuan in addition to the three thousand paid as the application and test fees. She e-mailed: "Sister, I must have a car. Yesterday Minmin, our little niece, came to town driving a brand-new Volkswagen. At the sight of that gorgeous machine, I felt as if a dozen awls were stabbing my heart. Everybody is doing better than me, and I don't want to live anymore!"

I realized she didn't simply want to impress her ex. She too had caught the national auto mania. I told her that was ridiculous, nuts. I knew she had some savings. She got a big bonus at the end of each year and freelanced at night. How had she become so vain and so unreasonable? I urged her to be rational. That was impossible, she claimed, because "everybody" drove a car in our hometown. I said she was not everybody and mustn't follow the trend. She wouldn't listen and asked me to remit her money as a loan. She already had a tidy sum in the bank, about eighty thousand yuan, she confessed.

Then why couldn't she just go ahead and buy a car if that was what she wanted? 5 She replied: "You don't get it, sister. I cannot drive a Chinese model. If I did, people would think I am cheap and laugh at me. Japanese and German cars are too expensive for me, so I might get a Hyundai Elantra or a Ford Focus. Please lend me $10,000. I'm begging you to help me out!"

That was insane. Foreign cars are double priced in China. A Ford Taurus sells for 250,000 yuan in my home province of Sichuan, more than $30,000. I told Yuchin an automobile was just a vehicle, no need to be fancy. She must drop her vanity. Certainly I wouldn't lend her the money, because that might amount to hitting a dog with a meatball—nothing would come back. So I said no. As it is, I'm still renting and have to save for the down payment on a small apartment somewhere in Queens. My family always assumes that I can pick up cash right and left here. No matter how hard I explain, they can't see how awful my job at a sushi house is. I waitress ten hours a day, seven days a week. My legs are swollen when I punch out at ten P.M. I might never be able to buy an apartment at all. I'm eager to leave my job and start something of my own—a snack bar or a nail salon or a video store. I must save every penny.

For two weeks Yuchin and I argued. How I hated the e-mail exchanges! Every morning I flicked on the computer and saw a new message from her, sometimes three or four. I often thought of ignoring them, but if I did, I'd fidget at work, as if I had eaten something that had upset my stomach. If only I had pretended I'd never gotten her e-mail at the outset so that we could have continued writing letters. I used to believe that in the United States you could always reshape your relationships with the people back home—you could restart your life on your own terms. But the Internet has spoiled everything—my family is able to get hold of me whenever they like. They might as well live nearby.

Four days ago Yuchin sent me this message; "Elder sister, since you refused to help me, I decided to act on my own. At any rate, I must have a car. Please don't be mad at me. Here is a website you should take a look at . . ."

I was late for work, so I didn't visit the site. For the whole day I kept wondering what she was up to, and my left eyelid twitched nonstop. She might have solicited donations. She was impulsive and could get outrageous. When I came back that night and turned on my computer, I was flabbergasted to see that she had put out an ad on a popular site. She announced: "Healthy young woman ready to offer you her organ(s) in order to buy a car. Willing to sell any part as long as I still can drive thereafter. Contact me and let us talk." She listed her phone number and e-mail address.

10   I wondered if she was just bluffing. Perhaps she was. On the other hand, she was such a hothead that for a damned car she might not hesitate to sell a kidney, or a cornea, or a piece of her liver. I couldn't help but call her names while rubbing my forehead.

I had to do something right away. Someone might take advantage of the situation and sign a contract with her. She was my only sibling—if she messed up her life, there would be nobody to care for our old parents. If I was living near them, I might have called her bluff, but now there was no way out. I wrote her back: "All right, my idiot sister, I will lend you $10,000. Remove your ad from the website. Now!"

In a couple of minutes she returned: "Thank you! Gonna take it off right away. I know you're the only person I can rely on in the whole world."

I responded: "I will lend you the money I made by working my ass off. You must pay it back within two years. I have kept a hard copy of our email exchanges, so do not assume you can write off the loan."

She came back: "Got it. Have a nice dream, sister!" She added a smile sign.

15   "Get out of my face!" I muttered.

If only I could shut her out of my life for a few weeks. If only I could go somewhere for some peace and quiet.

FRANZ KAFKA (1883–1924)

A Hunger Artist (1924)

Translated by Edwin and Willa Muir

During these last decades the interest in professional fasting has markedly diminished. It used to pay very well to stage such great performances under one's own management, but today that is quite impossible. We live in a different world now. At one time the whole town took a lively interest in the hunger artist; from day to day of his fast the excitement mounted; everybody wanted to see him at least once a day; there were people who bought season tickets for the last few days and sat from morning till night in front of his small barred cage; even in the nighttime there were visiting hours, when the whole effect was heightened by torch flares; on fine days the cage was set out in the open air, and then it was the children's special treat to see the hunger artist; for their elders he was often just a joke that happened to be in fashion, but the children stood open-mouthed, holding each other's hands for greater security, marveling at him as he sat there pallid in black tights, with his ribs sticking out so prominently, not even on a seat but down among straw on the ground, sometimes giving a courteous nod, answering questions with a constrained smile, or perhaps stretching an arm through the bars so that one might feel how thin it was, and then again withdrawing deep into himself, paying no attention to anyone or anything, not even to the all-important striking of the clock that was the only piece of furniture in his cage, but merely starting into vacancy with half shut eyes, now and then taking a sip from a tiny glass of water to moisten his lips.

Besides causal onlookers there were also relays of permanent watchers selected by the public, usually butchers, strangely enough, and it was their task to watch the hunger artist day and night, three of them at a time, in case he should have some secret recourse to nourishment. This was nothing but a formality, instituted to reassure the masses, for the initiates knew well enough that during his fast the artist would never in any circumstances, not even under forcible compulsion, swallow the smallest morsel of food: the honor of his profession forbade it. Not every watcher, of course, was capable of understanding this, there were often groups of night watchers who were very lax in carrying out their duties and deliberately huddled together in a retired corner to play cards with great absorption, obviously intending to give the hunger artist the chance of a little refreshment, which they supposed he could draw from some private hoard. Nothing annoyed the artist more than such watchers; they made him miserable; they made his fast seem unendurable; sometimes he mastered his feebleness sufficiently to sing during their watch for as long as he could keep going, to show them how unjust their suspicions were. But that was of little use; they only wondered at his cleverness in being able to fill his mouth even while singing. Much more to his taste were the watchers who sat close up to the bars, who were not content with the dim night lighting of the hall but focused him in the full glare of the electric pocket torch given them by the impresario. The harsh light did not trouble him at all, in any case he could never sleep properly, and he could always drowse a little, whatever the light, at any hour, even when the hall was thronged with noisy onlookers. He was quite happy at the prospect of spending a sleepless night with such watchers; he was ready to exchange jokes with them, to tell them stories out of his nomadic life, anything at all to keep them awake and demonstrate to them again that he had no eatables in his cage and that he was fasting as not one of them could fast. But his happiest moment was when the morning came and an enormous breakfast was brought them, at his expense, on which they flung themselves with the keen appetite of healthy men after a weary night of wakefulness. Of course there were people who argued that this breakfast was an unfair attempt to bribe the watchers, but that was going rather too far, and when they were invited to take on a night's vigil without a breakfast, merely for the sake of the cause, they made themselves scarce, although they stuck stubbornly to their suspicions.

Such suspicions, anyhow, were a necessary accompaniment to the profession of fasting. No one could possibly watch the hunger artist continuously, day and night, and so no one could produce first-hand evidence that the fast had really been rigorous and continuous; only the artist himself could know that, he was therefore bound to be the sole completely satisfied spectator of his own fast. Yet for other reasons he was never satisfied; it was not perhaps mere fasting that had brought him to such skeleton thinness that many people had regretfully to keep away from his exhibitions; because the sight of him was too much for them, perhaps it was dissatisfaction with himself that had worn him down. For he alone knew, what no other initiate knew, how easy it was to fast. It was the easiest thing in the world. He made no secret of this, yet people did not believe him, at the best they set him down as modest, most of them, however, thought he was out for publicity or else was some kind of cheat who found it easy to fast because he had discovered a way of making it easy, and then had the impudence to admit the fact, more or less. He had to put up with all that, and in the course of time had got used to it, but his inner dissatisfaction always rankled, and never yet, after any term of fasting—this must be granted to his credit—had he left the cage of his own free will. The longest period of fasting was fixed by his impresario at forty days, beyond that term he was not allowed to go, not even in great cities, and there was good reason for it, too. Experience had proved that for about forty days the interest of the public could be stimulated by a steadily increasing pressure of advertisement, but after that the town began to lose interest, sympathetic support began notably to fall off; there were of course local variations as between one town and another or one country and another, but as a general rule forty days marked the limit. So on the for-tieth day the flower-bedecked cage was opened, enthusiastic spectators filled the hall, a military band played, two doctors entered the cage to measure the results of the fast, which were announced through a megaphone, and finally two young ladies appeared, blissful at having been selected for the honor, to help the hunger artist down the few steps leading to a small table on which was spread a carefully chosen invalid repast. And at this very moment the artist always turned stubborn. True, he would entrust his bony arms to the outstretched helping hands of the ladies bending over him, but stand up he would not. Why stop fasting at this particular moment, after forty days of it? He had held out for a long time, an illimitably long time; why stop now, when he was in his best fasting form, or rather, not yet quite in his best fasting form? Why should he be cheated of the fame he would get for fasting longer, for being not only the record hunger artist of all time, which presumably he was already, but for beating his own record by a performance beyond human imagination, since he felt that there were no limits to his capacity for fasting? His public pretended to admire him so much, why should it have so little patience with him; if he could endure fasting longer, why shouldn't the public endure it? Besides, he was tired, he was comfortable sitting in the straw, and now he was supposed to lift himself to his full height and go down to a meal the very thought of which gave him a nausea that only the presence of the ladies kept him from betraying, and even that with an effort. And he looked up into the eyes of the ladies who were apparently so friendly and in reality so cruel, and shook his head, which felt too heavy on its strengthless neck. But then there happened yet again what always happened. The impresario came forward, without a word—for the band made speech impossible—lifted his arms in the air above the artist, as if inviting Heaven to look down upon its creature here in the straw, this suffering martyr, which indeed he was, although in quite another sense; grasped him round the emaciated waist, with exaggerated caution, so that the frail condition he was in might be appreciated; and committed him to the care of the blenching ladies, not without secretly giving him a shaking so that his legs and body tottered and swayed. The artist now submitted com-pletely; his head lolled on his breast as if it had landed there by chance; his body was hollowed out; his legs in a spasm of self-preservation clung close to each other at the knees, yet scraped on the ground as if it were not really solid ground, as if they were only trying to find solid ground; and the whole weight of his body, a feather-weight after all, relapsed onto one of the ladies, who, looking round for help and panting a little—this post of honor was not at all what she had expected it to be—first stretched her neck as far as she could to keep her face at least free from contact with the artist, when finding this impossible, and her more fortunate companion not coming to her aid but merely holding extended on her own trembling hand the little bunch of knuckle-bones that was the artist's, to the great delight of the spectators burst into tears and had to be replaced by an attendant who had long been stationed in readiness. Then came the food, a little of which the impresario managed to get between the artist's lips, while he sat in a kind of half-fainting trance, to the accompaniment of cheerful patter designed to distract the public's attention from the artist's condition; after that, a toast was drunk to the public, supposedly prompted by a whisper from the artist in the impresario's ear; the band confirmed it with a mighty flourish, the spectators melted away, and no one had any cause to be dissatisfied with the proceedings, no one except the hunger artist himself, he only, as always.

So he lived for many years, with small regular intervals of recuperation, in visible glory, honored by the world, yet in spite of that troubled in spirit, and all the more troubled because no one would take his trouble seriously. What comfort could he possibly need? What more could he possibly wish for? And if some good-natured person, feeling sorry for him, tried to console him by pointing out that his melancholy was probably caused by fasting, it could happen, especially when he had been fasting for some time, that he reacted with an outburst of fury and to the general alarm began to shake the bars of his cage like a wild animal. Yet the impresario had a way of punishing these outbreaks which he rather enjoyed putting into operation. He would apologize publicly for the artist's behavior, which was only to be excused, he admitted, because of the irritability caused by fasting: a condition hardly to be understood by well-fed people; then by natural transition he went on to mention the artist's equally incomprehensible boast that he could fast for much longer than he was doing; he praised the high ambition, the good will, the great self-denial undoubtedly implicit in such a statement; and then quite simply countered it by bringing out photographs, which were also on sale to the public, showing the artist on the fortieth day of a fast lying in bed almost dead from exhaustion. This perversion of the truth, familiar to the artist though it was, always unnerved him afresh and proved too much for him. What was a consequence of the premature ending of his fast was here presented as the cause of it! To fight against this lack of understanding, against a whole world of non-understanding, was impossible. Time and again in good faith he stood by the bars listening to the impresario, but as soon as the photographs appeared he always let go and sank with a groan back on to his straw, and the reassured public could once more come close and gaze at him.

A few years later when the witnesses of such scenes called them to mind, they often failed to understand themselves at all. For meanwhile the aforementioned change in public interest had set in; it seemed to happen almost overnight; there may have been profound causes for it, but who was going to bother about that; at any rate the pampered hunger artist suddenly found himself deserted one fine day by the amusement seekers, who went streaming past him to other more favored attractions. For the last time the impresario hurried him over half Europe to discover whether the old interest might still survive here and there; all in vain; everywhere, as if by secret agreement, a positive revulsion from professional fasting was in evidence. Of course it could not really have sprung up so suddenly as all that, and many premonitory symptoms which had not been sufficiently remarked or suppressed during the rush and glitter of success now came retrospectively to mind, but it was now too late to take any countermeasures. Fasting would surely come into fashion again at some future date, yet that was no comfort for those living in the present. What, then, was the hunger artist to do? He had been applauded by thousands in his time and could hardly come down to showing himself in a street booth at village fairs, and as for adopting another profession, he was not only too old for that but too fanatically devoted to fasting. So he took leave of the impresario, his partner in an unparalleled career, and hired himself to a large circus; in order to spare his own feelings he avoided reading the conditions of his contract.

A large circus with its enormous traffic in replacing and recruiting men, animals and apparatus can always find a use for people at any time, even for a hunger artist, provided of course that he does not ask too much, and in this particular case anyhow it was not only the artist who was taken on but his famous and long-known name as well, indeed considering the peculiar nature of his performance, which was not impaired by advancing age, it could not be objected that here was an artist past his prime, no longer at the height of his professional skill, seeking a refuge in some quiet corner of a circus; on the contrary, the hunger artist averred that he could fast as well as ever, which was entirely credible, he even alleged that if he were allowed to fast as he liked, and this was at once promised him without more ado, he could astound the world by establishing a record never yet achieved, a statement which certainly provoked a smile among the other professionals, since it left out of account the change in public opinion, which the hunger artist in his zeal conveniently forgot.

He had not, however, actually lost his sense of the real situation and took it as a matter of course that he and his cage should be stationed, not in the middle of the ring as a main attraction, but outside, near the animal cages, on a site that was after all easily accessible. Large and gaily painted placards made a frame for the cage and announced what was to be seen inside it. When the public came thronging out in the intervals to see the animals, they could hardly avoid passing the hunger artist's cage and stopping there for a moment, perhaps they might even have stayed longer had not those pressing behind them in the narrow gangway, who did not understand why they should be held up on their way toward the excitements of the menagerie, made it impossible for anyone to stand gazing quietly for any length of time. And that was the reason why the hunger artist, who had of course been looking forward to these visiting hours as the main achievement of his life, began instead to shrink from them. At first he could hardly wait for the intervals; it was exhilarating to watch the crowds come streaming his way, until only too soon—not even the most obstinate self-deception, clung to almost consciously, could hold out against the fact—the conviction was borne in upon him that these people, most of them, to judge from their actions, again and again, without exception, were all on their way to the menagerie. And the first sight of them from the distance remained the best. For when they reached his cage he was at once deafened by the storm of shouting and abuse that arose from the two contending factions, which renewed themselves continuously, of those who wanted to stop and stare at him—he soon began to dislike them more than the others—not out of real interest but only out of obstinate self-assertiveness, and those who wanted to go straight on to the animals: When the first great rush was past, the stragglers came along, and these, whom nothing could have prevented from stopping to look at him as long as they had breath, raced past with long strides, hardly even glancing at him, in their haste to get to the menagerie in time. And all too rarely did it happen that he had a stroke of luck, when some father of a family fetched up before him with his children, pointed a finger at the hunger artist and explained at length what the phenomenon meant, telling stories of earlier years when he himself had watched similar but much more thrilling performances, and the children, still rather uncomprehending, since neither inside nor outside school had they been sufficiently prepared for this lesson—what did they care about fasting?—yet showed by the brightness of their intent eyes that new and better times might be coming. Perhaps, said the hunger artist to himself many a time, things would be a little better if his cage were set not quite so near the menagerie. That made it too easy for people to make their choice, to say nothing of what he suffered from the stench of the menagerie, the animals' restlessness by night, the carrying past of raw lumps of flesh for the beasts of prey, the roaring at feeding times, which depressed him continually. But he did not dare to lodge a complaint with the management; after all, he had the animals to thank for the troops of people who passed his cage, among whom there might always be one here and there to take an interest in him, and who could tell where they might seclude him if he called attention to his existence and thereby to the fact that, strictly speaking, he was only an impediment on the way to the menagerie.

A small impediment, to be sure, one that grew steadily less. People grew familiar with the strange idea that they could be expected, in times like these, to take an interest in a hunger artist, and with this familiarity the verdict went out against him. He might fast as much as he could, and he did so; but nothing could save him now, people passed him by. Just try to explain to anyone the art of fasting! Anyone who has no feeling for it cannot be made to understand it. The fine placards grew dirty and illegible, they were torn down; the little notice board telling the number of fast days achieved, which at first was changed carefully every day, had long stayed at the same figure, for after the first few weeks even this small task seemed pointless to the staff; and so the artist simply fasted on and on, as he had once dreamed of doing, and it was no trouble to him, just as he had always foretold, but no one counted the days, no one, not even the artist himself, knew what records he was already breaking, and his heart grew heavy. And when once in a time some leisurely passer-by stopped, made merry over the old figure on the board and spoke of swindling, that was in its way the stupidest lie ever invented by indifference and inborn malice, since it was not the hunger artist who was cheating; he was working honestly, but the world was cheating him of his reward.

Many more days went by, however, and that too came to an end. An overseer's eye fell on the cage one day and he asked the attendants why this perfectly good cage should be left standing there unused with dirty straw inside it; nobody knew, until one man, helped out by the notice board, remembered about the hunger artist. They poked into the straw with sticks and found him in it. "Are you still fasting?" asked the overseer: "When on earth do you mean to stop?" "Forgive me, everybody," whispered the hunger artist; only the overseer, who had his ear to the bars, understood him.

"Of course," said the overseer, and tapped his forehead with a finger to let the attendants know what state the man was in, "we forgive you." "I always wanted you to admire my fasting," said the hunger artist. "We do admire it," said the overseer, affably. "But you shouldn't admire it," said the hunger artist. "Well, then we don't admire it," said the overseer, "but why shouldn't we admire it?" "Because I have to fast, I can't help it," said the hunger artist. "What a fellow you are," said the overseer, "and why can't you help it?" "Because," said the hunger artist, lifting his head a little and speaking, with his lips pursed, as if for a kiss, right into the overseer's ear, so that no syllable might be lost, "because I couldn't find the food I liked. If I had found it, believe me, I should have made no fuss and stuffed myself like you or anyone else." These were his last words, but in his dimming eyes remained the firm though no longer proud persuasion that he was still continuing to fast.

10   "Well, clear this out now!" said the overseer, and they buried the hunger artist, straw and all. Into the cage they put a young panther. Even the most insensitive felt it refreshing to see this wild creature leaping around the cage that had so long been dreary. The panther was all right. The food he liked was brought him without hesitation by the attendants; he seemed not even to miss his freedom; his noble body, furnished almost to the bursting point with all that it needed, seemed to carry freedom around with it too; somewhere in his jaws it seemed to lurk; and the joy of life streamed with such ardent passion from his throat that for the onlookers it was not easy to stand the shock of it. But they braced themselves, crowded round the cage, and did not want ever to move away.

LORRIE MOORE (1957–   )

Referential (2012)

Mania. For the third time in three years they talked in a frantic way about what would be a suitable birthday present for her deranged son. There was so little they were actually allowed to bring: almost everything could be transformed into a weapon and so most items had to be left at the front desk, and then, if requested, brought in later by a big blond aide, who would look the objects over beforehand for their wounding possibilities. Pete had bought a basket of jams, but they were in glass jars, and so not allowed. "I forgot about that," he said. They were arranged in colour from brightest marmalade to cloudberry to fig, as if they contained the urine tests of an increasingly ill person, and so she thought, *Just as well they will be confiscated.* They would find something else to bring.

By the time her son was twelve, and had begun his dazed and spellbound muttering, no longer brushing his teeth, Pete had been in their lives for four years, and now it was four years after that. The love they had for Pete was long and winding, not without hidden turns, but without any real halts. They thought of him as a kind of stepfather. Perhaps all three of them had gotten old together, although it showed mostly on her, the mother, with her black shirtdresses worn for slimming and her now greying hair undyed and often pinned up with strands hanging down like Spanish moss.

Once her son had been stripped and gowned and placed in the facility, she, too, removed her necklaces, earrings, scarves—all her prosthetic devices, she said to Pete, trying to amuse—and put them in a latched accordion file under her bed. She was not allowed to wear them when visiting so she would no longer wear them at all, a kind of solidarity with her child, a kind of new widowhood on top of the widowhood she already possessed. Unlike other women her age (who tried too hard with lurid lingerie and flashing jewellery), she now felt that sort of effort was ludicrous, and she went out into the world like an Amish woman, or perhaps, even worse, as when the unforgiving light of spring hit her face, an Amish man. If she were going to be old, let her be a full-fledged citizen of the old country! "To me you always look so beautiful," Pete no longer said.

Pete had lost his job in the new economic downturn. At one point he had been poised to live with her, but her child's deepening troubles had caused him to pull back—he believed he loved her but could not find the large space he needed for himself in her life or in her house (and did not blame her son, or did he?). He eyed with somewhat visible covetousness and sour remarks the front room that her son, when home, lived in with large blankets and empty ice-cream pints, an Xbox, and DVDs.

She no longer knew where Pete went, sometimes for weeks at a time. She thought it an act of vigilance and attachment that she would not ask, would try not to care. She once grew so hungry for touch she went to the Stressed Tress salon around the corner just to have her hair washed. The few times she had flown to Buffalo to see her brother and his family, at airport security she had chosen the pat-downs and the wandings rather than the scanning machine.

"Where is Pete?" her son cried out at visits she made alone, his face scarlet with acne, swollen and wide with the effects of medications that had been changed then changed again, and she said Pete was busy today, but soon, soon, maybe next week. A maternal vertigo beset her, the room circled, and the cutting scars on her son's arms sometimes seemed to spell out Pete's name in the thin lines there, the loss of fathers etched primitively in an algebra of skin. In the carousel spin of the room, the white webbed lines resembled coarse campfire writing, as when young people used to stiffly carve the words peace and f--- in park picnic tables and trees, the C three-quarters of a square. Mutilation was a language. And vice versa. The cutting endeared her boy to the girls, who were all cutters themselves and seldom saw a boy who was one as well, and so in the group sessions he became popular, which he seemed neither to mind nor perhaps really to notice. When no one was looking he cut the bottoms of his feet with crisp paper from crafts hour. He also pretended to read the girls' soles like palms, announcing the arrival of strangers and the progress toward romance—"toemances!" he called them—and detours, sometimes glimpsing his own fate in the words they had cut there.

Now she and Pete went to see her son without the jams but with a soft deckle-edged book about Daniel Boone, which was allowed, even if her son would believe it contained messages for him, believe that although it was a story about a long-ago person it was also the story of his own sorrow and heroism in the face of every manner of wilderness and defeat and abduction and that his own life could be draped over the book, which was noble armature for the revelation of tales of *him*. There would be

5

clues in the words on pages with numbers that added up to his age: 97, 88, 466. There were other veiled references to his existence. There always were.

They sat at the visitors' table together and her son set the book aside and did try to smile at both of them. There was still sweetness in his eyes, the sweetness he was born with, even if fury could dart in a scattershot fashion across them. Someone had cut his tawny hair—or at least had tried. Perhaps the staff person did not want the scissors near him for a prolonged period and had snipped quickly, then leaped away, then approached again, grabbed and snipped, then jumped back. At least that's what it looked like. It was wavy hair and had to be cut carefully. Now it no longer cascaded down but was close to his head, springing out at angles that seemed to matter to no one but a mother.

"So where have you been?" her son asked Pete, giving him a hard stare.

"Good question," said Pete, as if praising the thing would make it go away. How could people be mentally well in such a world?

10   "Do you miss us?" the boy asked.

Pete did not answer.

"Do you think of me when you look at the black capillaries of the trees at night?"

"I suppose I do." Pete stared back at him, so as not to shift in his seat. "I am always hoping you are OK and that they treat you well here."

"Do you think of my mom when staring up at the clouds and all they hold?"

15   Pete fell quiet again.

Her son continued, studying Pete. "Have you ever watched how sparrows can kill the offspring of others? Baby wrens, for instance? I've been watching out the windows. Did you know that sparrows can swoop into the wrens' house and pluck out the fledglings from their nests and hurl them to the ground with a force you would not think possible for a sparrow? Even a homicidal sparrow?"

"Nature can be cruel," said Pete.

"Nature can be one big horror movie! But murder is not something one would expect—from a sparrow. All things can be found in the world—but usually you have to look for them. You have to look! For instance, you have to look for us! We are sort of hidden but sort of not. We can be found. If you look in the obvious places, we can be found. We haven't disappeared, even if you want us to, we are there to—"

"That's enough," she said to her son, who turned to her with a change of expression.

20   "There's supposed to be cake this afternoon for someone's birthday," he said.

"That will be nice!" she said, smiling back.

"No candles, of course. Or forks. We will just have to grab the frosting and mash it into our eyes for blinding. Do you ever think about how at that moment of the candles time stands still, even as the moments carry away the smoke? It's like the fire of burning love. Do you ever wonder why so many people have things they don't deserve but how absurd all those things are to begin with? Do you really think a wish can come true if you never ever ever ever ever ever tell it to anyone?"

On the ride home she and Pete did not exchange a word, and every time she looked at his ageing hands, clasped arthritically around the steering wheel, the familiar thumbs slung low in their slightly simian way, she would understand anew the desperate place they both were in, though the desperations were separate, not joined, and her eyes would then feel the stabbing pressure of tears. The last time her son had tried to do it, his method had been, in the doctor's words, morbidly ingenious. He might have succeeded but a fellow patient, a girl from group, had stopped him at the last minute. There had been blood to be mopped. Once her son had only wanted a distracting pain, but then soon he had wanted to tear a hole in himself and flee through it. Life was full of spies and preoccupying espionage. Yet the spies sometimes would flee as well and someone might have to go after them in order, paradoxically, to escape them altogether, over the rolling fields of living dream, into the early morning mountains of dawning signification.

There was a storm in front and lightning did its quick, purposeful zigzag between and in the clouds. She did not need such stark illustration that horizons could be shattered, filled with messages, broken codes, yet there it was. A spring snow began to fall with the lightning still cracking, and Pete put the windshield wipers on so that they both could peer through the cleared semicircles at the darkening road before them. She knew that the world was not created to speak just to her, and yet, as with her son, sometimes things did. The fruit trees had bloomed early, for instance, and the orchards they passed were pink, but the early warmth precluded bees, and so there would be little fruit. Most of the dangling blossoms would fall in this very storm.

When they arrived at her house and went in, Pete glanced at himself in the hallway mirror. Perhaps he needed assurance that he was alive and not the ghost he seemed.

"Would you like a drink?" she asked, hoping he would stay. "I have some good vodka. I could make you a nice White Russian!"

"Just vodka," he said reluctantly. "Straight."

She opened the freezer to find the vodka, and when she closed it again, she stood waiting there for a moment, looking at the photos she'd attached with magnets to the refrigerator. As a baby her son had looked happier than most babies. As a six-year-old he was still smiling and hamming it up, his arms and legs shooting out like starbursts, his perfectly gapped teeth flashing, his hair curling in honeyed coils. At ten his expression was already vaguely brooding and fearful, though there was light in his eyes, his lovely cousins beside him. There he was a plumpish teenager, his arm around Pete. And there in the corner he was an infant again, held by his dignified, handsome father, whom her son did not recall because he had died so long ago. All this had to be accepted. Living did not mean one joy piled upon another. It was merely the hope for less pain, hope played like a playing card upon another hope, a wish for kindnesses and mercies to emerge like kings and queens in an unexpected change of the game. One could hold the cards oneself or not: they would land the same regardless. Tenderness did not enter except in a damaged way and by luck.

"You don't want ice?"

"No," said Pete. "No thank you."

She placed two glasses of vodka on the kitchen table and there they sat.

"Perhaps this will help you sleep," she said.

"Don't know if anything can do that," he said, with a swig. Insomnia plagued him.

"I am going to bring him home tomorrow," she said. "He needs his home back, his house, his room. He is no danger to anyone."

35   Pete drank some more, sipping noisily. She could see he wanted no part of this, but she felt she had no choice but to proceed. "Perhaps you could help. He looks up to you."

"Help how?" asked Pete with a flash of anger. There was the clink of his glass on the table.

"We could each spend part of the night near him," she said.

The telephone rang. The Radio Shack wall phone brought almost nothing but bad news, and so its ringing sound, especially in the evening, always startled her. She repressed a shudder but still her shoulders hunched and curved. She stood.

"Hello?" she said, answering it on the third ring, her heart pounding. But the person on the other end hung up. She sat back down. "I guess it was a wrong number," she said, adding, "Perhaps you would like more vodka."

40   "Only a little. Then I should go."

She poured him more. She had said what she'd wanted to say and did not want to have to persuade him. She would wait for him to step forward with the right words. Unlike some of her meaner friends, who kept warning her, she believed there was a deep good side of him and she was always patient for it. What else could she be?

The phone rang again.

"Probably telemarketers," he said.

"I hate them," she said. "Hello?" she said more loudly into the receiver.

45   This time when the caller hung up she glanced at the number on the phone, in the lit panel where the caller ID was supposed to reveal it.

She sat back down and poured herself more vodka. "Someone is calling here from your apartment," she said.

He threw back the rest of his vodka. "I should go," he said and got up and headed for the door. She followed him. At the door she watched him grasp the front knob and twist it firmly. He opened the door wide, blocking the mirror.

"Good night," he said. His expression had already forwarded itself to someplace far away.

She threw her arms around him to kiss him, but he turned his head abruptly so her mouth landed on his ear. She remembered he had done this evasive move eight years ago, at the beginning, when they had first met, and he was in a condition of romantic overlap.

50   "Thank you for coming with me," she said.

"You're welcome," he replied, then hurried down the steps to his car, which was parked at the curb out front. She did not attempt to walk him to it. She closed the door and locked it, as the telephone began to ring again. She turned off all the lights, including the porches'.

She went into the kitchen. She had not really been able to read the caller ID without reading glasses, and had invented the part about its being Pete's number, though he had made it the truth anyway, which was the black magic of lies, good guesses, and nimble bluffs. Now she braced herself. She planted her feet. "Hello?" she said, answering on the fifth ring. The plastic panel where the number should show was clouded as if by a scrim, a page of onionskin over the onion—or rather, over a picture of an onion. One depiction on top of another.

"Good evening," she said again loudly. What would burst forth? A monkey's paw. A lady. A tiger.

But there was nothing at all.

JOYCE CAROL OATES (1938–   )

Heat (1989)

It was midsummer, the heat rippling above the macadam roads, cicadas screaming out of the trees, and the sky like pewter, glaring.

The days were the same day, like the shallow mud-brown river moving always in the same direction but so slow you couldn't see it. Except for Sunday: church in the morning, then the fat Sunday newspaper, the color comics, and newsprint on your fingers.

Rhea and Rhoda Kunkel went flying on their rusted old bicycles, down the long hill toward the railroad yard, Whipple's Ice, the scrubby pastureland where dairy cows grazed. They'd stolen six dollars from their own grandmother who loved them. They were eleven years old; they were identical twins; they basked in their power.

Rhea and Rhoda Kunkel: it was always Rhea-and-Rhoda, never Rhoda-and-Rhea, I couldn't say why. You just wouldn't say the names that way. Not even the teachers at school would say them that way.

We went to see them in the funeral parlor where they were waked; we were made to. The twins in twin caskets, white, smooth, gleaming, perfect as plastic, with white satin lining puckered like the inside of a fancy candy box. And the waxy white lilies, and the smell of talcum powder and perfume. The room was crowded; there was only one way in and out.

Rhea and Rhoda were the same girl; they'd wanted it that way. Only looking from one to the other could you see they were two.

The heat was gauzy; you had to push your way through like swimming. On their bicycles Rhea and Rhoda flew through it hardly noticing, from their grandmother's place on Main Street to the end of South Main where the paved road turned to gravel leaving town. That was the summer before seventh grade, when they died. Death was coming for them, but they didn't know.

They thought the same thoughts sometimes at the same moment, had the same dream and went all day trying to remember it, bringing it back like something you'd be hauling out of the water on a tangled line. We watched them; we were jealous. None of us had a twin. Sometimes they were serious and sometimes, remembering, they shrieked and laughed like they were being killed. They stole things out of desks and lockers but if you caught them they'd hand them right back; it was like a game.

There were three floor fans in the funeral parlor that I could see, tall whirring fans with propeller blades turning fast to keep the warm air moving. Strange little gusts came from all directions, making your eyes water. By this time Roger Whipple was arrested, taken into police custody. No one had hurt him. He would never stand trial; he was ruled mentally unfit and would never be released from confinement.

5

10   He died there, in the state psychiatric hospital, years later, and was brought back home to be buried—the body of him, I mean. His earthly remains.

Rhea and Rhoda Kunkel were buried in the same cemetery, the First Methodist. The cemetery is just a field behind the church.

In the caskets the dead girls did not look like anyone we knew, really. They were placed on their backs with their eyes closed, and their mouths, the way you don't always look in life when you're sleeping. Their faces were too small. Every eyelash showed, too perfect. Like angels, everyone was saying, and it was strange it was *so*. I stared and stared.

What had been done to them, the lower parts of them, didn't show in the caskets.

Roger Whipple worked for his father at Whipple's Ice. In the newspaper it stated he was nineteen. He'd gone to DeWitt Clinton until he was sixteen; my mother's friend Sadie taught there and remembered him from the special education class. A big slow sweet-faced boy with these big hands and feet, thighs like hams. A shy gentle boy with good manners and a hushed voice.

15   He wasn't simpleminded exactly, like the others in that class, He was watchful, he held back.

Roger Whipple in overalls squatting in the rear of his father's truck, one of his older brothers driving. There would come the sound of the truck in the driveway, the heavy block of ice smelling of cold, ice tongs over his shoulder. He was strong, round-shouldered like an older man. Never staggered or grunted. Never dropped anything. Pale washed-looking eyes lifting out of a big face, a soft mouth wanting to smile. We giggled and looked away. They said he'd never been the kind to hurt even an animal; all the Whipples swore.

Sucking ice, the cold goes straight into your jaws and deep into the bone.

People spoke of them as the Kunkel twins. Mostly nobody tried to tell them apart: homely corkscrew-twisty girls you wouldn't know would turn up so quiet and solemn and almost beautiful, perfect little dolls' faces with the freckles powdered over, couches of rouge on the cheeks and mouths. I was tempted to whisper to them, kneeling by the coffins, *Hey, Rhea! Hey, Rhoda! Wake up!*

They had loud slip-sliding voices that were the same voice. They weren't shy. They were always first in line. One behind you and one in front of you and you'd better be wary of some trick. Flamey-orange hair and the bleached-out skin that goes with it, freckles like dirty raindrops splashed on their faces. Sharp green eyes they'd bug out until you begged them to stop.

20   Places meant to be serious, Rhea and Rhoda had a hard time sitting still. In church, in school, a sideways glance between them could do it. Jamming their knuckles into their mouths, choking back giggles. Sometimes laughter escaped through their fingers like steam hissing. Sometimes it came out like snorting and then none of us could hold back. The worst time was in assembly, the principal up there telling us that Miss Flagler had died, we would all miss her. Tears shining in the woman's eyes behind her goggle glasses and one of the twins gave a breathless little snort; you could feel it like flames running down the whole row of girls, none of us could hold back.

Sometimes the word "tickle" was enough to get us going, just that word.

I never dreamt about Rhea and Rhoda so strange in their caskets sleeping out in the middle of a room where people could stare at them, shed tears, and pray over them. I never dream about actual things, only things I don't know. Places I've never been, people I've never seen. Sometimes the person I am in the dream isn't me. Who it is, I don't know.

Rhea and Rhoda bounced up the drive on their bicycles behind Whipple's Ice. They were laughing like crazy and didn't mind the potholes jarring their teeth or the clouds of dust. If they'd had the same dream the night before, the hot sunlight erased it entirely.

When death comes for you, you sometimes know and sometimes don't.

Roger Whipple was by himself in the barn, working. Kids went down there to beg him for ice to suck or throw around or they'd tease him, not out of meanness bur for something to do. It was slow, the days not changing in the summer, heat sometimes all night long. He was happy with children that age, he was that age himself in his head—sixth-grade learning abilities, as the newspaper stated, though he could add and subtract quickly. Other kinds of arithmetic gave him trouble.

People were saying afterward he'd always been strange. Watchful like he was, those thick soft lips. The Whipples did wrong to let him run loose.

They said he'd always been a good gentle boy, went to Sunday school and sat still there and never gave anybody any trouble. He collected Bible cards; he hid them away under his mattress for safekeeping. Mr. Whipple started in early disciplining him the way you might discipline a big dog or a horse. Not letting the creature know he has any power to be himself exactly. Not giving him the opportunity to test his will.

Neighbors said the Whipples worked him like a horse, in fact. The older brothers were the most merciless. And why they all wore coveralls, heavy denim and long legs on days so hot, nobody knew. The thermometer above the First Midland Bank read 98 degrees F. on noon of that day, my mother said.

Nights afterward my mother would hug me before I went to bed. Pressing my face hard against her breasts and whispering things I didn't hear, like praying to Jesus to love and protect her little girl and keep her from harm, but I didn't hear; I shut my eyes tight and endured it. Sometimes we prayed together, all of us or just my mother and me kneeling by my bed. Even then I knew she was a good mother, there was this girl she loved as her daughter that was me and loved more than that girl deserved. There was nothing I could do about it.

Mrs. Kunkel would laugh and roll her eyes over the twins. In that house they were "double trouble"—you'd hear it all the time like a joke on the radio that keeps coming back. I wonder did she pray with them too. I wonder would they let her.

In the long night you forget about the day; it's like the other side of the world. Then the sun is there, and the heat. You forget.

We were running through the field behind school, a place where people dumped things sometimes, and there was a dead dog there, a collie with beautiful fur, but his eyes were gone from the sockets and the maggots had got him where somebody tried to lift him with her foot, and when Rhea and Rhoda saw they screamed a single scream and hid their eyes.

They did nice things—gave their friends candy bars, nail polish, some novelty key chains they'd taken from somewhere, movie stars' pictures framed in plastic. In the

25

30

movies they'd share a box of popcorn, not noticing where one or the other of them left off and a girl who wasn't any sister of theirs sat.

Once they made me strip off my clothes where we'd crawled under the Kunkels' veranda. This was a large hollowed-out space where the earth dropped away at one end and you could sit without bumping your head; it was cool and smelled of dirt and stone. Rhea said all of a sudden, *Strip!* and Rhoda said at once, *Strip! Come on!* So it happened. They wouldn't let me out unless I took off my clothes, my shirt and shorts, yes, and my panties too. *Come on,* they said, whispering and giggling; they were blocking the way out so I had no choice. I was scared but I was laughing too. This is to show our power over you, they said. But they stripped too just like me.

35   You have power over others you don't realize until you test it.

Under the Kunkels' veranda we stared at each other but we didn't touch each other. My teeth chattered, because what if somebody saw us, some boy, or Mrs. Kunkel herself? I was scared but I was happy too. Except for our faces, their face and mine, we could all be the same girl.

The Kunkel family lived in one side of a big old clapboard house by the river; you could hear the trucks rattling on the bridge, shifting their noisy gears on the hill. Mrs. Kunkel had eight children. Rhea and Rhoda were the youngest. Our mothers wondered why Mrs. Kunkel had let herself go; she had a moon-shaped pretty face but her hair was frizzed ratty; she must have weighed two hundred pounds, sweated and breathed so hard in the warm weather. They'd known her in school. Mr. Kunkel worked construction for the county. Summer evenings after work he'd be sitting on the veranda drinking beer, flicking cigarette butts out into the yard; you'd be fooled, almost thinking they were fireflies. He went bare-chested in the heat, his upper body dark like stained wood. Flat little purplish nipples inside his chest hair the girls giggled to see. Mr. Kunkel teased us all; he'd mix Rhea and Rhoda up the way he'd mix the rest of us up, like it was too much trouble to keep names straight.

Mr. Kunkel was in police custody; he didn't even come to the wake. Mrs. Kunkel was there in rolls of chin fat that glistened with sweat and tears, the makeup on her face so caked and discolored you were embarrassed to look. It scared me, the way she grabbed me as soon as my parents and I came in, hugging me against her big balloon breasts, sobbing. All the strength went out of me; I couldn't push away.

The police had Mr. Kunkel for his own good, they said. He'd gone to the Whipples, though the murderer had been taken away, saying he would kill anybody he could get his hands on: the old man, the brothers. They were all responsible, he said; his little girls were dead. Tear them apart with his bare hands, he said, but he had a tire iron.

40   Did it mean anything special, or was it just an accident Rhea and Rhoda had taken six dollars from their grandmother an hour before? Because death was coming for them; it had to happen one way or another.

If you believe in God you believe that. And if you don't believe in God it's obvious.

Their grandmother lived upstairs over a shoe store downtown, an apartment looking out on Main Street. They'd bicycle down there for something to do and she'd give them grape juice or lemonade and try to keep them awhile, a lonely old lady but she was nice, she was always nice to me; it was kind of nasty of Rhea and Rhoda to steal from her but they were like that. One was in the kitchen talking with her and without any plan or anything the other went to use the bathroom, then slipped into her bedroom, got the money out of her purse like it was something she did every day of the week, that easy. On the stairs going down to the street Rhoda whispered to Rhea, What did you *do?* knowing Rhea had done something she hadn't ought to have done but not knowing what it was or anyway how much money it was. They started in poking each other, trying to hold the giggles back until they were safe away.

On their bicycles they stood high on the pedals, coasting, going down the hill but not using their brakes. *What did you do! Oh, what did you do!*

Rhea and Rhoda always said they could never be apart. If one didn't know exactly where the other was that one could die. Or the other could die. Or both.

Once they'd gotten some money from somewhere, they wouldn't say where, and   45
paid for us all to go to the movies. And ice cream afterward too.

You could read the newspaper articles twice through and still not know what he did. Adults talked about it for a long time but not so we could hear. I thought probably he'd used an ice pick. Or maybe I heard somebody guess who didn't know any more than me.

We liked it that Rhea and Rhoda had been killed, and all the stuff in the paper, and everybody talking about it, but we didn't like it that they were dead; we missed them.

Later, in tenth grade, the Kaufmann twins moved into our school district; Doris and Diane. But it wasn't the same thing.

Roger Whipple said he didn't remember any of it. Whatever he did, he didn't remember. At first everybody thought he was lying; then they had to accept it as true, or true in some way: doctors from the state hospital examined him. He said over and over he hadn't done anything and be didn't remember the twins there that afternoon, but he couldn't explain why their bicycles were at the foot of his stairway and he couldn't explain why he'd taken a bath in the middle of the day. The Whipples admitted that wasn't a practice of Roger's or of any of them, ever, a bath in the middle of the day.

Roger Whipple was a clean boy, though. His hands always scrubbed so you actu-   50
ally noticed, swinging the block of ice off the truck and, inside the kitchen, helping to set it in the icebox. They said he'd go crazy if he got bits of straw under his nails from the icehouse or inside his clothes. He'd been taught to shave and he shaved every morning without fail; they said the sight of the beard growing in, the scratchy feel of it, seemed to scare him.

A few years later his sister Linda told us how Roger was built like a horse. She was our age, a lot younger than him; she made a gesture toward her crotch so we'd know what she meant. She'd happened to see him a few times, she said, by accident.

There he was squatting in the dust laughing, his head lowered, watching Rhea and Rhoda circle him on their bicycles. It was a rough game where the twins saw how close they could come to hitting him, brushing him with their bike fenders, and he'd lunge out, not seeming to notice if his fingers hit the spokes; it was all happening so fast you maybe wouldn't feel pain. Out back of the icehouse, the yard blended in with the yard of the old railroad depot next door that wasn't used any more. It was burning hot in the sun; dust rose in clouds behind the girls. Pretty soon they got bored with the game, though Roger Whipple even in his heavy overalls wanted to keep going. He was red-faced with all the excitement; he was a boy who loved to laugh and didn't have much chance. Rhea said she was thirsty, she wanted some ice, so Roger Whipple scrambled right up and went to get a big bag of ice cubes! He hadn't any more sense than that.

They sucked on the ice cubes and fooled around with them. He was panting and lolling his tongue pretending to be a dog, and Rhea and Rhoda cried. Here, doggie! Here, doggie-doggie! tossing ice cubes at Roger Whipple he tried to catch in his mouth. That went on for a while. In the end the twins just dumped the rest of the ice onto the dirt, then Roger Whipple was saying he had some secret things that belonged to his brother Eamon he could show them, hidden under his bed mattress; would they like to see what the things were?

He wasn't one who could tell Rhea from Rhoda or Rhoda from Rhea. There was a way some of us knew: the freckles on Rhea's face were a little darker than Rhoda's, and Rhea's eyes were just a little darker than Rhoda's. But you'd have to see the two side by side with no clowning around to know.

55   Rhea said OK, she'd like to see the secret things. She let her bike fall where she was straddling it.

Roger Whipple said he could only take one of them upstairs to his room at a time, he didn't say why.

OK, said Rhea. Of the Kunkel twins, Rhea always had to be first.

She'd been born first, she said. Weighed a pound or two more.

Roger Whipple's room was in a strange place: on the second floor of the Whipple house above an unheated storage space that had been added after the main part of the house was built. There was a way of getting to the room from the outside, up a flight of rickety wooden stairs. That way Roger could get in and out of his room without going through the rest of the house. People said the Whipples had him live there like some animal, they didn't want him tramping through the house, but they denied it. The room had an inside door too.

60   Roger Whipple weighed about one hundred ninety pounds that day. In the hospital he swelled up like a balloon, people said, bloated from the drugs; his skin was soft and white as bread dough and his hair fell out. He was an old man when he died aged thirty-one.

Exactly why he died, the Whipples never knew. The hospital just told them his heart had stopped in his sleep.

Rhoda shaded her eyes, watching her sister running up the stairs with Roger Whipple behind her, and felt the first pinch of fear, that something was wrong or was going to be wrong. She called after them in a whining voice that she wanted to come along too, she didn't want to wait down there all alone, but Rhea just called back to her to be quiet and wait her turn, so Rhoda waited, kicking at the ice cubes melting in the dirt, and after a while she got restless and shouted up to them—the door was shut, the shade on the window was drawn—saying she was going home, damn them, she was sick of waiting, she said, and she was going home. But nobody came to the door or looked out the window; it was like the place was empty. Wasps had built one of those nests that look like mud in layers under the eaves, and the only sound was wasps.

Rhoda bicycled toward the road so anybody who was watching would think she was going home; she was thinking she hated Rhea! hated her damn twin sister! wished she was dead and gone, God damn her! She was going home, and the first thing she'd tell their mother was that Rhea had stolen six dollars from Grandma: she had it in her pocket right that moment.

The Whipple house was an old farmhouse they'd tried to modernize by putting on red asphalt siding meant to look like brick. Downstairs the rooms were big and drafty; upstairs they were small, some of them unfinished and with bare floorboards, like Roger Whipple's room, which people would afterward say based on what the police said was like an animal's pen, nothing in it but a bed shoved into a corner and some furniture and boxes and things Mrs. Whipple stored there.

Of the Whipples—there were seven in the family still living at home—only 65 Mrs. Whipple and her daughter Iris were home that afternoon. They said they hadn't heard a sound except for kids playing in the back; they swore it.

Rhoda was bent on going home and leaving Rhea behind, but at the end of the driveway something made her turn her bicycle wheel back . . . so if you were watching you'd think she was just cruising around for something to do, a red-haired girl with whitish skin and freckles, skinny little body, pedaling fast, then slow, then coasting, then fast again, turning and dipping and crisscrossing her path, talking to herself as if she was angry. She hated Rhea! She was furious at Rhea! But feeling sort of scared too and sickish in the pit of her belly, knowing that she and Rhea shouldn't be in two places; something might happen to one of them or to both. Some things you know.

So she pedaled back to the house. Laid her bike down in the dirt next to Rhea's. The bikes were old hand-me-downs, the kickstands were broken. But their daddy had put on new Goodyear tires for them at the start of the summer, and he'd oiled them too.

You never would see just one of the twins' bicycles anywhere, you always saw both of them laid down on the ground and facing in the same direction with the pedals in about the same position.

Rhoda peered up at the second floor of the house, the shade drawn over the window, the door still closed. She called out, Rhea? Hey, Rhea? starting up the stairs, making a lot of noise so they'd hear her, pulling on the railing as if to break it the way a boy would. Still she was scared. But making noise like that and feeling so disgusted and mad helped her get stronger, and there was Roger Whipple with the door open staring down at her flush-faced and sweaty as if he was scared too. He seemed to have forgotten her. He was wiping his hands on his overalls. He just stared, a lemony light coming up in his eyes.

Afterward he would say he didn't remember anything. Just didn't remember 70 anything. The size of a grown man but round-shouldered so it was hard to judge how tall he was, or how old. His straw-colored hair falling in his eyes and his fingers twined together as if he was praying or trying with all the strength in him to keep his hands still. He didn't remember the twins in his room and couldn't explain the blood but he cried a lot, acted scared and guilty and sorry like a dog that's done bad, so they decided he shouldn't be made to stand trial; there was no point to it.

Afterward Mrs. Whipple kept to the house, never went out, not even to church or grocery shopping. She died of cancer just a few months before Roger died; she'd loved her boy, she always said; she said none of it was his fault in his heart, he wasn't the kind of boy to injure an animal; he loved kittens especially and was a good sweet obedient boy and religious too and Jesus was looking after him and whatever happened it must have been those girls teasing him; everybody knew what the Kunkel twins were like. Roger had had a lifetime of being teased and taunted by children, his heart broken by all the abuse, and something must have snapped that day, that was all.

The Whipples were the ones, though, who called the police. Mr. Whipple found the girls' bodies back in the icehouse hidden under some straw and canvas. Those two look-alike girls, side by side.

He found them around 9 P.M. that night. He knew, he said. Oh, he knew.

The way Roger was acting, and the fact that the Kunkel girls were missing: word had gotten around town. Roger taking a bath like that in the middle of the day and washing his hair too and nor answering when anyone said his name, just sitting there staring at the floor. So they went up to his room and saw the blood. So they knew.

75   The hardest minute of his life, Mr. Whipple said, was in the icehouse lifting that canvas to see what was under it.

He took it hard too; he never recovered. He hadn't any choice but to think what a lot of people thought—it had been his fault. He was an old-time Methodist, he took all that seriously, but none of it helped him. Believed Jesus Christ was his personal savior and He never stopped loving Roger or turned His face from him, and if Roger did truly repent in his heart he would be saved and they would be reunited in Heaven, all the Whipples reunited. He believed, but none of it helped in his life.

The icehouse is still there but boarded up and derelict, the Whipples' ice business ended long ago. Strangers live in the house, and the yard is littered with rusting hulks of cars and pickup trucks. Some Whipples live scattered around the county but none in town. The old train depot is still there too.

After I'd been married some years I got involved with this man, I won't say his name, his name is not a name I say, but we would meet back there sometimes, back in that old lot that's all weeds and scrub trees. Wild as kids and on the edge of being drunk. I was crazy for this guy, I mean crazy like I could hardly think of anybody but him or anything but the two of us making love the way we did; with him deep inside me I wanted it never to stop. Just fuck and fuck and fuck, I'd whisper to him, and this went on for a long time, two or three years, then ended the way these things do and looking back on it I'm not able to recognize that woman, as if she was someone not even not-me but a crazy woman I would despise, making so much of such a thing, risking her marriage and her kids finding out and her life being ruined for such a thing, my God. The things people do.

It's like living out a story that has to go its own way.

80   Behind the icehouse in his car I'd think of Rhea and Rhoda and what happened that day upstairs in Roger Whipple's room. And the funeral parlor with the twins like dolls laid out and their eyes like dolls' eyes too that shut when you tilt them back.

One night when I wasn't asleep but wasn't awake either I saw my parents standing in the doorway of my bedroom watching me and I knew their thoughts, how they were thinking of Rhea and Rhoda and of me their daughter wondering how they could keep me from harm, and there was no clear answer.

In his car in his arms I'd feel my mind drift, after we'd made love or at least after the first time. And I saw Rhoda Kunkel hesitating on the stairs a few steps down from Roger Whipple. I saw her white-faced and scared but deciding to keep going anyway, pushing by Roger Whipple to get inside the room, to find Rhea; she had to brush against him where he was standing as if he meant to block her but not having the nerve exactly to block her and he was smelling of his body and breathing hard but not in imitation of any dog now, not with his tongue flopping and lolling to make them laugh. Rhoda was asking where was Rhea? She couldn't see well at first in the dark little cubbyhole of a room because the sunshine had been so bright outside.

Roger Whipple said Rhea had gone home. His voice sounded scratchy as if it hadn't been used in some time. She'd gone home, he said, and Rhoda said right away that Rhea wouldn't go home without her and Roger Whipple came toward her saying, Yes she did, yes she *did*, as if he was getting angry she wouldn't believe him. Rhoda was calling, *Rhea, where are you?* Stumbling against something on the floor tangled with the bedclothes.

Behind her was this big boy saying again and again, Yes she did, yes she *did*, his voice rising, but it would never get loud enough so that anyone would hear and come save her.

I wasn't there, but some things you know.

FLANNERY O'CONNOR (1925–1964)

Everything That Rises Must Converge (1965)

Her doctor had told Julian's mother that she must lose twenty pounds on account of her blood pressure, so on Wednesday nights Julian had to take her downtown on the bus for a reducing class at the Y. The reducing class was designed for working girls over fifty, who weighed from 165 to 200 pounds. His mother was one of the slimmer ones, but she said ladies did not tell their age or weight. She would not ride the buses by herself at night since they had been integrated, and because the reducing class was one of her few pleasures, necessary for her health, and *free*, she said Julian could at least put himself out to take her, considering all she did for him. Julian did not like to consider all she did for him, but every Wednesday night he braced himself and took her.

She was almost ready to go, standing before the hall mirror, putting on her hat, while he, his hands behind him, appeared pinned to the door frame, waiting like Saint Sebastian[1] for the arrows to begin piercing him. The hat was new and had

---

[1] *Saint Sebastian:* A Roman Catholic Saint. Accused of being a Christian, Sebastian was tied to a tree, shot with arrows, and left for dead. He survived and recovered, returning to preach. The emperor then had him beaten to death.

cost her seven dollars and a half. She kept saying, "Maybe I shouldn't have paid that for it. No, I shouldn't have. I'll take it off and return it tomorrow. I shouldn't have bought it."

Julian raised his eyes to heaven. "Yes, you should have bought it," he said "Put it on and let's go." It was a hideous hat. A purple velvet flap came down on one side of it and stood up on the other; the rest of it was green and looked like a cushion with the stuffing out. He decided it was less comical than jaunty and pathetic. Everything that gave her pleasure was small and depressed him.

She lifted the hat one more time and set it down slowly on top of her head. Two wings of gray hair protruded on either side of her florid face, but her eyes, sky-blue, were as innocent and untouched by experience as they must have been when she was ten. Were it not that she was a widow who had struggled fiercely to feed and clothe and put him through school and who was supporting him still "until he got on his feet," she might have been a little girl that he had to take to town.

5   "It's all right, it's all right," he said. "Let's go." He opened the door himself and started down the walk to get her going. The sky was a dying violet and the houses stood out darkly against it, bulbous liver-colored monstrosities of a uniform ugliness though no two were alike. Since this had been a fashionable neighborhood forty years ago, his mother persisted in thinking they did well to have an apartment in it. Each house had a narrow collar of dirt around it in which sat, usually, a grubby child. Julian walked with his hands in his pockets, his head down and thrust forward and his eyes glazed with the determination to make himself completely numb during the time he would be sacrificed to her pleasure.

The door closed and he turned to find the dumpy figure, surmounted by the atrocious hat, coming toward him. "Well," she said, "you only live once and paying a little more for it, I at least won't meet myself coming and going."

"Some day I'll start making money," Julian said gloomily—he knew he never would—"and you can have one of those jokes whenever you take the fit." But first they would move. He visualized a place where the nearest neighbors would be three miles away on either side.

"I think you're doing fine," she said, drawing on her gloves. "You've only been out of school a year. Rome wasn't built in a day."

She was one of the few members of the Y reducing class who arrived in hat and gloves and who had a son who had been to college. "It takes time," she said, "and the world is in such a mess. This hat looked better on me than any of the others, though when she brought it out I said, 'Take that thing back. I wouldn't have it on my head,' and she said, 'Now wait till you see it on,' and when she put it on me, I said, 'We-ull,' and she said, 'If you ask me, that hat does something for you and you do something for the hat, and besides,' she said, 'with that hat, you won't meet yourself coming and going.'"

10   Julian thought he could have stood his lot better if she had been selfish, if she had been an old hag who drank and screamed at him. He walked along, saturated in depression, as if in the midst of his martyrdom he had lost his faith. Catching sight of his long, hopeless, irritated face, she stopped suddenly with a grief-stricken look, and pulled back on his arm. "Wait on me," she said. "I'm going back to the house and take this thing off and tomorrow I'm going to return it. I was out of my head. I can pay the gas bill with that seven-fifty."

He caught her arm in a vicious grip. "You are not going to take it back," he said. "I like it."

"Well," she said, "I don't think I ought . . ."

"Shut up and enjoy it," he muttered, more depressed than ever.

"With the world in the mess it's in," she said, "it's a wonder we can enjoy anything. I tell you, the bottom rail is on the top."

Julian sighed.

"Of course," she said, "if you know who are you, you can go anywhere." She said this every time he took her to the reducing class. "Most of them in it are not our kind of people," she said, "but I can be gracious to anybody. I know who I am."

"They don't give a damn for your graciousness," Julian said savagely. "Knowing who you are is good for one generation only. You haven't the foggiest idea where you stand now or who you are."

She stopped and allowed her eyes to flash at him. "I most certainly do know who I am," she said, "and if you don't know who you are, I'm ashamed of you."

"Oh hell," Julian said.

"Your great-grandfather was a former governor of this state," she said. "Your grandfather was a prosperous land-owner. Your grandmother was a Godhigh."

"Will you look around you," he said tensely, "and see where you are now?" and he swept his arm jerkily out to indicate the neighborhood, which the growing darkness at least made less dingy.

"You remain what you are," she said. "Your great-grandfather had a plantation and two hundred slaves."

"There are no more slaves," he said irritably.

"They were better off when they were," she said. He groaned to see that she was off on that topic. She rolled onto it every few days like a train on an open track. He knew every stop, every junction, every swamp along the way, and knew the exact point at which her conclusion would roll majestically into the station: "It's ridiculous. It's simply not realistic. They should rise, yes, but on their own side of the fence."

"Let's skip it," Julian said.

"The ones I feel sorry for," she said, "are the ones that are half white. They're tragic."

"Will you skip it?"

"Suppose we were half white. We would certainly have mixed feelings."

"I have mixed feelings now," he groaned.

"Well let's talk about something pleasant," she said. "I remember going to Grandpa's when I was a little girl. Then the house had double stairways that went up to what was really the second floor—all the cooking was done on the first. I used to like to stay down in the kitchen on account of the way the walls smelled. I would sit with my nose pressed against the plaster and take deep breaths. Actually the place belonged to the Godhighs but your grandfather Chestny paid the mortgage and saved it for them. They were in reduced circumstances," she said, "but reduced or not, they never forgot who they were."

"Doubtless that decayed mansion reminded them," Julian muttered. He never spoke of it without contempt or thought of it without longing. He had seen it once when he was a child before it had been sold. The double stairways had rotted and been torn down. Negroes were living in it. But it remained in his mind as his mother had known it. It appeared in his dreams regularly. He would stand on the wide porch, listening to the rustle of oak leaves, then wander through the high-ceilinged hall into the parlor that opened onto it and gaze at the worn rugs and faded draperies. It occurred to him that it was he, not she, who could have appreciated it. He preferred its threadbare elegance to anything he could name and it was because of it that all the neighborhoods they had lived in had been a torment to him—whereas she had hardly known the difference. She called her insensitivity "being adjustable."

"And I remember the old darky who was my nurse, Caroline. There was no better person in the world. I've always had a great respect for my colored friends," she said. "I'd do anything in the world for them and they'd . . ."

"Will you for God's sake get off that subject?" Julian said. When he got on a bus by himself, he made it a point to sit down beside a Negro, in reparation as it were for his mother's sins.

"You're mighty touchy tonight," she said. "Do you feel all right?"

35   "Yes I feel all right," he said. "Now lay off."

She pursed her lips. "Well, you certainly are in a vile humor," she observed. "I just won't speak to you at all."

They had reached the bus stop. There was no bus in sight and Julian, his hands still jammed in his pockets and his head thrust forward, scowled down the empty street. The frustration of having to wait on the bus as well as ride on it began to creep up his neck like a hot hand. The presence of his mother was borne in upon him as she gave a pained sigh. He looked at her bleakly. She was holding herself very erect under the preposterous hat, wearing it like a banner of her imaginary dignity. There was in him an evil urge to break her spirit. He suddenly unloosened his tie and pulled it off and put it in his pocket.

She stiffened. "Why must you look like *that* when you take me to town?" she said. "Why must you deliberately embarrass me?"

"If you'll never learn where you are," he said, "you can at least learn where I am."

40   "You look like a—thug," she said.

"Then I must be one," he murmured.

"I'll just go home," she said. "I will not bother you. If you can't do a little thing like that for me . . ."

Rolling his eyes upward, he put his tie back on. "Restored to my class," he muttered. He thrust his face toward her and hissed, "True culture is in the mind, the *mind*," he said, and tapped his head, "the mind."

"It's in the heart," she said, "and in how you do things and how you do things is because of who you *are*."

45   "Nobody in the damn bus cares who you are."

"I care who I am," she said icily.

The lighted bus appeared on top of the next hill and as it approached, they moved out into the street to meet it. He put his hand under her elbow and hoisted her up on the creaking step. She entered with a little smile, as if she were going into a drawing room where everyone had been waiting for her. While he put in the tokens, she sat down on one of the broad front seats for three which faced the aisle. A thin woman with protruding teeth and long yellow hair was sitting on the end of it. His mother moved up beside her and left room for Julian beside herself. He sat down and looked at the floor across the aisle where a pair of thin feet in red and white canvas sandals were planted.

His mother immediately began a general conversation meant to attract anyone who felt like talking. "Can it get any hotter?" she said and removed from her purse a folding fan, black with a Japanese scene on it, which she began to flutter before her.

"I reckon it might could," the woman with the protruding teeth said, "but I know for a fact my apartment couldn't get no hotter."

"It must get the afternoon sun," his mother said. She sat forward and looked up and down the bus. It was half filled. Everybody was white. "I see we have the bus to ourselves," she said. Julian cringed. 50

"For a change," said the woman across the aisle, the owner of the red and white canvas sandals. "I come on one the other day and they were thick as fleas—up front and all through."

"The world is in a mess everywhere," his mother said. "I don't know how we've let it get in this fix."

"What gets my goat is all those boys from good families stealing automobile tires," the woman with the protruding teeth said. "I told my boy, I said you may not be rich but you been raised right and if I ever catch you in any such mess, they can send you on to the reformatory. Be exactly where you belong."

"Training tells," his mother said. "Is your boy in high school?"

"Ninth grade," the woman said. 55

"My son just finished college last year. He wants to write but he's selling typewriters until he gets started," his mother said.

The woman leaned forward and peered at Julian. He threw her such a malevolent look that she subsided against the seat. On the floor across the aisle there was an abandoned newspaper. He got up and got it and opened it out in front of him. His mother discreetly continued the conversation in a lower tone but the woman across the aisle said in a loud voice, "Well that's nice. Selling typewriters is close to writing. He can go right from one to the other."

"I tell him," his mother said, "that Rome wasn't built in a day."

Behind the newspaper Julian was withdrawing into the inner compartment of his mind where he spent most of his time. This was a kind of mental bubble in which he established himself when he could not bear to be a part of what was going on around him. From it he could see out and judge but in it he was safe from any kind of penetration from without. It was the only place where he felt free of the general idiocy of his fellows. His mother had never entered it but from it he could see her with absolute clarity.

The old lady was clever enough and he thought that if she had started from any 60 of the right premises, more might have been expected of her. She lived according to the laws of her own fantasy world, outside of which he had never seen her set foot. The law of it was to sacrifice herself for him after she had first created the necessity to do so by making a mess of things. If he had permitted her sacrifices, it was only because her lack of foresight had made them necessary. All of her life had been a struggle to act like a Chestny without the Chestny goods, and to give him everything she thought a Chestny ought to have; but since, said she, it was fun to struggle, why complain? And when you had won, as she had won, what fun to look back on the hard times! He could not forgive her that she had enjoyed the struggle and that she thought *she* had won.

What she meant when she said she had won was that she had brought him up successfully and had sent him to college and that he had turned out so well—good looking (her teeth had gone unfilled so that his could be straightened), intelligent (he realized he was too intelligent to be a success), and with a future ahead of him (there was of course no future ahead of him). She excused his gloominess on the grounds that he was still growing up and his radical ideas on his lack of practical experience. She said he didn't yet know a thing about "life," that he hadn't even entered the real world—when already he was as disenchanted with it as a man of fifty.

The further irony of all this was that in spite of her, he had turned out so well. In spite of going to only a third-rate college, he had, on his own initiative, come out with a first-rate education; in spite of growing up dominated by a small mind, he had ended up with a large one; in spite of all her foolish views, he was free of prejudice and unafraid to face facts. Most miraculous of all, instead of being blinded by love for her as she was for him, he had cut himself emotionally free of her and could see her with complete objectivity. He was not dominated by his mother.

The bus stopped with a sudden jerk and shook him from his meditation. A woman from the back lurched forward with little steps and barely escaped falling in his newspaper as she righted herself. She got off and a large Negro got on. Julian kept his paper lowered to watch. It gave him a certain satisfaction to see injustice in daily operation. It confirmed his view that with a few exceptions there was no one worth knowing within a radius of three hundred miles. The Negro was well dressed and carried a briefcase. He looked around and then sat down on the other end of the seat where the woman with the red and white canvas sandals was sitting. He immediately unfolded a newspaper and obscured himself behind it. Julian's mother's elbow at once prodded insistently into his ribs. "Now you see why I won't ride on these buses by myself," she whispered.

The woman with the red and white canvas sandals had risen at the same time the Negro sat down and had gone further back in the bus and taken the seat of the woman who had got off. His mother leaned forward and cast her an approving look.

65   Julian rose, crossed the aisle, and sat down in the place of the woman with the canvas sandals. From this position, he looked serenely across at his mother. Her face had turned an angry red. He stared at her, making his eyes the eyes of a stranger. He felt his tension suddenly lift as if he had openly declared war on her.

He would have liked to get in conversation with the Negro and to talk with him about art or politics or any subject that would be above the comprehension of those around them, but the man remained entrenched behind his paper. He was either ignoring the change of seating or had never noticed it. There was no way for Julian to convey his sympathy.

His mother kept her eyes fixed reproachfully on his face. The woman with the protruding teeth was looking at him avidly as if he were a type of monster new to her.

"Do you have a light?" he asked the Negro.

Without looking away from his paper, the man reached in his pocket and handed him a packet of matches.

"Thanks," Julian said. For a moment he held the matches foolishly. A NO SMOKING sign looked down upon him from over the door. This alone would not have deterred him; he had no cigarettes. He had quit smoking some months before because he could not afford it. "Sorry," he muttered and handed back the matches. The Negro lowered the paper and gave him an annoyed look. He took the matches and raised the paper again.

His mother continued to gaze at him but she did not take advantage of his momentary discomfort. Her eyes retained their battered look. Her face seemed to be unnaturally red, as if her blood pressure had risen. Julian allowed no glimmer of sympathy to show on his face. Having got the advantage, he wanted desperately to keep it and carry it through. He would have liked to teach her a lesson that would last her a while, but there seemed no way to continue the point. The Negro refused to come out from behind his paper.

Julian folded his arms and looked stolidly before him, facing her but as if he did not see her, as if he had ceased to recognize her existence. He visualized a scene in which, the bus having reached their stop, he would remain in his seat and when she said, "Aren't you going to get off?" he would look at her as a stranger who had rashly addressed him. The corner they got off on was usually deserted, but it was well lighted and it would not hurt her to walk by herself the four blocks to the Y. He decided to wait until the time came and then decide whether or not he would let her get off by herself. He would have to be at the Y at ten to bring her back, but he could leave her wondering if he was going to show up. There was no reason for her to think she could always depend on him.

He retired again into the high-ceilinged room sparsely settled with large pieces of antique furniture. His soul expanded momentarily but then he became aware of his mother across from him and the vision shriveled. He studied her coldly. Her feet in little pumps dangled like a child's and did not quite reach the floor. She was training on him an exaggerated look of reproach. He felt completely detached from her. At that moment he could with pleasure have slapped her as he would have slapped a particularly obnoxious child in his charge.

He began to imagine various unlikely ways by which he could teach her a lesson. He might make friends with some distinguished Negro professor or lawyer and bring him home to spend the evening. He would be entirely justified but her blood pressure would rise to 300. He could not push her to the extent of making her have a stroke, and moreover, he had never been successful at making any Negro friends. He had tried to strike up an acquaintance on the bus with some of the better types, with ones that looked like professors or ministers or lawyers. One morning he had sat down next to a distinguished-looking dark brown man who had answered his questions with a sonorous solemnity but who had turned out to be an undertaker. Another day he had sat down beside a cigar-smoking Negro with a diamond ring on his finger, but after a few stilted pleasantries, the Negro had rung the buzzer and risen, slipping two lottery tickets into Julian's hand as he climbed over him to leave.

75   He imagined his mother lying desperately ill and his being able to secure only a Negro doctor for her. He toyed with that idea for a few minutes and then dropped it for a momentary vision of himself participating as a sympathizer in a sit-in demonstration. This was possible but he did not linger with it. Instead, he approached the ultimate horror. He brought home a beautiful suspiciously Negroid woman. Prepare yourself, he said. There is nothing you can do about it. This is the woman I've chosen. She's intelligent, dignified, even good, and she's suffered and she hasn't thought *fun.* Now persecute us, go ahead and persecute us. Drive her out of here, but remember, you're driving me too. His eyes were narrowed and through the indignation he had generated, he saw his mother across the aisle, purple-faced, shrunken to the dwarf-like proportions of her moral nature, sitting like a mummy beneath the ridiculous banner of her hat.

He was tilted out of his fantasy again as the bus stopped. The door opened with a sucking hiss and out of the dark a large, gaily dressed, sullen-looking colored woman got on with a little boy. The child, who might have been four, had on a short plaid suit and a Tyrolean hat with a blue feather in it. Julian hoped that he would sit down beside him and that the woman would push in beside his mother. He could think of no better arrangement.

As she waited for her tokens, the woman was surveying the seating possibilities—he hoped with the idea of sitting where she was least wanted. There was something familiar-looking about her but Julian could not place what it was. She was a giant of a woman. Her face was set not only to meet opposition but to seek it out. The downward tilt of her large lower lip was like a warning sign: DON'T TAMPER WITH ME. Her bulging figure was encased in a green crepe dress and her feet overflowed in red shoes. She had on a hideous hat. A purple velvet flap came down on one side of it and stood up on the other, the rest of it was green and looked like a cushion with the stuffing out. She carried a mammoth red pocket-book that bulged throughout as if it were stuffed with rocks.

To Julian's disappointment, the little boy climbed up on the empty seat beside his mother. His mother lumped all children, black and white, into the common category, "cute," and she thought little Negroes were on the whole cuter than little white children. She smiled at the little boy as he climbed on the seat.

Meanwhile the woman was bearing down upon the empty seat beside Julian. To his annoyance, she squeezed herself into it. He saw his mother's face change as the woman settled herself next to him and he realized with satisfaction that this was more objectionable to her than it was to him. Her face seemed almost gray and there was a look of dull recognition in her eyes, as if suddenly she had sickened at some awful confrontation. Julian saw that it was because she and the woman had, in a sense, swapped sons. Though his mother would not realize the symbolic significance of this, she would feel it. His amusement showed plainly on his face.

80   The woman next to him muttered something unintelligible to herself. He was conscious of a kind of bristling next to him, a muted growling like that of an angry cat. He could not see anything but the red pocketbook upright on the bulging green thighs. He visualized the woman as she had stood waiting for her tokens—the ponderous figure, rising from the red shoes upward over the solid hips, the mammoth bosom, the haughty face, to the green and purple hat.

His eyes widened.

The vision of the two hats, identical, broke upon him with the radiance of a brilliant sunrise. His face was suddenly lit with joy. He could not believe that Fate had thrust upon his mother such a lesson. He gave a loud chuckle so that she would look at him and see that he saw. She turned her eyes on him slowly. The blue in them seemed to have turned a bruised purple. For a moment he had an uncomfortable sense of her innocence, but it lasted only a second before principle rescued him. Justice entitled him to laugh. His grin hardened until it said to her as plainly as if he were saying aloud: Your punishment exactly fits your pettiness. This should teach you a permanent lesson.

Her eyes shifted to the woman. She seemed unable to bear looking at him and to find the woman preferable. He became conscious again of the bristling presence at his side. The woman was rumbling like a volcano about to become active. His mother's mouth began to twitch slightly at one corner. With a sinking heart, he saw incipient signs of recovery on her face and realized that this was going to strike her suddenly as funny and was going to be no lesson at all. She kept her eyes on the woman and an amused smile came over her face as if the woman were a monkey that had stolen her hat. The little Negro was looking up at her with large fascinated eyes. He had been trying to attract her attention for some time.

"Carver!" the woman said suddenly. "Come heah!"

When he saw that the spotlight was on him at last, Carver drew his feet up and turned himself toward Julian's mother and giggled. 85

"Carver!" the woman said. "You heah me? Come heah!"

Carver slid down from the seat but remained squatting with his back against the base of it, his head turned slyly around toward Julian's mother, who was smiling at him. The woman reached a hand across the aisle and snatched him to her. He righted himself and hung backwards on her knees, grinning at Julian's mother. "Isn't he cute?" Julian's mother said to the woman with the protruding teeth.

"I reckon he is," the woman said without conviction.

The Negress yanked him upright but he eased out of her grip and shot across the aisle and scrambled, giggling wildly, onto the seat beside his love.

"I think he likes me," Julian's mother said, and smiled at the woman. It was the 90 smile she used when she was being particularly gracious to an inferior. Julian saw everything was lost. The lesson had rolled off her like rain on a roof.

The woman stood up and yanked the little boy off the seat as if she were snatching him from contagion. Julian could feel the rage in her at having no weapon like his mother's smile. She gave the child a sharp slap across his leg. He howled once and then thrust his head into her stomach and kicked his feet against her shins. "Behave," she said vehemently.

The bus stopped and the Negro who had been reading the newspaper got off. The woman moved over and set the little boy down with a thump between herself and Julian. She held him firmly by the knee. In a moment he put his hands in front of his face and peeped at Julian's mother through his fingers.

"I see yoooooooo!" she said and put her hand in front of her face and peeped at him.

The woman slapped his hand down. "Quit yo' foolishness," she said, "before I knock the living Jesus out of you!"

95   Julian was thankful that the next stop was theirs. He reached up and pulled the cord. The woman reached up and pulled it at the same time. Oh my God, he thought. He had the terrible intuition that when they got off the bus together, his mother would open her purse and give the little boy a nickel. The gesture would be as natural to her as breathing. The bus stopped and the woman got up and lunged to the front, dragging the child, who wished to stay on, after her. Julian and his mother got up and followed. As they neared the door, Julian tried to relieve her of her pocketbook.

"No," she murmured, "I want to give the little boy a nickel."

"No!" Julian hissed. "No!"

She smiled down at the child and opened her bag. The bus door opened and the woman picked him up by the arm and descended with him, hanging at her hip. Once in the street she set him down and shook him.

Julian's mother had to close her purse while she got down the bus step but as soon as her feet were on the ground, she opened it again and began to rummage inside. "I can't find but a penny," she whispered, "but it looks like a new one."

100   "Don't do it!" Julian said fiercely between his teeth. There was a streetlight on the corner and she hurried to get under it so that she could better see into her pocketbook. The woman was heading off rapidly down the street with the child still hanging backward on her hand.

"Oh little boy!" Julian's mother called and took a few quick steps and caught up with them just beyond the lamppost. "Here's a bright new penny for you," and she held out the coin, which shone bronze in the dim light.

The huge woman turned and for a moment stood, her shoulders lifted and her face frozen with frustrated rage, and stared at Julian's mother. Then all at once she seemed to explode like a piece of machinery that had been given one ounce of pressure too much. Julian saw the black fist swing out with the red pocketbook. He shut his eyes and cringed as he heard the woman shout, "He don't take nobody's pennies!" When he opened his eyes, the woman was disappearing down the street with the little boy staring wide-eyed over her shoulder. Julian's mother was sitting on the sidewalk.

"I told you not to do that," Julian said angrily. "I told you not to do that!"

He stood over her for a minute, gritting his teeth. Her legs were stretched out in front of her and her hat was on her lap. He squatted down and looked her in the face. It was totally expressionless. "You got exactly what you deserved," he said. "Now get up."

105   He picked up her pocketbook and put what had fallen out back in it. He picked the hat up off her lap. The penny caught his eye on the sidewalk and he picked that up and let it drop before her eyes into the purse. Then he stood up and leaned over and held his hands out to pull her up. She remained immobile. He sighed. Rising above them on either side were black apartment buildings, marked with irregular rectangles of light. At the end of the block a man came out of a door and walked off in the opposite direction. "All right," he said, "suppose somebody happens by and wants to know why you're sitting on the sidewalk?"

She took the hand and, breathing hard, pulled heavily up on it and then stood for a moment, swaying slightly as if the spots of light in the darkness were circling around her. Her eyes, shadowed and confused, finally settled on his face. He did not try to conceal his irritation. "I hope this teaches you a lesson," he said. She leaned forward and her eyes raked his face. She seemed trying to determine his identity. Then, as if she found nothing familiar about him, she started off with a headlong movement in the wrong direction.

"Aren't you going on to the Y?" he asked.

"Home," she muttered.

"Well, are we walking?"

For answer she kept going. Julian followed along, his hands behind him. He saw   110
no reason to let the lesson she had had go without backing it up with an explanation of its meaning. She might as well be made to understand what had happened to her. "Don't think that was just an uppity Negro woman," he said. "That was the whole colored race which will no longer take your condescending pennies. That was your black double. She can wear the same hat as you, and to be sure," he added gratuitously (because he thought it was funny), "it looked better on her than it did on you. What all this means," he said, "is that the old world is gone. The old manners are obsolete and your graciousness is not worth a damn." He thought bitterly of the house that had been lost for him. "You aren't who you think you are," he said.

She continued to plow ahead, paying no attention to him. Her hair had come undone on one side. She dropped her pocketbook and took no notice. He stooped and picked it up and handed it to her but she did not take it.

"You needn't act as if the world had come to an end," he said, "because it hasn't. From now on you've got to live in a new world and face a few realities for a change. Buck up," he said, "it won't kill you."

She was breathing fast.

"Let's wait on the bus," he said.

"Home," she said thickly.   115

"I hate to see you behave like this," he said. "Just like a child. I should be able to expect more of you." He decided to stop where he was and make her stop and wait for a bus. "I'm not going any farther," he said stopping. "We're going on the bus."

She continued to go on as if she had not heard him. He took a few steps and caught her arm and stopped her. He looked into her face and caught his breath. He was looking into a face he had never seen before. "Tell Grandpa to come get me," she said.

He stared, stricken.

"Tell Caroline to come get me," she said.

Stunned, he let her go and she lurched forward again, walking as if one leg were   120
shorter than the other. A tide of darkness seemed to be sweeping her from him. "Mother!" he cried. "Darling, sweetheart, wait!" Crumpling, she fell to the pavement. He dashed forward and fell at her side, crying, "Mamma, Mamma!" He turned her over. Her face was fiercely distorted. One eye, large and staring, moved slightly to the left as if it had become unmoored. The other remained fixed on him, raked his face again, found nothing and closed.

"Wait here, wait here!" he cried and jumped up and began to run for help toward a cluster of lights he saw in the distance ahead of him. "Help, help!" he shouted, but his voice was thin, scarcely a thread of sound. The lights drifted farther away the faster he ran and his feet moved numbly as if they carried him nowhere. The tide of darkness seemed to sweep him back to her, postponing from moment to moment his entry into the world of guilt and sorrow.

EDGAR ALLAN POE (1809–1849)

The Tell-Tale Heart (1843)

True!—nervous—very, very dreadfully nervous I had been and am; but why *will* you say that I am mad? The disease had sharpened my senses—not destroyed—not dulled them. Above all was the sense of hearing acute. I heard all things in the heaven and in the earth. I heard many things in hell. How, then, am I mad? Hearken! and observe how healthily—how calmly I can tell you the whole story.

It is impossible to say how first the idea entered my brain; but once conceived, it haunted me day and night. Object there was none. Passion there was none. I loved the old man. He had never wronged me. He had never given me insult. For his gold I had no desire. I think it was his eye! yes, it was this! One of his eyes resembled that of a vulture—a pale eye, with a film over it. Whenever it fell upon me, my blood ran cold; and so by degrees—very gradually—I made up my mind to take the life of the old man, and thus rid myself of the eye forever.

Now this is the point. You fancy me mad. Madmen know nothing. But you should have seen *me*. You should have seen how wisely I proceeded—with what caution—with what foresight—with what dissimulation I went to work! I was never kinder to the old man than during the whole week before I killed him. And every night, about midnight, I turned the latch of his door and opened it—oh, so gently! And then, when I had made an opening sufficient for my head, I put in a dark lantern, all closed, closed, so that no light shone out, and then I thrust in my head. Oh, you would have laughed to see how cunningly I thrust it in! I moved it slowly—very, very slowly, so that I might not disturb the old man's sleep. It took me an hour to place my whole head within the opening so far that I could see him as he lay upon his bed. Ha!— would a madman have been so wise as this? And then, when my head was well in the room, I undid the lantern cautiously—oh, so cautiously—cautiously (for the hinges creaked)—I undid it just so much that a single thin ray fell upon the vulture eye. And this I did for seven long nights—every night just at midnight—but I found the eye always closed; and so it was impossible to do the work; for it was not the old man who vexed me, but his Evil Eye. And every morning, when the day broke, I went boldly into the chamber, and spoke courageously to him, calling him by name in a hearty tone, and inquiring how he had passed the night. So you see he would have been a very profound old man, indeed, to suspect that every night, just at twelve, I looked in upon him while he slept.

Upon the eighth night I was more than usually cautious in opening the door. A watch's minute hand moves more quickly than did mine. Never before that night had I *felt* the extent of my own powers—of my sagacity. I could scarcely contain my feelings of triumph. To think that there I was, opening the door little by little, and he not even to dream of my secret deeds or thoughts. I fairly chuckled at the idea; and perhaps he heard me; for he moved on the bed suddenly, as if startled. Now you may think that I drew back—but no. His room was as black as pitch with the thick darkness (for the shutters were close fastened through fear of robbers), and so I knew that he could not see the opening of the door, and I kept pushing it on steadily, steadily.

I had my head in, and was about to open the lantern, when my thumb slipped upon the tin fastening, and the old man sprang up in the bed, crying out—"Who's there?"

I kept quite still and said nothing. For a whole hour I did not move a muscle, and in the meantime I did not hear him lie down. He was still sitting up in the bed listening;—just as I have done, night after night, hearkening to the death watches[1] in the wall.

Presently I heard a slight groan, and I knew it was the groan of mortal terror. It was not a groan of pain or of grief—oh, no!—it was the low stifled sound that arises from the bottom of the soul when overcharged with awe. I knew the sound very well. Many a night, just at midnight, when all the world slept, it has welled up from my own bosom, deepening, with its dreadful echo, the terrors that distracted me. I say I knew it well. I knew what the old man felt, and pitied him, although I chuckled at heart. I knew that he had been lying awake ever since the first slight noise, when he had turned in the bed. His fears had been ever since growing upon him. He had been trying to fancy them causeless, but could not. He had been saying to himself—"It is nothing but the wind in the chimney—it is only a mouse crossing the floor," or "it is merely a cricket which has made a single chirp." Yes, he had been trying to comfort himself with these suppositions; but he had found all in vain. *All in vain*; because Death, in approaching him, had stalked with his black shadow before him, and enveloped the victim. And it was the mournful influence of the unperceived shadow that caused him to feel—although he neither saw nor heard—to *feel* the presence of my head within the room.

When I had waited a long time, very patiently, without hearing him lie down, I resolved to open a little—a very, very little crevice in the lantern. So I opened it—you cannot imagine how stealthily, stealthily—until, at length, a single dim ray, like the thread of the spider, shot from out of the crevice and fell upon the vulture eye.

It was open—wide, wide open—and I grew furious as I gazed upon it. I saw it with perfect distinctness—all a dull blue, with a hideous veil over it that chilled the very marrow in my bones; but I could see nothing else of the old man's face or person: for I had directed the ray as if by instinct, precisely upon the damned spot.

And now have I not told you that what you mistake for madness is but over-acuteness of the senses?—now, I say, there came to my ears a low, dull, quick sound, such as a watch makes when enveloped in cotton. I knew *that* sound well, too. It was the beating of the old man's heart. It increased my fury, as the beating of a drum stimulates the soldier into courage.

But even yet I refrained and kept still. I scarcely breathed. I held the lantern motionless. I tried how steadily I could maintain the ray upon the eye. Meantime the hellish tattoo of the heart increased. It grew quicker and quicker, and louder and louder every instant. The old man's terror *must* have been extreme! It grew louder, I say, louder every moment!—do you mark me well? I have told you that I am nervous: so I am. And now at the dead hour of the night, amid the dreadful silence of that old house, so strange a noise as this excited me to uncontrollable terror. Yet, for

---

[1]*death watches:* Wood-burrowing beetles. Their clicking sound was superstitiously thought of as an omen of death.

some minutes longer I refrained and stood still. But the beating grew louder, louder! I thought the heart must burst. And now a new anxiety seized me—the sound would be heard by a neighbor! The old man's hour had come! With a loud yell, I threw open the lantern and leaped into the room. He shrieked once—once only. In an instant I dragged him to the floor, and pulled the heavy bed over him. I then smiled gaily, to find the deed so far done. But, for many minutes, the heart beat on with a muffled sound. This, however, did not vex me; it would not be heard through the wall. At length it ceased. The old man was dead. I removed the bed and examined the corpse. Yes, he was stone, stone dead. I placed my hand upon the heart and held it there many minutes.

If still you think me mad, you will think so no longer when I describe the wise precautions I took for the concealment of the body. The night waned, and I worked hastily, but in silence. First of all I dismembered the corpse. I cut off the head and the arms and the legs.

I then took up three planks from the flooring of the chamber, and deposited all between the scantlings. I then replaced the boards so cleverly, so cunningly, that no human eye—not even *his*—could have detected anything wrong. There was nothing to wash out—no stain of any kind—no bloodspot whatever. I had been too wary for that. A tub had caught all—ha! ha!

When I had made an end of these labors, it was four o'clock—still dark as mid-night. As the bell sounded the hour, there came a knocking at the street door. I went down to open it with a light heart,—for what had I *now* to fear? There entered three men, who introduced themselves, with perfect suavity, as officers of the police. A shriek had been heard by a neighbor during the night; suspicion of foul play had been aroused, information had been lodged at the police office, and they (the officers) had been deputed to search the premises.

15   I smiled,—for *what* had I to fear? I bade the gentlemen welcome. The shriek, I said, was my own in a dream. The old man, I mentioned, was absent in the country. I took my visitors all over the house. I bade them search—search *well*. I led them, at length, to *his* chamber. I showed them his treasures, secure, undisturbed. In the enthusiasm of my confidence, I brought chairs into the room, and desired them *here* to rest from their fatigues, while I myself, in the wild audacity of my perfect triumph, placed my own seat upon the very spot beneath which reposed the corpse of the victim.

The officers were satisfied. My *manner* had convinced them. I was singularly at ease. They sat, and while I answered cheerily, they chatted of familiar things. But, ere long, I felt myself getting pale and wished them gone. My head ached, and I fancied a ringing in my ears: but still they sat and still they chatted. The ringing became more distinct:—it continued and became more distinct: I talked more freely to get rid of the feeling: but it continued and gained definitiveness—until, at length, I found that the noise was *not* within my ears.

No doubt I now grew *very* pale:—but I talked more fluently, and with a height-ened voice. Yet the sound increased—and what could I do? It was a *low, dull, quick sound—much such a sound as a watch makes when enveloped in cotton.* I gasped for breath—and yet the officers heard it not. I talked more quickly—more vehemently; but the noise steadily increased. I arose and argued about trifles, in a high key and with violent gesticulations; but the noise steadily increased. Why *would* they not be gone? I paced the floor to and fro with heavy strides, as if excited to fury by the observations of the men—but the noise steadily increased. Oh God! what *could* I do? I foamed—I raved—I swore! I swung the chair upon which I had been sitting, and grated it upon the boards, but the noise arose over all and continually increased. It grew louder—louder—*louder!* And still the men chatted pleasantly, and smiled. Was it possible they heard not? Almighty God!—no, no! They heard!—they suspected!—they *knew!*—they were making a mockery of my horror!—this I thought, and this I think. But anything was better than this agony! Anything was more tolerable than this derision! I could bear those hypocritical smiles no longer! I felt that I must scream or die!—and now—again!—hark! louder! louder! louder! *louder!*—

"Villains!" I shrieked, "dissemble no more! I admit the deed!—tear up the planks!—here, here!—it is the beating of his hideous heart!"

KATHERINE ANNE PORTER (1890–1980)

The Jilting of Granny Weatherall (1930)

She flicked her wrist neatly out of Doctor Harry's pudgy careful fingers and pulled the sheet up to her chin. The brat ought to be in knee breeches. Doctoring around the country with spectacles on his nose! "Get along now, take your schoolbooks and go. There's nothing wrong with me."

Doctor Harry spread a warm paw like a cushion on her forehead where the forked green vein danced and made her eyelids twitch. "Now, now, be a good girl, and we'll have you up in no time."

"That's no way to speak to a woman nearly eighty years old just because she's down. I'd have you respect your elders, young man."

"Well, Missy, excuse me." Doctor Harry patted her cheek. "But I've got to warn you, haven't I? You're a marvel, but you must be careful or you're going to be good and sorry."

"Don't tell me what I'm going to be. I'm on my feet now, morally speaking. It's Cornelia. I had to go to bed to get rid of her."

Her bones felt loose, and floated around in her skin, and Doctor Harry floated like a balloon around the foot of the bed. He floated and pulled down his waistcoat and swung his glasses on a cord. "Well, stay where you are, it certainly can't hurt you."

"Get along and doctor your sick," said Granny Weatherall. "Leave a well woman alone. I'll call for you when I want you. . . . Where were you forty years ago when I pulled through milk-leg and double pneumonia? You weren't even born. Don't let Cornelia lead you on," she shouted, because Doctor Harry appeared to float up to the ceiling and out. "I pay my own bills, and I don't throw my money away on nonsense!"

She meant to wave good-by, but it was too much trouble. Her eyes closed of themselves, it was like a dark curtain drawn around the bed. The pillow rose and

5

floated under her, pleasant as a hammock in a light wind. She listened to the leaves rustling outside the window. No, somebody was swishing newspapers: no, Cornelia and Doctor Harry were whispering together. She leaped broad awake, thinking they whispered in her ear.

"She was never like this, *never* like this!" "Well, what can we expect?" "Yes, eighty years old. . . ."

10   Well, and what if she was? She still had ears. It was like Cornelia to whisper around doors. She always kept things secret in such a public way. She was always being tactful and kind. Cornelia was dutiful; that was the trouble with her. Dutiful and good: "So good and dutiful," said Granny, "that I'd like to spank her." She saw herself spanking Cornelia and making a fine job of it.

"What'd you say, Mother?"

Granny felt her face tying up in hard knots.

"Can't a body think, I'd like to know?"

"I thought you might want something."

15   "I do. I want a lot of things. First off, go away and don't whisper."

She lay and drowsed, hoping in her sleep that the children would keep out and let her rest a minute. It had been a long day. Not that she was tired. It was always pleasant to snatch a minute now and then. There was always so much to be done, let me see: tomorrow.

Tomorrow was far away and there was nothing to trouble about. Things were finished somehow when the time came; thank God there was always a little margin over for peace: then a person could spread out the plan of life and tuck in the edges orderly. It was good to have everything clean and folded away, with the hair brushes and tonic bottles sitting straight on the white embroidered linen: the day started without fuss and the pantry shelves laid out with rows of jelly glasses and brown jugs and white stone-china jars with blue whirligigs and words painted on them: coffee, tea, sugar, ginger, cinnamon, allspice: and the bronze clock with the lion on top nicely dusted off. The dust that lion could collect in twenty-four hours! The box in the attic with all those letters tied up, well, she'd have to go through that tomorrow. All those letters—George's letters and John's letters and her letters to them both—lying around for the children to find afterwards made her uneasy. Yes, that would be tomorrow's business. No use to let them know how silly she had been once.

While she was rummaging around she found death in her mind and it felt clammy and unfamiliar. She had spent so much time preparing for death there was no need for bringing it up again. Let it take care of itself now. When she was sixty she had felt very old, finished, and went around making farewell trips to see her children and grandchildren, with a secret in her mind: This is the very last of your mother, children! Then she made her will and came down with a long fever. That was all just a notion like a lot of other things, but it was lucky too, for she had once and for all got over the idea of dying for a long time. Now she couldn't be worried. She hoped she had better sense now. Her father had lived to be one hundred and two years old and had drunk a noggin of strong hot toddy on his last birthday. He told the reporters it was his daily habit, and he owed his long life to that. He had made quite a scandal and was very pleased about it. She believed she'd just plague Cornelia a little.

"Cornelia! Cornelia!" No footsteps, but a sudden hand on her cheek. "Bless you, where have you been?"

"Here, Mother."   20

"Well, Cornelia, I want a noggin of hot toddy."

"Are you cold, darling?"

"I'm chilly, Cornelia. Lying in bed stops the circulation. I must have told you that a thousand times."

Well, she could just hear Cornelia telling her husband that Mother was getting a little childish and they'd have to humor her. The thing that most annoyed her was that Cornelia thought she was deaf, dumb, and blind. Little hasty glances and tiny gestures tossed around her and over her head saying, "Don't cross her, let her have her way, she's eighty years old," and she sitting there as if she lived in a thin glass cage. Sometimes Granny almost made up her mind to pack up and move back to her own house where nobody could remind her every minute that she was old. Wait, wait, Cornelia, till your own children whisper behind your back!

In her day she had kept a better house and had got more work done. She wasn't   25
too old yet for Lydia to be driving eighty miles for advice when one of the children jumped the track, and Jimmy still dropped in and talked things over: "Now, Mammy, you've a good business head, I want to know what you think of this? . . ." Old. Cornelia couldn't change the furniture around without asking. Little things, little things! They had been so sweet when they were little. Granny wished the old days were back again with the children young and everything to be done over. It had been a hard pull, but not too much for her. When she thought of all the food she had cooked, and all the clothes she had cut and sewed, and all the gardens she had made—well, the children showed it. There they were, made out of her, and they couldn't get away from that. Sometimes she wanted to see John again and point to them and say, Well, I didn't do so badly, did I? But that would have to wait. That was for tomorrow. She used to think of him as a man, but now all the children were older than their father, and he would be a child beside her if she saw him now. It seemed strange and there was something wrong in the idea. Why, he couldn't possibly recognize her. She had fenced in a hundred acres once, digging the post holes herself and clamping the wires with just a negro boy to help. That changed a woman. John would be looking for a young woman with the peaked Spanish comb in her hair and the painted fan. Digging post holes changed a woman. Riding country roads in the winter when women had their babies was another thing: sitting up nights with sick horses and sick negroes and sick children and hardly ever losing one. John, I hardly ever lost one of them! John would see that in a minute, that would be something he could understand, she wouldn't have to explain anything!

It made her feel like rolling up her sleeves and putting the whole place to rights again. No matter if Cornelia was determined to be everywhere at once, there were a great many things left undone on this place. She would start tomorrow and do them. It was good to be strong enough for everything, even if all you made melted and changed and slipped under your hands, so that by the time you finished you almost forgot what you were working for. What was it I set out to do? she asked herself intently, but she could not remember. A fog rose over the valley, she saw it marching across the creek swallowing the trees and moving up the hill like an army of ghosts.

Soon it would be at the near edge of the orchard, and then it was time to go in and light the lamps. Come in, children, don't stay out in the night air.

Lighting the lamps had been beautiful. The children huddled up to her and breathed like little calves waiting at the bars in the twilight. Their eyes followed the match and watched the flame rise and settle in a blue curve, then they moved away from her. The lamp was lit, they didn't have to be scared and hang on to mother any more. Never, never, never more. God, for all my life I thank Thee. Without Thee, my God, I could never have done it. Hail, Mary, full of grace.

I want you to pick all the fruit this year and see that nothing is wasted. There's always someone who can use it. Don't let good things rot for want of using. You waste life when you waste good food. Don't let things get lost. It's bitter to lose things. Now, don't let me get to thinking, not when I am tired and taking a little nap before supper. . . .

The pillow rose about her shoulders and pressed against her heart and the memory was being squeezed out of it: oh, push down the pillow, somebody: it would smother her if she tried to hold it. Such a fresh breeze blowing and such a green day with no threats in it. But he had not come, just the same. What does a woman do when she has put on the white veil and set out the white cake for a man and he doesn't come? She tried to remember. No, I swear he never harmed me but in that. He never harmed me but in that . . . and what if he did? There was the day, the day, but a whirl of dark smoke rose and covered it, crept up and over into the bright field where every-thing was planted so carefully in orderly rows. That was hell, she knew hell when she saw it. For sixty years she had prayed against remembering him and against losing her soul in the deep pit of hell, and now the two things were mingled in one and the thought of him was a smoky cloud from hell that moved and crept in her head when she had just got rid of Doctor Harry and was trying to rest a minute. Wounded vanity, Ellen, said a sharp voice in the top of her mind. Don't let your wounded vanity get the upper hand of you. Plenty of girls get jilted. You were jilted, weren't you? Then stand up to it. Her eyelids wavered and let in streamers of blue-gray light like tissue paper over her eyes. She must get up and pull the shades down or she'd never sleep. She was in bed again and the shades were not down. How could that happen? Better turn over, hide from the light, sleeping in the light gave you nightmares. "Mother, how do you feel now?" and a stinging wetness on her forehead. But I don't like having my face washed in cold water!

30   Hapsy? George? Lydia? Jimmy? No, Cornelia, and her features were swollen and full of little puddles. "They're coming, darling, they'll all be here soon." Go wash your face, child, you look funny.

Instead of obeying, Cornelia knelt down and put her head on the pillow. She seemed to be talking but there was no sound. "Well, are you tongue-tied? Whose birthday is it? Are you going to give a party?"

Cornelia's mouth moved urgently in strange shapes. "Don't do that, you bother me, daughter."

"O, no, Mother. Oh, no. . . ."

Nonsense. It was strange about children. They disputed your every word. "No what, Cornelia?"

35   "Here's Doctor Harry."

"I won't see that boy again. He just left five minutes ago."

"That was this morning, Mother. It's night now. Here's the nurse."

"This is Doctor Harry, Mrs. Weatherall. I never saw you look so young and happy!"

"Ah, I'll never be young again—but I'd be happy if they'd let me lie in peace and get rested."

She thought she spoke up loudly, but no one answered. A warm weight on her forehead, a warm bracelet on her wrist, and a breeze went on whispering, trying to tell her something. A shuffle of leaves in the everlasting hand of God. He blew on them and they danced and rattled. "Mother, don't mind, we're going to give you a little hypodermic." "Look here, daughter, how do ants get in this bed? I saw sugar ants yesterday." Did you send for Hapsy too?

It was Hapsy she really wanted. She had to go a long way back through a great many rooms to find Hapsy standing with a baby on her arm. She seemed to herself to be Hapsy also, and the baby on Hapsy's arm was Hapsy and himself and herself, all at once, and there was no surprise in the meeting. Then Hapsy melted from within and turned flimsy as gray gauze and the baby was a gauzy shadow, and Hapsy came up close and said, "I thought you'd never come." and looked at her very searchingly and said, "You haven't changed a bit!" They leaned forward to kiss, when Cornelia began whispering from a long way off, "Oh, is there anything you want to tell me? Is there anything I can do for you?"

Yes, she had changed her mind after sixty years and she would like to see George. I want you to find George. Find him and be sure to tell him I forgot him. I want him to know I had my husband just the same and my children and my house like any other woman. A good house too and a good husband that I loved and fine children out of him. Better than I hoped for even. Tell him I was given back everything he took away and more. Oh, no, oh, God, no, there was something else besides the house and the man and the children. Oh, surely they were not all? What was it? Something not given back. . . . Her breath crowded down under her ribs and grew into a monstrous frightening shape with cutting edges; it bored up into her head, and the agony was unbelievable: Yes, John, get the Doctor now, no more talk, my time has come.

When this one was born it should be the last. The last. It should have been born first, for it was the one she had truly wanted. Everything came in good time. Nothing left out, left over. She was strong, in three days she would be as well as ever. Better. A woman needed milk in her to have her full health.

"Mother, do you hear me?"

"I've been telling you—"

"Mother, Father Connolly's here."

"I went to Holy Communion last week. Tell him I'm not so sinful as all that."

"Father just wants to speak to you."

He could speak as much as he pleased. It was like him to drop in and inquire about her soul as if it were a teething baby, and then stay on for a cup of tea and a round of cards and gossip. He always had a funny story of some sort, usually about an Irishman who made his little mistakes and confessed them, and the point lay in some absurd thing he would blurtout in the confessional showing his struggles between native piety and original sin. Granny felt easy about her soul. Cornelia, where are your manners? Give Father Connolly a chair. She had her secret comfortable understanding with a few favorite saints who cleared a straight road to God for her. All as surely signed and sealed as the papers for the new Forty Acres. Forever . . . heirs and assigns forever. Since the day the wedding cake was not cut, but thrown out and wasted. The whole bottom dropped out of the world, and there she was blind and sweating with nothing under her feet and the walls falling away. His hand had caught her under the breast, she had not fallen, there was the freshly polished floor with the green rug on it, just as before. He had cursed like a sailor's parrot and said, "I'll kill him for you." Don't lay a hand on him, for my sake leave something to God. "Now, Ellen, you must believe what I tell you. . . ."

50   So there was nothing, nothing to worry about any more, except sometimes in the night one of the children screamed in a nightmare, and they both hustled out shaking and hunting for the matches and calling, "There, wait a minute, here we are!" John, get the doctor now, Hapsy's time has come. But there was Hapsy standing by the bed in a white cap. "Cornelia, tell Hapsy to take off her cap. I can't see her plain."

Her eyes opened very wide and the room stood out like a picture she had seen somewhere. Dark colors with the shadows rising towards the ceiling in long angles. The tall black dresser gleamed with nothing on it but John's picture, enlarged from a little one, with John's eyes very black when they should have been blue. You never saw him, so how do you know how he looked? But the man insisted the copy was perfect, it was very rich and handsome. For a picture, yes, but it's not my husband. The table by the bed had a linen cover and a candle and a crucifix. The light was blue from Cornelia's silk lampshades. No sort of light at all, just frippery. You had to live forty years with kerosene lamps to appreciate honest electricity. She felt very strong and she saw Doctor Harry with a rosy nimbus around him.

"You look like a saint, Doctor Harry, and I vow that's as near as you'll ever come to it."

"She's saying something."

"I heard you, Cornelia. What's all this carrying-on?"

55   "Father Connolly's saying—"

Cornelia's voice staggered and bumped like a cart in a bad road. It rounded corners and turned back again and arrived nowhere. Granny stepped up in the cart very lightly and reached for the reins, but a man sat beside her and she knew him by his hands, driving the cart. She did not look in his face, for she knew without seeing, but looked instead down the road where the trees leaned over and bowed to each other and a thousand birds were singing a Mass. She felt like singing too, but she put her hand in the bosom of her dress and pulled out a rosary, and Father Connolly murmured Latin in a very solemn voice and tickled her feet. My God, will you stop that nonsense? I'm a married woman. What if he did run away and leave me to face the priest by myself? I found another a whole world better. I wouldn't have exchanged my husband for anybody except St. Michael himself, and you may tell him that for me with a thank you in the bargain.

Light flashed on her closed eyelids, and a deep roaring shook her. Cornelia, is that lightning? I hear thunder. There's going to be a storm. Close all the windows. Call the children in. . . . "Mother, here we are, all of us." "Is that you, Hapsy?" "Oh, no, I'm Lydia. We drove as fast as we could." Their faces drifted above her, drifted away. The rosary fell out of her hands and Lydia put it back. Jimmy tried to help, their hands fumbled together, and Granny closed two fingers around Jimmy's thumb. Beads wouldn't do, it must be something alive. She was so amazed her thoughts ran round and round. So, my dear Lord, this is my death and I wasn't even thinking about it. My children have come to see me die. But I can't, it's not time. Oh, I always hated surprises. I wanted to give Cornelia the amethyst set—Cornelia, you're to have the amethyst set, but Hapsy's to wear it when she wants, and, Doctor Harry, do shut up. Nobody sent for you. Oh, my dear Lord, do wait a minute. I meant to do something about the Forty Acres, Jimmy doesn't need it and Lydia will later on, with that worthless husband of hers. I meant to finish the altar cloth and send six bottles of wine to Sister Borgia for her dyspepsia. I want to send six bottles of wine to Sister Borgia, Father Connolly, now don't let me forget.

Cornelia's voice made short turns and tilted over and crashed. "Oh, Mother, oh, Mother, oh, Mother. . . ."

"I'm not going, Cornelia. I'm taken by surprise. I can't go."

You'll see Hapsy again. What about her? "I thought you'd never come." Granny made a long journey outward, looking for Hapsy. What if I don't find her? What then? Her heart sank down and down, there was no bottom to death, she couldn't come to the end of it. The blue light from Cornelia's lampshade drew into a tiny point in the center of her brain, it flickered and winked like an eye, quietly it fluttered and dwindled. Granny lay curled down within herself, amazed and watchful, staring at the point of light that was herself; her body was now only a deeper mass of shadow in an endless darkness and this darkness would curl around the light and swallow it up. God, give a sign!

For the second time there was no sign. Again no bridegroom and the priest in the house. She could not remember any other sorrow because this grief wiped them all away. Oh, no, there's nothing more cruel than this—I'll never forgive it. She stretched herself with a deep breath and blew out the light.

JOHN STEINBECK (1902–1968)

The Chrysanthemums (1937)

The high grey-flannel fog of winter closed off the Salinas Valley from the sky and from all the rest of the world. On every side it sat like a lid on the mountains and made of the great valley a closed pot. On the broad, level land floor the gang plows bit deep and left the black earth shining like metal where the shares had cut. On the foothill ranches across the Salinas River, the yellow stubble fields seemed to be bathed in pale cold sunshine, but there was no sunshine in the valley now in December. The thick willow scrub along the river flamed with sharp and positive yellow leaves.

It was a game of quiet and of waiting. The air was cold and tender. A light wind blew up from the southwest so that the farmers were mildly hopeful of a good rain before long; but fog and rain do not go together.

Across the river, on Henry Allen's foothill ranch there was little work to be done, for the hay was cut and stored and the orchards were plowed up to receive the rain deeply when it should come. The cattle on the higher slopes were becoming shaggy and rough-coated.

Elisa Allen, working in her flower garden, looked down across the yard and saw Henry, her husband, talking to two men in business suits. The three of them stood by the tractor shed, each man with one foot on the side of the little Fordson. They smoked cigarettes and studied the machine as they talked.

5   Elisa watched them for a moment and then went back to her work. She was thirty-five. Her face was lean and strong and her eyes were as clear as water. Her figure looked blocked and heavy in her gardening costume, a man's black hat pulled low down over her eyes, clod-hopper shoes,[1] a figured print dress almost completely covered by a big corduroy apron with four big pockets to hold the snips, the trowel and scratcher, the seeds and the knife she worked with. She wore heavy leather gloves to protect her hands while she worked.

She was cutting down the old year's chrysanthemum stalks with a pair of short and powerful scissors. She looked down toward the men by the tractor shed now and then. Her face was eager and mature and handsome; even her work with the scissors was over-eager, over-powerful. The chrysanthemum stems seemed too small and easy for her energy.

She brushed a cloud of hair out of her eyes with the back of her glove, and left a smudge of earth on her cheek in doing it. Behind her stood the neat white farm house with red geraniums close-banked around it as high as the windows. It was a hard-swept looking little house with hard-polished windows, and a clean mud-mat on the front steps.

Elisa cast another glance toward the tractor shed. The strangers were getting into their Ford coupe. She took off a glove and put her strong fingers down into the forest of new green chrysanthemum sprouts that were growing around the old roots. She spread the leaves and looked down among the close-growing stems. No aphids were there, no sowbugs or snails or cutworms. Her terrier fingers destroyed such pests before they could get started.

Elisa started at the sound of her husband's voice. He had come near quietly, and he leaned over the wire fence that protected her flower garden from cattle and dogs and chickens.

10   "At it again," he said. "You've got a strong new crop coming."

Elisa straightened her back and pulled on the gardening glove again. "Yes. They'll be strong this coming year." In her tone and on her face there was a little smugness.

"You've got a gift with things," Henry observed. "Some of those yellow chrysanthemums you had this year were ten inches across. I wish you'd work out in the orchard and raise some apples that big."

Her eyes sharpened. "Maybe I could do it, too. I've a gift with things, all right. My mother had it. She could stick anything in the ground and make it grow. She said it was having planters' hands that knew how to do it."

---

[1] *clod-hopper shoes:* Heavy shoes, such as the ones that a plowman might wear.

"Well, it sure works with flowers," he said.

"Henry, who were those men you were talking to?"

"Why, sure, that's what I came to tell you. They were from the Western Meat Company. I sold those thirty head of three-year-old steers. Got nearly my own price, too."

"Good," she said. "Good for you."

"And I thought," he continued, "I thought how it's Saturday afternoon, and we might go into Salinas for dinner at a restaurant, and then to a picture show—to celebrate, you see."

"Good," she repeated. "Oh, yes. That will be good."

Henry put on his joking tone. "There's fights tonight. How'd you like to go to the fights?"

"Oh, no," she said breathlessly. "No, I wouldn't like fights."

"Just fooling, Elisa. We'll go to a movie. Let's see. It's two now. I'm going to take Scotty and bring down those steers from the hill. It'll take us maybe two hours. We'll go in town about five and have dinner at the Cominos Hotel. Like that?"

"Of course I'll like it. It's good to eat away from home."

"All right, then. I'll go get up a couple of horses."

She said, "I'll have plenty of time to transplant some of these sets, I guess."

She heard her husband calling Scotty down by the barn. And a little later she saw the two men ride up the pale yellow hillside in search of the steers.

There was a little square sandy bed kept for rooting the chrysanthemums. With her trowel she turned the soil over and over, and smoothed it and patted it firm. Then she dug ten parallel trenches to receive the sets. Back at the chrysanthemum bed she pulled out the little crisp shoots, trimmed off the leaves of each one with her scissors and laid it on a small orderly pile.

A squeak of wheels and plod of hoofs came from the road. Elisa looked up. The country road ran along the dense bank of willows and cottonwoods that bordered the river, and up this road came a curious vehicle, curiously drawn. It was an old spring-wagon, with a round canvas top on it like the cover of a prairie schooner.[2] It was drawn by an old bay horse and a little grey-and-white burro. A big stubble-bearded man sat between the cover flaps and drove the crawling team. Underneath the wagon, between the hind wheels, a lean and rangy mongrel dog walked sedately. Words were printed on the canvas, in clumsy, crooked letters. "Pots, pans, knives, sisors, lawn mores, Fixed." Two rows of articles, and the triumphantly definitive "Fixed" below. The black paint had run down in little sharp points beneath each letter.

Elisa, squatting on the ground, watched to see the crazy, loose-jointed wagon pass by. But it didn't pass. It turned into the farm road in front of her house, crooked old wheels skirling and squeaking. The rangy dog darted from between the wheels and ran ahead. Instantly the two ranch shepherds flew out at him. Then all three stopped, and with stiff and quivering tails, with taut straight legs, with ambassadorial dignity, they slowly circled, sniffing daintily. The caravan pulled up to Elisa's

[2]*prairie schooner:* Covered wagon used by American pioneers.

wire fence and stopped. Now the newcomer dog, feeling outnumbered, lowered his tail and retired under the wagon with raised hackles and bared teeth.

30   The man on the wagon seat called out, "That's a bad dog in a fight when he gets started."

Elisa laughed. "I see he is. How soon does he generally get started?"

The man caught up her laughter and echoed it heartily. "Sometimes not for weeks and weeks," he said. He climbed stiffly down, over the wheel. The horse and the donkey drooped like unwatered flowers.

Elisa saw that he was a very big man. Although his hair and beard were greying, he did not look old. His worn black suit was wrinkled and spotted with grease. The laughter had disappeared from his face and eyes the moment his laughing voice ceased. His eyes were dark, and they were full of the brooding that gets in the eyes of teamsters and of sailors. The calloused hands he rested on the wire fence were cracked, and every crack was a black line. He took off his battered hat.

"I'm off my general road, ma'am," he said. "Does this dirt road cut over across the river to the Los Angeles highway?"

35   Elisa stood up and shoved the thick scissors in her apron pocket. "Well, yes, it does, but it winds around and then fords the river. I don't think your team could pull through the sand."

He replied with some asperity. "It might surprise you what them beasts can pull through."

"When they get started?" she asked.

He smiled for a second. "Yes. When they get started."

"Well," said Elisa, "I think you'll save time if you go back to the Salinas road and pick up the highway there."

40   He drew a big finger down the chicken wire and made it sing. "I ain't in any hurry, ma'am. I go from Seattle to San Diego and back every year. Takes all my time. About six months each way. I aim to follow nice weather."

Elisa took off her gloves and stuffed them in the apron pocket with the scissors. She touched the under edge of her man's hat, searching for fugitive hairs. "That sounds like a nice kind of a way to live," she said.

He leaned confidentially over the fence. "Maybe you noticed the writing on my wagon. I mend pots and sharpen knives and scissors. You got any of them things to do?"

"Oh, no," she said quickly. "Nothing like that." Her eyes hardened with resistance.

"Scissors is the worst thing," he explained. "Most people just ruin scissors trying to sharpen 'em, but I know how. I got a special tool. It's a little bobbit kind of thing, and patented. But it sure does the trick."

45   "No. My scissors are all sharp."

"All right, then. Take a pot," he continued earnestly, "a bent pot, or a pot with a hole. I can make it like new so you don't have to buy no new ones. That's a saving for you."

"No," she said shortly. "I tell you I have nothing like that for you to do."

His face fell to an exaggerated sadness. His voice took on a whining undertone. "I ain't had a thing to do today. Maybe I won't have no supper tonight. You see I'm off my regular road. I know folks on the highway clear from Seattle to San Diego. They save their things for me to sharpen up because they know I do it so good and save them money."

"I'm sorry," Elisa said irritably. "I haven't anything for you to do."

His eyes left her face and fell to searching the ground. They roamed about until they came to the chrysanthemum bed where she had been working. "What's them plants, ma'am?"   50

The irritation and resistance melted from Elisa's face. "Oh, those are chrysanthemums, giant whites and yellows. I raise them every year, bigger than anybody around here."

"Kind of a long-stemmed flower? Looks like a quick puff of colored smoke?" he asked.

"That's it. What a nice way to describe them."

"They smell kind of nasty till you get used to them," he said.

"It's a good bitter smell," she retorted, "not nasty at all."   55

He changed his tone quickly. "I like the smell myself."

"I had ten-inch blooms this year," she said.

The man leaned farther over the fence. "Look. I know a lady down the road a piece, has got the nicest garden you ever seen. Got nearly every kind of flower but no chrysanthemums. Last time I was mending a copper-bottom washtub for her (that's a hard job but I do it good), she said to me, 'If you ever run acrost some nice chrysanthemums I wish you'd try to get me a few seeds.' That's what she told me."

Elisa's eyes grew alert and eager. "She couldn't have known much about chrysanthemums. You *can* raise them from seed, but it's much easier to root the little sprouts you see there."

"Oh," he said. "I s'pose I can't take none to her, then."   60

"Why yes you can," Elisa cried. "I can put some in damp sand, and you can carry them right along with you. They'll take root in the pot if you keep them damp. And then she can transplant them."

"She'd sure like to have some, ma'am. You say they're nice ones?"

"Beautiful," she said. "Oh, beautiful." Her eyes shone. She tore off the battered hat and shook out her dark pretty hair. "I'll put them in a flower pot, and you can take them right with you. Come into the yard."

While the man came through the picket gate Elisa ran excitedly along the geranium-bordered path to the back of the house. And she returned carrying a big red flower pot. The gloves were forgotten now. She kneeled on the ground by the starting bed and dug up the sandy soil with her fingers and scooped it into the bright new flower pot. Then she picked up the little pile of shoots she had prepared. With her strong fingers she pressed them into the sand and tamped around them with her knuckles. The man stood over her. "I'll tell you what to do," she said. "You remember so you can tell the lady."

"Yes, I'll try to remember."   65

"Well, look. These will take root in about a month. Then she must set them out, about a foot apart in good rich earth like this, see?" She lifted a handful of dark soil for him to look at. "They'll grow fast and tall. Now remember this: In July tell her to cut them down, about eight inches from the ground."

"Before they bloom?" he asked.

"Yes, before they bloom." Her face was tight with eagerness. "They'll grow right up again. About the last of September the buds will start."

She stopped and seemed perplexed. "It's the budding that takes the most care," she said hesitantly. "I don't know how to tell you." She looked deep into his eyes, searchingly. Her mouth opened a little, and she seemed to be listening. "I'll try to tell you," she said. "Did you ever hear of planting hands?"

70 "Can't say I have, ma'am."

"Well, I can only tell you what it feels like. It's when you're picking off the buds you don't want. Everything goes right down into your fingertips. You watch your fingers work. They do it themselves. You can feel how it is. They pick and pick the buds. They never make a mistake. They're with the plant. Do you see? Your fingers and the plant. You can feel that, right up your arm. They know. They never make a mistake. You can feel it. When you're like that you can't do anything wrong. Do you see that? Can you understand that?"

She was kneeling on the ground looking up at him. Her breast swelled passionately.

The man's eyes narrowed. He looked away self-consciously. "Maybe I know," he said. "Sometimes in the night in the wagon there—"

Elisa's voice grew husky. She broke in on him, "I've never lived as you do, but I know what you mean. When the night is dark—why, the stars are sharp-pointed, and there's quiet. Why, you rise up and up! Every pointed star gets driven into your body. It's like that. Hot and sharp and—lovely."

75 Kneeling there, her hand went out toward his legs in the greasy black trousers. Her hesitant fingers almost touched the cloth. Then her hand dropped to the ground. She crouched low like a fawning dog.

He said, "It's nice, just like you say. Only when you don't have no dinner, it ain't."

She stood up then, very straight, and her face was ashamed. She held the flower pot out to him and placed it gently in his arms. "Here. Put it in your wagon, on the seat, where you can watch it. Maybe I can find something for you to do."

At the back of the house she dug in the can pile and found two old and battered aluminum saucepans. She carried them back and gave them to him. "Here, maybe you can fix these."

His manner changed. He became professional. "Good as new I can fix them." At the back of his wagon he sat a little anvil, and out of an oily tool box dug a small machine hammer. Elisa came through the gate to watch him while he pounded out the dents in the kettles. His mouth grew sure and knowing. At a difficult part of the work he sucked his under-lip.

80 "You sleep right in the wagon?" Elisa asked.

"Right in the wagon, ma'am. Rain or shine I'm dry as a cow in there."

"It must be nice," she said. "It must be very nice. I wish women could do such things."

"It ain't the right kind of a life for a woman."

Her upper lip raised a little, showing her teeth. "How do you know? How can you tell?" she said.

85 "I don't know, ma'am," he protested. "Of course I don't know. Now here's your kettles, done. You don't have to buy no new ones."

"How much?"

"Oh, fifty cents'll do. I keep my prices down and my work good. That's why I have all them satisfied customers up and down the highway."

Elisa brought him a fifty-cent piece from the house and dropped it in his hand. "You might be surprised to have a rival some time. I can sharpen scissors, too. And I can beat the dents out of little pots. I could show you what a woman might do."

He put his hammer back in the oily box and shoved the little anvil out of sight. "It would be a lonely life for a woman, ma'am, and a scarey life, too, with animals creeping under the wagon all night." He climbed over the singletree,[3] steadying himself with a hand on the burro's white rump. He settled himself in the seat, picked up the lines. "Thank you kindly, ma'am," he said. "I'll do like you told me; I'll go back and catch the Salinas road."

"Mind," she called, "if you're long in getting there, keep the sand damp."   90

"Sand, ma'am? . . . Sand? Oh, sure. You mean around the chrysanthemums. Sure I will." He clucked his tongue. The beasts leaned luxuriously into their collars. The mongrel dog took his place between the back wheels. The wagon turned and crawled out the entrance road and back the way it had come, along the river.

Elisa stood in front of her wire fence watching the slow progress of the caravan. Her shoulders were straight, her head thrown back, her eyes half-closed, so that the scene came vaguely into them. Her lips moved silently, forming the words "Good-bye—good-bye." Then she whispered, "That's a bright direction. There's a glowing there." The sound of her whisper startled her. She shook herself free and looked about to see whether anyone had been listening. Only the dogs had heard. They lifted their heads toward her from their sleeping in the dust, and then stretched out their chins and settled asleep again. Elisa turned and ran hurriedly into the house.

In the kitchen she reached behind the stove and felt the water tank. It was full of hot water from the noonday cooking. In the bathroom she tore off her soiled clothes and flung them into the corner. And then she scrubbed herself with a little block of pumice, legs and thighs, loins and chest and arms, until her skin was scratched and red. When she had dried herself she stood in front of a mirror in her bedroom and looked at her body. She tightened her stomach and threw out her chest. She turned and looked over her shoulder at her back.

After a while she began to dress, slowly. She put on her newest underclothing and her nicest stockings and the dress which was the symbol of her prettiness. She worked carefully on her hair, penciled her eyebrows and rouged her lips.

Before she was finished she heard the little thunder of hoofs and the shouts of   65
Henry and his helper as they drove the red steers into the corral. She heard the gate bang shut and set herself for Henry's arrival.

His step sounded on the porch. He entered the house calling, "Elisa, where are you?"

"In my room, dressing. I'm not ready. There's hot water for your bath. Hurry up. It's getting late."

---

[3] *singletree:* A wooden bar that connects a wagon to the horses' harnesses.

When she heard him splashing in the tub, Elisa laid his dark suit on the bed, and shirt and socks and tie beside it. She stood his polished shoes on the floor beside the bed. Then she went to the porch and sat primly and stiffly down. She looked toward the river road where the willow-line was still yellow with frosted leaves so that under the high grey fog they seemed a thin band of sunshine. This was the only color in the grey afternoon. She sat unmoving for a long time. Her eyes blinked rarely.

Henry came banging out of the door, shoving his tie inside his vest as he came. Elisa stiffened and her face grew tight. Henry stopped short and looked at her. "Why—why, Elisa. You look so nice!"

100   "Nice? You think I look nice? What do you mean by 'nice'?"

Henry blundered on. "I don't know. I mean you look different, strong and happy."

"I am strong? Yes, strong. What do you mean 'strong'?"

He looked bewildered. "You're playing some kind of a game," he said helplessly. "It's a kind of a play. You look strong enough to break a calf over your knee, happy enough to eat it like a watermelon."

For a second she lost her rigidity. "Henry! Don't talk like that. You didn't know what you said." She grew complete again. "I'm strong," she boasted. "I never knew before how strong."

105   Henry looked down toward the tractor shed, and when he brought his eyes back to her, they were his own again. "I'll get out the car. You can put on your coat while I'm starting."

Elisa went into the house. She heard him drive to the gate and idle down his motor, and then she took a long time to put on her hat. She pulled it here and pressed it there. When Henry turned the motor off she slipped into her coat and went out.

The little roadster[4] bounced along on the dirt road by the river, raising the birds and driving the rabbits into the brush. Two cranes flapped heavily over the willow-line and dropped into the river-bed.

Far ahead on the road Elisa saw a dark speck. She knew.

She tried not to look as they passed it, but her eyes would not obey. She whispered to herself sadly, "He might have thrown them off the road. That wouldn't have been much trouble, not very much. But he kept the pot," she explained. "He had to keep the pot. That's why he couldn't get them off the road."

110   The roadster turned a bend and she saw the caravan ahead. She swung full around toward her husband so she could not see the little covered wagon and the mismatched team as the car passed them.

In a moment it was over. The thing was done. She did not look back.

She said loudly, to be heard above the motor, "It will be good, tonight, a good dinner."

"Now you're changed again," Henry complained. He took one hand from the wheel and patted her knee. "I ought to take you in to dinner oftener. It would be good for both of us. We get so heavy out on the ranch."

---

[4]*roadster:* An early roofless automobile, with a single seat for two or three passengers.

"Henry," she asked, "could we have wine at dinner?"

"Sure we could. Say! That will be fine."   115

She was silent for a while; then she said, "Henry, at those prize fights, do the men hurt each other very much?"

"Sometimes a little, not often. Why?"

"Well, I've read how they break noses, and blood runs down their chests. I've read how the fighting gloves get heavy and soggy with blood."

He looked around at her. "What's the matter, Elisa? I didn't know you read things like that." He brought the car to a stop, then turned to the right over the Salinas River bridge.

"Do any women ever go to the fights?" she asked.   120

"Oh, sure, some. What's the matter, Elisa? Do you want to go? I don't think you'd like it, but I'll take you if you really want to go."

She relaxed limply in the seat. "Oh, no. No. I don't want to go. I'm sure I don't." Her face was turned away from him. "It will be enough if we can have wine. It will be plenty." She turned up her coat collar so he could not see that she was crying weakly—like an old woman.

AMY TAN (1952–   )

Two Kinds (1989)

My mother believed you could be anything you wanted to be in America. You could open a restaurant. You could work for the government and get good retirement. You could buy a house with almost no money down. You could become rich. You could become instantly famous.

"Of course you can be prodigy, too," my mother told me when I was nine. "You can be best anything. What does Auntie Lindo know? Her daughter, she is only best tricky."

America was where all my mother's hopes lay. She had come here in 1949 after losing everything in China: her mother and father, her family home, her first husband, and two daughters, twin baby girls. But she never looked back with regret. There were so many ways for things to get better.

We didn't immediately pick the right kind of prodigy. At first my mother thought I could be a Chinese Shirley Temple. We'd watch Shirley's old movies on TV as though they were training films. My mother would poke my arm and say, "*Ni kan*"—You watch. And I would see Shirley tapping her feet, or singing a sailor song, or pursing her lips into a very round O while saying, "Oh my goodness."

"*Ni kan*," said my mother as Shirley's eyes flooded with tears. "You already know   5 how. Don't need talent for crying!"

Soon after my mother got this idea about Shirley Temple, she took me to a beauty training school in the Mission district and put me in the hands of a student who could barely hold the scissors without shaking. Instead of getting big fat curls, I emerged with an uneven mass of crinkly black fuzz. My mother dragged me off to the bathroom and tried to wet down my hair.

"You look like Negro Chinese," she lamented, as if I had done this on purpose.

The instructor of the beauty training school had to lop off these soggy clumps to make my hair even again. "Peter Pan is very popular these days," the instructor assured my mother. I now had hair the length of a boy's, with straight-across bangs that hung at a slant two inches above my eyebrows. I liked the haircut and it made me actually look forward to my future fame.

In fact, in the beginning, I was just as excited as my mother, maybe even more so. I pictured this prodigy part of me as many different images, trying each one on for size. I was a dainty ballerina girl standing by the curtains, waiting to hear the right music that would send me floating on my tiptoes. I was like the Christ child lifted out of the straw manger, crying with holy indignity. I was Cinderella stepping from her pumpkin carriage with sparkly cartoon music filling the air.

10   In all of my imaginings, I was filled with a sense that I would soon become *perfect*. My mother and father would adore me. I would be beyond reproach. I would never feel the need to sulk for anything.

But sometimes the prodigy in me became impatient. "If you don't hurry up and get me out of here, I'm disappearing for good," it warned. "And then you'll always be nothing."

Every night after dinner, my mother and I would sit at the Formica kitchen table. She would present new tests, taking her examples from stories of amazing children she had read in *Ripley's Believe It or Not*, or *Good Housekeeping*, *Reader's Digest*, and a dozen other magazines she kept in a pile in our bathroom. My mother got these magazines from people whose houses she cleaned. And since she cleaned many houses each week, we had a great assortment. She would look through them all, searching for stories about remarkable children.

The first night she brought out a story about a three-year-old boy who knew the capitals of all the states and even most of the European countries. A teacher was quoted as saying the little boy could also pronounce the names of the foreign cities correctly.

"What's the capital of Finland?" my mother asked me, looking at the magazine story.

15   All I knew was the capital of California, because Sacramento was the name of the street we lived on in Chinatown. "Nairobi!" I guessed, saying the most foreign word I could think of. She checked to see if that was possibly one way to pronounce "Helsinki" before showing me the answer.

The tests got harder—multiplying numbers in my head, finding the queen of hearts in a deck of cards, trying to stand on my head without using my hands, predicting the daily temperatures in Los Angeles, New York, and London.

One night I had to look at a page from the Bible for three minutes and then report everything I could remember. "Now Jehoshaphat had riches and honor in abundance and . . . that's all I remember, Ma," I said.

And after seeing my mother's disappointed face once again, something inside of me began to die. I hated the tests, the raised hopes and failed expectations. Before going to bed that night, I looked in the mirror above the bathroom sink and when I saw only my face staring back—and that it would always be this ordinary face—I began to cry. Such a sad, ugly girl! I made high-pitched noises like a crazed animal, trying to scratch out the face in the mirror.

And then I saw what seemed to be the prodigy side of me—because I had never seen that face before. I looked at my reflection, blinking so I could see more clearly. The girl staring back at me was angry, powerful. This girl and I were the same. I had new thoughts, willful thoughts, or rather thoughts filled with lots of won'ts. I won't let her change me, I promised myself. I won't be what I'm not.

So now on nights when my mother presented her tests, I performed listlessly, my   20
head propped on one arm. I pretended to be bored. And I was. I got so bored I started counting the bellows of the foghorns out on the bay while my mother drilled me in other areas. The sound was comforting and reminded me of the cow jumping over the moon. And the next day, I played a game with myself, seeing if my mother would give up on me before eight bellows. After a while I usually counted only one, maybe two bellows at most. At last she was beginning to give up hope.

Two or three months had gone by without any mention of my being a prodigy again. And then one day my mother was watching *The Ed Sullivan Show* on TV. The TV was old and the sound kept shorting out. Every time my mother got halfway up from the sofa to adjust the set, the sound would go back on and Ed would be talking. As soon as she sat down, Ed would go silent again. She got up, the TV broke into loud piano music. She sat down. Silence. Up and down, back and forth, quiet and loud. It was like a stiff embraceless dance between her and the TV set. Finally she stood by the set with her hand on the sound dial.

She seemed entranced by the music, a little frenzied piano piece with this mesmerizing quality, sort of quick passages and then teasing lilting ones before it returned to the quick playful parts.

"Ni kan," my mother said, calling me over with hurried hand gestures, "Look here."

I could see why my mother was fascinated by the music. It was being pounded out by a little Chinese girl, about nine years old, with a Peter Pan haircut. The girl had the sauciness of a Shirley Temple. She was proudly modest like a proper Chinese child. And she also did this fancy sweep of a curtsy, so that the fluffy skirt of her white dress cascaded slowly to the floor like the petals of a large carnation.

In spite of these warning signs, I wasn't worried. Our family had no piano and   25
we couldn't afford to buy one, let alone reams of sheet music and piano lessons. So I could be generous in my comments when my mother bad-mouthed the little girl on TV.

"Play note right, but doesn't sound good! No singing sound," complained my mother.

"What are you picking on her for?" I said carelessly. "She's pretty good. Maybe she's not the best, but she's trying hard." I knew almost immediately I would be sorry I said that.

"Just like you," she said. "Not the best. Because you not trying." She gave a little huff as she let go of the sound dial and sat down on the sofa.

The little Chinese girl sat down also to play an encore of "Anitra's Dance" by Grieg. I remember the song, because later on I had to learn how to play it.

30   Three days after watching *The Ed Sullivan Show*, my mother told me what my schedule would be for piano lessons and piano practice. She had talked to Mr. Chong, who lived on the first floor of our apartment building. Mr. Chong was a retired piano teacher and my mother had traded housecleaning services for weekly lessons and a piano for me to practice on every day, two hours a day, from four until six.

When my mother told me this, I felt as though I had been sent to hell. I whined and then kicked my foot a little when I couldn't stand it anymore.

"Why don't you like me the way I am? I'm *not* a genius! I can't play the piano. And even if I could, I wouldn't go on TV if you paid me a million dollars!" I cried.

My mother slapped me. "Who ask you be genius?" she shouted. "Only ask you be your best. For you sake. You think I want you be genius? Hnnh! What for! Who ask you!"

"So ungrateful," I heard her mutter in Chinese. "If she had as much talent as she has temper, she would be famous now."

35   Mr. Chong, whom I secretly nicknamed Old Chong, was very strange, always tapping his fingers to the silent music of an invisible orchestra. He looked ancient in my eyes. He had lost most of the hair on top of his head and he wore thick glasses and had eyes that always looked tired and sleepy. But he must have been younger than I thought, since he lived with his mother and was not yet married.

I met Old Lady Chong once and that was enough. She had this peculiar smell like a baby that had done something in its pants. And her fingers felt like a dead person's, like an old peach I once found in the back of the refrigerator; the skin just slid off the meat when I picked it up.

I soon found out why Old Chong had retired from teaching piano. He was deaf. "Like Beethoven!" he shouted to me. "We're both listening only in our head!" And he would start to conduct his frantic silent sonatas.

Our lessons went like this. He would open the book and point to different things, explaining their purpose: "Key! Treble! Bass! No sharps or flats! So this is C major! Listen now and play after me!"

And then he would play the C scale a few times, a simple chord, and then, as if inspired by an old, unreachable itch, he gradually added more notes and running trills and a pounding bass until the music was really something quite grand.

40   I would play after him, the simple scale, the simple chord, and then I just played some nonsense that sounded like a cat running up and down on top of garbage cans. Old Chong smiled and applauded and then said, "Very good! But now you must learn to keep time!"

So that's how I discovered that Old Chong's eyes were too slow to keep up with the wrong notes I was playing. He went through the motions in half-time. To help me keep rhythm, he stood behind me, pushing down on my right shoulder for every beat. He balanced pennies on top of my wrists so I would keep them still as I slowly played scales and arpeggios. He had me curve my hand around an apple and keep that shape when playing chords. He marched stiffly to show me how to make each finger dance up and down, staccato like an obedient little soldier.

He taught me all these things, and that was how I also learned I could be lazy and get away with mistakes, lots of mistakes. If I hit the wrong notes because I hadn't practiced enough, I never corrected myself. I just kept playing in rhythm. And Old Chong kept conducting his own private reverie.

So maybe I never really gave myself a fair chance. I did pick up the basics pretty quickly, and I might have become a good pianist at that young age. But I was so determined not to try, not to be anybody different that I learned to play only the most ear-splitting preludes, the most discordant hymns.

Over the next year, I practiced like this, dutifully in my own way. And then one day I heard my mother and her friend Lindo Jong both talking in a loud bragging tone of voice so others could hear. It was after church, and I was leaning against the brick wall wearing a dress with stiff white petticoats. Auntie Lindo's daughter, Waverly, who was about my age, was standing farther down the wall about five feet away. We had grown up together and shared all the closeness of two sisters squabbling over crayons and dolls. In other words, for the most part, we hated each other. I thought she was snotty. Waverly Jong had gained a certain amount of fame as "Chinatown's Littlest Chinese Chess Champion."

"She bring home too many trophy," lamented Auntie Lindo that Sunday. "All day she play chess. All day I have no time do nothing but dust off her winnings." She threw a scolding look at Waverly, who pretended not to see her.   45

"You lucky you don't have this problem," said Auntie Lindo with a sigh to my mother.

And my mother squared her shoulders and bragged: "Our problem worser than yours. If we ask Jing-mei wash dish, she hear nothing but music. It's like you can't stop this natural talent."

And right then, I was determined to put a stop to her foolish pride.

A few weeks later, Old Chong and my mother conspired to have me play in a talent show which would be held in the church hall. By then, my parents had saved up enough to buy me a secondhand piano, a black Wurlitzer spinet with a scarred bench. It was the showpiece of our living room.

For the talent show, I was to play a piece called "Pleading Child" from Schumann's   50
Scenes from Childhood. It was a simple, moody piece that sounded more difficult than it was. I was supposed to memorize the whole thing, playing the repeat parts twice to make the piece sound longer. But I dawdled over it, playing a few bars and then cheating, looking up to see what notes followed. I never really listened to what I was playing. I daydreamed about being somewhere else, about being someone else.

The part I liked to practice best was the fancy curtsy: right foot out, touch the rose on the carpet with a pointed foot, sweep to the side, left leg bends, look up and smile.

My parents invited all the couples from the Joy Luck Club[1] to witness my debut. Auntie Lindo and Uncle Tin were there. Waverly and her two older brothers had

---

[1]*Joy Luck Club:* A name denoting the mother's circle of friends, all of whom were Chinese immigrants to the United States.

also come. The first two rows were filled with children both younger and older than I was. The littlest ones got to go first. They recited simple nursery rhymes, squawked out tunes on miniature violins, twirled Hula Hoops, pranced in pink ballet tutus, and when they bowed or curtsied, the audience would sigh in unison, "Awww," and then clap enthusiastically.

When my turn came, I was very confident. I remember my childish excitement. It was as if I knew, without a doubt, that the prodigy side of me really did exist. I had no fear whatsoever, no nervousness. I remember thinking to myself, This is it! This is it! I looked out over the audience, at my mother's blank face, my father's yawn, Auntie Lindo's stiff-lipped smile, Waverly's sulky expression. I had on a white dress layered with sheets of lace, and a pink bow in my Peter Pan haircut. As I sat down I envisioned people jumping to their feet and Ed Sullivan rushing up to introduce me to everyone on TV.

And I started to play. It was so beautiful. I was so caught up in how lovely I looked that at first I didn't worry how I would sound. So it was a surprise to me when I hit the first wrong note and I realized something didn't sound quite right. And then I hit another and another followed that. A chill started at the top of my head and began to trickle down. Yet I couldn't stop playing, as though my hands were bewitched. I kept thinking my fingers would adjust themselves back, like a train switching to the right track. I played this strange jumble through two repeats, the sour notes staying with me all the way to the end.

55　　When I stood up, I discovered my legs were shaking. Maybe I had just been nervous and the audience, like Old Chong, had seen me go through the right motions and had not heard anything wrong at all. I swept my right foot out, went down on my knee, looked up and smiled. The room was quiet, except for Old Chong, who was beaming and shouting, "Bravo! Bravo! Well done!" But then I saw my mother's face, her stricken face. The audience clapped weakly, and as I walked back to my chair, with my whole face quivering as I tried not to cry, I heard a little boy whisper loudly to his mother, "That was awful," and the mother whispered back, "Well, she certainly tried."

And now I realized how many people were in the audience, the whole world it seemed. I was aware of eyes burning into my back. I felt the shame of my mother and father as they sat stiffly throughout the rest of the show.

We could have escaped during intermission. Pride and some strange sense of honor must have anchored my parents to their chairs. And so we watched it all: the eighteen-year-old boy with a fake mustache who did a magic show and juggled flaming hoops while riding a unicycle. The breasted girl with white makeup who sang from *Madama Butterfly* and got honorable mention. And the eleven-year-old boy who won first prize playing a tricky violin song that sounded like a busy bee.

After the show, the Hsus, the Jongs, and the St. Clairs from the Joy Luck Club came up to my mother and father.

"Lots of talented kids," Auntie Lindo said vaguely, smiling broadly.

60　　"That was somethin' else," said my father, and I wondered if he was referring to me in a humorous way, or whether he even remembered what I had done.

Waverly looked at me and shrugged her shoulders. "You aren't a genius like me," she said matter-of-factly. And if I hadn't felt so bad, I would have pulled her braids and punched her stomach.

But my mother's expression was what devastated me: a quiet, blank look that said she had lost everything. I felt the same way, and it seemed as if everybody were now coming up, like gawkers at the scene of an accident, to see what parts were actually missing. When we got on the bus to go home, my father was humming the busy-bee tune and my mother was silent. I kept thinking she wanted to wait until we got home before shouting at me. But when my father unlocked the door to our apartment, my mother walked in and then went to the back, into the bedroom. No accusations. No blame. And in a way, I felt disappointed. I had been waiting for her to start shouting, so I could shout back and cry and blame her for all my misery.

I assumed my talent-show fiasco meant I never had to play the piano again. But two days later, after school, my mother came out of the kitchen and saw me watching TV.

"Four clock," she reminded me as if it were any other day. I was stunned, as though she were asking me to go through the talent-show torture again. I wedged myself more tightly in front of the TV.

"Turn off TV," she called from the kitchen five minutes later. 65

I didn't budge. And then I decided. I didn't have to do what my mother said anymore. I wasn't her slave. This wasn't China. I had listened to her before and look what happened. She was the stupid one.

She came out from the kitchen and stood in the arched entryway of the living room. "Four clock," she said once again, louder.

"I'm not going to play anymore," I said nonchalantly. "Why should I? I'm not a genius."

She walked over and stood in front of the TV. I saw her chest was heaving up and down in an angry way.

"No!" I said, and I now felt stronger, as if my true self had finally emerged. So 70 this was what had been inside me all along.

"No! I won't!" I screamed.

She yanked me by the arm, pulled me off the floor, snapped off the TV. She was frighteningly strong, half pulling, half carrying me toward the piano as I kicked the throw rugs under my feet. She lifted me up and onto the hard bench. I was sobbing by now, looking at her bitterly. Her chest was heaving even more and her mouth was open, smiling crazily as if she were pleased I was crying.

"You want me to be someone that I'm not!" I sobbed. "I'll never be the kind of daughter you want me to be!"

"Only two kinds of daughters," she shouted in Chinese. "Those who are obedient and those who follow their own mind! Only one kind of daughter can live in this house. Obedient daughter!"

"Then I wish I wasn't your daughter. I wish you weren't my mother," I shouted. As 75 I said these things I got scared. It felt like worms and toads and slimy things crawling out of my chest, but it also felt good, as if this awful side of me had surfaced, at last.

"Too late change this," said my mother shrilly.

And I could sense her anger rising to its breaking point. I wanted to see it spill over. And that's when I remembered the babies she had lost in China, the ones we never talked about. "Then I wish I'd never been born!" I shouted. "I wish I were dead! Like them."

It was as if I had said the magic words. Alakazam!—and her face went blank, her mouth closed, her arms went slack, and she backed out of the room, stunned, as if she were blowing away like a small brown leaf, thin, brittle, lifeless.

It was not the only disappointment my mother felt in me. In the years that followed, I failed her so many times, each time asserting my own will, my right to fall short of expectations. I didn't get straight As. I didn't become class president. I didn't get into Stanford. I dropped out of college.

80   For unlike my mother, I did not believe I could be anything I wanted to be. I could only be me.

And for all those years, we never talked about the disaster at the recital or my terrible accusations afterward at the piano bench. All that remained unchecked, like a betrayal that was now unspeakable. So I never found a way to ask her why she had hoped for something so large that failure was inevitable.

And even worse, I never asked her what frightened me the most: Why had she given up hope?

For after our struggle at the piano, she never mentioned my playing again. The lessons stopped. The lid to the piano was closed, shutting out the dust, my misery, and her dreams.

So she surprised me. A few years ago, she offered to give me the piano, for my thirtieth birthday. I had not played in all those years. I saw the offer as a sign of forgiveness, a tremendous burden removed.

85   "Are you sure?" I asked shyly. "I mean, won't you and Dad miss it?"

"No, this your piano," she said firmly. "Always your piano. You only one can play."

"Well, I probably can't play anymore," I said. "It's been years."

"You pick up fast," said my mother, as if she knew this was certain. "You have natural talent. You could been genius if you want to."

"No I couldn't."

90   "You just not trying," said my mother. And she was neither angry nor sad. She said it as if to announce a fact that could never be disproved. "Take it," she said.

But I didn't at first. It was enough that she had offered it to me. And after that, every time I saw it in my parents' living room, standing in front of the bay windows, it made me feel proud, as if it were a shiny trophy I had won back.

Last week I sent a tuner over to my parents' apartment and had the piano reconditioned, for purely sentimental reasons. My mother had died a few months before and I had been getting things in order for my father, a little bit at a time. I put the jewelry in special silk pouches. The sweaters she had knitted in yellow, pink, bright orange—all the colors I hated—I put those in moth-proof boxes. I found some old Chinese silk dresses, the kind with little slits up the sides. I rubbed the old silk against my skin, then wrapped them in tissue and decided to take them home with me.

After I had the piano tuned, I opened the lid and touched the keys. It sounded even richer than I remembered. Really, it was a very good piano. Inside the bench were the same exercise notes with handwritten scales, the same secondhand music books with their covers held together with yellow tape.

I opened up the Schumann book to the dark little piece I had played at the recital. It was on the left-hand side of the page, "Pleading Child." It looked more difficult than I remembered. I played a few bars, surprised at how easily the notes came back to me.

And for the first time, or so it seemed, I noticed the piece on the right-hand side. It was called "Perfectly Contented." I tried to play this one as well. It had a lighter melody but the same flowing rhythm and turned out to be quite easy. "Pleading Child" was shorter but slower; "Perfectly Contented" was longer, but faster. And after I played them both a few times, I realized they were two halves of the same song.

95

3| POETRY

CHAPTER 22

UNDERSTANDING POETRY

The Granger Collection, NYC

MARIANNE MOORE (1887–1972)

Poetry (1921)

I, too, dislike it: there are things that are important beyond
    all this fiddle.
    Reading it, however, with a perfect contempt for it, one
    discovers in it after all, a place for the genuine.
        Hands that can grasp, eyes
        that can dilate, hair that can rise   5
            if it must, these things are important not because a

high-sounding interpretation can be put upon them but because
    they are useful. When they become so derivative as to become
    unintelligible, the same thing may be said for all of us, that we
        do not admire what   10
        we cannot understand: the bat
            holding on upside down or in quest of something to

eat, elephants pushing, a wild horse taking a roll, a tireless wolf under
    a tree, the immovable critic twitching his skin like a horse that feels
    a flea, the base-
    ball fan, the statistician—   15
        nor is it valid
        to discriminate against "business documents and

school-books";[1] all these phenomena are important. One must
    make a distinction
    however: when dragged into prominence by half poets, the result
    is not poetry,

---

[1] *"business documents and school-books"*: Moore quotes the *Diaries of Tolstoy* (New York, 1917): "Where the boundary between prose and poetry lies, I shall never be able to understand. . . . Poetry is verse; prose is not verse. Or else poetry is everything with the exception of business documents and school-books."

nor till the poets among us can be   20
    "literalists of
the imagination"[2]—above
    insolence and triviality and can present

for inspection, "imaginary gardens with real toads in them,"[3]
    shall we have
it. In the meantime, if you demand on the one hand,   25
the raw material of poetry in
    all its rawness and
    that which is on the other hand
        genuine, you are interested in poetry.

Pamela Spiro Wagner

PAMELA SPIRO WAGNER (1952   )

How to Read a Poem: Beginner's Manual*

First, forget everything you have learned,
that poetry is difficult,
that it cannot be appreciated by the likes of you,
with your high school equivalency diploma,
your steel-tipped boots,   5
or your white-collar misunderstandings.

Do not assume meanings hidden from you:
the best poems mean what they say and say it.

To read poetry requires only courage
enough to leap from the edge   10
and trust.

Treat a poem like dirt,
humus rich and heavy from the garden.
Later it will become the fat tomatoes
and golden squash piled high upon your kitchen table.   15

Poetry demands surrender,
language saying what is true,
doing holy things to the ordinary.

Read just one poem a day.
Someday a book of poems may open in your hands   20

---

[2] *"literalists of the imagination":* A reference (given by Moore) to W. B. Yeats's "William Blake and His Illustrations" (in *Ideas of Good and Evil*, 1903): "The limitation of his view was from the very intensity of his vision; he was a too literal realist of the imagination as others are of nature; and because he believed that the figures seen by the mind's eye, when exalted by inspiration, were 'external existences,' symbols of divine essences, he hated every grace of style that might obscure their lineaments."

[3] *"imaginary gardens with real toads in them":* Moore places these words in quotations, but the source is unknown.

*Publication date is unavailable.

like a daffodil offering its cup
to the sun.

When you can name five poets
without including Bob Dylan,
when you exceed your quota   25
and don't even notice,
close this manual.

Congratulations.
You can now read poetry.

Origins of Modern Poetry

The history of poetry begins where the history of all literature begins—with the **oral tradition**, information passed down from one generation to another by word of mouth. In a time before literacy and the printing press, the oral tradition was relied on as a way of preserving stories, histories, values, and beliefs. These stories were usually put into the form of rhyming poems, with repeated words and sounds used to make the poems easier to memorize and remember.

These extended narratives were eventually transcribed as **epics**—long poems depicting the actions of heroic figures who determine the fate of a nation or of an entire race. Early epics include Homer's *Iliad* and *Odyssey*, the *Epic of Gilgamesh*, the *Bhagavad Gita*, and Virgil's *Aeneid*. Early poetry can also be found in various religious texts, including ancient Hindu holy books like the Upanishads; sections of the Bible, including the Song of Solomon; and the Koran.

During the **Anglo-Saxon era** (late sixth to mid-eleventh centuries), poetry flourished as a literary form. Unfortunately, only about 30,000 lines of poetry survive from this period. Those poems that did survive are marked by violence, carnage, and heroic deeds as well as Pagan and Christian themes. The major texts of this time include *Beowulf*, *The Battle of Maldon*, and *The Dream of the Rood*, which is one of the earliest Christian poems. The theme of Christian morality in poetry continued into the Middle Ages with poems such as William Langland's *Piers Plowman*, which consists of three religious dream visions, and Chaucer's *Canterbury Tales*, a collection of narrative poems told by pilgrims as they travel to Canterbury, England. Using a slightly different approach to similar subject matter, Dante Alighieri wrote the Italian epic poem *The Divine Comedy*, which depicts an imaginary journey through hell, purgatory, and heaven.

Illustration of Trojan horse from Virgil's *Aenied*
Source: © Bettman/Corbis

In France, the **troubadours**, poets of the Provençal region, wrote complex lyric poems about courtly love.

The next major literary period, the **Renaissance** (late fourteenth to mid-sixteenth centuries), witnessed the rebirth of science, philosophy, and the classical arts. Perhaps the most important writer of this period was William Shakespeare. A prolific poet, Shakespeare also wrote plays in verse, continuing in the tradition of the ancient Greek tragedian Sophocles and the ancient Roman playwright Seneca. Other notable writers of the Renaissance included Sir Philip Sidney, Christopher Marlowe, and Edmund Spenser.

During the seventeenth century, several literary movements emerged that contributed to poetry's growing prevalence and influence. John Milton continued the tradition of Christian poetry with his epic *Paradise Lost*, which told the tale of Adam and Eve's exile from the Garden of Eden. The **metaphysical poets** (John Donne, Andrew Marvell, and George Herbert) used elaborate figures of speech and favored intellect over emotions in their writing. Their poems were characterized by reason, complex comparisons and allusions, and paradoxes, and they introduced the **meditative poem** (a poem that abstractly ponders a concept or idea) into the literary world.

In the early eighteenth century, British poets (such as Alexander Pope and Samuel Johnson) wrote poems, biographies, and literary criticism. Toward the end of the eighteenth century, the movement known as **Romanticism** began. Romantic poetry was marked by heightened emotion and sentiment; a strong sense

Image depicting the pilgrims from Geoffrey Chaucer's *The Canterbury Tales*

Title Roy 18 D II f.148 Lydgate and the Canterbury Pilgrims Leaving Canterbury from the 'Troy Book and the Siege of Thebes' by John Lydgate (c.1370-c.1451) 1412-22 (vellum) (detail of 8063) Creator English School, (15th century) Nationality English Location British Library, London, UK

Illuminated manuscript (fifteenth century) from Dante's *Divine Comedy* depicting Dante and Virgil in Hell

Alfredo Dagli Orti/The Art Archive/Fine Art/Corbis

of individualism; a fascination with nature, the Middle Ages, and mysticism; a rebellion against social and political norms; and a return to first-person lyric poems. The early British Romantics included Samuel Taylor Coleridge, William Wordsworth, and William Blake. This generation was followed by the later Romantics, including Percy Bysshe Shelley, John Keats, and George Gordon, Lord Byron. American Romantics (called **transcendentalists**) included Henry David Thoreau, Ralph Waldo Emerson, and Walt Whitman.

John Martin's painting *The Bard* (1817) illustrating the mystical view of nature characteristic of Romanticism

The Bard, c.1817 (oil on canvas), Martin, John (1789–1854) / Yale Center for British Art, Paul Mellon Collection, USA / Paul Mellon Collection/The Bridgeman Art Library

Illuminated manuscript from William Blake's "The Tyger"

Source: ©Fitzwilliam Museum, University of Cambridge, UK/Bridgeman Art Library

The nineteenth century was marked by yet another shift in poetic consciousness. This time, poets moved away from the contemplation of the self within nature that characterized Romanticism and returned to a more elevated sense of rhetoric and subject matter. Notable British poets included Matthew Arnold, Robert Browning, Elizabeth Barrett Browning, and Alfred, Lord Tennyson. American poets of the this period included Edgar Allan Poe, Henry Wadsworth Longfellow, Emily Dickinson, and Phillis Wheatley, a slave who became the first African American poet.

Undated engraving illustrating Edgar Allan Poe's "The Raven"

Source: ©Bettmann/CORBIS

The twentieth century had perhaps the largest number of literary movements to date, with each one reflecting its predecessors and influencing future generations of poets. In the early twentieth century, a literary movement that became known as **modernism** developed. As writers responded to the increasing complexity of a changing world, the overarching sentiment of modernism was that the "old ways" would no longer suffice in a world that had changed almost overnight as a result of the rise of industrialization and urbanization, as well as the devastation of World War I. Key modernist poets included W. H. Auden, William Butler Yeats, Ezra Pound, and T. S. Eliot, whose epic poem *The Waste Land* expressed the fragmentation of consciousness in the modern world.

After World War I, poets began to challenge the prevailing ideas of subject matter and form. Ezra Pound, along with Amy Lowell and other poets, founded

imagism, a poetic movement that emphasized free verse and the writer's response to a visual scene or an object. William Carlos Williams wrote poems that were often deceptively simple, while the poetry of Wallace Stevens was often opaque and difficult to grasp. Dylan Thomas and E. E. Cummings also experimented with form, with Cummings intentionally manipulating the accepted constructs of grammar, syntax, and punctuation.

In the 1920s, the United States experienced the **Harlem Renaissance.** This rebirth of arts and culture was centered in Harlem, an area in New York City where, by the mid-1920s, the African American population had reached 150,000. Harlem was teeming with creativity, especially in music (jazz and blues), literature, art, and drama. The poets who were part of the Harlem Renaissance—including Langston Hughes, Countee Cullen, James Weldon Johnson, and Jean Toomer—chose diverse subject matter and styles, but they were united in their celebration of African American culture.

In the early 1930s, a group of poets gathered at a college in Black Mountain, North Carolina, with the aim of teaching and writing about poetry in a new way. The **Black Mountain poets,** as they were called, stressed the process of writing poetry rather than the finished poem. Notable poets in this group included Robert Creeley, Denise Levertov, and Charles Olson. Meanwhile, in Latin America, poetry was growing in importance, with poets such as Pablo Neruda experimenting with subject matter, language, form, and imagery.

In the late 1940s, in the aftermath of World War II, a group of disillusioned American poets turned to eastern mysticism and newly available hallucinogenic drugs to achieve higher consciousness. They became known as the **Beat poets,** and their work was known

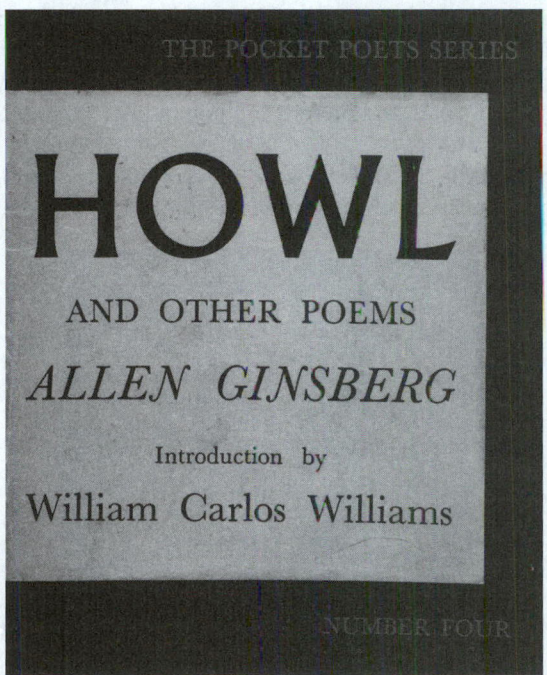

Cover of first edition of *Howl,* published by City Lights Books in 1956

for social and political criticism that challenged the established norms of the time. These poets included Allen Ginsberg, whose long poem *Howl* became an unofficial anthem of the revolutionary 1960s, and Lawrence Ferlinghetti.

Up until the late 1950s, subject matter in American poetry was largely impersonal, concentrating chiefly on symbols, ideas, and politics. This changed when a group of poets—including Robert Lowell, Anne Sexton, W. D. Snodgrass, and Sylvia Plath— began to write **confessional poems** about their own personal experiences, emotions, triumphs, and tragedies (including mental illness and attempted suicide). Although there was considerable backlash against these poets from writers who thought that such highly personal subjects were not suitable for poetry, contemporary poets such as Sharon Olds continue to write confessional poetry.

The early 1960s witnessed the rise of the **Black Arts Movement**, which had its roots in the ideas of the civil rights struggle, Malcolm X and the Nation of Islam, and the Black Power Movement. The Black Arts poets wrote political works that addressed the sociopolitical and cultural context of African American life. Notable authors in this group included Amiri Baraka, Gwendolyn Brooks, Jayne Cortez, and Etheridge Knight.

The next major literary movement in poetry had its beginnings in the mid to late 1980s with slam poetry. **Slam poetry**, with origins in the oral tradition, was influenced by the Beat poets, who stressed the live performance of poems. In a **slam**, poets compete either individually or in teams before an audience, which serves as the judge. (The structure of a traditional poetry slam was created by Marc Smith, a poet and construction worker, in 1986.) Slam poetry is concerned with current events and social and political themes, and often the winning poet is the one who best combines enthusiasm, presentation, and attitude with contemporary subject matter. A home base for slam poetry is the Nyuorican Poets Café in New York City, which has become a forum for poetry, music, video, and theater. Notable slam poets past and present include Miguel Piñero, Maggie Estep, Jeffrey McDaniel, and Bob Holman.

A spinoff of slam poetry is the **spoken word movement**, which, unlike slam poetry, is a rehearsed performance. Spoken word performances have captivated a broad audience due

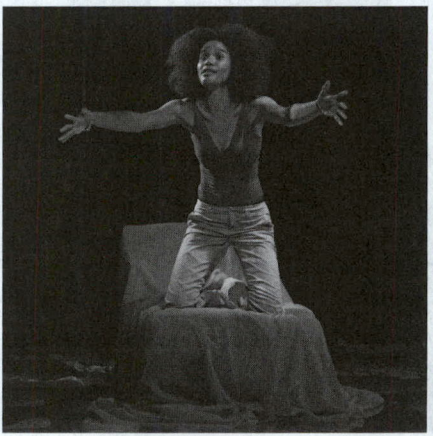

Staceyann Chin, acclaimed slam poet and the star of *Def Poetry Jam on Broadway*
Richard Termine/The New York Times/Redux

in part to television shows such as HBO's *Def Poetry Jam*, (2002–2007). **Hip-hop** and musical forms whose lyrics rely heavily on rhyme, alliteration, assonance, consonance, other poetic devices, also owe a debt to slam poetry and the spoken word movement.

Contemporary poetry *is* an extremely diverse genre whose practitioners have been influenced by the literary movements discussed above. Some contemporary poets embrace narrative poetry; others favor the lyric. Some write free verse; others experiment with traditional forms like the **sonnet** or the **villanelle**. Still others write **concrete poetry**, which uses well as varying type sizes and type fonts to form pictures on a page, or other forms of **visual poetry**.

With the advent of digital media, forms of poetry have emerged that use multimedia to create texts. Not just words, but also sound, images, and video combine to form poetic forms and new levels of aesthetic experience. For example, **hypertext** elements links to other texts (or visuals) that are available electronically. These links can at once on the screen, or they can be revealed gradually, creating multiple meaning. **Kinetic poetry** is a form in which letters (or words) drift around the gradually coalescing to form phrases, lines, and possibly entire poems. **Interactive** depends on readers contributing content that enhances and possibly determines meaning of the poem. **Code poetry** is programming code expressed as poetry. The famous code poem is "Black Perl," which is written in Perl programming language. other forms of digital poetry use digital technology to challenge and expand of what poetry is and should be.

Defining Poetry

history and across national and cultural boundaries, poetry has occupied an important place. In ancient China and Japan, for example, poetry was prized above all else. tells of a samurai warrior who, when defeated, asked for a pen and paper. Thinking wanted to write a will before being executed, his captor granted his wish. Instead of will, however, the warrior wrote a farewell poem that so moved his captor that he immediately released him.

the ancient Greeks and Romans, poetry was the medium of spiritual and philosophical expression. Today, throughout the world, poetry continues to delight and to inspire. many people in countless places, poetry is the language of the emotions, the medium expression they use when they speak from the heart.

But what exactly *is* poetry? Is it, as Pamela Spiro Wagner says, "language saying what true / doing holy things to the ordinary" (p. 651)? Or is a poem simply what Marianne Moore (p. 650) calls "all this fiddle"?

One way of defining poetry is to examine how it is different from other forms of literature, such as fiction or drama. The first and most important element of poetry that distinguishes it from other genres is its **form**. Unlike prose, which is written from margin to margin, poetry is made up of individual **lines**. A poetic line begins and ends where the poet chooses: it can start at the left margin or halfway across the page, and it can end at the right margin or after only a word or two. A poet chooses when to stop, or break, the line according to his or her sense of rhythm and meter.

Poets also use the **sound** of the words themselves, alone and in conjunction with the other words of the poem, to create a sense of rhythm and melody. **Alliteration** (the repetition of initial consonant sounds in consecutive or neighboring words), **assonance**

rap,
and

sounds), and **consonance** (the repetition of consonant sounds
e devices commonly used by poets to help create the music of a poem.
rhyme (either at the ends of lines or within the lines themselves), which
he pattern of sounds in a poem.

n, poets are more likely than writers of other kinds of liter
words or phrases that describe the senses. These vivid descrip e to rely on
er to connect with the poet's ideas in a tangible way. Poets also ma tails help
urative language, including metaphors and similes, to convey their id ive use
eir readers access these ideas.

Another way of defining poetry is to examine our assumptions about help
readers, different poets, different generations of readers and poets, and differe
often have different expectations about poetry. As a result, they have varying
tions about what poetry should be, and these assumptions raise questions. Mus
be written to delight or inspire, or can a poem have a political or social message
a poem's theme be conveyed subtly, embellished with imaginatively chosen soun
words, or can it be explicit and straightforward? Such questions, which have been d
by literary critics as well as by poets for many years, have no easy answers—and p
no answers at all. A **haiku**—a short poem, rich in imagery, adhering to a rigid
structure—is certainly poetry. To some Western readers, however, a haiku might
too plain or understated to be "poetic." Still, most of these readers would agree tha
following lines qualify as poetry.

WILLIAM SHAKESPEARE (1564–1616)

That time of year thou mayst in me behold (1609)

That time of year thou mayst in me behold
When yellow leaves, or none, or few, do hang
Upon those boughs which shake against the cold,
Bare ruined choirs, where late the sweet birds sang.
In me thou see'st the twilight of such day   5
As after sunset fadeth in the West,
Which by and by black night doth take away,
Death's second self that seals up all in rest.
In me thou see'st the glowing of such fire,
That on the ashes of his youth doth lie,   10
As the deathbed whereon it must expire,
Consumed with that which it was nourished by.
   This thou perceiv'st, which makes thy love more strong,
   To love that well which thou must leave ere long.

This poem includes many of the characteristics that Western readers commonly associate
with poetry. For instance, its lines have a regular pattern of rhyme and meter that identifies it as a **sonnet**. The poem also develops a complex network of related images and figures
of speech that compare the lost youth of the aging speaker to the sunset and to autumn.

Finally, the pair of rhyming lines at the end of the poem expresses a familiar poetic theme: the lovers' realization that they must eventually die makes their love stronger.

   Although most readers would classify Shakespeare's sonnet as a poem, they might be less certain about the following lines.

E. E. CUMMINGS (1894–1962)

l(a (1923)

```
l(a

le

af

fa

ll                 5

s)

one

l

iness
```

Unlike Shakespeare's poem, "l(a" does not seem to have any of the characteristics normally associated with poetry. It has no meter, rhyme, or imagery. It has no repeated sounds and no figures of speech. It cannot even be read aloud because its "lines" are fragments of words. In spite of its odd appearance, however, "l(a" does communicate a conventional poetic theme.

   When reconstructed, the words Cummings broke apart have the following appearance: "l (a leaf falls) one l iness." In a sense, this poem is a complex visual and verbal pun. If the parenthetical insertion "(a leaf falls)" is removed, the remaining letters spell "loneliness." Moreover, the form of the letter *l* in loneliness suggests the number *1*—which, in turn, suggests the loneliness and isolation of the individual, as reflected in nature (the single leaf). Like Shakespeare, Cummings uses an image of a leaf to express his ideas about life and human experience. At the same time, by breaking words into bits and pieces, Cummings suggests the flexibility of language and conveys the need to break out of customary ways of using words to define experience.

   As these two poems illustrate, defining what a poem is (and what it is not) can be difficult. Poems can rhyme or not rhyme. They can be divided into stanzas and have a distinct form, or they can flow freely and have no discernable form. These and other choices are what many poets find alluring about the process of writing poetry. As a form, poetry is compact and concise, and choosing the right words to convey ideas is a challenge. As a literary genre, it offers room for experimentation while at the same time remaining firmly grounded in a literary tradition that stretches back through time to antiquity.

▨ Recognizing Kinds of Poetry

Most poems are either **narrative** poems, which recount a story, or **lyric** poems, which communicate a speaker's mood, feelings, or state of mind.

Narrative Poetry

Although any brief poem that tells a story, such as Edwin Arlington Robinson's "Richard Cory" (p. 1011), may be considered a narrative poem, the two most familiar forms of narrative poetry are the *epic* and the *ballad*.

Epics are narrative poems that recount the accomplishments of heroic figures, typically including expansive settings, superhuman feats, and gods and supernatural beings. The language of epic poems tends to be formal, even elevated, and often quite elaborate. In ancient times, epics were handed down orally; more recently, poets have written literary epics, such as John Milton's *Paradise Lost* (1667) and Nobel Prize–winning poet Derek Walcott's *Omeros* (1990), that follow many of the same conventions.

The **ballad** is another type of narrative poetry with roots in an oral tradition. Originally intended to be sung, a ballad uses repeated words and phrases, including a refrain, to advance its story. Some—but not all—ballads use the **ballad stanza**. For an example of a traditional ballad in this book, see "Bonny Barbara Allan" (p. 954). Dudley Randall's "Ballad of Birmingham" (p. 708) is an example of a contemporary ballad.

Lyric Poetry

Like narrative poems, lyric poems take various forms.

An **elegy** is a poem in which a poet mourns the death of a specific person (or persons), as in Langston Hughes's "Birmingham Sunday (September 15, 1963) (p. 922), about four African American girls killed in the bombing of a church. Another example of this type of poem is A. E. Housman's "To an Athlete Dying Young" (p. 735).

An **ode** is a long lyric poem, formal and serious in style, tone, and subject matter. An ode typically has a fairly complex stanzaic pattern, such as the **terza rima** used by Percy Bysshe Shelley in "Ode to the West Wind" (p. 1013). Another ode in this text is John Keats's "Ode on a Grecian Urn" (p. 995).

An **aubade** is a poem about morning, usually celebrating the coming of dawn. For example, see Bill Coyle's "Aubade" (p. 970).

An **occasional poem** is written to celebrate a particular event or occasion. An example is Billy Collins's 2002 poem "The Names," read before a joint session of Congress to commemorate the first anniversary of the terrorist attacks on the World Trade Center.

A **meditation** is a lyric poem that focuses on a physical object, using this object as a vehicle for considering larger issues. Edmund Waller's seventeenth-century poem "Go, lovely rose" is a meditation.

A **pastoral**—for example, Christopher Marlowe's "The Passionate Shepherd to His Love" (p. 1003)—is a lyric poem that celebrates the simple, idyllic pleasures of country life.

A **dramatic monologue** is a poem whose speaker addresses one or more silent listeners, often revealing much more than he or she intends. Robert Browning's "My Last Duchess" (p. 679) and "Porphyria's Lover" (p. 696) and Alfred Lord Tennyson's "Ulysses" (p. 1017) are dramatic monologues.

As you read the poems in this text, you will encounter works with a wide variety of forms, styles, and themes. Some you will find appealing, amusing, uplifting, or moving; others may strike you as puzzling, intimidating, or depressing. But regardless of your critical reaction to the poems, one thing is certain: if you take the time to connect with the lines you are reading, you will come away from them thinking not just about the images and ideas they express but also about yourself and your world.

in part to television shows such as HBO's *Def Poetry Jam*, (2002–2007). **Hip-hop** and **rap**, musical forms whose lyrics rely heavily on rhyme, alliteration, assonance, consonance, and other poetic devices, also owe a debt to slam poetry and the spoken word movement.

Contemporary poetry is an extremely diverse genre whose practitioners have been influenced by many of the literary movements discussed above. Some contemporary poets embrace narrative poetry; others favor the lyric. Some write free verse; others experiment with traditional forms like the **sonnet** or the **villanelle**. Still others write **concrete poetry**, which uses words as well as varying type sizes and type fonts to form pictures on a page, or other forms of **visual poetry**.

With the advent of digital media, forms of poetry have emerged that use multimedia elements to create texts. Not just words, but also sound, images, and video combine to create new poetic forms and new levels of aesthetic experience. For example, **hypertext poetry** has links to other texts (or visuals) that are available electronically. These links can appear all at once on the screen, or they can be revealed gradually, creating multiple levels of meaning. **Kinetic poetry** is a form in which letters (or words) drift around the screen, gradually coalescing to form phrases, lines, and possibly entire poems. **Interactive poetry** depends on readers contributing content that enhances and possibly determines the meaning of the poem. **Code poetry** is programming code expressed as poetry. The most famous code poem is "Black Perl," which is written in Perl programming language. These and other forms of digital poetry use digital technology to challenge and expand the notion of what poetry is and should be.

Defining Poetry

Throughout history and across national and cultural boundaries, poetry has occupied an important place. In ancient China and Japan, for example, poetry was prized above all else. One story tells of a samurai warrior who, when defeated, asked for a pen and paper. Thinking that he wanted to write a will before being executed, his captor granted his wish. Instead of writing a will, however, the warrior wrote a farewell poem that so moved his captor that he immediately released him.

To the ancient Greeks and Romans, poetry was the medium of spiritual and philosophical expression. Today, throughout the world, poetry continues to delight and to inspire. For many people in countless places, poetry is the language of the emotions, the medium of expression they use when they speak from the heart.

But what exactly *is* poetry? Is it, as Pamela Spiro Wagner says, "language saying what is true / doing holy things to the ordinary" (p. 651)? Or is a poem simply what Marianne Moore (p. 650) calls "all this fiddle"?

One way of defining poetry is to examine how it is different from other forms of literature, such as fiction or drama. The first and most important element of poetry that distinguishes it from other genres is its **form**. Unlike prose, which is written from margin to margin, poetry is made up of individual **lines**. A poetic line begins and ends where the poet chooses: it can start at the left margin or halfway across the page, and it can end at the right margin or after only a word or two. A poet chooses when to stop, or break, the line according to his or her sense of rhythm and meter.

Poets also use the **sound** of the words themselves, alone and in conjunction with the other words of the poem, to create a sense of rhythm and melody. **Alliteration** (the repetition of initial consonant sounds in consecutive or neighboring words), **assonance** (the repetition of vowel sounds), and **consonance** (the repetition of consonant sounds within words) are three devices commonly used by poets to help create the music of a poem. Poets can also use **rhyme** (either at the ends of lines or within the lines themselves), which contributes to the pattern of sounds in a poem.

In addition, poets are more likely than writers of other kinds of literature to rely on **imagery**, words or phrases that describe the senses. These vivid descriptions or details help the reader to connect with the poet's ideas in a tangible way. Poets also make extensive use of **figurative language**, including metaphors and similes, to convey their ideas and to help their readers access these ideas.

Another way of defining poetry is to examine our assumptions about it. Different readers, different poets, different generations of readers and poets, and different cultures often have different expectations about poetry. As a result, they have varying assumptions about what poetry should be, and these assumptions raise questions. Must poetry be written to delight or inspire, or can a poem have a political or social message? Must a poem's theme be conveyed subtly, embellished with imaginatively chosen sounds and words, or can it be explicit and straightforward? Such questions, which have been debated by literary critics as well as by poets for many years, have no easy answers—and perhaps no answers at all. A **haiku**—a short poem, rich in imagery, adhering to a rigid formal structure—is certainly poetry. To some Western readers, however, a haiku might seem too plain or understated to be "poetic." Still, most of these readers would agree that the following lines qualify as poetry.

WILLIAM SHAKESPEARE (1564–1616)

That time of year thou mayst in me behold (1609)

That time of year thou mayst in me behold
When yellow leaves, or none, or few, do hang
Upon those boughs which shake against the cold,
Bare ruined choirs, where late the sweet birds sang.
In me thou see'st the twilight of such day   5
As after sunset fadeth in the West,
Which by and by black night doth take away,
Death's second self that seals up all in rest.
In me thou see'st the glowing of such fire,
That on the ashes of his youth doth lie,   10
As the deathbed whereon it must expire,
Consumed with that which it was nourished by.
    This thou perceiv'st, which makes thy love more strong,
    To love that well which thou must leave ere long.

This poem includes many of the characteristics that Western readers commonly associate with poetry. For instance, its lines have a regular pattern of rhyme and meter that identifies it as a **sonnet**. The poem also develops a complex network of related images and figures of speech that compare the lost youth of the aging speaker to the sunset and to autumn.

Finally, the pair of rhyming lines at the end of the poem expresses a familiar poetic theme: the lovers' realization that they must eventually die makes their love stronger.

Although most readers would classify Shakespeare's sonnet as a poem, they might be less certain about the following lines.

E. E. CUMMINGS (1894–1962)

l(a (1923)

```
l(a

le

af

fa

ll                5

s)

one

l

iness
```

Unlike Shakespeare's poem, "l(a" does not seem to have any of the characteristics normally associated with poetry. It has no meter, rhyme, or imagery. It has no repeated sounds and no figures of speech. It cannot even be read aloud because its "lines" are fragments of words. In spite of its odd appearance, however, "l(a" does communicate a conventional poetic theme.

When reconstructed, the words Cummings broke apart have the following appearance: "l (a leaf falls) one l iness." In a sense, this poem is a complex visual and verbal pun. If the parenthetical insertion "(a leaf falls)" is removed, the remaining letters spell "loneliness." Moreover, the form of the letter *l* in loneliness suggests the number *1*—which, in turn, suggests the loneliness and isolation of the individual, as reflected in nature (the single leaf). Like Shakespeare, Cummings uses an image of a leaf to express his ideas about life and human experience. At the same time, by breaking words into bits and pieces, Cummings suggests the flexibility of language and conveys the need to break out of customary ways of using words to define experience.

As these two poems illustrate, defining what a poem is (and what it is not) can be difficult. Poems can rhyme or not rhyme. They can be divided into stanzas and have a distinct form, or they can flow freely and have no discernable form. These and other choices are what many poets find alluring about the process of writing poetry. As a form, poetry is compact and concise, and choosing the right words to convey ideas is a challenge. As a literary genre, it offers room for experimentation while at the same time remaining firmly grounded in a literary tradition that stretches back through time to antiquity.

Recognizing Kinds of Poetry

Most poems are either **narrative** poems, which recount a story, or **lyric** poems, which communicate a speaker's mood, feelings, or state of mind.

Narrative Poetry

Although any brief poem that tells a story, such as Edwin Arlington Robinson's "Richard Cory" (p. 1011), may be considered a narrative poem, the two most familiar forms of narrative poetry are the *epic* and the *ballad*.

Epics are narrative poems that recount the accomplishments of heroic figures, typically including expansive settings, superhuman feats, and gods and supernatural beings. The language of epic poems tends to be formal, even elevated, and often quite elaborate. In ancient times, epics were handed down orally; more recently, poets have written literary epics, such as John Milton's *Paradise Lost* (1667) and Nobel Prize–winning poet Derek Walcott's *Omeros* (1990), that follow many of the same conventions.

The **ballad** is another type of narrative poetry with roots in an oral tradition. Originally intended to be sung, a ballad uses repeated words and phrases, including a refrain, to advance its story. Some—but not all—ballads use the **ballad stanza**. For an example of a traditional ballad in this book, see "Bonny Barbara Allan" (p. 954). Dudley Randall's "Ballad of Birmingham" (p. 708) is an example of a contemporary ballad.

Lyric Poetry

Like narrative poems, lyric poems take various forms.

An **elegy** is a poem in which a poet mourns the death of a specific person (or persons), as in Langston Hughes's "Birmingham Sunday (September 15, 1963) (p. 922), about four African American girls killed in the bombing of a church. Another example of this type of poem is A. E. Housman's "To an Athlete Dying Young" (p. 735).

An **ode** is a long lyric poem, formal and serious in style, tone, and subject matter. An ode typically has a fairly complex stanzaic pattern, such as the **terza rima** used by Percy Bysshe Shelley in "Ode to the West Wind" (p. 1013). Another ode in this text is John Keats's "Ode on a Grecian Urn" (p. 995).

An **aubade** is a poem about morning, usually celebrating the coming of dawn. For example, see Bill Coyle's "Aubade" (p. 970).

An **occasional poem** is written to celebrate a particular event or occasion. An example is Billy Collins's 2002 poem "The Names," read before a joint session of Congress to commemorate the first anniversary of the terrorist attacks on the World Trade Center.

A **meditation** is a lyric poem that focuses on a physical object, using this object as a vehicle for considering larger issues. Edmund Waller's seventeenth-century poem "Go, lovely rose" is a meditation.

A **pastoral**—for example, Christopher Marlowe's "The Passionate Shepherd to His Love" (p. 1003)—is a lyric poem that celebrates the simple, idyllic pleasures of country life.

A **dramatic monologue** is a poem whose speaker addresses one or more silent listeners, often revealing much more than he or she intends. Robert Browning's "My Last Duchess" (p. 679) and "Porphyria's Lover" (p. 696) and Alfred Lord Tennyson's "Ulysses" (p. 1017) are dramatic monologues.

As you read the poems in this text, you will encounter works with a wide variety of forms, styles, and themes. Some you will find appealing, amusing, uplifting, or moving; others may strike you as puzzling, intimidating, or depressing. But regardless of your critical reaction to the poems, one thing is certain: if you take the time to connect with the lines you are reading, you will come away from them thinking not just about the images and ideas they express but also about yourself and your world.

Waterlilies, 1914–17 (see detail 153601) (oil on canvas), Monet, Claude (1840–1926) / Musee Marmottan Monet, Paris, France / Bridgeman Images

POETRY SAMPLER: POETRY AND ART

Many poets have found visual art to be a source of inspiration for their poems. In fact, the ancient Greeks used the word *ekphrasis* to denote poetry that focused on paintings, artistic objects, and highly visual scenes. In the *Illiad*, for example, Homer vividly describes the shield of Achilles. The Ancient Romans also saw the connection between art and poetry. The Roman poet Horace made this point in *Ars Poetica* when he observed, "as in painting, so in poetry." Other more contemporary examples of *ekphrasis* occur in John Keats's "Ode on a Grecian Urn" (p. 995) and W. H. Auden's "Musée des Beaux Arts" (p. 876).

A poem about a work of art often expresses a poet's deep emotional response to the work. Sometimes the poet not only gives voice to his or her reactions but also gives voice to the work of art itself. This is true of Keats when he writes about a Grecian urn (which he probably saw in the British Museum in London). In this poem, Keats attempts to come to terms not only with the static images he sees on the urn but also with the effect the urn has on him. For Keats, the quiet majesty of the urn reflects a basic principle of art: "Heard melodies are sweet, but those unheard / Are sweeter; therefore, ye soft pipes, play on" (lines 11–12). For Keats, the message of the urn is simple and very direct: "'Beauty is truth, truth beauty,'—that is all / Ye know on earth, and all ye need to know" (lines 49–50).

A poem about a work of art can also try convey the work's essence to readers. Auden attempts to achieve this in his "Musée des Beaux Arts." By pointing out the inherent contradictions in the Brueghel painting his poem describes, Auden seeks to penetrate the painting and to interpret it for readers. As Icarus plunges to his death into the sea, "dogs go on with their doggy life" (line 12) and the ploughman goes on plowing, never having heard "the splash, the forsaken cry" (line 16). For Auden, Brueghel's painting expresses a truth that the old masters knew: that no matter how momentous an occurrence, life goes on. While someone is suffering—whether it be Christ or Icarus—"someone else is eating or opening a window or just walking dully along" (line 4).

Each of the poems in this sampler is accompanied by the art that inspired it. In "Sonnet in Primary Colors," Rita Dove explores her reactions to paintings by the artist Frida Kahlo. In "Van Gogh's Bed," Jane Flanders describes Vincent Van Gogh's painting of his bedroom in the southern French town of Arles. In "Cézanne's Ports," Alan Ginsberg uses a painting by a well-known impressionist as inspiration just as Robert Hayden does in "Monet's *Waterlilies*." In "The Starry Night," Anne Sexton attempts to convey the intensity of Van Gogh's powerful painting *The Starry Night*. Finally, in "Girl Powdering Her Neck," Cathy Song contemplates a portrait by Kitagawa Utamaro of a geisha preparing herself for her next assignation.

RITA DOVE (1952–   )

Sonnet in Primary Colors (1995)

This is for the woman with one black wing
perched over her eyes: lovely Frida,[1] erect
among parrots, in the stern petticoats of the peasant,
who painted herself a present—
wildflowers entwining the plaster corset   5
her spine resides in, that flaming pillar—
this priestess in the romance of mirrors.

Each night she lay down in pain and rose
to the celluloid butterflies of her Beloved Dead,
Lenin[2] and Marx[3] and Stalin[4] arrayed at the footstead.   10
And rose to her easel, the hundred dogs panting
like children along the graveled walks of the garden, Diego's[5]
love a skull in the circular window
of the thumbprint searing her immutable brow.

Self Portrait with Monkey and Parrot (1938) by
Frida Kahlo

[1] *Frida:* Frida Kahlo (1907–1954), Mexican painter, feminist and Communist.
[2] *Lenin:* Vladimir Ilyich Lenin (1870–1924), Communist revolutionary and first leader of the Soviet Union.
[3] *Marx:* Karl Marx (1818–1883), political theorist and author of *The Communist Manifesto.*
[4] *Stalin:* Joseph Stalin (1878–1953), second leader of the Soviet Union.
[5] *Diego's:* Diego Rivera (1886–1957), Communist Mexican artist, husband of Frida Kahlo.

JANE FLANDERS (1940–2001)

Van Gogh's Bed (1985)

is orange,
like Cinderella's coach, like
the sun when he looked it
straight in the eye.

is narrow, he sleeps alone, tossing
between two pillows, while it carried him
bumpily to the ball.

is clumsy,
but friendly. A peasant
built the frame; an old wife beat
the mattress till it rose like meringue.

is empty,
morning light pours in
like wine, melody, fragrance,
the memory of happiness.

The Bedroom (1888) by Vincent Van Gogh

DEA / G. DAGLI ORTI/Getty Images

ALLEN GINSBERG (1926–1997)

Cézanne's[1] Ports (1961)

In the foreground we see time and life
swept in a race
toward the left hand side of the picture
where shore meets shore.   5

But that meeting place
isn't represented;
it doesn't occur on the canvas.

For the other side of the bay
is Heaven and Eternity,
with a bleak white haze over its mountains.   10

And the immense water of L'Estaque[2] is a go-between
for minute rowboats.

L'Estaque (1883–1885) by Paul Cézanne
Source: ©The Metropolitan Museum of Art/Art Resource, NY

[1] *Cézanne's:* Paul Cézanne (1839–1906), French Postimpressionist painter.
[2] *L'Estaque:* Fishing village in France where Cézanne painted many views of the sea.

ROBERT HAYDEN (1913–1980)

Monet's *Waterlilies*[1] (1966)

Today as the news from Selma[2] and Saigon[3]
poisons the air like fallout,
I come again to see
the serene, great picture that I love.

Here space and time exist in light   5
the eye like the eye of faith believes.
The seen, the known
dissolve in iridescence, become
illusive flesh of light
that was not, was, forever is.   10

O light beheld as through refracting tears.
Here is the aura of that world
each of us has lost.
Here is the shadow of its joy.

Waterlilies (1914–1917) by Claude Monet
Waterlilies, 1914–17 (see detail 158601) (oil on canvas), Monet, Claude (1840–1926) / Musee Marmottan Monet, Paris, France / Bridgeman Images

[1] *"Waterlilies"*: A series of paintings by Claude Monet (1840–1926), a French impressionist painter.
[2] *Selma:* Selma, Alabama. The site of civil rights marches in the mid 1960s, one of which was ended by police violence.
[3] *Saigon:* Capital of South Vietnam from 1954 to 1975; now know as Ho Chi Minh City.

ANNE SEXTON (1928–1974)

The Starry Night[1] (1962)

That does not keep me from having a terrible need of—shall I say the word—
religion. Then I go out at night to paint the stars.
                                   —Vincent Van Gogh in a letter to his brother

The town does not exist
except where one black-haired tree slips
up like a drowned woman into the hot sky.
The town is silent. The night boils with eleven stars.
Oh starry starry night! This is how   5
I want to die.

It moves. They are all alive.
Even the moon bulges in its orange irons
to push children, like a god, from its eye.
The old unseen serpent swallows up the stars.   10
Oh starry starry night! This is how
I want to die:

into that rushing beast of the night,
sucked up by that great dragon, to split
from my life with no flag,   15
no belly,
no cry.

The Starry Night (1889) by Vincent Van Gogh

---

[1]*The Starry Night:* Famous painting (1889) by Dutch Postimpressionist painter Vincent Van Gogh (1853–1890).

CATHY SONG (1955–   )

Girl Powdering Her Neck (1983)

from a ukiyo-e[1] print by Utamaro[2]

The light is the inside
sheen of an oyster shell,
sponged with talc and vapor,
moisture from a bath.

A pair of slippers   5
are placed outside
the rice-paper doors.
She kneels at a low table
in the room,
her legs folded beneath her   10
as she sits on a buckwheat pillow.

Her hair is black
with hints of red,
the color of seaweed
spread over rocks.   15

Morning begins the ritual
wheel of the body,
the application of translucent skins.
She practices pleasure:
the pressure of three fingertips   20
applying powder.
Fingerprints of pollen
some other hand will trace.

The peach-dyed kimono
patterned with maple leaves   25
drifting across the silk,
falls from right to left
in a diagonal, revealing
the nape of her neck
and the curve of a shoulder   30
like the slope of a hill
set deep in snow in a country
of huge white solemn birds.
Her face appears in the mirror,

a reflection in a winter pond,   35
rising to meet itself.

She dips a corner of her sleeve
like a brush into water
to wipe the mirror;
she is about to paint herself.   40
The eyes narrow
in a moment of self-scrutiny.
The mouth parts
as if desiring to disturb
the placid plum face;   45
break the symmetry of silence.
But the berry-stained lips,
stenciled into the mask of beauty,
do not speak.

Two chrysanthemums   50
touch in the middle of the lake
and drift apart.

Girl Powdering Her Neck (1790) by
Kitagawa Utamaro
Source: Erich Lessing/Art Resource, NY

---

e woodblock print.

1806), Japanese printmaker.

Reading and Reacting

1. On which features of the work of art does the poet focus? Which aspects does the poet ignore?
2. What purpose is the poet trying to achieve? For example, is the poet expressing emotion, offering an analysis, or attempting to shed light on a particular characteristic or detail of the work?
3. What insight into the work of art do you gain from reading the poem? Do you think the poet is missing anything?
4. What questions about the work of art does the poem raise?
5. Do you disagree with the speaker's interpretation of the work of art? If so, with what do you disagree?

6. **CRITICAL PERSPECTIVE** Writing on the subject of ekphrastic poetry—poetry that takes as its subject a work of visual art—poet and critic Alfred Corn notes both the dangers and the potential rewards of this poetic strategy:

   > A disadvantage . . . of using very great works of visual art as a subject for ekphrasis is that the comparison between the original and the poem about it may prove too unfavorable. Readers may wonder why they should bother reading a moderately effective poem when they could instead look at the great painting it was based on. If the poem doesn't contain something more than was already available to the audience, it will strike the reader as superfluous, the secondary product of someone too dependent on the earlier, greater work. . . . Once the ambition of producing a complete and accurate description is put aside, a poem can provide new aspects for a work of visual art. It can provide a special angle of approach not usually brought to bear on the original.

   Do the ekphrastic poems in this chapter do what Corn says poems of this kind should do—that is, "provide new aspects for a work of visual art"?

WRITING SUGGESTIONS: Poetry and Art

1. Write a **response** (see Chapter 3) expressing your reactions to either "Monet's *Waterlilies*" or "Van Gogh's Bed."
2. Write an **explication** (see Chapter 3) of "The Starry Night" or "Cezanne's Ports."
3. Write a **comparison-contrast essay** (see Chapter 3) examining the ways the two women are presented in the poems "Sonnet in Primary Colors" and "Girl Powdering Her Neck."
4. Write a **character analysis** (see Chapter 3) of Frida Kahlo as she is depicted in "Sonnet in Primary Colors." Be sure to explore Kahlo's background as well as the hardships she faced. (To prepare for this assignment, do some research on the Web about Kahlo's life and art. Make sure you document the material that you borrow from your sources.)
5. Write an essay about the **cultural context** (see Chapter 3) of "Girl Powdering Her Neck."
6. Write a **comparison-contrast essay** (see Chapter 3) comparing any one of the poems in this chapter to the work of art that inspired it. What details about the work of art does the poet emphasize? Which does the poet downplay or ignore?

CATHY SONG (1955–   )

Girl Powdering Her Neck (1983)

from a ukiyo-e[1] print by Utamaro[2]

The light is the inside
sheen of an oyster shell,
sponged with talc and vapor,
moisture from a bath.

A pair of slippers   5
are placed outside
the rice-paper doors.
She kneels at a low table
in the room,
her legs folded beneath her   10
as she sits on a buckwheat pillow.

Her hair is black
with hints of red,
the color of seaweed
spread over rocks.   15

Morning begins the ritual
wheel of the body,
the application of translucent skins.
She practices pleasure:
the pressure of three fingertips   20
applying powder.
Fingerprints of pollen
some other hand will trace.

The peach-dyed kimono
patterned with maple leaves   25
drifting across the silk,
falls from right to left
in a diagonal, revealing
the nape of her neck
and the curve of a shoulder   30
like the slope of a hill
set deep in snow in a country
of huge white solemn birds.
Her face appears in the mirror,

a reflection in a winter pond,   35
rising to meet itself.

She dips a corner of her sleeve
like a brush into water
to wipe the mirror;
she is about to paint herself.   40
The eyes narrow
in a moment of self-scrutiny.
The mouth parts
as if desiring to disturb
the placid plum face;   45
break the symmetry of silence.
But the berry-stained lips,
stenciled into the mask of beauty,
do not speak.

Two chrysanthemums   50
touch in the middle of the lake
and drift apart.

Girl Powdering Her Neck (1790) by Kitagawa Utamaro
Source: Erich Lessing/Art Resource, NY

---

[1]ukiyo-e: A type of Japanese woodblock print.

[2]Utamaro: Kitagawa Utamaro (1754–1806), Japanese printmaker.

Reading and Reacting

1. On which features of the work of art does the poet focus? Which aspects does the poet ignore?

2. What purpose is the poet trying to achieve? For example, is the poet expressing emotion, offering an analysis, or attempting to shed light on a particular characteristic or detail of the work?

3. What insight into the work of art do you gain from reading the poem? Do you think the poet is missing anything?

4. What questions about the work of art does the poem raise?

5. Do you disagree with the speaker's interpretation of the work of art? If so, with what do you disagree?

6. **CRITICAL PERSPECTIVE** Writing on the subject of ekphrastic poetry—poetry that takes as its subject a work of visual art—poet and critic Alfred Corn notes both the dangers and the potential rewards of this poetic strategy:

   > A disadvantage . . . of using very great works of visual art as a subject for ekphrasis is that the comparison between the original and the poem about it may prove too unfavorable. Readers may wonder why they should bother reading a moderately effective poem when they could instead look at the great painting it was based on. If the poem doesn't contain something more than was already available to the audience, it will strike the reader as superfluous, the second-ary product of someone too dependent on the earlier, greater work. . . . Once the ambition of producing a complete and accurate description is put aside, a poem can provide new aspects for a work of visual art. It can provide a special angle of approach not usually brought to bear on the original.

Do the ekphrastic poems in this chapter do what Corn says poems of this kind should do— that is, "provide new aspects for a work of visual art"?

WRITING SUGGESTIONS: Poetry and Art

1. Write a **response** (see Chapter 3) expressing your reactions to either "Monet's *Waterlilies*" or "Van Gogh's Bed."

2. Write an **explication** (see Chapter 3) of "The Starry Night" or "Cezanne's Ports."

3. Write a **comparison-contrast essay** (see Chapter 3) examining the ways the two women are presented in the poems "Sonnet in Primary Colors" and "Girl Powdering Her Neck."

4. Write a **character analysis** (see Chapter 3) of Frida Kahlo as she is depicted in "Sonnet in Primary Colors." Be sure to explore Kahlo's background as well as the hardships she faced. (To prepare for this assignment, do some research on the Web about Kahlo's life and art. Make sure you document the material that you borrow from your sources.)

5. Write an essay about the **cultural context** (see Chapter 3) of "Girl Powdering Her Neck."

6. Write a **comparison-contrast essay** (see Chapter 3) comparing any one of the poems in this chapter to the work of art that inspired it. What details about the work of art does the poet emphasize? Which does the poet downplay or ignore?

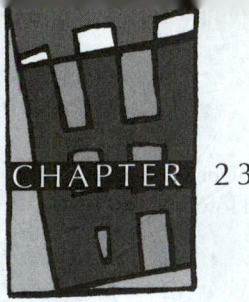

CHAPTER 23

READING AND WRITING ABOUT POETRY

 Reading Poetry

Sometimes readers approach poetry purely for pleasure. At other times, reading a poem is also the first step toward writing about it. The following guidelines, designed to help you explore poetic works, focus on issues explored in chapters to come:

- *Paraphrase the poem.* What does your paraphrase reveal about the poem's subject and central concerns? What is lost or gained in your paraphrase of the poem?

- *Consider the poem's* **voice.** Who is the poem's speaker? How would you characterize the poem's tone? Is the poem ironic? (See Chapter 24.)

- *Study the poem's* **diction.** Look up the meanings of any unfamiliar words. How does word choice affect your reaction to the poem? What do the connotations of words reveal about the poem? What level of diction is used? Is word order unusual or unexpected? How does the arrangement of words contribute to your understanding of the poem? (See Chapter 25.)

- *Examine the poem's* **imagery.** What kind of imagery predominates? What specific images are used? Is there a pattern of imagery? How does imagery enrich the poem? (See Chapter 26.)

- *Identify the poem's* **figures of speech.** Does the poet use metaphor? simile? personification? hyperbole? understatement? metonymy or synecdoche? apostrophe? How do figures of speech affect your reading of the poem? (See Chapter 27.)

- *Listen to the* **sound** *of the poem.* Are rhythm and meter regular or irregular? How do rhythm and meter reinforce the poem's central concerns? Does the poem use alliteration? assonance? rhyme? How do these elements enhance the poem? (See Chapter 28.)

- *Look at the poem's* **form.** Is the poem written in closed or open form? Is the poem constructed as a sonnet? a sestina? a villanelle? an epigram? a haiku? a prose poem? a concrete poem? How does the poem's form help to communicate (or reinforce) its ideas? (See Chapter 29.)

- *Consider the poem's use of* **symbol, allegory, allusion,** *or* **myth.** Does the poem make use of symbols? allusions? How do symbols or allusions support its theme? Is the poem an allegory? Does the poem retell or interpret a myth? (See Chapter 30.)

- *Consider the poem's **theme**.* Does the poem treat a conventional subject? What central theme does the poem explore? What other themes are examined? How are the themes expressed? (See Chapter 31.)

Active Reading

When you approach a poem that you plan to write about, you engage in the same **active reading** strategies you use when you read a short story or a play. When you finish recording your reactions to the poem, you focus on a topic, list possible ideas to explore, decide on a thesis, prepare an outline, and then go on to draft and revise your essay.

Catherine Whittaker, a student in an Introduction to Literature course, was asked to write a three- to five-page essay comparing any two of the poems that appear in "Poems about Parents" in Chapter 31 (pp. 884–892). Her instructor told the class that the essay should reflect students' own ideas about the poems, not the opinions of literary critics. As Catherine planned and wrote her essay, she was guided by the process described in Chapter 2, "Reading and Writing about Literature."

Previewing

Catherine began her work by previewing the poems, eliminating those she considered obscure or difficult and those whose portrait of the speaker's parent did not seem sympathetic. This process helped Catherine to narrow down her choices. As she looked through "Those Winter Sundays," two phrases in the opening lines ("Sundays too"; "blueblack cold") caught her eye; she also noticed the words "The squat pen rests; snug as a gun" in line 2 of "Digging." In each case, the words made Catherine want to examine the poem further. She noticed too that both poems focused on fathers and that both were divided into stanzas of varying lengths. Keeping these general parallels in mind, Catherine began a close reading of each poem.

Highlighting and Annotating

As Catherine read and reread "Those Winter Sundays" and "Digging," she recorded her comments and questions. The poems, with her highlighting and annotations, apappear below and on the following pages.

ROBERT HAYDEN (1913–1980)

<u>Those</u> Winter Sundays (1962)

Sundays(too)my father got up early

and put his clothes on <u>in the blueblack cold</u>,

then with cracked hands <u>that ached</u>

<u>from labor in the weekday</u> weather made

banked fires blaze. No one ever thanked him.   5

I'd wake and hear the cold splintering, breaking.

Annotations:

Were there many Sundays like these?

Like all other days of the week?

Why did he get up before dawn?

What kind of job did the father have?

Was there a large family?

When the rooms were warm, he'd call,

and slowly I would rise and dress,

fearing the chronic angers of that house,

were there problems in the family?

Speaking indifferently to him,   10

who had driven out the cold

and polished my good shoes as well.

Was there a mother around?

What did I know, what did I know

of love's austere and lonely offices?

Offices=duties or functions assigned to someone

Austere=without adornment or ornamentation, simple; harsh

SEAMUS HEANEY (1939–2013)

Digging (1966)

Between my finger and my thumb

The squat pen rests; snug as a gun.   *gun=snug?*

Why a "squat" pen?

Under my window, a clean rasping sound

When the spade sinks into gravelly ground:

My father, digging. I look down   5

Till his straining rump among the flowerbeds

Bends low, comes up twenty years away   *Is he thinking about the past?*

Stooping in rhythm through potato drills

Where he was digging.

The coarse boot nestled on the lug, the shaft   10

Against the inside knee was levered firmly.

Like the poet's pen?

He rooted out tall tops, buried the bright edge deep

To scatter new potatoes that we picked   *Was this a family task?*

Loving their cool hardness in our hands.

By God, the old man could handle a spade.   15

Just like his old man.

Two generations could "handle a spade." Can the poet dig?

My grandfather cut more turf in a day

Than any other man on Toner's bog.

Once I carried him milk in a bottle

Corked sloppily with paper. He straightened up   20

To drink it, then fell to right away ——→ *The grandfather was a hard worker*

Nicking and slicing neatly, heaving sods —→ *Digging was an art*

Over his shoulder, going down and down

For the good turf. Digging.

The cold smell of potato mould, the squelch and slap   25

Of soggy peat, the curt cuts of an edge

Through living roots awaken in my head.

→ *What does it make him remember?*

But I've no spade to follow men like them.

What are "men like them" like?

Same as first 2 lines { Between my finger and my thumb

The squat pen rests. → *Why is this repeated?*   30

I'll dig with it.

↳ *Dig for what?*

Catherine found the language of both poems appealing, and she believed her highlighting and annotating had given her some valuable insights. For example, she noticed some similarities between the two poems: both focus on the past, both portray fathers as hard workers, and neither mentions a mother.

 ## Writing about Poetry

Planning an Essay

Catherine still had to find a specific topic for her essay, and her preliminary work suggested some interesting possibilities. She was especially intrigued by the way both poems depicted fathers as actively engaged in physical tasks.

Choosing a Topic

One idea Catherine thought she might want to write about was the significance of the sons' attitudes toward their fathers: although both see their fathers as hard workers, the son in

"Those Winter Sundays" seems to have mixed feelings about his father's devotion to his family, whereas the son in "Digging" is more appreciative. Catherine explored this idea in two journal entries.

"Those Winter Sundays"

Why did the father get up early every morning? Maybe he had a large family and little money. There is no mention of a mother. The poems suggest the utter cold and "chronic angers" of the house. The father not only made fires to warm the house but also polished his child's (or children's) shoes—maybe for church. And yet, the child seemed not to care about or appreciate the father's efforts. Was he too young to say thank you, or were there other problems in the house for which the child blamed the father?

"Digging"

In the poem, the poet seems to be wondering what to write about when the sounds of digging capture his attention. He remembers the steady rhythm of his father's digging of the potatoes and how they (probably the poet and his brothers and sisters) picked out the cool potatoes. He seems to appreciate his father's and grandfather's hard work and skill. He does, however, feel regret that he is not like these dedicated men. Even though he cannot use a shovel, he hopes to use his pen to make his own contributions as a writer.

When Catherine reread her journal entries, she saw that her essay could focus on the two fathers' similar roles and the sons' contrasting attitudes toward their fathers. (In fact, she had so many ideas that she did not feel she had to brainstorm to generate more material.) Before she could write a draft of her essay, however, she needed to identify specific similarities and differences between the two poems.

Seeing Connections

Catherine reread the highlighted and annotated poems and then compiled the following lists of similarities and differences.

Differences

"Those Winter Sundays"	"Digging"
• memories of family problems	• only happy memories
• the child is ambivalent toward his father	• the child admires his father
• atmosphere of tension	• atmosphere of happiness and family unity

Similarities

- the fathers are hard workers
- the fathers appear to love their children
- the events seem to have happened years ago
- children, now grown, appreciate their fathers' dedication
- children, now grown, are inspired by their fathers' determination

At this point, as connections between the two poems came into focus, Catherine was able to decide on a thesis and on a possible order for her ideas.

Deciding on a Thesis

Catherine expressed her essay's main idea in the following thesis statement.

> Although their family backgrounds are different, both poets now realize the determination and dedication of their fathers and are consequently impassioned in their writing.

Preparing a Scratch Outline

Catherine reviewed her notes to help her identify the specific ideas she wanted to develop in her first draft. Then, she arranged those ideas in a logical order in a scratch outline.

"Those Winter Sundays"

Poet reflects on childhood
- father's hard work
- his own misunderstanding and lack of appreciation for everything his father did

Family's unhappiness
- tension in the house
- no mother mentioned in the poem

Poet's realization of father's love and dedication

"Digging"

Poet reminisces about childhood
- father's skill and hard work
- grandfather's cutting of turf
- children's participation and acceptance

Family's happiness

Poet's desire to continue the family tradition

Drafting an Essay

With a thesis statement and a scratch outline to guide her, Catherine wrote the following first draft of her essay. Her instructor's comments appear in the margins and at the end of the essay.

first draft

A Comparison of Two Poems about Fathers

Robert Hayden's "Those Winter Sundays" and "Digging" by Seamus Heaney are

careful!
you're
confus-
ing poet <
and
speaker

poems that were inspired by fathersand composed as tributes to fathers. Although

their family backgrounds are different, both poets now realize the determination and

dedication of their fathers and are consequently impassioned in their writing.

In "Those Winter Sundays," Hayden reflects back on his childhood. He

remembers the many Sundays when his father got up early to start the fires to make

the house warm for his children's awakening. The poet pictures his father's hands

what
do you
mean?

made rough by his weekday work. These same hands not only made the fires on

Sunday but also polished his son's good shoes, in preparation, no doubt, for church.

Hayden also quite clearly remembers that his father was never thanked for his

work. The reader imagines that the father had many children and may have been

poor. There were inner tensions in the house and, quite noticeably, there is no

mention of a mother.

Looking back, the poet now realizes the love and dedication with which his

father took care of the family. As a child, he never thanked his father, but now, as

an adult, the poet seems to appreciate the simple kindness of his father.

Quotations
from the
poem would
strengthen
your
discussion
in ¶s 3
and 4.

In a similar sense, Seamus Heaney's "Digging" is a tribute to his father and

grandfather. He also reminisces about his father and clearly remembers the skill

with which his father dug potatoes. The grandfather too is remembered, as is his

technique for "heaving sods." There is an atmosphere of happiness in this poem.

Add line
number
in paren-
theses.

With the children helping the father harvest the potatoes, a sense of family

togetherness is created. The reader feels that this family is a hardworking but

nevertheless happy one.

As the poet reminisces about his childhood, he realizes that, unlike his

father and grandfather, he will never be a master of digging or a person who uses physical strength to earn a living. He wishes to be like his father before him, desiring to accomplish and contribute. However, for the poet, any "digging" to be done will be by his pen, in the form of literature.

To conclude, the fathers in these poets' pasts inspire them to write. However, an appreciation for their fathers' dedication is achieved only after the children mature into adults. It is then that the fathers' impact on their children's lives is realized for its true importance.

Good start! When you revise, focus on the following:

- Edit use of "poet" and "speaker" carefully. You can't assume that these poems reflect the poets' own lives or attitudes toward their fathers.

- Add more specific references to the poems, particularly quotations. (Don't forget to give line numbers.)

- Consider adding brief references to other poems about parents. (check the textbook)

- Consider rearranging your material into a point-by-point comparison, which will make the specific similarities and differences clearer

Let's discuss this draft in a conference.

First Draft: Commentary

After submitting her first draft, Catherine met with her instructor. Together, they reviewed not only her first draft but also her annotations, journal entries, lists of similarities and differences, and scratch outline. During the conference, her instructor explained his written comments and, building on Catherine's own ideas, helped her develop a plan for revision.

Catherine's instructor agreed that the poems' similarities were worth exploring in detail. He thought, however, that her references to the poems' language and ideas needed to be much more specific and that her essay's subject-by-subject structure—discussing "Those Winter Sundays" first and then moving on to consider "Digging"—made the specific similarities between the two poems difficult to see. He also thought that her thesis statement should be more concrete and specific.

Because the class had studied other poems in which speakers try to resolve their ambivalent feelings toward their parents, Catherine's instructor also suggested that she consider referring to one or two of these poems to provide a wider context for her ideas. Finally, he explained the difference between the perspective of the poet and that of the **speaker**, a persona the poet creates.

As she reexamined her ideas in light of her discussion with her instructor, Catherine looked again at both the annotated poems and her notes about them. She then recorded her thoughts about her progress in an additional journal entry.

> After reviewing the poems again and talking to Professor Jackson, I discovered some additional points I want to include in my next draft. The connection between the poet's pen and the shovel is evident in "Digging," and so is the link between the cold and the tensions in the house in "Those Winter Sundays." The tone of each poem should also be discussed. For example, I think that the poet's choice of *austere* in "Those Winter Sundays" has significance and should be included. In my next draft, I'll expand my first draft—hopefully, without reading into the poems too much. I also need to reorganize my ideas so parallels between the two poems will be clearer.

Because this journal entry suggested a new arrangement for her ideas, Catherine prepared a new scratch outline to guide her revision.

> Reflections on their fathers
> > Both poems
> > - fathers' dedication
> > - fathers' hard work
> Family similarities and differences
> > "Digging"
> > - loving and caring
> > "Those Winter Sundays"
> > - family problems (tone of the poem)

Lessons learned from fathers
    "Digging"
        • inspiration (images of pen and shovel)
        • realization of father's inner strength
  "Those Winter Sundays"
        • "austere" caring (images of cold)
        • realization of father's inner strength

Brief discussion of other poems about fathers

Revising and Editing an Essay

After once again reviewing all the material she had accumulated, Catherine wrote a second draft.

A Comparison of Two Poems about Fathers

    Robert Hayden's "Those Winter Sundays" and Seamus Heaney's "Digging" are two literary pieces that are tributes to the speakers' fathers. The inspiration and admiration the speakers feel are evident in each poem. Although the nature of the two family relationships may differ, the common thread of the love of fathers for their children weaves through each poem.

    Reflections on one's childhood can bring assorted memories to light. Presumably, the speakers are now adults and reminisce about their childhoods with a mature sense of enlightenment not found in children. Both speakers describe their fathers' hard work and dedication to their families. Hayden's speaker remembers that even after working hard all week, his father would get up early on Sunday to warm the house in preparation for his children's rising. The speaker vividly portrays his father's hands, describing "cracked hands that ached / from labor in the weekday weather" (lines 3-4). And yet, these same hands not only built the fires that drove out the cold but also polished the children's good shoes.

    In a similar way, Heaney's speaker reminisces about his father's and grandfather's digging of turf, describing their skill and their dedication to their task.

    The fathers in these poems appear to be the hardest of workers, laborers who sought to support their families. Not only did they have a dedication to their work, but they also cared about and undoubtedly loved their children. Looking back, Hayden's speaker realizes that, although his childhood may not have been perfect nor his family life entirely without problems, his father loved him. Heaney's description of the potato picking makes us imagine a loving family led by a father and grandfather who worked together and included the children in both work and celebration. Heaney's speaker grows to become a man who has nothing but respect for his father and grandfather, wishing to be like them and somehow follow their greatness.

Although some similarities exist between the sons and fathers in the two poems, the family life is quite different. Perhaps it is the tone of the poems that best typifies the family atmosphere. The tone of "Digging" is wholesome, earthy, natural, and happy, emphasizing the healthy and caring nature of the poet's childhood. In reminiscing, Heaney's speaker seems to have no bad memories concerning his father or family. In contrast, the tone of Hayden's poem is very much like the coldness of the Sunday mornings. Even though the father warmed the house, the "chronic angers of that house" (9) did not leave with the cold. The speaker, as a child, seems full of resentment toward the father, no doubt blaming him for the family problems. (Curiously, it is the father and not the mother who polishes the children's good shoes. Was there no mother?) The reader senses that the father–son communication evident in Heaney's family is missing in Hayden's.

Many other poets have written about their fathers. Judith Ortiz Cofer in "My Father in the Navy: A Childhood Memory" writes a touching tribute to her father, whose homecomings were so eagerly awaited. In other poems, such as Theodore Roethke's "My Papa's Waltz," the fathers are depicted as imperfect, vulnerable people who try to cope with life as well as possible.

"Digging" and "Those Winter Sundays" are poems written from the inspirations of sons, admiring and appreciating their fathers. Childhood memories act not only as images of the past but also as aids for the speakers' self-realization and enlightenment. Even after childhood, the fathers' influence over their sons is evident; only now do the speakers appreciate its true importance.

Second Draft: Commentary

When she reread her second draft, Catherine thought she had accomplished much of what she had set out to do. For example, she had tightened her thesis statement, rearranged her discussion, added specific details, and changed *poet* to *speaker* where necessary.

However, she still was not satisfied with her analysis of the poems' language and tone (she had not, for example, considered the importance of the word *austere* or examined the significance of Heaney's equation of *spade* and *pen*). She also thought that the material in paragraph 6 about other poems, though interesting, was distracting, so she decided to try to move it to follow her introduction, where it could provide a context for the discussion to follow.

After making further revisions, Catherine prepared a final draft of her essay, which appears below.

Whittaker 1

Catherine Whittaker

Professor Jackson

English 102

10 April 2015

Digging for Memories

Robert Hayden's "Those Winter Sundays" and Seamus Heaney's "Digging" are two poems that are tributes to the speakers' fathers. Although the depiction of the families and the tones of the two poems are different, the common thread of love between fathers and children extends through the two poems, and each speaker is inspired by his father's example.

> Introduction

> Thesis statement

Many other poets have written about children and their fathers. Some of these poems express regret and gratitude. For example, Judith Ortiz Cofer in "My Father in the Navy: A Childhood Memory" writes a touching tribute to her father, whose homecomings were so eagerly awaited. In other poems, such as Theodore Roethke's "My Papa's Waltz," fathers are depicted as imperfect, vulnerable people who try to cope with life as well as possible.

> ¶6 from second draft has been relocated. References to poems in Chapter 32 of this text include complete authors' names and titles.

As these and other poems reveal, reflections on childhood can bring complex memories to light, as they do for Hayden's and Heaney's speakers. Now adults, they reminisce about their childhoods with a mature sense of enlightenment not found in children. Both speakers describe their fathers' hard work and dedication to their families. For example, Hayden's speaker remembers that even after working hard all week, his father would get up early on Sunday to warm the house in preparation for his sleeping children. The speaker vividly portrays his father's hands, describing "cracked hands that

> First point of similarity: both poems focus on memory

ached / from labor in the weekday weather" (lines 3-4). And yet, these same hands not only built the fires that drove out the cold but also polished his children's good shoes. In a similar way, Heaney's speaker reminisces about his father's and grandfather's digging of soil and sod, pointing out their skill and their dedication to their tasks.

> First reference to lines of poetry includes *line* or *lines*. Subsequent references include just line numbers.

The fathers in these poems appear to be hard workers, laborers who struggled to support their families. Not only were they dedicated to their work, but they also loved their children. Looking back, Hayden's speaker realizes that, although his childhood may not have been perfect and his family life was not entirely without problems, his father loved him. Heaney's description of the potato picking allows us to imagine a loving family led by a father and grandfather who worked together and included the children in both work and celebration. Heaney's speaker grows into a man who has nothing but respect for his father and grandfather, wishing to be like them and to somehow fill their shoes.

> Second point of similarity: both fathers are hard workers.

Although some similarities exist between the fathers (and the sons) in the poems, the family life the two poems depict is very different. Perhaps it is the tone of each poem that best reveals the family atmosphere. The tone of "Digging" is wholesome, earthy, natural, and happy, emphasizing the healthy and caring nature of the speaker's childhood. Heaney's speaker seems to have no bad memories of his father or family. In contrast, the tone of Hayden's poem is very much like the coldness of the Sunday mornings. Even though the father warmed the house, the "chronic angers of that house" (9) did not leave with the cold. The speaker, as a child, seems to have resented his father, blaming him for the family's problems. The warm relationship readers see between the father and the son in Heaney's poem is absent in Hayden's.

> Focus shifts to contrast between the two poems.

In spite of these differences, readers cannot go away from either poem without the impression that both speakers learned important lessons from their fathers. Both fathers had a great amount of inner strength and were dedicated to their families. As the years pass, Hayden's speaker has come to realize the depth of his father's devotion to his family. He uses the image of the "blueblack cold" (2) that was splintered and broken by the fires lovingly prepared by his father to suggest the father's efforts to keep his family free from harm. The cold suggests the tensions of the family, but the father is determined to force these tensions out of the house through his "austere and lonely offices" (14).

> Focus returns to parallels between the two poems. Third point of similarity: Both speakers learn from fathers (discussed in two paragraphs).

Whittaker 3

In Heaney's poem, the father—and the grandfather—also had a profound impact on the young speaker. As the memories come pouring back, the speaker's admiration for the men who came before him forces him to reflect on his own life and work. He realizes that he will never have the ability (or the desire) to do the physical labor of his relatives: "I've no spade to follow men like them" (28). However, just as the spade was the tool of his father and grandfather, the pen will be the tool with which the speaker will work. The shovel suggests the hard work, effort, and determination of the men who came before him, and the pen is the literary equivalent of the shovel. Heaney's speaker has been inspired by his father and grandfather, and he hopes to accomplish with a pen in the world of literature what they accomplished with a shovel on the land.

"Digging" and "Those Winter Sundays" are poems written from the perspective of adult sons who admire and appreciate their fathers. Childhood memories not only evoke vivid images of the past but also lead the speakers to insight and enlightenment. Long after childhood, the fathers' influence over their sons is evident; only now, however, do the speakers appreciate its true importance.

> Conclusion reinforces thesis.

Whittaker 4

Works Cited

Hayden, Robert. "Those Winter Sundays." Kirszner and Mandell, pp. 662–63.

Heaney, Seamus. "Digging." Kirszner and Mandell, pp. 663–64.

Kirszner, Laurie G. and Stephen R. Mandell, editors. *Compact Literature: Reading, Reacting, Writing*, 9th ed., Wadsworth, 2016.

Final Draft: Commentary

As she wrote her final draft, Catherine expanded her analysis, looking more closely at the language and tone of the two poems. To support and clarify her points, she added more quotations, taking care to reproduce words and punctuation marks accurately and to cite line numbers in parentheses after each quotation. She also moved her discussion of other poems to paragraph 2, where it provides a smooth transition from her introduction to her discussion of Hayden and Heaney. When she was satisfied with the content of her essay, she proofread it carefully and prepared a works-cited page.

CHAPTER 24

VOICE

Langston Hughes
AP Images

Robert Browning
AP Images

Louise Glück
AP Images/Library of Congress, Sigrid Estrada

Janice Mirikitani
David Paul Morris/ Getty Images Entertainment/
Getty Images

Source: ©Bettmann/Corbis

EMILY DICKINSON (1830–1886)

I'm nobody! Who are you? (1891)

I'm nobody! Who are you?
Are you—Nobody—Too?
Then there's a pair of us?
Don't tell! they'd advertise—you know!

How dreary—to be—Somebody!   5
How public—like a Frog—
To tell one's name—the livelong June—
To an admiring Bog!

The Speaker in the Poem

When they read a work of fiction, readers must decide whether the narrator is sophisticated or unsophisticated, trustworthy or untrustworthy, innocent or experienced. Just as fiction depends on a narrator, poetry depends on a **speaker** who describes events, feelings, and ideas to readers. Finding out as much as possible about this speaker can help readers to interpret a poem. For example, the speaker in Emily Dickinson's "I'm nobody! Who are you?" seems at first to be not just self-effacing but also playful, even flirtatious. As the poem continues, however, the speaker becomes more complex. In the first stanza, she reveals her private self—internal, isolated, with little desire to be well known; in the second stanza, she expresses disdain for those who seek to become "somebody," whom she sees as self-centered, self-promoting, and inevitably superficial. Far from being defeated by her isolation, the speaker rejects fame and celebrates her status as a "nobody."

One question readers might ask about "I'm nobody! Who are you?" is how close the speaker's voice is to the poet's. Readers who conclude that the poem is about the conflict between a poet's public and private selves may be tempted to see the speaker and the poet as one. But this is not necessarily the case. Like the narrator of a short story, the speaker of a poem is a **persona,** or mask, that the poet puts on. Granted, in some poems little distance exists between the poet and the speaker. Without hard evidence to support a link between speaker and poet, however, readers should not simply assume they are one and the same.

In many cases, the speaker is quite different from the poet—even when the speaker's voice conveys the attitude of the poet, either directly or indirectly. In the 1789 poem "The Chimney Sweeper" (p. 959), for example, William Blake assumes the voice of a child to criticize the system of child labor that existed in eighteenth-century England. Even though the child speaker does not understand the economic and social forces that cause his misery, readers sense the poet's anger as the trusting speaker describes the appalling conditions under which he works. The poet's indignation is especially apparent in the biting irony of the last line, in which the victimized speaker echoes the moral precepts of the time by innocently assuring readers that if all people do their duty, "they need not fear harm."

Sometimes the poem's speaker is anonymous. In such cases—as in William Carlos Williams's "Red Wheelbarrow" (p. 742), for instance—the first-person voice is absent, and the speaker remains outside the poem. At other times, the speaker has a set identity— a king, a beggar, a highwayman, a sheriff, a husband, a wife, a rich man, a murderer, a child, a mythical figure, an explorer, a teacher, a faithless lover, a saint—or even a flower, an animal, or a clod of earth. Whatever the case, the speaker is not the poet but rather a creation that the poet uses to convey his or her ideas. (For this reason, poems by a single poet may have very different voices. Compare Sylvia Plath's bitter and sardonic poem "Daddy" [p. 772] with her nurturing and celebratory work "Morning Song" [p. 693], for example.)

Sometimes a poem's title tells readers that the poet is assuming a particular persona. In the following poem, for example, the title identifies the speaker as a fictional character, Gretel from the fairy tale "Hansel and Gretel."

AP Images/Library of Congress. Sigrid Estrada

LOUISE GLÜCK (1943–   )

Gretel in Darkness (1971)

This is the world we wanted.
All who would have seen us dead
are dead. I hear the witch's cry
break in the moonlight through a sheet
of sugar: God rewards.   5
Her tongue shrivels into gas. . . .
Now, far from women's arms
And memory of women, in our father's hut
we sleep, are never hungry.
Why do I not forget?   10
My father bars the door, bars harm
from this house, and it is years.

No one remembers. Even you, my brother,
summer afternoons you look at me as though
you meant to leave,   15
as though it never happened.
But I killed for you. I see armed firs,
the spires of that gleaming kiln—

Nights I turn to you to hold me
but you are not there.   20
Am I alone? Spies
hiss in the stillness, Hansel
we are there still, and it is real, real,
that black forest, and the fire in earnest.

The speaker in this poem comments on her life after her encounter with the witch in the forest. Speaking to her brother, Gretel observes that they now live in the world they wanted: they live with their father in his hut, and the witch and the wicked stepmother are dead. Even so, the memory of the events in the forest haunts Gretel and makes it impossible for her to live "happily ever after."

By assuming the persona of Gretel, the poet is able to convey some interesting and complex ideas. On one level, Gretel represents any person who has lived through a traumatic experience. Memories of the event keep breaking through into the present, frustrating her attempts to reestablish her belief in the goodness of the world. The voice we hear is sad, alone, and frightened: "Nights I turn to you to hold me," she says, "but you are not there." Although the murder Gretel committed for her brother was justified, it seems to haunt her. "No one remembers," laments Gretel, not even her brother. At some level, she realizes that by killing the witch she has killed a part of herself, perhaps the part of women that men fear and consequently transform into witches and wicked stepmothers. The world that is left after the killing is her father's and her brother's, not her own, and she is now alone haunted by the memories of the black forest. In this sense, Gretel—"Now, far from women's arms / And

Illustration of "Hansel and Gretel" (1930)
AP Images

memory of women"—may be the voice of all victimized women who, because of men, act against their own best interests—and regret it.

As "Gretel in Darkness" illustrates, a title can identify a poem's speaker, but the speaker's words can provide even more information. In the next poem, the first line of each stanza establishes the identity of the speaker—and defines his perspective.

Source: ©AP Photo

LANGSTON HUGHES (1902–1967)

Negro (1926)

I am a Negro:
    Black as the night is black,
    Black like the depths of my Africa.

I've been a slave:
    Caesar told me to keep his door-steps clean.   5
    I brushed the boots of Washington.

I've been a worker:
    Under my hand the pyramids arose.
    I made mortar for the Woolworth Building.

I've been a singer: 10
    All the way from Africa to Georgia
    I carried my sorrow songs.
    I made ragtime.

I've been a victim:
    The Belgians cut off my hands in the Congo.   15
    They lynch me still in Mississippi.

I am a Negro:
    Black as the night is black,
    Black like the depths of my Africa.

Here the speaker, identifying himself as "a Negro," assumes each of the roles African Americans have historically played in Western society—slave, worker, singer, and victim. By so doing, he gives voice to his ancestors who, by being forced to serve others, were deprived of their identities. By presenting not only their suffering but also their accomplishments, the speaker asserts his pride in being black. The speaker also implies that the suffering of black people has been caused by economic exploitation: Romans, Egyptians, Belgians, and Americans all used black labor to help build their societies. In this context, the speaker's implied warning is clear: except for the United States, all the societies that have exploited blacks have declined, and long after the fall of those empires, black people still endure.

In each of the preceding poems, the speaker is alone. The following poem, a **dramatic monologue,** presents a more complex situation in which the poet creates a complete dramatic scene. The speaker is developed as a character whose distinctive personality is revealed through his words as he addresses a silent listener.

ROBERT BROWNING (1812–1889)

My Last Duchess (1842)

Ferrara

That's my last Duchess painted on the wall,
Looking as if she were alive. I call
That piece a wonder, now: Frà Pandolf's[1] hands
Worked busily a day, and there she stands.
Will't please you sit and look at her? I said   5
"Frà Pandolf" by design, for never read
Strangers like you that pictured countenance,
The depth and passion of its earnest glance,
But to myself they turned (since none puts by
The curtain I have drawn for you, but I)   10
And seemed as they would ask me, if they durst,

[1] *Frà Pandolf:* "Brother" Pandolf, a fictive painter.

How such a glance came there; so, not the first
Are you to turn and ask thus. Sir, 'twas not
Her husband's presence only, called that spot
Of joy into the Duchess' cheek: perhaps   15
Frà Pandolf chanced to say "Her mantle laps
Over my lady's wrist too much," or "Paint
Must never hope to reproduce the faint
Half-flush that dies along her throat": such stuff
Was courtesy, she thought, and cause enough   20
For calling up that spot of joy. She had
A heart—how shall I say?—too soon made glad,
Too easily impressed; she liked whate'er
She looked on, and her looks went everywhere.
Sir, 'twas all one! My favor at her breast,   25
The dropping of the daylight in the West,
The bough of cherries some officious fool
Broke in the orchard for her, the white mule
She rode with round the terrace—all and each
Would draw from her alike the approving speech,   30
Or blush, at least. She thanked men—good! but thanked
Somehow—I know not how—as if she ranked
My gift of a nine-hundred-years-old name
With anybody's gift. Who'd stoop to blame
This sort of trifling? Even had you skill   35
In speech—(which I have not)—to make your will
Quite clear to such an one, and say, "Just this
Or that in you disgusts me; here you miss,
Or there exceed the mark"—and if she let
Herself be lessoned so, nor plainly set   40
Her wits to yours, forsooth, and made excuse
—E'en then would be some stooping; and I choose
Never to stoop. Oh sir, she smiled, no doubt,
Whene'er I passed her; but who passed without
Much the same smile? This grew; I gave commands;   45
Then all smiles stopped together. There she stands
As if alive. Will't please you rise? We'll meet
The company below, then. I repeat,
The Count your master's known munificence
Is ample warrant that no just pretense   50
Of mine for dowry will be disallowed;
Though his fair daughter's self, as I avowed
At starting, is my object. Nay, we'll go
Together down, sir. Notice Neptune,[2] though,

---

[2]*Neptune:* In Roman mythology, the god of the sea.

Taming a sea horse, thought a rarity,   55
Which Claus of Innsbruck[3] cast in bronze for me!

Art gallery similar to setting of "My Last Duchess"
The King's Closet, Windsor Castle, from 'Royal Residences', engraved by William James Bennett
(1769–1844), published by William Henry Pyne (1769–1843), 1816, Wild, Charles (1781–1835) (after) /
Private Collection / The Stapleton Collection/The Bridgeman Art Library

The speaker in "My Last Duchess" is most likely Alfonso II, duke of Ferrara, Italy, whose young wife, Lucrezia, died in 1561 after only three years of marriage. Shortly after her death, the duke began negotiations to marry again. When the poem opens, the duke is showing a portrait of his late wife to an emissary of an unnamed count who is there to arrange a marriage between the duke and the count's daughter. The duke remarks that the artist, Frà Pandolf, has caught a certain look on the duchess's face. This look aroused the jealousy of the duke, who thought that it should have been for him alone. Eventually, the duke could tolerate the situation no longer; he "gave commands," and "all smiles stopped together."

Though silent, the listener plays a subtle but important role in the poem: his presence establishes the dramatic situation that allows the character of the duke to be revealed. The duke tells his story to communicate to the emissary exactly what he expects from his prospective bride and from her father. As he speaks, the duke provides only the information that he wants the emissary to take back to his master, the count. Although the duke appears vain and superficial, he is actually extraordinarily shrewd. Throughout the poem, he turns the conversation to his own ends and gains the advantage through flattery and false modesty. The success of the poem lies in the poet's ability to develop the voice of this complex character, who embodies both superficial elegance and shocking cruelty.

---

[3]*Claus of Innsbruck:* A fictive—or unidentified—sculptor. The count of Tyrol's capital was at Innsbrück, Austria.

FURTHER READING: The Speaker in the Poem

LESLIE MARMON SILKO (1948–   )

Where Mountain Lion Lay Down with Deer (1973)

I climb the black rock mountain
   stepping from day to day
          silently.
I smell the wind for my ancestors
    pale blue leaves
     crushed wild mountain smell.   5
Returning
  up the gray stone cliff
  where I descended
     a thousand years ago.   10
Returning to faded black stone.
  where mountain lion lay down with deer.
It is better to stay up here
        watching wind's reflection
       in tall yellow flowers.   15
The old ones who remember me are gone
   the old songs are all forgotten
and the story of my birth.
How I danced in snow-frost moonlight
    distant stars to the end of the Earth,   20
How I swam away
     in freezing mountain water
     narrow mossy canyon tumbling down
       out of the mountain
       out of the deep canyon stone   25
     down
      the memory
       spilling out
      into the world.

Reading and Reacting

1. Who is speaking in line 4? in line 9? Can you explain this shift?

2. From where is the speaker returning? What is she trying to recover?

3. **JOURNAL ENTRY** Is it important to know that the poet is Native American? How does this information affect your interpretation of the poem?

4. **CRITICAL PERSPECTIVE** In her 1983 essay "Answering the Deer," poet and critic Paula Gunn Allen observes that the possibility of cultural extinction is a reality Native

Americans must face. Native American women writers, says Allen, face this fact directly but with a kind of hope:

> The sense of hope . . . comes about when one has faced ultimate disaster time and time again over the ages and has emerged . . . stronger and more certain of the endurance of the people, the spirits, and the land from which they both arise and which informs both with life. Transformation, or more directly, metamorphosis, is the oldest tribal ceremonial theme. . . . And it comes once again into use within American Indian poetry of extinction and regeneration that is ultimately the only poetry any contemporary Indian woman can write.

Does Silko's poem address the issue of cultural extinction and the possibility of regeneration or metamorphosis? How?

Related Works: "This Is What It Means to Say Phoenix, Arizona" (p. 278), "Two Kinds" (p. 639), "We Wear the Mask" (p. 728), "Solemnly Over the Fertile Land" (p. 746)

David Paul Morris/ Getty Images Entertainment/Getty Images

JANICE MIRIKITANI (1942–   )

Suicide Note   1987)

> *. . . An Asian American college student was reported to have jumped to her death from her dormitory window. Her body was found two days later under a deep cover of snow. Her suicide note contained an apology to her parents for having received less than a perfect four point grade average. . . .*

How many notes written . . .
ink smeared like birdprints in snow.

  not good enough   not pretty enough   not smart enough
dear mother and father.
I apologize   5
for disappointing you.
I've worked very hard,
             not good enough
harder, perhaps to please you.
If only I were a son, shoulders broad   10
as the sunset threading through pine,
I would see the light in my mother's
eyes, or the golden pride reflected
in my father's dream
of my wide, male hands worthy of work   15
and comfort.
I would swagger through life
muscled and bold and assured,

drawing praises to me
like currents in the bed of wind, virile   20
with confidence.
   not good enough   not strong enough   not good enough

I apologize.
Tasks do not come easily.
Each failure, a glacier.   25
Each disapproval, a bootprint.
Each disappointment,
ice above my river.
So I have worked hard.
         not good enough   30
My sacrifice I will drop
bone by bone, perched
on the ledge of my womanhood,
fragile as wings.
         not strong enough   35
It is snowing steadily
surely not good weather
for flying—this sparrow
sillied and dizzied by the wind
on the edge.   40
        not smart enough
I make this ledge my altar
to offer penance.
This air will not hold me,
the snow burdens my crippled wings,   45
my tears drop like bitter cloth
softly into the gutter below.
   not good enough   not strong enough   not smart enough
         Choices thin as shaved
         ice. Notes shredded   50
         drift like snow
on my broken body,
cover me like whispers
of sorries
sorries.   55
Perhaps when they find me
they will bury
my bird bones beneath
a sturdy pine
and scatter my feathers like   60
unspoken song
over this white and cold and silent
breast of earth.

Reading and Reacting

1. This poem is a suicide note that contains an apology. Why does the speaker feel she must apologize? Do you agree that she needs to apologize?

2. What attitude does the speaker convey toward her parents?

3. **JOURNAL ENTRY** Is the college student who speaks in this poem a stranger to you, or is her voice in any way like that of students you know?

4. **CRITICAL PERSPECTIVE** In her essay "Reading Asian American Poetry," Juliana Chang discusses the reasons why Asian American prose, both fiction and nonfiction, has received more critical attention than Asian American poetry. In particular, she points to "the critical perception that poetry is to prose precisely as the private and individual are to the public and the social, and that the poetic therefore has less social relevance." Chang continues, "Anecdotally, I have heard consistently that poetry is considered 'difficult,' that readers often experience an anxiety over being equipped with the right 'key' to decipher a complex of images and patterns in order to gain access to a 'hidden,' and therefore private, meaning."

    Do you feel that "Suicide Note" has social relevance? Does the poem seem accessible or difficult? Does its meaning seem "hidden" in any way?

Related Works: "The Rocking-Horse Winner" (p. 484), "The Value of Education" (p. 727), "What Shall I Give My Children?" (p. 731), "Dreams of Suicide" (p. 864), "Death Be Not Proud" (p. 980), *The Cuban Swimmer* (p. 1416)

RAFAEL CAMPO (1964–   )

My Voice (1996)

To cure myself of wanting Cuban songs,
I wrote a Cuban song about the need
For people to suppress their fantasies,
Especially unhealthy ones. The song
Began by making reference to the sea,   5
Because the sea is like a need so great
And deep it never can be swallowed. Then
The song explores some common myths
About the Cuban people and their folklore:
The story of a little Carib[1] boy   10
Mistakenly abandoned to the sea;
The legend of a bird who wanted song
So desperately he gave up flight; a queen

---

[1] *Carib:* A member of the native people of the Caribbean islands.

Whose strength was greater than a rival king's.
The song goes on about morality,   15
And then there is a line about the sea,
How deep it is, how many creatures need
Its nourishment, how beautiful it is
To need. The song is ending now, because
I cannot bear to hear it any longer.   20
I call this song of needful love my voice.

Reading and Reacting

1. Why does the speaker want to cure himself "of wanting Cuban songs" (line 1)? To what songs is he referring? Why, at the end of the poem, can he no longer "bear to hear" his own Cuban song?

2. At one point in the poem, Campo refers to "the Cuban people and their folklore" (9). What examples of folklore does he give? Why are these stories important to Campo?

3. **JOURNAL ENTRY** Campo is a practicing physician. In what way does "My Voice" reflect his need to heal? What is the difference between *healing* and *curing*?

Related Works: "Araby" (p. 361), "Cathedral" (p. 435), "Evolution of My Block" (p. 808), "Mexican Almuerzo in New England" (p. 843), "Isla" (p. 860), *The Cuban Swimmer* (p. 1416)

 ## The Tone of the Poem

The **tone** of a poem conveys the speaker's attitude toward his or her subject or audience. In speech, this attitude can be conveyed easily: stressing a word in a sentence can modify or color a statement. For example, the statement "Of course, you would want to go to that restaurant" is quite straightforward, but changing the emphasis to "Of course *you* would want to go to *that* restaurant" transforms a neutral statement into a sarcastic one. For poets, however, conveying a particular tone to readers poses a challenge because readers rarely hear poets' spoken voices. Instead, poets indicate tone by using rhyme, meter, word choice, sentence structure, figures of speech, and imagery.

The range of possible tones is wide. For example, a poem's speaker may be joyful, sad, playful, serious, comic, intimate, formal, relaxed, condescending, or ironic. In the following poem, notice the speaker's detached, almost irreverent attitude toward his subject.

ROBERT FROST (1874–1963)

Fire and Ice (1923)

Some say the world will end in fire,
Some say in ice.
From what I've tasted of desire
I hold with those who favor fire.
But if it had to perish twice,   5

I think I know enough of hate
To say that for destruction ice
Is also great
And would suffice.

Here the speaker uses word choice, rhyme, and especially **understatement** to comment on the human condition. The conciseness as well as the simple, regular meter and rhyme suggest an **epigram**—a short poem that makes a pointed comment in an unusually clear, and often witty, manner. This pointedness is consistent with the speaker's glib, unemotional tone, as is the last line's wry understatement that ice "would suffice." The contrast between the poem's serious message—that hatred and indifference are equally destructive—and its informal style and offhand tone complement the speaker's detached, almost smug, posture.

Sometimes shifts in tone reveal changes in the speaker's attitude. In the next poem, subtle shifts in tone reveal a change in the speaker's attitude toward war.

Underwood And Underwood/The LIFE Images Collection/Getty Images

THOMAS HARDY (1840–1928)

The Man He Killed (1902)

"Had he and I but met
    By some old ancient inn,
We should have sat us down to wet
    Right many a nipperkin![1]

"But ranged as infantry,   5
    And staring face to face,
I shot at him as he at me,
    And killed him in his place.

"I shot him dead because—
    Because he was my foe,   10
Just so: my foe of course he was;
    That's clear enough; although

"He thought he'd 'list,[2] perhaps,
    Off-hand-like—just as I—
Was out of work—had sold his traps—   15
    No other reason why.

"Yes; quaint and curious war is!
    You shoot a fellow down
You'd treat if met where any bar is,
    Or help to half-a-crown."[3]   20

---

[1] *nipperkin:* A small container of liquor.

[2] *'list:* Enlist.

[3] *crown:* A unit of British currency.

British infantry fighting in South Africa during the Boer War

The speaker in this poem is a soldier relating a wartime experience. Quotation marks indicate that he is engaged in conversation—perhaps in a pub—and his dialect indicates that he is a member of the English working class. For him, at least at first, the object of war is simple: kill or be killed. To Hardy, this speaker represents all men who are thrust into a war without understanding its underlying social, economic, or ideological causes. In this sense, the speaker and his enemy are both victims of forces beyond their comprehension or control.

The tone of "The Man He Killed" changes as the speaker tells his story. In the first two stanzas, sentences are smooth and unbroken, establishing the speaker's matter-of-fact tone and reflecting his confidence that he has done what he had to do. In the third and fourth stanzas, broken syntax reflects the narrator's increasingly disturbed state of mind as he tells about the man he killed. The poem's singsong meter and regular rhyme scheme (*met/wet, inn/nipperkin*) suggest that the speaker is struggling to maintain his composure; the smooth sentence structure of the last stanza and the use of a cliché ("Yes; quaint and curious war is!") indicate that the speaker is trying to trivialize an incident that has seriously traumatized him.

Sometimes a poem's tone can establish an ironic contrast between the speaker and his or her subject. The speaker's abrupt change of tone at the end of the next poem establishes such a contrast.

AMY LOWELL (1874–1925)

Patterns (1915)

I walk down the garden-paths,
And all the daffodils
Are blowing, and the bright blue squills.

I walk down the patterned garden-paths
In my stiff, brocaded gown.
With my powdered hair and jewelled fan,   5
I too am a rare
Pattern. As I wander down
The garden-paths.

My dress is richly figured,   10
And the train
Makes a pink and silver stain
On the gravel, and the thrift
Of the borders.
Just a plate of current fashion   15
Tripping by in high-heeled, ribboned shoes.
Not a softness anywhere about me,
Only whalebone[1] and brocade.
And I sink on a seat in the shade
Of a lime tree. For my passion   20
Wars against the stiff brocade.
The daffodils and squills
Flutter in the breeze
As they please.
And I weep;   25
For the lime-tree is in blossom
And one small flower has dropped upon my bosom.

And the plashing of waterdrops
In the marble fountain
Comes down the garden-paths.   30
The dripping never stops.
Underneath my stiffened gown
Is the softness of a woman bathing in a marble basin,
A basin in the midst of hedges grown
So thick, she cannot see her lover hiding,   35
But she guesses he is near,
And the sliding of the water
Seems the stroking of a dear
Hand upon her.
What is Summer in a fine brocaded gown!   40
I should like to see it lying in a heap upon the ground.
All the pink and silver crumpled up on the ground.

I would be the pink and silver as I ran along the paths,
And he would stumble after,
Bewildered by my laughter.   45

---

[1] *whalebone:* The type of bone used to stiffen corsets.

I should see the sun flashing from his sword-hilt and buckles
    on his shoes.
I would choose
To lead him in a maze along the patterned paths,
A bright and laughing maze for my heavy-booted lover.
Till he caught me in the shade,   50
And the buttons of his waistcoat bruised my body as
    he clasped me,
Aching, melting, unafraid.
With the shadows of the leaves and the sundrops,
And the plopping of the waterdrops,
All about us in the open afternoon—   55
I am very like to swoon
With the weight of this brocade,
For the sun sifts through the shade.

Underneath the fallen blossom
In my bosom,   60
Is a letter I have hid.
It was brought to me this morning by a rider from the Duke.
Madam, we regret to inform you that Lord Hartwell
Died in action Thursday se'nnight.[2]
As I read it in the white, morning sunlight,   65
The letters squirmed like snakes.
"Any answer, Madam," said my footman.
"No," I told him.
"See that the messenger takes some refreshment.
No, no answer."   70
And I walked into the garden,
Up and down the patterned paths,
In my stiff, correct brocade.
The blue and yellow flowers stood up proudly in the sun,
Each one.   75
I stood upright too,
Held rigid to the pattern
By the stiffness of my gown.
Up and down I walked.
Up and down.   80
In a month he would have been my husband.
In a month, here, underneath this lime,
We would have broken the pattern;

---

[2] se'nnight: "Seven night," or a week ago Thursday.

He for me, and I for him,
He as Colonel, I as Lady,   85
On this shady seat.
He had a whim
That sunlight carried blessing.
And I answered, "It shall be as you have said."
Now he is dead.   90

In Summer and in Winter I shall walk
Up and down
The patterned garden-paths
In my stiff, brocaded gown.
The squills and daffodils   95
Will give place to pillared roses, and to asters, and to snow.
I shall go
Up and down,
In my gown.
Gorgeously arrayed,   100
Boned and stayed.
And the softness of my body will be guarded from embrace
By each button, hook, and lace.
For the man who should loose me is dead,
Fighting with the Duke in Flanders,[3]   105
In a pattern called a war.
Christ! What are patterns for?

The speaker begins by describing herself walking down garden paths. She wears a stiff bro-caded gown, has powdered hair, and carries a jeweled fan. By her own admission, she is "a plate of current fashion." Although her tone is controlled, she is preoccupied by sensual thoughts. Beneath her "stiffened gown / Is the softness of a woman bathing in a marble basin," and the "sliding of the water" in a fountain reminds the speaker of the stroking of her lover's hand. She imagines herself shedding her brocaded gown and running with her lover along the maze of "patterned paths." The sensuality of the speaker's thoughts stands in ironic contrast to the images of stiffness and control that dominate the poem: her passion "Wars against the stiff brocade." She is also full of repressed rage. She knows that her lover has been killed, and she realizes the meaninglessness of the patterns of her life, patterns to which she has conformed, just as her lover conformed by going to war. Throughout the poem, the speaker's tone reflects her barely contained anger and frustration. In the last line, when she finally lets out her rage, the poem's point about the senselessness of conformity and war becomes apparent.

---

[3]*Flanders:* A region in northwestern Europe, including part of northern France and western Belgium. Flanders was a site of prolonged fighting during World War I.

FURTHER READING: The Tone of the Poem

Triton blowing his horn (detail from Trevi fountain, Rome)
sootra/Shutterstock.com

WILLIAM WORDSWORTH (1770–1850)

The World Is Too Much with Us (1807)

The world is too much with us; late and soon,
Getting and spending, we lay waste our powers;
Little we see in Nature that is ours;
We have given our hearts away, a sordid boon!
This Sea that bares her bosom to the moon;   5
The winds that will be howling at all hours,
And are up-gathered now like sleeping flowers;
For this, for everything, we are out of tune;
It moves us not. Great God! I'd rather be
A Pagan suckled in a creed outworn;   10
So might I, standing on this pleasant lea,
Have glimpses that would make me less forlorn;
Have sight of Proteus[1] rising from the sea;
Or hear old Triton[2] blow his wreathèd horn.

Reading and Reacting

1. What is the speaker's attitude toward the contemporary world? How is this attitude revealed through the poem's tone?

2. This poem is a **sonnet**, a highly structured traditional form. How do the regular meter and rhyme scheme help to establish the poem's tone?

3. **JOURNAL ENTRY** Imagine you are a modern-day environmentalist, labor organizer, or corporate executive. Write a response to the sentiments expressed in this poem.

4. **CRITICAL PERSPECTIVE** In his 1972 essay "Two Roads to Wordsworth," M. H. Abrams notes that critics have tended to view Wordsworth in one of two ways:

   One Wordsworth is simple, elemental, forthright, the other is complex, paradoxical, problematic; one is an affirmative poet of life, love, and joy, the other is an equivocal or self-divided poet whose affirmations are implicitly qualified . . . by a pervasive sense of morality and an ever-incipient despair of life; . . . one is the Wordsworth of light, the other the Wordsworth of [shadow], or even darkness.

   Does your reading of "The World Is Too Much with Us" support one of these versions of Wordsworth over the other? Which one? Why?

---

[1] *Proteus:* Sometimes said to be Poseidon's son, this Greek sea-god had the ability to change shape at will and to tell the future.

[2] *Triton:* The trumpeter of the sea, this sea-god is usually pictured blowing on a conch shell. Triton was the son of Poseidon, ruler of the sea.

Related Works: "The Rocking-Horse Winner" (p. 484), "Morning Song" (p. 693), "Metaphors" (p. 764) "The Road Not Taken" (p. 805), "The Peace of Wild Things" (p. 897), "Dover Beach" (p. 956), "The Lake Isle of Innisfree" (p. 1027)

SYLVIA PLATH (1932–1963)

Morning Song (1962)

Love set you going like a fat gold watch.
The midwife slapped your footsoles, and your bald cry
Took its place among the elements.

Our voices echo, magnifying your arrival. New statue.
In a drafty museum, your nakedness   5
Shadows our safety. We stand round blankly as walls.

I'm no more your mother
Than the cloud that distills a mirror to reflect its own slow
Effacement at the wind's hand.

All night your moth-breath   10
Flickers among the flat pink roses. I wake to listen:
A far sea moves in my ear.

One cry, and I stumble from bed, cow-heavy and floral
In my Victorian nightgown.
Your mouth opens clean as a cat's. The window square   15

Whitens and swallows its dull stars. And now you try
Your handful of notes;
The clear vowels rise like balloons.

Reading and Reacting

1. Who is the speaker? To whom is she speaking? What does the poem reveal about her?
2. What is the poem's subject? What attitudes about this subject do you suppose the poet expects her readers to have?
3. How is the tone of the first stanza different from that of the third? How does the tone of each stanza reflect its content?

4. **JOURNAL ENTRY** In what sense does this poem reinforce traditional ideas about motherhood? How does it challenge them?

5. **CRITICAL PERSPECTIVE** Sylvia Plath's life, which ended in suicide, was marked by emotional turbulence and instability. As Anne Stevenson observes in *Bitter Fame*, her 1988 biography of Plath, in the weeks immediately preceding the composition of "Morning Song" a fit of rage over her husband's supposed infidelity caused Plath to destroy many of his books and poetic works in progress. Then, only a few days later, she suffered a miscarriage. According to Stevenson, "Morning Song" is about sleepless nights and

surely reflects Plath's depression. However, in a 1991 biography, *Rough Magic*, Paul Alexander says, "Beautiful, simple, touching, 'Morning Song' was Plath's—then—definitive statement of motherhood."

Which biographer's assessment of the poem do you think makes more sense? Why?

Related Works: "The Yellow Wallpaper" (p. 379), "Metaphors" (p. 764), "Daddy" (p. 772), "Those Winter Sundays" (p. 885), *Proof* (p. 1180)

CLAUDE MCKAY (1890–1948)

The White City (1922)

I will not toy with it nor bend an inch.
Deep in the secret chambers of my heart
I muse my life-long hate, and without flinch
I bear it nobly as I live my part.
My being would be a skeleton, a shell,   5
If this dark Passion that fills my every mood,
And makes my heaven in the white world's hell,
Did not forever feed me vital blood.
I see the mighty city through a mist—
The strident trains that speed the goaded mass,   10
The poles and spires and towers vapor-kissed,
The fortressed port through which the great ships pass,
The tides, the wharves, the dens I contemplate,
Are sweet like wanton loves because I hate.

Reading and Reacting

1. How would you characterize the tone of this sonnet?
2. How is the speaker's description of the city in the third quatrain consistent with the emotions he expresses in lines 1–8?
3. The closing couplet of a Shakespearean sonnet traditionally sums up the poem's concerns. Is this the case here? Explain.

4. **JOURNAL ENTRY** What possible meanings does the phrase "the white world's hell" (line 7) have? How does it express the poem's central theme?

5. **CRITICAL PERSPECTIVE** According to Cary Nelson in *Modern American Poetry*, "'The White City' is not an attack on white people but rather a critique of race-based economic and political power." Which parts of the poem support this assessment? Which do not?

Related Works: "Discovering America" (p. 135), from *American Born Chinese* (p. 176), "Battle Royal" (p. 287), "The Man He Killed" (p. 687), "Dinner Guest: Me" (p. 925), "If We Must Die" (p. 1003), *Fences* (p. 1548)

Gather Ye Rosebuds While Ye May (1909 oil painting)
'Gather Ye Rosebuds While Ye May', 1909 (oil on canvas), Waterhouse, John
William (1849–1917) / Private Collection / Photo © Odon Wagner Gallery,
Toronto, Canada/The Bridgeman Art Library

ROBERT HERRICK (1591–1674)

To the Virgins, to Make Much of Time (1646)

Gather ye rosebuds while ye may,
Old Time is still a-flying;
And this same flower that smiles today,
Tomorrow will be dying.

The glorious lamp of heaven, the sun,   5
The higher he's a-getting,
The sooner will his race be run,
And nearer he's to setting.

That age is best which is the first,
When youth and blood are warmer;   10
But being spent, the worse, and worst
Times still succeed the former.

Then be not coy, but use your time,
And while ye may, go marry;
For having lost but once your prime,   15
You may forever tarry.

Reading and Reacting

1. How would you characterize the speaker? Do you think he expects his listeners to share his views? How might his expectations affect his tone?

2. This poem is developed like an argument. What is the speaker's main point? How does he support it?

3. What effect does the poem's use of rhyme have on its tone?

4. **JOURNAL ENTRY** Whose side are you on—the speaker's or those he addresses?

5. **CRITICAL PERSPECTIVE** Critic Roger Rollin offers the following reading of the final stanza of "To the Virgins, to Make Much of Time":

> This last stanza makes it clear enough that to the speaker young women are coy by [custom or choice] rather than by nature. Their receptivity to love is under their control. The delaying tactics that social custom prescribes for them are self-defeating, threatening to waste life's most precious commodities—time, youth, and love.

Does Rollin's interpretation seem plausible to you? What evidence do you find in the final stanza, or elsewhere in the poem, that the virgins addressed are not naturally "coy" but rather are constrained by social convention?

Related Works: "Love and Other Catastrophes: A Mix Tape" (p. 127), "The Passionate Shepherd to His Love" (p. 1003), *The Brute* (p. 1048), *The Date* (p. 1411)

Irony

Just as in fiction and drama, **irony** occurs in poetry when a discrepancy exists between two levels of meaning or experience. Consider the tone of the following lines by Stephen Crane:

> Do not weep, maiden, for war is kind.
> Because your lover threw wild hands toward the sky
> And the afrightened steed ran on alone,
> Do not weep.
> War is kind.

Surely the speaker in this poem does not intend his words to be taken literally. How can war be "kind"? Isn't war exactly the opposite of "kind"? By making this ironic statement, the speaker actually conveys the opposite idea: war is a cruel, mindless exercise of violence.

Skillfully used, irony enables a poet to make a pointed comment about a situation or to manipulate a reader's emotions. Implicit in irony is the writer's assumption that readers will not be misled by the literal meaning of a statement. In order for irony to work, readers must recognize the disparity between what is said and what is meant, or between what a speaker thinks is occurring and what readers know to be occurring.

One kind of irony that appears in poetry is **dramatic irony**, which occurs when a speaker believes one thing and readers realize something else. In the following poem, the poet uses a deranged speaker to tell a story that is filled with irony.

ROBERT BROWNING (1812–1889)

Porphyria's Lover (1836)

> The rain set early in to-night,
>   The sullen wind was soon awake,
> It tore the elm-tops down for spite,
>   And did its worst to vex the lake:
>   I listened with heart fit to break.   5
> When glided in Porphyria; straight
>   She shut the cold out and the storm,
> And kneeled and made the cheerless grate
>   Blaze up, and all the cottage warm;
>   Which done, she rose, and from her form   10
> Withdrew the dripping cloak and shawl,
>   And laid her soiled gloves by, untied
> Her hat and let the damp hair fall,
>   And, last, she sat down by my side
>   And called me. When no voice replied,   15
> She put my arm about her waist,
>   And made her smooth white shoulder bare,

And all her yellow hair displaced,
    And, stooping, made my cheek lie there,
    And spread, o'er all, her yellow hair,   20
Murmuring how she loved me—she
    Too weak, for all her heart's endeavour,
To set its struggling passion free
    From pride, and vainer ties dissever,
    And give herself to me for ever.   25
But passion sometimes would prevail,
    Nor could to-night's gay feast restrain
A sudden thought of one so pale
    For love of her, and all in vain:
So, she was come through wind and rain.   30
Be sure I looked up at her eyes
    Happy and proud; at last I knew
Porphyria worshipped me; surprise
    Made my heart swell, and still it grew
    While I debated what to do.   35
That moment she was mine, mine, fair,
    Perfectly pure and good: I found
A thing to do, and all her hair
    In one long yellow string I wound
    Three times her little throat around,   40
And strangled her. No pain felt she;
    I am quite sure she felt no pain.
As a shut bud that holds a bee,
    I warily oped her lids: again
    Laughed the blue eyes without a stain.   45
And I untightened next the tress
    About her neck; her cheek once more
Blushed bright beneath my burning kiss:
    I propped her head up as before,
    Only, this time my shoulder bore   50
Her head, which droops upon it still:
    The smiling rosy little head,
So glad it has its utmost will,
    That all it scorned at once is fled,
    And I, its love, am gained instead!   55
Porphyria's love: she guessed not how
    Her darling one wish would be heard.
And thus we sit together now,
    And all night long we have not stirred,
And yet God has not said a word!   60

Like Browning's "My Last Duchess" (p. 679), this poem is a **dramatic monologue**, a poem that assumes an implied listener as well as a speaker. The speaker recounts his story in a straightforward manner, seemingly unaware of the horror of his tale. In fact, much of the effect of this poem comes from the speaker's telling his tale of murder in a flat, unemotional tone—and from readers' gradual realization that the speaker is mad.

The irony of the poem, as well as its title, becomes apparent as the monologue progresses. At first, the speaker fears that Porphyria is too weak to free herself from pride and vanity to love him. As he looks into her eyes, however, he comes to believe that she worships him. The moment the speaker realizes that Porphyria loves him, he feels compelled to kill her and keep her his forever. According to him, she is at this point "mine, mine, fair, / Perfectly pure and good," and he believes that by murdering her, he actually fulfills "Her darling one wish"—to stay with him forever. As he attempts to justify his actions, the speaker reveals himself to be a deluded psychopathic killer.

Another kind of irony is **situational irony**, which occurs when the situation itself contradicts readers' expectations. For example, in "Porphyria's Lover" the meeting of two lovers ironically results not in joy and passion but in murder.

In the next poem, the situation also creates irony.

PERCY BYSSHE SHELLEY (1792–1822)

Ozymandias[1] (1818)

I met a traveler from an antique land
Who said: Two vast and trunkless legs of stone
Stand in the desert. Near them, on the sand,
Half sunk, a shattered visage lies, whose frown,
And wrinkled lip, and sneer of cold command,   5
Tell that its sculptor well those passions read
Which yet survive, stamped on these lifeless things,
The hand that mocked them, and the heart that fed;
And on the pedestal these words appear:
"My name is Ozymandias, king of kings: 10
Look on my works, ye Mighty, and despair!"
Nothing beside remains. Round the decay
Of that colossal wreck, boundless and bare
The lone and level sands stretch far away.

The speaker in "Ozymandias" recounts a tale about a colossal statue that lies shattered in the desert. Its head lies separated from the trunk, and the face has a wrinkled lip and a "sneer of cold command." On the pedestal of the monument are words exhorting all those who pass: "Look on my works, ye Mighty, and despair!" The situational irony of the poem has its source in the contrast between the "colossal wreck" and the boastful inscription on its base: Ozymandias is a monument to the vanity of those who mistakenly think they can withstand the ravages of time.

---

[1]*Ozymandias:* The Greek name for Ramses II, ruler of Egypt in the thirteenth century B.C.

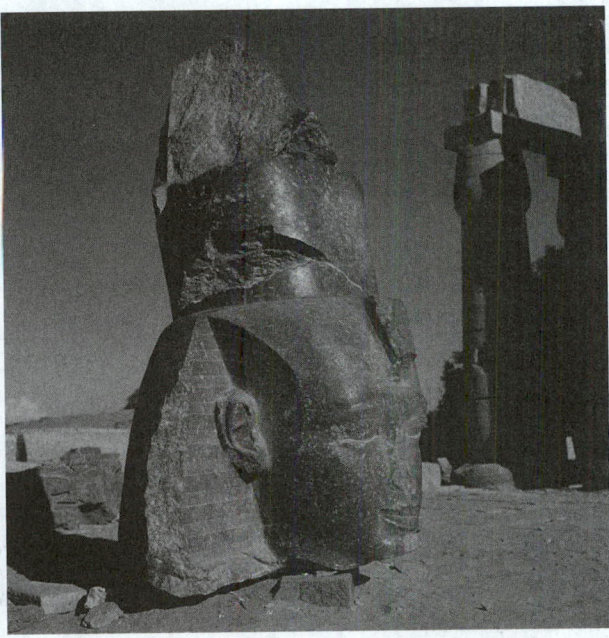

Head of Ramses II, possible inspiration for "Ozymandias"
© Roger Wood/CORBIS

Perhaps the most common kind of irony found in poetry is **verbal irony**, which is created when words say one thing but mean another, often exactly the opposite. When verbal irony is particularly biting, it is called **sarcasm**—for example, Stephen Crane's use of the word *kind* in his antiwar poem "War Is Kind." In speech, verbal irony is easy to detect through the speaker's change in tone or emphasis. In writing, when these signals are absent, verbal irony becomes more difficult to convey. Poets must depend on the context of a remark or on the contrast between a word and other images in the poem to create irony.

FURTHER READING: Irony

SHERMAN J. ALEXIE (1966–)

Evolution (1992)

Buffalo Bill[1] opens a pawn shop on the reservation
right across the border from the liquor store
and he stays open 24 hours a day, 7 days a week

and the Indians come running in with jewelry
television sets, a VCR, a full-length beaded buckskin outfit   5
it took Inez Muse 12 years to finish. Buffalo Bill

---

[1] *Buffalo Bill:* Nickname of William Frederick Cody (1846–1917), soldier, showman, and hunter.

takes everything the Indians have to offer, keeps it
all catalogued and filed in a storage room. The Indians
pawn their hands, saving the thumbs for last, they pawn

their skeletons, falling endlessly from the skin   10
and when the last Indian has pawned everything
but his heart, Buffalo Bill takes that for twenty bucks

closes up the pawn shop, paints a new sign over the old
calls his venture The museum of native american
    cultures
charges the Indians five bucks a head to enter.   15

Reading and Reacting

1. In this poem, what is Buffalo Bill's relationship with the Indians? Why do you think Alexie introduces this historical figure?
2. What is the significance of the poem's title? Is it ironic in any way?
3. Identify several examples of irony in this poem. What different kinds of irony are present?

4. **Journal Entry** What point do you think the speaker is making about American culture? about Native American culture?

5. **Critical Perspective** In an essay on Sherman J. Alexie's poetry, critic Jennifer Gillan notes that Alexie is "a Spokane/Coeur d'Alene Indian from Washington State" and goes on to discuss the ways in which this fact informs his work:

   > From a tribe neither Plains nor Pueblo, which few would associate with the Hollywood version of American Indians, Alexie wonders whether his people ever had access to the authenticity all America seems to associate with Indians. Alienated from their American Indian culture as well as from America, the characters in Alexie's poetry and prose collections want to believe in the wisdom of old Indian prophets, want to return to the "old ways," but know that doing so will just trap them inside another clichéd Hollywood narrative.

   In what sense, if any, are the Indians portrayed in "Evolution" "trapped"? Are they "alienated" from both their own culture and the broader American culture?

Related Works: "This Is What It Means to Say Phoenix, Arizona" (p. 278), Where Mountain Lion Lay Down with Deer" (p. 682), "The English Canon" (p. 725), "Buffalo Bill's" (p. 971), "Indian Boarding School: The Runaways" (p. 986), *The Cuban Swimmer* (p. 1416).

ANNE SEXTON (1928–1974)

Cinderella (1970)

You always read about it:
the plumber with twelve children
who wins the Irish Sweepstakes.
From toilets to riches.
That story.   5

Or the nursemaid,
some luscious sweet from Denmark
who captures the oldest son's heart.
From diapers to Dior.[1]
That story.   10

Or a milkman who serves the wealthy,
eggs, cream, butter, yogurt, milk,
the white truck like an ambulance
who goes into real estate
and makes a pile.   15
From homogenized to martinis at lunch.

Or the charwoman
who is on the bus when it cracks up
and collects enough from the insurance.
From mops to Bonwit Teller.[2]   20
That story.

Once
the wife of a rich man was on her deathbed
and she said to her daughter Cinderella:
Be devout. Be good. Then I will smile   25
down from heaven in the seam of a cloud.
The man took another wife who had
two daughters, pretty enough
but with hearts like blackjacks.
Cinderella was their maid.   30
She slept on the sooty hearth each night
and walked around looking like Al Jolson.[3]
Her father brought presents home from town,
jewels and gowns for the other women
but the twig of a tree for Cinderella.   35
She planted that twig on her mother's grave
and it grew to a tree where a white dove sat.
Whenever she wished for anything the dove
would drop it like an egg upon the ground.
The bird is important, my dears, so heed him.   40

Next came the ball, as you all know.
It was a marriage market.
The prince was looking for a wife.
All but Cinderella were preparing
and gussying up for the big event.   45

---

[1] *Dior:* The fashion designer Christian Dior.

[2] *Bonwit Teller:* An exclusive department store.

[3] *Al Jolson:* American entertainer and songwriter (1886–1950) famous for his blackface minstrel performances.

Cinderella begged to go too.
Her stepmother threw a dish of lentils
into the cinders and said: Pick them
up in an hour and you shall go.
The white dove brought all his friends;   50
all the warm wings of the fatherland came,
and picked up the lentils in a jiffy.
No, Cinderella, said the stepmother,
you have no clothes and cannot dance.
That's the way with stepmothers.   55

Cinderella went to the tree at the grave
and cried forth like a gospel singer:
Mama! Mama! My turtledove,
send me to the prince's ball!
The bird dropped down a golden dress   60
and delicate little gold slippers.
Rather a large package for a simple bird.
So she went. Which is no surprise.
Her stepmother and sisters didn't
recognize her without her cinder face   65
and the prince took her hand on the spot
and danced with no other the whole day.

As nightfall came she thought she'd better
get home. The prince walked her home
and she disappeared into the pigeon house   70
and although the prince took an axe and broke
it open she was gone. Back to her cinders.
These events repeated themselves for three days.
However on the third day the prince
covered the palace steps with cobbler's wax   75
and Cinderella's gold shoe stuck upon it.
Now he would find whom the shoe fit
and find his strange dancing girl for keeps.
He went to their house and the two sisters
were delighted because they had lovely feet.   80
The eldest went into a room to try the slipper on
but her big toe got in the way so she simply
sliced it off and put on the slipper.
The prince rode away with her until the white dove
told him to look at the blood pouring forth.   85
That is the way with amputations.
They don't just heal up like a wish.
The other sister cut off her heel
but the blood told as blood will.
The prince was getting tired.   90

He began to feel like a shoe salesman.
But he gave it one last try.
This time Cinderella fit into the shoe
like a love letter into its envelope.

At the wedding ceremony   95
the two sisters came to curry favor
and the white dove pecked their eyes out.
Two hollow spots were left
like soup spoons.

Cinderella and the prince   100
lived, they say, happily ever after,
like two dolls in a museum case
never bothered by diapers or dust,
never arguing over the timing of an egg,
never telling the same story twice,   105
never getting a middle-aged spread,
their darling smiles pasted on for eternity
Regular Bobbsey Twins.⁴
That story.

Reading and Reacting

1. The first twenty-one lines of the poem act as a prelude. How does this prelude help to establish the speaker's ironic tone?
2. At times, the speaker talks directly to readers. What effect do these statements have on you? Would the poem be stronger without them?
3. Throughout the poem, the speaker mixes contemporary colloquial expressions with the conventional language of a fairy tale. Find examples of these two kinds of language. How does their juxtaposition create irony?

4. **JOURNAL ENTRY** What details of the Cinderella fairy tale does Sexton change in her poem? Why do you think she makes these changes?

5. **CRITICAL PERSPECTIVE** In his 1973 book *Confessional Poets*, Robert Phillips comments on Anne Sexton's use of the Grimm Brothers' fairy tales in her book *Transformations*. According to Phillips, by transforming the Grimms' stories into symbols of our own time, Sexton "has managed to offer us understandable images of the world around us":

   ["Cinderella"] she takes to be a prototype of the old rags to riches theme ("From diapers to Dior. / That story."). Cinderella is said to have slept on the sooty hearth each night and "walked around looking like Al Jolson"—a comparison indicative of the level of invention and humor in the book. At the end, when Cinderella marries the handsome prince to live happily ever after, . . . Sexton pulls a double whammy and reveals that the ending, in itself, is another fairy tale within a fairy tale, totally unreal and unlikely.

---

⁴*Bobbsey Twins:* The two sets of twins—Nan and Bert, Flossie and Freddie—in a popular series of early twentieth-century children's books. They led an idealized, problem-free life.

Is the poem "Cinderella," written in 1970, still a "symbol of our own time"? Does it still offer us "understandable images of the world around us"?

Related Works: "Girl" (p. 137), "The Story of an Hour" (p. 201), "The Girl with Bangs" (p. 262), "Gretel in Darkness" (p. 677), *Beauty* (p. 1069), *Trifles* (p. 1604)

SANDRA M. CASTILLO (1962–   )

Castro[1] Moves into the Havana Hilton[*]

"History always dresses us for the wrong occasions."
—Ricardo Pau-Llosa

Camera Obscura[2]

The afternoon lightening his shadow,
Fidel descends from the mountains,
the clean-shaven lawyer turned guerilla,
his eyes focused on infinity,
El Jefe Máximo con sus Barbudos,[3]   5
rebels with rosary beads
on their 600-mile procession across the island
with campesinos[4] on horseback, flatbed trucks, tanks,
a new year's journey down the oldest roads
towards betrayal.   10

Ambient light.[5] Available light[6]

Light inside of them,
nameless isleños[7] line El Malecón[8] to touch Fidel,
already defining himself in black and white.
The dramatic sky moving in for the close-up
that will frame his all-night oratory,   15
he turns to the crowd,
variations on an enigma,

---

[*]Publication date unavailable.

[1]*Castro:* Fidel Castro (1962–   ), head of the Cuban government from 1959 to 2008.

[2]Camera Obscura: A simple device for projecting images.

[3]*El Jefe Máximo con sus Barbudos:* Spanish for "the big boss with his bearded companions."

[4]*campesinos:* Spanish for "farmers."

[5]Ambient light: A photographic term meaning either the natural light available in a given setting, or the minimal light from a single source provided by a photographer.

[6]Available light: A photographic term meaning the natural light available in a given setting.

[7]*isleños:* Spanish for "islanders."

[8]*El Malecón:* A long, wide street in Havana, Cuba.

waving from his pulpit with rehearsed eloquence,
a dove on his shoulder.

This is a photograph. This is not a sign.   20

Flash-on camera. Celebrity portraits.

1. Fidel on a balcony across the street
   from Grand Central Station,
   an American flag above his head,
   New York, 1959.

2. Fidel made small by the Lincoln Memorial,   25
   Washington D.C., 1959.

3. Fidel learning to ski,
   a minor black ball against a white landscape,
   Russia, 1962.

4. Fidel and shotgun,   30
   hunting with Nikita,[9]
   Russia, 1962.

Circles of Confusion

Beyond photographs,
Havana is looted and burned.
Women weep at out wailing wall,   35
El Paredón,[10] where traitors are taken,
and television cameras shoot
the executions, this blood soup,
the paradoxes of our lives,
three years before I am born.   40

Photoflood[11]

But it is late afternoon,
and a shower of confetti and serpentine[12]
falls from every floor of the Havana Hilton,
where history is a giant piñata,
where at midnight, Fidel will be photographed   45
eating a ham sandwich.

---

[9]*Nikita:* Nikita Khrushchev (1894–1971), leader of the Soviet Union from 1953 to 1964.

[10]*El Paredón:* A wall in Havana where executions were carried out.

[11]Photoflood: An extremely bright floodlight used in photography and cinematography.

[12]*serpentine:* A coiled type of party streamer.

Fidel Castro in New York, April 1959.

Reading and Reacting

1. The Havana Hilton was built in 1957. The majority of the hotel was owned by Meyer Lansky, a major organized crime figure, who paid the Cuban dictator, Fulgencio Batista, a share of the profits. When Fidel Castro overthrew Batista in 1959, Castro made the hotel his headquarters. Why do you think Castillo chooses to focus on this hotel? What point do you think that she is trying to make?

2. In the section of the poem entitled "Flash-on camera. Celebrity portraits," Castillo describes four pictures of Castro along with the dates they were taken. What do these pictures show about Castro?

3. What does Castillo mean when she says that at the Havana Hilton "history is a giant piñata"?

4. **JOURNAL ENTRY** What is Castillo's attitude toward Castro? How can you tell?

Related Works: from *Persepolis* (p. 162), "Hitler's First Photograph" (p. 709), *The Cuban Swimmer* (p. 1416)

AGHA SHAHID ALI (1949–2001)

The Wolf's Postscript to "Little Red Riding Hood"*

First, grant me my sense of history:
I did it for posterity,
for kindergarten teachers

---

*Publication date unavailable.

and a clear moral:
Little girls shouldn't wander off   5
in search of strange flowers,
and they mustn't speak to strangers.

And then grant me my generous sense of plot:
Couldn't I have gobbled her up
right there in the jungle?   10
Why did I ask her where her grandma lived?
As if I, a forest-dweller,
didn't know of the cottage
under the three oak trees
and the old woman lived there   15
all alone?
As if I couldn't have swallowed her years before?

And you may call me the Big Bad Wolf,
now my only reputation.
But I was no child-molester   20
though you'll agree she was pretty.

And the huntsman:
Was I sleeping while he snipped
my thick black fur
and filled me with garbage and stones?   25
I ran with that weight and fell down,
simply so children could laugh
at the noise of the stones
cutting through my belly,
at the garbage spilling out   30
with a perfect sense of timing,
just when the tale
should have come to an end.

Reading and Reacting

1. How does Ali portray the Big Bad Wolf? How is this characterization different from the one in the classic fairy tale "Little Red Riding Hood"?
2. How would you describe the tone of this poem? How does Ali create this tone?
3. The wolf says that he "did it for posterity" and "for kindergarten teachers." What does he mean?
4. Why does the wolf think that he needs to add a postscript to "Little Red Riding Hood"?

5. **JOURNAL ENTRY** What "clear moral" does the poem have? In what sense is this moral ironic?

Related Works: "Gretel in Darkness" (p. 677), "Porphyria's Lover" (p. 696), "The Chimney Sweeper" (p. 959), *Beauty* (p. 1069)

DUDLEY RANDALL (1914–2000)

Ballad of Birmingham (1969)

(On the bombing of a church in Birmingham, Alabama, 1963)

"Mother dear, may I go downtown
Instead of out to play,
And march the streets of Birmingham
In a Freedom March today?"

"No, baby, no, you may not go,   5
For the dogs are fierce and wild,
And clubs and hoses, guns and jails
Aren't good for a little child."

"But, mother, I won't be alone.
Other children will go with me,   10
And march the streets of Birmingham
To make our country free."

"No, baby, no, you may not go,
For I fear those guns will fire.
But you may go to church instead   15
And sing in the children's choir."

She has combed and brushed her night-dark hair,
And bathed rose petal sweet,
And drawn white gloves on her small brown hands,
And white shoes on her feet.   20

The mother smiled to know her child
Was in the sacred place,
But that smile was the last smile
To come upon her face.

For when she heard the explosion,   25
Her eyes grew wet and wild.
She raced through the streets of Birmingham
Calling for her child.

She clawed through bits of glass and brick,
Then lifted out a shoe.   30
"O, here's the shoe my baby wore,
But, baby, where are you?"

Reading and Reacting

1. Who are the speakers in the poem? How do their tones differ?
2. What kinds of irony are present in the poem? Give examples of each kind you identify.
3. What point do you think the poem makes about violence? about racial hatred? about the civil rights struggle?

4. This poem is a **ballad**, a form of poetry traditionally written to be sung or recited. Ballads typically repeat words and phrases and have regular meter and rhyme. How do the regular rhyme, repeated words, and singsong meter affect the poem's tone?

5. **JOURNAL ENTRY** This poem was written in response to the 1963 bombing of the 16th Street Baptist Church in Birmingham, Alabama, a bomb that killed four African American children (pictured on p. 923). How does this historical background help you to understand the irony of the poem?

6. **CRITICAL PERSPECTIVE** Speaking of "Ballad of Birmingham," critic James Sullivan says, "This poem uses the ballad convention of the innocent questioner and the wiser respondent (the pattern of, for example, 'Lord Randall' and 'La Belle Dame sans Merci': [p. 993]), but it changes the object of knowledge from fate to racial politics. The child is the conventional innocent, while the mother understands the violence of this political moment."
   How does Randall's use of these ballad conventions help him create irony?

Related Works: "Birmingham Sunday (September 15, 1963)" (p. 922), "Bonny Barbara Allan" (p. 954), "Emmett Till" (p. 985), "If We Must Die" (p. 1003), *Fences* (p. 1548)

Adolph Hitler as a baby

WISLAWA SZYMBORSKA (1923–2012)

Hitler's First Photograph (1986)

And who's this little fellow in his itty-bitty robe?
That's tiny baby Adolf, the Hitler's little boy!
Will he grow up to be an LL.D.?[1]
Or a tenor in Vienna's Opera House?
Whose teensy hand is this, whose little ear and eye and nose?   5
Whose tummy full of milk, we just don't know:
printer's, doctor's, merchant's, priest's?
Where will those tootsy-wootsies finally wander?
To garden, to school, to an office, to a bride,
maybe to the Burgermeister's[2] daughter?   10

Precious little angel, mommy's sunshine, honeybun,
while he was being born a year ago,
there was no dearth of signs on the earth and in the sky:
spring sun, geraniums in windows,
the organ-grinder's music in the yard,   15
a lucky fortune wrapped in rosy paper,
then just before the labor his mother's fateful dream:
a dove seen in dream means joyful news,

---

[1]*LL.D.: Legum Doctor,* or Doctor of Law.

[2]*Burgermeister:* An executive of a town in Germany.

if it is caught, a long-awaited guest will come.
Knock knock, who's there, it's Adolf's heartchen[3] knocking.   20

A little pacifier, diaper, rattle, bib,
our bouncing boy, thank God and knock on wood, is well,
looks just like his folks, like a kitten in a basket,
like the tots in every other family album.
Shush, let's not start crying, sugar,   25
the camera will click from under that black hood.

The Klinger Atelier,[4] Grabenstrasse,[5] Braunau,[6]
and Braunau is small but worthy town,
honest businesses, obliging neighbors,
smell of yeast dough, of gray soap.   30
No one hears howling dogs, or fate's footsteps.
A history teacher loosens his collar
and yawns over homework.

Reading and Reacting

1. What attitude toward her subject does the speaker expect readers to have? How do you know? How much information about Hitler does she expect readers to know?

2. Throughout the poem, the speaker speaks to baby Hitler as she would to any other baby. How do words like "angel," sunshine," "honeybun," and "sugar" create irony in the poem?

3. What does the speaker mean in line 31 of the poem when she says, "No one hears howling dogs, or fate's footsteps"?

4. Why does the poem end with the image of a history teacher loosening his tie and yawning? What effect does this image have on you?

5. **JOURNAL ENTRY** What point do you think Szymborska is making in this poem? How does irony help her make this point?

6. **CRITICAL PERSPECTIVE** Speaking of "Hitler's First Photograph," critic Alan Reid makes this observation:

> "Hitler's First Photograph" is one of the most chilling poetic inspections of the psychopathological phenomena associated with its namesake and Nazism ever written. By describing Hitler in his first year of life from the perspective of his parents (any parents), [Szymborska] jolts us out of our complacency around the question of how this could have happened. . . . She prods us to question whether the signs were there and, if they were not, to ask what gives rise to such abominations and to recognize the need to be vigilant.

Do you agree with Reid's assessment of the poem? Why, or why not?

---

[3] *heartchen:* A partial translation of a German word meaning "little heart."

[4] *Klinger Atelier:* Painting of Max Klinger's artist's studio.

[5] *Grabenstrasse:* Street in Austria.

[6] *Braunau:* Birthplace of Hitler in Austria-Hungary.

Related Works: "I Stand Here Ironing" (p. 299), "Young Goodman Brown" (p. 448), "A Blessing from My Six Years' Son" (p. 729), "What Shall I Give My Children?" (p. 731), "Daddy" (p. 772), "Those Winter Sundays" (p. 885), "The Lamb" (p. 960), *Proof* (p. 1180)

✔ **CHECKLIST   Writing about Voice**

The Speaker in the Poem

☐ What do we know about the speaker?

☐ Is the speaker anonymous, or does he or she have a particular identity?

☐ How does assuming a particular persona help the poet to convey his or her ideas?

☐ Does the title give readers any information about the speaker's identity?

☐ How does word choice provide information about the speaker?

☐ Does the speaker make any direct statements to readers that help establish his or her identity or character?

☐ Does the speaker address anyone? How can you tell? How does the presence of a listener affect the speaker?

The Tone of the Poem

☐ What is the speaker's attitude toward his or her subject?

☐ How do word choice, rhyme, meter, sentence structure, figures of speech, and imagery help to convey the attitude of the speaker?

☐ Is the poem's tone consistent? How do shifts in tone reveal the changing mood or attitude of the speaker?

Irony

☐ Does the poem include dramatic irony? situational irony? verbal irony?

WRITING SUGGESTIONS: Voice

1. The poet Robert Frost once said that he wanted to write "poetry that talked." According to Frost, "whenever I write a line it is because that line has already been spoken clearly by a voice within my mind, an audible voice." Choose some poems in this chapter (or from elsewhere in the book) that you consider "poetry that talks." Then, write an essay about how successful they are in communicating "an audible voice."

2. Compare the speakers' voices in "Patterns" (p. 688) and "Gretel in Darkness" (p. 677). How are their attitudes toward men similar? How are they different?

3. The theme of Herrick's poem "To the Virgins, to Make Much of Time" (p. 695) is known as **carpe diem**, or "seize the day." Read Andrew Marvell's "To His Coy Mistress" (p. 776), which has the same theme, and compare its tone with that of "To the Virgins, to Make Much of Time."

4. Many critics think that Langston Hughes's poem "I, Too" (p. 918) is a response to Walt Whitman's "I Hear America Singing" (p. 1022). Read both poems and compare the speakers' voices. How are they similar, and how are they different? How does the speaker's voice reinforce the major theme of each poem?

5. Because the speaker and the poet are not the same, poems by the same author can have different voices. Compare the voices of several poems by one poet—for example, Sylvia Plath, W. H. Auden, Robert Frost, or William Blake—whose works are included in this anthology.

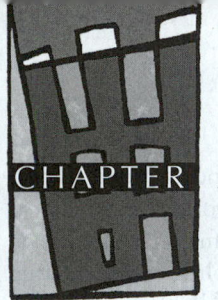

CHAPTER 25

WORD CHOICE, WORD ORDER

Adrienne Rich
AP Images/Chuck Knoblock

Margaret Atwood
AP Images/Dave Thomson

E. E. Cummings
Pictorial Press Ltd/Alamy

Gwendolyn Brooks
Bill Tague

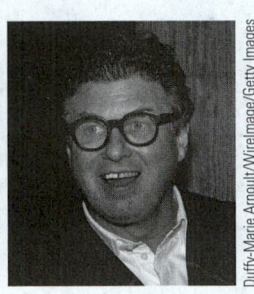

Duffy-Marie Arnoult/WireImage/Getty Images

BOB HOLMAN (1948–   )

Beautiful (2002)

January 3, 2002

Dear Bob,

You are not allowed to use
the word "beautiful" in a poem
this year.

Signed,
The Rest of the World
Except for You

713

Words identify and name, characterize and distinguish, compare and contrast. Words describe, limit, and embellish; words locate and measure. Even though words may be elusive and uncertain and changeable, a single word—such as Holman's "beautiful" in the poem on the preceding page—can also be meaningful. In poetry, as in love and in politics, words matter.

Beyond the quantitative—how many words, how many letters and syllables—is a much more important consideration: the *quality* of words. Which words are chosen, and why? Why are certain words placed next to others? What does a word suggest in a particular context? How are the words arranged? What exactly constitutes the "right word"?

 ## Word Choice

In poetry, even more than in fiction or drama, words are the focus—sometimes even the true subject—of a work. For this reason, the choice of one word over another can be crucial. Because poems are brief, they must compress many ideas into just a few lines; poets know how much weight each individual word carries, so they choose with great care, trying to select words that imply more than they state.

In general, poets (like prose writers) select words because they communicate particular ideas. However, poets may also choose words for their sound. For instance, a word may echo another word's sound, and such repetition may place emphasis on both words; a word may rhyme with another word and therefore be needed to preserve the poem's rhyme scheme; or a word may have a certain combination of stressed and unstressed syllables needed to maintain the poem's metrical pattern. Occasionally, a poet may even choose a word because of how it looks on the page.

At the same time, poets may choose words for their degree of concreteness or abstraction, specificity or generality. A **concrete** word refers to an item that is a perceivable, tangible entity—for example, a kiss or a flag. An **abstract** word refers to an intangible idea, condition, or quality, something that cannot be perceived by the senses—love or patriotism, for instance. **Specific** words refer to particular items; **general** words refer to entire classes or groups of items. The following sequence illustrates the movement from general to specific.

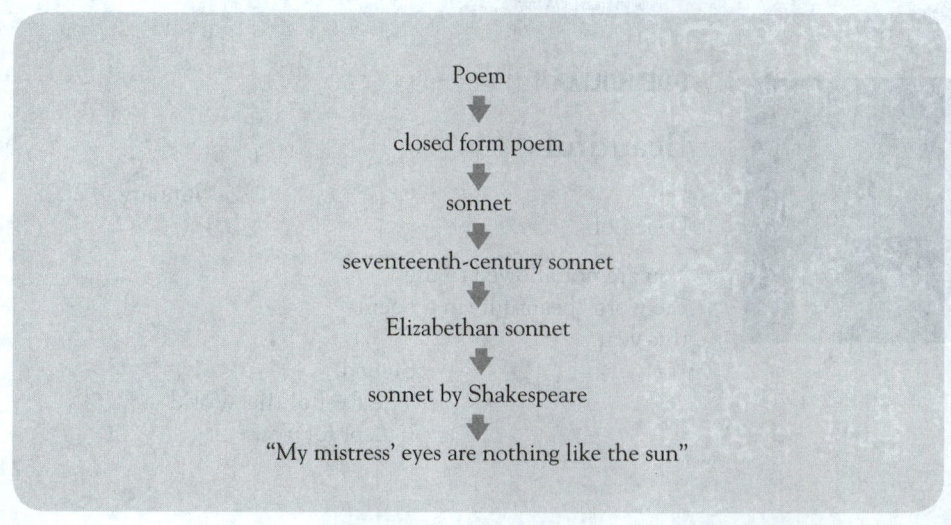

Poem

↓

closed form poem

↓

sonnet

↓

seventeenth-century sonnet

↓

Elizabethan sonnet

↓

sonnet by Shakespeare

↓

"My mistress' eyes are nothing like the sun"

Sometimes a poet wants a precise word, one that is both specific and concrete. At other times, a poet might prefer general or abstract language, which may allow for more subtlety—or even for intentional ambiguity.

Finally, a word may be chosen for its **connotation**—what it suggests. Every word has one or more **denotations**—what it signifies without emotional associations, judgments, or opinions. The word *family*, for example, denotes "a group of related things or people." Connotation is a more complex matter; after all, a single word may have many different associations. In general terms, a word may have a connotation that is positive, neutral, or negative. Thus, *family* may have a positive connotation when it describes a group of loving relatives, a neutral connotation when it describes a biological category, and an ironically negative connotation when it describes an organized crime family. Beyond this distinction, *family*, like any other word, may have a variety of emotional and social associations, suggesting loyalty, warmth, home, security, or duty. In fact, many words have somewhat different meanings in different contexts. When poets choose words, then, they must consider what a particular word may suggest to readers as well as what it denotes.

In the poem that follows, the poet chooses words for their sounds and for their relationships to other words as well as for their connotations.

WALT WHITMAN (1819–1892)

When I Heard the Learn'd Astronomer (1865)

When I heard the learn'd astronomer,
When the proofs, the figures, were ranged in columns before me,
When I was shown the charts and diagrams, to add, divide,
    and measure them,
When I sitting heard the astronomer where he lectured with much
    applause in the lecture-room,
How soon unaccountable I became tired and sick,   5
Till rising and gliding out I wander'd off by myself,
In the mystical moist night-air, and from time to time,
Look'd up in perfect silence at the stars.

This poem might be paraphrased as follows: "When I grew restless listening to an astronomy lecture, I went outside, where I found I learned more just by looking at the stars than I had learned inside." However, the paraphrase is obviously neither as rich nor as complex as the poem. Through careful use of diction, Whitman establishes a dichotomy that supports the poem's central theme about the relative merits of two ways of learning.

The poem can be divided into two groups of four lines each. The first four lines, unified by the repetition of "When," introduce the astronomer and his tools: "proofs," "figures," and "charts and diagrams" to be added, divided, or measured. In this section of the poem, the speaker is passive: he sits and listens ("I heard"; "I was shown"; "I sitting heard"). The repetition of "When" reinforces the dry monotony of the lecture. In the next four lines, the choice of words signals the change in the speaker's actions and reactions. The confined lecture hall is replaced by "the mystical moist night-air," and the dry lecture and the applause give way to "perfect silence"; instead of sitting passively, the speaker becomes active (he rises, glides, wanders); instead of listening, he looks. The mood of the first half of the poem is restrained:

the language is concrete and physical, and the speaker is passively receiving information from a "learn'd" authority. The rest of the poem, celebrating intuitive knowledge and feelings, is more abstract, freer. Throughout the poem, the lecture hall is set in sharp contrast to the natural world outside its walls.

After considering the poem as a whole, readers should not find it hard to understand why the poet selected certain words. Whitman's use of "lectured" in line 4 rather than a more neutral word like "spoke" is appropriate both because it suggests formality and distance and because it echoes "lecture-room" in the same line. The word "sick" in line 5 is striking because it connotes physical as well as emotional distress, more effectively conveying the extent of the speaker's discomfort than "bored" or "restless" would. "Rising" and "gliding" (line 6) are used rather than "standing" and "walking out" both because of the way their stressed vowel sounds echo each other (and echo "time to time" in the next line) and because of their connotation of dreaminess, which is consistent with "wander'd" (line 6) and "mystical" (line 7). The word "moist" (line 7) is chosen not only because its consonant sounds echo the *m* and *st* sounds in "mystical," but also because it establishes a contrast with the dry, airless lecture hall. Finally, line 8's "perfect silence" is a better choice than a reasonable substitute like "complete silence" or "total silence," either of which would suggest the degree of the silence but not its quality.

FURTHER READING: Word Choice

RHINA ESPAILLAT (1932–)

Bilingual/Bilingue (1998)

My father liked them separate, one there,
one here (allá y aquí), as if aware

that words might cut in two his daughter's heart
(el corazón) and lock the alien part

to what he was—his memory, his name   5
(su nombre)—with a key he could not claim.

"English outside this door, Spanish inside,"
he said, "y basta."[1] But who can divide

the world, the word (mundo y palabra) from
any child? I knew how to be dumb   10

and stubborn (testaruda); late, in bed,
I hoarded secret syllables I read

until my tongue (mi lengua) learned to run
where his stumbled. And still the heart was one.

I like to think he knew that, even when,   15
proud (orgulloso) of his daughter's pen,

he stood outside mis versos,[2] half in fear
of words he loved but wanted not to hear.

---

[1] "y basta.": and enough.

[2] *mis versos:* my poems.

Reading and Reacting

1. Why do you think the poet includes parenthetical Spanish translations in this poem? Are they necessary? Why do you think the Spanish words "y basta" (line 8) and "mis versos" (line 17) are not translated as the others are?

2. Some of the words in this poem might be seen as having more than one connotation. Consider, for example, "alien" (line 4), "word" (line 9), "dumb" (line 10), and "syllables" (line 12). What meanings could each of these words have? Which meaning do you think the poet intended them to have?

3. What is the relationship between "the word" and "the world" in this poem?

4. **JOURNAL ENTRY** What is the father's fear? Do you think this fear is justified? Why do you think he doesn't want to hear his daughter's words?

Related Works: "The Secret Lion" (p. 180), "Two Kinds" (p. 639), "My Voice" (p. 685), "Baca Grande" (p. 723), "'Find Work'" (p. 824), "My Father in the Navy: A Childhood Memory" (p. 887)

AP Images/Chuck Knoblock

ADRIENNE RICH (1929–2012)

Living in Sin (1955)

She had thought the studio would keep itself,
no dust upon the furniture of love.
Half heresy, to wish the taps less vocal,
the panes relieved of grime. A plate of pears,
a piano with a Persian shawl, a cat   5
stalking the picturesque amusing mouse
had risen at his urging.
Not that at five each separate stair would writhe
under the milkman's tramp; that morning light
so coldly would delineate the scraps   10
of last night's cheese and three sepulchral bottles;
that on the kitchen shelf among the saucers
a pair of beetle-eyes would fix her own—
envoy from some black village in the mouldings . . .
Meanwhile, he, with a yawn,   15
sounded a dozen notes upon the keyboard,
declared it out of tune, shrugged at the mirror,
rubbed at his beard, went out for cigarettes;
while she, jeered by the minor demons,
pulled back the sheets and made the bed and found   20
a towel to dust the table-top,
and let the coffee-pot boil over on the stove.
By evening she was back in love again,
though not so wholly but throughout the night
she woke sometimes to feel the daylight coming   25
like a relentless milkman up the stairs.

1950s milkman making delivery
Philip Gendreau/© Bettmann/Corbis

Reading and Reacting

1. How might the poem's impact change if each of these words were deleted: "Persian" (line 5), "picturesque" (line 6), "sepulchral" (line 11), "minor" (line 19), "sometimes" (line 25)?

2. What words in the poem have strongly negative connotations? What do these words suggest about the relationship the poem describes? How does the image of the "relentless milkman" (line 26) sum up this relationship?

3. This poem, about a woman in love, uses very few words conventionally associated with love poems. Instead, many of its words denote the everyday routine of housekeeping. Give examples of such words. Why do you think they are used?

4. **JOURNAL ENTRY** What connotations does the title have? What other phrases have similar denotative meanings? How do their connotations differ? Why do you think Rich chose the title "Living in Sin"?

5. **CRITICAL PERSPECTIVE** In "Her Cargo: Adrienne Rich and the Common Language," a 1979 essay examining the poet's work over almost thirty years, Alicia Ostriker offers the following analysis of Rich's early poems, including "Living in Sin":

They seem about to state explicitly . . . a connection between feminine subordination in male-dominated middle-class relationships, and emotionally lethal inarticulateness for both sexes. But the poetry . . . is minor because it is polite. It illustrates symptoms but does not probe sources. There is no disputing the ideas of the predecessors, and Adrienne Rich at this point is a cautious good poet in the sense of being a good girl, a quality noted with approval by her reviewers.

Does your reading of "Living in Sin" support Ostriker's characterization of the poem as "polite" and "cautious"? Do you think Rich is "being a good girl"?

Related Works: "Hills Like White Elephants" (p. 119), "Love and Other Catastrophies: A Mix Tape" (p. 127), "The Storm" (p. 273), "What lips my lips have kissed" (p. 899)

© Pictorial Press Ltd / Alamy

E. E. CUMMINGS (1894–1962)

in Just-[1] (1923)

in Just-
spring when the world is mud-
luscious the little
lame balloonman
whistles   far   and wee   5

and eddieandbill come
running from marbles and
piracies and it's
spring
when the world is puddle-wonderful   10
the queer
old balloonman whistles
far   and   wee

and bettyandisbel come dancing
from hop-scotch and jump-rope and   15
it's
spring
and
      the
            goat-footed   20

balloonMan whistles
far
and
wee

---

[1]*in Just-:* This poem is also known as "Chansons Innocentes I."

Reading and Reacting

1. In this poem, Cummings coins a number of words that he uses to modify other words. Identify these coinages. What other, more conventional, words could be used in their place? What does Cummings accomplish by using the coined words instead?

2. What do you think Cummings means by "far and wee" in lines 5, 13, and 22–24? Why do you think he arranges these three words in a different way on the page each time he uses them?

3. **JOURNAL ENTRY** Evaluate this poem. Do you like it? Is it memorable? moving? Or is it just clever?

4. **CRITICAL PERSPECTIVE** In "Latter-Day Notes on E. E. Cummings' Language" (1955), Robert E. Maurer suggests that Cummings often coined new words in the same way that children do: for example, "by adding the normal -er or -est (*beautifuler, chiefest*), or stepping up the power of a word such as *last*, which is already superlative, and saying *lastest*," creating words such as *givingest* and *whirlingest*. In addition to "combining two or more words to form a single new one . . . to give an effect of wholeness, of one quality" (for example, *yellowgreen*), "in the simplest of his word coinages, he merely creates a new word by analogy as a child would without adding any shade of meaning other than that inherent in the prefix or suffix he utilizes, as in the words *unstrength* and *untimid*. . . ." Many early reviewers, Maurer notes, criticized such coinages because they "convey a thrill but not a precise impression," a criticism also leveled at Cummings's poetry more broadly.

   Consider the coinages in "in Just-." Do you agree that many do not add "shades of meaning" or provide a "precise impression"? Or, do you find that the coinages contribute to the poem in a meaningful way?

Related Works: "The Secret Lion" (p. 180), "anyone lived in a pretty how town" (p. 734), "Constantly Risking Absurdity" (p. 760), "Jabberwocky" (p. 810), "the sky was can dy" (p. 840)

FRANCISCO X. ALARCÓN (1954–   )

"Mexican" Is Not a Noun (2002)

> to forty-six UC Santa Cruz students and
> seven faculty arrested in Watsonville for
> showing solidarity with two thousand
> striking cannery workers who were mostly
> Mexican women, October 27, 1985

"Mexican"
is not
a noun
or an
adjective   5

"Mexican"
is a life
long
low-paying
job   10

a check
mark on
a welfare
police
form   15

more than
a word
a nail in
the soul
but   20

it hurts
it points
it dreams
it offends
it cries   25

it moves
it strikes
it burns
just like
a verb   30

Reading and Reacting

1. According to the speaker, the word *Mexican* is "not / a noun / or an / adjective" (lines 3–5). What part of speech does he see it as? Why?

2. What does the poet gain by isolating the word *Mexican* on its own line in lines 1 and 6? by repeating the word?

3. In what sense is the word *Mexican* "a nail in / the soul" (18–19)? Why is it "more than / a word" (16–17)?

4. **JOURNAL ENTRY** Write a paragraph in which you define the word *Mexican* by elaborating on the speaker's characterizations.

Related Works: "The Secret Lion" (p. 180), "Reapers" (p. 751), "The Carpet Factory" (p. 822), "La Migra" (p. 1004)

 ## Levels of Diction

The diction of a poem may be formal or informal or fall anywhere in between, depending on the identity of the speaker and on the speaker's attitude toward the reader and toward his or her subject. At one extreme, very formal poems can seem lofty and dignified, far removed in style and vocabulary from everyday speech. At the other extreme, highly informal poems can be full of jargon, regionalisms, and slang. Many poems, of course, use language that falls somewhere between formal and informal diction.

Formal diction is characterized by a learned vocabulary and grammatically correct forms. In general, formal diction does not include colloquialisms, such as contractions and shortened word forms (*phone* for *telephone*). As the following poem illustrates, a speaker who uses formal diction can sound aloof and impersonal.

AP Images/Dave Thomson

MARGARET ATWOOD (1939–   )

The City Planners (1966)

Cruising these residential Sunday
streets in dry August sunlight:
what offends us is
the sanities:
the houses in pedantic rows, the planted   5
sanitary trees, assert
levelness of surface like a rebuke
to the dent in our car door.
No shouting here, or
shatter of glass; nothing more abrupt   10
than the rational whine of a power mower
cutting a straight swath in the discouraged grass.

But though the driveways neatly
sidestep hysteria
by being even, the roofs all display   15
the same slant of avoidance to the hot sky,
certain things:
the smell of spilled oil a faint

sickness lingering in the garages,
a splash of paint on brick surprising as a bruise,   20
a plastic hose poised in a vicious

coil; even the too-fixed stare of the wide windows
give momentary access to
the landscape behind or under
the future cracks in the plaster   25

when the houses, capsized, will slide
obliquely into the clay seas, gradual as glaciers
that right now nobody notices.

That is where the City Planners
with the insane faces of political conspirators   30
are scattered over unsurveyed
territories, concealed from each other,
each in his own private blizzard;

guessing directions, they sketch
transitory lines rigid as wooden borders   35
on a wall in the white vanishing air

tracing the panic of suburb
order in a bland madness of snows.

1950s suburban housing development
Masterfile

Atwood's speaker is clearly concerned about the poem's central issue, but rather than use *I*, the poem uses the first-person plural (*us*) to convey some degree of emotional detachment. Although phrases such as "sickness lingering in the garages" and "insane faces of political conspirators" clearly communicate the speaker's disapproval, formal words—"pedantic," "rebuke," "display," "poised," "obliquely," "conspirators," "transitory"—help her to maintain her distance. Both the speaker herself and her attack on the misguided city planners gain credibility through her balanced, measured tone and through her use of language that is as formal and "professional" as theirs.

Informal diction is the language closest to everyday conversation. It includes **colloquialisms**—contractions, shortened word forms, and the like—and may also include slang, regional expressions, and even nonstandard words.

In the poem that follows, the speaker uses informal diction to highlight the contrast between James Baca, a law student speaking to the graduating class of his old high school, and the graduating seniors.

JIM SAGEL (1947–1998)

Baca Grande[1] (1982)

> *Una vaca se topó con un ratón y le dice:*
> *"Tú—¿tan chiquito y con bigote?" Y le responde el ratón:*
> *"Y tú tan grandota—¿y sin brassiere?"[2]*

It was nearly a miracle
James Baca remembered anyone at all

---

[1] *Baca Grande: Baca* is both a phonetic spelling of the Spanish word *vaca* (cow) and the last name of one of the poem's characters. *Grande* means "large."

[2] *Una . . . brassiere?:* A cow ran into a rat and said: "You—so small and with a moustache?" The rat responded: "And you—so big and without a bra?"

from the old hometown gang
having been two years at Yale
    no less   5
and halfway through law school
at the University of California at Irvine
They hardly recognized him either
in his three-piece grey business suit
and surfer-swirl haircut   10
with just the menacing hint
of a tightly trimmed Zapata moustache
    for cultural balance
and relevance

He had come to deliver the keynote address   15
to the graduating class of 80
at his old alma mater
and show off his well-trained lips
which laboriously parted
    each Kennedyish "R"   20
and drilled the first person pronoun
through the microphone
like an oil bit
with the slick, elegantly honed phrases
that slid so smoothly   25
off his meticulously bleached
    tongue
He talked Big Bucks
with astronautish fervor and if he
    the former bootstrapless James A. Baca   30
could dazzle the ass
off the universe
then even you
    yes you

Joey Martinez toying with your yellow   35
    tassle
and staring dumbly into space
could emulate Mr. Baca someday
    possibly
well   40
there was of course
such a thing
as being an outrageously successful
gas station attendant too
    let us never forget   45
it doesn't really matter what you do
so long as you excel

James said
never believing a word
of it   50
for he had already risen
    as high as they go

Wasn't nobody else
from this deprived environment
who'd ever jumped   55
    straight out of college
into the Governor's office
and maybe one day
he'd sit in that big chair
    himself   60
and when he did
he'd forget this damned town
and all the petty little people
in it
once and for all   65

That much he promised himself

"Baca Grande" uses numerous colloquialisms, including contractions; conversational place-holders, such as "no less" and "well"; shortened word forms, such as "gas"; slang terms, such as "Big Bucks"; whimsical coinages ("Kennedyish," "astronautish," "bootstrapless"); non-standard grammatical constructions, such as "Wasn't nobody else"; and even profanity. The level of language is perfectly appropriate for the poem's speaker, one of the students Baca addresses—suspicious, streetwise, and unimpressed by Baca's "three-piece grey business suit" and "surfer-swirl haircut." In fact, the informal diction is a key element in the poem, expressing the gap between the slick James Baca, with "his well-trained lips / which laboriously parted / each Kennedyish 'R'" and members of his audience, with their unpretentious, forthright speech—and also the gap between Baca as he is today and the student he once was. In this sense, "Baca Grande" is as much a linguistic commentary as a social one.

FURTHER READING: Levels of Diction

ADRIENNE SU (1967–   )

The English Canon[1] (2000)

It's not that the first speakers left out women
Unless they were goddesses, harlots, or impossible loves
Seen from afar, often while bathing,
And it's not that the only parts my grandfathers
    could have played

---

[1] *English Canon:* Those works in English traditionally thought worthy of study.

Were as extras in Xanadu[2]   5
Nor that it gives no instructions for shopping or cooking.

The trouble is, I've spent my life
Getting over the lyrics
That taught me to brush my hair till it's gleaming,

Stay slim, dress tastefully, and not speak of sex,   10
Death, violence, or the desire for any of them,
And to let men do the talking and warring

And bringing of the news. I know a girl's got to protest
These days, but she also has to make money
And do her share of journalism and combat,   15

And she has to know from the gut whom to trust,
Because what do her teachers know, living in books,
And what does she know, starting from scratch?

Reading and Reacting

1. What criticisms does the speaker have of the traditional English literary canon?
2. List the words and expressions that identify this poem's diction as informal. Given the poem's subject and theme, do you think this informal language (and the speaker's use of contractions) is a strength or a weakness?
3. What does the speaker mean when she says, "The trouble is, I've spent my life / Getting over the lyrics" (7–8)?
4. **JOURNAL ENTRY** Reread the poem's last two lines. What does the speaker know that her teachers do not know? What do her teachers know that she does not know?
5. **CRITICAL PERSPECTIVE** In her essay "Teaching Literature: Canon, Controversy, and the Literary Anthology," Barbara Mujica discusses the way in which literary anthologies (like this one) tend naturally to create lists of works, known as **canons**, that are considered to be of especially high quality:

> "Anthology". . . is from the Greek word for "collection of flowers," a term implying selection. The very format of an anthology prompts canon formation . . . Anthologies convey the notion of evolution (the succession of literary movements) and hierarchy (the recognition of masterpieces). They create and reform canons, establish literary reputations, and help institutionalize the national culture, which they reflect.

How would you characterize the attitude of the speaker in "The English Canon" to the process that Mujica describes? What is your own attitude toward the idea of canons in literature? Do you think some works can be said to be indisputably better than others?

Related Works: "Gryphon" (p. 250), "The Secretary Chant" (p. 767), "Women" (p. 846), "Aristotle" (p. 865), "Theme for English B" (p. 920)

---

[2] *Xanadu:* The summer capital of the emperor Kublai Kahn; also the setting for the poem "Kubla Khan" (p. 968) by the English poet Samuel Taylor Coleridge.

MARK HALLIDAY (1949–   )

The Value of Education (2000)

I go now to the library. When I sit in the library
I am not illegally dumping bags of kitchen garbage
in the dumpster behind Clippinger Laboratory,
and a very pissed-off worker at Facilities Management
is not picking through my garbage and finding   5
several yogurt-stained and tomato-sauce-stained envelopes
with my name and address on them.
When I sit in the library,
I might doze off a little,
and what I read might not penetrate my head   10
which is mostly porridge in a bowl of bone.
However, when I sit there trying to read
I am not, you see, somewhere else being a hapless ass.
I am not leaning on the refrigerator
in the apartment of a young female colleague   15
chatting with oily pep
because I imagine she may suddenly decide to
do sex with me while her boyfriend is on a trip.
Instead I am in the library! Sitting still!
No one in town is approaching my chair   20
with a summons, or a bill, or a huge fist.
This is good. You may say,
"But this is merely a negative definition of
the value of education." Maybe so,
but would you be able to say that   25
if you hadn't been to the library?

Reading and Reacting

1. Who is the speaker? What does he reveal about himself? Whom might he be addressing?
2. How is the speaker's life outside the library different from the life he leads inside the library?
3. In lines 23–24, the speaker imagines a challenge to his comments. Do you think this challenge is valid? What do you think of the speaker's reply?
4. What phrases are repeated in this poem? Why?
5. JOURNAL ENTRY What argument is the speaker making for the benefits of the library (and for the value of education)? Is he joking, or is he serious?

Related Works: "Gryphon" (p. 250), "When I Heard the Learn'd Astronomer" (p. 715), "Why I Went to College" (p. 833)

PAUL LAURENCE DUNBAR (1872–1906)

We Wear the Mask (1896)

We wear the mask that grins and lies,
It hides our cheeks and shades our eyes—   5
This debt we pay to human guile;
With torn and bleeding hearts we smile,
And mouth with myriad subtleties.

Why should the world be over-wise,
In counting all our tears and sighs?
Nay, let them only see us, while
   We wear the mask.

We smile, but, O great Christ, our cries   10
To thee from tortured souls arise.
We sing, but oh the clay is vile
Beneath our feet, and long the mile;
But let the world dream otherwise,
   We wear the mask!   15

Reading and Reacting

1. Which of the following words and phrases do you see as formal? Why?

- "human guile" (line 3)
- "torn and bleeding hearts" (4)
- "myriad subtleties" (5)
- "over-wise" (6)
- "tortured souls" (11)
- "vile" (12)

2. Some choices of words and phrases listed in question 1 are determined at least in part by the poem's rhyme scheme and metrical pattern. If rhyme and meter were not an issue, what other words and phrases could you substitute for those listed? How would your substitutions change the poem's level of diction?

3. Do you think the poem's meter and rhyme make it seem more or less formal? Explain.

4. Given the poem's subject matter, is its relatively formal level of diction appropriate? Why or why not?

5. JOURNAL ENTRY What exactly is the mask to which the speaker refers? Who is the "we" who wears this mask? (Note that Dunbar is an African American poet writing in the late nineteenth century.)

6. CRITICAL PERSPECTIVE In his book *Paul Laurence Dunbar*, Peter Revell explains that "'We Wear the Mask' itself is 'masked'" in its hidden references to race. How does the poem's diction help mask its message?

Related Works: from *The Harlem Hellfighters* (p. 145), "Big Black Good Man" (p. 318), "Negro" (p. 678), "Yet Do I Marvel" (p. 869)

MARY KARR (1965–   )

A Blessing from My Sixteen Years' Son (2004)

I have this son who assembled inside me
during Hurricane Gloria. In a flash, he appeared,
in a heartbeat. Outside, pines toppled.

Phone lines snapped and hissed like cobras.
Inside, he was a raw pearl: microscopic, luminous.   5
Look at the muscled obelisk of him now

pawing through the icebox for more grapes.
Sixteen years and not a bone broken,
not a single stitch. By his age,

I was marked more ways, and small.   10
He's a slouching six foot three,
with implausible blue eyes, which settle

on the pages of Emerson's "Self-Reliance"
with profound belligerence.
A girl with a navel ring   15

could make his cell phone go brr,
or an Afro'd boy leaning on a mop at Taco Bell—
creatures strange as dragons or eels.

Balanced on a kitchen stool, each gives counsel
arcane as any oracle's. Bruce claims school   20
is harshing my mellow. Case longs to date

A tattooed girl because he wants a women
Willing to do stuff she'll regret
They've come to lead my son

into his broadening spiral.   25
Someday soon, the tether
will snap. I birthed my own mom

into oblivion. The night my son smashed
the car fender, then rode home
in the rain-streaked cop car, he asked, *Did you*   30

and Dad screw up so much?
He'd let me tuck him in,
my grandmother's wedding quilt

from 1912 drawn to his goateed chin. Don't
blame us, I said. You're your own   35
idiot now. At which he grinned.

The cop said the girl in the crimped Chevy
took it hard. He'd found my son
awkwardly holding her in the canted headlights,

where he'd draped his own coat   40
over her shaking shoulders. *My fault,*
he'd confessed right off.

Nice kid, said the cop.

Reading and Reacting

1. This poem uses both formal and informal diction. Identify three or four examples of formal and informal words and expressions. Why do you think Karr chose not to use a consistent level of diction throughout the poem?

2. What words and expressions does the speaker use to describe her son? What does her choice of words tell you about him? about her?

3. Define each of these words: *obelisk* (6); *oracle* (20); *tether* (26); *crimped* (37); *canted* (39). What connotations does each word have in the context in which it is used? Do any of these words seem unexpected or jarring?

4. What is the "blessing" referred to in the title?

5. **JOURNAL ENTRY** What kind of relationship do you think the speaker has with her son? How can you tell?

6. **CRITICAL PERSPECTIVE** Though she is a poet, Mary Karr is also well-known as the author of several memoirs in which she relates the details of a difficult, sometimes impoverished childhood. She discussed her childhood in an interview with the *Paris Review*:

   > Childhood was terrifying for me. A kid has no control. You're three feet tall, flat broke, unemployed, and illiterate. Terror snaps you awake. You pay keen attention. People can just pick you up and move you and put you down. Our little cracker box of a house could give you the adrenaline rush of fear. . . .

   How do Karr's comments about her childhood affect your response to "Blessing from My Sixteen Years' Son"? Does the knowledge that the poet's childhood was difficult and full of anxiety affect how you view the speaker's relationship with her son?

Related Works: "I Stand Here Ironing" (p. 299), "Referential" (p. 598), "What Shall I Give My Children?" (p. 731), "Mid-Term Break" (p. 991)

Source: ©Bill Tague

GWENDOLYN BROOKS (1917–2000)

We Real Cool (1959)

The Pool Players.
Seven at the Golden Shovel.

We real cool. We
Left School. We

Lurk late. We
Strike straight. We   5

Sing sin. We
Thin gin. We

Jazz June. We
Die soon.

Reading and Reacting

1. What elements of nonstandard English grammar appear in this poem? How does the use of such language affect your attitude toward the speaker?
2. Every word in this poem is a single syllable. Why?
3. Why do you think the poet begins with "We" only in the first line instead of isolating each complete sentence on its own line? How does this strategy change the poem's impact?
4. **JOURNAL ENTRY** Write a prose version of this poem, adding words, phrases, and sentences to expand the poem into a paragraph.
5. **CRITICAL PERSPECTIVE** In *Gwendolyn Brooks: Poetry and the Heroic Voice*, critic D. H. Malhem writes of "We Real Cool," "Despite presentation in the voice of the gang, this is a maternal poem, gently scolding yet deeply sorrowing for the hopelessness of the boys."

    Do you agree with Malhem that the speaker's attitude is "maternal"?

Players in a pool hall (1950s)
Mac Gramlich/Hulton Archive/Getty Images

Related Works: "Where Are You Going, Where Have You Been?" (p. 506), "Greasy Lake" (p. 569), "Ex-Basketball Player" (p. 764), "Why I Went to College" (p. 833)

GWENDOLYN BROOKS (1917–2000)

What Shall I Give My Children? (1949)

What shall I give my children? who are poor,
Who are adjudged the leastwise of the land,
Who are my sweetest lepers, who demand

No velvet and no velvety velour;
But who have begged me for a brisk contour,   5
Crying that they are quasi, contraband
Because unfinished, graven by a hand
Less than angelic, admirable or sure.
My hand is stuffed with mode, design, device.
But I lack access to my proper stone.   10
And plenitude of plan shall not suffice
Nor grief nor love shall be enough alone
To ratify my little halves who bear
Across an autumn freezing everywhere.

Reading and Reacting

1. Unlike "We Real Cool" (p. 730), also by Gwendolyn Brooks, this sonnet's diction is quite formal. Given the subject of each poem, do the poet's decisions about level of diction make sense to you?

2. Which words in this poem do you see as elevated—that is, not likely to be used in conversation?

3. Apart from individual words, what else strikes you as formal about this poem?

4. **JOURNAL ENTRY** Consulting a dictionary if necessary, write down a synonym for each of the formal words you identified in question 2. Then, write out three or four lines of this poem in more conversational language.

Related Work: "We Real Cool" (p. 730)

 ## Word Order

The order in which words are arranged in a poem is as important as the choice of words. Because English sentences nearly always have a subject-verb-object sequence, with adjectives preceding the nouns they modify, a departure from this order calls attention to itself. Thus, poets can use readers' expectations about word order to their advantage.

For example, poets often manipulate word order to place emphasis on a word. Sometimes they achieve this emphasis by using a very unconventional sequence; sometimes they simply place the word first or last in a line or place it in a stressed position in the line. Poets may also choose a particular word order to make two related—or startlingly unrelated—words fall in adjacent or parallel positions, calling attention to the similarity (or the difference) between them. In other cases, poets may manipulate syntax to preserve a poem's rhyme or meter or to highlight sound correspondences that might otherwise not be noticeable. Finally, irregular syntax may be used throughout a poem to reveal a speaker's mood—for example, to give a playful quality to a poem or to suggest a speaker's disoriented state.

In the poem that follows, word order frequently departs from conventional English syntax.

EDMUND SPENSER (1552–1599)

One day I wrote her name upon the strand (1595)

One day I wrote her name upon the strand,[1]
But came the waves and washed it away:
Again I wrote it with a second hand,
But came the tide and made my pains his prey.
"Vain man," said she, "that doest in vain assay,   5
A mortal thing so to immortalize,
For I myself shall like to this decay,
And eek[2] my name be wiped out likewise."
"Not so," quod[3] I, "let baser things devise,
To die in dust, but you shall live by fame: 10
My verse your virtues rare shall eternize,
And in the heavens write your glorious name.
Where whenas death shall all the world subdue,
Our love shall live, and later life renew."

"One day I wrote her name upon the strand," a sonnet, has a fixed metrical pattern and rhyme scheme. To accommodate the sonnet's rhyme and meter, Spenser makes a number of adjustments in syntax. For example, to make sure certain rhyming words fall at the ends of lines, the poet sometimes moves words out of their conventional order, as the following three comparisons illustrate.

<u>Conventional Word Order</u>	<u>Inverted Sequence</u>
"'Vain man,' she said, 'that doest *assay in vain.*'"	"'Vain man,' said she, 'that doest *in vain assay.*'" ("Assay" appears at end of line 5, to rhyme with line 7's "decay.")
"My verse shall *eternize your rare virtues.*"	"My verse *your virtues rare shall eternize.*" ("Eternize" appears at end of line 11 to rhyme with line 9's "devise.")
"Where whenas death shall *subdue all the world,* / Our love shall live, and *later renew life.*"	"Where whenas death shall *all the world subdue,* / Our love shall live, and *later life renew.*" (Rhyming words "subdue" and "renew" are placed at ends of lines.)

To make sure the metrical pattern stresses certain words, the poet occasionally moves a word out of conventional order and places it in a stressed position. The following comparison illustrates this technique.

----

[1] *strand:* Beach.
[2] *eek:* Also, indeed.
[3] *quod:* Said.

Conventional Word Order	Inverted Sequence
"But *the waves came* and washed it away."	"But *came the waves* and washed it away." (Stress in line 2 falls on "waves" rather than on "the.")

As the above comparisons show, Spenser's adjustments in syntax are motivated at least in part by a desire to preserve his sonnet's rhyme and meter.

The next poem does more than simply invert word order; it presents an intentionally disordered syntax.

E. E. CUMMINGS (1894–1962)

anyone lived in a pretty how town (1940)

anyone lived in a pretty how town
(with up so floating many bells down)
spring summer autumn winter
he sang his didn't he danced his did.

Women and men (both little and small)   5
cared for anyone not at all
they sowed their isn't they reaped their same
sun moon stars rain

children guessed (but only a few
and down they forgot as up they grew   10
autumn winter spring summer)
that noone loved him more by more

when by now and tree by leaf
she laughed his joy she cried his grief
bird by snow and stir by still   15
anyone's any was all to her

someones married their everyones
laughed their cryings and did their dance
(sleep wake hope and then) they
said their nevers they slept their dream   20

stars rain sun moon
(and only the snow can begin to explain
how children are apt to forget to remember
with up so floating many bells down)

one day anyone died i guess   25
(and noone stooped to kiss his face)
busy folk buried them side by side
little by little and was by was

all by all and deep by deep
and more by more they dream their sleep   30

noone and anyone earth by april
wish by spirit and if by yes.

Women and men (both dong and ding)
summer autumn winter spring
reaped their sowing and went their came   35
sun moon stars rain

Cummings, like Spenser, sometimes manipulates syntax in response to the demands of rhyme
and meter—for example, in line 10. But Cummings goes much further, using unconventional
syntax as part of a scheme that includes other unusual elements of the poem, such as its
unexpected departures from the musical metrical pattern (for example, in lines 3 and 8) and
from the rhyme scheme (for example, in lines 3 and 4) and its use of various parts of speech
in unfamiliar contexts. Together, these techniques give the poem a playful quality. The
refreshing disorder of the syntax (for instance, in lines 1–2, 10, and 24) adds to the poem's
whimsical effect.

FURTHER READING: Word Order

A. E. HOUSMAN (1859–1936)

To an Athlete Dying Young (1896)

The time you won your town the race
We chaired you through the market-place;
Man and boy stood cheering by,
And home we brought you shoulder-high.

Today, the road all runners come,   5
Shoulder-high we bring you home,
And set you at your threshold down,
Townsman of a stiller town.

Smart lad, to slip betimes away
From fields where glory does not stay,   10
And early though the laurel grows
It withers quicker than the rose.

Eyes the shady night has shut
Cannot see the record cut,
And silence sounds no worse than cheers   15
After earth has stopped the ears.

Now you will not swell the rout
Of lads that wore their honors out,
Runners whom renown outran
And the name died before the man.   20

So set, before its echoes fade,
The fleet foot on the sill of shade,
And hold to the low lintel up
The still-defended challenge-cup.

And round that early-laureled head   25
Will flock to gaze the strengthless dead,
And find unwithered on its curls
The garland briefer than a girl's.

Reading and Reacting

1. Where does the poem's meter or rhyme scheme require the poet to depart from conventional syntax?
2. Edit the poem so its word order is more conventional. Do your changes improve the poem?
3. JOURNAL ENTRY Who do you think the speaker might be? What might his relationship to the athlete be?

Related Works: "To the Virgins, to Make Much of Time" (p. 695), "Nothing Gold Can Stay" (p. 749), "Ex-Basketball Player" (p. 764), "Birmingham Sunday (September 15, 1963)" (p. 922)

CHARLES JENSEN (1977–   )

Poem in Which Words Have Been Left Out (2012)

—The "Miranda Rights," established 1966

You have the right to remain
anything you can and will be.

An attorney you cannot afford
will be provided to you.   5

You have silent will.
You can be against law.
You cannot afford one.

You remain silent. Anything you say
will be provided to you.

The right can and will be   10
against you. The right provided you.

Have anything you say be
right. Anything you say can be right.

Say you have the right attorney.
The right remain silent.   15

Be held. Court the one. Be provided.
You cannot be you.

Reading and Reacting

1. In the 1966 case of *Miranda v. Arizona*, the Supreme Court ruled that all suspects be advised of their rights. Look up the wording of the Miranda warning as it is used today. Then, identify specific lines of the poem that conform to and depart from this wording.
2. How is the word *right* used in this poem? What meanings does it have in different contexts?
3. What "words have been left out" of this poem?
4. How do you interpret the poem's last line? Does it contradict the first two lines? Explain.

5. **JOURNAL ENTRY** What commentary do you think this poem is making about the American judicial system?

Related Works: "Accident" (p. 131), "Bullet in the Brain" (p. 496), "A Blessing from My Sixteen Years' Son" (p. 729), "The Community College Revises Its Curriculum in Response to Changing Demographics" (p. 987), *Nine Ten* (p. 1108), *Trifles* (p. 1604)

✔ **CHECKLIST** **Writing about Word Choice and Word Order**

Word Choice

☐ Which words are of key importance in the poem? What is the denotative meaning of each of these key words?

☐ Which key words have neutral connotations? Which have negative connotations? Which have positive connotations? Beyond its literal meaning, what does each word suggest?

☐ Why is each word chosen instead of a synonym? (For example, is the word chosen for its sound? its connotation? its relationship to other words in the poem? its contribution to the poem's metrical pattern?)

☐ What other words could be effectively used in place of words now in the poem? How would substitutions change the poem's meaning?

☐ Are any words repeated? Why?

Levels of Diction

☐ How would you characterize the poem's level of diction? Why is this level of diction used? Is it appropriate?

☐ Does the poem mix different levels of diction? If so, why?

Word Order

☐ Is the poem's word order conventional, or are words arranged in unexpected order?

☐ What is the purpose of the unusual word order? (For example, does it preserve the poem's meter or rhyme scheme? Does it highlight particular sound correspondences? Does it place emphasis on a particular word or phrase? Does it reflect the speaker's mood?)

☐ How would the poem's impact change if conventional syntax were used?

WRITING SUGGESTIONS: Word Choice, Word Order

1. Reread the two poems in this chapter by E. E. Cummings—"in Just-" (p. 719) and "anyone lived in a pretty how town" (p. 734). If you like, you may also read one or two additional poems in this book by Cummings. Do you believe Cummings chose words primarily for their sound? for their appearance on the page? What other factors might have influenced his choices?

2. The tone of "We Real Cool" (p. 730) is flat and unemotional; the problem on which it focuses, however, is serious. Expand this concise poem into a few paragraphs that retain the poem's informal, colloquial tone but use more detailed, more emotional language to communicate the hopeless situation of the speaker and his friends. Include dialogue as well as narrative.

3. Reread "Living in Sin" (p. 717) and "The English Canon" (p. 725), and choose one or two other poems in this book whose speaker is a woman. Compare the speakers' levels of diction and choice of words. What does their language reveal about their lives?

4. Analyze the choice of words and the level of diction in several poems in this book that express social or political criticism. Poems that might work well include Claude McKay's "If We Must Die" (p. 1003) and Louise Erdrich's "Indian Boarding School: The Runaways" (p. 986).

5. Consider the words and expressions used by the speaker to describe her teenage son in "A Blessing from My Sixteen Years' Son" (p. 729). Choose several other works in this text that focus on teenagers, and compare the language used to characterize them with Karr's use of language in this poem.

CHAPTER 26

IMAGERY

Octavio Paz
Steve Northup/The LIFE Images
Collection/Getty Images

Ezra Pound
AP Images

William Carlos Williams
John D. Schiff/Bettmann/Corbis

Source: ©Steven Flanders

JANE FLANDERS (1940–2001)

Cloud Painter (1984)

Suggested by the life and art of John Constable[1]

At first, as you know, the sky is incidental—
a drape, a backdrop for trees and steeples.
Here an oak clutches a rock (already he works outdoors),

[1] *John Constable:* British painter (1776–1837) noted for his landscapes.

a wall buckles but does not break,
water pearls through a lock, a haywain[2] trembles.   5

The pleasures of landscape are endless. What we see
around us should be enough.
Horizons are typically high and far away.

Still, clouds let us drift and remember. He is, after all,
a miller's son, used to trying   10
to read the future in the sky, seeing instead
ships, horses, instruments of flight.
Is that his mother's wash flapping on the line?
His schoolbook, smudged, illegible?

In this period the sky becomes significant.   15
Cloud forms are technically correct—mares' tails,
sheep-in-the-meadow, thunderheads.
You can almost tell which scenes have been interrupted
by summer showers.

Now his young wife dies.   20
His landscapes achieve belated success.
He is invited to join the Academy. I forget
whether he accepts or not.

In any case, the literal forms give way
to something spectral, nameless. His palette shrinks   25
to gray, blue, white—the colors of charity.

Horizons sink and fade,
trees draw back till they are little more than frames,
then they too disappear.

Finally the canvas itself begins to vibrate   30
with waning light,
as if the wind could paint.
And we too, at last, stare into a space
which tells us nothing,
except that the world can vanish along with our need for it.   35

Because the purpose of poetry—and, for that matter, of all literature—is to expand the perception of readers, poets appeal to the senses. In "Cloud Painter," Jane Flanders uses **images**, such as the mother's wash on the line and the smudged schoolbook, to enable readers to visualize particular scenes in John Constable's early paintings. (For additional poems written in response to works of art, see the "Poetry Sampler: Poetry and Art," p. PS1). Clouds are described so readers can picture them—"mares' tails, / sheep-in-the-meadow, thunderheads." Thus, "Cloud Painter" is not only about the work of John Constable but also about

---

[2]*haywain:* An open horse-drawn wagon for carrying hay.

John Constable (1776–1837). *Landscape, Noon, The Haywain.* 1821. Oil on canvas,
130½ × 185½ cm. London, National Gallery.
The Hay Wain, 1821 (oil on canvas), Constable, John (1776–1837) / National Gallery, London, UK / Bridgeman Images

the ability of an artist—poet or painter—to call up images in the minds of an audience. To achieve this end, a poet uses **imagery,** language that evokes a physical sensation produced by one or more of the five senses—sight, hearing, taste, touch, smell.

Although the effect can be complex, the way images work is simple: when you read the word *red,* your memory of the various red things that you have seen determines how you picture the image. In addition, the word *red* may have **connotations**—emotional associations that define your response. A red sunset, for example, can have a positive connotation or a negative one, depending on whether it is associated with the end of a perfect day or with air pollution. By choosing images carefully, poets not only create pictures in a reader's mind but also create a great number of imaginative associations. These associations help poets to establish the **atmosphere** or **mood** of the poem. The image of softly falling snow in "Stopping by Woods on a Snowy Evening" (p. 9), for example, creates a quiet, almost mystical mood.

Readers come to a poem with their own unique experiences, so an image in a poem does not suggest exactly the same thing to all readers. In "Cloud Painter," for example, the poet presents the image of an oak tree clutching a rock. Although most readers will probably see a picture that is generally consistent with the one the poet sees, no two images will be identical. Every reader will have his or her own distinct mental image of a tree clinging to a rock; some images will be remembered experiences, whereas others will be imaginative creations. Some readers may even be familiar enough with the work of the painter John Constable to visualize a particular tree clinging to a particular rock in one of his paintings. By conveying what the poet imagines, images open readers' minds to perceptions and associations different from—and possibly more original and complex than—their own.

One advantage of imagery is its extreme economy. A few carefully chosen words enable poets to evoke a range of emotions and reactions. In the following poem, William Carlos Williams uses simple visual images to create a rich and compelling picture.

John D. Schiff/© Bettmann/Corbis

WILLIAM CARLOS WILLIAMS (1883–1963)

Red Wheelbarrow (1923)

so much depends
upon

a red wheel
barrow

glazed with rain   5
water

beside the white
chickens

What is immediately apparent in this poem is its verbal economy. The poet does not tell readers what the barnyard smells like or what sounds the animals make. In fact, he does not even present a detailed picture of the scene. How large is the wheelbarrow? What is its condition? How many chickens are in the barnyard? In this poem, the answers to these questions are not important.

Even without answering these questions, the poet is able to use simple imagery to create a scene on which, he says, "so much depends." The wheelbarrow establishes a momentary connection between the poet and his world. Like a still-life painting, the red wheelbarrow beside the white chickens gives order to a world that is full of seemingly unrelated objects. In this poem, the poet suggests that our ability to perceive the objects of this world gives our lives meaning and that our ability to convey our perceptions to others is central to our lives as well as to poetry.

Images enable poets to present ideas that would be difficult to convey in any other way. One look at a dictionary will illustrate that concepts such as *beauty* and *mystery* are so abstract that they are difficult to define, let alone to discuss in specific terms. However, by choosing an image or a series of images to embody these ideas, poets can effectively make their feelings known, as Ezra Pound does in the two-line poem that follows.

AP Images

EZRA POUND (1885–1972)

In a Station of the Metro (1916)

The apparition of these faces in the crowd;
Petals on a wet, black bough.

This poem is almost impossible to paraphrase because the information it communicates is less important than the feelings

Paris Metro station platform
Hulton Archive/ Archive Photos/Getty Images

associated with this information. The poem's title indicates that the first line is meant to suggest a group of people standing in a station of the Paris subway. The scene, however, is presented not as a clear picture but as an "apparition," suggesting that it is unexpected or even dreamlike. In contrast with the image of the subway platform is the image of the people's faces as flower petals on the dark branch of a tree. Thus, the subway platform—dark, cold, wet, subterranean (associated with baseness, death, and hell)—is juxtaposed with flower petals—delicate, pale, radiant, lovely (associated with the ideal, life, and heaven). These contrasting images, presented without comment, bear the entire weight of the poem.

Although images can be strikingly visual, they can also appeal to the senses of hearing, smell, taste, and touch. The following poem uses images of sound and taste as well as sight.

GARY SNYDER (1930–   )

Some Good Things to Be Said for the Iron Age (1970)

A ringing tire iron
    dropped on the pavement
Whang of a saw
brusht on limbs
the taste   5
of rust

Here Snyder presents two commonplace aural images: the ringing of a tire iron and the sound of a saw. These somewhat ordinary images gain power, however, through their visual isolation on separate lines in the poem. Together they produce a harsh and jarring chord that creates a sense of uneasiness in the reader. This poem does more than present sensory images, though; it also conveys the speaker's interpretations of these images. The last two lines imply not only that the time in which we live (the Iron Age) is base and mundane, but also that it is declining, decaying into an age of rust. The title of the poem makes an ironic comment, suggesting that compared to the time that is approaching, the age of iron may be "good." Thus, in the mind of the poet, ordinary events gain added significance, and images that spring from everyday experience become sources of insight.

Much visual imagery is **static**, freezing the moment and thereby giving it the timeless quality of painting or sculpture. ("Red Wheelbarrow" presents such a tableau, and so does "In a Station of the Metro.") In contrast, some imagery is **kinetic**, conveying a sense of motion or change.

WILLIAM CARLOS WILLIAMS (1883–1963)

The Great Figure (1938)

Among the rain
and lights
I saw the figure
in gold
on a red   5
firetruck
moving
tense
unheeded
to gong clangs   10
siren howls
and wheels rumbling
through the dark city.

Commenting on "The Great Figure" in his autobiography, Williams explained that while walking in New York, he heard the sound of a fire engine. As he turned the corner, he saw a golden figure 5 on a red background speed by. The impression was so forceful that he immediately jotted down a poem about it. In the poem, Williams attempts to recreate the sensation the figure 5 made as it moved into his consciousness. The poet presents images in the order in which he perceived them: first the 5, and then the red fire truck howling and clanging into the darkness. Thus, "The Great Figure" uses images of sight, sound, and movement to convey the poet's experience. The American painter Charles Demuth was fascinated by the poem. Working closely with Williams, he attempted to capture the poem's kinetic energy in a painting.

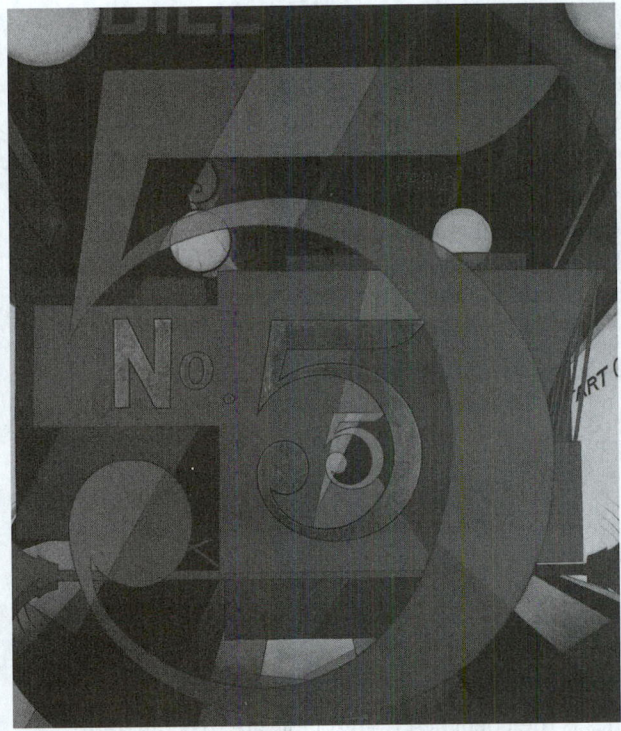

Charles Henry Demuth (1883–1935). *The Figure 5 in Gold*. Oil on
composition board, 36 × 29¾ in.
The Metropolitan Museum of Art/Image source/Art Resource, NY

NOTE A special use of imagery, called **synesthesia**, occurs when one sense is described
in terms of another sense—for instance, when a sound is described with color. When people say they are feeling *blue* or describe music as *hot* or *smooth*, they are using synesthesia.

FURTHER READING: Imagery

DAVID TRINIDAD (1953–   )

9773 Comanche Ave. (2010)

In color photographs, my childhood house looks
fresh as an uncut sheet cake—
pale yellow buttercream, ribbons of white trim

squeezed from the grooved tip of a pastry tube.
Whose dream was this confection?   5
This suburb of identical, pillow-mint homes?

The sky, too, is pastel. Children roller skate
down the new sidewalk. Fathers stake young trees.
Mothers plan baby showers and Tupperware parties.

The Avon Lady treks door to door.   10
Six or seven years old, I stand on the front porch,
hand on the decorative cast-iron trellis that frames it,

squinting in California sunlight,
striped short-sleeved shirt buttoned at the neck.
I sit in the backyard (this picture's black-and-white),   15

my Flintstones playset spread out on the grass.
I arrange each plastic character, each dinosaur,
each palm tree and round "granite" house.

Half a century later, I barely recognize it
when I search the address on Google Maps   20
and, via "Street view," find myself face to face—

foliage overgrown, facade remodeled and painted
a drab brown. I click to zoom: light hits
one of the windows. I can almost see what's inside.

Reading and Reacting

1. What two scenes is the poem describing? How are they different?
2. What is the main theme of this poem?
3. What different kinds of images does the poem present? How do they reinforce the central theme of the poem?
4. To what senses do the images of the poem appeal?
5. **Journal Entry** Search your address on Google Maps. How would you describe what you see?

Related Works: "The Secret Lion" (p. 180), "Evolution of My Block" (p. 808), "American Haiku" (p. 836), "Spring and All" (p. 842)

FERNANDO PESSOA (AS RICARDO REIS) (1888–1935)

Solemnly Over the Fertile Land (1927)

Translated by Richard Zenith

Solemnly over the fertile land
The brief and futile white cloud passes,
And for a black instant the fields are touched
    By a cold breeze

So too in my soul the slow thought soars   5
And darkens my mind, but I, like the field
That returns to itself, return to the day,
    The surface of life.

Reading and Reacting

1. What two things are being compared in the poem? Do you think that this comparison makes sense?
2. To what senses do the images in the poem appeal? Where does Pessoa use synesthesia?
3. What idea do you think Pessoa wants to convey in the poem's last line?

4. **JOURNAL ENTRY** Do you think that the tone of this poem is optimistic or pessimistic? Explain.

5. **CRITICAL PERSPECTIVE** In *The Book of Disquiet*, Pessoa makes the following observation:

> Life is an experimental journey undertaken involuntarily. It is a journey of the spirit through the material world and, since it is the spirit that travels, it is the spirit that is experienced. That is why there exist contemplative souls who have lived more intensely, more widely, more tumultuously than others who have lived their lives purely externally.

In what sense is "Solemnly Over the Fertile Land" an experimental journey?

Related Works: "Cloud Painter" (p. 739), "Pied Beauty" (p. 806), "Easter Wings" (p. 847), "To See a World in a Grain of Sand" (p. 961), "Death Be Not Proud" (p. 980), "God's Grandeur" (p. 992), "The Solitary Reaper" (p. 1026)

F. J. BERGMANN (1954–   )

An Apology (2003)

Forgive me
for backing over
and smashing
your red wheelbarrow.

It was raining   5
and the rear wiper
does not work on
my new plum-colored SUV.

I am also sorry
about the white   10
chickens.

Reading and Reacting

1. A **parody** is a literary work that imitates the style of another work for comic effect or ridicule. Bergmann's "An Apology" is a parody of William Carlos Williams's "Red Wheelbarrow" (p. 742). Why do you think Bergmann chose this poem to parody?
2. What aspects of "Red Wheelbarrow" does Bergmann parody? Do you think these elements deserve to be parodied, or do you think Bergmann's parody is unjustified or unfair?
3. Do you think Bergmann's purpose is to ridicule "Red Wheelbarrow" or just to amuse his readers? Explain.

4. **JOURNAL ENTRY** Write a parody of another poem in this book. Make sure you decide in advance what elements of the poem you want to parody.

5. **CRITICAL PERSPECTIVE** Blogger and critic Kerry Michael Wood observes that some readers think that critics have read too much into "The Red Wheelbarrow." According to him, however, "The Red Wheelbarrow" is a "sparkling gem" of the imagist school of poetry that "insisted on 'no ideas but in things.'"

Do you agree or disagree with Wood's assessment? Explain.

Related Works: "A Hunger Artist" (p. 151), "Red Wheelbarrow" (p. 742), "My mistress' eyes are nothing like the sun" (p. 754)

HART CRANE (1899–1932)

Echoes (1917)

1

Slivers of rain upon the pane,
Jade-green with sunlight, melt and flow
Upward again:—they leave no stain
Of all the storm an hour ago.

2

Over the hill a last cloud dips   5
And disappears, and I should go
As silently but that your lips
Are warmed with a redder glow.

3

Fresh and fragile, your arms now
Are circles of cool roses,—so . . .   10
In opal pools beneath your brow
I dream we quarreled long, long ago.

Reading and Reacting

1. What images does Crane use to describe the storm? What qualities of the storm does he stress?
2. "Echoes" consists of three stanzas. What ideas are presented in each stanza?
3. What do you think the poem's title means? In what sense does this poem deal with echoes?
4. How does the poem's last line suggest what happened before the storm? Is the speaker referring to a literal storm or to something else?
5. **JOURNAL ENTRY** Crane uses a metaphor in stanza 3. Find this metaphor and explain its significance.

Related Works: "Love and Other Catastrophes: A Mix Tape" (p. 127), "The Storm" (p. 273), "Porphyria's Lover" (p. 696), "To His Coy Mistress" (p. 776), "Four Haiku" (p. 835), "Parting at Morning" (p. 899)

LOLA RIDGE (1873–1941)

Wall Street at Night (1920)

Long vast shapes . . . cooled and flushed through with darkness . . .
Lidless windows
Glazed with a flashy luster
From some little pert café chirping up like a sparrow.
And down among iron guts   5
Piled silver
Throwing gray spatter of light . . . pale without heat . . .
Like the pallor[1] of dead bodies.

Reading and Reacting

1. What are the "long vast shapes" that the speaker mentions in line 1?
2. Find examples of **similes**, **metaphors**, and **personification**. How do these figures of speech reinforce the poem's theme?
3. What possible meanings could the poem's title have?
4. **JOURNAL ENTRY** This poem was written in 1893, a year when there was a serious economic depression in the United States. What images in "Wall Street at Night" suggest this economic turmoil?

Related Works: "Discovering America" (p. 135), "A Worn Path" (p. 463), "The World Is Too Much with Us" (p. 692), "The City Planners" (p. 722).

ROBERT FROST (1874–1963)

Nothing Gold Can Stay (1923)

Nature's first green is gold,
Her hardest hue to hold.
Her early leaf's a flower;
But only so an hour.
Then leaf subsides to leaf.   5
So Eden sank to grief.
So dawn goes down to day.
Nothing gold can stay.

[1]*pallor:* Paleness.

Painting of the Garden of Eden
© SuperStock

Reading and Reacting

1. What central idea does this poem express?
2. What do you think the first line of the poem means? In what sense is this line ironic?
3. What is the significance of the colors green and gold in this poem? What do these colors have to do with "Eden" and "dawn"?

4. **Journal Entry** How do the various images in the poem prepare readers for the last line? Do you think the title spoils the impact of the last line?

5. **Critical Perspective** In "The Figure a Poem Means," the introduction to the first edition of his *Collected Poems* (1930), Frost laid out a theory of poetry:

   > It begins in delight, it inclines to the impulse, it assumes direction with the first line laid down, it runs a course of lucky events, and ends in a clarification of life—not necessarily a great clarification . . . but a momentary stay against confusion. . . . Like a piece of ice on a hot stove the poem must ride on its own melting. . . . Read it a hundred times: it will forever keep its freshness as a metal keeps its fragrance. It can never lose its sense of a meaning that once unfolded by surprise as it went.

   Explain how Frost's remarks apply to "Nothing Gold Can Stay."

Related Works: "The Secret Lion" (p. 180), "Araby" (p. 361), "Greasy Lake" (p. 569), "Shall I compare thee to a summer's day?" (p. 758), "God's Grandeur" (p. 992)

JEAN TOOMER (1894–1967)

Reapers (1923)

Black reapers with the sound of steel on stones
Are sharpening scythes. I see them place the hones[1]
In their hip-pockets as a thing that's done,
And start their silent swinging, one by one.
Black horses drive a mower through the weeds,   5
And there, a field rat, startled, squealing bleeds,
His belly close to ground. I see the blade,
Blood-stained, continue cutting weeds and shade.

Reading and Reacting

1. What determines the order in which the speaker arranges the images in this poem? At what point does he comment on these images?

2. The first four lines of the poem seem to suggest that the workers are content. What image contradicts this impression? How does it do so?

3. What ideas are traditionally associated with the image of the reaper? the scythe? the harvest? (To answer these questions, you may want to consult a reference source, such as <http://www.symbols.com>.) In what way does the speaker rely on these conventional associations to help him convey his ideas? Can you appreciate the poem without understanding these associations?

4. **JOURNAL ENTRY** Who do you think the speaker might be? Why?

5. **CRITICAL PERSPECTIVE** As Brian Joseph Benson and Mabel Mayle Dillard point out in their 1980 study *Jean Toomer*, the poet disagreed with some other artists of the Harlem Renaissance choosing not to focus on "Negro" themes for a primarily black audience but rather to try to make his work universal in scope.

   Do you think he has achieved this goal in "Reapers"?

Related Works: "A Worn Path" (p. 463), "The Negro Speaks of Rivers" (p. 916), "Because I could not stop for Death—" (p. 973), "The Solitary Reaper" (p. 1026)

KOBAYASHI ISSA (1763–1827)

Haiku*

Not yet having become a Buddha,
The ancient pine-tree
Idly dreaming

---

[1]*hones:* Stones used to sharpen cutting instruments
*Publication date unavailable

Reading and Reacting

1. Buddhists believe that every person goes through cycles of death and rebirth until he or she reaches the state of nirvana. A key element in achieving this state is the extinction of all desire. In line 1 of the poem, who (or what) has not yet achieved nirvana and become a Buddha?

2. What two images are being compared in the poem? What insight or spiritual message is suggested by this comparison?

3. What is the tone of this poem? Do you think the speaker intends to be taken literally?

4. **JOURNAL ENTRY** Read the definition of *haiku* on page 834. In what respects is this poem a haiku? How is it unlike traditional haiku?

5. **CRITICAL PERSPECTIVE** In his essay series *Confessions of a Translator*, David G. Lanoue writes the following about Kobayashi Issa's haiku:

> Though Japanese children are made to memorize it, this haiku is no mere child's poem. It not only vocalizes Issa's Buddhist compassion for, and sense of karmic connection with, sentient life, it hints of a political meaning.

In what sense is this poem "political"? How does it express the Buddhist idea of "compassion for all life"?

Related Works: "Gryphon" (p. 250), "A Worn Path" (p. 463), "Four Haiku" (p. 835), "American Haiku" (p. 836), "Girl Powdering Her Neck" (p. PS7).

N. SCOTT MOMADAY (1934–   )

Long Shadows at Dulce (1976)

1.

September is a long
Illusion of itself;
The elders bide their time.

2.

The sheep camps are lively
With children. The slim girls,   5
The limber girls, recline.

3.

November is the flesh
And blood of the black bear,
Dusk its bone and marrow.

4.

In the huddled horses   10
That know of perfect cold
There is calm, like sorrow.

Reading and Reacting

1. What is the subject of each of the four stanzas of the poem? Could each one of these stanzas be considered a separate poem? Explain.
2. What does the speaker mean when he says, "September is a long / illusion of itself"?
3. Momaday wrote "Long Shadows at Dulce" after working for a short time as a school-teacher at Dulce, a small town on the Jicarilla Apache Reservation in Northern New Mexico. What images attempt to convey the character of Dulce?
4. **JOURNAL ENTRY** What things do you associate with September and November? How are they similar and different from the associations made by the speaker?

Related Works: "This Is What It Means to Say Phoenix, Arizona" (p. 278), "Where Mountain Lion Lay Down with Deer" (p. 682), "Evolution" (p. 699), "9773 Comanche Ave." (p. 745)

FREDERICK MORGAN (1922–2004)

The Busses (1995)

From our corner window
rainy winter mornings
nudging their way down Park
moistly glowing, puddled by the rain.

Stopping at doorways here and there   5
where children climb aboard
they merge into the traffic's flow
and dwindle from our sight.

We watch—then turn away,
and when in changing light   10
we look again, we see a stream
dark and serene in China,
down which sleek goldfish dart and gleam.

Reading and Reacting

1. Who is the speaker? Why do you think he uses the first-person plural pronoun *we*?
2. What words in the poem rhyme? What ideas do these rhyming words emphasize?
3. In the first two stanzas of the poem, the speaker describes school busses picking up children—probably along Park Avenue in New York City. In the third stanza, the imagery abruptly changes. How does this change expand the poem's meaning?
4. **JOURNAL ENTRY** What point is this poem making? How does the image in the last stanza help make this point?

Related Works: "The Secret Lion" (p. 180), "How to Talk to Girls at Parties" (p. 214), "Red Wheelbarrow" (p. 742), "In a Station of the Metro" (p. 742), "For Once, Then, Something" (p. 853), "Cézanne's Ports" (p. PS4)

WILLIAM SHAKESPEARE (1564–1616)

Red and white damasked rose
RMN-Grand Palais / Art Resource, NY

My mistress' eyes are nothing like the sun (1609)

My mistress' eyes are nothing like the sun;
Coral is far more red than her lips' red;
If snow be white, why then her breasts are dun;
If hairs be wires, black wires grow on her head.
I have seen roses damasked red and white,   5
But no such roses see I in her cheeks;
And in some perfumes is there more delight
Than in the breath that from my mistress reeks.
I love to hear her speak, yet well I know
That music hath a far more pleasing sound;   10
I grant I never saw a goddess go:
My mistress, when she walks, treads on the ground.
    And yet, by heaven, I think my love as rare
    As any she, belied with false compare.

Reading and Reacting

1. What point does Shakespeare make in the first twelve lines of his sonnet?
2. What point does the rhymed couplet at the end of the poem make?
3. How is Shakespeare's imagery like and unlike that of traditional love poems? For example, how is the imagery in this poem different from that in Elizabeth Barrett Browning's "How Do I Love Thee?" (p. 899).

4. **JOURNAL ENTRY** How do you think the woman to whom the poem is addressed will react?

5. **CRITICAL PERSPECTIVE** During the Renaissance, poets commonly used the "Petrarchan conceit" to praise their lovers. In this type of metaphor, the author draws elaborate comparisons between his beloved and one or more dissimilar things. According to critic Felicia Jean Steele, "Traditional readings of Shakespeare's Sonnet 130 argue that Shakespeare cunningly employs Petrarchan imagery while deliberately undermining it."

    How does this poem use the Petrarchan conceit? How does it undercut this convention?

Related Works: "A&P" (p. 238), "The Storm" (p. 273), "General Review of the Sex Situation" (p. 901), *The Brute* (p. 1048)

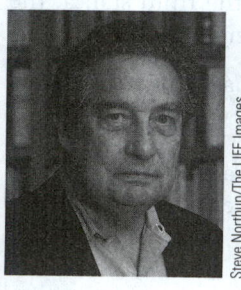

Steve Northup/The LIFE Images Collection/Getty Images

OCTAVIO PAZ (1914–1998)

Daybreak (1969)

Hands and lips of wind
heart of water
            eucalyptus
campground of the clouds

the life that is born every day   5
the death that is born every life

I rub my eyes:
the sky walks the land

Reading and Reacting

1. What are the connotations of the word *daybreak*?
2. What images does the speaker use to evoke daybreak? What other images could he
   have used?
3. The poem is visually divided into three parts. What idea does each part express?

4. **JOURNAL ENTRY** How would you describe the tone of this poem? How do the images
   help establish this tone?

Related Works: "Haiku" (p. 751), "Spring and All" (p. 842), "The Windhover" (p. 894),
"Parting at Morning" (p. 899), "Anecdote of the Jar" (p. 1016)

OCTAVIO PAZ (1914–1998)

Nightfall (1969)

What sustains it,
half-open, the clarity of nightfall,
the light let loose in the gardens?

All the branches,
conquered by the weight of birds,   5
lean toward the darkness.

Pure, self-absorbed moments
still gleam
on the fences.

Receiving night,   10
the groves become
hushed fountains.

A bird falls,
the grass grows dark,
edges blur, lime is black,   15
the world is less credible

Reading and Reacting

1. Does the speaker present nightfall as something that has positive or negative connotations? Explain.
2. Each of the five stanzas in the poem presents an image. What feature of nightfall does
   each image describe?

3. What does the speaker mean in the last line when he says that nightfall makes the world "less credible"?

4. JOURNAL ENTRY What images do you associate with nightfall? How are these images like and unlike those in the poem?

5. CRITICAL PERSPECTIVE The poetry critic Helen Vendler noted the following about the relationships between reality and fantasy in the work of Octavio Paz:

> For Paz, poetry is a brink, a precipice, an abyss, where silent before a void, the poet leaves historical time to reenter the time of desire, a time always with us, for which our myths of the Golden Age are only a representation.

How do "Daybreak" and "Nightfall" "leave historical time" to "reenter a time of desire"? What is desired in these poems? How do these desires differ from waking desires?

Related Works: "Araby" (p. 361), "Gretel in Darkness" (p. 677), "Harlem" (p. 760), "Meeting at Night" (p. 898), "Ode to The West Wind" (p. 1013)

> ✔ **CHECKLIST   Writing about Imagery**
>
> ☐ Do the images in the poem appeal to the sense of sight? hearing? taste? touch? smell?
>
> ☐ Does the poem depend on a single image or on several different images?
>
> ☐ Does the poem depend on a group of related images?
>
> ☐ What details make the images memorable?
>
> ☐ What mood do the images create?
>
> ☐ Are the images static or kinetic?
>
> ☐ How do the poem's images help to convey its theme?
>
> ☐ How effective are the images? How do they enhance your enjoyment of the poem?

WRITING SUGGESTIONS: Imagery

1. Read the definition of **haiku** on page 751. How are short poems such as "Some Good Things to Be Said for the Iron Age" (p. 743) and "In a Station of the Metro" (p. 742) like and unlike haiku?

2. After rereading "Cloud Painter" (p. 739) and "The Great Figure" (p. 744), read "Musée des Beaux Arts" (p. 876) and study the corresponding paintings *Landscape, Noon,* the *Haywain* (p. 741), *The Figure 5 in Gold* (p. 745), and *Landscape with the Fall of Icarus* (p. 877). Then, write an essay in which you draw some conclusions about the differences between artistic and poetic images. If you like, you may also consider the pictures and poems in the "Poetry Sampler: Poetry and Art," PS1–PS8.

3. Analyze the role of imagery in the depiction of the parent/child relationships in "My Papa's Waltz" (p. 885), "Digging" (p. 886), and "A Woman Mourned by Daughters" (p. 890). How does each poem's imagery convey the nature of the relationship it describes?

4. Write an essay in which you discuss the color imagery in "Nothing Gold Can Stay" (p. 749) and "My misstress' eyes are nothing like the sun" (p. 754). In what way does color reinforce the themes of these poems?

CHAPTER 27

FIGURES OF SPEECH

Martín Espada
AP Images/Daily Hampshire
Gazette, Kevin Gutting

Nancy Mercado
Ricardo Muniz

Sylvia Plath
Cleveland State University
Library / Everett Collection

Marge Piercy
AP Photo/Ben Barnhart

Source: ©Bettmann/Corbis

WILLIAM SHAKESPEARE (1564–1616)

Shall I compare thee to a summer's day? (1609)

Shall I compare thee to a summer's day?
Thou art more lovely and more temperate.
Rough winds do shake the darling buds of May,
And summer's lease hath all too short a date.
Sometime too hot the eye of heaven shines,   5
And often is his gold complexion dimmed;
And every fair from fair sometimes declines,
By chance, or nature's changing course, untrimmed.

But thy eternal summer shall not fade,
Nor lose possession of that fair thou ow'st;[1]   10
Nor shall death brag thou wand'rest in his shade,
When in eternal lines to time thou grow'st.
    So long as men can breathe or eyes can see,
    So long lives this, and this gives life to thee.

Although writers experiment with language in all kinds of literary works, poets in particular recognize the power of a figure of speech to take readers beyond the literal meaning of a word. For this reason, **figures of speech**—expressions that use words to achieve effects beyond the power of ordinary language—are more prominent in poetry than in other kinds of writing. For example, the sonnet above compares a loved one to a summer's day in order to make the point that, unlike the fleeting summer, the loved one will—within the poem—remain forever young. But this sonnet goes beyond the obvious equation (loved one = summer's day): the speaker's assertion that his loved one will live forever in his poem actually says more about his confidence in his own talent and reputation (and about the power of language) than about the loved one's beauty.

Simile, Metaphor, and Personification

When William Wordsworth opens a poem with "I wandered lonely as a cloud" (p. 893), he conveys a good deal more than he would if he simply began, "I wandered, lonely." By comparing himself in his loneliness to a cloud, the speaker suggests that like the cloud he is a part of nature and that he too is drifting, passive, blown by winds, and lacking will or substance. Thus, by using a figure of speech, the poet can suggest a wide variety of feelings and associations in very few words.

The phrase "I wandered lonely as a cloud" is a **simile**, a comparison between two unlike items that uses *like* or *as*. When an imaginative comparison between two unlike items does not use *like* or *as*—that is, when it says "a *is* b" rather than "a is *like* b"—it is a **metaphor**.

Accordingly, when the speaker in Adrienne Rich's "Living in Sin" (p. 717) speaks of "daylight coming / like a relentless milkman up the stairs," she is using a strikingly original simile to suggest that daylight brings not the conventional associations of promise and awakening but rather a stale, never-ending routine that is greeted without enthusiasm. This idea is consistent with the rest of the poem, an account of an unfulfilling relationship. However, when the speaker in the Audre Lorde poem on page 761 says, "Rooming houses are old women," she uses a metaphor, equating two elements to stress their common associations with emptiness, transience, and hopelessness. At the same time, by identifying rooming houses as old women, Lorde is using **personification**, a special kind of comparison, closely related to metaphor, that gives life or human characteristics to inanimate objects or abstract ideas.

Sometimes, as in Wordsworth's "I wandered lonely as a cloud," a single brief simile or metaphor can be appreciated for what it communicates on its own. At other times, however, a simile or metaphor may be one of several related figures of speech that work together to convey a poem's meaning. The following poem, for example, presents a series of related similes. Together, they suggest the depth of the problem the poem explores in a manner that each individual simile could not do on its own.

---

[1] *that fair thou ow'st:* That beauty you possess.

Harlem street scene, 1957
AP Photo/Robert Kradin

LANGSTON HUGHES (1902–1967)

Harlem (1951)

What happens to a dream deferred?

Does it dry up
like a raisin in the sun?
Or fester like a sore—
And then run?   5
Does it stink like rotten meat?
Or crust and sugar over—
like a syrupy sweet?

Maybe it just sags
like a heavy load.   10

Or does it explode?

The dream to which Hughes alludes in this poem is the dream of racial equality. It is also the American Dream—and, by extension, any important unrealized dream. His speaker offers six tentative answers to the question asked in the poem's first line, and five of the six are presented as similes. As the poem unfolds, the speaker considers different alternatives: the dream can shrivel up and die, fester, decay, crust over—or sag under the weight of the burden those who hold the dream must carry. In each case, the speaker transforms an abstract entity—a dream—into a concrete item—a raisin in the sun, a sore, rotten meat, syrupy candy, a heavy load. The final line, italicized for emphasis, gains power less from what it says than from what it leaves unsaid. Unlike the other alternatives explored in the poem, *"Or does it explode?"* is not presented as a simile. Nevertheless, because of the pattern of figurative language the poem has established, readers can supply the other, unspoken half of the comparison: ". . . like a bomb."

Sometimes a single extended simile or extended metaphor is developed throughout a poem. The following poem develops an **extended simile**, comparing a poet to an acrobat.

LAWRENCE FERLINGHETTI (1919–   )

Constantly Risking Absurdity (1958)

Constantly risking absurdity
                and death
      whenever he performs
            above the heads
                of his audience   5
   the poet like an acrobat
            climbs on rime
              to a high wire of his own making
   and balancing on eyebeams
             above a sea of faces   10
     paces his way
         to the other side of day

performing entrechats
>   and sleight-of-foot tricks
and other high theatrics   15
>   and all without mistaking
>   any thing
>   for what it may not be

>   For he's the super realist
>   who must perforce perceive   20
>   taut truth
>   before the taking of each stance or step
in his supposed advance
>   toward that still higher perch
where Beauty stands and waits   25
>   with gravity
>   to start her death-defying leap

And he
>   a little charleychaplin man
>   who may or may not catch   30
her fair eternal form
>   spreadeagled in the empty air
>   of existence

In his extended comparison of a poet and an acrobat, Ferlinghetti characterizes the poet as a circus performer, at once swinging recklessly on a trapeze and balancing carefully on a tightrope.

What the poem suggests is that the poet, like an acrobat, works hard at his craft but manages to make it all look easy. Something of an exhibitionist, the poet is innovative and creative, taking impossible chances yet also building on traditional skills in his quest for truth and beauty. Moreover, like an acrobat, the poet is balanced "on eyebeams / above a sea of faces," for he too depends on audience reaction to help him keep his performance focused. The poet may be "the super realist," but he also has plenty of playful tricks up his sleeve: "entrechats / and sleight-of-foot tricks / and other high theatrics," including puns ("above the heads / of his audience"), unexpected rhyme ("climbs on rime"), alliteration ("taut truth"), coinages ("a little charleychaplin man"), and all the other linguistic acrobatics available to poets. (Even the arrangement of the poem's lines on the page suggests the acrobatics it describes.) Like these tricks, the poem's central simile is a whimsical one, perhaps suggesting that Ferlinghetti is poking fun at poets who take their craft too seriously. In any case, the simile helps him to illustrate the acrobatic possibilities of language in a fresh and original manner.

The following poem develops an **extended metaphor**, personifying rooming houses as old women.

AUDRE LORDE (1934–1992)

Rooming houses are old women (1968)

Rooming houses are old women
rocking dark windows into their whens
waiting incomplete circles

rocking
rent office to stoop to   5
community bathrooms to gas rings and
under-bed boxes of once useful garbage
city issued with a twice monthly check
and the young men next door
with their loud midnight parties   10
and fishy rings left in the bathtub
no longer arouse them
from midnight to mealtime no stops inbetween
light breaking to pass through jumbled up windows
and who was it who married the widow that Buzzie's
    son messed with?   15

To Welfare and insult form the slow shuffle
from dayswork to shopping bags
heavy with leftovers
Rooming houses
are old women waiting   20
searching
through darkening windows
the end or beginning of agony
old women seen through half-ajar doors
hoping   25
they are not waiting
but being
the entrance to somewhere
unknown and desired
but not new.   30

So closely does Lorde equate rooming houses and old women in this poem that at times it is difficult to tell which of the two is actually the poem's subject. Despite the poem's assertion, rooming houses are *not* old women; however, they are *comparable to* the old women who live there because their walls enclose a lifetime of disappointments as well as the physical detritus of life. Like the old women, rooming houses are in decline, rocking away their remaining years. And, like the houses they inhabit, these women's boundaries are fixed—"rent office to stoop to / community bathrooms to gas rings"—and their hopes and expectations are few. They are surrounded by other people's loud parties, but their own lives have been reduced to a "slow shuffle" to nowhere, a hopeless, frightened—and perhaps pointless—"waiting / searching." Over time, the women and the places in which they live have become one. By using an unexpected comparison between two seemingly unrelated entities, the poem illuminates both the essence of the rooming houses and the essence of their elderly occupants.

FURTHER READING: Simile, Metaphor, and Personification

ROBERT BURNS (1759–1796)

Oh, my love is like a red, red rose (1796)

Oh, my love is like a red, red rose
    That's newly sprung in June;

My love is like the melody
    That's sweetly played in tune.

So fair art thou, my bonny lass,   5
    So deep in love am I;
And I will love thee still, my dear,
    Till a' the seas gang[1] dry.

Till a' the seas gang dry, my dear,
    And the rocks melt wi' the sun;   10
And I will love thee still, my dear,
    While the sands o' life shall run.

And fare thee weel, my only love!
    And fare thee weel awhile!
And I will come again, my love   15
    Though it were ten thousand mile.

Reading and Reacting

1. Why does the speaker compare his love to a rose? What other simile is used in the poem? For what purpose is it used?
2. Why do you suppose Burns begins his poem with similes? Would moving them to the end change the poem's impact?
3. Where does the speaker seem to exaggerate the extent of his love? Why does he exaggerate? Do you think this exaggeration weakens the poem? Explain.

4. JOURNAL ENTRY Create ten original similes that begin with, "My love is like _____."

Related Works: "Araby" (p. 361), "Baca Grande" (p. 723), "My mistress' eyes are nothing like the sun" (p. 754), "To His Coy Mistress" (p. 776), "How Do I Love Thee?" (p. 899), *The Brute* (p. 1048)

AP Images/Jacques Brinon

N. SCOTT MOMADAY (1934–   )

Simile (1974)

What did we say to each other
that now we are as the deer
who walk in single file
with heads high
with ears forward   5
with eyes watchful
with hooves always placed on firm ground
in whose limbs there is latent flight

Reading and Reacting

1. In what sense are the speaker and the person he is speaking to like the deer he describes in this extended simile? In what sense are their limbs in "latent flight" (line 8)?

[1]*gang:* Go.

2. Without using similes or metaphors, paraphrase this poem.

3. This entire poem consists of a single sentence, but it has no punctuation. Do you see this as a problem? What punctuation marks, if any, would you add? Why?

4. **JOURNAL ENTRY** What do you suppose the speaker and the person he addresses might have said to each other to inspire the feelings described in this poem?

Related Works: "Long Shadows at Dulce" (p. 752), "Comparatives" (p. 803), "Let me not to the marriage of true minds" (p. 1012)

SYLVIA PLATH (1932–1963)

Metaphors (1960)

I'm a riddle in nine syllables,
An elephant, a ponderous house,
A melon strolling on two tendrils.
O red fruit, ivory, fine timbers!
This loaf's big with its yeasty rising.   5
Money's new-minted in this fat purse.
I'm a means, a stage, a cow in calf.
I've eaten a bag of green apples,
Boarded the train there's no getting off.

Reading and Reacting

1. The speaker in this poem is a pregnant woman. Do all the metaphors she uses to characterize herself seem appropriate? For instance, in what sense is the speaker "a means, a stage" (line 7)?

2. If you were going to expand this poem, what other metaphors (or similes) would you add?

3. What are the "nine syllables" to which the speaker refers in the poem's first line? What significance does the number *nine* have in terms of the poem's subject? in terms of its form?

4. **JOURNAL ENTRY** Would you say the speaker has a positive, negative, or neutral attitude toward her pregnancy? Which metaphors give you this impression?

Related Works: "I Stand Here Ironing" (p. 299), "A Blessing from My Sixteen Years' Son" (p. 729)

AP Images/Bill Ulrich

JOHN UPDIKE (1932–2009)

Ex-Basketball Player (1958)

Pearl Avenue runs past the high-school lot,
Bends with the trolley tracks, and stops, cut off
Before it has a chance to go two blocks,
At Colonel McComsky Plaza. Berth's Garage
Is on the corner facing west, and there,   5

1950s gas pumps

AP Images/Seth Perlman

Most days, you'll find Flick Webb, who helps Berth out.

Flick stands tall among the idiot pumps—
Five on a side, the old bubble-head style,
Their rubber elbows hanging loose and low.
One's nostrils are two S's, and his eyes   10
An E and O.[1] And one is squat, without
A head at all—more of a football type.

Once Flick played for the high-school team,
    the Wizards.
He was good: in fact, the best. In '46
He bucketed three hundred ninety points,   15
A county record still. The ball loved Flick.
I saw him rack up thirty-eight or forty
In one home game. His hands were like wild birds.

He never learned a trade, he just sells gas,
Checks oil, and changes flats. Once in a while,   20
As a gag, he dribbles an inner tube,
But most of us remember anyway.
His hands are fine and nervous on the lug wrench.
It makes no difference to the lug wrench, though.

Off work, he hangs around Mae's luncheonette.   25
Grease-gray and kind of coiled, he plays pinball,
Smokes those thin cigars, nurses lemon phosphates.
Flick seldom says a word to Mae, just nods
Beyond her face toward bright applauding tiers
Of Necco Wafers, Nibs, and Juju Beads.   30

Reading and Reacting

1. Explain the use of personification in the second stanza and in the poem's last two lines. What two elements make up the comparison in each figure of speech? In what sense are the two elements in each pair comparable?

2. What other figures of speech can you identify in the poem? How do these figures of speech work together to communicate the poem's central theme?

3. **JOURNAL ENTRY** Who do you think this poem's speaker might be? What is his attitude toward Flick Webb? Do you think Flick himself shares this assessment? Explain.

Related Works: "A&P" (p. 238), "Miss Brill" (p. 245), "To an Athlete Dying Young" (p. 735), "Sadie and Maud" (p. 792), *Fences* (p. 1548)

---

[1] *ESSO:* Former name of Exxon.

RANDALL JARRELL (1914–1965)

The Death of the Ball Turret Gunner[1] (1945)

From my mother's sleep I fell into the State
And I hunched in its belly till my wet fur froze.
Six miles from earth, loosed from its dream of life,
I woke to black flak and the nightmare fighters.
When I died they washed me out of the turret with a hose.   5

Gunner in ball turret
Source: ©Cape Canaveral Hangar, United States Air Force

Reading and Reacting

1. Who is the speaker? To what does he compare himself in the poem's first two lines? What words establish this comparison?

2. Contrast the speaker's actual identity with the one he creates for himself in lines 1–2. What elements of his actual situation do you think lead him to characterize himself as he does in these lines?

3. **JOURNAL ENTRY** Both this poem and "Dulce et Decorum Est" (p. 902) use figures of speech to describe the horrors of war. Which poem has a greater impact on you? How does the poem's figurative language contribute to this impact?

4. **CRITICAL PERSPECTIVE** In a 1974 article, Frances Ferguson criticizes "The Death of the Ball Turret Gunner," arguing that the poem "thoroughly manifests the lack of a middle between the gunner's birth and his death. . . . Because the poem presents a man who seems to have lived in order to die, we forget the fiction that he must have lived." However, in a 1978 explication, Patrick J. Horner writes that the "manipulation of time reveals the stunning brevity of the gunner's waking life and the State's total disregard for that phenomenon. . . . Because of the telescoping of time, [the poem] resonates with powerful feeling."

   With which critic do you agree? Do you see the "lack of a middle" as a positive or negative quality of this poem?

---

[1] *Ball turret gunner:* World War II machine gunner positioned upside-down in a plexiglass sphere in the belly of a bomber.

Related Works: "The Things They Carried" (p. 392), "The Soldier" (p. 904), from *In Time of War* (p. 906), "Terza Rima" (p. 908).

MARGE PIERCY (1936–   )

The Secretary Chant (1973)

My hips are a desk.
From my ears hang
chains of paper clips.
Rubber bands form my hair.
My breasts are wells of mimeograph ink.   5
My feet bear casters.
Buzz. Click.
My head is a badly organized file.
My head is a switchboard
where crossed lines crackle.   10
Press my fingers
and in my eyes appear
credit and debit.
Zing. Tinkle.
My navel is a reject button.   15
From my mouth issue canceled reams.
Swollen, heavy, rectangular
I am about to be delivered
of a baby
Xerox machine.   20
File me under W
because I wonce
was
a woman.

Secretaries in typing pool, 1956
© TopFoto / The Image Works

Reading and Reacting

1. Examine each of the poem's figures of speech. Do they all make reasonable comparisons, or are some far-fetched or hard to visualize? Explain the relationship between the secretary and each item with which she is compared.

2. **JOURNAL ENTRY** Using as many metaphors and similes as you can, write a "chant" about a job you have held.

3. **CRITICAL PERSPECTIVE** In a review of a recent collection of Piercy's poetry, critic Sandra Gilbert notes instances of "a kind of bombast" (pompous language) and remarks, "As most poets realize, political verse is almost the hardest kind to write."

    In what sense can "The Secretary Chant" be seen as "political verse"? Do you think Piercy successfully achieves her political purpose, or does she undercut it with "bombast"?

Related Works: "A Hunger Artist" (p. 151), "A&P" (p. 238), "Battle Royal" (p. 287), "The Carpet Factory" (p. 822), "Women" (p. 846), *Applicant* (p. 1076).

JOHN DONNE (1572–1631)

A Valediction: Forbidding Mourning (1611)

As virtuous men pass mildly away,
    And whisper to their souls to go,
Whilst some of their sad friends do say
    The breath goes now, and some say no:

So let us melt, and make no noise,   5
    No tear-floods, nor sigh-tempests move;
'Twere profanation of our joys
    To tell the laity[1] our love.

Moving of th' earth brings harms and fears;
    Men reckon what it did and meant;   10
But trepidation of the spheres,
    Though greater far, is innocent.

Dull sublunary lovers' love
    (Whose soul is sense) cannot admit
Absence, because it doth remove   15
    Those things which elemented it.

But we, by a love so much refined
    That ourselves know not what it is,
Inter-assurèd of the mind,
    Care less, eyes, lips, and hands to miss.   20

---

[1] *laity:* Here, "common people."

Our two souls, therefore, which are one,
    Though I must go, endure not yet
A breach, but an expansion,
    Like gold to airy thinness beat.

If they be two, they are two so   25
    As stiff twin compasses[2] are two:
Thy soul, the fixed foot, makes no show
    To move, but doth, if th' other do.

And though it in the center sit,
    Yet when the other far doth roam,   30
It leans and harkens after it,
    And grows erect as that comes home.

Such wilt thou be to me, who must,
    Like th' other foot, obliquely run;
Thy firmness makes my circle just,[3]   35
    And makes me end where I begun.

Engraving of compass

---

[2] *compasses:* V-shaped instruments used for drawing circles.
[3] *just:* Perfect.

Reading and Reacting

1. Beginning with line 25, the poem develops an extended metaphor that compares the speaker and his loved one to "twin compasses" (line 26), attached yet separate. Why is the compass (pictured on the previous page) an especially apt metaphor? What physical characteristics of the compass does the poet emphasize?

2. The poem uses other figures of speech to characterize both the lovers' union and their separation. To what other events does the speaker compare his separation from his loved one? To what other elements does he compare their attachment? Do you think these comparisons make sense?

3. **JOURNAL ENTRY** To what other object could Donne have compared his loved one and himself? Explain the logic of the extended metaphor you suggest.

4. **CRITICAL PERSPECTIVE** In *John Donne and the Metaphysical Poets* (1970), Judah Stampfer writes of this poem's "thin, dry texture, its stanzas of pinched music," noting that its form "has too clipped a brevity to qualify as a song" and that its "music wobbles on a dry, measured beat." Yet, he argues, "the poem comes choked with emotional power" because "the speaker reads as a naturally reticent man, leaving his beloved in uncertainty and deep trouble." Stampfer concludes, "Easy self-expression here would be self-indulgent, if not reprehensible. . . . For all his careful dignity, we feel a heart is breaking here."

   Do you find such emotional power in this highly intellectual poem?

Related Works: "To My Dear and Loving Husband" (p. 775), "How Do I Love Thee?" (p. 899), *A Doll House* (p. 1113), *Post-its* (p. 1176)

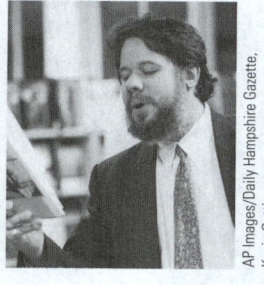

AP Images/Daily Hampshire Gazette, Kevin Gutting

MARTÍN ESPADA (1957–   )

My Father as a Guitar (2000)

The cardiologist prescribed
a new medication
and lectured my father
that he had to stop working.
And my father said: *I can't.*   5
The landlord won't let me.
The heart pills are dice
in my father's hand,
gambler who needs cash
by the first of the month.   10

On the night his mother died
in faraway Puerto Rico,
my father lurched upright in bed,
heart hammering
like the fist of a man at the door   15
with an eviction notice.

Minutes later,
the telephone sputtered
with news of the dead.

Sometimes I dream   20
my father is a guitar,
with a hole in his chest
where the music throbs
between my fingers.

Reading and Reacting

1. Where does this poem use simile? metaphor? personification?

2. What is the speaker's attitude toward his father? In what way does the poem's central comparison (between the father and a guitar) help the speaker express his feelings?

3. **JOURNAL ENTRY** Why do you suppose the speaker dreams that his father is a guitar? How might his dreams be related to his father's dreams about his own mother?

4. **CRITICAL PERSPECTIVE** In a review of one of Espada's earlier collections of poetry, Leslie Ullman discusses how the poet brings his characters to life:

   > The poems in this collection tell their stories and flesh out their characters deftly, without shrillness or rhetoric, and vividly enough to invite the reader into a shared sense of loss. Espada makes vanquished individuals and curtailed family histories present by offering us their remnants, their echoes, in such a way as to make us confront the ruined whole.

   Does "My Father as a Guitar" present the speaker's father in the way Ullman describes?

Related Works: "Nothing Gold Can Stay" (p. 749), "My Papa's Waltz" (p. 885), "Do not go gentle into that good night" (p. 891), *Proof* (p. 1180)

 ## Hyperbole and Understatement

Two additional kinds of figurative language, *hyperbole* and *understatement*, also give poets opportunities to suggest meaning beyond the literal level of language.

Hyperbole is intentional exaggeration—saying more than is actually meant. In the poem "Oh, my love is like a red, red rose" (p. 762), when the speaker says that he will love his lady until all the seas go dry, he is using hyperbole.

Understatement is the opposite—saying less than is meant. When the speaker in the poem "Fire and Ice" (p. 686), weighing two equally grim alternatives for the end of the world, says that "for destruction ice / Is also great / And would suffice," he is using understatement. In both cases, poets expect their readers to understand that their words are not to be taken literally.

By using hyperbole and understatement, poets enhance the impact of their poems. For example, poets can use hyperbole to convey exaggerated anger or graphic images of horror—and to ridicule and satirize as well as to inflame and shock. With understatement, poets can convey the same kind of powerful emotions subtly, without artifice or embellishment, thereby leading readers to read more closely than they might otherwise.

The emotionally charged poem that follows uses hyperbole to convey anger and bitterness that seem almost beyond the power of words.

SYLVIA PLATH (1932–1963)

Daddy (1965)

You do not do, you do not do
Any more, black shoe
In which I have lived like a foot
For thirty years, poor and white,
Barely daring to breathe or Achoo.   5

Daddy, I have had to kill you.
You died before I had time—
Marble-heavy, a bag full of God,
Ghastly statue with one grey toe
Big as a Frisco seal   10

And a head in the freakish Atlantic
Where it pours bean green over blue
In the waters off beautiful Nauset.
I used to pray to recover you.
Ach, du.[1]   15

In the German tongue, in the Polish town[2]
Scraped flat by the roller
Of wars, wars, wars.
But the name of the town is common.
My Polack friend   20

Says there are a dozen or two.
So I never could tell where you
Put your foot, your root,
I never could talk to you.
The tongue stuck in my jaw.   25

It stuck in a barb wire snare.
Ich, ich, ich, ich,[3]
I could hardly speak.
I thought every German was you.
And the language obscene   30

An engine, an engine
Chuffing me off like a Jew.

---

[1]*Ach, du:* "Ah, you" (German).

[2]*Polish town:* Grabôw, where Plath's father was born.

[3]*ich:* "I" (German).

A Jew to Dachau, Auschwitz, Belsen.[4]
I began to talk like a Jew.
I think I may well be a Jew.   35

The snows of the Tyrol, the clear beer of Vienna
Are not very pure or true.
With my gypsy ancestress and my weird luck
And my Taroc pack and my Taroc pack
I may be a bit of a Jew.   40

I have always been scared of *you*,
With your Luftwaffe,[5] your gobbledygoo.
And your neat moustache
And your Aryan eye, bright blue.
Panzer[6]-man, panzer-man, O You—   45

Not God but a swastika
So black no sky could squeak through.
Every woman adores a Fascist,
The boot in the face, the brute
Brute heart of a brute like you.   50

You stand at the blackboard, daddy,
In the picture I have of you,
A cleft in your chin instead of your foot
But no less a devil for that, no not
Any less the black man who   55

Bit my pretty red heart in two.
I was ten when they buried you.
At twenty I tried to die
And get back, back, back to you.
I thought even the bones would do.   60

But they pulled me out of the sack,
And they stuck me together with glue.
And then I knew what to do.
I made a model of you,
A man in black with a Meinkampf[7] look   65

And a love of the rack and the screw.
And I said I do, I do.
So daddy, I'm finally through.
The black telephone's off at the root,
The voices just can't worm through.   70

---

[4]*Dachau, Auschwitz, Belsen:* Nazi concentration camps.

[5]*Luftwaffe:* The German air force.

[6]*Panzer:* Protected by armor. The Panzer division was the German armored division.

[7]*Meinkampf: Mein Kampf* (My Struggle) is Adolf Hitler's autobiography.

If I've killed one man, I've killed two—
The vampire who said he was you
And drank my blood for a year,
Seven years, if you want to know.
Daddy, you can lie back now.   75

There's a stake in your fat black heart
And the villagers never liked you.
They are dancing and stamping on you.
They always *knew* it was you.
Daddy, daddy, you bastard, I'm through.   80

Nazi poster, 1941
Hulton Archive/Archive Photos/Getty Images

In her anger and frustration, the speaker sees herself as a helpless victim—a foot entrapped in a shoe, a Jew in a concentration camp—of her father's (and, later, her husband's) absolute tyranny. Thus, her hated father is characterized as a "black shoe," "a bag full of God," a "Ghastly statue," and, eventually, a Nazi, a torturer, the devil, a vampire. The poem "Daddy" is widely accepted by scholars as autobiographical, and the fact that Plath's own father was actually neither a Nazi nor a sadist (nor, obviously, the devil or a vampire) makes it clear that the figures of speech in the poem are wildly exaggerated. Even so, they may convey the poet's true feelings toward her father—and, perhaps, toward the patriarchal society in which she lived.

Plath uses hyperbole to communicate these emotions to readers who she knows cannot possibly feel the way she does. Her purpose, therefore, is not only to shock but also to enlighten, to persuade, and perhaps even to empower her readers. Throughout the poem, the inflammatory language is set in ironic opposition to the childish, affectionate term "Daddy"—most strikingly in the last line's choked out "Daddy, daddy, you bastard, I'm through." The result of the exaggerated rhetoric is a poem that is vivid and shocking. And, although some might believe that Plath's almost wild exaggeration undermines the poem's impact, others would argue that the powerful language is necessary to convey the extent of the speaker's rage.

Like "Daddy," the following poem describes a situation whose emotional impact is devastating. In this case, however, the poet does not use highly charged language; instead, she uses understatement, presenting her imagined scenario without embellishment.

EDNA ST. VINCENT MILLAY (1892–1950)

If I should learn, in some quite casual way (1931)

If I should learn, in some quite casual way,
That you were gone, not to return again—
Read from the back-page of a paper, say,
Held by a neighbor in a subway train,
How at a corner of this avenue   5
And such a street (so are the papers filled)
A hurrying man—who happened to be you—
At noon today had happened to be killed,
I should not cry aloud—could not cry
Aloud, or wring my hands in such a place—   10
I should but watch the station lights rush by
With a more careful interest on my face,
Or raise my eyes and read with greater care
Where to store furs and how to treat the hair.

Although this poem's speaker imagines a tragic scenario—receiving the news of her lover's death—her language is restrained. In the poem's first eight lines, words and expressions like "quite casual" (1), "say" (3), "this avenue / And such a street" (5–6), and "happened to be" (7, 8) convey a sense of randomness. The speaker's voice is detached and passive. In the remaining six lines, which describe her reaction to the news, she calmly explains her unwillingness to make a scene, telling what she will not do—"cry / Aloud, or wring my hands . . ." (9–10)—and expressing her determination to adopt an air of studied interest in the subway car's trivial advertisements. The poem's language and tone are consistently flat and unemotional, conveying a sense of detachment and resignation.

FURTHER READING: Hyperbole and Understatement

ANNE BRADSTREET (1612–1672)

To My Dear and Loving Husband (1678)

If ever two were one, then surely we.
If ever man were lov'd by wife, then thee;

If ever wife was happy in a man,
Compare with me ye women if you can.
I prize thy love more than whole Mines of gold,   5
Or all the riches that the East doth hold.
My love is such that Rivers cannot quench,
Nor ought but love from thee, give recompense.
Thy love is such I can no way repay,
The heavens reward thee manifold I pray.   10
Then while we live, in love let's so persever,
That when we live no more, we may live ever.

Reading and Reacting

1. Review the claims the poem's speaker makes about her love in lines 5–8. Are such exaggerated declarations of love necessary, or would the rest of the poem be sufficient to convey the extent of her devotion to her husband?

2. **JOURNAL ENTRY** Compare this poem's declarations of love to those of John Donne's speaker in "A Valediction: Forbidding Mourning" (p. 768). Which speaker do you find more convincing? Why?

Related Works: "A Rose for Emily" (p. 224), "How Do I Love Thee?" (p. 899), "Let me not to the marriage of true minds" (p. 1012)

ANDREW MARVELL (1621–1678)

To His Coy Mistress (1681)

Had we but world enough and time,
This coyness, lady, were no crime.
We would sit down and think which way
To walk, and pass our long love's day.
Thou by the Indian Ganges' side   5
Should'st rubies find; I by the tide
Of Humber[1] would complain. I would
Love you ten years before the Flood,
And you should, if you please, refuse
Till the conversion of the Jews.   10
My vegetable love should grow
Vaster than empires, and more slow.
An hundred years should go to praise
Thine eyes, and on thy forehead gaze,
Two hundred to adore each breast,   15
But thirty thousand to the rest.
An age at least to every part,

---

[1] *Humber:* An estuary on the east coast of England.

And the last age should show your heart.
For, lady, you deserve this state,
Nor would I love at lower rate.   20
    But at my back I always hear
Time's wingèd chariot hurrying near,
And yonder all before us lie
Deserts of vast eternity.
Thy beauty shall no more be found,   25
Nor in thy marble vault shall sound
My echoing song; then worms shall try
That long preserved virginity,
And your quaint honor turn to dust,
And into ashes all my lust.   30
The grave's a fine and private place,
But none, I think, do there embrace.
    Now therefore, while the youthful hue
Sits on thy skin like morning glew[2]
And while thy willing soul transpires   35
At every pore with instant fires,
Now let us sport us while we may;
And now, like amorous birds of prey,
Rather at once our time devour
Than languish in his slow-chapped[3] power.   40
Let us roll all our strength and all
Our sweetness up into one ball
And tear our pleasures with rough strife
Thorough the iron gates of life.
Thus, though we cannot make our sun   45
Stand still, yet we will make him run.

Winged horses pulling chariot
Helene Rogers /Art Directors & TRIP / Alamy

Reading and Reacting

1. In this poem, Marvell's speaker sets out to convince a reluctant woman to become his lover. In order to make his case more persuasive, he uses hyperbole, exaggerating time periods, sizes, spaces, and the possible fate of the woman if she refuses him. Identify as many examples of hyperbole as you can.

2. The tone of "To His Coy Mistress" is more whimsical than serious. Given this tone, what do you see as the purpose of Marvell's use of hyperbole?

3. **JOURNAL ENTRY** Using contemporary prose, paraphrase the first four lines of the poem. Then, beginning with the word *However*, compose a few new sentences of prose, continuing the argument Marvell's speaker makes.

4. **CRITICAL PERSPECTIVE** In her essay "Andrew Marvell's 'To His Coy Mistress': A Feminist Reading," critic Margaret Wald presents the following analysis of the poem:

---

[2]*glew:* Dew.

[3]*slow-chapped:* Slowly crushing.

Andrew Marvell's speaker in "To His Coy Mistress" invokes Petrarchan convention, a poetic mode originating in the fourteenth century in which a male lover uses exaggerated metaphors to appeal to his female beloved. Yet Marvell alludes to such excessive—and disempowering—pining only to defy this tradition of unrequited love. Instead of respectful adulation, he offers lustful invitation; rather than anticipating rejection, he assumes sexual dominion over the eponymous "mistress." The poem is as much a celebration of his rhetorical mastery as it is of his physical conquest.

In what sense is the speaker in this poem celebrating his beloved? In what sense is he celebrating himself? Is his portrayal of his loved one entirely positive? Which elements, if any, are negative?

Related Works: "Where Are You Going, Where Have You Been?" (p. 506), "To the Virgins, to Make Much of Time" (p. 695), "The Passionate Shepherd to His Love" (p. 1003), *The Brute* (p. 1048)

ROBERT FROST (1874–1963)

"Out, Out—" (1916)

The buzz saw snarled and rattled in the yard
And made dust and dropped stove-length sticks of wood,
Sweet-scented stuff when the breeze drew across it.
And from there those that lifted eyes could count
Five mountain ranges one behind the other   5
Under the sunset far into Vermont.
And the saw snarled and rattled, snarled and rattled,
As it ran light, or had to bear a load.
And nothing happened: day was all but done.
Call it a day, I wish they might have said   10
To please the boy by giving him the half hour
That a boy counts so much when saved from work.
His sister stood beside them in her apron
To tell them "Supper." At the word, the saw,
As if to prove saws knew what supper meant,   15
Leaped out at the boy's hand, or seemed to leap—
He must have given the hand. However it was,
Neither refused the meeting. But the hand!
The boy's first outcry was a rueful laugh,
As he swung toward them holding up the hand   20
Half in appeal, but half as if to keep
The life from spilling. Then the boy saw all—
Since he was old enough to know, big boy
Doing a man's work, though a child at heart—
He saw all spoiled. "Don't let him cut my hand off—   25
The doctor, when he comes. Don't let him, sister!"

So. But the hand was gone already.
The doctor put him in the dark of ether.
He lay and puffed his lips out with his breath.
And then—the watcher at his pulse took fright.   30
No one believed. They listened at his heart.
Little—less—nothing!—and that ended it.
No more to build on there. And they, since they
Were not the one dead, turned to their affairs.

Reading and Reacting

1. The poem's title is an **allusion** to a passage in Shakespeare's *Macbeth* (5.5.23–28) that addresses the brevity and meaninglessness of life in very emotional terms:

> Out, out brief candle!
> Life's but a walking shadow, a poor player,
> That struts and frets his hour upon the stage
> And then is heard no more. It is a tale
> Told by an idiot, full of sound and fury,
> Signifying nothing.

What idea do you think Frost wants to convey through the title "Out, Out—"?

2. Explain why each of the following qualifies as understatement:
   - "Neither refused the meeting." (line 18)
   - "He saw all spoiled." (line 25)
   - "—and that ended it." (line 32)
   - "No more to build on there." (line 33)

Can you identify any other examples of understatement in the poem?

3. **JOURNAL ENTRY** Do you think the poem's impact is strengthened or weakened by its understated tone?

4. **CRITICAL PERSPECTIVE** In an essay on Frost in his book *Affirming Limits*, poet and critic Robert Pack focuses on the single word "So" in line 27 of "Out, Out—":

> For a moment, his narration is reduced to the impotent word "So," and in that minimal word all his restrained grief is held. . . . That "So" is the narrator's cry of bearing witness to a story that must be what it is in a scene he cannot enter. He cannot rescue or protect the boy. . . . In the poem's sense of human helplessness in an indifferent universe, we are all "watchers," and what we see is death without redemption, "signifying nothing." So. So? So! How shall we read that enigmatic word?

How do you read this "enigmatic word"? Why?

Related Works: "The Lottery" (p. 419), "Happy Endings" (p. 545), "The Death of the Ball Turret Gunner" (p. 766), "Terza Rima" (p. 908)

COUNTEE CULLEN (1903–1946)

Incident (1925)

Once riding in old Baltimore,
Heart-filled, head-filled with glee;

I saw a Baltimorean
Keep looking straight at me.

Now I was eight and very small,   5
And he was no whit bigger,
And so I smiled, but he poked out
His tongue, and called me, "Nigger."

I saw the whole of Baltimore
From May until December;   10
Of all the things that happened there
That's all that I remember.

Reading and Reacting

1. This poem's last two lines are extremely understated. What words or lines in the poem are *not* understated? Does this use of both direct and understated language make sense? Explain.

2. What do you think the speaker might be referring to by "all the things that happened" in Baltimore (11)? Why?

3. JOURNAL ENTRY Retell the events of this poem in a paragraph, paraphrasing lines 1–10 but quoting the last two lines exactly. Include a few sentences that reveal the speaker's emotions.

4. CRITICAL PERSPECTIVE According to critic Jervis Anderson, Countee Cullen, although one of the most prominent African American poets of his time, placed relatively little emphasis in his work on race and racial politics:

> Cullen did not, could not, avoid entirely the question of race. But his view of himself as a poet did not permit him to make that question his main subject. . . . Usually, Cullen engaged the race problem obliquely—at times with deft jabs and glancing blows. . . . at times with understated amusement, as in "Incident."

Do you agree with Anderson that in "Incident," Cullen deals with race with "understated amusement"? What evidence for or against this interpretation do you see in the poem?

Related Works: "Battle Royal" (p. 287), "Big Black Good Man" (p. 318), "Negro" (p. 678), "Ethel's Sestina" (p. 828), "Yet Do I Marvel" (p. 869), "If We Must Die" (p. 1003)

MARGARET ATWOOD (1939–   )

You fit into me   (1971)

You fit into me
like a hook into an eye

a fish hook
an open eye

Reading and Reacting

1. What positive connotations does Atwood expect readers to associate with the phrase "you fit into me"? What does the speaker seem at first to mean by "like a hook into an eye" in line 2?

2. The speaker's shift to the brutal suggestions of lines 3 and 4 is calculated to shock readers. Does the use of hyperbole here have another purpose in the context of the poem? Explain.

3. **JOURNAL ENTRY** Do you find this poem unsettling? Do you think it is serious or just a joke?

Related Works: "Hills Like White Elephants" (p. 119), "Love and Other Catastrophes: A Mix Tape" (p. 127), "Daddy" (p. 772), *A Doll House* (p. 1113)

 Metonymy and Synecdoche

Metonymy and synecdoche are two related figures of speech. **Metonymy** is the substitution of the name of one thing for the name of another thing that most readers associate with the first—for example, using *hired gun* to mean "paid assassin" or *suits* to mean "business executives." A specific kind of metonymy, called **synecdoche**, is the substitution of a part for the whole (for example, using *wheels* to refer to an automobile or *bread*—as in "Give us this day our daily bread"—to mean "food") or the whole for a part (for example, using *the law* to refer to a police officer).

With metonymy and synecdoche, instead of describing something by saying it is like something else (as in simile) or by equating it with something else (as in metaphor), writers can characterize an object or concept by using a term that evokes it. The following poem illustrates the use of synecdoche.

RICHARD LOVELACE (1618–1658)

To Lucasta Going to the Wars (1649)

Tell me not, Sweet, I am unkind
    That from the nunnery
Of thy chaste breast and quiet mind,
    To war and arms I fly.

True, a new mistress now I chase,   5
    The first foe in the field;
And with a stronger faith embrace
    A sword, a horse, a shield.

Yet this inconstancy is such
    As you too shall adore;   10
I could not love thee, Dear, so much,
    Loved I not Honor more.

Prince Rupert's cavalry charging at Edgehill, 1642
The Print Collector / HIP / The Image Works

Here, Lovelace's use of synecdoche allows him to condense a number of complex ideas into a very few words. In line 3, when the speaker says that he is flying from his loved one's "chaste breast and quiet mind," he is using "breast" and "mind" to stand for all his loved one's physical and intellectual attributes. In line 8, when he says that he is embracing "A sword, a horse, a shield," he is using these three items to represent the trappings of war—and, thus, to represent war itself.

FURTHER READING: Metonymy and Synecdoche

DYLAN THOMAS (1914–1953)

The Hand That Signed the Paper (1936)

The hand that signed the paper felled a city;
Five sovereign fingers taxed the breath.
Doubled the globe of dead and halved a country;
These five kings did a king to death.

The mighty hand leads to a sloping shoulder   5
The finger joints are cramped with chalk;
A goose's quill has put an end to murder
That put an end to talk.

The hand that signed the treaty bred a fever,
And famine grew, and locusts came;   10
Great is the hand that holds dominion over
Man by a scribbled name.

The five kings count the dead but do not soften
The crusted wound nor stroke the brow;
A hand rules pity as a hand rules heaven;   15
Hands have no tears to flow.

Reading and Reacting

1. When the speaker uses the word *hand* in the expression, "the hand that signed the paper," to what larger entity is he referring? Why does he use *hand* instead of what it stands for?
2. Does *hand* stand for the same thing throughout the poem, or does its meaning change? Explain.
3. What are the "five sovereign fingers" (2)? What are the "five kings" (4, 13)? Do these two phrases refer to the same thing or to two different things? Explain.
4. Is this poem an example of synecdoche or metonymy? Explain.
5. **JOURNAL ENTRY** What do you think this poem might be saying about power and powerful rulers?

Related Works: "All about Suicide" (p. 7), "Ozymandias" (p. 698), "Terza Rima" (p. 908), "Dover Beach" (p. 956)

Apostrophe

With **apostrophe**, a poem's speaker addresses an absent person or thing—for example, a historical or literary figure or even an inanimate object or an abstract concept.

In the following poem, the speaker addresses the Twin Towers of the World Trade Center, destroyed in the terrorist attacks of September 11, 2001.

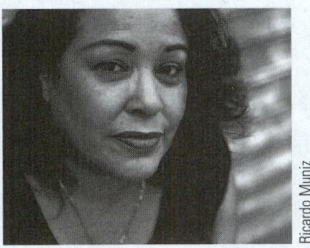

Ricardo Muniz

NANCY MERCADO (1959–   )

Going to Work (2001)

On their daily trips
Commuters shed tears now
Use American flags
Like veiled women
To hide their sorrows   5
Rush to buy throwaway cameras
To capture your twin ghosts

Frantically I too
Purchase your memory
On postcards & coffee mugs   10
In New York City souvenir shops
Afraid I'll forget your facade
Forget my hallowed Sunday
Morning PATH Train rides
My subway travels through   15
The center of your belly
Day after day

Afraid I'll forget your powers
To transform helicopters
Into ladybugs gliding in the air   20
To turn New York City
Into a breathing map
To display the curvature
Of our world

In "Going to Work," the poem's speaker describes her reactions in the aftermath of the September 11th attacks and remembers how, before the towers were destroyed, she traveled to work on the PATH (Port Authority Trans-Hudson) train that ran beneath them. Now, she says, commuters "Rush to buy throwaway cameras / To capture your twin ghosts." She continues, "Frantically I too / Purchase your memory" in the form of souvenirs. In the speaker's mind, the towers loom large; despite her fears, there is little danger of her forgetting them. In their remembered size and power, they still "display the curvature / Of our world."

FURTHER READING: Apostrophe

JOHN KEATS (1795–1821)

Ode to a Nightingale   (1819)

I

My heart aches, and a drowsy numbness pains
   My sense, as though of hemlock[1] I had drunk,
Or emptied some dull opiate[2] to the drains
   One minute past, and Lethe[3]–wards had sunk:
'Tis not through envy of thy happy lot.   5
   But being too happy in thine happiness,—
      That thou, light-wingèd Dryad[4] of the trees,
         In some melodious plot
Of beechen[5] green, and shadows numberless,
   Singest of summer in full-throated ease.   10

II

O for a draught[6] of vintage! that hath been
   Cool'd a long age in the deep-delvèd[7] earth,
Tasting of Flora[8] and the country-green,

---

[1] *hemlock:* A medicinal plant used as a sedative or, in higher doses, a deadly poison.

[2] *opiate:* A medicine containing opium, a substance derived from poppies, which aids sleep and relieves pain.

[3] *Lethe:* In Greek mythology, a river in Hades, the land of the dead. Those who drank its water lost all memory of the past.

[4] *Dryad:* A spirit believed to inhabit trees.

[5] *beechen:* Of or relating to a beech tree.

[6] *draught:* A large sip of liquid.

[7] *deep-delvèd:* Excavated.

[8] *Flora:* In Roman mythology, the goddess of flowers.

Dance, and Provençal[9] song, and sunburnt mirth!
O for a beaker full of the warm South!   15
   Full of the true, the blushful Hippocrene,[10]
     With beaded bubbles winking at the brim,
      And purple-stainèd mouth;
That I might drink, and leave the world unseen,
     And with thee fade away into the forest dim: 20

III

Fade far away, dissolve, and quite forget
   What thou among the leaves hast never known,
The weariness, the fever, and the fret
   Here, where men sit and hear each other groan;
Where palsy shakes a few, sad, last grey hairs,   25
   Where youth grows pale, and spectre-thin, and dies;
     Where but to think is to be full of sorrow
      And leaden-eyed despairs,
   Where beauty cannot keep her lustrous eyes,
     Or new Love pine at them beyond to-morrow.   30

IV

Away! away! for I will fly to thee,
   Not charioted by Bacchus[11] and his pards,[12]
But on the viewless wings of Poesy,
   Though the dull brain perplexes and retards:
Already with thee! tender is the night,   35
   And haply the Queen-Moon is on her throne,
     Cluster'd around by all her starry Fays;[13]
      But here there is no light,
Save what from heaven is with the breezes blown
   Through verdurous[14] glooms and winding mossy ways.   40

V

I cannot see what flowers are at my feet,
   Nor what soft incense hangs upon the boughs,
But, in embalmèd darkness, guess each sweet
   Wherewith the seasonable month endows
The grass, the thicket, and the fruit-tree wild;   45
   White hawthorn, and the pastoral eglantine;[15]

---

[9]*Provençal:* From Provence, a region of southern France.

[10]*Hippocrene:* A fountain on Mt. Helicon, in Greece, considered sacred to the Muses.

[11]*Bacchus:* The god of wine.

[12]*pards:* Leopards or panthers.

[13]*Fays:* Fairies.

[14]*verdurous:* Green with vegetation.

[15]*eglantine:* A plant also known as the sweet-briar.

Fast-fading violets cover'd up in leaves;
   And mid-May's eldest child,
The coming musk-rose, full of dewy wine,
   The murmurous haunt of flies on summer eves.   50

VI

Darkling I listen; and, for many a time
   I have been half in love with easeful Death,
Call'd him soft names in many a musèd rhyme,
   To take into the air my quiet breath;
Now more than ever seems it rich to die,   55
   To cease upon the midnight with no pain,
     While thou art pouring forth thy soul abroad
       In such an ecstasy!
Still wouldst thou sing, and I have ears in vain—
   To thy high requiem become a sod.   60

VII

Thou wast not born for death, immortal Bird!
   No hungry generations tread thee down;
The voice I hear this passing night was heard
   In ancient days by emperor and clown:
Perhaps the self-same song that found a path   65
   Through the sad heart of Ruth, when, sick for home,
     She stood in tears amid the alien corn;[16]
       The same that ofttimes hath
Charm'd magic casements,[17] opening on the foam
   Of perilous seas, in faery lands forlorn.[18]   70

VIII

Forlorn! the very word is like a bell
   To toll me back from thee to my sole self!
Adieu! the fancy cannot cheat so well
   As she is famed to do, deceiving elf.
Adieu![19] adieu! the plaintive anthem fades   75
   Past the near meadows, over the still stream,
   Up the hill-side; and now 'tis buried deep
     In the next valley-glades:
Was it a vision, or a waking dream?
   Fled is that music:—Do I wake or sleep?

---

[16]*corn:* Grain.

[17]*casements:* Windows.

[18]*forlorn:* Lost.

[19]*Adieu:* Farewell.

Lithograph of nightingale, c. 1830
The Nightingale of France, c.1830 (colour litho), Oudart, Paul
Louis (b.1796) (after) / Bibliothèque des Arts Décoratifs, Paris,
France / Archives Charmet / Bridgeman Images

Reading and Reacting

1. Where does the speaker first address the nightingale? Where else does he speak directly to the nightingale?

2. In lines 19–20, the speaker expresses his desire to "leave the world unseen, / And with thee fade away into the forest dim. . . ." Why does he want to "fade away"? What is it about the "forest dim" that attracts him? Give some examples from the poem to contrast the speaker's world with the world of the nightingale.

3. What is it that the speaker admires about the nightingale? In what sense does he see the nightingale as superior to human beings?

4. **JOURNAL ENTRY** If you were to write an **ode**—a long, serious, and formal poem—to a creature or an object, what would you choose as your subject? Why? How do you see your own world as different from (and inferior to) the world of your subject?

Related Works: "Young Goodman Brown" (p. 448),"Sonny's Blues" (p. 547), "The World Is Too Much with Us" (p. 692), "Death Be Not Proud" (p. 980)

ALLEN GINSBERG (1926–1997)

A Supermarket in California (1956)

What thoughts I have of you tonight, Walt Whitman,[1] for I walked down
the sidestreets under the trees with a headache self-conscious looking at the
full moon.

---

[1] *Walt Whitman:* American poet (1819–1892) whose poems frequently praise the commonplace and often contain lengthy "enumerations."

In my hungry fatigue, and shopping for images, I went into
the neon fruit supermarket, dreaming of your enumerations!

What peaches and what penumbras! Whole families shopping at night!
Aisles full of husbands! Wives in the avocados, babies in the tomatoes!—
and you, Garcia Lorca,[2] what were you doing down
by the watermelons?

I saw you, Walt Whitman, childless, lonely old grubber, poking among
the meats in the refrigerator and eyeing the grocery boys.[3]

I heard you asking questions of each: Who killed the pork chops?   5
What price bananas? Are you my Angel?

I wandered in and out of the brilliant stacks of cans following you, and
followed in my imagination by the store detective.

We strode down the open corridors together in our solitary fancy tasting
artichokes, possessing every frozen delicacy, and never passing the cashier.

Where are we going, Walt Whitman? The doors close in an hour.
Which way does your beard point tonight?

(I touch your book[4] and dream of our odyssey in the supermarket and
feel absurd.)

Will we walk all night through solitary streets? The trees add   10
shade to shade, lights out in the houses, we'll both be lonely.

Will we stroll dreaming of the lost America of love past blue automobiles
in driveways, home to our silent cottage?

Ah, dear father, graybeard, lonely old courage-teacher, what America
did you have when Charon[5] quit poling his ferry and you
got out on a smoking bank and stood watching the boat disappear on the
black waters of Lethe?[6]

Reading and Reacting

1. In this poem, Ginsberg's speaker wanders through the aisles of a supermarket, speaking to the nineteenth-century American poet Walt Whitman and asking Whitman a series of questions. Why do you think the speaker addresses Whitman? What kind of answers do you think he is looking for?

2. In paragraph 2, the speaker says he is "shopping for images." What does he mean? Why does he look for these images in a supermarket? Does he find them?

3. Is this poem about supermarkets? about Walt Whitman? about poetry? about love? about America? What do you see as its primary theme? Why?

[2]*Federico Garcia Lorca:* Spanish poet and dramatist (1899–1936).

[3]*eyeing the grocery boys:* Whitman's sexual orientation is the subject of much debate. Ginsberg is suggesting here that Whitman was homosexual.

[4]*your book: Leaves of Grass.*

[5]*Charon:* In Greek mythology, the ferryman who transported the dead over the river Styx to Hades.

[6]*Lethe:* In Greek mythology, the river of forgetfulness (one of five rivers in Hades).

4. JOURNAL ENTRY Does the incongruous image of the respected poet "poking / among the meats" (paragraph 4) in the supermarket strengthen the poem's impact, or does it undercut any serious "message" the poem might have? Explain.

5. CRITICAL PERSPECTIVE The critic Leslie Fiedler discusses some of the ways in which Ginsberg's style resembles that of Walt Whitman:

> Everything about Ginsberg is . . . blatantly Whitmanian: his meter is resolutely anti-iambic, his line groupings stubbornly anti-stanzaic, his diction aggressively colloquial and American, his voice public.

Does this characterization apply to "A Supermarket in California"? If so, how?

Related Works: "A&P" (p. 238), "Chicago" (p. 838), from "Out of the Cradle Endlessly Rocking" (p. 841), "Old Walt" (p. 923), "Defending Walt Whitman" (p. 952), "I Hear America Singing" (p. 1022), *from* "Song of Myself" (p. 1023), *The Cuban Swimmer* (p. 1416)

✔ CHECKLIST   Writing about Figures of Speech

☐ What figures of speech are used in the poem? Identify any examples of simile, metaphor, personification, hyperbole, understatement, metonymy, synecdoche, and apostrophe.

☐ What two elements are being compared in each use of simile, metaphor, and personification? What characteristics are shared by the two items being compared?

☐ Does the poet use hyperbole? Why? For example, is it used to move or to shock readers, or is its use intended to produce a humorous or satirical effect? Would more understated language be more effective?

☐ Does the poet use understatement? For what purpose? Would more emotionally charged language be more effective?

☐ If the poem includes metonymy or synecdoche, what term is being substituted for another? To what object or concept does the term refer?

☐ If the poem includes apostrophe, whom or what does the speaker address? What does the use of apostrophe accomplish?

☐ How do figures of speech contribute to the impact of the poem as a whole?

WRITING SUGGESTIONS: Figures of Speech

1. Various figures of speech are often used to describe characters in literary works. Choose two or three works that focus on a single character—for example, "A Rose for Emily" (p. 224), "Miss Brill" (p. 245), "Gryphon" (p. 250) or "Richard Cory" (p. 1011)—and explain how figures of speech are used to characterize each work's central figure. If you like, you may write about works that focus on real (rather than fictional) people—for example, "Emmett Till" (p. 985).

2. Write an essay in which you discuss the different ways poets use figures of speech to examine the nature of poetry itself. What kinds of figures of speech do poets use to describe their craft? (You might begin by reading the two poems about poetry that open Chapter 22.)

3. Write a letter (or a poem) replying to the speaker in the poem by Marvell, Bradstreet, Donne, or Burns that appears in this chapter. Use figures of speech to express the depth of your love and the extent of your devotion.

4. Choose three or four poems that have a common subject—for example, love or nature—and write an essay in which you draw some general conclusions about the relative effectiveness of the poems' use of figures of speech to examine that subject. (If you like, you may focus on the poems clustered under the heads "Poems about Parents," "Poems about Nature," "Poems about Love," and "Poems about War" in Chapter 31.)

5. Select a poem and a short story that deal with the same subject, and write an essay in which you compare their use of figures of speech.

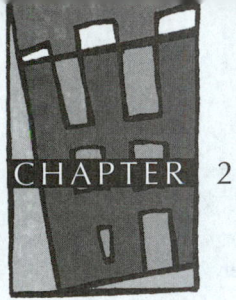

CHAPTER 28

SOUND

N. Scott Momaday
AP Images/Jacques Brinon

Jacob Saenz
Maryam Fakouri

Walt Whitman
© Bettmann/Corbis

Emily Dickinson
Bettmann/Corbis

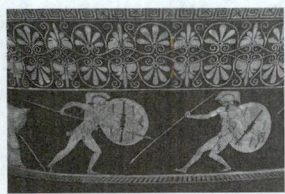

Detail of vase showing Achilles
killing Hector

© The Trustees of the British Museum / Art
Resource, NY

WALT WHITMAN (1819–1892)

Had I the Choice*

Had I the choice to tally greatest bards,
To limn[1] their portraits, stately, beautiful, and emulate at will,
Homer with all his wars and warriors—Hector, Achilles, Ajax,
Or Shakespeare's woe-entangled Hamlet, Lear,
    Othello—Tennyson's fair ladies,

---

*Publication date is not available.

[1]*limn:* To draw, depict.

Meter or wit the best, or choice conceit to wield in perfect   5
    rhyme, delight of singers;
These, these, O sea, all these I'd gladly barter,
Would you the undulation of one wave, its trick to me transfer,
Or breathe one breath of yours upon my verse,
And leave its odor there.

 ## Rhythm

Rhythm—the regular recurrence of sounds—is at the center of all natural phenomena: the beating of a heart, the lapping of waves against the shore, the croaking of frogs on a summer's night, the whispering of wheat swaying in the wind. Even mechanical phenomena, such as the movement of rush-hour traffic through a city's streets, have a kind of rhythm. Poetry, which explores these phenomena, often tries to reflect the same rhythms. Walt Whitman expresses this idea in "Had I the Choice" when he says that he would gladly trade the "perfect rhyme" of Shakespeare for the ability to reproduce "the undulation of one wave" in his verse.

Public speakers frequently repeat key words and phrases to create rhythm. In his "I Have a Dream" speech, for example, Martin Luther King Jr. repeats the phrase "I have a dream" to create a rhythm that ties the central section of the speech together:

> I say to you today, my friends, even though we face the difficulties of today and tomorrow, I still have a dream. It is a dream deeply rooted in the American dream. I have a dream that one day this nation will rise up and live out the true meaning of its creed: "We hold these truths to be self-evident, that all men are created equal." I have a dream that one day, on the red hills of Georgia, sons of former slaves and the sons of former slave owners will be able to sit down together at the table of brotherhood. I have a dream that one day even the state of Mississippi, a state sweltering with the heat of injustice, sweltering with the heat of oppression, will be transformed into an oasis of freedom and justice. I have a dream that my four little children will one day live in a nation where they will not be judged by the color of their skin, but by the content of their character.

Poets too create rhythm by using repeated words and phrases, as Gwendolyn Brooks does in the poem that follows.

GWENDOLYN BROOKS (1917–2000)

Sadie and Maud (1945)

Maud went to college.
Sadie stayed at home.
Sadie scraped life
With a fine-tooth comb.

She didn't leave a tangle in.   5
Her comb found every strand.
Sadie was one of the livingest chits
In all the land.

Sadie bore two babies
Under her maiden name.   10
Maud and Ma and Papa
Nearly died of shame.

When Sadie said her last so-long
Her girls struck out from home.
(Sadie had left as heritage   15
Her fine-tooth comb.)

Maud, who went to college,
Is a thin brown mouse.
She is living all alone
In this old house.   20

Much of the force of this poem comes from the repeated words "Sadie" and "Maud," which shift the focus from one subject to the other and back again ("Maud went to college / Sadie stayed home"). The poem's singsong rhythm recalls the rhymes children recite when jumping rope. This evocation of carefree childhood is ironically contrasted with the adult realities that both Sadie and Maud face as they grow up: Sadie stays at home and has two children out of wedlock; Maud goes to college and ends up "a thin brown mouse." The speaker implies that the alternatives Sadie and Maud represent are both undesirable. Although Sadie "scraped life / with a fine-tooth comb," she dies young and leaves nothing to her girls but her desire to experience life. Maud, who graduated from college, shuts out life and cuts herself off from her roots.

Just as the repetition of words and phrases can create rhythm, so can the appearance of words on the printed page. How a poem looks is especially important in **open form poetry** (see p. 837), which dispenses with traditional patterns of versification. In the following excerpt from "The Moon Is Hiding In" by E. E. Cummings, for example, an unusual arrangement of words forces readers to slow down and then to speed up, creating a rhythm that emphasizes a key phrase—"The / lily":

the moon is hiding
in her hair.
The
lily
of heaven
full of all dreams,
draws down.

 ## Meter

Although rhythm can be affected by the regular repetition of words and phrases or by the arrangement of words into lines, poetic rhythm is largely created by **meter**, the recurrence of regular units of stressed and unstressed syllables. A **stress** (or accent) occurs when one syllable is emphasized more than another, unstressed, syllable: *fór • ceps, bá • sic, il • lú • sion, ma • lár • i • a*. In a poem, even one-syllable words can be stressed to create a particular effect. For example, in Elizabeth Barrett Browning's line "How do I love thee? Let me count the ways," the metrical pattern that places stress on "love" creates one meaning; stressing "I" would create another.

Scansion is the analysis of patterns of stressed and unstressed syllables within a line. The most common method of poetic notation indicates stressed syllables with a ′ and unstressed syllables with a ˘. Although scanning lines gives readers the "beat" of the poem, scansion only generally suggests the sound of spoken language, which contains an infinite variety of stresses. By providing a graphic representation of the stressed and unstressed syllables of a poem, scansion aids understanding, but it is no substitute for reading the poem aloud and experimenting with various patterns of emphasis.

The basic unit of meter is a **foot**—a group of syllables with a fixed pattern of stressed and unstressed syllables. The chart that follows illustrates the most common types of metrical feet in English and American verse.

Foot	Stress Pattern	Example
Iamb	˘′	They pace | in sleek | chi val | ric cer | tain ty (Adrienne Rich)
Trochee	′˘	Thou, when | thou re | turn'st, wilt | tell me. (John Donne)
Anapest	˘˘′	With a hey, | and a ho, | and a hey | no ni no (William Shakespeare)
Dactyl	′˘˘	Constantly | risking ab | surdity (Lawrence Ferlinghetti)

Iambic and *anapestic* meters are called **rising meters** because they progress from unstressed to stressed syllables. *Trochaic* and *dactylic* meters are called **falling meters** because they progress from stressed to unstressed syllables.

The following types of metrical feet, less common than those listed above, are used to add emphasis or to provide variety rather than to create the dominant meter of a poem.

Foot	Stress Pattern	Example
Spondee	′ ′	′ ′ ⌣ Pomp, pride | and ′ ⌣ ′ ⌣ circumstance of ′ ⌣ ′ glorious war! (William Shakespeare)
Pyrrhic	⌣ ⌣	⌣ ′ ⌣ ′ A horse! a horse! ⌣ ′ ⌣ ⌣ My king | dom for | ⌣ ′ a horse! (William Shakespeare)

A metric line of poetry is measured by the number of feet it contains.

Monometer	one foot	**Pentameter**	five feet
Dimeter	two feet	**Hexameter**	six feet
Trimeter	three feet	**Heptameter**	seven feet
Tetrameter	four feet	**Octameter**	eight feet

The name for a metrical pattern of a line of verse identifies the name of the foot used and the number of feet the line contains. For example, the most common foot in English poetry is the **iamb**, most often occurring in lines of three or five feet.

Metrical Pattern	Example
Iambic trimeter	⌣ ′ ⌣ ′ ⌣ ′ Eight hun | dred of | the brave (William Cowper)
Iambic pentameter	⌣ ′ ⌣ ′ ⌣ O, how | much more | doth ′ ⌣ ′ ⌣ ′ beau | ty beau | teous seem (William Shakespeare)

Because **iambic pentameter** is so well suited to the rhythms of English speech, writers frequently use it in plays and poems. Shakespeare's plays, for example, are written in unrhymed lines of iambic pentameter called **blank verse** (see p. 816).

Many other metrical combinations are also possible; a few are illustrated on the next page.

Metrical Pattern	Example
Trochaic trimeter	´ ˘ ´ ˘ ´ ˘ Like a | high-born | maiden (Percy Bysshe Shelley)
Anapestic tetrameter	˘ ˘ ´ ˘ ˘ ´ The As sy | rian came down | ˘ ˘ ´ ˘ ˘ ´ like the wolf | on the fold (Lord Byron)
Dactylic hexameter	´ ˘ ˘ ´ ˘ ˘ Maid en most | beau ti ful | ´ ˘ ˘ ´ ˘ ˘ ´ moth er most | boun ti ful, | la ˘ ˘ ´ dy of | lands, (A. C. Swinburne)
Iambic heptameter	˘ ´ ˘ ´ ˘ ´ ˘ The yel | low fog | that rubs | its ´ ˘ ˘ ´ ˘ ˘ ´ back | up on | the win | ˘ ´ dow-panes (T. S. Eliot)

Scansion can be an extremely technical process, and when readers become bogged down with anapests and dactyls, they can easily forget that poetic scansion is not an end in itself. Meter should be appropriate for the ideas expressed by the poem, and it should help to create a suitable tone. A light, skipping rhythm, for example, would be inappropriate for an **elegy**, and a slow, heavy rhythm would surely be out of place in an **epigram** or a limerick. The following lines of a poem by Samuel Taylor Coleridge illustrate the uses of different types of metrical feet:

Trochee trips from long to short;
From long to long in solemn sort
Slow Spondee stalks; strong foot! yet ill able
Ever to come up with Dactyl trisyllable.
Iambics march from short to long—   5
With a leap and a bound the swift Anapests throng;
One syllable long, with one short at each side,
Amphibrachys hastes with a stately stride—
First and last being long, middle short, Amphimacer
Strikes his thundering hoofs like a proud high-bred Racer.   10

A poet may use one kind of meter—iambic meter, for example—throughout a poem, but may occasionally vary line length to relieve monotony or to accommodate the poem's meaning or emphasis. In the following poem, the poet uses iambic lines of different lengths.

EMILY DICKINSON (1830–1886)

I like to see it lap the Miles— (1891)

I like to see it lap the Miles—
And lick the Valleys up—
And stop to feed itself at Tanks—
And then—prodigious step

Around a Pile of Mountains—   5
And supercilious peer
In Shanties—by the sides of Roads—
And then a Quarry pare

To fit its Ribs
And crawl between   10
Complaining all the while
In horrid—hooting stanza—
Then chase itself down Hill—

And neigh like Boanerges[1]—
Then—punctual as a Star   15
Stop—docile and omnipotent
At its own stable door—

Dickinson's poem is a single sentence that, except for some pauses, stretches unbroken from beginning to end. Iambic lines of varying lengths actually suggest the movements of the train that the poet describes. Lines of iambic tetrameter, such as the first, give readers a sense of the train's steady, rhythmic movement across a flat landscape, and shorter lines ("To fit its Ribs / And crawl between") suggest the train's slowing motion. Beginning with two iambic dimeter lines and progressing to iambic trimeter lines, the third stanza increases in speed just like the train that is racing downhill "In horrid—hooting stanza—."

When a poet uses more than one type of metrical foot, any variation in a metrical pattern—the substitution of a trochee for an iamb, for instance—immediately calls attention to itself. For example, in line 16 of "I like to see it lap the Miles—," the poet departs from iambic meter by placing unexpected stress on the first word, *stop*. By emphasizing this word, the poet brings the flow of the poem to an abrupt halt, suggesting the jolt riders experience when a train comes to a stop.

Another way of varying the meter of a poem is to introduce a pause known as a **caesura**—a Latin word meaning "a cutting"—within a line. When scanning a poem, you indicate a caesura with two parallel lines: ‖. Unless a line of poetry is extremely short, it probably will contain a caesura.

---

[1]*Boanerges:* A vociferous preacher and orator. Also, the name, meaning "son of thunder," Jesus gave to apostles John and James because of their fiery zeal.

A caesura occurs after a punctuation mark or at a natural break in phrasing:

> How do I love thee? ‖ Let me count the ways.
> **Elizabeth Barrett Browning**

> Two loves I have ‖ of comfort and despair.
> **William Shakespeare**

> High on a throne of royal state, ‖ which far
> Outshone the wealth of Ormus ‖ and of Ind
> **John Milton**

Sometimes more than one caesura occurs in a single line:

> 'Tis good. ‖ Go to the gate. ‖ Somebody knocks.
> **William Shakespeare**

Although the end of a line may mark the end of a metrical unit, it does not always coincide with the end of a sentence. Lines that have distinct pauses at the end—usually signaled by punctuation—are called **end-stopped lines**. Lines that do not end with strong pauses are called **run-on lines**. (Sometimes the term **enjambment** is used to describe run-on lines.) End-stopped lines can sometimes seem formal, or even forced, because their length is rigidly dictated by the poem's meter, rhythm, and rhyme scheme. In the following excerpt from John Keats's "La Belle Dame sans Merci" (p. 993), for example, rhythm, meter, and rhyme dictate the pauses that occur at the ends of the lines:

> O, what can ail thee, knight-at-arms,
>   Alone and palely loitering?
> The sedge has wither'd from the lake,
>   And no birds sing.

In contrast to end-stopped lines, run-on lines often seem more natural. Because their ending points are determined by the rhythms of speech and by the meaning and emphasis the poet wishes to convey rather than by meter and rhyme, run-on lines are suited to the open form of much modern poetry. In the following lines from the poem "We Have Come Home," by Lenrie Peters, run-on lines give readers the sense of spoken language:

> We have come home
> From the bloodless war
> With sunken hearts
> Our boots full of pride—
> From the true massacre of the soul
> When we have asked
> "What does it cost
> To be loved and left alone?"

Rather than relying exclusively on end-stopped or run-on lines, poets often use a combination of the two to produce the effects they want.

FURTHER READING: Rhythm and Meter

ADRIENNE RICH (1929–2012)

Aunt Jennifer's Tigers (1951)

Aunt Jennifer's tigers prance across a screen,
Bright topaz denizens of a world of green.
They do not fear the men beneath the tree;
They pace in sleek chivalric certainty.[1]

Aunt Jennifer's fingers fluttering through her wool   5
Find even the ivory needle hard to pull.
The massive weight of Uncle's wedding band
Sits heavily upon Aunt Jennifer's hand.

When Aunt is dead, her terrified hands will lie
Still ringed with ordeals she was mastered by.   10
The tigers in the panel that she made
Will go on prancing, proud and unafraid.

Reading and Reacting

1. What is the dominant metrical pattern of the poem? How does the meter enhance the contrast the poem develops?

2. The lines in the first stanza are end-stopped, and those in the second and third stanzas combine end-stopped and run-on lines. What does the poet achieve by varying the rhythm?

3. What ideas do the caesuras in the first and fourth lines of the last stanza emphasize?

4. **JOURNAL ENTRY** What is the speaker's opinion of Aunt Jennifer's marriage? Do you think she is commenting on this particular marriage or on marriage in general?

5. **CRITICAL PERSPECTIVE** In *The Aesthetics of Power*, Claire Keyes writes of this poem that although it is formally beautiful, almost perfect, its voice creates problems:

   [T]he tone seldom approaches intimacy, the speaker seeming fairly detached from the fate of Aunt Jennifer. . . . The dominant voice of the poem asserts the traditional theme that art outlives the person who produces it. . . . The speaker is almost callous in her disregard for Aunt's death. . . . Who cares that Aunt Jennifer dies? The speaker does not seem to; she gets caught up in those gorgeous tigers. . . . Here lies the dominant voice: Aunt is not compelling; her creation is.

   Do you agree with Keyes's interpretation of the poem?

Related Works: "Miss Brill" (p. 245), "Everyday Use" (p. 426), "Happy Endings" (p. 545), "Rooming houses are old women" (p. 761)

---

[1]*chivalric certainty:* With pride and honor.

THOMAS LUX (1946–   )

A Little Tooth (1989)

Your baby grows a tooth, then two,
and four, and five, then she wants some meat
directly from bone. It's all

over: she'll learn some words she'll fall
in love with cretins, dolts, a sweet   5
talker on his way to jail. And you,

your wife, get old, flyblown, and rue
nothing. You did, you loved, your feet
are sore. It's dusk. Your daughter's tall.

Reading and Reacting

1. This poem was selected to be featured in the New York City's "Poetry in Motion" program, which posts poems in public busses and trains. What qualities make "A Little Tooth" suitable for this program?

2. What is the dominant metrical pattern of this poem? Do you think this meter is an appropriate choice here? Explain.

3. Where in the poem does Lux use caesuras? What effect do these pauses have?

4. **JOURNAL ENTRY** "A Little Tooth" is characterized by its extreme compression. What ideas does the poem express? Does the poem effectively communicate these ideas, or does it try to do too much in too few lines?

5. **CRITICAL PERSPECTIVE** Writing about Thomas Lux's work in the journal *Poetry*, Peter Campion makes the following observation:

> The problem is not simply that Lux knows the course his poems will take before he begins, though this probably contributes. It's that he writes from above his material. Reading Lux you rarely sense a consciousness moving down in the lines themselves. The poems are set speeches: their odd images or turns of phrase glimmer for moments then disappear as Lux glides on toward his desired effect.

Do you feel that Campion's criticisms apply to "A Little Tooth"? Why or why not?

Related Works: "Everyday Use" (p. 426), "Doe Season" (p. 472), "Where Are You Going, Where Have You Been?" (p. 506), "My Father as a Guitar" (p. 770), "Sadie and Maud" (p. 792), "Aristotle" (p. 865), "*What Are You Going to Be?*" (p. 1062).

LEWIS CARROLL (1832–1898)

A Boat Beneath a Sunny Sky (1872)

A boat beneath a sunny sky,
Lingering onward dreamily
In an evening of July—

Children three that nestle near,
Eager eye and willing ear,   5
Pleased a simple tale to hear—

Long has paled that sunny sky:
Echoes fade and memories die:
Autumn frosts have slain July.

Still she haunts me, phantomwise,   10
Alice moving under skies
Never seen by waking eyes.

Children yet, the tale to hear,
Eager eye and willing ear,
Lovingly shall nestle near.   15

In a Wonderland they lie,
Dreaming as the days go by,
Dreaming as the summers die:

Ever drifting down the stream—
Lingering in the golden gleam—   20
Life, what is it but a dream?

Reading and Reacting

1. Lewis Carroll (whose real name was Charles Lutwidge Dodgson) took three young sisters (including Alice Pleasance Liddell) on a boat trip in 1862. As he rowed, he told them a story of a girl named Alice, who follows a rabbit down a rabbit hole to Wonderland. The girls—especially Alice—were so captivated by the story, that they asked Carroll to write it down. Eventually, this story became *Alice's Adventures in Wonderland*. What specific references to this boat trip are in the poem?

2. What is the poem's primary metrical pattern? How does this pattern help establish the poem's mood?

3. Where in the poem are caesuras used? What effect does each of these pauses have?

4. What point is Carroll making about childhood? about Wonderland? What do you think Carroll means in the poem's last line: "Life, what is it but a dream?" (Notice the allusion to the children's nursery rhyme "Row, Row, Your Boat.")

5. **JOURNAL ENTRY** "A Boat Beneath a Sunny Sky" is an **acrostic poem**; that is, the first letter of each line spells out a word—in this case, *Alice Pleasance Liddell*. Is this technique just a clever device, or does it somehow add to the poem? Explain.

Related Works: "Encounters with Unexpected Animals" (p. 132), "A&P" (p. 238), "Gretel in Darkness" (p. 677), "What Shall I Give My Children?" (p. 731), "One day I wrote her name upon the strand" (p. 733), "Where the Sidewalk Ends" (p. 808), "Jabberwocky" (p. 810)

Alliteration and Assonance

Just as poetry depends on rhythm, it also depends on the sounds of individual words. An effect pleasing to the ear, such as "Did he who made the Lamb make thee?" from William Blake's "The Tyger" (p. 961), is called **euphony**. A jarring or discordant effect, such as "The vorpal blade went snicker-snack!" from Lewis Carroll's "Jabberwocky" (p. 810), is called **cacophony**.

One of the earliest, and perhaps the most primitive, methods of enhancing sound is **onomatopoeia**, which occurs when the sound of a word echoes its meaning, as it does in common words such as *bang, crash*, and *hiss*. Poets make broad application of this technique by using combinations of words that suggest a correspondence between sound and meaning, as Edgar Allan Poe does in these lines from his poem "The Bells":

> Yet the ear, it fully knows,
>   By the twanging
>   And the clanging,
> How the danger ebbs and flows;
> Yet the ear distinctly tells,
>   In the jangling
>   And the wrangling
> How the danger sinks and swells
> By the sinking or the swelling in the anger of the bells—
>   Of the bells,—
>   Of the bells, bells, bells, bells. . . .

Poe's primary objective in this poem is to re-create the sound of ringing bells. Although he succeeds, the aural effect throughout the 113-line poem is extremely tedious. A more subtle use of onomatopoetic words appears in the following passage from *An Essay on Criticism* by Alexander Pope:

> Soft is the strain when Zephyr gently blows,
> And the smooth stream in smoother numbers flows;
> But when the loud surges lash the sounding shore,
> The hoarse, rough verse should like the torrent roar:
> When Ajax strives some rock's vast weight to throw,
> The line too Labors, and the words move slow.

After earlier admonishing readers that sound must echo sense, Pope uses onomatopoetic words such as *lash* and *roar* to convey the fury of the sea, and he uses repeated consonants to echo the sounds these words suggest. Notice, for example, how the *s* and *m* sounds suggest the gently blowing Zephyr and the flowing of the smooth stream and how the series of *r* sounds echoes the torrent's roar.

Alliteration—the repetition of consonant sounds in consecutive or neighboring words, usually at the beginning of words—is another device used to enhance sound in a poem. Both Poe ("sinks and swells") and Pope ("smooth stream") make use of alliteration in the preceding excerpts, and so does N. Scott Momaday in the following poem.

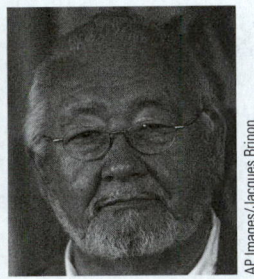

AP Images/Jacques Brinon

N. SCOTT MOMADAY (1934–   )

Comparatives (1976)

Sunlit sea,
the drift of fronds,
and banners
of bobbing boats—
the seaside   5
upon the planks,
the coil and
crescent of flesh
extending
just into death.   10

Even so,
in the distant,
inland sea,
a shadow runs,
radiant,   15
rude in the rock:
fossil fish,
fissure of bone
forever.
It is perhaps   20
the same thing,
an agony
twice perceived.

It is most like
wind on waves—   25
mere commotion,
mute and mean,
perceptible—
that is all.

Throughout the poem, Momaday uses alliteration to create a pleasing aural effect and to link certain words and ideas. Each stanza has its own alliterative pattern: the first stanza contains repeated s and b sounds, the second stanza contains repeated initial r and f sounds, and the third stanza contains repeated initial w and m sounds. Not only does this use of alliteration create a pleasing effect, it also reinforces the development of the poem's theme from stanza to stanza.

Assonance—the repetition of the same or similar vowel sounds, especially in stressed syllables—can also enrich a poem. When used effectively, assonance can create both mood and tone in a subtle, musical way. Consider, for example, the use of assonance in the following lines from Dylan Thomas's "Do not go gentle into that good night": "Old age should burn and rave at close of day; / Rage, rage, against the dying of the light."

Sometimes assonance unifies an entire poem. In the following poem, assonance emphasizes the thematic connections among words and thus links the poem's ideas.

ROBERT HERRICK (1591–1674)

Delight in Disorder (1648)

A sweet disorder in the dress
Kindles in clothes a wantonness.
A lawn[1] about the shoulders thrown
Into a fine distractión;
An erring lace, which here and there   5
Enthralls the crimson stomacher;[2]
A cuff neglectful, and thereby
Ribbons to flow confusedly;
A winning wave, deserving note,
In the tempestuous petticoat;   10
A careless shoestring, in whose tie
I see a wild civility;
Do more bewitch me than when art
Is too precise in every part.

Repeated vowel sounds extend throughout this poem—for instance, "shoulders" and "thrown" in line 3; and "tie," "wild," and "precise" in lines 11, 12, and 14. Using alliteration as well as assonance, Herrick subtly links certain words—"tempestuous petticoat," for example. By connecting these words, he calls attention to the pattern of imagery that helps to convey the poem's theme.

 Rhyme

In addition to alliteration and assonance, poets create sound patterns with **rhyme**—the use of matching sounds in two or more words: "tight" and "might"; "born" and "horn"; "sleep" and "deep." For a rhyme to be **perfect**, final vowel and consonant sounds must be the same, as they are in each of the preceding examples. **Imperfect rhyme** (also called *near rhyme, slant rhyme, approximate rhyme,* or **consonance**) occurs when the final consonant sounds in two words are the same but the preceding vowel sounds are different—"learn" / "barn" or "pads" / "lids," for example. Finally, **eye rhyme** occurs when two words look as if they should rhyme but do not—for example, "watch" and "catch."

Rhyme can also be classified according to the position of the rhyming syllables in a line of verse. The most common type of rhyme is **end rhyme**, which occurs at the end of a line:

Tyger! Tyger! burning <u>bright</u>
In the forests of the <u>night</u>
      William Blake, "The Tyger"

---

[1] *lawn:* A shawl made of fine fabric.
[2] *stomacher:* A heavily embroidered garment worn by females over the chest and stomach.

Internal rhyme occurs within a line:

> The Sun came up upon the left,
> Out of the <u>sea</u> came <u>he</u>!
> And he shone <u>bright</u> and on the <u>right</u>
> Went down into the sea.
>   **Samuel Taylor Coleridge**, "The Rime of the Ancient Mariner"

Beginning rhyme occurs at the beginning of a line:

> Red river, red river,
> <u>Slow</u> flow heat is silence
> <u>No</u> will is still as a river
>   **T. S. Eliot**, "Virginia"

Rhyme can also be classified according to the number of syllables that correspond. **Masculine rhyme** (also called **rising rhyme**) occurs when single syllables correspond ("can" / "ran"; "descend" / "contend"). **Feminine rhyme** (also called **double rhyme** or **falling rhyme**) occurs when two syllables, a stressed one followed by an unstressed one, correspond ("ocean" / "motion"; "leaping" / "sleeping"). **Triple rhyme** occurs when three syllables correspond. Less common than the other two, triple rhyme is often used for humorous or satiric purposes, as in the following lines from the long poem *Don Juan* by Lord Byron:

> Sagest of women, even of widows, she
>   Resolved that Juan should be quite a <u>paragon</u>,
> And worthy of the noblest pedigree:
>   (His sire of Castile, his dam from <u>Aragon</u>).

The conventional way to describe a poem's rhyme scheme is to chart rhyming sounds that appear at the ends of lines. The sound that ends the first line is designated *a*, and all subsequent lines that end in that sound are also labeled *a*. The next sound to appear at the end of a line is designated *b*, and all other lines whose last sounds rhyme with it are also designated *b*—and so on through the alphabet. The lines of the poem that follows are labeled in this manner.

ROBERT FROST (1874–1963)

The Road Not Taken (1915)

Two roads diverged in a yellow wood,	a
And sorry I could not travel both	b
And be one traveler, long I stood	a
And looked down one as far as I could	a
To where it bent in the undergrowth;	b 5
Then took the other, as just as fair	c
And having perhaps the better claim,	d
Because it was grassy and wanted wear;	c

Though as for that, the passing there	c	
Had worn them really about the same,	d	10
And both that morning equally lay	e	
In leaves no step had trodden black	f	
Oh, I kept the first for another day!	e	
Yet knowing how way leads on to way,	e	
I doubted if I should ever come back.	f	15
I shall be telling this with a sigh	g	
Somewhere ages and ages hence:	h	
two roads diverged in a wood, and I—	g	
I took the one less traveled by,	g	
And that has made all the difference.	h	20

The rhyme scheme of the four five-line stanzas in "The Road Not Taken" is the same in each stanza: *abaab, cdccd,* and so on. Except for the last line of the poem, all the rhymes are masculine. Despite its regular rhyme scheme, the poem sounds conversational, as if someone is speaking it without any effort or planning. The beauty of this poem comes from Frost's subtle use of rhyme, which makes the lines flow together, and from the alternating rhymes, which suggest the divergent roads that confront the speaker.

FURTHER READING: Alliteration, Assonance, and Rhyme

GERARD MANLEY HOPKINS (1844–1889)

Pied Beauty (1918)

Glory be to God for dappled things—
    For skies of couple-color as a brinded[1] cow;
      For rose-moles all in stipple upon trout that swim;
Fresh-firecoal chestnut-falls; finches' wings;
    Landscape plotted and pieced—fold, fallow, and plow;   5
      And áll trádes, their gear and tackle and trim.[2]

All things counter, original, spare, strange;
    Whatever is fickle, freckled (who knows how?)
      With swift, slow; sweet, sour; adazzle, dim;
He fathers-forth whose beauty is past change: 10
        Praise him.

---

[1] *brinded:* Brindled (streaked).

[2] *trim:* Equipment.

John Constable, *Summer Evening Near East Bergholt*, Suffolk (1806–09)
V&A Images, London / Art Resource, NY

Reading and Reacting

1. Identify examples of onomatopoeia, alliteration, assonance, imperfect rhyme, and perfect rhyme. Do you think all these techniques are essential to the poem? Are any of them annoying or distracting?

2. What is the central idea of this poem? How do the sounds of the poem help to communicate this idea?

2. Identify examples of masculine and feminine rhyme.

4. **JOURNAL ENTRY** Hopkins uses both pleasing and discordant sounds in his poem. Identify uses of euphony and cacophony, and explain how these techniques affect your reactions to the poem.

5. **CRITICAL PERSPECTIVE** In her essay "The Allegory of Form in Hopkins's Religious Sonnets," Jennifer A. Wagner discusses the ways in which Gerard Manley Hopkins saw relationships between what his poems were saying and how they expressed it:

> Hopkins's most profound perception with regard to the form lies precisely in his demand for the conventional integrity of the sonnet, in his "dogmatic" (his word) insistence on the division of the octave and sestet—and in his recognition of the revisionary movement in the sonnet structure. . . . For Hopkins the play between octave and sestet is not incidental; it creates a "turn" that becomes a trope of limitation or reduction.

Since "Pied Beauty" is what is known as a "curtal," or shortened, sonnet, it is not divided into sections of eight and six lines (the "octet" and "sestet" that Wagner mentions). Still, there is a turn, or change of emphasis between the poem's two parts. How does the poem change after that turn occurs?

Related Works: "Cathedral" (p. 435), "Women" (p. 846), "I wandered lonely as a cloud" (p. 893), "Loveliest of Trees" (p. 894), "Batter My Heart, Three-Personed God" (p. 979), *Beauty* (p. 1069)

SHEL SILVERSTEIN (1930–1999)

Where the Sidewalk Ends (1974)

There is a place where the sidewalk ends
And before the street begins,
And there the grass grows soft and white,
And there the sun burns crimson bright,
And there the moon-bird rests from his flight,   5
To cool in the peppermint wind.

Let us leave this place where the smoke blows black
And the dark street winds and bends.
Past the pits where the asphalt flowers grow
We shall walk with a walk that is measured and slow,   10
And watch where the chalk-white arrows go
To the place where the sidewalk ends.

Yes we'll walk with a walk that is measured and slow,
And we'll go where the chalk-white arrows go,
For the children, they mark, and the children, they know   15
The place where the sidewalk ends.

Reading and Reacting

1. Describe the rhyme scheme of this poem. How does the rhyme scheme contribute to the poem's overall effect?

2. What words does the poem repeat? What ideas does this repetition emphasize?

3. Where does the poem use alliteration and assonance? Do the alliteration and assonance contribute something vital to the poem, or are they just a distraction?

4. JOURNAL ENTRY Silverstein is primarily known as a children's poet. What message does "Where the Sidewalk Ends" have for children? What message do you think it has for adults?

Related Works: "Gryphon" (p. 250), "A Boat Beneath a Sunny Sky" (p. 800), "The Lamb" (p. 960)

Maryam Fakouri

JACOB SAENZ (1982–   )

Evolution of My Block (2010)

As a boy I bicycled the block
w/a brown mop top falling
into a tail bleached blond,

gold-like under golden light,
like colors of Noble Knights   5
'banging on corners, unconcerned

w/the colors I bore—a shorty
too small to war with, too brown
to be down for the block.

White Knights became brown   10
Kings still showing black & gold
on corners now crowned,

the block a branch branded
w/la corona graffitied on
garage doors by the pawns.   15

As a teen, I could've beamed
the crown, walked in w/out
the beat down custom,

warred w/my cousin
who claimed Two-Six,   20
the set on the next block

decked in black & beige.
But I preferred games to gangs,
books to crooks wearing hats

crooked to the left or right   25
fighting for a plot, a block
to spot & mark w/blood

of boys who knew no better
way to grow up than throw up
the crown & be down for whatever.   30

Reading and Reacting

1. Identify several different kinds of rhyme in this poem. Then, find examples of alliteration and assonance.
2. What image does the poem create? How do rhyme, alliteration, and assonance help Saenz convey this image?
3. What words are repeated throughout the poem? What is the purpose of this repetition?
4. Explain the poem's title. How has the speaker's block "evolved"?

5. **JOURNAL ENTRY** How is the speaker different from the other boys on his block? How do you account for these differences?

Related Works: "The Secret Lion" (p. 180), "Greasy Lake" (p. 569), "No Face" (p. 577), "My Voice" (p. 685), "9773 Comanche Ave." (p. 745), "The United Fruit Co." (p. 1006), *The Cuban Swimmer* (p. 1416)

"THE JABBERWOCK, WITH EYES OF FLAME,
CAME WHIFFLING THROUGH THE TULGEY WOOD"

Illustration of Jabberwock from *Alice in Wonderland*
© Mary Evans Picture Library / Alamy

LEWIS CARROLL (1832–1898)

Jabberwocky (1871)

'Twas brillig, and the slithy toves
    Did gyre and gimble in the wabe:
All mimsy were the borogoves,
    And the mome raths outgrabe.

"Beware the Jabberwock, my son!   5
    The jaws that bite, the claws that catch!
Beware the Jubjub bird, and shun
    The frumious Bandersnatch!"

He took his vorpal sword in hand;
    Long time the manxome foe he sought—   10
So rested he by the Tumtum tree
    And stood awhile in thought.

And, as in uffish thought he stood,
    The Jabberwock, with eyes of flame,
Came whiffling through the tulgey wood,   15
    And burbled as it came!

One, two! One, two! And through and through
    The vorpal blade went snicker-snack!
He left it dead, and with its head
    He went galumphing back.   20

"And hast thou slain the Jabberwock?
    Come to my arms, my beamish boy!
O frabjous day! Callooh, Callay!"
    He chortled in his joy.

'Twas brillig, and the slithy toves   25
    Did gyre and gimble in the wabe:
All mimsy were the borogoves,
    And the mome raths outgrabe.

Reading and Reacting

1. Many words in this poem may be unfamiliar to you. Are they actual words? Use a dictionary to check before you dismiss any. Do some words that do not appear in the dictionary nevertheless seem to have meaning in the context of the poem? Explain.

2. This poem contains many examples of onomatopoeia. What meanings does the sound of each of these words suggest?

3. JOURNAL ENTRY Summarize the story the poem tells. In what sense is this poem a story of a young man's initiation into adulthood?

4. **CRITICAL PERSPECTIVE** According to Humpty Dumpty in Carroll's *Alice in Wonderland*, the nonsense words in the poem are **portmanteau words** (that is, words whose form and meaning are derived from two other distinct words—as *smog* is a portmanteau of *smoke* and *fog*). Critic Elizabeth Sewell, however, rejects this explanation: "[F]*rumious*, for instance, is not a word, and does not have two meanings packed up in it; it is a group of letters without any meaning at all. . . . [I]t looks like other words, and almost certainly more than two."

Which nonsense words in the poem seem to you to be portmanteau words, and which do not? Can you suggest possible sources for the words that are not portmanteau words?

Related Works: "The Secret Lion" (p. 180), "A&P" (p. 238), "Gryphon" (p. 250), "To Lucasta Going to the Wars" (p. 781), "A Boat Beneath a Sunny Sky" (p. 800), "Ulysses" (p. 1017)

✔ **CHECKLIST   Writing about Sound**

Rhythm and Meter

☐ Does the poem contain repeated words and phrases? If so, how do they help to create rhythm?

☐ Does the poem use one kind of meter throughout, or does the meter vary from line to line?

☐ How does the meter contribute to the overall effect of the poem?

☐ Where do caesuras appear? What effect do they have?

☐ Are the lines of the poem end-stopped, run-on, or a combination of the two? What effects are created by the presence or absence of pauses at the ends of lines?

Alliteration, Assonance, and Rhyme

☐ Does the poem include alliteration or assonance?

☐ Does the poem have a regular rhyme scheme?

☐ Does the poem use internal rhyme? beginning rhyme?

☐ Does the poem include examples of masculine, feminine, or triple rhyme?

☐ How does rhyme unify the poem?

☐ How does rhyme reinforce the poem's ideas?

WRITING SUGGESTIONS: Sound

1. William Blake's "The Tyger" appeared in a collection entitled *Songs of Experience*. Compare this poem (p. 961) to "The Lamb" (p. 960), which appeared in a collection called *Songs of Innocence*. In what sense are the speakers in these two poems either "innocent" or "experienced"? How does sound help to convey the voice of the speakers in these two poems?

2. "Sadie and Maud" (p. 792), like "My Papa's Waltz" (p. 885) and "Daddy" (p. 772), communicates the speaker's attitude toward home and family. How does the presence or absence of rhyme in these poems help to convey the speakers' attitudes?

3. Robert Frost once said that writing **free verse** poems, which have no fixed metrical pattern, is like playing tennis without a net. What do you think he meant? Do you agree? After reading "Out, Out—" (p. 778), "Stopping by Woods on a Snowy Evening" (p. 9), and "The Road Not Taken" (p. 805), write an essay in which you discuss Frost's use of meter.

4. Select two or three contemporary poems that have no end rhyme. Write an essay in which you discuss what these poets gain and lose by not using end rhyme.

5. Prose writers as well as poets use assonance and alliteration. Choose two or three passages of prose—from "Araby" (p. 361), "Barn Burning" (p. 335), or "The Things They Carried" (p. 392), for example—and discuss their use of assonance and alliteration. Where are these techniques used? How do they help the writer create a mood?

CHAPTER 29

FORM

Alberto Alvaro Ríos
Courtesy of Alberto Alvaro Ríos

George Herbert
Michael Nicholson/Corbis

Elizabeth Bishop
The Granger Collection, NYC

Carl Sandburg
Bettmann/Corbis

JOHN KEATS (1795–1821)

On the Sonnet (1819)

If by dull rhymes our English must be chained,
And like Andromeda,[1] the sonnet sweet
Fettered, in spite of painéd loveliness,
Let us find, if we must be constrained,
Sandals more interwoven and complete   5

---

[1] *Andromeda:* In Greek mythology, an Ethiopian princess chained to a rock to appease a sea monster.

To fit the naked foot of Poesy:
Let us inspect the lyre, and weigh the stress
Of every chord, and see what may be gained
By ear industrious, and attention meet;
Misers of sound and syllable, no less   10
Than Midas[2] of his coinage, let us be
Jealous of dead leaves in the bay-wreath crown;
So, if we may not let the Muse be free,
She will be bound with garlands of her own.

Andromeda in Chains
Giorgio Vasari/Alinari Archives/Fine Art/Corbis

The **form** of a literary work is its structure or shape, the way its elements fit together to form a whole; **poetic form** is the design of a poem described in terms of rhyme, meter, and stanzaic pattern.

Until the twentieth century, most poetry was written in **closed form** (sometimes called **fixed form**), characterized by regular patterns of meter, rhyme, line length, and stanzaic divisions. Early poems that were passed down orally—epics and ballads, for example—relied on regular form to facilitate memorization. Even after poems began to be written down, poets tended to favor regular patterns. In fact, until relatively recently, regular form was what distinguished poetry from prose. Of course, strict adherence to regular patterns sometimes

---

[2]*Midas:* A legendary king of Phrygia whose wish that everything he touched would turn to gold was granted by the god Dionysus.

produced poems that were, in John Keats's words, "chained" by "dull rhymes" and "fettered" by the rules governing a particular form (p. 813). But rather than feeling "constrained" by form, many poets have experimented with imagery, figures of speech, allusion, and other techniques, moving away from rigid patterns of rhyme and meter and thus stretching closed form to its limits.

As they sought new ways in which to express themselves, poets also borrowed forms from other cultures, adapting them to the demands of their own languages. English and American poets, for example, adopted (and still use) early French forms, such as the **villanelle** and the **sestina**, and early Italian forms, such as the **Petrarchan sonnet** and **terza rima**. The nineteenth-century American poet Henry Wadsworth Longfellow studied Icelandic epics; the twentieth-century poet Ezra Pound studied the works of French troubadours; and Pound and other twentieth-century American poets, such as Richard Wright and Carolyn Kizer, were inspired by Japanese haiku. Other American poets, such as Vachel Lindsay, Langston Hughes, and Maya Angelou, looked closer to home—to the rhythms of blues, jazz, and spirituals—for inspiration.

As time went on, more and more poets moved away from closed form to experiment with **open form** poetry (sometimes called **free verse** or *vers libre*), varying line length within a poem, dispensing with meter and stanzaic divisions, breaking lines in unexpected places, and even abandoning any semblance of formal structure. In English, nineteenth-century poets—such as William Blake and Matthew Arnold—experimented with lines of irregular meter and length, and Walt Whitman and others wrote **prose poems**, poems whose lines extend from the left to the right margin, with no line breaks, so that they look like prose. (Well before this time, Asian poetry and some biblical passages had used a type of free verse.) In nineteenth-century France, symbolist poets, such as Baudelaire, Rimbaud, Verlaine, and Mallarmé, also used free verse. In the early twentieth century, a group of American poets—including Ezra Pound, William Carlos Williams, and Amy Lowell—who were associated with a movement known as **imagism** wrote poetry that dispensed with traditional principles of English versification, creating new rhythms and meters.

Although much contemporary English and American poetry is composed in open form, many poets also continue to write in closed form—even in very traditional, highly structured patterns. Still, new forms, and new variations of old forms, are being created all the time. And, because contemporary poets do not necessarily feel bound by rules or restrictions about what constitutes "acceptable" poetic form, they experiment freely, trying to discover the form that best suits the poem's purpose, subject, language, and theme.

Closed Form

A **closed form** poem has an identifiable, repeated pattern, with lines of similar length arranged in groups of two, three, four, or more. A closed form poem also tends to rely on a regular metrical pattern and rhyme scheme.

Despite what its name suggests, closed form poetry does not have to be confining or conservative. In fact, contemporary poets often experiment with closed form—for example, by using characteristics of open form poetry (such as lines of varying length) within a closed form. Sometimes poets move back and forth within a single poem from open to closed to open form; sometimes (like their eighteenth-century counterparts) they combine different stanzaic forms (stanzas of two and three lines, for example) within a single poem.

Even when poets work within a traditional closed form, such as a sonnet, sestina, or villanelle, they can break new ground. For example, they can write a sonnet with an unexpected meter or rhyme scheme (or with no consistent pattern of rhyme or meter at all), add an extra line or even extra stanzas to a traditional sonnet form, combine two different traditional sonnet forms in a single poem, or write an abbreviated version of a sestina or villanelle. In other words, poets can use traditional forms as building blocks, combining them in innovative ways to create new patterns and new forms.

Sometimes a pattern (such as **blank verse**) simply determines the meter of a poem's individual lines. At other times, the pattern extends to the level of the **stanza**, with lines arranged into groups (**couplets**, **quatrains**, and so on). At still other times, as in the case of traditional closed forms like sonnets, a poetic pattern gives shape to an entire poem.

Blank Verse

Blank verse is unrhymed poetry with each line written in a pattern of five stressed and five unstressed syllables called **iambic pentameter** (see p. 795). Many passages from Shakespeare's plays, such as the following lines from *Hamlet*, are written in blank verse:

> To sleep! perchance to dream:—ay, there's the rub;
> For in that sleep of death what dreams may come,
> When we have shuffled off this mortal coil,
> Must give us pause: there's the respect
> That makes calamity of so long life

For a contemporary use of blank verse, see John Updike's "Ex-Basketball Player" (p. 764).

Stanza

A **stanza** is a group of two or more lines with the same metrical pattern—and often with a regular rhyme scheme as well—separated by blank space from other such groups of lines. Stanzas in poetry are like paragraphs in prose: they group related ideas into units.

A two-line stanza with rhyming lines of similar length and meter is called a **couplet**. The **heroic couplet**, first used by Chaucer and later very popular throughout the eighteenth century, consists of two rhymed lines of iambic pentameter, with a weak pause after the first line and a strong pause after the second. The following example, from Alexander Pope's *An Essay on Criticism*, is a heroic couplet:

> True ease in writing comes from art, not chance,
> As those move easiest who have learned to dance.

A three-line stanza with lines of similar length and a set rhyme scheme is called a **tercet**. Percy Bysshe Shelley's "Ode to the West Wind" (p. 1013) is built largely of tercets:

> O wild West Wind, thou breath of Autumn's being,
> Thou, from whose unseen presence the leaves dead
> Are driven, like ghosts from an enchanter fleeing,
>
> Yellow, and black, and pale, and hectic red,
> Pestilence-stricken multitudes: O Thou,
> Who chariotest to their dark wintry bed

Although in many tercets all three lines rhyme, "Ode to the West Wind" uses a special rhyme scheme, also used by Dante, called **terza rima**. This rhyme scheme (*aba, bcb, cdc, ded,* and so on) creates an interlocking series of stanzas: line 2's *dead* looks ahead to the rhyming words *red* and *bed*, which close lines 4 and 6, and the pattern continues throughout the poem. Robert Frost's "Acquainted with the Night" (p. 787) is a contemporary example of terza rima.

A four-line stanza with lines of similar length and a set rhyme scheme is called a **quatrain**. The quatrain, the most widely used and versatile unit in English and American poetry, is used by William Wordsworth in the following excerpt from "She dwelt among the untrodden ways":

> A violet by a mossy stone
>   Half hidden from the eye!
> —Fair as a star, when only one
>   Is shining in the sky.

Quatrains are frequently used by contemporary poets as well—for instance, in Theodore Roethke's "My Papa's Waltz" (p. 885) and *Adrienne* Rich's "Aunt Jennifer's Tigers" (p. 799).

One special kind of quatrain, called the **ballad stanza**, alternates lines of eight and six syllables; typically, only the second and fourth lines rhyme. The following lines from the traditional Scottish ballad "Sir Patrick Spence" illustrate the ballad stanza:

> The king sits in Dumferling toune,
>   Drinking the blude-reid wine:
> "O whar will I get guid sailor
>   To sail this schip of mine?"

Common measure, a four-line stanzaic pattern closely related to the ballad stanza, is used in hymns as well as in poetry. It differs from the ballad stanza in that its rhyme scheme is *abab* rather than *abcb*.

Other stanzaic forms include **rhyme royal**, a seven-line stanza (*ababbcc*) set in iambic pentameter, used in Sir Thomas Wyatt's sixteenth-century poem "They Flee from Me That Sometimes Did Me Seke" as well as in Theodore Roethke's twentieth-century "I Knew a Woman"; **ottava rima**, an eight-line stanza (*abababcc*) set in iambic pentameter; and the **Spenserian stanza**, a nine-line form (*ababbcbcc*) whose first eight lines are set in iambic pentameter and whose last line is in iambic hexameter. The romantic poets John Keats and Percy Bysshe Shelley were among those who used the Spenserian stanza. (See Chapter 28 for definitions and examples of various metrical patterns.)

The Sonnet

Perhaps the most familiar kind of traditional closed form poem written in English is the **sonnet**, a fourteen-line poem with a distinctive rhyme scheme and metrical pattern. The English or **Shakespearean sonnet**, which consists of fourteen lines divided into three quatrains and a concluding couplet, is written in iambic pentameter and follows the rhyme scheme *abab cdcd efef gg*. The **Petrarchan sonnet**, popularized in the fourteenth century by the Italian poet Francesco Petrarch, also consists of fourteen lines of iambic pentameter, but these lines are divided into an eight-line unit called an **octave** and a six-line unit (composed of two tercets) called a **sestet**. The rhyme scheme of the octave is *abba abba*; the rhyme scheme of the sestet is *cde cde*.

The conventional structures of these sonnet forms reflect the arrangement of ideas within the poem. In the Shakespearean sonnet, the poet typically presents three "paragraphs" of related thoughts, introducing an idea in the first quatrain, developing it in the two remaining quatrains, and summing up in a succinct closing couplet. In the Petrarchan sonnet, the octave introduces a problem that is resolved in the sestet. (Many Shakespearean sonnets also have a problem–solution structure.) Some poets vary the traditional patterns somewhat to suit the poem's language or ideas. For example, they may depart from the pattern to sidestep a forced rhyme or unnatural stress on a syllable, or they may shift from problem to solution in a place other than between octave and sestet.

The following poem is a traditional English sonnet.

WILLIAM SHAKESPEARE (1564–1616)

When, in disgrace with Fortune and men's eyes (1609)

When, in disgrace with Fortune and men's eyes,
I all alone beweep my outcast state,
And trouble deaf heaven with my bootless[1] cries,
And look upon myself and curse my fate,
Wishing me like to one more rich in hope,   5
Featured like him, like him with friends possessed,
Desiring this man's art, and that man's scope,
With what I most enjoy contented least,
Yet in these thoughts myself almost despising,
Haply[2] I think on thee, and then my state,   10
Like to the lark at break of day arising
From sullen earth, sings hymns at heaven's gate;
For thy sweet love rememb'red such wealth brings
That then I scorn to change my state with kings.

Shakespeare's sonnet is written in iambic pentameter and has a conventional rhyme scheme: *abab* (eyes-state-cries-fate), *cdcd* (hope-possessed-scope-least), *efef* (despising-state-arising-gate), *gg* (brings-kings). In this poem, in which the speaker explains how thoughts of his loved one can rescue him from despair, each quatrain is unified by subject matter as well as by rhyme.

In the first quatrain, the speaker presents his problem: he is down on his luck and out of favor with his peers, isolated in self-pity and cursing his fate. In the second quatrain, he develops this idea further: he is envious of others and dissatisfied with things that usually

---

[1] *bootless:* Futile.
[2] *Haply:* Luckily.

Goddess of Fortune turning wheel
©Charles Walker / Topfoto / The Image Works

please him. In the third quatrain, the focus shifts. The first two quatrains have developed a dependent clause ("When . . .") that introduces a problem, and now line 9 begins to present the solution. In the third quatrain, the speaker explains how, in the midst of his despair and self-hatred, he thinks of his loved one, and his spirits soar. The closing couplet sums up the mood transformation the poem describes and explains its significance: when the speaker realizes the emotional riches his loved one gives him, he is no longer envious of others.

FURTHER READING: The Sonnet

JOHN KEATS (1795–1821)

On First Looking into Chapman's Homer[1] (1816)

Much have I traveled in the realms of gold,
    And many goodly states and kingdoms seen;
    Round many western islands have I been
Which bards in fealty to Apollo[2] hold.
Oft of one wide expanse had I been told   5
    That deep-browed Homer ruled as his demesne,[3]
    Yet did I never breathe its pure serene[4]

---

[1]*Chapman's Homer:* The translation of Homer's works by Elizabethan poet George Chapman.

[2]*Apollo:* Greek god of light, truth, reason, male beauty; associated with music and poetry.

[3]*demesne:* Realm, domain.

[4]*serene:* Air, atmosphere.

Till I heard Chapman speak out loud and bold.
Then felt I like some watcher of the skies
   When a new planet swims into his ken;   10
Or like stout Cortez[5] when with eagle eyes
   He stared at the Pacific—and all his men
Looked at each other with a wild surmise—
   Silent, upon a peak in Darien.[6]

Bust of Homer
Portrait bust of Homer (marble), Greek, (9th century BC)
/ Private Collection / Photo © Boltin Picture Library /
Bridgeman Images

Reading and Reacting

1. Is this a Petrarchan or a Shakespearean sonnet? Explain.

2. **JOURNAL ENTRY** The sestet's change of focus is introduced with the word *Then* in line 9. How does the mood of the sestet differ from the mood of the octave? How does the language differ?

3. **CRITICAL PERSPECTIVE** As Keats's biographer Aileen Ward observes, Homer's epic tales of gods and heroes were known to most readers of Keats's day only in a very formal eighteenth-century translation by Alexander Pope. Here is Pope's description of Ulysses escaping from a shipwreck:

> his knees no more
> Perform'd their office, or his weight upheld:
> His swoln heart heav'd, his bloated body swell'd:
> From mouth to nose the briny torrent ran,

---

[5] *Cortez:* It was Vasco de Balboa (not Hernando Cortez as Keats suggests) who first saw the Pacific Ocean, from "a peak in Darien."

[6] *Darien:* Former name of the Isthmus of Panama.

And lost in lassitude lay all the man,
Deprived of voice, of motion, and of breath,
The soul scarce waking in the arms of death . . .

In a rare 1616 edition of Chapman's translation, Keats discovered a very different poem:

both knees falt'ring, both
His strong hands hanging down, and all with froth
His cheeks and nostrils flowing, voice and breath
Spent to all use, and down he sank to death.
The sea had soak'd his heart through. . . .

This, as Ward notes, was "poetry of a kind that had not been written in England for two hundred years."

Can you understand why Keats was so moved by Chapman's translation? Do you think Keats's own poem seems closer in its form and language to Pope or to Chapman?

Related Works: "Snow" (p. 126), "Gryphon" (p. 250), "Araby" (p. 361), "When I Heard the Learn'd Astronomer" (p. 715), *Trifles* (p. 1604)

EDNA ST. VINCENT MILLAY (1892–1950)

Love is not all (1931)

Love is not all: it is not meat nor drink
Nor slumber nor a roof against the rain;
Nor yet a floating spar to men that sink
And rise and sink and rise and sink again;
Love can not fill the thickened lung with breath,   5
Nor clean the blood, nor set the fractured bone;
Yet many a man is making friends with death
Even as I speak, for lack of love alone.
It well may be that in a difficult hour,
Pinned down by pain and moaning for release,   10
Or nagged by want past resolution's power,
I might be driven to sell your love for peace,
Or trade the memory of this night for food.
It well may be. I do not think I would.

Reading and Reacting

1. Describe the poem's rhyme scheme. Is it a Petrarchan or a Shakespearean sonnet?
2. Does this poem have a problem–solution structure, or is there some other thematic distinction between its octave and its sestet?
3. Why are the words "It well may be" repeated in lines 9 and 14?

4. **JOURNAL ENTRY** The poem's first six lines list all the things that love is *not* and what it *cannot* do. Why do you think the poet chose not to enumerate what love *is* and what it *can* do?

5. CRITICAL PERSPECTIVE In an essay on Edna St. Vincent Millay's love sonnets, poet and critic Anna Evans notes the ways in which Millay's unconventional lifestyle provided material for her poetry:

> Some of Millay's finest sonnets written during her marriage are presumed to be addressed to her younger poet lover George Dillon, who became part of a ménage a trois in the Millay household. . . The narrator of "Love is not all: it is not meat or drink" demonstrates Millay's newest philosophy of romantic love. There is no doubt that the speaker is expressing love for the object of the poem, yet there is no commitment, the love is spoken of already almost as of something in the past, and the poem lacks an absolute conviction of permanence.

What evidence can you find in the poem to support Evans's claims that there is no romantic "commitment," and that the speaker "lacks an absolute conviction of permanence"?

Related Works: "Love and Other Catastrophes: A Mix Tape" (p. 127), "If I should learn, in some quite casual way" (p. 775), "When, in disgrace with Fortune and men's eyes" (p. 818), "How Do I Love Thee?" (p. 899), "What lips my lips have kissed" (p. 899), "General Review of the Sex Situation" (p. 901)

LYNN AARTI CHANDHOK (1963–   )

The Carpet Factory (2001)

A wood shack on the riverbank. Inside,
through dust-filled shafts of light, bright colors rise
and drown the warps, transforming their brown threads
to poppy fields, the Tree of Life, a wide
sun hemmed by cartwheeled tulips, fountainheads   5
that spew blue waterfalls of peacock eyes.

With furious fingers mothlike at the weft,
the children tie and cut and tie and cut
and tamp the knots down, turning blade to gavel.
Each pull's a dust-cloud *plink*—bereft   10
of music. Toothless men spit betelnut
in blood-red stains. Everywhere, reds unravel.

The bended limbs of saplings twist and part
and weave into the prayer rug's pale silk heart.

Reading and Reacting

1. Look carefully at this poem's rhyme scheme and at the way its lines are divided into stanzas. Is it more like a Shakespearean or a Petrarchan sonnet? Explain.
2. This poem uses color imagery to describe a prayer rug. Identify the references to color. Do they all describe the rug?
3. What point does this poem make about the carpet factory? How does the closing couplet sum up this point?

4. **JOURNAL ENTRY** How are the descriptions of the factory—and of its child laborers—different from the descriptions of the carpets produced there?

5. **CRITICAL PERSPECTIVE** Reviewing Lynn Aarti Chandhok's book *The View from Zero Bridge*, Patty Paine focuses on the poem "The Carpet Factory":

> This poem itself is meticulously crafted and beautifully realized. The form and the content merge seamlessly. . . One can see the slants of light, the children's fingers darting at the weft, hear the plink and watch the blood-red spittle seep into the ground. By taking such care with her images, the poet has created an intimacy and familiarity that transports the reader into a world that is fully formed. . . The specter of child labor hovers over "The Carpet Factory," and Chandhok confronts the issue through imagery rather than polemics.

Given its focus on the issue of child labor, do you see this poem as social protest? Or, do you see the poem's content as less important than its form and imagery? How does Paine's reading of the poem affect your own interpretation of it? Do the poem's "form and content merge seamlessly"?

Related Works: "Girl" (p. 137), "Gretel in Darkness" (p. 677), "The Secretary Chant" (p. 767), "Aunt Jennifer's Tigers" (p. 799), "Indian Boarding School: The Runaways" (p. 986), *Trifles* (p. 1604)

GWENDOLYN BROOKS (1917–2000)

First Fight. Then Fiddle (1949)

First fight. Then fiddle. Ply the slipping string
With feathery sorcery; muzzle the note
With hurting love; the music that they wrote
Bewitch, bewilder. Qualify to sing
Threadwise. Devise no salt, no hempen thing   5
For the dear instrument to bear. Devote
The bow to silks and honey. Be remote
A while from malice and from murdering.
But first to arms, to armor. Carry hate
In front of you and harmony behind.   10
Be deaf to music and to beauty blind.
Win war. Rise bloody, maybe not too late
For having first to civilize a space
Wherein to play your violin with grace.

Reading and Reacting

1. What is the subject of Brooks's poem?
2. Explain the poem's rhyme scheme. Is this rhyme scheme an essential element of the poem? Would the poem be equally effective if it did not include end rhyme? Why or why not?

3. Study the poem's use of capitalization and punctuation carefully. Why do you think Brooks chooses to end many of her sentences in midline? How do her decisions determine how you read the poem?

4. JOURNAL ENTRY What do you think Brooks means by "fight" and "fiddle"?

Related Works: "The White City" (p. 694), "The Soldier" (p. 904)

RHINA ESPAILLAT (1932–   )

"Find Work" (1999)

> *I tie my Hat—I crease my Shawl—*
> *Life's little duties do—precisely*
> *As the very least*
> *Were infinite—to me—*
> —Emily Dickinson, #443

My mother's mother, widowed very young
of her first love, and of that love's first fruit,
moved through her father's farm, her country tongue
and country heart anaesthetized and mute
with labor. So her kind was taught to do—   5
"Find work," she would reply to every grief—
and her one dictum, whether false or true,
tolled heavy with her passionate belief.
Widowed again, with children, in her prime,
she spoke so little it was hard to bear   10
so much composure, such a truce with time
spent in the lifelong practice of despair.
But I recall her floors, scrubbed white as bone,
her dishes, and how painfully they shone.

Reading and Reacting

1. Explain the meaning of each of the following in the context of the poem:
- "that love's first fruit" (line 2)
- "her kind" (5)
- "truce with time" (11)

2. Why does the poet choose the words "anaesthetized" (4) and "painfully" (14)? What other words would work with the poem's content and meter?

3. Why do you think the poet introduces the poem with lines from Emily Dickinson? How are these lines related to the poem's content?

4. JOURNAL ENTRY Do you think the sonnet form suits this poem's subject matter? Why or why not?

Related Works: "I Stand Here Ironing" (p. 299), "A Worn Path" (p. 463), "Mexican Almuerzo in New England" (p. 843), "Dusting" (p. 886), "Not Waving but Drowning" (p. 1015), *Trifles* (p. 1604)

The Sestina

The **sestina**, introduced in thirteenth-century France, is composed of six 6-line stanzas and a three-line conclusion called an **envoi**. The sestina does not require end rhyme; however, it requires that each line end with one of six key words, which are repeated throughout the poem in a fixed order. The alternation of these six words in different positions—but always at the ends of lines—in each of the poem's six stanzas creates a rhythmic verbal pattern that unifies the poem, as the key words do in the poem that follows.

ALBERTO ALVARO RÍOS (1952–   )

Nani (1982)

Sitting at her table, she serves
the sopa de arroz[1] to me
instinctively, and I watch her,
the absolute mamá, and eat words
I might have had to say more   5
out of embarrassment. To speak,
now-foreign words I used to speak,
too, dribble down her mouth as she serves
me albóndigas.[2] No more
than a third are easy to me.   10
By the stove she does something with words
and looks at me only with her
back. I am full. I tell her
I taste the mint, and watch her speak
smiles at the stove. All my words   15
make her smile. Nani never serves
herself, she only watches me
with her skin, her hair. I ask for more.

I watch the mamá warming more
tortillas for me. I watch her   20
fingers in the flame for me.
Near her mouth, I see a wrinkle speak
of a man whose body serves

---

[1] *sopa de arroz:* Rice soup.

[2] *albóndigas:* Meatballs.

the ants like she serves me, then more words
from more wrinkles about children, words   25
about this and that, flowing more
easily from these other mouths. Each serves
as a tremendous string around her,
holding her together. They speak
nani was this and that to me   30
and I wonder just how much of me
will die with her, what were the words
I could have been, was. Her insides speak
through a hundred wrinkles, now, more
than she can bear, steel around her,   35
shouting, then, What is this thing she serves?

She asks me if I want more.
I own no words to stop her.
Even before I speak, she serves.

In many respects, Ríos's poem closely follows the form of the traditional sestina. For instance, it interweaves six key words—"serves," "me," "her," "words," "more," and "speak"—through six groups of six lines each, rearranging the order in which the words appear so that the first line of each group of six lines ends with the same key word that also ended the preceding group of lines. The poem repeats the key words in exactly the order prescribed: *abcdef, faebdc, cfdabe,* and so on. In addition, the sestina closes with a three-line envoi that includes all six of the poem's key words, three at the ends of lines and three within the lines. Despite this generally strict adherence to the sestina form, Ríos departs from the form by grouping his six sets of six lines not into six separate stanzas but rather into two eighteen-line stanzas.

The sestina form suits Ríos's subject matter. The focus of the poem, on the verbal and nonverbal interaction between the poem's "me" and "her," is reinforced by each of the related words. "Nani" is a poem about communication, and the key words return to probe this theme again and again. Throughout the poem, these repeated words help to create a fluid, melodic, and tightly woven work.

FURTHER READING: The Sestina

ELIZABETH BISHOP (1911–1979)

Sestina (1965)

September rain falls on the house.
In the failing light, the old grandmother
sits in the kitchen with the child
beside the Little Marvel Stove,
reading the jokes from the almanac,   5
laughing and talking to hide her tears.

She thinks that her equinoctial tears
and the rain that beats on the roof of the house
were both foretold by the almanac,
but only known to a grandmother.   10
The iron kettle sings on the stove.
She cuts some bread and says to the child,

It's time for tea now; but the child
is watching the teakettle's small hard tears
dance like mad on the hot black stove,   15
the way the rain must dance on the house.
Tidying up, the old grandmother
hangs up the clever almanac

on its string. Birdlike, the almanac
hovers half open above the child,   20
hovers above the old grandmother
and her teacup full of dark brown tears.
She shivers and says she thinks the house
feels chilly, and puts more wood in the stove.

It was to be, says the Marvel Stove.   25
I know what I know, says the almanac.
With crayons the child draws a rigid house
and a winding pathway. Then the child
puts in a man with buttons like tears
and shows it proudly to the grandmother.   30

But secretly, while the grandmother
busies herself about the stove,
the little moons fall down like tears
from between the pages of the almanac
into the flower bed the child   35
has carefully placed in the front of the house.

Time to plant tears, says the almanac.
The grandmother sings to the marvellous stove
and the child draws another inscrutable house.

Reading and Reacting

1. Does the poet's adherence to the traditional sestina form create any problems? For example, do you think word order seems forced at any point?
2. Consider the adjectives used in this poem. Which of them are unexpected? What is the effect of these surprising choices? Do you find them distracting, or do you think they strengthen the poem?

3. **JOURNAL ENTRY** What are the poem's six key words? How are these words related to the poem's theme?

4. CRITICAL PERSPECTIVE In his essay "Elizabeth Bishop's Surrealist Inheritance," Richard Mullen writes the following:

> Some of the enchanted mystery which permeates Elizabeth Bishop's poetry arises from her preoccupation with dreams, sleep, and the borders between sleeping and waking. Her poems contain much of the magic, uncanniness and displacement associated with the works of the surrealists, for she too explores the workings of the unconscious and the interplay between conscious perception and dream.

What examples can you find in "Sestina" of "the enchanted mystery" to which Mullen refers? In what ways is the poem dreamlike?

Related Works: "Nani" (p. 825), "My Papa's Waltz" (p. 885), "The Fish" (p. 957)

PATRICIA SMITH (1955–   )

Ethel's Sestina (2006)

Ethel Freeman's body sat for days in her wheelchair outside the New Orleans Convention Center. Her son Herbert, who has assured his mother that help was on the way, was forced to leave her there once she died.

Gon' be obedient in this there chair,
gon's bide my time, fanning against this sun.
I ask my boy, and all he says is *Wait*.
He wipes my brow with steam, says I should sleep.
I trust his every word. Herbert my son.   5
I believe him when he says help gon' come

Been so long since all these suffrin' folks come
to this place. Now on the ground 'round my chair,
they sweat in my shade, keep asking my son
could that be a bus they see. It's the sun   10
foolin' them, shining much too loud for sleep,
making us hear engines, wheels. Not yet. Wait.

Lawd, some folks prayin' for rain while they wait,
forgetting what rain can do. When it come,
it smashes living flat, wakes you from sleep,   15
eats streets, washes you clean out of the chair
you be sittin' in. Best to praise this sun,
shinin' its dry shine *Lawd have mercy, son.*

Is it coming? Such a strong man, my son.
Can't help but believe when he tells us, *Wait.*   20
Wait some more. Wish some trees would block this sun.
We wait. Ain't no white men or buses come,
but look—see that there? Get me out this chair,
help me stand on up. No time for sleepin',

cause look what's rumbling this way. If you sleep   25
you gon' miss it. *Look there*, I tell my son.
He don't hear. I'm 'bout to get out this chair,
but the ghost in my legs tells me to wait,
wait for the salvation that's sho to come.
I see my savior's face 'longside that sun.   30

Nobody sees me running toward the sun.
Lawd, they think I done gone and fell asleep.
They don't hear *Come*.

Come.
Come.   35
Come.
Come.
Come.
Come.

Ain't but one power make me leave my son.   40
I can't wait, Herbert. Lawd knows I can't wait.
Don't cry, boy, I ain't in that chair no more.

Wish you coulda come on this journey, son,
seen that ol' sweet sun lift me out of sleep.
Didn't have to wait. And see my golden chair?   45

People waiting for help outside the New Orleans Convention Center
after Hurricane Katrina in 2005

Mario Tama/Getty Images News/Getty Images

Reading and Reacting

1. What six key words are repeated in this poem? What other words are repeated? Why?
2. Where does this sestina depart from its required form? Is this departure justified by the poem's theme or subject matter? Does it strengthen or weaken the poem's impact?
3. **JOURNAL ENTRY** Write a few sentences—or a few lines of poetry—from Herbert's point of view, expressing what you think he would like to tell his mother.

4. CRITICAL PERSPECTIVE In an interview with Cherryl Floyd-Miller for the Webzine *Torch*, Patricia Smith talked about the qualities of a good "persona poem":

> I think the persona poem moves us out of our space, moves us out of our comfort zone where we're almost forced to take a really hard look at another life. Whether it be something you're just doing for the fun of it, like, you know, wow, what's it like to be Little Richard for a day, or you're sitting next to some woman who is clutching like twenty bags or something on the subway, you know that her whole life is in those bags, and you realize just how close everyone's life is to your own.

Does "Ethel's Sestina" take you "out of [your] comfort zone"? Does it make you "realize just how close everyone's life is to your own"?

Related Works: "Girl" (p. 137), "Everyday Use" (p. 426), "Incident" (p. 779), "Do not go gentle into that good night" (p. 891), "I, Too" (p. 918), *Fences* (p. 1548)

The Villanelle

The villanelle, first introduced in France during the Middle Ages, is a nineteen-line poem composed of five tercets and a concluding quatrain; its rhyme scheme is *aba aba aba aba aba abaa*. Two different lines are systematically repeated in the poem: line 1 appears again in lines 6, 12, and 18, and line 3 reappears as lines 9, 15, and 19. Thus, each tercet concludes with an exact (or close) duplication of either line 1 or line 3, and the final quatrain concludes by repeating both line 1 and line 3.

Earth Mother, painting of Mother Nature by Sir Edward Burne-Jones, 1882

Earth Mother, 1882 (encaustic on panel), Burne-Jones, Sir Edward Coley (1833–98) / Worcester Art Museum, Massachusetts, USA/The Bridgeman Art Library

THEODORE ROETHKE (1908–1963)

The Waking (1953)

I wake to sleep, and take my waking slow.
I feel my fate in what I cannot fear.
I learn by going where I have to go.

We think by feeling. What is there to know?
I hear my being dance from ear to ear.   5
I wake to sleep, and take my waking slow.

Of those so close beside me, which are you?
God bless the Ground! I shall walk softly there,
And learn by going where I have to go.

Light takes the Tree; but who can tell us how?   10
The lowly worm climbs up a winding stair;
I wake to sleep, and take my waking slow.

Great Nature has another thing to do
To you and me; so take the lively air,
And, lovely, learn by going where to go.   15

This shaking keeps me steady. I should know.
What falls away is always. And is near.
I wake to sleep, and take my waking slow.
I learn by going where I have to go.

"The Waking," like all villanelles, closely intertwines threads of sounds and words. The repeated lines and the very regular rhyme and meter give the poem a monotonous, almost hypnotic, rhythm. This poem uses end rhyme and repeats entire lines. It also makes extensive use of alliteration ("I feel my fate in what I cannot fear") and internal rhyme ("I hear my being dance from ear to ear"; "I wake to sleep and take my waking slow"). The result is a tightly constructed poem of overlapping sounds and images.

DEBORAH PAREDEZ (1970–   )

Wife's Disaster Manual (2012)

When the forsaken city starts to burn,
after the men and children have fled,
stand still, silent as prey, and slowly turn

back. Behold the curse. Stay and mourn
the collapsing doorways, the unbroken bread   5
in the forsaken city starting to burn.

Don't flinch. Don't join in.
Resist the righteous scurry and instead
stand still, silent as prey. Slowly turn

your thoughts away from escape: the iron   10
gates unlatched, the responsibilities shed.
When the forsaken city starts to burn,

surrender to your calling, show concern
for those who remain. Come to a dead
standstill. Silent as prey, slowly turn   15

into something essential. Learn
the names of the fallen. Refuse to run ahead
when the forsaken city starts to burn.
Stand still and silent. Pray. Return.

Reading and Reacting

1. This poem is a series of commands. To whom are these commands addressed? What reaction do you think the speaker expects?
2. What does the word *forsaken* mean? What is the "forsaken city"?
3. What two lines are repeated in this villanelle? What is the poem's rhyme scheme? Does it depart form the traditional structure of the villanelle in any respects? Explain.

4. **JOURNAL ENTRY** What do you think this poem is about? What makes you think so?

Related Works: "Fire and Ice" (p. 686), "The World Is Too Much with Us" (p. 692), "Going to Work" (p. 783), "Aristotle" (p. 865), "The End and the Beginning" (p. 908)

The Epigram

Originally, an epigram was an inscription carved in stone on a monument or statue. As a literary form, an **epigram** is a very brief poem that makes a pointed, often sarcastic, comment in a surprising twist at the end. In a sense, it is a poem with a punch line. Although some epigrams rhyme, others do not. Many are only two lines long, but others are somewhat longer. What they have in common is their economy of language and their tone.

FURTHER READING: The Epigram

SAMUEL TAYLOR COLERIDGE (1772–1834)

What Is an Epigram? (1802)

What is an epigram? a dwarfish whole,
Its body brevity, and wit its soul.

DOROTHY PARKER (1893–1967)

News Item (1937)

Men seldom make passes
At girls who wear glasses.

CAROL ANN DUFFY (1955–   )

Mrs. Darwin (2001)

7 April 1852
Went to the Zoo.
I said to Him—
Something about that Chimpanzee over there reminds me of you.

Reading and Reacting

1. Explain the point made in each of the epigrams above.
2. Evaluate each poem. What qualities do you conclude make an epigram effective?

3. **JOURNAL ENTRY** In what respects are short-short stories (see Chapter 10) and ten-minute plays (see Chapter 36) like epigrams?

4. **CRITICAL PERSPECTIVE** In "Making Love Modern: Dorothy Parker and Her Public," Nina Miller explains why Dorothy Parker's poetry achieved its considerable popularity during the 1920s:

   Sophistication—that highly prized commodity which was to define the Jazz Age—meant cynicism and a barbed wit, and women like Parker were perfectly situated to dominate this discourse. In the twenties, as a wisecracking member of the celebrated Algonquin Round Table,

Parker would be at the cutting edge of a mannered and satirical wittiness, one which determined the shape of her poetry in important ways.

What is it that makes "News Item" witty? If it is satirical, what attitudes in society does it satirize?

Related Works: "Love and Other Catastrophes: A Mix Tape" (p. 127), "Fire and Ice" (p. 686), "You fit into me" (p. 780), "Shakespearean Sonnet" (p. 868), "General Review of the Sex Situation" (p. 901), *Nine Ten* (p. 1108)

MARTÍN ESPADA (1957–   )

Why I Went to College (2000)

> If you don't,
> my father said,
> you better learn
> to eat soup
> through a straw,   5
> 'cause I'm gonna
> break your jaw

Reading and Reacting

1. How is "Why I Went to College" different from the three epigrams on page 832? How is it similar to them?
2. What function does the poem's title serve? Is it the epigram's "punch line," or does it serve another purpose?
3. What can you infer about the speaker's father from this poem? Why, for example, do you think he wants his son to go to college?
4. **JOURNAL ENTRY** Exactly why did the speaker go to college? Expand this short poem into a paragraph written from the speaker's point of view.

Related Works: "Baca Grande" (p. 723), "My Father as a Guitar" (p. 770), "My Papa's Waltz" (p. 885), "'Faith' is a fine invention" (p. 973), "Marks" (p. 1008)

A. R. AMMONS (1926–2001)

Both Ways (1990)

> One can't
> have it
>
> both ways
> and both

ways is   5
the only

way I
want it.

Reading and Reacting

1. Is this poem actually an epigram, or is it just a short poem? Explain your conclusion.
2. Why do you think the speaker uses "one" in line 1 and "I" in line 7? Try substituting other pronouns for these two. How do your substitutions change the poem's meaning?

3. **JOURNAL ENTRY** Write three original epigrams: one about love, one about school or work, and one about a social or political issue.

4. **CRITICAL PERSPECTIVE** In reviewing *The Really Short Poems of A. R. Ammons*, poet and critic Fred Chappell criticizes some of the individual poems as trivial or even confusing but then goes on to add the following:

   [A]t his best [Ammons] is incomparable. No one else is so cheerfully quirky, so slyly sensible, so oxymoronically accurate. Most of us think in clichés, I'm afraid, but Ammons appears to think in reversed clichés; it's hard to believe he ever met a thought he didn't want to stand on its head. When he has done so, the effect may be merely clumsy. But it may also be utterly fresh and original, witty, unexpected, serious, and even profound.

   Is "Both Ways" an example of one of the "reversed clichés" that Chappell discusses? Is the poem "witty"? Could it be considered "serious, and even profound"?

Related Works: "The Story of an Hour" (p. 201), "Two Kinds" (p. 639) "The Road Not Taken" (p. 805), *Beauty* (p. 1069)

Haiku

Like an epigram, a haiku compresses words into a very small package. Unlike an epigram, however, a haiku focuses on an image, not an idea. A traditional Japanese form, the **haiku** is a brief unrhymed poem that presents the essence of some aspect of nature, concentrating a vivid image in three lines. Although in the strictest sense a haiku consists of seventeen syllables divided into three lines of five, seven, and five syllables, respectively, not all poets conform to this rigid structure.

The following poem is a translation of a classic Japanese haiku by Matsuo Bashō:

Silent and still: then
Even sinking into the rocks,
The cicada's screech.

Notice that this poem conforms to the haiku's three-line structure and traditional subject matter, vividly depicting a natural scene without comment or analysis.

FURTHER READING: Haiku

MATSUO BASHŌ (1644–1694)

Four Haiku*

Translated by Geoffrey Bownas and Anthony Thwaite

Spring:
A hill without a name
Veiled in morning mist.

The beginning of autumn:
Sea and emerald paddy   5
Both the same green.

The winds of autumn
Blow: yet still green
The chestnut husks.

A flash of lightning: 10
Into the gloom
Goes the heron's cry.

Reading and Reacting

1. Haiku are admired for their extreme economy and their striking images. What are the central images in each of Bashō's haiku? To what senses do these images appeal?

2. In another poem, Bashō says that art begins with "The depths of the country / and a rice-planting song." What do you think he means? How do these four haiku exemplify this idea?

3. Do you think the conciseness of these poems increases or decreases the impact of their images? Explain.

4. **JOURNAL ENTRY** "In a Station of the Metro" (p. 742) is Ezra Pound's version of a haiku. How successful do you think his poem is as a haiku? Do you think a longer poem could have conveyed the images more effectively?

Related Works: "Where Mountain Lion Lay Down with Deer" (p. 682), "Some Good Things to Be Said for the Iron Age" (p. 743), "the sky was can dy" (p. 840), "Easter Wings" (p. 847), "Birches" (p. 895), "Fog" (p. 895), "Meeting at Night" (p. 898)

---

*Publication date is not available.

JACK KEROUAC (1922–1969)

American Haiku*

Early morning yellow flowers,
thinking about
the drunkards of Mexico.

No telegram today
only more leaves   5
fell.

Nightfall,
boy smashing dandelions
with a stick.

Holding up my   10
purring cat to the moon
I sighed.

Drunk as a hoot owl,
writing letters
by thunderstorm.   15

Empty baseball field
a robin
hops along the bench.

All day long
wearing a hat   20
that wasn't on my head.

Crossing the football field
coming home from work—
the lonely businessman.

After the shower   25
among the drenched roses
the bird thrashing in the bath.

Snap your finger
stop the world—
rain falls harder.   30

Nightfall,
too dark to read the page
too cold.

Following each other
my cats stop   35
when it thunders.

*Publication date is not available.

Wash hung out
by moonlight
Friday night in May.

The bottoms of my shoes   40
are clean
from walking in the rain.

Glow worm
sleeping on this flower—
your light's on.   45

Reading and Reacting

1. How are these haiku different from those by Matsuo Bashō (p. 835)? Do they fit the definition of *haiku* on page 834?

2. What, if anything, makes these poems "American"? Is it their language? their subject
   matter? something else?

3. **JOURNAL ENTRY** Try writing a few "American haiku" of your own. Then, evaluate the
   success of your efforts. What problems did you encounter?

4. **CRITICAL PERSPECTIVE** Writing about his experiments with haiku, Jack Kerouac said,
   "Above all, a Haiku must be very simple and free of all poetic trickery and make a little
   picture and yet be as airy and graceful as a Vivaldi Pastorella."

   Do you think Kerouac's haiku satisfy these conditions?

Related Works: "Love and Other Catastrophes: A Mix Tape" (p. 127), "Comparatives"
(p. 803), "Chicago" (p. 838), *from* "Song of Myself" (p. 1023)

 ## Open Form

Although an **open form** poem may make occasional use of rhyme and meter, it has no
familiar pattern or design: no conventional stanzaic divisions, no consistent metrical pattern or line length, no repeated rhyme scheme. Still, open form poetry is not necessarily
shapeless, untidy, or randomly ordered. All poems have form, and the form of a poem
may be determined by factors such as repeated sounds, the appearance of words on the
printed page, or pauses in natural speech as well as by a conventional metrical pattern or
rhyme scheme.

Open form poetry invites readers to participate in the creative process, to discover the
relationship between form and meaning. In fact, some modern poets believe that only open
form offers them freedom to express their ideas or that the subject matter or mood of their
poetry demands a relaxed, experimental approach to form. For example, when Lawrence
Ferlinghetti portrays the poet as an acrobat who "climbs on rime" (p. 760), he constructs his
poem in a way that is consistent with the poet/acrobat's willingness to take risks. Thus, the
poem's idiosyncratic form supports its ideas about the limitless possibilities of poetry and the
poet as experimenter.

Without a conventional pattern, however, poets must create forms that suit their needs, and they must continue to shape and reshape the look of the poem on the page as they revise its words. Thus, open form is a challenge, but it is also a way for poets to experiment with fresh arrangements of words and new juxtapositions of ideas, as Carl Sandburg does in the following poem.

Source: ©Bettmann/Corbis

CARL SANDBURG (1878–1967)

Chicago (1914)

Hog Butcher for the World,
Tool Maker, Stacker of Wheat,
Player with Railroads and the Nation's Freight Handler;
Stormy, husky, brawling,
City of the Big Shoulders: 5
They tell me you are wicked and I believe them, for I have seen
    your painted women under the gas lamps luring the farm boys.
And they tell me you are crooked and I answer: Yes, it is true
    I have seen the gunman kill and go free to kill again.
And they tell me you are brutal and my reply is: On the faces of
    women and children I have seen the marks of wanton hunger.
And having answered so I turn once more to those who sneer at
    this my city, and I give them back the sneer and say to them:
Come and show me another city with lifted head singing so
    proud to be alive and coarse and strong and cunning.   10
Flinging magnetic curses amid the toil of piling job on job,
    here is a tall bold slugger set vivid against the little soft cities;
Fierce as a dog with tongue lapping for action, cunning as a
    savage pitted against the wilderness,
    Bareheaded,
      Shoveling,
      Wrecking,   15
      Planning,
      Building, breaking, rebuilding,
Under the smoke, dust all over his mouth, laughing with white
    teeth,
Under the terrible burden of destiny laughing as a young man
    laughs,
Laughing even as an ignorant fighter laughs who has never lost
    a battle,   20
Bragging and laughing that under his wrist is the pulse, and under
    his ribs the heart of the people,
                  Laughing!
Laughing the stormy, husky, brawling laughter of Youth,
    half-naked, sweating, proud to be Hog Butcher, Tool Maker,
    Stacker of Wheat, Player with Railroads and Freight Handler
    to the Nation.

Chicago street scene, 1925
Hulton-Deutsch Collection/Historical/Corbis

"Chicago" uses capitalization and punctuation conventionally, and it generally (though not always) arranges words in lines in a way that is consistent with the natural divisions of phrases and sentences. However, the poem is not divided into stanzas, and its lines vary widely in length—from a single word isolated on a line to a line crowded with words—and follow no particular metrical pattern. Instead, its form is created through its pattern of alternating sections of long and short lines; through its repeated words and phrases ("They tell me" in lines 6–8, "under" in lines 18–19, and "laughing" in lines 18–23, for example); through **alliteration** (for instance, "slugger set vivid against the little soft cities" in line 11); and, most of all, through the piling up of words and images into catalogs in lines 1–5, 13–17, and 22.

In order to understand Sandburg's reasons for choosing such a form, readers need to consider the poem's subject matter and theme. "Chicago" celebrates the scope and power of a "Stormy, husky, brawling" city, one that is exuberant and outgoing, not sedate and civilized. Chicago is a city that does not follow anyone else's rules; it is, after all, "Bareheaded, / Shoveling, / Wrecking, / Planning, / Building, breaking, rebuilding," constantly active, in flux, on the move, "proud to be alive." "Fierce as a dog . . . cunning as a savage," the city is characterized as, among other things, a worker, a fighter, and a harborer of "painted women" and killers and hungry women and children. Just as Chicago itself does not conform to the rules, the poem departs from the orderly confines of stanzaic form and measured rhyme and meter, a kind of form that is, after all, better suited to "the little soft cities" than to the "tall bold slugger" that is Chicago.

Of course, open form poetry does not have to look like Sandburg's prose poem. The following poem, an extreme example of open form, looks almost as if it has spilled out of a box of words.

E. E. CUMMINGS (1894–1962)

the sky was can dy (1925)

the
    sky
        was
can dy lu
minous   5
        edible
spry
      pinks shy
lemons
greens   coo l choc   10
olate
s.

  un der,
  a lo
co   15
mo
  tive   s pout
         ing
           vi
             o   20
         lets

Like many of Cummings's poems, this one seems ready to skip off the page. Its irregular line length and its unconventional capitalization, punctuation, and word divisions immediately draw readers' attention to its form. Despite these oddities, and despite the absence of orderly rhyme and meter, the poem does have its conventional elements.

A closer examination reveals that the poem's theme—the beauty of the sky—is quite conventional; that the poem is divided, though somewhat crudely, into two sections; and that the poet does use some rhyme—"spry" and "shy," for example. However, Cummings's sky is described not in traditional terms but rather as something "edible," not only in terms of color but of flavor as well. The breaks within words ("can dy lu / minous"; "coo l choc / olate / s") seem to expand the words' possibilities, visually stretching them to the limit, extending their taste and visual image over several lines and, in the case of the poem's last two words, visually reinforcing the picture the words describe. In addition, the isolation of syllables exposes hidden rhyme, as in "lo / co / mo" and "lu" / "coo." Thus, by using open form, Cummings illustrates the capacity of a poem to move beyond the traditional boundaries set by words and lines.

FURTHER READING: Open Form

WALT WHITMAN (1819–1892)

from "Out of the Cradle Endlessly Rocking" (1881)

Out of the cradle endlessly rocking,
Out of the mocking-bird's throat, the musical shuttle,
Out of the Ninth-month[1] midnight,
Over the sterile sands and the fields beyond, where the child
    leaving his bed wander'd alone, bareheaded, barefoot,
Down from the shower'd halo,   5
Up from the mystic play of shadows twining and twisting as if
    they were alive,
Out from the patches of briers and blackberries,
From the memories of the bird that chanted to me,
From your memories sad brother, from the fitful risings and
    fallings I heard,
From under that yellow half-moon late-risen and swollen as if
    with tears,   10
From those beginning notes of yearning and love there in the
    mist,
From the thousand responses of my heart never to cease,
From the myriad thence-arous'd words,
From the word stronger and more delicious than any,
From such as now they start the scene revisiting,   15
As a flock, twittering, rising, or overhead passing,
Borne hither, ere all eludes me, hurriedly,
A man, yet by these tears a little boy again,
Throwing myself on the sand, confronting the waves,
I, chanter of pains and joys, uniter of here and hereafter,   20
Taking all hints to use them, but swiftly leaping beyond them,
A reminiscence sing.

---

[1]*Ninth-month:* The Quaker designation for September; in context, an allusion to the human birth cycle.

Reading and Reacting

1. This excerpt, the first twenty-two lines of a poem nearly two hundred lines long, has no regular metrical pattern or rhyme scheme. What gives it its form?

2. How might you explain why the poem's lines vary in length?

3. JOURNAL ENTRY Compare this excerpt with the excerpt from Whitman's "Song of Myself" (p. 1023). In what respects are the forms of the two poems similar?

Related Works: "Chicago" (p. 838), "Old Walt" (p. 923), "Defending Walt Whitman" (p. 952), *from* "Song of Myself" (p. 1023)

WILLIAM CARLOS WILLIAMS (1883–1963)

Spring and All (1923)

By the road to the contagious hospital
under the surge of the blue
mottled clouds driven from the
northeast—a cold wind. Beyond, the
waste of broad, muddy fields   5
brown with dried weeds, standing and fallen

patches of standing water
the scattering of tall trees

All along the road the reddish
purplish, forked, upstanding, twiggy   10
stuff of bushes and small trees
with dead, brown leaves under them
leafless vines—

Lifeless in appearance, sluggish
dazed spring approaches—   15

They enter the new world naked,
cold, uncertain of all
save that they enter. All about them
the cold, familiar wind—

Now the grass, tomorrow   20
the stiff curl of wildcarrot leaf
One by one objects are defined—
It quickens: clarity, outline of leaf

But now the stark dignity of
entrance—Still, the profound change   25
has come upon them: rooted, they
grip down and begin to awaken

Contagious Hospital, Brookline, MA, 1909
© Brookline Historical Society, Brookline, Massachussetts

Reading and Reacting

1. Although this poem is written in free verse and lacks a definite pattern of meter or rhyme, it includes some characteristics of closed form poetry. Explain.
2. What does Williams accomplish by visually isolating lines 7–8 and lines 14–15?
3. "Spring and All" includes assonance, alliteration, and repetition. Give several examples of each technique, and explain what each adds to the poem.

4. **JOURNAL ENTRY** What do you think the word *All* means in the poem's title?

5. **CRITICAL PERSPECTIVE** According to critic Bonnie Costello, "Williams thought about the creative process in painters' terms, and he asks us to experience the work as we might experience a modern painting. His great achievement was to bring some of its qualities into poetry."

   Consider the images Williams uses in this poem. In what ways is this poem like a painting? Which images are conveyed in "painters' terms"? How does he use these images to create meaning in the poem?

Related Works: "l(a" (p. 659), "Comparatives" (p. 803), "Pied Beauty" (p. 806), "I wandered lonely as a cloud" (p. 893), "Monet's *Waterlillies*" (p. PS5)

RICHARD BLANCO (1968–   )

Mexican Almuerzo in New England (2002)

Word is praise for Marina, up past 3:00 a.m. the night before her flight, preparing and packing the *platos tradicionales* she's now heating up in the oven while the *tortillas* steam like full moons on the stovetop. Dish by dish she tries to recreate Mexico in her son's New England kitchen, taste-testing *el mole* from the pot,

stirring every thing: *el chorizo-con-papas, el picadillo, el guacamole*. The spirals of 5
her stirs match the spirals in her eyes, the scented steam coils around her like
incense, suffusing the air with her folklore. She loves Alfredo, as she loves all her
sons, as she loves all things: *seashells, cacti, plumes, artichokes*. Her hand waves us
to circle around the kitchen island, where she demonstrates how to fold tacos for
the *gringo* guests, explaining what is *hot* and what is *not*, trying to describe tastes 10
with English words she cannot savor. As we eat, she apologizes: *not as good as at
home, pero bueno. . .* It is the best she can do in this strange kitchen which Sele
has tried to disguise with *papel picado* banners of colored tissue paper displaying
our names in piñata pink, maíz yellow, and Guadalupe green—strung across the
lintels of the patio filled with talk of an early spring and *do you remembers* that 15
leave an after-taste even the *flan* and *café negro* don't cleanse. Marina has finished. She sleeps in the guest room while Alfredo's paintings confess in the living
room, while the papier-mâché skeletons giggle on the shelves, and shadows lean
on the porch with rain about to fall. Tomorrow our names will be taken down
and Marina will leave with her empty clay pots, feeling as she feels all things: 20
velvet, branches, honey, stones. Feeling what we all feel: home is a forgotten recipe,
a spice we can find nowhere, a taste we can never reproduce, exactly.

Reading and Reacting

1. What does the word *almuerzo* mean? Translate all the Spanish words in this poem. Which
   meanings are essential to your understanding of the poem, and which are not? Why?
2. Blanco, who is of Cuban heritage, says that he wrote this poem "in homage" to a Mexican
   American family and its matriarch, Marina. What does *homage* mean? In what sense is
   this poem written "in homage"?
3. Does the form of this **prose poem** suit its subject matter? Why or why not?
4. At the end of the poem, the speaker says that Marina feels "what we all feel: home is a
   forgotten recipe, a spice we can find nowhere, a taste we can never reproduce, exactly."
   What does he mean? Do you see this as a pessimistic sentiment? Explain.
5. **JOURNAL ENTRY** Rewrite this poem so its lines look like lines of poetry. Or, rewrite the
   poem as a short-short story divided into paragraphs. How does your rewrite change the
   poem? Is it an improvement?

Related Works: "Pilón" (p. 128), "Bilingual/Bilingue" (p. 716), "Dusting" (p. 886), "Papa's
Bridge" (p. 889), "Mosul" (p. 907)

CLAIRE LEE (1997–   )

Living in Numbers (2013)

Sunday, August 22, 2010:
Number of times I've woken up after
oversleeping and sprung out of bed like a ninja: 959

Number of broken bones: 3
Number of scars, physical: 4; emotional: 947
Number of funerals attended: 7   5
Number of friends, Facebook: 744, real: 9
Number of cavities filled: 0

Percentage of people I can stand in the world: 3.5
Number of times I've laughed so hard my sides would bruise: 2,972
Number of times I've wanted to bawl my eyes out: 320   10
Number of things I regret: 11
Number of things I know: 918,394

Monday, August 23, 2010:
Number of times I've woken up after oversleeping and sprung out of bed like
   a ninja: 960
Number of broken bones: 3
Number of scars, physical: 4; emotional: 1,293   15
Number of funerals attended: 7
Number of friends, Facebook: 800, real: 7
Number of cavities filled: 0

Percentage of people I can stand in the world: 3.4
Number of times I've laughed so hard my sides would bruise: 2,973   20
Number of times I've wanted to bawl my eyes out: 321
Number of things I regret: 13
Number of things I know: 918,390

Reading and Reacting

1. This poem's lines vary in length, and it is not divided into conventional stanzas; it also lacks a regular rhyme scheme and metrical pattern. What elements give it its form?

2. In what sense is the poem's speaker "living in numbers"? What function do the numbers serve in her life?

3. JOURNAL ENTRY What do you know about the life of this poem's speaker? What don't you know?

Related Works: "Love and Other Catastrophes: A Mix Tape" (p. 127), "Referential" (p. 598), "Suicide Note" (p. 683)

 ## Concrete Poetry

With roots in the ancient Greek pattern poems and the sixteenth- and seventeenth-century **emblem poems**, contemporary **concrete poetry** uses words—sometimes, different fonts and type sizes—to shape a picture on the page.

MAY SWENSON (1913–1989)

Women (1970)

Women	Or they
should be	should be
pedestals	little horses
moving	those wooden
pedestals	sweet 5
moving	oldfashioned
to the	painted
motions	rocking
of men	horses

the gladdest things in the toyroom 10

The	feelingly
pegs	and then
of their	unfeelingly
ears	To be
so familiar	joyfully 15
and dear	ridden
to the trusting	rockingly
fists	ridden until
To be chafed	the restored

egos dismount and the legs stride away 20

Immobile	willing
sweetlipped	to be set
sturdy	into motion
and smiling	Women
women	should be 25
should always	pedestals
be waiting	to men

The form of a concrete poem is not something that emerges from the poem's words and images; it is something predetermined by the visual image the poet has decided to create. Although some concrete poems are little more than novelties, others—like the poem above—can be original and enlightening.

The curved shape of Swenson's poem immediately reinforces its title, and the arrangement of words on the page suggests a variety of visual directions readers might follow. The two columns seem at first to suggest two alternatives: "Women should be . . ." / "Or they should be. . . ." A closer look, however, reveals that the poem's central figures of speech, such as woman as rocking horse and woman as pedestal, move back and forth between the two columns of images. This exchange of positions might suggest that the two possibilities are really just two ways of looking at one limited role. Thus, the experimental form of the poem visually challenges the apparent complacency of its words, suggesting that women, like words, need not fall into traditional roles or satisfy conventional expectations.

Source: ©Michael Nicholson/Corbis

FURTHER READING: Concrete Poetry

GEORGE HERBERT (1593–1633)

Easter Wings (1633)

Lord, who createdst man in wealth and store,
Though foolishly he lost the same,
Decaying more and more
Till he became
Most poor,   *5*
With thee
Oh, let me rise
As larks, harmoniously,
And sing this day thy victories;
Then shall the fall further the flight in me.   *10*

My tender age in sorrow did begin;
And still with sicknesses and shame
Thou didst so punish sin,
That I became
Most thin.   *15*
With thee
Let me combine,
And feel this day thy victory;
For if I imp my wing on thine,
Affliction shall advance the flight in me.   *20*

Reading and Reacting

1. In this example of a seventeenth-century emblem poem, lines are arranged so that shape and subject matter reinforce each other. Explain how this is accomplished. (For example, how does line length support the poem's images and ideas?)
2. This poem has a definite rhyme scheme. How would you describe it? What relationship do you see between the rhyme scheme and the poem's visual divisions?

Related Works: "l(a" (p. 659), "A Valediction: Forbidding Mourning" (p. 768), "Batter My Heart, Three-Personed God" (p. 979), "When I Have Fears" (p. 997)

JOHN HOLLENDER (1929–2013)

Skeleton Key[1] (1969)

O with what key
shall I unlock this
heart Tight in a coffer
of chest something awaits a
jab a click a sharp turn yes an   5
opening Out with it then Let it
pour into forms it molds itself
Much like an escape of dreaming
prisoners taking shape out in a
relenting air in bright volumes   10
unimaginable even amid anterior
blacknesses let mine run out in
the sunny roads Let them be
released by modulations
of point by bend of   15
line too tiny for
planning out back
in hopeful dark
times or places
How to hold on   20
to a part flat
or wide enough
to grasp was
not too hard
formerly and   25
patterned
edges cut
themselves
What midget
forms shall   30
fall in
line or
row beyond
this wall
of self A   35
key can
open a car
Why not me
O let me
get in   40

---

[1] *skeleton key:* A key capable of opening a number of different locks.

Reading and Reacting

1. In addition to the word *I*, what other words are capitalized in this poem? Why? Should any other words be capitalized? Explain.

2. Do you think this poem's lack of punctuation is a problem? If so, why? Where might you add punctuation marks?

3. What relationship, if any, do you see between this poem's content and its form? Do you think this actually *is* a poem? Explain.

4. **JOURNAL ENTRY** Compare this poem's form with the form of "Easter Wings" (p. 847). How are they alike? How are they different?

5. **CRITICAL PERSPECTIVE** In praising the poetry of John Hollander, Phoebe Pettingell asserts the following:

   > He has consistently been one of the most innovative poets writing during the last forty years. In part, I think, this may be attributed to his enjoying artfully arranging patterns.
   >
   > To sit down with a collection of his poems is almost like entering the alternative universes of an artist like the Dutch M.C. Escher. All those intersecting planes and superimposed perspectives help us notice fresh relationships between things in our own world—things that had previously escaped our eye until the engraver's insight highlighted the pattern for us.

   How does "Skeleton Key" demonstrate Hollander's playfulness? How does the relationship between its form and its content help the reader to "notice fresh relationships between things in our own world"?

Related Works: "Love and Other Catastrophes: A Mix Tape" (p. 127), "l(a" (p. 659), "The Great Figure" (p. 744)

✔ **CHECKLIST   Writing about Form**

☐ Is the poem written in open or closed form? On what characteristics do you base your conclusion?

☐ Why did the poet choose open or closed form? For example, is the poem's form consistent with its subject matter, tone, or theme? Is it determined by the conventions of the historical period in which it was written?

☐ If the poem is arranged in closed form, does the pattern apply to single lines, to groups of lines, or to the entire poem? What factors determine the breaks between groups of lines?

☐ Is the poem a sonnet? a sestina? a villanelle? an epigram? a haiku? How do the traditional form's conventions suit the poet's language and theme? Does the poem follow the rules of the form at all times, or does it break any new ground?

☐ If the poem is arranged in open form, what determines the breaks at the ends of lines?

continued on next page

- ☐ Are certain words or phrases isolated on lines? Why?

- ☐ How do elements such as assonance, alliteration, rhyme, and repetition of words give the poem form?

- ☐ What use does the poet make of punctuation and capitalization? of white space on the page?

- ☐ Is the poem a prose poem? How does this form support the poem's subject matter?

- ☐ Is the poem a concrete poem? How does the poet use the visual shape of the poem to convey meaning?

WRITING SUGGESTIONS: Form

1. Reread the definitions of closed form and open form in this chapter. Based on these definitions, do you think concrete poems are "open" or "closed"? Explain your position in a short essay, supporting your thesis with specific references to the concrete poems in this chapter.

2. Some poets—for example, Emily Dickinson and Robert Frost—write both open and closed form poems. Choose one open and one closed form poem by a single poet, and analyze the two poems, explaining the poet's possible reasons for choosing each type of form.

3. Do you see complex forms, such as the villanelle and the sestina, as exercises or even merely as opportunities for poets to show off their skills—or do you believe the special demands of the forms add something valuable to a poem? To help you answer this question, read Dylan Thomas's "Do not go gentle into that good night" (p. 891), and Elizabeth Bishop's "Sestina" (p. 826).

4. The following poem is an alternate version of May Swenson's "Women" (p. 846). Read the two versions carefully, and write an essay in which you compare them. What differences do you notice? Which do you think was written first? Why? Do the two poems make the same point? Which makes the point with less ambiguity? Which is more effective? Why?

Women Should Be Pedestals

Women should be pedestals
moving pedestals
moving to the motions of men
Or they should be little horses
those wooden sweet oldfashioned painted rocking horses   5
the gladdest things in the toyroom
The pegs of their ears so familiar and dear
to the trusting fists
To be chafed feelingly

and then unfeelingly   10
To be joyfully ridden
until the restored egos dismount and the legs stride away
Immobile sweetlipped sturdy and smiling
women should always be waiting
willing to be set into motion   15
Women should be pedestals to men

CHAPTER 30

SYMBOL, ALLEGORY, ALLUSION, MYTH

William Butler Yeats
Bettmann/Corbis

Christina Rossetti
The Granger Collection, NYC

W. H. Auden
Mary Evans Picture Library/Alamy

Edgar Allan Poe
AP Images

Bettmann/Corbis

WILLIAM BLAKE (1757–1827)

The Sick Rose (1794)

O Rose thou art sick
The invisible worm
That flies in the night,
In the howling storm:
Has found out thy bed   5
Of crimson joy:
And his dark secret love
Does thy life destroy.

▦ Symbol

A **symbol** is an idea or image that suggests something else—but not in the simple way that a dollar sign stands for money or a flag represents a country. A symbol is an image that transcends its literal, or denotative, meaning in a complex way. For instance, if someone gives a rose to a loved one, it could simply be a sign of love. But in the poem "The Sick Rose," the rose has a range of contradictory and complementary meanings. What does the rose represent? Beauty? Perfection? Passion? Something else? Blake further complicates the matter by saying that the rose is "sick," infected by a worm that could symbolize death, decay, or sexuality. As this poem illustrates, the distinctive trait of a symbol is that its meaning cannot easily be pinned down or defined.

Such ambiguity can be frustrating, but it is precisely this characteristic of a symbol that enriches a poem by giving it additional layers of meaning. As Robert Frost has said, a symbol is a little thing that touches a larger thing. In the poem of his that follows, the central symbol does just this.

ROBERT FROST (1874–1963)

For Once, Then, Something (1923)

Others taunt me with having knelt at well-curbs
Always wrong to the light, so never seeing
Deeper down in the well than where the water
Gives me back in a shining surface picture
Me myself in the summer heaven, godlike,   5
Looking out of a wreath of fern and cloud puffs.
Once, when trying with chin against a well-curb,
I discerned, as I thought, beyond the picture,
Through the picture, a something white, uncertain,
Something more of the depths—and then I lost it.   10
Water came to rebuke the too clear water.
One drop fell from a fern, and lo, a ripple
Shook whatever it was lay there at bottom,
Blurred it, blotted it out. What was that whiteness?
Truth? A pebble of quartz? For once, then, something.   15

The central symbol in this poem is the "something" that the speaker thinks he sees at the bottom of a well. Traditionally, the act of looking down a well suggests a search for truth. In this poem, the speaker says that he always seems to look down the well at the wrong angle, so that all he can see is his own reflection—the surface, not the depths. Once, however, the speaker thought he saw something "beyond the picture," something "white, uncertain," but the image remained indistinct, disappearing when a drop of water from a fern caused the water to ripple. The poem ends with the speaker questioning the significance of what he saw. Like a reader encountering a symbol, the speaker is left trying to come to terms with images that cannot be clearly perceived and associations that cannot be readily understood. In light of the elusive nature of truth, all the speaker can do is ask questions that have no definite answers.

Symbols that appear in poetic works can be *conventional* or *universal*. **Conventional symbols** are those recognized by people who share certain cultural and social assumptions. For example, national flags evoke a general and agreed-upon response in most people of a particular country and—for better or for worse—American children have for years perceived the golden arches of McDonald's as a symbol of food and fun. **Universal symbols** are those likely to be recognized by people regardless of their culture. In 1890, the noted Scottish anthropologist Sir James George Frazer wrote the first version of his work *The Golden Bough*, in which he identified parallels between the rites and beliefs of early pagan cultures and those of Christianity. Fascinated by Frazer's work, the psychologist Carl Jung sought to explain these parallels by formulating a theory of **archetypes**, which held that certain images or ideas reside in the subconscious of all people. According to Jung, archetypal symbols include water, symbolizing rebirth; spring, symbolizing growth; and winter, symbolizing death.

Sometimes symbols that appear in poems can be obscure or highly idiosyncratic. William Blake is one of many poets (William Butler Yeats is another) whose works combine symbols from different cultural, theological, and philosophical sources to form complex networks of personal symbolic associations. To Blake, for example, the scientist Isaac Newton represents the tendency of scientists to quantify experience while ignoring the beauty and mystery of nature. Readers cannot begin to understand his use of Newton as a symbol until they have read a number of Blake's more difficult poems.

How do you know when an idea or image in a poem is a symbol? At what point do you decide that a particular object or idea goes beyond the literal level and takes on symbolic significance? When is a rose more than a rose or a well more than a well? Frequently you can recognize a symbol by its prominence or repetition. In "For Once, Then, Something," for example, the well is introduced in the first line of the poem, and it is the poem's focal point; in "The Sick Rose," the importance of the rose is emphasized by the title.

It is not enough, however, to identify an image or idea that seems to suggest something else. Your decision that a particular item has symbolic significance must be supported by the details of the poem and make sense in light of the ideas the poem develops. In the following poem, the symbolic significance of the volcano helps readers to understand the poem's central theme.

EMILY DICKINSON (1830–1886)

Volcanoes be in Sicily (1914)

Volcanoes be in Sicily
And South America
I judge from my Geography—
Volcanoes nearer here
A Lava step at any time   5
Am I inclined to climb—
A Crater I may contemplate
Vesuvius at Home.

This poem opens with a statement of fact: volcanoes are located in Sicily and South America. In line 3, however, the speaker introduces the improbable idea that volcanoes

Eruption of Mt. Etna (Sicily), 2001
Tony Gentile/Reuters/Corbis

are located near where she is at the moment. Readers familiar with Dickinson know that her poems are highly autobiographical and that she lived in Amherst, Massachusetts, where there are no volcanoes. This information leads readers to suspect that they should not take the speaker's observation literally and that in the context of the poem volcanoes may have symbolic significance. But what do volcanoes suggest here?

On the one hand, volcanoes represent the awesome creative power of nature; on the other hand, they suggest its destructiveness. The speaker's contemplation of the crater of Vesuvius—the volcano that buried the ancient Roman city of Pompeii in A.D. 79—is therefore filled with contradictory associations. Because Dickinson was a recluse, volcanoes—active, destructive, unpredictable, and dangerous—may be seen as symbolic of everything she fears in the outside world—and, perhaps, within herself. Volcanoes may even suggest her own creative power, which, like a volcano, is something to be feared as well as contemplated. Dickinson seems to have a voyeur's attraction to danger and power, but she also fears them. For this reason, Dickinson keeps real volcanoes at a distance but uses her imagination to visit a symbolic, but no less terrifying, "Vesuvius at Home."

FURTHER READING: Symbol

LANGSTON HUGHES (1902–1967)

Island (1951)

Wave of sorrow,
Do not drown me now:

I see the island
Still ahead somehow.

I see the island   5
And its sands are fair:

Wave of sorrow,
Take me there.

Reading and Reacting

1. What makes you suspect that the island has symbolic significance in this poem?

2. Is the "wave of sorrow" also a symbol?

3. JOURNAL ENTRY Beyond its literal meaning, what might the island in this poem suggest? Consider several possibilities.

4. CRITICAL PERSPECTIVE James Baldwin, a preeminent African American writer, wrote the following about the poetry of Langston Hughes:

> Hughes, in his sermons, blues and prayers, has working for him the power and the beat of Negro speech and Negro music. Negro speech is vivid largely because it is private. It is a kind of emotional shorthand—or sleight-of-hand—by means of which Negroes express, not only their relationship to each other, but their judgment of the white world.

Can a symbol—such as the island in this poem—also function as "emotional shorthand"? What kind of judgment do you think it might reveal about the "white world"?

Related Works: "A Worn Path" (p. 463), "The White City" (p. 694), "Isla" (p. 860), "Acquainted with the Night" (p. 987), *The Cuban Swimmer* (p. 1416), *Fences* (p. 1548)

EDGAR ALLAN POE (1809–1849)

The Raven (1844)

Once upon a midnight dreary, while I pondered, weak and weary
Over many a quaint and curious volume of forgotten lore,
While I nodded, nearly napping, suddenly there came a tapping,
As of some one gently rapping, rapping at my chamber door.
"'Tis some visitor," I muttered, "tapping at my chamber door—   5
                Only this, and nothing more."

Ah, distinctly I remember it was in the bleak December,
And each separate dying ember wrought its ghost upon the floor.
Eagerly I wished the morrow;—vainly I had sought to borrow
From my books surcease of sorrow—sorrow for the lost Lenore—   10
For the rare and radiant maiden whom the angels name Lenore—
                Nameless here for evermore.

And the silken sad uncertain rustling of each purple curtain
Thrilled me—filled me with fantastic terrors never felt before;
so that now, to still the beating of my heart, I stood repeating   15
"'Tis some visitor entreating entrance at my chamber door;—
Some late visitor entreating entrance at my chamber door;
                This it is, and nothing more."

Presently my soul grew stronger; hesitating then no longer,
"Sir," said I, "or Madam, truly your forgiveness I implore;   20
But the fact is I was napping, and so gently you came rapping,

And so faintly you came tapping, tapping at my chamber door,
That I scarce was sure I heard you"—here I opened wide the door;—
Darkness there, and nothing more.

Deep into that darkness peering, long I stood there wondering, fearing,   25
Doubting, dreaming dreams no mortal ever dared to dream before;
But the silence was unbroken, and the darkness gave no token,
And the only word there spoken was the whispered word, "Lenore!"
This I whispered, and an echo murmured back the word, "Lenore!"—
Merely this, and nothing more.   30

Back into the chamber turning, all my soul within me burning,
Soon I heard again a tapping somewhat louder than before.
"Surely," said I, "surely that is something at my window lattice;
Let me see, then, what thereat is, and this mystery explore—
Let my heart be still a moment and this mystery explore;—   35
'Tis the wind and nothing more!"

Open here I flung the shutter, when, with many a flirt and flutter,
In there stepped a stately raven of the saintly days of yore;
Not the least obeisance made he; not an instant stopped or stayed he;
But, with mien of lord or lady, perched above my chamber door—   40
Perched upon a bust of Pallas[1] just above my chamber door—
Perched, and sat, and nothing more.

Then this ebony bird beguiling my sad fancy into smiling,
By the grave and stern decorum of the countenance it wore,
"Though thy crest be shorn and shaven, thou," I said, "art sure no craven,   45
Ghastly grim and ancient raven wandering from the Nightly shore—
Tell me what thy lordly name is on the Night's Plutonian[2] shore!"
Quoth the raven, "Nevermore."

Much I marvelled this ungainly fowl to hear discourse so plainly,
Though its answer little meaning—little relevancy bore,   50
For we cannot help agreeing that no living human being
Ever yet was blessed with seeing bird above his chamber door—
Bird or beat upon the sculptured bust above his chamber door,
With such name as "Nevermore."

But the raven, sitting lonely on the placid bust, spoke only   55
That one word, as if his soul in that one word he did outpour.
Nothing farther then he uttered—not a feather then he fluttered—
Till I scarcely more than muttered "Other friends have flown before—
On the morrow *he* will leave me, as my hopes have flown before."
Then the bird said "Nevermore."   60

---

[1]*Pallas:* Athena, Greek goddess of wisdom.
[2]*Plutonian:* Dark; Pluto was the Greek god of the dead and ruler of the underworld.

Startled at the stillness broken by reply so aptly spoken,
"Doubtless," said I, "what it utters is its only stock and store
Caught from some unhappy master whom unmerciful Disaster
Followed fast and followed faster till his songs one burden bore—
Till the dirges of his Hope that melancholy burden bore   65
                Of 'Never—nevermore.'"

But the raven still beguiling all my sad soul into smiling,
Straight I wheeled a cushioned seat in front of bird and bust and door;
Then, upon the velvet sinking, I betook myself to linking
Fancy unto fancy, thinking what this ominous bird of yore—   70
What this grim, ungainly, ghastly, gaunt, and ominous bird of yore
                Meant in croaking "Nevermore."

This I sat engaged in guessing, but no syllable expressing
To the fowl whose fiery eyes now burned into my bosom's core;
This and more I sat divining, with my head at ease reclining   75
On the cushion's velvet lining that the lamplight gloated o'er,
But whose velvet violet lining with the lamplight gloating o'er,
            she shall press, ah, nevermore!

Then, methought, the air grew denser, perfumed from an unseen censer
Swung by angels whose faint foot-falls tinkled on the tufted floor.   80
"Wretch," I cried, "thy God hath lent thee—by these angels he hath sent thee
Respite—respite and nepenthe[3] from thy memories of Lenore!
Quaff, oh quaff this kind nepenthe and forget this lost Lenore!"
            Quoth the raven, "Nevermore."

"Prophet!" said I, "thing of evil!—prophet still, if bird or devil!—   85
Whether Tempter sent, or whether tempest tossed thee here ashore,
Desolate, yet all undaunted, on this desert land enchanted—
On this home by Horror haunted—tell me truly, I implore—
Is there—*is* there balm in Gilead?[4]—tell me—tell me, I implore!"
            Quoth the raven, "Nevermore."   90

"Prophet!" said I, "thing of evil—prophet still, if bird or devil!
By that Heaven that bends above us—by that God we both adore—
Tell this soul with sorrow laden if, within the distant Aidenn,[5]
It shall clasp a sainted maiden whom the angels name Lenore—
Clasp a rare and radiant maiden whom the angels name Lenore."   95
            Quoth the raven, "Nevermore."

"Be that word our sign of parting, bird or fiend!" I shrieked upstarting—
"Get thee back into the tempest and the Night's Plutonian shore!
Leave no black plume as a token of that lie thy soul hath spoken!
Leave my loneliness unbroken!—quit the bust above my door!   100
Take thy beak from out my heart, and take thy form from off my door!"
            Quoth the raven, "Nevermore."

---

[3]*nepenthe:* A drug mentioned in the *Odessy* as a remedy for grief.

[4]*Gilead:* A region mentioned in the Bible; noted for its soothing ointments.

[5]*Aidenn:* A variation of Eden, the home of Adam and Eve.

And the raven, never flitting, still is sitting, still is sitting
On the pallid bust of Pallas just above my chamber door;
And his eyes have all the seeming of a demon's that is dreaming,   105
And the lamp-light o'er him streaming throws his shadow on the floor;
And my soul from out that shadow that lies floating on the floor
Shall be lifted—nevermore!

Raven
Ivan Bliznetsov/Dreamstime.com

Reading and Reacting

1. Who is the speaker in the poem? What is his state of mind? How does the raven mirror the speaker's mental state?

2. "The Raven" contains a good deal of alliteration. Identify some examples. How does this use of repeated initial consonant sounds help to convey the mood of the poem?

3. The speaker refers to the raven in a number of different ways. At one point, it is simply "an ebony bird" (line 42); at another, it is a "prophet" and "a thing of evil" (85). How else does the speaker characterize the raven?

4. **JOURNAL ENTRY** What is the symbolic significance of the raven? Of the repeated word "nevermore"? Of the bust of Pallas, the ancient Greek god of wisdom?

5. **CRITICAL PERSPECTIVE** According to Christoffer Nilsson, who maintains a website dedicated to the works of Poe, "The Raven" was composed with almost mathematical precision. When writing the stanza in which the interrogation of the raven reaches its climax (third stanza from the end), Poe wanted to make certain that no preceding stanza would "surpass this in rhythmical effect":

> Poe then worked backwards from this stanza and used the word "Nevermore" in many different ways, so that even with the repetition of this word, it would not prove to be monotonous.

Poe builds the tension in this poem up, stanza by stanza, but after the climaxing stanza he tears the whole thing down, and lets the narrator know that there is no meaning in searching for a moral in the raven's "nevermore."

Do you agree with Nilsson that it makes no sense to look for a moral in the raven's "nevermore"? What kind of moral, if any, do you think "Nevermore" implies for the speaker?

Related Works: "A Hunger Artist" (p. 151), "Rooming houses are old women" (p. 761), "Ode to a Nightingale" (p. 784), "The Fish" (p. 957), "The Tyger" (p. 961), *Hamlet* (p. 1016)

VIRGIL SUÁREZ (1962–   )

Isla (2000)

In Los Angeles I grew up watching *The Three Stooges*,
The Little Rascals, *Speed Racer*, and the Godzilla movies,

those my mother called *"Los monstruos,"* and though I didn't
yet speak English, I understood why such a creature would,

upon being woken up from its centuries-long slumber, rise   5
and destroy Tokyo's buildings, cars, people—I understood

by the age of twelve what it meant to be unwanted, exiled,
how you move from one country to another where nobody

wants you, nobody knows you, and I sat in front of the TV,
transfixed by the snow-fizz on our old black and white,   10

and when Godzilla bellows his eardrum-crushing growl,
I screamed back, this victory-holler from one so rejected

and cursed to another. When the monster whipped its tail
and destroyed, I threw a pillow across my room; each time

my mother stormed into the room and asked me what,   15
what I thought I was doing throwing things at the walls.

"¡Ese monstruo, esa isla!" she'd say. That monster, that island,
and I knew she wasn't talking about the movie. She meant

her country, mine, that island in the Caribbean we left behind,
itself a reptile-looking mass on each map, on my globe,   20

a crocodile-like creature rising again, eating us so completely.

—*for Jarret Keene*

Reading and Reacting

1. What specific elements in the poem make you think that the island is a symbol?
2. Why does the speaker discuss Godzilla? What relation does Godzilla have to Cuba—the island the speaker "left behind"?

3. What does the island symbolize to the speaker? to his mother? to you?

4. JOURNAL ENTRY The speaker uses Spanish in two places (as well as the title) in the poem. Why? What would be lost if these phrases were written in English?

Related Works: "Sticks" (p. 141), "New York Day Women" (p. 348), "Metaphors" (p. 764), "Mexican Almuerzo in New England" (p. 843), "Papa's Bridge" (p. 889), "I Hear America Singing" (p. 1022), *The Cuban Swimmer* (p. 1416)

Allegory

Allegory is a form of narrative that conveys a message or doctrine (usually moral or political) by using people, places, or things to stand for abstract ideas. **Allegorical figures**, each with a strict equivalent, form an **allegorical framework**, a set of ideas that conveys the allegory's message or lesson. Thus, the allegory takes place on two levels: a **literal level** that tells a story and a **figurative level** on which the allegorical figures in the story stand for ideas, concepts, and other qualities.

Like symbols, allegorical figures suggest other things. But unlike symbols, which have a range of possible meanings, allegorical figures can always be assigned specific meanings. (Because writers use allegory to instruct, they gain nothing by hiding its significance.) Thus, symbols open up possibilities for interpretation, whereas allegories tend to restrict possibilities.

Quite often an allegory involves a journey or an adventure, as in the case of Dante's *Divine Comedy*, which traces a journey through Hell, Purgatory, and Heaven. Within an allegory, everything can have meaning: the road on which the characters walk, the people they encounter, or a phrase that one of them repeats throughout the journey. Once you understand the allegorical framework, your main task is to see how the various elements fit within this system. Some allegorical poems can be relatively straightforward, but others can be so complicated that it takes a great deal of effort to unlock their meaning. In the following poem, a journey is central to the allegory.

CHRISTINA ROSSETTI (1830–1894)

Uphill (1861)

Does the road wind up-hill all the way?
    Yes, to the very end.
Will the day's journey take the whole long day?
    From morn to night, my friend.

But is there for the night a resting-place?   5
    A roof for when the slow dark hours begin.
May not the darkness hide it from my face?
    You cannot miss that inn.

Shall I meet other wayfarers at night?
    Those who have gone before.   10

Then must I knock, or call when just in sight?
    They will not keep you standing at that door.

Shall I find comfort, travel-sore and weak?
    Of labor you shall find the sum.
Will there be beds for me and all who seek?   15
    Yea, beds for all who come.

The Pilgrims going up the hill Difficulty.

Illustration from 1776 printing of
The Pilgrim's Progress
© Lebrecht / The Image Works

"Uphill" uses a question-and-answer structure to describe a journey along an uphill road. Like the one described in John Bunyan's seventeenth-century allegory *The Pilgrim's Progress*, this is a spiritual journey, one that suggests the challenges a person faces throughout life. The day-and-night duration of the journey stands for life and death, and the inn at the end of the road stands for the grave, the final resting place.

FURTHER READING: Allegory

CARL DENNIS (1939–   )

At the Border (2004)

At the border between the past and the future
No sign on a post warns you that your passport

Won't let you return to your native land
As a citizen, just as a tourist
Who won't be allowed to fraternize with the locals.   5

No guard steps out of a booth to explain
You can't bring gifts back, however modest,
Can't even pass a note to a few friends
That suggests what worries of theirs are misguided,
What expectations too ambitious.   10

Are you sure you're ready to leave,
To cross the bridge that begins
Under a clear sky and ends in fog?
But look, you've started across already
And it's one-lane wide, with no room for U-turns.   15

No time even to pause as drivers behind you
Lean on their horns, those who've convinced themselves
Their home awaits them on the other side.

Reading and Reacting

1. On one level, this poem is about a trip. What details suggest that the poem is about something more?
2. In this poem, the border separates the past and the future. Why does the speaker call the distance between the past and the future a border?
3. What is the allegorical significance of each of the following items?

   - The passport
   - The bridge
   - The guard
   - The fog
   - The one-lane road
   - The drivers

4. **JOURNAL ENTRY** How does this poem describe the past? How is the past different from the future?

5. **CRITICAL PERSPECTIVE** In a review of "At the Border," poet Robert Pinsky makes the following observation:

   > Dennis gives a dreamy urgency to his compact allegory. . . . The feeling is not gloomy, but a gentle and haunted metaphysical teasing. Unornamented and intimate, the poem's even voice describes the humdrum details of tourism—the passport, the bridge, the guard, the traffic—as emblems of a perpetual journey from one misty idea of home to another—one behind, beyond return and the other envisioned ahead, but receding into the fog.

   What is the "perpetual journey" to which Pinsky refers? Do you agree that the poem has "a dreamy urgency"?

Related Works: "The Secret Lion" (p. 180), "Young Goodman Brown" (p. 448), "A Worn Path" (p. 463), "Rooming houses are old women" (p. 761), "Uphill" (p. 861)

Allusion

An **allusion** is a brief reference to a person, place, or event (fictional or actual) that readers are expected to recognize. Like symbols and allegories, allusions enrich a work by introducing associations from another context.

Although most poets expect readers to recognize their references, some use allusions to exclude certain readers from their work. In his 1922 poem "The Waste Land," for example, T. S. Eliot alludes to historical events, ancient languages, and obscure literary works. He even includes a set of notes to accompany his poem, but they do little more than complicate an already difficult text. (As you might expect, initial critical response to this poem was mixed: some critics said that it was a work of genius, while others thought that it was arcane and pretentious.)

In a sense, allusions favor those readers who have the background or knowledge to recognize them and excludes those who do not. At one time, writers could expect educated readers to recognize allusions to the Bible and to Greek and Roman classics. For example, when Christopher Marlowe referred to "Olympus' top" in his sixteenth-century play *Doctor Faustus*, he expected his readers to know that he was alluding to Mount Olympus, the home of the gods in Greek mythology. Today, this assumption is not valid, but with the advent of search engines such as *Google*, interpreting an allusion requires nothing more than entering a keyword (or keywords) into a Web browser. If, when reading a poem, you come across a reference to which you are not familiar, take the time to look it up. Your understanding and appreciation of a poem will be enhanced by your ability to interpret an unfamiliar reference.

Allusions can come from any source: history, the arts, other works of literature, the Bible, current events, or even the personal life of the poet. Notice how the following poem uses allusions to prominent literary figures as well as to myth to develop its theme.

WILLIAM MEREDITH (1919–2007)

Dreams of Suicide (1980)

(in sorrowful memory of Ernest Hemingway, Sylvia Plath, and John Berryman)

I

I reach for the awkward shotgun not to disarm
you, but to feel the metal horn,
furred with the downy membrane of dream.
More surely than the unicorn,
you are the mythical beast.   5

II

Or I am sniffing an oven. On all fours
I am imitating a totemic animal
but she is not my totem or the totem
of my people, this is not my magic oven.

III

If I hold you tight by the ankles,   10
still you fly upward from the iron railing.

> Your father made these wings,
> after he made his own, and now from beyond
> he tells you *fly down*, in the voice
> my own father might say *walk, boy*.   15

This poem is dedicated to the memory of three writers who committed suicide. In each stanza, the speaker envisions in a dream the death of one of the writers. In the first stanza, he dreams of Ernest Hemingway, who killed himself with a shotgun. The speaker grasps the "metal horn" of Hemingway's shotgun and transforms Hemingway into a mythical beast who, like a unicorn, represents the rare, unique talent of the artist. In the second stanza, the speaker dreams of Sylvia Plath, who asphyxiated herself in a gas oven. He sees himself, like Plath, on his knees imitating an animal sniffing an oven. In the third stanza, the speaker dreams of John Berryman, who leaped to his death. Berryman is characterized as Icarus, a mythological figure who, along with his father Daedalus, fled Crete by building wings made of feathers and wax. Together they flew away; however, ignoring his father's warning, Icarus flew so close to the sun that the wax melted, and he fell to his death in the sea. In this poem, then, the speaker uses allusions to make a point about the difficult lives of writers—and, perhaps, to convey his own empathy for those who could not survive the struggle to reconcile art and life.

FURTHER READING: Allusion

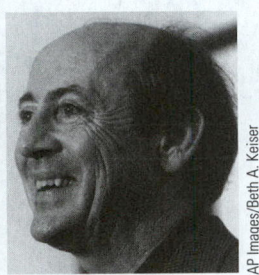

AP Images/Beth A. Keiser

BILLY COLLINS (1941–   )

Aristotle[1] (1998)

This is the beginning.
Almost anything can happen.
This is where you find
the creation of light, a fish wriggling onto land,
the first word of Paradise Lost[2] on an empty page.   5
Think of an egg, the letter A,
a woman ironing on a bare stage as the heavy curtain rises.
This is the very beginning.
The first-person narrator introduces himself,
tells us about his lineage.   10
The mezzo-soprano[3] stands in the wings.
Here the climbers are studying a map
or pulling on their long woolen socks.
This is early on, years before the Ark, dawn.
The profile of an animal is being smeared   15
on the wall of a cave,
and you have not yet learned to crawl.

---

[1] *Aristotle:* Greek philosopher (384–322 BC).

[2] *Paradise Lost:* Epic poem by John Milton (1608–1674).

[3] *mezzo-soprano:* Meaning "middle soprano," a type of female opera singer.

This is the opening, the gambit,
a pawn moving forward an inch.
This is your first night with her, your first night without her   20
This is the first part
where the wheels begin to turn,
where the elevator begins its ascent,
before the doors lurch apart.

This is the middle.   25
Things have had time to get complicated,
messy, really. Nothing is simple anymore.
Cities have sprouted up along the rivers
teeming with people at cross-purposes—
a million schemes, a million wild looks.   30
Disappointment unshoulders his knapsack
here and pitches his ragged tent.
This is the sticky part where the plot congeals,
where the action suddenly reverses
or swerves off in an outrageous direction.   35
Here the narrator devotes a long paragraph
to why Miriam does not want Edward's child.
Someone hides a letter under a pillow.
Here the aria[4] rises to a pitch,
a song of betrayal, salted with revenge,   40
And the climbing party is stuck on a ledge
halfway up the mountain.
This is the bridge, the painful modulation.
This is the thick of things.
So much is crowded into the middle—   45
the guitars of Spain, piles of ripe avocados,
Russian uniforms, noisy parties,
lakeside kisses, arguments heard through a wall
too much to name, too much to think about.

And this is the end,   50
the car running out of road,
the river losing its name in an ocean,
the long nose of the photographed horse
touching the white electronic line.
This is the colophon,[5] the last elephant in the parade,   55
the empty wheelchair, and pigeons floating down in the evening.
Here the stage is littered with bodies,

---

[4]*aria:* A musical piece for one voice, often performed in the context of an opera.
[5]*colophon:* The finishing touch.

the narrator leads the characters to their cells,
and the climbers are in their graves.
It is me hitting the period   60
and you closing the book.
It is Sylvia Plath[6] in the kitchen
and St. Clement[7] with an anchor around his neck.
This is the final bit
thinning away to nothing.   65
This is the end, according to Aristotle,
what we have all been waiting for,
what everything comes down to,
the destination we cannot help imagining,
a streak of light in the sky,   70
a hat on a peg, and outside the cabin, falling leaves.

Reading and Reacting

1. According to Aristotle, the plot of a tragedy must be "whole"—it must have a beginning, a middle, and an end. Do you think the poem's title is appropriate? Explain.
2. In what sense is this poem a tragedy? In what sense is it not?
3. What allusions does the speaker make in the last stanza? What is the significance of these allusions?

4. **JOURNAL ENTRY** Does Collins expect readers to be familiar with his allusions? Do you think he expects too much of readers? Or, do you think the effort is worth the gain?

5. **CRITICAL PERSPECTIVE** Critic John Taylor praises the work of Billy Collins in the following terms:

> Rarely has anyone written poems that appear so transparent on the surface yet become so ambiguous, thought-provoking or simply wise once the reader has peered into the depths. Collins's pellucid style greatly facilitates this kind of meditative peering into the unknown, yet this clarity is hard-won. It takes a sure hand indeed to guide readers so often and respectfully into an unobstructed communion with reverie, drollery, gentle mischievousness, or a subdued but genuine joy.

Do you think this description applies to the poem "Aristotle"? For example, is "Aristotle" "transparent on the surface"? Is it in any way "ambiguous"? Which aspects of the poem might be considered "wise" or "thought-provoking"?

Related Works: "Love and Other Catastrophes: A Mix Tape" (p. 127), "Araby" (p. 361), "The Things They Carried" (p. 392), "My Last Duchess" (p. 679), "Daddy" (p. 772), *Oedipus the King* (p. 1430)

---

[6] *Sylvia Plath:* American poet (1932–1963) who committed suicide by inhaling the gas from her oven.

[7] *St. Clement:* First of the Apostolic Fathers and Pope of Rome from 88 to 97 AD or from 92 to 101 AD, Clement was supposedly martyred by being tied to an anchor and thrown into the sea.

R. S. GWYNN (1948–   )

Shakespearean Sonnet (2005)

(With a first line taken from the TV listings)

A man is haunted by his father's ghost.
A boy and girl love while their families fight.
A Scottish king is murdered by his host.
Two couples get lost on a summer night.
A hunchback murders all who block his way.   5
A ruler's rivals plot against his life.
A fat man and a prince make rebels pay.
A noble Moor has doubts about his wife.
An English king decides to conquer France.
A duke learns that his best friend is a she,   10
A forest sets the scene for this romance.
An old man and his daughters disagree.
A Roman leader makes a big mistake.
A sexy queen is bitten by a snake.

Reading and Reacting

1. Why does Gwynn write his poem in the form of a Shakespearean sonnet?
2. Each line of the poem summarizes the plot of a Shakespeare play in the form of a TV listing. What do you think Gwynn hopes to accomplish with these summaries?
3. Where does Gwynn use alliteration? At what point does he use irony?
4. JOURNAL ENTRY Try to identify all the plays Gwynn alludes to in his poem.
5. CRITICAL PERSPECTIVE According to critic Bruce Bawer, R. S. Gwynn's recurrent theme is "the decay of Western civilization—trash culture, fashionable politics, education made E-Z—and the enduring faults, frailties, fallacies, foibles, and fraudulencies of the human comedy." In what sense, if any, do you think "Shakespearean Sonnet" is about "the decay of Western civilization"?

Related Works: "Cathedral" (p. 435), "The English Canon" (p. 725)," An Apology" (p. 747), "Shall I compare thee to a summer's day?" (p. 758), "When, in disgrace with Fortune and men's eyes" (p. 818), *Hamlet* (p. 1016)

 Myth

A **myth** is a narrative that embodies—and in some cases helps to explain—the religious, philosophical, moral, and political values of a culture. Using gods and supernatural beings, myths try to make sense of occurrences in the natural world. (The term *myth* can also refer to a private belief system devised by an individual poet as well as to any fully realized fictitious setting in which a literary work takes place, such as the myths of William Faulkner's Yoknapatawpha County or of novelist Lawrence Durrell's Alexandria.) Contrary to popular usage, *myth* does not mean "falsehood." In the broadest sense, myths are stories—usually whole groups of stories—that can be true or partly true as well as false; regardless of their degree of accuracy, however, myths frequently express the deepest beliefs of a culture. According to this definition, the *Iliad* and the *Odyssey*, the Koran, and the Old and New Testaments can all be referred to as myths.

The mythologist Joseph Campbell observed that myths contain truths that link people together, whether they live today or lived 2,500 years ago. Myths attempt to explain phenomena that human beings care about, regardless of when and where they live. It is not surprising, then, that myths frequently contain **archetypal images**—images that cut across cultural and racial boundaries and touch us at a very deep level. Many Greek myths illustrate this power. For example, when Orpheus descends into Hades to rescue his wife, Eurydice, he acts out the universal human desire to transcend death; and when Telemachus sets out in search of his father, Odysseus, he reminds readers that we are all lost children searching for parents. When Icarus ignores his father and flies too near the sun and when Pandora cannot resist looking into a box that she has been told not to open, we are reminded of the human weaknesses we all share.

When poets use myths, they are making allusions. They expect readers to bring to the poem the cultural, emotional, and ethical context of the myths to which they are alluding. At one time, when all educated individuals studied the Greek and Latin classics as well as the Bible and other religious texts, poets could safely assume that readers would recognize the mythological allusions they made. Today, many readers are unable to understand the full significance of an allusion or its application within a poem. Many of the poems in this anthology are accompanied by notes, but these may not provide all the information you will need to understand the full significance of each mythological allusion. Occasionally, you may have to look elsewhere for answers, turning to dictionaries, encyclopedias, online information sites such as <http://www.answers.com>, or collections of myths such as the *New Larousse Encyclopedia of Mythology* or *Bulfinch's Mythology*.

Sometimes a poet alludes to a myth in a title; sometimes references to various myths appear throughout a poem; at other times, an entire poem focuses on a single myth. In each case, as in the following poem, the use of myth helps to develop the poem's theme.

COUNTEE CULLEN (1903–1946)

Yet Do I Marvel (1925)

I doubt not God is good, well-meaning, kind,
And did He stoop to quibble could tell why
The little buried mole continues blind,
Why flesh that mirrors Him must some day die,
Make plain the reason tortured Tantalus   5
Is baited by the fickle fruit, declare
If merely brute caprice dooms Sisyphus
To struggle up a never-ending stair.
Inscrutable His ways are, and immune
To catechism by a mind too strewn   10

With petty cares to slightly understand
What awful brain compels His awful hand.
Yet do I marvel at this curious thing:
To make a poet black, and bid him sing!

Engraving of Tantalus reaching for fruit
©The Print Collector / HIP / The Image Works

The speaker begins by affirming his belief in the benevolence of God but then questions why God engages in what appear to be capricious acts. As part of his catalog of questions, the speaker alludes to Tantalus and Sisyphus, two figures from Greek mythology. Tantalus was a king who was condemned to Hades for his crimes. There, he was forced to stand in a pool of water up to his chin. Overhead hung a tree branch laden with fruit. When Tantalus got thirsty and tried to drink, the level of the water dropped, and when he got hungry and reached for fruit, it moved just out of reach. Thus, Tantalus was doomed to be near what he most desired but forever unable to obtain it. Sisyphus also was condemned to Hades. For his disrespect of Zeus, he was sentenced to endless toil. Every day, Sisyphus pushed a boulder up a steep hill. Every time he neared the top, the boulder rolled back down the hill, and Sisyphus had to begin again. Like Tantalus, the speaker in "Yet Do I Marvel" cannot have what he wants; like Sisyphus, he is forced to toil in vain. He wonders why a well-meaning God would "make a poet black, and bid him sing" in a racist society that does not listen to his voice. Thus, the poet's two allusions to Greek mythology enrich the poem by connecting the suffering of the speaker to a universal drama that has been acted out again and again.

FURTHER READING: Myth

MAY SWENSON (1919–1995)

The Centaur (1995)

The summer that I was ten—
Can it be there was only one
summer that I was ten?

It must have been a long one then—
each day I'd go out to choose   5
a fresh horse from my stable

which was a willow grove
down by the old canal.
I'd go on my two bare feet.

But when, with my brother's jack-knife,   10
I had cut me a long limber horse
with a good thick knob for a head,

and peeled him slick and clean
except a few leaves for the tail,
and cinched my brother's belt   15

around his head for a rein,
I'd straddle and canter[1] him fast
up the grass bank to the path,

trot along in the lovely dust
that talcumed over his hoofs,   20
hiding my toes, and turning

his feet to swift half-moons.
The willow knob with the strap
jouncing between my thighs

was the pommel[2] and yet the poll[3]   25
of my nickering[4] pony's head.
My head and my neck were mine,

yet they were shaped like a horse.
My hair flopped to the side
like the mane of a horse in the wind.   30

---

[1] *canter:* A horse's style of walking (faster than a trot, but slower than a gallop).

[2] *pommel:* The raised part at the front of a horse's saddle.

[3] *poll:* The back of a horse's skull.

[4] *nickering:* Neighing or whinnying softly.

My forelock swung in my eyes,
my neck arched and I snorted.
I shied and skittered and reared,

stopped and raised my knees,
pawed at the ground and quivered.   35
My teeth bared as we wheeled

and swished through the dust again.
I was the horse and the rider,
and the leather I slapped to his rump

spanked my own behind.   40
Doubled, my two hoofs beat
a gallop along the bank,

the wind twanged in my mane,
my mouth squared to the bit.
And yet I sat on my steed   45

quiet, negligent riding,
my toes standing the stirrups,
my thighs hugging his ribs.

At a walk we drew up to the porch.
I tethered him to a paling.⁵   50
Dismounting, I smoothed my skirt

and entered the dusky hall.
My feet on the clean linoleum
left ghostly toes in the hall.

Where have you been? said my mother.   55
Been riding, I said from the sink,
and filled me a glass of water.

What's that in your pocket? she said.
Just my knife. It weighted my pocket
and stretched my dress awry.   60

Go tie back your hair, said my mother,
and Why is your mouth all green?
Rob Roy⁶, he pulled some clover
as we crossed the field, I told her.

---

⁵*paling:* One of the vertical wooden pieces making up a fence.
⁶*Rob Roy:* One of the horses in the 1877 novel *Black Beauty.*

Statue of a centaur

Reading and Reacting

1. In Greek mythology, centaurs were a primitive tribe of half-horse half-men, who lived in the mountains and forests. What do they represent to the speaker in the poem?

2. On the surface, the poem describes a child's fantasy of riding a stick horse. What else does it suggest?

3. As the poem progresses, the child speaker becomes more and more like a horse. Find some images that convey this transformation.

4. JOURNAL ENTRY "The Centaur" begins with an adult speaker reminiscing about events that took place when she was ten. Why do you think these events are so important to her?

5. CRITICAL PERSPECTIVE According to William Stafford, Swenson's poems have a cumulative effect on readers. She defines things, "but the definitions have a stealthy trend; what she chooses and the way she progresses heap upon the reader a consistent, incremental effect." How does this comment apply to "The Centaur"?

Related Works: "Gryphon" (p. 250), "Young Goodman Brown" (p. 448), "The Negro Speaks of Rivers" (p. 916), "Go Down, Moses" (p. 955), "The Nymph's Reply to the Shepherd" (p. 1009), "Ulysses" (p. 1017), "The Second Coming" (p. 1029)

Source: ©Bettmann/Corbis

WILLIAM BUTLER YEATS (1865–1939)

Leda and the Swan (1924)

A sudden blow: the great wings beating still
Above the staggering girl, her thighs caressed
By the dark webs, her nape caught in his bill,
He holds her helpless breast upon his breast.

How can those terrified vague fingers push   5
The feathered glory from her loosening thighs?
And how can body, laid in that white rush,
But feel the strange heart beating where it lies?

A shudder in the loins engenders there
The broken wall, the burning roof and tower   10
And Agamemnon dead.
                                        Being so caught up,
So mastered by the brute blood of the air,
Did she put on his knowledge with his power
Before the indifferent beak could let her drop?   15

Peter Paul Rubens, *Leda and the Swan*, 1598
bpk, Berlin / Art Resource, NY

Reading and Reacting

1. What event is described in this poem? What is the mythological significance of this event?
2. How is Leda portrayed? Why is the swan described as a "feathered glory" (line 6)? Why in the poem's last line is Leda dropped by his "indifferent beak"?
3. The third stanza refers to the Trojan War, which was indirectly caused by the event described in the poem. How does the allusion to the Trojan War help develop the theme of the poem?

4. **JOURNAL ENTRY** Does the poem answer the question asked in its last two lines? Explain.

5. **CRITICAL PERSPECTIVE** According to Richard Ellmann, this poem deals with "transcendence of opposites." The bird's "rape of the human, the coupling of god and woman, the moment at which one epoch ended and another began . . . in the act which included all these Yeats had the violent symbol for the transcendence of opposites which he needed."

   What opposite or contrary forces exist in the myth of Leda and the swan? Do you think the poem implies that these forces can be reconciled?

Related Works: "Where Are You Going, Where Have You Been?" (p. 506), "Greasy Lake" (p. 569), "Easter Wings" (p. 847), "The Second Coming" (p. 1029)

SEAMUS HEANEY (1939–2013)

Anything Can Happen (2006)

Anything can happen. You know how Jupiter
Will mostly wait for clouds to gather head
Before he hurls the lightning? Well, just now
He galloped his thunder cart and his horses

Across a clear blue sky. It shook the earth   5
And the clogged underearth, the River Styx,[1]
The winding streams, the Atlantic shore itself.
Anything can happen, the tallest towers

Be overturned, those in high places daunted,
Those overlooked regarded. Stropped-beak Fortune[2]   10
Swoops, making the air gasp, tearing the crest off one,
Setting it down bleeding on the next.

Ground gives. The heaven's weight
Lifts up off Atlas[3] like a kettle-lid.
Capstones shift, nothing resettles right.   15
Telluric[4] ash and fire-spores boil away.

Reading and Reacting

1. According to Heaney, he wrote "Anything Can Happen" in response to the destruction of the Twin Towers of the World Trade Center on September 11th, 2001. Why do you think he used Jupiter, chief deity of the Roman religion, in this poem?

---

[1] *the River Styx:* In classical mythology, a river that formed the boundary between this world and the underworld.

[2] *Stropped-beak Fortune:* The Roman goddess of luck (also called Fortuna) with a sharpened beak.

[3] *Atlas:* In classical mythology, a Titan, or giant, who was punished by Jupiter by being made to hold up the heavens.

[4] *Telluric:* Relating to the earth.

Andromeda in Chains
Alinari Archives/Corbis

2. The speaker says that usually Jupiter will "wait for clouds to gather" before "he hurls his lightening." What is different about this occasion?

3. What does the speaker mean when he says, "nothing resettles right"?

4. What other references to mythology appear in the poem? What function do they serve?

5. JOURNAL ENTRY What is the significance of the poem's title? How does it reflect the poem's theme?

6. CRITICAL PERSPECTIVE According to David Flawbert, who posted an analysis of "Anything Can Happen" on a blog dedicated to the work of Seamus Heaney, the phrase "Those overlooked regarded" may be referring to the people trapped in the towers as gesturing aggressively at their attacker. Do you think that Flawbert's interpretation is justified by the rest of the poem? Why or why not?

Related Works: from *The Harlem Hellfighters* (p. 145), "Bullet in the Brain" (p. 496), "Digging" (p. 663), "Fire and Ice" (p. 686), "Dulce et Decorum Est" (p. 902), "The End and the Beginning" (p. 908), *Nine Ten* (p. 1108)

© Mary Evans Picture Library / Alamy

W. H. AUDEN (1907–1973)

Musée des Beaux Arts (1940)

About suffering they were never wrong,
The Old Masters: how well they understood
Its human position; how it takes place
While someone else is eating or opening a window or just
    walking dully along

How, when the aged are reverently, passionately waiting   5
For the miraculous birth, there always must be
Children who did not specially want it to happen, skating
On a pond at the edge of the wood:
They never forgot
That even the dreadful martyrdom must run its course   10
Anyhow in a corner, some untidy spot
Where the dogs go on with their doggy life and the torturer's horse
Scratches its innocent behind on a tree.
In Brueghel's *Icarus*, for instance: how everything turns away
Quite leisurely from the disaster; the ploughman may   15
Have heard the splash, the forsaken cry,
But for him it was not an important failure; the sun shone
As it had to on the white legs disappearing into the green
Water; and the expensive delicate ship that must have seen
Something amazing, a boy falling out of the sky,   20
Had somewhere to get to and sailed calmly on.

Brueghel, Pieter the Elder (1525?–1569). *Landscape with the Fall of Icarus*
Scala / Art Resource, NY

Reading and Reacting

1. Reread the summary of the myth of Icarus on page 865. What does Auden's interpretation of this myth contribute to the poem?

2. What point does the poet make by referring to the "Old Masters" (line 2)?

3. **JOURNAL ENTRY** Brueghel's painting *Landscape with the Fall of Icarus* is shown above. How does looking at this painting help you to understand the poem? To what specific details in the painting does the poet refer?

Related Works: "The Lottery" (p. 419), "One day I wrote her name upon the strand" (p. 733), "Shall I compare thee to a summer's day?" (p. 758), "Not Waving but Drowning" (p. 1015), "The Second Coming" (p. 1029)

AP Images

T. S. ELIOT (1888–1965)

Journey of the Magi[1] (1927)

"A cold coming we had of it,
Just the worst time of the year
For a journey, and such a long journey:
The ways deep and the weather sharp,
The very dead of winter."*   5
And the camels galled, sore-footed, refractory,
Lying down in the melting snow.
There were times we regretted
The summer palaces on slopes, the terraces,
And the silken girls bringing sherbet.   10
Then the camel men cursing and grumbling
And running away, and wanting their liquor and women,
And the night-fires going out, and the lack of shelters,
And the cities hostile and the towns unfriendly
And the villages dirty and charging high prices: 15
A hard time we had of it.
At the end we preferred to travel all night,
Sleeping in snatches,
With the voices singing in our ears, saying
That this was all folly.   20
Then at dawn we came down to a temperate valley,
Wet, below the snow line, smelling of vegetation;
With a running stream and a water-mill beating the darkness,
And three trees[2] on the low sky,
And an old white horse[3] galloped away in the meadow.   25
Then we came to a tavern with vine-leaves over the lintel,
Six hands at an open door dicing for pieces of silver,[4]
And feet kicking the empty wine-skins.
But there was no information, and so we continued
And arrived at evening, not a moment too soon   30
Finding the place; it was (you may say) satisfactory.

[1] *Magi:* The three wise men who ventured east to pay tribute to the infant Jesus (see Matthew 12.1–12)

*The five quoted lines are adapted from a passage in a 1622 Christmas Day sermon by Bishop Lancelot Andrewes.

[2] *three trees:* The three crosses at Calvary (see Luke 23.32–33).

[3] *white horse:* The horse ridden by the conquering Christ in Revelation 19.11–16.

[4] *dicing . . . silver:* Echoes the soldiers dicing for Christ's garments, as well as his betrayal by Judas Iscariot for thirty pieces of silver (see Matthew 27.35 and 26.14–16).

All this was a long time ago, I remember,
And I would do it again, but set down
This set down
This: were we led all that way for   35
Birth or Death? There was a Birth, certainly,
We had evidence and no doubt. I had seen birth and death,
But had thought they were different; this Birth was
Hard and bitter agony for us, like Death, our death.
We returned to our places, these Kingdoms,   40
But no longer at ease here, in the old dispensation,
With an alien people clutching their gods.
I should be glad of another death.

Adoration of the Magi by Lavinia Hamer
Adoration of the Magi (w/c), Hamer, Lavinia (Contemporary Artist)/
Private Collection / Bridgeman Images

Reading and Reacting

1. The speaker in this poem is one of the three wise men who came to pay tribute to the infant Jesus. In what way are his recollections unexpected? How would you have expected him to react to the birth of Jesus?

2. In what way do the mythical references in the poem allude to future events? Do you need to understand these allusions in order to appreciate the poem?

3. What does the speaker mean in line 41 when he says that the three wise men were "no longer at ease here, in the old dispensation"? What has changed for them? Why does the speaker say that he would be glad for "another death" (line 43)?

4. **JOURNAL ENTRY** How is this poem similar to and different from the story of the three wise men told in the New Testament (Matthew 2.1–18)?

5. CRITICAL PERSPECTIVE In an analysis of "Journey of the Magi," poet and critic Anthony Hecht discusses the most common interpretation of the poem, pointing to "a consensus of critical feeling about the tone of the conclusion of this poem, which, it is said, appears to border on despair and exhaustion of hope." Hecht, however, suspects that something more subtle is going on—namely, that Eliot is using the speaker of the poem to express his own imperfect acceptance of Christianity:

> Again, if I am right about this, the poem might have a deeply personal meaning for Eliot himself, and might represent a kind of "confession," an acknowledgment that he had not yet perfectly embraced the fate to which he nominally adhered, that his imperfect spiritual status was, like the Magus's, that of a person whose faith was incomplete.

Which of the two interpretations given above seems more plausible to you? Is the speaker of the poem wrestling with an incomplete faith, or is he experiencing "despair and exhaustion of hope"?

Related Works: "Araby" (p. 361), "Cathedral" (p. 435), "The World Is Too Much with Us" (p. 692), "On First Looking into Chapman's Homer" (p. 819), "Do not go gentle into that good night" (p. 891), "The Love Song of J. Alfred Prufrock" (p. 981)

✔ **CHECKLIST**   **Writing about Symbol, Allegory, Allusion, Myth**

Symbol

- [ ] Are there any symbols in the poem? What leads you to believe they are symbols?
- [ ] Are these symbols conventional?
- [ ] Are they universal or archetypal?
- [ ] Are any symbols obscure or highly idiosyncratic?
- [ ] What is the literal meaning of each symbol in the context of the poem?
- [ ] Beyond its literal meaning, what else could each symbol suggest?
- [ ] How does your interpretation of each symbol enhance your understanding of the poem?

Allegory

- [ ] Is the poem an allegory?
- [ ] Are there any allegorical figures within the poem? How can you tell?
- [ ] What do the allegorical figures signify on a literal level?
- [ ] What lesson does the allegory illustrate?

Allusion

- Are there any allusions in the poem?

- Do you recognize the names, places, historical events, or literary works to which the poet alludes?

- In what way does each allusion deepen the poem's meaning? Does any allusion interfere with your understanding or enjoyment of the poem? If so, how?

- Would the poem be more effective without a particular allusion?

Myth

- What myths or mythological figures are alluded to?

- How does the poem use myth to convey its meaning?

- How faithful is the poem to the myth? Does the poet add material to the myth? Are any details from the original myth omitted? Is any information distorted? Why?

WRITING SUGGESTIONS: Symbol, Allegory, Allusion, Myth

1. Read "Aunt Jennifer's Tigers" (p. 799), "A Woman Mourned by Daughters" (p. 890), and "Living in Sin" (p. 717) by Adrienne Rich. Then write an essay in which you discuss the similarities and differences in Rich's use of symbols in these poems.

2. Many popular songs make use of allusion. Choose one or two popular songs that you know well, and analyze their use of allusion, paying particular attention to whether the allusions expand the impact and meaning of the song or create barriers to listeners' understanding.

3. Read the Emily Dickinson poem "Because I could not stop for Death—" (p. 973), and then write an interpretation of the poem, identifying its allegorical figures.

4. What applications do the lessons of myth have for life today? Analyze a poem in which myth is central, and then discuss how you might use myth to make generalizations about your own life.

5. Both Judith Ortiz Cofer's "My Father in the Navy: A Childhood Memory" (p. 887) and Alfred, Lord Tennyson's "Ulysses" (p. 1017) allude to Homer's *Odyssey*. Read a summary of the *Odyssey*, and then write an essay in which you compare the poets' treatment of Homer's tale.

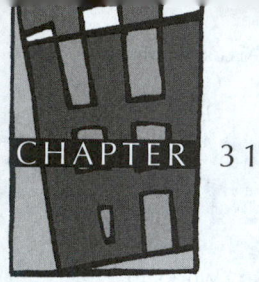

CHAPTER 31

DISCOVERING THEMES IN POETRY

Yusef Komunyakaa
Yusef Komunyakaa, New York City, 2010
(b/w photo),./© Chris Felver/The
Bridgeman Art Library

Dylan Thomas
AP Images

Judith Ortiz Cofer
Dorothy Alexander

Edna St. Vincent Millay
Library of Congress Prints and
Photographs Division[LC-USZ62-42479]

ROBERT HERRICK (1591–1674)

The Argument of His Book (1648)

I sing of brooks, of blossoms, birds, and bowers,
Of April, May, of June, and July-flowers;
I sing of May-poles, hock-carts, wassails, wakes,
Of bridegrooms, brides and of their bridal-cakes;
I write of youth, of love, and have access   5

By these to sing of cleanly wantonness;
I sing of dews, of rains, and piece by piece
Of balm, of oil, of spice and ambergris;
I sing of times trans-shifting, and I write
How roses first came red and lilies white;   10
I write of groves, of twilights, and I sing
The court of Mab,[1] and of the fairy king;
I write of Hell; I sing (and ever shall)
Of Heaven, and hope to have it after all.

Dance around Maypole
Wadsworth Hulton Archive/Getty Images

As the poem above makes clear, a poem can be about anything, from the mysteries of the universe to poetry itself. Although no subject is really inappropriate for poetic treatment, certain conventional subjects—family, nature, love, war, death, the folly of human desires, and the inevitability of growing old—recur frequently.

A poem's theme, however, is more than its subject. In general terms, *theme* refers to the ideas that the poet explores, the concerns that the poem examines. More specifically, a poem's **theme** is its main point or idea. Poems "about death," for example, may examine the difficulty of facing one's own mortality, eulogize a friend, assert the need for the acceptance of life's cycles, or cry out against death's inevitability. Such poems may also explore the **carpe diem** theme—the belief that life is brief, so we must "seize the day."

In order to understand the theme of a poem, readers should consider its form, voice, tone, language, images, allusions, sound—all of its individual elements. Together, these elements

[1] *Mab:* Queen of the fairies.

communicate the ideas that are important in the poem. Keep in mind, however, that a poem may not mean the same thing to every reader. Different readers will bring different backgrounds, attitudes, and experiences to a poem and will therefore see things in various ways. Moreover, various poets may approach the same subject in drastically different ways, emphasizing different elements as they view the subject matter from their own unique perspectives. Ultimately, there are as many different themes, and ways to approach these themes, as there are writers (and readers) of poetry.

 ## Poems about Parents

Although a poet's individual experience may be vastly different from the experiences of his or her readers, certain ideas seem universal in poems about parents. On the one hand, such poems can express positive sentiments: love, joy, wistfulness, nostalgia, and gratitude for childhood's happy memories and a parent's unconditional love. On the other hand, they may express negative emotions: detachment, frustration, resentment, regret, or even anger. When they write about parents, poets may be emotionally engaged or distant, curious or apathetic, remorseful or grateful; they may idealize parents or attack them. Regardless of the particulars of the poem's specific theme, however, virtually all poems about parents address one basic concept: the influence of a parent over his or her child.

For as long as poets have been writing poetry, their personal experiences (and childhoods) have influenced their subject matter and their poems. In American poetry, poems about parents became more common with the advent of **confessionalism**, a movement in the mid 1950s in which poets began to write subjective verse about their personal experiences. Poems in Robert Lowell's *Life Studies* and W. D. Snodgrass's *Heart's Needle* both addressed the positive and negative aspects of the poets' families (including their parents and children), thus opening the door for an influx of poems about similar themes. Poems by Sylvia Plath and Anne Sexton dealt with previously taboo subjects such as abortion, suicide, and mental illness. Though confessional poets often adapted or fictionalized their experiences when putting them into verse, the line between art and life could be thin, sometimes dangerously so: both Plath and Sexton committed suicide.

The poems in this section all deal with issues related to parents and family, but their styles, voices, and focuses are very different. Sometimes the speakers' voices express ambivalence, communicating conventional sentiments of love and admiration alongside perplexity, frustration, and even anger. This ambivalence is apparent in Theodore Roethke's "My Papa's Waltz" (p. 885), Robert Hayden's "Those Winter Sundays" (p. 885), and Julia Alvarez's "Dusting" (p. 886) as adult speakers struggle to make peace with their parents' long-ago behavior. In Seamus Heaney's "Digging" (p. 886), the speaker is more positive, finding traits in his father (and grandfather) that he would like to emulate. Judith Ortiz Cofer's "My Father in the Navy: A Childhood Memory" (p. 887) explores visual images of the speaker's father, while Mitsuye Yamada's "The Night Before Goodbye" (p. 888) considers a mother's quiet sacrifice, and Richard Blanco's "Papa's Bridge" (p. 889) focuses on a symbol that connects father and son. Finally, Andrew Hudgins's "Elegy for My Father, Who Is Not Dead" (p. 890), Adrienne Rich's "A Woman Mourned by Daughters" (p. 890), and Dylan Thomas's "Do not go gentle into that good night" (p. 891) examine the speakers' emotional reactions to the idea of their parents' deaths.

Source: ©Bettmann/Corbis

THEODORE ROETHKE (1908–1963)

My Papa's Waltz (1948)

The whiskey on your breath
Could make a small boy dizzy;
But I hung on like death:
Such waltzing was not easy.

We romped until the pans   5
Slid from the kitchen shelf;
My mother's countenance
Could not unfrown itself.

The hand that held my wrist
Was battered on one knuckle;   10
At every step you missed
My right ear scraped a buckle.

You beat time on my head
With a palm caked hard by dirt,
Then waltzed me off to bed   15
Still clinging to your shirt.

Oscar White/Pach Brothers/Historical/Corbis

ROBERT HAYDEN (1913–1980)

Those Winter Sundays (1962)

Sundays too my father got up early
and put his clothes on in the blueblack cold,
then with cracked hands that ached
from labor in the weekday weather made
banked fires blaze. No one ever thanked him.   5

I'd wake and hear the cold splintering,
    breaking.
When the rooms were warm, he'd call,
and slowly I would rise and dress,
fearing the chronic angers of that house,

Speaking indifferently to him,   10
who had driven out the cold
and polished my good shoes as well.
What did I know, what did I know
of love's austere and lonely offices?

JULIA ALVAREZ (1950–   )

Dusting (1996)

Each morning I wrote my name
On the dusty cabinet, then crossed
The dining table in script, scrawled
In capitals on the backs of chairs,
Practicing signatures like scales   5
While mother followed, squirting
Linseed from a burping can
Into a crumpled-up flannel.

She erased my fingerprints
From the bookshelf and rocker,   10
Polished mirrors on the desk
Scribbled with my alphabets.
My name was swallowed in the towel
With which she jeweled the table tops.
The grain surfaced in the oak   15
And the pine grew luminous.
But I refused with every mark
To be like her, anonymous.

Jeff Morgan 12/Alamy

SEAMUS HEANEY (1939–2013)

Digging (1966)

Between my finger and my thumb
The squat pen rests; snug as a gun.

Under my window, a clean rasping sound
When the spade sinks into gravelly ground:
My father, digging. I look down   5

Till his straining rump among the flowerbeds
Bends low, comes up twenty years away
Stooping in rhythm through potato drills
Where he was digging.

The coarse boot nestled on the lug, the shaft   10
Against the inside knee was levered firmly.
He rooted out tall tops, buried the bright edge deep
To scatter new potatoes that we picked
Loving their cool hardness in our hands.

By God, the old man could handle a spade.   15
Just like his old man.

My grandfather cut more turf in a day
Than any other man on Toner's bog.
Once I carried him milk in a bottle
Corked sloppily with paper. He straightened up   20
To drink it, then fell to right away

Nicking and slicing neatly, heaving sods
Over his shoulder, going down and down
For the good turf. Digging.

The cold smell of potato mould, the squelch and slap   25
Of soggy peat, the curt cuts of an edge
Through living roots awaken in my head.
But I've no spade to follow men like them.

Between my finger and my thumb
The squat pen rests.   30
I'll dig with it.

Source: ©Dorothy Alexander

JUDITH ORTIZ COFER (1952–   )

My Father in the Navy:
A Childhood Memory (1982)

Stiff and immaculate
in the white cloth of his uniform
and a round cap on his head like a halo,
he was an apparition on leave from a shadow-world
and only flesh and blood when he rose from below   5
the waterline where he kept watch over the engines
and dials making sure the ship parted the waters
on a straight course.
Mother, brother and I kept vigil
on the nights and dawns of his arrivals,   10
watching the corner beyond the neon sign of a quasar
for the flash of white our father like an angel
heralding a new day.
His homecomings were the verses
we composed over the years making up   15
the siren's song that kept him coming back
from the bellies of iron whales
and into our nights
like the evening prayer.

MITSUYE YAMADA (1923–   )

The Night Before Goodbye (1976)

Mama is mending
my underwear
while my brothers sleep.
Her husband taken away by the FBI
one son lured away by the Army   5
now another son and daughter
lusting for the free world outside.
She must let go.
The war goes on.
She will take one still small son   10
and join Papa in internment[1]
to make a family.
Still sewing
squinting in the dim light
in room C barrack 4 block 4   15
she whispers
Remember
keep your underwear
in good repair
in case of accident   20
don't bring shame
on us.

Manzanar Relocation Center, 1943
Ansel Adams's *Photographs of Japanese-American Internment at Manzanar*, Library of Congress,
#LC-DIG-ppprs-00284

---

[1]*internment:* Shortly after the attack on Pearl Harbor, President Roosevelt ordered that all people of Japanese ancestry—even
American citizens—be removed from the West Coast. About 112,000 people were relocated to "internment camps," where they
remained until after the war's end.

RICHARD BLANCO (1968–   )

Papa's Bridge (1998)

Morning, driving west again, away from the sun
rising in the slit of the rearview mirror, as I climb
on slabs of concrete and steel bent into a bridge
arcing with all its parabolic[1] y-squared splendor.
I rise to meet the shimmering faces of buildings   5
above tree tops meshed into a calico[2] of greens,
forgetting the river below runs, insists on running
and scouring the earth, moving it grain by grain.

And for a few inclined seconds every morning
I am twelve years old with my father standing   10
at the tenth floor window of his hospital room,
gazing at this same bridge like a mammoth bone
aching with the gravity of its own dense weight.
The glass dosed by a tepid[3] light reviving the city
as I watched and read his sleeping, wondering   15
if he could even dream in such dreamless white:

Was he falling? Was he flying? Who was he, who
was I underneath his eyes, flitting like the birds
across the rooftops and early stars wasting away,
the rush-hour cars pushing through the avenues   20
like the tiny blood cells through his vein, the I.V.
spiraling down like a string of clear licorice feeding
his forearm, bruised pearl and lavender, colors
of the morning haze and the pills on his tongue.

The stitches healed, while the room kept sterile   25
with the usual silence between us. For three days
I served him water or juice in wilting paper cups,
flipped through muted soap operas and game shows,
and filled out the menu cards stamped *Bland Diet*.
For three nights I wedged flat and strange pillows   30
around his body like a fallen S shaped by the bed
and mortared in place by layers of stiff percale.[4]

When he was ordered to walk, I took his hand,
together we stepped to the window and he spoke
—*You'll know how to build bridges like that someday*—   35

---

[1] *parabolic:* Having a curved, bowl-like surface.

[2] *calico:* Patchwork.

[3] *tepid:* Weak or lukewarm.

[4] *percale:* Close-woven cotton fabric.

today, I cross this city, this bridge, still spanning
the silent distance between us with the memory
of a father and son holding hands, secretly in love.

ANDREW HUDGINS (1951–   )

Elegy for My Father, Who Is Not Dead (1987)

One day I'll lift the telephone
and be told my father's dead. He's ready.
In the sureness of his faith, he talks
about the world beyond this world
as though his reservations have   5
been made. I think he wants to go,
a little bit—a new desire
to travel building up, an itch
to see fresh worlds. Or older ones.
He thinks that when I follow him   10
he'll wrap me in his arms and laugh,
they way he did when I arrived
on earth. I do not think he's right.
He's ready. I am not. I can't
just say goodbye as cheerfully   15
as if he were embarking on a trip
to make my later trip go well.
I see myself on deck, convinced
his ship's gone down, while he's convinced
I'll see him standing on the dock   20
and waving, shouting, Welcome back.

ADRIENNE RICH (1929–2012)

A Woman Mourned by Daughters (1984)

Now, not a tear begun,
we sit here in your kitchen,
spent, you see, already.
You are swollen till you strain
this house and the whole sky.   5
You, whom we so often
succeeded in ignoring!
You are puffed up in death
like a corpse pulled from the sea;
we groan beneath your weight.   10
And yet you were a leaf,

a straw blown on the bed,
you had long since become
crisp as a dead insect.
What is it, if not you,   15
that settles on us now
like satins you pulled down
over our bridal heads?
What rises in our throats
like food you prodded in?   20
Nothing could be enough.
You breathe upon us now
through solid assertions
of yourself: teaspoons, goblets,
seas of carpet, a forest   25
of old plants to be watered,
an old man in an adjoining
room to be touched and fed.
And all this universe
dares us to lay a finger   30
anywhere, save exactly
as you would wish it done.

AP Images

DYLAN THOMAS (1914–1953)

Do not go gentle into that good night* (1952)

Do not go gentle into that good night,
Old age should burn and rave at close of day;
Rage, rage against the dying of the light.

Though wise men at their end know dark is right,
Because their words had forked no lightning they   5
Do not go gentle into that good night.

Good men, the last wave by, crying how bright
Their frail deeds might have danced in a green bay,
Rage, rage against the dying of the light.

Wild men who caught and sang the sun in flight,   10
And learn, too late, they grieved it on its way,
Do not go gentle into that good night.

---

*This poem was written during the last illness of the poet's father.

Grave men, near death, who see with blinding sight
Blind eyes could blaze like meteors and be gay,
Rage, rage against the dying of the light.   15

And you, my father, there on the sad height,
Curse, bless, me now with your fierce tears, I pray,
Do not go gentle into that good night.
Rage, rage against the dying of the light.

Reading and Reacting: Poems about Parents

1. What is each speaker's attitude toward his or her parent?
2. Which words, images, and figures of speech in each poem have positive associations? Which create a negative impression?
3. How would you characterize each poem's tone? For example, is the tone sentimental? playful? angry? resentful? regretful? admiring?
4. What problems are explored in each poem?
5. What does each poem say about the parent? What does each poem reveal about the child?
6. What is each poem's central theme?

Related Works: "I Stand Here Ironing" (p. 299), "New York Day Women" (p. 348), "Two Kinds" (p. 639), "Daddy" (p. 772), "*What Are You Going to Be?*" (p. 1062), *Proof* (p. 1180), *Fences* (p. 1548)

 ## Poems about Nature

In his 1913 poem "Trees," the American poet Joyce Kilmer neatly summarized the symbiotic relationship that exists between poetry and nature: "I think that I shall never see / A poem lovely as a tree." Poets have always found inspiration in the beauty, majesty, and grandeur of the natural world; in fact, some forms of poetry are dedicated solely to the subject of nature. For example, a **pastoral** is a literary form that deals nostalgically with a simple rural life. Many of the early Greek and Roman pastorals were about shepherds who passed the time writing about love while watching their flocks. In these poems, the shepherd's life is idealized; thus, the pastoral tradition celebrates simple times and the beauty of the rural life. Similarly, an **idyll**, a short work in verse or prose (or a painting or a piece of music), depicts simple pastoral or rural scenes, often in idealized terms.

Certain literary movements also focused on the subject of nature. For the **romantic poets**, nature was a source of inspiration, authenticity, and spiritual refreshment, qualities they by and large saw as lacking in the lives of Europeans—both the educated classes and those working in the mills and factories that came with industrialization. Later, the American **transcendentalists**, including Ralph Waldo Emerson and Henry David Thoreau, examined the relationships between philosophy, religion, and nature. In *Walden*, for example, Thoreau wrote about the pleasures and rewards of withdrawing from mainstream life in order to live simply in the woods.

Although all poems about nature deal with the same general subject, their approaches, and their focuses, can differ greatly. Poems "about nature" may focus on the seasons, the weather, mountains or the sea, birds or animals, or trees and flowers. They may praise the beauty of nature, assert the superiority of its simplest creatures, consider nature's evanescence, or mourn its destruction. In the pages that follow, romantic poet William Wordsworth's "I wandered lonely as a cloud" (below) extols the virtue of nature and the value of immersing oneself in its beauty, while in "The Windhover" (p. 894), Gerard Manley Hopkins celebrates the divinity of God's natural kingdom, and in "Loveliest of Trees" (p. 894), A. E. Housman's speaker acknowledges the importance of appreciating nature's simple beauty while he still has time. Some poems about nature focus on a single image. For example, in Carl Sandburg's "Fog" (p. 895), the speaker focuses on the image of fog hanging over the city. Other nature poems convey the pull of memory, as in Robert Frost's "Birches" (p. 895), where the speaker recalls the childhood pleasure of climbing trees and longs for the simplicity of those times. Both Denise Levertov's "Living" (p. 896) and Wendell Berry's "The Peace of Wild Things" (p. 897) express a oneness with nature and its creatures. Finally, Carl Sandburg's bittersweet "Autumn Movement" (p. 897) examines the idea that "no beautiful thing lasts."

WILLIAM WORDSWORTH (1770–1850)

I wandered lonely as a cloud (1807)

I wandered lonely as a cloud
    That floats on high o'er vales and hills,
When all at once I saw a crowd,
    A host, of golden daffodils,
Beside the lake, beneath the trees,   5
Fluttering and dancing in the breeze.

Continuous as the stars that shine
    And twinkle on the milky way,
They stretched in never-ending line
    Along the margin of a bay: 10
Ten thousand saw I at a glance,
Tossing their heads in sprightly dance.

The waves beside them danced; but they
    Out-did the sparkling waves in glee;
A poet could not but be gay,   15
    In such a jocund company;
I gazed—and gazed—but little thought
What wealth the show to me had brought:

For oft, when on my couch I lie
    In vacant or in pensive mood,   20
They flash upon that inward eye
    Which is the bliss of solitude;
And then my heart with pleasure fills,
And dances with the daffodils.

GERARD MANLEY HOPKINS (1844–1889)

The Windhover[1] (1877)

To Christ Our Lord

I caught this morning morning's minion,[2] kingdom
  of daylight's dauphin, dapple-dawn-drawn Falcon,
    in his riding
Of the rolling level underneath him steady air, and striding
High there, how he rung upon the rein[3] of a wimpling[4] wing
In his ecstasy! then off, off forth on swing,   5
  As a skate's heel sweeps smooth on a bow-bend: the hurl and
    gliding
Rebuffed the big wind. My heart in hiding
Stirred for a bird,—the achieve of, the mastery of the thing!

Brute beauty and valor and act, oh, air, pride, plume, here
  Buckle! and the fire that breaks from thee then, a billion   10
Times told lovelier, more dangerous, O my chevalier!

No wonder of it: shéer plód, makes plow down sillion[5]
Shine, and blue-bleak embers, ah my dear,
  Fall, gall themselves, and gash gold-vermilion.

A. E. HOUSMAN (1859–1936)

Loveliest of Trees (1896)

Loveliest of trees, the cherry now
Is hung with bloom along the bough,
And stands about the woodland ride
Wearing white for Eastertide.

Now, of my threescore years and ten,   5
Twenty will not come again,
And take from seventy springs a score,
It only leaves me fifty more.

And since to look at things in bloom
Fifty springs are little room,   10
About the woodlands I will go
To see the cherry hung with snow.

---

[1] *Windhover:* A kestrel, a European falcon able to hover in the air with its head to the wind.
[2] *minion:* Favorite.
[3] *rung upon the rein:* A horse is "rung upon the rein" when it circles at the end of a long rein held by the trainer.
[4] *wimpling:* Rippling.
[5] *sillion:* The ridge between two furrows.

CARL SANDBURG (1878–1967)

Fog (1961)

The fog comes
on little cat feet.

It sits looking
over harbor and city
on silent haunches   5
and then moves on.

Source: ©Bettmann/Corbis

ROBERT FROST (1874–1963)

Birches (1915)

When I see birches bend to left and right
Across the lines of straighter darker trees,
I like to think some boy's been swinging them.
But swinging doesn't bend them down to stay
As ice-storms do. Often you must have seen them   5
Loaded with ice a sunny winter morning
After a rain. They click upon themselves
As the breeze rises, and turn many-colored
As the stir cracks and crazes their enamel.
Soon the sun's warmth makes them shed crystal shells   10
Shattering and avalanching on the snow-crust—
Such heaps of broken glass to sweep away
You'd think the inner dome of heaven had fallen.
They are dragged to the withered bracken by the load,
And they seem not to break; though once they are bowed 15
So low for long, they never right themselves:
You may see their trunks arching in the woods
Years afterwards, trailing their leaves on the ground
Like girls on hands and knees that throw their hair
Before them over their heads to dry in the sun.   20
But I was going to say when Truth broke in
With all her matter-of-fact about the ice-storm
I should prefer to have some boy bend them
As he went out and in to fetch the cows—
Some boy too far from town to learn baseball,   25
Whose only play was what he found himself,
Summer or winter, and could play alone.
One by one he subdued his father's trees
By riding them down over and over again
Until he took the stiffness out of them,   30
And not one but hung limp, not one was left
For him to conquer. He learned all there was

To learn about not launching out too soon
And so not carrying the tree away
Clear to the ground. He always kept his poise   35
To the top branches, climbing carefully
With the same pains you use to fill a cup
Up to the brim, and even above the brim.
Then he flung outward, feet first, with a swish,
Kicking his way down through the air to the ground.   40
So was I once myself a swinger of birches.
And so I dream of going back to be.
It's when I'm weary of considerations,
And life is too much like a pathless wood
Where your face burns and tickles with the cobwebs   45
Broken across it, and one eye is weeping
From a twig's having lashed across it open.
I'd like to get away from earth awhile
And then come back to it and begin over.
May no fate willfully misunderstand me   50
And half grant what I wish and snatch me away
Not to return. Earth's the right place for love:
I don't know where it's likely to go better.
I'd like to go by climbing a birch tree,
And climb black branches up a snow-white trunk   55
Toward Heaven, till the tree could bear no more,
But dipped its top and set me down again.
That would be good both going and coming back.
One could do worse than be a swinger of birches.

DENISE LEVERTOV (1923–1997)

Living (1967)

The fire in leaf and grass
so green it seems
each summer the last summer.

The wind blowing, the leaves
shivering in the sun,   5
each day the last day.

A red salamander
so cold and so
easy to catch, dreamily

moves his delicate feet   10
and long tail. I hold
my hand open for him to go.

Each minute the last minute.

WENDELL BERRY (1934–   )

The Peace of Wild Things (1968)

When despair for the world grows in me
and I wake in the night at the least sound
in fear of what my life and my children's lives may be,
I go and lie down where the wood drake[1]
rests in his beauty on the water, and the great heron feeds.   5
I come into the peace of wild things
who do not tax their lives with forethought
of grief. I come into the presence of still water.
And I feel above me the day-blind stars
waiting with their light. For a time   10
I rest in the grace of the world, and am free.

CARL SANDBURG (1878–1967)

Autumn Movement (1918)

I cried over beautiful things knowing no beautiful thing lasts.

The field of cornflower yellow is a scarf at the neck of the copper sunburned woman,
    the mother of the year, the taker of seeds.

The northwest wind comes and the yellow is torn full of holes, new beautiful things
    come in the first spit of snow on the northwest wind, and the old things go,   5
    not one lasts.

Reading and Reacting: Poems about Nature

1. What aspect of nature does the poem focus on?
2. What is the speaker's attitude toward nature? For example, is nature seen as a benevolent, comforting, threatening, awe-inspiring, or overwhelming force?
3. Which words, images, and figures of speech in the poem have positive associations? Which create a negative impression of nature?
4. How would you characterize each poem's tone? For example, is the speaker hopeful? thoughtful? humbled? frightened?
5. Is the natural world the poem's true subject, or is it just the setting? Explain.
6. What is each poem's central theme?

Related Works: "Snow" (p. 126), "Doe Season" (p. 472), "Greasy Lake" (p. 569), "Cézanne's Ports" (p. PS4), "Nothing Gold Can Stay" (p. 749), "Comparatives" (p. 803), "Four Haiku" (p. 835)

---

[1] *wood drake:* A male wood duck, a species inhabiting North American forested areas.

Poems about Love

Since the earliest times, romantic love has been one of the great themes of poetry. In the European tradition, Sappho, whose works exist largely in fragments, is one of the early classic Greek poets. Even more influential, in part because most of their works survived, were the Romans Catullus and Ovid. Although the Bible may strike some as an unlikely place to find love poetry, the *Song of Songs* is just that (although it is also commonly interpreted as an allegory of the love between God and his people). In *La Vita Nuova* (*The New Life*), Dante wrote about the life-changing effect of his meeting with Beatrice, a beautiful young woman who was to die young. It is this same Beatrice with whose help Dante embarks on his journey from hell to heaven in *The Divine Comedy*.

Love has played an equally important part in English poetry. During the Middle Ages, poems such as *Sir Gawain and the Green Knight* and *Le Morte d'Arthur* employed the conventions of "courtly love," in which a protagonist performs gallant deeds to win the hand of a fair maiden. Examples of Renaissance love poems include many of the sonnets of William Shakespeare and Edmund Spenser as well as Christopher Marlowe's "The Passionate Shepherd to His Love" (p. 1003), which was answered by Sir Walter Raleigh's "The Nymph's Reply to the Shepherd" (p. 1009).

Although the Renaissance may arguably be considered the high point of love poetry in English, the tradition has continued to the present day. Increased opportunities for women to read, write, and publish poetry have brought new perspectives to what was once a male-dominated field. **Confessional poetry** has allowed a more direct, frank discussion of love. And, of course, love songs today are as much in fashion as they were in the time of Shakespeare, Dante, or Sappho—and heard by more people than ever.

In each of the poems in this section, the poets address the subject of love in their own unique ways. Husband and wife Robert Browning and Elizabeth Barrett Browning are represented by the traditional love poems "Meeting at Night" (p. 898), "Parting at Morning" (p. 899), and "How Do I Love Thee?" (p. 899), which is one of the most frequently quoted poems in the English language.

In Edna St. Vincent Millay's "What lips my lips have kissed" (p. 899), the speaker reminisces about her past lovers with a mixture of nostalgia and wistfulness, and the speaker in Jehanne Dubrow's "Before the Deployment" (p. 900) relives her soldier–lover's departure. On a lighter note, Leigh Hunt's "Jenny Kissed Me" (p. 900) expresses the joy a kiss can bring, and Dorothy Parker's "General Review of the Sex Situation" (p. 901) is a tongue-in-cheek comment on the differences between the sexes.

ROBERT BROWNING (1812–1889)

Meeting at Night (1845)

The gray sea and the long black land;
And the yellow half-moon large and low;
And the startled little waves that leap
In fiery ringlets from their sleep,

As I gain the cove with pushing prow,   5
And quench its speed i' the slushy sand.

Then a mile of warm sea-scented beach;
Three fields to cross till a farm appears;
A tap at the pane, the quick sharp scratch
And blue spurt of a lighted match,   10
And a voice less loud, through its joys and fears,
Than the two hearts beating each to each!

Parting at Morning   (1845)

Round the cape of a sudden came the sea,
And the sun looked over the mountain's rim:
And straight was a path of gold for him,
And the need of a world of men for me.

ELIZABETH BARRETT BROWNING (1806–1861)

How Do I Love Thee?   (1850)

How do I love thee? Let me count the ways.
I love thee to the depth and breadth and height
My soul can reach, when feeling out of sight
For the ends of being and ideal grace.
I love thee to the level of every day's   5
Most quiet need, by sun and candle-light.
I love thee freely, as men strive for right.
I love thee purely, as they turn from praise.
I love thee with the passion put to use
In my old griefs, and with my childhood's faith.   10
I love thee with a love I seemed to lose
With my lost saints. I love thee with the breath,
Smiles, tears, of all my life; and, if God choose,
I shall but love thee better after death.

EDNA ST. VINCENT MILLAY (1892–1950)

What lips my lips have kissed   (1923)

What lips my lips have kissed, and where, and why,
I have forgotten, and what arms have lain
Under my head till morning; but the rain
Is full of ghosts tonight, that tap and sigh
Upon the glass and listen for reply,   5

And in my heart there stirs a quiet pain
For unremembered lads that not again
Will turn to me at midnight with a cry.
Thus in the winter stands the lonely tree,
Nor knows what birds have vanished one by one,
Yet knows its boughs more silent than before: 10
I cannot say what loves have come and gone,
I only know that summer sang in me
A little while, that in me sings no more.

JEHANNE DUBROW (1975–   )

Before the Deployment (2010)

He kisses me before he goes. While I,
still dozing, half-asleep, laugh and rub my face

against the sueded surface of the sheets,
thinking it's him I touch, his skin beneath

my hands, my body curving in to meet   5
his body there. I never hear him leave.

But I believe he shuts the bedroom door,
as though unsure if he should change his mind,

pull off his boots, crawl beneath the blankets
left behind, his hand a heat against my breast,   10

our heart rates slowing into rest. Perhaps
all good-byes should whisper like a piece of silk—

and then the quick surprise of waking, alone
except for the citrus ghost of his cologne.

LEIGH HUNT (1784–1859)

Jenny Kissed Me (1838)

Jenny kissed me when we met,
Jumping from the chair she sat in.
Time, you thief! who love to get
Sweets into your list, put that in.
Say I'm weary, say I'm sad;   5
Say that health and wealth have missed me;
Say I'm growing old, but add—
Jenny kissed me!

DOROTHY PARKER (1893–1967)

General Review of the Sex Situation (1933)

Woman wants monogamy;
Man delights in novelty.
Love is woman's moon and sun;
Man has other forms of fun.

Woman lives but in her lord;   5
Count to ten, and man is bored.
With this the gist and sum of it,
What earthly good can come of it?

Reading and Reacting: Poems about Love

1. What general ideas about love are expressed in each poem?
2. What conventional images and figures of speech are used to express feelings of love?
3. Does any poet use any unexpected (or even shocking) images or figures of speech?
4. How would you characterize the tone of each poem? For example, is the tone happy? sad? celebratory? regretful? ambivalent?
5. What does each poem reveal about the speaker? about the person to whom the poem is addressed?
6. What is each poem's central theme?

Related Works: "Hills Like White Elephants" (p. 119), "Love and Other Catastrophes: A Mix Tape" (p. 127), "The Storm" (p. 273), "Living in Sin" (p. 717), "My mistress' eyes are nothing like the sun" (p. 754), "Shall I compare thee to a summer's day?" (p. 758), "A Valediction: Forbidding Mourning" (p. 768), "To My Dear and Loving Husband" (p. 775), "You fit into me" (p. 780), *The Brute* (p. 1048).

 Poems about War

In poetry, war is as ancient a theme as love and nature. In fact, the earliest poems, including Homer's *Iliad* and *Odyssey* and Virgil's *Aeneid*, have at their centers epic battles and struggles. These poems were created in metered verse so they could be remembered and passed down from one generation to the next. Portions of them would be recited at public gatherings and festivals, making them analogous to the war movies of today. Epic poems reflected the belief that war could be a noble and glorious endeavor, and they often glorified the heroes of the wars and battles they described. Even in the earliest of these poems, however, there is a sense of the futility and devastation that war brings with it; for example, in the *Iliad*, many of the Greeks laying siege to the city of Troy are sick of the war and want to go home. In the *Aeneid*, the scene where Aeneas witnesses the destruction of his native Troy by the Greeks, and by the gods aiding them, is one of the most moving in literature.

In modern times, poets have tended to concentrate on the horrors of war, no doubt in part because technology has allowed armies to do more damage more quickly than ever before. World War I, which saw the first widespread use of aircraft, poison gas, and machine guns in warfare, marked a turning point in war and in poetic responses to it. One of the best-known poems to come out of this war is "Dulce et Decorum Est" (p. 902), written toward the end of the war by Wilfred Owen, a soldier who was killed on the Western Front in 1918. The poem, which was not published until after Owen's death, includes graphic images and ends with a bitterly ironic quotation that summarizes the mentality that fuels war: "It is sweet and fitting to die for one's country." In "Atrocities" (p. 903), Siegfried Sassoon, a contemporary of Owens's, offers a similarly cynical look at war (and warriors).

Of course, not all poems about war are poems of protest. For example, "The Soldier," by Rupert Brooke (p. 904), a contemporary of both Owen's and Sassoon's, celebrates the nobility of fighting for the sake of one's beloved country; Joel McCrea's classic "In Flanders Fields" (p. 904) mourns the inevitable losses war brings yet expresses the sentiment that the fight must go on; and Radiohead's lyrics "Harry Patch (In Memory of)" (p. 905) honor the death of the last surviving British soldier of World War I.

Modern poems about war do not always focus on soldiers. For example, although Henry Reed's "Naming of Parts" (p. 905) focuses on the grim realities of a soldier's training for war, W. H. Auden's poem from "In Time of War" (p. 906) examines the evils of the Nanking Massacre and the Dachau concentration camp.

In the post–World War II years, enemies were not as clearly defined as they had been in the past. The war in Vietnam unfolded before the American people on their television screens and, as a result, many Americans (including American soldiers) came to question the war and its goals. This attempt to come to terms with the war and its aftermath carried over into poems about the war, as seen in Yusef Komunyakaa's "Facing It" (p. 906), in which a Vietnam veteran visits the Vietnam War Memorial in Washington D. C.

The post-Vietnam years have seen troops from various nations take part in conflicts around the globe—conflicts whose costs have been high and whose goals have not always been as clear-cut as they were in past conflicts. Writing about one such conflict—the Iraq war—in his prose poem "Mosul" (p. 907), David Hernandez focuses on the physical realities of war. Finally, Richard Wilbur's "Terza Rima" (p. 908) comments on the difficulty of expressing the horrors of war, and Wislawa Szymborska's "The End and the Beginning" (p. 908) addresses the problem of cleaning up the damage left behind.

WILFRED OWEN (1893–1918)

Dulce et Decorum Est[1] (1920)

Bent double, like old beggars under sacks,
Knock-kneed, coughing like hags, we cursed through sludge,
Till on the haunting flares we turned our backs
And towards our distant rest began to trudge.
Men marched asleep. Many had lost their boots   5

---

[1] *Dulce et Decorum Est:* The title and last two lines are from Horace, *Odes* 3.2: "Sweet and fitting it is to die for one's country."

But limped on, blood-shod. All went lame; all blind;
Drunk with fatigue; deaf even to the hoots
Of tired, outstripped Five-Nines² that dropped behind.

Gas! GAS Quick, boys!—An ecstasy of fumbling,
Fitting the clumsy helmets just in time;   10
But someone still was yelling out and stumbling
And flound'ring like a man in fire or lime . . .
Dim, through the misty panes and thick green light,
As under a green sea, I saw him drowning.
In all my dreams, before my helpless sight,   15
He plunges at me, guttering, choking, drowning.

If in some smothering dreams you too could pace
Behind the wagon that we flung him in,
And watch the white eyes writhing in his face,
His hanging face, like a devil's sick of sin;   20
If you could hear, at every jolt, the blood
Come gargling from the froth-corrupted lungs,
Obscene as cancer, bitter as the cud
Of vile, incurable sores on innocent tongues,—
My friend, you would not tell with such high zest   25
To children ardent for some desperate glory,
The old Lie: Dulce et decorum est
Pro patria mori.

SILEGFRIED SASSOON (1886–1967)

Atrocities (1919)

You told me, in your drunken-boasting mood,
How once you butchered prisoners. That was good!
I'm sure you felt no pity while they stood
Patient and cowed and scared, as prisoners should.

How did you do them in? Come, don't be shy: 5
You know I love to hear how Germans die,
Downstairs in dug-outs. 'Camerad! they cry;
Then squeal like stoats when bombs begin to fly.

And you? I know your record. You went sick
When orders looked unwholesome: then, with trick   10
And lie, you wangled home. And here you are,
Still talking big and boozing in a bar.

---

²*Five-Nines:* Shells that explode on impact and release poison gas.

British soldier, WWI
©SSPL / The Image Works

RUPERT BROOKE (1887–1915)

The Soldier (1915)

If I should die, think only this of me;
    That there's some corner of a foreign field
That is forever England. There shall be
    In that rich earth a richer dust concealed;
A dust whom England bore, shaped, made aware,   5
    Gave, once, her flowers to love, her ways to roam,
A body of England's breathing English air,
    Washed by the rivers, blest by suns of home.
And think, this heart, all evil shed away,
    A pulse in the eternal mind, no less   10
        Gives somewhere back the thoughts by England given;
Her sights and sounds; dreams happy as her day;
    And laughter, learnt of friends; and gentleness,
        In hearts at peace, under an English heaven.

JOHN MCCRAE (1872–1918)

In Flanders[1] Fields (1915)

In Flanders fields the poppies blow
Between the crosses row on row,
That mark our place; and in the sky
The larks, still bravely singing, fly
Scarce heard amid the guns below.   5

We are the Dead. Short days ago
We lived, felt dawn, saw sunset glow,
Loved and were loved, and now we lie
In Flanders fields.

Take up our quarrel with the foe: 10
To you from failing hands we throw
The torch; be yours to hold it high.
If ye break faith with us who die
We shall not sleep, though poppies grow
In Flanders fields.   15

---

[1] *Flanders:* The Dutch-speaking region of Belgium, where some of the bloodiest battles of World War I were fought.

RADIOHEAD

Harry Patch (In Memory of) (2009)

"i am the only one that got through
the others died where ever they fell
it was an ambush
they came up from all sides
give your leaders each a gun and then let them fight it out themselves   5
i've seen devils coming up from the ground
i've seen hell upon this earth
the next will be chemical but they will never learn"

HENRY REED (1914–1986)

Naming of Parts (1946)

Today we have naming of parts. Yesterday,
We had daily cleaning. And tomorrow morning,
We shall have what to do after firing. But today,
Today we have naming of parts. Japonica[1]
Glistens like coral in all of the neighboring gardens,   5
   And today we have naming of parts.

This is the lower sling swivel. And this
Is the upper sling swivel, whose use you will see,
When you are given your slings. And this is the piling swivel,
Which in your case you have not got. The branches   10
Hold in the gardens their silent, eloquent gestures,
   Which in our case we have not got.

This is the safety-catch, which is always released
With an easy flick of the thumb. And please do not let me
See anyone using his finger. You can do it quite easy   15
If you have any strength in your thumb. The blossoms
Are fragile and motionless, never letting anyone see
   Any of them using their finger.

And this you can see is the bolt. The purpose of this
Is to open the breech, as you see. We can slide it   20
Rapidly backwards and forwards: we call this
Easing the spring. And rapidly backwards and forwards
The early bees are assaulting and fumbling the flowers:
   They call it easing the Spring.

---

[1] *Japonica:* A shrub having waxy flowers in a variety of colors.

They call it easing the Spring: it is perfectly easy   25
If you have any strength in your thumb: like the bolt,
And the breech, and the cocking-piece, and the point of balance,
Which in our case we have not got; and the almond-blossom
Silent in all of the gardens and the bees going backwards and forwards,
    For today we have the naming of parts.   30

W. H. AUDEN (1907–1973)

from "In Time of War" (1939)

XVI

Here war is simple like a monument:
A telephone is speaking to a man;
Flags on a map assert that troops were sent;
A boy brings milk in bowls. There is a plan

For living men in terror of their lives,   5
Who thirst at nine who were to thirst at noon,
And can be lost and are, and miss their wives,
And, unlike an idea, can die too soon.

But ideas can be true although men die,
And we can watch a thousand faces   10
Made active by one lie:

And maps can really point to places
Where life is evil now:
Nanking[1] Dachau.[2]

Yusef Komunyakaa, New York City, 2010 (b/w photo), / © Chris Felver/ The Bridgeman Art Library

YUSEF KOMUNYAKAA (1947–   )

Facing It (1988)

My black face fades,
hiding inside the black granite.
I said I wouldn't,
dammit: No tears.
I'm stone. I'm flesh.   5

---

[1]*Nanking*: A city in China where, in 1937, massacres and rapes were committed on a massive scale by the Japanese Imperial Army.

[2]*Dachau*: A concentration camp in Germany, opened in 1933 and liberated by American forces in 1945.

Hand tracing names of the dead on
the Vietnam War Memorial.
AP Images/Dennis Cook

My clouded reflection eyes me
like a bird of prey, the profile of night
slanted against morning. I turn
this way—the stone lets me go.
I turn that way—I'm inside   10
the Vietnam Veterans Memorial
again, depending on the light
to make a difference.
I go down the 58,022 names,
half-expecting to find   15
my own in letters like smoke.
I touch the name Andrew Johnson;
I see the booby trap's white flash.
Names shimmer on a woman's blouse
but when she walks away   20
the names stay on the wall.
Brushstrokes flash, a red bird's
wings cutting across my stare.
The sky. A plane in the sky.
A white vet's image floats   25
closer to me, then his pale eyes
look through mine. I'm a window.
He's lost his right arm
inside the stone. In the black mirror
a woman's trying to erase names: 30
No, she's brushing a boy's hair.

DAVID HERNANDEZ (1971–   )

Mosul[1] (2011)

The donkey. The donkey pulling the cart.
The caravan of dust. The cart made of plywood,
of crossbeam and junkyard tires. The donkey
made of donkey. The long face. The long ears.
The curled lashes. The obsidian eyes blinking   5
in the dust. The cart rolling, cracking the knuckles
of pebbles. The dust. The blanket over the cart.
The hidden mortar shells. The veins of wires.
The remote device. The red light. The donkey
trotting. The blue sky. The rolling cart. The dust   10
smudging the blue sky. The silent bell of the sun.

---

[1] *Mosul:* The second largest city in Iraq.

The Humvee. The soldiers. The dust-colored
uniforms. The boy from Montgomery, the boy
from Little Falls. The donkey cart approaching.
The dust. The laughter on their lips. The dust   15
on their lips. The moment before the moment.
The shockwave. The dust. The dust. The dust.

AP Images/Nancy Palmieri

RICHARD WILBUR (1921–   )

Terza Rima[1] (2008)

In this great form, as Dante proved in Hell,
There is no dreadful thing that can't be said
In passing. Here, for instance, one could tell

How our jeep skidded sideways toward the dead
Enemy soldier with the staring eyes,   5
Bumping a little as it struck his head,

And then flew on, as if toward Paradise.

Alberto Cristofani A3/Contrasto/Redux

WISLAWA SZYMBORSKA (1923–2012)

The End and the Beginning (1993)

After every war
someone has to clean up.
Things won't
straighten themselves up, after all.

Someone has to push the rubble   5
to the side of the road.
so the corpse-filled wagons
can pass.

Someone has to get mired
in scum and ashes,   10
sofa springs,
splintered glass,
and bloody rags.

Someone has to drag in a girder
to prop up a wall,   15
Someone has to glaze a window,
rehang a door.

---

[1]*Terza Rima:* The interlocking rhyme scheme that Dante Alighieri devised for his *Divine Comedy,* the first third of which deals with hell.

Photogenic it's not,
and takes years.
All the cameras have left   20
for another war.

We'll need the bridges back,
and new railway stations.
Sleeves will go ragged
from rolling them up.   25
Someone, broom in hand,
still recalls the way it was.

Someone else listens
and nods with unsevered head.
But already there are those nearby   30
starting to mill about
who will find it dull.

From out of the bushes
sometimes someone still unearths
rusted-out arguments   35
and carries them to the garbage pile.

Those who knew
what was going on here
must make way for
those who know little.   40
And less than little.
And finally as little as nothing.

In the grass that has overgrown
causes and effects,
someone must be stretched out   45
blade of grass in his mouth
gazing at the clouds.

Reading and Reacting: Poems about War

1. What is each speaker's attitude toward war? Does the speaker seem to be focusing on a particular war or on war in general?
2. What conventional images and figures of speech does each poem use to express its ideas about war?
3. Do any of the poems use unusual, unexpected, or shocking images or figures of speech?
4. How would you describe each poem's tone? For example, is the tone angry? cynical? sad? disillusioned? resigned?
5. How does each poem's form help to communicate the speaker's attitude toward war?
6. What is each poem's central theme?

Related Works: "The Things They Carried" (p. 392), "The Man He Killed" (p. 687), "Patterns" (p. 688), "The Death of the Ball Turret Gunner" (p. 766), *Nine Ten* (p. 1108)

WRITING SUGGESTIONS: Discovering Themes in Poetry

1. Compare any two poems in this chapter about parents, nature, love, or war.

2. Write an **explication** (see Chapter 3) of one of the poems in this chapter.

3. Write an essay in which you compare one of the poems in this chapter to a short story or play on the same general subject. (For possible topics, consult the Related Works list that follows each group of poems.)

4. Some poets write multiple poems on the same general subject. For example, Shakespeare wrote many love poems, and Robert Frost wrote a number of poems about nature. Choose two poems by a single poet that explore the same subject, and compare and contrast the two poems' treatment of this subject.

5. A number of poems in this book focus on the theme of poetry itself. Choose three poems that explore this theme, and write an essay that compares the poems' ideas about reading and writing poetry.

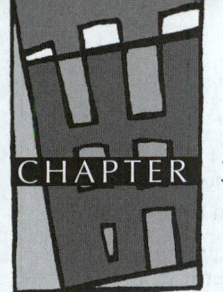

CHAPTER 32

THE POETRY OF LANGSTON HUGHES: A CASEBOOK FOR READING, RESEARCH, AND WRITING

This chapter provides all the materials you will need to develop a research project about Langston Hughes. It includes the following sources:

Background

Critical Perspectives

Other poems by Hughes that appear elsewhere in this anthology are "Negro" (p. 678), "Harlem" (p. 760), and "Island" (p. 855).

Each of the sources in this casebook offers insights into the poems included here. Three are Hughes's own words, one is largely biographical, and others discuss Hughes's use of poetic devices and his influences. All were selected to help you appreciate this poet as well as the themes and devices in his poetry. Other kinds of sources can also enrich your understanding of Hughes's accomplishments—for example, other poems by Hughes, biographical data about the writer, and works of literature by other writers dealing with similar themes.

In preparation for writing an essay on a topic of your choice, read the poems carefully. Then, consider the Reading and Reacting questions that follow them (p. 928) in light of what you have read. Use your responses to help you find a topic you can develop in a three- to six-page essay. When you write your essay, be sure to document any words or ideas that you borrow from your sources and to enclose words that are not your own in quotation marks. (For guidelines on evaluating literary criticism, see p. 14; for guidelines on using source materials, see Chapters 6 and 7.)

About the Author

Library of Congress Prints and Photographs Division[LC-USZ62-43605]

LANGSTON HUGHES (1902–1967) was one of the best-known American writers of the twentieth century. As a member of the Harlem Renaissance in the 1920s, he helped create a vital African American literature. His earliest book of poetry, *The Weary Blues* (1926), established him as one of the most important poets of his generation. His first novel, *Not Without Laughter*, was published in 1930. Not only did Hughes deal honestly in this novel with the daily lives and struggles of African Americans but he also wrote poems that owed much to African American musical forms, such as jazz and blues. Art and politics were inseparable for Hughes, and he was active throughout his life in the struggle for racial and economic justice.

Hughes was born in Joplin, Missouri, in 1902, and during his early life, he experienced the racial and economic inequities that would become the focus of his writing and social activism. His father, James Hughes, wanted to be a lawyer, but racial prejudice prevented him from going to law school. Eventually he decided to leave the United States for Mexico, where he thought he would have more opportunities to succeed. Hughes's mother, Carrie, refused to follow her husband, so the young Langston had little contact with his father until he was in his late teens. As a child, Hughes was a voracious reader. While attending Central High School in Cleveland, Ohio, he began to write poetry, with Carl Sandburg as one of his chief influences. Upon leaving high school, Hughes began the travels that would have such a great effect on his work. In 1920, he went to live with his father in Mexico City. On the way there, he wrote what was to become one of his best-known poems, "The Negro Speaks of Rivers." Father and son had little in common, so the trip

Langston Hughes as a young boy
AP Images

was not successful on a personal level. (At one point, Hughes even considered suicide.) When he returned to the United States, he enrolled at Columbia University to study engineering, but his classes were of little interest to him, and he spent most of his time writing and absorbing the cultural life of New York's African American community.

With the publication of his first book of poetry, *The Weary Blues*, in 1926, Hughes became a visible member of the Harlem Renaissance, a major literary movement of the twentieth century. Centered in the Harlem section

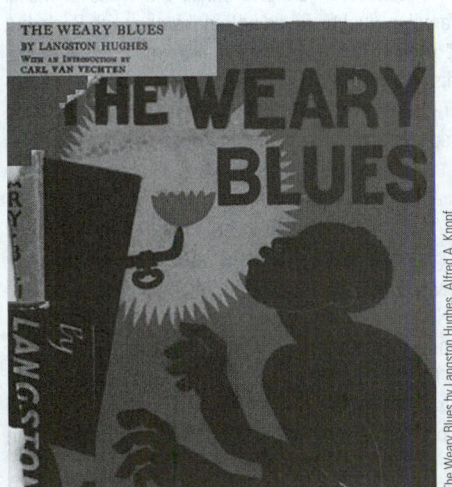

The Weary Blues by Langston Hughes, Alfred A. Knopf

Book jacket for *The Weary Blues* by Langston Hughes

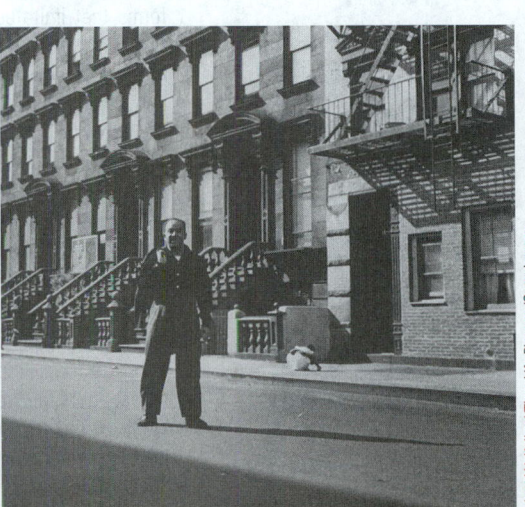

Robert W. Kelley//Time Life Pictures/Getty Images

Langston Hughes in Harlem in 1958.

of New York City, the movement represented the first great flowering of African American literature and included writers such as James Weldon Johnson, Claude McKay, and Countee Cullen. This creative period ended with the onset of the Great Depression in the 1930s.

Although he would become arguably the best-known writer of the Harlem Renaissance, Hughes's work was not universally praised. In fact, many of the elements that have given his work its staying power—his use of African American vernacular, his imitation of the forms of popular music, his concern for the economically disadvantaged—were seen as controversial. Many critics thought that African American writing ought to deal primarily

Lafayette Theater, Harlem, ca. 1929
© John Springer Collection/Corbis

with uplifting stories and follow the conventions of white literature. These critics believed that Hughes's work was undercutting the advances African Americans were achieving in both literary and social life.

Hughes's response to his critics was straightforward. "I sympathized deeply," he later said, "with those critics and those intellectuals, and I saw clearly the need for some of the kinds of books they wanted." He insisted, however, that not every book by an African American could or should be about subjects that middle- or upper-class whites and blacks would find palatable: "I didn't know the upper-class Negroes well enough to write much about them. I knew only the people I had grown up with, and they weren't people whose shoes were always shined, who had been to Harvard, or who had heard of Bach. But they seemed to me good people, too."

In portraying these "good people," Hughes did not shy away from depicting the details of their difficult lives. His subjects are often poor and frequently face racism. Sometimes they are in trouble with the law, and they are typically less interested in intellectual discussion than in paying the rent. The poor had been portrayed before in poetry: T. S. Eliot's long poem *The Waste Land*, published in 1922, just four years before *The Weary Blues*, includes a pointed exchange between two "lower-class" women. What distinguished Hughes's approach from Eliot's, apart from his direct style, was his sympathy for his subjects and his intimate familiarity with their living conditions.

In writing about lower-class African Americans, people who had never "heard of Bach," Hughes devised poetic

Langston Hughes commemorative stamp (2002)

forms that imitated the cadences of jazz and blues, the types of music with which they were familiar. Hughes found nothing wrong with Bach, but he was convinced that African Americans had their own composers and performers. Nor was this simply a self-conscious attempt to find an appropriate poetic vehicle for his subject matter or to promote the art of African Americans; Hughes loved jazz and blues and nothing could have been more natural for him than to use their rhythms in his poetry. His later move into writing song lyrics was a natural transition.

In 1932, Hughes traveled to the Soviet Union and observed many aspects of the Soviet system that he felt were admirable. He was especially impressed by what he saw as the lack of racial injustice and economic inequality. He learned the Uzbek language while recuperating from an illness and began writing on a regular basis for Soviet newspapers, including *Izvestia*. He published a book devoted to impressions of the trip, *A Negro Looks at Soviet Central Asia* in 1934, and he also reflected on his experiences in newspaper columns for the *Chicago Defender*.

Hughes left the Soviet Union after a little more than a year, but he did not abandon his commitment to radical social change. Back in the United States, he settled for a time in California, where he devoted himself to a number of social causes. It would be a mistake, however, to suppose that Hughes was hostile to America. During World War II, when the United States was allied with the Soviet Union against Nazi Germany, Fascist Italy, and Imperial Japan, Hughes used his writing to support the American war effort even as he encouraged America to live up to its democratic ideals.

As part of his effort to depict the lives of average African Americans, Hughes invented a character, Jesse B. Semple, later known as Simple. Simple first appeared in newspaper columns that were so popular they were later anthologized in a series of books, beginning in 1950 with *Simple Speaks His Mind*. Here, Hughes uses a fictional narrator who talks with, and buys drinks for, his friend Semple. The popularity of the pieces derived in part from their humor and straightforward examination of racial issues and partly from Hughes's skillful use of African American vernacular. Since his first publications, Hughes had included the actual speech of the black lower class in his work, and the "Simple" books brought this strategy to a wide audience.

During the cold war in the 1950s, his sympathetic comments on communism and the Soviet Union caused Hughes great political difficulties. His activities were monitored by the House Un-American Activities Committee (HUAC), and in 1953 he was called to testify before Senator Joseph McCarthy's Subcommittees on Subversive Activities. In his testimony to the committee, Hughes denied being a communist but explained why he felt communism appealed to some African Americans. There is some debate about Hughes's actual political views during this period. Commentators who maintain that Hughes had never been a communist also assume that his statements to the Committee were

Langston Hughes testifying before the House Un-American Activities Committee in Washington, D.C., in March of 1953
AP Images

an accurate reflection of his political views. Others, however, are convinced that Hughes, afraid that the writing career he had worked so hard to establish would be destroyed, was downplaying the communist views he still held.

Despite the disruption to his career caused by the Committee's investigation, Hughes remained an important literary and political figure for the remainder of his life. In 1961, he published *Ask Your Mama*, a work that addressed many of the racial and cultural issues that would be so important in the 1960s. He also traveled widely, often as an official representative of the United States. When Hughes died in 1967, he was completing work on his last volume of poetry, *The Panther and the Lash*.

Today, Hughes is remembered chiefly as a poet, but he made important contributions to virtually every genre of writing. He was an accomplished dramatist who also founded several theaters. He wrote novels, short stories, newspaper articles, song lyrics, translations, and fiction for children. In addition to his work as a writer, Hughes edited numerous books and helped encourage and promote the work of younger African American writers. In the years since his death, his reputation has become solidly established. Plain-spoken and highly rhythmic, his poetry continues to appeal to new readers and to provide an example of the ways in which social commitment and literary art can be combined.

 Poems

The Negro Speaks of Rivers (1921)

I've known rivers:
I've known rivers ancient as the world and old as the flow of
    human blood in human veins.

My soul has grown deep like the rivers.

I bathed in the Euphrates[1] when dawns were young.
I built my hut near the Congo[2] and it lulled me to sleep.   5
I looked upon the Nile and raised the pyramids above it.
I heard the singing of the Mississippi when Abe Lincoln went
    down to New Orleans, and I've seen its muddy bosom turn
    all golden in the sunset.

I've known rivers:
Ancient, dusky rivers.

My soul has grown deep like the rivers.   10

Dream Variations (1924)

To fling my arms wide
In some place of the sun,
To whirl and to dance
Till the white day is done.
Then rest at cool evening   5

---

[1]*Euphrates:* Major river of southwest Asia; with the Tigris, the Euphrates forms a valley sometimes referred to as the "cradle of civilization."

[2]*Congo:* River in equatorial Africa, the continent's second longest.

Beneath a tall tree
While night comes on gently,
    Dark like me—
That is my dream!

To fling my arms wide   10
In the face of the sun,
Dance! Whirl! Whirl!
Till the quick day is done.
Rest at pale evening . . .
A tall, slim tree . . .   15
Night coming tenderly
    Black like me.

The Weary Blues (1926)

Droning a drowsy syncopated tune,
Rocking back and forth to a mellow croon,
    I heard a Negro play.
Down on Lenox Avenue[1] the other night
By the pale dull pallor of an old gas light   5
    He did a lazy sway . . .
    He did a lazy sway . . .
To the tune o' those Weary Blues.
With his ebony hands on each ivory key
He made that poor piano moan with melody.   10
    O Blues!
Swaying to and fro on his rickety stool
He played that sad raggy tune like a musical fool.
    Sweet Blues!
Coming from a black man's soul.   15
    O Blues!
In a deep song voice with a melancholy tone
I heard that Negro sing, that old piano moan—
    "Ain't got nobody in all this world,
    Ain't got nobody but ma self.   20
    I's gwine to quit ma frownin'
    And put ma troubles on the shelf."
Thump, thump, thump, went his foot on the floor.
He played a few chords then he sang some more—
    "I got the Weary Blues   25
    And I can't be satisfied,

---

[1] *Lenox Avenue:* Street in Harlem noted for nightlife and music during the 1920s.

> Got the Weary Blues
> And can't be satisfied—
> I ain't happy no mo'
> And I wish that I had died."   30
And far into the night he crooned that tune.
The stars went out and so did the moon.
The singer stopped playing and went to bed
While the Weary Blues echoed through his head.
He slept like a rock or a man that's dead.   35

Dancers and musicians at the Savoy Ballroom in Harlem, 1947
Source: ©Bettmann/Corbis

I, Too[1] (1925)

I, too, sing America.

I am the darker brother.
They send me to eat in the kitchen
When company comes,
But I laugh,   5
And eat well,
And grow strong.

Tomorrow,
I'll be at the table
When company comes.   10

---

[1] *I, Too:* This poem is a direct response to Walt Whitman's poem "I Hear America Singing" (p. 1022).

Nobody'll dare
Say to me,
"Eat in the kitchen,"
Then.

Besides,
They'll see how beautiful I am
And be ashamed—

I too, am America.

Song for a Dark Girl (1927)

Way Down South in Dixie
    (Break the heart of me)
They hung my black young lover
    To a cross roads tree.

Way Down South in Dixie   5
    (Bruised body high in air)
I asked the white Lord Jesus
    What was the use of prayer.

Way down South in Dixie
    (Break the heart of me)   10
Love is a naked shadow
    On a gnarled and naked tree.

Ballad of the Landlord (1940)

Landlord, landlord,
My roof has sprung a leak.
Don't you 'member I told you about it
Way last week?

Landlord, landlord,   5
These steps is broken down.
When you come up yourself
It's a wonder you don't fall down.

Ten Bucks you say I owe you?
Ten Bucks you say is due?   10
Well, that's Ten Bucks more'n I'll pay you
Till you fix this house up new.

What? You gonna get eviction orders?
You gonna cut off my heat?
You gonna take my furniture and   15
Throw it in the street?

An exposed wall in a tenement like the one
referred to in "Ballad of a Landlord"
Masaaki Toyoura/amana images/Getty Images

Um-huh! You talking high and mighty.
Talk on—till you get through.
You ain't gonna be able to say a word
If I land my fist on you.   20

Police! Police!
Come and get this man!
He's trying to ruin the government
And overturn the land!

Copper's whistle!   25
Patrol bell!
Arrest.

Precinct Station.

Iron cell.
Headlines in press: 30

MAN THREATENS LANDLORD

TENANT HELD NO BAIL

JUDGE GIVES NEGRO 90 DAYS IN COUNTY JAIL

Theme for English B (1949)

The instructor said,

> Go home and write
> a page tonight.
> And let that page come out of you—
> Then, it will be true.   5

I wonder if it's that simple?
I am twenty-two, colored, born in Winston-Salem.
I went to school there, then Durham, then here
to this college on the hill above Harlem.
I am the only colored student in my class.   10
The steps from the hill lead down into Harlem,
through a park, then I cross St. Nicholas,
Eighth Avenue, Seventh, and I come to the Y,
the Harlem Branch Y, where I take the elevator
up to my room, sit down and write this page: 15

It's not easy to know what is true for you or me
at twenty-two, my age. But I guess I'm what
I feel and see and hear, Harlem, I hear you:
hear you, hear me—we two—you, me, talk on this page.
(I hear New York, too) Me—who?   20

Well, I like to eat, sleep, drink, and be in love.
I like to work, read, learn, and understand life.
I like a pipe for a Christmas present,
or records—Bessie,[1] bop,[2] or Bach.
I guess being colored doesn't make me *not* like   25
the same things other folks like who are other races.
So will my page be colored that I write?
Being me, it will not be white.
But it will be
a part of you, instructor.   30
You are white—
yet a part of me, as I am a part of you.
That's American.
Sometimes perhaps you don't want to be a part of me.
Nor do I often want to be a part of you.   35
But we are, that's true!
As I learn from you,
I guess you learn from me—
although you're older—and white—
and somewhat more free.   40

This is my page for English B.

Dream Boogie (1951)

Good morning, daddy!
Ain't you heard
The boogie-woogie[3] rumble
Of a dream deferred?

Listen closely: 5
You'll hear their feet
Beating out and beating out a—

> *You think*
> *It's a happy beat?*

Listen to it closely: 10
Ain't you heard
something underneath
like a—

> *What did I say?*

---

[1] *Bessie:* Bessie Smith (1894–1937), blues singer.

[2] *bop:* Short for "bebop," a jazz style developed in the early 1940s by Charlie Parker, Dizzy Gillespie, and others.

[3] *boogie-woogie:* A popular black musical style with variants in both blues and jazz; more specifically, a vigorous piano style marked by heavy and repeated bass figures.

```
Sure,                                        15
I'm happy!
Take it away!

    Hey, pop!
    Re-bop!
    Mop!                                     20

    Y-e-a-h!
```

Birmingham Sunday (September 15, 1963)[1] (1967)

```
  Four little girls
Who went to Sunday School that day
And never came back home at all
But left instead
Their blood upon the wall                     5
With spattered flesh
And bloodied Sunday dresses
Torn to shreds by dynamite
That China made aeons ago—
Did not know                                 10
That what China made
Before China was ever Red at all
Would redden with their blood
This Birmingham-on-Sunday wall.

    Four tiny girls                          15
Who left their blood upon that wall,
In little graves today await
The dynamite that might ignite
The fuse of centuries of Dragon Kings[2]
Whose tomorrow sings a hymn                   20
The missionaries never taught Chinese
In Christian Sunday School
To implement the Golden Rule.
    Four little girls
Might be awakened someday soon               25
By songs upon the breeze
As yet unfelt among magnolia trees.
```

Sixteenth Street Baptist Church, Birmingham, Alabama; site of the September 15, 1963 firebombing
Kevin Fleming/Documentary Value/Corbis

---

[1] *September 15, 1963:* On this date, only weeks after Martin Luther King Jr.'s historic March on Washington, four young African American girls were killed at their Sunday school in Birmingham, Alabama, by a bomb, likely in response to recent civil rights activities in the area.

[2] *Dragon Kings:* In Chinese myth and lore, the dragon is a beneficent force that dispenses blessings in both the natural and supernatural worlds. Eventually, the dragon became a symbol of imperial China. The dragon has also been used in the mythology of white supremacist groups like the Ku Klux Klan.

Photos taken in 1963 of the four girls killed in the bombing of the Sixteenth Street Baptist Church (clockwise from top left: Addie Mae Collins, 14; Cynthia Wesley, 14; Carole Robertson, 14; and Denise McNair, 11)
AP Images

Old Walt (1954)

Old Walt Whitman
Went finding and seeking,
Finding less than sought
Seeking more than found,
Every detail minding   5
Of the seeking or the finding.

Pleasured equally
In seeking as in finding,
Each detail minding,
Old Walt went seeking   10
And finding.

Lenox Avenue: Midnight (1926)

The rhythm of life
Is a jazz rhythm,
Honey.
The gods are laughing at us.

The broken heart of love,   5
The weary, weary heart of pain,—
    Overtones,
    Undertones,
To the rumble of street cars,
To the swish of rain.   10

Lenox Avenue,
Honey.
Midnight,
And the gods are laughing at us.

Un-American Investigators (1953)

The committee's fat,
Smug, almost secure
Co-religionists
Shiver with delight
In warm manure   5
As those investigated—
Too brave to name a name—
Have pseudonyms revealed
In Gentile game
    Of who,   10
    Born Jew,
    Is who?
Is not your name Lipshitz?
    Yes.
Did you not change it   15
For subversive purposes?
    No.
For nefarious gain?
    Not so.
Are you sure?   20

The committee shivers
With delight in
Its manure.

Dinner Guest: Me (1965)

I know I am
The Negro Problem
Being wined and dined,
Answering the usual questions
That come to white mind   5
Which seeks demurely
To probe in polite way
The why and wherewithal
Of darkness U.S.A.—
Wondering how things got this way   10
In current democratic night,
Murmuring gently
Over *fraises du bois*,
"I'm so ashamed of being white."

The lobster is delicious,   15
The wine divine,
And center of attention
At the damask table, mine.
To be a Problem on
Park Avenue at eight   20
Is not so bad.
Solutions to the Problem,
Of course, wait.

Ballad of Booker T. (1941)

Booker T.
Was a practical man.
He said, Till the soil
And learn from the land.
Let down your bucket   5

Where you are.
Your fate is here
And not afar.
To help yourself
And your fellow man,   10
Train your head,
Your heart, and your hand.
For smartness alone's
Surely not meet—
If you haven't at the same time   15
Got something to eat.
Thus at Tuskegee
He built a school
With book-learning there.
And the workman's tool.   20
He started out
In a simple way—
For yesterday
Was not today.
Sometimes he had   25
Compromise in his talk—
For a man must crawl
Before he can walk—
And in Alabama in '85
A joker was lucky   30
To be alive.
But Booker T.
Was nobody's fool;
You may carve a dream
With an humble tool.   35
The tallest tower
Can tumble down
If it be not rooted
In solid ground,
So, being a far-seeing   40
Practical man,
He said, Train your head,
Your heart, and your hand.
Your fate is here
And not afar,   45
So let down your bucket
Where you are.

BALLAD OF BOOKER T.

1st draft
May 30, 1941

Old Booker T.

Was a practical man.

He said, Till the soil,

and Learn from the land.

Let down your buckets

Where you are:

In your own backyard,
~~Contan~~ There could
~~Right~~ be a star.

Train you ~~head~~ *head,*
Your ~~head~~, *heart* ~~and~~ your hand.

To help yourself

And your fellowman

~~Thus Booker T.~~

~~Built a school,~~

~~With~~ book-learning there

And the workman's tool.

For ~~to~~ smart *ness* alone
Is ~~not~~ meet--- *surely*
~~If~~ ~~and~~ *got*
~~KMEM~~/you haven't ~~got~~
/something to eat.

He started out

In a simple way,--

For ~~X~~Yesterday

Was not today.

Sometimes he had *com* —

~~Co~~mpromise in his talk,---

For a man must crawl

Before he can walk.

And in Alabama in '85

A joker was lucky
be
To ~~stay~~ alive.

But ~~mix~~ Booker T.

Was nobody's fool:

You may carve a dream

From an humble tool---

And the tallest tower

Can tumble down

If ~~is~~ *the* not rooted

In solid ground.

He said, Train your ~~heart~~, *head,*

Your head, and your ~~h~~

~~Train your~~ *head*
~~heart~~
Your ~~head~~, and your hand--
heart
For Booke**r** T.

Was a practical man.

[AC7059]

This draft of the poem "Ballad of Booker T." was hand edited by Langston Hughes in 1941.

Reading and Reacting

1. How does Hughes use music and musical allusions? Are the poems themselves meant to be musical?
2. Which poems are poems of protest? Does Hughes seem to place his social or political goals above literary concerns?
3. How do historical and geographic allusions contribute to the power of "The Negro Speaks of Rivers"?
4. How is the question of identity (especially racial identity) handled in "The Negro Speaks of Rivers" and "Theme for English B"? Explain any differences you see.
5. How would you characterize Hughes's attitude toward America in "Theme for English B" and "I, Too"? Do you think these poems are patriotic? Explain.
6. Hughes is often celebrated for his ability to express complex human dilemmas in accessible language and forms. Does he do this successfully in "Harlem" (p. 760)? Explain.
7. In the poem "Birmingham Sunday," why does Hughes include statements about Chinese mythology and history?
8. Is the "dream" in "Harlem" (p. 760) the same as the dream in "Dream Boogie"? Do you think the poems were meant to be read side by side? Do they shed light on each other? Do they represent different approaches to a similar problem?
9. In which poems do you think the first-person voice is autobiographical? In which poems do you think Hughes is creating a speaker?
10. What do you think Hughes expects of those who read his poetry? Reflection? a change of heart? action? something else?

11. **JOURNAL ENTRY** Are Langston Hughes's poems relevant only to African Americans, or do they also have relevance for other Americans—and even for readers in other countries?

12. **CRITICAL PERSPECTIVE** In his essay "The Negro Artist and the Racial Mountain" (p. 929), Hughes asserts his respect for the "common people," those he admires for their lack of self-importance:

> But then there are the low-down folks, the so-called common element, and they are the major-ity—may the Lord be praised! The people who have their nip of gin on Saturday nights are not too important to themselves or the community, or too well fed, or too learned to watch the lazy world go round. They live on Seventh Street in Washington or State Street in Chicago and they do not particularly care whether they are like white folks or anybody else. . . . They furnish a wealth of colorful, distinctive material for any artist because they still hold their own individuality in the face of American standardizations.

How does Hughes depict the "common people" in his poetry? What are their concerns? How have America's "standardizations" attempted to shape and change the common people, and what has been the result of those attempts?

Related Works: "Big Black Good Man" (p. 318), "A Worn Path" (p. 463), "Ballad of Birmingham" (p. 708), "We Real Cool" (p. 730), "Sadie and Maud" (p. 792), *Fences* (p. 1548)

Sources

Background

LANGSTON HUGHES*

from The Negro Artist and the Racial Mountain

One of the most promising of the young Negro poets said to me once, "I want to be a poet—not a Negro poet," meaning, I believe, "I want to write like a white poet": meaning subconsciously, "I would like to be a white poet," meaning behind that, "I would like to be white." And I was sorry the young man said that, for no great poet has ever been afraid of being himself. And I doubted then that, with his desire to run away spiritually from his race, this boy would ever be a great poet. But this is the mountain standing in the way of any true Negro art in America—this urge within the race toward whiteness, the desire to pour racial individuality into the mold of American standardization, and to be as little Negro and as much American as possible.

But let us look at the immediate background of this young poet. His family is of what I suppose one would call the Negro middle class: people who are by no means rich yet never uncomfortable nor hungry—smug, contented, respectable folk, members of the Baptist church. The father goes to work every morning. He is a chief steward at a large white club. The mother sometimes does fancy sewing or supervises parties for the rich families of the town. The children go to a mixed school. In the home they read white papers and magazines. And the mother often says, "Don't be like niggers" when the children are bad. A frequent phrase from the father is, "Look how well a white man does things." And so the word white comes to be unconsciously a symbol of all the virtues. It holds for the children beauty, morality, and money. The whisper of "I want to be white" runs silently through their minds. This young poet's home is, I believe, a fairly typical home of the colored middle class. One sees immediately how difficult it would be for an artist born in such a home to interest himself in interpreting the beauty of his own people. He is never taught to see that beauty. He is taught rather not to see it, or if he does, to be ashamed of it when it is not according to Caucasian patterns.

For racial culture the home of a self-styled "high-class" Negro has nothing better to offer. Instead there will perhaps be more aping of things white than in a less cultured or less wealthy home. The father is perhaps a doctor, lawyer, landowner, or politician. The mother may be a social worker, or a teacher, or she may do nothing and have a maid. Father is often dark but he has usually married the lightest woman he could find. The family attend a fashionable church where few really colored faces are to be found. And they themselves draw a color line. In the North they go to white theaters and white movies.

The Nation 23 June 1926. Print.

And in the South they have at least two cars and a house "like white folks." Nordic manners, Nordic faces, Nordic hair, Nordic art (if any), and an Episcopal heaven. A very high mountain indeed for the would-be racial artist to climb in order to discover himself and his people.

But then there are the low-down folks, the so-called common element, and they are the majority—may the Lord be praised! The people who have their nip of gin on Saturday nights are not too important to themselves or the community, or too well fed, or too learned to watch the lazy world go round. They live on Seventh Street in Washington or State Street in Chicago and they do not particularly care whether they are like white folks or anybody else. Their joy runs, bang! into ecstasy. Their religion soars to a shout. Work maybe a little today, rest a little tomorrow. Play awhile. Sing awhile. O, let's dance! These common people are not afraid of spirituals, as for a long time their more intellectual brethren were, and jazz is their child. They furnish a wealth of colorful, distinctive material for any artist because they still hold their own individuality in the face of American standardizations. And perhaps these common people will give to the world its truly great Negro artist, the one who is not afraid to be himself. Whereas the better-class Negro would tell the artist what to do, the people at least let him alone when he does appear. And they are not ashamed of him—if they know he exists at all. And they accept what beauty is their own without question.

Certainly there is, for the American Negro artist who can escape the restric-   5
tions the more advanced among his own group would put upon him, a great field of unused material ready for his art. Without going outside his race, and even among the better classes with their "white" culture and conscious American manners, but still Negro enough to be different, there is sufficient matter to furnish a black artist with a lifetime of creative work. And when he chooses to touch on the relations between Negroes and whites in this country with their innumerable overtones and undertones, surely, and especially for literature and the drama, there is an inexhaustible supply of themes at hand. To these the Negro artist can give his racial individuality, his heritage of rhythm and warmth, and his incongruous humor that so often, as in the Blues, becomes ironic laughter mixed with tears. . . .

Let the blare of Negro jazz bands and the bellowing voice of Bessie Smith singing Blues penetrate the closed ears of the colored near-intellectuals until they listen and perhaps understand. Let Paul Robeson singing Water Boy, and Rudolph Fisher writing about the streets of Harlem, and Jean Toomer holding the heart of Georgia in his hands, and Aaron Douglas drawing strange black fantasies cause the smug Negro middle class to turn from their white, respectable, ordinary books and papers to catch a glimmer of their own beauty. We younger Negro artists who create now intend to express our individual dark-skinned selves without fear or shame. If white people are pleased we are glad. If they are not, it doesn't matter. We know we are beautiful. And ugly too. The tom-tom cries and the tom-tom laughs. If colored people are pleased we are glad. If they are not, their displeasure doesn't matter either. We build our temples for tomorrow, strong as we know how, and we stand on top of the mountain, free within ourselves.

LANGSTON HUGHES

To Negro Writers*

There are certain practical things American Negro writers can do through their work.

We can reveal to the Negro masses, from which we come, our potential power to transform the now ugly face of the Southland into a region of peace and plenty.

We can reveal to the white masses those Negro qualities which go beyond the mere ability to laugh and sing and dance and make music, and which are a part of the useful heritage that we place at the disposal of a future free America.

Negro writers can seek to unite blacks and whites in our country, not on the nebulous basis of an inter-racial meeting, or the shifting sands of religious brotherhood, but on the solid ground of the daily working-class struggle to wipe out, now and forever, all the old inequalities of the past.

5   Furthermore, by way of exposure, Negro writers can reveal in their novels, stories, poems, and articles:

The lovely grinning face of Philanthropy—which gives a million dollars to a Jim Crow school, but not one job to a graduate of that school; which builds a Negro hospital with second-rate equipment, then commands black patients and student-doctors to go there whether they will or no; or which, out of the kindness of its heart, erects yet another separate, segregated, shut-off, Jim Crow Y.M.C.A.

Negro writers can expose those white labor leaders who keep their unions closed against Negro workers and prevent the betterment of all workers.

We can expose, too, the sick-sweet smile of organized religion—which lies about what it doesn't know, and about what it *does* know. And the half-voodoo, half-clown, face of revivalism, dulling the mind with the clap of its empty hands.

Expose, also, the false leadership that besets the Negro people—bought and paid for leadership, owned by capital, afraid to open its mouth except in the old conciliatory way so advantageous to the exploiters.

10   And all the economic roots of race hatred and race fear.

And the Contentment Tradition of the O-lovely-Negroes school of American fiction, which makes an ignorant black face and a Carolina head filled with superstition, appear more desirable than a crown of gold; the jazz-band; and the O-so-gay writers who make of the Negro's poverty and misery a dusky funny paper.

And expose war. And the old My-Country-'Tis-of-Thee lie. And the colored American Legion posts strutting around talking about the privilege of dying for the nobel Red, White and Blue, when they aren't even permitted the privilege of living for it. Or voting for it in Texas. Or working for it in the diplomatic service. Or even rising, like every other good little boy, from the log cabin to the White House.

White House is right!

Dear colored American Legion, you can swing from a lynching tree, uniform and all, with pleasure—and nobody'll fight for you. Don't you know that? Nobody even

*American Writers' Congress. Ed. Henry Hart. New York: International Publishers, 1935. Print.

salutes you down South, dead or alive, medals or no medals, chevrons[1] or not, no matter how many wars you've fought in.

Let Negro writers write about the irony and pathos of the *colored* American Legion.   15
    "Salute, Mr. White Man!"
    "Salute, hell! . . . You're a nigger."
Or would you rather write about the moon?
Sure, the moon still shines over Harlem. Shines over Scottsboro. Shines over Birmingham, too, I reckon. Shines over Cordie Cheek's grave, down South.

Write about the moon if you want to. Go ahead. This is a free country.
But there are certain very practical things American Negro writers can do. And must do. There's a song that says, "the time ain't long." That song is right. Something has got to change in America—and change soon. We must help that change to come.
The moon's still shining as poetically as ever, but all the stars on the flag are dull.   20
(And the stripes, too.)
We want a new and better America, where there won't be any poor, where there won't be any more Jim Crow, where there won't be any lynchings, where there won't be any munition makers, where we won't need philanthropy, nor charity, nor the New Deal, nor Home Relief.
We want an America that will be ours, a world that will be ours—we Negro workers and white workers! Black writers and white! We'll make that world!

LANGSTON HUGHES

from My Adventures as a Social Poet[*]

Some of my earliest poems were social poems in that they were about people's problems—whole groups of people's problems—rather than my own personal difficulties. Sometimes, though, certain aspects of my personal problems happened to be also common to many other people. And certainly, racially speaking, my own problems of adjustment to American life were the same as those of millions of other segregated Negroes. The moon belongs to everybody, but not this American earth of ours. That is perhaps why poems about the moon perturb no one, but poems about color and poverty do perturb many citizens. Social forces pull backwards or forwards, right or left, and social poems get caught in the pulling and hauling. Sometimes the poet himself gets pulled and hauled—even hauled off to jail. . . .

My adventures as a social poet are mild indeed compared to the body-breaking, soul-searing experiences of poets in the recent Fascist countries or of the resistance poets of the Nazi-invaded lands during the war. For that reason, I can use so light a word as "adventure" in regard to my own skirmishes with reaction and censorship.

My adventures as a social poet began in a colored church in Atlantic City shortly after my first book, *The Weary Blues*, was published in 1926. I had been invited to come down to the shore from Lincoln University where I was a student, to give a program of my poems in the church. During the course of my program I read several of my poems in the form of the

---

[1] *chevrons:* Stripes on a military uniform denoting rank.
[*] *Python* Third Quarter, 1947. Print.

Negro folk songs, including some blues poems about hard luck and hard work. As I read I noticed a deacon approach the pulpit with a note which he placed on the rostrum beside me, but I did not stop to open the note until I had finished and had acknowledged the applause of a cordial audience. The note read, "Do not read any more blues in my pulpit." It was signed by the minister. That was my first experience with censorship.

The kind and generous woman who sponsored my writing for a few years after my college days did not come to the point quite so directly as did the minister who disliked blues. Perhaps, had it not been in the midst of the great depression of the late '20's and '30's, the kind of poems that I am afraid helped to end her patronage might not have been written. But it was impossible for me to travel from hungry Harlem to the lovely homes on Park Avenue without feeling in my soul the great gulf between the very poor and the very rich in our society. In those days, on the way to visit this kind lady I would see the homeless sleeping in subways and the hungry begging in doorways on sleet-stung winter days. It was then that I wrote a poem called "Advertisement for the Waldorf-Astoria," satirizing the slick-paper magazine advertisements of the opening of that deluxe hotel. Also I wrote:

> PARK BENCH
>
> I live on a park bench,
> You, Park Avenue.
> Hell of a distance
> Between us two.
>
> I beg a dime for dinner—
> You got a butler and maid.
> But I'm wakin' up!
> Say, ain't you afraid
>
> That I might, just maybe,
> In a year or two,
> Move on over
> To Park Avenue?

In a little while I did not have a patron any more.

5   But that year I won a prize, the Harmon Gold Award for Literature, which consisted of a medal and four hundred dollars. With the four hundred dollars I went to Haiti. On the way I stopped in Cuba and I was cordially received by the writers and artists. I had written poems about the exploitation of Cuba by the sugar barons and I had translated many poems of Nicolás Guillén such as:

> CANE
>
> Negro
> In the cane fields.
> White man
> Above the cane fields
> Earth
> Beneath the cane fields.
> Blood
> That flows from us.

This was during the days of the dictatorial Machado regime. Perhaps someone called his attention to these poems and translations because, when I came back from Haiti weeks later, I was not allowed to land in Cuba, but was detained by the immigration authorities at Santiago and put on an island until the American consul came, after three days, to get me off with the provision that I cross the country to Havana and leave Cuban soil at once.

That was my first time being put out of any place. But since that time I have been put out of or barred from quite a number of places, all because of my poetry—not the roses and moonlight poems (which I write, too) but because of poems about poverty, oppression, and segregation. Nine Negro boys in Alabama were on trial for their lives when I got back from Cuba and Haiti. The famous Scottsboro "rape" case was in full session. I visited those boys in the death house at Kilby Prison, and I wrote many poems about them. One of these poems was:

CHRIST IN ALABAMA

Christ is a Nigger,
Beaten and black—
O, bare your back.

Mary is His Mother—
Mammy of the South,
Silence your mouth.

God's His Father—
White Master above,
Grant us your love.

Most holy bastard
Of the bleeding mouth:
Nigger Christ
On the cross of the South.

Contempo, a publication of some of the students at the University of North Carolina, published the poem on its front page on the very day that I was being presented in a program of my poems at the University in Chapel Hill. That evening there were police outside the building in which I spoke, and in the air the rising tension of race that is peculiar to the South. It had been rumored that some of the local citizenry were saying that I should be run out of town, and that one of the sheriffs agreed, saying, "Sure, he ought to be run out! It's bad enough to call Christ a *bastard*. But when he calls him a *nigger*, he's gone too far!"

The next morning a third of my fee was missing when I was handed my check. One of the departments of the university jointly sponsoring my program had refused to come through with its portion of the money. Nevertheless, I remember with pleasure the courtesy and kindness of many of the students and faculty at Chapel Hill and their lack of agreement with the anti-Negro elements of the town. There I began to learn at the University of North Carolina how hard it is to be a white liberal in the South.

10   It was not until I had been to Russia and around the world as a writer and journalist that censorship and opposition to my poems reached the point of completely
preventing me from appearing in public programs on a few occasions. It happened first
in Los Angeles shortly after my return from the Soviet Union. I was to have been one
of several speakers on a memorial program to be held at the colored branch Y.M.C.A.
for a young Negro journalist of the community. At the behest of white higher-ups, no
doubt, some reactionary Negro politicians informed the Negro Y.M.C.A. that I was
a Communist. The secretary of the Negro Branch Y then informed the committee of
young people in charge of the memorial that they could have their program only if I
did not appear.

I have never been a Communist, but I soon learned that anyone visiting the
Soviet Union and speaking with favor of it upon returning is liable to be so labeled.
Indeed when Mrs. Roosevelt, Walter White, and so Christian a lady as Mrs. Bethune
who has never been in Moscow, are so labeled, I should hardly be surprised! I wasn't
surprised. And the young people's committee informed the Y secretary that since
the Y was a public community center which they helped to support, they saw no
reason why it should censor their memorial program to the extent of eliminating
any speaker.

Since I had been allotted but a few moments on the program, it was my intention
simply to read this short poem of mine:

> Dear lovely death
> That taketh all things under wing,
> Never to kill,
> Only to change into some other thing
> This suffering flesh—
> To make it either more or less
> But not again the same,
> Dear lovely death,
> Change is thy other name.

But the Negro branch Y, egged on by the reactionary politicians (whose incomes,
incidentally, were allegedly derived largely from gambling houses and other underworld activities), informed the young people's committee that the police would be at
the door to prevent my entering the Y on the afternoon of the scheduled program. So
when the crowd gathered, the memorial was not held that Sunday. The young people
simply informed the audience of the situation and said that the memorial would be
postponed until a place could be found where all the participants could be heard. The
program was held elsewhere a few Sundays later. . . .

So goes the life of a social poet. I am sure none of these things would ever have
happened to me had I limited the subject matter of my poems to roses and moonlight.
But, unfortunately, I was born poor—and colored—and almost all the prettiest roses
I have seen have been in rich white people's yards—not in mine. That is why I
cannot write exclusively about roses and moonlight—for sometimes in the moonlight my brothers see a fiery cross and a circle of Klansmen's hoods. Sometimes in
the moonlight a dark body sways from a lynching tree—but for his funeral there are
no roses.

Critical Perspectives

ARNOLD RAMPERSAD

from The Origins of Poetry in Langston Hughes*

Revealing an increase in skill, Hughes's early poetry nevertheless gives no sign of a major poetic talent in the making. At some point in his development, however, something happened to Hughes that was as mysterious and as wonderful, in its own way, as the miracle that overtook John Keats after the watchful night spent with his friend Charles Cowden Clarke and a copy of Chapman's translation. With "The Negro Speaks of Rivers" the creativity in Langston Hughes, hitherto unexpressed, suddenly created itself.

In writing thus about Hughes, are we taking him too seriously? With a few exceptions, literary critics have resisted offering even a modestly complicated theory concerning his creativity. His relentless affability and charm, his deep, open love of the black masses, his devotion to their folk forms, and his insistence on writing poetry that they could understand, all have contributed to the notion that Langston Hughes was intellectually and emotionally shallow. One wonders, then, at the source of the creative energy that drove him from 1921 to 1967 to write so many poems, novels, short stories, plays, operas, popular histories, children's books, and assorted other work. As a poet, Hughes virtually reinvented Afro-American poetry with his pioneering use of the blues and other folk forms; as Howard Mumford Jones marveled in a 1927 review, Hughes added the verse form of the blues to poetry in English (a form that continues to attract the best black poets, including Michael Harper, Sherley Anne Williams, and Raymond Patterson). One wonders, too, in his aspect as a poet, why this apparently happy, apparently shallow man defined his creativity in terms of unhappiness. "I felt bad for the next three or four years," he would write in *The Big Sea* about the period beginning more or less with the publication of "The Negro Speaks of Rivers," and "those were the years when I wrote most of my poetry. (For my best poems were all written when I felt the worst. When I was happy, I didn't write anything)." . . .

The first of [Hughes's] two illnesses took place in the summer of 1919, when Hughes (at seventeen) saw his father for the first time in a dozen years. In 1903, James Hughes had gone to Mexico, where he would become a prosperous property owner. In a lonely, impoverished, passed-around childhood in the Midwest, his son had fantasized about the man "as a kind of strong, bronze cowboy, in a big Mexican hat, going back and forth from his business in the city to his ranch in the mountains, free—in a land where there were no white folks to draw the color line, and no tenements with rent always due—just mountains and cacti: Mexico!" Elated to be invited suddenly to Mexico in 1919 at the end of his junior year in high school, Langston left the United States with high hopes for his visit.

The summer was a disaster. James Hughes proved to be an unfeeling, domineering, and materialistic man, scornful of Indians and blacks (he was himself black) and the poor in general; and contemptuous of his son's gentler pace and artistic temperament. One day, Langston could take no more: "Suddenly my stomach began to turn over and over.

The Southern Review 21.3 (1985): 695–705. Print.

And I could not swallow another mouthful. Waves of heat engulfed me. My eyes burned. My body shook. I wanted more than anything on earth to hit my father, but instead I got up from the table and went back to bed. The bed went round and round and the room turned dark. Anger clotted in every vein, and my tongue tasted like dry blood." But the boy, ill for a long time, never confessed the true cause of his affliction. Having been moved to Mexico City, he declined to help his doctors: "I never told them . . . that I was sick because I hated my father." He recovered only when it was time to return to the United States.

5   Hughes's second major illness came eleven years later. By this time he had finished high school, returned to Mexico to live with his father for a year, attended Columbia University for one year (supported grudgingly by James Hughes), dropped out of school, and served as a messman on voyages to Africa and to Europe, where he spent several months in 1924 as a dishwasher. All the while, however, Hughes was publishing poetry in a variety of places, especially in important black journals. This activity culminated in books of verse published in 1926 (*The Weary Blues*) and 1927 (*Fine Clothes to the Jew*) that established him, with Countee Cullen, as one of two major black poets of the decade. In 1929, he graduated after three and a half years at black Lincoln University, Pennsylvania. In 1930, Hughes published his first novel, *Not Without Laughter*.

This book had been virtually dragged out of him by his patron of the preceding three years, "Godmother" (as she wished to be called), an old, white, very generous but eccentric woman who ruled Hughes with a benevolent despotism inspired by her volatile beliefs in African spirituality, folk culture, mental telepathy, and the potential of his genius. But the result of her largesse was a paradox: the more comfortable he grew, the less Hughes was inclined to create. Estranged by his apparent languor, his patron finally seized on an episode of conflict to banish him once and for all. Hughes was devastated. Surviving drafts of his letters to "Godmother" reveal him deep in self-abasement before a woman with whom he was clearly in love. Ten years later, he confessed in *The Big Sea*: "I cannot write here about that last half-hour in the big bright drawing-room high above Park Avenue . . . because when I think about it, even now, something happens in the pit of my stomach that makes me ill. That beautiful room . . . suddenly became like a trap closing in, faster and faster, the room darker and darker, until the light went out with a sudden crash in the dark, and everything became like . . . that morning in Mexico when I suddenly hated my father.

"I was violently and physically ill, with my stomach turning over and over. . . . And there was no rationalizing anything. I couldn't." For several months, according to my research (Hughes erroneously presents a far briefer time frame in *The Big Sea*), he waited in excruciating hope for a reconciliation. As in Mexico, he wasted time and money on doctors without revealing to them the source of his chronic illness (which one very ingenious Harlem physician diagnosed as a Japanese tapeworm). Rather than break his silence, Hughes even agreed to have his tonsils removed. Gradually it became clear that reconciliation was impossible. Winning a prize of four hundred dollars for his novel, Hughes fled to seclusion in hot, remote Haiti. When his money ran out some months later, he returned home, healed at last but badly scarred.

Although they occurred more than a decade apart, the two illnesses were similar. Both showed a normally placid Hughes driven into deep rage by an opponent, a rage which he was unable to ventilate because the easy expression of personal anger and indignation was anathema to him. In both cases, he developed physical symptoms of hyperventilation and, eventually, anemia. More importantly, both were triggered in a period of relatively low poetic creativity (as when he was still a juvenile poet) or outright poetic inactivity (as with his patron). In each instance, Hughes had become satisfied with this low creativity or inactivity. At both times, a certain powerful figure, first his father, then "Godmother," had opposed his right to be content. His father had opposed any poetic activity at all; "Godmother" had opposed his right to enjoy the poetical state without true poetical action, or writing. In other words, a powerful will presented itself in forceful opposition to what was, in one sense, a vacuum of expressive will on Hughes's part. (Needless to say, the *apparent* absence of will in an individual can easily be a token of the presence of a very powerful will.) The result on both occasions, which was extraordinary, was first Hughes's endurance of, then his violent rebellion against, a force of will that challenged his deepest vision of the poetic life. . . .

In his bitter struggles with his father and "Godmother," Hughes turned to the black race for direction. But one needs to remember that this appeal in itself hardly gave Hughes distinction as a poet; what made Hughes distinct was the highly original manner in which he internalized the Afro-American racial dilemma and expressed it in poems such as "When Sue Wears Red," "The Negro Speaks of Rivers," "Mother to Son," "Dream Variations," and "The Weary Blues," poems of Hughes's young manhood on which his career would rest. Of these, the most important was "The Negro Speaks of Rivers."

> I've known rivers.
> I've known rivers ancient as the world and old
>   as the flow of human blood in human veins.
>
> My soul has grown deep like the rivers.
>
> I bathed in the Euphrates when dawns were young.
> I built my hut near the Congo and it lulled me to sleep.
> I looked upon the Nile and raised the pyramids above it.
> I heard the singing of the Mississippi when Abe Lincoln went down
>   to New Orleans, and I've seen its muddy bosom turn all golden
>   in the sunset.
>
> I've known rivers:
> Ancient, dusky rivers.
>
> My soul has grown deep like the rivers.

Here, the persona moves steadily from dimly starred personal memory ("I've known rivers") toward a rendezvous with modern history (Lincoln going down the Mississippi and seeing the horror of slavery that, according to legend, would make him one day free the slaves). The death wish, benign but suffusing, of its images of rivers older than human blood, of souls grown as deep as these rivers, gives way steadily to an altering, ennobling vision whose final effect gleams in the evocation of the Mississippi's "muddy bosom" turning at last "all golden in the sunset." Personal anguish has been alchemized by the poet into a gracious meditation on his race, whose despised ("muddy") culture and history, irradiated by the poet's vision, changes within the poem from mud into gold. This is a classic example of the essential process of creativity in Hughes.

10   The poem came to him, according to Hughes (accurately, it seems clear) about ten months after his Mexican illness, when he was riding a train from Cleveland to Mexico to rejoin his father. The time was sundown, the place the Mississippi outside St. Louis. "All day on the train I had been thinking of my father," he would write in *The Big Sea*. "Now it was just sunset and we crossed the Mississippi, slowly, over a long bridge. I looked out of the window of the Pullman at the great muddy river flowing down toward the heart of the South, and I began to think what that river, the old Mississippi, had meant to Negroes in the past—how to be sold down the river was the worst fate that could overtake a slave in bondage. Then I remembered reading how Abraham Lincoln had made a trip down the Mississippi on a raft, and how he had seen slavery at its worst, and had decided within himself that it should be removed from American life. Then I began to think of other rivers in our past—the Congo, and the Niger, and the Nile in Africa—and the thought came to me: 'I've known rivers,' and I put it down on the back of an envelope I had in my pocket, and within the space of ten or fifteen minutes, as the train gathered speed in the dusk, I had written this poem."

Here, starting with anguish over his father, Hughes discovered the compressed ritual of passivity, challenge, turmoil, and transcendence he would probably have to re-create, doubtless in variant forms, during the great poetic trysts of his life. Even after he became a successful, published poet, the basic process remained the same, because his psychology remained largely the same even though he had become technically expert. In his second major illness, caused by his patron "Godmother," Hughes wrote poetry as he struggled for a transcendence that would be long in coming. The nature of that interim poetry is telling. When he sent some poems to a friend for a little book to be printed privately, she noticed at once that many spoke of death— "Dear lovely Death / That taketh all things under wing— / Never to kill. . . ." She called the booklet *Dear Lovely Death*. In "Afro-American Fragment," unlike in "The Negro Speaks of Rivers," Africa is seen plaintively:

> . . . Subdued and time-lost
> Are the drums—and yet
> Through some vast mist of race
> There comes this song
> I do not understand,
> This song of atavistic land,
> Of bitter yearnings lost
> Without a place—
> So long,
> So far away
> Is Africa's
> Dark face.

But when Hughes returned home, scarred but healed, after months in seclusion in Haiti, he no longer thought of loss and death. Instead, he plunged directly into the life of the black masses with a seven-month tour of the South in which he read his poetry in their churches and schools. Then he set out for the Soviet Union, where he would spend more than a year. Hughes then reached the zenith of his revolutionary ardor with poems (or verse) such as "Good Morning Revolution," "Goodbye Christ," and "Put One More 'S' in the USA."

POETRY FOUNDATION

from Langston Hughes 1902–1967*

Langston Hughes was first recognized as an important literary figure during the 1920s, a period known as the "Harlem Renaissance" because of the number of emerging black writers. Du Bose Heyward wrote in the *New York Herald Tribune* in 1926: "Langston Hughes, although only twenty-four years old, is already conspicuous in the group of Negro intellectuals who are dignifying Harlem with a genuine art life. . . . It is, however, as an individual poet, not as a member of a new and interesting literary group, or as a spokesman for a race that Langston Hughes must stand or fall. . . . Always intensely subjective, passionate, keenly sensitive to beauty and possessed of an unfaltering musical sense, Langston Hughes has given us a 'first book' that marks the opening of a career well worth watching."

Despite Heyward's statement, much of Hughes's early work was roundly criticized by many black intellectuals for portraying what they thought to be an unattractive view of black life. In his autobiographical *The Big Sea*, Hughes commented: "*Fine Clothes to the Jew* was well received by the literary magazines and the white press, but the Negro critics did not like it at all. The Pittsburgh *Courier* ran a big headline across the top of the page, *LANGSTON HUGHES' BOOK OF POEMS TRASH*. The headline in the New York *Amsterdam News* was *LANGSTON HUGHES—THE SEWER DWELLER*. The Chicago *Whip* characterized me as 'the poet low-rate of Harlem.' Others called the book a disgrace to the race, a return to the dialect tradition, and a parading of all our racial defects before the public. . . . The Negro critics and many of the intellectuals were very sensitive about their race in books. (And still are.) In anything that white people were likely to read, they wanted to put their best foot forward, their politely polished and cultural foot—and only that foot."

An example of the type of criticism of which Hughes was writing is Estace Gay's comments on *Fine Clothes to the Jew*. "It does not matter to me whether every poem in the book is true to life," Gay wrote. "Why should it be paraded before the American public by a Negro author as being typical or representative of the Negro? Bad enough to have white authors holding up our imperfections to public gaze. Our aim ought to be [to] present to the general public, already misinformed both by well meaning and malicious writers, our higher aims and aspirations, and our better selves." Commenting on reviewers like Gay, Hughes wrote: "I sympathized deeply with those critics and those intellectuals, and I saw clearly the need for some of the kinds of books they wanted. But I did not see how they could expect every Negro author to write such books. Certainly, I personally knew very few people anywhere who were wholly beautiful and wholly good. Besides I felt that the masses of our people had as much in their lives to put into books as did those more fortunate ones who had been born with some

*The Poetry Foundation. Poetry Foundation, 2014. Web.

means and the ability to work up to a master's degree at a Northern college. Anyway, I didn't know the upper class Negroes well enough to write much about them. I knew only the people I had grown up with, and they weren't people whose shoes were always shined, who had been to Harvard, or who had heard of Bach. But they seemed to me good people, too."

Hoyt W. Fuller commented that Hughes "chose to identify with plain black people—not because it required less effort and sophistication, but precisely because he saw more truth and profound significance in doing so. Perhaps in this he was inversely influenced by his father—who, frustrated by being the object of scorn in his native land, rejected his own people. Perhaps the poet's reaction to his father's flight from the American racial reality drove him to embrace it with extra fervor." (Langston Hughes's parents separated shortly after his birth and his father moved to Mexico. The elder Hughes came to feel a deep dislike and revulsion for other American blacks.) In Hughes's own words, his poetry is about "workers, roustabouts, and singers, and job hunters on Lenox Avenue in New York, or Seventh Street in Washington or South State in Chicago—people up today and down tomorrow, working this week and fired the next, beaten and baffled, but determined not to be wholly beaten, buying furniture on the installment plan, filling the house with roomers to help pay the rent, hoping to get a new suit for Easter—and pawning that suit before the Fourth of July." . . .

5   Hughes, more than any other black poet or writer, recorded faithfully the nuances of black life and its frustrations. Although Hughes had trouble with both black and white critics, he was the first black American to earn his living solely from his writing and public lectures. Part of the reason he was able to do this was the phenomenal acceptance and love he received from average black people. A reviewer for *Black World* noted in 1970: "Those whose prerogative it is to determine the rank of writers have never rated him highly, but if the weight of public response is any gauge then Langston Hughes stands at the apex of literary relevance among Black people. The poet occupies such a position in the memory of his people precisely because he recognized that 'we possess within ourselves a great reservoir of physical and spiritual strength,' and because he used his artistry to reflect this back to the people. He used his poetry and prose to illustrate that 'there is no lack within the Negro people of beauty, strength and power,' and he chose to do so on their own level, on their own terms." . . .

It was Hughes's belief in humanity and his hope for a world in which people could sanely and with understanding live together that led to his decline in popularity in the racially turbulent latter years of his life. Unlike younger and more militant writers, Hughes never lost his conviction that "*most* people are generally good, in every race and in every country where I have been." Reviewing *The Panther and the Lash: Poems of Our Times in Poetry*, Laurence Lieberman recognized that Hughes's "sensibility [had] kept pace with the times," but he criticized his lack of a personal political stance. "Regrettably, in different poems, he is fatally prone to sympathize with starkly antithetical politics of race," Lieberman commented. "A reader can appreciate his catholicity, his tolerance of all the rival—and mutually hostile—views of his outspoken compatriots, from Martin Luther King to Stokely Carmichael,* but we are

---

*Stokely Carmichael: Civil rights activist (1941–1998).

tempted to ask, what are Hughes' politics? And if he has none, why not? The age demands intellectual commitment from its spokesmen. A poetry whose chief claim on our attention is moral, rather than aesthetic, must take sides politically."

Despite some recent criticism, Hughes's position in the American literary scene seems to be secure. David Littlejohn wrote that Hughes is "the one sure Negro classic, more certain of permanence than even Baldwin or Ellison or Wright. . . . His voice is as sure, his manner as original, his position as secure as, say Edwin Arlington Robinson's or Robinson Jeffers'. . . . By molding his verse always on the sounds of Negro talk, the rhythms of Negro music, by retaining his own keen honesty and directness, his poetic sense and ironic intelligence, he maintained through four decades a readable newness distinctly his own." . . .

Donald B. Gibson noted in the introduction to *Modern Black Poets: A Collection of Critical Essays* that Hughes "has perhaps the greatest reputation (worldwide) that any black writer has ever had. Hughes differed from most of his predecessors among black poets, and (until recently) from those who followed him as well, in that he addressed his poetry to the people, specifically to black people. During the twenties when most American poets were turning inward, writing obscure and esoteric poetry to an ever decreasing audience of readers, Hughes was turning outward, using language and themes, attitudes and ideas familiar to anyone who had the ability simply to read. He has been, unlike most nonblack poets other than Walt Whitman, Vachel Lindsay, and Carl Sandburg, a poet of the people. . . . Until the time of his death, he spread his message humorously—though always seriously—to audiences throughout the country, having read his poetry to more people (possibly) than any other American poet."

RICK BROWN

Bitter Jazz in Langston Hughes's "Dream Boogie"*

Langston Hughes's "Dream Boogie" is a poem that exposes the racial misery underlying the musical revelry of jazz, laying bare the agony that begets the art form even as the work exalts in it. The opening selection from Hughes's celebrated 1951 long poem *Montage of a Dream Deferred*, the piece presents an ethereal scene in which an African-American speaker tries and fails to conjure an understanding of racial injustice in an indifferent listener. Though the entreaty fails, the speaker continues to feign happiness (Hughes, "Dream Boogie" lines 15–17), and the interactions of the two voices merge into syncopated jazz scatting (18–21). The paradoxical synergy and disconnection of the speakers form the heart of the piece, which exemplifies Hughes's conception of the dualistic nature of jazz as "the tom-tom of joy and laughter, and pain swallowed in a smile" ("The Negro Artist" 694).

That painful duality influences every aspect of "Dream Boogie," which Benjamin R. Lempert describes as "perhaps the consummate bebop poem" for its sharp dichotomy between speech and meaning (1073). Even the poem's title, "Dream Boogie," is wildly divergent in its allusions. The "dream" of the selection is an unrealized one:

the singular, African-American "dream deferred" (line 4) of the long poem itself.[1] Yet the dream is also a more universal vision of a fleeting image that may never coalesce. Both meanings are encapsulated in the jazzy connotations of the title's "boogie," a colloquial term that connotes both a social gathering and a style of blues ("boogie, n.[2]," def. 1a, 1b). Hughes's title choice is thus purposeful and twofold, suggesting the paradoxical idea that an unrealizable dream could foster festivities and music.[2]

Hughes explores just such an idea in the piece through a framework of bebop jazz, using quick, seemingly improvisational lines and sudden changes in rhythm and voice in a way that exemplifies the spirit of bebop's culturally subversive "aesthetic of speed and displacement . . . dedicated to reorienting perception," as described by Eric Lott (600–01). That style is evident in the very first lines of "Dream Boogie," a quatrain that immediately establishes the work's diction, rhythm, and viewpoint:

> Good morning, daddy!
> Ain't you heard
> The boogie-woogie rumble
> Of a dream deferred? (1–4)

The poem's opening line is a call to attention that immediately establishes the voice of a jazz speaker through its employment of the word *daddy*, a term of male address in jazz slang ("daddy, n.," def. 3). So too is the musical rhythm of the speaker's swinging, irregular, but roughly rhyming speech pattern that of jazz, although the actual subject matter of the speaker's words is rather more profound. Though seeminglymerely reveling in inconsequential, jazzy assonance ("boogie-woogie") and slight alliteration ("dream deferred"), the speaker is actually exhorting his audience to recognize the metaphorical discontent that rumbles beneath his music (lines 2–4).

Subversion reverberates in the speaker's message, which continues in the poem's second stanza, an abbreviated quatrain that uses violent, intensely aural imagery that rises with a threatening impetus, becoming audible "both in the literal and figural sense" (Lempert 1073). The speaker exhorts the listener to "Listen closely: / You'll hear their feet / Beating out and beating out a—" (lines 5–7). If the speaker's entreaties in the poem's first stanza suggest the presence of a "rumble" beneath a bebop melody, the speaker's following words emphatically confirm it, ascending to a fever pitch in the pounding rhythm of the seventh line. Hughes's construction of the last line of the stanza is particularly powerful, its repetition of "beating out" creating a drumming, cacophonous beat that sharply contrasts with the shorter, more relaxed lines preceding it (line 7). The first stanza's "dream deferred" may rumble, but the second stanza's discontent pounds in a fierce bebop rhythm, its synecdochic image of people's feet thrumming out a beat that wells with anger, threatening to "explode" like its "festering" counterpart in Hughes's more famous "Harlem" (4, 11).

5   One imagines it would, if not for the third stanza, in which the listener uncomprehendingly questions the speaker's earnest evocation of jazz's underlying discontent. The listener's question is as simple as it is unintentionally subversive: "You think / It's a happy beat?" (8–9). If the listener hears the "boogie-woogie rumble" underlying the music, he does not betray that comprehension. Rather, the listener seemingly

perceives only the mirth of jazz for literal happiness, a disconnect that implies a gap in race and experience between the two.

Nevertheless, the listener's statement pierces the speaker's entreaty, and the jarring juxtaposition of the two voices signals the breakdown of the quatrains of the first two stanzas for more irregular jazz verse. As that verse proliferates, the dialogue of the two speakers, like many others in *Montage*, begins to "function like improvised solos and duets," according to Hokanson (73).

The halting breakdown of meaningful communication soon reaches its nadir as the speaker's repeated entreaty in the fourth stanza is again interrupted by another interjection from the listener, fully realizing the "disruptive, dialogic, interrogative pattern" that characterizes the poem (Lowney 371). Critically, at the end of the fourth stanza, Hughes cuts the line just before one would expect the critical phrase "dream deferred" to return (line 13). The speaker's inability to say it before the listener interjects constitutes a literal, aural deferral of speech that metaphorically echoes the disenfranchisement of his people. Furthermore, the listener's speech in the fifth stanza is now sharp; whereas his earlier question was merely uncomprehending, his new response—"What did I say?"—simply recalls his earlier statement, ignoring the speaker's new entreaty altogether (line 14). As the final quatrain of the work is broken, the chance for understanding is lost.

Ironically, Hughes's jazz artistry in the poem reaches its synergistic height even as the disconnection between the two speakers grows complete. The sixth stanza is a feignedly happy response from the narrator—"Sure, / I'm happy! / Take it away!" (Hughes 15–17)—that forms a strangely effective rhyming quatrain with the listener's earlier interjection in the poem's fourteenth line. Although the speaker's response is a facile, frustrated concession—"an attendant acquiescence to an ironic . . . mask of minstrel performance," in Lempert's description (1073)—his words nevertheless become a uniquely musical response to the listener's words, mimicking the "call and response" patterns of jazz. The speaker's quick, short-lined responses are nothing like his earlier quatrains, symbolizing the end of his attempts to reach the listener. When the speaker says, "Take it away!" (line 17), Hughes gives the reader an obvious double meaning—an exhortation for the listener to lead the music, and a metaphorical wish on the speaker's part to escape his burdens. The speaker is hardly "happy," and his turn toward stylistically artful but otherwise meaningless vocal music is a biting concession—one typical of the art form.[3]

Paradoxically bitter yet cathartic jazz reigns in the final stanza of the piece, an intellectually meaningless but musically adept merging of the two voices for the final, scatting break that leads the poem out. Nonsensical bebop syllables ultimately belie any chance for understanding, yet the two speakers nevertheless unite in jazz. That is, of course, Hughes's point. Upon a rereading of the work, the reader realizes that the poet structured the entire poem as a bebop line, complete with dueling solos (stanzas one, two, four, and six for the speaker, and stanzas three and five for the listener) and an ultimate merging of the two voices into combined music in the final stanzas. Hughes's "Dream Boogie" is thus not only an anecdote of two speakers' disconnection but also the rising, rumbling rhythm of a people's discontent, an apt starting point for a *Montage of a Dream Deferred.*

Notes

[1]Indeed, as Günter H. Lenz writes, the poem "delineates the force-field in which all the elements" (275) of the long poem operate. Though worthy of consideration in its own right, the piece is properly seen as the opening selection of what Hughes intended to be read as a single long poem. For a broader analysis of jazz elements in *Montage of a Dream Deferred*, see Hokanson.

[2]That paradox runs throughout *Montage*. John Lowney notes that the poem's discordant bebop "nonsense" motifs create a "sense of anxiety, fragmentation, and urgency" that illuminates the sharp divide between surface rhythms and deeper "dreams deferred" (370).

[3]Lempert asserts that the eclipse of reasoned pleas by otherwise meaningless bebop syllables conveys a "profound disillusionment with music's communicative potentials" (1073) that arises naturally from bebop's insistence on being received materially.

Works Cited

"Boogie, n.²" Def. 1a, 1b. *The Oxford English Dictionary*. 2nd ed. 1989. *OED Online*. Web. 7 Feb. 2012.

"Daddy, n." Def. 3. *The Oxford English Dictionary*. 2nd ed. 1989. *OED Online*. Web. 7 Feb. 2012.

Hokanson, Robert O'Brien. "Jazzing It Up: The Be-Bop Modernism of Langston Hughes." *Mosaic: A Journal for the Interdisciplinary Study of Literature* 31.4 (1998): 61–82. Print.

Hughes, Langston. "Dream Boogie." *Montage of a Dream Deferred*. New York: Holt, 1951. 3. Print.

———. "Harlem." *Montage of a Dream Deferred*. New York: Holt, 1951. 71. Print.

———. "The Negro Artist and the Racial Mountain." *The Nation* 23 June 1926: 692–94. Print.

Lempert, Benjamin R. "Harryette Mullen and the Contemporary Jazz Voice." *Callaloo* 33.4 (2010): 1059–78. *ProQuest*. Web. 2 Feb. 2012.

Lenz, Günter H. "'The Riffs, Runs, Breaks, and Distortions of the Music of a Community in Transition:' Redefining African American Modernism and the Jazz Aesthetic in Langston Hughes' *Montage of a Dream Deferred* and *Ask Your Mama*." *Massachusetts Review* 44.1/2 (2003): 269–82. *ProQuest*. Web. 2 Feb. 2012.

Lott, Eric. "Double V, Double-Time: Bebop's Politics of Style." *Callaloo* 36 (1988): 597–605. JSTOR. Web. 2 Feb. 2012.

Lowney, John. "Langston Hughes and the 'Nonsense' of Bebop." *American Literature* 72.2 (2000): 357–85. Print.

KAREN JACKSON FORD

from Do Right to Write Right: Langston Hughes's Aesthetics of Simplicity[*]

The one thing most readers of twentieth-century American poetry can say about Langston Hughes is that he has known rivers. "The Negro Speaks of Rivers" has become memorable for its lofty, oratorical tone, mythic scope, and powerful rhythmic repetitions.

* *Twentieth-Century Literature* 38.4 (1992): 435–56. Print.

> I've known rivers:
> I've known rivers ancient as the world and old as the flow of human
>   blood in human veins.

But however beautiful its cadences, the poem is remembered primarily because it is Hughes's most frequently anthologized work. The fact is, "The Negro Speaks of Rivers" is one of Hughes's most uncharacteristic poems, and yet it has defined his reputation, along with a small but constant selection of other poems included in anthologies. "The Negro Speaks of Rivers," "A House in Taos," "The Weary Blues," "Montage of a Dream Deferred," "Theme for English B," "Refugee in America," and "I, Too"—these poems invariably comprise his anthology repertoire despite the fact that none of them typifies his writing. What makes these poems atypical is exactly what makes them appealing and intelligible to the scholars who edit anthologies—their complexity. True, anthologies produced in the current market, which is hospitable to the African-American tradition and to canon reform, now include a brief selection of poems in black folk forms. But even though Hughes has fared better in anthologies than most African-American writers, only a small and predictable segment of his poetry has been preserved. A look back through the original volumes of poetry, and even through the severely redrawn *Selected Poems*, reveals a wealth of simpler poems we ought to be reading.[1]

Admittedly, an account of Hughes's poetic simplicity requires some qualification. Most obvious is the fact that he wrote poems that are not simple. "The Negro Speaks of Rivers" is oracular; "The Weary Blues" concludes enigmatically; "A House in Taos" is classically modernist in both its fragmented form and its decadent sensibility. Even more to the point, many of the poems that have been deemed simple are only ironically so. "The Black Christ," for example, is a little jingle that invokes monstrous cultural complexity. Likewise, two later books, *Ask Your Mama* (1961) and *The Panther and the Lash* (1967), contain an intricate vision of American history beneath their simple surfaces.[2] Nevertheless, the overwhelming proportion of poems in the Hughes canon consists of work in the simpler style, and even those poems that can yield complexities make use of simplicity in ways that ought not to be ignored.

The repression of the great bulk of Hughes's poems is the result of chronic critical scorn for their simplicity. Throughout his long career, but especially after his first two volumes of poetry (readers were at first willing to assume that a youthful poet might grow to be more complex), his books received their harshest reviews for a variety of "flaws" that all originate in an aesthetics of simplicity. From his first book, *The Weary Blues* (1926), to his last one, *The Panther and the Lash* (1967), the reviews invoke a litany of faults: the poems are superficial, infantile, silly, small, unpoetic, common, jejune, iterative, and, of course, simple.[3] Even his admirers reluctantly conclude that Hughes's poetics failed. Saunders Redding flatly opposes simplicity and artfulness. "While Hughes's rejection of his own growth shows an admirable loyalty to his self-commitment as the poet of the 'simple, Negro commonfolk' . . . it does a disservice to his art" (Mullen 74). James Baldwin, who recognizes the potential of simplicity as an artistic principle, faults the poems for "tak[ing] refuge . . . in a fake simplicity in order to avoid the very difficult simplicity of the experience" (Mullen 85).

Despite a lifetime of critical disappointments, then, Hughes remained loyal to the aesthetic program he had outlined in 1926 in his decisive poetic treatise, "The Negro Artist and the Racial Mountain." There he had predicted that the common people would "give to this world its truly great Negro artist, the one who is not afraid to be himself," a poet who would explore the "great field of unused [folk] material ready for his art" and recognize that this source would provide "sufficient matter to furnish a black artist with a lifetime of creative work" (692).* This is clearly a portrait of the poet Hughes would become, and he maintained his fidelity to this ideal at great cost to his literary reputation. . . .

In his column in the *Chicago Defender* on February 13, 1943, Hughes first introduced the prototype of the humorous and beloved fictional character Jesse B. Semple, nicknamed by his Harlem friends "Simple." For the next twenty-three years Hughes would continue to publish Simple stories both in the *Defender* and in several volumes of collected and edited pieces.[4] Hughes called Simple his "ace-boy," and it is surely not coincidental that the Simple stories span the years, the 1940s to the 1960s, when Langston Hughes needed a literary ace in the hole.[5] The success of the Simple stories was an important consolation of the writer's later years, when his poetry was reviewed with disappointment, his autobiography dismissed as "chit-chat," his plays refused on Broadway, and his fiction diminished in importance next to Richard Wright's *Native Son* (1940) and Ralph Ellison's *Invisible Man* (1952).[6]

It seems obvious, however, that in the long association with his ace-boy Hughes found more than popularity and financial success. In fact, his prefatory sketches of Simple attest to the character's importance, in the sheer number of times Hughes sets out to explain him and in the specific details these explanations provide.[7] All of them depict Simple as an African American Everyman, the authentic—even unmediated—voice of the community that engendered him. For instance, in "Who Is Simple?" Hughes emphasizes the authenticity of his creation: "[Simple's] first words came directly out of the mouth of a young man who lived just down the block from me" (*Best* vii). Here and elsewhere Hughes asserts a vital connection between the fictional character and the people he represents: "If there were not a lot of genial souls in Harlem as talkative as Simple, I would never have these tales to write down that are 'just like him'" (*Best* viii). The author's dedication to Simple is surely rooted in his conviction that Simple embodies and speaks for the very people to whom Hughes had committed himself back in the 1920s.

Notes

[1]Easily ninety per cent of the poems in Hughes's canon are of the sort that I am describing as simple.

[2]Jemie, Hudson, and Miller, among others, have persuasively demonstrated the intricacies of Hughes's jazz structures in these two late books.

[3]Reviews in which these epithets appear are collected in Mullen.

[4]The stories are collected in five volumes, *The Best of Simple, Simple Speaks His Mind, Simple Stakes a Claim, Simple Takes a Wife,* and *Simple's Uncle Sam*. Additionally, Hughes takes Simple to the stage with *Simply Heavenly*, a comedy about Simple's marriage.

*See pages 929–930 for the quoted passage in its entirety.

[5]In "Who Is Simple?"—the foreword to *The Best of Simple*—Hughes concludes, "He is my ace-boy, Simple. I hope you like him, too" (viii).

[6]For a chronicle of Hughes's disappointments during these years, see Rampersad, especially chapter 8 of the second volume "In Warm Manure: 1951 to 1953." Ellison characterized *The Big Sea* as a "chit-chat" book during an interview with Rampersad in 1983 (202).

[7]Hughes wrote at least four explanations of Simple: "The Happy Journey of 'Simply Heavenly,'" "Simple and Me," "Who Is Simple?" and the "Character Notes" to *Simply Heavenly*.

GEORGE B. HUTCHINSON

from Langston Hughes and the "Other" Whitman[*]

At various points in his long career, Hughes put together no fewer than three separate anthologies of Whitman's poetry (one of them for children), included several Whitman poems in an anthology on *The Poetry of the Negro*, wrote a poem entitled "Old Walt" for the one hundredth anniversary of *Leaves of Grass*, and repeatedly—in lectures, newspaper columns, and introductions—encouraged black Americans to read his work. He called Whitman "America's greatest poet" and spoke of *Leaves of Grass* as the greatest expression of "the real meaning of democracy ever made on our shores." Feeling that Whitman had been ignored and, in current parlance, marginalized by the custodians of culture, Hughes indeed attempted in his own way to canonize the poet he considered "the Lincoln of our Letters" (*Chicago Defender*, July 4, 1953). . . .

One reason Whitman's poetry has resonated in the sensibilities of black American writers is that in certain of his poems he uses the condition of the slave as representative of the condition of his audience. The "you" of his songs, if it is to apply to *all* readers, must apply to slaves, those most graphically denied the right to self-determination. The poem "To You (Whoever You Are)" at times seems directly addressed to a slave:

> None has done justice to you, you have not done justice to yourself,
> None but has found you imperfect, I only find no imperfection
>   in you,
> None but would subordinate you, I only am he who will never consent
>   to subordinate you,
> I only am he who places over you no master, owner, better, God,
>   beyond what waits intrinsically in yourself. (14–17)

Arguably, Whitman here distills the specific oppression of black people in the antebellum United States into a metaphor for the hidden condition of all people—"you, whoever you are." But his slave is not just any slave—his slave is the *most* enslaved, the one rejected by all others and even by himself or herself. . . . Hughes was the first African-American poet to sense the affinity between the inclusive "I" of Whitman (which Whitman claimed as his most important innovation—"the quite changed attitude of the ego, the one chanting or talking, towards himself and towards his fellow humanity") ("A Backward Glance," 564) and the "I" of the blues and even of the

---

[*]*The Continuing Presence of Walt Whitman: The Life after the Life*. Ed. Robert K. Martin. Iowa City: U of Iowa P, 1992. Print.

spirituals. The result of Hughes's appropriation of this triply descended "I" is amply demonstrated in one of his first published poems, "The Negro Speaks of Rivers":

> I've known rivers ancient as the world and old as the flow of human
>   blood in human veins.
>
> My soul has grown deep like the rivers.
>
> I bathed in the Euphrates when dawns were young.
> I built my hut near the Congo and it lulled me to sleep.
> I looked upon the Nile and raised the pyramids above it.
> I heard the singing of the Mississippi when Abe Lincoln went down to
>   New Orleans, and I've seen its muddy bosom turn all golden in the
>   sunset. (*Weary Blues*, 51)

Though Hughes would later, for the most part, turn away from the Whitmanesque style of free verse, the example of Whitman's break with traditional definitions of the poetic, his attempts to achieve an orally based poetics with the cadence and diction of the voice on the street, at the pond-side, or at the pulpit, provided a partial model for the young black poet looking for a way to sing his own song, which would be at the same time a song of his people.

YUSEF KOMUNYAKAA

from Langston Hughes + Poetry = The Blues*

> And far into the night he crooned that tune.
> The stars went out and so did the moon.
> The singer stopped playing and went to bed.
> While the Weary Blues echoed through his head.

—Langston Hughes, *The Weary Blues*

When we analyze and weigh the most innovative voices of the Harlem Renaissance, Langston Hughes—alongside Zora Neale Hurston, Jean Toomer, and Helene Johnson—remains at the axis. Where Countee Cullen and Claude McKay embraced the archaism of the Keatian ode and the Elizabethan sonnet[1] respectively, Hughes grafted on to his modernist vision traditional blues as well as the Chicago Renaissance (Vachel Lindsay and Carl Sandburg).[2] So, as the other voices grew silent during the Great Depression of 1929—with modernism[3] and imagism[4] having taken a firm hold and reshaped the tongue and heart of American poetry—the 1930s found a prolific Hughes. From the outset an American-ness had been at the center of Hughes's work, which is one of the reasons he has endured. Even his benchmark poem "The Negro Speaks of Rivers" plumbs* the "muddy bosom" of the Mississippi after its narrator praises the Euphrates and the Congo (i.e., after taking readers on a tour through African heritage, the poem focuses on racial tensions in America).

Callaloo 25.4 (2002): 1140–43. Print.
*From *Blue Notes: Essays, Interviews and Commentaries*. (University of Michigan Press, 2000). Originally published in *Nexus* (1996). Reprinted by permission of the author.
* *plumbs:* Examines.

Like Walt Whitman, the pulse and throb of Hughes's vision is driven by an acute sense of beauty and tragedy in America's history. Arnold Rampersad says in *The Life of Langston Hughes* that "On a visit to Kansas City he became aware of yet another aspect of black culture on which he would draw later as an artist and an individual. At an open air theatre on Independence Avenue, from an orchestra of blind musicians, Hughes first heard the blues. The music seemed to cry, but the words somehow laughed." Where Whitman had embraced the aria of the Italian opera (horizontal music), Hughes's divining rod quivered over the bedrock of the blues (vertical music).[5] The short lines of the blues poems create a syncopated insistence and urgency. Art has to have tension. And it is the simultaneous laughter and crying that create the tension in Hughes's blues poetry.[6] Hughes writes in "Homesick Blues":

> Homesick blues is / A terrible thing to have. / To keep from cryin' / I opens ma mouth an' laughs.

In "Midwinter Blues" we find the same tension:

> Don't know's I'd mind his goin'
> But he left me when the coal was low.
> Don't know's I'd mind his goin'
> But he left when the coal was low.
> Now, if a man loves a woman
> That ain't no time to go.

Hughes also incorporates a jagged lyricism and modulation into his poetry by using short lines—a modern feeling that depends on a vertical movement that sidesteps contemplation but invites action/motion. There is confrontation in the blues. Stephen Henderson states in *Understanding the New Black Poetry*: "In oral tradition, the dogged determination of the work songs, the tough-minded power of the blues, the inventive energy of jazz, and the transcendent vision of God in the spirituals and the sermons, all energize the idea of Freedom, of Liberation, which is itself liberated from the temporal, the societal, and the political."

Hughes seems to have set out to take poetry off the page and toss it up into the air we breathe; he desired to bring poetry into our daily lives. In essence, he wanted his blues chants to parallel the improvisation in the lives of African Americans:

> To fling my arms wide
> In the face of the sun.
> Dance! Whirl! Whirl!
> Till the quick day is done.
> Rest at pale evening. . .
> A tall, slim tree. . .
> Night coming tenderly
>   Black like me.

Hughes speaks here about daring joy to enter black life. The poem, "Dream Variations," is more than the speaker day-dreaming about bringing images of nature into Harlem (the first black metropolis of the modern world): this is celebration and revolution in the same breath. Hughes addresses the future, forging through imagery and metaphor, the possibility of a new black culture in literature, music, and the arts.

Notes

[1]Cullen modeled his poetry on the verse of the nineteenth-century British poet John Keats; McKay's models were the seventeenth-century Elizabethan poets, including William Shakespeare.

[2]According to Hughes's biographer, Faith Berry, Hughes's high school English teacher (at Central High in Cleveland), "introduced her class to the Chicago school of poets: Vachel Lindsay, Edgar Lee Masters, and—the poet Hughes admired most, and eventually his greatest influence in the matter of form—Carl Sandburg."

[3]Modernist poets like T.S. Eliot, Wallace Stevens, and Ezra Pound broke away from poetic traditions of the nineteenth century, such as rhyme and "flowery" language, the kind of poetry Cullen and Claude McKay continued to write.

[4]Imagism was a post–World War I literary movement that rebelled against nineteenth-century Romanticism and promoted the use of free verse and precise, concentrated imagery. The early poems of William Carlos Williams and the poetry of H.D. exemplify this tradition.

[5]The lines of Whitman's verse are very long, giving his poetry a horizontal feel. Hughes's lines are short, so the reader's eyes move quickly down the page, giving the poetry a sense of verticalness.

[6]In a review of W.C. Handy's *Blues: An Anthology* Langston Hughes says the blues grew out of "the racial hurt and the racial ecstasy," out of "trouble with incongruous overtones of laughter [and] joy with strange undertones of pain."

Topics for Further Research

1. As Hughes's own essays in this chapter suggest, much of his life was spent actively campaigning for various causes. Research his social and political activities and their effect on his poetry. How did his social and political work change between 1935 and 1955?

2. Investigate the ways in which Hughes's poetry was inspired by African American music. For example, how did the different musical forms of the female blues singers of the 1920s and the bebop musicians of the 1940s affect his poetry?

3. Hughes was a primary inspiration for the artistic movement known as *negritude*. Poets and writers like Nicolás Guillén, Jacques Roumain, Aimé Cesaire, and Leopold Senghor all acknowledged Hughes's influence. Find out what the negritude poets stood for, and write an essay in which you discuss why Hughes was so important to this movement.

4. Hughes's work was distinct from that of his two most important contemporaries, Gwendolyn Brooks and Robert Hayden, who were influenced by modernism. Is *modernism* a useful term for discussing what distinguishes Brooks and Hayden from Hughes? Why might Hughes be skeptical about some aspects of modernism? (Before answering these questions, look up the term *modernism* in an encyclopedia or dictionary of literary terms.) Read the poems by Brooks and Hayden in this anthology. Then, read some additional poems by one of these poets, and compare some of these poems to Hughes's poems.

5. Hughes was a central figure in a period of African American artistic flowering called the Harlem Renaissance. Find out as much as you can about the Harlem Renaissance and Hughes's involvement with it. Then, write an essay in which you assess how the Harlem Renaissance was important to Hughes's development as a poet.

6. Read a collection of Hughes's "Simple" stories, newspaper columns that were later collected in book form. What is he able to do in fiction that he is unable to do in poetry? What is he able to do in poetry that he is unable to do in fiction?

CHAPTER 33

POETRY FOR FURTHER READING

Samuel Taylor Coleridge
The Granger Collection

Linda Pastan
Goodman/Van Riper Photography

Edwin Arlington Robinson
Bettmann/Corbis

Wallace Stevens
AP Images/Hartford Courant

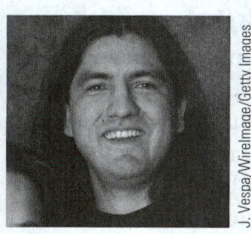

J. Vespa/WireImage/Getty Images

SHERMAN J. ALEXIE (1966–   )

Defending Walt Whitman (1996)

Basketball is like this for young Indian boys, all arms and legs
and serious stomach muscles. Every body is brown!
These are the twentieth-century warriors who will never kill,
although a few sat quietly in the deserts of Kuwait,
waiting for orders to do something, do something.   5

God, there is nothing as beautiful as a jump shot
on a reservation summer basketball court

where the ball is moist with sweat
and makes a sound when it swishes through the net
that causes Walt Whitman to weep because it is so perfect.   10

There are veterans of foreign wars here,
whose bodies are still dominated
by collarbones and knees, whose bodies still respond
in the ways that bodies are supposed to respond when we
    are young.

Every body is brown! Look there, that boy can run   15
up and down this court forever. He can leap for a rebound
with his back arched like a salmon, all meat and bone
synchronized, magnetic, as if the court were a river,
as if the rim were a dam, as if the air were a ladder
leading the Indian boy toward home.   20

Some of the Indian boys still wear their military haircuts
while a few have let their hair grow back.
It will never be the same as it was before!
One Indian boy has never cut his hair, not once, and he braids it
into wild patterns that do not measure anything.   25
He is just a boy with too much time on his hands.
Look at him. He wants to play this game in bare feet.

God, the sun is so bright! There is no place like this.
Walt Whitman stretches his calf muscles
on the sidelines. He has the next game.   30
His huge beard is ridiculous on the reservation.
Some body throws a crazy pass and Walt Whitman catches it
    with quick hands.
He brings the ball close to his nose
and breathes in all of its smells: leather, brown skin, sweat,
    black hair,
burning oil, twisted ankle, long drink of warm water,   35
gunpowder, pine tree. Walt Whitman squeezes the ball tightly.
He wants to run. He hardly has the patience to wait for his turn.
"What's the score?" he asks. He asks, "What's the score?"

Basketball is like this for Walt Whitman. He watches these
    Indian boys
as if they were the last bodies on earth. Every body is brown!   40
Walt Whitman shakes because he believes in God.
Walt Whitman dreams of the Indian boy who will defend him,
trapping him in the corner, all flailing arms and legs
and legendary stomach muscles. Walt Whitman shakes
because he believes in God. Walt Whitman dreams   45
of the first jump shot he will take, the ball arcing clumsily
from his fingers, striking the rim so hard that it sparks.

Walt Whitman shakes because he believes in God.
Walt Whitman closes his eyes. He is a small man and his beard
is ludicrous on the reservation, absolutely insane.   50
His beard makes the Indian boys laugh righteously. His beard
   frightens
the smallest Indian boys. His beard tickles the skin
of the Indian boys who dribble past him. His beard, his beard!

God, there is beauty in every body. Walt Whitman stands
at center court while the Indian boys run from basket to basket.   55
Walt Whitman cannot tell the difference between
offense and defense. He does not care if he touches the ball.
Half of the Indian boys wear T-shirts damp with sweat
and the other half are barebacked, skin slick and shiny.
There is no place like this. Walt Whitman smiles.   60
Walt Whitman shakes. This game belongs to him.

ANONYMOUS

Bonny Barbara Allan

(Traditional Scottish ballad)

It was in and about the Martinmas[1] time,
   When the green leaves were afalling,
That Sir John Graeme, in the West Country,
   Fell in love with Barbara Allan.

He sent his men down through the town,   5
   To the place where she was dwelling;
"O haste and come to my master dear,
   Gin[2] ye be Barbara Allan."

O hooly,[3] hooly rose she up,
   To the place where he was lying,   10
And when she drew the curtain by:
   "Young man, I think you're dying."

"O it's I'm sick, and very, very sick,
   And 'tis a' for Barbara Allan."—
"O the better for me ye's never be,   15
   Tho your heart's blood were aspilling."

---

[1] *Martinmas:* Saint Martin's Day, November 11.

[2] *Gin:* If.

[3] *hooly:* Slowly.

"O dinna ye mind,⁴ young man," said she,
  "When ye was in the tavern adrinking,
That ye made the health gae round and round,
  And slighted Barbara Allan?"   20

He turned his face unto the wall,
  And death was with him dealing:
"Adieu, adieu, my dear friends all,
  And be kind to Barbara Allan."

And slowly, slowly raise she up,   25
  And slowly, slowly left him,
And sighing said she could not stay,
  Since death of life had reft him.

She had not gane a mile but twa,⁵
  When she heard the dead-bell ringing,   30
And every jow⁶ that the dead-bell geid,
  It cried, "Woe to Barbara Allan!"

"O mother, mother, make my bed!
  O make it saft and narrow!
Since my love died for me today,   35
  I'll die for him tomorrow."

ANONYMOUS

Go Down, Moses*

Go down, Moses,
Way down in Egyptland
Tell old Pharaoh
To let my people go.

When Israel was in Egyptland   5
Let my people go
Oppressed so hard they could not stand
Let my people go.

---

⁴*O dinna ye mind:* Don't you remember?

⁵*twa:* Two.

⁶*jow:* Stroke.

*Music, especially religious songs, or "spirituals," was one of the few means of expression permitted for slaves. Many of these spirituals contained coded messages conveying antislavery sentiments or even directions on how to use the Underground Railroad. For example, the spiritual "Wade in the Water" seemed, on the surface, to be about crossing the River Jordan to reach the Promised Land. But its lyrics contained vital information, including the idea that crossing streams was a good way for runaway slaves to cover their scent and thus to lose the bloodhounds used to track them.

Go down, Moses,
Way down in Egyptland   10
Tell old Pharaoh
"Let my people go."

"Thus saith the Lord," bold Moses said,
"Let my people go;
If not I'll smite your first-born dead   15
Let my people go.

"No more shall they in bondage toil,
Let my people go;
Let them come out with Egypt's spoil,
Let my people go."   20

The Lord told Moses what to do
Let my people go;
To lead the children of Israel through,
Let my people go.

Go down, Moses,
Way down in Egyptland,   25
Tell old Pharaoh,
"Let my people go!"

MATTHEW ARNOLD (1822–1888)

Dover Beach (1867)

The sea is calm tonight.
The tide is full, the moon lies fair
Upon the straits;—on the French coast the light
Gleams and is gone; the cliffs of England stand,
Glimmering and vast, out in the tranquil bay.   5
Come to the window, sweet is the night-air!
Only, from the long line of spray
Where the sea meets the moon-blanched[1] land,
Listen! you hear the grating roar
Of pebbles which the waves draw back, and fling,   10
At their return, up the high strand,[2]
Begin, and cease, and then again begin,
With tremulous cadence slow, and bring
The eternal note of sadness in.

---

[1] *moon-blanched:* Whitened by moonlight.
[2] *strand:* Beach.

Sophocles[3] long ago   15
Heard it on the Aegean,[4] and it brought
Into his mind the turbid ebb and flow
Of human misery; we
Find also in the sound a thought,
Hearing it by this distant northern sea.   20

The Sea of Faith
Was once, too, at the full, and round earth's shore
Lay like the folds of a bright girdle furled.
But now I only hear
Its melancholy, long, withdrawing roar,   25
Retreating, to the breath
Of the night-wind, down the vast edges drear
And naked shingles[5] of the world.

Ah, love, let us be true
To one another! for the world, which seems   30
To lie before us like a land of dreams,
So various, so beautiful, so new,
Hath really neither joy, nor love, nor light,
Nor certitude, nor peace, nor help for pain;
And we are here as on a darkling[6] plain   35
Swept with confused alarms of struggle and flight,
Where ignorant armies clash by night.

ELIZABETH BISHOP (1911–1979)

The Fish (1946)

I caught a tremendous fish
and held him beside the boat
half out of water, with my hook
fast in a corner of his mouth.
He didn't fight.   5
He hadn't fought at all.
He hung a grunting weight,
battered and venerable
and homely. Here and there
his brown skin hung in strips   10

---

[3] *Sophocles:* Greek playwright (496–406 B.C.), author of tragedies such as *Oedipus the King* and *Antigone.*
[4] *Aegean:* Sea between Greece and Turkey.
[5] *shingles:* Gravel beaches.
[6] *darkling:* Darkening.

like ancient wallpaper,
and its pattern of darker brown
was like wallpaper:
shapes like full-blown roses
stained and lost through age.   15
He was speckled with barnacles,
fine rosettes of lime,
and infested
with tiny white sea-lice,
and underneath two or three   20
rags of green weed hung down.
While his gills were breathing in
the terrible oxygen
—the frightening gills,
fresh and crisp with blood,   25
that can cut so badly—
I thought of the coarse white flesh
packed in like feathers,
the big bones and the little bonies,
the dramatic reds and blacks   30
of his shiny entrails,
and the pink swim-bladder
like a big peony.
I looked into his eyes
which were far larger than mine   35
but shallower, and yellowed,
the irises backed and packed
with tarnished tinfoil
seen through the lenses
of old scratched isinglass.   40
They shifted a little, but not
to return my stare.
—It was more like the tipping
of an object toward the light.
I admired his sullen face,   45
the mechanism of his jaw,
and then I saw
that from his lower lip
—if you could call it a lip—
grim, wet, and weaponlike,   50
hung five old pieces of fish-line,
or four and a wire leader
with the swivel still attached,
with all their five big hooks
grown firmly in his mouth.   55
A green line, frayed at the end
and crimped from the strain and snap

when it broke and he got away.
Like medals with their ribbons
frayed and wavering,   60
a five-haired beard of wisdom
trailing from his aching jaw.
I stared and stared
and victory filled up
the little rented boat,   65
from the pool of bilge
where oil had spread a rainbow
around the rusted engine
to the bailer rusted orange,
the sun-cracked thwarts,   70
the oarlocks on their strings,
the gunnels—until everything
was rainbow, rainbow, rainbow!
And I let the fish go.

WILLIAM BLAKE (1757–1827)

The Chimney Sweeper[1] (1789)

When my mother died I was very young,
And my father sold me while yet my tongue
Could scarcely cry "'weep! 'weep! 'weep! 'weep!"
So your chimneys I sweep, and in soot I sleep.

There's little Tom Dacre, who cried when his head,   5
That curled like a lamb's back, was shaved: so I said
"Hush, Tom! never mind it, for when your head's bare
You know that the soot cannot spoil your white hair."

And so he was quiet, and that very night,
As Tom was a-sleeping, he had such a sight!   10
That thousands of sweepers, Dick, Joe, Ned, and Jack,
Were all of them locked up in coffins of black.

And by came an Angel who had a bright key,
And he opened the coffins and set them all free;
Then down a green plain leaping, laughing, they run,   15
And wash in a river, and shine in the sun.

Then naked and white, all their bags left behind,
They rise upon clouds and sport in the wind;
And the Angel told Tom, if he'd be a good boy,
He'd have God for his father, and never want joy.   20

---

[1]During the eighteenth and early nineteenth centuries, orphans as young as four years old were apprenticed to chimney
sweepers.

And so Tom awoke; and we rose in the dark,
And got with our bags and our brushes to work.
Though the morning was cold, Tom was happy and warm;
So if all do their duty they need not fear harm.

WILLIAM BLAKE (1757–1827)

The Lamb (1789)

   Little Lamb, who made thee?
   Dost thou know who made thee?
Gave thee life & bid thee feed,
By the stream & o'er the mead;
Gave thee clothing of delight,   5
Softest clothing wooly bright;
Gave thee such a tender voice,
Making all the vales rejoice!
   Little Lamb who made thee?
   Dost thou know who made thee?   10

   Little Lamb I'll tell thee,
   Little Lamb I'll tell thee!
He is calléd by thy name,
For he calls himself a Lamb:
He is meek & he is mild,   15
He became a little child:
I a child & thou a lamb,
We are calléd by his name.
   Little Lamb God bless thee.
   Little Lamb God bless thee.   20

WILLIAM BLAKE (1757–1827)

London (1794)

I wander through each chartered street,
Near where the chartered Thames does flow,
And mark in every face I meet
Marks of weakness, marks of woe.

In every cry of every man,   5
In every infant's cry of fear,
In every voice, in every ban,
The mind-forged manacles I hear.

How the chimney-sweeper's cry
Every black'ning church appalls;   10

And the hapless soldier's sigh
Runs in blood down palace walls.

But most through midnight streets I hear
How the youthful harlot's curse
Blasts the new born infant's tear,   15
And blights with plagues the marriage hearse.

WILLIAM BLAKE (1757–1827)

To see a World in a Grain of Sand (1803)

To see a World in a Grain of Sand
And a Heaven in a Wild Flower,
Hold Infinity in the palm of your hand
And Eternity in an hour.

WILLIAM BLAKE (1757–1827)

The Tyger (1794)

Tyger! Tyger! burning bright
In the forests of the night,
What immortal hand or eye
Could frame thy fearful symmetry?

In what distant deeps or skies   5
Burnt the fire of thine eyes?
On what wings dare he aspire?
What the hand dare seize the fire?

And what shoulder, and what art,
Could twist the sinews of thy heart?   10
And when thy heart began to beat,
What dread hand? and what dread feet?

What the hammer? what the chain?
In what furnace was thy brain?
What the anvil? what dread grasp   15
Dare its deadly terrors clasp?

When the stars threw down their spears,
And watered heaven with their tears,
Did he smile his work to see?
Did he who made the Lamb make thee?   20

Tyger! Tyger! burning bright
In the forests of the night,
What immortal hand or eye
Dare frame thy fearful symmetry?

ELIZABETH BRADFIELD

Why They Went (2010)

that men might learn what the world is like at the
spot where the sun does not decline in the heavens.
*   —Apsley Cherry-Garrard*

Frost bitten. Snow blind. Hungry. Craving
fresh pie and hot toddies,[1] a whole roasted
unflippered thing to carve. Craving a bed
that had, an hour before entering,
been warmed with a stone from the hearth.   5

Always back to Eden—to the time when we knew
with certainty that something watched and loved us.
That the very air was miraculous and ours.
That all we had to do was show up.

The sun rolled along the horizon. The light never left them.   10
The air from their warm mouths became diamonds.
And they longed for everything they did not have.
And they came home and longed again.

ANNE BRADSTREET (1612–1672)

The Author to Her Book[1] (1678)

Thou ill-formed offspring of my feeble brain,
Who after birth did'st by my side remain,
Till snatched from thence by friends, less wise than true,
Who thee abroad exposed to public view;
Made thee in rags, halting, to the press to trudge,   5
Where errors were not lessened, all may judge.
At thy return my blushing was not small,
My rambling brat (in print) should mother call;
I cast thee by as one unfit for light,
Thy visage was so irksome in my sight   10
Yet being mine own, at length affection would
Thy blemishes amend, if so I could:
I washed thy face, but more defects I saw,
And rubbing off a spot, still made a flaw.
I stretched thy joints to make thee even feet,[2]   15
Yet still thou run'st more hobbling than is meet;[3]

---

[1] *hot toddies:* Alcoholic drinks consisting of liquor, hot water, sugar, and spices.
[1] *Her Book:* Bradstreet addresses *The Tenth Muse*, a collection of her poetry published without her consent in 1650.
[2] *even feet:* Metrical feet.
[3] *meet:* Appropriate or decorous.

In better dress to trim thee was my mind,
But nought save homespun cloth in the house I find.
In this array, 'mongst vulgars[4] may'st thou roam;
In critics' hands beware thou dost not come;   20
And take thy way where yet thou are not known.
If for thy Father asked, say thou had'st none;
And for thy Mother, she alas is poor,
Which caused her thus to send thee out of door.

GWENDOLYN BROOKS (1917–2000)

The *Chicago Defender*[1] Sends a Man to Little Rock (1960)

Fall, 1957[2]

In Little Rock the people bear
Babes, and comb and part their hair
And watch the want ads, put repair
To roof and latch. While wheat toast burns
A woman waters multiferns.   5

Time upholds or overturns
The many, tight, and small concerns.

In Little Rock the people sing
Sunday hymns like anything,
Through Sunday pomp and polishing.   10

And after testament and tunes,
Some soften Sunday afternoons
With lemon tea and Lorna Doones.

I forecast
And I believe   15
Come Christmas Little Rock will cleave
To Christmas tree and trifle, weave,
From laugh and tinsel, texture fast.

In Little Rock is baseball; Barcarolle.[3]
That hotness in July . . . the uniformed figures raw and implacable   20

---

[4]*vulgars:* Common people.

[1]Chicago Defender: A weekly newspaper for African American readers.

[2]*Fall, 1957:* When b ack students first entered the public high school in Little Rock, Arkansas, in 1957, the city erupted in race riots protesting desegregation.

[3]*Barcarolle:* A Venetian gondolier's song, or a song suggesting the rhythm of rowing.

And not intellectual,
Batting the hotness or clawing the suffering dust.
The Open Air Concert, on the special twilight green. . . .
When Beethoven is brutal or whispers to lady-like air.
Blanket-sitters are solemn, as Johann troubles to lean   25
To tell them what to mean. . . .

There is love, too, in Little Rock. Soft women softly
Opening themselves in kindness,
Or, pitying one's blindness,
Awaiting one's pleasure   30
In azure
Glory with anguished rose at the root. . . .
To wash away old semi-discomfitures.
They re-teach purple and unsullen blue.
The wispy soils go. And uncertain   35
Half-havings have they clarified to sures.

In Little Rock they know
Not answering the telephone is a way of rejecting life,
That it is our business to be bothered, is our business
To cherish bores or boredom, be polite   40
To lies and love and many-faceted fuzziness.

I scratch my head, massage the hate-I-had.
I blink across my prim and pencilled pad.
The saga I was sent for is not down.
Because there is a puzzle in this town.   45

The biggest News I do not dare
Telegraph to the Editor's chair:
"They are like people everywhere."

The angry Editor would reply
In hundred harryings of Why.   50

And true, they are hurling spittle, rock,
Garbage and fruit in Little Rock.
And I saw coiling storm a-writhe
On bright madonnas. And a scythe
Of men harassing brownish girls.   55
(The bows and barrettes in the curls
And braids declined away from joy.)

I saw a bleeding brownish boy. . . .

The lariat lynch-wish I deplored.

The loveliest lynchee was our Lord.   60

GWENDOLYN BROOKS (1917–2000)

Medgar Evers[1] (1964)

For Charles Evers[2]

The man whose height his fear improved he
arranged to fear no further. The raw
intoxicated time was time for better birth or a final death.

Old styles, old tempos, all the engagement of
the day—the sedate, the regulated fray—   5
the antique light, the Moral rose, old gusts,
tight whistlings from the past, the mothballs
in the Love at last our man forswore.

Medgar Evers annoyed confetti and assorted
brands of businessmen's eyes.   10

The shows came down: to maxims and surprise.
And palsy.

Roaring no rapt arise-ye to the dead, he
leaned across tomorrow. People said that
he was holding clean globes in his hands.   15

CHARLES BUKOWSKI (1920–1994)

so you want to be a writer? (2003)

if it doesn't come bursting out of you
in spite of everything,
don't do it.
unless it comes unasked out of your
heart and your mind and your mouth   5
and your gut,
don't do it.
if you have to sit for hours
staring at your computer screen
or hunched over your   10
typewriter
searching for words,
don't do it.
if you're doing it for money or
fame,   15

---

[1] *Medgar Evers:* African American civil rights leader who was killed by a sniper in 1963.
[2] *Charles Evers:* Medgar Evers's brother.

don't do it.
if you're doing it because you want
women in your bed,
don't do it.
if you have to sit there and   20
rewrite it again and again,
don't do it.
if it's hard work just thinking about doing it,
don't do it.
if you're trying to write like somebody   25
else,
forget about it.

if you have to wait for it to roar out of
you,
then wait patiently.   30
if it never does roar out of you,
do something else.

if you first have to read it to your wife
or your girlfriend or your boyfriend
or your parents or to anybody at all,   35
you're not ready.

don't be like so many writers,
don't be like so many thousands of
people who call themselves writers,
don't be dull and boring and   40
pretentious, don't be consumed with self-
love.
the libraries of the world have
yawned themselves to
sleep   45
over your kind.
don't add to that.
don't do it.
unless it comes out of
your soul like a rocket,   50
unless being still would
drive you to madness or
suicide or murder,
don't do it.
unless the sun inside you is   60
burning your gut,
don't do it.

when it is truly time,
and if you have been chosen,

it will do it by   65
itself and it will keep on doing it
until you die or it dies in you.

there is no other way.

and there never was.

GEORGE GORDON, LORD BYRON (1788–1824)

She Walks in Beauty (1815)

1

She walks in beauty, like the night
  Of cloudless climes and starry skies;
And all that's best of dark and bright
  Meet in her aspect and her eyes:
Thus mellowed to that tender light   5
  Which heaven to gaudy day denies.

2

One shade the more, one ray the less,
  Had half impaired the nameless grace
Which waves in every raven tress,
  Or softly lightens o'er her face;   10
Where thoughts serenely sweet express
  How pure, how dear their dwelling place.

3

And on that cheek, and o'er that brow,
  So soft, so calm, yet eloquent,
The smiles that win, the tints that glow,   15
  But tell of days in goodness spent,
A mind at peace with all below,
  A heart whose love is innocent!

JUDITH ORTIZ COFER (1952–   )

Lessons of the Past (1990)

For my daughter

I was born the year my father learned to march in step
with other men, to hit bull's eyes, to pose for sepia photos
in dress uniform outside Panamanian nightspots—pictures
he would send home to his pregnant teenage bride inscribed:
To my best girl.   5

My birth
made her a madonna, a husbandless young woman
with a legitimate child, envied by all the tired women
of the pueblo as she strolled my carriage down dirt roads,
both of us dressed in fine clothes bought with army checks.   10

When he came home,
he bore gifts: silk pajamas from the orient for her; a pink
iron crib for me. People filled our house to welcome him.
He played Elvis loud and sang along in his new English.
She sat on his lap and laughed at everything.   15
They roasted a suckling pig out on the patio. Later,
no one could explain how I had climbed over the iron bars
and into the fire. Hands lifted me up quickly but not before
the tongues had licked my curls.

There is a picture of me   20
taken soon after: my hair clipped close to my head,
my eyes enormous—about to overflow with fear.
I look like a miniature of one of those women
in Paris after World War II, hair shorn,
being paraded down the streets in shame,   25
for having loved the enemy.

But then things changed,
and some nights he didn't come home. I remember
hearing her cry in the kitchen. I sat on the rocking chair
waiting for my cocoa, learning how to count, *uno, dos, tres,*   30
cuatro, cinco on my toes. So that when he came in,
smelling strong and sweet as sugarcane syrup,
I could surprise my *papsito*—
who liked his girls smart, who didn't like crybabies—
with a new lesson, learned well.   35

SAMUEL TAYLOR COLERIDGE (1772–1834)

Kubla Khan[1] (1797, 1798)

Or, a Vision in a Dream. A Fragment.

In Xanadu did Kubla Khan
A stately pleasure-dome decree:
Where Alph,[2] the sacred river, ran
Through caverns measureless to man

---

[1] *Kubla Khan:* Coleridge mythologizes the actual Kublai Khan, a thirteenth-century Mongol emperor, as well as the Chinese city of Xanadu.

[2] *Alph:* Probably derived from the Greek river Alpheus, whose waters, according to legend, rose from the Ionian Sea in Sicily as the fountain of Arethusa.

Down to a sunless sea.   5
So twice five miles of fertile ground
With walls and towers were girdled round;
And there were gardens bright with sinuous rills,
Where blossomed many an incense-bearing tree;
And here were forests ancient as the hills,   10
Enfolding sunny spots of greenery.

But oh! that deep romantic chasm which slanted
Down the green hill athwart a cedarn cover!
A savage place! as holy and enchanted
As e'er beneath a waning moon was haunted   15
By woman wailing for her demon-lover!
And from this chasm, with ceaseless turmoil seething,
As if this earth in fast thick pants were breathing,
A mighty fountain momently was forced:
Amid whose swift half-intermitted burst   20
Huge fragments vaulted like rebounding hail,
Or chaffy grain beneath the thresher's flail:
And 'mid these dancing rocks at once and ever
It flung up momently the sacred river.
Five miles meandering with a mazy motion   25
Through wood and dale the sacred river ran,
Then reached the caverns measureless to man,
And sank in tumult to a lifeless ocean:
And 'mid this tumult Kubla heard from far
Ancestral voices prophesying war!   30

    The shadow of the dome of pleasure
    Floated midway on the waves;
    Where was heard the mingled measure
    From the fountain and the caves.
It was a miracle of rare device,   35
A sunny pleasure-dome with caves of ice!

    A damsel with a dulcimer
    In a vision once I saw:
    It was an Abyssinian maid,
    And on her dulcimer she played,   40
    Singing of Mount Abora.[3]
    Could I revive within me
    Her symphony and song,

---

[3] *Mount Abora:* Some scholars see a reminiscence here of John Milton's *Paradise Lost* 4.280–82: "where Abassin kings their issue guard / Mount Amara, though this by some supposed / True Paradise under the Ethiop Line."

To such a deep delight 'twould win me,
That with music loud and long,   45
I would build that dome in air,
That sunny dome! those caves of ice!
And all who heard should see them there,
And all should cry, Beware! Beware!
His flashing eyes, his floating hair   50
Weave a circle round him thrice,[4]
And close your eyes with holy dread,
For he on honey-dew hath fed,
And drunk the milk of Paradise.

BILLY COLLINS (1941–   )

Introduction to Poetry (1988)

I ask them to take a poem
and hold it up to the light
like a color slide

or press an ear against its hive.

I say drop a mouse into a poem   5
and watch him probe his way out,

or walk inside the poem's room
and feel the walls for a light switch.

I want them to waterski
across the surface of a poem   10
waving at the author's name on the shore.

But all they want to do
is tie the poem to a chair with rope
and torture a confession out of it.

They begin beating it with a hose   15
to find out what it really means.

BILL COYLE (1968–   )

Aubade[1] (2005)

On a dead street
in a high wall

---

[4]*Weave . . . thrice:* A magic ritual to keep away intruding spirits.
[1]*Aubade:* A song for the morning.

a wooden gate
I don't recall

ever seeing open   5
is today
and I who happen
to pass this way

in passing glimpse
a garden lit   10
by dark lamps
at the heart of it.

E. E. CUMMINGS (1894–1962)

Buffalo Bill's (1923)

Buffalo Bill's
defunct
    who used to
    ride a watersmooth-silver
                  stallion   5
and break onetwothreefourfive pigeonsjustlikethat
                            Jesus
he was a handsome man
             and what i want to know is
how do you like your blueeyed boy   10
Mister Death

E. E. CUMMINGS (1894–1962)

next to of course god america i (1926)

"next to of course god america i
love you land of the pilgrims' and so forth oh
say can you see by the dawn's early my
country 'tis of centuries come and go
and are no more what of it we should worry   5
in every language even deafanddumb
thy sons acclaim your glorious name by gorry
by jingo by gee by gosh by gum
why talk of beauty what could be more beautiful than these heroic happy dead   10
who rushed like lions to the roaring slaughter
they did not stop to think they died instead
then shall the voice of liberty be mute?"

He spoke. And drank rapidly a glass of water

JIM DANIELS (1956–   )

Short-Order Cook (1985)

An average joe comes in
and orders thirty cheeseburgers and thirty fries.

I wait for him to pay before I start cooking.
He pays.
He ain't no average joe.   5

The grill is just big enough for ten rows of three.
I slap the burgers down
throw two buckets of fries in the deep frier
and they pop pop, spit spit . . .
pssss . . .   10
The counter girls laugh.
I concentrate.
It is the crucial point—
they are ready for the cheese:
my fingers shake as I tear off slices   15
toss them on the burgers/fries done/dump
refill buckets/burgers ready/flip into buns/
beat that melting cheese/wrap burgers in plastic/
into paper bags/fried done/dump/fill thirty bags/
bring them to the counter/wipe sweat on sleeve   20
and smile at the counter girls.
I puff my chest out and bellow:
Thirty cheeseburgers! Thirty fries!
I grab a handful of ice, toss it in my mouth
do a little dance and walk back to the grill.   25
Pressure, responsibility, success.
Thirty cheeseburgers, thirty fries.

EMILY DICKINSON (1830–1886)

After great pain, a formal feeling comes— (1862)

After great pain, a formal feeling comes—
The Nerves sit ceremonious, like Tombs—
The stiff Heart questions was it He, that bore,
And Yesterday, or Centuries before?

The Feet, mechanical, go round—   5
Of Ground, or Air, or Ought—
A Wooden way
Regardless grown,
A Quartz contentment, like a stone—

This is the Hour of Lead—   10
Remembered, if outlived,
As Freezing persons, recollect the Snow—
First—Chill—then Stupor—then the letting go—

EMILY DICKINSON (1830–1886)

Because I could not stop for Death— (1863)

Because I could not stop for Death—
He kindly stopped for me—
The Carriage held but just Ourselves—
And Immortality.

We slowly drove—He knew no haste   5
And I had put away
My labor and my leisure too,
For His Civility—

We passed the School, where Children strove
At Recess—in the Ring—   10
We passed the Fields of Gazing Grain—
We passed the Setting Sun—

Or rather—He passed Us—
The Dews drew quivering and chill—
For only Gossamer, my Gown—   15
My Tippet[1]—only Tulle—

We passed before a House that seemed
A Swelling of the Ground—
The Roof was scarcely visible—
The Cornice—in the Ground—   20

Since then—'tis Centuries—and yet
Feels shorter than the Day
I first surmised the Horses' Heads
Were toward Eternity—

EMILY DICKINSON (1830–1886)

"Faith" is a fine invention (1860)

"Faith" is a fine invention
When Gentlemen can *see*—
But *Microscopes* are prudent
In an Emergency.

---

[1]*Tippet:* A short cape or scarf.

EMILY DICKINSON (1830–1886)

"Hope" is the thing with feathers— (1861)

"Hope" is the thing with feathers—
That perches in the soul—
And sings the tune without the words—
And never stops—at all—

And sweetest—in the Gale—is heard—   5
And sore must be the storm—
That could abash the little Bird—
That kept so many warm—

I've heard it in the chillest land—
And on the strangest Sea—   10
Yet, never, in Extremity,
It asked a crumb—of Me.

EMILY DICKINSON (1830–1886)

I dwell in Possibility— (1862)

I dwell in Possibility—
A fairer House than Prose—
More numerous of Windows—
Superior—for Doors—

Of Chambers as the Cedars—   5
Impregnable of Eye—
And for an Everlasting Roof
The Gambrels[1] of the Sky—

Of Visitors—the fairest—
For Occupation—This—   10
The spreading wide my narrow Hands
To gather Paradise—

EMILY DICKINSON (1830–1886)

I heard a Fly buzz—when I died— (1862)

I heard a Fly buzz—when I died—
The Stillness in the Room
Was like the Stillness in the Air—
Between the Heaves of Storm—

---

[1]*Gambrels:* A gambrel roof; a ridged roof with two slopes on each side.

The Eyes around—had wrung them dry—   5
And Breaths were gathering firm
For that last Onset—when the King
Be witnessed—in the Room—

I willed my Keepsakes—Signed away
What portion of me be   10
Assignable—and then it was
There interposed a Fly—

With Blue—uncertain stumbling Buzz—
Between the light—and me—
And then the Windows failed—and then   15
I could not see to see—

EMILY DICKINSON (1830–1886)

I never saw a Moor—   (1865)

I never saw a Moor—
I never saw the Sea—
Yet know I how the Heather looks
And what a Billow be.

I never spoke with God   5
Nor visited in Heaven—
Yet certain am I of the spot
As if the Checks were given—

EMILY DICKINSON (1830–1886)

I taste a liquor never brewed—   (1861)

I taste a liquor never brewed—
From Tankards scooped in Pearl—
Not all the Frankfort Berries[1]
Yield such an Alcohol!

Inebriate of Air—am I—   5
and Debauchee of Dew—
Reeling—thro endless summer days—
From inns of Molten Blue—

When "Landlords" turn the drunken Bee
Out of the Foxglove's door—   10

---

[1] *Frankfort Berries:* The 1890 Higginson and Todd edition *Poems* changed "Frankfort Berries" to "vats upon the Rhine."

When Butterflies—renounce their "drams"—
I shall but drink the more!

Till Seraphs swing their snowy Hats—
And Saints—to windows run—
To see the little Tippler   15
From Manzanilla come!

EMILY DICKINSON (1830–1886)

Much Madness is divinest Sense— (1862)

Much Madness is divinest Sense—
To a discerning Eye—
Much Sense—the starkest Madness—
'Tis the Majority
In this, as All, prevail—   5

Assent—and you are sane—
Demur—you're straightway dangerous—
And handled with a Chain—

EMILY DICKINSON (1830–1886)

My Life had stood—a Loaded Gun (c. 1863)

My Life had stood—a Loaded Gun—
In Corners—till a Day
The Owner passed—identified—
And carried Me away—

And now We roam in Sovereign Woods—   5
And now We hunt the Doe—
And every time I speak for Him—
The Mountains straight reply—

And do I smile, such cordial light
Upon the Valley glow—   10
It is as a Vesuvian[1] face
Had let its pleasure through—

And when at Night—Our good Day done—
I guard My Master's Head—
'Tis better than the Eider-Duck's[2]   15
Deep Pillow—to have shared—

---

[1] *Vesuvian:* The volcano Mount Vesuvius erupted in A.D. 79, destroying the city of Pompeii.

[2] *Eider-Duck's:* Eider ducks produce a soft down (eiderdown) used as pillow stuffing.

To foe of His—I'm deadly foe—
None stir the second time—
On whom I lay a Yellow Eye—
Or an emphatic Thumb—   20

Though I than He—may longer live
He longer must—than I—
For I have but the power to kill,
Without—the power to die—

EMILY DICKINSON (1830–1886)

The Soul selects her own Society— (1862)

The Soul selects her own Society—
Then—shuts the Door—
To her divine Majority—
Present no more—

Unmoved—she notes the Chariots—pausing—   5
At her low Gate—
Unmoved—an Emperor be kneeling
Upon her Mat—

I've known her—from an ample nation—
Choose One—
Then—close the Valves of her attention—   10
Like Stone—

EMILY DICKINSON (1830–1886)

Success is counted sweetest (1859)

Success is counted sweetest
By those who ne'er succeed.
To comprehend a nectar[1]
Requires sorest need.

Not one of all the purple Host   5
Who took the Flag today
Can tell the definition
So clear of Victory

As he defeated—dying—
On whose forbidden ear   10
The distant strains of triumph
Burst agonized and clear!

---

[1] *nectar:* In Greek mythology, the drink of the gods.

EMILY DICKINSON (1830–1886)

Tell all the Truth but tell it slant— (1868)

Tell all the Truth but tell it slant—
Success in Circuit lies
Too bright for our infirm Delight
The Truth's superb surprise
As Lightning to the Children eased   5
With explanation kind
The Truth must dazzle gradually
Or every man be blind—

EMILY DICKINSON (1830–1886)

There is no Frigate like a Book (1873)

There is no Frigate like a Book
To take us Lands away
Nor any Coursers like a Page
Of prancing Poetry—
This Traverse may the poorest take   5
Without oppress of Toll—
How frugal is the Chariot
That bears the Human soul.

EMILY DICKINSON (1830–1886)

There's a certain Slant of light (c. 1861)

There's a certain Slant of light,
Winter Afternoons—
That oppresses, like the Heft
Of Cathedral Tunes—

Heavenly Hurt, it gives us—   5
We can find no scar,
But internal difference,
Where the Meanings, are—

None may teach it—Any—
'Tis the Seal Despair—   10
An imperial affliction
Sent us of the Air—

When it comes, the landscape listens—
Shadows—hold their breath—
When it goes, 'tis like the Distance   15
On the look of Death—

EMILY DICKINSON (1830–1886)

This is my letter to the World (1862)

This is my letter to the World
That never wrote to Me—
The simple News that Nature told—
With tender Majesty

Her Message is committed   5
To Hands I cannot see
For love of Her—Sweet—countrymen—
Judge tenderly—of Me

EMILY DICKINSON (1830–1886)

Wild Nights—Wild Nights! (1861)

Wild Nights—Wild Nights!
Were I with thee
Wild Nights should be
Our luxury!

Futile—the Winds—   5
To a Heart in port—
Done with the Compass—
Done with the Chart!

Rowing in Eden—
Ah, the Sea!   10
Might I but moor—Tonight—
In Thee!

JOHN DONNE (1572–1631)

Batter My Heart, Three-Personed God (c. 1610)

Batter my heart, three-personed God, for You
As yet but knock, breathe, shine, and seek to mend.
That I may rise and stand, o'erthrow me, and bend
Your force to break, blow, burn, and make me new.
I, like an usurped town to another due,   5
Labor to admit You, but Oh! to no end.
Reason, Your viceroy in me, me should defend,
But is captived, and proves weak or untrue.
Yet dearly I love You, and would be lovèd fain,
But am betrothed unto Your enemy;   10

Divorce me, untie or break that knot again;
Take me to You, imprison me, for I,
Except You enthrall me, never shall be free,
Nor ever chaste, except You ravish me.

JOHN DONNE (1572–1631)

Death Be Not Proud (c. 1610)

Death be not proud, though some have callèd thee
Mighty and dreadful, for thou art not so;
For those whom thou think'st thou dost overthrow
Die not, poor death, nor yet canst thou kill me.
From rest and sleep, which but thy pictures be,   5
Much pleasure, then from thee much more must flow,
And soonest our best men with thee do go,
Rest of their bones, and soul's delivery.
Thou art slave to fate, chance, kings, and desperate men,
And dost with poison, war, and sickness dwell,   10
And poppy, or charms can make us sleep as well,
And better than thy stroke; why swell'st thou then?
One short sleep past, we wake eternally,
And death shall be no more; death, thou shalt die.

JOHN DONNE (1572–1631)

The Flea (1633)

Mark but this flea, and mark in this[1]
How little that which thou deny'st me is;
It sucked me first, and now sucks thee,
And in this flea our two bloods mingled be;
Thou know'st that this cannot be said   5
A sin, nor shame, nor loss of maidenhead,
    Yet this enjoys before it woo,
    And pampered swells with one blood made of two,
    And this, alas, is more than we would do.[2]

Oh stay, three lives in one flea spare,   10
Where we almost, yea more than, married are.
This flea is you and I, and this
Our marriage bed, and marriage temple is;

[1] *mark in this:* Note the moral lesson in it.
[2] *more than we would do:* If we do not join our blood.

Though parents grudge, and you, we're met
And cloistered in these living walls of jet. 15
    Though use make you apt to kill me,
    Let not to that, self-murder added be,
    And sacrilege, three sins in killing three.

Cruel and sudden, hast thou since
Purpled thy nail in blood of innocence? 20
Wherein could this flea guilty be,
Except in that drop which it sucked from thee?
Yet thou triumph'st, and say'st that thou
Find'st not thyself, nor me, the weaker now;
    'Tis true; then learn how false, fears be; 25
    Just so much honor, when thou yield'st to me,
    Will waste, as this flea's death took life from thee.

DENISE DUHAMEL (1961–   )

Buddhist Barbie (1997)

In the 5th century B.C.
an Indian philosopher
Gautama teaches "All is emptiness"
and "There is no self."
In the 20th century A.D. 5
Barbie agrees, but wonders how a man
with such a belly could pose,
smiling, and without a shirt.

T. S. ELIOT (1888–1965)

The Love Song of J. Alfred Prufrock (1917)

S'io credessi che mia risposta fosse
A persona che mai tornasse al mondo,
Questa fiamma staria senza piu scosse.
Ma perciocche giammai di questo fondo
Non torno vivo alcun, s'i'odo il vero,
Senza tema d'infamia ti rispondo.[1]

Let us go then, you and I,
When the evening is spread out against the sky

[1]*S'io . . . rispondo:* The epigraph is from Dante's *Inferno*, Canto 27. In response to the poet's question about his identity, Guido da Montefelto, who for his sin of fraud must spend eternity wrapped in flames, replies: "If I thought that I was speaking to someone who could go back to the world, this flame would shake me no more. But since from this place nobody ever returns alive, if what I hear is true, I answer you without fear of infamy."

Like a patient etherized upon a table;
Let us go, through certain half-deserted streets,
The muttering retreats   5
Of restless nights in one-night cheap hotels
And sawdust restaurants with oyster-shells:
Streets that follow like a tedious argument
Of insidious intent
To lead you to an overwhelming question . . .   10
Oh, do not ask, "What is it?"
Let us go and make our visit.

In the room the women come and go
Talking of Michelangelo.

The yellow fog that rubs its back upon the window-panes,   15
The yellow smoke that rubs its muzzle on the window-panes
Licked its tongue into the corners of the evening,
Lingered upon the pools that stand in drains,
Let fall upon its back the soot that falls from chimneys,
Slipped by the terrace, made a sudden leap,   20
And seeing that it was a soft October night,
Curled once about the house, and fell asleep.

And indeed there will be time
For the yellow smoke that slides along the street,
Rubbing its back upon the window-panes;   25
There will be time, there will be time
To prepare a face to meet the faces that you meet;
There will be time to murder and create,
And time for all the works and days² of hands
That lift and drop a question on your plate;   30
Time for you and time for me,
And time yet for a hundred indecisions,
And for a hundred visions and revisions,
Before the taking of a toast and tea.

In the room the women come and go   35
Talking of Michelangelo.

And indeed there will be time
To wonder, "Do I dare?" and, "Do I dare?"
Time to turn back and descend the stair,
With a bald spot in the middle of my hair—   40
(They will say: "How his hair is growing thin!")
My morning coat, my collar mounting firmly to the chin,

---

²*works and days: Works and Days,* by the eighth-century B.C. Greek poet Hesiod, is a poem that celebrates farm life.

My necktie rich and modest, but asserted by a simple pin—
(They will say: "But how his arms and legs are thin!")
Do I dare   45
Disturb the universe?
In a minute there is time
For decisions and revisions which a minute will reverse.

For I have known them all already, known them all—
Have known the evenings, mornings, afternoons,   50
I have measured out my life with coffee spoons;
I know the voices dying with a dying fall³
Beneath the music from a farther room.
    So how should I presume?

And I have known the eyes already, known them all—   55
The eyes that fix you in a formulated phrase,
And when I am formulated, sprawling on a pin,
When I am pinned and wriggling on the wall,
Then how should I begin
To spit out all the butt-ends of my days and ways?   60
    And how should I presume?

And I have known the arms already, known them all—
Arms that are braceleted and white and bare
(But in the lamplight, downed with light brown hair!)
Is it perfume from a dress   65
That makes me so digress?
Arms that lie along a table, or wrap about a shawl.
    And should I then presume?
    And how should I begin?

       • • • • •

Shall I say, I have gone at dusk through narrow streets   70
And watched the smoke that rises from the pipes
Of lonely men in shirt-sleeves, leaning out of windows? . . .

I should have been a pair of ragged claws
Scuttling across the floors of silent seas.

       • • • • •

And the afternoon, the evening, sleeps so peacefully!   75
Smoothed by long fingers,
Asleep . . . tired . . . or it malingers,

---

³*dying fall:* An allusion to Orsino's speech in *Twelfth Night* (1.1): "That strain again! It had a dying fall."

Stretched on the floor, here beside you and me.
Should I, after tea and cakes and ices,
Have the strength to force the moment to its crisis?   80
But though I have wept and fasted, wept and prayed,
Though I have seen my head (grown slightly bald) brought in
    upon a platter,[4]
I am no prophet—and here's no great matter;
I have seen the moment of my greatness flicker,
And I have seen the eternal Footman[5] hold my coat, and   85
    snicker,
And in short, I was afraid.

And would it have been worth it, after all,
After the cups, the marmalade, the tea,
Among the porcelain, among some talk of you and me,
Would it have been worth while,   90
To have bitten off the matter with a smile,
To have squeezed the universe into a ball
To roll it toward some overwhelming question,
To say: "I am Lazarus,[6] come from the dead,
Come back to tell you all, I shall tell you all"—   95
If one, settling a pillow by her head,
    Should say: "That is not what I meant at all.
    That is not it, at all."

And would it have been worth it, after all,
Would it have been worth while,   100
After the sunsets and the dooryards and the sprinkled streets,
After the novels, after the teacups, after the skirts that trail
    along the floor—
And this, and so much more?—
It is impossible to say just what I mean!
But as if a magic lantern threw the nerves in patterns on a   105
    screen:
Would it have been worth while
If one, settling a pillow or throwing off a shawl,
And turning toward the window, should say:
    "That is not it at all,
    That is not what I meant, at all."   110

---

[4] *head . . . platter:* Like John the Baptist, who was beheaded by King Herod (see Matthew 14.3–11).

[5] *eternal Footman:* Perhaps death or fate.

[6] *Lazarus:* A man whom Christ raised from the dead (see John 11.1–44).

• • • • •

No! I am not Prince Hamlet, nor was meant to be;
Am an attendant lord, one that will do
To swell a progress,[7] start a scene or two,
Advise the prince; no doubt, an easy tool,
Deferential, glad to be of use,   115
Politic, cautious, and meticulous;
Full of high sentence,[8] but a bit obtuse;
At times, indeed, almost ridiculous—
Almost, at times, the Fool.

I grow old . . . I grow old . . .   120
I shall wear the bottoms of my trousers rolled.

Shall I part my hair behind? Do I dare to eat a peach?
I shall wear white flannel trousers, and walk upon the beach.
I have heard the mermaids singing, each to each.

I do not think that they will sing to me.   125

I have seen them riding seaward on the waves
Combing the white hair of the waves blown back
When the wind blows the water white and black.

We have lingered in the chambers of the sea
By sea-girls wreathed with seaweed red and brown   130
Till human voices wake us, and we drown.

JAMES A. EMANUEL (1921–   )

Emmett Till[1] (1968)

I hear a whistling
Through the water.
Little Emmett
Won't be still.
He keeps floating   5
Round the darkness,

---

[7]*a progress:* Here, in the Elizabethan sense of a royal journey.

[8]*sentence:* Opinions.

[1]*Emmett Till:* Emmett Till, a fourteen-year-old African American boy from Chicago, was visiting relatives in Mississippi when he allegedly whistled at a white woman who ran a local store. Unfamiliar with the racial climate of the South, he did not realize that his actions would generate a savage response. Several days later, he was kidnapped, and his severely beaten and mutilated body was later found in the river with a heavy cotton gin fan tied around his neck with barbed wire. His death prompted a new chapter in the Civil Rights struggle; the investigation into his murder was reopened in 2004.

Edging through
The silent chill.
Tell me, please,
That bedtime story   10
Of the fairy
River Boy
Who swims forever,
Deep in treasures,
Necklaced in   15
A coral toy.

LOUISE ERDRICH (1954–   )

Indian Boarding School: The Runaways (1984)

Home's the place we head for in our sleep.
Boxcars stumbling north in dreams
don't wait for us. We catch them on the run.
The rails, old lacerations that we love,
shoot parallel across the face and break   5
just under Turtle Mountains.[1] Riding scars
you can't get lost. Home is the place they cross.

The lame guard strikes a match and makes the dark
less tolerant. We watch through cracks in boards
as the land starts rolling, rolling till it hurts   10
to be here, cold in regulation clothes.
We know the sheriff's waiting at midrun
to take us back. His car is dumb and warm.
The highway doesn't rock, it only hums
like a wing of long insults. The worn-down welts   15
of ancient punishments lead back and forth.

All runaways wear dresses, long green ones,
the color you would think shame was. We scrub
the sidewalks down because it's shameful work.
Our brushes cut the stone in watered arcs   20
and in the soak frail outlines shiver clear
a moment, things us kids pressed on the dark
face before it hardened, pale, remembering
delicate old injuries, the spines of names and leaves.

---

[1] *Turtle Mountains:* Erdrich is a descendant of the Turtle Mountain band of the Chippewa.

MARTÍN ESPADA (1957–   )

The Community College Revises Its Curriculum in Response to Changing Demographics (2000)

SPA 100 Conversational Spanish
2 credits

The course
is especially concerned
with giving police
the ability
to express themselves   5
tersely
in matters of interest
to them

ROBERT FROST (1874–1963)

Acquainted with the Night (1928)

I have been one acquainted with the night.
I have walked out in rain—and back in rain.
I have outwalked the furthest city light.

I have looked down the saddest city lane.
I have passed by the watchman on his beat   5
And dropped my eyes, unwilling to explain.

I have stood still and stopped the sound of feet
When far away an interrupted cry
Came over houses from another street,

But not to call me back or say good-by;   10
And further still at an unearthly height,
One luminary clock against the sky

Proclaimed the time was neither wrong nor right.
I have been one acquainted with the night.

ROBERT FROST (1874–1963)

Design (1936)

I found a dimpled spider, fat and white,
On a white heal-all,[1] holding up a moth

---

[1] *heal-all:* A perennial weed with flowers ranging from light blue to purple in color.

Like a white piece of rigid satin cloth—
Assorted characters of death and blight
Mixed ready to begin to morning right,   5
Like the ingredients of a witches' broth—
A snow-drop spider, a flower like a froth,
And dead wings carried like a paper kite.

What had the flower to do with being white,
The wayside blue and innocent heal-all?   10
What brought the kindred spider to that height,
Then steered the white moth thither in the night?
What but design of darkness to appall?—
If design govern in a thing so small.

ROBERT FROST (1874 –1963)

Mending Wall (1914)

Something there is that doesn't love a wall,
That sends the frozen-ground-swell under it,
And spills the upper boulders in the sun;
And makes gaps even two can pass abreast.
The work of hunters is another thing: 5
I have come after them and made repair
Where they have left not one stone on a stone,
But they would have the rabbit out of hiding,
To please the yelping dogs. The gaps I mean,
No one has seen them made or heard them made,   10
But at spring mending-time we find them there.
I let my neighbor know beyond the hill;
And on a day we meet to walk the line
And set the wall between us once again.
We keep the wall between us as we go.   15
To each the boulders that have fallen to each.
And some are loaves and some so nearly balls
We have to use a spell to make them balance:
"Stay where you are until our backs are turned!"
We wear our fingers rough with handling them.   20
Oh, just another kind of outdoor game,
One on a side. It comes to little more:
There where it is we do not need the wall:
He is all pine and I am apple orchard.
My apple trees will never get across   25
And eat the cones under his pines, I tell him.
He only says, "Good fences make good neighbors."

Spring is the mischief in me, and I wonder
If I could put a notion in his head:
"*Why* do they make good neighbors? Isn't it   30
Where there are cows? But here there are no cows.
Before I built a wall I'd ask to know
What I was walling in or walling out,
And to whom I was like to give offense.
Something there is that doesn't love a wall,   35
That wants it down." I could say "Elves" to him,
But it's not elves exactly, and I'd rather
He said it for himself. I see him there
Bringing a stone grasped firmly by the top
In each hand, like an old-stone savage armed.   40
He moves in darkness as it seems to me,
Not of woods only and the shade of trees.
He will not go behind his father's saying,
And he likes having thought of it so well
He says again, "Good fences make good neighbors."   45

THOMAS HARDY (1840–1928)

The Convergence of the Twain (1912)

(Lines on the loss of the "Titanic")

I

    In a solitude of the sea
        Deep from human vanity,
And the Pride of Life that planned her, stilly couches she.

II

    Steel chambers, late the pyres[1]
        Of her salamandrine fires,[2]   5
Cold currents thrid,[3] and turn to rhythmic tidal lyres.

III

    Over the mirrors meant
        To glass the opulent
The sea-worm crawls—grotesque, slimed, dumb, indifferent.

---

[1] *pyres:* Funeral pyres; piles of wood on which corpses were burned in ancient rites.

[2] *salamandrine fires:* An allusion to the old belief that salamanders could live in fire.

[3] *thrid:* Thread (archaic verb form).

IV

Jewels in joy designed
  To ravish the sensuous mind
Lie lightless, all their sparkles bleared and black and blind.   10

V

Dim moon-eyed fishes near
  Gaze at the gilded gear
And query: "What does this vaingloriousness down here?" . . .   15

VI

Well: while was fashioning
  This creature of cleaving wing,
The Immanent[4] Will that stirs and urges everything

VII

Prepared a sinister mate
  For her—so gaily great—   20
A Shape of Ice, for the time far and dissociate.

VIII

And as the smart ship grew
  In stature, grace, and hue,
In shadowy silent distance grew the Iceberg too.

IX

Alien they seemed to be: 25
  No mortal eye could see
The intimate welding of their later history,

X

Or sign that they were bent
  By paths coincident
On being anon[5] twin halves of one august[6] event,   30

XI

Till the Spinner of the Years
  Said "Now!" And each one hears,
And consummation comes, and jars two hemispheres.

---

[4] *Immanent:* Inherent, dwelling within.
[5] *anon:* Soon.
[6] *august:* Awe-inspiring, majestic.

SEAMUS HEANEY (1939–2013)

Mid-Term Break (1966)

I sat all morning in the college sick bay
Counting bells knelling classes to a close.
At two o'clock our neighbors drove me home.

In the porch I met my father crying—
He had always taken funerals in his stride—   5
And Big Jim Evans saying it was a hard blow.

The baby cooed and laughed and rocked the pram
When I came in, and I was embarrassed
By old men standing up to shake my hand

And tell me they were "sorry for my trouble,"   10
Whispers informed strangers I was the eldest,
Away at school, as my mother held my hand

In hers and coughed out angry tearless sighs.
At ten o'clock the ambulance arrived
With the corpse, stanched and bandaged by the nurses.   15

Next morning I went up into the room. Snowdrops
And candles soothed the bedside; I saw him
For the first time in six weeks. Paler now,

Wearing a poppy bruise on his left temple,
He lay in the four foot box as in his cot.   20
No gaudy scars, the bumper knocked him clear.

A four foot box, a foot for every year.

WILLIAM ERNEST HENLEY (1849–1903)

Invictus (1888)

Out of the night that covers me,
Black as the Pit from pole to pole,
I thank whatever gods may be
For my unconquerable soul.

In the fell clutch of circumstance   5
I have not winced nor cried aloud.
Under the bludgeonings of chance
My head is bloody, but unbowed.

Beyond this place of wrath and tears
Looms but the Horror of the shade,   10
And yet the menace of the years
Finds, and shall find, me unafraid.

It matters not how strait the gate,
How charged with punishments the scroll.
I am the master of my fate: 15
I am the captain of my soul.

GERARD MANLEY HOPKINS (1844–1889)

God's Grandeur (1877)

The world is charged with the grandeur of God.
   It will flame out, like shining from shook foil;
   It gathers to a greatness, like the ooze of oil
Crushed. Why do men then now not reck his rod?
Generations have trod, have trod, have trod;   5
   And all is seared with trade; bleared, smeared with toil;
   And wears man's smudge and shares man's smell: the soil
Is bare now, nor can foot feel, being shod.

And for all this, nature is never spent;
   There lives the dearest freshness deep down things;
And though the last lights off the black West went   10
   Oh, morning, at the brown brink eastward, springs—
Because the Holy Ghost over the bent
   World broods with warm breast and with ah! bright wings.

A. E. HOUSMAN (1859–1936)

When I Was One-and-Twenty (1896)

When I was one-and-twenty
   I heard a wise man say,
"Give crowns and pounds and guineas
   But not your heart away;
Give pearls away and rubies   5
   But keep your fancy free."
But I was one-and-twenty,
   No use to talk to me.

When I was one-and-twenty
   I heard him say again,   10

The heart out of the bosom
    Was never given in vain;
'Tis paid with sighs a plenty
    And sold for endless rue."
And I am two-and-twenty,   15
    And oh, 'tis true, 'tis true.

DONALD JUSTICE (1925–2004)

Men at Forty (1967)

Men at forty
Learn to close softly
The doors to rooms they will not be
Coming back to.

At rest on a stair landing,   5
They feel it
Moving beneath them now like the deck of a ship,
Though the swell is gentle.

And deep in mirrors
They rediscover   10
The face of the boy as he practices tying
His father's tie there in secret

And the face of that father,
Still warm with the mystery of lather.
They are more fathers than sons themselves now.   15
Something is filling them, something

That is like the twilight sound
Of the crickets, immense,
Filling the woods at the foot of the slope
Behind their mortgaged houses.   20

JOHN KEATS (1795–1821)

La Belle Dame sans Merci: A Ballad[1] (1819, 1820)

1

O what can ail thee, knight at arms,
    Alone and palely loitering?
The sedge has wither'd from the lake,
    And no birds sing.

---

[1] *"La Belle Dame sans Merci"*: The title, which means "The Lovely Lady without Pity," was taken from a medieval poem by Alain Chartier.

2

O what can ail thee, knight at arms,
   So haggard and so woe-begone?   5
The squirrel's granary is full,
   And the harvest's done.

3

I see a lily on thy brow
   With anguish moist and fever dew,   10
And on thy cheeks a fading rose
   Fast withereth too.

4

I met a lady in the meads,
   Full beautiful, a fairy's child;
Her hair was long, her foot was light,   15
   And her eyes were wild.

5

I made a garland for her head,
   And bracelets too, and fragrant zone;[2]
She look'd at me as she did love,
   And made sweet moan.   20

6

I set her on my pacing steed,
   And nothing else saw all day long,
For sidelong would she bend, and sing
   A fairy's song.

7

She found me roots of relish sweet,   25
   And honey wild, and manna dew,
And sure in language strange she said—
   I love thee true.

8

She took me to her elfin grot,[3]
   And there she wept, and sigh'd full sore,   30
And there I shut her wild wild eyes
   With kisses four.

9

And there she lullèd me asleep,
   And there I dream'd—Ah! woe betide!

---

[2] *fragrant zone:* Belt.

[3] *grot:* Grotto.

The latest[4] dream I ever dream'd   35
   On the cold hill's side.

10

I saw pale kings, and princes too,
   Pale warriors, death pale were they all;
They cried—"La belle dame sans merci
    Hath thee in thrall!"   40

11

I saw their starv'd lips in the gloam[5]
   With horrid warning gapèd wide,
And I awoke and found me here
    On the cold hill's side.

12

And this is why I sojourn here,   45
   Alone and palely loitering,
Though the sedge is wither'd from the lake,
    And no birds sing.

JOHN KEATS (1795–1821)

Ode on a Grecian Urn (1819)

1

Thou still unravish'd bride of quietness,
   Thou foster-child of silence and slow time,
Sylvan[1] historian, who canst thus express
A flowery tale more sweetly than our rhyme:
What leaf-fring'd legend haunts about thy shape   5
   Of deities or mortals, or of both,
    In Tempe[2] or the dales of Arcady?[3]
   What men or gods are these? What maidens loth?
What mad pursuit? What struggle to escape?
What pipes and timbrels? What wild ecstasy?   10

2

Heard melodies are sweet, but those unheard
   Are sweeter; therefore, ye soft pipes, play on;

---

[4] *latest:* Last.

[5] *gloam:* Twilight.

[1] *Sylvan:* Pertaining to woods or forests.

[2] *Tempe:* A beautiful valley in Greece.

[3] *Arcady:* The valleys of Arcadia, a mountainous region on the Greek peninsula. Like Tempe, they represent a rustic pastoral ideal.

Sketch by John Keats of the Sosibios Vase that
may have inspired "Ode on a Grecian Urn"
Keats-Shelley House, Rome, Italy

Not to the sensual ear, but, more endear'd,
  Pipe to the spirit ditties of no tone:
Fair youth, beneath the trees, thou canst not leave   15
  Thy song, nor ever can those trees be bare;
    Bold lover, never, never canst thou kiss,
Though winning near the goal—yet, do not grieve;
    She cannot fade, though thou hast not thy bliss,
For ever wilt thou love, and she be fair!   20

3

Ah, happy, happy boughs! that cannot shed
  Your leaves, nor ever bid the spring adieu;
And, happy melodist, unwearied,
  For ever piping songs for ever new;
More happy love! more happy, happy love!   25
  For ever warm and still to be enjoy'd,
    For ever panting, and for ever young;
All breathing human passion far above,
  That leaves a heart high-sorrowful and cloy'd,
A burning forehead, and a parching tongue.   30

4

Who are these coming to the sacrifice?
  To what green altar, O mysterious priest,
Lead'st thou that heifer lowing at the skies,
  And all her silken flanks with garlands drest?
What little town by river or sea shore,   35
  Or mountain-built with peaceful citadel,
    Is emptied of this folk, this pious morn?
And, little town, thy streets for evermore
  Will silent be; and not a soul to tell
    Why thou art desolate, can e'er return.   40

5

O Attic[4] shape! Fair attitude! with brede[5]
  Of marble men and maidens overwrought,[6]
With forest branches and the trodden weed;
  Thou, silent form, dost tease us out of thought
As doth eternity: Cold Pastoral!   45
  When old age shall this generation waste,
    Thou shalt remain, in midst of other woe
Than ours, a friend to man, to whom thou say'st,
"Beauty is truth, truth beauty,"—that is all
Ye know on earth, and all ye need to know.   50

---

[4]*Attic:* Characteristic of Athens or Athenians.
[5]*brede:* Braid.
[6]*overwrought:* Elaborately ornamented.

JOHN KEATS (1795–1821)

When I Have Fears (1818)

When I have fears that I may cease to be
    Before my pen has gleaned my teeming brain,
Before high-piléd books, in charact'ry,[1]
    Hold like rich garners the full-ripened grain;
When I behold, upon the night's starred face,   5
    Huge cloudy symbols of a high romance,
And think that I may never live to trace
    Their shadows, with the magic hand of chance;
And when I feel, fair creature of an hour,
    That I shall never look upon thee more,   10
Never have relish in the faery power
    Of unreflecting love!—then on the shore
Of the wide world I stand alone, and think
Till Love and Fame to nothingness do sink.

DAVID KEPLINGER (1968–   )

Wave (2013)

Lincoln, leaving Springfield,[1] 1861,
    boards a train with a salute: but it is weak.
To correct it, he slides his hand away
    from his face as if waving, as if brushing
the snows of childhood from his eyes.   5
The train is coming east. In the window
    Lincoln watches his face. You'll grow old
the moment you arrive, he says to this face.
    But you will never reach great age. The train
speeds like the cortical[2] pressure wave   10

in the left lateral sinus,[3] say, a bullet
    in the skull. Then he will have his salute.
Then they will love him. Then eternity will slow, fall
    like snow. Then the treaty with huge silence
which he, his face exhausted, must sign.   15

---

[1] *charact'ry:* Print.

[1] *Springfield:* The capital of Illinois, where Abraham Lincoln lived before being elected president.

[2] *cortical:* Relating to the cerebral cortex, the outer layer of tissue in the brain (Lincoln was shot in the head by his assassin).

[3] *lateral sinus:* A channel that drains blood from the brain.

STEVE KOWIT (1938–   )

The Grammar Lesson (1995)

A noun's a thing. A verb's the thing it does.
An adjective is what describes the noun.
In "The can of beets is filled with purple fuzz"

of and *with* are prepositions. *The*'s
an article, a *can*'s a noun,   5
a noun's a thing. A verb's the thing it does.

A can *can* roll—or not. What isn't was
or might be, *might* meaning not yet known.
"Our can of beets *is* filled with purple fuzz"

is present tense. While words like *our* and *us*   10
are pronouns—i.e. *it* is moldy, *they* are icky brown.
A noun's a thing; a verb's the thing it does.

Is is a helping verb. It helps because
filled isn't a full verb. *Can*'s what *our* owns
in "Our can of beets is filled with purple fuzz."   15

See? There's almost nothing to it. Just
memorize these rules . . . or write them down!
A noun's a thing, a verb's the thing it does.
The can of beets is filled with purple fuzz.

LAM THI MY DA (1949–   )

Bomb Crater Sky (2005)

Translated by Martha Collins and Thuy Dinh

They say that you, a road builder
Had such love for our country
You rushed out and waved your torch
To call the bombs down on yourself
And save the road for the troops   5

As my unit passed on that worn road
The bomb crater reminded us of your story
Your grave is radiant with bright-colored stones
Piled high with love for you, a young girl

As I looked in the bomb crater where you died   10
The rain water became a patch of sky
Our country is kind
Water from the sky washes pain away

Now you lie down deep in the earth
As the sky lay down in that earthen crater   15
At night your soul sheds light
Like the dazzling stars
Did your soft white skin
Become a bank of white clouds?

By day I pass under a sun-flooded sky   20
And it is your sky
And that anxious, wakeful disc
Is it the sun, or is it your heart
Lighting my way
As I walk down the long road?   25

The name of the road is your name
Your death is a young girl's patch of blue sky
My soul is lit by your life

And my friends, who never saw you
Each has a different image of your face   30

PHILIP LARKIN (1922–1985)

The Explosion (1974)

On the day of the explosion
Shadows pointed towards the pithead:
In the sun the slagheap slept.

Down the lane came men in pitboots
Coughing oath-edged talk and pipe-smoke,   5
Shouldering off the freshened silence.

One chased after rabbits; lost them;
Came back with a nest of lark's eggs;
Showed them; lodged them in the grasses.

So they passed in beards and moleskins,   10
Fathers, brothers, nicknames, laughter,
Through the tall gates standing open.

At noon, there came a tremor; cows
Stopped chewing for a second; sun,
Scarfed as in a heat-haze, dimmed.   15

The dead go on before us, they
Are sitting in God's house in comfort,
We shall see them face to face—

Plain as lettering in the chapels
It was said, and for a second   20
Wives saw men of the explosion

Larger than in life they managed—
Gold as on a coin, or walking
Somehow from the sun towards them,

One showing the eggs unbroken.   25

LI-YOUNG LEE (1957–   )

From Blossoms (1986)

From blossoms comes
this brown paper bag of peaches
we bought from the boy
at the bend in the road where we turned toward
signs painted Peaches.   5

From laden boughs, from hands,
from sweet fellowship in the bins,
comes nectar at the roadside, succulent
peaches we devour, dusty skin and all,
comes the familiar dust of summer, dust we eat.   10

O, to take what we love inside,
to carry within us an orchard, to eat
not only the skin, but the shade,
not only the sugar, but the days, to hold
the fruit in our hands, adore it, then bite into   15
the round jubilance of peach.

There are days we live
as if death were nowhere
in the background; from joy
to joy to joy, from wing to wing,   20
from blossom to blossom to
impossible blossom, to sweet impossible blossom.

ROBERT LOWELL (1917–1977)

Skunk Hour (1959)

(For Elizabeth Bishop)

Nautilus Island's hermit
heiress still lives through winter in her Spartan[1] cottage;

---

[1] *Spartan:* Minimal, severe, plain.

her sheep still graze above the sea.
Her son's a bishop. Her farmer
is first selectman in our village;   5
she's in her dotage.

Thirsting for
the hierarchie² privacy
of Queen Victoria's³ century,
she buys up all   10
the eyesores facing her shore,
and lets them fall.

The season's ill—
we've lost our summer millionaire,
who seemed to leap from an L. L. Bean   15
catalogue. His nine-knot yawl
was auctioned off to lobstermen.
A red fox stain covers Blue Hill.

And now our fairy
decorator brightens his shop for fall;   20
his fishnet's filled with orange cork,
orange, his cobbler's⁴ bench and awl;⁵
there is no money in his work,
he'd rather marry.

One dark night,   25
my Tudor Ford climbed the hill's skull;
I watched for love-cars. Lights turned down,
they lay together, hull to hull,
where the graveyard shelves on the town. . . .
My mind's not right.   30

A car radio bleats,
"Love, O careless Love. . . ."⁶ hear
my ill-spirit sob in each blood cell,
as if my hand were at its throat. . . .
I myself am hell;   35
nobody's here—
only skunks, that search
in the moonlight for a bite to eat.
They march on their soles up Main Street:

---

²*Hierachie:* Having to do with hierarchies, or orderings of people or things from higher to lower.

³*Queen Victoria:* Monarch of Great Britain from 1837–1901.

⁴*Cobbler:* One who mends shoes.

⁵*awl:* A tool for making holes in leather.

⁶"*Love, O careless Love. . . .*": Lyrics to a traditional song.

white stripes, moonstruck eyes' red fire   40
under the chalk-dry and spar spire
of the Trinitarian Church.

I stand on top
of our back steps and breathe the rich air—
a mother skunk with her column of kittens swills the garbage pail.   45
She jabs her wedge-head in a cup
of sour cream, drops her ostrich tail,
and will not scare.

ARCHIBALD MACLEISH (1892–1982)

Ars Poetica[1] (1926)

A poem should be palpable and mute
As a globed fruit,

Dumb
As old medallions to the thumb,

Silent as the sleeve-worn stone   5
Of casement ledges where the moss has grown—

A poem should be wordless
As the flight of birds.

A poem should be motionless in time
As the moon climbs,   10

Leaving, as the moon releases
Twig by twig the night-entangled trees,

Leaving, as the moon behind the winter leaves,
Memory by memory the mind—

A poem should be motionless in time   15
As the moon climbs.

A poem should be equal to:
Not true.

For all the history of grief
An empty doorway and a maple leaf.   20

For love
The leaning grasses and two lights above the sea—

A poem should not mean
But be.

---

[1] *Ars Poetica:* "The Art of Poetry" (Latin).

CHRISTOPHER MARLOWE (1564–1593)

The Passionate Shepherd to His Love (1600)

Come live with me and be my love,
And we will all the pleasures prove
That valleys, groves, hills, and fields,
Woods, or steepy mountain yields.

And we will sit upon the rocks,   5
Seeing the shepherds feed their flocks
By shallow rivers, to whose falls
Melodious birds sing madrigals.

And I will make thee beds of roses
And a thousand fragrant posies,   10
A cap of flowers and a kirtle[1]
Embroidered all with leaves of myrtle;

A gown made of the finest wool
Which from our pretty lambs we pull;
Fair-linèd slippers for the cold,   15
With buckles of the purest gold;

A belt of straw and ivy buds,
With coral clasps and amber studs.
And if these pleasures may thee move,
Come live with me and be my love.   20

The shepherds' swains shall dance and sing
For thy delight each May morning.
If these delights thy mind may move,
Then live with me and be my love.

CLAUDE MCKAY (1890–1948)

If We Must Die (1922)

If we must die, let it not be like hogs
Hunted and penned in an inglorious spot,
While round us bark the mad and hungry dogs,
Making their mock at our accursed lot.
If we must die, O let us nobly die,   5
So that our precious blood may not be shed
In vain; then even the monsters we defy
Shall be constrained to honor us though dead!
O kinsmen! we must meet the common foe!

---

[1] *kirtle:* Skirt.

Though far outnumbered let us show us brave,   10
And for their thousand blows deal one deathblow!
What though before us lies the open grave?
Like men we'll face the murderous, cowardly pack,
Pressed to the wall, dying, but fighting back!

JOHN MILTON (1608–1674)

When I consider how my light is spent[1] (1655?)

When I consider how my light is spent,
　　Ere half my days in this dark world and wide,
　　And that one talent[2] which is death to hide
Lodged with me useless, though my soul more bent
To serve therewith my Maker, and present   5
　　My true account, lest He returning chide;
　　"Doth God exact day-labor, light denied?"
I fondly[3] ask. But Patience, to prevent
That murmur, soon replies, "God doth not need
　　Either man's work or His own gifts. Who best   10
　　Bear His mild yoke, they serve Him best. His state
Is kingly: thousands at His bidding speed,
And post o'er land and ocean without rest;
They also serve who only stand and wait."

PAT MORA (1942–   )

La Migra[1] (1993)

I

Let's play *La Migra*
I'll be the Border Patrol.
You be the Mexican maid.
I get the badge and sunglasses.
You can hide and run,   5
but you can't get away
because I have a jeep.
I can take you wherever
I want, but don't ask
questions because   10
I don't speak Spanish.

---

[1] *how my light is spent:* A meditation on his blindness.

[2] *one talent:* See Jesus' parable of the talents in Matthew 25.14–30.

[3] *fondly:* Foolishly.

[1] *La Migra:* Mexican slang for U.S. border patrol.

I can touch you wherever
I want but don't complain
too much because I've got
boots and kick—if I have to,   15
and I have handcuffs.
Oh, and a gun.
Get ready, get set, run.

II

Let's play *La Migra*
You be the Border Patrol.   20
I'll be the Mexican woman.
Your jeep has a flat,
and you have been spotted
by the sun.
All you have is heavy: hat   25
glasses, badge, shoes, gun.
I know this desert,
where to rest,
where to drink.
Oh, I am not alone.   30
You hear us singing
and laughing with the wind,
Agua dulce brota aqui,
aqui, aqui[2] but since you
can't speak Spanish,   35
you do not understand.
Get ready.

PABLO NERUDA (1904–1973)

Tonight I Can Write (1924)

Translated by W. S. Merwin

Tonight I can write the saddest lines.

Write, for example, 'The night is starry
and the stars are blue and shiver in the distance.'
The night wind revolves in the sky and sings.

Tonight I can write the saddest lines.   5
I loved her, and sometimes she loved me too.

Through nights like this one I held her in my arms.
I kissed her again and again under the endless sky.

---

[2] *Agua . . . aqui:* Sweet water springs here, here, here.

She loved me, sometimes I loved her too.
How could one not have loved her great still eyes.   10

Tonight I can write the saddest lines.
To think that I do not have her. To feel that I have lost her,

To hear the immense night, still more immense without her,
And the verse falls to the soul like dew to the pasture.

What does it matter that my love could not keep her.   15
The night is starry and she is not with me.

This is all. In the distance someone is singing. In the distance.
My soul is not satisfied that it has lost her.

My sight tries to find her as though to bring her closer.
My heart looks for her, and she is not with me.   20

The same night whitening the same trees.
We, of that time, are no longer the same.

I no longer love her, that's certain, but how I loved her.
My voice tried to find the wind to touch her hearing.

Another's. She will be another's. As she was before my kisses.   25
Her voice, her bright body. Her infinite eyes.

I no longer love her, that's certain, but maybe I love her.
Love is so short, forgetting is so long.

Because through nights like this one I held her in my arms
my soul is not satisfied that it has lost her.   30

Though this be the last pain that she makes me suffer
And these the last verses that I write for her.

PABLO NERUDA (1904–1973)

The United Fruit Co.[1] (1950)

Translated by Robert Bly

When the trumpet sounded, it was
all prepared on the earth,
and Jehovah parceled out the earth
to Coca-Cola, Inc., Anaconda,
Ford Motors, and other entities: 5
The Fruit Company, Inc.
reserved for itself the most succulent,
the central coast of my own land,
the delicate waist of America.

---

[1] *United Fruit Co.:* Incorporated in New Jersey in 1899 by Andrew Preston and Minor C. Keith, United Fruit became a major force in growing, transporting, and merchandising Latin American produce, especially bananas. The company is notorious for its involvement in politics, and as a result its name came to represent "Yankee" imperialism and oppression.

It rechristened its territories   10
as the "Banana Republics"
and over the sleeping dead,
over the restless heroes
who brought about the greatness,
the liberty and the flags,   15
it established the comic opera:
abolished the independencies,
presented crowns of Caesar,
unsheathed envy, attracted
the dictatorship of the flies,   20
Trujillo flies, Tacho flies,
Carias flies, Martinez flies,
Ubico flies,[2] damp flies
of modest blood and marmalade,
drunken flies who zoom   25
over the ordinary graves,
circus flies, wise flies
well trained in tyranny.
Among the bloodthirsty flies
the Fruit Company lands its ships,   30
taking off the coffee and the fruit;
the treasure of our submerged
territories flows as though
on plates into the ships.
Meanwhile Indians are falling   35
into the sugared chasms
of the harbors, wrapped
for burial in the mist of the dawn:
a body rolls, a thing
that has no name, a fallen cipher,   40
a cluster of dead fruit
thrown down on the dump.

Source: ©Goodman/Van Riper Photography

LINDA PASTAN (1932–   )

Ethics (1980)

In ethics class so many years ago
our teacher asked this question every fall:
if there were a fire in a museum
which would you save, a Rembrandt painting
or an old woman who hadn't many   5
years left anyhow? Restless on hard chairs
caring little for pictures or old age

---

[2]*Trujillo, Tacho, Carias, Martinez, Ubico:* Political dictators.

we'd opt one year for life, the next for art
and always half-heartedly. Sometimes
the woman borrowed my grandmother's face   10
leaving her usual kitchen to wander
some drafty, half imagined museum.
One year, feeling clever, I replied
why not let the woman decide herself?
Linda, the teacher would report, eschews   15
the burdens of responsibility.
This fall in a real museum I stand
before a real Rembrandt, old woman,
or nearly so, myself. The colors
within this frame are darker than autumn,   20
darker even than winter—the browns of earth,
though earth's most radiant elements burn
through the canvas. I know now that woman
and painting and season are almost one
and all beyond saving by children.   25

LINDA PASTAN (1932–   )

Marks (1978)

My husband gives me an A
for last night's supper,
an incomplete for my ironing,
a B plus in bed.
My son says I am average,   5
an average mother, but if
I put my mind to it
I could improve.
My daughter believes
in Pass/Fail and tells me   10
I pass. Wait 'til they learn
I'm dropping out.

LEROY V. QUINTANA (1944–   )

Poem for Salt (1999)

The biggest snowstorm to hit Denver in twenty years.
What is the world to do, freed from the shackles
of the eight hours needed to earn its daily salary?

Only on a day such as this does salt overshadow gold.
Salt, with its lips of blue fire, common as gossip,   5

ordinary as sin. Like true love and gasoline,
missed only when they run out. Salt spilling
from a blue container a young girl is holding,
along with an umbrella, on the label of a blue
container of salt that the woman across the street,   10
under her umbrella is pouring behind her left rear wheel;
to no avail this discontented, unbuttoned December
    morning.

SIR WALTER RALEIGH (1552–1618)

The Nymph's Reply to the Shepherd (1600)

If all the world and love were young,
And truth in every shepherd's tongue,
These pretty pleasures might me move
To live with thee and be thy love.

Time drives the flocks from field to fold,   5
When rivers rage and rocks grow cold;
And Philomel[1] becometh dumb;
The rest complains of cares to come.

The flowers do fade, and wanton fields
To wayward winter reckoning yields: 10
A honey tongue, a heart of gall,
Is fancy's spring, but sorrow's fall.

Thy gowns, thy shoes, thy beds of roses,
Thy cap, thy kirtle, and thy posies
Soon break, soon wither, soon forgotten,   15
In folly ripe, in reason rotten.

Thy belt of straw and ivy buds,
Thy coral clasps and amber studs.
All these in me no means can move
To come to thee and be thy love.   20

But could youth last, and love still breed,
Had joys no date, nor age no need,
Then these delights my mind might move
To live with thee and be thy love.

---

[1] *Philomel:* The nightingale.

Bettmann/Corbis

EDWIN ARLINGTON ROBINSON (1869–1935)

Miniver Cheevy (1910)

Miniver Cheevy, child of scorn,
   Grew lean while he assailed the seasons;
He wept that he was ever born,
   And he had reasons.

Miniver loved the days of old   5
   When swords were bright and steeds were prancing;
The vision of a warrior bold
   Would set him dancing.

Miniver sighed for what was not,
   And dreamed, and rested from his labors;   10
He dreamed of Thebes[1] and Camelot,[2]
   And Priam's neighbors.[3]

Miniver mourned the ripe renown
   That made so many a name so fragrant;
He mourned Romance, now on the town,   15
   And Art, a vagrant.

Miniver loved the Medici,[4]
   Albeit he had never seen one;
He would have sinned incessantly
   Could he have been one.   20

Miniver cursed the commonplace
   And eyed a khaki suit with loathing;
He missed the medieval grace
   Of iron clothing.

Miniver scorned the gold he sought,   25
   But sore annoyed was he without it;
Miniver thought, and thought, and thought,
   And thought about it.

Miniver Cheevy, born too late,
   Scratched his head and kept on thinking;   30
Miniver coughed, and called it fate,
   And kept on drinking.

---

[1] *Thebes:* The setting of many Greek legends, including that of Oedipus.

[2] *Camelot:* The legendary site of King Arthur's court.

[3] *Priam's neighbors:* Priam was the last king of Troy; his "neighbors" included Helen, Aeneas, and Hector.

[4] *Medici:* Rulers of Florence, Italy, from the fifteenth through the eighteenth centuries. During the Renaissance, Lorenzo de Medici was a renowned patron of the arts.

EDWIN ARLINGTON ROBINSON (1869–1935)

Richard Cory (1897)

Whenever Richard Cory went down town,
We people on the pavement looked at him:
He was a gentleman from sole to crown,
Clean favored, and imperially slim.

And he was always quietly arrayed,   5
And he was always human when he talked;
But still he fluttered pulses when he said,
"Good-morning," and he glittered when he walked.

And he was rich—yes, richer than a king—
And admirably schooled in every grace: 10
In fine, we thought that he was everything
To make us wish that we were in his place.

So on we worked, and waited for the light,
And went without the meat, and cursed the bread;
And Richard Cory, one calm summer night,   15
Went home and put a bullet through his head.

CYNTHIA RYLANT (1954–   )

God Went to Beauty School (2003)

He went there to learn how
to give a good perm
and ended up just crazy
about nails
so He opened up His own shop.   5
"Nails by Jim" He called it.
He was afraid to call it
Nails by God.
He was sure people would
think He was being   10
disrespectful and using
His own name in vain
and nobody would tip.
He got into nails, of course,
because He'd always loved   15
hands—
hands were some of the best things
He'd ever done
and this way He could just
hold one in His   20

and admire those delicate
bones just above the knuckles,
delicate as birds' wings,
and after He'd done that
awhile,   25
He could paint all the nails
any color He wanted,
then say,
"Beautiful,"
and mean it.   30

WILLIAM SHAKESPEARE (1564–1616)

Let me not to the marriage of true minds (1609)

Let me not to the marriage of true minds
Admit impediments.[1] Love is not love
Which alters when it alteration finds,
Or bends with the remover to remove:
Oh, no! it is an ever-fixéd mark,   5
That looks on tempests and is never shaken;
It is the star to every wandering bark,
Whose worth's unknown, although his height be taken.[2]
Love's not Time's fool,[3] though rosy lips and cheeks
Within his bending sickle's compass come;   10
Love alters not with his brief hours and weeks,
But bears it out even to the edge of doom.[4]
    If this be error and upon me proved,
    I never writ, nor no man ever loved.

WILLIAM SHAKESPEARE (1564–1616)

Not marble, nor the gilded monuments (1609)

Not marble, nor the gilded monuments
Of princes, shall outlive this powerful rhyme;

---

[1]*Admit impediments:* A reference to "The Order of Solemnization of Matrimony" in the Anglican Book of Common Prayer: "I require that if either of you know any impediments why ye may not be lawfully joined together in Matrimony, ye do now confess it."

[2]*Whose worth's . . . taken:* Although the altitude of a star may be measured, its worth is unknowable.

[3]*Love's not Time's fool:* Love is not mocked by Time.

[4]*doom:* Doomsday.

But you shall shine more bright in these contents
Than unswept stone, besmeared with sluttish time.
When wasteful war shall statues overturn,   5
And broils root out the work of masonry,
Nor Mars[1] his sword nor war's quick fire shall burn
The living record of your memory.
'Gainst death and all-oblivious enmity
Shall you pace forth; your praise shall still find room   10
Even in the eyes of all posterity
That wear this world out to the ending doom.
   So, till the judgment that yourself arise,
   You live in this, and dwell in lovers' eyes.

PERCY BYSSHE SHELLEY (1792–1822)

Ode to the West Wind (1820)

I

O wild West Wind, thou breath of Autumn's being,
Thou, from whose unseen presence the leaves dead
Are driven, like ghosts from an enchanter fleeing,

Yellow, and black, and pale, and hectic red,[1]
Pestilence-stricken multitudes: O Thou,   5
Who chariotest to their dark wintry bed

The winged seeds, where they lie cold and low,
Each like a corpse within its grave, until
Thine azure sister of the Spring[2] shall blow

Her clarion o'er the dreaming earth, and fill   10
(Driving sweet buds like flocks to feed in air)
With living hues and odours plain and hill:

Wild Spirit, which art moving everywhere;
Destroyer and Preserver; hear, O hear!

II

Thou on whose stream, mid the steep sky's commotion,   15
Loose clouds like Earth's decaying leaves are shed,
Shook from the tangled boughs of Heaven and Ocean,

---

[1] *Mars:* The Roman god of war.

[1] *Yellow . . . hectic red:* A reference to a tubercular fever that produces flushed cheeks.

[2] *azure . . . Spring:* The west wind of the spring.

Angels of rain and lightning: there are spread
On the blue surface of thine aery surge,
Like the bright hair uplifted from the head   20

Of some fierce Maenad,[3] even from the dim verge
Of the horizon to the zenith's height,
The locks of the approaching storm. Thou Dirge

Of the dying year, to which this closing night
Will be the dome of a vast sepulchre,   25
Vaulted with all thy congregated might

Of vapours, from whose solid atmosphere
Black rain and fire and hail will burst: O hear!

III

Thou who didst waken from his summer dreams
The blue Mediterranean, where he lay,   30
Lulled by the coil of his crystalline streams,

Beside a pumice isle in Baiae's bay,[4]
And saw in sleep old palaces and towers
Quivering within the wave's intenser day,

All overgrown with azure moss and flowers   35
So sweet, the sense faints picturing them! Thou
For whose path the Atlantic's level powers

Cleave themselves into chasms, while far below
The sea-blooms and the oozy woods which wear
The sapless foliage of the ocean, know   40

Thy voice, and suddenly grow grey with fear,
And tremble and despoil themselves: O hear!

IV

If I were a dead leaf thou mightest bear;
If I were a swift cloud to fly with thee;
A wave to pant beneath thy power, and share   45

The impulse of thy strength, only less free
Than thou, O Uncontrollable! If even
I were as in my boyhood, and could be

The comrade of thy wanderings over Heaven,
As then, when to outstrip thy skiey speed   50
Scarce seemed a vision; I would ne'er have striven

---

[3]*Maenad:* A female votary who danced wildly in ceremonies for Dionysus (or Bacchus), Greek god of wine and vegetation, who according to legend died in the fall and was reborn in the spring.

[4]*Baiae's bay:* A bay in the Mediterranean Sea, west of Naples. It was known for the opulent villas built by Roman emperors along its shores.

As thus with thee in prayer in my sore need,
Oh! lift me as a wave, a leaf, a cloud!
I fall upon the thorns of life! I bleed!

A heavy weight of hours has chained and bowed   55
One too like thee: tameless, and swift, and proud.

V

Make me thy lyre,[5] even as the forest is:
What if my leaves are falling like its own!
The tumult of thy mighty harmonies

Will take from both a deep, autumnal tone,   60
Sweet though in sadness. Be thou, Spirit fierce,
My spirit! Be thou me, impetuous one!

Drive my dead thoughts over the universe
Like withered leaves to quicken a new birth!
And, by the incantation of this verse,   65

Scatter, as from an unextinguished hearth
Ashes and sparks, my words among mankind!
Be through my lips to unawakened Earth

The trumpet of a prophecy! O Wind,
If Winter comes, can Spring be far behind?   70

STEVIE SMITH (1902–1971)

Not Waving but Drowning (1957)

Nobody heard him, the dead man,
But still he lay moaning:
I was much further out than you thought
And not waving but drowning.

Poor chap, he always loved larking   5
And now he's dead
It must have been too cold for him his heart gave way,
They said.

Oh, no no no, it was too cold always
(Still the dead one lay moaning)   10
I was much too far out all my life
And not waving but drowning.

---

[5]*lyre:* An Aeolian harp, a stringed instrument that produces musical sounds when exposed to the wind.

WOLE SOYINKA (1934–   )

Hamlet (1972)

He stilled his doubts, they rose to halt and lame
A resolution on the rack. Passion's flame
Was doused in fear of error, his mind's unease
Bred indulgence to the state's disease
Ghosts embowelled his earth; he clung to rails   5
In a gallery of abstractions, dissecting tales
As "told by an idiot." Passionless he set a stage
Of passion for the guilt he would engage.

Justice despaired. The turn and turn abouts
Of reason danced default to duty's counterpoint   10
Till treachery scratched the slate of primal clay
Then Metaphysics waived a thought's delay—
It took the salt in the wound, the "point
Envenom'd too" to steel the prince of doubts.

WALLACE STEVENS (1879–1955)

Anecdote of the Jar (1923)

I placed a jar in Tennessee,
And round it was, upon a hill.
It made the slovenly wilderness
Surround that hill.

The wilderness rose up to it,   5
And sprawled around, no longer wild.
The jar was round upon the ground
And tall and of a port in air.

It took dominion everywhere.
The jar was gray and bare.   10
It did not give of bird or bush,
Like nothing else in Tennessee.

WALLACE STEVENS (1879–1955)

The Emperor of Ice-Cream (1923)

Call the roller of big cigars,
The muscular one, and bid him whip
In kitchen cups concupiscent curds.
Let the wenches dawdle in such dress
As they are used to wear, and let the boys   5

Bring flowers in last month's newspapers.
Let be be finale of seem.
The only emperor is the emperor of ice-cream.

Take from the dresser of deal,[1]
Lacking the three glass knobs, that sheet   10
On which she embroidered fantails[2] once
And spread it so as to cover her face.
If her horny feet protrude, they come
To show how cold she is, and dumb.
Let the lamp affix its beam.   15
The only emperor is the emperor of ice-cream.

AP Images

ALFRED, LORD TENNYSON (1809–1897)

The Eagle (1851)

He clasps the crag with crooked hands;
Close to the sun in lonely lands,
Ring'd with the azure world, he stands.

The wrinkled sea beneath him crawls;
He watches from his mountain walls,   5
And like a thunderbolt he falls.

ALFRED, LORD TENNYSON (1809–1892)

Ulysses[1] (1833)

It little profits that an idle king,
By this still hearth, among these barren crags,
Matched with an agèd wife, I mete and dole
Unequal laws unto a savage race
That hoard, and sleep, and feed, and know not me.   5
I cannot rest from travel; I will drink
Life to the lees. All times I have enjoyed
Greatly, have suffered greatly, both with those
That loved me, and alone; on shore, and when
Through scudding drifts the rainy Hyades[2]   10

---

[1] *deal:* Fir or pine wood.

[2] *fantails:* According to Stevens, "the word fantails does not mean fans, but fantail pigeons."

[1] *Ulysses:* A legendary Greek king of Ithaca and hero of Homer's *Odyssey*, Ulysses (or Odysseus) is noted for his daring and cunning. After his many adventures—including encounters with the Cyclops, the cannibalistic Laestrygones, and the enchantress Circe—Ulysses returned home to his faithful wife, Penelope. Tennyson portrays an older Ulysses pondering his situation.

[2] *Hyades:* A group of stars whose rising was supposedly followed by rain and thus stormy seas.

Vexed the dim sea. I am become a name;
For always roaming with a hungry heart
Much have I seen and known—cities of men
And manners, climates, councils, governments,
Myself not least, but honored of them all—   15
And drunk delight of battle with my peers,
Far on the ringing plains of windy Troy.[3]
I am a part of all that I have met;
Yet all experience is an arch wherethrough
Gleams that untraveled world whose margin fades   20
Forever and forever when I move.
How dull it is to pause, to make an end,
To rust unburnished, not to shine in use!
As though to breathe were life! Life piled on life
Were all too little, and of one to me   25
Little remains; but every hour is saved
From that eternal silence, something more,
A bringer of new things; and vile it were
For some three suns to store and hoard myself,
And this grey spirit yearning in desire   30
To follow knowledge like a sinking star,
Beyond the utmost bound of human thought.

    This is my son, mine own Telemachus,
To whom I leave the scepter and the isle—
Well-loved of me, discerning to fulfill   35
This labor, by slow prudence to make mild
A rugged people, and through soft degrees
Subdue them to the useful and the good.
Most blameless is he, centered in the sphere
Of common duties, decent not to fail   40
In offices of tenderness, and pay
Meet adoration to my household gods,
When I am gone. He works his work, I mine.

    There lies the port; the vessel puffs her sail;
There gloom the dark, broad seas. My mariners,   45
Souls that have toiled, and wrought, and thought with me—
That ever with a frolic welcome took
The thunder and the sunshine, and opposed
Free hearts, free foreheads—you and I are old;
Old age hath yet his honor and his toil.   50
Death closes all; but something ere the end,
Some work of noble note, may yet be done,

---

[3] *Troy:* An ancient city in Asia Minor. According to legend, Paris, king of Troy, abducted Helen, the beautiful wife of Menelaus, king of Sparta, initiating the Trojan War, in which numerous Greek heroes, including Ulysses, fought.

Not unbecoming men that strove with Gods.
The lights begin to twinkle from the rocks;
The long day wanes; the low moon climbs; the deep　　　55
Moans round with many voices. Come, my friends,
'Tis not too late to seek a newer world.
Push off, and sitting well in order smite
The sounding furrows; for my purpose holds
To sail beyond the sunset, and the baths　　　60
Of all the western stars, until I die.
It may be that the gulfs will wash us down;
It may be we shall touch the Happy Isles,[4]
And see the great Achilles,[5] whom we knew.
Though much is taken, much abides; and though　　　65
We are not now that strength which in old days
Moved earth and heaven, that which we are, we are—
One equal temper of heroic hearts,
Made weak by time and fate, but strong in will
To strive, to seek, to find, and not to yield.　　　70

DYLAN THOMAS (1914–1953)

Fern Hill (1946)

Now as I was young and easy under the apple boughs
About the lilting house and happy as the grass was green,
　　　The night above the dingle[1] starry,
　　　　Time let me hail and climb
　　　Golden in the heydays of his eyes,　　　5
And honoured among wagons I was prince of the apple towns
And once below a time I lordly had the trees and leaves
　　　　Trail with daisies and barley
　　　Down the rivers of the windfall light.

And as I was green and carefree, famous among the barns　　　10
About the happy yard and singing as the farm was home,
　　　In the sun that is young once only,
　　　　Time let me play and be
　　　Golden in the mercy of his means,
And green and golden I was huntsman and herdsman, the calves　　　15
Sang to my horn, the foxes on the hills barked clear and cold,

---

[4]*Happy Isles:* Elysium, or Paradise, believed to be in the far western ocean.
[5]*Achilles:* Greek hero of the Trojan War.
[1]*dingle:* A small valley or dell, typically wooded.

And the sabbath rang slowly
    In the pebbles of the holy streams.

All the sun long it was running, it was lovely, the hay
Fields high as the house, the tunes from the chimneys, it was air   20
    And playing, lovely and watery
        And fire green as grass.
    And nightly under the simple stars
As I rode to sleep the owls were bearing the farm away,
All the moon long I heard, blessed among stables, the nightjars[2]   25
    Flying with the ricks,[3] and the horses
        Flashing into the dark.

And then to awake, and the farm, like a wanderer white
With the dew, come back, the cock on his shoulder: it was all
    Shining, it was Adam and maiden,   30
        The sky gathered again
    And the sun grew round that very day.
So it must have been after the birth of the simple light
In the first, spinning place, the spellbound horses walking warm
    Out of the whinnying green stable   35
        On to the fields of praise.

And honoured among foxes and pheasants by the gay house
Under the new made clouds and happy as the heart was long,
    In the sun born over and over,
        I ran my heedless ways,   40
    My wishes raced through the house high hay
And nothing I cared, at my sky blue trades, that time allows
In all his tuneful turning so few and such morning songs
    Before the children green and golden
        Follow him out of grace,   45

Nothing I cared, in the lamb white days, that time would take me
Up to the swallow thronged loft by the shadow of my hand,
    In the moon that is always rising,
        Nor that riding to sleep
    I should hear him fly with the high fields   50
And wake to the farm forever fled from the childless land.
Oh as I was young and easy in the mercy of his means,
    Time held me green and dying
        Though I sang in my chains like the sea.

---

[2]*nightjars:* A type of nocturnal bird.
[3]*ricks:* A pile of hay or straw.

KO UN (1933–   )

In the old days a poet once said (2008)

Translated by Brother Anthony, Young-moo Kim, and Gary Gach

In the old days a poet once said
our nation is destroyed
yet the mountains and rivers survive

Today's poet says
the mountains and rivers are destroyed   5
yet our nation survives

Tomorrow's poet will say
the mountains and rivers are destroyed
our nation is destroyed and Alas!
you and I are completely destroyed   10

CHARLES WEBB (1939–   )

The Death of Santa Claus (1997)

He's had the chest pains for weeks,
but doctors don't make house
calls to the North Pole,

he's let his Blue Cross lapse,
blood tests make him faint,   5
hospital gown always flap

open, waiting rooms upset
his stomach, and it's only
indigestion anyway, he thinks,

until, feeding the reindeer,   10
he feels as if a monster fist
has grabbed his heart and won't
stop squeezing. He can't
breathe, and the beautiful white
world he loves goes black,   15

and he drops on his jelly belly
in the snow and Mrs. Claus
tears out of the toy factory

wailing, and the elves wring
their little hands, and Rudolph's   20
nose blinks like a sad ambulance

light, and in a tract house
in Houston, Texas, I'm 8,
telling my mom that stupid

kids at school say Santa's a big   25
fake, and she sits with me
on our purple-flowered couch,

and takes my hand, tears
in her throat, the terrible
news rising in her eyes.   30

PHILLIS WHEATLEY (1753–1784)

On Being Brought from Africa to America (1773)

'Twas mercy brought me from my *Pagan* land,
Taught my benighted soul to understand
That there's a God, that there's a *Saviour* too:
Once I redemption neither sought nor knew.
Some view our sable race with scornful eye,   5
"Their colour is a diabolic die."
Remember, *Christians*, *Negroes*, black as *Cain*,
May be refin'd, and join th' angelic train.

WALT WHITMAN (1819–1892)

I Hear America Singing (1867)

I hear America singing, the varied carols I hear,
Those of mechanics, each one singing his as it should be blithe
    and strong,
The carpenter singing his as he measures his plank or beam,
The mason singing his as he makes ready for work, or leaves
    off work,
The boatman singing what belongs to him in his boat, the   5
    deckhand singing on the steamboat deck,
The shoemaker singing as he sits on his bench, the hatter
    singing as he stands,
The wood-cutter's song, the ploughboy's on his way in the
    morning, or at noon intermission or at sundown,
The delicious singing of the mother, or of the young wife at
    work, or of the girl sewing or washing,
Each singing what belongs to him or her and to none else,
The day what belongs to the day—at night the party of young   10
    fellows, robust, friendly,
Singing with open mouths their strong melodious songs.

WALT WHITMAN (1819–1892)

A Noiseless Patient Spider (1881)

A noiseless patient spider,
I mark'd where on a little promontory it stood isolated,
Mark'd how to explore the vacant vast surrounding,
It launch'd forth filament, filament, filament, out of itself,
Ever unreeling them, ever tirelessly speeding them.   5

And you O my soul where you stand,
Surrounded, detached, in measureless oceans of space,
Ceaselessly musing, venturing, throwing, seeking the spheres to
    connect them,
Till the bridge you will need be form'd, till the ductile anchor
    hold,
Till the gossamer thread you fling catch somewhere, O my soul.   10

WALT WHITMAN (1819–1892)

from "Song of Myself" (1855)

1

I celebrate myself, and sing myself,
And what I assume you shall assume,
For every atom belonging to me as good belongs to you.

I loafe and invite my soul,
I lean and loafe at my ease observing a spear of summer grass.   5

My tongue, every atom of my blood, form'd from this soil, this air,
Born here of parents born here from parents the same, and their
    parents the same,
I, now thirty-seven years old in perfect health begin,
Hoping to cease not till death.

Creeds and schools in abeyance,   10
Retiring back a while sufficed at what they are, but never
    forgotten,
I harbor for good or bad, I permit to speak at every hazard,
Nature without check with original energy.

2

Houses and rooms are full of perfumes, the shelves are crowded
    with perfumes,
I breathe the fragrance myself and know it and like it,   15
The distillation would intoxicate me also, but I shall not let it.

The atmosphere is not a perfume, it has no taste of the distillation,

    it is odorless,
It is for my mouth forever, I am in love with it,
I will go to the bank by the wood and become undisguised
    and naked,
I am mad for it to be in contact with me.   20

The smoke of my own breath,
Echoes, ripples, buzz'd whispers, love-root, silk-thread, crotch
    and vine,
My respiration and inspiration, the beating of my heart, the
    passing of blood and air through my lungs,
The sniff of green leaves and dry leaves, and of the shore and
    dark-color'd sea-rocks, and of hay in the barn,
The sound of the belch'd words of my voice loos'd to the eddies
    of the wind,   25
A few light kisses, a few embraces, a reaching around of arms,
The play of shine and shade on the trees as the supple
    boughs wag,
The delight alone or in the rush of the streets, or along the fields
    and hill-sides,
The feeling of health, the full-noon trill, the song of me rising
    from bed and meeting the sun.

Have you reckon'd a thousand acres much? have you
    reckon'd the
        earth much?   30
Have you practis'd so long to learn to read?
Have you felt so proud to get at the meaning of poems?

Stop this day and night with me and you shall possess the origin
    of all poems,
You shall possess the good of the earth and sun, (there are millions
        of suns left,)
You shall no longer take things at second or third hand, nor look
    through the eyes of the dead, nor feed on the
        spectres in books,   35
You shall not look through my eyes either, nor take things
    from me,
You shall listen to all sides and filter them from your self.

WILLIAM WORDSWORTH (1770–1850)

Composed upon Westminster Bridge, September 3, 1802 (1807)

Earth has not anything to show more fair:
Dull would he be of soul who could pass by

A sight so touching in its majesty:
This City now doth, like a garment, wear
The beauty of the morning; silent, bare,   5
Ships, towers, domes, theatres, and temples lie
Open unto the fields, and to the sky;
All bright and glittering in the smokeless air.
Never did sun more beautifully steep
In his first splendor, valley, rock, or hill;   10
Ne'er saw I, never felt, a calm so deep!
The river glideth at his own sweet will:
Dear God! the very houses seem asleep;
And all that mighty heart is lying still!

WILLIAM WORDSWORTH (1770–1850)

London, 1802 (1802)

Milton![1] thou should'st be living at this hour:
England hath need of thee: she is a fen
Of stagnant waters: altar, sword and pen,
Fireside, the heroic wealth of hall and bower,
Have forfeited their ancient English dower   5
Of inward happiness. We are selfish men;
Oh! raise us up, return to us again;
And give us manners, virtue, freedom, power.
Thy soul was like a star, and dwelt apart:
Thou hadst a voice whose sound was like the sea: 10
Pure as the naked heavens, majestic, free,
So didst thou travel on life's common way,
In cheerful godliness; and yet thy heart
The lowliest duties on herself did lay.

WILLIAM WORDSWORTH (1770–1850)

My heart leaps up when I behold (1807)

My heart leaps up when I behold
    A rainbow in the sky:
So was it when my life began;
So is it now I am a man;
So be it when I shall grow old,   5
    Or let me die!
The Child is father of the Man;

---

[1] *Milton:* John Milton (1608–1674), poet, best known for *Paradise Lost*.

And I could wish my days to be
Bound each to each by natural piety.

WILLIAM WORDSWORTH (1770–1850)

The Solitary Reaper[1] (1807)

Behold her, single in the field,
Yon solitary Highland lass!
Reaping and singing by herself;
Stop here, or gently pass!
Alone she cuts and binds the grain,   5
And sings a melancholy strain;
O listen! for the vale profound
Is overflowing with the sound.

No nightingale did ever chaunt
More welcome notes to weary bands   10
Of travelers in some shady haunt
Among Arabian sands.
A voice so thrilling ne'er was heard
In springtime from the cuckoo-bird,
Breaking the silence of the seas   15
Among the farthest Hebrides.[2]

Will no one tell me what she sings?—
Perhaps the plaintive numbers flow
For old, unhappy, far-off things,
And battles long ago.   20
Or is it some more humble lay,
Familiar matter of today?
Some natural sorrow, loss, or pain,
That has been, and may be again?

Whate'er the theme, the maiden sang   25
As if her song could have no ending;
I saw her singing at her work,
And o'er the sickle[3] bending—
I listened, motionless and still;
And, as I mounted up the hill,   30
The music in my heart I bore
Long after it was heard no more.

---

[1] *Reaper:* A worker who harvests grain.
[2] *Hebrides:* A group of islands off the west coast of Scotland.
[3] *sickle:* A curved blade used for harvesting grain or cutting grass.

WILLIAM BUTLER YEATS (1865–1939)

An Irish Airman Foresees His Death (1919)

I know that I shall meet my fate
Somewhere among the clouds above;
Those that I fight I do not hate,
Those that I guard I do not love;
My country is Kiltartan Cross   5
My countrymen Kiltartan's poor,
No likely end could bring them loss
Or leave them happier than before.
Nor law, nor duty bade me fight,
Nor public men, nor cheering crowds,   10
A lonely impulse of delight
Drove to this tumult in the clouds;
I balanced all, brought all to mind,
The years to come seemed waste of breath,
A waste of breath the years behind   15
In balance with this life, this death.

WILLIAM BUTLER YEATS (1865–1939)

The Lake Isle of Innisfree (1892)

I will arise and go now, and go to Innisfree,[1]
And a small cabin build there, of clay and wattles[2] made:
Nine bean-rows will I have there, a hive for the honey-bee,
And live alone in the bee-loud glade.

And I shall have some peace there, for peace comes
    dropping slow,
Dropping from the veils of the morning to where the   5
    cricket sings;
There midnight's all a glimmer, and noon a purple glow,
And evening full of the linnet's wings.

I will arise and go now, for always night and day
I hear lake water lapping with low sounds by the shore;
While I stand on the roadway, or on the pavements grey,   10
I hear it in the deep heart's core.

---

[1] *Innisfree:* An island in Lough (Lake) Gill, County Sligo, in Ireland.
[2] *wattles:* Stakes interwoven with twigs or branches, used for walls and roofing.

WILLIAM BUTLER YEATS (1865–1939)

Sailing to Byzantium[1]   (1927)

That is no country for old men. The young
In one another's arms, birds in the trees
—Those dying generations—at their song,
The salmon-falls, the mackerel-crowded seas,
Fish, flesh, or fowl, commend all summer long   5
Whatever is begotten, born, and dies.
Caught in that sensual music all neglect
Monuments of unaging intellect.

An aged man is but a paltry thing,
A tattered coat upon a stick, unless   10
Soul clap its hands and sing, and louder sing
For every tatter in its mortal dress,
Nor is there singing school but studying
Monuments of its own magnificence;
And therefore I have sailed the seas and come   15
To the holy city of Byzantium.

O sages standing in God's holy fire
As in the gold mosaic of a wall,
Come from the holy fire, perne in a gyre,
And be the singing-masters of my soul.   20
Consume my heart away; sick with desire
And fastened to a dying animal
It knows not what it is; and gather me
Into the artifice of eternity.

Once out of nature I shall never take   25
My bodily form from any natural thing,
But such a form as Grecian goldsmiths make
Of hammered gold and gold enameling
To keep a drowsy Emperor awake;
Or set upon a golden bough to sing   30
To lords and ladies of Byzantium
Of what is past, or passing, or to come.

---

[1] *Byzantium:* Ancient Greek city later rebuilt as Constantinople (now Istanbul).

WILLIAM BUTLER YEATS (1865–1939)

The Second Coming[1]   (1921)

Turning and turning in the widening gyre[2]
The falcon cannot hear the falconer;
Things fall apart; the center cannot hold;
Mere anarchy is loosed upon the world,
The blood-dimmed tide is loosed, and everywhere   5
The ceremony of innocence is drowned;
The best lack all conviction, while the worst
Are full of passionate intensity.[3]

Surely some revelation is at hand;
Surely the Second Coming is at hand;   10
The Second Coming! Hardly are those words out
When a vast image out of *Spiritus Mundi*[4]
Troubles my sight: somewhere in sands of the desert
A shape with lion body and the head of a man,
A gaze blank and pitiless as the sun,   15
Is moving its slow thighs, while all about it
Reel shadows of the indignant desert birds.
The darkness drops again; but now I know
That twenty centuries[5] of stony sleep
Were vexed to nightmare by a rocking cradle,   20
And what rough beast, its hour come round at last,
Slouches towards Bethlehem to be born?

KEVIN YOUNG (1970–   )

Song of Smoke   (2005)

To watch you walk
cross the room in your black

corduroys is to see
civilization start—

---

[1] *The Second Coming:* The phrase usually refers to the return of Christ. Yeats theorized cycles of history, much like the turning of a wheel. Here he offers a poetic comment on his view of the dissolution of civilization at the end of one such cycle.

[2] *gyre:* Spiral.

[3] *Mere . . . intensity:* Lines 4–8 refer to the Russian Revolution of 1917.

[4] Spiritus Mundi: Literally, "Spirit of the World" (Latin). Yeats believed all souls to be connected by a "Great Memory."

[5] *twenty centuries:* The centuries between the birth of Christ and the twentieth century, in which Yeats was writing.

the *wish . . .*   5
whish-whisk

of your strut is flint
striking rock—the spark

of a length of cord
rubbed till   10

smoke starts—you stir
me like coal

and for days smoulder.
I am no more

a Boy Scout and, besides,   15
could never

put you out—you
keep me on

all day like an iron, out
of habit—   20

you threaten, brick . . .
house, to burn

all this down. You leave me
only a chimney.

4| D R A M A

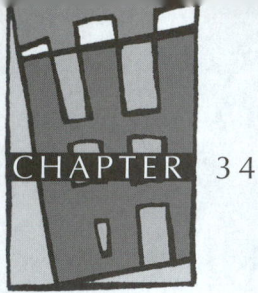

CHAPTER 34

UNDERSTANDING DRAMA

 Dramatic Literature

The distinctive appearance of a script, with its divisions into acts and scenes, identifies **drama** as a unique form of literature. A play is written to be performed in front of an audience by actors who take on the roles of the characters and who present the story through dialogue and action. (An exception is a **closet drama**, which is meant to be read, not performed.) In fact, the term *theater* comes from the Greek word *theasthai*, which means "to view" or "to see." Thus, drama is different from novels and short stories, which are meant to be read.

 Origins of Modern Drama

The Ancient Greek Theater

The dramatic presentations of ancient Greece developed out of religious rites performed to honor gods or to mark the coming of spring. Playwrights such as Aeschylus (525–456 B.C.), Sophocles (496–406 B.C.), and Euripides (480?–406 B.C.) wrote plays to be performed and judged at competitions held during the yearly Dionysian festivals. Works were chosen by a selection board and evaluated by a panel of judges. To compete in the contest, writers had to submit three tragedies, which could either be based on a common theme or unrelated, and one comedy. Unfortunately, very few of these ancient Greek plays survive today.

The open-air, semicircular ancient Greek theater, built into the side of a hill, looked much like a primitive version of a modern sports stadium. Some Greek theaters, such as the Athenian theater, could seat almost seventeen thousand spectators. Sitting in tiered seats, the audience would look down on the **orchestra**, or "dancing place," occupied by the **chorus**—originally a group of men (led by an individual called the **choragos**) who danced and chanted and later a group of onlookers who commented on the drama.

Raised a few steps above the orchestra was a platform on which the actors performed. Behind this platform was a **skene**, or building, that originally served as a resting place or dressing room. (The modern word *scene* is derived from the Greek *skene*.) Behind the skene

Grand Theater at Ephesus (3rd century B.C.), a Greek settlement in what is now Turkey
Dave G. Houser/Documentary Value/Corbis

was a line of pillars called a **colonnade**, which was covered by a roof. Actors used the skene for entrances and exits; beginning with the plays of Sophocles, painted backdrops were hung there. These backdrops, however, were most likely more decorative than realistic. Historians believe that realistic props and scenery were probably absent from the ancient Greek theater. Instead, the setting was suggested by the play's dialogue, and the audience had to imagine the physical details of a scene.

Two mechanical devices were used. One, a rolling cart or platform, was sometimes employed to introduce action that had occurred offstage. For example, actors frozen in position could be rolled onto the roof of the skene to illustrate an event such as the killing of Oedipus's father, which occurred before the play began. Another mechanical device, a small crane, was used to show gods ascending to or descending from heaven. Such devices enabled playwrights to dramatize the myths that were celebrated at the Dionysian festivals.

The ancient Greek theater was designed to enhance acoustics. The flat stone wall of the skene reflected the sound from the orchestra and the stage, and the curved shape of the amphitheater captured the sound, enabling the audience to hear the lines spoken by the actors. Each actor wore a stylized mask, or **persona**, to convey to the audience the personality traits of the particular character being portrayed—a king, a soldier, a wise old man, a young girl (female roles were played by men). The mouths of these masks were probably constructed so they amplified the voice and projected it into the audience. In addition, the actors wore *kothorni*, high shoes that elevated them above the stage, perhaps also helping to project their voices. Due to the excellent acoustics, audiences who see plays performed in these ancient theaters today can hear clearly without the aid of microphones or speaker systems.

Because actors wore masks and because males played the parts of women and gods as well as men, acting methods in the ancient Greek theater were probably not realistic. In their masks, high shoes, and full-length tunics (called *chiton*), actors could not hope to appear natural or to mimic the attitudes of everyday life. Instead, they probably recited their lines while standing in stylized poses, with emotions conveyed more by gesture and tone than by action. Typically, three actors had all the speaking roles. One actor—the **protagonist**—would play the central role and have the largest speaking part. Two other actors would divide the remaining lines between them. Although other characters would come on and off the stage, they would usually not have speaking roles.

Ancient Greek tragedies were typically divided into five parts. The first part was the **prologos**, or prologue, in which an actor gave the background or explanations that the audience needed to follow the rest of the drama. Then came the **párodos**, in which the chorus entered and commented on the events presented in the prologue. Following this were several **episodia**, or episodes, in which characters spoke to one another on the stage and developed the central conflict of the play. Alternating with episodes were **stasimon** (choral odes), in which the chorus commented on the exchanges that had taken place during the preceding episode. Frequently, the choral odes were divided into *strophes*, or stanzas, which were recited or sung as the chorus moved across the orchestra in one direction, and *antistrophes*, which were recited as it moved in the opposite direction. (Interestingly, the chorus stood between the audience and the actors, often functioning as an additional audience, expressing the political, social, and moral views of the community.) The fifth part was the **exodos**, the last scene of the play, during which the conflict was resolved and the actors left the stage.

Using music, dance, and verse—as well as a variety of architectural and technical innovations—the ancient Greek theater was able to convey the traditional themes of tragedy. Thus, the Greek theater powerfully expressed ideas that were central to the religious festivals in which they first appeared: the reverence for the cycles of life and death, the unavoidable dictates of the gods, and the inscrutable workings of fate.

The Elizabethan Theater

The Elizabethan theater, influenced by the classical traditions of Roman and Greek dramatists, traces its roots back to local religious pageants performed at medieval festivals during the twelfth and thirteenth centuries. Town **guilds**—organizations of craftsmen who worked in the same profession—reenacted Old and New Testament stories: the fall of man, Noah and the flood, David and Goliath, and the crucifixion of Christ, for example. Church fathers encouraged these plays because they brought the Bible to a largely illiterate audience. Sometimes these spectacles, called **mystery plays**, were presented in the market square or on the church steps, and at other times actors appeared on movable stages or wagons called **pageants**, which could be wheeled to a given location. (Some of these wagons were quite elaborate, with trapdoors and pulleys and an upper tier that simulated heaven.) As mystery plays became more popular, they were performed in series over several days, presenting an entire cycle of a holiday—the crucifixion and resurrection of Christ during Easter, for example.

Performance of a mystery play
Art Resource

Related to mystery plays are **morality plays**, which developed in the fourteenth and fifteenth centuries. Unlike mystery plays, which depict scenes from the Bible, morality plays allegorize the Christian way of life. Typically, characters representing various virtues and vices struggle or debate over the soul of man. *Everyman* (1500), the best known of these plays, dramatizes the good and bad qualities of Everyman and shows his struggle to determine what is of value to him as he journeys toward death.

By the middle of the sixteenth century, mystery and morality plays had lost ground to a new secular drama. One reason for this decline was that mystery and morality plays were associated with Catholicism and consequently discouraged by the Anglican clergy. In addition, newly discovered plays of ancient Greece and Rome introduced a dramatic tradition that supplanted the traditions of religious drama. English plays that followed the classic model were sensational and bombastic, often dealing with murder, revenge, and blood retribution. Appealing to privileged classes and commoners alike, these plays were extremely popular. (One source estimates that in London, between 20,000 and 25,000 people attended performances each week.)

In spite of the popularity of the theater, actors and playwrights encountered a number of difficulties. First, they faced opposition from city officials who were averse to theatrical presentations because they thought that the crowds attending these performances spread disease. Puritans opposed the theater because they thought plays were immoral and sinful. Finally, some people attached to the royal court opposed the theater because they thought that the playwrights undermined the authority of Queen Elizabeth by spreading seditious ideas. As a result, during Elizabeth's reign, performances were placed under the strict control of the **Master of Revels**, a public official who had the power to censor plays (and did so with great regularity) and to grant licenses for performances.

Acting companies that wanted to put on a performance had to obtain a license—possible only with the patronage of a powerful nobleman—and to perform the play in an area designated by the queen. Despite these difficulties, a number of actors and playwrights gained a measure of financial independence by joining together and forming acting companies. These companies of professional actors performed works such as Christopher Marlowe's *Tamburlaine* and Thomas Kyd's *The Spanish Tragedy* in tavern courtyards and then eventually in permanent theaters. According to scholars, the structures of the Elizabethan theater evolved from these tavern courtyards.

William Shakespeare's plays were performed at the Globe Theatre (a corner of which was unearthed in December 1988). Although scholars do not know the exact design of the original Globe, drawings from the period provide a good idea of its physical features. The major difference between the Globe and today's theaters is the multiple stages on which action could be performed. The Globe consisted of a large main **stage** that extended out into the open-air **yard** where the **groundlings**, or common people, stood. Spectators who paid more sat on small stools in two or three levels of galleries that extended in front of and around the stage. (The theater could probably seat almost two thousand people at a performance.) Most of the play's action occurred on the stage, which had no curtain and could be seen from three sides. Beneath the stage was a space called the **hell**, which could be reached when the floorboards were removed. This space enabled actors to "disappear" or descend into a hole or grave when the play called for such action. Above the stage was a roof called the **heavens**, which protected the actors from the weather and contained ropes and pulleys used to lower props or to create special effects.

At the rear of the stage was a narrow **alcove** covered by a curtain that could be open or closed. This curtain, often painted, functioned as a decorative rather than a realistic backdrop. The main function of this alcove was to enable actors to hide or disappear when the script called for them to do so. Some Elizabethan theaters contained a **rear stage** instead of an alcove. Because the rear stage was concealed by a curtain, props could be arranged on it ahead of time. When the action on the rear stage was finished, the curtain would be closed and the action would continue on the front stage.

On either side of the rear stage was a door through which the actors could enter and exit the front stage. Above the rear stage was a curtained stage called the **chamber**, which functioned as a balcony or as any other setting located above the action taking place on the stage below. On either side of the chamber were casement windows, which actors could use when a play called for a conversation with someone leaning out a window or standing on a balcony. Above the chamber was the **music gallery**, a balcony that housed the musicians who provided musical interludes throughout the play (and that doubled as a stage if the play required it). The **huts**, windows located above the music gallery, could be used by characters playing lookouts or sentries. Because of the many acting sites, more than one action could take place simultaneously. For example,

The Globe Playhouse,
1599-1613

A CONJECTURAL

RECONSTRUCTION

KEY

AA Main entrance
B   The Yard
CC Entrances to lowest gallery
D   Entrances to staircase and upper
    galleries
E   Corridor serving the different sections
    of the middle gallery
F   Middle gallery ('Twopenny Rooms')
G   'Gentlemen's Rooms' or 'Lords' Rooms'
H   The stage

J   The hanging being put up round the
    stage
K   The 'Hell' under the stage
L   The stage trap, leading down to the
    Hell
MM Stage doors
N   Curtained 'place behind the stage'
O   Gallery above the stage, used as re-
    quired sometimes by musicians, some-
    times by spectators, and often as part
    of the play
P   Back-stage area (the tiring-house)
Q   Tiring-house door
R   Dressing-rooms
S   Wardrobe and storage
T   The hut housing the machine for
    lowering enthroned gods, etc., to the
    stage
U   The 'Heavens'
W   Hoisting the playhouse flag

The Globe Playhouse, 1599–1613; a conjectural reconstruction. From C. Walter Hodges
The Globe Restored: A Study of the Elizabethan Theatre. New York: Norton, 1973.
Source: C.W. Hodges. Conjectural Reconstruction of the Globe Playhouse, 1965. Pen & ink.

lookouts could stand in the towers of Hamlet's castle while Hamlet and Horatio walked the walls below.

During Shakespeare's time, the theater had many limitations that challenged the audience's imagination. First, young boys—usually between the ages of ten and twelve—played all the women's parts. In addition, there was no artificial lighting, so plays had to be performed in daylight. Rain, wind, or clouds could disrupt a performance or ruin an image—such as "the morn in russet mantle clad"—that the audience was asked to imagine. Finally, because few sets and props were used, the audience often had to visualize the high walls of a castle or the trees of a forest. The plays were performed without intermission, except for musical interludes that occurred at various points. Thus, the experience of seeing one of Shakespeare's plays staged in the Elizabethan theater was different from seeing it staged in a modern theater.

Today, a reconstruction of the Globe Theatre (below) stands on the south bank of the Thames River in London. In the 1940s, the American actor Sam Wanamaker visited London and was shocked to find nothing that commemorated the site of the original Globe. He eventually decided to try to raise enough money to reconstruct the Globe in its original location. The Globe Playhouse Trust was founded in the 1970s, but the actual construction of the new theater did not begin until the 1980s. After a number of setbacks—for example, the Trust ran out of funds after the construction of a large underground "diaphragm" wall needed to keep out the river water—the project was finally completed. The first performance at the reconstructed Globe was given on June 14, 1996, which would have been the late Sam Wanamaker's 77th birthday.

Aerial view of the reconstructed Globe Theatre in London
Jason Hawkes/Latitude/Corbis

The Modern Theater

Unlike the theaters of ancient Greece and Elizabethan England, seventeenth- and eighteenth-century theaters—such as the Palais Royal, where the great French playwright Molière presented many of his plays—were covered by a roof, beautifully decorated, and illuminated by candles so that plays could be performed at night. The theater remained brightly lit even during performances, partly because there was no easy way to extinguish hundreds of candles and partly because people went to the theater as much to see each other as to see the play.

A curtain opened and closed between acts, and the audience of about five hundred spectators sat in a long room and viewed the play on a **picture-frame stage**. This type of stage, which resembles the stages on which plays are performed today, contained the action within a **proscenium arch** that surrounded the opening through which the audience viewed the performance. Thus, the action seemed to take place in an adjoining room with one of its walls cut away. Painted scenery (some of it quite elaborate), intricately detailed costumes, and stage makeup were commonplace, and for the first time women performed female roles. In addition, a complicated series of ropes, pulleys, and cranks enabled stagehands to change scenery quickly, and sound-effects machines could give audiences the impression that they were hearing a galloping horse or a raging thunderstorm. Because the theaters were small, audiences were relatively close to the stage, so actors could use subtle movements and facial expressions to enhance their performances.

Many of the first innovations in the theater were quite basic. For example, the first stage lighting was produced by candles lining the front of the stage. This method of lighting was not only ineffective—actors were lit from below and had to step forward to be fully illuminated—but also dangerous. Costumes and even entire theaters could (and did) catch fire. Later, covered lanterns with reflectors provided better and safer lighting. In the nineteenth century, a device that used an oxyhydrogen flame directed on a cylinder of lime created extremely bright illumination that could, with the aid of a lens, be concentrated into a spotlight. (It is from this method of stage lighting that we get the expression *to be in the limelight.*)

Eventually, in the twentieth century, electric lights provided a dependable and safe way of lighting the stage. Electric spotlights, footlights, and ceiling light bars made the actors clearly visible and enabled playwrights to create special effects. In Arthur Miller's *Death of a Salesman* (p. 1233), for example, lighting focuses attention on action in certain areas of the stage while other areas are left in complete darkness.

Along with electric lighting came other innovations, such as electronic amplification. Microphones made it possible for actors to speak conversationally and to avoid using unnaturally loud "stage diction" to project their voices to the rear of the theater. Microphones placed at various points around the stage enabled actors and actresses to interact naturally and to deliver their lines audibly even without facing the audience. More recently, small wireless microphones have eliminated the unwieldy wires and the "dead spaces" left between upright or hanging microphones, allowing characters to move freely around the stage.

The true revolutions in staging came with the advent of **realism** in the middle of the nineteenth century. Until this time, scenery had been painted on canvas backdrops that trembled visibly, especially when they were intersected by doors through which actors and actresses entered. With realism came settings that were accurate down to the smallest detail. (Improved lighting, which revealed the inadequacies of painted backdrops, made such realistic stage settings necessary.) Backdrops were replaced by the **box set**, three flat panels arranged to form connected walls, with the fourth wall removed to give the audience the illusion of looking into a room. The room itself was decorated with real furniture, plants, and pictures on the walls; the door of one room might connect to another completely furnished room, or a window might open to a garden filled with realistic foliage. In addition, new methods of changing scenery were employed. Elevator stages, hydraulic lifts, and moving platforms enabled directors to make complicated changes in scenery out of the audience's view.

During the late nineteenth and early twentieth centuries, however, some playwrights reacted against what they saw as the excesses of realism. They introduced **surrealistic stage settings**, in which color and scenery mirrored the uncontrolled images of dreams, and **expressionistic stage settings**, in which costumes and scenery were exaggerated and distorted to reflect the workings of a troubled, even unbalanced mind. In addition, playwrights used lighting to create areas of light, shadow, and color that reinforced the themes of the play or reflected the emotions of the protagonist. Eugene O'Neill's 1920 play *The Emperor Jones*, for example, used a series of expressionistic scenes to show the deteriorating mental state of the terrified protagonist.

Sets in contemporary plays run the gamut from realistic to fantastic, from a detailed re-creation of a room in a production of Tennessee Williams's *The Glass Menagerie* (1945) to dreamlike sets for Eugene O'Neill's *The Emperor Jones* (1920) and Edward Albee's *The Sandbox* (1959). Motorized devices, such as revolving turntables, and *wagons*—scenery mounted on wheels—make possible rapid changes of scenery. The Broadway musical *Les Misérables*, for example, required scores of elaborate sets—Parisian slums, barricades, walled

Thrust-Stage Theater. Rendering of the thrust stage at the Guthrie Theatre in Minneapolis. With seats on three sides of the stage area, the thrust stage and its background can assume many forms. Entrances can be made from the aisles, from the sides, through the stage floor, and from the back.
Alvis Upitis/Hulton Archive/Getty Images

gardens—to be shifted as the audience watched. A gigantic barricade constructed on stage at one point in the play was later rotated to show the carnage that had taken place on both sides of a battle. Light, sound, and smoke were used to heighten the impact of the scene.

Today, as dramatists attempt to break down the barriers that separate audiences from the action they are viewing, plays are not limited to the picture-frame stage; in fact, they are performed on many different kinds of stages. Some plays take place on a **thrust stage** (pictured on the previous page), which has an area that projects out into the audience. Other plays are performed on an **arena stage**, with the audience surrounding the actors. (This kind of performance is often called **theater in the round**.) In addition, experiments have been done with **environmental staging**, in which the stage surrounds the audience or several stages are situated at various locations throughout the audience. Plays may also be performed outdoors, in settings ranging from parks to city streets.

Some playwrights even try to blur the line that divides the audience from the stage by having actors move through or sit in the audience—or even by eliminating the stage entirely. For example, *Tony 'n Tina's Wedding*, a **participatory drama** created in 1988 by the theater group Artificial Intelligence, takes place not in a theater but at a church where a wedding is performed and then at a catering hall where the wedding reception is held. Throughout the play, the members of the audience function as guests, joining in the wedding celebration and mingling with the actors, who improvise freely.

A more recent example of participatory drama is *Sleep No More*, which takes place in a block of warehouses (which has been transformed into the McKittrick Hotel) in the Chelsea neighborhood of New York City. The play is a wordless production of Shakespeare's

Arena-Stage Theater. The arena theater at the Riverside Community Players in Riverside, California. The audience surrounds the stage area, which may or may not be raised. Use of scenery is limited—perhaps to a single piece of scenery standing alone in the middle of the stage.
Source: Courtesy The Arena Theatre, Riverside Community Players, Riverside, CA

Scene from the participatory drama *Sleep No More*
Credit: Lucas Jackson/Reuters/Corbis

Macbeth. Audience members, who must wear white Venetian carnival masks and remain silent at all times, are taken by elevator to various floors of the "hotel." Once deposited, they are free to follow any of the actors, who appear and disappear at will, or to explore the hotel's many rooms. The action can be intense, with audience members chasing actors down dark, narrow hallways or up and down stairs to other floors of the hotel, and at times, being pulled into the action of the play.

Today, no single architectural form defines the theater. The modern stage is a flexible space suited to the many varieties of contemporary theatrical production.

 Tragedy and Comedy

Tragedy

In his *Poetics*, Aristotle (384–322 B.C.) sums up ancient Greek thinking about drama when he defines a **tragedy**—a drama treating a serious subject and involving persons of significance. According to Aristotle, when the members of an audience see a tragedy, they should feel both pity (and thus closeness to the protagonist) and fear (and thus revulsion) because they recognize in themselves the potential for similar reactions. The purging of these emotions that audience members experience as they see the dramatic action unfold is called **catharsis**. For catharsis to occur, the protagonist of a tragedy must be worthy of the audience's attention and sympathy.

Sergey Tarasov/Shutterstock.com

Because of his or her exalted position, the fall of a tragic protagonist is greater than that of an average person; therefore, it arouses more pity and fear in the audience. Often the entire society suffers as a result of the actions of the protagonist. Before the action of Sophocles' *Oedipus the King* (p. 1430), for example, Oedipus has freed Thebes from the deadly grasp of the Sphinx by answering her riddle and, as a result, has been welcomed as king. But because of his sins, Oedipus is an affront to the gods and brings famine and pestilence to the city. When his fall finally comes, it is sudden and absolute.

According to Aristotle, the protagonist of a tragedy is neither all good nor all evil, but a mixture of the two. The protagonist is like the rest of us—only more exalted and possessing some weakness or flaw (**hamartia**). This tragic flaw—perhaps narrowness of vision or overwhelming pride (**hubris**)—is typically the element that creates the conditions for tragedy. Shakespeare's Romeo and Juliet, for example, are so much in love they think they can ignore the blood feud that rages between their two families. However, their naive efforts to sustain their love despite the feud lead them to their tragic deaths. Similarly, Richard III's blind ambition to gain the throne causes him to murder all those who stand in his way. His unscrupulousness sets into motion the forces that eventually cause his death.

Irony—a discrepancy between what characters say and what the audience believes to be true—is central to tragedy. **Dramatic irony** (also called **tragic irony**) emerges from a situation in which the audience knows more about the dramatic situation than a character does. As a result, the character's words and actions may be consistent with what he or she expects but at odds with what the audience knows will happen. Thus, a character may say or do something that causes the audience to infer a meaning beyond what the character intends or realizes. The dramatic irony is clear, for example, when Oedipus announces that whoever has disobeyed the dictates of the gods will be exiled. The audience knows, although Oedipus does not, that he has just condemned himself. **Cosmic irony**, also called **irony of fate**, occurs when God, fate, or some larger, uncontrollable force seems to be intentionally deceiving characters into believing they can escape their fate. Too late, they realize that trying to avoid their destiny is futile. Years before Oedipus was born, for example, the oracle of Apollo foretold that Oedipus would kill his parents. Naturally, his parents attempted to thwart the prophecy, but ironically, their actions ensured that the prophecy would be fulfilled.

At some point in a tragedy—after the climax—the protagonist begins to recognize and understand the reasons for his or her downfall. This moment of recognition (called the **catastrophe**) elevates tragic protagonists to grandeur and gives their suffering meaning. Without this recognition, there would be no tragedy, just **pathos**—suffering that exists simply to satisfy the sentimental or morbid sensibilities of the audience. In spite of the death of the protagonist, then, tragedy enables the audience to see the nobility of the character and thus to experience a sense of elation. In Shakespeare's *King Lear*, for example, a king at the height of his powers decides to divide his kingdom among his three daughters. Later, he realizes that without his power, he is just a bothersome old man to his ambitious children. Only after going mad does he understand the vanity of his former existence; he dies a humbled but enlightened man.

According to Aristotle, a tragedy achieves the illusion of reality when it has **unity of action**—that is, when the play contains only those actions that lead to its tragic outcome. Later critics interpreted this constraint to mean that including subplots or mixing tragic and comic elements would destroy this unity. To the concept of unity of action, these later critics added two other requirements: **unity of place**—the requirement that the play have a single setting—and **unity of time**—the requirement that the events depicted by the play take no longer than the actual duration of the play (or, at most, a single day).

The **three unities** have had a long and rather uneven history. For example, although Shakespeare observed the unities in some of his plays—such as *The Tempest* and *The Comedy of Errors*—he had no compunctions about writing plays with subplots and frequent changes of location. He also wrote **tragicomedies**, such as *The Merchant of Venice*, which have a serious theme appropriate for tragedy but end happily, usually because of a sudden turn of events. During the eighteenth century, with its emphasis on classic form, the unities were adhered to quite strictly. In the late eighteenth and early nineteenth centuries, with the onset of romanticism and its emphasis on the natural, interest in the unities of place and time waned. Even though some modern plays (particularly one-act plays) do observe the unities—*Trifles* (p. 1604), for instance, has a single setting and takes place during a period of time that corresponds to the length of the play—few modern dramatists strictly adhere to them.

Ideas about appropriate subjects for tragedy have also changed. For Aristotle, the protagonist of a tragedy had to be exceptional—a king, for example. The protagonists of Greek tragedies were usually historical or mythical figures. Shakespeare often used kings and princes as protagonists—Richard II and Hamlet, for example—but he also used people of lesser rank, as in *Romeo and Juliet* and *A Midsummer Night's Dream*. In our times, interest in the lives of monarchs has been overshadowed by involvement in the lives of ordinary people. Modern tragedies—*Death of a Salesman*, for example—are more likely to focus on a traveling salesman than on a king.

With the rise of the middle class in the nineteenth century, ideas about the nature of tragedy changed. Responding to the age's desire for sentimentality, playwrights produced **melodramas**, sensational plays that appealed mainly to the emotions. Melodramas include many of the elements of tragedy but end happily and often rely on conventional plots and stock characters. Because the protagonists in melodramas—often totally virtuous heroines suffering at the hands of impossibly wicked villains—helplessly endure their tribulations without ever gaining insight or enlightenment, they never achieve tragic status. As a result, they remain cardboard cutouts who exist only to exploit the emotions of the audience. Melodrama survives today in many films and in television soap operas.

Realism, which arose in the late nineteenth century as a response to the artificiality of melodrama, presented serious (and sometimes tragic) themes and believable characters in the context of everyday contemporary life. Writers of realistic drama used their plays to educate their audiences about the problems of the society in which they lived. For this reason, realistic drama focuses on the commonplace and eliminates the unlikely coincidences and excessive sentimentality of melodrama. Dramatists such as Henrik Ibsen scrutinize the lives of ordinary people, not larger-than-life characters. After great suffering, these characters rise above the limitations of their mediocre lives and exhibit courage or emotional strength. The insight they gain often focuses attention on a social problem—the restrictive social conventions that define the behavior of women in nineteenth-century marriages, for example. Realistic drama also features settings and props similar to those used in people's daily lives and includes dialogue that reflects the way people actually speak.

Developing alongside realism was a literary movement called **naturalism**. Like realism, naturalism rejected the unrealistic plots and sentimentality of melodrama, but unlike realism, naturalism sought to explore the depths of the human condition. Influenced by Charles Darwin's ideas about evolution and natural selection and Karl Marx's ideas about economic forces that shape people's lives, naturalism is a pessimistic philosophy that presents a world that is at worst hostile and at best indifferent to human concerns. It portrays human beings as higher-order animals who are driven by basic instincts—especially hunger, fear, greed, and sexuality—and who are subject to economic, social, and biological forces beyond their understanding or control. For these reasons, it is well suited to tragic themes.

The nineteenth-century French writer Émile Zola did much to develop the theory of naturalism, as did the American writers Stephen Crane, Frank Norris, and Theodore Dreiser. Naturalism also finds its way into the work of contemporary dramatists, such as Arthur Miller. Unlike other tragic characters, the protagonists of naturalist works are crushed not by the gods or by fate but by poverty, animal drives, or social class. Willy Loman in *Death of a Salesman*, (p. 1233), for example, is subject to the economic forces of a society that does not value its workers and discards those it no longer finds useful.

Comedy

A **comedy** treats themes and characters with humor and typically has a happy ending. Whereas tragedy focuses on the hidden dimensions of the tragic hero's character, comedy focuses on the public persona, the protagonist as a social being. Tragic figures are typically seen in isolation, questioning the meaning of their lives and trying to comprehend their suffering. Hamlet—draped in sable, longing for death, and self-consciously contemplating his duty—epitomizes the isolation of the tragic hero.

Sergey Tarasov/Shutterstock.com

Unlike tragic heroes, comic figures are seen in the public arena, where people intentionally assume the masks of pretension and self-importance. The purpose of comedy is to strip away these masks and expose human beings for what they are. Whereas tragedy reveals the nobility of the human condition, comedy reveals its inherent folly, portraying human beings as selfish, hypocritical, vain, weak, irrational, and capable of self-delusion. Thus, the basic function of comedy is critical—to tell people that things are not what they seem and that appearances are not necessarily reality. In the comic world, nothing is solid or predictable, and accidents and coincidences are more important to the plot than reason. Many of Shakespeare's comedies, for example, depend on exchanged or confused identities. The wordplay and verbal nonsense of comedy add to this general confusion.

Comedies typically rely on certain familiar plot devices. Many comedies begin with a startling or unusual situation that attracts the audience's attention. In Shakespeare's *A Midsummer Night's Dream*, for example, Theseus, the duke of Athens, rules that Hermia will either marry the man her father has chosen for her or be put to death. Such an event could lead to tragedy if comedy did not intervene to save the day.

Comedy often depends on obstacles and hindrances to further its plot: the more difficult the problems the lovers face, the more satisfying their eventual triumph will be. For this reason, the plot of a comedy is usually more complex than the plot of a tragedy. Compare the rather straightforward plot of *Hamlet* (p. 1304)—a prince ordered to avenge his murdered father's death is driven mad with indecision and, after finally acting decisively, is killed himself—with the mix-ups, mistaken identities, and general confusion of *A Midsummer Night's Dream*.

Finally, comedies have happy endings. Whereas tragedy ends with death, comedy ends with an affirmation of life. Eventually, the confusion and misunderstandings reach a point where some resolution must be achieved: the difficulties of the lovers are overcome, the villains are banished, and the lovers marry—or at least express their intention to do so. In this way, the lovers establish their connection with the rest of society, and its values are affirmed.

The first comedies, written in Greece in the fifth century B.C., heavily satirized the religious and social issues of the day and were characterized by bawdy humor. In the fourth and third centuries B.C., this **Old Comedy** gave way to **New Comedy**, a comedy of romance with stock characters—lovers and untrustworthy servants, for example—and conventional settings. Lacking the bitter satire and bawdiness of Old Comedy, New Comedy depends on outrageous plots, mistaken identities, young lovers, interfering parents, and conniving servants. Ultimately, the young lovers outwit all those who stand between them and, in so doing, affirm the primacy of youth and love over old age and death.

Old and New Comedy represent two distinct lines of humor that extend to modern times. Old Comedy depends on **satire**—biting humor that diminishes a person, idea, or institution by ridiculing it or holding it up to scorn. Unlike most comedy, which exists simply to make people laugh, satire is social criticism, deriding hypocrisy, pretension, and vanity or condemning vice. At its best, satire appeals to the intellect, has a serious purpose, and arouses thoughtful laughter. New Comedy may also be satiric, but the satire is often tempered by elements of **farce**, comedy in which stereotypical characters engage in boisterous horseplay and slapstick humor, all the while making jokes and sexual innuendoes—as they do in Anton Chekhov's *The Brute* (p. 1048).

English comedy got its start in the sixteenth century in the form of farcical episodes that appeared in morality plays. During the Renaissance, comedy developed rapidly, beginning in 1533 with Nicholas Udall's *Ralph Roister Doister* and eventually evolving into Shakespeare's **romantic comedy**—such as *A Midsummer Night's Dream*—in which love is the main subject and idealized heroines and lovers endure great difficulties until the inevitable happy ending is reached.

Also during the Renaissance, particularly in the seventeenth century, writers such as Ben Jonson experimented with a different type of comedy—the **comedy of humours**, which focused on characters whose behavior was controlled by a characteristic trait, or *humour*. During the Renaissance, a person's temperament was thought to be determined by the mix of fluids, or humours, in the body. When one humour dominated, a certain type of disposition resulted. Playwrights capitalized on this belief, writing comedies in which characters are motivated by stereotypical behaviors that result from the imbalance of the humours. In comedies such as Jonson's *Volpone* and *The Alchemist*, characters such as the suspicious husband and the miser can be manipulated by others because of their predictable dispositions.

Closely related to the comedy of humours is the satiric **comedy of manners**, which developed during the sixteenth and seventeenth centuries and achieved great popularity in the nineteenth century. This form focused on the manners and customs of society and directed its satire against characters who violated social conventions and rules of behavior. The comedy comes from players striving to maintain appearances while at the same time revealing the truth behind artificial codes of conduct. These plays tend to be memorable more for their witty dialogue than for their development of characters or setting. Oliver Goldsmith's *She Stoops to Conquer*, George Bernard Shaw's *Pygmalion*, and even some of the television sitcoms of today are examples of this type of comedy.

In the eighteenth century, a reaction against the perceived immorality of the comedy of manners led to **sentimental comedy**, which eventually achieved great popularity. This kind of comedy relied on sentimental emotion rather than on wit or humor to move an audience. It also dwelled on the virtues rather than on the vices of life. The heroes of sentimental comedy are unimpeachably noble, moral, and honorable; the pure, virtuous, middle-class heroines suffer trials and tribulations calculated to move the audience to tears rather than to laughter. Eventually, the distress of the hero and heroine is resolved in a sometimes contrived (but always happy) ending. Sir Richard Steele's *The Conscious Lovers* (1722) is an example of sentimental comedy.

In his 1877 essay *The Idea of Comedy*, novelist and critic George Meredith suggests that comedy that appeals to the intellect should be called **high comedy**. Thus, Shakespeare's *As You Like It* and George Bernard Shaw's *Pygmalion* can be characterized as high comedy. When comedy has little or no intellectual appeal, according to Meredith, it is **low comedy**. Low comedy appears in parts of Shakespeare's *The Taming of the Shrew* and as comic relief in *Macbeth*.

The twentieth century developed its own characteristic comic forms, reflecting the uncertainty and pessimism of a period marked by two world wars, the Holocaust, and nuclear destruction, as well as threats posed by environmental pollution and ethnic and racial conflict—and, in this century, the terrorist attacks of September 11, 2001. Combining laughter and hints of tragedy, these modern tragicomedies feature **antiheroes**, characters who, instead of manifesting dignity and power, are ineffectual or petty. Their plight frequently elicits laughter, not pity and fear, from the audience. **Black** or **dark comedies**, for example, rely on the morbid and the absurd. These works are usually so satiric and bitter that they threaten to slip over into tragedy. The screenplay of Joseph Heller's novel *Catch-22*, which ends with a character dropping bombs on his own men, is a classic example of such comedy. **Theater of the absurd**, which includes comedies such as Samuel Beckett's *Waiting for Godot* and Tom Stoppard's *Rosencrantz and Guildenstern Are Dead*, begins with the assumption that the human condition is irrational. Typically, this type of drama does not have a conventional plot; instead, it presents a series of apparently unrelated images and illogical exchanges of dialogue meant to reinforce the idea that human beings live in a remote, confusing, and often incomprehensible universe. Absurdist dramas seem to go in circles, never progressing to a climax or achieving a resolution, thus reinforcing the theme of the endless and meaningless repetition that characterizes modern life.

Defining Drama

Dramatic works differ from other prose works in a number of fairly obvious ways. For one thing, plays look different on the page: generally, they are divided into **acts** and **scenes**; they include **stage directions** that specify characters' entrances and exits and describe what settings look like and how characters look and act; and they consist primarily of **dialogue**, lines spoken by the characters. And, of course, plays are different from other prose works in that they are written not to be read but to be performed in front of an audience.

Unlike novels and short stories, plays do not usually have narrators to tell the audience what a character is thinking or what happened in the past; for the most part, the audience knows only what characters reveal. To compensate for the absence of a narrator, playwrights can use **monologues** (extended speeches by one character), **soliloquies** (monologues in which a character expresses private thoughts while alone on stage), or **asides** (brief comments by a character who reveals thoughts by speaking directly to the audience without being heard by the other characters). In addition to these dramatic techniques, a play can also use costumes, scenery, props, music, lighting, and other techniques to enhance its impact on the audience.

The play that follows, Anton Chekhov's *The Brute* (1888), is typical of modern drama in many respects. A one-act play translated from Russian, it is essentially a struggle of wills between two headstrong characters, a man and a woman, with action escalating through the characters' increasingly heated exchanges of dialogue. Stage directions briefly describe the setting—"the drawing room of a country house"—and announce the appearance of various props. They also describe the major characters' appearances as well as their actions, gestures, and emotions. Because the play is a **farce,** it features broad physical comedy, asides, wild dramatic gestures, and elaborate figures of speech, all designed to enhance its comic effect.

Source: ©Bettmann/Corbis

ANTON CHEKHOV (1860–1904) is an important nineteenth-century Russian playwright and short story writer. He became a doctor and, as a young adult, supported the rest of his family after his father's bankruptcy. After his early adult years in Moscow, Chekhov spent the rest of his life in the country, moving to Yalta, a resort town in Crimea, for his health (he suffered from tuberculosis). He continued to write plays, mostly for the Moscow Art Theatre, although he could not supervise their production as he would have wished. His plays include *The Seagull* (1896), *Uncle Vanya* (1898), *The Three Sisters* (1901), and *The Cherry Orchard* (1904).

The Brute, or *The Bear* (1888), is one of a number of one-act farces Chekhov wrote just before his major plays. It is based on a French farce *(Les Jurons de Cadillac* by Pierre Breton) about a man who cannot refrain from swearing. The woman he loves offers to marry him if he can avoid swearing for one hour; he is unable to do it, but he fails so charmingly that she agrees to marry him anyway.

Cultural Context The custom of dueling has been popular throughout history in many countries. Generally speaking, as in *The Brute*, duels are fought as a matter of honor—in response to an insult, an offense to one's character, or an affront to one's dignity. Once a challenge to a duel has been issued, negotiators (called *seconds*) agree on the time, place, and weaponry involved, as well as the point of surrender (first blood drawn or death). In a pistol duel, the participants stand back to back, count off a predetermined number of paces, turn, and fire. Today, dueling is illegal in most countries, and killing someone in the course of a duel is considered murder.

The Brute

A JOKE IN ONE ACT (1888)

Translated by Eric Bentley

CHARACTERS

Mrs. Popov, *widow and landowner,*
small, with dimpled cheeks
Mr. Grigory S. Smirnov, *gentleman*
farmer, middle-aged
Luka, *Mrs. Popov's footman, an old man*

Gardener
Coachman
Hired Men

SCENE

The drawing room of a country house. Mrs. Popov, in deep mourning, is staring hard at a photograph. Luka is with her.

LUKA: It's not right, ma'am, you're killing yourself. The cook has gone off with the maid to pick berries. The cat's having a high old time in the yard catching birds. Every living thing is happy. But you stay moping here in the house like it was a convent, taking no pleasure in nothing. I mean it, ma'am! It must be a full year since you set foot out of doors.

MRS. POPOV: I must never set foot out of doors again, Luka. Never! I have nothing to set foot out of doors *for*. My life is done. *He* is in his grave. I have buried myself alive in this house. We are *both* in our graves.

LUKA: You're off again, ma'am. I just won't listen to you no more. Mr. Popov is dead, but what can we do about that? It's God's doing. God's will be done. You've cried over him, you've done your share of mourning, haven't you? There's a limit to everything. You can't go on weeping and wailing forever. My old lady died, for that matter, and I wept and wailed over her a whole month long. Well, that was it. I couldn't weep and wail all my life. She just wasn't worth it. (*He sighs.*) As for the neighbors, you've forgotten all about them, ma'am. You don't visit them and you don't let them visit you. You and I are like a pair of spiders—excuse the expression, ma'am—here we are in this house like a pair of spiders, we never see the light of day. And it isn't like there was no nice people around either. The whole county's swarming with 'em. There's a regiment quartered at Riblov, and the officers are so good-looking! The girls can't take their eyes off them—There's a ball at the camp every Friday—The military band plays most every day of the week—What do you say, ma'am? You're young, you're pretty, you could enjoy yourself! Ten years from now you may want to strut and show your feathers to the officers, and it'll be too late.

MRS. POPOV: (*firmly*) You must never bring this subject up again, Luka. Since Popov died, life has been an empty dream to me, you know that. *You* may think I am alive. Poor ignorant Luka! You are wrong. I am dead. I'm in my grave. Never more shall I see the light of day, never strip from my body this . . . raiment of death! Are you listening, Luka? Let his ghost learn how I love him! Yes, *I* know, and *you* know, he was often unfair to me, he was cruel to me, and he was unfaithful to me. What of it? *I* shall be faithful to *him*, that's all. I will show him how *I* can love. Hereafter, in a better world than this, he will welcome me back, the same loyal girl I always was—

LUKA: Instead of carrying on this way, ma'am, you should go out in the garden and take a bit of a walk, ma'am. Or why not harness Toby and take a drive? Call on a couple of the neighbours, ma'am? 5

MRS. POPOV: (*breaking down*) Oh, Luka!

LUKA: Yes, ma'am? What have I said, ma'am? Oh, dear!

MRS. POPOV: Toby! You said Toby! He adored that horse. When he drove me out to the Korchagins and the Vlasovs, it was always with Toby! He was a wonderful driver, do you remember, Luka? So graceful! So strong! I can see him now, pulling at those reins with all his might and main! Toby! Luka, tell them to give Toby an extra portion of oats today.

LUKA: Yes, ma'am.

A bell rings.

10 MRS. POPOV: Who is that? Tell them I'm not at home.

LUKA: Very good, ma'am. (*Exit.*)

MRS. POPOV: (*gazing again at the photograph*) You shall see, my Popov, how a wife can love and forgive. Till death do us part. Longer than that. Till death re-unite us forever! (*Suddenly a titter breaks through her tears.*) Aren't you ashamed of yourself, Popov? Here's your little wife, being good, being faithful, so faithful she's locked up here waiting for her own funeral, while you—doesn't it make you ashamed, you naughty boy? You were terrible, you know. You were unfaithful, and you made those awful scenes about it, you stormed out and left me alone for weeks—

Enter Luka.

LUKA: (*upset*) There's someone asking for you, ma'am. Says he must—

MRS. POPOV: I suppose you told him that since my husband's death I see no one?

15 LUKA: Yes, ma'am. I did, ma'am. But he wouldn't listen, ma'am. He says it's urgent.

MRS. POPOV: (*shrilly*) I see no one!!

LUKA: He won't take no for an answer, ma'am. He just curses and swears and comes in anyway. He's a perfect monster, ma'am. He's in the dining room right now.

MRS. POPOV: In the dining room, is he? I'll give him his come-uppance. Bring him in here this minute.

Exit Luka.

(*Suddenly sad again.*) Why do they do this to me? Why? Insulting my grief, intruding on my solitude? (*She sighs.*) I'm afraid I'll have to enter a convent. I will, I *must* enter a convent!

Enter Mr. Smirnov and Luka.

SMIRNOV: (*to Luka*) Dolt! Idiot! You talk too much! (*Seeing Mrs. Popov. With dignity.*) May I have the honor of introducing myself, madam? Grigory S. Smirnov, landowner and lieutenant of artillery, retired. Forgive me, madam, if I disturb your peace and quiet, but my business is both urgent and weighty.

20 MRS. POPOV: (*declining to offer him her hand*) What is it you wish, sir?

SMIRNOV: At the time of his death, your late husband—with whom I had the honor to be acquainted, ma'am—was in my debt to the tune of twelve hundred rubles. I have two notes to prove it. Tomorrow, ma'am, I must pay the interest on a bank loan. I have therefore no alternative, ma'am, but to ask you to pay me the money today.

MRS. POPOV: Twelve hundred rubles? But what did my husband owe it to you for?

SMIRNOV: He used to buy his oats from me, madam.

MRS. POPOV: (*to Luka, with a sigh*) Remember what I said, Luka: tell them to give Toby an extra portion of oats today!

Exit Luka.

My dear Mr.—what was the name again?

SMIRNOV: Smirnov, ma'am.   25

MRS. POPOV: My dear Mr. Smirnov, if Mr. Popov owed you money, you shall be
    paid—to the last ruble, to the last kopeck. But today—you must excuse me,
    Mr.—what was it?

SMIRNOV: Smirnov, ma'am.

MRS. POPOV: Today, Mr. Smirnov, I have no ready cash in the house. (*Smirnov
    starts to speak.*) Tomorrow, Mr. Smirnov, no, the day after tomorrow, all
    will be well. My steward will be back from town. I shall see that he pays
    what is owing. Today, no. In any case, today is exactly seven months from
    Mr. Popov's death. On such a day you will understand that I am in no mood
    to think of money.

SMIRNOV: Madam, if you don't pay up now, you can carry me out feet foremost.
    They'll seize my estate.

MRS. POPOV: You can have your money. (*He starts to thank her.*) Tomorrow. (*He*   30
    again starts to speak.) That is: the day after tomorrow.

SMIRNOV: I don't need the money the day after tomorrow. I need it today.

MRS. POPOV: I'm sorry, Mr.—

SMIRNOV: (*shouting*) Smirnov!

MRS. POPOV: (*sweetly*) Yes, of course. But you can't have it today.

SMIRNOV: But I can't wait for it any longer!   35

MRS. POPOV: Be sensible, Mr. Smirnov. How can I pay you if I don't have it?

SMIRNOV: You don't have it?

MRS. POPOV: I don't have it.

SMIRNOV: Sure?

MRS. POPOV: Positive.   40

SMIRNOV: Very well. I'll make a note to that effect. (*Shrugging.*) And then they
    want me to keep cool. I meet the tax commissioner on the street, and he says,
    "Why are you always in such a bad humor, Smirnov?" Bad humor! How can I
    help it, in God's name? I need money, I need it desperately. Take yesterday: I
    leave home at the crack of dawn, I call on all my debtors. Not a one of them
    pays up. Footsore and weary, I creep at midnight into some little dive, and try to
    snatch a few winks of sleep on the floor by the vodka barrel. Then today, I come
    here, fifty miles from home, saying to myself, "At last, at last, I can be sure of
    something," and you're not in the mood! You give me a mood! Christ, how can
    I help getting all worked up?

MRS. POPOV: I thought I'd made it clear, Mr. Smirnov, that you'll get your money
    the minute my steward is back from town.

SMIRNOV: What the hell do I care about your steward? Pardon the expression,
    ma'am. But it was you I came to see.

MRS. POPOV: What language! What a tone to take to a lady! I refuse to hear an-
    other word. (*Quickly, exit.*)

SMIRNOV: Not in the mood, huh? "Exactly seven months since Popov's death," huh?   45
    How about me? (*Shouting after her.*) Is there this interest to pay, or isn't there?
    I'm asking you a question: is there this interest to pay, or isn't there? So your
    husband died, and you're not in the mood, and your steward's gone off some

place, and so forth and so on, but what can *I* do about all that, huh? What do *you* think I should do? Take a running jump and shove my head through the wall? Take off in a balloon? You don't know my *other* debtors. I call on Gruzdeff. Not at home. I look for Yaroshevitch. He's hiding out. I find Kooritsin. He kicks up a row, and I have to throw him through the window. I work my way right down the list. Not a kopeck. Then I come to you, and God damn it to hell, if you'll pardon the expression, you're not in the mood! (*Quietly, as he realizes he's talking to air.*) I've spoiled them all, that's what, I've let them play me for a sucker. Well, I'll show them. I'll show this one. I'll stay right here till she pays up. Ugh! (*He shudders with rage.*) I'm in a rage! I'm in a positively towering rage! Every nerve in my body is trembling at forty to the dozen! I can't breathe, I feel ill, I think I'm going to faint, hey, you there!

Enter Luka.

LUKA: Yes, sir? Is there anything you wish, sir?
SMIRNOV: Water! Water! No, make it vodka.

Exit Luka.

Consider the logic of it. A fellow creature is desperately in need of cash, so desperately in need that he has to seriously contemplate hanging himself, and this woman, this mere chit of a girl, won't pay up, and why not? Because, forsooth, she isn't in the mood! Oh, the logic of women! Come to that, I never have liked them, I could do without the whole sex. Talk to a woman? I'd rather sit on a barrel of dynamite, the very thought gives me gooseflesh. Women! Creatures of poetry and romance! Just to see one in the distance gets me mad. My legs start twitching with rage. I feel like yelling for help.

Enter Luka, handing Smirnov a glass of water.

LUKA: Mrs. Popov is indisposed, sir. She is seeing no one.
SMIRNOV: Get out.

Exit Luka.

Indisposed, is she? Seeing no one, huh? Well, she can see me or not, but I'll be here, I'll be right here till she pays up. If you're sick for a week, I'll be here for a week. If you're sick for a year, I'll be here for a year. You won't get around *me* with your widow's weeds and your schoolgirl dimples. I know all about dimples. (*Shouting through the window.*) Semyon, let the horses out of those shafts, we're not leaving, we're staying, and tell them to give the horses some oats, yes, oats, you fool, what do you think? (*Walking away from the window.*) What a mess, what an unholy mess! I didn't sleep last night, the heat is terrific today, not a damn one of 'em has paid up, and here's this—this skirt in mourning that's not in the mood! My head aches, where's that—(*He drinks from the glass.*) Water, ugh! You there!

Enter Luka.

50 LUKA: Yes, sir. You wish for something, sir?

SMIRNOV: Where's that confounded vodka I asked for?

Exit Luka.

> (*Smirnov sits and looks himself over.*) Oof! A fine figure of a man I am! Un-
> washed, uncombed, unshaven, straw on my vest, dust all over me. The little
> woman must've taken me for a highwayman. (*Yawns.*) I suppose it wouldn't be
> considered polite to barge into a drawing room in this state, but who cares? I'm
> not a visitor, I'm a creditor—most unwelcome of guests, second only to Death.

Enter Luka.

LUKA: (*handing him the vodka*) If I may say so, sir, you take too many liberties, sir.
SMIRNOV: What?!
LUKA: Oh, nothing, sir, nothing.
SMIRNOV: Who in hell do you think you're talking to? Shut your mouth!   55
LUKA: (*aside*) There's an evil spirit abroad. The Devil must have sent him. Oh!
> (*Exit Luka.*)
SMIRNOV: What a rage I'm in! I'll grind the whole world to powder. Oh, I feel ill
> again. You there!

Enter Mrs. Popov.

MRS. POPOV: (*looking at the floor*) In the solitude of my rural retreat, Mr. Smirnov,
> I've long since grown unaccustomed to the sound of the human voice. Above
> all, I cannot bear shouting. I must beg you not to break the silence.
SMIRNOV: Very well. Pay me my money and I'll go.
MRS. POPOV: I told you before, and I tell you again, Mr. Smirnov. I have no cash,   60
> you'll have to wait till the day after tomorrow. Can I express myself more plainly?
SMIRNOV: And I told you before, and I tell you again, that I need the money today,
> that the day after tomorrow is too late, and that if you don't pay, and pay now,
> I'll have to hang myself in the morning!
MRS. POPOV: But I have no cash. This is quite a puzzle.
SMIRNOV: You won't pay, huh?
MRS. POPOV: I can't pay, Mr. Smirnov.
SMIRNOV: In that case, I'm going to sit here and wait. (*Sits down.*) You'll pay up the   65
> day after tomorrow? Very good. Till the day after tomorrow, here I sit. (*Pause.*
> *He jumps up.*) Now look, do I have to pay that interest tomorrow, or don't I? Or
> do you think I'm joking?
MRS. POPOV: I must ask you not to raise your voice, Mr. Smirnov. This is not a stable.
SMIRNOV: Who said it was? Do I have to pay the interest tomorrow or not?
MRS. POPOV: Mr. Smirnov, do you know how to behave in the presence of a lady?
SMIRNOV: No, madam, I do not know how to behave in the presence of a lady.
MRS. POPOV: Just what I thought. I look at you, and I say: ugh! I hear you talk, and   70
> I say to myself: "That man doesn't know how to talk to a lady."
SMIRNOV: You'd like me to come simpering to you in French, I suppose. "*Enchanté,*
> *madame! Merci beaucoup* for not paying zee money, *madame! Pardonnez-moi* if I
> 'ave disturbed you, *madame!* How *charmante* you look in mourning, *madame!*"

MRS. POPOV: Now you're being silly, Mr. Smirnov.

SMIRNOV: *(mimicking)* "Now you're being silly, Mr. Smirnov." "You don't know how to talk to a lady, Mr. Smirnov." Look here, Mrs. Popov, I've known more women than you've known pussy cats. I've fought three duels on their account. I've jilted twelve, and been jilted by nine others. Oh, yes, Mrs. Popov, I've played the fool in my time, whispered sweet nothings, bowed and scraped and endeavored to please. Don't tell me I don't know what it is to love, to pine away with longing, to have the blues, to melt like butter, to be weak as water. I was full of tender emotion. I was carried away with passion. I squandered half my fortune on the sex. I chattered about women's emancipation. But there's an end to everything, dear madam. Burning eyes, dark eyelashes, ripe, red lips, dimpled cheeks, heaving bosoms, soft whisperings, the moon above; the lake below—I don't give a rap for that sort of nonsense any more, Mrs. Popov. I've found out about women. Present company excepted, they're liars. Their behavior is mere play acting; their conversation is sheer gossip. Yes, dear lady, women, young or old, are false, petty, vain, cruel, malicious, unreasonable. As for intelligence, any sparrow could give them points. Appearances, I admit, can be deceptive. In appearance, a woman may be all poetry and romance, goddess and angel, muslin and fluff. To look at her exterior is to be transported to heaven. But I have looked at her interior, Mrs. Popov, and what did I find there—in her very soul? A crocodile. *(He has gripped the back of the chair so firmly that it snaps.)* And, what is more revolting, a crocodile with an illusion, a crocodile that imagines tender sentiments are its own special province, a crocodile that thinks itself queen of the realm of love! Whereas, in sober fact, dear madam, if a woman can love anything except a lapdog you can hang me by the feet on that nail. For a man, love is suffering, love is sacrifice. A woman just swishes her train around and tightens her grip on your nose. Now, you're a woman, aren't you, Mrs. Popov? You must be an expert on some of this. Tell me, quite frankly, did you ever know a woman to be—faithful, for instance? Or even sincere? Only old hags, huh? Though some women are old hags from birth. But as for the others? You're right: a faithful woman is a freak of nature—like a cat with horns.

MRS. POPOV: Who *is* faithful, then? Who *have* you cast for the faithful lover? Not man?

75   SMIRNOV: Right first time, Mrs. Popov: man.

MRS. POPOV: *(going off into a peal of bitter laughter)* Man! Man is faithful! That's a new one! *(Fiercely.)* What right do you have to say this, Mr. Smirnov? Men faithful? Let me tell you something. Of all the men I have ever known my late husband Popov was the best. I loved him, and there are women who know how to love, Mr. Smirnov. I gave him my youth, my happiness, my life, my fortune. I worshipped the ground he trod on—and what happened? The best of men was unfaithful to me, Mr. Smirnov. Not once in a while. All the time. After he died, I found his desk drawer full of love letters. While he was alive, he was always going away for the week-end. He squandered my money. He made love to other women before my very eyes. But, in spite of all, Mr. Smirnov, *I* was faithful. Unto death. And beyond. I am *still* faithful, Mr. Smirnov! Buried alive in this house, I shall wear mourning till the day I, too, am called to my eternal rest.

SMIRNOV: (*laughing scornfully*) Expect me to believe that? As if I couldn't see through all this hocus-pocus. Buried alive! Till you're called to your eternal rest! Till when? Till some little poet—or some little subaltern with his first moustache—comes riding by and asks: "Can that be the house of the mysterious Tamara who for love of her late husband has buried herself alive, vowing to see no man?" Ha!

MRS. POPOV: (*flaring up*) How dare you? How dare you insinuate—?

SMIRNOV: You may have buried yourself alive, Mrs. Popov, but you haven't forgotten to powder your nose.

MRS. POPOV: (*incoherent*) How dare you? How—? 80

SMIRNOV: Who's raising his voice now? Just because I call a spade a spade. Because I shoot straight from the shoulder. Well, don't shout at me, I'm not your steward.

MRS. POPOV: I'm not shouting, you're shouting! Oh, leave me alone!

SMIRNOV: Pay me the money, and I will.

MRS. POPOV: You'll get no money out of me!

SMIRNOV: Oh, so that's it! 85

MRS. POPOV: Not a ruble, not a kopeck. Get out! Leave me alone!

SMIRNOV: Not being your husband, I must ask you not to make scenes with me. (*He sits.*) I don't like scenes.

MRS. POPOV: (*choking with rage*) You're sitting down?

SMIRNOV: Correct, I'm sitting down.

MRS. POPOV: I asked you to leave! 90

SMIRNOV: Then give me the money. (*Aside.*) Oh, what a rage I'm in, what a rage!

MRS. POPOV: The impudence of the man! I won't talk to you a moment longer. Get out. (*Pause.*) Are you going?

SMIRNOV: No.

MRS. POPOV: No?!

SMIRNOV: No. 95

MRS. POPOV: On your head be it. Luka!

Enter Luka.

    Show the gentleman out, Luka.

LUKA: (*approaching*) I'm afraid, sir, I'll have to ask you, um, to leave, sir, now, um—

SMIRNOV: (*jumping up*) Shut your mouth, you old idiot! Who do you think you're talking to? I'll make mincemeat of you.

LUKA: (*clutching his heart*) Mercy on us! Holy saints above! (*He falls into an armchair.*) I'm taken sick! I can't breathe!!

MRS. POPOV: Then where's Dasha? Dasha! Dasha! Come here at once! (*She rings.*) 100

LUKA: They gone picking berries, ma'am, I'm alone here—Water, water, I'm taken sick!

MRS. POPOV: (*to Smirnov*) Get out, you!

SMIRNOV: Can't you even be polite with me, Mrs. Popov?

MRS. POPOV: (*clenching her fists and stamping her feet*) With you? You're a wild animal, you were never house-broken!

105 SMIRNOV: What? What did you say?

MRS. POPOV: I said you were a wild animal, you were never house-broken.

SMIRNOV: *(advancing upon her)* And what right do you have to talk to me like that?

MRS. POPOV: Like what?

SMIRNOV: You have insulted me, madam.

110 MRS. POPOV: What of it? Do you think I'm scared of you?

SMIRNOV: So you think you can get away with it because you're a woman. A creature of poetry and romance, huh? Well, it doesn't go down with me. I hereby challenge you to a duel.

LUKA: Mercy on us! Holy saints alive! Water!

SMIRNOV: I propose we shoot it out.

MRS. POPOV: Trying to scare me again? Just because you have big fists and a voice like a bull? You're a brute.

115 SMIRNOV: No one insults Grigory S. Smirnov with impunity! And I don't care if you *are* a female.

MRS. POPOV: *(trying to outshout him)* Brute, brute, brute!

SMIRNOV: The sexes are equal, are they? Fine: then it's just prejudice to expect men alone to pay for insults. I hereby challenge—

MRS. POPOV: *(screaming)* All right! You want to shoot it out? All right! Let's shoot it out!

SMIRNOV: And let it be here and now!

120 MRS. POPOV: Here and now! All right! I'll have Popov's pistols here in one minute! *(Walks away, then turns.)* Putting one of Popov's bullets through your silly head will be a pleasure! Au revoir. *(Exit.)*

SMIRNOV: I'll bring her down like a duck, a sitting duck. I'm not one of your little poets, I'm no little subaltern with his first moustache. No, sir, there's no weaker sex where I'm concerned!

LUKA: Sir! Master! *(He goes down on his knees.)* Take pity on a poor old man, and do me a favor: go away. It was bad enough before, you nearly scared me to death. But a duel—!

SMIRNOV: *(ignoring him)* A duel! That's equality of the sexes for you! That's women's emancipation! Just as a matter of principle I'll bring her down like a duck. But what a woman! "Putting one of Popov's bullets through your silly head . . ." Her cheeks were flushed, her eyes were gleaming! And, by God, she's accepted the challenge! I never knew a woman like this before!

LUKA: Sir! Master! Please go away! I'll always pray for you!

125 SMIRNOV: *(again ignoring him)* What a woman! Phew!! *She's* no sour puss, *she's* no cry baby. She's fire and brimstone. She's a human cannon ball. What a shame I have to kill her!

LUKA: *(weeping)* Please, kind sir, please, go away!

SMIRNOV: *(as before)* I like her, isn't that funny? With those dimples and all? I like her. I'm even prepared to consider letting her off that debt. And where's my rage? It's gone. I never knew a woman like this before.

Enter Mrs. Popov with pistols.

MRS. POPOV: (*boldly*) Pistols, Mr. Smirnov! (*Matter of fact.*) But before we start, you'd better show me how it's done. I'm not too familiar with these things. In fact I never gave a pistol a second look.

LUKA: Lord, have mercy on us, I must go hunt up the gardener and the coachman. Why has this catastrophe fallen upon us, O Lord? (*Exit.*)

SMIRNOV: (*examining the pistols*) Well, it's like this. There are several makes: one is   130
the Mortimer, with capsules, especially constructed for dueling. What you have here are Smith and Wesson triple-action revolvers, with extractor, first-rate job, worth ninety rubles at the very least. You hold it this way. (*Aside.*) My God, what eyes she has! They're setting me on fire.

MRS. POPOV: This way?

SMIRNOV: Yes, that's right. You cock the trigger, take aim like this, head up, arm out like this. Then you just press with this finger here, and it's all over. The main thing is, keep cool, take slow aim, and don't let your arm jump.

MRS. POPOV: I see. And if it's inconvenient to do the job here, we can go out in the garden.

SMIRNOV: Very good. Of course, I should warn you: I'll be firing in the air.

MRS. POPOV: What? This is the end. Why?   135

SMIRNOV: Oh, well—because—for private reasons.

MRS. POPOV: Scared, huh? (*She laughs heartily.*) Now don't you try to get out of it, Mr. Smirnov. My blood is up. I won't be happy till I've drilled a hole through that skull of yours. Follow me. What's the matter? Scared?

SMIRNOV: That's right. I'm scared.

MRS. POPOV: Oh, come on, what's the matter with you?

SMIRNOV: Well, um, Mrs. Popov, I, um, I like you.   140

MRS. POPOV: (*laughing bitterly*) Good God! He likes me, does he? The gall of the man. (*Showing him the door.*) You may leave, Mr. Smirnov.

SMIRNOV: (*Quietly puts the gun down, takes his hat, and walks to the door. Then he stops and the pair look at each other without a word. Then, approaching gingerly.*) Listen, Mrs. Popov. Are you still mad at me? I'm in the devil of a temper myself, of course. But then, you see—what I mean is—it's this way—the fact is— (*Roaring.*) Well, is it my fault, damn it, if I like you? (*Clutches the back of a chair. It breaks.*) Christ, what fragile furniture you have here. I like you. Know what I mean? I could fall in love with you.

MRS. POPOV: I hate you. Get out!

SMIRNOV: What a woman! I never saw anything like it. Oh, I'm lost, I'm done for, I'm a mouse in a trap.

MRS. POPOV: Leave this house, or I shoot!   145

SMIRNOV: Shoot away! What bliss to die of a shot that was fired by that little velvet hand! To die gazing into those enchanting eyes. I'm out of my mind. I know: you must decide at once. Think for one second, then decide. Because if I leave now, I'll never be back. Decide! I'm a pretty decent chap. Landed gentleman, I should say. Ten thousand a year. Good stable. Throw a kopeck up in the air, and I'll put a bullet through it. Will you marry me?

MRS. POPOV: *(indignant, brandishing the gun)* We'll shoot it out! Get going! Take your pistol!

SMIRNOV: I'm out of my mind. I don't understand anything any more. *(Shouting.)* You there! That vodka!

MRS. POPOV: No excuses! No delays! We'll shoot it out!

150   **SMIRNOV:** I'm out of my mind. I'm falling in love. I *have* fallen in love. *(He takes her hand vigorously; she squeals.)* I love you. *(He goes down on his knees.)* I love you as I've never loved before. I jilted twelve, and was jilted by nine others. But I didn't love a one of them as I love you. I'm full of tender emotion. I'm melting like butter. I'm weak as water. I'm on my knees like a fool, and I offer you my hand. It's a shame, it's a disgrace. I haven't been in love in five years. I took a vow against it. And now, all of a sudden, to be swept off my feet, it's a scandal. I offer you my hand, dear lady. Will you or won't you? You won't? Then don't! *(He rises and walks toward the door.)*

MRS. POPOV: I didn't say anything.

SMIRNOV: *(stopping)* What?

MRS. POPOV: Oh, nothing, you can go. Well, no, just a minute. No, you can go. Go! I detest you! But, just a moment. Oh, if you knew how furious I feel! *(Throws the gun on the table.)* My fingers have gone to sleep holding that horrid thing. *(She is tearing her handkerchief to shreds.)* And what are you standing around for? Get out of here!

SMIRNOV: Goodbye.

MRS. POPOV: Go, go, go! *(Shouting.)* Where are you going? Wait a minute! No, no, it's all right, just go. I'm fighting mad. Don't come near me, don't come near me!

SMIRNOV: *(who is coming near her)* I'm pretty disgusted with myself—falling in love like a kid, going down on my knees like some moongazing whippersnapper, the very thought gives me gooseflesh. *(Rudely.)* I love you. But it doesn't make sense. Tomorrow, I have to pay that interest, and we've already started mowing. *(He puts his arm about her waist.)* I shall never forgive myself for this.

MRS. POPOV: Take your hands off me, I hate you! Let's shoot it out!

A long kiss. Enter Luka with an axe, the Gardener with a rake, the coachman with a pitch fork, hired men with sticks.

LUKA: *(seeing the kiss)* Mercy on us! Holy saints above!

MRS. POPOV: *(dropping her eyes)* Luka, tell them in the stable that Toby is *not* to have any oats today.

*   *   *

 A Note on Translations

Many dramatic works that we read or see are translations from other languages. For example, Ibsen wrote in Norwegian, Sophocles in Greek, Molière in French, and Chekhov in Russian. Before English-speaking viewers or readers can evaluate the language of a translated play, they must understand that the language they hear or read is the translator's interpretation of what the playwright intended to communicate. For example, certain words do not have corresponding words in English. In addition, some phrases are idiomatic and cannot be understood outside their original cultural contexts. Finally, some words have specific **connotations**—emotional associations—that the equivalent words in English do not have. For this reason, a translation is always an interpretation, not just a search for literal equivalents; this means that a translation is always different from the original. Moreover, because different translators make different choices when they try to convey a sense of the original, two translations of the same work can vary considerably.

Compare these two versions of an exchange of dialogue from two translations of the same Chekhov play, called *The Brute* in the translation that begins on page 1048 and *The Bear* in the alternate version.

From *The Brute*

SMIRNOV: You'd like me to come simpering to you in French, I suppose. "*Enchanté, madame! Merci beaucoup* for not paying zee money, *madame! Pardonnez-moi* if I 've disturbed you, *madame!* How *charmante* you look in mourning, *madame!*"

MRS. POPOV: Now you're being silly, Mr. Smirnov.

SMIRNOV: (*mimicking*) "Now you're being silly, Mr. Smirnov." "You don't know how to talk to a lady, Mr. Smirnov." Look here, Mrs. Popov. I've known more women than you've known pussy cats. I've fought three duels on their account. I've jilted twelve, and been jilted by nine others. Oh, yes, Mrs. Popov, I've played the fool in my time, whispered sweet nothings, bowed and scraped and endeavored to please. Don't tell me I don't know what it is to love, to pine away with longing, to have the blues, to melt like butter, to be weak as water. I was full of tender emotion. I was carried away with passion. I squandered half my fortune on the sex. I chattered about women's emancipation. But there's an end to everything, dear madam. . . . (1.71–73)

From *The Bear*

SMIRNOV: Ach, it's astonishing! How would you like me to talk to you? In French, perhaps? (*Lisps in anger.*) Madame, *je vous prie.* . . . How happy I am that you're not paying me the money. . . . Ah, pardon, I've made you uneasy! Such lovely weather we're having today! And you look so becoming in your mourning dress. (*Bows and scrapes.*)

MRS. POPOV: That's rude and not very clever!

SMIRNOV: (*teasing*) Rude and not very clever! I don't know how to behave in the company of ladies. Madam, in my time I've seen far more women than you've seen sparrows. Three times I've fought duels over women; I've jilted twelve women, nine have jilted me! Yes! There was a time when I played the fool; I became sentimental over women, used honeyed words, fawned on them, bowed and scraped. . . . I loved, suffered, sighed at the moon; I became limp, melted, shivered. . .I loved passionately, madly, every which way, devil take me, I chattered away like a magpie about the emancipation of women, ran through half my fortune as a result of my tender feelings; but now, if you will excuse me, I'm on to your ways! I've had enough!

Although both translations convey Smirnov's anger and frustration, they use different words (with different connotations), different phrasing, and even different stage directions. In

The Bear, for instance, only one French phrase is used, whereas *The Brute* uses several and specifies a French accent as well; other differences between the two translations include *The Bear*'s use of "teasing," "sparrows," and "I've had enough!" where *The Brute* uses "mimicking," "pussy cats," and "But there's an end to everything, dear madam." (Elsewhere in the play, *The Bear* uses profanity while *The Brute* uses more polite language.)

 ## Recognizing Kinds of Drama

The dramatic tradition stretches back to antiquity, with some of the earliest known plays dating back to the sixth century B.C. This long lifespan has produced numerous developments in the form and conventions of drama.

Traditionally, plays are divided into **acts** and **scenes**. Between acts, there is sometimes an **intermission**, a pause in the action that can be used to heighten the dramatic tension created at the end of the previous scene (as well as to represent the passage of time between one act and the next). The number of acts in a play can range from one to five, depending on the length and scope of the play itself. Shakespeare's *Hamlet* and *A Midsummer Night's Dream* both have five acts, but most full-length contemporary plays have just two or three.

Some shorter plays have only one act. In a **one-act play** such as Chekov's *The Brute*, the playwright is faced with the challenge of creating a dramatic work that includes all the elements that are part of longer plays—exposition, conflict, climax, and resolution. Because these plays are shorter, their imagery and dialogue are often more concise. In fact, because there is less time to devote to character development, subtext, or the consequences of events, one-act plays differ from full-length plays in the same way that short stories differ from novels.

An even more recent development in drama is the **ten-minute play**—a play in which all the actors are onstage and all events take place within a ten-minute time period (see Chapter 35). On an even smaller scale, a **monologue**—an extended speech delivered by one character—can stand alone as a complete dramatic work, as in Joyce Carol Oates's *When I Was a Little Girl and My Mother Didn't Want Me* (1997). Some contemporary plays—including Eve Ensler's *The Vagina Monologues* (1996) and Claudia Shear's *Blown Sideways Through Life* (1994) are composed entirely of a series of interrelated dramatic monologues.

Some contemporary drama is **improvisational**, which means that it is either partially or completely unscripted. This dramatic tradition is a descendant of **commedia dell'arte**, an Italian form of improvisational theater that began in the sixteenth century and was popular until the eighteenth century. Today, many theater actors are trained in "improv" work, which challenges them to sharpen their concentration and to trust in their own instincts rather than relying solely on a script. Some improvisational plays rely on audience participation, requiring actors to improvise in response to audience members' spontaneous contributions to the play.

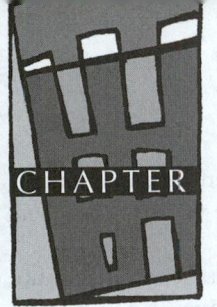

CHAPTER 35

DRAMA SAMPLER: TEN-MINUTE PLAYS

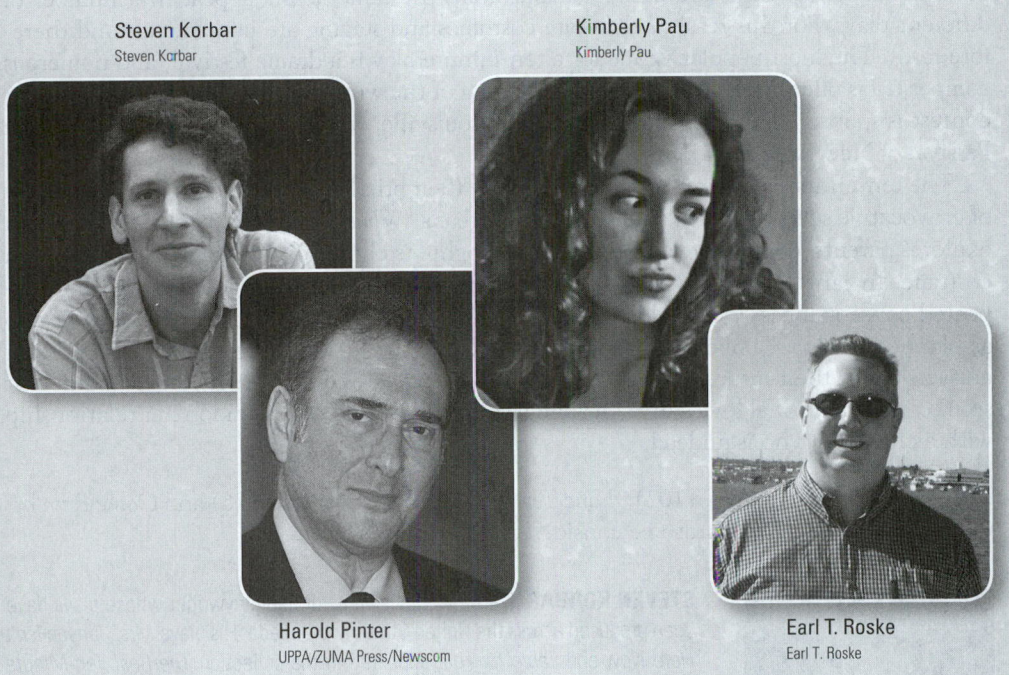

Steven Korbar
Steven Korbar

Kimberly Pau
Kimberly Pau

Harold Pinter
UPPA/ZUMA Press/Newscom

Earl T. Roske
Earl T. Roske

Throughout the long history of playwriting, many types and forms of drama have emerged. In recent years, theater has become more experimental, as evidenced by the proliferation of one-act and ten-minute plays, which strive to convey complex ideas in a short amount of time. While traditional one-act plays such as Anton Chekhov's *The Brute* (p. 1048) and Susan Glaspell's *Trifles* (p. 1604) may have the luxury of unfolding in a more extended period, the **ten-minute play**, which must be performed in ten minutes or less, offers a very small window of opportunity in which the playwright can create meaning. In fact, as director Jon Jory has noted, the ten-minute play is in a sense the dramatic equivalent of the **haiku** in that it is intended to be taken in all at once and thus to have a particularly intense effect on the audience. According to Jory, considered to be the father of the ten-minute play genre, these plays "must, by nature, imply rather than explain. They often depend on metaphor to extend their reach. They stick like glue in the mind because the viewer remembers the *whole* play."

Since a page of script roughly translates into a minute of time onstage, a ten-minute play is generally limited to about ten pages. Despite its brevity, however, a ten-minute play is more than just a scene or an excerpt from a longer play: it is written to stand alone as a complete dramatic work. Although its brief length means it has little or no room for **exposition**, it must introduce a **conflict** (usually relatively early in the play), and it must provide a **resolution**, just as any other play does.

Ten-minute plays are generally staged in groups, allowing the audience to watch several plays in sequence. Casts are usually small; often, the same actors appear in a number of different plays. For this reason, elaborate costumes and staging are impractical (and therefore rare). The most popular venue for a ten-minute play is a drama festival, and numerous competitions offer prizes that include the staging of the winning play. The most prominent contest is sponsored by the Actors Theatre of Louisville, which stages the annual Humana Festival of New American Plays.

The ten-minute plays in this sampler, despite their brief length, manage to treat a variety of provocative subjects. For example, Steven Korbar's *"What Are You Going to Be?"* (p. 1062) explores parents' complex reactions to their daughter's choice of a burka as her Halloween costume. In Jane Martin's *Beauty* (p. 1069), the two protagonists trade lives, with unexpected consequences; in Harold Pinter's *Applicant* (p. 1076), a job interview does not go as planned; and in Kimberly Pau's *Magic 8 Ball* (p. 1073), two college students search for answers about their future. Finally, Earl T. Roske's *Zombie Love* (p. 1079) offers a different spin on the traditional love story as a young woman is pressured to abandon her relationship with a character who is undead.

NOTE *The Blizzard* (p. 1102), *Nine Ten* (p. 1108), *Post-its* (p. 1176) and *Come Rain or Come Shine* (p. 1477) can also be considered ten-minute plays.

Steven Korbar

STEVEN KORBAR (1967–   ) is an actor and playwright whose plays have been produced across the United States and Canada. His plays *Mrs. Jansen Isn't Here Now* and *Table for Four* appeared in the collection *The Best Ten-Minute Plays 2010*, and his work was featured in the 2013 Queer Theatre Festival in Washington DC. Published in the collection *The Best Ten-Minute Plays 2013*, the following play won the Merce award at the Secret Rose Theatre's 2011 10-Minute Play Festival in Los Angeles.

"What Are You Going to Be?" (2011)

CHARACTERS

Greg: *thirties to forties*
Carol: *thirties to forties*
Natalie: *an adolescent girl*

SETTING:
An upper middle class home—decorated for Halloween.

TIME:
Early evening

Lights come up to find CAROL *seated in a living room setting. She is very still and appears rather stunned. After a moment* GREG *enters. He is carrying a grocery bag and is in high spirits.*

GREG: Okay, don't get mad at me, but I broke my promise —I bought more Hallow-
    een candy! I know we already have a ton but A) they were having an incredible
    sale and B) and most importantly . . . they're "Junior Mints"! I figure we can
    just put them in the back of the cupboard and conveniently forget them till
    Trick or Treating is over tomorrow night. Oh don't be all angry. "Junior
    Mints"! . . . What's the matter?

CAROL: *(A choked voice)* . . . Natalie . . .

GREG: *(Stricken)* What? . . . What!? *(Quickly becoming hysterical. Dropping the bag)*
    Oh God! Natalie. NATALIE!
    Where is she, where . . .

CAROL: No. No, she's fine. She's not hurt or sick or anything.

GREG: Then why did you . . . Oh my God! What is wrong with you!? Why did you   5
    say "Natalie" like something horrible happened?

CAROL: *(Flatly)* I'm sorry.

GREG: You scared the living . . . you don't joke around like that—you took ten
    years off my life, you, you made me drop my "Junior Mints."

CAROL: I'm very sorry, I should have phrased what I had to say differently.

GREG: What could you have to say that was worth giving me a cardiac infarction?

CAROL: Natalie . . . finally decided what she's going to be for Halloween.   10

GREG: *(A beat)* Her Halloween costume. Carol, what is the point of all this family
    therapy if you're just going to keep overreacting to every little thing? You know
    what Dr. Penelope told you; perspective is what we have to strive for. If you just
    take a step back and a deep cleansing breath, pretty soon you're going to see
    that what seemed so dire really wasn't such a terrible . . .

NATALIE *enters. We assume she is a normal adolescent girl, though it is hard to tell as she is dressed in the burka[1] of a Muslim woman from the Middle East. Her costume is heavy, black and very constricting.* GREG *stares at her for a long moment. He looks at* CAROL *and then back to* NATALIE, *trying desperately not to overreact.*

    . . . Hey princess.

NATALIE: Hi Dad.

GREG: What'cha doing?

NATALIE: Just trying on my Halloween costume.

GREG: So you decided against the ballerina?   15

NATALIE: Yeah. I'm going to be a Muslim woman from the Middle East instead.

GREG: Why . . . did you decide to be that?

NATALIE: Cause I wanted a costume not a lot of other girls would have.

GREG: . . . Good job.

NATALIE: There isn't any reason you don't want me wearing this . . . is there?   20

---

[1]*burka:* A full-body garment worn by some Muslim women when they are out in public.

GREG: I . . . can't think of any.

NATALIE: Good. Well, I'm going to go back to my room, figure out which way is Mecca[2] and practice lying face down on the floor.

NATALIE exits

GREG: (*A long beat. Trying desperately to sound reasonable*) Well . . . we said no Lady Gaga.

CAROL: This is not my fault. I am a good mother—there are no preservatives in anything I feed that girl.

25 GREG: This is not about fault. This can be an opportunity; to learn more about our daughter and try to understand her thought process.

NATALIE: (OFF STAGE) I can hear every word you're saying.

GREG: (*Yelling towards the direction of her room*) Well then shut your door Missy! (*To* CAROL. *More quietly*)

Let's just try to discuss this quietly. Now, where did she get the . . .

CAROL: Burka is the word you're trying to sound casual saying. And I don't know where she got it—I was too terrified to look through her browsing history.

GREG: There is no reason to be terrified. There is nothing wrong with being Middle Eastern. We cannot let her feel we have a problem with that. Muslims are human beings just like you and me—we see them every day on "Anderson Cooper." We just have to figure out why Natalie wants to dress like one.

30 CAROL: I know why—to destroy me. She's rejecting everything I've ever taught her about being a modern, post-feminist woman and chosen the most subservient, oppressed female role model she could find. My God, she might as well just be dressing up as my mother for Halloween!

GREG: Those are a completely different set of issues. What matters now is that if we decide it's better for her not to wear this costume, she doesn't think it's because we have any sort of discriminatory . . .

NATALIE enters

NATALIE: Hey mom, can I have a needle and thread to fix my costume; I think too much of my face is showing.

GREG: You know sweetie, we actually wanted to talk to you about your costume and what you'll be wearing tomorrow night.

NATALIE: I'll be wearing this.

GREG: Maybe . . . but your mom and I would like you to be aware of all your options. For instance, you could reexamine the whole line of Disney princesses—there's Jasmine from *Aladdin*. All the same ethnicity and you could look so pretty.

---

[2]*Mecca:* Islamic holy city in Saudi Arabia.

NATALIE: No. Nobody my age is going to wear a princess costume. And even if   35
    I did it sure wouldn't be Jasmine—she's a total infidel. Anyway, who cares what
    I wear, it's just a costume and the costumes we wear shouldn't matter . . . right Dad?
GREG: Right! . . . right.
CAROL: Natalie, it's just that we feel it might seem disrespectful to people of the
    Muslim faith for you to be wearing this as a costume for Halloween.
GREG: (*Impressed with* CAROL'S *ruse*) Good! (*Immediately to* NATALIE. *Earnestly*)
    Right. Halloween is more of a secular holiday and it's just better to keep religion
    out of it.
CAROL: Remember how the Davis's passed out bible quotes instead of candy last
    Halloween; their house got TP'd for four straight nights.
NATALIE: (*Suspiciously*) Tell me the truth; this really isn't because the two of you   40
    have got some weird thing against Islam, is it?
GREG: No!
CAROL: No!
GREG: No!
CAROL: No!
GREG: It's just; you don't want to belittle anyone's faith sweetie. I mean, you   45
    wouldn't run around asking for candy dressed as a Catholic nun, would you?
CAROL: Well honey, some people do go out dressed as nuns. It's a costume; they go
    out dressed as slutty nuns.
GREG: . . . Those are slutty nurses.
NATALIE: No, she's right. Some are nurses but a lot of them are slutty nuns too.
GREG: Okay, fine. There are slutty nun costumes; but you wouldn't go out dressed
    in one would you?
NATALIE: No. I already know two girls who are going as that.   50
GREG: (*More frustrated*) I think it is just culturally insensitive to these people as a
    group. And by these people I do not mean . . . (*Catching himself and making air
    quotes*) "These People." I just, I don't feel comfortable with you dressing this
    way.
NATALIE: When Lauren Nakamura went dressed as a geisha last year, the two of you
    wouldn't stop gushing about how adorable she looked.
GREG: That is completely different.
NATALIE: Why, because Arabs frighten you but you find Asians all cute and
    non-threatening?
GREG: Absolutely not!   55
CAROL: No!
GREG: Do not put words in my mouth! The image of the passive Asian is nothing
    but a ridiculous, antiquated racial stereotype!
CAROL: Of course it is.
GREG: Just look at Pearl Harbor. (*After realizing what he's said, putting a discrete hand
    over his mouth*)
CAROL: What your father means is he would like you to find another costume to   60
    wear.
NATALIE: What would he like me to be; a white, male, Protestant who can prove
    he's straight?

GREG *instinctively moves to attack* NATALIE, *muttering something like "You miserable little . . . ." Carol restrains him.*

CAROL: This is not a judgment on anyone's religion or race.

NATALIE: Then why is Dad getting all freaked out?

GREG: I am not getting freaked out: nobody ever even mentioned terrorism.

65 NATALIE: What!?

GREG: I mean; it is wrong to ascribe the worst in human nature to any one particular people. And anybody who does that is ignorant and we should just feel sorry for them.

NATALIE: Then I can go like this?

GREG: I will lock you in the crawl space first.

NATALIE: Well my friend Lele really is Muslim and she likes this costume and she's totally cool with me wearing it.

70 GREG: I don't care what your friend thinks. You are not wearing that costume. It is inappropriate; it's thoughtless and wearing it would just be plain insulting to the people and culture of Islam!

NATALIE: Is that what all of your Muslim friends say Dad?

GREG *tries to answer but is left with his mouth open.* NATALIE *stares at him for a beat, turns and exits in triumphant silence*

GREG: (*A beat, then erupting in frustration*) What is going on here! I don't understand, why is she doing this to us!

NATALIE: (*Off stage*) I can still hear you!

75 GREG: I am going to remove that door from its hinges!

NATALIE: (*Off stage*) That doesn't even make sense—I could hear you better then!

GREG: I know that! (*Moving to* CAROL. *Whispering*) She used to be so sweet when she was little.

CAROL: I told you we shouldn't have let her have all those inoculations.

GREG: We could just cram her into a stuffed pumpkin and that was her costume.

80 CAROL: Polio and Rubella; fine. But she was never right again after that Smallpox vaccine.

GREG: (*Humiliated*) I said terrorist.

CAROL: And Pearl Harbor.

GREG: Since the day she was born I've tried to teach her to respect diversity. She has been to every church, heard every philosophy; we introduced her to that school friend of yours who's a Wiccan[3] and a lesbian. I've taken that girl to so many Bat mitzvahs[4] in the last year I could practically poach a salmon all by myself. I paid $125.00 for a dress so she could look right at her friend's quinceañera[5] and another $15.00 to the gardener to learn how to pronounce *quinceañera*! What in the hell more do I have to do—she wouldn't go with me to the Tyler Perry movie!

---

[3] *Wiccan:* A follower of Wicca, a religion rooted in magic and nature.

[4] *Bat mitzvah:* A rite of passage for Jewish girls passing into womanhood.

[5] *quinceañera:* A rite of passage for Hispanic girls passing into womanhood.

CAROL: If you ask me this whole place is just crawling with Radon.

GREG: Will you stop blaming everything on hazardous materials.   85

CAROL: Well I told you; it's not me. I breast fed that kid for fourteen months and stayed gluten free the whole time—I did my part.

GREG: Well all I know is I left a peaceful home this morning, worked hard all day for my family and when I walked back through the front door this evening suddenly it's a Jihad![6] Where did that come from?

CAROL: Well not my side of the family—she didn't inherit any of that gamy, exotic blood from me.

GREG: . . . And what in the hell is that supposed to mean?

CAROL *does not respond*

I'm part Dutch, part Scots/Irish and 1/8th Armenian.

CAROL *points at him as if to say "Bingo"*

Armenia is in Europe.

CAROL: Oh no it's not. Not real Europe. Not *Sound of Music* Europe. You've always   90
had a little smudge of the Third World on you; I knew it the first time I saw that dusky little mother of yours—I mean, no offence, but the woman's always looked like she just finished carrying a jug of water on her head.

GREG: Are you out of your mind?

CAROL: And there's another trait that's straight out of the Casbah[7]—your condescending manner towards women. So archaic and primitive—it's downright patriarchal.

GREG: Oh really, is that what your Wiccan friend would call it?

CAROL: And a homophobe to boot.

GREG: You are making me very angry!   95

CAROL: Oh boy, start gathering up your stones everybody: I feel an honor killing coming on!

GREG: Do you even understand the sociopolitical implications of what you're saying? This is the kind of thinking that fostered colonialism for the last two centuries.

NATALIE *enters no longer wearing the burka*

NATALIE: Okay, okay, okay—just stop the arguing, alright! If this is what it's going to do to you, fine; I won't wear the stupid costume. If my parents can't handle somebody dressing a little different then I guess I was just expecting too much! Everyone has their secret little hates and prejudices, even my own mother and father. That's just how it is. So I'll just do what you want. I'll go back to wearing my original Lady Gaga costume . . . unless you have something against her religion too?

CAROL *and* GREG *simultaneously shake their heads*

---

[6] *Jihad:* Islamic holy war.

[7] *Casbah:* North African fortress or walled quarter of a city.

Okay then. That's how it's going to be and we won't even talk about it anymore. I'm not a baby—it's not like I can't stand disappointment. I guess I have to start getting used to it sometime, don't I?

GREG: *(Earnestly)* Natalie . . . I want you to know I think you've shown a lot of maturity tonight. And maturity is a rare thing at any age.

100 NATALIE: Thanks Dad—I bet that's just how Anderson Cooper would have put it.

NATALIE exits. There is a silence

GREG: Well, I think it all worked out for the best.

CAROL: In the long run I think so.

GREG: It's good she made the decision by herself.

CAROL: It wouldn't have been right if we'd had to force her.

105 GREG: These are volatile times; it's just better not to broach certain subjects.

GREG: *(Suddenly aware)* . . . Did she just play us?

CAROL: Played us like a violin.

GREG: She was never going to wear that as a costume, was she?

CAROL: She was going as Lady Gaga if she'd had to slit our throats.

110 GREG: We really did kind of raise a terrorist, didn't we?

CAROL: Utterly remorseless.

GREG: It's just stunning. How she manipulated us. The way she preyed on our irrational fears and exploited our ingrained prejudices. And for no other reason but to get what she wanted from us.

CAROL: I always did tell her she could be the first woman president of the United States.

GREG: Well, she sure had my number. If anyone asks me, I guess I know what I'm going to be for Halloween.

115 CAROL: Your own adolescent daughter's little bitch?

GREG: I was going to say a hypocrite. How can I ever look another Arab American in the eye again?

CAROL: Well, since I don't think there are any in our "Emotional Eating" class, I doubt it will be a problem. Anyway, Halloween will be over and done with tomorrow night, and if we're lucky we can just put the whole horrible thing behind us.

GREG: Can we? Christmas is only two months away.

CAROL: *(Remembering a horrible fact)* . . . Oh my God.

120 GREG: She's still got her heart set on that puppy.

CAROL: Oh no! The dander . . . the dander. We can't have it in the house!

GREG: *(Low and fatalistic)* We may not have a choice Carol. We may not have a choice. *(A distraught beat. Then yelling in the direction of NATALIE's bedroom)* I know you can hear me!

NATALIE is heard laughing off stage CAROL and GREG cower together.

*   *   *

JANE MARTIN, a prize-winning playwright, has never made a public appearance or spoken about any of her works. In fact, she has never given an interview, and no picture of her has ever been published. As one critic wryly observed, Martin is "America's best known, unknown playwright." Martin first came to the attention of American theater audiences with her collection of monologues, *Talking With . . .* , a work that premiered at the 1981 Humana Festival of New American Plays at the Actors Theatre of Louisville, Kentucky. Her other works include *Vital Signs; What Mama Don't Know; Cementville*; the Pulitzer Prize–nominated *Keely and Du* (winner of the 1994 American Theatre Critics Association New Play Award); *Criminal Hearts; Middle Aged White Guys; Jack and Jill; Mr. Bundy; Flaming Guns of the Purple Sage; Good Boys; Flags*; and *Sez She*. Martin's name is widely believed to be a pseudonym. Jon Jory, former artistic director of the Actors Theatre of Louisville—and director of the premieres of all of Martin's plays—is spokesperson for the playwright and, according to some people, may actually be the playwright behind the pen name. Jory has repeatedly denied this; in a 1994 interview, he said that Martin "feels she could not write plays if people knew who she was, regardless of her identity or gender." In Jory's opinion, "The point in the end is the plays themselves. . . . But if Jane's anonymity is a P. T. Barnum publicity stunt, it's one of the longest circus acts going."

Beauty (2000)

CHARACTERS
Carla
Bethany

An apartment. Minimalist set. A young woman, Carla, on the phone.

CARLA: In love with me? You're in love with me? Could you describe yourself again? Uh-huh. Uh-huh. And you spoke to me? (*A knock at the door.*) Listen, I always hate to interrupt a marriage proposal, but . . . could you possibly hold that thought? (*Puts phone down and goes to door. Bethany, the same age as Carla and a friend, is there. She carries the sort of Mideastern lamp we know of from Aladdin.*)

BETHANY: Thank God you were home. I mean, you're not going to believe this!

CARLA: Somebody on the phone. (*Goes back to it.*)

BETHANY: I mean, I just had a beach urge, so I told them at work my uncle was dying . . .

CARLA: (*motions to Bethany for quiet*) And you were the one in the leather jacket   5
with the tattoo? What was the tattoo? (*Carla again asks Bethany, who is gesturing wildly that she should hang up, to cool it.*) Look, a screaming eagle from shoulder to shoulder, maybe. There were a lot of people in the bar.

BETHANY: (*gesturing and mouthing*) I have to get back to work.

CARLA: (*on phone*) See, the thing is, I'm probably not going to marry someone I can't remember . . . particularly when I don't drink. Sorry. Sorry. Sorry. (*She hangs up.*) Madness.

BETHANY: So I ran out to the beach . . .

CARLA: This was some guy I never met who apparently offered me a beer . . .

BETHANY: . . . low tide and this . . . (*The lamp.*) . . . was just sitting there, lying   10
there . . .

CARLA: . . . and he tracks me down . . .

BETHANY: . . . on the beach, and I lift this lid thing . . .

CARLA: . . . and seriously proposes marriage.

BETHANY: . . . and a genie comes out.

CARLA: I mean, that's twice in a . . . what?   15

BETHANY: A genie comes out of this thing.

CARLA: A genie?

BETHANY: I'm not kidding, the whole Disney kind of thing, swirling smoke, and then this twenty-foot-high, see-through guy in like an Arabian outfit.

CARLA: Very funny.

20 BETHANY: Yes, funny, but twenty feet high! I look up and down the beach, I'm alone. I don't have my pepper spray or my hand alarm. You know me, when I'm petrified I joke. I say his voice is too high for Robin Williams, and he says he's a castrati. Naturally. Who else would I meet?

CARLA: What's a castrati?

BETHANY: You know . . .

The appropriate gesture.

CARLA: Bethany, dear one, I have three modeling calls. I am meeting Ralph Lauren!

BETHANY: Okay, good. Ralph Lauren. Look, I am not kidding!

25 CARLA: You're not kidding what?!

BETHANY: There is a genie in this thingamajig.

CARLA: Uh-huh. I'll be back around eight.

BETHANY: And he offered me *wishes!*

CARLA: Is this some elaborate practical joke because it's my birthday?

30 BETHANY: No, happy birthday, but I'm like crazed because I'm on this deserted beach with a twenty-foot-high, see-through genie, so like sarcastically . . . you know how I need a new car . . . I said fine, gimme 25,000 dollars . . .

CARLA: On the beach with the genie?

BETHANY: Yeah, right, exactly, and it rains down out of the sky.

CARLA: Oh sure.

BETHANY: *(pulling a wad out of her purse)* Count it, those are thousands. I lost one in the surf.

Carla sees the top bill. Looks at Bethany, who nods encouragement. Carla thumbs through them.

35 CARLA: These look real.

BETHANY: Yeah.

CARLA: And they rained down out of the sky?

BETHANY: Yeah.

CARLA: You've been really strange lately, are you dealing?

40 BETHANY: Dealing what, I've even given up chocolate.

CARLA: Let me see the genie.

BETHANY: Wait, wait.

CARLA: Bethany, I don't have time to screw around. Let me see the genie or let me go on my appointments.

BETHANY: Wait! So I pick up the money . . . see, there's sand on the money . . . and I'm like nuts so I say, you know, "Okay, look, ummm, big guy, my uncle is in the hospital" . . . because as you know when I said to the people at work my uncle was dying, I was on one level telling the truth although it had nothing to do with the beach, but he was in Intensive Care after the accident, and that's on

my mind, so I say, okay, Genie, heal my uncle . . . which is like impossible given
he was hit by two trucks, and the genie says, "Yes, Master" . . . like they're supposed to say, and he goes into this like kind of whirlwind, kicking up sand and
stuff, and I'm like, "Oh my God!" and the air clears, and he bows, you know,
and says, "It is done, Master," and I say, "Okay, whatever-you-are, I'm calling
on my cell phone," and I get it out and I get this doctor who is like dumbstruck
who says my uncle came to, walked out of Intensive Care and left the hospital!
I'm not kidding, Carla.

CARLA: On your mother's grave?   45

BETHANY: On my mother's grave.

They look at each other.

CARLA: Let me see the genie.

BETHANY: No, no, look, that's the whole thing . . . I was just, like, reacting, you
know, responding, and that's already two wishes . . . although I'm really pleased
about my uncle, the $25,000 thing, I could have asked for $10 million, and
there is only one wish left.

CARLA: So ask for $10 million.

BETHANY: I don't think so. I don't think so. I mean, I gotta focus in here. Do you   50
have a sparkling water?

CARLA: No. Bethany, I'm missing Ralph Lauren now. Very possibly my one chance
to go from catalogue model to the very, very big time, so, if you are joking, stop
joking.

BETHANY: Not joking. See, see, the thing is, I know what I want. In my guts.
Yes. Underneath my entire bitch of a life is this unspoken, ferocious, all-
consuming urge . . .

CARLA: *(trying to get her to move this along)* Ferocious, all-consuming urge . . .

BETHANY: I want to be like you.

CARLA: Me?   55

BETHANY: Yes.

CARLA: Half the time you don't even like me.

BETHANY: Jealous. The ogre of jealousy.

CARLA: You're the one with the $40,000 job straight out of school. You're the one
who has published short stories. I'm the one hanging on by her fingernails in
modeling. The one who has creeps calling her on the phone. The one who had
to have a nose job.

BETHANY: I want to be beautiful.   60

CARLA: You are beautiful.

BETHANY: Carla, I'm not beautiful.

CARLA: You have charm. You have personality. You know perfectly well you're
pretty.

BETHANY: "Pretty," see, that's it. Pretty is the minor leagues of beautiful. Pretty is
what people discover about you after they know you. Beautiful is what knocks
them out across the room. Pretty, you get called a couple of times a year;
beautiful is twenty-four hours a day.

CARLA: Yeah? So?   65

BETHANY: So?! We're talking *beauty* here. Don't say "So?" Beauty is the real deal. You are the center of any moment of your life. People stare. Men flock. I've seen you get offered discounts on makeup for no reason. Parents treat beautiful children better. Studies show your income goes up. You can have sex anytime you want it. Men have to know me. That takes up to a year. I'm continually horny.

CARLA: Bethany, I don't even like sex. I can't have a conversation without men coming on to me. I have no privacy. I get hassled on the street. They start pressuring me from the beginning. Half the time, it never occurs to them to start with a conversation. Smart guys like you. You've had three long-term relationships, and you're only twenty-three. I haven't had one. The good guys, the smart guys are scared to death of me. I'm surrounded by male bimbos who think a preposition is when you go to school away from home. I have no woman friends except you. I don't even want to talk about this!

BETHANY: I knew you'd say something like this. See, you're "in the club" so you can say this. It's the way beauty functions as an elite. You're trying to keep it all for yourself.

CARLA: I'm trying to tell you it's no picnic.

70 BETHANY: But it's what everybody wants. It's the nasty secret at large in the world. It's the unspoken tidal desire in every room and on every street. It's the unspoken, the soundless whisper . . . millions upon millions of people longing hopelessly and forever to stop being whatever they are and be beautiful, but the difference between those ardent multitudes and me is that I have a goddamn genie and one more wish!

CARLA: Well, it's not what I want. This is me, Carla. I have never read a whole book. Page six, I can't remember page four. The last thing I read was *The Complete Idiot's Guide to WordPerfect*. I leave dinner parties right after the dessert because I'm out of conversation. You know the dumb blond joke about the application where it says, "Sign here," she put Sagittarius? I've done that. Only beautiful guys approach me, and that's because they want to borrow my eye shadow. I barely exist outside a mirror! You don't want to *be* me.

BETHANY: None of you tell the truth. That's why you have no friends. We can all see you're just trying to make us feel better because we aren't in your league. This only proves to me it should be my third wish. Money can only buy things. Beauty makes you the center of the universe.

Bethany picks up the lamp.

CARLA: Don't do it. Bethany, don't wish it! I am telling you you'll regret it.

Bethany lifts the lid. There is a tremendous crash, and the lights go out. Then they flicker and come back up, revealing Bethany and Carla on the floor where they have been thrown by the explosion. We don't realize it at first, but they have exchanged places.

CARLA/BETHANY: Oh God.

75 BETHANY/CARLA: Oh God.

CARLA/BETHANY: Am I bleeding? Am I dying?

BETHANY/CARLA: I'm so dizzy. You're not bleeding.

CARLA/BETHANY: Neither are you.

BETHANY/CARLA: I feel so weird.

CARLA/BETHANY: Me too. I feel . . . (*Looking at her hands.*) Oh, my God, I'm   80
wearing your jewelry. I'm wearing your nail polish.

BETHANY/CARLA: I know I'm over here, but I can see myself over there.

CARLA/BETHANY: I'm wearing your dress. I have your legs!!

BETHANY/CARLA: These aren't my shoes. I can't meet Ralph Lauren wearing
these shoes!

CARLA/BETHANY: I wanted to be beautiful, but I didn't want to be you.

BETHANY/CARLA: Thanks a lot!!   85

CARLA/BETHANY: I've got to go. I want to pick someone out and get laid.

BETHANY/CARLA: You can't just walk out of here in my body!

CARLA/BETHANY: Wait a minute. Wait a minute. What's eleven eighteenths
of 1,726?

BETHANY/CARLA: Why?

CARLA/BETHANY: I'm a public accountant. I want to know if you have my brain.   90

BETHANY/CARLA: One hundred thirty-two and a half.

CARLA/BETHANY: You have my brain.

BETHANY/CARLA: What shade of Rubenstein lipstick does Cindy Crawford wear
with teal blue?

CARLA/BETHANY: Raging Storm.

BETHANY/CARLA: You have my brain. You poor bastard.   95

CARLA/BETHANY: I don't care. Don't you see?

BETHANY/CARLA: See what?

CARLA/BETHANY: We both have the one thing, the one and only thing everybody
wants.

BETHANY/CARLA: What is that?

CARLA/BETHANY: It's better than beauty for me; it's better than brains for you.   100

BETHANY/CARLA: What? What?!

CARLA/BETHANY: Different problems.

Blackout.

*   *   *

KIMBERLY PAU (1981–   ) is a writer and producer of a range of
plays, including the experimental one-act play *Bomb Shelter*, which
was nominated for eight awards, and the "sci-farce" comedy *Deacti-
vated*, which was a finalist for the 2014 Leah Ryan Fund for Emerging
Women Writers. Pau's work also includes a libretto, a music video,
and two experimental short films. A founding member of the New
York City artistic collective Ouroboros Co., Pau was recognized as
one of the Top Ten Off-Off Broadway Theatre Professionals of 2011
by reviewfix.com.

Kimberly Pau

Magic 8 Ball (2012)

CHARACTERS

ELIZABETH and MELISSA are both twenty years old. They are nice girls who grew up well and attend college. They are dressed in somewhat sexy nighties that don't quite flatter them but were probably quite expensive from Victoria's Secret or somewhere else at the mall. They have North Dakota accents.

SETTING: This script was created for the Tiny Theater Festival at the Brick Theater where the pieces were performed in a 6' × 6' × 6' box constructed of PVC pipe—performers and scenic elements were instructed to not exist outside the box at any point during each piece.

The Magic 8 Ball is about 500x larger than the regular toy ones, and it will be used as a device to add in movement. When the characters shake the Magic 8 Ball they are moving together. The movement is non-literal.

Lights up on a 20 year old girl's bedroom.

OFF STAGE VOICE: The Magic 8 Ball is a hollow plastic sphere resembling an oversized, black and white 8-ball. Inside is a cylindrical reservoir containing a white, plastic, icosahedral[1] die floating in alcohol with dissolved dark blue dye. A random selection device comprising a sealed container having relatively flat window means at least a portion of which is adapted to be substantially horizontally disposed.

Melissa and Elizabeth, both 20, in sexy ill-fitting pajamas play with a giant Magic 8 Ball. They take sexy pics of themselves with their smart phones.

MELISSA: I'm at odds. But I don't know if I should believe in this thing. I know. Oh jeez, ok I know to trust you. I could just trust you couldn't I? Right. I know. I don't know what to ask. (*Pause.*) I do. I do know what to ask. Ready? Do you.

ELIZABETH (*interrupting*): You have to call it Magic 8 Ball, the first time, it doesn't start to work unless you conjure it by name.

MELISSA: Right. Magic 8 Ball, do you predict the future? (*She shakes the ball*)

5   **MAGIC 8 BALL V.O.:** It is decidedly so.

ELIZABETH: See I told you so. Watch me. You can get creative with it. Like, am I going to have 4 children with Bradley? (*shakes the ball*)

MAGIC 8 BALL V.O.: Better not tell you now.

ELIZABETH: Darn. See? It's too clever.

MELISSA: Uh, you probably won't even know Bradley's name by the time you're old enough to have a kid. No. 20's not old enough. It's not. Am I going to have kids? No, wait, better, am I the spinster type? (*shakes the ball*)

10   **MAGIC 8 BALL V.O.:** You may rely on it.

---

[1] *icosahedral:* Having twenty triangular faces.

MELISSA: Huh. Is that an answer to the first question or the second? I guess we have to defer to the latter right? Yeah. Aw jeez.

ELIZABETH: I think you can still have kids if you're a spinster these days.

MELISSA: Oh yeah? Thanks. You go.

ELIZABETH: Should we order pizza? (*shakes the ball*)

MAGIC 8 BALL V.O.: My reply is no.   15

MELISSA: Oh yeah, looking out for our best interest. And our thighs.

ELIZABETH: You see?

MELISSA: We should ask it something important.

ELIZABETH: Oh yeah, like something meaningful.

MELISSA: Yeah. Will the world end in our lifetime? (*shakes the ball*)   20

MAGIC 8 BALL V.O.: Reply hazy, try again.

ELIZABETH: That question is confusing to me and I'm a human. I think if you're a crystal ball you like to keep it simple.

MELISSA: Oh yeah. Okay. Will we be friends with the robots? (*shakes the ball*)

MAGIC 8 BALL V.O.: My sources say no.

MELISSA: Oh darn.   25

ELIZABETH: We're not going to like the robots and they're not going to like us. Boring. And predictable! Gosh there's so much I need to know. Is Bradley desperately in love with me? (*shakes the ball*)

MAGIC 8 BALL V.O.: As I see it, yes.

ELIZABETH: YES!!!

MELISSA: As I see it? That's very non-committal.

ELIZABETH: Is he going to propose? (*shakes the ball*)   30

MAGIC 8 BALL V.O.: As I see it, yes.

ELIZABETH: Oh yeah, creepy, twice in a row!

MELISSA: Oh yeah? Did you shake it enough?

ELIZABETH: Um, yeah. Will he do it tomorrow? (*shakes the ball*)

MAGIC 8 BALL V.O.: Don't count on it.   35

ELIZABETH: The next day? (*shakes the ball*)

MAGIC 8 BALL V.O.: Outlook not so good.

ELIZABETH: Darnit! The day after that? (*shakes the ball*)

MAGIC 8 BALL V.O.: Signs point to yes.

ELIZABETH: Uh, thank Gosh.   40

MELISSA: Magic 8 Ball is a mister and he's leading you on.

ELIZABETH: I don't care what you say! It's true! I believe that it's true. Do you want to ask about James?

MELISSA: No. No. I don't want that to be tainted by voodoo.

ELIZABETH: Don't you want to know if you are going to die together?

MELISSA: You think Magic 8 Ball can tell me that?   45

ELIZABETH: Yes, obviously. Magic 8 Ball, are me and Bradley going to die together on the same day in our sleep on the same porch swing? (*shakes the ball*)

MAGIC 8 BALL V.O.: Concentrate and ask again.

ELIZABETH: Magic 8 Ball, are me and Bradley going to die together? (*shakes the ball*)

MAGIC 8 BALL V.O.: Cannot predict now.

MELISSA: Oh jeez, well that's smart. Magic 8 Ball, are you wise and all-knowing?   50
I mean, do you give good advice?

MAGIC 8 BALL V.O.: Yes—definitely.

MELISSA: Then why are you lying to Elizabeth about Bradley like this? (*shakes the ball*)

ELIZABETH: What do you mean?!

MAGIC 8 BALL V.O.: Ask again later.

55 **MELISSA:** Oh ok, fair enough, but will you at least admit that you know very well that Bradley and James have discovered this past weekend that they like to have sex with each other better than us and that's why they haven't even responded to our text pics of us in our new fabulous nighties? (*shakes the ball*)

MAGIC 8 BALL V.O.: It is certain.

ELIZABETH: What! No! You liar! Magic 8 Ball you lie!

MELISSA: Oh yeah? Is Elizabeth going to blame me for this? Specifically according to what you once referred to as my gangly lack of sex appeal? (*shakes the ball*)

MAGIC 8 BALL V.O.: Without a doubt.

60 **ELIZABETH:** Of course it's because of your chopsticks for legs!

MELISSA: Is Elizabeth going to find a new boyfriend first or am I? Oh, wait that's not a yes or no question. Oh jeez. Am I going to fall in real love first, before Elizabeth? (*shakes the ball*)

MAGIC 8 BALL V.O.: Yes.

ELIZABETH: It's totally broken!

MELISSA: Oh yeah? Is Elizabeth going to give up on love after her next boyfriend goes gay too? (*shakes the ball*)

65 **MAGIC 8 BALL V.O.:** Most likely.

ELIZABETH: Is Melissa going to be sad when I fling myself from the roof and fall splat on the asphalt? (*shakes the ball*)

MELISSA: Oh jeez. Oh crap. Of course I would be devastated!

MAGIC 8 BALL V.O.: Very doubtful.

ELIZABETH: That's it. Now I have absolutely no way of predicting anything.

70 **MELISSA:** Dear Magic 8 Ball, will we be able to find happiness without knowing what's predetermined even if our poor boyfriends like each other more than they like us? (*shakes the ball*)

MAGIC 8 BALL V.O.: Outlook good.

OFF STAGE VOICE: A single transparent, fluid bubble is formed in the liquid between the face carrying the displayed insignia and the horizontal portion of the window, said single bubble having a predetermined volume such that substantially the entire face carrying the displayed insignia can be viewed through the bubble and the horizontally disposed portion of the window.

*   *   *

HAROLD PINTER (1930–2008) was an English playwright, screenwriter, director, actor, and poet. He won numerous awards, including the 2005 Nobel Prize in Literature, and held several honorary university degrees. His work has appeared in numerous collections, including most recently *Various Voices: Sixty Years of Prose, Poetry, Politics, 1948–2008* (2009). A vocal political activist, Pinter often explored absurd and dark subjects in his work.

UPPA/ZUMA Press/Newscom

Applicant (1961)

An office. Lamb, a young man, eager, cheerful, enthusiastic, is sitting nervously, alone. The door opens. Miss Piffs comes in. She is the essence of efficiency.

PIFFS: Ah, good morning.

LAMB: Oh, good morning, miss.

PIFFS: Are you Mr. Lamb?

LAMB: That's right.

PIFFS (*studying a sheet of paper*): Yes. You're applying for this vacant post, aren't   5
  you?

LAMB: I am actually, yes.

PIFFS: Are you a physicist?

LAMB: Oh yes, indeed. It's my whole life.

PIFFS (*languidly*): Good, Now our procedure is, that before we discuss the
  applicant's qualifications we like to subject him to a little test to determine
  his psychological suitability. You've no objection?

LAMB: Oh, good heavens, no.   10

PIFFS: Jolly good.

Miss Piffs has taken some objects out of a drawer and goes to Lamb. She places a chair for him.

PIFFS: Please sit down. (*He sits*) Can I fit these to your palms?

LAMB (*affably*): What are they?

PIFFS: Electrodes.

LAMB: Oh yes, of course. Funny little things.   15

She attaches them to his palms.

PIFFS: Now the earphones.

She attaches earphones to his head.

LAMB: I say, how amusing.

PIFFS: Now I plug in.

She plugs in to the wall.

LAMB (*a trifle nervously*): Plug in, do you? Oh yes, of course. Yes, you'd have to,
  wouldn't you?

Miss Piffs perches on a high stool and looks down on Lamb.

  This helps to determine my . . . my suitability does it?

PIFFS: Unquestionably. Now relax. Just relax. Don't think about a thing.   20

LAMB: No.

PIFFS: Relax completely. Rela-a-a-x. Quite relaxed?

Lamb nods. Miss Piffs presses a button on the side of her stool. A piercing high pitched buzz-hum is heard. Lamb jolts rigid. His hands go to his earphones. He is propelled from the chair. He tries to crawl under the chair. Miss Piffs watches, impassive. The noise stops.

Lamb peeps out from under the chair, crawls out, stands, twitches, emits a short chuckle and collapses in the chair.

PIFFS: Would you say you were an excitable person?

LAMB: Not—not unduly, no. Of course, I—

25 PIFFS: Would you say you were a moody person?

LAMB: Moody? No, I wouldn't say I was moody—well, sometimes occasionally—

PIFFS: Do you ever get fits of depression?

LAMB: Well, I wouldn't call them depression exactly—

PIFFS: Do you often do things you regret in the morning?

30 LAMB: Regret? Things I regret? Well, it depends what you mean by often, really—
   I mean when you say often—

PIFFS: Are you often puzzled by women?

LAMB: Women?

PIFFS: Men.

LAMB: Men? Well, I was just going to answer the question about women—

35 PIFFS: Do you often feel puzzled?

LAMB: Puzzled?

PIFFS: By women.

LAMB: Women?

PIFFS: Men.

40 LAMB: Oh, now just a minute, I . . . Look, do you want separate answers or a joint
   answer?

PIFFS: After your day's work do you ever feel tired? Edgy? Fretty? Irritable? At a
   loose end? Morose? Frustrated? Morbid? Unable to concentrate? Unable to
   sleep? Unable to eat? Unable to remain seated? Unable to remain upright?
   Lustful? Indolent? On heat? Randy? Full of desire? Full of energy? Full of dread?
   Drained? of energy, of dread? of desire?

Pause.

LAMB (**thinking**): Well, it's difficult to say really . . .

PIFFS: Are you a good mixer?

LAMB: Well, you've touched on quite an interesting point there—

45 PIFFS: Do you suffer from eczema, listlessness, or falling coat?

LAMB: Er . . .

PIFFS: Are you virgo intacta?[1]

LAMB: I beg your pardon?

PIFFS: Are you virgo intacta?

50 LAMB: Oh, I say, that's rather embarrassing. I mean—in front of a lady—

PIFFS: Are you virgo intacta?

LAMB: Yes, I am, actually. I'll make no secret of it.

PIFFS: Have you always been virgo intacta?

LAMB: Oh yes, always. Always.

55 PIFFS: From the word go?

---

[1]*Virgo intacta:* A virgin.

LAMB: Go? Oh yes, from the word go.

PIFFS: Do women frighten you?

She presses a button on the other side of her stool. The stage is plunged into redness, which flashes on and off in time with her questions.

PIFFS (*building*): Their clothes? Their shoes? Their voices? Their laughter? Their stares? Their way of walking? Their way of sitting? Their way of smiling? Their way of talking? Their mouths? Their hands? Their feet? Their shins? Their thighs? Their knees? Their eyes? Their (*Drumbeat*). Their (*Drumbeat*). Their (*Cymbal bang*). Their (*Trombone chord*). Their (*Bass note*).

LAMB (*in a high voice*): Well it depends what you mean really—

The light still flashes. She presses the other button and the piercing buzz-hum is heard again. Lamb's hands go to his earphones. He is propelled from the chair, falls, rolls, crawls, totters and collapses.

Silence.

He lies face upwards. Miss Piffs looks at him then walks to Lamb and bends over him.

PIFFS: Thank you very much, Mr. Lamb. We'll let you know.　60

*　　*　　*

EARL T. ROSKE is a playwright, short story writer, novelist, and poet. In 2012, he independently published his first novel, *Tale of the Music-Thief*. Roske has written numerous ten-minute plays, which have been produced all over the world. The following play appeared in the 2013 Short + Sweet Festival in Sydney, Australia, the 2013 New Works Winter Festival in Massachusetts, the 2012 Autumn One-Acts in New York, and the Pan Theater's 2011 Ten-Minute Play Festival in California.

Zombie Love (2011)

CHARACTERS

Emily: *Female, early twenties*

Kathy: *Female, early twenties*

Walter: *Male, early twenties, undead*

TIME. PLACE, AND TECHNICAL REQUIREMENTS: Current era, time is now. Park bench, rising moon light, a dead rat, some dying flowers that are edible. Zombie make-up.

Lights up on a park. There is—at minimum—a bench. Emily enters with Walter, a zombie, in tow.

EMILY: Right here! This is perfect, Walter. A bench to sit on and a clear view of the rising moon.

WALTER: (*Always speaks in drawn out syllables and without the use of lips or teeth. The intention is to go with the stereotype.*) Oh. Okay.

EMILY: Come and sit with me. This will be so romantic. You. Me. The moon rising over the hills.

WALTER: Kathy.

50   EMILY: Kathy? No, it's okay. She has no idea—

KATHY: (*Entering*) There you are.

WALTER: Ew . . . nar . . .

WALTER: Trouble.

EMILY: Hello, Kathy.

(*Beat*)

Lovely evening.

55   KATHY: No hardly. Why are you out here with that?

WALTER: Aw . . .

EMILY: With "him." I'm with "him," Kathy.

KATHY: Whatever. It's not like it has feelings.

WALTER: Do, too . . . .

60   EMILY: See. If you'd just take the time to get to know him.

KATHY: I don't want to know a zombie.

WALTER: It's okay . . . .

EMILY: No it's not, Walter, dear. I'm sorry she doesn't understand.

KATHY: Listen. Emily. We need to talk.

65   EMILY: So talk.

KATHY: In private.

EMILY: This is private.

KATHY: Not in front of—of him. Okay?

EMILY: (*Pause*) Fine. Walter, honey. Give us a moment.

70   WALTER: Um . . . Okay . . .

KATHY: Yeah, go eat a bug or something.

WALTER: I like bugs . . . .

KATHY: Gross!

EMILY: Walter. Remember to chew or they'll just crawl back out.

75   WALTER: Okay . . . .

KATHY: Doubly gross!

EMILY: So . . . ?

KATHY: You need to come home.

EMILY: I will. Right after Walter and I watch the moon rise.

Walter sees something moving around on the ground. He follows it, grunting/moaning/groaning every few lines of dialogue that follows.

80   KATHY: Now.

EMILY: Really, Kathy, since when are you the boss of me.

KATHY: Someone has to look out for you. Since you've started dating a dead guy.

EMILY: Undead. And you're going to hold that against him?

KATHY: Yes!

EMILY: It's not his fault. He didn't choose to be a zombie. It's just a part of who   85
    he is.
KATHY: Part? Huge part!
EMILY: Good.
KATHY: I just don't think he's the right guy for you.
EMILY: Well I happen to disagree.
KATHY: People are talking, Emily. You're losing friends.   90

Walter falls onto a small object on the ground and strangles it with his hands. Pleased grunt-ing/moaning/groaning sounds. He gets to his feet holding a dead rat during the next few lines of dialogue. Emily and Kathy are unaware of what has been happening with Walter.

EMILY: Let them talk. Walter and I are happy together.
KATHY: Oh. come on, Emily! You Can't let this thing—
EMILY: Walter. His name is Walter.
KATHY: This undead Walter come between you and your friends. Between you and
    your family.
EMILY: Well they'd better not force me to choose, because—   95
WALTER: (*Presents dead rat to Emily.*) Ook!
KATHY: Ohmygod!
EMILY: Aw, thank you, honey.
WALTER: Or . . . ew . . .
KATHY: It's a dead rat!   100
EMILY: Yes it is. Walter, dear, just put it down over there, sweety.

    (*Points to base of bench. Walter puts dead rat next to bench leg.*)

    We'll play with it later.
WALTER: Oodie . . . !
KATHY: That's . . . Oh, it's disgusting.
EMILY: It isn't.

    (*To Walter*)

    (Kathy and I are still talking. Just a bit longer, okay?
WALTER: Oon . . . ?   105
EMILY: (*Looking up.*) The moon hasn't started yet. It'll be okay. Soon. I promise.
WALTER: Kay . . .

Moves off to one side

KATHY: How can you stand it?
EMILY: What? He brought me a present.
KATHY: A dead rat!   110
EMILY: Well at least he put some effort into it. His own brain power.
WALTER: Bwains . . . !
EMILY: Not now. sweety.

    (*To Kathy*)

It wasn't some cheesey crushed velvet rose bought at some quicky-mart as an afterthought.

KATHY: Dead. Rat.

115 EMILY: You just don't get it. He's not like other guys. He really cares about me.

KATHY: The undead can't care. Except caring about eating brains.

WALTER: Bwains . . . ?

KATHY: Oh, hush!

EMILY: Don't talk to him like that. At least I know Walter will be there when I need him. He'll listen when I just need to talk. Can you say that about other guys?

120 KATHY: Other guys still have a pulse!

Walter finds some half-dead flowers and "bunches" them into a bouquet.

EMILY: I don't have to worry about Walter going out and getting drunk—

KATHY: 'Cause he's dead.

EMILY: Forgetting to come home. Sleeping with my best friend.

KATHY: That'd never happen. Thank god.

125 EMILY: Or just sitting on the couch, hand in his pants, watching sports all day.

Walter hands Emily the "bunched" flowers.

Thank you! Walter likes to take walks with me.

KATHY: 'Cause you order him to go.

EMILY: I don't have to order him.

WALTER: Ind . . . oad . . . ill . . . !

KATHY: Find road-kill? That's disgusting.

130 EMILY: No guy is perfect, but at least I have something real with Walter.

KATHY: Whatever. No one's happy about this but you, Emily. You're driving your friends away. You family is hurt because you won't date somebody nice, and living. Pretty soon all you're going to have left is smelly, undead, rat killing Walter! You won't be happy. You'll grow old regretting your decision.

EMILY: You're the one who sounds unhappy.

KATHY: I'm unhappy that I'm losing my best friend.

EMILY: You haven't lost me, Kathy. I'm right here.

135 KATHY: I don't think I can stay your friend if you continue to date that!

EMILY: Geez, Kathy, you can be such a killjoy. I guess I have no choice.

KATHY: I knew you'd see reason.

EMILY: Walter, dear.

WALTER: Uh . . . ?

140 EMILY: Kill Kathy for me, please? There's a sweetheart.

KATHY: What? No! Wait!

Walter grabs Kathy who screams. Her scream is choked off as Walter strangles her as they fall to the ground.

WALTER: Bwains . . . !

EMILY: No, no, Walter. No brains.

WALTER: No . . . bwains . . . ?

145 EMILY: Just kill her, don't eat her. Okay, honey.

WALTER: Aw . . . O . . . A . . .

EMILY: We want to keep her as a friend.
WALTER: Ake . . . end . . . !

Walter gets up.

EMILY: The eclipse is about to start, Walter. Come join me?
WALTER: E . . . ips . . .

Sits with Emily

EMILY: Come join us, Kathy?
KATHY: (*Slowly sitting up. Talks like Walter now.*) Uh . . . ha . . . een . . . ?
EMILY: What happened? Just keeping you as my best friend. Come. Sit with us.
KATHY: O . . . ay . . .

Kathy sits next to Emily.

EMILY: There. Isn't this perfect?

   (*Links arms with Kathy and Walter*)

   What could be better than this?
KATHY & WALTER: Bwains!!!
EMILY: Oh, you, two. Look. It's starting.

They all watch the lunar eclipse.

Lights out

*   *   *

Reading and Reacting

1. Do you think any of the characters in the five plays in this chapter are fully developed, or do you see most (or all) of them as stereotypes? Given the limits of its form, do you think a ten-minute play can ever really develop a character?

2. Most of the plays in this chapter have only one or two characters. Should any additional parts have been written for these plays? Explain.

3. Could the roles in this chapter's plays be portrayed by actors of any gender? of any age? of any race? Why or why not?

4. Identify the central conflict in each play. What do you see as the **climax**, or highest point of tension, in each? Where does the climax generally occur in these plays?

5. Each play in this chapter has a single setting, and each of these settings is described only minimally. Do any settings seem to require more detailed descriptions? If you were going to expand each play, what additional settings might you show?

6. Considering the subject matter of each of the plays in this chapter, what kinds of topics seem to be most appropriate for ten-minute plays? Why do you think this is so? What kinds of topics would *not* be suitable for ten-minute plays?

7. CRITICAL PERSPECIVE The website *10-Minute-Plays.com*, whose slogan is "High-octane drama for a fast-food nation," summarizes the structure of a ten-minute play as follows:

> Pages 1 to 2: Set up the world of your main character.
> Pages 2 to 3: Something happens to throw your character's world out of balance.
> Pages 4 to 7: Your character struggles to restore order to his world.
> Page 8: Just when your character is about to restore order, something happens to complicate matters.
> Pages 9 to 10: Your character either succeeds or fails in his attempt to restore order.

Although not every play in this chapter is exactly ten pages long, do they all nevertheless conform to the general structure outlined above?

WRITING SUGGESTIONS: Ten-Minute Plays

1. Write a **response** (see Chapter 3) expressing your reactions to either *Magic 8 Ball* or *Zombie Love*.
2. Write an **explication** (see Chapter 3) of *Applicant*.
3. Assume you are a director providing background for an actor who is to play the role of Carla or Bethany in *Beauty*. Write a **character analysis** (see Chapter 3) of one of these characters, outlining her background and explaining her emotions, actions, conflicts, and motivation.
4. Write an essay about the **cultural context** (see Chapter 3) of *"What Are You Going to Be?"*
5. Choose a scene from one of the longer plays in this text that has a definite beginning, middle, and end. Rewrite this scene as a self-contained ten-minute play. (If you like, you can update the scene to the present time, change the characters' names or genders, and make other changes you see as necessary.)
6. Write an original ten-minute play for two characters.

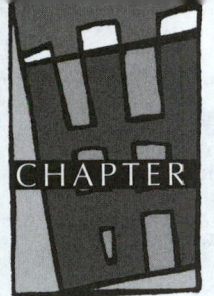

CHAPTER 36

READING AND WRITING ABOUT DRAMA

 ## Reading Drama

When you read a play, you will notice features it shares with works of fiction—for instance, the use of figurative language and symbols, the interaction among characters, and the development of a theme or themes. However, you will also notice features that mark a play as different from a short story or a novel—for example, the inclusion of stage directions and the presence of acts and scenes.

The following guidelines, designed to help you explore works of dramatic literature, focus on issues that are examined in depth in chapters to come:

- *Trace the play's* **plot**. What conflicts are present? Where does the rising action reach a climax? Where does the falling action begin? What techniques move the action along? (See Chapter 37.)
- *Analyze the play's* **characters**. Who are the central characters? What are their most distinctive traits? How do you learn about their personalities, backgrounds, appearances, and strengths and weaknesses? (See Chapter 38.)
- *Consider how the characters act—and how they interact with one another.* Do the characters change and grow in response to the play's events, or do they remain essentially unchanged? (See Chapter 38.)
- *Examine the play's* **language**. How does **dialogue** reveal characters' emotions, conflicts, opinions, and motivations? (See Chapter 38.)
- *Look for* **soliloquies** *or* **asides**. What do they contribute to your knowledge of the play's characters and events? (See Chapter 38.)
- *Read the play's* **stage directions**. What do you learn from the descriptions of the characters, including their dress, gestures, and facial expressions? (See Chapter 38.) What information do you gain from studying the playwright's descriptions of the play's setting? Do the stage directions include information about lighting, props, music, or sound effects? (See Chapter 39.)
- *Consider the play's* **staging**. Where and when does the action take place? What techniques are used to convey a sense of time and place to the audience? (See Chapter 39.)

- *Try to identify the play's **themes**.* What main idea does the play communicate? What additional themes are explored? (See Chapter 40.)
- *Identify any **symbols** in the play.* How do these symbols help you to understand the play's themes? (See Chapter 40.)

Active Reading

As you read a play about which you plan to write, you follow the same process that guides you when you read any work of literature. You read actively, marking the text as you proceed. Then, you go on to select a topic and develop ideas about it, decide on a thesis, prepare an outline, and write and revise several drafts.

Kimberly Allison, a student in an Introduction to Literature course, was given the following assignment.

> Without consulting any outside sources, write a three- to five-page essay about any one-act play in our literature anthology. You may focus on action, character, staging, or theme, or you may consider more than one of these elements.

Previewing

Kim decided to write her essay on Susan Glaspell's play *Trifles*, which appears in Chapter 41. She began by previewing *Trifles*, noting its brief length, its one-act structure, its list of characters, and its setting in John Wright's farmhouse. Kim noticed immediately that John Wright does not appear in the play, and his absence aroused her curiosity.

Highlighting and Annotating

As Kim read *Trifles*, she highlighted the dialogue and stage directions she thought she might later want to examine more closely, noted possible links among ideas, identified patterns of action and language, and jotted down her own observations and questions. She found herself especially interested in the female and male characters' different reactions to the objects discovered in the house and in the interaction between the women and the men.

The following highlighted and annotated passage illustrates some of her responses to the play.

The men laugh; the women looked abashed.   Why do the men and women react so differently?

COUNTY ATTORNEY: (*rubbing his hands over the stove*) Frank's fire didn't do much up there, did it? Well, let's go out to the barn and get that cleared up.

→The men go outside.

Why
do the
men
go and
the
women
stay?

MRS. HALE : ((*resentfully*)) I don't know as there's anything

so strange, our takin' up our time with(little things)

while we're waiting for them to get the evidence.

(*She sits down at the big table smoothing out a block with*

decision.) I don't see as it's anything to laugh about.

MRS. PETERS : (*apologetically*) Of course they've got

awful important things on their minds.

Like what?

Why does she make excuses for the men?

→ Pulls up a chair and joins Mrs. Hale at the table.

Kim's highlighting and annotations of the entire play—most of which, like those above, focused on the play's characters—suggested some interesting possibilities for her essay.

Writing about Drama

Planning an Essay

Even after Kim decided to write about the play's characters, she knew she had to narrow her focus. Her notes suggested that gender roles in general, and the role of the women in particular, would make an interesting topic, so she decided to explore this idea further.

Choosing a Topic

To help her decide on a direction for her essay, Kim wrote the following entry in her journal.

What is the role of the women in this play? Although the two women have gone with their husbands to pick up some items for Mrs. Wright, they seem to be primarily interested in why Mrs. Wright would leave her house in such disarray. They find several objects that suggest that Mrs. Wright was lonely and that she was dominated by her husband. But these women are left on their own and seem to band together. Their guilt about not visiting Mrs. Wright also seems to connect them with the murder suspect. The women find the details, or "trifles," of Mrs. Wright's life interesting and learn from them the facts surrounding the murder; the men wander aimlessly around the house and yard. The real clue to the murder appears to be Mrs. Wright's messy house, but the men do not seem to understand the implications of the disorder. The women have an understanding that comes from their own experiences as women, which the men are unable to tap into.

At this point, Kim concluded that the role of the women in *Trifles* would be the best focus for her essay. As she went on to gather ideas to write about, she also planned to examine the ways in which the women interacted with the men.

Finding Something to Say: Brainstorming

Kim's next step was to develop the specific ideas to discuss in her essay. She reread the play and her annotations, keeping her topic (the role of women) in mind as she made the following brainstorming notes.

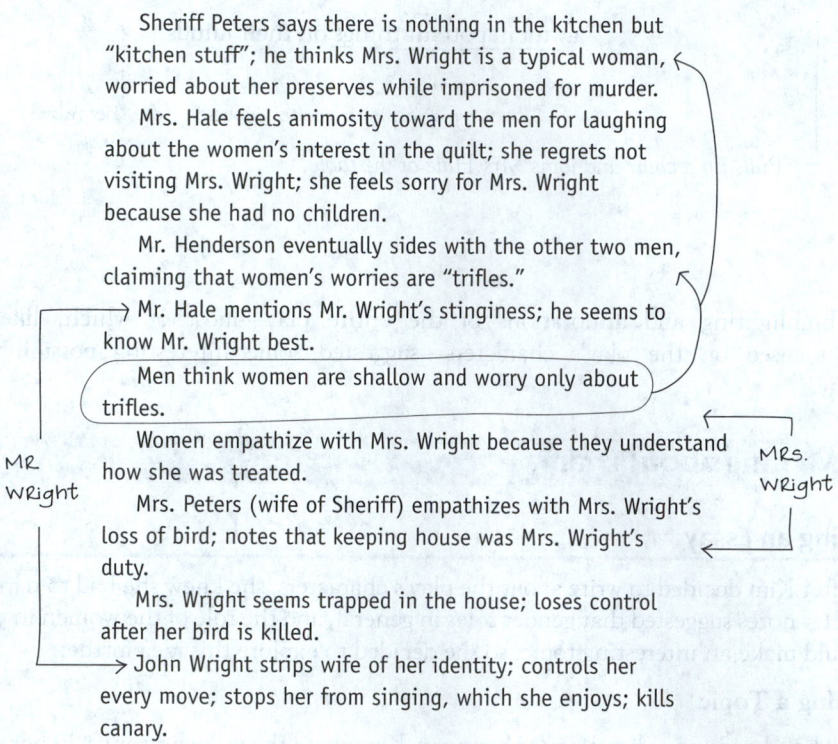

Sheriff Peters says there is nothing in the kitchen but "kitchen stuff"; he thinks Mrs. Wright is a typical woman, worried about her preserves while imprisoned for murder.

Mrs. Hale feels animosity toward the men for laughing about the women's interest in the quilt; she regrets not visiting Mrs. Wright; she feels sorry for Mrs. Wright because she had no children.

Mr. Henderson eventually sides with the other two men, claiming that women's worries are "trifles."

Mr. Hale mentions Mr. Wright's stinginess; he seems to know Mr. Wright best.

Men think women are shallow and worry only about trifles.

Women empathize with Mrs. Wright because they understand how she was treated.

Mrs. Peters (wife of Sheriff) empathizes with Mrs. Wright's loss of bird; notes that keeping house was Mrs. Wright's duty.

Mrs. Wright seems trapped in the house; loses control after her bird is killed.

John Wright strips wife of her identity; controls her every move; stops her from singing, which she enjoys; kills canary.

MR WRIGHT

MRS. WRIGHT

When she reread her notes, the first thing Kim noticed was that the female and male characters have two entirely different attitudes about women's lives and concerns: the men think their own work is much more important than that of the women, which they see as trivial; the women realize they are not much different from Mrs. Wright. Now, Kim saw that in order to discuss the role of women in the play, she first had to define that role in relation to the role of the men.

Seeing Connections: Listing

At this point, Kim decided that listing ideas under the heads *Men* and *Women* could help her clarify the differences between men's and women's roles.

Men	**Women**
Work outside the home	Make preserves
Make decisions about financial expenditures	Clean house
	Make quilts
Think women should do just housework	Raise children
Create and enforce law	Go to ladies' clubs for socializing
Dictate wives' actions	Follow laws that men create
Have separate identities and power	Subordinate their desires to their husbands'
Act in ways that are accepted by society	Act defiantly to break boundaries set by social role

Making these two lists enabled Kim to confirm her idea that the men's and the women's roles are defined very differently in *Trifles*. In fact, the men and women seem to agree that they have different responsibilities, and both seem to understand and accept the fact that power is unevenly distributed.

Deciding on a Thesis

Kim's work clarified her understanding of the limited role women have in the society portrayed in *Trifles*. This, in turn, enabled her to develop the following **thesis statement**.

The central focus of *Trifles* is not on finding out who killed Mr. Wright but on defining the limited, even subservient, role of women like Mrs. Wright.

Preparing an Outline

Guided by her thesis statement and the information she had collected in her notes, Kim made a scratch outline, arranging her supporting details in a logical order under appropriate headings.

Mrs. Hale and Mrs. Peters had limited roles

- Subservient to husbands
- Restricted to performing domestic chores
- Confined to kitchen
- Identified with Minnie Wright's loneliness

Minnie Wright had limited role

- Did what husband told her to do
- Had no link with outside world
- Couldn't sing
- Had no friends
- Had no identity

Drafting an Essay

Following her tentative thesis and her scratch outline, Kim wrote the following first draft of her essay. Before she began, she reviewed her notes and her highlighting of the play to look for details that would illustrate and support her generalizations about it.

---

fiRst dRaft

The Women's Role in *Trifles*

Susan Glaspell's *Trifles* seems to focus on the murder of John Wright. Mr. Wright had little concern for his wife's opinions. Mr. Hale suggested that Minnie Wright was powerless against her husband, and Sheriff Henry Peters questioned whether Minnie was allowed to quilt her log cabin pattern. Perhaps, because Mr. Wright did not spend his money freely, he would have made Minnie knot the quilt because it cost less. Minnie was controlled by her husband. He forced her to perform repetitive domestic chores. The central focus of *Trifles* is not on finding out who killed Mr. Wright but on defining the limited, even subservient role of women like Mrs. Wright.

Mrs. Peters and Mrs. Hale were similar to Minnie. Mrs. Peters and Mrs. Hale also performed domestic chores and had to do what their husbands wanted them to do, and they too were confined to Mrs. Wright's kitchen. The kitchen was the focal point of the play. Mrs. Peters and Mrs. Hale remained confined to the kitchen while their husbands exercised their freedom to enter and exit the house at will. This mirrored Minnie's life because she stayed home while her husband went to work and into town. The two women discussed Minnie's isolation. Beginning to identify with Minnie's loneliness, Mrs. Peters and Mrs. Hale recognized that while they were busy in their own homes, they had, in fact, participated in isolating and confining Minnie.

Eventually, the women found that the kitchen held the clues to Mrs. Wright's loneliness and to the details of the murder. The two women discovered that Minnie's only connection to the outside world was her bird. Minnie too was a caged bird because she was kept from singing and communicating with others by her husband. And piecing together the evidence, the women came to believe that John Wright had broken the bird's neck.

At the same time, Mrs. Peters and Mrs. Hale discovered the connection between the dead canary and Minnie's situation, and they began to recognize that they had to band together in order to exert their strength against the men. They realized that Minnie's independence and identity were crushed by her husband and that their own husbands believed women's lives were trivial and unimportant. The revelation that Mrs. Peters and Mrs. Hale experienced encouraged them to commit an act as rebellious as the one that got Minnie in trouble: they concealed their discovery from their husbands and from the law.

   Because Mrs. Hale and Mrs. Peters empathized with Minnie's situation, they suppressed the evidence they found and endured the men's insults. And in this way, the women attempted to break through the boundaries of their social roles, just as Minnie had done before them.

First Draft: Commentary

When Kim reread her first draft, she realized that she had gone beyond the scope of her tentative thesis statement and scratch outline, considering not just the women's subservient role but also the actions they take to break free of this role. She decided to revise her thesis statement to reflect this new emphasis—and then to expand her essay to develop this aspect of her revised thesis more fully.

   Kim's peer review group made the general suggestion that she develop her essay further. In addition, they thought that her essay's sentences seemed choppy—many needed to be linked with transitional words and phrases—and that her introduction was unfocused.

   When Kim met with her instructor to discuss her revision plans, he encouraged her to expand her essay's focus and to use quotations and specific examples to support her ideas. He also reminded her to use the present tense in her essay—not "Mrs. Peters and Mrs. Hale *were* similar to Minnie" but "Mrs. Peters and Mrs. Hale *are* similar to Minnie." (Only events that occurred *before* the time in which the play takes place—for example, the murder itself or Minnie's girlhood experiences—should be described in past tense.)

   After meeting with her instructor, Kim made a new scratch outline to guide her as she continued to revise.

Subservient role of women
- Minnie's husband didn't respect her opinion
- Her husband didn't let her sing
- Minnie could perform only domestic chores

Confinement of women in home
- Mrs. Hale and Mrs. Peters are confined to kitchen
- Minnie was lonely at home because she had no children
- Minnie didn't belong to Ladies Aid
- Minnie was a caged bird

Women's defiance
- Mrs. Hale and Mrs. Peters solve "mystery"
- They realize they must band together
- They take action
- They defy men's law

Revising and Editing an Essay

Before she wrote her next draft, Kim reviewed the suggestions she had recorded in meetings with classmates and with her instructor. Then, she incorporated this material, along with her own new ideas, into her second draft, which follows.

---

second dRaft

Confinement and Rebellion in *Trifles*

Susan Glaspell's play *Trifles* involves the solving of a murder. Two women, Mrs. Peters and Mrs. Hale, discover that Mrs. Wright, who remains in jail throughout the play, has indeed murdered her husband. Interestingly, the women make this discovery through the examination of evidence in Mrs. Wright's kitchen, which their husbands, Sheriff Henry Peters and farmer Lewis Hale, along with the county attorney, Mr. Henderson, dismiss as women's "trifles." The focus of *Trifles*, however, is not on the murder of John Wright but on the subservient role of women, the confinement of the wife in the home, and the desperate measures women must take to achieve autonomy.

The role of Minnie Wright becomes evident in the first few minutes of the play, when Mr. Hale declares, "I didn't know as what his wife wanted made much difference to John—" (1605). Minnie's powerlessness is further revealed when the women discuss how Mr. Wright forced her to give up the thing she loved—singing. Both of these observations suggest that Minnie's every action was controlled and stifled by her husband. She was not allowed to make decisions or be an individual; instead, she was expected only to perform domestic chores.

Doing domestic chores was the only part of life that Minnie was allowed to exert some power over, a condition that is shared by Mrs. Peters and Mrs. Hale, whom we assume work only in the home and whose behavior as wives is determined by their husbands.

The men are free to walk throughout the house and outside of it while the women are, not surprisingly, confined to the kitchen, just as Mrs. Wright had been confined to the house. Early in the play, Mrs. Hale refers to Minnie's isolation, saying she "kept so much to herself. She didn't even belong to the Ladies Aid" (1609). Mrs. Hale goes on to mention Mrs. Wright's lack of nice clothing, which further suggests her confinement in the home: if she never left her home, she wouldn't need to look nice, and why would she want to leave home if she had no nice clothes? Minnie's isolation is further revealed when Mrs. Hale mentions her lack of children: "Not having children makes less work—but it makes a quiet house, and Wright out to work all day, and no company when he did come in" (1612). Minnie's only connection to the outside world was her bird, which becomes the symbol of her confinement because she herself was a caged bird. In a sense, Mr. Wright strangled her, as he did the bird, by preventing her from talking to other people in the community. Unlike the men, Mrs. Peters and Mrs. Hale realize the connection between the dead canary and Minnie's situation as *"Their eyes meet"* and they share *"A look of growing comprehension, of horror"* (1612).

The comprehension that Mrs. Peters and Mrs. Hale experience urges them to rebel by concealing their discovery from their husbands and from the law. Mrs. Peters does concede that "the law is the law" (1610), but she also seems to believe that because Mr. Wright treated his wife badly, treating her as a domestic slave and isolating her from the world, Minnie was justified in killing him. And Mrs. Peters knows that even if Minnie had been able to communicate the abuse she suffered, the law would not take the abuse into account because the men on the jury would not be sympathetic to a woman's complaints about how her husband treated her.

The dialogue in *Trifles* reveals a huge difference in how women and men view their experiences. From the opening of the play, the gulf between the men and women emerges, and as the play progresses, the polarization of the male and female characters becomes clearer. Once the men leave the kitchen to find what they consider to be significant criminal evidence, the men and women are divided physically as well as emotionally. The men create their own community, as do the women. With the women alone in the kitchen, the focus of the dialogue is on the female experience. The women discuss the preserves, the quilt, and the disarray in the kitchen, emphasizing that Mrs. Wright would not have left her home in disorder unless she had been distracted by some more pressing situation.

Minnie Wright seems to have accepted her servitude voluntarily, making work in the home her main interest. But the men trivialize Mrs. Wright's and other women's significance when they criticize her role as a homemaker. The county attorney condemns her, sarcastically observing, "I shouldn't say she had the homemaking instinct" (1608). Minnie attempted to keep her home clean and do her chores, but the cold exploded her preserves, and her husband dirtied the towels. What caused Minnie to neglect her chores is something of great importance: her longing for independence and freedom from the servitude she once accepted voluntarily.

What makes this play most interesting is that Mrs. Hale and Mrs. Peters come to realize that they too have volunteered to be subservient to their husbands. They understand that their husbands will trivialize their discovery about the murder, as the men earlier trivialized their discussions of Minnie's daily tasks. Therefore, the women band together and conceal the information, breaking through their subservient roles as wives. And, in the end, they find their own independence and significance in society.

Second Draft: Commentary

When she read her second draft, Kim had mixed feelings about it. She thought it was an improvement over her first draft, primarily because she had expanded the focus of her discussion and added specific details and quotations to support her points. She also believed her essay was now clearer, with a more specific thesis statement and smoother transitions.

Still, Kim thought that the logic of her discussion was somewhat difficult to follow, and she thought clearer topic sentences might correct this problem by guiding readers more smoothly through her essay. She also felt that her organization, which did not follow her revised scratch outline, was somewhat confusing. (For example, she discussed the women's subservient role in two different parts of her essay—paragraphs 2 and 7.) In addition, Kim thought her third paragraph could be developed further, and she believed her essay needed additional supporting details and quotations throughout. After rereading her notes, she wrote her final draft, which appears on the following pages.

Allison 1

Kimberly Allison

Professor Johnson

English 1013

13 April 2015

Desperate Measures: Acts of Defiance in *Trifles*

Opening sentence identifies author and work.

Susan Glaspell wrote her best-known play, *Trifles*, in 1916, at a time when married women were beginning to challenge their socially defined roles, realizing that their identities as wives kept them in a subordinate position in society. Because women were demanding more autonomy, traditional institutions such as marriage, which

Introduction places play in historical context.

confined women to the home and made them mere extensions of their husbands, were beginning to be reexamined.

Evidently touched by these concerns, Glaspell chose as her play's protagonist a married woman, Minnie Wright, who challenged society's expectations in a very extreme way: by murdering her husband. Minnie's defiant act has occurred before the action begins; during the play, two women, Mrs. Peters and Mrs. Hale, who accompany their husbands on an investigation of the murder scene, piece together the details of the situation surrounding the murder. As the events unfold, however, it becomes clear that the focus of *Trifles* is not on who killed John Wright but on the themes of the subordinate role of women, the confinement of the wife in the home, and the experiences all women share. With these themes, Glaspell shows her audience the desperate measures women had to take to achieve autonomy.

> **Thesis statement**

   The subordinate role of women, particularly Minnie's role in her marriage, becomes evident in the first few minutes of the play, when Mr. Hale observes that the victim, John Wright, had little concern for his wife's opinions: "I didn't know as what his wife wanted made much difference to John—" (1605). Here Mr. Hale suggests that Mrs. Wright was powerless against the wishes of her husband. Indeed, as these characters imply, Mrs. Wright's every act and thought was controlled by her husband, who tried to break her spirit by forcing her to stay alone in the house, performing repetitive domestic chores. Mrs. Wright's only source of power in the household was her kitchen work, a situation that Mrs. Peters and Mrs. Hale understand because their own behavior is also determined by their husbands. Therefore, when Sheriff Peters makes fun of Minnie's concern about her preserves, saying, "Well, can you beat the women! Held for murder and worryin' about her preserves" (1607), he is, in a sense, criticizing all three of the women for worrying about domestic matters rather than about the murder that has been committed. Indeed, the sheriff's comment suggests that he assumes women's lives are trivial, an attitude that influences the thoughts and speech of all three men.

> **Topic sentence identifies first point essay will discuss: women's subordinate role.**

   Mrs. Peters and Mrs. Hale are similar to Minnie Wright in another way as well: throughout the play, they are confined to the kitchen of the Wrights' house. As a result, the kitchen becomes the focal point of the play—and, ironically, the women find that the kitchen holds the clues to Mrs. Wright's loneliness and to the details of the murder. Mrs. Peters and Mrs. Hale remain confined to the kitchen while their husbands enter and exit the house at will. This situation mirrors Minnie Wright's daily life, as she remained in the home while her husband went to work and into town. As they move about the kitchen, the two women discuss Minnie Wright's isolation: "Not having children makes less work— but it makes a quiet house, and Wright out to work all day, and no company when he did come in" (1612). Beginning to identify with Mrs. Wright's loneliness, Mrs. Peters and Mrs. Hale recognize that, busy in their own homes, they have participated in isolating and confining Minnie Wright. Mrs. Hale declares, "Oh, I wish I'd come over here once in a while! That was a crime! That was a crime! Who's going to punish that? . . . I might have known she needed help!" (1614).

> **Topic sentence introduces second point essay will discuss: women's confinement in the home.**

Allison 3

Soon the two women discover that Mrs. Wright's only connection to the outside world was her bird, the symbol of her confinement; she herself was a caged bird who was kept from singing and communicating with others because of her husband. And piecing together the evidence—the disorderly kitchen, the misstitched quilt pieces, and the dead canary—the women come to believe that John Wright broke the bird's neck, just as he had broken his wife's spirit. At this point, Mrs. Peters and Mrs. Hale understand the connection between the dead canary and Minnie Wright's motivation. The stage directions describe the moment when the women become aware of the truth behind the murder: *"Their eyes meet,"* and the women share *"A look of growing comprehension, of horror"* (1612).

Through their observations and discussions in Mrs. Wright's kitchen, Mrs. Hale and Mrs. Peters come to understand the commonality of women's experiences. Mrs. Hale speaks for both of them when she says, "I know how things can be—for women. . . . We all go through the same things—it's all just a different kind of the same thing" (1614). And once the two women realize the experiences they share, they begin to recognize that they must join together in order to challenge their male-oriented society; although their experiences may seem trivial to the men, the "trifles" of their lives are significant to them. They realize that Minnie's independence and identity were crushed by her husband and that their own husbands also believe that women's lives are trivial and unimportant. This realization leads them to commit an act as defiant as the one that got Minnie into trouble: they conceal their discovery from their husbands and from the law.

Significantly, Mrs. Peters does acknowledge that "the law is the law" (1610), yet she still seems to believe that because Mr. Wright treated his wife badly, she is justified in killing him. They also realize, however, that for men the law is black and white and that an all-male jury will not take into account the extenuating circumstances that prompted Minnie Wright to kill her husband. And even if Mrs. Wright were allowed to communicate to the all-male court the psychological abuse she has suffered, the law would undoubtedly view her experience as trivial because a woman who complained about how her husband treated her would be seen as ungrateful.

Nevertheless, because Mrs. Hale and Mrs. Peters empathize with Mrs. Wright's situation, they suppress the evidence they find, enduring their husbands' condescension rather than standing up to them. And through this desperate action, the women break

Allison 4

through the boundaries of their social role, just as Minnie Wright has done. Although Mrs. Wright is imprisoned for her crime, she has freed herself; and although Mrs. Peters and Mrs. Hale conceal their knowledge, fearing the men will laugh at them, these women are really challenging society and, in this way, freeing themselves as well.

In *Trifles*, Susan Glaspell addresses many of the problems shared by early-twentieth-century women, including their subordinate status and their confinement in the home. In order to emphasize the pervasiveness of these problems and the desperate measures women had to take to break out of restrictive social roles, Glaspell does more than focus on the plight of a woman who has ended her isolation and loneliness by committing a heinous crime against society. By presenting characters who demonstrate the vast differences between male and female experience, she illustrates how men define the roles of women and how women must challenge these roles in search of their own significance in society and their eventual independence.

> Conclusion places play in historical context.

Allison 5

Work Cited

Glaspell, Susan. *Trifles. Compact Literature: Reading, Reacting, Writing*. Ed. Laurie G. Kirszner and Stephen R. Mandell. 9th ed. Boston: Wadsworth, 2016. 1604-15. Print.

Final Draft: Commentary

Kim made many changes in her final draft. Although her focus is much the same as it was in her previous draft, she expanded her essay considerably. Most important, she added a discussion of the commonality of women's experience in paragraph 6 and elsewhere, and this material helps to explain what motivates Mrs. Hale and Mrs. Peters to conceal evidence from their husbands.

As she expanded her essay, Kim added explanations, details, and quotations, taking care to provide accurate page numbers in parentheses after each quotation and to include a work-cited page. She also worked hard to make her topic sentences clearer, and she used information from her class notes to help her write a new introduction and conclusion that discussed the status of women at the time in which *Trifles* was written. Finally, she added a new title and revised her thesis statement again to emphasize the focus of her essay on the "desperate measures" all three women are driven to in response to their social situation.

CHAPTER 37

PLOT

David Ives
Evan Agostini/Getty Images Entertainment/
Getty Images

Warren Leight
Scott Gries/Getty Images Entertainment/
Getty Images

Henrik Ibsen
Hulton Archive/Getty Images

Plot denotes the way events are arranged in a work of literature. Although the conventions of drama require that the plot of a play be presented somewhat differently from the plot of a short story, the same components of plot are present in both. Plot in a dramatic work, like plot in a short story, is shaped by conflicts that are revealed, intensified, and resolved through the characters' actions. (See Chapter 13 for a discussion of conflict.)

 Plot Structure

In 1863, the German novelist and playwright Gustav Freytag devised a pyramid to represent a prototype for the plot of a dramatic work. According to Freytag, a play typically begins with **exposition**, which presents characters and setting and introduces the basic situation in which the characters are involved. Then, during the **rising action**, complications develop, conflicts emerge, suspense builds, and crises occur. The rising action culminates in a **climax**, a point at which the plot's tension peaks. Finally, during the **falling action**, the intensity subsides, eventually winding down to a **resolution**, or **denouement**, in which all loose ends are tied up.

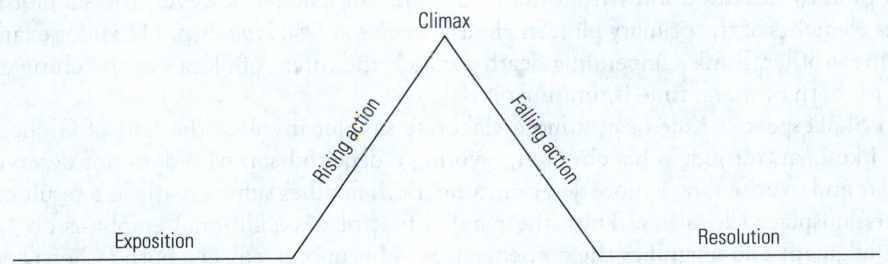

The familiar plot of a detective story follows Freytag's concept of plot: the exposition section includes the introduction of the detective and the explanation of the crime; the rising action develops as the investigation of the crime proceeds, with suspense increasing as the solution approaches; the high point of the action, the climax, comes with the revelation of the crime's solution; and the falling action presents the detective's explanation of the solution. The story concludes with a resolution that typically includes the capture of the criminal and the restoration of order.

The action of Susan Glaspell's one-act play *Trifles* (p. 1604), which in many ways resembles a detective story, can be diagrammed like this:

Of course, the plot of a complex dramatic work rarely conforms to the neat pattern represented by Freytag's pyramid. For example, a play can lack exposition entirely. Because long stretches of exposition can be dull, a playwright may decide to arouse audience interest by moving directly into conflict, as Sophocles does in *Oedipus the King* (p. 1430) and as Milcha Sanchez-Scott does in *The Cuban Swimmer* (p. 1416). Similarly, because audiences tend to lose interest after the play's climax is reached, a playwright may choose to dispense with extended falling action. Thus, after Hamlet's death, the play ends quite abruptly, with no real resolution.

Plot and Subplot

While the main plot is developing, a parallel plot, called a **subplot**, may be developing alongside it. This structural device is common in the works of Shakespeare and in many other plays as well. The subplot's function may not immediately be clear, so at first it may seem to draw attention away from the main plot. Ultimately, however, the subplot reinforces elements of the primary plot. In Henrik Ibsen's *A Doll House* (p. 1113), for example, the threat of Dr. Rank's impending death parallels the threat of Nora's approaching exposure; for both of them, time is running out.

In Shakespeare's *King Lear*, a more elaborate subplot involves the Earl of Gloucester, who, like Lear, misjudges his children, favoring a deceitful son who does not deserve his support and overlooking a more deserving one. Both families suffer greatly as a result of the fathers' misplaced loyalties. Thus, the parallel plot places additional emphasis on Lear's poor judgment and magnifies the consequences of his misguided acts: both fathers, and all but one of the five children, are dead by the play's end. A subplot can also set up a contrast with the main plot—as it does in *Hamlet* (p. 1304), where Fortinbras acts decisively to avenge his father, an action that underscores Hamlet's hesitation and procrastination when faced with a similar challenge.

Plot Development

In a dramatic work, plot unfolds through **action**: what characters say and do. Generally, a play does not include a narrator. Instead, dialogue, stage directions, and various staging techniques work together to move the play's action along.

Exchanges of **dialogue** reveal what is happening—and, sometimes, indicate what happened in the past or suggest what will happen in the future. Characters can recount past events to other characters, announce an intention to take some action in the future, or summarize events that are occurring offstage. Thus, dialogue takes the place of formal narrative.

On the printed page, **stage directions** efficiently move readers from one location and time period to another by specifying entrances and exits and identifying the play's structural divisions—acts and scenes—and their accompanying changes of setting.

Staging techniques can also advance a play's action. For example, a change in lighting can shift the focus to another part of the stage—and thus to another place and time. An adjustment of scenery or props—for instance, a breakfast table, complete with morning paper, replacing a bedtime setting—can indicate that the action has moved forward in time, as can a change of costumes. Music can also move a play's action along, predicting excitement or doom or a romantic interlude—or a particular character's entrance.

Occasionally, a play does have a formal narrator to move the plot along. For example, in Thornton Wilder's play *Our Town* (1938), a character known as the Stage Manager functions as a narrator, not only describing the play's setting and introducing the characters to the audience but also soliciting questions from characters scattered around the audience, prompting characters, and interrupting dialogue.

Flashbacks

Many plays—such as Arthur Miller's *Death of a Salesman* (p. 1233)—include **flashbacks**, which depict events that occurred before the play's main action. Dialogue can also summarize events that occurred earlier, thereby overcoming the limitations set by the time frame in which the play's action unfolds. Thus, Mr. Hale in *Trifles* tells the other characters how he discovered John Wright's murder, and Nora in *A Doll House* confides her secret past to her friend Kristine. As characters on stage are brought up to date, the audience is also given necessary information—facts that are essential to an understanding of the characters' motivation. (In less realistic dramas, characters can interrupt the action to deliver long monologues or soliloquies that fill in background details—or even address the audience directly, as Tom does in Tennessee Williams's *The Glass Menagerie*.)

Foreshadowing

In addition to revealing past events, dialogue can **foreshadow**, or look ahead to, future action. In many cases, seemingly unimportant comments have significance that becomes clear as the play develops. For example, in act 3 of *A Doll House*, Torvald Helmer says to Kristine, "An exit should always be effective, Mrs. Linde, but that's what I can't get Nora to grasp." At the end of the play, Nora's exit is not only effective but also memorable.

Elements of staging—such as props, scenery, lighting, music, and sound effects—can also foreshadow events to come. Finally, various bits of **stage business**—gestures or movements designed to attract the audience's attention—may also foreshadow future events. In *A Doll House*, for example, Nora's sneaking forbidden macaroons seems at first to suggest her fear of her husband, but her actions actually foreshadow her eventual defiance of his authority.

✔ CHECKLIST   Writing about Plot

- What happens in the play?

- What is the play's central conflict? How is it resolved? What other conflicts are present?

- What section of the play constitutes its rising action?

- Where does the play's climax occur?

- What crises can you identify?

- How is suspense created?

- What section of the play constitutes its falling action?

- Does the play contain a subplot? What is its purpose? How is it related to the main plot?

continued on next page

- How do characters' actions advance the play's plot?

- How does dialogue advance the play's plot?

- How do stage directions advance the play's plot?

- How do staging techniques advance the play's plot?

- Does the play include a narrator?

- Does the play include flashbacks? foreshadowing? Does the play's dialogue contain summaries of past events or references to events in the future? How does the use of flashbacks or foreshadowing advance the play's plot?

DAVID IVES (1950–   ), recipient of a Guggenheim Fellowship in playwriting, has published and produced numerous plays, many of which are one-act comedies. His plays are collected in *All in the Timing* (1994), *Mere Mortals* (1998), *Time Flies and Other Short Plays* (2001), *Polish Joke and Other Plays* (2004), and *The Other Woman and Other Short Pieces* (2008). His play *Don Juan in Chicago* (1995) won the Outer Critics Circle Playwriting Award.

Cultural Context The isolated country house is a familiar convention of English and American crime fiction—particularly in classical detective stories in which the number of suspects is limited by the enclosed setting. This genre was defined and popularized by the prolific English mystery writer (and creator of the iconic detective Hercule Poirot) Agatha Christie (1890–1976), who was known as the "queen of crime." By referring to Christie, the characters in this play evoke the well-established tradition of the murder mystery.

The Blizzard (2006)

CHARACTERS

Jenny

Neil

Salim

Natasha

A country house, toward evening. Cold winter light in the windows. In the course of the play, the lights gradually dim around center stage to nighttime. At curtain, Jenny is onstage alone.

JENNY: *(Calls.)* Neil? — Neil! *(Neil enters from outside, stage right.)*

NEIL: It's still coming down. Some of those drifts are three feet deep already. What's the matter?

JENNY: Nothing. I just wondered what happened to you.

NEIL: Got scared, huh?

JENNY: No, I wasn't *scared*. The food's all ready. Do you really think they'll make it   5
   up here in this?

NEIL: Joe's got those new chains on the car. The ones that Sandy made him fork
   out for? Just what you'd expect from Miss Rationality.

JENNY: Right. Mr. *List Maker*. Mr. My-Pencils-Have-To-Be-Laid-Out-In-The-
   Right-Order-On-My-Desk. No, you're not rational. Sandy is rational.

NEIL: What about the TV?

JENNY: Nothing. Not a thing.

NEIL: The electricity's on. You'd think with a satellite dish we'd pick up *something*.   10

JENNY: The telephone's still out.

NEIL: They've probably been trying us since they left the city.

JENNY: There's no radio either.

NEIL: No *radio?*

JENNY: Isn't it *great?* It's just like an Agatha Christie.   15

NEIL: Thanks for that. I'm still not used to it. Being so remote. Nature's always
   scared the living crap out of me. Now I'm living in it. Or visiting it on
   weekends, anyway. You know I saw a bat flapping around out there? I didn't
   know there were bats in blizzards. No *radio?* The world could be ending
   out there, for Christ's sake. And we'd be the last ones to hear about it. No
   radio . . .

JENNY: Yes, we have no radio and a beautiful blizzard and a house and woods and a
   mountain that are all ours.

NEIL: All ours in twenty-nine years and three months.

JENNY: I kind of wish they weren't coming up tonight. It's so cozy. I wouldn't mind
   curling up with a book.

NEIL: I wish you hadn't said "Agatha Christie."   20

JENNY: You inflict *Torturama* One, Two and Three on people and I can't say
   "Agatha Christie"?

NEIL: Those are movies, not a real house in the middle of the real country with the
   lines down. And *Torturama* paid for our little mansion on a hill, babe.

JENNY: You know what it is about murder mysteries? No, listen. I think the reason
   people like murder mysteries is that, in a murder mystery, everything is *signifi-*
   cant. The people in murder mysteries are living in a *significant world*. A world
   where everything is there for a reason. Even before the murder's happened,
   you know that one is going to happen and you know that everything is a *clue*.
   Or rather, you know that some things are clues and some things are just obfus-
   cation, they're snow. And you know that everybody has a secret of some kind.
   A secret that's like a soul. Murder mysteries are religious, in a way. Don't
   laugh. They're life the way you feel it when you're in love. When everything's
   in a special light. Incandescent. They're a couple of hours of everything *mean-*
   ing something, for God's sake. And then they're over and you're back to your
   old life, to real life. To mortgages and pork loin and potatoes and making a
   cherry pie.

NEIL: So real life doesn't feel like it means something to you these days?

25 JENNY: Sure it does. I'm just saying . . . Well, don't we all wish for that in real life? One of those moments when everything feels charged with meaning? When the air is electric?

NEIL: Well here's your opportunity. Listen, we're probably going to be totally snowed in. Why don't we all do something different this weekend.

JENNY: Different, what does different mean?

NEIL: I don't know. Something unusual. Something unexpected. Not you and Sandy holing yourself up in the kitchen and talking about whatever you talk about, not me and Joe sitting around talking about Mom and Dad and what happened in the third grade. Not the usual pour-a-glass-of-Jack-Daniels, bullshit bullshit bullshit, what've you guys been doing, go in to dinner and break out the Margaux '01, have you seen any movies, did you catch that episode of blah blah blah. I don't know, something we've never done before, or let's talk about something we've never talked about before. Anything, instead of all the things we usually talk about.

JENNY: Okay. Something unusual. I love it.

30 SALIM: *(Offstage.)* Hello — ? Neil?

NEIL: There they are. *(Salim and Natasha enter from the front door at stage left. Salim carries a black plastic valise.)*

SALIM: Hello! Neil and Jenny, right? Sorry for the cold hand, I'm freezing. God, you're just like Joe and Sandy described you. I can't believe I'm finally meeting you, Neil. I am such a fan of *Torturama*. All of them. Natasha can't watch them, herself. Natasha is squeamish.

NEIL: I'm sorry, I don't understand . . .

SALIM: Salim. And Natasha.

35 NATASHA: Hello. I'm so happy to encounter you at last. And you, Jenny, you are just as beautiful as Sandy told me. You are exquisite.

SALIM: And God, what a place up here! But so remote! Wow! We brought this for you. *(Holds up the black valise.)* A little housewarming gift.

NEIL: Whoa, whoa, whoa. I'm sorry, maybe there's been a mistake . . .

SALIM: I mean, this is the place, isn't it? You're Neil and Jenny? Oh, right, right. *Where are Joe and Sandy.* Middle of a snowstorm. Two strange people walk in. You're spooked. Totally natural. Natasha?

NATASHA: Joe and Sandy couldn't make it, so they sent us instead.

40 NEIL: They sent you instead. Wait a minute. They sent *you* instead . . .

SALIM: They caught some kind of bug. God, Joe and Sandy have been telling us all about you two for I don't know how long.

NATASHA: A long time.

SALIM: A very long time.

NEIL: I don't think Joe and Sandy ever mentioned knowing a . . . I'm sorry . . .

45 SALIM: Salim.

NEIL: A Salim and a Natasha.

SALIM: You've been out of touch with your brother for too long, brother. They were really broken up they couldn't make it tonight. I'd say call them up and ask them but hey, are your cellphones as down as ours up here?

JENNY: How do you know Joe and Sandy?

SALIM: *(The black valise.)* You know what's in here? Just for showing us your hospitality? It's this new tequila, a hundred bucks a bottle. Olé, right? Let's support those oppressed brothers churning this stuff out for ten pesos a day. Neil, you want to pour?

JENNY: You didn't answer me.   50

NATASHA: How do we know Joe and Sandy.

SALIM: How do we know Joe and Sandy. How do we know them, Natasha?

NATASHA: Intimately.

SALIM: Intimately. Good word. We know them intimately.

JENNY: Neil . . . *Neil* . . .   55

NEIL: Look, I'm very sorry, but I'm going to have to ask you to leave.

SALIM: To leave? But . . . okay, I get it, I get it, you want some kind of proof that we're not just what . . .

NATASHA: Imposters.

SALIM: Imposters. Ten points, Natasha. We're not imposters! We're the real thing! I'm sorry if I'm coming on kind of strong, it's my personality, you know what I mean? God, how do you prove that you know somebody? Let's see. Where do I start? Do I start with Joe or Sandy? You know she made him get these hotshot snowchains for the car. That is so Sandy. No imagination, but always thinking ahead. So *rational. (Pause.)* Listen. Listen, I'm sorry we barged in on you like this. Maybe we should leave, but . . . hey, are you really going to turn two freezing strangers back out into the storm? Neil, you're the guy who inflicted *Torturama* on the world, more killings per square frame than any movie in history. You're pouring blood in the aisles, man. Don't tell me you're scared. What are you scared of? What am I, the wrong color? And what am I going to do to you, huh? If I was going to do something to you I'd've done it already, wouldn't I? *(Pause.)* So do we leave? Or do we stay? Aw, have a heart, Neil.

NEIL: Well, we can't turn you out in this weather . . .   60

JENNY: Turn them out, Neil.

NEIL: Honey, I . . .

JENNY: Turn them out.

NEIL: It's a blizzard out there, honey.

SALIM: Your wife is so sweet. Really. She is a doll.   65

NATASHA: You know, with so much snow, it's like we're in a murder mystery here.

SALIM: Natasha adores Agatha Christie. You know what I hate about murder mysteries? It's that everybody in them's got a secret. People don't have secrets. People are open books. I don't know you personally, Neil, but just looking at you I'd say you're probably the kind of guy who makes lists, for example. Lines his pencils up on the desk. Likes things neat and tidy. Am I right? A Jack Daniels before dinner kinda guy. You're not the kind of guy who, what, secretly worked for the CIA once upon a time, you're not a guy with a secret history of killing people, I mean *really* killing people, off screen, you don't have any real blood on your hands. You're in the entertainment industry. You have nothing to hide.

JENNY: Send them away, Neil.

SALIM: And Jenny, she probably made her usual dinner for tonight, let's see what would it be, pork loin and some kind of special potato recipe and a cherry-rhubarb pie for dessert. The perfect American housewife. Nothing to conceal. I'm sorry, I'm sorry, there's that personality of mine again. I'm brash. I'm insensitive. I'm loud. Call me American.

70 NEIL: You know I have a gun in the house.

SALIM: Oh, that's rich. What a liar! "I have a gun in the house." Right. That's so cute. This isn't a movie, this is *real life*, Neil. And I'm your brother for the night. I'm a stand-in for Joe. Remember me? Your brother?

JENNY: Where are Joe and Sandy?

SALIM: They're very sick in bed is where they are.

JENNY: What have you done with them?

75 SALIM: They can't move is what they are. Aren't I your brother? Neil? Come on. *(He puts his arm around Neil's waist.)* Am I your brother?

NEIL: Sure . . .

SALIM: Am I your brother? Am I your brother? Am I your brother?

NEIL: You're my brother.

SALIM: There you see? How hard was that? Now we can talk about all those kids we used to beat up in third grade. Just like old times. Well, brother, what do you say? We're here for the duration. You gonna play the good host here or what? You want to show me around the grounds?

80 NEIL: Sure.

SALIM: Sure what?

NEIL: Sure, brother.

SALIM: Attaboy! *(Salim follows Neil off through the back door. A pause.)*

NATASHA: You know what I love about murder mysteries? Is that everything in them seems to mean something. The people in murder mysteries are living in a significant world. Everything holding it's breath. Waiting. The air is electric. And then, bang, it happens. The irrevocable. Whatever that is. Changing everything. It's a kind of poetry. To me, it's almost a religious feeling.

85 JENNY: I don't want any more fucking significance. I don't want it. I don't want it.

NATASHA: Poor Jenny. Afraid over nothing. Why? Why?

JENNY: You have the wrong people.

NATASHA: You're the right people. Neil and Jenny. We're just here for dinner with you. And you have nothing to be afraid of. Really. Absolutely nothing.

JENNY: *(Calls out.)* Neil . . . ? *Neil* . . . ?

50 NATASHA: Absolutely nothing . . . *(The lights fade.)*

*   *   *

Reading and Reacting

1. Using Freytag's pyramid (p. 1098) as a model, outline the plot of *The Blizzard*. Does it include all five stages of plot?

2. Neil is a writer whose credits include *Torturama* (presumably a horror movie). Why is this information significant? What else do you know about Neil and Jenny? What more would you like to know?

3. Review the play's stage directions. What kind of information do they provide? Do you think readers need more information? Explain.

4. Which of the following can be considered foreshadowing:

- The blizzard
- The fact that, according to the opening stage directions, "*the lights gradually dim*" during the course of the play as night approaches
- Jenny's statement: "I wish they weren't coming up tonight."
- Neil's statement: "Why don't we all do something different this weekend."

5. Describe the play's setting. Is the blizzard essential to the play's action and outcome, or could events have unfolded in the same way without it?

6. Jenny says people like murder mysteries because "in a murder mystery, everything is significant"; Natasha later echoes this sentiment. What do they mean? Does this characterization apply to *The Blizzard*?

7. Salim says, "You know what I hate about murder mysteries? It's that everybody in them's got a secret." What secrets might the characters in *The Blizzard* be hiding? Is *The Blizzard* a murder mystery?

8. What do you think might happen to the characters after the play ends? Why? Do you think this outcome is inevitable? Why or why not?

9. **JOURNAL ENTRY** What is the significance of the black valise (the play's only prop)? Do you see it as a symbol?

10. **CRITICAL PERSPECTIVE** In a review of Ives's plays, *New York Times* theater critic Ben Brantley makes the following point:

> Mr. Ives's theories may owe much to the philosophical arcana of such dense thinkers as Einstein and Derrida, but he is no coolly detached academic. His obsessions with randomness and relativity are translated into revuelike sketches that percolate with comic brio and zesty bits of stagecraft.

Do you see evidence in *The Blizzard* that Ives is obsessed with "randomness and relativity"?

Related Works: "Stopping by Woods on a Snowy Evening" (p. 9), "Accident" (p. 131), "Encounters with Unexpected Animals" (p. 132), "A Good Man Is Hard to Find" (p. 367)

Scott Gries/Getty Images Entertainment/
Getty Images

WARREN LEIGHT (1957–   ), a widely acclaimed writer and director, was a writer/producer for the television series *Law and Order: Criminal Intent*. His play *Side Man* (1998) was nominated for a Pulitzer Prize and won Broadway's 1999 Tony Award for Best Play. His other plays include *Glimmer, Glimmer* and *Shine* (2001) and *No Foreigners Beyond This Point* (2006). His screen credits include *The Night We Never Met* (1993), *Dear God* (1996), and *Mother's Day* (2010).

Cultural Context The right of the accused to a trial by jury is stated in the Sixth Amendment to the United States Constitution as well as in the constitutions of individual states. However, even though it is a civic duty and an important cultural mainstay, many Americans see jury duty as a burden because it requires them to take time off from their work and family responsibilities to serve. Although failing to appear for jury service is a crime, a study conducted by the American Judicature Society reported that, on any given day, an average of twenty percent of Americans summoned for jury duty do not appear. (That number drops to fewer than ten percent in some urban areas.) Some common excuses people use to try to get out of serving include obligations at school, work, or home; child or elder care; illness or disability; and bias (which may result from prior knowledge of the case or having a previous or ongoing relationship with someone involved in the case). In one 2007 criminal case in Miami, Florida, a prospective juror was dismissed after she told the judge that, if she served, her pet ferret would be left home alone.

Nine Ten (2001)

CHARACTERS

Leslie
John
Kearrie
Nick
Lyris

Jury Duty Grand Hall. Morning.
John, a slightly awkward bond trader, sits on a bench. Very neat, buttoned down. He reads a perfectly folded Wall Street Journal. *Lyris Touzet, a dancer, enters, almost spills her coffee on him.*

LYRIS: Is this Part B?
JOHN: What?
LYRIS: Part B, or not part B?
JOHN: Ah . . . that is the question.
5   LYRIS: Are you making fun of me?
JOHN: No no. Um, let me look at your . . . (*She hands him a slip of paper, he reads it.*)
      Where you are is where you're supposed to be.

She sits next to him. He needs a little more personal space than she does.

LYRIS: Why do they call us at eight-thirty? It's like, nine already, and they haven't
      said anything.
JOHN: They build in a grace period.
LYRIS: They what?

JOHN: They say eight-thirty so that most people get here by nine. And around nine   10
 ten they start calling names.
LYRIS: You knew this, and you came at eight-thirty?
JOHN: Eight actually.
LYRIS: Eight A.M.? You must hate your wife.
JOHN: I don't see her much. We both have to be at work at six.
LYRIS: You punch in at six?   15
JOHN: Well, I don't . . . punch in exactly. But, the desk opens at six so . . . .
LYRIS: Your desk opens?
JOHN: Sorry. Trading desk. Bonds. Euros, mostly. From my desk, I'm up so high, on
 a clear day, you can see Europe.

At a bench opposite, Nick Theron works the Times *crossword puzzle as Leslie Rudin arrives,
pissed off and hyper.*

LESLIE: Part B?
NICK: Must be.   20
LYRIS: Have they called any—
NICK: Does it look like it? (*She looks to the court officer's desk, downstage left.*)
 Every once in a while this guy comes out and says we should wait. Which
 is . . . helpful.
LESLIE: I tried to get out of it on the phone and they said it was my third postponement and I had to come down here in person on the day of and that I wasn't
 going to get out anyway. And I finally get here—do they just change the
 names of the subway lines for spite lately?—and there's a line a mile long to
 get through security and they go through my purse like I'm a serial killer and it
 turns out if I want to smoke I'm going to have to go down and outside, and then
 wait on line again for them to check my bag. This just sucks.
NICK: I'm going to tell the judge that I'm a felon. He won't even question it. And
 he'll tell me felons can't serve. I'll act offended at this. And then he'll just let
 me go back to my life.
LESLIE: (*impressed*) That's good.   25
NICK: Racial profiling. A two-way street.

Over to John and Lyris.

LYRIS: My brother's in the same building. Security guard. You probably don't
 know him.

Kearrie, a tough businesswoman, enters, rushed.

KEARRIE: Part B?
LYRIS AND JOHN: Or not part B?
KEARRIE: It's too early for cute. (*They look at her, she means it.*) Have they started to   30
 give out postponements yet?
LYRIS: No one gets postponement.
KEARRIE: I'm on a flight tomorrow. (*Pulls something out of her bag.*) I've got a ticket.

John takes another look at her.

JOHN: Kearrie?

KEARRIE: What?

35 JOHN: It's me, John. . . .

KEARRIE: Right. John. That narrows it down.

JOHN: John McCormack. From Wharton.

Kearrie still doesn't place him.

LYRIS: *(to John)* You sure leave an impression.

JOHN: Story of my life. *(To Kearrie.)* Case study. Euro-economic unity.

40 KEARRIE: You got an A, I got a B plus. Even though we worked together.

JOHN: *(to Lyris)* You know about Irish Alzheimer's . . . you forget everything except
    your grudges.

KEARRIE: You went to Gold and Strauss when we graduated, right?

JOHN: Still there.

KEARRIE: *(grades him a loser)* You're kidding. You are not still at—

45 JOHN: Just the last ten years. Kearrie this is—

LYRIS: Lyris Touzet. Spiritual dancer. And healer.

JOHN: Lyris this is Kearrie Whitman. We went to Wharton together. Class of 91.

LYRIS: I must have missed you two by like . . . one year.

Leslie and Nick. He has no hope of attending to his crossword puzzle. Leslie must talk or die.

LESLIE: I'm out in the Hamptons. One week after Labor Day. Paradise found. The
    assholes are gone. The beaches are empty. The water is warm.

50 NICK: Sharks are hungry.

LESLIE: No sharks in the Hamptons. Professional courtesy.

NICK: Touché.

LESLIE: I think I'll stay another day. Then I remember . . . fuck me—eight-thirty
    summons. Drive in at midnight. Get stuck in traffic. The L.I.E. has got to be the
    only road in the world that has traffic jams at two A.M. By the time I get to my
    garage it's locked for the night. You ever try to find a space on the right side of
    the street at two A.M.?

Back to John and Lyris chatting. Kearrie plays with her Palm Pilot.

JOHN: It's funny, I always wanted to be a spiritual dancer.

55 LYRIS: You're making fun of me.

JOHN: I'm not. . . . swear to god. But what is a—

LYRIS: I heal people, through movement. Rhythm. Every person has their
    own . . . pulse. Below the surface, that—

KEARRIE: Fuck me!

LYRIS: I help them to get in touch with their inner—

60 KEARRIE: *(Turns to them.)* Fuck me fuck me fuck . . .

JOHN: What's hers?

Kearrie now rants in their direction, about her Palm Pilot.

KEARRIE: Money on the table. I've got a watch list. It's programmed to signal
    me when there's a discrepancy between euro prices and ADRs. The spread is

sitting there. Sitting there. It's blinking—buy me. Buy me. I try to buy and my damn signal fades. What's the point of fucking having a watch list if you can't follow up on it. This whole building should be wired. This city is . . . in the stone ages.

LYRIS: (*to John*) Some people are harder cases than others.

Over to Nick and Leslie.

NICK: My neighborhood, downtown, they're *always* filming. Some sequel to a sequel to a disaster flick. *Mortal Danger Times Four.* Whatever. Which means like—

LESLIE: They take every parking place. Big lights up—   65

NICK: —all night long.

LESLIE: Idiots on walkie-talkies saying don't walk there. On your own street. Call the cops to complain, they don't care. No one in this city cares. The film crew can be, like, setting off concussion bombs, and nobody does anything.

Back to John and Lyris.

JOHN: (*to Lyris*) I can't.

LYRIS: Everybody can move. Even you . . . Stand up.

He doesn't.

LYRIS: (*loud*) STAND UP!   70

Nick and Leslie hear this. Look over to John and Lyris. John doesn't want to attract attention, so he stands. John and Lyris now overlap with Nick and Leslie. Kearrie is in her own world.

LYRIS: (*to John*) Just start to, sway a little . . . from your hips.

LESLIE: (*to Nick*) That is sick the way he's flirting with her.

John sits back down.

JOHN: I can't.

LYRIS: Yes you can.

NICK: (*to Leslie*) How do you know it's his fault?   75

LESLIE: (*to Nick*) It's always the guy's fault. I date cops. Believe me. I know.

JOHN: (*to Lyris*) I don't like to. Move. I like things as they are. I've had the same job for ten years.

KEARRIE: (*on her cell phone, to her office*) Here? It's a fucking hellhole. What do you think? Ah-huh. Ah-huh. Ah-huh. Look—keep that on hold.

JOHN: (*to Lyris, oblivious to Kearrie*) Same office, same view. Married my junior high school sweetheart. We take the same train to work. We have the same lunch. Tuna. On rye. No mayo.

LYRIS: No mayo?   80

JOHN: It's not so bad, once you get used to it.

KEARRIE: (*into phone*) Yeah as soon as they call roll, I show my plane ticket . . . and I'm out of here.

Now, from downstage left, a court officer enters.

COURT OFFICER: Hello folks. Welcome to New York County Jury Duty. Before you all come up to me . . .

KEARRIE: Excuse me, I have a flight to—

85 NICK: I have a record—

COURT OFFICER: (*He drowns her out.*)—with your reasons for why you shouldn't be here, let me tell you: I've heard them all. On the bright side, most of you will get to go back to your life in two or three days.

Leslie, Nick, Kearrie, John, and Lyris all groan. Two days is eternity.

COURT OFFICER: And we are as happy to have you, as you are happy to be here. First things first. Check your summons, and be sure you're in the right place. This is Civil Court. Part B. 60 Centre Street. Today is Monday, September 10th . . . Two thousand and one.

Blackout.

*   *   *

Reading and Reacting

1. The exposition provided in the play's stage directions is quite minimal, giving few clues about setting. How do you picture the setting?

2. What basic information does the audience learn about each character? Given the revelation at the end of the play, why is this information important?

3. In the absence of a narrator, how do we learn about each character?

4. This play has a single setting and very little physical action. What moves the plot along?

5. What preconceived ideas do you think most people have about jury duty? How do the characters reinforce these ideas? How does the play use the audience's stereotypical assumptions about jury duty to advance the plot?

6. John complains that he is bored with his life, stuck in a routine. Given the play's ending, these complaints are deeply ironic. What other examples of irony can you identify in this play?

7. Foreshadowing is extremely important in *Nine Ten*. Consider how each of the following details foreshadows the play's ending: John works on a very high floor of his building; Lyris's brother is a security guard in John's building; Kearrie has a ticket for a flight the following day; Nick lives downtown; Leslie dates cops. What is the probable significance of each of these details?

8. At the beginning of the play, John explains the rules for jury duty, saying, "around nine ten they start calling names." Does this statement have any significance beyond its literal meaning?

9. JOURNAL ENTRY Do you think the play's title gives the ending away? Explain. What alternate titles might be appropriate, and why?

10. CRITICAL PERSPECTIVE In her article on literature about the 9/11 terrorist attacks, award-winning novelist Julia Glass tries to find common ground among writers who address her era's "most resounding moments":

> Storytellers who dramatize their own era embrace its most resounding moments, moments when the spiritual compass by which we live (and write) has spun out of alignment. Realigning that compass, searching for a new magnetic north, is some of the best work fiction writers do. We seize something that everyone around us has taken for granted and, whether tenderly or violently, ironically or tragically, we upend it, dissect or shatter it. We write not about *you or them* or *then*. We write about *us*; we write about *now*. *Reader*, we say, *the view has changed; let me show you how.*

In what sense does *Nine Ten* "upend," "dissect," or "shatter" common perceptions of the world as it was before 9/11?

Related Works: "Going to Work" (p. 783), "The End and the Beginning" (p. 908), *Trifles* (p. 1604)

HENRIK IBSEN (1828–1906), Norway's foremost dramatist, was born into a prosperous family; however, his father lost his fortune when Ibsen was six. When Ibsen was fifteen, he was apprenticed to an apothecary away from home and was permanently estranged from his family. During his apprenticeship, he studied to enter the university and wrote plays. Although he did not pass the university entrance exam, his second play, *The Warrior's Barrow* (1850), was produced by the Christiania Theatre in 1850. He began a life in the theater, writing plays and serving as artistic director of a theatrical company. Disillusioned by the public's lack of interest in theater, he left Norway, living with his wife and son in Italy and Germany between 1864 and 1891. By the time he returned to Norway, he was famous and revered. Ibsen's most notable plays include *Brand* (1865), *Peer Gynt* (1867), *A Doll House* (1879), *Ghosts* (1881), *An Enemy of the People* (1882), *The Wild Duck* (1884), *Hedda Gabler* (1890), and *When We Dead Awaken* (1899).

Photo credit (vertical): Hulton Archive/Getty Images

A Doll House marks the beginning of Ibsen's successful realist period, during which he explored the ordinary lives of small-town people—in this case, writing what he called "a modern tragedy." Ibsen based the play on a true story, which closely paralleled the main events of the play: a wife borrows money to finance a trip for an ailing husband, repayment is demanded, she forges a check and is discovered. (In the real-life story, however, the husband demanded a divorce, and the wife had a nervous breakdown and was committed to a mental institution.) The issue in *A Doll House*, he said, is that there are "two kinds of moral law, . . . one in man and a completely different one in woman. They do not understand each other. . . ." Nora and Helmer's marriage is destroyed because they cannot comprehend or accept their differences. The play begins conventionally but does not fulfill the audience's expectations for a tidy resolution; as a result, it was not a success when it was first performed. Nevertheless, the publication of *A Doll House* made Ibsen internationally famous.

Cultural Context During the nineteenth century, the law treated women only a little better than it treated children. Women could not vote, and they were not considered able to handle their own financial affairs. A woman could not borrow money in her own name, and when she married, her finances were placed under the control of her husband. Moreover, working outside the home was out of the question for a middle-class woman. So, if a woman were to leave her husband, she was not likely to have any way of supporting herself, and she would lose the custody of her children. At the time when *A Doll House* was first performed, most viewers were offended by the way Nora spoke to her husband, and Ibsen was considered an anarchist for suggesting that a woman could leave her family in search of herself. However, Ibsen argued that he was merely asking people to look at, and think about, the social structure they supported.

A Doll House (1879)

Translated by Rolf Fjelde

CHARACTERS

Torvald Helmer, *a lawyer*	**Nils Krogstad,** *a bank clerk*
Nora, *his wife*	**The Helmers' three small children**
Dr. Rank	**Anne-Marie,** *their nurse*
Mrs. Linde	**Helene,** *a maid*
A Delivery Boy	

The action takes place in Helmer's residence.

ACT 1

A comfortable room, tastefully but not expensively furnished. A door to the right in the back wall leads to the entryway; another to the left leads to Helmer's study. Between these doors, a piano. Midway in the left-hand wall a door, and further back a window. Near the window a round table with an armchair and a small sofa. In the right-hand wall, toward the rear, a door, and nearer the foreground a porcelain stove with two armchairs and a rocking chair beside it. Between the stove and the side door, a small table. Engravings on the walls. An étagère with china figures and other small art objects; a small bookcase with richly bound books; the floor carpeted; a fire burning in the stove. It is a winter day.

A bell rings in the entryway; shortly after we hear the door being unlocked. Nora comes into the room, humming happily to herself; she is wearing street clothes and carries an armload of packages, which she puts down on the table to the right. She has left the hall door open; and through it a Delivery Boy is seen, holding a Christmas tree and a basket, which he gives to the Maid who let them in.

NORA: Hide the tree well, Helene. The children mustn't get a glimpse of it till this evening, after it's trimmed. (*To the Delivery Boy, taking out her purse.*) How much?

DELIVERY BOY: Fifty, ma'am.

NORA: There's a crown. No, keep the change. (*The Boy thanks her and leaves. Nora shuts the door. She laughs softly to herself while taking off her street things. Drawing a bag of macaroons from her pocket, she eats a couple, then steals over and listens at her husband's study door.*) Yes, he's home. (*Hums again as she moves to the table right.*)

HELMER: (*from the study*) Is that my little lark twittering out there?

5 NORA: (*busy opening some packages*) Yes, it is.

HELMER: Is that my squirrel rummaging around?

NORA: Yes!

HELMER: When did my squirrel get in?

NORA: Just now. (*Putting the macaroon bag in her pocket and wiping her mouth.*) Do come in, Torvald, and see what I've bought.

HELMER: Can't be disturbed. (*After a moment he opens the door and peers in, pen in hand.*) Bought, you say? All that there? Has the little spendthrift been out throwing money around again? 10

NORA: Oh, but Torvald, this year we really should let ourselves go a bit. It's the first Christmas we haven't had to economize.

HELMER: But you know we can't go squandering.

NORA: Oh yes, Torvald, we can squander a little now. Can't we? Just a tiny, wee bit. Now that you've got a big salary and are going to make piles and piles of money.

HELMER: Yes—starting New Year's. But then it's a full three months till the raise comes through.

Scene from *A Doll House* with Toby Stephens (as Torvald Helmer) and Gillian Anderson (as Nora) at The Donmar Warehouse, London, UK in May 2009
Source: Nigel Norrington/ArenaPal/TopFoto/The Image Works

NORA: Pooh! We can borrow that long. 15

HELMER: Nora! (*Goes over and playfully takes her by the ear.*) Are your scatterbrains off again? What if today I borrowed a thousand crowns, and you squandered them over Christmas week, and then on New Year's Eve a roof tile fell on my head, and I lay there—

NORA: (*putting her hand on his mouth*) Oh! Don't say such things!

HELMER: Yes, but what if it happened—then what?

N‍ORA: If anything so awful happened, then it just wouldn't matter if I had debts or not.

20   H‍ELMER: Well, but the people I'd borrowed from?

N‍ORA: Them? Who cares about them! They're strangers.

H‍ELMER: Nora, Nora, how like a woman! No, but seriously, Nora, you know what I think about that. No debts! Never borrow! Something of freedom's lost—and something of beauty, too—from a home that's founded on borrowing and debt. We've made a brave stand up to now, the two of us; and we'll go right on like that the little while we have to.

N‍ORA: *(going toward the stove)* Yes, whatever you say, Torvald.

H‍ELMER: *(following her)* Now, now, the little lark's wings mustn't droop. Come on, don't be a sulky squirrel. *(Taking out his wallet.)* Nora, guess what I have here.

25   N‍ORA: *(turning quickly)* Money!

H‍ELMER: There, see. *(Hands her some notes.)* Good grief, I know how costs go up in a house at Christmastime.

N‍ORA: Ten—twenty—thirty—forty. Oh, thank you, Torvald; I can manage no end on this.

H‍ELMER: You really will have to.

N‍ORA: Oh yes, I promise I will! But come here so I can show you everything I bought. And so cheap! Look, new clothes for Ivar here—and a sword. Here a horse and a trumpet for Bob. And a doll and a doll's bed here for Emmy; they're nothing much, but she'll tear them to bits in no time anyway. And here I have dress material and handkerchiefs for the maids. Old Anne-Marie really deserves something more.

30   H‍ELMER: And what's in that package there?

N‍ORA: *(with a cry)* Torvald, no! You can't see that till tonight!

H‍ELMER: I see. But tell me now, you little prodigal, what have you thought of for yourself?

N‍ORA: For myself? Oh, I don't want anything at all.

H‍ELMER: Of course you do. Tell me just what—within reason—you'd most like to have.

35   N‍ORA: I honestly don't know. Oh, listen, Torvald—

H‍ELMER: Well?

N‍ORA: *(fumbling at his coat buttons, without looking at him)* If you want to give me something, then maybe you could—you could—

H‍ELMER: Come on, out with it.

N‍ORA: *(hurriedly)* You could give me money, Torvald. No more than you think you can spare; then one of these days I'll buy something with it.

40   H‍ELMER: But Nora—

N‍ORA: Oh, please, Torvald darling, do that! I beg you, please. Then I could hang the bills in pretty gilt paper on the Christmas tree. Wouldn't that be fun?

H‍ELMER: What are those little birds called that always fly through their fortunes?

N‍ORA: Oh yes, spendthrifts; I know all that. But let's do as I say, Torvald; then I'll have time to decide what I really need most. That's very sensible, isn't it?

H‍ELMER: *(smiling)* Yes, very—that is, if you actually hung onto the money I give you, and you actually used it to buy yourself something. But it goes for the house and for all sorts of foolish things, and then I only have to lay out some more.

NORA: Oh, but Torvald—   45

HELMER: Don't deny it, my dear little Nora. (*Putting his arm around her waist.*)
Spendthrifts are sweet, but they use up a frightful amount of money. It's incredible what it costs a man to feed such birds.

NORA: Oh, how can you say that! Really, I save everything I can.

HELMER: (*laughing*) Yes, that's the truth. Everything you can. But that's nothing
at all.

NORA: (*humming, with a smile of quiet satisfaction*) Hm, if you only knew what
expenses we larks and squirrels have, Torvald.

HELMER: You're an odd little one. Exactly the way your father was. You're never   50
at a loss for scaring up money; but the moment you have it, it runs right out
through your fingers; you never know what you've done with it. Well, one takes
you as you are. It's deep in your blood. Yes, these things are hereditary, Nora.

NORA: Ah, I could wish I'd inherited many of Papa's qualities.

HELMER: And I couldn't wish you anything but just what you are, my sweet little
lark. But wait; it seems to me you have a very—what should I call it?—a very
suspicious look today—

NORA: I do?

HELMER: You certainly do. Look me straight in the eye.

NORA: (*looking at him*) Well?   55

HELMER: (*shaking an admonitory finger*) Surely my sweet tooth hasn't been running
riot in town today, has she?

NORA: No. Why do you imagine that?

HELMER: My sweet tooth really didn't make a little detour through the confectioner's?

NORA: No, I assure you, Torvald—

HELMER: Hasn't nibbled some pastry?   60

NORA: No, not at all.

HELMER: Nor even munched a macaroon or two?

NORA: No, Torvald, I assure you, really—

HELMER: There, there now. Of course I'm only joking.

NORA: (*going to the table, right*) You know I could never think of going against you.   65

HELMER: No, I understand that; and you *have* given me your word. (*Going over to
her.*) Well, you keep your little Christmas secrets to yourself, Nora darling. I
expect they'll come to light this evening, when the tree is lit.

NORA: Did you remember to ask Dr. Rank?

HELMER: No. But there's no need for that; it's assumed he'll be dining with us. All
the same, I'll ask him when he stops by here this morning. I've ordered some
fine wine. Nora, you can't imagine how I'm looking forward to this evening.

NORA: So am I. And what fun for the children, Torvald!

HELMER: Ah, it's so gratifying to know that one's gotten a safe, secure job, and with   70
a comfortable salary. It's a great satisfaction, isn't it?

NORA: Oh, it's wonderful!

HELMER: Remember last Christmas? Three whole weeks before, you shut yourself
in every evening till long after midnight, making flowers for the Christmas tree,
and all the other decorations to surprise us. Ugh, that was the dullest time I've
ever lived through.

NORA: It wasn't at all dull for me.

HELMER: *(smiling)* But the outcome *was* pretty sorry, Nora.

75 NORA: Oh, don't tease me with that again. How could I help it that the cat came in and tore everything to shreds.

HELMER: No, poor thing, you certainly couldn't. You wanted so much to please us all, and that's what counts. But it's just as well that the hard times are past.

NORA: Yes, it's really wonderful.

HELMER: Now I don't have to sit here alone, boring myself, and you don't have to tire your precious eyes and your fair little delicate hands—

NORA: *(clapping her hands)* No, is it really true, Torvald, I don't have to? Oh, how wonderfully lovely to hear! *(Taking his arm.)* Now I'll tell you just how I've thought we should plan things. Right after Christmas—*(The doorbell rings.)* Oh, the bell. *(Straightening the room up a bit.)* Somebody would have to come. What a bore!

80 HELMER: I'm not at home to visitors, don't forget.

MAID: *(from the hall doorway)* Ma'am, a lady to see you—

NORA: All right, let her come in.

MAID: *(to Helmer)* And the doctor's just come too.

HELMER: Did he go right to my study?

85 MAID: Yes, he did.

Helmer goes into his room. The Maid shows in Mrs. Linde, dressed in traveling clothes, and shuts the door after her.

MRS. LINDE: *(in a dispirited and somewhat hesitant voice)* Hello, Nora.

NORA: *(uncertain)* Hello—

MRS. LINDE: You don't recognize me.

NORA: No, I don't know—but wait, I think—*(Exclaiming.)* What! Kristine! Is it really you?

90 MRS. LINDE: Yes, it's me.

NORA: Kristine! To think I didn't recognize you. But then, how could I? *(More quietly.)* How you've changed, Kristine!

MRS. LINDE: Yes, no doubt I have. In nine—ten long years.

NORA: Is it so long since we met! Yes, it's all of that. Oh, these last eight years have been a happy time, believe me. And so now you've come in to town, too. Made the long trip in the winter. That took courage.

MRS. LINDE: I just got here by ship this morning.

95 NORA: To enjoy yourself over Christmas, of course. Oh, how lovely! Yes, enjoy ourselves, we'll do that. But take your coat off. You're not still cold? *(Helping her.)* There now, let's get cozy here by the stove. No, the easy chair there! I'll take the rocker here. *(Seizing her hands.)* Yes, now you have your old look again; it was only in that first moment. You're a bit more pale, Kristine—and maybe a bit thinner.

MRS. LINDE: And much, much older, Nora.

NORA: Yes, perhaps a bit older; a tiny, tiny bit; not much at all. *(Stopping short; suddenly serious.)* Oh, but thoughtless me, to sit here, chattering away. Sweet, good Kristine, can you forgive me?

MRS. LINDE: What do you mean, Nora?

NORA: *(softly)* Poor Kristine, you've become a widow.

MRS. LINDE: Yes, three years ago. 100

NORA: Oh, I knew it, of course: I read it in the papers. Oh, Kristine, you must believe me; I often thought of writing you then, but I kept postponing it, and something always interfered.

MRS. LINDE: Nora dear, I understand completely.

NORA: No, it was awful of me, Kristine. You poor thing, how much you must have gone through. And he left you nothing?

MRS. LINDE: No.

NORA: And no children? 105

MRS. LINDE: No.

NORA: Nothing at all, then?

MRS. LINDE: Not even a sense of loss to feed on.

NORA: *(looking incredulously at her)* But Kristine, how could that be?

MRS. LINDE: *(smiling wearily and smoothing her hair)* Oh, sometimes it happens, 110 Nora.

NORA: So completely alone. How terribly hard that must be for you. I have three lovely children. You can't see them now; they're out with the maid. But now you must tell me everything—

MRS. LINDE: No, no, no, tell me about yourself.

NORA: No, you begin. Today I don't want to be selfish. I want to think only of you today. But there *is* something I must tell you. Did you hear of the wonderful luck we had recently?

MRS. LINDE: No, what's that?

NORA: My husband's been made manager in the bank, just think! 115

MRS. LINDE: Your husband? How marvelous!

NORA: Isn't it? Being a lawyer is such an uncertain living, you know, especially if one won't touch any cases that aren't clean and decent. And of course Torvald would never do that, and I'm with him completely there. Oh, we're simply delighted, believe me! He'll join the bank right after New Year's and start getting a huge salary and lots of commissions. From now on we can live quite differently—just as we want. Oh, Kristine, I feel so light and happy! Won't it be lovely to have stacks of money and not a care in the world?

MRS. LINDE: Well, anyway, it would be lovely to have enough for necessities.

NORA: No, not just for necessities, but stacks and stacks of money!

MRS. LINDE: *(smiling)* Nora, Nora, aren't you sensible yet? Back in school you were 120 such a free spender.

NORA: *(with a quiet laugh)* Yes, that's what Torvald still says. *(Shaking her finger.)* But "Nora, Nora" isn't as silly as you all think. Really, we've been in no position for me to go squandering. We've had to work, both of us.

MRS. LINDE: You too?

NORA: Yes, at odd jobs—needlework, crocheting, embroidery, and such—*(casually)* and other things too. You remember that Torvald left the department when we were married? There was no chance of promotion in his office, and of course he needed to earn more money. But that first year he drove himself terribly. He took on all kinds of extra work that kept him going morning and night. It wore him down, and then he fell deathly ill. The doctors said it was essential for him to travel south.

MRS. LINDE: Yes, didn't you spend a whole year in Italy?

125 NORA: That's right. It wasn't easy to get away, you know. Ivar had just been born. But of course we had to go. Oh, that was a beautiful trip, and it saved Torvald's life. But it cost a frightful sum, Kristine.

MRS. LINDE: I can well imagine.

NORA: Four thousand, eight hundred crowns it cost. That's really a lot of money.

MRS. LINDE: But it's lucky you had it when you needed it.

NORA: Well, as it was, we got it from Papa.

130 MRS. LINDE: I see. It was just about the time your father died.

NORA: Yes, just about then. And, you know, I couldn't make that trip out to nurse him. I had to stay here, expecting Ivar any moment, and with my poor sick Torvald to care for. Dearest Papa, I never saw him again, Kristine. Oh, that was the worst time I've known in all my marriage.

MRS. LINDE: I know how you loved him. And then you went off to Italy?

NORA: Yes. We had the means now, and the doctors urged us. So we left a month after.

MRS. LINDE: And your husband came back completely cured?

135 NORA: Sound as a drum!

MRS. LINDE: But—the doctor?

NORA: Who?

MRS. LINDE: I thought the maid said he was a doctor, the man who came in with me.

NORA: Yes, that was Dr. Rank—but he's not making a sick call. He's our closest friend, and he stops by at least once a day. No, Torvald hasn't had a sick moment since, and the children are fit and strong, and I am, too. (*Jumping up and clapping her hands.*) Oh, dear God, Kristine, what a lovely thing to live and be happy! But how disgusting of me—I'm talking of nothing but my own affairs. (*Sits on a stool close by Kristine, arms resting across her knees.*) Oh, don't be angry with me! Tell me, is it really true that you weren't in love with your husband? Why did you marry him, then?

140 MRS. LINDE: My mother was still alive, but bedridden and helpless—and I had my two younger brothers to look after. In all conscience, I didn't think I could turn him down.

NORA: No, you were right there. But was he rich at the time?

MRS. LINDE: He was very well off, I'd say. But the business was shaky, Nora. When he died, it all fell apart, and nothing was left.

NORA: And then—?

MRS. LINDE: Yes, so I had to scrape up a living with a little shop and a little teaching and whatever else I could find. The last three years have been like one endless workday without a rest for me. Now it's over, Nora. My poor mother doesn't need me, for she's passed on. Nor the boys, either; they're working now and can take care of themselves.

145 NORA: How free you must feel—

MRS. LINDE: No—only unspeakably empty. Nothing to live for now. (*Standing up anxiously.*) That's why I couldn't take it any longer out in that desolate hole.

Maybe here it'll be easier to find something to do and keep my mind occupied. If I could only be lucky enough to get a steady job, some office work—

NORA: Oh, but Kristine, that's so dreadfully tiring, and you already look so tired. It would be much better for you if you could go off to a bathing resort.

MRS. LINDE: *(going toward the window)* I have no father to give me travel money, Nora.

NORA: *(rising)* Oh, don't be angry with me.

MRS. LINDE: *(going to her)* Nora dear, don't you be angry with me. The worst of my   150
kind of situation is all the bitterness that's stored away. No one to work for, and yet you're always having to snap up your opportunities. You have to live; and so you grow selfish. When you told me the happy change in your lot, do you know I was delighted less for your sakes than for mine?

NORA: How so? Oh, I see. You think Torvald could do something for you.

MRS. LINDE: Yes, that's what I thought.

NORA: And he will, Kristine! Just leave it to me; I'll bring it up so delicately—find something attractive to humor him with. Oh, I'm so eager to help you.

MRS. LINDE: How very kind of you, Nora, to be so concerned over me—doubly kind, considering you really know so little of life's burdens yourself.

NORA: I—? I know so little—?   155

MRS. LINDE: *(smiling)* Well my heavens—a little needlework and such—Nora, you're just a child.

NORA: *(tossing her head and pacing the floor)* You don't have to act so superior.

MRS. LINDE: Oh?

NORA: You're just like the others. You all think I'm incapable of anything serious—

MRS. LINDE: Come now—   160

NORA: That I've never had to face the raw world.

MRS. LINDE: Nora dear, you've just been telling me all your troubles.

NORA: Hm! Trivial! *(Quietly.)* I haven't told you the big thing.

MRS. LINDE: Big thing? What do you mean?

NORA: You look down on me so, Kristine, but you shouldn't. You're proud that you   165
worked so long and hard for your mother.

MRS. LINDE: I don't look down on a soul. But it *is* true: I'm proud—and happy, too—to think it was given to me to make my mother's last days almost free of care.

NORA: And you're also proud thinking of what you've done for your brothers.

MRS. LINDE: I feel I've a right to be.

NORA: I agree. But listen to this, Kristine—I've also got something to be proud and happy for.

MRS. LINDE: I don't doubt it. But whatever do you mean?   170

NORA: Not so loud. What if Torvald heard! He mustn't, not for anything in the world. Nobody must know, Kristine. No one but you.

MRS. LINDE: But what is it, then?

NORA: Come here. *(Drawing her down beside her on the sofa.)* It's true—I've also got something to be proud and happy for. I'm the one who saved Torvald's life.

MRS. LINDE: Saved—? Saved how?

175   **NORA:** I told you about the trip to Italy. Torvald never would have lived if he
       hadn't gone south—

  MRS. LINDE: Of course; your father gave you the means—

  NORA: *(smiling)* That's what Torvald and all the rest think, but—

  MRS. LINDE: But—?

  NORA: Papa didn't give us a pin. I was the one who raised the money.

180   **MRS. LINDE:** You? That whole amount?

  NORA: Four thousand, eight hundred crowns. What do you say to that?

  MRS. LINDE: But Nora, how was it possible? Did you win the lottery?

  NORA: *(disdainfully)* The lottery? Pooh! No art to that.

  MRS. LINDE: But where did you get it from then?

185   **NORA:** *(humming, with a mysterious smile)* Hmm, tra-la-la-la.

  MRS. LINDE: Because you couldn't have borrowed it.

  NORA: No? Why not?

  MRS. LINDE: A wife can't borrow without her husband's consent.

  NORA: *(tossing her head)* Oh, but a wife with a little business sense, a wife who
       knows how to manage—

190   **MRS. LINDE:** Nora, I simply don't understand—

  NORA: You don't have to. Whoever said I *borrowed* the money? I could have gotten
       it other ways. *(Throwing herself back on the sofa.)* I could have gotten it from
       some admirer or other. After all, a girl with my ravishing appeal—

  MRS. LINDE: You lunatic.

  NORA: I'll bet you're eaten up with curiosity, Kristine.

  MRS. LINDE: Now listen here, Nora—you haven't done something indiscreet?

195   **NORA:** *(sitting up again)* Is it indiscreet to save your husband's life?

  MRS. LINDE: I think it's indiscreet that without his knowledge you—

  NORA: But that's the point: he mustn't know! My Lord, can't you understand? He
       mustn't ever know the close call he had. It was to *me* the doctors came to say his
       life was in danger—that nothing could save him but a stay in the south. Didn't
       I try strategy then! I began talking about how lovely it would be for me to travel
       abroad like other young wives; I begged and I cried; I told him please to remem-
       ber my condition, to be kind and indulge me; and then I dropped a hint that he
       could easily take out a loan. But at that, Kristine, he nearly exploded. He said
       I was frivolous, and it was his duty as man of the house not to indulge me in
       whims and fancies—as I think he called them. Aha, I thought, now you'll just
       have to be saved—and that's when I saw my chance.

  MRS. LINDE: And your father never told Torvald the money wasn't from him?

  NORA: No, never. Papa died right about then. I'd considered bringing him into my
       secret and begging him never to tell. But he was too sick at the time—and then,
       sadly, it didn't matter.

200   **MRS. LINDE:** And you've never confided in your husband since?

  NORA: For heaven's sake, no! Are you serious? He's so strict on that subject.
       Besides—Torvald, with all his masculine pride—how painfully humiliating for
       him if he ever found out he was in debt to me. That would just ruin our rela-
       tionship. Our beautiful, happy home would never be the same.

  MRS. LINDE: Won't you ever tell him?

NORA: (*thoughtfully, half smiling*) Yes—maybe sometime, years from now, when I'm no longer so attractive. Don't laugh! I only mean when Torvald loves me less than now, when he stops enjoying my dancing and dressing up and reciting for him. Then it might be wise to have something in reserve—(*Breaking off.*) How ridiculous! That'll never happen—Well, Kristine, what do you think of my big secret? I'm capable of something too, hm? You can imagine, of course, how this thing hangs over me. It really hasn't been easy meeting the payments on time. In the business world there's what they call quarterly interest and what they call amortization, and these are always so terribly hard to manage. I've had to skimp a little here and there, wherever I could, you know. I could hardly spare anything from my house allowance, because Torvald has to live well. I couldn't let the children go poorly dressed; whatever I got for them, I felt I had to use up completely—the darlings!

MRS. LINDE: Poor Nora, so it had to come out of your own budget, then?

NORA: Yes, of course. But I was the one most responsible, too. Every time Torvald gave me money for new clothes and such, I never used more than half; always bought the simplest, cheapest outfits. It was a godsend that everything looks so well on me that Torvald never noticed. But it did weigh me down at times, Kristine. It *is* such a joy to wear fine things. You understand.   205

MRS. LINDE: Oh, of course.

NORA: And then I found other ways of making money. Last winter I was lucky enough to get a lot of copying to do. I locked myself in and sat writing every evening till late in the night. Ah, I was tired so often, dead tired. But still it was wonderful fun, sitting and working like that, earning money. It was almost like being a man.

MRS. LINDE: But how much have you paid off this way so far?

NORA: That's hard to say, exactly. These accounts, you know, aren't easy to figure. I only know that I've paid out all I could scrape together. Time and again I haven't known where to turn. (*Smiling.*) Then I'd sit here dreaming of a rich old gentleman who had fallen in love with me—

MRS. LINDE: What! Who is he?   210

NORA: Oh, really! And that he'd died, and when his will was opened, there in big letters it said, "All my fortune shall be paid over in cash, immediately, to that enchanting Mrs. Nora Helmer."

MRS. LINDE: But Nora dear—who *was* this gentleman?

NORA: Good grief, can't you understand? The old man never existed; that was only something I'd dream up time and again whenever I was at my wits' end for money. But it makes no difference now; the old fossil can go where he pleases for all I care; I don't need him or his will—because now I'm free. (*Jumping up.*) Oh, how lovely to think of that, Kristine! Carefree! To know you're carefree, utterly carefree; to be able to romp and play with the children, and to keep up a beautiful, charming home—everything just the way Torvald likes it! And think, spring is coming, with big blue skies. Maybe we can travel a little then. Maybe I'll see the ocean again. Oh yes, it *is* so marvelous to live and be happy!

The front doorbell rings.

MRS. LINDE: *(rising)* There's the bell. It's probably best that I go.
215 NORA: No, stay. No one's expected. It must be for Torvald.
MAID: *(from the hall doorway)* Excuse me, ma'am—there's a gentleman here to see
    Mr. Helmer, but I didn't know—since the doctor's with him—
NORA: Who is the gentleman?
KROGSTAD: *(from the doorway)* It's me, Mrs. Helmer.

Mrs. Linde starts and turns away toward the window.

NORA: *(stepping toward him, tense, her voice a whisper)* You? What is it? Why do you
    want to speak to my husband?
220 KROGSTAD: Bank business—after a fashion. I have a small job in the investment
    bank, and I hear now your husband is going to be our chief—
NORA: In other words, it's—
KROGSTAD: Just dry business, Mrs. Helmer. Nothing but that.
NORA: Yes, then please be good enough to step into the study. *(She nods indifferently
    as she sees him out by the hall door, then returns and begins stirring up the stove.)*
MRS. LINDE: Nora—who was that man?
225 NORA: That was a Mr. Krogstad—a lawyer.
MRS. LINDE: Then it really was him.
NORA: Do you know that person?
MRS. LINDE: I did once—many years ago. For a time he was a law clerk in our town.
NORA: Yes, he's been that.
230 MRS. LINDE: How he's changed.
NORA: I understand he had a very unhappy marriage.
MRS. LINDE: He's a widower now.
NORA: With a number of children. There now, it's burning. *(She closes the stove door
    and moves the rocker a bit to one side.)*
MRS. LINDE: They say he has a hand in all kinds of business.
235 NORA: Oh? That may be true: I wouldn't know. But let's not think about business.
    It's so dull.

Dr. Rank enters from Helmer's study.

RANK: *(still in the doorway)* No, no, really—I don't want to intrude, I'd just as soon
    talk a little while with your wife. *(Shuts the door, then notices Mrs. Linde.)* Oh,
    beg pardon. I'm intruding here too.
NORA: No, not at all. *(Introducing him.)* Dr. Rank, Mrs. Linde.
RANK: Well now, that's a name much heard in this house. I believe I passed the
    lady on the stairs as I came.
MRS. LINDE: Yes, I take the stairs very slowly. They're rather hard on me.
240 RANK: Uh-hm, some touch of internal weakness?
MRS. LINDE: More overexertion, I'd say.
RANK: Nothing else? Then you're probably here in town to rest up in a round of
    parties?
MRS. LINDE: I'm here to look for work.
RANK: Is that the best cure for overexertion?
245 MRS. LINDE: One has to live, Doctor.

RANK: Yes, there's a common prejudice to that effect.

NORA: Oh, come on, Dr. Rank—you really do want to live yourself.

RANK: Yes, I really do. Wretched as I am, I'll gladly prolong my torment indefinitely. All my patients feel like that. And it's quite the same, too, with the morally sick. Right at this moment there's one of those moral invalids in there with Helmer—

MRS. LINDE: (*softly*) Ah!

NORA: Who do you mean?   250

RANK: Oh, it's a lawyer, Krogstad, a type you wouldn't know. His character is rotten to the root—but even he began chattering all-importantly about how he had to *live.*

NORA: Oh? What did he want to talk to Torvald about?

RANK: I really don't know. I only heard something about the bank.

NORA: I didn't know that Krog—that this man Krogstad had anything to do with the bank.

RANK: Yes, he's gotten some kind of berth down there. (*To Mrs. Linde.*) I don't   255
know if you also have, in your neck of the woods, a type of person who scuttles about breathlessly, sniffing out hints of moral corruption, and then maneuvers his victim into some sort of key position where he can keep an eye on him. It's the healthy these days that are out in the cold.

MRS. LINDE: All the same, it's the sick who most need to be taken in.

RANK: (*with a shrug*) Yes, there we have it. That's the concept that's turning society into a sanatorium.

Nora, lost in her thoughts, breaks out into quiet laughter and claps her hands.

RANK: Why do you laugh at that? Do you have any real idea of what society is?

NORA: What do I care about dreary old society? I was laughing at something quite different—something terribly funny. Tell me, Doctor—is everyone who works in the bank dependent now on Torvald?

RANK: Is that what you find so terribly funny?   260

NORA: (*smiling and humming*) Never mind, never mind! (*Pacing the floor.*) Yes, that's really immensely amusing: that we—that Torvald has so much power now over all those people. (*Taking the bag out of her pocket.*) Dr. Rank, a little macaroon on that?

RANK: See here, macaroons! I thought they were contraband here.

NORA: Yes, but these are some that Kristine gave me.

MRS. LINDE: What? I—?

NORA: Now, now, don't be afraid. You couldn't possibly know that Torvald had   265
forbidden them. You see, he's worried they'll ruin my teeth. But hmp! Just this once! Isn't that so, Dr. Rank? Help yourself! (*Puts a macaroon in his mouth.*) And you too, Kristine. And I'll also have one, only a little one—or two, at the most. (*Walking about again.*) Now I'm really tremendously happy. Now there's just one last thing in the world that I have an enormous desire to do.

RANK: Well! And what's that?

NORA: It's something I have such a consuming desire to say so Torvald could hear.

RANK: And why can't you say it?

NORA: I don't dare. It's quite shocking.

270 MRS. LINDE: Shocking?

RANK: Well, then it isn't advisable. But in front of us you certainly can. What do you have such a desire to say so Torvald could hear?

NORA: I have such a huge desire to say—to hell and be damned!

RANK: Are you crazy?

MRS. LINDE: My goodness, Nora!

275 RANK: Go on, say it. Here he is.

NORA: (hiding the macaroon bag) Shh, shh, shh!

Helmer comes in from his study, hat in hand, overcoat over his arm.

NORA: (going toward him) Well, Torvald dear, are you through with him?

HELMER: Yes, he just left.

NORA: Let me introduce you—this is Kristine, who's arrived here in town.

280 HELMER: Kristine—? I'm sorry, but I don't know—

NORA: Mrs. Linde, Torvald dear. Mrs. Kristine Linde.

HELMER: Of course. A childhood friend of my wife's, no doubt?

MRS. LINDE: Yes, we knew each other in those days.

NORA: And just think, she made the long trip down here in order to talk with you.

285 HELMER: What's this?

MRS. LINDE: Well, not exactly—

NORA: You see, Kristine is remarkably clever in office work, and so she's terribly eager to come under a capable man's supervision and add more to what she already knows—

HELMER: Very wise, Mrs. Linde.

NORA: And then when she heard that you'd become a bank manager—the story was wired out to the papers—then she came in as fast as she could and—Really, Torvald, for my sake you can do a little something for Kristine, can't you?

290 HELMER: Yes, it's not at all impossible. Mrs. Linde, I suppose you're a widow?

MRS. LINDE: Yes.

HELMER: Any experience in office work?

MRS. LINDE: Yes, a good deal.

HELMER: Well, it's quite likely that I can make an opening for you—

295 NORA: (clapping her hands) You see, you see!

HELMER: You've come at a lucky moment, Mrs. Linde.

MRS. LINDE: Oh, how can I thank you?

HELMER: Not necessary. (Putting his overcoat on.) But today you'll have to excuse me—

RANK: Wait, I'll go with you. (He fetches his coat from the hall and warms it at the stove.)

300 NORA: Don't stay out long, dear.

HELMER: An hour; no more.

NORA: Are you going too, Kristine?

MRS. LINDE: (putting on her winter garments) Yes, I have to see about a room now.

HELMER: Then perhaps we can all walk together.

305 NORA: (helping her) What a shame we're so cramped here, but it's quite impossible for us to—

MRS. LINDE: Oh, don't even think of it! Good-bye, Nora dear, and thanks for everything.

NORA: Good-bye for now. Of course you'll be back this evening. And you too, Dr. Rank. What? If you're well enough? Oh, you've got to be! Wrap up tight now.

In a ripple of small talk the company moves out into the hall; children's voices are heard outside on the steps.

NORA: There they are! There they are! (*She runs to open the door. The children come in with their nurse, Anne-Marie.*) Come in, come in! (*Bends down and kisses them.*) Oh, you darlings—! Look at them, Kristine. Aren't they lovely!

RANK: No loitering in the draft here.

HELMER: Come, Mrs. Linde—this place is unbearable now for anyone but mothers.   310

Dr. Rank, Helmer, and Mrs. Linde go down the stairs. Anne-Marie goes into the living room with the children. Nora follows, after closing the hall door.

NORA: How fresh and strong you look. Oh, such red cheeks you have! Like apples and roses. (*The children interrupt her throughout the following.*) And it was so much fun? That's wonderful. Really? You pulled both Emmy and Bob on the sled? Imagine, all together! Yes, you're a clever boy, Ivar. Oh, let me hold her a bit, Anne-Marie. My sweet little doll baby! (*Takes the smallest from the nurse and dances with her.*) Yes, yes, Mama will dance with Bob as well. What? Did you throw snowballs? Oh, if I'd only been there! No, don't bother, Anne-Marie— I'll undress them myself. Oh yes, let me. It's such fun. Go in and rest; you look half frozen. There's hot coffee waiting for you on the stove. (*The nurse goes into the room to the left. Nora takes the children's winter things off, throwing them about, while the children talk to her all at once.*) Is that so? A big dog chased you? But it didn't bite? No, dogs never bite little, lovely doll babies. Don't peek in the packages, Ivar! What is it? Yes, wouldn't you like to know. No, no, it's an ugly something. Well? Shall we play? What shall we play? Hide-and-seek? Yes, let's play hide-and-seek. Bob must hide first. I must? Yes, let me hide first. (*Laughing and shouting, she and the children play in and out of the living room and the adjoining room to the right. At last Nora hides under the table. The children come storming in, search, but cannot find her, then hear her muffled laughter, dash over to the table, lift the cloth up and find her. Wild shouting. She creeps forward as if to scare them. More shouts. Meanwhile, a knock at the hall door; no one has noticed it. Now the door half opens, and Krogstad appears. He waits a moment; the game goes on.*)

KROGSTAD: Beg pardon, Mrs. Helmer—

NORA: (*with a strangled cry, turning and scrambling to her knees*) Oh! What do you want?

KROGSTAD: Excuse me. The outer door was ajar; it must be someone forgot to shut it—

NORA: (*rising*) My husband isn't home, Mr. Krogstad.   315

KROGSTAD: I know that.

NORA: Yes—then what do you want here?

KROGSTAD: A word with you.

NORA: With—? (*To the children, quietly.*) Go in to Anne-Marie. What? No, the strange man won't hurt Mama. When he's gone, we'll play some more.

(*She leads the children into the room to the left and shuts the door after them. Then, tense and nervous.*) You want to speak to me?

320 KROGSTAD: Yes, I want to.

NORA: Today? But it's not yet the first of the month—

KROGSTAD: No, it's Christmas Eve. It's going to be up to you how merry a Christmas you have.

NORA: What is it you want? Today I absolutely can't—

KROGSTAD: We won't talk about that till later. This is something else. You do have a moment to spare, I suppose?

325 NORA: Oh yes, of course—I do, except—

KROGSTAD: Good. I was sitting over at Olsen's Restaurant when I saw your husband go down the street—

NORA: Yes?

KROGSTAD: With a lady.

NORA: Yes. So?

330 KROGSTAD: If you'll pardon my asking: wasn't that lady a Mrs. Linde?

NORA: Yes.

KROGSTAD: Just now come into town?

NORA: Yes, today.

KROGSTAD: She's a good friend of yours?

335 NORA: Yes, she is. But I don't see—

KROGSTAD: I also knew her once.

NORA: I'm aware of that.

KROGSTAD: Oh? You know all about it. I thought so. Well, then let me ask you short and sweet: is Mrs. Linde getting a job in the bank?

NORA: What makes you think you can cross-examine me, Mr. Krogstad—you, one of my husband's employees? But since you ask, you might as well know—yes, Mrs. Linde's going to be taken on at the bank. And I'm the one who spoke for her, Mr. Krogstad. Now you know.

340 KROGSTAD: So I guessed right.

NORA: (*pacing up and down*) Oh, one does have a tiny bit of influence, I should hope. Just because I am a woman, don't think it means that—When one has a subordinate position, Mr. Krogstad, one really ought to be careful about pushing somebody who—hm—

KROGSTAD: Who has influence?

NORA: That's right.

KROGSTAD: (*in a different tone*) Mrs. Helmer, would you be good enough to use your influence on my behalf?

345 NORA: What? What do you mean?

KROGSTAD: Would you please make sure that I keep my subordinate position in the bank?

NORA: What does that mean? Who's thinking of taking away your position?

KROGSTAD: Oh, don't play the innocent with me. I'm quite aware that your friend would hardly relish the chance of running into me again; and I'm also aware now whom I can thank for being turned out.

NORA: But I promise you—

KROGSTAD: Yes, yes, yes, to the point: there's still time, and I'm advising you to use   350
your influence to prevent it.

NORA: But Mr. Krogstad, I have absolutely no influence.

KROGSTAD: You haven't? I thought you were just saying—

NORA: You shouldn't take me so literally. I! How can you believe that I have any
such influence over my husband?

KROGSTAD: Oh, I've known your husband from our student days. I don't think the
great bank manager's more steadfast than any other married man.

NORA: You speak insolently about my husband, and I'll show you the door.   355

KROGSTAD: The lady has spirit.

NORA: I'm not afraid of you any longer. After New Year's, I'll soon be done with
the whole business.

KROGSTAD: (restraining himself) Now listen to me, Mrs. Helmer. If necessary, I'll
fight for my little job in the bank as if it were life itself.

NORA: Yes, so it seems.

KROGSTAD: It's not just a matter of income; that's the least of it. It's something   360
else—All right, out with it! Look, this is the thing. You know, just like all
the others, of course, that once, a good many years ago, I did something
rather rash.

NORA: I've heard rumors to that effect.

KROGSTAD: The case never got into court; but all the same, every door was closed
in my face from then on. So I took up those various activities you know about.
I had to grab hold somewhere; and I dare say I haven't been among the worst.
But now I want to drop all that. My boys are growing up. For their sakes, I'll
have to win back as much respect as possible here in town. That job in the bank
was like the first rung in my ladder. And now your husband wants to kick me
right back down in the mud again.

NORA: But for heaven's sake, Mr. Krogstad, it's simply not in my power to help you.

KROGSTAD: That's because you haven't the will to—but I have the means to make
you.

NORA: You certainly won't tell my husband that I owe you money?   365

KROGSTAD: Hm—what if I told him that?

NORA: That would be shameful of you. (Nearly in tears.) This secret—my joy and
my pride—that he should learn it in such a crude and disgusting way—learn it
from you. You'd expose me to the most horrible unpleasantness—

KROGSTAD: Only unpleasantness?

NORA: (vehemently) But go on and try. It'll turn out the worse for you, because then
my husband will really see what a crook you are, and then you'll never be able to
hold your job.

KROGSTAD: I asked if it was just domestic unpleasantness you were afraid of.   370

NORA: If my husband finds out, then of course he'll pay what I owe at once, and
then we'd be through with you for good.

KROGSTAD: (a step closer) Listen, Mrs. Helmer—you've either got a very bad memory, or else no head at all for business. I'd better put you a little more in touch
with the facts.

NORA: What do you mean?

KROGSTAD: When your husband was sick, you came to me for a loan of four thousand, eight hundred crowns.

375 NORA: Where else could I go?

KROGSTAD: I promised to get you that sum—

NORA: And you got it.

KROGSTAD: I promised to get you that sum, on certain conditions. You were so
involved in your husband's illness, and so eager to finance your trip, that I guess
you didn't think out all the details. It might just be a good idea to remind you.
I promised you the money on the strength of a note I drew up.

NORA: Yes, and that I signed.

380 KROGSTAD: Right. But at the bottom I added some lines for your father to guarantee
the loan. He was supposed to sign down there.

NORA: Supposed to? He did sign.

KROGSTAD: I left the date blank. In other words, your father would have dated his
signature himself. Do you remember that?

NORA: Yes, I think—

KROGSTAD: Then I gave you the note for you to mail to your father. Isn't that so?

385 NORA: Yes.

KROGSTAD: And naturally you sent it at once—because only some five, six days
later you brought me the note, properly signed. And with that, the money
was yours.

NORA: Well, then; I've made my payments regularly, haven't I?

KROGSTAD: More or less. But—getting back to the point—those were hard times for
you then, Mrs. Helmer.

NORA: Yes, they were.

390 KROGSTAD: Your father was very ill, I believe.

NORA: He was near the end.

KROGSTAD: He died soon after?

NORA: Yes.

KROGSTAD: Tell me, Mrs. Helmer, do you happen to recall the date of your father's
death? The day of the month, I mean.

395 NORA: Papa died the twenty-ninth of September.

KROGSTAD: That's quite correct; I've already looked into that. And now we come to
a curious thing—(*taking out a paper*) which I simply cannot comprehend.

NORA: Curious thing? I don't know—

KROGSTAD: This is the curious thing: that your father co-signed the note for your
loan three days after his death.

NORA: How—? I don't understand.

400 KROGSTAD: Your father died the twenty-ninth of September. But look. Here your
father dated his signature October second. Isn't that curious, Mrs. Helmer?
(*Nora is silent.*) Can you explain it to me? (*Nora remains silent.*) It's also remarkable that the words "October second" and the year aren't written in your
father's hand, but rather in one that I think I know. Well, it's easy to understand. Your father forgot perhaps to date his signature, and then someone or
other added it, a bit sloppily, before anyone knew of his death. There's nothing wrong in that. It all comes down to the signature. And there's no question

about *that*, Mrs. Helmer. It really *was* your father who signed his own name here, wasn't it?

NORA: *(after a short silence, throwing her head back and looking squarely at him)* No, it wasn't. I signed Papa's name.

KROGSTAD: Wait, now—are you fully aware that this is a dangerous confession?

NORA: Why? You'll soon get your money.

KROGSTAD: Let me ask you a question—why didn't you send the paper to your father?

NORA: That was impossible. Papa was so sick. If I'd asked him for his signature,   405
I also would have had to tell him what the money was for. But I couldn't tell him, sick as he was, that my husband's life was in danger. That was just impossible.

KROGSTAD: Then it would have been better if you'd given up the trip abroad.

NORA: I couldn't possibly. The trip was to save my husband's life. I couldn't give that up.

KROGSTAD: But didn't you ever consider that this was a fraud against me?

NORA: I couldn't let myself be bothered by that. You weren't any concern of mine. I couldn't stand you, with all those cold complications you made, even though you knew how badly off my husband was.

KROGSTAD: Mrs. Helmer, obviously you haven't the vaguest idea of what you've   410
involved yourself in. But I can tell you this: it was nothing more and nothing worse than I once did—and it wrecked my whole reputation.

NORA: You? Do you expect me to believe that you ever acted bravely to save your wife's life?

KROGSTAD: Laws don't inquire into motives.

NORA: Then they must be very poor laws.

KROGSTAD: Poor or not—if I introduce this paper in court, you'll be judged according to law.

NORA: This I refuse to believe. A daughter hasn't a right to protect her dying father   415
from anxiety and care? A wife hasn't a right to save her husband's life? I don't know much about laws, but I'm sure that somewhere in the books these things are allowed. And you don't know anything about it—you who practice the law? You must be an awful lawyer, Mr. Krogstad.

KROGSTAD: Could be. But business—the kind of business we two mixed up in— don't you think I know about that? All right. Do what you want now. But I'm telling you *this:* if I get shoved down a second time, you're going to keep me company. *(He bows and goes out through the hall.)*

NORA: *(pensive for a moment, then tossing her head)* Oh, really! Trying to frighten me! I'm not so silly as all that. *(Begins gathering up the children's clothes, but soon stops.)* But—? No, but that's impossible! I did it out of love.

THE CHILDREN: *(in the doorway, left)* Mama, that strange man's gone out the door.

NORA: Yes, yes, I know it. But don't tell anyone about the strange man. Do you hear? Not even Papa!

THE CHILDREN: No, Mama. But now will you play again?   420

NORA: No, not now.

THE CHILDREN: Oh, but Mama, you promised.

NORA: Yes, but I can't now. Go inside; I have too much to do. Go in, go in, my sweet darlings. (*She herds them gently back in the room and shuts the door after them. Settling on the sofa, she takes up a piece of embroidery and makes some stitches, but soon stops abruptly.*) No! (*Throws the work aside, rises, goes to the hall door and calls out.*) Helene! Let me have the tree in here. (*Goes to the table, left, opens the table drawer, and stops again.*) No, but that's utterly impossible!

MAID: (*with the Christmas tree*) Where should I put it, ma'am?

425   NORA: There. The middle of the floor.

MAID: Should I bring anything else?

NORA: No, thanks. I have what I need.

The Maid, who has set the tree down, goes out.

NORA: (*absorbed in trimming the tree*) Candles here—and flowers here. That terrible creature! Talk, talk, talk! There's nothing to it at all. The tree's going to be lovely. I'll do anything to please you, Torvald. I'll sing for you, dance for you—

Helmer comes in from the hall, with a sheaf of papers under his arm.

NORA: Oh! You're back so soon?

430   HELMER: Yes. Has anyone been here?

NORA: Here? No.

HELMER: That's odd. I saw Krogstad leaving the front door.

NORA: So? Oh yes, that's true. Krogstad was here a moment.

HELMER: Nora, I can see by your face that he's been here, begging you to put in a good word for him.

435   NORA: Yes.

HELMER: And it was supposed to seem like your own idea? You were to hide it from me that he'd been here. He asked you that, too, didn't he?

NORA: Yes, Torvald, but—

HELMER: Nora, Nora, and you could fall for that? Talk with that sort of person and promise him anything? And then in the bargain, tell me an untruth.

NORA: An untruth—?

440   HELMER: Didn't you say that no one had been here? (*Wagging his finger.*) My little songbird must never do that again. A songbird needs a clean beak to warble with. No false notes. (*Putting his arm about her waist.*) That's the way it should be, isn't it? Yes, I'm sure of it. (*Releasing her.*) And so, enough of that. (*Sitting by the stove.*) Ah, how snug and cozy it is here. (*Leafing among his papers.*)

NORA: (*busy with the tree, after a short pause*) Torvald!

HELMER: Yes.

NORA: I'm so much looking forward to the Stenborgs' costume party, day after tomorrow.

HELMER: And I can't wait to see what you'll surprise me with.

445   NORA: Oh, that stupid business!

HELMER: What?

NORA: I can't find anything that's right. Everything seems so ridiculous, so inane.

HELMER: So my little Nora's come to *that* recognition?

NORA: (*going behind his chair, her arms resting on its back*) Are you very busy, Torvald?

HELMER: Oh—   450
NORA: What papers are those?
HELMER: Bank matters.
NORA: Already?
HELMER: I've gotten full authority from the retiring management to make all neces-
     sary changes in personnel and procedure. I'll need Christmas week for that. I
     want to have everything in order by New Year's.
NORA: So that was the reason this poor Krogstad—   455
HELMER: Hm.
NORA: (*still leaning on the chair and slowly stroking the nape of his neck*) If you weren't
     so very busy, I would have asked you an enormous favor, Torvald.
HELMER: Let's hear. What is it?
NORA: You know, there isn't anyone who has your good taste—and I want so much
     to look well at the costume party. Torvald, couldn't you take over and decide
     what I should be and plan my costume?
HELMER: Ah, is my stubborn little creature calling for a lifeguard?   460
NORA: Yes, Torvald, I can't get anywhere without your help.
HELMER: All right—I'll think it over. We'll hit on something.
NORA: Oh, how sweet of you. (*Goes to the tree again. Pause.*) Aren't the red flowers
     pretty—? But tell me, was it really such a crime that this Krogstad committed?
HELMER: Forgery. Do you have any idea what that means?
NORA: Couldn't he have done it out of need?   465
HELMER: Yes, or thoughtlessness, like so many others. I'm not so heartless that I'd
     condemn a man categorically for just one mistake.
NORA: No, of course not, Torvald!
HELMER: Plenty of men have redeemed themselves by openly confessing their
     crimes and taking their punishment.
NORA: Punishment—?
HELMER: But now Krogstad didn't go that way. He got himself out by sharp practices,   470
     and that's the real cause of his moral breakdown.
NORA: Do you really think that would—?
HELMER: Just imagine how a man with that sort of guilt in him has to lie and cheat
     and deceive on all sides, has to wear a mask even with the nearest and dearest
     he has, even with his own wife and children. And with the children, Nora—
     that's where it's most horrible.
NORA: Why?
HELMER: Because that kind of atmosphere of lies infects the whole life of a home.
     Every breath the children take in is filled with the germs of something degenerate.
NORA: (*coming closer behind him*) Are you sure of that?   475
HELMER: Oh, I've seen it often enough as a lawyer. Almost everyone who goes bad
     early in life has a mother who's a chronic liar.
NORA: Why just—the mother?
HELMER: It's usually the mother's influence that's dominant, but the father's works
     in the same way, of course. Every lawyer is quite familiar with it. And still this
     Krogstad's been going home year in, year out, poisoning his own children with
     lies and pretense; that's why I call him morally lost. (*Reaching his hands out*

toward her.) So my sweet little Nora must promise me never to plead his cause. Your hand on it. Come, come, what's this? Give me your hand. There, now. All settled. I can tell you it'd be impossible for me to work alongside of him. I literally feel physically revolted when I'm anywhere near such a person.

NORA: (*withdraws her hand and goes to the other side of the Christmas tree*) How hot it is here! And I've got so much to do.

480 HELMER: (*getting up and gathering his papers*) Yes, and I have to think about getting some of these read through before dinner. I'll think about your costume, too. And something to hang on the tree in gilt paper, I may even see about that. (*Putting his hand on her head.*) Oh you, my darling little songbird. (*He goes into his study and closes the door after him.*)

NORA: (*softly, after a silence*) Oh, really! It isn't so. It's impossible. It must be impossible.

ANNE-MARIE: (*in the doorway, left*) The children are begging so hard to come in to Mama.

NORA: No, no, no, don't let them in to me! You stay with them, Anne-Marie.

ANNE-MARIE: Of course, ma'am. (*Closes the door.*)

485 NORA: (*pale with terror*) Hurt my children—! Poison my home? (*A moment's pause; then she tosses her head.*) That's not true. Never. Never in all the world.

ACT 2

Same room. Beside the piano the Christmas tree now stands stripped of ornaments, burned-down candle stubs on its ragged branches. Nora's street clothes lie on the sofa. Nora, alone in the room, moves restlessly about; at last she stops at the sofa and picks up her coat.

NORA: (*dropping the coat again*) Someone's coming! (*Goes toward the door, listens.*) No—there's no one. Of course—nobody's coming today, Christmas Day—or tomorrow, either. But maybe—(*Opens the door and looks out.*) No, nothing in the mailbox. Quite empty. (*Coming forward.*) What nonsense! He won't do anything serious. Nothing terrible could happen. It's impossible. Why, I have three small children.

Anne-Marie, with a large carton, comes in from the room to the left.

ANNE-MARIE: Well, at last I found the box with the masquerade clothes.

NORA: Thanks. Put it on the table.

ANNE-MARIE: (*does so*) But they're all pretty much of a mess.

5 NORA: Ahh! I'd love to rip them in a million pieces!

ANNE-MARIE: Oh, mercy, they can be fixed right up. Just a little patience.

NORA: Yes, I'll go get Mrs. Linde to help me.

ANNE-MARIE: Out again now? In this nasty weather? Miss Nora will catch cold— get sick.

NORA: Oh, worse things could happen—How are the children?

10 ANNE-MARIE: The poor mites are playing with their Christmas presents, but—

NORA: Do they ask for me much?

ANNE-MARIE: They're so used to having Mama around, you know.

NORA: Yes. But Anne-Marie, I *can't* be together with them as much as I was.

ANNE-MARIE: Well, small children get used to anything.

NORA: You think so? Do you think they'd forget their mother if she was gone   15
for good?

ANNE-MARIE: Oh, mercy—gone for good!

NORA: Wait, tell me, Anne-Marie—I've wondered so often—how could you ever
have the heart to give your child over to strangers?

ANNE-MARIE: But I had to, you know, to become little Nora's nurse.

NORA: Yes, but how could you *do* it?

ANNE-MARIE: When I could get such a good place? A girl who's poor and who's   20
gotten in trouble is glad enough for that. Because that slippery fish, he didn't do
a thing for me, you know.

NORA: But your daughter's surely forgotten you.

ANNE-MARIE: Oh, she certainly has not. She's written to me, both when she was
confirmed and when she was married.

NORA: (*clasping her about the neck*) You old Anne-Marie, you were a good mother
for me when I was little.

ANNE-MARIE: Poor little Nora, with no other mother but me.

NORA: And if the babies didn't have one, then I know that you'd—What silly talk!   25
(*Opening the carton.*) Go in to them. Now I'll have to—Tomorrow you can see
how lovely I'll look.

ANNE-MARIE: Oh, there won't be anyone at the party as lovely as Miss Nora. (*She
goes off into the room, left.*)

NORA: (*begins unpacking the box, but soon throws it aside*) Oh, if I dared to go out.
If only nobody would come. If only nothing would happen here while I'm out.
What craziness—nobody's coming. Just don't think. This muff—needs a
brushing. Beautiful gloves, beautiful gloves. Let it go. Let it go! One, two, three,
four, five, six—(*With a cry.*) Oh, there they are! (*Poises to move toward the door,
but remains irresolutely standing. Mrs. Linde enters from the hall, where she has
removed her street clothes.*)

NORA: Oh, it's you, Kristine. There's no one else out there? How good that
you've come.

MRS. LINDE: I hear you were up asking for me.

NORA: Yes, I just stopped by. There's something you really can help me with. Let's   30
get settled on the sofa. Look, there's going to be a costume party tomorrow
evening at the Stenborgs' right above us, and now Torvald wants me to go as a
Neapolitan peasant girl and dance the tarantella that I learned in Capri.

MRS. LINDE: Really, are you giving a whole performance?

NORA: Torvald says yes, I should. See, here's the dress. Torvald had it made for me
down there; but now it's all so tattered that I just don't know—

MRS. LINDE: Oh, we'll fix that up in no time. It's nothing more than the trimmings—
they're a bit loose here and there. Needle and thread? Good, now we have what
we need.

NORA: Oh, how sweet of you!

MRS. LINDE: (*sewing*) So you'll be in disguise tomorrow, Nora. You know what? I'll   35
stop by then for a moment and have a look at you all dressed up. But listen, I've
absolutely forgotten to thank you for that pleasant evening yesterday.

NORA: *(getting up and walking about)* I don't think it was as pleasant as usual yesterday. You should have come to town a bit sooner, Kristine—Yes, Torvald really
knows how to give a home elegance and charm.

MRS. LINDE: And you do, too, if you ask me. You're not your father's daughter
for nothing. But tell me, is Dr. Rank always so down in the mouth as
yesterday?

NORA: No, that was quite an exception. But he goes around critically ill all the
time—tuberculosis of the spine, poor man. You know, his father was a disgusting thing who kept mistresses and so on—and that's why the son's been sickly
from birth.

MRS. LINDE: *(lets her sewing fall to her lap)* But my dearest Nora, how do you know
about such things?

40 NORA: *(walking more jauntily)* Hmp! When you've had three children, then you've
had a few visits from—from women who know something of medicine, and they
tell you this and that.

MRS. LINDE: *(resumes sewing; a short pause)* Does Dr. Rank come here every day?

NORA: Every blessed day. He's Torvald's best friend from childhood, and my good
friend, too. Dr. Rank almost belongs to this house.

MRS. LINDE: But tell me—is he quite sincere? I mean, doesn't he rather enjoy flattering people?

NORA: Just the opposite. Why do you think that?

45 MRS. LINDE: When you introduced us yesterday, he was proclaiming that he'd often
heard my name in this house; but later I noticed that your husband hadn't the
slightest idea who I really was. So how could Dr. Rank—?

NORA: But it's all true, Kristine. You see, Torvald loves me beyond words, and, as
he puts it, he'd like to keep me all to himself. For a long time he'd almost be
jealous if I even mentioned any of my old friends back home. So of course I
dropped that. But with Dr. Rank I talk a lot about such things, because he likes
hearing about them.

MRS. LINDE: Now listen, Nora; in many ways you're still like a child. I'm a good
deal older than you, with a little more experience. I'll tell you something: you
ought to put an end to all this with Dr. Rank.

NORA: What should I put an end to?

MRS. LINDE: Both parts of it, I think. Yesterday you said something about a rich
admirer who'd provide you with money—

50 NORA: Yes, one who doesn't exist—worse luck. So?

MRS. LINDE: Is Dr. Rank well off?

NORA: Yes, he is.

MRS. LINDE: With no dependents?

NORA: No, no one. But—

55 MRS. LINDE: And he's over here every day?

NORA: Yes, I told you that.

MRS. LINDE: How can a man of such refinement be so grasping?

NORA: I don't follow you at all.

MRS. LINDE: Now don't try to hide it, Nora. You think I can't guess who loaned you
the forty-eight hundred crowns?

NORA: Are you out of your mind? How could you think such a thing! A friend   60
of ours, who comes here every single day. What an intolerable situation that
would have been!

MRS. LINDE: Then it really wasn't him.

NORA: No, absolutely not. It never even crossed my mind for a moment—And he
had nothing to lend in those days; his inheritance came later.

MRS. LINDE: Well, I think that was a stroke of luck for you, Nora dear.

NORA: No, it never would have occurred to me to ask Dr. Rank—Still, I'm quite
sure that if I had asked him—

MRS. LINDE: Which you won't, of course.   65

NORA: No, of course not. I can't see that I'd ever need to. But I'm quite positive
that if I talked to Dr. Rank—

MRS. LINDE: Behind your husband's back?

NORA: I've got to clear up this other thing; *that's* also behind his back. I've *got* to
clear it all up.

MRS. LINDE: Yes, I was saying that yesterday, but—

NORA: (*pacing up and down*) A man handles these problems so much better than   70
a woman—

MRS. LINDE: One's husband does, yes.

NORA: Nonsense. (*Stopping.*) When you pay everything you owe, then you get your
note back, right?

MRS. LINDE: Yes, naturally.

NORA: And can rip it into a million pieces and burn it up—that filthy scrap
of paper!

MRS. LINDE: (*looking hard at her, laying her sewing aside, and rising slowly*) Nora,   75
you're hiding something from me.

NORA: You can see it in my face?

MRS. LINDE: Something's happened to you since yesterday morning. Nora, what is it?

NORA: (*hurrying toward her*) Kristine! (*Listening.*) Shh! Torvald's home. Look, go in
with the children a while. Torvald can't bear all this snipping and stitching. Let
Anne-Marie help you.

MRS. LINDE: (*gathering up some of the things*) All right, but I'm not leaving here
until we've talked this out. (*She disappears into the room, left, as Torvald enters
from the hall.*)

NORA: Oh, how I've been waiting for you, Torvald dear.   80

HELMER: Was that the dressmaker?

NORA: No, that was Kristine. She's helping me fix up my costume. You know, it's
going to be quite attractive.

HELMER: Yes, wasn't that a bright idea I had?

NORA: Brilliant! But then wasn't I good as well to give in to you?

HELMER: Good—because you give in to your husband's judgment? All right, you   85
little goose, I know you didn't mean it like that. But I won't disturb you. You'll
want to have a fitting, I suppose.

NORA: And you'll be working?

HELMER: Yes. (*Indicating a bundle of papers.*) See. I've been down to the bank. (*Starts
toward his study.*)

NORA: Torvald.

HELMER: *(stops)* Yes.

90 NORA: If your little squirrel begged you, with all her heart and soul, for something—?

HELMER: What's that?

NORA: Then would you do it?

HELMER: First, naturally, I'd have to know what it was.

NORA: Your squirrel would scamper about and do tricks, if you'd only be sweet and give in.

95 HELMER: Out with it.

NORA: Your lark would be singing high and low in every room—

HELMER: Come on, she does that anyway.

NORA: I'd be a wood nymph and dance for you in the moonlight.

HELMER: Nora—don't tell me it's that same business from this morning?

100 NORA: *(coming closer)* Yes, Torvald, I beg you, please!

HELMER: And you actually have the nerve to drag that up again?

NORA: Yes, yes, you've got to give in to me; you *have* to let Krogstad keep his job in the bank.

HELMER: My dear Nora, I've slated his job for Mrs. Linde.

NORA: That's awfully kind of you. But you could just fire another clerk instead of Krogstad.

105 HELMER: This is the most incredible stubbornness! Because you go and give an impulsive promise to speak up for him, I'm expected to—

NORA: That's not the reason, Torvald. It's for your own sake. That man does writing for the worst papers; you said it yourself. He could do you any amount of harm. I'm scared to death of him—

HELMER: Ah, I understand. It's the old memories haunting you.

NORA: What do you mean by that?

HELMER: Of course, you're thinking about your father.

110 NORA: Yes, all right. Just remember how those nasty gossips wrote in the papers about Papa and slandered him so cruelly. I think they'd have had him dismissed if the department hadn't sent you up to investigate, and if you hadn't been so kind and open-minded toward him.

HELMER: My dear Nora, there's a notable difference between your father and me. Your father's official career was hardly above reproach. But mine is; and I hope it'll stay that way as long as I hold my position.

NORA: Oh, who can ever tell what vicious minds can invent? We could be so snug and happy now in our quiet, carefree home—you and I and the children, Torvald! That's why I'm pleading with you so—

HELMER: And just by pleading for him you make it impossible for me to keep him on. It's already known at the bank that I'm firing Krogstad. What if it's rumored around now that the new bank manager was vetoed by his wife—

NORA: Yes, what then—?

115 HELMER: Oh yes—as long as our little bundle of stubbornness gets her way—! I should go and make myself ridiculous in front of the whole office—give people the idea I can be swayed by all kinds of outside pressure. Oh, you can bet I'd feel the effects of that soon enough! Besides—there's something that rules Krogstad right out at the bank as long as I'm the manager.

NORA: What's that?

HELMER: His moral failings I could maybe overlook if I had to—

NORA: Yes, Torvald, why not?

HELMER: And I hear he's quite efficient on the job. But he was a crony of mine back in my teens—one of those rash friendships that crop up again and again to embarrass you later in life. Well, I might as well say it straight out: we're on a first-name basis. And that tactless fool makes no effort at all to hide it in front of others. Quite the contrary—he thinks that entitles him to take a familiar air around me, and so every other second he comes booming out with his "Yes, Torvald!" and "Sure thing, Torvald!" I tell you, it's been excruciating for me. He's out to make my place in the bank unbearable.

NORA: Torvald, you can't be serious about all this.   120

HELMER: Oh no? Why not?

NORA: Because these are such petty considerations.

HELMER: What are you saying? Petty? You think I'm petty!

NORA: No, just the opposite, Torvald dear. That's exactly why—

HELMER: Never mind. You call my motives petty; then I might as well be just that.   125
Petty! All right! We'll put a stop to this for good. (*Goes to the hall door and calls.*) Helene!

NORA: What do you want?

HELMER: (*searching among his papers*) A decision. (*The Maid comes in.*) Look here; take this letter; go out with it at once. Get hold of a messenger and have him deliver it. Quick now. It's already addressed. Wait, here's some money.

MAID: Yes, sir. (*She leaves with the letter.*)

HELMER: (*straightening his papers*) There, now, little Miss Willful.

NORA: (*breathlessly*) Torvald, what was that letter?   130

HELMER: Krogstad's notice.

NORA: Call it back, Torvald! There's still time. Oh, Torvald, call it back! Do it for my sake—for your sake, for the children's sake! Do you hear, Torvald; do it! You don't know how this can harm us.

HELMER: Too late.

NORA: Yes, too late.

HELMER: Nora dear, I can forgive you this panic, even though basically you're   135
insulting me. Yes, you are! Or isn't it an insult to think that *I* should be afraid of a courtroom hack's revenge? But I forgive you anyway, because this shows so beautifully how much you love me. (*Takes her in his arms.*) This is the way it should be, my darling Nora. Whatever comes, you'll see: when it really counts, I have strength and courage enough as a man to take on the whole weight myself.

NORA: (*terrified*) What do you mean by that?

HELMER: The whole weight, I said.

NORA: (*resolutely*) No, never in all the world.

HELMER: Good. So we'll share it, Nora, as man and wife. That's as it should be. (*Fondling her.*) Are you happy now? There, there, there—not these frightened dove's eyes. It's nothing at all but empty fantasies—Now you should run through your tarantella and practice your tambourine. I'll go to the inner office and shut both doors, so I won't hear a thing; you can make all the noise you like.

(*Turning in the doorway.*) And when Rank comes, just tell him where he can find me. (*He nods to her and goes with his papers into the study, closing the door.*)

140   NORA: (*standing as though rooted, dazed with fright, in a whisper*) He really could do it. He will do it. He'll do it in spite of everything. No, not that, never, never! Anything but that! Escape! A way out—(*The doorbell rings.*) Dr. Rank! Anything but that! *Anything*, whatever it is! (*Her hands pass over her face, smoothing it; she pulls herself together, goes over and opens the hall door. Dr. Rank stands outside, hanging his fur coat up. During the following scene, it begins getting dark.*)

NORA: Hello, Dr. Rank. I recognized your ring. But you mustn't go in to Torvald yet; I believe he's working.

RANK: And you?

NORA: For you, I always have an hour to spare—you know that. (*He has entered, and she shuts the door after him.*)

RANK: Many thanks. I'll make use of these hours while I can.

145   NORA: What do you mean by that? While you can?

RANK: Does that disturb you?

NORA: Well, it's such an odd phrase. Is anything going to happen?

RANK: What's going to happen is what I've been expecting so long—but I honestly didn't think it would come so soon.

NORA: (*gripping his arm*) What is it you've found out? Dr. Rank, you have to tell me!

150   RANK: (*sitting by the stove*) It's all over with me. There's nothing to be done about it.

NORA: (*breathing easier*) Is it you—then—?

RANK: Who else? There's no point in lying to one's self. I'm the most miserable of all my patients, Mrs. Helmer. These past few days I've been auditing my internal accounts. Bankrupt! Within a month I'll probably be laid out and rotting in the churchyard.

NORA: Oh, what a horrible thing to say.

RANK: The thing itself is horrible. But the worst of it is all the other horror before it's over. There's only one final examination left; when I'm finished with that, I'll know about when my disintegration will begin. There's something I want to say. Helmer with his sensitivity has such a sharp distaste for anything ugly. I don't want him near my sickroom.

155   NORA: Oh, but Dr. Rank—

RANK: I won't have him in there. Under no condition. I'll lock my door to him—As soon as I'm completely sure of the worst, I'll send you my calling card marked with a black cross, and you'll know then the wreck has started to come apart.

NORA: No, today you're completely unreasonable. And I wanted you so much to be in a really good humor.

RANK: With death up my sleeve? And then to suffer this way for somebody else's sins. Is there any justice in that? And in every single family, in some way or another, this inevitable retribution of nature goes on—

NORA: (*her hands pressed over her ears*) Oh, stuff! Cheer up! Please—be gay!

160   RANK: Yes, I'd just as soon laugh at it all. My poor, innocent spine, serving time for my father's gay army days.

NORA: (*by the table, left*) He was so infatuated with asparagus tips and *pâté de foie gras*, wasn't that it?

RANK: Yes—and with truffles.

NORA: Truffles, yes. And then with oysters, I suppose?

RANK: Yes, tons of oysters, naturally.

NORA: And then the port and champagne to go with it. It's so sad that all these   165
delectable things have to strike at our bones.

RANK: Especially when they strike at the unhappy bones that never shared in
the fun.

NORA: Ah, that's the saddest of all.

RANK: (looks searchingly at her) Hm.

NORA: (after a moment) Why did you smile?

RANK: No, it was you who laughed.   170

NORA: No, it was you who smiled, Dr. Rank!

RANK: (getting up) You're even a bigger tease than I'd thought.

NORA: I'm full of wild ideas today.

RANK: That's obvious.

NORA: (putting both hands on his shoulders) Dear, dear Dr. Rank, you'll never die for   175
Torvald and me.

RANK: Oh, that loss you'll easily get over. Those who go away are soon forgotten.

NORA: (looks fearfully at him) You believe that?

RANK: One makes new connections, and then—

NORA: Who makes new connections?

RANK: Both you and Torvald will when I'm gone. I'd say you're well under way   180
already. What was that Mrs. Linde doing here last evening?

NORA: Oh, come—you can't be jealous of poor Kristine?

RANK: Oh yes, I am. She'll be my successor here in the house. When I'm down
under, that woman will probably—

NORA: Shh! Not so loud. She's right in there.

RANK: Today as well. So you see.

NORA: Only to sew on my dress. Good gracious, how unreasonable you are. (Sitting   185
on the sofa.) Be nice now, Dr. Rank. Tomorrow you'll see how beautifully I'll
dance; and you can imagine then that I'm dancing only for you—yes, and of
course for Torvald, too—that's understood. (Takes various items out of the
carton.) Dr. Rank, sit over here and I'll show you something.

RANK: (sitting) What's that?

NORA: Look here. Look.

RANK: Silk stockings.

NORA: Flesh-colored. Aren't they lovely? Now it's so dark here, but tomorrow—
No, no, no, just look at the feet. Oh well, you might as well look at the rest.

RANK: Hm—   190

NORA: Why do you look so critical? Don't you believe they'll fit?

RANK: I've never had any chance to form an opinion on that.

NORA: (glancing at him a moment) Shame on you. (Hits him lightly on the ear with the
stockings.) That's for you. (Puts them away again.)

RANK: And what other splendors am I going to see now?

NORA: Not the least bit more, because you've been naughty. (She hums a little and   195
rummages among her things.)

RANK: (*after a short silence*) When I sit here together with you like this, completely easy and open, then I don't know—I simply can't imagine—whatever would have become of me if I'd never come into this house.

NORA: (*smiling*) Yes, I really think you feel completely at ease with us.

RANK: (*more quietly, staring straight ahead*) And then to have to go away from it all—

NORA: Nonsense, you're not going away.

200 RANK: (*his voice unchanged*)—and not even be able to leave some poor show of gratitude behind, scarcely a fleeting regret—no more than a vacant place that anyone can fill.

NORA: And if I asked you now for—? No—

RANK: For what?

NORA: For a great proof of your friendship—

RANK: Yes, yes?

205 NORA: No, I mean—for an exceptionally big favor—

RANK: Would you really, for once, make me so happy?

NORA: Oh, you haven't the vaguest idea what it is.

RANK: All right, then tell me.

NORA: No, but I can't, Dr. Rank—it's all out of reason. It's advice and help, too—and a favor—

210 RANK: So much the better. I can't fathom what you're hinting at. Just speak out. Don't you trust me?

NORA: Of course. More than anyone else. You're my best and truest friend, I'm sure. That's why I want to talk to you. All right, then, Dr. Rank: there's something you can help me prevent. You know how deeply, how inexpressibly dearly Torvald loves me; he'd never hesitate a second to give up his life for me.

RANK: (*leaning close to her*) Nora—do you think he's the only one—

NORA: (*with a slight start*) Who—?

RANK: Who'd gladly give up his life for you.

215 NORA: (*heavily*) I see.

RANK: I swore to myself you should know this before I'm gone. I'll never find a better chance. Yes, Nora, now you know. And also you know now that you can trust me beyond anyone else.

NORA: (*rising, natural and calm*) Let me by.

RANK: (*making room for her, but still sitting*) Nora—

NORA: (*in the hall doorway*) Helene, bring the lamp in. (*Goes over to the stove.*) Ah, dear Dr. Rank, that was really mean of you.

220 RANK: (*getting up*) That I've loved you just as deeply as somebody else? Was *that* mean?

NORA: No, but that you came out and told me. That was quite unnecessary—

RANK: What do you mean? Have you known—?

The Maid comes in with the lamp, sets it on the table, and goes out again.

RANK: Nora—Mrs. Helmer—I'm asking you: have you known about it?

NORA: Oh, how can I tell what I know or don't know? Really, I don't know what to say—Why did you have to be so clumsy, Dr. Rank! Everything was so good.

RANK: Well, in any case, you now have the knowledge that my body and soul are at   225
    your command. So won't you speak out?

NORA: *(looking at him)* After that?

RANK: Please, just let me know what it is.

NORA: You can't know anything now.

RANK: I have to. You mustn't punish me like this. Give me the chance to do what-
    ever is humanly possible for you.

NORA: Now there's nothing you can do for me. Besides, actually, I don't need any   230
    help. You'll see—it's only my fantasies. That's what it is. Of course! *(Sits in the*
    rocker, looks at him, and smiles.) What a nice one you are, Dr. Rank. Aren't you
    a little bit ashamed, now that the lamp is here?

RANK: No, not exactly. But perhaps I'd better go—for good?

NORA: No, you certainly can't do that. You must come here just as you always have.
    You know Torvald can't do without you.

RANK: Yes, but *you?*

NORA: You know how much I enjoy it when you're here.

RANK: That's precisely what threw me off. You're a mystery to me. So many times   235
    I've felt you'd almost rather be with me than with Helmer.

NORA: Yes—you see, there are some people that one loves most and other people
    that one would almost prefer being with.

RANK: Yes, there's something to that.

NORA: When I was back home, of course I loved Papa most. But I always thought it
    was so much fun when I could sneak down to the maids' quarters, because they
    never tried to improve me, and it was always so amusing, the way they talked to
    each other.

RANK: Aha, so it's *their* place that I've filled.

NORA: *(jumping up and going to him)* Oh, dear, sweet Dr. Rank, that's not what   240
    I mean at all. But you can understand that with Torvald it's just the same as
    with Papa—

The Maid enters from the hall.

MAID: Ma'am—please! *(She whispers to Nora and hands her a calling card.)*

NORA: *(glancing at the card)* Ah! *(Slips it into her pocket.)*

RANK: Anything wrong?

NORA: No, no, not at all. It's only some—it's my new dress—

RANK: Really? But—there's your dress.   245

NORA: Oh, that. But this is another one—I ordered it—Torvald mustn't know—

RANK: Ah, now we have the big secret.

NORA: That's right. Just go in with him—he's back in the inner study. Keep him
    there as long as—

RANK: Don't worry. He won't get away. *(Goes into the study.)*

NORA: *(to the Maid)* And he's standing waiting in the kitchen?   250

MAID: Yes, he came up by the back stairs.

NORA: But didn't you tell him somebody was here?

MAID: Yes, but that didn't do any good.

NORA: He won't leave?

255   MAID: No, he won't go till he's talked with you, ma'am.

NORA: Let him come in, then—but quietly. Helene, don't breathe a word about this. It's a surprise for my husband.

MAID: Yes, yes, I understand—(*Goes out.*)

NORA: This horror—it's going to happen. No, no, no, it can't happen, it mustn't. (*She goes and bolts Helmer's door. The Maid opens the hall door for Krogstad and shuts it behind him. He is dressed for travel in a fur coat, boots, and a fur cap.*)

NORA: (*going toward him*) Talk softly. My husband's home.

260   KROGSTAD: Well, good for him.

NORA: What do you want?

KROGSTAD: Some information.

NORA: Hurry up, then. What is it?

KROGSTAD: You know, of course, that I got my notice.

265   NORA: I couldn't prevent it, Mr. Krogstad. I fought for you to the bitter end, but nothing worked.

KROGSTAD: Does your husband's love for you run so thin? He knows everything I can expose you to, and all the same he dares to—

NORA: How can you imagine he knows anything about this?

KROGSTAD: Ah, no—I can't imagine it either, now. It's not at all like my fine Torvald Helmer to have so much guts—

NORA: Mr. Krogstad, I demand respect for my husband!

270   KROGSTAD: Why, of course—all due respect. But since the lady's keeping it so carefully hidden, may I presume to ask if you're also a bit better informed than yesterday about what you've actually done?

NORA: More than you ever could teach me.

KROGSTAD: Yes, I *am* such an awful lawyer.

NORA: What is it you want from me?

KROGSTAD: Just a glimpse of how you are, Mrs. Helmer. I've been thinking about you all day long. A cashier, a night-court scribbler, a—well, a type like me also has a little of what they call a heart, you know.

275   NORA: Then show it. Think of my children.

KROGSTAD: Did you or your husband ever think of mine? But never mind. I simply wanted to tell you that you don't need to take this thing too seriously. For the present, I'm not proceeding with any action.

NORA: Oh no, really! Well—I knew that.

KROGSTAD: Everything can be settled in a friendly spirit. It doesn't have to get around town at all; it can stay just among us three.

NORA: My husband must never know anything of this.

280   KROGSTAD: How can you manage that? Perhaps you can pay me the balance?

NORA: No, not right now.

KROGSTAD: Or you know some way of raising the money in a day or two?

NORA: No way that I'm willing to use.

KROGSTAD: Well, it wouldn't have done you any good, anyway. If you stood in front of me with a fistful of bills, you still couldn't buy your signature back.

285   NORA: Then tell me what you're going to do with it.

KROGSTAD: I'll just hold onto it—keep it on file. There's no outsider who'll even get wind of it. So if you've been thinking of taking some desperate step—

NORA: I have.

KROGSTAD: Been thinking of running away from home—

NORA: I have!

KROGSTAD: Or even of something worse—   290

NORA: How could you guess that?

KROGSTAD: You can drop those thoughts.

NORA: How could you guess I was thinking of *that*?

KROGSTAD: Most of us think about *that* at first. I thought about it too, but I discov-
     ered I hadn't the courage—

NORA: (*lifelessly*) I don't either.   295

KROGSTAD: (*relieved*) That's true, you haven't the courage? You too?

NORA: I don't have it—I don't have it.

KROGSTAD: It would be terribly stupid, anyway. After that first storm at home blows
     out, why, then—I have here in my pocket a letter for your husband—

NORA: Telling everything?

KROGSTAD: As charitably as possible.   300

NORA: (*quickly*) He mustn't ever get that letter. Tear it up. I'll find some way to
     get money.

KROGSTAD: Beg pardon, Mrs. Helmer, but I think I just told you—

NORA: Oh, I don't mean the money I owe you. Let me know how much you want
     from my husband, and I'll manage it.

KROGSTAD: I don't want any money from your husband.

NORA: What do you want, then?   305

KROGSTAD: I'll tell you what. I want to recoup, Mrs. Helmer; I want to get on in
     the world—and there's where your husband can help me. For a year and a half
     I've kept myself clean of anything disreputable—all that time struggling with
     the worst conditions; but I was satisfied, working my way up step by step. Now
     I've been written right off, and I'm just not in the mood to come crawling back.
     I tell you, I want to move on. I want to get back in the bank—in a better
     position. Your husband can set up a job for me—

NORA: He'll never do that!

KROGSTAD: He'll do it. I know him. He won't dare breathe a word of protest. And
     once I'm in there together with him, you just wait and see! Inside of a year, I'll
     be the manager's right-hand man. It'll be Nils Krogstad, not Torvald Helmer,
     who runs the bank.

NORA: You'll never see the day!

KROGSTAD: Maybe you think you can—   310

NORA: I have the courage now—for *that*.

KROGSTAD: Oh, you don't scare me. A smart, spoiled lady like you—

NORA: You'll see; you'll see!

KROGSTAD: Under the ice, maybe? Down in the freezing, coal-black water?
     There, till you float up in the spring, ugly, unrecognizable, with your hair
     falling out—

NORA: You don't frighten me.   315

KROGSTAD: Nor do you frighten me. One doesn't do these things, Mrs. Helmer.
     Besides, what good would it be? I'd still have him safe in my pocket.

NORA: Afterwards? When I'm no longer—?

KROGSTAD: Are you forgetting that *I'll* be in control then over your final reputation? (*Nora stands speechless, staring at him.*) Good; now I've warned you. Don't
do anything stupid. When Helmer's read my letter, I'll be waiting for his reply.
And bear in mind that it's your husband himself who's forced me back to my
old ways. I'll never forgive him for that. Good-bye, Mrs. Helmer. (*He goes out
through the hall.*)

NORA: (*goes to the hall door, opens it a crack, and listens*) He's gone. Didn't leave
the letter. Oh no, no, that's impossible too! (*Opening the door more and more.*)
What's that? He's standing outside—not going downstairs. He's thinking it
over? Maybe he'll—? (*A letter falls in the mailbox; then Krogstad's footsteps are
heard, dying away down a flight of stairs. Nora gives a muffled cry and runs over
toward the sofa table. A short pause.*) In the mailbox. (*Slips warily over to the hall
door.*) It's lying there. Torvald, Torvald—now we're lost!

320   MRS. LINDE: (*entering with the costume from the room, left*) There now, I can't see
anything else to mend. Perhaps you'd like to try—

NORA: (*in a hoarse whisper*) Kristine, come here.

MRS. LINDE: (*tossing the dress on the sofa*) What's wrong? You look upset.

NORA: Come here. See that letter? *There!* Look—through the glass in the mailbox.

MRS. LINDE: Yes, yes, I see it.

325   NORA: That letter's from Krogstad—

MRS. LINDE: Nora—it's Krogstad who loaned you the money!

NORA: Yes, and now Torvald will find out everything.

MRS. LINDE: Believe me, Nora, it's best for both of you.

NORA: There's more you don't know. I forged a name.

330   MRS. LINDE: But for heaven's sake—?

NORA: I only want to tell you that, Kristine, so that you can be my witness.

MRS. LINDE: Witness? Why should I—?

NORA: If I should go out of my mind—it could easily happen—

MRS. LINDE: Nora!

335   NORA: Or anything else occurred—so I couldn't be present here—

MRS. LINDE: Nora, Nora, you aren't yourself at all!

NORA: And someone should try to take on the whole weight, all of the guilt, you
follow me—

MRS. LINDE: Yes, of course, but why do you think—?

NORA: Then you're the witness that it isn't true, Kristine. I'm very much myself; my
mind right now is perfectly clear; and I'm telling you: nobody else has known
about this; I alone did everything. Remember that.

340   MRS. LINDE: I will. But I don't understand all this.

NORA: Oh, how could you ever understand it? It's the miracle now that's going to
take place.

MRS. LINDE: The miracle?

NORA: Yes, the miracle. But it's so awful, Kristine. It mustn't take place, not for
anything in the world.

MRS. LINDE: I'm going right over and talk with Krogstad.

345   NORA: Don't go near him; he'll do you some terrible harm!

MRS. LINDE: There was a time once when he'd gladly have done anything for me.

NORA: He?

MRS. LINDE: Where does he live?

NORA: Oh, how do I know? Yes. (*Searches in her pocket.*) Here's his card. But the letter, the letter—!

HELMER: (*from the study, knocking on the door*) Nora!   350

NORA: (*with a cry of fear*) Oh! What is it? What do you want?

HELMER: Now, now, don't be so frightened. We're not coming in. You locked the door—are you trying on the dress?

NORA: Yes, I'm trying it. I'll look just beautiful, Torvald.

MRS. LINDE: (*who has read the card*) He's living right around the corner.

NORA: Yes, but what's the use? We're lost. The letter's in the box.   355

MRS. LINDE: And your husband has the key?

NORA: Yes, always.

MRS. LINDE: Krogstad can ask for his letter back unread; he can find some excuse—

NORA: But it's just this time that Torvald usually—

MRS. LINDE: Stall him. Keep him in there. I'll be back as quick as I can. (*She hurries* 360
out through the hall entrance.*)

NORA: (*goes to Helmer's door, opens it, and peers in*) Torvald!

HELMER: (*from the inner study*) Well—does one dare set foot in one's own living room at last? Come on, Rank, now we'll get a look—(*In the doorway.*) But what's this?

NORA: What, Torvald dear?

HELMER: Rank had me expecting some grand masquerade.

RANK: (*in the doorway*) That was my impression, but I must have been wrong.   365

NORA: No one can admire me in my splendor—not till tomorrow.

HELMER: But Nora dear, you look so exhausted. Have you practiced too hard?

NORA: No, I haven't practiced at all yet.

HELMER: You know, it's necessary—

NORA: Oh, it's absolutely necessary, Torvald. But I can't get anywhere without your   370
help. I've forgotten the whole thing completely.

HELMER: Ah, we'll soon take care of that.

NORA: Yes, take care of me, Torvald, please! Promise me that? Oh, I'm so nervous. That big party—You must give up everything this evening for me. No business— don't even touch your pen. Yes? Dear Torvald, promise?

HELMER: It's a promise. Tonight I'm totally at your service—you little helpless thing. Hm—but first there's one thing I want to—(*Goes toward the hall door.*)

NORA: What are you looking for?

HELMER: Just to see if there's any mail.   375

NORA: No, no, don't do that, Torvald!

HELMER: Now what?

NORA: Torvald, please. There isn't any.

HELMER: Let me look, though. (*Starts out. Nora, at the piano, strikes the first notes of the tarantella. Helmer, at the door, stops.*) Aha!

NORA: I can't dance tomorrow if I don't practice with you.   380

HELMER: (*going over to her*) Nora dear, are you really so frightened?

NORA: Yes, so terribly frightened. Let me practice right now; there's still time before dinner. Oh, sit down and play for me, Torvald. Direct me. Teach me, the way you always have.

HELMER: Gladly, if it's what you want. (*Sits at the piano.*)

NORA: (*snatches the tambourine up from the box, then a long, varicolored shawl, which she throws around herself, whereupon she springs forward and cries out*) Play for me now! Now I'll dance!

Helmer plays and Nora dances. Rank stands behind Helmer at the piano and looks on.

385 HELMER: (*as he plays*) Slower. Slow down.

NORA: Can't change it.

HELMER: Not so violent, Nora!

NORA: Has to be just like this.

HELMER: (*stopping*) No, no, that won't do at all.

390 NORA: (*laughing and swinging her tambourine*) Isn't that what I told you?

RANK: Let me play for her.

HELMER: (*getting up*) Yes, go on. I can teach her more easily then.

Rank sits at the piano and plays; Nora dances more and more wildly. Helmer has stationed himself by the stove and repeatedly gives her directions; she seems not to hear them; her hair loosens and falls over her shoulders; she does not notice, but goes on dancing. Mrs. Linde enters.

MRS. LINDE: (*standing dumbfounded at the door*) Ah—!

NORA: (*still dancing*) See what fun, Kristine!

395 HELMER: But Nora darling, you dance as if your life were at stake.

NORA: And it is.

HELMER: Rank, stop! This is pure madness. Stop it, I say!

Rank breaks off playing, and Nora halts abruptly.

HELMER: (*going over to her*) I never would have believed it. You've forgotten everything I taught you.

NORA: (*throwing away the tambourine*) You see for yourself.

400 HELMER: Well, there's certainly room for instruction here.

NORA: Yes, you see how important it is. You've got to teach me to the very last minute. Promise me that, Torvald?

HELMER: You can bet on it.

NORA: You mustn't, either today or tomorrow, think about anything else but me; you mustn't open any letters—or the mailbox—

HELMER: Ah, it's still the fear of that man—

405 NORA: Oh yes, yes, that too.

HELMER: Nora, it's written all over you—there's already a letter from him out there.

NORA: I don't know. I guess so. But you mustn't read such things now; there mustn't be anything ugly between us before it's all over.

RANK: (*quietly to Helmer*) You shouldn't deny her.

HELMER: (*putting his arm around her*) The child can have her way. But tomorrow night, after you've danced—

NORA: Then you'll be free.   410

MAID: *(in the doorway, right)* Ma'am, dinner is served.

NORA: We'll be wanting champagne, Helene.

MAID: Very good, ma'am. *(Goes out.)*

HELMER: So—a regular banquet, hm?

NORA: Yes, a banquet—champagne till daybreak! *(Calling out.)* And some macaroons,   415
    Helene. Heaps of them—just this once.

HELMER: *(taking her hands)* Now, now, now—no hysterics. Be my own little lark again.

NORA: Oh, I will soon enough. But go on in—and you, Dr. Rank. Kristine, help me
    put up my hair.

RANK: *(whispering, as they go)* There's nothing wrong—really wrong, is there?

HELMER: Oh, of course not. It's nothing more than this childish anxiety I was telling
    you about. *(They go out, right.)*

NORA: Well?   420

MRS. LINDE: Left town.

NORA: I could see by your face.

MRS. LINDE: He'll be home tomorrow evening. I wrote him a note.

NORA: You shouldn't have. Don't try to stop anything now. After all, it's a wonder-
    ful joy, this waiting here for the miracle.

MRS. LINDE: What is it you're waiting for?   425

NORA: Oh, you can't understand that. Go in to them: I'll be along in a moment.

*Mrs. Linde goes into the dining room. Nora stands a short while as if composing herself; then
she looks at her watch.*

NORA: Five. Seven hours to midnight. Twenty-four hours to the midnight after, and
    then the tarantella's done. Seven and twenty-four? Thirty-one hours to live.

HELMER: *(in the doorway, right)* What's become of the little lark?

NORA: *(going toward him with open arms)* Here's your lark!

ACT 3

*Same scene. The table, with chairs around it, has been moved to the center of the room. A
lamp on the table is lit. The hall door stands open. Dance music drifts down from the floor
above. Mrs. Linde sits at the table, absently paging through a book, trying to read, but apparently unable to focus her thoughts. Once or twice she pauses, tensely listening for a sound
at the outer entrance.*

MRS. LINDE: *(glancing at her watch)* Not yet—and there's hardly any time left. If
    only he's not—(*Listening again.*) Ah, there he is. *(She goes out in the hall and
    cautiously opens the outer door. Quiet footsteps are heard on the stairs. She whispers:)*
    Come in. Nobody's here.

KROGSTAD: *(in the doorway)* I found a note from you at home. What's back of all this?

MRS. LINDE: I just *had* to talk to you.

KROGSTAD: Oh? And it just *had* to be here in this house?

MRS. LINDE: At my place it was impossible; my room hasn't a private entrance.   5
    Come in; we're all alone. The maid's asleep, and the Helmers are at the
    dance upstairs.

KROGSTAD: (*entering the room*) Well, well, the Helmers are dancing tonight? Really?

MRS. LINDE: Yes, why not?

KROGSTAD: How true—why not?

MRS. LINDE: All right, Krogstad, let's talk.

10 KROGSTAD: Do we two have anything more to talk about?

MRS. LINDE: We have a great deal to talk about.

KROGSTAD: I wouldn't have thought so.

MRS. LINDE: No, because you've never understood me, really.

KROGSTAD: Was there anything more to understand—except what's all too common in life? A calculating woman throws over a man the moment a better catch comes by.

15 MRS. LINDE: You think I'm so thoroughly calculating? You think I broke it off lightly?

KROGSTAD: Didn't you?

MRS. LINDE: Nils—is that what you really thought?

KROGSTAD: If you cared, then why did you write me the way you did?

MRS. LINDE: What else could I do? If I had to break off with you, then it was my job as well to root out everything you felt for me.

20 KROGSTAD: (*wringing his hands*) So that was it. And this—all this, simply for money!

MRS. LINDE: Don't forget I had a helpless mother and two small brothers. We couldn't wait for you, Nils; you had such a long road ahead of you then.

KROGSTAD: That may be; but you still hadn't the right to abandon me for somebody else's sake.

MRS. LINDE: Yes—I don't know. So many, many times I've asked myself if I did have that right.

KROGSTAD: (*more softly*) When I lost you, it was as if all the solid ground dissolved from under my feet. Look at me; I'm a half-drowned man now, hanging onto a wreck.

25 MRS. LINDE: Help may be near.

KROGSTAD: It was near—but then you came and blocked it off.

MRS. LINDE: Without my knowing it, Nils. Today for the first time I learned that it's you I'm replacing at the bank.

KROGSTAD: All right—I believe you. But now that you know, will you step aside?

MRS. LINDE: No, because that wouldn't benefit you in the slightest.

30 KROGSTAD: Not "benefit" me, hm! I'd step aside anyway.

MRS. LINDE: I've learned to be realistic. Life and hard, bitter necessity have taught me that.

KROGSTAD: And life's taught me never to trust fine phrases.

MRS. LINDE: Then life's taught you a very sound thing. But you do have to trust in actions, don't you?

KROGSTAD: What does that mean?

35 MRS. LINDE: You said you were hanging on like a half-drowned man to a wreck.

KROGSTAD: I've good reason to say that.

MRS. LINDE: I'm also like a half-drowned woman on a wreck. No one to suffer with; no one to care for.

KROGSTAD: You made your choice.

MRS. LINDE: There wasn't any choice then.

KROGSTAD: So—what of it?   40

MRS. LINDE: Nils, if only we two shipwrecked people could reach across to each other.

KROGSTAD: What are you saying?

MRS. LINDE: Two on one wreck are at least better off than each on his own.

KROGSTAD: Kristine!

MRS. LINDE: Why do you think I came into town?   45

KROGSTAD: Did you really have some thought of me?

MRS. LINDE: I have to work to go on living. All my born days, as long as I can remember, I've worked, and it's been my best and my only joy. But now I'm completely alone in the world; it frightens me to be so empty and lost. To work for yourself—there's no joy in that. Nils, give me something—someone to work for.

KROGSTAD: I don't believe all this. It's just some hysterical feminine urge to go out and make a noble sacrifice.

MRS. LINDE: Have you ever found me to be hysterical?

KROGSTAD: Can you honestly mean this? Tell me—do you know everything about   50
my past?

MRS. LINDE: Yes.

KROGSTAD: And you know what they think I'm worth around here.

MRS. LINDE: From what you were saying before, it would seem that with me you could have been another person.

KROGSTAD: I'm positive of that.

MRS. LINDE: Couldn't it happen still?   55

KROGSTAD: Kristine—you're saying this in all seriousness? Yes, you are! I can see it in you. And do you really have the courage, then—?

MRS. LINDE: I need to have someone to care for; and your children need a mother. We both need each other. Nils, I have faith that you're good at heart—I'll risk everything together with you.

KROGSTAD: *(gripping her hands)* Kristine, thank you, thank you—Now I know I can win back a place in their eyes. Yes—but I forgot—

MRS. LINDE: *(listening)* Shh! The tarantella. Go now! Go on!

KROGSTAD: Why? What is it?   60

MRS. LINDE: Hear the dance up there? When that's over, they'll be coming down.

KROGSTAD: Oh, then I'll go. But—it's all pointless. Of course, you don't know the move I made against the Helmers.

MRS. LINDE: Yes, Nils, I know.

KROGSTAD: And all the same, you have the courage to—?

MRS. LINDE: I know how far despair can drive a man like you.   65

KROGSTAD: Oh, if I only could take it all back.

MRS. LINDE: You easily could—your letter's still lying in the mailbox.

KROGSTAD: Are you sure of that?

MRS. LINDE: Positive. But—

KROGSTAD: *(looks at her searchingly)* Is that the meaning of it, then? You'll save your   70
friend at any price. Tell me straight out. Is that it?

MRS. LINDE: Nils—anyone who's sold herself for somebody else once isn't going to do it again.

KROGSTAD: I'll demand my letter back.

MRS. LINDE: No, no.

KROGSTAD: Yes, of course. I'll stay here till Helmer comes down; I'll tell him to give me my letter again—that it only involves my dismissal—that he shouldn't read it—

75   MRS. LINDE: No, Nils, don't call the letter back.

KROGSTAD: But wasn't that exactly why you wrote me to come here?

MRS. LINDE: Yes, in that first panic. But it's been a whole day and night since then, and in that time I've seen such incredible things in this house. Helmer's got to learn everything; this dreadful secret has to be aired; those two have to come to a full understanding; all these lies and evasions can't go on.

KROGSTAD: Well, then, if you want to chance it. But at least there's one thing I can do, and do right away—

MRS. LINDE: (listening) Go now, go, quick! The dance is over. We're not safe another second.

80   KROGSTAD: I'll wait for you downstairs.

MRS. LINDE: Yes, please do; take me home.

KROGSTAD: I can't believe it; I've never been so happy. (He leaves by way of the outer door; the door between the room and the hall stays open.)

MRS. LINDE: (straightening up a bit and getting together her street clothes) How different now! How different! Someone to work for, to live for—a home to build. Well, it is worth the try! Oh, if they'd only come! (Listening.) Ah, there they are. Bundle up. (She picks up her hat and coat. Nora's and Helmer's voices can be heard outside; a key turns in the lock, and Helmer brings Nora into the hall almost by force. She is wearing the Italian costume with a large black shawl about her; he has on evening dress, with a black domino open over it.)

NORA: (struggling in the doorway) No, no, no, not inside! I'm going up again. I don't want to leave so soon.

85   HELMER: But Nora dear—

NORA: Oh, I beg you, please, Torvald. From the bottom of my heart, please—only an hour more!

HELMER: Not a single minute, Nora darling. You know our agreement. Come on, in we go; you'll catch cold out here. (In spite of her resistance, he gently draws her into the room.)

MRS. LINDE: Good evening.

NORA: Kristine!

90   HELMER: Why, Mrs. Linde—are you here so late?

MRS. LINDE: Yes, I'm sorry, but I did want to see Nora in costume.

NORA: Have you been sitting here, waiting for me?

MRS. LINDE: Yes. I didn't come early enough; you were all upstairs; and then I thought I really couldn't leave without seeing you.

HELMER: (removing Nora's shawl) Yes, take a good look. She's worth looking at, I can tell you that, Mrs. Linde. Isn't she lovely?

95   MRS. LINDE: Yes, I should say—

HELMER: A dream of loveliness, isn't she? That's what everyone thought at the party, too. But she's horribly stubborn—this sweet little thing. What's to be done with her? Can you imagine, I almost had to use force to pry her away.

NORA: Oh, Torvald, you're going to regret you didn't indulge me, even for just a half hour more.

HELMER: There, you see. She danced her tarantella and got a tumultuous hand—which was well earned, although the performance may have been a bit too naturalistic—I mean it rather overstepped the proprieties of art. But never mind—what's important is, she made a success, an overwhelming success. You think I could let her stay on after that and spoil the effect? Oh no; I took my lovely little Capri girl—my capricious little Capri girl, I should say—took her under my arm; one quick tour of the ballroom, a curtsy to every side, and then—as they say in novels—the beautiful vision disappeared. An exit should always be effective, Mrs. Linde, but that's what I can't get Nora to grasp. Phew, it's hot in here. (*Flings the domino on a chair and opens the door to his room.*) Why's it dark in here? Oh yes, of course. Excuse me. (*He goes in and lights a couple of candles.*)

NORA: (*in a sharp, breathless whisper*) So?

MRS. LINDE: (*quietly*) I talked with him.   100

NORA: And—?

MRS. LINDE: Nora—you must tell your husband everything.

NORA: (*dully*) I knew it.

MRS. LINDE: You've got nothing to fear from Krogstad, but you have to speak out.

NORA: I won't tell.   105

MRS. LINDE: Then the letter will.

NORA: Thanks, Kristine. I know now what's to be done. Shh!

HELMER: (*reentering*) Well, then, Mrs. Linde—have you admired her?

MRS. LINDE: Yes, and now I'll say good night.

HELMER: Oh, come, so soon? Is this yours, this knitting?   110

MRS. LINDE: Yes, thanks. I nearly forgot it.

HELMER: Do you knit, then?

MRS. LINDE: Oh yes.

HELMER: You know what? You should embroider instead.

MRS. LINDE: Really? Why?   115

HELMER: Yes, because it's a lot prettier. See here, one holds the embroidery so, in the left hand, and then one guides the needle with the right—so—in an easy, sweeping curve—right?

MRS. LINDE: Yes, I guess that's—

HELMER: But, on the other hand, knitting—it can never be anything but ugly. Look, see here, the arms tucked in, the knitting needles going up and down—there's something Chinese about it. Ah, that was really a glorious champagne they served.

MRS. LINDE: Yes, good night, Nora, and don't be stubborn any more.

HELMER: Well put, Mrs. Linde!   120

MRS. LINDE: Good night, Mr. Helmer.

HELMER: (*accompanying her to the door*) Good night, good night. I hope you get home all right. I'd be very happy to—but you don't have far to go. Good night, good night. (*She leaves. He shuts the door after her and returns.*) There, now, at last we got her out the door. She's a deadly bore, that creature.

NORA: Aren't you pretty tired, Torvald?

HELMER: No, not a bit.

125 NORA: You're not sleepy?

HELMER: Not at all. On the contrary, I'm feeling quite exhilarated. But you? Yes, you really look tired and sleepy.

NORA: Yes, I'm very tired. Soon now I'll sleep.

HELMER: See! You see! I was right all along that we shouldn't stay longer.

NORA: Whatever you do is always right.

130 HELMER: (*kissing her brow*) Now my little lark talks sense. Say, did you notice what a time Rank was having tonight?

NORA: Oh, was he? I didn't get to speak with him.

HELMER: I scarcely did either, but it's a long time since I've seen him in such high spirits. (*Gazes at her a moment, then comes nearer her.*) Hm—it's marvelous, though, to be back home again—to be completely alone with you. Oh, you bewitchingly lovely young woman!

NORA: Torvald, don't look at me like that!

HELMER: Can't I look at my richest treasure? At all that beauty that's mine, mine alone—completely and utterly.

135 NORA: (*moving around to the other side of the table*) You mustn't talk to me that way tonight.

HELMER: (*following her*) The tarantella is still in your blood, I can see—and it makes you even more enticing. Listen. The guests are beginning to go. (*Dropping his voice.*) Nora—it'll soon be quiet through this whole house.

NORA: Yes, I hope so.

HELMER: You do, don't you, my love? Do you realize—when I'm out at a party like this with you—do you know why I talk to you so little, and keep such a distance away; just send you a stolen look now and then—you know why I do it? It's because I'm imagining then that you're my secret darling, my secret young bride-to-be, and that no one suspects there's anything between us.

NORA: Yes, yes; oh, yes, I know you're always thinking of me.

140 HELMER: And then when we leave and I place the shawl over those fine young rounded shoulders—over that wonderful curving neck—then I pretend that you're my young bride, that we're just coming from the wedding, that for the first time I'm bringing you into my house—that for the first time I'm alone with you—completely alone with you, your trembling young beauty! All this evening I've longed for nothing but you. When I saw you turn and sway in the tarantella—my blood was pounding till I couldn't stand it—that's why I brought you down here so early—

NORA: Go away, Torvald! Leave me alone. I don't want all this.

HELMER: What do you mean? Nora, you're teasing me. You will, won't you? Aren't I your husband—?

A knock at the outside door.

NORA: (*startled*) What's that?

HELMER: (*going toward the hall*) Who is it?

RANK: (*outside*) It's me. May I come in a moment?   145

HELMER: (*with quiet irritation*) Oh, what does he want now? (*Aloud.*) Hold on. (*Goes and opens the door.*) Oh, how nice that you didn't just pass us by!

RANK: I thought I heard your voice, and then I wanted so badly to have a look in. (*Lightly glancing about.*) Ah, me, these old familiar haunts. You have it snug and cozy in here, you two.

HELMER: You seemed to be having it pretty cozy upstairs, too.

RANK: Absolutely. Why shouldn't I? Why not take in everything in life? As much as you can, anyway, and as long as you can. The wine was superb—

HELMER: The champagne especially.   150

RANK: You noticed that too? It's amazing how much I could guzzle down.

NORA: Torvald also drank a lot of champagne this evening.

RANK: Oh?

NORA: Yes, and that always makes him so entertaining.

RANK: Well, why shouldn't one have a pleasant evening after a well spent day?   155

HELMER: Well spent? I'm afraid I can't claim that.

RANK: (*slapping him on the back*) But I can, you see!

NORA: Dr. Rank, you must have done some scientific research today.

RANK: Quite so.

HELMER: Come now—little Nora talking about scientific research!   160

NORA: And can I congratulate you on the results?

RANK: Indeed you may.

NORA: Then they were good?

RANK: The best possible for both doctor and patient—certainty.

NORA: (*quickly and searchingly*) Certainty?   165

RANK: Complete certainty. So don't I owe myself a gay evening afterwards?

NORA: Yes, you're right, Dr. Rank.

HELMER: I'm with you—just so long as you don't have to suffer for it in the morning.

RANK: Well, one never gets something for nothing in life.

NORA: Dr. Rank—are you very fond of masquerade parties?   170

RANK: Yes, if there's a good array of odd disguises—

NORA: Tell me, what should we two go as at the next masquerade?

HELMER: You little featherhead—already thinking of the next!

RANK: We two? I'll tell you what: you must go as Charmed Life—

HELMER: Yes, but find a costume for *that!*   175

RANK: Your wife can appear just as she looks every day.

HELMER: That was nicely put. But don't you know what you're going to be?

RANK: Yes, Helmer, I've made up my mind.

HELMER: Well?

RANK: At the next masquerade I'm going to be invisible.   180

HELMER: That's a funny idea.

RANK: They say there's a hat—black, huge—have you never heard of the hat that makes you invisible? You put it on, and then no one on earth can see you.

HELMER: (*suppressing a smile*) Ah, of course.

RANK: But I'm quite forgetting what I came for. Helmer, give me a cigar, one of the dark Havanas.

185 HELMER: With the greatest of pleasure. (*Holds out his case.*)

RANK: Thanks. (*Takes one and cuts off the tip.*)

NORA: (*striking a match*) Let me give you a light.

RANK: Thank you. (*She holds the match for him; he lights the cigar.*) And now good-bye.

HELMER: Good-bye, good-bye, old friend.

190 NORA: Sleep well, Doctor.

RANK: Thanks for that wish.

NORA: Wish me the same.

RANK: You? All right, if you like—Sleep well. And thanks for the light. (*He nods to them both and leaves.*)

HELMER: (*his voice subdued*) He's been drinking heavily.

195 NORA: (*absently*) Could be. (*Helmer takes his keys from his pocket and goes out in the hall.*) Torvald—what are you after?

HELMER: Got to empty the mailbox; it's nearly full. There won't be room for the morning papers.

NORA: Are you working tonight?

HELMER: You know I'm not. Why—what's this? Someone's been at the lock.

NORA: At the lock—?

200 HELMER: Yes, I'm positive. What do you suppose—? I can't imagine one of the maids—? Here's a broken hairpin. Nora, it's yours—

NORA: (*quickly*) Then it must be the children—

HELMER: You'd better break them of that. Hm, hm—well, opened it after all. (*Takes the contents out and calls into the kitchen.*) Helene! Helene, would you put out the lamp in the hall. (*He returns to the room, shutting the hall door, then displays the handful of mail.*) Look how it's piled up. (*Sorting through them.*) Now what's this?

NORA: (*at the window*) The letter! Oh, Torvald, no!

HELMER: Two calling cards—from Rank.

205 NORA: From Dr. Rank?

HELMER: (*examining them*) "Dr. Rank, Consulting Physician." They were on top. He must have dropped them in as he left.

NORA: Is there anything on them?

HELMER: There's a black cross over the name. See? That's a gruesome notion. He could almost be announcing his own death.

NORA: That's just what he's doing.

210 HELMER: What! You've heard something? Something he's told you?

NORA: Yes. That when those cards came, he'd be taking his leave of us. He'll shut himself in now and die.

HELMER: Ah, my poor friend! Of course I knew he wouldn't be here much longer. But so soon—And then to hide himself away like a wounded animal.

NORA: If it has to happen, then it's best it happens in silence—don't you think so, Torvald?

HELMER: (*pacing up and down*) He'd grown right into our lives. I simply can't imagine him gone. He with his suffering and loneliness—like a dark cloud setting off our sunlit happiness. Well, maybe it's best this way. For him, at least. (*Standing still.*)

And maybe for us too, Nora. Now we're thrown back on each other, completely. (*Embracing her.*) Oh you, my darling wife, how can I hold you close enough? You know what, Nora—time and again I've wished you were in some terrible danger, just so I could stake my life and soul and everything, for your sake.

NORA: (*tearing herself away, her voice firm and decisive*) Now you must read your   215
mail, Torvald.

HELMER: No, no, not tonight. I want to stay with you, dearest.

NORA: With a dying friend on your mind?

HELMER: You're right. We've both had a shock. There's ugliness between us—these thoughts of death and corruption. We'll have to get free of them first. Until then—we'll stay apart.

NORA: (*clinging about his neck*) Torvald—good night! Good night!

HELMER: (*kissing her on the cheek*) Good night, little songbird. Sleep well, Nora.   220
I'll be reading my mail now. (*He takes the letters into his room and shuts the door after him.*)

NORA: (*with bewildered glances, groping about, seizing Helmer's domino, throwing it around her, and speaking in short, hoarse, broken whispers*) Never see him again. Never, never. (*Putting her shawl over her head.*) Never see the children either—them, too. Never, never. Oh, the freezing black water! The depths—down—Oh, I wish it were over—He has it now; he's reading it—now. Oh no, no, not yet. Torvald, good-bye, you and the children—(*She starts for the hall; as she does, Helmer throws open his door and stands with an open letter in his hand.*)

HELMER: Nora!

NORA: (*screams*) Oh—!

HELMER: What is this? You know what's in this letter?

NORA: Yes, I know. Let me go! Let me out!   225

HELMER: (*holding her back*) Where are you going?

NORA: (*struggling to break loose*) You can't save me, Torvald!

HELMER: (*slumping back*) True! Then it's true what he writes? How horrible! No, no, it's impossible—it can't be true.

NORA: It *is* true. I've loved you more than all this world.

HELMER: Ah, none of your slippery tricks.   230

NORA: (*taking one step toward him*) Torvald—!

HELMER: What *is* this you've blundered into!

NORA: Just let me loose. You're not going to suffer for my sake. You're not going to take on my guilt.

HELMER: No more playacting. (*Locks the hall door.*) You stay right here and give me a reckoning. You understand what you've done? Answer! You understand?

NORA: (*looking squarely at him, her face hardening*) Yes. I'm beginning to understand   235
everything now.

HELMER: (*striding about*) Oh, what an awful awakening! In all these eight years—she who was my pride and joy—a hypocrite, a liar—worse, worse—a criminal! How infinitely disgusting it all is! The shame! (*Nora says nothing and goes on looking straight at him. He stops in front of her.*) I should have suspected something of the kind. I should have known. All your father's flimsy values—Be still! All your father's flimsy values have come out in you. No religion, no morals, no sense of duty—Oh, how I'm punished for letting him off! I did it for your sake, and you repay me like this.

NORA: Yes, like this.

HELMER: Now you've wrecked all my happiness—ruined my whole future. Oh, it's awful to think of. I'm in a cheap little grafter's hands; he can do anything he wants with me, ask for anything, play with me like a puppet—and I can't breathe a word. I'll be swept down miserably into the depths on account of a featherbrained woman.

NORA: When I'm gone from this world, you'll be free.

240 HELMER: Oh, quit posing. Your father had a mess of those speeches too. What good would that ever do me if you were gone from this world, as you say? Not the slightest. He can still make the whole thing known; and if he does, I could be falsely suspected as your accomplice. They might even think that I was behind it—that I put you up to it. And all that I can thank you for—you that I've coddled the whole of our marriage. Can you see now what you've done to me?

NORA: (icily calm) Yes.

HELMER: It's so incredible, I just can't grasp it. But we'll have to patch up whatever we can. Take off the shawl. I said, take if off! I've got to appease him somehow or other. The thing has to be hushed up at any cost. And as for you and me, it's got to seem like everything between us is just as it was—to the outside world, that is. You'll go right on living in this house, of course. But you can't be allowed to bring up the children; I don't dare trust you with them—Oh, to have to say this to someone I've loved so much! Well, that's done with. From now on happiness doesn't matter; all that matters is saving the bits and pieces, the appearance—(*The doorbell rings. Helmer starts.*) What's that? And so late. Maybe the worst—? You think he'd—? Hide, Nora! Say you're sick. (*Nora remains standing motionless. Helmer goes and opens the door.*)

MAID: (*half dressed, in the hall*) A letter for Mrs. Helmer.

HELMER: I'll take it. (*Snatches the letter and shuts the door.*) Yes, it's from him. You don't get it; I'm reading it myself.

245 NORA: Then read it.

HELMER: (*by the lamp*) I hardly dare. We may be ruined, you and I. But—I've got to know. (*Rips open the letter, skims through a few lines, glances at an enclosure, then cries out joyfully.*) Nora! (*Nora looks inquiringly at him.*) Nora! Wait—better check it again—Yes, yes, it's true. I'm saved. Nora, I'm saved!

NORA: And I?

HELMER: You too, of course. We're both saved, both of us. Look. He's sent back your note. He says he's sorry and ashamed—that a happy development in his life—oh, who cares what he says! Nora, we're saved! No one can hurt you. Oh, Nora, Nora—but first, this ugliness all has to go. Let me see—(*Takes a look at the note.*) No, I don't want to see it; I want the whole thing to fade like a dream. (*Tears the note and both letters to pieces, throws them into the stove and watches them burn.*) There—now there's nothing left—He wrote that since Christmas Eve you—Oh, they must have been three terrible days for you, Nora.

NORA: I fought a hard fight.

250 HELMER: And suffered pain and saw no escape but—No, we're not going to dwell on anything unpleasant. We'll just be grateful and keep on repeating: it's over

now, it's over! You hear me, Nora? You don't seem to realize—it's over. What's
it mean—that frozen look? Oh, poor little Nora, I understand. You can't believe
I've forgiven you. But I have, Nora; I swear I have. I know that what you did,
you did out of love for me.

NORA: That's true.

HELMER: You loved me the way a wife ought to love her husband. It's simply the
means that you couldn't judge. But you think I love you any the less for not
knowing how to handle your affairs? No, no—just lean on me; I'll guide you and
teach you. I wouldn't be a man if this feminine helplessness didn't make you
twice as attractive to me. You mustn't mind those sharp words I said—that was
all in the first confusion of thinking my world had collapsed. I've forgiven you,
Nora; I swear I've forgiven you.

NORA: My thanks for your forgiveness. (*She goes out through the door, right.*)

HELMER: No, wait—(*Peers in.*) What are you doing in there?

NORA: (*inside*) Getting out of my costume.   255

HELMER: (*by the open door*) Yes, do that. Try to calm yourself and collect your
thoughts again, my frightened little songbird. You can rest easy now; I've got
wide wings to shelter you with. (*Walking about close by the door.*) How snug and
nice our home is, Nora. You're safe here; I'll keep you like a hunted dove I've
rescued out of a hawk's claws. I'll bring peace to your poor, shuddering heart.
Gradually it'll happen, Nora; you'll see. Tomorrow all this will look different to
you; then everything will be as it was. I won't have to go on repeating I forgive
you; you'll feel it for yourself. How can you imagine I'd ever conceivably want
to disown you—or even blame you in any way? Ah, you don't know a man's
heart, Nora. For a man there's something indescribably sweet and satisfying in
knowing he's forgiven his wife—and forgiven her out of a full and open heart.
It's as if she belongs to him in two ways now: in a sense he's given her fresh
into the world again, and she's become his wife and his child as well. From now
on that's what you'll be to me—you little, bewildered, helpless thing. Don't be
afraid of anything, Nora; just open your heart to me, and I'll be conscience and
will to you both—(*Nora enters in her regular clothes.*) What's this? Not in bed?
You've changed your dress?

NORA: Yes, Torvald, I've changed my dress.

HELMER: But why now, so late?

NORA: Tonight I'm not sleeping.

HELMER: But Nora dear—   260

NORA: (*looking at her watch*) It's still not so very late. Sit down, Torvald; we have a
lot to talk over. (*She sits at one side of the table.*)

HELMER: Nora—what is this? That hard expression—

NORA: Sit down. This'll take some time. I have a lot to say.

HELMER: (*sitting at the table directly opposite her*) You worry me, Nora. And I don't
understand you.

NORA: No, that's exactly it. You don't understand me. And I've never understood   265
you either—until tonight. No, don't interrupt. You can just listen to what I say.
We're closing out accounts, Torvald.

HELMER: How do you mean that?

NORA: (*after a short pause*) Doesn't anything strike you about our sitting here like this?

HELMER: What's that?

NORA: We've been married now eight years. Doesn't it occur to you that this is the first time we two, you and I, man and wife, have ever talked seriously together?

270 HELMER: What do you mean—seriously?

NORA: In eight whole years—longer even—right from our first acquaintance, we've never exchanged a serious word on any serious thing.

HELMER: You mean I should constantly go and involve you in problems you couldn't possibly help me with?

NORA: I'm not talking of problems. I'm saying that we've never sat down seriously together and tried to get to the bottom of anything.

HELMER: But dearest, what good would that ever do you?

275 NORA: That's the point right there: you've never understood me. I've been wronged greatly, Torvald—first by Papa, and then by you.

HELMER: What! By us—the two people who've loved you more than anyone else?

NORA: (shaking her head) You never loved me. You've thought it fun to be in love with me, that's all.

HELMER: Nora, what a thing to say!

NORA: Yes, it's true now, Torvald. When I lived at home with Papa, he told me all his opinions, so I had the same ones too; or if they were different I hid them, since he wouldn't have cared for that. He used to call me his doll-child, and he played with me the way I played with my dolls. Then I came into your house—

280 HELMER: How can you speak of our marriage like that?

NORA: (unperturbed) I mean, then I went from Papa's hands into yours. You arranged everything to your own taste, and so I got the same taste as you—or I pretended to; I can't remember. I guess a little of both, first one, then the other. Now when I look back, it seems as if I'd lived here like a beggar—just from hand to mouth. I've lived by doing tricks for you, Torvald. But that's the way you wanted it. It's a great sin what you and Papa did to me. You're to blame that nothing's become of me.

HELMER: Nora, how unfair and ungrateful you are! Haven't you been happy here?

NORA: No, never. I thought so—but I never have.

HELMER: Not—not happy!

285 NORA: No, only lighthearted. And you've always been so kind to me. But our home's been nothing but a playpen. I've been your doll-wife here, just as at home I was Papa's doll-child. And in turn the children have been my dolls. I thought it was fun when you played with me, just as they thought it fun when I played with them. That's been our marriage, Torvald.

HELMER: There's some truth in what you're saying—under all the raving exaggeration. But it'll all be different after this. Playtime's over; now for the schooling.

NORA: Whose schooling—mine or the children's?

HELMER: Both yours and the children's, dearest.

NORA: Oh, Torvald, you're not the man to teach me to be a good wife to you.

290 HELMER: And you can say that?

NORA: And I—how am I equipped to bring up children?

HELMER: Nora!

NORA: Didn't you say a moment ago that that was no job to trust me with?

HELMER: In a flare of temper! Why fasten on that?

NORA: Yes, but you were so very right. I'm not up to the job. There's another job   295
    I have to do first. I have to try to educate myself. You can't help me with that.
    I've got to do it alone. And that's why I'm leaving you now.

HELMER: *(jumping up)* What's that?

NORA: I have to stand completely alone, if I'm ever going to discover myself and
    the world out there. So I can't go on living with you.

HELMER: Nora, Nora!

NORA: I want to leave right away. Kristine should put me up for the night—

HELMER: You're insane! You've no right! I forbid you!   300

NORA: From here on, there's no use forbidding me anything. I'll take with me
    whatever is mine. I don't want a thing from you, either now or later.

HELMER: What kind of madness is this!

NORA: Tomorrow I'm going home—I mean, home where I came from. It'll be easier
    up there to find something to do.

HELMER: Oh, you blind, incompetent child!

NORA: I must learn to be competent, Torvald.   305

HELMER: Abandon your home, your husband, your children! And you're not even
    thinking what people will say.

NORA: I can't be concerned about that. I only know how essential this is.

HELMER: Oh, it's outrageous. So you'll run out like this on your most sacred vows.

NORA: What do you think are my most sacred vows?

HELMER: And I have to tell you that! Aren't they your duties to your husband and   310
    children?

NORA: I have other duties equally sacred.

HELMER: That isn't true. What duties are they?

NORA: Duties to myself.

HELMER: Before all else, you're a wife and a mother.

NORA: I don't believe in that any more. I believe that, before all else, I'm a human   315
    being, no less than you—or anyway, I ought to try to become one. I know the
    majority thinks you're right, Torvald, and plenty of books agree with you, too.
    But I can't go on believing what the majority says, or what's written in books.
    I have to think over these things myself and try to understand them.

HELMER: Why can't you understand your place in your own home? On a point like
    that, isn't there one everlasting guide you can turn to? Where's your religion?

NORA: Oh, Torvald, I'm really not sure what religion is.

HELMER: What—?

NORA: I only know what the minister said when I was confirmed. He told me reli-
    gion was this thing and that. When I get clear and away by myself, I'll go into
    that problem too. I'll see if what the minister said was right, or, in any case, if
    it's right for me.

HELMER: A young woman your age shouldn't talk like that. If religion can't move   320
    you, I can try to rouse your conscience. You do have some moral feeling? Or,
    tell me—has that gone too?

NORA: It's not easy to answer that, Torvald. I simply don't know. I'm all confused
    about these things. I just know I see them so differently from you. I find out, for

one thing, that the law's not at all what I'd thought—but I can't get it through
my head that the law is fair. A woman hasn't a right to protect her dying father
or save her husband's life! I can't believe that.

HELMER: You talk like a child. You don't know anything of the world you live in.

NORA: No, I don't. But now I'll begin to learn for myself. I'll try to discover who's
right, the world or I.

HELMER: Nora, you're sick; you've got a fever. I almost think you're out of your
head.

325 NORA: I've never felt more clearheaded and sure in my life.

HELMER: And—clearheaded and sure—you're leaving your husband and children?

NORA: Yes.

HELMER: Then there's only one possible reason.

NORA: What?

330 HELMER: You no longer love me.

NORA: No. That's exactly it.

HELMER: Nora! You can't be serious!

NORA: Oh, this is so hard, Torvald—you've been so kind to me always. But I can't
help it. I don't love you any more.

HELMER: (*struggling for composure*) Are you also clearheaded and sure about that?

335 NORA: Yes, completely. That's why I can't go on staying here.

HELMER: Can you tell me what I did to lose your love?

NORA: Yes, I can tell you. It was this evening when the miraculous thing didn't
come—then I knew you weren't the man I'd imagined.

HELMER: Be more explicit; I don't follow you.

NORA: I've waited now so patiently eight long years—for, my Lord, I know miracles
don't come every day. Then this crisis broke over me, and such a certainty filled
me: *now* the miraculous event would occur. While Krogstad's letter was lying
out there, I never for an instant dreamed that you could give in to his terms.
I was so utterly sure you'd say to him: go on, tell your tale to the whole wide
world. And when he'd done that—

340 HELMER: Yes, what then? When I'd delivered my own wife into shame and
disgrace—!

NORA: When he'd done that, I was so utterly sure that you'd step forward, take the
blame on yourself and say: I am the guilty one.

HELMER: Nora—!

NORA: You're thinking I'd never accept such a sacrifice from you? No, of course
not. But what good would my protests be against you? That was the miracle I
was waiting for, in terror and hope. And to stave that off, I would have taken
my life.

HELMER: I'd gladly work for you day and night, Nora—and take on pain and depri-
vation. But there's no one who gives up honor for love.

345 NORA: Millions of women have done just that.

HELMER: Oh, you think and talk like a silly child.

NORA: Perhaps. But you neither think nor talk like the man I could join myself to.
When your big fright was over—and it wasn't from any threat against me, only
for what might damage you—when all the danger was past, for you it was just as

if nothing had happened. I was exactly the same, your little lark, your doll, that you'd have to handle with double care now that I'd turned out so brittle and frail. (*Gets up.*) Torvald—in that instant it dawned on me that for eight years I've been living here with a stranger, and that I'd even conceived three children—oh, I can't stand the thought of it! I could tear myself to bits.

HELMER: (*heavily*) I see. There's a gulf that's opened between us—that's clear. Oh, but Nora, can't we bridge it somehow?

NORA: The way I am now, I'm no wife for you.

HELMER: I have the strength to make myself over.   350

NORA: Maybe—if your doll gets taken away.

HELMER: But to part! To part from you! No, Nora, no—I can't imagine it.

NORA: (*going out, right*) All the more reason why it has to be. (*She reenters with her coat and a small overnight bag, which she puts on a chair by the table.*)

HELMER: Nora, Nora, not now! Wait till tomorrow.

NORA: I can't spend the night in a strange man's room.   355

HELMER: But couldn't we live here like brother and sister—

NORA: You know very well how long that would last. (*Throws her shawl about her.*) Good-bye, Torvald. I won't look in on the children. I know they're in better hands than mine. The way I am now, I'm no use to them.

HELMER: But someday, Nora—someday—?

NORA: How can I tell? I haven't the least idea what'll become of me.

HELMER: But you're my wife, now and wherever you go.   360

NORA: Listen, Torvald—I've heard that when a wife deserts her husband's house just as I'm doing, then the law frees him from all responsibility. In any case, I'm freeing you from being responsible. Don't feel yourself bound, any more than I will. There has to be absolute freedom for us both. Here, take your ring back. Give me mine.

HELMER: That too?

NORA: That too.

HELMER: There it is.

NORA: Good. Well, now it's all over. I'm putting the keys here. The maids know all   365
about keeping up the house—better than I do. Tomorrow, after I've left town, Kristine will stop by to pack up everything that's mine from home. I'd like those things shipped up to me.

HELMER: Over! All over! Nora, won't you ever think about me?

NORA: I'm sure I'll think of you often, and about the children and the house here.

HELMER: May I write you?

NORA: No—never. You're not to do that.

HELMER: Oh, but let me send you—   370

NORA: Nothing. Nothing.

HELMER: Or help you if you need it.

NORA: No. I accept nothing from strangers.

HELMER: Nora—can I never be more than a stranger to you?

NORA: (*picking up the overnight bag*) Ah, Torvald—it would take the greatest miracle   375
of all—

HELMER: Tell me the greatest miracle!

NORA: You and I both would have to transform ourselves to the point that—Oh, Torvald, I've stopped believing in miracles.

HELMER: But I'll believe. Tell me! Transform ourselves to the point that—?

NORA: That our living together could be a true marriage. (*She goes out down the hall.*)

380 HELMER: (*sinks down on a chair by the door, face buried in his hands*) Nora! Nora! (*Looking about and rising.*) Empty. She's gone. (*A sudden hope leaps in him.*) The greatest miracle—?

From below, the sound of a door slamming shut.

*   *   *

Reading and Reacting

1. What is your attitude toward Nora at the beginning of the play? How does your attitude toward her change as the play progresses? What actions and lines of dialogue change your assessment of her?

2. List the key events that occurred before the start of the play. How do we learn of each event?

3. Explain the role of each of the following in advancing the play's action: the Christmas tree, the locked mailbox, the telegram Dr. Rank receives, Dr. Rank's calling cards.

4. In act 2, Torvald says, "Whatever comes, you'll see: when it really counts, I have strength and courage enough as a man to take on the whole weight myself." How does this statement influence Nora's subsequent actions?

5. Explain how each of the following foreshadows events that will occur later in the play: Torvald's comments about Krogstad's children (act 1); Torvald's attitude toward Nora's father (act 2); Krogstad's suggestions about suicide (act 2).

6. In addition to the play's main plot—which concerns the blackmail of Nora by Krogstad and her attempts to keep her crime secret from Torvald—the play contains several subplots. Some of them began to develop before the start of the play, and some unfold alongside the main plot. Identify these subplots. How do they advance the themes of survival, debt, sacrifice, and duty that run through the play?

7. Is Kristine Linde as much of a "modern woman" as Nora? Is she actually *more* of a modern woman? Is she essential to the play? How might the play be different without her?

8. **JOURNAL ENTRY** Do you see *A Doll House* as primarily about the struggle between the needs of the individual and the needs of society or about the conflict between women's roles in the family and in the larger society? Explain.

9. **CRITICAL PERSPECTIVE** Since its earliest performances, there has been much comment on the conclusion of *A Doll House*. Many viewers have found the play's ending unrealistically harsh. In fact, a famous German actress refused to play the scene as written because she insisted she would never leave her children. (Ibsen reluctantly rewrote the ending for her; in this version, Helmer forces Nora to the doorway of the children's bedroom, and she sinks to the floor as the curtain falls.) Moreover, many critics have found it hard to accept Nora's sudden transformation from, in the words of Elizabeth Hardwick in her essay "Ibsen's Women," "the girlish, charming wife to the radical, courageous heroine setting out alone."

What is your response to the play's ending? Do you think it makes sense in light of what we have learned about Nora and her marriage? Or, do you agree with Hardwick that Nora's abandonment of her children is not only implausible but also a "rather casual" gesture that "drops a stain on our admiration of Nora"?

Related Works: "The Story of an Hour" (p. 201), "The Yellow Wallpaper" (p. 379), "The Rocking-Horse Winner" (p. 484), "The Chrysanthemums" (p. 631), "Marks" (p. 1008)

WRITING SUGGESTIONS: Plot

1. Central to the plot of *A Doll House* is a woman who commits a crime. Compare and contrast the desperate situation that motivates Nora with the situation faced by Mrs. Hale in *Trifles* (p. 1604). Then, consider the reactions of other characters in the two plays to each woman's crime. If you like, you may also discuss the crime committed by Emily Grierson in "A Rose for Emily" (p. 224).
2. In *The Blizzard*, the action unfolds in a confined, isolated space. Consider this play alongside some other works in which one or more characters are similarly confined—for example, the two people in the car in "Encounters with Unexpected Animals" (p. 132) or the people waiting for jury duty in *Nine Ten* (p. 1108). How does the confined setting influence the characters' actions and reactions?
3. Write an essay in which you compare the influence of Nora's father on the plot of *A Doll House* with the influence of Catherine's father on the plot of *Proof* (p. 1180).
4. Write a monologue for Nora in *A Doll House*, including everything you think she would like to tell her children.
5. Write a play called *Nine Twelve*. Keep all the major characters of *Nine Ten*, but put them together on September 12 in another setting, where they discuss what happened to them since they last met and how their attitudes toward jury duty, work, and life in general have changed as a result.

CHAPTER 38

CHARACTER

Paul Dooley
s_bukley/Shutterstock

Winnie Holzman
Everett Collection Inc/Alamy

David Auburn
AP Images

Arthur Miller
AP Images

William Shakespeare
Bettmann/Corbis

In Tennessee Williams's 1945 play *The Glass Menagerie*, the protagonist, Tom Wingfield, functions as the play's narrator. Stepping out of his role as a character and speaking directly to the audience, he directs the play's action, music, lighting, and other elements. In addition, he summarizes characters' actions, explains what motivates them, and discusses the significance of their behavior in the context of the play—commenting on his own character's actions as well. As narrator, Tom also presents useful background information about the characters. For instance, when he introduces his coworker, Jim, he prepares the audience for Jim's entrance and helps them to understand his subsequent actions:

> In high school Jim was a hero. He had tremendous Irish good nature and vitality with the scrubbed and polished look of white chinaware. He seemed to move in a continual spotlight. . . . But Jim apparently ran into more interference after his graduation. . . . His speed had definitely slowed. Six years after he left high school he was holding a job that wasn't much better than mine. (scene 6)

Most plays, however, do not include narrators who present background. Instead, the audience learns about characters from their own words and from comments by others about them, as well as from the characters' actions. When reading a play, we learn about the characters from the playwright's stage directions; when watching a performance, we gain insight into characters from the way actors interpret them.

Characters in plays, like characters in novels and short stories, may be **round** or **flat**, **static** or **dynamic**. Generally speaking, major characters are likely to be round, whereas minor characters are likely to be flat. Through the language and the actions of the characters, audiences learn whether the characters are multidimensional, skimpily developed, or perhaps merely **foils**, players whose main purpose is to shed light on more important characters. Audiences also learn about the emotions, attitudes, and values that help to shape the characters—their hopes and fears, their strengths and weaknesses. In addition, by comparing characters' early words and actions with later ones, audiences learn whether characters grow and change emotionally.

Characters' Words

Characters' words reveal the most about their attitudes, feelings, beliefs, and values. Sometimes information is communicated (to other characters as well as to the audience) in a **monologue**—an extended speech by one character. A **soliloquy**—a monologue revealing a character's thoughts and feelings, directed at the audience and presumed not to be heard by other characters—can also convey information about a character. For example, Hamlet's well-known soliloquy that begins "To be or not to be" eloquently communicates his distraught mental state—his resentment of his mother and uncle, his confusion about what course of action to take, and his suicidal thoughts. Finally, **dialogue**—an exchange of words between two characters—can reveal misunderstanding or conflict between them, or it can show their agreement, mutual support, or similar beliefs.

In Henrik Ibsen's *A Doll House* (p. 1113), dialogue reveals a good deal about the characters. Nora Helmer, the spoiled young wife, has broken the law and kept her crime secret from her husband. Through her words, we learn about her motivation, her values, her emotions, and her reactions to other characters and to her potentially dangerous situation. We learn, for instance, that she is flirtatious: "If your little squirrel begged you, with all her heart and soul . . ." We also see that she is childishly unrealistic about the consequences of her actions. When her husband, Torvald, asks what she would do if he was seriously injured, leaving her in debt, she says, "If anything so awful happened, then it just wouldn't matter if I had debts or not." When Torvald presses, "Well, but the people I'd borrowed from?" she dismisses them: "Them? Who cares about them! They're strangers." As the play progresses, Nora's lack of understanding of the power of the law becomes more and more significant as she struggles with her moral and ethical dilemma.

The inability of both Nora and Torvald to confront ugly truths is also revealed through their words. When, in act 1, Nora tells Krogstad, her blackmailer, that his revealing her secret could expose her to "the most horrible unpleasantness," he responds, "Only unpleasantness?" Yet later on, in act 3, Torvald echoes her language, fastidiously dismissing the horror with, "No, we're not going to dwell on anything unpleasant."

The ease with which Torvald is able to dismiss his dying friend Dr. Rank in act 3 ("He with his suffering and loneliness—like a dark cloud setting off our sunlit happiness. Well, maybe it's best this way.") foreshadows the lack of support he will give Nora immediately thereafter. Especially revealing is his use of *I* and *my* and *me*, which convey his self-centeredness:

> Now you've wrecked all my happiness—ruined my whole future. Oh, it's awful to think
> of. I'm in a cheap little grafter's hands; he can do anything he wants with me, ask for
> anything, play with me like a puppet—and I can't breathe a word. I'll be swept down
> miserably into the depths on account of a featherbrained woman.

Just as Torvald's words reveal that he has not been changed by the play's events, Nora's words show that she has changed significantly. Her dialogue near the end of act 3 shows that she has become a responsible, determined woman—one who understands her situation and her options and is no longer blithely oblivious to her duties. When she says, "I've never felt more clearheaded and sure in my life," she is calm and decisive. When she says, "Our home's been nothing but a playpen. I've been your doll-wife here, just as at home I was Papa's doll-child," she reveals a new self-awareness. And, when she confronts her husband, she displays—perhaps for the first time in their relationship—complete honesty.

Sometimes what other characters say to (or about) a character can reveal more to an audience than the character's own words. For instance, in *A Doll House*, when the dying Dr. Rank says, apparently without malice, "[Torvald] Helmer with his sensitivity has such a sharp distaste for anything ugly," the audience not only thinks ill of the man who is too "sensitive" to visit his sick friend but also questions his ability to withstand situations that may be emotionally or morally "ugly" as well.

When a character is offstage for much (or even all) of the action, the audience must rely on other characters' assessments of the absent character. In Susan Glaspell's *Trifles* (p. 1604), the play's focus is on an absent character, Minnie Wright, who is described solely through other characters' comments. The evidence suggests that Mrs. Wright killed her husband, and only Mrs. Hale's and Mrs. Peters's comments about Mrs. Wright's dreary life can delineate her character and suggest a likely motive for the murder. Although Mrs. Wright never appears on stage, we learn essential information from the other women about her: that as a young girl she liked to sing and that more recently she was so distraught about the lack of beauty in her life that even her sewing revealed her distress.

Whether a character's words are in the form of a monologue, a soliloquy, or dialogue—and whether they reveal information about the character who is speaking or about someone else—words are always revealing. Explicitly or implicitly, they convey a character's nature, attitudes, and relationships with other characters.

Keep in mind that the kind of language characters use can vary widely. A character may, for instance, use learned words, foreign words, elaborate figures of speech, irony or sarcasm, regionalisms, slang, jargon, clichés, or profanity. Words can also be used to indicate tone—for example, to express irony. Any of these uses of language may communicate vital information to the audience about a character's background, attitudes, and motivation. And, of course, a character's language may change as a play progresses, and this change too may be revealing.

Formal and Informal Language

The level of diction a character uses can give audiences a good deal of information. One character in a dramatic work may speak very formally, using absolutely correct grammar, a learned vocabulary, and long, complex sentences; another may speak in an informal style,

CHARACTERS' WORDS   **1169**

using conversational speech, colloquialisms, and slang. At times, two characters with different levels of language may be set in opposition for dramatic effect, as they are in Irish playwright George Bernard Shaw's classic play *Pygmalion* (1912), which updates the ancient Greek myth of a sculptor who creates (and falls in love with) a statue of a woman. In Shaw's version, a linguistics professor sets out to teach "proper" speech and manners to a woman who sells flowers on the street. Throughout the play, the contrasting language of Henry Higgins, the professor, and Eliza Doolittle, the flower seller, reveals their differing social standing. The following exchange illustrates this contrast:

LIZA: I ain't got no mother. Her that turned me out was my sixth stepmother. But I done without them. And I'm a good girl, I am.

HIGGINS: Very well, then, what on earth is all this fuss about?

A character's accent or dialect may also be significant. In **comedies of manners**, for instance, rustic or provincial characters, identified by their speech, are often objects of humor. In *Pygmalion*, Eliza Doolittle uses cockney dialect, the dialect spoken in the East End of London. At first, her colorful, distinctive language (complete with expressions like *Nah-ow*, *garn*, and *ah-ah-ah-ow-ow-ow-oo*) and her nonstandard grammatical constructions make her an object of ridicule; later, the transformation of her speech reveals the dramatic changes in her character.

Plain and Elaborate Language

A character's speech may be simple and straightforward or complex and convoluted; it may be plain and unadorned or embellished with elaborate **figures of speech**. The relative complexity or lack of complexity of a character's speech may have different effects on the audience. For example, a character whose language is simple and unsophisticated may seem to be unintelligent, unenlightened, gullible, or naive—especially if he or she also uses slang, dialect, or colloquial expressions. Conversely, a character's plain, down-to-earth language may convey common sense or intelligence. Plain language may also be quite emotionally powerful. For example, Willy Loman's speech in act 2 of *Death of a Salesman* (p. 1233), about an eighty-four-year-old salesman named Dave Singleman, moves the audience with its sincerity and directness:

> Do you know? When he died—and by the way he died the death of a salesman, in his green velvet slippers in the smoker of the New York, New Haven and Hartford, going into Boston—when he died, hundreds of salesmen and buyers were at his funeral. Things were sad on a lotta trains for months after that.

Like plain speech, elaborate language may have different effects in different contexts. Sometimes, use of figures of speech can make a character seem to have depth and insight and analytical skills absent in other characters. In the following excerpt from a soliloquy in act 1 scene 2 of *Hamlet*, for example, complex language reveals the depth of Hamlet's anguished self-analysis:

HAMLET: O, that this too too solid flesh would melt,
　　Thaw, and resolve itself into a dew!
　　Or that the Everlasting had not fix'd
　　His canon 'gainst self-slaughter! O God! O God!

> How weary, stale, flat, and unprofitable
> Seem to me all the uses of this world!
> Fie on't, O fie, 'tis an unweeded garden,
> That grows to seed. . . .

In these lines, Hamlet compares the world to a garden gone to seed. His use of imagery and figures of speech vividly communicates his feelings about the world and his internal struggle against the temptation to commit suicide.

Sometimes, however, elaborate language may make a character seem aloof, pompous, or even untrustworthy. In the following passages from Shakespeare's *King Lear*, Goneril and Regan, the deceitful daughters, use complicated verbal constructions to conceal their true feelings from their father, King Lear. In contrast, Cordelia—the loyal, loving daughter—uses simple, straightforward language that suggests her sincerity and lack of artifice. Compare the three speeches:

> GONERIL: Sir, I love you more than words can wield the matter;
>   Dearer than eyesight, space, and liberty;
>   Beyond what can be valued, rich or rare;
>   No less than life, with grace, health, beauty, honour;
>   As much as child e'er lov'd, or father found;
>   A love that makes breath poor, and speech unable.
>   Beyond all manner of so much I love you. . . .
>
> REGAN: Sir, I am made
>   Of the selfsame metal that my sister is,
>   And prize me at her worth. In my true heart
>   I find she names my very deed of love;
>   Only she comes too short, that I profess
>   Myself an enemy to all other joys
>   Which the most precious square of sense possesses,
>   And find I am alone felicitate
>   In your dear Highness' love. . . .
>
> CORDELIA: Unhappy that I am, I cannot heave
>   My heart into my mouth. I love your Majesty
>   According to my bond; no more no less. . . .

Cordelia's unwillingness, even when she is prodded by Lear, to exaggerate her feelings or misrepresent her love through inflated language shows the audience her honesty and nobility. The contrast between her language and that of her sisters makes their very different motives clear.

Tone

Tone reveals a character's mood or attitude. Tone can be flat or emotional, bitter or accepting, affectionate or aloof, anxious or calm. Contrasts in tone can indicate differences in outlook or emotional state between two characters; changes in tone from one point in a play to another can suggest corresponding changes within a character. At the end of *A Doll*

House, for instance, Nora is resigned to what she must do, and her language is appropriately controlled. Her husband, however, is desperate to change her mind, and his language reflects this desperation. The following exchanges of dialogue from the end of act 3 illustrate the two characters' contrasting emotional states:

HELMER: But to part! To part from you! No, Nora, no—I can't imagine it.
NORA: *(going out, right)* All the more reason why it has to be.

HELMER: Over! All over! Nora, won't you ever think about me?
NORA: I'm sure I'll think of you often, and about the children and the house here.

In earlier scenes between the two characters, Nora is emotional—at times, hysterical—and her husband is considerably more controlled. As the exchanges above indicate, both Nora and Torvald Helmer change drastically during the course of the play.

Irony

Irony, a contradiction or discrepancy between two levels of meaning, can reveal a great deal about character. **Verbal irony**—a contradiction between what a character says and what he or she means—is very important in drama, where the verbal interplay between characters may carry the weight of the play. For example, when Nora and Dr. Rank discuss the latest news about his health in *A Doll House*, there is deep irony in his use of the phrase "complete certainty." Although the phrase usually suggests reassuring news, here it is meant to suggest death, and both Nora and Dr. Rank understand this.

   Dramatic irony depends on the audience's knowing something that a character has not yet realized, or on one character's knowing something that other characters do not know. In some cases, dramatic irony is created by an audience's awareness of historical background or events of which characters are unaware. Familiar with the story of Oedipus, for instance, the audience knows that the man who has caused all the problems in Thebes—the man Oedipus vows to find and take revenge on—is Oedipus himself. In other cases, dramatic irony emerges when the audience learns something—something the characters do not yet know or comprehend—from a play's unfolding action. The central irony in *A Doll House*, for example, is that the family's "happy home" rests on a foundation of secrets, lies, and deception. Torvald does not know about the secrets, and Nora does not understand how they have poisoned her marriage. The audience, however, quickly becomes aware of the atmosphere of deceit—and aware of how it threatens the family's happiness.

   Dramatic irony may also be conveyed through dialogue. Typically, dramatic irony is revealed when a character says something that gives the audience information that other characters, offstage at the time, do not know. In *A Doll House*, the audience knows—because Nora has explained her situation to Kristine—that Nora spent the previous Christmas season hard at work, earning money to pay her secret debt. Torvald, however, remains unaware of her activities and believes her story that she was using the time to make holiday decorations, which the cat destroyed. This belief is consistent with his impression of Nora as an irresponsible child, yet the audience has quite a different impression of her. This discrepancy, one of many contradictions between the audience's view of Nora and Torvald's view of her, helps to create dramatic tension in the play.

   Finally, **asides** (comments to the audience that other characters do not hear) can create dramatic irony by undercutting dialogue, providing ironic contrast between what the characters on stage know and what the audience knows. In Anton Chekhov's *The Brute* (p. 1048), for example, the audience knows that Mr. Smirnov is succumbing to Mrs. Popov's charms because he says, in an aside, "My God, what eyes she has! They're setting me on fire." Mrs. Popov, however, is not yet aware of his infatuation. The discrepancy between the audience's awareness and the character's adds to the play's humor.

 ## Characters' Actions

Through their actions, characters convey their values and attitudes to the audience. Actions also reveal aspects of a character's personality. For example, when Nora in *A Doll House* plays hide-and-seek with her children, eats forbidden macaroons, and takes childish joy in Christmas, her immaturity is apparent.

Audiences also learn about characters from what they do *not* do. Thus, Nora's failure to remain in touch with her friend Kristine, who has had a hard life, reveals her selfishness, and the decision by Mrs. Peters and Mrs. Hale in *Trifles* not to give their evidence to the sheriff indicates their defiant support for Mrs. Wright and their understanding of what motivated her to take such drastic action.

Finally, audiences learn a good deal about characters by observing how they interact with other characters. In William Shakespeare's *Othello*, Iago is the embodiment of evil, and as the play's action unfolds, we discover his true nature. He reveals the secret marriage of Othello and Desdemona to her father; he schemes to arouse Othello's jealousy, making him believe Desdemona has been unfaithful with his lieutenant, Cassio; he persuades Cassio to ask Desdemona to plead his case with Othello, knowing this act will further arouse Othello's suspicions; he encourages Othello to be suspicious of Desdemona's defense of Cassio; he plants Desdemona's handkerchief in Cassio's room; and, finally, he persuades Othello to kill Desdemona and then kills his own wife, Emilia, to prevent her from exposing his role in the intrigue. As the play progresses, then, Iago's dealings with others consistently reveal him to be evil and corrupt.

 ## Stage Directions

When we read a play (rather than see it performed), we also read the playwright's italicized **stage directions**, the notes that concern **staging**—the scenery, props, lighting, music, sound effects, costumes, and other elements that contribute to the way the play looks and sounds to an audience (see Chapter 40). In addition to commenting on staging, stage directions may supply physical details about the characters, suggesting their age, appearance, movements, gestures, and facial expressions. These details may in turn convey additional information about characters: appearance may reveal social position or economic status, expressions may reveal attitudes, and so on. Stage directions may also indicate the manner in which a line of dialogue is to be delivered—*confidently* or *hesitantly*, for instance. The way a line is spoken may reveal a character to be excited, upset, angry, shy, or disappointed. Finally, stage directions may indicate changes in characters—for instance, a character whose speech is described as timid in early scenes may deliver lines emphatically and forcefully later on in the play.

Some stage directions provide a good deal of detail about character; others do little more than list characters' names. Arthur Miller is one playwright who often provides detailed information about character through stage directions. In *Death of a Salesman*, for instance, Miller's stage directions at the beginning of act 1 characterize Willy Loman immediately and specifically:

> He is past sixty years of age, dressed quietly. Even as he crosses the stage to the doorway of the house, his exhaustion is apparent. He unlocks the door, comes into the kitchen, and thankfully lets his burden down, feeling the soreness of his palms. A word-sigh escapes his lips . . .

Subsequent stage directions indicate how lines are to be spoken. For example, in the play's opening lines, Willy's wife Linda calls out to him "*with some trepidation*"; Linda speaks "*very carefully, delicately,*" and Willy speaks "*with casual irritation.*" These instructions to readers (and actors) are meant to suggest the strained relationship between the two characters.

George Bernard Shaw is well known for the full character description in his stage directions. In these directions—seen by readers of the play but of course not heard by audiences—he communicates complex information about characters' attitudes and values, motivation and reactions, and relationships with other characters. In doing so, Shaw himself functions as a kind of narrator, explicitly communicating his own attitudes toward various characters. (The voice in Shaw's stage directions is not the voice of a character in the play; it is the voice of the playwright.) Shaw's stage directions for *Pygmalion* initially describe Eliza Doolittle as follows:

> She is not at all an attractive person. She is perhaps eighteen, perhaps twenty, hardly older. She wears a little sailor hat of black straw that has long been exposed to the dust and soot of London and has seldom if ever been brushed. Her hair needs washing rather badly; its mousy color can hardly be natural. She wears a shoddy black coat that reaches nearly to her knees and is shaped to her waist. She has a brown skirt with a coarse apron. Her boots are much the worse for wear. She is no doubt as clean as she can afford to be; but compared to the ladies she is very dirty. Her features are no worse than theirs; but their condition leaves something to be desired; and she needs the services of a dentist.

Rather than providing an objective summary of the character's most notable physical attributes, Shaw injects subjective comments ("*seldom if ever brushed*"; "*color can hardly be natural*"; "*no doubt as clean as she can afford to be*") that reveal his attitude toward Eliza. This initially supercilious attitude, which he has in common with Professor Higgins, is tempered considerably by the end of the play, helping to make Eliza's transformation more obvious to readers than it would be if measured by her words and actions alone. By act 5, the tone of the stage directions characterizing Eliza has changed to admiration: "*Eliza enters, sunny, self-possessed, and giving a staggeringly convincing exhibition of ease of manner.*"

Stage directions in most other plays are not nearly as comprehensive. In *Hamlet*, for example, characters are introduced with only the barest identifying tags: "Claudius, *King of Denmark*"; "Hamlet, *Son to the former, and nephew to the present King*"; "Gertrude, *Queen of Denmark, mother to Hamlet.*" Most of the play's stage directions do little more than chronicle the various characters' entrances and exits or specify particular physical actions: "*Enter Ghost*"; "*Spreads his arms*"; "*Ghost beckons Hamlet*"; "*He kneels*"; "*Sheathes his sword*"; "*Leaps in the grave.*" Occasionally, stage directions specify a prop ("*Puts down the skull*"); a sound effect ("*A noise within*"); or a costume ("*Enter the ghost in his night-gown*"). Such brevity is typical of Shakespeare's plays, in which characters are delineated almost solely by their words—and, not incidentally, by the way actors have interpreted the characters over the years. In fact, because Shakespeare's stage directions only suggest characters' gestures, physical reactions, movements, and facial expressions, actors have been left quite free to experiment, reading various interpretations into Shakespeare's characters.

 ## Actors' Interpretations

When we see a play performed, we gain insight into a character not merely through what the character says and does or how other characters react but also through the way an actor interprets the role. If a playwright does not specify a character's mannerisms, gestures, or movements, or does not indicate how a line is to be delivered, an actor is free to interpret the role as he or she believes it should be played. Even when a playwright *does* specify such actions, the actor has a good deal of freedom to decide which gestures or expressions will convey a particular emotion.

In "Some Thoughts on Playwriting" (1941), American dramatist Thornton Wilder argues that "the theatre is an art which reposes upon the work of many collaborators" rather than on "one governing selecting will." Citing examples from Shakespeare and Ibsen, Wilder illustrates the great degree of "intervention" that may occur in dramatic productions. For instance, Wilder observes, Shakespeare's Shylock (a character in *The Merchant of Venice*) has been portrayed by two different actors as "noble, wronged and indignant" and as "a vengeful and hysterical buffoon"—and both performances were considered plausible interpretations. As noted earlier, the absence of detailed stage directions in Shakespeare's plays makes possible (and perhaps even encourages) such widely divergent interpretations. However, as Wilder points out, even when playing roles created by a dramatist such as Ibsen, whose stage directions are typically quite specific, actors and directors have a good deal of leeway. Thus, actress Janet McTeer, who played the part of Ibsen's Nora in the 1997 London production of *A Doll House*, saw Nora and Torvald, despite their many problems, as "the perfect couple," deeply in love and involved in a passionate marriage. "You have to make that marriage sexually credible," McTeer told the *New York Times*, "to imagine they have a wonderful time in bed, so there becomes something to lose. If you play them as already past it or no longer attracted to each other, then there is no play." This interpretation is not inconsistent with the play, but it does go beyond what Ibsen actually wrote.

Similarly, the role of Catherine in David Auburn's *Proof* (p. 1180) has been played by several actresses—among them Mary-Louise Parker, Jennifer Jason Leigh, Anne Heche, Gwyneth Paltrow, and Lea Salonga—and each actress has interpreted this complex character in a different way. As *New York Times* theater critic John Rockwell observes, "Catherine can be loopy-ethereal-sexy (Ms. Parker), earthy and even a little bitter (Ms. Leigh), or adorable-needy-fragile (Ms. Heche), and Mr. Auburn's structure and characters and ideas still work."

Irish playwright Samuel Beckett devotes a good deal of attention to indicating actors' movements and gestures and their physical reactions to one another. In his 1952 play *Waiting for Godot*, for example, Beckett's stage directions seem to choreograph every gesture, every emotion, every intention:

- *(he looks at them ostentatiously in turn to make it clear they are both meant)*
- *Vladimir seizes Lucky's hat. Silence of Lucky. He falls. Silence. Panting of the victors.*
- *Estragon hands him the boot. Vladimir inspects it, throws it down angrily.*
- *Estragon pulls, stumbles, falls. Long silence.*
- *He goes feverishly to and fro, halts finally at extreme left, broods.*

Beckett provides full and obviously carefully thought-out stage directions and, in so doing, attempts to retain a good deal of control over his characters. Still, in a 1988 production of *Godot*, director Mike Nichols and comic actors Robin Williams and Steve Martin felt free to improvise, adding gestures and movements not specified or even hinted at—and most critics believed that this production remained true to the tragicomic spirit of Beckett's existentialist play. In a sense, then, the playwright's words on the page are just the beginning of the characters' lives on the stage.

✔ CHECKLIST Writing about Character

- Does any character serve as a narrator? If so, what information does this narrator supply about the other characters? How reliable is the narrator?

- Who are the major characters? What do we know about them?

- Do the major characters change and grow during the course of the play, or do they remain essentially unchanged?

- What do the minor characters contribute to the play?

- Does the play include monologues or soliloquies? What do these extended speeches reveal about the characters?

- What is revealed about the characters through dialogue?

- Do characters use foreign words, regionalisms, slang, jargon, clichés, or profanity? What does such use of language reveal about the characters? about the play's theme?

- Is the characters' language formal or informal?

- Do characters speak in dialect? Do they have accents?

- Is the characters' language plain or elaborate?

- Do different characters use different kinds of language? What is the significance of these differences?

- How does language reveal characters' emotional states?

- Does the tone of any character's language change significantly as the play progresses? What does this change reveal?

- Does the play include verbal irony? dramatic irony? How is irony conveyed? What purpose does irony achieve?

- What is revealed about the characters through what others say about them?

- What is revealed about characters through their actions?

- What is revealed about characters through the play's stage directions?

- How might different actors' interpretations change an audience's understanding of the characters?

PAUL DOOLEY (1928–   ) **AND WINNIE HOLZMAN** (1954–   ) are a husband-and-wife playwriting team. Dooley was the co-creator and head writer of the 1970s children's television series *The Electric Company*. He has acted in numerous television shows and films, including *Scrubs* (2009), *Grey's Anatomy* (2008), *Grace under Fire* (1993), *Star Trek: Deep Space Nine* (1993), and *Sixteen Candles* (1984). Holzman wrote the book for the Broadway hit *Wicked* (2003), which was nominated for a 2004 Tony Award. An actor and a screenwriter for numerous television shows, Holzman received a 1995 Emmy Award nomination for writing the television series *My So-Called Life* (1994).

Cultural Context: The Post-it® brand changed the way Americans wrote notes and reminders. In 1980, Post-it launched the sticky note as a new consumer product. Initially intended for business use, Post-its quickly became a national household staple. Post-it's website touts the product's literal and figurative staying power, pointing out, for example, that a Post-it stuck to an evacuated home stayed put for three days during Hurricane Hugo in 1989. Since popularizing sticky notes more than thirty years ago, Post-it has created a wide range of related products, including digital notes.

Post-its (Notes on a Marriage) (1998)

Post-its (Notes on a Marriage) premiered at a benefit performance for the Gilda Radner Cancer Fund, 1998. The cast was as follows:

> **ACTOR**   Paul Dooley
> **ACTRESS**   Winnie Holzman

There is a chair with a small table and a glass of water on either side of the stage, a la A. R. Gurney's Love Letters. *The Actor and Actress enter simultaneously from either wing, dressed simply. Each grasps a handful of Post-its as if it were a script. They sit, modestly acknowledging each other and the audience. Each takes out a pair of reading glasses, puts them on. The Actor lifts his first Post-it to begin . . . and reads. Every line is read from a Post-it.*

ACTOR: Had an early meeting, couldn't bear to wake you. Close front door hard or it won't lock. PS: Last night was incredible.

ACTRESS: Helped myself to breakfast. You need milk. PS: Next time, wake me.

ACTOR: Hey, sleepyhead. Tried to wake you. Not easy. Left you some coffee, hope you like it black.

ACTRESS: Thought 1 should spend at least one night this week at my place. Picked up some milk; you don't have to pay me back.

5   ACTOR: Off to work, extra set of keys on hall table.

ACTRESS: Darling: Went jogging with Lila. If you go out, we need milk. Wow. I can't believe we're a "we"!

ACTOR: Hon: If you have time, could you pick up my shirts? Ticket on hall table. Thanks. PS: Milk.

ACTRESS: Shirts are in your closet. Your mother called. She seemed surprised to hear my voice. You obviously never mentioned me. (*Icy*) Your shirts came to fourteen-fifty.

ACTOR: Gone to florist. Back soon. Hope you liked the chocolates.

ACTRESS: Darling, don't go in the den.   10

ACTOR: Sweetheart, I understand how much it means to you, but at this stage of our relationship I'm just not ready. . . to have a dog.

ACTRESS: (*After a beat.*) We need Milk-Bones. (*Next Post-it.*) Your mother called; call her. (*Next Post-it.*) Did you call your mother? (*Next Post-it.*) Went to lunch with your mother. Back soon.

ACTOR: Your new best friend my mother called. Call her.

ACTRESS: We need milk. Also, your mom mentioned how much you hate Eugene. I don't think Eugene's so bad. You should hear *my* middle name. Thank God *my* mother's dead!

ACTOR: Please do not mention the name Eugene to me ever again. Thank you.   15

ACTRESS: Shopping list: Pistachio ice cream. Sardines. Those tiny little cheeses that come in that cute little net bag. . . They're so adorable, they make me cry.

ACTRESS: We need Pampers. And baby wipes. And we need to get married.

ACTOR: Meet me City Hall, six sharp. You bring old and borrowed; I'll do new and blue. Mom will stay with Eugenia.

ACTRESS: Note to self: Find breast pump.

ACTOR: Take cold shower.   20

ACTRESS: Lose forty pounds.

ACTOR: Redirect sex drive into career. (*Next Post-it.*) Home late. Don't wait up.

ACTRESS: Hey. stranger, if you're not too busy, could you call Eugenia tonight, around bedtime? Just to see if she recognizes your voice?

ACTOR: Hon: Sorry about your birthday. PS: I got the raise!

ACTRESS: To the new vice president in charge of marketing. We need milk.   25
Please advise.

ACTOR: Hon: I think we're out of milk. (*Next Post-it.*) Still no milk!

ACTRESS: If you want it so bad, get it yourself. The milk train doesn't stop here anymore.

ACTOR: If you can't even manage to get to the store—get some household help!

ACTRESS: (*Icy.*) Have gone to bed. Dinner is in fridge. If there is something in particular you wish for dinner tomorrow night, please leave note to that effect, and I will have Ursula or Carla or *Jose*, if it's *heavy*, pick it up. (*Beat.*) I can't take this anymore! We barely—(*Turns Post-it over.*)—communicate! There's got to be more to this marriage than a few hastily scribbled words on a small square of pastel paper! (*Beat.*) By the way, we're out of Post-its.

ACTOR: You think I *want* to spend every night at the office? You have absolutely no   30
concept of how a business is run.

ACTRESS: To Whom It May Concern: Regarding your Post-it of June the tenth, allow me to clarify my position—up yours. Eugenia and I will be at your mother's. PS: *You* need milk.

The Actor glances over at the Actress, she sips her water, coolly avoids his gaze. Finally . . .

ACTOR: Call her at my mother's. (*Next Post-it.*) Must call her. (*Next Post-it.*) Reminder: Take out garbage. Call her. (*Next Post-it.*) People to call: Her.

The Actor looks over again at the Actress. She continues to ignore him.

ACTOR: Shopping list: Small loaf bread. Half pint milk. Soup for one. (*Next Post-it.*) Scotch for one. (*Next Post-it.*) Inflatable doll. (*Next Post-it.*) Scotch for two.

The Actress looks at him. He catches her eye. Caught, she hastily looks away.

ACTOR: Things to tell her. That I'm sorry. That I miss her. That all I want—all I ever wanted—for her to be happy.

The Actress turns to him, touched by this. Then. . . takes the next Post-it. Reads.

35 ACTRESS: We need milk.
ACTOR: Dearest—have gone down to the end of the driveway to get the paper. Back soon.
ACTRESS: Honey, that therapist called back. He can see you Monday.
ACTOR: Sweetie, your therapist says your Tuesday is now Friday.
ACTRESS: What a session! Dr. K. believes that part of me is locked in unconscious competition with you, and envious of your of masculine role. By the way, we need cucumbers, sausages, and a really big zucchini.
40 ACTOR: At last—a breakthrough today with Dr. G. It all became crystal clear. My mother. My father. *His* mother. You. *Your* mother. (*Turns Post-it over, continues,*) I see our entire marriage in a new light! I must free myself from the past so we can truly have a future. This changes everything.
ACTRESS: Hon: A Diet Coke exploded all over that note you left. Hope it wasn't important.

He stares at her. Oblivious to his reaction, she reads the next Post-it.

Took Eugenia to Brownies. Back soon.
ACTOR: Took Eugenia to kickboxing. Back soon.
ACTRESS: Took Eugenia to therapy. Could be a while.
ACTOR: Someone named Olaf called. Needs your résumé. What résumé?
45 ACTRESS: I landed the job! I start Monday! (*Next Post-it.*) Last-minute meeting. I'll try to call. (*Next Post-it.*) I'll be working late, don't wait up. (*Next Post-it.*) I'm glad you waited. Last night was incredible.
ACTOR: Drove Eugenia to DMV. Hope she doesn't drive me home.
ACTRESS: Eugenia called. Loves college. Mentioned someone named Tyrone. Doesn't miss us at all.
ACTOR: Pick up travel brochures.
ACTRESS: Eugenia called. When can we meet Tyrone?
50 ACTOR: Schedule trip to campus when we get back.
ACTRESS: Sweetheart: Travel agent called. Cruise is confirmed! The honeymoon we never had! A time for us to leave all this behind and enjoy ten glorious days of total togetherness.

A long, silent beat. Very long. Very silent. They both look straight ahead. Finally he lifts the next Post-it.

ACTOR: (*With great relief.*) God, it's good to be home! (*Next Post-it.*) Dinner
  Wednesday with Eugenia and what's-his-name.
ACTRESS: Tyrone called—it's a boy. Kareem Eugene.
ACTOR: Eugenia called. Loves being a mom.
ACTRESS: Off to throw pots! Back soon! (*Next Post-it.*) Don't forget—we're bird-   55
  watching Thursday! (*Next Post-it.*) What night is good for square dancing?
ACTOR: Any night you want—we're free! Nothing to tie us down.
ACTOR: Eugenia called. Could we take Kareem for the weekend?
ACTRESS: Tyrone called. Could we take Kareem for spring break?
ACTOR: Kareem called. Could he spend the summer with us? Again. (*Next Post-it.*)
  Took Kareem to DMV.
ACTRESS: Honey—last night was incredible. I couldn't believe how long it went on.   60
  You've got to do something about your snoring.
ACTOR: Shopping list: Bengay, Dentucreme. Viagra.
ACTRESS: Wrinkles Away. I-Can't-Believe-It's-Support-Hose. Estrogen in a Drum.
ACTOR: We need milk of magnesia.
ACTRESS: Call Medicare.
ACTOR: You left your keys in the door again.   65
ACTRESS: Do you have my keys?
ACTOR: I can't find my glasses.
ACTRESS: Have you seen my cane?
ACTOR: How can I see your cane if I can't find my glasses?
ACTRESS: Gone for walk.   70
ACTOR: Where are you? Next time you go out, leave me a note!
ACTRESS: Sweetheart—dinner in oven. Taking nap. Love ya.

There's a pause as lights slowly fade on the Actress. *Then . . .*

ACTOR: Call Emily. Also cousin Ruthie. Send note to Father McKay and everyone
  who sent flowers. (*Beat.*) The service was lovely. Everybody said so. (*Beat.*)
  I was looking through your things for that locket you said Eugenia should have.
  I could hardly believe what I found. You'd saved every Post-it I ever wrote you.
  I wish I'd saved yours. I could be reading them now. (*Beat.*) Back soon. Going
  to the store. We need milk.

*   *   *

Reading and Reacting

1. Summarize the plot of *Post-its*. What actually happens in this play?
2. What events occur offstage? Identify the references to these events in the characters' dialogue.
3. Read the stage direction at the beginning of the play. What information about the
   two characters do you get from these stage directions?
4. What facts are revealed in the course of the play about the two characters? What
   more can you infer about them?
5. In this play, the actors read every line from Post-it notes. What are the advantages
   and disadvantages of this format?

6. What props are used in this play? What purpose does each prop serve? If you were staging this play, would you use any additional props?

7. Do you think the fact that this play has only two speaking parts is a handicap? Can you suggest a way to add other characters while retaining the "Post-it" format? What other characters do you think could have speaking parts?

8. How much time passes in the course of this play? How can you tell?

9. Do the two characters grow and change over the years? Does their relationship grow and change? Explain.

10. Why is the reference to needing milk repeated over and over again? Is this an effective use of repetition, or does it become annoying? Explain.

11. JOURNAL ENTRY Write a series of text messages between this play's two characters, using shorthand and abbreviations as needed. (If you like, you can "translate" some of the play's Post-it messages into text messages.) Does the change of format change the nature of the conversation? If so, how?

12. CRITICAL PERSPECTIVE Savanna Dooley, a screenwriter who is also Dooley and Holzman's daughter, describes Holzman's book for the musical *Wicked* as follows: "It is rich with her trademarks: a story about an outsider, fully realized characters, and some subversive political commentary." Does *Post-its* also demonstrate Holzman's "trademarks" as described by Dooley?

Related Works: "Hills Like White Elephants" (p. 119), "Love and Other Catastrophes: A Mix Tape" (p. 127), "The Story of an Hour" (p. 201), "Meeting at Night" (p. 898), "Parting at Morning" (p. 899), "How Do I Love Thee?" (p. 899), *The Brute* (p. 1048)

Source: ©AP Photo/Alan Solomon

DAVID AUBURN (1969–   ) was born in Chicago and grew up in Columbus, Ohio, and in Arkansas before returning to Chicago for college. Having spent time in Los Angeles on a screenwriting fellowship, Auburn moved to New York to become a playwright. He enrolled in the playwriting program at Juilliard and had his first full-length play, *Skyscraper* (1998), produced off-Broadway in 1997. The production attracted the attention of the Manhattan Theatre Club, which told Auburn, "Keep us in mind for your next play and send it to us." He did, and that play was *Proof* (2000), his first Broadway production. *Proof* was awarded the 2001 Pulitzer Prize for drama and the 2001 Tony Award; Auburn also received a Dramatists Guild's Hull-Warriner Award. He adapted *Proof* into the 2005 feature film of the same name. His other plays include *Fifth Planet* (1998), *Miss You* (1998), and *The Next Life*. His short play *What Do You Believe about the Future?* (1996) appeared in *Harper's* magazine and was adapted for the screen. Auburn also wrote the screenplays for the 2006 feature film *The Lake House* and for the 2007 feature film *The Girl in the Park* (which he also directed). Winner of the Joseph Kesselring Prize for drama, Auburn has also received the Helen Merrill Playwriting Award and a Guggenheim Foundation Fellowship.

Cultural Context *Proof* is a play about mathematics, traditionally a male-dominated field, yet its central character is a young woman. The number of women in mathematics has grown slowly but steadily in the last thirty years. According to the U.S. Census Bureau's 2011 Statistical Abstract, since 2000, women have been earning more bachelor's degrees than men in science and engineering fields from colleges and universities in the United States. The percentage of American women earning PhDs in science and engineering fields has also risen, approaching forty percent. Despite these gains, the notion that women can excel in math and science is still not universally accepted. In January 2005, Dr. Lawrence Summers, then president of Harvard University, hypothesized that innate genetic differences between men and women might be one reason why "fewer women succeed in math and science careers." These comments—from the leader of a prestigious university—sparked international controversy.

Proof (2001)

SETTING

The back porch of a house in chicago

CHARACTERS

Robert, *fifties*   **Hal,** *twenty-eight*
Catherine, *twenty-five*   **Claire,** *twenty-nine*

ACT 1
SCENE 1

Night. Catherine sits in a chair. She is exhausted, haphazardly dressed. Eyes closed. Robert is standing behind her. He is Catherine's father. Rumpled academic look. Catherine does not know he is there. After a moment:

ROBERT: Can't sleep?
CATHERINE: Jesus, you scared me.
ROBERT: Sorry.
CATHERINE: What are you doing here?
ROBERT: I thought I'd check up on you. Why aren't you in bed?   5

Gwyneth Paltrow as Catherine and Jake Gyllenhaal as Hal in the 2005 film adaptation of *Proof*
Miramax/The Kobal Collection/Picture-Desk

CATHERINE: Your student is still here. He's up in your study.

ROBERT: He can let himself out.

CATHERINE: I might as well wait up till he's done.

ROBERT: He's not my student anymore. He's teaching now. Bright kid.

Beat.

10 CATHERINE: What time is it?

ROBERT: It's almost one.

CATHERINE: Huh.

ROBERT: After midnight . . .

CATHERINE: So?

15 ROBERT: So: (*He indicates something on the table behind him: a bottle of champagne.*) Happy birthday.

CATHERINE: Dad.

ROBERT: Do I ever forget?

CATHERINE: Thank you.

ROBERT: Twenty-five. I can't believe it.

20 CATHERINE: Neither can I. Should we have it now?

ROBERT: It's up to you.

CATHERINE: Yes.

ROBERT: You want me to open it?

CATHERINE: Let me. Last time you opened a bottle of champagne out here you broke a window.

25 ROBERT: That was a long time ago. I resent your bringing it up.

CATHERINE: You're lucky you didn't lose an eye.

Pop. The bottle foams.

ROBERT: Twenty-five!

CATHERINE: I feel old.

ROBERT: You're a kid.

30 CATHERINE: Glasses?

ROBERT: Goddamn it, I forgot the glasses. Do you want me to—

CATHERINE: Nah.

Catherine drinks from the bottle. A long pull. Robert watches her.

ROBERT: I hope you like it. I wasn't sure what to get you.

CATHERINE: This is the worst champagne I have ever tasted.

35 ROBERT: I am proud to say I don't know anything about wines. I hate those kind of people who are always talking about "vintages."

CATHERINE: It's not even champagne.

ROBERT: The bottle was the right shape.

CATHERINE: "Great Lakes Vineyards." I didn't know they made wine in Wisconsin.

ROBERT: A girl who's drinking from the bottle shouldn't complain. Don't guzzle it. It's an elegant beverage. Sip.

40 CATHERINE: (*offering the bottle*) Do you—

ROBERT: No, go ahead.

CATHERINE: You sure?

ROBERT: Yeah. It's your birthday.

CATHERINE: Happy birthday to me.

ROBERT: What are you going to do on your birthday?   45

CATHERINE: Drink this. Have some.

ROBERT: No. I hope you're not spending your birthday alone.

CATHERINE: I'm not alone.

ROBERT: I don't count.

CATHERINE: Why not?   50

ROBERT: I'm your old man. Go out with some friends.

CATHERINE: Right.

ROBERT: Your friends aren't taking you out?

CATHERINE: No.

ROBERT: Why not?   55

CATHERINE: Because in order for your friends to take you out you generally have
    to have friends.

ROBERT: *(dismissive)* Oh—

CATHERINE: It's funny how that works.

ROBERT: You have friends. What about that cute blonde, what was her name?

CATHERINE: What?   60

ROBERT: She lives over on Ellis Avenue—you used to spend every minute together.

CATHERINE: Cindy Jacobsen?

ROBERT: Cindy Jacobsen!

CATHERINE: That was in *third grade*, Dad. Her family moved to Florida in 1983.

ROBERT: What about Claire?   65

CATHERINE: She's not my friend, she's my sister. And she's in New York. And
    I don't like her.

ROBERT: I thought she was coming in.

CATHERINE: Not till tomorrow.

Beat.

ROBERT: My advice, if you find yourself awake late at night, is to sit down and do
    some mathematics.

CATHERINE: Oh please.   70

ROBERT: We could do some together.

CATHERINE: No.

ROBERT: Why not?

CATHERINE: I can't think of anything worse. You sure you don't want any?

ROBERT: Yeah, thanks. You used to love it.   75

CATHERINE: Not anymore.

ROBERT: You knew what a prime number was before you could read.

CATHERINE: Well now I've forgotten.

ROBERT: *(Hard)* Don't waste your talent, Catherine.

Beat.

CATHERINE: I knew you'd say something like that.   80

ROBERT: I realize you've had a difficult time.

CATHERINE: Thanks.

ROBERT: That's not an excuse. Don't be lazy.

CATHERINE: I haven't been lazy, I've been taking care of you.

85   ROBERT: Kid, I've seen you. You sleep till noon, you eat junk, you don't work, the dishes pile up in the sink. If you go out it's to buy magazines. You come back with a stack of magazines this high—I don't know how you read that crap. And those are the good days. Some days you don't get up, you don't get out of bed.

CATHERINE: Those are the good days.

ROBERT: Bullshit. Those days are lost. You threw them away. And you'll never know what else you threw away with them—the work you lost, the ideas you didn't have, discoveries you never made because you were moping in your bed at four in the afternoon. (*Beat.*) You know I'm right. (*Beat.*)

CATHERINE: I've lost a few days.

ROBERT: How many?

90   CATHERINE: Oh, I don't know.

ROBERT: I bet you do.

CATHERINE: What?

ROBERT: I bet you count.

CATHERINE: Knock it off.

95   ROBERT: Well do you know or don't you?

CATHERINE: I don't.

ROBERT: Of course you do. How many days have you lost?

CATHERINE: A month. Around a month.

ROBERT: Exactly.

100   CATHERINE: Goddamn it, I don't—

ROBERT: *How many?*

CATHERINE: Thirty-three days.

ROBERT: Exactly?

CATHERINE: I don't know.

105   ROBERT: Be precise, for Chrissake.

CATHERINE: I slept till noon today.

ROBERT: Call it thirty-three and a quarter days.

CATHERINE: Yes, all right.

ROBERT: You're kidding!

110   CATHERINE: No.

ROBERT: Amazing number!

CATHERINE: It's a depressing fucking number.

ROBERT: Catherine, if every day you say you've lost were a year, it would be a very interesting fucking number.

CATHERINE: Thirty-three and a quarter years is not interesting.

115   ROBERT: Stop it. You know exactly what I mean.

CATHERINE: (*conceding*) 1729 weeks.

ROBERT: 1729. Great number. The smallest number expressible—

CATHERINE: —expressible as the sum of two cubes in two different ways.

ROBERT: 12 cubed plus 1 cubed equals 1729.

CATHERINE: And 10 cubed plus 9 cubed. Yes, we've got it, thank you.   120
ROBERT: You see? Even your depression is mathematical. Stop moping and get to
    work. The kind of potential you have—
CATHERINE: I haven't done anything good.
ROBERT: You're young. You've got time.
CATHERINE: I do?   125
ROBERT: Yes.
CATHERINE: By the time you were my age you were famous.
ROBERT: By the time I was your age I'd already done my best work.

Beat.

CATHERINE: What about after?
ROBERT: After what?
CATHERINE: After you got sick.   130
ROBERT: What about it?
CATHERINE: You couldn't work then.
ROBERT: No, if anything I was sharper.
CATHERINE: (*She can't help it: she laughs.*) Dad.
ROBERT: I was. Hey, it's true. The clarity—that was the amazing thing. No doubts.   135
CATHERINE: You were happy?
ROBERT: Yeah, I was busy.
CATHERINE: Not the same thing.
ROBERT: I don't see the difference. I knew what I wanted to do and I did it.
    If I wanted to work a problem all day long, I did it.
    If I wanted to look for information—secrets, complex and tantalizing messages—
I could find them all around me. In the air. In a pile of fallen leaves some neighbor
raked together. In box scores in the paper, written in the steam coming up off a cup
of coffee. The whole world was talking to me.
    If I just wanted to close my eyes, sit quietly on the porch and listen for the
messages, I did that.
    It was wonderful.

Beat.

CATHERINE: How old were you? When it started.   140
ROBERT: Mid-twenties. Twenty-three, four. (*Beat.*) Is that what you're worried
    about?
CATHERINE: I've thought about it.
ROBERT: Just getting a year older means nothing, Catherine.
CATHERINE: It's not just getting older.
ROBERT: It's me.   145

Beat.

CATHERINE: I've thought about it.
ROBERT: Really?
CATHERINE: How could I not?

ROBERT: Well if that's why you're worried you're not keeping up with the medical literature. There are all kinds of factors. It's not simply something you inherit. Just because I went bughouse doesn't mean you will.

150 CATHERINE: Dad . . .

ROBERT: Listen to me. Life changes fast in your early twenties and it shakes you up. You're feeling down. It's been a bad week. You've had a lousy couple years, no one knows that better than me. But you're gonna be okay.

CATHERINE: Yeah?

ROBERT: Yes. I promise you. Push yourself. Don't read so many magazines. Sit down and get the machinery going and I swear to God you'll feel fine. The simple fact that we can talk about this together is a good sign.

CATHERINE: A good sign?

155 ROBERT: Yes!

CATHERINE: How could it be a good sign?

ROBERT: Because! Crazy people don't sit around wondering if they're nuts.

CATHERINE: They don't?

ROBERT: Of course not. They've got better things to do. Take it from me. A very good sign that you're crazy is an inability to ask the question "Am I crazy?"

160 CATHERINE: Even if the answer is yes?

ROBERT: Crazy people don't ask. You see?

CATHERINE: Yes.

ROBERT: So if you're asking . . .

CATHERINE: I'm not.

165 ROBERT: But if you were, it would be a very good sign.

CATHERINE: A good sign . . .

ROBERT: A good sign that you're fine.

CATHERINE: Right.

ROBERT: You see? You've just gotta think these things through. Now come on, what do you say? Let's call it a night; you go up, get some sleep, and then in the morning you can—

170 CATHERINE: Wait. No.

ROBERT: What's the matter?

CATHERINE: It doesn't work.

ROBERT: Why not?

CATHERINE: It doesn't make sense.

175 ROBERT: Sure it does.

CATHERINE: No.

ROBERT: Where's the problem?

CATHERINE: The problem is you are crazy!

ROBERT: What difference does that make?

180 CATHERINE: You admitted—You just told me that you are.

ROBERT: So?

CATHERINE: You said a crazy person would never admit that.

ROBERT: Yeah, but it's . . . Oh. I see.

CATHERINE: So?

185 ROBERT: It's a point.

CATHERINE: So how can you admit it?
ROBERT: Well. Because I'm also dead. (*Beat.*) Aren't I?
CATHERINE: You died a week ago.
ROBERT: Heart failure. Quick. The funeral's tomorrow.
CATHERINE: That's why Claire's flying in from New York.   190
ROBERT: Yes.
CATHERINE: You're sitting here. You're giving me advice. You brought me
    champagne.
ROBERT: Yes.

Beat.

CATHERINE: Which means . . .
ROBERT: For you?   195
CATHERINE: Yes.
ROBERT: For you, Catherine, my daughter, who I love very much . . . It could be
    a bad sign.

They sit together for a moment. Noise off. Hal enters, semi-hip clothes. He carries a backpack and a jacket, folded. He lets the door go and it bangs shut. Catherine sits up with a jolt.

CATHERINE: What?
HAL: Oh God, sorry—did I wake you?
CATHERINE: What?   200
HAL: Were you asleep?

Beat. Robert is gone.

CATHERINE: You scared me, for Chrissake. What are you doing?
HAL: I'm sorry. I didn't realize it had gotten so late. I'm done for the night.
CATHERINE: Good.
HAL: Drinking alone?   205

Catherine realizes she is holding the champagne bottle. She puts it down quickly.

CATHERINE: Yes.
HAL: Champagne, huh?
CATHERINE: Yes.
HAL: Celebrating?
CATHERINE: No. I just like champagne.   210
HAL: It's festive.
CATHERINE: What?
HAL: Festive. (*He makes an awkward "party" gesture.*)
CATHERINE: Do you want some?
HAL: Sure.   215
CATHERINE: (*gives him the bottle*) I'm done. You can take the rest with you.
HAL: Oh. No thanks.
CATHERINE: Take it, I'm done.
HAL: No, I shouldn't. I'm driving. (*Beat.*) Well I can let myself out.
CATHERINE: Good.   220

HAL: When should I come back?

CATHERINE: Come back?

HAL: Yeah. I'm nowhere near finished. Maybe tomorrow?

CATHERINE: We have a funeral tomorrow.

225 HAL: God, you're right, I'm sorry. I was going to attend, if that's all right.

CATHERINE: Yes.

HAL: What about Sunday? Will you be around?

CATHERINE: You've had three days.

HAL: I'd love to get in some more time up there.

230 CATHERINE: How much longer do you need?

HAL: Another week. At least.

CATHERINE: Are you joking?

HAL: No. Do you know how much stuff there is?

CATHERINE: A week?

235 HAL: I know you don't need anybody in your hair right now. Look, I spent the last couple days getting everything sorted out. It's mostly notebooks. He dated them all; now that I've got them in order I don't have to work here. I could take some stuff home, read it, bring it back.

CATHERINE: No.

HAL: I'll be careful.

CATHERINE: My father wouldn't want anything moved and I don't want anything to leave this house.

HAL: Then I should work here. I'll stay out of the way.

240 CATHERINE: You're wasting your time.

HAL: Someone needs to go through your dad's papers.

CATHERINE: There's nothing up there. It's garbage.

HAL: There are a hundred and three notebooks.

CATHERINE: I've looked at those. It's gibberish.

245 HAL: Someone should read them.

CATHERINE: He was crazy.

HAL: Yes, but he wrote them.

CATHERINE: He was a graphomaniac, Harold. Do you know what that is?

HAL: I know. He wrote compulsively. Call me Hal.

250 CATHERINE: There's no connection between the ideas. There's no ideas. It's like a monkey at a typewriter. A hundred and three notebooks full of bullshit.

HAL: Let's make sure they're bullshit.

CATHERINE: I'm sure.

HAL: I'm prepared to look at every page. Are you?

CATHERINE: No. I'm not crazy.

Beat.

255 HAL: Well, I'm gonna be late . . . Some friends of mine are in this band. They're playing at a bar up on Diversey. Way down the bill, they're probably going on around two, two-thirty. I said I'd be there.

CATHERINE: Great.

HAL: They're all in the math department. They're really good. They have this great song—you'd like it—called "i"—lower-case I. They just stand there and don't play anything for three minutes.

CATHERINE: "Imaginary Number."

HAL: It's a math joke. You see why they're way down the bill.

CATHERINE: Long drive to see some nerds in a band.   260

HAL: God I hate when people say that. It is not that long a drive.

CATHERINE: So they are nerds.

HAL: Oh they're raging geeks. But they're geeks who, you know, can dress themselves . . . hold down a job at a major university . . . Some of them have switched from glasses to contacts. They play sports, they play in a band, they get laid surprisingly often, so in that sense they sort of make you question the whole set of terms: geek, nerd, wonk, dweeb, dilbert, paste-eater.

CATHERINE: You're in this band, aren't you?

HAL: Okay, yes. I play drums. You want to come? I never sing, I swear to God.   265

CATHERINE: No thanks.

HAL: All right. Look, Catherine, Monday: what do you say?

CATHERINE: Don't you have a job?

HAL: Yeah, I have a full teaching load this quarter plus my own work.

CATHERINE: Plus band practice.   270

HAL: I don't have time to do this but I'm going to. If you'll let me. (*Beat.*) I loved your dad. I don't believe a mind like his can just shut down. He had lucid moments. He had a lucid year, a whole year four years ago.

CATHERINE: It wasn't a year. It was more like nine months.

HAL: A school year. He was advising students . . . I was stalled on my Ph.D. I was this close to quitting. I met with your dad and he put me on the right track with my research. I owe him.

CATHERINE: Sorry.

HAL: Look. Let me—You're twenty-five, right?   275

CATHERINE: How old are you?

HAL: It doesn't matter. Listen.

CATHERINE: Fuck you, how old are you?

HAL: I'm twenty-eight, all right? When your dad was younger than both of us, he made major contributions to three fields: game theory, algebraic geometry, and nonlinear operator theory. Most of us never get our heads around one. He basically invented the mathematical techniques for studying rational behavior, and he gave the astrophysicists plenty to work over too. Okay?

CATHERINE: Don't lecture me.   280

HAL: I'm not. I'm telling you, if I came up with one-tenth of the shit your dad produced, I could write my own ticket to any math department in the country.

Beat.

CATHERINE: Give me your backpack.

HAL: What?

CATHERINE: Give me your backpack.

285   **HAL:** Why?

       CATHERINE: I want to look inside it.

       HAL: What?

       CATHERINE: Open it and give it to me.

       HAL: Oh come on.

290   **CATHERINE:** You're not taking anything out of this house.

       HAL: I wouldn't do that.

       CATHERINE: You're hoping to find something upstairs that you can publish.

       HAL: Sure.

       CATHERINE: Then you can write your own ticket.

295   **HAL:** What? No! It would be under your dad's name. It would be for your dad.

       CATHERINE: I don't believe you. You have a notebook in that backpack.

       HAL: What are you talking about?

       CATHERINE: Give it to me.

       HAL: You're being a little bit paranoid.

300   **CATHERINE:** *Paranoid?*

       HAL: Maybe a little.

       CATHERINE: Fuck you, *Hal. I know* you have one of my notebooks.

       HAL: I think you should calm down and think about what you're saying.

       CATHERINE: I'm saying you're lying to me and stealing my family's property.

305   **HAL:** And I think that sounds paranoid.

       CATHERINE: Just because I'm paranoid doesn't mean there isn't something in that backpack.

       HAL: *You just said yourself there's nothing up there.* Didn't you?

       CATHERINE: I—

310   **HAL:** Didn't you say that?

       CATHERINE: Yes.

       HAL: So what would I take? Right?

Beat.

       CATHERINE: You're right.

       HAL: Thank you.

315   **CATHERINE:** So you don't need to come back.

       HAL: *(Sighs.)* Please. Someone should know for sure whether—

       CATHERINE: *I lived with him.* I spent my life with him. I fed him. Talked to him. Tried to listen when he talked. Talked to people who weren't there . . . Watched him shuffling around like a ghost. A very smelly ghost. He was filthy. I had to make sure he bathed. My own father.

       HAL: I'm sorry. I shouldn't have . . .

       CATHERINE: After my mother died it was just me here. I tried to keep him happy no matter what idiotic project he was doing. He used to read all day. He kept demanding more and more books. I took them out of the library by the carload. We had hundreds upstairs. Then I realized he wasn't reading: he believed aliens were sending him messages through the Dewey decimal numbers on the library books. He was trying to work out the code.

320   **HAL:** What kind of messages?

CATHERINE: Beautiful mathematics. The most elegant proofs, perfect proofs, proofs like music.

HAL: Sounds good.

CATHERINE: Plus fashion tips, knock-knock jokes—I mean it was *nuts*, okay?

HAL: He was ill. It was a tragedy.

CATHERINE: Later the writing phase: scribbling nineteen, twenty hours a day . . . I   325
ordered him a case of notebooks and he used every one.

    I dropped out of school . . .

    I'm glad he's dead.

HAL: I understand why you'd feel that way.

CATHERINE: Fuck you.

HAL: You're right. I can't imagine dealing with that. It must have been awful. I know you—

CATHERINE: You don't know me. I want to be alone. I don't want him around.

HAL: *(confused)* Him? I don't—   330

CATHERINE: You. I don't want you here.

HAL: Why?

CATHERINE: He's dead.

HAL: But I'm not—

CATHERINE: *He's* dead; I don't need any *protégés* around.   335

HAL: There will be others.

CATHERINE: What?

HAL: You think I'm the only one? People are already working over his stuff.
Someone's gonna read those notebooks.

CATHERINE: I'll do it.

HAL: No, you—   340

CATHERINE: He's my father, I'll do it.

HAL: You can't.

CATHERINE: Why not?

HAL: You don't have the math. It's all just squiggles on a page. You wouldn't know the good stuff from the junk.

CATHERINE: It's all junk.   345

HAL: If it's not we can't afford to miss any through carelessness.

CATHERINE: I know mathematics.

HAL: If there was anything up there it would be pretty high-order. It would take a professional to recognize it.

CATHERINE: I think I could recognize it.

HAL: *(Patient)* Cathy . . .   350

CATHERINE: *What?*

HAL: I know your dad taught you some basic stuff, but come on.

CATHERINE: You don't think I could do it.

HAL: I'm sorry: I know that you couldn't. (*Beat. Catherine snatches his backpack.*)
Hey! Oh come on. Give me a break. (*Catherine opens the backpack and rifles through it.*) This isn't an airport.

Catherine removes items one by one. A water bottle. Some workout clothes. An orange. Drumsticks. Nothing else. She puts everything back in and gives it back. Beat.

355   CATHERINE: You can come tomorrow.

Beat. They are both embarrassed.

HAL: The university health service is uh very good.
      My mom died a couple years ago and I was pretty broken up. Also my work
      wasn't going that well . . . I went over and talked to this doctor. I saw her for a
      couple months and it really helped.
CATHERINE: I'm fine.

Beat.

HAL: Also exercise is great. I run along the lake a couple of mornings a week. It's
      not too cold yet. If you wanted to come sometime I could pick you up. We
      wouldn't have to talk . . .
CATHERINE: No thanks.
360   HAL: All right. I'm gonna be late for the show. I better go.
CATHERINE: Okay.

Beat.

HAL: It's seriously like twenty minutes up to the club. We go on, we play, we're ter-
      rible but we buy everyone drinks afterward to make up for it. You're home by
      four, four-thirty, tops . . .
CATHERINE: Good night.
HAL: Good night. (*He starts to exit. He has forgotten his jacket.*)
365   CATHERINE: Wait, your coat.
HAL: No, you don't have to—

*Catherine picks up his jacket. As she does, a composition book that was folded up in the coat
falls to the floor. Beat. She picks it up, trembling with rage.*

CATHERINE: I'm *paranoid*?
HAL: Wait.
CATHERINE: You think I should go *jogging*?
370   HAL: Just hold on.
CATHERINE: Get out!
HAL: Can I please just—
CATHERINE: Get the fuck out of my house.
HAL: Listen to me for a *minute*.
375   CATHERINE: (*Waving the book*) You stole this!
HAL: Let me *explain*!
CATHERINE: You stole it from *me*, you stole it from my *father*—

Hal snatches the book.

HAL: I want to show you something. Will you calm down?
CATHERINE: Give it back.
380   HAL: Just wait a minute.
CATHERINE: I'm calling the police. (*She picks up the phone and dials.*)

HAL: Don't. Look, I borrowed the book, all right? I'm sorry, I just picked it up before I came downstairs and thought I'd—

CATHERINE: *(On phone)* Hello?

HAL: I did it for a reason.

CATHERINE: Hello, police? I—Yes, I'd like to report a robbery in progress.   385

HAL: I noticed something—something your father wrote. All right? Not math, something he *wrote*. Here, let me show you.

CATHERINE: A *robbery*.

HAL: Will you put the fucking phone down and listen to me?

CATHERINE: *(On phone)* Yes, I'm at 5724 South—

HAL: It's about you. See? *You*. It was written about you. Here's your name: *Cathy*.   390
See?

CATHERINE: South . . .

Catherine pauses. She seems to be listening. Hal reads.

HAL: "A good day. Some very good news from Catherine." I didn't know what that referred to, but I thought you might . . .

CATHERINE: When did he write this?

HAL: I think four years ago. The handwriting is steady. It must have been during his remission. There's more. *(A moment. Catherine hangs up the phone.)* "Machinery not working yet but I am patient." "The machinery" is what he called his mind, his ability to do mathematics.

CATHERINE: I know.   395

HAL: *(reads)* "I know I'll get there. I am an auto mechanic who after years of greasy work on a hopeless wreck turns the ignition and hears a faint cough. I am not driving yet, but there's cause for optimism. Talking with students helps. So does being outside, eating meals in restaurants, riding buses, all the activities of 'normal' life.

"Most of all Cathy. The years she has lost caring for me. I almost wrote 'wasted.' Yet her refusal to let me be institutionalized—her keeping me at home, caring for me herself, has certainly saved my life. Made writing this possible. Made it possible to imagine doing math again. Where does her strength come from? I can never repay her.

"Today is her birthday: she is twenty-one. I'm taking her to dinner." Dated September 4. That's tomorrow.

CATHERINE: It's today.

HAL: You're right. *(He gives her the book.)* I thought you might want to see it. I shouldn't have tried to sneak it out. Tomorrow I was going to—it sounds stupid now. I was going to wrap it. Happy birthday.

Hal exits. Catherine is alone. She puts her head in her hands. She weeps. Eventually she stops, wipes her eyes. From off: a police siren, drawing closer.

CATHERINE: Shit.   400

Fade

SCENE 2

The next morning. Claire, stylish, attractive, drinks coffee from a mug. She has brought bagels and fruit on a tray out to the porch. She arranges them on two plates. She notices the champagne bottle lying on the floor. She picks it up and sets it on a table. Catherine enters. Her hair is wet from a shower.

CLAIRE: Better. Much.
CATHERINE: Thanks.
CLAIRE: Feel better?
CATHERINE: Yeah.
5   CLAIRE: You look a million times better. Have some coffee.
CATHERINE: Okay.
CLAIRE: How do you take it?
CATHERINE: Black.
CLAIRE: Have a little milk. (*She pours.*) Want a banana? It's a good thing I brought
    food: there was nothing in the house.
10   CATHERINE: I've been meaning to go shopping.
CLAIRE: Have a bagel.
CATHERINE: No. I hate breakfast. (*Beat.*)
CLAIRE: You didn't put on the dress.
CATHERINE: Didn't really feel like it.
15   CLAIRE: Don't you want to try it on? See if it fits?
CATHERINE: I'll put it on later.

Beat.

CLAIRE: If you want to dry your hair I have a hair dryer.
CATHERINE: Nah.
CLAIRE: Did you use that conditioner I brought you?
20   CATHERINE: No, shit, I forgot.
CLAIRE: It's my favorite. You'll love it, Katie. I want you to try it.
CATHERINE: I'll use it next time.
CLAIRE: You'll like it. It has jojoba.
CATHERINE: What is "jojoba"?
25   CLAIRE: It's something they put in for healthy hair.
CATHERINE: Hair is dead.
CLAIRE: What?
CATHERINE: It's dead tissue. You can't make it "healthy."
CLAIRE: Whatever, it's something that's good for your hair.
30   CATHERINE: What, a chemical?
CLAIRE: No, it's organic.
CATHERINE: Well it can be organic and still be a chemical.
CLAIRE: I don't know what it is.
CATHERINE: Haven't you ever heard of organic chemistry?
35   CLAIRE: It makes my hair feel, look, and smell good. That's the extent of my
    information about it. You might like it if you decide to use it.
CATHERINE: Thanks, I'll try it.

CLAIRE: Good. (*Beat.*) If the dress doesn't fit we can go downtown and exchange it.
CATHERINE: Okay.
CLAIRE: I'll take you to lunch.
CATHERINE: Great.   40
CLAIRE: Maybe Sunday before I go back. Do you need anything?
CATHERINE: Like clothes?
CLAIRE: Or anything. While I'm here.
CATHERINE: Nah, I'm cool.

Beat.

CLAIRE: I thought we'd have some people over tonight. If you're feeling okay.   45
CATHERINE: I'm feeling okay, Claire, stop saying that.
CLAIRE: You don't have any plans?
CATHERINE: No.
CLAIRE: I ordered some food. Wine, beer.
CATHERINE: We are burying Dad this afternoon.   50
CLAIRE: I think it will be all right. Anyone who's been to the funeral and wants to
    come over for something to eat can. And it's the only time I can see any old
    Chicago friends. It'll be nice. It's a funeral but we don't have to be completely
    grim about it. *If* it's okay with you.
CATHERINE: Yes, sure.
CLAIRE: It's been a stressful time. It would be good to relax in a low-key way. Mitch
    says Hi.
CATHERINE: Hi Mitch.
CLAIRE: He's really sorry he couldn't come.   55
CATHERINE: Yeah, he's gonna miss all the fun.
CLAIRE: He wanted to see you. He sends his love. I told him you'd see him soon
    enough. (*Beat.*) We're getting married.
CATHERINE: No shit.
CLAIRE: Yes! We just decided.
CATHERINE: Yikes.   60
CLAIRE: Yes!
CATHERINE: When?
CLAIRE: January.
CATHERINE: Huh.
CLAIRE: We're not going to do a huge thing. His folks are gone too. Just City Hall,   65
    then a big dinner at our favorite restaurant for all our friends. And you, of
    course. I hope you'll be in the wedding.
CATHERINE: Yeah. Of course. Congratulations, Claire, I'm really happy for you.
CLAIRE: Thanks. Me too. We just decided it was time. His job is great. I just got
    promoted . . .
CATHERINE: Huh.
CLAIRE: You will come?
CATHERINE: Yes, sure. January? I mean, I don't have to check my calendar or   70
    anything. Sure.
CLAIRE: That makes me very happy. (*Beat. From here on Claire treads gingerly.*)

CLAIRE: How are you?

CATHERINE: Okay.

CLAIRE: How are you feeling about everything?

75 CATHERINE: About "everything"?

CLAIRE: About Dad.

CATHERINE: What about him?

CLAIRE: How are you feeling about his death? Are you all right?

CATHERINE: Yes, I am.

80 CLAIRE: Honestly?

CATHERINE: Yes.

CLAIRE: I think in some ways it was the "right time." If there is ever a right time.
        Do you know what you want to do now?

CATHERINE: No.

CLAIRE: Do you want to stay here?

85 CATHERINE: I don't know.

CLAIRE: Do you want to go back to school?

CATHERINE: I haven't thought about it.

CLAIRE: Well there's a lot to think about.
        How do you feel?

CATHERINE: Physically? Great. Except my hair seems kind of unhealthy, I wish
        there were something I could do about that.

90 CLAIRE: Come on, Catherine.

CATHERINE: What is the point of all these questions?

Beat.

CLAIRE: Katie, some policemen came by while you were in the shower.

CATHERINE: Yeah?

CLAIRE: They said they were "checking up" on things here. Seeing how everything
        was this morning.

95 CATHERINE: *(neutral)* That was nice.

CLAIRE: They told me they responded to a call last night and came to the house.

CATHERINE: Yeah?

CLAIRE: Did you call the police last night?

CATHERINE: Yeah.

100 CLAIRE: Why?

CATHERINE: I thought the house was being robbed.

CLAIRE: But it wasn't.

CATHERINE: No. I changed my mind.

Beat.

CLAIRE: First you call 911 with an emergency and then you hang up on them—

105 CATHERINE: I didn't really want them to come.

CLAIRE: So why did you call?

CATHERINE: I was trying to get this guy out of the house.

CLAIRE: Who?

CATHERINE: One of Dad's students.

CLAIRE: Dad hasn't had any students for years. 110
CATHERINE: No, he *was* Dad's student. Now he's—he's a mathematician.
CLAIRE: Why was he in the house in the first place?
CATHERINE: Well he's been coming here to look at Dad's notebooks.
CLAIRE: In the middle of the night?
CATHERINE: It was late. I was waiting for him to finish, and last night I thought he 115
might have been stealing them.
CLAIRE: Stealing the notebooks.
CATHERINE: *Yes.* So I told him to go.
CLAIRE: Was he stealing them?
CATHERINE: Yes. That's why I called the police—
CLAIRE: What is this man's name? 120
CATHERINE: Hal. Harold. Harold Dobbs.
CLAIRE: The police said you were the only one here.
CATHERINE: He left before they got here.
CLAIRE: With the notebooks?
CATHERINE: No, Claire, don't be stupid, there are over a hundred notebooks. He 125
was only stealing *one*, but he was stealing it so he could give it *back* to me, so
I let him go so he could play with his band on the north side.
CLAIRE: His band?
CATHERINE: He was late. He wanted me to come with him but I was like, Yeah, right.

Beat.

CLAIRE: *(gently)* Is "Harold Dobbs" your boyfriend?
CATHERINE: No!
CLAIRE: Are you sleeping with him? 130
CATHERINE: What? Euughh! No! He's a math geek!
CLAIRE: And he's in a band? A rock band?
CATHERINE: No, a marching band. He plays trombone. Yes, a rock band!
CLAIRE: What is the name of his band?
CATHERINE: How should I know? 135
CLAIRE: "Harold Dobbs" didn't tell you the name of his rock band?
CATHERINE: No. I don't know. Look in the paper. They were playing last night.
They do a song called "Imaginary Number" that doesn't exist.

Beat.

CLAIRE: I'm sorry, I'm just trying to understand: is "Harold Dobbs"—
CATHERINE: Stop saying "Harold Dobbs."
CLAIRE: Is this . . . person . . . 140
CATHERINE: *Harold Dobbs exists.*
CLAIRE: I'm sure he does.
CATHERINE: He's a mathematician at the University of Chicago. Call the fucking
math department.
CLAIRE: Don't get upset. I'm just trying to understand! I mean if you found out
some creepy grad student was trying to take some of Dad's papers and you called
the police, I'd understand, and if you were out here partying, drinking with your
boyfriend, I'd understand. But the two stories don't go together.

145   CATHERINE: Because you made up the "boyfriend" story. I was here *alone*.
CLAIRE: Harold Dobbs wasn't here?
CATHERINE: No, he—*Yes*, he was here, but we weren't partying!
CLAIRE: You weren't drinking with him?
CATHERINE: No!
150   CLAIRE: *(She holds up the champagne bottle.)* This was sitting right here. Who were
   you drinking champagne with?

Catherine hesitates.

CATHERINE: With no one.
CLAIRE: Are you sure?
CATHERINE: Yes.

Beat.

CLAIRE: The police said you were abusive. *(Catherine doesn't say anything.)* They
   said you're lucky they didn't haul you in.
155   CATHERINE: These guys were assholes, Claire. They wouldn't go away. They wanted
   me to fill out a report . . .
CLAIRE: Were you abusive?
CATHERINE: This one cop kept spitting on me when he talked. It was disgusting.
CLAIRE: Did you use the word "dickhead"?
CATHERINE: Oh I don't remember.
160   CLAIRE: Did you tell one cop . . . to go fuck the other cop's mother?
CATHERINE: *No.*
CLAIRE: That's what they said.
CATHERINE: Not with that phrasing.
CLAIRE: Did you strike one of them?
165   CATHERINE: They were trying to come in the house!
CLAIRE: Oh my God.
CATHERINE: I might have *pushed* him a little.
CLAIRE: They said you were either drunk or disturbed.
CATHERINE: They wanted to come in here and *search my house*—
170   CLAIRE: *You* called *them*.
CATHERINE: Yes but I didn't actually *want* them to come. But they did come and
   then they started acting like they owned the place, pushing me around, calling
   me "girly," smirking at me, laughing: they were assholes.
CLAIRE: These guys seemed perfectly nice. They were off-duty and they took the
   trouble to come back here at the end of their shift to check up on you. They
   were very polite.
CATHERINE: Well people are nicer to you.

Beat.

CLAIRE: Katie. Would you like to come to New York?
175   CATHERINE: Yes, I told you, I'll come in January.
CLAIRE: You could come sooner. We'd love to have you. You could stay with us.
   It'd be fun.

CATHERINE: I don't want to.

CLAIRE: Mitch has become an *excellent* cook. It's like his hobby now. He buys all these gadgets. Garlic press, olive oil sprayer . . . Every night there's something new. Delicious, wonderful meals. The other day he made vegetarian chili!

CATHERINE: What the fuck are you talking about?

CLAIRE: Stay with us for a while. We would have so much fun.   180

CATHERINE: Thanks, I'm okay here.

CLAIRE: Chicago is dead. New York is so much more fun, you can't believe it.

CATHERINE: The "fun" thing is really not where my focus is at the moment.

CLAIRE: I think New York would be a really fun and . . . safe . . . place for you to—

CATHERINE: I don't need a safe place and I don't want to have any fun! I'm   185
perfectly fine here.

CLAIRE: You look tired. I think you could use some downtime.

CATHERINE: Downtime?

CLAIRE: Katie, please. You've had a very hard time.

CATHERINE: I'm *perfectly okay*.

CLAIRE: I think you're upset and exhausted.   190

CATHERINE: I was *fine* till you got here.

CLAIRE: Yes, but you—

HAL: (*from off*) Catherine?

CLAIRE: Who is that?

Beat. Hal enters.

HAL: Hey, I—   195

Catherine stands and points triumphantly at him.

CATHERINE: *Harold Dobbs!*

HAL: (*confused*) Hi.

CATHERINE: Okay? I really don't need this, Claire. I'm fine, you know, I'm totally fine, and then you swoop in here with these questions, and "Are you okay?" and your soothing tone of voice and "Oh, the poor policemen"—I think the police can handle themselves!—and bagels and bananas and jojoba and "Come to New York" and vegetarian *chili*. I mean it really pisses me off so just *save it*.

Beat.

CLAIRE: (*Smoothly, to Hal*) I'm Claire. Catherine's sister.

HAL: Oh, hi. Hal. Nice to meet you. (*Uncomfortable beat.*) I . . . hope it's not too   200
early. I was just going to try to get some work done before the uh—if uh if . . .

CLAIRE: Yes!

CATHERINE: Sure, okay.

Hal exits. A moment.

CLAIRE: That's Harold Dobbs?

CATHERINE: Yes.

CLAIRE: He's cute.   205

CATHERINE: (*disgusted*) Eugh.

CLAIRE: He's a mathematician?

CATHERINE: I think you owe me an apology, Claire.

CLAIRE: We need to make some decisions. But I shouldn't have tried to start first thing in the morning. I don't want an argument. (*Beat.*) Maybe Hal would like a bagel?

Beat. Catherine doesn't take the hint. She exits.

Fade

SCENE 3

Night. Inside the house a party is in progress. Loud music from a not-very-good but enthusiastic band. Catherine is alone on the porch. She wears a flattering black dress. Inside, the band finishes a number. Cheers, applause. After a moment Hal comes out. He wears a dark suit. He has taken off his tie. He is sweaty and revved up from playing. He holds two bottles of beer. Catherine regards him. A beat.

CATHERINE: I feel that for a funeral reception this might have gotten a bit out of control.

HAL: Aw come on. It's great. Come on in.

CATHERINE: I'm okay.

HAL: We're done playing, I promise.

5   CATHERINE: No thanks.

HAL: Do you want a beer?

CATHERINE: I'm okay.

HAL: I brought you one.

Beat. Catherine hesitates.

CATHERINE: Okay. (*She takes it, sips.*) How many people are in there?

10   HAL: It's down to about forty.

CATHERINE: Forty?

HAL: Just the hardcore partyers.

CATHERINE: My sister's friends.

HAL: No, mathematicians. Your sister's friends left hours ago. The guys were really pleased to be asked to participate. They worshipped your dad.

15   CATHERINE: It was Claire's idea.

HAL: It was good.

CATHERINE: (*concedes*) The performance of "Imaginary Number" was . . . sort of . . . moving.

HAL: Good funeral. I mean not "good," but—

CATHERINE: No. Yeah.

20   HAL: Can you believe how many people came?

CATHERINE: I was surprised.

HAL: I think he would have liked it. (*Catherine looks at him.*) Sorry, it's not my place to—

CATHERINE: No, you're right. Everything was better than I thought.

Beat.

HAL: You look great.
CATHERINE: (*indicates the dress*) Claire gave it to me.   25
HAL: I like it.
CATHERINE: It doesn't really fit.
HAL: No, Catherine, it's good.

A moment. Noise from inside.

CATHERINE: When do you think they'll leave?
HAL: No way to know. Mathematicians are insane. I went to this conference in   30
    Toronto last fall. I'm young, right? I'm in shape, I thought I could hang with the
    big boys. Wrong. I've never been so exhausted in my life. Forty-eight straight
    hours of partying, drinking, drugs, papers, lectures . . .
CATHERINE: Drugs?
HAL: Yeah. Amphetamines mostly. I mean, I don't. Some of the older guys are
    really hooked.
CATHERINE: Really?
HAL: Yeah, they think they need it.
CATHERINE: Why?   35
HAL: They think math's a young man's game. Speed keeps them racing, makes
    them feel sharp. There's this fear that your creativity peaks around twenty-three
    and it's all downhill from there. Once you hit fifty it's over, you might as well
    teach high school.
CATHERINE: That's what my father thought.
HAL: I dunno. Some people stay prolific.
CATHERINE: Not many.
HAL: No, you're right. Really original work—it's all young guys.   40
CATHERINE: Young guys.
HAL: Young people.
CATHERINE: But it is men, mostly.
HAL: There are some women.
CATHERINE: Who?   45
HAL: There's a woman at Stanford, I can't remember her name.
CATHERINE: Sophie Germain.
HAL: Yeah? I've probably seen her at meetings, I just don't think I've met her.
CATHERINE: She was born in Paris in 1776.

Beat.

HAL: So I've definitely never met her.   50
CATHERINE: She was trapped in her house.
    The French Revolution was going on, the Terror. She had to stay inside for
    safety and she passed the time reading in her father's study. The Greeks . . . Later
    she tried to get a real education but the schools didn't allow women. So she
    wrote letters. She wrote to Gauss. She used a man's name. Uh—Antoine-August
    Le Blanc. She sent him some proofs involving a certain kind of prime number,
    important work. He was delighted to correspond with such a brilliant young
    man. Dad gave me a book about her.

HAL: I'm stupid. Sophie Germain, of course.

CATHERINE: You know her?

HAL: Germain Primes.

55 CATHERINE: Right.

HAL: They're famous. Double them and add one, and you get another prime. Like two. Two is prime, doubled plus one is five: also prime.

CATHERINE: Right. Or $92,305 \times 2^{16,998} + 1$.

HAL: *(startled)* Right.

CATHERINE: That's the biggest one. The biggest one known . . .

Beat.

60 HAL: Did he ever find out who she was? Gauss.

CATHERINE: Yeah. Later a mutual friend told him the brilliant young man was a woman.

He wrote to her: "A taste for the mysteries of numbers is excessively rare, but when a person of the sex which, according to our customs and prejudices, must encounter infinitely more difficulties than men to familiarize herself with these thorny researches, succeeds nevertheless in penetrating the most obscure parts of them, then without a doubt she must have the noblest courage, quite extraordinary talents, and superior genius."

(Now self-conscious.) I memorized it . . .

Hal stares at her. He suddenly kisses her, then stops, embarrassed. He moves away.

HAL: Sorry. I'm a little drunk.

CATHERINE: It's okay. *(Uncomfortable beat.)* I'm sorry about yesterday. I wasn't helpful. About the work you're doing. Take as long as you need upstairs.

65 HAL: You were fine. I was pushy.

CATHERINE: I was awful.

HAL: No. My timing was terrible. Anyway, you're probably right.

CATHERINE: What?

HAL: About it being junk.

70 CATHERINE: *(nods)* Yes.

HAL: I read through a lot of stuff today, just skimming. Except for the book I stole—

CATHERINE: Oh God, I'm sorry about that.

HAL: No, you were right.

CATHERINE: I shouldn't have called the police.

75 HAL: It was my fault.

CATHERINE: No.

HAL: The point is, that book—I'm starting to think it's the only lucid one, really. And there's no math in it.

CATHERINE: No.

HAL: I mean, I'll keep reading, but if I don't find anything in a couple of days . . .

80 CATHERINE: Back to the drums.

HAL: Yeah.

CATHERINE: And your own research.

HAL: Such as it is.

CATHERINE: What's wrong with it?

HAL: It's not exactly setting the world on fire.   85

CATHERINE: Oh come on.

HAL: It sucks, basically.

CATHERINE: Harold.

HAL: My papers get turned down. For the right reasons—my stuff is trivial. The big
    ideas aren't there.

CATHERINE: It's not about big ideas. It's work. You've got to chip away at a problem.   90

HAL: That's not what your dad did.

CATHERINE: I think it was, in a way. He'd attack a question from the side, from
    some weird angle, sneak up on it, grind away at it. He was slogging. He was just
    so much faster than anyone else that from the outside it looked magical.

HAL: I don't know.

CATHERINE: I'm just guessing.

HAL: Plus the work was beautiful. You can read it for pleasure. It's streamlined: no   95
    wasted moves, like a ninety-five-mile-an-hour fastball. It's just . . . elegant.

CATHERINE: Yeah.

HAL: And that's what you can never duplicate. At least I can't. It's okay. At a
    certain point you realize it's not going to happen, you readjust your expecta-
    tions. I enjoy teaching.

CATHERINE: You might come up with something.

HAL: I'm twenty-eight, remember? On the downhill slope.

CATHERINE: Have you tried speed? I've heard it helps.   100

HAL: (*laughs*) Yeah.

Beat.

CATHERINE: So, Hal.

HAL: Yeah?

CATHERINE: What do you do for sex?

HAL: What?   105

CATHERINE: At your conferences.

HAL: Uh, I uh—

CATHERINE: Isn't that why people hold conferences? Travel. Room service.
    Tax-deductible sex in big hotel beds.

HAL: (*laughs, nervous*) Maybe. I don't know.   110

CATHERINE: So what do you do? All you guys.

Beat. Is she flirting with him? Hal is not sure.

HAL: Well we are scientists.

CATHERINE: So?

HAL: So there's a lot of experimentation.

CATHERINE: (*laughs*) I see.   115

*Beat. Catherine goes to him. She kisses him. A longer kiss. It ends. Hal is surprised and
pleased.*

HAL: Huh.

CATHERINE: That was nice.

HAL: Really?

CATHERINE: Yes.

120 HAL: Again?

CATHERINE: Yes.

Kiss.

HAL: I always liked you.

CATHERINE: You did?

HAL: Even before I knew you. I'd catch glimpses of you when you visited your dad's office at school. I wanted to talk to you, but I thought, No, you do not flirt with your doctoral adviser's daughter.

125 CATHERINE: Especially when your adviser's crazy.

HAL: Especially then.

Kiss.

CATHERINE: You came here once. Four years ago. Remember?

HAL: Sure. I can't believe you do. I was dropping off a draft of my thesis for your dad. Jesus I was nervous.

CATHERINE: You looked nervous.

130 HAL: I can't believe you remember that.

CATHERINE: I remember you. *(Kiss.)* I thought you seemed . . . not boring.

They continue to kiss.

Fade

SCENE 4

The next morning. Catherine alone on the porch, in a robe. Hal enters, half-dressed. He walks up behind her quietly. She hears him and turns.

HAL: How long have you been up?

CATHERINE: A while.

HAL: Did I oversleep?

CATHERINE: No.

Beat. Morning-after awkwardness.

5 HAL: Is your sister up?

CATHERINE: No. She's flying home in a couple hours. I should probably wake her.

HAL: Let her sleep. She was doing some pretty serious drinking with the theoretical physicists last night.

CATHERINE: I'll make her some coffee when she gets up.

Beat.

HAL: Sunday mornings I usually go out. Get the paper, have some breakfast.

10 CATHERINE: Okay.

Beat.

HAL: Do you want to come?

CATHERINE: Oh. No. I ought to stick around until Claire leaves.

HAL: All right. Do you mind if I stay?

CATHERINE: No. You can work if you want.

HAL: *(Taken aback)* Okay.   15

CATHERINE: Okay.

HAL: Should I?

CATHERINE: If you want to.

HAL: Do you want me to go?

CATHERINE: Do you want to go?   20

HAL: I want to stay here with you.

CATHERINE: Oh . . .

HAL: I want to spend the day with you if possible. I'd like to spend as much time
with you as I can unless of course I'm coming on *way* too strong right now and
scaring you in which case I'll begin backpedaling immediately . . . (*Catherine
laughs. Her relief is evident; so is his. They kiss.*) How embarrassing is it if I say last
night was wonderful?

CATHERINE: It's only embarrassing if I don't agree.

HAL: Uh, so . . .   25

CATHERINE: Don't be embarrassed. (*They kiss. After a moment she breaks off. She
hesitates, making a decision. Then she takes a chain from around her neck. There is a
key on the chain. She tosses it to Hal.*) Here.

HAL: What's this?

CATHERINE: It's a key.

HAL: Ah.

CATHERINE: Try it.   30

HAL: Where?

CATHERINE: Bottom drawer of the desk in my dad's office.

HAL: What's in there?

CATHERINE: There's one way to find out, Professor.

HAL: Now? (*Catherine shrugs. He laughs, unsure if this is a joke or not.*) Okay.   35

*Hal kisses her quickly, then goes inside. Catherine smiles to herself. She is happy, on the edge
of being giddy. Claire enters, hungover. She sits down, squinting.*

CATHERINE: Good morning.

CLAIRE: Please don't yell please!

CATHERINE: Are you all right?

CLAIRE: No. (*Beat. She clutches her head.*) Those fucking physicists.

CATHERINE: What happened?   40

CLAIRE: Thanks a *lot* for leaving me all alone with them.

CATHERINE: Where were your friends?

CLAIRE: My stupid friends left—it was only eleven o'clock!—they all had to get
home and pay their babysitters or bake bread or something. I'm left alone with
these lunatics . . .

CATHERINE: Why did you drink so much?

45   CLAIRE: I thought I could keep up with them. I thought they'd stop. They didn't.
        Oh God. "Have another tequila . . ."
    CATHERINE: Do you want some coffee?
    CLAIRE: In a minute. *(Beat.)* That *band.*
    CATHERINE: Yeah.
    CLAIRE: They were terrible.
50   CATHERINE: They were okay. They had fun. I think.
    CLAIRE: Well as long as everyone had fun. *(Beat.)* Your dress turned out
        all right.
    CATHERINE: I love it.
    CLAIRE: You do.
    CATHERINE: Yeah, it's wonderful.
55   CLAIRE: I was surprised you even wore it.
    CATHERINE: I love it, Claire. Thanks.
    CLAIRE: *(surprised)* You're welcome. You're in a good mood.
    CATHERINE: Should I not be?
    CLAIRE: Are you kidding? No. I'm thrilled. *(Beat.)* I'm leaving in a few hours.
60   CATHERINE: I know.
    CLAIRE: The house is a wreck. Don't clean it up yourself. I'll hire someone to
        come in.
    CATHERINE: Thanks. You want your coffee?
    CLAIRE: No, thanks.
    CATHERINE: *(starting in)* It's no trouble.
65   CLAIRE: Hold on a sec, Katie. I just . . . *(She takes a breath.)* I'm leaving soon. I—
    CATHERINE: You said. I know.
    CLAIRE: I'd still like you to come to New York.
    CATHERINE: Yes: January.
    CLAIRE: I'd like you to move to New York.
70   CATHERINE: Move?
    CLAIRE: Would you think about it? For me? You could stay with me and Mitch at
        first. There's plenty of room. Then you could get your own place. I've already
        scouted some apartments for you, really cute places.
    CATHERINE: What would I do in New York?
    CLAIRE: What are you doing here?
    CATHERINE: I live here.
75   CLAIRE: You could do whatever you want. You could work, you could go to school.
    CATHERINE: I don't know, Claire. This is pretty major.
    CLAIRE: I realize that.
    CATHERINE: I know you mean well. I'm just not sure what I want to do. I mean
        to be honest you were right yesterday. I do feel a little confused. I'm tired. It's
        been a pretty weird couple of years. I think I'd like to take some time to figure
        things out.
    CLAIRE: You could do that in New York.
80   CATHERINE: And I could do it here.
    CLAIRE: But it would be much easier for me to get you set up in an apartment in
        New York, and—

CATHERINE: I don't need an apartment, I'll stay in the house.

CLAIRE: We're selling the house.

Beat.

CATHERINE: What?

CLAIRE: We—I'm selling it.   85

CATHERINE: When?

CLAIRE: I'm hoping to do the paperwork this week. I know it seems sudden.

CATHERINE: No one was here looking at the place, who are you selling it to?

CLAIRE: The university. They've wanted the block for years.

CATHERINE: *I live here.*   90

CLAIRE: Honey, now that Dad's gone it doesn't make sense. It's in bad shape. It
     costs a fortune to heat. It's time to let it go. Mitch agrees, it's a very smart move.
     We're lucky, we have a great offer—

CATHERINE: Where am I supposed to live?

CLAIRE: Come to New York.

CATHERINE: I can't believe this.

CLAIRE: It'll be so good. You deserve a change. This would be a whole new adven-   95
     ture for you.

CATHERINE: Why are you doing this?

CLAIRE: I want to help.

CATHERINE: By kicking me out of my *house?*

CLAIRE: It was my house too.

CATHERINE: You haven't lived here for years.   100

CLAIRE: I know that. You were on your own. I really regret that, Katie.

CATHERINE: Don't.

CLAIRE: I know I let you down. I feel awful about it. Now I'm trying to help.

CATHERINE: You want to help *now?*

CLAIRE: Yes.   105

CATHERINE: Dad is dead.

CLAIRE: I know.

CATHERINE: He's dead. Now that he's dead you fly in for the weekend and decide
     you want to help? *You're late.* Where have you been?

CLAIRE: I—

CATHERINE: Where were you five years ago? You weren't helping then.   110

CLAIRE: I was working.

CATHERINE: I was here. I lived with him *alone.*

CLAIRE: I was working fourteen-hour days. I paid every bill here. I paid off the mort-
     gage on this three-bedroom house while I was living in a studio in Brooklyn.

CATHERINE: You had your life. You got to finish school.

CLAIRE: You could have stayed in school!   115

CATHERINE: How?

CLAIRE: I would have done anything—I told you that. I told you a million times to
     do anything you wanted.

CATHERINE: What about Dad? Someone had to take care of him.

CLAIRE: He was ill. He should have been in a full-time professional-care situation.

120   CATHERINE: He didn't belong in the nuthouse.

       CLAIRE: He might have been better off.

       CATHERINE: How can you say that?

       CLAIRE: This is where I'm meant to feel guilty, right?

       CATHERINE: Sure, go for it.

125   CLAIRE: I'm heartless. My own father.

       CATHERINE: He needed to be here. In his own house, near the university, near his students, near everything that made him happy.

       CLAIRE: Maybe. Or maybe some real professional care would have done him more good than rattling around in a filthy house with *you* looking after him.

          I'm sorry, Catherine, it's not your fault. It's my fault for letting you do it.

       CATHERINE: I was right to keep him here.

       CLAIRE: No.

130   CATHERINE: What about his remission? Four years ago. He was healthy for almost a year.

       CLAIRE: And then he went right downhill again.

       CATHERINE: He might have been worse in a hospital.

       CLAIRE: And he *might* have been *better*. Did he ever do any work again?

       CATHERINE: No.

135   CLAIRE: No. (*Beat.*) And you might have been better.

       CATHERINE: (*keeping her voice under control*) Better than what?

       CLAIRE: Living here with him didn't do you any good. You said that yourself. You had so much talent . . .

       CATHERINE: You think I'm like Dad.

       CLAIRE: I think you have some of his talent and some of his tendency toward . . . instability.

Beat.

140   CATHERINE: Claire, in addition to the "cute apartments" that you've "scouted" for me in New York, would you by any chance also have devoted some of your considerable energies toward scouting out another type of—

       CLAIRE: *No.*

       CATHERINE: —living facility for your bughouse little sister?

       CLAIRE: *No!* Absolutely not. That is not what this is about.

       CATHERINE: Don't lie to me, Claire. I'm smarter than you.

Beat.

145   CLAIRE: The resources . . . I've investigated—

       CATHERINE: Oh my *God.*

       CLAIRE: —if you *wanted* to, all I'm saying is, the doctors in New York and the people are the *best*, and they—

       CATHERINE: *Fuck you.*

       CLAIRE: It would be entirely up to you. You wouldn't *live* anywhere, you can—

150   CATHERINE: I hate you.

       CLAIRE: Don't yell, please. Calm down.

       CATHERINE: *I hate you.* I—

Hal enters, holding a notebook. Claire and Catherine stop suddenly. Beat.

CLAIRE: What are you doing here? . . .

Claire stares at Catherine

HAL: How long have you known about this?
CATHERINE: A while.   155
HAL: Why didn't you tell me about it?
CATHERINE: I wasn't sure I wanted to.

Beat.

HAL: Thank you.
CATHERINE: You're welcome.
CLAIRE: What's going on?   160
HAL: God, Catherine, thank you.
CATHERINE: I thought you'd like to see it.
CLAIRE: What is it?
HAL: It's incredible.
CLAIRE: What *is* it?   165
HAL: Oh, uh, it's a result. A proof. I mean it looks like a proof. I mean it is a proof,
    a very long proof, I haven't read it all of course, or checked it, I don't even
    know if I *could* check it, but if it *is* a proof of what I think it's a proof of, it's . . . a
    very . . . *important* . . . proof.
CLAIRE: What does it prove?
HAL: It looks like it proves a theorem . . . a mathematical theorem about prime
    numbers, something mathematicians have been trying to prove since . . . since
    there were mathematicians, basically. Most people thought it couldn't be done.
CLAIRE: Where did you find it?
HAL: In your father's desk. Cathy told me about it.   170
CLAIRE: You know what this is?
CATHERINE: Sure.
CLAIRE: Is it good?
CATHERINE: Yes.
HAL: It's historic. If it checks out.   175
CLAIRE: What does it say?
HAL: I don't know yet. I've just read the first few pages.
CLAIRE: But what does it mean?
HAL: It means that during a time when everyone thought your dad was crazy . . . or
    barely functioning . . . he was doing some of the most important mathematics
    in the world. If it checks out, it means you publish instantly. It means newspa-
    pers all over the world are going to want to talk to the person who found this
    notebook.
CLAIRE: Cathy.   180
HAL: Cathy.
CATHERINE: I didn't find it.
HAL: Yes you did.

CATHERINE: No.

185 CLAIRE: Well did you find it or did Hal find it?

HAL: I didn't find it.

CATHERINE: I didn't find it.

I wrote it.

Curtain

ACT 2

SCENE 1

Robert is alone on the porch. He sits quietly, enjoying a drink, the quiet, the September afternoon. A notebook nearby, unopened. He closes his eyes, apparently dozing. It is four years earlier than the events in Act One. Catherine enters quietly. She stands behind her father for a moment.

ROBERT: Hello.

CATHERINE: How did you know I was here?

ROBERT: I heard you.

CATHERINE: I thought you were asleep.

5 ROBERT: On an afternoon like this? No.

CATHERINE: Do you need anything?

ROBERT: No.

CATHERINE: I'm going to the store.

ROBERT: What's for dinner?

10 CATHERINE: What do you want?

ROBERT: Not spaghetti.

CATHERINE: All right.

ROBERT: Disgusting stuff.

CATHERINE: That's what I was going to make.

15 ROBERT: I had a feeling. Good thing I spoke up. You make it too much.

CATHERINE: What do you want?

ROBERT: What do you have a taste for?

CATHERINE: Nothing.

ROBERT: Nothing at all?

20 CATHERINE: I don't care. I thought pasta would be easy.

ROBERT: Pasta, oh God, don't even say the word "pasta." It sounds so hopeless, like surrender: "Pasta would be easy." Yes, yes, it would. Pasta. It doesn't *mean* anything. It's just a euphemism people invented when they got sick of eating spaghetti.

CATHERINE: Dad, what do you want to eat?

ROBERT: I don't know.

CATHERINE: Well I don't know what to get.

25 ROBERT: I'll shop.

CATHERINE: No.

ROBERT: I'll do it.

CATHERINE: No, Dad, rest.

ROBERT: I wanted to take a walk anyway.

CATHERINE: Are you sure?   30

ROBERT: Yes. What about a walk to the lake? You and me.

CATHERINE: All right.

ROBERT: I would love to go to the lake. Then on the way home we'll stop at the
    store, see what jumps out at us.

CATHERINE: It's warm. It would be nice, if you're up for it.

ROBERT: You're damn right I'm up for it. We'll work up an appetite. Give me ten   35
    seconds, let me put this stuff away and we're out the door.

CATHERINE: I'm going to school.

Beat.

ROBERT: When?

CATHERINE: I'm gonna start at Northwestern at the end of the month.

ROBERT: Northwestern?

CATHERINE: They were great about my credits. They're taking me in as a sopho-   40
    more. I wasn't sure when to talk to you about it.

ROBERT: Northwestern?

CATHERINE: Yes.

ROBERT: What's wrong with Chicago?

CATHERINE: You still teach there. I'm sorry, it's too weird, taking classes in your
    department.

ROBERT: It's a long drive.   45

CATHERINE: Not that long, half an hour.

ROBERT: Still, twice a day . . .

CATHERINE: Dad, I'd live there.

Beat.

ROBERT: You'd actually want to live in Evanston?

CATHERINE: Yes. I'll still be close. I can come home whenever you want.   50
    You've been well—really well—for almost seven months.
    I don't think you need me here every minute of the day.

Beat.

ROBERT: This is all a done deal? You're in.

CATHERINE: Yes.

ROBERT: You're sure.

CATHERINE: *Yes.*

ROBERT: Who pays for it?   55

CATHERINE: They're giving me a free ride, Dad. They've been great.

ROBERT: On tuition, sure. What about food, books, clothes, gas, meals out—do you
    plan to have a social life?

CATHERINE: I don't know.

ROBERT: You gotta pay your own way on dates, at least the early dates, say the first
    three, otherwise they expect something.

CATHERINE: The money will be fine. Claire's gonna help out.   60

ROBERT: When did you talk to Claire?

CATHERINE: I don't know, a couple weeks ago.

ROBERT: You talk to her before you talk to me?

CATHERINE: There were a lot of details to work out. She was great, she offered to take care of all the expenses.

65 ROBERT: This is a big step. A different *city*—

CATHERINE: It's not even a long-distance phone call.

ROBERT: It's a huge place. They're serious up there. I mean serious. Yeah the football's a disaster but the math guys don't kid around. You haven't been in school. You sure you're ready? You can get buried up there.

CATHERINE: I'll be all right.

ROBERT: You're way behind.

70 CATHERINE: I know.

ROBERT: A year, at least.

CATHERINE: Thank you, *I know.* Look, I don't know if this is a good idea. I don't know if I can handle the work. I don't know if I can handle *any* of it.

ROBERT: For Chrissake, Catherine, you should have talked to me.

CATHERINE: Dad. Listen. If you ever . . . if for any reason it ever turned out that you needed me here full-time again—

75 ROBERT: *I won't.* That's not—

CATHERINE: I can always take a semester off, or—

ROBERT: No. Stop it. I just—the end of the *month?* Why didn't you say something before?

CATHERINE: Dad, come on. It took a while to set this up, and until recently, until very recently, you weren't—

ROBERT: You just said yourself I've been fine.

80 CATHERINE: Yes, but I didn't know—*I hoped,* but I didn't *know,* no one knew if this would last. I told myself to wait until I was sure about you. That you were feeling okay again. Consistently okay.

ROBERT: So I'm to take this conversation as a vote of confidence? I'm honored.

CATHERINE: Take it however you want. I believed you'd get better.

ROBERT: Well thank you very much.

CATHERINE: Don't thank me. I had to. I was living with you.

85 ROBERT: All right, that's enough, Catherine. Let's stay on the subject.

CATHERINE: This is the subject! There were *library books* upstairs stacked up to the ceiling, do you remember that? You were trying to decode *messages*—

ROBERT: The fucking books are gone, I took them back myself. Why do you bring that garbage up?

Knocking offstage. Beat. Catherine goes inside to answer the door. She returns with Hal. He carries a manila envelope. He is nervous.

ROBERT: Mr. Dobbs.

HAL: Hi. I hope it's not a bad time.

90 ROBERT: Yes it is, actually, you couldn't have picked worse.

HAL: Oh, I uh—

ROBERT: You interrupted an argument.

HAL: I'm sorry. I can come back.

ROBERT: It's all right. We needed a break.

HAL: Are you sure?   95

ROBERT: Yes. The argument was about dinner. We don't know what to eat. What's your suggestion?

A beat while Hal is on the spot.

HAL: Uh, there's a great pasta place not too far from here.

ROBERT: *No!*

CATHERINE: *(with Robert):* That is a *brilliant* idea.

ROBERT: Oh dear Jesus God, no.   100

CATHERINE: *(with Robert):* What's it called? Give me the address.

ROBERT: No! Sorry. Wrong answer, but thank you for trying.

Hal stands there, looking at both of them.

HAL: I can come back.

ROBERT: Stay. *(To Catherine.)* Where are you going?

CATHERINE: Inside.   105

ROBERT: What about dinner?

CATHERINE: What about him?

ROBERT: What are you doing here, Dobbs?

HAL: My timing sucks. I am really sorry.

ROBERT: Don't be silly.   110

HAL: I'll come to your office.

ROBERT: Stop. Sit down. Glad you're here. Don't let the dinner thing throw you, you'll bounce back. *(To Catherine.)* This should be easier. Let's back off the problem, let it breathe, come at it again when it's not looking.

CATHERINE: Fine. *(Exiting.)* Excuse me.

ROBERT: Sorry, I'm rude. Hal, this is my daughter Catherine. *(To Catherine.)* Don't go, have a drink with us. Catherine, Harold Dobbs.

CATHERINE: Hi.   115

HAL: Hi.

ROBERT: Hal is a grad student. He's doing his Ph.D., very promising stuff. Unfortunately for him, his work coincided with my return to the department and he got stuck with me.

HAL: No, no, it's been—I've been very lucky.

CATHERINE: How long have you been at U. of C.?

HAL: Well I've been working on my thesis for—   120

ROBERT: Hal's in our "Infinite" program. As he approaches completion of his dissertation, time approaches infinity. Would you like a drink, Hal?

HAL: Yes I would. And uh, with all due respect . . .

Hal hands Robert the envelope.

ROBERT: Really? *(He opens it and looks inside.)* You must have had an interesting few months.

HAL: *(cheerfully)* Worst summer of my life.

ROBERT: Congratulations.   125

HAL: It's just a draft. Based on everything we talked about last spring. (*Robert pours a drink. Hal babbles.*) I wasn't sure if I should wait till the quarter started, or if I should give it to you *now*, or hold off, do another draft, but I figured fuck it, I, I mean I just . . . let's just get it *over* with, so I thought I'd just come over and see if you were home, and—

ROBERT: Drink this.

HAL: Thanks. (*He drinks.*) I decided, I don't know, if it feels done, maybe it is.

ROBERT: Wrong. If it feels done, there are major errors.

130   HAL: Uh, I—

ROBERT: That's okay, that's good, we'll find them and fix them. Don't worry. You're on your way to a solid career, you'll be teaching younger, more irritating versions of yourself in no time.

HAL: Thank you.

ROBERT: Catherine's in the math department at Northwestern, Hal.

Catherine looks up, startled.

HAL: Oh, who are you working with?

135   CATHERINE: I'm just starting this fall. Undergrad.

ROBERT: She's starting in . . . three weeks?

CATHERINE: A little more.

Beat.

ROBERT: They have some good people at Northwestern. O'Donohue. Kaminsky.

CATHERINE: Yes.

140   ROBERT: They will work your ass off.

CATHERINE: I know.

ROBERT: You'll have to run pretty hard to catch up.

CATHERINE: I think I can do it.

ROBERT: Of course you can. (*Beat.*)

145   HAL: You must be excited.

CATHERINE: I am.

HAL: First year of school can be great.

CATHERINE: Yeah?

HAL: Sure, all the new people, new places, getting out of the house.

150   CATHERINE: (*Embarrassed*) Yes.

HAL: (*Embarrassed*) Or, no I—

ROBERT: Absolutely, getting the hell out of here, thank God, it's about time. I'll be glad to see the back of her.

CATHERINE: You will?

ROBERT: Of course. Maybe I want to have the place to myself for a while, did that ever occur to you? (*To Hal.*) It's awful the way children sentimentalize their parents. (*To Catherine.*) We could use some quiet around here.

155   CATHERINE: Oh don't worry, I'll come back. I'll be here every Sunday cooking up big vats of pasta to last you through the week.

ROBERT: And I'll drive up, strut around Evanston, embarrass you in front of your classmates.

CATHERINE: Good. So we'll be in touch.

ROBERT: Sure. And if you get stuck with a problem, give me a call.

CATHERINE: Okay. Same to you.

ROBERT: Fine. Make sure to get me your number. *(To Hal.)* I'm actually looking   160
forward to getting some work done.

HAL: Oh, what are you working on?

ROBERT: Nothing. *(Beat.)* Nothing at the moment.

    Which I'm glad of, really. This is the time of year when you don't want
to be tied down to anything. You want to be outside. I love Chicago in
September. Perfect skies. Sailboats on the water. Cubs losing. Warm, the
sun still hot . . . with the occasional blast of Arctic wind to keep you on your
toes, remind you of winter. Students coming back, bookstores full, everybody
busy.

    I was in a bookstore yesterday. Completely full, students buying books . . .
browsing . . . Students do a hell of a lot of browsing, don't they? Just browsing. You see them shuffling around with their backpacks, goofing off, taking
up space. You'd call it loitering except every once in a while they pick up a
book and flip the pages: "browsing." I admire it. It's an honest way to kill an
afternoon. In the back of a used bookstore, or going through a crate of somebody's old record albums—not looking for anything, just looking, what the hell,
touching the old book jackets, seeing what somebody threw out, seeing what
they underlined . . . Maybe you find something great, like an old thriller with a
painted cover from the forties, or a textbook one of your professors used when *he*
was a student—his name is written in it very carefully . . . Yeah, I like it. I like
watching the students. Wondering what they're gonna buy, what they're gonna
read. What kind of ideas they'll come up with when they settle down and get to
work . . .

    I'm not doing much right now. It does get harder. It's a stereotype that hap-
pens to be true, unfortunately for me—unfortunately for you, for all of us.

CATHERINE: Maybe you'll get lucky.

ROBERT: Maybe I will. Maybe you'll pick up where I left off.

CATHERINE: Don't hold your breath.   165

ROBERT: Don't underestimate yourself.

CATHERINE: Anyway.

Beat.

ROBERT: Another drink? Cathy? Hal?

CATHERINE: No thanks.

HAL: Thanks, I really should get going.   170

ROBERT: Are you sure?

HAL: Yes.

ROBERT: I'll call you when I've looked at this. Don't think about it till then. Enjoy
yourself, see some movies.

HAL: Okay.

ROBERT: You can come by my office in a week. Call it—   175

HAL: The eleventh?

ROBERT: Yes, we'll . . . (*Beat. He turns to Catherine. Grave*) I am sorry. I used to have a pretty good memory for numbers. Happy birthday.

CATHERINE: Thank you.

ROBERT: I am so sorry. I'm embarrassed.

180 CATHERINE: Dad, don't be stupid.

ROBERT: I didn't get you anything.

CATHERINE: Don't worry about it.

ROBERT: I'm taking you out.

CATHERINE: You don't have to.

185 ROBERT: We are going out. I didn't want to shop and cook. Let's go to dinner. Let's get the hell out of this neighborhood. What do you want to eat? Let's go to the North Side. Or Chinatown. Or Greektown. I don't know what's good anymore.

CATHERINE: Whatever you want.

ROBERT: Whatever *you* want goddamnit, Catherine, it's your birthday.

Beat.

CATHERINE: Steak.

ROBERT: Steak. Yes.

190 CATHERINE: No, first beer, really cold beer. Really cheap beer.

ROBERT: Done.

CATHERINE: That Chicago beer that's watery with no flavor and you can just drink *gallons* of it.

ROBERT: They just pump the water out of Lake Michigan and bottle it.

CATHERINE: It's so awful.

195 ROBERT: I have a taste for it myself.

CATHERINE: Then the steak, grilled really black, and potatoes and creamed spinach.

ROBERT: I remember a place. If it's still there I think it will do the trick.

CATHERINE: And dessert.

ROBERT: That goes without saying. It's your birthday, hooray. And there's the solution to our dinner problem. Thank you for reminding me, Harold Dobbs.

200 CATHERINE: (*To Hal.*) We're being rude. Do you want to come?

HAL: Oh, no, I shouldn't.

ROBERT: Why not? Please, come.

CATHERINE: Come on.

A tiny moment between Hal and Catherine. Hal wavers, then

HAL: No, I can't, I have plans. Thank you, though. Happy birthday.

CATHERINE: Thanks. Well. I'll let you out.

ROBERT: I'll see you on the eleventh, Hal.

HAL: Great.

CATHERINE: I'm gonna change my clothes, Dad. I'll be ready in a sec.

Hal and Catherine exit. A moment. It's darker. Robert looks out at the evening. Eventually he picks up the notebook and a pen. He sits down. He opens to a blank page. He writes.

ROBERT: "September fourth. A good day . . ." (*He continues to write.*)

Fade

SCENE 2

Morning. An instant after the end of Act One: Catherine, Claire, and Hal.

HAL: You wrote this?
CATHERINE: Yes.
CLAIRE: You mean Dad dictated it to you?
CATHERINE: No, its my proof. It's mine, I wrote it.
CLAIRE: When?   5
CATHERINE: I started after I quit school. I finished a few months before Dad died.
CLAIRE: Did he see it?
CATHERINE: No. He didn't know I was working on it. It wouldn't have mattered to
     him anyway, he was too sick.
HAL: I don't understand—you did this by yourself?
CATHERINE: Yes.   10
CLAIRE: It's in Dad's notebook.
CATHERINE: I used one of his blank books. There were a bunch of them upstairs.

Beat.

CLAIRE: (*To Hal.*) Tell me exactly where you found this.
HAL: In his study.
CATHERINE: In his desk. I gave him the—   15
CLAIRE: (*To Catherine.*) Hold on. (*To Hal.*) Where did you find it?
HAL: In the bottom drawer of the desk in the study, a locked drawer: Catherine
     gave me the key.
CLAIRE: Why was the drawer locked?
CATHERINE: It's mine, it's the drawer I keep my private things in. I've used it for
     years.
CLAIRE: (*To Hal.*) Was there anything else in the drawer?   20
HAL: No.
CATHERINE: No, that's the only—
CLAIRE: Can I see it? (*Hal gives Claire the book. She pages through it. Beat.*) I'm sorry,
     I just . . . (*To Catherine.*) The book was in the . . . You told him where to find
     it . . . You gave him the key . . . You wrote this incredible thing and you didn't
     tell anyone?
CATHERINE: I'm telling you both now. After I dropped out of school I had
     nothing to do. I was depressed, really depressed, but at a certain point
     I decided, Fuck it, I don't need them. It's just math, I can do it on my own.
     So I kept working here. I worked at night, after Dad had gone to sleep.
     It was hard but I did it.

Beat.

CLAIRE: Catherine, I'm sorry but I just find this very hard to believe.   25
CATHERINE: Claire. I wrote. The proof.

CLAIRE: I'm sorry, I—

CATHERINE: Claire . . .

CLAIRE: This is Dad's handwriting.

30 CATHERINE: It's not.

CLAIRE: It looks exactly like it.

CATHERINE: It's my writing.

CLAIRE: I'm sorry—

CATHERINE: Ask Hal, he's been looking at Dad's writing for weeks.

Claire gives Hal the book. He looks at it. Beat.

35 HAL: I don't know.

CATHERINE: Hal, come on.

CLAIRE: What does it look like?

HAL: It looks . . . I don't know what Catherine's handwriting looks like.

CATHERINE: It *looks* like *that.*

40 HAL: Okay. It . . . Okay. (*Beat. He hands the book back.*)

CLAIRE: I think—you know what? I think it's early, and people are tired and not in the best state to make decisions about emotional things, so maybe we should all just take a breath . . .

CATHERINE: You don't believe me?

CLAIRE: I don't know. I really don't know anything about this.

CATHERINE: Never mind. I don't know why I expected you to believe me about *anything.*

45 CLAIRE: Could you *tell* us the proof? That would show it was yours.

CATHERINE: You wouldn't understand it.

CLAIRE: Tell it to Hal.

CATHERINE: (*taking the book*) We could talk through it together. It might take a while.

CLAIRE: (*taking the book*) You can't use the book.

50 CATHERINE: For God's sake, it's forty pages long. I didn't *memorize* it. It's not a muffin recipe.

This is stupid. It's my book, my writing, my key, my drawer, my proof. Hal, tell her!

HAL: Tell her what?

CATHERINE: Whose book is that?

HAL: I don't know.

CATHERINE: What is the matter with you? You've been looking at his other stuff, you know there's nothing even remotely like this!

55 HAL: Look, Catherine—

CATHERINE: We'll go through the proof together. We'll sit down—if Claire will *please* let me have my book back—

CLAIRE: (*giving her the book*) All right, talk him through it.

HAL: That might take days and it still wouldn't show that she wrote it.

CATHERINE: Why not?

60 HAL: Your dad might have written it and explained it to you later. I'm not saying he did, I'm just saying there's no proof that you wrote this.

CATHERINE: Of course there isn't, but come on! He didn't do this, he couldn't have. He didn't do any mathematics at all for years. Even in the good year he couldn't work: you *know* that. You're supposed to be a scientist.

Beat.

HAL: You're right. Okay. Here's my suggestion. I know three or four guys at the department, very sharp, disinterested people who knew your father, knew his work. Let me take this to them.

CATHERINE: What?

HAL: I'll tell them we've found something, something potentially major, we're not sure about the authorship; I'll sit down with them. We'll go through the thing carefully—

CLAIRE: Good.   65

HAL: —and figure out exactly what we've got. It would only take a couple of days, probably, and then we'd have a lot more information.

CLAIRE: I think that's an excellent suggestion.

CATHERINE: You can't.

CLAIRE: Catherine.

CATHERINE: No! You can't take it.   70

HAL: I'm not "taking" it.

CATHERINE: This is what you wanted.

HAL: Oh come on, Jesus.

CATHERINE: You don't waste any time, do you? No hesitation.
     You can't wait to show them your brilliant discovery.

HAL: I'm trying to determine what this is.   75

CATHERINE: I'm telling you what it is.

HAL: You don't know!

CATHERINE: *I wrote it.*

HAL: *It's your father's handwriting.* (*Beat. Pained.*) At least it looks an awful lot like the writing in the other books. Maybe your writing looks exactly like his, I don't know.

CATHERINE: (*softly*) It does look like his.   80
     I didn't show this to anyone else. I could have. I wanted you to be the first to see it. I didn't know I wanted that until last night. It's *me.* I trusted you.

HAL: I know.

CATHERINE: Was I wrong?

HAL: No. I—

CATHERINE: I should have known she wouldn't believe me but why don't you?

HAL: This is one of his notebooks. The exact same kind he used.   85

CATHERINE: I told you. I just used one of his blank books. There were extras.

HAL: There aren't any extra books in the study.

CATHERINE: There were when I started writing the proof. I bought them for him. He must have used the rest up later.

HAL: And the writing.

CATHERINE: You want to test the handwriting?   90

HAL: No. It doesn't matter. He could have dictated it to you for Chrissake. It still doesn't make sense.

CATHERINE: Why not?

HAL: I'm a mathematician.

CATHERINE: Yes.

95   HAL: I know how hard it would be to come up with something like this. I mean it's impossible. You'd have to be . . . you'd have to be your dad, basically. Your dad at the peak of his powers.

CATHERINE: I'm a mathematician too.

HAL: Not like your dad.

CATHERINE: Oh, he's the only one who could have done this?

HAL: The only one I know.

100 CATHERINE: Are you sure?

HAL: Your father was the most—

CATHERINE: Just because you and the rest of the geeks worshipped him doesn't mean he wrote this proof, Hal!

HAL: He was the *best*. My generation hasn't produced anything like him. He revolutionized the field twice before he was twenty-two. I'm sorry, Catherine, but you took some classes at Northwestern for a few months.

CATHERINE: My education wasn't at Northwestern. It was living in this house for twenty-five years.

105 HAL: Even so, it doesn't matter. This is too advanced. I don't even understand most of it.

CATHERINE: You think it's too advanced.

HAL: Yes.

CATHERINE: It's too advanced for *you*.

HAL: You could not have done this work.

110 CATHERINE: But what if I did?

HAL: Well what if?

CATHERINE: It would be a real disaster for you, wouldn't it? And for the other geeks who *barely* finished their Ph.D.'s, who are marking time doing *lame* research, bragging about the conferences they go to—*wow*—playing in an *awful* band, and whining that they're intellectually past it at twenty-eight, *because they are*.

Beat. Hal hesitates, then abruptly exits. Beat. Catherine is furious and so upset she looks dazed.

CLAIRE: Katie. Let's go inside. Katie?

Catherine opens the book, tries to rip out the pages, destroy it. Claire goes to take it from her. They struggle. Catherine gets the book away. They stand apart, breathing hard. After a moment, Catherine throws the book to the floor. She exits.

Fade

SCENE 3

The next day. The porch is empty. Knocking off. No one appears. After a moment Hal comes around the side of the porch and knocks on the back door.

HAL: Catherine?

Claire enters.

HAL: I thought you were leaving.
CLAIRE: I had to delay my flight.

Beat.

HAL: Is Catherine here?
CLAIRE: I don't think this is a good time, Hal.   5
HAL: Could I see her?
CLAIRE: Not now.
HAL: What's the matter?
CLAIRE: She's sleeping.
HAL: Can I wait here until she gets up?   10
CLAIRE: She's been sleeping since yesterday. She won't get up. She won't eat, won't
    talk to me. I couldn't go home. I'm going to wait until she seems okay to travel.
HAL: Jesus, I'm sorry.
CLAIRE: Yes.
HAL: I'd like to talk to her.
CLAIRE: I don't think that's a good idea.   15
HAL: Has she said anything?
CLAIRE: About you? No.
HAL: Yesterday . . . I know I didn't do what she wanted.
CLAIRE: Neither of us did.
HAL: I didn't know what to say. I feel awful.   20
CLAIRE: Why did you sleep with her?

Beat.

HAL: I'm sorry, that's none of your business.
CLAIRE: Bullshit. I have to take care of her. It's a little bit harder with you jerking
    her around.
HAL: I wasn't jerking her around. It just happened.
CLAIRE: Your timing was not great.   25
HAL: It wasn't *my* timing, it was *both* of our—
CLAIRE: Why'd you do it? You know what she's like. She's fragile and you took
    advantage of her.
HAL: No. It's what we both wanted. I didn't mean to hurt her.
CLAIRE: You did.
HAL: I'd like to talk to Catherine, please.   30
CLAIRE: You can't.
HAL: Are you taking her away?
CLAIRE: Yes.
HAL: To New York.
CLAIRE: Yes.   35
HAL: Just going to drag her to New York.
CLAIRE: If I have to.
HAL: Don't you think she should have some say in whether or not she goes?
CLAIRE: If she's not going to speak, what else can I do?

40   Hal: Let me try. Let me talk to her.

      Claire: Hal, give up. This has nothing to do with you.

      Hal: I know her. She's tougher than you think, Claire.

      Claire: What?

      Hal: She can handle herself. She can handle talking to me—maybe it would help. Maybe she'd like it.

45   Claire: Maybe she'd *like* it? Are you out of your *mind*? You're the reason she's up there right now! You have *no idea* what she needs. You don't know her! She's my sister. Jesus, you fucking mathematicians: you *don't think*. You don't know what you're doing. You stagger around creating these catastrophes and it's people like me who end up flying in to clean them up. (*Beat.*) She needs to get out of Chicago, out of this house. I'll give you my number in New York. You can call her once she's settled there. That's it, that's the deal.

      Hal: Okay. (*Beat. He doesn't move.*)

      Claire: I don't mean to be rude but I have a lot to do.

      Hal: There's one more thing. You're not going to like it.

      Claire: Sure, take the notebook.

50   Hal: (*startled*) I—

      Claire: Hold on a sec, I'll get it for you. (*She goes inside and returns with the notebook. She gives it to Hal.*)

      Hal: I thought this would be harder.

      Claire: Don't worry, I understand. It's very sweet you want to see Catherine but of course you'd like to see the notebook too.

      Hal: (*Huffy*) It's—No, it's my responsibility—as a professional I can't turn my back on the necessity of the—

55   Claire: Relax. I don't care. Take it. What would I do with it?

      Hal: You sure?

      Claire: Yes, of course.

      Hal: You trust me with this?

      Claire: Yes.

60   Hal: You just said I don't know what I'm doing.

      Claire: I think you're a little bit of an idiot but you're not dishonest. Someone needs to figure out what's in there. I can't do it. It should be done here, at Chicago: my father would like that. When you decide what we've got let me know what the family should do.

      Hal: Thanks.

      Claire: Don't thank me, it's by far the most convenient option available. I put my card in there, call me whenever you want.

      Hal: Okay.

Hal starts to exit. Claire hesitates, then

65   Claire: Hal.

      Hal: Yeah?

      Claire: Can you tell me about it? The proof. I'm just curious.

      Hal: It would take some time. How much math have you got?

Beat.

CLAIRE: I'm a currency analyst. It helps to be very quick with numbers. I am.
  I probably inherited about one one-thousandth of my father's ability. It's enough.
    Catherine got more. I'm not sure how much.

Fade

SCENE 4

Winter. About three and a half years earlier. Robert is on the porch. He wears a T-shirt. He writes in a notebook. After a moment we hear Catherine's voice from offstage.

CATHERINE: Dad? (*She enters wearing a parka. She sees her father and stops.*) What are
  you doing out here?
ROBERT: Working.
CATHERINE: It's December. It's thirty degrees.
ROBERT: I know.

Catherine stares at him, baffled.

CATHERINE: Don't you need a coat?   5
ROBERT: Don't you think I can make that assessment for myself?

Beat.

CATHERINE: Aren't you cold?
ROBERT: Of course I am! I'm freezing my ass off!
CATHERINE: So what are you *doing* out here?
ROBERT: Thinking! Writing!   10
CATHERINE: You're gonna freeze.
ROBERT: It's too hot in the house. The radiators dry out the air. Also the
  clanking—I can't concentrate. If the house weren't so old, we'd have central
  air heating, but we don't, so I have to come out here to get any work done.
CATHERINE: I'll turn off the radiators. They won't make any noise. Come inside,
  it isn't safe.
ROBERT: I'm okay.
CATHERINE: I've been calling. Didn't you hear the phone?   15
ROBERT: It's a distraction.
CATHERINE: I didn't know what was going on. I had to drive all the way down here.
ROBERT: I can see that.
CATHERINE: I had to skip class. (*She brings Robert a coat and he puts it on.*) Why
  don't you answer the phone?
ROBERT: Well I'm sorry, Catherine, but it's a question of priorities, and work takes 20
  priority, you know that.
CATHERINE: You're working?
ROBERT: Goddamnit, I am working! I say "I"—The machinery. The machinery is
  working. Catherine, it's on full-blast. All the cylinders are firing, I'm on fire.
  That's why I came out here, to cool off. I haven't felt like this for years.
CATHERINE: You're kidding.
ROBERT: No!
CATHERINE: I don't believe it.   25

ROBERT: I don't believe it either! But it's true. It started about a week ago. I woke up, came downstairs, made a cup of coffee, and before I could pour in the milk it was like someone turned the *light* on in my head.

CATHERINE: Really?

ROBERT: Not the light, the whole *power grid*. *I lit up*, and it's like no time has passed since I was twenty-one.

CATHERINE: You're kidding!

30　ROBERT: No! I'm back! I'm back in touch with the source—the font, the—whatever the source of my creativity was all those years ago. I'm in contact with it again. I'm *sitting* on it. It's a geyser and I'm shooting right up into the air on top of it.

CATHERINE: My God.

ROBERT: I'm not talking about divine inspiration. It's not funneling down into my head and onto the page. It'll take *work* to shape these things; I'm not saying it won't be a tremendous amount of work. It *will* be a tremendous amount of work. It's not going to be easy. But the raw material is there. It's like I've been driving in traffic and now the lanes are opening up before me and I can *accelerate*.
I see whole landscapes—places for the work to go, new techniques, revolutionary possibilities. I'm going to get whole branches of the profession talking to each other. I—I'm sorry, I'm being rude. How's school?

CATHERINE: *(taken aback)* Fine.

ROBERT: You're working hard?

35　CATHERINE: Sure.

ROBERT: Faculty treating you all right?

CATHERINE: Yes. Dad—

ROBERT: Made any friends?

CATHERINE: Of course. I—

40　ROBERT: Dating?

CATHERINE: Dad, hold on.

ROBERT: No details necessary if you don't want to provide them. I'm just interested.

CATHERINE: School's great. I want to talk about what you're doing.

ROBERT: Great, let's talk.

45　CATHERINE: This work.

ROBERT: Yes.

CATHERINE: *(indicating the notebooks)* Is it here?

ROBERT: Part of it, yes.

CATHERINE: Can I see it?

50　ROBERT: It's all at a very early stage.

CATHERINE: I don't mind.

ROBERT: Nothing's actually complete, to be honest. It's all in progress. I think we're talking years.

CATHERINE: That's okay. I don't care. Just let me see anything.

ROBERT: You really want to?

55　CATHERINE: Yes.

ROBERT: You're genuinely interested.

CATHERINE: Dad, of course!

ROBERT: Of course. It's your field.

CATHERINE: Yes.
ROBERT: You know how happy that makes me.   60

Beat.

CATHERINE: Yes.
ROBERT: I think there's enough here to keep me working the rest of my life.
      Not just me.
      I was starting to imagine I was finished, Catherine. Really finished. Don't get
   me wrong, I was grateful I could go to my office, have a life, but secretly I was
   terrified I'd never work again. Did you know that?
CATHERINE: I wondered.
ROBERT: I was absolutely fucking terrified.
      Then I remembered something and a part of the terror went away. I remem-
   bered you.
      Your creative years were just beginning. You'd get your degree, do your own
   work. You were just getting started. If you hadn't gone into math, that would have
   been all right. Claire's done well for herself. I'm satisfied with her.
      I'm proud of you.
      I don't mean to embarrass you. It's part of the reason we have children. We hope
   they'll survive us, accomplish what we can't.
      Now that I'm back in the game I admit I've got another idea, a better one.
CATHERINE: What?   65
ROBERT: I know you've got your own work. I don't want you to neglect that. You
   can't neglect it. But I could probably use some help. Work with me. If you want
   to, if you can work it out with your class schedule and everything else, I could
   help you with that, make some calls, talk to your teachers . . .
      I'm getting ahead of myself.
      Well, Jesus, look, enough bullshit. You asked to see something. Let's start
   with this. I've roughed something out. General outline for a proof. Major result.
   Important. It's not finished but you can see where it's going. Let's see. (*He selects
   a notebook.*) Here. (*He gives it to Catherine. She opens it and reads.*) It's very rough.

After a long moment Catherine closes the notebook. A beat. She sits down next to Robert.

CATHERINE: Dad. Let's go inside.
ROBERT: The gaps might make it hard to follow. We can talk it through.
CATHERINE: You're cold. Let's go in.
ROBERT: Maybe we could work on this together. This might be a great place to   70
   start. What about it? What do you think? Let's talk it through.
CATHERINE: Not now. I'm cold too. It's really freezing out here. Let's go inside.
ROBERT: I'm telling you it's stifling in there, goddamn it. The radiators. Look, read
   out the first couple of lines. That's how we start: you read, and we go line by
   line, out loud, through the argument. See if there's a better way, a shorter way.
   Let's collaborate.
CATHERINE: No. Come on.
ROBERT: I've been waiting years for this. This is something I want to do. Come on,
   let's do some work together.

75 CATHERINE: We can't do it out here. It's freezing cold. I'm taking you in.
ROBERT: Not until we *talk about the proof.*
CATHERINE: No.
ROBERT: Goddamnit, Catherine, open the goddamn book and read me the lines.

Beat. Catherine, opens the book. She reads slowly, without inflection.

CATHERINE: "Let X equal the quantity of all quantities of X. Let X equal the cold.
It is cold in December. The months of cold equal November through February.
There are four months of cold and four of heat, leaving four months of indeter-
minate temperature. In February it snows. In March the lake is a lake of ice.
In September the students come back and the bookstores are full. Let X equal
the month of full bookstores. The number of books approaches infinity as the
number of months of cold approaches four. I will never be as cold now as I will
in the future. The future of cold is infinite. The future of heat is the future of
cold. The bookstores are infinite and so are never full except in September . . ."
*(She stops reading and slowly closes the book. Robert is shivering uncontrollably. She
puts her arms around him and helps him to his feet.)* It's all right. We'll go inside.
80 ROBERT: I'm cold.
CATHERINE: We'll warm you up.
ROBERT: Don't leave. Please.
CATHERINE: I won't. Let's go inside.

Fade

SCENE 5

*The present. A week after the events in Scene 3. Claire on the porch. Coffee in takeout cups.
Claire takes a plane ticket out of her purse, checks the itinerary. A moment. Catherine enters
with bags for travel. Claire gives her a cup of coffee. Catherine drinks in silence. Beat.*

CATHERINE: Good coffee.
CLAIRE: It's all right, isn't it? *(Beat.)* We have a place where we buy all our coffee.
They roast it themselves, they have an old roaster down in the basement. You
can smell it on the street. Some mornings you can smell it from our place, four
stories up. It's wonderful. "Manhattan's Best": some magazine wrote it up. Who
knows. But it is very good.
CATHERINE: Sounds good.
CLAIRE: You'll like it.
5 CATHERINE: Good.

Beat.

CLAIRE: You look nice.
CATHERINE: Thanks, so do you.

Beat.

CLAIRE: It's bright.
CATHERINE: Yes.

CLAIRE: It's one of the things I do miss. All the space, the light. You could sit out   10
    here all morning.
CATHERINE: It's not that warm.
CLAIRE: Are you cold?
CATHERINE: Not really. I just—
CLAIRE: It has gotten chilly. I'm sorry. Do you want to go in?
CATHERINE: I'm okay.   15
CLAIRE: I just thought it might be nice to have a quick cup of coffee out here.
CATHERINE: No, it is.
CLAIRE: Plus the kitchen's all put away. If you're cold—
CATHERINE: I'm not. Not really.
CLAIRE: Want your jacket?   20
CATHERINE: Yeah, okay. (*Claire gives it to her. She puts it on.*) Thanks.
CLAIRE: It's that time of year.
CATHERINE: Yes. You can feel it coming. (*Beat. She stares out at the yard.*)
CLAIRE: Honey, there's no hurry.
CATHERINE: I know.   25
CLAIRE: If you want to hang out, be alone for a while—
CATHERINE: No. It's no big deal.
CLAIRE: We don't have to leave for twenty minutes or so.
CATHERINE: I know. Thanks, Claire.
CLAIRE: You're all packed.   30
CATHERINE: Yes.
CLAIRE: If you missed anything it doesn't really matter. The movers will send us
    everything next month. (*Catherine doesn't move. Beat.*) I know this is hard.
CATHERINE: It's fine.
CLAIRE: This is the right decision.
CATHERINE: I know . . .   35
CLAIRE: I want to do everything I can to make this a smooth transition for you. So
    does Mitch.
CATHERINE: Good.
CLAIRE: The actual departure is the hardest part. Once we get there we can relax.
    Enjoy ourselves.
CATHERINE: I know.

Beat.

CLAIRE: You'll love New York.   40
CATHERINE: I can't wait.
CLAIRE: You'll love it. It's the most exciting city.
CATHERINE: I know.
CLAIRE: It's not like Chicago, it's really alive.
CATHERINE: I've read about that.   45
CLAIRE: I think you'll truly feel at home there.
CATHERINE: You know what I'm looking forward to?
CLAIRE: What?
CATHERINE: Seeing Broadway musicals.

Beat.

50 CLAIRE: Mitch can get us tickets to whatever you'd like.
CATHERINE: And Rockefeller Center in winter—all the skaters!
CLAIRE: Well, you—
CATHERINE: Also, the many fine museums!

Beat.

CLAIRE: I know how hard this is for you.
55 CATHERINE: Listening to you say how hard it is for me is what's hard for me.
CLAIRE: Once you're there you'll see all the possibilities that are available.
CATHERINE: Restraints, lithium, electroshock.
CLAIRE: *Schools.* In the New York area alone there's NYU, Columbia—
CATHERINE: Bright college days! Football games, road trips, necking on the "quad."
60 CLAIRE: Or if that's not what you want we can help you find a job. Mitch has
         terrific contacts all over town.
CATHERINE: Does he know anyone in the phone-sex industry?
CLAIRE: I want to make this as easy a transition as I can.
CATHERINE: It's going to be *easy*, Claire, it's gonna be so fucking easy you won't
         believe it.
CLAIRE: Thank you.
65 CATHERINE: I'm going to sit quietly on the plane to New York. And live quietly in a
         cute apartment. And answer Dr. Von Heimlich's questions very politely.
CLAIRE: You can see any doctor you like, or you can see no doctor.
CATHERINE: I would like to see a doctor called Dr. Von Heimlich: please find one.
         And I would like him to wear a monocle. And I'd like him to have a very soft,
         very well-upholstered couch, so that I'll be perfectly comfortable while I'm
         blaming everything on you.

Beat.

CLAIRE: Don't come.
CATHERINE: No, I'm coming.
70 CLAIRE: Stay here, see how you do.
CATHERINE: I could.
CLAIRE: You can't take care of yourself for *five days.*
CATHERINE: Bullshit!
CLAIRE: You *slept all week.* I had to cancel my flight. I missed a week of work—I was
         this close to taking you to the hospital! I couldn't believe it when you finally
         dragged yourself up.
75 CATHERINE: I was tired!
CLAIRE: You were completely out of it, Catherine, you weren't speaking!
CATHERINE: I didn't want to talk to you.

Beat.

CLAIRE: Stay here if you hate me so much.
CATHERINE: And do what?

CLAIRE: You're the genius, figure it out.   80

Claire is upset, near tears. She digs in her bag, pulls out a plane ticket, throws it on the table. She exits. Catherine is alone. She can't quite bring herself to leave the porch. A moment. Hal enters—not through the house, from the side. He is badly dressed and looks very tired. He is breathless from running.

HAL: You're still here. (*Catherine is surprised. She doesn't speak.*) I saw Claire leaving out front. I wasn't sure if you—(*He holds up the notebook.*) This fucking thing . . . checks out.

   I have been over it, *twice*, with two different sets of guys, old geeks *and* young geeks. It is *weird*. I don't know where the techniques came from. Some of the moves are very hard to follow. But we can't find anything wrong with it! There might be something wrong with it but we can't find it. I have not slept. (*He catches his breath.*) It works. I thought you might want to know.

CATHERINE: I already knew.

Beat.

HAL: I had to swear these guys to secrecy. They were jumping out of their skins. See, one e-mail and it's all over. I threatened them. I think we're safe, they're physical cowards. (*Beat.*) I had to see you.

CATHERINE: I'm leaving.

HAL: I know. Just wait for a minute, please?   85

CATHERINE: What do you want? You have the book. She told me you came by for it and she gave it to you. You can do whatever you want with it. Publish it.

HAL: Catherine.

CATHERINE: Get Claire's permission and publish it. She doesn't care. She doesn't know anything about it anyway.

HAL: I don't want Claire's permission.

CATHERINE: You want mine? Publish. Go for it. Have a press conference. Tell the   90
world what my father discovered.

HAL: I don't want to.

CATHERINE: Or fuck my father, pass it off as your own work. Who cares? Write your own ticket to any math department in the country.

HAL: I don't think your father wrote it.

Beat.

CATHERINE: You thought so last week.

HAL: That was last week. I spent this week reading the proof. I think I understand   95
it, more or less. It uses a lot of newer mathematical techniques, things that were developed in the last decade. Elliptic curves. Modular forms. I think I learned more mathematics this week than I did in four years of grad school.

CATHERINE: So?

HAL: So the proof is very . . . hip.

CATHERINE: Get some sleep, Hal.

HAL: What was your father doing the last ten years? He wasn't well, was he?

CATHERINE: Are you done?   100

HAL: I don't think he would have been able to master those new techniques.

CATHERINE: But he was a genius.

HAL: But he was nuts.

CATHERINE: So he read about them later.

105   HAL: Maybe. The books he would have needed are upstairs.

Beat.

Your dad dated everything. Even his most incoherent entries he dated. There are no dates in this.

CATHERINE: The handwriting—

HAL: —looks like your dad's. Parents and children sometimes have similar handwriting, especially if they've spent a lot of time together.

CATHERINE: Interesting theory.

HAL: I like it.

110   CATHERINE: I like it too. It's what I told you last week.

HAL: I know.

CATHERINE: You blew it.

HAL: I—

CATHERINE: It's too bad, the rest of it was really good. All of it: "I loved your dad." "I always liked you." "I'd like to spend every minute with you . . ." It's killer stuff. You got laid *and* you got the notebook! You're a genius!

115   HAL: You're giving me way too much credit. *(Beat.)* I don't expect you to be happy with me. I just wanted . . . I don't know. I was hoping to discuss some of this with you before you left. Purely professional. I don't expect anything else.

CATHERINE: Forget it.

HAL: I mean we have questions. Working on this must have been amazing. I'd love just to hear you talk about some of it.

CATHERINE: No.

HAL: You'll have to deal with it eventually, you know. You can't ignore it, you'll have to get it published. You'll have to talk to someone.

Take it, at least. Then I'll go. Here.

120   CATHERINE: I don't want it.

HAL: Come on, Catherine. I'm trying to correct things.

CATHERINE: You *can't*. Do you hear me?

You think you've figured something out? You run over here so pleased with yourself because you changed your mind. Now you're certain. You're so . . . *sloppy*. You don't know anything. The book, the math, the dates, the writing, all that stuff you decided with your buddies, it's just evidence. It doesn't finish the job. It doesn't prove anything.

HAL: Okay, what would?

CATHERINE: *Nothing.*

You should have trusted me.

Beat.

125   HAL: I know *(Beat. Catherine gathers her things.)* So Claire sold the house?

CATHERINE: Yes.

HAL: Stay in Chicago. You're an adult.

CATHERINE: She wants me in New York. She wants to look after me.

HAL: Do you need looking after?

CATHERINE: She thinks I do.

HAL: You looked after your dad for five years.   130

CATHERINE: So maybe it's my turn.

    I kick and scream, but I don't know. Being taken care of, it doesn't sound so bad. I'm tired.

    And the house is a wreck, let's face it. It was my dad's house . . .

Beat.

HAL: Nice house.

CATHERINE: It's old.

HAL: I guess.

CATHERINE: It's drafty as hell. The winters are rough.   135

HAL: That's just Chicago.

CATHERINE: Either it's freezing inside, or the steam's on full-blast and you're stifling.

HAL: I don't mind cold weather. Keeps you alert.

CATHERINE: Wait a few years.

HAL: I've lived here all my life.   140

CATHERINE: Yeah?

HAL: Sure. Just like you.

CATHERINE: Still. I don't think I should spend another winter here.

Beat.

HAL: There is nothing wrong with you.

CATHERINE: I think I'm like my dad.   145

HAL: I think you are too.

CATHERINE: I'm . . . *afraid* I'm like my dad.

HAL: You're not him.

CATHERINE: Maybe I will be.

HAL: Maybe. Maybe you'll be better.   150

Pause. Hal hands her the book. This time Catherine takes it. She sits. She looks down at the book, runs her fingers over the cover.

CATHERINE: It didn't feel "amazing" or—what word did you use?

HAL: Yeah, amazing.

CATHERINE: Yeah. It was just connecting the dots.

    Some nights I could connect three or four. Some nights they'd be really far apart, I'd have no idea how to get to the next one, if there was a next one.

HAL: He really never knew?

CATHERINE: No. I worked after midnight. He was usually in bed.   155

HAL: Every night?

CATHERINE: No. When I got stuck I watched TV. Sometimes if he couldn't sleep he'd come downstairs, sit with me. We'd talk. Not about math, he couldn't. About the movie we were watching. I'd explain the stories.

Or about fixing the heat. Decide we didn't want to. We liked the radiators even though they clanked in the middle of the night, made the air dry.

Or we'd plan breakfast, talk about what we were gonna eat together in the morning.

Those nights were usually pretty good.

I know . . . it works . . . But all I can see are the compromises, the approximations, places where it's stitched together. It's lumpy. Dad's stuff was way more elegant. When he was young.

Beat.

HAL: Talk me through it? Whatever's bothering you. Maybe you'll improve it.
CATHERINE: I don't know . . .
160 **HAL:** Pick anything. Give it a shot? Maybe you'll discover something elegant.

A moment, Hal sits next to Catherine. Eventually she opens the book, turns the pages slowly, finding a section. She looks at him.

CATHERINE: Here.

She begins to speak.

Curtain

*   *   *

Reading and Reacting

1. How are Catherine and her father alike? Why are their similarities important?
2. What role does the academic discipline of mathematics play in *Proof*? How would the play be different if Catherine and Robert shared another academic or professional interest instead of mathematics?
3. Robert had a mental breakdown when he was in his mid-twenties; now, Catherine is afraid the same thing is happening to her. Do you think her fears are justified? Why, or why not?
4. How do you interpret the play's title? Consider all its possible meanings.
5. Why do you think Hal doubts that Catherine could have written the proof? Could it be because he worships Robert? because Catherine is so young? because she has no reputation as a mathematician? because she does not have a PhD? because she is female? because she has a family history of mental illness? Which of these explanations seems most likely? Which seems least likely? Why?
6. Is Claire essential to the play? Do you see her as a fully developed character or merely as a foil for Catherine?
7. Act 1 ends with Catherine announcing, "I wrote it." What stage directions would you write for this dramatic moment if you wanted to indicate Catherine's gestures, expression, and tone—and Hal's and Claire's reactions?
8. Which stereotypes about mathematicians does this play promote? Which does it challenge? For example, are Hal and his friends "typical" mathematicians? is Robert? is Catherine?

9. In act 1, scene 3, Hal explains why some mathematicians take amphetamines:

> They think math's a young man's game. Speed keeps them racing, makes them feel sharp. There's this fear that your creativity peaks around twenty-three and it's all downhill from there. Once you hit fifty it's over, you might as well teach high school.

How does this speech provide insight into the motivation of the three mathematicians in this play (Robert, Hal, and Catherine)?

10. What purpose does Catherine's story about Sophie Germain (act 1, scene 3) serve in the play?

11. Robert is dead when the play begins, yet he functions as a character who interacts with his daughter. Would the play have worked without him? Would it have been more effective? What, if anything, does his presence add?

12. What do you see as the central theme of this play? For example, is its focus on mathematics? genius? heredity? family relationships? professional rivalry? feminism? mental illness? Explain your reasoning.

13. Do you think *Proof* has a happy ending? Explain.

14. JOURNAL ENTRY Do you believe Catherine really wrote the proof? Why, or why not?

15. CRITICAL PERSPECTIVE In his review of *Proof* for the *New York Times*, critic Bruce Weber discusses the play's characterizations of mathematicians:

> Without any baffling erudition—if you know what a prime number is, there won't be a single line of dialogue you find perplexing—the play presents mathematicians as both blessed and bedeviled by the gift for abstraction that ties them achingly to one another and separates them, also achingly, from concrete-minded folks like you and me. And perhaps most satisfying of all, it does so without a moment of meanness.

In what sense are the play's characters "blessed" by mathematics? How are they "bedeviled" by it? How does mathematics unite them? How does it separate them from ordinary people?

Related Works: "Gryphon" (p. 250), "Doe Season" (p. 472), "Digging" (p. 663), "My Father as a Guitar" (p. 770), "Living in Numbers" (p. 844), "Elegy for My Father, Who Is Not Dead" (p. 890), "Do not go gentle into that good night" (p. 891), *Doubt: A Parable* (p. 1516), *Trifles* (p. 1604)

ARTHUR MILLER (1915–2005) was born in New York City and graduated in 1938 from the University of Michigan, where he began to write plays. His first big success, which won the New York Drama Critics Circle Award, was *All My Sons* (1947), about a man who has knowingly manufactured faulty airplane parts during World War II. Other significant plays are *The Crucible* (1953), based on the Salem witch trials of 1692, which Miller saw as parallel to contemporary investigations of suspected Communists by the House Un-American Activities Committee; *A View from the Bridge* (1955); and *After the Fall* (1955). He was married for a time to actress Marilyn Monroe and wrote the screenplay for her movie *The Misfits* (1961). His play *The Last Yankee* opened off-Broadway in 1993, *Broken Glass* was both published and performed in 1994, and *Mr. Peter's Connection* was published in 1998. In 2001, Miller was awarded an NEH fellowship and the John H. Finney Award for Exemplary Service to New York City.

AP Images

Death of a Salesman is Miller's most significant work, a play that quickly became an American classic. Miller said he was very much influenced by the structure of Greek tragedy, and in his play he shows that a tragedy can also be the story of an ordinary person told in realistic terms. The play is frequently produced, and each production interprets it a bit differently. When Miller directed *Death of a Salesman* in China in 1983, audiences perceived it as primarily the story of the mother. In the 1983 Broadway production, Miller himself realized "at a certain point that it was far more the story of Biff, the son, than it was of Willy Loman, the salesman of the title."

Cultural Context At the time *Death of a Salesman* was written in 1949, the United States was experiencing the largest economic expansion in its history. After World War II, soldiers returned home, women left the factory jobs they had held while men were at war, and more and more consumer goods were developed and manufactured. As companies expanded and were consolidated, large, impersonal corporations began to replace the mom-and-pop businesses that had dominated the American scene before the war. The foot soldiers of these corporations were the traveling salesmen (today often called "manufacturers' representatives") who moved from town to town and covered large territories in a relentless effort to sign up clients and generate sales. During the same period, the American suburbs began to appear, with a mass movement of population from older urban neighborhoods to massive housing developments such as those constructed in Levittown, Long Island, in 1946. It is against this background that the events of *Death of a Salesman* unfold.

Death of a Salesman (1949)

CHARACTERS

Willy Loman	**The Woman**
Linda, *his wife*	**Howard Wagner**
Biff ⎫	**Jenny**
Happy ⎬ *his sons*	**Stanley**
Uncle Ben	**Miss Forsythe**
Charley	**Letta**
Bernard	

The action takes place in Willy Loman's house and yard and in various places he visits in the New York and Boston of today.

Throughout the play, in the stage directions, left and right mean stage left and stage right.

ACT 1

A melody is heard, played upon a flute. It is small and fine, telling of grass and trees and the horizon. The curtain rises.

Before us is the Salesman's house. We are aware of towering, angular shapes behind it, surrounding it on all sides. Only the blue light of the sky falls upon the house and forestage; the surrounding area shows an angry glow of orange. As more light appears, we see a solid vault of apartment houses around the small, fragile-seeming home. An air of the dream clings to the place, a dream rising out of reality. The kitchen at center seems actual enough, for there is a kitchen table with three chairs, and a refrigerator. But no other fixtures are seen. At the back of the kitchen there is a draped entrance, which leads to the living room. To the right of the kitchen, on a level raised two feet, is a bedroom furnished only with a brass bedstead and a straight chair. On a shelf over the bed a silver athletic trophy stands. A window opens onto the apartment house at the side.

Lee J. Cobb, Mildred Dunnock, Arthur Kennedy, and Cameron Michael in
original Broadway production directed by Elia Kazan (1949–50)
© Photofest

Behind the kitchen, on a level raised six and a half feet, is the boys' bedroom, at present barely visible. Two beds are dimly seen, and at the back of the room a dormer window. (This bedroom is above the unseen living room.) At the left a stairway curves up to it from the kitchen.

The entire setting is wholly or, in some places, partially transparent. The roofline of the house is one-dimensional; under and over it we see the apartment buildings. Before the house lies an apron, curving beyond the forestage into the orchestra. This forward area serves as the back yard as well as the locale of all Willy's imaginings and of his city scenes. Whenever the action is in the present the actors observe the imaginary wall-lines, entering the house only through the door at the left. But in the scenes of the past these boundaries are broken, and characters enter or leave a room by stepping "through" a wall onto the forestage.

From the right, Willy Loman, the Salesman, enters, carrying two large sample cases. The flute plays on. He hears but is not aware of it. He is past sixty years of age, dressed quietly. Even as he crosses the stage to the doorway of the house, his exhaustion is apparent. He unlocks the door, comes into the kitchen, and thankfully lets his burden down, feeling the soreness of his palms. A word-sigh escapes his lips—it might be "Oh, boy, oh, boy." He closes the door, then carries his cases out into the living room, through the draped kitchen doorway.

Linda, his wife, has stirred in her bed at the right. She gets out and puts on a robe, listening. Most often jovial, she has developed an iron repression of her exceptions to Willy's behavior—she *more than loves him, she admires him, as though his mercurial nature, his temper, his massive dreams and little cruelties, served her only as sharp reminders of the turbulent longings within him, longings which she shares but lacks the temperament to utter and follow to their end.*

LINDA: *(hearing Willy outside the bedroom, calls with some trepidation)* Willy!

WILLY: It's all right. I came back.

LINDA: Why? What happened? *(Slight pause.)* Did something happen, Willy?

WILLY: No, nothing happened.

5   LINDA: You didn't smash the car, did you?

WILLY: *(with casual irritation)* I said nothing happened. Didn't you hear me?

LINDA: Don't you feel well?

WILLY: I am tired to the death. *(The flute has faded away. He sits on the bed beside her, a little numb.)* I couldn't make it. I just couldn't make it, Linda.

LINDA: *(very carefully, delicately)* Where were you all day? You look terrible.

10   WILLY: I got as far as a little above Yonkers. I stopped for a cup of coffee. Maybe it was the coffee.

LINDA: What?

WILLY: *(after a pause)* I suddenly couldn't drive any more. The car kept going onto the shoulder, y'know?

LINDA: *(helpfully)* Oh. Maybe it was the steering again. I don't think Angelo knows the Studebaker.

WILLY: No, it's me, it's me. Suddenly I realize I'm goin' sixty miles an hour and I don't remember the last five minutes. I'm—I can't seem to—keep my mind to it.

15   LINDA: Maybe it's your glasses. You never went for your new glasses.

WILLY: No, I see everything. I came back ten miles an hour. It took me nearly four hours from Yonkers.

LINDA: *(resigned)* Well, you'll just have to take a rest, Willy, you can't continue this way.

WILLY: I just got back from Florida.

LINDA: But you didn't rest your mind. Your mind is overactive, and the mind is what counts, dear.

20   WILLY: I'll start out in the morning. Maybe I'll feel better in the morning. *(She is taking off his shoes.)* These goddam arch supports are killing me.

LINDA: Take an aspirin. Should I get you an aspirin? It'll soothe you.

WILLY: *(with wonder)* I was driving along, you understand? And I was fine. I was even observing the scenery. You can imagine, me looking at scenery, on the road every week of my life. But it's so beautiful up there, Linda, the trees are so thick, and the sun is warm. I opened the windshield and just let the warm air bathe over me. And then all of a sudden I'm goin' off the road! I'm tellin' ya, I absolutely forgot I was driving. If I'd've gone the other way over the white line I might've killed somebody. So I went on again—and five minutes later I'm dreamin' again, and I nearly—*(He presses two fingers against his eyes.)* I have such thoughts, I have such strange thoughts.

LINDA: Willy, dear. Talk to them again. There's no reason why you can't work in New York.

WILLY: They don't need me in New York. I'm the New England man. I'm vital in New England.

LINDA: But you're sixty years old. They can't expect you to keep traveling every week.   25

WILLY: I'll have to send a wire to Portland. I'm supposed to see Brown and Morrison tomorrow morning at ten o'clock to show the line. Goddammit, I could sell them! (*He starts putting on his jacket.*)

LINDA: (*taking the jacket from him*) Why don't you go down to the place tomorrow and tell Howard you've simply got to work in New York? You're too accommodating, dear.

WILLY: If old man Wagner was alive I'd a been in charge of New York now! That man was a prince, he was a masterful man. But that boy of his, that Howard, he don't appreciate. When I went north the first time, the Wagner Company didn't know where New England was!

LINDA: Why don't you tell those things to Howard, dear?

WILLY: (*encouraged*) I will, I definitely will. Is there any cheese?   30

LINDA: I'll make you a sandwich.

WILLY: No, go to sleep. I'll take some milk. I'll be up right away. The boys in?

LINDA: They're sleeping. Happy took Biff on a date tonight.

WILLY: (*interested*) That so?

LINDA: It was so nice to see them shaving together, one behind the other, in the bathroom. And going out together. You notice? The whole house smells of shaving lotion.   35

WILLY: Figure it out. Work a lifetime to pay off a house. You finally own it, and there's nobody to live in it.

LINDA: Well, dear, life is a casting off. It's always that way.

WILLY: No, no, some people—some people accomplish something. Did Biff say anything after I went this morning?

LINDA: You shouldn't have criticized him, Willy, especially after he just got off the train. You mustn't lose your temper with him.

WILLY: When the hell did I lose my temper? I simply asked him if he was making any money. Is that a criticism?   40

LINDA: But, dear, how could he make any money?

WILLY: (*worried and angered*) There's such an undercurrent in him. He became a moody man. Did he apologize when I left this morning?

LINDA: He was crestfallen, Willy. You know how he admires you. I think if he finds himself, then you'll both be happier and not fight any more.

WILLY: How can he find himself on a farm? Is that a life? A farmhand? In the beginning, when he was young, I thought, well, a young man, it's good for him to tramp around, take a lot of different jobs. But it's more than ten years now and he has yet to make thirty-five dollars a week!

LINDA: He's finding himself, Willy.   45

WILLY: Not finding yourself at the age of thirty-four is a disgrace!

LINDA: Shh!

WILLY: The trouble is he's lazy, goddammit!

LINDA: Willy, please!

WILLY: Biff is a lazy bum!   50

LINDA: They're sleeping. Get something to eat. Go on down.

WILLY: Why did he come home? I would like to know what brought him home.

LINDA: I don't know. I think he's still lost, Willy. I think he's very lost.

WILLY: Biff Loman is lost. In the greatest country in the world a young man with such—personal attractiveness, gets lost. And such a hard worker. There's one thing about Biff—he's not lazy.

55 LINDA: Never.

WILLY: (*with pity and resolve*) I'll see him in the morning; I'll have a nice talk with him. I'll get him a job selling. He could be big in no time. My God! Remember how they used to follow him around in high school? When he smiled at one of them their faces lit up. When he walked down the street . . . (*He loses himself in reminiscences.*)

LINDA: (*trying to bring him out of it*) Willy, dear, I got a new kind of American-type cheese today. It's whipped.

WILLY: Why do you get American when I like Swiss?

LINDA: I just thought you'd like a change—

60 WILLY: I don't want a change! I want Swiss cheese. Why am I always being contradicted?

LINDA: (*with a covering laugh*) I thought it would be a surprise.

WILLY: Why don't you open a window in here, for God's sake?

LINDA: (*with infinite patience*) They're all open, dear.

WILLY: The way they boxed us in here. Bricks and windows, windows and bricks.

65 LINDA: We should've bought the land next door.

WILLY: The street is lined with cars. There's not a breath of fresh air in the neighborhood. The grass don't grow any more, you can't raise a carrot in the back yard. They should've had a law against apartment houses. Remember those two beautiful elm trees out there? When I and Biff hung the swing between them?

LINDA: Yeah, like being a million miles from the city.

WILLY: They should've arrested the builder for cutting those down. They massacred the neighborhood. (*Lost.*) More and more I think of those days, Linda. This time of year it was lilac and wisteria. And then the peonies would come out, and the daffodils. What fragrance in this room!

LINDA: Well, after all, people had to move somewhere.

70 WILLY: No, there's more people now.

LINDA: I don't think there's more people. I think—

WILLY: There's more people! That's what's ruining this country! Population is getting out of control. The competition is maddening! Smell the stink from that apartment house! And another on the other side . . . How can they whip cheese?

On Willy's last line, Biff and Happy raise themselves up in their beds, listening.

LINDA: Go down, try it. And be quiet.

WILLY: (*turning to Linda, guiltily*) You're not worried about me, are you, sweetheart?

75 BIFF: What's the matter?

HAPPY: Listen!

LINDA: You've got too much on the ball to worry about.

WILLY: You're my foundation and my support, Linda.

LINDA: Just try to relax, dear. You make mountains out of molehills.

80 WILLY: I won't fight with him any more. If he wants to go back to Texas, let him go.

LINDA: He'll find his way.

WILLY: Sure. Certain men just don't get started till later in life. Like Thomas Edison, I think. Or B. F. Goodrich. One of them was deaf. (*He starts for the bedroom doorway.*) I'll put my money on Biff.

LINDA: And Willy—if it's warm Sunday we'll drive in the country. And we'll open the windshield, and take lunch.

WILLY: No, the windshields don't open on the new cars.

LINDA: But you opened it today.   85

WILLY: Me? I didn't. (*He stops.*) Now isn't that peculiar! Isn't that remarkable— (*He breaks off in amazement and fright as the flute is heard distantly.*)

LINDA: What, darling?

WILLY: That is the most remarkable thing.

LINDA: What, dear?

WILLY: I was thinking of the Chevvy. (*Slight pause.*) Nineteen twenty-eight . . .   90
when I had that red Chevvy—(*Breaks off.*) That funny? I coulda sworn I was driving that Chevvy today.

LINDA: Well, that's nothing. Something must've reminded you.

WILLY: Remarkable. Ts. Remember those days? The way Biff used to simonize that car? The dealer refused to believe there was eighty thousand miles on it. (*He shakes his head.*) Heh! (*To Linda.*) Close your eyes, I'll be right up. (*He walks out of the bedroom.*)

HAPPY: (*to Biff*) Jesus, maybe he smashed up the car again!

LINDA: (*calling after Willy*) Be careful on the stairs, dear! The cheese is on the middle shelf! (*She turns, goes over to the bed, takes his jacket, and goes out of the bedroom.*)

Light has risen on the boys' room. Unseen, Willy is heard talking to himself, "Eighty thousand miles," and a little laugh. Biff gets out of bed, comes downstage a bit, and stands attentively. Biff is two years older than his brother Happy, well built, but in these days bears a worn air and seems less self-assured. He has succeeded less, and his dreams are stronger and less acceptable than Happy's. Happy is tall, powerfully made. Sexuality is like a visible color on him, or a scent that many women have discovered. He, like his brother, is lost, but in a different way, for he has never allowed himself to turn his face toward defeat and is thus more confused and hardskinned, although seemingly more content.

HAPPY: (*getting out of bed*) He's going to get his license taken away if he keeps that   95
up. I'm getting nervous about him, y'know, Biff?

BIFF: His eyes are going.

HAPPY: No, I've driven with him. He sees all right. He just doesn't keep his mind on it. I drove into the city with him last week. He stops at a green light and then it turns red and he goes. (*He laughs.*)

BIFF: Maybe he's color-blind.

HAPPY: Pop? Why he's got the finest eye for color in the business. You know that.

BIFF: (*sitting down on his bed*) I'm going to sleep.   100

HAPPY: You're not still sour on Dad, are you, Biff?

BIFF: He's all right, I guess.

WILLY: (*underneath them, in the living room*) Yes, sir, eighty thousand miles— eighty-two thousand!

BIFF: You smoking?

105 HAPPY: *(holding out a pack of cigarettes)* Want one?

BIFF: *(taking a cigarette)* I can never sleep when I smell it.

WILLY: What a simonizing job, heh!

HAPPY: *(with deep sentiment)* Funny, Biff, y'know? Us sleeping in here again? The old beds. *(He pats his bed affectionately.)* All the talk that went across those two beds, huh? Our whole lives.

BIFF: Yeah. Lotta dreams and plans.

110 HAPPY: *(with a deep and masculine laugh)* About five hundred women would like to know what was said in this room.

They share a soft laugh.

BIFF: Remember that big Betsy something—what the hell was her name—over on Bushwick Avenue?

HAPPY: *(combing his hair)* With the collie dog!

BIFF: That's the one. I got you in there, remember?

HAPPY: Yeah, that was my first time—I think. Boy, there was a pig! *(They laugh, almost crudely.)* You taught me everything I know about women. Don't forget that.

115 BIFF: I bet you forgot how bashful you used to be. Especially with girls.

HAPPY: Oh, I still am, Biff.

BIFF: Oh, go on.

HAPPY: I just control it, that's all. I think I got less bashful and you got more so. What happened, Biff? Where's the old humor, the old confidence? *(He shakes Biff's knee. Biff gets up and moves restlessly about the room.)* What's the matter?

BIFF: Why does Dad mock me all the time?

120 HAPPY: He's not mocking you, he—

BIFF: Everything I say there's a twist of mockery on his face. I can't get near him.

HAPPY: He just wants you to make good, that's all. I wanted to talk to you about Dad for a long time, Biff. Something's—happening to him. He—talks to himself.

BIFF: I noticed that this morning. But he always mumbled.

HAPPY: But not so noticeable. It got so embarrassing I sent him to Florida. And you know something? Most of the time he's talking to you.

125 BIFF: What's he say about me?

HAPPY: I can't make it out.

BIFF: What's he say about me?

HAPPY: I think the fact that you're not settled, that you're still kind of up in the air . . .

BIFF: There's one or two other things depressing him, Happy.

130 HAPPY: What do you mean?

BIFF: Never mind. Just don't lay it all to me.

HAPPY: But I think if you just got started—I mean—is there any future for you out there?

BIFF: I tell ya, Hap, I don't know what the future is. I don't know—what I'm supposed to want.

HAPPY: What do you mean?

135 BIFF: Well, I spent six or seven years after high school trying to work myself up. Shipping clerk, salesman, business of one kind or another. And it's a measly

manner of existence. To get on that subway on the hot mornings in summer. To devote your whole life to keeping stock, or making phone calls, or selling or buying. To suffer fifty weeks of the year for the sake of a two-week vacation, when all you really desire is to be outdoors, with your shirt off. And always to have to get ahead of the next fella. And still—that's how you build a future.

HAPPY: Well, you really enjoy it on a farm? Are you content out there?

BIFF: *(with rising agitation)* Hap, I've had twenty or thirty different kinds of jobs since I left home before the war, and it always turns out the same. I just realized it lately. In Nebraska when I herded cattle, and the Dakotas, and Arizona, and now in Texas. It's why I came home now, I guess, because I realized it. This farm I work on, it's spring there now, see? And they've got about fifteen new colts. There's nothing more inspiring or—beautiful than the sight of a mare and a new colt. And it's cool there now, see? Texas is cool now, and it's spring. And whenever spring comes to where I am, I suddenly get the feeling, my God, I'm not gettin' anywhere! What the hell am I doing, playing around with horses, twenty-eight dollars a week! I'm thirty-four years old, I oughta be makin' my future. That's when I come running home. And now, I get here, and I don't know what to do with myself. *(After a pause.)* I've always made a point of not wasting my life, and every time I come back here I know that all I've done is to waste my life.

HAPPY: You're a poet, you know that, Biff? You're a—you're an idealist!

BIFF: No, I'm mixed up very bad. Maybe I oughta get married. Maybe I oughta get stuck into something. Maybe that's my trouble. I'm like a boy. I'm not married, I'm not in business, I just—I'm like a boy. Are you content, Hap? You're a success, aren't you? Are you content?

HAPPY: Hell, no!   140

BIFF: Why? You're making money, aren't you?

HAPPY: *(moving about with energy, expressiveness)* All I can do now is wait for the merchandise manager to die. And suppose I get to be merchandise manager? He's a good friend of mine, and he just built a terrific estate on Long Island. And he lived there about two months and sold it, and now he's building another one. He can't enjoy it once it's finished. And I know that's just what I would do. I don't know what the hell I'm workin' for. Sometimes I sit in my apartment—all alone. And I think of the rent I'm paying. And it's crazy. But then, it's what I always wanted. My own apartment, a car, and plenty of women. And still, goddammit, I'm lonely.

BIFF: *(with enthusiasm)* Listen, why don't you come out West with me?

HAPPY: You and I, heh?

BIFF: Sure, maybe we could buy a ranch. Raise cattle, use our muscles. Men built   145
like we are should be working out in the open.

HAPPY: *(avidly)* The Loman Brothers, heh?

BIFF: *(with vast affection)* Sure, we'd be known all over the counties!

HAPPY: *(enthralled)* That's what I dream about, Biff. Sometimes I want to just rip my clothes off in the middle of the store and outbox that goddam merchandise manager. I mean I can outbox, outrun, and outlift anybody in that store, and I have to take orders from those common, petty sons-of-bitches till I can't stand it any more.

BIFF: I'm telln' you, kid, if you were with me I'd be happy out there.

150 HAPPY: *(enthused)* See, Biff, everybody around me is so false that I'm constantly
lowering my ideals . . .

BIFF: Baby, together we'd stand up for one another, we'd have someone to trust.

HAPPY: If I were around you—

BIFF: Hap, the trouble is we weren't brought up to grub for money. I don't know
how to do it.

HAPPY: Neither can I!

155 BIFF: Then let's go!

HAPPY: The only thing is—what can you make out there?

BIFF: But look at your friend. Builds an estate and then hasn't the peace of mind to
live in it.

HAPPY: Yeah, but when he walks into the store the waves part in front of him.
That's fifty-two thousand dollars a year coming through the revolving door, and
I got more in my pinky finger than he's got in his head.

BIFF: Yeah, but you just said—

160 HAPPY: I gotta show some of those pompous, self-important executives over there
that Hap Loman can make the grade. I want to walk into the store the way he
walks in. Then I'll go with you, Biff. We'll be together yet, I swear. But take
those two we had tonight. Now weren't they gorgeous creatures?

BIFF: Yeah, yeah, most gorgeous I've had in years.

HAPPY: I get that any time I want, Biff. Whenever I feel disgusted. The only trouble
is, it gets like bowling or something. I just keep knockin' them over and it
doesn't mean anything. You still run around a lot?

BIFF: Naa. I'd like to find a girl—steady, somebody with substance.

HAPPY: That's what I long for.

165 BIFF: Go on! You'd never come home.

HAPPY: I would! Somebody with character, with resistance! Like Mom, y'know?
You're gonna call me a bastard when I tell you this. That girl Charlotte I was
with tonight is engaged to be married in five weeks. *(He tries on his new hat.)*

BIFF: No kiddin'!

HAPPY: Sure, the guy's in line for the vice-presidency of the store. I don't know
what gets into me, maybe I just have an overdeveloped sense of competition
or something, but I went and ruined her, and furthermore I can't get rid of her.
And he's the third executive I've done that to. Isn't that a crummy characteristic? And to top it all, I go to their weddings! *(Indignantly, but laughing.)* Like I'm
not supposed to take bribes. Manufacturers offer me a hundred-dollar bill now
and then to throw an order their way. You know how honest I am, but it's like
this girl, see. I hate myself for it. Because I don't want the girl, and, still, I take
it and—I love it!

BIFF: Let's go to sleep.

170 HAPPY: I guess we didn't settle anything, heh?

BIFF: I just got one idea that I think I'm going to try.

HAPPY: What's that?

BIFF: Remember Bill Oliver?

HAPPY: Sure, Oliver is very big now. You want to work for him again?

BIFF: No, but when I quit he said something to me. He put his arm on my shoulder,   175
and he said, "Biff, if you ever need anything, come to me."

HAPPY: I remember that. That sounds good.

BIFF: I think I'll go to see him. If I could get ten thousand or even seven or eight
thousand dollars I could buy a beautiful ranch.

HAPPY: I bet he'd back you. 'Cause he thought highly of you, Biff, I mean, they all
do. You're well liked, Biff. That's why I say to come back here, and we both
have the apartment. And I'm telln' you, Biff, any babe you want . . .

BIFF: No, with a ranch I could do the work I like and still be something. I just wonder though. I wonder if Oliver still thinks I stole that carton of basketballs.

HAPPY: Oh, he probably forgot that long ago. It's almost ten years. You're too sensi-   180
tive. Anyway, he didn't really fire you.

BIFF: Well, I think he was going to. I think that's why I quit. I was never sure
whether he knew or not. I know he thought the world of me, though. I was the
only one he'd let lock up the place.

WILLY: *(below)* You gonna wash the engine, Biff?

HAPPY: Shh!

Biff looks at Happy, who is gazing down, listening. Willy is mumbling in the parlor.

HAPPY: You hear that?

They listen. Willy laughs warmly.

BIFF: *(growing angry)* Doesn't he know Mom can hear that?   185

WILLY: Don't get your sweater dirty, Biff!

A look of pain crosses Biff's face.

HAPPY: Isn't that terrible? Don't leave again, will you? You'll find a job here. You
gotta stick around. I don't know what to do about him, it's getting embarrassing.

WILLY: What a simonizing job!

BIFF: Mom's hearing that!

WILLY: No kiddin', Biff, you got a date? Wonderful!   190

HAPPY: Go on to sleep. But talk to him in the morning, will you?

BIFF: *(reluctantly getting into bed)* With her in the house. Brother!

HAPPY: *(getting into bed)* I wish you'd have a good talk with him.

The light on their room begins to fade.

BIFF: *(to himself in bed)* That selfish, stupid . . .

HAPPY: Sh . . . Sleep, Biff.   195

*Their light is out. Well before they have finished speaking, Willy's form is dimly seen below
in the darkened kitchen. He opens the refrigerator, searches in there, and takes out a bottle
of milk. The apartment houses are fading out, and the entire house and surroundings become
covered with leaves. Music insinuates itself as the leaves appear.*

WILLY: Just wanna be careful with those girls, Biff, that's all. Don't make any promises.
No promises of any kind. Because a girl, y'know, they always believe what you
tell'em, and you're very young, Biff, you're too young to be talking seriously to girls.

Light rises on the kitchen. Willy, talking, shuts the refrigerator door and comes downstage to the kitchen table. He pours milk into a glass. He is totally immersed in himself, smiling faintly.

WILLY: Too young entirely, Biff. You want to watch your schooling first. Then when you're all set, there'll be plenty of girls for a boy like you. (*He smiles broadly at a kitchen chair.*) That so? The girls pay for you? (*He laughs.*) Boy, you must really be makin' a hit.

Willy is gradually addressing—physically—a point offstage, speaking through the wall of the kitchen, and his voice has been rising in volume to that of a normal conversation.

WILLY: I been wondering why you polish the car so careful. Ha! Don't leave the hubcaps, boys. Get the chamois to the hubcaps. Happy, use newspaper on the windows, it's the easiest thing. Show him how to do it, Biff! You see, Happy? Pad it up, use it like a pad. That's it, that's it, good work. You're doin' all right, Hap. (*He pauses, then nods in approbation for a few seconds, then looks upward.*) Biff, first thing we gotta do when we get time is clip that big branch over the house. Afraid it's gonna fall in a storm and hit the roof. Tell you what. We get a rope and sling her around, and then we climb up there with a couple of saws and take her down. Soon as you finish the car, boys, I wanna see ya. I got a surprise for you, boys.

BIFF: (*offstage*) Whatta ya got, Dad?

200 WILLY: No, you finish first. Never leave a job till you're finished—remember that. (*Looking toward the "big trees."*) Biff, up in Albany I saw a beautiful hammock. I think I'll buy it next trip, and we'll hang it right between those two elms. Wouldn't that be something? Just swingin' there under those branches. Boy, that would be . . .

Young Biff and Young Happy appear from the direction Willy was addressing. Happy carries rags and a pail of water. Biff, wearing a sweater with a block "S," carries a football.

BIFF: (*pointing in the direction of the car offstage*) How's that, Pop, professional?
WILLY: Terrific. Terrific job, boys. Good work, Biff.
HAPPY: Where's the surprise, Pop?
WILLY: In the back seat of the car.
205 HAPPY: Boy! (*He runs off.*)
BIFF: What is it, Dad? Tell me, what'd you buy?
WILLY: (*laughing, cuffs him*) Never mind, something I want you to have.
BIFF: (*turns and starts off*) What is it, Hap?
HAPPY: (*offstage*) It's a punching bag!
210 BIFF: Oh, Pop!
WILLY: It's got Gene Tunney's[1] signature on it!

Happy runs onstage with a punching bag.

BIFF: Gee, how'd you know we wanted a punching bag?

---

[1] *Gene Tunney's:* James Joseph ("Gene") Tunney (1897–1978)—American boxer, world heavyweight champion from his defeat of Jack Dempsey in 1926 until his retirement in 1928.

WILLY: Well, it's the finest thing for the timing.

HAPPY: (*lies down on his back and pedals with his feet*) I'm losing weight, you notice, Pop?

WILLY: (*to Happy*) Jumping rope is good too.   215

BIFF: Did you see the new football I got?

WILLY: (*examining the ball*) Where'd you get a new ball?

BIFF: The coach told me to practice my passing.

WILLY: That so? And he gave you the ball, heh?

BIFF: Well, I borrowed it from the locker room. (*He laughs confidentially.*)   220

WILLY: (*laughing with him at the theft*) I want you to return that.

HAPPY: I told you he wouldn't like it!

BIFF: (*angrily*) Well, I'm bringing it back!

WILLY: (*stopping the incipient argument, to Happy*) Sure, he's gotta practice with a regulation ball, doesn't he? (*To Biff.*) Coach'll probably congratulate you on your initiative!

BIFF: Oh, he keeps congratulating my initiative all the time, Pop.   225

WILLY: That's because he likes you. If somebody else took that ball there'd be an uproar. So what's the report, boys, what's the report?

BIFF: Where'd you go this time, Dad? Gee we were lonesome for you.

WILLY: (*pleased, puts an arm around each boy and they come down to the apron*) Lonesome, heh?

BIFF: Missed you every minute.

WILLY: Don't say? Tell you a secret, boys. Don't breathe it to a soul. Someday I'll   230
have my own business, and I'll never have to leave home any more.

HAPPY: Like Uncle Charley, heh?

WILLY: Bigger than Uncle Charley! Because Charley is not—liked. He's liked, but he's not—well liked.

BIFF: Where'd you go this time, Dad?

WILLY: Well, I got on the road, and I went north to Providence. Met the Mayor.

BIFF: The Mayor of Providence!   235

WILLY: He was sitting in the hotel lobby.

BIFF: What'd he say?

WILLY: He said, "Morning!" And I said, "You've got a fine city here, Mayor." And then he had coffee with me. And then I went to Waterbury. Waterbury is a fine city. Big clock city, the famous Waterbury clock. Sold a nice bill there. And then Boston—Boston is the cradle of the Revolution. A fine city. And a couple of other towns in Mass., and on to Portland and Bangor and straight home!

BIFF: Gee, I'd love to go with you sometime, Dad.

WILLY: Soon as summer comes.   240

HAPPY: Promise?

WILLY: You and Hap and I, and I'll show you all the towns. America is full of beautiful towns and fine, upstanding people. And they know me, boys, they know me up and down New England. The finest people. And when I bring you fellas up, there'll be open sesame for all of us, 'cause one thing, boys: I have friends. I can park my car in any street in New England, and the cops protect it like their own. This summer, heh?

BIFF AND HAPPY: (*together*) Yeah! You bet!

WILLY: We'll take our bathing suits.

245 HAPPY: We'll carry your bags, Pop!

WILLY: Oh, won't that be something! Me comin' into the Boston store with you boys carryin' my bags. What a sensation!

Biff is prancing around, practicing passing the ball.

WILLY: You nervous, Biff, about the game?

BIFF: Not if you're gonna be there.

WILLY: What do they say about you in school, now that they made you captain?

250 HAPPY: There's a crowd of girls behind him everytime the classes change.

BIFF: *(taking Willy's hand)* This Saturday, Pop, this Saturday—just for you, I'm going to break through for a touchdown.

HAPPY: You're supposed to pass.

BIFF: I'm takin' one play for Pop. You watch me, Pop, and when I take off my helmet, that means I'm breakin' out. Then you watch me crash through that line!

WILLY: *(kisses Biff)* Oh, wait'll I tell this in Boston!

Bernard enters in knickers. He is younger than Biff, earnest and loyal, a worried boy.

255 BERNARD: Biff, where are you? You're supposed to study with me today.

WILLY: Hey, looka Bernard. What're you lookin' so anemic about, Bernard?

BERNARD: He's gotta study, Uncle Willy. He's got Regents next week.

HAPPY: *(tauntingly, spinning Bernard around)* Let's box, Bernard!

BERNARD: Biff! *(He gets away from Happy.)* Listen, Biff, I heard Mr. Birnbaum say that if you don't start studyin' math he's gonna flunk you, and you won't graduate. I heard him!

260 WILLY: You better study with him, Biff. Go ahead now.

BERNARD: I heard him!

BIFF: Oh, Pop, you didn't see my sneakers! *(He holds up a foot for Willy to look at.)*

WILLY: Hey, that's a beautiful job of printing!

BERNARD: *(wiping his glasses)* Just because he printed University of Virginia on his sneakers doesn't mean they've got to graduate him, Uncle Willy!

265 WILLY: *(angrily)* What're you talking about? With scholarships to three universities they're gonna flunk him?

BERNARD: But I heard Mr. Birnbaum say—

WILLY: Don't be a pest, Bernard! *(To his boys.)* What an anemic!

BERNARD: Okay, I'm waiting for you in my house, Biff.

Bernard goes off. The Lomans laugh.

WILLY: Bernard is not well liked, is he?

270 BIFF: He's liked, but he's not well liked.

HAPPY: That's right, Pop.

WILLY: That's just what I mean. Bernard can get the best marks in school, y'understand, but when he gets out in the business world, y'understand, you are going to be five times ahead of him. That's why I thank Almighty God you're both built like Adonises. Because the man who makes an appearance in the business world, the man who creates personal interest, is the man who gets ahead. Be liked and you will never want. You take me, for instance. I never have to wait in line to see a buyer. "Willy Loman is here!" That's all they have to know, and I go right through.

BIFF: Did you knock them dead, Pop?

WILLY: Knocked 'em cold in Providence, slaughtered 'em in Boston.

HAPPY: (*on his back, pedaling again*) I'm losing weight, you notice, Pop?   275

Linda enters, as of old, a ribbon in her hair, carrying a basket of washing.

LINDA: (*with youthful energy*) Hello, dear!

WILLY: Sweetheart!

LINDA: How'd the Chevvy run?

WILLY: Chevrolet, Linda, is the greatest car ever built. (*To the boys.*) Since when do you let your mother carry wash up the stairs?

BIFF: Grab hold there, boy!   280

HAPPY: Where to, Mom?

LINDA: Hang them up on the line. And you better go down to your friends, Biff. The cellar is full of boys. They don't know what to do with themselves.

BIFF: Ah, when Pop comes home they can wait!

WILLY: (*laughs appreciatively*) You better go down and tell them what to do, Biff.

BIFF: I think I'll have them sweep out the furnace room.   285

WILLY: Good work, Biff.

BIFF: (*goes through wall-line of kitchen to doorway at back and calls down*) Fellas! Everybody sweep out the furnace room! I'll be right down!

VOICES: All right! Okay, Biff.

BIFF: George and Sam and Frank, come out back! We're hangin' up the wash! Come on, Hap, on the double! (*He and Happy carry out the basket.*)

LINDA: The way they obey him!   290

WILLY: Well, that's training, the training. I'm tellin' you, I was sellin' thousands and thousands, but I had to come home.

LINDA: Oh, the whole block'll be at that game. Did you sell anything?

WILLY: I did five hundred gross in Providence and seven hundred gross in Boston.

LINDA: No! Wait a minute, I've got a pencil. (*She pulls pencil and paper out of her apron pocket.*) That makes your commission . . . Two hundred—my God! Two hundred and twelve dollars!

WILLY: Well, I didn't figure it yet, but . . .   295

LINDA: How much did you do?

WILLY: Well, I—I did—about a hundred and eighty gross in Providence. Well, no—it came to—roughly two hundred gross on the whole trip.

LINDA: (*without hesitation*) Two hundred gross. That's . . . (*She figures.*)

WILLY: The trouble was that three of the stores were half closed for inventory in Boston. Otherwise I woulda broke records.

LINDA: Well, it makes seventy dollars and some pennies. That's very good.   300

WILLY: What do we owe?

LINDA: Well, on the first there's sixteen dollars on the refrigerator—

WILLY: Why sixteen?

LINDA: Well, the fan belt broke, so it was a dollar eighty.

305   WILLY: But it's brand new.
    LINDA: Well, the man said that's the way it is. Till they work themselves in,
       y'know.

They move through the wall-line into the kitchen.

    WILLY: I hope we didn't get stuck on that machine.
    LINDA: They got the biggest ads of any of them!
    WILLY: I know, it's a fine machine. What else?
310   LINDA: Well, there's nine-sixty for the washing machine. And for the vacuum
       cleaner there's three and a half due on the fifteenth. Then the roof, you got
       twenty-one dollars remaining.
    WILLY: It don't leak, does it?
    LINDA: No, they did a wonderful job. Then you owe Frank for the carburetor.
    WILLY: I'm not going to pay that man! That goddam Chevrolet, they ought to pro-
       hibit the manufacture of that car!
    LINDA: Well, you owe him three and a half. And odds and ends, comes to around a
       hundred and twenty dollars by the fifteenth.
315   WILLY: A hundred and twenty dollars! My God, if business don't pick up I don't
       know what I'm gonna do!
    LINDA: Well, next week you'll do better.
    WILLY: Oh, I'll knock them dead next week. I'll go to Hartford. I'm very well liked
       in Hartford. You know, the trouble is, Linda, people don't seem to take to me.

They move onto the forestage.

    LINDA: Oh, don't be foolish.
    WILLY: I know it when I walk in. They seem to laugh at me.
320   LINDA: Why? Why would they laugh at you? Don't talk that way, Willy.

Willy moves to the edge of the stage. Linda goes into the kitchen and starts to darn stockings.

    WILLY: I don't know the reason for it, but they just pass me by. I'm not noticed.
    LINDA: But you're doing wonderful, dear. You're making seventy to a hundred dol-
       lars a week.
    WILLY: But I gotta be at it ten, twelve hours a day. Other men—I don't know—
       they do it easier. I don't know why—I can't stop myself—I talk too much.
       A man oughta come in with a few words. One thing about Charley. He's a man
       of few words, and they respect him.
    LINDA: You don't talk too much, you're just lively.
325   WILLY: *(smiling)* Well, I figure, what the hell, life is short, a couple of jokes. *(To
       himself.)* I joke too much! *(The smile goes.)*
    LINDA: Why? You're—
    WILLY: I'm fat. I'm very—foolish to look at, Linda. I didn't tell you, but Christmas
       time I happened to be calling on F. H. Stewarts, and a salesman I know, as I was
       going in to see the buyer, I heard him say something about—walrus. And I—I
       cracked him right across the face. I won't take that. I simply will not take that.
       But they do laugh at me. I know that.
    LINDA: Darling . . .

WILLY: I gotta overcome it. I know I gotta overcome it. I'm not dressing to advantage, maybe.

LINDA: Willy, darling, you're the handsomest man in the world— 330

WILLY: Oh, no, Linda.

LINDA: To me you are. (*Slight pause.*) The handsomest.

From the darkness is heard the laughter of a woman. Willy doesn't turn to it, but it continues through Linda's lines.

LINDA: And the boys, Willy. Few men are idolized by their children the way you are.

Music is heard as behind a scrim, to the left of the house. The Woman, dimly seen, is dressing.

WILLY: (*with great feeling*) You're the best there is, Linda, you're a pal, you know that? On the road—on the road I want to grab you sometimes and just kiss the life outa you.

The laughter is loud now, and he moves into a brightening area at the left, where The Woman has come from behind the scrim and is standing, putting on her hat, looking into a "mirror" and laughing.

WILLY: 'Cause I get so lonely—especially when business is bad and there's nobody 335
to talk to. I get the feeling that I'll never sell anything again, that I won't make a living for you, or a business, a business for the boys. (*He talks through The Woman's subsiding laughter; The Woman primps at the "mirror."*) There's so much I want to make for—

THE WOMAN: Me? You didn't make me, Willy. I picked you.

WILLY: (*pleased*) You picked me?

THE WOMAN: (*who is quite proper-looking, Willy's age*) I did. I've been sitting at that desk watching all the salesmen go by, day in, day out. But you've got such a sense of humor, and we do have such a good time together, don't we?

WILLY: Sure, sure. (*He takes her in his arms.*) Why do you have to go now?

THE WOMAN: It's two o'clock . . . 340

WILLY: No, come on in! (*He pulls her.*)

THE WOMAN: . . . my sisters'll be scandalized. When'll you be back?

WILLY: Oh, two weeks about. Will you come up again?

THE WOMAN: Sure thing. You do make me laugh. It's good for me. (*She squeezes his arm, kisses him.*) And I think you're a wonderful man.

WILLY: You picked me, heh? 345

THE WOMAN: Sure. Because you're so sweet. And such a kidder.

WILLY: Well, I'll see you next time I'm in Boston.

THE WOMAN: I'll put you right through to the buyers.

WILLY: (*slapping her bottom*) Right. Well, bottoms up!

THE WOMAN: (*slaps him gently and laughs*) You just kill me, Willy. (*He suddenly grabs* 350
her and kisses her roughly.) You kill me. And thanks for the stockings. I love a lot of stockings. Well, good night.

WILLY: Good night. And keep your pores open!

THE WOMAN: Oh, Willy!

The Woman bursts out laughing, and Linda's laughter blends in. The Woman disappears into the dark. Now the area at the kitchen table brightens. Linda is sitting where she was at the kitchen table, but now is mending a pair of silk stockings.

LINDA: You are, Willy. The handsomest man. You've got no reason to feel that—
WILLY: (*coming out of The Woman's dimming area and going over to Linda*) I'll make it all up to you, Linda, I'll—
355 LINDA: There's nothing to make up, dear. You're doing fine, better than—
WILLY: (*noticing her mending*) What's that?
LINDA: Just mending my stockings. They're so expensive—
WILLY: (*angrily, taking them from her*) I won't have you mending stockings in this house! Now throw them out!

Linda puts the stockings in her pocket.

BERNARD: (*entering on the run*) Where is he? If he doesn't study!
360 WILLY: (*moving to the forestage, with great agitation*) You'll give him the answers!
BERNARD: I do, but I can't on a Regents! That's a state exam! They're liable to arrest me!
WILLY: Where is he? I'll whip him, I'll whip him!
LINDA: And he'd better give back that football, Willy, it's not nice.
WILLY: Biff! Where is he? Why is he taking everything?
365 LINDA: He's too tough with the girls, Willy. All the mothers are afraid of him!
WILLY: I'll whip him!
BERNARD: He's driving the car without a license!

The Woman's laugh is heard.

WILLY: Shut up!
LINDA: All the mothers—
370 WILLY: Shut up!
BERNARD: (*backing quietly away and out*) Mr. Birnbaum says he's stuck up.
WILLY: Get outa here!
BERNARD: If he doesn't buckle down he'll flunk math! (*He goes off.*)
LINDA: He's right, Willy, you've gotta—
375 WILLY: (*exploding at her*) There's nothing the matter with him! You want him to be a worm like Bernard? He's got spirit, personality . . .

As he speaks, Linda, almost in tears, exits into the living room. Willy is alone in the kitchen, wilting and staring. The leaves are gone. It is night again, and the apartment houses look down from behind.

WILLY: Loaded with it. Loaded! What is he stealing? He's giving it back, isn't he? Why is he stealing? What did I tell him? I never in my life told him anything but decent things.

Happy in pajamas has come down the stairs; Willy suddenly becomes aware of Happy's presence.

HAPPY: Let's go now, come on.

WILLY: (*sitting down at the kitchen table*) Huh! Why did she have to wax the floors herself? Everytime she waxes the floors she keels over. She knows that!

HAPPY: Shh! Take it easy. What brought you back tonight?

WILLY: I got an awful scare. Nearly hit a kid in Yonkers. God! Why didn't I go to   380
Alaska with my brother Ben that time! Ben! That man was a genius, that man was success incarnate! What a mistake! He begged me to go.

HAPPY: Well, there's no use in—

WILLY: You guys! There was a man started with the clothes on his back and ended up with diamond mines!

HAPPY: Boy, someday I'd like to know how he did it.

WILLY: What's the mystery? The man knew what he wanted and went out and got it! Walked into a jungle, and comes out, the age of twenty-one, and he's rich! The world is an oyster, but you don't crack it open on a mattress!

HAPPY: Pop, I told you I'm gonna retire you for life.   385

WILLY: You'll retire me for life on seventy goddam dollars a week? And your women and your car and your apartment, and you'll retire me for life! Christ's sake, I couldn't get past Yonkers today! Where are you guys, where are you? The woods are burning! I can't drive a car!

Charley has appeared in the doorway. He is a large man, slow of speech, laconic, immovable. In all he says, despite what he says, there is pity, and now, trepidation. He has a robe over his pajamas, slippers on his feet. He enters the kitchen.

CHARLEY: Everything all right?

HAPPY: Yeah, Charley, everything's . . .

WILLY: What's the matter?

CHARLEY: I heard some noise. I thought something happened. Can't we do something   390
about the walls? You sneeze in here, and in my house hats blow off.

HAPPY: Let's go to bed, Dad. Come on.

Charley signals to Happy to go.

WILLY: You go ahead, I'm not tired at the moment.

HAPPY: (*to Willy*) Take it easy, huh? (*He exits.*)

WILLY: What're you doin' up?

CHARLEY: (*sitting down at the kitchen table opposite Willy*) Couldn't sleep good. I had   395
a heartburn.

WILLY: Well, you don't know how to eat.

CHARLEY: I eat with my mouth.

WILLY: No, you're ignorant. You gotta know about vitamins and things like that.

CHARLEY: Come on, let's shoot. Tire you out a little.

WILLY: (*hesitantly*) All right. You got cards?   400

CHARLEY: (*taking a deck from his pocket*) Yeah, I got them. Someplace. What is it with those vitamins?

WILLY: (*dealing*) They build up your bones. Chemistry.

CHARLEY: Yeah, but there's no bones in a heartburn.

WILLY: What are you talkin' about? Do you know the first thing about it?

CHARLEY: Don't get insulted.   405

WILLY: Don't talk about something you don't know anything about.

They are playing. Pause.

CHARLEY: What're you doin' home?

WILLY: A little trouble with the car.

CHARLEY: Oh. *(Pause.)* I'd like to take a trip to California.

410 WILLY: Don't say.

CHARLEY: You want a job?

WILLY: I got a job, I told you that. *(After a slight pause.)* What the hell are you offering me a job for?

CHARLEY: Don't get insulted.

WILLY: Don't insult me.

415 CHARLEY: I don't see no sense in it. You don't have to go on this way.

WILLY: I got a good job. *(Slight pause.)* What do you keep comin' in here for?

CHARLEY: You want me to go?

WILLY: *(after a pause, withering)* I can't understand it. He's going back to Texas again. What the hell is that?

CHARLEY: Let him go.

420 WILLY: I got nothin' to give him, Charley, I'm clean, I'm clean.

CHARLEY: He won't starve. None a them starve. Forget about him.

WILLY: Then what have I got to remember?

CHARLEY: You take it too hard. To hell with it. When a deposit bottle is broken you don't get your nickel back.

WILLY: That's easy enough for you to say.

425 CHARLEY: That ain't easy for me to say.

WILLY: Did you see the ceiling I put up in the living room?

CHARLEY: Yeah, that's a piece of work. To put up a ceiling is a mystery to me. How do you do it?

WILLY: What's the difference?

CHARLEY: Well, talk about it.

430 WILLY: You gonna put up a ceiling?

CHARLEY: How could I put up a ceiling?

WILLY: Then what the hell are you bothering me for?

CHARLEY: You're insulted again.

WILLY: A man who can't handle tools is not a man. You're disgusting.

435 CHARLEY: Don't call me disgusting, Willy.

Uncle Ben, carrying a valise and an umbrella, enters the forestage from around the right corner of the house. He is a stolid man, in his sixties, with a mustache and an authoritative air. He is utterly certain of his destiny, and there is an aura of far places about him. He enters exactly as Willy speaks.

WILLY: I'm getting awfully tired, Ben.

Ben's music is heard. Ben looks around at everything.

CHARLEY: Good, keep playing; you'll sleep better. Did you call me Ben?

Ben looks at his watch.

WILLY: That's funny. For a second there you reminded me of my brother Ben.

BEN: I have only a few minutes. (*He strolls, inspecting the place. Willy and Charley continue playing.*)

CHARLEY: You never heard from him again, heh? Since that time?   440

WILLY: Didn't Linda tell you? Couple of weeks ago we got a letter from his wife in Africa. He died.

CHARLEY: That so.

BEN: (*chuckling*) So this is Brooklyn, eh?

CHARLEY: Maybe you're in for some of his money.

WILLY: Naa, he had seven sons. There's just one opportunity I had with that man . . .   445

BEN: I must make a train, William. There are several properties I'm looking at in Alaska.

WILLY: Sure, sure! If I'd gone with him to Alaska that time, everything would've been totally different.

CHARLEY: Go on, you'd froze to death up there.

WILLY: What're you talking about?

BEN: Opportunity is tremendous in Alaska, William. Surprised you're not up there.   450

WILLY: Sure, tremendous.

CHARLEY: Heh?

WILLY: There was the only man I ever met who knew the answers.

CHARLEY: Who?

BEN: How are you all?   455

WILLY: (*taking a pot, smiling*) Fine, fine.

CHARLEY: Pretty sharp tonight.

BEN: Is Mother living with you?

WILLY: No, she died a long time ago.

CHARLEY: Who?   460

BEN: That's too bad. Fine specimen of a lady, Mother.

WILLY: (*to Charley*) Heh?

BEN: I'd hoped to see the old girl.

CHARLEY: Who died?

BEN: Heard anything from Father, have you?   465

WILLY: (*unnerved*) What do you mean, who died?

CHARLEY: (*taking a pot*) What're you talkin' about?

BEN: (*looking at his watch*) William, it's half-past eight!

WILLY: (*as though to dispel his confusion he angrily stops Charley's hand*) That's my build!

CHARLEY: I put the ace—   470

WILLY: If you don't know how to play the game I'm not gonna throw my money away on you!

CHARLEY: (*rising*) It was my ace, for God's sake!

WILLY: I'm through, I'm through!

BEN: When did Mother die?

WILLY: Long ago. Since the beginning you never knew how to play cards.   475

CHARLEY: (*picks up the cards and goes to the door*) All right! Next time I'll bring a deck with five aces.

WILLY: I don't play that kind of game!

CHARLEY: *(turning to him)* You should be ashamed of yourself!

WILLY: Yeah?

480 CHARLEY: Yeah! *(He goes out.)*

WILLY: *(slamming the door after him)* Ignoramus!

BEN: *(as Willy comes toward him through the wall-line of the kitchen)* So you're William.

WILLY: *(shaking Ben's hand)* Ben! I've been waiting for you so long! What's the answer? How did you do it?

BEN: Oh, there's a story in that.

Linda enters the forestage, as of old, carrying the wash basket.

485 LINDA: Is this Ben?

BEN: *(gallantly)* How do you do, my dear.

LINDA: Where've you been all these years? Willy's always wondered why you—

WILLY: *(pulling Ben away from her impatiently)* Where is Dad? Didn't you follow him? How did you get started?

BEN: Well, I don't know how much you remember.

490 WILLY: Well, I was just a baby, of course, only three or four years old—

BEN: Three years and eleven months.

WILLY: What a memory, Ben!

BEN: I have many enterprises, William, and I have never kept books.

WILLY: I remember I was sitting under the wagon in—was it Nebraska?

495 BEN: It was South Dakota, and I gave you a bunch of wild flowers.

WILLY: I remember you walking away down some open road.

BEN: *(laughing)* I was going to find Father in Alaska.

WILLY: Where is he?

BEN: At that age I had a very faulty view of geography, William. I discovered after a few days that I was heading due south, so instead of Alaska, I ended up in Africa.

500 LINDA: Africa!

WILLY: The Gold Coast!

BEN: Principally, diamond mines.

LINDA: Diamond mines!

BEN: Yes, my dear. But I've only a few minutes—

505 WILLY: No! Boys! Boys! *(Young Biff and Happy appear.)* Listen to this. This is your Uncle Ben, a great man! Tell my boys, Ben!

BEN: Why, boys, when I was seventeen I walked into the jungle, and when I was twenty-one I walked out. *(He laughs.)* And by God I was rich.

WILLY: *(to the boys)* You see what I been talking about? The greatest things can happen!

BEN: *(glancing at his watch)* I have an appointment in Ketchikan Tuesday week.

WILLY: No, Ben! Please tell about Dad. I want my boys to hear. I want them to know the kind of stock they spring from. All I remember is a man with a big beard, and I was in Mamma's lap, sitting around a fire, and some kind of high music.

510 BEN: His flute. He played the flute.

WILLY: Sure, the flute, that's right!

New music is heard, a high, rollicking tune.

BEN: Father was a very great and a very wild-hearted man. We would start in Boston, and he'd toss the whole family into the wagon, and then he'd drive the team right across the country; through Ohio, and Indiana, Michigan, Illinois, and all the Western states. And we'd stop in the towns and sell the flutes that he'd made on the way. Great inventor, Father. With one gadget he made more in a week than a man like you could make in a lifetime.

WILLY: That's just the way I'm bringing them up, Ben—rugged, well liked, all-around.

BEN: Yeah? (*To Biff.*) Hit that, boy—hard as you can. (*He pounds his stomach.*)   515

BIFF: Oh, no, sir!

BEN: (*taking boxing stance*) Come on, get to me! (*He laughs.*)

WILLY: Go to it, Biff! Go ahead, show him!

BIFF: Okay! (*He cocks his fist and starts in.*)

LINDA: (*to Willy*) Why must he fight, dear?

BEN: (*sparring with Biff*) Good boy! Good boy!   520

WILLY: How's that, Ben, heh?

HAPPY: Give him the left, Biff!

LINDA: Why are you fighting?

BEN: Good boy! (*Suddenly comes in, trips Biff, and stands over him, the point of his umbrella poised over Biff's eye.*)

LINDA: Look out, Biff!   525

BIFF: Gee!

BEN: (*patting Biff's knee*) Never fight fair with a stranger, boy. You'll never get out of the jungle that way. (*Taking Linda's hand and bowing.*) It was an honor and a pleasure to meet you, Linda.

LINDA: (*withdrawing her hand coldly, frightened*) Have a nice—trip.

BEN: (*to Willy*) And good luck with your—what do you do?

WILLY: Selling.   530

BEN: Yes. Well . . . (*He raises his hand in farewell to all.*)

WILLY: No, Ben, I don't want you to think . . . (*He takes Ben's arm to show him.*) It's Brooklyn, I know, but we hunt too.

BEN: Really, now.

WILLY: Oh, sure, there's snakes and rabbits and—that's why I moved out here. Why, Biff can fell any one of these trees in no time! Boys! Go right over to where they're building the apartment house and get some sand. We're gonna rebuild the entire front stoop right now! Watch this, Ben!

BIFF: Yes, sir! On the double, Hap!   535

HAPPY: (*as he and Biff run off*) I lost weight, Pop, you notice?

Charley enters in knickers, even before the boys are gone.

CHARLEY: Listen, if they steal any more from that building the watchman'll put the cops on them!

LINDA: (*to Willy*) Don't let Biff . . .

Ben laughs lustily.

WILLY: You shoulda seen the lumber they brought home last week. At least a dozen six-by-tens worth all kinds of money.

540   CHARLEY: Listen, if that watchman—
     WILLY: I gave them hell, understand. But I got a couple of fearless characters there.
     CHARLEY: Willy, the jails are full of fearless characters.
     BEN: (clapping Willy on the back, with a laugh at Charley) And the stock exchange, friend!
     WILLY: (joining in Ben's laughter) Where are the rest of your pants?
545   CHARLEY: My wife bought them.
     WILLY: Now all you need is a golf club and you can go upstairs and go to sleep. (To Ben.) Great athlete! Between him and his son Bernard they can't hammer a nail!
     BERNARD: (rushing in) The watchman's chasing Biff!
     WILLY: (angrily) Shut up! He's not stealing anything!
     LINDA: (alarmed, hurrying off left) Where is he? Biff, dear! (She exits.)
550   WILLY: (moving toward the left, away from Ben) There's nothing wrong. What's the matter with you?
     BEN: Nervy boy. Good!
     WILLY: (laughing) Oh, nerves of iron, that Biff!
     CHARLEY: Don't know what it is. My New England man comes back and he's bleedin', they murdered him up there.
     WILLY: It's contacts, Charley, I got important contacts!
555   CHARLEY: (sarcastically) Glad to hear it, Willy. Come in later, we'll shoot a little casino. I'll take some of your Portland money. (He laughs at Willy and exits.)
     WILLY: (turning to Ben) Business is bad, it's murderous. But not for me, of course.
     BEN: I'll stop by on my way back to Africa.
     WILLY: (longingly) Can't you stay a few days? You're just what I need, Ben, because I—I have a fine position here, but I—well, Dad left when I was such a baby and I never had a chance to talk to him and I still feel—kind of temporary about myself.
     BEN: I'll be late for my train.

They are at opposite ends of the stage.

560   WILLY: Ben, my boys—can't we talk? They'd go into the jaws of hell for me, see, but I—
     BEN: William, you're being first-rate with your boys. Outstanding, manly chaps!
     WILLY: (hanging on to his words) Oh, Ben, that's good to hear! Because sometimes I'm afraid that I'm not teaching them the right kind of—Ben, how should I teach them?
     BEN: (giving great weight to each word, and with a certain vicious audacity) William, when I walked into the jungle, I was seventeen. When I walked out I was twenty-one. And, by God, I was rich! (He goes off into darkness around the right corner of the house.)
     WILLY: . . . was rich! That's just the spirit I want to imbue them with! To walk into a jungle! I was right! I was right! I was right!

Ben is gone, but Willy is still speaking to him as Linda, in nightgown and robe, enters the kitchen, glances around for Willy, then goes to the door of the house, looks out and sees him. Comes down to his left. He looks at her.

LINDA: Willy, dear? Willy?   565

WILLY: I was right!

LINDA: Did you have some cheese? (*He can't answer.*) It's very late, darling. Come
to bed, heh?

WILLY: (*looking straight up*) Gotta break your neck to see a star in this yard.

LINDA: You coming in?

WILLY: What ever happened to that diamond watch fob? Remember? When Ben   570
came from Africa that time? Didn't he give me a watch fob with a diamond in it?

LINDA: You pawned it, dear. Twelve, thirteen years ago. For Biff's radio correspondence course.

WILLY: Gee, that was a beautiful thing. I'll take a walk.

LINDA: But you're in your slippers.

WILLY: (*starting to go around the house at the left*) I was right! I was! (*Half to Linda,
as he goes, shaking his head.*) What a man! There was a man worth talking to.
I was right!

LINDA: (*calling after Willy*) But in your slippers, Willy!   575

Willy is almost gone when Biff, in his pajamas, comes down the stairs and enters the kitchen.

BIFF: What is he doing out there?

LINDA: Sh!

BIFF: God Almighty, Mom, how long has he been doing this?

LINDA: Don't, he'll hear you.

BIFF: What the hell is the matter with him?   580

LINDA: It'll pass by morning.

BIFF: Shouldn't we do anything?

LINDA: Oh, my dear, you should do a lot of things, but there's nothing to do, so go
to sleep.

Happy comes down the stairs and sits on the steps.

HAPPY: I never heard him so loud, Mom.

LINDA: Well, come around more often; you'll hear him. (*She sits down at the table*   585
and mends the lining of Willy's jacket.)

BIFF: Why didn't you ever write me about this, Mom?

LINDA: How would I write to you? For over three months you had no address.

BIFF: I was on the move. But you know I thought of you all the time. You know
that, don't you, pal?

LINDA: I know, dear, I know. But he likes to have a letter. Just to know that there's
still a possibility for better things.

BIFF: He's not like this all the time, is he?   590

LINDA: It's when you come home he's always the worst.

BIFF: When I come home?

LINDA: When you write you're coming, he's all smiles, and talks about the future,
and—he's just wonderful. And then the closer you seem to come, the more
shaky he gets, and then, by the time you get here, he's arguing, and he seems
angry at you. I think it's just that maybe he can't bring himself to—to open up
to you. Why are you so hateful to each other? Why is that?

Biff: (evasively) I'm not hateful, Mom.

595   Linda: But you no sooner come in the door than you're fighting!

Biff: I don't know why. I mean to change. I'm tryin', Mom, you understand?

Linda: Are you home to stay now?

Biff: I don't know. I want to look around, see what's doin'.

Linda: Biff, you can't look around all your life, can you?

600   Biff: I just can't take hold, Mom. I can't take hold of some kind of a life.

Linda: Biff, a man is not a bird, to come and go with the springtime.

Biff: Your hair . . . (He touches her hair.) Your hair got so gray.

Linda: Oh, it's been gray since you were in high school. I just stopped dyeing it, that's all.

Biff: Dye it again, will ya? I don't want my pal looking old. (He smiles.)

605   Linda: You're such a boy! You think you can go away for a year and . . . You've got to get it into your head now that one day you'll knock on this door and there'll be strange people here—

Biff: What are you talking about? You're not even sixty, Mom.

Linda: But what about your father?

Biff: (lamely) Well, I meant him too.

Happy: He admires Pop.

610   Linda: Biff, dear, if you don't have any feeling for him, then you can't have any feeling for me.

Biff: Sure I can, Mom.

Linda: No. You can't just come to see me, because I love him. (With a threat, but only a threat, of tears.) He's the dearest man in the world to me, and I won't have anyone making him feel unwanted and low and blue. You've got to make up your mind now, darling, there's no leeway any more. Either he's your father and you pay him that respect, or else you're not to come here. I know he's not easy to get along with—nobody knows that better than me—but . . .

Willy: (from the left, with a laugh) Hey, hey, Biffo!

Biff: (starting to go out after Willy) What the hell is the matter with him? (Happy stops him.)

615   Linda: Don't—don't go near him!

Biff: Stop making excuses for him! He always, always wiped the floor with you. Never had an ounce of respect for you.

Happy: He's always had respect for—

Biff: What the hell do you know about it?

Happy: (surlily) Just don't call him crazy!

620   Biff: He's got no character—Charley wouldn't do this. Not in his own house— spewing out that vomit from his mind.

Happy: Charley never had to cope with what he's got to.

Biff: People are worse off than Willy Loman. Believe me, I've seen them!

Linda: Then make Charley your father, Biff. You can't do that, can you? I don't say he's a great man. Willy Loman never made a lot of money. His name was never in the paper. He's not the finest character that ever lived. But he's a human being, and a terrible thing is happening to him. So attention must be paid. He's not to be allowed to fall into his grave like an old dog. Attention, attention must be finally paid to such a person. You called him crazy—

BIFF: I didn't mean—

LINDA: No, a lot of people think he's lost his—balance. But you don't have to be very smart to know what his trouble is. The man is exhausted.   625

HAPPY: Sure!

LINDA: A small man can be just as exhausted as a great man. He works for a company thirty-six years this March, opens up unheard-of territories to their trademark, and now in his old age they take his salary away.

HAPPY: *(indignantly)* I didn't know that, Mom.

LINDA: You never asked, my dear! Now that you get your spending money someplace else you don't trouble your mind with him.

HAPPY: But I gave you money last—   630

LINDA: Christmas time, fifty dollars! To fix the hot water it cost ninety-seven fifty! For five weeks he's been on straight commission, like a beginner, an unknown!

BIFF: Those ungrateful bastards!

LINDA: Are they any worse than his sons? When he brought them business, when he was young, they were glad to see him. But now his old friends, the old buyers that loved him so and always found some order to hand him in a pinch—they're all dead, retired. He used to be able to make six, seven calls a day in Boston. Now he takes his valises out of the car and puts them back and takes them out again and he's exhausted. Instead of walking he talks now. He drives seven hundred miles, and when he gets there no one knows him any more, no one welcomes him. And what goes through a man's mind, driving seven hundred miles home without having earned a cent? Why shouldn't he talk to himself? Why? When he has to go to Charley and borrow fifty dollars a week and pretend to me that it's his pay? How long can that go on? How long? You see what I'm sitting here and waiting for? And you tell me he has no character? The man who never worked a day but for your benefit? When does he get the medal for that? Is this his reward—to turn around at the age of sixty-three and find his sons, who he loved better than his life, one a philandering bum—

HAPPY: Mom!

LINDA: That's all you are, my baby! *(To Biff.)* And you! What happened to the love you had for him? You were such pals! How you used to talk to him on the phone every night! How lonely he was till he could come home to you!   635

BIFF: All right, Mom. I'll live here in my room, and I'll get a job. I'll keep away from him, that's all.

LINDA: No, Biff. You can't stay here and fight all the time.

BIFF: He threw me out of this house, remember that.

LINDA: Why did he do that? I never knew why.

BIFF: Because I know he's a fake and he doesn't like anybody around who knows!   640

LINDA: Why a fake? In what way? What do you mean?

BIFF: Just don't lay it all at my feet. It's between me and him—that's all I have to say. I'll chip in from now on. He'll settle for half my pay check. He'll be all right. I'm going to bed. *(He starts for the stairs.)*

LINDA: He won't be all right.

BIFF: *(turning on the stairs, furiously)* I hate this city and I'll stay here. Now what do you want?

LINDA: He's dying, Biff.   645

Happy turns quickly to her, shocked.

Biff: *(after a pause)* Why is he dying?

Linda: He's been trying to kill himself.

Biff: *(with great horror)* How?

Linda: I live from day to day.

650 **Biff:** What're you talking about?

Linda: Remember I wrote you that he smashed up the car again? In February?

Biff: Well?

Linda: The insurance inspector came. He said that they have evidence. That all these accidents in the last year—weren't—weren't—accidents.

Happy: How can they tell that? That's a lie.

655 **Linda:** It seems there's a woman . . . *(She takes a breath as—)*

Biff: *(sharply but contained)* What woman?

Linda: *(simultaneously)* . . . and this woman . . .

Linda: What?

Biff: Nothing. Go ahead.

660 **Linda:** What did you say?

Biff: Nothing. I just said what woman?

Happy: What about her?

Linda: Well, it seems she was walking down the road and saw his car. She says that he wasn't driving fast at all, and that he didn't skid. She says he came to that little bridge, and then deliberately smashed into the railing, and it was only the shallowness of the water that saved him.

Biff: Oh, no, he probably just fell asleep again.

665 **Linda:** I don't think he fell asleep.

Biff: Why not?

Linda: Last month . . . *(With great difficulty.)* Oh, boys, it's so hard to say a thing like this! He's just a big stupid man to you, but I tell you there's more good in him than in many other people. *(She chokes, wipes her eyes.)* I was looking for a fuse. The lights blew out, and I went down the cellar. And behind the fuse box—it happened to fall out—was a length of rubber pipe—just short.

Happy: No kidding?

Linda: There's a little attachment on the end of it. I knew right away. And sure enough, on the bottom of the water heater there's a new little nipple on the gas pipe.

670 **Happy:** *(angrily)* That—jerk.

Biff: Did you have it taken off?

Linda: I'm—I'm ashamed to. How can I mention it to him? Every day I go down and take away that little rubber pipe. But, when he comes home, I put it back where it was. How can I insult him that way? I don't know what to do. I live from day to day, boys. I tell you, I know every thought in his mind. It sounds so old-fashioned and silly, but I tell you he put his whole life into you and you've turned your backs on him. *(She is bent over in the chair, weeping, her face in her hands.)* Biff, I swear to God! Biff, his life is in your hands!

Happy: *(to Biff)* How do you like that damned fool!

BIFF: *(kissing her)* All right, pal, all right. It's all settled now. I've been remiss. I know that, Mom, but now I'll stay, and I swear to you, I'll apply myself. *(Kneeling in front of her, in a fever of self-reproach.)* It's just—you see, Mom, I don't fit in business. Not that I won't try. I'll try, and I'll make good.

HAPPY: Sure you will. The trouble with you in business was you never tried to please people.   675

BIFF: I know, I—

HAPPY: Like when you worked for Harrison's. Bob Harrison said you were tops, and then you go and do some damn fool thing like whistling whole songs in the elevator like a comedian.

BIFF: *(against Happy)* So what? I like to whistle sometimes.

HAPPY: You don't raise a guy to a responsible job who whistles in the elevator!

LINDA: Well, don't argue about it now.   680

HAPPY: Like when you'd go off and swim in the middle of the day instead of taking the line around.

BIFF: *(his resentment rising)* Well, don't you run off? You take off sometimes, don't you? On a nice summer day?

HAPPY: Yeah, but I cover myself!

LINDA: Boys!

HAPPY: If I'm going to take a fade the boss can call any number where I'm supposed   685
to be and they'll swear to him that I just left. I'll tell you something that I hate to say, Biff, but in the business world some of them think you're crazy.

BIFF: *(angered)* Screw the business world!

HAPPY: All right, screw it! Great, but cover yourself!

LINDA: Hap, Hap!

BIFF: I don't care what they think! They've laughed at Dad for years, and you know why? Because we don't belong in this nut-house of a city! We should be mixing cement on some open plain, or—or carpenters. A carpenter is allowed to whistle!

Willy walks in from the entrance of the house, at left.

WILLY: Even your grandfather was better than a carpenter. *(Pause. They watch him.)*   690
You never grew up. Bernard does not whistle in the elevator, I assure you.

BIFF: *(as though to laugh Willy out of it)* Yeah, but you do, Pop.

WILLY: I never in my life whistled in an elevator! And who in the business world thinks I'm crazy?

BIFF: I didn't mean it like that, Pop. Now don't make a whole thing out of it, will ya?

WILLY: Go back to the West! Be a carpenter, a cowboy, enjoy yourself!

LINDA: Willy, he was just saying—   695

WILLY: I heard what he said!

HAPPY: *(trying to quiet Willy)* Hey, Pop, come on now . . .

WILLY: *(continuing over Happy's line)* They laugh at me, heh? Go to Filene's, go to the Hub, go to Slattery's, Boston. Call out the name Willy Loman and see what happens! Big shot!

BIFF: All right, Pop.

WILLY: Big!   700

BIFF: All right!

WILLY: Why do you always insult me?

BIFF: I didn't say a word. (*To Linda.*) Did I say a word?

LINDA: He didn't say anything, Willy.

705   WILLY: (*going to the doorway of the living room*) All right, good night, good night.

LINDA: Willy, dear, he just decided . . .

WILLY: (*to Biff*) If you get tired hanging around tomorrow, paint the ceiling I put up in the living room.

BIFF: I'm leaving early tomorrow.

HAPPY: He's going to see Bill Oliver, Pop.

710   WILLY: (*interestedly*) Oliver? For what?

BIFF: (*with reserve, but trying, trying*) He always said he'd stake me. I'd like to go into business, so maybe I can take him up on it.

LINDA: Isn't that wonderful?

WILLY: Don't interrupt. What's wonderful about it? There's fifty men in the City of New York who'd stake him. (*To Biff.*) Sporting goods?

BIFF: I guess so. I know something about it and—

715   WILLY: He knows something about it! You know sporting goods better than Spalding, for God's sake! How much is he giving you?

BIFF: I don't know, I didn't even see him yet, but—

WILLY: Then what're you talkin' about?

BIFF: (*getting angry*) Well, all I said was I'm gonna see him, that's all!

WILLY: (*turning away*) Ah, you're counting your chickens again.

720   BIFF: (*starting left for the stairs*) Oh, Jesus, I'm going to sleep!

WILLY: (*calling after him*) Don't curse in this house!

BIFF: (*turning*) Since when did you get so clean!

HAPPY: (*trying to stop them*) Wait a . . .

WILLY: Don't use that language to me! I won't have it!

725   HAPPY: (*grabbing Biff, shouts*) Wait a minute! I got an idea. I got a feasible idea. Come here, Biff, let's talk this over now, let's talk some sense here. When I was down in Florida last time, I thought of a great idea to sell sporting goods. It just came back to me. You and I, Biff—we have a line, the Loman Line. We train a couple of weeks, and put on a couple of exhibitions, see?

WILLY: That's an idea!

HAPPY: Wait! We form two basketball teams, see? Two water-polo teams. We play each other. It's a million dollars' worth of publicity. Two brothers, see? The Loman Brothers. Displays in the Royal Palms—all the hotels. And banners over the ring and the basketball court: "Loman Brothers." Baby, we could sell sporting goods!

WILLY: That is a one-million-dollar idea.

LINDA: Marvelous!

730   BIFF: I'm in great shape as far as that's concerned.

HAPPY: And the beauty of it is, Biff, it wouldn't be like a business. We'd be out playin' ball again . . .

BIFF: (*enthused*) Yeah, that's . . .

WILLY: Million-dollar . . .

HAPPY: And you wouldn't get fed up with it, Biff. It'd be the family again. There'd be the old honor, and comradeship, and if you wanted to go off for a swim or somethin'—well, you'd do it! Without some smart cooky gettin' up ahead of you!

WILLY: Lick the world! You guys together could absolutely lick the civilized world.   735

BIFF: I'll see Oliver tomorrow. Hap, if we could work that out . . .

LINDA: Maybe things are beginning to—

WILLY: *(wildly enthused, to Linda)* Stop interrupting! *(To Biff.)* But don't wear sport jacket and slacks when you see Oliver.

BIFF: No, I'll—

WILLY: A business suit, and talk as little as possible, and don't crack any jokes.   740

BIFF: He did like me. Always liked me.

LINDA: He loved you!

WILLY: *(to Linda)* Will you stop! *(To Biff.)* Walk in very serious. You are not applying for a boy's job. Money is to pass. Be quiet, fine, and serious. Everybody likes a kidder, but nobody lends him money.

HAPPY: I'll try to get some myself, Biff. I'm sure I can.

WILLY: I can see great things for you, kids, I think your troubles are over. But remem-   745
ber, start big and you'll end big. Ask for fifteen. How much you gonna ask for?

BIFF: Gee, I don't know—

WILLY: And don't say "Gee." "Gee" is a boy's word. A man walking in for fifteen thousand dollars does not say "Gee!"

BIFF: Ten, I think, would be top though.

WILLY: Don't be so modest. You always started too low. Walk in with a big laugh. Don't look worried. Start off with a couple of your good stories to lighten things up. It's not what you say, it's how you say it—because personality always wins the day.

LINDA: Oliver always thought the highest of him—   750

WILLY: Will you let me talk?

BIFF: Don't yell at her, Pop, will ya?

WILLY: *(angrily)* I was talking, wasn't I!

BIFF: I don't like you yelling at her all the time, and I'm tellin' you, that's all.

WILLY: What're you, takin' over this house?   755

LINDA: Willy—

WILLY: *(turning on her)* Don't take his side all the time, goddammit!

BIFF: *(furiously)* Stop yelling at her!

WILLY: *(suddenly pulling on his cheek, beaten down, guilt ridden)* Give my best to Bill Oliver—he may remember me. *(He exits through the living room doorway.)*

LINDA: *(her voice subdued)* What'd you have to start that for? *(Biff turns away.)* You   760
see how sweet he was as soon as you talked hopefully? *(She goes over to Biff.)* Come up and say good night to him. Don't let him go to bed that way.

HAPPY: Come on, Biff, let's buck him up.

LINDA: Please, dear. Just say good night. It takes so little to make him happy. Come. *(She goes through the living room doorway, calling upstairs from within the living room.)* Your pajamas are hanging in the bathroom. Willy!

HAPPY: (*looking toward where Linda went out*) What a woman! They broke the mold when they made her. You know that, Biff?

BIFF: He's off salary. My God, working on commission!

765 **HAPPY:** Well, let's face it: he's no hot-shot selling man. Except that sometimes, you have to admit, he's a sweet personality.

BIFF: (*deciding*) Lend me ten bucks, will ya? I want to buy some new ties.

HAPPY: I'll take you to a place I know. Beautiful stuff. Wear one of my striped shirts tomorrow.

BIFF: She got gray. Mom got awful old. Gee, I'm gonna go in to Oliver tomorrow and knock him for a—

HAPPY: Come on up. Tell that to Dad. Let's give him a whirl. Come on.

770 **BIFF:** (*steamed up*) You know, with ten thousand bucks, boy!

HAPPY: (*as they go into the living room*) That's the talk, Biff, that's the first time I've heard the old confidence out of you! (*From within the living room, fading off.*) You're gonna live with me, kid, and any babe you want you just say the word . . . (*The last lines are hardly heard. They are mounting the stairs to their parents' bedroom.*)

LINDA: (*entering her bedroom and addressing Willy, who is in the bathroom. She is straightening the bed for him*) Can you do anything about the shower? It drips.

WILLY: (*from the bathroom*) All of a sudden everything falls to pieces! Goddam plumbing, oughta be sued, those people. I hardly finished putting it in and the thing . . . (*His words rumble off.*)

LINDA: I'm just wondering if Oliver will remember him. You think he might?

775 **WILLY:** (*coming out of the bathroom in his pajamas*) Remember him? What's the matter with you, you crazy? If he'd've stayed with Oliver he'd be on top by now! Wait'll Oliver gets a look at him. You don't know the average caliber any more. The average young man today—(*he is getting into bed*)—is got a caliber of zero. Greatest thing in the world for him was to bum around.

Biff and Happy enter the bedroom. Slight pause.

WILLY: (*stops short, looking at Biff*) Glad to hear it, boy.

HAPPY: He wanted to say good night to you, sport.

WILLY: (*to Biff*) Yeah. Knock him dead, boy. What'd you want to tell me?

BIFF: Just take it easy, Pop. Good night. (*He turns to go.*)

780 **WILLY:** (*unable to resist*) And if anything falls off the desk while you're talking to him—like a package or something—don't you pick it up. They have office boys for that.

LINDA: I'll make a big breakfast—

WILLY: Will you let me finish? (*To Biff.*) Tell him you were in the business in the West. Not farm work.

BIFF: All right, Dad.

LINDA: I think everything—

785 **WILLY:** (*going right through her speech*) And don't undersell yourself. No less than fifteen thousand dollars.

BIFF: (*unable to bear him*) Okay. Good night, Mom. (*He starts moving.*)

WILLY: Because you got a greatness in you, Biff, remember that. You got all kinds a greatness . . . (*He lies back, exhausted. Biff walks out.*)

LINDA: (*calling after Biff*) Sleep well, darling!

HAPPY: I'm gonna get married, Mom. I wanted to tell you.

LINDA: Go to sleep, dear.   790

HAPPY: (*going*) I just wanted to tell you.

WILLY: Keep up the good work. (*Happy exits.*) God . . . remember that Ebbets Field game? The championship of the city?

LINDA: Just rest. Should I sing to you?

WILLY: Yeah. Sing to me. (*Linda hums a soft lullaby.*) When that team came out—he was the tallest, remember?

LINDA: Oh, yes. And in gold.   795

Biff enters the darkened kitchen, takes a cigarette, and leaves the house. He comes downstage into a golden pool of light. He smokes, staring at the night.

WILLY: Like a young god. Hercules—something like that. And the sun, the sun all around him. Remember how he waved to me? Right up from the field, with the representatives of three colleges standing by? And the buyers I brought, and the cheers when he came out—Loman, Loman, Loman! God Almighty, he'll be great yet. A star like that, magnificent, can never really fade away!

The light on Willy is fading. The gas heater begins to glow through the kitchen wall, near the stairs, a blue flame beneath red coils.

LINDA: (*timidly*) Willy, dear, what has he got against you?

WILLY: I'm so tired. Don't talk any more.

Biff slowly returns to the kitchen. He stops, stares toward the heater.

LINDA: Will you ask Howard to let you work in New York?

WILLY: First thing in the morning. Everything'll be all right.   800

Biff reaches behind the heater and draws out a length of rubber tubing. He is horrified and turns his head toward Willy's room, still dimly lit, from which the strains of Linda's desperate but monotonous humming rise.

WILLY: (*staring through the window into the moonlight*) Gee, look at the moon moving between the buildings!

Biff wraps the tubing around his hand and quickly goes up the stairs. Curtain.

ACT 2

Music is heard, gay and bright. The curtain rises as the music fades away. Willy, in shirt sleeves, is sitting at the kitchen table, sipping coffee, his hat in his lap. Linda is filling his cup when she can.

WILLY: Wonderful coffee. Meal in itself.

LINDA: Can I make you some eggs?

WILLY: No. Take a breath.

LINDA: You look so rested, dear.

5   WILLY: I slept like a dead one. First time in months. Imagine, sleeping till ten on a Tuesday morning. Boys left nice and early, heh?

LINDA: They were out of here by eight o'clock.

WILLY: Good work!

LINDA: It was so thrilling to see them leaving together. I can't get over the shaving lotion in this house.

WILLY: (smiling) Mmm—

10   LINDA: Biff was very changed this morning. His whole attitude seemed to be hopeful. He couldn't wait to get downtown to see Oliver.

WILLY: He's heading for a change. There's no question, there simply are certain men that take longer to get—solidified. How did he dress?

LINDA: His blue suit. He's so handsome in that suit. He could be a—anything in that suit!

Willy gets up from the table. Linda holds his jacket for him.

WILLY: There's no question, no question at all. Gee, on the way home tonight I'd like to buy some seeds.

LINDA: (laughing) That'd be wonderful. But not enough sun gets back there. Nothing'll grow any more.

15   WILLY: You wait, kid, before it's all over we're gonna get a little place out in the country, and I'll raise some vegetables, a couple of chickens . . .

LINDA: You'll do it yet, dear.

Willy walks out of his jacket. Linda follows him.

WILLY: And they'll get married, and come for a weekend. I'd build a little guest house. 'Cause I got so many fine tools, all I'd need would be a little lumber and some peace of mind.

LINDA: (joyfully) I sewed the lining . . .

WILLY: I could build two guest houses, so they'd both come. Did he decide how much he's going to ask Oliver for?

20   LINDA: (getting him into the jacket) He didn't mention it, but I imagine ten or fifteen thousand. You going to talk to Howard today?

WILLY: Yeah. I'll put it to him straight and simple. He'll just have to take me off the road.

LINDA: And Willy, don't forget to ask for a little advance, because we've got the insurance premium. It's the grace period now.

WILLY: That's a hundred . . . ?

LINDA: A hundred and eight, sixty-eight. Because we're a little short again.

25   WILLY: Why are we short?

LINDA: Well, you had the motor job on the car . . .

WILLY: That goddam Studebaker!

LINDA: And you got one more payment on the refrigerator . . .

WILLY: But it just broke again!

30   LINDA: Well, it's old, dear.

WILLY: I told you we should've bought a well-advertised machine. Charley bought a General Electric and it's twenty years old and it's still good, that son-of-a-bitch.

LINDA: But, Willy—

WILLY: Whoever heard of a Hastings refrigerator? Once in my life I would like to own something outright before it's broken! I'm always in a race with the junk-yard! I just finished paying for the car and it's on its last legs. The refrigerator consumes belts like a goddam maniac. They time those things. They time them so when you finally paid for them, they're used up.

LINDA: (*buttoning up his jacket as he unbuttons it*) All told, about two hundred dollars would carry us, dear. But that includes the last payment on the mortgage. After this payment, Willy, the house belongs to us.

WILLY: It's twenty-five years!   35

LINDA: Biff was nine years old when we bought it.

WILLY: Well, that's a great thing. To weather a twenty-five year mortgage is—

LINDA: It's an accomplishment.

WILLY: All the cement, the lumber, the reconstruction I put in this house! There ain't a crack to be found in it any more.

LINDA: Well, it served its purpose.   40

WILLY: What purpose? Some stranger'll come along, move in, and that's that. If only Biff would take this house, and raise a family . . . (*He starts to go.*) Good-by, I'm late.

LINDA: (*suddenly remembering*) Oh, I forgot! You're supposed to meet them for dinner.

WILLY: Me?

LINDA: At Frank's Chop House on Forty-eighth near Sixth Avenue.

WILLY: Is that so! How about you?   45

LINDA: No, just the three of you. They're gonna blow you to a big meal!

WILLY: Don't say! Who thought of that?

LINDA: Biff came to me this morning, Willy, and he said, "Tell Dad, we want to blow him to a big meal." Be there six o'clock. You and your two boys are going to have dinner.

WILLY: Gee whiz! That's really somethin'. I'm gonna knock Howard for a loop, kid. I'll get an advance, and I'll come home with a New York job. Goddammit, now I'm gonna do it!

LINDA: Oh, that's the spirit, Willy!   50

WILLY: I will never get behind a wheel the rest of my life!

LINDA: It's changing, Willy, I can feel it changing!

WILLY: Beyond a question. G'by, I'm late. (*He starts to go again.*)

LINDA: (*calling after him as she runs to the kitchen table for a handkerchief*) You got your glasses?

WILLY: (*feels for them, then comes back in*) Yeah, yeah, got my glasses.   55

LINDA: (*giving him the handkerchief*) And a handkerchief.

WILLY: Yeah, handkerchief.

LINDA: And your saccharine?

WILLY: Yeah, my saccharine.

LINDA: Be careful on the subway stairs.   60

She kisses him, and a silk stocking is seen hanging from her hand. Willy notices it.

WILLY: Will you stop mending stockings? At least while I'm in the house. It gets me nervous. I can't tell you. Please.

Linda hides the stocking in her hand as she follows Willy across the forestage in front of the house.

LINDA: Remember, Frank's Chop House.
WILLY: *(passing the apron)* Maybe beets would grow out there.
LINDA: *(laughing)* But you tried so many times.
65 **WILLY:** Yeah. Well, don't work hard today. *(He disappears around the right corner of the house.)*
LINDA: Be careful!

As Willy vanishes, Linda waves to him. Suddenly the phone rings. She runs across the stage and into the kitchen and lifts it.

LINDA: Hello? Oh, Biff! I'm so glad you called, I just . . . Yes, sure, I just told him. Yes, he'll be there for dinner at six o'clock, I didn't forget. Listen, I was just dying to tell you. You know that little rubber pipe I told you about? That he connected to the gas heater? I finally decided to go down the cellar this morning and take it away and destroy it. But it's gone! Imagine? He took it away himself, it isn't there! *(She listens.)* When? Oh, then you took it. Oh—nothing, it's just that I'd hoped he'd taken it away himself. Oh, I'm not worried, darling, because this morning he left in such high spirits, it was like the old days! I'm not afraid any more. Did Mr. Oliver see you? . . . Well, you wait there then. And make a nice impression on him, darling. Just don't perspire too much before you see him. And have a nice time with Dad. He may have big news too! . . . That's right, a New York job. And be sweet to him tonight, dear. Be loving to him. Because he's only a little boat looking for a harbor. *(She is trembling with sorrow and joy.)* Oh, that's wonderful, Biff, you'll save his life. Thanks, darling. Just put your arm around him when he comes into the restaurant. Give him a smile. That's the boy . . . Good-by, dear. . . . You got your comb? . . . That's fine. Good-by, Biff dear.

In the middle of her speech, Howard Wagner, thirty-six, wheels in a small typewriter table on which is a wire-recording machine and proceeds to plug it in. This is on the left forestage. Light slowly fades on Linda as it rises on Howard. Howard is intent on threading the machine and only glances over his shoulder as Willy appears.

WILLY: Pst! Pst!
HOWARD: Hello, Willy, come in.
70 **WILLY:** Like to have a little talk with you, Howard.
HOWARD: Sorry to keep you waiting. I'll be with you in a minute.
WILLY: What's that, Howard?
HOWARD: Didn't you ever see one of these? Wire recorder.
WILLY: Oh. Can we talk a minute?
75 **HOWARD:** Records things. Just got delivery yesterday. Been driving me crazy, the most terrific machine I ever saw in my life. I was up all night with it.
WILLY: What do you do with it?
HOWARD: I bought it for dictation, but you can do anything with it. Listen to this. I had it home last night. Listen to what I picked up. The first one is my daughter.

Get this. (*He flicks the switch and "Roll out the Barrel" is heard being whistled.*) Listen to that kid whistle.

WILLY: That is lifelike, isn't it?

HOWARD: Seven years old. Get that tone.

WILLY: Ts, ts. Like to ask a little favor if you . . .   80

The whistling breaks off, and the voice of Howard's Daughter is heard.

HIS DAUGHTER: "Now you, Daddy."

HOWARD: She's crazy for me! (*Again the same song is whistled.*) That's me! Ha! (*He winks.*)

WILLY: You're very good!

The whistling breaks off again. The machine runs silent for a moment.

HOWARD: Sh! Get this now, this is my son.

HIS SON: "The capital of Alabama is Montgomery; the capital of Arizona is   85
    Phoenix; the capital of Arkansas is Little Rock; the capital of California is
    Sacramento . . ." (*And on, and on.*)

HOWARD: (*holding up five fingers*) Five years old, Willy!

WILLY: He'll make an announcer some day!

HIS SON: (*continuing*) "The capital . . ."

HOWARD: Get that—alphabetical order! (*The machine breaks off suddenly.*) Wait a
    minute. The maid kicked the plug out.

WILLY: It certainly is a—   90

HOWARD: Sh, for God's sake!

HIS SON: "It's nine o'clock, Bulova watch time. So I have to go to sleep."

WILLY: That really is—

HOWARD: Wait a minute! The next is my wife.

They wait.

HOWARD'S VOICE: "Go on, say something." (*Pause.*) "Well, you gonna talk?"   95

HIS WIFE: "I can't think of anything."

HOWARD'S VOICE: "Well, talk—it's turning."

HIS WIFE: (*shyly, beaten*) "Hello." (*Silence.*) "Oh, Howard, I can't talk into this . . ."

HOWARD: (*snapping the machine off*) That was my wife.

WILLY: That is a wonderful machine. Can we—   100

HOWARD: I tell you, Willy, I'm gonna take my camera, and my bandsaw, and all my
    hobbies, and out they go. This is the most fascinating relaxation I ever found.

WILLY: I think I'll get one myself.

HOWARD: Sure, they're only a hundred and a half. You can't do without it. Supposing you wanna hear Jack Benny, see? But you can't be at home at that hour.
    So you tell the maid to turn the radio on when Jack Benny comes on, and this
    automatically goes on with the radio . . .

WILLY: And when you come home you . . .

HOWARD: You can come home twelve o'clock, one o'clock, any time you like, and   105
    you get yourself a Coke and sit yourself down, throw the switch, and there's Jack
    Benny's program in the middle of the night!

WILLY: I'm definitely going to get one. Because lots of time I'm on the road, and
    I think to myself, what I must be missing on the radio!

HOWARD: Don't you have a radio in the car?

WILLY: Well, yeah, but who ever thinks of turning it on?

HOWARD: Say, aren't you supposed to be in Boston?

110   WILLY: That's what I want to talk to you about, Howard. You got a minute?

He draws a chair in from the wing.

HOWARD: What happened? What're you doing here?

WILLY: Well . . .

HOWARD: You didn't crack up again, did you?

WILLY: Oh, no. No . . .

115   HOWARD: Geez, you had me worried there for a minute. What's the trouble?

WILLY: Well, to tell you the truth, Howard, I've come to the decision that I'd
    rather not travel any more.

HOWARD: Not travel! Well, what'll you do?

WILLY: Remember, Christmas time, when you had the party here? You said you'd
    try to think of some spot for me here in town.

HOWARD: With us?

120   WILLY: Well, sure.

HOWARD: Oh, yeah, yeah. I remember. Well, I couldn't think of anything for you,
    Willy.

WILLY: I tell ya, Howard. The kids are all grown up, y'know. I don't need much any
    more. If I could take home—well, sixty-five dollars a week, I could swing it.

HOWARD: Yeah, but Willy, see I—

WILLY: I tell ya why, Howard. Speaking frankly and between the two of us,
    y'know—I'm just a little tired.

125   HOWARD: Oh, I could understand that, Willy. But you're a road man, Willy, and we
    do a road business. We've only got a half-dozen salesmen on the floor here.

WILLY: God knows, Howard, I never asked a favor of any man. But I was with the
    firm when your father used to carry you in here in his arms.

HOWARD: I know that, Willy, but—

WILLY: Your father came to me the day you were born and asked me what I thought
    of the name of Howard, may he rest in peace.

HOWARD: I appreciate that, Willy, but there just is no spot here for you. If I had a
    spot I'd slam you right in, but I just don't have a single, solitary spot.

He looks for his lighter. Willy has picked it up and gives it to him. Pause.

130   WILLY: *(with increasing anger)* Howard, all I need to set my table is fifty dollars a week.

HOWARD: But where am I going to put you, kid?

WILLY: Look, it isn't a question of whether I can sell merchandise, is it?

HOWARD: No, but it's a business, kid, and everybody's gotta pull his own weight.

WILLY: *(desperately)* Just let me tell you a story, Howard—

135   HOWARD: 'Cause you gotta admit, business is business.

WILLY: *(angrily)* Business is definitely business, but just listen for a minute. You
    don't understand this. When I was a boy—eighteen, nineteen—I was already

on the road. And there was a question in my mind as to whether selling had a future for me. Because in those days I had a yearning to go to Alaska. See, there were three gold strikes in one month in Alaska, and I felt like going out. Just for the ride, you might say.

HOWARD: *(barely interested)* Don't say.

WILLY: Oh, yeah, my father lived many years in Alaska. He was an adventurous man. We've got quite a little streak of self-reliance in our family. I thought I'd go out with my older brother and try to locate him, and maybe settle in the North with the old man. And I was almost decided to go, when I met a salesman in the Parker House. His name was Dave Singleman. And he was eighty-four years old, and he'd drummed merchandise in thirty-one states. And old Dave, he'd go up to his room, y'understand, put on his green velvet slippers—I'll never forget—and pick up his phone and call the buyers, and without ever leaving his room, at the age of eighty-four, he made his living. And when I saw that, I realized that selling was the greatest career a man could want. 'Cause what could be more satisfying than to be able to go, at the age of eighty-four, into twenty or thirty different cities, and pick up a phone, and be remembered and loved and helped by so many different people? Do you know? when he died—and by the way he died the death of a salesman, in his green velvet slippers in the smoker of the New York, New Haven and Hartford, going into Boston—when he died, hundreds of salesmen and buyers were at his funeral. Things were sad on a lotta trains for months after that. *(He stands up. Howard has not looked at him.)* In those days there was personality in it, Howard. There was respect, and comradeship, and gratitude in it. Today, it's all cut and dried, and there's no chance for bringing friendship to bear—or personality. You see what I mean? They don't know me any more.

HOWARD: *(moving away, to the right)* That's just the thing, Willy.

WILLY: If I had forty dollars a week—that's all I'd need. Forty dollars, Howard.   140

HOWARD: Kid, I can't take blood from a stone, I—

WILLY: *(desperation is on him now)* Howard, the year Al Smith was nominated, your father came to me and—

HOWARD: *(starting to go off)* I've got to see some people, kid.

WILLY: *(stopping him)* I'm talking about your father! There were promises made across this desk! You mustn't tell me you've got people to see—I put thirty-four years into this firm, Howard, and now I can't pay my insurance! You can't eat the orange and throw the peel away—a man is not a piece of fruit! *(After a pause.)* Now pay attention. Your father—in 1928 I had a big year. I averaged a hundred and seventy dollars a week in commissions.

HOWARD: *(impatiently)* Now, Willy, you never averaged—   145

WILLY: *(banging his hand on the desk)* I averaged a hundred and seventy dollars a week in the year of 1928! And your father came to me—or rather, I was in the office here—it was right over this desk—and he put his hand on my shoulder—

HOWARD: *(getting up)* You'll have to excuse me, Willy, I gotta see some people. Pull yourself together. *(Going out.)* I'll be back in a little while.

On Howard's exit, the light on his chair grows very bright and strange.

WILLY: Pull myself together! What the hell did I say to him? My God, I was yelling at him! How could I! (*Willy breaks off, staring at the light, which occupies the chair, animating it. He approaches this chair, standing across the desk from it.*) Frank, Frank, don't you remember what you told me that time? How you put your hand on my shoulder, and Frank . . . (*He leans on the desk and as he speaks the dead man's name he accidentally switches on the recorder, and instantly—*)

HOWARD'S SON: ". . . of New York is Albany. The capital of Ohio is Cincinnati, the capital of Rhode Island is . . ." (*The recitation continues.*)

150 WILLY: (*leaping away with fright, shouting*) Ha! Howard! Howard! Howard!

HOWARD: (*rushing in*) What happened?

WILLY: (*pointing at the machine, which continues nasally, childishly, with the capital cities*) Shut it off! Shut it off!

HOWARD: (*pulling the plug out*) Look, Willy . . .

WILLY: (*pressing his hands to his eyes*) I gotta get myself some coffee. I'll get some coffee . . .

Willy starts to walk out. Howard stops him.

155 HOWARD: (*rolling up the cord*) Willy, look . . .

WILLY: I'll go to Boston.

HOWARD: Willy, you can't go to Boston for us.

WILLY: Why can't I go?

HOWARD: I don't want you to represent us. I've been meaning to tell you for a long time now.

160 WILLY: Howard, are you firing me?

HOWARD: I think you need a good long rest, Willy.

WILLY: Howard—

HOWARD: And when you feel better, come back, and we'll see if we can work something out.

WILLY: But I gotta earn money, Howard. I'm in no position—

165 HOWARD: Where are your sons? Why don't your sons give you a hand?

WILLY: They're working on a very big deal.

HOWARD: This is no time for false pride, Willy. You go to your sons and tell them that you're tired. You've got two great boys, haven't you?

WILLY: Oh, no question, no question, but in the meantime . . .

HOWARD: Then that's that, heh?

170 WILLY: All right, I'll go to Boston tomorrow.

HOWARD: No, no.

WILLY: I can't throw myself on my sons. I'm not a cripple!

HOWARD: Look, kid, I'm busy this morning.

WILLY: (*grasping Howard's arm*) Howard, you've got to let me go to Boston!

175 HOWARD: (*hard, keeping himself under control*) I've got a line of people to see this morning. Sit down, take five minutes, and pull yourself together, and then go home, will ya? I need the office, Willy. (*He starts to go, turns, remembering the recorder, starts to push off the table holding the recorder.*) Oh, yeah. Whenever you can this week, stop by and drop off the samples. You'll feel better, Willy, and then come back and we'll talk. Pull yourself together, kid, there's people outside.

Howard exits, pushing the table off left. Willy stares into space, exhausted. Now the music is heard—Ben's music—first distantly, then closer, closer. As Willy speaks, Ben enters from the right. He carries valise and umbrella.

WILLY: Oh, Ben, how did you do it? What is the answer? Did you wind up the Alaska deal already?

BEN: Doesn't take much time if you know what you're doing. Just a short business trip. Boarding ship in an hour. Wanted to say good-by.

WILLY: Ben, I've got to talk to you.

BEN: *(glancing at his watch)* Haven't the time, William.

WILLY: *(crossing the apron to Ben)* Ben, nothing's working out. I don't know what to do.   180

BEN: Now, look here, William. I've bought timberland in Alaska and I need a man to look after things for me.

WILLY: God, timberland! Me and my boys in those grand outdoors!

BEN: You've a new continent at your doorstep, William. Get out of these cities, they're full of talk and time payments and courts of law. Screw on your fists and you can fight for a fortune up there.

WILLY: Yes, yes! Linda! Linda!

Linda enters as of old, with the wash.

LINDA: Oh, you're back?   185

BEN: I haven't much time.

WILLY: No, wait! Linda, he's got a proposition for me in Alaska.

LINDA: But you've got—*(To Ben.)* He's got a beautiful job here.

WILLY: But in Alaska, kid, I could—

LINDA: You're doing well enough, Willy!   190

BEN: *(to Linda)* Enough for what, my dear?

LINDA: *(frightened of Ben and angry at him)* Don't say those things to him! Enough to be happy right here, right now. *(To Willy, while Ben laughs.)* Why must everybody conquer the world? You're well liked, and the boys love you, and someday—*(to Ben)*—why, old man Wagner told him just the other day that if he keeps it up he'll be a member of the firm, didn't he, Willy?

WILLY: Sure, sure. I am building something with this firm, Ben, and if a man is building something he must be on the right track, mustn't he?

BEN: What are you building? Lay your hand on it. Where is it?

WILLY: *(hesitantly)* That's true, Linda, there's nothing.   195

LINDA: Why? *(To Ben.)* There's a man eighty-four years old—

WILLY: That's right, Ben, that's right. When I look at that man I say, what is there to worry about?

BEN: Bah!

WILLY: It's true, Ben. All he has to do is go into any city, pick up the phone, and he's making his living and you know why?

BEN: *(picking up his valise)* I've got to go.   200

WILLY: *(holding Ben back)* Look at this boy!

Biff, in his high school sweater, enters carrying suitcase. Happy carries Biff's shoulder guards, gold helmet, and football pants.

WILLY: Without a penny to his name, three great universities are begging for him, and from there the sky's the limit, because it's not what you do, Ben. It's who you know and the smile on your face! It's contacts, Ben, contacts! The whole wealth of Alaska passes over the lunch table at the Commodore Hotel, and that's the wonder, the wonder of this country, that a man can end with diamonds here on the basis of being liked! *(He turns to Biff.)* And that's why when you get out on that field today it's important. Because thousands of people will be rooting for you and loving you. *(To Ben, who has again begun to leave.)* And Ben! when he walks into a business office his name will sound out like a bell and all the doors will open to him! I've seen it, Ben, I've seen it a thousand times! You can't feel it with your hand like timber, but it's there!

BEN: Good-by, William.

WILLY: Ben, am I right? Don't you think I'm right? I value your advice.

205   BEN: There's a new continent at your doorstep, William. You could walk out rich. Rich. *(He is gone.)*

WILLY: We'll do it here, Ben! You hear me? We're gonna do it here!

Young Bernard rushes in. The gay music of the boys is heard.

BERNARD: Oh, gee, I was afraid you left already!

WILLY: Why? What time is it?

BERNARD: It's half-past one!

210   WILLY: Well, come on, everybody! Ebbets Field[1] next stop! Where's the pennants? *(He rushes through the wall-line of the kitchen and out into the living room.)*

LINDA: *(to Biff)* Did you pack fresh underwear?

BIFF: *(who has been limbering up)* I want to go!

BERNARD: Biff, I'm carrying your helmet, ain't I?

HAPPY: No, I'm carrying the helmet.

215   BERNARD: Oh, Biff, you promised me.

HAPPY: I'm carrying the helmet.

BERNARD: How am I going to get in the locker room?

LINDA: Let him carry the shoulder guards. *(She puts her coat and hat on in the kitchen.)*

BERNARD: Can I, Biff? 'Cause I told everybody I'm going to be in the locker room.

220   HAPPY: In Ebbets Field it's the clubhouse.

BERNARD: I meant the clubhouse. Biff!

HAPPY: Biff!

BIFF: *(grandly, after a slight pause)* Let him carry the shoulder guards.

HAPPY: *(as he gives Bernard the shoulder guards)* Stay close to us now.

Willy rushes in with the pennants.

225   WILLY: *(handing them out)* Everybody wave when Biff comes out on the field. *(Happy and Bernard run off.)* You set now, boy?

The music has died away.

---

[1] *Ebbets Field:* The home park of the Brooklyn Dodgers.

BIFF: Ready to go, Pop. Every muscle is ready.

WILLY: *(at the edge of the apron)* You realize what this means?

BIFF: That's right, Pop.

WILLY: *(feeling Biff's muscles)* You're comin' home this afternoon captain of the All-Scholastic Championship Team of the City of New York.

BIFF: I got it, Pop. And remember, pal, when I take off my helmet, that touchdown is for you. 230

WILLY: Let's go! *(He is starting out, with his arm around Biff, when Charley enters, as of old, in knickers.)* I got no room for you, Charley.

CHARLEY: Room? For what?

WILLY: In the car.

CHARLEY: You goin' for a ride? I wanted to shoot some casino.

WILLY: *(furiously)* Casino! *(Incredulously.)* Don't you realize what today is? 235

LINDA: Oh, he knows, Willy. He's just kidding you.

WILLY: That's nothing to kid about!

CHARLEY: No, Linda, what's goin' on?

LINDA: He's playing in Ebbets Field.

CHARLEY: Baseball in this weather? 240

WILLY: Don't talk to him. Come on, come on! *(He is pushing them out.)*

CHARLEY: Wait a minute, didn't you hear the news?

WILLY: What?

CHARLEY: Don't you listen to the radio? Ebbets Field just blew up.

WILLY: You go to hell! *(Charley laughs. Pushing them out.)* Come on, come on! 245
We're late.

CHARLEY: *(as they go)* Knock a homer, Biff, knock a homer!

WILLY: *(the last to leave, turning to Charley)* I don't think that was funny, Charley. This is the greatest day of his life.

CHARLEY: Willy, when are you going to grow up?

WILLY: Yeah, heh? When this game is over, Charley, you'll be laughing out of the other side of your face. They'll be calling him another Red Grange.[2] Twenty-five thousand a year.

CHARLEY: *(kidding)* Is that so? 250

WILLY: Yeah, that's so.

CHARLEY: Well, then, I'm sorry, Willy. But tell me something.

WILLY: What?

CHARLEY: Who is Red Grange?

WILLY: Put up your hands. Goddam you, put up your hands! 255

Charley, chuckling, shakes his head and walks away, around the left corner of the stage. Willy follows him. The music rises to a mocking frenzy.

WILLY: Who the hell do you think you are, better than everybody else? You don't know everything, you big, ignorant, stupid . . . Put up your hands!

---

[2]*Red Grange:* Harold Edward ("Red") Grange (1903–1991)—American football player. A running back for the New York Giants football team and the Chicago Bears, Grange was elected to the Football Hall of Fame in 1963.

Light rises, on the right side of the forestage, on a small table in the reception room of Charley's office. Traffic sounds are heard. Bernard, now mature, sits whistling to himself. A pair of tennis rackets and an overnight bag are on the floor beside him.

WILLY: *(offstage)* What are you walking away for? Don't walk away! If you're going to say something say it to my face! I know you laugh at me behind my back. You'll laugh out of the other side of your goddam face after this game. Touchdown! Touchdown! Eighty thousand people! Touchdown! Right between the goal posts.

Bernard is a quiet, earnest, but self-assured young man. Willy's voice is coming from right upstage now. Bernard lowers his feet off the table and listens. Jenny, his father's secretary, enters.

JENNY: *(distressed)* Say, Bernard, will you go out in the hall?

BERNARD: What is that noise? Who is it?

260   JENNY: Mr. Loman. He just got off the elevator.

BERNARD: *(getting up)* Who's he arguing with?

JENNY: Nobody. There's nobody with him. I can't deal with him any more, and your father gets all upset everytime he comes. I've got a lot of typing to do, and your father's waiting to sign it. Will you see him?

WILLY: *(entering)* Touchdown! Touch—*(He sees Jenny.)* Jenny, Jenny, good to see you. How're ya? Workin'? Or still honest?

JENNY: Fine. How've you been feeling?

265   WILLY: Not much any more, Jenny. Ha, ha! *(He is surprised to see the rackets.)*

BERNARD: Hello, Uncle Willy.

WILLY: *(almost shocked)* Bernard! Well, look who's here! *(He comes quickly, guiltily, to Bernard and warmly shakes his hand.)*

BERNARD: How are you? Good to see you.

WILLY: What are you doing here?

270   BERNARD: Oh, just stopped by to see Pop. Get off my feet till my train leaves. I'm going to Washington in a few minutes.

WILLY: Is he in?

BERNARD: Yes, he's in his office with the accountant. Sit down.

WILLY: *(sitting down)* What're you going to do in Washington?

BERNARD: Oh, just a case I've got there, Willy.

275   WILLY: That so? *(indicating the rackets)* You going to play tennis there?

BERNARD: I'm staying with a friend who's got a court.

WILLY: Don't say. His own tennis court. Must be fine people, I bet.

BERNARD: They are, very nice. Dad tells me Biff's in town.

WILLY: *(with a big smile)* Yeah, Biff's in. Working on a very big deal, Bernard.

280   BERNARD: What's Biff doing?

WILLY: Well, he's been doing very big things in the West. But he decided to establish himself here. Very big. We're having dinner. Did I hear your wife had a boy?

BERNARD: That's right. Our second.

WILLY: Two boys! What do you know!

BERNARD: What kind of a deal has Biff got?

WILLY: Well, Bill Oliver—very big sporting-goods man—he wants Biff very badly.   285
Called him in from the West. Long distance, carte blanche, special deliveries.
Your friends have their own private tennis court?

BERNARD: You still with the old firm, Willy?

WILLY: (*after a pause*) I'm—I'm overjoyed to see how you made the grade, Bernard,
overjoyed. It's an encouraging thing to see a young man really—really—Looks
very good for Biff—very—(*He breaks off, then.*) Bernard—(*He is so full of emotion,
he breaks off again.*)

BERNARD: What is it, Willy?

WILLY: (*small and alone*) What—what's the secret?

BERNARD: What secret?   290

WILLY: How—how did you? Why didn't he ever catch on?

BERNARD: I wouldn't know that, Willy.

WILLY: (*confidentially, desperately*) You were his friend, his boyhood friend. There's
something I don't understand about it. His life ended after that Ebbets Field
game. From the age of seventeen nothing good ever happened to him.

BERNARD: He never trained himself for anything.

WILLY: But he did, he did. After high school he took so many correspondence courses.   295
Radio mechanics; television; God knows what, and never made the slightest mark.

BERNARD: (*taking off his glasses*) Willy, do you want to talk candidly?

WILLY: (*rising, faces Bernard*) I regard you as a very brilliant man, Bernard. I value
your advice.

BERNARD: Oh, the hell with the advice, Willy. I couldn't advise you. There's just
one thing I've always wanted to ask you. When he was supposed to graduate,
and the math teacher flunked him—

WILLY: Oh, that son-of-a-bitch ruined his life.

BERNARD: Yeah, but, Willy, all he had to do was go to summer school and make up   300
that subject.

WILLY: That's right, that's right.

BERNARD: Did you tell him not to go to summer school?

WILLY: Me? I begged him to go. I ordered him to go!

BERNARD: Then why wouldn't he go?

WILLY: Why? Why! Bernard, that question has been trailing me like a ghost for the   305
last fifteen years. He flunked the subject, and laid down and died like a hammer
hit him!

BERNARD: Take it easy, kid.

WILLY: Let me talk to you—I got nobody to talk to. Bernard, Bernard, was it my
fault? Y'see? It keeps going around in my mind, maybe I did something to him.
I got nothing to give him.

BERNARD: Don't take it so hard.

WILLY: Why did he lay down? What is the story there? You were his friend!

BERNARD: Willy, I remember, it was June, and our grades came out. And he'd   310
flunked math.

WILLY: That son-of-a-bitch!

BERNARD: No, it wasn't right then. Biff just got very angry, I remember, and he was
ready to enroll in summer school.

WILLY: (*surprised*) He was?

BERNARD: He wasn't beaten by it at all. But then, Willy, he disappeared from the block for almost a month. And I got the idea that he'd gone up to New England to see you. Did he have a talk with you then?

Willy stares in silence.

315 BERNARD: Willy?

WILLY: (*with a strong edge of resentment in his voice*) Yeah, he came to Boston. What about it?

BERNARD: Well, just that when he came back—I'll never forget this, it always mystifies me. Because I'd thought so well of Biff, even though he'd always taken advantage of me. I loved him, Willy, y'know? And he came back after that month and took his sneakers—remember those sneakers with "University of Virginia" printed on them? He was so proud of those, wore them every day. And he took them down in the cellar, and burned them up in the furnace. We had a fist fight. It lasted at least half an hour. Just the two of us, punching each other down the cellar, and crying right through it. I've often thought of how strange it was that I knew he'd given up his life. What happened in Boston, Willy?

Willy looks at him as at an intruder.

BERNARD: I just bring it up because you asked me.

WILLY: (*angrily*) Nothing. What do you mean, "What happened?" What's that got to do with anything?

320 BERNARD: Well, don't get sore.

WILLY: What are you trying to do, blame it on me? If a boy lays down is that my fault?

BERNARD: Now, Willy, don't get—

WILLY: Well, don't—don't talk to me that way! What does that mean, "What happened?"

Charley enters. He is in his vest, and he carries a bottle of bourbon.

CHARLEY: Hey, you're going to miss that train. (*He waves the bottle.*)

325 BERNARD: Yeah, I'm going. (*He takes the bottle.*) Thanks, Pop. (*He picks up his rackets and bag.*) Good-by, Willy, and don't worry about it. You know, "If at first you don't succeed . . ."

WILLY: Yes, I believe in that.

BERNARD: But sometimes, Willy, it's better for a man just to walk away.

WILLY: Walk away?

BERNARD: That's right.

330 WILLY: But if you can't walk away?

BERNARD: (*after a slight pause*) I guess that's when it's tough. (*Extending his hand.*) Good-by, Willy.

WILLY: (*shaking Bernard's hand*) Good-by, boy.

CHARLEY: (*an arm on Bernard's shoulder*) How do you like this kid? Gonna argue a case in front of the Supreme Court.

BERNARD: (*protesting*) Pop!

335 WILLY: (*genuinely shocked, pained, and happy*) No! The Supreme Court!

BERNARD: I gotta run, 'By, Dad!

CHARLEY: Knock 'em dead, Bernard!

Bernard goes off.

WILLY: (*as Charley takes out his wallet*) The Supreme Court! And he didn't even
  mention it!

CHARLEY: (*counting out money on the desk*) He don't have to—he's gonna do it.

WILLY: And you never told him what to do, did you? You never took any interest   340
  in him.

CHARLEY: My salvation is that I never took any interest in anything. There's some
  money—fifty dollars. I got an accountant inside.

WILLY: Charley, look . . . (*With difficulty.*) I got my insurance to pay. If you can
  manage it—I need a hundred and ten dollars.

Charley doesn't reply for a moment; merely stops moving.

WILLY: I'd draw it from my bank but Linda would know, and I . . .

CHARLEY: Sit down, Willy.

WILLY: (*moving toward the chair*) I'm keeping an account of everything, remember.   345
  I'll pay every penny back. (*He sits.*)

CHARLEY: Now listen to me, Willy.

WILLY: I want you to know I appreciate . . .

CHARLEY: (*sitting down on the table*) Willy, what're you doin'? What the hell is goin'
  on in your head?

WILLY: Why? I'm simply . . .

CHARLEY: I offered you a job. You can make fifty dollars a week. And I won't send   350
  you on the road.

WILLY: I've got a job.

CHARLEY: Without pay? What kind of a job is a job without pay? (*He rises.*) Now,
  look, kid, enough is enough. I'm no genius but I know when I'm being insulted.

WILLY: Insulted!

CHARLEY: Why don't you want to work for me?

WILLY: What's the matter with you? I've got a job.   355

CHARLEY: Then what're you walkin' in here every week for?

WILLY: (*getting up*) Well, if you don't want me to walk in here—

CHARLEY: I am offering you a job.

WILLY: I don't want your goddam job!

CHARLEY: When the hell are you going to grow up?   360

WILLY: (*furiously*) You big ignoramus, if you say that to me again I'll rap you one!
  I don't care how big you are! (*He's ready to fight.*)

Pause.

CHARLEY: (*kindly, going to him*) How much do you need, Willy?

WILLY: Charley, I'm strapped. I'm strapped. I don't know what to do. I was
  just fired.

CHARLEY: Howard fired you?

WILLY: That snotnose. Imagine that? I named him. I named him Howard.   365

CHARLEY: Willy, when're you gonna realize that them things don't mean anything? You named him Howard, but you can't sell that. The only thing you got in this world is what you can sell. And the funny thing is that you're a salesman, and you don't know that.

WILLY: I've always tried to think otherwise, I guess. I always felt that if a man was impressive, and well liked, that nothing—

CHARLEY: Why must everybody like you? Who liked J. P. Morgan?[3] Was he impressive? In a Turkish bath he'd look like a butcher. But with his pockets on he was very well liked. Now listen, Willy, I know you don't like me, and nobody can say I'm in love with you, but I'll give you a job because—just for the hell of it, put it that way. Now what do you say?

WILLY: I—I just can't work for you, Charley.

370   CHARLEY: What're you, jealous of me?

WILLY: I can't work for you, that's all, don't ask me why.

CHARLEY: (angered, takes out more bills) You been jealous of me all your life, you damned fool! Here, pay your insurance. (He puts the money in Willy's hand.)

WILLY: I'm keeping strict accounts.

CHARLEY: I've got some work to do. Take care of yourself. And pay your insurance.

375   WILLY: (moving to the right) Funny, y'know? After all the highways, and the trains, and the appointments, and the years, you end up worth more dead than alive.

CHARLEY: Willy, nobody's worth nothin' dead. (After a slight pause.) Did you hear what I said?

Willy stands still, dreaming.

CHARLEY: Willy!

WILLY: Apologize to Bernard for me when you see him. I didn't mean to argue with him. He's a fine boy. They're all fine boys, and they'll end up big—all of them. Someday they'll all play tennis together. Wish me luck, Charley. He saw Bill Oliver today.

CHARLEY: Good luck.

380   WILLY: (on the verge of tears) Charley, you're the only friend I got. Isn't that a remarkable thing? (He goes out.)

CHARLEY: Jesus!

Charley stares after him a moment and follows. All light blacks out. Suddenly raucous music is heard, and a red glow rises behind the screen at right. Stanley, a young waiter, appears, carrying a table, followed by Happy, who is carrying two chairs.

STANLEY: (putting the table down) That's all right, Mr. Loman, I can handle it myself. (He turns and takes the chairs from Happy and places them at the table.)

HAPPY: (glancing around) Oh, this is better.

STANLEY: Sure, in the front there you're in the middle of all kinds a noise. Whenever you got a party, Mr. Loman, you just tell me and I'll put you back here. Y'know, there's a lotta people they don't like it private, because when they go

---

[3] *J. P. Morgan:* John Pierpont Morgan (1837–1913)—American financier.

out they like to see a lotta action around them because they're sick and tired to stay in the house by theirself. But I know you, you ain't from Hackensack. You know what I mean?

HAPPY: (*sitting down*) So, how's it coming, Stanley?   385

STANLEY: Ah, it's a dog's life. I only wish during the war they'd a took me in the Army. I coulda been dead by now.

HAPPY: My brother's back, Stanley.

STANLEY: Oh, he come back, heh? From the Far West.

HAPPY: Yeah, big cattle man, my brother, so treat him right. And my father's coming too.

STANLEY: Oh, your father too!   390

HAPPY: You got a couple of nice lobsters?

STANLEY: Hundred per cent, big.

HAPPY: I want them with the claws.

STANLEY: Don't worry, I don't give you no mice. (*Happy laughs.*) How about some wine? It'll put a head on the meal.

HAPPY: No. You remember, Stanley, that recipe I brought you from overseas? With   395
the champagne in it?

STANLEY: Oh, yeah, sure. I still got it tacked up yet in the kitchen. But that'll have to cost a buck apiece anyways.

HAPPY: That's all right.

STANLEY: What'd you, hit a number or somethin'?

HAPPY: No, it's a little celebration. My brother is—I think he pulled off a big deal today. I think we're going into business together.

STANLEY: Great! That's the best for you. Because a family business, you know what   400
I mean?—that's the best.

HAPPY: That's what I think.

STANLEY: 'Cause what's the difference? Somebody steals? It's in the family. Know what I mean? (*Sotto voce.*) Like this bartender here. The boss is goin' crazy what kinda leak he's got in the cash register. You put it in but it don't come out.

HAPPY: (*raising his head*) Sh!

STANLEY: What?

HAPPY: You notice I wasn't lookin' right or left, was I?   405

STANLEY: No.

HAPPY: And my eyes are closed.

STANLEY: So what's the—

HAPPY: Strudel's comin'.

STANLEY: (*catching on, looks around*) Ah, no, there's no—   410

He breaks off as a furred, lavishly dressed Girl enters and sits at the next table. Both follow her with their eyes.

STANLEY: Geez, how'd ya know?

HAPPY: I got radar or something. (*Staring directly at her profile.*) Oooooooo . . . Stanley.

STANLEY: I think that's for you, Mr. Loman.

HAPPY: Look at that mouth. Oh, God. And the binoculars.

STANLEY: Geez, you got a life, Mr. Loman.   415

HAPPY: Wait on her.

STANLEY: *(going to The Girl's table)* Would you like a menu, ma'am?

GIRL: I'm expecting someone, but I'd like a—

HAPPY: Why don't you bring her—excuse me, miss, do you mind? I sell champagne, and I'd like you to try my brand. Bring her a champagne, Stanley.

420　GIRL: That's awfully nice of you.

HAPPY: Don't mention it. It's all company money. *(He laughs.)*

GIRL: That's a charming product to be selling, isn't it?

HAPPY: Oh, gets to be like everything else. Selling is selling, y'know.

GIRL: I suppose.

425　HAPPY: You don't happen to sell, do you?

GIRL: No, I don't sell.

HAPPY: Would you object to a compliment from a stranger? You ought to be on a magazine cover.

GIRL: *(looking at him a little archly)* I have been.

Stanley comes in with a glass of champagne.

HAPPY: What'd I say before, Stanley? You see? She's a cover girl.

430　STANLEY: Oh, I could see, I could see.

HAPPY: *(to The Girl)* What magazine?

GIRL: Oh, a lot of them. *(She takes the drink.)* Thank you.

HAPPY: You know what they say in France, don't you? "Champagne is the drink of the complexion"—Hya, Biff!

Biff has entered and sits with Happy.

BIFF: Hello, kid. Sorry I'm late.

435　HAPPY: I just got here. Uh, Miss—?

GIRL: Forsythe.

HAPPY: Miss Forsythe, this is my brother.

BIFF: Is Dad here?

HAPPY: His name is Biff. You might've heard of him. Great football player.

440　GIRL: Really? What team?

HAPPY: Are you familiar with football?

GIRL: No, I'm afraid I'm not.

HAPPY: Biff is quarterback with the New York Giants.

GIRL: Well, that is nice, isn't it? *(She drinks.)*

445　HAPPY: Good health.

GIRL: I'm happy to meet you.

HAPPY: That's my name. Hap. It's really Harold, but at West Point they called me Happy.

GIRL: *(now really impressed)* Oh, I see. How do you do? *(She turns her profile.)*

BIFF: Isn't Dad coming?

450　HAPPY: You want her?

BIFF: Oh, I could never make that.

HAPPY: I remember the time that idea would never come into your head. Where's the old confidence, Biff?

BIFF: I just saw Oliver—

HAPPY: Wait a minute. I've got to see that old confidence again. Do you want her? She's on call.

BIFF: Oh, no. (*He turns to look at The Girl.*)

HAPPY: I'm telling you. Watch this. (*Turning to The Girl.*) Honey? (*She turns to him.*) Are you busy?

GIRL: Well, I am . . . but I could make a phone call.

HAPPY: Do that, will you, honey? And see if you can get a friend. We'll be here for a while. Biff is one of the greatest football players in the country.

GIRL: (*standing up*) Well, I'm certainly happy to meet you.

HAPPY: Come back soon.

GIRL: I'll try.

HAPPY: Don't try, honey, try hard.

The Girl exits. Stanley follows, shaking his head in bewildered admiration.

HAPPY: Isn't that a shame now? A beautiful girl like that? That's why I can't get married. There's not a good woman in a thousand. New York is loaded with them, kid!

BIFF: Hap, look—

HAPPY: I told you she was on call!

BIFF: (*strangely unnerved*) Cut it out, will ya? I want to say something to you.

HAPPY: Did you see Oliver?

BIFF: I saw him all right. Now look, I want to tell Dad a couple of things and I want you to help me.

HAPPY: What? Is he going to back you?

BIFF: Are you crazy? You're out of your goddam head, you know that?

HAPPY: Why? What happened?

BIFF: (*breathlessly*) I did a terrible thing today, Hap. It's been the strangest day I ever went through. I'm all numb, I swear.

HAPPY: You mean he wouldn't see you?

BIFF: Well, I waited six hours for him, see? All day. Kept sending my name in. Even tried to date his secretary so she'd get me to him, but no soap.

HAPPY: Because you're not showin' the old confidence, Biff. He remembered you, didn't he?

BIFF: (*stopping Happy with a gesture*) Finally, about five o'clock, he comes out. Didn't remember who I was or anything. I felt like such an idiot, Hap.

HAPPY: Did you tell him my Florida idea?

BIFF: He walked away. I saw him for one minute. I got so mad I could've torn the walls down! How the hell did I ever get the idea I was a salesman there? I even believed myself that I'd been a salesman for him! And then he gave me one look and—I realized what a ridiculous lie my whole life has been! We've been talking in a dream for fifteen years. I was a shipping clerk.

HAPPY: What'd you do?

BIFF: (*with great tension and wonder*) Well, he left, see. And the secretary went out. I was all alone in the waiting-room. I don't know what came over me, Hap. The next thing I know I'm in his office—paneled walls, everything. I can't explain it. I—Hap, I took his fountain pen.

Happy: Geez, did he catch you?

Biff: I ran out. I ran down all eleven flights. I ran and ran and ran.

Happy: That was an awful dumb—what'd you do that for?

Biff: (*agonized*) I don't know, I just—wanted to take something, I don't know. You gotta help me, Hap. I'm gonna tell Pop.

485   Happy: You crazy? What for?

Biff: Hap, he's got to understand that I'm not the man somebody lends that kind of money to. He thinks I've been spiting him all these years and it's eating him up.

Happy: That's just it. You tell him something nice.

Biff: I can't.

Happy: Say you got a lunch date with Oliver tomorrow.

490   Biff: So what do I do tomorrow?

Happy: You leave the house tomorrow and come back at night and say Oliver is thinking it over. And he thinks it over for a couple of weeks, and gradually it fades away and nobody's the worse.

Biff: But it'll go on forever!

Happy: Dad is never so happy as when he's looking forward to something!

Willy enters.

Happy: Hello, scout!

495   Willy: Gee, I haven't been here in years!

Stanley has followed Willy in and sets a chair for him. Stanley starts off but Happy stops him.

Happy: Stanley!

Stanley stands by, waiting for an order.

Biff: (*going to Willy with guilt, as to an invalid*) Sit down, Pop. You want a drink?

Willy: Sure, I don't mind.

Biff: Let's get a load on.

500   Willy: You look worried.

Biff: N-no. (*To Stanley.*) Scotch all around. Make it doubles.

Stanley: Doubles, right. (*He goes.*)

Willy: You had a couple already, didn't you?

Biff: Just a couple, yeah.

505   Willy: Well, what happened, boy? (*Nodding affirmatively, with a smile.*) Everything go all right?

Biff: (*takes a breath, then reaches out and grasps Willy's hand*) Pal . . . (*He is smiling bravely, and Willy is smiling too.*) I had an experience today.

Happy: Terrific, Pop.

Willy: That so? What happened?

Biff: (*high, slightly alcoholic, above the earth*) I'm going to tell you everything from first to last. It's been a strange day. (*Silence. He looks around, composes himself as best he can, but his breath keeps breaking the rhythm of his voice.*) I had to wait quite a while for him, and—

510   Willy: Oliver?

BIFF: Yeah, Oliver. All day, as a matter of cold fact. And a lot of—instances—facts, Pop, facts about my life came back to me. Who was it, Pop? Who ever said I was a salesman with Oliver?

WILLY: Well, you were.

BIFF: No, Dad, I was a shipping clerk.

WILLY: But you were practically—

BIFF: (*with determination*) Dad, I don't know who said it first, but I was never a salesman for Bill Oliver.

WILLY: What're you talking about?

BIFF: Let's hold on to the facts tonight, Pop. We're not going to get anywhere bullin' around. I was a shipping clerk.

WILLY: (*angrily*) All right, now listen to me—

BIFF: Why don't you let me finish?

WILLY: I'm not interested in stories about the past or any crap of that kind because the woods are burning, boys, you understand? There's a big blaze going on all around. I was fired today.

BIFF: (*shocked*) How could you be?

WILLY: I was fired, and I'm looking for a little good news to tell your mother, because the woman has waited and the woman has suffered. The gist of it is that I haven't got a story left in my head, Biff. So don't give me a lecture about facts and aspects. I am not interested. Now what've you got to say to me?

Stanley enters with three drinks. They wait until he leaves.

WILLY: Did you see Oliver?

BIFF: Jesus, Dad!

WILLY: You mean you didn't go up there?

HAPPY: Sure he went up there.

BIFF: I did. I—saw him. How could they fire you?

WILLY: (*on the edge of his chair*) What kind of a welcome did he give you?

BIFF: He won't even let you work on commission?

WILLY: I'm out! (*Driving.*) So tell me, he gave you a warm welcome?

HAPPY: Sure, Pop, sure!

BIFF: (*driven*) Well, it was kind of—

WILLY: I was wondering if he'd remember you. (*To Happy.*) Imagine, man doesn't see him for ten, twelve years and gives him that kind of a welcome!

HAPPY: Damn right!

BIFF: (*trying to return to the offensive*) Pop, look—

WILLY: You know why he remembered you, don't you? Because you impressed him in those days.

BIFF: Let's talk quietly and get this down to the facts, huh?

WILLY: (*as though Biff had been interrupting*) Well, what happened? It's great news, Biff. Did he take you into his office or'd you talk in the waiting-room?

BIFF: Well, he came in, see, and—

WILLY: (*with a big smile*) What'd he say? Betcha he threw his arm around you.

BIFF: Well, he kinda—

WILLY: He's a fine man. (*To Happy.*) Very hard man to see, y'know.

HAPPY: *(agreeing)* Oh, I know.

WILLY: *(to Biff)* Is that where you had the drinks?

545 **BIFF:** Yeah, he gave me a couple of—no, no!

HAPPY: *(cutting in)* He told him my Florida idea.

WILLY: Don't interrupt. *(To Biff.)* How'd he react to the Florida idea?

BIFF: Dad, will you give me a minute to explain?

WILLY: I've been waiting for you to explain since I sat down here! What happened? He took you into his office and what?

550 **BIFF:** Well—I talked. And—and he listened, see.

WILLY: Famous for the way he listens, y'know. What was his answer?

BIFF: His answer was—*(He breaks off, suddenly angry.)* Dad, you're not letting me tell you what I want to tell you!

WILLY: *(accusing, angered)* You didn't see him, did you?

BIFF: I did see him!

555 **WILLY:** What'd you insult him or something? You insulted him, didn't you?

BIFF: Listen, will you let me out of it, will you just let me out of it!

HAPPY: What the hell!

WILLY: Tell me what happened!

BIFF: *(to Happy)* I can't talk to him!

A single trumpet note jars the ear. The light of green leaves stains the house, which holds the air of night and a dream. Young Bernard enters and knocks on the door of the house.

560 **YOUNG BERNARD:** *(frantically)* Mrs. Loman, Mrs. Loman!

HAPPY: Tell him what happened!

BIFF: *(to Happy)* Shut up and leave me alone!

WILLY: No, no! You had to go and flunk math!

BIFF: What math? What're you talking about?

565 **YOUNG BERNARD:** Mrs. Loman, Mrs. Loman!

Linda appears in the house, as of old.

WILLY: *(wildly)* Math, math, math!

BIFF: Take it easy, Pop!

YOUNG BERNARD: Mrs. Loman!

WILLY: *(furiously)* If you hadn't flunked you'd've been set by now!

570 **BIFF:** Now, look, I'm gonna tell you what happened, and you're going to listen to me.

YOUNG BERNARD: Mrs. Loman!

BIFF: I waited six hours—

HAPPY: What the hell are you saying?

BIFF: I kept sending in my name but he wouldn't see me. So finally he . . . *(He continues unheard as light fades low on the restaurant.)*

575 **YOUNG BERNARD:** Biff flunked math!

LINDA: No!

YOUNG BERNARD: Birnbaum flunked him! They won't graduate him!

LINDA: But they have to. He's gotta go to the university. Where is he? Biff! Biff!

YOUNG BERNARD: No, he left. He went to Grand Central.

LINDA: Grand—You mean he went to Boston!   580
YOUNG BERNARD: Is Uncle Willy in Boston?
LINDA: Oh, maybe Willy can talk to the teacher. Oh, the poor, poor boy!

Light on house area snaps out.

BIFF: (*at the table, now audible, holding up a gold fountain pen*) . . . so I'm washed up
    with Oliver, you understand? Are you listening to me?
WILLY: (*at a loss*) Yeah, sure. If you hadn't flunked—
BIFF: Flunked what? What're you talking about?   585
WILLY: Don't blame everything on me! I didn't flunk math—you did! What pen?
HAPPY: That was awful dumb, Biff, a pen like that is worth—
WILLY: (*seeing the pen for the first time*) You took Oliver's pen?
BIFF: (*weakening*) Dad, I just explained it to you.
WILLY: You stole Bill Oliver's fountain pen!   590
BIFF: I didn't exactly steal it! That's just what I've been explaining to you!
HAPPY: He had it in his hand and just then Oliver walked in, so he got nervous and
    stuck it in his pocket!
WILLY: My God, Biff!
BIFF: I never intended to do it, Dad!
OPERATOR'S VOICE: Standish Arms, good evening!   595
WILLY: (*shouting*) I'm not in my room!
BIFF: (*frightened*) Dad, what's the matter? (*He and Happy stand up.*)
OPERATOR: Ringing Mr. Loman for you!
WILLY: I'm not there, stop it!
BIFF: (*horrified, gets down on one knee before Willy*) Dad, I'll make good, I'll make   600
    good. (*Willy tries to get to his feet. Biff holds him down.*) Sit down now.
WILLY: No, you're no good, you're no good for anything.
BIFF: I am, Dad, I'll find something else, you understand? Now don't worry about
    anything. (*He holds up Willy's face.*) Talk to me, Dad.
OPERATOR: Mr. Loman does not answer. Shall I page him?
WILLY: (*attempting to stand, as though to rush and silence the Operator*) No, no, no!
HAPPY: He'll strike something, Pop.   605
WILLY: No, no . . .
BIFF: (*desperately, standing over Willy*) Pop, listen! Listen to me! I'm telling you
    something good. Oliver talked to his partner about the Florida idea. You listen-
    ing? He—he talked to his partner, and he came to me . . . I'm going to be all
    right, you hear? Dad, listen to me, he said it was just a question of the amount!
WILLY: Then you . . . got it?
HAPPY: He's gonna be terrific, Pop!
WILLY: (*trying to stand*) Then you got it, haven't you? You got it! You got it!   610
BIFF: (*agonized, holds Willy down*) No, no. Look, Pop. I'm supposed to have lunch
    with them tomorrow. I'm just telling you this so you'll know that I can still
    make an impression, Pop. And I'll make good somewhere, but I can't go
    tomorrow, see?
WILLY: Why not? You simply—
BIFF: But the pen, Pop!

WILLY: You give it to him and tell him it was an oversight!

615   HAPPY: Sure, have lunch tomorrow!

BIFF: I can't say that—

WILLY: You were doing a crossword puzzle and accidentally used his pen!

BIFF: Listen, kid, I took those balls years ago, now I walk in with his fountain pen? That clinches it, don't you see? I can't face him like that! I'll try elsewhere.

PAGE'S VOICE: Paging Mr. Loman!

620   WILLY: Don't you want to be anything?

BIFF: Pop, how can I go back?

WILLY: You don't want to be anything, is that what's behind it?

BIFF: (now angry at Willy for not crediting his sympathy) Don't take it that way! You think it was easy walking into that office after what I'd done to him? A team of horses couldn't have dragged me back to Bill Oliver!

WILLY: Then why'd you go?

625   BIFF: Why did I go? Why did I go? Look at you! Look at what's become of you!

Off left, The Woman laughs.

WILLY: Biff, you're going to go to that lunch tomorrow, or—

BIFF: I can't go. I've got no appointment!

HAPPY: Biff, for . . .!

WILLY: Are you spiting me?

630   BIFF: Don't take it that way! Goddammit!

WILLY: (strikes Biff and falters away from the table) You rotten little louse! Are you spiting me?

THE WOMAN: Someone's at the door, Willy!

BIFF: I'm no good, can't you see what I am?

HAPPY: (separating them) Hey, you're in a restaurant! Now cut it out, both of you! (The Girls enter.) Hello, girls, sit down.

The Woman laughs, off left.

635   MISS FORSYTHE: I guess we might as well. This is Letta.

THE WOMAN: Willy, are you going to wake up?

BIFF: (ignoring Willy) How're ya, miss, sit down. What do you drink?

MISS FORSYTHE: Letta might not be able to stay long.

LETTA: I gotta get up very early tomorrow. I got jury duty. I'm so excited! Were you fellows ever on a jury?

640   BIFF: No, but I been in front of them! (The Girls laugh.) This is my father.

LETTA: Isn't he cute? Sit down with us, Pop.

HAPPY: Sit him down, Biff!

BIFF: (going to him) Come on, slugger, drink us under the table. To hell with it! Come on, sit down, pal.

On Biff's last insistence, Willy is about to sit.

THE WOMAN: (now urgently) Willy, are you going to answer the door!

The Woman's call pulls Willy back. He starts right, befuddled.

BIFF: Hey, where are you going?   645
WILLY: Open the door.
BIFF: The door?
WILLY: The washroom . . . the door . . . where's the door?
BIFF: (*leading Willy to the left*) Just go straight down.

Willy moves left.

THE WOMAN: Willy, Willy, are you going to get up, get up, get up, get up?   650

Willy exits left.

LETTA: I think it's sweet you bring your daddy along.
MISS FORSYTHE: Oh, he isn't really your father!
BIFF: (*at left, turning to her resentfully*) Miss Forsythe, you've just seen a prince walk
   by. A fine, troubled prince. A hard-working, unappreciated prince. A pal, you
   understand? A good companion. Always for his boys.
LETTA: That's so sweet.
HAPPY: Well, girls, what's the program? We're wasting time. Come on, Biff. Gather   655
   round. Where would you like to go?
BIFF: Why don't you do something for him?
HAPPY: Me!
BIFF: Don't you give a damn for him, Hap?
HAPPY: What're you talking about? I'm the one who—
BIFF: I sense it, you don't give a good goddam about him. (*He takes the rolled-up hose*   660
   from his pocket and puts it on the table in front of Happy.) Look what I found in the
   cellar, for Christ's sake. How can you bear to let it go on?
HAPPY: Me? Who goes away? Who runs off and—
BIFF: Yeah, but he doesn't mean anything to you. You could help him—I can't!
   Don't you understand what I'm talking about? He's going to kill himself, don't
   you know that?
HAPPY: Don't I know it! Me!
BIFF: Hap, help him! Jesus . . . help him . . . Help me, help me, I can't bear to look
   at his face. (*Ready to weep, he hurries out, up right.*)
HAPPY: (*starting after him*) Where are you going?   665
MISS FORSYTHE: What's he so mad about?
HAPPY: Come on, girls, we'll catch up with him.
MISS FORSYTHE: (*as Happy pushes her out*) Say, I don't like that temper of his!
HAPPY: He's just a little overstrung, he'll be all right!
WILLY: (*off left, as The Woman laughs*) Don't answer! Don't answer!   670
LETTA: Don't you want to tell your father—
HAPPY: No, that's not my father. He's just a guy. Come on, we'll catch Biff,
   and, honey, we're going to paint this town! Stanley, where's the check!
   Hey, Stanley!

They exit. Stanley looks toward left.

STANLEY: (*calling to Happy indignantly*) Mr. Loman! Mr. Loman!

Stanley picks up a chair and follows them off. Knocking is heard off left. The Woman enters, laughing. Willy follows her. She is in a black slip; he is buttoning his shirt. Raw, sensuous music accompanies their speech.

WILLY: Will you stop laughing? Will you stop?

675 **THE WOMAN:** Aren't you going to answer the door? He'll wake the whole hotel.

WILLY: I'm not expecting anybody.

THE WOMAN: Whyn't you have another drink, honey, and stop being so damn self-centered?

WILLY: I'm so lonely.

THE WOMAN: You know you ruined me, Willy? From now on, whenever you come to the office, I'll see that you go right through to the buyers. No waiting at my desk any more, Willy. You ruined me.

680 **WILLY:** That's nice of you to say that.

THE WOMAN: Gee, you are self-centered! Why so sad? You are the saddest self-centeredest soul I ever did see-saw. (*She laughs. He kisses her.*) Come on inside, drummer boy. It's silly to be dressing in the middle of the night. (*As knocking is heard.*) Aren't you going to answer the door?

WILLY: They're knocking on the wrong door.

THE WOMAN: But I felt the knocking. And he heard us talking in here. Maybe the hotel's on fire!

WILLY: (*his terror rising*) It's a mistake.

685 **THE WOMAN:** Then tell him to go away!

WILLY: There's nobody there.

THE WOMAN: It's getting on my nerves, Willy. There's somebody standing out there and it's getting on my nerves!

WILLY: (*pushing her away from him*) All right, stay in the bathroom here, and don't come out. I think there's a law in Massachusetts about it, so don't come out. It may be that new room clerk. He looked very mean. So don't come out. It's a mistake, there's no fire.

The knocking is heard again. He takes a few steps away from her, and she vanishes into the wing. The light follows him, and now he is facing Young Biff, who carries a suitcase. Biff steps toward him. The music is gone.

BIFF: Why didn't you answer?

690 **WILLY:** Biff! What are you doing in Boston?

BIFF: Why didn't you answer? I've been knocking for five minutes, I called you on the phone—

WILLY: I just heard you. I was in the bathroom and had the door shut. Did anything happen home?

BIFF: Dad—I let you down.

WILLY: What do you mean?

695 **BIFF:** Dad . . .

WILLY: Biffo, what's this about? (*Putting his arm around Biff.*) Come on, let's go downstairs and get you a malted.

BIFF: Dad, I flunked math.

WILLY: Not for the term?

BIFF: The term. I haven't got enough credits to graduate.

WILLY: You mean to say Bernard wouldn't give you the answers?   700

BIFF: He did, he tried, but I only got a sixty-one.

WILLY: And they wouldn't give you four points?

BIFF: Birnbaum refused absolutely. I begged him, Pop, but he won't give me those points. You gotta talk to him before they close the school. Because if he saw the kind of man you are, and you just talked to him in your way, I'm sure he'd come through for me. The class came right before practice, see, and I didn't go enough. Would you talk to him? He'd like you, Pop. You know the way you could talk.

WILLY: You're on. We'll drive right back.

BIFF: Oh, Dad, good work! I'm sure he'll change it for you!   705

WILLY: Go downstairs and tell the clerk I'm checkin' out. Go right down.

BIFF: Yes, Sir! See, the reason he hates me, Pop—one day he was late for class so I got up at the blackboard and imitated him. I crossed my eyes and talked with a lithp.

WILLY: (*laughing*) You did? The kids like it?

BIFF: They nearly died laughing!

WILLY: Yeah? What'd you do?   710

BIFF: The thquare root of thixthy twee is . . . (*Willy bursts out laughing; Biff joins him.*) And in the middle of it he walked in!

Willy laughs and The Woman joins in offstage.

WILLY: (*without hesitating*) Hurry downstairs and—

BIFF: Somebody in there?

WILLY: No, that was next door.

The Woman laughs offstage.

BIFF: Somebody got in your bathroom!   715

WILLY: No, it's the next room, there's a party—

THE WOMAN: (*enters, laughing. She lisps this*) Can I come in? There's something in the bathtub, Willy, and it's moving!

Willy looks at Biff, who is staring open-mouthed and horrified at The Woman.

WILLY: Ah—you better go back to your room. They must be finished painting by now. They're painting her room so I let her take a shower here. Go back, go back . . . (*He pushes her.*)

THE WOMAN: (*resisting*) But I've got to get dressed, Willy, I can't—

WILLY: Get out of here! Go back, go back . . . (*Suddenly striving for the ordinary.*)   720
This is Miss Francis, Biff, she's a buyer. They're painting her room. Go back, Miss Francis, go back . . .

THE WOMAN: But my clothes, I can't go out naked in the hall!

WILLY: (*pushing her offstage*) Get outa here! Go back, go back!

Biff slowly sits down on his suitcase as the argument continues offstage.

THE WOMAN: Where's my stockings? You promised me stockings, Willy!

WILLY: I have no stockings here!

725 THE WOMAN: You had two boxes of size nine sheers for me, and I want them!

WILLY: Here, for God's sake, will you get outa here!

THE WOMAN: *(enters holding a box of stockings)* I just hope there's nobody in the hall. That's all I hope. *(To Biff.)* Are you football or baseball?

BIFF: Football.

THE WOMAN: *(angry, humiliated)* That's me too. G'night. *(She snatches her clothes from Willy, and walks out.)*

730 WILLY: *(after a pause)* Well, better get going. I want to get to the school first thing in the morning. Get my suits out of the closet. I'll get my valise. *(Biff doesn't move.)* What's the matter? *(Biff remains motionless, tears falling.)* She's a buyer. Buys for J. H. Simmons. She lives down the hall—they're painting. You don't imagine—*(He breaks off. After a pause.)* Now listen, pal, she's just a buyer. She sees merchandise in her room and they have to keep it looking just so . . . *(Pause. Assuming command.)* All right, get my suits. *(Biff doesn't move.)* Now stop crying and do as I say. I gave you an order. Biff, I gave you an order! Is that what you do when I give you an order? How dare you cry! *(Putting his arm around Biff.)* Now look, Biff, when you grow up you'll understand about these things. You mustn't—you mustn't overemphasize a thing like this. I'll see Birnbaum first thing in the morning.

BIFF: Never mind.

WILLY: *(getting down beside Biff)* Never mind! He's going to give you those points. I'll see to it.

BIFF: He wouldn't listen to you.

WILLY: He certainly will listen to me. You need those points for the U. of Virginia.

735 BIFF: I'm not going there.

WILLY: Heh? If I can't get him to change that mark you'll make it up in summer school. You've got all summer to—

BIFF: *(his weeping breaking from him)* Dad . . .

WILLY: *(infected by it)* Oh, my boy . . .

BIFF: Dad . . .

740 WILLY: She's nothing to me, Biff. I was lonely, I was terribly lonely.

BIFF: You—you gave her Mama's stockings! *(His tears break through and he rises to go.)*

WILLY: *(grabbing for Biff)* I gave you an order!

BIFF: Don't touch me, you—liar!

WILLY: Apologize for that!

745 BIFF: You fake! You phony little fake! You fake! *(Overcome, he turns quickly and weeping fully goes out with his suitcase. Willy is left on the floor on his knees.)*

WILLY: I gave you an order! Biff, come back here or I'll beat you! Come back here! I'll whip you!

Stanley comes quickly in from the right and stands in front of Willy.

WILLY: *(shouts at Stanley)* I gave you an order . . .

STANLEY: Hey, let's pick it up, pick it up, Mr. Loman. *(He helps Willy to his feet.)* Your boys left with the chippies. They said they'll see you home.

A second waiter watches some distance away.

WILLY: But we were supposed to have dinner together.

Music is heard, Willy's theme.

STANLEY: Can you make it?   750

WILLY: I'll—sure, I can make it. (*Suddenly concerned about his clothes.*) Do I—I look
all right?

STANLEY: Sure, you look all right. (*He flicks a speck off Willy's lapel.*)

WILLY: Here—here's a dollar.

STANLEY: Oh, your son paid me. It's all right.

WILLY: (*putting it in Stanley's hand*) No, take it. You're a good boy.   755

STANLEY: Oh, no, you don't have to . . .

WILLY: Here—here's some more, I don't need it any more. (*After a slight pause.*)
Tell me—is there a seed store in the neighborhood?

STANLEY: Seeds? You mean like to plant?

As Willy turns, Stanley slips the money back into his jacket pocket.

WILLY: Yes. Carrots, peas . . .

STANLEY: Well, there's hardware stores on Sixth Avenue, but it may be too late now.   760

WILLY: (*anxiously*) Oh, I'd better hurry. I've got to get some seeds. (*He starts off to
the right.*) I've got to get some seeds, right away. Nothing's planted. I don't have
a thing in the ground.

*Willy hurries out as the light goes down. Stanley moves over to the right after him, watches
him off. The other waiter has been staring at Willy.*

STANLEY: (*to the waiter*) Well, whatta you looking at?

*The waiter picks up the chairs and moves off right. Stanley takes the table and follows him.
The light fades on this area. There is a long pause, the sound of the flute coming over. The
light gradually rises on the kitchen, which is empty. Happy appears at the door of the house,
followed by Biff. Happy is carrying a large bunch of long-stemmed roses. He enters the kitchen,
looks around for Linda. Not seeing her, he turns to Biff, who is just outside the house door,
and makes a gesture with his hands, indicating "Not here, I guess." He looks into the living
room and freezes. Inside, Linda, unseen, is seated, Willy's coat on her lap. She rises
ominously and quietly and moves toward Happy, who backs up into the kitchen, afraid.*

HAPPY: Hey, what're you doing up? (*Linda says nothing but moves toward him impla-
cably.*) Where's Pop? (*He keeps backing to the right, and now Linda is in full view in
the doorway to the living room.*) Is he sleeping?

LINDA: Where were you?

HAPPY: (*trying to laugh it off*) We met two girls, Mom, very fine types. Here, we   765
brought you some flowers. (*Offering them to her.*) Put them in your room, Ma.

*She knocks them to the floor at Biff's feet. He has now come inside and closed the door behind
him. She stares at Biff, silent.*

HAPPY: Now what'd you do that for? Mom, I want you to have some flowers—

LINDA: (*cutting Happy off, violently to Biff*) Don't you care whether he lives or dies?

HAPPY: (*going to the stairs*) Come upstairs, Biff.

BIFF: *(with a flare of disgust, to Happy)* Go away from me! *(To Linda.)* What do you
    mean, lives or dies? Nobody's dying around here, pal.

770   LINDA: Get out of my sight! Get out of here!

BIFF: I wanna see the boss.

LINDA: You're not going near him!

BIFF: Where is he? *(He moves into the living room and Linda follows.)*

LINDA: *(shouting after Biff)* You invite him for dinner. He looks forward to it all
    day—*(Biff appears in his parents' bedroom, looks around, and exits)*—and then you
    desert him there. There's no stranger you'd do that to!

775   HAPPY: Why? He had a swell time with us. Listen, when I—*(Linda comes back into
    the kitchen)*—desert him I hope I don't outlive the day!

LINDA: Get out of here!

HAPPY: Now look, Mom . . .

LINDA: Did you have to go to women tonight? You and your lousy rotten whores!

Biff re-enters the kitchen.

HAPPY: Mom, all we did was follow Biff around trying to cheer him up! *(To Biff.)*
    Boy, what a night you gave me!

780   LINDA: Get out of here, both of you, and don't come back! I don't want you tor-
    menting him any more. Go on now, get your things together! *(To Biff.)* You
    can sleep in his apartment. *(She starts to pick up the flowers and stops herself.)* Pick
    up this stuff, I'm not your maid any more. Pick it up, you bum, you!

*Happy turns his back to her in refusal. Biff slowly moves over and gets down on his knees,
picking up the flowers.*

LINDA: You're a pair of animals! Not one, not another living soul would have had
    the cruelty to walk out on that man in a restaurant!

BIFF: *(not looking at her)* Is that what he said?

LINDA: He didn't have to say anything. He was so humiliated he nearly limped
    when he came in.

HAPPY: But, Mom he had a great time with us—

785   BIFF: *(cutting him off violently)* Shut up!

Without another word, Happy goes upstairs.

LINDA: You! You didn't even go in to see if he was all right!

BIFF: *(still on the floor in front of Linda, the flowers in his hand; with self-loathing)* No.
    Didn't. Didn't do a damned thing. How do you like that, heh? Left him
    babbling in a toilet.

LINDA: You louse. You . . .

BIFF: Now you hit it on the nose! *(He gets up, throws the flowers in the wastebasket.)*
    The scum of the earth, and you're looking at him!

790   LINDA: Get out of here!

BIFF: I gotta talk to the boss, Mom. Where is he?

LINDA: You're not going near him. Get out of this house!

BIFF: *(with absolute assurance, determination)* No. We're gonna have an abrupt
    conversation, him and me.

LINDA: You're not talking to him!

Hammering is heard from outside the house, off right. Biff turns toward the noise.

LINDA: (*suddenly pleading*) Will you please leave him alone?   795
BIFF: What's he doing out there?
LINDA: He's planting the garden!
BIFF: (*quietly*) Now? Oh, my God!

Biff moves outside, Linda following. The light dies down on them and comes up on the center of the apron as Willy walks into it. He is carrying a flashlight, a hoe and a handful of seed packets. He raps the top of the hoe sharply to fix it firmly, and then moves to the left, measuring off the distance with his foot. He holds the flashlight to look at the seed packets, reading off the instructions. He is in the blue of night.

WILLY: Carrots . . . quarter-inch apart. Rows . . . one-foot rows. (*He measures it off.*) One foot. (*He puts down a package and measures off.*) Beets. (*He puts down another package and measures again.*) Lettuce. (*He reads the package, puts it down.*) One foot—(*He breaks off as Ben appears at the right and moves slowly down to him.*) What a proposition, ts, ts. Terrific, terrific. 'Cause she's suffered, Ben, the woman has suffered. You understand me? A man can't go out the way he came in, Ben, a man has got to add up to something. You can't, you can't—(*Ben moves toward him as though to interrupt.*) You gotta consider, now. Don't answer so quick. Remember, it's a guaranteed twenty-thousand-dollar proposition. Now look, Ben, I want you to go through the ins and outs of this thing with me. I've got nobody to talk to, Ben, and the woman has suffered, you hear me?
BEN: (*standing still, considering*) What's the proposition?   800
WILLY: It's twenty thousand dollars on the barrelhead. Guaranteed, gilt-edged, you understand?
BEN: You don't want to make a fool of yourself. They might not honor the policy.
WILLY: How can they dare refuse? Didn't I work like a coolie to meet every premium on the nose? And now they don't pay off? Impossible!
BEN: It's called a cowardly thing, William.
WILLY: Why? Does it take more guts to stand here the rest of my life ringing up a zero?   805
BEN: (*yielding*) That's a point, William. (*He moves, thinking, turns.*) And twenty thousand—that *is* something one can feel with the hand, it is there.
WILLY: (*now assured, with rising power*) Oh, Ben, that's the whole beauty of it! I see it like a diamond, shining in the dark, hard and rough, that I can pick up and touch in my hand. Not like—like an appointment! This would not be another damned-fool appointment, Ben, and it changes all the aspects. Because he thinks I'm nothing, see, and so he spites me. But the funeral—(*Straightening up.*) Ben, that funeral will be massive! They'll come from Maine, Massachusetts, Vermont, New Hampshire! All the old-timers with the strange license plates— that boy will be thunder-struck, Ben, because he never realized—I am known! Rhode Island, New York, New Jersey—I am known, Ben, and he'll see it with his eyes once and for all. He'll see what I am, Ben! He's in for a shock, that boy!
BEN: (*coming down to the edge of the garden*) He'll call you a coward.
WILLY: (*suddenly fearful*) No, that would be terrible.

810 **BEN:** Yes. And a damned fool.

WILLY: No, no, he mustn't, I won't have that! (*He is broken and desperate.*)

BEN: He'll hate you, William.

The gay music of the boys is heard.

WILLY: Oh, Ben, how do we get back to all the great times? Used to be so full of light, and comradeship, the sleigh-riding in winter, and the ruddiness on his cheeks. And always some kind of good news coming up, always something nice coming up ahead. And never even let me carry the valises in the house, and simonizing, simonizing that little red car! Why, why can't I give him something and not have him hate me?

BEN: Let me think about it. (*He glances at his watch.*) I still have a little time. Remarkable proposition, but you've got to be sure you're not making a fool of yourself.

Ben drifts off upstage and goes out of sight. Biff comes down from the left.

815 **WILLY:** (*suddenly conscious of Biff, turns and looks up at him, then begins picking up the packages of seeds in confusion*) Where the hell is that seed? (*Indignantly.*) You can't see nothing out here! They boxed in the whole goddam neighborhood!

BIFF: There are people all around here. Don't you realize that?

WILLY: I'm busy. Don't bother me.

BIFF: (*taking the hoe from Willy*) I'm saying good-by to you, Pop. (*Willy looks at him, silent, unable to move.*) I'm not coming back any more.

WILLY: You're not going to see Oliver tomorrow?

820 **BIFF:** I've got no appointment, Dad.

WILLY: He put his arm around you, and you've got no appointment?

BIFF: Pop, get this now, will you? Everytime I've left it's been a fight that sent me out of here. Today I realized something about myself and I tried to explain it to you and I—I think I'm just not smart enough to make any sense out of it for you. To hell with whose fault it is or anything like that. (*He takes Willy's arm.*) Let's just wrap it up, heh? Come on in, we'll tell Mom. (*He gently tries to pull Willy to the left.*)

WILLY: (*frozen, immobile, with guilt in his voice*) No, I don't want to see her.

BIFF: Come on! (*He pulls again, and Willy tries to pull away.*)

825 **WILLY:** (*highly nervous*) No, no, I don't want to see her.

BIFF: (*tries to look into Willy's face, as if to find the answer there*) Why don't you want to see her?

WILLY: (*more harshly now*) Don't bother me, will you?

BIFF: What do you mean, you don't want to see her? You don't want them calling you yellow, do you? This isn't your fault; it's me, I'm a bum. Now come inside! (*Willy strains to get away.*) Did you hear what I said to you?

Willy pulls away and quickly goes by himself into the house. Biff follows.

LINDA: (*to Willy*) Did you plant, dear?

830 **BIFF:** (*at the door, to Linda*) All right, we had it out. I'm going and I'm not writing any more.

LINDA: *(going to Willy in the kitchen)* I think that's the best way, dear. 'Cause there's no use drawing it out, you'll just never get along.

Willy doesn't respond.

BIFF: People ask where I am and what I'm doing, you don't know, and you don't care. That way it'll be off your mind and you can start brightening up again. All right? That clears it, doesn't it? *(Willy is silent, and Biff goes to him.)* You gonna wish me luck, scout? *(He extends his hand.)* What do you say?

LINDA: Shake his hand, Willy.

WILLY: *(turning to her, seething with hurt)* There's no necessity to mention the pen at all, y'know.

BIFF: *(gently)* I've got no appointment, Dad.   835

WILLY: *(erupting fiercely)* He put his arm around . . . ?

BIFF: Dad, you're never going to see what I am, so what's the use of arguing? If I strike oil I'll send you a check. Meantime forget I'm alive.

WILLY: *(to Linda)* Spite, see?

BIFF: Shake hands, Dad.

WILLY: Not my hand.   840

BIFF: I was hoping not to go this way.

WILLY: Well, this is the way you're going. Good-by.

Biff looks at him a moment, then turns sharply and goes to the stairs.

WILLY: *(stops him with)* May you rot in hell if you leave this house!

BIFF: *(turning)* Exactly what is it that you want from me?

WILLY: I want you to know, on the train, in the mountains, in the valleys, wherever   845
you go, that you cut down your life for spite!

BIFF: No, no.

WILLY: Spite, spite, is the word of your undoing! And when you're down and out, remember what did it. When you're rotting somewhere beside the railroad tracks, remember, and don't you dare blame it on me!

BIFF: I'm not blaming it on you!

WILLY: I won't take the rap for this, you hear?

Happy comes down the stairs and stands on the bottom step, watching.

BIFF: That's just what I'm telling you!   850

WILLY: *(sinking into a chair at the table, with full accusation)* You're trying to put a knife in me—don't think I don't know what you're doing!

BIFF: All right, phony! Then let's lay it on the line. *(He whips the rubber tube out of his pocket and puts it on the table.)*

HAPPY: You crazy—

LINDA: Biff! *(She moves to grab the hose, but Biff holds it down with his hand.)*

BIFF: Leave it there! Don't move it!   855

WILLY: *(not looking at it)* What is that?

BIFF: You know goddam well what that is.

WILLY: *(caged, wanting to escape)* I never saw that.

BIFF: You saw it. The mice didn't bring it into the cellar! What is this supposed to do, make a hero out of you? This supposed to make me sorry for you?

860   WILLY: Never heard of it.

BIFF: There'll be no pity for you, you hear it? No pity!

WILLY: (*to Linda*) You hear the spite!

BIFF: No, you're going to hear the truth—what you are and what I am!

LINDA: Stop it!

865   WILLY: Spite!

HAPPY: (*coming down toward Biff*) You cut it now!

BIFF: (*to Happy*) The man don't know who we are! The man is gonna know!
    (*To Willy.*) We never told the truth for ten minutes in this house!

HAPPY: We always told the truth!

BIFF: (*turning on him*) You big blow, are you the assistant buyer? You're one of the
    two assistants to the assistant, aren't you?

870   HAPPY: Well, I'm practically—

BIFF: You're practically full of it! We all are! And I'm through with it. (*To Willy.*)
    Now hear this, Willy, this is me.

WILLY: I know you!

BIFF: You know why I had no address for three months? I stole a suit in Kansas City
    and I was in jail. (*To Linda, who is sobbing.*) Stop crying. I'm through with it.

Linda turns away from them, her hands covering her face.

WILLY: I suppose that's my fault!

875   BIFF: I stole myself out of every good job since high school!

WILLY: And whose fault is that?

BIFF: And I never got anywhere because you blew me so full of hot air I could never
    stand taking orders from anybody! That's whose fault it is!

WILLY: I hear that!

LINDA: Don't, Biff!

880   BIFF: It's goddam time you heard that! I had to be boss big shot in two weeks, and
    I'm through with it!

WILLY: Then hang yourself! For spite, hang yourself!

BIFF: No! Nobody's hanging himself, Willy! I ran down eleven flights with a pen
    in my hand today. And suddenly I stopped, you hear me? And in the middle of
    that office building, do you hear this? I stopped in the middle of that building
    and I saw—the sky. I saw the things that I love in this world. The work and
    the food and time to sit and smoke. And I looked at the pen and said to myself,
    what the hell am I grabbing this for? Why am I trying to become what I don't
    want to be? What am I doing in an office, making a contemptuous, begging fool
    of myself, when all I want is out there, waiting for me the minute I say I know
    who I am! Why can't I say that, Willy? (*He tries to make Willy face him, but Willy
    pulls away and moves to the left.*)

WILLY: (*with hatred, threateningly*) The door of your life is wide open!

BIFF: Pop! I'm a dime a dozen, and so are you!

885   WILLY: (*turning on him now in an uncontrolled outburst*) I am not a dime a dozen!
    I am Willy Loman, and you are Biff Loman!

Biff starts for Willy, but is blocked by Happy. In his fury, Biff seems on the verge of attacking his father.

BIFF: I am not a leader of men, Willy, and neither are you. You were never anything but a hard-working drummer who landed in the ash can like all the rest of them! I'm one dollar an hour, Willy! I tried seven states and couldn't raise it. A buck an hour! Do you gather my meaning? I'm not bringing home any prizes any more, and you're going to stop waiting for me to bring them home!

WILLY: (*directly to Biff*) You vengeful, spiteful mutt!

Biff breaks from Happy. Willy, in fright, starts up the stairs. Biff grabs him.

BIFF: (*at the peak of his fury*) Pop, I'm nothing! I'm nothing, Pop. Can't you understand that? There's no spite in it any more. I'm just what I am, that's all.

Biff's fury has spent itself, and he breaks down, sobbing, holding on to Willy, who dumbly fumbles for Biff's face.

WILLY: (*astonished*) What're you doing? What're you doing? (*To Linda.*) Why is he crying?

BIFF: (*crying, broken*) Will you let me go, for Christ's sake? Will you take that phony dream and burn it before something happens? (*Struggling to contain himself, he pulls away and moves to the stairs.*) I'll go in the morning. Put him—put him to bed. (*Exhausted, Biff moves up the stairs to his room.*) 890

WILLY: (*after a long pause, astonished, elevated*) Isn't that remarkable? Biff—he likes me!

LINDA: He loves you, Willy!

HAPPY: (*deeply moved*) Always did, Pop.

WILLY: Oh, Biff! (*Staring wildly.*) He cried! Cried to me! (*He is choking with his love, and now cries out his promise.*) That boy—that boy is going to be magnificent!

Ben appears in the light just outside the kitchen.

BEN: Yes, outstanding, with twenty thousand behind him. 895

LINDA: (*sensing the racing of his mind, fearfully, carefully*) Now come to bed, Willy. It's all settled now.

WILLY: (*finding it difficult not to rush out of the house*) Yes, we'll sleep. Come on. Go to sleep, Hap.

BEN: And it does take a great kind of man to crack the jungle.

In accents of dread, Ben's idyllic music starts up.

HAPPY: (*his arm around Linda*) I'm getting married, Pop, don't forget it. I'm changing everything. I'm gonna run that department before the year is up. You'll see, Mom. (*He kisses her.*)

BEN: The jungle is dark but full of diamonds, Willy. 900

Willy turns, moves, listening to Ben.

LINDA: Be good. You're both good boys, just act that way, that's all.

HAPPY: 'Night, Pop. (*He goes upstairs.*)

LINDA: *(to Willy)* Come, dear.

BEN: *(with greater force)* One must go in to fetch a diamond out.

905   WILLY: *(to Linda, as he moves slowly along the edge of the kitchen, toward the door)* I just want to get settled down, Linda. Let me sit alone for a little.

LINDA: *(almost uttering her fear)* I want you upstairs.

WILLY: *(taking her in his arms)* In a few minutes, Linda. I couldn't sleep right now. Go on, you look awful tired. *(He kisses her.)*

BEN: Not like an appointment at all. A diamond is rough and hard to the touch.

WILLY: Go on now. I'll be right up.

910   LINDA: I think this is the only way, Willy.

WILLY: Sure, it's the best thing.

BEN: Best thing!

WILLY: The only way. Everything is gonna be—go on, kid, get to bed. You look so tired.

LINDA: Come right up.

915   WILLY: Two minutes.

Linda goes into the living room, then reappears in her bedroom. Willy moves just outside the kitchen door.

WILLY: Loves me. *(Wonderingly.)* Always loved me. Isn't that a remarkable thing? Ben, he'll worship me for it!

BEN: *(with promise)* It's dark there, but full of diamonds.

WILLY: Can you imagine that magnificence with twenty thousand dollars in his pocket?

LINDA: *(calling from her room)* Willy! Come up!

920   WILLY: *(calling from the kitchen)* Yes! Yes! Coming! It's very smart, you realize that, don't you, sweetheart? Even Ben sees it. I gotta go, baby. 'By! By! *(Going over to Ben, almost dancing.)* Imagine? When the mail comes he'll be ahead of Bernard again!

BEN: A perfect proposition all around.

WILLY: Did you see how he cried to me? Oh, if I could kiss him, Ben!

BEN: Time, William, time!

WILLY: Oh, Ben, I always knew one way or another we were gonna make it, Biff and I!

925   BEN: *(looking at his watch)* The boat. We'll be late. *(He moves slowly off into the darkness.)*

WILLY: *(elegiacally, turning to the house)* Now when you kick off, boy, I want a seventy-yard boot, and get right down the field under the ball, and when you hit, hit low and hit hard, because it's important, boy. *(He swings around and faces the audience.)* There's all kinds of important people in the stands, and the first thing you know . . . *(Suddenly realizing he is alone.)* Ben! Ben, where do I . . . ? *(He makes a sudden movement of search.)* Ben, how do I . . . ?

LINDA: *(calling)* Willy, you coming up?

WILLY: *(uttering a gasp of fear, whirling about as if to quiet her)* Sh! *(He turns around as if to find his way; sounds, faces, voices, seem to be swarming in upon him and he flicks at them, crying.)* Sh! Sh! *(Suddenly music, faint and high, stops him. It rises in intensity, almost to an unbearable scream. He goes up and down on his toes, and rushes off around the house.)* Shhh!

LINDA: Willy?

There is no answer. Linda waits. Biff gets up off his bed. He is still in his clothes. Happy sits up. Biff stands listening.

LINDA: *(with real fear)* Willy, answer me! Willy!   930

There is the sound of a car starting and moving away at full speed.

LINDA: No!
BIFF: *(rushing down the stairs)* Pop!

As the car speeds off, the music crashes down in a frenzy of sound, which becomes the soft pulsation of a single cello string. Biff slowly returns to his bedroom. He and Happy gravely don their jackets. Linda slowly walks out of her room. The music has developed into a dead march. The leaves of day are appearing over everything. Charley and Bernard, somberly dressed, appear and knock on the kitchen door. Biff and Happy slowly descend the stairs to the kitchen as Charley and Bernard enter. All stop a moment when Linda, in clothes of mourning, bearing a little bunch of roses, comes through the draped doorway into the kitchen. She goes to Charley and takes his arm. Now all move toward the audience, through the wall-line of the kitchen. At the limit of the apron, Linda lays down the flowers, kneels, and sits back on her heels. All stare down at the grave.

REQUIEM

CHARLEY: It's getting dark, Linda.

Linda doesn't react. She stares at the grave.

BIFF: How about it, Mom? Better get some rest, heh? They'll be closing the gate soon.

Linda makes no move. Pause.

HAPPY: *(deeply angered)* He had no right to do that! There was no necessity for it. We would've helped him.
CHARLEY: *(grunting)* Hmmm.
BIFF: Come along, Mom.   5
LINDA: Why didn't anybody come?
CHARLEY: It was a very nice funeral.
LINDA: But where are all the people he knew? Maybe they blame him.
CHARLEY: Naa. It's a rough world, Linda. They wouldn't blame him.
LINDA: I can't understand it. At this time especially. First time in thirty-five years   10
    we were just about free and clear. He only needed a little salary. He was even
    finished with the dentist.
CHARLEY: No man only needs a little salary.
LINDA: I can't understand it.
BIFF: There were a lot of nice days. When he'd come home from a trip; or on Sundays,
    making the stoop; finishing the cellar; putting on the new porch; when he built
    the extra bathroom; and put up the garage. You know something, Charley, there's
    more of him in that front stoop than in all the sales he ever made.

Charley: Yeah. He was a happy man with a batch of cement.

15   Linda: He was so wonderful with his hands.

Biff: He had the wrong dreams. All, all, wrong.

Happy: *(almost ready to fight Biff)* Don't say that!

Biff: He never knew who he was.

Charley: *(stopping Happy's movement and reply. To Biff.)* Nobody dast blame this man. You don't understand: Willy was a salesman. And for a salesman, there is no rock bottom to the life. He don't put a bolt to a nut, he don't tell you the law or give you medicine. He's a man out there in the blue, riding on a smile and a shoeshine. And when they start not smiling back—that's an earthquake. And then you get yourself a couple of spots on your hat, and you're finished. Nobody dast blame this man. A salesman is got to dream, boy. It comes with the territory.

20   Biff: Charley, the man didn't know who he was.

Happy: *(infuriated)* Don't say that!

Biff: Why don't you come with me, Happy?

Happy: I'm not licked that easily. I'm staying right in this city, and I'm gonna beat this racket! *(He looks at Biff, his chin set.)* The Loman Brothers!

Biff: I know who I am, kid.

25   Happy: All right, boy. I'm gonna show you and everybody else that Willy Loman did not die in vain. He had a good dream. It's the only dream you can have—to come out number-one man. He fought it out here, and this is where I'm gonna win it for him.

Biff: *(with a hopeless glance at Happy, bends toward his mother)* Let's go, Mom.

Linda: I'll be with you in a minute. Go on, Charley. *(He hesitates.)* I want to, just for a minute. I never had a chance to say good-by.

Charley moves away, followed by Happy. Biff remains a slight distance up and left of Linda. She sits there, summoning herself. The flute begins, not far away, playing behind her speech.

Linda: Forgive me, dear. I can't cry. I don't know what it is, but I can't cry. I don't understand it. Why did you ever do that? Help me, Willy, I can't cry. It seems to me that you're just on another trip. I keep expecting you. Willy, dear, I can't cry. Why did you do it? I search and search and I search, and I can't understand it, Willy. I made the last payment on the house today. Today, dear. And there'll be nobody home. *(A sob rises in her throat.)* We're free and clear. *(Sobbing more fully, released.)* We're free. *(Biff comes slowly toward her.)* We're free . . . We're free . . .

Biff lifts her to her feet and moves out up right with her in his arms. Linda sobs quietly. Bernard and Charley come together and follow them, followed by Happy. Only the music of the flute is left on the darkening stage as over the house the hard towers of the apartment buildings rise into sharp focus, and—

The Curtain Falls

*   *   *

Reading and Reacting

1. Is Willy a likeable character? What words and actions—both Willy's and those of other characters—help you to reach your conclusion?
2. How does the existence of The Woman affect your overall impression of Willy? What does she reveal about his character?
3. What does Willy's attitude toward his sons indicate about his character? How is this attitude revealed?
4. In the absence of a narrator, what devices does Miller use to provide exposition—basic information about character and setting?
5. The conversation between Biff and Happy in act 1 reveals many of their differences. List some of the differences between these two characters.
6. In numerous remarks, Willy expresses his philosophy of business. Summarize some of his key ideas about the business world. How realistic do you think these ideas are? How do these ideas help to delineate his character?
7. In act 1, Linda tells Willy, "Few men are idolized by their children the way you are." Is she sincere, is she being ironic, or is she just trying to make Willy feel better?
8. How do the frequent flashbacks help to explain what motivates Willy? How else could this background information have been presented in the play? Are there advantages to using flashbacks instead of the alternative you suggest?
9. Is Linda simply a stereotype of the long-suffering wife, or is she a multidimensional character? Explain.
10. Willy Loman lives in Brooklyn, New York; his "territory" is New England. What is the significance to him of the "faraway places"—Africa, Alaska, California, Texas, and the like—mentioned in the play?
11. What purpose does Bernard serve in the play?
12. The play concludes with a requiem. What is a requiem? What information about each of the major characters is supplied in this brief section? Is this information essential to your understanding or appreciation of the play, or would the play have been equally effective without the requiem? Explain.

13. **JOURNAL ENTRY** Do you believe Willy Loman is an innocent victim of the society in which he lives, or do you believe there are flaws in his character that make him at least partially responsible for his own misfortune? Explain.

14. **CRITICAL PERSPECTIVE** Writing just after Miller's death in 2005, playwright David Mamet notes that at the end of *Death of a Salesman*, Miller has offered no solution to Willy's problems but instead "has reconciled us to the notion that there is no solution—that it is the human lot to try and fail, and that no one is immune from self-deception." Mamet goes on to explain the value of Miller's plays by comparing "bad drama" and "good drama":

    > Bad drama reinforces our prejudices. It informs us of what we knew when we came into the theater. . . .
    >
    > The good drama survives because it appeals not to the fashion of the moment, but to the problems both universal and eternal, as they are insoluble.
    >
    > To find beauty in the sad, hope in the midst of loss, and dignity in failure is great poetic art.

According to Mamet's criteria, does *Death of a Salesman* qualify as "good drama"? Do you think it is great drama?

Related Works: "Those Winter Sundays" (p. 885), "Do not go gentle into that good night" (p. 891), *Oedipus the King* (p. 1430), *Fences* (p. 1548)

Source: ©Bettmann/Corbis

WILLIAM SHAKESPEARE (1564–1616) is recognized as the greatest of English writers, but many details about his life are based on conjecture or tradition. The earliest dependable information concerning Shakespeare is found in the parish registers of Stratford-upon-Avon's Holy Trinity Church, where his baptism was recorded on April 26, 1564. Although his date of birth cannot be determined with certainty, tradition has assigned it to April 23, 1564. Little is known about his early life, but reliable information about significant events is available in church documents. For example, he married Ann Hathaway in 1582 and had three children—Susanna in 1583 and the twins Judith and Hamnet in 1585.

Soon after the birth of his children, Shakespeare left Stratford for London. Upon his arrival in the capital, he set out to establish himself in London's literary world. His first step toward achieving this goal occurred in 1592, when he published his narrative poem *Venus and Adonis*; the following year, he published a second poem, *The Rape of Lucrece*.

By 1594, Shakespeare had become quite involved with the London stage. For approximately twenty years, he enjoyed a successful professional career in London—as actor, playwright, shareholder in the Lord Chamberlain's Men (an acting company), part owner of the Globe Theatre (from 1599), and author of at least thirty-six plays. The income derived from these activities brought him significant wealth and enabled him, sometime between 1610 and 1613, to retire from the theater and to return to Stratford-upon-Avon, where he owned considerable property. On April 23, 1616, Shakespeare died at age fifty-two in Stratford and was buried two days later in Holy Trinity Church.

It is difficult to date many of Shakespeare's plays exactly because they must be dated by records of their first performance (often hard to come by) and by topical references in the text. Shakespeare's company probably first staged *Hamlet* at the Globe Theatre in 1600 or 1601, but some scholars believe the play was composed as early as 1598.

Hamlet has been called Shakespeare's most complex and most confusing play, yet it is also the play most frequently performed, read, and written about. Shakespeare's audience would have recognized *Hamlet* as a **revenge tragedy**—a play in which the hero discovers that a close relative has been murdered, experiences considerable trouble in identifying the murderer, and, after overcoming numerous obstacles, avenges the death by killing the

An audience at the reconstructed Globe Theatre in London
Source: © Andreas Hub/laif/Redux Pictures

murderer. Frequently, revenge tragedies featured murders, physical mutilations, and ghosts, all enacted with grand style and bold rhetoric. These plays were extremely popular productions that were the action movies of their day.

Hamlet, however, is different from the typical revenge tragedy. Because the ghost gives him the necessary information, Hamlet has no need to search for the cause of his father's death or find the murderer. In fact, the only impediments to Hamlet's revenge are those he himself creates. And, by the time the delay ends and Hamlet avenges his father's death, the loss is immense: his mother, the woman he loves, her father and brother, and Hamlet himself are all dead. Although the argument that there would be no play if Hamlet had immediately avenged his father may be valid, it fails to satisfy those who ponder the tragic cost of Hamlet's inaction.

Cultural Context The appearance of a ghost was a longstanding tradition in Renaissance drama. The ghost appeared in Elizabethan revenge tragedies as a plot device to help further the action and prompt a reaction from the hero. For a Renaissance audience, the dramatic representation of a ghost from purgatory would evoke a rich context of legends and lore derived from paintings, illuminated manuscripts, prints, and narratives. Moreover, stories involving ghosts were a frequent element of medieval sermons. However, the ghost in *Hamlet* transcends the traditions of the revenge tragedy. Here, Shakespeare's use of the ghost not only as a plot device but also as a character who may or may not be telling the truth adds depth and complexity to the play.

Hamlet

Prince of Denmark* (c. 1600)

CHARACTERS

Claudius, *King of Denmark*
Hamlet, *son to the former and nephew to the present King*
Polonius, *Lord Chamberlain*
Horatio, *friend to Hamlet*
Laertes, *son to Polonius*

Courtiers {
Voltimand
Cornelius
Rosencrantz
Guildenstern
Osric
}

A Gentleman
A Priest
Francisco, *a soldier*

Officers {
Marcellus
Bernardo
}

Reynaldo, *servant to Polonius*
Players
Two Clowns, *grave-diggers*
Fortinbras, *Prince of Norway*
A Captain
English Ambassadors
Ghost of Hamlet's Father
Gertrude, *Queen of Denmark and mother of Hamlet*
Ophelia, *daughter to Polonius*
Lords, Ladies, Officers, Soldiers, Sailors, Messengers, and other Attendants

---

*Note that individual lines are numbered in the following play. When a line is shared by one or more characters, it is counted as one line.

Richard Burton as Hamlet
©Bettmann/Corbis

Laurence Olivier as Hamlet
©Bettmann/Corbis,

Mel Gibson as Hamlet
©Paramount/The Kobal Collection

ACT 1

SCENE 1

Elsinore. A platform before the castle.

Francisco at his post. Enter to him Bernardo.

BERNARDO: Who's there?
FRANCISCO: Nay, answer me: stand, and unfold yourself.
BERNARDO: Long live the king!
FRANCISCO: Bernardo?
5   BERNARDO: He.
FRANCISCO: You come most carefully upon your hour.

BERNARDO: 'Tis now struck twelve; get thee to bed, Francisco.
FRANCISCO: For this relief much thanks: 'tis bitter cold,
        And I am sick at heart.
10 BERNARDO: Have you had quiet guard?
FRANCISCO: Not a mouse stirring.
BERNARDO: Well, good-night.
        If you do meet Horatio and Marcellus,
        The rivals of my watch, bid them make haste.
15 FRANCISCO: I think I hear them.—Stand, ho! Who is there?

Enter Horatio and Marcellus.

HORATIO: Friends to this ground.
MARCELLUS: And liegemen to the Dane.
FRANCISCO: Give you good-night.
MARCELLUS: O, farewell, honest soldier:
20   Who hath reliev'd you?
FRANCISCO: Bernardo has my place.
        Give you good-night.

Exit.

MARCELLUS: Holla! Bernardo!

BERNARDO: Say.

    What, is Horatio there?   25

HORATIO: A piece of him.

BERNARDO: Welcome, Horatio:—welcome, good Marcellus.

MARCELLUS: What, has this thing appear'd again to-night?

BERNARDO: I have seen nothing.

MARCELLUS: Horatio says 'tis but our fantasy,   30

    And will not let belief take hold of him

    Touching this dreaded sight, twice seen of us:

    Therefore I have entreated him along

    With us to watch the minutes of this night;

    That, if again this apparition come   35

    He may approve our eyes and speak to it.

HORATIO: Tush, tush, 'twill not appear.

BERNARDO: Sit down awhile,

    And let us once again assail your ears,

    That are so fortified against our story,   40

    What we two nights have seen.

HORATIO: Well, sit we down,

    And let us hear Bernardo speak of this.

BERNARDO: Last night of all,

    When yon same star that's westward from the pole   45

    Had made his course to illume that part of heaven

    Where now it burns, Marcellus and myself,

    The bell then beating one,—

MARCELLUS: Peace, break thee off; look where it comes again!

Enter Ghost, armed.

BERNARDO: In the same figure, like the king that's dead.   50

MARCELLUS: Thou art a scholar; speak to it, Horatio.

BERNARDO: Looks it not like the king? mark it, Horatio.

HORATIO: Most like:—it harrows me with fear and wonder.

BERNARDO: It would be spoke to.

MARCELLUS: Question it, Horatio.   55

HORATIO: What art thou, that usurp'st this time of night,

    Together with that fair and warlike form

    In which the majesty of buried Denmark

    Did sometimes march? by heaven I charge thee, speak!

MARCELLUS: It is offended.   60

BERNARDO: See, it stalks away!

HORATIO: Stay! speak, speak! I charge thee, speak!

Exit Ghost.

MARCELLUS: 'Tis gone, and will not answer.

BERNARDO: How now, Horatio! you tremble and look pale:

65   Is not this something more than fantasy?
        What think you on't?

HORATIO: Before my God, I might not this believe
        Without the sensible and true avouch
        Of mine own eyes.

70 MARCELLUS: Is it not like the king?

HORATIO: As thou art to thyself:
        Such was the very armor he had on
        When he the ambitious Norway combated;
        So frown'd he once when, in an angry parle,[1]
75   He smote the sledded Polacks on the ice.
        'Tis strange.

MARCELLUS: Thus twice before, and just at this dead hour,
        With martial stalk hath he gone by our watch.

HORATIO: In what particular thought to work I know not;
80   But, in the gross and scope of my opinion,
        This bodes some strange eruption to our state.

MARCELLUS: Good now, sit down, and tell me, he that knows,
        Why this same strict and most observant watch
        So nightly toils the subject of the land;
85   And why such daily cast of brazen cannon,
        And foreign mart for implements of war;
        Why such impress of shipwrights, whose sore task
        Does not divide the Sunday from the week;
        What might be toward, that this sweaty haste
90   Doth make the night joint-laborer with the day:
        Who is't that can inform me?

HORATIO: That can I;
        At least, the whisper goes so. Our last king,
        Whose image even but now appear'd to us,
95   Was, as you know, by Fortinbras of Norway,
        Thereto prick'd on by a most emulate pride,
        Dar'd to the combat; in which our valiant Hamlet,—
        For so this side of our known world esteem'd him,—
        Did slay this Fortinbras; who, by a seal'd compact,
100   Well ratified by law and heraldry,
        Did forfeit, with his life, all those his lands.
        Which he stood seiz'd of,[2] to the conqueror:
        Against the which, a moiety competent[3]
        Was gagéd[4] by our king; which had return'd

---

[1]*parle:* Parley, or conference.   [2]*seiz'd of:* Possessed.   [3]*moiety competent:* A sufficient portion of his lands.
[4]*gagéd:* Engaged or pledged.

To the inheritance of Fortinbras,   105
Had he been vanquisher; as by the same cov'nant,
And carriage of the article design'd,
His fell to Hamlet. Now, sir, young Fortinbras,
Of unimproved mettle hot and full,
Hath in the skirts of Norway, here and there,   110
Shark'd up a list of landless resolutes,
For food and diet, to some enterprise
That hath a stomach in't: which is no other,—
As it doth well appear unto our state,—
But to recover of us by strong hand,   115
And terms compulsatory, those foresaid lands
So by his father lost: and this, I take it,
Is the main motive of our preparations,
The source of this our watch, and the chief head
Of this post-haste and romage⁵ in the land.   120

BERNARDO: I think it be no other, but e'en so:
Well may it sort that this portentous figure
Comes armed through our watch; so like the king
That was and is the question of these wars.

HORATIO: A mote it is to trouble the mind's eye.   125
In the most high and palmy state of Rome,
A little ere the mightiest Julius fell,
The graves stood tenantless, and the sheeted dead
Did squeak and gibber in the Roman streets:
As, stars with trains of fire and dews of blood,   130
Disasters in the sun; and the moist star,
Upon whose influence Neptune's empire stands,
Was sick almost to doomsday with eclipse:
And even the like precurse of fierce events,—
As harbingers preceding still the fates,   135
And prologue to the omen coming on,—
Have heaven and earth together demonstrated
Unto our climature and countrymen.—
But, soft, behold! lo, where it comes again!

Re-enter Ghost.

I'll cross it, though it blast me.—Stay, illusion!   140
If thou hast any sound or use of voice,
Speak to me:
If there be any good thing to be done,
That may to thee do ease, and grace to me,
Speak to me: 145

---

⁵*post-haste and romage:* General activity.

If thou art privy to thy country's fate,
Which, happily,[6] foreknowing may avoid,
O, speak!
Or if thou has uphoarded in thy life
150 Extorted treasure in the womb of earth,
For which, they say, you spirits oft walk in death,

Cock crows.

Speak of it:—stay, and speak!—Stop it, Marcellus.
MARCELLUS: Shall I strike at it with my partisan?[7]
HORATIO: Do, if it will not stand.
155 BERNARDO: 'Tis here!
HORATIO: 'Tis here!
MARCELLUS: 'Tis gone!

Exit Ghost.

We do it wrong, being so majestical,
To offer it the show of violence;
160 For it is, as the air, invulnerable,
And our vain blows malicious mockery.
BERNARDO: It was about to speak when the cock crew.
HORATIO: And then it started like a guilty thing
Upon a fearful summons. I have heard,
165 The cock, that is the trumpet to the morn,
Doth with his lofty and shrill-sounding throat
Awake the god of day; and at his warning,
Whether in sea or fire, in earth or air,
The extravagant and erring spirit hies
170 To his confine: and of the truth herein
This present object made probation.[8]
MARCELLUS: It faded on the crowing of the cock.
Some say that ever 'gainst that season comes
Wherein our Saviour's birth is celebrated,
175 The bird of dawning singeth all night long:
And then, they say, no spirit can walk abroad;
The nights are wholesome; then no planets strike,
No fairy takes, nor witch hath power to charm;
So hallow'd and so gracious is the time.
180 HORATIO: So have I heard, and do in part believe.
But, look, the morn, in russet mantle clad,
Walks o'er the dew of yon high eastern hill:
Break we our watch up: and, by my advice,
Let us impart what we have seen to-night

6*happily:* Haply, or perhaps.   7*partisan:* Pike.   8*probation:* Proof.

Unto young Hamlet; for, upon my life,   185
This spirit, dumb to us, will speak to him:
Do you consent we shall acquaint him with it,
As needful in our loves, fitting our duty?
MARCELLUS: Let's do't, I pray; and I this morning know
Where we shall find him most conveniently.   190

Exeunt.

SCENE 2

Elsinore. A room of state in the castle.

*Enter the King, Queen, Hamlet, Polonius, Laertes, Voltimand, Cornelius, Lords, and
Attendants.*

KING: Though yet of Hamlet our dear brother's death
The memory be green; and that it us befitted
To bear our hearts in grief, and our whole kingdom
To be contracted in one brow of woe;
Yet so far hath discretion fought with nature   5
That we with wisest sorrow think on him,
Together with remembrance of ourselves.
Therefore our sometime sister, now our queen,
The imperial jointress of this warlike state,
Have we, as 'twere with defeated joy,—   10
With one auspicious and one dropping eye,
With mirth and funeral, and with dirge in marriage,
In equal scale weighing delight and dole,—
Taken to wife: nor have we herein barr'd
Your better wisdoms, which have freely gone   15
With this affair along:—for all, our thanks.
Now follows that you know, young Fortinbras,
Holding a weak supposal of our worth,
Or thinking by our late dear brother's death
Our state to be disjoint and out of frame,   20
Colleagued with the dream of his advantage,
He hath not fail'd to pester us with message,
Importing the surrender of those lands
Lost by his father, with all bonds of law,
To our most valiant brother. So much for him.—   25
Now for ourself, and for this time of meeting:
Thus much the business is:—we have here writ
To Norway, uncle of young Fortinbras,—
Who, impotent and bed-rid, scarcely hears
Of this his nephew's purpose,—to suppress   30
His further gait herein; in that the levies,
The lists, and full proportions, are all made

Out of his subject:—and we here despatch
You, good Cornelius, and you, Voltimand,
35   For bearers of this greeting to old Norway;
Giving to you no further personal power
To business with the king more than the scope
Of these dilated articles allow.
Farewell; and let your haste commend your duty.

40   CORNELIUS AND VOLTIMAND: In that and all things will we show
     our duty.

KING: We doubt it nothing: heartily farewell.

Exeunt Voltimand and Cornelius.

And now, Laertes, what's the news with you?
You told us of some suit; what is't, Laertes?
You cannot speak of reason to the Dane,
45   And lose your voice: what wouldst thou beg, Laertes,
That shall not be my offer, nor thy asking?
The head is not more native to the heart,
The hand more instrumental to the mouth,
Than is the throne of Denmark to thy father.
50   What wouldst thou have, Laertes?

LAERTES: Dread my lord,
Your leave and favor to return to France;
From whence though willingly I came to Denmark,
To show my duty in your coronation;
55   Yet now, I must confess, that duty done,
My thoughts and wishes bend again toward France.
And bow them to your gracious leave and pardon.

KING: Have you your father's leave? What says Polonius?

POLONIUS: He hath, my lord, wrung from me my slow leave
60   By laborsome petition; and at last
Upon his will I seal'd my hard consent:
I do beseech you, give him leave to go.

KING: Take thy fair hour, Laertes; time be thine,
And thy best graces spend it at thy will!—
65   But now, my cousin Hamlet, and my son,—

HAMLET: [*Aside*] A little more than kin, and less than kind.

KING: How is it that the clouds still hang on you?

HAMLET: Not so, my lord; I am too much i' the sun.

QUEEN: Good Hamlet, cast thy nighted color off,
70   And let thine eye look like a friend on Denmark.
Do not for ever with thy vailed[1] lids
Seek for thy noble father in the dust:

---

[1] *vailed:* Downcast.

Thou know'st 'tis common,—all that live must die,
Passing through nature to eternity.

HAMLET: Ay, madam, it is common.   75

QUEEN: If it be,
Why seems it so particular with thee?

HAMLET: Seems, madam! nay, it is; I know not seems.
'Tis not alone my inky cloak, good mother,
Nor customary suits of solemn black,   80
Nor windy suspiration of forc'd breath,
No, nor the fruitful river in the eye,
Nor the dejected 'havior of the visage,
Together with all forms, moods, shows of grief,
That can denote me truly: these, indeed, seem;   85
For they are actions that a man might play:
But I have that within which passeth show;
These but the trappings and the suits of woe.

KING: 'Tis sweet and cómmendable in your nature, Hamlet,
To give these mourning duties to your father: 90
But, you must know, your father lost a father;
That father lost, lost his; and the survivor bound,
In filial obligation, for some term
To do obsequious sorrow: but to persever
In obstinate condolement is a course   95
Of impious stubbornness; 'tis unmanly grief:
It shows a will most incorrect to heaven;
A heart unfortified, a mind impatient;
An understanding simple and unschool'd:
For what we know must be, and is as common   100
As any the most vulgar thing to sense,[2]
Why should we, in our peevish opposition,
Take it to heart? Fie! 'tis a fault to heaven,
A fault against the dead, a fault to nature,
To reason most absurd; whose common theme   105
Is death of fathers, and who still[3] hath cried,
From the first corse till he that died to-day,
This must be so. We pray you, throw to earth
This unprevailing woe; and think of us
As of a father: for let the world take note   110
You are the most immediate to our throne;
And with no less nobility of love
Than that which dearest father bears his son
Do I impart toward you. For your intent
In going back to school in Wittenberg,   115

---

[2]*any . . . sense:* Anything that is very commonly seen or heard.   [3]*still:* Ever, or always.

It is most retrograde to our desire:
And we beseech you bend you to remain
.   Here, in the cheer and comfort of our eye,
Our chiefest courtier, cousin, and our son.

120   QUEEN: Let not thy mother lose her prayers, Hamlet:
I pray thee, stay with us; go not to Wittenberg.
HAMLET: I shall in all my best obey you, madam.
KING: Why, 'tis a loving and a fair reply:
Be as ourself in Denmark.—Madam, come;
125   This gentle and unforc'd accord of Hamlet
Sits smiling to my heart: in grace whereof,
No jocund health that Denmark drinks to-day
But the great cannon to the clouds shall tell;
And the king's rouse[4] the heavens shall bruit[5] again,
130   Re-speaking earthly thunder. Come away.

Exeunt all but Hamlet.

HAMLET: O, that this too too solid flesh would melt,
Thaw, and resolve itself into a dew!
Or that the Everlasting had not fix'd
His canon 'gainst self-slaughter! O God! O God!
135   How weary, stale, flat, and unprofitable
Seem to me all the uses of this world!
Fie on't! O fie! 'tis an unweeded garden,
That grows to seed; things rank and gross in nature
Possess it merely. That it should come to this!
140   But two months dead!—nay, not so much, not two:
So excellent a king; that was, to this,
Hyperion[6] to a satyr: so loving to my mother,
That he might not beteem the winds of heaven
Visit her face too roughly. Heaven and earth!
145   Must I remember? why, she would hang on him
As if increase of appetite had grown
By what it fed on: and yet, within a month,—
Let me not think on't,—Frailty, thy name is woman!—
A little month; or ere those shoes were old
150   With which she follow'd my poor father's body
Like Niobe, all tears;—why she, even she,—
O God! a beast, that wants discourse of reason,
Would have mourn'd longer,—married with mine uncle,
My father's brother; but no more like my father
155   Than I to Hercules: within a month;
Ere yet the salt of most unrighteous tears

---

[4]*rouse:* Drink.   [5]*bruit:* Echo.   [6]*Hyperion:* The Greek sun-god, the brightest and most beautiful of the gods.

Had left the flushing in her galled eyes,
She married:—O, most wicked speed, to post
With such dexterity to incestuous sheets!
It is not, nor it cannot come to good;
But break, my heart,—for I must hold my tongue!   160

Enter Horatio, Marcellus, and Bernardo.

HORATIO: Hail to your lordship!
HAMLET: I am glad to see you well:
    Horatio,—or I do forget myself.
HORATIO: The same, my lord, and your poor servant ever.   165
HAMLET: Sir, my good friend; I'll change that name with you:
    And what make you from Wittenberg, Horatio?—Marcellus?
MARCELLUS: My good lord,—
HAMLET: I am very glad to see you.—Good even, sir.—
    But what, in faith, make you from Wittenberg?   170
HORATIO: A truant disposition, good my lord.
HAMLET: I would not hear your enemy say so;
    Nor shall you do mine ear that violence,
    To make it truster of your own report
    Against yourself: I know you are no truant.   175
    But what is your affair in Elsinore?
    We'll teach you to drink deep ere you depart.
HORATIO: My lord, I came to see your father's funeral.
HAMLET: I pray thee, do not mock me, fellow-student;
    I think it was to see my mother's wedding.   180
HORATIO: Indeed, my lord, it follow'd hard upon.
HAMLET: Thrift, thrift, Horatio! the funeral-bak'd meats
    Did coldly furnish forth the marriage tables.
    Would I had met my dearest foe[7] in heaven
    Ere I had ever seen that day, Horatio!—   185
    My father,—methinks I see my father.
HORATIO: Where, my lord?
HAMLET: In my mind's eye, Horatio.
HORATIO: I saw him once; he was a goodly[8] king.
HAMLET: He was a man, take him for all in all,   190
    I shall not look upon his like again.
HORATIO: My lord, I think I saw him yester-night.
HAMLET: Saw who?
HORATIO: My lord, the king your father.
HAMLET: The king my father!   195
HORATIO: Season your admiration[9] for awhile
    With an attent ear, till I may deliver,

---

[7]*dearest foe:* Worst enemy.   [8]*goodly:* Handsome.   [9]*admiration:* Astonishment.

Upon the witness of these gentlemen,
This marvel to you.

200   HAMLET: For God's love, let me hear.
HORATIO: Two nights together had these gentlemen,
Marcellus and Bernardo, in their watch,
In the dead vast and middle of the night,
Been thus encounter'd. A figure like your father,
205   Arm'd at all points exactly, cap-a-pe,[10]
Appears before them, and with solemn march
Goes slow and stately by them: thrice he walk'd
By their oppress'd[11] and fear-surprised eyes,
Within his truncheon's length; whilst they, distill'd
210   Almost to jelly with the act of fear,
Stand dumb, and speak not to him. This to me
In dreadful secrecy impart they did;
And I with them the third night kept the watch:
Where, as they had deliver'd, both in time,
215   Form of the thing, each word made true and good,
The apparition comes: I knew your father;
These hands are not more like.
HAMLET: But where was this?
MARCELLUS: My lord, upon the platform where we watch'd.
220   HAMLET: Did you not speak to it?
HORATIO: My lord, I did;
But answer made it none: yet once methought
It lifted up its head, and did address
Itself to motion, like as it would speak:
225   But even then the morning cock crew loud,
And at the sound it shrunk in haste away,
And vanish'd from our sight.
HAMLET: 'Tis very strange.
HORATIO: As I do live, my honor'd lord, 'tis true;
230   And we did think it writ down in our duty
To let you know of it.
HAMLET: Indeed, indeed, sirs, but this troubles me.
Hold you the watch to-night?
MARCELLUS AND BERNARDO: We do, my lord.
235   HAMLET: Arm'd, say you?
MARCELLUS AND BERNARDO: Arm'd, my lord.
HAMLET: From top to toe?
MARCELLUS AND BERNARDO: My lord, from head to foot.
HAMLET: Then saw you not his face?
240   HORATIO: O yes, my lord; he wore his beaver up.

---

[10]*cap-a-pe:* From head to toe.   [11]*oppress'd:* Overwhelmed.

HAMLET: What, look'd he frowningly?

HORATIO: A countenance more in sorrow than in anger.

HAMLET: Pale or red?

HORATIO: Nay, very pale.

HAMLET: And fix'd his eyes upon you?   245

HORATIO: Most constantly.

HAMLET: I would I had been there.

HORATIO: It would have much amaz'd you.

HAMLET: Very like, very like. Stay'd it long?

HORATIO: While one with moderate haste might tell[12] a hundred.   250

MARCELLUS AND BERNARDO: Longer, longer.

HORATIO: Not when I saw't.

HAMLET: His beard was grizzled,—no?

HORATIO: It was, as I have seen it in his life,
    A sable silver'd.   255

HAMLET: I will watch to-night;
    Perchance 'twill walk again.

HORATIO: I warrant it will.

HAMLET: If it assume my noble father's person
    I'll speak to it, though hell itself should gape   260
    And bid me hold my peace. I pray you all,
    If you have hitherto conceal'd this sight,
    Let it be tenable in your silence still;
    And whatsoever else shall hap to-night,
    Give it an understanding, but no tongue: 265
    I will requite your loves. So, fare ye well:
    Upon the platform, 'twixt eleven and twelve,
    I'll visit you.

ALL: Our duty to your honor.

HAMLET: Your loves, as mine to you: farewell.   270

Exeunt Horatio, Marcellus, and Bernardo.

    My father's spirit in arms; all is not well;
    I doubt some foul play: would the night were come!
    Till then sit still, my soul: foul deeds will rise,
    Though all the earth o'erwhelm them, to men's eyes.

Exit.

SCENE 3

A room in Polonius' house.

Enter Laertes and Ophelia.

LAERTES: My necessaries are embark'd: farewell:
    And, sister, as the winds give benefit,

---

[12]*tell:* Count

And convoy[1] is assistant, do not sleep,
But let me hear from you.

5   OPHELIA: Do you doubt that?

LAERTES: For Hamlet, and the trifling of his favor,
Hold it a fashion and a toy in blood:
A violet in the youth of primy nature,
Forward, not permanent, sweet, not lasting,
10   The perfume and suppliance of a minute;
No more.

OPHELIA: No more but so?

LAERTES: Think it no more:
For nature, crescent,[2] does not grow alone
15   In thews and bulk; but as this temple[3] waxes,
The inward service of the mind and soul
Grows wide withal. Perhaps he loves you now;
And now no soil nor cautel[4] doth besmirch
The virtue of his will: but you must fear,
20   His greatness weigh'd, his will is not his own;
For he himself is subject to his birth:
He may not, as unvalu'd persons do,
Carve for himself; for on his choice depends
The safety and the health of the whole state;
25   And therefore must his choice be circumscrib'd
Unto the voice and yielding of that body
Whereof he is the head. Then if he says he loves you,
It fits your wisdom so far to believe it
As he in his particular act and place
30 ➤ May give his saying deed; which is no further
Than the main[5] voice of Denmark goes withal.
Then weigh what loss your honor may sustain
If with too credent ear you list his songs,
Or lose your heart, or your chaste treasure open
35   To his unmaster'd importunity.
Fear it, Ophelia, fear it, my dear sister;
And keep within the rear of your affection,
Out of the shot and danger of desire.
The chariest maid is prodigal enough
40   If she unmask her beauty to the moon:
Virtue itself scrapes not calumnious strokes:
The canker galls the infants of the spring
Too oft before their buttons be disclos'd;
And in the morn and liquid dew of youth
45   Contagious blastments are most imminent.

---

[1]*convoy:* Means of conveyance.   [2]*crescent:* Growing.   [3]*temple:* Body.   [4]*cautel:* Deceit.
[5]*main:* Strong, or mighty.

Be wary, then; best safety lies in fear:
Youth to itself rebels, though none else near.

OPHELIA: I shall the effect of this good lesson keep
As watchman to my heart. But, good my brother,
Do not, as some ungracious pastors do,   50
Show me the steep and thorny way to heaven;
Whilst like a puff'd and reckless libertine,
Himself the primrose path of dalliance treads,
And recks not his own rede.[6]

LAERTES: O, fear me not.   55
I stay too long:—but here my father comes.

Enter Polonius.

A double blessing is a double grace;
Occasion smiles upon a second leave.

POLONIUS: Yet here, Laertes! aboard, aboard, for shame!
The wind sits in the shoulder of your sail,   60
And you are stay'd for. There,—my blessing with you!

Laying his hand on Laertes' head.

And these few precepts in thy memory
See thou character.[7] Give thy thoughts no tongue,
Nor any unproportion'd thought his act.
Be thou familiar, but by no means vulgar.   65
The friends thou hast, and their adoption tried,
Grapple them to thy soul with hoops of steel;
But do not dull thy palm with entertainment
Of each new-hatch'd, unfledg'd comrade. Beware
Of entrance to a quarrel; but, being in,   70
Bear't that the opposéd may beware of thee.
Give every man thine ear, but few thy voice:
Take each man's censure,[8] but reserve thy judgment.
Costly thy habit as thy purse can buy,
But not express'd in fancy; rich, not gaudy: 75
For the apparel oft proclaims the man;
And they in France of the best rank and station
Are most select and generous chief in that.
Neither a borrower nor a lender be:
For a loan oft loses both itself and friend;   80
And borrowing dulls the edge of husbandry.
This above all,—to thine own self be true;
And it must follow, as the night the day,
Thou canst not then be false to any man.
Farewell: my blessing season this in thee!   85

---

[6]*rede:* Counsel.   [7]*in . . . character:* Engrave in your mind.   [8]*censure:* Opinion.

Laertes: Most humbly do I take my leave, my lord.

Polonius: The time invites you; go, your servants tend.[9]

Laertes: Farewell, Ophelia; and remember well
What I have said to you.

90 **Ophelia:**   'Tis in my memory lock'd,
And you yourself shall keep the key of it.

Laertes: Farewell. [*Exit.*]

Polonius: What is't, Ophelia, he hath said to you?

Ophelia: So please you, something touching the Lord Hamlet.

95 **Polonius:** Marry, well bethought:
'Tis told me he hath very oft of late
Given private time to you; and you yourself
Have of your audience been most free and bounteous:
If it be so,—as so 'tis put on me,
100 And that in way of caution,—I must tell you,
You do not understand yourself so clearly
As it behoves my daughter and your honor.
What is between you? give me up the truth.

Ophelia: He hath, my lord, of late made many tenders
105 Of his affection to me.

Polonius: Affection! pooh! you speak like a green girl,
Unsifted in such perilous circumstance.
Do you believe his tenders,[10] as you call them?

Ophelia: I do not know, my lord, what I should think.

110 **Polonius:** Marry, I'll teach you: think yourself a baby;
That you have ta'en these tenders for true pay,
Which are not sterling. Tender yourself more dearly;
Or,—not to crack the wind of the poor phrase,
Wronging it thus,—you'll tender me a fool.

115 **Ophelia:** My lord, he hath impórtun'd me with love
In honorable fashion.

Polonius: Ay, fashion you may call it; go to, go to.

Ophelia: And hath given countenance to his speech, my lord,
With almost all the holy vows of heaven.

120 **Polonius:** Ay, springes to catch woodcocks. I do know,
When the blood burns, how prodigal the soul
Lends the tongue vows: these blazes, daughter,
Giving more light than heat,—extinct in both,
Even in their promise, as it is a-making,—
125 You must not take for fire. From this time
Be somewhat scanter of your maiden presence;
Set your entreatments at a higher rate
Than a command to parley. For Lord Hamlet,

---

[9]*tend:* Wait.   [10]*tenders:* Offers.

Believe so much in him, that he is young;
And with a larger tether may he walk   130
Than may be given you: in few, Ophelia,
Do not believe his vows; for they are brokers,[11]—
Not of that die which their investments show,
But mere implorators of unholy suits,
Breathing like sanctified and pious bawds,   135
The better to beguile. This is for all,—
I would not, in plain terms, from this time forth,
Have you so slander any moment leisure
As to give words or talk with the Lord Hamlet.
Look to't, I charge you; come your ways.   140

OPHELIA: I shall obey, my lord.

Exeunt.

SCENE 4

The platform.

Enter Hamlet, Horatio, and Marcellus.

HAMLET: The air bites shrewdly; it is very cold.
HORATIO: It is a nipping and an eager air.
HAMLET: What hour now?
HORATIO: I think it lacks of twelve.
MARCELLUS: No, it is struck.   5
HORATIO: Indeed? I heard it not: then it draws near the season
      Wherein the spirit held his wont to walk.

A flourish of trumpets, and ordnance shot off within.

      What does this mean, my lord?
HAMLET: The king doth wake to-night, and takes his rouse,
      Keeps wassail, and the swaggering upspring[1] reels; 10
      And, as he drains his draughts of Rhenish down,
      The kettle-drum and trumpet thus bray out
      The triumph of his pledge.[2]
HORATIO: Is it a custom?
HAMLET: Ay, marry, is't: 15
      But to my mind,—though I am native here,
      And to the manner born,—it is a custom
      More honor'd in the breach than the observance.
      This heavy-headed revel east and west
      Makes us traduc'd and tax'd of other nations: 20
      They clepe us drunkards, and with swinish phrase

---

[11]*brokers:* Procurers.   [1]*upspring:* A dance.   [2]*triumph . . . pledge:* The glory of his toasts.

Soil our addition³; and, indeed, it takes
From our achievements, though perform'd at height,
The pith and marrow of our attribute.

25 So oft it chances in particular men
That, for some vicious mole of nature in them,
As in their birth,—wherein they are not guilty,
Since nature cannot choose his origin,—
By the o'ergrowth of some complexion,

30 Oft breaking down the pales and forts of reason;
Or by some habit, that too much o'erleavens
The form of plausive⁴ manners;—that these men,—
Carrying, I say, the stamp of one defect,
Being nature's livery or fortune's star,—

35 Their virtues else,—be they as pure as grace,
As infinite as man may undergo,—
Shall in the general censure take corruption
From that particular fault: the dram of evil
Doth all the noble substance of a doubt

40 To his own scandal.

HORATIO: Look, my lord, it comes!

Enter Ghost.

HAMLET: Angels and ministers of grace defend us!—
Be thou a spirit of health or goblin damn'd,
Bring with thee airs from heaven or blasts from hell,

45 Be thy intents wicked or charitable,
Thou com'st in such a questionable shape
That I will speak to thee: I'll call thee Hamlet,
King, father, royal Dane: O, answer me!
Let me not burst in ignorance; but tell

50 Why thy canóniz'd bones, hearsèd in death,
Have burst their cerements;⁵ why the sepulchre,
Wherein we saw thee quietly in-urn'd,
Hath op'd his ponderous and marble jaws
To cast thee up again! What may this mean,

55 That thou, dead corpse, again in còmplete steel,
Revisit'st thus the glimpses of the moon,
Making night hideous and we⁶ fools of nature
So horridly to shake our disposition
With thoughts beyond the reaches of our souls?

60 Say, why is this? wherefore? what should we do?

Ghost beckons Hamlet.

---

³*addition:* Reputation.   ⁴*plausive:* Pleasing.   ⁵*cerements:* Burial garments.   ⁶*we:* Us.

HORATIO: It beckons you to go away with it,
    As if it some impartment did desire
    To you alone.
MARCELLUS: Look, with what courteous action
    It waves you to a more removed ground: 65
    But do not go with it.
HORATIO: No, by no means.
HAMLET: It will not speak; then will I follow it.
HORATIO: Do not, my lord.
HAMLET: Why, what should be the fear?   70
    I do not set my life at a pin's fee;
    And for my soul, what can it do to that,
    Being a thing immortal as itself?
    It waves me forth again;—I'll follow it.
HORATIO: What if it tempt you toward the flood, my lord.   75
    Or to the dreadful summit of the cliff
    That beetles o'er his base into the sea,
    And there assume some other horrible form,
    Which might deprive your sovereignty of reason,
    And draw you into madness? think of it: 80
    The very place puts toys of desperation,
    Without more motive, into every brain
    That looks so many fathoms to the sea
    And hears it roar beneath.
HAMLET: It waves me still.—   85
    Go on; I'll follow thee.
MARCELLUS: You shall not go, my lord.
HAMLET: Hold off your hands.
HORATIO: Be rul'd; you shall not go.
HAMLET: My fate cries out,   90
    And makes each petty artery in this body
    As hardy as the Némean lion's[7] nerve.—

Ghost beckons.

    Still am I call'd;—unhand me, gentlemen;—[*Breaking from them*]
    By heaven, I'll make a ghost of him that lets[8] me.
    I say, away!—Go on; I'll follow thee.   95

Exeunt Ghost and Hamlet.

HORATIO: He waxes desperate with imagination.
MARCELLUS: Let's follow; 'tis not fit thus to obey him.
HORATIO: Have after.—To what issue will this come?
MARCELLUS: Something is rotten in the state of Denmark.

---

[7] *Némean lion's:* The fierce lion that Hercules was called upon to slay as one of his "twelve labors."   [8] *lets:* Hinders.

100   HORATIO: Heaven will direct it.
    MARCELLUS: Nay, let's follow him.

Exeunt.

SCENE 5

A more remote part of the platform.

Enter Ghost and Hamlet.

  HAMLET: Where wilt thou lead me? speak, I'll go no further.
  GHOST: Mark me.
  HAMLET: I will.
  GHOST: My hour is almost come,
5   When I to sulphurous and tormenting flames
      Must render up myself.
  HAMLET: Alas, poor ghost!
  GHOST: Pity me not, but lend thy serious hearing
      To what I shall unfold.
10 HAMLET: Speak; I am bound to hear.
  GHOST: So art thou to revenge, when thou shalt hear.
  HAMLET: What?
  GHOST: I am thy father's spirit;
      Doom'd for a certain term to walk the night,
15   And, for the day, confin'd to waste in fires
      Till the foul crimes[1] done in my days of nature
      Are burnt and purg'd away. But that I am forbid
      To tell the secrets of my prison-house,
      I could a tale unfold whose lightest word
20   Would harrow up thy soul; freeze thy young blood;
      Make thy two eyes, like stars, start from their spheres;
      Thy knotted and combined locks to part,
      And each particular hair to stand on end,
      Like quills upon the fretful porcupine:
25   But this eternal blazon[2] must not be
      To ears of flesh and blood.—List, list, O, list!—
      If thou didst ever thy dear father love,—
  HAMLET: O God!
  GHOST: Revenge his foul and most unnatural murder.
30 HAMLET: Murder!
  GHOST: Murder—most foul, as in the best it is;
      But this most foul, strange, and unnatural.
  HAMLET: Haste me to know't, that I, with wings as swift
      As meditation or the thoughts of love,
35   May sweep to my revenge.

---

[1] *foul crimes:* Sins or faults.   [2] *eternal blazon:* Disclosure of information concerning the other world.

GHOST: I find thee apt;
  And duller shouldst thou be than the fat weed
  That rots itself in ease on Lethe³ wharf,
  Wouldst thou not stir in this. Now, Hamlet,
  'Tis given out that, sleeping in mine orchard,   40
  A serpent stung me; so the whole ear of Denmark
  Is by a forged process of my death
  Rankly abus'd: but know, thou noble youth,
  The serpent that did sting thy father's life
  Now wears his crown.   45
HAMLET: O my prophetic soul! mine uncle!
GHOST: Ay, that incestuous, that adulterate beast,
  With witchcraft of his wit, with traitorous gifts,—
  O wicked wit and gifts that have the power
  So to seduce!—won to his shameful lust   50
  The will of my most seeming virtuous queen:
  O Hamlet, what a falling-off was there!
  From me, whose love was of that dignity
  That it went hand in hand even with the vow
  I made to her in marriage: and to decline   55
  Upon a wretch whose natural gifts were poor
  To those of mine!
  But virtue, as it never will be mov'd,
  Though lewdness court it in a shape of heaven;
  So lust, though to a radiant angel link'd,   60
  Will sate itself in a celestial bed
  And prey on garbage.
  But, soft! methinks I scent the morning air;
  Brief let me be.—Sleeping within mine orchard,
  My custom always in the afternoon,   65
  Upon my sécure hour thy uncle stole,
  With juice of cursed hebenon⁴ in a vial,
  And in the porches of mine ears did pour
  The leperous distilment; whose effect
  Holds such an enmity with blood of man   70
  That, swift as quicksilver, it courses through
  The natural gates and alleys of the body;
  And with a sudden vigor it doth posset⁵
  And curd, like eager⁶ droppings into milk,
  The thin and wholesome blood: so did it mine;   75
  And a most instant tetter bark'd about,
  Most lazar-like,⁷ with vile and loathsome crust,
  All my smooth body.

---

³*Lethe:* The river of forgetfulness of the past, out of which the dead drink.   ⁴*hebenon:* Ebony.   ⁵*posset:* Coagulate.
⁶*eager:* Acid.   ⁷*lazar-like:* Like a leper, whose skin is rough.

Thus was I, sleeping, by a brother's hand,
80   Of life, of crown, of queen, at once despatch'd:
Cut off even in the blossoms of my sin,
Unhousel'd, unanointed, unanel'd;
No reckoning made, but sent to my account
With all my imperfections on my head:
85   O, horrible! O, horrible! most horrible!
If thou hast nature in thee, bear it not;
Let not the royal bed of Denmark be
A couch for luxury[8] and damned incest.
But, howsoever thou pursu'st this act,
90   Taint not thy mind, nor let thy soul contrive
Against thy mother aught: leave her to heaven,
And to those thorns that in her bosom lodge,
To prick and sting her. Fare thee well at once!
The glowworm shows the matin to be near,
95   And 'gins to pale his uneffectual fire:
Adieu, adieu! Hamlet, remember me. [Exit.]
HAMLET: O all you host of heaven! O earth! what else?
And shall I couple hell?—O, fie!—Hold, my heart;
And you, my sinews, grow not instant old,
100   But bear me stiffly up.—Remember thee!
Ay, thou poor ghost, while memory holds a seat
In this distracted globe. Remember thee!
Yea, from the table of my memory
I'll wipe away all trivial fond[9] recórds,
105   All saws of books, all forms, all pressures past,
That youth and observation copied there;
And thy commandment all alone shall live
Within the book and volume of my brain,
Unmix'd with baser matter: yes, by heaven.—
110   O most pernicious woman!
O villain, villain, smiling, damned villain!
My tables,—meet it is I set it down,
That one may smile, and smile, and be a villain;
At least, I am sure, it may be so in Denmark:

Writing.

115   So, uncle, there you are. Now to my word;
It is, *Adieu, adieu! remember me:*
I have sworn't.
HORATIO: [*Within*] My lord, my lord,—
MARCELLUS: [*Within*]   Lord Hamlet,—
120   HORATIO: [*Within*]   Heaven secure him!

---

[8] *luxury:* Lechery.   [9] *fond:* Foolish.

MARCELLUS: [*Within*] So be it!
HORATIO: [*Within*] Illo, ho, ho, my lord!
HAMLET: Hillo, ho, ho, boy! come, bird, come.[10]

Enter Horatio and Marcellus.

MARCELLUS: How is't, my noble lord?
HORATIO: What news, my lord?   125
HAMLET: O, wonderful!
HORATIO: Good my lord, tell it.
HAMLET: No; you'll reveal it.
HORATIO: Not I, my lord, by heaven.
MARCELLUS: Nor I, my lord.   130
HAMLET: How say you, then; would heart of man once think it?—
     But you'll be secret?
HORATIO AND MARCELLUS: Ay, by heaven, my lord.
HAMLET: There's ne'er a villain dwelling in all Denmark
     But he's an arrant knave.   135
HORATIO: There needs no ghost, my lord, come from the grave
     To tell us this.
HAMLET: Why, right; you are i' the right;
     And so, without more circumstance at all,
     I hold it fit that we shake hands and part: 140
     You, as your business and desire shall point you,—
     For every man has business and desire,
     Such as it is;—and for mine own poor part,
     Look you, I'll go pray.
HORATIO: These are but wild and whirling words, my lord.   145
HAMLET: I'm sorry they offend you, heartily;
     Yes, faith, heartily.
HORATIO: There's no offence, my lord.
HAMLET: Yes, by Saint Patrick, but there is, Horatio,
     And much offence too. Touching this vision here,—   150
     It is an honest ghost, that let me tell you:
     For you desire to know what is between us,
     O'ermaster't as you may. And now, good friends,
     As you are friends, scholars, and soldiers,
     Give me one poor request.   155
HORATIO: What is't, my lord? we will.
HAMLET: Never make known what you have seen to-night.
HORATIO AND MARCELLUS: My lord, we will not.
HAMLET: Nay, but swear't.
HORATIO: In faith,   160
     My lord, not I.

---

[10]*Hillo . . . come:* Hamlet uses the word "bird" because this is a falconer's call.

MARCELLUS: Nor I, my lord, in faith.

HAMLET: Upon my sword.

MARCELLUS: We have sworn, my lord, already.

165 HAMLET: Indeed, upon my sword, indeed.

GHOST: [*Beneath*] Swear.

HAMLET: Ha, ha, boy! say'st thou so? art thou there, truepenny?—
  Come on,—you hear this fellow in the cellarage,—
  Consent to swear.

170 HORATIO: Propose the oath, my lord.

HAMLET: Never to speak of this that you have seen,
  Swear by my sword.

GHOST: [*Beneath*] Swear.

HAMLET: Hic et ubique?[11] then we'll shift our ground.—

175   Come hither, gentlemen,
  And lay your hands again upon my sword:
  Never to speak of this that you have heard,
  Swear by my sword.

GHOST: [*Beneath*] Swear.

180 HAMLET: Well said! old mole! canst work i' the earth so fast?
  A worthy pioneer![12]—Once more remove, good friends.

HORATIO: O day and night, but this is wondrous strange!

HAMLET: And therefore as a stranger give it welcome.
  There are more things in heaven and earth, Horatio,

185   Than are dreamt of in your philosophy.
  But come;—
  Here, as before, never, so help you mercy,
  How strange or odd soe'er I bear myself,—
  As I, perchance, hereafter shall think meet

190   To put an antic disposition on,—
  That you, at such times seeing me, never shall,
  With arms encumber'd[13] thus, or this headshake,
  Or by pronouncing of some doubtful phrase,
  As, *Well, well, we know;*—or, *We could, an if we would;*—

195   Or, *If we list to speak;*—or, *There be, an if they might;*—
  Or such ambiguous giving out, to note
  That you know aught of me:—this not to do,
  So grace and mercy at your most need help you,
  Swear.

200 GHOST: [*Beneath*] Swear.

HAMLET: Rest, rest, perturbed spirit!—So, gentlemen,
  With all my love I do commend to you:
  And what so poor a man as Hamlet is

---

[11]Hic et ubique?: "Here and everywhere" (Latin). [12]*pioneer:* A soldier who digs trenches and undermines fortresses.
[13]*encumber'd:* Folded.

May do, to express his love and friending to you,
God willing, shall not lack. Let us go in together;   205
And still your fingers on your lips, I pray.
The time is out of joint:—O cursed spite,
That ever I was born to set it right!—
Nay, come, let's go together.

Exeunt.

ACT 2

SCENE 1

A room in Polonius' house.

Enter Polonius and Reynaldo.

POLONIUS: Give him this money and these notes, Reynaldo.
REYNALDO: I will, my lord.
POLONIUS: You shall do marvelous wisely, good Reynaldo,
Before you visit him, to make inquiry
On his behavior.   5
REYNALDO: My lord, I did intend it.
POLONIUS: Marry, well said; very well said. Look you, sir,
Inquire me first what Danskers[1] are in Paris;
And how, and who, what means, and where they keep,
What company, at what expense; and finding,   10
By this encompassment and drift of question,
That they do know my son, come you more nearer
Than your particular demands will touch it:
Take you, as 'twere, some distant knowledge of him;
As thus, *I know his father and his friends,*   15
And in part him;—do you mark this, Reynaldo?
REYNALDO: Ay, very well, my lord.
POLONIUS: *And in part him;—but, you may say, not well:*
But if't be he I mean, he's very wild;
Addicted so and so; and there put on him   20
What forgeries you please; marry, none so rank
As may dishonor him; take heed of that;
But, sir, such wanton, wild, and usual slips
As are companions noted and most known
To youth and liberty.   25
REYNALDO: As gaming, my lord.
POLONIUS: Ay, or drinking, fencing, swearing, quarreling,
Drabbing:[2]—you may go so far.
REYNALDO: My lord, that would dishonor him.

---

[1]*Danskers:* Danes.   [2]*Drabbing:* Going about with loose women.

30   POLONIUS: Faith, no; as you may season it in the charge.
          You must not put another scandal on him,
          That he is open to incontinency;
          That's not my meaning: but breathe his faults so quaintly
          That they may seem the taints of liberty;
35   The flash and outbreak of a fiery mind;
          A savageness in unreclaimed blood,
          Of general assault.
     REYNALDO: But, my good lord,—
     POLONIUS: Wherefore should you do this?
40   REYNALDO: Ay, my lord,
          I would know that.
     POLONIUS: Marry, sir, here's my drift;
          And I believe it is a fetch of warrant:[3]
          You laying these slight sullies on my son.
45   As 'twere a thing a little soil'd i' the working,
          Mark you,
          Your party in converse, him you would sound,
          Having ever seen in the prenominate crimes
          The youth you breathe of guilty, be assur'd
50   He closes with you in this consequence;
          Good sir, or so; or *friend*, or *gentleman*,—
          According to the phrase or the addition[4]
          Of man and country.
     REYNALDO: Very good, my lord.
55   POLONIUS: And then, sir, does he this,—he does,—
          What was I about to say?—By the mass, I was
          About to say something:—where did I leave?
     REYNALDO: At *closes in the consequence*,
          At *friend or so*, and *gentleman*.
60   POLONIUS: At—*closes in the consequence*,—ay, marry;
          He closes with you thus:—*I know the gentleman;*
          I saw him yesterday, or t'other day,
          Or then, or then; with such, or such; and, as you say,
          There was he gaming; there o'ertook in's rouse;
65   *There falling out at tennis: or perchance,*
          I saw him enter such a house of sale,—
          Videlicet,[5] a brothel,—or so forth.—
          See you now;
          Your bait of falsehood takes this carp of truth:
70   And thus do we of wisdom and of reach,
          With windlasses, and with assays of bias,
          By indirections find directions out:

---

[3] *fetch of warrant:* A good device.   [4] *addition:* Form of address.   [5] *Videlicet:* That is; namely (Latin).

So, by my former lecture and advice,
Shall you my son. You have me, have you not?
REYNALDO: My lord, I have.   75
POLONIUS: God b' wi' you; fare you well.
REYNALDO: Good my lord!
POLONIUS: Observe his inclination in yourself.
REYNALDO: I shall, my lord.
POLONIUS: And let him ply his music.   80
REYNALDO: Well, my lord.
POLONIUS: Farewell!

Exit Reynaldo.

Enter Ophelia.

How now, Ophelia! what's the matter?
OPHELIA: Alas, my lord, I have been so affrighted.
POLONIUS: With what, i' the name of God?   85
OPHELIA: My lord, as I was sewing in my chamber,
Lord Hamlet,—with his doublet all unbrac'd;
No hat upon his head; his stockings foul'd,
Ungarter'd, and down-gyved[6] to his ankle;
Pale as his shirt; his knees knocking each other;   90
And with a look so piteous in purport
As if he had been loosed out of hell
To speak of horrors,—he comes before me.
POLONIUS: Mad for thy love?
OPHELIA: My lord, I do not know;   95
But truly I do fear it.
POLONIUS: What said he?
OPHELIA: He took me by the wrist, and held me hard;
Then goes he to the length of all his arm;
And with his other hand thus o'er his brow,   100
He falls to such perusal of my face
As he would draw it. Long stay'd he so;
At last,—a little shaking of mine arm,
And thrice his head thus waving up and down,—
He rais'd a sigh so piteous and profound   105
That it did seem to shatter all his bulk
And end his being; that done, he lets me go:
And, with his head over his shoulder turn'd,
He seem'd to find his way without his eyes;
For out o' doors he went without their help,   110
And to the last bended their light on me.

---

[6]*down-gyved:* Dangling like chains.

POLONIUS: Come, go with me: I will go seek the king.
This is the very ecstasy[7] of love;
Whose violent property fordoes itself,[8]

115

And leads the will to desperate undertakings,
As oft as any passion under heaven
That does afflict our nature. I am sorry,—
What, have you given him any hard words of late?

OPHELIA: No, my good lord; but, as you did command,

120

I did repel his letters, and denied
His access to me.

POLONIUS: That hath made him mad.
I am sorry that with better heed and judgment
I had not quoted him: I fear'd he did but trifle,

125

And meant to wreck thee; but, beshrew my jealousy!
It seems it is as proper to our age
To cast beyond ourselves in our opinions
As it is common for the younger sort
To lack discretion. Come, go we to the king:

130

This must be known; which, being kept close, might move
More grief to hide than hate to utter love.

Exeunt.

SCENE 2

A room in the castle.

Enter King, Queen, Rosencrantz, Guildenstern, and Attendants.

KING: Welcome, dear Rosencrantz and Guildenstern!
Moreover that we much did long to see you,
The need we have to use you did provoke
Our hasty sending. Something have you heard

5

Of Hamlet's transformation; so I call it,
Since nor the exterior nor the inward man
Resembles that it was. What it should be,
More than his father's death, that thus hath put him
So much from the understanding of himself,

10

I cannot dream of: I entreat you both,
That being of so young days brought up with him,
And since so neighbor'd to his youth and humor,
That you vouchsafe your rest here in our court
Some little time: so by your companies

15

To draw him on to pleasures, and to gather,
So much as from occasion you may glean,

---

[7]*ecstasy:* Madness.   [8]*fordoes itself:* Destroys itself.

Whether aught, to us unknown, afflicts him thus,
That, open'd, lies within our remedy.

QUEEN: Good gentlemen, he hath much talk'd of you;   20
And sure I am two men there are not living
To whom he more adheres. If it will please you
To show us so much gentry and good-will
As to expend your time with us awhile,
For the supply and profit of our hope,
Your visitation shall receive such thanks   25
As fits a king's remembrance.

ROSENCRANTZ: Both your majesties
Might, by the sovereign power you have of us,
Put your dread pleasures more into command
Than to entreaty.   30

GUILDENSTERN: We both obey,
And here give up ourselves, in the full bent,
To lay our service freely at your feet,
To be commanded.

KING: Thanks, Rosencrantz and gentle Guildenstern.   35
QUEEN: Thanks, Guildenstern and gentle Rosencrantz:
And I beseech you instantly to visit
My too-much-changed son.—Go, some of you,
And bring these gentlemen where Hamlet is.

GUILDENSTERN: Heavens make our presence and our practices   40
Pleasant and helpful to him!

QUEEN: Ay, amen!

Exeunt Rosencrantz, Guildenstern, and some Attendants.

Enter Polonius.

POLONIUS: The ambassadors from Norway, my good lord,
Are joyfully return'd.

KING: Thou still has been the father of good news.   45
POLONIUS: Have I, my lord? Assure you, my good liege,
I hold my duty, as I hold my soul,
Both to my God and to my gracious king:
And I do think,—or else this brain of mine
Hunts not the trail of policy[1] so sure   50
As it hath us'd to do,—that I have found
The very cause of Hamlet's lunacy.

KING: O, speak of that; that do I long to hear.
POLONIUS: Give first admittance to the ambassadors;
My news shall be the fruit to that great feast.   55
KING: Thyself do grace to them, and bring them in.

----

[1] *trail of policy:* Statecraft.

Exit Polonius.

> He tells me, my sweet queen, that he hath found
> The head and source of all your son's distemper.

QUEEN: I doubt it is no other but the main,—

60   His father's death and our o'erhasty marriage.

KING: Well, we shall sift him.

Re-enter Polonius, with Voltimand and Cornelius.

>   Welcome, my good friends!
> Say, Voltimand, what from our brother Norway?

VOLTIMAND: Most fair return of greetings and desires.

65   Upon our first, he sent out to suppress
> His nephew's levies; which to him appear'd
> To be a preparation 'gainst the Polack;
> But, better look'd into, he truly found
> It was against your highness: whereat griev'd,—

70   That so his sickness, age, and impotence
> Was falsely borne in hand,—sends out arrests
> On Fortinbras; which he, in brief, obeys;
> Receives rebuke from Norway; and, in fine,
> Makes vows before his uncle never more

75   To give the assay of arms against your majesty.
> Whereon old Norway, overcome with joy,
> Gives him three thousand crowns in annual fee;
> And his commission to employ those soldiers,
> So levied as before, against the Polack:

80   With an entreaty, herein further shown, [*gives a paper*]
> That it might please you to give quiet pass
> Through your dominions for this enterprise,
> On such regards of safety and allowance
> As therein are set down.

85 KING: It likes us well;

> And at our more consider'd time we'll read,
> Answer, and think upon this business.
> Meantime we thank you for your well-took labor:
> Go to your rest; at night we'll feast together:

90   Most welcome home!

Exeunt Voltimand and Cornelius.

POLONIUS: This business is well ended.—

> My liege, and madam,—to expostulate
> What majesty should be, what duty is,
> Why day is day, night night, and time is time,

95   Were nothing but to waste night, day, and time.
> Therefore, since brevity is the soul of wit,
> And tediousness the limbs and outward flourishes,

I will be brief:—your noble son is mad:
Mad call I it; for to define true madness,
What is't but to be nothing else but mad?   100
But let that go.
QUEEN: More matter with less art.
POLONIUS: Madam, I swear I use no art at all.
That he is mad, 'tis true 'tis pity;
And pity 'tis 'tis true: a foolish figure;   105
But farewell it, for I will use no art.
Mad let us grant him, then: and now remains
That we find out the cause of this effect;
Or rather say, the cause of this defect,
For this effect defective comes by cause: 110
Thus it remains, and the remainder thus.
Perpend.
I have a daughter,—have whilst she is mine,—
Who, in her duty and obedience, mark,
Hath given me this: now gather, and surmise   115

[Reads]

    To the celestial, and my soul's idol, the most beautified Ophelia,—

That's an ill phrase, a vile phrase,—beautified is a vile phrase: but you shall
hear. Thus:

[Reads]

    In her excellent white bosom, these, &c.

QUEEN: Came this from Hamlet to her?   120
POLONIUS: Good madam, stay a while; I will be faithful.

[Reads]

    Doubt thou the stars are fire;
      Doubt that the sun doth move;
    Doubt truth to be a liar;   125
      But never doubt I love.

    *O dear Ophelia, I am ill at these numbers, I have not art to reckon my groans: but
that I love thee best, O most best, believe it. Adieu.*
    Thine evermore, most dear lady, whilst this machine is to him,
                                    Hamlet

This, in obedience, hath my daughter show'd me:
And more above, hath his solicitings,   130
As they fell out by time, by means, and place,
All given to mine ear.
KING: But how hath she
Receiv'd his love?
POLONIUS: What do you think of me?   135

KING: As of a man faithful and honorable.

POLONIUS: I would fain prove so. But what might you think,
When I had seen this hot love on the wing,—
As I perceiv'd it, I must tell you that,
140   Before my daughter told me,—what might you,
Or my dear majesty your queen here, think,
If I had play'd the desk or table-book;[2]
Or given my heart a winking, mute and dumb;
Or look'd upon this love with idle sight;—
145   What might you think? No, I went round to work,
And my young mistress thus I did bespeak:
Lord Hamlet is a prince out of thy sphere;
This must not be: and then I precepts gave her,
That she should lock herself from his resort,
150   Admit no messengers, receive no tokens.
Which done, she took the fruits of my advice;
And he, repulsed,—a short tale to make,—
Fell into a sadness; then into a fast;
Thence to a watch; thence into a weakness;
155   Thence to a lightness; and, by this declension,
Into the madness wherein now he raves
And all we wail for.

KING: Do you think 'tis this?

QUEEN: It may be, very likely.

160 POLONIUS: Hath there been such a time,—I'd fain know that,—
That I have positively said, *'Tis so,*
When it prov'd otherwise?

KING: Not that I know.

POLONIUS: Take this from this, if this be otherwise: [*Pointing to his head and shoulder*]
165   If circumstances lead me, I will find
Where truth is hid, though it were hid indeed
Within the center.

KING: How may we try it further?

POLONIUS: You know, sometimes he walks for hours together
170   Here in the lobby.

QUEEN: So he does, indeed.

POLONIUS: At such a time I'll loose my daughter to him:
Be you and I behind an arras[3] then;
Mark the encounter: if he love her not,
175   And be not from his reason fall'n thereon,
Let me be no assistant for a state,
But keep a farm and carters.

KING: We will try it.

---

[2]*table-book:* Memorandum pad.   [3]*arras:* Tapestry, hung some distance away from a wall.

QUEEN: But look, where sadly the poor wretch comes reading.
POLONIUS: Away, I do beseech you, both away: 180
    I'll board[4] him presently:—O, give me leave.

Exeunt King, Queen, and Attendants.

Enter Hamlet, reading.

    How does my good Lord Hamlet?
HAMLET: Well, God-a-mercy.
POLONIUS: Do you know me, my lord?
HAMLET: Excellent, excellent well; you're a fishmonger.   185
POLONIUS: Not I, my lord.
HAMLET: Then I would you were so honest a man.
POLONIUS: Honest, my lord!
HAMLET: Ay, sir; to be honest, as this world goes, is to be one man picked out of
    ten thousand.   190
POLONIUS: That's very true, my lord.
HAMLET: For if the sun breed maggots in a dead dog, being a god kissing
    carrion,—Have you a daughter?
POLONIUS: I have, my lord.
HAMLET: Let her not walk i' the sun: conception is a blessing; but not as your   195
    daughter may conceive:—friend, look to't.
POLONIUS: How say you by that?—[*Aside*] Still harping on my daughter:—yet he
    knew me not at first; he said I was a fishmonger: he is far gone, far gone: and
    truly in my youth I suffered much extremity for love; very near this. I'll speak to
    him again.—What do you read, my lord?   200
HAMLET: Words, words, words.
POLONIUS: What is the matter, my lord?
HAMLET: Between who?
POLONIUS: I mean, the matter that you read, my lord.
HAMLET: Slanders, sir: for the satirical slave says here that old men have gray   205
    beards; that their faces are wrinkled; their eyes purging thick amber and plum-
    tree gum; and that they have a plentiful lack of wit, together with most weak
    hams: all which, sir, though I most powerfully and potently believe, yet I hold it
    not honesty to have it thus set down; for you yourself, sir, should be old as I am,
    if, like a crab, you could go backward.   210
POLONIUS: [*Aside*] Though this be madness, yet there is method in't.—Will you walk
    out of the air, my lord?
HAMLET: Into my grave?
POLONIUS: Indeed, that is out o' the air.—[*Aside*] How pregnant[5] sometimes his
    replies are! a happiness that often madness hits on, which reason and sanity   215
    could not so prosperously be delivered of. I will leave him, and suddenly con-
    trive the means of meeting between him and my daughter.—More honorable
    lord, I will most humbly take my leave of you.

---

[4]*board:* Address.   [5]*pregnant:* Ready, and clever.

HAMLET: You cannot, sir, take from me anything that I will more willingly part
220   withal,—except my life, except my life, except my life.
POLONIUS: Fare you well, my lord.
HAMLET: These tedious old fools!

Enter Rosencrantz and Guildenstern.

POLONIUS: You go to seek the Lord Hamlet; there he is.
ROSENCRANTZ: [*To Polonius*] God save you, sir!

Exit Polonius.

225 GUILDENSTERN: Mine honored lord!
ROSENCRANTZ: My most dear lord!
HAMLET: My excellent good friends! How dost thou, Guildenstern? Ah,
        Rosencrantz? Good lads, how do ye both?
ROSENCRANTZ: As the indifferent children of the earth.
230 GUILDENSTERN: Happy in that we are not overhappy; on fortune's cap we are not
        the very button.
HAMLET: Nor the soles of her shoe?
ROSENCRANTZ: Neither, my lord.
HAMLET: Then you live about her waist, or in the middle of her favors?
235 GUILDENSTERN: Faith, her privates we.
HAMLET: In the secret parts of fortune? O, most true; she is a strumpet. What's
        the news?
ROSENCRANTZ: None, my lord, but that the world's grown honest.
HAMLET: Then is doomsday near: but your news is not true. Let me question more
240   in particular: what have you, my good friends, deserved at the hands of fortune,
        that she sends you to prison hither?
GUILDENSTERN: Prison, my lord!
HAMLET: Denmark's a prison.
ROSENCRANTZ: Then is the world one.
245 HAMLET: A goodly one; in which there are many confines, wards, and dungeons,
        Denmark being one o' the worst.
ROSENCRANTZ: We think not so, my lord.
HAMLET: Why, then, 'tis none to you; for there is nothing either good or bad, but
        thinking makes it so: to me it is a prison.
250 ROSENCRANTZ: Why, then, your ambition makes it one; 'tis too narrow for
        your mind.
HAMLET: O God, I could be bounded in a nutshell, and count myself a king of
        infinite space, were it not that I have bad dreams.
GUILDENSTERN: Which dreams, indeed, are ambition; for the very substance of the
255   ambitious is merely the shadow of a dream.
HAMLET: A dream itself is but a shadow.
ROSENCRANTZ: Truly, and I hold ambition of so airy and light a quality that it is but
        a shadow's shadow.
HAMLET: Then are our beggars bodies, and our monarchs and outstretched heroes
260   the beggars' shadows. Shall we to the court? for, by my fay, I cannot reason.

ROSENCRANTZ AND GUILDENSTERN: We'll wait upon you.

HAMLET: No such matter: I will not sort you with the rest of my servants, for, to
speak to you like an honest man, I am most dreadfully attended. But, in the
beaten way of friendship, what make you at Elsinore?

ROSENCRANTZ: To visit you, my lord; no other occasion.   265

HAMLET: Beggar that I am, I am even poor in thanks; but I thank you: and sure,
dear friends, my thanks are too dear a halfpenny. Were you not sent for? Is it
your own inclining? Is it a free visitation? Come, deal justly with me: come,
come; nay, speak.

GUILDENSTERN: What should we say, my lord?   270

HAMLET: Why, anything—but to the purpose. You were sent for; and there is a
kind of confession in your looks, which your modesties have not craft enough to
color: I know the good king and queen have sent for you.

ROSENCRANTZ: To what end, my lord?

HAMLET: That you must teach me. But let me conjure you, by the rights of our fellow-   275
ship, by the consonancy of our youth, by the obligation of our ever-preserved love,
and by what more dear a better proposer could charge you withal, be even and
direct with me, whether you were sent for or no?

ROSENCRANTZ: What say you? [*To Guildenstern*]

HAMLET: [*Aside*] Nay, then, I have an eye of you.—If you love me, hold not off.   280

GUILDENSTERN: My lord, we were sent for.

HAMLET: I will tell you why; so shall my anticipation prevent your discovery,
and your secrecy to the king and queen moult no feather. I have of late,—but
wherefore I know not,—lost all my mirth, forgone all custom of exercises; and,
indeed, it goes so heavily with my disposition that this goodly frame, the earth,   285
seems to me a sterile promontory; this most excellent canopy, the air, look
you, this brave o'erhanging firmament, this majestical roof fretted[6] with golden
fire,—why, it appears no other thing to me than a foul and pestilent congregation of vapors. What a piece of work is man! How noble in reason! how infinite
in faculties! in form and moving, how express and admirable! in action, how   290
like an angel! in apprehension, how like a god! the beauty of the world! the par-
agon of animals! And yet, to me, what is this quintessence of dust? man delights
not me; no, nor woman neither, though by your smiling you seem to say so.

ROSENCRANTZ: My lord, there was no such stuff in my thoughts.

HAMLET: Why did you laugh, then, when I said, *Man delights not me?*   295

ROSENCRANTZ: To think, my lord, if you delight not in man, what lenten
entertainment[7] the players shall receive from you: we coted[8] them on the
way; and hither are they coming, to offer you service.

HAMLET: He that plays the king shall be welcome,—his majesty shall have tribute
of me; the adventurous knight shall use his foil and target; the lover shall not   300
sigh gratis; the humorous[9] man shall end his part in peace; the clown shall make
those laugh whose lungs are tickled o' the sere;[10] and the lady shall say her mind
freely, or the blank verse shall halt[11] for't.—What players are they?

---

[6]*roof fretted:* A roof with fretwork.   [7]*lenten entertainment:* Poor reception.   [8]*coted:* Passed.
[9]*humorous:* Eccentric.   [10]*whose lungs . . . sere:* Whose lungs, for laughter, are easily tickled.   [11]*halt:* Limp.

ROSENCRANTZ: Even those you were wont to take delight in,—the tragedians of
305   the city.

HAMLET: How chances it they travel? their residence, both in reputation and profit,
    was better both ways.

ROSENCRANTZ: I think their inhibition[12] comes by the means of the late
    innovation.

310 HAMLET: Do they hold the same estimation they did when I was in the city? Are
    they so followed?

ROSENCRANTZ: No, indeed, they are not.

HAMLET: How comes it? do they grow rusty?

ROSENCRANTZ: Nay, their endeavor keeps in the wonted pace; but there is, sir, an
315   aery[13] of children, little eyases,[14] that cry out on the top of question, and are most
    tyrannically clapped for't: these are now the fashion; and so berattle the common
    stages,—so they call them,—that many wearing rapiers are afraid of goose-quills,
    and dare scarce come thither.

HAMLET: What, are they children? who maintains 'em? how are they escoted?[15] Will
320   they pursue the quality[16] no longer than they can sing? will they not say afterwards,
    if they should grow themselves to common players,—as it is most like, if their
    means are no better,—their writers do them wrong, to make them exclaim against
    their own succession?

ROSENCRANTZ: Faith, there has been much to do on both sides; and the nation
325   holds it no sin to tarre[17] them to controversy: there was for awhile no money bid
    for argument, unless the poet and the player went to cuffs in the question.

HAMLET: Is't possible?

GUILDENSTERN: O, there has been much throwing about of brains.

HAMLET: Do the boys carry it away?

330 ROSENCRANTZ: Ay, that they do, my lord; Hercules and his load[18] too.

HAMLET: It is not strange; for mine uncle is king of Denmark, and those that would
    make mouths at him while my father lived, give twenty, forty, fifty, an hundred
    ducats a-piece for his picture in little. 'Sblood, there is something in this more
    than natural, if philosophy could find it out.

Flourish of trumpets within.

335 GUILDENSTERN: There are the players.

HAMLET: Gentlemen, you are welcome to Elsinore. Your hands, come: the appur-
    tenance of welcome is fashion and ceremony: let me comply with you in this
    garb; lest my extent[19] to the players, which, I tell you, must show fairly outward,
    should more appear like entertainment[20] than yours. You are welcome: but my
340   uncle-father and aunt-mother are deceived.

GUILDENSTERN: In what, my dear lord?

---

[12]*inhibition:* Difficulty, preventing them from remaining in the capital.   [13]*aery:* Brood of birds of prey.
[14]*little eyases:* Young hawks; a reference to the boys' companies that became popular rivals of Shakespeare's company
of players.   [15]*escoted:* Financially supported.   [16]*quality:* Profession.   [17]*to tarre:* To egg them on.
[18]*his load:* The globe, or the world.   [19]*extent:* Show of friendliness.   [20]*entertainment:* Welcome.

HAMLET: I am but mad north-north-west: when the wind is southerly I know a
   hawk from a handsaw.

Enter Polonius.

POLONIUS: Well be with you, gentlemen!
HAMLET: Hark you, Guildenstern;—and you too;—at each ear a hearer: that great   345
   baby you see there is not yet out of his swathing-clouts.
ROSENCRANTZ: Happily he's the second time come to them; for they say an old man
   is twice a child.
HAMLET: I will prophesy he comes to tell me of the players; mark it. You say right,
   sir: o' Monday morning; 'twas so indeed.   350
POLONIUS: My lord, I have news to tell you.
HAMLET: My lord, I have news to tell you. When Roscius was an actor in
   Rome,—
POLONIUS: The actors are come hither, my lord.
HAMLET: Buzz, buzz!   355
POLONIUS: Upon mine honor,—
HAMLET: Then came each actor on his ass,—
POLONIUS: The best actors in the world, either for tragedy, comedy, history,
   pastoral, pastoral-comical, historical-pastoral, tragical-historical, tragical
   comical-historical-pastoral, scene individable,[21] or poem unlimited:[22] Seneca   360
   cannot be too heavy nor Plautus too light. For the law of writ and the lib-
   erty,[23] these are the only men.
HAMLET: O Jephthah, judge of Israel, what a treasure hadst thou!
POLONIUS: What a treasure had he, my lord?
HAMLET: Why—   365

> One fair daughter, and no more,
> The which he loved passing well.

POLONIUS: [*Aside*] Still on my daughter.
HAMLET: Am I not i' the right, old Jephthah?
POLONIUS: If you call me Jephthah, my lord, I have a daughter that I love passing well.   370
HAMLET: Nay, that follows not.
POLONIUS: What follows, then, my lord?
HAMLET: Why—

> As by lot, God wot,
> and then, you know,   375
> It came to pass, as most like it was,

the first row of the pious chanson will show you more; for look where my
abridgement comes.

---

[21]*scene individable:* A play that observes the unities of time and place.   [22]*poem unlimited:* A typical multiscene
Elizabethan drama, not restricted by the unities; examples are *Hamlet, Macbeth, King Lear,* and nearly any other play
by Shakespeare.   [23]*For the law . . . liberty:* For the laws of the unities and for playwriting that is not so restricted.

Enter four or five Players.

380
You are welcome, masters; welcome, all:—I am glad to see thee well:—welcome, good friends.—O, my old friend! Thy face is valanced since I saw thee last; comest thou to beard me in Denmark?—What, my young lady and mistress! By'r lady, your ladyship is nearer heaven than when I saw you last, by the altitude of a chopine.[24] Pray God, your voice, like a piece of uncurrent gold, be not cracked within the ring.—Masters, you are all welcome. We'll e'en to't like French falcon-

385
ers, fly at anything we see: we'll have a speech straight: come, give us a taste of your quality; come, a passionate speech.

1st Player: What speech, my lord?

Hamlet: I heard thee speak me a speech once,—but it was never acted; or, if it was, not above once; for the play, I remember, pleased not the million; 'twas

390
caviare to the general: but it was,—as I received it, and others whose judgments in such matters cried in the top of mine,—an excellent play, well digested in the scenes, set down with as much modesty as cunning. I remember, one said there were no sallets in the lines to make the matter savory, nor no matter in the phrase that might indite the author of affectation; but called it an honest

395
method, as wholesome as sweet, and by very much more handsome than fine. One speech in it I chiefly loved: 'twas Aeneas' tale to Dido; and thereabout of it especially where he speaks of Priam's slaughter: if it live in your memory, begin at this line;—let me see, let me see:—

The rugged Pyrrhus, like the Hyrcanian beast,[25]

400
—it is not so:—it begins with Pyrrhus:—

The rugged Pyrrhus,—he whose sable arms,
Black as his purpose, did the night resemble
When he lay couched in the ominous horse,—
Hath now this dread and black complexion smear'd

405
With heraldry more dismal; head to foot
Now is he total gules; horridly trick'd
With blood of fathers, mothers, daughters, sons,
Bak'd and impasted with the parching streets,
That lend a tyrannous and damned light

410
To their vile murders: roasted in wrath and fire,
And thus o'er-sized with coagulate gore,
With eyes like carbuncles, the hellish Pyrrhus
Old grandsire Priam seeks.—

So proceed you.

415
Polonius: 'Fore God, my lord, well spoken, with good accent and good discretion.

---

[24] *chopine:* A wooden stilt more than a foot high used under a woman's shoe; a Venetian fashion introduced into England.
[25] *The rugged . . . :* This speech is an example of the declamatory style of drama, which Shakespeare surely must have considered outmoded.

1ST PLAYER: Anon he finds him
    Striking too short at Greeks; his antique sword,
    Rebellious to his arm, lies where it falls,
    Repugnant to command: unequal match'd,
    Pyrrhus at Priam drives; in rage strikes wide;   420
    But with the whiff and wind of his fell sword
    The unnerved father falls. Then senseless Ilium,
    Seeming to feel this blow, with flaming top
    Stoops to his base; and with a hideous crash
    Takes prisoner Pyrrhus' ear: for, lo! his sword,   425
    Which was declining on the milky head
    Of reverend Priam, seem'd i' the air to stick:
    So, as a painted tyrant, Pyrrhus stood;
    And, like a neutral to his will and matter,
    Did nothing.   430
    But as we often see, against some storm,
    A silence in the heavens, the rack stand still,
    The blood winds speechless, and the orb below
    As hush as death, anon the dreadful thunder
    Doth rend the region; so, after Pyrrhus' pause,   435
    A roused vengeance sets him new a-work;
    And never did the Cyclops' hammers fall
    On Mars his armor, forg'd for proof eterne,
    With less remorse than Pyrrhus' bleeding sword
    Now falls on Priam.—   440
    Out, out, thou strumpet, Fortune! All you gods,
    In general synod, take away her power;
    Break all the spokes and fellies from her wheel,
    And bowl the round knave down the hill of heaven,
    As low as to the fiends!   445
POLONIUS: This is too long.
HAMLET: It shall to the barber's, with your beard.—Pr'ythee, say on.—He's for a jig,
    or a tale of bawdry, or he sleeps:—say on; come to Hecuba.
1ST PLAYER: But who, O, who had seen the mobled queen,—
HAMLET: *The mobled queen?*   450
POLONIUS: That's good; *mobled queen* is good.
1ST PLAYER: Run barefoot up and down, threatening the flames
    With bissom rheum; a clout upon that head
    Where late the diadem stood; and, for a robe,
    About her lank and all o'er-teemed loins,   455
    A blanket, in the alarm of fear caught up;—
    Who this had seen, with tongue in venom steep'd,
    'Gainst Fortune's state would treason have pronounc'd:
    But if the gods themselves did see her then,
    When she saw Pyrrhus make malicious sport   460
    In mincing with his sword her husband's limbs,

The instant burst of clamor that she made,—
Unless things mortal move them not at all,—
Would have made milch the burning eyes of heaven,
465   And passion in the gods.

POLONIUS: Look, whether he has not turn'd his color, and has tears in's eyes.—Pray
     you, no more.

HAMLET: 'Tis well; I'll have thee speak out the rest soon.—Good my lord, will you
470   see the players well bestowed? Do you hear, let them be well used; for they are
     the abstracts and brief chronicles of the time; after your death you were better
     have a bad epitaph than their ill report while you live.

POLONIUS: My lord, I will use them according to their desert.

HAMLET: God's bodikin, man, better: use every man after his desert, and who
     should scape whipping? Use them after your own honor and dignity: the less
475   they deserve the more merit is in your bounty. Take them in.

POLONIUS: Come, sirs.

HAMLET: Follow him, friends: we'll hear a play to-morrow.

Exit Polonius with all the Players but the First.

     Dost thou hear me, old friend; can you play the Murder of Gonzago?

1ST PLAYER: Ay, my lord.

480   HAMLET: We'll ha't to-morrow night. You could, for a need, study a speech of some
     dozen or sixteen lines which I would set down and insert in't? could you not?

1ST PLAYER: Ay, my lord.

HAMLET: Very well.—Follow that lord; and look you mock him not.

Exit First Player.

     —My good friends, [*to Rosencrantz and Guildenstern*] I'll leave you till night:
485   you are welcome to Elsinore.

ROSENCRANTZ: Good my lord!

Exeunt Rosencrantz and Guildenstern.

HAMLET: Ay, so God b' wi' ye!—Now I am alone.
     O, what a rogue[26] and peasant slave am I!
     Is it not monstrous that this player here,
490   But in a fiction, in a dream of passion,
     Could force his soul so to his own conceit[27]
     That from her working all his visage wan'd;
     Tears in his eyes, distraction in's aspéct,
     A broken voice, and his whole function suiting
495   With forms to his conceit? And all for nothing!
     For Hecuba!
     What's Hecuba to him or he to Hecuba,
     That he should weep for her? What would he do,

---

[26]*rogue:* Wretched creature.   [27]*conceit:* Conception.

Had he the motive and the cue for passion
That I have? He would drown the stage with tears,   500
And cleave the general ear with horrid speech;
Make mad the guilty, and appal the free;
Confound the ignorant, and amaze, indeed,
The very faculties of eyes and ears.
Yet I,   505
A dull and muddy-mettled rascal, peak,
Like John-a-dreams, unpregnant of my cause,
And can say nothing; no, not for a king
Upon whose property and most dear life
A damn'd defeat was made. Am I a coward?   510
Who calls me villain? breaks my pate across?
Plucks off my beard and blows it in my face?
Tweaks me by the nose? gives me the lie i' the throat,
As deep as to the lungs? who does me this, ha?
'Swounds, I should take it: for it cannot be   515
But I am pigeon-liver'd, and lack gall
To make oppression bitter; or ere this
I should have fatted all the region kites
With this slave's offal:—bloody, bawdy villain!
Remorseless, treacherous, lecherous, kindless villain!   520
O, vengeance!
Why, what an ass am I! This is most brave,
That I, the son of a dear father murder'd,
Prompted to my revenge by heaven and hell,
Must, like a whore, unpack my heart with words,   525
And fall a-cursing like a very drab,
A scullion!
Fie upon't! foh!—About, my brain! I have heard
That guilty creatures, sitting at a play,
Have by the very cunning of the scene   530
Been struck so to the soul that presently
They have proclaim'd their malefactions;
For murder, though it have no tongue, will speak
With most miraculous organ. I'll have these players
Play something like the murder of my father   535
Before mine uncle: I'll observe his looks;
I'll tent[28] him to the quick: if he but blench,
I know my course. The spirit that I have seen
May be the devil: and the devil hath power
To assume a pleasing shape; yea, and perhaps   540
Out of my weakness and my melancholy,—

---

[28] *tent*: Probe.

As he is very potent with such spirits,—
Abuses me to damn me: I'll have grounds
More relative than this:—the play's the thing
545   Wherein I'll catch the conscience of the king. [*Exit.*]

ACT 3

SCENE 1

A room in the castle.

Enter King, Queen, Polonius, Ophelia, Rosencrantz, and Guildenstern.

KING: And can you, by no drift of circumstance,
    Get from him why he puts on this confusion,
    Grating so harshly all his days of quiet
    With turbulent and dangerous lunacy?
5 ROSENCRANTZ: He does confess he feels himself distracted;
    But from what cause he will by no means speak.
GUILDENSTERN: Nor do we find him forward to be sounded;
    But, with a crafty madness, keeps aloof
    When we would bring him on to some confession
10   Of his true state.
QUEEN: Did he receive you well?
ROSENCRANTZ: Most like a gentleman.
GUILDENSTERN: But with much forcing of his disposition.
ROSENCRANTZ: Niggard of question; but, of our demands,
15   Most free in his reply.
QUEEN: Did you assay him
    To any pastime?
ROSENCRANTZ: Madam, it so fell out that certain players
    We o'er-raught on the way: of these we told him;
20   And there did seem in him a kind of joy
    To hear of it: they are about the court;
    And, as I think, they have already order
    This night to play before him.
POLONIUS: 'Tis most true:
25   And he beseech'd me to entreat your majesties
    To hear and see the matter.
KING: With all my heart; and it doth much content me
    To hear him so inclin'd.
    Good gentlemen, give him a further edge,
30   And drive his purpose on to these delights.
ROSENCRANTZ: We shall, my lord.

Exeunt Rosencrantz and Guildenstern.

KING: Sweet Gertrude, leave us too;
    For we have closely sent for Hamlet hither
    That he, as 'twere by accident, may here

Affront Ophelia: 35
Her father and myself,—lawful espials,[1]—
Will so bestow ourselves that, seeing, unseen,
We may of their encounter frankly judge;
And gather by him, as he is behav'd,
If't be the affliction of his love or no 40
That thus he suffers for.

QUEEN: I shall obey you:—
And for your part, Ophelia, I do wish
That your good beauties be the happy cause
Of Hamlet's wildness: so shall I hope your virtues 45
Will bring him to his wonted way again,
To both your honors.

OPHELIA: Madam, I wish it may.

Exit Queen.

POLONIUS: Ophelia, walk you here.—Gracious, so please you,
We will bestow ourselves.—[*To Ophelia*] Read on this book; 50
That show of such an exercise may color
Your loneliness.—We are oft to blame in this,—
'Tis too much prov'd,—that with devotion's visage
And pious action we do sugar o'er
The devil himself. 55

KING: [*Aside*]   O, 'tis too true!
How smart a lash that speech doth give my conscience!
The harlot's cheek, beautied with plastering art,
Is not more ugly to the thing that helps it
Than is my deed to my most painted word: 60
O heavy burden!

POLONIUS: I hear him coming: let's withdraw, my lord.

Exeunt King and Polonius.

Enter Hamlet.

HAMLET: To be, or not to be,—that is the question:
Whether 'tis nobler in the mind to suffer
The slings and arrows of outrageous fortune, 65
Or to take arms against a sea of troubles,
And by opposing end them?—To die,—to sleep,—
No more; and by a sleep to say we end
The heart-ache and the thousand natural shocks
That flesh is heir to,—'tis a consummation 70
Devoutly to be wish'd. To die,—to sleep;—
To sleep! perchance to dream:—ay, there's the rub;

---

[1]*espials:* Spies.

For in that sleep of death what dreams may come,
When we have shuffled off this mortal coil,
75   Must give us pause: there's the respect
That makes a calamity of so long life;
For who would bear the whips and scorns of time,
The oppressor's wrong, the proud man's contumely,
The pangs of déspis'd love, the law's delay,
80   The insolence of office, and the spurns
That patient merit of the unworthy takes,
When he himself might his quietus make
With a bare bodkin?² who would fardels³ bear,
To grunt⁴ and sweat under a weary life,
85   But that the dread of something after death,—
The undiscover'd country, from whose bourn⁵
No traveler returns,—puzzles the will,
And makes us rather bear those ills we have
Than to fly to others that we know not of?
90   Thus conscience does make cowards of us all;
And thus the native hue of resolution
Is sicklied o'er with the pale cast of thought;
And enterprises of great pith and moment,
With this regard, their currents turn awry,
95   And lose the name of action.—Soft you now!
The fair Ophelia.—Nymph, in thy orisons⁶
Be all my sins remember'd.

OPHELIA: Good my lord,
How does your honor for this many a day?
100 HAMLET: I humbly thank you; well, well, well.
OPHELIA: My lord, I have remembrances of yours,
That I have longed long to re-deliver;
I pray you, now receive them.
HAMLET: No, not I;
105 I never gave you aught.
OPHELIA: My honor'd lord, you know right well you did;
And with them, words of so sweet breath compos'd
As made the things more rich: their perfume lost,
Take these again; for to the noble mind
110 Rich gifts wax poor when givers prove unkind.
There, my lord.
HAMLET: Ha, ha! are you honest?
OPHELIA: My lord?
HAMLET: Are you fair?
115 OPHELIA: What means your lordship?

---

²bodkin: Stiletto.   ³fardels: Burdens.   ⁴grunt: Groan.   ⁵bourn: Boundary.   ⁶orisons: Prayers.

HAMLET: That if you be honest and fair, your honesty should admit no discourse to
    your beauty.

OPHELIA: Could beauty, my lord, have better commerce than with honesty?

HAMLET: Ay, truly; for the power of beauty will sooner transform honesty from what
    it is to a bawd than the force of honesty can translate beauty into his likeness: 120
    this was sometime a paradox, but now the time gives it proof. I did love you once.

OPHELIA: Indeed, my lord, you made me believe so.

HAMLET: You should not have believed me; for virtue cannot so inoculate our old
    stock but we shall relish of it: I loved you not.

OPHELIA: I was the more deceived.   125

HAMLET: Get thee to a nunnery: why wouldst thou be a breeder of sinners? I am
    myself indifferent[7] honest; but yet I could accuse me of such things that it were
    better my mother had not borne me: I am very proud, revengeful, ambitious;
    with more offences at my beck than I have thoughts to put them in, imagination
    to give them shape, or time to act them in. What should such fellows as I do   130
    crawling between heaven and earth? We are arrant knaves, all; believe none of
    us. Go thy ways to a nunnery. Where's your father?

OPHELIA: At home, my lord.

HAMLET: Let the doors be shut upon him, that he may play the fool nowhere but
    in's own house. Farewell.   135

OPHELIA: O, help him, you sweet heavens!

HAMLET: If thou dost marry, I'll give thee this plague for thy dowry,—be thou as
    chaste as ice, as pure as snow, thou shalt not escape calumny. Get thee to a
    nunnery, go: farewell. Or, if thou wilt needs marry, marry a fool; for wise men
    know well enough what monsters you make of them. To a nunnery, go; and   140
    quickly too. Farewell.

OPHELIA: O heavenly powers, restore him!

HAMLET: I have heard of your paintings too, well enough; God has given you one
    face and you make yourselves another: you jig, you amble, and you lisp, and
    nickname God's creatures, and make your wantonness your ignorance. Go to,   145
    I'll no more on't; it hath made me mad. I say, we will have no more marriages:
    those that are married already, all but one, shall live; the rest shall keep as they
    are. To a nunnery, go. [*Exit.*]

OPHELIA: O, what a noble mind is here o'erthrown!
    The courtier's, soldier's, scholar's eye, tongue, sword: 150
    The expectancy and rose of the fair state,
    The glass of fashion and the mould of form,
    The observ'd of all observers,—quite, quite down!
    And I, of ladies most deject and wretched
    That suck'd the honey of his music vows,   155
    Now see that noble and most sovereign reason,
    Like sweet bells jangled, out of tune and harsh;
    That unmatch'd form and feature of blown[8] youth

---

[7] *indifferent:* Tolerably.   [8] *blown:* Full-blown.

160 Blasted with ecstasy: O, woe is me,
To have seen what I have seen, see what I see!

Re-enter King and Polonius.

KING: Love! his affections do not that way tend;
Nor what he spake, though it lack'd form a little,
Was not like madness. There's something in his soul
O'er which his melancholy sits on brood;
165 And I do doubt⁹ the hatch and the disclose
Will be some danger: which for to prevent,
I have in quick determination
Thus set it down:—he shall with speed to England
For the demand of our neglected tribute:
170 Haply, the seas and countries different,
With variable objects, shall expel
This something-settled matter in his heart;
Whereon his brains still beating puts him thus
From fashion of himself. What think you on't?
175 POLONIUS: It shall do well: but yet do I believe
The origin and commencement of his grief
Sprung from neglected love.—How now, Ophelia!
You need not tell us what Lord Hamlet said;
We heard it all.—My lord, do as you please;
180 But if you hold it fit, after the play,
Let his queen mother all alone entreat him
To show his grief: let her be round with him;
And I'll be plac'd, so please you, in the ear
Of all their conference. If she finds him not,¹⁰
185 To England send him; or confine him where
Your wisdom best shall think.
KING: It shall be so:
Madness in great ones must not unwatch'd go.

Exeunt.

SCENE 2

A hall in the castle.

Enter Hamlet and certain Players.

HAMLET: Speak the speech, I pray you, as I pronounced it to you, trippingly on the
tongue: but if you mouth it, as many of your players do, I had as lief the town-crier
spoke my lines. Nor do not saw the air too much with your hand, thus; but use all
gently: for in the very torrent, tempest, and, as I may say, the whirlwind of pas-
5   sion, you must acquire and beget a temperance that may give it smoothness. O, it

---

⁹*doubt:* Fear.   ¹⁰*finds him not:* Does not find him out.

offends me to the soul, to hear a robustious periwigpated fellow tear a passion to
tatters, to very rags, to split the ears of the groundlings, who, for the most part, are
capable of nothing but inexplicable dumb shows and noise: I could have such a
fellow whipped for o'erdoing Termagant;[1] it out-herods Herod:[2] pray you, avoid it.

1ST PLAYER: I warrant your honor.   10

HAMLET: Be not too tame neither, but let your own discretion be your tutor; suit the
action to the word, the word to the action; with this special observance, that you
o'erstep not the modesty of nature: for anything so overdone is from the purpose
of playing, whose end, both at the first and now, was and is, to hold, as 'twere, the
mirror up to nature; to show virtue her own feature, scorn her own image, and the   15
very age and body of the time his form and pressure. Now, this overdone or come
tardy off, though it make the unskilful laugh, cannot but make the judicious grieve;
the censure of the which one must, in your allowance, o'erweigh a whole theater of
others. O, there be players that I have seen play,—and heard others praise, and that
highly,—not to speak it profanely, that, neither having the accent of Christians,   20
nor the gait of Christian, pagan, nor man, have so strutted and bellowed that I have
thought some of nature's journeymen had made men, and not made them well,
they imitated humanity so abominably.

1ST PLAYER: I hope we have reformed that indifferently with us, sir.

HAMLET: O, reform it altogether. And let those that play your clowns speak no more   25
than is set down for them: for there be of them that will themselves laugh, to set
on some quantity of barren spectators to laugh too; though, in the meantime,
some necessary question of the play be then to be considered: that's villainous,
and shows a most pitiful ambition in the fool that uses it. Go, make you ready.

Exeunt Players.

Enter Polonius, Rosencrantz, and Guildenstern.

How now, my lord! will the king hear this piece of work?   30
POLONIUS: And the queen, too, and that presently.
HAMLET: Bid the players make haste.

Exit Polonius.

Will you two help to hasten them?
ROSENCRANTZ AND GUILDENSTERN: We will, my lord. [*Exeunt.*]
HAMLET: What, ho, Horatio!   35

Enter Horatio.

HORATIO: Here, sweet lord, at your service.
HAMLET: Horatio, thou art e'en as just a man
    As e'er my conversation cop'd withal.
HORATIO: O, my dear lord,—
HAMLET: Nay, do not think I flatter;   40

---

[1] *Termagant:* A violent pagan deity, supposedly Mohammedan.   [2] *out-herods Herod:* Outrants the ranting Herod, who
figures in medieval drama.

For what advancement may I hope from thee,
That no revénue hast, but thy good spirits,
To feed and clothe thee? Why should the poor be flatter'd?
No, let the candied tongue lick ábsurd pomp;

45   And crook the pregnant hinges of the knee
Where thrift may follow fawning. Dost thou hear?
Since my dear soul was mistress of her choice,
And could of men distinguish, her election
Hath seal'd thee for herself: for thou hast been

50   As one, in suffering all, that suffers nothing;
A man that Fortune's buffets and rewards
Hast ta'en with equal thanks: and bless'd are those
Whose blood and judgment are so well commingled
That they are not a pipe for Fortune's finger

55   To sound what stop she please. Give me that man
That is not passion's slave, and I will wear him
In my heart's core, ay, in my heart of heart,
As I do thee.—Something too much of this.—
There is a play to-night before the king;

60   One scene of it comes near the circumstance
Which I have told thee of my father's death:
I pr'ythee, when thou see'st that act a-foot,
Even with the very comment of thy soul
Observe mine uncle: if this his occulted guilt

65   Do not itself unkennel in one speech,
It is a damned ghost that we have seen;
And my imaginations are as foul
As Vulcan's stithy.[3] Give him heedful note:
For I mine eyes will rivet to his face;

70   And, after, we will both our judgments join
In censure of his seeming.

HORATIO: Well, my lord:
If he steal aught the whilst this play is playing,
And scape detecting, I will pay the theft.

75   HAMLET: They are coming to the play; I must be idle:[4]
Get you a place.

Danish march. A flourish. Enter King, Queen, Polonius, Ophelia, Rosencrantz, Guilden-
stern, and others.

KING: How fares our cousin Hamlet?

HAMLET: Excellent, i'faith; of the chameleon's dish: I eat the air,[5]
promise-crammed: you cannot feed capons so.

80   KING: I have nothing with this answer, Hamlet; these words are not mine.

HAMLET: No, nor mine now. [*To Polonius*] My lord, you played once i' the university,
you say?

---

[3] *stithy:* Smithy.   [4] *idle:* Foolish.   [5] *of the chameleon's . . . the air:* Chameleons were believed to live on air.

POLONIUS: That did I, my lord, and was accounted a good actor.

HAMLET: And what did you enact?

POLONIUS: I did enact Julius Caesar: I was killed i' the Capitol; Brutus killed me.   85

HAMLET: It was a brute part of him to kill so capital a calf there.—Be the players ready.

ROSENCRANTZ: Ay, my lord; they stay upon your patience.

QUEEN: Come hither, my good Hamlet, sit by me.

HAMLET: No, good mother, here's metal more attractive.   90

POLONIUS: O, ho! do you mark that? [*To the King*]

HAMLET: Lady, shall I lie in your lap? [*Lying down at Ophelia's feet*]

OPHELIA: No, my lord.

HAMLET: I mean, my head upon your lap?

OPHELIA: Ay, my lord.   95

HAMLET: Do you think I meant country matters?

OPHELIA: I think nothing, my lord.

HAMLET: That's a fair thought to lie between maids' legs.

OPHELIA: What is, my lord?

HAMLET: Nothing.   100

OPHELIA: You are merry, my lord.

HAMLET: Who, I?

OPHELIA: Ay, my lord.

HAMLET: O, your only jig-maker. What should a man do but be merry? for, look you, how cheerfully my mother looks, and my father died within's two hours.   105

OPHELIA: Nay, 'tis twice two months, my lord.

HAMLET: So long? Nay, then, let the devil wear black, for I'll have a suit of sables. O heavens! die two months ago, and not forgotten yet? Then there's hope a great man's memory may outlive his life half a year: but, by'r lady, he must build churches, then; or else shall he suffer not thinking on, with the hobby-horse,   110 whose epitaph is, *For, O, for, O, the hobby-horse is forgot.*

Trumpets sound. The dumb show enters.

Enter a King and a Queen, very lovingly; the Queen embracing him and he her. She kneels, and makes show of protestation unto him. He takes her up, and declines his head upon her neck: lays him down upon a bank of flowers: she, seeing him asleep, leaves him. Anon comes in a fellow, takes off his crown, kisses it, and pours poison in the King's ears, and exit. The Queen returns; finds the King dead, and makes passionate action. The Poisoner, with some two or three Mutes, comes in again, seeming to lament with her. The dead body is carried away. The Poisoner woos the Queen with gifts: she seems loth and unwilling awhile, but in the end accepts his love.

Exeunt.

OPHELIA: What means this, my lord?

HAMLET: Marry, this is miching mallecho;[6] it means mischief.

OPHELIA: Belike this show imports the argument of the play.

---

[6]*miching mallecho*: A sneaking misdeed.

Enter Prologue.

115   **Hamlet:** We shall know by this fellow: the players cannot keep counsel; they'll tell all.

Ophelia: Will he tell us what this show meant?

Hamlet: Ay, or any show that you'll show him: be not you ashamed to show, he'll
　　　　not shame to tell you what it means.

Ophelia: You are naught, you are naught: I'll mark the play.

120   **Prologue:**

> For us, and for our tragedy,
> Here stooping to your clemency,
> We beg your hearing patiently.

Hamlet: Is this a prologue, or the posy[7] of a ring?

125   **Ophelia:** 'Tis brief, my lord.

Hamlet: As woman's love.

Enter a King and a Queen.

Prologue King: Full thirty times hath Phoebus' cart gone round
　　　　Neptune's salt wash and Tellus' orbed ground,[8]
　　　　And thirty dozen moons with borrow'd sheen
130　　　About the world have times twelve thirties been,
　　　　Since love our hearts, and Hymen did our hands
　　　　Unite commutual in most sacred bands.

Prologue Queen: So many journeys may the sun and moon
　　　　Make us again count o'er ere love be done!
135　　　But, woe is me, you are so sick of late,
　　　　So far from cheer and from your former state
　　　　That I distrust you.[9] Yet, though I distrust,
　　　　Discomfort you, my lord, it nothing must:
　　　　For women's fear and love holds quantity,[10]
140　　　In neither aught, or in extremity.
　　　　Now, what my love is, proof hath made you know;
　　　　And as my love is siz'd, my fear is so:
　　　　Where love is great, the littlest doubts are fear;
　　　　Where little fears grow great, great love grows there.

145   **Prologue King:** Faith, I must leave thee, love, and shortly too;
　　　　My operant powers their functions leave[11] to do:
　　　　And thou shalt live in this fair world behind,
　　　　Honor'd, belov'd; and haply one as kind
　　　　For husband shalt thou,—

150   **Prologue Queen:**　　　　　　O, confound the rest!
　　　　Such love must needs be treason in my breast:
　　　　In second husband let me be accurst!
　　　　None wed the second but who kill'd the first.

---

[7]*posy:* Motto or inscription.　　[8]*orbed ground:* The globe.　　[9]*distrust you:* Worry about you.
[10]*holds quantity:* Correspond in degree.　　[11]*leave:* Cease.

HAMLET: [*Aside*] Wormwood, wormwood.
PROLOGUE QUEEN: The instances that second marriage move   155
    Are base respects of thrift, but none of love:
    A second time I kill my husband, dead,
    When second husband kisses me in bed.
PROLOGUE KING: I do believe you think what now you speak;
    But what we do determine oft we break.   160
    Purpose is but the slave to memory;
    Of violent birth, but poor validity:
    Which now, like fruit unripe, sticks on the tree;
    But fall unshaken when they mellow be.
    Most necessary 'tis that we forget   165
    To pay ourselves what to ourselves is debt:
    What to ourselves in passion we propose,
    The passion ending, doth the purpose lose.
    The violence of either grief or joy
    Their own enactures with themselves destroy: 170
    Where joy most revels grief doth most lament;
    Grief joys, joy grieves, on slender accident.
    This world is not for aye; nor 'tis not strange
    That even our loves should with our fortunes change;
    For 'tis a question left us yet to prove   175
    Whether love lead fortune or else fortune love.
    The great man down, you mark his favorite flies;
    The poor advanc'd makes friends of enemies.
    And hitherto doth love on fortune tend:
    For who not needs shall never lack a friend;   180
    And who in want a hollow friend doth try,
    Directly seasons him his enemy.
    But, orderly to end where I begun,—
    Our wills and fates do so contrary run
    That our devices still are overthrown;   185
    Our thoughts are ours, their ends none of our own:
    So think thou wilt no second husband wed;
    But die thy thoughts when thy first lord is dead.
PROLOGUE QUEEN: Nor earth to me give food, nor heaven light!
    Sport and repose lock from me day and night!   190
    To desperation turn my trust and hope!
    An anchor's[12] cheer in prison be my scope!
    Each opposite, that blanks the face of joy,
    Meet what I would have well, and it destroy!
    Both here and hence, pursue me lasting strife,   195
    If, once a widow, ever I be wife!
HAMLET: If she should break it now! [*To Ophelia*]

---

[12]*anchor's*: Anchorite's, or hermit's.

PROLOGUE KING: 'Tis deeply sworn. Sweet, leave me here awhile;
My spirits grow dull, and fain I would beguile
200   The tedious day with sleep. [*Sleeps*]
PROLOGUE QUEEN: Sleep rock thy brain,
And never come mischance between us twain! [*Exit.*]
HAMLET: Madam, how like you this play?
QUEEN: The lady doth protest too much, methinks.
205   HAMLET: O, but she'll keep her word.
KING: Have you heard the argument? Is there no offence in't?
HAMLET: No, no, they do but jest, poison in jest; no offence i' the world.
KING: What do you call the play?
HAMLET: The Mouse-trap. Marry, how? Tropically.[13] This play is the image of a murder
210   done in Vienna: Gonzago is the duke's name: his wife, Baptista: you shall see anon;
'tis a knavish piece of work: but what o' that? your majesty, and we that have free
souls, it touches us not: let the galled jade wince, our withers are unwrung.

Enter Lucianus.

This is one Lucianus, nephew to the king.
OPHELIA: You are a good chorus, my lord.
215   HAMLET: I could interpret between you and your love, if I could see the puppets
dallying.
OPHELIA: You are keen, my lord, you are keen.
HAMLET: It would cost you a groaning to take off my edge.
OPHELIA: Still better, and worse.
220   HAMLET: So you must take your husbands.—Begin, murderer; pox, leave thy
damnable faces and begin. Come:—*The croaking raven doth bellow for revenge.*
LUCIANUS: Thoughts black, hands apt, drugs fit, and time agreeing;
Confederate season, else no creature seeing;
Thou mixture rank, of midnight weeds collected,
225   With Hecate's ban[14] thrice blasted, thrice infected,
Thy natural magic and dire property
On wholesome life usurp immediately.

Pours the poison into the sleeper's ears.

HAMLET: He poisons him i' the garden for's estate. His name's Gonzago: the story is
extant, and writ in choice Italian: you shall see anon how the murderer gets the
230   love of Gonzago's wife.
OPHELIA: The king rises.
HAMLET: What, frighted with false fire!
QUEEN: How fares my lord?
POLONIUS: Give o'er the play.
235   KING: Give me some light:—away!
ALL: Lights, lights, lights!

---

[13]*Tropically:* Figuratively, or metaphorically; by means of a "trope."   [14]*Hecate's ban:* The spell of the goddess of witchcraft.

Exeunt all but Hamlet and Horatio.

HAMLET:

> Why, let the stricken deer go weep,
> The hart ungalled play;
> For some must watch, while some must sleep: 240
> So runs the world away.—

Would not this, sir, and a forest of feathers, if the rest of my fortunes turn Turk with me, with two Provencial roses on my razed shoes, get me a fellowship in a cry[15] of players, sir?

HORATIO: Half a share.   245

HAMLET: A whole one, I.

> For thou dost know, O Damon dear,
>   This realm dismantled was
> Of Jove himself; and now reigns here
>   A very, very—pajock.[16]   250

HORATIO: You might have rhymed.

HAMLET: O good Horatio, I'll take the ghost's word for a thousand pound. Didst perceive?

HORATIO: Very well, my lord.

HAMLET: Upon the talk of the poisoning,—   255

HORATIO: I did very well note him.

HAMLET: Ah, ha!—Come, some music! come, the recorders!—

> For if the king like not the comedy,
> Why, then, belike,—he likes it not, perdy.

Come, some music!   260

Re-enter Rosencrantz and Guildenstern.

GUILDENSTERN: Good my lord, vouchsafe me a word with you.

HAMLET: Sir, a whole history.

GUILDENSTERN: The king, sir,—

HAMLET: Ay, sir, what of him?

GUILDENSTERN: Is, in his retirement, marvelous distempered.   265

HAMLET: With drink, sir?

GUILDENSTERN: No, my lord, rather with choler.

HAMLET: Your wisdom should show itself more richer to signify this to his doctor; for, for me to put him to his purgation would perhaps plunge him into far more choler.

GUILDENSTERN: Good my lord, put your discourse into some frame, and start not so   270
wildly from my affair.

HAMLET: I am tame, sir:—pronounce.

---

[15]*cry:* Company.   [16]*pajock:* Peacock.

GUILDENSTERN: The queen, your mother, in most great affliction of spirit, hath sent
      me to you.

275   HAMLET: You are welcome.

GUILDENSTERN: Nay, good my lord, this courtesy is not of the right breed. If it shall
      please you to make me a wholesome answer, I will do you mother's commandment:
      if not, your pardon and my return shall be the end of my business.

HAMLET: Sir, I cannot.

280   GUILDENSTERN: What, my lord?

HAMLET: Make you a wholesome answer; my wit's diseas'd: but, sir, such answer as
      I can make, you shall command; or, rather, as you say, my mother: therefore no
      more, but to the matter: my mother, you say,—

ROSENCRANTZ: Then thus she says: your behavior hath struck her into amazement
285   and admiration.

HAMLET: O wonderful son, that can so astonish a mother!—But is there no sequel
      at the heels of this mother's admiration?

ROSENCRANTZ: She desires to speak with you in her closet[17] ere you go to bed.

HAMLET: We shall obey, were she ten times our mother. Have you any further
290   trade with us?

ROSENCRANTZ: My lord, you once did love me.

HAMLET: So I do still, by these pickers and stealers.[18]

ROSENCRANTZ: Good, my lord, what is your cause of distemper? you do, surely, bar
      the door upon your own liberty if you deny your griefs to your friend.

295   HAMLET: Sir, I lack advancement.

ROSENCRANTZ: How can that be, when you have the voice of the king himself for
      your succession in Denmark?

HAMLET: Ay, but While the grass grows,—the proverb is something musty.

Re-enter the Players, with recorders.

      O, the recorders:—let me see one.—To withdraw with you:—why do you go
300   about to recover the wind of me, as if you would drive me into a toil?

GUILDENSTERN: O, my lord, if my duty be too bold, my love is too unmannerly.

HAMLET: I do not well understand that. Will you play upon this pipe?

GUILDENSTERN: My lord, I cannot.

HAMLET: I pray you.

305   GUILDENSTERN: Believe me, I cannot.

HAMLET: I do beseech you.

GUILDENSTERN: I know no touch of it, my lord.

HAMLET: 'Tis as easy as lying: govern these ventages[19] with your finger and thumb,
      give it breath with your mouth, and it will discourse most eloquent music. Look
310   you, these are the stops.

GUILDENSTERN: But these cannot I command to any utterance of harmony; I have
      not the skill.

HAMLET: Why, look you now, how unworthy a thing you make of me! You would
      play upon me; you would seem to know my stops; you would pluck out the heart of

---

[17]*closet:* Boudoir.   [18]*pickers and stealers:* Fingers.   [19]*ventages:* Holes.

my mystery; you would sound me from my lowest note to the top of my compass: 315
and there is much music, excellent voice, in this little organ; yet cannot you make
it speak. 'Sblood, do you think that I am easier to be played on than a pipe? Call
me what instrument you will, though you can fret me you cannot play upon me.

Enter Polonius.

    God bless you, sir!
POLONIUS: My lord, the queen would speak with you, and presently.   320
HAMLET: Do you see yonder cloud that's almost in shape of a camel?
POLONIUS: By the mass, and 'tis like a camel indeed.
HAMLET: Methinks it is like a weasel.
POLONIUS: It is backed like a weasel.
HAMLET: Or like a whale?   325
POLONIUS: Very like a whale.
HAMLET: Then will I come to my mother by and by.—They fool me to the top of
    my bent.—I will come by and by.
POLONIUS: I will say so.
HAMLET: By and by is easily said.   330

Exit Polonius.

    Leave me, friends.

Exeunt Rosencrantz, Guildenstern, Horatio, and Players.

    'Tis now the very witching time of night,
    When churchyards yawn, and hell itself breathes out
    Contagion to this world: now could I drink hot blood,
    And do such bitter business as the day   335
    Would quake to look on. Soft! now to my mother.—
    O heart, lose not thy nature; let not ever
    The soul of Nero[20] enter this firm bosom:
    Let me be cruel, not unnatural:
    I will speak daggers to her, but use none;   340
    My tongue and soul in this be hypocrites,—
    How in my words soever she be shent,
    To give them seals never, my soul, consent! [*Exit.*]

SCENE 3

A room in the castle.

Enter King, Rosencrantz, and Guildenstern.

KING: I like him not; nor stands it safe with us
    To let his madness range. Therefore prepare you;
    I your commission with forthwith despatch,
    And he to England shall along with you:

---

[20]*Nero:* The Roman emperor Nero killed his mother, a crime of which Hamlet does not want to be guilty.

5   The terms of our estate may not endure
       Hazard so dangerous as doth hourly grow
       Out of his lunacies.
     GUILDENSTERN: We will ourselves provide:
       Most holy and religious fear it is
10   To keep those many many bodies safe
       That live and feed upon your majesty.
     ROSENCRANTZ: The single and peculiar life is bound,
       With all the strength and armor of the mind,
       To keep itself from 'noyance; but much more
15   That spirit upon whose weal depend and rest
       The lives of many. The cease of majesty
       Dies not alone; but like a gulf doth draw
       What's near it with it: it is a massy wheel,
       Fix'd on the summit of the highest mount,
20   To whose huge spokes ten thousand lesser things
       Are mortis'd and adjoin'd; which, when it falls,
       Each small annexment, petty consequence,
       Attends the boisterous ruin. Never alone
       Did the king sigh, but with a general groan.
25   KING: Arm you, I pray you, to this speedy voyage;
       For we will fetters put upon this fear,
       Which now goes too free-footed.
     ROSENCRANTZ AND GUILDENSTERN: We will haste us.

Exeunt Rosencrantz and Guildenstern.

Enter Polonius.

     POLONIUS: My lord, he's going to his mother's closet:
30   Behind the arras I'll convey myself
       To hear the process; I'll warrant she'll tax him home:[1]
       And, as you said, and wisely was it said,
       'Tis meet that some more audience than a mother,
       Since nature makes them partial, should o'erhear
35   The speech, of vantage. Fare you well, my liege:
       I'll call upon you ere you go to bed,
       And tell you what I know.
     KING: Thanks, dear my lord.

Exit Polonius.

       O, my offence is rank, it smells to heaven;
40   It hath the primal eldest curse upon't,—
       A brother's murder!—Pray can I not,
       Though inclination be as sharp as will:

---

[1]*tax him home:* Reprove him properly.

My stronger guilt defeats my strong intent;
And, like a man to double business bound,
I stand in pause where I shall first begin,   45
And both neglect. What if this cursed hand
Were thicker than itself with brother's blood,—
Is there not rain enough in the sweet heavens
To wash it white as snow? Whereto serves mercy
But to confront the visage of offence?   50
And what's in prayer but this twofold force,—
To be forestalled ere we come to fall,
Or pardon'd being down? Then I'll look up;
My fault is past. But, O, what form of prayer
Can serve my turn? Forgive me my foul murder?—   55
That cannot be; since I am still possess'd
Of those effects for which I did the murder,—
My crown, mine own ambition, and my queen.
May one be pardon'd and retain the offence?[2]
In the corrupted currents of this world   60
Offence's gilded hand may shove by justice;
And oft 'tis seen the wicked prize itself
Buys out the law: but 'tis not so above;
There is no shuffling,—there the action lies
In his true nature; and we ourselves compell'd,   65
Even to the teeth and forehead of our faults,
To give in evidence. What then? what rests?[3]
Try what repentance can: what can it not?
Yet what can it when one can not repent?
O wretched state! O bosom black as death!   70
O limed[4] soul, that, struggling to be free,
Art more engag'd! Help, angels! make assay:
Bow, stubborn knees; and, heart, with strings of steel,
Be soft as sinews of the new-born babe!
All may be well. [*Retires and kneels*]   75

Enter Hamlet.

HAMLET: Now might I do it pat, now he is praying;
And now I'll do't—and so he goes to heaven;
And so am I reveng'd:—that would be scann'd:
A villain kills my father; and for that,
I, his sole son, do this same villain send   80
To heaven.
O, this is hire and salary, not revenge.
He took my father grossly, full of bread;

---

[2] *retain the offence:* Retain the gains won by the offense.   [3] *rests:* Remains.   [4] *limed:* Snared.

With all his crimes broad blown, as flush as May;
85 And how his audit stands who knows save heaven?
But in our circumstance and course of thought
'Tis heavy with him: and am I, then, reveng'd,
To take him in the purging of his soul,
When he is fit and season'd for his passage?
90 No.
Up, sword; and know thou a more horrid hent:[5]
When he is drunk, asleep, or in his rage;
Or in the incestuous pleasure of his bed;
At gaming, swearing; or about some act
95 That has no relish of salvation in't;—
Then trip him, that his heels may kick at heaven;
And that his soul may be as damn'd and black
As hell, whereto it goes. My mother stays:
This physic but prolongs thy sickly days. [*Exit.*]

The King rises and advances.

100 KING: My words fly up, my thoughts remain below:
Words without thoughts never to heaven go. [*Exit.*]

SCENE 4

Another room in the castle.

Enter Queen and Polonius.

POLONIUS: He will come straight. Look you lay home to him:
Tell him his pranks have been too broad to bear with,
And that your grace hath screen'd and stood between
Much heat and him. I'll silence me e'en here.
5 Pray you, be round with him.
HAMLET: [*Within*] Mother, mother, mother!
QUEEN: I'll warrant you:
Fear me not:—withdraw, I hear him coming.

Polonius goes behind the arras. Enter Hamlet.

HAMLET: Now, mother, what's the matter?
10 QUEEN: Hamlet, thou hast thy father much offended.
HAMLET: Mother, you have my father much offended.
QUEEN: Come, come, you answer with an idle tongue.
HAMLET: Go, go, you question with a wicked tongue.
QUEEN: Why, how now, Hamlet!
15 HAMLET: What's the matter now?
QUEEN: Have you forgot me?
HAMLET: No, by the rood, not so:

[5]*hent:* Opportunity.

You are the queen, your husband's brother's wife;
And,—would it were not so!—you are my mother.

QUEEN: Nay, then, I'll set those to you that can speak.   20

HAMLET: Come, come, and sit you down; you shall not budge;
You go not till I set you up a glass
Where you may see the inmost part of you.

QUEEN: What wilt thou do? thou wilt not murder me?—
Help, help, ho!   25

POLONIUS: [Behind] What, ho! help, help, help!

HAMLET: How now! a rat?
[Draws.]
Dead, for a ducat, dead! [Makes a pass through the arras]

POLONIUS: [Behind] O, I am slain! [Falls and dies.]   30

QUEEN: O me, what hast thou done?

HAMLET: Nay, I know not:
Is it the king? [Draws forth Polonius]

QUEEN: O, what a rash and bloody deed is this!

HAMLET: A bloody deed!—almost as bad, good mother,   35
As kill a king and marry with his brother.

QUEEN: As kill a king!

HAMLET: Ay, lady, 'twas my word.—
Thou wretched, rash, intruding fool, farewell! [To Polonius]
I took thee for thy better: take thy fortune;   40
Thou find'st to be too busy is some danger.—
Leave wringing of your hands: peace; sit you down,
And let me wring your heart: for so I shall,
If it be made of penetrable stuff;
If damned custom have not braz'd it so   45
That it is proof and bulwark against sense.

QUEEN: What have I done, that thou dar'st wag thy tongue
In noise so rude against me?

HAMLET: Such an act
That blurs the grace and blush of modesty;   50
Calls virtue hypocrite; takes off the rose
From the fair forehead of an innocent love,
And sets a blister there; makes marriage-vows
As false as dicers' oaths: O, such a deed
As from the body of contraction plucks   55
The very soul, and sweet religion makes
A rhapsody of words: heaven's face doth glow;
Yea, this solidity and compound mass,
With tristful[1] visage, as against the doom,
Is thought-sick at the act.   60

QUEEN: Ah me, what act,

---

[1] *tristful:* Gloomy.

That roars so loud, and thunders in the index?
HAMLET: Look here upon this picture and on this,—
    The counterfeit presentment of two brothers.
65   See what grace was seated on this brow;
    Hyperion's curls; the front of Jove himself;
    An eye like Mars, to threaten and command;
    A station like the herald Mercury
    New-lighted on a heaven-kissing hill;
70   A combination and a form, indeed,
    Where every god did seem to set his seal,
    To give the world assurance of a man:
    This was your husband.—Look you now, what follows:
    Here is your husband, like a mildew'd ear
75   Blasting his wholesome brother. Have you eyes?
    Could you on this fair mountain leave to feed,
    And batten on this moor? Ha! have you eyes?
    You cannot call it love; for at your age
    The hey-day in the blood is tame, it's humble,
80   And waits upon the judgment: and what judgment
    Would step from this to this? Sense, sure, you have,
    Else could you not have motion: but sure that sense
    Is apoplex'd: for madness would not err;
    Nor sense to ecstasy was ne'er so thrill'd
85   But it reserv'd some quantity of choice
    To serve in such a difference. What devil was't
    That thus hath cozen'd you at hoodman-blind?[2]
    Eyes without feeling, feeling without sight,
    Ears without hand or eyes, smelling sans all,
90   Or but a sickly part of one true sense
    Could not so mope.
    O shame! where is thy blush! Rebellious hell,
    If thou canst mutine in a matron's bones,
    To flaming youth let virtue be as wax,
95   And melt in her own fire: proclaim no shame
    When the compulsive ardor gives the charge,
    Since frost itself as actively doth burn,
    And reason panders[3] will.
QUEEN: O Hamlet, speak no more:
100   Thou turn'st mine eyes into my very soul;
    And there I see such black and grained spots
    As will not leave their tinct.[4]
HAMLET: Nay, but to live
    In the rank sweat of an enseamed bed,
105   Stew'd in corruption, honeying and making love

---

[2]*cozen'd . . . hoodman-blind:* Tricked you at blindman's buff.   [3]*panders:* Becomes subservient to.
[4]*As will not . . . tinct:* As will not yield up their color.

Over the nasty sty,—

QUEEN: O, speak to me no more;
These words like daggers enter in mine ears;
No more, sweet Hamlet.

HAMLET: A murderer and a villain;   110
A slave that is not twentieth part the tithe
Of your precedent lord; a vice of kings;[5]
A cutpurse of the empire and the rule,
That from a shelf the precious diadem stole,
And put it in his pocket!   115

QUEEN: No more.

HAMLET: A king of shreds and patches,—

Enter Ghost.

Save me, and hover o'er me with your wings,
You heavenly guards!—What would your gracious figure?

QUEEN: Alas, he's mad!   120

HAMLET: Do you not come your tardy son to chide,
That, laps'd in time and passion, lets go by
The important acting of your dread command?
O, say!

GHOST: Do not forget: this visitation   125
Is but to whet thy almost blunted purpose.
But, look, amazement on thy mother sits:
O, step between her and her fighting soul,—
Conceit in weakest bodies strongest works,—
Speak to her, Hamlet.   130

HAMLET: How is it with you, lady?

QUEEN: Alas, how is't with you,
That you do bend your eye on vacancy,
And with the incorporal air do hold discourse?
Forth at your eyes your spirits wildly peep;   135
And, as the sleeping soldiers in the alarm,
Your bedded hair, like life in excrements,[6]
Starts up and stands on end. O gentle son,
Upon the heat and flame of thy distemper
Sprinkle cool patience. Whereon do you look?   140

HAMLET: On him, on him! Look you, how pale he glares!
His form and cause conjoin'd, preaching to stones,
Would make them capable.—Do not look upon me;
Lest with this piteous action you convert
My stern effects: then what I have to do   145
Will want true color; tears perchance for blood.

---

[5]*a vice of kings:* A buffoon among kings; the character "Vice" in morality plays.   [6]*in excrements:* In outgrowths or extremities.

QUEEN: To whom do you speak this?
HAMLET: Do you see nothing there?
QUEEN: Nothing at all; yet all that is I see.
150 HAMLET: Nor did you nothing hear?
QUEEN: No, nothing but ourselves.
HAMLET: Why, look you there! look, how it steals away!
    My father, in his habit as he liv'd!
    Look, where he goes, even now, out at the portal!

Exit Ghost.

155 QUEEN: This is the very coinage of your brain:
    This bodiless creation ecstasy
    Is very cunning in.
HAMLET: Ecstasy!
    My pulse, as yours, doth temperately keep time.
160   And makes as healthful music: it is not madness
    That I have utter'd: bring me to the test,
    And I the matter will re-word; which madness
    Would gambol from. Mother, for love of grace,
    Lay not that flattering unction to your soul,
165   That not your trespass, but my madness speaks:
    It will but skin and film the ulcerous place,
    Whilst rank corruption, mining all within,
    Infects unseen. Confess yourself to Heaven;
    Repent what's past; avoid what is to come;
170   And do not spread the compost on the weeds,
    To make them ranker. Forgive me this my virtue;
    For in the fatness[7] of these pursy times
    Virtue itself of vice must pardon beg,
    Yea, curb and woo for leave to do him good.
175 QUEEN: O Hamlet, thou hast cleft my heart in twain.
HAMLET: O, throw away the worser part of it,
    And live the purer with the other half.
    Good-night: but go not to mine uncle's bed;
    Assume a virtue, if you have it not.
180   That monster custom, who all sense doth eat,
    Of habits devil, is angel yet in this,—
    That to the use of actions fair and good
    He likewise gives a frock or livery
    That aptly is put on. Refrain to-night;
185   And that shall lend a kind of easiness
    To the next abstinence: the next more easy;
    For use almost can change the stamp of nature,
    And either curb the devil, or throw him out

---

[7]*fatness:* Corruption.

With wondrous potency. Once more, good-night:
And when you are desirous to be bless'd,   190
I'll blessing beg of you.—For this same lord [*pointing to Polonius*]
I do repent: but Heaven hath pleas'd it so,
To punish me with this, and this with me,
That I must be their[8] scourge and minister.
I will bestow him, and will answer well   195
The death I gave him. So, again, good-night.—
I must be cruel only to be kind:
Thus bad begins and worse remains behind.—
One word more, good lady.

QUEEN: What shall I do?   200

HAMLET: Not this, by no means, that I bid you do:
Let the bloat king tempt you again to bed;
Pinch wanton on your cheek; call you his mouse;
And let him, for a pair of reechy kisses,
Or paddling in your neck with his damn'd fingers,   205
Make you to ravel all this matter out,
That I essentially am not in madness,
But mad in craft. 'Twere good you let him know;
For who that's but a queen, fair, sober, wise,
Would from a paddock,[9] from a bat, a gib,[10]   210
Such dear concernings hide? who would do so?
No, in despite of sense and secrecy,
Unpeg the basket on the house's top,
Let the birds fly, and, like the famous ape,
To try conclusions, in the basket creep,   215
And break your own neck down.

QUEEN: Be thou assur'd, if words be made of breath
And breath of life, I have not life to breathe
What thou hast said to me.

HAMLET: I must to England; you know that?   220

QUEEN: Alack,
I had forgot: 'tis so concluded on.

HAMLET: There's letters seal'd: and my two school-fellows,—
Whom I will trust as I will adders fang'd,
They bear the mandate; they must sweep my way,   225
And marshal me to knavery. Let it work;
For 'tis the sport to have the éngineer
Hoist with his own petard: and't shall go hard
But I will delve one yard below their mines,
And blow them at the moon: O, 'tis most sweet,   230
When in one line two crafts directly meet.—
This man shall set me packing:

---

[8] *their:* Heaven's, or the heavens'.   [9] *paddock:* Toad.   [10] *gib:* Tomcat.

I'll lug the guts into the neighbor room.—
Mother, good-night.—Indeed, this counsellor
235   Is now most still, most secret, and most grave,
Who was in life a foolish prating knave.
Come, sir, to draw toward an end with you:—
Good-night, mother.

Exeunt severally; Hamlet dragging out Polonius.

ACT 4

SCENE 1

A room in the castle.

Enter King, Queen, Rosencrantz, and Guildenstern.

KING: There's matter in these sighs, these prófound heaves:
    You must translate: 'tis fit we understand them.
    Where is your son?
QUEEN: Bestow this place on us a little while. [*To Rosencrantz and Guildenstern,*
5   *who go out*]
    Ah, my good lord, what have I seen to-night!
KING: What, Gertrude? How does Hamlet?
QUEEN: Mad as the sea and wind, when both contend
    Which is the mightier: in his lawless fit,
10   Behind the arras hearing something stir,
    He whips his rapier out, and cries, A *rat, a rat!*
    And, in this brainish apprehension,[1] kills
    The unseen good old man.
KING: O heavy deed!
15   It had been so with us had we been there:
    His liberty is full of threats to all;
    To you yourself, to us, to every one.
    Alas, how shall this bloody deed be answer'd?
    It will be laid to us, whose providence
20   Should have kept short, restrain'd, and out of haunt
    This mad young man: but so much was our love,
    We would not understand what was most fit;
    But, like the owner of a foul disease,
    To keep it from divulging, let it feed
25   Even on the pith of life. Where is he gone?
QUEEN: To draw apart the body he hath kill'd:
    O'er whom his very madness, like some ore
    Among a mineral of metals base,
    Shows itself pure; he weeps for what is done.

---

[1] *brainish apprehension:* Mad notion.

KING: O Gertrude, come away!   30
 The sun no sooner shall the mountains touch
 But we will ship him hence: and this vile deed
 We must, with all our majesty and skill,
 Both countenance and excuse.—Ho, Guildenstern!

Enter Rosencrantz and Guildenstern.

 Friends both, go join you with some further aid: 35
 Hamlet in madness hath Polonius slain,
 And from his mother's closet hath he dragg'd him:
 Go seek him out; speak fair, and bring the body
 Into the chapel. I pray you, haste in this.

Exeunt Rosencrantz and Guildenstern.

 Come, Gertrude, we'll call up our wisest friends;   40
 And let them know both what we mean to do
 And what's untimely done: so haply slander,—
 Whose whisper o'er the world's diameter,
 As level as the cannon to his blank,
 Transports his poison'd shot,—may amiss our name,   45
 And hit the woundless air.—O, come away!
 My soul is full of discord and dismay.

Exeunt.

SCENE 2

Another room in the castle.

Enter Hamlet.

HAMLET: Safely stowed.
ROSENCRANTZ AND GUILDENSTERN: [*Within*] Hamlet! Lord Hamlet!
HAMLET: What noise? who calls on Hamlet?
 O, here they come.

Enter Rosencrantz and Guildenstern.

ROSENCRANTZ: What have you done, my lord, with the dead body?   5
HAMLET: Compounded it with dust, whereto 'tis kin.
ROSENCRANTZ: Tell us where 'tis, that we may take it thence,
 And bear it to the chapel.
HAMLET: Do not believe it.
ROSENCRANTZ: Believe what?   10
HAMLET: That I can keep your counsel, and not mine own. Besides, to be demanded
 of a sponge!—what replication should be made by the son of a king?
ROSENCRANTZ: Take you me for a sponge, my lord?
HAMLET: Ay, sir; that soaks up the king's countenance, his rewards, his authorities.
 But such officers do the king best service in the end: he keeps them, like an ape,   15

in the corner of his jaw; first mouthed, to be last swallowed: when he needs what
you have gleaned, it is but squeezing you, and, sponge, you shall be dry again.

ROSENCRANTZ: I understand you not, my lord.

HAMLET: I am glad of it: a knavish speech sleeps in a foolish ear.

20   ROSENCRANTZ: My lord, you must tell us where the body is, and go with us to the king.

HAMLET: The body is with the king, but the king is not with the body. The king is
 a thing,—

GUILDENSTERN: A thing, my lord!

HAMLET: Of nothing: bring me to him.

25   Hide fox, and all after.

Exeunt.

SCENE 3

Another room in the castle.

Enter King, attended.

KING: I have sent to seek him, and to find the body.
 How dangerous is it that this man goes loose!
 Yet must not we put the strong law on him:
 He's lov'd of the distracted multitude,
5   Who like not in their judgment, but their eyes;
 And where 'tis so, the offender's scourge is weigh'd,
 But never the offence. To bear all smooth and even,
 This sudden sending him away must seem
 Deliberate pause: diseases desperate grown
10   By desperate appliance are reliev'd,
 Or not at all.

Enter Rosencrantz.

How now! what hath befallen!

ROSENCRANTZ: Where the dead body is bestow'd, my lord,
 We cannot get from him.

15   KING: But where is he?

ROSENCRANTZ: Without, my lord; guarded, to know your pleasure.

KING: Bring him before us.

ROSENCRANTZ: Ho, Guildenstern! bring in my lord.

Enter Hamlet and Guildenstern.

KING: Now, Hamlet, where's Polonius?

20   HAMLET: At supper.

KING: At supper! where?

HAMLET: Not where he eats, but where he is eaten: a certain convocation of politic
 worms are e'en at him. Your worm is your only emperor for diet: we fat all creatures else to fat us, and we fat ourselves for maggots: your fat king and your lean
25   beggar is but variable service,—two dishes, but to one table: that's the end.

KING: Alas, alas!

HAMLET: A man may fish with the worm that hath eat of a king, and eat of the fish
    that hath fed of that worm.

KING: What does thou mean by this?

HAMLET: Nothing but to show you how a king may go a progress through the guts   30
    of a beggar.

KING: Where is Polonius?

HAMLET: In heaven; send thither to see: if your messenger find him not there,
    seek him i' the other place yourself. But, indeed, if you find him not within this
    month, you shall nose him as you go up the stairs into the lobby.   35

KING: Go seek him there. [*To some Attendants*]

HAMLET: He will stay till ye come.

Exeunt Attendants.

KING: Hamlet, this deed, for thine especial safety,—
    Which we do tender, as we dearly grieve
    For that which thou hast done,—must send thee hence   40
    With fiery quickness: therefore prepare thyself;
    The bark is ready, and the wind at help,
    The associates tend, and everything is bent
    For England.

HAMLET: For England!   45

KING: Ay, Hamlet.

HAMLET: Good.

KING: So is it, if thou knew'st our purposes.

HAMLET: I see a cherub that sees them.—But, come; for England!—
    Farewell, dear mother.   50

KING: Thy loving father, Hamlet.

HAMLET: My mother: father and mother is man and wife; man and wife is one flesh;
    and so, my mother.—Come, for England! [*Exit.*]

KING: Follow him at foot; tempt him with speed aboard;
    Delay it not; I'll have him hence to-night: 55
    Away! for everything is seal'd and done
    That else leans on the affair, pray you, make haste.

Exeunt Rosencrantz and Guildenstern.

And, England, if my love thou hold'st at aught,—
    As my great power thereof may give the sense,
    Since yet thy cicatrice looks raw and red   60
    After the Danish sword, and thy free awe
    Pays homage to us,—thou mayst not coldly set
    Our sovereign process; which imports at full,
    By letters conjuring to that effect,
    The present death of Hamlet. Do it, England;   65
    For like the hectic in my blood he rages,

And thou must cure me: till I know 'tis done,
Howe'er my haps, my joys will ne'er begin. [*Exit.*]

SCENE 4

A plain in Denmark.

Enter Fortinbras, and Forces marching.

FORTINBRAS: Go, from me greet the Danish king:
    Tell him that, by his license, Fortinbras
    Craves the conveyance of a promis'd march
    Over his kingdom. You know the rendezvous,
5   If that his majesty would aught with us,
    We shall express our duty in his eye,
    And let him know so.
CAPTAIN: I will do't, my lord.
FORTINBRAS: Go softly on.

Exeunt Fortinbras and Forces.

Enter Hamlet, Rosencrantz, Guildenstern, &c.

10 HAMLET: Good sir, whose powers are these?
CAPTAIN: They are of Norway, sir.
HAMLET: How purpos'd, sir, I pray you?
CAPTAIN: Against some part of Poland.
HAMLET: Who commands them, sir?
15 CAPTAIN: The nephew to old Norway, Fortinbras.
HAMLET: Goes it against the main of Poland, sir,
    Or for some frontier?
CAPTAIN: Truly to speak, and with no addition,
    We go to gain a little patch of ground
20   That hath in it no profit but the name.
    To pay five ducats, five, I would not farm it;
    Nor will it yield to Norway or the Pole
    A ranker[1] rate should it be sold in fee.
HAMLET: Why, then the Polack never will defend it.
25 CAPTAIN: Yes, it is already garrison'd.
HAMLET: Two thousand souls and twenty thousand ducats
    Will not debate the question of this straw:
    This is the imposthume[2] of much wealth and peace,
    That inward breaks, and shows no cause without
30   Why the man dies.—I humbly thank you, sir.
CAPTAIN: God b' wi' you, sir. [*Exit.*]
ROSENCRANTZ: Will't please you go, my lord?
HAMLET: I'll be with you straight. Go a little before.

---

[1]*ranker:* Dearer.   [2]*imposthume:* Ulcer.

Exeunt all but Hamlet.

How all occasions do inform against me,
And spur my dull revenge! What is a man,   35
If his chief good and market of his time
Be but to sleep and feed? a beast, no more.
Sure he that made us with such large discourse,[3]
Looking before and after, gave us not
That capability and godlike reason   40
To fust[4] in us unus'd. Now, whether it be
Bestial oblivion or some craven scruple
Of thinking too precisely on the event,—
A thought which, quarter'd, hath but one part wisdom
And ever three parts coward,—I do not know   45
Why yet I live to say, *This thing's to do;*
Sith[5] I have cause, and will, and strength, and means
To do't. Examples, gross as earth, exhort me:
Witness this army, of such mass and charge,
Led by a delicate and tender prince;   50
Whose spirit, with divine ambition puff'd,
Makes mouths at the invisible event;
Exposing what is mortal and unsure
To all that fortune, death, and danger dare,
Even for an egg-shell. Rightly to be great   55
Is not to stir without great argument,
But greatly to find quarrel in a straw
When honor's at the stake. How stand I, then,
That have a father kill'd, a mother stain'd,
Excitements of my reason and my blood,   60
And let all sleep? while, to my shame, I see
The imminent death of twenty thousand men,
That, for a fantasy and trick of fame,
Go to their graves like beds; fight for a plot
Whereon the numbers cannot try the cause,   65
Which is not tomb enough and continent[6]
To hide the slain?—O, from this time forth,
My thoughts be bloody, or be nothing worth! [*Exit.*]

SCENE 5

Elsinore. A room in the castle.

Enter Queen and Horatio.

QUEEN: I will not speak with her.
HORATIO: She is importunate; indeed, distract:
Her mood will needs be pitied.

---

[3]*discourse:* Reasoning faculty.   [4]*fust:* Grow musty.   [5]*Sith:* Since.   [6]*continent:* Container.

	QUEEN:	What would she have?
5	HORATIO:	She speaks much of her father; says she hears

QUEEN: What would she have?

5   HORATIO: She speaks much of her father; says she hears
     There's tricks i' the world; and hems, and beats her heart;
     Spurns enviously at straws; speaks things in doubt,
     That carry but half sense: her speech is nothing,
     Yet the unshapèd use of it doth move
10   The hearers to collection; they aim at it,
     And botch the words up fit to their own thoughts;
     Which, as her winks, and nods, and gestures yield them,
     Indeed would make one think there might be thought,
     Though nothing sure, yet much unhappily.
15   'Twere good she were spoken with; for she may strew
     Dangerous conjectures in ill-breeding minds.
     QUEEN: Let her come in.

Exit Horatio.

     To my sick soul, as sin's true nature is,
     Each toy seems prologue to some great amiss:
20   So full of artless jealousy is guilt,
     It spills itself in fearing to be spilt.

Re-enter Horatio and Ophelia.

     OPHELIA: Where is the beauteous majesty of Denmark?
     QUEEN: How now, Ophelia!
     OPHELIA: [*Sings*]

25   How should I your true love know
                  From another one?
              By his cockle hat and staff,
                  And his sandal shoon.

     QUEEN: Alas, sweet lady, what imports this song?
30   OPHELIA: Say you? nay, pray you, mark.

     [*Sings*]

              He is dead and gone, lady,
                  He is dead and gone;
              At his head a grass green turf,
                  At his heels a stone.

35   QUEEN: Nay, but, Ophelia,—
     OPHELIA: Pray you, mark.

     [*Sings*]

              White his shroud as the mountain snow,

Enter King.

QUEEN: Alas, look here, my lord.
OPHELIA: [*Sings*]

> Larded with sweet flowers;
> Which bewept to the grave did go
> With true-love showers.   40

KING: How do you, pretty lady?
OPHELIA: Well, God 'ild you![1] They say the owl was a baker's daughter.
    Lord, we know what we are, but know not what we may be.   45
    God be at your table!
KING: Conceit upon her father.
OPHELIA: Pray you, let's have no words of this; but when they ask you what it
    means, say you this:

[*Sings*]

> To-morrow is Saint Valentine's day   50
>   All in the morning betime,
> And I a maid at your window,
>   To be your Valentine.
> Then up he rose, and donn'd his clothes,
>   And dupp'd the chamber-door;   55
> Let in the maid, that out a maid
>   Never departed more.

KING: Pretty Ophelia!
OPHELIA: Indeed, la, without an oath, I'll make an end on't;

[*Sings*]

> By Gis[2] and by Saint Charity,   60
>   Alack, and fie for shame!
> Young men will do't, if they come to't;
>   By cock, they are to blame.
> Quoth she, before you tumbled me,
>   You promis'd me to wed.   65
> So would I ha' done, by yonder sun,
>   An thou hadst not come to my bed.

KING: How long hath she been thus?
OPHELIA: I hope all will be well. We must be patient: but I cannot choose but
    weep, to think they should lay him i' the cold ground. My brother shall know of   70
    it: and so I thank you; for your good counsel.—Come, my coach!—Good-night,
    ladies; good-night, sweet ladies; good-night, good-night. [*Exit.*]
KING: Follow her close; give her good watch, I pray you.

Exit Horatio.

---

[1]*ild you:* Yield you—i.e., reward you.   [2]*Gis:* A contraction for "by Jesus."

O, this is the poison of deep grief; it springs
75 All from her father's death. O Gertrude, Gertrude,
When sorrows come, they come not single spies,
But in battalions! First, her father slain:
Next, your son gone; and he most violent author
Of his own just remove: the people muddied,
80 Thick and unwholesome in their thoughts and whispers
For good Polonius' death; and we have done but greenly
In hugger-mugger[3] to inter him: poor Ophelia
Divided from herself and her fair judgment,
Without the which we are pictures, or mere beasts:
85 Last, and as much containing as all these,
Her brother is in secret come from France;
Feeds on his wonder, keeps himself in clouds,
And wants not buzzers to infect his ear
With pestilent speeches of his father's death;
90 Wherein necessity, of matter beggar'd,
Will nothing stick our person to arraign
In ear and ear. O my dear Gertrude, this,
Like to a murdering piece,[4] in many places
Gives me superfluous death.

A noise within.

95 QUEEN: Alack, what noise is this?
KING: Where are my Switzers?[5] let them guard the door.

Enter a Gentleman.

What is the matter?

GENTLEMAN: Save yourself, my lord:
The ocean, overpeering of his list,
100 Eats not the flats with more impetuous haste
Than young Laertes, in a riotous head,
O'erbears your officers. The rabble call him lord;
And, as the world were now but to begin,
Antiquity forgot, custom not known,
105 The ratifiers and props of every word,
They cry, *Choose we, Laertes shall be king!*
Caps, hands, and tongues applaud it to the clouds,
Laertes shall be king, Laertes king!
QUEEN: How cheerfully on the false trail they cry!
110 O, this is counter, you false Danish dogs!

---

[3]*in hugger-mugger:* In great secrecy and haste.   [4]*murdering piece:* A cannon.   [5]*Switzers:* Bodyguard of Swiss mercenaries.

KING: The doors are broke.

Noise within.

Enter Laertes armed; Danes following.

LAERTES: Where is this king?—Sirs, stand you all without.

DANES: No, let's come in.

LAERTES: I pray you, give me leave.

DANES: We will, we will. [*They retire without the door.*]   115

LAERTES: I thank you:—keep the door.—O thou vile king,
    Give me my father!

QUEEN: Calmly, good Laertes.

LAERTES: That drop of blood that's calm proclaims me bastard;
    Cries cuckold to my father; brands the harlot   120
    Even here, between the chaste unsmirched brow
    Of my true mother.

KING: What is the cause, Laertes,
    That thy rebellion looks so giant-like?—
    Let him go, Gertrude; do not fear our person: 125
    There's such divinity doth hedge a king,
    That treason can but peep to what it would,
    Acts little of his will.—Tell me, Laertes,
    Why thou art thus incens'd.—Let him go, Gertrude:—
    Speak, man.   130

LAERTES: Where is my father?

KING: Dead.

QUEEN: But not by him.

KING: Let him demand his fill.

LAERTES: How came he dead? I'll not be juggled with: 135
    To hell, allegiance! vows, to the blackest devil!
    Conscience and grace, to the profoundest pit!
    I dare damnation:—to this point I stand,—
    That both the worlds I give to negligence,
    Let come what comes; only I'll be reveng'd   140
    Most thoroughly for my father.

KING: Who shall stay you?

LAERTES: My will, not all the world:
    And for my means, I'll husband them so well,
    They shall go far with little.   145

KING: Good Laertes,
    If you desire to know the certainty
    Of your dear father's death, is't writ in your revenge
    That, sweepstake, you will draw both friend and foe,
    Winner or loser?   150

LAERTES: None but his enemies.

KING: Will you know them, then?
LAERTES: To his good friends thus wide I'll ope my arms;
    And, like the kind life-rendering pelican,[6]
155   Repast them with my blood.
KING: Why, now you speak
    Like a good child and a true gentleman.
    That I am guiltless of your father's death,
    And am most sensible in grief for it,
160   It shall as level to your judgment pierce
    As day does to your eye.
DANES: [*Within*]   Let her come in.
LAERTES: How now! what noise is that?

Re-enter Ophelia, fantastically dressed with straws and flowers.

    O heat, dry up my brains! tears seven times salt
165   Burn out the sense and virtue of mine eyes!—
    By heaven, thy madness shall be paid by weight
    Till our scale turn the beam. O rose of May!
    Dear maid, kind sister, sweet Ophelia!—
    O heavens! is't possible a young maid's wits
170   Should be as mortal as an old man's life!
    Nature is fine in love; and where 'tis fine
    It sends some precious instance of itself
    After the thing it loves.
OPHELIA: [*Sings*]

175   They bore him barefac'd on the bier;
            Hey no nonny, nonny, hey nonny;
          And on his grave rain'd many a tear,—
            Fare you well, my dove!

LAERTES: Hadst thou thy wits, and didst persuade revenge,
180   It could not move thus.
OPHELIA: You must sing, *Down-a-down, and you call him a-down-a.* O, how the
    wheel becomes it! It is the false steward, that stole his master's daughter.
LAERTES: This nothing's more than matter.
OPHELIA: There's rosemary, that's for remembrance; pray, love, remember: and
185   there is pansies that's for thoughts.
LAERTES: A document in madness,—thoughts and remembrance fitted.
OPHELIA: There's fennel for you, and columbines:—there's rue for you; and here's
    some for me:—we may call it herb-grace o' Sundays:—
    O, you must wear your rue with a difference.—There's a daisy:—I would give
190   you some violets, but they withered all when my father died:—they say, he
    made a good end,—

---

[6]*life-rendering pelican:* The mother pelican was believed to draw blood from herself to feed her young.

[*Sings*]

    For bonny sweet Robin is all my joy,—

Laertes: Thoughts and affliction, passion, hell itself,
   She turns to favor and to prettiness.

Ophelia: [*Sings*]   195

    And will he not come again?
    And will he not come again?
      No, no, he is dead,
      Go to thy death-bed,
    He never will come again.   200
    His beard was as white as snow
    All flaxen was his poll:
      He is gone, he is gone,
      And we cast away moan:
    God ha' mercy on his soul!   205

And of all Christian souls, I pray God.—God b' wi' ye. [*Exit.*]

Laertes: Do you see this, O God?

King: Laertes, I must commune with your grief,
   Or you deny me right. Go but apart,
   Make choice of whom your wisest friends you will,   210
   And they shall hear and judge 'twixt you and me:
   If by direct or by collateral hand
   They find us touch'd, we will our kingdom give,
   Our crown, our life, and all that we call ours,
   To you in satisfaction; but if not,   215
   Be you content to lend your patience to us,
   And we shall jointly labor with your soul
   To give it due content.

Laertes: Let this be so;
   His means of death, his obscure burial,—   220
   No trophy, sword, nor hatchment[7] o'er his bones
   No noble rite nor formal ostentation,—
   Cry to be heard, as 'twere from heaven to earth,
   That I must call't in question.

King: So you shall;   225
   And where the offence is, let the great axe fall.
   I pray you, go with me.

Exeunt.

---

[7] *hatchment:* A tablet with coat of arms.

SCENE 6

Another room in the castle.

Enter Horatio and a Servant.

Horatio: What are they that would speak with me?
Servant: Sailors, sir: they say they have letters for you.
Horatio: Let them come in.—

Exit Servant.

5   I do not know from what part of the world
       I should be greeted, if not from Lord Hamlet.

Enter Sailors.

1st Sailor: God bless you, sir.
Horatio: Let him bless thee too.
1st Sailor: He shall, sir, an't please him. There's a letter for you, sir; it comes from
       the ambassador that was bound for England; if your name be Horatio, as I am let
10   to know it is.
Horatio: [Reads] *Horatio, when thou shalt have overlooked this, give these fellows some
       means to the king: they have letters for him. Ere we were two days old at sea, a pirate
       of very warlike appointment gave us chase. Finding ourselves too slow of sail, we put
       on a compelled valor; and in the grapple I boarded them; on the instant they got clear
15   of our ship; so I alone became their prisoner. They have dealt with me like thieves of
       mercy: but they knew what they did; I am to do a good turn for them. Let the king
       have the letters I have sent; and repair thou to me with as much haste as thou wouldst
       fly death. I have words to speak in thine ear will make thee dumb; yet are they much
       too light for the bore of the matter. These good fellows will bring thee where I am.*
20   *Rosencrantz and Guildenstern hold their course for England: of them I have much to
       tell thee. Farewell. He that thou knowest thine.*

Hamlet

       Come, I will give you way for these your letters;
       And do't the speedier, that you may direct me
25   To him from whom you brought them.

Exeunt.

SCENE 7

Another room in the castle.

Enter King and Laertes.

King: Now must your conscience my acquittance seal,
       And you must put me in your heart for friend,
       Sith you have heard, and with a knowing ear,
       That he which hath your noble father slain
5   Pursu'd my life.
Laertes: It well appears:—but tell me
       Why you proceeded not against these feats,

So crimeful and so capital in nature.
As by your safety, wisdom, all things else,
You mainly were stirr'd up.   10

KING: O, for two special reasons;
Which may to you, perhaps, seem much unsinew'd,
But yet to me they are strong. The queen his mother
Lives almost by his looks; and for myself,—
My virtue or my plague, be it either which,—   15
She's so conjunctive to my life and soul,
That, as the star moves not but in his sphere,
I could not but by her. The other motive,
Why to a public count I might not go,
Is the great love the general gender bear him;   20
Who, dipping all his faults in their affection,
Would, like the spring that turneth wood to stone,
Convert his gyves to graces; so that my arrows,
Too slightly timber'd for so loud a wind,
Would have reverted to my bow again,   25
And not where I had aim'd them.

LAERTES: And so have I a noble father lost;
A sister driven into desperate terms,—
Whose worth, if praises may go back again,
Stood challenger on mount of all the age   30
For her perfections:—but my revenge will come.

KING: Break not your sleeps for that: you must not think
That we are made of stuff so flat and dull
That we can let our beard be shook with danger,
And think it pastime. You shortly shall hear more: 35
I lov'd your father, and we love ourself;
And that, I hope, will teach you to imagine,—

Enter a Messenger.

How now! what news?
MESSENGER: Letters, my lord, from Hamlet:
This to your majesty; this to the queen.   40
KING: From Hamlet! Who brought them?
MESSENGER: Sailors, my lord, they say; I saw them not:
They were given me by Claudio,—he receiv'd them
Of him that brought them.
KING: Laertes, you shall hear them.—Leave us.   45

Exit Messenger.

[*Reads*] *High and mighty,—You shall know I am set naked on your kingdom.*
To-morrow shall I beg leave to see your kingly eyes: when I shall, first asking your
pardon thereunto, recount the occasions of my sudden and more strange return.
                                                                  Hamlet

What should this mean? Are all the rest come back?   50

Or is it some abuse,[1] and no such thing?

LAERTES: Know you the hand?

KING: 'Tis Hamlet's character:[2]—*Naked*,—
And in a postscript here, he says, *alone*.
55 Can you advise me?

LAERTES: I am lost in it, my lord. But let him come;
It warms the very sickness in my heart,
That I shall live, and tell him to his teeth,
Thus diddest thou.

60 KING: If it be so, Laertes,—
As how should it be so? how otherwise?—
Will you be rul'd by me?

LAERTES: Ay, my lord:
So you will not o'errule me to a peace.

65 KING: To thine own peace. If he be now return'd,—
As checking at his voyage, and that he means
No more to undertake it,—I will work him
To an exploit, now ripe in my device,
Under the which he shall not choose but fall:
70 And for his death no wind of blame shall breathe;
But even his mother shall uncharge the practice
And call it accident.

LAERTES: My lord, I will be rul'd;
The rather if you could devise it so
75 That I might be the organ.

KING: It falls right.
You have been talk'd of since your travel much,
And that in Hamlet's hearing, for a quality
Wherein they say you shine: your sum of parts
80 Did not together pluck such envy from him
As did that one; and that, in my regard,
Of the unworthiest siege.

LAERTES: What part is that, my lord?

KING: A very riband in the cap of youth,
85 Yet needful too; for youth no less becomes
The light and careless livery that it wears
Than settled age his sables and his weeds,
Importing health and graveness.—Two months since,
Here was a gentleman of Normandy,—
90 I've seen myself, and serv'd against, the French,
And they can well on horseback: but this gallant
Had witchcraft in't; he grew unto his seat;
And to such wondrous doing brought his horse,

---

[1] *abuse*: Ruse.   [2] *character*: Handwriting.

As he had been incorps'd and demi-natur'd[3]
With the brave beast: so far he topp'd my thought,   95
That I, in forgery of shapes and tricks,[4]
Come short of what he did.

LAERTES: A Norman was't?

KING: A Norman.

LAERTES: Upon my life, Lamond.   100

KING: The very same.

LAERTES: I know him well: he is the brooch, indeed,
   And gem of all the nation.

KING: He made confession of you;
   And gave you such a masterly report   105
   For art and exercise in your defence,
   And for your rapier most especially,
   That he cried out, 'twould be a sight indeed
   If one could match you: the scrimers[5] of their nation,
   He swore, had neither motion, guard, nor eye,   110
   If you oppos'd them. Sir, this report of his
   Did Hamlet so envenom with his envy,
   That he could nothing do but wish and beg
   Your sudden coming o'er, to play with him.
   Now, out of this,—   115

LAERTES: What out of this, my lord?

KING: Laertes, was your father dear to you?
   Or are you like the painting of a sorrow,
   A face without a heart?

LAERTES: Why ask you this?   120

KING: Not that I think you did not love your father;
   But that I know love is begun by time;
   And that I see, in passages of proof,[6]
   Time qualifies the spark and fire of it.
   There lives within the very flame of love   125
   A kind of wick or snuff that will abate it;
   And nothing is at a like goodness still;
   For goodness, growing to a pleurisy,[7]
   Dies in his own too much: that we would do
   We should do when we would; for this *would* changes,   130
   And hath abatements and delays as many
   As there are tongues, or hands, or accidents;
   And then this *should* is like a spendthrift sigh
   That hurts by easing. But to the quick o' the ulcer:
   Hamlet comes back: what would you undertake   135

---

[3]*As . . . demi-natur'd:* Made as one body and formed into half man, half horse—or centaur.   [4]*in forgery . . . tricks:*
In imagining tricks of horsemanship.   [5]*scrimers:* Fencers.   [6]*passages of proof:* The evidence of experience.
[7]*pleurisy:* Plethora, an excess of blood.

> To show yourself your father's son in deed
> More than in words?
> LAERTES: To cut his throat i' the church.
> KING: No place, indeed, should murder sanctuarize;
> 140   Revenge should have no bounds. But, good Laertes,
> Will you do this, keep close within your chamber.
> Hamlet return'd shall know you are come home:
> We'll put on those shall praise your excellence,
> And set a double varnish on the fame
> 145   The Frenchman gave you; bring you, in fine, together,
> And wager on yours heads: he, being remiss,[8]
> Most generous, and free from all contriving,
> Will not peruse the foils; so that, with ease,
> Or with a little shuffling, you may choose
> 150   A sword unbated, and, in a pass of practice,
> Requite him for your father.
> LAERTES: I will do't it:
> And, for that purpose, I'll anoint my sword.
> I bought an unction of a mountebank,
> 155   So mortal that but dip a knife in it,
> Where it draws blood no cataplasm so rare,[9]
> Collected from all simples that have virtue
> Under the moon, can save the thing from death
> That is but scratch'd withal: I'll touch my point
> 160   With this contagion, that, if I gall him slightly,
> It may be death.
> KING: Let's further think of this;
> Weigh what convenience both of time and means
> May fit us to our shape: if this should fail,
> 165   And that our drift look through our bad performance,
> 'Twere better not assay'd: therefore this project
> Should have a back or second, that might hold
> If this should blast in proof. Soft! let me see:—
> We'll make a solemn wager on your cunnings,—
> 170   I ha't:
> When in your motion you are hot and dry,—
> As make your bouts more violent to that end,—
> And that he calls for drink, I'll have prepar'd him
> A chalice for the nonce;[10] whereon but sipping,
> 175   If he by chance escape your venom'd stuck
> Our purpose may hold there.

Enter Queen.

> How now, sweet queen!

---

[8]*remiss:* Unguarded and free from suspicion.   [9]*no cataplasm so rare:* No poultice, however remarkably efficacious.
[10]*nonce:* Purpose.

QUEEN: One woe doth tread upon another's heel,
    So fast they follow:—your sister's drown'd, Laertes.
LAERTES: Drown'd! O, where? 180
QUEEN: There is a willow grows aslant a brook,
    That shows his hoar leaves in the glassy stream;
    There with fantastic garlands did she come
    Of crowflowers, nettles, daisies, and long purples,
    That liberal shepherds give a grosser name, 185
    But our cold maids do dead men's fingers call them.
    There, on the pendant boughs her coronet weeds
    Clambering to hang, an envious[11] sliver broke;
    When down her weedy trophies and herself
    Fell in the weeping brook. Her clothes spread wide; 190
    And, mermaid-like, awhile they bore her up:
    Which time she chanted snatches of old tunes;
    As one incapable of her own distress,
    Or like a creature native and indu'd
    Unto that element: but long it could not be 195
    Till that her garments, heavy with their drink,
    Pull'd the poor wretch from her melodious lay
    To muddy death.
LAERTES: Alas, then, she is drown'd?
QUEEN: Drown'd, drown'd. 200
LAERTES: Too much of water hast thou, poor Ophelia,
    And therefore I forbid my tears: but yet
    It is our trick; nature her custom holds,
    Let shame say what it will: when these are gone,
    The woman will be out.[12]—Adieu, my lord: 205
    I have a speech of fire, that fain would blaze,
    But that this folly douts it.[13] [*Exit.*]
KING: Let's follow, Gertrude;
    How much I had to do to calm his rage!
    Now fear I this will give it start again; 210
    Therefore let's follow.

Exeunt.

ACT 5

SCENE 1

A churchyard.

Enter two Clowns[1] with spades, &c.

1ST CLOWN: Is she to be buried in Christian burial that wilfully seeks her own
    salvation?

---

[11]*envious*: Malicious.   [12]*The woman . . . out*: I.e., "I shall be ruthless."   [13]*douts it*: Drowns it.
[1]*Clowns*: Rustic fellows.

2ND CLOWN: I tell thee she is; and therefore make her grave straight: the crowner[2] hath sat on her, and finds it Christian burial.

5   1ST CLOWN: How can that be, unless she drowned herself in her own defence?

2ND CLOWN: Why, 'tis found so.

1ST CLOWN: It must be *se offendendo*,[3] it cannot be else. For here lies the point: if I drown myself wittingly, it argues an act: and an act hath three branches; it is to act, to do, and to perform: argal,[4] she drowned herself wittingly.

10   2ND CLOWN: Nay, but hear you, goodman delver,—

1ST CLOWN: Give me leave. Here lies the water; good: here stands the man; good: if the man go to this water and drown himself, it is, will he, nill he, he goes,—mark you that: but if the water come to him and drown him, he drowns not himself: argal, he that is not guilty of his own death shortens not his own life.

15   2ND CLOWN: But is this law?

1ST CLOWN: Ay, marry, is't; crowner's quest law.

2ND CLOWN: Will you ha' the truth on't? If this had not been a gentlewoman she should have been buried out of Christian burial.

1ST CLOWN: Why, there thou say'st: and the more pity that great folks should have
20   countenance in this world to drown or hang themselves more than their even Christian.[5]—Come, my spade. There is no ancient gentlemen but gardeners, ditchers, and grave-makers; they hold up Adam's profession.

2ND CLOWN: Was he a gentleman?

1ST CLOWN: He was the first that ever bore arms.

25   2ND CLOWN: Why, he had none.

1ST CLOWN: What, art a heathen? How dost thou understand the Scripture? The Scripture says, Adam digged: could he dig without arms? I'll put another question to thee: if thou answerest me not to the purpose, confess thyself,[6]—

2ND CLOWN: Go to.

30   1ST CLOWN: What is he that builds stronger than either the mason, the shipwright, or the carpenter?

2ND CLOWN: The gallows-maker; for that frame outlives a thousand tenants.

1ST CLOWN: I like thy wit well, in good faith: the gallows does well; but how does it well? it does well to those that do ill: now thou dost ill to say the gallows is built
35   stronger than the church: argal, the gallows may do well to thee. To't again, come.

2ND CLOWN: Who builds stronger than a mason, a shipwright, or a carpenter?

1ST CLOWN: Ay, tell me that, and unyoke.

2ND CLOWN: Marry, now I can tell.

1ST CLOWN: To't.

40   2ND CLOWN: Mass, I cannot tell.

Enter Hamlet and Horatio, at a distance.

1ST CLOWN: Cudgel thy brains no more about it, for your dull ass will not mend his pace with beating; and when you are asked this question next, say a gravemaker;

---

[2]*crowner:* Coroner.   [3]*se offendendo:* In self-offense; he means *se defendendo,* in self-defense.
[4]*argal:* He means *ergo,* therefore.   [5]*even-Christian:* Fellow Christian.   [6]*confess thyself:* "Confess thyself an ass," perhaps.

the houses that he makes last till doomsday. Go, get thee to Yaughan: fetch me
a stoup of liquor.

Exit Second Clown.

Digs and sings.

> In youth, when I did love, did love, 45
>   Methought it was very sweet,
> To contract, O, the time, for, ah, my behove,[7]
>   O, methought there was nothing meet.

HAMLET: Has this fellow no feeling of his business, that he sings at grave-making?
HORATIO: Custom hath made it in him a property of easiness. 50
HAMLET: 'Tis e'en so: the hand of little employment hath the daintier sense.
1ST CLOWN: [*Sings*]

> But age, with his stealing steps,
>   Hath claw'd me in his clutch,
> And hath shipp'd me intil the land, 55
>   As if I had never been such.

Throws up a skull.

HAMLET: That skull had a tongue in it, and could sing once: how the knave joels[8]
it to the ground, as if it were Cain's jawbone, that did the first murder! This
might be the pate of a politician, which this ass now o'erreaches; one that
would circumvent God, might it not? 60
HORATIO: It might, my lord.
HAMLET: Or of a courtier; which could say, *Good-morrow, sweet lord! How dost
thou, good lord?* This might be my lord such-a-one, that praised my lord such-a-
one's horse, when he meant to beg it,—might it not?
HORATIO: Ay, my lord. 65
HAMLET: Why, e'en so: and now my Lady Worm's; chapless,[9] and knocked about
the mazard[10] with a sexton's spade: here's fine revolution, an we had the trick to
see't. Did these bones cost no more the breeding but to play at loggats[11] with
'em? Mine ache to think on't.
1ST CLOWN: [*Sings*] 70

> A pick-axe and a spade, a spade,
>   For and a shrouding sheet:
> O, a pit of clay for to be made
>   For such a guest is meet.

Throws up another.

HAMLET: There's another: why may not that be the skull of a lawyer? Where be his 75
quiddits[12] now, his quillets,[13] his cases, his tenures, and his tricks? why does he

---

[7]*behove:* Behoof, or advantage.   [8]*joels:* Throws.   [9]*chapless:* Without a lower jaw.   [10]*mazard:* Head.
[11]*loggats:* A game in which small pieces of wood are hurled at a stake.   [12]*quiddits:* Quiddities, "whatnesses"—
that is, hair-splittings.   [13]*quillets:* Quibbling distinctions.

suffer this rude knave now to knock him about the sconce with a dirty shovel, and will not tell him of his action of battery? Hum! This fellow might be in's time a great buyer of land, with his statutes, his recognizances, his fines, his

80 double vouchers, his recoveries: is this the fine of his fines, and the recovery of his recoveries, to have his fine pate full of fine dirt? will his vouchers vouch him no more of his purchases, and double ones too, than the length and breadth of a pair of indentures? The very conveyances of his lands will hardly lie in this box; and must the inheritor himself have no more, ha?

85 HORATIO: Not a jot more, my lord.

HAMLET: Is not parchment made of sheep-skins?

HORATIO: Ay, my lord, and of calf-skins too.

HAMLET: They are sheep and calves which seek out assurance in that. I will speak to this fellow.—Whose grave's this, sir?

90 1ST CLOWN: Mine, sir.—[*Sings*]

> O, a pit of clay for to be made
>   For such a guest is meet.

HAMLET: I think it be thine indeed; for thou liest in't.

1ST CLOWN: You lie out on't, sir, and therefore it is not yours: for my part, I do not

95 lie in't, and yet it is mine.

HAMLET: Thou dost lie in't, to be in't, and say it is thine: 'tis for the dead, not for the quick; therefore thou liest.

1ST CLOWN: 'Tis a quick lie, sir: 'twill away again from me to you.

HAMLET: What man dost thou dig it for?

100 1ST CLOWN: For no man, sir.

HAMLET: What woman, then?

1ST CLOWN: For none, neither.

HAMLET: Who is to be buried in't?

1ST CLOWN: One that was a woman, sir; but, rest her soul, she's dead.

105 HAMLET: How absolute the knave is! we must speak by the card, or equivocation will undo us. By the Lord, Horatio, these three years I have taken note of it; the age is grown so picked[14] that the toe of the peasant comes so near the heel of the courtier, he galls his kibe.[15]—How long hast thou been a grave-maker?

1ST CLOWN: Of all the days i' the year, I came to't that day that our last King

110 Hamlet o'ercame Fortinbras.

HAMLET: How long is that since?

1ST CLOWN: Cannot you tell that? every fool can tell that: it was the very day that young Hamlet was born,—he that is mad, and sent into England.

HAMLET: Ay, marry, why was he sent into England?

115 1ST CLOWN: Why, because he was mad: he shall recover his wits there; or, if he do not, it's no great matter there.

HAMLET: Why?

1ST CLOWN: 'Twill not be seen in him there; there the men are as mad as he.

---

[14]*picked*: Refined or educated.   [15]*galls his kibe*: Rubs and irritates the chilblain sore on the courtier's heel.

HAMLET: How came he mad?

1ST CLOWN: Very strangely, they say.   120

HAMLET: How strangely?

1ST CLOWN: Faith, e'en with losing his wits.

HAMLET: Upon what ground?

1ST CLOWN: Why, here in Denmark: I have been sexton here, man and boy, thirty
    years.   125

HAMLET: How long will a man lie i' the earth ere he rot?

1ST CLOWN: Faith, if he be not rotten before he die,—as we have many pocky
    corses now-a-days, that will scarce hold the laying in,—he will last you some
    eight year or nine year: a tanner will last you nine year.

HAMLET: Why he more than another?   130

1ST CLOWN: Why, sir, his hide is so tanned with his trade that he will keep out water
    a great while; and your water is a sore decayer of your whoreson dead body.
    Here's a skull now; this skull has lain in the earth three-and-twenty years.

HAMLET: Whose was it?

1ST CLOWN: A whoreson mad fellow's it was: whose do you think it was?   135

HAMLET: Nay, I know not.

1ST CLOWN: A pestilence on him for a mad rogue! 'a poured a flagon of Rhenish on
    my head once. This same skull, sir, was Yorick's skull, the king's jester.

HAMLET: This?

1ST CLOWN: E'en that.   140

HAMLET: Let me see. [*Takes the skull*]—Alas, poor Yorick!—I knew him, Horatio;
    a fellow of infinite jest, of most excellent fancy: he hath borne me on his
    back a thousand times; and now, how abhorred in my imagination it is! my
    gorge rises at it. Here hung those lips that I have kissed I know not how oft.
    Where be your gibes now? your gambols? your songs? your flashes of merriment,   145
    that were wont to set the table on a roar? Not one now, to mock your own grin-
    ning? quite chap-fallen? Now get you to my lady's chamber, and tell her, let her
    paint an inch thick, to this favor[16] she must come; make her laugh at that.—
    Pr'ythee, Horatio, tell me one thing.

HORATIO: What's that, my lord?   150

HAMLET: Dost thou think Alexander looked o' this fashion i' the earth?

HORATIO: E'en so.

HAMLET: And smelt so? pah! [*Throws down the skull*]

HORATIO: E'en so, my lord.

HAMLET: To what base uses we may return, Horatio! Why may not imagination   155
    trace the noble dust of Alexander till he find it stopping a bung-hole?

HORATIO: 'Twere to consider too curiously to consider so.

HAMLET: No, faith, not a jot; but to follow him thither with modesty enough, and
    likelihood to lead it: as thus; Alexander died, Alexander was buried, Alexander
    returneth into dust; the dust is earth; of earth we make loam; and why of that   160
    loam whereto he was converted might they not stop a beer-barrel?

---

[16]*favor*: Face.

Imperious Caesar, dead and turn'd to clay,
    Might stop a hole to keep the wind away:
    O, that that earth which kept the world in awe
165   Should patch a wall to expel the winter's flaw!—

But soft! but soft! aside.—Here comes the king.

Enter Priests, &c., in procession; the corpse of Ophelia, Laertes and Mourners following;
King, Queen, their Trains, &c.

The queen, the courtiers: who is that they follow?
And with such maimed rites? This doth betoken
The corpse they follow did with desperate hand
170 Fordo its own life: 'twas of some estate.
Couch we awhile and mark. [*Retiring with Horatio*]

LAERTES: What ceremony else?
HAMLET: That is Laertes,
  A very noble youth: mark.
175 LAERTES: What ceremony else?
1ST PRIEST: Her obsequies have been as far enlarg'd
  As we have warrantise: her death was doubtful,
  And, but that great command o'ersways the order,
  She should in ground unsanctified have lodg'd
180 Till the last trumpet; for charitable prayers,
  Shards, flints, and pebbles, should be thrown on her,
  Yet here she is allowed her virgin rites,
  Her maiden strewments, and the bringing home
  Of bell and burial.
185 LAERTES: Must there no more be done?
1ST PRIEST: No more be done:
  We should profane the service of the dead
  To sing a requiem, and such rest to her
  As to peace-parted souls.
190 LAERTES: Lay her i' the earth;—
  And from her fair and unpolluted flesh
  May violets spring!—I tell thee, churlish priest,
  A ministering angel shall my sister be
  When thou liest howling.
195 HAMLET: What, the fair Ophelia!
QUEEN: Sweets to the sweet: farewell! [*Scattering flowers*]
  I hop'd thou shouldst have been my Hamlet's wife;
  I thought thy bride-bed to have deck'd, sweet maid,
  And not have strew'd thy grave.
200 LAERTES: O, treble woe
  Fall ten times treble on that cursed head
  Whose wicked deed thy most ingenious sense
  Depriv'd thee of!—Hold off the earth awhile,

Till I have caught her once more in mine arms:

Leaps into the grave.

Now pile your dust upon the quick and dead,   205
Till of this flat a mountain you have made,
To o'er-top old Pelion[17] or the skyish head
Of blue Olympus.

HAMLET: [*Advancing*] What is he whose grief
    Bears such an emphasis? whose phrase of sorrow   210
    Conjures the wandering stars, and makes them stand
    Like wonder-wounded hearers? this is I, Hamlet the
    Dane. [*Leaps into the grave*]

LAERTES: The devil take thy soul! [*Grappling with him*]

HAMLET: Thou pray'st not well.   215
    I pr'ythee, take thy fingers from my throat;
    For, though I am not splenitive and rash,
    Yet have I in me something dangerous,
    Which let thy wiseness fear: away thy hand.

KING: Pluck them asunder.   220

QUEEN: Hamlet! Hamlet!

ALL: Gentlemen,—

HORATIO: Good my lord, be quiet.

The Attendants part them, and they come out of the grave.

HAMLET: Why, I will fight with him upon this theme
    Until my eyelids will no longer wag.   225

QUEEN: O my son, what theme?

HAMLET: I lov'd Ophelia; forty thousand brothers
    Could not, with all their quantity of love,
    Make up my sum.—What wilt thou do for her?

KING: O, he is mad, Laertes.   230

QUEEN: For love of God, forbear him.

HAMLET: 'Swounds, show me what thou'lt do:
    Woul't weep? woul't fight? woul't fast? woul't tear thyself?
    Woul't drink up eisel?[18] eat a crocodile?
    I'll do't.—Dost thou come here to whine?   235
    To outface me with leaping in her grave?
    Be buried quick[19] with her, and so will I:
    And, if thou prate of mountains, let them throw
    Millions of acres on us, till our ground,
    Singeing his pate against the burning zone,[20]   240
    Make Ossa[21] like a wart! Nay, an thou'lt mouth,
    I'll rant as well as thou.

---

[17]*Pelion:* A mountain in Greece.   [18]*eisel:* Vinegar.   [19]*quick:* Alive.   [20]*burning zone:* The fiery zone of the celestial sphere.   [21]*Ossa:* A high mountain in Greece.

QUEEN: This is mere madness:
        And thus awhile the fit will work on him;
245   Anon, as patient as the female dove,
        When that her golden couplets are disclos'd,²²
        His silence will sit drooping.
    HAMLET: Hear you, sir;
        What is the reason that you use me thus?
250   I lov'd you ever: but it is no matter;
        Let Hercules himself do what he may,
        The cat will mew, and dog will have his day. [Exit.]
    KING: I pray thee, good Horatio, wait upon him.—

    Exit Horatio.

        [To Laertes] Strengthen your patience in our last night's speech;
255   We'll put the matter to the present push.—
        Good Gertrude, set some watch over your son.—
        This grave shall have a living monument:
        An hour of quiet shortly shall we see;
        Till then, in patience our proceeding be.

    Exeunt.

SCENE 2

A hall in the castle.

Enter Hamlet and Horatio.

    HAMLET: So much for this, sir: now let me see the other;
        You do remember all the circumstance?
    HORATIO: Remember it, my lord!
    HAMLET: Sir, in my heart there was a kind of fighting
5   That would not let me sleep: methought I lay
        Worse than the mutines in the bilboes.¹ Rashly,
        And prais'd be rashness for it,—let us know,
        Our indiscretion sometimes serves us well,
        When our deep plots do fail: and that should teach us
10   There's a divinity that shapes our ends,
        Rough-hew them how we will.
    HORATIO: This is most certain.
    HAMLET: Up from my cabin,
        My sea-gown scarf'd about me, in the dark
15   Grop'd I to find out them: had my desire;
        Finger'd their packet; and, in fine, withdrew
        To mine own room again: making so bold,

---

²²When . . . are disclos'd: When the golden twins are hatched.   ¹mutines . . . bilboes: Mutineers in the iron stocks
on board ship.

My fears forgetting manners, to unseal
Their grand commission; where I found, Horatio,
O royal knavery! an exact command,—   20
Larded with many several sorts of reasons,
Importing Denmark's health and England's too,
With, ho! such bugs[2] and goblins in my life,—
That, on the supervise, no leisure bated,
No, not to stay the grinding of the axe,   25
My head should be struck off.

HORATIO: Is't possible?

HAMLET: Here's the commission: read it at more leisure.
But wilt thou hear me how I did proceed?

HORATIO: I beseech you.   30

HAMLET: Being thus benetted round with villainies,—
Ere I could make a prologue to my brains,
They had begun the play,—I sat me down;
Devis'd a new commission; wrote it fair:
I once did hold it, as our statists do,   35
A baseness to write fair, and labor'd much
How to forget that learning; but, sir, now
It did me yeoman's service. Wilt thou know
The effect of what I wrote?

HORATIO: Ay, good my lord.   40

HAMLET: An earnest conjuration from the king,—
As England was his faithful tributary;
As love between them like the palm might flourish;
As peace should still her wheaten garland wear
And stand a comma[3] 'tween their amities;   45
And many such like as's of great charge,—
That, on the view and know of these contents,
Without debatement further, more or less,
He should the bearers put to sudden death,
Not shriving-time allow'd.   50

HORATIO: How was this seal'd?

HAMLET: Why, even in that was heaven ordinant.
I had my father's signet in my purse,
Which was the model of that Danish seal:
Folded the writ up in form of the other;   55
Subscrib'd it; gav't the impression; plac'd it safely,
The changeling never known. Now, the next day
Was our sea-fight; and what to this was sequent
Thou know'st already.

HORATIO: So Guildenstern and Rosencrantz go to't.   60

---

[2]*bugs:* Bugbears.   [3]*comma:* Link.

HAMLET: Why, man, they did make love to this employment;
    They are not near my conscience; their defeat
    Does by their own insinuation[4] grow:
    'Tis dangerous when the baser nature[5] comes
65   Between the pass and fell[6] incensed points
    Of mighty opposites.
HORATIO: Why, what a king is this!
HAMLET: Does it not, think'st thee, stand me now upon,[7]
    He that hath kill'd my king and whor'd my mother;
70   Popp'd in between the election and my hopes;
    Thrown out his angle for my proper life,
    And with such cozenage,[8]—is't not perfect conscience
    To quit him with this arm? and is't not to be damn'd,
    To let this canker of our nature come
75   In further evil?
HORATIO: It must be shortly known to him from England
    What is the issue of the business there.
HAMLET: It will be short: the interim is mine;
    And a man's life's no more than to say One.
80   But I am very sorry, good Horatio,
    That to Laertes I forgot myself;
    For by the image of my cause I see
    The portraiture of his: I'll court his favors:
    But, sure, the bravery[9] of his grief did put me
85   Into a towering passion.
HORATIO: Peace; who comes here?

Enter Osric.

OSRIC: Your lordship is right welcome back to Denmark.
HAMLET: I humbly thank you, sir.—Dost know this water-fly?
HORATIO: No, my good lord.
90 HAMLET: Thy state is the more gracious; for 'tis a vice to know him. He hath much
    land, and fertile: let a beast be lord of beasts, and his crib shall stand at the
    king's mess: 'tis a chough;[10] but, as I say, spacious in the possession of dirt.
OSRIC: Sweet lord, if your lordship were at leisure, I should impart a thing to you
    from his majesty.
95 HAMLET: I will receive it with all diligence of spirit. Put your bonnet to his right
    use; 'tis for the head.
OSRIC: I thank your lordship, 'tis very hot.
HAMLET: No, believe me, 'tis very cold; the wind is northerly.
OSRIC: It is indifferent cold, my lord, indeed.
100 HAMLET: Methinks it is very sultry and hot for my complexion.

---

[4]*insinuation:* By their own "sticking their noses" into the business.   [5]*baser nature:* Men of lower rank.
[6]*fell:* Fierce.   [7]*Does . . . upon:* I.e., "Don't you think it is my duty?"   [8]*cozenage:* Deceit.
[9]*bravery:* Ostentation.   [10]*his crib . . . chough:* He shall have his trough at the king's table: he is a chattering fool.

OSRIC: Exceedingly, my lord; it is very sultry,—as't were,—I cannot tell how.—But, my lord, his majesty bade me signify to you that he has laid a great wager on your head. Sir, this is the matter,—

HAMLET: I beseech you, remember,—

Hamlet moves him to put on his hat.

OSRIC: Nay, in good faith; for mine ease, in good faith. Sir, here is newly come to court Laertes; believe me, an absolute gentleman, full of most excellent differences, of very soft society and great showing: indeed, to speak feelingly of him, he is the card or calendar of gentry, for you shall find in him the continent of what part a gentleman would see. 105

HAMLET: Sir, his definement suffers no perdition in you;—though, I know, to divide him inventorially would dizzy the arithmetic of memory, and yet but yaw neither, in respect of his quick sail. But, in the verity of extolment, I take him to be a soul of great article; and his infusion of such dearth[11] and rareness as, to make true diction of him, his semblable is his mirror; and who else would trace him, his umbrage,[12] nothing more. 110 / 115

OSRIC: Your lordship speaks most infallibly of him.

HAMLET: The concernancy, sir? why do we wrap the gentleman in our more rawer breath?

OSRIC: Sir?

HORATIO: Is't not possible to understand in another tongue? You will do't sir, really. 120

HAMLET: What imports the nomination[13] of this gentleman?

OSRIC: Of Laertes?

HORATIO: His purse is empty already; all's golden words are spent.

HAMLET: Of him, sir.

OSRIC: I know, you are not ignorant,— 125

HAMLET: I would you did, sir; yet, in faith, if you did, it would not much approve me.[14]—Well, sir.

OSRIC: You are not ignorant of what excellence Laertes is,—

HAMLET: I dare not confess that, lest I should compare with him in excellence; but to know a man well were to know himself. 130

OSRIC: I mean, sir, for his weapon; but in the imputation laid on him by them, in his meed he's unfellowed.[15]

HAMLET: What's his weapon?

OSRIC: Rapier and dagger.

HAMLET: That's two of his weapons: but, well. 135

OSRIC: The king, sir, hath wagered with him six Barbary horses: against the which he has imponed,[16] as I take it, six French rapiers and poniards, with their assigns, as girdle, hangers, and so: three of the carriages, in faith, are very dear to fancy, very responsive to the hilts, most delicate carriages, and of very liberal conceit. 140

---

[11]*dearth:* Rareness, or excellence.   [12]*umbrage:* Shadow.   [13]*nomination:* Naming.   [14]*if you . . . approve me:* If you, who are a fool, thought me not ignorant, that would not be particularly to my credit.   [15]*in . . . unfellowed:* In his worth he has no equal.   [16]*imponed:* Staked.

HAMLET: What call you the carriages?

HORATIO: I knew you must be edified by the margent[17] ere you had done.

OSRIC: The carriages, sir, are the hangers.

HAMLET: The phrase would be more german to the matter if we could carry cannon
by our sides: I would it might be hangers till then. But, on: six Barbary horses
against six French swords, their assigns, and three liberal conceited carriages;
that's the French bet against the Danish: why is this imponed, as you call it?

OSRIC: The king, sir, hath laid, that in a dozen passes between you and him he shall
not exceed you three hits: he hath laid on twelve for nine; and it would come to
immediate trial if your lordship would vouchsafe the answer.

HAMLET: How if I answer no?

OSRIC: I mean, my lord, the opposition of your person in trial.[18]

HAMLET: Sir, I will walk here in the hall: if it please his majesty, it is the breathing
time of day with me: let the foils be brought, the gentleman willing, and the
king hold his purpose, I will win for him if I can; if not, I will gain nothing
but my shame and the odd hits.

OSRIC: Shall I re-deliver you[19] e'en so?

HAMLET: To this effect, sir; after what flourish your nature will.

OSRIC: I commend my duty to your lordship.

HAMLET: Yours, yours.

Exit Osric.

He does well to commend it himself; there are no tongues else for's turn.

HORATIO: This lapwing runs away with the shell on his head.[20]

HAMLET: He did comply with his dug before he sucked it.[21] Thus has he,—and
many more of the same bevy, that I know the drossy age dotes on,—only got
the tune of the time, and outward habit of encounter; a kind of yesty collection,[22] which carries them through and through the most fanned and win-
nowed opinions; and do but blow them to their trial, the bubbles are out.

Enter a Lord.

LORD: My lord, his majesty commended him to you by young Osric, who brings
back to him that you attend him in the hall: he sends to know if your pleasure
hold to play with Laertes, or that you will take longer time.

HAMLET: I am constant to my purposes; they follow the king's pleasure: if his fitness
speaks, mine is ready; now or whensoever, provided I be so able as now.

LORD: The king and queen and all are coming down.

HAMLET: In happy time.

LORD: The queen desires you to use some gentle entertainment to Laertes before
you fall to play.

---

[17]*edified . . . margent:* Informed by a note in the margin of your instructions.   [18]*the opposition . . . trial:* The presence of your person as Laertes' opponent in the fencing contest.   [19]*re-deliver you:* Carry back your answer.
[20]*This lapwing . . . head:* This precocious fellow is like a lapwing that starts running when it is barely out of the shell.
[21]*He . . . sucked it:* He paid compliments to his mother's breast before he sucked it.   [22]*yesty collection:* Yeasty or
frothy affair.

HAMLET: She well instructs me.

Exit Lord.

HORATIO: You will lose this wager, my lord.

HAMLET: I do not think so; since he went into France I have been in continual
   practice: I shall win at the odds. But thou wouldst not think how ill all's here   180
   about my heart: but it is no matter.

HORATIO: Nay, good my lord,—

HAMLET: It is but foolery; but it is such a kind of gain-giving[23] as would perhaps
   trouble a woman.

HORATIO: If your mind dislike anything, obey it: I will forestall their repair hither,   185
   and say you are not fit.

HAMLET: Not a whit, we defy augury: there's a special providence in the fall of a
   sparrow. If it be now, 'tis not to come; if it be not to come, it will be now; if it
   be not now, yet it will come: the readiness is all. Since no man has aught of
   what he leaves, what is't to leave betimes?[24]   190

Enter King, Queen, Laertes, Lords, Osric, and Attendants with foils, &c.

KING: Come, Hamlet, come, and take this hand from me.

The King puts Laertes' hand into Hamlet's.

HAMLET: Give me your pardon, sir: I have done you wrong:
   But pardon't, as you are a gentleman.
   This presence knows, and you must needs have heard,
   How I am punish'd with sore distraction.   195
   What I have done,
   That might your nature, honor, and exception
   Roughly awake, I here proclaim was madness.
   Was't Hamlet wrong'd Laertes? Never Hamlet:
   If Hamlet from himself be ta'en away,   200
   And when he's not himself does wrong Laertes,
   Then Hamlet does it not, Hamlet denies it.
   Who does it, then? His madness: if't be so,
   Hamlet is of the faction that is wrong'd;
   His madness is poor Hamlet's enemy.   205
   Sir, in this audience,
   Let my disclaiming from a purpos'd evil
   Free me so far in your most generous thoughts
   That I have shot mine arrow o'er the house
   And hurt my brother.   210

LAERTES: I am satisfied in nature,
   Whose motive, in this case, should stir me most
   To my revenge: but in my terms of honor
   I stand aloof; and will no reconcilement

---

[23]*gain-giving:* Misgiving.   [24]*what . . . betimes?:* What does an early death matter?

215   Till by some elder masters of known honor
          I have a voice and precedent of peace
          To keep my name ungor'd. But till that time
          I do receive your offer'd love like love,
          And will not wrong it.

220   **HAMLET:**   I embrace it freely;
          And will this brother's wager frankly play.[25]—
          Give us the foils; come on.

      LAERTES: Come, one for me.

      HAMLET: I'll be your foil, Laertes; in mine ignorance

225   Your skill shall, like a star in the darkest night,
          Stick fiery off indeed.

      LAERTES: You mock me, sir.

      HAMLET: No, by this hand.

      KING: Give them the foils, young Osric.

230   Cousin Hamlet,
          You know the wager?

      HAMLET: Very well, my lord;
          Your grace hath laid the odds o' the weaker side.

      KING: I do not fear it; I have seen you both;

235   But since he's better'd, we have therefore odds.

      LAERTES: This is too heavy, let me see another.

      HAMLET: This likes me well. These foils have all a length?

They prepare to play.

      OSRIC: Ay, my good lord.

      KING: Set me the stoups of wine upon that table,—

240   If Hamlet give the first or second hit,
          Or quit in answer of the third exchange,
          Let all the battlements their ordnance fire;
          The king shall drink to Hamlet's better breath;
          And in the cup an union[26] shall he throw,

245   Richer than that which four successive kings
          In Denmark's crown have worn. Give me the cups;
          And let the kettle[27] to the trumpet speak,
          The trumpet to the cannoneer without,
          The cannons to the heavens, the heavens to earth,

250   Now the king drinks to Hamlet.—Come, begin;—
          And you, the judges, bear a wary eye.

      HAMLET: Come on, sir.

      LAERTES: Come, my lord.

They play.

---

[25] *frankly play:* Fence with a heart free from resentment.   [26] *an union:* A pearl.   [27] *kettle:* Kettledrum.

HAMLET: One.
LAERTES: No.   255
HAMLET: Judgment.
OSRIC: A hit, a very palpable hit.
LAERTES: Well;—again.
KING: Stay, give me a drink.—Hamlet, this pearl is thine;
   Here's to thy health.—   260

Trumpets sound, and cannon shot off within.

   Give him the cup.
HAMLET: I'll play this bout first; set it by awhile.—
   Come.—Another hit; what say you?

They play.

LAERTES: A touch, a touch, I do confess.
KING: Our son shall win.   265
QUEEN: He's fat, and scant of breath.—
   Here, Hamlet, take my napkin, rub thy brows:
   The queen carouses to thy fortune, Hamlet.
HAMLET: Good madam!
KING: Gertrude, do not drink.   270
QUEEN: I will, my lord; I pray you, pardon me.
KING: [*Aside*] It is the poison'd cup; it is too late.
HAMLET: I dare not drink yet, madam; by and by.
QUEEN: Come, let me wipe thy face.
LAERTES: My lord, I'll hit him now.   275
KING: I do not think't.
LAERTES: [*Aside*] And yet 'tis almost 'gainst my conscience.
HAMLET: Come, for the third, Laertes: you but dally;
   I pray you, pass with your best violence:
   I am afeard you make a wanton of me.   280
LAERTES: Say you so? come on.

They play.

OSRIC: Nothing, neither way.
LAERTES: Have at you now!

Laertes wounds Hamlet; then, in scuffling, they change rapiers, and Hamlet wounds Laertes.

KING: Part them; they are incens'd.
HAMLET: Nay, come, again.   285

The Queen falls.

OSRIC: Look to the queen there, ho!
HORATIO: They bleed on both sides.—How is it, my lord?
OSRIC: How is't, Laertes?

LAERTES: Why, as a woodcock to my own springe, Osric;
290   I am justly kill'd with mine own treachery.
HAMLET: How does the queen?
KING: She swoons to see them bleed.
QUEEN: No, no, the drink, the drink,—O my dear Hamlet,—
         The drink, the drink!—I am poison'd. [Dies.]
295 HAMLET: O villainy!—Ho! let the door be lock'd:
         Treachery! seek it out.

Laertes falls.

LAERTES: It is here, Hamlet: Hamlet, thou art slain;
         No medicine in the world can do thee good;
         In thee there is not half an hour of life;
300   The treacherous instrument is in thy hand,
         Unbated and envenom'd: the foul practice
         Hath turn'd itself on me; lo, here I lie,
         Never to rise again: thy mother's poison'd:
         I can no more:—the king, the king's to blame.
305 HAMLET: The point envenom'd too!—
         Then venom to thy work. [Stabs the King.]
OSRIC AND LORDS: Treason! treason!
KING: O, yet defend me, friends; I am but hurt.
HAMLET: Here, thou incestuous, murderous, damned Dane,
310   Drink off this potion.—Is thy union here?
         Follow my mother.

King dies.

LAERTES: He is justly serv'd;
         It is a poison temper'd by himself.—
         Exchange forgiveness with me, noble Hamlet:
315   Mine and my father's death come not upon thee,
         Nor thine on me! [Dies.]
HAMLET: Heaven make thee free of it! I follow thee.—
         I am dead, Horatio.—Wretched queen, adieu!—
         You that look pale and tremble at this chance,
320   That art but mutes or audience to this act,
         Had I but time,—as this fell sergeant, death,
         Is strict in his arrest,—O, I could tell you,—
         But let it be.—Horatio, I am dead;
         Thou liv'st; report me and my cause aright
325   To the unsatisfied.[28]

---

[28] *the unsatisfied:* The uninformed.

HORATIO: Never believe it:
   I am more an antique Roman than a Dane,—
   Here's yet some liquor left.
HAMLET: As thou'rt a man,
   Give me the cup; let go; by heaven, I'll have't.—   330
   O good Horatio, what a wounded name,
   Things standing thus unknown, shall live behind me!
   If thou didst ever hold me in thy heart,
   Absent thee from felicity awhile,
   And in this harsh world draw thy breath in pain,   335
   To tell my story.—

March afar off, and shot within.

                    What warlike noise is this?
OSRIC: Young Fortinbras, with conquest come from Poland,
   To the ambassadors of England gives
   This warlike volley.   340
HAMLET: O, I die, Horatio;
   The potent poison quite o'er-crows my spirit:
   I cannot live to hear the news from England;
   But I do prophesy the election lights
   On Fortinbras: he has my dying voice;   345
   So tell him, with the occurrents, more and less,
   Which have solicited.[29]—The rest is silence. [*Dies.*]
HORATIO: Now cracks a noble heart.—Good-night, sweet prince,
   And flights of angels sing thee to thy rest!
   Why does the drum come hither?   350

March within. Enter Fortinbras, the English Ambassadors, and others.

FORTINBRAS: Where is this sight?
HORATIO: What is it you would see?
   If aught of woe or wonder, cease your search.
FORTINBRAS: This quarry cries on havoc.[30]—O proud death,
   What feast is toward in thine eternal cell,   355
   That thou so many princes at a shot
   So bloodily hast struck?
1ST AMBASSADOR: The sight is dismal;
   And our affairs from England come too late:
   The ears are senseless that should give us hearing,   360
   To tell him his commandment is fulfill'd,

---

[29] *So tell him . . . solicited:* So tell him, together with the events, more or less, that have brought on this tragic affair.
[30] *This quarry . . . havoc:* This collection of dead bodies cries out havoc.

That Rosencrantz and Guildenstern are dead:
Where should we have our thanks?

HORATIO: Not from his mouth,
365   Had it the ability of life to thank you:
He never gave commandment for their death.
But since, so jump³¹ upon this bloody question,
You from the Polack wars, and you from England,
Are here arriv'd, give order that these bodies
370   High on a stage be placed to the view;
And let me speak to the yet unknowing world
How these things came about: so shall you hear
Of carnal, bloody, and unnatural acts;
Of accidental judgments, casual slaughters;
375   Of deaths put on by cunning and forc'd cause;
And, in this upshot, purposes mistook
Fall'n on the inventors' heads: all this can I
Truly deliver.

FORTINBRAS: Let us haste to hear it,
380   And call the noblest to the audience.
For me, with sorrow I embrace my fortune:
I have some rights of memory in this kingdom,³²
Which now to claim my vantage doth invite me.

HORATIO: Of that I shall have also cause to speak,
385   And from his mouth whose voice will draw on more:
But let this same be presently perform'd,
Even while men's minds are wild: lest more mischance
On plots and errors happen.

FORTINBRAS: Let four captains
390   Bear Hamlet like a soldier to the stage;
For he was likely, had he been put on,³³
To have prov'd most royally: and, for his passage,
The soldier's music and the rites of war
Speak loudly for him.—
395   Take up the bodies.—Such a sight as this
Becomes the field, but here shows much amiss.
Go, bid the soldiers shoot.

A dead march.

Exeunt, bearing off the dead bodies: after which a peal of ordnance is shot off.

*   *   *

---

³¹ *so jump:* So opportunely.   ³² *I have . . . kingdom:* I have some unforgotten rights to this kingdom.
³³ *put on:* Tested by succession to the throne.

Reading and Reacting

1. What are Hamlet's most notable character traits? Do you see these traits as generally positive or negative?
2. Review each of Hamlet's soliloquies. Do you believe his assessments of his own problems are accurate? Are his assessments of other characters' behavior accurate? Point to examples from the soliloquies that reveal Hamlet's insight or lack of insight.
3. Is Hamlet a sympathetic character? Where (if anywhere) do you find yourself growing impatient with him or disagreeing with him?
4. Why does Hamlet behave so cruelly toward Ophelia after his "To be or not to be" soliloquy (act 3, scene 1)? How does this behavior affect your view of his character?
5. What do other characters' comments reveal about Hamlet's character *before* the key events in the play begin to unfold? For example, in what way has Hamlet changed since he returned to the castle and found out about his father's death?
6. Claudius is presented as the play's villain. Is he all bad, or does he have any redeeming qualities?
7. List those in the play whom you believe to be flat characters. Why do you characterize each individual in this way? What does each of these flat characters contribute to the play?
8. Is Fortinbras simply Hamlet's foil, or does he have another essential role? Explain.
9. Each of the play's major characters has one or more character flaws that influence plot development. What specific weaknesses do you see in Claudius, Gertrude, Polonius, Laertes, Ophelia, and Hamlet himself? Through what words or actions is each weakness revealed? How does each weakness contribute to the play's plot?
10. Why doesn't Hamlet kill Claudius as soon as the ghost tells him what Claudius did? Why doesn't he kill him when he has the chance in act 3? What words and actions reveal Hamlet's motivation for hesitating? What are the implications of his failure to act?
11. Why does Hamlet pretend to be insane? Why does he arrange for the "play within a play" to be performed? Why does he agree to the duel with Laertes? In each case, what words or actions reveal his motivation to the audience?
12. Is the ghost an essential character, or could the information he reveals and the reactions he arouses come from another source? Explain. (Keep in mind that the ghost is a stock character in Elizabethan revenge tragedies.)
13. Describe Hamlet's relationship with his mother. Do you consider this a typical mother/son relationship? Why, or why not?
14. In the graveyard scene (act 5, scene 1), the gravediggers make many ironic comments. How do these comments shed light on the events taking place in the play?

15. **JOURNAL ENTRY** Both Gertrude and Ophelia are usually seen as weak women, firmly under the influence of the men in their lives. Do you think this characterization of them as passive and dependent is accurate? Explain your views.

16. **CRITICAL PERSPECTIVE** In *The Meaning of Shakespeare*, (1951), Harold Goddard reads *Hamlet* as, in part, a play about war, with a grimly ironic conclusion in that "all the Elder Hamlet's conquests have been for nothing—for less than nothing. Fortinbras, his

former enemy, is to inherit the kingdom! Such is the end to which the ghost's thirst for vengeance has led." Goddard goes on to describe the play's ending:

> The dead Hamlet is borne out "like a soldier" and the last rites over his body are to be the rites of war. The final word of the text is "shoot." The last sounds we hear are a dead march and the reverberations of ordnance being shot off. The end crowns the whole. The sarcasm of fate could go no further. Hamlet, who aspired to nobler things, is treated at death as if he were the mere image of his father: a warrior. Shakespeare knew what he was about in making the conclusion of his play martial. Its theme has been war as well as revenge. It is the story of the Minotaur over again, of that monster who from the beginning of human strife has exacted his annual tribute of youth. No sacrifice ever offered to it was more precious than Hamlet. But he was not the last.

> If ever a play seems expressly written for the twentieth century, it is *Hamlet*. It should be unnecessary to underscore its pertinence to an age in which, twice within three decades, the older generation has called on the younger generation to settle a quarrel with the making of which it had nothing to do. So taken, *Hamlet* is an allegory of our time. Imagination or violence, Shakespeare seems to say, there is no other alternative.

Can you find other evidence in the play to support the idea that war (and, more specifically, the futility of war) is one of its major themes? Do you agree that the play is, in this respect, "an allegory of our time"?

Related Works: "The Cask of Amontillado" (p. 328), "Young Goodman Brown" (p. 448), "Referential" (p. 598), *Oedipus the King* (p. 1430)

WRITING SUGGESTIONS: Character

1. In *Death of a Salesman*, each character pursues his or her version of the American Dream. Choose two characters, define their concept of the American Dream, and explain how each tries to make the dream a reality. In each case, consider the obstacles the character encounters, and try to account for the character's success or lack of success. If you like, you may also consider other works in which the American Dream is central—for example, "Two Kinds" (p. 639), *The Cuban Swimmer* (p. 1416), or *Fences* (p. 1548).

2. The key female characters in this chapter's plays—the wife in *Post-its*, Catherine in *Proof*, Linda in *Death of a Salesman*, and Ophelia in *Hamlet*—are, in one way or another, in conflict with men. Focusing on female characters in two different plays, define each conflict, and consider whether it is resolved in the play. (If you like, you may also discuss a female character who appears in a play in another chapter.)

3. Minor characters are often flat characters; in many cases, their sole function is to advance the plot or to highlight a particular trait in a major character. Sometimes, however, minor characters may be of more than minor importance. Choose one minor character from *Death of a Salesman* or *Hamlet* (or from a play in another chapter), and write an essay in which you discuss what this character contributes and how the play would be different without him or her.

4. Watch a film version of one of the plays in this chapter, and write an essay in which you evaluate the actor's interpretation of the central character.

5. Three of this chapter's four plays explore complex relationships between parents and children. Write an essay in which you compare and contrast two of these three relationships: Catherine's relationship with her father, Willy Loman's relationships with his sons, or Hamlet's relationship with his mother.

6. In several other plays in this anthology, as in *Proof*, the past is an important influence on characters' lives in the present. Write an essay in which you discuss the impact of the past on the present in *Proof* and one or two other plays—for example, *A Doll House* (p. 1113) or *Doubt: A Parable* (p. 1516).

CHAPTER 39

STAGING

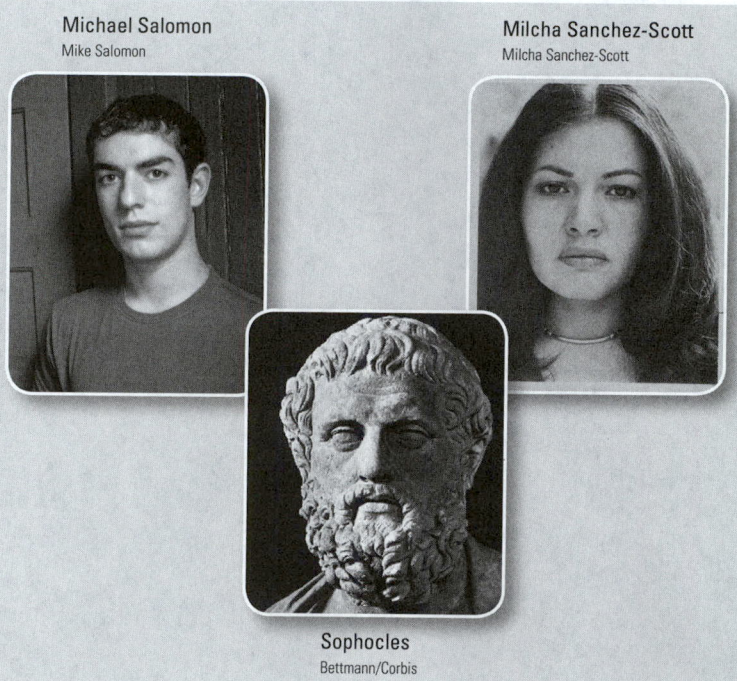

Michael Salomon
Mike Salomon

Milcha Sanchez-Scott
Milcha Sanchez-Scott

Sophocles
Bettmann/Corbis

Staging refers to the physical elements of a play's production that determine how the play looks and sounds to an audience. It encompasses the **stage settings**, or **sets**—furnishings, scenery, props, and lighting—as well as the costumes, sound effects, and music that bring the play to life on the stage. In short, staging is everything that goes into making a written script a performance.

Contemporary staging in the West has traditionally concentrated on recreating the real world. This concept of staging, which has dominated Western theatrical productions for centuries, would seem alien in many non-Western theaters. Japanese **Kabuki dramas** and **No plays**, for example, depend on staging conventions that make no attempt to mirror reality. Scenery and costumes are largely symbolic, and often actors wear highly stylized makeup or masks. Although some European and American playwrights have been strongly influenced by non-Western staging, the majority of plays being produced in the West still try to create the illusion of reality.

Stage Directions

Usually a playwright presents instructions for the staging of a play in **stage directions**—notes that comment on the scenery, the movements of the performers, the lighting, and the placement of props. (In the absence of detailed stage directions, dialogue can provide information about staging.) Sometimes these stage directions are quite simple, leaving much to the discretion (and imagination) of the director. Consider how little specific information about the setting of the play is provided in these stage directions from act 1 of Samuel Beckett's 1952 absurdist play *Waiting for Godot*:

> *A country road. A tree. Evening.*

Often, however, playwrights furnish more detailed information about staging. Consider these stage directions from act 1 of Anton Chekhov's *The Cherry Orchard*:

> *A room, which has always been called the nursery. One of the doors leads into Anya's room. Dawn, sun rises during the scene. May, the cherry trees in flower, but it is cold in the garden with the frost of the early morning. Windows closed.*
> *Enter Dunyasha with a candle and Lopahin with a book in his hand.*

These comments indicate that the first act takes place in a room with more than one door and that several windows reveal cherry trees in bloom. They also specify that the lighting should simulate the sun rising at dawn and that characters should enter carrying certain props. Still, Chekhov leaves it up to those staging the play to decide on the costumes for the characters and on the furniture to be placed around the room.

Some stage directions are even more specific. Irish playwright George Bernard Shaw's long, complex stage directions are legendary in the theater. Note the degree of detail he provides in these stage directions from his 1906 comedy *The Doctor's Dilemma*:

> *The consulting-room has two windows looking on Queen Anne Street. Between the two is a marble-topped console, with haunched gilt legs ending in sphinx claws. The huge pier-glass [a long narrow mirror that fits between two windows] which surmounts it is mostly disabled from reflection by elaborate painting on its surface of palms, ferns, lilies, tulips, and sunflowers. The adjoining wall contains the fireplace, with two arm-chairs before it. As we happen to face the corner we see nothing of the other two walls. On the right of the fireplace, or rather on the right of any person facing the fireplace, is the door. On the left is the writing-table at which Redpenny [a medical student] sits. It is an untidy table with a microscope, several test tubes, and a spirit lamp [an alcohol burner] standing up through its litter of papers. There is a couch in the middle of the room, at right angles to the console, and parallel to the fireplace. A chair stands between the couch and the window. Another in the corner. Another at the other end of the windowed wall. . . . The wallpaper and carpets are mostly green. . . . The house, in fact, was so well furnished in the middle of the XIXth century that it stands unaltered to this day and is still quite presentable.*

Not only does Shaw indicate exactly what furniture is to be placed on stage, but he also includes a good deal of physical description—specifying, for example, "gilt legs ending in sphinx claws" and "test tubes and a spirit lamp" that clutter the writing table. In addition, he defines furniture placement and specifies color.

Regardless of how detailed the stage directions are, they do not eliminate the need for creative interpretations on the part of the producer, director, set designers, and actors (see "Actors' Interpretations," p. 1174). Many directors see stage directions as simply suggestions, not requirements, and some consider them more confusing than helpful. Therefore, some directors may choose to interpret a play's stage directions quite loosely—or even to ignore them entirely. For example, in 2007, the Classical Theater of Harlem staged Samuel Beckett's 1952 existentialist drama *Waiting for Godot* in New Orleans. The performances were held outdoors in areas of the city that had been seriously damaged by Hurricane Katrina, and the still-devastated setting gave new power to Beckett's drama of characters' search for meaning against a backdrop of emptiness and despair.

 ## The Uses of Staging

Various elements of staging provide important information about characters and their motivations as well as about the play's theme.

Costumes

Costumes establish the historical period in which a play is set and provide insight into the characters who wear them. For example, when Hamlet first appears on stage, he is profoundly disillusioned and quite melancholy. This fact was immediately apparent to Shakespeare's audience because Hamlet is dressed in sable, which to the Elizabethans signified a melancholy nature. In Tennessee Williams's *The Glass Menagerie* (1945), Laura's dress of soft violet material and her hair ribbon reflect her delicate, childlike innocence. In contrast, her mother's "*imitation velvety-looking cloth [coat] with imitation fur collar*" and her "*enormous black patent-leather pocketbook*" reveal her somewhat pathetic attempt to achieve respectability. Later in the play, awaiting the "gentleman caller," Laura's mother wears a dress that is both outdated and inappropriately youthful, suggesting both her need to relive her own past and her increasingly desperate desire to marry off her daughter.

Props and Furnishings

Props (short for *properties*) can also help audiences interpret a play's characters and themes. For example, the handkerchief in Shakespeare's *Othello* gains significance as the play progresses: it begins as an innocent object and ends as the piece of evidence that convinces Othello his wife is committing adultery. Sometimes props can have symbolic significance. During the Renaissance, for example, flowers had symbolic meaning. In act 4 of *Hamlet*, Ophelia, who is mad, gives flowers to various characters. In a note to the play, the critic Thomas Parrott points out the symbolic significance of her gifts: to Claudius, the murderer of Hamlet's father, she gives fennel and columbines, which signify flattery and ingratitude; to the Queen, she gives rue and daisies, which symbolize sadness and unfaithfulness. Although modern audiences would not understand the significance of these flowers, many people in Shakespeare's Elizabethan audience would have been aware of their meaning.

The **furnishings** in a room can also reveal a lot about a play's characters and themes. Willy Loman's house in Arthur Miller's *Death of a Salesman* (p. 1233) is sparsely furnished, revealing the declining financial status of the family. The kitchen contains a table and three chairs and the bedroom only a brass bed and a straight chair. Over the bed on a shelf is Willy's son's silver athletic trophy, a constant reminder of his loss of status. Like Willie Lowman's house, the Helmer's living room in *A Doll's House*, suggests its inhabitant's social status. The furnishings are typical of "respectable" middle-class families in nineteenth-century Norway. According to the stage directions, the living room is, "*A comfortable room, tastefully but not expensively furnished.*" Everything in it—from the round table with an armchair, to the porcelain stove, to the carpeted floor—is practical and efficient. These furnishings immediately convey to audiences the apparent stability of the family as well as its core values.

Scenery and Lighting

Playwrights often use **scenery** and **lighting** to create imaginative stage settings. In *Death of a Salesman*, the house is surrounded by "*towering angular shapes*" of apartment houses that emphasize the "*small, fragile-seeming home.*" Arthur Miller calls for a set that is "*wholly, or in some places, transparent.*" Whenever the action is in the present, the actors observe the imaginary boundaries that separate rooms or mark the exterior walls of the house. When the characters reenact past events, however, they walk over the boundaries and come to the front of the stage. By lighting up and darkening different parts of the stage, Miller shifts from the present to the past and back again.

Contemporary playwrights often use sets that combine realistic and nonrealistic elements. In his Tony Award–winning play M. *Butterfly*, for example, David Henry Hwang employs not only scrims but also a large red lacquered ramp that runs from the bottom to the top of the stage. The action takes place beneath, on, and above the ramp, creating an effect not unlike that created by Shakespeare's multiple stages. At several points in the play, a character who acts as the narrator sits beneath the ramp, addressing the audience, while at the same time a character on top of the ramp acts out the narrator's words.

Music and Sound Effects

Staging involves more than visual elements such as costumes and scenery; it also involves **music** and **sound effects**. The stage directions for *Death of a Salesman*, for example, begin, "*A melody is heard, played upon a flute.*" Although not specifically identified, the music is described as "*small and fine, telling of grass and trees and the horizon.*" Significantly, this music stands in stark contrast to the claustrophobic urban setting of the play. Music also plays a major role in *The Glass Menagerie*, where a single recurring tune, like circus music, weaves in and out of the play. This musical motif gives emotional impact to certain lines and suggests the fantasy world into which Laura has retreated.

Sound effects play an important part in Henrik Ibsen's *A Doll House* (p. 1113). At the very end of the play, after his wife has left him, Torvald Helmer sits alone on the stage. In the following stage directions, the final sound effect cuts short Helmer's attempt at self-deluding optimism:

HELMER: (*sinks down on a chair by the door, face buried in his hands*) Nora! Nora! (*Looking about and rising.*) Empty. She's gone. (*A sudden hope leaps in him.*) The greatest miracle—?

From below, the sound of a door slamming shut.

When you read a play, it may be difficult to appreciate the effect that staging can have on a performance. As you read, pay particular attention to the stage directions, and use your imagination to visualize the scenes the playwright describes. In addition, try to imagine the play's sights and sounds, and consider the options for staging that are suggested as characters speak to one another. Although careful reading cannot substitute for seeing a play performed, it can help you imagine the play as it might appear on the stage.

 ## A Final Note

Because of a play's limited performance time, and because of space and financial limitations, not every action or event can be represented on stage. Frequently, incidents that would involve many actors or require elaborate scenery are only suggested. For example, a violent riot may be suggested by a single scuffle, a full-scale wedding by the kiss between bride and groom, a gala evening at the opera by a well-dressed group in box seats, and a trip to an exotic locale by a departure scene. Other events may be suggested by sounds offstage—for example, the roar of a crowd may suggest an athletic event.

✔ **CHECKLIST**   **Writing about Staging**

☐ What information about staging is specified in the stage directions of the play?

☐ What information about staging is suggested by the play's dialogue?

☐ What information about staging is left to the imagination?

☐ How might different decisions about staging change the play?

☐ Do the stage directions provide information about how characters are supposed to look or behave?

☐ What costumes are specified? In what ways do costumes provide insight into the characters who wear them?

☐ What props play an important part in the play? Do these props have symbolic meaning?

☐ Is the scenery special or unusual in any way?

☐ What kind of lighting is specified by the stage directions? In what way does this lighting affect your reaction to the play?

☐ How are music and sound effects used in the play? Are musical themes associated with any characters? Do music or sound effects heighten the emotional impact of certain lines?

☐ What events occur offstage? Why? How are they suggested?

☐ How does staging help to communicate the play's themes?

Mike Salomon

MICHAEL SALOMON (1988–   ) is a playwright, screenwriter, and short story writer. His plays include *The Tragedy of King James the First* / (read by sportscaster Bob Costas on *Slate's* "Hang Up and Listen" podcast) and *RMEO + JULEZ* (winner of the Manhattan Theatre Club's 2009 REALationships Playwright Competition and included in the collection *25 10-Minute Plays for Teens*). The following play appeared in the collection *The Best Ten-Minute Plays 2013*.

Cultural Context In *The Date*, the characters refer to "alternative casting," a practice in theater and film in which an actor is cast for a role originally intended for someone else. Some examples of alternative casting include the role of Marty McFly in the 1985 movie *Back to the Future* (originally offered to Eric Stoltz, but played by Michael J. Fox) and the role of Clarice Starling in the 1991 movie *The Silence of the Lambs* (played by Jodie Foster, but originally offered to Michelle Pfeiffer). In these examples, the alternative actors are as suited to the roles as the actors they replaced. Some critics, however, have objected to a kind of alternative casting known as "color-blind casting" (and sometimes attacked as "politically correct casting"), a practice in which roles are assigned without regard to race, ethnicity, or even gender. *The Date* tests the boundaries of alternative casting and makes fun of tightly scripted roles—both on and off the stage.

The Date (2012)

CHARACTERS

JACKIE, *female, early twenties, black*
DUQUAN, *male, late fifties, white*
STAGE DIRECTIONS, *male, twenties or thirties (any race except black)*

SETTING

A dimly lit, romantic restaurant.

LIGHTS UP ON JACKIE AND DUQUAN, *sitting at opposite ends of a small, elegantly set dinner table. Both are dressed to the nines. Duquan's sport coat hangs neatly over the back of his chair. On the table are a basket of bread-sticks, a long, burning candle, salt and pepper shakers, and two table settings. Both Jackie and Duquan are reading menus. STAGE DIRECTIONS sits in a folding chair in the front corner of the stage—apart from the others. He faces the audience with a script in hand.*

STAGE DIRECTIONS: (*Reading.*) Setting: a dimly lit, romantic restaurant. At one end of the table sits Jackie, a well-dressed, twenty-four year old African American woman. At the other end sits Duquan, a twenty-five year old African American man wearing a shirt and tie.

DUQUAN: See anything that looks good?

Jackie looks up, shocked to see Duquan sitting across from her. She says nothing but stares at him in confusion. Duquan clears his throat.

DUQUAN: (*cont'd*) See anything that looks good?

Jackie glances around the restaurant, unsettled, then back at Duquan. He clears his throat again.

DUQUAN: (*cont'd*) Do you see anything—

5 JACKIE: I'm—I'm sorry. Is this—? Are you—? Who are you?
 DUQUAN: I'm Duquan.
 JACKIE: Right . . . Seriously, who are you?
 DUQUAN: I'm Duquan.

A beat.

 DUQUAN: *(cont'd)* So, see anything that looks—
10 JACKIE: Wait, wait, wait. Hold up. I'm sorry. *You're* Duquan?
 DUQUAN: Yeah.
 JACKIE: Aren't you supposed to be, like, twenty-five? And black?
 DUQUAN: Uh-huh.
 JACKIE: So . . .
15 DUQUAN: So what?
 JACKIE: So why aren't you?
 DUQUAN: I am.
 JACKIE: You're a black twenty-five year old?
 DUQUAN: Mm-hmm.
20 JACKIE: Really? *You're* a black twenty-five year old?
 DUQUAN: Yes, ma'am.
 JACKIE: *Really?*
 DUQUAN: I, um . . .

Duquan begrudgingly stands up and walks over to Stage Directions.

 DUQUAN: *(cont'd)* May I?

Duquan takes the script out of Stage Directions hands and flips to the front. He turns to Jackie.

25 DUQUAN: *(cont'd)* Let's see . . . Yup, that's what it says right here: "Duquan, a
  twenty-five year old African American man. Wearing a shirt and tie."

He gestures down to his own shirt and tie, then returns the script to Stage Directions and heads back to his seat.

 JACKIE: Right, right, right. But *you're* not black.
 DUQUAN: I beg your pardon.
 JACKIE: You're like some fifty year old white guy.
 DUQUAN: Oh. *Oooh!* I see. Yeah, this is a . . . uh . . . oh what do they call it?
  Alternative casting!
30 JACKIE: What?
 DUQUAN: Yeah, I've been alternatively cast.
 JACKIE: For our date?
 DUQUAN: Mm-hmm.
 JACKIE: I'm confused.
35 DUQUAN: Ok, well see, you *are* on a date with a twenty-five-year-old black man,
  and *I* am that black man. You get it?
 JACKIE: Not particularly.
 DUQUAN: Ok. Ok. Uh, let's say this pepper shaker is you, and this salt shaker is
  me, and so you're on a date with the salt shaker, but it's really a pepper shaker,

and—wait, no, that's not right. Hang on. What if *I'm* the pepper shaker and *you're* the—

JACKIE: Hold up. Hold up. I get what you're saying. I just don't understand why.

DUQUAN: Oh. Well it's—I think it's got something to do with the whole date setting and, you know, love, and the way there's, um, deception, and—

STAGE DIRECTIONS: It's symbolic of the misrepresentations that we, as humans, purvey in our romantic endeavors.

DUQUAN: Ah. See, there you go. It's symbolism.

JACKIE: It's a date.

DUQUAN: Yes, but it's symbolism too.

JACKIE: Ok. Well what am I symbolic of?

DUQUAN: Oh. I don't know. Maybe nothing. Breadstick?

He offers her a breadstick. She doesn't take it.

JACKIE: Nothing?

DUQUAN: Or something. I mean we all have our own layers. I guess you could say mine are just a little more forthright.

JACKIE: I guess so.

DUQUAN: So you're cool, then? Everything settled?

JACKIE: What? No. I don't know. I mean, this all still seems kind of messed up to me. Don't get me wrong. I've been on some pretty wacked out dates before, but *this*?

DUQUAN: Hey, you're preaching to the choir here. Talk about your identity crisis, right? I mean, I vote republican.

JACKIE: Yeah, but wait—hang on. This—it is a date, right?

DUQUAN: Uh huh.

JACKIE: And we're supposed to sit here and have a real conversation and, like, really connect like two people, right?

DUQUAN: That's what *I* had in mind. Yeah.

JACKIE: Well doesn't it change everything—I mean, doesn't it make any hope of real connection impossible—if you aren't who you're supposed to be?

DUQUAN: But I'm exactly who I'm supposed to be.

JACKIE: You're not a twenty-five year old black man!

DUQUAN: But I *am* a twenty-five year old black man.

JACKIE: Really? Then who's Lil Wayne?

DUQUAN: I don't know. A Muppet?

JACKIE: See!

DUQUAN: Look, is it really that big a deal?

JACKIE: Of course it is. I don't want to be on a date with—

DUQUAN: Oh. I see. A white guy?

JACKIE: A guy three times my age! And yes, if I'm *supposed* to be on a date with a black guy in the first place, I think it is a little weird to show up and have that black guy be a white guy who apparently *is* a black guy, but he's not really, and he's just been alternatively cast as—

To Stage Directions

I mean, what the hell? Was this *your* idea?

Stage Directions shrugs.

Duquan: Look, it's just a simple conceit. You know, like a magic show, or professional wrestling, or fake breasts . . .

Jackie: I don't want my romantic life to be anything like fake breasts, thank you.

Duquan: Ok, well think about it this way: Let's say there really was a twenty-five year old black man sitting here across from you. Does that make the situation any less deceptive? Isn't he just as liable to mislead you about the particular nuances or intricacies of his personality and life? I mean, at least I'm wearing my deceit on my skin.

70 Jackie: But how does that make it any better?

Duquan: Well now you know you can't trust me.

Jackie: But I want to be able to trust you.

Duquan: Ok, then trust me.

Jackie: How?

75 Duquan: I don't know. Just concede to the illusion.

Jackie: The illusion that you're twenty-five and black?

Duquan: That's the one.

Jackie: But you're not.

Duquan: Would it help if I spoke in ebonics?

80 Jackie: No. What is wrong with you?

Duquan: Hey, I will have you know I'm actually a very fun guy. Even for a black man in his twenties. People say I'm quite hip.

Jackie: No. You aren't. You aren't any of that. Just stop it.

Duquan: Fine. I'm sorry, ok? I'm—I'm trying my best here. You know, in a lot of ways I'm probably being more honest than any other guy you'd be out with right now.

Jackie: Yeah? Well I don't care about that.

85 Duquan: Well you probably should care or someone's gonna wind up getting herself into some prickly situations.

Jackie: But I *don't* care. Look, guy—

Duquan: Duquan.

Jackie: Look, Duquan, I'm sure you're a terrific person and all. Honestly, I do. But I can't deal with all these messed up layers and symbolisms and alternative anythings right now. I just want to be on a normal date with a regular guy, you know? Someone who's roughly my age and has similar interests. Someone I can tell about myself and who can tell me about himself, and then maybe we'll hit it off—or maybe we won't. And yeah, maybe everything he says isn't gonna be the whole honest truth. Maybe he's got a secret drug problem or some creepy fetish or even a wife and kids waiting for him at home, but all of that's up to me to find out for myself. And until I do, I just have to trust him, right? Believe in whatever it is he makes himself out to be and just pray that it's for real.

Duquan: Sure, I guess. So then the issue with me is . . . ?

90 Jackie: I can't believe in you. You're not . . . you're not real.

DUQUAN: So, what you're saying is you'd rather you didn't know if you were being lied to?

JACKIE: In a way.

DUQUAN: I see. Ignorance is bliss, huh?

JACKIE: In this case it is.

DUQUAN: I guess so. And so this whole wearing my dishonesty on my sleeve thing: 95
it's a little too much, isn't it?

JACKIE: I'm sorry. I know you were excited to be all symbolic.

DUQUAN: No, no, it's fine. It kind of does all make sense, in a way.

JACKIE: Yeah?

He nods. Beat.

DUQUAN: Hey, what if you just closed your eyes? Tried to pretend—

JACKIE: Believe me, I've tried. So many times . . . 100

DUQUAN: No luck?

JACKIE: No luck.

DUQUAN: I get it. So then all this . . . ?

JACKIE: I can't do it. I'm sorry.

She stands and starts to gather her things.

DUQUAN: Well maybe some other time then. 105

JACKIE: Yeah, maybe.

DUQUAN: And maybe I could just be a fifty-eight year old white guy. Named Norm.

JACKIE: And maybe I'll be a twenty-four year-old black girl named Jackie.

A beat.

DUQUAN: For what it's worth, I don't have any creepy fetishes. Or a wife.
Or fake breasts.

Jackie smiles and nods. She exits.

DUQUAN: *(cont'd)* Right. 110

*A long pause. Duquan begins to look around uncomfortably—unsure of what to do next.
Stage Directions appears equally confounded. At last the two make eye contact. A beat
passes. Getting an idea, Stage Directions stands and walks over to the table, sitting himself
in Jackie's former chair.*

STAGE DIRECTIONS: *(Reading from his script.)* Setting: a dimly lit, romantic restaurant.
At one end of the table sits Jackie . . .

He gestures to himself. Duquan nods understandingly.

Still reading.
. . . a well-dressed, twenty-four year old African American woman. At the other
end sits Duquan, a twenty-five year old African American man wearing a shirt
and tie.

Pause.

DUQUAN: See anything that looks good?

STAGE DIRECTIONS: Oh, everything looks amazing. I don't think I'll ever be able to choose.

*   *   *

Reading and Reacting

1. Which elements of the play's staging do you consider experimental? Why? Which do you see as conventional?
2. Why does Salomon make the stage directions a character in the play?
3. What difficulties do you think someone staging this play would face? How would you address these difficulties?
4. What is the significance of the play's title? Is it in any way ironic?
5. *The Date* begins with Duquan sitting at a table with Jackie. It ends with Duquan sitting with Stage Directions. What is the significance of this change?
6. What is the central conflict of the play? Can it ever be resolved? Explain.
7. In what ways are the beginning and end of the play similar? How are they different?
8. What is the central theme of *The Date*? Is the play making a point about drama? about race? about dating? about relationships? about something else?

9. **JOURNAL ENTRY** Assume that there are no stage directions for *The Date*. Write your own set of stage directions, making sure that they reflect your own interpretation of the play.

10. **CRITICAL PERSPECTIVE** Writing for Northwestern University's online publication *North by Northwestern*, Jennifer Schaefer reviews Michael Solomon's ten-minute play *RMEO + JULEZ*, which won the Manhattan Theater Club's 2009 REALationships Playwright competition. In her review, Schaefer observes that the play explores ideas about how technology—especially social media—affects "relationships in the digital age." In what way is the "date" depicted in this play a critique of contemporary romantic relationships? How, if at all, does technology undercut the ability of Jackie and Duquan to relate to each other?

Related Works: "Love and Other Catastrophes: A Mix Tape" (p. 127), "How to Talk to Girls at Parties" (p. 214), "Cathedral" (p. 435), "Castro Moves into the Havana Hilton" (p. 704)

Milcha Sanchez-Scott

MILCHA SANCHEZ-SCOTT (1955–   ) is a Los Angeles–based writer of plays that include *Dog Lady* and *The Cuban Swimmer*, both one-act plays (1984); *Roosters*, published in *On New Ground: Contemporary Hispanic American Plays* (1987) and adapted into the 1993 feature film of the same name; and *Stone Wedding*, produced at the Los Angeles Theater Center (1988). Also produced by the Los Angeles Theater Center was her play *Carmen*, adapted from Georges Bizet's opera of the same title.

Born in Bali, Sanchez-Scott is the daughter of an Indonesian mother and a Colombian-Mexican father. Her early childhood was spent in Mexico, South America, and Britain; her family moved to San Diego when she was fourteen.

Writing in *Time* magazine, William A. Henry observes that the visionary or hallucinatory elements in Sanchez-Scott's plays derive from the Latin American "magic realism" tradition of Jorge Luis Borges and Gabriel García Márquez. For example, Henry notes that in *Roosters*, what seems "a straightforward depiction of the life of farmlands gives way to mysterious visitations, symbolic cockfights enacted by dancers, virginal girls wearing wings, archetypal confrontations between father and son."

In 1984, the New York production of *The Cuban Swimmer* was noteworthy for an ingeniously designed set that realistically re-created on stage Pacific Ocean waves, a helicopter, and a boat. According to the *New York Times*, "The audience [could] almost feel the resisting tides and the California oil slick . . . represented by a watery-blue floor and curtain." Jeannette Mirabel, as the Cuban swimmer, made an "auspicious" debut in the play, according to the *Times*: "In a tour de force of balletic movements, she [kept] her arms fluttering in the imaginary waters throughout the play."

Cultural Context In 1980, in the wake of numerous incidences of dissent and rebellion, Fidel Castro deported a large number of Cubans and encouraged many others to leave. In the resulting exodus, which became known as the Mariel boatlift, more than 120,000 Cuban refugees arrived in Florida, placing tremendous strain on United States resources. In 1984, an agreement was made between the two countries that limited the number of Cuban immigrants to 20,000 per year. Over time, the United States relaxed this quota, but the resulting abundance of refugees prompted the United States government to reinstate the quota in the mid-1990s. In 1996, the Cuban Adjustment Act was passed, stating that Cubans who reached dry land would be allowed to become permanent residents of the United States, but those who were intercepted while still at sea would be returned to Cuba. In 1999, the plight of Cuban refugees was reflected in the story of Elian Gonzalez, a six-year-old boy who was found clinging to an inner tube but was later returned to Cuba in accordance with the 1996 act. Starting in 2009, President Barack Obama, in an effort to open a dialogue with Cuba, eased some travel and economic restrictions.

The Cuban Swimmer (1984)

CHARACTERS

Margarita Suárez, *the swimmer* **Abuela,** *her grandmother*
Eduardo Suárez, *her father, the coach* **Voice of Mel Munson**
Simón Suárez, *her brother* **Voice of Mary Beth White**
Aída Suárez, *her mother* **Voice of Radio Operator**

SETTING

The Pacific Ocean between San Pedro and Catalina Island.

TIME

Summer.

Live conga drums can be used to punctuate the action of the play.

SCENE 1

Pacific Ocean. Midday. On the horizon, in perspective, a small boat enters upstage left, crosses to upstage right, and exits. Pause. Lower on the horizon, the same boat, in larger perspective, enters upstage right, crosses and exits upstage left. Blackout.

Joanna Liao as Margarita Suárez in a production of *The Cuban Swimmer*
Source: Milcha Sanchez-Scott's THE CUBAN SWIMMER at People's Light & Theatre Company. Photo by Mark Garvin.

SCENE 2

*Pacific Ocean. Midday. The swimmer, Margarita Suárez, is swimming. On the boat fol-
lowing behind her are her father, Eduardo Suárez, holding a megaphone, and Simón, her
brother, sitting on top of the cabin with his shirt off, punk sunglasses on, binoculars hanging
on his chest.*

EDUARDO: (*leaning forward, shouting in time to Margarita's swimming*) Uno, dos, uno,
    dos. Y uno, dos . . . keep your shoulders parallel to the water.
SIMÓN: I'm gonna take these glasses off and look straight into the sun.
EDUARDO: (*through megaphone*) Muy bien, muy bien . . . but punch those arms in, baby.
SIMÓN: (*looking directly at the sun through binoculars*) Come on, come on, zap me.
    Show me something. (*He looks behind at the shoreline and ahead at the sea.*) Stop!
    Stop, *Papi!* Stop!

*Aída Suárez and Abuela, the swimmer's mother and grandmother, enter running from the
back of the boat.*

5   AÍDA AND ABUELA: *Qué? Qué es?*
    AÍDA: *Es un shark?*
    EDUARDO: Eh?
    ABUELA: *Que es un shark dicen?*

Eduardo blows whistle. Margarita looks up at the boat.

SIMÓN: No, *Papi*, no shark, no shark. We've reached the halfway mark.
10   ABUELA: (*looking into the water*) A dónde está?

AÍDA: It's not in the water.

ABUELA: Oh, no? Oh, no?

AÍDA: No! A *poco* do you think they're gonna have signs in the water to say you are halfway to Santa Catalina? No. It's done very scientific. *A ver, hijo*, explain it to your grandma.

SIMÓN: Well, you see, Abuela—(*He points behind.*) There's San Pedro. (*He points ahead.*) And there's Santa Catalina. Looks halfway to me.

Abuela shakes her head and is looking back and forth, trying to make the decision, when suddenly the sound of a helicopter is heard.

ABUELA: (*looking up*) *Virgencita de la Caridad del Cobre. Qué es eso?*   15

Sound of helicopter gets closer. Margarita looks up.

MARGARITA: *Papi, Papi!*

A small commotion on the boat, with everybody pointing at the helicopter above. Shadows of the helicopter fall on the boat. Simón looks up at it through binoculars.

Papi—qué es? What is it?

EDUARDO: (*through megaphone*) Uh . . . uh . . . uh, *un momentico* . . . *mi hija.* . . . Your *papi's* got everything under control, understand? Uh . . . you just keep stroking. And stay . . . uh . . . close to the boat.

SIMÓN: Wow, *Papi!* We're on TV, man! Holy Christ, we're all over the fucking U.S.A.! It's Mel Munson and Mary Beth White!

AÍDA: *Por Dios!* Simón, don't swear. And put on your shirt.

Aída fluffs her hair, puts on her sunglasses and waves to the helicopter. Simón leans over the side of the boat and yells to Margarita.

SIMÓN: Yo, Margo! You're on TV, man.   20

EDUARDO: Leave your sister alone. Turn on the radio.

MARGARITA: *Papi! Qué está pasando?*

ABUELA: *Que es la televisión dicen?* (*She shakes her head.*) *Porque como yo no puedo ver nada sin mis espejuelos.*

Abuela rummages through the boat, looking for her glasses. Voices of Mel Munson and Mary Beth White are heard over the boat's radio.

MEL'S VOICE: As we take a closer look at the gallant crew of *La Havana* . . . and there . . . yes, there she is . . . the little Cuban swimmer from Long Beach, California, nineteen-year-old Margarita Suárez. The unknown swimmer is our Cinderella entry . . . a bundle of tenacity, battling her way through the choppy, murky waters of the cold Pacific to reach the Island of Romance . . . Santa Catalina . . . where should she be the first to arrive, two thousand dollars and a gold cup will be waiting for her.

AÍDA: Doesn't even cover our expenses.   25

ABUELA: *Qué dice?*

EDUARDO: Shhhh!

MARY BETH'S VOICE: This is really a family effort, Mel, and—

MEL'S VOICE: Indeed it is. Her trainer, her coach, her mentor, is her father, Eduardo Suárez. Not a swimmer himself, it says here, Mr. Suárez is head usher of the Holy Name Society and the owner-operator of Suárez Treasures of the Sea and Salvage Yard. I guess it's one of those places—

30   MARY BETH'S VOICE: If I might interject a fact here, Mel, assisting in this swim is Mrs. Suárez, who is a former Miss Cuba.

MEL'S VOICE: And a beautiful woman in her own right. Let's try and get a closer look.

Helicopter sound gets louder. Margarita, frightened, looks up again.

MARGARITA: *Papi!*

EDUARDO: *(through megaphone) Mi hija,* don't get nervous . . . it's the press. I'm handling it.

AÍDA: I see how you're handling it.

35   EDUARDO: *(through megaphone)* Do you hear? Everything is under control. Get back into your rhythm. Keep your elbows high and kick and kick and kick and kick . . .

ABUELA: *(finds her glasses and puts them on) Ay sí, es la televisión* . . . *(She points to helicopter.) Qué lindo mira* . . . *(She fluffs her hair, gives a big wave.) Aló América! Viva mi Margarita, viva todo los Cubanos en los Estados Unidos!*

AÍDA: *Ay por Dios,* Cecilia, the man didn't come all this way in his helicopter to look at you jumping up and down, making a fool of yourself.

ABUELA: I don't care. I'm proud.

AÍDA: He can't understand you anyway.

40   ABUELA: *Viva* . . . *(She stops.) Simón, comó se dice viva?*

SIMÓN: Hurray.

ABUELA: Hurray for *mi* Margarita *y* for all the Cubans living *en* the United States, *y un abrazo* . . . *Simón, abrazo* . . .

SIMÓN: A big hug.

ABUELA: *Sí,* a big hug to all my friends in Miami, Long Beach, Union City, except for my son Carlos, who lives in New York in sin! He lives . . . *(she crosses herself)* in Brooklyn with a Puerto Rican woman in sin! *No decente* . . .

45   SIMÓN: Decent.

ABUELA: Carlos, *no decente.* This family, *decente.*

AÍDA: Cecilia, *por Dios.*

MEL'S VOICE: Look at that enthusiasm. The whole family has turned out to cheer little Margarita on to victory! I hope they won't be too disappointed.

MARY BETH'S VOICE: She seems to be making good time, Mel.

50   MEL'S VOICE: Yes, it takes all kinds to make a race. And it's a testimonial to the all-encompassing fairness . . . the greatness of this, the Wrigley Invitational Women's Swim to Catalina, where among all the professionals there is still room for the amateurs . . . like these, the simple people we see below us on the ragtag *La Havana,* taking their long-shot chance to victory. *Vaya con Dios!*

Helicopter sound fading as family, including Margarita, watch silently. Static as Simón turns radio off. Eduardo walks to bow of boat, looks out on the horizon.

EDUARDO: *(to himself)* Amateurs.

AÍDA: Eduardo, that person insulted us. Did you hear, Eduardo? That he called us a simple people in a ragtag boat? Did you hear . . . ?

ABUELA: (*clenching her fist at departing helicopter*) Mal-Rayo los parta!

SIMÓN: (*same gesture*) Asshole!

Aída follows Eduardo as he goes to side of boat and stares at Margarita.

AÍDA: This person comes in his helicopter to insult your wife, your family, your   55
daughter . . .

MARGARITA: (*pops her head out of the water*) Papi?

AÍDA: Do you hear me, Eduardo? I am not simple.

ABUELA: Sí.

AÍDA: I am complicated.

ABUELA: Sí, demasiada complicada.   60

AÍDA: Me and my family are not so simple.

SIMÓN: Mom, the guy's an asshole.

ABUELA: (*shaking her fist at helicopter*) Asshole!

AÍDA: If my daughter was simple, she would not be in that water swimming.

MARGARITA: Simple? Papi . . . ?   65

AÍDA: Ahora, Eduardo, this is what I want you to do. When we get to Santa Catalina, I want you to call the TV station and demand an apology.

EDUARDO: Cállete mujer! Aquí mando yo. I will decide what is to be done.

MARGARITA: Papi, tell me what's going on.

EDUARDO: Do you understand what I am saying to you, Aída?

SIMÓN: (*leaning over side of boat, to Margarita*) Yo Margo! You know that Mel Munson   70
guy on TV? He called you a simple amateur and said you didn't have a chance.

ABUELA: (*leaning directly behind Simón.*) Mi hija, insultó a la familia. Desgraciado!

AÍDA: (*leaning in behind Abuela*) He called us peasants! And your father is not doing anything about it. He just knows how to yell at me.

EDUARDO: (*through megaphone*) Shut up! All of you! Do you want to break her concentration? Is that what you are after? Eh?

Abuela, Aída, and Simón shrink back. Eduardo paces before them.

Swimming is rhythm and concentration. You win a race aquí. (*Pointing to his head.*) Now . . . (*to Simón*) you, take care of the boat, Aída y Mama . . . do something. Anything. Something practical.

Abuela and Aída get on knees and pray in Spanish.

Hija, give it everything, eh? . . . por la familia. Uno . . . dos. . . . You must win.

Simón goes into cabin. The prayers continue as lights change to indicate bright sunlight, later in the afternoon.

SCENE 3

Tableau for a couple of beats. Eduardo on bow with timer in one hand as he counts strokes per minute. Simón is in the cabin steering, wearing his sunglasses, baseball cap on backward. Abuela and Aída are at the side of the boat, heads down, hands folded, still muttering prayers in Spanish.

AÍDA AND ABUELA: *(crossing themselves)* En el nombre del Padre, del Hijo y del Espíritu Santo amén.

EDUARDO: *(through megaphone)* You're stroking seventy-two!

SIMÓN: *(singing)* Mama's stroking, Mama's stroking seventy-two. . . .

EDUARDO: *(through megaphone)* You comfortable with it?

5   SIMÓN: *(singing)* Seventy-two, seventy-two, seventy-two for you.

AÍDA: *(looking at the heavens)* Ay, Eduardo, *ven acá*, we should be grateful that *Nuestro Señor* gave us such a beautiful day.

ABUELA: *(crosses herself)* Si, gracias a Dios.

EDUARDO: She's stroking seventy-two, with no problem. *(He throws a kiss to the sky.)* It's a beautiful day to win.

AÍDA: *Qué hermoso!* So clear and bright. Not a cloud in the sky. *Mira! Mira!* Even rainbows on the water . . . a sign from God.

10   SIMÓN: *(singing)* Rainbows on the water . . . you in my arms . . .

ABUELA AND EDUARDO: *(Looking the wrong way.)* Dónde?

AÍDA: *(pointing toward Margarita)* There, dancing in front of Margarita, leading her on . . .

EDUARDO: Rainbows on . . . *Ay coño!* It's an oil slick! You . . . you . . . *(To Simón.)* Stop the boat. *(Runs to bow, yelling.)* Margarita! Margarita!

On the next stroke, Margarita comes up all covered in black oil.

MARGARITA: *Papi! Papi* . . . !

Everybody goes to the side and stares at Margarita, who stares back. Eduardo freezes.

15   AÍDA: *Apúrate*, Eduardo, move . . . what's wrong with you . . . *no me oíste*, get my daughter out of the water.

EDUARDO: *(softly)* We can't touch her. If we touch her, she's disqualified.

AÍDA: But I'm her mother.

EDUARDO: Not even by her own mother. Especially by her own mother. . . . You always want the rules to be different for you, you always want to be the exception. *(To Simón.)* And you . . . you didn't see it, eh? You were playing again?

SIMÓN: *Papi*, I was watching . . .

20   AÍDA: *(interrupting) Pues*, do something Eduardo. You are the big coach, the monitor.

SIMÓN: Mentor! Mentor!

EDUARDO: How can a person think around you? *(He walks off to bow, puts head in hands.)*

ABUELA: *(looking over side)* Mira como todos los little birds are dead. *(She crosses herself.)*

AÍDA: Their little wings are glued to their sides.

25   SIMÓN: Christ, this is like the La Brea tar pits.

AÍDA: They can't move their little wings.

ABUELA: *Esa niña tiene que moverse.*

SIMÓN: Yeah, Margo, you gotta move, man.

Abuela and Simón gesture for Margarita to move. Aída gestures for her to swim.

ABUELA: *Anda niña, muévete.*

AÍDA: Swim, *hija*, swim or the *aceite* will stick to your wings.   30
MARGARITA: *Papi?*
ABUELA: *(taking megaphone)* Your *papi* say "move it!"

Margarita with difficulty starts moving.

ABUELA, AÍDA AND SIMÓN: *(laboriously counting)* Uno, dos . . . uno, dos . . .
   anda . . . uno, dos.
EDUARDO: *(running to take megaphone from Abuela)* Uno, dos . . .

Simón races into cabin and starts the engine. Abuela, Aída and Eduardo count together.

SIMÓN: *(looking ahead)* Papi, it's over there!   35
EDUARDO: Eh?
SIMÓN: *(pointing ahead and to the right)* It's getting clearer over there.
EDUARDO: *(through megaphone)* Now pay attention to me. Go to the right.

Simón, Abuela, Aída and Eduardo all lean over side. They point ahead and to the right, except Abuela, who points to the left.

FAMILY: *(shouting together)* Para yá! Para yá!

Lights go down on boat. A special light on Margarita, swimming through the oil, and on Abuela, watching her.

ABUELA: *Sangre de mi sangre*, you will be another to save us. En Bolondron, where   40
   your great-grandmother Luz Suárez was born, they say one day it rained blood.
   All the people, they run into their houses. They cry, they pray, *pero* your great-
   grandmother Luz she had *cojones* like a man. She run outside. She look straight
   at the sky. She shake her fist. And she say to the evil one, "*Mira . . . (beating her
   chest) coño, Diablo, aquí estoy si me quieres.*" And she open her mouth, and she
   drunk the blood.

Blackout

SCENE 4

Lights up on boat. Aída and Eduardo are on deck watching Margarita swim. We hear the gentle, rhythmic lap, lap, lap of the water, then the sound of inhaling and exhaling as Margarita's breathing becomes louder. Then Margarita's heartbeat is heard, with the lapping of the water and the breathing under it. These sounds continue beneath the dialogue to the end of the scene.

AÍDA: *Dios mío.* Look how she moves through the water. . . .
EDUARDO: You see, it's very simple. It is a matter of concentration.
AÍDA: The first time I put her in water she came to life, she grew before my eyes.
   She moved, she smiled, she loved it more than me. She didn't want my breast
   any longer. She wanted the water.
EDUARDO: And of course, the rhythm. The rhythm takes away the pain and helps
   the concentration.

Pause. Aída and Eduardo watch Margarita.

5   AÍDA: Is that my child or a seal. . . .

EDUARDO: Ah, a seal, the reason for that is that she's keeping her arms very close to her body. She cups her hands, and then she reaches and digs, reaches and digs.

AÍDA: To think that a daughter of mine . . .

EDUARDO: It's the training, the hours in the water. I used to tie weights around her little wrists and ankles.

AÍDA: A spirit, an ocean spirit, must have entered my body when I was carrying her.

10   EDUARDO: *(to Margarita)* Your stroke is slowing down.

Pause. We hear Margarita's heartbeat with the breathing under, faster now.

AÍDA: Eduardo, that night, the night on the boat . . .

EDUARDO: Ah, the night on the boat again . . . the moon was . . .

AÍDA: The moon was full. We were coming to America. . . . *Qué romantico.*

Heartbeat and breathing continue.

EDUARDO: We were cold, afraid, with no money, and on top of everything, you were hysterical, yelling at me, tearing at me with your nails. *(Opens his shirt, points to the base of his neck.)* Look, I still bear the scars . . . telling me that I didn't know what I was doing . . . saying that we were going to die. . . .

15   AÍDA: You took me, you stole me from my home . . . you didn't give me a chance to prepare. You just said we have to go now, now! Now, you said. You didn't let me take anything. I left everything behind. . . . I left everything behind.

EDUARDO: Saying that I wasn't good enough, that your father didn't raise you so that I could drown you in the sea.

AÍDA: You didn't let me say even a good-bye. You took me, you stole me, you tore me from my home.

EDUARDO: I took you so we could be married.

AÍDA: That was in Miami. But that night on the boat, Eduardo. . . . We were not married, that night on the boat.

20   EDUARDO: *No pasó nada!* Once and for all get it out of your head, it was cold, you hated me, and we were afraid. . . .

AÍDA: *Mentiroso!*

EDUARDO: A man can't do it when he is afraid.

AÍDA: Liar! You did it very well.

EDUARDO: I did?

25   AÍDA: *Sí.* Gentle. You were so gentle and then strong . . . my passion for you so deep. Standing next to you . . . I would ache . . . looking at your hands I would forget to breathe, you were irresistible.

EDUARDO: I was?

AÍDA: You took me into your arms, you touched my face with your fingertips . . . you kissed my eyes . . . *la esquina de la boca y . . .*

EDUARDO: *Sí, sí,* and then . . .

AÍDA: I look at your face on top of mine, and I see the lights of Havana in your eyes. That's when you seduced me.

30   EDUARDO: Shhh, they're gonna hear you.

Lights go down. Special on Aída.

AÍDA: That was the night. A woman doesn't forget those things . . . and later that night was the dream . . . the dream of a big country with fields of fertile land and big, giant things growing. And there by a green, slimy pond I found a giant pea pod and when I opened it, it was full of little, tiny baby frogs.

Aída crosses herself as she watches Margarita. We hear louder breathing and heartbeat.

MARGARITA: Santa Teresa. Little Flower of God, pray for me. San Martín de Porres, pray for me. Santa Rosa de Lima, *Virgencita de la Caridad del Cobre*, pray for me. . . . Mother pray for me.

SCENE 5

Loud howling of wind is heard, as lights change to indicate unstable weather, fog and mist. Family on deck, braced and huddled against the wind. Simón is at the helm.

AÍDA: Ay Dios mío, qué viento.
EDUARDO: *(through megaphone)* Don't drift out . . . that wind is pushing you out.
    (To Simón.) You! Slow down. Can't you see your sister is drifting out?
SIMÓN: It's the wind, *Papi.*
AÍDA: Baby, don't go so far. . . .
ABUELA: *(to heaven)* Ay Gran Poder de Dios, quita este maldito viento.   5
SIMÓN: Margo! Margo! Stay close to the boat.
EDUARDO: Dig in. Dig in hard. . . . Reach down from your guts and dig in.
ABUELA: *(to heaven)* Ay Virgen de la Caridad del Cobre, por lo más tú quieres a pararla.
AÍDA: *(putting her hand out, reaching for Margarita)* Baby, don't go far.

Abuela crosses herself. Action freezes. Lights get dimmer, special on Margarita. She keeps swimming, stops, starts again, stops, then, finally exhausted, stops altogether. The boat stops moving.

EDUARDO: What's going on here? Why are we stopping?   10
SIMÓN: *Papi*, she's not moving! Yo Margo!

The family all run to the side.

EDUARDO: Hija! . . . Hijita! You're tired, eh?
AÍDA: *Por supuesto* she's tired. I like to see you get in the water, waving your arms and legs from San Pedro to Santa Catalina. A person isn't a machine, a person has to rest.
SIMÓN: Yo, Mama! Cool out, it ain't fucking brain surgery.
EDUARDO: *(to Simón)* Shut up, you. *(Louder to Margarita.)* I guess your mother's   15
right for once, huh? . . . I guess you had to stop, eh? . . . Give your brother, the idiot . . . a chance to catch up with you.
SIMÓN: *(clowning like Mortimer Snerd)* Dum dee dum dee dum ooops, ah shucks . . .
EDUARDO: I don't think he's Cuban.
SIMÓN: *(like Ricky Ricardo)* Oye, Lucy! I'm home! Ba ba lu!

EDUARDO: *(joins in clowning, grabbing Simón in a headlock)* What am I gonna do with this idiot, eh? I don't understand this idiot. He's not like us, Margarita. *(Laughing.)* You think if we put him into your bathing suit with a cap on his head . . . *(He laughs hysterically.)* You think anyone would know . . . huh? Do you think anyone would know? *(Laughs.)*

20   SIMÓN: *(vamping)* Ay, mi amor. Anybody looking for tits would know.

Eduardo slaps Simón across the face, knocking him down. Aída runs to Simón's aid. Abuela holds Eduardo back.

MARGARITA: *Mía culpa! Mía culpa!*

ABUELA: *Qué dices hija?*

MARGARITA: *Papi,* it's my fault, it's all my fault. . . . I'm so cold, I can't move. . . . I put my face in the water . . . and I hear them whispering . . . laughing at me. . . .

AÍDA: Who is laughing at you?

25   MARGARITA: The fish are all biting me . . . they hate me . . . they whisper about me. She can't swim, they say. She can't glide. She has no grace. . . . Yellowtails, bonita, tuna, man-o'-war, snub-nose sharks, *los baracudas* . . . they all hate me . . . only the dolphins care . . . and sometimes I hear the whales crying . . . she is lost, she is dead. I'm so numb, I can't feel. *Papi! Papi!* Am I dead?

EDUARDO: *Vamos,* baby, punch those arms in. Come on . . . do you hear me?

MARGARITA: *Papi* . . . *Papi* . . . forgive me. . . .

All is silent on the boat. Eduardo drops his megaphone, his head bent down in dejection. Abuela, Aída, Simón, all leaning over the side of the boat. Simón slowly walks away.

AÍDA: *Mi hija, qué tienes?*

SIMÓN: Oh, Christ, don't make her say it. Please don't make her say it.

30   ABUELA: Say what? *Qué cosa?*

SIMÓN: She wants to quit, can't you see she's had enough?

ABUELA: *Mira, para eso. Esta niña* is turning blue.

AÍDA: *Oyeme, mi hija.* Do you want to come out of the water?

MARGARITA: *Papi?*

35   SIMÓN: *(to Eduardo)* She won't come out until *you* tell her.

AÍDA: Eduardo . . . answer your daughter.

EDUARDO: *Le dije* to concentrate . . . concentrate on your rhythm. Then the rhythm would carry her . . . ay, it's a beautiful thing, Aída. It's like yoga, like meditation, the mind over matter . . . the mind controlling the body . . . that's how the great things in the world have been done. I wish you . . . I wish my wife could understand.

MARGARITA: *Papi?*

SIMÓN: *(to Margarita)* Forget him.

40   AÍDA: *(imploring)* Eduardo, *por favor.*

EDUARDO: *(walking in circles)* Why didn't you let her concentrate? Don't you understand, the concentration, the rhythm is everything. But no, you wouldn't listen. *(Screaming to the ocean.)* Goddamn Cubans, why, God, why do you make us go everywhere with our families? *(He goes to back of boat.)*

AÍDA: *(opening her arms)* Mi hija, ven, come to Mami. *(Rocking.)* Your *mami* knows.

Abuela has taken the training bottle, puts it in a net. She and Simón lower it to Margarita.

SIMÓN: Take this. Drink it. (*As Margarita drinks, Abuela crosses herself.*)

ABUELA: *Sangre de mi sangre.*

Music comes up softly. Margarita drinks, gives the bottle back, stretches out her arms, as if on a cross. Floats on her back. She begins a graceful backstroke. Lights fade on boat as special lights come up on Margarita. She stops. Slowly turns over and starts to swim, gradually picking up speed. Suddenly as if in pain she stops, tries again, then stops in pain again. She becomes disoriented and falls to the bottom of the sea. Special on Margarita at the bottom of the sea.

MARGARITA: *Ya no puedo* . . . I can't. . . . A person isn't a machine . . . *es mi culpa* . . . Father forgive me . . . *Papi! Papi!* One, two. *Uno, dos.* (*Pause.*) *Papi! A dónde estás?* (*Pause.*) One, two, one, two. *Papi! Ay, Papi!* Where are you . . . ? Don't leave me. . . . Why don't you answer me? (*Pause. She starts to swim, slowly.*) *Uno, dos, uno, dos.* Dig in, dig in. (*Stops swimming.*) *Por favor, Papi!* (*Starts to swim again.*) One, two, one, two. Kick from your hip, kick from your hip. (*Stops swimming. Starts to cry.*) Oh God, please. . . . (*Pause.*) Hail Mary, full of grace . . . dig in, dig in . . . the Lord is with thee. . . . (*She swims to the rhythm of her Hail Mary.*) Hail Mary, full of grace . . . dig in, dig in . . . the Lord is with thee . . . dig in, dig in. . . . Blessed art thou among women. . . . *Mami,* it hurts. You let go of my hand. I'm lost. . . . And blessed is the fruit of thy womb, now and at the hour of our death. Amen. I don't want to die, I don't want to die.

Margarita is still swimming. Blackout. She is gone.

SCENE 6

Lights up on boat, we hear radio static. There is a heavy mist. On deck we see only black outline of Abuela with shawl over her head. We hear the voices of Eduardo, Aída, and Radio Operator.

EDUARDO'S VOICE: *La Havana!* Coming from San Pedro. Over.

RADIO OPERATOR'S VOICE: Right, DT6-6, you say you've lost a swimmer.

AÍDA'S VOICE: Our child, our only daughter . . . listen to me. Her name is Margarita Inez Suárez, she is wearing a black one-piece bathing suit cut high in the legs with a white racing stripe down the sides, a white bathing cap with goggles and her whole body covered with a . . . with a . . .

EDUARDO'S VOICE: With lanolin and paraffin.

AÍDA'S VOICE: *Sí* . . . con lanolin and paraffin.

More radio static. Special on Simón, on the edge of the boat.

SIMÓN: Margo! Yo Margo! (*Pause.*) Man don't do this. (*Pause.*) Come on. . . . Come on. . . . (*Pause.*) God, why does everything have to be so hard? (*Pause.*) Stupid. You know you're not supposed to die for this. Stupid. It's his dream and he can't even swim. (*Pause.*) Punch those arms in. Come home. Come home. I'm your little brother. Don't forget what Mama said. You're not supposed to leave me behind. *Vamos,* Margarita, take your little brother, hold his hand tight when you cross the street. He's so little. (*Pause.*) Oh, Christ, give us a sign. . . . I know! I know! Margo, I'll send you a message . . . like mental telepathy. I'll hold my breath, close my eyes, and I'll bring you home. (*He takes a deep breath; a few beats.*) This time I'll beep . . . I'll send out sonar signals like a dolphin. (*He imitates dolphin sounds.*)

The sound of real dolphins takes over from Simón, then fades into sound of Abuela saying the Hail Mary in Spanish, as full lights come up slowly.

SCENE 7

Eduardo coming out of cabin, sobbing, Aída holding him. Simón anxiously scanning the horizon. Abuela looking calmly ahead.

EDUARDO: *Es mi culpa, sí, es mi culpa.* (*He hits his chest.*)
AÍDA: *Ya, ya viejo* . . . it was my sin . . . I left my home.
EDUARDO: Forgive me, forgive me. I've lost our daughter, our sister, our grand-daughter, *mi carne, mi sangre, mis ilusiones.* (*To heaven.*) *Dios mío,* take me . . . take me, I say . . . Goddammit, take me!
SIMÓN: I'm going in.
5 **AÍDA AND EDUARDO:** No!
EDUARDO: (*grabbing and holding Simón, speaking to heaven*) God, take me, not my children. They are my dreams, my illusions . . . and not this one, this one is my mystery . . . he has my secret dreams. In him are the parts of me I cannot see.

Eduardo embraces Simón. Radio static becomes louder.

AÍDA: I . . . I think I see her.
SIMÓN: No, it's just a seal.
ABUELA: (*looking out with binoculars*) *Mi nietacita, dónde estás?* (*She feels her heart.*) I don't feel the knife in my heart . . . my little fish is not lost.

Radio crackles with static. As lights dim on boat, Voices of Mel and Mary Beth are heard over the radio.

10 **MEL'S VOICE:** Tragedy has marred the face of the Wrigley Invitational Women's Race to Catalina. The Cuban swimmer, little Margarita Suárez, has reportedly been lost at sea. Coast Guard and divers are looking for her as we speak. Yet in spite of this tragedy the race must go on because . . .
MARY BETH'S VOICE: (*interrupting loudly*) Mel!
MEL'S VOICE: (*startled*) What!
MARY BETH'S VOICE: Ah . . . excuse me, Mel . . . we have a winner. We've just received word from Catalina that one of the swimmers is just fifty yards from the breakers . . . it's, oh, it's . . . Margarita Suárez!

Special on family in cabin listening to radio.

MEL'S VOICE: What? I thought she died!

Special on Margarita, taking off bathing cap, trophy in hand, walking on the water.

MARY BETH'S VOICE: Ahh . . . unless . . . unless this is a tragic . . . No . . . there she   15
is, Mel. Margarita Suárez! The only one in the race wearing a black bathing suit
cut high in the legs with a racing stripe down the side.

Family cheering, embracing.

SIMÓN: *(screaming)* Way to go, Margo!

MEL'S VOICE: This is indeed a miracle! It's a resurrection! Margarita Suárez, with a
flotilla of boats to meet her, is now walking on the waters, through the breakers . . . onto the beach, with crowds of people cheering her on. What a jubila-
tion! This is a miracle!

Sound of crowds cheering. Lights and cheering sounds fade.

Blackout

*   *   *

Reading and Reacting

1. What lighting and sound effects do the stage directions specify? In what way do
these effects advance the action of the play? How do they help to communicate
the play's theme?

2. Although most of the play is in English, the characters frequently speak Spanish.
What are the advantages and disadvantages of this use of Spanish? How does the
mixing of English and Spanish reflect one of the play's themes?

3. What function do the voices of Mel and Mary Beth serve in the play?

4. What conflicts develop among the family members as the play proceeds? Do you
think these conflicts are meant to represent the problems of other immigrant
groups?

5. In what sense is Mel's final comment "This is a miracle!" true? In what sense is it
ironic?

6. Could this play be seen as an allegory? What is the value of seeing it in this way?

7. During much of the play, Margarita is swimming in full view of the audience. Suggest three ways in which a director could convey this effect on stage. Which way
would you choose if you were directing the play? Why?

8. As the headnote to the play explains, the 1984 New York production of *The
Cuban Swimmer* had an extremely realistic set. Could the play be staged unrealistically, with the characters on a raised platform instead of a boat? How do you think
this kind of set would change the audience's reaction?

9. **JOURNAL ENTRY** Are you able to empathize with Margarita's struggle? What elements of the play make it easy (or difficult) for you to do so?

10. **CRITICAL PERSPECTIVE** In a 1998 article in the *New York Times*, theater critic Brooks
Atkinson said, "Nothing is better for good actors than a stage with no scenery."
    How do you interpret Atkinson's comment? Do you think this remark could be
applied to the staging of *The Cuban Swimmer*?

Related Works: "Snow" (p. 126), "The Secret Lion" (p. 180), "Two Kinds" (p. 639),
"My Voice" (p. 685), "Baca Grande" (p. 723), "Harlem" (p. 760), "Mexican Almuerzo
in New England" (p. 843), "Isla" (p. 860)

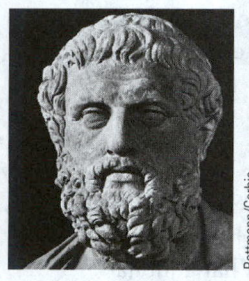

Bettmann/Corbis

SOPHOCLES (496–406 B.C.), along with Aeschylus and Euripides, is one of the three great ancient Greek tragic dramatists. He lived during the flowering and subsequent decline of fifth-century B.C. Athens—the high point of Greek civilization. Born as Greece struggled against the Persian Empire and moved to adopt democracy, he lived as an adult under Pericles during the golden age of Athens and died as it became clear that Athens would lose the Peloponnesian War. Sophocles was an active participant in the public life of Athens, serving as a collector of tribute from Athenian subjects and later as a general. He wrote at least 120 plays, but only seven have survived, including three plays about Oedipus: *Oedipus the King* (c. 430 B.C.), *Oedipus at Colonus* (411? B.C.), and *Antigone* (441 B.C.).

   Oedipus the King, or *Oedipus Rex* (sometimes called *Oedipus the Tyrant*), was performed shortly after a great plague in Athens (probably in 429 or 425 B.C.) and as Athens was falling into decline. The play opens with an account of a plague in Thebes, Oedipus's kingdom. Over the years, *Oedipus the King* has attracted impressive critical attention, from Aristotle's use of it as a model for his definition of tragedy to Freud's use of it when he discusses the Oedipus complex.

Cultural Context During the period in which *Oedipus* was written, the Greeks were especially interested in the relationship between greatness and *hubris*, the excessive pride and ambition that leads to the downfall of a hero in classical tragedy. They were fascinated by the idea that hubris can bring destruction: that the same traits that can elevate a person to greatness can also cause his or her ruin. This theme recurs throughout classical literature and was especially relevant between 431 and 404 B.C., when the second Peloponnesian War (which Athens lost) was being fought between Athens and Sparta. After a Spartan army invaded Attica in 431 B.C., the Athenians retreated behind the walls of their city while the Athenian fleet began raids. Between 430 and 428 B.C., a plague (which the Athenians believed was inflicted upon them by the gods) wiped out at least a quarter of the Athenian population. It was during this tumultuous time that Sophocles wrote of Oedipus and his troubles.

Oedipus the King* (c. 430 B.C.)

Translated by Thomas Gould

CHARACTERS

Oedipus,[1] *the King of Thebes*	**Tiresias,** *a blind seer or prophet*
Priest of Zeus, *leader of the suppliants*	**Jocasta,** *the queen of Thebes*
Creon, *Oedipus's brother-in-law*	**Messenger,** *from Corinth, once a shepherd*
Chorus, *a group of Theban elders*	**Herdsman,** *once a servant of Laius*
Choragos, *spokesman of the Chorus*	**Second Messenger,** *a servant of Oedipus*

MUTES

Suppliants, *Thebans seeking Oedipus's help*
Attendants, *for the Royal Family*
Servants, *to lead Tiresias and Oedipus*
Antigone, *daughter of Oedipus and Jocasta*
Ismene, *daughter of Oedipus and Jocasta*

---

*Note that individual lines are numbered in the following play. When a line is shared by two or more characters, it is counted as one line.

[1] *Oedipus:* The name, meaning "swollen foot," refers to the mutilation of Oedipus's feet by his father, Laius, before the infant was sent to Mount Cithaeron to be put to death by exposure.

The action takes place during the day in front of the royal palace in Thebes. There are two altars (left and right) on the proscenium and several steps leading down to the orchestra. As the play opens, Thebans of various ages who have come to beg Oedipus for help are sitting on these steps and in part of the orchestra. These suppliants are holding branches of laurel or olive which have strips of wool[2] wrapped around them. Oedipus enters from the palace (the central door of the skene).

Laurence Olivier as Oedipus
Merlyn Severn/Picture Post/Getty Images

<u>PROLOGUE[3]</u>

OEDIPUS: My children, ancient Cadmus'[4] newest care,
    why have you hurried to those seats, your boughs
    wound with the emblems of the suppliant?
    The city is weighed down with fragrant smoke,
    with hymns to the Healer[5] and the cries of mourners.   5
    I thought it wrong, my sons, to hear your words
    through emissaries, and have come out myself,
    I, Oedipus, a name that all men know.

Oedipus addresses the Priest.

    Old man—for it is fitting that you speak
    for all—what is your mood as you entreat me,   10

---

[2] *wool:* Branches wrapped with wool are traditional symbols of prayer or supplication.

[3] *Prologue:* The portion of the play containing the exposition, or explanation, of what has gone before and what is now happening.

[4] *Cadmus:* Oedipus's great-great-grandfather (although Oedipus does not know this) and the founder of Thebes.

[5] *Healer:* Apollo, god of prophecy, light, healing, justice, purification, and destruction.

fear or trust? You may be confident
that I'll do anything. How hard of heart
if an appeal like this did not rouse my pity!
PRIEST: You, Oedipus, who hold the power here,

15   you see our several ages, we who sit
before your altars—some not strong enough
to take long flight, some heavy in old age,
the priests, as I of Zeus,[6] and from our youths
a chosen band. The rest sit with their windings

20   in the markets, at the twin shrines of Pallas,[7]
and the prophetic embers of Ismēnos.[8]
Our city, as you see yourself, is tossed
too much, and can no longer lift its head
above the troughs of billows red with death.

25   It dies in the fruitful flowers of the soil,
it dies in its pastured herds, and in its women's
barren pangs. And the fire-bearing god[9]
has swooped upon the city, hateful plague,
and he has left the house of Cadmus empty.

30   Black Hades[10] is made rich with moans and weeping.
Not judging you an equal of the gods,
do I and the children sit here at your hearth,
but as the first of men, in troubled times
and in encounters with divinities.

35   You came to Cadmus' city and unbound
the tax we had to pay to the harsh singer,[11]
did it without a helpful word from us,
with no instruction; with a god's assistance
you raised up our life, so we believe.

40   Again now Oedipus, our greatest power,
we plead with you, as suppliants, all of us,
to find us strength, whether from a god's response,

---

[6]*Zeus:* Father and king of the gods.

[7]*Pallas:* Athena, goddess of wisdom, arts, crafts, and war.

[8]*Ismēnos:* A reference to the temple of Apollo near the river Ismēnos in Thebes. Prophecies were made here by "reading" the ashes of the altar fires.

[9]*fire-bearing god:* Contagious fever viewed as a god.

[10]*Black Hades:* Refers both to the underworld where the spirits of the dead go and to the god of the underworld.

[11]*harsh singer:* The Sphinx, a monster with a woman's head, a lion's body, and wings. The "tax" from which Oedipus freed Thebes was the destruction of all the young men who failed to solve the Sphinx's riddle and were subsequently devoured. The Sphinx always asked the same riddle: "What goes on four legs in the morning, two legs at noon, and three legs in the evening, and yet is weakest when supported by the largest number of feet?" Oedipus discovered the correct answer—man, who crawls in infancy, walks in his prime, and uses a stick in old age—and thus ended the Sphinx's reign of terror. The Sphinx destroyed herself when Oedipus answered the riddle. Oedipus's reward for freeing Thebes of the Sphinx was the throne and the hand of the recently widowed Jocasta.

or learned in some way from another man.
I know that the experienced among men
give counsels that will prosper best of all.   45
Noblest of men, lift up our land again!
Think also of yourself; since now the land
calls you its Savior for your zeal of old,
oh let us never look back at your rule
as men helped up only to fall again!   50
Do not stumble! Put our land on firm feet!
The bird of omen was auspicious then,
when you brought that luck; be that same man again!
The power is yours; if you will rule our country,
rule over men, not in an empty land.   55
A towered city or a ship is nothing
if desolate and no man lives within.

OEDIPUS: Pitiable children, oh I know, I know
the yearnings that have brought you. Yes, I know
that you are sick. And yet, though you are sick,   60
there is not one of you so sick as I.
For your affliction comes to each alone,
for him and no one else, but my soul mourns
for me and for you, too, and for the city.
You do not waken me as from a sleep,   65
for I have wept, bitterly and long,
tried many paths in the wanderings of thought,
and the single cure I found by careful search
I've acted on: I sent Menoeceus' son,
Creon, brother of my wife, to the Pythian   70
halls of Phoebus,[12] so that I might learn
what I must do or say to save this city.
Already, when I think what day this is,
I wonder anxiously what he is doing.
Too long, more than is right, he's been away.   75
But when he comes, then I shall be a traitor
if I do not do all that the god reveals.

PRIEST: Welcome words! But look, those men have signaled
that it is Creon who is now approaching!

OEDIPUS: Lord Apollo! May he bring Savior Luck,   80
a Luck as brilliant as his eyes are now!

PRIEST: His news is happy, it appears. He comes,
forehead crowned with thickly berried laurel.[13]

OEDIPUS: We'll know, for he is near enough to hear us.

---

[12] *Pythian halls . . . Phoebus:* The temple of Phoebus, Apollo's oracle or prophet at Delphi.
[13] *laurel:* Creon is wearing a garland of laurel leaves, sacred to Apollo.

Enter Creon along one of the parados.

85   Lord, brother in marriage, son of Menoeceus!
            What is the god's pronouncement that you bring?
      CREON: It's good. For even troubles, if they chance
            to turn out well, I always count as lucky.
      OEDIPUS: But what was the response? You seem to say
90   I'm not to fear—but not to take heart either.
      CREON: If you will hear me with these men present,
            I'm ready to report—or go inside.

Creon moves up the steps toward the palace.

      OEDIPUS: Speak out to all! The grief that burdens me
            concerns these men more than it does my life.
95   CREON: Then I shall tell you what I heard from the god.
            The task Lord Phoebus sets for us is clear:
            drive out pollution sheltered in our land,
            and do not shelter what is incurable.
      OEDIPUS: What is our trouble? How shall we cleanse ourselves?
100   CREON: We must banish or murder to free ourselves
            from a murder that blows storms through the city.
      OEDIPUS: What man's bad luck does he accuse in this?
      CREON: My Lord, a king named Laius ruled our land
            before you came to steer the city straight.
105   OEDIPUS: I know. So I was told—I never saw him.
      CREON: Since he was murdered, you must raise your hand
            against the men who killed him with their hands.
      OEDIPUS: Where are they now? And how can we ever find
            the track of ancient guilt now hard to read?
110   CREON: In our own land, he said. What we pursue,
            that can be caught; but not what we neglect.
      OEDIPUS: Was Laius home, or in the countryside—
            or was he murdered in some foreign land?
      CREON: He left to see a sacred rite, he said;
115   He left, but never came home from his journey.
      OEDIPUS: Did none of his party see it and report—
            someone we might profitably question?
      CREON: They were all killed but one, who fled in fear,
            and he could tell us only one clear fact.
120   OEDIPUS: What fact? One thing could lead us on to more
            if we could get a small start on our hope.
      CREON: He said that bandits chanced on them and killed him—
            with the force of many hands, not one alone.
      OEDIPUS: How could a bandit dare so great an act—
125   unless this was a plot paid off from here!
      CREON: We thought of that, but when Laius was killed,
            we had no one to help us in our troubles.

OEDIPUS: It was your very kingship that was killed!
   What kind of trouble blocked you from a search?
CREON: The subtle-singing Sphinx asked us to turn   130
   from the obscure to what lay at our feet.
OEDIPUS: Then I shall begin again and make it plain.
   It was quite worthy of Phoebus, and worthy of you,
   to turn our thoughts back to the murdered man,
   and right that you should see me join the battle   135
   for justice to our land and to the god.
   Not on behalf of any distant kinships,
   it's for myself I will dispel this stain.
   Whoever murdered him may also wish
   to punish me—and with the selfsame hand.   140
   In helping him I also serve myself.
   Now quickly, children: up from the altar steps,
   and raise the branches of the suppliant!
   Let someone go and summon Cadmus' people:
   say I'll do anything.

Exit an Attendant along one of the parados.

                   Our luck will prosper   145
   if the god is with us, or we have already fallen.
PRIEST: Rise, my children; that for which we came,
   he has himself proclaimed he will accomplish.
   May Phoebus, who announced this, also come
   as Savior and reliever from the plague.   150

Exit Oedipus and Creon into the palace. The Priest and the Suppliants exit left and right along the parados. After a brief pause, the Chorus (including the Choragos) enters the orchestra from the parados.

PARADOS[1]

STROPHE 1[2]

CHORUS: Voice from Zeus,[3] sweetly spoken, what are you
   that have arrived from golden
   Pytho[4] to our shining
   Thebes? I am on the rack, terror
      shakes my soul.   155
   Delian Healer,[5] summoned by "iē!"

---

[1] *Parados:* A song sung by the Chorus on first entering.

[2] *Strophe:* Probably refers to the direction in which the Chorus danced while reciting specific stanzas. *Strophe* may have indicated dance steps to stage left, *antistrophe* to stage right.

[3] *Voice from Zeus:* A reference to Apollo's prophecy. Zeus taught Apollo how to prophesy.

[4] *Pytho:* Delphi.

[5] *Delian Healer:* Apollo.

I await in holy dread what obligation, something new
or something back once more with the revolving years,
    you'll bring about for me.
160   Oh tell me, child of golden Hope,
        deathless Response!

ANTISTROPHE 1

I appeal to you first, daughter of Zeus,
    deathless Athena,
    and to your sister who protects this land,
165   Artemis,[6] whose famous throne is the whole circle
        of the marketplace,
and Phoebus, who shoots from afar: iō–!
Three-fold defenders against death, appear!
If ever in the past, to stop blind ruin
170   sent against the city,
you banished utterly the fires of suffering,
        come now again!

STROPHE 2

Ah! Ah! Unnumbered are the miseries
I bear. The plague claims all
175   our comrades. Nor has thought found yet a spear
by which a man shall be protected. What our glorious
earth gives birth to does not grow. Without a birth
from cries of labor
        do the women rise.
180   One person after another
        you may see, like flying birds,
faster than indomitable fire, sped
to the shore of the god that is the sunset.[7]

ANTISTROPHE 2

And with their deaths unnumbered dies the city.
185   Her children lie unpitied on the ground,
    spreading death, unmourned.
Meanwhile young wives, and gray-haired mothers with them,
on the shores of the altars, from this side and that,
suppliants from mournful trouble,
190   cry out their grief.
A hymn to the Healer shines,
    the flute a mourner's voice.
Against which, golden goddess, daughter of Zeus,
    send lovely Strength.

---

[6] *Artemis:* Goddess of virginity, childbirth, and hunting.
[7] *god . . . sunset:* Hades, god of the underworld.

STROPHE 3

Causing raging Ares[8]—who,   195
    armed now with no shield of bronze,
burns me, coming on amid loud cries—
to turn his back and run from my land,
with a fair wind behind, to the great
    hall of Amphitritē,[9]   200
or to the anchorage that welcomes no one,
Thrace's troubled sea!
If night lets something get away at last,
    it comes by day.
Fire-bearing god . . .   205
    you who dispense the might of lightning,
Zeus! Father! Destroy him with your thunderbolt!

Enter Oedipus from the palace.

ANTISTROPHE 3

Lycēan Lord![10] From your looped
    bowstring, twisted gold,
I wish indomitable missiles might be scattered   210
and stand forward, our protectors; also fire-bearing
radiance of Artemis, with which
    she darts across the Lycian mountains.
I call the god whose head is bound in gold,
with whom this country shares its name,   215
Bacchus,[11] wine-flushed, summoned by "euoi!,"
    Maenads' comrade,
to approach ablaze
    with gleaming . . .
pine, opposed to that god-hated god.   220

EPISODE 1[1]

OEDIPUS: I hear your prayer. Submit to what I say
    and to the labors that the plague demands
    and you'll get help and a relief from evils.
    I'll make the proclamation, though a stranger
    to the report and to the deed. Alone,   225
    had I no key, I would soon lose the track.

---

[8] *Ares:* God of war and destruction.

[9] *Amphitritē:* The Atlantic Ocean.

[10] *Lycēan Lord:* Apollo.

[11] *Bacchus:* Dionysus, god of fertility and wine.

[1] *Episode:* The portion of ancient Greek plays that appears between choric songs.

Since it was only later that I joined you,
to all the sons of Cadmus I say this:
230   whoever has clear knowledge of the man
who murdered Laius, son of Labdacus,
I command him to reveal it all to me—
nor fear if, to remove the charge, he must
accuse himself: his fate will not be cruel—
235   he will depart unstumbling into exile.
But if you know another, or a stranger,
to be the one whose hand is guilty, speak:
I shall reward you and remember you.
But if you keep your peace because of fear,
240   and shield yourself or kin from my command,
hear you what I shall do in that event:
I charge all in this land where I have throne
and power, shut out that man—no matter who—
both from your shelter and all spoken words,
nor in your prayers or sacrifices make
245   him partner, nor allot him lustral[2] water.
All men shall drive him from their homes: for he
is the pollution that the god-sent Pythian
response has only now revealed to me.
In this way I ally myself in war
250   with the divinity and the deceased.[3]
And this curse, too, against the one who did it,
whether alone in secrecy, or with others:
may he wear out his life unblest and evil!
I pray this, too: if he is at my hearth
255   and in my home, and I have knowledge of him,
may the curse pronounced on others come to me.
All this I lay to you to execute,
for my sake, for the god's, and for this land
now ruined, barren, abandoned by the gods.
260   Even if no god had driven you to it,
you ought not to have left this stain uncleansed,
the murdered man a nobleman, a king!
You should have looked! But now, since, as it happens,
It's I who have the power that he had once,
265   and have his bed, and a wife who shares our seed,
and common bond had we had common children
(had not his hope of offspring had bad luck—

---

[2] *lustral:* Purifying.

[3] *the deceased:* Laius.

but as it happened, luck lunged at his head);
because of this, as if for my own father,
I'll fight for him, I'll leave no means untried, 270
to catch the one who did it with his hand,
for the son of Labdacus, of Polydōrus,
of Cadmus before him, and of Agēnor.[4]
This prayer against all those who disobey:
the gods send out no harvest from their soil, 275
nor children from their wives. Oh, let them die
victims of this plague, or of something worse.
Yet for the rest of us, people of Cadmus,
we the obedient, may Justice, our ally,
and all the gods, be always on our side! 280
CHORAGOS:[5] I speak because I feel the grip of your curse:
the killer is not I. Nor can I point
to him. The one who set us to this search,
Phoebus, should also name the guilty man.
OEDIPUS: Quite right, but to compel unwilling gods— 285
no man has ever had that kind of power.
CHORAGOS: May I suggest to you a second way?
OEDIPUS: A second or a third—pass over nothing!
CHORAGOS: I know of no one who sees more of what
Lord Phoebus sees than Lord Tiresias. 290
My Lord, one might learn brilliantly from him.
OEDIPUS: Nor is this something I have been slow to do.
At Creon's word I sent an escort—twice now!
I am astonished that he has not come.
CHORAGOS: The old account is useless. It told us nothing. 295
OEDIPUS: But tell it to me. I'll scrutinize all stories.
CHORAGOS: He is said to have been killed by travelers.
OEDIPUS: I have heard, but the one who did it no one sees.
CHORAGOS: If there is any fear in him at all,
he won't stay here once he has heard that curse. 300
OEDIPUS: He won't fear words: he had no fear when he did it.

Enter Tiresias from the right, led by a Servant and two of Oedipus's Attendants.

CHORAGOS: Look there! There is the man who will convict him!
It's the god's prophet they are leading here,
one gifted with the truth as no one else.
OEDIPUS: Tiresias, master of all omens— 305
public and secret, in the sky and on the earth—
your mind, if not your eyes, sees how the city

---

[4]*son . . . Agēnor:* Refers to Laius by citing his genealogy.

[5]*Choragos:* Leader of the Chorus and principal commentator on the play's action.

lives with a plague, against which Thebes can find
no Saviour or protector, Lord, but you.

310   For Phoebus, as the attendants surely told you,
returned this answer to us: liberation
from the disease would never come unless
we learned without a doubt who murdered Laius—
put them to death, or sent them into exile.

315   Do not begrudge us what you may learn from birds
or any other prophet's path you know!
Care for yourself, the city, care for me,
care for the whole pollution of the dead!
We're in your hands. To do all that he can

320   to help another is man's noblest labor.

TIRESIAS: How terrible to understand and get
no profit from the knowledge! I knew this,
but I forgot, or I had never come.

OEDIPUS: What's this? You've come with very little zeal.

325   TIRESIAS: Let me go home! If you will listen to me,
You will endure your troubles better—and I mine.

OEDIPUS: A strange request, not very kind to the land
that cared for you—to hold back this oracle!

TIRESIAS: I see your understanding comes to you

330   inopportunely. So that won't happen to me . . .

OEDIPUS: Oh, by the gods, if you understand about this,
don't turn away! We're on our knees to you.

TIRESIAS: None of you understands! I'll never bring
my grief to light—I will not speak of yours.

335   OEDIPUS: You know and won't declare it! Is your purpose
to betray us and to destroy this land!

TIRESIAS: I will grieve neither of us. Stop this futile
cross-examination. I'll tell you nothing!

OEDIPUS: Nothing? You vile traitor! You could provoke

340   a stone to anger! You still refuse to tell?
Can nothing soften you, nothing convince you?

TIRESIAS: You blamed anger in me—you haven't seen.
The kind that lives with you, so you blame me.

OEDIPUS: Who wouldn't fill with anger, listening

345   to words like yours which now disgrace this city?

TIRESIAS: It will come, even if my silence hides it.

OEDIPUS: If it will come, then why won't you declare it?

TIRESIAS: I'd rather say no more. Now if you wish,
respond to that with all your fiercest anger!

350   OEDIPUS: Now I am angry enough to come right out
with this conjecture: you, I think, helped plot
the deed; you did it—even if your hand,
cannot have struck the blow. If you could see,
I should have said the deed was yours alone.

TIRESIAS: Is that right! Then I charge you to abide   355
    by the decree you have announced: from this day
    say no word to either these or me,
    for you are the vile polluter of this land!
OEDIPUS: Aren't you appalled to let a charge like that
    come bounding forth? How will you get away?   360
TIRESIAS: You cannot catch me. I have the strength of truth.
OEDIPUS: Who taught you this? Not your prophetic craft!
TIRESIAS: You did. You made me say it. I didn't want to.
OEDIPUS: Say what? Repeat it so I'll understand.
TIRESIAS: I made no sense? Or are you trying me?   365
OEDIPUS: No sense I understood. Say it again!
TIRESIAS: I say you are the murderer you seek.
OEDIPUS: Again that horror! You'll wish you hadn't said that.
TIRESIAS: Shall I say more, and raise your anger higher?
OEDIPUS: Anything you like! Your words are powerless.   370
TIRESIAS: You live, unknowing, with those nearest to you
    in the greatest shame. You do not see the evil.
OEDIPUS: You won't go on like that and never pay!
TIRESIAS: I can if there is any strength in truth.
OEDIPUS: In truth, but not in you! You have no strength,   375
    blind in your ears, your reason, and your eyes.
TIRESIAS: Unhappy man! Those jeers you hurl at me
    before long all these men will hurl at you.
OEDIPUS: You are the child of endless night; it's not
    for me or anyone who sees to hurt you.   380
TIRESIAS: It's not my fate to be struck down by you.
    Apollo is enough. That's his concern.
OEDIPUS: Are these inventions Creon's or your own?
TIRESIAS: No, your affliction is yourself, not Creon.
OEDIPUS: Oh success!—in wealth, kingship, artistry,   385
    in any life that wins much admiration—
    the envious ill will stored up for you!
    to get at my command, a gift I did not
    seek, which the city put into my hands,
    my loyal Creon, colleague from the start,   390
    longs to sneak up in secret and dethrone me.
    So he's suborned this fortuneteller—schemer!
    deceitful beggar-priest!—who has good eyes
    for gains alone, though in his craft he's blind.
    Where were your prophet's powers ever proved?   395
    Why, when the dog who chanted verse[6] was here,
    did you not speak and liberate this city?
    Her riddle wasn't for a man chancing by
    to interpret; prophetic art was needed,

---

[6]*dog . . . verse:* The Sphinx.

400   but you had none, it seems—learned from birds
        or from a god. I came along, yes I,
        Oedipus the ignorant, and stopped her—
        by using thought, not augury from birds.
        And it is I whom you now wish to banish,
405   so you'll be close to the Creontian throne.
        You—and the plot's concocter—will drive out
        pollution to your grief: you look quite old
        or you would be the victim of that plot!
CHORAGOS: It seems to us that this man's words were said
410   in anger, Oedipus, and yours as well.
        Insight, not angry words, is what we need,
        the best solution to the god's response.
TIRESIAS: You are the king, and yet I am your equal
        in my right to speak. In that I too am Lord.
415   for I belong to Loxias,[7] not you.
        I am not Creon's man. He's nothing to me.
        Hear this, since you have thrown my blindness at me:
        Your eyes can't see the evil to which you've come,
        nor where you live, nor who is in your house.
420   Do you know your parents? Not knowing, you are
        their enemy, in the underworld and here.
        A mother's and a father's double-lashing
        terrible-footed curse will soon drive you out.
        Now you can see, then you will stare into darkness.
425   What place will not be harbor to your cry,
        or what Cithaeron[8] not reverberate
        when you have heard the bride-song in your palace
        to which you sailed? Fair wind to evil harbor!
        Nor do you see how many other woes
430   will level you to yourself and to your children.
        So, at my message, and at Creon, too,
        splatter muck! There will never be a man
        ground into wretchedness as you will be.
OEDIPUS: Am I to listen to such things from him!
435   May you be damned! Get out of here at once!
        Go! Leave my palace! Turn around and go!

Tiresias begins to move away from Oedipus.

TIRESIAS: I wouldn't have come had you not sent for me.
OEDIPUS: I did not know you'd talk stupidity,
        or I wouldn't have rushed to bring you to my house.

---

[7]*Loxias:* Apollo.

[8]*Cithaeron:* The mountain on which Oedipus was to be exposed as an infant.

Tiresias: Stupid I seem to you, yet to your parents 440
    who gave you natural birth I seemed quite shrewd.
Oedipus: Who? Wait! Who is the one who gave me birth?
Tiresias: This day will give you birth,[9] and ruin too.
Oedipus: What murky, riddling things you always say!
Tiresias: Don't you surpass us all at finding out? 445
Oedipus: You sneer at what you'll find has brought me greatness.
Tiresias: And that's the very luck that ruined you.
Oedipus: I wouldn't care, just so I saved the city.
Tiresias: In that case I shall go. Boy, lead the way!
Oedipus: Yes, let him lead you off. Here, underfoot, 450
    you irk me. Gone, you'll cause no further pain.
Tiresias: I'll go when I have said what I was sent for.
    Your face won't scare me. You can't ruin me.
    I say to you, the man whom you have looked for
    as you pronounced your curses, your decrees 455
    on the bloody death of Laius—he is here!
    A seeming stranger, he shall be shown to be
    a Theban born, though he'll take no delight
    in that solution. Blind, who once could see,
    a beggar who was rich, through foreign lands 460
    he'll go and point before him with a stick.
    To his beloved children, he'll be shown
    a father who is also brother; to the one
    who bore him, son and husband; to his father,
    his seed-fellow and killer. Go in 465
    and think this out; and if you find I've lied,
    say then I have no prophet's understanding!

Exit Tiresias, led by a Servant. Oedipus exits into the palace with his Attendants.

STASIMON 1[1]
STROPHE 1

Chorus: Who is the man of whom the inspired
    rock of Delphi[2] said
he has committed the unspeakable 470
    with blood-stained hands?
Time for him to ply a foot
mightier than those of the horses
    of the storm in his escape;
upon him mounts and plunges the weaponed 475

---

[9] *This day . . . birth:* On this day, you will learn who your parents are.
[1] *Stasimon:* Greek choral ode between episodes.
[2] *rock of Delphi:* Apollo's oracle at Delphi.

son of Zeus,[3] with fire and thunderbolts,
and in his train the dreaded goddesses
of Death, who never miss.

ANTISTROPHE 1

480
The message has just blazed,
    gleaming from the snows
of Mount Parnassus: we must track
    everywhere the unseen man.
He wanders, hidden by wild
forests, up through caves

485
    and rocks, like a bull,
anxious, with an anxious foot, forlorn.
He puts away from him the mantic[4] words come from earth's
navel,[5] at its center, yet these live
forever and still hover round him.

STROPHE 2

490
Terribly he troubles me,
    the skilled interpreter of birds![6]
I can't assent, nor speak against him.
    Both paths are closed to me.
I hover on the wings of doubt,

495
    not seeing what is here nor what's to come.
What quarrel started in the house of Labdacus[7]
or in the house of Polybus,[8]
    either ever in the past
    or now, I never

500
heard, so that . . . with this fact for my touchstone
I could attack the public
    fame of Oedipus, by the side of the Labdaceans
an ally, against the dark assassination.

ANTISTROPHE 2

No, Zeus and Apollo

505
    understand and know things
mortal; but that another man
    can do more as a prophet than I can—
for that there is no certain test,
    though, skill to skill,

---

[3]*son of Zeus:* Apollo.

[4]*mantic:* Prophetic.

[5]*earth's navel:* Delphi.

[6]*interpreter of birds:* Tiresias. The Chorus is troubled by his accusations.

[7]*house of Labdacus:* The line of Laius.

[8]*Polybus:* Oedipus's foster father.

one man might overtake another.   510
No, never, not until
   I see the charges proved,
when someone blames him shall I nod assent.
For once, as we all saw, the winged maiden[9] came
against him: he was seen then to be skilled,   515
   proved, by that touchstone, dear to the people. So,
never will my mind convict him of the evil.

EPISODE 2

Enter Creon from the right door of the skene and speaks to the Chorus.

CREON: Citizens, I hear that a fearful charge
   is made against me by King Oedipus!
   I had to come. If, in this crisis,   520
   he thinks that he has suffered injury
   from anything that I have said or done,
   I have no appetite for a long life—
   bearing a blame like that! It's no slight blow
   the punishment I'd take from what he said: 525
   it's the ultimate hurt to be called traitor
   by the city, by you, by my own people!
CHORAGOS: The thing that forced that accusation out
   could have been anger, not the power of thought.
CREON: But who persuaded him that thoughts of mine   530
   had led the prophet into telling lies?
CHORAGOS: I do not know the thought behind his words.
CREON: But did he look straight at you? Was his mind right
   when he said that I was guilty of this charge?
CHORAGOS: I have no eyes to see what rulers do.   535
   But here he comes himself out of the house.

Enter Oedipus from the palace.

OEDIPUS: What? You here? And can you really have
   the face and daring to approach my house
   when you're exposed as its master's murderer
   and caught, too, as the robber of my kingship?   540
   Did you see cowardice in me, by the gods,
   or foolishness, when you began this plot?
   Did you suppose that I would not detect
   your stealthy moves, or that I'd not fight back?
   It's your attempt that's folly, isn't it—   545
   tracking without followers or connections,
   kingship which is caught with wealth and numbers?

---

[9]*winged maiden:* The Sphinx.

CREON: Now wait! Give me as long to answer back!
    Judge me for yourself when you have heard me!
550 OEDIPUS: You're eloquent, but I'd be slow to learn
    from you, now that I've seen your malice toward me.
CREON: That I deny. Hear what I have to say.
OEDIPUS: Don't you deny it! You are the traitor here!
CREON: If you consider mindless willfulness
555   a prized possession, you are not thinking sense.
OEDIPUS: If you think you can wrong a relative
    and get off free, you are not thinking sense.
CREON: Perfectly just, I won't say no. And yet
    what is this injury you say I did you?
560 OEDIPUS: Did you persuade me, yes or no, to send
    someone to bring that solemn prophet here?
CREON: And I still hold to the advice I gave.
OEDIPUS: How many years ago did your King Laius . . .
CREON: Laius! Do what? Now I don't understand.
565 OEDIPUS: Vanish—victim of a murderous violence?
CREON: That is a long count back into the past.
OEDIPUS: Well, was this seer then practicing his art?
CREON: Yes, skilled and honored just as he is today.
OEDIPUS: Did he, back then, ever refer to me?
570 CREON: He did not do so in my presence ever.
OEDIPUS: You did inquire into the murder then.
CREON: We had to, surely, though we discovered nothing.
OEDIPUS: But the "skilled" one did not say this then? Why not?
CREON: I never talk when I am ignorant.
575 OEDIPUS: But you're not ignorant of your own part.
CREON: What do you mean? I'll tell you if I know.
OEDIPUS: Just this: if he had not conferred with you
    he'd not have told about my murdering Laius.
CREON: If he said that, you are the one who knows.
580   But now it's fair that you should answer me.
OEDIPUS: Ask on! You won't convict me as the killer.
CREON: Well then, answer. My sister is your wife?
OEDIPUS: Now there's a statement that I can't deny.
CREON: You two have equal power in this country?
585 OEDIPUS: She gets from me whatever she desires.
CREON: And I'm a third? The three of us are equals?
OEDIPUS: That's where you're treacherous to your kinsman!
CREON: But think about this rationally, as I do.
    First look at this: do you think anyone
590   prefers the anxieties of being king
    to untroubled sleep—if he has equal power?
    I'm not the kind of man who falls in love
    with kingship. I am content with a king's power.

And so would any man who's wise and prudent.
I get all things from you, with no distress;   595
as king I would have onerous duties, too.
How could the kingship bring me more delight
than this untroubled power and influence?
I'm not misguided yet to such a point
that profitable honors aren't enough.   600
As it is, all wish me well and all salute;
those begging you for something have me summoned,
for their success depends on that alone.
Why should I lose all this to become king?
A prudent mind is never traitorous.   605
Treason's a thought I'm not enamored of;
nor could I join a man who acted so.
In proof of this, first go yourself to Pytho
and ask if I brought back the true response.
Then, if you find I plotted with that portent   610
reader,[1] don't have me put to death by your vote
only—I'll vote myself for my conviction.
Don't let an unsupported thought convict me!
It's not right mindlessly to take the bad
for good or to suppose the good are traitors.   615
Rejecting a relation who is loyal
is like rejecting life, our greatest love.
In time you'll know securely without stumbling,
for time alone can prove a just man just,
though you can know a bad man in a day.   620
CHORAGOS: Well said, to one who's anxious not to fall.
    Swift thinkers, Lord, are never safe from stumbling.
OEDIPUS: But when a swift and secret plotter moves
    against me, I must make swift counterplot.
    If I lie quiet and await his move,   625
    he'll have achieved his aims and I'll have missed.
CREON: You surely cannot mean you want me exiled!
OEDIPUS: Not exiled, no. Your death is what I want!
CREON: If you would first define what envy is . . .
OEDIPUS: Are you still stubborn? Still disobedient?   630
CREON: I see you cannot think!
OEDIPUS: For me I can.
CREON: You should for me as well!
OEDIPUS: But you're a traitor!
CREON: What if you're wrong?
OEDIPUS: Authority must be maintained.

---

[1] *portent reader:* Apollo's oracle or prophet.

CREON: Not if the ruler's evil.

OEDIPUS: Hear that, Thebes!

635 CREON: It is my city too, not yours alone!

CHORAGOS: Please don't, my Lords! Ah, just in time, I see
      Jocasta there, coming from the palace.
      With her help you must settle your quarrel.

Enter Jocasta from the palace.

JOCASTA: Wretched men! What has provoked this ill-

640   advised dispute? Have you no sense of shame,
      with Thebes so sick, to stir up private troubles?
      Now go inside! And Creon, you go home!
      Don't make a general anguish out of nothing!

CREON: My sister, Oedipus your husband here

645   sees fit to do one of two hideous things:
      to have me banished from the land—or killed!

OEDIPUS: That's right: I caught him, Lady, plotting harm
      against my person—with a malignant science.

CREON: May my life fail, may I die cursed, if I

650   did any of the things you said I did!

JOCASTA: Believe his words, for the god's sake, Oedipus,
      in deference above all to his oath
      to the gods. Also for me, and for these men!

KOMMOS[1]

STROPHE 1

CHORUS: Consent, with will and mind,

655   my king, I beg of you!

OEDIPUS: What do you wish me to surrender?

CHORUS: Show deference to him who was not feeble in time past
      and is now great in the power of his oath!

OEDIPUS: Do you know what you're asking?

CHORUS: Yes.

OEDIPUS: Tell me then.

660 CHORUS: Never to cast into dishonored guilt, with an unproved
      assumption, a kinsman who has bound himself by curse.

OEDIPUS: Now you must understand, when you ask this,
      you ask my death or banishment from the land.

STROPHE 2

CHORUS: No, by the god who is the foremost of all gods,

665   the Sun! No! Godless,
            friendless, whatever death is worst of all,

---

[1]*Kommos:* A dirge or lament sung by the Chorus and one or more of the chief characters.

let that be my destruction, if this
    thought ever moved me!
But my ill-fated soul
    this dying land   670
wears out—the more if to these older troubles
she adds new troubles from the two of you!
OEDIPUS: Then let him go, though it must mean my death,
    or else disgrace and exile from the land.
    My pity is moved by your words, not by his—   675
    he'll only have my hate, wherever he goes.
CREON: You're sullen as you yield; you'll be depressed
    when you've passed through this anger. Natures like yours
    are hardest on themselves. That's as it should be.
OEDIPUS: Then won't you go and let me be?   680
CREON: I'll go.
    Though you're unreasonable, they know I'm righteous.

Exit Creon.

ANTISTROPHE 1

CHORUS: Why are you waiting, Lady?
    Conduct him back into the palace!
JOCASTA: I will, when I have heard what chanced.
CHORUS: Conjectures—words alone, and nothing based on thought. 685
    But even an injustice can devour a man.
JOCASTA: Did the words come from both sides?
CHORUS: Yes.
JOCASTA: What was said?
CHORUS: To me it seems enough! enough! the land already troubled,
    that this should rest where it has stopped.
OEDIPUS: See what you've come to in your honest thought,   690
    in seeking to relax and blunt my heart?

ANTISTROPHE 2

CHORUS: I have not said this only once, my Lord.
    That I had lost my sanity,
        without a path in thinking—
be sure this would be clear   695
    if I put you away
who, when my cherished land
    wandered crazed
with suffering, brought her back on course.
Now, too, be a lucky helmsman!   700
JOCASTA: Please, for the god's sake, Lord, explain to me
    the reason why you have conceived this wrath?

OEDIPUS: I honor you, not them,[2] and I'll explain
    to you how Creon has conspired against me.

705 JOCASTA: All right, if that will explain how the quarrel started.

OEDIPUS: He says I am the murderer of Laius!

JOCASTA: Did he claim knowledge or that someone told him?

OEDIPUS: Here's what he did: he sent that vicious seer
    so he could keep his own mouth innocent.

710 JOCASTA: Ah then, absolve yourself of what he charges!
    Listen to this and you'll agree, no mortal
    is ever given skill in prophecy.
    I'll prove this quickly with one incident.
    It was foretold to Laius—I shall not say

715   by Phoebus himself, but by his ministers—
    that when his fate arrived he would be killed
    by a son who would be born to him and me.
    And yet, so it is told, foreign robbers
    murdered him, at a place where three roads meet.

720   As for the child I bore him, not three days passed
    before he yoked the ball-joints of its feet,[3]
    then cast it, by others' hands, on a trackless mountain.
    That time Apollo did not make our child
    a patricide, or bring about what Laius

725   feared, that he be killed by his own son.
    That's how prophetic words determined things!
    Forget them. The things a god must track
    he will himself painlessly reveal.

OEDIPUS: Just now, as I was listening to you, Lady,

730   what a profound distraction seized my mind!

JOCASTA: What made you turn around so anxiously?

OEDIPUS: I thought you said that Laius was attacked
    and butchered at a place where three roads meet.

JOCASTA: That is the story, and it is told so still.

735 OEDIPUS: Where is the place where this was done to him?

JOCASTA: The land's called Phocis, where a two-forked road
    comes in from Delphi and from Daulia.

OEDIPUS: And how much time has passed since these events?

JOCASTA: Just prior to your presentation here

740   as king this news was published to the city.

OEDIPUS: Oh, Zeus, what have you willed to do to me?

JOCASTA: Oedipus, what makes your heart so heavy?

OEDIPUS: No, tell me first of Laius' appearance,
    what peak of youthful vigor he had reached.

---

[2]*them:* The Chorus.

[3]*ball-joints of its feet:* The ankles.

JOCASTA: A tall man, showing his first growth of white.
    He had a figure not unlike your own.
OEDIPUS: Alas! It seems that in my ignorance
    I laid those fearful curses on myself.
JOCASTA: What is it, Lord? I flinch to see your face.
OEDIPUS: I'm dreadfully afraid the prophet sees.   750
    But I'll know better with one more detail.
JOCASTA: I'm frightened too. But ask: I'll answer you.
OEDIPUS: Was his retinue small, or did he travel
    with a great troop, as would befit a prince?
JOCASTA: There were just five in all, one a herald.   755
    There was a carriage, too, bearing Laius.
OEDIPUS: Alas! Now I see it! But who was it,
    Lady, who told you what you know about this?
JOCASTA: A servant who alone was saved unharmed.
OEDIPUS: By chance, could he be now in the palace?   760
JOCASTA: No, he is not. When he returned and saw
    you had the power of the murdered Laius,
    he touched my hand and begged me formally
    to send him to the fields and to the pastures,
    so he'd be out of sight, far from the city.   765
    I did. Although a slave, he well deserved
    to win this favor, and indeed far more.
OEDIPUS: Let's have him called back in immediately.
JOCASTA: That can be done, but why do you desire it?
OEDIPUS: I fear, Lady, I have already said   770
    too much. That's why I wish to see him now.
JOCASTA: Then he shall come; but it is right somehow
    that I, too, Lord, should know what troubles you.
OEDIPUS: I've gone so deep into the things I feared
    I'll tell you everything. Who has a right   775
    greater than yours, while I cross through this chance?
    Polybus of Corinth was my father,
    my mother was the Dorian Meropē.
    I was first citizen, until this chance
    attacked me—striking enough, to be sure,   780
    but not worth all the gravity I gave it.
    This: at a feast a man who'd drunk too much
    denied, at the wine, I was my father's son.
    I was depressed and all that day I barely
    held it in. Next day I put the question   785
    to my mother and father. They were enraged
    at the man who'd let this fiction fly at me.
    I was much cheered by them. And yet it kept
    grinding into me. His words kept coming back.
    Without my mother's or my father's knowledge   790

I went to Pytho. But Phoebus sent me away
dishonoring my demand. Instead, other
wretched horrors he flashed forth in speech.
He said that I would be my mother's lover,
795   show offspring to mankind they could not look at,
and be his murderer whose seed I am.[4]
When I heard this, and ever since, I gauged
the way to Corinth by the stars alone,
running to a place where I would never see
800   the disgrace in the oracle's words come true.
But I soon came to the exact location
where, as you tell of it, the king was killed.
Lady, here is the truth. As I went on,
when I was just approaching those three roads,
805   a herald and a man like him you spoke of
came on, riding a carriage drawn by colts.
Both the man out front and the old man himself[5]
tried violently to force me off the road.
The driver, when he tried to push me off,
810   I struck in anger. The old man saw this, watched
me approach, then leaned out and lunged down
with twin prongs[6] at the middle of my head!
He got more than he gave. Abruptly—struck
once by the staff in this my hand—he tumbled
815   out, head first, from the middle of the carriage.
And then I killed them all. But if there is
a kinship between Laius and this stranger,
who is more wretched than the man you see?
Who was there born more hated by the gods?
820   For neither citizen nor foreigner
may take me in his home or speak to me.
No, they must drive me off. And it is I
who have pronounced these curses on myself!
I stain the dead man's bed with these my hands,
825   by which he died. Is not my nature vile?
Unclean?—if I am banished and even
in exile I may not see my own parents,
or set foot in my homeland, or else be yoked
in marriage to my mother, and kill my father,
830   Polybus, who raised me and gave me birth?
If someone judged a cruel divinity

---

[4]*be . . . am:* I would murder my father.

[5]*old man himself:* Laius.

[6]*lunged . . . prongs:* Laius strikes Oedipus with a two-pronged horse goad, or whip.

did this to me, would he not speak the truth?
You pure and awful gods, may I not ever
see that day, may I be swept away
from men before I see so great and so   835
calamitous a stain fixed on my person!

CHORAGOS: These things seem fearful to us, Lord, and yet,
until you hear it from the witness, keep hope!

OEDIPUS: That is the single hope that's left to me,
to wait for him, that herdsman—until he comes.   840

JOCASTA: When he appears, what are you eager for?

OEDIPUS: Just this: if his account agrees with yours
then I shall have escaped this misery.

JOCASTA: But what was it that struck you in my story?

OEDIPUS: You said he spoke of robbers as the ones   845
who killed him. Now: if he continues still
to speak of many, then I could not have killed him.
One man and many men just do not jibe.
But if he says one belted man, the doubt
is gone. The balance tips toward me. I did it.   850

JOCASTA: No! He told it as I told you. Be certain.
He can't reject that and reverse himself.
The city heard these things, not I alone.
But even if he swerves from what he said,
he'll never show that Laius' murder, Lord,   855
occurred just as predicted. For Loxias
expressly said my son was doomed to kill him.
The boy—poor boy—he never had a chance
to cut him down, for he was cut down first.
Never again, just for some oracle   860
will I shoot frightened glances right and left.

OEDIPUS: That's full of sense. Nonetheless, send a man
to bring that farm hand here. Will you do it?

JOCASTA: I'll send one right away. But let's go in.
Would I do anything against your wishes?   865

Exit Oedipus and Jocasta through the central door into the palace.

STASIMON 2
STROPHE 1

CHORUS: May there accompany me
the fate to keep a reverential purity in what I say,
in all I do, for which the laws have been set forth
and walk on high, born to traverse the brightest,
highest upper air; Olympus[1] only   870

---

[1] *Olympus:* Mount Olympus, home of the gods, and treated as a god itself.

is their father, nor was it
mortal nature
that fathered them, and never will
oblivion lull them into sleep;
875   the god in them is great and never ages.

ANTISTROPHE 1

The will to violate, seed of the tyrant,
if it has drunk mindlessly of wealth and power,
without a sense of time or true advantage,
mounts to a peak, then
880   plunges to an abrupt . . . destiny,
where the useful foot
is of no use. But the kind
of struggling that is good for the city
I ask the god never to abolish.
885   The god is my protector: never will I give that up.

STROPHE 2

But if a man proceeds disdainfully
    in deeds of hand or word
and has no fear of Justice
    or reverence for shrines of the divinities
890   (may a bad fate catch him
        for his luckless wantonness!),
if he'll not gain what he gains with justice
and deny himself what is unholy,
or if he clings, in foolishness, to the untouchable
895   (what man, finally, in such an action, will have strength
    enough to fend off passion's arrows from his soul?),
if, I say, this kind of
    deed is held in honor—
why should I join the sacred dance?

ANTISTROPHE 2

900   No longer shall I visit and revere
        Earth's navel,[2] the untouchable,
nor visit Abae's[3] temple,
        or Olympia,[4]
if the prophecies are not matched by events
905   for all the world to point to.
No, you who hold the power, if you are rightly called

---

[2] *Earth's navel:* Delphi.

[3] *Abae's:* Abae was a town in Phocis where there was another oracle of Apollo.

[4] *Olympia:* Site of the oracle of Zeus.

Zeus the king of all, let this matter not escape you
and your ever-deathless rule,
for the prophecies to Laius fade . . .
and men already disregard them;   910
nor is Apollo anywhere
    glorified with honors.
Religion slips away.

EPISODE 3

Enter Jocasta from the palace carrying a branch wound with wool and a jar of incense. She is attended by two women.

JOCASTA: Lords of the realm, the thought has come to me
    to visit shrines of the divinities   915
    with suppliant's branch in hand and fragrant smoke.
    For Oedipus excites his soul too much
    with alarms of all kinds. He will not judge
    the present by the past, like a man of sense.   920
    He's at the mercy of all terror-mongers.

Jocasta approaches the altar on the right and kneels.

    Since I can do no good by counseling,
    Apollo the Lycēan!—you are the closest—
    I come a suppliant, with these my vows,
    for a cleansing that will not pollute him.   925
    For when we see him shaken we are all
    afraid, like people looking at their helmsman.

Enter a Messenger along one of the parados. He sees Jocasta at the altar and then addresses the Chorus.

MESSENGER: I would be pleased if you would help me, stranger.
    Where is the palace of King Oedipus?
    Or tell me where he is himself, if you know.
CHORUS: This is his house, stranger. He is within.   930
    This is his wife and mother of his children.
MESSENGER: May she and her family find prosperity,
    if, as you say, her marriage is fulfilled.
JOCASTA: You also, stranger, for you deserve as much
    for your gracious words. But tell me why you've come.   935
    What do you wish? Or what have you to tell us?
MESSENGER: Good news, my Lady, both for your house and husband.
JOCASTA: What is your news? And who has sent you to us?
MESSENGER: I come from Corinth. When you have heard my news
    you will rejoice, I'm sure—and grieve perhaps.   940
JOCASTA: What is it? How can it have this double power?

MESSENGER: They will establish him their king, so say
        the people of the land of Isthmia.[1]
JOCASTA: But is old Polybus not still in power?
945 MESSENGER: He's not, for death has clasped him in the tomb.
JOCASTA: What's this? Has Oedipus' father died?
MESSENGER: If I have lied then I deserve to die.
JOCASTA: Attendant! Go quickly to your master,
        and tell him this.

Exit an Attendant into the palace.

                    Oracles of the gods!
950 Where are you now? The man whom Oedipus
    fled long ago, for fear that he should kill him—
    he's been destroyed by chance and not by him!

Enter Oedipus from the palace.

OEDIPUS: Darling Jocasta, my beloved wife,
    Why have you called me from the palace?
955 JOCASTA: First hear what this man has to say. Then see
        what the god's grave oracle has come to now!
OEDIPUS: Where is he from? What is this news he brings me?
JOCASTA: From Corinth. He brings news about your father:
        that Polybus is no more! that he is dead!
960 OEDIPUS: What's this, old man? I want to hear you say it.
MESSENGER: If this is what must first be clarified,
        please be assured that he is dead and gone.
OEDIPUS: By treachery or by the touch of sickness?
MESSENGER: Light pressures tip agéd frames into their sleep.
965 OEDIPUS: You mean the poor man died of some disease.
MESSENGER: And of the length of years that he had tallied.
OEDIPUS: Aha! Then why should we look to Pytho's vapors,[2]
        or to the birds that scream above our heads?[3]
    If we could really take those things for guides,
970 I would have killed my father. But he's dead!
    He is beneath the earth, and here am I,
    who never touched a spear. Unless he died
    of longing for me and I "killed" him that way!
    No, in this case, Polybus, by dying, took
975 the worthless oracle to Hades with him.
JOCASTA: And wasn't I telling you that just now?
OEDIPUS: You were indeed. I was misled by fear.

---

[1]*land of Isthmia:* Corinth, Greek city-state situated on an isthmus.
[2]*Pytho's vapors:* Prophecies of the oracle at Delphi.
[3]*birds . . . heads:* Prophecies derived from interpreting the flights of birds.

JOCASTA: You should not care about this anymore.

OEDIPUS: I must care. I must stay clear of my mother's bed.

JOCASTA: What's there for man to fear? The realm of chance   980
  prevails. True foresight isn't possible.
  His life is best who lives without a plan.
  This marriage with your mother—don't fear it.
  How many times have men in dreams, too, slept
  with their own mothers! Those who believe such things   985
  mean nothing endure their lives most easily.

OEDIPUS: A fine, bold speech, and you are right, perhaps,
  except that my mother is still living,
  so I must fear her, however well you argue.

JOCASTA: And yet your father's tomb is a great eye.   990

OEDIPUS: Illuminating, yes. But I still fear the living.

MESSENGER: Who is the woman who inspires this fear?

OEDIPUS: Merope, Polybus' wife, old man.

MESSENGER: And what is there about her that alarms you?

OEDIPUS: An oracle, god-sent and fearful, stranger.   995

MESSENGER: Is it permitted that another know?

OEDIPUS: It is. Loxias once said to me
  I must have intercourse with my own mother
  and take my father's blood with these my hands.
  So I have long lived far away from Corinth.   1000
  This has indeed brought much good luck, and yet,
  to see one's parents' eyes is happiest.

MESSENGER: Was it for this that you have lived in exile?

OEDIPUS: So I'd not be my father's killer, sir.

MESSENGER: Had I not better free you from this fear,   1005
  my Lord? That's why I came—to do you service.

OEDIPUS: Indeed, what a reward you'd get for that!

MESSENGER: Indeed, this is the main point of my trip,
  to be rewarded when you get back home.

OEDIPUS: I'll never rejoin the givers of my seed![4]   1010

MESSENGER: My son, clearly you don't know what you're doing.

OEDIPUS: But how is that, old man? For the gods' sake, tell me!

MESSENGER: If it's because of them you won't go home.

OEDIPUS: I fear that Phoebus will have told the truth.

MESSENGER: Pollution from the ones who gave you seed?   1015

OEDIPUS: That is the thing, old man, I always fear.

MESSENGER: Your fear is groundless. Understand that.

OEDIPUS: Groundless? Not if I was born their son.

MESSENGER: But Polybus is not related to you.

---

[4]*givers of my seed:* i.e., "my parents." Oedipus still thinks Merope and Polybus are his parents.

1020   OEDIPUS: Do you mean Polybus was not my father?

MESSENGER: No more than I. We're both the same to you.

OEDIPUS: Same? One who begot me and one who didn't?

MESSENGER: He didn't beget you any more than I did.

OEDIPUS: But then, why did he say I was his son?

1025   MESSENGER: He got you as a gift from my own hands.

OEDIPUS: He loved me so, though from another's hands?

MESSENGER: His former childlessness persuaded him.

OEDIPUS: But had you bought me, or begotten me?

MESSENGER: Found you. In the forest hallows of Cithaeron.

1030   OEDIPUS: What were you doing traveling in that region?

MESSENGER: I was in charge of flocks which grazed those mountains.

OEDIPUS: A wanderer who worked the flocks for hire?

MESSENGER: Ah, but that day I was your savior, son.

OEDIPUS: From what? What was my trouble when you took me?

1035   MESSENGER: The ball-joints of your feet might testify.

OEDIPUS: What's that? What makes you name that ancient trouble?

MESSENGER: Your feet were pierced and I am your rescuer.

OEDIPUS: A fearful rebuke those tokens left for me!

MESSENGER: That was the chance that names you who you are.

1040   OEDIPUS: By the gods, did my mother or my father do this?

MESSENGER: That I don't know. He might who gave you to me.

OEDIPUS: From someone else? You didn't chance on me?

MESSENGER: Another shepherd handed you to me.

OEDIPUS: Who was he? Do you know? Will you explain!

1045   MESSENGER: They called him one of the men of—was it Laius?

OEDIPUS: The one who once was king here long ago?

MESSENGER: That is the one! The man was shepherd to him.

OEDIPUS: And is he still alive so I can see him?

MESSENGER: But you who live here ought to know that best.

1050   OEDIPUS: Does any one of you now present know
        about the shepherd whom this man has named?
        Have you seen him in town or in the fields? Speak out!
        The time has come for the discovery!

CHORAGOS: The man he speaks of, I believe, is the same

1055   as the field hand you have already asked to see.
        But it's Jocasta who would know this best.

OEDIPUS: Lady, do you remember the man we just
        now sent for—is that the man he speaks of?

JOCASTA: What? The man he spoke of? Pay no attention!

1060   His words are not worth thinking about. It's nothing.

OEDIPUS: With clues like this within my grasp, give up?
        Fail to solve the mystery of my birth?

JOCASTA: For the love of the gods, and if you love your life,
        give up this search! My sickness is enough.

1065   OEDIPUS: Come! Though my mothers for three generations
        were in slavery, you'd not be lowborn!

JOCASTA: No, listen to me! Please! Don't do this thing!
OEDIPUS: I will not listen; I will search out the truth.
JOCASTA: My thinking is for you—it would be best.
OEDIPUS: This "best" of yours is starting to annoy me.   1070
JOCASTA: Doomed man! Never find out who you are!
OEDIPUS: Will someone go and bring that shepherd here?
    Leave her to glory in her wealthy birth!
JOCASTA: Man of misery! No other name
    shall I address you by, ever again.   1075

Exit Jocasta into the palace after a long pause.

CHORAGOS: Why has your lady left, Oedipus,
    hurled by a savage grief? I am afraid
    disaster will come bursting from this silence.
OEDIPUS: Let it burst forth! However low this seed
    of mine may be, yet I desire to see it.   1080
    She, perhaps—she has a woman's pride—
    is mortified by my base origins.
    But I who count myself the child of Chance,
    the giver of good, shall never know dishonor.
    She is my mother,[5] and the months my brothers   1085
    who first marked out my lowness, then my greatness.
    I shall not prove untrue to such a nature
    by giving up the search for my own birth.

STASIMON 3

STROPHE

CHORUS: If I have mantic power[1]
    and excellence in thought,   1090
    by Olympus,
        you shall not, Cithaeron, at tomorrow's
    full moon,
    fail to hear us celebrate you as the countryman
    of Oedipus, his nurse and mother,   1095
    or fail to be the subject of our dance,
        since you have given pleasure
    to our king.
    Phoebus, whom we summon by "iē!,"
    may this be pleasing to you!   1100

ANTISTROPHE

Who was your mother, son?
which of the long-lived nymphs

---

[5]*She . . . mother:* Chance is my mother.
[1]*If . . . mantic power:* If I am a prophet.

after lying with Pan,[2]
   the mountain roaming . . . Or was it a bride
1105   of Loxias?[3]
For dear to him are all the upland pastures.
Or was it Mount Cyllēnē's lord,[4]
or the Bacchic god,[5]
   dweller of the mountain peaks,
1110   who received you as a joyous find
from one of the nymphs of Helicon,
the favorite sharers of his sport?

EPISODE 4

OEDIPUS: If someone like myself, who never met him,
   may calculate—elders, I think I see
1115   the very herdsman we've been waiting for.
His many years would fit that man's age,
and those who bring him on, if I am right,
are my own men. And yet, in real knowledge,
you can outstrip me, surely: you've seen him.

Enter the old Herdsman escorted by two of Oedipus's Attendants. At first, the Herdsman will not look at Oedipus.

1120 CHORAGOS: I know him, yes, a man of the house of Laius,
   a trusty herdsman if he ever had one.
OEDIPUS: I ask you first, the stranger come from Corinth:
   is this the man you spoke of?
MESSENGER: That's he you see.
OEDIPUS: Then you, old man. First look at me! Now answer:
1125   did you belong to Laius' household once?
HERDSMAN: I did. Not a purchased slave but raised in the palace.
OEDIPUS: How have you spent your life? What is your work?
HERDSMAN: Most of my life now I have tended sheep.
OEDIPUS: Where is the usual place you stay with them?
1130 HERDSMAN: On Mount Cithaeron. Or in that district.
OEDIPUS: Do you recall observing this man there?
HERDSMAN: Doing what? Which is the man you mean?
OEDIPUS: This man right here. Have you had dealings with him?
HERDSMAN: I can't say right away. I don't remember.
1135 MESSENGER: No wonder, master. I'll bring clear memory
   to his ignorance. I'm absolutely sure

---

[2]*Pan:* God of shepherds and woodlands, half man and half goat.

[3]*Loxias:* Apollo.

[4]*Mount Cyllēnē's lord:* Hermes, messenger of the gods.

[5]*Bacchic god:* Dionysus.

he can recall it, the district was Cithaeron,
he with a double flock, and I, with one,
lived close to him, for three entire seasons,
six months along, from spring right to Arcturus.[1]   1140
Then for the winter I'd drive mine to my fold,
and he'd drive his to Laius' pen again.
Did any of the things I say take place?

HERDSMAN: You speak the truth, though it's from long ago.

MESSENGER: Do you remember giving me, back then,   1145
    a boy I was to care for as my own?

HERDSMAN: What are you saying? Why do you ask me that?

MESSENGER: There, sir, is the man who was that boy!

HERDSMAN: Damn you! Shut your mouth! Keep your silence!

OEDIPUS: Stop! Don't you rebuke his words.   1150
    Your words ask for rebuke far more than his.

HERDSMAN: But what have I done wrong, most royal master?

OEDIPUS: Not telling of the boy of whom he asked.

HERDSMAN: He's ignorant and blundering toward ruin.

OEDIPUS: Tell it willingly—or under torture.   1155

HERDSMAN: Oh god! Don't—I am old—don't torture me!

OEDIPUS: Here! Someone put his hands behind his back!

HERDSMAN: But why? What else would you find out, poor man?

OEDIPUS: Did you give him the child he asks about?

HERDSMAN: I did. I wish that I had died that day!   1160

OEDIPUS: You'll come to that if you don't speak the truth.

HERDSMAN: It's if I speak that I shall be destroyed.

OEDIPUS: I think this fellow struggles for delay.

HERDSMAN: No, no! I said already that I gave him.

OEDIPUS: From your own home, or got from someone else?   1165

HERDSMAN: Not from my own. I got him from another.

OEDIPUS: Which of these citizens? What sort of house?

HERDSMAN: Don't—by the gods!—don't, master, ask me more!

OEDIPUS: It means your death if I must ask again.

HERDSMAN: One of the children of the house of Laius.   1170

OEDIPUS: A slave—or born into the family?

HERDSMAN: I have come to the dreaded thing, and I shall say it.

OEDIPUS: And I to hearing it, but hear I must.

HERDSMAN: He was reported to have been—his son.
    Your lady in the house could tell you best.   1175

OEDIPUS: Because she gave him to you?

HERDSMAN: Yes, my lord.

OEDIPUS: What was her purpose?

HERDSMAN: I was to kill the boy.

---

[1] *Arcturus:* A star that is first seen in September in the sky over Greece.

OEDIPUS: The child she bore?

HERDSMAN: She dreaded prophecies.

OEDIPUS: What were they?

HERDSMAN: The word was that he'd kill his parents.

1180 OEDIPUS: Then why did you give him up to this old man?

HERDSMAN: In pity, master—so he would take him home,
      to another land. But what he did was save him
      for this supreme disaster. If you are the one
      he speaks of—know your evil birth and fate!

1185 OEDIPUS: Ah! All of it was destined to be true!
      Oh light, now may I look my last upon you,
      shown monstrous in my birth, in marriage monstrous,
      a murderer monstrous in those I killed.

Exit Oedipus, running into the palace.

STASIMON 4
STROPHE 1

CHORUS: Oh generations of mortal men,
1190   while you are living, I will
          appraise your lives at zero!
      What man
      comes closer to seizing lasting blessedness
      than merely to seize its semblance,
1195   and after living in this semblance, to plunge?
      With your example before us,
      with your destiny, yours,
          suffering Oedipus, no mortal
      can I judge fortunate.

ANTISTROPHE 1

1200 For he,[1] outranging everybody,
      shot his arrow[2] and became the lord
          of wide prosperity and blessedness,
      oh Zeus, after destroying
      the virgin with the crooked talons,[3]
1205   singer of oracles; and against death,
      in my land, he arose a tower of defense.
      From which time you were called my king
      and granted privileges supreme—in mighty
      Thebes the ruling lord.

---

[1] *he:* Oedipus.

[2] *shot his arrow:* Took his chances; made a guess at the Sphinx's riddle.

[3] *virgin . . . talons:* The Sphinx.

STROPHE 2

But now—whose story is more sorrowful than yours?   1210
Who is more intimate with fierce calamities,
with labors, now that your life is altered?
Alas, my Oedipus, whom all men know:
one great harbor[4]—
one alone sufficed for you,   1215
as son and father,
when you tumbled,[5] plowman[6] of the woman's chamber.
How, how could your paternal
     furrows, wretched man,
endure you silently so long.   1220

ANTISTROPHE 2

Time, all-seeing, surprised you living an unwilled life
and sits from of old in judgment on the marriage, not a marriage,
where the begetter is the begot as well.
Ah, son of Laius . . . ,
would that—oh, would that   1225
I had never seen you!
I wail, my scream climbing beyond itself
from my whole power of voice. To say it straight:
     from you I got new breath—
but I also lulled my eye to sleep.[7]   1230

EXODOS[1]

Enter the Second Messenger from the palace.

SECOND MESSENGER: You who are first among the citizens,
    what deeds you are about to hear and see!
    What grief you'll carry, if, true to your birth,
    you still respect the house of Labdacus!
    Neither the Ister nor the Phasis river   1235
    could purify this house, such suffering
    does it conceal, or soon must bring to light—
    willed this time, not unwilled. Griefs hurt worst
    which we perceive to be self-chosen ones.
CHORAGOS: They were sufficient, the things we knew before,   1240
    to make us grieve. What can you add to those?

---

[4]*one great harbor:* Metaphorical allusion to Jocasta's body.

[5]*tumbled:* Were born and had sex.

[6]*plowman:* Plowing is used here as a sexual metaphor.

[7]*I . . . sleep:* I failed to see the corruption you brought.

[1]*Exodos:* The final scene, containing the play's resolution.

SECOND MESSENGER: The thing that's quickest said and quickest heard:
  our own, our royal one, Jocasta's dead.
  CHORAGOS: Unhappy queen! What was responsible?
1245 SECOND MESSENGER: Herself. The bitterest of these events
  is not for you, you were not there to see,
  but yet, exactly as I can recall it,
  you'll hear what happened to that wretched lady.
  She came in anger through the outer hall,
1250 and then she ran straight to her marriage bed,
  tearing her hair with the fingers of both hands.
  Then, slamming shut the doors when she was in,
  she called to Laius, dead so many years,
  remembering the ancient seed which caused
1255 his death, leaving the mother to the son
  to breed again an ill-born progeny.
  She mourned the bed where she, alas, bred double—
  husband by husband, children by her child.
  From this point on I don't know how she died,
1260 for Oedipus then burst in with a cry,
  and did not let us watch her final evil.
  Our eyes were fixed on him. Wildly he ran
  to each of us, asking for his spear
  and for his wife—no wife: where he might find
1265 the double mother-field, his and his children's.
  He raved, and some divinity then showed him—
  for none of us did so who stood close by.
  With a dreadful shout—as if some guide were leading—
  he lunged through the double doors; he bent the hollow
1270 bolts from the sockets, burst into the room,
  and there we saw her, hanging from above,
  entangled in some twisted hanging strands.
  He saw, was stricken, and with a wild roar
  ripped down the dangling noose. When she, poor woman,
1275 lay on the ground, there came a fearful sight:
  he snatched the pins of worked gold from her dress,
  with which her clothes were fastened: these he raised
  and struck into the ball-joints of his eyes.[2]
  He shouted that they would no longer see
1280 the evils he had suffered or had done,
  see in the dark those he should not have seen,
  and know no more those he once sought to know.
  While chanting this, not once but many times
  he raised his hand and struck into his eyes.

---

[2]*ball-joints of his eyes:* His eyeballs. Oedipus blinds himself in both eyes at the same time.

Blood from his wounded eyes poured down his chin, 1285
not freed in moistening drops, but all at once
a stormy rain of black blood burst like hail.
These evils, coupling them, making them one,
have broken loose upon both man and wife.
The old prosperity that they had once 1290
was true prosperity, and yet today,
mourning, ruin, death, disgrace, and every
evil you could name—not one is absent.

CHORAGOS: Has he allowed himself some peace from all this grief?

SECOND MESSENGER: He shouts that someone slide the bolts and show 1295
to all the Cadmeians the patricide,
his mother's—I can't say it, it's unholy—
so he can cast himself out of the land,
not stay and curse his house by his own curse.
He lacks the strength, though, and he needs a guide, 1300
for his is a sickness that's too great to bear.
Now you yourself will see: the bolts of the doors
are opening. You are about to see
a vision even one who hates must pity.

Enter the blinded Oedipus from the palace, led in by a household Servant.

CHORAGOS: Terrifying suffering for men to see, 1305
more terrifying than any I've ever
come upon. Oh man of pain
what madness reached you? Which god from far off,
surpassing in range his longest spring,
struck hard against your god-abandoned fate? 1310
Oh man of pain,
I cannot look upon you—though there's so much
I would ask you, so much to hear,
so much that holds my eyes—
such is the shudder you produce in me. 1315

OEDIPUS: Ah! Ah! I am a man of misery.
Where am I carried? Pity me! Where
is my voice scattered abroad on wings?
Divinity, where has your lunge transported me?

CHORAGOS: To something horrible, not to be heard or seen. 1320

KOMMOS

STROPHE 1

OEDIPUS: Oh, my cloud
of darkness, abominable, unspeakable as it attacks me,
not to be turned away, brought by an evil wind!
Alas!

1325   Again alas! Both enter me at once:
        the sting of the prongs,[1] the memory of evils!
        CHORUS: I do not marvel that in these afflictions
            you carry double griefs and double evils.

ANTISTROPHE 1

        OEDIPUS: Ah, friend,
1330   so you at least are there, resolute servant!
            Still with a heart to care for me, the blind man.
            Oh! Oh!
            I know that you are there. I recognize
            even inside my darkness, that voice of yours.
1335   CHORUS: Doer of horror, how did you bear to quench
            your vision? What divinity raised your hand?

STROPHE 2

        OEDIPUS: It was Apollo there, Apollo, friends,
            who brought my sorrows, vile sorrows to their perfection,
                these evils that were done to me.
1340   But the one who struck them with his hand,
                that one was none but I, in wretchedness.
            For why was I to see
                when nothing I could see would bring me joy?
        CHORUS: Yes, that is how it was.
1345   OEDIPUS: What could I see, indeed,
            or what enjoy—what greeting
            is there I could hear with pleasure, friends?
            Conduct me out of the land
                as quickly as you can!
1350   Conduct me out, my friends,
                the man utterly ruined,
            supremely cursed,
                the man who is by gods
            the most detested of all men!
1355   CHORUS: Wretched in disaster and in knowledge:
            oh, I could wish you'd never come to know!

ANTISTROPHE 2

        OEDIPUS: May he be destroyed, whoever freed the savage shackles
            from my feet when I'd been sent to the wild pasture,
                whoever rescued me from murder
1360   and became my savior—
                a bitter gift:
            if I had died then,
            I'd not have been such grief to self and kin.

---

[1] *prongs:* Refers both to the whip that Laius used and to the two gold pins that Oedipus used to blind himself.

Chorus: I also would have had it so.

Oedipus: I'd not have returned to be my father's   1365
    murderer; I'd not be called by men
    my mother's bridegroom.
    Now I'm without a god,
        child of a polluted parent,
    fellow progenitor with him   1370
        who gave me birth in misery.
    If there's an evil that
        surpasses evils, that
    has fallen to the lot of Oedipus.

Choragos: How can I say that you have counseled well?   1375
    Better not to be than live a blind man.

Oedipus: That this was not the best thing I could do—
    don't tell me that, or advise me any more!
    Should I descend to Hades and endure
    to see my father with these eyes? Or see   1380
    my poor unhappy mother? For I have done,
    to both of these, things too great for hanging.
    Or is the sight of children to be yearned for,
    to see new shoots that sprouted as these did?
    Never, never with these eyes of mine!   1385
    Nor city, nor tower, nor holy images
    of the divinities! For I, all-wretched,
    most nobly raised—as no one else in Thebes—
    deprived myself of these when I ordained
    that all expel the impious one—god-shown   1390
    to be polluted, and the dead king's son![2]
    Once I exposed this great stain upon me,
    could I have looked on these with steady eyes?
    No! No! And if there were a way to block
    the source of hearing in my ears, I'd gladly   1395
    have locked up my pitiable body,
    so I'd be blind and deaf. Evils shut out—
    that way my mind could live in sweetness.
    Alas, Cithaeron, why did you receive me?
    Or when you had me, not killed me instantly?   1400
    I'd not have had to show my birth to mankind.
    Polybus, Corinth, halls—ancestral,
    they told me—how beautiful was your ward,
    a scar that held back festering disease!
    Evil my nature, evil my origin.   1405
    You, three roads, and you, secret ravine,

---

[2] *I . . . son:* Oedipus refers to his own curse against the murderer as well as his sins of patricide and incest.

you oak grove, narrow place of those three paths
that drank my blood[3] from these hands, from him
who fathered me, do you remember still
1410   the things I did to you? When I'd come here,
what I then did once more? Oh marriages! Marriages!
You gave us life and when you'd planted us
you sent the same seed up, and then revealed
fathers, brothers, sons, and kinsman's blood,
1415   and brides, and wives, and mothers, all the most
atrocious things that happen to mankind!
One should not name what never should have been.
Somewhere out there, then, quickly, by the gods,
cover me up, or murder me, or throw me
1420   to the ocean where you will never see me more!

Oedipus moves toward the Chorus and they back away from him.

Come! Don't shrink to touch this wretched man!
Believe me, do not be frightened! I alone
of all mankind can carry these afflictions.

Enter Creon from the palace with Attendants.

1425   CHORAGOS: Tell Creon what you wish for. Just when we need him
he's here. He can act, he can advise you.
He's now the land's sole guardian in your place.
OEDIPUS: Ah! Are there words that I can speak to him?
What ground for trust can I present? It's proved
that I was false to him in everything.
1430   CREON: I have not come to mock you, Oedipus,
nor to reproach you for your former falseness.
You men, if you have no respect for sons
of mortals, let your awe for the all-feeding
flames of lordy Hēlius[4] prevent
1435   your showing unconcealed so great a stain,
abhorred by earth and sacred rain and light.
Escort him quickly back into the house!
If blood kin only see and hear their own
afflictions, we'll have no impious defilement.
1440   OEDIPUS: By the gods, you've freed me from one terrible fear,
so nobly meeting my unworthiness:
grant me something—not for me; for you!
CREON: What do you want that you should beg me so?
OEDIPUS: To drive me from the land at once, to a place
1445   where there will be no man to speak to me!

---

[3] *my blood:* i.e., "the blood of my father, Laius."
[4] *Hēlius:* The sun.

CREON: I would have done just that—had I not wished
    to ask first of the god what I should do.
OEDIPUS: His answer was revealed in full—that I,
    the patricide, unholy, be destroyed.
CREON: He said that, but our need is so extreme,   1450
    it's best to have sure knowledge what must be done.
OEDIPUS: You'll ask about a wretched man like me?
CREON: Is it not time you put your trust in the god?
OEDIPUS: But I bid you as well, and shall entreat you.
    Give her who is within what burial   1455
    you will—you'll give your own her proper rites;
    but me—do not condemn my fathers' land
    to have me dwelling here while I'm alive,
    but let me live on mountains—on Cithaeron
    famed as mine, for my mother and my father,   1460
    while they yet lived, made it my destined tomb,
    and I'll be killed by those who wished my ruin!
    And yet I know: no sickness will destroy me,
    nothing will: I'd never have been saved
    when left to die unless for some dread evil.   1465
    Then let my fate continue where it will!
    As for my children, Creon, take no pains
    for my sons—they're men and they will never lack
    the means to live, wherever they may be—
    but my two wretched, pitiable girls,   1470
    who never ate but at my table, never
    were without me—everything that I
    would touch, they'd always have a share of it—
    please care for them! Above all, let me touch
    them with my hands and weep aloud my woes!   1475
    Please, my Lord!
    Please, noble heart! Touching with my hands,
    I'd think I held them as when I could see.

Enter Antigone and Ismene from the palace with Attendants.

    What's this?
    Oh gods! Do I hear, somewhere, my two dear ones   1480
    sobbing? Has Creon really pitied me
    and sent to me my dearest ones, my children?
    Is that it?
CREON: Yes, I prepared this for you, for I knew
    you'd feel this joy, as you have always done.   1485
OEDIPUS: Good fortune, then, and, for your care, be guarded
    far better by divinity than I was!
    Where are you, children? Come to me! Come here

1490
to these my hands, hands of your brother, hands
of him who gave you seed, hands that made
these once bright eyes to see now in this fashion.

Oedipus embraces his daughters.

He, children, seeing nothing, knowing nothing,
he fathered you where his own seed was plowed.
I weep for you as well, though I can't see you,
1495
imagining your bitter life to come,
the life you will be forced by men to live.
What gatherings of townsmen will you join,
what festivals, without returning home
in tears instead of watching holy rites?
1500
And when you've reached the time for marrying,
where, children, is the man who'll run the risk
of taking on himself the infamy
that will wound you as it did my parents?
What evil is not here? Your father killed
1505
his father, plowed the one who gave him birth,
and from the place where he was sown, from there
he got you, from the place he too was born.
These are the wounds: then who will marry you?
No man, my children. No, it's clear that you
1510
must wither in dry barrenness, unmarried.

Oedipus addresses Creon.

Son of Menoeceus! You are the only father
left to them—we two who gave them seed
are both destroyed: watch that they don't become
poor, wanderers, unmarried—they are your kin.
1515
Let not my ruin be their ruin, too!
No, pity them! You see how young they are,
bereft of everyone, except for you.
Consent, kind heart, and touch me with your hand!

Creon grasps Oedipus's right hand.

You, children, if you had reached an age of sense,
1520
I would have counseled much. Now, pray you may live
always where it's allowed, finding a life
better than his was, who gave you seed.
CREON: Stop this now. Quiet your weeping. Move away, into the house.
OEDIPUS: Bitter words, but I obey them.
CREON: There's an end to all things.
OEDIPUS: I have first this request.
1525
CREON: Tell me. I shall judge when I will hear it.

OEDIPUS: Banish me from my homeland.
CREON: You must ask that of the god.
OEDIPUS: But I am the gods' most hated man!
CREON: Then you will soon get what you want.
OEDIPUS: Do you consent?
CREON: I never promise when, as now, I'm ignorant.
OEDIPUS: Then lead me in.
CREON: Come. But let your hold fall from your children.
OEDIPUS: Do not take them from me, ever!
CREON: Do not wish to keep all of the power. 1530
    You had power, but that power did not follow you through life.

Oedipus's daughters are taken from him and led into the palace by Attendants. Oedipus is led into the palace by a Servant. Creon and the other Attendants follow. Only the Chorus remains.

CHORUS: People of Thebes, my country, see: here is that Oedipus—
    he who "knew" the famous riddle, and attained the highest power,
    whom all citizens admired, even envying his luck!
    See the billows of wild troubles which he has entered now! 1535
    Here is the truth of each man's life: we must wait, and see his end,
    scrutinize his dying day, and refuse to call him happy
    till he has crossed the border of his life without pain.

Exit the Chorus along each of the parados.

*   *   *

Reading and Reacting

1. The ancient Greeks used no scenery in their theatrical productions. In the absence of scenery, how is the setting established at the beginning of *Oedipus the King*?

2. In some recent productions of *Oedipus the King*, actors wear copies of ancient Greek masks. What are the advantages and disadvantages of using such masks in a contemporary production of the play?

3. In the ancient Greek theater, the *strophe* and *antistrophe* were sung or chanted by the chorus as it danced back and forth across the stage. If you were staging the play today, would you retain the chorus or do away with it entirely? What would be gained or lost with each alternative?

4. Why does Sophocles have Oedipus blind himself offstage? What would be the effect of having Oedipus perform this act in full view of the audience?

5. How does Sophocles observe the unities of time, place, and action? How does Sophocles manage to present information about what happened years before the action of the play while still maintaining the three unities?

6. The ancient Greek audience that viewed *Oedipus the King* was familiar with the plot of the play. Given this situation, how does Sophocles create suspense? What are the advantages and disadvantages of using a story that the audience already knows?

7. By the end of the play, what has Oedipus learned about himself? about the gods? about the quest for truth? Is he a tragic or a pathetic figure? (See pages 1042–45 for a discussion of **tragedy** and **pathos**.)

8. Today, many directors employ **color-blind casting**—that is, they cast an actor in a role without regard to his or her race. Do you think this practice could be used in casting *Oedipus the King*? How, for example, would you react to an African American Oedipus or to an Asian Creon?

9. **JOURNAL ENTRY** Do you think Oedipus deserves his fate? Why, or why not?

10. **CRITICAL PERSPECTIVE** In "On Misunderstanding the *Oedipus Rex*," F. R. Dodds argues that Sophocles did not intend that Oedipus's tragedy be seen as rising from a "grave moral flaw." Neither, says Dodds, was Oedipus a "mere puppet" of the gods. Rather, "what fascinates us is the spectacle of a man freely choosing, from the highest motives, a series of actions which lead to his own ruin":

> Oedipus is great, not in virtue of a great worldly position—for his worldly position is an illusion which will vanish like a dream—but in virtue of his inner strength: strength to pursue the truth at whatever personal cost, and strength to accept and endure it when found. . . . Oedipus is great because he accepts the responsibility for all his acts, including those which are objectively most horrible, though subjectively innocent.

Do you agree with Dodds's arguments? Do you see Oedipus as someone who has inner strength or as a morally flawed victim of the gods?

Related Works: "Barn Burning" (p. 335), "Young Goodman Brown" (p. 448), "'Out, Out—'" (p. 778), "Leda and the Swan" (p. 874), "Ulysses" (p. 1017), *Hamlet* (p. 1304)

WRITING SUGGESTIONS: Staging

1. Discuss the problems that the original staging of *Oedipus the King* poses for contemporary audiences, and offer some possible solutions.
2. The simplicity of the ancient Greek theater was one of its main strengths. If a scene called for a particular setting—a palace, for example—the setting could be established with dialogue. Find some examples of this technique, and write an essay in which you discuss whether or not such suggestions are as effective in the staging of *Oedipus the King* than special effects or realistic settings would be.
3. Discuss and analyze the staging options for *The Date*—or for a play that is not in this chapter, such as *Beauty* (p. 1069) or *Magic 8 Ball* (p. 1073).
4. Choose a short story that appears in this anthology, and explain how you would stage it if it were a play. What furnishings, props, costumes, lighting, and sound effects would you choose? What events would occur offstage? Possible subjects for this essay might include "The Story of an Hour" (p. 201), "A&P" (p. 238), or "The Storm" (p. 273).
5. Assume you have a very limited budget for staging *The Cuban Swimmer*. What challenges would you face? Write an essay in which you outline your plans for staging *The Cuban Swimmer*.

CHAPTER 40

THEME

Sophocles
Bettmann/Corbis

August Wilson
AP Images

Jeni Mahoney
Photo by Sarah Jessup

John Patrick Shanley
Joe Seer/Shutterstock.com

Like a short story or a poem, a play is open to interpretation. Readers' reactions are influenced by the language of the text, and audiences' reactions are influenced by the performance on stage. As in all works of literature, every element of a play—its title, its conflicts, its dialogue, its characters, and its staging—can shed light on its themes.

Titles

The **title** of a play can provide insight into its themes. The ironic title of Susan Glaspell's *Trifles* (p. 1604), for example, suggests that women's concerns with "trifles" may get to the truth more effectively than the preoccupations of self-important men do. Lorraine Hansberry's *A Raisin in the Sun* (1959), is another title that offers clues to the theme of a play. An allusion to Langston Hughes's poem "Harlem" (p. 760)—which asks, "what happens to a dream deferred? / Does it dry up / like a raisin in the sun?"—the title suggests what happens to an African American family whose dreams are repeatedly crushed. Likewise, the title *Fences* (p. 1548) offers clues to a major theme of August Wilson's play, suggesting that the main character is kept from his goals by barriers that are constructed by himself as well as by society. Finally, the title of Anton Chekhov's *The Brute* (p. 1048) calls attention to the play's ideas about male–female relationships. The title may refer to Smirnov, who says that he has never liked women—whom he characterizes as "creatures of poetry and romance." Or, it may refer to Mrs. Popov's late husband, to whose memory she has dedicated her life despite the fact that he was unfaithful. Either alternative reinforces the play's tongue-in-cheek characterization of men as "brutes."

 Conflicts

The unfolding plot of a play—especially the **conflicts** that develop—can reveal the play's themes. In Henrik Ibsen's *A Doll House* (p. 1113), for example, at least three major conflicts are present: one between Nora and her husband Torvald, one between Nora and Krogstad (an old acquaintance), and one between Nora and society. Each of these conflicts sheds light on the themes of the play.

Through Nora's conflict with Torvald, Ibsen examines the constraints placed on women and men by marriage in the nineteenth century. Both Nora and Torvald are imprisoned within their respective roles: Nora must be passive and childlike, and Torvald must be honorable and always in control. Nora, therefore, expects her husband to be noble and generous and, in a crisis, to sacrifice himself for her. When he fails to live up to her high expectations, she is profoundly disillusioned.

Nora's conflict with Krogstad underscores Ibsen's criticisms of the class system in nineteenth-century Norway. At the beginning of the play, Nora finds it "immensely amusing: that we—that Torvald has so much power over . . . people." Krogstad, a bank clerk who is in the employ of Torvald, visits Nora in act 1 to enlist her aid in saving his job. It is clear that she sees him as her social inferior. For example, when Krogstad questions her about a woman with whom he has seen her, she replies, "What makes you think you can cross-examine me, Mr. Krogstad—you, one of my husband's employees?" Nora does not realize that she and Krogstad are, ironically, very much alike: both occupy subordinate positions and therefore have no power to determine their own destinies.

Finally, through Nora's conflict with society, Ibsen examines the destructive nature of the forces that subjugate women. Nineteenth-century society was male dominated. A married woman had the same legal status as one of her children. She could not borrow money without her husband's signature, own real estate in her own name, or enter into contracts. In addition, all her assets—including inheritances and trust funds—automatically became the property of her husband at the time of marriage. As a result of her sheltered life, Nora at the beginning of the play is completely unaware of the consequences of her actions. Most readers share Dr. Rank's confusion when he asks Nora, "Why do you laugh at that? Do you have any idea of what society is?" It is Nora's disillusionment at finding out that Torvald and the rest of society are not what she has been led to believe they are that ultimately causes her to rebel. By walking out the door at the end of the play, Nora rejects not only her husband and her children (to whom she has no legal right once she leaves), but also society and its laws.

These three conflicts underscore many of the themes that dominate *A Doll House*. First, the conflicts show that marriage in the nineteenth century imprisons both men and women in narrow, constricting roles. They also show that middle-class Norwegian society is narrow, smug, and judgmental. (Krogstad is looked down upon for a crime years after he committed it, and Nora is looked down upon because she borrows money to save her husband's life.) Finally, the conflicts show that society does not offer individuals—especially women—the freedom to lead happy and fulfilling lives. Only when the social and economic conditions that govern society change, Ibsen suggests, can both women and men live together in mutual esteem.

 ## Dialogue

Dialogue can also give insight into a play's themes. Sometimes a character suggests—or even explicitly states—a theme. In act 3 of *A Doll House*, for example, Nora's friend, Mrs. Linde, comes as close as any character to expressing the central concern of the play when she says, "Helmer's got to learn everything; this dreadful secret has to be aired; those two have to come to a full understanding; all these lies can't go on." As the play goes on to demonstrate, the lies that exist both in marriage and in society are obstacles to love and happiness.

One of the main themes of Arthur Miller's *Death of a Salesman* (p. 1233)—the questionable validity of the American Dream, given the nation's social, political, and economic realities—is suggested by the play's dialogue. As his son Biff points out, Willy Loman's stubborn belief in upward mobility and material success is based more on fantasy than on fact:

WILLY: (*with hatred, threatening*) The door of your life is wide open!
BIFF: Pop! I am a dime a dozen, and so are you!
WILLY: (*turning on him now in an uncontrolled outburst*) I am not a dime a dozen! I am Willy Loman, and you are Biff Loman!

Biff starts for Willy, but is blocked by Happy. In his fury, Biff seems on the verge of attacking his father.

BIFF: I am not a leader of men, Willy, and neither are you. You were never anything but a hard-working drummer who landed in the ash can like all the rest of them! I'm one dollar an hour, Willy! I tried seven states and couldn't raise it. A buck an hour! Do you gather my meaning? I'm not bringing home any prizes any more, and you're going to stop waiting for me to bring them home!

Although it does not explicitly state the theme of the play, this exchange strongly suggests that Biff rejects the desperate optimism to which Willy clings.

 ## Characters

Because a dramatic work focuses on a central character, or **protagonist**, the development of this character can shed light on a play's themes. Willy Loman in *Death of a Salesman* is developed in great detail. At the beginning of the play, he feels trapped, exhausted, and estranged from his surroundings. As Willy gradually sinks from depression into despair, the action of the play shifts from the present to the past, showing the events that shaped his life.

His attitudes, beliefs, dreams, and dashed hopes reveal him to be an embodiment of the major theme of the play—that an unquestioning belief in the American Dream of success is both unrealistic and destructive.

Nora in *A Doll House* changes a great deal during the course of the play. At the beginning, she is more her husband's possession than an adult capable of shaping her own destiny. Nora's status becomes apparent in the first act when Torvald gently scolds his "little spendthrift" and refers to her as his "little lark" and his "squirrel." She is reduced to childish deceptions, such as hiding her macaroons when her husband enters the room. After Krogstad accuses her of committing forgery and threatens to expose her, she expects her husband to rise to the occasion and take the blame for her. When Torvald instead accuses her of being a hypocrite, a liar, and a criminal, Nora's neat little world comes crashing down. As a result of this experience, Nora changes; no longer is she the submissive and obedient wife. Instead, she becomes assertive—even rebellious—ultimately telling Torvald that their marriage is a sham and that she can no longer stay with him. This abrupt shift in Nora's personality gives the audience a clear understanding of the major themes of the play.

Unlike Willy and Nora, Antigone in Sophocles's *Antigone* (p. 1484) is a character who changes very little during the course of the play. Fiercely devoted to her brother, Antigone decides to bury her brother's body in violation of Creon's decree that his corpse must be left to rot. Antigone's loyalty to her brother and to the gods makes it impossible for her to compromise. Her stubborn refusal to bend to the will of the king causes her downfall as well as her death. Antigone's inability to change highlights the central conflict of the play: Is a person's main duty to the king, to the gods, or to him- or herself?

 Staging

Various staging elements, such as props and furnishings, may also convey the themes of a play. In *Death of a Salesman*, Biff's trophy, which is constantly in the audience's view, is a prop that ironically underscores the futility of Willy's efforts to achieve success. Similarly, the miniature animals in *The Glass Menagerie* suggest the fragility of Laura's character and the futility of her efforts to fit into the modern world. And, in *Trifles*, the depressing farm house, the broken birdcage, and the dead canary hint at Mrs. Wright's misery and the reason she murdered her husband.

Special lighting effects and music can also suggest a play's themes. Throughout *The Glass Menagerie*, for example, words and pictures are projected onto a section of the set between the front room and dining room walls. In scene 1, as Tom's mother, Amanda, tells him about her experiences with her "gentlemen callers," an image of her as a girl greeting callers appears on the screen. As Amanda continues, the words "*Où sont Les Neiges*"—"Where are the snows [of yesteryear]?"—appear on the screen. Later in the play, when Laura and her mother discuss a boy Laura knew, his picture is projected on the screen, showing him as a high school hero carrying a silver cup. In addition to the slides, Williams uses music—a recurring tune, dance music, and "Ave Maria"—to increase the emotional impact of certain scenes. He also uses shafts of light focused on selected areas or characters to create a dreamlike atmosphere for the play. Collectively, the slides, music, and lighting reinforce the theme that those who retreat into the past inevitably become estranged from the present.

A Final Note

As you read, your own values and beliefs influence your interpretation of a play's themes. For instance, your interest in the changing status of women could lead you to focus on the submissive, almost passive, role of Willy's wife, Linda, in *Death of a Salesman*. As a result, you could conclude that the play shows how, in the post–World War II United States, women like Linda often sacrificed their own happiness for that of their husbands. Remember, however, that the play itself, not just your own feelings or assumptions about it, must support your interpretation.

✔ **CHECKLIST   Writing about Theme**

☐ What is the central theme of the play?

☐ What other themes can you identify?

☐ Does the title of the play suggest a theme?

☐ What conflicts exist in the play? How do they shed light on the themes of the play?

☐ Do any characters' statements express or imply a theme of the play?

☐ Do any characters change during the play? How do these changes suggest the play's themes?

☐ Do certain characters resist change? How does their failure to change suggest a theme of the play?

☐ Do scenery and props help to communicate the play's themes?

☐ Does music reinforce certain ideas in the play?

☐ Does lighting underscore the themes of the play?

Photo by Sarah Jessup

JENI MAHONEY (1964–   ) has published many plays as well as a feature-length screenplay. She directs the Playwriting program at Playwrights Horizons Theater School at New York University's Tisch School of the Arts and is the founding artistic director of Seven Devils Playwrights Conference and co-artistic director of id Theatre Company. Mahoney is the recipient of the Field's Independent Artist Challenge Program Grant and Columbia University's Woolrich Postgraduate Fellowship.

Cultural Context This play critiques the collective ideological beliefs that are held by many members of a particular political group. The 24-7 commentary by political pundits on cable news shows often reinforces viewers' preconceived political beliefs instead of challenging them. As a result, both Republicans and Democrats have become increasingly polarized. Intense debates about key social issues, such as gay rights, abortion, and immigration, have increased the ideological rift between these two groups. In this play, the complexities (and significance) of the characters' deeply held political and social beliefs are revealed in a surprising and unexpected way.

Come Rain or Come Shine (2005)

CHARACTERS
Mom, *40s*
Luke, *her son, 20s*
Chris, *Luke's friend, 20s*

PLACE
Mom's house

Scene from a 2014 production of *Come Rain or Come Shine*
Paula Marchiel

Mom, a 40-ish woman, urban hippie comfy in her casual clothes and middle-aged body, cleans (hides the mess) and talks on the phone. Liza Minelli sings "Come Rain or Come Shine" in the background. She is on the phone.

MOM: No, you're right. No, I don't know what I was thinking.

Mom reaches for a stack of new CDs still in the plastic wrap and sorts through them.

Um . . . Sara Brightman, *Best of Broadway, Les Mis.* Too much, right? No, I'll return 'em. Hey, what about *Rent*—that's something I might actually be listening to, right?

She makes a face, obviously not the response she wanted. Mom opens a nearby drawer and drops the CDs in.

I know. I just want to be supportive. As long as he's happy, right? That's all any mother can ask for.

Mom spots someone walking up to the driveway.

Oh! There they are! What? Yeah, nice-looking, in a sort of corporate way. Okay. Bye.

She hangs up the phone, puts it down—any old place, not in the charger, and sits on the couch and picks up a magazine—trying to look casual. The door opens slightly. Luke, 20s, young, impeccably neat, much more conservative than his mother, peeks in. Shy by nature, he hesitates at the door before entering.

LUKE: Mom—?
MOM: (*Pretending casual surprise.*) Boo-key!

She goes to him warmly and hugs him. A second figure lingers behind Luke.

Lukey, Boo-key. My gosh, is it three already?
LUKE: We're a little early.
MOM: Of course you are. Always punctual. Oh, I missed you so much!   5
LUKE: Good to see you too, Mom.
MOM: Well, come in already, you big goof!

Luke indicates his friend.

LUKE: Mom, this Chris. Chris, my Mom.

Chris leans into the room. Like Luke, he is dressed conservatively, obviously particular about his appearance and more well-practiced socially than Luke. Chris reaches out a hand to Mom.

CHRIS: Pleased to meet you, Mrs. Wilson.
MOM: Chris.   10

She stares at him meaningfully, then confides playfully—

MOM: It's Ms., actually—but you can just call me Mom.
CHRIS: Thanks, that's very . . . friendly, Ms. Wilson.
MOM: Yes. Well. Come in. Sit down. Tell me all about the drive!

The two men sit on the couch.

LUKE: Are you alright. Mom?
MOM: No, I'm not "alright," I'm thrilled! My long-lost Lukey Boo-key is here with   15
    his friend. Chris. See? Isn't this nice?
LUKE: 'Cause you might want to cut down on the caffeine. . . .
MOM: Drinks! You boys must be parched. What can I get you? Would you like a
    Cosmopolitan?
LUKE: A what???
MOM: I hear they're all the rage.
LUKE: When did you start drinking?   20
MOM: Me? No. I just thought you and Chris might want a drink.
CHRIS: No thanks, Ms. Wilson. I don't drink.

Mom smiles warmly.

MOM: Good for you, Chris. I can't tell you how glad I am to hear that. Really.
    Knowing that you respect your body, makes me respect you that much more.

CHRIS: Thank you, Ms. Wilson.

25   MOM: Oh, Luke. I like your friend very much.

LUKE: You know, I think I'll take that drink—Como, Commic, whatever-you-call-it.

CHRIS: Luke, do you think that's a good idea?

LUKE: Oh . . . yes.

MOM: Okay, then.

Mom flits—as best she can—to the kitchen. As soon as she is gone, Luke makes a bee line for the front door.

30   CHRIS: Hey!

LUKE: I can't do this.

CHRIS: It's just cold feet.

Chris goes to Luke and puts his arm around him and turns him back toward the room. Luke hyperventilates.

LUKE: . . . can't . . . breathe. . . .

CHRIS: That's totally normal. Luke, your mom seems very sweet.

35   LUKE: You don't understand. THAT is not my mom! I don't know who that charming lady is. I've never, EVER heard my mom offer anybody a mixed drink that didn't include wheat germ and flax seed oil.

CHRIS: She's nervous, Luke, just like you. It's clear she misses you. She wants to be a part of your life. That's a great start. Hey, maybe offering you a drink is just her way of treating you like a grown-up.

LUKE: You think?

Chris nods. A loud crash and a curse from the kitchen—Luke smiles: of course Chris is right.

LUKE: Everything okay—

MOM: Fine, fine! Just . . . ah, why don't you put on some music! There are some CDs in the junk drawer!

Before Luke can get to the CD drawer, Chris stops him.

40   CHRIS: Remember what we talked about, Luke: you gotta be who you are and be proud of it.

Luke nods in agreement.

How many of us there are, hiding the shadows—afraid to tell our parents, our bosses, our friends? Afraid of what? This is America. We have as much right to be here as they do. More! And it's about time we stood up and got counted.

Mom enters proudly with a pink Cosmo in a martini glass. She hands it to Luke. He puts it down without drinking it.

MOM: Aren't you going to try it?

LUKE: Mom, look.

Luke is stuck. Chris jumps in.

CHRIS: Why don't you have a seat, Mrs. Wilson. I think Luke has something he
wants to say.

Mom sits.

MOM: Of course. What did you want to say, Luke?
LUKE: Mom, I . . .   45
MOM: I love you, Luke. You can tell me anything. Don't you know that by now?
LUKE: It's just that . . . I've been afraid that—
MOM: Afraid? Of me?
LUKE: You gotta admit you're acting a bit . . . strange.
MOM: Maybe I did go a bit overboard. I just wanted you to know that I support   50
you—whatever choices you make for your self and your life. Haven't I always
lived a life of tolerance and acceptance—why should my son be any different?
CHRIS: I know that is a comfort for Luke. He was a little nervous about coming here
today.
MOM: And seeing you here with Chris . . . well, I just couldn't be happier. You're a
lovely man, Chris—just the kind of partner I would pick for my son.
LUKE: What?
MOM: He obviously loves you, Luke.
CHRIS: Well, I—   55
LUKE: Mom! Chris is not my lover!
CHRIS: Your what???
MOM: It's alright, Luke—
LUKE: I can't believe you—
CHRIS: Are you implying that I'm—?   60
LUKE: You think I'm gay!
MOM: I love you no matter what you are.
LUKE: I'm not gay! Why would you—I can't believe—That's why you told Chris to
call you Mom, isn't it? Isn't it! You think he's your new son-in-law!
MOM: Well, then who the hell is he??
LUKE: He's my roommate, Mom.   65
CHRIS: Housemate—we're not—we don't—we don't share a *room*.
MOM: So . . . then . . . what's this all about?
LUKE: Have a seat, Mom.
MOM: Are you okay, Lukey?
LUKE: Just sit, Mom.   70

Mom sits nervously.

MOM: Now you're scaring me.
CHRIS: You'll be laughing in few minutes. Trust me. We all will.
LUKE: Don't you get it? She wants me to be gay. *That* she could accept. She could
be the proud "out" mother of her "I'm queer, I'm here" son—she could buy
T-shirts, and join parent groups and march on Washington . . .

To Mom.

But I'm not gay, Mom. I'm not. I'm sorry. I'm . . . a Republican.

Beat. Mom laughs, but her laughter quickly shifts from disbelief to shock. She searches Luke's eyes for any sign.

MOM: You're—

75 LUKE: Republican. Come on, Mom. John Kerry? I just couldn't do it any more. He was . . . a weasel, Mom. I'm sorry.

MOM: A . . . a . . . weasel?? John Kerry is a weasel? Compared to Bush?

LUKE: He's a leader, Mom. And that's the long and short of it. He's got convictions, he knows what they are and he's not afraid to stand up for what he believes in.

MOM: I—can't believe what I'm hearing.

CHRIS: We're at war, Mrs. Wilson, in case you hadn't noticed. You don't change doctors in the middle of an operation.

80 MOM: You do if the doctor is killing you.

LUKE: But you don't replace the doctor with a philosophy professor.

MOM: You're both . . .

CHRIS: . . . Republican . . .

She looks at Luke. He is a stranger to her. She gets up and crosses to the kitchen as if to leave.

LUKE: Mom—

Chris goes to Mom. Takes her arm to stop her. Mom looks at Chris pointedly—he releases her. She spots the Cosmo on the table and decides to take it.

85 MOM: Okay, I'm going to need some time to sit with this.

She is about to exit when—

CHRIS: Hold up—

Mom turns to face Chris and Luke. Luke stares dejectedly at his feet.

Let me get this straight—you would accept Luke being gay, but you can't accept him being a Republican?

MOM: You're not born Republican. Luke was raised with solid LIBERAL values. He was raised to have a complex and nuanced understanding of national and international policy. We took him on Peace Corp vacations, spent holidays working soup kitchens! I poured my life and soul into this boy—what did I do wrong, Luke? Is it me? Is it my fault?

LUKE: It's nobody's fault, Mom. It's just what I am.

MOM: It is not "what you are." It's a choice—a choice, I might add, that is going to kill your father, Luke, KILL HIM—

CHRIS: Now, Ms. Wilson, we all know that's an exaggeration—

MOM: Do you know where your father is right now, Luke? Do you know where he is? He is out protesting the reclassification of farmed salmon to inflate the administration's so-called environmental policy!

CHRIS: Why should farmed salmon be prejudiced against?

Mom looks at Chris as if he's an idiot.

MOM: And to think, just moments ago you looked so smart.

LUKE: Mom, lay off him.

MOM: Tell me, Luke, is this the kind of thinking you aspire to? Is this what you think? Is global warming a myth? Is Alaskan oil going to save the SUV? I knew we never should have let you go to college in the Midwest!

LUKE: Mom! Did you ever stop to think that maybe . . . just maybe . . . if everyone disagrees with you, you might be wrong?

MOM: Everybody does not disagree with me.

LUKE: Okay. Let's say 4 million more people agree with me.

MOM: Luke, those people are—

LUKE: What? Stupid? Is that what you were going to call "those people"? Is that what you're calling me?

MOM: I was going to say . . . reactionaries.

CHRIS: Do you know why people voted in droves this year, Mrs. Wilson? To put an end once and for all to this nonsense about the Democratic Party being the "silent majority." It's not. THAT is the lesson here. THAT is why people like Luke and myself have to come out of the shadows and make our voices heard. Welcome to the real America, Mrs. Wilson. This is it.

MOM: You don't know me. How dare you come into my house and lecture me about the "real" America.

CHRIS: So much for tolerance, right?

MOM: I think you should go now.

CHRIS: I was just leaving anyway, can't stand the smell of hypocrisy. Come on—

Chris nods to Luke and heads out the door, but Luke holds his ground.

LUKE: Well, what about it, Mom? Should I go too?

Mom stands frozen. Miserable. There is nothing more to say. Luke turns to Chris, who disappears out the door, leaving it open. Luke goes to the door and takes the handle as if to shut the door behind Chris. He turns to Mom. She smiles: maybe he'll stay.

LUKE: I'm not stupid, Mom.

Luke exits, leaving the door open behind him. Mom remains frozen, Cosmo untouched in her hand.

"Come Rain or Come Shine" plays as the lights fade to black.

*   *   *

Reading and Reacting

1. What impression of Mom do the stage directions give? How do the following props reinforce this impression?

   - The telephone
   - The CDs
   - The pink Cosmo

2. When Chris meets Mom for the first time, he calls her "Mrs. Wilson." She corrects him saying, "It's Ms. actually—but you can just call me Mom." What does this exchange tell you about Mom? about Chris?

3. At one point in the play, Luke says, "THAT is not my mom! I don't know who that charming lady is." What does he mean? Why do you think his mother behaves the way she does?

4. According to Luke, his mother wants him to be gay. What does he mean? Why is Luke afraid to tell his mother that he is a Republican?

5. How does Mom see herself? How do Chris and Luke see her?

6. What point is the play making about gays? about Republicans? about tolerance?

7. At the end of the play Luke leaves. Why doesn't he stay? Why does Mom "remain frozen"?

8. What is the significance of the play's title? Before you answer, look up the lyrics of the song "Come Rain or Come Shine."

9. JOURNAL ENTRY Do you think Mahoney's play is insulting to gays? Republicans? both? neither? Explain.

10. CRITICAL PERSPECTIVE Artistic director of Atlanta's Alliance Theatre, Susan V. Booth praises Jeni Mahoney's ability to combine humor with self-reflection in her plays. In your opinion, does *Come Rain or Come Shine* achieve this goal? Why or why not?

Related Works: "Discovering America" (p. 135), "Young Goodman Brown" (p. 448), "My Voice" (p. 685), "Patterns" (p. 688), "We Wear the Mask" (p. 728), "Wall Street at Night" (p. 749), "*What Are You Going to Be?*" (p. 1062), *A Doll House* (p. 1113)

SOPHOCLES (496–406 B.C.) (picture and biography on p. 1430) was one of nine generals elected for a military campaign against Samos, a Greek island that was in revolt against Athens. Sophocles' election was due at least in part to the popularity of his play *Antigone*. (Greek plays often centered on problems of the city-state, and the theater was in many ways the center of the state's religious and political life.)

Even though it was written long before *Oedipus the King*, *Antigone* traces the events that befall Oedipus's younger daughter after his banishment from Thebes. Caught between the laws of the gods and the edict of her uncle the king, Antigone follows her conscience despite the fatal consequences to herself. In the 1960s, the story of Antigone was especially meaningful to those Americans who engaged in civil disobedience in struggles for civil rights and in protest against the war in Vietnam.

CULTURAL CONTEXT The central struggle in this play revolves around Antigone's desire to bury her brother in an honorable way. The ancient Greeks believed that at the moment of death, the spirit of the dead person left the body as a little puff of wind. The body was then prepared for burial according to certain rituals, which were primarily performed by female relatives. The burial rituals consisted of three parts: the *prothesis*, or laying out of the body; the *ekphora*, or funeral procession; and the interment of the body or cremated remains of the deceased. Coins were placed over the eyelids of the deceased as payment for the ferryman who would usher the body across the River Styx and into the underworld. The ancient Greeks believed that if the correct methods of burial were not followed, the soul of the deceased would roam between worlds until the proscribed rites were completed.

Antigone* (441 B.C.)

Translated by F. Storr, BA, Former Scholar of Trinity College, Cambridge

DRAMATIS PERSONAE

ANTIGONE and ISMENE: *Daughters of Oedipus and sisters of Polyneices and Eteocles*
CREON: *King of Thebes*
HAEMON: *Son of Creon, betrothed to Antigone*
EURYDICE: *Wife of Creon*
TEIRESIAS: *The prophet*
CHORUS: *Theban elders*

A WATCHMAN
A MESSENGER
A SECOND MESSENGER

Scene from a 1999 production of *Antigone* at London's Old Vic Theater
John Haynes/Lebrecht Music & Arts

PROLOGUE

ANTIGONE and ISMENE before the Palace gates.

ANTIGONE: Ismene, sister of my blood and heart,
See'st thou how Zeus would in our lives fulfill
The weird of Oedipus, a world of woes!
For what of pain, affliction, outrage, shame,
Is lacking in our fortunes, thine and mine?   5

---

*Note that individual lines are numbered in the following play. When a line is shared by two or more characters, it is counted as one line.

And now this proclamation of today
Made by our Captain-General to the State,
What can its purport be? Didst hear and heed,
Or art thou deaf when friends are banned as foes?

10   ISMENE: To me, Antigone, no word of friends
Has come, or glad or grievous, since we twain
Were reft of our two brethren in one day
By double fratricide; and since i' the night
Our Argive leaguers fled, no later news
15   Has reached me, to inspirit or deject.

ANTIGONE: I know 'twas so, and therefore summoned thee
Beyond the gates to breathe it in thine ear.

ISMENE: What is it? Some dark secret stirs thy breast.

ANTIGONE: What but the thought of our two brothers dead,
20   The one by Creon graced with funeral rites,
The other disappointed? Eteocles
He hath consigned to earth (as fame reports)
With obsequies that use and wont ordain,
So gracing him among the dead below.
25   But Polyneices, a dishonored corse,
(So by report the royal edict runs)
No man may bury him or make lament—
Must leave him tombless and unwept, a feast
For kites to scent afar and swoop upon.
30   Such is the edict (if report speak true)
Of Creon, our most noble Creon, aimed
At thee and me, aye me too; and anon
He will be here to promulgate, for such
As have not heard, his mandate; 'tis in sooth
35   No passing humor, for the edict says
Whoe'er transgresses shall be stoned to death.
So stands it with us; now 'tis thine to show
If thou art worthy of thy blood or base.

ISMENE: But how, my rash, fond sister, in such case
40   Can I do anything to make or mar?

ANTIGONE: Say, wilt thou aid me and abet? Decide.

ISMENE: In what bold venture? What is in thy thought?

ANTIGONE: Lend me a hand to bear the corpse away.

ISMENE: What, bury him despite the interdict?

45   ANTIGONE: My brother, and, though thou deny him, thine
No man shall say that *I* betrayed a brother.

ISMENE: Wilt thou persist, though Creon has forbid?

ANTIGONE: What right has he to keep me from my own?

ISMENE: Bethink thee, sister, of our father's fate,
50   Abhorred, dishonored, self-convinced of sin,
Blinded, himself his executioner.
Think of his mother-wife (ill sorted names)

Done by a noose herself had twined to death
And last, our hapless brethren in one day,
Both in a mutual destiny involved,   55
Self-slaughtered, both the slayer and the slain.
Bethink thee, sister, we are left alone;
Shall we not perish wretchedest of all,
If in defiance of the law we cross
A monarch's will? —weak women, think of that,   60
Not framed by nature to contend with men.
Remember this too that the stronger rules;
We must obey his orders, these or worse.
Therefore I plead compulsion and entreat
The dead to pardon. I perforce obey   65
The powers that be. 'Tis foolishness, I ween,
To overstep in aught the golden mean.

ANTIGONE: I urge no more; nay, wert thou willing still,
 I would not welcome such a fellowship.
 Go thine own way; myself will bury him.   70
 How sweet to die in such employ, to rest,—
 Sister and brother linked in love's embrace—
 A sinless sinner, banned awhile on earth,
 But by the dead commended; and with them
 I shall abide for ever. As for thee,   75
 Scorn, if thou wilt, the eternal laws of Heaven.

ISMENE: I scorn them not, but to defy the State
 Or break her ordinance I have no skill.

ANTIGONE: A specious pretext. I will go alone
 To lap my dearest brother in the grave.   80

ISMENE: My poor, fond sister, how I fear for thee!

ANTIGONE: O waste no fears on me; look to thyself.

ISMENE: At least let no man know of thine intent,
 But keep it close and secret, as will I.

ANTIGONE: O tell it, sister; I shall hate thee more   85
 If thou proclaim it not to all the town.

ISMENE: Thou hast a fiery soul for numbing work.

ANTIGONE: I pleasure those whom I would liefest please.

ISMENE: If thou succeed; but thou art doomed to fail.

ANTIGONE: When strength shall fail me, yes, but not before.   90

ISMENE: But, if the venture's hopeless, why essay?

ANTIGONE: Sister, forbear, or I shall hate thee soon,
 And the dead man will hate thee too, with cause.
 Say I am mad and give my madness rein
 To wreck itself; the worst that can befall   95
 Is but to die an honorable death.

ISMENE: Have thine own way then; 'tis a mad endeavor,
 Yet to thy lovers thou art dear as ever.

[Exeunt]

PÁRODOS[1]

STROPHE[2] 1

CHORUS: Sunbeam, of all that ever dawn upon
        Our seven-gated Thebes the brightest ray,
          O eye of golden day,
    How fair thy light o'er Dirce's fountain shone,
5   Speeding upon their headlong homeward course,
    Far quicker than they came, the Argive force;
          Putting to flight
    The argent shields, the host with scutcheons white.
    Against our land the proud invader came
10   To vindicate fell Polyneices' claim.
        Like to an eagle swooping low,
        On pinions white as new fall'n snow.
    With clanging scream, a horsetail plume his crest,
    The aspiring lord of Argos onward pressed.

ANTISTROPHE[3] 1

15   Hovering around our city walls he waits,
    His spearmen raven at our seven gates.
    But ere a torch our crown of towers could burn,
    Ere they had tasted of our blood, they turn
    Forced by the Dragon; in their rear
20   The din of Ares panic-struck they hear.
    For Zeus who hates the braggart's boast
    Beheld that gold-bespangled host;
    As at the goal the paean they upraise,
    He struck them with his forked lightning blaze.

STROPHE 2

25   To earthy from earth rebounding, down he crashed;
        The fire-brand from his impious hand was dashed,
    As like a Bacchic reveler on he came,
    Outbreathing hate and flame,
    And tottered. Elsewhere in the field,
30   Here, there, great Area like a war-horse wheeled;
        Beneath his car down thrust
        Our foemen bit the dust.
    Seven captains at our seven gates
    Thundered; for each a champion waits,
35   Each left behind his armor bright,
    Trophy for Zeus who turns the fight;

---

[1] *Párados:* The song that signifies the entrance of the chorus.

[2] *Strophe:* The first half of an ode, sung by the chorus.

[3] *Antistrophe:* The second half of an ode. Typically a response to the strophe, and also sung by the chorus.

Save two alone, that ill-starred pair
One mother to one father bare,
Who lance in rest, one 'gainst the other
Drave, and both perished, brother slain by brother.   40

ANTISTROPHE 2

Now Victory to Thebes returns again
And smiles upon her chariot-circled plain.
    Now let feast and festal should
    Memories of war blot out.
    Let us to the temples throng,   45
    Dance and sing the live night long.

SCENE 1

    God of Thebes, lead thou the round.
    Bacchus, shaker of the ground!
    Let us end our revels here;
    Lo! Creon our new lord draws near,
    Crowned by this strange chance, our king.   5
    What, I marvel, pondering?
    Why this summons? Wherefore call
    Us, his elders, one and all,
    Bidding us with him debate,
    On some grave concern of State?   10

[Enter CREON]

CREON: Elders, the gods have righted one again
    Our storm-tossed ship of state, now safe in port.
    But you by special summons I convened
    As my most trusted councilors; first, because
    I knew you loyal to Laius[1] of old;   15
    Again, when Oedipus restored our State,
    Both while he ruled and when his rule was o'er,
    Ye still were constant to the royal line.
    Now that his two sons perished in one day,
    Brother by brother murderously slain,   20
    By right of kinship to the Princes dead,
    I claim and hold the throne and sovereignty.
    Yet 'tis no easy matter to discern
    The temper of a man, his mind and will,
    Till he be proved by exercise of power;   25
    And in my case, if one who reigns supreme
    Swerve from the highest policy, tongue-tied
    By fear of consequence, that man I hold,
    And ever held, the basest of the base.

---

[1]*Laius:* A previous King of Thebes, and Oepdius' father.

30 And I contemn the man who sets his friend
    Before his country. For myself, I call
    To witness Zeus, whose eyes are everywhere,
    If I perceive some mischievous design
    To sap the State, I will not hold my tongue;
35 Nor would I reckon as my private friend
    A public foe, well knowing that the State
    Is the good ship that holds our fortunes all:
    Farewell to friendship, if she suffers wreck.
    Such is the policy by which I seek
40 To serve the Commons and conformably
    I have proclaimed an edict as concerns
    The sons of Oedipus; Eteocles
    Who in his country's battle fought and fell,
    The foremost champion—duly bury him
45 With all observances and ceremonies
    That are the guerdon of the heroic dead.
    But for the miscreant exile who returned
    Minded in flames and ashes to blot out
    His father's city and his father's gods,
50 And glut his vengeance with his kinsmen's blood,
    Or drag them captive at his chariot wheels—
    For Polyneices 'tis ordained that none
    Shall give him burial or make mourn for him,
    But leave his corpse unburied, to be meat
55 For dogs and carrion crows, a ghastly sight.
    So am I purposed; never by my will
    Shall miscreants take precedence of true men,
    But all good patriots, alive or dead,
    Shall be by me preferred and honored.
60 CHORUS: Son of Menoeceus[2], thus thou will'st to deal
    With him who loathed and him who loved our State.
    Thy word is law; thou canst dispose of us
    The living, as thou will'st, as of the dead.
    CREON: See then ye execute what I ordain.
65 CHORUS: On younger shoulders lay this grievous charge.
    CREON: Fear not, I've posted guards to watch the corpse.
    CHORUS: What further duty would'st thou lay on us?
    CREON: Not to connive at disobedience.
    CHORUS: No man is mad enough to court his death.
70 CREON: The penalty *is* death: yet hope of gain
    Hath lured men to their ruin oftentimes.

[Enter GUARD]

GUARD: My lord, I will not make pretense to pant
    And puff as some light-footed messenger.

---

[2]*Menoeceus:* Father of Creon and father-in-law of Oedipus.

In sooth my soul beneath its pack of thought
Made many a halt and turned and turned again;   75
For conscience plied her spur and curb by turns.
"Why hurry headlong to thy fate, poor fool?"
She whispered. Then again, "If Creon learn
This from another, thou wilt rue it worse."
Thus leisurely I hastened on my road;   80
Much thought extends a furlong to a league.
But in the end the forward voice prevailed,
To face thee. I will speak though I say nothing.
For plucking courage from despair methought,
"Let the worst hap, thou canst but meet thy fate."   85
CREON: What is thy news? Why this despondency?
GUARD: Let me premise a word about myself?
    I neither did the deed nor saw it done,
    Nor were it just that I should come to harm.
CREON: Thou art good at parry, and canst fence about   90
    Some matter of grave import, as is plain.
GUARD: The bearer of dread tidings needs must quake.
CREON: Then, sirrah, shoot thy bolt and get thee gone.
GUARD: Well, it must out; the corpse is buried; someone
    E'en now besprinkled it with thirsty dust,   95
    Performed the proper ritual[3]—and was gone.
CREON: What say'st thou? Who hath dared to do this thing?
GUARD: I cannot tell, for there was ne'er a trace
    Of pick or mattock—hard unbroken ground,
    Without a scratch or rut of chariot wheels,   100
    No sign that human hands had been at work.
    When the first sentry of the morning watch
    Gave the alarm, we all were terror-stricken.
    The corpse had vanished, not interred in earth,
    But strewn with dust, as if by one who sought   105
    To avert the curse that haunts the unburied dead:
    Of hound or ravening jackal, not a sign.
    Thereat arose an angry war of words;
    Guard railed at guard and blows were like to end it,
    For none was there to part us, each in turn   110
    Suspected, but the guilt brought home to none,
    From lack of evidence. We challenged each
    The ordeal, or to handle red-hot iron,
    Or pass through fire, affirming on our oath
    Our innocence—we neither did the deed   115
    Ourselves, nor know who did or compassed it.
    Our quest was at a standstill, when one spake
    And bowed us all to earth like quivering reeds,

---

[3]*proper ritual:* Rituals and the way they are performed are important in Greek tragedies, especially rituals for death.

For there was no gainsaying him nor way
120   To escape perdition: Ye are bound to tell
The King ye cannot hide it; so he spake.
And he convinced us all; so lots were cast,
And I, unlucky scapegoat, drew the prize.
So here I am unwilling and withal
125   Unwelcome; no man cares to hear ill news.

CHORUS: I had misgivings from the first, my liege,
Of something more than natural at work.

CREON: O cease, you vex me with your babblement;
I am like to think you dote in your old age.
130   Is it not arrant folly to pretend
That gods would have a thought for this dead man?
Did they forsooth award him special grace,
And as some benefactor bury him,
Who came to fire their hallowed sanctuaries,
135   To sack their shrines, to desolate their land,
And scout their ordinances? Or perchance
The gods bestow their favors on the bad.
No! no! I have long noted malcontents
Who wagged their heads, and kicked against the yoke,
140   Misliking these my orders, and my rule.
'Tis they, I warrant, who suborned my guards
By bribes. Of evils current upon earth
The worst is money. Money 'tis that sacks
Cities, and drives men forth from hearth and home;
145   Warps and seduces native innocence,
And breeds a habit of dishonesty.
But they who sold themselves shall find their greed
Out-shot the mark, and rue it soon or late.
Yea, as I still revere the dread of Zeus,
150   By Zeus I swear, except ye find and bring
Before my presence here the very man
Who carried out this lawless burial,
Death for your punishment shall not suffice.
Hanged on a cross, alive ye first shall make
155   Confession of this outrage. This will teach you
What practices are like to serve your turn.
There are some villainies that bring no gain.
For by dishonesty the few may thrive,
The many come to ruin and disgrace.

GUARD: May I not speak, or must I turn and go
160   Without a word?—

CREON: Begone! canst thou not see
That e'en this question irks me?

GUARD: Where, my lord?
165   Is it thy ears that suffer, or thy heart?

CREON: Why seek to probe and find the seat of pain?
GUARD: I gall thine ears—this miscreant thy mind.
CREON: What an inveterate babbler! Get thee gone!
GUARD: Babbler perchance, but innocent of the crime.
CREON: Twice guilty, having sold thy soul for gain.   170
GUARD: Alas! How sad when reasoners reason wrong.
CREON: Go, quibble with thy reason. If thou fail'st
   To find these malefactors, thou shalt own
   The wages of ill-gotten gains is death.

[Exit CREON]

GUARD: I pray he may be found. But caught or not   175
   (And fortune must determine that) thou never
   Shalt see me here returning; that is sure.
   For past all hope or thought I have escaped,
   And for my safety owe the gods much thanks.

ODE[1] 1
STROPHE 1

CHORUS: Many wonders there be, but naught more wondrous than man;
   Over the surging sea, with a whitening south wind wan,
   Through the foam of the firth, man makes his perilous way;
   And the eldest of deities Earth that knows not toil nor decay
   Ever he furrows and scores, as his team, year in year out,   5
   With breed of the yoked horse, the ploughshare turneth about.

ANTISTROPHE 1

The light-witted birds of the air, the beasts of the weald and the wood
He traps with his woven snare, and the brood of the briny flood.
Master of cunning he: the savage bull, and the hart
Who roams the mountain free, are tamed by his infinite art;   10
And the shaggy rough-maned steed is broken to bear the bit.

STROPHE 2

Speech and the wind-swift speed of counsel and civic wit,
He hath learnt for himself all these; and the arrowy rain to fly
And the nipping airs that freeze, 'neath the open winter sky.
He hath provision for all: fell plague he hath learnt to endure;   15
Safe whate'er may befall: yet for death he hath found no cure.

ANTISTROPHE 2

Passing the wildest flight thought are the cunning and skill,
That guide man now to the light, but now to counsels of ill.
If he honors the laws of the land, and reveres the Gods of the State
Proudly his city shall stand; but a cityless outcast I rate   20
Whoso bold in his pride from the path of right doth depart;

---

[1]*Ode:* A type of lyrical stanza that is comprised of three parts: the strophe, the antistrophe, and the epode.

Ne'er may I sit by his side, or share the thoughts of his heart.

What strange vision meets my eyes,
Fills me with a wild surprise?
25 Sure I know her, sure 'tis she,
The maid Antigone.
Hapless child of hapless sire,
Didst thou recklessly conspire,
Madly brave the King's decree?
30 Therefore are they haling thee?

SCENE II

[Enter GUARD bringing ANTIGONE]

GUARD: Here is the culprit taken in the act
Of giving burial. But where's the King?
CHORUS: There from the palace he returns in time.

[Enter CREON]

CREON: Why is my presence timely? What has chanced?
5 GUARD: No man, my lord, should make a vow, for if
He ever swears he will not do a thing,
His afterthoughts belie his first resolve.
When from the hail-storm of thy threats I fled
I sware thou wouldst not see me here again;
10 But the wild rapture of a glad surprise
Intoxicates, and so I'm here forsworn.
And here's my prisoner, caught in the very act,
Decking the grave. No lottery this time;
This prize is mine by right of treasure-trove.
15 So take her, judge her, rack her, if thou wilt.
She's thine, my liege; but I may rightly claim
Hence to depart well quit of all these ills.
CREON: Say, how didst thou arrest the maid, and where?
GUARD: Burying the man. There's nothing more to tell.
20 CREON: Hast thou thy wits? Or know'st thou what thou say'st?
GUARD: I saw this woman burying the corpse
Against thy orders. Is that clear and plain?
CREON: But how was she surprised and caught in the act?
GUARD: It happened thus. No sooner had we come,
25 Driven from thy presence by those awful threats,
Than straight we swept away all trace of dust,
And bared the clammy body. Then we sat
High on the ridge to windward of the stench,
While each man kept he fellow alert and rated
30 Roundly the sluggard if he chanced to nap.
So all night long we watched, until the sun
Stood high in heaven, and his blazing beams
Smote us. A sudden whirlwind then upraised

A cloud of dust that blotted out the sky,
And swept the plain, and stripped the woodlands bare,   35
And shook the firmament. We closed our eyes
And waited till the heaven-sent plague should pass.
At last it ceased, and lo! There stood this maid.
A piercing cry she uttered, sad and shrill,
As when the mother bird beholds her nest   40
Robbed of its nestlings; even so the maid
Wailed as she saw the body stripped and bare,
And cursed the ruffians who had done this deed.
Anon she gathered handfuls of dry dust,
Then, holding high a well-wrought brazen urn,   45
Thrice on the dead she poured a lustral stream.
We at the sight swooped down on her and seized
Our quarry. Undismayed she stood, and when
We taxed her with the former crime and this,
She disowned nothing. I was glad—and grieved;   50
For 'tis most sweet to 'scape oneself scot-free,
And yet to bring disaster to a friend
Is grievous. Take it all in all, I deem
A man's first duty is to serve himself.
CREON: Speak, girl, with head bent low and downcast eyes,   55
   Does thou plead guilty or deny the deed?
ANTIGONE: Guilty. I did it, I deny it not.
CREON: (*to GUARD*) Sirrah, begone whither thou wilt, and thank
   Thy luck that thou hast 'scaped a heavy charge.

(*To ANTIGONE*)

   Now answer this plain question, yes or no,   60
   Wast thou acquainted with the interdict?
ANTIGONE: I knew, all knew; how should I fail to know?
CREON: And yet wert bold enough to break the law?
ANTIGONE: Yea, for these laws were not ordained of Zeus,
   And she who sits enthroned with gods below,   65
Justice, enacted not these human laws.
Nor did I deem that thou, a mortal man,
Could'st by a breath annul and override
The immutable unwritten laws of Heaven.
They were not born today nor yesterday;   70
They die not; and none knoweth whence they sprang.
I was not like, who feared no mortal's frown,
To disobey these laws and so provoke
The wrath of Heaven. I knew that I must die,
E'en hadst thou not proclaimed it; and if death   75
Is thereby hastened, I shall count it gain.
For death is gain to him whose life, like mine,
Is full of misery. Thus my lot appears

Not sad, but blissful; for had I endured
80   To leave my mother's son unburied there,
I should have grieved with reason, but not now.
And if in this thou judgest me a fool,
Methinks the judge of folly's not acquit.
CHORUS: A stubborn daughter of a stubborn sire,
85   This ill-starred maiden kicks against the pricks.
CREON: Well, let her know the stubbornest of wills
Are soonest bended, as the hardest iron,
O'er-heated in the fire to brittleness,
Flies soonest into fragments, shivered through.
90   A snaffle curbs the fieriest steed, and he
Who in subjection lives must needs be meek.
But this proud girl, in insolence well-schooled,
First overstepped the established law, and then—
A second and worse act of insolence—
95   She boasts and glories in her wickedness.
Now if she thus can flout authority
Unpunished, I am woman, she the man.
But though she be my sister's child or nearer
Of kin than all who worship at my hearth,
100   Nor she nor yet her sister shall escape
The utmost penalty, for both I hold,
As arch-conspirators, of equal guilt.
Bring forth the older; even now I saw her
Within the palace, frenzied and distraught.
105   The workings of the mind discover oft
Dark deeds in darkness schemed, before the act.
More hateful still the miscreant who seeks
When caught, to make a virtue of a crime.
ANTIGONE: Would'st thou do more than slay thy prisoner?
110   CREON: Not I, thy life is mine, and that's enough.
ANTIGONE: Why dally then? To me no word of thine
Is pleasant: God forbid it e'er should please;
Nor am I more acceptable to thee.
And yet how otherwise had I achieved
115   A name so glorious as by burying
A brother? so my townsmen all would say,
Where they not gagged by terror, Manifold
A king's prerogatives, and not the least
That all his acts and all his words are law.
120   CREON: Of all these Thebans none so deems but thou.
ANTIGONE: These think as I, but bate their breath to thee.
CREON: Hast thou no shame to differ from all these?
ANTIGONE: To reverence kith and kin[1] can bring no shame.

---

[1] *Kith and kin:* friends and family

CREON: Was his dead foeman not thy kinsman too?
ANTIGONE: One mother bare them and the self-same sire. 125
CREON: Why cast a slur on one by honoring one?
ANTIGONE: The dead man will not bear thee out in this.
CREON: Surely, if good and evil fare alive.
ANTIGONE: The slain man was no villain but a brother.
CREON: The patriot perished by the outlaw's brand. 130
ANTIGONE: Nathless the realms below these rites require.
CREON: Not that the base should fare as do the brave.
ANTIGONE: Who knows if this world's crimes are virtues there?
CREON: Not even death can make a foe a friend.
ANTIGONE: My nature is for mutual love, not hate. 135
CREON: Die then, and love the dead if thou must;
    No woman shall be the master while I live.

[Enter ISMENE]

CHORUS: Lo from out the palace gate,
           Weeping o'er her sister's fate,
           Comes Ismene; see her brow, 140
           Once serene, beclouded now,
           See her beauteous face o'erspread
           With a flush of angry red.
CREON: Woman, who like a viper unperceived
    Didst harbor in my house and drain my blood, 145
    Two plagues I nurtured blindly, so it proved,
    To sap my throne. Say, didst thou too abet
    This crime, or dost abjure all privity?
    Ismene:I did the deed, if she will have it so,
    And with my sister claim to share the guilt. 150
ANTIGONE: That were unjust. Thou would'st not act with me
    At first, and I refused thy partnership.
ISMENE: But now thy bark is stranded, I am bold
    To claim my share as partner in the loss.
ANTIGONE: Who did the deed the under-world knows well: 155
    A friend in word is never friend of mine.
ISMENE: O sister, scorn me not, let me but share
    Thy work of piety, and with thee die.
ANTIGONE: Claim not a work in which thou hadst no hand;
    One death sufficeth. Wherefore should'st thou die? 160
ISMENE: What would life profit me bereft of thee?
ANTIGONE: Ask Creon, he's thy kinsman and best friend.
ISMENE: Why taunt me? Find'st thou pleasure in these gibes?
ANTIGONE: 'Tis a sad mockery, if indeed I mock.
ISMENE: O say if I can help thee even now. 165
ANTIGONE: No, save thyself; I grudge not thy escape.
ISMENE: Is e'en this boon denied, to share thy lot?
ANTIGONE: Yea, for thou chosed'st life, and I to die.

ISMENE: Thou canst not say that I did not protest.

170   ANTIGONE: Well, some approved thy wisdom, others mine.

ISMENE: But now we stand convicted, both alike.

ANTIGONE: Fear not; thou livest, I died long ago
     Then when I gave my life to save the dead.

CREON: Both maids, methinks, are crazed. One suddenly

175   Has lost her wits, the other was born mad.

ISMENE: Yea, so it falls, sire, when misfortune comes,
     The wisest even lose their mother wit.

CREON: I' faith thy wit forsook thee when thou mad'st
     Thy choice with evil-doers to do ill.

180   ISMENE: What life for me without my sister here?

CREON: Say not thy sister *here*: thy sister's dead.

ISMENE: What, wilt thou slay thy own son's plighted bride?

CREON: Aye, let him raise him seed from other fields.

ISMENE: No new espousal can be like the old.

185   CREON: A plague on trulls who court and woo our sons.

ANTIGONE: O Haemon, how thy sire dishonors thee!

CREON: A plague on thee and thy accursed bride!

CHORUS: What, wilt thou rob thine own son of his bride?

CREON: 'Tis death that bars this marriage, not his sire.

190   CHORUS: So her death-warrant, it would seem, is sealed.

CREON: By you, as first by me; off with them, guards,
     And keep them close. Henceforward let them learn
     To live as women use, not roam at large.
     For e'en the bravest spirits run away

195   When they perceive death pressing on life's heels.

ODE II

STROPHE 1

CHORUS: Thrice blest are they who never tasted pain!
     If once the curse of Heaven attaint a race,
       The infection lingers on and speeds apace,
     Age after age, and each the cup must drain.

5   So when Etesian blasts from Thrace downpour
     Sweep o'er the blackening main and whirl to land
       From Ocean's cavernous depths his ooze and sand,
     Billow on billow thunders on the shore.

ANTISTROPHE 1

On the Labdacidae I see descending

10   Woe upon woe; from days of old some god
     Laid on the race a malison, and his rod
     Scourges each age with sorrows never ending.

The light that dawned upon its last born son
     Is vanished, and the bloody axe of Fate

15   Has felled the goodly tree that blossomed late.
     O Oedipus, by reckless pride undone!

STROPHE 2

Thy might, O Zeus, what mortal power can quell?
Not sleep that lays all else beneath its spell,
Nor moons that never tire: untouched by Time,
    Throned in the dazzling light   20
    That crowns Olympus' height,
Thou reignest King, omnipotent, sublime.

    Past, present, and to be,
    All bow to thy decree,
    All that exceeds the mean by Fate   25
    Is punished, Love or Hate.

ANTISTROPHE 2

Hope flits about never-wearying wings;
Profit to some, to some light loves she brings,
But no man knoweth how her gifts may turn,
Till 'neath his feet the treacherous ashes burn.   30
Sure 'twas a sage inspired that spake this word;
    If evil good appear
    To any, Fate is near;
And brief the respite from her flaming sword.

SCENE III

    Hither comes in angry mood
    Haemon, latest of thy brood;
    Is it for his bride he's grieved,
    Or her marriage-bed deceived,
    Doth he make his mourn for thee,   5
    Maid forlorn, Antigone?

[Enter HAEMON]

CREON: Soon shall we know, better than seer can tell.
    Learning may fixed decree anent thy bride,
    Thou mean'st not, son, to rave against thy sire?
    Know'st not whate'er we do is done in love?   10
HAEMON: O father, I am thine, and I will take
    Thy wisdom as the helm to steer withal.
    Therefore no wedlock shall by me be held
    More precious than thy loving goverance.
CREON: Well spoken: so right-minded sons should feel,   15
    In all deferring to a father's will.
    For 'tis the hope of parents they may rear
    A brood of sons submissive, keen to avenge
    Their father's wrongs, and count his friends their own.
    But who begets unprofitable sons,   20
    He verily breeds trouble for himself,
    And for his foes much laughter. Son, be warned

And let no woman fool away thy wits.
Ill fares the husband mated with a shrew,
25   And her embraces very soon wax cold.
For what can wound so surely to the quick
As a false friend? So spue and cast her off,
Bid her go find a husband with the dead.
For since I caught her openly rebelling,
30   Of all my subjects the one malcontent,
I will not prove a traitor to the State.
She surely dies. Go, let her, if she will,
Appeal to Zeus the God of Kindred, for
If thus I nurse rebellion in my house,
35   Shall not I foster mutiny without?
For whoso rules his household worthily,
Will prove in civic matters no less wise.
But he who overbears the laws, or thinks
To overrule his rulers, such as one
40   I never will allow. Whome'er the State
Appoints must be obeyed in everything,
But small and great, just and unjust alike.
I warrant such a one in either case
Would shine, as King or subject; such a man
45   Would in the storm of battle stand his ground,
A comrade leal and true; but Anarchy—
What evils are not wrought by Anarchy!
She ruins States, and overthrows the home,
She dissipates and routs the embattled host;
50   While discipline preserves the ordered ranks.
Therefore we must maintain authority
And yield to title to a woman's will.
Better, if needs be, men should cast us out
Than hear it said, a woman proved his match.
55   **CHORUS:** To me, unless old age have dulled wits,
Thy words appear both reasonable and wise.
HAEMON: Father, the gods implant in mortal men
Reason, the choicest gift bestowed by heaven.
'Tis not for me to say thou errest, nor
60   Would I arraign thy wisdom, if I could;
And yet wise thoughts may come to other men
And, as thy son, it falls to me to mark
The acts, the words, the comments of the crowd.
The commons stand in terror of thy frown,
65   And dare not utter aught that might offend,
But I can overhear their muttered plaints,
Know how the people mourn this maiden doomed
For noblest deeds to die the worst of deaths.
When her own brother slain in battle lay
70   Unsepulchered, she suffered not his corse

To lie for carrion birds and dogs to maul:
Should not her name (they cry) be writ in gold?
Such the low murmurings that reach my ear.
O father, nothing is by me more prized
Than thy well-being, for what higher good   75
Can children covet than their sire's fair fame,
As fathers too take pride in glorious sons?
Therefore, my father, cling not to one mood,
And deemed not thou art right, all others wrong.
For whoso thinks that wisdom dwells with him,   80
That he alone can speak or think aright,
Such oracles are empty breath when tried.
The wisest man will let himself be swayed
By others' wisdom and relax in time.
See how the trees beside a stream in flood   85
Save, if they yield to force, each spray unharmed,
But by resisting perish root and branch.
The mariner who keeps his mainsheet taut,
And will not slacken in the gale, is like
To sail with thwarts reversed, keel uppermost.   90
Relent then and repent thee of thy wrath;
For, if one young in years may claim some sense,
I'll say 'tis best of all to be endowed
With absolute wisdom; but, if that's denied,
(And nature takes not readily that ply)   95
Next wise is he who lists to sage advice.
CHORUS: If he says aught in season, heed him, King.

(To HAEMON)

Heed thou thy sire too; both have spoken well.

CREON: What, would you have us at our age be schooled,
    Lessoned in prudence by a beardless boy?   100
HAEMON: I plead for justice, father, nothing more.
    Weigh me upon my merit, not my years.
CREON: Strange merit this to sanction lawlessness!
HAEMON: For evil-doers I would urge no plea.
CREON: Is not this maid an arrant law-breaker?   105
HAEMON: The Theban commons with one voice say, No.
CREON: What, shall the mob dictate my policy?
HAEMON: 'Tis thou, methinks, who speakest like a boy.
CREON: Am I to rule for others, or myself?
HAEMON: A State for one man is no State at all.   110
CREON: The State is his who rules it, so 'tis held.
HAEMON: As monarch of a desert thou wouldst shine.
CREON: This boy, methinks, maintains the woman's cause.
HAEMON: If thou be'st woman, yes. My thought's for thee.
CREON: O reprobate, would'st wrangle with thy sire?   115

HAEMON: Because I see thee wrongfully perverse.
CREON: And am I wrong, if I maintain my rights?
HAEMON: Talk not of rights; thou spurn'st the due of Heaven
CREON: O heart corrupt, a woman's minion thou!
120 HAEMON: Slave to dishonor thou wilt never find me.
CREON: Thy speech at least was all a plea for her.
HAEMON: And thee and me, and for the gods below.
CREON: Living the maid shall never be thy bride.
HAEMON: So she shall die, but one will die with her.
125 CREON: Hast come to such a pass as threaten me?
HAEMON: What threat is this, vain counsels to reprove?
CREON: Vain fool to instruct thy betters; thou shall rue it.
HAEMON: Wert not my father, I had said thou err'st.
CREON: Play not the spaniel, thou a woman's slave.
130 HAEMON: When thou dost speak, must no man make reply?
CREON: This passes bounds. By heaven, thou shalt not rate
       And jeer and flout me with impunity.
       Off with the hateful thing that she may die
       At once, beside her bridegroom, in his sight.
135 HAEMON: Think not that in my sight the maid shall die,
       Or by my side; never shalt thou again
       Behold my face hereafter. Go, consort
       With friends who like a madman for their mate.

[Exit HAEMON]

CHORUS: Thy son has gone, my liege, in angry haste.
140   Fell is the wrath of youth beneath a smart.
CREON: Let him go vent his fury like a fiend:
       These sisters twain he shall not save from death.
CHORUS: Surely, thou meanest not to slay them both?
CREON: I stand corrected; only her who touched
145   The body.
CHORUS: And what death is she to die?
CREON: She shall be taken to some desert place
       By man untrod, and in a rock-hewn cave,
       With food no more than to avoid the taint
150   That homicide might bring on all the State,
       Buried alive. There let her call in aid
       The King of Death, the one god she reveres,
       Or learn too late a lesson learnt at last:
       'Tis labor lost, to reverence the dead.

ODE III
STROPHE

CHORUS: Love resistless in fight, all yield at a glance of thine eye,
       Love who pillowed all night on a maiden's cheek dost lie,
       Over the upland holds. Shall mortals not yield to thee?

ANTISTROPHE

Mad are thy subjects all, and even the wisest heart
Straight to folly will fall, at a touch of thy poisoned dart.   5
Thou didst kindle the strife, this feud of kinsman with kin,
By the eyes of a winsome wife, and the yearning her heart to win.
For as her consort still, enthroned with Justice above,
Thou bendest man to thy will, O all invincible Love.

SCENE IV

Lo I myself am borne aside,
From Justice, as I view this bride.
(O sight an eye in tears to drown)
Antigone, so young, so fair,
   Thus hurried down   5
Death's bower with the dead to share.

STROPHE 1

ANTIGONE: Friends, countrymen, my last farewell I make;
   My journey's done.
One last fond, lingering, longing look I take
   At the bright sun.   10
For Death who puts to sleep both young and old
   Hales my young life,
And beckons me to Acheron's dark fold,
   An unwed wife.
No youths have sung the marriage song for me,   15
   My bridal bed
No maids have strewn with flowers from the lea,
   'Tis Death I wed.
CHORUS: But bethink thee, thou art sped,
   Great and glorious, to the dead.   20
   Thou the sword's edge hast not tasted,
   No disease thy frame hath wasted.
   Freely thou alone shalt go
   Living to the dead below.

ANTISTROPHE 1

ANTIGONE: Nay, but the piteous tale I've heard men tell   25
   Of Tantalus' doomed child,
Chained upon Siphylus' high rocky fell,
   That clung like ivy wild,
Drenched by the pelting rain and whirling snow,
   Left there to pine,   30
While on her frozen breast the tears aye flow—
   Her fate is mine.

CHORUS: She was sprung of gods, divine,
                    Mortals we of mortal line.
35   Like renown with gods to gain
                    Recompenses all thy pain.
                    Take this solace to thy tomb
                    Hers in life and death thy doom.

STROPHE 2

ANTIGONE: Alack, alack! Ye mock me. Is it meet
40   Thus to insult me living, to my face?
        Cease, by our country's altars I entreat,
           Ye lordly rulers of a lordly race.
        O fount of Dirce, wood-embowered plain
           Where Theban chariots to victory speed,
45   Mark ye the cruel laws that now have wrought my bane,
           The friends who show no pity in my need!
        Was ever fate like mine? O monstrous doom,
           Within a rock-built prison sepulchered,
        To fade and wither in a living tomb,
50   And alien midst the living and the dead.

STROPHE 3

CHORUS: In thy boldness over-rash
                    Madly thou thy foot didst dash
                    'Gainst high Justice' altar stair.
                    Thou a father's guild dost bear.

ANTISTROPHE 2

55 ANTIGONE: At this thou touchest my most poignant pain,
           My ill-starred father's piteous disgrace,
        The taint of blood, the hereditary stain,
           That clings to all of Labdacus' famed race.
        Woe worth the monstrous marriage-bed where lay
60   A mother with the son her womb had borne,
        Therein I was conceived, woe worth the day,
           Fruit of incestuous sheets, a maid forlorn,
        And now I pass, accursed and unwed,
           To meet them as an alien there below;
65   And thee, O brother, in marriage ill-bestead,
           'Twas thy dead hand that dealt me this death-blow.

CHORUS: Religion has her chains, 'tis true,
                    Let rite be paid when rites are due.
                    Yet is it ill to disobey
70   The powers who hold by might the sway.
                    Thou hast withstood authority,
                    A self-willed rebel, thou must die.

EPODE[1]

ANTIGONE: Unwept, unwed, unfriended, hence I go,
    No longer may I see the day's bright eye;
Not one friend left to share my bitter woe,   75
    And o'er my ashes heave one passing sigh.

CREON: If wail and lamentation aught availed
    To stave off death, I trow they'd never end.
    Away with her, and having walled her up
    In a rock-vaulted tomb, as I ordained,   80
    Leave her alone at liberty to die,
    Or, if she choose, to live in solitude,
    The tomb her dwelling. We in either case
    Are guiltless as concerns this maiden's blood,
    Only on earth no lodging shall she find.   85

ANTIGONE: O grave, O bridal bower, O prison house
    Hewn from the rock, my everlasting home,
    Whither I go to join the mighty host
    Of kinsfolk, Persephassa's[2] guests long dead,
    The last of all, of all more miserable,   90
    I pass, my destined span of years cut short.
    And yet good hope is mine that I shall find
    A welcome from my sire, a welcome too,
    From thee, my mother, and my brother dear;
    From with these hands, I laved and decked your limbs   95
    In death, and poured libations on your grave.
    And last, my Polyneices, unto thee
    I paid due rites, and this my recompense!
    Yet am I justified in wisdom's eyes.
    For even had it been some child of mine,   100
    Or husband mouldering in death's decay,
    I had not wrought this deed despite the State.
    What is the law I call in aid? 'Tis thus
    I argue. Had it been a husband dead
    I might have wed another, and have borne   105
    Another child, to take the dead child's place.
    But, now my sire and mother both are dead,
    No second brother can be born for me.
    Thus by the law of conscience I was led
    To honor thee, dear brother, and was judged   110
    By Creon guilty of a heinous crime.
    And now he drags me like a criminal,
    A bride unwed, amerced of marriage-song
    And marriage-bed and joys of motherhood,
    By friends deserted to a living grave.   115

---

[1] *Epode:* The third part of an ode.
[2] *Persephassa:* Daughter of Zeus, also know as Persephone.

What ordinance of heaven have I transgressed?
Hereafter can I look to any god
For succor, call on any man for help?
Alas, my piety is impious deemed.
120   Well, if such justice is approved of heaven,
I shall be taught by suffering my sin;
But if the sin is theirs, O may they suffer
No worse ills than the wrongs they do to me.
CHORUS: The same ungovernable will
125   Drives like a gale the maiden still.
CREON: Therefore, my guards who let her stay
Shall smart full sore for their delay.
ANTIGONE: Ah, woe is me! This word I hear
Brings death most near.
130 CHORUS: I have no comfort. What he saith,
Portends no other thing than death.
ANTIGONE: My fatherland, city of Thebes divine,
Ye gods of Thebes whence sprang my line,
Look, puissant lords of Thebes, on me;
135   The last of all your royal house ye see.
Martyred by men of sin, undone.
Such meed my piety hath won.

[Exit ANTIGONE]

ODE IV

STROPHE 1

CHORUS: Like to thee that maiden bright,
Danae, in her brass-bound tower,
Once exchanged the glad sunlight
For a cell, her bridal bower.
5   And yet she sprang of royal line,
My child, like thine,
And nursed the seed
By her conceived
Of Zeus descending in a golden shower.
10   Strange are the ways of Fate, her power
Nor wealth, nor arms withstand, nor tower;
Nor brass-prowed ships, that breast the sea
From Fate can flee.

ANTISTROPHE 1

Thus Dryas' child, the rash Edonian King,
15   For words of high disdain
Did Bacchus[1] to a rocky dungeon bring,

---

[1] *Bacchus:* Another name for Dionysis, God of wine.

To cool the madness of a fevered brain.
     His frenzy passed,
     He learnt at last
'Twas madness gibes against a god to fling.   20
For once he fain had quenched the Maenad's fire;
And of the tuneful Nine[2] provoked the ire.

STROPHE 2

By the Iron Rocks that guard the double main,
     On Bosporus' lone strand,
Where stretcheth Salmydessus' plain   25
     In the wild Thracian land,
There on his borders Ares[3] witnessed
     The vengeance by a jealous step-dame ta'en
The gore that trickled from a spindle red,
     The sightless orbits of her step-sons twain.   30

ANTISTROPHE 2

Wasting away they mourned their piteous doom,
The blasted issue of their mother's womb.
But she her lineage could trace
     To great Erecththeus' race;
Daughter of Boreas in her sire's vast caves   35
     Reared, where the tempest raves,
Swift as his horses o'er the hills she sped;
A child of gods; yet she, my child, like thee,
     By Destiny
That knows not death nor age—she too was vanquished.   40

SCENE V

[Enter TEIRESIAS and BOY]

TEIRESIAS:[1] Princes of Thebes, two wayfarers as one,
     Having betwixt us eyes for one, we are here.
     The blind man cannot move without a guide.
CREON: Why tidings, old Teiresias?
TEIRESIAS: I will tell thee;   5
     And when thou hearest thou must heed the seer.
CREON: Thus far I ne'er have disobeyed thy rede.
TEIRESIAS: So hast thou steered the ship of State aright.
CREON: I know it, and I gladly own my debt.
TEIRESIAS: Bethink thee that thou treadest once again   10
     The razor edge of peril.

---

[2] *Nine:* The nine muses, who represent knowledge and art.

[3] *Ares:* The Greek god of war.

[1] *Teiresias:* A blind seer whose visions of the future are often ignored or misinterpreted.

CREON: What is this?
            Thy words inspire a dread presentiment.
TEIRESIAS: The divination of my arts shall tell.
15   Sitting upon my throne of augury,
                As is my wont, where every fowl of heaven
                Find harborage, upon mine ears was borne
                A jargon strange of twitterings, hoots, and screams;
                So knew I that each bird at the other tare
20   With bloody talons, for the whirr of wings
                Could signify naught else. Perturbed in soul,
                I straight essayed the sacrifice by fire
                On blazing altars, but the God of Fire
                Came not in flame, and from the thigh bones dripped
25   And sputtered in the ashes a foul ooze;
                Gall-bladders cracked and spurted up: the fat
                Melted and fell and left the thigh bones bare.
                Such are the signs, taught by this lad, I read—
                As I guide others, so the boy guides me—
30   The frustrate signs of oracles grown dumb.
                O King, thy willful temper ails the State,
                For all our shrines and altars are profaned
                By what has filled the maw of dogs and crows,
                The flesh of Oedipus' unburied son.
35   Therefore the angry gods abominate
                Our litanies and our burnt offerings;
                Therefore no birds trill out a happy note,
                Gorged with the carnival of human gore.
                O ponder this, my son. To err is common
40   To all men, but the man who having erred
                Hugs not his errors, but repents and seeks
                The cure, is not a wastrel nor unwise.
                No fool, the saw goes, like the obstinate fool.
                Let death disarm thy vengeance. O forbear
45   To vex the dead. What glory wilt thou win
                By slaying twice the slain? I mean thee well;
                Counsel's most welcome if I promise gain.
CREON: Old man, ye all let fly at me your shafts
            Like anchors at a target; yea, ye set
50   Your soothsayer on me. Peddlers are ye all
                And I the merchandise ye buy and sell.
                Go to, and make your profit where ye will,
                Silver of Sardis change for gold of Ind;
                Ye will not purchase this man's burial,
55   Not though the winged ministers of Zeus
                Should bear him in their talons to his throne;
                Not e'en in awe of prodigy so dire
                Would I permit his burial, for I know
                No human soilure can assail the gods;

This too I know, Teiresias, dire's the fall　　　　　　60
　　Of craft and cunning when it tries to gloss
　　Foul treachery with fair words for filthy gain.
TEIRESIAS: Alas! doth any know and lay to heart—
CREON: Is this the prelude to some hackneyed saw?
TEIRESIAS: How far good counsel is the best of goods?　　65
CREON: True, as unwisdom is the worst of ills.
TEIRESIAS: Thou art infected with that ill thyself.
CREON: I will not bandy insults with thee, seer.
TEIRESIAS: And yet thou say'st my prophesies are frauds.
CREON: Prophets are all a money-getting tribe.　　70
TEIRESIAS: And kings are all a lucre-loving race.
CREON: Dost know at whom thou glancest, me thy lord?
TEIRESIAS: Lord of the State and savior, thanks to me.
CREON: Skilled prophet art thou, but to wrong inclined.
TEIRESIAS: Take heed, thou wilt provoke me to reveal　　75
　　The mystery deep hidden in my breast.
CREON: Say on, but see it be not said for gain.
TEIRESIAS: Such thou, methinks, till now hast judged my words.
CREON: Be sure thou wilt not traffic on my wits.
TEIRESIAS: Know then for sure, the coursers of the sun　　80
　　Not many times shall run their race, before
　　Thou shalt have given the fruit of thine own loins
　　In quittance of thy murder, life for life;
　　For that thou hast entombed a living soul,
　　And sent below a denizen of earth,　　85
　　And wronged the nether gods by leaving here
　　A corpse unlaved, unwept, unsepulchered.
　　Herein thou hast no part, nor e'en the gods
　　In heaven; and thou usurp'st a power not thine.
　　For this the avenging spirits of Heaven and Hell　　90
　　Who dog the steps of sin are on thy trail:
　　What these have suffered thou shalt suffer too.
　　And now, consider whether bought by gold
　　I prophesy. For, yet a little while,
　　And sound of lamentation shall be heard,　　95
　　Of men and women through thy desolate halls;
　　And all thy neighbor States are leagues to avenge
　　Their mangled warriors who have found a grave
　　I' the maw of wolf or hound, or winged bird
　　That flying homewards taints their city's air.　　100
　　These are the shafts, that like a bowman I
　　Provoked to anger, loosen at thy breast,
　　Unerring, and their smart thou shalt not shun.
　　Boy, lead me home, that he may vent his spleen
　　On younger men, and learn to curb his tongue　　105
　　With gentler manners than his present mood.

[Exit TEIRESIAS]

CHORUS: My liege, that man hath gone, foretelling woe.
        And, O believe me, since these grizzled locks
        Were like the raven, never have I known
110   The prophet's warning to the State to fail.
CREON: I know it too, and it perplexes me.
        To yield is grievous, but the obstinate soul
        That fights with Fate, is smitten grievously.
CHORUS: Son of Menoeceus, list to good advice.
115 CHORUS: What should I do. Advise me. I will heed.
CHORUS: Go, free the maiden from her rocky cell;
        And for the unburied outlaw build a tomb.
CREON: Is that your counsel? You would have me yield?
CHORUS: Yea, king, this instant. Vengeance of the gods
120   Is swift to overtake the impenitent.
CREON: Ah! what a wrench it is to sacrifice
        My heart's resolve; but Fate is ill to fight.
CHORUS: Go, trust not others. Do it quick thyself.
CREON: I go hot-foot. Bestir ye one and all,
125   My henchmen! Get ye axes! Speed away
        To yonder eminence! I too will go,
        For all my resolution this way sways.
        'Twas I that bound, I too will set her free.
        Almost I am persuaded it is best
130   To keep through life the law ordained of old.

[Exit CREON]

PAEAN

STROPHE 1

CHORUS: Thou by many names adored,
        Child of Zeus the God of thunder,
        Of a Theban bride the wonder,
    Fair Italia's guardian lord;
5   In the deep-embosomed glades
        Of the Eleusinian Queen
    Haunt of revelers, men and maids,
        Dionysus[1], thou art seen.
    Where Ismenus rolls his waters,
10   Where the Dragon's teeth were sown,
    Where the Bacchanals thy daughters
        Round thee roam,
        There thy home;
    Thebes, O Bacchus, is thine own.

---

[1]*Dionysus:* God of wine.

ANTISTROPHE 1

Thee on the two-crested rock   15
    Lurid-flaming torches see;
Where Corisian maidens flock,
    Thee the springs of Castaly.
By Nysa's bastion ivy-clad,
By shores with clustered vineyards glad,   20
There to thee the hymn rings out,
And through our streets we Thebans shout,
    All hail to thee
    Evoe, Evoe![2]

STROPHE 2

Oh, as thou lov'st this city best of all,   25
To thee, and to thy Mother levin-stricken,
In our dire need we call;
Thou see'st with what a plague our townsfolk sicken.
    Thy ready help we crave,
Whether adown Parnassian heights descending,   30
Or o'er the roaring straits thy swift was wending,
    Save us, O save!

ANTISTROPHE 2

Brightest of all the orbs that breathe forth light,
    Authentic son of Zeus, immortal king,
Leader of all the voices of the night,   35
    Come, and thy train of Thyiads with thee bring,
    Thy maddened rout
Who dance before thee all night long, and shout,
    Thy handmaids we,
    Evoe, Evoe!   40

EXODOS[1]

[Enter MESSENGER]

MESSENGER: Attend all ye who dwell beside the halls
    Of Cadmus and Amphion. No man's life
    As of one tenor would I praise or blame,
    For Fortune with a constant ebb and rise
    Casts down and raises high and low alike,   5
    And none can read a mortal's horoscope.
    Take Creon; he, methought, if any man,
    Was enviable. He had saved this land
    Of Cadmus from our enemies and attained

---

[2]*Evoe, Evoe!:* An exclamation indicating joy.

[1]*Exodus:* The closing of the play.

10 A monarch's powers and ruled the state supreme,
    While a right noble issue crowned his bliss.
    Now all is gone and wasted, for a life
    Without life's joys I count a living death.
    You'll tell me he has ample store of wealth,
15 The pomp and circumstance of kings; but if
    These give no pleasure, all the rest I count
    The shadow of a shade, nor would I weigh
    His wealth and power 'gainst a dram of joy.

CHORUS: What fresh woes bring'st thou to the royal house?
20 MESSENGER: Both dead, and they who live deserve to die.
CHORUS: Who is the slayer, who the victim? speak.
MESSENGER: Haemon; his blood shed by no stranger hand.
CHORUS: What mean ye? by his father's or his own?
MESSENGER: His own; in anger for his father's crime.
25 CHORUS: O prophet, what thou spakest comes to pass.
MESSENGER: So stands the case; now 'tis for you to act.
CHORUS: Lo! from the palace gates I see approaching
    Creon's unhappy wife, Eurydice.
    Comes she by chance or learning her son's fate?

[Enter EURYDICE]

30 EURYDICE: Ye men of Thebes, I overheard your talk.
    As I passed out to offer up my prayer
    To Pallas[2], and was drawing back the bar
    To open wide the door, upon my ears
    There broke a wail that told of household woe
35 Stricken with terror in my handmaids' arms
    I fell and fainted. But repeat your tale
    To one not unacquaint with misery.

MESSENGER: Dear mistress, I was there and will relate
    The perfect truth, omitting not one word.
40 Why should we gloze and flatter, to be proved
    Liars hereafter? Truth is ever best.
    Well, in attendance on my liege, your lord,
    I crossed the plain to its utmost margin, where
    The corse of Polyneices, gnawn and mauled,
45 Was lying yet. We offered first a prayer
    To Pluto[3] and the goddess of cross-ways,
    With contrite hearts, to deprecate their ire.
    Then laved with lustral waves the mangled corse,
    Laid it on fresh-lopped branches, lit a pyre,
50 And to his memory piled a mighty mound

---

[2]*Pallas:* The Greek goddess Athena.
[3]*Pluto:* The Greek god of the underworld, more commonly known as Hades.

Of mother earth. Then to the caverned rock,
The bridal chamber of the maid and Death,
We sped, about to enter. But a guard
Heard from that godless shrine a far shrill wail,
And ran back to our lord to tell the news.   55
But as he nearer drew a hollow sound
Of lamentation to the King was borne.
He groaned and uttered then this bitter plaint:
"Am I a prophet? miserable me!
Is this the saddest path I ever trod?   60
'Tis my son's voice that calls me. On press on,
My henchmen, haste with double speed to the tomb
Where rocks down-torn have made a gap, look in
And tell me if in truth I recognize
The voice of Haemon or am heaven-deceived."   65
So at the bidding of our distraught lord
We looked, and in the craven's vaulted gloom
I saw the maiden lying strangled there,
A noose of linen twined about her neck;
And hard beside her, clasping her cold form,   70
Her lover lay bewailing his dead bride
Death-wedded, and his father's cruelty.
When the King saw him, with a terrible groan
He moved towards him, crying, "O my son
What hast thou done? What ailed thee? What mischance   75
Has reft thee of thy reason? O come forth,
Come forth, my son; thy father supplicates."
But the son glared at him with tiger eyes,
Spat in his face, and then, without a word,
Drew his two-hilted sword and smote, but missed   80
His father flying backwards. Then the boy,
Wroth with himself, poor wretch, incontinent
Fell on his sword and drove it through his side
Home, but yet breathing clasped in his lax arms
The maid, her pallid cheek incarnadined   85
With his expiring gasps. So there they lay
Two corpses, one in death. His marriage rites
Are consummated in the halls of Death:
A witness that of ills whate'er befall
Mortals' unwisdom is the worst of all.   90

[Exit EURYDICE]

Chorus: What makest thou of this? The Queen has gone
    Without a word importing good or ill.
Messenger: I marvel too, but entertain good hope.
    'Tis that she shrinks in public to lament

95   Her son's sad ending, and in privacy
           Would with her maidens mourn a private loss.
           Trust me, she is discreet and will not err.
    CHORUS: I know not, but strained silence, so I deem,
           Is no less ominous than excessive grief.
100   MESSENGER: Well, let us to the house and solve our doubts,
           Whether the tumult of her heart conceals
           Some fell design. It may be thou art right:
           Unnatural silence signifies no good.
    CHORUS: Lo! the King himself appears.
105   Evidence he with him bears
               'Gainst himself (ah me! I quake
               'Gainst a king such charge to make)
               But all must own,
               The guilt is his and his alone.
110   CREON: Woe for sin of minds perverse,
               Deadly fraught with mortal curse.
               Behold us slain and slayers, all akin.
               Woe for my counsel dire, conceived in sin.
               Alas, my son,
115   Life scarce begun,
               Thou wast undone.
               The fault was mine, mine only, O my son!
    CHORUS: Too late thou seemest to perceive the truth.
    CREON: By sorrow schooled. Heavy the hand of God,
120   Thorny and rough the paths my feet have trod,
           Humbled my pride, my pleasure turned to pain;
           Poor mortals, how we labor all in vain!

[Enter SECOND MESSENGER]

SECOND MESSENGER: Sorrows are thine, my lord, and more to come,
           One lying at thy feet, another yet
125   More grievous waits thee, when thou comest home.
    CREON: What woe is lacking to my tale of woes?
    SECOND MESSENGER: Thy wife, the mother of thy dead son here,
           Lies stricken by a fresh inflicted blow.
    CREON: How bottomless the pit!
130   Does claim me too, O Death?
               What is this word he saith,
              This woeful messenger? Say, is it fit
             To slay anew a man already slain?
               Is Death at work again,
135   Stroke upon stroke, first son, then mother slain?
    CHORUS: Look for thyself. She lies for all to view.
    CREON: Alas! another added woe I see.
           What more remains to crown my agony?
           A minute past I clasped a lifeless son,

And now another victim Death hath won.   140
    Unhappy mother, most unhappy son!
SECOND MESSENGER: Beside the altar on a keen-edged sword
    She fell and closed her eyes in night, but erst
    She mourned for Megareus who nobly died
    Long since, then for her son; with her last breath   145
    She cursed thee, the slayer of her child.
CREON: I shudder with affright
    O for a two-edged sword to slay outright
        A wretch like me,
          Made one with misery.   150
SECOND MESSENGER: 'Tis true that thou wert charged by the dead Queen
    As author of both deaths, hers and her son's.
CREON: In what wise was her self-destruction wrought?
SECOND MESSENGER: Hearing the loud lament above her son
    With her own hand she stabbed herself to the heart.   155
CREON: I am the guilty cause. I did the deed,
    Thy murderer. Yea, I guilty plead.
    My henchmen, lead me hence, away, away,
    A cipher, less than nothing; no delay!
CHORUS: Well said, if in disaster aught is well   160
    His past endure demand the speediest cure.
CREON: Come, Fate, a friend at need,
        Come with all speed!
        Come, my best friend,
        And speed my end!   165
        Away, away!
    Let me not look upon another day!
CHORUS: This for the morrow; to us are present needs
    That they whom it concerns must take in hand.
CREON: I join your prayer that echoes my desire.   170
CHORUS: O pray not, prayers are idle; from the doom
    Of fate for mortals refuge is there none.
CREON: Away with me, a worthless wretch who slew
    Unwitting thee, my son, thy mother too.
    Whither to turn I know now; every way   175
        Leads but astray,
    And on my head I feel the heavy weight
        Of crushing Fate.
CHORUS: Of happiness the chiefest part
        Is a wise heart: 180
    And to defraud the gods in aught
        With peril's fraught.
        Swelling words of high-flown might
    Mightily the gods do smite.
    Chastisement for errors past   185
    Wisdom brings to age at last.

Reading and Reacting

1. What ideas does *Antigone* express about duty? about obedience? How do these ideas con form (or fail to conform) to your own concepts of duty and obedience?

2. According to Aristotle, the main character in a tragedy possess a flaw that leads to his or her downfall. Write an essay in which you discuss Antigone's tragic flaw. How does this flaw set up (or make inevitable) the series events that lead to the tragic resolution of the play?

3. Both Creon and Antigone defend rights that they believe are sacred. What rights are in con flict? Is there any room for compromise? Do you sympathize with Antigone or with Creon?

4. Aristotle believed that to be effective, tragic heroes must have elements of both good and evil. Does Antigone conform to Aristotle's requirement? Explain.

5. What is Antigone's fatal flaw? How does this flaw lead to the tragic resolution of the play?

6. As the play progresses, do Creon and Antigone change, or do they remain essentially un changed by events?

7. At the very end of *Antigone*, the Chorus says, "Chastisement for errors past / Wisdom brings to age at last." Do you think Creon has gained wisdom from his experi ences? Why, or why not?

8. How does Antigone's gender affect her actions? How does it determine how she is treated? Are the play's attitudes toward women consistent with those of contemporary American society? Explain.

9. **JOURNAL ENTRY** If you were Antigone, would you have stuck to your principles, or would you have given in? Explain your reasoning.

10. **CRITICAL PERSPECTIVE** In *Sophocles the Playwright*, S. M. Adams argues that, to the ancient Greek audience, Antigone and Creon were both tragic heroes. Do you agree? If so, do you see the fact that the play has two tragic heroes as a problem?

Related Works: "A Hunger Artist" (p. 151), from *Persepolis* (p. 162), "A Worn Path" (p. 463), "Do not go gentle into that good night" (p. 891), "Medgar Evers" (p. 965), *Hamlet* (p. 1304), *Oedipus the King* (p. 1430)

Joe Seer/Shutterstock.com

JOHN PATRICK SHANLEY (1950–   ) is a playwright, screenwriter, and director. He has written numerous plays and screenplays, including the recent plays *Pirate (2010)* and *Outside Mullingar* (2014), as well as the Academy Award–winning film *Moonstruck* (1987) and the Emmy Award–nominated film *Alive* (1993). The recipient of numerous honors, Shanley adapted his Pulitzer Prize–winning play *Doubt: A Parable* into the critically acclaimed 2008 feature film *Doubt*. Describing the play, Shanley explained, "I am interested in hierarchies. I think they reveal societies. . . . I'm interested very much in where authority comes from, which is always a central element of hierarchy."

CULTURAL CONTEXT The early 1960s marked a seismic shift in the history of Catholicism. With Pope John XXIII at the helm, Catholic leaders convened in Rome to discuss the state of the Catholic Church. These meetings, called the Second Vatican Council (Vatican II), brought about a series of changes in church policy and culture, including the shift from delivering Mass in Latin to delivering it in English. According to Reverend Mark Massa, dean of Boston College's School of Theology and Ministry, "Starting with Vatican II, Catholics became aware that the church, its worship, and its beliefs change—that the church develops over history. The current battles between the left and the right are really between those who want to press a historical awareness of change and those who want to view the church as timeless."

Doubt: A Parable (2004)

CHARACTERS

Father Brendan Flynn, *late thirties*
Sister Aloysius Beauvier, *fifties / sixties*
Sister James, *twenties*
Mrs. Muller, *around thirty-eight*

PLACE

*St. Nicholas, a Catholic church
and school in the Bronx, New York.*

TIME

1964

"The bad sleep well"

—*Title of Kurosawa film*

"In much wisdom is much grief: and be that increaseth knowledge increaseth sorrow."

—*Ecclesiastes*

"Everything that is hard to attain is easily assailed by the mob."

—*Ptolemy*

ONE

A priest, Father Flynn, in his late thirties, in green and gold vestments, gives a sermon. He is working class, from the Northeast.

FLYNN: What do you do when you're not sure? That's the topic of my sermon today. You look for God's direction and can't find it. Last year when President Kennedy was assassinated, who among us did not experience the most profound disorientation. Despair. "What now? Which way? What do I say to my kids? What do I tell myself?" It was a time of people sitting together, bound together by a common feeling of hopelessness. But think of that! Your *bond* with your fellow beings was your *despair*. It was a public experience, shared by everyone in our society. It was awful, but we were in it together! How much worse is it then for the lone man, the lone woman, stricken by a private calamity? "No one knows I'm sick. No one knows I've lost my last real friend. No one knows I've done something wrong." Imagine the isolation. You see the world as through a window. On the one side of the glass: happy, untroubled people. On the other side: you. Something has happened, you have to carry it, and it's incommunicable. For those so afflicted, only God knows their pain. Their secret. The secret of their alienating sorrow. And when such a person, as they must, howls to the sky, to God: "Help me!" What if no answer comes? Silence. I want to tell you a story. A cargo ship sank, and all her crew was drowned. Only this one sailor survived. He made a raft of some spars and, being of a nautical discipline, turned his eyes to the Heavens and read the stars. He set a course for his home and, exhausted, fell asleep. Clouds rolled in and blanketed the sky. For the next twenty nights, as he floated on the vast ocean, he could no longer see the stars. He thought he was on course, but there was no way to be certain. As the days rolled on, and he wasted away with fevers, thirst and starvation,

Bran F. O'Byrne as Father Flynn and Cherry Jones as
Sister Aloysius at the Manhattan Theatre Club, 2004
© Joan Marcus

he began to have doubts. Had he set his course right? Was he still going on towards his home? Or was he horribly lost and doomed to a terrible death? No way to know. The message of the constellations—had he imagined it because of his desperate circumstance? Or had he seen Truth once and now had to hold on to it without further reassurance? That was his dilemma on a voyage without apparent end. There are those of you in church today who know exactly the crisis of faith I describe. I want to say to you, doubt can be a bond as powerful and sustaining as certainty. When you are lost, you are not alone. In the name of the Father, the Son, and the Holy Ghost. Amen. (*He exits.*)

TWO

The lights crossfade to a corner office in a Catholic school in the Bronx. The principal, Sister Aloysius Beauvier, sits at her desk, writing in a ledger with a fountain pen. She is in her fifties or sixties. She is watchful, reserved, unsentimental. She is of the order of the Sisters of Charity. She wears a black bonnet and floor-length black habit,[1] rimless glasses. A knock at the door.

SISTER ALOYSIUS: Come in. (*Sister James, also of the Sisters Charity, pokes her head in. She is in her twenties. There's a bit of sunshine in her heart, though she's reserved as well.*)

---

[1] *habit:* A garment.

SISTER JAMES: Have you a moment, Sister Aloysius?

SISTER ALOYSIUS: Come in, Sister James. (*She enters.*) Who's watching your class?

SISTER JAMES: They're having Art.

SISTER ALOYSIUS: Art. Waste of time.   5

SISTER JAMES: It's only an hour a week.

SISTER ALOYSIUS: Much can be accomplished in sixty minutes.

SISTER JAMES: Yes, Sister Aloysius. I wondered if I might know what you did about William London?

SISTER ALOYSIUS: I sent him home.   10

SISTER JAMES: Oh dear. So he's still bleeding?

SISTER ALOYSIUS: Oh yes.

SISTER JAMES: His nose just let loose and started gushing during the Pledge of Allegiance.

SISTER ALOYSIUS: Was it spontaneous?

SISTER JAMES: What else would it be?   15

SISTER ALOYSIUS: Self-induced.

SISTER JAMES: You mean, you think he might've intentionally given himself a nosebleed?

SISTER ALOYSIUS: Exactly.

SISTER JAMES: No!

SISTER ALOYSIUS: You are a very innocent person, Sister James. William London is   20
    a fidgety boy and if you do not keep right on him, he will do anything to escape
    his chair. He would set his foot on fire for half a day out of school.

SISTER JAMES: But why?

SISTER ALOYSIUS: He has a restless mind.

SISTER JAMES: But that's good.

SISTER ALOYSIUS: No, it's not. His father's a policeman, and the last thing he wants
    is a rowdy boy. William London is headed for trouble. Puberty has got hold of
    him. He will be imagining all the wrong things, and I strongly suspect he will
    not graduate high school. But that's beyond our jurisdiction. We simply have to
    get him through, out the door, and then he's somebody else's project. Ordinar-
    ily, I assign my most experienced sisters to eighth grade, but I'm working within
    constraints. Are you in control of your class?

SISTER JAMES: I think so.   25

SISTER ALOYSIUS: Usually more children are sent down to me.

SISTER JAMES: I try to take care of things myself.

SISTER ALOYSIUS: That can be an error. You are answerable to me, I to the mon-
    signor, he to the bishop, and so on up to the Holy Father. There's a chain of
    discipline. Make use of it.

SISTER JAMES: Yes, Sister.

SISTER ALOYSIUS: How's Donald Muller doing?   30

SISTER JAMES: Steady.

SISTER ALOYSIUS: Good. Has anyone hit him?

SISTER JAMES: No.

SISTER ALOYSIUS: Good. That girl, Linda Conte, have you seated her away from the boys?

SISTER JAMES: As far as space permits. It doesn't do much good.   35

SISTER ALOYSIUS: Just get her through. Intact. (*Pause. Sister Aloysius is staring absently at Sister James. A silence falls.*)

SISTER JAMES: So. Should I go? (*No answer.*) Is something the matter?

SISTER ALOYSIUS: No. Why? Is something the matter?

SISTER JAMES: I don't think so.

40 SISTER ALOYSIUS: Then nothing's the matter then.

SISTER JAMES: Well. Thank you, Sister. I just wanted to check on William's nose. (*She starts to go.*)

SISTER ALOYSIUS: He had a ballpoint pen.

SISTER JAMES: Excuse me, Sister?

SISTER ALOYSIUS: William London had a ballpoint pen. He was fiddling with it while he waited for his mother. He's not using it for assignments, I hope.

45 SISTER JAMES: No, of course not.

SISTER ALOYSIUS: I'm sorry I allowed even cartridge pens into the school. The students really should only be learning script with true fountain pens. Always the easy way out these days. What does that teach? Every easy choice today will have its consequence tomorrow. Mark my words.

SISTER JAMES: Yes, Sister.

SISTER ALOYSIUS: Ballpoints make them press down, and when they press down, they write like monkeys.

SISTER JAMES. I don't allow them ballpoint pens.

50 SISTER ALOYSIUS: Good. Penmanship is dying all across the country. You have some time. Sit down. (*Sister James hesitates and sits down.*) We might as well have a talk. I've been meaning to talk to you. I observed your lesson on the New Deal at the beginning of the term. Not bad. But I caution you. Do not idealize Franklin Delano Roosevelt. He was a good president, but he did attempt to pack the Supreme Court. I do not approve of making heroes of lay historical figures. If you want to talk about saints, do it in Religion.

SISTER JAMES: Yes, Sister.

SISTER ALOYSIUS: Also. I question your enthusiasm for History.

SISTER JAMES: But I love History!

SISTER ALOYSIUS: That is exactly my meaning. You favor History and risk swaying the children to value it over their other subjects. I think this is a mistake.

55 SISTER JAMES: I never thought of that. I'll try to treat my other lessons with more enthusiasm.

SISTER ALOYSIUS: No. Give them their History without putting sugar all over it. That's the point. Now. Tell me about your class. How would you characterize the condition of 8-B?

SISTER JAMES: I don't know where to begin. What do you want to know?

SISTER ALOYSIUS: Let's begin with Stephen Inzio.

SISTER JAMES: Stephen Inzio has the highest marks in the class.

60 SISTER ALOYSIUS: Noreen Horan?

SISTER JAMES: Second highest marks.

SISTER ALOYSIUS: Brenda McNulty?

SISTER JAMES: Third highest.

SISTER ALOYSIUS: You see, I am making a point, Sister James. I know that Stephen Inzio, Noreen Horan, and Brenda McNulty are one, two, and three in your class. School-wide, there are forty-eight such students each grade period. I make it my business to know all forty-eight of their names. I do not say this to aggrandize myself, but to illustrate the importance of paying attention. You must pay attention as well.

SISTER JAMES: Yes Sister Aloysius.   65

SISTER ALOYSIUS: I cannot be everywhere.

SISTER JAMES: Am I falling short, Sister?

SISTER ALOYSIUS: These three students with the highest marks. Are they the most intelligent children in your class?

SISTER JAMES: No, I wouldn't say they are. But they work the hardest.

SISTER ALOYSIUS: Very good! That's right! That's the ethic. What good's a gift if it's 70 left in the box? What good is a high IQ if you're staring out the window with your mouth agape? Be hard on the bright ones, Sister James. Don't be charmed by cleverness. Not theirs. And not yours. I think you are a competent teacher, Sister James, but maybe not our best teacher. The best teachers do not perform, they cause the students to perform.

SISTER JAMES: Do I perform?

SISTER ALOYSIUS: As if on a Broadway stage.

SISTER JAMES: Oh dear. I had no conception.

SISTER ALOYSIUS: You're showing off. You like to see yourself ten feet tall in their eyes. Another thing occurs to me. Where were you before?

SISTER JAMES: Mount St. Margaret's.   75

SISTER ALOYSIUS: All girls.

SISTER. JAMES: Yes.

SISTER ALOYSIUS: I feel I must remind you. Boys are made of gravel, soot, and tar paper. Boys are a different breed.

SISTER JAMES: I feel I know how to handle them.

SISTER ALOYSIUS: But perhaps you are wrong. And perhaps you are not working 80 hard enough.

SISTER JAMES: Oh. (*Sister James cries a little.*)

SISTER ALOYSIUS: No tears.

SISTER JAMES: I thought you were satisfied with me.

SISTER ALOYSIUS: Satisfaction is a vice. Do you have a handkerchief?

SISTER JAMES: Yes.   85

SISTER ALOYSIUS: Use it. Do you think that Socrates was satisfied? Good teachers are never content. We have some three hundred and seventy-two students in this school. It is a society which requires constant educational, spiritual and human vigilance. I can not afford an excessively innocent instructor in my eighth grade class. It's self-indulgent. Innocence is a form of laziness. Innocent teachers are easily duped. You must be canny, Sister James.

SISTER JAMES: Yes, Sister.

SISTER ALOYSIUS: When William London gets a nosebleed, be skeptical. Don't let a little blood fuddle your judgment. God gave you a brain and a heart. The heart is warm, but your wits must be cold. Liars should be frightened to lie to you. They should be uncomfortable in your presence. I doubt they are.

SISTER JAMES: I don't know. I've never thought about it.

SISTER ALOYSIUS: The children should think you see right through them.   90

SISTER JAMES: Wouldn't that be a little frightening?

SISTER ALOYSIUS: Only to the ones that are up to no good.

SISTER JAMES: But I want my students to feel they can talk to me.

SISTER ALOYSIUS: They're children. They can talk to each other. It's more important they have a fierce moral guardian. You stand at the door, Sister. You are
the gatekeeper. If you are vigilant, they will not need to be.

95 SISTER JAMES: I'm not sure what you want me to do.

SISTER ALOYSIUS: And if things occur in your classroom which you sense require
understanding, but you don't understand, come to me.

SISTER JAMES: Yes, Sister.

SISTER ALOYSIUS: That's why I'm here. That's why I'm the principal of this school.
Do you stay when the specialty instructors come in?

SISTER JAMES: Yes.

100 SISTER ALOYSIUS: But you're here now while the Art class is going on.

SISTER JAMES: I was a little concerned about William's nose.

SISTER ALOYSIUS: Right. So you have Art in class.

SISTER JAMES: She comes in, Mrs. Bell. Yes.

SISTER ALOYSIUS: And you take them down to the basement for Dance with Mrs.
Shields.

105 SISTER JAMES: On Thursdays.

SISTER ALOYSIUS: Another waste of time.

SISTER JAMES: Oh, but everyone loves the Christmas pageant.

SISTER ALOYSIUS: I don't love it. Frankly it offends me. Last year the girl playing
Our Lady was wearing lipstick. I was waiting in the wings for that little jade.

SISTER JAMES: Then there's Music.

110 SISTER ALOYSIUS: That strange woman with the portable piano. What's wrong with
her neck?

SISTER JAMES: Some kind of goiter. Poor woman.

SISTER ALOYSIUS: Yes. Mrs. Carolyn.

SISTER JAMES: That's right.

SISTER ALOYSIUS: We used to have a Sister teaching that. Not enough Sisters.
What else?

115 SISTER JAMES: Physical Education and Religion.

SISTER ALOYSIUS: And for that we have Father Flynn. Two hours a week. And you
stay for those?

SISTER JAMES: Mostly. Unless I have reports to fill out or . . .

SISTER ALOYSIUS: What do you think of Father Flynn?

120 SISTER JAMES: Oh, he's a brilliant man. What a speaker!

SISTER ALOYSIUS: Yes. His sermon this past Sunday was poetic.

SISTER JAMES: He's actually very good, too, at teaching basketball. I was surprised. I
wouldn't think a man of the cloth the personality type for basketball, but he has
a way he has, very natural with dribbling and shooting.

SISTER ALOYSIUS: What do you think that sermon was about?

SISTER JAMES: What?

125 SISTER ALOYSIUS: This past Sunday. What was he talking about?

SISTER JAMES: Well, Doubt. He was talking about Doubt.

SISTER ALOYSIUS: Why?

SISTER JAMES: Excuse me, Sister?

SISTER ALOYSIUS: Well, sermons come from somewhere, don't they? Is Father Flynn in Doubt, is he concerned that someone else is in Doubt?

SISTER JAMES: I suppose you'd have to ask him.   130

SISTER ALOYSIUS: No. That would not be appropriate. He is my superior. And if he were troubled, he should confess it to a fellow priest, or the monsignor. We do not share intimate information with priests. (A *pause*.)

SISTER JAMES: I'm a little concerned. (*Sister Aloysius leans forward*.)

SISTER ALOYSIUS: About what?

SISTER JAMES: The time, Art class will be over in a few minutes. I should go up.

SISTER ALOYSIUS: Have you noticed anything, Sister James?   135

SISTER JAMES: About what?

SISTER ALOYSIUS: I want you to be alert.

SISTER JAMES: I don't believe I'm following you, Sister.

SISTER ALOYSIUS: I'm sorry I'm not more forthright, but I must be careful not to create something by saying it. I can only say I am concerned, perhaps needlessly, about matters in St. Nicholas School.

SISTER JAMES: Academically?   140

SISTER ALOYSIUS: I wasn't inviting a guessing game. I want you to pay attention to your class.

SISTER JAMES: Well, of course I'll pay attention to my class, Sister. And I'll try not to perform. And I'll try to be less innocent. I'm sorry you're disappointed in me. Please know that I will try my best. Honestly.

SISTER ALOYSIUS: Look at you. You'd trade anything for a warm look. I'm telling you here and now, I want to see the starch in your character cultivated. If you are looking for reassurance, you can be fooled. If you forget yourself and study others, you will not be fooled. It's important. One final matter and then you really must get back. Sister Veronica is going blind.

SISTER JAMES: Oh how horrible!

SISTER ALOYSIUS: This is not generally known, and I don't want it known. If they   145
find out in the rectory, she'll be gone. I cannot afford to lose her. But now if you see her making her way down those stone stairs into the courtyard, for the love of Heaven, lightly take her hand as if in fellowship and see that she doesn't destroy herself. All right, go.

THREE

The lights crossfade to Father Flynn, whistle around his neck, in a sweatshirt and pants, holding a basketball.

FLYNN: All right, settle down, boys. Now the thing about shooting from the foul line: It's psychological. The rest of the game you're cooperating with your teammates, you're competing against the other team. But at the foul line, it's you against yourself. And the danger is: You start to think. When you think, you stop breathing. Your body locks up. So you have to remember to relax. Take a breath, unlock your knees—this is something for you to watch, Jimmy. You stand like a parking meter. Come up with a routine of what you do. Shift your weight, move your hips . . . You think that's funny, Ralph? What's funny is you never getting a foul shot. Don't worry if you look silly. They won't think you're silly if you get the basket. Come up with a routine, concentrate on the routine, and you'll forget to get tensed up. Now on another matter, I've noticed several of you guys have dirty nails. I don't want to see that. I'm not talking about the length of your nails. I'm talking about cleanliness. See? Look at my nails. They're long, I like them a little long, but look at how clean they are. That makes it okay. There was a kid I grew up with, Timmy Mathisson, never had clean nails, and he'd stick his fingers up his nose, in his mouth.—This is a true story, learn to listen! He got spinal meningitis and died a horrible death. Sometimes it's the little things that get you. You try to talk to a girl with those filthy paws, Mr. Conroy, she's gonna take off like she's being chased by the Red Chinese! (*Reacting generally to laughter*) All right, all right. You guys, what am I gonna do with you? Get dressed, come on over to the rectory, have some Kool-Aid and cookies, we'll have a bull session. (*Blows his whistle.*) Go!

FOUR

Crossfade to a bit of garden, a bench, brick wall. Sister Aloysius, in full habit and a black shawl, is wrapping a pruned rosebush in burlap. Sister James enters.

SISTER JAMES: Good afternoon, Sister.

SISTER ALOYSIUS: Good afternoon, Sister James. Mr. McGinn pruned this bush, which was the right thing to do, but he neglected to protect it from the frost.

SISTER JAMES: Have we had a frost?

SISTER ALOYSIUS: When it comes, its too late.

5 SISTER JAMES: You know about gardening?

SISTER ALOYSIUS: A little. Where is your class?

SISTER JAMES: The girls are having Music.

SISTER ALOYSIUS: And the boys?

SISTER JAMES: They're in the rectory. (*Sister James indicates the rectory, which is out of view, just on the other side of the garden.*)

10 SISTER ALOYSIUS: With Father Flynn.

SISTER JAMES: Yes. He's giving them a talk.

SISTER ALOYSIUS: On what subject?

SISTER JAMES: How to be a man.

SISTER ALOYSIUS: Well, if Sisters were permitted in the rectory, I would be interested to hear that talk. I don't know how to be a man. I would like to know what's involved. Have you ever given the girls a talk on how to be a woman?

15 SISTER JAMES: No. I wouldn't be competent.

SISTER ALOYSIUS: Why not?

SISTER JAMES: I just don't think I would. I took my vows at the beginning . . . Before . . . At the beginning.

SISTER ALOYSIUS: The founder of our order, the Blessed Mother Seton, was married and had five children before embarking on her vows.

SISTER JAMES: I've often wondered how she managed so much in one life.

SISTER ALOYSIUS: Life perhaps is longer than you think and the dictates of the soul   20
more numerous. I was married.

SISTER JAMES: You were! (*Sister Aloysius smiles for the first time.*)

SISTER ALOYSIUS: You could at least hide your astonishment.

SISTER JAMES: I . . . didn't know.

SISTER ALOYSIUS: When one takes on the habit, one must close the door on secular
things. My husband died in the war against Adolph Hitler.

SISTER JAMES: Really! Excuse me, Sister.   25

SISTER ALOYSIUS: But I'm like you. I'm not sure I would feel competent to lecture
tittering girls on the subject of womanhood. I don't come into this garden often.
What is it, forty feet across? The convent here, the rectory there. We might as
well be separated by the Atlantic Ocean. I used to potter around out here, but
Monsignor Benedict does his reverie at quixotic times, and we are rightly discouraged from crossing paths with priests unattended. He is seventy-nine, but
nevertheless.

SISTER JAMES: The monsignor is very good, isn't he?

SISTER ALOYSIUS: Yes. But he is oblivious.

SISTER JAMES: To what?

SISTER ALOYSIUS: I don't believe he knows who's President of the United States. I   30
mean him no disrespect of course. It's just that he's otherworldly in the extreme.

SISTER JAMES: Is it that he's innocent, Sister Aloysius?

SISTER ALOYSIUS: You have a slyness at work, Sister James. Be careful of it. How is
your class? How is Donald Muller?

SISTER JAMES: He is thirteenth in class.

SISTER ALOYSIUS: I know. That's sufficient. Is he being accepted?

SISTER JAMES: He has no friends.   35

SISTER ALOYSIUS: That would be a lot to expect after only two months. Has anyone
hit him?

SISTER JAMES: No.

SISTER ALOYSIUS: Someone will. And when it happens, send them right down to
me.

SISTER JAMES: I'm not so sure anyone will.

SISTER ALOYSIUS: There is a statue of St. Patrick on one side of the church altar and   40
a statue of St. Anthony on the other. This parish serves Irish and Italian families. Someone will hit Donald Muller.

SISTER JAMES: He has a protector.

SISTER ALOYSIUS: Who?

SISTER JAMES: Father Flynn. (*Sister Aloysius, who has been fussing with mulch, is suddenly rigid. She rises.*)

SISTER ALOYSIUS: What?

SISTER JAMES: He's taken an interest. Since Donald went on the altar boys. (*Pause.*)   45
I thought I should tell you.

SISTER ALOYSIUS: I told you to come to me, but I hoped you never would.

SISTER JAMES: Maybe I shouldn't have.

SISTER ALOYSIUS: I knew once you did, something would be set in motion. So it's
happened.

SISTER JAMES: What?! I'm not telling you that! I'm not even certain what you mean.

50   SISTER ALOYSIUS: Yes, you are.

SISTER JAMES: I've been trying to become more cold in my thinking as you suggested . . . I feel as if I've lost my way a little, Sister Aloysius. I had the most terrible dream last night. I want to be guided by you and responsible to the children, but I want my peace of mind. I must tell you I have been longing for the return of my peace of mind.

SISTER ALOYSIUS: You may not have it. It is not your place to be complacent. That's for the children. That's what we give them.

SISTER JAMES: I think I'm starting to understand you a little. But it's so unsettling to look at things and people with suspicion. It feels as if I'm less close to God.

SISTER ALOYSIUS: When you take a step to address wrongdoing, you are taking a step away from God, but in his service. Dealing with such matters is hard and thankless work.

55   SISTER JAMES: I've become more reserved in class. I feel separated from the children.

SISTER ALOYSIUS: That's as it should be.

SISTER JAMES: But I feel, wrong. And about this other matter, I don't have any evidence. I'm not at all certain that anything's happened.

SISTER ALOYSIUS: We can't wait for that.

SISTER JAMES: But what if it's nothing?

60   SISTER ALOYSIUS: Then it's nothing. I wouldn't mind being wrong. But I doubt I am.

SISTER JAMES: Then what's to be done?

SISTER ALOYSIUS: I don't know.

SISTER JAMES: You'll know what to do.

65   SISTER ALOYSIUS: I don't know what to do. There are parameters which protect him and hinder me.

SISTER JAMES: But he can't be safe if it's established. I doubt he could recover from the shame.

SISTER ALOYSIUS: What have you seen?

SISTER JAMES: I don't know.

SISTER ALOYSIUS: What have you seen?

70   SISTER JAMES: He took Donald to the rectory.

SISTER ALOYSIUS: What for?

SISTER JAMES: A talk.

SISTER ALOYSIUS: Alone?

SISTER JAMES: Yes.

75   SISTER ALOYSIUS: When?

SISTER JAMES: A week ago.

SISTER ALOYSIUS: Why didn't you tell me?

SISTER JAMES: I didn't think there was anything wrong with it. It never came into my mind that he . . . that there could be anything wrong.

SISTER ALOYSIUS: Of all the children. Donald Muller. I suppose it makes sense.

80   SISTER JAMES: How does it make sense?

SISTER ALOYSIUS: He's isolated. The little sheep lagging behind is the one the wolf goes for.

SISTER JAMES: I don't know that anything's wrong!

SISTER ALOYSIUS: Our first Negro student. I thought there'd be fighting, a parent or two to deal with . . . should've foreseen this possibility.

SISTER JAMES: How could you imagine it?

SISTER ALOYSIUS: It is my job to outshine the fox in cleverness! That's my job!   85

SISTER JAMES: But maybe it's nothing!

SISTER ALOYSIUS: Then why do you look like you've seen the Devil?

SISTER JAMES: It's just the way the boy acted when he came back to class.

SISTER ALOYSIUS: He said something?

SISTER JAMES: No. It was his expression. He looked frightened and . . . he put his   90
head on the desk in the most peculiar way. (*Struggles.*) And one other thing. I
think there was alcohol on his breath. There was alcohol on his breath. (*Sister
Aloysius looks toward the rectory*)

SISTER ALOYSIUS: Eight years ago at St. Boniface we had a priest who had to be
stopped. But I had Monsignor Scully then . . . whom I could rely on. Here,
there's no man I can go to, and men run everything. We are going to have to
stop him ourselves.

SISTER JAMES: Can't you just . . . report your suspicions?

SISTER ALOYSIUS: To Monsignor Benedict? The man's guileless! He would just ask
Father Flynn!

SISTER JAMES: Well, would that be such a bad idea?

SISTER ALOYSIUS: And he would believe whatever Father Flynn told him. He would   95
think the matter settled.

SISTER JAMES: But maybe that is all that needs to be done. If it's true. If I had done
something awful, and I was confronted with it, I'd be so repentant.

SISTER ALOYSIUS: Sister James, my dear, you must try to imagine a very different
kind of person than yourself. A man who would do this has already denied a
great deal. If I tell the monsignor and he is satisfied with Father Flynn's rebuttal,
the matter is suppressed.

SISTER JAMES: Well then, tell the bishop.

SISTER ALOYSIUS: The hierarchy of the Church does not permit my going to the
bishop. No. Once I tell the monsignor, it's out of my hands, I'm helpless. I'm
going to have to come up with a pretext, get Father Flynn into my office. Try to
force it. You'll have to be there.

SISTER JAMES: Me? No! Why? Oh no, Sister! I couldn't!   100

SISTER ALOYSIUS: I can't be closeted alone with a priest. Another Sister must be in
attendance, and it has to be you. The circle of confidence mustn't be made any
wider. Think of the boy if this gets out.

SISTER JAMES: I can't do it!

SISTER ALOYSIUS: Why not? You're squeamish?

SISTER JAMES: I'm not equipped! It's . . . I would be embarrassed. I couldn't possibly
be present if the topic were spoken of!

SISTER ALOYSIUS: Please, Sister, do not indulge yourself in witless adolescent scru-   105
ples. I assure you I would prefer a more seasoned confederate. But you are the
one who came to me.

SISTER JAMES: You told me to!

SISTER ALOYSIUS: Would you rather leave the boy to be exploited? And don't think this will be the only story. If you close your eyes, you will be a party to all that comes after.

SISTER JAMES: You're supposed to tell the monsignor!

SISTER ALOYSIUS: That you saw a look in a boy's eye? That perhaps you smelled something on his breath? Monsignor Benedict thinks the sun rises and sets on Father Flynn. You'd be branded an hysteric and transferred.

110   SISTER JAMES: We can ask him.

SISTER ALOYSIUS: Who?

SISTER JAMES: The boy, Donald Muller.

SISTER ALOYSIUS: He'll deny it.

SISTER JAMES: Why?

115   SISTER ALOYSIUS: Shame.

SISTER JAMES: You can't know that.

SISTER ALOYSIUS: And if he does point the finger, how do you think that will be received in this community? A black child. (*No answer.*) I am going to think this through. Then I'm going to invite Father Flynn to my office on an unrelated matter. You will be there.

SISTER JAMES: But what good can I do?

SISTER ALOYSIUS: Aside from the unacceptability of a priest and nun being alone, I need a witness.

120   SISTER JAMES: To what?

SISTER ALOYSIUS: He may tell the truth and lie afterwards. (*Sister James looks toward the rectory.*)

SISTER JAMES: The boys are coming out of the rectory. They look happy enough.

SISTER ALOYSIUS: They look smug. Like they have a secret.

SISTER JAMES: There he is.

125   SISTER ALOYSIUS: If I could, Sister James, I would certainly choose to live in innocence. But innocence can only be wisdom in a world without evil. Situations arise, and we are confronted with wrongdoing and the need to act.

SISTER JAMES: I have to take the boys up to class.

SISTER ALOYSIUS: Go on, then. Take them. I will be talking to you. (*The sound of wind, Sister Aloysius pulls her shawl tightly about her and goes. After a moment, Sister James goes as well.*)

FIVE

The principal's office. A phone rings. Sister Aloysius enters with a pot of tea, walking quickly to answer the phone.

SISTER ALOYSIUS: Hello, St. Nicholas School? Oh yes, Mr. McGinn. Thank you for calling back. That was quite a windstorm we had last night. No, I didn't know there was a Great Wind in Ireland and you were there for it. That's fascinating. Yes. I was wondering if you would be so kind as to remove a free limb that's fallen in the courtyard of the church. Sister Veronica tripped on it this morning and fell on her face. I think she's all right. She doesn't look any worse, Mr. McGinn. Thank you, Mr. McGinn. (*She hangs up the phone and looks at her* watch, a bit anxious. A knock at the door.) Come in. (*The door opens. Father Flynn is standing there in his black cassock.*[2] *He doesn't come in.*)

FLYNN: Good morning, Sister Aloysius! How are you today?

SISTER ALOYSIUS: Good morning, Father Flynn. Very well. Good of you to come by. (*Father Flynn takes a step into the office.*)

FLYNN: Are we ready for the meeting?

SISTER ALOYSIUS: We're just short Sister James. (*Father Flynn steps back into the doorway.*) Did you hear that wind last night?

FLYNN: I certainly did. Imagine what it must've been like in the frontier days when a man alone in the woods sat by a fire in his buckskins and listened to a sound like that. Imagine the loneliness! The immense darkness pressing in! How frightening if must've been!

SISTER ALOYSIUS: If one lacked faith in God's protection, I suppose it would be frightening.

FLYNN: Did I hear Sister Veronica had an accident?

SISTER ALOYSIUS: Yes, Sister Veronica fell on a piece of wood this morning and practically killed herself.

FLYNN: Is she all right?

SISTER ALOYSIUS: Oh, she's fine.

FLYNN: Her sight isn't good, is it?

SISTER ALOYSIUS: Her sight is fine. Nuns fall, you know.

FLYNN: No, I didn't know that.

SISTER ALOYSIUS: It's the habit. It catches us up more often than not. What with our being in black and white, and so prone to falling, we're more like dominos than anything else. (*Sister James appears at the door, breathless.*)

SISTER JAMES: Am I past the time? (*Father Flynn takes a step into the office.*)

FLYNN: Not at all. Sister Aloysius and I were just having a nice chat.

SISTER JAMES: Good morning, Father Flynn. Good morning, Sister. I'm sorry I was delayed. Mr. McGinn has closed the courtyard to fix something so I had to go back through the convent and out the side door, and then I ran into Sister Veronica.

FLYNN: How is she?

SISTER JAMES: She has a bit of a bloody nose.

SISTER ALOYSIUS: I'm beginning to think you're punching people.

SISTER JAMES: Sister?

SISTER ALOYSIUS: Well, after the incident with . . . Never mind. Well, come in, please. Sit down. (*They come in and sit down. Father Flynn takes Sister Aloysius's chair. He is sitting at her desk. She reacts but says nothing.*) I actually have a hot pot of tea. (*Closes the door but for an inch.*) And close this but not quite, for form's sake. Would you have a cup of tea, Father?

FLYNN: I would love a cup of tea.

SISTER ALOYSIUS: Perhaps you could serve him, Sister?

SISTER JAMES: Of course.

SISTER ALOYSIUS: And yourself, of course.

---

[2]*cassock:* A full-length garment.

SISTER JAMES: Would you like tea, Sister Aloysius?

SISTER ALOYSIUS: I've already had my cup.

30 FLYNN: Is there sugar?

SISTER ALOYSIUS: Sugar? Yes! (*Rummages in her desk.*) It's here somewhere. I put it in the drawer for Lent last year and never remembered to take it out.

FLYNN: It mustn't have been much to give up then.

SISTER ALOYSIUS: No, I'm sure you're right. Here it is. I'll serve you, though for want of practice, I'm . . . [clumsy] (*She's got the sugar bowl and is poised to serve him a lump of sugar with a small pair of tongs when she sees his nails.*) Your fingernails.

FLYNN: I wear them a little long. The sugar?

35 SISTER ALOYSIUS: Oh yes. One?

FLYNN: Three.

SISTER ALOYSIUS: Three. (*She's appalled but tries to hide it.*)

FLYNN: Sweet tooth.

SISTER ALOYSIUS: One, two, three. Sister, do you take sugar? (*Sister Aloysius looks at Sister James.*)

40 SISTER JAMES: (*To Sister Aloysius.*) Never! (*To Father Flynn.*) Not that there's anything wrong with sugar. (*To Sister Aloysius again.*) Thank you. (*Sister Aloysius puts the sugar away in her desk.*)

SISTER ALOYSIUS: Well, thank you, Father, for making the time for us. We're at our wit's end.

FLYNN: I think it's an excellent idea to rethink the Christmas pageant. Last year's effort was a little woebegone.

SISTER JAMES: No! I loved it! (*Becomes self-conscious*) But I love all Christmas pageants. I just love the Nativity. The birth of the Savior. And the hymns of course. "O Little Town of Bethlehem," "O Come, O Come, Emmanuel" . . .

SISTER ALOYSIUS: Thank you, Sister James. Sister James will be co-directing the pageant with Mrs. Shields, this year. So what do you think, Father Flynn? Is there something new we could do?

45 FLYNN: Well, we all love the Christmas hymns, but it might be jolly to include a secular song.

SISTER ALOYSIUS: Secular.

FLYNN: Yes. "It's Beginning to Look a Lot Like Christmas." Something like that.

SISTER ALOYSIUS: What would be the point of performing a secular song?

FLYNN: Fun.

50 SISTER JAMES: Or "Frosty the Snowman."

FLYNN: That's a good one. We could have one of the boys dress as a snowman and dance around.

SISTER ALOYSIUS: Which boy?

FLYNN: We'd do tryouts.

SISTER ALOYSIUS: "Frosty the Snowman" espouses a pagan belief in magic. The snowman comes to life when an enchanted hat is put on his head. If the music were more somber, people would realize the images are disturbing and the song heretical. (*Sister James and Father Flynn exchange a look.*)

55 SISTER JAMES: I've never thought about "Frosty the Snowman" like that.

SISTER ALOYSIUS: It should be banned from the airwaves.

FLYNN: So. Not "Frosty the Snowman." (*Father Flynn writes something in a small notebook.*)

SISTER ALOYSIUS: I don't think so. "It's Beginning to Look a Lot Like Christmas" would be fine, I suppose. The parents would like it. May I ask what you wrote down? With that ballpoint pen.

FLYNN: Oh. Nothing. An idea for a sermon.

SISTER ALOYSIUS: You had one just now?   60

FLYNN: I get them all the time.

SISTER ALOYSIUS: How fortunate.

FLYNN: I forget them, so I write them down.

SISTER ALOYSIUS: What is the idea?

FLYNN: Intolerance. (*Sister James tries to break a bit of tension.*)   65

SISTER JAMES: Would you like a little more tea, Father?

FLYNN: Not yet. I think a message of the Second Ecumenical Council was that the Church needs to take on a more familiar face. Reflect the local community. We should sing a song from the radio now and then. Take the kids out for ice cream.

SISTER ALOYSIUS: Ice cream.

FLYNN: Maybe take the boys on a camping trip. We should be friendlier. The children and the parents should see us as members of their family rather than emissaries from Rome. I think the pageant should be charming, like a community theatre doing a show.

SISTER ALOYSIUS: But we are not members of their family. We're different.   70

FLYNN: Why? Because of our vows?

SISTER ALOYSIUS: Precisely.

FLYNN: I don't think we're so different. (*To Sister James.*) You know, I would take some more tea, Sister. Thank you.

SISTER ALOYSIUS: And they think we're different. The working-class people of this parish trust us to be different.

FLYNN: I think we're getting off the subject.   75

SISTER ALOYSIUS: Yes, you're right, back to it. The Christmas pageant. We must be careful how Donald Muller is used in the pageant. (*Sister James shakes as she pours the tea.*)

FLYNN: Easy there, Sister, you don't spill.

SISTER JAMES: Oh, uh, yes, Father.

FLYNN: What about Donald Muller?

SISTER ALOYSIUS: We must be careful, in the pageant, that we neither hide Donald   80
Muller nor put him forward.

FLYNN: Because of the color of his skin.

SISTER ALOYSIUS: That's right.

FLYNN: Why?

SISTER ALOYSIUS: Come, Father. You're being disingenuous.

FLYNN: I think he should be treated like every other boy.   85

SISTER ALOYSIUS: You yourself singled the boy out for special attention. You held a private meeting with him at the rectory. (*Turning to Sister James.*) A week ago?

SISTER JAMES: Yes. (*He realizes something's up*)

FLYNN: What are we talking about?

SISTER JAMES: Donald Muller?

90 SISTER ALOYSIUS: The boy acted strangely when he returned to class. (*Father Flynn turns to Sister James.*)

FLYNN: He did?

SISTER JAMES: When he returned from the rectory. A little odd, yes.

SISTER ALOYSIUS: Can you tell us why?

FLYNN: How did he act strangely?

95 SISTER JAMES: I'm not sure how to explain it. He laid his head on his desk . . .

FLYNN: You mean you had some impression?

SISTER JAMES: Yes.

FLYNN: And he'd come from the rectory so you're asking me if I know anything about it?

SISTER JAMES: That's it.

100 FLYNN: Hmmm. Did you want to discuss the pageant. Is that why I'm here, or is this what you wanted to discuss?

SISTER ALOYSIUS: This.

FLYNN: Well. I feel a hide uncomfortable.

SISTER ALOYSIUS: Why?

FLYNN: Why do you think? Something about your tone.

105 SISTER ALOYSIUS: I would prefer a discussion of fact rather than tone.

FLYNN: Well. If I had judged my conversation with Donald Muller to be of concern to you, Sister, I would have sat you down and talked to you about it. But I did not judge it to be of concern to you.

SISTER ALOYSIUS: Perhaps you are mistaken in your understanding of what concerns me. The boy is in my school, and his well-being is my responsibility.

FLYNN: His well-being is not at issue.

SISTER ALOYSIUS: I am not satisfied that that is true. He was upset when he returned to class.

110 FLYNN: Did he say something?

SISTER JAMES: No.

SISTER ALOYSIUS: What happened in the rectory?

FLYNN: Happened? Nothing happened. I had a talk with a boy.

SISTER ALOYSIUS: What about?

115 FLYNN: It was a private matter.

SISTER ALOYSIUS: He is twelve years old. What could be private?

FLYNN: I'll say it again. Sister, I object to your tone.

SISTER ALOYSIUS: This is not about my tone or your tone, Father Flynn. It's about arriving at the truth.

FLYNN: Of what?

120 SISTER ALOYSIUS: You know what I'm talking about. Don't you? You're controlling the expression on your face right now. Aren't you?

FLYNN: My face? You said you wanted to talk about the pageant, Sister. That's why I'm here. Am I to understand that you brought me into your office to confront me in some way? It's outrageous. I'm not answerable to you. What exactly are you accusing me of?

SISTER ALOYSIUS: I am not accusing you of anything, Father Flynn. I am asking you to tell me what happened in the rectory. (*Father Flynn stands.*)

FLYNN: I don't wish to continue this conversation at all further. And if you are dissatisfied with that, I suggest you speak to Monsignor Benedict. I can only imagine that your unfortunate behavior this morning is the result of overwork. Perhaps you need a leave of absence. I may suggest it. Have a good morning. (*To Sister James.*) Sister?

SISTER JAMES: Good morning, Father. (*Sister Aloysius's next words stop him.*)

SISTER ALOYSIUS: There was alcohol on his breath. (*He turns.*) When he returned   125
from his meeting with you. (*He comes back and sits down. He rubs his eyes.*)

FLYNN: Alcohol.

SISTER JAMES: I did smell it on his breath.

SISTER ALOYSIUS: Well?

FLYNN: Can't you let this alone?

SISTER ALOYSIUS: No.   130

FLYNN: I see there's no way out of this.

SISTER JAMES: Take your time, Father. Would you like some more tea?

FLYNN: You should've let it alone.

SISTER ALOYSIUS: Not possible.

FLYNN: Donald Muller served as altar boy last Tuesday morning. After Mass,   135
Mr. McGinn caught him in the sacristy drinking altar wine. When I found out,
I sent for him. There were tears. He begged not to be removed from the altar
boys. And I took pity on him, I told him if no one else found out, I would let
him stay on. (*Sister James is overjoyed, Sister Aloysius is unmoved.*)

SISTER JAMES: Oh, what a relief! That explains everything! Thanks be to God! Oh,
Sister, look, it's all a mistake!

SISTER ALOYSIUS: And if I talk to Mr. McGinn?

FLYNN: Talk to Mr. McGinn by all means. But now that the boy's secret's out, I'm
going to have to remove him from the altar boys. Which I think is too bad.
That's what I was trying to avoid.

SISTER JAMES: You were trying to protect the boy!

FLYNN: That's right.   140

SISTER JAMES: I might've done the same thing! (*To Sister Aloysius.*) Is there a way
Donald could stay on the altar boys?

SISTER ALOYSIUS: No. If the boy drank altar wine, he cannot continue as an altar
boy.

FLYNN: Of course you're right. I'm just not the disciplinarian you are, Sister. And
he is the only Negro in the school. That did affect my thinking on the matter.
It will be commented on that he's no longer serving at Mass. It's a public thing.
A certain ignorant element in the parish will be confirmed in their beliefs.

SISTER ALOYSIUS: He must be held to the same standard as the others.

FLYNN: Of course. Do we need to discuss the pageant or was that just . . .   145

SISTER ALOYSIUS: No, this was the issue.

FLYNN: Are you satisfied?

SISTER ALOYSIUS: Yes.

FLYNN: Then I'll be going. I have some writing to do.

150   SISTER ALOYSIUS: Intolerance.

FLYNN: That's right. (*He goes, then stops at the door.*) I'm not pleased with how you handled this, Sister. Next time you are troubled by dark ideas, I suggest you speak to the monsignor. (*He goes. After a moment, Sister James weakly launches into optimism.*)

SISTER JAMES: Well. What a relief. He cleared it all up.

SISTER ALOYSIUS: You believe him?

SISTER JAMES: Of course.

155   SISTER ALOYSIUS: Isn't it more that it's easier to believe him?

SISTER JAMES: But we can corroborate his story with Mr. McGinn!

SISTER ALOYSIUS: Yes. These types of people are clever. They're not so easily undone.

SISTER JAMES: Well, I'm convinced!

SISTER ALOYSIUS: You're not. You just want things to be resolved so you can have simplicity back.

160   SISTER JAMES: I want no further part of this.

SISTER ALOYSIUS: I'll bring him down. With or without your help.

SISTER JAMES: How can you be so sure he's lying?

SISTER ALOYSIUS: Experience.

SISTER JAMES: You just don't like him! You don't like it that he uses a ballpoint pen. You don't like it that he takes three lumps of sugar in his tea. You don't like it that he likes "Frosty the Snowman." And you're letting that convince you of something terrible, just terrible! Well, I like "Frosty the Snowman"! And it would be nice if this school weren't run like a prison! And I think it's a good thing that I love to teach History and that I might inspire my students to love it, too! And if you judge that to mean I'm not fit to be a teacher, then so be it!

165   SISTER ALOYSIUS: Sit down. (*Sister James does.*) In ancient Sparta, important matters were decided by who shouted loudest. Fortunately, we are not in ancient Sparta. Now, do you honestly find the students in this school to be treated like inmates in a prison?

SISTER JAMES: (*Relating.*) No, I don't. Actually, by and large, they seem to be fairly happy. But they're all uniformly terrified of you!

SISTER ALOYSIUS: Yes. That's how it works. Sit there. (*Sister Aloysius looks in a notebook, picks up the phones dials.*) Hello, this is Sister Aloysius Beauvier, the principal of St. Nicholas. Is this Mrs. Muller? I'm calling about your son, Donald. I would like you and your husband to come down here for a talk. When would be convenient? (*Lights fade.*)

SIX

Father Flynn, in blue and white vestments, is at the pulpit.

FLYNN: A woman was gossiping with a friend about a man she hardly knew—I know none of you have ever done this—and that night she had a dream. A great hand appeared over her and pointed down at her. She was immediately seized with an overwhelming sense of guilt. The next day she went to confession. She got the old parish priest, Father O'Rourke, and she told him the whole thing. "Is gossiping a sin?" she asked the old man. "Was that the Hand of God Almighty pointing a finger at me? Should I be asking your absolution? Father, tell me, have I done something wrong?" *(Irish brogue.)* "Yes!" Father O'Rourke answered her, "Yes, you ignorant, badly brought-up female! You have borne false witness against your neighbor, you have played fast and loose with his reputation, and you should be heartily ashamed!" So the woman said she was sorry and asked forgiveness. "Not so fast!" says O'Rourke. "I want you to go home, take a pillow up on your roof, cut it open with a knife, and return here to me!" So she went home, took the pillow off her bed, a knife from the drawer, went up the fire escape to the roof, and stabbed the pillow. Then she went back to the old priest as instructed. "Did you gut the pillow with the knife?" he says. "Yes, Father." "And what was the result?" "Feathers," she said. "Feathers?" he repeated. "Feathers everywhere, Father!" "Now I want you to go back and gather up every last feather that flew out on the wind!" "Well," she says, "it can't be done. I don't know where they went. The wind took them all over." "And that," said Father O'Rourke, "is gossip!" In the name of the Father, Son, and the Holy Ghost, Amen.

SEVEN

The lights crossfade to the garden. A crow caws. Sister James sits on the bench, deep in thought. Father Flynn enters.

FLYNN: Good afternoon, Sister James.

SISTER JAMES: Good afternoon, Father.

FLYNN: What is that bird complaining about? What kind of bird is that? A starling? A grackle?

SISTER JAMES: A crow?

FLYNN: Of course it is. Are you praying? I didn't mean to interrupt.   5

SISTER JAMES: I'm not praying, no.

FLYNN: You seem subdued.

SISTER JAMES: Oh, I can't sleep.

FLYNN: Why not?

SISTER JAMES: Bad dreams. Actually one bad dream, and then I haven't slept   10
   right since.

FLYNN: What about?

SISTER JAMES: I looked in a mirror and there was a darkness where my face should
   be. It frightened me.

FLYNN: I can't sleep on occasion.

SISTER JAMES: No? Do you see that big hand pointing a finger at you?

FLYNN: Yes, sometimes.   15

SISTER JAMES: Was your sermon directed at anyone in particular?

FLYNN: What do you think?

SISTER JAMES: Did you make up that story about the pillow?

FLYNN: Yes. You make up little stories to illustrate. In the tradition of the parable.

SISTER JAMES: Aren't the things that actually happen in life more worthy of inter-   20
   pretation than a make-up story?

FLYNN: No. What actually happens in life is beyond interpretation. The truth makes for a bad sermon. It tends to be confusing and have no clear conclusion.

SISTER JAMES: I received a letter from my brother in Maryland yesterday. He's very sick.

FLYNN: Maybe you should go and see him.

SISTER JAMES: I can't leave my class.

25   FLYNN: How's Donald Muller doing?

SISTER JAMES: I don't know.

FLYNN: You don't see him?

SISTER JAMES: I see him every day, but I don't know how he's doing. I don't know how to judge these things. Now.

FLYNN: I stopped speaking to him for fear of it being misunderstood. Isn't that a shame? I actually avoided him the other day when I might've passed him in the hall. He doesn't understand why. I noticed you didn't come to me for confession.

30   SISTER JAMES: No. I went to Monsignor Benedict. He's very kind.

FLYNN: I wasn't?

SISTER JAMES: It wasn't that. As you know. You know why.

FLYNN: You're against me?

SISTER JAMES: No.

35   FLYNN: You're not convinced?

SISTER JAMES: It's not for me to be convinced, one way or the other. It's Sister Aloysius.

FLYNN: Are you just an extension of her?

SISTER JAMES: She's my superior.

FLYNN: But what about you?

40   SISTER JAMES: I wish I knew nothing whatever about it. I wish the idea had never entered my mind.

FLYNN: How did it enter your mind?

SISTER JAMES: Sister Aloysius.

FLYNN: I feel as if my reputation has been damaged through no fault of my own. But I'm reluctant to take the steps necessary to repair it for fear of doing further harm. It's frustrating, I can tell you that.

SISTER JAMES: Is it true?

45   FLYNN: What?

SISTER JAMES: You know what I'm asking.

FLYNN: No, it's not true.

SISTER JAMES: Oh, I don't know what to believe.

FLYNN: How can you take sides against me?

50   SISTER JAMES: It doesn't matter.

FLYNN: It does matter! I've done nothing. There's no substance to any of this. The most innocent actions can appear sinister to the poisoned mind. I had to throw that poor boy off the altar. He's devastated. The only reason I haven't gone to the monsignor is I don't want to tear apart the school. Sister Aloysius would most certainly lose her position as principal if I made her accusations known. Since they're baseless. You might lose your place as well.

SISTER JAMES: Are you threatening me?

FLYNN: What do you take me for? No.

SISTER JAMES: I want to believe you.

FLYNN: Then do. It's as simple as that.   55

SISTER JAMES: It's not me that has to be convinced.

FLYNN: I don't have to prove anything to her.

SISTER JAMES: She's determined.

FLYNN: To what?

SISTER JAMES: Protect the boy.   60

FLYNN: It's me that cares about that boy, not her. Has she ever reached out a hand
to that child or any child in this school? She's like a block of ice! Children need
warmth, kindness, understanding! What does she give them? Rules. That black
boy needs a helping hand or he's not going to make it here! But if she has her
way, he'll be left to his own undoing. Why do you think he was in the sacristy
drinking wine that day? He's in trouble! She sees me talk in a human way to
these children and she immediately assumes there must be something wrong
with it. Something dirty. Well, I'm not going to let her keep this parish in the
Dark Ages! And I'm not going to let her destroy my spirit or compassion!

SISTER JAMES: I'm sure that's not her intent.

FLYNN: I care about this congregation!

SISTER JAMES: I know you do.

FLYNN: Like you care about your class! You love them, don't you?   65

SISTER JAMES: Yes.

FLYNN: That's natural. How else would you relate to children? I can look at your
face and know your philosophy: kindness.

SISTER JAMES: I don't know. I mean, of course.

FLYNN: What is Sister Aloysius's philosophy do you suppose? (*A pause.*)

SISTER JAMES: I don't have to suppose. She's told me. She discourages . . . warmth.   70
She's suggested I be more . . . formal.

FLYNN: There are people who go after your humanity, Sister James, who tell you
the light in your heart is a weakness. That your soft feelings betray you. I don't
believe that. It's an old tactic of cruel people to kill kindness to the name of virtue. Don't believe it. There's nothing wrong with love.

SISTER JAMES: Of course not, but.. . .

FLYNN: Have you forgotten that was the message of the Savior to us all. Love. Not
suspicion, disapproval and judgment. Love of people. Have you found Sister
Aloysius a positive inspiration?

SISTER JAMES: I don't want to misspeak, but no. She's taken away my joy of teaching. And I loved teaching more than anything. (*She cries a little. He pats her
uneasily, looking around.*)

FLYNN: It's all right. You're going to be all right.   75

SISTER JAMES: I feel as if everything is upside down.

FLYNN: It isn't though. There are just times in life when we feel lost. You're not
alone with it. It happens to many of us.

SISTER JAMES: A bond. (*Becomes self-conscious.*) I'd better go in.

FLYNN: I'm sorry your brother is ill.

80 SISTER JAMES: Thank you, Father. (*Starts to go, stops.*) I don't believe it!

FLYNN: You don't?

SISTER JAMES: No.

FLYNN: Thank you, Sister. That's a great relief to me. Thank you very much. (*She goes. He takes out his little black book and writes in it. The crow caws. He yells at it:*) Oh, be quiet. (*Then he opens a prayer book and walks away.*)

EIGHT

Crossfade to the principal's office. Sister Aloysius is sitting looking out the window, very still. A knock at the door. She doesn't react. A second knock, louder. She pulls a small earplug out of her ear and scurries to the door. She opens it. There stands Mrs. Muller, a black woman of about thirty-eight, in her Sunday best, dressed for church. She's on red alert.

SISTER ALOYSIUS: Mrs. Muller?

MRS. MULLER: Yes.

SISTER ALOYSIUS: Come in. (*Sister Aloysius closes the door.*) Please have a seat.

MRS. MULLER: I thought I might a had the wrong day when you didn't answer the door.

5 SISTER ALOYSIUS: Oh, yes. Well, just between us, I was listening to a transistor radio with an earpiece. (*She shows Mrs. Muller a very small transistor radio.*) Look at how tiny they're making them now. I confiscated it from one of the students, and now I can't stop using it.

MRS. MULLER: You like music?

SISTER ALOYSIUS: Not really. News reports. Years ago I used to listen to all the news reports because my husband was in Italy in the war. When I came into possession of this little radio, I found myself doing it again. Though there is no war and the voices have changed.

MRS. MULLER: You were a married woman?

SISTER ALOYSIUS: Yes. But then he was killed. Is your husband coming?

10 MRS. MULLER: Couldn't get off work.

SISTER ALOYSIUS: I see. Of course. It was a lot to ask.

MRS. MULLER: How's Donald doing?

SISTER ALOYSIUS: He's passing his subjects. He has average grades.

MRS. MULLER: Oh. Good. He was upset about getting taken off the altar boys.

15 SISTER ALOYSIUS: Did he explain why?

MRS. MULLER: He said he was caught drinking wine.

SISTER ALOYSIUS: That is the reason.

MRS. MULLER: Well, that seems fair. But he's a good boy, Sister. He fell down there, but he's a good boy pretty much down the line. And he knows what an opportunity he has here. I think the whole thing was just a bit much for him.

SISTER ALOYSIUS: What do you mean, the whole thing?

20 MRS. MULLER: He's the only colored here. He's the first in this school. That'd be a lot for a boy.

SISTER ALOYSIUS: I suppose it is. But he has to do the work of course.

MRS. MULLER: He is doing it though, right?

SISTER ALOYSIUS: Yes. He's getting by. He's getting through. How is he at home?

MRS. MULLER: His father beat the hell out of him over that wine.

SISTER ALOYSIUS: He shouldn't do that.   25

MRS. MULLER: You don't tell my husband what to do. You just stand back. He didn't want Donald to come here.

SISTER ALOYSIUS: Why not?

MRS. MULLER: Thought he'd have a lot of trouble with the other boys. But that hasn't really happened as far as I can make out.

SISTER ALOYSIUS: Good.

MRS. MULLER: That priest, Father Flynn, been watching out for him.   30

SISTER ALOYSIUS: Yes. Have you met Father Flynn?

MRS. MULLER: Not exactly, no. I seen him on the altar, but I haven't met him face to face. No. Just, you know, heard from Donald.

SISTER ALOYSIUS: What does he say?

MRS. MULLER: You know, Father Flynn, Father Flynn. He looks up to him. The man gives him his time, which is what the boy needs. He needs that.

SISTER ALOYSIUS: Mrs. Muller, we may have a problem.   35

MRS. MULLER: Well, I thought you must a had a reason for asking me to come in. Principal's a big job. If you stop your day to talk to me, must be something. I just want to say though, it's just till June.

SISTER ALOYSIUS: Excuse me?

MRS. MULLER: Whatever the problem is, Donald just has to make it here till June. Then he's off into high school.

SISTER ALOYSIUS: Right.

MRS. MULLER: If Donald can graduate from here, he has a better chance of getting   40 into a good high school. And that would mean an opportunity at college. I believe he has the intelligence. And he wants it, too.

SISTER ALOYSIUS: I don't see anything at this time standing in the way of his graduating with his class.

MRS. MULLER: Well, that's all I care about. Anything else is all right with me.

SISTER ALOYSIUS: I doubt that.

MRS. MULLER: Try me.

SISTER ALOYSIUS: I'm concerned about the relationship between Father Flynn and   45 your son.

MRS. MULLER: You don't say. Concerned. What do you mean, concerned?

SISTER ALOYSIUS: That it may not be right.

MRS. MULLER: Uh-huh. Well, there's something wrong with everybody, isn't that so? Got to be forgiving.

SISTER ALOYSIUS: I'm concerned, to be frank, that Father Flynn may have made advances on your son.

MRS. MULLER: *May* have made.   50

SISTER ALOYSIUS: I can't be certain.

MRS. MULLER: No evidence?

SISTER ALOYSIUS: No.

MRS. MULLER: Then maybe there's nothing to it?

SISTER ALOYSIUS: I think there is something to it.   55

MRS. MULLER: Well, I would prefer not to see it that way if you don't mind.

SISTER ALOYSIUS: I can understand that this is hard to hear. I think Father Flynn
    gave Donald that altar wine.

MRS. MULLER: Why would he do that?

SISTER ALOYSIUS: Has Donald been acting strangely?

60   MRS. MULLER: No.

SISTER ALOYSIUS: Nothing out of the ordinary?

MRS. MULLER: He's been himself.

SISTER ALOYSIUS: All right.

MRS. MULLER: Look, Sister. I don't want any trouble, and I feel like you're on the
    match somehow.

65   SISTER ALOYSIUS: I'm not sure you completely understand.

MRS. MULLER: I think I understand the kind of thing you're talking about. But I
    don't want to get into it.

SISTER ALOYSIUS: What's that?

MRS. MULLER: Not to be disagreeing with you, but if we're talking about something
    floating around between this priest and my son, that ain't my son's fault.

SISTER ALOYSIUS: I'm not suggesting it is.

70   MRS. MULLER: He's just a boy.

SISTER ALOYSIUS: I know.

MRS. MULLER: Twelve years old. If somebody should be taking blame for anything,
    it should be the man, not the boy.

SISTER ALOYSIUS: I agree with you completely.

MRS. MULLER: You're agreeing with me but I'm sitting in the principal's office talk-
    ing about my son. Why isn't the priest in the principal's office, if you know what
    I'm saying and you'll excuse my bringing it up.

75   SISTER ALOYSIUS: You're here because I'm concerned about Donald's welfare.

MRS. MULLER: You think I'm not?

SISTER ALOYSIUS: Of course you are.

MRS. MULLER: Let me ask you something. You honestly think that priest gave Don-
    ald that wine to drink?

SISTER ALOYSIUS: Yes, I do.

80   MRS. MULLER: Then how come my son got kicked off the altar boys if it was the
    man that gave it to him?

SISTER ALOYSIUS: The boy got caught, the man didn't.

MRS. MULLER: How come the priest didn't get kicked off the priesthood?

SISTER ALOYSIUS: He's a grown man, educated. And he knows what's at stake. It's
    not so easy to pin someone like that down.

MRS. MULLER: So you give my son the whole blame. No problem my son getting
    blamed and punished. That's easy. You know why that is?

85   SISTER ALOYSIUS: Perhaps you should let me talk. I think you're getting upset.

MRS. MULLER: That's because that's the way it is. You're just finding out about it,
    but that's the way it is and the way it's been, Sister. You're not going against no
    man in a *robe* and win, Sister. He's got the position.

SISTER ALOYSIUS: And he's got your son.

MRS. MULLER: Let him have 'im then.

SISTER ALOYSIUS: What?

MRS. MULLER: It's just till June.   90
SISTER ALOYSIUS: Do you know what you're saying?
MRS. MULLER: Know more about it than you.
SISTER ALOYSIUS: I believe this man is creating or has already brought about an im-
    proper relationship with your son.
MRS. MULLER: I don't know.
SISTER ALOYSIUS: I know I'm right.   95
MRS. MULLER: Why you need to know something like that for sure when you don't?
    Please, Sister. You got some kind a righteous cause going with this priest, and
    now you want to drag my boy into it. My son doesn't need additional difficul-
    ties. Let him take the good and leave the rest when he leaves this place in June.
    He knows how to do that, I taught him how to do that.
SISTER ALOYSIUS: What kind of mother are you?
MRS. MULLER: Excuse me, but you don't know enough about life to say a thing like
    that, Sister.
SISTER ALOYSIUS: I know enough.
MRS. MULLER: You know the rules maybe, but that don't cover it.   100
SISTER ALOYSIUS: I know what I won't accept!
MRS. MULLER: You accept what you gotta accept and you work with it. That's the
    truth I know. Sorry to be so sharp, but you're in here in this room . . .
SISTER ALOYSIUS: This man is in my school.
MRS. MULLER: Well, he's gotta be somewhere, and maybe he's doing some good
    too. You ever think of that?
SISTER ALOYSIUS: He's after the boys.   105
MRS. MULLER: Well, maybe some of them boys want to get caught. Maybe what you
    don't know maybe is my son is . . . that way. That's why his father beat him up.
    Not the wine. He beat Donald for being what he is.
SISTER ALOYSIUS: What are you telling me?
MRS. MULLER: I'm his mother. I'm talking about his nature now, not anything he's
    done. But you can't hold a child responsible for what God gave him to be.
SISTER ALOYSIUS: Listen to me with care, Mrs. Muller. I'm only interested in ac-
    tions. It's hopeless to discuss a child's possible inclination. I'm finding it difficult
    enough to address a man's deeds. This isn't about what the boy may be, but
    what the man is. It's about the man.
MRS. MULLER: But there's the boy's nature.   110
SISTER ALOYSIUS: Let's leave that out of it.
MRS. MULLER: Forget it then. You're the one forcing people to say these things out
    loud. Things are in the air and you leave them alone if you can. That's what I
    know. My boy came to this school cause they were gonna kill him at the public
    school. So we were lucky enough to get him in here for his last year. Good. His
    father don't like him. He comes here, the kids don't like him. One man is good
    to him. This priest. Puts out a hand to the boy. Does the man have his reasons?
    Yes. Everybody has their reasons. *You* have your reasons. But do I ask the man
    why he's good to my son? No, I don't care why. My son needs some man to care
    about him and see him through to where he wants to go. And thank God, this
    educated man with some kindness in him wants to do just that.

SISTER ALOYSIUS: This will not do.

MRS. MULLER: It's just till June. Sometimes things aren't black and white.

115   SISTER ALOYSIUS: And sometimes they are. I'll throw your son out of this school. Make no mistake.

MRS. MULLER: But why would you do that? If nothing started with him?

SISTER ALOYSIUS: Because I will stop this whatever way I must.

MRS. MULLER: You'd hurt my son to get your way?

SISTER ALOYSIUS: It won't end with your son. There will be others, if there aren't already.

120   MRS. MULLER: Throw the priest out then.

SISTER ALOYSIUS: I'm trying to do just that.

MRS. MULLER: Well, what do you want from me? (A pause.)

SISTER ALOYSIUS: Nothing. As it turns out. I was hoping you might know something that would help me, but it seems you don't.

125   MRS. MULLER: Please leave my son out of this. My husband would kill that child over a thing like this.

SISTER ALOYSIUS: I'll try. (Mrs. Muller stands up.)

MRS. MULLER: I don't know, Sister. You may think you're doing good, but the world's a hard place. I don't know that you and me are on the same side. I'll be standing with my son and those who are good with my son. It'd be nice to see you there. Nice talking with you, Sister. Good morning. (She goes, leaving the door open behind her. Sister Aloysius is shaken. After a moment, Father Flynn appears at the door. He's in a controlled fury.)

FLYNN: May I come in?

SISTER ALOYSIUS: We would require a third party.

130   FLYNN: What was Donald's mother doing here?

SISTER ALOYSIUS: We were having a chat.

FLYNN: About what?

SISTER ALOYSIUS: A third party is truly required, Father.

FLYNN: No, Sister. No third party. You and me are due for a talk. (He comes in and slams the door behind him. They face each other.) You have to stop this campaign against me!

135   SISTER ALOYSIUS: You can stop it at any time.

FLYNN: How?

SISTER ALOYSIUS: Confess and resign.

FLYNN: You are attempting to destroy my reputation! But the result of all this is going to be your removal, not mine!

SISTER ALOYSIUS: What are you doing in this school?

140   FLYNN: I am trying to do good!

SISTER ALOYSIUS: Or even more to the point, what are you doing in the priesthood?

FLYNN: You are single-handedly holding this school and this parish back!

SISTER ALOYSIUS: From what?

FLYNN: Progressive education and a welcoming church.

145   SISTER ALOYSIUS: You can't distract me, Father Flynn. This isn't about my behavior, it's about yours.

FLYNN: It's about your unfounded suspicions.

SISTER ALOYSIUS: That's right. I have suspicions.

FLYNN: You know what I haven't understood through all this? Why do you suspect me? What have I done?

SISTER ALOYSIUS: You gave that boy wine to drink. And you let him take the blame.

FLYNN: That's completely untrue! Did you talk to Mr. McGinn?   150

SISTER ALOYSIUS: All McGinn knows is the boy drank wine. He doesn't how he came to drink it.

FLYNN: Did his mother have something to add to that?

SISTER ALOYSIUS: No.

FLYNN: So that's it. There's nothing there.

SISTER ALOYSIUS: I'm not satisfied.   155

FLYNN: Well, if you're not satisfied, ask the boy then!

SISTER ALOYSIUS: No, he'd protect you. That's what he's been doing.

FLYNN: Oh, and why would he do that?

SISTER ALOYSIUS: Because you have seduced him.

FLYNN: You're insane! You've got it in your head that I've corrupted this child after   160
giving him wine, and nothing I say will change that.

SISTER ALOYSIUS: That's right.

FLYNN: But correct me if I'm wrong. This has nothing to do with the wine, not
really. You had a fundamental mistrust of me before this incident! It was you
that warned Sister James to be on the lookout, wasn't it?

SISTER ALOYSIUS: That's true.

FLYNN: So you admit it

SISTER ALOYSIUS: Certainly.   165

FLYNN: Why?

SISTER ALOYSIUS: I know people.

FLYNN: That's not good enough!

SISTER ALOYSIUS: It won't have to be.

FLYNN: How's that?   170

SISTER ALOYSIUS: You will tell me what you've done.

FLYNN: Oh I will?

SISTER ALOYSIUS: Yes.

FLYNN: I'm not one of your truant boys, you know. Sister James is convinced I'm
innocent.

SISTER ALOYSIUS: So you talked to Sister James? Well, of course you talked to Sister   175
James.

FLYNN: Did you know that Donald's father beats him?

SISTER ALOYSIUS: Yes.

FLYNN: And might that not account for the odd behavior Sister James noticed in
the boy?

SISTER ALOYSIUS: It might.

FLYNN: Then what is it? What? What did you hear, what did you see that con-   180
vinced you so thoroughly?

SISTER ALOYSIUS: What does it matter?

FLYNN: I want to know.

SISTER ALOYSIUS: On the first day of the school year, I saw you touch William
        London's wrist. And I saw him pull away.
FLYNN: That's all?
185 SISTER ALOYSIUS: That was all.
FLYNN: But that's nothing. (*He writes in his book.*)
SISTER ALOYSIUS: What are you writing now?
FLYNN. You leave me no choice. I'm writing down what you say. I tend to get too
        flustered to remember the details of an upsetting conversation, and this may be
        important. When I talk to the monsignor and explain why you have to be re-
        moved as the principal of this school.
SISTER ALOYSIUS: This morning, before I spoke with Mrs. Muller, I took the precau-
        tion of calling the last parish to which you were assigned.
190 FLYNN: What did he say?
SISTER ALOYSIUS: Who?
FLYNN. The pastor?
SISTER ALOYSIUS: I did not speak to the pastor. I spoke to one of the nuns.
FLYNN. You should've spoken to the pastor.
195 SISTER ALOYSIUS: I spoke to a nun.
FLYNN: That's not the proper route for you to have taken, Sister! The Church is
        very clear. You're supposed to go through the pastor.
SISTER ALOYSIUS: Why? Do you have an understanding, you and he? Father Flynn,
        you have a history.
FLYNN: You have no right to go rummaging through my past!
SISTER ALOYSIUS: This is your third parish in five years.
200 FLYNN: Call the pastor and ask him why I left! It was perfectly innocent.
SISTER ALOYSIUS: I'm not calling the pastor.
FLYNN: I am a good priest! And there is nothing in my record to suggest otherwise.
SISTER ALOYSIUS: You will go after another child and another, until you are
        stopped.
FLYNN: What nun did you speak to?
205 SISTER ALOYSIUS: I won't say.
FLYNN: I've not touched a child.
SISTER ALOYSIUS: You have.
FLYNN: You have not the slightest proof of anything.
SISTER ALOYSIUS: But I have my certainty, and armed with that, I will go to your
        last parish, and the one before that if necessary. I will find a parent, Father
        Flynn! Trust me I will. A parent who probably doesn't know that you are still
        working with children! And once I do that, you will be exposed. You may even
        be attacked, metaphorically or otherwise.
210 FLYNN: You have no right to act on your own! You are a member of a religious or-
        der. You have taken vows, obedience being one! You answer to us! You have no
        right to step outside the Church!
SISTER ALOYSIUS: I will step outside the Church if that's what needs to be done,
        though the door should shut behind me! I will do what needs to be done, Fa-
        ther, if it means I'm damned to Hell! You should understand that, or you will
        mistake me. Now, did you give Donald Muller wine to drink?

FLYNN: Have you never done anything wrong?

SISTER ALOYSIUS: I have.

FLYNN: Mortal sin?

SISTER ALOYSIUS: Yes.

FLYNN: And?

SISTER ALOYSIUS: I confessed it! Did you give Donald Muller wine to drink?

FLYNN: Whatever I have done, I have left in the healing hands of my confessor. As have you! We are the same!

SISTER ALOYSIUS: We are not the same! A dog that bites is a dog that bites! I do not justify what I do wrong and go on. I admit it, desist, and take my medicine. Did you give Donald Muller wine to drink?

FLYNN: No.

SISTER ALOYSIUS: Mental reservation?

FLYNN: No.

SISTER ALOYSIUS: You lie. Very well then. If you won't leave my office, I will. And once I go, I will not stop. (*She goes to the door. Suddenly, a new tone comes into his voice.*)

FLYNN: Wait!

SISTER ALOYSIUS: You will request a transfer from this parish. You will take a leave of absence until it is granted.

FLYNN: And do what for the love of God? My life is here.

SISTER ALOYSIUS: Don't.

FLYNN: Please! Are we people? Am I a person flesh and blood like you? Or are we just ideas and convictions? I can't say everything. Do you understand? There are things I can't say. Even if you can't imagine the explanation, Sister, remember that there are circumstances beyond your knowledge. Even if you feel certainty, it is an emotion and not a fact. In the spirit of charity, I appeal to you. On behalf of my life's work. You have to behave responsibly. I put myself in your hands.

SISTER ALOYSIUS: I don't want you.

FLYNN: My reputation is at stake.

SISTER ALOYSIUS: You can preserve your reputation.

FLYNN: If you say these things, I won't be able to do my work in the community.

SISTER ALOYSIUS: Your work in the community should be discontinued.

FLYNN: You'd leave me with nothing.

SISTER ALOYSIUS: That's not true. It's Donald Muller who has nothing, and you took full advantage of that.

FLYNN: I have not done anything wrong. I care about that boy, very much.

SISTER ALOYSIUS: Because you smile at him and sympathize with him, and talk to him as if you were the same?

FLYNN: That child needed a friend!

SISTER ALOYSIUS: You are a cheat. The warm feeling you experienced when that boy looked at you with trust was not the sensation of virtue. It can be got by a drunkard from his tot of rum. You're a disgrace to the collar. The only reason you haven't been thrown out of the Church is the decline in vocations.

FLYNN: I can fight you.

SISTER ALOYSIUS: You will lose.

FLYNN: You can't know that.

SISTER ALOYSIUS: I know.

FLYNN: Where's your compassion?

245 SISTER ALOYSIUS: Nowhere you can get at it. Stay here. Compose yourself. Use the phone if you like. Good day, Father. I have no sympathy for you. I know you're invulnerable to true regret. (*Starts to go. Pause.*) And cut your nails. (*She goes, closing the door behind her. After a moment, he goes to the phone and dials.*)

FLYNN: Yes. This is Father Brendan Flynn of St. Nicholas parish. I need to make an appointment to see the bishop. (*Lights fade.*)

NINE

The lights crossfade to Sister Aloysius, walking into garden. It's a sunny day. She sits on the bench. Sister James enters.

SISTER ALOYSIUS: How's your brother?

SISTER JAMES: Better. Much better.

SISTER ALOYSIUS: I'm very glad. I prayed for him.

SISTER JAMES: It was good to get away. I needed to see my family. It had been too long.

5 SISTER ALOYSIUS: Then I'm glad you did it.

SISTER JAMES: And Father Flynn is gone.

SISTER ALOYSIUS: Yes.

SISTER JAMES: Where?

SISTER ALOYSIUS: St. Jerome's.

10 SISTER JAMES: So you did it. You got him out.

SISTER ALOYSIUS: Yes.

SISTER JAMES: Donald Muller is heartbroken that he's gone.

SISTER ALOYSIUS: Can't be helped. It's just till June.

SISTER JAMES: I don't think Father Flynn did anything wrong.

15 SISTER ALOYSIUS: No? He convinced you?

SISTER JAMES: Yes, he did.

SISTER ALOYSIUS: Hmmm.

SISTER JAMES: Did you ever prove it?

SISTER ALOYSIUS: What?

20 SISTER JAMES: That he interfered with Donald Muller?

SISTER ALOYSIUS: Did I ever prove it to whom?

SISTER JAMES: Anyone but yourself?

SISTER ALOYSIUS: No.

SISTER JAMES: But you were sure.

25 SISTER ALOYSIUS: Yes.

SISTER JAMES: I wish I could be like you.

SISTER ALOYSIUS: Why?

SISTER JAMES: Because I can't sleep at night anymore. Everything seems uncertain to me.

SISTER ALOYSIUS: Maybe we're not supposed to sleep so well. They've made Father Flynn the pastor of St. Jerome.

SISTER JAMES: Who?   30
SISTER ALOYSIUS: The bishop appointed Father Flynn the pastor of St. Jerome
   Church and School. It's a promotion.
SISTER JAMES: You didn't tell them?
SISTER ALOYSIUS: I told our good Monsignor Benedict. I crossed the garden and
   told him. He did not believe it to be true.
SISTER JAMES: Then why did Father Flynn leave? What did you say to him to make
   him go?
SISTER ALOYSIUS: That I had called a nun in his previous parish. That I had found   35
   out his prior history of infringements.
SISTER JAMES: So you did prove it!
SISTER ALOYSIUS: I was lying. I made no such call.
SISTER JAMES: You lied?
SISTER ALOYSIUS: Yes. But if he had no such history, the lie wouldn't have worked.
   His resignation was his confession. He was what I thought he was. And he's gone.
SISTER JAMES: I can't believe you lied.   40
SISTER ALOYSIUS: In the pursuit of wrongdoing, one steps away from God. Of course
   there's a price.
SISTER JAMES: I see. So now he's in another school.
SISTER ALOYSIUS: Yes. Oh, Sister James!
SISTER JAMES: What is it, Sister?
SISTER ALOYSIUS: I have doubts! I have such doubts! (*Sister Aloysius is bent with*   45
   emotion. Sister James comfort her. Lights fade.)

*   *   *

Reading and Reacting

1. In what year is the play set? How do you know?
2. What key themes are introduced in the sermon Father Flynn delivers at the beginning of the play? How are these themes developed throughout the play?
3. How, according to Father Flynn, did the assassination of President Kennedy bring
   people together?
4. In his sermon at the beginning of the play, Father Flynn says, "Doubt can be a
   bond as powerful and as sustaining as certainty." What does he mean? How does
   this view of doubt differ from the view of doubt (and its consequences) developed
   in the play?
5. A **parable** is a brief story—often seen in the Bible or in religious sermons—
   intended to teach a moral or religious lesson. What parables do Father Flynn's
   sermons contain? What lessons do these parables teach?
6. What evidence does Sister Aloysius have to support her accusations against Father
   Flynn? Do you think her accusations are justified?
7. How does Father Flynn's view of the church differ from that of Sister Aloysius?
   How do their respective views reflect the changes that the Catholic Church was
   undergoing at the time the play takes place?
8. Sister James and Mrs. Muller are minor characters in the play. How do they change
   as the play progresses?

9. Early in the play, Father Flynn and Sister Aloysius have the following exchange:

> Sister A.: Sister Veronica fell on a piece of wood this morning and practically
>   killed herself.
> Flynn: Is she all right?
> Sister A.: Oh, she's fine.
> Flynn: Her sight isn't good, is it?
> Sister A.: Her sight is fine. Nuns fall, you know.
> Flynn: No, I didn't know that.
> Sister A.: It's the habit. It catches us more often than not. What with our being in black and
>   white, and so prone to falling, we are more like dominoes than anything else.

How do Sister Aloysius's comments foreshadow events that occur later in the play?

10. JOURNAL ENTRY In what sense is *Doubt* a parable? What lesson does the play teach?

11. CRITICAL PERSPECTIVE In a *New York Times* review of *Doubt*, theater critic John Simon made the following observation:

> *Doubt* may well be Shanley's best play to date. It goes back to his days in a Catholic school in the Bronx run by Sisters of Charity, and while it does not seem patently autobiographical, eight years at that school surely left their mark on the playwright. Another influence must be the recent revelations of pederasty in the priesthood. But what makes the play particularly absorbing is its enlightened objectivity.

Do you agree with Simon that the play is objective? Or, do you think that Shanley favors the position of one of the characters over that of another? Explain.

Related Works: "Gryphon" (p. 250), "Cathedral" (p. 435), "The Value of Education" (p. 727), "Theme for English B" (p. 920), *Proof* (p. 1180)

AUGUST WILSON (1945–2005) was born in Pittsburgh, Pennsylvania, to a German immigrant father and a black mother and lived in the African American neighborhood known as the Hill District. After leaving school at fifteen when he was accused of plagiarizing a paper, he participated in the Black Arts movement in Pittsburgh, submitting poems to local African American publications. In 1969, Wilson and his friend Rob Penny founded the Black Horizons Theatre Company, for which Wilson produced and directed plays. Although Wilson wrote plays while living in Pittsburgh, his work began to gain recognition only after 1978, when he moved to St. Paul, Minnesota. There, in 1982, Lloyd Richards, dean of the Yale School of Drama and artistic director of the Yale Repertory Company, staged a performance of Wilson's *Ma Rainey's Black Bottom*.

Wilson's achievement was epic. Beginning with *Ma Rainey's Black Bottom* in 1984, he wrote a ten-play cycle that chronicled the African American experience in the United States decade by decade. In addition to *Ma Rainey's Black Bottom*, a Tony Award winner, the plays in this cycle include *Fences* (1985), which won a Pulitzer Prize in 1987; *Joe Turner's Come and Gone* (1986); *Two Trains Running* (1989), which won Wilson his fifth New York Drama Critics Circle Award; *The Piano Lesson* (1987), which won a second Pulitzer Prize for Wilson in 1990; *Seven Guitars* (1996); and *Radio Golf*, the last play in the cycle, which opened in 2005, the year of Wilson's death. To honor his achievements, Broadway's Virginia Theater was renamed the August Wilson Theater.

Fences explores how the long-upheld color barrier in professional baseball affected the main character, Troy, who struggles with the pain of never realizing his dream of becoming a big-league player. Throughout the play, Troy retreats behind literal and figurative barriers that impair his relationships with his family.

CULTURAL CONTEXT The history of African Americans in baseball began in the period between emancipation and the civil rights movement. Banned from professional baseball, African American players formed the Negro

Leagues, with stars such as Satchel Paige and Josh Gibson emerging in the 1930s. Then, in 1946, Branch Rickey, the club president and general manager of the Brooklyn Dodgers, changed everything when he set out to sign the Negro Leagues' top players to his team. The first player he chose was Jackie Robinson, who broke the racial barrier and debuted at first base for the Dodgers on April 15, 1947, at the age of 28. Robinson's performance earned him the Rookie of the Year award. In 1957, the year in which *Fences* is set, Robinson announced his retirement from baseball after he was traded to the New York Giants. In 1962, he was inducted into the Baseball Hall of Fame.

Fences (1985)

CHARACTERS

Troy Maxson

Jim Bono, *Troy's friend*

Rose, *Troy's wife*

Lyons, *Troy's oldest son by previous marriage*

Gabriel, *Troy's brother*

Cory, *Troy and Rose's son*

Raynell, *Troy's daughter*

SETTING

The setting is the yard which fronts the only entrance to the Maxson household, an ancient two-story brick house set back off a small alley in a big-city neighborhood. The entrance to the house is gained by two or three steps leading to a wooden porch badly in need of paint.

A relatively recent addition to the house and running its full width, the porch lacks congruence. It is a sturdy porch with a flat roof. One or two chairs of dubious value sit at one end where the kitchen window opens onto the porch. An old-fashioned icebox stands silent guard at the opposite end.

The yard is a small dirt yard, partially fenced, except for the last scene, with a wooden sawhorse, a pile of lumber, and other fence-building equipment set off to the side. Opposite is a tree from which hangs a ball made of rags. A baseball bat leans against the tree. Two oil drums serve as garbage receptacles and sit near the house at right to complete the setting.

THE PLAY

Near the turn of the century, the destitute of Europe sprang on the city with tenacious claws and an honest and solid dream. The city devoured them. They swelled its belly until it burst into a thousand furnaces and sewing machines, a thousand butcher shops and bakers' ovens, a thousand churches and hospitals and funeral parlors and money-lenders. The city grew. It nourished itself and offered each man a partnership limited only by his talent, his guile, and his willingness and capacity for hard work. For the immigrants of Europe, a dream dared and won true.

The descendants of African slaves were offered no such welcome or participation. They came from places called the Carolinas and the Virginias, Georgia, Alabama, Mississippi, and Tennessee. They came strong, eager, searching. The city rejected them and they fled and settled along the riverbanks and under bridges in shallow, ramshackle houses made of sticks and tarpaper. They collected rags and wood. They sold the use of their muscles and their bodies. They cleaned houses and washed clothes, they shined shoes, and in quiet desperation and vengeful pride, they stole, and lived in pursuit of their own dream. That they could breathe free, finally, and stand to meet life with the force of dignity and whatever eloquence the heart could call upon.

By 1957, the hard-won victories of the European immigrants had solidified the industrial might of America. War had been confronted and won with new energies that used loyalty and patriotism as its fuel. Life was rich, full, and flourishing. The Milwaukee Braves won the World Series, and the hot winds of change that would make the sixties a turbulent, racing, dangerous, and provocative decade had not yet begun to blow full.

ACT 1
SCENE 1

It is 1957. Troy and Bono enter the yard, engaged in conversation. Troy is fifty-three years old, a large man with thick, heavy hands; it is this largeness that he strives to fill out and make an accommodation with. Together with his blackness, his largeness informs his sensibilities and the choices he has made in his life.

Of the two men, Bono is obviously the follower. His commitment to their friendship of thirty-odd years is rooted in his admiration of Troy's honesty, capacity for hard work, and his strength, which Bono seeks to emulate.

Scene from the 1987 Broadway production of *Fences* starring James Earl Jones as Troy
© 1987 Ron Scherl/StageImage/The Image Works

It is Friday night, payday, and the one night of the week the two men engage in a ritual of talk and drink. Troy is usually the most talkative and at times he can be crude and almost vulgar, though he is capable of rising to profound heights of expression. The men carry lunch buckets and wear or carry burlap aprons and are dressed in clothes suitable to their jobs as garbage collectors.

BONO: Troy, you ought to stop that lying!
TROY: I ain't lying! The nigger had a watermelon this big. *(He indicates with his hands.)* Talking about . . . "What watermelon, Mr. Rand?" I liked to fell out! "What watermelon, Mr. Rand?" . . . And it sitting there big as life.

BONO: What did Mr. Rand say?

TROY: Ain't said nothing. Figure if the nigger too dumb to know he carrying a watermelon, he wasn't gonna get much sense out of him. Trying to hide that great
big old watermelon under his coat. Afraid to let the white man see him carry it
home.

BONO: I'm like you . . . I ain't got no time for them kind of people.   5

TROY: Now what he look like getting mad 'cause he see the man from the union
talking to Mr. Rand?

BONO: He come to me talking about . . . "Maxson gonna get us fired." I told him
to get away from me with that. He walked away from me calling you a trouble-
maker. What Mr. Rand say?

TROY: Ain't said nothing. He told me to go down the Commissioner's office next
Friday. They called me down there to see them.

BONO: Well, as long as you got your complaint filed, they can't fire you. That's what
one of them white fellows tell me.

TROY: I ain't worried about them firing me. They gonna fire me 'cause I asked a   10
question? That's all I did. I went to Mr. Rand and asked him, "Why? Why you
got the white mens driving and the colored lifting?" Told him, "what's the matter, don't I count? You think only white fellows got sense enough to drive a
truck. That ain't no paper job! Hell, anybody can drive a truck. How come you
got all whites driving and the colored lifting?" He told me "take it to the union."
Well, hell, that's what I done! Now they wanna come up with this pack of lies.

BONO: I told Brownie if the man come and ask him any questions . . . just tell the
truth! It ain't nothing but something they done trumped up on you 'cause you
filed a complaint on them.

TROY: Brownie don't understand nothing. All I want them to do is change the job
description. Give everybody a chance to drive the truck. Brownie can't see that.
He ain't got that much sense.

BONO: How you figure he be making out with that gal be up at Taylors' all the time
. . . that Alberta gal?

TROY: Same as you and me. Getting just as much as we is. Which is to say nothing.

BONO: It is, huh? I figure you doing a little better than me . . . and I ain't saying   15
what I'm doing.

TROY: Aw, nigger, look here . . . I know you. If you had got anywhere near that gal,
twenty minutes later you be looking to tell somebody. And the first one you
gonna tell . . . that you gonna want to brag to . . . is me.

BONO: I ain't saying that. I see where you be eyeing her.

TROY: I eye all the women. I don't miss nothing. Don't never let nobody tell you
Troy Maxson don't eye the women.

BONO: You been doing more than eyeing her. You done bought her a drink or two.

TROY: Hell yeah, I bought her a drink! What that mean? I bought you one, too.   20
What that mean 'cause I buy her a drink? I'm just being polite.

BONO: It's all right to buy her one drink. That's what you call being polite. But
when you wanna be buying two or three . . . that's what you call eyeing her.

TROY: Look here, as long as you known me . . . you ever known me to chase after
women?

BONO: Hell yeah! Long as I done known you. You forgetting I knew you when.

TROY: Naw, I'm talking about since I been married to Rose?

25 BONO: Oh, not since you been married to Rose. Now, that's the truth, there. I can say that.

TROY: All right then! Case closed.

BONO: I see you be walking up around Alberta's house. You supposed to be at Taylors' and you be walking up around there.

TROY: What you watching where I'm walking for? I ain't watching after you.

BONO: I seen you walking around there more than once.

30 TROY: Hell, you liable to see me walking anywhere! That don't mean nothing cause you see me walking around there.

BONO: Where she come from anyway? She just kinda showed up one day.

TROY: Tallahassee. You can look at her and tell she one of them Florida gals. They got some big healthy women down there. Grow them right up out the ground. Got a little bit of Indian in her. Most of them niggers down in Florida got some Indian in them.

BONO: I don't know about that Indian part. But she damn sure big and healthy. Woman wear some big stockings. Got them great big old legs and hips as wide as the Mississippi River.

TROY: Legs don't mean nothing. You don't do nothing but push them out of the way. But them hips cushion the ride!

35 BONO: Troy, you ain't got no sense.

TROY: It's the truth! Like you riding on Goodyears!

Rose enters from the house. She is ten years younger than Troy, her devotion to him stems from her recognition of the possibilities of her life without him: a succession of abusive men and their babies, a life of partying and running the streets, the Church, or aloneness with its attendant pain and frustration. She recognizes Troy's spirit as a fine and illuminating one and she either ignores or forgives his faults, only some of which she recognizes. Though she doesn't drink, her presence is an integral part of the Friday night rituals. She alternates between the porch and the kitchen, where supper preparations are under way.

ROSE: What you all out here getting into?

TROY: What you worried about what we getting into for? This is men talk, woman.

ROSE: What I care what you all talking about? Bono, you gonna stay for supper?

40 BONO: No, I thank you, Rose. But Lucille say she cooking up a pot of pigfeet.

TROY: Pigfeet! Hell, I'm going home with you! Might even stay the night if you got some pigfeet. You got something in there to top them pigfeet, Rose?

ROSE: I'm cooking up some chicken. I got some chicken and collard greens.[1]

TROY: Well, go on back in the house and let me and Bono finish what we was talking about. This is men talk. I got some talk for you later. You know what kind of talk I mean. You go on and powder it up.

ROSE: Troy Maxson, don't you start that now!

---

[1]*collard greens:* A leafy green vegetable.

TROY: *(puts his arm around her)* Aw, woman . . . come here. Look here, Bono . . .   45
    when I met this woman . . . I got out that place, say, "Hitch up my pony, saddle
    up my mare . . . there's a woman out there for me somewhere." I looked here.
    Looked there. Saw Rose and latched on to her. I latched on to her and told
    her—I'm gonna tell you the truth—I told her, "Baby, I don't wanna marry, I
    just wanna be your man." Rose told me . . . tell him what you told me, Rose.

ROSE: I told him if he wasn't the marrying kind, then move out the way so the mar-
    rying kind could find me.

TROY: That's what she told me. "Nigger, you in my way. You blocking the view!
    Move out the way so I can find me a husband." I thought it over two or three
    days. Come back—

ROSE: Ain't no two or three days nothing. You was back the same night.

TROY: Come back, told her . . . "Okay, baby . . . but I'm gonna buy me a banty
    rooster and put him out there in the backyard . . . and when he see a stranger
    come, he'll flap his wings and crow . . ." Look here, Bono, I could watch the
    front door by myself . . . it was that back door I was worried about.

ROSE: Troy, you ought not talk like that. Troy ain't doing nothing but telling a lie.   50

TROY: Only thing is . . . when we first got married . . . forget the rooster . . . we ain't
    had no yard!

BONO: I hear you tell it. Me and Lucille was staying down there on Logan Street.
    Had two rooms with the outhouse in the back. I ain't mind the outhouse none.
    But when that goddamn wind blow through there in the winter . . . that's what
    I'm talking about! To this day I wonder why in the hell I ever stayed down
    there for six long years. But see, I didn't know I could do no better. I thought
    only white folks had inside toilets and things.

ROSE: There's a lot of people don't know they can do no better than they doing
    now. That's just something you got to learn. A lot of folks still shop at Bella's.

TROY: Ain't nothing wrong with shopping at Bella's. She got fresh food.

ROSE: I ain't said nothing about if she got fresh food. I'm talking about what she   55
    charge. She charge ten cents more than the A&P.

TROY: The A&P ain't never done nothing for me. I spends my money where I'm
    treated right. I go down to Bella, say, "I need a loaf of bread, I'll pay you Friday."
    She give it to me. What sense that make when I got money to go and spend it
    somewhere else and ignore the person who done right by me? That ain't in the
    Bible.

ROSE: We ain't talking about what's in the Bible. What sense it make to shop there
    when she overcharge?

TROY: You shop where you want to. I'll do my shopping where the people been
    good to me.

ROSE: Well, I don't think it's right for her to overcharge. That's all I was saying.

BONO: Look here . . . I got to get on. Lucille going be raising all kind of hell.   60

TROY: Where you going, nigger? We ain't finished this pint. Come here, finish this
    pint.

BONO: Well, hell, I am . . . if you ever turn the bottle loose.

TROY: *(hands him the bottle)* The only thing I say about the A&P is I'm glad Cory
    got that job down there. Help him take care of his school clothes and things.

Gabe done moved out and things getting tight around here. He got that job . . . He can start to look out for himself.

ROSE: Cory done went and got recruited by a college football team.

65   **TROY:** I told that boy about that football stuff. The white man ain't gonna let him get nowhere with that football. I told him when he first come to me with it. Now you come telling me he done went and got more tied up in it. He ought to go and get recruited in how to fix cars or something where he can make a living.

ROSE: He ain't talking about making no living playing football. It's just something the boys in school do. They gonna send a recruiter by to talk to you. He'll tell you he ain't talking about making no living playing football. It's a honor to be recruited.

TROY: It ain't gonna get him nowhere. Bono'll tell you that.

BONO: If he be like you in the sports . . . he's gonna be all right. Ain't but two men ever played baseball as good as you. That's Babe Ruth[2] and Josh Gibson.[3] Them's the only two men ever hit more home runs than you.

TROY: What it ever get me? Ain't got a pot to piss in or a window to throw it out of.

70   **ROSE:** Times have changed since you was playing baseball, Troy. That was before the war. Times have changed a lot since then.

TROY: How in hell they done changed?

ROSE: They got lots of colored boys playing ball now. Baseball and football.

BONO: You right about that, Rose. Times have changed, Troy. You just come along too early.

TROY: There ought not never have been no time called too early! Now you take that fellow . . . what's that fellow they had playing right field for the Yankees back then? You know who I'm talking about, Bono. Used to play right field for the Yankees.

75   **ROSE:** Selkirk?

TROY: Selkirk! That's it! Man batting .269, understand? .269. What kind of sense that make? I was hitting .432 with thirty-seven home runs! Man batting .269 and playing right field for the Yankees! I saw Josh Gibson's daughter yesterday. She walking around with raggedy shoes on her feet. Now I bet you Selkirk's daughter ain't walking around with raggedy shoes on her feet! I bet you that!

ROSE: They got a lot of colored baseball players now. Jackie Robinson[4] was the first. Folks had to wait for Jackie Robinson.

TROY: I done seen a hundred niggers play baseball better than Jackie Robinson. Hell, I know some teams Jackie Robinson couldn't even make! What you talking about Jackie Robinson. Jackie Robinson wasn't nobody. I'm talking about if

---

[2]*Babe Ruth:* George Herman Ruth (1895–1948), American baseball player. He played for the New York Yankees during the 1910s and 1920s and is remembered for his home-run hitting and flamboyant lifestyle.

[3]*Josh Gibson:* (1911–1947), American baseball player. He played in the Negro Leagues between the 1920s and 1940s and was known as "the Negro Babe Ruth." An unwritten rule against hiring black players kept him out of the major leagues.

[4]*Jackie Robinson:* John Roosevelt Robinson (1919–1972). He became the first African American to play major-league baseball when he was hired by the Brooklyn Dodgers in 1947.

you could play ball then they ought to have let you play. Don't care what color you were. Come telling me I come along too early. If you could play . . . then they ought to have let you play.

Troy takes a long drink from the bottle.

ROSE: You gonna drink yourself to death. You don't need to be drinking like that.

TROY: Death ain't nothing. I done seen him. Done wrassled with him. You can't tell me nothing about death. Death ain't nothing but a fastball on the outside corner. And you know what I'll do to that! Lookee here, Bono . . . am I lying? You get one of them fastballs, about waist high, over the outside corner of the plate where you can get the meat of the bat on it . . . and good god! You can kiss it goodbye. Now, am I lying?

BONO: Naw, you telling the truth there. I seen you do it.

TROY: If I'm lying . . . that 450 feet worth of lying! (*Pause.*) That's all death is to me. A fastball on the outside corner.

ROSE: I don't know why you want to get on talking about death.

TROY: Ain't nothing wrong with talking about death. That's part of life. Everybody gonna die. You gonna die, I'm gonna die. Bono's gonna die. Hell, we all gonna die.

ROSE: But you ain't got to talk about it. I don't like to talk about it.

TROY: You the one brought it up. Me and Bono was talking about baseball . . . you tell me I'm gonna drink myself to death. Ain't that right, Bono? You know I don't drink this but one night out of the week. That's Friday night. I'm gonna drink just enough to where I can handle it. Then I cuts it loose. I leave it alone. So don't you worry about me drinking myself to death. 'Cause I ain't worried about Death. I done seen him. I done wrestled with him.

Look here, Bono . . . I looked up one day and Death was marching straight at me. Like Soldiers on Parade! The Army of Death was marching straight at me. The middle of July, 1941. It got real cold just like it be winter. It seem like Death himself reached out and touched me on the shoulder. He touch me just like I touch you. I got cold as ice and Death standing there grinning at me.

ROSE: Troy, why don't you hush that talk.

TROY: I say . . . what you want, Mr. Death? You be wanting me? You done brought your army to be getting me? I looked him dead in the eye. I wasn't fearing nothing. I was ready to tangle. Just like I'm ready to tangle now. The Bible say be ever vigilant. That's why I don't get but so drunk. I got to keep watch.

ROSE: Troy was right down there in Mercy Hospital. You remember he had pneumonia? Laying there with a fever talking plumb out of his head.

TROY: Death standing there staring at me . . . carrying that sickle in his hand. Finally he say, "You want bound over for another year?" See, just like that . . . "You want bound over for another year?" I told him, "Bound over hell! Let's settle this now!"

It seem like he kinda fell back when I said that, and all the cold went out of me. I reached down and grabbed that sickle and threw it just as far as I could throw it . . . and me and him commenced to wrestling.

We wrestled for three days and three nights. I can't say where I found the strength from. Every time it seemed like he was gonna get the best of me, I'd reach way down deep inside myself and find the strength to do him one better.

ROSE: Every time Troy tell that story he find different ways to tell it. Different things to make up about it.

TROY: I ain't making up nothing. I'm telling you the facts of what happened. I wrestled with Death for three days and three nights and I'm standing here to tell you about it. *(Pause.)* All right. At the end of the third night we done weakened each other to where we can't hardly move. Death stood up, throwed on his robe . . . had him a white robe with a hood on it. He throwed on that robe and went off to look for his sickle. Say, "I'll be back." Just like that. "I'll be back." I told him, say, "Yeah, but . . . you gonna have to find me!" I wasn't no fool. I wan't going looking for him. Death ain't nothing to play with. And I know he's gonna get me. I know I got to join his army . . . his camp followers. But as long as I keep my strength and see him coming . . . . as long as I keep up my vigilance . . . he's gonna have to fight to get me. I ain't going easy.

BONO: Well, look here, since you got to keep up your vigilance . . . let me have the bottle.

TROY: Aw hell, I shouldn't have told you that part. I should have left out that part.

95 ROSE: Troy be talking that stuff and half the time don't even know what he be talking about.

TROY: Bono know me better than that.

BONO: That's right. I know you. I know you got some Uncle Remus[5] in your blood. You got more stories than the devil got sinners.

TROY: Aw hell, I done seen him too! Done talked with the devil.

ROSE: Troy, don't nobody wanna be hearing all that stuff.

Lyons enters the yard from the street. Thirty-four years old, Troy's son by a previous marriage, he sports a neatly trimmed goatee, sport coat, white shirt, tieless and buttoned at the collar. Though he fancies himself a musician, he is more caught up in the rituals and "idea" of being a musician than in the actual practice of the music. He has come to borrow money from Troy, and while he knows he will be successful, he is uncertain as to what extent his lifestyle will be held up to scrutiny and ridicule.

100 LYONS: Hey, Pop.

TROY: What you come "Hey, Popping" me for?

LYONS: How you doing, Rose? *(He kisses her.)* Mr. Bono. How you doing?

BONO: Hey, Lyons . . . how you been?

TROY: He must have been doing all right. I ain't seen him around here last week.

105 ROSE: Troy, leave your boy alone. He come by to see you and you wanna start all that nonsense.

TROY: I ain't bothering Lyons. *(Offers him the bottle.)* Here . . . get you a drink. We got an understanding. I know why he come by to see me and he know I know.

---

[5]*Uncle Remus:* The fictional narrator of *Uncle Remus: His Songs and His Sayings* (1880) and a number of sequels by Joel Chandler Harris. Uncle Remus tells tales about characters such as Brer Rabbit and the Tarbaby in exaggerated dialect, now widely considered to be a derogatory representation of African Americans.

LYONS: Come on, Pop . . . I just stopped by to say hi . . . see how you was doing.

TROY: You ain't stopped by yesterday.

ROSE: You gonna stay for supper, Lyons? I got some chicken cooking in the oven.

LYONS: No, Rose . . . thanks. I was just in the neighborhood and thought I'd stop by   110
for a minute.

TROY: You was in the neighborhood all right, nigger. You telling the truth there.
You was in the neighborhood cause it's my payday.

LYONS: Well, hell, since you mentioned it . . . let me have ten dollars.

TROY: I'll be damned! I'll die and go to hell and play blackjack with the devil before I give you ten dollars.

BONO: That's what I wanna know about . . . that devil you done seen.

LYONS: What . . . Pop done seen the devil? You too much, Pops.   115

TROY: Yeah, I done seen him. Talked to him too!

ROSE: You ain't seen no devil. I done told you that man ain't had nothing to do
with the devil. Anything you can't understand, you want to call it the devil.

TROY: Look here, Bono . . . I went down to see Hertzberger about some furniture.
Got three rooms for two-ninety-eight. That what it say on the radio. "Three
rooms . . . two-ninety-eight." Even made up a little song about it. Go down
there . . . man tell me I can't get no credit. I'm working every day and can't get
no credit. What to do? I got an empty house with some raggedy furniture in
it. Cory ain't got no bed. He's sleeping on a pile of rags on the floor. Working
every day and can't get no credit. Come back here—Rose'll tell you—madder
than hell. Sit down . . . try to figure what I'm gonna do. Come a knock on the
door. Ain't been living here but three days. Who know I'm here? Open the door
. . . devil standing there bigger than life. White fellow . . . white fellow . . . got
on good clothes and everything. Standing there with a clipboard in his hand.
I ain't had to say nothing. First words come out of his mouth was . . . "I understand you need some furniture and can't get no credit." I liked to fell over. He
say, "I'll give you all the credit you want, but you got to pay the interest on it."
I told him, "Give me three rooms worth and charge whatever you want." Next
day a truck pulled up here and two men unloaded them three rooms. Man what
drove the truck give me a book. Say send ten dollars, first of every month to the
address in the book and everything will be all right. Say if I miss a payment the
devil was coming back and it'll be hell to pay. That was fifteen years ago. To
this day . . . the first of the month I send my ten dollars, Rose'll tell you.

ROSE: Troy lying.

TROY: I ain't never seen that man since. Now you tell me who else that could have   120
been but the devil? I ain't sold my soul or nothing like that, you understand.
Naw, I wouldn't have truck with the devil about nothing like that. I got my furniture and pays my ten dollars the first of the month just like clockwork.

BONO: How long you say you been paying this ten dollars a month?

TROY: Fifteen years!

BONO: Hell, ain't you finished paying for it yet? How much the man done charged
you?

TROY: Ah hell, I done paid for it. I done paid for it ten times over! The fact is I'm
scared to stop paying it.

125   **Rose:** Troy lying. We got that furniture from Mr. Glickman. He ain't paying no ten
dollars a month to nobody.

Troy: Aw hell, woman. Bono know I ain't that big a fool.

Lyons: I was just getting ready to say . . . I know where there's a bridge for sale.

Troy: Look here, I'll tell you this . . . it don't matter to me if he was the devil. It
don't matter if the devil give credit. Somebody has got to give it.

Rose: It ought to matter. You going around talking about having truck with the
devil . . . God's the one you gonna have to answer to. He's the one gonna be at
the Judgment.

130   **Lyons:** Yeah, well, look here, Pop . . . let me have that ten dollars. I'll give it back
to you. Bonnie got a job working at the hospital.

Troy: What I tell you, Bono? The only time I see this nigger is when he wants
something. That's the only time I see him.

Lyons: Come on, Pop, Mr. Bono don't want to hear all that. Let me have the ten
dollars. I told you Bonnie working.

Troy: What that mean to me? "Bonnie working." I don't care if she working. Go
ask her for the ten dollars if she working. Talking about "Bonnie working." Why
ain't you working?

Lyons: Aw, Pop, you know I can't find no decent job. Where am I gonna get a job
at? You know I can't get no job.

135   **Troy:** I told you I know some people down there. I can get you on the rubbish if
you want to work. I told you that the last time you came by here asking me for
something.

Lyons: Naw, Pop . . . thanks. That ain't for me. I don't wanna be carrying nobody's
rubbish. I don't wanna be punching nobody's time clock.

Troy: What's the matter, you too good to carry people's rubbish? Where you think
that ten dollars you talking about come from? I'm just supposed to haul people's
rubbish and give my money to you 'cause you too lazy to work. You too lazy to
work and wanna know why you ain't got what I got.

Rose: What hospital Bonnie working at? Mercy?

Lyons: She's down at Passavant working in the laundry.

140   **Troy:** I ain't got nothing as it is. I give you that ten dollars and I got to eat beans
the rest of the week. Naw . . . you ain't getting no ten dollars here.

Lyons: You ain't got to be eating no beans. I don't know why you wanna say
that.

Troy: I ain't got no extra money. Gabe done moved over to Miss Pearl's paying her
the rent and things done got tight around here. I can't afford to be giving you
every payday.

Lyons: I ain't asked you to give me nothing. I asked you to loan me ten dollars. I
know you got ten dollars.

Troy: Yeah, I got it. You know why I got it? 'Cause I don't throw my money away
out there in the streets. You living the fast life . . . wanna be a musician . . . running around in them clubs and things . . . then, you learn to take care of yourself. You ain't gonna find me going and asking nobody for nothing. I done spent
too many years without.

145   **Lyons:** You and me is two different people, Pop.

TROY: I done learned my mistake and learned to do what's right by it. You still trying to get something for nothing. Life don't owe you nothing. You owe it to
yourself. Ask Bono. He'll tell you I'm right.

LYONS: You got your way of dealing with the world . . . I got mine. The only thing
that matters to me is the music.

TROY: Yeah, I can see that! It don't matter how you gonna eat . . . where your next
dollar is coming from. You telling the truth there.

LYONS: I know I got to eat. But I got to live too. I need something that gonna help
me to get out of the bed in the morning. Make me feel like I belong in the
world. I don't bother nobody. I just stay with the music 'cause that's the only
way I can find to live in the world. Otherwise there ain't no telling what I might
do. Now I don't come criticizing you and how you live. I just come by to ask you
for ten dollars. I don't wanna hear all that about how I live.

TROY: Boy, your mama did a hell of a job raising you.   150

LYONS: You can't change me, Pop. I'm thirty-four years old. If you wanted to
change me, you should have been there when I was growing up. I come by to
see you . . . ask for ten dollars and you want to talk about how I was raised. You
don't know nothing about how I was raised.

ROSE: Let the boy have ten dollars, Troy.

TROY: (to Lyons) What the hell you looking at me for? I ain't got no ten dollars.
You know what I do with my money. (To Rose.) Give him ten dollars if you
want him to have it.

ROSE: I will. Just as soon as you turn it loose.

TROY: (handing Rose the money) There it is. Seventy-six dollars and forty-two cents.   155
You see this, Bono? Now, I ain't gonna get but six of that back.

ROSE: You ought to stop telling that lie. Here, Lyons. (She hands him the money.)

LYONS: Thanks, Rose. Look . . . I got to run . . . I'll see you later.

TROY: Wait a minute. You gonna say "thanks, Rose" and ain't gonna look to see
where she got that ten dollars from? See how they do me, Bono?

LYONS: I know she got it from you, Pop. Thanks. I'll give it back to you.

TROY: There he go telling another lie. Time I see that ten dollars . . . he'll be owing   160
me thirty more.

LYONS: See you, Mr. Bono.

BONO: Take care, Lyons!

LYONS: Thanks, Pop. I'll see you again.

Lyons exits the yard.

TROY: I don't know why he don't go and get him a decent job and take care of that
woman he got.

BONO: He'll be all right, Troy. The boy is still young.   165

TROY: The *boy* is thirty-four years old.

ROSE: Let's not get off into all that.

BONO: Look here . . . I got to be going. I got to be getting on. Lucille gonna be
waiting.

TROY: (puts his arm around Rose) See this woman, Bono? I love this woman. I love
this woman so much it hurts. I love her so much . . . I done run out of ways of

loving her. So I got to go back to basics. Don't you come by my house Monday
morning talking about time to go to work . . . 'cause I'm still gonna be stroking!

170   ROSE: Troy! Stop it now!

BONO: I ain't paying him no mind, Rose. That ain't nothing but gin-talk. Go on,
Troy. I'll see you Monday.

TROY: Don't you come by my house, nigger! I done told you what I'm gonna be
doing.

The lights go down to black.

SCENE 2

*The lights come up on Rose hanging up clothes. She hums and sings softly to herself. It is the
following morning.*

ROSE: *(sings)*

> Jesus, be a fence all around me every day
> Jesus, I want you to protect me as I travel on my way.
> Jesus, be a fence all around me every day.

Troy enters from the house.

> Jesus, I want you to protect me
> As I travel on my way.

(To Troy.) 'Morning, You ready for breakfast? I can fix it soon as I finish
hanging up these clothes?

TROY: I got the coffee on. That'll be all right. I'll just drink some of that this
morning.

ROSE: That 651 hit yesterday. That's the second time this month. Miss Pearl hit for
a dollar . . . seem like those that need the least always get lucky. Poor folks can't
get nothing.

TROY: Them numbers don't know nobody. I don't know why you fool with them.
You and Lyons both.

5   ROSE: It's something to do.

TROY: You ain't doing nothing but throwing your money away.

ROSE: Troy, you know I don't play foolishly. I just play a nickel here and a nickel
there.

TROY: That's two nickels you done thrown away.

ROSE: Now I hit sometimes . . . that makes up for it. It always comes in handy when
I do hit. I don't hear you complaining then.

10   TROY: I ain't complaining now. I just say it's foolish. Trying to guess out of six hundred ways which way the number gonna come. If I had all the money niggers,
these Negroes, throw away on numbers for one week—just one week—I'd be a
rich man.

ROSE: Well, you wishing and calling it foolish ain't gonna stop folks from playing
numbers. That's one thing for sure. Besides . . . some good things come from
playing numbers. Look where Pope done bought him that restaurant off of
numbers.

TROY: I can't stand niggers like that. Man ain't had two dimes to rub together. He walking around with his shoes all run over bumming money for cigarettes. All right. Got lucky there and hit the numbers . . .

ROSE: Troy, I know all about it.

TROY: Had good sense, I'll say that for him. He ain't throwing his money away. I seen niggers hit the numbers and go through two thousand dollars in four days. Man bought him that restaurant down there . . . fixed it up real nice . . . and then didn't want nobody to come in it! A Negro go in there and can't get no kind of service. I seen a white fellow come in there and order a bowl of stew. Pope picked all the meat out the pot for him. Man ain't had nothing but a bowl of meat! Negro come behind him and ain't got nothing but the potatoes and carrots. Talking about what numbers do for people, you picked a wrong example. Ain't done nothing but make a worser fool out of him than he was before.

ROSE: Troy, you ought to stop worrying about what happened at work yesterday.   15

TROY: I ain't worried. Just told me to be down there at the Commissioner's office on Friday. Everybody think they gonna fire me. I ain't worried about them firing me. You ain't got to worry about that. (*Pause.*) Where's Cory? Cory in the house? (*Calls.*) Cory?

ROSE: He gone out.

TROY: Out, huh? He gone out 'cause he know I want him to help me with this fence. I know how he is. That boy scared of work.

Gabriel enters. He comes halfway down the alley and, hearing Troy's voice, stops.

TROY: (*continues*) He ain't done a lick of work in his life.

ROSE: He had to go to football practice. Coach wanted them to get in a little extra   20
practice before the season start.

TROY: I got his practice . . . running out of here before he get his chores done.

ROSE: Troy, what is wrong with you this morning? Don't nothing set right with you. Go on back in there and go to bed . . . get up on the other side.

TROY: Why something got to be wrong with me? I ain't said nothing wrong with me.

ROSE: You got something to say about everything. First it's the numbers . . . then it's the way the man runs his restaurant . . . then you done got on Cory. What's it gonna be next? Take a look up there and see if the weather suits you . . . or is it gonna be how you gonna put up the fence with the clothes hanging in the yard.

TROY: You hit the nail on the head then.   25

ROSE: I know you like I know the back of my hand. Go on in there and get you some coffee . . . see if that straighten you up. 'Cause you ain't right this morning.

Troy starts into the house and sees Gabriel. Gabriel starts singing. Troy's brother, he is seven years younger than Troy. Injured in World War II, he has a metal plate in his head. He carries an old trumpet tied around his waist and believes with every fiber of his being that he is the Archangel Gabriel.[1] He carries a chipped basket with an assortment of discarded fruits and vegetables he has picked up in the strip district and which he attempts to sell.

Archangel Gabriel: A messenger of God.

GABRIEL: *(singing)*

> Yes, ma'am, I got plums
> You ask me how I sell them
> Oh ten cents apiece
> Three for a quarter
> Come and buy now
> 'Cause I'm here today
> And tomorrow I'll be gone

Gabriel enters.

Hey, Rose!

ROSE: How you doing, Gabe?

GABRIEL: There's Troy . . . Hey, Troy!

30 TROY: Hey, Gabe.

Exit into kitchen.

ROSE: *(To Gabriel.)* What you got there?

GABRIEL: You know what I got, Rose. I got fruits and vegetables.

ROSE: *(looking in basket)* Where's all these plums you talking about?

GABRIEL: I ain't got no plums today, Rose. I was just singing that. Have some tomorrow. Put me in a big order for plums. Have enough plums tomorrow for St. Peter and everybody.

Troy reenters from kitchen, crosses to steps.

(To Rose.) Troy's mad at me.

35 TROY: I ain't mad at you. What I got to be mad at you about? You ain't done nothing to me.

GABRIEL: I just moved over to Miss Pearl's to keep out from in your way. I ain't mean no harm by it.

TROY: Who said anything about that? I ain't said anything about that.

GABRIEL: You ain't mad at me, is you?

TROY: Naw . . . I ain't mad at you, Gabe. If I was mad at you I'd tell you about it.

40 GABRIEL: Got me two rooms. In the basement. Got my own door too. Wanna see my key? *(He holds up a key.)* That's my own key! Ain't nobody else got a key like that. That's my key! My two rooms!

TROY: Well, that's good, Gabe. You got your own key . . . that's good.

ROSE: You hungry, Gabe? I was just fixing to cook Troy his breakfast.

GABRIEL: I'll take some biscuits. You got some biscuits? Did you know when I was in heaven . . . every morning me and St. Peter[2] would sit down by the gate and eat some big fat biscuits? Oh, yeah! We had us a good time. We'd sit there and eat us them biscuits and then St. Peter would go off to sleep and tell me to wake him up when it's time to open the gates for the judgment.

ROSE: Well, come on . . . I'll make up a batch of biscuits.

Rose exits into the house.

---

[2]*St. Peter:* Disciple of Christ, believed to be the guard at the gates of heaven.

GABRIEL: Troy . . . St. Peter got your name in the book. I seen it. It say . . . Troy   45
Maxson. I say . . . I know him! He got the same name like what I got. That's my
brother!

TROY: How many times you gonna tell me that, Gabe?

GABRIEL: Ain't got my name in the book. Don't have to have my name. I done
died and went to heaven. He got your name though. One morning St. Peter was
looking at his book . . . marking it up for the judgment . . . and he let me see
your name. Got it in there under M. Got Rose's name . . . I ain't seen it like I
seen yours . . . but I know it's in there. He got a great big book. Got everybody's
name what was ever been born. That's what he told me. But I seen your name.
Seen it with my own eyes.

TROY: Go on in the house there. Rose going to fix you something to eat.

GABRIEL: Oh, I ain't hungry. I done had breakfast with Aunt Jemima. She come
by and cooked me up a whole mess of flapjacks. Remember how we used to eat
them flapjacks?

TROY: Go on in the house and get you something to eat now.   50

GABRIEL: I got to sell my plums. I done sold some tomatoes. Got me two quarters.
Wanna see? (*He shows Troy his quarters.*) I'm gonna save them and buy me a
new horn so St. Peter can hear me when it's time to open the gates. (*Gabriel
stops suddenly. Listens.*) Hear that? That's the hellhounds. I got to chase them
out of here. Go on get out of here! Get out!

Gabriel exits singing.

> Better get ready for the Judgment
> Better get ready for the Judgment
> My Lord is coming down

Rose enters from the house.

TROY: He's gone off somewhere.

GABRIEL: (*offstage*)

> Better get ready for the Judgment
> Better get ready for the Judgment morning
> Better get ready for the Judgment
> My God is coming down

ROSE: He ain't eating right. Miss Pearl say she can't get him to eat nothing.

TROY: What you want me to do about it, Rose? I done did everything I can for the   55
man. I can't make him get well. Man got half his head blown away . . . what you
expect?

ROSE: Seem like something ought to be done to help him.

TROY: Man don't bother nobody. He just mixed up from that metal plate he got in
his head. Ain't no sense for him to go back into the hospital.

ROSE: Least he be eating right. They can help him take care of himself.

TROY: Don't nobody wanna be locked up, Rose. What you wanna lock him up for?
Man go over there and fight the war . . . messin' around with them Japs, get half
his head blown off . . . and they give him a lousy three thousand dollars. And I
had to swoop down on that.

60   ROSE: Is you fixing to go into that again?

TROY: That's the only way I got a roof over my head . . . 'cause of that metal plate.

ROSE: Ain't no sense you blaming yourself for nothing. Gabe wasn't in no condition to manage that money. You done what was right by him. Can't nobody say you ain't done what was right by him. Look how long you took care of him . . . till he wanted to have his own place and moved over there with Miss Pearl.

TROY: That ain't what I'm saying, woman! I'm just stating the facts. If my brother didn't have that metal plate in his head . . . I wouldn't have a pot to piss in or a window to throw it out of. And I'm fifty-three years old. Now see if you can understand that!

Troy gets up from the porch and starts to exit the yard.

ROSE: Where you going off to? You been running out of here every Saturday for weeks. I thought you was gonna work on this fence?

65   TROY: I'm gonna walk down to Taylors'. Listen to the ball game. I'll be back in a bit. I'll work on it when I get back.

He exits the yard. The lights go to black.

SCENE 3

The lights come up on the yard. It is four hours later. Rose is taking down the clothes from the line. Cory enters carrying his football equipment.

ROSE: Your daddy like to had a fit with you running out of here this morning without doing your chores.

CORY: I told you I had to go to practice.

ROSE: He say you were supposed to help him with this fence.

CORY: He been saying that the last four or five Saturdays, and then he don't never do nothing, but go down to Taylors'. Did you tell him about the recruiter?

5   ROSE: Yeah, I told him.

CORY: What he say?

ROSE: He ain't said nothing too much. You get in there and get started on your chores before he gets back. Go on and scrub down them steps before he gets back here hollering and carrying on.

CORY: I'm hungry. What you got to eat, Mama?

ROSE: Go on and get started on your chores. I got some meat loaf in there. Go on and make you a sandwich . . . and don't leave no mess in there.

Cory exits into the house. Rose continues to take down the clothes. Troy enters the yard and sneaks up and grabs her from behind.

Troy! Go on, now. You liked to scared me to death. What was the score of the game? Lucille had me on the phone and I couldn't keep up with it.

10   TROY: What I care about the game? Come here, woman. *(He tries to kiss her.)*

ROSE: I thought you went down Taylors' to listen to the game. Go on, Troy! You supposed to be putting up this fence.

TROY: *(attempting to kiss her again)* I'll put it up when I finish with what is at hand.

ROSE: Go on, Troy. I ain't studying you.

TROY: *(chasing after her)* I'm studying you . . . fixing to do my homework!

ROSE: Troy, you better leave me alone.

TROY: Where's Cory? That boy brought his butt home yet?

ROSE: He's in the house doing his chores.

TROY: *(calling)* Cory! Get your butt out here, boy!

Rose exits into the house with the laundry. Troy goes over to the pile of wood, picks up a board, and starts sawing. Cory enters from the house.

TROY: You just now coming in here from leaving this morning?

CORY: Yeah, I had to go to football practice.

TROY: Yeah, what?

CORY: Yessir.

TROY: I ain't but two seconds off you noway. The garbage sitting in there overflowing . . . you ain't done none of your chores . . . and you come in here talking about "Yeah."

CORY: I was just getting ready to do my chores now, Pop . . .

TROY: Your first chore is to help me with this fence on Saturday. Everything else come after that. Now get that saw and cut them boards.

Cory takes the saw and begins cutting the boards. Troy continues working. There is a long pause.

CORY: Hey, Pop . . . why don't you buy a TV?

TROY: What I want with a TV? What I want one of them for?

CORY: Everybody got one. Earl, Ba Bra . . . Jesse!

TROY: I ain't asked you who had one. I say what I want with one?

CORY: So you can watch it. They got lots of things on TV. Baseball games and everything. We could watch the World Series.

TROY: Yeah . . . and how much this TV cost?

CORY: I don't know. They got them on sale for around two hundred dollars.

TROY: Two hundred dollars, huh?

CORY: That ain't that much, Pop.

TROY: Naw, it's just two hundred dollars. See that roof you got over your head at night? Let me tell you something about that roof. It's been over ten years since that roof was last tarred. See now . . . the snow comes this winter and sit up there on that roof like it is . . . and it's gonna seep inside. It's just gonna be a little bit . . . ain't gonna hardly notice it. Then the next thing you know, it's gonna be leaking all over the house. Then the wood rot from all that water and you gonna need a whole new roof. Now, how much you think it cost to get that roof tarred?

CORY: I don't know.

TROY: Two hundred and sixty-four dollars . . . cash money. While you thinking about a TV, I got to be thinking about the roof . . . and whatever else go wrong here. Now if you had two hundred dollars, what would you do . . . fix the roof or buy a TV?

CORY: I'd buy a TV. Then when the roof started to leak . . . when it needed fixing . . . I'd fix it.

TROY: Where you gonna get the money from? You done spent it for a TV. You gonna sit up and watch the water run all over your brand new TV.

40 CORY: Aw, Pop. You got money. I know you do.

TROY: Where I got it at, huh?

CORY: You got it in the bank.

TROY: You wanna see my bankbook? You wanna see that seventy-three dollars and twenty-two cents I got sitting up in there?

CORY: You ain't got to pay for it all at one time. You can put a down payment on it and carry it on home with you.

45 TROY: Not me. I ain't gonna owe nobody nothing if I can help it. Miss a payment and they come and snatch it right out your house. Then what you got? Now, soon as I get two hundred dollars clear, then I'll buy a TV. Right now, as soon as I get two hundred and sixty-four dollars, I'm gonna have this roof tarred.

CORY: Aw . . . Pop!

TROY: You go on and get you two hundred and buy one if ya want it. I got better things to do with my money.

CORY: I can't get no two hundred dollars. I ain't never seen two hundred dollars.

TROY: I'll tell you what . . . you get you a hundred dollars and I'll put the other hundred with it.

50 CORY: All right, I'm gonna show you.

TROY: You gonna show me how you can cut them boards right now.

Cory begins to cut the boards. There is a long pause.

CORY: The Pirates won today. That makes five in a row.

TROY: I ain't thinking about the Pirates. Got an all-white team. Got that boy . . . that Puerto Rican boy . . . Clemente.[1] Don't even half-play him. That boy could be something if they give him a chance. Play him one day and sit him on the bench the next.

CORY: He gets a lot of chances to play.

55 TROY: I'm talking about playing regular. Playing every day so you can get your timing. That's what I'm talking about.

CORY: They got some white guys on the team that don't play every day. You can't play everybody at the same time.

TROY: If they got a white fellow sitting on the bench . . . you can bet your last dollar he can't play! The colored guy got to be twice as good before he get on the team. That's why I don't want you to get all tied up in them sports. Man on the team and what it get him? They got colored on the team and don't use them. Same as not having them. All them teams the same.

---

[1]*Clemente:* Roberto Clemente (1934–1972), Major League baseball player for the Pittsburg Pirates, known as much for his humanitarianism as his unique batting style and ability. Clemente received the Most Valuable Player Award in 1966 and died in a plane crash in 1972 while shuttling supplies to Nicaraguan earthquake victims.

CORY: The Braves got Hank Aaron[2] and Wes Covington.[3] Hank Aaron hit two home runs today. That makes forty-three.

TROY: Hank Aaron ain't nobody. That what you supposed to do. That's how you supposed to play the game. Ain't nothing to it. It's just a matter of timing . . . getting the right follow-through. Hell, I can hit forty-three home runs right now!

CORY: Not off no major-league pitching, you couldn't.   60

TROY: We had better pitching in the Negro leagues. I hit seven home runs off of Satchel Paige.[4] You can't get no better than that!

CORY: Sandy Koufax.[5] He's leading the league in strikeouts.

TROY: I ain't thinking of no Sandy Koufax.

CORY: You got Warren Spahn[6] and Lew Burdette.[7] I bet you couldn't hit no home runs off of Warren Spahn.

TROY: I'm through with it now. You go on and cut them boards. (*Pause.*) Your   65
mama tell me you done got recruited by a college football team? Is that right?

CORY: Yeah. Coach Zellman say the recruiter gonna be coming by to talk to you. Get you to sign the permission papers.

TROY: I thought you supposed to be working down there at the A&P. Ain't you suppose to be working down there after school?

CORY: Mr. Stawicki say he gonna hold my job for me until after the football season. Say starting next week I can work weekends.

TROY: I thought we had an understanding about this football stuff? You suppose to keep up with your chores and hold that job down at the A&P. Ain't been around here all day on a Saturday. Ain't none of your chores done . . . and now you telling me you done quit your job.

CORY: I'm going to be working weekends.   70

TROY: You damn right you are! And ain't no need for nobody coming around here to talk to me about signing nothing.

---

[2]*Hank Aaron:* Henry Aaron (1934–   ), American baseball player who broke Babe Ruth's career home run record with a lifetime total of 755 home runs. The holder of 12 other Major League records, Aaron spent his Major League career with the Braves, first in Milwaukee and later in their hometown of Atlanta.

[3]*Wes Covington:* John Wesley Covington (1932–   ), American baseball player known for his ability to frustrate pitchers by wasting time at the plate. In an eleven-year career, Covington played for six Major League teams, beginning with the Milwaukee Braves and retiring with the Los Angeles Dodgers in 1966.

[4]*Satchel Page:* Leroy Robert Paige (1906–1982), American baseball player. He played in the Negro Leagues from the 1920s until 1948, when he joined the Cleveland Indians; he reportedly pitched 55 no-hit games during his career. Joe DiMaggio called him "the best pitcher I have ever faced."

[5]*Sandy Koufax:* Sanford Koufax (1935–   ), left-handed pitcher who won 129 games and lost only 47 for the Los Angeles Dodgers in the six seasons between 1961 and 1966; he won three Cy Young Awards and pitched four no-hit games, the last of which (1965) was a perfect game.

[6]*Warren Spahn:* (1921–2003), left-handed pitcher who at the time of his retirement in 1966 held the National League record of 363 wins; he won 20 or more games in four consecutive seasons (1947–1950) and in several other seasons during the 1950s.

[7]*Lew Burdette:* Selva Lewis Burdette (1926–2007), American baseball player who pitched and won three games for the Milwaukee Braves against the New York Yankees in the 1957 World Series; for that Series, his ERA was an amazingly low .067.

CORY: Hey, Pop . . . you can't do that. He's coming all the way from North Carolina.

TROY: I don't care where he coming from. The white man ain't gonna let you get nowhere with that football noway. You go on and get your book-learning so you can work yourself up in that A&P or learn how to fix cars or build houses or something, get you a trade. That way you have something can't nobody take away from you. You go on and learn how to put your hands to some good use. Besides hauling people's garbage.

CORY: I get good grades, Pop. That's why the recruiter wants to talk with you. You got to keep up your grades to get recruited. This way I'll be going to college. I'll get a chance . . .

75   TROY: First you gonna get your butt down there to the A&P and get your job back.

CORY: Mr. Stawicki done already hired somebody else 'cause I told him I was playing football.

TROY: You a bigger fool than I thought . . . to let somebody take away your job so you can play some football. Where you gonna get your money to take out your girlfriend and whatnot? What kind of foolishness is that to let somebody take away your job?

CORY: I'm still gonna be working weekends.

TROY: Naw . . . naw. You getting your butt out of here and finding you another job.

80   CORY: Come on, Pop! I got to practice. I can't work after school and play football too. The team needs me. That's what Coach Zellman say . . .

TROY: I don't care what nobody else say. I'm the boss . . . you understand? I'm the boss around here. I do the only saying what counts.

CORY: Come on, Pop!

TROY: I asked you . . . did you understand?

CORY: Yeah . . .

85   TROY: What?!

CORY: Yessir.

TROY: You go on down there to that A&P and see if you can get your job back. If you can't do both . . . then you quit the football team. You've got to take the crookeds with the straights.

CORY: Yessir. (*Pause.*) Can I ask you a question?

TROY: What the hell you wanna ask me? Mr. Stawicki the one you got the questions for.

90   CORY: How come you ain't never liked me?

TROY: Liked you? Who the hell say I got to like you? What law is there say I got to like you? Wanna stand up in my face and ask a damn fool-ass question like that. Talking about liking somebody. Come here, boy, when I talk to you.

Cory comes over to where Troy is working. He stands slouched over and Troy shoves him on his shoulder.

Straighten up, goddammit! I asked you a question . . . what law is there say I got to like you?

CORY: None.

TROY: Well, all right then! Don't you eat every day? (*Pause.*) Answer me when I talk to you! Don't you eat every day?

CORY: Yeah.

TROY: Nigger, as long as you in my house, you put that sir on the end of it when   95
you talk to me!

CORY: Yes . . . sir.

TROY: You eat every day.

CORY: Yessir!

TROY: Got a roof over your head.

CORY: Yessir!   100

TROY: Got clothes on your back.

CORY: Yessir.

TROY: Why you think that is?

CORY: 'Cause of you.

TROY: Ah, hell I know it's 'cause of me . . . but why do you think that is?   105

CORY: (hesitant) 'Cause you like me.

TROY: Like you? I go out of here every morning . . . bust my butt . . . putting up
with them crackers[8] every day . . . 'cause I like you? You are the biggest fool I
ever saw. (Pause.) It's my job. It's my responsibility! You understand that? A
man got to take care of his family. You live in my house . . . sleep you behind on
my bedclothes . . . fill you belly up with my food . . . 'cause you my son. You my
flesh and blood. Not 'cause I like you! 'Cause it's my duty to take care of you.
I owe a responsibility to you! Let's get this straight right here . . . before it go
along any further . . . I ain't got to like you. Mr. Rand don't give me my money
come payday cause he likes me. He give me 'cause he owe me. I done give you
everything I had to give you. I gave you your life! Me and your mama worked
that out between us. And liking your black ass wasn't part of the bargain. Don't
you try and go through life worrying about if somebody like you or not. You best
be making sure they doing right by you. You understand what I'm saying, boy?

CORY: Yessir.

TROY: Then get the hell out of my face, and get on down to that A&P.

Rose has been standing behind the screen door for much of the scene. She enters as Cory exits.

ROSE: Why don't you let the boy go ahead and play football, Troy? Ain't no harm   110
in that. He's just trying to be like you with the sports.

TROY: I don't want him to be like me! I want him to move as far away from my life
as he can get. You the only decent thing that ever happened to me. I wish him
that. But I don't wish him a thing else from my life. I decided seventeen years
ago that boy wasn't getting involved in no sports. Not after what they did to me
in the sports.

ROSE: Troy, why don't you admit you was too old to play in the major leagues? For
once . . . why don't you admit that?

TROY: What do you mean too old? Don't come telling me I was too old. I just
wasn't the right color. Hell, I'm fifty-three years old and can do better than
Selkirk's .269 right now!

---

[8]*crackers:* Derogatory term for white people, generally poor southern whites.

ROSE: How's was you gonna play ball when you were over forty? Sometimes I can't go no sense out of you.

115 TROY: I got good sense, woman. I got sense enough not to let my boy get hurt over playing no sports. You been mothering that boy too much. Worried about if people like him.

ROSE: Everything that boy do . . . he do for you. He wants you to say "Good job, son." That's all.

TROY: Rose, I ain't got time for that. He's alive. He's healthy. He's got to make his own way. I made mine. Ain't nobody gonna hold his hand when he get out there in that world.

ROSE: Times have changed from when you was young, Troy. People change. The world's changing around you and you can't even see it.

TROY: (slow, methodical) Woman . . . I do the best I can do. I come in here every Friday. I carry a sack of potatoes and a bucket of lard. You all line up at the door with your hands out. I give you the lint from my pockets. I give you my sweat and my blood. I ain't got no tears. I done spent them. We go upstairs in that room at night . . . and I fall down on you and try to blast a hole into forever. I get up Monday morning . . . find my lunch on the table. I go out. Make my way. Find my strength to carry me through to the next Friday. (Pause.) That's all I got, Rose. That's all I got to give. I can't give nothing else.

Troy exits into the house. The lights go down to black.

SCENE 4

It is Friday. Two weeks later. Cory starts out of the house with his football equipment. The phone rings.

CORY: (calling) I got it! (He answers the phone and stands in the screen door talking.) Hello? Hey, Jesse. Naw . . . I was just getting ready to leave now.

ROSE: (calling) Cory!

CORY: I told you, man, them spikes[1] is all tore up. You can use them if you want, but they ain't no good. Earl got some spikes.

ROSE: (calling) Cory!

5 CORY: (calling to Rose) Mam? I'm talking to Jesse. (Into phone.) When she say that? (Pause.) Aw, you lying, man. I'm gonna tell her you said that.

ROSE: (calling) Cory, don't you go nowhere!

CORY: I got to go to the game, Ma! (Into the phone.) Yeah, hey, look, I'll talk to you later. Yeah, I'll meet you over Earl's house. Later. Bye, Ma.

Cory exits the house and starts out the yard.

ROSE: Cory, where you going off to? You got that stuff all pulled out and thrown all over your room.

CORY: (in the yard) I was looking for my spikes. Jesse wanted to borrow my spikes.

10 ROSE: Get up there and get that cleaned up before your daddy get back in here.

---

[1]*spikes:* Athletic shoes with sharp metal grips set into the soles.

CORY: I got to go to the game! I'll clean it up *when I get back.*

Cory exits.

ROSE: That's all he need to do is see that room all messed up.

Rose exits into the house. Troy and Bono enter the yard. Troy is dressed in clothes other than his work clothes.

BONO: He told him the same thing he told you. Take it to the union.

TROY: Brownie ain't got that much sense. Man wasn't thinking about nothing. He wait until I confront them on it . . . then he wanna come crying seniority. *(Calls.)* Hey, Rose!

BONO: I wish I could have seen Mr. Rand's face when he told you.   15

TROY: He couldn't get it out of his mouth! Liked to bit his tongue! When they called me down there to the Commissioner's office . . . he thought they was gonna fire me. Like everybody else.

BONO: I didn't think they was gonna fire you. I thought they was gonna put you on the warning paper.

TROY: Hey, Rose! *(To Bono.)* Yeah, Mr. Rand like to bit his tongue.

Troy breaks the seal on the bottle, takes a drink, and hands it to Bono.

BONO: I see you run right down to Taylors' and told that Alberta gal.

TROY: *(calling)* Hey, Rose! *(To Bono.)* I told everybody. Hey, Rose! I went down   20
there to cash my check.

ROSE: *(entering from the house)* Hush all that hollering, man! I know you out here. What they say down there at the Commissioner's office?

TROY: You supposed to come when I call you, woman. Bono'll tell you that. *(To Bono.)* Don't Lucille come when you call her?

ROSE: Man, hush your mouth, I ain't no dog . . . talk about "come when you call me."

TROY: *(puts his arm around Rose)* You hear this, Bono? I had me an old dog used to get uppity like that. You say, "C'mere, Blue!" . . . and he just lay there and look at you. End up getting a stick and chasing him away trying to make him come.

ROSE: I ain't studying you and your dog. I remember you used to sing that old song.   25

TROY: *(he sings)*

Hear it ring! Hear it ring!
I had a dog his name was Blue.

ROSE: Don't nobody wanna hear you sing that old song.

TROY: *(sings)*

You know Blue was mighty true.

ROSE: Used to have Cory running around here singing that song.

BONO: Hell, I remember that song myself.   30

TROY: *(sings)*

You know Blue was a good old dog.
Blue treed a possum in a hollow log.

That was my daddy's song. My daddy made up that song.

ROSE: I don't care who made it up. Don't nobody wanna hear you sing it.

TROY: *(makes a song like calling a dog)* Come here, woman.

ROSE: You come in here carrying on, I reckon they ain't fired you. What they say down there at the Commissioner's office?

35   **TROY:** Look here, Rose . . . Mr. Rand called me into his office today when I got back from talking to them people down there . . . it come from up top . . . he called me in and told me they was making me a driver.

ROSE: Troy, you kidding!

TROY: No I ain't. Ask Bono.

ROSE: Well, that's great, Troy. Now you don't have to hassle them people no more.

Lyons enters from the street.

TROY: Aw hell, I wasn't looking to see you today. I thought you was in jail. Got it all over the front page of the *Courier* about them raiding Sefus's place . . . where you be hanging out with all them thugs.

40   **LYONS:** Hey, Pop . . . that ain't got nothing to do with me. I don't go down there gambling. I go down there to sit in with the band. I ain't got nothing to do with the gambling part. They got some good music down there.

TROY: They got some rogues . . . is what they got.

LYONS: How you been, Mr. Bono? Hi, Rose.

BONO: I see where you playing down at the Crawford Grill tonight.

ROSE: How come you ain't brought Bonnie like I told you? You should have brought Bonnie with you, she ain't been over in a month of Sundays.

45   **LYONS:** I was just in the neighborhood . . . thought I'd stop by.

TROY: Here he come . . .

BONO: Your daddy got a promotion on the rubbish. He's gonna be the first colored driver. Ain't got to do nothing but sit up there and read the paper like them white fellows.

LYONS: Hey, Pop . . . if you knew how to read you'd be all right.

BONO: Naw . . . naw . . . you mean if the nigger knew how to *drive* he'd be all right. Been fighting with them people about driving and ain't even got a license. Mr. Rand know you ain't got no driver's license?

50   **TROY:** Driving ain't nothing. All you do is point the truck where you want it to go. Driving ain't nothing.

BONO: Do Mr. Rand know you ain't got no driver's license? That's what I'm talking about. I ain't asked if driving was easy. I asked if Mr. Rand know you ain't got no driver's license.

TROY: He ain't got to know. The man ain't got to know my business. Time he find out, I have two or three driver's licenses.

LYONS: *(going into his pocket)* Say, look here, Pop . . .

TROY: I knew it was coming. Didn't I tell you, Bono? I know what kind of "Look here, Pop" that was. The nigger fixing to ask me for some money. It's Friday night. It's my payday. All them rogues down there on the avenue . . . the ones that ain't in jail . . . and Lyons is hopping in his shoes to get down there with them.

LYONS: See, Pop . . . if you give somebody else a chance to talk sometimes, you'd see   55
that I was fixing to pay you back your ten dollars like I told you. Here . . . I told
you I'd pay you when Bonnie got paid.

TROY: Naw . . . you go ahead and keep that ten dollars. Put it in the bank. The next
time you feel like you wanna come by here and ask me for something . . . you go
on down there and get that.

LYONS: Here's your ten dollars, Pop. I told you I don't want you to give me nothing.
I just wanted to borrow ten dollars.

TROY: Naw . . . you go on and keep that for the next time you want to ask me.

LYONS: Come on, Pop . . . here go your ten dollars.

ROSE: Why don't you go on and let the boy pay you back, Troy?   60

LYONS: Here you go, Rose. If you don't take it I'm gonna have to hear about it for
the next six months. (*He hands her the money.*)

ROSE: You can hand yours over here too, Troy.

TROY: You see this, Bono. You see how they do me.

BONO: Yeah, Lucille do me the same way.

Gabriel is heard singing offstage. He enters.

GABRIEL: Better get ready for the Judgment! Better get ready for . . . Hey! . . . Hey!   65
. . . There's Troy's boy!

LYONS: How are you doing, Uncle Gabe?

GABRIEL: Lyons . . . The King of the Jungle! Rose . . . hey, Rose. Got a flower for
you. (*He takes a rose from his pocket.*) Picked it myself. That's the same rose like
you is!

ROSE: That's right nice of you, Gabe.

LYONS: What you been doing, Uncle Gabe?

GABRIEL: Oh, I been chasing hellhounds and waiting on the time to tell St. Peter to   70
open the gates.

LYONS: You been chasing hellhounds, huh? Well . . . you doing the right thing,
Uncle Gabe. Somebody got to chase them.

GABRIEL: Oh, yeah . . . I know it. The devil's strong. The devil ain't no pushover.
Hellhounds snipping at everybody's heels. But I got my trumpet waiting on the
judgment time.

LYONS: Waiting on the Battle of Armageddon, huh?

GABRIEL: Ain't gonna be too much of a battle when God get to waving that Judgment sword. But the people's gonna have a hell of a time trying to get into
heaven if them gates ain't open.

LYONS: (*putting his arm around Gabriel*) You hear this, Pop. Uncle Gabe, you all   75
right!

GABRIEL: (*laughing with Lyons*) Lyons! King of the Jungle.

ROSE: You gonna stay for supper, Gabe? Want me to fix you a plate?

GABRIEL: I'll take a sandwich, Rose. Don't want no plate. Just wanna eat with my
hands. I'll take a sandwich.

ROSE: How about you, Lyons? You staying? Got some short ribs cooking.

LYONS: Naw, I won't eat nothing till after we finished playing. (*Pause.*) You ought   80
to come down and listen to me play, Pop.

TROY: I don't like that Chinese music. All that noise.

ROSE: Go on in the house and wash up, Gabe . . . I'll fix you a sandwich.

GABRIEL: *(to Lyons, as he exits)* Troy's mad at me.

LYONS: What you mad at Uncle Gabe for, Pop?

85 ROSE: He thinks Troy's mad at him cause he moved over to Miss Pearl's.

TROY: I ain't mad at the man. He can live where he want to live at.

LYONS: What he move over there for? Miss Pearl don't like nobody.

ROSE: She don't mind him none. She treats him real nice. She just don't allow all that singing.

TROY: She don't mind that rent he be paying . . . that's what she don't mind.

90 ROSE: Troy, I ain't going through that with you no more. He's over there cause he want to have his own place. He can come and go as he please.

TROY: Hell, he could come and go as he please here. I wasn't stopping him. I ain't put no rules on him.

ROSE: It ain't the same thing, Troy. And you know it.

Gabriel comes to the door.

Now, that's the last I wanna hear about that. I don't wanna hear nothing else about Gabe and Miss Pearl. And next week . . .

GABRIEL: I'm ready for my sandwich, Rose.

ROSE: And next week . . . when that recruiter come from that school . . . I want you to sign that paper and go on and let Cory play football. Then that'll be the last I have to hear about that.

95 TROY: *(to Rose as she exits into the house)* I ain't thinking about Cory nothing.

LYONS: What . . . Cory got recruited? What school he going to?

TROY: That boy walking around here smelling his piss . . . thinking he's grown. Thinking he's gonna do what he want, irrespective of what I say. Look here, Bono . . . I left the Commissioner's office and went down to the A&P . . . that boy ain't working down there. He lying to me. Telling me he got his job back . . . telling me he working weekends . . . telling me he working after school . . . Mr. Stawicki tell me he ain't working down there at all!

LYONS: Cory just growing up. He's just busting at the seams trying to fill out your shoes.

TROY: I don't care what he's doing. When he get to the point where he wanna disobey me . . . then it's time for him to move on. Bono'll tell you that. I bet he ain't never disobeyed his daddy without paying the consequences.

100 BONO: I ain't never had a chance. My daddy came on through . . . but I ain't never knew him to see him . . . or what he had on his mind or where he went. Just moving on through. Searching out the New Land. That's what the old folks used to call it. See a fellow moving around from place to place . . . woman to woman . . . called it searching out the New Land. Can't say if he ever found it. I come along, didn't want no kids. Didn't know if I was gonna be in one place long enough to fix on them right as their daddy. I figured I was going searching too. As it turned out I been hooked up with Lucille near about as long as your daddy been with Rose. Going on sixteen years.

TROY: Sometimes I wish I hadn't known my daddy. He ain't cared nothing about no kids. A kid to him wasn't nothing. All he wanted was for you to learn how to walk so he could start you to working. When it come time for eating . . . he ate first. If there was anything left over, that's what you got. Man would sit down and eat two chickens and give you the wing.

LYONS: You ought to stop that, Pop. Everybody feed their kids. No matter how hard times is . . . everybody care about their kids. Make sure they have something to eat.

TROY: The only thing my daddy cared about was getting them bales of cotton in to Mr. Lubin. That's the only thing that mattered to him. Sometimes I used to wonder why he was living. Wonder why the devil hadn't come and got him. "Get them bales of cotton in to Mr. Lubin" and find out he owe him money . . .

LYONS: He should have just went on and left when he saw he couldn't get nowhere. That's what I would have done.

TROY: How he gonna leave with eleven kids? And where he gonna go? He ain't knew how to do nothing but farm. No, he was trapped and I think he knew it. But I'll say this for him . . . he felt a responsibility toward us. Maybe he ain't treated us the way I felt he should have . . . but without that responsibility he could have walked off and left us . . . made his own way.

BONO: A lot of them did. Back in those days what you talking about . . . they walk out their front door and just take on down one road or another and keep on walking.

LYONS: There you go? That's what I'm talking about.

BONO: Just keep on walking till you come to something else. Ain't you never heard of nobody having the walking blues? Well, that's what you call it when you just take off like that.

TROY: My daddy ain't had them walking blues! What you talking about? He stayed right there with his family. But he was just as evil as he could be. My mama couldn't stand him. Couldn't stand that evilness. She run off when I was about eight. She sneaked off one night after he had gone to sleep. Told me she was coming back for me. I ain't never seen her no more. All his women run off and left him. He wasn't good for nobody.

When my turn come to head out, I was fourteen and got to sniffing around Joe Canewell's daughter. Had us an old mule we called Greyboy. My daddy sent me out to do some plowing and tied up Greyboy and went to fooling around with Joe Canewell's daughter. We done found us a nice little spot, got real cozy with each other. She about thirteen and we done figured we was grown anyway . . . so we down there enjoying ourselves . . . ain't thinking about nothing. We didn't know Greyboy had got loose and wandered back to the house and my daddy was looking for me. We down there by the creek enjoying ourselves when my daddy come up on us. Surprised us. He had them leather straps off the mule and commenced to whupping me like there was no tomorrow. I jumped up, mad and embarrassed. I was scared of my daddy. When he commenced to whupping on me . . . quite naturally I run to get out of the way. (*Pause.*) Now I thought he was mad 'cause I ain't done my work. But I see where he was chasing me off so he could have that gal for himself. When I see what the matter of it was, I lost

105

all fear of my daddy. Right there is where I become a man . . . at fourteen years of age. *(Pause.)* Now it was my turn to run him off. I picked up them same reins that he had used on me. I picked up them reins and commenced to whupping on him. The gal jumped up and run off . . . and when my daddy turned to face me, I could see why the devil had never come to get him . . . cause he was the devil himself. I don't know what happened. When I woke up, I was laying right there by the creek, and Blue . . . this old dog we had . . . was licking my face. I thought I was blind. I couldn't see nothing. Both my eyes were swollen shut. I laid there and cried. I didn't know what I was gonna do. The only thing I knew was the time had come for me to leave my daddy's house. And right there the world suddenly got big. And it was a long time before I could cut it down to where I could handle it.

Part of that cutting down was when I got to the place where I could feel him kicking in my blood and knew that the only thing that separated us was the matter of a few years.

Gabriel enters from the house with a sandwich.

110   Lyons: What you got there, Uncle Gabe?

Gabriel: Got me a ham sandwich. Rose gave me a ham sandwich.

Troy: I don't know what happened to him. I done lost touch with everybody except Gabriel. But I hope he's dead. I hope he found some peace.

Lyons: That's a heavy story, Pop. I didn't know you left home when you was fourteen.

Troy: And didn't know nothing. The only part of the world I knew was the forty-two acres of Mr. Lubin's land. That's all I knew about life.

115   Lyons: Fourteen's kinda young to be out on your own. *(Phone rings.)* I don't even think I was ready to be out on my own at fourteen. I don't know what I would have done.

Troy: I got up from the creek and walked on down to Mobile.[2] I was through with farming. Figured I could do better in the city. So I walked the two hundred miles to Mobile.

Lyons: Wait a minute . . . you ain't walked no two hundred miles, Pop. Ain't nobody gonna walk no two hundred miles. You talking about some walking there.

Bono: That's the only way you got anywhere back in them days.

Lyons: Shhh. Damn if I wouldn't have hitched a ride with somebody!

120   Troy: Who you gonna hitch it with? They ain't got no cars and things like they got now. We talking about 1918.

Rose: *(entering)* What you all out here getting into?

Troy: *(to Rose)* I'm telling Lyons how good he got it. He don't know nothing about this I'm talking.

Rose: Lyons, that was Bonnie on the phone. She say you supposed to pick her up.

Lyons: Yeah, okay, Rose.

---

[2] *Mobile:* City and seaport in southwestern Alabama.

TROY: I walked on down to Mobile and hitched up with some of them fellows that   125
was heading this way. Got up here and found out . . . not only couldn't you get
a job . . . you couldn't find no place to live. I thought I was in freedom. Shhh.
Colored folks living down there on the riverbanks in whatever kind of shelter
they could find for themselves. Right down there under the Brady Street Bridge.
Living in shacks made of sticks and tarpaper. Messed around there and went
from bad to worse. Started stealing. First it was food. Then I figured, hell, if I
steal money I can buy me some food. Buy me some shoes too! One thing led to
another. Met your mama. I was young and anxious to be a man. Met your mama
and had you. What I do that for? Now I got to worry about feeding you and
her. Got to steal three times as much. Went out one day looking for somebody
to rob . . . that's what I was, a robber. I'll tell you the truth. I'm ashamed of it
today. But it's the truth. Went to rob this fellow . . . pulled out my knife . . . and
he pulled out a gun. Shot me in the chest. I felt just like somebody had taken a
hot branding iron and laid it on me. When he shot me I jumped at him with my
knife. They told me I killed him and they put me in the penitentiary and locked
me up for fifteen years. That's where I met Bono. That's where I learned how
to play baseball. Got out that place and your mama had taken you and went
on to make life without me. Fifteen years was a long time for her to wait. But
that fifteen years cured me of that robbing stuff. Rose'll tell you. She asked me
when I met her if I had gotten all that foolishness out of my system. And I told
her, "Baby, it's you and baseball all what count with me." You hear me, Bono? I
meant it too. She say, "Which one comes first?" I told her, "Baby, ain't no doubt
it's baseball . . . but you stick and get old with me and we'll both outlive this
baseball." Am I right, Rose? And it's true.

ROSE: Man, hush your mouth. You ain't said no such thing. Talking about "Baby,
you know you'll always be number one with me." That's what you was talking.

TROY: You hear that, Bono. That's why I love her.

BONO: Rose'll keep you straight. You get off the track, she'll straighten you up.

ROSE: Lyons, you better get on up and get Bonnie. She waiting on you.

LYONS: *(gets up to go)* Hey, Pop, why don't you come on down to the Grill and hear   130
me play.

TROY: I ain't going down there. I'm too old to be sitting around in them clubs.

BONO: You got to be good to play down at the Grill.

LYONS: Come on, Pop . . .

TROY: I got to get up in the morning.

LYONS: You ain't got to stay long.   135

TROY: Naw, I'm gonna get my supper and go on to bed.

LYONS: Well, I got to go. I'll see you again.

TROY: Don't you come around my house on my payday.

ROSE: Pick up the phone and let somebody know you coming. And bring Bonnie
with you. You know I'm always glad to see her.

LYONS: Yeah, I'll do that, Rose. You take care now. See you, Pop. See you, Mr.   140
Bono. See you, Uncle Gabe.

GABRIEL: Lyons! King of the Jungle!

Lyons exits.

Troy: Is supper ready, woman? Me and you got some business to take care of. I'm
    gonna tear it up too.

Rose: Troy, I done told you now!

Troy: (*puts his arm around Bono*) Aw hell, woman . . . this is Bono. Bono like fam-
    ily. I done known this nigger since . . . how long I done know you?

145 **Bono:** It's been a long time.

Troy: I done know this nigger since Skippy was a pup. Me and him done been
    through some times.

Bono: You sure right about that.

Troy: Hell, I done know him longer than I known you. And we still standing
    shoulder to shoulder. Hey, look here, Bono . . . a man can't ask for no more
    than that. (*Drinks to him.*) I love you, nigger.

Bono: Hell, I love you too . . . I got to get home see my woman. You got yours in
    hand. I got to go get mine.

*Bono starts to exit as Cory enters the yard, dressed in his football uniform. He gives Troy a
hard, uncompromising look.*

150 **Cory:** What you do that for, Pop?

He throws his helmet down in the direction of Troy.

Rose: What's the matter? Cory . . . what's the matter?

Cory: Papa done went up to the school and told Coach Zellman I can't play foot-
    ball no more. Wouldn't even let me play the game. Told him to tell the re-
    cruiter not to come.

Rose: Troy . . .

Troy: What you Troying me for. Yeah, I did it. And the boy know why I did it.

155 **Cory:** Why you wanna do that to me? That was the one chance I had.

Rose: Ain't nothing wrong with Cory playing football, Troy.

Troy: The boy lied to me. I told the nigger if he wanna play football . . . to keep
    up his chores and hold down that job at the A&P. That was the conditions.
    Stopped down there to see Mr. Stawicki . . .

Cory: I can't work after school during the football season, Pop! I tried to tell you
    that Mr. Stawicki's holding my job for me. You don't never want to listen to
    nobody. And then you wanna go and do this to me!

Troy: I ain't done nothing to you. You done it to yourself.

160 **Cory:** Just cause you didn't have a chance! You just scared I'm gonna be better
    than you, that's all.

Troy: Come here.

Rose: Troy . . .

Cory reluctantly crosses over to Troy.

Troy: All right! See. You done made a mistake.

Cory: I didn't even do nothing!

165 **Troy:** I'm gonna tell you what your mistake was. See . . . you swung at the ball and
    didn't hit it. That's strike one. See, you in the batter's box now. You swung and
    you missed. That's strike one. Don't you strike out!

Lights fade to black.

ACT 2

SCENE 1

The following morning. Cory is at the tree hitting the ball with the bat. He tries to mimic Troy, but his swing is awkward, less sure. Rose enters from the house.

ROSE: Cory, I want you to help me with this cupboard.

CORY: I ain't quitting the team. I don't care what Poppa say.

ROSE: I'll talk to him when he gets back. He had to go see about your Uncle Gabe. The police done arrested him. Say he was disturbing the peace. He'll be back directly. Come on in here and help me clean out the top of this cupboard.

Cory exits into the house. Rose sees Troy and Bono coming down the alley.

Troy . . . what they say down there?

TROY: Ain't said nothing. I give them fifty dollars and they let him go. I'll talk to you about it. Where's Cory?

ROSE: He's in there helping me clean out these cupboards.   5

TROY: Tell him to get his butt out here.

Troy and Bono go over to the pile of wood. Bono picks up the saw and begins sawing.

TROY: *(to Bono)* All they want is the money. That makes six or seven times I done went down there and got him. See me coming they stick out their *hands*.

BONO: Yeah. I know what you mean. That's all they care about . . . that money. They don't care about what's right. *(Pause.)* Nigger, why you got to go and get some hard wood? You ain't doing nothing but building a little old fence. Get you some soft pine wood. That's all you need.

TROY: I know what I'm doing. This is outside wood. You put pine wood inside the house. Pine wood is inside wood. This here is outside wood. Now you tell me where the fence is gonna be?

BONO: You don't need this wood. You can put it up with pine wood and it'll stand   10
as long as you gonna be here looking at it.

TROY: How you know how long I'm gonna be here, nigger? Hell, I might just live forever. Live longer than old man Horsely.

BONO: That's what Magee used to say.

TROY: Magee's a damn fool. Now you tell me who you ever heard of gonna pull their own teeth with a pair of rusty pliers.

BONO: The old folks . . . my granddaddy used to pull his teeth with pliers. They ain't had no dentists for the colored folks back then.

TROY: Get clean pliers! You understand? Clean pliers! Sterilize them! Besides we   15
ain't living back then. All Magee had to do was walk over to Doc Goldblum's.

BONO: I see where you and that Tallahassee gal . . . that Alberta . . . I see where you all done got tight.

TROY: What you mean "got tight"?

BONO: I see where you be laughing and joking with her all the time.

TROY: I laughs and jokes with all of them, Bono. You know me.

BONO: That ain't the kind of laughing and joking I'm talking about.   20

Cory enters from the house.

CORY: How you doing, Mr. Bono?

TROY: Cory? Get that saw from Bono and cut some wood. He talking about the wood's too hard to cut. Stand back there, Jim, and let that young boy show you how it's done.

BONO: He's sure welcome to it.

Cory takes the saw and begins to cut the wood.

Whew-e-e! Look at that. Big old strong boy. Look like Joe Louis.[1] Hell, must be getting old the way I'm watching that boy whip through that wood.

CORY: I don't see why Mama want a fence around the yard noways.

25   TROY: Damn if I know either. What the hell she keeping out with it? She ain't got nothing nobody want.

BONO: Some people build fences to keep people out . . . and other people build fences to keep people in. Rose wants to hold on to you all. She loves you.

TROY: Hell, nigger, I don't need nobody to tell me my wife loves me. Cory . . . go on in the house and see if you can find that other saw.

CORY: Where's it at?

TROY: I said find it! Look for it till you find it!

Cory exits into the house.

What's that supposed to mean? Wanna keep us in?

30   BONO: Troy . . . I done known you seem like damn near my whole life. You and Rose both. I done know both of you all for a long time. I remember when you met Rose. When you was hitting them baseballs out the park. A lot of them gals was after you then. You had the pick of the litter. When you picked Rose, I was happy for you. That was the first time I knew you had any sense. I said . . . My man Troy knows what he's doing . . . I'm gonna follow this nigger . . . he might take me somewhere. I been following you too. I done learned a whole heap of things about life watching you. I done learned how to tell where the shit lies. How to tell it from the alfalfa. You done learned me a lot of things. You showed me how to not make the same mistakes . . . to take life as it comes along and keep putting one foot in front of the other. *(Pause.)* Rose a good woman, Troy.

TROY: Hell, nigger, I know she a good woman. I been married to her for eighteen years. What you got on your mind, Bono?

BONO: I just say she a good woman. Just like I say anything. I ain't got to have nothing on your mind.

TROY: You just gonna say she a good woman and leave it hanging out there like that? Why you telling me she a good woman?

BONO: She loves you, Troy. Rose loves you.

35   TROY: You saying I don't measure up. That's what you trying to say. I don't measure up 'cause I'm seeing this other gal. I know what you trying to say.

---

[1]*Joe Louis:* Joseph Louis Barrow (1914–1981), American boxer known as the "Brown Bomber." In 1937, he became the youngest boxer ever to win the Heavyweight Championship, which he defended twenty-five times; he retired undefeated in 1949.

BONO: I know what Rose means to you, Troy. I'm just trying to say I don't want to see you mess up.

TROY: Yeah, I appreciate that, Bono. If you was messing around on Lucille I'd be telling you the same thing.

BONO: Well, that's all I got to say. I just say that because I love you both.

TROY: Hell, you know me . . . I wasn't out there looking for nothing. You can't find a better woman than Rose. I know that. But seems like this woman just stuck onto me where I can't shake her loose. I done wrestled with it, tried to throw her off me . . . but she just stuck on tighter. Now she's stuck on for good.

BONO: You's in control . . . that's what you tell me all the time. You responsible for   40
what you do.

TROY: I ain't ducking the responsibility of it. As long as it sets right in my heart . . . then I'm okay. 'Cause that's all I listen to. It'll tell me right from wrong every time. And I ain't talking about doing Rose no bad turn. I love Rose. She done carried me a long ways and I love and respect her for that.

BONO: I know you do. That's why I don't want to see you hurt her. But what you gonna do when she find out? What you got then? If you try and juggle both of them . . . sooner or later you gonna drop one of them. That's common sense.

TROY: Yeah, I hear what you saying, Bono. I been trying to figure a way to work it out.

BONO: Work it out right, Troy. I don't want to be getting all up between you and Rose's business . . . but work it so it come out right.

TROY: Ah hell, I get all up between you and Lucille's business. When you gonna get   45
that woman that refrigerator she been wanting? Don't tell me you ain't got no money now. I know who your banker is. Mellon don't need that money bad as Lucille want that refrigerator. I'll tell you that.

BONO: Tell you what I'll do . . . when you finish building this fence for Rose . . . I'll buy Lucille that refrigerator.

TROY: You done stuck your foot in your mouth now!

Troy grabs up a board and begins to saw. Bono starts to walk out the yard.

Hey, nigger . . . where you going?

BONO: I'm going home. I know you don't expect me to help you now. I'm protecting my money. I wanna see you put that fence up by yourself. That's what I want to see. You'll be here another six months without me.

TROY: Nigger, you ain't right.

BONO: When it comes to my money . . . I'm right as fireworks on the Fourth of July.   50

TROY: All right, we gonna see now. You better get out your bankbook.

Bono exits, and Troy continues to work. Rose enters from the house.

ROSE: What they say down there? What's happening with Gabe?

TROY: I went down there and got him out. Cost me fifty dollars. Say he was disturbing the peace. Judge set up a hearing for him in three weeks. Say to show cause why he shouldn't be recommitted.

ROSE: What was he doing that cause them to arrest him?

TROY: Some kids were teasing him and he run them off home. Say he was howling   55
and carrying on. Some folks seen him and called the police. That's all it was.

ROSE: Well, what's you say? What'd you tell the judge?

TROY: Told him I'd look after him. It didn't make no sense to recommit the man. He stuck out his big greasy palm and told me to give him fifty dollars and take him on home.

ROSE: Where's he at now? Where'd he go off to?

TROY: He's gone about his business. He don't need nobody to hold his hand.

60 ROSE: Well, I don't know. Seem like that would be the best place for him if they did put him into the hospital. I know what you're gonna say. But that's what I think would be best.

TROY: The man done had his life ruined fighting for what? And they wanna take and lock him up. Let him be free. He don't bother nobody.

ROSE: Well, everybody got their own way of looking at it I guess. Come on and get your lunch. I got a bowl of lima beans and some cornbread in the oven. Come and get something to eat. Ain't no sense you fretting over Gabe.

Rose turns to go into the house.

TROY: Rose . . . got something to tell you.

ROSE: Well, come on . . . wait till I get this food on the table.

65 TROY: Rose!

She stops and turns around.

I don't know how to say this. (*Pause.*) I can't explain it none. It just sort of grows on you till it gets out of hand. It starts out like a little bush . . . and the next thing you know it's a whole forest.

ROSE: Troy . . . what is you talking about?

TROY: I'm talking, woman, let me talk. I'm trying to find a way to tell you . . . I'm gonna be a daddy. I'm gonna be somebody's daddy.

ROSE: Troy . . . you're not telling me this? You're gonna be . . . what?

TROY: Rose . . . now . . . see . . .

70 ROSE: You telling me you gonna be somebody's daddy? You telling your *wife* this?

Gabriel enters from the street. He carries a rose in his hand.

GABRIEL: Hey, Troy! Hey, Rose!

ROSE: I have to wait eighteen years to hear something like this.

GABRIEL: Hey, Rose . . . I got a flower for you. (*He hands it to her.*) That's a rose. Same rose like you is.

ROSE: Thanks, Gabe.

75 GABRIEL: Troy, you ain't mad at me is you? Them bad mens come and put me away. You ain't mad at me is you?

TROY: Naw, Gabe, I ain't mad at you.

ROSE: Eighteen years and you wanna come with this.

GABRIEL: (*takes a quarter out of his pocket*) See what I got? Got a brand new quarter.

TROY: Rose . . . it's just . . .

80 ROSE: Ain't nothing you can say, Troy. Ain't no way of explaining that.

GABRIEL: Fellow that give me this quarter had a whole mess of them. I'm gonna keep this quarter till it stop shining.

ROSE: Gabe, go on in the house there. I got some watermelon in the Frigidaire. Go on and get you a piece.

GABRIEL: Say, Rose . . . you know I was chasing hellhounds and them bad mens come and get me and take me away. Troy helped me. He come down there and told them they better let me go before he beat them up. Yeah, he did!

ROSE: You go on and get you a piece of watermelon, Gabe. Them bad mens is gone now.

GABRIEL: Okay, Rose . . . gonna get me some watermelon. The kind with the stripes   65
on it.

Gabriel exits into the house.

ROSE: Why, Troy? Why? After all these years to come dragging this in to me now. It don't make no sense at your age. I could have expected this ten or fifteen years ago, but not now.

TROY: Age ain't got nothing to do with it, Rose.

ROSE: I done tried to be everything a wife should be. Everything a wife could be. Been married eighteen years and I got to live to see the day you tell me you been seeing another woman and done fathered a child by her. And you know I ain't never wanted no half nothing in my family. My whole family is half. Everybody got different fathers and mothers . . . my two sisters and my brother. Can't hardly tell who's who. Can't never sit down and talk about Papa and Mama. It's your papa and your mama and my papa and my mama . . .

TROY: Rose . . . stop it now.

ROSE: I ain't never wanted that for none of my children. And now you wanna drag   90
your behind in here and tell me something like this.

TROY: You ought to know. It's time for you to know.

ROSE: Well, I don't want to know, goddamn it!

TROY: I can't just make it go away. It's done now. I can't wish the circumstance of the thing away.

ROSE: And you don't want to either. Maybe you want to wish me and my boy away. Maybe that's what you want? Well, you can't wish us away. I've got eighteen years of my life invested in you. You ought to have stayed upstairs in my bed where you belong.

TROY: Rose . . . now listen to me . . . we can get a handle on this thing. We can talk   95
this out . . . come to an understanding.

ROSE: All of a sudden it's "we." Where was "we" at when you was down there rolling around with some godforsaken woman? "We" should have come to an understanding before you started making a damn fool of yourself. You're a day late and a dollar short when it comes to an understanding with me.

TROY: It's just . . . She gives me a different idea . . . a different understanding about myself. I can step out of this house and get away from the pressures and problems . . . be a different man. I ain't got to wonder how I'm gonna pay the bills or get the roof fixed. I can just be a part of myself that I ain't never been.

ROSE: What I want to know . . . is do you plan to continue seeing her. That's all you can say to me.

TROY: I can sit up in her house and laugh. Do you understand what I'm saying. I can laugh out loud . . . and it feels good. It reaches all the way down to the bottom of my shoes. (*Pause.*) Rose, I can't give that up.

100 **ROSE:** Maybe you ought to go on and stay down there with her . . . if she's a better woman than me.

TROY: It ain't about nobody being a better woman or nothing. Rose, you ain't the blame. A man couldn't ask for no woman to be a better wife than you've been. I'm responsible for it. I done locked myself into a pattern trying to take care of you all that I forgot about myself.

ROSE: What the hell was I there for? That was my job, not somebody else's.

TROY: Rose, I done tried all my life to live decent . . . to live a clean . . . hard . . . useful life. I tried to be a good husband to you. In every way I knew how. Maybe I come into the world backwards, I don't know. But . . . you born with two strikes on you before you come to the plate. You got to guard it closely . . . always looking for the curve ball on the inside corner. You can't afford to let none get past you. You can't afford a call strike. If you going down . . . you going down swinging. Everything lined up against you. What you gonna do. I fooled them, Rose. I bunted. When I found you and Cory and a halfway decent job . . . I was safe. Couldn't nothing touch me. I wasn't gonna strike out no more. I wasn't going back to the penitentiary. I wasn't gonna lay in the streets with a bottle of wine. I was safe. I had me a family. A job. I wasn't gonna get that last strike. I was on first looking for one of them boys to knock me in. To get me home.

ROSE: You should have stayed in my bed, Troy.

105 **TROY:** Then when I saw that gal . . . she firmed up my backbone. And I got to thinking that if I tried . . . I just might be able to steal second. Do you understand after eighteen years I wanted to steal second.

ROSE: You should have held me tight. You should have grabbed me and held on.

TROY: I stood on first base for eighteen years and I thought . . . well, goddamn it . . . go on for it!

ROSE: We're not talking about baseball! We're talking about you going off to lay in bed with another woman . . . and then bring it home to me. That's what we're talking about. We ain't talking about no baseball.

TROY: Rose, you're not listening to me. I'm trying the best I can to explain it to you. It's not easy for me to admit that I been standing in the same place for eighteen years.

110 **ROSE:** I been standing with you! I been right here with you, Troy. I got a life too. I gave eighteen years of my life to stand in the same spot with you. Don't you think I ever wanted other things? Don't you think I had dreams and hopes? What about my life? What about me. Don't you think it ever crossed my mind to want to know other men? That I wanted to lay up somewhere and forget about my responsibilities? That I wanted someone to make me laugh so I could feel good? You not the only one who's got wants and needs. But I held on to you, Troy. I took all my feelings, my wants and needs, my dreams . . . and I buried them inside you. I planted a seed and watched and prayed over it. I planted myself inside you and waited to bloom. And it didn't take me no eighteen years to find out the soil was hard and rocky and it wasn't never gonna bloom.

But I held on to you, Troy. I held you tighter. You was my husband. I owed you everything I had. Every part of me I could find to give you. And upstairs in that room . . . with the darkness falling in on me . . . I gave everything I had to try and erase the doubt that you wasn't the finest man in the world. And wherever you was going . . . I wanted to be there with you. 'Cause you was my husband. 'Cause that's the only way I was gonna survive as your wife. You always talking about what you give . . . and what you don't have to give. But you take too. You take . . . and don't even know nobody's giving!

Rose turns to exit into the house; Troy grabs her arm.

TROY: You say I take and don't give!
ROSE: Troy! You're hurting me!
TROY: You say I take and don't give!
ROSE: Troy . . . you're hurting my arm! Let go!
TROY: I done give you everything I got. Don't you tell that lie on me.   115
ROSE: Troy!
TROY: Don't you tell that lie on me!

Cory enters from the house.

CORY: Mama!
ROSE: Troy. You're hurting me.
TROY: Don't you tell me about no taking and giving.   120

Cory comes up behind Troy and grabs him. Troy, surprised, is thrown off balance just as Cory throws a glancing blow that catches him on the chest and knocks him down. Troy is stunned, as is Cory.

ROSE: Troy. Troy. No!

Troy gets to his feet and starts at Cory.

   Troy . . . no. Please! Troy!

Rose pulls on Troy to hold him back. Troy stops himself.

TROY: *(to Cory)* All right. That's strike two. You stay away from around me, boy. Don't you strike out. You living with a full count. Don't you strike out.

Troy exits out the yard as the lights go down.

SCENE 2

It is six months later, early afternoon. Troy enters from the house and starts to exit the yard. Rose enters from the house.

ROSE: Troy, I want to talk to you.
TROY: All of a sudden, after all this time, you want to talk to me, huh? You ain't wanted to talk to me for months. You ain't wanted to talk to me last night. You ain't wanted no part of me then. What you wanna talk to me about now?
ROSE: Tomorrow's Friday.   5

TROY: I know what day tomorrow is. You think I don't know tomorrow's Friday?
My whole life I ain't done nothing but look to see Friday coming and you got to
tell me it's Friday.

ROSE: I want to know if you're coming home.

TROY: I always come home, Rose. You know that. There ain't never been a night I
ain't come home.

ROSE: That ain't what I mean . . . and you know it. I want to know if you're coming
straight home after work.

10   TROY: I figure I'd cash my check . . . hang out at Taylors' with the boys . . . maybe
play a game of checkers . . .

ROSE: Troy, I can't live like this. I won't live like this. You livin' on borrowed time
with me. It's been going on six months now you ain't been coming home.

TROY: I be here every Friday. Every night of the year. That's 365 days.

ROSE: I want you to come home tomorrow after work.

TROY: Rose . . . I don't mess up my pay. You know that now. I take my pay and I
give it to you. I don't have no money but what you give me back. I just want to
have a little time to myself . . . a little time to enjoy life.

15   ROSE: What about me? When's my time to enjoy life?

TROY: I don't know what to tell you, Rose. I'm doing the best I can.

ROSE: You ain't been home from work but time enough to change your clothes and
run out . . . and you wanna call that the best you can do?

TROY: I'm going over to the hospital to see Alberta. She went into the hospital this
afternoon. Look like she might have the baby early. I won't be gone long.

ROSE: Well, you ought to know. They went over to Miss Pearl's and got Gabe today. She said you told them to go ahead and lock him up.

20   TROY: I ain't said no such thing. Whoever told you that is telling a lie. Pearl ain't
doing nothing but telling a big fat lie.

ROSE: She ain't had to tell me. I read it on the papers.

TROY: I ain't told them nothing of the kind.

ROSE: I saw it right there on the papers.

TROY: What it say, huh?

25   ROSE: It said you told them to take him.

TROY: Then they screwed that up, just the way they screw up everything. I ain't
worried about what they got on the paper.

ROSE: Say the government send part of his check to the hospital and the other part
to you.

TROY: I ain't got nothing to do with that if that's the way it works. I ain't made up
the rules about how it work.

ROSE: You did Gabe just like you did Cory. You wouldn't sign the paper for Cory . . .
but you signed for Gabe. You signed that paper.

The telephone is heard ringing inside the house.

30   TROY: I told you I ain't signed nothing, woman! The only thing I signed was the release form. Hell, I can't read. I don't know what they had on that paper! I ain't
signed nothing about sending Gabe away.

ROSE: I said send him to the hospital . . . you said let him be free . . . now you done went down there and signed him to the hospital for half his money. You went back on yourself, Troy. You gonna have to answer for that.

TROY: See now . . . you been over there talking to Miss Pearl. She done got mad cause she ain't getting Gabe's rent money. That's all it is. She's liable to say anything.

ROSE: Troy, I seen where you signed the paper.

TROY: You ain't seen nothing I signed. What she doing got papers on my brother anyway? Miss Pearl telling a big fat lie. And I'm gonna tell her about it too! You ain't seen nothing I signed. Say . . . you ain't seen nothing I signed.

Rose exits into the house to answer the telephone. Presently she returns.

ROSE: Troy . . . that was the hospital. Alberta had the baby.   35

TROY: What she have? What is it?

ROSE: It's a girl.

TROY: I better get on down to the hospital to see her.

ROSE: Troy . . .

TROY: Rose . . . I got to go see her now. That's only right . . . what's the matter . . .   40
the baby's all right, ain't it?

ROSE: Alberta died having the baby.

TROY: Died . . . you say she's dead? Alberta's dead?

ROSE: They said they done all they could. They couldn't do nothing for her.

TROY: The baby? How's the baby?

ROSE: They say it's healthy. I wonder who's gonna bury her.   45

TROY: She had family, Rose. She wasn't living in the world by herself.

ROSE: I know she wasn't living in the world by herself.

TROY: Next thing you gonna want to know if she had any insurance.

ROSE: Troy, you ain't got to talk like that.

TROY: That's the first thing that jumped out your mouth. "Who's gonna bury her?"   50
Like I'm fixing to take on that task for myself.

ROSE: I am your wife. Don't push me away.

TROY: I ain't pushing nobody away. Just give me some space. That's all. Just give me some room to breathe.

Rose exits into the house. Troy walks about the yard.

TROY: (*with a quiet rage that threatens to consume him*) All right . . . Mr. Death. See now . . . I'm gonna tell you what I'm gonna do. I'm gonna take and build me a fence around this yard. See? I'm gonna build me a fence around what belongs to me. And then I want you to stay on the other side. See? You stay over there until you're ready for me. Then you come on. Bring your army. Bring your sickle. Bring your wrestling clothes. I ain't gonna fall down on my vigilance this time. You ain't gonna sneak up on me no more. When you ready for me . . . when the top of your list say Troy Maxson . . . that's when you come around here. You come up and knock on the front door. Ain't nobody else got nothing to do with this. This is between you and me. Man to man. You stay on the other side of the fence until you ready for me. Then you come up and knock on the front door. Anytime you want. I'll be ready for you.

The lights go down to black.

SCENE 3

The lights come up on the porch. It is late evening three days later. Rose sits listening to the ball game waiting for Troy. The final out of the game is made and Rose switches off the radio. Troy enters the yard carrying an infant wrapped in blankets. He stands back from the house and calls.

Rose enters and stands on the porch. There is a long, awkward silence, the weight of which grows heavier with each passing second.

TROY: Rose . . . I'm standing here with my daughter in my arms. She ain't but a wee bittie little old thing. She don't know nothing about grownups' business. She innocent . . . and she ain't got no mama.

ROSE: What you telling me for, Troy?

She turns and exits into the house.

TROY: Well . . . I guess we'll just sit out here on the porch.

He sits down on the porch. There is an awkward indelicateness about the way he handles the baby. His largeness engulfs and seems to swallow it. He speaks loud enough for Rose to hear.

A man's got to do what's right for him. I ain't sorry for nothing I done. It felt right in my heart. (*To the baby.*) What you smiling at? Your daddy's a big man. Got these great big old hands. But sometimes he's scared. And right now your daddy's scared 'cause we sitting out here and ain't got no home. Oh, I been homeless before. I ain't had no little baby with me. But I been homeless. You just be out on the road by your lonesome and you see one of them trains coming and you just kinda go like this . . .

He sings a lullaby.

> Please, Mr. Engineer let a man ride the line
> Please, Mr. Engineer let a man ride the line
> I ain't got no ticket please let me ride the blinds

Rose enters from the house. Troy, hearing her steps behind him, stands and faces her.

She's my daughter, Rose. My own flesh and blood. I can't deny her no more than I can deny them boys. (*Pause.*) You and them boys is my family. You and them and this child is all I got in the world. So I guess what I'm saying is . . . I'd appreciate it if you'd help me take care of her.

ROSE: Okay, Troy . . . you're right. I'll take care of your baby for you . . . 'cause . . . like you say . . . she's innocent . . . and you can't visit the sins of the father upon the child. A motherless child has got a hard time. (*She takes the baby from him.*) From right now . . . this child got a mother. But you a womanless man.

Rose turns and exits into the house with the baby. Lights go down to black.

SCENE 4

It is two months later. Lyons enters from the street. He knocks on the door and calls.

LYONS: Hey, Rose! (*Pause.*) Rose!

ROSE: (*from inside the house*) Stop that yelling. You gonna wake up Raynell. I just got her to sleep.

LYONS: I just stopped by to pay Papa this twenty dollars I owe him. Where's Papa at?

ROSE: He should be here in a minute. I'm getting ready to go down to the church. Sit down and wait on him.

LYONS: I got to go pick up Bonnie over her mother's house.   5

ROSE: Well, sit it down there on the table. He'll get it.

LYONS: (*enters the house and sets the money on the table*) Tell Papa I said thanks. I'll see you again.

ROSE: All right, Lyons. We'll see you.

Lyons starts to exit as Cory enters.

CORY: Hey, Lyons.

LYONS: What's happening, Cory? Say man, I'm sorry I missed your graduation. You   10
know I had a gig and couldn't get away. Otherwise, I would have been there, man. So what you doing?

CORY: I'm trying to find a job.

LYONS: Yeah I know how that go, man. It's rough out there. Jobs are scarce.

CORY: Yeah, I know.

LYONS: Look here, I got to run. Talk to Papa . . . he know some people. He'll be able to help get you a job. Talk to him . . . see what he say.

CORY: Yeah . . . all right, Lyons.   15

LYONS: You take care. I'll talk to you soon. We'll find some time to talk.

Lyons exits the yard. Cory wanders over to the tree, picks up the bat, and assumes a batting stance. He studies an imaginary pitcher and swings. Dissatisfied with the result, he tries again. Troy enters. They eye each other for a beat. Cory puts the bat down and exits the yard. Troy starts into the house as Rose exits with Raynell. She is carrying a cake.

TROY: I'm coming in and everybody's going out.

ROSE: I'm taking this cake down to the church for the bake sale. Lyons was by to see you. He stopped by to pay you your twenty dollars. It's laying in there on the table.

TROY: (*going into his pocket*) Well . . . here go this money.

ROSE: Put it in there on the table, Troy. I'll get it.   20

TROY: What time you coming back?

ROSE: Ain't no use in you studying me. It don't matter what time I come back.

TROY: I just asked you a question, woman. What's the matter . . . can't I ask you a question?

ROSE: Troy, I don't want to go into it. Your dinner's in there on the stove. All you got to do is heat it up. And don't you be eating the rest of them cakes in there. I'm coming back for them. We having a bake sale at the church tomorrow.

Rose exits the yard. Troy sits down on the steps, takes a pint bottle from his pocket, opens it, and drinks. He begins to sing.

25 TROY:

> Hear it ring! Hear it ring!
> Had an old dog his name was Blue
> You know Blue was mighty true
> You know Blue was a good old dog
> Blue treed a possum in a hollow log
> You know from that he was a good old dog

Bono enters the yard.

BONO: Hey, Troy.

TROY: Hey, what's happening, Bono?

BONO: I just thought I'd stop by to see you.

TROY: What you stop by and see me for? You ain't stopped by in a month of Sundays. Hell, I must owe you money or something.

30 BONO: Since you got your promotion I can't keep up with you. Used to see you every day. Now I don't even know what route you working.

TROY: They keep switching me around. Got me out in Greentree now . . . hauling white folks' garbage.

BONO: Greentree, huh? You lucky, at least you ain't got to be lifting them barrels. Damn if they ain't getting heavier. I'm gonna put in my two years and call it quits.

TROY: I'm thinking about retiring myself.

BONO: You got it easy. You can *drive* for another five years.

35 TROY: It ain't the same, Bono. It ain't like working the back of the truck. Ain't got nobody to talk to . . . feel like you working by yourself. Naw, I'm thinking about retiring. How's Lucille?

BONO: She all right. Her arthritis get to acting up on her sometime. Saw Rose on my way in. She going down to the church, huh?

TROY: Yeah, she took up going down there. All them preachers looking for somebody to fatten their pockets. *(Pause.)* Got some gin here.

BONO: Naw, thanks. I just stopped by to say hello.

TROY: Hell, nigger . . . you can take a drink. I ain't never known you to say no to a drink. You ain't got to work tomorrow.

40 BONO: I just stopped by. I'm fixing to go over to Skinner's. We got us a domino game going over his house every Friday.

TROY: Nigger, you can't play no dominoes. I used to whup you four games out of five.

BONO: Well, that learned me. I'm getting better.

TROY: Yeah? Well, that's all right.

BONO: Look here . . . I got to be getting on. Stop by sometime, huh?

45 TROY: Yeah, I'll do that, Bono. Lucille told Rose you bought her a new refrigerator.

BONO: Yeah, Rose told Lucille you had finally built your fence . . . so I figured we'd call it even.

TROY: I knew you would.

BONO: Yeah . . . okay. I'll be talking to you.
TROY: Yeah, take care, Bono. Good to see you. I'm gonna stop over.
BONO: Yeah. Okay, Troy.   50

Bono exits. Troy drinks from the bottle.

TROY:

> Old Blue died and I dig his grave
> Let him down with a golden chain
> Every night when I hear old Blue bark
> I know Blue treed a possum in Noah's Ark.
> Hear it ring! Hear it ring!

Cory enters the yard. They eye each other for a beat. Troy is sitting in the middle of the steps. Cory walks over.

CORY: I got to get by.
TROY: Say what? What's you say?
CORY: You in my way. I got to get by.
TROY: You got to get by where? This is my house. Bought and paid for. In full. Took   55
  me fifteen years. And if you wanna go in my house and I'm sitting on the steps . . .
  you say excuse me. Like your mama taught you.
CORY: Come on, Pop . . . I got to get by.

Cory starts to maneuver his way past Troy. Troy grabs his leg and shoves him back.

TROY: You just gonna walk over top of me?
CORY: I live here too!
TROY: *(advancing toward him)* You just gonna walk over top of me in my own house?
CORY: I ain't scared of you.   60
TROY: I ain't asked if you was scared of me. I asked you if you was fixing to walk
  over top of me in my own house? That's the question. You ain't gonna say ex-
  cuse me? You just gonna walk over top of me?
CORY: If you wanna put it like that.
TROY: How else am I gonna put it?
CORY: I was walking by you to go into the house 'cause you sitting on the steps
  drunk, singing to yourself. You can put it like that.
TROY: Without saying excuse me???   65

Cory doesn't respond.

  I asked you a question. Without saying excuse me???
CORY: I ain't got to say excuse me to you. You don't count around here no more.
TROY: Oh, I see . . . I don't count around here no more. You ain't got to say excuse
  me to your daddy. All of a sudden you done got so grown that your daddy don't
  count around here no more . . . Around here in his own house and yard that he
  done paid for with the sweat of his brow. You done got so grown to where you
  gonna take over. You gonna take over my house. Is that right? You gonna wear
  my pants. You gonna go in there and stretch out on my bed. You ain't got to say
  excuse me 'cause I don't count around here no more. Is that right?

CORY: That's right. You always talking this dumb stuff. Now, why don't you just get out my way?

TROY: I guess you got someplace to sleep and something to put in your belly. You got that, huh? You got that? That's what you need. You got that, huh?

70 CORY: You don't know what I got. You ain't got to worry about what I got.

TROY: You right! You one hundred percent right! I done spent the last seventeen years worrying about what you got. Now it's your turn, see? I'll tell you what to do. You grown . . . we done established that. You a man. Now, let's see you act like one. Turn your behind around and walk out this yard. And when you get out there in the alley . . . you can forget about this house. See? 'Cause this is my house. You go on and be a man and get your own house. You can forget about this. 'Cause this is mine. You go on and get yours 'cause I'm through with doing for you.

CORY: You talking about what you did for me . . . what'd you ever give me?

TROY: Them feet and bones! That pumping heart, nigger! I give you more than anybody else is ever gonna give you.

CORY: You ain't never gave me nothing! You ain't never done nothing but hold me back. Afraid I was gonna be better than you. All you ever did was try and make me scared of you. I used to tremble every time you called my name. Every time I heard your footsteps in the house. Wondering all the time . . . what's Papa gonna say if I do this? . . . What's he gonna say if I do that? . . . What's Papa gonna say if I turn on the radio? And Mama, too . . . she tries . . . but she's scared of you.

75 TROY: You leave your mama out of this. She ain't got nothing to do with this.

CORY: I don't know how she stand you . . . after what you did to her.

TROY: I told you to leave your mama out of this!

He advances toward Cory.

CORY: What you gonna do . . . give me a whupping? You can't whup me no more. You're too old. You just an old man.

TROY: (*shoves him on his shoulder*) Nigger! That's what you are. You just another nigger on the street to me!

80 CORY: You crazy! You know that?

TROY: Go on now! You got the devil in you. Get on away from me!

CORY: You just a crazy old man . . . talking about I got the devil in me.

TROY: Yeah, I'm crazy! If you don't get on the other side of that yard . . . I'm gonna show you how crazy I am! Go on . . . get the hell out of my yard.

CORY: It ain't your yard. You took Uncle Gabe's money he got from the army to buy this house and then you put him out.

85 TROY: (*advances on Cory*) Get your black ass out of my yard!

Troy's advance backs Cory up against the tree. Cory grabs up the bat.

CORY: I ain't going nowhere! Come on . . . put me out! I ain't scared of you.

TROY: That's my bat!

CORY: Come on!

TROY: Put my bat down!

CORY: Come on, put me out.

Cory swings at Troy, who backs across the yard.

   What's the matter? You so bad . . . put me out!

Troy advances toward Cory.

CORY: *(backing up)* Come on! Come on!
TROY: You're gonna have to use it! You wanna draw that bat back on me . . . you're
   gonna have to use it.
CORY: Come on! . . . Come on!

*Cory swings the bat at Troy a second time. He misses. Troy continues to advance toward
him.*

TROY: You're gonna have to kill me! You wanna draw that bat back on me. You're
   gonna have to kill me.

*Cory, backed up against the tree, can go no farther. Troy taunts him. He sticks out his head
and offers him a target.*

   Come on! Come on!

Cory is unable to swing the bat. Troy grabs it.

TROY: Then I'll show you.

*Cory and Troy struggle over the bat. The struggle is fierce and fully engaged. Troy ultimately
is the stronger and takes the bat away from Cory and stands over him ready to swing. He
stops himself.*

   Go on and get away from around my house.

Cory, stung by his defeat, picks himself up, walks slowly out of the yard and up the alley.

CORY: Tell Mama I'll be back for my things.
TROY: They'll be on the other side of that fence.

Cory exits.

TROY: I can't taste nothing. Helluljah! I can't taste nothing no more. (*Troy assumes
   a batting posture and begins to taunt Death, the fastball on the outside corner.*) Come
   on! It's between you and me now! Come on! Anytime you want! Come on! I be
   ready for you . . . but I ain't gonna be easy.

The lights go down on the scene.

SCENE 5

*The time is 1965. The lights come up in the yard. It is the morning of Troy's funeral. A
funeral plaque with a light hangs beside the door. There is a small garden plot off to the side.
There is noise and activity in the house as Rose, Gabriel, and Bono have gathered. The door
opens and Raynell, seven years old, enters dressed in a flannel nightgown. She crosses to the
garden and pokes around with a stick. Rose calls from the house.*

ROSE: Raynell!
RAYNELL: Mam?
ROSE: What you doing out there?
RAYNELL: Nothing.

Rose comes to the door.

5   ROSE: Girl, get in here and get dressed. What you doing?
RAYNELL: Seeing if my garden growed.
ROSE: I told you it ain't gonna grow overnight. You got to wait.
RAYNELL: It don't look like it never gonna grow. Dag!
ROSE: I told you a watched pot never boils. Get in here and get dressed.
10   RAYNELL: This ain't even no pot, Mama.
ROSE: You just have to give it a chance. It'll grow. Now you come on and do what
      I told you. We got to be getting ready. This ain't no morning to be playing
      around. You hear me?
RAYNELL: Yes, mam.

*Rose exits into the house. Raynell continues to poke at her garden with a stick. Cory enters.
He is dressed in a Marine corporal's uniform, and carries a duffel bag. His posture is that of
a military man, and his speech has a clipped sternness.*

CORY: (to Raynell) Hi. (Pause.) I bet your name is Raynell.
RAYNELL: Uh huh.
15   CORY: Is your mama home?

Raynell runs up on the porch and calls through the screen door.

RAYNELL: Mama . . . there's some man out here. Mama?

Rose comes to the door.

ROSE: Cory? Lord have mercy! Look here, you all!

*Rose and Cory embrace in a tearful reunion as Bono and Lyons enter from the house dressed
in funeral clothes.*

BONO: Aw, looka here . . .
ROSE: Done got all grown up!
20   CORY: Don't cry, Mama. What you crying about?
ROSE: I'm just so glad you made it.
CORY: Hey Lyons. How you doing, Mr. Bono.

Lyons goes to embrace Cory.

LYONS: Look at you, man. Look at you. Don't he look good, Rose. Got them Corpo-
      ral stripes.
ROSE: What took you so long?
25   CORY: You know how the Marines are, Mama. They got to get all their paperwork
      straight before they let you do anything.

ROSE: Well, I'm sure glad you made it. They let Lyons come. Your Uncle Gabe's still in the hospital. They don't know if they gonna let him out or not. I just talked to them a little while ago.

LYONS: A Corporal in the United States Marines.

BONO: Your daddy knew you had it in you. He used to tell me all the time.

LYONS: Don't he look good, Mr. Bono?

BONO: Yeah, he remind me of Troy when I first met him. *(Pause.)* Say, Rose, Lucille's down at the church with the choir. I'm gonna go down and get the pallbearers lined up. I'll be back to get you all.

ROSE: Thanks, Jim.

CORY: See you, Mr. Bono.

LYONS: *(with his arm around Raynell)* Cory . . . look at Raynell. Ain't she precious? She gonna break a whole lot of hearts.

ROSE: Raynell, come and say hello to your brother. This is your brother, Cory. You remember Cory.

RAYNELL: No, Mam.

CORY: She don't remember me, Mama.

ROSE: Well, we talk about you. She heard us talk about you. *(To Raynell.)* This is your brother, Cory. Come on and say hello.

RAYNELL: Hi.

CORY: Hi. So you're Raynell. Mama told me a lot about you.

ROSE: You all come on into the house and let me fix you some breakfast. Keep up your strength.

CORY: I ain't hungry, Mama.

LYONS: You can fix me something, Rose. I'll be in there in a minute.

ROSE: Cory, you sure you don't want nothing? I know they ain't feeding you right.

CORY: No, Mama . . . thanks. I don't feel like eating. I'll get something later.

ROSE: Raynell . . . get on upstairs and get that dress on like I told you.

Rose and Raynell exit into the house.

LYONS: So . . . I hear you thinking about getting married.

CORY: Yeah, I done found the right one, Lyons. It's about time.

LYONS: Me and Bonnie been split up about four years now. About the time Papa retired. I guess she just got tired of all them changes I was putting her through. *(Pause.)* I always knew you was gonna make something out yourself. Your head was always in the right direction. So . . . you gonna stay in . . . make it a career . . . put in your twenty years?

CORY: I don't know. I got six already, I think that's enough.

LYONS: Stick with Uncle Sam and retire early. Ain't nothing out here. I guess Rose told you what happened with me. They got me down the workhouse. I thought I was being slick cashing other people's checks.

CORY: How much time you doing?

LYONS: They give me three years. I got that beat now. I ain't got but nine more months. It ain't so bad. You learn to deal with it like anything else. You got to take the crookeds with the straights. That's what Papa used to say. He used to say that when he struck out. I seen him strike out three times in a row . . . and

the next time up he hit the ball over the grandstand. Right out there in Home-
stead Field. He wasn't satisfied hitting in the seats . . . he want to hit it over
everything! After the game he had two hundred people standing around waiting
to shake his hand. You got to take the crookeds with the straights. Yeah, Papa
was something else.

CORY: You still playing?

LYONS: Cory . . . you know I'm gonna do that. There's some fellows down there we
got us a band . . . we gonna try and stay together when we get out . . . but yeah,
I'm still playing. It still helps me to get out of bed in the morning. As long as it
do that I'm gonna be right there playing and trying to make some sense out of it.

55 ROSE: (calling) Lyons, I got these eggs in the pan.

LYONS: Let me go on and get these eggs, man. Get ready to go bury Papa. (Pause.)
How you doing? You doing all right?

*Cory nods. Lyons touches him on the shoulder and they share a moment of silent grief. Lyons
exits into the house. Cory wanders about the yard. Raynell enters.*

RAYNELL: Hi.

CORY: Hi.

RAYNELL: Did you used to sleep in my room?

60 CORY: Yeah . . . that used to be my room.

RAYNELL: That's what Papa call it. "Cory's room." It got your football in the closet.

Rose comes to the door.

ROSE: Raynell, get in there and get them good shoes on.

RAYNELL: Mama, can't I wear these? Them other ones hurt my feet.

ROSE: Well, they just gonna have to hurt your feet for a while. You ain't said they
hurt your feet when you went down to the store and got them.

65 RAYNELL: They didn't hurt then. My feet done got bigger.

ROSE: Don't you give me no backtalk now. You get in there and get them shoes on.

Raynell exits into the house.

Ain't too much changed. He still got that piece of rag tied to that tree. He was
out here swinging that bat. I was just ready to go back in the house. He swung
that bat and then he just fell over. Seem like he swung it and stood there with
this grin on his face . . . and then he just fell over. They carried him on down to
the hospital, but I knew there wasn't no need . . . why don't you come on in the
house?

CORY: Mama . . . I got something to tell you. I don't know how to tell you this . . .
but I've got to tell you . . . I'm not going to Papa's funeral.

ROSE: Boy, hush your mouth. That's your daddy you talking about. I don't want
hear that kind of talk this morning. I done raised you to come to this? You
standing there all healthy and grown talking about you ain't going to your
daddy's funeral?

CORY: Mama . . . listen . . .

70 ROSE: I don't want to hear it, Cory. You just get that thought out of your head.

CORY: I can't drag Papa with me everywhere I go. I've got to say no to him. One
time in my life I've got to say no.

ROSE: Don't nobody have to listen to nothing like that. I know you and your daddy
ain't seen eye to eye, but I ain't got to listen to that kind of talk this morning.
Whatever was between you and your daddy . . . the time has come to put it aside.
Just take it and set it over there on the shelf and forget about it. Disrespecting
your daddy ain't gonna make you a man, Cory. You got to find a way to come to
that on your own. Not going to your daddy's funeral ain't gonna make you a man.

CORY: The whole time I was growing up . . . living in his house . . . Papa was like
a shadow that followed you everywhere. It weighed on you and sunk into your
flesh. It would wrap around you and lay there until you couldn't tell which one
was you anymore. That shadow digging in your flesh. Trying to crawl in. Trying
to live through you. Everywhere I looked, Troy Maxson was staring back at me
. . . hiding under the bed . . . in the closet. I'm just saying I've got to find a way
to get rid of that shadow, Mama.

ROSE: You just like him. You got him in you good.

CORY: Don't tell me that, Mama.

ROSE: You Troy Maxson all over again.

CORY: I don't want to be Troy Maxson. I want to be me.

ROSE: You can't be nobody but who you are, Cory. That shadow wasn't nothing
but you growing into yourself. You either got to grow into it or cut it down to
fit you. But that's all you got to make life with. That's all you got to measure
yourself against that world out there. Your daddy wanted you to be everything
he wasn't . . . and at the same time he tried to make you into everything he was.
I don't know if he was right or wrong . . . but I do know he meant to do more
good than he meant to do harm. He wasn't always right. Sometimes when he
touched he bruised. And sometimes when he took me in his arms he cut.

When I first met your daddy I thought . . . Here is a man I can lay down with
and make a baby. That's the first thing I thought when I seen him. I was thirty
years old and had done seen my share of men. But when he walked up to me
and said, "I can dance a waltz that'll make you dizzy." I thought, Rose Lee, here
is a man that you can open yourself up to and be filled to bursting. Here is a
man that can fill all them empty spaces you been tipping around the edges of.
One of them empty spaces was being somebody's mother.

I married your daddy and settled down to cooking his supper and keeping
clean sheets on the bed. When your daddy walked through the house he was so
big he filled it up. That was my first mistake. Not to make him leave some room
for me. For my part in the matter. But at that time I wanted that. I wanted a
house that I could sing in. And that's what your daddy gave me. I didn't know
to keep up his strength I had to give up little pieces of mine. I did that. I took
on his life as mine and mixed up the pieces so that you couldn't hardly tell
which was which anymore. It was my choice. It was my life and I didn't have to
live it like that. But that's what life offered me in the way of being a woman and
I took it. I grabbed hold of it with both hands.

By the time Raynell came into the house, me and your daddy had done lost
touch with one another. I didn't want to make my blessing off of nobody's misfortune . . . but I took on to Raynell like she was all them babies I had wanted
and never had.

75

The phone rings.

Like I'd been blessed to relive a part of my life. And if the Lord see fit to keep up my strength . . . I'm gonna do her just like your daddy did you . . . I'm gonna give her the best of what's in me.

RAYNELL: *(entering, still with her old shoes)* Mama . . . Reverend Tollivier on the phone.

Rose exits into the house.

80 RAYNELL: Hi.

CORY: Hi.

RAYNELL: You in the Army or the Marines?

CORY: Marines.

RAYNELL: Papa said it was the Army. Did you know Blue?

85 CORY: Blue? Who's Blue?

RAYNELL: Papa's dog what he sing about all the time.

CORY: *(singing)*

> Hear it ring! Hear it ring!
> I had a dog his name was Blue
> You know Blue was mighty true
> You know Blue was a good old dog
> Blue treed a possum in a hollow log
> You know from that he was a good old dog.
> Hear it ring! Hear it ring!

Raynell joins in singing.

CORY AND RAYNELL:

> Blue treed a possum out on a limb
> Blue looked at me and I looked at him
> Grabbed that possum and put him in a sack
> Blue stayed there till I came back
> Old Blue's feets was big and round
> Never allowed a possum to touch the ground.
> Old Blue died and I dug his grave
> I dug his grave with a silver spade
> Let him down with a golden chain
> And every night I call his name
> Go on Blue, you good dog you
> Go on Blue, you good dog you

RAYNELL:

> Blue laid down and died like a man
> Blue laid down and died . . .

90 BOTH:

> Blue laid down and died like a man
> Now he's treeing possums in the Promised Land
> I'm gonna tell you this to let you know
> Blue's gone where the good dogs go

When I hear old Blue bark
When I hear old Blue bark
Blue treed a possum in Noah's Ark[1]
Blue treed a possum in Noah's Ark.

Rose comes to the screen door.

ROSE: Cory, we gonna be ready to go in a minute.
CORY: *(to Raynell)* You go on in the house and change them shoes like Mama told
   you so we can go to Papa's funeral.
RAYNELL: Okay, I'll be back.

*Raynell exits into the house. Cory gets up and crosses over to the tree. Rose stands in the
screen door watching him. Gabriel enters from the alley.*

GABRIEL: *(calling)* Hey, Rose!
ROSE: Gabe?   95
GABRIEL: I'm here, Rose. Hey Rose, I'm here!

Rose enters from the house.

ROSE: Lord . . . Look here, Lyons!
LYONS: See, I told you, Rose . . . I told you they'd let him come.
CORY: How you doing, Uncle Gabe?
LYONS: How you doing, Uncle Gabe?   100
GABRIEL: Hey, Rose. It's time. It's time to tell St. Peter to open the gates. Troy, you
   ready? You ready, Troy. I'm gonna tell St. Peter to open the gates. You get ready
   now.

*Gabriel, with great fanfare, braces himself to blow.t The trumpet is without a mouthpiece.
He puts the end of it into his mouth and blows with great force, like a man who has been
waiting some twenty-odd years for this single moment. No sound comes out of the trumpet.
He braces himself and blows again with the same result. A third time he blows. There is a
weight of impossible description that falls away and leaves him bare and exposed to a frightful
realization. It is a trauma that a sane and normal mind would be unable to withstand. He
begins to dance. A slow, strange dance, eerie and life-giving. A dance of atavistic signature
and ritual. Lyons attempts to embrace him. Gabriel pushes Lyons away. He begins to howl in
what is an attempt at song, or perhaps a song turning back into itself in an attempt at speech.
He finishes his dance and the gates of heaven stand open as wide as God's closet.*

   That's the way that go!

                    *   *   *

Reading and Reacting

1. Obviously, fences are a central metaphor in this play. To what different kinds of fences
   does the play's title refer?
2. How are the fathers and sons in this play alike? How are they different? Does the play
   imply that sons must inevitably follow in their fathers' footsteps?

---

[1] *Noah's Ark:* See Genesis 6.14–20.

3. This play is set in 1957. Given the racial climate of the country at that time, how realistic are Cory's ambitions? How reasonable are his father's criticisms?

4. In what ways has Troy's character been shaped by his contact with the white world?

5. Is Troy a tragic hero? If so, what is his flaw?

6. Which of the play's characters, if any, do you consider to be stereotypes? What comment do you think the play makes about stereotypes?

7. How does the conflict between Troy and Cory reflect conflicts within the African American community? Does the play suggest any possibilities for compromise?

8. Do you consider the message of this play to be optimistic or pessimistic? Explain.

9. **JOURNAL ENTRY** Which characters do you like? Which do you dislike? Why?

10. **CRITICAL PERSPECTIVE** Robert Brustein, theater critic and artistic director of Harvard's American Repertory Theater, has criticized Wilson on the ground that "his recurrent theme is the familiar American charge of victimization"; in *Fences*, he argues, "Wilson's larger purpose depends on his conviction that Troy's potential was stunted not [by] 'his own behavior' but by centuries of racist oppression."

  Do you see the central theme of *Fences* as "the familiar American charge of victimization," or do you think another theme is more important?

Related Works: "Discovering America" (p. 135), "Big Black Good Man" (p. 318), "Ex-Basketball Player" (p. 764), "Yet Do I Marvel" (p. 869), *Death of a Salesman* (p. 1233)

WRITING SUGGESTIONS: Theme

1. In an interview, writer Lorrie Moore calls *Fences* "an African American *Death of a Salesman*." What do you think she means? Do you agree? Write an essay in which you examine the two plays in light of Moore's comment.

2. Write an essay in which you analyze the baseball images in *Fences*. How do the references to baseball help to develop the play's themes?

3. One of the themes of *Fences* is the dream parents have for their children. Compare the development of this theme in *Fences* and in another play in this book—for example, *The Cuban Swimmer* (p. 1416) or *Hamlet* (p. 1304).

4. *Doubt* explores the grey area that exists between right and wrong, between truth and lies: Sister Aloysius questions Father Flynn's interactions with his charges; meanwhile Sister James (as well as the audience) has doubts. Do you think Sister Aloysius was right to act as she did, or do you think she should have given Father Flynn the benefit of the doubt?

5. Like *Come Rain or Come Shine*, "*What Are You Going to Be?*" (p. 1062) deals with parents who try to control or manipulate their children. Compare the parent–child relationships in both these plays, considering how successful the parents in each play are in their endeavors.

CHAPTER 41

SUSAN GLASPELL'S *TRIFLES*: A CASEBOOK FOR READING, RESEARCH, AND WRITING

This chapter provides all the materials you will need to develop a research project about Susan Glaspell's one-act play *Trifles*. It includes the following resources:

Background

Critical Perspectives

---

*Note that some of the critical articles in this casebook were written before the current MLA documentation style was adopted. See Chapter 7 for current MLA format.

Each of the sources in this casebook offers insights that can help you to understand, enjoy, and write about *Trifles*. Some offer historical perspectives; some are biographical; others offer critical interpretations. All were selected to help you to understand the play and appreciate its characters and themes. Other kinds of sources (included here) can also enrich your understanding of Glaspell's accomplishments—for example, the short story that Glaspell wrote about the same subject as *Trifles* and factual accounts of the real murder case on which both works were based.

In preparation for writing an essay on a topic of your choice about *Trifles*, read the play and the accompanying source materials carefully. After doing so, explore—in your journal, in group discussions, or in brainstorming notes—the possibilities suggested by the Reading and Reacting questions on page 1615. Think about the ideas expressed in the critical articles, biographical information, and other materials as well as those in the play itself. Your goal is to decide on a topic you can develop in a four- to six-page essay. Remember to document any words or ideas that you borrow from the play or from other sources, enclosing any borrowed words in quotation marks. (For guidelines on evaluating literary criticism, see p. 14; for guidelines on using source materials, see Chapter 6, "Using Sources in Your Writing," and Chapter 7, "Documenting Sources and Avoiding Plagiarism.")

Also note that a number of websites can offer insights into Glaspell's work. The International Susan Glaspell Society maintains a comprehensive website on her life and work. Project Gutenberg makes free eBooks of her plays available online, and the website for Patricia Bryan and Thomas Wolf's book about the John Hossack murder, *Midnight Assassin*, is an invaluable source for articles that Glaspell wrote about the case while she was a reporter in Davenport, Iowa.

About the Author

AP Images

The career of playwright and fiction writer **Susan Glaspell** (1876–1948) has in some ways paralleled that of her African American contemporary Zora Neale Hurston. Although Glaspell's works received more recognition during her lifetime than did Hurston's, both women's works went out of print before being "resurrected" during the last decades of the twentieth century through the efforts of feminists who sought to rediscover the works of America's lost women writers. Hurston's flamboyant lifestyle sometimes attracted attention that should have gone to her work; after she died in relative obscurity in Florida, her fame was reestablished largely through the efforts of fellow novelist Alice Walker. Glaspell's bohemian lifestyle led her from staid Davenport, Iowa, where she was born, first to Chicago and then eventually to Greenwich Village. It was a desire to escape with her husband, George Cram "Jig" Cook, from the heat of New York summers that led Glaspell to take a temporary break from her fiction writing to immerse herself in the world of the theater.

Glaspell left Davenport to attend Drake University but returned in 1901 to work as a reporter for a local newspaper. Her duties included covering the legislature and the social scene. Soon they also included reporting on the Hossack murder case, about which she wrote numerous articles that showed an increasing sympathy for the woman accused of murdering her husband with two ax blows to the head, particularly after she heard Mrs. Hossack's testimony and visited the Hossack home. Memories of the murder scene that she visited in 1901 would return to her in 1915 when her husband encouraged her to take up playwriting.

By the time Glaspell married Cook in 1913, she was already a successful writer. She had published short stories in periodicals and in a collection entitled *Lifted Masks* (1912), as well as two novels, *The Glory of the Conquered* (1909) and *The Visioning* (1911). Cook had a flair for the dramatic, however, that led to his dream of founding a community theater in Provincetown, Massachusetts, where he and his wife spent their summers with other refugees from New York. Glaspell and Cook found Broadway theater disappointing and shared a desire to establish in Provincetown a theater that would showcase American plays and that would not be limited by financial concerns.

Since Glaspell did not feel bound by the need to make her plays profitable, she felt free to experiment with new forms. After the success of the first season of the Provincetown Players, Cook announced a play by Glaspell for the next bill. Although for the first season Glaspell and Cook had enjoyed coauthoring *Suppressed Desires*, which poked gentle fun at the recent popularity of the theories of Sigmund Freud, now Glaspell undertook writing a play on her own. As she sat in the deserted fish-house, she saw taking shape on the stage

The Provincetown Theatre, Provincetown, Massachusetts, 1936.
Carl Van Vechten Photographs/Library of Congress

before her the kitchen of the Hossack home she had visited as a reporter. Writing at a time when women did not yet have the right to serve on juries, Glaspell chose to have two female characters serve as judge and jury for a woman accused of murdering her husband. She named the one-act play *Trifles* because the men in the play who seek a motivation for the murder see women's work as too "trifling" to be of any significance, too much of the world of women, while the women realize that the very "trifles" the men disparage reveal just the motivation they seek.

Trifles was first produced in 1916 and first published in 1920 in a collection that included Glaspell's other one-act plays and her first full-length drama, *Bernice*. By that time the Provincetown Players had moved to New York to become the Playwrights' Theater. Two more of Glaspell's plays, *Inheritors* (1921) and *Chains of Dew* (unpublished) were produced at the New York location, but by the time the latter was produced in 1922, Glaspell and Cook were on their way to Greece, where Cook died in 1924. Three years later, in 1927, Glaspell published her memoir of her husband, *The Road to the Temple*.

Glaspell never reestablished a close relationship to the Playwrights' Theater after her husband's death. She did, however, become lovers with Normal Matson and together, in 1928, they wrote a play called *The Comic Artist*. Her playwriting career peaked in 1930 when her play *Alison's House* was awarded the Pulitzer Prize in drama. By that time she had largely turned away from playwriting and back to fiction. She continued to write novels until she died of viral pneumonia in 1948.

 Play

Trifles (1916)

CHARACTERS

George Henderson, *county attorney*
Henry Peters, *sheriff*
Lewis Hale, *a neighboring farmer*
Mrs. Peters
Mrs. Hale

SCENE

The kitchen in the now abandoned farmhouse of John Wright, a gloomy kitchen, and left without having been put in order—unwashed pans under the sink, a loaf of bread outside the breadbox, a dish towel on the table—other signs of incompleted work. At the rear the outer door opens and the Sheriff comes in followed by the County Attorney and Hale. The Sheriff and Hale are men in middle life, the County Attorney is a young man; all are much bundled up and go at once to the stove. They are followed by two women—the Sheriff's wife first; she is a slight wiry woman, a thin nervous face. Mrs. Hale is larger and would ordinarily be called more comfortable looking, but she is disturbed now and looks fearfully about as she enters. The women have come in slowly, and stand close together near the door.

COUNTY ATTORNEY: *(rubbing his hands)* This feels good. Come up to the fire, ladies.
MRS. PETERS: *(after taking a step forward)* I'm not—cold.

SHERIFF: (*unbuttoning his overcoat and stepping away from the stove as if to mark the beginning of official business*) Now, Mr. Hale, before we move things about, you explain to Mr. Henderson just what you saw when you came here yesterday morning.

COUNTY ATTORNEY: By the way, has anything been moved? Are things just as you left them yesterday?

SHERIFF: (*looking about*) It's just the same. When it dropped below zero last night I thought I'd better send Frank out this morning to make a fire for us—no use getting pneumonia with a big case on, but I told him not to touch anything except the stove—and you know Frank.

COUNTY ATTORNEY: Somebody should have been left here yesterday.

SHERIFF: Oh—yesterday. When I had to send Frank to Morris Center for that man who went crazy—I want you to know I had my hands full yesterday. I knew you could get back from Omaha by today and as long as I went over everything here myself—

COUNTY ATTORNEY: Well, Mr. Hale, tell just what happened when you came here yesterday morning.

HALE: Harry and I had started to town with a load of potatoes. We came along the road from my place and as I got here I said, "I'm going to see if I can't get John Wright to go in with me on a party telephone." I spoke to Wright about it once before and he put me off, saying folks talked too much anyway, and all he asked was peace and quiet—I guess you know about how much he talked himself; but I thought maybe if I went to the house and talked about it before his wife, though I said to Harry that I didn't know as what his wife wanted made much difference to John—

COUNTY ATTORNEY: Let's talk about that later, Mr. Hale. I do want to talk about that, but tell now just what happened when you got to the house.

In this scene from the Provincetown Players' 1917 production of Susan Glaspell's *Trifles*, the three men discuss the crime while Mrs. Peters and Mrs. Hale look on.

Photo by: Prudence Katze

HALE: I didn't hear or see anything; I knocked at the door, and still it was all quiet inside. I knew they must be up, it was past eight o'clock. So I knocked again, and I thought I heard somebody say, "Come in." I wasn't sure, I'm not sure yet, but I opened the door—this door (*indicating the door by which the two woman are still standing*) and there in that rocker—(*pointing to it*) sat Mrs. Wright.

They all look at the rocker.

COUNTY ATTORNEY: What—was she doing?

HALE: She was rockin' back and forth. She had her apron in her hand and was kind of—pleating it.

COUNTY ATTORNEY: And how did she—look?

15 HALE: Well, she looked queer.

COUNTY ATTORNEY: How do you mean—queer?

HALE: Well, as if she didn't know what she was going to do next. And kind of done up.

COUNTY ATTORNEY: How did she seem to feel about your coming?

HALE: Why I don't think she minded—one way or other. She didn't pay much attention. I said, "How do, Mrs. Wright, it's cold, ain't it?" And she said, "Is it?"—and went on kind of pleating at her apron. Well, I was surprised; she didn't ask me to come up to the stove, or to set down, but just sat there, not even looking at me, so I said, "I want to see John." And then she—laughed. I guess you would call it a laugh. I thought of Harry and the team outside, so I said a little sharp: "Can't I see John?" "No," she says, kind o' dull like. "Ain't he home?" says I. "Yes," says she, "he's home." "Then why can't I see him?" I asked her, out of patience. "'Cause he's dead," says she. "*Dead?*" says I. She just nodded her head, not getting a bit excited, but rockin' back and forth. "Why—where is he?" says I, not knowing what to say. She just pointed upstairs—like that. (*Himself pointing to the room above.*) I got up, with the idea of going up there. I walked from there to here—then I says, "Why, what did he die of?" "He died of a rope around his neck," says she, and just went on pleatin' at her apron. Well, I went out and called Harry. I thought I might—need help. We went upstairs and there he was lyin'—

20 COUNTY ATTORNEY: I think I'd rather have you go into that upstairs, where you can point it all out. Just go on now with the rest of the story.

HALE: Well, my first thought was to get that rope off. It looked . . . (*stops, his face twitched*) . . . but Harry, he went up to him, and he said, "No, he's dead all right, and we'd better not touch anything." So we went back down stairs. She was still sitting that same way. "Has anybody been notified?" I asked. "No," says she, unconcerned. "Who did this, Mrs. Wright?" said Harry. He said it businesslike—and she stopped pleatin' of her apron. "I don't know," she says. "You don't *know?*" says Harry. "No," says she. "Weren't you sleepin' in the bed with him?" says Harry. "Yes," says she, "but I was on the inside." "Somebody slipped a rope round his neck and strangled him and you didn't wake up?" says Harry. "I didn't wake up," she said after him. We must 'a looked as if we didn't see how that could be, for after a minute she said, "I sleep sound." Harry was going to ask her more questions but I said maybe we ought to let her tell her story first to the coroner, or the sheriff, so Harry went fast as he could to Rivers' place, where there's a telephone.

COUNTY ATTORNEY: And what did Mrs. Wright do when she knew that you had gone for the coroner?

HALE: She moved from that chair to this one over here (*pointing to a small chair in the corner*) and just sat there with her hands held together and looking down. I got a feeling that I ought to make some conversation, so I said I had come in to see if John wanted to put in a telephone, and at that she started to laugh, and then she stopped and looked at me—scared. (*The County Attorney, who has had his notebook out, makes a note.*) I dunno, maybe it wasn't scared. I wouldn't like to say it was. Soon Harry got back, and then Dr. Lloyd came, and you, Mr. Peters, and so I guess that's all I know that you don't.

COUNTY ATTORNEY: (*looking around*) I guess we'll go upstairs first—and then out to the barn and around there. (*To the Sheriff.*) You're convinced that there was nothing important here—nothing that would point to any motive.

SHERIFF: Nothing here but kitchen things.   25

The County Attorney, after again looking around the kitchen, opens the door of a cupboard closet. He gets up on a chair and looks on a shelf. Pulls his hand away, sticky.

COUNTY ATTORNEY: Here's a nice mess.

The women draw nearer.

MRS. PETERS: (*to the other woman*) Oh, her fruit; it did freeze. (*To the County Attorney.*) She worried about that when it turned so cold. She said the fire'd go out and her jars would break.

SHERIFF: Well, can you beat the woman! Held for murder and worryin' about her preserves.

COUNTY ATTORNEY: I guess before we're through she may have something more serious than preserves to worry about.

HALE: Well, women are used to worrying over trifles.   30

The two women move a little closer together.

COUNTY ATTORNEY: (*with the gallantry of a young politician*) And yet, for all their worries, what would we do without the ladies? (*The women do not unbend. He goes to the sink, takes a dipperful of water from the pail and pouring it into a basin, washes his hands. Starts to wipe them on the roller towel, turns it for a cleaner place.*) Dirty towels! (*Kicks his foot against the pans under the sink.*) Not much of a housekeeper, would you say, ladies?

MRS. HALE: (*stiffly*) There's a great deal of work to be done on a farm.

COUNTY ATTORNEY: To be sure. And yet (*with a little bow to her*) I know there are some Dickson county farmhouses which do not have such roller towels.

He gives it a pull to expose its full length again.

MRS. HALE: Those towels get dirty awful quick. Men's hands aren't always as clean as they might be.

COUNTY ATTORNEY: Ah, loyal to your sex, I see. But you and Mrs. Wright were   35
neighbors. I suppose you were friends, too.

MRS. HALE: (*shaking her head*) I've not seen much of her of late years. I've not been in this house—it's more than a year.

COUNTY ATTORNEY: And why was that? You didn't like her?

MRS. HALE: I liked her well enough. Farmer's wives have their hands full, Mr. Henderson. And then—

COUNTY ATTORNEY: Yes—?

40   MRS. HALE: *(looking about)* It never seemed a very cheerful place.

COUNTY ATTORNEY: No—it's not cheerful. I shouldn't say she had the homemaking instinct.

MRS. HALE: Well, I don't know as Wright had, either.

COUNTY ATTORNEY: You mean that they didn't get on very well?

MRS. HALE: No, I don't mean anything. But I don't think a place'd be any cheerfuller for John Wright's being in it.

45   COUNTY ATTORNEY: I'd like to talk more of that a little later. I want to get the lay of things upstairs now.

He goes to the left, where three steps lead to a stair door.

SHERIFF: I suppose anything Mrs. Peters does'll be all right. She was to take in some clothes for her, you know, and a few little things. We left in such a hurry yesterday.

COUNTY ATTORNEY: Yes, but I would like to see what you take, Mrs. Peters, and keep an eye out for anything that might be of use to us.

MRS. PETERS: Yes, Mr. Henderson.

The women listen to the men's steps on the stairs, then look about the kitchen.

MRS. HALE: I'd hate to have men coming into my kitchen, snooping around and criticizing.

She arranges the pans under the sink which the County Attorney had shoved out of place.

50   MRS. PETERS: Of course it's no more than their duty.

MRS. HALE: Duty's all right, but I guess that deputy sheriff that came out to make the fire might have got a little of this on. *(Gives the roller towel a pull.)* Wish I'd thought of that a little sooner. Seems mean to talk about her for not having things slicked up when she had to come away in such a hurry.

MRS. PETERS: *(who has gone to a small table in the left rear of the room, and lifted one end of a towel that covers a pan)* She had bread set.

Stands still.

MRS. HALE: *(eyes fixed on a loaf of bread beside the breadbox, which is on a low shelf at the other side of the room. Moves slowly toward it.)* She was going to put this in there. *(Picks up loaf, then abruptly drops it. In a manner of returning to familiar things.)* It's a shame about her fruit. I wonder if it's all gone. *(Gets up on the chair and looks.)* I think there's some here that's all right, Mrs. Peters. Yes—here; *(holding it toward the window)* this is cherries, too. *(Looking again.)* I declare I believe that's the only one. *(Gets down, bottle in her hand. Goes to the sink and wipes it off on the outside.)* She'll feel awful bad after all her hard work in the hot weather. I remember the afternoon I put up my cherries last summer.

She puts the bottle on the big kitchen table, center of the room. With a sigh, is about to sit down in the rocking-chair. Before she is seated realizes what chair it is; with a slow look at it, steps back. The chair which she has touched rocks back and forth.

MRS. PETERS: Well, I must get those things from the front room closet. (*She goes to the door at the right, but after looking into the other room, steps back.*) You coming with me, Mrs. Hale? You could help me carry them.

They go in the other room; reappear, Mrs. Peters carrying a dress and skirt, Mrs. Hale following with a pair of shoes.

MRS. PETERS: My, it's cold in there.   55

She puts the clothes on the big table, and hurries to the stove.

MRS. HALE: (*examining her skirt*) Wright was close. I think maybe that's why she kept so much to herself. She didn't even belong to the Ladies Aid. I suppose she felt she couldn't do her part, and then you don't enjoy things when you feel shabby. She used to wear pretty clothes and be lively, when she was Minnie Foster, one of the town girls singing in the choir. But that—oh, that was thirty years ago. This all you was to take in?

MRS. PETERS: She said she wanted an apron. Funny thing to want, for there isn't much to get you dirty in jail, goodness knows. But I suppose just to make her feel more natural. She said they was in the top drawer in this cupboard. Yes, here. And then her little shawl that always hung behind the door. (*Opens stair door and looks.*) Yes, here it is.

Quickly shuts door leading upstairs.

MRS. HALE: (*abruptly moving toward her*) Mrs. Peters?
MRS. PETERS: Yes, Mrs. Hale?
MRS. HALE: Do you think she did it?   60
MRS. PETERS: (*in a frightened voice*) Oh, I don't know.
MRS. HALE: Well, I don't think she did. Asking for an apron and her little shawl. Worrying about her fruit.
MRS. PETERS: (*starts to speak, glances up, where footsteps are heard in the room above. In a low voice.*) Mr. Peters says it looks bad for her. Mr. Henderson is awful sarcastic in a speech and he'll make fun of her sayin' she didn't wake up.
MRS. HALE: Well, I guess John Wright didn't wake up when they was slipping that rope under his neck.
MRS. PETERS: No, it's strange. It must have been done awful crafty and still. They   65
say it was such a—funny way to kill a man, rigging it all up like that.
MRS. HALE: That's just what Mr. Hale said. There was a gun in the house. He says that's what he can't understand.
MRS. PETERS: Mr. Henderson said coming out that what was needed for the case was a motive; something to show anger, or—sudden feeling.
MRS. HALE: (*who is standing by the table*) Well, I don't see any signs of anger around here. (*She puts her hand on the dish towel which lies on the table, stands looking down at table, one half of which is clean, the other half messy.*) It's wiped to here. (*Makes

a move as if to finish work, then turns and looks at loaf of bread outside the breadbox. Drops towel. In that voice of coming back to familiar things.) Wonder how they are finding things upstairs. I hope she had it a little more red-up[1] up there. You know, it seems kind of sneaking. Locking her up in town and then coming out here and trying to get her own house to turn against her!

MRS. PETERS: But Mrs. Hale, the law is the law.

70 MRS. HALE: I s'pose 'tis. *(Unbuttoning her coat.)* Better loosen up your things, Mrs. Peters. You won't feel them when you go out.

Mrs. Peters takes off her fur tippet, goes to hang it on the hook at back of room, stands looking at the under part of the small corner table.

MRS. PETERS: She was piecing a quilt.

She brings the large sewing basket and they look at the bright pieces.

MRS. HALE: It's log cabin pattern. Pretty, isn't it? I wonder if she was goin' to quilt it or just knot it?

Footsteps have been heard coming down the stairs. The Sheriff enters followed by Hale and the County Attorney.

SHERIFF: They wonder if she was going to quilt it or just knot it!

The men laugh; the women look abashed.

COUNTY ATTORNEY: *(rubbing his hands over the stove)* Frank's fire didn't do much up there, did it? Well, let's go out to the barn and get that cleared up.

The men go outside.

75 MRS. HALE: *(resentfully)* I don't know as there's anything so strange, our takin' up time with little things while we're waiting for them to get the evidence. *(She sits down at the big table smoothing out a block with decision.)* I don't see as it's anything to laugh about.

MRS. PETERS: *(apologetically)* Of course they've got awful important things on their minds.

Pulls up a chair and joins Mrs. Hale at the table.

MRS. HALE: *(examining another block)* Mrs. Peters, look at this one. Here, this is the one she was working on, and look at the sewing! All the rest of it has been so nice and even. And look at this! It's all over the place! Why, it looks as if she didn't know what she was about!

After she has said this they look at each other, then start to glance back at the door. After an instant Mrs. Hale has pulled at a knot and ripped the sewing.

MRS. PETERS: Oh, what are you doing, Mrs. Hale?

MRS. HALE: *(mildly)* Just pulling out a stitch or two that's not sewed very good. *(Threading a needle.)* Bad sewing always made me fidgety.

[1] *red-up*: Spruced-up (slang).

MRS. PETERS: *(nervously)* I don't think we ought to touch things.   80

MRS. HALE: I'll just finish up this end. (*Suddenly stopping and leaning forward.*) Mrs. Peters?

MRS. PETERS: Yes, Mrs. Hale?

MRS. HALE: What do you suppose she was so nervous about?

MRS. PETERS: Oh—I don't know. I don't know as she was nervous. I sometimes sew awful queer when I'm just tired. (*Mrs. Hale starts to say something, looks at Mrs. Peters, then goes on sewing.*) Well, I must get these things wrapped up. They may be through sooner than we think. (*Putting apron and other things together.*) I wonder where I can find a piece of paper, and string.

MRS. HALE: In that cupboard, maybe.   85

MRS. PETERS: *(looking in cupboard)* Why, here's a birdcage. (*Holds it up.*) Did she have a bird, Mrs. Hale?

MRS. HALE: Why, I don't know whether she did or not—I've not been here for so long. There was a man around last year selling canaries cheap, but I don't know as she took one; maybe she did. She used to sing real pretty herself.

MRS. PETERS: *(glancing around)* Seems funny to think of a bird here. But she must have had one, or why would she have a cage? I wonder what happened to it.

MRS. HALE: I s'pose maybe the cat got it.

MRS. PETERS: No, she didn't have a cat. She's got that feeling some people have   90 about cats—being afraid of them. My cat got in her room and she was real upset and asked me to take it out.

MRS. HALE: My sister Bessie was like that. Queer, ain't it?

MRS. PETERS: *(examining the cage)* Why, look at this door. It's broke. One hinge is pulled apart.

MRS. HALE: *(looking too)* Looks as if someone must have been rough with it.

MRS. PETERS: Why, yes.

She brings the cage forward and puts it on the table.

MRS. HALE: I wish if they're going to find any evidence they'd be about it. I don't   95 like this place.

MRS. PETERS: But I'm awful glad you came with me, Mrs. Hale. It would be lonesome for me sitting here alone.

MRS. HALE: It would, wouldn't it? (*Dropping her sewing.*) But I tell you what I do wish, Mrs. Peters. I wish I had come over sometimes when *she* was here. I— (*looking around the room*)—wish I had.

MRS. PETERS: But of course you were awful busy, Mrs. Hale—your house and your children.

MRS. HALE: I could've come. I stayed away because it weren't cheerful—and that's why I ought to have come. I—I've never liked this place. Maybe because it's down in a hollow and you don't see the road. I dunno what it is but it's a lonesome place and always was. I wish I had come over to see Minnie Foster sometimes. I can see now—

Shakes her head.

MRS. PETERS: Well, you mustn't reproach yourself, Mrs. Hale. Somehow we just   100 don't see how it is with other folks until—something comes up.

MRS. HALE: Not having children makes less work—but it makes a quiet house, and Wright out to work all day, and no company when he did come in. Did you know John Wright, Mrs. Peters?

MRS. PETERS: Not to know him; I've seen him in town. They say he was a good man.

MRS. HALE: Yes—good; he didn't drink, and kept his word as well as most, I guess, and paid his debts. But he was a hard man, Mrs. Peters. Just to pass the time of day with him—(*Shivers.*) Like a raw wind that gets to the bone. (*Pauses, her eye falling on the cage.*) I should think she would 'a wanted a bird. But what do you suppose went with it?

MRS. PETERS: I don't know, unless it got sick and died.

She reaches over and swings the broken door, swings it again. Both women watch it.

105 MRS. HALE: You weren't raised round here, were you? (*Mrs. Peters shakes her head.*) You didn't know—her?

MRS. PETERS: Not till they brought her yesterday.

MRS. HALE: She—come to think of it, she was kind of like a bird herself—real sweet and pretty, but kind of timid and—fluttery. How—she—did—change. (*Silence; then as if struck by a happy thought and relieved to get back to everyday things.*) Tell you what, Mrs. Peters, why don't you take the quilt with you? It might take up her mind.

MRS. PETERS: Why, I think that's a real nice idea, Mrs. Hale. There couldn't possibly be any objection to it, could there? Now, just what would I take? I wonder if her patches are in here—and her things.

They look in the sewing basket.

MRS. HALE: Here's some red. I expect this has got sewing things in it. (*Brings out a fancy box.*) What a pretty box. Looks like something somebody would give you. Maybe her scissors are in here. (*Opens box. Suddenly puts her hand to her nose.*) Why—(*Mrs. Peters bends nearer, then turns her face away.*) There's something wrapped up in this piece of silk.

110 MRS. PETERS: Why, this isn't her scissors.

MRS. HALE: (*lifting the silk*) Oh, Mrs. Peters—it's—

Mrs. Peters bends closer.

MRS. PETERS: It's the bird.

MRS. HALE: (*jumping up*) But, Mrs. Peters—look at it! Look at its neck! It's all—other side *to*.

MRS. PETERS: Somebody—wrung—its—neck.

Their eyes meet. A look of growing comprehension, of horror. Steps are heard outside. Mrs. Hale slips box under quilt pieces, and sinks into her chair. Enter Sheriff and County Attorney. Mrs. Peters rises.

115 COUNTY ATTORNEY: (*as one turning from serious things to little pleasantries*) Well, ladies, have you decided whether she was going to quilt it or knot it?

MRS. PETERS: We think she was going to—knot it.

COUNTY ATTORNEY: Well, that's interesting, I'm sure. (*Seeing the birdcage.*) Has the bird flown?

MRS. HALE: *(putting more quilt pieces over the box)* We think the—cat got it.
COUNTY ATTORNEY: *(preoccupied)* Is there a cat?

Mrs. Hale glances in a quick covert way at Mrs. Peters.

MRS. PETERS: Well, not *now*. They're superstitious, you know. They leave.   120
COUNTY ATTORNEY: *(to Sheriff Peters, continuing an interrupted conversation)* No sign
    at all of anyone having come from the outside. Their own rope. Now let's go up
    again and go over it piece by piece. *(They start upstairs.)* It would have to have
    been someone who knew just the—

*Mrs. Peters sits down. The two women sit there not looking at one another, but as if peering
into something and at the same time holding back. When they talk now it is in the manner of
feeling their way over strange ground, as if afraid of what they are saying, but as if they can
not help saying it.*

MRS. HALE: She liked the bird. She was going to bury it in that pretty box.
MRS. PETERS: *(in a whisper)* When I was a girl—my kitten—there was a boy took
    a hatchet, and before my eyes—and before I could get there—*(Covers her face
    an instant.)* If they hadn't held me back I would have—*(catches herself, looks up-
    stairs where steps are heard, falters weakly)*—hurt him.
MRS. HALE: *(with a slow look around her)* I wonder how it would seem never to have
    had any children around. *(Pause.)* No, Wright wouldn't like the bird—a thing
    that sang. She used to sing. He killed that, too.
MRS. PETERS: *(moving uneasily)* We don't know who killed the bird.   125
MRS. HALE: I knew John Wright.
MRS. PETERS: It was an awful thing was done in this house that night, Mrs. Hale.
    Killing a man while he slept, slipping a rope around his neck that choked the
    life out of him.
MRS. HALE: His neck. Choked the life out of him.

Her hand goes out and rests on the birdcage.

MRS. PETERS: *(with rising voice)* We don't know who killed him. We don't know.
MRS. HALE: *(her own feeling not interrupted)* If there'd been years and years of noth-   130
    ing, then a bird to sing to you, it would be awful—still, after the bird was still.
MRS. PETERS: *(something within her speaking)* I know what stillness is. When we
    homesteaded in Dakota, and my first baby died—after he was two years old, and
    me with no other then—
MRS. HALE: *(moving)* How soon do you suppose they'll be through, looking for the
    evidence?
MRS. PETERS: I know what stillness is. *(Pulling herself back.)* The law has got to pun-
    ish crime, Mrs. Hale.
MRS. HALE: *(not as if answering that)* I wish you'd seen Minnie Foster when she wore
    a white dress with blue ribbons and stood up there in the choir and sang. *(A
    look around the room.)* Oh, I wish I'd come over here once in a while! That was a
    crime! That was a crime! Who's going to punish that?
MRS. PETERS: *(looking upstairs)* We mustn't—take on.   135

MRS. HALE: I might have known she needed help! I know how things can be—for women. I tell you, it's queer, Mrs. Peters. We live close together and we live far apart. We all go through the same things—it's all just a different kind of the same thing. (*Brushes her eyes; noticing the bottle of fruit, reaches out for it.*) If I was you I wouldn't tell her her fruit was gone. Tell her it *ain't.* Tell her it's all right. Take this in to prove it to her. She—she may never know whether it was broke or not.

MRS. PETERS: (*takes the bottle, looks about for something to wrap it in; takes petticoat from the clothes brought from the other room, very nervously begins winding this around the bottle. In a false voice*) My, its a good thing the men couldn't hear us. Wouldn't they just laugh! getting all stirred up over a little thing like this—a dead canary. As if that could have anything to do with—with—wouldn't they *laugh!*

The men are heard coming down stairs.

MRS. HALE: (*under her breath*) Maybe they would—maybe they wouldn't.

COUNTY ATTORNEY: No, Peters, it's all perfectly clear except a reason for doing it. But you know juries when it comes to women. If there was some definite thing. Something to show—something to make a story about—a thing that would connect up with this strange way of doing it—

The women's eyes meet for an instant. Enter Hale from outer door.

140   HALE: Well, I've got the team around. Pretty cold out there.

COUNTY ATTORNEY: I'm going to stay here a while by myself. (*To the Sheriff.*) You can send Frank out for me, can't you? I want to go over everything. I'm not satisfied that we can't do better.

SHERIFF: Do you want to see what Mrs. Peters is going to take in?

The County Attorney goes to the table, picks up the apron, laughs.

COUNTY ATTORNEY: Oh, I guess they're not very dangerous things the ladies have picked out. (*Moves a few things about, disturbing the quilt pieces which cover the box. Steps back.*) No, Mrs. Peters doesn't need supervising. For that matter, a sheriff's wife is married to the law. Ever think of it that way, Mrs. Peters?

MRS. PETERS: Not—just that way.

145   SHERIFF: (*chuckling*) Married to the law. (*Moves toward the other room.*) I just want you to come in here a minute, George. We ought to take a look at these windows.

COUNTY ATTORNEY: (*scoffingly*) Oh, windows!

SHERIFF: We'll be right out, Mr. Hale.

Hale goes outside. The Sheriff follows the County Attorney into the other room. Then Mrs. Hale rises, hands tight together, looking intensely at Mrs. Peters, whose eyes make a slow turn, finally meeting Mrs. Hale's. A moment Mrs. Hale holds her, then her own eyes point the way to where the box is concealed. Suddenly Mrs. Peters throws back quilt pieces and tries to put the box in the bag she is wearing. It is too big. She opens box, starts to take bird out, cannot touch it, goes to pieces, stands there helpless. Sound of a knob turning in the other room. Mrs. Hale snatches the box and puts it in the pocket of her big coat. Enter County Attorney and Sheriff.

COUNTY ATTORNEY: *(facetiously)* Well, Henry, at least we found out that she was not going to quilt it. She was going to—what is it you call it, ladies?

MRS. HALE: *(her hand against her pocket)* We call it—knot it, Mr. Henderson.

*   *   *

Reading and Reacting

1. Consider why Glaspell might have chosen the kitchen of the Wright home as the setting for *Trifles*. What details of that setting reflect plot and theme?

2. To what extent is the play a product of the time in which it was written and initially produced, and to what extent could the events of the play happen today?

3. Whom do you see as the play's protagonist? Why?

4. In spite of the fact that we never see John Wright on stage, we tend to form an impression of the type of person he was. How do we obtain information about him? What impression does that information add up to regarding the type of person that he is?

5. Why does some conflict arise between the male and the female characters as they all look about the kitchen? Is that conflict ever resolved? Are we allowed insight into internal conflict going on within any of the characters?

6. Early in the play, when the County Attorney ridicules women for "worrying over trifles," Mrs. Hale and Mrs. Peters "move a little closer together" (1607). In what ways do the two women move "closer together" in more than a physical sense before the play is over? How does the relationship between the two women—along with their relationship with the absent Minnie Foster—reveal the theme of the work?

7. What "trifles" do the women discover as they wait downstairs, and how do those "trifles" provide the motive for murder that the men, at the same time, are looking for upstairs?

8. Discuss the symbolism of the dead bird and its cage.

9. When *Trifles* was rewritten as a short story, Glaspell changed the title to "A Jury of Her Peers." Which title do you think better captures the theme of the play? Why?

10. There are numerous references in the play to quilting and knotting. Explain how these references suggest more than simply technical terms for two ways of making a quilt. What weight and meaning do all of those references give to Mrs. Hale's last words?

11. **JOURNAL ENTRY** Mrs. Hale and Mrs. Peters may literally be helping Mrs. Wright get away with murder. Do you think their actions are justified, or do you condemn them for breaking the law? Explain.

12. **CRITICAL PERSPECTIVE** In her book *Susan Glaspell: Her Life and Times*, Linda Ben-Zvi writes that when Glaspell wrote the short story "A Jury of Her Peers" (p. 1631) a year after the play "for a more conservative readership around the country, she added certain details designed to gain their empathy for Minnie." What details in the short story did she add to make her readers sympathize more with Minnie?

Related Works: "I Stand Here Ironing" (p. 299), "The Yellow Wallpaper" (p. 379), "Everyday Use" (p. 426), "Harlem" (p. 760), "Daddy" (p. 772), "After great pain, a formal feeling comes—" (p. 972), *A Doll House* (p. 1113)

Sources

Background

LINDA BEN-ZVI

from "Murder, She Wrote": The Genesis of Susan Glaspell's *Trifles**

In the preface of her book *Women Who Kill* Ann Jones explains that her massive study of women murderers began with a quip. After working through a reading list that included *The Awakening*, *The House of Mirth*, and *The Bell Jar*, a student asked: "Isn't there anything a woman can do but kill herself?" Jones responded, "She can always kill somebody else" (xv).

Women killing somebody else, especially when that somebody is male, has fascinated criminologists, lawyers, psychologists, and writers. Fascinated and frightened them. Fear is the subtext of Jones's book: "The fears of men who, even as they shape society, are desperately afraid of women, and so have fashioned a world in which women come and go only in certain rooms; and about the fears of those women who, finding the rooms too narrow and the door still locked, lie in wait or set the place afire" (xvi). Or kill.

Women who kill evoke fear because they challenge societal constructs of femininity—passivity, restraint, and nurture—thus the rush to isolate and label the female offender, to cauterize her act. Her behavior *must* be aberrant, or crazed, if it is to be explicable. And explicable it must be; her crime cannot be seen as societally driven if the cultural stereotypes are to remain unchallenged.[1]

Theater loves a good murder story: violence, passion, and purpose. The stuff of tragedy is the stuff of the whodunit; *Oedipus* is, among other things, the Ur-detective story. Therefore, it is not surprising that contemporary dramatists should turn to murder—specifically, murder by women—as sources for plays. And following the thesis of Jones's book, it is also not surprising that the most powerful of the dramas—those that are more than exempla, docudramas, or hysterogenic flights—should be written by women who share with Jones an awareness that often the murderer, like the feminist, in her own way, "tests society's established boundaries" (13). . . .

The case at first glance seemed simple. Sometime after midnight on December 2, 1900, John Hossack, a well-to-do farmer, was struck twice on the head with an ax while he slept in bed. Margaret Hossack, his wife of thirty-three years, who was sleeping beside him, reported that a strange sound, "like two pieces of wood striking," wakened her; she jumped out of bed, went into the adjoining sitting room, saw a light shining on a wall, and heard the door to the front porch slowly closing. Only then did she hear her husband's groans. Assembling the five of her nine children who were still residing at home, she lit a lamp, reentered the bedroom, and discovered Hossack bleeding profusely, the walls and bedsheets spattered, his brain matter oozing from a five-inch gash, his head crushed. One of her sons claimed that the mortally

* *Theatre Journal* 44.2 (1992): 141–62. Print.

injured man was still able to speak. When he said to his father, "Well pa, you are badly hurt," Hossack replied, "No, I'm not hurt, but I'm not feeling well" (Dec. 4).

It was assumed that prowlers must have committed the crime, but, when a search of the farmhouse failed to reveal any missing items, a coroner's inquest was called. Its findings were inconclusive. However, after discovering the presumed murder weapon smeared with blood under the family corn crib, and listening to reports and innuendos from neighbors, who hinted at a history of marital and family trouble, the sheriff arrested Mrs. Hossack, "as a matter of precaution" (Dec. 5), while the funeral was still in progress, or, as Glaspell would more vividly report, "just as the sexton was throwing the last clods on the grave of her murdered husband" (Jan. 14). . . .

Employing the techniques of "Gonzo" journalism sixty years before Hunter Thompson, Glaspell filed twenty-six stories on the Hossack case, from the fifteen-line item on page 3, dated December 3, 1900, that summarily described the event of the murder, to the page 1, full-column story on April 11, 1901, that reported the jury's decision at the trial. Most are indistinguishable from her own unsigned "Newsgirl" features running in the paper at the time. They make ready use of hyperbole, invention, and supposition, all filtered through one of Glaspell's common devices in her column: a lively, often opinionated persona. Whether labeled "your correspondent," "a representative from the *News*," or "a member of the press," she is a constructed presence who invites the reader to share some privileged information, intriguing rumor, and running assessment of the case and of the guilt or innocence of the accused.

In her first extended coverage of the crime, under the headline "Coroner's Jury Returns Its Verdict This Morning—Mrs. Hossack Thought to Be Crazy," Glaspell announces the imminent arrest of the woman, a fact "secretly revealed to your correspondent." She also provides the first of many rumors that become increasingly more prominent in her coverage although never attributed to specific sources: "Friends of Mrs. Hossack are beginning to suggest that she is insane, and that she has been in this condition for a year and a half, under the constant surveillance of members of the family," and "the members of the Hossack family were not on pleasant relations with each other," information that comes as "a complete surprise, as Hossack was not supposed to have an enemy in the world." She concludes by citing the most damaging evidence used against the accused woman throughout her trial: Mrs. Hossack's claim that she lay asleep beside her husband and was not awakened while the murder was taking place (Dec. 5).

Glaspell continues to mix fact, rumor, and commentary with a superfluity of rousing language and imagery, opening her next report with the reminder that Mrs. Hossack has been arrested for the death of her husband, "on charge of having beaten out his brains with an axe"; that the accused woman has employed the legal services of Mr. Henderson and State Senator Berry; that when arrested she showed no emotion and absolutely declined to make any statement concerning her guilt or innocence; and that, while her family supported her, "the public sentiment is overwhelmingly against her." How she gleaned this information or arrived at these conclusions Glaspell does not say. She does, however, provide her first description of the accused woman: "Though past 50 years of age, she is tall and powerful and looks like she would be dangerous if aroused to a point of hatred." She again repeats the rumors of domestic tensions and quotes a neighbor named Haines, a witness at the inquest, who implied that Mrs. Hossack had years before asked him to get her husband "out of the way" (Dec. 6). . . .

In the months before the trial Glaspell filed only three small articles about the case, each one using the opportunity of a new piece of news to summarize the details of the murder, the grisly events becoming more grisly with the retelling. On March 23 she reports that new evidence has emerged "and that in all probability it would result in Mrs. Hossack's acquittal at an early date." She does not say what the evidence is, but she offers an important turn in the case. Mr. Haines, the primary source of information about trouble in the Hossack home and the party to whom, it is believed, Mrs. Hossack turned to get rid of her husband, "had gone insane brooding over the tragedy, and was yesterday sentenced to the insane asylum."

Although there had been talk of moving the venue of the trial because of the strong feelings against Margaret Hossack and the fear that an impartial jury could not be found (Jan. 14), the trial finally began in the Polk County Courthouse on April 1, 1901, and was held every day except Sundays for the next ten days. Glaspell had apparently been success-ful in stirring public interest because she reports that on the first day over twelve hundred people attended, far more than the tiny rural court could accommodate, and that on the day the jury returned its verdict more than two thousand were present. Noting the composition of the observers, she says: "The conspicuous feature so far is the large attendance of women in court. Over half of the spectators present today belong to the gentler sex. The bright array of Easter hats lent a novelty to the scene, giving it much the appearance of some social func-tion" (Apr. 2).[2]

The seventy-eight witnesses, fifty-three for the prosecution and twenty-five for the defense, focused on seven specific questions during the trial: (1) Would it have been possible, as his son testified, for John Hossack, who had sustained two traumatic blows—one made with the ax head, the second with the blunt handle—to talk and call for his wife and children? (2) Were the blood found on the ax and the hairs later discovered nearby human, or were they, as claimed by the family, the residue of the turkey killed two days earlier for Thanksgiving? (3) How had the ax, which the youngest son said he placed inside the corn crib after killing the turkey, come to be found under it, in its usual place? (4) Had the ax and Mrs. Hossack's nightclothes been washed to remove incriminating stains of blood? (5) Was the dog, who always barked when strangers appeared, drugged on the night of the crime, as family mem-bers testified? (6) Had earlier domestic troubles in the Hossack house been resolved and all dissension ceased for over a year before the murder, as the family stated? and (7) Would it have been possible for an intruder or intruders to enter the house through the bedroom win-dow, stand at the foot of the bed, and reach up to strike the fatal blows without rousing the woman who slept by her husband's side? An eighth question—what prompted Mrs. Hossack to leave home and wish her husband "out of the way"?—only entered the testimony twice. One neighbor, the wife of Mr. Haines, stated that she and her husband had come to aid Mrs. Hossack, who thought her husband would kill the family (Apr. 3). Another neighbor testi-fied that he had to act as protector when Mrs. Hossack returned to her home "in case her husband again maltreated her as she had reason for believing" (Apr. 2).

Glaspell's reports do not suggest that the prosecution or the defense pursued the possibil-ity of violence in the home, and she does not broach the subject herself. Instead, her stories of the trial tend to be summaries of testimony by experts and lay people who describe the structure of the brain, the disposition of the body in the bed, and the configuration of the blood spots on the walls. She does pause to describe the shock caused when the Hossack bed was brought into the courtroom, complete with bloodstained bedding, and when two vials of hairs were displayed—one found near the ax, the other obtained by exhuming John Hossack.

Interspersed between these accounts are her descriptions of the accused and of those attending the trial. During day one, for example, Glaspell describes Mrs. Hossack's reaction to the recital of counts against her: "Her eyes frequently filled with tears and her frame shook with emotion" (Apr. 2). On the next day, when the murder scene was again invoked, she notes that Mrs. Hossack, who occupied a seat by the sheriff's wife, surrounded by three of her daughters and all but one of her sons, broke down and wept bitterly: "Grief was not confined to her alone, it spread until the weeping group embraced the family and the sympathetic wife of Sheriff Hodson who frequently applied her handkerchief to her eyes" (Apr. 3).

Since there were no witnesses to the crime, the prosecution's case was based entirely on circumstantial evidence, and Glaspell often stops in her narration of testimony to weigh the success of the unsubstantiated arguments and to prod her readers to keep following the case. After one lengthy argument about how well Mrs. Hossack was able to wield an ax, Glaspell comments: "It must be admitted, however, that the prosecution has not thus far furnished any direct evidence and it is extremely doubtful if the chain of circumstantial evidence thus far offered will be sufficient to eliminate all doubt of the defendant's guilt from the minds of the jurors . . . on the other hand it is claimed by the prosecution attorney that the best evidence is yet to come" (Apr. 4). When Mrs. Hossack took the stand in her own defense and repeated the story she had held since the inquest, describing how she and her husband had spent a typical evening together the night of the crime—"He sat in the kitchen reading . . . later played with his whip . . . [while] I was patching and darning"—Glaspell observes, "When she left the stand, there seemed to be an impression on the audience that she had told the truth" (Apr. 8). Earlier questions of Mrs. Hossack's sanity apparently were dispelled by her composed appearance in court.

Like the novelist she would soon become, Glaspell saves her most impassioned descriptions for the climax of the trial, the summations by the lawyers. Of State Senator Berry, the defense counsel, she writes:

> It is said to be the master effort of his life . . . at times the jury without an exception was moved to tears. Strong men who had not shed a tear in years sat in their seats mopping their eyes and compressing their lips in a vain effort to suppress the emotion caused by the Senator's eloquent pleas. (Apr. 9)

This lachrymose display, she says, even extended to the prosecution attorneys, who were "seen to turn away their heads fearful lest the anguish of the family would unman them and the jury would have an impression which they could not afterward remove." The spectators were also moved. When the court was adjourned at noon, she writes, "fully two thousand people went out in the sunshine, their faces stained by the tears which had coursed down their cheeks."

Aside from tears Berry's chief strategy was to charge that Mr. Haines, "the insane man," was the real murderer. When he had been asked by the Hossack children to come to the house on the night of the murder, he had refused, saying that there were tramps about. It was he who had first implicated Mrs. Hossack by suggesting that she had wanted her husband dead and had sought his aid. And it was Mrs. Haines who had provided some of the most damning evidence about dissension in the Hossack home.

As successful as Berry may have been in concluding for the defense, Glaspell warns her readers that "it is certain that when attorney McNeal closes the argument for the prosecution the effect of Senator Berry's eloquence will have been lost and the verdict, if any at all is reached, can hardly be acquittal" (Apr. 9). Why, she does not say.

On the last day of the trial County Attorney Clammer and Mr. McNeal summarized for the prosecution, and, as Glaspell predicted, McNeal was able to rouse the audience with his indictment—"She did it, gentlemen, and I ask you to return it to her in kind . . . she has forfeited her right to live and she should be as John Hossack, who lies rotting beneath the ground." He, too, had his own bombshell: Margaret Hossack had been pregnant and given birth to a child before their marriage. This, McNeal claimed, was the dark secret often referred to in the trial, the story Hossack said he would take to his grave, and the reason for the unhappiness in the Hossack home. Just how a pregnancy thirty-three years earlier could have been the sole cause of trouble in the marriage and how it proved Mrs. Hossack's guilt in the murder of her husband was not clear, but, as Glaspell reports, it provided the jury with the impression that she was a woman who could not be trusted. It was with this revelation that the trial ended (Apr. 10).

The case went to the jury on April 10, the judge presenting the following charge: "When evidence consists of a chain of well authenticated circumstances, it is often more convincing and satisfactory and gives a stronger ground of assurance of the defendant's guilt than the direct testimony of witnesses unconfirmed by circumstances" (Apr. 11). In less than twenty-four hours the jury returned its verdict. Margaret Hossack was found guilty as charged and was sentenced to life imprisonment at hard labor. Glaspell reported the outcome but made no comment on the finding.

It was the last story she filed in the case; it was also the last story she filed as a reporter for the *Des Moines Daily News*. Immediately after the trial she resigned and returned home to Davenport to begin writing fiction, and by the summer of 1901 she had moved to Chicago and enrolled in the graduate English program at the University of Chicago. Therefore, she may never have learned the final disposition of the Hossack case, for the story was not yet over. In April 1901 Lawyers Henderson and Berry lost an appeal with a lower court, but in April 1902 the Supreme Court of the State of Iowa agreed to hear the case. Citing several instances in which the trial judge had ruled incorrectly on the evidence, the higher court overturned the original conviction and requested a new trial.[3] A second trial took place in Madison County in February 1903. This time the jury, after twenty-seven hours of deliberation, was unable to reach a verdict: nine voting for conviction and three for acquittal. In papers filed in April 1903 the prosecutor stated that, since no further information had surfaced, if would be a waste of taxpayers' money to ask a third jury to hear the case. Mrs. Hossack, then near sixty and in failing health, was ordered released and was allowed to return to her home, her guilt or innocence still in question. . . .

Trifles begins at home. A murder has been committed—a man strangled while he slept—and his wife, who claimed to be sleeping beside him at the time, has been accused of the crime and been taken to jail to await trial. Those prosecuting the case, County Attorney Henderson and Sheriff Peters, have returned to the scene to search for clues that will provide "a motive; something to show anger, or—sudden feeling" and explain "the funny way" the man was murdered, "rigging it all up like that." Accompanying them are Mr. Hale, who found the body; Mrs. Peters, the sheriff's wife, charged with bringing the accused woman some of her things; and Mrs. Hale, who keeps her company in the kitchen below while the men move around the upstairs bedroom and perimeter of the farmhouse searching for clues.

In the absence of the wife the women, like quilters, patch together the scenario of her life and of her guilt. As they imagine her, Minnie Foster Wright is a lonely, childless woman, married to a taciturn husband, isolated from neighbors because of the rigors of farm life. When they discover a bird cage, its door ripped off and a canary, its neck wrung, they have no trouble making the connection. The husband has killed the bird, the wife's only comfort, as he killed the birdlike spirit of the woman. The motive and method of murder become as clear to them as the signs of sudden anger they infer from the half-wiped kitchen table and Minnie's erratic quilt stitching. Based on such circumstantial evidence, the women try the case, find the accused guilty, but dismiss the charge, recognizing the exigencies that led her to the act. In the process of judging they become compeers, Mrs. Peters recognizing her own disenfranchisement under the law and her own potential for violence, Mrs. Hale recognizing her failure to sustain her neighbor and thus her culpability in driving the desperate woman to kill.

This brief summary indicates how few specific details remain in Glaspell's re-visioning of the Hossack case. There is mention of "that man who went crazy," but he is not named or connected to the events.[4] Of the names of the participants only Henderson is used, assigned to the county attorney rather than the defense lawyer. Margaret Hossack has been renamed Minnie Foster Wright, the pun on the surname marking her lack of "rights" and implying her right to free herself against the societally sanctioned right of her husband to control the family, a right implicit in the Hossack case.

Glaspell's most striking alterations are her excision of Minnie and the change of venue. The accused woman has been taken away to jail before *Trifles* begins, her place signified by the empty rocking chair that remains in her kitchen. By not physically representing Minnie on the stage, the playwright is able to focus on issues that move beyond the guilt or innocence of one person. Since the audience never actually sees Minnie, it is not swayed by her person, but, instead, by her condition, a condition shared by other women who can be imagined in the empty subject position. And by situating her play in the kitchen not the court, in the private space in which Minnie lived rather than the public space in which she will be tried, Glaspell is able to offer the audience a composite picture of the life of Minnie Wright, Margaret Hossack, and countless women whose experiences were not represented in court because their lives were not deemed relevant to the adjudication of their cases. Most important in her shift of venue, Glaspell can focus on the central question never asked in the original Hossack case, that concerning the motives for murder: Why do women kill?

Motives are writ large in *Trifles*. The mise-en-scène suggests the harshness of Minnie's life. The house is isolated, "down in a hollow and you don't see the road"—dark, foreboding, a kind of rural, Gothic scene.

The interior of the kitchen replicates this barrenness and the commensurate disjunctions in the family, as the woman experienced them. Things are broken, cold, imprisoning; they are also violent. "Preserves" explode from lack of heat, a punning reminder of the causal relationship between isolation and violence. The mutilated cage and bird signify the brutal nature of Wright and the physical abuse the wife has borne. Employing expressionistic techniques, Glaspell externalizes Minnie's desperation and the conditions that caused it.[5] She also finds the dramatic correlative for revenge. Rather than use an ax, this abused wife strangles her husband: a punishment to fit his crime. So powerfully does Glaspell marshal the evidence of Minnie's strangled life that the jury on the stage and the jury who observe them from the audience presume the wife's right to take violent action in the face of the violence done to her. They see what might cause women to kill.

When Glaspell turns to the characters in her play she again reworks the figures from the Hossack case, offering a revisionary reading of their roles in the original trial. The lawmen in *Trifles* bear traces of the original investigators, the county attorney and the sheriff. Mr. Hale is Glaspell's invention, a composite of the Indianola farmers who testified at the Hossack trial, his name possibly derived from Mr. Haines. By introducing a man not directly charged with prosecution of the case, Glaspell is able to show a patriarchal power and privilege, the united front that judged Margaret Hossack. She also illustrates the process through which an individual joins the ranks.

In "A Jury of Her Peers" she goes to great lengths to indicate Mr. Hale's awkwardness at the beginning of the story, as he relates the details of the case, and how easily he is intimidated by the county attorney. Yet when he is allowed—by virtue of his gender—to go upstairs with the men of law, it is Hale, not they, who directly taunts the women: "But would the women know a clue if they did come upon it?" It is also he whom Glaspell ironically says speaks "with good natured superiority" when he declares that "women are used to worrying over trifles." Gender transcends class here, as it did in the original trial, in which the farmers, jurors, and lawyers had a common connection: they were male, and, as such, they were in control of the court and the direction of the testimony. She also indicates, however, that the privileged club does have a pecking order. Mr. Hale is recently admitted—or, more likely, only temporarily admitted—and, therefore, more likely to chide those below him in order to gain favor with those above. A similar desire to ingratiate themselves with the law and to establish a camaraderie that temporarily suspended class was clearly apparent among the farmers of Indianola, eager to play a part in convicting Mrs. Hossack, some so ready that their zeal in intruding themselves into the investigation was cited in the Supreme Court reversal.

Constructing her category of men across class lines, establishing their connectedness based on legal empowerment and rights, Glaspell summarily dismisses them to roam about on the periphery of the tale, their presence theatrically marked by shuffling sounds above the heads of the women and occasional appearances as they scurry out to the barn. With her deft parody Glaspell undercuts the authority they wielded in the original case and throws into question their sanctioned preserve of power. They physically crisscross the stage as they verbally crisscross the details of the crime, both actions leading nowhere, staged to show ineffectuality and incompetence.

In her version of the Hossack case it is the women, also drawn across class lines, who occupy their place, standing in stage center and functioning as the composite shaping consciousness that structures the play.[6] Glaspell carefully chooses the two women who will usurp legal agency. Mrs. Peters is the wife of the sheriff, patterned after Sheriff Hodson's wife, whose acts of kindness to Margaret Hossack seem to have stayed in Glaspell's memory. At first Mrs. Peters parrots the masculinist view and voice of her husband, defending the search of the home as men's "duty." She gradually comes to recognize, however, that marital designation—wife of the sheriff—offers her no more freedom than it does Minnie; in fact, it completely effaces her as an individual. Glaspell illustrates this condition by having the women identified only by their surnames, while, at the same time, they seek to particularize Minnie, referring to her by both her first and her maiden name.[7]

To the men, however, Minnie is John Wright's wife, just as Mrs. Peters is the sheriff's wife: "married to the law," "one of us," "not in need of supervision." Even Mrs. Hale, at the beginning of "Jury," assumes that Mrs. Peters will be an extension of her husband and will share his views of the murder. Yet as Mrs. Peters slowly ferrets out the facts of Minnie's life—the childlessness, the isolation—and conflates the experiences with her own early married days, she begins to identify with Minnie. It is when she comes upon the bird cage and the dead canary that she makes the most important connection: an understanding of female violence in the face of male brutality: "When I was a girl—my kitten—there was a boy took a hatchet, and before my eyes—and before I could get there—(*covers her face an instant*) If they hadn't held me back I would—(*catches herself, looks upstairs where steps are heard, falters weakly*)—hurt him."

It is significant that Glaspell attributes to Mrs. Peters, the sheriff's wife, the memory of a murder with an ax, the murder weapon in the Hossack case, and offers as sign of brutality the dismemberment of an animal, a trace, perhaps of the turkey in the original case. In the reversal of roles that Glaspell stages—in having Mrs. Peters act in lieu of her husband, dispensing her verdict based on her reading of the case and the motives for murder—she destroys the notion that a woman is her husband. She also stages what a woman may become when given legal power: a subject acting under her own volition, her decisions not necessarily coinciding with her husband's or with the male hegemony. She becomes self-deputized.

If Mrs. Peters is taken from life, so too is Mrs. Hale, a possible surrogate for the young reporter Susan Glaspell.[8] Just as Mrs. Peters recognizes her own potential for murder in the face of powerlessness, and this recognition motivates her to act and to seize the juridical position, Mrs. Hale comes to her own awareness in the course of the play. What she discovers in the kitchen of the Wright home is her own complicity in Minnie's situation, because of the aid she has withheld. "We live close together and we live far apart. We all go through the same thing, it's just a different kind of the same thing," she says, summarizing her insight about "how it is for women." In light of the Hossack case and Glaspell's role in sensationalizing the proceedings and in shaping public opinion, the lines appear to be confessional; thus, to her question "Who will punish that?" Mrs. Hale's words seem to indicate that Glaspell's awareness in 1916 of her omissions and commissions in 1901, of her failure to act in Margaret Hossack's behalf, and of her failure to recognize the implications of the trial for her own life.

Given this awareness, it may seem strange that, when Glaspell has the opportunity to retry Margaret Hossack and change the outcome of the case, she does not acquit the woman, or, as Kayann Short argues, give her "her day in court" (9) to prove her innocence. Instead, she has Mrs. Peters and Mrs. Hale assume Minnie's guilt and, as in the original trial, base their findings on circumstantial evidence instead of incontrovertible proof. When approaching *Trifles* in relation to the Hossack case, however, it becomes clear that acquittal is not Glaspell's intention, not why she wrote the play. Whether Margaret Hossack or Minnie Wright committed murder is moot; what is incontrovertible is the brutality of their lives, the lack of options they had to redress grievances or to escape abusive husbands, and the complete disregard of their plight by the courts and by society. Instead of arguing their innocence, Glaspell concretizes the conditions under which these women live and the circumstances that might cause them to kill. She thus presents the subtext that was excised from the original trial and that undergirds so many of the cases cited in Ann Jones's study: men's fears of women who might kill and women's fears of the murder they might be forced to commit. In so doing, she stages one of the first modern arguments for justifiable homicide.[9] By having Mrs. Peters and Mrs. Hale unequivocally assume Minnie's guilt and also assume justification for her act, Glaspell presents her audience/jury with a defense that forces it to confront the central issues of female powerlessness and disenfranchisement and the need for laws to address such issues.[10]

Yet Glaspell does not actually present the victimization of women or the violent acts such treatment may engender; instead, she stages the potential for female action and the usurpation of power.[11] By having the women assume the central positions and conduct the investigation and the trial, she actualizes an empowerment that suggests that there are options short of murder that can be imagined for women. Mrs. Peters and Mrs. Hale may seem to conduct their trial sub rosa because they do not actively confront the men, but in Mrs. Hale's final words, "We call it—knot it," ostensibly referring to a form of quilting but clearly addressed to the actions the women have taken, they become both actors and namers. Even if the men do not understand the pun—either through ignorance or, as Judith Fetterley suggests, through self-preservation—the audience certainly does. It recognizes that the women have achieved an important political victory: they have wrested control of language, a first step in political ascendancy, and they have wrested control of the case and the stage. Not waiting to be given the vote or the right to serve on juries, Glaspell's women have taken the right for themselves. Her audience in 1916 would get the point. It would also understand that Glaspell is deconstructing the very assumptions about the incontrovertibility of the law and about its absolutist position. Mrs. Peters and Mrs. Hale, by suturing into their deliberations their own experiences and fears—just as the men in the Hossack case did—illustrate the subjective nature of the reading of evidence and, by implication, of all essentialist readings.

In 1916 it would be clearer than it often is to contemporary audiences that Glaspell is more concerned with legal and social empowerment than with replacing one hierarchy with another; that women acting surreptitiously may be less a comment on their natures than on the political systems that breed such behavior; not that women speak "in a different voice" but, rather, that they speak in a manner deriving from their different position under the law, from their common erasure. Her depiction of the conditions of her women is close to what Catherine MacKinnon describes in her book *Feminism Unmodified:* women's actions—their voices—deriving not from some innate nature but from the ways they have been forced to speak and to act. MacKinnon suggests that, if legal and social changes could occur, it would then be time to decide how a woman "talks."[12] When women are powerless, she argues, "you don't just speak differently. A lot, you don't speak. Your speech is not differently articulated, it is silenced" (39). In *Trifles* Glaspell, like MacKinnon, posits gender as a production of the inequality of power under law, "a social status based on who is permitted to do what to whom" (MacKinnon 8). . . .

At the time she wrote *Trifles* Glaspell was living in a community passionately concerned with socialism and feminism; she herself was a founding member of Heterodoxy, the New York-based group of women whose numbers included activists Marie Jenny Howe, Crystal Eastman, Elizabeth Irwin, Mary Heaton Vorse, and, for a time, Charlotte Perkins Gilman.[13] The audience for the Provincetown Players was already a body of the committed, who in 1916 worked for suffrage and for social reform that would redress class distinctions in the United States and who, for the most part, were opposed to Wilson and the war. Unlike many suffragists, their arguments were usually posited on a materialist rather than an essentialist reading of gender, concerned either with class struggles of which gender limitations were part or enlightenment ideals of individualism applicable to both women and men. They did not romanticize femininity; most debunked the "cult of the home." Their major concern was in insuring "that women shall have the same right as man to be different, to be individuals, not merely a social unit," and that this individualism would manifest itself in legal and social freedom.[14] It was for this audience and at this time that Glaspell returned to the Hossack case.

Trifles, therefore, is grounded in a double-focused historical context: the Iowa of 1901 and the Provincetown of 1916, the two periods leaving traces and providing many of the tensions and fissures that produce the contemporary feel to Glaspell's best works. Thus positioned, her writing acts as a palimpsest for the shifting roles of women in the early twentieth century and for her own shifts in attitudes toward the possibilities for women and herself. It is either a testament to the skill with which Glaspell constructed *Trifles* and "A Jury of Her Peers" or proof of how little women's lives have changed since 1916 that contemporary feminist critics still use the play and story as palimpsests for their own readings of contemporary feminist issues, and these readings still point to some of the dilemmas that faced Glaspell and her personae in 1901 and in 1916: how to free women from the stereotypic roles into which they have been cast, how to articulate their lives and their rights without reinscribing them in the very roles against which they inveigh, how to represent female power not victimization—in short, how to represent Margaret Hossack. Yet in reading the works through a contemporary grid, critics should be careful of turning them into contemporary tracts, assuming that, just because Glaspell offers a picture of two women who bond, she is arguing for a higher moral ground for women, romanticizing femininity and home, arguing sexual difference, or the categorization of women under a fixed moral genus.[15] Given her own interests and concerns at the time, and her own relation to the Hossack case, it is more likely that her play and story are illustrating the need to provide both male and female voices in court—and in art—if human experience is not to be forever subsumed under the male pronoun and if women's voices are to be heard not as difference but as equally registered.

Notes

[1] At the turn of the century the father of modern criminology, Cesare Lombroso, offered a checklist of the physical qualities that would identify women who might kill: "approximate more to males . . . than to normal women, especially in the superciliary arches in the seam of sutures, in the lower jaw-bones, and in peculiarities of the occipital region" (Jones 6).

[2] The Hossack case was not unique in the number of women in attendance. Jones offers examples of irate ministers commenting on the large numbers of women who attended celebrated murder trials around the same period. In one case a minister comments that, "It is a strange thing that women, under no compulsion whatever, are found in large numbers in every notorious trial everywhere, and the dirtier the trial the more woman usually will be found in attendance" (138). He does not conjecture about this phenomenon.

[3] There were seven procedural points upon which the Supreme Court of Iowa based its reversal, the most significant of which were the following: that the hairs found under the corn crib were not proved to be from the murder weapon and had been taken by the county attorney and given to the sheriff and could not, therefore, be introduced as evidence; that the dissension in the Hossack house had abated at least a year prior to the murder and could not, therefore, be introduced in the case. See *State v. Hossack*, Supreme Court of Iowa, April 9, 1902, *Northwestern Reporter*, 1077–81.

[4] See Hedges for a discussion of insanity in rural American life and the practice by women on the plains of having canaries to provide them company.

[5] Glaspell often used expressionistic techniques in her plays. See Ben-Zvi, "Susan Glaspell and Eugene O'Neill" (1982 and 1986), for a discussion of *The Verge* as an expressionistic drama.

[6] Mrs. Peters and Mrs. Hale are of different classes, a fact visually captured by the filmmaker Sally Heckel in her version of "A Jury of Her Peers" (Texture Films). Mrs. Hale wears a plain, cloth coat and head scarf; Mrs. Peters has a fur tippet and large, feathered hat.

Their language also bears signs of their class, a technique Glaspell often repeats. In *Trifles* Mrs. Hale makes grammatical errors, has unfinished sentences, drops letters. Mrs. Peters speaks in a grammatically correct manner befitting the sheriff's wife. For example, Mrs. Hale's comment, "I wonder if she was goin' to quilt it or just knot it" becomes Mrs. Peters's "We think she was going to—knot it," the omitted *g* signifying for Glaspell different education and position. What joins them is the men's categorization of them, predicated on gender, erasing difference, dismissing individuality.

[7] At the time Glaspell was writing the play, the question of women taking their husbands' names was a political issue. One of Glaspell's friends, Ruth Hale, launched a movement called the Lucy Stone League, which supported married women who chose to keep their maiden names. (See Schwarz 14, 58, 83.) Glaspell, like her contemporaries Neith Boyce, Mary Heaton Vorse, and others, never assumed her husband's name.

[8] When the Provincetown Players staged the play Glaspell chose to play Mrs. Hale and had her husband, George Cram Cook, play Hale.

[9] One could argue that the precedent for staging a case of justifiable homicide for women was established in *The Oresteia*, in which the motives leading to Clytemnestra's murder of Agamemnon are delineated, or would be if one affixed to the work the murder of Iphigenia, as Ariane Mnouchkine did in a production of the Aeschylus' trilogy at the Théâtre du Soleil that is prefaced by Euripides' *Iphigenia in Aulis*. (See *New York Times*, March 27, 1981, B3, for a description of this performance.) For a discussion of contemporary wife battering cases and the plea of justifiable homicide, see Jones (chap. 6).

[10] In most of Glaspell's plays there is a political component directly connected to particular events of her period that would have been immediately evident to her audience but is often lost in contemporary discussions of her works. In *Suppressed Desires*, for instance, she takes on a noted antifeminist of the period, one Professor Sedwick, who had said, "All women were hens." In the play Glaspell and Cook play on the name Stephen (Step-hen), parodying both Freudianism and Cook's childhood pronunciation of the word (*Road* 25). Yet they are also answering Sedwick, a reference her audience would immediately have understood. Even more overtly, *Inheritors* challenges contemporary issues such as the Alien and Sedition laws and the Red Scare.

[11] See Butler on the problems of staging victimization and thus representing the very condition the writer may wish to dismantle.

[12] MacKinnon, while acknowledging the work of such people as Carol Gilligan, argues that Gilligan "achieves for moral reasoning what the special protection rule achieves in law: the affirmative rather than the negative valuation of that which has accurately distinguished women from men, by making it seem as though those attributes, with their consequences, really are somehow ours, rather than what male supremacy has attributed to us for its own use": "For women to affirm difference, when difference means dominance, as it does with gender, means to affirm the qualities and characteristics of powerlessness" (38–39). What is relevant about MacKinnon in relation to *Trifles* and "Jury" is her emphasis on law and enfranchisement. Reading Glaspell through MacKinnon allows the critics to move beyond the questions of "different voice" that were the critical bulwarks of the first moment of Glaspell criticism (see, e.g., Ben-Zvi, Stein, Alkalay-Gut, and Malpede) or critiqued in the more recent materialist readings (see Carroll, Hart, Nelligan [in *Susan Glaspell*], Short, Stephens, and Williams). It is hard to imagine, however, that Glaspell would have supported MacKinnon's stance on censorship as a way of alleviating pornography. Repeatedly in her writing, Glaspell objected to any form of censorship, for whatever reason.

[13] See Judith Schwarz's description of Heterodoxy, in which she lists Glaspell as a founding member; also see Nancy Cott's detailed study of the feminist movement in New York in the years 1910–1920; and June Sochen's descriptions of the period and of Glaspell's relation to feminists in Greenwich Village. In *Women and American Socialism, 1870–1920* Buhle discusses how Glaspell "created female characters as working-class women with capacities to feel intensely, to understand

injustice rather than internalizing oppression, and when conditions allowed to strike back at their oppressors" (203).

[14] These quotations are taken from the same *New York Times* report (February 18, 1914) concerning a meeting organized by Heterodoxy president, Marie Jenny Howe, at Cooper Union, billed as "the first feminist meeting ever convened." At the time Glaspell was in Davenport, after suffering a miscarriage, but many of her friends were there, and she would most likely have been in the audience, if not on the dais. For other references to articles on feminism written between 1913–16, see Cott.

[15] Five years later she would write *The Verge*, her most powerful and feminist play. Her persona, Claire Archer, would demand a life not circumscribed by the traditional roles assigned to women—mother, caregiver, hostess—and would stand in juxtaposition to her daughter and her sister, who represent conventional women whose gender does not provide them with an insight into Claire's life or her aspiration. In *The Verge* Glaspell also pursues feminism as a "transvaluation of values" on a Nietzschean model. See Cott (296) in relation to Dora Marsden and a similar position; also see Carroll.

Works Cited

Alkalay-Gut, Karen. "'A Jury of Her Peers': The Importance of *Trifles*." *Studies in Short Fiction* 21 (1984): 3–11.

Barlow, Judith, ed. *Plays by American Women: 1900–1930*. New York: Applause Books, 1985.

Ben-Zvi, Linda. "Susan Glaspell and Eugene O'Neill." *Eugene O'Neill Newsletter* 6 (1982): 22–29.

———. "Susan Glaspell, Eugene O'Neill, and the Imagery of Gender." *Eugene O'Neill Newsletter* 10 (1986): 22–28.

———. "Susan Glaspell's Contributions to Contemporary Women Playwrights." In *Feminine Focus: The New Women Playwrights*. Ed. Enoch Brater. New York: Oxford University Press, 1989. 147–66.

Bigsby, C. W. E., ed. *Plays by Susan Glaspell*. Cambridge: Cambridge University Press, 1987.

Buhle, Mari Jo. *Women and American Socialism, 1870–1920*. Urbana: University of Illinois Press, 1981.

Butler, Judith. "Performing Acts and Gender Constitution: An Essay in Phenomenology and Feminist Theory." In *Performing Feminisms: Feminist Critical Theory and Theatre*. Ed. Sue-Ellen Case. Baltimore: Johns Hopkins University Press, 1990. 270–82.

Carroll, Kathleen. "Centering Women Onstage: Susan Glaspell's Dialogic Strategy of Resistance." PhD diss. University of Maryland, 1990.

Cott, Nancy. *The Grounding of Modern Feminism*. New Haven: Yale University Press, 1987.

Gilligan, Carol. *In a Different Voice: Psychological Theory and Women's Development*. Cambridge: Harvard University Press, 1982.

Glaspell, Susan. "The Hossack Case." *Des Moines Daily News*, December 2, 1900–April 13, 1901.

———. "A Jury of Her Peers." *Everyweek*, March 5, 1917.

———. *Trifles*. New York: Frank Shay/Washington Square Players, 1916; rpt. in Bigsby.

Hedges, Elaine. "Small Things Reconsidered: Susan Glaspell's 'A Jury of Her Peers.'" *Women's Studies* 12 (1986): 89–110.

Heilbrun, Carolyn. *Writing a Woman's Life*. New York: W. W. Norton, 1988.

Jones, Ann. *Women Who Kill*. New York: Holt, Rinehart and Winston, 1980.

Kolodny, Annette. "A Map for Re-Reading: Gender and the Interpretation of Literary Texts." In *The New Feminist Criticism*. Ed. Elaine Showalter. New York: Pantheon, 1985. 46–62.

Larabee, Ann. "Death in Delphi: Susan Glaspell and the Companionate Marriage." *Mid-American Review* 7. no. 2 (1987): 93–106.

MacKinnon, Catherine. *Feminism Unmodified: Discourses on Life and Law*. Cambridge: Harvard University Press, 1987.

Malpede, Karen. "Introduction." *Women in Theatre*. New York: Drama Books, 1983.

Murphy, Jeanette. "A Question of Silence." In *Films for Women*. Ed. Charlotte Brunsdon. London: British Film Institute, 1986. 99–108.

Noe, Marcia. *Susan Glaspell: Voice from the Heartland*. Macomb: Western Illinois Monograph Series, 1983.

Northwestern Reporter, April 9, 1902: 1077–81.

Polk County Transcripts of Court Records, case no. 805, April 2, 1901–March 3, 1903.

Rockwell, John. "An *Oresteia* Using Non-Western Techniques." *New York Times*. March 27, 1981.

Schwarz, Judith. *Radical Feminists of Heterodoxy: Greenwich Village, 1912–1940*. Lebanon, N.H.: New Victoria Publishers, 1982.

Short, Kayann. "A Different Kind of the Same Thing: The Erasure of Difference in 'A Jury of Her Peers.'" In *Trifles and "A Jury of Her Peers" Casebook*. Ed. Linda Ben-Zvi, forthcoming.

Sochen, June. *The New Woman in Greenwich Village, 1910–1920*. New York:Quadrangle, 1972.

Stein, Karen. "The Women's World of Glaspell's *Trifles*." In *Women in American Theatre*. Ed. Helen Krich Chinoy and Linda Walsh Jenkins. New York: Theatre Communications Group, 1987. 253–56.

Stephens, Judith. "Gender Ideology and Dramatic Convention in Progressive Era Plays, 1890–1920." In *Performing Feminisms: Feminist Critical Theory and Theatre*. Ed. Sue-Ellen Case. Baltimore: Johns Hopkins University Press, 1990. 283-93.

Supreme Court of Iowa, April 9, 1902. *Northwestern Reporter*: 1077–81.

"Talk on Feminism Stirs Great Crowd." *New York Times*. February 18, 1914.

Warren County Court Records. Hossack trial, April 1903.

Williams, Linda. "A Jury of Their Peers: Marlene Gorris's 'A Question of Silence.'" In *Postmodernism and Its Discontents: Theories and Practices*. Ed. E. Ann Kaplan. London: Verso, 1988. 107–15.

SUSAN GLASPELL

Surrounded by Mystery: Murder of John Hossack Was Not for Money*

Persons who went to the home of John Hossack Monday and saw the murdered man in his bed, and heard portions of the testimony before the coroner's jury, are all at sea as to who killed Hossack or for what reason. There is no evidence of burglary. The murderer came through a porch and front room to the bed room where Mr. and Mrs. Hossack slept. He evidently reached across the bed with an ax and struck two blows. One crushed in the skull and the other made a deep cut, yet Hossack lived from Saturday night until 10 a.m. Sunday, though he did not regain consciousness, and no one has yet been found who can give a clue to the murder. The ax was found under a shed about fifty feet from the house. Mrs. Hossack swore before the jury that she was awakened about midnight by the slamming of a door, saw a flash of light and then all was dark. She called to her husband but as he did not respond, she got up and lighted a lamp. Then she discovered him on the bed, with blood all over the clothing. She said she did not hear the blows nor see any one. The officers are investigating.

Des Moines Daily News 4 Dec. 1900: n. pag. Print.

It is rumored that trouble had arisen in the Hossack household and that possibly some relative committed the murder.

The funeral of Mr. Hossack was set for Wednesday at 1 p.m. from the First M.E. church at New Virginia. The family consisted of wife, and four children, who were at home.

Burt Osborn and Harry Hartman of Indianola went to the Hossack home Sunday afternoon and took flashlight photographs of the remains of Hossack as they lay on the bed. The left temple is crushed in, probably by the butt end of the ax; while the upper part of the head is deeply gashed.

The ax, which was found under a shed and covered with blood, has been sent to a chemist, who is to report whether or not the blood is human or from chickens, as stated by some members of the family.

The report that Hossack did not regain consciousness is contradicted. One of his sons testified before the coroner's jury that he said to his father, "Well, pa, you are badly hurt," and that he replied: "No, I'm not hurt, but I'm not feeling well."

It is said that Hossack did not make any statement as to whom he suspected of the crime.

ANONYMOUS

Wife Charged with Murder*

While attending her husband's funeral, Mrs. Margaret Hossack yesterday was arrested by Sheriff Lewis Hudson of Warren county, charged with the murder of her husband, John Hossack, who was killed in cold blood Saturday night at the Hossack home, six miles northwest of this place.

The attendance at the funeral was unusually large, farmers coming for miles around to attend. But when the sheriff stepped up to Mrs. Hossack, shortly after the last chunk of dirt had been thrown upon the newly made grave, and she was on her way to town with her children by her side, the arrest caused a tremendous sensation. Mrs. Hossack took the arrest calmly, evidently having anticipated the event. She expressed a desire to go first to her home to get a few things and within an hour the sheriff and the accused were on their way to the county jail at Indianola.

More than twenty witnesses were examined by the coroner and his jury before the evidence was closed. Almost the last witness, and by far the most important one examined, was Mrs. Hossack herself. She reiterated her former statements of the crime, and although she was under examination for nearly three hours nothing in the way of causing her to break down or to cross herself in her evidence resulted.

The evidence upon which Mrs. Hossack was arrested is purely circumstantial, the only testimony being to the effect that Hossack and his wife had frequent quarrels, and the improbability of the woman's story that she slept peacefully by the side of the murdered man and heard no sounds until after it was all over and the murderer had escaped through the front door.

Cedar Rapids Republican 6 Dec. 1900: n. pag. Print.

SUSAN GLASPELL

Surprise Is Expected: Rumored Developments in Hossack Murder Case[*]

Senator Berry of Indianola, counsel for Mrs. Hossack who is accused of murdering her aged husband on the night of December 1, 1900, was in the city a few days ago. While here the Senator intimated that new and valuable evidence has been discovered for the defendant and that in all probability it would result in her acquittal at an early date. Just what the nature of this evidence is the Senator did not say. However, enough is known to warrant the belief that surprises will be the order of the Hossack trial. County Attorney Clammer is said to have intimated that he was expecting a surprise from the opposing counsel, but he, too, refused to disclose the nature of the surprises, if there are any in store.

W.T. Haines, the man who testified before the grand jury that Mrs. Hossack tried to hire him to murder her husband, is reported to have gone insane brooding over the tragedy, and was yesterday sentenced to the insane asylum.

The Hossack trial comes on for hearing next Tuesday. Both the counsel for the state and defense have been working industriously since Mrs. Hossack was bound over to the grand jury for the murder of her husband, and one of the most sensational trials that has ever occupied the attention of a Warren county criminal court is promised when the case opens; Judge Applegate is on the bench. He is said to be one of the fairest minded judges in the circuit and there will be no objection from either source. For a time it was thought that a change of venue would be asked and Polk county courts expected the famous trial to come here. Both Senator Berry and County Attorney Clammer have made statements, however, to the effect that no such a change will be asked.

Bloody Evidences of Murder

No one has ever been able to gain access to the exhibits which will be introduced as evidence at the trial. The bloody ax, the pole and blade of which are covered with the life blood of John Hossack, is kept locked in the vaults of the state attorney. Four finger marks appear on the handle and it is understood these will be used as damaging evidence against the defendant. The marks are plainly visible and the imprint made by the lines on the finger tips can be traced. It may be that this celebrated case will employ the hobby of Mark Twain's "Puddinhead Wilson"[*] in ferreting out the murder of the old defenseless man.

Locked up in the attorney's vaults is also the chemical analysis of the blood found on the blade of the ax. There is a question as to whether or not this blood is human. The ax was sent to Chemist Floyd Davis for his analysis and he, together with County Attorney Clammer, and the midnight assassin, are the only persons who know whether the blood is that of John Hossack or, as has been claimed by the defense, a chicken, which had been slaughtered the day previous to the murder.

---

[*]*Des Moines Daily News* 23 Mar. 1901: n. pag. Print.
[*] *the hobby of . . .* : Gathering fingerprints.

Story Told Again

Everyone remembers the foul murder of John Hossack, who was killed while sleeping by the side of his aged wife on the night of December 1. The story is old, but as the trial approaches a curiosity revives and the incidents on that eventful night are vividly recalled. Hossack was a wealthy farmer residing in the vicinity of New Virginia, a small village thirteen miles south of Indianola. About 2 o'clock on the night of December 1 the Hossack household was aroused by screams from Mrs. Hossack who declared her husband had been murdered. Soon lights were gleaming through the rooms and members of the family were horrified to see the dead body of their parent lying in a pool of blood on the bed, a deep gash extending along the base of the right ear, one side of the incision mashed, and the brains slowly oozing from the gaping wound. Neighbors were aroused and a physician summoned, but the old man was mortally wounded. The laceration of the brain by the blade of an ax paralyzed the right side of his body rendering him unable to talk. He died the following morning and the secret of his death was buried with him a day later.

Arrested at Open Grave

But Mrs. Hossack was suspected. No one could have struck the fatal blow seemingly without arousing her. The suspicion grew until a coroner's jury was empanelled. They deliberated, adjourning without returning a verdict. County Attorney Clammer of Warren county was present at the session. He believed the wife was guilty of the crime and at once proceeded to Indianola swearing out a warrant for her arrest. It was served the next day just as they were throwing the last shovel of dirt on her husband's grave. She offered no resistance and showed no emotion. Four months in the county jail has not changed her. She is the same square jawed, determined looking woman as she was when Sheriff Hodson arrested her for the murder of her husband; the same as when she was dragged into a justice court and held to the grand jury under heavy bonds; the same as when an indictment, charging her with murder in the first degree, was returned and the same as she will be when led into the court room for final indictment.

SUSAN GLASPELL

A Jury of Her Peers (1917)

When Martha Hale opened the storm door and got a cut of the north wind, she ran back for her big woolen scarf. As she hurriedly wound that round her head her eye made a scandalized sweep of her kitchen. It was no ordinary thing that called her away—it was probably farther from ordinary than anything that had ever happened in Dickson County. But what her eye took in was that her kitchen was in no shape for leaving: her bread all ready for mixing, half the flour sifted and half unsifted.

She hated to see things half done; but she had been at that when the team from town stopped to get Mr. Hale, and then the sheriff came running in to say his wife wished Mrs. Hale would come too—adding, with a grin, that he guessed she was getting scarey and wanted another woman along. So she had dropped everything right where it was.

"Martha!" now came her husband's impatient voice. "Don't keep folks waiting out here in the cold."

She again opened the storm door, and this time joined the three men and the one woman waiting for her in the big two-seated buggy.

5   After she had the robes tucked around her she took another look at the woman who sat beside her on the back seat. She had met Mrs. Peters the year before at the county fair, and the thing she remembered about her was that she didn't seem like a sheriff's wife. She was small and thin and didn't have a strong voice. Mrs. Gorman, sheriff's wife before Gorman went out and Peters came in, had a voice that somehow seemed to be backing up the law with every word. But if Mrs. Peters didn't look like a sheriff's wife, Peters made it up in looking like a sheriff. He was to a dot the kind of man who could get himself elected sheriff—a heavy man with a big voice, who was particularly genial with the law-abiding, as if to make it plain that he knew the difference between criminals and non-criminals. And right there it came to Mrs. Hale's mind, with a stab, that this man who was so pleasant and lively with all of them was going to the Wrights' now as a sheriff.

"The country's not very pleasant this time of year," Mrs. Peters at last ventured, as if she felt they ought to be talking as well as the men.

Mrs. Hale scarcely finished her reply, for they had gone up a little hill and could see the Wright place now, and seeing it did not make her feel like talking. It looked very lonesome this cold March morning. It had always been a lonesome-looking place. It was down in a hollow, and the poplar trees around it were lonesome-looking trees. The men were looking at it and talking about what had happened. The county attorney was bending to one side of the buggy, and kept looking steadily at the place as they drew up to it.

"I'm glad you came with me," Mrs. Peters said nervously, as the two women were about to follow the men in through the kitchen door.

Even after she had her foot on the doorstep, her hand on the knob, Martha Hale had a moment of feeling she could not cross the threshold. And the reason it seemed she couldn't cross it now was simply because she hadn't crossed it before. Time and time again it had been in her mind, "I ought to go over and see Minnie Foster"—she still thought of her as Minnie Foster, though for twenty years she had been Mrs. Wright. And then there was always something to do and Minnie Foster would go from her mind. But *now* she could come.

10   The men went over to the stove. The women stood close together by the door. Young Henderson, the county attorney, turned around and said, "Come up to the fire, ladies."

Mrs. Peters took a step forward, then stopped. "I'm not—cold," she said.

And so the two women stood by the door, at first not even so much as looking around the kitchen.

The men talked for a minute about what a good thing it was the sheriff sent his deputy out that morning to make a fire for them, and then Sheriff Peters stepped back from the stove, unbuttoned his outer coat, and leaned his hands on the kitchen table in a way that seemed to mark the beginning of official business. "Now, Mr. Hale," he said in a sort of semiofficial voice, "before we move things about, you tell Mr. Henderson just what it was you saw when you came here yesterday morning."

The county attorney was looking around the kitchen.

"By the way," he said, "has anything been moved?" He turned to the sheriff. "Are   15
things just as you left them yesterday?"

Peters looked from cupboard to sink; from that to a small worn rocker a little to
one side of the kitchen table.

"It's just the same."

"Somebody should have been left here yesterday," said the county attorney.

"Oh—yesterday," returned the sheriff, with a little gesture as of yesterday having been more than he could bear to think of. "When I had to send Frank to Morris
Center for that man who went crazy—let me tell you, I had my hands full *yesterday*.
I knew you could get back from Omaha by today, George, and as long as I went over
everything here myself—"

"Well, Mr. Hale," said the county attorney, in a way of letting what was past and   20
gone go, "tell just what happened when you came here yesterday morning."

Mrs. Hale, still leaning against the door, had that sinking feeling of the mother
whose child is about to speak a piece. Lewis often wandered along and got things
mixed up in a story. She hoped that he would tell this straight and plain, and not say
unnecessary things that would just make things harder for Minnie Foster. He didn't
begin at once, and she noticed that he looked queer—as if standing in that kitchen
and having to tell what he had seen there yesterday morning made him almost sick.

"Yes, Mr. Hale?" the county attorney reminded.

"Harry and I had started to town with a load of potatoes," Mrs. Hale's husband
began.

Harry was Mrs. Hale's oldest boy. He wasn't with them now, for the very good   25
reason that those potatoes never got to town yesterday and he was taking them this
morning, so he hadn't been home when the sheriff stopped to say he wanted Mr. Hale
to come over to the Wright place and tell the county attorney his story there, where
he could point it all out. With all Mrs. Hale's other emotions came the fear that maybe
Harry wasn't dressed warm enough—they hadn't any of them realized how that north
wind did bite.

"We come along this road," Hale was going on, with a motion of his hand to the
road over which they had just come, "and as we got in sight of the house I says to
Harry, 'I'm goin' to see if I can't get John Wright to take a telephone.' You see," he
explained to Henderson, "unless I can get somebody to go in with me they won't come
out this branch road except for a price I can't pay. I'd spoke to Wright about it once
before; but he put me off, saying folks talked too much anyway, and all he asked was
peace and quiet—guess you know about how much he talked himself. But I thought
maybe if I went to the house and talked about it before his wife, and said all the
women-folks liked the telephones, and that in this lonesome stretch of road it would
be a good thing—well, I said to Harry that that was what I was going to say—though
I said at the same time that I didn't know as what his wife wanted made much difference to John—"

Now, there he was!—saying things he didn't need to say. Mrs. Hale tried to catch
her husband's eye, but fortunately the county attorney interrupted with:

"Let's talk about that a little later, Mr. Hale. I do want to talk about that, but I'm
anxious now to get along to just what happened when you got here."

When he began this time, it was very deliberately and carefully:

"I didn't see or hear anything. I knocked at the door. And still it was all quiet inside. I knew they must be up—it was past eight o'clock. So I knocked again, louder, and I thought I heard somebody say 'Come in.' I wasn't sure—I'm not sure yet. But I opened the door—this door," jerking a hand toward the door by which the two women stood, "and there, in that rocker"—pointing to it—"sat Mrs. Wright."

30   Every one in the kitchen looked at the rocker. It came into Mrs. Hale's mind that that rocker didn't look in the least like Minnie Foster—the Minnie Foster of twenty years before. It was a dingy red, with wooden rungs up the back, and the middle rung was gone, and the chair sagged to one side.

"How did she—look?" the county attorney was inquiring.

"Well," said Hale, "she looked—queer."

"How do you mean—queer?"

As he asked it he took out a notebook and pencil. Mrs. Hale did not like the sight of that pencil. She kept her eye fixed on her husband, as if to keep him from saying unnecessary things that would go into that notebook and make trouble.

35   Hale did speak guardedly, as if the pencil had affected him too.

"Well, as if she didn't know what she was going to do next. And kind of—done up."

"How did she seem to feel about your coming?"

"Why, I don't think she minded—one way or other. She didn't pay much attention. I said, 'Ho' do, Mrs. Wright? It's cold, ain't it?' And she said, 'Is it?'—and went on pleatin' at her apron.

"Well, I was surprised. She didn't ask me to come up to the stove, or to sit down, but just set there, not even lookin' at me. And so I said: 'I want to see John.'

40   "And then she—laughed. I guess you would call it a laugh.

"I thought of Harry and the team outside, so I said, a little sharp, 'Can I see John?' 'No,' says she—kind of dull like. 'Ain't he home?' says I. Then she looked at me. 'Yes,' says she, 'he's home.' 'Then why can't I see him?' I asked her, out of patience with her now. ''Cause he's dead,' says she, just as quiet and dull—and fell to pleatin' her apron. 'Dead?' says I, like you do when you can't take in what you've heard.

"She just nodded her head, not getting a bit excited, but rockin' back and forth.

"'Why—where is he?' says I, not knowing *what* to say.

"She just pointed upstairs—like this"—pointing to the room above.

45   "I got up, with the idea of going up there myself. By this time I—didn't know what to do. I walked from there to here; then I says: 'Why, what did he die of?'

"'He died of a rope around his neck,' says she; and just went on pleatin' at her apron."

Hale stopped speaking, and stood staring at the rocker, as if he were still seeing the woman who had sat there the morning before. Nobody spoke; it was as if every one were seeing the woman who had sat there the morning before.

"And what did you do then?" the county attorney at last broke the silence.

"I went out and called Harry. I thought I might—need help. I got Harry in, and we went upstairs." His voice fell almost to a whisper. "There he was—lying over the—"

50   "I think I'd rather have you go into that upstairs," the county attorney interrupted, "where you can point it all out. Just go on now with the rest of the story."

"Well, my first thought was to get that rope off. It looked—" He stopped, his face twitching.

"But Harry, he went up to him, and he said, 'No, he's dead all right, and we'd better not touch anything.' So we went downstairs.

"She was still sitting that same way. 'Has anybody been notified?' I asked. 'No,' says she, unconcerned.

" 'Who did this, Mrs. Wright?' said Harry. He said it businesslike, and she stopped pleatin' at her apron. 'I don't know,' she says. 'You don't *know?*' says Harry. 'Weren't you sleepin' in the bed with him?' 'Yes,' says she, 'but I was on the inside.' 'Somebody slipped a rope round his neck and strangled him, and you didn't wake up?' says Harry. 'I didn't wake up,' she said after him.

"We may have looked as if we didn't see how that could be, for after a minute she said, 'I sleep sound.'

"Harry was going to ask her more questions, but I said maybe that weren't our business; maybe we ought to let her tell her story first to the coroner or the sheriff. So Harry went fast as he could over to High Road—the Rivers's place, where there's a telephone."

"And what did she do when she knew you had gone for the coroner?" The attorney got his pencil in his hand all ready for writing.

"She moved from that chair to this one over here"—Hale pointed to a small chair in the corner—"and just sat there with her hands held together and looking down. I got a feeling that I ought to make some conversation, so I said I had come in to see if John wanted to put in a telephone; and at that she started to laugh, and then she stopped and looked at me—scared."

At the sound of the moving pencil the man who was telling the story looked up.

"I dunno—maybe it wasn't scared," he hastened; "I wouldn't like to say it was. Soon Harry got back, and then Dr. Lloyd came, and you, Mr. Peters, and so I guess that's all I know that you don't."

He said that last with relief, and moved a little, as if relaxing. Every one moved a little. The county attorney walked toward the stair door.

"I guess we'll go upstairs first—then out to the barn and around there."

He paused and looked around the kitchen.

"You're convinced there was nothing important here?" he asked the sheriff. "Nothing that would—point to any motive?"

The sheriff too looked all around, as if to re-convince himself.

"Nothing here but kitchen things," he said, with a little laugh for the insignificance of kitchen things.

The county attorney was looking at the cupboard—a peculiar, ungainly structure, half closet and half cupboard, the upper part of it being built in the wall, and the lower part just the old-fashioned kitchen cupboard. As if its queerness attracted him, he got a chair and opened the upper part and looked in. After a moment he drew his hand away sticky.

"Here's a nice mess," he said resentfully.

The two women had drawn nearer, and now the sheriff's wife spoke.

"Oh—her fruit," she said, looking to Mrs. Hale for sympathetic understanding. She turned back to the county attorney and explained. "She worried about that when it turned so cold last night. She said the fire would go out and her jars might burst."

Mrs. Peters's husband broke into a laugh.

"Well, can you beat the women! Held for murder, and worrying about her preserves!"

The young attorney set his lips.

"I guess before we're through with her she may have something more serious than preserves to worry about."

75   "Oh, well," said Mrs. Hale's husband, with good-natured superiority, "women are used to worrying over trifles."

The two women moved a little closer together. Neither of them spoke. The county attorney seemed suddenly to remember his manners—and think of his future.

"And yet," said he, with the gallantry of a young politician, "for all their worries, what would we do without the ladies?"

The women did not speak, did not unbend. He went to the sink and began washing his hands. He turned to wipe them on the roller wheel—whirled it for a cleaner place.

"Dirty towels! Not much of a housekeeper, would you say, ladies?"

80   He kicked his foot against some dirty pans under the sink.

"There's a great deal of work to be done on a farm," said Mrs. Hale stiffly.

"To be sure. And yet"—with a little bow to her—"I know there are some Dickson County farmhouses that do not have such roller towels." He gave it a pull to expose its full length again.

"Those towels get dirty awful quick. Men's hands aren't always as clean as they might be."

"Ah, loyal to your sex, I see," he laughed. He stopped and gave her a keen look. "But you and Mrs. Wright were neighbors. I suppose you were friends, too."

85   Martha Hale shook her head.

"I've seen little enough of her of late years. I've not been in this house—it's more than a year."

"And why was that? You didn't like her?"

"I liked her well enough," she replied with spirit. "Farmer's wives have their hands full, Mr. Henderson. And then—" She looked around the kitchen.

"Yes?" he encouraged.

90   "It never seemed a very cheerful place," said she, more to herself than to him.

"No," he agreed; "I don't think any one would call it cheerful. I shouldn't say she had the homemaking instinct."

"Well, I don't know as Wright had, either," she muttered.

"You mean they didn't get on very well?" he was very quick to ask.

"No; I don't mean anything," she answered, with decision. As she turned a little away from him, she added: "But I don't think a place would be any the cheerfuler for John Wright's bein' in it."

95   "I'd like to talk to you about that a little later, Mrs. Hale," he said. "I'm anxious to get the lay of things upstairs now."

He moved toward the stair door, followed by the two men.

"I suppose anything Mrs. Peters does'll be all right?" the sheriff inquired. "She was supposed to take in some clothes for her, you know—and a few little things. We left in such a hurry yesterday."

The county attorney looked at the two women whom they were leaving alone among the kitchen things.

"Yes—Mrs. Peters," he said, his glance resting on the woman who was not Mrs. Peters, the big farmer woman who stood behind the sheriff's wife. "Of course Mrs.

Peters is one of us," he said, in a manner of entrusting responsibility. "And keep your
eye out, Mrs. Peters, for anything that might be of use. No telling; you women might
come upon a clue to the motive—and that's the thing we need."

Mr. Hale rubbed his face after the fashion of a show man getting ready for a pleas-   100
antry.

"But would the women know a clue if they did come upon it?" he said; and, having
delivered himself of this, he followed the others through the stair door.

The women stood motionless and silent, listening to the footsteps, first upon the
stairs, then in the room above them.

Then, as if releasing herself from something strange, Mrs. Hale began to arrange
the dirty pans under the sink, which the county attorney's disdainful push of the foot
had deranged.

"I'd hate to have men comin' into my kitchen," she said testily—"snoopin' round
and criticizin'."

"Of course it's no more than their duty," said the sheriff's wife, in her manner of   105
timid acquiescence.

"Duty's all right," replied Mrs. Hale bluffly; "but I guess that deputy sheriff that
come out to make the fire might have got a little of this on." She gave the roller towel
a pull. "Wish I'd thought of that sooner! Seems mean to talk about her for not having
things slicked up, when she had to come away in such a hurry."

She looked around the kitchen. Certainly it was not "slicked up." Her eye was held
by a bucket of sugar on a low shelf. The cover was off the wooden bucket, and beside
it was a paper bag—half full.

Mrs. Hale moved toward it.

"She was putting this in here," she said to herself—slowly.

She thought of the flour in her kitchen at home—half sifted, half not sifted. She   110
had been interrupted, and had left things half done. What had interrupted Minnie
Foster? Why had that work been left half done? She made a move as if to finish it,—
unfinished things always bothered her,—and then she glanced around and saw that
Mrs. Peters was watching her—and she didn't want Mrs. Peters to get that feeling she
had got of work begun and then—for some reason—not finished.

"It's a shame about her fruit," she said, and walked toward the cupboard that the
county attorney had opened, and got on the chair, murmuring: "I wonder if it's all gone."

It was a sorry enough looking sight, but "Here's one that's all right," she said at
last. She held it toward the light. "This is cherries, too." She looked again. "I declare
I believe that's the only one."

With a sigh, she got down from the chair, went to the sink, and wiped off the
bottle.

"She'll feel awful bad, after all her hard work in the hot weather. I remember the
afternoon I put up my cherries last summer."

She set the bottle on the table, and, with another sigh, started to sit down in the   115
rocker. But she did not sit down. Something kept her from sitting down in that chair.
She straightened—stepped back, and half turned away, stood looking at it, seeing the
woman who sat there "pleatin' at her apron."

The thin voice of the sheriff's wife broke in upon her: "I must be getting those
things from the front room closet." She opened the door into the other room, started

in, stepped back. "You coming with me, Mrs. Hale?" she asked nervously. "You—you could help me get them."

They were soon back—the stark coldness of that shut-up room was not a thing to linger in.

"My!" said Mrs. Peters, dropping the things on the table and hurrying to the stove.

Mrs. Hale stood examining the clothes the woman who was being detained in town had said she wanted.

120 "Wright was close!" she exclaimed, holding up a shabby black skirt that bore the marks of much making over. "I think maybe that's why she kept so much to herself. I s'pose she felt she couldn't do her part; and then, you don't enjoy things when you feel shabby. She used to wear pretty clothes and be lively—when she was Minnie Foster, one of the town girls, singing in the choir. But that—oh, that was twenty years ago."

With a carefulness in which there was something tender, she folded the shabby clothes and piled them at one corner of the table. She looked at Mrs. Peters, and there was something in the other woman's look that irritated her.

"She don't care," she said to herself. "Much difference it makes to her whether Minnie Foster had pretty clothes when she was a girl."

Then she looked again, and she wasn't so sure; in fact, she hadn't at any time been perfectly sure about Mrs. Peters. She had that shrinking manner, and yet her eyes looked as if they could see a long way into things.

"This all you was to take in?" asked Mrs. Hale.

125 "No," said the sheriff's wife; "she said she wanted an apron. Funny thing to want," she ventured in her nervous little way, "for there's not much to get you dirty in jail, goodness knows. But I suppose just to make her feel more natural. If you're used to wearing an apron—. She said they were in the bottom drawer of this cupboard. Yes— here they are. And then her little shawl that always hung on the stair door."

She took the small gray shawl from behind the door leading upstairs, and stood a minute looking at it.

Suddenly Mrs. Hale took a quick step toward the other woman.

"Mrs. Peters!"

"Yes, Mrs. Hale?"

130 "Do you think she—did it?"

A frightened look blurred the other things in Mrs. Peter's eyes.

"Oh, I don't know," she said, in a voice that seemed to shrink away from the subject.

"Well, I don't think she did," affirmed Mrs. Hale stoutly. "Asking for an apron, and her little shawl. Worryin' about her fruit."

"Mr. Peters says—." Footsteps were heard in the room above; she stopped, looked up, then went on in a lowered voice: "Mr. Peters says—it looks bad for her. Mr. Henderson is awful sarcastic in a speech, and he's going to make fun of her saying she didn't—wake up."

135 For a moment Mrs. Hale had no answer. Then, "Well, I guess John Wright didn't wake up—when they was slippin' that rope under his neck," she muttered.

"No, it's *strange*," breathed Mrs. Peters. "They think it was such a—funny way to kill a man."

She began to laugh; at the sound of the laugh, abruptly stopped.

"That's just what Mr. Hale said," said Mrs. Hale, in a resolutely natural voice. "There was a gun in the house. He says that's what he can't understand."

"Mr. Henderson said, coming out, that what was needed for the case was a motive. Something to show anger—or sudden feeling."

"Well, I don't see any signs of anger around here," said Mrs. Hale. "I don't—"   140

She stopped. It was as if her mind tripped on something. Her eye was caught by a dish-towel in the middle of the kitchen table. Slowly she moved toward the table. One half of it was wiped clean, the other half messy. Her eyes made a slow, almost unwilling turn to the bucket of sugar and the half empty bag beside it. Things begun—and not finished.

After a moment she stepped back, and said, in that manner of releasing herself:

"Wonder how they're finding things upstairs? I hope she had it a little more red up up there. You know,"—she paused, and feeling gathered,—"it seems kind *of sneaking*; locking her up in town and coming out here to get her own house to turn against her!"

"But, Mrs. Hale," said the sheriff's wife, "the law is the law."

"I s'pose 'tis," answered Mrs. Hale shortly.   145

She turned to the stove, saying something about that fire not being much to brag of. She worked with it a minute, and when she straightened up she said aggressively:

"The law is the law—and a bad stove is a bad stove. How'd you like to cook on this?"—pointing with a poker to the broken lining. She opened the oven door and started to express her opinion of the oven; but she was swept into her own thoughts, thinking of what it would mean, year after year, to have that stove to wrestle with. The thought of Minnie Foster trying to bake in that oven—and the thought of her never going over to see Minnie Foster—.

She was startled by hearing Mrs. Peters say: "A person gets discouraged—and loses heart."

The sheriff's wife had looked from the stove to the sink—to the pail of water which had been carried in from outside. The two women stood there silent, above them the footsteps of the men who were looking for evidence against the woman who had worked in that kitchen. That look of seeing into things, of seeing through a thing to something else, was in the eyes of the sheriff's wife now. When Mrs. Hale next spoke to her, it was gently:

"Better loosen up your things, Mrs. Peters. We'll not feel them when we go out."   150

Mrs. Peters went to the back of the room to hang up the fur tippet she was wearing. A moment later she exclaimed, "Why, she was piecing a quilt," and held up a large sewing basket piled high with quilt pieces.

Mrs. Hale spread some of the blocks on the table.

"It's log-cabin pattern," she said, putting several of them together. "Pretty, isn't it?"

They were so engaged with the quilt that they did not hear the footsteps on the stairs. Just as the stair door opened Mrs. Hale was saying:

"Do you suppose she was going to quilt it or just knot it?" The sheriff threw up his hands.

"They wonder whether she was going to quilt it or just knot it!"   155

There was a laugh for the ways of women, a warming of hands over the stove, and then the county attorney said briskly:

"Well, let's go right out to the barn and get that cleared up."

"I don't see as there's anything so strange," Mrs. Hale said resentfully, after the outside door had closed on the three men—"our taking up our time with little things while we're waiting for them to get the evidence. I don't see as it's anything to laugh about."

"Of course they've got awful important things on their minds," said the sheriff's wife apologetically.

160   They returned to the inspection of the blocks for the quilt. Mrs. Hale was looking at the fine, even sewing, and preoccupied with thoughts of the woman who had done that sewing, when she heard the sheriff's wife say, in a queer tone:

"Why, look at this one."

She turned to take the block held out to her.

"The sewing," said Mrs. Peters, in a troubled way. "All the rest of them have been so nice and even—but—this one. Why, it looks as if she didn't know what she was about!"

Their eyes met—something flashed to life, passed between them; then, as if with an effort, they seemed to pull away from each other. A moment Mrs. Hale sat there, her hands folded over that sewing which was so unlike all the rest of the sewing. Then she had pulled a knot and drawn the threads.

165   "Oh, what are you doing, Mrs. Hale?" asked the sheriff's wife, startled.

"Just pulling out a stitch or two that's not sewed very good," said Mrs. Hale mildly.

"I don't think we ought to touch things," Mrs. Peters said, a little helplessly.

"I'll just finish up this end," answered Mrs. Hale, still in that mild, matter-of-fact faction.

She threaded a needle and started to replace bad sewing with good. For a little while she sewed in silence. Then, in that thin, timid voice, she heard:

"Mrs. Hale!"

170   "Yes, Mrs. Peters?"

"What do you suppose she was so—nervous about?"

"Oh, *I* don't know," said Mrs. Hale, as if dismissing a thing not important enough to spend much time on. "I don't know as she was—nervous. I sew awful queer sometimes when I'm just tired."

She cut a thread, and out of the corner of her eye looked up at Mrs. Peters. The small, lean face of the sheriff's wife seemed to have tightened up. Her eyes had that look of peering into something. But the next moment she moved, and said in her thin, indecisive way:

"Well, I must get those clothes wrapped. They may be through sooner than we think. I wonder where I could find a piece of paper—and string."

175   "In that cupboard, maybe," suggested Mrs. Hale, after a glance around.

One piece of the crazy sewing remained unripped. Mrs. Peters's back turned, Martha Hale now scrutinized that piece, compared it with the dainty, accurate sewing of the other blocks. The difference was startling. Holding this block made her feel queer, as if the distracted thoughts of the woman who had perhaps turned to it to try and quiet herself were communicating themselves to her.

Mrs. Peter's voice roused her.

"Here's a birdcage," she said. "Did she have a bird, Mrs. Hale?"

"Why, I don't know whether she did or not." She turned to look at the cage Mrs. Peters was holding up. "I've not been here in so long." She sighed. "There was a man around last year selling canaries cheap—but I don't know as she took one. Maybe she did. She used to sing real pretty herself."

Mrs. Peters looked around the kitchen.   180

"Seems kind of funny to think of a bird here." She half laughed—an attempt to put up a barrier. "But she must have had one—or why would she have a cage? I wonder what happened to it?"

"I suppose maybe the cat got it," suggested Mrs. Hale, resuming her sewing.

"No, she didn't have a cat. She's got that feeling some people have about cats—being afraid of them. When they brought her to our house yesterday, my cat got in the room, and she was real upset and asked me to take it out."

"My sister Bessie was like that," laughed Mrs. Hale.

The sheriff's wife did not reply. The silence made Mrs. Hale turn around. Mrs.   185
Peters was examining the birdcage.

"Look at this door," she said slowly. "It's broke. One hinge has been pulled apart."

Mrs. Hale came nearer.

"Looks as if some one must have been—rough with it."

Again their eyes met—startled, questioning, apprehensive. For a moment neither spoke nor stirred. Then Mrs. Hale, turning away, said brusquely:

"If they're going to find any evidence, I wish they'd be about it. I don't like this place.   190

"But I'm awful glad you came with me, Mrs. Hale." Mrs. Peters put the birdcage on the table and sat down. "It would be lonesome for me—sitting here alone.

"Yes, it would, wouldn't it?" agreed Mrs. Hale, a certain determined naturalness in her voice. She picked up the sewing, but now it dropped in her lap, and she murmured in a different voice: "But I tell you what I *do* wish, Mrs. Peters. I wish I had come over sometimes when she was here. I wish—I had."

"But of course you were awful busy, Mrs. Hale. Your house—and your children."

"I could've come," retorted Mrs. Hale shortly. "I stayed away because it weren't cheerful—and that's why I ought to have come. I"—she looked around—"I've never liked this place. Maybe because it's down in a hollow and you don't see the road. I don't know what it is, but it's a lonesome place, and always was. I wish I had come over to see Minnie Foster sometimes. I can see now—" She did not put it into words.

"Well, you mustn't reproach yourself," counseled Mrs. Peters. "Somehow, we just   195
don't see how it is with other folks till—something comes up."

"Not having children makes less work," mused Mrs. Hale, after a silence, "but it makes a quiet house—and Wright out to work all day—and no company when he did come in. Did you know John Wright, Mrs. Peters?"

"Not to know him. I've seen him in town. They say he was a good man."

"Yes—good," conceded John Wright's neighbor grimly. "He didn't drink, and kept his word as well as most, I guess, and paid his debts. But he was a hard man, Mrs. Peters. Just to pass the time of day with him—." She stopped, shivered a little. "Like a raw wind that gets to the bone." Her eye fell upon the cage on the table before her, and she added, almost bitterly: "I should think she would've wanted a bird!"

Suddenly she leaned forward, looking intently at the cage. "But what do you s'pose went wrong with it?"

200 "I don't know," returned Mrs. Peters; "unless it got sick and died."

But after she said it she reached over and swung the broken door. Both women watched it as if somehow held by it.

"You didn't know—her?" Mrs. Hale asked, a gentler note in her voice.

"Not till they brought her yesterday," said the sheriff's wife.

"She—come to think of it, she was kind of like a bird herself. Real sweet and pretty, but kind of timid and—fluttery. How—she—did—change."

205 That held her for a long time. Finally, as if struck with a happy thought and relieved to get back to everyday things, she exclaimed:

"Tell you what, Mrs. Peters, why don't you take the quilt in with you? It might take up her mind."

"Why, I think that's a real nice idea, Mrs. Hale," agreed the sheriff's wife, as if she too were glad to come into the atmosphere of a simple kindness. "There couldn't possibly be any objection to that, could there? Now, just what will I take? I wonder if her patches are here—and her things."

They turned to the sewing basket.

"Here's some red," said Mrs. Hale, bringing out a roll of cloth. Underneath that was a box. "Here, maybe her scissors are in here—and her things." She held it up. "What a pretty box! I'll warrant that was something she had a long time ago—when she was a girl."

210 She held it in her hand a moment; then, with a little sigh, opened it.

Instantly her hand went to her nose.

"Why—!"

Mrs. Peters drew nearer—then turned away.

"There's something wrapped up in this piece of silk," faltered Mrs. Hale.

215 "This isn't her scissors," said Mrs. Peters in a shrinking voice.

Her hand not steady, Mrs. Hale raised the piece of silk. "Oh, Mrs. Peters!" she cried. "It's—"

Mrs. Peters bent closer.

"It's the bird," she whispered.

"But, Mrs. Peters!" cried Mrs. Hale. "*Look* at it! Its neck—look at its neck! It's all—other side *to*."

220 She held the box away from her.

The sheriff's wife again bent closer.

"Somebody wrung its neck," said she, in a voice that was slow and deep.

And then again the eyes of the two women met—this time clung together in a look of dawning comprehension, of growing horror. Mrs. Peters looked from the dead bird to the broken door of the cage. Again their eyes met. And just then there was a sound at the outside door.

Mrs. Hale slipped the box under the quilt pieces in the basket, and sank into the chair before it. Mrs. Peters stood holding to the table. The county attorney and the sheriff came in from outside.

225 "Well, ladies," said the county attorney, as one turning from serious things to little pleasantries, "have you decided whether she was going to quilt it or knot it?"

"We think," began the sheriff's wife in a flurried voice, "that she was going to—knot it."

He was too preoccupied to notice the change that came in her voice on that last.

"Well, that's very interesting, I'm sure," he said tolerantly. He caught sight of the birdcage. "Has the bird flown?"

"We think the cat got it," said Mrs. Hale in a voice curiously even.

He was walking up and down, as if thinking something out.   230

"Is there a cat?" he asked absently.

Mrs. Hale shot a look up at the sheriff's wife.

"Well, not *now*," said Mrs. Peters. "They're superstitious, you know, they leave."

She sank into the chair.

The county attorney did not heed her. "No sign at all of any one having come in   235
from the outside," he said to Peters, in the manner of continuing an interrupted conversation. "Their own rope. Now let's go upstairs again and go over it, piece by piece. It would have to have been some one who knew just the—"

The stair door closed behind them and their voices were lost.

The two women sat motionless, not looking at each other, but as if peering into something and at the same time holding back. When they spoke now it was if they were afraid of what they were saying, but as if they could not help saying it.

"She liked the bird," said Martha Hale, low and slowly. "She was going to bury it in that pretty box."

"When I was a girl," said Mrs. Peters, under her breath, "my kitten—there was a boy took a hatchet, and before my eyes—before I could get there—" She covered her face an instant. "If they hadn't held me back I would have"—she caught herself, looked upstairs where footsteps were heard, and finished weakly—"hurt him."

Then they sat without speaking or moving.   240

"I wonder how it would seem," Mrs. Hale at last began, as if feeling her way over strange ground—"never to have had any children around?" Her eyes made a slow sweep of the kitchen, as if seeing what that kitchen had meant through all the years. "No, Wright wouldn't like the bird," she said after that—"a thing that sang. She used to sing. He killed that too." Her voice tightened.

Mrs. Peters moved uneasily.

"Of course we don't know who killed the bird."

"I knew John Wright," was Mrs. Hale's answer.

"It was an awful thing was done in the house that night, Mrs. Hale," said the   245
sheriff's wife. "Killing a man while he slept—slipping a thing round his neck that choked the life out of him."

Mrs. Hale's hand went out to the birdcage.

"His neck. Choked the life out of him."

"We don't *know* who killed him," whispered Mrs. Peters wildly. "We don't *know*!"

Mrs. Hale had not moved. "If there had been years and years of—nothing, then a bird to sing to you, it would be awful—still—after the bird was still."

It was as if something within her not herself had spoken, and it found in Mrs.   250
Peters something she did not know as herself.

"I know what stillness is," she said, in a queer, monotonous voice. "When we homesteaded in Dakota, and my first baby died—after he was two years old—and me with no other then—"

Mrs. Hale stirred.

"How soon do you suppose they'll be through looking for evidence?"

"I know what stillness is," repeated Mrs. Peters, in just that same way. Then she too pulled back. "The law has got to punish crime, Mrs. Hale," she said in her tight little way.

255   "I wish you'd seen Minnie Foster," was the answer, "when she wore a white dress with blue ribbons, and stood up there in the choir and sang."

The picture of that girl, the fact that she had lived neighbor to that girl for twenty years, and had let her die for lack of life, was suddenly more than she could bear.

"Oh, I *wish* I'd come over here once in a while!" she cried. "That was a crime! That was a crime! Who's going to punish that?"

"We mustn't take on," said Mrs. Peters, with a frightened look toward the stairs.

"I might 'a' *known* she needed help! I tell you, it's *queer*, Mrs. Peters. We live close together, and we live far apart. We all go through the same things—it's all just a different kind of the same thing! If it weren't—why do you and I *understand*? Why do we *know*—what we know this minute?"

260   She dashed her hand across her eyes. Then, seeing the jar of fruit on the table, she reached for it and choked out:

"If I was you I wouldn't *tell* her her fruit was gone! tell her it *ain't*. Tell her it's all right—all of it. Here—take this in to prove it to her! She—she may never know whether it was broke or not."

She turned away.

Mrs. Peters reached out for the bottle of fruit as if she were glad to take it—as if touching a familiar thing, having something to do, could keep her from something else. She got up, looked about for something to wrap the fruit in, took a petticoat from the pile of clothes she had brought from the front room, and nervously started winding that round the bottle.

"My!" she began, in a high, false voice, "it's a good thing the men couldn't hear us! Getting all stirred up over a little thing like a—dead canary." She hurried over that. "As if that could have anything to do with—with—My, wouldn't they *laugh*?"

265   Footsteps were heard on the stairs.

"Maybe they would," muttered Mrs. Hale—"maybe they wouldn't."

"No, Peters," said the county attorney incisively; "it's all perfectly clear, except the reason for doing it. But you know juries when it comes to women. If there was a definite thing—something to show. Something to make a story about. A thing that would connect up with this clumsy way of doing it."

In a covert way Mrs. Hale looked at Mrs. Peters. Mrs. Peters was looking at her. Quickly they looked away from each other. The outer door opened and Mr. Hale came in.

"I've got the team round now," he said. "Pretty cold out there."

270   "I'm going to stay here awhile by myself," the county attorney suddenly announced. "You can send Frank out for me, can't you?" he asked the sheriff. "I want to go over everything. I'm not satisfied we can't do better."

Again, for one brief moment, the two women's eyes found one another.

The sheriff came up to the table.

"Did you want to see what Mrs. Peters was going to take in?"

The county attorney picked up the apron. He laughed.

"Oh, I guess they're not very dangerous things the ladies have picked out."

Mrs. Hale's hand was on the sewing basket in which the box was concealed. She felt that she ought to take her hand off the basket. She did not seem able to. He picked up one of the quilt blocks which she had piled on to cover the box. Her eyes felt like fire. She had a feeling that if he took up the basket she would snatch it from him.

But he did not take it up. With another little laugh, he turned away, saying:

"No; Mrs. Peters doesn't need supervising. For that matter, a sheriff's wife is married to the law. Ever think of it that way, Mrs. Peters?"

Mrs. Peters was standing beside the table. Mrs. Hale shot a look up at her, but she could not see her face. Mrs. Peters had turned away. When she spoke, her voice was muffled.

"Not—just that way," she said.

"Married to the law!" chuckled Mrs. Peter's husband. He moved toward the door into the front room, and said to the county attorney:

"I just want you to come in here a minute, George. We ought to take a look at these windows."

"Oh—windows," said the county attorney scoffingly.

"We'll be right out, Mr. Hale," said the sheriff to the farmer, who was still waiting by the door.

Hale went to look after the horses. The sheriff followed the county attorney into the other room. Again—for one moment—the two women were alone in that kitchen.

Martha Hale sprang up, her hands tight together, looking at that other woman, with whom it rested. At first she could not see her eyes, for the sheriff's wife had not turned back since she turned away at that suggestion of being married to the law. But now Mrs. Hale made her turn back. Her eyes made her turn back. Slowly, unwillingly, Mrs. Peters turned her head until her eyes met the eyes of the other woman. There was a moment when they held each other in a steady, burning look in which there was no evasion nor flinching. Then Martha Hale's eyes pointed the way to the basket in which was hidden the thing that would make certain the conviction of the other woman—that woman who was not there and yet who had been there with them all through the hour.

For a moment Mrs. Peters did not move. And then she did it. With a rush forward, she threw back the quilt pieces, got the box, tried to put it in her handbag. It was too big. Desperately she opened it, started to take the bird out. But there she broke—she could not touch the bird. She stood helpless, foolish.

There was the sound of a knob turning in the inner door. Martha Hale snatched the box from the sheriff's wife, and got it in the pocket of her big coat just as the sheriff and the county attorney came back into the kitchen.

"Well, Henry," said the county attorney facetiously, "at least we found out that she was not going to quilt it. She was going to—what is it you call it, ladies?"

Mrs. Hale's hand was against the pocket of her coat.

"We call it—knot it, Mr. Henderson."

275

280

285

290

Critical Perspectives

SUZY CLARKSON HOLSTEIN

from Silent Justice in a Different Key: Glaspell's "Trifles"*

Susan Glaspell's "Trifles" is a deceptive play: deceptive because, like its title, it *seems* simple, almost inconsequential. Yet the play represents a profound conflict between two models of perception and behavior. An exploration of the play reveals a fundamental difference between the women's actions and the men's, a difference grounded in varying understandings of the home space. That difference culminates, finally, in the establishing of two competing ethical paradigms. . . .

[I]t is in fact no accident that the women discover the evidence. Their *method* from the very beginning of the play leads not only to the discovery that eludes the men, but also to their ultimate moral choice, a choice which radically separates them from the men. That is, their *way* of knowing leads them not simply to knowledge; it also leads to the decision about how to act on that knowledge.

From the very outset, the men and women of the play perceive the setting, the lonely farmhouse, from diverging perspectives. The men come to the scene of a crime and attempt to look through the eyes of legal investigators. They stride into the room, and, with the exception of three words, we hear only male voices for the first quarter of the play. The county attorney conducts his investigation by the book. He interviews the key witness, asking for only facts (interpretations, he indicates, will receive attention later). The strict linear process also applies to spaces: the men go methodically from room to room, following the preset plan of the search. The sheriff and attorney are certain that they have left nothing out, "nothing of importance" ("Trifles," 8). Yet at the end of the play, they know no more than at the beginning. The motive for the crime remains obscure.

By contrast, the women arrive at a *home*. Although neither they nor the men realize it, they too are conducting an investigation. Their process seems formless as they move through the kitchen, talking and reflecting. The men patronize them and gently ridicule their concerns while the women themselves, at least at the outset, characterize their activity in the house as relatively unimportant. But as Mrs. Hale and Mrs. Peters gather household goods for Minnie Wright, the two characters begin to reconstruct the accused woman's life. They do so through several means: memories of her, memories of their own lives (similar to hers in many ways), and speculation about her feelings and responses to the conditions of her life. Instead of following a predetermined schedule of inquiry, they begin, almost instinctively, to put themselves into Minnie Wright's place. In her sewing box, they discover Minnie's dead pet bird, and this discovery would be the missing piece to the men's "puzzle." As they recognize that the bird has been violently strangled and then lovingly set inside a piece of rich

The Midwest Quarterly 44.3 (2003): 282–90. Print.

material, the stage directions reveal their incipient knowledge: "[the women's] eyes meet. A look of growing comprehension, of horror" ("Trifles," 24). They then reflect her husband would not have liked a thing that sang and would have silenced it as he silenced the singing Minnie. As they share and ponder, the mundane details of Minnie's life lead Mrs. Hale and Mrs. Peters to comprehend what their husbands do not: the motive for the murder. Far more importantly, the details that allow them this insight—details overlooked as unimportant by the men—lead the women to understand the almost tangible oppression of Minnie Wright's everyday life. In one of the play's many ironies, Mrs. Hale says, resentfully, "I don't know as there's anything so strange, our takin' up our time with little things while we're waiting for them to get the evidence" ("Trifles," 17). Evidence, of course, *is* generally comprised of "little things," as we have witnessed graphically in our twentieth-century crime labs. None of the play's characters ever recognizes the irony, for the women accept the designation of their concerns as mere "trifles." But in another ironic turn, Mrs. Hale and Mrs. Peters ultimately find power in being devalued, for their low status allows them to keep quiet at the play's end. Much like servants and other discounted groups, the women are permitted access to knowledge because it is assumed they will not be able to make intelligent use of it. . . .

Though this silence sounds no different to the men than the women's initial speech-lessness, we as an audience hear a completely new tone in the quiet. In the beginning, the women are silent from the powerlessness Belenky has described (23–24); their final refusal to speak rings with the power of intention and choice. . . .

Clearly, as several feminist commentators have noted, the women are able to empathize with Minnie Wright because they share her experience. Annette Kolodny points out that the men cannot "read" the messages Minnie Wright sends silently through the details of her house since the men don't "share her context" (Kolodny, 462). But the men's *method* of reading, I would argue, is fundamentally different from the women's. The plot of the play is not simply the women reading Minnie's experience while the men read John's, not simply a rural version of "he said, she said." The county attorney, Mr. Peters, and Mr. Hale never attempt to identify with John Wright or even consider him as a distinct individual with specific behaviors. Instead, they view him as they do his wife, an abstraction. He is the victim of a crime, she the criminal. (Today, she would be a "perpetrator," in our even more abstract language of criminology.) The men, ignoring the context or "web" as Carol Gilligan might describe it, can make no sense of a seemingly aberrant moment (62).

The women's approach and their recognition of the web of experience also propel Mrs. Hale to another stage unthinkable to the men. She takes direct responsibility for the desperation that led to the murder. Early in the play, she regrets not visiting "Minnie Foster" (significantly using the woman's maiden name). After the women have found the dead bird, she responds emphatically to Mrs. Peters as they discuss Minnie's guilt and their pending decision:

> Mrs. Peters: The law has got to punish crime, Mrs. Hale.
> Mrs. Hale: . . . I wish you'd seen Minnie Foster when she wore a white dress with blue ribbons and stood up in the choir and sang. [A look around the room.] Oh, I *wish* I'd come over here once in a while! That was a crime! That was a crime! Who's going to punish that? (27)

From Mrs. Hale's perspective, people are linked together through fragile, sometimes imperceptible strands. The tiny trifles of life—a neighbor's visit, a bird's song, the sewing of a quilt—have profound reverberations. Further, Mrs. Hale observes, "We live close together and we live far apart. We all go through the same things—it's all just a different kind of the same thing" ("Trifles," 27). . . .

Much popular and theoretical exploration has been made of the differences between genders. Some have tried to untangle the biological and environmental strands of the puzzle but we are far from being able to isolate essentially "feminine" or essentially "masculine" behavior as distinct from cultural conditioned performance. Certainly, during the early part of the twentieth century, the duties and structures of women's lives would have predisposed them to approach a problem from a different angle than that of the men. As many commentators have noted, even today, despite the significant changes in women's lives and opportunities since mid-century, women's responsibilities and concerns *tend* to remain somewhat distinct from men's.

Whether these differences between men and women are primarily based in biology (sex) or culture (gender), they remain evident in current culture. We recognize Glaspell's women constructing an alternative paradigm of justice and care, for they posit it on different grounds than the tradition of rights and rules, the standards used in the dominant culture. The ethic of care, the notion of responsibility *within* relationships especially, takes precedence in such a construction over strict formulations of justice based on precise reciprocity (Gilligan, 73). Therefore, unlike some moral development schemas whose highest stage strives for principles which are universal in application (e.g., Piaget and Kohlberg, cited in Gilligan), the women in this play develop a highly differentiated and reflective moral schema. The paradigm is probably not exclusively the domain of women but it *is* the domain of those who have been shaped since birth by conventions that support an ethic based on a "psychological logic of relationships" rather than a "formal logic of fairness" (Gilligan, 73). Although an individual might appropriate the logic most closely associated with the other gender, to do so requires overcoming intense cultural conditioning. Indeed, it is likely that individual women have attempted to adopt the "fairness" ideology Gilligan describes so as to succeed in the dominant masculine culture. The pattern is familiar: just as members of minority cultures often must study "mainstream" culture and embrace new ideologies to succeed, so some women have worked to place themselves within the predominantly masculine logic. For even though Glaspell's play was written more than eighty years ago, social critics still document the devaluing of women's alternative patterns. In *The Difference*, Judith Mann observed the divergence between the two ethics visible in men and women making decisions and in the responses to those decisions. The men, Mann argues, operated from an ethos of self-reliance and competition and therefore strove to be first with a quick, firm answer. Women on the other hand valued cooperation and worked to interconnect, taking time to make up their minds. Such behavior was "dismissed as indecisive" instead of being understood as a separate model that promoted integrated thinking (Mann, 382). The distinction Mann observed echoes what we hear in Glaspell's play.

Early in the two women's discussion, Mrs. Hale expresses discomfort at the men's violation (from her perspective) of Mrs. Wright's house. Mrs. Peters counters matter-of-factly, "But Mrs. Hale, the law is the law" ("Trifles," 16). Yet as Mrs. Peters begins to follow Mrs. Hale's lead, her perspective also begins to shift. By the end of the play, both women operate in a contextual rather than an abstract mode: in Gilligan's terms, they are concerned more with relationships than with rules. The neat, rigid order of criminal law, an order defined and upheld by their husbands and the county attorney, has given way to the messier pattern of day-to-day life and shared responsibilities and experience. Significantly, Mrs. Peter's final action of the play goes far beyond mere silent complicity with Mrs. Hale's concealment of evidence. It is the sheriff's wife herself, the woman the county attorney deems to be "married to the law" ("Trifles," 29), who frantically tries to hide the bird. Of course, the women's choice to adopt an alternative model of perception can succeed only in silence, but it is no longer a silence of powerlessness. In the play's final line, a line replete with several puns, Mrs. Hale and Mrs. Peters intentionally "knot" their knowledge and do "not" share it. Their silence has become a mark of their solidarity, a refusal to endanger a sister. For the men in the play, their secret remains an undiscovered trifle.

Bibliography

Belenky, Mary, et al. *Women's Ways of Knowing: The Development of Self, Voice, and Mind.* New York: Basic Books, 1986.

Gilligan, Carol. *In a Different Voice: Psychological Theory and Women's Development.* Cambridge: Harvard University Press, 1982.

Glaspell, Susan. "Trifles." *Plays.* Boston: Small, Maynard and Company, 1920. 7–29.

——. *The Inheritors. Plays.* Cambridge: Cambridge University Press, 1989. 103–57.

Kolodny, Annette. "A Map for Rereading: or, Gender and the Interpretation of Literary Texts." *New Literary History*, 11 (1980), 457–71.

Mann, Judith. *The Difference: Growing Up Female in America.* New York, N.Y.: Warner, 1994.

LEONARD MUSTAZZA

Generic Translation and Thematic Shift in Susan Glaspell's *Trifles* and "A Jury of Her Peers"[*]

Commentators on Susan Glaspell's classic feminist short story, "A Jury of Her Peers" (1917), and the one-act play from which it derives, *Trifles* (1916), have tended to regard the two works as essentially alike. And even those few who have noticed the changes that Glaspell made in the process of generic translation have done so only in passing. In his monograph on Glaspell, Arthur Waterman, who seems to have a higher regard for the story than for the play, suggests that [the] story is a "moving fictional experience" because of the progressive honing of the author's skills, the story's vivid realism owing to her work as a local-color writer for the *Des Moines Daily News*, and its unified plot due to its dramatic origin (Waterman 29–30). More specifically, Elaine Hedges appropriately notes the significance of Glaspell's change in titles from *Trifles*, which emphasizes the supposedly trivial household items with which the women "acquit" their accused peer, to "A Jury of Her Peers," which emphasizes the question of legality. In 1917, Hedges observes, women were engaged in the final years of their fight for the vote, and Glaspell's change in titles thus "emphasizes the story's comtemporaneity, by calling attention to its references to the issue of women's legal place in American society" (Hedges 106). Apart from these and a few other passing remarks, however, critics have chosen to focus on one work or the other. Indeed, thematic criticisms of the respective pieces are virtually indistinguishable, most of these commentaries focusing on the question of assumed "roles" in the works.[1]

Studies in Short Fiction 26.4 (1989): 489–96. Print.

On one level, there is good reason for this lack of differentiation. Not only is the overall narrative movement of the works similar, but Glaspell incorporated in the short story virtually every single line of the dialogue from *Trifles*.[2] By the same token, though, she also added much to the short story, which is about twice as long as the play. The nature of the additions is twofold, the first and most obvious being her descriptions of locales, modes of utterance, characters, props, and so on—the kinds of descriptions that the prose writer's form will allow but the dramatist's will not. The other type of alteration is more subtle, and it involves the revisions, embellishments, and redirections that occur when an existent story is retold. When, for instance, a novel is turned into a film of a play, the best that can be said about the generic translation is that it is "faithful," but never is it identical. So it is with "Jury." It is certainly faithful to the play, but it is also different in a variety of ways, and it is these differences, which took place in the act of generic translation, that I would like to consider here.

In her articles on *Trifles*, Beverly Smith makes an interesting observation. Noting that the women in the play, Mrs. Hale and Mrs. Peters, function as defense counsel for and jury of their accused peer, Minnie Foster Wright, she goes on to suggest that the men's role, their official capacities notwithstanding, are comparable to that of a Greek Chorus, "the voice of the community's conscience," entering at various points to reiterate their major themes—Minnie's guilt and the triviality of the women's occupations, avocations, and preoccupations (Smith 175). This equation is, I think, quite useful, for the periodic entries, commentaries, and exits of the male characters in both Glaspell works do in fact mark the progressive stages of the narrative, which primarily concerns the women, including the absent Minnie Foster.[3] Though not on stage for the entire drama, as is the Greek Chorus, the men nevertheless function in much the same way, providing commentary and separating the major movements of the narrative. What is more, if we regard the men's exits from the stage as marking these movements, we will recognize the first principal difference between the play and the story—namely, that the latter contains twice as many movements as the former and is therefore necessarily a more developed and complex work.

Trifles opens with Mr. Hale's account of what he found when he arrived at the Wright farm the day before. Of the women themselves, we know almost nothing beyond their general appearances as described in the opening stage directions—that Mrs. Peters, the sheriff's wife, is "a slight, wiry woman [with] a thin nervous face"; and that Mrs. Hale, the witness's wife, is larger than Mrs. Peters and "comfortable looking," though now appearing fearful and disturbed as she enters the scene of the crime (Glaspell, *Trifles* 15). Standing close together as they enter the Wright's home, the women remain almost completely undifferentiated until, some time later, they begin to speak. Thus, Glaspell underscores here the male/female polarities that she will explore in the course of the play.

Her entire narrative technique is different in the prose version. That story begins in Mrs. Hale's disordered kitchen, which will later serve as a point of comparison with the major scene of the story, Mrs. Wright's kitchen. Annoyed at being called away from her housework, she nevertheless agrees to Sheriff Peter's request that she come along to accompany Mrs. Peters, who is there to fetch some personal effects for the jailed woman. Quite unlike the play's opening, which emphasizes the physical closeness of and the attitudinal similarities between the women, "Jury," taking us as it does into Mrs. Hale's thoughts, emphasizes the women's apartness:

> She had met Mrs. Peters the year before at the county fair, and the thing she remembered about her was that *she didn't seem like the sheriff's wife*. She was small and thin and didn't

have a strong voice. Mrs. Gorman, the sheriff's wife before Gorman went out and Peters came in, had a voice that somehow seemed to be backing up the law with every word. But if Mrs. Peters didn't look like a sheriff's wife, Peters made up for it in looking like a sheriff—a heavy man with a big voice, who was particularly genial with the law-abiding, as if to make it plain that he knew the difference between criminals and non-criminals. (Glaspell, "Jury" 70; emphasis added)

Interestingly, for all the added material here, Glaspell omits mention of what the women look like. In fact, we will get no explicit statements on their appearance.

Ironically, however despite her seeming mismatch with her husband, her lack of corporeal "presence," Mrs. Peters turns out to be more suited to her assumed public role than Mrs. Hale had suspected—all too suited, in fact, since she perfectly assumes her male-approved role. "Of course Mrs. Peters is one of us" (77), the county attorney asserts prior to getting on with his investigation of the house, and that statement turns out to be laden with meaning in the story. In *Trifles*, when the men leave to go about their investigative business, the women, we are told, "listen to the men's steps, then look about the kitchen" (19). In "Jury," however, we get much more. Again here, the women stand motionless, listening to the men's footsteps, but this momentary stasis is followed by a significant gesture: "Then, *as if releasing herself from something strange*, Mrs. Hale began to arrange the dirty pans under the sink, which the county attorney's disdainful push of the foot had deranged" (77; emphasis added). One is prompted here to ask: what is this "something strange" from which she releases herself? Though the actions described in the play and the story are the same, why does Glaspell not include in the stage directions to the play an indication of Mrs. Hale's facial expression?

The answer, I think, lies again in the expanded and altered context of "Jury," where the author continually stresses the distance between the women. If Mrs. Peters is, as the county attorney has suggested, one of "them," Mrs. Hale certainly is not, and she distances herself from her male-approved peer in word and deed. The something strange from which she releases herself is, in this context, her reflexive movement towards Mrs. Peters. Mrs. Hale is, in fact, both extricating herself from the male strictures placed upon all of the women and asserting her intellectual independence. Karen Alkalay-Gut has correctly observed that, to the men, the disorder of Mrs. Wright's kitchen implies her "potential homicidal tendencies, inconceivable in a good wife" (3). For her part, Mrs. Hale is rejecting the men's specious reasoning, complaining about the lawyer's disdainful treatment of the kitchen things and asserting, "I'd hate to have men comin' into my kitchen, snoopin' round and criticizin' " (77), obviously recalling the disorder in her kitchen and resenting the conclusions about her that could be drawn. Lacking that opening scene, the play simply does not resonate so profoundly.

Even more telling is a subtle but important change that Glaspell made following Mrs. Hale's testy assertion. In both the play and the story, Mrs. Peters offers the meek defense, "Of course it's no more than their duty" (*Trifles*, 19; "Jury," 77), and then the two works diverge. In *Trifles*, Mrs. Peters manages to change the subject. Noticing some dough that Mrs. Wright had been preparing the day before, she says flatly, "she had bread set" (20), and that statement directs Mrs. Hale's attention to the half-done and ruined kitchen chores. In effect, the flow of conversation is mutually directed in the play, and the distance between the women is thus minimized. When she wrote the story, however, Glaspell omitted mention of the bread and instead took us into Mrs. Hale's thoughts, as she does at the beginning of the story:

She thought of the flour in her kitchen at home—half sifted, half not sifted. She had been interrupted, and had left things half done. What had interrupted Minnie Foster? Why had that work been left half done? She made a move as if to finish it,—unfinished things always bothered her,—and then she glanced around and saw that Mrs. Peters was watching her—and she didn't want Mrs. Peters to get that feeling she got of work begun and then—for some reason—not finished.

   "It's a shame about her fruit," she said. . . . (77–78)

Although mention of the ruined fruit preserved is included in the play as well, two significant additions are made in the above passage. First, there is the continual comparison between Mrs. Hale's life and Mrs. Wright's. Second, and more important, we get the clear sense here of Mrs. Hale's suspicion of Mrs. Peters, her not wanting to call attention to the unfinished job for fear that the sheriff's wife will get the wrong idea—or, in this case, the right idea, for the evidence of disturbance, however circumstantial, is something the men may be able to use against Mrs. Wright. In other words, unlike the play, the story posits a different set of polarities, with Mrs. Peters presumably occupying a place within the official party and Mrs. Hale taking the side of the accused against all of them.

   We come at this point to a crossroads in the story. Mrs. Hale can leave things as they are and keep information to herself, or she can recruit Mrs. Peters as a fellow "juror" in the case, moving the sheriff's wife away from her sympathy for her husband's position and towards identification with the accused woman. Mrs. Hale chooses the latter course and sets about persuading Mrs. Peters to emerge, in Alkalay-Gut's words, "as an individual distinct from her role as sheriff's wife." Once that happens, "her identification with Minnie is rapid and becomes complete" (6).

   The persuasive process begins easily but effectively, with Mrs. Hale reflecting upon the change in Minnie Foster Wright over the thirty or so years she has known her—the change, to use the metaphor that Glaspell will develop, from singing bird to muted caged bird. She follows this reminiscence with a direct question to Mrs. Peters about whether the latter thinks that Minnie killed her husband. "Oh, I don't know," is the frightened response in both works (*Trifles*, 21; "Jury," 79), but, as always, the story provides more insight and tension than does the drama. Still emphasizing in her revision the distance between the two women, Glaspell has Mrs. Hale believe that her talk of the youthful Minnie has fallen on deaf ears: "Much difference it makes to her whether Minnie Foster had pretty clothes when she was a girl" (78). This sense of the other woman's indifference to such irrelevant trivialities is occasioned not only by Mrs. Hale's persistent belief in the other woman's official role but also by an odd look that crosses Mrs. Peters' face. At the second glance, however, Mrs. Hale notices something else that melts her annoyance and undercuts her suspicions about the sheriff's wife: "Then she looked again, and she wasn't so sure; in fact, she hadn't at any time been perfectly sure about Mrs. Peters. She had that shrinking manner, and yet her eyes looked as if they could see a long way into things" (79). Whereas the play shows the women meandering towards concurrence, the short story is here seen to evolve—and part of that evolution, we must conclude, is due to Mrs. Hale's ability to persuade her peer to regard the case from her perspective. The look that she sees in Mrs. Peters' eyes suggests to her that she might be able to persuade her, that the potential for identification is there. Hence, when she asks whether Mrs. Peters thinks Minnie is guilty, the question resonates here in ways the play does not.

   Accordingly, Mrs. Hale will become much more aggressive in her arguments hereafter, taking on something of the persuader's hopeful hostility, which, in the case of the story, stands in marked contrast to the hostility she felt for Mrs. Peters' official role earlier. Thus, when Mrs. Peters tries to retreat into a male argument, weakly asserting that "the law is the law," (*Trifles*, 22; "Jury," 80), the Mrs. Hale of the short story does not let the remark pass, as the one in *Trifles* does: "the law is the law—and a bad stove is a bad stove. How'd you like to cook on this?" Even she, however, is startled by Mrs. Peters' immediate response to her homey analogy and *ad hominem* attack: "A person gets discouraged—and loses heart," Mrs. Peters says—"That look of seeing . . . through a thing to something else" (80) back on her face.

As far as I am concerned, the addition of this passage is the most important change that Glaspell made in her generic translation. Having used this direct personal attack and having noted the ambivalence that Mrs. Peters feels for her role as sheriff's wife, Mrs. Hale will now proceed to effect closure of the gap between them—again, a gap that is never this widely opened in *Trifles*. Now Mrs. Hale will change her entire mode of attack, pushing the limits, doing things she hesitated doing earlier, assailing Mrs. Peters whenever she lapses into her easy conventional attitudes. For instance, when Mrs. Peters objects to Mrs. Hale's repair of a badly knitted quilt block—in effect, tampering with circumstantial evidence of Minnie's mental disturbance the day before—Mrs. Hale proceeds to do it anyway. As a measure of how much she has changed, we have only to compare this act with her earlier hesitation to finish another chore for fear of what Mrs. Peters might think. She has no reason to be distrustful of Mrs. Peters any longer, for the process of identification is now well underway.

That identification becomes quite evident by the time the women find the most compelling piece of circumstantial evidence against Mrs. Wright—the broken bird cage and the dead bird, its neck wrung and its body placed in a pretty box in Mrs. Wright's sewing basket. When the men notice the cage and Mrs. Hale misleadingly speculates that a cat may have been at it, it is Mrs. Peters who confirms the matter. Asked by the county attorney whether a cat was on the premises, Mrs. Peters—fully aware that there is no cat and never has been—quickly and evasively replies, "Well not *now*. . . . They're superstitious, you know; they leave" (85). Not only is Mrs. Peters deliberately lying here, but, more important, she is assuming quite another role from the one she played earlier. Uttering a banality, she plays at being the shallow woman who believes in superstitions, thus consciously playing one of the roles the men expect her to assume and concealing her keen intellect from them, her ability to extrapolate facts from small details.

From this point forward, the play and the short story are essentially the same. Mrs. Hale will continue her persuasive assault, and Mrs. Peters will continue to struggle inwardly. The culmination of this struggle occurs when, late in the story, the county sheriff says that "a sheriff's wife is married to the law," and she responds, "Not—just that way" (*Trifles*, 27; "Jury," 88). In "Jury," however, this protest carries much greater force than it does in *Trifles* for the simple reason that it is a measure of how far Mrs. Peters has come in the course of the short story.

Appropriately enough, too, Mrs. Hale has the final word in both narratives. Asked derisively by the county attorney what stitch Mrs. Wright had been using to make her quilt, Mrs. Hale responds with false sincerity, "We call it—knot it, Mr. Henderson" (*Trifles*, 28; "Jury," 88). Most critics have read this line as an ironic reference to the women's solidarity at this point.[4] That is quite true, but, as I have been suggesting here, the progress towards this solidarity varies subtly but unmistakably in the two narratives. Whereas *Trifles*, opening as it does with the women's close physical proximity, reveals the dichotomy between male and female concepts of justice and social roles, "A Jury of Her Peers" is much more concerned with the separateness of the women themselves and their self-injurious acquiescence in male-defined roles. Hence, in her reworking of the narrative, Glaspell did much more than translate the material from one genre to another. Rather, she subtly changed its theme, and, in so doing, she wrote a story that is much more interesting, resonant, and disturbing than the slighter drama from which it derives.

Notes

[1] Rachel France notes that *Trifles* reveals "the dichotomy between men and women in rural life," an important feature of that dichotomy being the men's "proclivity for the letter of the law" as opposed to the women's more humane understanding of justice ("Apropos of Women and the Folk Play," in *Women in American Theatre: Careers, Images, Movements*, ed. Helen Krich Chinoy and Linda Walsh Jenkins [New York: Crown, 1981], p. 151). Karen Alkalay-Gut observes three polarities in "Jury": the opposition between the large external male world and the women's more circumscribed place within the home; the attitudes of men and women generally; and the distinction between *law*, which is identified with "the imposition of abstractions on individual circumstances," and *justice*, "the extrapolation of judgment from individual circumstances" ("'A Jury of Her Peers': The Importance of *Trifles*," *Studies in Short Fiction*, 21 [Winter 1984], 2). Karen Stein calls the play "an anomaly in the murder mystery genre, which is predominantly a male tour de force." By bonding together, she goes on, the women act in a manner that is "diametrically opposed to the solo virtuosity usually displayed by male detectives" ("The Women's World of Glaspell's *Trifles*," in *Women in American Theatre*, ed. Helen Krich Chinoy and Linda Walsh Jenkins [New York: Crown, 1981], p. 254). Judith Fetterley also advances an interesting and imaginative interpretation. She sees the characters in "Jury" as readers and the trivial household items as their text. The men fail to read the same meanings in that text that the women do because they are committed to "the equation of textuality with masculine subject matter and masculine point of view" ("Reading about Reading: 'A Jury of Her Peers,' 'The Murders in the Rue Morgue,' and 'The Yellow Wallpaper,'" in *Gender and Reading: Essays on Readers, Texts and Contexts*, ed. Elizabeth A. Flynn and Patrocinio P. Schweickart [Baltimore: Johns Hopkins Univ. Press, 1986], pp. 147–48).

[2] Elaine Hedges notes that one reference included in the play but omitted from "Jury" is Mrs. Hale's lament that, because of Mr. Wright's parsimony, Minnie could not join the Ladies' Aid, a society in which women cooperated with the local church to make items like carpets and quilts. These items were then sold to support ministers' salaries and to aid foreign missions. Minnie is thus denied not only the company of other women but also one of the few public roles that farm women were allowed to play ("Small Things Reconsidered," p. 102). In this regard, the story reveals, as Jeannie McKnight suggests, "a kind of classic 'cabin fever' as motivation for the homicide . . ." ("American Dream, Nightmare Underside: Diaries, Letters, and Fiction of Women on the American Frontier,"
in *Women, Women Writers, and the West*, ed. L. L. Lee and Merrill Lewis [Troy, NY: Whitson, 1979], p. 31).

[3] Cynthia Sutherland aptly observes that the story's effect depends to a large extent upon the removal of Minnie from the sight of the audience, thus focusing our attention on the facts of her plight rather than on her appearance and mannerisms ("American Women Playwrights as Mediators of the 'Woman Problem,'" *Modern Drama*, 21 [September 1978], 323).

[4] Beverly Smith sees "the bond among women [as] the essential knot" ("Women's Work," p. 179). Cynthia Sutherland regards the reference to knotting as "a subdued, ironic, and grisly reminder of the manner in which a stifled wife has enacted her desperate retaliation" ("American Women Playwrights," p. 323). And Elaine Hedges argues that the reference has three meanings: the rope that Minnie knotted around her husband's neck; the bond among the women; and the fact that the women have tied the men in knots ("Small Things Reconsidered," p. 107).

Works Cited

Alkalay-Gut, Karen. "'A Jury of Her Peers': The Importance of *Trifles!" Studies in Short Fiction* 21 (Winter 1984): 1–9.

Glaspell, Susan. "A Jury of Her Peers." *The Wadsworth Casebook Series for Reading, Research, and Writing: Trifles.* Ed. Donna Winchell. Boston: Wadsworth, 2004. 70–88.

—. *Trifles. The Wadsworth Casebook Series for Reading, Research, and Writing: Trifles.* Ed. Donna Winchell. Boston: Wadsworth, 2004. 15–28.

Hedges, Elaine. "Small Things Reconsidered: Susan Glaspell's 'A Jury of Her Peers.'" *Women's Studies* 12.1 (1986): 89–110.

Smith, Beverly, A. "Women's Work—*Trifles?* The Skill and Insight of Playwright Susan Glaspell." *International Journal of Women's Studies* 5 (March–April 1982): 175.

Waterman, Arthur E. *Susan Glaspell.* New York: Twayne, 1966.

LILLIAN SCHANFIELD

from The Case of the Battered Wife: Susan Glaspell's *Trifles* and "A Jury of Her Peers"*

One conceptualization of the nature of domestic violence places battery in the larger context of a symbolic wheel called "The Power and Control Circle," the spokes of which radiate outward from a hub, creating segments that constitute nine of the most controlling and abusive tactics reported by battered women.[1] Often inter-related, these tactics include not only physical and sexual abuse, but also emotional, economic, verbal abuse and isolation as methods of control and domination.

Thinking of battery in terms of these power strategies facilitates recognition of certain abusive behaviors that would otherwise go unidentified as battery, especially if looked at discretely. For example, economic control, which typically involves requiring a woman to ask her spouse for any money she spends, keeping her ignorant about income, and thus dependent and financially helpless, would not normally be construed as battery. These activities, however, take on a different hue when coupled with isolating tactics, which include excessive possessiveness, control of all social contacts, and severe limitation of her involvement with the world outside the home. The same synergy is true for other behaviors: verbal abuse (humiliation such as disparagement and name calling), threats to hurt her or others, intimidation (looks or gestures such as upraised fists, smashing objects or abusing pets), and emotional abuse, which has an extremely broad scope. . . .

That Mr. Wright was a physical batterer is not unlikely. A particular kind of volatility resulted in the birdcage door ripped off its hinges and the bird's neck twisted and broken. In light of this, we may ask whether there is evidence of Mr. Wright's violent temper and an inclination to harm or kill his wife. Furthermore, Glaspell is insistent on our identifying Mrs. Wright as a "songbird" herself. "No, Wright wouldn't like the bird—a thing that sang. She used to sing. He killed that, too" (Glaspell, "Jury" 390), muses Mrs. Hale, underscoring the analogy between the murdered-bird and the victim-wife. And if Mrs. Wright had ever

---

* *Circles* 5 (1997): 69–82. Print.

sported bruises, they would never have been seen by anyone because of her isolation. Indeed, studies show that physical battering often comes as a surprise to people who know the victims because shamefully they often tend to hide the evidence of the violence.

In placing the behavior of Mr. Wright within the "Power and Control Wheel," the story provides evidence of Mr. Wright's economic domination and his physical and emotional isolation of his wife. Although he is not a poor man, Mr. Wright's miserliness permeates the grim farmhouse and is symbolized most poignantly by the broken stove, a source of nurturance and warmth for farm families. When the visiting ladies enter the house, they are gripped by its austerity. Mrs. Wright's clothes, which they reluctantly handle, are shabby. The black skirt, for example, "bore the marks of much making over" (Glaspell, "Jury" 384), and Mrs. Hale connects the loss of pride in her appearance with her isolation. "Wright was close! I think maybe that's why she kept so much to herself . . . you don't enjoy things when you feel shabby" (Glaspell, "Jury" 384). Ironically, Mrs. Wright has requested an apron to wear in prison over her everyday clothing. The women react to the cold, spartan surroundings in careful understatements that define things by what they are not but ought to be: the fire was not "much to brag of" (Glaspell, "Jury" 385); "the stark coldness of that shut-up room was not a thing to linger in" (Glaspell, "Jury" 385). "I don't think a place would be any the cheerfuler for John Wright's bein' in it" (Glaspell, "Jury" 382). The coldness of the house is associated with Mr. Wright's withholding personality. Mrs. Hale sums him up with a simile drawn from the harsh physical environment: "A hard man . . . like a raw wind that gets to the bone" (Glaspell, "Jury" 388).

Mrs. Hale reminisces about Minnie Foster, regressing to the suspect's maiden name. She remembers her as a lively girl with pretty clothes, wearing a "white dress with blue ribbons" (Glaspell, "Jury" 391), and a member of the church choir. We can infer that Minnie was once a gregarious, lively young woman, well taken care of by her family and accustomed to town living. How did twenty years of marriage reduce her to a depressed, shabby, hermit-like Minnie Wright? Her dilapidated rocker seems to symbolize her: "a dingy red, with wooden rungs up the back, and the middle rung was gone, and the chair sagged to one side" (Glaspell, "Jury" 379). "[It] didn't look in the least like Minnie Foster" (Glaspell, "Jury" 379), thinks Mrs. Hale. Like many self-descriptions by battered women, the chair reflects a sense of hopelessness—irreparable, damaged, worn out. Perhaps out of feelings of guilt for her own complicity in the tragedy, Mrs. Hale has difficulty sitting down in the chair, thereby putting herself in Mrs. Wright's place.

The various isolating behaviors experienced by Mrs. Wright are similar to those reported by battered women who often describe the downward path from what had earlier been perceived as a romantic kind of possessiveness to the ultimate condition of being a possession.[2] Mr. Wright had succeeded apparently in isolating his wife from everything that fed her spirit. The narrator of "A Jury of Her Peers" insistently underscores the remoteness of the Wright farmhouse—"It looked very lonesome . . . it was down in a hollow," adding gratuitously, "the poplar trees around it were lonesome-looking trees" (Glaspell 377). Later, Mrs. Hale echoes the narrator's exact words: "down in a hollow and you don't see the road," and identifies with the feelings of the isolated woman: "I dunno what it is, but it's a lonesome place and always was" (Glaspell, "Jury" 388). Mr. Wright's systematic physical isolation of his wife is made clear from the outset of the story by his refusal to participate in a telephone party line, ironically the reason for Mr. Hale's stopping by for a chat. Mr. Wright's resistance may have been due to his cheapness. Also a telephone, especially a party line, would have meant additional noise, anathema to a man described as having a passion for peace and quiet. Most significantly, a telephone would have given his wife access to the outside world.

The men in the story are easy on their neighbor. In their eyes he is a "good man," and his well known "passion" is collegially interpreted by them as an idiosyncratic kind of masculine taciturnity. Even Mr. Hale, who seems the most sympathetic of the men, is quite nonjudgmental in his assessment: what Mrs. Wright might have wanted would not have "made much difference to John" (Glaspell, "Jury" 379). This kind of fraternal "forgiveness" reminds us that a major problem in understanding the nature of domestic violence is that battered women's experiences have traditionally been filtered through male police officers, judges or clergy and diluted or slanted to a male perspective. Indeed, this is the reason that battered women often need spokespersons or advocates to tell their stories.[3]

Unfortunately, Mrs. Wright's childlessness exacerbated her isolation and loneliness. Surprisingly, both women focus on the silence of a childless home more than the nurturing aspect of motherhood. Mrs. Hale sees it in social terms: "Not having children . . . makes a quiet house, and Wright out to work all day, and no company when he did come in" (Glaspell, "Jury" 388). Mrs. Peters, who had lost a child, disjointedly draws a parallel between the strangled bird and her dead baby: "I know what stillness is. When we homesteaded in Dakota, and my first baby died—after he was two years old, and me with no other then— . . ." (Glaspell, "Jury" 391). "If there had been years and years of—nothing, then a bird to sing to you, it would be awful—still—after the bird was still" (Glaspell, "Jury" 391).

Mrs. Wright's loneliness was magnified by her separation from the support provided by female company, and all that that would have signified in this rural community. In farming areas communal activities such as quilting bees and church activities would have provided opportunities for female camaraderie and networking as well as an opportunity to test her reality. Studies of battered women demonstrate that isolation places them at increased risk because of the reduced opportunity for intervention from the community. In contrast to her earlier social lifestyle, the married Mrs. Wright "didn't even belong to the Ladies' Aid" (Glaspell, *Trifles* 393).

The quilting blocks upon which Mrs. Wright was working may represent an attempt to impose order on the meaningless patchwork of her life but also ironically underscore her aloneness. Since quilting is associated with female group activity, when were these squares to have been sewn together and by whom? One woman reminiscing about her grandmother working on a quilt wrote: "Each piece she sewed brought back another memory. 'This was a piece of my first party dress. I danced till the rooster crowed! Here's a piece of your father's first baby bunting, and Aunt Beulah's communion dress.'"[4] One can only wonder what memories were evoked by Mrs. Wright's scraps. Indeed, needlework has the last word in both play and story; Glaspell ends both ironically with technical terminology as the men, trying to trivialize women's concerns, ask mockingly whether the women have figured out whether Mrs. Wright had been intending "to quilt it or just knot it" ("Jury" 389). . . .

Notes

1 See generally, Ellen Pence, "Power Control Wheel," The Domestic Abuse Intervention Project in Duluth, MN, 1987.

2 Angela Browne, *When Battered Women Kill* 43 (1987).

3 See e.g., Shirley Ardener, Introduction, *Perceiving Women*, (Shirley Ardener ed. 1975), discussing dominant ideology, muted subgroups and language. See generally Linda Ben-Zvi, "Susan Glaspell's Contributions to Contemporary Women Playwrights," *Feminine Focus: The New Women Playwrights* 47 (Enoch Brater ed. 1989), on voice and language in Glaspell; and Lenore Walker, *The Battered Woman* 258 (1979).

4 Juanene Rhodes, Letter to the Editor, *Reminisce*, Sept. 1992, 11.

Works Cited

Glaspell, Susan. "A Jury of Her Peers." *Literature: Structure, Sound and Sense* 377–92 (Laurence Perrine ed. 1956).

——. *Trifles. The Norton Anthology of Literature by Women: The Tradition in English* 1389–99 (Sandra M. Gilbert and Susan Gubar eds. 1985).

JUDITH KAY RUSSELL

Glaspell's *Trifles**

On the surface, Susan Glaspell's one-act play *Trifles* focuses on the death of an oppressive husband at the hands of his emotionally abused wife in an isolated and remote farm in the midwest. Beneath the surface, the collective behaviors of Mrs. Hale, Mrs. Peters, and Mrs. Wright in Glaspell's play bear strong resemblance to those of the Fates (Clotho the Spinner, Lachesis the Disposer of Lots, and Atropos the Cutter of the Thread) in Greek mythology. Although Glaspell brings new vigor to the myth, the attention given to Mrs. Hale's resewing the quilt, the change in Mrs. Peters's perspective on law and justice, and the rope placed by Mrs. Wright around her husband's neck are nonetheless grounded in the story of the Three Sisters who control the fate of men.

Mrs. Hale embodies the qualities of Clotho the Spinner, the sister who spins the thread of life. Mrs. Hale subtly suggests that Mrs. Wright is not the sole agent in the death of Mr. Wright. On the surface, Mrs. Hale's ungrammatical reference to that event, "when they was slipping the rope under his neck" (79), can be attributed to improper subject and verb agreement, which is not uncommon in certain regional dialects. However, the use of the plural pronoun and singular verb subtly suggests the involvement of more than one in a single outcome, and it foreshadows the conspiracy of the three women and their efforts to control the outcome or the fate of all characters. Furthermore, the information concerning the domestic life of the Wrights is supplied, or spun, mainly by Mrs. Hale; she describes Mr. Wright as "a hard man," and with her recollections of the young Minnie Foster (now Mrs. Wright) as "kind of like a bird" (82), she establishes the connection of Mr. Wright's involvement in the physical death of the canary and spiritual death of his wife. The condescending manner in which the men joke about the women's concern regarding Mrs. Wright's intention "to quilt or just knot" the quilt evokes a defensive remark from Mrs. Hale in which she hints that it is unwise to tempt fate; she asserts, "I don't see as it's anything to laugh about" (79–80). Finally, by "just pulling out a stitch or two that's not sewed very good" and replacing it with her own stitching (80), Mrs. Hale symbolically claims her position as the person who spins the thread of life.

The second member of the Three Sisters, Lachesis the Disposer of Lots is personified by Mrs. Peters. The viability of the thread spun by Mrs. Hale depends on the actions and reactions of Mrs. Peters. To claim her position as the member of the Fates responsible for assigning destiny, she must abandon objectivity and move toward subjectivity. Her objectivity is exemplified by her assertion that "the law is the law" and her view on physical evidence as she informs Mrs. Hale, " I don't think we ought to touch things" (79–80). The sight of the dead canary and the recognition that "somebody—wrung—its—neck" marks Mrs. Peters's initiation into subjectivity and the sisterhood (83). The discovery of the dead bird awakens Mrs. Peters's suppressed childhood memories of rage toward the "boy [who] took a hatchet" and brutally killed her kitten (83). In her mind, the kitten, Mrs. Wright, and the bird become enmeshed. Mrs. Peters realizes that the dead bird will be used to stereotype Mrs. Wright as a madwoman who overreacts to "trifles." At this point, Mrs. Peters emerges from the shadow of her role as the sheriff's wife and becomes "married to the law" (85). Her new concept of law subjectively favors justice over procedure. She claims her position as the sister who dispenses the lots in life when she moves to hide the bird and thus denies the men "something to make a story about" (85).

Mrs. Wright represents Atropos the Cutter of the Thread. Symbolically, Mrs. Wright is first linked to Atropos in Mr. Hale's description of her "rockin' back and forth" (73), a motion similar to that made by cutting with scissors. The connection to Atropos is further established when Mrs. Peters discovers the dead bird in Mrs. Wright's sewing box and exclaims, "Why, this isn't her scissors" (83). Ironically, the dead canary takes the place of the scissors: The death of the bird is directly tied to the fate of Mr. Wright. In addition, Mrs. Wright assumes mythical status through her spiritual presence and physical absence from the stage. Mr. Hale relates that in his questioning of Mrs. Wright, she admits that her husband "died of a rope around his neck," but she doesn't know how it happened because she "didn't wake up"; she is a sound sleeper (74–75). Mrs. Wright denies personal involvement in the death of her husband, yet she acknowledges that he died while she slept beside him in the bed. Mrs. Wright says, "I was on the inside" (75). Although she may be referring to her routine "inside" position of sleep behind her husband in the bed placed along the wall, Mrs. Wright's statement suggests a movement from the outside (her individual consciousness) to the inside (the collective consciousness of the Fates). Her involvement with the rope of death is the equivalent of severing the thread of life. She did not spin the thread, nor did she assign the lot; she merely contributed a part to the whole, and that collective whole becomes greater than the sum of its parts. For this reason, Mrs. Wright is correct in denying individual knowledge or responsibility in the death of her husband.

In *Trifles*, Mrs. Hale weaves the story or describes the circumstances, Mrs. Peters weighs the evidence and determines the direction of justice, and Mrs. Wright carries out the verdict; although the procedure is somewhat reversed, the mythic ritual is performed nevertheless. Susan Glaspell's use of the Fates, or the Three Sisters, does not weaken her dramatization of women who are oppressed by men. Although some believe that the power of the Three Sisters rivals that of Zeus, Glaspell reminds her audience that, regardless of myth or twentieth-century law, it still takes three women to equal one man. That is the inequality on which she focuses.

Work Cited

Glaspell, Susan. "Trifles." *Plays By American Women: 1900–1930*. Ed. Judith E. Barlow. New York: Applause Theater Book, 1994. 70–86.

Topics for Further Research

1. Write an essay analyzing the differences between the facts of the Hossack case as described by Ben-Zvi and in Glaspell's fictionalized account of the murder and the resulting trial. How did Glaspell reshape the facts to suit her artistic purposes, and to what effect?

2. Read one of Glaspell's other plays, and discuss in an essay any similarities you see in her treatment of women and their role in society between that work and *Trifles*.

3. Research the role that Glaspell played in the founding of the Provincetown Players, and write an essay explaining why that role gave her the status of a major figure in the history of American drama.

4. When were women in Iowa first allowed to serve on juries? How does that bit of background information affect your reading of *Trifles*? How might it have affected how the play was viewed by Glaspell's contemporaries? Write an essay exploring how limitations on women's rights at the time the play is set have affected its reception.

5. Read some contemporary reviews of productions of Glaspell's plays, and write an essay in which you summarize their reception and draw some conclusions about why they were received as they were.

6. Explain in an essay why Glaspell's work was brought back into prominence in the second half of the twentieth century by feminist scholars.

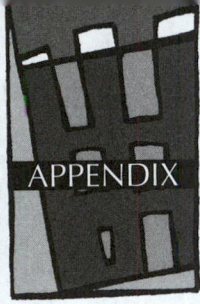

USING LITERARY CRITICISM IN YOUR WRITING

As you become aware of various schools of literary criticism, you see new ways to think—and to write—about fiction, poetry, and drama. Just as you value the opinions of your peers and your instructors, you also will find that the ideas of literary critics can enrich your own reactions to and evaluations of literature. Keep in mind that no single school of literary criticism offers the "right" way of approaching what you read; moreover, no single critic provides the definitive analysis of any short story, poem, or play. As you become aware of the richly varied possibilities of literary criticism, you will begin to ask new questions and discover new insights about the works you read.

Formalism and New Criticism

Formalism stresses the importance of literary form to the meaning of a work. Formalist scholars consider each work of literature in isolation. They consider biographical, historical, and social matters to be irrelevant to the real meaning of a play, short story, novel, or poem. For example, a formalist would see the relationship between Adam and Eve in *Paradise Lost* as entirely unrelated to John Milton's own marital concerns, and they would view theological themes in the same work as entirely separate from Milton's deep involvement with the Puritan religious and political cause in seventeenth-century England. Formalists would also regard Milton's intentions and readers' responses to the epic poem as irrelevant. Instead, formalists would read the text closely, paying attention to organization and structure, to verbal nuances (suggested by word choice and use of figurative language), and to multiple meanings (often created through the writer's use of paradox and irony). Formalist critics try to reconcile the tensions and oppositions inherent in the text in order to develop a unified reading.

The formalist movement in English-language criticism began in England with I. A. Richards's *Practical Criticism* (1929). To explain and introduce his theory, Richards asked students to interpret famous poems without telling them the poets' names. This strategy encouraged close reading of the text rather than reliance on information about a poet's reputation, the details of a poet's life, or the poem's historical context. The American formalist movement, called **New Criticism**, was made popular by college instructors who realized that formalist criticism provided a useful way for students to work along with an instructor in interpreting a literary work rather than passively listening to a lecture on biographical, literary, and historical influences. The New Critical theorists Cleanth Brooks and Robert Penn Warren put together a series of textbooks (*Understanding Poetry*, *Understanding Fiction*, and *Understanding Drama*, first published in the late 1930s) that were used in colleges for years. After the 1950s, many New Critics began to reevaluate their theories and to broaden their approaches. Although few scholars currently maintain a strictly formalist approach, nearly every critical movement, including feminist, Marxist, psychoanalytic, structuralist, and deconstructionist criticism, owes a debt to the close reading techniques introduced by the formalists.

A New Critical Reading: Kate Chopin's "The Storm" (p. 273)

If you were to apply formalist criticism to Chopin's "The Storm," you might begin by noting the story's three distinctive sections. What relationship do the sections bear to one another? What do we learn from the word choice, the figures of speech, and the symbols in these sections? And, most important, how do these considerations lead readers to a unified view of the story?

In the first section of "The Storm," readers meet Bobinôt and his son Bibi. The description of the approaching clouds as "sombre," "sinister," and "sullen" (273) suggests an atmosphere of foreboding, yet the alliteration of these words also introduces a poetic tone. The conversation between father and son in the final part of this section contrasts, yet does not conflict, with the rather formal language of the introduction. Both Bobinôt and Bibi speak in Cajun dialect, suggesting their humble origins, yet their words have a rhythm that echoes the poetic notes struck in the description of the storm. As the section closes, Bobinôt, thinking of his wife, Calixta, at home, buys a can of the shrimp he knows she likes and holds the treasure "stolidly" (273), ironically suggesting the protection he cannot offer his wife in his separation from her during the coming storm.

The long second section brings readers to the story's central events. Calixta, as she watches the rain, sees her former lover, Alcée, riding up to seek shelter. As in the first section, the language of the narrator is somewhat formal and always poetic, filled with sensuous diction and images. For instance, we see Calixta "unfasten[ing] her white sacque at the throat" (274) and, later, Alcée envisions her lips "as red and moist as pomegranate seed" (275). Again, as in the first section, the conversation of the characters is carried on in dialect, suggesting their lack of sophistication and their connection to the powerful natural forces that surround them. The lovemaking that follows, then, seems both natural and poetic. There is nothing sordid about this interlude and, as the final sections of the story suggest through their rather ordinary, matter-of-fact language, nothing has been harmed by Calixta and Alcée's yielding to passion.

In the third section, Bobinôt brings home the shrimp, a symbol of his love for Calixta, and, although we recognize the tension between Bobinôt's shy, gentle approach and Alcée's passion, readers can accept the final sentence as literal rather than ironic. The "storms" (both the rain and the storm of passion) have passed, and no one has been hurt. The threat suggested in the opening sentences has been diffused; both the power and the danger evoked by the poetic diction of the first two sections have disappeared, to be replaced entirely by the rhythms of daily life and speech.

For Further Reading: Formalism and New Criticism

Brooks, Cleanth. *The Well Wrought Urn.* 1947.
Empson, William. *Seven Types of Ambiguity.* 1930.
Hartman, Geoffrey H. *Beyond Formalism.* 1970.
Stallman, Robert W. *Critiques and Essays in Criticism. 1920–1948.* 1949.
Wellek, René. *A History of Modern Criticism.* Vol. 6. 1986.
Wimsatt, W. K. *The Verbal Icon.* 1954.

Reader-Response Criticism

Reader-response criticism opposes formalism, seeing the reader's interaction with the text as central to interpretation. Unlike formalists, reader-response critics do not believe that a work of literature exists as a separate, closed entity. Instead, they consider the reader's contribution to the text as essential. A poem, short story, novel, or play is not a solid piece of fabric but rather a series of threads separated by gaps that readers must fill in, drawing on their own experiences and knowledge.

As readers approach a literary text, they contribute their own interpretations. As they read one sentence and then the next, they develop expectations; and, in realistic stories, these expectations are generally met. Nevertheless, nearly every reader supplies personal meanings and observations, making each reader's experience of a work unique and distinctive from every other reader's experience of the same work. For example, imagine Shakespeare's *Romeo and Juliet* as it might be read by a fourteen-year-old high school student and by her father. The young woman, whose age is the same as Juliet's, is almost certain to identify closely with the female protagonist and to "read" Lord Capulet, Juliet's father, as overbearing and rigid. The young reader's father, however, may be drawn to the poignant passage where Capulet talks with a prospective suitor, urging that he wait while Juliet has time to enjoy her youth. Capulet describes the loss of his other children and calls Juliet "the hopeful lady of my earth." Although the young woman reading this line may interpret it as yet another indication of Capulet's possessiveness, her father may see it as a sign of love and even generosity. The twenty-first-century father may "read" Capulet as a man willing to risk offending a friend in order to keep his daughter safe from the rigors of early marriage (and early childbearing). Whose interpretation is correct? Reader-response theorists would say that both readings are entirely plausible and therefore equally "right."

The differing interpretations produced by different readers can be seen as simply the effect of the different personalities (and personal histories) involved in constructing meaning from the same series of clues. Not only does the reader "create" the work of literature, in large part, but the literature itself may work on the reader as he or she reads, altering the reader's experience and thus the reader's interpretation. For example, the father reading *Romeo and Juliet* may alter his sympathetic view of Capulet as he continues through the play and observes Capulet's later, angry exchanges with Juliet.

Reader-response theorists believe in the importance of **recursive reading**—that is, reading and rereading with the idea that no interpretation is carved in stone. A second or third interaction with the text may well produce a new interpretation. This changing view is particularly likely when the rereading takes place significantly later than the initial reading. For example, if the young woman just described reread *Romeo and Juliet* when she was middle-aged and herself the mother of teenage children, her reaction to Capulet would quite likely be different from her reaction when she read the work at age fourteen.

In one particular application of reader-response theory, called **reception theory**, the idea of developing readings is applied to the general reading public rather than to individual readers. Reception theory, as proposed by Hans Robert Jauss ("Literary History as a Challenge to Literary Theory," *New Literary History*, Vol. 2 [1970–1971]), suggests that each new generation reads the same works of literature differently. Because each generation of readers has experienced different historical events, read different books, and been aware of different critical theories, each generation will view the same works very differently from its predecessors. (Consider, for example, the changing views toward Shakespeare from the seventeenth century to the present.)

Reader-response criticism has received serious attention since the 1960s, when Norman Holland formulated the theory in *The Dynamics of Literary Response* (1968). The German critic Wolfgang Iser (*The Implied Reader*, 1974) argued that in order to be an effective reader, one must be familiar with the conventions and "codes" of writing. This, then, is one reason for studying literature in a classroom: not to produce approved interpretations but to develop strategies and information that will help readers to make sense of a text. Stanley Fish, an American critic, goes even further, arguing that there may not be any "objective" text at all (*Is There a Text in This Class?*, 1980). Fish says that no two readers read the same book, though readers can be trained to have relatively similar life responses to a text if they have had relatively similar experiences. For instance, readers who went to college and took an Introduction to Literature course in which they learned to respond to the various elements of literature, such as character, theme, irony, and figurative language, are likely to have similar responses to a text.

Reader-Response Readings: Kate Chopin's "The Storm" (p. 273)

To demonstrate possible reader-response readings, we can look at the same story previously considered from a formalist perspective. (Of course, if several formalist critics read the story, they too would each write a somewhat different interpretation.)

Written by a twenty-five-year-old man who has studied American literature

> In Kate Chopin's "The Storm," attention must be paid to the two adult male characters, Bobinôt and Alcée. Usually, in a love triangle situation, one man is portrayed more sympathetically than the other. But Chopin provides us with a dilemma. Alcée is not a cavalier seducer; he genuinely cares for Calixta. Neither is he a brooding hero. There is nothing gruff or angry about Alcée, and he returns to his family home with no apparent harm done following the passionate interlude. On the other hand, Bobinôt is not a cruel or abusive husband. We can see no clear reason for Calixta's affair except for her desire to fulfill a sexual longing for Alcée.

Written by an eighteen-year-old male student in a first-year literature course

> Bibi doesn't seem to be a very important character in the story, but we should pay attention to him as a reflection of his father. At the beginning of the story, Bibi worries about his mother and he expresses his concern to his father. Bobinôt tries to reassure his son, but he gets up and buys a treat for Calixta as much to comfort himself as to get something for her. Then Bibi sits with his father, and it seems as if he has transferred all his worries to Bobinôt. In the third section of the story, after Calixta and Alcée have had their love affair, Bibi and Bobinôt come home. They both seem like children, worried about how Calixta will react. She, of course, is nice to them because she feels so guilty. At the end of the third section, both father and son are happy and enjoying themselves. You can't help but feel great sympathy for them both because they are so loving and simple and because they have been betrayed by Calixta, who has not behaved the way a loving mother and wife should.

Written by a forty-five-year-old woman who has studied Kate Chopin's life and work

> A decade after the controversial novel *The Awakening* was published in 1899, one critic protested, "To think of Kate Chopin, who once contented herself with mild yarns about

genteel Creole life . . . blowing us a hot blast like that!" (qtd. in Gilbert and Gubar 981). This literary observer was shocked, as one might expect from an early-twentieth-century reader, by Chopin's frank picture of sexual relations, and particularly of the sexual feelings of the novel's heroine. One cannot help but wonder, however, whether the scandalized reader was really widely acquainted with Chopin.

Certainly he could not have read "The Storm." This short story is surprising for many reasons, but primarily because it defies the sexual mores of the late nineteenth century by showing a woman who is neither evil nor doomed enjoying, even glorying in, her sexuality. Calixta is presented as a good wife and loving mother, concerned about her husband and son who are away from home during the storm. Yet her connection to Bobinôt and Bibi does not keep her from passionately enjoying her interlude with Alcée. She goes to his arms unhesitatingly, with no false modesty or guilt (feigned or real) to hold her back. Somehow, this scenario does not seem to fit the definition of "a mild yarn about genteel Creole life."

For Further Reading: Reader-Response Criticism

Bleich, David. *Subjective Criticism*. 1978.
Fish, Stanley. *Is There a Text in This Class?* 1980.
Holland, Norman. *The Dynamics of Literary Response*. 1968.
Iser, Wolfgang. *The Implied Reader*. 1974.
———. *The Act of Reading: A Theory of Aesthetic Response*. 1978.
Rosenblatt, Louise. *The Reader, the Text, the Poem*. 1978.
Sulleiman, Susan, and Inge Crosman, eds. *The Reader in the Text*. 1980.
Tomkins, Jane P., ed. *Reader-Response Criticism*. 1980.

 ## Feminist Criticism

Throughout the nineteenth century, women such as the Brontë sisters, George Eliot (Mary Ann Evans), Elizabeth Barrett Browning, and Christina Rossetti struggled for the right to be taken as seriously as their male counterparts. Then, in 1929, Virginia Woolf, an experimental novelist and literary critic, published *A Room of One's Own*, which described the difficulties that women writers faced and defined a tradition of literature written by women.

Feminist criticism emerged as a distinct approach to literature only in the late 1960s. Modern feminist criticism began with works such as Mary Ellman's *Thinking about Women* (1968), which focuses on the negative female stereotypes in books authored by men and points out alternative female characteristics suggested by women authors. Another pioneering feminist work was Kate Millet's *Sexual Politics* (1969), which analyzes the societal mechanisms that perpetuate male domination of women. Since that time, feminist writings, though not unified in one theory or methodology, have appeared in ever-growing numbers. Some feminist critics have adapted psychoanalytic, Marxist, or other poststructuralist theories, and others have broken new ground. In general, feminist critics take the view that our culture—and by extension our literature—is primarily patriarchal (controlled by males).

According to feminist critics, what is at issue is not anatomical sex but gender. As Simone de Beauvoir explained, a person is not born feminine, as our society defines it, but rather becomes so because of cultural conditioning. According to feminist critics, paternalist Western culture has defined the feminine as "other" to the male, as passive and emotional in opposition to the dominating and rational masculine.

Feminist critics claim that paternalist cultural stereotypes pervade works of literature in the **canon**—those works generally acknowledged to be the best and most significant. Feminists point out that the traditional canon typically consisted of works written by males and about male experiences. Female characters, when they did appear, were often subordinated to male characters. A female reader of these works must either identify with the male protagonist or accept a marginalized role.

One response of feminist critics is to reinterpret works in the traditional canon. As Judith Fetterley explains in *The Resisting Reader* (1978), the reader "revisions" the text, focusing on the covert sexual bias in a literary work. For example, a feminist scholar studying Shakespeare's *Macbeth* might look closely at the role played by Lady Macbeth and argue that she was not simply a cold-hearted villain but a victim of the circumstances of her time: women in her day were not permitted to follow their own ambitions but were relegated to supporting roles, living their lives vicariously through the achievements of their husbands and sons.

A second focus of feminist scholars has been the redefinition of the canon. By seeking out, analyzing, and evaluating little-known works by women, feminist scholars have rediscovered women writers who were ignored or shunned by the reading public and by critics of their own times. Thus, writers such as Kate Chopin and Charlotte Perkins Gilman (see "The Yellow Wallpaper," p. 379), who wrote during the late nineteenth and early twentieth centuries, are now recognized as worthy of serious consideration and study.

A Feminist Reading: Tillie Olsen's "I Stand Here Ironing" (p. 299)

To approach Tillie Olsen's "I Stand Here Ironing" from a feminist perspective, you might focus on the passages in which the narrator describes her relationships and encounters with men.

Some readings of Tillie Olsen's "I Stand Here Ironing" suggest that the narrator made choices that doomed her oldest daughter to a life of confusion. If we look at the narrator's relationships with the men in her life, however, we can see that she herself is the story's primary victim.

At nineteen, the narrator was a mother abandoned by her husband, who left her a note saying that he "could no longer endure . . . sharing want" (300) with his wife and infant daughter. This is the first desertion we hear about in the narrator's life, and although she agonizingly describes her painful decisions and the mistakes she made with her daughter Emily, we cannot help but recognize that she was the one who stayed and tried to make things right. Her actions contrast sharply with those of her husband, who ran away, saying that his wife and daughter were burdens too great for him to bear.

The second abandonment is more subtle than the first but no less devastating. After the narrator remarried, she was again left alone to cope with a growing family when her second husband went off to war. True, this desertion was for a "noble" purpose and probably was not voluntary, but the narrator, nevertheless, had to seek one of the low-paying jobs available to women to supplement her allotment checks. She was again forced to leave her children because her husband had to serve the needs of the male-dominated military establishment.

The narrator was alone at crucial points in Emily's life and had to turn away from her daughter in order to survive. She has been brought up in a world that teaches women to depend on men, but she learns that she is ultimately alone. Although the desertions she endured were not always intentional, she had to bear the brunt of circumstances that were not her choice but were foisted on her by the patriarchal society in which she lives.

For Further Reading: Feminist Criticism

Benstock, Shari, ed. *Feminist Issues in Literary Scholarship*. 1987.

Engleton, Mary, ed. *Feminist Issues in Literary Theory: A Reader*. 1986.

Gilbert, Sandra, and Susan Gubar. *The Madwoman in the Attic*. 1979.

————. *No Man's Land*. 3 vols. 1988, 1989, 1994.

————, eds. *The Norton Anthology of Literature by Women*. 1985.

Heilbrun, Carolyn G. *Hamlet's Mother and Other Women*. 1990.

Jacobus, Mary. *Reading Woman: Essays in Feminist Criticism*. 1986.

Miller, Nancy, K., ed. *The Poetics of Gender*. 1986.

————. *Subject to Change*. 1988.

Showalter, Elaine. *A Literature of Their Own*. 1977.

————. *Sister's Choice: Tradition and Change in American Women's Writing*. 1991.

 ## Marxist Criticism

Marxist criticism bases interpretations of literature on the social and economic theories of Karl Marx (*Das Kapital*, 1867–94) and his colleague and coauthor Friedrich Engels (*The Communist Manifesto*, 1884). Marx and Engels believed that the dominant capitalist middle class would eventually be challenged and overthrown by the working class. In the meantime, however, middle-class capitalists would continue to exploit the working class, who produce excess products and profits yet do not share in the benefits of their labor. Marx and Engels further regarded all parts of the society in which they lived—religious, legal, educational, governmental—as tainted by what they saw as the corrupt values of middle-class capitalists.

Marxist critics apply these views about class struggle to their readings of poetry, fiction, and drama. They tend to analyze the literary works of any historical era as products of the ideology, or network of concepts, that supports the interests of the cultural elite and suppresses those of the working class. Some Marxist critics see all Western literature as distorted by the privileged views of the elite class, but most believe that a few creative writers reject the distorted views of their society and see clearly the wrongs to which working-class people have been subjected. For example, George Lukacs, a Hungarian Marxist critic, proposed that great works of literature create their own worlds and reflect life with clarity. These great works, though not written by Marxists, can be studied for their revealing examples of class conflict and other Marxist concerns. A Marxist critic would look with favor on Charles Dickens, who in nearly every novel pointed out inequities in the political, legal, and educational establishments of his time. Readers who remember Oliver Twist's pitiful plea for "more" workhouse porridge (refused by evil Mr. Bumble, who skims money from funds intended to feed the impoverished inmates) cannot help but see fertile ground for the Marxist critic, who would certainly applaud Dickens's scathing criticism of Victorian social and economic inequality.

Marxist criticism developed in the 1920s and 1930s in Germany and the Soviet Union. Since 1960, British and American Marxism has received greatest attention, with works such as Raymond Williams's *Culture and Society, 1780–1950* (1960) and Terry Eagleton's *Criticism and Ideology* (1976).

A Marxist Reading: Tillie Olsen's "I Stand Here Ironing" (p. 299)

In a Marxist reading of Tillie Olsen's "I Stand Here Ironing," you might concentrate on events that demonstrate how the narrator's and Emily's fates have been directly affected by the capitalist society of the United States.

Tillie Olsen's "I Stand Here Ironing" stands as a powerful indictment of the capitalist system. The narrator and her daughter Emily are repeatedly exploited and defeated by the pressures of the economic system in which they live.

The narrator's first child, Emily, is born into the world of the 1930s depression—an economic disaster brought on by the excesses and greed of Wall Street. When the young mother is deserted by her first husband, there are no government programs in place to help her. She says it was the "pre-relief, pre-WPA world of the depression" that forced her away from her child and into "a job hashing at night" (300). Although she is willing to work, she is paid so poorly that she must finally send Emily to live with her husband's family. Raising the money to bring Emily back takes a long time; and after this separation, Emily's health, both physical and emotional, is precarious.

When Emily gets the measles, we get a hard look at what the few social programs that existed during the Depression were like. The child is sent—at the urging of a government social worker—to a convalescent home. The narrator notes bitterly, "They still send children to that place. I see pictures on the society page of sleek young women planning affairs to raise money for it, or dancing at the affairs, or decorating Easter eggs or filling Christmas stockings for the children" (302). The privileged class basks in the artificial glow of their charity work for the poor, yet the newspapers never show pictures of the hospitalized children who are kept isolated from everyone they loved and forced to eat "runny eggs . . . or mush with lumps" (302). Once again the mother is separated from her daughter by a system that discriminates against the poor. Because the family cannot afford private treatment, Emily is forced to undergo treatment in a public institution that not only denies her any contact with her family but also cruelly forbids her to save the letters she receives from home. Normal family relationships are severely disrupted by an uncaring economic structure that only grudgingly offers aid to the poor.

It is clear that the division between mother and daughter is created by, and worsened by, the social conditions in which they live. Because they are poor, they are separated at crucial times and, therefore, never get to know each other fully. Thus, neither can truly understand the ordeals the other has been forced to endure.

For Further Reading: Marxist Criticism

Agger, Ben. *The Discourse of Domination*. 1992.

Bullock, Chris, and David Peck, eds. *Guide to Marxist Literary Criticism*. 1980.

Eagleton, Terry. *Marxism and Literary Criticism*. 1976.

Frow, John. *Marxism and Literary History*. 1986.

Holub, Renate, and Antonio Gramsci. *Beyond Marxism and Postmodernism*. 1992.

Jameson, Fredric. *Marxism and Form*. 1971.

Lentricchia, Frank. *Criticism and Social Change*. 1983.

Ohmann, Richard M. *Politics of Letters*. 1987.

Strelka, Joseph P., ed. *Literary Criticism and Sociology*. 1973.

Williams, Raymond. *Culture and Society, 1780–1950*. 1960.

———. *Marxism and Literature*. 1977.

Psychoanalytic Criticism

Psychoanalytic criticism focuses on a work of literature as an expression in fictional form of the inner workings of the human mind. The premises and procedures used in psychoanalytic criticism were developed by Sigmund Freud (1846–1939), though some critics disagree strongly with his conclusions and their therapeutic and literary applications. Feminists, for example, take issue with Freud's notion that women are inherently masochistic.

Some of the major points of Freud's theories depend on the idea that much of what is most significant to us does not take place in our conscious life. Freud believed that we are forced (mostly by the rigors of having to live in harmony with other people) to repress much of our experience and many of our desires in order to coexist peacefully with others. Some of this repressed experience Freud saw as available to us through dreams and other unconscious structures. He believed that literature could often be interpreted as the reflection of our unconscious life.

Freud was among the first psychoanalytic critics, often using techniques developed for interpreting dreams to interpret literature. Among other analyses, he wrote an insightful study of Dostoevsky's *The Brothers Karamazov* as well as brief commentaries on several of Shakespeare's plays, including *A Midsummer Night's Dream*, *Macbeth*, *King Lear*, and *Hamlet*. The study of *Hamlet* may have inspired a classic of psychoanalytic criticism: Ernest Jones's *Hamlet and Oedipus* (1949), in which Jones explains Hamlet's strange reluctance to act against his uncle Claudius as resulting from Hamlet's unresolved longings for his mother and subsequent drive to eliminate his father. Because Hamlet's own father is dead, Jones argues, Claudius becomes, in the young man's subconscious mind, a father substitute. Hamlet, then, cannot make up his mind to kill his uncle because he sees not a simple case of revenge (for Claudius's murder of his father) but rather a complex web that includes incestuous desire for his own mother (now wed to Claudius). Jones extends his analysis to include the suggestion that Shakespeare himself experienced such a conflict and reflected his own Oedipal feelings in *Hamlet*.

A French psychoanalyst, Jacques Lacan (1901–1981), combined Freudian theories with structuralist literary theories to argue that the essential alienating experience of the human psyche is the acquisition of language. Lacan believed that once you can name yourself and distinguish yourself from others, you enter the difficult social world that requires you to repress your instincts. Like Lacan, who modified and adapted psychoanalytic criticism to connect it to structuralism, many twentieth-century literary scholars, including Marxists and feminists, have found useful approaches in psychoanalytic literary theory (for example, see Mary Jacobus's *Reading Woman: Essays in Feminist Criticism*, 1986).

Psychoanalytic Terms

To fully appreciate psychoanalytic criticism, readers need to understand the following terms:

- *id*—The part of the mind that determines sexual drives and other unconscious compulsions that urge individuals to unthinking gratification.
- *ego*—The conscious mind that strives to deal with the demands of the id and to balance its needs with messages from the superego.

- *superego*—The part of the unconscious that seeks to repress the demands of the id and to prevent gratification of basic physical appetites. The superego is a sort of censor that represents the prohibitions of society, religion, family beliefs, and so on.
- *condensation*—A process that takes place in dreams (and in literature) when several elements from the repressed unconscious are linked together to form a new yet disguised whole.
- *symbolism*—The use of representative objects to stand for forbidden (often sexual) objects. This process takes place in dreams and in literature. For instance, a pole, knife, or gun may stand for the penis.
- *displacement*—The substitution of a socially acceptable desire for a desire that is not acceptable. This process takes place in dreams or in literature. For example, a woman who experiences sexual desires for her son may instead dream of being intimate with a neighbor who has the same first name as (or who looks like) her son.
- *Oedipus complex*—The repressed desire of a son to unite sexually with his mother and kill his father. According to Freud, all young boys go through this stage, but most resolve these conflicts before puberty.
- *projection*—A defense mechanism in which people mistakenly see in others antisocial impulses they fail to recognize in themselves.
- *subject*—The term used in Lacanian theory to designate a speaking person, or a person who has assumed a position within language. The Lacanian subject of language is split, or characterized by unresolvable tension between the conscious perception of the self (Freud's ego) and the unconscious desires that motivate behavior.

A Psychoanalytic Reading: Edgar Allan Poe's "The Cask of Amontillado" (p. 328)

Edgar Allan Poe died in 1849, six years before Freud was born, so Poe could not possibly have known Freud's work. Nevertheless, psychoanalytic critics argue that the principles discovered by Freud and those who followed him are inherent in human nature. Therefore, they believe it is perfectly plausible to use modern psychiatric terms when analyzing a work written before their invention. If you approached Poe's "The Cask of Amontillado" from a psychoanalytic perspective, you might write the following interpretation.

> Montresor, the protagonist of Poe's "The Cask of Amontillado," has long fascinated readers who have puzzled over his motives for the story's climactic action when he imprisons his rival, Fortunato, and leaves him to die. Montresor claims that Fortunato insulted him and dealt him a "thousand injuries" (329). Yet when we meet Fortunato, although he appears something of a pompous fool, none of his actions—or even his comments—seems powerful enough to motivate Montresor's thirst for revenge.
>
> If, however, we consider a defense mechanism, first named "projection" and described by Sigmund Freud, we gain a clearer picture of Montresor. Those who employ projection are often people who experience antisocial impulses yet are not conscious of these impulses. It seems highly likely that Fortunato did not persecute Montresor; rather, Montresor himself experienced the impulse to act in a hostile manner toward Fortunato. We know, for

instance, that Fortunato belongs to the exclusive Order of Masons because he gives Montresor the secret Masonic sign. Montresor's failure to recognize the sign shows that he is a mason only in the grimmest literal sense. Montresor clearly resents Fortunato's high standing and projects onto Fortunato all of his own hostility toward those who (he thinks) have more or know more than he does. Thus, he imagines that Fortunato's main business in life is to persecute and insult him.

Montresor's obsessive behavior further indicates his pathology. He plans Fortunato's punishment with the cunning one might ordinarily reserve for a major battle, cleverly figuring out a way to keep his servants from the house and to lure the ironically named Fortunato to his death. Each step of the revenge is carefully plotted. This is no sudden crime of passion but rather the diabolically planned act of a deeply disturbed mind.

If we understand Montresor's need to take all of the hatred and anger that is inside himself and to rid himself of those socially unacceptable emotions by projecting them onto someone else, then we can see how he rationalizes a crime that seems otherwise nearly unmotivated. By killing Fortunato, Montresor symbolically kills the evil in himself. It is interesting to note that the final lines of the story support this reading. Montresor observes that "For the half of a century no mortal has disturbed" the bones (334). In other words, the unacceptable emotions have not again been aroused. His last words, a Latin phrase from the Mass for the Dead meaning "rest in peace," suggest that only through his heinous crime has he found release from the torment of his own hatred.

For Further Reading: Psychoanalytic Criticism

Freud, Sigmund. *The Interpretation of Dreams.* 1900.

Gardner, Shirley N., ed. *The (M)other Tongue: Essays in Feminist Psychoanalytic Interpretation.* 1985.

Hartman, Geoffrey H., ed. *Psychoanalysis and the Question of the Text.* 1979.

Kris, Ernst. *Psychoanalytic Explorations in Art.* 1952.

Kristeva, Julia. *Desire in Language.* 1980.

Nelson, Benjamin, ed. *Sigmund Freud on Creativity and the Unconscious.* 1958.

Wright, Elizabeth. *Psychoanalytic Criticism: Theory in Practice.* 1984.

 ## Structuralism

Structuralism, a literary movement with roots in linguistics and anthropology, concentrates on literature as a system of signs that have no inherent meaning except in their agreed-upon or conventional relation to one another. Structuralism is usually described by its proponents not as a new way to interpret literary works but rather as a way to understand how works of literature come to have meaning. Because structuralism developed from linguistic theory, some structuralists use linguistic approaches to literature. When they talk about literary texts, they use the terms (such as *morpheme* and *phoneme*) that linguists use as they study the nature of language. Many structuralists, however, use the linguistic model as an analogy. To understand the analogy, you need to know a bit of linguistic theory.

The French linguist Ferdinand de Saussure (*Course in General Linguistics*, 1915) suggested that the relationship between an object and the name we use to designate it is purely arbitrary. What, for example, makes "C-A-T" signify a small, furry animal with pointed ears and whiskers? Only our learned expectation makes us associate *cat* with the family feline pet.

Had we grown up in France, we would make the same association with *chat,* or in Mexico with *gato.* The words we use to designate objects (linguists call these words *signs*) make sense only within the large context of our entire language system and will not be understood as meaningful by someone who does not know that language system. Further, Saussure pointed out, signs become truly useful only when we use them to designate difference. For instance, the word *cat* becomes useful when we want to differentiate a small furry animal that meows from a small furry animal that barks. Saussure was interested in how language, as a structure of conventions, worked. He asked intriguing questions about the underlying rules that allow this made-up structure of signs to work, and, as a result, his pioneering study caught the interest of scholars in many fields.

Many literary scholars saw linguistic structuralism as analogous to the study of literary works. Literary structuralism leads readers to think of poems, short stories, novels, and plays not as self-contained and individual entities that have some kind of inherent meaning but rather as part of a larger literary system. To fully appreciate and analyze the work, the reader must understand the system within which it operates. Like linguistic structuralism, literary structuralism focuses on the importance of difference. We must, for example, understand the difference between the structure of poetry and the structure of prose before we can make sense of William Carlos Williams's "Red Wheelbarrow" (p. 742):

> so much depends
> upon
> a red wheel
> barrow

Readers unacquainted with the conventions of poetry would find those lines meaningless and confusing, although if they knew the conventions of prose, they would readily understand this sentence:

> So much depends upon a red wheelbarrow.

The way we interpret any group of "signs," then, depends on how they are structured and on the way we understand the system that governs their structure.

Structuralists believe that literature is basically artificial because although it uses the same "signs" as everyday language, whose purpose is to give information, the purpose of literature is *not* primarily to relay data. For example, a poem like Dylan Thomas's "Do not go gentle into that good night" (p. 891) is written in the linguistic form of a series of commands, yet the poem goes much further than that. Its meaning is created not only by our understanding the lines as a series of commands but also by our recognition of the poetic form, the rhyming conventions, and the figures of speech that Thomas uses. We can only fully discuss the poem within the larger context of our literary knowledge.

Structuralism also provides the foundation for poststructuralism, a theoretical movement that informs the fields of deconstructionist and New Historicist criticism and has influenced the work of many psychoanalytic and sociological critics. Although structuralists claim that language functions by arbitrarily connecting words (signifiers) to ideas (signifieds), poststructuralists develop the implications of this claim, arguing that because the connection of a word to an idea is purely arbitrary, any operation of language is inherently unstable. Poststructuralists believe that to study a literary text is to study a continuously shifting set of meanings.

A Structuralist Reading: William Faulkner's "Barn Burning" (p. 335)

A structuralist reading tries to bring to light some of the assumptions about language and form that we are likely to take for granted. Looking at the opening paragraph of Faulkner's "Barn Burning," from the point of view of structuralist criticism, you might first look at an interpretation that reads the passage as a stream of Sarty's thoughts. The structuralist critic might then consider the assumptions a reader would have to make to see what Faulkner has written as the thoughts of an illiterate child. Next, the structuralist might look at evidence to suggest the language in this section operates outside the system of language that would be available to Sarty and that, therefore, "Barn Burning" opens not with a simple recounting of the main character's thoughts but rather with something far more complex.

> The opening paragraph of William Faulkner's "Barn Burning" is often read as an excursion into the mind of Sarty, the story's young protagonist. When we read the passage closely, however, we note that a supposedly simple consciousness is represented in a highly complex way. For Sarty—uneducated and illiterate—the "scarlet devils" and "silver curve of fish" on the labels of food tins serve as direct signs appealing to his hunger. It is unlikely, however, that Sarty could consciously understand what he sees and express it as metaphor. We cannot, then, read this opening passage as a recounting of the thoughts that pass through Sarty's mind. Instead, these complex sentences and images offer possibilities that reach beyond the limits of Sarty's linguistic system.
>
> Because our own knowledge is wider than Sarty's, the visual images the narrator describes take on meanings for us that are unavailable to the young boy. For example, like Sarty, we know that the "scarlet devils" stand for deviled ham. Yet the devils also carry another possible connotation. They may indicate evil and thus serve to emphasize the despair and grief Sarty feels are ever present. So we are given images that flash through the mind of an illiterate young boy, apparently intended to suggest his poverty and ignorance (he cannot read the words on the labels), yet we are led to see a highly complicated set of meanings. When we encounter later in the passage Sarty's articulated thought, "*our enemy . . . ourn! mine and hisn both! . . . ,*" his down-to-earth dialect shows clearly the sharp distinction between the system of language the narrator uses to describe Sarty's view of the store shelves and the system of language Sarty uses to describe what he sees and feels.

For Further Reading: Structuralism

Barthes, Roland. *Critical Essays.* 1964.

Culler, Jonathan. *Structuralist Poetics.* 1975.

Greimas, A. J. *Structured Semantics: An Attempt at a Method.* Trans. McDowell, Schleifer, and Velie. 1983.

Hawkes, Terence. *Structuralism and Semiotics.* 1977.

Lentricchia, Frank. *After the New Criticism.* 1980.

Pettit, Philip. *The Concept of Structuralism: A Critical Analysis.* 1975.

Scholes, Robert. *Structuralism in Literature: An Introduction.* 1974.

Deconstruction

Deconstruction is a literary movement that developed from structuralism. Deconstructionists argue that every text contains within it some ingredient undermining its purported system of meaning. In other words, the structure that seems to hold the text together is unstable because it depends on the conclusions of a particular ideology (for instance, the idea that women are inferior to men or that peasants are content with their lowly position in life), conclusions that are not as natural as the text may pretend. The practice of finding the point at which the text falls apart because of these internal inconsistencies is called deconstruction.

Deconstructive theorists share with formalists and structuralists a concern for the work itself rather than for biographical, historical, or ideological influences. Like formalists, deconstructionists focus on possibilities for multiple meanings within texts. However, while formalists seek to explain paradox by discovering tensions and ironies that can lead to a unified reading, deconstructionists insist on the primacy of multiple possibilities. They maintain that any given text is capable of yielding many divergent readings, all of which are equally valid yet may in some way undermine and oppose one another.

Like structuralists, deconstructionists see literary texts as part of larger systems of discourse. A key structuralist technique is identifying opposites in an attempt to show the structure of language used in a work. Having identified the opposites, the structuralist rests the case. Deconstructionists, however, go further. Jacques Derrida, a French philosopher, noticed that these oppositions do not simply reflect linguistic structures but are the linguistic response to the way people deal with their beliefs (their ideologies). For instance, if you believe strongly that democracy is the best possible form of government, you tend to lump other forms of government into the category "nondemocracies." If a government is nondemocratic, that—not its other distinguishing characteristics—would be significant to you. This typical ideological response operates in all kinds of areas of belief, even ones we are not aware of. Deconstructionists contend that texts tend to give away their ideological biases by means of this opposition.

Derrida called this distinction between "A" and "Not-A" (rather than between "A" and "B") *différance*, a word he coined to suggest a concept represented by the French verb *différer*, which has two meanings: "to be different" and "to defer." (Note that in Derrida's new term an *a* is substituted for an *e*—a distinction that can be seen in writing but not heard in speaking.) When a deconstructionist uncovers *différance* through careful examination of a text, he or she also finds an (often unwitting) ideological bias. Deconstructionists argue that the reader must transcend such ideological biases and must instead acknowledge contradictory possibilities as equally worthy of consideration. No one meaning can or should be designated as correct.

Deconstruction, then, is not really a system of criticism (and, in fact, deconstructionists resist being labeled as a school of criticism). Rather, deconstruction offers a way to take apart a literary text and thereby reveal its separate layers. Deconstructionists often focus on the metaphorical nature of language, claiming that all language is basically metaphoric because the sign we use to designate any given object or action stands apart from the object itself. In fact, deconstructionists believe that all writing is essentially literary and metaphorical because language, by its very nature, can only *stand for* what we call reality or truth; it cannot *be* reality or truth.

A major contribution of deconstructive critics lies in their playful approach to language and to literary criticism. They refuse to accept as absolute any one way of reading poetry, fiction, or drama, and they guard against what they see as the fixed conclusions and arbitrary operating assumptions of many schools of criticism.

A Deconstructionist Reading: Flannery O'Connor's "A Good Man Is Hard to Find" (p. 367)

A deconstructionist reading of Flannery O'Connor's "A Good Man Is Hard to Find" might challenge the essentially religious interpretations the author offered of her own stories in essays and letters. If you were applying deconstructionist criticism to the story, you might argue that the author's reading of the story is no more valid than anyone else's, and that the story can just as legitimately be read as an investigation of the functions of irony in language.

Flannery O'Connor explained that the grotesque and violent aspects of her stories are intended to shock the reader into recognizing the inhospitable nature of the world and thereby recognizing the universal human need for divine grace. The last sentence of "A Good Man Is Hard to Find" is spoken by The Misfit, who has just murdered a family of travelers: "It's no real pleasure in life" (378). However, the language of O'Connor's stories is extremely ironic—that is, her narrators and characters often say one thing but mean another. So, it is possible that their statements are not empirically true but are representations of a persona or elements of a story they have created using language.

The Grandmother, for example, lives almost entirely in fictions—newspaper clippings, stories for the grandchildren, her belief that The Misfit is a good man. In contrast, The Misfit is more literal than the Grandmother in his perception of reality. He knows, for example, whether the car turned over once or twice. But he too is posing, at first as the tough guy who rejects religious and societal norms by saying, ". . . it's nothing for you to do but enjoy the few minutes you got left the best way you can—by killing somebody or burning down his house or doing some other meanness to him. No pleasure but meanness . . ." (377). Finally, he poses as the pessimist—or, according to O'Connor's reading, the Christian—who claims, "It's no real pleasure in life." The contradictions in The Misfit's language make it impossible to tell which of these facades is "real."

For Further Reading: Deconstruction

Abrams, M. H. "Rationality and the Imagination in Cultural History." *Critical Inquiry* 2 (1976): 447–64. (Abrams claims deconstructionists are parasites who depend on other critics to come up with interpretations that can be deconstructed.)

Arac, Jonathan, Wlad Godzich, and Wallace Martin, eds. *The Yale Critics: Deconstruction in America.* 1983.

Berman, Art. *From the New Criticism to Deconstruction.* 1988.

Culler, Jonathan. *On Deconstruction: Theory and Criticism after Structuralism.* 1982.

Jefferson, Ann. "Structuralism and Post-Structuralism." *Modern Literary Theory: A Comparative Introduction.* 1982.

Johnson, Barbara. *The Critical Difference: Essays in the Contemporary Rhetoric of Reading.* 1980.

Leitsch, Vincent B. *Deconstructive Theory and Practice.* 1982.

Lynn, Steven. "A Passage into Critical Theory." *College English* 52 (1990): 258–71.

Miller, J. Hillis. "The Critic as Host." *Deconstruction and Criticism.* Ed. Harold Bloom et al. 1979. (a response to Abrams's article, listed above)

Norris, Christopher. *Deconstruction: Theory and Practice.* 1982.

Cultural Studies

Cultural studies is a particularly difficult field of criticism to define for a number of reasons. Chief among these is the scope of the field. Literary theory has typically focused on literature—however defined—while bringing in knowledge about a work's historical context or the life and views of the author as a means of better understanding the work. Cultural studies, on the other hand, treats any and all objects produced by a society as worthy of the same kind of analysis that literary texts receive. Thus, the advertisements for Arthur Miller's *Death of a Salesman*, or the diary of an actual traveling salesman might, to a cultural critic, be as interesting and complex as Miller's play itself.

Given that the work of art no longer occupies a privileged position relative to other artifacts, it is not surprising that cultural critics have tended to call into question the relative merit of what we have traditionally thought of as masterpieces. To say that one work is "better" than another, such critics would argue, is an almost meaningless statement, and one that reveals more about the values of the person making it than about the work itself. Many cultural critics would therefore reject altogether the idea of a literary canon, or a list of great works that an educated person should know. At the very least, cultural critics would argue, any canon must be subject to constant examination and revision.

Cultural studies has roots in both the French structuralism of critics such as Roland Barthes and the Cultural Materialism of British critics such as Raymond Williams. In his classic text *Mythologies* (1957), Barthes began to apply structural analysis not simply to texts but to phenomena in popular culture—professional wrestling, for example. Williams came at similar subject matter from a different angle. Mass culture has traditionally been viewed by Marxists as something imposed on the working classes and the disadvantaged by upper and bourgeoisie classes seeking to maintain their own position. Williams, while acknowledging the truth in such an assertion, distinguished between mass culture and popular culture, noting that the latter can be used by those outside of power as a means of self-expression and even rebellion. It is not surprising that there is a distinctly political edge to cultural studies, and that many of its practitioners see themselves as activists and their research as a means to effect social change.

There are a number of distinct schools—New Historicism, postcolonialism, American multiculturalism, and queer theory—that are often, though not always, placed under the heading of cultural studies. Of these four, the broadest is New Historicism. Its assumptions—that a work cannot be discussed in isolation from the culture that gave rise to it—are shared by most critics in the other schools, and it might be described as much as a method as a school. Postcolonialism, American multiculturalism, and queer theory can all be seen as applications of the principles of cultural studies—particularly its awareness of power relationships and its questioning of traditional canons—to specific geographical areas and cultures.

New Historicism

New Historicism relates a text to the historical and cultural contexts of the period in which it was created and the periods in which it was critically evaluated. These contexts are not considered simply as "background" but as integral parts of a text. According to the New Historicists, history is not objective facts; rather, like literature, history is subject to interpretation and reinterpretation depending on the power structure of a society. Louis Althusser, for example, suggests that ideology intrudes in the discourse of an era, subjecting readers to the interests of the ruling establishment. Michel Foucault argues that the discourse of an era defines the nature of "truth" and what behaviors are acceptable, sane, or criminal. "Truth," according to Foucault, is produced by the interaction of power and the systems in which the power flows, and it changes as society changes. Mikhail Bakhtin suggests that all discourse is dialogic, containing within it many independent and sometimes conflicting voices.

Literature, in the opinion of the New Historicist critics, cannot be interpreted without reference to the time and place in which it was written. Criticism likewise cannot be evaluated without reference to the time and place in which it was written. A flaw of much criticism, according to the New Historicists, is the consideration of a literary text as if it were an organic whole. Such an approach ignores the diversity of conflicting voices in a text and in the cultural context in which a text is embedded. Indeed, Stephen Greenblatt prefers the term "cultural poetics" to New Historicism because it acknowledges the integral role that literature and art play in the culture of any era. Works of art and literature, according to Greenblatt, actively foster subversive elements or voices but somehow constrain those forces in ways that defuse challenges to the dominant culture.

New Historicists also point out that readers, like texts, are influenced and shaped by the cultural context of their eras and that a thoroughly objective "reading" of a text is therefore impossible. Acknowledging that all readers to some degree "appropriate" a text, some New Historicists present their criticism of texts as "negotiations" between past and present contexts. Thus, criticism of a particular work of literature would draw from both the cultural context of the era in which the text was written and the critic's present cultural context, and the critic would acknowledge how the latter context influences interpretation of the former.

Since the early 1970s, feminist critics have adopted some New Historicist positions, focusing on male–female power conflicts. And critics interested in multicultural texts have stressed the role of the dominant white culture in suppressing or marginalizing the texts of nonwhites. Marxist critics, including Raymond Williams, have adopted the term "cultural materialism" in discussing their mode of New Historicism, which focuses on the political significance of a literary text.

A New Historicist Reading: Charlotte Perkins Gilman's "The Yellow Wallpaper" (p. 379)

A New Historicist scholar might write an essay about "The Yellow Wallpaper" as an illustration of the destructive effects of the patriarchal culture of the late nineteenth century on women. This reading would be vastly different from that of most nineteenth-century critics, who interpreted the story as a harrowing case study of female mental illness. Even some early-twentieth-century readings posited that the narrator's mental illness is the result of her individual psychological problems. In a New Historicist reading, however, you might focus on the social conventions of the time, which produced conflicting discourses that drove the narrator to madness.

> The female narrator of "The Yellow Wallpaper," who is writing in her private journal (which is the text of the short story), explains that her husband, a physician, has diagnosed her as having a "temporary nervous depression—a slight hysterical tendency" (380). She says she should believe such a physician "of high standing" (380) and cooperate with his treatment, which is to confine her to a room in an isolated country estate and compel her to rest and have no visitors and not to write. The "cure" is intended to reduce her nervous-

ness, she further explains. But as the story unfolds, the narrator reveals that she suspects the treatment will not cure her because it leaves her alone with her thoughts without even her writing to occupy her mind. Her husband's "cure" forces her into a passive role and eliminates any possibility of asserting her own personality. However, she guiltily suggests that her own lack of confidence in her husband's diagnosis may be what is preventing her cure.

The text of "The Yellow Wallpaper" can be divided into at least two conflicting discourses: (1) the masculine discourse of the husband, who has the authority both of a highly respected physician and of a husband, two positions reinforced by the patriarchal culture of the time; and (2) the feminine discourse of the narrator, whose hesitant personal voice contradicts the masculine voice but undermines itself because it keeps reminding her that women should obey their husbands and their physicians. A third discourse underlies the two dominant ones—that of the gothic horror tale, a popular genre of the late nineteenth century. The narrator in "The Yellow Wallpaper" is isolated against her will in a room with barred windows in an almost deserted palatial country mansion she describes as "The most beautiful place!" (380). She is at the mercy of her captor, in this case her husband. She is not sure whether she is hallucinating, and she thinks the mansion may be haunted. She does not know whom to trust, not being sure whether her husband really wants to "cure" her or to punish her for expressing her rebellion.

The narrator learns to hide her awareness of the conflicting discourses. She avoids mentioning her thoughts and fears about her illness or her fancies about the house being haunted, and she hides her writing. She speaks reasonably and in "a very quiet voice" (387). But this inability to speak freely to anyone is a kind of torture, and alone in her room with the barred windows, she takes up discourse with the wallpaper. At first she describes it as "One of those sprawling flamboyant patterns committing every artistic sin" (381). But she is fascinated by the pattern, which has been distorted by mildew and by the tearing away of some sections. The narrator begins to strip off the wallpaper to free a woman she thinks is trapped inside; and, eventually, she visualizes herself as that woman, trapped yet freed by the destruction of the wallpaper. The narrator retreats, or escapes into madness, driven there by the multiple discourses she cannot resolve.

For Further Reading: New Historicist Criticism

Brook, Thomas. *The New Historicism and Other Old Fashioned Topics*. 1991.

Coates, Christopher. "What Was the New Historicism?" *Centennial Review* 32.2 (Spring 1993): 267–80.

Geertz, Clifford. "Thick Description: Toward an Interpretive Theory of Culture." *The Interpretation of Cultures*. By Clifford Geertz. 1973.

Greenblatt, Stephen, ed. *Representing the English Renaissance*. 1988.

Levin, David. "American Historicism: Old and New." *American Literary History* 6.3 (Fall 1994): 527–38.

Rabinov, Paul, ed. *The Foucault Reader*. 1986.

Veeser, H. Aram, ed. *The New Historicism*. 1989.

Queer Theory

The roots of queer theory go back to the 1960s and 1970s, when movements for gay liberation and changing attitudes toward sexuality in general made it easier for artists and critics to identify themselves as gay and lesbian and to deal directly with gay and lesbian themes in their work. Critical examination of these subjects intensified during the 1980s, partly in response to the AIDS crisis. By the early 1990s, the term "queer theory," coined by Teresa de Lauretis, came to be used as an umbrella term for the work being done by critics such as Eve Kosofsky Sedgwick and Judith Butler.

The actual scope of queer theory is significantly broader than the name might imply: queer theorists tend to doubt prevailing notions of sexual identity as something fixed by biology or even by personal inclination since a person might find different means of sexual expression appealing at different points. Queer theory therefore calls into question terms such as *homosexual, heterosexual, bisexual, transsexual,* and *transgender*. It also examines sympathetically those aspects of sexuality that, while not necessarily "queer" in the sense of "gay," have nonetheless been marginalized—cross-dressing, for example, or sadomasochism.

When applying queer theory to texts, critics tend to be particularly interested in those ways in which the text blurs or subverts traditional notions of sexual identity, notions that tend to rely on "heteronormativity"—the idea that heterosexuality is the statistical, and even moral, standard and that all departures from it are perverse or problematic. These blurrings in the text occur not only in contemporary literature but also in works from the past, where they were perhaps missed because of the ideological prejudices of earlier critics.

Given queer theory's emphasis on gender, there are inevitably points of contact with feminist criticism. Critics such as Judith Butler, however, have argued that feminists have been too quick to regard gender, however defined, as something fixed. Queer theory has connections to gay and lesbian activism, but those connections are sometimes strained because activists are often trying to gain recognition or respect for those with a given sexual identity, while queer theorists are more likely to call into question *all* identities. Like other schools within the field of cultural studies, critics employing queer theory often examine cultural artifacts such as film, music, and television programs, in this case for messages that may subtly subvert heteronormativity. For example, there has been considerable interest within queer studies in the ways that Madonna has portrayed sexuality.

In theoretical terms, queer theory's biggest debt has been to the deconstructionists, particularly to Michel Foucault, and to his groundbreaking work, *The History of Sexuality*. Among the foundational works in the field are Butler's *Gender Trouble* and Sedgwick's *Epistemology of the Closet*.

A Queer Theory Reading: Zadie Smith's "The Girl with Bangs" (p. 262)

A queer theory reading of Zadie Smith's "The Girl with Bangs" might focus on the ways in which sexual desire in the story seems related less to gender as it is commonly conceived than to the attraction between individuals. A critic might argue, in fact, that the story as a whole calls into question the validity of gender roles.

> In Zadie Smith's "The Girl with Bangs," the narrator enters into her first relationship with another woman, one that leaves her with a new perspective on sexual relationships and on herself. However, the narrator does not think in terms of gay and straight. Rather, she describes herself as being "a boy" in her relationship with Charlotte Greaves.
>
> Male and female, in the eyes of the narrator, are designations that have less to do with physical gender than with gender roles. Because she is the one who pursues Charlotte, and because she is the one who figuratively waits beneath Charlotte's window, she sees herself in the male role, that of the pursuer. Because she finds herself helpless to resist Charlotte— a situation she has never encountered with a man—she thinks, "So this is what it's like being a boy" (265). When Maurice comes to ask her to give up Charlotte, she describes their talk—with only partial irony—as "man-to-man."

The narrator agrees to end her relationship with Charlotte, but when she and Maurice go to speak with Charlotte, they find her in bed with another man. Charlotte's sexual openness—she apparently has sex with anyone, of either gender, whenever she wants—represents another challenge to the heteronormativity of society and to its conventions of monogamy. Her eventual marriage to Maurice might seem at first a surrender to that norm, but the story certainly hints that Maurice will regret the marriage because nothing indicates that Charlotte will suddenly stop sleeping with other people.

Interestingly, the story concludes with the narrator identifying not—as she has during the affair with Charlotte—with men, but with a woman, the woman Maurice has been sleeping with in Thailand. For the duration of the affair, she viewed men as helpless, a view at odds with much of the stereotypical rhetoric of manliness—though not with the conventions of traditional courting. She pictured men, and herself with them, as standing beneath the beloved's window, waiting to catch whatever she might throw down. Now she says that "in the real world, or so it seems to me, it is almost always women and not men who are waiting under windows, and they are almost always disappointed. In this matter Charlotte was unusual" (266).

To say that Charlotte was "unusual" is to say that she was odd, or, in the broadest sense of the word, "queer." What is "queerest" about Charlotte, then, may not be her bisexuality or promiscuity, but her ability to remain free of the negative emotional consequences her existence as a woman in a male-dominated society would typically bring with it.

For Further Reading: Queer Theory

Butler, Judith. *Bodies That Matter: On the Discursive Limits of "Sex."* 1993.

Halperin, David. *Homosexuality: A Cultural Construct.* 1990.

———. *One Hundred Years of Homosexuality.* 1990.

Jagose, Annamarie. *Queer Theory: An Introduction.* 1997.

Parker, Andrew. *After Sex?: On Writing Since Queer Theory.* 2007.

Sedgwick, Eve Kosofsky. *Between Men: English Literature and Male Homosocial Desire.* 1985.

Spargo, Tamsin. *Foucault and Queer Theory.* 1999.

Thomas, Calvin (ed.). *Straight with a Twist: Queer Theory and the Subject of Heterosexuality.* 1999.

Postcolonial Studies

In the years following World War II, the period of European colonization came to a close as first one country and then another gained its independence from the countries—England, France, Belgium—that had controlled them. In most cases, these newly independent countries were substantially different from how they had been prior to colonization; some, in fact, had actually been created by colonization, their borders having been determined by foreign powers. The colonial powers typically introduced their own languages as the languages of government in these countries, and the educational systems they introduced for both the European and native populations of the colonies were likewise modeled on those in Europe.

Writers in former colonies who began to write after the end of colonial rule, then, inherited an often uncomfortable mix of cultural tools and assumptions. On the one hand, many of them had been educated to appreciate European works of literature, and many of them wrote most naturally in European languages. On the other hand, they saw everywhere around them a culture that was very different from that of its former European masters, and which those masters tended to regard as inferior and less civilized. The tension that results from this cultural mix is one of the chief subjects of postcolonial theory and research. In addition, although colonialism has more or less formally ended, many critics would argue that European and other western countries continue to dominate their former colonial possessions in a cultural and economic sense, a domination called **neo-colonialism**.

Postcolonial critics do not necessarily restrict themselves to the literatures of those countries that the European powers have left. Australia, New Zealand, and Canada, for example, were all colonies, and some critics would regard any literature produced in such countries, including that by authors of European descent, to be an appropriate subject of study for postcolonialism. Others would argue that such writers belong to a European tradition and would use the adjective *postcolonial* to describe only the works written by authors from the indigenous populations of those countries.

Nor do postcolonial critics restrict themselves to looking at works produced since the end of the colonial period. Canonical European texts are of special interest to these critics, especially for the light they shed on the ways in which the colonizers viewed the colonized. The character of Caliban in Shakespeare's *The Tempest*, for instance, has been the focus of much debate about what his brutish nature reveals about the views of Shakespeare and the England in which he lived toward the native peoples being encountered by European explorers.

One of the foundational texts of postcolonialism is Edward Said's *Orientalism* (1978), which examined the ways in which Europeans and Americans view, and have viewed, peoples in developing nations (often known as the Third World). Other important works include *The Location of Culture* (1994) by Homi Bhaba and the essay "Under Western Eyes" (1986) by Chandra Talpade Mohanty.

A Postcolonial Reading: Jhumpa Lahiri's 2000 short story "The Third and Final Continent"

A postcolonial reading of "The Third and Final Continent" by Jhumpa Lahiri might look at the differences the narrator notices between his native culture and those of England and the United States. It might also examine the process of his gradual assimilation to American culture, and his own sense of the cultural distance he has traveled.

> Jhumpa Lahiri's short story "The Third and Final Continent" relates the thoughts of an Indian emigrant as he adjusts to western society. As a citizen of a country that gained its independence from Great Britain less than twenty years earlier—and after his own birth—the narrator is very much in the position of a provincial visiting the imperial homeland. He lives with other Indians—specifically with other Bengalis—and they eat Indian food and listen to Indian music, but many of their habits are English. For example, they drink tea, smoke English cigarettes, and watch cricket matches.
>
> The narrator arrives in the United States on the day of the first moon landing. The symbolism of this is particularly appropriate since the American astronauts have literally gone to another world, something the narrator does metaphorically. The moment also marks, again literally, the height of American power. At that moment, America is the most powerful country in the world, much as Great Britain was when it first subjugated India. To plant a flag on a piece of land has traditionally been a way of claiming that land for the country represented by the flag.

In the time the narrator spends with Mrs. Croft each evening while staying in her house, the acknowledgement of American supremacy becomes a kind of religious ritual. Each time Mrs. Croft observes that there is an American flag on the moon, the narrator is expected to reply, loudly enough so that the old women can hear him, "Splendid!" The narrator himself had not thought very much about the moon landing despite the reports of it in the paper—and despite the fact that he is a librarian at the Massachusetts Institute of Technology. His values and the values of the American culture in which he finds himself are very different.

His stay with Mrs. Croft also reveals to him the enormous difference between Indian and American attitudes toward family. It shocks the narrator to learn that a woman one hundred and three years old would be living alone, and the story of her fortitude after the death of her husband is in marked contrast to his own mother's descent into madness after the death of her husband. At the same time, the narrator and Mrs. Croft seem to have a special understanding. The culture he comes from, with its strict rules of propriety, is in some ways reminiscent of the America in which Mrs. Croft lived as a young woman, a point made clear when the old woman, on seeing the narrator's new wife dressed in her traditional Indian clothes, acknowledges that she is truly a lady.

For Further Reading: Postcolonial Studies

Ashcroft, Bill, Gareth Griffiths, and Helen Tiffin. *The Empire Writes Back: Theory and Practice in Post-Colonial Literatures.* 1989.

Chaterjee, Para. *Nationalist Thought in the Colonial World: A Derivative Discourse.* 1993.

Gandhi, Leela. *Postcolonial Theory: A Critical Introduction.* 1998.

Loomba, Ania. *Colonialism/Postcolonialism.* 1998.

Nandy, Ashis. *The Intimate Enemy: Loss and Recovery of Self under Colonialism.* 1983.

Poddar, Prem, and David Johnson. *A Historical Companion of Postcolonial Thought.* 2005.

Said, Edward. *Culture and Imperialism.* 1994.

Williams, Patrick, and Laura Chrisman, eds. *Colonial Discourse and Post-colonial Theory: A Reader.* 1994.

Young, Robert. *Colonial Desire: Hybridity in Theory, Culture, and Race.* 1995.

——— *Postcolonialism: An Historical Introduction.* 2001.

American Multiculturalism

Since its beginnings, America has been home to people from an increasing number of different cultures, many of which have retained distinct identities and traditions over time. Many of these groups came willingly, as immigrants from Europe and other places, while others—African slaves in particular—did not. And, of course, the Native Americans were here before any of the waves of European immigration. That America is multiethnic has long been recognized—it is an unarguable fact. That America is, and ought to be, multicultural—that is, that it is not one culture but many, and that all its cultures are equally valuable—is a position that has gained increasing support in recent decades, particularly since the civil rights movements of the 1950s and 1960s.

One of the chief goals of multicultural critics has been to increase the visibility of literature produced by members of minority groups in the United States. Another has been to create a critical environment in which these works can be properly appreciated. (Since many works by minority authors were written out of a set of assumptions different from those of the dominant culture, such a critical environment could not be assumed.) Multicultural critics have drawn attention to those features of writing by different groups that are distinctive.

Much multicultural criticism so far has focused on the writing of African Americans. The emphasis on this group has been due in part to the sheer number of its members, and in part to the sense that they had been excluded from American public life in a more profound and violent way than any other group. No doubt a further reason is that the *African American struggle* for equality and freedom has been so central to America's attempts at self-definition. At the same time, Native American, Asian American, and Latino writers, as well as writers of other backgrounds, have attracted an increasing amount of both critical attention and popular success. More recently, the field of ethnic studies has brought attention to the unique accomplishments of groups such *as Irish, Italian, and Arab Americans.* At the same time, religious studies scholars have looked at the cultures and cultural products of different religious groups, groups that often cut across ethnic and racial boundaries.

Multiculturalism shares many points of contact with cultural studies in general—for example, a willingness to investigate literature traditionally excluded from the canon and a suspicion of the categories of "high" and "low" art. Along with Marxist and New Historicist criticism, it shares an awareness of the ways in which writers and the texts they produce are shaped by societal conditions, and the ways in which those conditions are enforced and defended by those in power.

Important texts in the study of multicultural literature include Henry Louis Gates's *The Signifying Monkey: A Theory of African-American Literary Criticism* (1988), *Beyond Ethnicity: Consent and Descent in American Culture* (1987) by Werner Sollar, and Robert Allen Warrior's *Tribal Secrets: Recovering American Indian Intellectual Traditions* (1995).

An American Multicultural Reading: Alice Walker's "Everyday Use" (p. 426)

A multicultural reading of "Everyday Use" might focus on the quilt that the narrator decides to give to Maggie, rather than to Dee, and on its connection to *African American history.* Such a reading might also look at the ways in which the narrator's relationship to that history differs from Dee's.

> *African American art* has often been functional—that is, it is meant to be used. The quilts that become the subject of contention in Alice Walker's "Everyday Use" are an example of this type of art. In fact, the title of the story is a specific reference to the functionality of the handmade things that Dee wants to take with her from her family home. Given Dee's newfound interest in African and *African American culture,* it is striking that she is unable to appreciate this fact, which seems so obvious to her mother and sister.
>
> Dee seems interested in the history of her people, and of her family, chiefly when she is able to view them as exotic. At times, it seems that she has come to visit her family largely because she sees their home as a kind of museum of black culture. She wants nearly everything in and around the house that she lays eyes on, but she wants them as curios or decorations, not as the functioning butter churns, dashers, and quilts that they are. She was named after her mother's sister, and after her grandmother, but she has taken a new, supposedly more African name: Wangero. She wants the artifacts these women have left behind but not their name.
>
> It would be going too far to say that Walker is simply condemning Dee as shallow. Dee does genuinely admire the artifacts she wants to take with her, and she does want them in

part because of the connection they have to members of her own family. Her failing—and this is where the story is at its most subtle—is that, in contrast with Maggie, she *needs* these artifacts to maintain a connection with her family's past. What convinces the narrator of the story to save the quilts for Maggie is the way in which Maggie relinquishes her claim to them: "She can have them, Mama . . . I can 'member Grandma Dee without the quilts" (432).

Dee's last words to her mother and sister neatly sum up her contradictory relationship to them and to the tradition they represent. After saying that her mother doesn't understand her own heritage, she turns to Dee and says, "You ought to try to make something of yourself, too, Maggie. It's really a new day for us. But from the way you and mama still live you'd never know it" (433). Dee wants to be free of all the negative aspects that have defined the African American experience, yet at the same time she wants to position herself as the heir to that culture. It isn't—it can't be—that simple.

For Further Reading: American Multiculturalism

Allen, Paula Gunn. *The Sacred Hoop: Recovering the Feminine in American Indian Traditions.* 1986.

Anzaldúa, Gloria. *Borderlands/La Frontera: The New Mestiza.* 1987.

Awkward, Michael. *Inspiriting Influences: Tradition, Revision, and Afro-American Literature.* 1989.

Berkovitch, Sacvan. *The Rites of Ascent: Transformations in the Symbolic Construction of America.* 1981.

Ferraro, Thomas J. *Ethnic Passages: Literary Immigrants in Twentieth-Century America.* 1993.

Gates, Henry Louis, Jr. (ed.). *Race, Writing and Difference.* 1985.

Goldberg, David Theo, ed. *Multiculturalism: A Critical Reader.* 1994.

Morrison, Toni. *Playing in the Dark: Whiteness and the Literary Imagination.* 1993.

Pulitano, Elvira. *Toward a Native American Critical Theory.* 2003.

West, Thomas R. *Signs of Struggle: The Rhetorical Politics of Cultural Difference.* 2002.

TEXT CREDITS

Chinua Achebe "Dead Men's Path" copyright © 1972, 1973 by Chinua Achebe, from GIRLS AT WAR AND OTHER STORIES. Used by permission of Doubleday, a division of Random House, Inc.

Francisco X. Alarcón "'Mexican' Is Not A Noun" from *The Other Side of Night/Del otro lado de la noche.* Copyright © 2002 by Francisco X. Alarcón. Reprinted by permission of University of Arizona Press.

Sherman Alexie reprinted from "The Summer of Black Widows" © 1996 by Sherman Alexie, by permission of Hanging Loose Press.

Sherman Alexie "This Is What It Means to Say Phoenix, Arizona" from THE LONE RANGER AND TONTO FISTFIGHT IN HEAVEN. Copyright © 1993 by Sherman Alexie. Used by permission of Grove/Atlantic, Inc.

Agha Shahid Ali from *A Walk Through the Yellow Pages* by Agha Shahid Ali, published by SUN-Gemini Press. © 1987 by Agha Shahid Ali. Used with permission. All rights reserved.

Julia Alvarez from HOMECOMING. Copyright © 1984, 1996 by Julia Alvarez. Published by Plume, an imprint of The Penguin Group (USA), and originally published by Grove Press. By permission of Susan Bergholz Literary Services, New York, NY and Lamy, NM. All rights reserved.

Julia Alvarez from HOW THE GARCIA GIRLS LOST THEIR ACCENTS. Copyright © 1991 by Julia Alvarez. Published by Algonquin Books of Chapel Hill. By permission of Susan Bergholz Literary Services, New York, NY and Lamy, NM. All rights reserved.

A. R. Ammons "Coming Right Up," from THE REALLY SHORT POEMS OF A. R. AMMONS by A. R. Ammons. Copyright © 1990 by A. R. Ammons. Used by permission of W.W. Norton & Company.

Margaret Atwood "Happy Endings"" from *Good Bones and Simple Murders* by Margaret Atwood © 1983, 1992, 1994. Published in Canada by McClelland & Stewart. Used with permission of the Author and the publisher.

Margaret Atwood "The City Planners" from THE CIRCLE GAME. Copyright © 1966, 1998 by Margaret Atwood. Reprinted with the permission of House of Anansi Press, Toronto.

Margaret Atwood "you fit into me" from SELECTED POEMS 1965–1975. Copyright © 1976 by Margaret Atwood. Reprinted with the permission of House of Anansi Press, Toronto.

W. H. Auden "*Musée* des Beaux Arts," copyright © 1940 and renewed 1968 by W. H. Auden, from COLLECTED POEMS OF W. H. AUDEN by W. H. Auden. Used by permission of Random House, Inc.

James Baldwin "Sonny's Blues" © 1957 by James Baldwin was originally published in PARTISAN REVIEW. Copyright renewed. Collected in GOING TO MEET THE MAN, published by Vintage Books. Reprinted by arrangement with the James Baldwin Estate.

Matsuo Bashō "[Silent and still: then]" from THE PENGUIN BOOK OF JAPANESE VERSE, translated by Geoffrey Bownas and Anthony Thwaite. Translation copyright © 1964, 1998 by Geoffrey Bownas and Anthony

Fernando Pessoa "Solemnly Over the Fertile Land." Fernando Pessoa & Co.: Selected Poems (ed. and trans. Richard Zenith, New York: Grove Press, 1998, 128). Reprinted with permission.

Marge Piercy "The secretary chant" from CIRCLES ON THE WATER by Marge Piercy, copyright © 1982 by Middlemarsh, Inc. Used by permission of Alfred A. Knopf, a division of Random House, Inc.

Harold Pinter "Applicant" from REVUE SKETCHES, copyright © 1961 Harold Pinter. Used by permission of Grove/Atlantic, Inc.

Sylvia Plath "Daddy" from ARIEL. Copyright © 1963 by Ted Hughes. Reprinted by permission of HarperCollins Publishers and Faber and Faber, Ltd.

Sylvia Plath "Morning Song" from ARIEL. Copyright © 1961, 1963 by Ted Hughes. Reprinted by permission of HarperCollins Publishers and Faber and Faber, Ltd.

Katherine Anne Porter "The Jilting of Granny Weatherall" from FLOWERING JUDAS AND OTHER STORIES. Copyright 1930 and renewed © 1956 by Katherine Anne Porter. Reprinted by permission of Houghton Mifflin Harcourt Publishing Company.

Dick Pothier and Thomas Gibbons "A Woman's Wintry Death Leads to a Long-Dead Friend" from THE PHILADELPHIA INQUIRER (1987). Reprinted with the permission of The Philadelphia Inquirer.

Ezra Pound from THE CANTOS OF EZRA POUND, copyright © 1948 by Ezra Pound. Reprinted by permission of New Directions Publishing Corp.

Ezra Pound from PERSONAE, copyright © 1926 by Ezra Pound. Reprinted by permission of New Directions Publishing Corp.

Leroy Quintana "Poem for Salt" from *The Great Whirl of Exile: Poems by Leroy Quintana*. Copyright © 1999 by Curbstone Press. Reprinted with permission.

Radiohead "Harry Patch (in Memory of)" written by Colin Greenwood, Jonathan Greenwood, Edward O'Brien, Philip Selway, and Thomas Yorke. Reprinted with permission of Kobalt Music Publishing America, Inc.

Henry Reed "Naming of Parts" from HENRY REED: COLLECTED POEMS, edited by Jon Stallworthy. Copyright © 1991. Reprinted with the permission of Oxford University Press, Ltd.

Adrienne Rich "Aunt Jennifer's Tigers." Copyright © 2002, 1951 by Adrienne Rich from THE FACT OF A DOORFRAME: SELECTED POEMS 1950–2001. Used by permission of the author and W. W. Norton & Company, Inc.

Adrienne Rich "Living in Sin." Copyright © 2002, 1955 by Adrienne Rich from THE FACT OF A DOORFRAME: SELECTED POEMS 1950-2001. Used by permission of the author and W. W. Norton & Company, Inc.

Adrienne Rich "A Woman Mourned by Daughters." Copyright © 1993, 1967, 1963 by Adrienne Rich from COLLECTED EARLY POEMS: 1950-1970. Used by permission of the author and W. W. Norton & Company, Inc.

Alberto Alvaro Ríos "Nani" from WHISPERING TO FOOL THE WIND. Copyright © 1982 by Alberto Alvaro Ríos. Reprinted with the permission of the author.

Alberto Alvaro Ríos "The Secret Lion" from THE IGUANA KILLER: TWELVE STORIES OF THE HEART. Copyright © 1984 by Alberto Alvaro Ríos. Reprinted with the permission of Confluence Press, www.confluencepress.com.

Theodore Roethke "My Papa's Waltz," copyright 1942 by Hearst Magazines, Inc., from THE COLLECTED POEMS OF THEODORE ROETHKE by Theodore Roethke. Used by permission of Doubleday, a division of Random House, Inc.

Earl T. Roske © 2011 by Earl T. Roske. Reprinted by permission of the author. For performance rights, contact Earl T. Roske (earltroske@yahoo.com).

Cynthia Rylant from *God Went to Beauty School* by Cynthia Rylant. Copyright © 2003 by Cynthia Rylant. Reprinted by permission of HarperCollins Children's Books. All rights reserved.

GLOSSARY OF LITERARY TERMS

Action What happens in a drama.

Alexandrine Verse with six iambic feet (iambic hexameter), a common form in French poetry but relatively rare in English poetry.

Allegorical figure or framework See **Allegory**.

Allegory Story with two parallel and consistent levels of meaning, one literal and one figurative, in which the figurative level offers a moral or political lesson; John Bunyan's *The Pilgrim's Progress* and Nathaniel Hawthorne's "Young Goodman Brown" are examples of moral allegory. An **allegorical figure** has only one meaning (for instance, it may represent good or evil), as opposed to a **symbol,** which may suggest a complex network of meanings. An **allegorical framework** is the system of ideas that conveys the allegory's message.

Alliteration Repetition of consonant sounds (usually the initial sounds) in a series of words, as in Blake's "The Chimney Sweeper": "So your chimneys I sweep, and in soot I sleep." Alliteration may be reinforced by repeated sounds within and at the ends of words.

Allusion Reference, often to literature, history, mythology, or the Bible, that is unacknowledged in the text but that the author expects a reader to recognize.

Ambiguity Device in which authors intentionally evoke a number of possible meanings of a word or grammatical structure by leaving unclear which meaning they intend.

Anapest See **Meter**.

Antagonist Character who is in conflict with or opposition to the protagonist; the villain. Some-times the antagonist may be a force or situation (war or poverty) rather than a person.

Antihero Modern character who possesses the opposite attributes of a hero. Rather than being dignified and powerful, the antihero tends to be passive and ineffectual. Willy Loman, the main character in Arthur Miller's *Death of a Salesman*, is an antihero.

Apostrophe Figure of speech in which an absent character or a personified force or object is addressed directly, as if it were present or could comprehend: "O Rose, thou art sick!"

Archetype Image or symbol that is so common or important that it seems to have universal significance. Many archetypes appear in classical myths (for example, a journey to the underworld).

Arena stage Stage on which the actors are surrounded by the audience; also called **theater in the round**.

Aside Brief comment spoken by an actor to the audience (such as, "Here she comes. I'll play a fine trick on her now!") and assumed not to be heard by the other characters.

Assonance Repetition of the same or similar vowel sounds in a series of words: "creep three feet."

Atmosphere Tone or mood of a literary work, often established by the setting and language. Atmosphere is the emotional aura that determines readers' expectations about a work—for example, the sense of doom established at the beginning of Shakespeare's *Macbeth*.

Aubade Poem about morning, usually celebrating the dawn.

Ballad Narrative poem, rooted in an oral tradition, usually arranged in quatrains rhyming *abcb* and containing a refrain.

Ballad stanza See **Stanza**.

Beast fable Short tale, usually including a moral, in which animals assume human characteristics—for example, Aesop's "The Tortoise and the Hare."

Beginning rhyme See **Rhyme**.

Black comedy Comedy that relies on the morbid and absurd. Often black comedies (also called *dark comedies*) are so satiric that they become ironic and tragic; examples are Joseph Heller's novel *Catch 22* and Edward Albee's play *The Sandbox*.

Blank verse Lines of unrhymed iambic pentameter in no particular stanzaic form. Because iambic pentameter resembles the rhythms of ordinary English speech, blank verse is often unobtrusive; for instance, Shakespeare's noble characters usually use it, though they may seem to us at first reading to be speaking in prose. See **Meter**.

Blocking Decisions about how characters move and where they stand on stage in a dramatic production.

Box set Stage setting that gives the audience the illusion of looking into a room.

Cacophony Harsh or unpleasant spoken sound created by clashing consonants such as "The vorpal blade went snicker-snack!" in Lewis Carroll's "Jabberwocky."

Caesura Strong or long pause in the middle of a poetic line, created by punctuation or by the sense of the poem, as in Yeats's "Leda and the Swan": "And Agamemnon dead. Being so caught up. . . ."

Carpe diem Latin for "seize the day"; the philosophy arguing that one should enjoy life today before it passes by, as seen in Herrick's "To the Virgins, to Make Much of Time."

Catastrophe The moment in a tragedy after the climax, when the rising action has ended and the falling action has begun, when the protagonist begins to understand the implications of events that will lead to his or her downfall.

Catharsis Aristotle's term for the emotional reaction or "purgation" that takes place in an audience watching a tragedy.

Character Fictional representation of a person, usually but not necessarily in a psychologically realistic way. E. M. Forster classified characters as **round** (well developed, closely involved in the action and responsive to it) or **flat** (static, stereotypical, or operating as **foils** for the protagonist). Characters can also be classified as **dynamic** (growing and changing in the course of the action) or **static** (remaining unchanged).

Characterization Way in which writers develop their characters and reveal those characters' traits to readers.

Choragos See **Chorus**.

Chorus Group of actors in classical Greek drama who comment in unison on the action and the hero; they are led by the **Choragos**.

Classicism Attitude toward art that values symmetry, clarity, discipline, and objectivity. **Neoclassicism**, practiced in eighteenth–century Europe, appreciated those qualities as found in Greek and Roman art and culture.

Cliché Overused phrase or expression.

Climax Point of greatest tension or importance, where the decisive action of a play or story takes place.

Closed form Type of poetic structure that has a recognizable rhyme scheme, meter, or stanzaic pattern; also called *fixed form*.

Closet drama Play meant to be read instead of performed—for example, Shelley's *Prometheus Unbound*.

Comedy Any literary work, but especially a play, in which events end happily, a character's fortunes are reversed for the better, and a community is drawn more closely together, often by the marriage of one or more protagonists at the end.

Comedy of humours Comedy that focuses on characters whose behavior is controlled by a single characteristic trait, or humour, such as *Volpone* (1606) by Ben Jonson.

Comedy of manners Satiric comedy that achieved great popularity in the nineteenth century. This form focuses on the manners and customs of society and directs its satire against the characters who violate its social conventions and norms. *The Importance of Being Earnest* (1895) by Oscar Wilde is a comedy of manners.

Common measure See **Stanza**.

Conceit See **Metaphor**.

Concrete poem Poem whose typographical appearance on the page reinforces its theme, as with George Herbert's "Easter Wings."

Conflict Struggle between opposing forces (protagonist and antagonist) in a work of literature.

Connotation Meaning that a word suggests beyond its literal, dictionary meaning; its emotional associations, judgments, or opinions. Connotations can be positive, neutral, or negative.

Consonance See **Rhyme**.

Convention See **Literary convention**.

Conventional symbol See **Symbol**.

Cosmic irony See **Irony**.

Couplet See **Stanza**.

Crisis Point at which the decisive action of the plot occurs.

Dactyl See **Meter**.

Denotation Dictionary meaning of a word; its explicit, literal meaning.

Denouement See **Resolution**.

Deus ex machina "God from a machine": any improbable resolution of plot involving the intervention of some force or agent from outside the story.

Dialect Particular regional variety of language, which may differ from the more widely used standard or written language in its pronunciation, grammar, or vocabulary. Eliza Doolittle's cockney dialect in the George Bernard Shaw play *Pygmalion* is an example.

Dialogue Conversation between two or more characters.

Diction Word choice that determines the level of language used in a piece of literature. **Formal diction** is lofty and elaborate (typical of Shakespearean nobility); **informal diction** is idiomatic and relaxed (like the narrative in John Updike's "A&P").

Jargon is the specialized diction of a professional or occupational group (such as computer scientists). **Idioms** are the colloquial expressions, including slang, of a particular group or society.

Didactic poetry Poetry whose purpose is to make a point or teach a lesson, particularly common in the eighteenth century.

Double entendre Phrase or word with a deliberate double meaning, one of which is usually sexual.

Double plot See **Plot**.

Drama Literature written to be performed.

Dramatic irony See **Irony**.

Dramatic monologue Type of poem perfected by Robert Browning that consists of a single speaker talking to one or more listeners and often revealing much more about the speaker than he or she seems to intend; Browning's "My Last Duchess" is an example of this form.

Dramatis personae Characters in a play.

Dynamic character See **Character**.

Elegy Poem commemorating someone's death, usually in a reflective or mournful tone, such as A. E. Housman's "To an Athlete Dying Young."

Elision Leaving out an unstressed syllable or vowel, usually in order to keep a regular meter in a line of poetry ("o'er" instead of "over," for example).

End rhyme See **Rhyme**.

End-stopped line Line of poetry that has a full pause at the end, typically indicated by a period or semicolon.

Enjambment See **Run-on line**.

Envoi Three-line conclusion to a sestina that includes all six of the poem's key words, three placed at the ends of lines and three within the lines. See **Sestina**.

Epic Long narrative poem, such as the *Iliad* or the *Aeneid*, recounting the adventures of heroes on whose actions the fate of a nation or race depends. Frequently the gods or other supernatural beings take active interest in the events.

Epigram Short pithy poem or statement—for example, Dorothy Parker's comment on an actress's performance, "She runs the gamut of emotions from A to B."

Epiphany Term first applied to literature by James Joyce to describe a sudden moment of revelation about the deep meaning of something, such as the boy's realization at the end of "Araby."

Euphemism Word consciously chosen for its pleasant **connotations**; often used for subjects such as sex and death, whose frank discussion is somewhat taboo in our society. For example, a euphemism for *die* is *pass away*.

Euphony Pleasant spoken sound created by smooth consonants such as "ripple" or "pleasure."

Exposition First stage of a plot, where the author presents the information about characters or setting that a reader or viewer will need to understand the subsequent action.

Expressionism Artistic and literary movement that attempts to portray inner experience. It moves away from realistic portrayals of life and is characterized by violent exaggeration of objective reality and extremes of mood and feeling. In drama, expressionistic stage sets mirror the inner states of the character.

Extended metaphor See **Metaphor**.

Extended simile See **Metaphor**. Also see **Conceit**.

Eye rhyme See **Rhyme**.

Fable Short tale, often involving animals or supernatural beings and stressing plot above character development, whose object is to teach a pragmatic or moral lesson. See **Beast fable**.

Fairy tale See **Folktale**.

Falling action Stage in a play's plot during which the intensity of the climax subsides.

Falling meter Trochaic and dactylic meters, so called because they move from stressed to unstressed syllables. See **Rising meter**.

Fantasy Work of literature that takes place in an unreal world or contains unreal or incredible characters. J. R. R. Tolkien's *The Lord of the Rings* is one example.

Farce Comedy in which stereotypical characters engage in boisterous horseplay and slapstick humor, as in Chekhov's *The Brute*.

Feminine rhyme See **Rhyme**.

Fiction Form of narrative that is primarily imaginative although its form may resemble that of factual writing like history and biography.

Figures of speech Expressions—such as **hyperbole, metaphor, metonymy, personification, simile, synechdoche,** and **understatement**—that use words to achieve effects beyond ordinary language.

Flashback Departure from chronological order that presents an event or situation that occurred before the time in which the story's action takes place.

Flat character See **Character**.

Foil Minor character whose role is to highlight the main character by presenting a contrast with him or her.

Folktale Contemporary version of an old, even ancient, oral tale that can be traced back centuries through many different cultures. Folktales include fairy tales, myths, and fables.

Foot See **Meter**.

Foreshadowing Introduction early in a story of situations, characters, or objects that seem to have no special importance but in fact are later revealed to have great significance.

Form Structure or shape of a literary work; the way a work's parts fit together to form a whole. In poetry, form is described in terms of the presence (or absence) of elements like rhyme, meter, and stanzaic pattern. See **Open form** and **Closed form**.

Formal diction See **Diction**.

Free verse See **Open form**.

Freytag's pyramid In his *Technique of the Drama* (1863) Gustav Freytag suggested that the stages of a classic dramatic plot resemble a pyramid, with rising action leading to the climax and giving way to falling action.

Genre Category of literature. Fiction, drama, and poetry are the three major genres; subgenres include the novel, the farce, and the lyric poem.

Haiku Seventeen-syllable, three-line form of Japanese verse that almost always uses concrete imagery and deals with the natural world.

Hamartia Aristotle's term for the "tragic flaw" in characters that eventually causes their downfall in Greek tragedy.

Hermeneutics Traditionally, the use of the Bible to interpret other historical or current events; in current critical theory, the principles and procedures followed to determine the meaning of a text.

Heroic couplet See **Stanza**.

High comedy Term introduced in 1877 by George Meredith to denote comedy that appeals to the intellect, such as Shakespeare's *As You Like It*. See **Low comedy**.

Hubris Tragic flaw of overwhelming pride that exists in the protagonist of a tragedy.

Hyperbole Figurative language that depends on intentional overstatement; Mark Twain often used it to create humor; Jonathan Swift used it for **satire**.

Iamb See **Meter**.

Imagery Words and phrases that describe the concrete experience of the five senses, most often sight. A **pattern of imagery** is a group of related images developed throughout a work. **Synesthesia** is a form of imagery that mixes the experience of the senses (hearing something visual, smelling something audible, and so on): "He smelled the blue fumes of her scent." **Static imagery** freezes the moment to give it the timeless quality of painting or sculpture. **Kinetic imagery** attempts to show motion or change.

Imagism Movement in modern poetry stressing terseness and concrete imagery. **Imagists** were a group of early twentieth-century American poets, including Ezra Pound, William Carlos Williams, and Amy Lowell, who focused on visual images and created new rhythms and meters.

Imperfect rhyme See **Rhyme**.

In medias res Latin phrase describing works like Homer's *Iliad* that begin in the middle of the action in order to catch a reader's interest.

Informal diction See **Diction**.

Internal rhyme See **Rhyme**.

Irony Literary device or situation that depends on the existence of at least two separate and contrasting levels of meaning or experience. **Dramatic** or **tragic irony**, such as that found in *Oedipus the King*, depends on the audience's knowing something the protagonist has not yet realized. **Situational irony** exists when what happens is at odds with what the story's situation leads readers to expect will happen, as in Browning's "Porphyria's Lover." **Cosmic irony** (or irony of fate) exists when fate frustrates any effort a character might make to control or reverse his or her destiny. **Verbal irony** occurs when what is said is in contrast with what is meant. Verbal irony can be expressed as **understatement, hyperbole,** or **sarcasm**.

Jargon Specialized language associated with a particular trade or profession.

Kinetic imagery Imagery that attempts to show motion or change. See, for example, William Carlos Williams's "The Great Figure."

Literary canon Group of literary works generally acknowledged by critics and teachers to be the best and most significant to have emerged from our history. In recent years, the canon has been expanded to include works by women and by writers of color.

Literary convention Something whose meaning is so widely understood within a society that authors can expect their audiences to accept and comprehend it unquestioningly—for example, the division of plays into acts or the fact that stepmothers in fairy tales are likely to be wicked.

Literary criticism Descriptions, analyses, interpretations, or evaluations of works of literature by experts in the field.

Literary symbol See **Symbol**.

Low comedy Introduced by George Meredith, it refers to comedy with little or no intellectual appeal. Low comedy is used as comic relief in *Macbeth*. See **High comedy**.

Lyric Form of poetry, usually brief and intense, that expresses a poet's subjective response to the world. In classical times, lyrics were set to music. The romantic poets, particularly Keats, often wrote lyrics about love, death, and nature.

Masculine rhyme See **Rhyme**.

Meditation Lyric poem that focuses on a physical object—for example, Keats's "Ode on a Grecian Urn"—using this object as a vehicle for considering larger issues.

Melodrama Sensational play that appeals shamelessly to the emotions, contains elements of tragedy but ends happily, and often relies on set plots and stock characters.

Metaphor Concise form of comparison equating two things that may at first seem completely dissimilar, often an abstraction and a concrete image—for example, "My love's a fortress." An **extended metaphor** (or **conceit**) is a comparison used throughout a work; in Tillie Olsen's "I Stand Here Ironing," the mother compares her daughter to a dress waiting to be ironed, thus conveying her daughter's passivity and vulnerability. See **Simile**.

Meter Regular pattern of stressed and unstressed syllables, each repeated unit of which is called a **foot:** an **anapest** has three syllables, two unstressed and the third stressed; a **dactyl** has three syllables, the first stressed and the subsequent ones unstressed. An **iamb** has two syllables, unstressed followed by stressed; a **trochee** has a stressed syllable followed by an unstressed one; a **spondee** has two stressed syllables; and a **pyrrhic** has two unstressed syllables. A poem's meter is described in terms of the kind of foot (anapest, for example) and the number of feet found in each line. The number of feet is designated by the Greek prefix for the number, so one foot per line is called *monometer*, two feet is *dimeter*, followed by *trimeter, tetrameter, pentameter, hexameter*, and so on. The most common meter in English is *iambic pentameter*. See also **Rising meter** and **Falling meter**.

Metonymy Figure of speech in which the term for one thing can be applied to another with which it is closely associated—for example, using "defend the flag" to mean "defend the nation."

Mimesis Aristotle's term for the purpose of literature, which he felt was "imitation" of life.

Monologue Extended speech by one character.

Mood Atmosphere created by the elements of a literary work (setting, characterization, imagery, tone, and so on).

Morality play Medieval Christian allegory, in which personified abstractions, such as Selfishness and Pride, struggle for a person's soul.

Motivation Reasons behind a character's behavior that make us accept or believe that character.

Mystery play Medieval play depicting biblical stories.

Myth Anonymous story reflecting the religious and social values of a culture or explaining natural phenomena, often involving gods and heroes.

Narrative The "storytelling" of a piece of fiction; the forward-moving recounting of episode and description. When an event that occurred earlier is told during a later sequence of events, it is called a **flashback**; suggesting earlier in a narration something that will occur later on is called **foreshadowing**.

Narrator Person who tells the story. See **Point of view**.

Naturalism Nineteenth-century movement whose followers believed that life should not be idealized when depicted in literature. Rather, literature should show that human experience is a continual (and for the most part losing) struggle against the natural world. Émile Zola, Jack London, and Stephen Crane are important practitioners of naturalism.

New Comedy Greek comedies of the fourth and third centuries B.C. that followed **Old Comedy**. They were comedies of romance with stock characters and conventional settings. They lacked the satire, abusive language, and bawdiness of Old Comedy.

Novel Fictional narrative, traditionally realistic, relating a series of events or following the history of a character or group of characters through a period of time.

Novella Extended short story, usually concentrated in episode and action (like a short story) but involving greater character development (like a novel); Franz Kafka's "The Metamorphosis" is a novella.

Octave See **Sonnet**.

Ode Relatively long lyric poem, common in antiquity and adapted by the romantic poets, for whom it was a serious poem of formal diction, often addressed to some significant object (such as a nightingale or the west wind) that has stimulated the poet's imagination.

Old Comedy The first comedies, written in Greece in the fifth century B.C., which heavily satirized the religious and social issues of the day. The chief practitioner of Old Comedy was Aristophanes. See **New Comedy**.

Onomatopoeia Word whose sound resembles what it describes: "snap, crackle, pop." Lewis Carroll's "Jabberwocky" uses onomatopoeia.

Open form Form of poetry that makes use of varying line lengths, abandoning stanzaic divisions, breaking lines in unexpected places, and even dispensing with any pretense of formal structure. Sometimes called *free verse* or *vers libre*. See **Form**.

Ottava rima See **Stanza**.

Oxymoron Phrase combining two seemingly incompatible elements: "crashing silence."

Parable Story that teaches a lesson, such as the parable of the prodigal son in the New Testament.

Paradox Seemingly contradictory situation. Adrienne Rich's "A Woman Mourned by Daughters" uses paradox.

Parody Exaggerated imitation of a serious piece of literature for humorous effect. Shakespeare's "My mistress' eyes are nothing like the sun" is a parody of traditional Renaissance love poetry.

Pastoral Literary work, such as Christopher Marlowe's lyric poem "The Passionate Shepherd to His Love," that deals nostalgically and usually unrealistically with a simple, preindustrial rural life; the name comes from the fact that traditionally pastorals feature shepherds.

Pastoral romance Prose tale set in an idealized rural world; popular in Renaissance England.

Pathos Suffering that exists simply to satisfy the sentimental or morbid sensibilities of the audience.

Pattern of imagery See **Imagery**.

Perfect rhyme See **Rhyme**.

Persona Narrator or speaker of a poem or story; in Greek tragedy, a persona was a mask worn by an actor.

Personification A figure of speech that endows inanimate objects or abstract ideas with life or human characteristics: "the river wept."

Petrarchan sonnet See **Sonnet**.

Picaresque Episodic, often satirical work, presenting the life story of a rogue or rascal—for example, Cervantes' *Don Quixote*. The form emerged in sixteenth-century Spain.

Picture-frame stage Stage that looks like a room with a missing fourth wall through which the audience views the play. The **proscenium arch** separates the audience from the play.

Plot Way in which the events of the story are arranged. When there are two stories of more or less equal importance, the work has a **double plot**; when there is more than one story but one string of events is clearly the most significant, the other stories are called **subplots**. Plot in fiction often follows the pattern of action in drama, rising to a **climax** and then falling to a **resolution**.

Poetic rhythm See **Rhythm**.

Point of view Perspective from which a story is told. The storyteller may be a major character in the story or a character who witnesses the story's events (*first-person narrator*) or someone who does not figure in the action at all (*third-person narrator*), in which case he or she may know the actions and internal doings of everyone in the story (*omniscient narrator*) or just know some part of these (*limited omniscient narrator*).

The narrator may be an *observer* or a *participant*. If he or she is untrustworthy (stupid or bad, for instance), the story has an *unreliable narrator*; narrators who are unreliable because they do not understand what they are reporting (children, for instance) are called *naïve narrators*. If the perspective on the events is the same as one would get by simply watching the action unfold on stage, the point of view is *dramatic* or *objective*.

Popular fiction Works aimed at a mass audience.

Prologue First part of a play (originally of a Greek tragedy) in which the actor gives the background or explanations that the audience needs to follow the rest of the drama.

Props (short for **properties**) Pictures, furnishings, and so on that decorate the stage for a play.

Proscenium arch Arch that surrounds the opening in a **picture-frame stage**;

through this arch the audience views the performances.

Prose poem Open form poem whose long lines appear to be prose set in paragraphs—for example, Yusef Komunyakaa's "Nude Interrogation."

Protagonist Principal character of a drama or a work of fiction; the hero. The *tragic hero* is the noble protagonist in classical Greek drama who falls because of a tragic flaw.

Pyrrhic See **Meter**.

Quatrain See **Stanza**.

Realism Writing that stresses life as it really is. Realism relies on careful description of setting and the trappings of daily life, psychological probability, and the lives of ordinary people. Ibsen's *A Doll House* is an example.

Resolution Also called the **denouement**, this is the final stage in the plot of a drama or work of fiction. Here the action comes to an end, and remaining loose ends are tied up.

Rhyme Repetition of concluding sounds in different words, often intentionally used at the ends of poetic lines. In **masculine rhyme** (also called *rising rhyme*) single syllables correspond. In **feminine rhyme** (also called *double rhyme* or *falling rhyme*) two syllables correspond, the second of which is stressed. In **triple rhyme**, three syllables correspond. **Eye rhyme** occurs when words look as though they should rhyme but are pronounced differently ("cough/ tough"). In **perfect rhyme**, the corresponding vowel and consonant sounds of accented syllables must be preceded by different consonants—for example, the *b* and *h* in "born" and "horn." **Imperfect rhyme**, also called *near rhyme*, *slant rhyme*, or *consonance* occurs when consonants in two words are the same but intervening vowels are different—for example, "pick/pack," "lads/lids." The most common type of rhyme within a poem is **end rhyme**, where the rhyming syllables are placed at the end of a line. **Internal rhyme** consists of rhyming words found within a line of poetry. **Beginning rhyme** occurs in the first syllable or syllables of a line.

Rhyme royal See **Stanza**.

Rhythm Regular recurrence of sounds in a poem. Ordinarily, rhythm is determined by the arrangement of metrical feet in a line, but sometimes *sprung rhythm*, introduced by Gerard Manley Hopkins, is used. In this type of rhythm, the number of strong stresses in a line determines the rhythm, regardless of how many weak stresses there might be.

Rising action Stage in a play's plot during which the action builds in intensity. See **Freytag's pyramid**.

Rising meter Iambic and anapestic meters, so called because they move from unstressed to stressed syllables. See **Falling meter**.

Romance Type of narrative that deals with love and adventure in a nonrealistic way, most popular in the Middle Ages but sometimes used by more modern authors, such as Hawthorne.

Romantic comedy Comedy such as Shakespeare's *Much Ado about Nothing* in which love is the main subject and idealized lovers endure great difficulties to get to the inevitable happy ending.

Romanticism Eighteenth- and nineteenth-century literary movement that valued subjectivity, individuality, the imagination, nature, excess, the exotic, and the mysterious.

Round character See **Character**.

Run-on line Line of poetry that ends with no punctuation or natural pause and consequently runs over into the next line; also called *enjambment*.

Sarcasm Form of irony in which apparent praise is used to convey strong, bitter criticism.

Satire Literary attack on folly or vanity by means of humor; usually intended to improve society.

Scansion Process of determining the meter of a poem by analyzing the strong and weak stresses in a line to find the unit of **meter** (each recurring pattern of stresses) and the number of these units (or **feet**) in each line.

Scrim Curtain that when illuminated from the front appears solid but when lit from the back becomes transparent.

Sentimental comedy Reaction against the **comedy of manners**. This type of comedy relies on sentimental emotion rather than on wit or humor and focuses on the virtues of life.

Sestet See **Sonnet**.

Sestina Poem composed of six six-line stanzas and a three-line conclusion called an **envoi**. Each line ends with one of six key words. The alternation of these six words in different positions—but always at the ends of lines—in the poem's six stanzas creates a rhythmic verbal pattern that unifies the poem.

Setting Background against which the action of a work takes place: the historical time, locale, season, time of day, weather, and so on.

Shakespearean sonnet See **Sonnet**.

Short-short story Short fictional narrative that is generally under five pages (or fifteen hundred words) in length.

Short story Fictional narrative centered on one climatic event and usually developing only one character in depth; its scope is narrower than that of the **novel**, and it often uses setting and characterization more directly to make its theme clear.

Simile Comparison of two seemingly unlike things using the words *like* or *as*: "My love is like an arrow through my heart." See **Metaphor**.

Situational irony See **Irony**.

Soliloquy Convention of drama in which a character speaks directly to the audience, revealing thoughts and feelings that other characters present on stage are assumed not to hear.

Sonnet Fourteen-line poem, usually a **lyric** in *iambic pentameter* (see **Meter**). It has a strict rhyme scheme in one of two forms: the *Italian*, or **Petrarchan sonnet** (an eight-line **octave** rhymed *abba/abba* with a six-line **sestet** rhymed *cdc/cdc* or a variation) and the *English*, or **Shakespearean sonnet** (three quatrains rhymed *abab/cdcd/efef* with a concluding couplet rhymed *gg*).

Speaker See **Persona**.

Spenserian stanza See **Stanza**.

Spondee See **Meter**.

Stage directions Words in a play that describe an actor's role apart from the dialogue, dealing with movements, attitudes, and so on.

Stage setting (set) Scenery and props in the production of a play. In *expressionist* stage settings, scenery and props are exaggerated and distorted to reflect the workings of a troubled, even abnormal mind. *Surrealistic* stage settings are designed to mirror the uncontrolled images of dreams or nightmares. See **Staging**.

Staging Overall production of a play in performance: the sets, costumes, lighting, sound, music, and so on.

Stanza Group of lines in a poem that forms a metrical or thematic unit. Each stanza is usually separated from others by a blank space on the page. Some common stanzaic forms are the **couplet** (two lines), **tercet** (three lines), **quatrain** (four lines), **sestet** (six lines), and **octave** (eight lines). The **heroic couplet**, first used by Chaucer and especially popular throughout the eighteenth century, notably in Alexander Pope's poetry, consists of two rhymed lines of iambic pentameter, with a weak pause after the first line and a strong pause after the second. **Terza rima**, a form used by Dante, has a rhyme scheme (*aba, bcb, ded*) that creates an interlocking series of stanzas. The **ballad stanza** alternates lines of eight and six syllables. Typically, only the second and fourth lines rhyme. **Common measure** is a four-line stanzaic pattern closely related to the ballad stanza. It differs in that its rhyme scheme is *abab* rather than *abcb*. **Rhyme royal** is a seven-line stanza (*ababbcc*) set in iambic pentameter. **Ottava rima** is an eight-line stanza (*abababcc*) set in iambic pentameter. The **Spenserian stanza** is a nine-line form (*ababbcbcc*) with the first eight lines in iambic pentameter and the last line in iambic hexameter.

Static character See **Character**.

Static imagery Imagery that freezes a moment to give it the timeless quality of painting or sculpture. Much visual imagery is static.

Stock character Stereotypical character who behaves consistently and whom the audience of a play can recognize and classify instantly: the town drunk, the nerd, and so on.

Stream of consciousness Form of narration controlled not by external events but by the thoughts and subjective impressions of the narrator, commonly found in modern literature, such as the work of Virginia Woolf and James Joyce.

Stress Accent or emphasis, either strong or weak, given to each syllable in a piece of writing, as determined by conventional pronunciation (cárpĕt, not cărpét) and intended emphasis ("going dówn, dówn, dówn tŏ thĕ bóttŏm ŏf thĕ ócĕan"). Strong stresses are marked with a ´ and weak ones with a ˘.

Structure Formal pattern or arrangement of elements to form a whole in a piece of literature.

Style How an author selects and arranges words to express ideas and, ultimately, theme.

Subplot See **Plot**.

Surrealism Literary movement that allows unconventional use of syntax; chronology; juxtaposition; and bizarre, dreamlike images in prose and poetry.

Symbol Person, object, action, or idea whose meaning transcends its literal or denotative sense in a complex way. A symbol is invested with significance beyond what it could carry on its own. **Universal symbols,** such as the grim reaper, may be called **archetypes; conventional symbols,** such as national flags, evoke a general and agreed-upon response from most people. There are also *private symbols*, such as the "gyre" created by Yeats, which the poet himself invested with extraordinary significance.

Synecdoche Figure of speech in which a part of something is used to represent the whole—for example, "hired hand" represents a laborer.

Synesthesia See **Imagery**.

Tale Short story often involving mysterious atmosphere and supernatural or inexplicable events, such as "The Tell-Tale Heart" by Edgar Allan Poe.

Ten-minute play Short play that can be performed in ten minutes or less.

Tercet See **Stanza**.

Terza rima See **Stanza**.

Theater in the round See **Arena stage**.

Theater of the Absurd Type of drama that discards conventions of plot, character, and motivation in order to depict a world in which nothing makes sense. Edward Albee's *The Sandbox* is an example.

Theme Central or dominant idea of a piece of literature, made concrete by the details and emphasis in the work itself.

Thrust stage Stage that juts out into the audience so the action may be viewed from three sides.

Tone Attitude of the speaker or author of a work toward the subject itself or the audience, as determined by the word choice and arrangement of the piece.

Tragedy Literary work, especially a play, that recounts the downfall of an individual. *Greek tragedy* demanded a noble protagonist whose fall could be traced to a *tragic personal flaw*. *Shakespearean tragedy* also treats noble figures, but the reasons for their tragedies may be less clear-cut than in Greek drama. *Domestic* or *modern tragedy* tends to deal with the fates of ordinary people.

Tragic irony See **Irony**.

Tragicomedy Type of Elizabethan and Jacobean drama that uses elements of both tragedy and comedy.

Triple rhyme See **Rhyme**.

Trochee See **Meter**.

Understatement Intentional downplaying of a situation's significance, often for ironic or humorous effect, as in Mark Twain's famous comment on reading his own obituary, "The reports of my death are greatly exaggerated."

Unities Rules that require a dramatic work to be unified in terms of its time, place, and action. *Oedipus the King* illustrates the three unities.

Universal symbol See **Symbol**.

Verbal irony See **Irony**.

Villanelle A nineteen-line poem composed of five tercets and a concluding quatrain; its rhyme scheme is *aba aba aba aba aba abaa*. Two different lines are systematically repeated in the poem: line 1 appears again in lines 6, 12, and 18, and line 3 reappears as lines 9, 15, and 19. Thus, each tercet concludes with an exact (or close) duplication of either line 1 or line 3, and the final quatrain concludes by repeating both line 1 and line 3.

Visual poetry Poetry that focuses as much on the words' appearance on the page as on what the words say, using a combination of media that may include video, photography, and even sound as well as text.

Wagons Sets mounted on wheels, which make rapid changes of scenery possible.

INDEX OF FIRST LINES OF POETRY

INDEX OF AUTHORS
AND TITLES

INDEX OF LITERARY TERMS